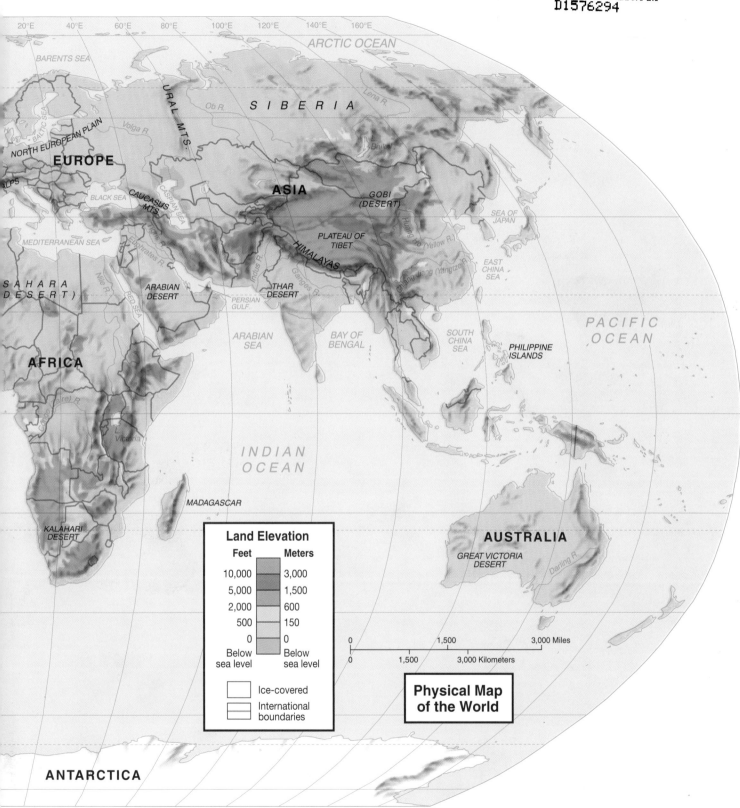

20°E 40°E 60°E 80°E 100°E 120°E 140°E 160°E

ARCTIC OCEAN

BARENTS SEA

URAL MTS.

Ob R.

SIBERIA

Lena R.

Volga R.

NORTH EUROPEAN PLAIN

EUROPE

ALPS

BALTIC SEA

BLACK SEA

CAUCASUS MTS.

CASPIAN SEA

Baikal

ASIA

GOBI
(DESERT)

SEA OF
JAPAN

MEDITERRANEAN SEA

Tigris R.

Euphrates R.

PLATEAU OF
TIBET

HIMALAYAS

Huang Ho (Yellow R.)

Chang Jiang (Yangtze R.)

EAST
CHINA
SEA

SAHARA
DESERT)

Nile R.

RED SEA

ARABIAN
DESERT

PERSIAN
GULF

Indus R.

THAR
DESERT

Ganges R.

AFRICA

ARABIAN
SEA

BAY OF
BENGAL

SOUTH
CHINA
SEA

PHILIPPINE
ISLANDS

PACIFIC
OCEAN

Congo (Zaire) R.

L.
Victoria

INDIAN
OCEAN

MADAGASCAR

KALAHARI
DESERT

AUSTRALIA

GREAT VICTORIA
DESERT

Darling R.

Land Elevation

Feet		Meters
10,000		3,000
5,000		1,500
2,000		600
500		150
0		0
Below sea level		Below sea level

Ice-covered

International boundaries

0	1,500	3,000 Miles
0	1,500	3,000 Kilometers

Physical Map of the World

ANTARCTICA

Civilization

PAST & PRESENT

Civilization

PAST & PRESENT

Ninth Edition

Palmira Brummett
UNIVERSITY OF TENNESSEE

Robert B. Edgar
HOWARD UNIVERSITY

Neil J. Hackett
OKLAHOMA STATE UNIVERSITY

George F. Jewsbury
CENTRE D'ÉTUDES DU MONDE RUSSE
ÉCOLE DES HAUTES ÉTUDES EN SCIENCES SOCIALES

Alastair M. Taylor
EMERITUS, QUEENS UNIVERSITY

Nels M. Bailkey
EMERITUS, TULANE UNIVERSITY

Clyde J. Lewis
EMERITUS, EASTERN KENTUCKY UNIVERSITY

T. Walter Wallbank (Late)

 LONGMAN

An imprint of Addison Wesley Longman, Inc.

New York • Reading, Massachusetts • Menlo Park, California • Harlow, England
Don Mills, Ontario • Sydney • Mexico City • Madrid • Amsterdam

Editor in Chief: Priscilla McGeehon
Director of Development: Betty Slack
Developmental Editor: Barbara A. Conover
Executive Marketing Manager: Sue Westmoreland
Supplements Editor: Joy Hilgendorf
Project Manager: Ellen MacElree
Design Manager: John Callahan
Cover and Text Designer: John Callahan
Cover Photograph: Thai Buddha Statue, courtesy of PhotoDisc, Inc.
Art Studio: Mapping Specialists Limited
Photo Researcher: PhotoSearch, Inc.
Electronic Production Specialist: Sarah Johnson
Electronic Page Makeup: York Graphic Services
Printer and Binder: Von Hoffmann Press
Cover Printer: The Lehigh Press, Inc.

For permission to use copyrighted material, grateful acknowledgment is made to the copyright holders on pp. C-1–C-5, which are hereby made part of this copyright page.

Please visit our website at http://www.awlonline.com

ISBN 0-321-00529-5
ISBN 0-321-00531-7 (Volume One)
ISBN 0-321-00533-3 (Volume Two)

2345678910—VH—0302010099

Brief Contents

Detailed Contents

*Each chapter ends with a Conclusion, Suggestions for Reading, Suggestions for Web Browsing, and Notes.

Documents

Maps

Endpaper Maps: Physical Map of the World, Contemporary Political Map of the World

xviii Maps

Discovery Through Maps

To the Instructor

The ninth edition of *Civilization Past & Present* continues to present a survey of world history, treating the development and growth of civilization not as a unique European experience but as a global one through which all the great culture systems have interacted to produce the present-day world. This edition includes all the elements of history—social, economic, political, military, religious, aesthetic, legal, and technological—to illustrate that global interaction.

The authors acknowledge that for our predominantly Western audience, an appreciation of their civilization is an essential aim of education, but this alone is no longer adequate. With the accelerating tempo of developments in business, communication, and technology, every day each part of the world is brought into closer contact with other parts: economic and political events that happen in even the most remote corner of the world affect each of us individually.

Changes to Organization and Content

The ninth edition maintains the strengths that have made *Civilization Past & Present* a highly respected textbook. As they revised, the authors used the latest historical scholarship and profited from many helpful suggestions from both adopters of the text and reviewers. Maintained throughout the text is a consistent writing style and level of presentation seldom found in multiauthored texts. In addition, the text introduces two new authors: Palmira Brummett of the University of Tennessee writes about Islam and West and South Asia, and Robert B. Edgar of Howard University provides coverage of Africa. While the ninth edition retains the basic organization and approach of its predecessors, all chapters have been reviewed and revised in light of the globalization of a rapidly changing world. Without increasing the number of chapters, the authors have carefully evaluated, revised, and rewritten chapters to provide balanced coverage of all parts of the world throughout history.

The new edition features the following specific changes:

- Chapter 1, on prelithic to neolithic societies, has been rewritten to reflect recent scholarship in prehistory.

- Chapter 2, "Early Civilizations: The Near East and Western Asia," is a new chapter featuring substantial information on Nubia.
- Chapter 5, "Classical China: From Origins to Empire, Prehistory to 220 C.E.," is a new, full chapter on early Chinese history.
- Chapter 6, "Ancient India: From Origins to 300 C.E.," is a new, full chapter on the early history of India.
- Chapter 10, "Islam: From Its Origins to 1300," rewritten by our scholar-author on Middle Eastern studies, offers expanded discussion of early Islam.
- Chapter 11, "The African Genesis: African Civilizations to 1500," rewritten by our scholar-author on Africian studies, features expanded coverage of early African history.
- Chapter 12, "The Growth and Spread of Asian Culture, 300–1300," has been updated and expanded.
- Chapter 13, "The Americas to 1492," includes a new section on the Amerindians of North America, in addition to already strong coverage of Central and South American civilizations.
- Chapter 15, "The Christian Reformations and the Emergence of the Modern Political System: Faith and State in Europe, 1517–1648," provides an improved analysis of the interrelationship of religious and political developments.
- Chapter 17, "The Islamic Gunpowder Empires, 1300–1650," is a newly written chapter.
- Chapter 18, "Ming China and National Development in Korea, Japan, and Southeast Asia, 1300–1650," provides coverage of these Asian civilizations.
- Chapter 19, "From Absolutism to the Old Regime: Centralized Power in Europe, 1648–1774," is reorganized and features expanded treatment of the origins and crises of central power.
- Chapter 20, "Limited Central Power in the Capitalist World, 1600–1789," emphasizes the interrelationship between decentralized political power and the world market.
- Chapter 21, "The Scientific Revolution and the Enlightenment: New Ideas and Their Consequences," discusses the interaction of scientific discovery and new political and social thought

and the consequence of that fusion in enlightened despotism and the American Revolution.

- Chapter 22, "The French and Napoleonic Revolutions and Their Impact on Europe and the Americas, 1789–1825," illustrates the impact of the quarter century of French dominance and its role in introducing the modern world.
- Chapter 23, "Africa, Asia, and European Penetration, 1650–1815," newly written and expanded, presents the European advances from a global rather than a Eurocentric view.
- Chapter 24, "Foundations of Western Dominance: Industrial, Scientific, Technological, Business, and Cultural Developments, 1815–1914," provides an enhanced overview of the material and of the intellectual forces fueling the Industrial Revolution and a century of European domination.
- Chapter 25, "The Politics of Ideas in the Western World, 1815–1861," and Chapter 26, "Power Politics in the West, 1861–1914," consider Western political developments in two stages: the politics of ideology to 1861 and the politics of Realpolitik to 1914.
- Chapter 27, "Africa and the Middle East, 1800–1914," an entirely new chapter, gives an account of non-Western affairs of that century from a non-Western point of view.
- Chapter 28, "Four Faces of Nineteenth-Century Imperialism," offers an analysis of the various forms of Western colonialism.
- Chapter 29, "The Perils of 'Progress': Middle-Class Thought and the Failure of European Diplomacy, 1878–1914," is a study of the complacency, misreading of science, and racism that permitted Europeans to ignore ticking time bombs such as the crisis in the Balkans.
- Chapter 30, "Winning the War and Losing the Peace: The Democracies, 1914–1939," discusses the end of the liberal dream in Europe after the disaster of World War I.
- Chapter 32, "Emerging National Movements in Asia and Africa, 1920s to 1950s," a new chapter, offers expanded treatment of Asia and Africa during the period between World Wars I and II.
- The final three chapters, Chapter 34, "The Cold War and After: Russia and Eastern Europe, 1945–1999," Chapter 35, "The 'Developed World' Since 1945," and Chapter 36, "The Developing World: The Struggle for Survival," have all been updated and expanded to reflect events of the late 1990s.

New Split

The split for the two-volume edition has changed: Volume 1, To 1650, contains Chapters 1–18; Volume 2, From 1300, contains Chapters 14–36. The start of

Volume 2 has been moved back to accommodate courses that cover material beginning earlier than 1650.

Pedagogical Features

The text has been developed with the dual purpose of helping students acquire a solid knowledge of past events and, equally important, of helping them think more constructively about the significance of those events for the complex times in which we now live. A number of pedagogical features—some well tested in earlier editions and a number of new ones—will assist students in achieving these goals.

New

Full-Color Format: The full-color format design of the ninth edition is intended to make *Civilization Past & Present* more "user-friendly" to its readers. *Photographs:* The text's more than 500 photos, most in full color, have been carefully selected to present a mix of Western and non-Western images. Special care has been taken to include images illustrating the lifestyles and contributions of women for all eras and areas. *Maps:* The use of full color allows students more readily to see distinctions on the more than 120 maps in the text. Some maps make clear the nature of a single distinctive event; others illustrate larger trends. The caption accompanying each map highlights the significance of the map and its relevance to a specific text topic.

Discovery Through Maps: A special new feature focusing on primary maps in each chapter offers a unique historical view—be it local, city, country, world, or constellation— of the way in which a particular culture looked at the world at a particular time. For example, a 4000-year-old Chinese map shows the major facts of life for the time: rivers and where they run, mountains, and provinces that paid tribute to the emperor; while an elaborate seventeenth-century map of Amsterdam makes clear that it was the Golden Age not only for the Netherlands but also for the Dutch cartographers who depicted its world.

Part Opening Essays: New essays at the beginning of each part relate the various chapters one to the other and emphasize thematic development within the book. These essays allow students to take stock of where they have been in their study of global history and to discover where the flow of history will take them.

Suggested Web Sites: Following the Suggestions for Reading is a listing of Web sites related to major topics of the chapter, offering access to differing interpretations, images, sounds, and discussion groups.

Chronology Tables: Short chronology tables within the chapter narrative allow the reader a quick recap of the important events or trends of a specific period.

Revised

Excerpts from Primary Source Documents: These excerpts from original sources represent a mix of the best of the old and a strengthening of the new, particularly non-Western documents. The selections have been chosen to give a variety of testimonies—political, economic, legal, religious, artistic, social, and popular—to show students the kinds of materials historians use to understand and interpret the past.

Chapter Opening Pages: Redesigned chapter opening pages feature an illustration relevant to the chapter topics, a chapter outline, and a streamlined, easy-to-read time line of key events that are discussed in the chapter.

Suggestions for Reading: Detailed annotated bibliographies list general interpretations, monographs, and collections of source materials that students can consult to expand their understanding of a particular topic or to prepare reports and papers.

Pronunciation Guide: The general index at the back of the text includes a pronunciation for most proper names. Students should find it easy, as well as helpful, to look up the correct pronunciation of the names and places they encounter in the text. The index also provides pronunciation guides for unfamiliar, difficult, or foreign words.

The ninth edition of *Civilization Past & Present* is a thorough revision in both its text narrative and its pedagogical features. It is intended to provide the reader with an understanding of the legacies of past eras and to illuminate the way in which the study of world history gives insights into the genesis, nature, and direction of our global civilization. The need for this kind of perspective has never been greater.

For Qualified College Adopters: Supplements for Instructors

Annotated Instructor's Edition by Paul Bischoff of Oklahoma State University. This unique edition helps instructors cover cultures and periods outside their areas of expertise with teaching suggestions, project ideas, chapter comparisons, additional background, and suggestions for further reading. It is an especial-ly valuable resource for both new instructors and more experienced faculty in search of new ideas and for all professors who struggle to teach cultures outside their areas of expertise.

BrummettOnline, http://www.awlonline.com/brummett, by Richard Rothaus of St. Cloud State University. This course companion provides text-specific resources for students and instructors and includes our on-line syllabus manager. Students will find it easy to learn and study with the chapter outlines, self-testing programs, Web activities, primary sources, Internet links, and glossary. Instructors will love it for the teaching ideas and aids, on-line images, links, and syllabus manager.

Instructor's Resource Manual revised by Patricia Ali of Morris College. This collection of resources includes chapter outlines, definitions, discussion suggestions, critical thinking exercises, term paper and essay topics, and audiovisual suggestions. It also includes special *African Perspectives* essays by Robert Edgar and *Genocide in History* essays by George Jewsbury.

Brummett Presentation Maker These easy-to-customize PowerPoint slides outline key points of each chapter of the text and are available as transparency masters and on dual platform CD-ROM and Windows or Macintosh disks.

Guide to Teaching World History by Palmira Brummett of the University of Tennessee at Knoxville. This new guide offers explanations of major issues and themes in world history, sample syllabi and instructions on how to create a manageable syllabus, ideas for cross-cultural and cross-temporal connections, a pronunciation guide, and tips on getting through all the material.

Test Bank and Test Generator by Susan Hellert of the University of Wisconsin at Platteville. This easy-to-customize test bank presents a wealth of multiple-choice, true-false, short-answer, and essay questions.

Discovering World History Through Maps and Views Overhead Transparency Acetates by Gerald Danzer of the University of Illinois at Chicago. This unique resource contains more than 100 full-color acetates of beautiful reference maps, source maps, urban plans, views, photos, art, and building diagrams.

Longman World History Atlas Overhead Transparency Acetates These acetates are available to instructors who select the *Longman World History Atlas* for their students.

Overhead Transparency Acetates to Accompany *Civilization Past & Present* These text-specific acetates are available to all adopters.

IRC World History Videodisk Instructional Resources Corporation's library of 2400 still images, 71 historical maps, and 12 narrative section overviews is especially flexible for classroom lectures and presentations.

Historical Newsreel Video This 90-minute video contains newsreel excerpts examining U.S. involvement in world affairs over the past 60 years.

Longman-Penguin Putnam Inc. Value Bundles Students and professors alike will love the value and quality of the Penguin books offered at a deep discount when bundled with *Civilization Past & Present,* Ninth Edition.

Supplements for Students

Interactive Edition CD-ROM This new CD-ROM is an electronic version of the text that contains the entire text, maps, and charts, as well as photos, glossary, and electronic student study guide. Its easy-to-use navigation makes it simple to search by topic or name, take notes on-line, and link to the Internet.

Brummett Online, http://www.awlonline.com/brummett, by Richard Rothaus of St. Cloud State University. This course companion provides text-specific resources for students and instructors and includes our on-line syllabus manager. Students will find it easy to learn and study with the chapter outlines, self-testing programs, Web activities, primary sources, Internet links, and glossary. Instructors will love it for the teaching ideas and aids, on-line images, Web links, and syllabus manager.

Student Study Guide in two volumes: Volume 1 (Chapters 1–18) and Volume 2 (Chapters 14–36) prepared by Sterling Kernek and David G. Egler of Western Illinois University, and Melvin Lyttaker III of Southeastern Community College. Each chapter includes chapter overviews, lists of themes and concepts, map exercises, multiple-choice practice tests, and critical thinking and essay questions.

StudyWizard Computerized Tutorial prepared by Paul George of Miami-Dade Community College. This interactive program features chapter outlines and multiple-choice, true-false, and short-answer questions. It also contains a glossary and gives users immediate test scores and answer explanations.

Everything You Need to Know About *Civilization Past & Present* This is a concise guide to the textbook's organization, pedagogy, themes, and special features.

Everything You Need to Know About Your History Course by Sandra Mathews-Lamb of Nebraska Wesleyan University. This guide helps students succeed in history courses by describing good techniques for taking notes, researching and writing papers, reading primary and secondary sources, reading maps, charts, and graphs, taking exams, learning from lectures, and using the textbook.

Guide to Internet and Advanced Media Resources for World History, Second Edition, by Richard Rothaus of St. Cloud State University. This guide shows students how to make the most of the Internet in their world history course and includes a comprehensive listing of Web resources for all areas of world history.

Documents in World History, Second Edition, edited by Peter N. Stearns et al. This two-volume collection of primary sources makes history come to life with first-hand accounts from all areas of the world.

World History Map Workbooks, Second Edition, by Glee Wilson of Kent State University. This two-volume workbook includes over 80 maps accompanied by a contextual overview and exercises in making, reading, and understanding maps. The exercises teach the locations of and relationships among various countries.

Longman World History Atlas This full-color, easy-to-read atlas contains 56 maps designed especially for the world history course. It is free when bundled with the text.

Longman World History Series These books focus on the world historical significance of a particular movement, experience, or interaction. Concise and inexpensive, they bring the global connections and consequences of these events to the fore, showing students how events that happened long ago or far away can still affect them.

Environmentalism: A Global History by Ramachandra Guha. Discusses the global and interconnected nature of the environmental movement from the Romantics to today with clear language and organization.

Colonial Encounters in the Age of High Imperialism by Scott B. Cook of the Rhode Island School of Design. Examines the world-transforming experience of Western imperialism from 1870 to 1914, focusing specifically on Belgium and the Congo, the United States and Hawaii, and Britain and India.

Timelink: World History Computerized Atlas by William Hamblin of Brigham Young University. A highly graphic, Hypercard-based computerized atlas and historical geography tutorial for Macintosh computers.

Acknowledgments

We are most grateful to the following reviewers who gave generously of their time and knowledge to provide thoughtful evaluations and many helpful suggestions for the revision of this edition.

Wayne Ackerson
Salisbury State University

Joseph Appiah
J. Sargeant Reynolds Community College

Mark C. Bartusis
Northern State University

Mauricio Borrero
St. John's University

Demoral Davis
Jackson State University

Paul George
Miami-Community College, Dade

David Gleason
Armstrong Atlantic State University

Christopher Guthrie
Tarleton State University

Janine Hartman
University of Cincinnati

Thomas Hegarty
University of Tampa

David Hill
McHenry County College

Thomas Howell
Louisiana College

Clark Hultquist
University of Montevallo

Daniel R. Kazmer
Georgetown University

Teresa Lafer
Pennsylvania State University

Robert McCormick
Newman University

David A. Meier
Dickinson State University

David Owusu-Ansah
James Madison University

George Pesely
Austin-Peay State

Charles Risher
Montreat College

Bill Schell
Murray State University

Paul J. Smith
Haverford College

Edward Tabri
Columbus State Community College

Joseph A. Tomberlin
Valdosta State University

Chris Warren
Copiah-Lincoln Community College

Mary Watrous
Washington State University

David L. White
Appalachian State University

We also thank the many conscientious reviewers who reviewed previous editions of this book.

Jay Pascal Anglin
University of Southern Mississippi

Joel Berlatsky
Wilkes College

Jackie R. Booker
Kent State University

Darwin F. Bostwick
Old Dominion University

Robert F. Brinson, Jr.
Santa Fe Community College

Robert H. Buchanan
Adams State College

Michael L. Carrafiello
East Carolina University

James O. Catron, Jr.
North Florida Junior College

William H. Cobb
East Carolina University

J. L. Collins
Allan Hancock College

J. R. Crawford
Montreat-Anderson College

Edward R. Crowther
Adams State College

Lawrence J. Daly
Bowling Green State University

William Edward Ezzell
DeKalb College–Central Campus

John D. Fair
Auburn University at Montgomery

Robert B. Florian
Salem-Teikyo University

Nels W. Forde
University of Nebraska

Joseph T. Fuhrmann
Murray State University

Robert J. Gentry
University of Southwestern Louisiana

Jeffrey S. Hamilton
Old Dominion University

Donald E. Harpster
College of St. Joseph

Gordon K. Harrington
Weber State University

J. Drew Harrington
Western Kentucky University

Geoff Haywood
Beaver College

Conrad C. Holcomb, Jr.
Surry Community College

Roger L. Jungmeyer
Lincoln University of Missouri

Bernard Kiernan
Concord College

Michael L. Krenn
University of Miami

Harral E. Landry
Texas Women's University

Marsha K. Marks
Alabama A&M University

Caroline T. Marshall
James Madison University

Eleanor McCluskey
Broward Community College

Arlin Migliazzo
Whitworth College

William C. Moose
Mitchell Community College

Wayne Morris
Lees-McRae College

John G. Muncie
East Stroudsburg University

Sr. Jeannette Plante, CSC
Notre Dame College

Norman Pollock
Old Dominion University

J. Graham Provan
Millikin University

George B. Pruden, Jr.
Armstrong State College

John D. Ramsbottom
Northeast Missouri State University

Ruth Richard
College of Lake County

Hugh I. Rodgers
Columbus College

Patrick J. Rollins
Old Dominion University

Chad Ronnander
University of Minnesota

Barry T. Ryan
Westmont College

Louis E. Schmier
Valdosta State College

William M. Simpson
Louisiana College

Barbara G. Sniffen
University of Wisconsin-Oshkosh

Lawrence Squeri
East Stroudsburg University

Terrence S. Sullivan
University of Nebraska at Omaha

Gordon L. Teffeteller
Valdosta State College

Malcolm R. Thorp
Brigham Young University

Helen M. Tierney
University of Wisconsin-Platteville

Leslie Tischauser
Prairie State College

Arthur L. Tolson
Southern University

Thomas Dwight Veve
Dalton College

John R. Willertz
Saginaw Valley State University

To the Student

We set two goals for ourselves when we wrote *Civilization Past & Present*. The first is to provide you with an understanding of the contributions of past eras in all parts of the globe to the shaping of subsequent events. The second is to illuminate the way in which the study of world history gives us insights into the genesis, nature, and direction of our own civilization.

These are challenging tasks. However, given the globalization of all aspects of our lives, they are essential. When economies in East Asia are in a state of crisis, the impact is felt on Wall Street. The culture of the New World—especially music and movies—has spread around the globe. When tragedies occur in the Balkans, we are all affected. Long gone are the days when an occurrence that took place far away could be isolated.

Now you are taking a course in world history to understand the development of the cultures of the world—cultures that are coming together to form a multifaceted world civilization. Understanding how and why other civilizations have chosen differing routes to their future, you can gain an understanding of why your part of civilization has succeeded or failed in attaining its potential. With an understanding of world history, you will be able to respond more knowledgeably to the changes through which you will live and make informed choices as a world citizen.

History is the study of change over time. A historian is a person who focuses on one aspect of changes in the past, poses questions about why a particular event has taken place, proposes answers—hypotheses—and tests those hypotheses against the evidence—all of the evidence. We do not expect you to be historians at this point in your career—to form your own hypotheses and write monographs. We have written this book, however, to enable you to study change over time in seven major chronological stages:

- Part 1, "The Ancient World," takes you from prehistory to the development of civilizations in Africa, Southwest Asia, South Asia, and East Asia to the third century of this era.
- Part 2, "The Middle Ages," studies the formative stages of the world's peoples at this pivotal time. Here we examine the establishment of the political,

religious, social, and cultural frameworks that would characterize Europe, Southwest Asia, Africa, Asia, and the Americas to the fifteenth century.

- Part 3, "The Transition to Modern Times," examines the impact of new intellectual frameworks, new modes of technology, and new economic systems in the world to the middle of the seventeenth century.
- Part 4, "The Rising European Tide," traces the interrelated burst of political, economic, scientific, and ideological energy that propelled the European continent to prominence by the end of the eighteenth century.
- Part 5, "The Century of Western Dominance," concentrates on the West's ascendency during the nineteenth century. The wave of technological, scientific, business, and intellectual exploration swept over, but did not overwhelm, the non-Western world.
- Part 6, "The New Thirty Years' War," discusses the end of the liberal dream during the three decades that witnessed the bloody catastrophes of the two world wars, the advent of authoritarian states, and the horrors of the Holocaust and nuclear weapons.
- Part 7, "From Bipolar Ideology to Global Competition," discusses the globalization of the world since 1945, first as part of the bipolar conflict known as the Cold War and then with the economic unification of the world and its vast disparity between the very rich and the extremely poor.

The authors have included a number of tools to help you on your voyage through this text. At the beginning of each part, a brief **essay** summarizes the major events and accomplishments occurring in its time frame and relates the chapters, and their world regions, to each other. These essays will give you a helpful overall perspective of the chapters included in each part.

As you begin the chapter, take five or ten minutes to look at the **chapter opening pages.** These two pages at the beginning of each chapter telegraph what is to come: a photo conceptualizes the main themes of the chapter, and a chapter outline and a time line allow you to fix beginning and end points in this part of your trip. Take time to read the introduction and then thumb to the end of the chapter to read the conclusion. Next, go through the chapter reading only the main and secondary headlines. Finally, return to the beginning of the chapter and start to read—knowing in advance where you have come from and which way you are going.

Within each chapter we offer you other tools to gain an understanding of the past. Events take place in a location, and each location has particular features that affect what will happen. Thus the text includes more than 120 four-color **maps,** each with its own explanatory caption. Some maps are designed to make clear the nature of a single distinctive event; others illustrate larger trends.

Different civilizations have different visions of themselves and their place in the world. The **Discovery Through Maps** boxes will give you a notion of the way that various cultures in the world have seen themselves and their relation to the rest of the globe. For example, in "A Korean-Centered View of the World," dating from around 1600, Japan shrivels away to a distant, tiny archipelago; and the labeling of non-Western areas of "An American View of the World in the 1820s" makes American intolerance toward the non-Western world immediately clear.

We also include two or more excerpts from **primary source documents** in each chapter. These excerpts from original sources offer you a window into the way that the people of the time expressed themselves. The documents cover a variety of viewpoints: political, economic, legal, religious, social, artistic, and popular. As examples, an ancient Roman text gives

advice on how to "Avoid Enticements into the Snares of Love"; in "Louis XIV to His Son," the Sun King of France instructs his son, a young man who never does become king; and in "That Was No Brother," two documents— one by an African chief and the other by the English explorer Henry Morton Stanley—give two very different perceptions of the same battle.

Short **chronology tables** within the chapter narrative will give you a quick view of the important events in a specific period.

The text's 500 **photos,** most in full color, give balanced pictorial coverage of all parts of the world. They enhance the reading of each chapter by giving additional context and bringing the matters under discussion to life. For this edition, we have paid special attention in these photos to the lifestyles and contributions of women.

After you have finished each chapter you will find two features to help you prepare a paper or project, or simply to learn more about a particular topic. The annotated bibliographies of **suggestions for reading** indicate useful general studies, monographs, and source materials. Also provided is a list of **suggested Web sites** to allow you to hook up to databases, sounds, images, or discussion groups dealing with the topics under consideration.

Finally, you will encounter numerous terms and names in your reading. The **pronunciation key** in the index will help you pronounce these often perplexing words. Say the words aloud so that you will become familiar with how the words sound as well as how they look.

Prologue
Perspective on Humanity

If the time span of our planet—now estimated at some 5 billion years—were telescoped into a single year, the first eight months would be devoid of any life. The next two months would be taken up with plant and very primitive animal forms, and not until well into December would any mammals appear. In this "year," members of *Homo erectus*, our ancient predecessors, would mount the global stage only between 10 and 11 P.M. on December 31. And how has the human species spent that brief allotment? Most of it—the equivalent of more than half a million years—has been given over to making tools out of stone. The revolutionary changeover from food-hunting nomads to farmers who raised grain and domesticated animals would occur in the last 60 seconds. And into that final minute would be crowded all of humanity's other accomplishments so far: the use of metal; the creation of civilizations; the mastery of the oceans; and the harnessing of steam, then gas, electricity, oil, and, finally, nuclear energy. Brief though it has been, humanity's time on the globe reveals a rich tapestry of science, industry, religion, and art. This accumulated experience of the human species is our *history*.

Past and Present

As we read and learn about early societies and their members, we discover them to be very different from us and the world in which we live. Yet we are linked by more than curiosity to our ancient predecessors. Why? Because we are of the same species, and we share a fundamental commonality that connects present with past: the human-environment nexus. It is the dynamic interplay of environmental factors and human activities that accounts for the process known as history. The biological continuity of our species, coupled with humanity's unflagging inventiveness, has enabled each generation to build on the experiences and contributions of its forebears so that continuity and change in human affairs proceed together.

The Universal Culture Pattern

In the interplay of humans with their environment and fellow beings, certain fundamental needs are always present. Six needs, common to people at all times and in all places, form the basis of a "universal culture pattern":

1. *The need to survive.* Men and women must have food, shelter, clothing, and the means to provide for their offsprings' survival.
2. *The need for social organization.* For people to make a living, raise families, and maintain order, a social structure is essential. Views about the relative importance of the group and the individual within it may vary with any such social structure.
3. *The need for stability and protection.* From earliest times, communities have had to keep peace among their members, defend themselves against external attack, and protect community assets.
4. *The need for knowledge and learning.* Since earliest times, humankind has transmitted knowledge acquired through experience, first orally, then by means of writing systems, and now by electronic means as well. As societies grow more complex, there is increasing need to preserve knowledge and transmit it through education to as many people as possible.
5. *The need for self-expression.* People responded creatively to their environment even before the days when they decorated the walls of Paleolithic caves with paintings of the animals they hunted. The arts appear to have a lineage as old as human experience.
6. *The need for religious expression.* Equally old is humanity's attempt to answer the "why" of its existence. What early peoples considered supernatural in their environment could often, at a later time, be explained by science in terms of natural phenomena. Yet today, no less than in archaic times, men and women continue to search for answers to the ultimate questions of existence.

Culture Change and Culture Lag

When people in a group behave similarly and share the same institutions and ways of life, they can be said to have a common *culture*. Throughout this text we will be looking at a number of different cultures, some of which are designated as *civilizations*. (If all societies have culture, then civilization is a particular *kind* of culture.) "A culture is the way of life of a human group; it includes all the learned and standardized forms of behavior which one uses and others in one's group expect and recognize. . . . Civilization is that kind of culture which includes the use of writing, the presence of cities and of wide political organization, and the development of occupational specialization."[1]

Cultures are never wholly static or wholly isolated. A particular culture may have an individuality that sets it off sharply from other cultures, but invariably it has been influenced by external contacts. Such contacts may be either peaceful or warlike, and they meet with varying degrees of acceptance. Through these contacts occurs the process of culture *diffusion*. Geography, too, has profoundly influenced the development of cultures, although we should not exaggerate its importance. Environmental influences tend to become less marked as people gain technological skill and mastery over the land. The domestication of animals and cereals, for example, took place in both the Old and New Worlds, but the animals and grains were different because of dissimilar ecological factors. Invention is another important source of culture change, although it is not clear to what extent external physical contact is required in the process of invention. However, men and women in different times and places have reached similar solutions to the challenges posed by their respective environments—resulting in the phenomenon known as *parallel invention*.

Some parts of a culture pattern change more rapidly than others, so that one institution sometimes becomes outmoded in relation to others in a single society. When different parts of a society fail to mesh harmoniously, the condition is often called *culture lag*. Numerous examples of this lag could be cited: the exploitation of child laborers during the nineteenth century, the failure to allow women to vote until the twentieth century, and the tragedy of hunger in the midst of plenty.

Past and Present as Prologue

What can the past and present—as history—suggest to us for tomorrow's world? Changes in the physical and social environments will probably accelerate as a result of continued technological innovation. These changes can result in increased disequilibrium and tensions among the various segments comprising the universal culture pattern—in other words, in increased culture lag.

Has the past anything to tell the future about the consequences of cultural disequilibrium—anything that we might profitably use in present-day planning for the decades ahead? Because our planet and its resources are finite, at some point a society must expect to shift progressively from exponential growth toward an overall global equilibrium. By that term, we mean the setting of maximal levels on the number of humans who can inhabit this planet with an assured minimal standard of life and on the exploitation of the earth's resources required to provide that standard. Otherwise, environmental disaster on an unprecedented scale could result in the decades ahead. Past and present conjoin to alert us to the need to engage in new forms of planning for the years ahead and also to the need to rethink our existing social goals and value systems. We need as long and as accurate a perspective as possible to make realistic analyses and to take the appropriate actions to improve our quality of life.

The "How" of History

History is the record of the past actions of humankind, based on surviving evidence. History shows that all patterns and problems in human affairs are the products of a complex process of growth. By shedding light on that process, history provides a means for us to benefit from human experience.

History as a Science

There is more than one way to treat the past. In dealing with the American or Russian Revolution or the Meiji Restoration, for example, the historian may describe events in narrative form or, instead, analyze general causes and compare stages with the patterns of similar events in other countries. Unlike the scientist, who attempts to verify hypotheses by repeating experiments under controlled conditions in the laboratory and to classify phenomena in a general group or category, the historian has to pay special attention to the *uniqueness* of data, because each event takes place at a particular time and in a particular place. And since that time is now past, the historian cannot verify conclusions by duplicating the circumstances in which the event occurred.

Nevertheless, historians insist that history be written as "scientifically" as possible and that evidence be analyzed with the same objective attitude employed by scientists examining natural phenomena. This scientific spirit requires historians to handle evidence according to established rules of historical analysis, to recognize biases and attempt to eliminate their effects, and to draw only such conclusions as the evidence seems to warrant.

The Historical Method

To meet these requirements, historians have evolved the "historical method." The first step is the search for *sources*, which may be material remains, oral traditions, pictorial data, or written records. From the source the historian must infer the facts. This process has two parts. *External criticism* tests the genuineness of the source. *Internal criticism* evaluates the source to ascertain the author's meaning and the accuracy of the work.

The final step in the historical method is *synthesis*. Here the historian must determine which factors in a given situation are most relevant to the purpose at hand, since obviously one cannot include everything that occurred. This delicate process of selection underscores the role that subjectivity plays in the writing of history. Furthermore, the more complex the events involved, the more crucial the historian's judgment becomes.[2]

Periodization

Can we really categorize history as "ancient," "medieval," or "modern"? Clearly, what is "modern" in the twentieth century will conceivably be considered "medieval" in the twenty-fifth century and eventually "ancient" in the thirty-fifth century. Yet not to break up the account would be akin to reading this book without the benefit of parts, chapters, paragraphs, or even separate sentences. Like time itself, history would then become a ceaseless flow of consciousness and events. To simplify the task and to manage materials more easily, the historian divides time into periods. The divisions chosen and the lines drawn reveal the distinctive way in which the historian regards the past.

The "Why" of History

The historian seeks to describe not only *what* has happened and *how* it happened but also *why* society undergoes change. Any search of this kind raises a number of fundamental questions: the impact of long-term geographical, economic, and social forces; the role of the individual; the power of the group in the extent to which events are unique or, conversely, can fit into patterns; and the problem of progress in human affairs. The answers vary with different philosophical views of the universe and the human role therein.

People who hold the teleological view see in history the guidance of a Divine Will, directing human destinies according to a cosmic purpose. Other thinkers have exalted the role of the individual in the historical process, contending that major figures chiefly determined the course of human events. Opponents of this thesis argue that history is determined by "forces" and "laws" and by the actions of entire societies. Sociologists approach history primarily by analyzing the origins, institutions, and functions of groups. Economists tend to look at the historical record from the standpoint of group action and especially the impact of economic forces.

To Karl Marx irresistible economic forces governed human beings and determined the trend of events. Marx contended that the shift from one economic stage to another—such as the shift from feudalism to capitalism—is attained by upheavals, or revolutions, which occur because the class controlling the methods of production eventually resists further progress in order to maintain its vested interests.

Numerous other attempts have been made to explain societal processes according to a set of principles. Writing at the time of World War I, the German Oswald Spengler maintained that civilizations were like organisms; each grew with the "superb aimlessness" of a flower and passed through a cycle of spring, summer, autumn, and winter. Charles Darwin's evolutionary hypothesis made a strong impact on nineteenth-century thought and gave rise to the concept that the principle of "survival of the fittest" must also apply to human societies. This line of thought—known as social Darwinism—raises social and ethical questions of major importance.

Does history obey impersonal laws and forces so that its course is inevitable? Or, at the other extreme, since every event is a unique act, is history simply the record of unforeseen and unrelated episodes? Can this apparent dilemma be avoided? We believe it can. Although all events are, in various respects, unique, they also contain elements that invite comparison. The comparative approach permits us to seek relationships between historical phenomena and to group them into movements or patterns or civilizations. We eschew any "theory" of history, preferring to see merit in a number of basic concepts. These include the effects of physical environment on social organization and institutions; the roles played by economic, political, and religious factors; and the individual impact exerted by men and women occupying key positions in various societies.

The Challenge of History

Progress and growth are continuous factors. They depend on, and contribute to, the maintenance of peace and security, the peaceful settlement of international disputes, and worldwide improvement in economic and social standards. Surely an indispensable step toward solving contemporary humanity's dilemma—technology without the requisite control and power without commensurate wisdom—must be a better understanding of how the world and its people came to be what they are today. Only by understanding the past can we assess both the perils and the opportunities of the present—and move courageously and compassionately into the future.

Notes

1. David G. Mandelbaum, "Concepts of Civilization and Culture," *Encyclopaedia Britannica*, 1967 ed., Vol. 5, p. 831A.

2. See P. Gardiner, *The Nature of Historical Explanation* (London: Oxford University Press, 1952), p. 98.

Civilization
PAST & PRESENT

The Ancient World

The origin and age of the universe may never be known precisely, but modern scientists believe that our world has been circling the sun for 5 billion years. During that incredibly long time, the earth changed from a gaseous to a liquid and finally to a solid state, waters formed on the earth's shell, and in their depths life took form. Remains of early humanlike creatures unearthed in Africa may be 3 to 4 million years old. The time span from those remote days to about 3500 B.C.E. is usually referred to as *prehistoric* or *preliterate* times. By far the greatest part of that time span was taken up by the human struggle for survival—a struggle in which human beings learned to shape crude tools from stone, make fire, and domesticate plants and animals.

The stage was now set for a progressively rapid extension of human control over the environment. We find the first civilizations widely scattered along the banks of rivers. Mesopotamia straddled the Tigris and the Euphrates; Egypt and Nubia stretched along the Nile; China expanded eastward from the region of the Wei and the Huang Ho; India arose along the Indus and the Ganges. Prolific in their gifts to the human race and so dynamic that two of them—China and India—have retained unbroken continuity to our own day, these civilizations possessed similarities at least as arresting as their differences. In all four, political systems developed, crafts flourished and commerce expanded, calendars and systems of writing were invented, art and literature of extraordinary beauty were created, and religions and philosophies came into being to satisfy people's inner yearnings.

Indebted to the Egyptians and Mesopotamians, Minoan and Mycenaean Greece fashioned a wealthy, sophisticated, commercial culture. Much of this Aegean civilization—the first advanced culture to appear in Europe—was destroyed by the end of the second millennium B.C.E., but enough remained to serve as the foundation for Greek civilization. Insatiably curious about their world, the Greeks enjoyed a freedom of thought and expression unknown in earlier societies. Their fierce passion to remain independent, however, was too often unrestrained. The failure of the Greek city-states to find a workable basis for cooperation doomed them to political disaster. Although the conquest of the city-states by King Philip of Macedonia ended the Hellenic Age, the influence of the Greeks was destined to increase. The establishment of a vast empire in the Near East by Philip's son, Alexander the Great, ushered in the Hellenistic Age and the widespread diffusion of Greek culture.

Meanwhile, a new power—Rome—had been developing on the Italian peninsula. After five centuries of modest growth, this city-state embarked on a career of unprecedented expansion. The splendor of Roman arms was matched by skill in administration, wisdom in law, and ingenuity in the practical arts of engineering and communication. These talents and abilities enabled the Romans to erect a Mediterranean empire, which survived until the fifth century C.E. Probably the greatest achievement of the Roman Empire was the skillful governing of a diversity of cultures within a political unity. To the Romans we owe a debt for preserving and disseminating classical culture, for the legacy of Greco-Roman culture is the foundation of Western civilization.

Despite often cataclysmic disasters during its formative period, China pursued ambitious innovations in all aspects of its society, from philosophy to economics. Throughout China the state established a theoretical focus toward the amelioration of social evils and the relief of distress. This was the ever-changing product of two of the main ingredients in the Chinese tradition—Confucianism, with its concern for a humane society, and Legalism, with its stress on the power of the state, always modified by the underlying, unified civilization. And by means of this civilization China was able to erect a fundamental frame of identity in which all other activities took place.

During India's formative age, three major religions were evolving on the subcontinent. Hinduism became the dominant social and religious force in India, with its notions of *dharma* allocated by caste. Jainism fostered the notion of *ahimsa* (nonviolence), which would play a powerful role in the twentieth-century Indian independence movement. Buddhism challenged the Brahmin order and spread beyond the frontiers of India, ultimately to become a world religion. India today is the heir of one of the longest-living civilizations in the world, one that has produced a set of religious, philosophical, and literary traditions that endures up to the present day.

Now let us survey the glorious classical age of civilization.

Prehistoric art in Los Toldos Cave,
Argentina, includes representations
of deer and hands. Archaeologists
have dated the art to around
15,000 B.C.E.

Prelithic to
Neolithic Societies
In the Beginning . . .

Today we speak about the advent of a new millennium and its significance. But what happened in the preceding thousands of years to shape our existence and direct our present and future actions? Without some knowledge of the opening chapter of the human story—just when and where our ancestors came to exist—we have no sense of how human history began.

This introductory chapter provides an overview of the longest period in which our ancestors existed on the planet, a time when they developed the basic tools and forms of social structure and behavior on which all succeeding cultures would build. Indeed, our Stone Age ancestors created the plot and tenuous story line that we continue both to follow and to expand, with novel twists and creative additions.

The Development of Humankind

Did God create humanity "in his own image," or was our species itself the product of physical change and adaptation neither more nor less than the rocks, plants, and animals of this planet? The controversy surrounding the theory of human evolution continues into the third millennium of the Common Era, although with decreasing intensity as more fossil evidence comes to light. Of course, the fossil record can probably never be complete, and paleontologists have only skeletal

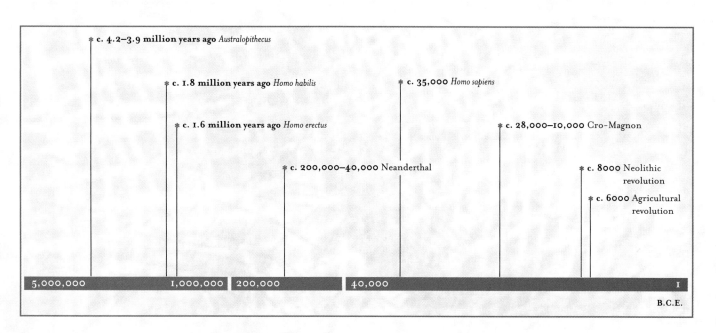

* c. 4.2–3.9 million years ago *Australopithecus*

* c. 1.8 million years ago *Homo habilis*

* c. 1.6 million years ago *Homo erectus*

* c. 200,000–40,000 *Neanderthal*

* c. 35,000 *Homo sapiens*

* c. 28,000–10,000 Cro-Magnon

* c. 8000 Neolithic revolution

* c. 6000 Agricultural revolution

| 5,000,000 | 1,000,000 | 200,000 | 40,000 | I |

B.C.E.

remains (usually partial ones) to analyze. Nevertheless, the evidence for evolution appears overwhelming, but the theory does not preclude the presence of a guiding intelligence ultimately responsible for the progressive development of organic life from simple to more complex forms, culminating in the intelligence and creativity of our own species.

According to the theory of evolution, humans belong to the Primate order, which also includes the lemurs, tarsiers, monkeys, and apes. The primates possess a similar skeletal structure, their hands and feet can grasp and retain objects, and compared with other creatures, they have a relatively large brain, excellent stereoscopic vision, and a mediocre sense of smell. The earliest primates, living perhaps 60 million years ago, were small mouselike creatures resembling the modern tree shrew that inhabited trees and hunted insects at night. Their way of life encouraged the development of mobile thumbs, flexible forelimbs, keen eyesight, and eye-hand coordination. Many species of these first primates became extinct, but tarsierlike and lemurlike types survived and became the ancestors of higher forms of primates.

As we can see from the geological table below, important developments occurred among the primates during the Tertiary period. In the Oligocene epoch, different lines of monkeys evolved, as well as primitive forms of anthropoid apes; in the next epoch, the Miocene, the ape family grew in size and variety and spread over much of Africa, Asia, and Europe. Before the end of this epoch (that is, no later than 28 million years ago), a development of the first magnitude occurred when the ape family became differentiated. One line evolved into the tree-dwelling apes, while the second led to ground-dwelling types known as hominids, or what we may arbitrarily call *prehumans* or *protohumans*. In time these prehumans learned to walk upright, their legs grew longer than their arms, and their hands—no longer required for locomotion—became more dexterous. Most important, the prehuman head gradually shifted toward a more upright position, rendering superfluous much of the muscle at the back of the neck. This development favored the progressive expansion of the brain, which in turn ultimately led to modern "thinking man" *(Homo sapiens),* the only survivor of the many-branched hominid tree.

Development of the Genus *Homo*

No conclusive fossil evidence bearing on prehuman evolution during the Pliocene epoch, which followed the Miocene, has yet been found. However, the Pleistocene epoch provides us with increasing data on the dynamic development of our genus, *Homo*. Remains of the Australopithecines ("southern apes") who lived

Geological Time Chart and Development of Primates

Epoch	Millions of Years Ago	First Primates to Appear
Quarternary Period		
Holocene	Present	
Pleistocene	0.01–3*	
Glacial phase: 4		*Homo sapiens,* Neanderthal Man
3		*Homo erectus; Homo ergaster*
2		
1		*Homo habilis; Australopithecus* ("Lucy")
Tertiary Period		
Pliocene	3–12	
Miocene	12–28	Apelike forms
Oligocene	28–40	Monkeys
Eocene	40–60	Earliest primates: tarsierlike and lemurlike types

*The Pleistocene epoch probably lasted 2 to 3 million years and ended about 10,000 years ago.

in Africa were discovered in 1924. No more than 4 feet in height, *Australopithecus* had an erect posture but an apelike brain, with a cranial volume measuring no more than 500 cubic centimeters.

Over the past 40 years, our knowledge of hominids and their relation to the genus *Homo* has been growing rapidly. In December 1998 the world learned of the discovery in South Africa of a skeleton that could rewrite human history. Some 20 miles northwest of Johannesburg, in a limestone cave, paleontologists discovered a fossilized hominid 4 feet tall and some 3.5 million years old. Described as "probably the most momentous paleoanthropological find ever made in Africa," its virtually complete remains provide uniquely detailed information on the transition from ape to human. This Australopithecine hominid had heels adapted for standing upright, walked on two legs, and used distended big toes to climb trees. Once the entire fossil has been fully examined, the ratio of brain size to the rest of its body will help determine if the specimen is a direct ancestor of humans.[1]

The first representative of the genus *Homo*, which was to succeed the Australopithecines, had been discovered in 1960 by Louis S. B. Leakey at Olduvai Gorge in Tanzania at a site some 1.75 million years old. His find was less than 5 feet tall, weighed less than 100 pounds, walked erect, had a well-developed thumb, and had a cranial capacity of 656 cubic centimeters (considerably more than *Australopithecus*). Significantly, these fossil remains were found in association with crude tools—rocks cracked and flaked into shapes used to cut meat killed by lions and leopards. Leakey named his find *Homo habilis* ("skillful man").

The succeeding millennia were notable for changes in body structure and for complexifying the number of species in the human fossil record. In 1984 paleontologists discovered in northern Kenya a species recognizably like our own, as illustrated by a remarkably complete 1.6 million–year–old skeleton known as the Turkana Boy. These humans possessed an essentially modern body structure and gait and long and slender limbs, had brains double the size of those of apes (though not much above half the modern human average), and were capable of growing to 6 feet tall. The Boy and his relatives were initially assigned to a new and more advanced species, *Homo erectus*, but distinctive differences in braincase construction have given them a separate status, *Homo ergaster*.

Evidence of *Homo erectus* was discovered in 1891 in Java (Java Man) and in 1927 in China (Peking Man). Since the 1950s, many *Homo erectus* fossils, dating back at least 1.6 million years, have also been uncovered in Africa. *Erectus* was the first species of *Homo* to migrate out of Africa, into the Near East

Hominid footprints at Laetoli, Tanzania, document a child walking northward in the footsteps of a bipedal adult.

and Europe and eventually to the Pacific Ocean— probably, it is conjectured, because they were active hunters of wild game and sought ever-larger ranges. Recent evidence indicates that *Homo erectus* possibly took no more than 100,000 years to reach Java from Africa. Its members had a cranial volume larger than *Homo habilis* but much less than modern humans, whose brain capacity averages between 1300 and 1600 cubic centimeters. They were about 5 feet 6 inches tall and had heavy brows and a receding forehead. They developed the ability to control and use fire, a major step in mastering the environment and extending human habitation into colder latitudes— and this skill set humans apart from the rest of the natural world. They also perfected the first major standardized all-purpose tool, the hand ax, made by striking flakes from a flint stone that had been hardened in fire to make it flake easily. Its cutting edge could be as effective as steel for cutting meat. The hand ax remained a favored tool long after the extinction of *Homo erectus*, which occurred well before the end of the Pleistocene epoch, and the gradual emergence of modern humans, *Homo sapiens*.

From about 200,000 to 40,000 years ago, during the last ice age, the Neanderthals were the principal inhabitants of Europe and adjacent parts of Asia and Africa. Named after the Neander Valley in western Germany where their remains were unearthed, they were the first specimens of fossil humans to be

Aerial view of Olduvai Gorge in Tanzania, the site of findings by Mary and Louis S. B. Leakey, including the first representative fossils of the genus Homo.

found. Somewhat taller than 5 feet, the Neanderthals had sloping foreheads with prominent brow ridges and thickset bodies. They invented a variety of specialized stone tools and adapted to extreme cold by using fire, wearing furs, and living in caves and rock shelters. With their stone-tipped spears, they became able hunters.

Despite a brain size averaging slightly larger than our own, Neanderthals were long considered to be brutish, dimwitted, slouching creatures—the stereotypical "cave man" of modern cartoonists. Were they a subspecies of *Homo sapiens* or a separate species? Recent mitochondrial DNA testing of an arm bone from a Neanderthal skeleton (found in the Neander Valley in 1857) showed very little overlap with the DNA of *Homo sapiens*. The conclusion is that *Homo sapiens* and Neanderthals may have had a common ancestor, but the Neanderthals are definitely not a subspecies of *Homo sapiens*. Yet their similarities are noteworthy. If a Neanderthal "could be reincarnated and placed in a New York subway—provided he was bathed, shaved, and dressed in modern clothing—it is doubtful whether he would attract any more attention than some of its other denizens."[2]

The culminating phase of the development of the genus *Homo* occurred some 40,000 years ago when the Cro-Magnons replaced the Neanderthals in Europe. What happened to the latter can only be conjectured. Named after the locality in southern France where their bones were first unearthed in 1868, Cro-Magnon skeletons are virtually indistinguishable from human skeletons of today. Skillfully made flints and bone tools, along with polychrome paintings found on the walls of caves, reflect an advanced culture. By 20,000 B.C.E. Cro-Magnon and other representatives of *Homo sapiens* inhabited Europe, Asia, Africa, and Australia and had migrated across the Bering Strait into North America. Today there is but one existing species of the genus *Homo*.

Preliterate Cultures and Societies

In many respects we humans are eclipsed in physical endowments by numerous other creatures—in an all-species Olympic Games, we might never qualify for a medal. We cannot compete with the strength of the elephant or the speed of the antelope on land or any number of animals that live in the sea. Our ability to defy gravity is dwarfed by insects that can jump farther and higher in terms of their size, to say nothing of birds whose specialized structures enable them to fly and to soar. Nor can we claim to have the acute sight of a hawk. However, in certain particulars humans are biologically superior to other inhabitants of the earth. What are the essential attributes that enable our species to forge far ahead of all others? Erect posture is certainly one characteristic. Although other primates also possess opposable thumbs, in humans the thumb is longer and more powerful than in apes and monkeys, making it ideal for purposive action, such as making tools, where manual dexterity is mainly of cerebral origin. And although apes and monkeys have eyes capable of stereoscopic and color vision, apparently only humankind has the capacity for close visual attention.

Refined vision and manual dexterity result not solely from our muscular apparatus but in large part from our finely attuned nervous system. This nervous system, in which the brain is the vital hub, has enabled humans to outdo all other animals in both adjusting to our immediate environment and progressively modifying it to our own needs and goals. So significant are the size and multiple capabilities of the human brain as a factor differentiating us from other primates that it has been termed the "organ of civilization."

Human intelligence is also unique because of the quality this intelligence displays. It enables humans to reason and apply imagination and to make tools to a set and regular pattern. At the same time, we should recognize that many animals are also capable of solving problems in adjusting to their environments and display imagination in the process. Furthermore, some nonhuman primates are tool users or even engage in patterned tool manufacture. For example, chimpanzee bands in East Africa have been observed to make more than five types of tools, with the young learning how to fashion them by copying from their mothers.[3] But even though these primates can make tools, they lack a type of intelligence and imagination that functions by means of symbols, which seems to be unique to our species.

Like other creatures, humans possess a practical intelligence by which to make meaningful responses to the environment. In addition, however, we have the capability of both thinking and communicating symbolically. The principle of symbolism operates so as to give everything a name and to make its functioning universally applicable rather than restrict it to local or particular cases. A symbol is not only universal but also versatile, since the same meaning can be expressed in various languages or in different contexts with the same language. By means of this capability to engage in symbolic thought and communication, humankind has created patterns of behavior and learning that can be termed *culture*. Compared with other animals, we live also in a symbolic universe, with its new dimension of reality. "Language, myth, art, and religion are parts of this universe. They are the varied threads which weave the symbolic net, the tangled web of human experience. All human progress in thought and experience refines upon and strengthens this net."[4]

Dawn of Paleolithic Cultures

Benjamin Franklin is credited with first defining human beings as "toolmaking animals." Yet this attribute is based on a tradition that began in the Pleistocene epoch when a distinct evolution occurred in the use and manufacture of tools among hominids. Australopithecine sites in South Africa indicate that

while these contemporaries of early *Homo* may not have fashioned tools, they at least made use of objects as improvised tools or weapons. Improvisation would have played an important role also among the first humans—even as today some Native Australians carve wooden implements with naturally fractured stone pieces.

At this early stage we find *eoliths* ("dawn stones"), odd bits of stone picked up to perform an immediate job. This simple utilization of what was at hand has been described as the first of three major steps in the formative history of toolmaking. The second stage consisted of *fashioning*, the haphazard preparation of a tool as need arose. The third step was *standardization*, the making of implements according to certain set traditions.[5] It is with this third stage that we see the importance of symbolic thought in creating patterns of learning and behavior—as illustrated by the Acheulean hand ax, whose design was so uniform that specimens from southern Africa, Kenya, South India, and England's Thames Valley are nearly identical.

Since the fashioning of tools by striking pieces of rock with other stones was the most distinctive feature of humankind's earliest societies, the first stage in its cultural development is known as the Paleolithic, or Old Stone, Age. Strictly speaking, *Paleolithic* is a cultural and not a chronological term. In fact, much of our knowledge of Paleolithic culture comes from groups surviving into modern times—for example, indigenous peoples in the rain forests of Brazil. From an economic standpoint, the Paleolithic is also a food-collecting stage, when humans hunted, fished, and collected wild fruits, nuts, and berries on which to survive.

Let us consider a technological phenomenon associated with the invention and development of computers. Many of the first machines filled an entire room, and their capabilities were unreliable and limited. But scientists progressively miniaturized them while increasing their reliability and specialized capabilities. This is but the latest example of a phenomenon that recurs through the history of technology and began with the invention and subsequent sophistication of tools in Stone Age cultures.

At first, toolmaking was haphazard and associated with pebble tools, made of split pebbles or shattered chunks of stone the size of one's fist or a bit larger. Such occasional toolmaking has been substantiated by finds in early Pleistocene geological beds in Africa, including the Olduvai Gorge. Standardized toolmaking resulted in better-made pebble tools with sharp edges. Found at the Lake Rudolph site in East Africa, some 600 knifelike tools carefully fashioned from smooth volcanic rock date back 2.6 million years. Another early tradition occurred in East and South Asia, where Peking Man made standardized

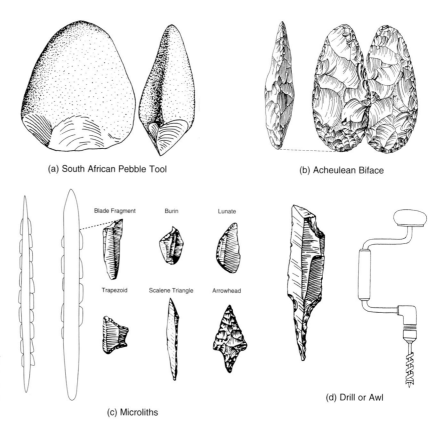

(a) South African Pebble Tool

(b) Acheulean Biface

Blade Fragment   Burin   Lunate

Trapezoid   Scalene Triangle   Arrowhead

(d) Drill or Awl

(c) Microliths

As human beings faced an ever-expanding set of challenges to their existence, they invented even more sophisticated tools, as evidenced by these examples of Paleolithic toolmaking.

chopper tools: broad heavy scrapers or cleavers and tools with an adzlike cutting edge.

The next standardized cultural tradition comprises core-biface tools. Here the implements are large pear-shaped pieces, made by flaking a stone slab around its edges from both sides. This produces a pointed core tool trimmed flat on the two opposite sides, or faces. The resulting hand ax (though the term may give an erroneous impression because to us an ax is not a pointed tool) was the first major standardized, all-purpose implement, equipped with two sharp cutting edges and employed probably as a hunter's knife as well as for chopping, cutting, scraping, and digging up grubs and roots. Hand axes, typified by the Acheulean tool industries in Europe, are associated with *Homo erectus*. They were "the predominant tool of a cultural tradition which not only spread over nearly one-fifth of the land area of the globe, but persisted for more than a hundred thousand years."[6]

Middle and Late Paleolithic Cultures

From about 70,000 to 35,000 years ago, the European and western Asian landscape was inhabited by Neanderthals who, as mentioned earlier, learned to adapt themselves to colder climatic conditions by living in caves and rock shelters. Their toolmaking industries involved the rudimentary beginnings of spe-

cialized tools and weapons. For example, the Neanderthals made side-scrapers, small heart-shaped hand axes, and invented stone-tipped spears to hunt their quarry.

About 35,000 B.C.E. the middle Paleolithic in Europe gave way to late Paleolithic cultures. By the end of the glacial phases, around 10,000 years ago, humans had inhabited Europe, western Asia, Africa, and Australia—and subsequently migrated into the Americas. *Homo sapiens*'s technology was marked by a wide range of new specialized tools and weapons. These included blade tools—narrow, parallel-sided flakes. The degree of toolmaking sophistication that had now been reached is marked by the invention of tools whose primary purpose was to make other tools. Noteworthy was the burin, shaped like a chisel, which worked bone, antlers, ivory, and wood into implements for particular purposes. The fashioning of small, specialized flints, known as *microliths*, represent a compact use of materials—indeed, the ancestor of present-day technological miniaturization. In late Paleolithic cultures, too, we find humans "taking to the air" by applying mechanical principles to the movement of weapons and tools. Throwers were made to launch spears; these worked on the lever principle and increased the propelling power of a hunter's arm. Late in this period, the bow was also invented, probably in North Africa. "It was the first means of concentrating muscular energy for the propulsion of an arrow, but it was soon discovered that it also provided a means of twirling a stick, and this led to the invention of the rotary drill."[7]

To withstand the cold weather, late Paleolithic peoples fashioned garments from sewn skins—bone needles with eyes, belt fashioners, and even buttons have been found in their sites—and they erected the first manmade buildings in areas where natural caves did not exist. The reindeer and mammoth hunters of what is present-day Russia lived in tents and huts made of hides and brush or in communal houses partially sunk into the ground with a mammoth's ribs for roof supports. There is also evidence that coal was used for fuel.

A special achievement of late Paleolithic cultures was their aesthetic expression. In 1879 a Spanish nobleman named Sautuola discovered a long procession of magnificently drawn bison on the ceiling of a cave on his Altamira estate in northern Spain. Archaeologists scoffed at Sautuola's discovery: the paintings were "too modern" and "too realistic." In a few years, however, Sautuola was vindicated with the discovery of more than a hundred Cro-Magnon caves in Spain and France, dating from about 28,000 to 10,000 B.C.E. In those caves were found animated paintings of bison, reindeer, primitive horses, and other animals, colored in shades of black, red, yellow, and brown.

Cave art rivals that of civilized artists not only stylistically but also as an expression of significant human experience. Universal in appeal, the drawings reflect a complete dependence on game animals and

success in hunting them. By drawing pictures of food animals—sometimes shown pregnant or pierced by spears and arrows—the artists may have believed that they could wield a magical power over the spirits of animals to ensure their multiplication. "A clue to the meaning of cave art can perhaps be obtained from the famous dancing figure found in Les Trois Frères in the Ariège. . . . It is a painting in black of a bearded figure wearing a mask and antlers of a red deer, the skin of a horse or wolf and a long, bushy tail. The suggestion that the dance was part of a magic ritual is inescapable."[8] Paleolithic artists also chiseled pictures on rock and bone and modeled figures out of clay.

Mesolithic, or Transitional, Cultures

Sweeping climatic changes that ended the fourth glacial phase initiated the Holocene, or Recent, epoch. With the final retreat of glaciers about 10,000 years B.C.E, alterations in the sea level greatly changed coastlines, and dense forests replaced areas in Europe marked previously by sparse vegetation, or tundra. Because of their highly specialized adaptation to cold weather, the reindeer moved north, and the hairy mammoth and other animals hunted by late Paleolithic peoples became extinct. The savannas of the Near East and North Africa were transformed into deserts dotted with occasional oases.

Humans adjusted to postglacial conditions by developing new cultures called Mesolithic, or Transitional. In Europe, many of these Mesolithic groups

The Conception of Space in Primeval Art

Primeval art never places objects in an immediate surrounding. Primeval art has no background. This is apparent in such large murals as the ceiling of Altamira as well as the small ritual objects of *art mobilier.* It is inherent in the prehistoric conception of space: all linear directions have equal right, and likewise all surfaces, whether they be regular or irregular. They can be tilted at any angle to the horizon throughout the entire 360-degree range. Animals that to us appear to be standing on their heads do not appear inverted to the eye of primeval man, because they existed, as it were, in space free from forces of gravity. . . .

The complete freedom and independence of vision of primeval art has never since been attained. It was its distinguishing characteristic. In our sense, there was no up and no down, no above and no below. Whether an animal appeared in a vertical position or in any other position was irrelevant to the eye of pre-

historic man. Nor was there a clear distinction or separation of one object from another. . . . Violent juxtaposition in size as well as in time were accepted as a matter of course. All was displayed within an eternal present, the perpetual interflow of today, yesterday, and tomorrow. . . .

Whether one looks at the Hall of the Hieroglyphs of Pech-Merle, with its intertwining figurations, or at the Altamira ceiling, with its powerful sequence of animals intimately associated with undecipherable symbols, the space conception of primeval art remains the same. It is not chaos. It approaches rather to the order of the stars, which move about in endless space, unconfined and universal in their relations.

From Sigfried Giedion, *The Eternal Present: The Beginnings of Art,* Bollingen Series 35.6.1 (New York: Pantheon Books, 1962), pp. 532–538.

lived along the coasts, fishing, seal-hunting, and gathering shellfish. Whereas Paleolithic peoples lived a largely nomadic life, Mesolithic groups followed a semisedentary existence, as attested by the large mounds of seashells and other debris, known as *kitchen middens,* found in Denmark and elsewhere along the Baltic seacoast. Other Mesolithic peoples lived inland, where in the plentiful forests they chopped wood with stone axes equipped with handles, made bows and arrows for hunting, and devised such forms of transport as skis, sleds, and dugout canoes. To provide propulsion for these sleds, our Mesolithic forebears domesticated the dog—the first of the many animals brought into a special symbiotic relationship with humans.

Mesolithic peoples were not able to produce their own food supply. However, while some groups retained the traditional food-gathering pattern of existence in Europe, Africa, and Australia, others—in southwestern Asia, for example—augmented their food resources with edible grasses that they found growing seasonally. Here a significant transition began to take place: the shift toward a food-producing economy, associated with the Neolithic Age. Paleolithic and Mesolithic peoples were hunters and fishers; our Neolithic ancestors were also farmers and herdsmen. The overall result comprised what has been described as the "first economic revolution"—and in the view of some scholars, perhaps the most far-reaching breakthrough in the ever-dynamic relationship of our species with its physical environment.

The Neolithic Revolution and the Advent of Agriculture

Neolithic cultures are usually characterized by the cultivation of grains, domestication of animals, pottery making, and use of polished stone tools (hence the name Neolithic, or New Stone, Age applied to these cultures). Actually, all four characteristics are not always present in a given Neolithic culture. Furthermore, certain advances usually associated with the Neolithic had been anticipated by Mesolithic groups (such as the domestication of dogs). Like *Paleolithic, Neolithic* is a technological and economic stage rather than an age or chronological period. For example, whereas Neolithic settlements in the Near East date back some 9000 years, the domestication of animals in Britain did not occur until thousands of years later.

Remains of a community dating to between 8000 and 6000 B.C.E.—older than any previously known settlement—have been unearthed at Jericho. Whereas early farming settlements were mainly small villages of 100 or 200 people, Jericho's location at an oasis enabled it to occupy an area of 74 acres, and it was protected by an enclosing fortification

wall as early as 7000 B.C.E.[9] Farming was possible because wild grains grew well there, and the local spring provided a continuous source of water.

Some authorities hold, however, that agriculture originated not at oases but in sites, such as Jarmo and Hassuna, in the mountainous uplands of what is now northern Iraq. Jarmo's 250 people lived in 20 mud-walled houses, reaped their grain with stone sickles, stored their food in stone bowls, and possessed domesticated goats, sheep, and dogs. Later levels of settlement contain evidence of domesticated pigs and clay pottery. The many tools made of obsidian, a volcanic rock from beds 300 miles away, indicate that a primitive form of commerce must have existed.

The wild ancestors of wheat and barley are thought to be highland forms—rainfall was greater there than on the arid lowlands—and wildlife was abundant. Neolithic farmers generally settled near a reliable water supply and combined agriculture with additional sources of food. The domestication of animals provided ready food, clothing, and transport. Tending herds instead of having to hunt them made a more settled existence possible. In southern Asia, in turn, water buffalo and elephants were domesticated, as were the llama and alpaca in the Peruvian highlands.

The best-preserved early village so far uncovered is Çatal Hüyük in southern Turkey, first excavated in 1961. This 32-acre site, occupied shortly before 6000 B.C.E., contains some of the most advanced features of Neolithic culture: pottery, woven textiles, mud-brick houses, shrines honoring a mother goddess, and plastered walls decorated with murals and carved reliefs.

Domestic Skills, Economic and Social Changes

Neolithic artisans ground and polished stones to produce axes, adzes, and chisels with strong and sharp cutting edges. They devised methods for drilling holes in stone, used boulders for grinding grain, and made stone bowls for storage. These stone artifacts show a much greater interest in design than had previously been the case. Moreover, when Neolithic peoples ceased to roam in search of food, they were better able to make pottery in quantity and to decorate it with geometric designs. Clothing and baskets had been fashioned in pre-Neolithic cultures, but the pattern of Neolithic life gave women more time to develop skills in the domestic arts. Similarly, Neolithic men paid more attention to the art of constructing shelters than their semisedentary Mesolithic forebears did. In Europe, where wood was abundant, rectangular timber houses were constructed; some had two rooms, a gabled roof, and walls of split saplings.

Discovery Through Maps

Oldest Known Map: Çatal Hüyük

This wall painting is perhaps the oldest known map. It is also, for modern viewers, one of the most easily understood ancient maps. It is a city plan painted on two walls of a room in a Neolithic community in south-central Anatolia, near what is still the major land route in Turkey between Europe and the Near East. Radiocarbon dating has placed the image around 6200 B.C.E. It is a very large figure, nearly 9 feet wide.

By the 1960s archaeologists had uncovered 139 rooms in the complex and decided that at least 40 were used for special rites, probably of a religious nature. One of these special rooms, whose walls had often been replastered, contained this large image featuring rows of boxlike shapes. Archaeologists were amazed at the similarity between their own carefully drawn site maps and the painting on the wall. It soon became apparent that the Neolithic image was a map of the community or perhaps of the town that immediately preceded the one the dig was uncovering.

A great deal of information can be gleaned from this map:

- The town site was on a slope, with rows of houses or buildings set on graded terraces.
- The rectangular buildings and the streets set at right angles provide a gridiron look that has characterized much town planning throughout history.
- The elongated, or linear, pattern of the settlement may reflect an orientation to a major road.
- The large figure that looks like a mountain with two peaks beyond the town is, no doubt, Hasan Dāg, a volcano that was active until about 2000 B.C.E. The volcano was the source of the obsidian that was the basis of the settlement's wealth. The glassy, volcanic rock was used for making cutting tools, knives, scrapers, weapons, jewelry, ornaments, and a variety of other artifacts.

The complete map contains about 80 rooms or buildings, somewhat fewer structures than were found in the actual town that was excavated. Since the wall was replastered several times, perhaps the map was "updated." Or it may have served a ceremonial purpose for which the absolute accuracy of a civic map was unnecessary.

Remains found near Swiss lakes show that even on soft, swampy earth the builders could erect houses by placing them on wooden foundations or on piles sunk into the ground.

Neolithic cultures brought profound economic and social changes. Paleolithic and Mesolithic peoples could not develop any permanent settlements or accumulate an excess of food, whereas a food-producing economy was radically different. By cultivating plants and breeding stock, villagers could now add to the food traditionally acquired by hunting. As a consequence, they greatly increased their control over the external environment. Also, a food-producing way of life that required permanent settlements enabled larger populations to be sustained. Any food surplus could be put aside for planting the following year's crops or was available to trade for commodities not produced locally. In addition, this food surplus helped support specialists who could now engage full time in toolmaking and other crafts.

Inevitably, the culture pattern was becoming more complex and interdependent. Within the community, a division of labor existed between the sexes. While the men made the tools and weapons, tended the herds, hunted, and built the dwellings, the women grew and prepared the food, wove baskets, fashioned clothing and pottery, and reared the young. Social anthropologists have found a strong correlation between communal ownership and female rights and high status, on the one hand, and individual ownership and male dominance, on the other. The first of these connections existed in early Neolithic times, as reflected in a social order in which descent was matrilineal (through the mother's line) and domicile was matrilocal (the husband lived with his wife's family or clan). "Indeed, it is tempting to be convinced that the earliest Neolithic societies throughout their range in time and space gave woman the highest status she has ever known. The way of life and its values, the skills demanded, were ideally suited to her."[10]

Each Neolithic village was largely self-supporting, growing its own food and using local materials for its tools, weapons, and houses. Because the people in Neolithic settlements had only limited contacts with the outside world, each village tended to develop its own localized culture. This condition of isolation permitted two types of settlement at different cultural and technological stages—a Mesolithic and a Neolithic, for example—to coexist for centuries with little interchange and consequently few modifications in their respective patterns of living.

The Neolithic revolution spread from its regional origins to the Balkan Peninsula by 5000 B.C.E., to Egypt and central Europe by 4000 B.C.E., and to Britain and northwestern India by 3000 B.C.E. The Neolithic cultures of western and northeastern Africa, Mesoamerica, and the Andes are later independent developments; cultural transference between the Near East and China is now doubted.

Preliterate Thought and Customs

Perhaps it is natural for most of us, living in a highly complex urban and mechanized society, to assume that preliterate peoples, ancient or modern, would possess few laws, little education, and only the simplest codes of conduct. But this is far from true. The organization of preliterate societies may have been as complex as our own. Rules regarding the role of parents, the treatment of children, the punishment of evildoers, the conduct of business, the worship of divine beings, and the conventions of eating and recreation have existed for scores of millennia, along with methods to influence or coerce individual members of society to do the "correct thing."

We cannot know with certainty about features of early peoples that are not apparent from the remains of tools and other objects. But we can speculate about these preliterate cultures by applying the conclusions that anthropologists have drawn from studies of present-day nonliterate societies. Yet a word of caution is necessary. That the general level of technological development in a modern-day nonliterate society appears to be similar to the stage reached in an ancient one does not mean that all aspects of the two cultures are comparable. Furthermore, it is often dif-

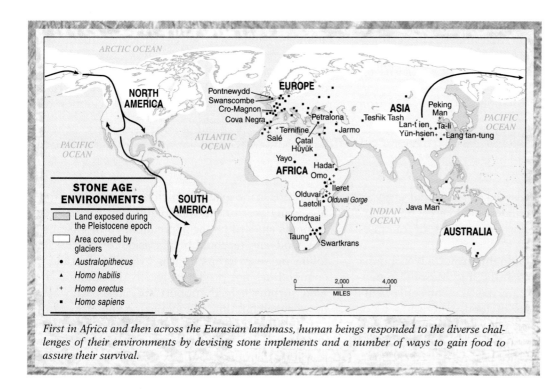

First in Africa and then across the Eurasian landmass, human beings responded to the diverse challenges of their environments by devising stone implements and a number of ways to gain food to assure their survival.

ficult to measure to what degree modern nonliterate societies have been affected by literate ones.

Forms of Social Organization

Among all peoples, past and present, the basic social unit appears to be the *elementary family*—parents and their offspring. Anthropologists cannot be certain what marriage customs were prevalent in the earliest societies, but monogamy was probably most common. The *extended family*—an individual family together with a circle of related persons who usually trace their descent through their mothers and are bound together by mutual loyalty—is often found in primitive social groupings. The extended family strengthens the elementary unit both in obtaining food and in protecting its members against other groups. Land is communally owned but allocated to separate families. Because of its economic and social advantages, this form of organization probably existed in ancient times.

A third preliterate social unit is the *clan*—a group of individuals within a community who believe that they have a common ancestor and therefore are "of one blood, of one soul." A clan is patrilineal if its members trace their relationship through the male line, matrilineal if through the female. Many preliterate peoples identify their clans by a *totem*—an animal or some natural object—that is revered and made the subject for amulets of various sorts. Nearly everyone is acquainted with the totem poles made by the Indians of British Columbia and Alaska. Forms of totemism in modern-day society include the insignia worn by a particular military unit, the emblems of such organizations as the Elks and Moose, and animal mascots used by college football teams.

A fourth grouping among some preliterate peoples is the *tribe*. This term lacks a precise definition, but it may be thought of as a community characterized by a common speech or distinctive dialect, a common cultural heritage, and a specific inhabited territory. Group loyalty is a strong trait among members of a tribe, and it is often accompanied by contempt for the peoples and customs of other communities.

Collective Responsibility in Law and Government

In preliterate societies, ethical behavior consists of not violating custom. The close relationships that exist in extended families and clans encourage conformity. Justice among individuals of a primitive group is synonymous with maintaining equilibrium. If one person steals another's property, the economic equilibrium has been disturbed. Such a theft constitutes a wrong against the victim; but where modern legal procedure calls for punishment of the thief, in these societies justice is achieved by a settlement between the injured person and the thief. If the latter restores what has been stolen or its equivalent, the victim is satisfied and the thief is not punished. More serious offenses, like murder and wounding, are also private matters, to be avenged by the next of kin on the principle of "an eye for an eye." Certain acts, however, are considered dangerous to the whole group and require punishment by the entire community. Treason, witchcraft, and incest are typical offenses in this category. Such acts cannot be settled by compensation; the punishment meted out is usually death. If a clan member gets into trouble too often, others will regard that person as a social nuisance and an economic liability, to be banished from the group or even executed.

Scholars theorize that in food-gathering and the earliest food-producing societies, as in nonliterate societies today, the governing political body was small and egalitarian. The adults participated in the decisions of the group, with special deference being paid to the views of older tribal members because of their greater experience and knowledge of the community's traditions and ceremonies. Serious decisions, such as going to war or electing a chief, required the consent of a general assembly of all adult males. The elected chief of the tribe was pledged to rule in accordance with custom and in consultation with the council of elders. Because of the strong element of representation present, this early form of government has been called "primitive democracy." Among more advanced food-producing communities, however, government tended to fall increasingly under the control of the richest members. In time there emerged strong individuals claiming political and religious leadership; we shall encounter them in the following chapters on early civilizations.

Religion and Magic

Perhaps the strongest single force in the life of preliterate peoples, past and present, is religion. Religious sensibilities apparently originated in feelings of awe that arose as our ancestors became conscious of the universe about them. Awe and wonder led to the belief, usually called *animism*, that life exists in everything in nature—winds, stones, trees, animals, and humans themselves. A natural extension is a belief in the existence of spirits separable from material bodies. Many spirits became objects of reverence, the human spirit being among the first. Neanderthal people placed food and implements alongside their carefully buried dead, an indication that they believed in an afterlife and treated their forebears with affection and respect.

We know also that late Paleolithic people revered the spirits of the animals they hunted for food, as

Stone Age fertility figurines have been throught the world. Shown here are three examples dating from around 25,000 B.C.E.: the limestone Venus of Willendorf, a mammoth ivory carving from Russia, and the ivory Venus of Lespugue.

well as the spirit of fertility on which both human and animal life depended. Such reverence was associated with totemism and in particular with the worship of a fertility deity, the Earth Mother (or Mother Goddess), who is known to us from many carved and modeled female figures with exaggerated sexual features. These fertility figurines have been excavated from Stone Age sites all over the world.

At Çatal Hüyük, 33 representations of the Mother Goddess have been found, but only eight of a god. The latter represented either the son of the goddess or her consort. The relative scarcity of male deities, together with evidence that the cult of the goddess was administered by priestesses rather than by priests, supports the view that women occupied a central position in Neolithic society.

Closely associated with primitive religion is the practice of magic. In addition to revering spirits, primitive people wanted to compel them to provide favors. For this purpose they employed magic. They turned to shamans to ward off droughts, famines, floods, and plagues through what they believed to be magic powers of communication with the spirits.

Neolithic "Science"

Traditionally, magic has been regarded as diametrically opposed to science. The former claims supernatural powers over natural forces, whereas the latter rejects any such determinism and studies natural phenomena by open-ended methods in its search for general laws. Yet as scholars are increasingly recognizing, both preliterate peoples and scientists believe that nature is orderly and that what is immediately apprehended by the senses can be systematically

classified. For example, the Hanunóo of the Philippines have recorded 461 animal types and have classified insect forms into 108 named categories, including 13 for ants and termites. They have more than 150 terms for the parts and properties of plants, which provide categories for "discussing the hundreds of characteristics which differentiate plant types and often indicate significant features of medicinal or nutritional value."[11]

Examples like these can be found in Stone Age societies all over the world. They point to the overall conclusion that the efforts of these "primitive" investigators and classifiers were not directed solely to economic or "useful" ends. Rather, plants and animals were deemed to be of value and interest in their own right, in turn inspiring a desire for knowledge for its own sake. The great contributions of Stone Age men and women—domestication of plants and animals, invention of tools, pottery, and weaving—involved centuries of methodical observation and often-repeated experiments. "This thirst for objective knowledge is one of the most neglected aspects of the thought of people we call 'primitive.' Even if it is rarely directed toward facts of the same level as those with which modern science is concerned, it implies comparable intellectual application and methods of observation. In both cases the universe is an object of thought at least as much as it is a means of satisfying needs."[12]

Further indications of the desire by early people to acquire knowledge have been provided by studies of Neolithic large stone monuments *(megaliths)*. The megalithic complex of Stonehenge in England has traditionally been considered a religious structure. However, an American astronomer, aided by a computer, found an "astonishing" number of correlations between the alignments of recognized Stonehenge positions—stones, holes, mounds—and the solar and lunar positions around 1500 B.C.E., when Stonehenge was built.[13] This knowledge would assist in developing a more accurate calendar, particularly useful when it came to planting crops.

The construction of Neolithic astronomical structures had occurred long before Stonehenge. Ancient sandstone monuments in southern Egypt indicate that their builders possessed a surprisingly complex knowledge of geometry and astronomy. These monuments are between 5000 and 7000 years old and represent the earliest known astronomical complex. A satellite survey of the Nabta Playa depression shows slabs in various configurations, including a circle that would have allowed the inhabitants to anticipate sunrise during the summer solstice. The ceremonial complex has alignments to cardinal and solstitial directions, while five alignments within the playa deposits radiate outward from megalithic structures, which may have served funerary purposes. The area would

Skara Brae in the Orkney Islands is an excellent example of a late Neolithic settlement that dates from 1500 B.C.E.

have been partly submerged by monsoon floodwaters during rainy seasons at the time; this placement suggests that the site may have been primarily "an expression of the interconnections between sun, water, death, and the fertile earth."[14]

Conclusion

Scientists and religionists have long debated who or what was responsible for the origin of our universe. Although evidence for evolution appears overwhelming, the theory does not preclude the presence of a guiding intelligence responsible for both the universe's creation and our planet's geological and biological development, culminating in the intelligence and behavior of our own species. During vast geological ages, organic life developed from single-celled organisms to multicelled creatures of extraordinary complexity. The earliest primates appeared in the Tertiary period. During the Oligocene epoch, different lines of monkeys and primitive forms of anthropoid apes evolved. Before the end of the Miocene epoch, one line of apes developed into tree-dwellers; another led to the ground-dwelling hominids, or prehumans. A considerable gap exists in our knowledge of prehuman development during the following Pliocene epoch.

The Pleistocene epoch provides us with rich data on the evolution of the genus *Homo*. In Africa emerged an apelike hominid, *Australopithecus,* that is not in modern mankind's line of descent. There was also *Homo habilis,* associated with the earliest

making of tools. Next appeared the *Homo erectus* group, including both Java Man and Peking Man, followed by Neanderthal Man and *Homo sapiens.* With their ability to think and communicate in symbolic terms, coupled with a toolmaking capability, early humans began, slowly but progressively, to acquire control over their terrestrial environment and in so doing to lay the foundations for the technological order so dominant in our lives today.

Thus paralleling its biological evolution began the first great period of humankind's cultural evolution, called the Paleolithic, or Old Stone, Age. We have seen how our ancestors' toolmaking capability advanced from reliance on very simple implements—such as the standardized, all-purpose hand ax, in use for 100,000 years or longer—to ever more specialized and sophisticated tools and techniques of operation. This technological evolution enabled *Homo* in turn to move into and adapt to different environments, whether the higher latitudes of Eurasia and North America, the rain forests of Southeast Asia, or the deserts of Australia. By the end of the last glacial phase, our forebears had spread over most of the world, and in the postglacial period they developed a semisedentary form of existence as found in the Mesolithic, or Transitional, cultures.

Paleolithic and Mesolithic cultures had food-gathering economies. Then, perhaps around 10,000 years ago, the Neolithic, or New Stone, Age emerged with the appearance of food-producing communities in western Asia and elsewhere. Neolithic cultures are usually characterized by the cultivation of grains, the domestication of animals, pottery making, and the fashioning of polished stone tools. These advances occurred in various places on earth and at different times. The revolutionary change from a food-gathering to a food-producing type of economy made possible the next stage in humankind's cultural evolution, riverine civilizations.

Suggestions for Reading

For a comprehensive and attractively written account of the human fossil record, the evolution of the human brain and cognitive powers, and the significance of lithic art, see Ian Tattersall, *Becoming Human: Evolution and Human Uniqueness* (Harcourt Brace, 1998); this might also be read in conjunction with Donald C. Johanson and Blake Edgar, *From Lucy to Language* (Simon & Schuster, 1996).

Delta Willis, *The Hominid Gang: Behind the Scenes in the Search for Human Origins* (Viking, 1989), is a popular account of the state of the art of human paleontology. Brian Fagan, *World Prehistory: A Brief Introduction* (HarperCollins, 1993), and J. Cowlett, *Ascent to Civilization: The Archeology of Early Man* (Knopf, 1984), are brief conventional accounts. See also Richard E. Leakey, *The Making of Mankind* (Michael Joseph, 1981); an interesting account of the life and work of his father, Louis S. B. Leakey, discoverer of *Homo habilis*, is found in the elder Leakey's book *By the Evidence: Memoirs, 1932–1951* (Harcourt Brace, 1974).

On genetic research and human origins, see Robert Shapiro, *The Human Blueprint: The Race to Unlock the Secret of Our Genetic Script* (St. Martin's Press, 1991). On human evolution and the spread of humankind from Africa to the rest of the world, see Noel T. Boaz, *Eco Homo: How the Human Being Emerged from the Cataclysmic History of the World* (Harper-Collins, 1997); Jared Diamond, *The Third Chimpanzee: The Evolution and Future of the Human Animal* (HarperCollins, 1992); Roger Lewin, *Bones of Contention: Controversies in the Search for Human Origins* (Simon & Schuster, 1987); Christopher Stringer and Robin McKie, *African Exodus: The Origins of Modern Humanity* (Henry Holt, 1997); and Alan Walker and Pat Shipman, *The Wisdom of the Bones: In Search of Human Origins* (Knopf, 1996).

Two works dealing with the origins of toolmaking in a broad cultural matrix are Kenneth P. Oakley, "Skill as a Human Possession," in *A History of Technology*, Vol. 1 (Clarendon Press, 1956), and Robert J. Braidwood, *Prehistoric Men* (Scott, Foresman, 1967); both are well illustrated with pictures of lithic implements, from pebble tools to microliths. For two accounts of perhaps the most famous of all megaliths, see Rodney Castleden, *The Making of Stonehenge* (Routledge, 1993), and Gerald S. Hawkins and John B. White, *Stonehenge Decoded* (Dell, 1966). An interesting and informative analysis of an early key Neolithic settlement is found in James Mellaart, *Çatal Hüyük: A Neolithic Town in Anatolia* (McGraw-Hill, 1967). On early communities, see Tim Megarry, *Society in Prehistory: The Origins of Human Culture* (New York University Press, 1995), and Jared Diamond, *Guns, Germs, and Steel: The Fates of Human Societies* (Norton, 1997).

Fundamental forms of expression in primeval art, symbolization, the role of animals, depiction of the human figure (including fertility figurines), and the conception of space in prehistory are dealt with in detail in Sigfried Giedion's profusely illustrated book *The Eternal Present: The Beginnings of Art* (Pan-theon, 1962). For a study of religious concepts in Stone Age art and their influence on European thought, see Gertrude Rachel Levy, *The Gate of Horn* (Faber & Faber, 1948). The role and significance of the Earth Mother cult in lithic cultures is analyzed and illustrated in Erich Neumann, *The Great Mother: An Analysis of the Archetype* (Pantheon, 1963), and perceived within a feminist critique in the opening chapters of Riane Eisler, *The Chalice and the Blade: Our History, Our Future* (Harper & Row, 1987). On religion and rock art, see David Lewis-Williams and Thomas Dowson, *Images of Power: Understanding Bushman Rock Art* (Southern Book Publishers, 1989), and David Lewis-Williams, *Believing and Seeing: Symbolic Meanings in Southern San Rock Paintings* (Academic Press, 1981).

Suggestions for Web Browsing

Fossil Hominids: Mary Leakey
http://www.talkorigins.org/faqs/homs/mleakey.html/

Discussion, with images, of the life and findings of one of the twentieth century's most famous archaeologists. Links to husband Louis Leakey, son Richard Leakey, Olduvai Gorge, and fossil findings.

Human Prehistory: An Exhibition
http://users.hol.gr/~dilos/prehis.htm

Walk through six rooms of text and vivid images that discuss the works of Lyell, Huxley, and Darwin; the first humans; the first human creations; the first villages, including Çatal Hüyük; and artworks of Neolithic Greece.

Chauvet Cave
http://www.culture.fr/culture/arcnat/chuvet/en/gvpda-d.htm

A French government site on a major discovery of prehistoric cave art. Contains information about the findings and many views of cave paintings at both this location and others in France.

Neanderthal Museum
http://www.neanderthal.de/

Site of a German museum whose goals are to maintain and popularize the cultural heritage of the Neanderthals.

Notes

1. BBC World Service, Dec. 10, 1998.
2. Richard E. Leakey, *The Making of Mankind* (London: Michael Joseph, 1981), p. 148.
3. See Jane Goodall, "Chimpanzees on the Gombe Stream Reserve," in *Primate Behavior*, ed. Irven De Vore et al. (New York: Holt, Rinehart and Winston, 1965), pp. 425–473.
4. Ernst Cassirer, *An Essay on Man: An Introduction to a Philosophy of Human Culture* (New Haven, Conn.: Yale University Press, 1965), pp. 24–25.
5. Robert J. Braidwood, *Prehistoric Men*, 7th ed. (Chicago: Scott, Foresman, 1967), p. 34.
6. Kenneth P. Oakley, "Skill as a Human Possession," in *A History of Technology*, Vol. 1 (Oxford: Clarendon Press, 1956), p. 25.
7. Ibid., p. 33.
8. Stuart Piggott, ed., *The Dawn of Civilization* (London: Thames & Hudson, 1961), p. 28.

9. Colin Renfrew, "The Emergence of Civilization," in *The Encyclopedia of Ancient Civilizations,* ed. Arthur Cotterell (New York: Viking, 1980), p. 13.

10. Jacquetta Hawkes and Leonard Woolley, "History of Mankind: Cultural and Scientific Development," in *Prehistory and the Beginnings of Civilization,* Vol. 1 (Paris: UNESCO, 1963), p. 264. For more on the status of women in Neolithic cultures, see Riane Eisler, *The Chalice and the Blade: Our History, Our Future* (San Francisco: Harper & Row, 1987), ch. 1.

11. Harold C. Conklin, *The Relation of Hanunóo Culture to the Plant World,* doctoral dissertation, Yale University, 1954 (microfilm), p. 97.

12. Claude Lévi-Strauss, *The Savage Mind* (Chicago: University of Chicago Press, 1970), p. 3.

13. Gerald S. Hawkins and John B. White, *Stonehenge Decoded* (New York: Dell, 1966), pp. 117–118, cited approvingly in Jacques Briard, *The Bronze Age in Barbarian Europe: From the Megaliths to the Celts,* trans. Mary Turton (Boston: Routledge & Kegan Paul, 1979).

14. Rob Stein, *Archaeology: Astronomical Structures in Ancient Egypt* (Washington, D.C.: Washington Post Company, 1998); J. M. Malville, F. Wendorf, A. A. Mazar, and R. Schild, "Megaliths and Neolithic Astronomy in Southern Egypt," *Nature,* April 2, 1998.

Head of a bull (c. 2430 B.C.E.) fashioned of lapis lazuli, this finely made creature decorated a lyre, which was found in the Royal Cemetery at Ur.

Early Civilizations
The Near East and Western Asia

H istorians do not agree on how best to define the term *civilization*. But most would accept the view that a civilization is a culture that has attained a degree of complexity, characterized by urban life. In other words, a civilization is a culture capable of sustaining a great number of specialists to cope with the economic, social, political, and religious needs of a large social unit. Other hallmarks of civilization are a system of writing (originating from the need to keep records), monumental architecture in place of simple buildings, and art that is not merely decorative, like that on Neolithic pottery, but is representative of people and their activities. All these characteristics of civilization first appeared together in the southern part of Mesopotamia, the land called Sumer.

Mesopotamia: The First Civilization

Around 6000 B.C.E., after the agricultural revolution had begun to spread from its place of origin on the northern fringes of the Fertile Crescent, an area of rich soil stretching northeast from the Nile River to the Tigris in what is now northern Iraq and then southeast to the Persian Gulf, Neolithic farmers started filtering into the Fertile Crescent itself. Although this broad plain received insufficient regular rainfall to support agriculture, the eastern section benefited from the Tigris and

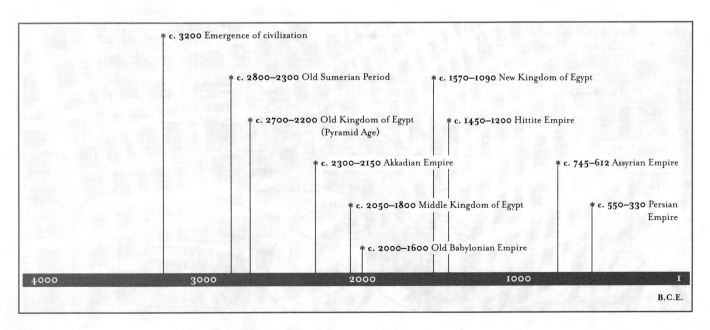

* **c. 3200** Emergence of civilization

* **c. 2800–2300** Old Sumerian Period

* **c. 1570–1090** New Kingdom of Egypt

* **c. 2700–2200** Old Kingdom of Egypt (Pyramid Age)

* **c. 1450–1200** Hittite Empire

* **c. 2300–2150** Akkadian Empire

* **c. 745–612** Assyrian Empire

* **c. 2050–1800** Middle Kingdom of Egypt

* **c. 550–330** Persian Empire

* **c. 2000–1600** Old Babylonian Empire

| 4000 | 3000 | 2000 | 1000 | I |

B.C.E.

Early Sumer and Akkad

c. 3200–2800 B.C.E.	Protoliterate period in Sumer
c. 2800–2300 B.C.E.	Old Sumerian period
c. 2370–2315 B.C.E.	Reign of Sargon of Akkad
c. 2300–2150 B.C.E.	Akkadian dominance
c. 2150–2000 B.C.E.	Neo-Sumerian period
c. 2000–1600 B.C.E.	Old Babylonian period
c. 1792–1750 B.C.E.	Reign of Hammurabi
c. 1595 B.C.E.	Sack of Babylon by Hittites

Euphrates Rivers as sources of irrigation. Known to the Greeks as Mesopotamia (Greek for "between the rivers"), the lower reaches of this plain, beginning near the point where the two rivers nearly converge, was called Babylonia. Babylonia included two geographical areas—Akkad in the north and Sumer, the delta of this river system, in the south.

Broken by river channels teeming with fish and refertilized frequently by alluvial silt laid down by uncontrolled floods, Sumer had tremendous agricultural potential if the environmental problems could be solved: swamps had to be drained, canals had to be dug to bring water to remote fields, and safeguards had to be constructed against flooding. In the course of the several successive cultural phases that followed the arrival of the first Neolithic farmers, these and other related problems were solved by co-operative effort. Between 3500 and 3100 B.C.E. the foundations were established for a type of economy and social order markedly different from anything previously known. This far more complex culture, based on large urban centers populated by interdependent and specialized workers, is what we associate with civilization.

Prelude to Civilization

Late Neolithic artisans discovered how to extract copper from oxide ores by heating them with charcoal. Then, about 3100 B.C.E., metal workers discovered that copper was improved by the addition of tin. The resulting alloy, bronze, was harder than copper and provided a sharper cutting edge. Thus the advent of civilization in Sumer is associated with the beginning of the Bronze Age, and this technology soon spread to Egypt, Europe, and Asia. The Bronze Age lasted until about 1200 B.C.E., when iron weapons and tools began to replace those made of bronze.

The first plow was probably a stick that the farmer pulled through the soil by a rope. In time,

however, domesticated cattle were harnessed to drag the plow. Yoked, harnessed oxen pulled plows in the Mesopotamian soil by 3000 B.C.E.

Since the Mesopotamian plain had no stone, no metals, and no timber except its soft palm trees, these materials had to be transported from Syria and Asia Minor. Water transport down the Tigris and Euphrates assisted this process. The oldest sailing boat known is represented by a model found in a Sumerian grave of about 3500 B.C.E. Soon after this date, wheeled vehicles appear in the form of war chariots drawn by donkeys.

Another important invention was the potter's wheel, first used in Sumer soon after 3500 B.C.E. Earlier, people had fashioned pots by molding or coiling clay by hand, but now a symmetrical product could be produced in a much shorter time. A pivoted clay disk heavy enough to revolve from its own momentum, the potter's wheel has been called the first true mechanical device.

The Emergence of Civilization in Sumer, c. 3200–2800 B.C.E.

By 3200 B.C.E. the population of Sumer had increased to the point where people were living in cities and had developed the majority of the characteristics of a civilization. Because these included the first evidence of writing, this first phase of Sumerian civilization, to about 2800 B.C.E., is called the Protoliterate period.

The Sumerian language is not related to Semitic or Indo-European, the major language families that appear later in the Near East. The original home of the Semitic-speaking peoples may have been the Arabian peninsula, and the Indo-Europeans seem to have migrated from regions around the Black and Caspian Seas. A third, much smaller language family, sometimes called Hamitic, included the Egyptians and other peoples of northeastern Africa.

Certain technical inventions of Protoliterate Sumer eventually made their way to both the Nile and the Indus valleys. Chief among these were the wheeled vehicle and the potter's wheel. The discovery in Egypt of cylinder seals similar in shape to those used in Sumer attests to contact between the two areas toward the end of the fourth millennium B.C.E. Certain early Egyptian art motifs and architectural forms are also thought to be of Sumerian origin. And it is probable that the example of Sumerian writing stimulated the Egyptians to develop a script of their own.

The symbols on the oldest Sumerian clay tablets, the world's first writing, were pictures of concrete things such as a person's face, a sheep, a star, or a measure of grain. Some of these pictographs also represented ideas; for example, the picture of a foot was used to represent the idea of walking, and a picture of a mouth joined to that for water meant "to

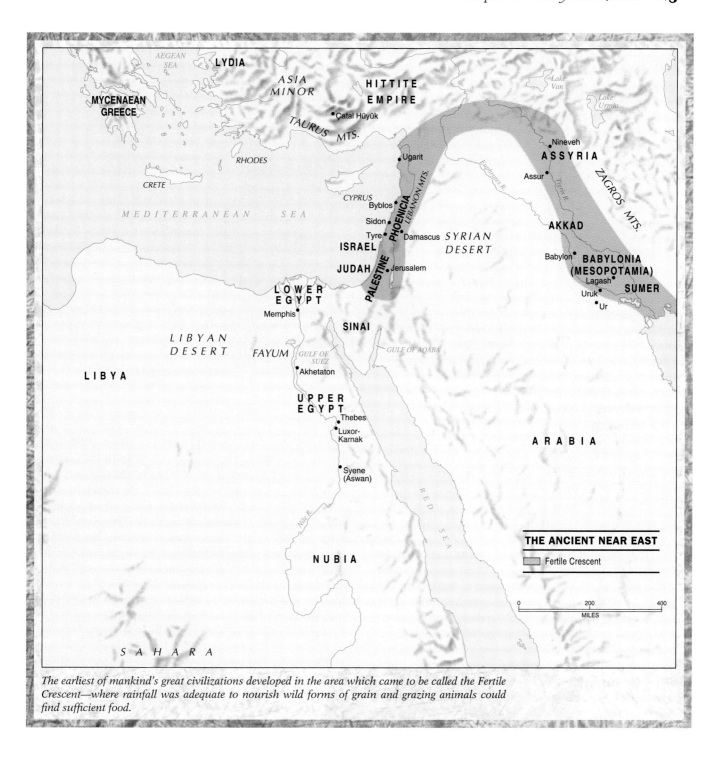

The earliest of mankind's great civilizations developed in the area which came to be called the Fertile Crescent—where rainfall was adequate to nourish wild forms of grain and grazing animals could find sufficient food.

drink." This early pictographic writing developed into phonetic (or syllabic) writing when the scribes realized that a sign could represent a sound as well as an object or idea. Thus the personal name Kuraka could be written by combining the pictographs for mountain *(kur)*, water *(a)*, and mouth *(ka)*. By 2800 B.C.E. the use of syllabic writing had reduced the number of Sumerian signs from nearly 2000 to 600.

When writing, Mesopotamian scribes used a reed stylus to make wedge-shaped impressions in soft clay tablets. This *cuneiform* system of writing (from the Latin *cuneus,* "wedge") was adopted by many other peoples of the Near East, including the Babylonians, the Assyrians, the Hittites, and the Persians.

The Old Sumerian Period, c. 2800–2300 B.C.E.

By 2800 B.C.E. the Sumerian cities had fully emerged into complex civilizations. This first historical age, called the Old Sumerian period, was characterized by constant warfare as each city attempted to protect or

Discovery Through Maps

Map of Nippur

Why do we make maps? Certainly one of the primary reasons is to establish one's perception of the world graphically—to give ourselves a security of knowing where we are located and what surrounds us. Our ancestors probably made maps before they invented any other form of written communication. But dating very old maps is a difficult task, for much of the record has been lost to the ravages of time.

Many of the world's oldest maps come to us from the ruins of Mesopotamia and from ancient Anatolia, the region now known as Turkey. These maps are most commonly engraved on clay tablets, and most vary greatly in scale—from very small perceptions of the world to larger inscriptions describing local features, such as a particular city or even individual fields or buildings. Scholars still are unsure as to the antiquity of many of these early efforts at cartography; dates given for some Mesopotamian maps may vary by as much as 1500 years, and the interpretation of their contents, size, symbols, and even colors differs widely.

One of the oldest examples of mapmaking is the Babylonian clay tablet inscribed with a map of Nippur. That ancient city, near the old capital of Babylon, was an important religious center for both the Sumerians and the Babylonians, who believed that Nippur was the holy city of their god Enlil. On the right side of the tablet can be found the temple and its storehouses, a park enclosed by a wall. The Euphrates River runs through the city, and two canals branch off from it—one leading to fields on the right side of the tablet and the other running through the center of the city. A wall encloses the city, and seven gates, each one named, are depicted. Archaeologists who study the ancient site of Nippur believe that this map was drawn to scale—if so, this tablet is our earliest known town plan drawn to such scale. The primary purpose of the map is not known, although a good possibility is that the map was intended to help in repairing the defenses of the city's walls.

enlarge its land and guarantee its access to water and irrigation. Each city-state was a theocracy, for the chief local god was believed to be the actual ruler. The god's earthly representative was the *ensi*, the high priest and city governor, who acted as the god's caretaker in both religious and civil functions. Though given the power to act for the god by virtue of being the human agent or the divine ruler, the ensi was not himself considered a divine being.

The ensis were powerful and sometimes autocratic rulers. Most familiar is the semilegendary Gilgamesh, ruler of Uruk about 2700 B.C.E., who is

known only from several epic tales. Like all Sumerian monarchs, Gilgamesh had to contend with the frequent opposition of the nobility who sat in his council. "The nobles of Uruk are gloomy in their chambers," begins the *Epic of Gilgamesh*, because "day and night is unbridled his [Gilgamesh's] arrogance." They appeal to the gods to create a hero who will be a "match" for Gilgamesh: "Let them contend, that Uruk may have peace." This tactic fails when the two heroes, after fighting to a draw, become fast friends. In another epic tale, Gilgamesh is able to overcome the refusal of his council to approve his decision not to submit to the ensi of Kish. He appeals to "the convened assembly of the men of his city," who readily support him: "Do not submit to the house of Kish, let us smite it with weapons."[1]

Early Sumerian society was highly collectivized, with the temples of the city god and subordinate deities assuming a central role. "Each temple owned lands which formed the estate of its divine owners. Each citizen belonged to one of the temples, and the whole of a temple community—the officials and priests, herdsmen and fishermen, gardeners, craftsmen, stonecutters, merchants, and even slaves—was referred to as 'the people of the god *X*.'"[2] The part of the temple land called "common" was worked by all members of the community, while the remaining land was divided among the citizens for their support at a rental of from one-third to one-sixth of the crop. Priests and temple administrators, however, held rent-free lands.

In addition to the temple lands, a considerable part of a city's territory originally consisted of land collectively owned by clans, kinship groups comprising a number of extended families. By 2600 B.C.E. these clan lands were becoming the private property of great landowners called *lugals* (literally, "great men"). Deeds of sale record the transfer of clan lands to private owners in return for substantial payments in copper to a few clan leaders and insignificant grants of food to the remaining clan members. These private estates were worked by "clients" whose status resembled that of the dependents of the temples.

In time, priests, administrators, and ensis began usurping temple land and other property and oppressing the common people. Their arrogance frequently led to the rise of despots who came to power on a wave of popular discontent. Since these despots were usually lugals, the term *lugal* became a political title and is generally translated as "king."

The Sumerian lugals made the general welfare their major concern. Best known is Urukagina, who declared himself lugal of Lagash near the end of the Old Sumerian period and ended the rule of priests and "powerful men," each of whom, he claimed, was guilty of acting "for his own benefit." Urukagina's inscriptions describe his many reforms and conclude: "He freed the inhabitants of Lagash from usury, burdensome controls, hunger, theft, murder, and seizure [of their property and persons]. He established freedom. The widow and the orphan were no longer at the mercy of the powerful man."[3]

The Sumerians, like their Mesopotamian successors, made extensive use of the institution of slavery, and slaves are recorded to have worked in many capacities—as farm and urban laborers, as servants in homes and temples, and in civic positions, such as in public administration. In certain cities, slaves accounted for 40 to 50 percent of the population. Slaves in Mesopotamia were not without rights, and in many cases they were treated with care. Slavery was not based on racial characteristics or cultural differences; people of the same culture became enslaved through conquest or to pay off debt. Perhaps because of the possibility that any city-state might be overtaken and its residents enslaved at the whims of the gods, the treatment of slaves in Mesopotamia seems generally to have been more humane than at other times and places in human history.

The Akkadian Period, c. 2300–2150 B.C.E.

Immediately north of Sumer lay the narrow region of Akkad, inhabited by Semites who had adopted much of Sumerian culture. Appearing late in the fourth millennium B.C.E., the Akkadians were among the earliest of the Semitic peoples who migrated into Mesopotamia from Arabia. A generation after Urukagina, Sargon I (2370–2315 B.C.E.),* an outstanding Akkadian ruler, conquered Sumer and went on to establish an empire that extended from the Persian Gulf almost to the Mediterranean Sea.

Very proud of his lower-class origins, Sargon boasted that his humble, unwed mother had been forced to abandon him: "She set me in a basket of rushes . . . [and] cast me into the river." Rescued and brought up by a gardener, Sargon rose to power through the army. As lugal, Sargon looked after the welfare of the lower classes and aided the rising class of private merchants. At the merchants' request, he once sent his army to far-off Asia Minor to protect a colony of them from interference by a local ruler. We are told that Sargon "did not sleep" in his efforts to promote prosperity and that in this new free enterprise economy, trade moved as freely "as the Tigris where it flows into the sea, . . . all lands lie in peace, their inhabitants prosperous and contented."[4]

Sargon's successors, however, were unable either to repel the attacks of less civilized mountain peoples or to overcome the desire for independence of the priest-dominated Sumerian cities. As a result, the dynasty founded by Sargon collapsed about 2150 B.C.E.

The Neo-Sumerian Period, c. 2150–2000 B.C.E.

Order and prosperity were restored by the lugals of the Third Dynasty of Ur. By creating a highly centralized administration in Sumer and Akkad, these rulers solved the problem of internal rebellion that had been of such concern for Sargon and his successors. The formerly temple-dominated cities became provinces administered by closely regulated governors. Religion became an arm of the state: the high priests were state appointees, and the temple economic organization was used as the state's agent in

Akkadian art is noted for its realism, perhaps best illustrated by this life-size head, cast in bronze, found at Nineveh and often conjectured to be Sargon. The head was deliberately mutilated in antiquity.

rigidly controlling the newly developing free enterprise economy that Sargon had encouraged.

At the head of this bureaucratic state stood the lugal of Ur, now considered a living god and celebrated in hymns as a heaven-sent authority who "brings splendor to the land, . . . savior of orphans whose misery he relieves, . . . the vigilant shepherd who conducts the people unto cooling shade."[5] Much of what we call social legislation was passed by these "vigilant shepherds." Their objective was the righting of wrongs that were not covered by the old customary law (*nig-ge-na*, "truth"), because the prologue to the law code of Ur-Nammu, founder of the dynasty, declared that it was the king's purpose to see that "the orphan did not fall a prey to the wealthy" and that "the man of one shekel did not fall a prey to the man of one mina [sixty shekels]."[6]

Disaster struck Ur about 2000 B.C.E., when Elamites from what is now Iran destroyed the city. The Sumerians were never again a dominant element politically, but their culture persisted as the foundation for all subsequent civilizations in the Tigris-Euphrates valley.

For more than two centuries following the destruction of Ur, disunity and warfare again plagued

Mesopotamia, along with economic stress, inflation, and acute hardship for the lower classes. Merchants, however, used the absence of state controls to become full-fledged capitalists who amassed fortunes that they invested in banking operations and land. The stronger local rulers of the period freed the poor from debt slavery and issued a variety of reform laws best illustrated by the legislation of Hammurabi.

The Old Babylonian Period, c. 2000–1600 B.C.E.

Semitic Amorites (from the Sumerian word *Amurru*, "West"), under the rule of their king, Hammurabi (c. 1792–1750 B.C.E.) of Babylon in Akkad, brought most of Mesopotamia under one rule by 1760 B.C.E. Hammurabi was a successful warrior who succeeded in expanding and securing Babylon's military power north into Assyria and south into Sumer.

Hammurabi is best known for his code of nearly 300 laws whose stated objective was "to cause justice to prevail in the land, to destroy the wicked and evil, to prevent the strong from oppressing the weak, . . . and to further the welfare of the people."[7] Hammurabi's legislation reestablished a state-controlled economy in which merchants were required to obtain a "royal permit," interest was limited to 20 percent, and prices were set for basic commodities and for fees charged by physicians, veterinarians, and builders. Minimum wages were established, and debt slavery was limited to three years. Other laws protected wives and children; but a wife who had "set her face to go out and play the part of a fool, neglect her house, belittle her husband" could be divorced without alimony, or the husband could take another wife and force the first to remain as a servant. Unless a son committed some grave offense, his father could not disinherit him. If the state failed to maintain law and order, the victim of that failure received compensation from the state: the value of the property stolen, or one mina of silver to the relatives of a murder victim.

Punishments were graded in their severity; the higher the guilty party on the social scale, the more severe the penalty. If an upper-class person, for example, knocked out the tooth of a social equal, his tooth would be knocked out; but if he did the same to a commoner, he paid a fine.

In the epilogue to the code, Hammurabi eloquently summed up his efforts to provide social justice for his people:

Let any oppressed man, who has a cause, come before my image as king of righteousness! Let him read the inscription on my monument! Let him give heed to my weighty words! And may my monument enlighten him as to his cause and may he understand his case! May he set his heart at ease! (and he will exclaim): "Hammurabi indeed is a ruler who is like a real father to his people. . . ."[8]

The Babylonians achieved little that today can accurately be called pure science. They did observe nature and collect data, which is the first requirement of science; but to explain natural phenomena, they did not go beyond the formulation of myths that defined things in terms of the unpredictable whims of the gods. The sun, moon, and five visible planets were thought to be gods who were able to influence human lives; accordingly, their movements were watched, recorded, and interpreted. Thus was born the pseudoscience of astrology.

Literature and Religion

The Babylonians took over from the Sumerians a body of literature ranging from heroic epics that compare favorably with the *Iliad* and the *Odyssey* to wisdom writings that have their counterparts in the Hebrew Old Testament. The Sumerian *Epic of Gilgamesh* recounts the exploits of the heroic ruler of Uruk who lived about 2700 B.C.E. Like all early folk epics, it reflects the values of a heroic age. The supreme value is the fame achieved through the performance of heroic deeds. After Gilgamesh slays the fierce Bull of Heaven, the "lyre maidens" of Uruk chant:

> *Who is most splendid among the heroes?*
> *Who is most glorious among men?*
> *Gilgamesh is most splendid among the heroes,*
> *Gilgamesh is most glorious among men.*

Since what these heroic heroes fear most is death, which replaces a glorious life on earth with a dismal existence in the House of Dust, "where dust is their fare and clay their food," the epic's central theme is Gilgamesh's hope for everlasting life. He seeks out and questions Utnapishtim, who was granted eternal life because he saved all living creatures from a great flood. (Utnapishtim's story has numerous similarities with the Hebrew account of Noah and the Flood.) But Gilgamesh's quest is hopeless, and he is so informed on several occasions:

> *Gilgamesh, whither rovest thou?*
> *The life thou pursuest thou shalt not find.*
> *When the gods created mankind,*
> *Death for mankind they set aside,*
> *Life in their own hands retaining.*
> *Thou, Gilgamesh, let full be thy belly.*
> *Make thou merry by day and by night.*
> *Of each day make thou a feast of rejoicing,*
> *Day and night dance thou and play! . . .*
> *Pay heed to the little one that holds on to thy hand,*
> *Let thy spouse delight in thy bosom!*
> *For this is the task of mankind!*[9]

The ancient Mesopotamians never progressed beyond this early view that immortality is reserved for the gods. Unlike the Egyptians, they did not go on

This scene is atop the nearly 8-foot stele, now in the Louvre, on which Hammurabi's code of laws is inscribed. It shows the self-styled "king of justice" saluting Shamash, the god of justice, who extends to him a rod and a ring, the symbols of royal authority.

Mathematics and Science

Building on the work of the Sumerians, the Babylonians made advances in arithmetic, geometry, and algebra. For ease of computation with both whole numbers and fractions, they compiled tables for multiplication and division and for square and cube roots. They knew how to solve linear and quadratic equations, and their knowledge of geometry included the theorem later formulated by the Greek philosopher Pythagoras: the square of the hypotenuse of a right-angled triangle is equal to the sum of the squares of the other two sides. They took over the Sumerian sexagismal system of counting based on the unit 60. This system is still used today in computing divisions of time and angles. They also adopted the Sumerian principle of place-value notation that gave numbers a value according to their position in a series. To represent zero, they employed the character for "not," which is the same as our "naught," still used orally for "zero."

to develop a belief in an attractive life after death as a reward for good behavior on earth. They did come to believe in divine rewards for moral conduct, but these were rewards to be enjoyed in this life—increased worldly goods, numerous offspring, long life. Thus they celebrated the sun-god Shamash in hymns that proclaimed that "the honest merchant . . . is pleasing to Shamash, and he will prolong his life. He will enlarge his family, gain wealth . . . and his descendants will never fail." The dishonest merchant, by contrast "is disappointed in the matter of profit and loses his capital."[10]

The ethical content of Babylonian religion was largely lost when the numerous priesthoods—more than 30 different types of priests and priestesses are known—became preoccupied with an elaborate set of rituals, particularly those designed to ward off evil demons and divine the future. Good deeds, the priests insisted, could not protect a person from demons that have the power to make their part-human and part-animal bodies invisible:

> Doors and bolts do not stop them;
> High walls and thick walls they cross like waves;
> They leap from house to house . . . ;
> Under the doors they slip like serpents.[11]

While one large class of priests provided amulets inscribed with incantations and magic formulas to exorcise demons, another group dealt with divining the future. Almost anything could be viewed as an omen, but most popular were dreams, the movements of birds and animals, the internal organs of sacrificed animals, the shape taken by oil poured on the surface of water, the casting of lots, and astronomical phenomena. Some of these methods of divination have survived virtually unchanged through the ages.

Ancient Egypt

c. 3100 B.C.E.	Menes unites Upper Egypt
c. 2700 B.C.E.	Construction of Step Pyramid
c. 1720 B.C.E.	Hyksos conquer Egypt
c. 1600 B.C.E.	Oldest medical text
c. 1479–1458 B.C.E.	Regency of Queen Hatshepsut
c. 1458–1436 B.C.E.	Reign of Thutmose III
c. 1363–1347 B.C.E.	Reign of Amenhotep IV (Akhenaton)
c. 1290–1224 B.C.E.	Reign of Ramses II
c. 700s B.C.E.	Conquest of Egypt by Kush

The End of an Era

The pattern of disunity and warfare, all too familiar in Mesopotamia, reasserted itself following Hammurabi's death. In 1595 B.C.E. the Hittites, an Indo-European people who had established themselves in Asia Minor, mounted a daring raid down the Euphrates, sacking Babylon and destroying the weakened dynasty of Hammurabi. The swift success of the Hittite raid was made possible by a new means of waging war: the use of lightweight chariots drawn by horses instead of donkeys or oxen. The next five centuries in Mesopotamia were an age of disorder about which little is known; nevertheless, the cultural heritage left by the Sumerians and Babylonians survived. Meanwhile, in a neighboring river valley, another civilization had emerged.

Egypt: Gift of the Nile

Egypt, one of Africa's earliest civilizations, is literally "the gift of the [Nile] river," as the ancient Greek historian Herodotus observed. The Nile River stretches for 4100 miles, but it is its last valley, extending 750 miles from the First Cataract to the Nile Delta, that was the heartland of Egyptian civilization. Egyptians called the Nile valley Kemet ("the black land") because its soils were renewed annually by the rich black silt deposited by the floodwaters of the Blue Nile and the Atbara, rivers descending from the Ethiopian highlands. Unlike the unpredictable floods of Mesopotamia, the Nile's floods rose and fell with unusual precision, reaching Aswan by late June and peaking in September before beginning to subside. The perennial key to successful farming was controlling the Nile by diverting its floodwaters along the 10- to 20-mile-wide floodplain for irrigation. Egyptian farmers achieved this by building an elaborate network of dikes and canals.

Predynastic Egypt

By 4800 B.C.E. the earliest farming communities began to appear in the western Nile Delta and spread to the rest of Egypt over the next eight centuries. Recognizing the advantages of creating larger social groupings and the need to cushion themselves from the impact of droughts, floods, and plagues, farming communities started banding together to form regional chiefdoms. Two distinct kingdoms gradually emerged. Lower Egypt comprised the broad Nile Delta north of Memphis, and Upper Egypt extended southward along the narrow Nile valley as far as the First Cataract, a rocky stretch of rapids that disrupted the flow of the river, at Aswan. Each kingdom contained about a score of districts (later called *nomes*) that had formerly been ruled by independent chieftains.

The Predynastic period ended soon after 3100 B.C.E. when King Menes united Upper Egypt and started gradually incorporating Lower Egypt into a new kingdom with its capital at Memphis. This period has become known as the First Dynasty, and it marks the beginning of one of the longest-lasting civilizations in history, flourishing for 3000 years.

The Old Kingdom,
c. 2700–2200 B.C.E.

The kings of the Third through Sixth Dynasties—the period called the Old Kingdom or Pyramid Age—firmly established order and stability, as well as the basic elements of Egyptian civilization. The nobility lost its independence, and all power was centered in the king, or *pharaoh* (*per-ao*, "great house," originally signified the royal palace but during the New Kingdom began to refer to the king). The king had a character both divine and human. Considered a god, he also represented humans before the gods. As the god of Egypt, the king, with his relatives, owned extensive tracts of land (from which he made frequent grants to temples, royal funerary cults, and private persons) and received the surplus from the crops produced on the huge royal estates. This surplus supported a large corps of specialists—administrators, priests, scribes, artists, artisans, and merchants—who labored in the service of the pharaoh. The people's welfare was thought to rest on absolute devotion to the god-king. "If you want to know what to do in life," advised one Egyptian writer, "cling to the pharaoh and be loyal." As a consequence, Egyptians felt a sense of security that was rare in Mesopotamia.

The belief that the pharaoh was divine led to the practice of mummification and the construction of colossal tombs—*pyramids*—to preserve the pharaoh's embalmed body for eternity. The ritual of mummification was believed to restore vigor and activity to the dead pharaoh; it was his passport to eternity. "You live again, you live again forever, here you are young once more forever." The pyramid tombs, especially those of the Fourth Dynasty at Giza near Memphis, which are the most celebrated of all ancient monuments, reflect the great power and wealth of the Old Kingdom pharaohs. Although pyramid construction was ordinarily concentrated during the four months of the year when the land was flooded by the Nile, the Egyptian masses performed it primarily as an act of fidelity to their god-king, on whom the security and prosperity of Egypt depended.

Security and prosperity came to an end late in the Sixth Dynasty. The burden of building and maintaining pyramid tombs for each new king exhausted the state. The Nile floods failed and crops were di-

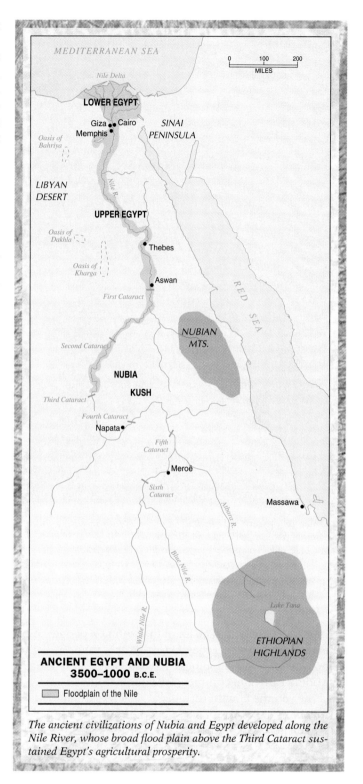

The ancient civilizations of Nubia and Egypt developed along the Nile River, whose broad flood plain above the Third Cataract sustained Egypt's agricultural prosperity.

minished, yet taxes were increased. As the state and its god-king lost credibility, provincial rulers assumed the prerogatives of the pharaohs, including the claim to immortality, and districts became independent.

For about a century and a half, known as the First Intermediate Period (c. 2200–2050 B.C.E.), the central authority of the pharaoh weakened as civil war raged among contenders for the throne and local rulers reasserted themselves. Outsiders raided and

Menkaure (Mycerinus), the builder of the Fourth Dynasty's third pyramid, and his wife, Queen Kamerernebly. The portrait statues of Old Kingdom pharaohs express a classical maturity of technique and of content—dignity, authority, and the certainty of eternal life.

Pair Statue of Mycerinus and Queen Kha-merer-nebty II, Egypt, Dynasty IV, Giza, Valley Temple of Mycerinus. Museum of Fine Arts, Boston, Harvard-Museum Expedition, 11.1738.

infiltrated the land. The lot of the common people became unbearable as they faced famine, robbery, and oppression. "All happiness has vanished," related a Middle Kingdom commentary on this troubled era. "I show you the land in turmoil. . . . Each man's heart is for himself. . . . A man sits with his back turned, while one slays another."[12]

The Middle Kingdom,
c. 2050–1800 B.C.E.

Stability was restored by the pharaohs of the Eleventh and Twelfth Dynasties, who reunited the kingdom and ruled from Thebes for a century. Stressing their role as watchful shepherds of the people, the Middle Kingdom pharaohs promoted the welfare of the downtrodden. One of them claimed, "I gave to the beggar and brought up the orphan. I gave success to the poor as to the wealthy."[13] The pharaohs of the Twelfth Dynasty revived the building of pyramids as

well as the construction of public works. The largest of these, a drainage and irrigation project in the marshy Fayum district south of Memphis, resulted in the reclamation of thousands of acres of arable land. Moreover, a concession gave a wider group of people the right to have their bodies mummified and erect private tombs and thereby, like the pharaohs and the nobility, to enjoy immortality.

During the Thirteenth Dynasty, the Hyksos ("rulers of foreign lands"), a Semitic people from western Asia, assumed power over much of Egypt. The Hyksos are often portrayed as invaders who conquered Egypt around 1720 B.C.E., but now it is understood that the Hyksos migrated into Lower Egypt during the Middle Kingdom and established trading networks. During the Second Intermediate Period (c. 1800–1570 B.C.E.), they took advantage of weaknesses in the Egyptian state and gradually took control over all of Lower Egypt and many parts of Upper Egypt. The Hyksos did not sweep aside Egyptian institutions and culture. They adapted to existing Egyptian government structures, copied architectural styles and the hieroglyphic ("sacred carvings") system of writing, and incorporated Egyptian cults into their religious pantheon. The Hyksos army also introduced new weaponry to the Egyptians: the horse-drawn chariot and bronze weapons such as the curved sword and body armor and helmets.

The New Kingdom or Empire,
c. 1570–1090 B.C.E.

Hyksos rule over Egypt lasted several centuries before a resurgent Egyptian dynasty based at Thebes challenged it. To nationalistic Egyptians, the Hyksos conquest was a great humiliation imposed on them by detestable barbarians. The Egyptian prince of Thebes proclaimed, "No man can settle down, when despoiled by the taxes of the Asiatics. I will grapple with him, that I may rip open his belly! My wish is to save Egypt and to smite the Asiatics!"[14] Adopting the new weapons introduced by their rulers, the Egyptians expelled the Hyksos and pursued them into Palestine. The pharaohs of the Eighteenth Dynasty, who reunited Egypt and founded the New Kingdom, made Palestine the nucleus of an Egyptian empire in western Asia.

The outstanding representative of this aggressive state was Thutmose III. Thutmose II had married his half-sister, Hatshepsut, but when their union failed to produce a male heir, Thutmose II fathered Thutmose III with a concubine. When Thutmose II died in 1479 B.C.E., Thutmose was still a child, and Hatshepsut was to act as co-regent until he came of age. However, she had her own ambitions. Supported by the powerful priests of the sun-god Amon, Hatshepsut proclaimed herself "king" and legitimized her succession by claiming that she was the designated successor and depicting herself as a daughter of Amon in many of her statues and helmets—sometimes even sporting the royal beard! She adopted all the customary royal titles.

Thutmose III had to wait for more than two decades before he assumed the throne on his own. Toward the end of his reign, he ordered Hatshepsut's name and inscriptions erased, her reliefs effaced, and her statues broken and thrown into a quarry. Historians still speculate whether he was expressing his anger at Hatshepsut or promoting his own accomplishments. This "Napoleon of Egypt," as Thutmose III has been called, is most noted for leading his army on 17 campaigns as far as Syria, where he set up his boundary markers on the banks of the Euphrates, called by the Egyptians "the river that runs backwards." Under his sway, Thutmose III allowed the existing rulers of conquered states to remain on their thrones, but their sons were taken as hostages to Egypt, where they were brought up, thoroughly Egyptianized, and eventually sent home to succeed their fathers as loyal vassals of Egyptian rule. Thutmose III erected *obelisks*—tall, pointed shafts of stone—to commemorate his reign and to record his wish that "his name might endure throughout the future forever and ever." Four of his obelisks survived in Egypt and today adorn the cities of Istanbul, Rome, London, and New York.

The Egyptian Empire reached its peak under Amenhotep III (c. 1402–1363 B.C.E.). The restored capital at Thebes, with its temples built for the sun-god Amon east of the Nile at Luxor and Karnak, became the most magnificent city in the world. Tribute flowed in from conquered lands, and relations were expanded with Asia and the Mediterranean. To improve ties, the kings of Mitanni and Babylonia offered daughters in marriage to Amenhotep III. In return, they asked the pharaoh for gold, "for gold is as common as dust in your land."

During the reign of the succeeding pharaoh, Amenhotep IV (c. 1363–1347 B.C.E.), however, the empire went into a sharp decline as the result of an internal struggle between the pharaoh and the powerful and wealthy priests of Amon, "king of the gods." The pharaoh undertook to revolutionize Egypt's religion by proclaiming the worship of the sun's disk, Aton, in place of Amon and all the other deities. Often called the first monotheist (although, as Aton's son, the pharaoh was also a god and he, not Aton, was worshipped by the Egyptians), Amenhotep changed his name to Akhenaton ("agreeable to Aton"), left Amon's city to found a new capital (Akhetaton), and concentrated on religious reform. Most of Egypt's tributary princes in Asia defected when their appeals for aid against invaders went unheeded. At home the Amon priesthood encouraged dissension. When Akhenaton died, his 9-year-old brother, Tutankhamen ("King Tut," c. 1347–1338 B.C.E.)—now best remembered for his small but richly furnished tomb, discovered in 1922—returned to the worship of Amon and to Memphis, where he

Sections of a wall painting from the tomb chapel of the treasurer Sebekhotep at Thebes show Nubians presenting gold nuggets and rings to King Thutmose IV. The painting dates from around 1400 B.C.E.

The largest of the colossal columns of the Hypostyle Hall of the temple of Karnak rise more than 70 feet and are more than 20 feet in diameter.

came under the influence of the priests of Amon. At this point the generals of the army took control of Egypt.

One of the new army leaders founded the Nineteenth Dynasty (c. 1305–1200 B.C.E.), which sought to reestablish Egyptian control over Palestine and Syria. The result was a long struggle with the Hittites, who in the meantime had pushed south from Asia Minor into Syria. This struggle reached a climax in the reign of Ramses II (c. 1290–1224 B.C.E.), the pharaoh of the Hebrew Exodus from Egypt under Moses (although Moses is not mentioned in Egyptian records). Ramses II regained Palestine, but when he failed to dislodge the Hittites from Syria, he agreed to a treaty. Its strikingly modern character is revealed in clauses providing for nonaggression, mutual assistance, and extradition of fugitives.

The long reign of Ramses II was one of Egypt's last periods of national grandeur. The number and size of Ramses' monuments rival those of the Pyramid Age. Outstanding among them are the great Hypostyle Hall, built for Amon at Karnak, and the temple at Abu Simbel in Nubia, with its four colossal statues of Ramses, which has been raised to save it from inundation by the waters of the High Dam at

Aswan. After Ramses II, royal authority gradually decayed as the power of the priests of Amon rose.

Third Intermediate Period, 1090–332 B.C.E.

The Third Intermediate Period was another period of transition in which the Amon priesthood at Thebes became so strong that the high priest was able to found his own dynasty and to rule over Upper Egypt. At the same time, merchant princes set up a dynasty of their own in the Delta. Libyans from the west moved into central Egypt, where in 940 B.C.E. they established a dynasty whose founder, Shoshenq, was a contemporary of King Solomon of Israel. Two centuries later, Egypt was conquered by the rulers of the kingdom of Kush, who established the Twenty-Fifth Dynasty. Kush's rule came to an end around 670 B.C.E. when the Assyrians of Mesopotamia made Egypt a province of their empire.

Egypt enjoyed a brief reprise of revived glory during the Twenty-Sixth Dynasty (c. 663–525 B.C.E.), which expelled the Assyrians with the aid of Greek mercenaries. The revival of ancient artistic and literary forms proved to be one of the most creative periods in Egyptian history. After attempts to expand into Syria were blocked by Nebuchadnezzar's Babylonians, Egypt's rulers concentrated on expanding their commercial linkages throughout the region. To achieve this end, Pharaoh Necho II (c. 610–595 B.C.E.) created the first Egyptian navy. He encouraged the Greeks to establish trading colonies in the Nile Delta; he put 12,000 laborers to work, digging a canal between the Nile mouth and the Red Sea (it was completed later by the Persians); and he commissioned a Phoenician expedition to search for new African trade routes.

Egypt passed under Persian rule in 525 B.C.E. but was able to regain its independence in 404 B.C.E. After three brief dynasties, Egypt again fell under the Persians before coming within the domain of Alexander the Great.

Nubia and the Kingdom of Kush

Egypt's most enduring relationship was with its neighbor to the south, Nubia, an area that stretches almost 900 miles from the town of Aswan to Khartoum, the point where the Blue and White Niles converge. The Nile gave Nubian civilization a distinctive character but in ways different from those in Egypt. As the Nile flows northward, its course is interrupted six times by cataracts that served as barriers to river traffic and Nubia's commercial contacts with Egypt. Moreover, the Nile did not contribute significantly to Nubia's agricultural life. The Nile's floodplain is about 2 miles wide, and many sections of the land are barren.

Emerging around 4000 B.C.E., the earliest Nubian culture was made up of hunters, fishermen, farmers, and seminomadic pastoralists. This culture was distinguished for its highly skilled sculptures, ceramics, and clay figurines. Nubia also developed a healthy trade with Egypt. Nubia exchanged animals and animal hides, incense, timber, gold, rare gems, and ebony and ivory for Egyptian honey, cloth, pearls, copper chisels, and alabaster vases.

After a centralized state emerged in Egypt, Egyptian dynasties regarded Nubia as a source of raw materials and slaves and made several attempts to colonize Nubia. During Egypt's First Intermediate Period, Egyptian soldiers invaded Lower Nubia (between the First and Second Cataracts) and built 11 fortresses with imposing names such as "Subduing the Oasis-Dwellers" and "Warding Off the Bow-Men." This state of hostility did not prevent Nubians from marrying into Egyptian royal families and the Egyptian state and army from recruiting Nubian administrators and archers.

Around 2300–2100 B.C.E. a new group of people, most likely herders from desert areas west of the Nile, migrated into Nubia. Around 1600 B.C.E. Egyptian records began referring to a "kingdom of Kush" that was centered in a fertile area of the Nile around the Third Cataract. Kush's capital was at Kerma, an urban center renowned for its sophisticated temples and palaces. Although the basis of Kush's society was agriculture and animal husbandry, Kush engaged in extensive trade with Egypt to the north and African societies to the south and east.

When the Hyksos dominated Egypt, Kushites regained control of Lower Nubia. After expelling the Hyksos, Egyptian forces reasserted their dominion over northern Nubia as far south as the Fourth Cataract, including Kerma. For the next four centuries, Egyptian administrators exploited Nubian gold to finance military campaigns in Asia and created an "Egyptianized" Nubian elite that adopted Egyptian deities and ritual and burial practices.

Kush did not regain its autonomy until the eighth century B.C.E., when a new line of rulers established themselves at Meroë in a fertile stretch of the Nile between the Fifth and Sixth Cataracts. The high point of Kush's power came a short time later. Taking advantage of strife in Egypt, the armies of Kush's King Piye swept through Egypt, conquering territory as far north as the Nile Delta. Although Piye proclaimed himself pharaoh over Egypt and Nubia, he allowed local rulers in Egypt a measure of independence. His successor, Shabaqo, was not so benign. He brought Egypt under the direct control of Kush. He and the three pharaohs who succeeded him estab-

lished the Twenty-Fifth Dynasty, which ruled Kush and Egypt for the next half century until they were forced to retreat following an Assyrian invasion.

Kush remained in existence until 400 C.E., when it was absorbed into the Ethiopian kingdom of Aksum. Around the second century B.C.E. Kush's rulers started recording their royal annals in a script that was part hieroglyphics and part shorthand cursive script. To this day, this language has not been translated.

Egyptian Society and Economy

Although most Egyptians were virtual serfs subject to forced labor, class stratification was not rigid, and people of merit could rise to a higher rank in the service of the pharaoh. The best avenue for advancement was education. The pharaoh's administration needed many scribes, and young men were urged to attend a scribal school. "Be a scribe, who is freed from forced labor, and protected from all work. . . . He directeth every work that is in this land." Yet then as now, the education of a young man was beset with pitfalls. "I am told thou forsakest writing, that thou givest thyself up to pleasures; thou goest from street to street, where it smelleth of beer, to destruction. Beer, it scareth man from thee, it sendeth thy soul to perdition."[15]

Compared with the Greeks and Romans, Egyptian women enjoyed more rights, although their status at all levels of society was generally lower than that of men. Few women could qualify as scribes and thus were largely excluded from administrative positions. However, women could serve as temple priestesses, musicians, gardeners, farmers, and bakers. Some royal women, because of their positions as wives or mothers of pharaohs, had great influence in royal courts. Business and legal documents show that women shared many of the economic and legal rights of men. Women generally had rights to own, buy, sell, and inherit property without reliance on male legal guardians, to engage in business deals, to make wills, and to testify in court.

The economy of Egypt was dominated by the divine pharaoh and his state, which owned most of the land and monopolized its commerce and industry. Because of the Nile and the proximity to the Mediterranean and Red Seas, most of Egypt's trade was carried out by ships. Boats regularly plied up and down the Nile, which, unlike the Tigris and the Euphrates, is easily navigable in both directions up to the First Cataract at Aswan. The current carries ships downstream, and the prevailing north wind enables them to sail upstream easily. Trade reached its height during the empire (c. 1570–1090 B.C.E.), when commerce traveled along four main routes: the Nile River to and from the south; the Red Sea, which was connected by

Many tomb paintings depict everyday life in Egypt. Here two servants pick figs at the tomb of Khnumhotpes at Bani Hasan.

caravan to the Nile bend near Thebes; a caravan route to Mesopotamia and southern Syria; and the Mediterranean Sea, connecting northern Syria, Cyprus, Crete, and Greece with the Nile Delta. Egypt's indispensable exports were timber, copper, tin, and olive oil, paid for with gold from its rich mines, linens, wheat, and papyrus rolls made from reeds—the preferred writing materials of the ancient world (the word *paper* is derived from the Greek *papyros*).

Egyptian Religion

During the Old Kingdom, Egyptian religion was lacking in ethical content. Relations between people and gods were based on material, not moral, considerations—the gods were thought to reward those who brought them gifts of sacrifice. But widespread suffering during the First Intermediate Period led to a revolution in religious thought. It was now believed that instead of sacrificial offerings, the gods were interested in good characters and love for one's fellows: "More acceptable [to the gods] is the character of one upright of heart than the ox of the evildoer.... Give the love of thyself to the whole world, a good character is a remembrance."[16]

Osiris, the mythical fertility god of the Nile whose death and resurrection explained the annual rise and fall of the river, became the center of Egypt's most popular religious cult when the new emphasis on moral character was combined with the supreme reward of an attractive afterlife. "Do justice whilst

thou endurest upon earth," people were told. "A man remains over after death, and his deeds are placed beside him in heaps. However, existence yonder is for eternity.... He who reaches it without wrongdoing shall exist yonder like a god."[17] The original premoral nature myth told how Osiris had been murdered by Seth, his brother, who cut the victim's body into many pieces and scattered them around Egypt. When Isis, his bereaved widow, collected all the pieces and wrapped them in linen, Osiris was resurrected, the Nile floods resumed, and vegetation revived. The moralized Osiris cult taught that Seth was the god of evil, that Osiris was the first mummy, and that every mummified Egyptian could become another Osiris, capable of resurrection from the dead and a blessed eternal life.

However, only a soul free of sin would be permitted to live forever in what was described as the "Field of the Blessed, an ideal land where there is no wailing and nothing evil, where barley grows four cubits high . . . ; where, even better, one has to do no work in the field oneself, but can let others take care of it."[18] In a ceremony called "counting up character," Osiris weighed the heart of the deceased against the Feather of Truth. If the heart was heavy with sin and outweighed the Feather of Truth, a horrible creature devoured it. During the empire the priesthood of Osiris became corrupt and claimed that it knew clever methods of surviving the soul testing, even if a person's heart were heavy with sin. Charms and magical prayers and formulas were sold to the living as insurance policies guaranteeing them a happy out-

In this scene from the Book of the Dead, a princess stands in the Hall of Judgment in the Underworld before a set of scales on which the jackal-headed god Anubis weighs her heart against the Feather of Truth. The baboonlike god Thoth records the result.

come in the judgment before Osiris. They constitute much of what is known as the Book of the Dead, which was placed in the tomb.

Mathematics and Science

The Egyptians were much less skilled in mathematics than the Mesopotamians. Their arithmetic was limited to addition and subtraction, which also served them when they needed to multiply and divide. They could cope with only simple algebra, but they did have considerable knowledge of practical geometry; the obliteration of field boundaries by the annual flooding of the Nile made the measurement of land a necessity. A knowledge of geometry was also essential in computing the dimensions of ramps for raising stones during the construction of pyramids. In these and other engineering projects the Egyptians were superior to their Mesopotamian contemporaries. Like the Mesopotamians, the Egyptians acquired a "necessary" technology without developing a truly scientific method. Yet what has been called the oldest known scientific treatise (c. 1600 B.C.E.) was composed during the New Kingdom. Its author, possibly a military surgeon or a doctor who treated pyramid-building laborers, described cases of dislocations and broken bones and recommended treatments or, in the case of more serious complications, nothing at all. In advising the physician to "measure for the heart" that "speaks" in various parts of the body, he

recognized the importance of the pulse and speculated about the circulation of the blood. Other medical writings considered a range of ailments, from pregnancy complications to hippopotamus bites. To Egyptian practitioners, the causes of medical conditions had to be dealt with holistically on a spiritual as well as a physical level. Thus they prescribed a combination of medicines, rituals, magical spells, and amulets.

The Old Kingdom also produced the world's first known solar calendar, the direct ancestor of our own. In order to plan their farming operations in accordance with the annual flooding of the Nile, the Egyptians kept records and discovered that the average period between floods was 365 days. They observed that the Nile flood coincided with the annual appearance of the Dog Star (Sirius) on the eastern horizon at dawn, and they soon associated the two phenomena. They also calculated that since the year was six hours short, an extra day had to be added every four years.

Monumentalism in Architecture

Because of their impressive, enduring tombs and temples, the Egyptians have been called the greatest builders in history. The earliest tomb was the mud-brick Arab *mastaba*, so called because of its resemblance to a low bench. By the beginning of the Third Dynasty, stone began to replace brick, and an architectural genius named Imhotep, now honored as the "father of architecture in stone," constructed the first pyramid by piling six huge stone mastabas one on top of the other. Adjoining this Step Pyramid was a temple complex whose stone columns were not freestanding but attached to a wall, as though the architect were tentatively feeling his way in the use of the new medium.

The most celebrated of the true pyramids were built for the Fourth Dynasty pharaohs Khufu, Khafre, and Menkaure. Khufu's pyramid, the largest of the three, covers 13 acres and originally rose 481 feet. It is composed of 2.3 million limestone bricks, some weighing 15 tons and all pushed and pulled into place by human muscle. This stupendous monument was built without mortar, yet some of the stones were so perfectly fitted that a knife cannot be inserted in the joints. The Old Kingdom's 80 pyramids are a striking expression of Egyptian civilization. Their dignity and massiveness reflect the religious basis of Egyptian society—the dogma that the king was a god who owned the nation and that serving him was the most important task of the people.

Just as the glory and serenity of the Old Kingdom can be seen in its pyramids, constructed as an act of loyalty by its subjects, so the power and wealth of the empire survive in the Amon temples at Thebes, made possible by the booty and tribute of conquest. On the east side of the Nile were built the magnificent temples of Karnak and Luxor. The Hypostyle Hall of the temple of Karnak, built by Ramses II, is larger than the cathedral of Notre Dame in Paris. Its forest of 134 columns is arranged in 16 rows, with the roof over the two broader central aisles raised to allow the entry of light. This technique was later used in Roman basilicas and in Christian churches.

Sculpture and Painting

Egyptian art was essentially religious. Tomb paintings and relief sculpture depict the everyday activities that the deceased wished to continue enjoying in the afterlife, and statues glorify the god-kings in all their serenity and eternity. Since religious art is inherently conservative, Egyptian art seldom departed from the classical tradition established during the vigorous and self-assured Old Kingdom. Sculptors idealized and standardized their subjects, and the human figure is shown either looking directly ahead or in profile, with a rigidity very much in keeping with the austere architectural settings of the statues.

Yet on two occasions an unprecedented realism appeared in Egyptian sculpture. The faces of some of the Middle Kingdom rulers appear drawn and weary, seemingly reflecting the burden of reconstructing Egypt after the collapse of the Old Kingdom. An even greater realism is seen in the portraits of Akhenaton and his queen, Nefertiti, which continued into the following reign of Tutankhamen. The pharaoh's brooding countenance is realistically portrayed, as is his ungainly paunch and his happy but far from god-like family life as he holds one of his young daughters on his knee or munches on a bone. The "heretic" pharaoh, who insisted on what he called "truth" in religion, seems also to have insisted on truth in art.

Painting shows the same precision and mastery of technique that are evident in sculpture. No attempt was made to show objects in perspective, and the scenes

The Step Pyramid (Third Dynasty, c. 2700 B.C.E.) was the first pyramid built of stone. The few remaining columns of the adjoining temple, also the first to be constructed of stone, are fluted to resemble the bundles of mud-smeared reeds that were formerly used as building materials.

The brooding and careworn countenance of this Middle Kingdom, pharaoh King Sesostris III, contrasts sharply with the confidence and vitality that characterize the portrait statues of Old Kingdom pharaohs.

Fragment of a head of King Sesostris III. The Metropolitan Museum of Art, Carnarvon Collection, Gift of Edward S. Harkness, 1926 (26.7.1394). All rights reserved. The Metropolitan Museum of Art.

This famous painted bust of Queen Nefertiti ("the beautiful one has come"), the wife and sister of Akhenaton, illustrates why she has been called "the most beautiful woman in history." Despite her dreamy expression, she had a forceful personality. She ultimately broke with her husband and moved out of the palace to another part of the capital.

seem flat. The effect of distance was conveyed by making objects in a series or by putting one object above another. Another convention employed was to depict everything from its most characteristic angle. Often the head, arms, and legs were shown in side view while the eyes, shoulders, and chest were shown in front view.

Writing and Literary Texts

In Egypt, as in Sumer, writing began with pictures. But unlike the Mesopotamian signs, the Egyptian hieroglyphics remained primarily pictorial. At first the hieroglyphics represented only objects, but later they came to stand for ideas and syllables. Early in the Old Kingdom the Egyptians took the further step of using alphabetical characters for 24 consonant sounds. Although they also continued to use the old pictographic and syllabic signs, the use of sound symbols had far-reaching consequences. It influenced their Semitic neighbors in Syria to produce an alphabet that, in its Phoenician form, became the forerunner of our own.

Among the earliest Egyptian literary works are the Pyramid Texts, a collection of magic spells and ritual texts inscribed on the walls of the burial chambers of Old Kingdom pharaohs. Their recurrent theme is an affirmation that the dead pharaoh is really a god and that no obstacle can prevent him from joining his fellow gods in the heavens.

Old Kingdom literature went on to achieve a classical maturity of style and content—it stresses a "truth" that is "everlasting." Hence *The Instructions of Ptah-hotep*, addressed to the author's sons, insists that "it is the strength of truth that it endures long, and a man can say, 'I learned it from my father.'" Ptah-hotep's maxims stress the values and virtues that are important in fostering positive human relationships. To him, honesty is a good policy because it will gain one wealth and position, while affairs with other men's wives is a bad policy because it will impede one's path to success in life.[19]

The troubled times that followed the collapse of the Old Kingdom produced the highly personal writings of the First Intermediate Period and the Middle Kingdom. They contain protests against the ills of the day, demands for social justice, and praise for a new value, romantic love, as a means of forgetting misery. The universal appeal of this literature is illustrated by the following lines from a love poem in which the beloved is called "sister."

*I behold how my sister cometh, and my heart is in
   gladness.
Mine arms open wide to embrace her; my heart exul-
   teth within me; for my lady has come to me. . . .
She kisseth me, she openeth her lips to me; then am I
   joyful even without beer.*[20]

A notable example of Egyptian literature is
Akhenaton's *Hymn to the Sun*, which is similar in
spirit to Psalm 104 in the Old Testament ("O Lord,
how manifold are thy works!"). A few lines indicate
its lyric beauty and its conception of one omnipotent
and beneficent Creator:

*Splendid you rise in heaven's lightland,
O living Aton, creator of life! . . .
How many are your deeds,
Though hidden from sight;
O Sole God beside whom there is none!
You made the earth as you wished, you alone.*[21]

The Hittites,
c. 2000—1200 B.C.E.

Except for a brief mention in the Old Testament
(Uriah the Hittite, for example, whose wife, Bath-
sheba, had an affair with King David), very little was
known about the Hittites until archaeologists began
to unearth the remains of their civilization in Asia
Minor in 1906. By 1920 Hittite writing had been deciphered, and it proved to be the earliest example of a
written Indo-European language. The Hittites are
thought to have entered Asia Minor from the north
about 2000 B.C.E., and their superior military ability—particularly demonstrated by the horse-drawn
chariot—enabled them to conquer the native people
of central Asia Minor.

The kings of the early Hittite kingdom were aggressive monarchs who were frequently at odds with
their nobles and were unable to establish an orderly
succession to the throne. One early Hittite king tells
how his grandfather's choice of his son as heir to the
throne was "spurned" by "the leading citizens," and
he goes on to warn his own son "not [to] relax," for
otherwise "it will mean the same old mischief."[22]

The Hittite Empire

After 1450 B.C.E. a series of energetic Hittite kings
succeeded in ending the "old mischief" of their nobles and created a more powerful government and an
empire that included Syria, which had been left virtually undefended by the Egyptian pharaoh Akhenaton. Ramses II moved north from Palestine in an
unsuccessful attempt to reconquer the region. Am-
bushed and forced back to Palestine after a bloody
battle, Ramses agreed to a treaty of "good peace and

good brotherhood" with the Hittites in 1269 B.C.E.
The Hittites may have been eager for peace with
Egypt because of the threat posed by a new movement of Indo-European peoples. Many survivors of
the resulting upheavals, which possibly included the
fall of Troy (c. 1150 B.C.E.), fled by sea seeking new
lands to plunder or settle. Collectively known as
the Sea Peoples, these uprooted people included
Philistines, Sicilians, Sardinians, and Etruscans.
They left their names in the areas where they eventually settled. The collapse of the Hittite Empire,
shortly after 1200 B.C.E., was partially a result of
these migrations.

Hittite Civilization

The Hittite state under the empire was based on the
models of the older monarchies of Mesopotamia and
Egypt. The king claimed to represent the sun-god and
was deified after death. The nobles held large estates
granted by the king and in return provided warriors,
who were armed increasingly with iron weapons. The
Hittites were among the first people to manufacture
iron weapons and use them effectively. Not until after
1200 B.C.E. did iron metallurgy become widespread
throughout the eastern Mediterranean area.

The Hittites adopted the Mesopotamian cuneiform script, together with some works of Babylonian literature. While their law code showed some
similarity to the code of Hammurabi, it differed in
prescribing more humane punishments. Instead of
retaliation ("an eye for an eye"), the Hittite code
made greater use of restitution and compensation.

The Hittites left their mark primarily as intermediaries. Their skills in metalworking, especially in
iron, were passed quickly to their neighbors. Not especially creative in the formulation of law or literature and art, they borrowed extensively from other
cultures and in turn passed their knowledge on to
others, in particular to the neighboring Phrygians,
Lydians, and Greeks.

The Era of Small States,
c. 1200—700 B.C.E.

After 1200 B.C.E., with the Hittite Empire destroyed
and Egypt in decline, the Semitic peoples of Syria
and Palestine were able to assert their territorial
claims in the power vacuum created by the weakness
of the dominant states. For nearly 500 years, until
they were conquered by the Assyrians, these peoples
played a significant role in history.

The Phoenicians

Phoenicians is a name the Greeks gave to those
Canaanites who lived along the Mediterranean coast

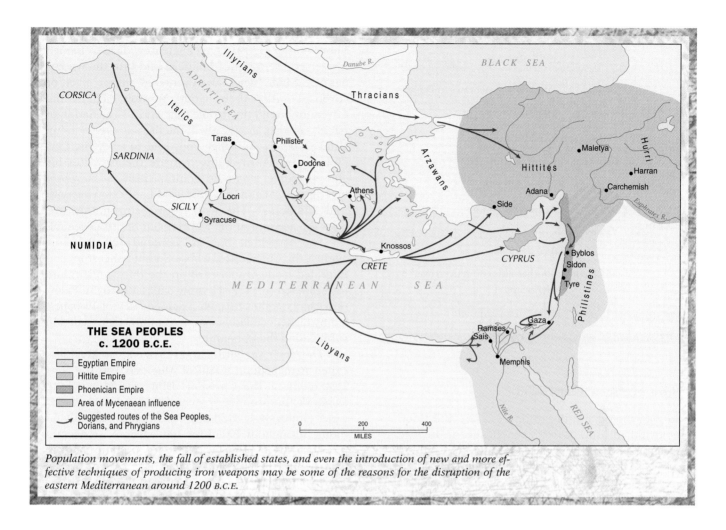

Population movements, the fall of established states, and even the introduction of new and more effective techniques of producing iron weapons may be some of the reasons for the disruption of the eastern Mediterranean around 1200 B.C.E.

of Syria, an area that is today Lebanon. Hemmed in by the Lebanon Mountains to the east, the Phoenicians turned to the sea for their livelihood and empire and by the eleventh century B.C.E. had become the Mediterranean's greatest traders, shipbuilders, navigators, and colonizers before the Greeks. To obtain silver and copper from Spain and tin from Britain, they established Gades (Cadiz) on the Atlantic coast of Spain. Carthage, one of a number of Phoenician trading posts on the shores of the Mediterranean, was destined to become Rome's chief rival in the third century B.C.E.

Although the Phoenicians were essentially traders, their home cities—notably Tyre, Sidon, and Byblos—also produced manufactured goods. Their most famous export was woolen cloth dyed with the purple dye obtained from shellfish found along their coast. They were also skilled makers of furniture (made from the famous cedars of Lebanon), metalware, glassware, and jewelry. The Greeks called Egyptian papyrus rolls *biblia* ("books") because Byblos was the shipping point for this widely used writing material; later the Hebrew and Christian Scriptures were called "the Book" (Bible).

Culturally, the Phoenicians were not particularly original. They left behind no literature and little in-

novative art. Yet they made one of the greatest contributions to human progress, the perfection of the alphabet, which, along with the Babylonian sexagesimal system of notation, they carried westward. Between 1800 and 1600 B.C.E. various Canaanite peoples, influenced by Egypt's semialphabetical writing, started to evolve a simplified method of writing. The Phoenician alphabet of 22 consonant symbols (the Greeks later added signs for vowels) is related to the 30-character alphabet of Ugarit, a Canaanite city, which was destroyed about 1200 B.C.E. by the raiding Sea Peoples.

The half-dozen Phoenician cities never united to form a strong state, and in the second half of the eighth century B.C.E. all but Tyre were conquered by the Assyrians. When Tyre finally fell to the Chaldeans in 571 B.C.E., the Hebrew prophet Ezekiel spoke what reads like an epitaph to the once great role played by the Phoenicians:

When your wares came from the seas, you satisfied many peoples; with your abundant wealth and merchandise, you enriched the kings of the earth. Now you are wrecked by the seas, in the depths of the waters; your merchandise and all your crew have sunk with you. (Ezekiel 27:33–34)

The Hebrews

c. 1800 B.C.E.	Migration of Hebrews to Palestine
c. 1550 B.C.E.	Migration to Egypt
c. 1300–1200 B.C.E.	Exodus from Egypt
c. 1020–1000 B.C.E.	Reign of Saul
c. 1000–961 B.C.E.	Reign of David
961–922 B.C.E.	Reign of Solomon
722 B.C.E.	Northern kingdom destroyed by Assyria
586 B.C.E.	Southern kingdom destroyed by Chaldeans
586–538 B.C.E.	Babylonian Captivity

The Hebrew Kingdoms

In war, diplomacy, inventions, and art, the Hebrews contributed little of great significance to history; in religion and ethics, however, their contribution to world civilization was tremendous. Out of their experience grew three great religions: Judaism, Christianity, and Islam.

Much of Hebrew experience is recorded in the Holy Writ of Israel (the Old Testament), whose present content was approved about 90 C.E. by a council of rabbis. As a work of literature it is outstanding; but it is more than that. "It is Israel's life story—a story that cannot be told adequately apart from the conviction that God had called this people in his grace, separated them from the nations for a special responsibility, and commissioned them with the task of being his servant in the accomplishment of his purpose."[23]

The biblical account of the history of the Hebrews (later called Israelites and then Jews) begins with the patriarchal clan leader Abraham, called in Genesis 14:13 "the Hebrew" (a nomad or wanderer). About 1800 B.C.E. Abraham led his people out of Ur in Sumer, where they had settled for a time in their wanderings, and eventually they arrived in the land of Canaan, later called Palestine.

About 1550 B.C.E., driven by famine, some Hebrews followed Abraham's great-grandson Joseph, son of Israel (also called Jacob), into Egypt. Joseph's rise to power in Egypt, and the hospitable reception of his people there, is attributed to the presence of the largely Semitic Hyksos, who had conquered Egypt about 1720 B.C.E. Following the expulsion of the Hyksos by the pharaohs of the Eighteenth Dy-

nasty, the Hebrews were enslaved by the Egyptians. Shortly after 1300 B.C.E. a Hebrew leader named Moses led them out of bondage and into the wilderness of Sinai, where they entered into a pact or covenant with their God, Yahweh. The Sinai Covenant bound the people as a whole—the nation of Israel, as they now called themselves—to worship Yahweh before all other gods and to obey his Law (Torah). In return, Yahweh made the Israelites his chosen people, whom he would protect and to whom he granted Canaan, the Promised Land "flowing with milk and honey." The history of Israel from this time on is the account of the working out of this covenant.

The Israelites had to contend for Palestine against the Canaanites, whose Semitic ancestors had migrated from Arabia early in the third millennium B.C.E. Joined by other Hebrew tribes already in Palestine, the Israelites formed a confederacy of 12 tribes, led by leaders called *judges*, and in time succeeded in subjugating the Canaanites.

The decisive battle in 1125 B.C.E. at Megiddo, called Armageddon ("Hill of Megiddo") in the New Testament of the Christian Bible, owed much to Deborah the prophetess, who "judged Israel at that time" (Judges 4:4). God ordered Deborah, already famous throughout Israel for her wisdom, to accompany the discouraged war leaders and stir them to victory. For this reason she has been called the Hebrew Joan of Arc.

The vigorous and decisive role played by Deborah and other Israelite women (Moses' sister Miriam, for example) reflects the great influence of women in early Israel. Genesis describes the two sexes as being equal and necessary for human livelihood: "So God created mankind in his image, . . . male and female he created them. And God blessed them and said to them, 'Be fruitful and multiply and fill the earth and subdue it [together]'" (1:27–28). And in the Song of Songs the maiden and the youth share equally in the desire and expression of love; there is no sense of subordination of one to the other. But the continuing dangers that faced the nation led to the creation of a strong centralized monarchy, and with it came male domination and female subordination. Deborah was the last recorded Israelite woman who played an obvious and public leadership role.

Soon after the Canaanites were defeated, a far more formidable opponent appeared. The Philistines, one of the Sea Peoples who had tried unsuccessfully to invade Egypt and from whom the name *Palestine* comes, settled along the coast about 1175 B.C.E. Aided by the use of iron weapons, which were new to the region and the Hebrews, the Philistines captured the Ark of the Covenant, the sacred chest described as having mysterious powers, in which Moses had placed stone tablets inscribed with the Ten Commandments entrusted to him by Yahweh. By the mid-

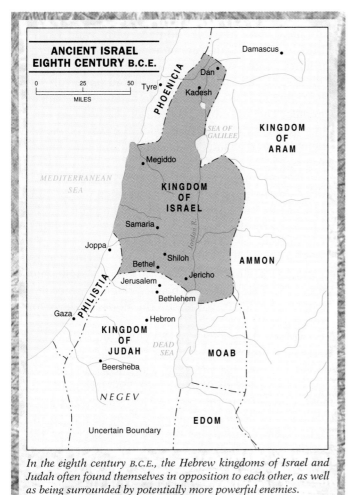

**ANCIENT ISRAEL
EIGHTH CENTURY B.C.E.**

In the eighth century B.C.E., the Hebrew kingdoms of Israel and Judah often found themselves in opposition to each other, as well as being surrounded by potentially more powerful enemies.

led by Samuel and overshadowed by the fame of the boy hero David, who had slain the Philistine giant Goliath in single combat, Saul made no attempt to transform Israel into a centralized state. He collected no taxes, and his army was composed of volunteers. A victim also of his own unsteady and moody nature, Saul finally committed suicide after an unsuccessful battle with the Philistines.

Saul's successor, the popular David (c. 1000–961 B.C.E.), not only restricted the Philistines to a narrow coastal strip but also became the ruler of the largest state in the ancient history of the area, stretching from the Euphrates to the Gulf of Aqaba. David also wrested Jerusalem from the Canaanites and made it the private domain of his royal court, separate from the existing 12 tribes. His popularity was enhanced when he deposited the recovered Ark of the Covenant in his royal chapel, to which he attached a priesthood. The priests in turn proclaimed that God had made a special covenant with David as "the Lord's servant" and with the throne of David through all generations to come.

David's work was completed by his son Solomon (961–922 B.C.E.), under whom Israel reached its high point of worldly power and splendor as a powerful monarchy. In the words of the Bible:

> *Solomon ruled over all the kingdoms from the Euphrates to the land of the Philistines and to the border of Egypt; they brought tribute and served Solomon all the days of his life. . . . And Judah and Israel dwelt in safety, from Dan even to Beersheba, every man under his vine and under his fig tree, all the days of Solomon. . . . And God gave Solomon wisdom and understanding beyond measure, and largeness of mind. . . .*
>
> *Now the weight of gold that came to Solomon in one year was six hundred and sixty-six talents of gold, besides that which came from the traders and from the traffic of the merchants, and from all the kings of Arabia and from the governors of the land. . . . The king also made a great ivory throne, and overlaid it with the finest gold. (1 Kings 5:1, 5, 9; 10:14–15, 18)*

But the price of Solomon's vast bureaucracy, building projects (especially the palace complex and the Temple at Jerusalem), standing army (1400 chariots and 12,000 horses), and harem (700 wives and 300 concubines) was great. High taxes, forced labor, and the loss of tribal independence led to dissension. The Old Testament attributed this dissension to Solomon's feeble old age:

> *For when Solomon was old, his wives turned away his heart after other gods; and his heart was not wholly true to the Lord his God, as was the heart of David his father. . . . Therefore the Lord said to Solomon, "Since . . . you have not kept my covenant and my statutes, which I have commanded you, I will surely tear the kingdom from you . . . ." (1 Kings 11:4, 11)*

dle of the eleventh century B.C.E. the Philistines were well on their way to dominating the entire land.

Lacking central authority, the loose 12-tribe confederacy of Israel could not cope with the Philistine danger. "Give us a king to govern us," the people demanded, "that we also may be like all the nations, and that our king may govern us and go before us and fight our battles" (1 Samuel 8:6, 20). This move was strongly opposed by the conservative upper class, led by the prophet-judge Samuel. He warned the assembled Israelites that if they set up a king they would reject the "rule of God" and suffer divine disapproval. He predicted that a king would subject them to despotic tyranny. But the Israelite assembly rejected Samuel's advice and elected Saul as their first king. At that point "the Lord said to Samuel, 'Hearken to the voice of the people in all that they say to you; for they have not rejected you, but they have rejected me from being king over them'" (1 Samuel 8:7). This statement appears to have been a grudging concession on God's part, like that of a father who allows his wayward son to learn from experience the folly of his ways.

Saul's reign (c. 1020–1000 B.C.E.) was not successful. Continuously undercut by the conservatives

When Solomon died in 922 B.C.E., the kingdom split in two—Israel in the north and Judah in the south. These two weak kingdoms were in no position to defend themselves when new, powerful empires rose again in Mesopotamia. In 722 B.C.E. the Assyrians captured Samaria, the capital of the northern kingdom, taking 27,290 Israelites into captivity (the famous "ten lost tribes" of Israel; two remained in the southern kingdom) and settling foreign peoples in their place. The resulting population, called Samaritans, was ethnically, culturally, and religiously mixed, as well as politically incapacitated.

The southern kingdom of Judah held out until 586 B.C.E., when Nebuchadnezzar, Chaldean ruler of Babylon, destroyed Jerusalem and carried away an estimated 15,000 captives; "none remained, except the poorest people of the land" (2 Kings 24:14). Thus began the famous Babylonian Captivity of the Jews (Judeans), which lasted until 538 B.C.E. when Cyrus, the king of Persia, having conquered Babylon, allowed them to return to Jerusalem, where they rebuilt the Temple destroyed by Nebuchadnezzar.

Generally peaceful Persian rule was followed by that of the Hellenistic Greeks and Romans. Then from 66 to 70 C.E. the Jews rebelled against Rome, and Jerusalem was largely destroyed in the savage fighting that resulted. The Jews were again driven into exile, known as the Diaspora (Greek for "scattering").

Hebrew Religion

From the time of Abraham, the Hebrews worshipped one god, a stern, warlike tribal deity whose name, Yahweh (Jehovah), was first revealed to Moses. Yahweh differed from the many Near Eastern nature gods in being completely separate from the physical universe that he had created. This view of Yahweh as the creator of all things everywhere eventually led to the monotheistic belief that Yahweh was the sole God in the universe.

After their entrance into Palestine, many Hebrews adopted the fertility dieties of the Canaanites as well as the luxurious Canaanite manner of living. As a result, prophets arose who "spoke for" Yahweh (*prophētēs* is Greek for "to speak"), insisting on strict adherence to the Sinai Covenant and condemning the "whoring" after other gods, the selfish pursuit of wealth, and the growth of social injustice.

Between 750 and 550 B.C.E. appeared a series of great prophets who wrote down their messages. They sought to purge the religion of Israel of all corrupting influences and to refine the concept of Yahweh. As summed up by Micah (c. 750 B.C.E.) in a statement often cited as the essence of all higher religions, "He has shown you, O man, what is good; and what does the Lord require of you but to do justice, and to love kindness, and to walk humbly with your God?" (Micah 6:8). Micah's contemporary, the shepherd-prophet Amos, stressed the need for social justice: "Thus saith the Lord: . . . [the rich and powerful] sell the righteous for silver, and the needy for a pair of sandals. They trample the head of the poor into the dust of the earth, and turn aside the way of the afflicted . . . so that they have profaned my holy name" (Amos 2:6–7).

The prophets viewed the course of Hebrew history as being governed by the sovereign will of Yahweh, seeing the Assyrians and the Chaldeans as "the rod of Yahweh's anger" to punish his stubborn, wayward people. They also developed the idea of a coming Messiah (the "anointed one" of God), a descendant of King David. As "a king in righteousness," the Messiah would begin a reign of peace and justice. This ideal would stir the hopes of Jews for centuries.

Among the greatest of the Hebrew prophets are Jeremiah and the anonymous Second Isaiah, so called because his message was incorporated into the Book of Isaiah (chapters 40–55). Jeremiah witnessed the events that led to Nebuchadnezzar's destruction of Jerusalem and the Temple and to the Babylonian Captivity of the Jews. He prepared the people for these disasters by affirming that Yahweh would forgive their sins and restore "a remnant" of his people by proclaiming a "new covenant." The old Sinai Covenant had been between Yahweh and the nation, which no longer existed. It had become overlaid with ritual and ceremony and centered in the Temple, which had been destroyed. The new covenant was between Yahweh and each individual; religion was now a matter of one's own heart and conscience, and both the nation and the Temple were considered unnecessary. Second Isaiah, who lived at the end of the Babylonian Captivity, capped the work of his predecessors by proclaiming Israel to be Yahweh's "righteous servant," purified and enlightened by suffering and ready to guide the world to the worship of the one, eternal, supreme God. Thus the Jews who returned from the Captivity were provided a renewed faith in their destiny and a new understanding of their religion that would gain strength through the centuries.

The Aramaeans

Closely related to the Hebrews were the Aramaeans, who occupied Syria east of the Lebanon Mountains. The most important of their little kingdoms was centered on Damascus, one of the oldest continuously inhabited cities in the world. The Aramaeans dominated the camel caravan trade connecting Mesopotamia, Phoenicia, and Egypt and

Assyria

c. 1350 B.C.E.	Assyrian rise to power
704–681 B.C.E.	Military power at height
669–626 B.C.E.	Reign of Ashurbanipal
612 B.C.E.	Fall of Nineveh

Later Empires of Western Asia, c. 700–500 B.C.E.

By 700 B.C.E. the era of small states had ended with the emergence of the Assyrian Empire. The two great contributions of the Assyrians were the forcible unification of weak, unstable nations and the establishment of an efficient imperial organization.

The Assyrian Empire

For two centuries before 700 B.C.E. the Assyrians had been attempting to transform the growing economic unity of the Near East—evidenced by Solomon's trading operations and even more by the activities of Aramaean merchants—into political unity. The Assyrian move to dominate the Mediterranean began in the ninth century B.C.E. and after a period of weakness was resumed in the eighth century, when they also took over Babylon. By 671 B.C.E. the Assyrians had annexed Egypt and were the masters of the entire Fertile Crescent.

continued to do so even after Damascus fell to the Assyrians in 732 B.C.E. The Aramaic language, which used an alphabet similar to the Phoenician, became the international language of the Near East. In Judea it was more commonly spoken than Hebrew among the lower classes and was used by Jesus and his disciples.

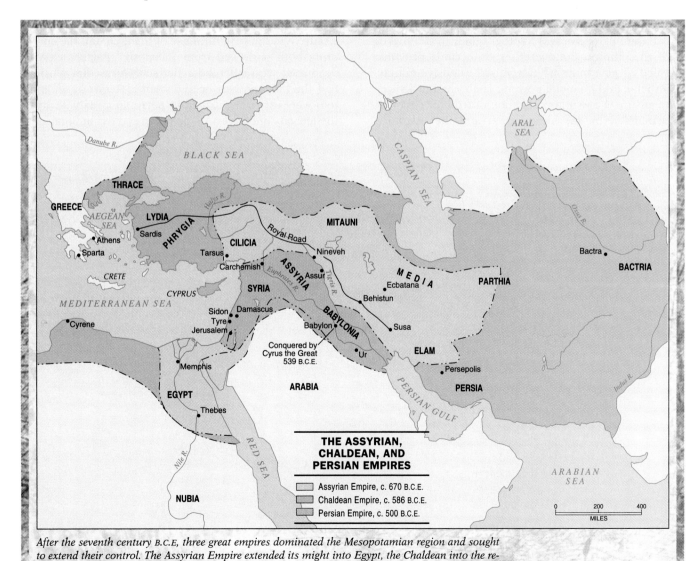

THE ASSYRIAN, CHALDEAN, AND PERSIAN EMPIRES

Assyrian Empire, c. 670 B.C.E.
Chaldean Empire, c. 586 B.C.E.
Persian Empire, c. 500 B.C.E.

After the seventh century B.C.E, three great empires dominated the Mesopotamian region and sought to extend their control. The Assyrian Empire extended its might into Egypt, the Chaldean into the region of the Fertile Crescent, and the Persian from Egypt in the West to the Indus River in the East.

A Semitic people long established in the hilly region of the upper Tigris, the Assyrians had experienced a thousand years of constant warfare. But their matchless army was only one of several factors that explain the success of Assyrian imperialism: a policy of calculated terrorism, an efficient system of political administration, and the support of the commercial classes that wanted political stability and unrestricted trade over large areas.

The Assyrian army, with its chariots, mounted cavalry, and sophisticated siege engines, was the most powerful yet seen in the ancient world. Neither troops nor walls could long resist the Assyrians, whose military might seemed unstoppable. Conquered peoples were held firmly in control by systematic policies designed to terrorize. A typical statement from the Assyrian royal inscriptions reads: "From some I cut off their noses, their ears and their fingers, of many I put out the eyes. . . . I bound their heads to tree trunks round about the city."[24] Mass deportations, like that of the Israelites, were employed as an effective means of destroying national feeling.

The well-coordinated Assyrian system of political administration was another factor in the success of the empire. Conquered lands became provinces ruled by governors who exercised extensive military, judicial, and financial powers. Their chief tasks were to ensure the regular collection of tribute (payments demanded by the conquerors) and the raising of troops for the permanent army that eventually replaced the native militia of sturdy Assyrian peasants. An efficient system of communications carried the "king's word" to the governors as well as the latter's reports to the royal court—including one prophetic dispatch reading: "The king knows that all lands hate us." Nevertheless, the Assyrians must be credited with laying the foundations for some elements of the later more humane administrative systems of their successors, the Persians and Alexander the Great of Macedonia.

Assyrian Culture

The Assyrians borrowed from the cultures of other peoples and unified the elements into a new product. This is evident in Assyrian architecture and sculpture, the work of subject artisans and artists. Both arts glorified the power of the Assyrian king. The palace, serving as both residence and administrative center, replaced the temple as the characteristic architectural form. A feature of Assyrian palace architecture was the structural use of the arch and the column, both borrowed from Babylonia. Palaces were decorated with splendid relief sculptures that glorified the king as warrior and hunter. Assyrian sculptors were especially skilled in portraying realistically the ferocity and agony of charging and dying lions.

This ancient Assyrian statue, "The Dying Lion," is an example of a common theme in royal Assyrian sculpture. The prowess of the Assyrian king as hunter and leader was often emphasized through such artistic themes.

Assyrian kings were interested in preserving written as well as pictorial records of their reigns, and King Ashurbanipal (669–626 B.C.E.) left a record of his great efforts in collecting the literary heritage of Sumer and Babylon. The 22,000 clay tablets found in the ruins of his palace at Nineveh provided modern scholars with their first direct knowledge of the bulk of this literature, which included the Sumerian *Epic of Gilgamesh.*

Downfall of the Assyrian Empire

Revolt against Assyrian terror and tribute was inevitable when Assyria's strength weakened and effective opposition to Assyrian terror arose. By the middle of the seventh century B.C.E. the Assyrians had been decimated by wars, and the Assyrian kings had to use unreliable mercenary troops and conscripted subject peoples. Egypt regained its independence under the Twenty-Sixth Dynasty, and the Medes to the north refused to pay further tribute. The Chaldeans, a new group of Semites who had migrated into Babylonia, revolted in 626 B.C.E. In 612 B.C.E. they joined the Medes in destroying Nineveh, the Assyrian capital. From one end of the Fertile Crescent to the other, people rejoiced: "Nineveh is laid waste; who will bemoan her? . . . All who hear the news of you clap their hands over you. For upon whom has not come your unceasing evil?" (Nahum 3:7, 19).

The Lydians and the Medes

The fall of Assyria left four states to struggle over the crumbs of empire: Chaldea and Egypt fought over Syria and Palestine, and Media and Lydia clashed over eastern Asia Minor.

After the collapse of the Hittite Empire about 1200 B.C.E., the Lydians had followed the Phrygians, whose last king was the legendary Midas, who died around 680 B.C.E., in establishing a kingdom in western Asia Minor. When Assyria fell, the Lydians expanded eastward until stopped by the Medes at the Halys River. Lydia profited from being in control of part of the commercial land route between Mesopotamia and the Aegean and from the possession of valuable gold-bearing streams. About 675 B.C.E. the Lydians invented coinage, which replaced the silver bars in general use up to that time. Lydia's most famous king was Croesus, and the phrase "rich as Croesus" is a reminder of Lydia's legendary wealth. With the king's defeat by the Persians in 547 B.C.E., Lydia ceased to exist as an independent state.

The Medes were an Indo-European people who by 1000 B.C.E. had established themselves on the Iranian plateau east of Assyria. By the seventh century B.C.E. they had created a strong kingdom with Ecbatana as its capital and with the Persians, their

kinsmen to the south, as their subjects. Following the collapse of Assyria, the Medes expanded into Armenia and eastern Asia Minor, but their short-lived empire ended in 550 B.C.E. when they, too, were absorbed by the Persians.

The Chaldean (Neo-Babylonian) Empire

While the Median kingdom controlled the highland region, the Chaldeans, with their capital at Babylon, were masters of the Fertile Crescent. Nebuchadnezzar, who had become king of the Chaldeans in 604 B.C.E., raised Babylonia to another epoch of brilliance after more than a thousand years of eclipse. By defeating the Egyptians in Syria, Nebuchadnezzar ended their hopes of re-creating their empire. As we have seen, he destroyed Jerusalem in 586 B.C.E. and took thousands of captured Jews to Babylonia.

Nebuchadnezzar rebuilt Babylon, making it the largest and most impressive city of its day. The tremendous city walls were wide enough at the top to have rows of small houses on either side. In the center of Babylon ran the famous Procession Street, which passed through the Ishtar Gate. This arch, which was adorned with brilliant tile animals, is the best remaining example of Babylonian architecture. The immense palace of Nebuchadnezzar towered terrace upon terrace, each decorated with masses of ferns, flowers, and trees. These roof gardens, the famous Hanging Gardens of Babylon, were so beautiful that they were regarded by the Greeks as one of the seven wonders of the ancient world.

Nebuchadnezzar also rebuilt the great temple-tower, or *ziggurat* (a Sumerian invention), the biblical "Tower of Babel," which the Greek historian Herodotus described a century later as

> a tower of solid masonry, a furlong [220 yards] in length and breadth, upon which was raised a second tower, and on that a third, and so on up to eight. The ascent to the top is on the outside, by a path which winds round all the towers.[25]

Nebuchadnezzar was the last great Mesopotamian ruler, and Chaldean power quickly crumbled after his death in 562 B.C.E. Chaldean priests, whose interests included political intrigue as well as astrology, continually undermined the monarchy. Finally, in 539 B.C.E. they opened the gates of Babylon to Cyrus the Persian, allowing him to add Babylon to his impressive new empire.

The Persian Empire

Cyrus the Persian was the greatest conqueror in the history of the ancient Near East. In 550 B.C.E. he

The brilliantly glazed bricks of the Ishtar Gate suggest the splendor of the Neo-Babylonian Empire during the reign of Nebuchadnezzar (604–562 B.C.E.). Adorning the brick is a stately procession of realistic-looking bulls and fantastic dragons, which feature a serpent's head and tail, a lion's body and forelegs, and a falcon's hind legs. Separately molded and glazed bricks were used to form the animals, which appear in raised relief on the gate.

ended Persian subjugation to the Medes by capturing Ecbatana and ending the Median dynasty. The Medes readily accepted their vigorous new ruler, who soon demonstrated that he deserved to be called "the Great." When King Croesus of Lydia moved across the Halys River in 547 B.C.E. to pick up some of the pieces of the collapsed Median Empire, Cyrus defeated him and annexed Lydia, including Greek cities on the coast of Asia Minor that were under Lydia's nominal control. Then he turned his attention eastward, establishing his power as far as the frontier of India. Babylon and its empire were next on his list. After Cyrus died, his son Cambyses (530–522 B.C.E.) conquered Egypt. The next ruler, Darius I (522–486

B.C.E.), added the Punjab region in India and Thrace in Europe. He also began a conflict with the Greeks that continued intermittently for more than 150 years until the Persians were conquered by Alexander the Great. Long before this event, the Persian nobility had forgotten Cyrus the Great's answer to their suggestion that they "leave this small and barren country of ours" and move to fertile Babylonia:

> *Do so if you wish, but if you do, be ready to find yourselves no longer governors but governed; for soft lands breed soft men; it does not happen that the same land brings forth wonderful crops and good fighting men.*[26]

Persian Government

Built on the Assyrian model, the Persian administrative system was far more efficient and humane. The empire was divided into 20 *satrapies,* or provinces, each ruled by a governor called a *satrap.* To check the satraps, a secretary and a military official representing the "Great King, King of Kings" were installed in every province. Also, special inspectors, "the Eyes and Ears of the King," traveled throughout the realm.

Imperial post roads connected the important cities. Along the Royal Road between Sardis and Susa there was a post station every 14 miles, where the king's couriers could obtain fresh horses, enabling them to cover the 1600-mile route in a week.

Persia

c. 600 B.C.E.	Union under Achaemenid kings
559–530 B.C.E.	Reign of Cyrus the Great
550 B.C.E.	Conquest of Median Empire
539 B.C.E.	Conquest of Babylon
530–522 B.C.E.	Reign of Cambyses
522–486 B.C.E.	Reign of Darius I

The Majesty of Darius the Great: A Persian Royal Inscription

The Persian kings ruled their vast empire with absolute authority. But the power of the king had to be used in a responsible and ethical manner and in agreement with the purposes of the great god of the Persians, Ahura-Mazda. The following inscription was intended to show the Persian people that the king was able and powerful but also just and honorable.

A great god is Ahuramazda who created this excellent work which one sees; who created happiness for man; who bestowed wisdom and energy upon Darius the king. Says Darius the king: by the favour of Ahuramazda I am of such a kind that I am a friend to what is right, I am no friend to what is wrong. It is not my wish that to the weak is done wrong because of the mighty, it is not my wish that the weak is hurt because of the mighty, that the mighty is hurt because of the weak. What is right, that is my wish. I am no friend of the man who is a follower of the lie. I am not hot-tempered. When I feel anger rising, I keep that under control by my thinking power. I control firmly my impulses. The man who co-operates, him do I reward according to his co-operation. He who

does harm, him I punish according to the damage. It is not my wish that a man does harm, it is certainly not my wish that a man if he causes damage be not punished. What a man says against a man, that does not convince me, until I have heard testimony(?) from both parties. What a man does or performs according to his powers, satisfies me, therewith I am satisfied and it gives me great pleasure and I am very satisfied and I give much to faithful men.

I am trained with both hands and feet. As a horseman I am a good horseman. As a bowman I am a good bowman, both afoot and on horseback. As a spearman I am a good spearman, both afoot and on horseback. And the skills which Ahuramazda has bestowed upon me and I have had the strength to use them, by the favour of Ahuramazda, what has been done by me, I have done with these skills which Ahuramazda has bestowed upon me.

From B. Gharib, "A Newly Found Inscription of Xerxes," *Franica Antiqua*, 1968, as quoted in Amélie Kuhrt, *The Ancient Near East: c. 3000–330 B.C.*, Vol. 2 (London: Routledge, 1995), p. 681.

"Nothing mortal travels so fast as these Persian messengers," wrote Herodotus. "These men will not be hindered . . . , either by snow, or rain, or heat, or by the darkness of night."[27]

The Persian Empire was the first to attempt to govern many different racial groups on the principle of equal responsibilities and rights for all peoples. So long as subjects paid their taxes and kept the peace, the king did not interfere with local religion, customs, or trade. Indeed, Darius was called "the shopkeeper" because he stimulated trade by introducing a uniform system of gold and silver coinage on the Lydian model.

Persian Religion and Art

The humaneness of the Persian rulers may have stemmed from the ethical religion founded by the prophet Zoroaster, who lived in the early sixth century B.C.E. Zoroaster attempted to replace what he called "the lie"—ritualistic, idol-worshiping cults and their Magi priests—with a religion centered on the sole god Ahura-Mazda ("Wise Lord"). This "father of Justice" demanded "good thoughts of the mind, good deeds of the hand, and good words of the tongue" from those who would attain paradise (a

Persian word). This new higher religion made little progress until first Darius and then the Magi adopted it. The Magi revived many old gods as lesser deities, added much ritual, and replaced monotheism with dualism by transforming what Zoroaster had called the principle or spirit of evil into the powerful god Ahriman (the model for the Jewish Satan), the rival of Ahura-Mazda, "between which each man must choose for himself." The complicated evolution of Zoroastrianism is revealed in its holy book, the Avesta ("The Law"), assembled in its present form between the fourth and sixth centuries C.E. Zoroastrian eschatology—the "doctrine of final things" such as the resurrection of the dead and a last judgment—influenced later Judaism. Following the Muslim conquest of Persia in the seventh century C.E., Zoroastrianism died out in its homeland. It exists today among the Parsees in India and in scattered communities worldwide.

In art the Persians borrowed largely from their predecessors in the Fertile Crescent, particularly the Assyrians. Their most important contribution was in palace architecture, the best remains of which are at Persepolis. Built on a high terrace, the royal residence was reached by a grand stairway faced with beautiful reliefs. Instead of the warfare and violence that characterized Assyrian sculpture, these reliefs

This scene, on a Greek vase (c. 330 B.C.E.), depicts King Darius (center) listening to his advisers as they confer on the eve of the battle of Marathon, which the Persians lost to the Greeks in 490 B.C.E.

depict hundreds of soldiers, courtiers, and representatives of 23 nations of the empire bringing gifts to the king for the festival of the new year.

Conclusion

Historians have determined that civilization—interdependent urban living—developed in Mesopotamia and Egypt in the second half of the fourth millennium B.C.E. Both of these civilizations originated in river valleys: one by the Tigris and Euphrates and one by the Nile. In each instance, the complex society we call a civilization was the result of organized and cooperative efforts that were necessary to make the rivers useful to humans living along them.

Mesopotamian civilization originated in the land called Sumer. The achievements of the Sumerians served as a foundation for later Mesopotamian civilizations established by Semitic peoples migrating into the river valleys. The most significant of these

later Semitic civilizations was the Babylonian Empire ruled by Hammurabi. Babylon was sacked by the Indo-European Hittites of Asia Minor, who went on to duel with Egypt over control of Syria and Palestine.

In Egypt a great civilization arose on the banks of the Nile, a civilization both monumental and timeless. The temples and tombs of the Egyptian monarchs were designed to endure forever and to preserve the satisfying and stable existence of this world into eternity. Egypt centered on the absolute rule of the pharaohs—god-kings who eventually extended their domain from Nubia to the Euphrates River.

By 1200 B.C.E. the great Near Eastern empires—Babylonian, Egyptian, and Hittite—had weakened, allowing the Semitic peoples of Syria and Palestine more opportunity to make their own cultural contributions, the most significant being the ethical monotheism of the Hebrews. Political diversity was ended by the rise of the Assyrian Empire, which unified all of the ancient Near East for the first time. After the fall of Assyria, the Chaldean Nebuchadnezzar constructed a new Babylonian Empire, but it was soon engulfed by the expansion of Persia. Stretching from India to Europe, the Persian Empire gave the Near East its greatest extension and power.

The achievements of these early civilizations would become the inheritance of the Greeks and eventually the Romans. Much of the social and cultural legacy of the ancient Near East remains preserved in the fabric of those Mediterranean societies, which rose to political and cultural prominence after the first civilizations declined in vitality.

Suggestions for Reading

Amélie Kuhrt, *The Ancient Near East*, 2 vols. (Routledge, 1995), is an outstanding overview. William W. Hallo and William Kelly Simpson, *The Ancient Near East: A History* (Harcourt Brace, 1998), is also excellent. See also Charles A. Burney, *From Village to Empire: An Introduction to Near Eastern Archaeology* (Phaidon, 1977), and Michael Roaf, *Cultural Atlas of Mesopotamia and the Ancient Near East* (Facts on File, 1990).

Nicholas Postgate, *Early Mesopotamia: Economy and Society at the Dawn of History* (Routledge, 1994), is a most valuable survey. See also Georges Roux, *Ancient Iraq*, 3rd ed. (Penguin, 1992); Samuel N. Kramer, *The Sumerians: Their History, Culture, and Character* (University of Chicago Press, 1971), and the same author's excellent *History Begins at Sumer* (University of Pennsylvania Press, 1981). Joan Oates, *Babylon* (Thames & Hudson, 1979); H. W. F. Saggs, *The Greatness That Was Babylon* (Hawthorne Books, 1962); and Mare van de Mieroop, *The Ancient Mesopotamian City* (Oxford University Press, 1997), are other good sources.

Henri Frankfort et al., *The Intellectual Adventure of Ancient Man* (University of Chicago Press, 1946), is a highly regarded interpretation of Mesopotamian, Egyptian, and Hebrew thought. See also Thorkild Jacobsen, *The Treasures of Darkness:*

A History of Mesopotamian Religion (Yale University Press, 1976).

Survey histories of Egyptian history include Nicolas Grimal, *A History of Ancient Egypt,* trans. Ian Shaw (Blackwell, 1992); *The Cambridge Ancient History* (Cambridge University Press, 1970–1997); Barry J. Kemp, *Ancient Egypt: Anatomy of a Civilization* (Routledge, 1989); Bruce Trigger et al., *Ancient Egypt: A Social History* (Cambridge University Press, 1983); T. G. H. James, *An Introduction to Ancient Egypt* (Harper & Row, 1990); Stephen Quirke and Jeffrey Spencer, eds., *The British Museum Book of Ancient Egypt* (Thames & Hudson, 1992); Guillemette Andrew, *Egypt in the Age of the Pyramids* (Cornell University Press, 1997); Sergio Donadoni, ed., *The Egyptians* (University of Chicago Press, 1997); and Ian Shaw and Paul Nicholson, *The Dictionary of Ancient Egypt* (Abrams, 1995). The position of women in Egyptian society is covered in Gay Robins, *Women in Ancient Egypt* (Harvard University Press, 1993); Barbara Patterson, *Women in Ancient Egypt* (St. Martin's Press, 1991); and Joyce Tyldesley, *Daughters of Isis: Women of Ancient Egypt* (Viking, 1994).

Selections of Egyptian literature are presented in John Foster, *Echoes of Egyptian Voices: An Anthology of Ancient Egyptian Poetry* (University of Oklahoma Press, 1992); R. B. Parkinson, trans. and ed., *Voices from Ancient Egypt: An Anthology of Middle Kingdom Writings* (University of Oklahoma Press, 1991); and Miriam Lichtheim, *Ancient Egyptian Literature,* 3 vols. (University of California Press, 1975).

The history of Nubia and the kingdom of Kush is examined in Derek Welsby, *The Kingdom of Kush* (Wiener, 1998); Stanley Burstein, ed., *Ancient African Civilizations: Kush and Axum* (Wiener, 1998); David O'Connor, *Ancient Nubia: Egypt's Rival in Africa* (University of Pennsylvania Press, 1993); P. L. Shinnie, *Ancient Nubia* (Kegan Paul, 1996); John Taylor, *Egypt and Nubia* (Harvard University Press, 1991); and William Y. Adams, *Nubia: Corridor to Africa* (Princeton University Press, 1977).

For Syrian art, see Harvey Weiss, ed., *Ebla to Damascus: Art and Architecture of Ancient Syria* (Smithsonian Institution, 1985). O. R. Gurney, *The Hittites,* 2nd ed. (Penguin, 1980) is an excellent work. See also Trevor Bryce, *The Kingdom of the Hittites* (Oxford University Press, 1998). Gerhard Herm, *The Phoenicians: The Purple Empire of the Ancient World,* trans. Caroline Hillier (Morrow, 1975), and Nancy K. Sandars, *The Sea Peoples: Warriors of the Ancient Mediterranean, 1250–1150 B.C.* (Thames & Hudson, 1978), are excellent accounts of the seafaring peoples of the Near East.

David J. Goldberg and John D. Rayner, *The Jewish People: Their History and Their Religion* (Viking, 1987), and Harry M. Orlinsky, *Ancient Israel* (Cornell University Press, 1960), are succinct overviews. Excellent longer surveys are Bernhard W. Anderson, *Understanding the Old Testament,* 4th ed. (Prentice Hall, 1986); Michael Grant, *The History of Ancient Israel* (Macmillan, 1984); and John Bright, *A History of Israel,* 3rd ed. (Westminster, 1981).

A. T. Olmstead's *History of Assyria* (Scribner, 1923) and *History of the Persian Empire* (Phoenix, 1948) are the standard accounts. See also Rustom Masani, *Zoroastrianism: The Religion of the Good Life* (Macmillan, 1968); Richard Frye, *The Heritage of Persia* (Mazda Publishing, 1993); and Jean-Louis Huot, *Persia: From the Origins to the Achaemenids* (World, 1965).

On ancient Near Eastern art and architecture, see Seton Lloyd, *The Art of the Ancient Near East* (Oxford University Press, 1961); Henri Frankfort, *The Art and Architecture of the Ancient Orient* (Penguin, 1978); Pierre Amiet, *Art of the Ancient Near East* (Abrams, 1980); and Ann C. Gunter, ed., *Investigating Artistic Environments in the Ancient Near East* (Smithsonian Institution, 1990).

For significant source readings, see James B. Pritchard, ed., *The Ancient Near East: An Anthology of Texts and Pictures* (Princeton University Press, 1958).

Suggestions for Web Browsing

Oriental Institute Virtual Museum
http://www-oi.uchicago.edu/OI/MUS/QTVR96/QTVR96.html

An integral part of the University of Chicago's Oriental Institute, the Oriental Institute Museum offers a virtual showcase of the history, art, and archaeology of the ancient Near East.

Life in Early Mesopotamia
http://www.hum.ku.dk/cni/mashnaqa/index.html

This site offers glimpses into a recent archaeological expedition to Tell Mashnaqa, a settlement nearly 7000 years old. Images of finds and of archaeologists at work.

Hammurabi
http://home.echo-on.net/~smithda/hammurabi.html

A short biography of Hammurabi, in addition to a discussion of the legal concepts he espoused in his code and a virtual recreation of the Hanging Gardens of Babylon.

Egyptian Museum
http://www.idsc.gov.eg/culture/egy_mus.htm

Web site of the Egyptian Museum in Cairo, highlighting images of accessories and jewelry, sculptures, furniture, mummies, and written documents of ancient Egypt from the museum's enormous collection.

Museums of the Vatican: Gregorian Egyptian Museum
http://christusrex.org/www1/vaticano/EG-Egiziano.html

The Vatican Museum's Egyptian Museum provides images and descriptions of many of the significant objects in one of the world's best ancient Egyptian museums.

Nubia: The Land Upriver
http://www.library.nwu.edu/class/history/B94/B94nubia.html

The geography and early history of the Nubian peoples, from prehistoric times to the kingdom of Kush.

Creative Impulse: Mesopotamia
http://history.evansville.net/meso.html

The University of Evansville's impressive site on all things about ancient Mesopotamia—images and documents on various aspects of Mesopotamia's ancient civilizations.

World Cultures: Mesopotamia and Persia
http://www.wsu.edu:8080/~dee/MESO/PERSIANS.HTM

This site gives valuable information on the influence of geography on early Persian civilization, reviews Persian military history, and discusses the importance of Persian religion.

Notes

1. "Gilgamesh and Agga," in Samuel N. Kramer, *The Sumerians: Their History, Culture, and Character* (Chicago: University of Chicago Press, 1971), pp. 187–190.
2. Henri Frankfort, *The Birth of Civilization in the Near East* (London: Williams & Norgate, 1951), p. 60.
3. "The Reforms of Urukagina," in Nels M. Bailkey, ed., *Readings in Ancient History: Thought and Experience from Gilgamesh to St. Augustine,* 4th ed. (Lexington, Mass.: Heath, 1992), p. 21.

4. Adam Falkenstein and W. von Soden, *Sumerische und Akkadische Hymnen und Gebete* (Zurich: Artemis-Verlag, 1953), p. 188. For a partial translation and full discussion of this text, see Samuel N. Kramer, *History Begins at Sumer* (Garden City, N.Y.: Doubleday/Anchor Books, 1959), pp. 228–232.

5. H. de Genouillac, trans., in *Revue d'Assyriologe* 25 (Paris, 1928), p. 148.

6. Quoted in Kramer, *History Begins at Sumer,* p. 53.

7. R. F. Harper, *The Code of Hammurabi* (Chicago: University of Chicago Press, 1904), p. 3.

8. Ibid., p. 101.

9. From *Epic of Gilgamesh,* trans. E. A. Speiser, in *Ancient Near Eastern Texts Relating to the Old Testament,* 2nd ed., ed. James B. Pritchard (Princeton, N.J.: Princeton University Press, 1955), p. 90.

10. Bailkey, *Readings in Ancient History,* p. 29.

11. Quoted in Sabatino Moscati, *The Face of the Ancient Orient* (Garden City, N.Y.: Doubleday/Anchor Books, 1962), p. 71.

12. Miriam Lichtheim, *Ancient Egyptian Literature,* Vol. 1 (Berkeley: University of California Press, 1975), pp. 141–142.

13. John A. Wilson, *The Burden of Egypt* (Chicago: University of Chicago Press, 1951), p. 117.

14. Ibid., p. 164.

15. Adolf Erman, *The Literature of the Ancient Egyptians,* trans. Aylward M. Blackman (London: Methuen, 1927), pp. 190, 196, 197.

16. "The Instruction of Meri-ka-Re," in Wilson, *The Burden of Egypt,* p. 120.

17. Ibid., p. 119.

18. Quoted in George Steindorff and George Hoyingen-Huene. *Egypt* (Locust Valley, N.Y.: Augustin, 1943), p. 23.

19. Bailkey, *Readings in Ancient History,* pp. 39–43.

20. George Steindorff and Keith E. Steel, *When Egypt Ruled the East* (Chicago: University of Chicago Press, 1942), p. 125.

21. Miriam Lichtheim, *Ancient Egyptian Literature,* Vol. 2 (Berkeley: University of California Press, 1975), pp. 96, 98.

22. O. R. Gurney, *The Hittites* (New York: Penguin, 1932), p. 172.

23. Bernhard W. Anderson, *Understanding the Old Testament,* 2nd ed. (Englewood Cliffs, N.J.: Prentice Hall, 1966), p. 559.

24. Daniel D. Luckenbill, *Ancient Records of Assyria and Babylonia,* Vol. 1 (Chicago: University of Chicago Press, 1926), p. 147.

25. Herodotus, *History of the Persian Wars,* 1.181.

26. Ibid., 9.122.

27. Ibid., 8.88.

The theater at Delphi, where the
god Apollo was thought to speak to
the Greeks by taking over the body
of his priestess.

The Greek
Achievement

*Minoan, Mycenaean, Hellenic,
and Hellenistic Civilizations*

Scarred by time, weather, and modern pollution, the ruins of the Athenian Acropolis today stand under a smog-laden sky and overlook the trees and buildings of a bustling modern city sprawled beneath. These ruins are striking symbols of a great civilization whose principal center was Athens.

In the fifth century B.C.E. the temples and statues of the Acropolis were new and gleaming, fresh from the hands of confident architects and sculptors. Five hundred years later, when Greece was a province of the Roman Empire, they still impressed the writer Plutarch:

> *The works . . . are wonderful; they were quickly created and they have lasted for ages. In beauty each one appeared venerable as soon as it was finished, but in freshness and vigor it looks even now new and lately built. They bloom with an eternal freshness that seems untouched by time, as though they had been inspired by an unfading spirit of youth.*[1]

Today the Acropolis no longer appears to be "untouched by time"; yet for us no less than for Plutarch, ancient Athens and the civilization that was centered there has retained an "eternal freshness." Greece's accomplishments were to prove enduring. Its magnificent intellectual and artistic legacy would provide much of the cultural heritage of Western civilization. And when we look at the Greek experience as a whole—political, economic, social, religious, and cultural—we can see the great impact of the ancient Greeks on the development of civilization in the West.

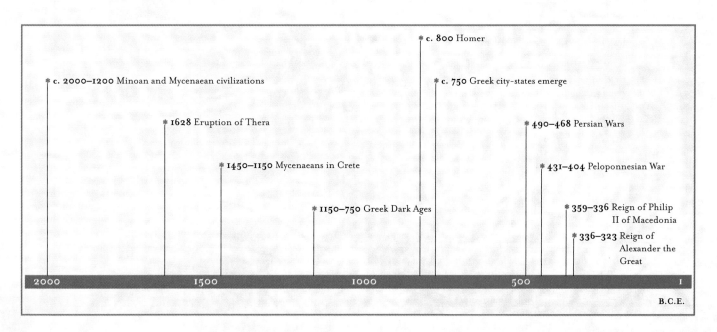

- c. 800 Homer
- c. 2000–1200 Minoan and Mycenaean civilizations
- c. 750 Greek city-states emerge
- 1628 Eruption of Thera
- 490–468 Persian Wars
- 1450–1150 Mycenaeans in Crete
- 431–404 Peloponnesian War
- 1150–750 Greek Dark Ages
- 359–336 Reign of Philip II of Macedonia
- 336–323 Reign of Alexander the Great

2000   1500   1000   500   1

B.C.E.

Minoan and Mycenaean Civilizations, c. 2000–1200 B.C.E.

Classical Greek civilization was preceded by two advanced cultures on the lands surrounding the Aegean Sea. Minoan civilization came into full flower about 2000 B.C.E.; Mycenaean civilization seems to have exerted its greatest power between 1450 and 1200 B.C.E. And both civilizations appear to have collapsed suddenly following 1200 B.C.E.

<table>
<tr><td colspan="2">**Preclassical Greece**</td></tr>
<tr><td>c. 2000–1200 B.C.E.</td><td>Minoan and Mycenaean civilizations</td></tr>
<tr><td>1628 B.C.E.</td><td>Eruption of Thera</td></tr>
<tr><td>1450–1150 B.C.E.</td><td>Mycenaeans in Crete</td></tr>
<tr><td>1150–750 B.C.E.</td><td>Greek Dark Ages</td></tr>
</table>

The Minoans

The first of these early cultures of the Aegean area to develop is now referred to as Minoan, after the legendary King Minos of Crete. Crete was the center of Minoan civilization, which spread to the Aegean Islands, the coast of Asia Minor, and mainland Greece. A narrow, 160-mile-long island, Crete served as a stepping-stone between Europe, Asia, and Africa.

Stimulated by immigrants from Asia Minor and by economic and cultural contacts with Mesopotamia, Egypt, and more southern Africa, a brilliant civilization emerged here by 2000 B.C.E.

Minoan prosperity was based on large-scale trade that ranged from Sicily, Greece, and Asia Minor to Syria and Africa. The Minoans employed the first ships capable of long voyages over the open sea.

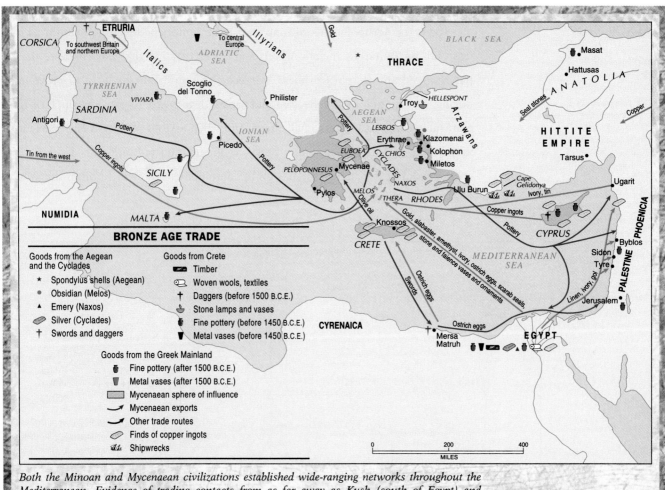

Both the Minoan and Mycenaean civilizations established wide-ranging networks throughout the Mediterranean. Evidence of trading contacts from as far away as Kush (south of Egypt) and Afghanistan has been found in Aegean Bronze Age archaeological sites.

Chief exports were olive oil, wine, metalware, and magnificent pottery. This trade was the monopoly of an efficient bureaucratic government under a powerful ruler whose administrative records were written on clay tablets, first in a form of picture writing (hieroglyphic) and later in a script known as Linear A, whose 87 signs represented syllables. As neither script has been deciphered, our knowledge of Minoan civilization is incomplete and imprecise; most of it is derived from the material remains—walls, temples, houses, and pottery and tablet fragments—uncovered by archaeologists.

The spectacular discoveries of the English archaeologist Sir Arthur Evans a century ago first brought to light this impressive civilization, whose existence had previously only been hinted at in the epics of Homer and in Greek legends such as that of the Minotaur, half bull and half man, who devoured young men and women sent as tribute from Greece. Between 1900 and 1905 Evans excavated the ruins of a great palace at Knossos, the dominant city in Crete after 1700 B.C.E. Rising at least three stories high and sprawling over nearly 6 acres, this "Palace of Minos," built of brick and limestone and employing unusual downward-tapering columns of wood, was a maze of royal apartments, storerooms, corridors, open courtyards, and broad stairways. Equipped with running water, the palace had a sanitation system that surpassed anything else constructed in Europe until Roman times. Walls were painted with elaborate frescoes in which the Minoans appear as a happy, peaceful people with a pronounced liking for dancing, festivals, and athletic contests. Women are shown enjoying a freedom and dignity unknown elsewhere in the ancient Near East or classical Greece. They are not secluded in the home but are seen sitting with men and taking an equal part in public festivities—even as athletes and bullfighters. Their dresses are very elaborate, with bright patterns and colors, pleats, puffed sleeves, and flounces. Bodices are open in front to the waist, and hair is elaborately fashioned with ringlets over the forehead and around the ears.

One of the most notable features of Minoan culture was its art, unrestrained and full of rhythmic motion. Art seems to have been an essential part of everyday life and not, as in the ancient Near East, an adjunct to religion and the state. What little is known of Minoan religion also contrasts sharply with other religious patterns in the Near East: there were no great temples, powerful priesthoods, or large cult statues of the gods. The principal deity was probably a Mother Goddess; her importance reflected the important position held by women in Minoan society. A number of recovered statuettes show her dressed like a fashionable Minoan woman with flounced skirts; a tightly laced, low-cut bodice; and elaborately arranged hair. She was perhaps the early inspiration for such later Greek goddesses as Athena, Demeter, and Aphrodite.

The Mycenaeans

About 2000 B.C.E. or shortly thereafter, the first Indo-European Greek tribes, collectively called Achaeans, entered Greece, where they absorbed the earlier settlers and ruled from fortified citadels at Mycenae, Pylos, Athens, and other sites in the south of Greece. By 1600 B.C.E. the Achaeans—or Mycenaeans, as they are usually called—had adopted much of the advanced culture of the Minoans. However, unlike the Minoans, the Mycenaeans seemed to have been a

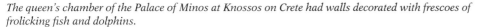

The queen's chamber of the Palace of Minos at Knossos on Crete had walls decorated with frescoes of frolicking fish and dolphins.

In contrast to some of the rigid and grandiose Mesopotamian and Egyptian statues, those of the Minoans were small and animated. This little priestess holds snakes, possibly reflecting Minoan religious rituals.

more warlike people and sailed the seas as raiders as well as traders. Mycenaean women adopted Minoan fashions and added a variety of sumptuous jewelry, from bracelets to earrings.

Some of the wealth accumulated by the kings of Mycenae—the greatest single hoard of gold, silver, and ivory objects found anywhere before the discovery of Tutankhamen's tomb—was unearthed in 1876 by Heinrich Schliemann, a few years after his sensational discoveries at Troy. The royal palace on the acropolis, or citadel, of Mycenae had well-proportioned audience rooms and apartments, fresco-lined walls, floors of painted stucco, and large storerooms. Impressive also were the royal "beehive" tombs, constructed of cut stone and covered with earth, near the citadel.

The expansive force of Mycenaean civilization led to the planting of colonies in the eastern Mediterranean (Hittite sources refer to Achaeans in Asia Minor) and even to the conquest of Knossos about 1450

B.C.E. This Mycenaean takeover was made possible by the destruction of the mazelike palace at Knossos by fire, perhaps the aftermath of an earthquake. Minoan dominance in the Aegean and prosperity on Crete had already been lessened by the devastation caused by the catastrophic eruption of the volcanic island of Thera (modern Santorini), 80 miles north of Crete, and a massive tidal wave that may have struck the northern shore of the island at a height of nearly half a mile. Archaeologists and volcanologists now place this great eruption in 1628 B.C.E., but the resulting damage to structures, crops, and the merchant fleet of the Minoans may have contributed to making the civilization vulnerable to Mycenaean raids. The palace at Knossos was rebuilt by the Mycenaeans only to be destroyed about 1380 B.C.E. by earthquake and fire, and the center of civilization in the Aegean shifted to the Greek mainland.

Much about the specifics of Minoan-Mycenaean relations was unclear until after 1952, when a young English architect, Michael Ventris, startled the scholarly world by deciphering a late type of Minoan script known as Linear B, many examples of which had been found by Evans at Knossos and by later archaeologists at mainland Greek sites such as Pylos, Mycenae, and Thebes. When Linear B turned out to be an early form of Greek written in syllabic characters, it followed that the rulers of Knossos after 1450 B.C.E. must have been Achaean Greeks who had adopted the Minoan script to write their own language.

The Linear B texts, which are administrative documents and inventories, add greatly to our knowledge of Mycenaean life. The Mycenaean centers were fortified palaces and administrative offices and not, as in Crete, true cities. The bulk of the population lived in scattered villages where they worked either communal land or land held by nobles or kings. The nobles were under the close control of the kings, whose administrative records were kept daily by a large number of scribes. Prominent in these records are details of the disbursement of grain and wine as wages and the collection of taxes in kind. The most important item of income was olive oil, the major article in the wide-ranging Mycenaean trade, which was operated as a royal monopoly. Perhaps it was their role as merchant adventurers that led the Achaean kings about 1250 B.C.E. to launch an expedition against Troy to eliminate a powerful commercial rival.

Troy, Site of Homer's *Iliad*

The city of Troy occupied a strategic position on the Hellespont (the strait from the Aegean to the Black Sea, now known as the Dardanelles). In this location, Troy could command both sea traffic through the straits and land routes between Asia and Europe. For many years scholars thought this city existed only in the epic poems of Homer. Heinrich Schliemann (1822–1890), a German romantic dreamer and amateur archaeologist, believed otherwise. As a youth he had read Homer's *Iliad,* and he became firmly convinced that Troy had actually existed. At the age of 48, having made a fortune in the California gold rush and in worldwide trade, Schliemann retired from business to prove that his dreams of ancient Troy's existence were true.

In 1870 Schliemann began excavations at the legendary site of Troy, where he unearthed nine buried cities, built one on top of the other. He discovered a treasure of golden earrings, hairpins, and bracelets in the second city (Troy II), which led him to believe that this was the city of Homer's epics. Excavations in the 1930s, however, showed that Troy II had been destroyed about 2200 B.C.E., far too early to have been the scene of the Trojan War. Scholars now believe that Troy VI or VII was probably the city made famous by Homer.

Neither the view that Troy was the victim of commercial rivalry nor the other widely held theory that it was destroyed by Achaean pirates seeking wealth corresponds to Homer's view that the Trojan War was caused by the abduction of Helen, queen of Sparta, by the Trojan prince Paris. Led by Agamemnon, king of Mycenae, the wrathful Achaeans besieged Troy for ten long years. Homer's *Iliad* deals only with a few weeks during the tenth year of the siege.

The Fall of Mycenaean Civilization

Greek traditions recorded that around 1200 B.C.E. a new wave of Greek invaders, materially aided by weapons made of iron instead of bronze, invaded Greece from the north and conquered the Mycenaean strongholds. These newcomers may have followed in the wake of the devastation caused by raiding Sea Peoples (see Chapter 2); some archaeologists suggest that invasions of new peoples caused less damage to Mycenaean sites than did revolts of the lower classes against their powerful and autocratic overlords. First of the Mycenaean strongholds to fall was Pylos, whose Linear B archives contain numerous references to quickly undertaken preparations to meet military emergencies. We find orders directing women and children to places of safety; instructions to armorers, "rowers," and food suppliers; and a report titled "How the Watchers Are Guarding the Coastal Regions."[2] The preparations were in vain, however. Pylos was sacked and burned, and all of the other major Mycenaean citadels were likewise destroyed.

In 1876, when Heinrich Schliemann found this gold death mask at Mycenae, he excitedly telegraphed a friend: "I have looked upon the face of Agamemnon." The mask, however, dates from about 1500 B.C.E., nearly three centuries before the Trojan War, during which Agamemnon is said to have reigned.

The Rise of Hellenic Civilization, c. 1150–500 B.C.E.

The four centuries from around 1150 to 750 B.C.E., the Greek Dark Ages, were marked by drastic depopulation and the disappearance of the major characteristics of Mycenaean civilization—centralized and bureaucratic administration, wide-ranging commerce, sophisticated art forms, monumental architecture, and writing. Although the fall of Mycenaean civilization was a catastrophic event, the passing of the Mycenaeans eventually gave rise to the development of a new and different civilization, the Hellenic. Hellenic civilization derives its name from the Greek god Hellen, who is credited with bringing humans to first inhabit Greece (Greeks ancient and modern call their country Hellas).

The Influence of Geography

Geographical factors played an important part in shaping the events of Greek history. The numerous mountain ranges that crisscross the peninsula, which is about the size of the state of Maine, severely restricted internal communication and led to the development of fiercely independent city-states and the reluctance of the Greeks to unite into a single nation. The mountains cover two-thirds of the peninsula, and along the west coast they come close to the sea, leaving few harbors or arable plains. Elsewhere the deeply indented coast provides many natural harbors. A narrow isthmus at the Gulf of Corinth made southern Greece almost an island—in fact, it was called the Peloponnesus ("Pelop's island"). The jagged coastline and the many islands offshore stimulated seagoing trade, and the rocky soil (less than a fifth of Greece is arable) and few natural resources encouraged the Greeks to establish colonies abroad.

The Homeric Age

Most of our information about the Greek Dark Ages is derived from the epics put in written form around 750 B.C.E. and attributed to a supposedly blind Ionian poet named Homer. Controversy surrounds the question of Homer's existence and whether he alone or several poets composed the *Iliad* and the *Odyssey*. The Homeric epics retain something of the material side of the Mycenaean period, handed down to Homer's time by a continuous oral tradition. But in terms of the details of political, economic, and social life, the religious beliefs and practices, and the ideals that gave meaning to life, the poet could only describe what was familiar to him in his own age, probably soon after 800 B.C.E.

The values held by Homer to give meaning to life in the Homeric Age were predominantly heroic values—the strength, skill, and valor of the dominating warrior. Such was the earliest meaning of *aretē*, "excellence" or "virtue," a key term whose meaning changed as values changed during the course of Greek culture. To obtain *aretē*—defined by one

Homeric hero as "to fight ever in the forefront and outdo my companions"—and the undying fame that was its reward, men welcomed hardship, struggle, and even death. Honor, like fame, was a measure of *aretē*, and the greatest of human tragedies was the denial of honor due to a great warrior. Homer makes such a denial the theme of the *Iliad:* "The ruinous wrath of Achilles that brought countless ills upon the Achaeans" when Achilles, insulted by Agamemnon, withdraws from battle.

The Homeric king was essentially a war leader, hardly more than a leader among his companions, fellow nobles who sat in his council to advise him and to check any attempt he might make to exercise arbitrary power. There was also a popular assembly of all arms-bearing men, whose consent was needed whenever a crisis occurred, such as war or the election of a new king.

Society was clearly aristocratic—only the *aristoi* ("best") possessed *aretē*—and the common man was reprimanded and beaten when he dared to question his superiors. Yet the commoners had certain political rights as members of the popular assembly.

The economy was a simple, self-sufficient agricultural system in which private ownership of land replaced the collective group ownership of Mycenaean times. One Homeric hero states that as a reward for leadership and heroism, he holds "a large estate by the banks of the river Zanthus, fair with orchard lawns and wheat-growing land."[3] The Greek word for "large estate" is *temenos*, a "cutting," which apparently indicates that the estate had been "cut out" of the common land.

From Oligarchy to Tyranny

The *polis*, or city-state—the political unit consisting of the city and its people—did not exist in the Greek Dark Ages. The nucleus of every polis was the high, fortified site, the *acropolis*, where people could take refuge from attack. In time this defensive center took on added significance as the focus of political and religious life. When commerce revived in the eighth and seventh centuries B.C.E., a trading center (*agora*) developed below the acropolis. The two areas and the surrounding territory, usually smaller than a modern county, formed the polis (the plural is *poleis*), from which our word *politics* is derived.

The political development of the polis was so rich and varied that it is difficult to think of a form of government not experienced—and given a lasting name—by the Greeks: monarchy, oligarchy, tyranny, and democracy.

By the middle of the eighth century B.C.E., the nobles, who wished to share in the authority exercised by monarchs, had taken over the government of most city-states, ushering in an age of aristocracy ("govern-

Greek civilization flourished in the mountainous lands of the eastern Mediterranean. Mainland Greece lacked arable land and navigable rivers, but its extensive coastline and fine harbors drew the Greeks to the sea for sustenance and commerce.

ment by the best") or oligarchy ("government by the few," a limited number of aristocrats). Exercising their superior power, the nobles in many locations abolished the popular assembly, acquired a monopoly of the best land, reduced many commoners to virtual serfdom, and forced others to seek a living on rocky, barren soil.

The hard lot of common people under aristocracy or oligarchy is recorded in the poet Hesiod's *Works and Days* (c. 700 B.C.E.). A commoner who had been cheated out of his parcel of land by his evil brother in league with "bribe-swallowing" aristocratic judges, Hesiod was the prophet of a moralized conception of the gods and a new age of social justice. To establish a just society, Hesiod argued, people must learn to pursue moderation *(sophrosynē)* in all things—apparently the first written expression of this famous Greek ideal—and realize that "far-seeing" Zeus and the other gods punish evildoers and reward the righteous. In contrast to Homer, with his aristocratic heroes, Hesiod defined human excellence, or *aretē*, in a way to make it attainable by common people. Its essential ingredients were righteousness and

work—honest work in competition with one's fellows being a desirable goal. "Gods and men hate him who lives without work," Hesiod insisted. "His nature is like the drones who sit idle and eat the labor of the bees." Furthermore, "work is no shame, but idleness is a shame," and "esteem," "glory," and "riches" follow work.[4]

Hesiod's newly written ideals of moderation and justice were slow to take root. Often the poor found relief only by emigrating overseas. As Plato later noted, the wealthy promoted colonization as a safety valve to ward off a threatened political and economic explosion:

> *When men who have nothing, and are in want of food, show a disposition to follow their leaders in an attack on the property of the rich—these, who are the natural plague of the state, are sent away by the legislator in a friendly spirit as far as he is able; and this dismissal of them is euphemistically termed a colony.[5]*

From 750 to 550 B.C.E. the Greeks planted colonies throughout much of the Mediterranean world. Colonies were founded along the northern coast of the Aegean and around the Black Sea. So many Greeks migrated to southern Italy and eastern Sicily that the region became known as *Magna Graecia,* Great Greece. Colonies were also founded as far west as present-day France—at Massilia (modern Marseilles), for example—and Spain and on parts of the African coast. Unique was Naucratis in Egypt, not a true colony but a trading post whose residents gained extraterritorial rights (their own magistrates and law courts) from the Egyptians.

In time colonization lessened some of Greece's economic and social problems. By 600 B.C.E. economic progress and the use of coined money, probably inspired by the Lydians, had created the beginnings of a middle class. The Greek poleis gradually became "industrialized" as a result of concentrating on the production of specialized goods—vases, metal products, textiles, olive oil, and wine—for export in exchange for food and raw materials. But before this economic revolution was completed, the continuing land hunger of the poor and landless contributed to a political revolution.

After 650 B.C.E. rulers known as *tyrants* seized power in many Greek states and, supported by both the desperately poor and the rising merchant classes, took the reins of government from the nobility. They were supported also by a new heavily armed infantry force (the hoplite phalanx), composed of middle-class citizens wealthy enough to furnish their own equipment. These tyrants (the word meant simply "one who usurps power" and did not at first have to-

day's connotation of brutality) sometimes distributed land to the landless poor and, by promoting further colonization, trade, and industry, increased economic development and generally made their poleis better places to live for all residents.

Athens to 500 B.C.E.

Athens and Sparta, the two city-states destined to dominate the political history of Greece during the classical period (the fifth century B.C.E. and most of the fourth), underwent markedly different courses of development during the period prior to 500 B.C.E. Whereas the political, economic, and social evolution of Athens was typical of most Greek states, Sparta's development produced a unique way of life that elicited the wonder and often the admiration of other Greeks.

In Athens during the seventh century B.C.E., the council of nobles became supreme. The popular assembly rarely met, and the king's authority was replaced by that of nine magistrates, called *archons* ("rulers"), chosen annually by the aristocratic council to exercise the king's civil, military, and religious powers. While the nobles on their large estates prospered, the small farmers and sharecroppers suffered. Bad years forced them to borrow seed from their rich neighbors, and when they were unable to repay their debts, they were sold into slavery. To the small farmers' clamor for the cancellation of debts and the end to debt slavery was added the voice of the landless for the redistribution of land.

A sixth-century B.C.E. oil container produced in Corinth. Corinthian pottery was the most popular of all such work for over 200 years, and many examples of it are found throughout the Mediterranean region.

When the Athenian nobles finally realized that their failure to address the cry for reform might result in the rise of a tyrant, they agreed to the policy of compromise advocated by the aristocrat Solon. In 594 B.C.E. Solon was made sole archon, with broad authority to revise the constitution of Athens in order to avoid class conflict. Inspired by the ideals of moderation and justice promoted by Hesiod a century earlier, Solon instituted middle-of-the-road reforms that have made his name a byword for wise statesmanship.

For the lower classes, Solon agreed to canceling all debts and forbidding future debt slavery, but he rejected as too radical the demand for the redivision of the land. His long-range solution to the economic problem was to seek full employment by stimulating trade and industry. To achieve this goal, Solon required fathers to teach their sons a trade, granted citizenship to foreign artisans and merchants who settled in Athens, and encouraged the intensive production of wine and olive oil for export.

Moderation also characterized Solon's political reforms—the common people were granted important political rights, but not complete equality. Although laws continued to originate in the new aristocratic Council of Four Hundred, they now had to be ratified by the popular assembly, which Solon revived. And since wealth, not birth, became the qualification for membership in the new council and for the archonships, wealthy commoners could acquire full political equality. Furthermore, the assembly could now act as a court to hear appeals from the decisions of the archons and to try the archons for misdeeds in office.

Unfortunately, Solon's moderate reforms did not completely satisfy the rich or the poor. The poor had received neither land nor full political equality, while the nobles thought Solon a radical who had betrayed his class. Deeply discouraged, Solon described what is too often the lot of moderate reformers: "Formerly their eyes sparkled when they saw me; now they coldly scorn me, no longer friends but enemies."[6]

Solon had warned the Athenians to accept his reforms unless "the people in its ignorance comes into the power of a tyrant." He lived to see his prediction fulfilled. In 560 B.C.E., after a period of anarchy, Pisistratus, a military hero and champion of the commoners, seized power as tyrant. He addressed the economic problem by banishing many nobles, whose lands he distributed among the poor, and by promoting commerce and industry. Together with extensive public works and the patronage of culture—starting Athens on the road to cultural leadership in Greece—these reforms gave rise to a popular saying that "life under Pisistratus was paradise on earth."

Pisistratus was succeeded by his two sons, one of whom was assassinated and the other exiled after he became tyrannical in the modern sense of the word. When the nobles, aided by a Spartan army, took the opportunity to restore aristocracy, a noble named Cleisthenes temporarily seized power and resisted Spartan interference. From 508 to 502 B.C.E. Cleisthenes put through constitutional reforms that greatly reduced the remaining power of the nobility. He disregarded the old noble-dominated tribes and created ten new ones, each embracing citizens of all classes from widely scattered districts. The popular assembly soon acquired the right to initiate legislation and became the sovereign power in the state; there could be no appeal from its decisions. The new democratic Council of Five Hundred, selected by lot from the ten tribes, advised the assembly and supervised the administrative actions of the archons. Cleisthenes' final reform was the peculiar institution of *ostracism,* an annual referendum in which a quorum of citizens could vote to exile for ten years any individual thought to be a threat to the new Athenian democracy. (A quorum consisted of 6000 of the 50,000 male citizens over the age of 18. The average attendance at an Athenian assembly, whose ordinary meetings were held every ten days, was about 5000.) By 500 B.C.E. the Athenian polis had established a form of democratic government more thorough than in any other city in the ancient world.

Sparta to 500 B.C.E.

Like many other Greek city-states, Sparta had moved from monarchy to oligarchy when the nobles installed five annual aristocratic magistrates, called *ephors* ("overseers"), to supervise the kings' activities. Instead of sending out colonists to solve the common problems of overpopulation and land hunger, the Spartan oligarchs turned to a simpler solution: the conquest of their Greek neighbors in Messenia, who were forced to become state slaves *(helots).* Around 650 B.C.E., however, the Messenians revolted, and it took nearly 20 years to crush the uprising, during which the aristocrats were forced to seek the aid of the Spartan commoners. In return, the nobles agreed to the commoners' demand for land division and political equality. Private ownership of land was abolished, and the land was divided equally among the 9000 Spartan citizens. In addition, the nobles established a popular assembly of all Spartan citizens with the right to elect the ephors and to approve or veto the proposals of the 30-member Council of Elders. While the Athenian state required only two years of military training for young men, the Spartan system—traditionally attributed to a legendary lawgiver named Lycurgus—was designed to make every Spartan man a professional soldier and to keep him in a constant state of readiness for war, especially the ever-present danger of a helot revolt. To this end,

No Adulterers in Sparta

Adultery was regarded among them as an impossible crime. A story is told of a very old Spartan named Geradas, who, when asked by a stranger what was done to adulterers in Sparta, answered, "Stranger, there are no adulterers among us." "And if there were one?" asked the stranger. "Then," said Geradas, "he would have to pay as compensation a bull big enough to stand on Mount Taygetus and drink from the river Eurotas." The stranger, astonished, asked, "Where can you find so big a bull?" "Where can you find an adulterer in Sparta?" answered Geradas.

From Plutarch, *Lives*, "Lycurgus," 15.

Sparta's totalitarian state enforced absolute subordination of the individual to its will.

State officials examined all newborn children, and any found sickly or deformed were abandoned to die. At the age of 7 a boy was taken from his family and placed in the charge of state educators, who taught him to bear hardship, endure discipline, and devote his life to the state. At 20 the young Spartan enrolled in the army and lived in barracks, where he contributed food from his allotment of land granted by the state and worked by helots. At 30 he was allowed to marry, but he continued to live in barracks, sneaking back to visit his wife only at night. Finally, at 60, he was released from the army and could live at home with his family.

This lifelong discipline produced formidable soldiers and inspired them with the spirit of obedience and respect for Spartan law. Plutarch reports in his biography of Lycurgus that Spartan training "accustomed the citizens to have neither the will nor the ability to lead a private life, but, like bees, to be organic parts of their community, clinging together around their leader, forgetting themselves in their enthusiastic patriotism, and belonging wholly to their country."[7]

Although many Greeks admired the Spartan way of life, the typical Spartan was an unsophisticated, uncultured fighting machine who exaggerated his masculinity, took few baths, and spoke few words. According to Plutarch, "When one of them was invited to hear a man imitate a nightingale, he answered, 'I have heard the original.'" Plutarch's description of their marriages is equally revealing:

Their marriage custom was for the husband to carry off his bride by force. They did not carry off little immature girls, but grown-up women who were ripe for marriage. After the bride had been carried off, . . . the bridegroom . . . comes into the room, unties her girdle, and takes her to himself. After spending a short time with her, he returns composedly to his usual quarters to sleep with the other young men. And so he continues afterwards, passing his days with his companions and visiting his wife by stealth, feeling ashamed and afraid that some one in the house might hear him. . . . This went on for a long time, and some even had children born to them before they ever saw their wives by daylight.[8]

Spartan girls also received state training in order to become healthy mothers of warrior sons. Clad in short tunics, which other Greeks thought immodest, they engaged in running, wrestling, and throwing the discus and javelin. As their men marched off to war, Spartan women bade them a laconic farewell (Laconia was the Spartan homeland): "Come back *with* your shield—or *on* it." Plutarch also reports that the Spartans

did away with all seclusion and retirement for women, and ordained that girls, no less than boys, should go naked in processions, and dance and sing at festivals in the presence of the young men. . . . This nakedness of the maidens had in it nothing disgraceful. It was done modestly, not licentiously, and it produced habits of simplicity and taught them to desire good health and beauty of body, and to love honor and courage no less than the men. This it was that made them speak and think as Gorgo, the wife of Leonidas, is said to have done. Some foreign lady, it seems, said to her, "You Spartan women are the only ones who rule men." She answered, "Yes, for we are the only ones who give birth to men."[9]

While Sparta developed the finest military machine in Greece, it remained backward culturally and economically. Trade and travel were prohibited because the city fathers feared that foreign ideas might threaten Spartan discipline. Sparta is a classic example of how intellectual stagnation accompanies rigid social conformity and military regimentation.

To provide additional assurance that its helots remained uncontaminated by democratic ideas, Sparta allied itself with oligarchic parties in other Peloponnesian states and aided them in suppressing their democratic opponents. The resulting Spartan League of oligarchic states, in operation by the end of the

Bronze statuette of a Spartan girl exercising (c. 500 B.C.E.).

sixth century B.C.E., was shortly to be opposed by an Athenian-led union of democratic states.

Unity and Strife in the Hellenic World, 500–336 B.C.E.

The leaders of a Greek economic and cultural revival after 750 B.C.E. were the Ionian Greeks, descendants of Mycenaeans who had fled the so-called Dorian invaders and settled the Aegean coast of Asia Minor, its offshore islands, and the mainland region of Attica, whose major city was Athens. Influenced by contacts with Phoenician traders (from whom they borrowed the alphabet in the eighth century B.C.E.) and neighboring Lydia and Egypt, the Ionians became innovators in art, science, philosophy, and literature; they were said to have "first kindled the torch of Hellenism." Ionian creativity was also evident in their commercial ventures, which spread throughout the Aegean region. It was especially because of their economic prosperity that they became the first of the Greeks to face threats from the great powers of the Near East.

The Persian Wars

When the Persians conquered Lydia in 547 B.C.E., they also took over Ionia, which had been under moderate Lydian rule. In open opposition to their Persian-appointed tyrants, the Ionian cities revolted in 499 B.C.E., established democratic regimes, and appealed to the Athenians, who were also Ionians, for aid. Athens sent 20 ships—token help, but far too few to prevail over the Persians. By 494 B.C.E. the Persian king Darius I had crushed the revolt, burning the Greek polis of Miletus in revenge.

Darius knew that Ionia was insecure as long as Athens remained free to incite the Ionian Greeks to revolt again. Thus in 490 B.C.E. a Persian force of about 20,000 infantry and cavalry sailed across the Aegean, conquering Greek island states in their path, and finally encamped on the plain of Marathon near Athens. Darius's aim of forcing the Athenians to accept the exiled son of Pisistratus as a pro-Persian tyrant was ended when the Athenian army, half the size of the Persian, won an overwhelming victory, slaying 6400 of the invaders while losing only 192.

The battle of Marathon was one of the most decisive in history. It destroyed the belief in Persian invincibility and demonstrated, according to the Greek historian Herodotus, that "free men fight better than slaves." Ten years later the Greeks were forced to prepare for a new Persian invasion under Xerxes, Darius's successor, whose objective was the subjection of all of Greece. Athens now had 200 warships, the largest fleet in Greece, and Sparta had agreed to head a defensive alliance of 31 states.

The Persian army was too huge to be transported by ship. Crossing the swift-flowing, mile-wide Hellespont near Troy on two pontoon bridges—a notable feat of engineering—the army marched along the Aegean coast accompanied by a great fleet carrying provisions. The Spartans wanted to abandon all of Greece except the Peloponnesus to the invaders but finally agreed to a holding action at the narrow pass of Thermopylae. Here 300 Spartans and a few

Persian Wars

before c. 540 B.C.E.	Persian control of Greek cities in Asia Minor
499–495 B.C.E.	Rebellion of Greek cities in Asia Minor
490 B.C.E.	Battle of Marathon
480–479 B.C.E.	Xerxes' invasion of Greece
480 B.C.E.	Battles of Thermopylae and Salamis
479 B.C.E.	Battles of Plataea

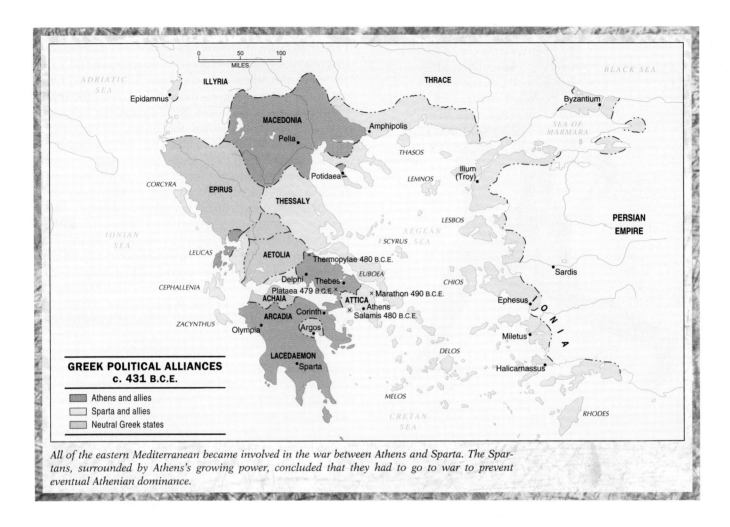

**GREEK POLITICAL ALLIANCES
c. 431 B.C.E.**

- ▪ Athens and allies
- ▫ Sparta and allies
- ▪ Neutral Greek states

All of the eastern Mediterranean became involved in the war between Athens and Sparta. The Spartans, surrounded by Athens's growing power, concluded that they had to go to war to prevent eventual Athenian dominance.

thousand other Greeks held back the Persians for three days until the Persians discovered a mountain path to the rear of the Greek position. The Spartans fought magnificently until all were slain, together with 700 other Greeks. The Spartan dead were immortalized on a monument erected at the pass: "Go tell the Spartans, you who pass us by, that here, obedient to their laws, we lie."

The Persians then sacked Athens, whose inhabitants had been evacuated, for they placed their faith in "wooden walls"—their fleet. Their faith was not misplaced; in the Bay of Salamis the Greek fleet, largely Athenian, turned the tide of victory with the shout: "On, sons of the Greeks! Set free your country, set your children free, your wives, the temples of your country's gods, your fathers' tombs; now they are all at stake." With 200 of his 350 ships destroyed and his lines of communication cut, Xerxes had no alternative but to retreat to Asia, although he left a strong force in Greece. The following summer (479 B.C.E.) the Greek army, with the Spartan army in the forefront, defeated the Persian force at Plataea, and Greece was for the time being safe from invasion.

Culmination of Athenian Democracy

The part they played in the Greek victory over the mighty Persian Empire exhilarated the Athenians and gave them the confidence and energy that made them the leaders of the Greek world during most of the remainder of the fifth century B.C.E. During this period, known as the Golden Age of Greece, the Athenians "attempted more and achieved more in a wider variety of fields than any nation great or small has ever attempted or achieved in a similar space of time."[10]

For more than 30 years (461–429 B.C.E.) during this period, the great statesman Pericles guided Athenian policy. In Pericles' time actual executive power no longer resided in the archons, who were chosen by lot, but in a board of ten elected generals. The generals urged the popular assembly to adopt specific measures, and the success or failure of their policies determined whether they would be reelected at the end of their annual term. Pericles failed in reelection only once, and so great was his influence on the Athenians that, in the words of his contemporary, the historian Thucydides, "what was in name a democracy was virtually a government by its greatest citizen."[11]

To enable even the poorest citizen to participate in government, Pericles extended payment to jurors (a panel of 6000 citizens chosen annually by lot) and to members of the assembly. Although his conservative opponents called this political bribery, Pericles insisted that it was essential to the success of democracy:

> *Our constitution is named a democracy, because it is in the hands not of the few but of the many. . . . [Athenians] do not allow absorption in their own various affairs to interfere with their knowledge of the city's. We differ from other states in regarding the man who holds aloof from public life not as "quiet" but as useless; we decide or debate, carefully and in person, all matters of policy, holding, not that words and deeds go ill together, but that acts are foredoomed to failure when undertaken undiscussed."[12]*

Athenian Society

The majority of the inhabitants of Athens, however, were not recognized as participating citizens. Women, slaves, and resident aliens were denied citizenship and had no voice in the government. Legally, women were first the property of their fathers and then of their husbands. They could not possess property in their own name or, as the law expressly stated, "make a contract about anything worth more than a bushel of barley."

Athens was distinctly a man's world. A wife's function was to bear children and manage the home, where she was restricted to the women's quarters when her husband entertained his friends. Men did not marry until they were about 30, and they usually married girls half their age. Marriages were normally arranged by the families, and prospective brides and bridegrooms seldom met before their marriage was arranged. Families were rather small, and infanticide, usually by exposure, of unwanted infants (especially girls) was practiced as a primitive form of population control. The average life expectancy was little more than 30 years, but if one were able to survive childhood, a longer life could be anticipated.

Athenian society allowed a double moral standard, and the sexual activity of a husband outside of marriage was not a matter for negative public comment. An acceptable social institution intended to serve the needs and desires of upper-class Athenian men was that of the female "companions" *(hetaerae)*. They were normally resident aliens and therefore not subject to the social restrictions imposed on Athenian women. A few of the *hetaerae*, such as Aspasia, the mistress and later wife of Pericles, were cultivated women who entertained at gatherings fre-

quented by Athenian political and cultural leaders. Generally speaking, however, champions of the social emancipation of Athenian women were almost nonexistent, and the women themselves accepted their status. Aside from a few cases in which wives murdered their husbands (usually by poison), married life seems to have been stable and peaceful. Attic (Athenian) gravestones in particular attest to the love spouses felt for one another. The tie to their children was strong, and the community set high store by the honor owed by sons and daughters to their parents.

Homosexuality was an acceptable form of social conduct for Athenian men during certain periods of their lives. A sexual relationship between a mature man and a young boy just before the youth attained puberty was common practice. This relationship was viewed as pedagogical—a rite of initiation into adult society—and such relationships were most common among Athenian soldiers. However, male homosexuality that continued into the years when Athenians were expected to marry and produce children, as well as homosexual prostitution at any time, was not socially acceptable. Such relationships were regarded as unnatural, and the Athenian government issued strong legal prohibitions against them.

In fifth-century Athens it is estimated that one out of every four persons was a slave. Some were war captives and others were children of slaves, but most came from outside Greece through slave dealers. No large slave gangs were employed on plantations, as they were on later Roman estates and state labor projects. Small landowners owned one or more slaves, who worked in the fields alongside their masters. Those who owned many slaves—one rich Athenian owned a thousand—hired them out to private individuals or to the state, where they worked beside Athenian citizens and received the same wages.

Other slaves were taught a trade and set up in business. They were allowed to keep one-sixth of their wages, and many of them were able to purchase their freedom. Although a very few voices argued that slavery was contrary to nature and that all people were equal, the Greek world as a whole agreed with Aristotle that some people—non-Greeks in particular—were incapable of full human reason; thus they were by nature slaves who needed the guidance of a master.

Athenian Imperialism

The Greek victory over Persia had been made possible by a temporary cooperation of leading Greek city-states, but that unity quickly dissolved after the war when Sparta, fearful of helot rebellion at home, recalled its troops and resumed its policy of isolation. Because the Persians still ruled the Ionian cities and another invasion of Greece seemed possible, Athens in 478 B.C.E. invited the city-states bordering the Aegean to form a defensive alliance called the Delian League. To maintain a 200-ship navy that would police the seas, each state was assessed ships or money in proportion to its wealth. From the beginning, Athens dominated the league. Since almost all of the 173 member states paid their assessments in money, which Athens was eager to collect, the Athenians furnished the necessary ships by building them to Athenian specifications in Athenian harbors, with cash collected from their allies.

By 468 B.C.E., after the Ionian cities had been set free and the Persian fleet had been destroyed, various league members thought it unnecessary to continue league membership. In putting down all attempts to withdraw from the league, the Athenians were motivated to a certain extent by the fear that the Persian danger still existed but mainly by the desire to maintain and protect the large free trade area necessary for Greek—and especially Athenian—commerce and industry. The Athenians created an empire because they dared not disband the Delian League. By aiding in the suppression of local aristocratic factions within its subject states and at times imposing democratic governments on the allied states, Athens both eased the task of controlling its empire and emerged as the leader of a union of democratic states.

To many Greeks—above all to the members of the oligarchic Spartan League and the suppressed aristocratic factions within the Athenian Empire—Athens had become a "tyrant city" and an "enslaver of Greek liberties." Pericles, however, justified Athenian imperialism on the grounds that it brought "freedom"—freedom from fear and want to the Greek world:

> We secure our friends not by accepting favors but by doing them. . . . We are alone among mankind in doing men benefits, not on calculations of self-interest, but in the fearless confidence of freedom. In a word, I claim that our city as a whole is an education to Greece.[13]

The Peloponnesian War

In 431 B.C.E. the Peloponnesian War broke out between the Spartan League and the Athenian Empire. Although commercial rivalry between Athens and Sparta's major ally, Corinth, was an important factor, the conflict is a classic example of how fear can generate a war unwanted by either side. The contemporary historian Thucydides wrote, "The real but unavowed cause I consider to have been the growth of the power of Athens, and the alarm which it inspired in Lacedaemon [Sparta]; this made war inevitable."[14] Several incidents served to ignite the underlying tension, and Sparta finally felt it necessary to declare war on the "aggressors."

Sparta's hope for victory lay in its army's ability to besiege Athens and destroy the crops in the Athenian countryside. Pericles, for his part, relied on Athens's unrivaled navy to import sufficient food and to harass its enemies' coasts. Fate took a hand in this game, however. In the second year of the war a plague, probably an outbreak of typhus, killed a third of the Athenian population, including Pericles. His death was a great blow to Athens, for leadership of the government passed to leaders of lesser vision and talent. In the words of Thucydides:

> Pericles, by his rank, ability, and known integrity, was able to exercise an independent control over the masses—to lead them instead of being led by them. . . . With his successors it was different. More on a level with one another, and each grasping at supremacy, they ended by committing even the conduct of state affairs to the whims of the multitude. This, as might have been expected in a great imperial state, produced a host of blunders.[15]

These blunders would lead Thucydides to conclude that "a democracy is incapable of [running an] empire."[16]

Eight more years of indecisive warfare ended in 421 B.C.E. with a compromise peace. During the succeeding period Athenian imperialism manifested itself in its worst form through the actions of Pericles' less able successors. In 416 B.C.E. an expedition embarked for Melos, a neutral Aegean island, to force it to join the Athenian Empire. Thucydides reports the Athenian argument used to justify their obvious imperialism:

> We believe that Heaven, and we know that men, by a natural law, always rule where they are stronger. We did not make that law, nor were we the first to act on it; we found it existing, and it will exist forever, after we are gone; and we know that you and anyone else as strong as we are would do as we do.[17]

The Athenians executed all Melians of military age and sold the women and children into slavery.

The war was resumed in 415 B.C.E. with an Athenian expedition against Syracuse, the major Greek state in Sicily, that ended in complete disaster. Acting on the invitation of states that feared Syracusan expansion, the Athenians hoped to add Sicily to their empire and so become powerful enough "to rule the whole of the Greek world."[18] But bad luck and incompetent leadership resulted in the destruction of two Athenian fleets and a large army by the Syracusans, who were also supported by Sparta. The war dragged on until 404 B.C.E., when Athens capitulated after its last fleet was destroyed by a Spartan fleet built with money received from Persia in exchange for possession of the Greek cities in Ionia. At home, Athens had been weakened by the plots and schemes of oligarchic politicians to whom Sparta now turned over the government. The once great city-state was also stripped of its empire, its fleet, the defense walls that led to the port, and its army and navy.

Aftermath of the War

Anarchy and depression were the political and economic legacies of the Peloponnesian War. Having ended the "tyranny" of Athens over Greece, the Spartans substituted their own form of rule that made the Athenian Empire's seem mild in comparison. Everywhere democracies were replaced by oligarchies supported by Spartan troops. The bloody regimes of these unimaginative oligarchs soon led to successful democratic revolutions at Athens and elsewhere. As one of their generals admitted, the Spartans did not know how to govern free people. Incessant warfare between a bewildering series of shifting alliances became typical of the fourth century B.C.E. Some alliances were even financed by Persia, which wanted to keep Greece disunited and weak.

Political instability in turn contributed to the economic and social ills that plagued Greece during this period. Commerce and industry lagged, and the unemployed who did not go abroad as soldiers of fortune supported authoritarian leaders and their radical schemes for the redivision of wealth. The wealthy, for their part, became increasingly reactionary and uncompromising. Most intellectuals—including Plato and Aristotle—lost faith in democracy and joined with the wealthy in looking for "a champion powerful in action" who would bring order and security to Greece. They found him, finally, in the person of the king of Macedonia.

The Macedonian Unification of Greece

To the north of Greece lay Macedonia, inhabited by hardy peasants, powerful nobles, and weak kings who were related to the Greeks. Macedonia had just emerged as a centralized, powerful state under their young and brilliant King Philip II (359–336 B.C.E.), who created the most formidable army yet known by joining the well-trained Macedonian cavalry of nobles with the hoplite infantry used by the Greeks. In his youth, Philip had been a hostage at Thebes, where he acquired an appreciation of Greek culture, an understanding of Greek political weakness, and a desire to win for Macedonia a place of honor in the Hellenic world. After unifying all of his home country—including a string of Greek colonies that had been established along its coast during the earlier centuries of Macedonia's weakness—Philip turned to the Greek city-states, whose wars afforded him the opportunity first to intervene and then to dominate.

Forensic facial reconstruction of Philip II, father of Alexander the Great, based on remains of his skull found in his tomb in Macedonia. The king had suffered an arrow wound to the eye during battle.

Demosthenes, a great Athenian orator and champion of democracy, warned in vain that "democracies and dictators cannot exist together" and urged the Athenians and other Greeks to stop Philip before it was too late. Ultimately, Athens and Thebes did act to stop Philip's advance, but their combined forces were shattered at Chaeronea in 338 B.C.E. Philip then forced the Greeks to form a league in which each state, while retaining self-government, swore to "make war upon him who violates the general peace" and to furnish Philip with men and supplies for a campaign against Persia. Two years later, before setting out for Asia Minor, Philip was assassinated by a noble with a personal grudge, leaving the war against Persia as a legacy for his gifted son Alexander.

Incapable of finding a solution to the anarchy that tore their world to shreds, the Greeks ended as political failures and at the mercy of a great outside power, first Macedonia and later Rome. They retained their cultural leadership, however, and the culture of the new Hellenistic Age and its successor, the world of Rome, was to be largely Greek.

The Greek Genius

The Greeks were the first to formulate many of the Western world's fundamental concepts in politics, philosophy, science, and art. How was it that a relatively small number of people could leave such a great legacy to later civilizations? The definitive answer may always elude historians, but a good part of the explanation may lie in environmental and social factors.

Unlike the Near Eastern monarchies, the polis was not governed by a "divine" ruler, nor were the thoughts and activities of its citizens limited by powerful priesthoods. Many Greeks, and most notably the Athenians, were fond of good conversation and loved debate and argument. As late as the first century C.E., St. Paul was welcomed by the Athenians because they "liked to spend all their time telling and listening to the latest new thing" (Acts 17:21).

The Greek Character

The Greeks felt a need to discover order and meaning both in nature and in human life. This outlook pro-

Classical Greek Literature and Culture

c. 800 B.C.E.	Homer
c. 700–480 B.C.E.	Archaic period of Greek art
c. 700 B.C.E.	Hesiod, *Works and Days*
c. 600 B.C.E.	Thales of Miletus, "father of philosophy"
525–456 B.C.E.	Aeschylus
c. 496–406 B.C.E.	Sophocles
c. 484–c. 425 B.C.E.	Herodotus, "father of history"
c. 480–406 B.C.E.	Euripides
c. 470–399 B.C.E.	Socrates
460–400 B.C.E.	Thucydides
c. 445–385 B.C.E.	Aristophanes
427–347 B.C.E.	Plato
c. 420 B.C.E.	Hippocrates' medical school
384–322 B.C.E.	Aristotle
342–270 B.C.E.	Epicurus
c. 336–c. 264 B.C.E.	Zeno

duced exceptional results in science, philosophy, and the arts. Beginning with Hesiod, the Greeks stressed the virtue of *sophrosynē* (moderation, self-control) as the key to happiness and fulfillment in life. Its opposite was *hubris,* meaning pride, arrogance, and unbridled ambition. The result of human excess and the basic cause of personal misfortune and social injustice, hubris invariably provoked *nemesis,* or retribution. According to the Greeks, an unavoidable law would cause the downfall or disgrace of anyone guilty of hubris. The Athenian dramatists employed this theme in their tragedies, and Herodotus attributed the Persian defeat by the Greeks to Xerxes' overpowering pride, for "Zeus tolerates pride in none but himself."[19]

The Greeks had all the human frailties and failings—at times they were irrational, vindictive, and cruel. But at their best they were guided by the ideals that permeate their intellectual and artistic legacy. The philosopher Protagoras is credited with the statement, "Man is the measure of all things"—a saying that sums up the humanistic character of Greek thought and art.

Greek Religious Development

Early Greek religion, like almost all early religious expressions, abounded in gods and goddesses who personified the forces of nature. Zeus, sky-god and wielder of thunderbolts, ruled the world from Mount Olympus in nearby Thessaly with the aid of lesser deities, many of whom were his children. His power was limited only by the mysterious decrees of Fate. Homer's gods act like humans, capable of evil deeds, favoritism, and jealousy, differing from ordinary people only in their immortality. Zeus was often the undignified victim of the plots of his wife, Hera, and other deities, and he asserted his authority through threats of violence. Hades, the place of the dead, was a subterranean land of dust and darkness, and Achilles, as Homer tells us in the *Odyssey,* would prefer to be a slave on earth than a king in Hades.

By the time of Hesiod (c. 700 B.C.E.), a religious reformation had begun that changed the vengeful and capricious gods of Homer into more sophisticated dispensers of justice who rewarded the good and punished the wicked. Zeus's stature was increased when he was newly identified as the source of Fate, which was no longer considered a separate mysterious power. And from the famous oracle at Delphi the voice of Zeus's son Apollo urged all Greeks to follow the ideal of moderation: "Nothing in excess" and "Know thyself" (meaning "know your limitations").

A century after Hesiod, the Orphic and Eleusinian mystery cults emerged as a type of Greek higher religion. Their initiates (*mystae*) were promised salvation in an afterlife of bliss in Elysium, formerly the home after death of a few heroes only. The basis of the Orphic cult was an old myth about Dionysus, a son of Zeus, who was killed and eaten by the evil Titans before Zeus arrived on the scene and burned them to ashes with his lightning bolts. Orpheus, a legendary figure, taught that Zeus then created man from the Titans' ashes. Human nature, therefore, is composed of two distinct and opposing elements: the evil titanic element (the body) and the divine Dionysian element (the soul). Death, which frees the divine soul from the evil body, is therefore to be welcomed. "Happy and blessed one!" reads a typical Orphic tomb inscription. "Thou shalt be god instead of mortal."

Early Greek Philosophy

What the Greeks were the first to call *philosophy* ("love of wisdom") arose from their curiosity about nature. The early Greek philosophers were called *physikoi* ("physicists") because their main interest was the investigation of the physical world. ("It is according to their wonder," wrote Aristotle, "that men begin to philosophize, pursuing science in order to know.") Only later, beginning with Socrates, would the chief concern of philosophy be not natural science but *ethics*—how people ought to act in light of moral principles.

The Mesopotamians, as noted in Chapter 2, were skilled observers of astronomical phenomena, which, like the Greeks, they attributed to the action of the gods. The early Greek philosophers, beginning with Thales of Miletus around 600 B.C.E., changed the course of human knowledge by insisting that the phenomena of the universe could be explained by natural rather than supernatural causes. This rejection of mythological explanations and the use of reason to explain natural phenomena have been called the "Greek miracle."

Called the "father of philosophy," Thales speculated on the nature of the basic substance of which everything in the universe is composed. He concluded that it was water, which exists in different states and is indispensable to the maintenance and growth of organisms. Thales' successors in Ionia proposed elements other than water as this primal substance in the universe. One called it the "boundless," apparently a general concept for matter; another proposed "air," out of which all things come by a process of "rarefying and condensing"; a third asserted that fire was the "most mobile, most transformable, most active, most life-giving" element. This search for a material substance as the first principle or cause of all things culminated two centuries after Thales in the atomic theory of Democritus (c. 460–370 B.C.E.). To Democritus, reality was the mechanical motion of indivisible atoms, which dif-

fered in shape, size, position, and arrangement but not in quality. Moving about continuously, atoms combined to create objects.

While these and other early Greek philosophers were proposing some form of matter as the basic element in nature, Pythagoras of Samos (c. 582–500 B.C.E.) countered with the profoundly significant idea that the "nature of things" was something nonmaterial: numbers. By experimenting with a vibrating chord, Pythagoras discovered that musical harmony is based on arithmetical proportions, and he intuitively concluded that the universe was constructed of numbers and their relationships. His mystical, nonmaterial interpretation of nature, together with his belief that the human body was distinct from the soul, greatly influenced Plato.

An important result of early Greek philosophical speculation was the undermining of conventional beliefs and traditions. In religion, for example, Anaximander argued that thunder and lightning were caused by blasts of wind and not by Zeus's thunderbolts. Xenophanes went on to ridicule the traditional view of the gods: "If oxen and lions had hands, . . . they would make portraits and statues of their gods in their own image."

The eroding of traditional beliefs was intensified during the last half of the fifth century B.C.E. by the activity of professional teachers, called Sophists ("intellectuals"). They taught a variety of subjects—the nucleus of our present arts and sciences—which they claimed would lead to material success. The most popular subject was *rhetoric,* the art of persuasion, or how to take either side of an argument. The Sophists tried to put all conventional beliefs to the test of rational criticism. Concluding that truth was relative, they denied the existence of universal standards to guide human actions.

Socrates, a Martyr to Truth

A contemporary of the early Sophists but opposed to their conclusions was the Athenian Socrates (c. 470–399 B.C.E.). Like the Sophists, Socrates turned from concern with the gods to human affairs; in the words of the Roman statesman Cicero, Socrates was "the first to call philosophy down from the heavens and to set her in the cities of men, bringing her into their homes and compelling her to ask questions about life and morality and things good and evil." But unlike the Sophists, Socrates believed that by asking meaningful questions and subjecting the answers to logical analysis, agreement could be reached about ethical standards and rules of conduct. And so he would question passersby in his function of "midwife assisting in the birth of correct ideas" (to use his own figure of speech). Taking as his motto the famous inscription on the temple of Apollo at Delphi,

"Know thyself," he insisted that "the unexamined life is not worth living." To Socrates, human excellence or virtue *(aretē)* is not Homer's heroic action or simply Hesiod's moral character but intellectual activity—knowledge. Evil and error are the result of ignorance.

In time Socrates' quest for truth led to his undoing. The Athenians, unnerved by their defeat in the Peloponnesian War and viewing Socrates as just another subversive Sophist, arrested him "because he does not believe in the gods recognized by the state . . . and . . . because he corrupts the youth." By a slim majority, a jury of citizens condemned Socrates to die, a fate he accepted without bitterness and with a last request:

> When my sons are grown up, I would ask you, my friends, to punish them, and I would have you trouble them, as I have troubled you, if they seem to care about riches, or anything, more than about virtue; or if they pretend to be something when they are really nothing, then reprove them, as I have reproved you, for not caring about that for which they ought to care, and thinking that they are something when they are really nothing. And if you do this, both I and my sons will have received justice at your hands.[20]

Plato and His Theory of Ideas

After Socrates' death, philosophical leadership passed to his most famous disciple, Plato (427–347 B.C.E.). Like Socrates, Plato believed that truth exists, but only in the realm of thought, the spiritual world of ideas or forms. Such universal truths as beauty, good, and justice exist apart from the material world, and the beauty, good, and justice encountered in the world of the senses are only imperfect reflections of eternal and changeless ideas. The task for humans is to come to know the true reality—the eternal ideas—behind these imperfect reflections. Only the soul, and the "soul's pilot," reason, can accomplish this goal, for the human soul is spiritual and immortal, and in its prenatal state it existed "beyond the heavens" where "true Being dwells."[21]

Disillusioned with the democracy that had led Athens to ruin in the Peloponnesian War and that had condemned Socrates to death, Plato put forward his concept of an ideal state in the *Republic*, the first systematic work on political science. The state's basic function, founded on the idea of justice, was the satisfaction of the common good. Plato described a kind of "spiritualized Sparta" in which the state regulated every aspect of life, including thought. Accordingly, poets and forms of music considered unworthy were banished from the state. Private property was abolished on the grounds that it bred selfishness. Plato believed there was no essential difference between men and women; therefore, women received the same education and held the same occupations as men, including "the art of war, which they must practice like men."[22] Individuals belonged to one of three classes and found happiness only through their contribution to the community: workers by producing the necessities of life, warriors by guarding the state, and philosophers by ruling in the best interests of all the people.

Plato founded the Academy in Athens, the famous school that existed from about 388 B.C.E. until 529 C.E., when it was closed by the Christian emperor Justinian. Here Plato taught and encouraged his students, whom he expected to become the intellectual elite who would go forth and reform society.

Aristotle, the Encyclopedic Philosopher

Plato's greatest pupil was Aristotle (384–322 B.C.E.), who set up his own school, the Lyceum, at Athens. Reacting against the otherworldly tendencies of Plato's thought, Aristotle insisted that ideas have no separate existence apart from the material world; knowledge of universal ideas is the result of the painstaking collection and organization of particular facts. Aristotle's Lyceum, accordingly, became a center for the analysis of data from many branches of learning.

Today, Aristotle's most significant works are the *Ethics* and the *Politics*. They deal with what he called the "philosophy of human affairs," whose object is the acquisition and maintenance of human happiness. Two kinds of virtue *(aretē)*, intellectual and moral, which produce two types of happiness, are described in the *Ethics*. Intellectual virtue is the product of reason, and only such people as philosophers and scientists ever attain it. Much more important for the good of society is moral virtue—virtues of character, such as justice, bravery, and temperance—which is the product less of reason than of habit and thus can be acquired by all. In this connection Aristotle introduced his "doctrine of the mean" as a guide for good conduct. He considered all moral virtues to be means between extremes; courage, for example, is the mean between cowardice and rashness. In the *Politics* Aristotle viewed the state as necessary "for the sake of the good life," because its laws and educational system provide the most effective training needed for the attainment of moral virtue and hence happiness. Thus to Aristotle, the viewpoint popular today that the state stands in opposition to the individual would be unthinkable.

There have probably been few geniuses whose interests were as widespread as Aristotle's. He investigated such diverse fields as biology (his minute observations include the life cycle of the gnat), mathematics, astronomy, physics, literary criticism (the concept of *catharsis*—art as a release of emotion), rhetoric, logic (deductive and inductive), politics (he

Aristotle Criticizes Communism

Aristotle foreshadows the failure of communist regimes.

Next let us consider what should be our arrangements about property: should the citizens of the perfect state have their possessions in common or not? . . .

There is always a difficulty in men living together and having things in common, but especially in their having common property. . . .

The present arrangement, if improved as it might be by good customs and laws, would be far better, and would have the advantages of both systems. Property should be in a certain sense common, but, as a general rule, private; for, when every one has a distinct interest, men will not complain of one another and they will make more progress, because every one will be attending to his own business. . . .

. . . Again, how immeasurably greater is the pleasure, when a man feels a thing to be his own; for the love of self is a feeling implanted by nature and not given in vain, although selfishness is rightly censured; this, however, is not the mere love of self, but the love of self in excess, like the miser's love of money; for all, or almost all, men love money, and other such objects in a measure. And further, there is the greatest pleasure in doing a kindness or service to friends or guests or companions, which can only be rendered when a man has private property. The advantage is lost by the excessive unification of the state. . . . No one, when men have all things in common, will any

longer set an example of liberality or do any liberal action; for liberality consists in the use which is made of property.

[Communistic] legislation may have a specious appearance of benevolence; men readily listen to it, and are easily induced to believe that in some wonderful manner everybody will become everybody's friend, especially when some one is heard denouncing the evils now existing in states, . . . which are said to arise out of the possession of private property. These evils, however, are due to a very different cause—the wickedness of human nature.

. . . The error of Socrates [i.e., Plato] must be attributed to the false notion of unity from which he starts. Unity there should be, both of the family and of the state, but in some respects only. For there is a point at which a state may attain such a degree of unity as to be no longer a state, or at which, without actually ceasing to exist, it will become an inferior state, like harmony passing into unison, or rhythm which has been reduced to a single foot. The state, as I was saying, is a plurality, which should be united and made into a community by education. . . . Let us remember that we should not disregard the experience of ages.

From Aristotle, *Politics*, trans. Benjamin Jowett (Oxford: Clarendon Press, 1908), pp. 60–64.

---

analyzed 158 Greek and foreign constitutions), ethics, and metaphysics. His knowledge was so encyclopedic that there is hardly a college course today that does not take note of what Aristotle had to say on the subject. Although his works on natural science are now little more than historical curiosities, they held a place of undisputed authority until the scientific revolution of the sixteenth and seventeenth centuries. But in no important sense are his humanistic studies, such as the *Ethics* and the *Politics*, out of date.

Medicine

Superstitions about the human body blocked the development of medical science until 420 B.C.E., when Hippocrates, the "father of medicine," founded a school in which he emphasized the value of observation and the careful interpretation of symptoms. Such modern medical terms as *crisis, acute,* and

chronic were first used by Hippocrates. He was firmly convinced that disease resulted from natural, not supernatural, causes. Writing of epilepsy, considered at the time a "sacred" or supernaturally inspired sickness, one Hippocratic writer observed:

It seems to me that this disease is no more divine than any other. It has a natural cause just as other diseases have. Men think it supernatural because they do not understand it. But if they called everything supernatural which they do not understand, why, there would be no end of such thing![23]

The Hippocratic school also gave medicine a sense of service to humanity that it has never lost. All members took the famous Hippocratic Oath, still in use today. One section states: "I will adopt the regimen which in my best judgment is beneficial to my patients, and not for their injury or for any wrongful purpose. I will not give poison to anyone, though I be asked . . . nor will I procure abortion."[24]

Despite their empirical approach, the Hippocratic school adopted the theory that the body contained four liquids or *humors*—blood, phlegm, black bile, and yellow bile—whose proper balance was the basis of health. This doctrine was to impede medical progress until modern times.

The Writing of History

If history is defined as an honest attempt to find out what happened and then to explain why it happened, Herodotus of Halicarnassus (c. 484–c. 425 B.C.E.) deserves to be called the "father of history." In his highly entertaining history of the Persian Wars, he identified the clash of two distinct civilizations, the Hellenic and the Near Eastern. His portrayal of both the Greeks and the Persians was in most cases highly impartial, but his fondness for a good story often led him to include tall tales in his work. As he stated more than once, "My duty is to report what has been said, but I do not have to believe it."

The first truly scientific historian was Thucydides (460–400 B.C.E.), who wrote a notably objective account of the Peloponnesian War. Although Thucydides was a contemporary of the events and a loyal Athenian, a reader can scarcely detect whether he favored Athens or Sparta. Thucydides believed that his history would become "an everlasting possession" for those who desire a clear picture of what has happened and, human nature being as it is, what is likely to be repeated in the future. His belief was based on his remarkable ability to analyze and explain human behavior. (Three examples were quoted in our account of the Peloponnesian War on p. 66.) In describing the character and purpose of his work, Thucydides probably had Herodotus in mind:

> *The absence of romance in my history will, I fear, detract somewhat from its interest; but I shall be content if it is judged useful by those inquirers who desire an exact knowledge of the past as an aid to the interpretation of the future, which will according to human nature recur in much the same way. My history has been composed to be an everlasting possession, not the show-piece of an hour.*[25]

Hellenic Poetry and Drama

Greek literary periods can be classified according to the dominant poetic forms that reflect particular stages of cultural development in Greece. First came the time of great epics, followed by periods in which lyric poetry and then drama flourished.

Sometime during the eighth century B.C.E. in Ionia, the *Iliad* and the *Odyssey*, the two great epics attributed to Homer, were set down in their present form. The *Iliad*, describing the clash of arms between the Greeks and Trojans "on the ringing plains of windy Troy," glorifies heroic bravery and physical strength against a background of divine intervention in human affairs. The *Odyssey*, relating the adventure-filled wanderings of Odysseus on his return to Greece after Troy's fall, places less stress on divine intervention and more on the cool resourcefulness of the hero in escaping from danger and in regaining his kingdom. These stirring epics have provided inspiration and source material for generations of poets in the Western world.

As Greek society continued to develop and seek new varieties of artistic expression, a new type of poetry, written to be sung to the accompaniment of a small stringed instrument called a lyre, became popular among the Ionian Greeks. Unlike Homer, authors of this lyric poetry sang not of legendary events but of present delights and sorrows. This new note, personal and passionate, can be seen in the following examples, in which the contrast between the new values of what is called the Greek Renaissance and those of Homer's heroic age is sharply clear. Unlike Homer's heroes, Archilochus of Paros (seventh century B.C.E) unashamedly throws away his shield and runs from the battlefield:

> *My trusty shield adorns some Thracian foe;*
> *I left it in a bush—not as I would!*
> *But I have saved my life; so let it go.*
> *Soon I will get another just as good.*[26]

And in contrast to Homer's view of an unromantic, purely physical attraction between Paris and the abducted Helen ("He led the way to the couch and the lady followed willingly"), Sappho of Lesbos (sixth century B.C.E.), one of the first and greatest of all female poets, saw Helen as the helpless, unresisting victim of romantic love:

> *Did not Helen, who was queen of mortal*
> *beauty, choose as first among mankind*
> *the very scourge of Trojan honor?*
> *Haunted by Love, she forgot kinsmen,*
> *her own dear child, and wandered off to a remote*
> *   country.*
> *Weak and fitful woman bending before any man!*[27]

Drama (also in verse) developed from the religious rites of Dionysus (son of Zeus from an affair with the daughter of the king of Tyre) in which a large chorus and its leader sang and danced. Thespis, a contemporary of Solon, added an actor called the "answerer" (*hypocrites*, the origin of our word *hypocrite*) to converse with the chorus and its leader. This innovation made dramatic dialogue possible. By the fifth century B.C.E. in Athens, two distinct forms, tragedy and comedy, had evolved. Borrowing from the old familiar legends of gods and heroes for their

Discovery Through Maps

The World According to Herodotus, c. 450 B.C.E.

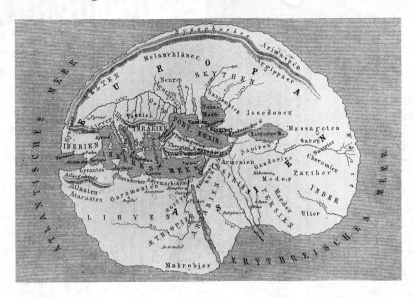

This map depicts the known world at the time of the Greek historian Herodotus, who lived and worked around 450–425 B.C.E. The map is a modern rendition of what we know Herodotus thought to be the world, as described in his writings, the *Histories*. The *Histories* was written to describe the events and circumstances that led the Greeks and the Persians to engage in war—a war that Herodotus believed changed the direction of human history. To understand why these two great powers came to conflict, the historian believed he would have to examine the origins, geographical setting, culture, and traditions of the whole empire of the Persians, as well as the background of the Greek city-states. The *Histories* became not just a listing of chronological events but an exploration of geography, sociology, and anthropology as well.

We are certain that Herodotus himself traveled extensively throughout his world in order to learn firsthand of the people he described. Most of his geographical knowledge came from his own observations or from interviews with the people he met. He seems to have believed that the earth was a flat disk, although he must have been familiar with contemporary theories that the world might be a sphere. He differed from most of his contemporaries in not picturing Europe, Africa (which he called Libya), and Asia as approximately the same size. He described Europe as being as long as both Asia and Africa put together. And yet Herodotus did not travel to the farthest reaches of the continent but relied on accounts of others; he knew nothing of the existence of Britain or Scandinavia, for example, and he did not know if Europe was surrounded by water to the west or north. His knowledge of Asia was limited to the lands of the Persian Empire. He knew that the Caspian Sea was an inland sea and not, as most of his contemporaries believed, a sea that emptied into the band of ocean that encircled the earth. He also knew that Africa was surrounded by water—a fact that the geographer Ptolemy missed 500 years later.

plots, the tragedians reinterpreted them from the point of view of the values and problems of their own times.

In reworking the old legends of the heroic age, Aeschylus (525–456 B.C.E.) attempted to spread the new values being presented about Greek religion, first expressed by Hesiod, by showing how following the old unsophisticated beliefs leads to suffering. In his trilogy, the *Oresteia*, for example, he concerned

himself with hubris as applied to the murder of the hero Agamemnon by his queen following his return from the Trojan War. Aeschylus then proceeded to work out its ramifications—murder piled on murder until people through suffering learn to substitute the moral law of Zeus for the primitive law of the blood feud. Like the prophets of Israel, Aeschylus taught that while "sin brings misery," misery in turn leads to wisdom:

Aristophanes on the Shortcomings of Athenian Democracy

In *The Frogs,* Aristophanes exhorts the Athenians to elect better-quality leaders.

[The leader of the chorus comes forward and addresses the audience.]

We chorus folk two privileges prize:
To amuse you, citizens, and to advise.
So, mid the fun that marks this sacred day,
We'll put on serious looks, and say our say. . . .
But if we choose to strut and put on airs
While Athens founders in a sea of cares,
In days to come, when history is penned,
They'll say we must have gone clean round the
*   bend. . . .*
I'll tell you what I think about the way
This city treats her soundest men today:
By a coincidence more sad than funny,
It's very like the way we treat our money.
The noble silver drachma, that of old
We were so proud of, and the recent gold,
Coins that rang true, clean-stamped and worth their
*   weight*

Throughout the world, have ceased to circulate.
Instead, the purses of Athenian shoppers
Are full of shoddy silver-plated coppers.
Just so, when men are needed by the nation,
The best have been withdrawn from circulation.
Men of good birth and breeding, men of parts,
Well schooled in wrestling and in gentler arts,
These we abuse, and trust instead to knaves,
Newcomers, aliens, copper-pated slaves,
All rascals—honestly, what men to choose!
There was a time when you'd have scorned to use
Men so debased, so far beyond the pale,
Even as scapegoats to be dragged from jail
And flogged to death outside the city gate.
My foolish friends, change now, it's not too late!
Try the good ones again: if they succeed,
You will have proved that you have sense indeed.

From Aristophanes, *The Frogs and Other Plays,* trans. David Barrett (Baltimore: Penguin, 1964), pp. 181–183.

Zeus the Guide, who made man turn
Thought-ward, Zeus, who did ordain
Man by Suffering shall Learn.
So the heart of him, again
Aching with remembered pain,
Bleeds and sleepeth not, until
Wisdom comes against his will.[28]

A generation later, Sophocles (c. 496–406 B.C.E.) largely abandoned Aeschylus's concern for the working out of divine justice and concentrated on character. To Sophocles, a certain amount of suffering was inevitable in life. No one is perfect; even in the best people there is a tragic flaw that causes them to make mistakes. Sophocles dwelled mainly on the way in which human beings react to suffering. Like his contemporary, the sculptor Phidias, Sophocles viewed humans as ideal creatures—"Many are the wonders of the world, and none so wonderful as Man"—and he displayed human greatness by depicting people experiencing great tragedy without whimpering. It has been said that to Sophocles—and to Shakespeare—"tragedy is essentially an expression, not of despair, but of the triumph over despair and of confidence in the value of human life."[29]

Euripides (c. 480–406 B.C.E.), the last of the great Athenian tragedians, reflects the rationalism and critical spirit of the late fifth century B.C.E. Gone is Sophocles' idealized view of humanity. To Euripides, human life was pathetic, and the ways of the gods were ridiculous. His recurrent theme was "Since life began, hath there in God's eye stood one happy man?"

For this he has been called the "poet of the world's grief." Euripides has also been called the first psychologist, for he looked deep into the human soul and described what he saw with intense realism. His *Medea,* for example, is a startling and moving account of a woman's exploitation and her retaliatory rage. When Medea's overly ambitious husband discards her for a young heiress, she kills her children out of a bitter hatred that is the dark side of her once passionate love:

He, even he,
Whom to know well was all the world to me,
The man I loved, hath proved most evil. Oh,
Of all things upon earth that bleed and grow,
A herb most bruised is woman.
. . . but once spoil her of her right
In man's love, and there moves, I warn thee well,
No bloodier spirit between heaven and hell.[30]

Far more than those of Aeschylus or even Sophocles, the themes of Euripides still remain relevant to the modern world.

Comedies were bawdy and spirited. There were no libel laws in Athens, and Aristophanes (c. 445–385 B.C.E.), the famous comic-dramatist and a conservative in outlook, brilliantly satirized Athenian democracy as a mob led by demagogues, the Sophists (among whom he included Socrates) as subversive, and Euripides as an underminer of civic spirit and traditional faith. Another favorite object of Aristophanes' satire was the youth of Athens; in the following lines from *The Wasps,* they are lampooned by the chorus of old men:

Yes, we may be poor old crocks,
But the whiteness of our locks
Does the City better credit, I would say,
Than the ringlets and the fashions
And the pederastic passions
Of the namby-pamby youngsters of today.[31]

Hellenic Architecture

During the archaic period of Greek art (c. 700–480 B.C.E.), architecture flourished in Ionia, Greece, and the Greek colonies in Sicily and southern Italy. Reflecting the prosperity produced by colonization, large stone temples were constructed. Their form may have developed from wooden structures that had been influenced by the remains of Mycenaean palaces or perhaps Egyptian temples.

The classical phase of Greek architecture reached its zenith in Athens during the second half of the fifth century B.C.E. The Parthenon, the Erechtheum, and the other temples on the Acropolis in Athens exhibit the highly developed features that make Greek structures so pleasing to the eye. All relationships, such as column spacing and height and the slight curvature of floor and roof lines, were calculated and executed with remarkable precision to achieve a perfect balance, both structurally and visually. The three orders, or styles, usually identified by the characteristics of the columns, were the Doric, which was used in the Parthenon; the Ionic, seen in the Erechtheum; and the later and more ornate Corinthian.

Greek temples afford an interesting comparison with those of Egypt. Whereas the Egyptian temple was enclosed by walls and only priests and royalty could

An ornate capital of the third Greek order, the Corinthian, which was more popular with the Hellenistic Greeks and the Romans.

In the Parthenon, great care was taken to design a perfect building, both structurally and visually. The topics of the Doric columns lean toward the center, and the columns are more widely spaced in the middle of each row than at the ends. All these refinements create an illusion of perfect regularity that would be lacking if the parts were actually regular. Sculpture adorned the triangular gables and part of the frieze just below the gables; another sculptured frieze ran around the walls inside the colonnade. The whole building was once painted in bright colors.

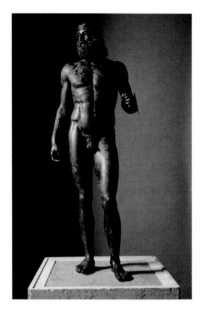

These statues illustrate the three major phases of Greek art. The kouros *("youth") statue (c. 540 B.C.E.) on the left is typically archaic, the statue of the warrior has all the characteristics of classical art, and the Laocoön group on the right illustrates the striving for effect of much of postclassical Hellenistic sculpture. This last statue depicts the legend that Laocoön and his two sons were strangled by a huge snake sent by Apollo as punishment for warning the unbelieving Trojans about the Trojan horse, a device used by the Greeks to gain entrance to Troy and destroy the city.*

Kouros, Statue of a youth, c. 610–600 B.C.E. The Metropolitan Museum of Art, New York. Fletcher Fund, 1932. (32.11.1). Photograph © 1993 The Metropolitan Museum of Art.

enter its inner rooms, the Greek temple was open, with a colonnade porch and an inside room containing a statue of the god or goddess. Sacrifice and ritual took place outside the temple, where the altar was placed.

Other types of buildings, notably the theaters, stadiums, and gymnasiums, also express the Greek spirit and way of life. In the open-air theaters, the circular shape of the spectators' sections and the plan of the orchestra section set a style that has survived to the present day.

Hellenic Sculpture and Pottery

Greek sculpture is usually described as having passed through three stages of development: the archaic period, the classical, and the Hellenistic. Greek sculpture of the archaic period, although crude in its representation of human anatomy, has the freshness and liveliness of youth. Influenced partly by Egyptian models, the statues of nude youths and draped maidens usually stand stiffly with clenched fists and with one foot thrust awkwardly forward. The fixed smile and formalized treatment of hair and drapery also reveal the sculptors' struggle to master the technique of their art.

The mastery of technique by 480 B.C.E. brought in the classical period of fifth-century Greek sculpture, whose principles of harmony and proportion have shaped the course of Western art. Sculpture from this period displays both the end of technical immaturity and the beginning of idealization of the human form, which reached its culmination in the dignity and poise of Phidias's figures in the continu-

ous frieze and pediments of the Parthenon. Carved with restraint and "calm exaltation," the frieze represents the citizens of Athens participating in a procession in honor of their patron goddess, Athena, which took place every four years.

The more relaxed nature of fourth-century B.C.E. Hellenic sculpture, while still considered classical, lacks some of the grandeur and dignity of fifth-century art. Charm, grace, and individuality characterize the work of Praxiteles, the most famous sculptor of the century. These qualities can be seen in his flowing statues of the god Hermes holding the young Dionysus and of Aphrodite stepping into her bath.

The making of pottery, the oldest Greek art, started at the beginning of the Greek Dark Ages (c. 1150 B.C.E.) with crude imitations of late Mycenaean forms. Soon the old Mycenaean patterns were replaced by abstract geometrical designs. With the coming of the archaic period came paintings of scenes from mythology and daily life. We can get an idea of what Greek painting, now lost, must have been like from surviving Greek pottery and mosaics.

The Hellenistic Age, 336–30 B.C.E.

The Hellenistic Age is the three-century period from Alexander the Great to Augustus, the first of the Roman emperors, who completed Rome's domination of the Mediterranean world by adding Egypt to Rome's empire in 30 B.C.E. The Hellenistic Age was

Macedonia and Alexander

359–336 B.C.E.	Reign of Philip II
338 B.C.E.	Philip conquers Greek city-states
336–323 B.C.E.	Reign of Alexander the Great
334 B.C.E.	Alexander invades Persian Empire
331 B.C.E.	Final battle at Gaugamela
327 B.C.E.	Alexander enters India
323 B.C.E.	Alexander dies

a period of economic expansion, cosmopolitanism, striking intellectual and artistic achievements, and the wide distribution of Greek culture.

Alexander the Great

When Philip of Macedonia was assassinated in 336 B.C.E., his authority was claimed by his 20-year-old son Alexander, who proved himself a resolute king from the very beginning of his reign by gaining the support of the Macedonian nobles, even though some of them suspected the young man of being involved in Philip's murder. Alexander persuaded his father's old generals and comrades to swear their loyalty to him and proceeded to demand the loyalty of the Greek League, which had been founded by his father. When the Greek city of Thebes responded to a rumor that Alexander had been killed in battle in the north by rebelling against the Macedonians, Alexander marched his army quickly to the south and ruthlessly crushed the city, selling its remaining inhabitants into slavery. The Greeks were horrified at such brutal action, but a lesson was learned, and few states dared consider rebellion in the years ahead.

Alexander was one of history's most remarkable individuals. Of average height and looks for a Macedonian, he nevertheless impressed his contemporaries as a gifted athlete, a charismatic personality, and a natural leader. Both his father, Philip, and his mother, Olympias, a princess from Illyria, were strong influences on him. Philip earned his son's respect as a king and a general, and Olympias was a forceful woman who wished great things for her son and who constantly assured the boy that his true father was not Philip but the god Zeus.

Having been tutored by Aristotle, Alexander was aware of the glories of Hellenic culture and wished to be the fulfillment of the Greek ideal. Reveling in the heroic deeds of the *Iliad*, which he always kept at his bedside, Alexander saw himself as a new Achilles waging war against barbarians when he planned to complete his father's plans to avenge the Persian attacks on Greece by conquering the Persian Empire. In 334 B.C.E. he set out with an army of 35,000 soldiers recruited from Macedonia and the Greek League. In quick succession he subdued Asia Minor, Syria, and Palestine, defeating the Persians in two great battles. He marched into Egypt, where the Egyptians welcomed him as a deliverer from their Persian masters and recognized the Macedonian as pharaoh, the living god-king of Egypt.

Alexander the Great in his first battle against Darius III in 333 B.C.E. This detail, from a late Hellenistic mosaic at Pompeii, is based on a Greek painting made around 300 B.C.E.

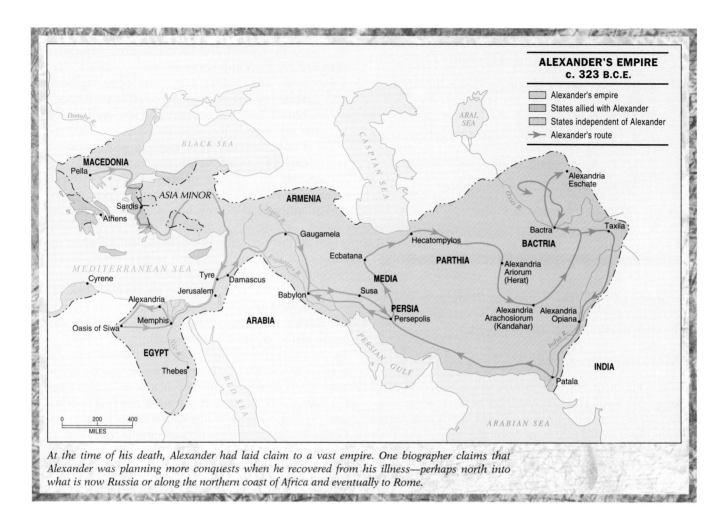

At the time of his death, Alexander had laid claim to a vast empire. One biographer claims that Alexander was planning more conquests when he recovered from his illness—perhaps north into what is now Russia or along the northern coast of Africa and eventually to Rome.

Greatly impressed with Egypt and its traditions, Alexander wished to spend more time there. But Darius III, the Persian king, was gathering one more great army to oppose the invader, and Alexander marched into Mesopotamia to meet the Persian armies for a final battle. In 331 B.C.E., at Gaugamela, near the ancient city of Nineveh, the Macedonians defeated the Persians. Darius III was executed by his own relatives as he fled, and Alexander became Great King of the Persian Empire. Alexander led his victorious troops to the ancient Persian capital city of Persepolis, but his campaigns did not end there. He wished to demand the loyalty of all Persian lands and to extend the great empire. He led his troops north through Media, then south and east into present-day Afghanistan, finally venturing as far east as the rich river valleys of India. There his weary and frightened soldiers, many of whom had been away from home for more than ten years, forced him to turn back.

In 323 B.C.E. Alexander fell ill with a mysterious fever. Perhaps he had contracted malaria in India; perhaps he fell victim to his accumulated battle wounds; perhaps his years of heavy drinking had taken their toll; perhaps, as rumor had it, he had been slowly poisoned by his enemies in the Macedonian camp. Whatever the case, after a short illness,

and without designating an heir to his empire, Alexander died in Babylon at the age of 32.

Alexander the Great is a puzzling figure to modern historians. Some view him as a ruthless conqueror who never lost a battle and a despot who ordered even his fellow Macedonians to prostrate themselves in his presence. Others, however, influenced by Greek and Roman writers and perhaps by their own idealism, picture him as a farsighted visionary hoping to unite East and West in one world and seeking the eventual "brotherhood of man" by establishing universal equality through a common Greek culture.

Some of Alexander's military and administrative policies sought to unify the lands he conquered and to promote what he himself called "concord and partnership in the empire" between easterners and westerners. He blended Persians with Greeks and Macedonians in his army and administration; he founded numerous cities—70, according to tradition—in the East and settled many of his followers in them; and he married two oriental princesses and encouraged his officers and men to take foreign wives. Finally, for perhaps egotistical and certainly for political reasons, he ordered the Greek city-states to accord him "divine honors."

Alexander was a remarkable blend of the romantic idealist and the practical realist, contrasting traits that he inherited from his parents. His mother, Olympias, who practiced the rites of the cult of Dionysus and claimed to be a descendant of the Greek hero Achilles, instilled in her son a consciousness of a divine mission that drove him onward, even to seeking the end of the earth beyond India. From his father he inherited his remarkable abilities as military commander, expert diplomat, and able political administrator. Alexander was a self-confident idealist who was excited by challenges, but meeting those challenges forced him to take actions that were practical and pragmatic. For example, he could not merely conquer the Great King of Persia; he had to act as his successor as well. Alexander ruled for only 13 years, but in many ways the world was never the same again.

The Division of Alexander's Empire

With the Greeks now masters of the ancient Near East, a new and distinctly cosmopolitan period in their history and culture began—the Hellenistic ("Greek-like") Age. For several decades following Alexander's sudden death, his generals rivaled each other for the spoils of empire. Three major Hellenistic kingdoms emerged and maintained an uneasy balance of power until the Roman conquests of the second and first centuries B.C.E.: Egypt, ruled by Alexander's friend and general Ptolemy and his successors; Asia, comprising most of the remaining provinces of the Persian Empire and held together with great difficulty by the dynasty founded by Seleucus; and Macedonia and Greece, ruled by the descendants of Antigonus the One-Eyed.

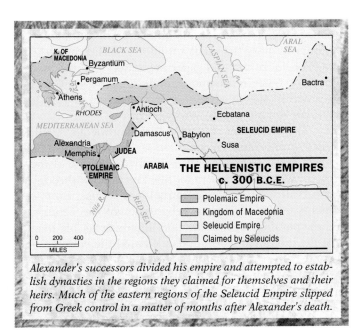

Alexander's successors divided his empire and attempted to establish dynasties in the regions they claimed for themselves and their heirs. Much of the eastern regions of the Seleucid Empire slipped from Greek control in a matter of months after Alexander's death.

While the Antigonids in Macedonia followed the model of Alexander's father, Philip, in ruling as national kings selected by the army, the Ptolemies ruled Egypt as divine pharaohs, and some of the Seleucids attempted to have themselves recognized as "saviors" and "benefactors" of their subjects. Ptolemaic and Seleucid administrations were centralized in bureaucracies staffed mainly by Greeks, an arrangement that created a vast gulf between rulers and ruled:

"What a mob!" [the Greek poet Theocritus has a Greek woman residing in Alexandria say to her friend]. "They're like ants, no one can count them. Ptolemy, you've done many good things. . . . No more hoods creep up on you nowadays and do you in—an old Egyptian habit. The tricks those scoundrels used to play! They're all alike—dirty, lazy, good-for-nothings!"[32]

Plagued by native revolts, dynastic troubles, and civil war, the Hellenistic kingdoms eventually began to crumble. Macedonia lost effective control of Greece by 250 B.C.E. when Athens asserted its independence and most of the other Greek states resisted Macedonian domination by forming two federal leagues, the Achaean and the Aetolian. Their constitutions have long commanded the attention of students of federal unions, including the writers of the United States Constitution.

The eastern reaches of Alexander's empire—India, Bactria, and Parthia—gradually broke out of Seleucid control. Pergamum, in northwestern Asia Minor, renounced its allegiance to the Seleucids and became an independent kingdom famous for its artists and scholars. In 200 B.C.E. the new power of Rome entered the scene, and by 30 B.C.E. Rome had annexed all but the last remaining Hellenistic state, Egypt; in that very year Cleopatra, the last reigning member of the dynasty founded by Ptolemy, was captured by the Romans and committed suicide.

Hellenistic Economy and Society

The Hellenistic Age was a time of economic expansion and social change. In the wake of Alexander's conquests, thousands of Greeks moved eastward to begin a new era of Greek colonization, ending the long economic depression that followed the breakup of the Athenian Empire. An economic union of East and West permitted the free flow of trade, and prosperity was stimulated further when Alexander put into circulation huge amounts of Persian gold and silver and introduced a uniform coinage. The result was a much larger and more affluent middle class than had existed previously. The condition of the poor, however, was made worse by rising prices.

By the third century B.C.E. the center of trade had shifted from Greece to the Near East. Largest of the

Hellenistic cities, and much larger than any cities in Greece itself, were Antioch, in northern Syria, and Alexandria, in Egypt. The riches of India, Persia, Arabia, and the Fertile Crescent were brought by sea and land to these Mediterranean ports.

Alexandria outdistanced all other Hellenistic cities as a commercial center. Its merchants supplied the ancient world with wheat, linen, papyrus, glass, and jewelry. Boasting a population of nearly a million, the city had a double harbor in which a great lighthouse, judged one of the wonders of the ancient world, rose to a height estimated at 370 feet. Its busy streets were filled with a mixture of peoples—Greeks, Macedonians, Jews, and Egyptians. As in all other Hellenistic cities in the Near East, the privileged Greeks and Macedonians were at the top of the social scale and the mass of natives at the bottom; the large Jewish population lived apart and was allowed a large degree of self-government. Labor was so cheap that slavery hardly existed in Hellenistic Egypt. As a consequence, worker-organized strikes were frequent.

Hellenistic Philosophy

Developments in philosophical thought reflected the changed conditions of the Hellenistic Age. With the growing loss of political freedom and the common condition of internal disorder, philosophers concerned themselves less with the reform of society and more with the attainment of happiness for the individual. "There is no point in saving the Greeks" is the way one Hellenistic philosopher summed up the new outlook, quite in contrast to that of Socrates, Plato, and Aristotle. This emphasis on peace of mind for the individual living in an insecure world led to the rise of four principal schools of Hellenistic philosophy, all of which had their start at Athens.

The Skeptics and Cynics reflected most clearly the doubts and misgivings of the times. The Skeptics hoped to achieve freedom from anxiety by denying the possibility of finding truth. The wise, they argued, will suspend judgment and not preach to others because they have learned that sensory experience, the only source of knowledge, is deceptive. The Skeptics were like modern pragmatists in substituting probability for certainty and insisting that even the probable must be tested by experience and exposed to the possibility of contradiction. To drive the point home, they were famous for arguing both sides of the same question.

To make their point, the Cynics carried this negativism further; their ideal was nonattachment to the values and conventions of society. Cynic philosophers, including Diogenes, wandered from city to city, calling for the public to pursue a nonconformist concept of *aretē*: "Look at me, I am without house or city, property or slave. I sleep on the ground. I have no wife, no children. What do I lack? Am I not without distress or fear? Am I not free?"[33]

More practical and popular were Epicureanism and Stoicism. The Athenian Epicurus (342–270 B.C.E.) taught that happiness could be achieved simply by freeing the body from pain and the mind from fear—particularly the fear of death. To reach this dual goal, people must avoid bodily excesses, including sensual pleasures, and accept the scientific teaching of Democritus that both body and soul are composed of atoms that fall apart at death. Beyond death there is no existence and nothing to fear. Epicurus maintained that the finest pleasures are intellectual and that the gods do not concern themselves with humans but spend their time pursuing true pleasure like good Epicureans.

The Stoics, followers of Zeno (c. 336–c. 264 B.C.E.), a Semite who settled in Athens, argued in contrast to Epicureanism that the universe is controlled by some power—variously called destiny, reason, natural law, providence, or God—that determines everything that happens. Fortified by this knowledge, wise Stoics conform their will to the "world will" and "stoically" accept whatever part fortune gives to them in the drama of life. The Epicurean retreated from worldly responsibilities, but the Stoic urged participation. Stoicism's stern sense of duty and belief in the equality of all people under a single ruling force made it particularly attractive to the Roman conquerors of the ancient world.

Science and Mathematics

The Greek concern for rational, impartial inquiry reached its highest level in the Hellenistic period, particularly in Alexandria, where the Ptolemies subsidized a great research institute, the Museum, and a library of more than half a million books. Emphasizing specialization and experimentation and enriched by Near Eastern astronomy and mathematics, Greek science in the third century B.C.E. achieved results unmatched until early modern times.

The expansion of geographical knowledge resulting from Alexander's conquests inspired scientists to make accurate maps and to estimate the size of the earth, which had been identified as a globe through observation of its shadow in a lunar eclipse. Eratosthenes, the outstanding geographer of the century, drew parallels of latitude and longitude on his map of the inhabited world and calculated the circumference of the globe (within 1 percent, an error of 195 miles) by measuring the difference in the angles of the noonday sun's shadows at Aswan and Alexandria. In astronomy, Aristarchus put forward the radical theory that the earth rotates on its axis and moves in an orbit around the sun. Most of his contemporaries adhered, however, to the prevailing geocentric theory, which stated that the earth was stationary and the sun revolved around it. Not only was this view supported by the powerful authority of Aristotle, but it also seemed to explain all the known facts of celestial motion. This was particularly true after Hipparchus in the next century added the new idea of *epicycles*—each planet revolves in its own small orbit while moving around the earth. Aristarchus's heliocentric theory was forgotten until the sixteenth century C.E., when it was revived by Copernicus.

Mathematics also made great advances in the third century B.C.E. Euclid systematized the theorems of plane and solid geometry, and Archimedes of Syracuse, who had studied at Alexandria, calculated the value of *pi*, invented a terminology for expressing numbers up to any magnitude, and established the rudiments of calculus. Archimedes also discovered specific gravity by noticing that he displaced water when submerged in his bath. And despite his dislike for making practical use of his knowledge, he invented the compound pulley, the windlass, and the endless screw for raising water.

The Hellenistic Greeks also extended the advances in medicine made earlier by Hippocrates and his school. By dissecting bodies of dead criminals, they were able to trace the outlines of the nervous system, to understand the principle of the circulation of the blood, and to ascertain that the brain, not the heart, is the true center of consciousness.

Hellenistic Art and Literature

The host of new cities that sprang up in Hellenistic times served as a tremendous impetus to new developments and experiments in architecture. The new cities benefited from town planning; the streets were laid out on a rectangular grid. The great public buildings were elaborate and highly ornamented; this was an age that preferred the ornate Corinthian column to the simpler Doric and Ionic styles of decoration.

Hellenistic sculptors continued and intensified the realistic, dramatic, and emotional approach that began to appear in late classical sculpture. Supported by rulers and other rich patrons in such affluent cities as Alexandria, Antioch, Rhodes, and Pergamum, they displayed their technical virtuosity by representing violent scenes, writhing forms, and dramatic poses, all with a realism that could make stone simulate flesh. Like most postclassical art, little evidence remained of the balance and restraint of classical Greek sculpture. The famous Laocoön group, with its twisted poses, contorted faces, and swollen muscles, stands in obvious contrast to the works of classical Greece seeking balance, harmony, and restraint.

In this second-century B.C.E. marble sculpture found on the island of Delos, Aphrodite defends herself with her sandal against the unwanted advances of the lecherous god Pan. The goddess is assisted by the winged god Eros (Cupid).

The quality of literature from the Hellenistic Age was generally inferior to that of the Hellenic Age. Scholarship flourished, and we are in debt for the preservation of much of Greek classical literature to the subsidized scholars at the Alexandrine library—"fatted fowls in a coop," as a Skeptic philosopher called them. They composed epics in imitation of Homer (one new feature was romantic love, not found in Homer), long poems on dreary subjects like the weather, and short, witty epigrams—all in a highly polished style. These sophisticated scholars also invented a new type of romantic, escapist literature: pastoral poetry extolling the unspoiled life and loves of shepherds and their rustic love interests. (Later both Roman and modern poets and painters would adopt this Hellenistic tradition of celebrating the charms of unsophisticated country life.) The best of the new poetry was written at Alexandria in the third century B.C.E. by Theocritus, who also composed very realistic poetry. The following short example, written by a contemporary, illustrates its character and appeal:

> Would that my father had taught me the craft of a
>   keeper of sheep,
> For so in the shade of the elm tree, or under the rocks
>   on the steep,
> Piping on reeds I had sat, and had lulled my sorrow to
>   sleep.[34]

The Hellenistic Contribution

The greatest contribution of the Hellenistic Age was the diffusion of Greek culture throughout the ancient East and the newly rising Roman West. In the East, the cities that Alexander and his successors built were the agents for spreading Hellenistic culture from the Aegean Sea to India. Literate Asians learned Greek to facilitate trade and to read Greek literature. In Judea, upper-class Jews built Greek theaters and gymnasiums and adopted Greek speech, dress, and names.

For a time the Seleucid Empire provided the peace and economic stability necessary to ensure the partial Hellenization of a vast area. But with an insufficient number of Greeks to colonize so large an area as the Near East, the Greek cities remained only islands in an Asian ocean. As time passed, this ocean encroached more and more on the Hellenized outposts.

The gradual weakening of the loosely knit Seleucid Empire eventually resulted in the creation of independent kingdoms on the edge of the Hellenistic world. In the middle of the third century, a nomad chieftain founded the kingdom of Parthia, situated between the Seleucid and Bactrian kingdoms. Claiming to be the heirs of the more ancient Persians, the Parthians expanded until by 130 B.C.E. they had wrested Babylonia from the Seleucids. Although Parthia was essentially a native Iranian state, its inhabitants absorbed some Hellenistic culture. Cut off from Seleucid rule by the Parthian kingdom, Bactria also became independent. Its Greek rulers, descendants of Alexander's veterans, controlled the caravan route to India and issued some of the most beautiful of Greek coins. In 183 B.C.E. the Bactrians crossed into India and conquered the province of Gandhara. One result of the conquest was a strong Greek influence on Indian art (see Chapter 6).

In the history of Western civilization, there is little of greater significance than Rome's absorption of Greek civilization and its transference of that heritage to later European culture. The stage on which this story began was the cosmopolitan Hellenistic Age, which "longed and strove for *Homonoia*, Concord between man and man ... [and] proclaimed a conception of the world as One Great City."[35] The process by which the Roman West was Hellenized will be described in the next chapter.

Conclusion

The two most important centers of the Aegean maritime civilization were Knossos, on the island of Crete, and Mycenae, on the Greek mainland. Aegean civilization reached its highest development first in Crete (2000–1450 B.C.E.), where these island dwellers fashioned a sophisticated urban culture, drawing on original creativity as well as influences from the Near East and Africa. After 1450 B.C.E. the center of Aegean culture shifted to Mycenae. The Mycenaean dominance lasted until nearly 1100 B.C.E., when migrations of peoples and possibly internal revolt ended their control, bringing about yet more migrations and displacement that probably forced the Mycenaeans eastward to Ionia and Asia Minor. There, and on the Greek mainland, fiercely independent city-states evolved a distinctly Hellenic culture that was to come to full fruition in the Hellenic Age (eighth to fourth centuries B.C.E.).

The Greek achievement reached its zenith in fifth-century B.C.E. Athens. During that time, the Athenians saved Greece from conquest by Persia and went on to unify most of Greece under their leadership. During its short existence, the Athenian Empire brought peace and prosperity to the Greek world. Athens also made itself the center of Greece's Golden Age of art, literature, and philosophy. We can therefore understand the assessment made by Pericles: "I claim that our city as a whole is an education to Greece."[36]

We can also paraphrase Pericles' statement and say that the history of Greece as a whole is an education to us. All aspects of Greek civilization—political, economic, social, cultural, and religious—appear to have gone through a complete development. (For example, is there any form of government that the Greeks did not experience?) With an understanding of Greek civilization from its beginning in the Greek Middle Ages, we are better able to understand European civilization from its beginning in the Middle Ages. We will also be inclined to say of Greek history what Thucydides said of his *History of the Peloponnesian War*: that it can be "judged useful by those inquirers who desire an exact knowledge of the past as an aid to the interpretation of the future, which will according to human nature recur in much the same way."[37]

Fortunately for the Greeks, and for us, Philip II of Macedonia, who conquered the city-states and ended their independence, sincerely admired Hellenic culture—an admiration shared by his son, Alexander the Great. It was the ambitious and charismatic Alexander who conquered the Near East and set up the empire that was eventually carved into three great successor states at the time of Alexander's death. The Hellenistic Age, which began with those successor states, was a period of economic expansion, cosmopolitanism, striking intellectual and artistic achievements, and the wide diffusion of Greek culture.

Suggestions for Reading

John Boardman, Jasper Griffin, and Oswyn Murray, eds., *The Oxford History of the Classical World* (Oxford University Press, 1986); Alan Samuel, *Promise of the West: The Greek World, Rome, and Judaism* (Routledge, 1988); and Peter Green, *Classical Bearings: Interpreting Ancient History and Culture* (Thames & Hudson, 1990), are valuable treatments.

Paul MacKendrick, *The Greek Stones Speak: The Story of Archaeology in Greek Lands,* 2nd ed. (Norton, 1981), is a popular account of the great archaeological discoveries in the Aegean area. See also Rodney Castleden, *Minoans: Life in Bronze Age Crete* (Routledge, 1990); Michael Wood, *In Search of the Trojan War* (New American Library, 1985); William McDonald and Carol Thomas, *Progress into the Past: The Rediscovery of Mycenaean Civilization* (Indiana University Press, 1990); Emily Vermeule, *Greece in the Bronze Age* (University of Chicago Press, 1972); Chester G. Starr, *The Origins of Greek Civilization, 1100–650 B.C.* (Knopf, 1961); Carl William Blegen, *Troy and Trojans* (Praeger, 1963); and A. J. B. Wace, *Mycenae* (Princeton University Press, 1949). Mary Renault, *The King Must Die* (Bantam, 1974), is an absorbing novel set in Mycenaean times.

John V. A. Fine, *The Ancient Greeks: A Critical History* (Belknap/Harvard University Press, 1983); A. R. Burn, *The Pelican History of Greece* (Penguin, 1966); M. I. Finley, *The Ancient Greeks: An Introduction to Their Life and Thoughts* (Viking, 1963); and Antony Andrewes, *The Greeks* (Norton, 1978), are valuable analyses. J. B. Bury and Russell Meiggs, *A History of Greece to the Death of Alexander the Great,* 4th ed. (St. Martin's Press, 1975), is a standard detailed history. M. I. Finley, *The World of Odysseus,* 2nd ed. (Viking, 1977), is excellent on the historical value of Homer. On the transition from oligarchy to democracy, see Antony Andrewes, *The Greek Tyrants* (Humanities Press, 1956), and W. G. Forrest, *The Emergence of Greek Democracy, 800–400 B.C.* (McGraw-Hill, 1966).

Valuable special studies on politics, economics, and society include A. R. Burn, *Persia and the Greeks: The Defense of the West, 546–478 B.C.,* 2nd ed. (Stanford University Press, 1984); Humphrey Mitchell, *Sparta* (Cambridge University Press, 1952); A. H. M. Jones, *Athenian Democracy* (Johns Hopkins University Press, 1986); Michel M. Austin and Pierre Vidal-Naquet, *Economic and Social History of Ancient Greece* (University of California Press, 1979); John Boardman, *The Greeks Overseas: Their Early Colonies and Trade,* 3rd ed. (Thames & Hudson, 1982); Russell Meiggs, *The Athenian Empire* (Oxford University Press, 1980); Cyril E. Robinson, *Everyday Life in Ancient Greece* (Greenwood Press, 1978); Frank Frost, *Greek Society,* 3rd ed. (Heath, 1987); M. I. Finley, *Ancient Slavery and Modern Ideology* (Penguin, 1983); H. A. Harris, *Sport in Greece and Rome* (Cornell University Press, 1972); K. J. Dover, *Greek Homosexuality,* 2nd ed. (MJF Books, 1997); and Chester G. Starr, *The Influence of Sea Power in Ancient History* (Oxford University Press, 1989). Martin Bernal, *Black Athena: The Afroasiatic Roots of Classical Civilization,* 2 vols. (Rutgers University Press, 1987, 1991), claims that Greek civilization had African and Near Eastern origins. For some critical reviews, see the *Journal of Mediterranean Archaeology,* vol. 3, no. 2 (June 1990).

Sarah Pomeroy, *Goddesses, Whores, Wives, and Slaves: Women in Classical Antiquity* (Schocken, 1976), is a short popular account. Bonnie S. Anderson and Judith P. Zinsser, *A History of Their Own: Women in Europe from Prehistory to the Present,* Vol. 1 (Harper & Row, 1988), and Mary Kinnear, *Daughters of Time: Women in the Western Tradition* (University of Michigan Press, 1982), are outstanding studies. See also Eva Cantarella, *Pandora's Daughters: The Role and Status of Women in Greek and Roman Antiquity* (Johns Hopkins University Press, 1988).

Edith Hamilton, *The Greek Way* (Norton, 1930), is a popular appreciation of Hellenic literature. Werner Jaeger, *Paideia: The Ideals of Greek Culture,* 2nd ed., Vol. 1: *Archaic Greece: The Mind of Athens* (Oxford University Press, 1986), has been called "the most illuminating work on Greece." See also Albin Lesky, *A History of Greek Literature* (Hackett, 1996).

Walter Burkert, *Greek Religion* (Harvard University Press, 1985), is a standard work. See also Walter F. Otto, *The Homeric Gods: The Spiritual Significance of Greek Religion* (Octagon Books, 1978); Michael Grant, *Myths of the Greeks and Romans* (Meridian, 1995); A. W. H. Adkins, *Moral Values and Political Behavior in Ancient Greece: From Homer to the End of the Fifth Century* (Norton, 1972); Eric R. Dodds, *The Greeks and the Irrational* (University of California Press, 1983); and Joseph Fontenrose, *The Delphic Oracle, Its Responses and Operations* (University of California Press, 1978).

Good introductions to Greek philosophy and science include W. K. C. Guthrie, *The Greek Philosophers from Thales to Aristotle* (Routledge, 1989); Francis M. Cornford, *Before and After Socrates* (Cambridge University Press, n.d.); G. E. R. Lloyd, *Early Greek Science: Thales to Aristotle* (Norton, 1970); G. E. R. Lloyd, *Greek Science After Aristotle* (Norton, 1973); and Erwin H. Ackerknecht, *A Short History of Medicine,* rev. ed. (Johns Hopkins University Press, 1982).

J. J. Pollitt, *Art and Experience in Classical Greece* (Cambridge University Press, 1972), is outstanding. See also Blanche R. Brown, *Anticlassicism in Greek Sculpture of the Fourth Century B.C.* (New York University Press, 1973); R. M. Cook, *Greek Art: Its Development, Character and Influence* (Penguin, 1991); A. W. Lawrence, *Greek Architecture,* 5th ed. (Yale University Press, 1996); Margarete Bieber, *The Sculpture of the Hellenistic Age,* 2nd ed. (Hacker, 1980); and Graham Ley, *A Short Introduction to the Ancient Greek Theater* (University of Chicago Press, 1991).

William W. Tarn, *Hellenistic Civilisation,* 3rd ed. (Methuen, 1966), is a detailed survey. See also F. W. Walbank, *The Hellenistic World* (Harvard University Press, 1982); John Onians, *Art and Thought in the Hellenistic Age: The Greek World View, 350–50 B.C.* (Thames & Hudson, 1979); and A. A. Long, *Hellenistic Philosophy: Stoics, Epicureans, Sceptics,* 2nd ed. (University of California Press, 1986). On the career and motives of Alexander the Great, see the biographies by Peter Green (Praeger, 1970), Ulrich Wilcken (Norton, 1932), J. R. Hamilton (University of Pittsburgh Press, 1974), and William W. Tarn (Beacon Press, 1948).

Suggestions for Web Browsing

Minoan Palaces
http://dilos.com/region/crete/minoan_pictures.html

Images and text from major Minoan archaeological sites, including Knossos.

Ancient Greek World
http://www.museum.upenn.edu/Greek_World/Intro.html

A presentation by the University of Pennsylvania Museum of Archaeology and Anthropology. Text and museum artifacts tell the vivid story of life in ancient Greece: land and time; daily life, economy, religion, and death.

Perseus Project
http://www.perseus.tufts.edu/

An impressive compilation of information on Greek art, architecture, and literature. One of the most useful but also scholarly sites dealing with ancient Greece.

Vatican Museum: Greek Collection
http://christusrex.org/www1/vaticano/GP-Profano.html

The excellent works in the Vatican's Greek collection are displayed and discussed in this outstanding site.

Daily Life in Ancient Greece
http://members.aol.com/Donnclass/Greeklife.html

A wonderfully entertaining site on ancient Greek life—gives a feel for what life would be like in a variety of Greek city-states.

Women's Life in Greece and Rome
http://www.uky.edu/ArtsSciences/Classics/wlgr/wlgr-index.html

Details about the private life and legal status of women, in addition to biographies of prominent women of ancient Rome.

Diotima: Women and Gender in the Ancient World
http://www.uky.edu/ArtsSciences/Classics/gender.html

An excellent site for information on women in ancient Greece—their political influence, occupations, dress, diet. A great range of information.

Alexander the Great
http://www.erc.msstate.edu/~vkire/faq/history/11.3.html

Web page detailing the life of the king of Macedonia and conqueror of the Persian Empire. Text and images describe his early life, ascension to the throne, major battles, travels, and death.

Ancient Olympics
http://olympics.tufts.edu/

Compare ancient and modern Olympic sports and read about the Olympic athletes who were famous in those earlier times.

Notes

1. Plutarch, *Lives*, "Pericles," 13.
2. See Leonard R. Palmer, *Mycenaeans and Minoans: Aegean Prehistory in the Light of the Linear B Tablets* (New York: Knopf, 1961), ch. 5.
3. Homer, *Iliad*, 12.360.
4. Quoted in Werner Jaeger, *Paideia: The Ideals of Greek Culture*, Vol. 1: *Archaic Greece: The Mind of Athens* (New York: Oxford University Press, 1939), p. 70.
5. Plato, *Laws* 5.735.
6. Plutarch, *Lives*, "Solon," 16.
7. Plutarch, *Lives*, "Lycurgus," 15.
8. Ibid.
9. Ibid.
10. Cyril E. Robinson, *Hellas: A Short History of Ancient Greece* (Boston: Beacon Press, 1955), p. 68.
11. Thucydides, *History of the Peloponnesian War* 2.65.
12. Ibid., 2.37, 40.
13. Ibid., 2.40, 41.
14. Ibid., 1.23.
15. Ibid., 2.65.
16. Ibid., 3.37.
17. Ibid., 5.105.
18. Ibid., 6.90.
19. Herodotus, *History of the Persian Wars* 7.10.
20. Plato, *Apology* 41.
21. Plato, *Phaedrus* 247.
22. Plato, *Republic* 451.
23. Quoted in Max Cary and T. J. Haarhoff, *Life and Thought in the Greek and Roman World*, 5th ed. (London: Methuen, 1959), p. 192.
24. Quoted in A. R. Burn, *The Pelican History of Greece* (Baltimore: Penguin, 1966), p. 272.
25. Thucydides, *History of the Peloponnesian War* 1.22.
26. Quoted in A. R. Burn, *The Lyric Age of Greece* (New York: St. Martin's Press, 1960), p. 166.
27. Sappho, "To Anaktoria," trans. Willis Barnstone, ll. 6–13, in *Sappho* (New York: Anchor Books, 1965).
28. Aeschylus, *Agamemnon*, in *Ten Greek Plays*, trans. Gilbert Murray, ed. Lane Cooper (New York: Oxford University Press, 1929), p. 96.
29. Joseph Wood Krutch, *The Modern Temper* (New York: Harcourt Brace, 1956), p. 84.
30. Euripides, *Medea*, in *Ten Greek Plays*, pp. 320, 321.
31. Aristophanes, *The Wasps*, ll. 1065–1070, in *The Frogs and Other Plays*, trans. David Barrett (Baltimore: Penguin, 1964), p. 77.
32. Theocritus, *Idyl* 15, trans. Nels M. Bailkey.
33. Quoted in I. E. S. Edwards and John Boardman, eds., *The Cambridge Ancient History*, Vol. 11 (Cambridge: Cambridge University Press, 1936), p. 696.
34. Moschus, *Idyl* 9, trans. Andrew Lang.
35. Gilbert Murray, *Hellenism and the Modern World* (Boston: Beacon Press, 1953), pp. 56–57.
36. Thucydides, *History of the Peloponnesian War* 2.41.
37. Ibid., 1.22.

The ruins of the Roman Carthage in modern Tunisia stand today as memorials to the splendor and might of Rome in its glory. Carthage, once the greatest rival to Rome's advance, gave way to conquest and was rebuilt under Roman dominance.

Roman Civilization
The Roman World, 509 B.C.E.–568 C.E.

Chapter Contents

As the Athenians saw the symbol of their city-state's democracy and culture in the Acropolis, so the Romans viewed the Forum as the symbol of world dominance. Temples were to be found there, but in contrast to the Acropolis, the Forum was dominated by secular buildings—meetinghouses used for judicial, financial, and other sorts of public business; the Senate House; the nearby Colosseum, used for gladiatorial shows; and the great palaces of the emperors rising on the neighboring Palatine Hill. While the Acropolis was crowned with statues to Athena, the Forum was adorned with triumphal arches and columns commemorating military conquests. Rome was the capital of a world-state, extending from Britain to the Euphrates, and its citizens were proud of their imperial position.

Although the buildings in the Forum appear Greek in style, they are more monumental and immense. Here, then, are two clues in understanding the Romans: they borrowed much from others, especially the Greeks, and often they modified what they took. The Romans replaced the chaos of the Hellenistic Age with law and order and embraced the intellectual and artistic legacy of the conquered Greeks. As Rome's empire expanded, this legacy was spread westward throughout most of Europe.

Throughout a history that led from a simple farming community in the plain of Latium to a strong state that became the master of the Mediterranean world as well as of Gaul, Britain, and parts of Germany, the Romans met one challenge

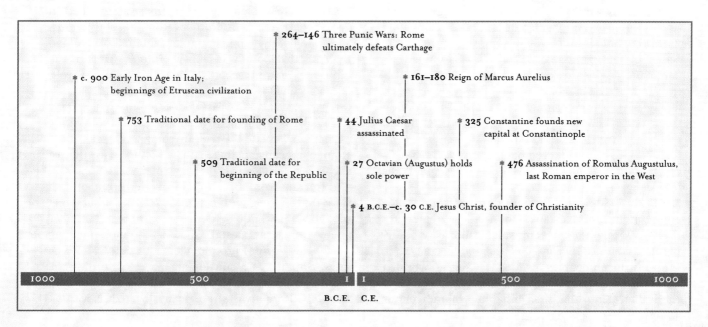

* 264–146 Three Punic Wars: Rome ultimately defeats Carthage

* c. 900 Early Iron Age in Italy; beginnings of Etruscan civilization

* 161–180 Reign of Marcus Aurelius

* 753 Traditional date for founding of Rome

* 44 Julius Caesar assassinated

* 325 Constantine founds new capital at Constantinople

* 509 Traditional date for beginning of the Republic

* 27 Octavian (Augustus) holds sole power

* 476 Assassination of Romulus Augustulus, last Roman emperor in the West

* 4 B.C.E.–c. 30 C.E. Jesus Christ, founder of Christianity

1000   500   I | I   500   1000

B.C.E.   C.E.

after another with practicality and efficiency. In the company of its marching legions went engineers and architects, so that today, scattered throughout the lands that once were part of the Roman world, the remains of roads, walls, baths, basilicas, amphitheaters, and aqueducts survive as symbols of the Roman contribution to Western civilization.

Rome to 509 B.C.E.

The history of Rome extends from 753 B.C.E., the traditional date for the founding of the city by Romulus, Rome's legendary first king, to 568 C.E., shortly after the death of Justinian. The first period in this span of more than a thousand years ended in 509 B.C.E. with the expulsion of the Etruscan monarch Tarquin the Proud, the seventh and last of Rome's kings, and the establishment of an aristocratic republic.

Geography and Early Settlers of Italy

Geography did much to shape the course of events in Italy. The Italian peninsula is 600 miles long and about four times the size of Greece, or two-thirds that of California. A great mountainous backbone, the Apennine range, runs almost the entire length of the peninsula. But the land is not so rugged as in Greece, and the mountains do not constitute a formidable barrier to political unification. Unlike in Greece, a network of roads could be built to link the regions. Furthermore, the plain of Latium and its major city, Rome, occupied a strategic position. It was relatively easy to defend, and once the Romans had begun to establish themselves as successful conquerors, they occupied a central position on the peninsula, which made it difficult for their enemies to unite successfully against them. The strategic position of Rome was duplicated on a larger scale by Italy itself. Italy juts into the Mediterranean almost in the center of that great sea. Once Italy was unified, its commanding position aided it in dominating the entire Mediterranean world.

Italy's most imposing valleys and harbors are on the western slopes of the Apennines. The Italian peninsula faced west, not east. For a long time, therefore, culture in Italy lagged behind that of Greece because cultural contact between the two peoples was long delayed.

Both Greeks and Romans were offshoots of a common Indo-European stock, and settlement of the Greek and Italian peninsulas followed broadly parallel stages. Between 2000 and 1000 B.C.E., when Indo-European peoples invaded the Aegean world, a western wing of this nomadic migration filtered into the Italian peninsula, then inhabited by indigenous Neolithic tribes. The first invaders, skilled in the use of copper and bronze, settled in the Po valley. Another wave of Indo-Europeans, equipped with iron weapons and tools, followed; in time the newer and older settlers intermingled and spread throughout the peninsula. One group, the Latins, settled in the plain of Latium, in the lower valley of the Tiber River.

As the Iron Age dawned in the western Mediterranean, the cultures of Italy became increasingly significant. During the ninth century B.C.E. the Etruscans established a dominant culture throughout much of Italy. The exact origin of the Etruscans remains uncertain. Some experts believe them to have been a non-Indo-European people who came to Italy by sea from Asia Minor. Others believe that their origin is explained through a rapid and creative growth of already resident iron-using peoples in northern Italy. Perhaps a combination of the two explanations is most likely—that native creativity fueled by contact with immigrants from the East resulted in a distinctly aggressive and creative culture. Expanding from the west coast up to the Po valley and south to the Bay of Naples, the Etruscans organized the backward Italic peoples into a loose confederation of Etruscan-dominated city-states.

After 750 B.C.E. Greek colonists migrated to southern Italy and Sicily, where they served as a protective buffer against powerful and prosperous Carthage, a Phoenician colony established in North Africa about 800 B.C.E. Yet the future was not to belong to these various invaders but to an insignificant village on the Tiber River, then in the shadows of Etruscan expansion. This was Rome, destined to be ruler of the ancient world.

Rome's Origins

According to ancient legend, Rome was founded in 753 B.C.E. by the twin brothers Romulus and Remus, sons of a nearby king's daughter who had been raped by Mars, the god of war. Thrown into the Tiber by the king, they were rescued and suckled by a she-wolf. Other legends further related that Romulus's ancestor was Aeneas, a Trojan who after the fall of Troy founded a settlement in Latium. The Aeneas story, perhaps invented by Greek mythmakers, pleased the Romans because it linked their history with that of the Greeks.

Turning from fable to fact, modern scholars believe that in the eighth century B.C.E. the inhabitants of some small Latin settlements on hills in the Tiber valley united and established a common meeting place, the Forum, around which the city of Rome grew. Situated at a convenient place for fording the river and protected from invaders by the hills and marshes, Rome was strategically located. Neverthe-

ITALY BEFORE
THE ROMAN EMPIRE

The Italian peninsula has little arable land and few navigable rivers and is crisscrossed with mountains. The Romans' ability to impose unity on this fragmented "boot" attests to their military and cultural strength and determination.

less, the expanding Etruscans conquered Rome about 625 B.C.E., and under their direction Rome became an important city-state.

Some features of Etruscan culture were original contributions; some were borrowed from the Greek colonies in southern Italy, and much of these, including the alphabet, was passed on to the Romans. (Etruscan writing can be read phonetically, but it is still not completely understood.) From their Etruscan overlords, the Romans acquired some of their gods and the practice of prophesying by examining animal entrails and observing the flight of birds. From the conquerors, too, the conquered learned the art of building (especially the arch), the practice of making statues of their gods, and the staging of gladiatorial combats. Even the name *Roma* appears to be an Etruscan word.

The Roman Monarchy, 753–509 B.C.E.

Rome's political growth followed a line of development similar to that of the Greek city-states: monarchy of the sort described by Homer, oligarchy, democracy, and, finally, the permanent dictatorship of the Roman emperors. For reasons that are both clear and instructive, in moving from oligarchy to democracy the Romans succeeded in avoiding the intermediate stage of tyranny.

The executive power, both civil and military, of Rome's seven kings (the last three were Etruscans) was called the *imperium*, which was symbolized by an ax bound in a bundle of rods *(fasces)*. In the twentieth century C.E. the fasces provided both the symbol and the name for Italian dictator Benito Mussolini's political creed, *fascism*.

Etruscan tombs were often elaborately painted with scenes of feasting and entertainment. On this tomb youths celebrate with music and wine.

Although the imperium was officially conferred on the monarch by a popular assembly made up of all arms-bearing citizens, the king turned for advice to a council of nobles called the Senate. Senators held their positions for life, and they and their families belonged to the *patrician* class, the fathers of the state (*pater* means "father"). The other class of Romans, the *plebeians*, or commoners, included small farmers, artisans, and many clients, or dependents, of patrician landowners.

In 509 B.C.E. the patricians overthrew the Etruscan monarchy and established an aristocratic form of government, known as the Republic.

The Early Republic, 509–133 B.C.E.: Domestic Affairs

The history of the Roman Republic can be divided into two distinct periods. During the first, from 509 to 133 B.C.E., two themes are dominant: a constitutional change from aristocracy to democracy, the result of the gradual extension of political and social equality to the plebeian lower class; and the expansion of Rome, first in Italy and then in the Mediterranean area.

Establishment of the Republic

In 509 B.C.E. the patricians forced out the last Etruscan king, Tarquin the Proud (Tarquinius Superbus), claiming he had acted despotically. (According to the Roman historian Livy, Tarquin was called "the Proud" because he "was the first king of Rome to break the established tradition of consulting the Senate on all matters of public business, and to govern by the mere authority of himself and his household.")[1] The patricians replaced the monarchy with an aristocracy they called a *republic* (res publica, "commonwealth"). The imperium was transferred to two new magistrates, called *consuls*. Elected annually from the patrician class, the consuls invariably exercised power in the interest of that class. In the event of war or serious domestic emergency, an "extraordinary" magistrate called *dictator* could be substituted for the two consuls, but he was given absolute power for six months only. The popular assembly was retained because the patricians could control it by means of their plebeian clients who, in return for a livelihood, voted as their patrons directed them.

Struggle for Equal Rights

For more than two centuries following the establishment of the Republic, the plebeians struggled for political and social equality. Outright civil war was avoided by the willingness, however reluctant and delayed, of the patricians to accept the demands of the plebeians. This largely explains why it was unnecessary for the plebeians to resort to tyrants to help them gain their goals, as had happened in the Greek city-states, or to revolt. Much of the plebeians' success in this struggle was due to their having been granted the right to organize themselves as a corporate body capable of collective action. This concession, granted by the Senate early in the fifth century B.C.E. after the plebeians threatened to leave Rome and found a city elsewhere, established a sort of state within a state known as the *Concilium Plebis* ("gathering of the plebeians"), which was presided over by plebeian leaders called *tribunes* and could pass *plebiscites* ("plebeian decrees") that were binding only on the plebeian community. The tribunes also received the right to stop unjust or oppressive acts of the patrician consuls and Senate by uttering the word *veto* ("I forbid").

The next major concession was in the field of law. Because the consuls often interpreted Rome's unwritten customary law to suit patrician interests, the plebeians demanded that it be written down and made available for all to see. As a result, about 450 B.C.E. the law was inscribed on a dozen tablets of bronze and set up publicly in the Forum. This Law of the Twelve Tables was the first landmark in the long history of Roman law, and Roman schoolchildren were required to memorize it.

In time the plebeians acquired other fundamental rights and safeguards: the rights to appeal a death sentence imposed by a consul and to be retried before the popular assembly were secured; marriage between patricians and plebeians, prohibited by the Law of the Twelve Tables, was legalized; and the enslavement of citizens for debt was abolished.

That their service in the Roman army was indispensable to the patricians greatly increased the plebeians' bargaining position in the state. Since Rome was almost constantly at war during these years, the patrician leaders of the state were more ready to accommodate plebeian demands than to face the possibility of a withdrawal of military participation by the commoners.

Little by little the plebeians acquired more power in the government. In 367 B.C.E. one consulship was reserved for the plebeians, and before the end of the century plebeians were eligible to hold other important magistracies that the patricians had created in the meantime. Among these new offices, whose powers had originally been held by the consuls, were the *praetor* (in charge of the administration of justice), *quaestor* (treasurer), and *censor* (supervisor of public morals and the letting of state contracts).

The long struggle for equality ended in 287 B.C.E. when the Concilium Plebis was recognized as a constitutional body, which then became known as the Tribal Assembly, and its plebiscites became laws *(leges)* binding on all citizens, patricians as well as plebeians. The Roman Republic was technically a democracy, although in actual practice a senatorial aristocracy of noble patricians and rich plebeians continued to control the state. Having gained political and social equality, the plebeians were usually willing to allow the more experienced Senate to run

the government from this time until 133 B.C.E., a period of almost constant warfare.

After 287 B.C.E. conflict in Roman society gradually assumed a new form. Before this time, the issue of greatest domestic importance had primarily been social and political inequality between the classes of patricians and plebeians. After equality was achieved, many rich plebeians were elected to the highest offices and became members of an expanded senatorial aristocracy. The new Roman "establishment" was prepared to guard its privileges even more fiercely than the old patricians had done. This fact became evident in 133 B.C.E. when a popular leader, Tiberius Gracchus, arose to challenge the establishment. But

This statue of a patrician with busts of his ancestors dates from either the first century B.C.E. or the first century C.E. The patricians were the aristocracy of Rome, and during the later Republic they came increasingly into conflict with senators and generals who took the part of the plebeians.

by this time the Roman populace had lost many of the characteristics that the citizens of the early Republic had demonstrated.

Society and Religion

The most important unit of early Roman society was the family. The power of the family father *(pater familias)* was absolute, and strict discipline was imposed to instill in children the virtues to which the Romans attached particular importance—loyalty, courage, self-control, and respect for laws and ancestral customs. The Romans of the early Republic were stern, hardworking, and practical. Cato the Elder (d. 149 B.C.E.), for example, took inspiration from frequent visits to view the small farm and humble cottage of a former consul who,

> though he had become the greatest of Romans, had subdued the most warlike nations, and driven Pyrrhus out of Italy, nevertheless tilled this little patch of ground with his own hands and occupied this cottage, after three triumphs. Here it was that the ambassadors of the Samnites once found him seated at his hearth cooking turnips, and offered him much gold; but he dismissed them, saying that a man whom such a meal satisfied had no need of gold.[2]

In contrast to the frequency of divorce in the late Republic, marriage in the early Republic was viewed as a lifelong union; patrician marriages were usually arranged between families and were undertaken primarily for the creation of children, but on many occasions such unions resulted in mutual affection between husband and wife. An early epitaph from the second century B.C.E. reads:

> Stranger, what I say is short, stay and read. Here is the unbeautiful grave of a beautiful woman. Her parents named her Claudia. She loved her husband with her whole heart. She bore two sons: one of whom she left alive on earth, the other she buried in the earth. Her speech was gay, but her bearing seemly. She kept the home. She made the wool. I have spoken. Go away.[3]

The religion of the early Romans had as yet little or no connection with ethics, and views concerning life after death were very vague. Religious practices were confined to placating the spirits *(numina)* of the family and the state by the repetition of complicated formulas, or spells. Mispronunciation of even a single syllable was enough to cause the spell to lose its power. Under Etruscan influence the major spirits were personified. The sky-spirit Jupiter became the patron god of Rome; Mars, spirit of vegetation, became god of war; and Janus, whose temple doors remained open when the army was away at war, was originally the spirit of the city gate.

Although early Roman religion had little to do with morals, it had much to do with morale. It strengthened family solidarity and enhanced a patriotic devotion to the state and its gods. But the early Romans' respect for hard work, frugality, and family and state gods was to be challenged by the effects of Rome's expansion in Italy and over much of the Mediterranean area during the early Republic.

The Early Republic, 509–133 B.C.E.: Foreign Affairs

The growth of Rome from a small city-state to the dominant power in the Mediterranean world in less than 400 years (509–133 B.C.E.) was a remarkable achievement. Roman expansion was not deliberately planned; rather, it was the result of dealing with unsettled conditions, first in Italy and then abroad, which were thought to threaten Rome's security. Rome always claimed that its wars were defensive, waged to protect itself from potentially hostile neighbors.

By 270 B.C.E. the first phase of Roman expansion had been accomplished. Ringed by hostile peoples—Etruscans in the north, land-hungry hill tribes in central Italy, and Greeks in the south—Rome subdued them all after long, determined effort and found itself master of all Italy south of the Po valley. In the process the Romans developed the administrative skills and traits of character—both fair-mindedness and ruthlessness—that would lead to the acquisition of an empire with possessions on three continents by 133 B.C.E.

Roman Conquest of Italy

Soon after driving out their Etruscan overlords in 509 B.C.E., Rome and the Latin League, composed of

---

The Early Wars of Rome

509 B.C.E.	Etruscans expelled from Rome
390 B.C.E.	Gauls attack and plunder Rome
338 B.C.E.	Rome emerges victor in wars with members of the Latin League
264–241 B.C.E.	Rome wins Sicily in First Punic War
218–201 B.C.E.	Rome defeats Hannibal in Second Punic War
149–146 B.C.E.	Carthage destroyed in Third Punic War

Livy: Horatius at the Bridge

Livy relates how one man saved Rome from reconquest by the Etruscans, about 506 B.C.E.

On the approach of the Etruscan army, the Romans abandoned their farmsteads and moved into the city. Garrisons were posted. In some sections the city walls seemed sufficient protection, in others the barrier of the Tiber. The most vulnerable point was the wooden bridge, and the Etruscans would have crossed it and forced an entrance into the city, had it not been for the courage of one man, Horatius Cocles—that great soldier whom the fortune of Rome gave to be her shield on that day of peril. . . . Proudly [Horatius] took his stand at the outer end of the bridge; conspicuous amongst the rout of fugitives, sword and shield ready for action, he prepared himself for close combat, one man against an army. The advancing enemy paused in sheer astonishment at such reckless courage. Two other men, Spurius Lartius and Titus Herminius, both aristocrats with a fine military record, were ashamed to leave Horatius alone, and with their support he won through the first few minutes of desperate danger. Soon, however, he forced them to save themselves and leave him; for little was now left of the bridge, and the demolition squads were calling them back before it was too late. Once more Horatius stood alone; with defiance in his eyes he confronted the Etruscan chivalry, challenging one after another to single combat, and mocking them all as tyrants' slaves who, careless of their own liberty, were coming to destroy the liberty of others. For a while they hung back, each waiting for his neighbour to make the first move, until shame at the unequal battle drove them to action, and with a fierce cry they hurled their spears at the solitary figure which barred their way. Horatius caught the missiles on his shield and, resolute as ever, straddled the bridge and held his ground. The Etruscans moved forward, and would have thrust him aside by the sheer weight of numbers, but their advance was suddenly checked by the crash of the falling bridge and the simultaneous shout of triumph from the Roman soldiers who had done their work in time. The Etruscans could only stare in bewilderment as Horatius, with a prayer to Father Tiber to bless him and his sword, plunged fully armed into the water and swam, through the missiles which fell thick about him, safely to the other side where his friends were waiting to receive him. It was a noble piece of work—legendary, maybe, but destined to be celebrated in story through the years to come.

From Livy, *The Early History of Rome*, trans. Aubrey de Sélincourt (Hammondsworth, England: Penguin, 1960), bk. 2, ch. 10.

other Latin peoples in Latium, entered into a defensive alliance against the Etruscans. This new combination was so successful that by the beginning of the fourth century B.C.E. it had become the chief power in central Italy. But at this time (390 B.C.E.) a major disaster almost ended the history of Rome. A raiding army of Celts, called Gauls by the Romans, invaded Italy from central Europe, wiped out the Roman army, and almost destroyed the city by fire. The elderly members of the Senate, according to the traditional account, sat awaiting their fate with quiet dignity before they were massacred. Only a garrison on the Capitoline Hill held out under siege. After seven months and the receipt of a huge ransom in gold, the Gauls withdrew. The stubborn Romans rebuilt their city and protected it with a stone wall, part of which still stands. They also remodeled their army by replacing the solid line of fixed spears of the phalanx formation, borrowed from the Etruscans and Greeks, with much more maneuverable small units of 120 men, called *maniples*, armed with javelins instead of spears. It would be 800 years before another barbarian army would be able to conquer the city of Rome.

The Latin League grew alarmed at Rome's increasing strength, and war broke out between the former allies. Upon Rome's victory in 338 B.C.E. the league was dissolved, and the Latin cities were forced to sign individual treaties with Rome. Thus the same year that saw the domination of Macedonia over Greece also saw the rise of a new power in Italy.

Border clashes with aggressive mountain tribes of Samnium led to three fiercely fought Samnite wars and the extension of Rome's frontiers to the Greek colonies in southern Italy by 290 B.C.E. Fearing Roman conquest, the Greeks prepared for war and called in the mercenary army of the Greek king, Pyrrhus of Epirus, who dreamed of becoming a second Alexander the Great. Pyrrhus's war elephants, unknown in Italy, twice routed the Romans, but at so heavy a cost that such a triumph is still called a "Pyrrhic victory." When a third battle failed to persuade the Romans to make peace, Pyrrhus is reported to have remarked, "The discipline of these barbarians is not barbarous," and returned to his homeland. By 270 B.C.E. the Roman army had subdued the Greek city-states in southern Italy.

Treatment of Conquered Peoples

Instead of slaughtering or enslaving their defeated foes in Italy, the Romans treated them fairly, in time creating a strong loyalty to Rome throughout the peninsula. Roman citizenship was a prized possession that was not extended to all peoples in Italy until the first century B.C.E. Most defeated states were required to sign a treaty of alliance with Rome, which bound them to accept Rome's foreign policy and to supply troops for the Roman army. No tribute was required, and each allied state retained local self-government. Rome did, however, annex about one-fifth of the conquered lands, on which nearly 30 colonies were established by 250 B.C.E.

The First Punic War

After 270 B.C.E. only Carthage remained as Rome's rival in the West. Much more wealthy and populous than Rome, with a magnificent navy that controlled the western Mediterranean and with a domain that included the northern coast of Africa, Sardinia, Corsica, western Sicily, and much of Spain, Carthage seemed more than a match for Rome. But Carthage was governed by a commercial oligarchy, which hired mercenaries to do its fighting. In the long run, the lack of a loyal body of citizens and allies, such as Rome had, proved to be Carthage's fatal weakness.

The First Punic War (from *punicus*, Latin for "Phoenician") broke out in 264 B.C.E. when Rome attempted to throw out a Carthaginian force that had occupied Messina, on the northeastern tip of Sicily, just across from Roman Italy. According to Polybius, a Hellenistic Greek historian, the Romans "felt it was absolutely necessary not to let Messina fall, or allow the Carthaginians to secure what would be like a bridge to enable them to cross into Italy."[4] Rome and its Italian allies lost more than 500 ships in naval engagements and storms before Carthage asked for peace in 241 B.C.E. (The Romans won only after they had invented the *corvus*, or "crow," a boarding bridge at the bow of a ship that, when lowered, turned a naval battle into a land battle.) Sicily, Sardinia, and Corsica were annexed as the first acquisitions in Rome's overseas empire, regulated and taxed—in contrast to Rome's allies in Italy—by Roman officials called *governors*.

The Contest with Hannibal

Stunned by its defeat, Carthage concentrated on enlarging its empire in Spain. Rome's determination to prevent this led to the greatest and most difficult war in Roman history. While both powers sought a position of advantage, a young Carthaginian general, Hannibal, precipitated the Second Punic War by attacking Saguntum, a Spanish town claimed by Rome as an ally. Rome declared war, and Hannibal, seizing the initiative, in 218 B.C.E. led an army of about 40,000 men, 9000 cavalry troops, and a detachment of African elephants across the Alps into Italy. Although the crossing had cost him nearly half of his men and all but one of his elephants, Hannibal defeated the Romans three times within three years.

Hannibal's forces never matched those of the Romans in numbers. At Cannae, for example, where Hannibal won his greatest victory, some 70,000 Romans were wiped out by nearly 50,000 Carthaginians. On the whole, Rome's allies remained loyal in spite of these losses—testimony to Rome's fair and statesmanlike treatment of its Italian subjects. Because the Romans controlled the seas, Hannibal received little aid from Carthage. As a result, Hannibal was unable to inflict a mortal blow against the Romans.

The Romans finally produced a general, Scipio, who was Hannibal's match in military strategy and who was bold enough to invade Africa. Asked to return home after 15 years spent on Italian soil, Hannibal clashed with Scipio's legions at Zama, where the Carthaginians suffered a complete defeat. The power of Carthage was broken forever by a harsh treaty imposed in 201 B.C.E. Carthage was forced to pay a huge war indemnity, disarm its forces, and turn Spain over to the Romans. Hannibal fled to the Seleucid Empire, where he stirred up anti-Roman sentiment.

Roman Intervention in the East

The defeat of Carthage left Rome free to turn eastward and deal with King Philip V of Macedonia. Fearful of the new power that had risen in the west, Philip had allied himself with Hannibal during the darkest days of the Second Punic War. (He sent no aid, however, because of an uprising in Greece.) Now, in 200 B.C.E., Rome was ready to act, following an appeal from Pergamum and Rhodes for aid in protecting the smaller Hellenistic states from Philip, who was advancing in the Aegean, and from the Seleucid emperor, who was moving into Asia Minor. The heavy Macedonian phalanxes were no match for the mobile Roman legions, and in 197 B.C.E. Philip was soundly defeated in Macedonia. His dreams of empire were ended when Rome deprived him of his warships and military bases in Greece. The Romans then proclaimed the independence of Greece and were praised as liberators by the grateful Greeks. According to the Roman historian Livy:

There was one people in the world which would fight for others' liberties at its own cost, to its own peril,

Hannibal's Character

The Roman historian Livy wrote the following character sketch of the great Carthaginian leader Hannibal. In Livy's brief profile, both the respect and the hatred the Romans held for their formidable enemy are quite obvious.

Hannibal was sent to Spain, where the troops received him with unanimous enthusiasm, the old soldiers feeling that in the person of this young man Hamilcar himself was restored to them. In the features and expression of the son's face they saw the father once again, the same vigour in his look, the same fire in his eyes. Very soon he no longer needed to rely upon his father's memory to make himself beloved and obeyed: his own qualities were sufficient. Power to command and readiness to obey are rare associates; but in Hannibal they were perfectly united, and their union made him as much valued by his commander as by his men. . . . Reckless in courting danger, he showed superb tactical ability once it was upon him. Indefatigable both physically and mentally, he could endure with equal ease excessive heat or excessive cold; he ate and drank not to flatter his appetites but only so much as would sustain his bodily strength. His time for waking, like his time for sleeping, was never determined by daylight or darkness: when his work was done, then, and then only, he rested, without need, moreover, of silence or a soft bed to woo sleep to his eyes. Often he was seen lying in his cloak on the bare ground amongst the common soldiers on sentry or picket duty. His accoutrement, like the horses he rode, was always conspicuous, but not his clothes, which were like those of any other officer of his rank and standing. Mounted or unmounted he was unequalled as a fighting man, always the first to attack, the last to leave the field. So much for his virtues—and they were great; but no less great were his faults: inhuman cruelty, a more than Punic perfidy, a total disregard of truth, honour, and religion, of the sanctity of an oath and of all that other men hold sacred. Such was the complex character of the man . . . doing and seeing everything which could help to equip him as a great military leader.

From Livy, *History of Rome,* 21.4, in Livy, *The War with Hannibal,* trans. Aubrey de Sélincourt (New York: Penguin, 1986).

and with its own toil, not limiting its guaranties of freedom to its neighbors, to men of the immediate vicinity, or to countries that lay close at hand, but ready to cross the sea that there might be no unjust empire anywhere and that everywhere justice, right, and law might prevail.[5]

A few years later Rome declared war on the Seleucid emperor, who had moved into Greece, urged on by Hannibal and a few greedy Greek states that resented Rome's refusal to dismember Macedonia. The Romans forced the emperor to leave Greece and Asia Minor, pay a huge indemnity, and give up his warships and war elephants. The Seleucids were checked again in 168 B.C.E. when a Roman ultimatum halted their invasion of Egypt. A Roman envoy met the advancing Seleucid army and, drawing a ring in the sand around the emperor, demanded that he decide on war or peace with Rome before stepping out of it. Egypt was declared a Roman protectorate. A year later Rome supported the Jews in their successful revolt against the Seleucids by addressing this message to the Seleucid ruler: "Wherefore hast thou made thy yoke heavy upon our friends and confederates the Jews? If therefore they complain any more against thee, we will do them justice, and fight with thee by sea and by land" (1 Maccabees 9:31–32).

Most of the East was now a Roman protectorate, the result of a policy—revealed again in Rome's action in stopping Seleucid aggression—in which Roman self-interest was combined with idealism. But Roman idealism turned sour when anti-Romanism became widespread in Greece, particularly among the poorer classes, who resented Rome's support of conservative governments and the status quo in general. The new policy was clearly revealed in 146 B.C.E. when, after many Greeks had supported an attempted Macedonian revival, Rome destroyed Corinth, a hotbed of anti-Romanism, as an object lesson. The Romans also supported the oligarchic factions in all Greek states and placed Greece under the watchful eye of the governor of Macedonia, which had been made a Roman province two years earlier. The idealistic Roman was fast becoming an ugly Roman.

Destruction of Carthage

In the West, meanwhile, Rome's hardening policy led to suspicion of Carthage's reviving prosperity and to a demand by Roman extremists for war—*Carthago delenda est* ("Carthage must be obliterated"). Obviously provoking the Third Punic War, the Romans besieged Carthage, which resisted heroically for

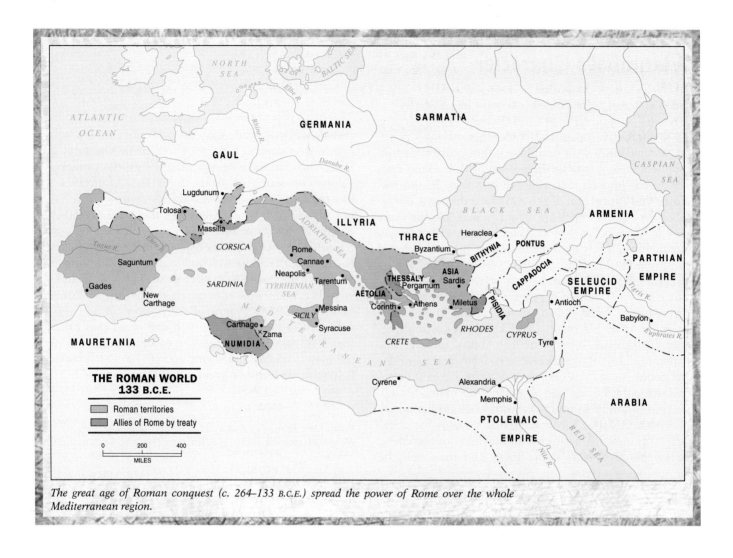

The great age of Roman conquest (c. 264–133 B.C.E.) spread the power of Rome over the whole Mediterranean region.

three years. They destroyed the city in 146 B.C.E., the same year they destroyed Corinth, and annexed the territory as a province.

Rome, Supreme in the Ancient World

In 133 B.C.E. Rome acquired its first province in Asia when the king of Pergamum, dying without an heir, left his kingdom to Rome. Apparently he feared that the discontented masses would revolt after his death unless Rome, with its reputation for maintaining law and order in the interest of the propertied classes, took over. Rome accepted the bequest and then spent the next three years suppressing a revolution of the poorer classes in the new province, called Asia. With provinces on three continents—Europe, Africa, and Asia—the once obscure Roman Republic was now supreme in the ancient world.

The Late Republic, 133–30 B.C.E.

The century following 133 B.C.E., during which Rome's frontiers reached the Euphrates and the

Rhine, witnessed the failure of the Republic to solve problems generated in part by the acquisition of an empire. These years serve as a good example of the failure of a democracy and its replacement by a dictatorship. The experience of the late Republic illustrates Thucydides' verdict that a democracy is incapable of running an empire. Athens kept its democracy but lost its empire; Rome would keep its empire and lose its democracy.

Effects of Roman Expansion

The political history of Rome thus far has consisted of two dominant themes: the gradual extension of equal rights for all male citizens and the expansion of Roman dominion over the Mediterranean world. Largely as a result of this expansion, Rome faced critical social and economic problems by the middle of the second century B.C.E.

One of the most pressing problems was the decline in the number of small landowners, whose spirit and devotion had made Rome great. Burdened by frequent military service, their farms and buildings destroyed by Hannibal, and unable to

The Late Republic

compete with the cheap grain imported from the new Roman province of Sicily, small farmers sold out and moved to the great city. Here they joined the unemployed and discontented *proletariat*, so called because their only contribution was *proles*, "children." The proletariat comprised a majority of the citizens in the city.

At the same time, improved farming methods learned from the Greeks and Carthaginians encouraged rich aristocrats to buy more and more land. Abandoning the cultivation of grain, they introduced large-scale scientific production of olive oil and wine, sheep and cattle. This change was especially profitable because an abundance of cheap slaves from conquered territory was available to work on the estates. These large slave plantations, called *latifundia,* were now common in many parts of Italy.

The land problem was further complicated by the government's practice of leasing part of the territory acquired in the conquest of the Italian peninsula to anyone willing to pay a percentage of the crop or animals raised on it. Only the wealthy could afford to lease large tracts of this public land, and in time they treated it as if it were their own property. Plebeian protests led to an attempt to limit the holdings of a single individual to 320 acres of public land, but the law enacted for that purpose was never enforced.

Corruption in the government was another mark of the growing weakness of the Roman Republic. Provincial officials took advantage of the opportunity to engage in graft for great profit, and a new sort of Roman businessmen scrambled selfishly for the profitable state contracts to supply the armies, collect taxes and loan money in the provinces, and lease state-owned mines and forests. An early example of corrupt business practices occurred during the Second Punic War. According to Livy, "Two scoundrels, taking advantage of the assumption by the state of all risks from tempest in the case of goods carried by sea

to armies in the field," fabricated false accounts of shipwrecks. "Their method was to load small and more or less worthless cargoes into old, rotten vessels, sink them at sea . . . , and then, in reporting the loss, enormously exaggerate the value of the cargoes." When the swindle was reported to the Senate, it took no action because it "did not wish at a time of such national danger to make enemies of the capitalists."[6]

Although in theory the government was a democracy, in practice it remained a senatorial oligarchy. Wars tend to strengthen the executive power in a state, and in Rome the Senate traditionally had such power. Even the tribunes, guardians of the people's rights, became for the most part puppets of the Senate. By the middle of the second century B.C.E. the government was in the hands of a wealthy, self-serving Senate, which became increasingly incapable of coping with the problems of governing a world-state. Ordinary citizens were for the most part impoverished and landless, and Rome swarmed with fortune hunters, imported slaves, unemployed farmers, and discontented war veterans. The poverty of the many, coupled with the great wealth of the few, hastened the decay of the old Roman traits of discipline, simplicity, and respect for authority. The next century (133–30 B.C.E.) saw Rome torn apart by internal conflict, which led to the establishment of a permanent dictatorship and the end of the Republic.

Reform Movement of the Gracchi

An awareness of Rome's profound social and economic problems led to the reform program of an idealistic and ambitious young aristocrat named Tiberius Gracchus. His reforming spirit was partly the product of the newly imported philosophical learning of Greece and an awareness that the old Roman character and way of life were fast slipping away. He sought to arrest Roman decline by restoring the backbone of the old Roman society, the small landowner. Supported by a faction of senators, Tiberius was elected tribune for the year 133 B.C.E. at the age of 29.

Tiberius proposed to the Tribal Assembly that the act limiting the holding of public land to 320 acres per citizen, plus 160 acres for each of two grown-up sons, be reenacted. Much of the public land would in the future continue to be held by the present occupants and their heirs as private property, but the rest was to be taken back and granted to the poor in small plots of 9 to 18 acres. The recipients were to pay a small rent and could not sell their holdings. In his address to the assembly Tiberius noted that

it is with lying lips that their commanders exhort the soldiers in their battles to defend sepulchres and shrines from the enemy; . . . they fight and die to support others in wealth and luxury, and though they are styled masters of the world, they have not a single clod of earth that is their own.[7]

When it became evident that the Tribal Assembly would adopt Tiberius's proposal, the Senate persuaded one of the other tribunes to veto the measure. On the ground that a tribune who opposed the will of the people had no right to his office, Tiberius took a fateful—and, the Senate claimed, unconstitutional—step by having the assembly depose the tribune in question. The agrarian bill was then passed.

To ensure the implementation of his agrarian reform, Tiberius again violated custom by standing for reelection in the Tribal Assembly after completing his one-year term. Claiming that he sought to make himself king, partisans of the Senate murdered Tiberius and 300 of his followers. The Republic's failure at this point to solve its problems without bloodshed stands in striking contrast to its earlier history of peaceful reform.

Tiberius's work was taken up by his younger brother, Gaius Gracchus, who was elected tribune for 123 B.C.E. In addition to the allocation of public land to the poor, Gaius proposed establishing Roman colonies in southern Italy and in Africa—his enemies said near the site of Carthage. To protect the poor against speculation in the grain market (especially in times of famine), Gaius committed the government to the purchase, storage, and subsequent distribution of wheat to the urban masses at about half the actual market price. Unfortunately, what Gaius intended as a relief measure later became a dole, whereby nearly free food was distributed—all too often for the advancement of astute politicians—to the entire proletariat.

Another of Gaius's proposals would have granted citizenship to Rome's Italian allies, who felt they were being mistreated by Roman officials. This proposal cost Gaius the support of the Roman proletariat, which did not wish to share the privileges of citizenship or share its control of the Tribal Assembly. Consequently, in 121 B.C.E. Gaius failed to be reelected to a third term as tribune when his opponents packed the Tribal Assembly with their followers on election day, and the Senate again resorted to force. It decreed what is today called martial law by authorizing the consuls to take any action deemed necessary "to protect the state and suppress the tyrants." Three thousand of Gaius's followers were killed in rioting or arrested and executed, a fate Gaius avoided by committing suicide.

The Senate had shown that it had no intention of initiating needed domestic reforms or of allowing others to do so, and the Gracchi's deaths were ominous signals of the way the Republic would decide its internal disputes in the future.

In foreign affairs as well, the Senate soon demonstrated ineptness. Rome was forced to grant citizenship to its Italian allies after the Senate's failure to deal with their grievances pushed them into open revolt (90–88 B.C.E.). Other shortsighted actions led to the first of the three civil wars that assisted in the destruction of the Republic.

The First Civil War: Marius Versus Sulla

Between 111 and 105 B.C.E. Roman armies, dispatched by the Senate and commanded by senators, failed to protect Roman business interests in Numidia, a kingdom in North Africa allied to Rome. Nor were they able to prevent Germanic tribes from overrunning southern Gaul, then a Roman province, and threatening Italy itself. Accusing the Senate of neglect and incompetence in directing Rome's foreign affairs, the Roman commercial class and common people joined together to elect Gaius Marius consul in 107 B.C.E., and the Tribal Assembly commissioned him to raise an army to put down the foreign danger. Marius first pacified North Africa and then crushed the first German threat to Rome. In the process he created a new-style Roman army that was destined to play a major role in the turbulent history of the late Republic.

Unlike the old Roman army, which was composed of conscripts who owned their own land and thought of themselves as loyal citizens of the Republic, the new army created by Marius was recruited from landless citizens for long terms of service. These professional soldiers identified their own interests with those of their commanders, to whom they swore loyalty and looked to for bonuses of land and money, since the Senate refused their requests for such support. Thus the character of the army changed from a militia of draftees to a career service in which loyalty to the state was replaced with loyalty to the commander. Ambitious generals were in a position to use their military power to seize the government.

In 88 B.C.E. the king of Pontus, in Asia Minor, encouraged by growing anti-Roman sentiment in the province of Asia and in Greece caused by corrupt governors, tax collectors, and moneylenders, declared war on Rome. The Senate ordered Cornelius Sulla, an able general and a strong supporter of the Senate's authority, to march east and restore order. As a countermove, the Tribal Assembly chose Marius for the eastern command. In effect both the Senate and the Tribal Assembly, whose power the Gracchi had revived, claimed to be the ultimate authority in the state. The result was the first of a series of civil wars between rival generals, each claiming to champion the cause of either the Senate or the Tribal Assembly. The first civil war ended in a complete victory for Sulla, who in 82 B.C.E. was appointed by the Senate to the seldom employed special office of dictator, not for a maximum of six months but for an unlimited term as "dictator for the revision of the constitution."

Sulla intended to restore the preeminence of the Senate. He drastically reduced the powers of the tribunes and the Tribal Assembly, giving the Senate virtually complete control of all legislation. Having massacred several thousand of the opposition, Sulla was convinced that his constitutional improvements would be permanent, and in 79 B.C.E. he voluntarily resigned his dictatorship and retired from public life. His reactionary changes, however, were not to last.

The Second Civil War: Pompey Versus Caesar

The first of the civil wars and its aftermath increased both division and discontent in the state and fueled the ambitions of younger individuals eager for personal power. The first of these men to come forward was Pompey, who had won fame as a military leader. In 70 B.C.E. he was elected consul. Although he was a former supporter of Sulla, he won popularity with the commoners by repealing Sulla's laws limiting the power of the tribunes and the Tribal Assembly. Pompey then put an end to disorder in the East caused by piracy (the result of the Senate's neglect of the Roman navy), the continuing threats of the king of Pontus, and the political uncertainty caused by the collapse of the Seleucid Empire. New Roman provinces and client states set up by Pompey brought order eastward as far as the Euphrates. These included the province of Syria—the last remnant of the once vast Seleucid Empire—and the client state of Judea, supervised by the governor of Syria.

Still another ambitious and able leader made his major impact in 59 B.C.E. Julius Caesar allied himself politically with Pompey and was elected consul. Following his consulship, Caesar spent nine years conquering Gaul, under the pretext of protecting the Gauls from the Germans across the Rhine. He accumulated a fortune in plunder and trained a loyal army of veterans. During his absence from Rome, he kept his name before the citizens by publishing an attractively written account of his military feats, *Commentaries on the Gallic War.*

Caesar's conquest of Gaul was to have tremendous consequences for the course of Western civilization, for its inhabitants quickly assimilated Roman culture. Consequently, when the Roman Empire collapsed in the West in the fifth century C.E., Romanized Gaul (France) ultimately took its place as a center of medieval civilization.

Fearful of Caesar's growing power, Pompey associated himself with the Senate in order to ruin him. When the Senate demanded in 49 B.C.E. that Caesar

disband his army, he crossed the Rubicon, the river in northern Italy that formed the boundary of his province. By crossing the Rubicon—a phrase employed today for any step that commits a person to a given course of action—Caesar in effect declared war on Pompey and the Senate. He marched on Rome while Pompey and most of the Senate fled to Greece, where Caesar defeated them at Pharsalus in 48 B.C.E. "They would have it so" was Caesar's curt comment as he walked among the Roman dead after the battle. Pompey was killed in Egypt when he sought refuge there, but the last Pompeian army was not defeated until 45 B.C.E. (After one battle, Caesar sent a friend a three-word letter: *Veni, vidi, vici*—"I came, I saw, I conquered.")

As he assumed the title of "dictator for the administration of public affairs," Caesar initiated far-reaching reforms. He granted citizenship to the Gauls and packed the Senate with many new non-Italian members, in this way making it a more truly representative body as well as a rubber stamp for his policies. In the interest of the poorer citizens, he reduced debts, inaugurated a public works program, established colonies outside Italy, and decreed that one-third of the laborers on the slave-worked estates in Italy be persons of free birth. As a result, he was able to reduce from 320,000 to 150,000 the number of people in the city of Rome receiving free grain. (The population of Rome is estimated to have been 500,000.) His most enduring act was the reform of the calendar in the light of Egyptian knowledge; with minor changes, this calendar of 365¼ days is still in use today.

Caesar realized that the Republic was dead. In his own words, "The Republic is merely a name, without form or substance." He believed that only intelligent autocratic leadership could save Rome from continued civil war and collapse. But Caesar inspired the hatred of many, particularly those who viewed him as a tyrant who had destroyed the Republic. On the Ides (fifteenth day) of March, 44 B.C.E., a group of conspirators, led by Brutus and other ex-Pompeians whom Caesar had pardoned, stabbed him to death in the Senate, and Rome was once more drawn into conflict.

Caesar's assassins had been offended by certain of his actions that seemed to fall just short of monarchy—his purple robe, the statues erected in his honor, the coins bearing his portrait—and they assumed that with his death the Republic would be restored to its traditional status. But the people of Rome remained unmoved by the conspirators' cry of "Liberty! Freedom! Tyranny is dead!" The majority of them were prepared to accept a successor to Caesar whose power and position stopped just short of a royal title. The real question was, who was to be Caesar's successor?

The Third Civil War: Antony Versus Octavian

Following Caesar's death, his 18-year-old grand-nephew and heir, Octavian, allied himself with Caesar's chief lieutenant, Mark Antony, against the conspirators and the Senate. The conspirators' armies were routed, and Cicero, a renowned orator and champion of the Senate, was put to death for his hostility toward Antony. Then for more than a decade Octavian and Antony exercised dictatorial power and divided the Roman world between them. But the ambitions of each man proved too great for the alliance to endure.

Antony, who took charge of the eastern half of the empire, became completely infatuated with Cleopatra, the last of the Egyptian Ptolemies. He even went so far as to transfer Roman territories to her control. Octavian took advantage of Antony's blunders to propagandize Rome and Italy against Antony and his foreign lover queen "with her polluted crew of creatures foul with lust." The resulting struggle was portrayed by Octavian as a war between the Roman West and the "oriental" East. When Octavian's fleet met Antony's near Actium in Greece, first Cleopatra and then Antony deserted the battle and fled to Egypt. There Antony committed suicide, as Cleopatra did soon afterward when Alexandria was captured in 30 B.C.E.

The Early Empire, 30 B.C.E.–180 C.E.

At the end of a century of civil violence, Rome was at last united under one leader, Octavian, who was hailed by the grateful Romans as the "father of his country." The Republic gave way to the permanent dictatorship of the empire, and two centuries of imperial greatness, known as the *Pax Romana* ("Roman Peace"), followed.

Reconstruction Under Augustus

Following his triumphal return to Rome, Octavian in 27 B.C.E. announced that he would "restore the Republic." But he did so only outwardly by blending republican institutions with his own strong personal leadership. He consulted the Senate on important issues, allowed it to retain control over Italy and half of the provinces, and gave it the legislative functions of the nearly unused Tribal Assembly. The Senate in return bestowed on Octavian the title *Augustus* ("The Revered," a title previously used for gods), by which he was known thereafter.

During the rest of his 45-year rule, Augustus never again held the office of dictator, and he seldom held the consulship. Where, then, did his strength lie? Throughout his career he kept the powers of a tribune, which gave him the right to initiate legislation and to veto the legislative and administrative acts of others. He also kept for himself the governorship of the frontier provinces, where the armies were stationed. Augustus's nearly total control of the army meant that his power could not be successfully challenged. From his military title, *imperator* ("victorious general"), is derived our modern term *emperor*.

Augustus thus effected a compromise "between the need for a monarchical head of the empire and the sentiment which enshrined Rome's republican constitution in the minds of his contemporaries."[8] He preferred the modest title of *princeps*, "first citizen" or "leader," which he felt best described his position, and his form of disguised dictatorship is therefore known as the Principate. At the beginning of the empire, then, political power was ostensibly divided between the princeps and the senatorial aristocrats. This arrangement was continued by most of Augustus's successors during the next two centuries.

Seeking to efface the scars of more than a century of civil strife, Augustus concentrated on internal reform. He did annex Egypt and extend the Roman frontier to the Danube as a defense against barbarian invasions, but he failed in an attempt to conquer Germany up to the Elbe River. As a result of this failure, the Germans were never Romanized, like the Celts of Gaul and Spain, and the boundary between their language and the Roman-based Romance languages of France and Spain is still the Rhine.

Augustus also sought to cure a sick society—to end the mood of utter hopelessness felt by many concerned Romans, among them the poet Horace:

> *Time corrupts all. What has it not made worse?*
> *Our grandfathers sired feebler children; theirs*
> *Were weaker still—ourselves; and now our curse*
> *Must be to breed even more degenerate heirs.*[9]

Through legislation and propaganda, Augustus sought with some success to check moral and social decline and revive the old Roman ideals and traditions. He rebuilt deteriorated temples, revived old priesthoods, and restored religious festivals. He attempted to reestablish the integrity of the family by legislating against adultery, the chief grounds for divorce, which had become quite common during the late Republic. A permanent court was set up to prosecute adulterous wives and their lovers. Among those found guilty and banished from Rome were Augustus's own daughter and granddaughter. Finally, to disarm the gangs that had been terrorizing citizens, he outlawed the carrying of daggers.

Augustus greatly reduced the corruption and exploitation that had flourished in the late Republic by creating a well-paid civil service, open to all classes. He also established a permanent standing army, stationed in the frontier provinces and kept out of politics. More than 40 colonies of retired soldiers were founded throughout the empire; among them were Palermo in Sicily, Patras in Greece, and Baalbek in Syria.

Augustus's reforms also gave rise to a new optimism and patriotism that were reflected in the art and literature of the Augustan Age (discussed later in this chapter).

The Julio-Claudian and Flavian Emperors

Augustus was followed by four descendants from among his family, the line of the Julio-Claudians, who ruled from 14 to 68 C.E. Augustus's stepson Tiberius, whom the Senate accepted as his successor, and Claudius were fairly efficient and devoted rulers; in Claudius's reign the Roman occupation of Britain began in 43 C.E. The other two rulers of this imperial line disregarded the appearance that they were only the first among all citizens: Caligula was a madman who demanded to be worshipped as a god and toyed with the idea of having his favorite horse elected to high office in Rome; Nero was infamous for his immorality, the murder of his wife and his mother, and his persecution of Christians in Rome. (See Chapter 7 for a discussion of the rise and spread of Christianity.)

In 64 C.E. a great fire raged for nine days, destroying more than half of the capital. The Roman historian Tacitus has left us a vivid account of how Nero made the unpopular Christians scapegoats for the fire:

Large numbers . . . were condemned—not so much for incendiarism as for their anti-social tendencies. Their deaths were made farcical. Dressed in wild animals' skins, they were torn to pieces by dogs, or crucified, or made into torches to be ignited after dark. . . . Nero provided his Gardens for the spectacle, and exhibited displays in the Circus. . . . Despite their guilt as Christians, and the ruthless punishment it deserved, the victims were pitied. For it was felt they were being sacrificed to one man's brutality rather than to the national interest.[10]

The Julio-Claudian line ended in 68 C.E. when Nero, declared a public enemy by the Senate and facing army revolts, committed suicide. In the following year four emperors were proclaimed by rival armies, with Vespasian the final victor. For nearly 30 years (69–96 C.E.) the Flavian dynasty (Vespasian followed by his two sons, Titus and Domitian) provided the empire with effective but autocratic rule. The fiction of republican institutions gave way to a scarcely veiled monarchy as the Flavians openly treated the office of emperor as theirs by right of conquest and inheritance.

The Antonines: "Five Good Emperors"

An end to autocracy and a return to the Augustan principle of an administration of equals—emperor and Senate—characterized the rule of the Antonine emperors (96–180 C.E.), under whom the empire reached the height of its prosperity and power. Selected on the basis of proven ability, these "good emperors" succeeded, according to Tacitus, in establishing "the rare happiness of times, when we may think what we please, and express what we think."[11] Two of these emperors are especially worthy of note.

Hadrian reigned from 117 to 138 C.E. His first important act was to stabilize the boundaries of the empire. He gave up as indefensible recently conquered Armenia and Mesopotamia and erected protective walls in Germany and Britain, the latter an imposing structure of stone 20 feet high. Hadrian traveled extensively, inspecting almost every province of the empire. New cities were founded, old ones were restored, and many public works were constructed, among them the famous Pantheon, still standing in Rome.

The last of the "five good emperors" was Marcus Aurelius, who ruled from 161 to 180 C.E. He preferred the study of philosophy and the quiet contemplation of his books to the blood and brutality of the battlefield. Yet he was repeatedly troubled by the invasions of the Parthians from the east and Germans from across the Danube. While engaged in his Germanic campaigns, he wrote his *Meditations*, a collection of personal thoughts notable for its lofty Stoic idealism and love of humanity. Ironically, the Stoic manner in which Christian martyrs accepted death did not impress him:

What an admirable soul that is which is ready, if at any moment it must be separated from the body. . . . This readiness must come from a man's own judgment, not from mere obstinacy, as with the Christians, but with reason and dignity if it is to persuade another, and without tragic show.[12]

Like a good Stoic, Marcus Aurelius died at his post at Vindobona (Vienna); at Rome his equestrian statue still stands on the Capitoline Hill.

The Pax Romana

In its finest period, the empire was a vast area stretching from Britain to the Euphrates and containing

The villa of the emperor Hadrian at Tivoli, a short distance away from Rome's congestion. Hadrian had the villa landscaped and decorated with replicas of famous Greek and oriental monuments.

The praetorian guard, the emperors' elite bodyguards, are shown here in a relief carving from Rome.

more than 100 million people. It was welded together into what Pliny the Elder, in the first century C.E., termed the "immense majesty of the Roman Peace." Writing during the rule of Augustus, the Roman poet Virgil was the spokesman for what enlightened Romans felt to be the mission of Rome:

> Others, doubtless, will mould lifelike bronze with greater delicacy, will win from marble the look of life, will plead cases better, chart the motions of the sky with the rod and foretell the risings of the stars. You, O Roman, remember to rule the nations with might. This will be your genius—to impose the way of peace, to spare the conquered and crush the proud.[13]

Non-Romans were equally conscious of the rich benefits derived from the Pax Romana, which began with Augustus and reached its fullest development under the Five Good Emperors. They welcomed the peace, prosperity, and administrative efficiency of the empire. Cities increased in number and were largely self-governed by their own upper-class magistrates and senates. In the mid-second century C.E., a Greek orator declared that the Romans "have linked together the nations of the world in one great family."[14]

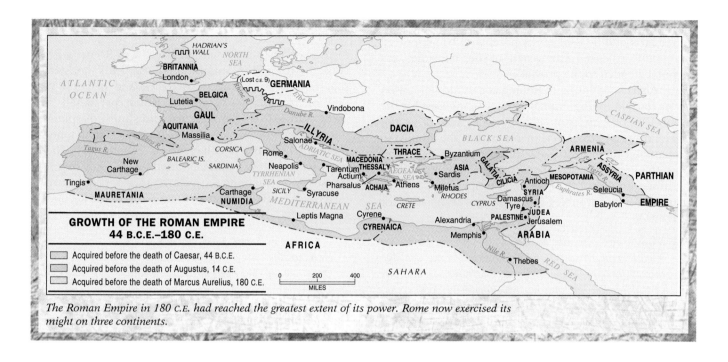

GROWTH OF THE ROMAN EMPIRE
44 B.C.E.–180 C.E.

☐ Acquired before the death of Caesar, 44 B.C.E.
☐ Acquired before the death of Augustus, 14 C.E.
☐ Acquired before the death of Marcus Aurelius, 180 C.E.

0   200   400
MILES

The Roman Empire in 180 C.E. had reached the greatest extent of its power. Rome now exercised its might on three continents.

The "True Democracy" of the Roman Empire

At the head of this huge world-state stood the emperor, its defender and symbol of unity as well as an object of worship. "The whole world speaks in unison," proclaimed the same Greek orator, "more distinctly than a chorus; and so well does it harmonize under this director-in-chief that it joins in praying this empire may last for all time."[15] The major theme of the many accounts written to celebrate the generally enlightened government of the Principate was that liberty had been exchanged for order and prosperity. The empire was said to represent a new kind of democracy: "the true democracy and the freedom that does not fail," "a democracy under the one man that can rule and govern best." The last century of the Republic, by contrast, exhibited

> *the evils found in every democracy. . . . The cause is the multitude of our population and the magnitude of the business of our government; for the population embraces men of every kind, . . . and the business of the state has become so vast that it can be administered only with the greatest difficulty.[16]*

Economic Prosperity

Rome's unification of the ancient world had far-reaching economic consequences. The Pax Romana was responsible for the elimination of tolls and other artificial barriers, the suppression of piracy and lawlessness, and the establishment of a reliable coinage. Such factors, in addition to the longest period of peace the West has ever enjoyed, explain in large measure the great expansion of commerce that occurred in the first and second centuries C.E. Industry was also stimulated, but its expansion was limited since wealth remained concentrated and no mass market for industrial goods was created. Industry remained organized on a small-shop basis, with producers widely scattered, resulting in self-sufficiency.

The economy of the empire remained basically agricultural, and huge estates, the *latifundia*, prospered. On these tracts, usually belonging to absentee owners, large numbers of *coloni*, free tenants, tilled the soil as sharecroppers. The *coloni* were replacing slave labor, which was becoming increasingly hard to secure with the disappearance of the flow of war captives.

Early Evidence of Economic Stagnation

Late in the first century C.E. the first sign of economic stagnation appeared in Italy. Italian agriculture began to suffer from overproduction as a result of the loss of Italy's markets for wine and olive oil in Roman Gaul, Spain, and North Africa, which were becoming self-sufficient in those products. To aid the Italian wine producers, the Flavian emperor Domitian created an artificial scarcity by forbidding the planting of new vineyards in Italy and by ordering half the existing vineyards in the provinces to be plowed under. A century later the Five Good Emperors sought to solve the continuing problem of overproduction in Italy by subsidizing the buying power of consumers. Loans at 5 percent interest were made to ailing landowners, with the interest to be paid into the treasuries of Italian municipalities and earmarked "for girls and boys of needy parents to be supported at public expense." This system of state subsidies was soon extended to the provinces.

Also contributing to Roman economic stagnation was the continuing drain of money to the East for the purchase of such luxury goods as silks and spices and the failure of city governments within the empire to keep their finances in order, thus making it necessary for the imperial government to intervene. As an official sent by one of the Five Good Emperors to investigate the fiscal troubles of some cities in Asia Minor reported:

> *Many sums of money are detained in private hands for a variety of reasons, and in addition some are disbursed for quite illegitimate expenditures. . . . The city of Nicomedia, my lord, has expended 3,329,000 sesterces on an aqueduct, which has been abandoned still unfinished and has even been torn down. Again they disbursed 200,000 sesterces for another aqueduct, but this, too, has been abandoned. So now, after throwing away all that money they must make a new expenditure in order to have water.[17]*

Such early evidence of declining prosperity foreshadowed the economic crisis of the third century C.E., when political anarchy and monetary inflation caused the economy of the empire to collapse (see Chapter 7).

Rome, Imperial Capital

At the hub of the sprawling empire was Rome, with close to a million inhabitants. Augustus boasted that he had found a city of brick and had left it one of marble. Nonetheless, Rome presented a great contrast of magnificence and slums, of splendid public buildings and poorly constructed tenements, which often collapsed or caught fire. The crowded narrow streets, lined with apartment houses and swarming with all manner of people, are described by the satirist Juvenal early in the second century C.E.:

> *. . . Hurry as I may, I am blocked*
> *By a surging crowd in front, while a vast mass*
> *Of people crushes onto me from behind.*
> *One with his elbow punches me, another*
> *With a hard litter-pole; one bangs a beam*
> *Against my head, a wine-cask someone else.*
> *With mud my legs are plastered; from all sides*
> *Huge feet trample upon me, and a soldier's*
> *Hobnails are firmly planted on my toes.[18]*

Social Life

At the top of the social order were the old senatorial families who lived as absentee owners of huge es-

A typically furnished bedroom in a villa near Pompeii (first century B.C.E.) illustrates the Roman view of domestic comfort. Though sparsely furnished, the room retains an elegant atmosphere, created in part by the elaborate murals and intricate mosaic floor pavement.

tates and left commerce and finance to a large and wealthy middle class. In contrast to the tenements of the poor, the homes of the rich were palatial, as revealed by excavations at Pompeii, which was buried and so preserved by the eruption of the volcano Vesuvius in 79 C.E. These elaborate villas contained courts and gardens with fountains, rooms with marble walls, mosaics on the floors, and numerous frescoes and other works of art. An interesting feature of Roman furniture was the abundance of couches and the scarcity of chairs. People usually reclined, even at meals.

The lower classes in the cities found a refuge from the dullness of their existence in social clubs, or guilds, called *collegia,* each comprising the workers of one trade. The activity of the collegia did not center on economic goals, like modern trade unions, but on the worship of a god and on feasts, celebrations, and decent burials for members.

The living conditions of slaves varied greatly. Those in domestic service were often treated humanely, with their years of efficient service frequently rewarded by emancipation. Nor was it uncommon for freed slaves to rise to positions of significance in business, letters, and the imperial service. However, conditions among slaves on the large estates could be indescribably harsh. Beginning with Augustus, however, numerous enactments protected slaves from mistreatment; Hadrian, for example, forbade private prisons and the killing of a slave without judicial approval.

Recreation played a key role in Roman social life. Both rich and poor were exceedingly fond of their public baths, which in the capital alone numbered 800 during the early days of the empire. The baths served the same purpose as modern-day athletic clubs. The larger baths contained enclosed gardens, promenades, gymnasiums, libraries, and famous works of art as well as a sequence of cleansing rooms through which one moved—the sweat room, the warm room where sweat was scraped off by a slave (soap was unknown), the tepid room for cooling off, and the invigorating cold bath. Another popular room was the lavatory, with its long row of marble toilets equipped with comfortable arm rests. Here Romans liked to sit and chat for an hour or more.

Footraces, boxing, and wrestling were minor sports; chariot racing and gladiatorial contests were the chief amusements. The cry for "bread and circuses" reached such proportions that by the first century C.E. the Roman calendar had as many as 100 days set aside as holidays, the majority of which were given over to games furnished at public expense. The most spectacular sport was chariot racing. The largest of six racecourses at Rome was the

A fresco portrait of a young woman from Pompeii. She seems to be caught in thought as she prepares to make an entry in her diary.

Circus Maximus, a huge marble-faced structure seating about 150,000 spectators. The games, which included as many as 24 races each day, were presided over by the emperor or his representative. The crowds bet furiously on their favorite charioteers, whose fame equaled that of the sports heroes of our own day.

Of equal or greater popularity were the gladiatorial contests, organized by both emperors and private promoters as regular features on the amusement calendar. These cruel spectacles, which have no exact counterpart in any other civilization, were held in arenas, the largest and most famous of which was the Colosseum, opened in 80 C.E. The contests took various forms. Ferocious animals were pitted against armed combatants or occasionally even against unarmed men and women who had been condemned to death. Another type of contest was the fight to the death between gladiators, generally equipped with different types of weapons but matched on equal terms. It was not uncommon for the life of a defeated gladiator who had fought courageously to be spared at the request of the spectators. Although many Romans considered these bloodletting contests barbaric, they continued until the fifth century, when Christianity forbade them.

A mosaic from the third century B.C.E. depicting gladiators. Introduced to Rome by the Etruscans, gladiatorial contests grew in popularity and cruelty as Rome grew older.

The Roman Crisis of the Third Century

In the third century C.E., internal anarchy and foreign invasion drastically transformed the Roman Empire. Augustus's constitutional monarchy in which the emperor shared power with the Senate changed to a despotic absolute monarchy in which the emperors made no attempt to hide the fact that they were backed by the military and would tolerate no senatorial influence. By the late third century, the emperor was no longer adressed as *princeps,* "first among equals," but as *dominus et deus,* "lord and god." The Principate had been replaced by the absolute rule known as the Dominate.

The transformation of the Roman Empire in the third century was foreshadowed by the reign of Commodus, who in 180 C.E. began a 12-year rule characterized by incompetence, corruption, cruelty, and neglect of affairs of state. He was strangled in 192, and civil war followed for a year until the establishment of the Severan dynasty (193–235). The Severan dynasty was intimidated by the military, just as the Principate had been. After 235, when the last member of the Severan dynasty was murdered by his own troops, 50 years of bloody civil wars, Germanic invasions, and new foreign threats ensued. Of the 26 men who claimed the title of emperor during this time, only one died a natural death.

Equally deadly to the well-being of the empire as military anarchy and foreign invasions was prolonged economic decline. The economy became static, inflation set in, and the concentration of land ownership in the hands of the few destroyed the small farming classes. The *latifundia,* with their fortified villas, grew as the number of *coloni* grew. As the rural tax base declined, chaotic conditions took their toll on trade, and by the end of the period the government refused to accept its own money for taxes and required payment in goods and services.

A much needed reconstruction of the empire was accomplished by Diocletian (285–305), a rough-hewn soldier and shrewd administrator. To increase the strength of the government, he completed the trend toward an autocracy of an oriental type featuring the Senate in a diminished role. He attempted to restructure the empire to ensure better government and an

The Roman Empire

14–68 C.E.	Period of the Julio-Claudian emperors
64 C.E.	Rome destroyed by fire; Emperor Nero attributes fire to Christians
69–96 C.E.	Period of the Flavian emperors
79 C.E.	Mount Vesuvius erupts, destroying Pompeii
96–180 C.E.	Period of the Antonine emperors
313 C.E.	Emperor Constantine issues Edict of Milan; Christians free to worship
378 C.E.	Battle of Adrianople; Germanic invasions into Roman Empire begin
395 C.E.	Roman Empire divided into eastern and western empires
476 C.E.	Last Roman emperor in the West assassinated

efficient succession scheme. Diocletian also tried to stop the economic decay of the empire by issuing new coins based on silver and gold and by imposing a freeze on prices and wages.

His succession scheme collapsed when Constantine (306–337) overcame his rivals to take power. He believed that the Christian God helped him during a battle for the city of Rome, and in return he actively supported Christianity by issuing in 313 the Edict of Milan, an order which decreed that Christianity would be tolerated throughout the empire. He continued the basic trends of Diocletian's work to ensure the production of essential goods and services as well as the collection of taxes. He imposed decrees tying people and their children to the same occupation in the same place. Most important, he moved the capital to the site of the old Greek colony of Byzantium (renaming it Constantinople). By doing so he in effect left Rome open to the attacks of the advancing Germanic peoples but ensured the continuation of Roman government in a new, safer location.

The Germanic Tribes

Waves of restless and diverse Germanic tribes were drawn into the power vacuum created during the two centuries of Rome's decline. While the westernmost German tribes (Franks, Angles, and Saxons) had achieved a settled agricultural life in the third and early fourth centuries, the Goths, Vandals, and Lombards remained largely nomadic.

The economic and legal practices of the Germanic tribes set them apart from the Romans. They engaged in so little commerce that cattle, rather than money, sufficed as a measure of value. A basic factor behind Germanic restlessness seems to have been land hunger. Their numbers were increasing, much of their land was forest and swamp, and their agricultural methods were inefficient. In an effort to eliminate blood feuds, the tribal law codes of the Germans encouraged the payment of compensation as an alternative for an aggrieved kin or family seeking vengeance. For the infliction of specific injuries, a stipulated payment, termed a *bot,* was required. The amount of compensation varied according to the severity of the crime and the social position of the victim.

Lack of written laws made it necessary to hold trials to determine guilt or innocence. A person standing trial could produce oath-helpers who would swear to his innocence. If unable to obtain oath-helpers, the accused was subjected to trial by ordeal, of which there were three kinds. In the first, the defendant had to lift a small stone out of a vessel of boiling water; unless his scalded arm healed within a prescribed number of days, he was judged guilty. In the second, he had to walk blindfolded and barefoot across a floor on which lay pieces of red-hot metal; success in avoiding the metal was a sign of inno-

cence. In the third, the bound defendant was thrown into a stream; if he sank he was innocent, but if he floated he was guilty because water was considered a divine element that would not accept a guilty person. Trial by ordeal lasted until the thirteenth century, when it was outlawed by Pope Innocent III and various secular rulers.

According to the Roman historian Tacitus, the Germans were notorious as heavy drinkers and gamblers, but Tacitus praised their courage, respect for women, and freedom from many Roman vices. A favorite amusement was listening to the tribal bards recite old tales of heroes and gods. Each warrior leader had a retinue of followers who were linked to him by personal loyalty. The war band—*comitatus* in Latin—had an important bearing on the origin of medieval feudalism, which was based on a similar personal bond between knights and their feudal lords. The heroic values associated with the *comitatus* also continued into the Middle Ages, where they formed the basis of the value system of the feudal nobility.

During the many centuries that the Romans and Germans faced each other across the Rhine-Danube frontier, there was much contact—peaceful as well as warlike—between the two peoples. Roman trade reached into German territory, and Germans entered the Roman Empire as slaves. During the troubled third century, many Germans were invited to settle on vacated lands within the empire or to serve in the Roman legions. By the fourth century the bulk of the Roman army and its generals in the west were German.

The Germans beyond the frontiers were kept in check by force of arms, by frontier walls, by diplomacy and gifts, and by playing off one tribe against another. In the last decades of the fourth century, however, these methods proved insufficient to prevent a series of great new invasions.

The Germanic Invasions

The impetus behind the increasing German activity on the frontiers in the late fourth century was the approach of the Huns. These nomads, superb horsemen and fighters from central Asia, had plundered and slain their Asian neighbors for centuries. In 372 they crossed the Volga and soon subjugated the easternmost Germanic tribe, the Ostrogoths. Terrified at the prospect of being conquered, the Visigoths, who found themselves next in the path of the advancing Huns, petitioned the Romans to allow them to settle as allies inside the empire. Permission was granted, and in 376 the entire tribe of Visigoths crossed the Danube into Roman territory. But soon corrupt Roman officials cheated and mistreated them, and the proud Germanic tribe went on a rampage. Valens, the East Roman emperor, tried to stop them, but he lost both his army and his life in the battle of Adrianople in 378.

Adrianople has been described as one of history's decisive battles, since it destroyed the legend of the invincibility of the Roman legions and ushered in a century and a half of chaos. For a few years the emperor Theodosius I held back the Visigoths, but after his death in 395 they began to migrate and pillage under their leader, Alaric. He invaded Italy, and in 410 his followers sacked Rome. The weak West Roman emperor ceded southern Gaul to the Visigoths, who soon expanded into Spain. Their Spanish kingdom lasted until the Muslim conquest of the eighth century.

To counter Alaric's threat to Italy, the Romans had withdrawn most of their troops from the Rhine frontier in 406 and from Britain the following year. A flood of Germanic tribes soon surged across the unguarded frontiers. The Vandals pushed their way through Gaul to Spain and, after pressure from the Visigoths, moved on to Africa, the granary of the empire. In 455 a Vandal raiding force sailed over from Africa, and Rome was sacked a second time. Meanwhile the Burgundians settled in the Rhone valley, the Franks gradually spread across Gaul, and the Angles, Saxons, and Jutes invaded Britain. Although each of these tribes set up a German-ruled kingdom within the confines of the empire, only the Franks in Gaul and the Angles and Sax-

ons in Britain managed to establish kingdoms that lasted longer than a few generations.

Meanwhile the Huns pushed farther into Europe. Led by Attila, the "scourge of God," the mounted nomads crossed the Rhine in 451. The remaining Roman forces in Gaul, joined by the Visigoths, defeated the Huns near Troyes. Attila then plundered northern Italy and planned to take Rome, but disease, lack of supplies, and the dramatic appeal of Pope Leo I, whose actions brought great prestige to the papacy, caused him to return to the plains of eastern Europe. The Huns' threat disintegrated after 453, when Attila died on the night of his marriage to a Germanic princess.

The End of the West Roman Empire, 395–568 C.E.

After the death of Theodosius I in 395, the Roman Empire was divided between his two sons. The decline of Roman rule in the West was hastened as a series of weakened emperors abandoned Rome and sought safety behind the marshes at the northern Italian city of Ravenna. The leaders of the imperial

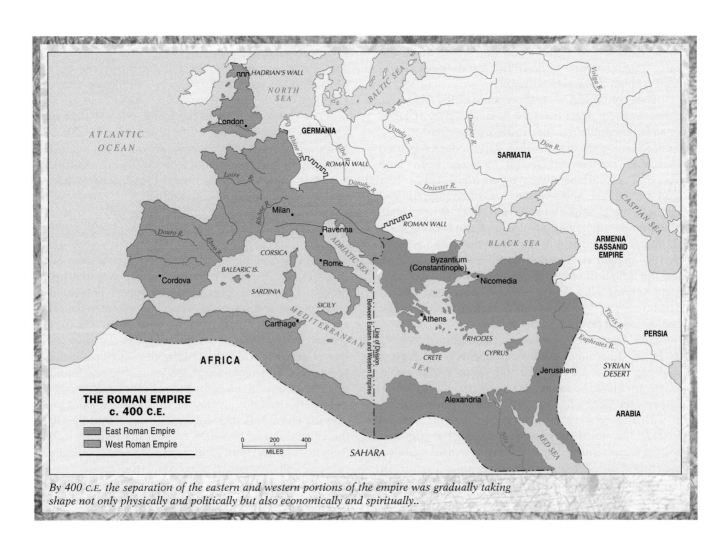

By 400 C.E. the separation of the eastern and western portions of the empire was gradually taking shape not only physically and politically but also economically and spiritually..

army, whose ranks were now mainly German, exercised the real power.

In 475 Orestes, the German commander of the troops, forced the Senate to elect his young son Romulus Augustulus ("Little Augustus") emperor in the West. The following year another German commander, Odovacar, killed Orestes. Seeing no reason to continue the powerless imperial line in the West, he deposed Romulus Augustulus and named himself head of the government. The deposition of this boy, who ironically bore the names of the legendary founder of Rome and the founder of the empire, marks the traditional "fall" of the Roman Empire.

The disintegration of the Huns' empire following the death of Attila freed the Ostrogoths to migrate as other tribes were doing. Under their energetic king, Theodoric (c. 454–526), the Ostrogoths were moved into action. Theodoric accepted a commission from the emperor in Constantinople to reimpose imperial authority over Italy, now in Odovacar's hands. In 488 Theodoric led his people into the Italian peninsula, where, after hard fighting, Odovacar sued for peace. After Odovacar was treacherously murdered, Theodoric established a strong Ostrogothic kingdom in Italy with its capital at Ravenna. Because he appreci-

ated the culture he had seen at Constantinople, Theodoric maintained classical culture on a high level. Following his death without a male heir in 526, civil war broke out in Italy, paving the way for a 20-year war of reconquest (535–555) by the armies of the East Roman emperor, Justinian. Italy was ravaged from end to end by the fighting, and the classical civilization that Theodoric had carefully preserved was in large part destroyed.

In 568, three years after the death of Justinian, the last wave of Germanic invaders, the Lombards, reputed to have been the most brutal and fierce of all the Germans, poured into Italy. The emperor in the East held on to southern Italy, as well as Ravenna and Venice, and the pope became virtual ruler of Rome. Not until the late nineteenth century would Italy again be united under one government.

The Roman Contribution

Unlike the Greeks, the Romans were not greatly interested in abstract thought. They constructed no original system of philosophy, invented no major new literary forms, and made no outstanding scientific

By about 481 C.E. the Germanic invasions had virtually eliminated the unity of the West Roman Empire, but the fate of the East was quite different.

discoveries. They excelled in the art of government. The Romans created a workable world-state and developed a skill in administration, law, and practical affairs. The Pax Romana was fashioned and maintained by a people who were, on the whole, conscious of their responsibilities to others.

The Roman Spirit

The Roman spirit was composed of many factors. Never completely forgotten was the tradition of plain living that stemmed from Rome's early history as a nation of farmers. Geography was another factor; for centuries the Romans faced the need to conquer or be conquered, and they had to stress discipline and duty to the state. But the Roman spirit also had another side. It could be arrogant and cruel, and its sense of justice was often untempered with mercy. In 84 C.E., a Scottish chieftain is reported to have said of his Roman conquerors, "To robbery, slaughter, plunder, they give the lying name of empire; they create a desert and call it peace."[19]

Rome's answer to such criticism was delivered a few years earlier by a Roman general to some tribes in Gaul that had revolted after the infamous emperor Nero had arrested some of their leaders:

Gaul always had its petty kingdoms and internecine wars, until you submitted to our authority. We, though so often provoked, have used the right of conquest to burden you only with the cost of maintaining peace. . . . You often command our legions. You rule these and other provinces. There is no privilege, no exclusion. . . . Endure the passions and rapacity of your masters, just as you bear barren seasons . . . and other natural evils. There will be vices as long as there are men. But they are not perpetual. . . .

Should the Roman be driven out . . . what can result but wars between all these nations? . . . Let the lessons of fortune . . . teach you not to prefer rebellion and ruin to submission and safety.[20]

Evolution of Roman Law

Of the contributions made by the Romans in government, Roman law is one of the most significant. Two great legal systems, Roman law and English common law, still remain the foundation of legal systems in most modern Western nations. Roman law is the basis for the law codes of Italy, France, Scotland, the Latin American countries, and Louisiana. Where English common law is used, as in the United States (except in Louisiana), there is also a basic heritage of great legal principles developed by ancient Roman jurists.

Roman law evolved slowly over a period of about a thousand years. At first, as in all early societies, the law was unwritten custom, handed down from a remote past, and harsh in its judgments. As noted earlier, in the fifth century B.C.E. this law was put in writing in the Law of the Twelve Tables, as the result of plebeian demand. During the remainder of the Republic the body of Roman law (*jus civile*, "law of the citizen") was enlarged by legislation passed by the Senate and the assembly and by judicial interpretation of existing law to meet new conditions. By the second century C.E. the emperor had become the sole source of law, a responsibility he entrusted to scholars "skilled in the law" (*jurisprudentes*). These scholars stuck fast to the principle of equity ("Follow the beneficial interpretation"; "Letter of law is height of injustice") and to Stoic philosophy with its concept of a "law of nature" (*jus naturale*) common to all people and assessable by human reason. As a result, the power of the father over the family was weakened, women gained control over their property, and the principle that an accused person was innocent until proven guilty was established. Finally, in the sixth century C.E. the enormous bulk of Roman law from all sources was codified and so preserved for the future.

Roman Engineering and Architecture

The empire's needs required a communication system of paved roads and bridges as well as huge public buildings and aqueducts. As road builders, the Romans surpassed all previous peoples. Constructed of layers of stone and gravel according to sound engineering principles, their roads were planned for the use of armies and messengers and were kept in constant repair. The earliest and best-known main Roman highway was the Appian Way. Running from Rome to the Bay of Naples, it was built about 300 B.C.E. to facilitate Rome's expansion southward. It has been said that the speed of travel possible on Roman highways was not surpassed until the early nineteenth century.

In designing their bridges and aqueducts, the Romans placed a series of stone arches next to one another to provide mutual support. At times several tiers of arches were used, one above the other. Fourteen aqueducts, stretching a total of 265 miles, supplied some 50 gallons of water daily for each inhabitant of Rome. They were proudly described by Rome's superintendent of aqueducts as "a signal testimony to the greatness of the Roman Empire," to be contrasted with "the idle pyramids or all the useless, though famous, works of the Greeks."[21]

At first the Romans copied Etruscan architectural models, but later they combined basic Greek elements with distinctly Roman innovations. By using concrete—a Roman invention—faced with brick or stone, they developed new methods for enclosing space. The Greeks' static post-and-lintel system was replaced by the more dynamic techniques of vaulting derived from the arch, borrowed from the Etruscans.

This splendid aqueduct, built under Augustus, spans the Gard River near Nîmes, in southern France. Its three massive tiers of arches are both majestic and beautiful. The topmost level served as a road.

Perhaps the most famous Roman building is the Colosseum, a huge amphitheater about $\frac{1}{4}$ mile around on the outside and with a seating capacity of about 45,000. On the exterior, its arches are decorated with Doric, Ionic, and Corinthian columns.

Sculpture and Painting

After the conquest of Greece, many Romans acquired a passion for Greek art. The homes of the wealthy were filled with statues, either brought to Rome as plunder or copied in Greece and shipped to Rome in great number.

Although strongly influenced by Etruscan and Greek models, the Romans developed a distinctive sculpture of their own, particularly portrait sculpture, which was remarkably realistic. Their skill in portraiture probably originated in the early practice of making and preserving wax images of the heads of important deceased family members. During the Principate, portraiture and relief sculpture tended to idealize the likenesses of the emperors. The Romans developed a great fund of decorative motifs, such as

Heavy concrete barrel vaults, cross (or groin) vaults, and domes—all so solid that they exerted no sidewise thrust—made possible the vast interiors that distinguish Roman architecture. The barrel vault was essentially a series of connected arches resembling a tunnel, and the cross vault consisted of two barrel vaults intersecting at right angles. The largest Roman domed structure is the Pantheon, the oldest important roofed building in the world that is still intact. As its name indicates, it was dedicated to "all the gods" by the emperor Hadrian as a symbol of the union of Greeks and Romans on equal terms. The massive dome rests on thick round walls of poured concrete with no window openings to weaken them. The only light enters through a great hole, 30 feet wide, at the top of the dome. The size of the dome remained unsurpassed until the twentieth century.

The typical Roman basilica, which served as a social and commercial center and as a law court, was not domed or vaulted. It was a rectangular structure with a light wooden ceiling held up by rows of columns that divided the interior into a central nave and side aisles. The roof over the nave was raised to admit light, creating a clerestory like that found in the temple at Karnak, in Egypt. The Roman basilica would eventually evolve into the Christian church.

Roman buildings were built to last, and their size, grandeur, and decorative richness aptly symbolized the proud imperial spirit of Rome. Whereas the Greeks evolved the temple, theater, and stadium, the Romans contributed the triumphal arch, bath, basilica, amphitheater, and multistoried apartment house.

Marble representation of a dying Gallic woman and her husband committing suicide rather than be taken prisoner by the Romans. The Romans regarded the Gauls as courageous but unsophisticated in politics and culture.

cupids, garlands of flowers, and scrolls of various patterns, which are still used today.

What little Roman painting has been preserved clearly reflects the influence of Hellenistic Greek models. The Romans were particularly skilled in producing floor mosaics—often copies of Hellenistic paintings—and in painting frescoes. The frescoes still to be seen in Pompeii and elsewhere show that the artists drew objects in clear though idealized perspective.

Literary Rome

In literature as in art, the Romans turned to the Greeks for their models. Roman epic, dramatic, and lyric poetry forms were usually written in conscious imitation of the Greek masterpieces. Although Latin literature is for the most part inferior to its Greek models, it remains one of the world's great literatures largely because of its influence on medieval, Renaissance, and modern culture.

Formal Latin literature did not begin until the mid-third century B.C.E. when a Greek slave named Livius Andronicus translated Homer's *Odyssey* and several Greek plays into Latin. By the end of the same century the first of a series of Latin epics dealing with Rome's past was composed. Only a few fragments have survived.

The oldest examples of Latin literature to survive intact are the 21 comedies of Plautus (c. 254–184 B.C.E.), which were adapted from Hellenistic Greek originals but with many Roman allusions, colloquialisms, and customs added. Plautus's comedies are bawdy and vigorously humorous, and their rollicking plots of illicit love and sarcastic characters such as a nagging wife ("Look at you! Gadding about, reeking of scent; you ought to know better, at your time of life"), timid husband ("But dear, I was only helping a friend buy a bottle of perfume"), lovelorn youth, clever slave, and swashbuckling soldier reveal the level of culture and taste in early Rome. The works of Plautus suggest many of the types that modern comedy has assumed, including farce, burlesque, and comedy of manners.

The Golden and Silver Ages of Latin Literature

Latin literature came of age in the first century B.C.E., when an outpouring of intellectual effort coincided with the last years of the Republic. This period marks the first half of the Golden Age of Latin literature, known as the Ciceronian period because of the stature of Marcus Tullius Cicero (106–43 B.C.E.), the greatest master of Latin prose and an outstanding intellectual force in Roman history.

Acclaimed as the greatest orator of his day, Cicero found time during his busy public life to write

The Golden and Silver Ages of Latin Literature, c. 100 B.C.E.–138 C.E.

106–43 B.C.E.	Cicero: Orations and letters
c. 87–54 B.C.E.	Catullus: Poems and epigrams
c. 99–55 B.C.E.	Lucretius: Philosophical poem *On the Nature of Things*
70–19 B.C.E.	Virgil: Epic poem *Aeneid*
65–8 B.C.E.	Horace: Poems
43 B.C.E.–17 C.E.	Ovid: *The Art of Love; Metamorphoses*
59 B.C.E.–17 C.E.	Livy: *History of Rome*
c. 55 B.C.E.–117 C.E.	Tacitus: *Annals, Histories, Agricula*
c. 50 B.C.E.–127 C.E.	Juvenal: *Satires*
c. 46–c. 126 C.E.	Plutarch: *Parallel Lives*

extensively on philosophy, political theory, and rhetoric. Some 900 of his letters survive. Together with 58 speeches, they give us insight into Cicero's personality as well as life in the late Republic. Cicero also made a rich contribution by passing on to the Romans and to later ages much of Greek thought—especially that of Plato and the Stoics—and at the same time interpreting philosophical concepts from the standpoint of a Roman intellectual and practical man of affairs. He did more than any other Roman to make Latin a great literary language.

Two notable poets of the Ciceronian period were Catullus and Lucretius. Catullus (c. 87–54 B.C.E.) was a socially active young man who wrote highly personal lyric poetry. His best-known poems are addressed to "Lesbia," an unprincipled noblewoman ten years his senior with whom he carried on a tempestuous affair: "I hate and love—the why I cannot tell, / But by my tortures know the fact too well."[22]

Catullus's contemporary Lucretius (c. 99–55 B.C.E.) found in the philosophy of Epicurus an antidote to his profound disillusionment with his fellow citizens who, he wrote, "in their greed of gain . . . amass a fortune out of civil bloodshed: piling wealth on wealth, they heap carnage on carnage. With heartless glee they welcome a brother's tragic death."[23]

Augustus provided the Roman world with a stability and confidence that encouraged a further outpouring of literary creativity. The second phase of the Golden Age of Latin literature, the Augustan Age, was notable particularly for its excellent poetry. Virgil (70–19 B.C.E.) is considered the greatest of all Roman poets. His masterpiece, a great national epic called the *Aeneid*, glorifies the work of Augustus and eloquently asserts Rome's destiny to conquer and rule the world. Using Homer's *Odyssey* as his model, Virgil recounted the fortunes of Aeneas, the legendary founder of the Latin people, who came from burning Troy to Italy. Throughout the *Aeneid* runs Virgil's deep and enthusiastic patriotism—but at a price: unlike Homer's resourceful and spirited Odysseus, Virgil's Aeneas is decidedly wooden, a piece of imperial symbolism about as animated as a triumphal arch. He abruptly leaves Carthage where the queen, Dido, has fallen passionately in love with him (Virgil is adept at describing the emotions of romantic love, a value unknown in Homer); he must stop "idling and fiddling" around in Africa and hurry on to fulfill his "high destiny" in Italy. As he puts out to sea he tells the weeping Dido, "God's will, not mine, says 'Italy.'"[24] (One can understand why some Romans would claim that Carthaginian outrage over Aeneas's treatment of Dido led to the Punic Wars.)

As the most noted poet after the death of Virgil, Horace (65–8 B.C.E.) often sincerely praised the emperor's achievements:

> *Now Parthia fears the fist of Rome, the fasces*
> *Potent on land and sea; now the once haughty*
> *Ambassadors from the Caspian and the Indus*
> *Sue for a soft reply.*
> *Now Faith and Peace and Honor and old-fashioned*
> *Conscience and unremembered Virtue venture*
> *To walk again, and with them blessed Plenty,*
> *Pouring her brimming horn.*[25]

Most of Horace's poetry, however, is concerned with everyday human interests and moods, and succeeding generations up to the present have been attracted by his serene outlook on life:

> *Happy the man, and happy he alone,*
> *He, who can call today his own:*
> *He who secure within, can say,*
> *Tomorrow do thy worst, for I have lived today.*[26]

Quite a different sort of poet was Ovid (43 B.C.E.–17 C.E.). His preference for themes of sensual love in his *Art of Love* and other poems ("There she stood, faultless beauty in front of me, naked") caused Augustus to exile him to the shores of the Black Sea, Rome's equivalent to Communist Russia's Siberia. But Ovid was also a first-rate storyteller, and it is largely through his *Metamorphoses*, a witty verse collection of Greek stories about the life of the gods—not neglecting their love lives—that classical mythology was transmitted to the modern world.

The literature of the Silver Age, the period between the deaths of Augustus and Hadrian (14–138 C.E.), substituted a more critical and negative spirit for the patriotism and optimism of the Augustan Age. Despite a great emphasis on artificial stylistic devices, the Silver Age was memorable for its moral emphasis, seen in Tacitus, Plutarch, Seneca, and especially Juvenal (c. 50 B.C.E.–127 C.E.), who has been called the greatest satiric poet who ever lived. With moral indignation and bitter irony he attacked the shortcomings of Roman society: the common people of the city, no longer having votes to sell, are interested only in free "bread and circuses"; a good woman is a "rare bird," as "uncommon as a black swan," but "worse still is the well-read menace" who "with antiquarian zeal quotes poets I've never heard of."[27]

The Writing of History

Two Roman historians produced notable works during the Golden and Silver Ages. The first, Livy (59 B.C.E.–17 C.E.), was a contemporary of Virgil. His immense *History of Rome*, like the latter's *Aeneid*, is of epic proportions and glorifies Rome's conquests and ancestral ways. By assembling the legends and traditions of early Roman history and folding them into a continuous narrative, Livy, like Virgil, intended to advance Augustus's program of moral and social regeneration. He praised the virtues of the ancient Romans and sought to draw moral lessons from an idealized past:

> *What chiefly makes the study of history wholesome and profitable is this, that you behold the lessons of every kind of experience set forth as on a conspicuous monument; from these you may choose for yourself and for your own state what to imitate, from these mark for avoidance what is shameful in the conception and shameful in the result.*[28]

Tacitus (55–117 C.E.), like his contemporary Juvenal, was concerned with improving society. In his *Germania* he contrasted the life of the idealized, simple Germanic tribes with the corrupt and immoral existence of the Roman upper classes. In the *Annals* and *Histories* he used his vivid, epigrammatic prose to depict the shortcomings of the emperors and their courts from the death of Augustus to 96 C.E. Tacitus idealized the earlier Republic, and because he viewed the emperors as tyrants, he could not do justice to the positive contributions of imperial government.

The most famous Greek author in the empire was Plutarch (c. 46–c. 126 C.E.). He lectured on philosophy in Rome before retiring to his small hometown to pursue research on the outstanding figures in Roman and Greek history in order to discover what qualities make people great or unworthy. His *Parallel Lives*, containing 46 biographies of famous Greeks and Romans arranged in pairs for the purpose of comparison, is one of the great readable classics of world literature. Because many of the sources Plutarch used have been lost, his *Lives* is a mine of valuable information for the historian.

Lucretius: "Avoid Enticement into the Snares of Love"

Epicurean philosophers regarded love as one of many vain pursuits that lead to unhappiness. "By clinging to it," Lucretius writes, "you assure yourself of heartsickness and pain."

To avoid enticement into the snares of love is not so difficult as, once entrapped, to escape out of the toils and snap the tenacious knots of Venus. And yet, be you never so tightly entangled and embrangled, you can still free yourself from the curse unless you stand in the way of your own freedom. First, you should concentrate on all the faults of mind or body of her whom you covet and sigh for. For men often behave as though blinded by love and credit the beloved with charms to which she has no valid title. How often do we see blemished and unsightly women basking in a lover's adoration! . . . A sallow wench is acclaimed as a nut-brown maid. A sluttish slattern is admired for her "sweet disorder." Her eyes are never green, but grey as Athene's. If she is stringy and woody, she is lithe as a gazelle. A stunted runt is a sprite, a sheer delight from top to toe. A clumsy giantess is "a daughter of the gods divinely tall." She has an impediment in her speech—a charming lisp, of course. She's as mute as a stockfish—what modesty! A waspish, fiery-tempered scold—she "burns with a gem-like flame." She becomes "svelte" and "willowy" when she is almost too skinny to live; "delicate" when she is half-dead with coughing. Her breasts are swollen and protuberant: she is "Ceres suckling Bacchus." Her nose is snub—"a Faun," then, or "a child of the Satyrs." Her lips bulge: she is "all kiss." It would be a wearisome task to run through the whole catalogue. But suppose her face in fact is all that could be desired and the charm of Venus radiates from her whole body. Even so, there are still others. Even so, we lived without her before.

From Lucretius, *On the Nature of the Universe*, trans. Ronald Latham (Harmondsworth, England: Penguin, 1951), bk. 4, ll. 1146 ff.

Religion and Philosophy

The turmoil of the late Republic helped erode the traditions, values, and religion of earlier Rome. For spiritual satisfaction and salvation, many Romans turned increasingly to the mystery cults of Greece (see Chapter 3) or the Near East. Among the latter were Cybele, the Great Mother, and the Egyptian Isis, who attracted the greatest number of women followers. A faithful mother herself, she extended a mother's arms to the weary of this world:

> Behold, I am come; thy weeping and prayer hath moved me to succor thee. . . . Thou shalt live blessed in this world . . . and when after thine allotted span of life . . . thou as a dweller in the Elysian Fields shalt worship me as one that hath been favorable to thee.[29]

The more intellectually sophisticated of Romans turned to Greek philosophy, particularly Epicureanism and Stoicism, for meaning. As young men, both Virgil and Horace embraced Epicureanism, but Lucretius was the most important Roman interpreter of this philosophy. In *On the Nature of Things*, Lucretius followed Epicurus in basing his explanation of the "nature of things" on materialism and atomism. He called on people to free themselves from the fear of death—which was drawing them to the emotional mystery religions of Greece and the East—since souls, like bodies, are composed of atoms that fall apart when death comes: "What has this bugbear Death to frighten man / If souls can die, as well as bodies can?"[30] Lucretius exhorted his readers to seek pleasure in the study of philosophy and not in material gain or such sensual excitements as love.

More in line with Roman taste, especially in the days of the empire, was Stoicism. The emphasis of Roman Stoicism was on living a just life, constancy to duty, courage in adversity, and service to humanity. Stoic influence had a humanizing effect on Roman law by introducing such concepts as the law of nature and the brotherhood of all, including slaves. The law of nature, as defined by Cicero, "is not a product of human thought, nor is it any enactment of peoples, but something eternal which rules the whole universe by its wisdom in command and prohibition." It is the source of "the rational principles on which our laws must be based."[31]

One of the outstanding Roman Stoics was Seneca (4 B.C.E.–65 C.E.), Nero's tutor and a writer of moral essays and tragedies. He was regarded with high favor by the leaders of the early Christian church, for his Stoicism, like that of the ex-slave Epictetus (d. 135 C.E.) and the emperor Marcus Aurelius, had the appearance of a religious creed. He stressed an all-wise Providence, or God, and believed that each person possessed a spark of the divine:

Discovery Through Maps

The Farnese Atlas

In this Roman sculpture from the first century C.E., now in the Archaeological Museum in Naples, the Greek god Atlas is represented as supporting a heavenly globe inscribed with the symbols for the Roman constellations. Atlas was credited by both the Greeks and the Romans not only with supporting the heavens but also with working out the "science" of astrology and discovering the spherical nature of the stars. He is represented in this sculpture as supporting the vault of the sky, which surrounds the earth.

Atlas was said to be one of the Titans, a race of gods who dominated the heavens and earth and whose dominance was threatened by another race of god, the Olympians. The gigantic god reigned over a great kingdom located in the west—Atlantis, larger than Europe and Africa combined, graced with beautiful temples, palaces, homes, and gardens. Atlas ruled Atlantis with wisdom and justice; he also knew all the secrets of the seas and the heavens. But the race of Olympians grew jealous and sent a great deluge, which destroyed Atlantis. Atlas survived and joined his brothers in rebellion against the Olympians. They were defeated, and the god Zeus, leader of the Olympic gods, spared Atlas's life but condemned him to bear the burden of supporting the heavens on his shoulders for all eternity. The Romans, firm believers in the influence of the heavens on human activities, made Atlas a popular subject of painting and sculpture.

God is near you, he is with you, he is within you. This is what I mean, Lucilius: a holy spirit dwells within us, one who marks our good and bad deeds, and is our guardian. . . . No man can be good without the help of God.[32]

Christians assumed that Seneca must have been influenced by St. Paul during the latter's stay in Rome. By 400 C.E. a fictitious collection of letters between the two was being circulated.

Science in the Roman Empire

The Romans had little scientific curiosity, but by putting the findings of Hellenistic science to practical use, they became masters in engineering, applied medicine, and public health.

The Romans pioneered in public health service and developed the extensive practice of *hydrotherapy,* the use of mineral baths for healing. Beginning in the early empire, doctors were employed in infirmaries where soldiers, officials, and the poor could obtain free medical care. Great aqueducts and admirable drainage systems also indicate Roman concern for public health.

Characteristic of their utilitarian approach to science was their interest in amassing large encyclopedias. The most important of these was the *Natural History,* compiled by Pliny the Elder (23–79 C.E), an enthusiastic collector of all kinds of scientific odds and ends. In writing his massive work, Pliny is reputed to have read more than 2000 books. The result is an intriguing mixture of fact and fable thrown together with scarcely any method of classification. Nevertheless, it was the most widely read work on science during the empire and the early Middle Ages.

Pliny was well aware of the lack of creative scientific activity in his day. "In these glad times of peace," he wrote, "no addition whatever is being made to knowledge by means of original research, and in fact even the discoveries of our predecessors are not being thoroughly studied." To Pliny, the cause of this state of affairs was "blind engrossment with avarice," and he cited this example: "Now that every sea has been opened up . . . , an immense multitude goes on voyages—but their object is profit not knowledge."[33] Pliny himself was suffocated by a rain of hot ashes while observing the eruption of Mount Vesuvius near Pompeii, an awesome event that killed roughly 2000 people and was described by Pliny's nephew: "Many lifted up their hands to the gods, but a great number believed there were no gods, and that this night was to be the world's last, eternal one."[34]

The last great scientific minds of the ancient world were two Greeks, Claudius Ptolemy and Galen, both of whom lived in the second century C.E. Ptolemy resided at Alexandria, where he became celebrated as a geographer, astronomer, and mathematician. His maps show a comparatively accurate knowledge of a broad section of the known world, and he used an excellent projection system. But he exaggerated the size of Asia, an error that influenced Columbus to underestimate the width of the Atlantic and to set sail from Spain in search of Asia. His work on astronomy, usually called the *Almagest* ("The Great Work") from the title of the Arabic translation, presented the geocentric (earth-centered) view of the universe that prevailed until the sixteenth century. In mathematics, Ptolemy's work in improving and developing trigonometry became the basis for modern knowledge of the subject.

Galen, born in Pergamum, in Asia Minor, was a physician for a school of gladiators. His fame spread, and he was called to Rome, where he became physician to the emperor Marcus Aurelius. Galen was responsible for notable advances in physiology and anatomy; for example, he was the first to explain the mechanism of respiration. Forbidden by the Roman government to dissect human bodies, Galen experimented with animals and demonstrated that an excised heart can continue to beat outside the body and that injuries to one side of the brain produce effects in the opposite side of the body.

Galen's account of how he discovered the cause of a Roman woman's chronic insomnia shows that he was aware of the psychosomatic factor in illness: he noted that the lady's pulse "suddenly became extremely irregular" whenever the name of a famous actor was mentioned. "Now what was it that escaped the notice of previous physicians when examining the aforesaid woman?" Galen wrote. "They have no clear conception of how the body tends to be affected by mental conditions."[35] Galen's medical encyclopedia, in which he summarized the medical knowledge of antiquity, remained the standard authority until the sixteenth century.

Conclusion

The story of Rome's rise from an insignificant and unsophisticated village along the banks of the Tiber to the mighty capital of an empire that included most of western Europe, the Mediterranean area, and the Near East will always remain one of the most fascinating stories in world history. Rome's expansion was accompanied by much devastation and suffering, yet it was less disastrous than continued international anarchy would have been.

Through the Roman achievement of a single empire and a cosmopolitan culture, the Greek legacy was preserved, synthesized, and disseminated—and the Romans were able to make important advances of their own. They excelled in political theory, governmental administration, and jurisprudence. Whereas the Greeks were individualistic, the Romans put a higher value on conformity, and their essentially conservative and judicious character more than compensated for their lack of creativity.

Rome's greatest achievement was the establishment of peace and prosperity over a vast area for long periods under a stable and acceptable government. The Roman citizens who accomplished this task were characterized by Livy, Rome's great historian at the end of the Republican period, in words that anticipate what modern Americans have often said of themselves:

I hope that my passion for Rome's past has not impaired my judgment; for I do honestly believe that no country has ever been greater or purer than ours or richer in good citizens and noble deeds; none has been free for so many generations from the vices of avarice and luxury; nowhere have thrift and plain living been for so long held in such esteem.[36]

Suggestions for Reading

Kare Christ, *The Romans: An Introduction to Their History and Civilization* (University of California Press, 1984), and Michael Grant, *History of Rome* (Scribner, 1979), are highly recommended general accounts. Also excellent are Donald R. Dudley, *The Civilization of Rome* (Mentor, 1960); Reginald H. Barrow, *The Romans* (Penguin, 1975); T. J. Cornell, *The Beginnings of Rome* (Routledge, 1995); and Peter D. Arnott, *The Romans and Their World* (St. Martin's Press, 1970). Max Cary and Howard H. Scullard, *A History of Rome: Down to the Reign of Constantine*, 3rd ed. (St. Martin's Press, 1976), is an outstanding account.

Massimo Pallotino, *The Etruscans*, rev. ed. (Penguin, 1975), and Emeline Hill Richardson, *The Etruscans: Their Art and Civilization* (University of Chicago Press, 1964), are excellent works. See also Michael Grant, *The Etruscans* (Scribner, 1981); Paul MacKendrick, *The Mute Stones Speak: The Story of Archaelogy in Italy* (Norton, 1976); and Alexandre Grandazzi, *The Foundation of Rome: Myth and History* (Cornell University Press, 1997).

Recommended special studies are Serge Lancel, *Carthage: A History* (Oxford University Press, 1997); Robert Malcolm Errington, *The Dawn of Empire: Rome's Rise to World Power* (Cornell University Press, 1972); William V. Harris, *War and Imperialism in Republican Rome, 327–70 B.C.* (Oxford University Press, 1978), which argues that Rome was deliberately imperialistic; Edward Luttwak, *The Grand Strategy of the Roman Empire* (Johns Hopkins University Press, 1977), a groundbreaking work of military history; Ramsay MacMullen, *The Enemies of the Roman Order: Treason, Unrest, and Alienation in the Empire* (Routledge, 1993); David Stockton, *The Gracchi* (Oxford University Press, 1979); Matthias Gelzer, *Caesar: Politician and Statesman* (Harvard University Press, 1985); Lily R. Taylor, *Party Politics in the Age of Caesar* (University of California Press, 1961); Ronald Syme, *The Roman Revolution* (Oxford University Press, 1939); P. A. Brunt, *Social Conflicts in the Roman Republic* (Norton, 1974); Arnold Hugh Martin Jones, *Augustus* (Norton, 1972); Fergus Millar, *The Emperor in the Roman World, 31 B.C.–A.D. 337* (Cornell University Press, 1977); Averil Cameron, *The Later Roman Empire* (Harvard University Press, 1993); William K. Klingaman, *The First Century: Emperors, Gods, and Everyman* (HarperCollins, 1990); and Olga Tellegen-Couperus, *A Short History of Roman Law* (Routledge, 1993).

Michael Grant, *Cities of Vesuvius: Pompeii and Herculaneum* (Penguin, 1978), re-creates the daily life of these buried cities. See also Claude Nicolet, *The World of the Citizen in Republican Rome* (University of California Press, 1980); John E. Stambaugh, *The Ancient Roman City* (Johns Hopkins University Press, 1988); John P. V. D. Balsdon, *Life and Leisure in Ancient Rome* (McGraw-Hill, 1969), and *Roman Women: Their History and Habits* (Knopf, 1975); Mary Lefkowitz and Maureen Fant, eds., *Women's Life in Greece and Rome: A Source Book in Translation*, rev. ed. (Johns Hopkins University Press, 1992); Keith Bradley, *Slavery and Society in Rome* (Cambridge University Press, 1994) and *Discovering the Roman Family* (Oxford University Press, 1991); Henry Charles Boren, *Roman Society: A Social, Economic, and Cultural History*, 2nd ed. (Heath, 1992); Florence Dupont, *Daily Life in Ancient Rome* (Oxford University Press, 1992); Beryl Rawson, ed., *The Family in Ancient Rome: New Perspectives* (Cornell University Press, 1986); Judith Hallett, *Fathers and Daughters in Roman Society* (Princeton University Press, 1984); Harold B. Mattingly, *The Man in the Roman Street* (Norton, 1966); and Michael Grant, *The Jews in the Roman World* (Scribner, 1973). Roland Auguet, *Cruelty and Civilization: The Roman Games* (Routledge, 1994), and Carlin Barton, *The Sorrows of the Ancient Romans* (Princeton University Press, 1993), both deal with games and gladiatorial combats.

Other books of interest are Martin L. Clarke, *The Roman Mind: Studies in the History of Thought from Cicero to Marcus Aurelius* (Norton, 1968); Chester G. Starr, *Civilization and the Caesars: The Intellectual Revolution in the Roman Empire* (Cornell University Press, 1954); Max Ludwig Wolfram Laistner, *The Greater Roman Historians* (University of California Press, 1963); Stanley Frederick Bonner, *Education in Ancient Rome* (University of California Press, 1978); John G. Landels, *Engineering in the Ancient World* (University of California Press, 1978); Martin Henig, ed., *A Handbook of Roman Art* (Oxford University Press, 1983); Mortimer Wheeler, *Roman Art and Architecture* (Thames & Hudson, 1985); Herbert Jennings Rose, *Religion in Greece and Rome* (Harper Torchbooks, 1959); and Robert Turcan, *The Cults of the Roman Empire* (Oxford University Press, 1996).

Recommended historical novels are Winifred Bryher, *Coin of Carthage* (Harvest, 1965); Thornton Wilder, *The Ides of March* (Avon, 1975); John Williams, *Augustus* (Penguin, 1979); Robert Graves, *I Claudius* (Vintage, 1977); Marguerite Yourcenar, *Memoirs of Hadrian* (Modern Library, 1984); Lindsey Davis, *Time to Depart* (Warner, 1995); and a continuing series of novels dealing with the Roman Republic by Colleen McCullough, beginning with *The First Man in Rome* (Morrow, 1990).

Suggestions for Web Browsing

Museums of the Vatican: Gregorian Estruscan Museum
http://christusrex.org/www1/vaticano/ET1-Etrusco.html
http://christusrex.org/www1/vaticano/ET2-Etrusco.html

Two sites within the extensive pages of the Museums of the Vatican offer numerous images from the Etruscan period.

Timeline
http://www.exovedate.com/ancient_timeline_one.html

The history of ancient Rome, with a chronological index and links to Internet resources. Emphasis is placed on the roles of women in ancient times.

Roman Empire
http://library.advanced.org/10805/rome/html

The history of the empire is illustrated through maps and time lines. Examinations of the sources of our knowledge through Roman writers is emphasized. An extensive history of ancient Rome.

Online Encyclopedia of the Roman Empire
http://www.salve.edu/~dmaaiom/deimprom.html

A massive site emphasizing the study of Roman history through coins and through maps of the empire.

Pompeii Forum Project
http://jefferson.village.virginia.edu/pompeii/forummap.htmp

Constructed by historians and archaeologists from the University of Virginia, this site examines ancient Pompeii through a variety of photographs.

Vesuvius
http://volcano.und.nodak.edu

A beautiful exploration of Mount Vesuvius in ancient Rome and as it appears today. Speculation on the next eruption as well.

Pompeii
http://www.tulane.edu/lester/text/Western.Architect/Pompeii/Pompeii.html

One hundred images from this Tulane University site provide a virtual tour of ancient Pompeii.

Women's Life in Greece and Rome
http://www.uky/edu/ArtsSciences/Classics/wlgr/wlgr-index.html

Details about the private life and legal status of women, in addition to biographies of prominent women of ancient Rome.

Roman Art and Architecture
http://harpy.uccs.edu/roman/html/romarch.html

A collection of images of Roman architecture.

Notes

1. Livy, *History of Rome*, 1.51, trans. Aubrey de Sélincourt, in *Livy: The Early History of Rome* (Baltimore: Penguin, 1988), p. 89.
2. Plutarch, *Lives*, "Cato the Elder," 2.2, trans. Bernadotte Perrin, Loeb Classical Library, Vol. 47 (Cambridge, Mass.: Harvard University Press, 1948), p. 307.
3. Quoted in Donald R. Dudley, *The Civilization of Rome* (New York: New American Library, 1962), p. 21.
4. Polybius, *Histories* 1.10, trans. Evelyn S. Shuckburgh, in *The Histories of Polybius*, Vol. I (Bloomington: University of Indiana Press, 1962), p. 10.
5. Livy, *Roman History* 33, trans. E. T. Sage, Loeb Classical Library, Vol. 9 (Cambridge, Mass.: Harvard University Press, 1979), p. 367.
6. Livy, *Roman History* 25.3, trans. Aubrey de Sélincourt, in *Livy: The War with Hannibal* (Baltimore: Penguin, 1965), p. 296.
7. Plutarch, *Lives*, "Tiberius Gracchus" 9.5, trans. Bernadotte Perrin, Loeb Classical Library, Vol. 10 (Cambridge, Mass.: Harvard University Press, 1948), pp. 165, 167.
8. Mason Hammond, *City-State and World State in Greek and Roman Political Theory Until Augustus* (Cambridge, Mass.: Harvard University Press, 1951), p. 153.
9. Horace, *Odes* 3.6, trans. James Michie, in *The Odes of Horace* (Indianapolis: Bobbs-Merrill, 1965), p. 138.
10. Tacitus, *Annals* 15:44, trans. Michael Grant (Baltimore: Penguin, 1959), p. 354.
11. Tacitus, *History* 1.1, trans. Alfread S. Church and William S. Brodribb, *The Complete Works of Tacitus* (New York: Random House, 1992), p. 420.
12. Marcus Aurelius, *Meditations* 11.3, trans. A. S. L. Farquarson, in *The Meditations of the Emperor Marcus Antoninus* Vol. I, (Oxford: Oxford University Press, 1944), p. 217.
13. Virgil, *Aeneid* 6.847–853, in Naphtali Lewis and Meyer Reinhold, eds., *Roman Civilization: Selected Readings*, Vol. 2 (New York: Columbia University Press, 1955), p. 23.
14. Aelius Aristides, *To Rome*, Oration 26, trans. S. Levin (Glencoe, Ill.: Free Press, 1950), p. 126.
15. Ibid., p. 126.
16. The advice of Maecenas, Rome's richest capitalist, to Augustus in Dio Cassius, *Roman History* 52, 14–15, trans. Earnest Cary, Loeb Classical Library, Vol. 6 (Cambridge, Mass.: Harvard University Press, 1925), pp. 109 ff.
17. Pliny the Younger, *Letters* 10.17a, in Naphtali Lewis and Meyer Reinhold, eds., *Roman Civilization: Selected Readings*, Vol. 2 (New York: Columbia University Press, 1955), p. 342.
18. Juvenal, *Satires* 3, in R. C. Trevelyan, *Translations from Horace, Juvenal, and Montaigne* (New York: Cambridge University Press, 1941), p. 129.
19. Tacitus, *Agricola* 30.
20. Tacitus, *Histories* 4. 74.
21. Frontinus, quoted in Michael Grant, *The World of Rome* (New York: New American Library, 1960), p. 298.
22. Catullus, *Carmen* 85, trans. Theodore Martin.
23. Lucretius, *On the Nature of the Universe* 3.70, trans. Ronald Latham (Baltimore: Penguin, 1951), p. 98.
24. Virgil, *Aeneid* 4.1, trans. C. Day Lewis.
25. Horace, "The Centennial Hymn," trans. James Michie, in *The Odes of Horace* (Indianapolis: Bobbs-Merrill, 1965), p. 227.
26. Horace, *Odes* 3.29, trans. John Dryden.
27. Juvenal, *Satires* 6, trans by Peter Green, in *The Sixteen Satires* (Baltimore: Penguin, 1974), p. 146.
28. Livy, *History of Rome* 1.10, trans. B. O. Foster, Loeb Classical Library, Vol. 1, (Cambridge, Mass.: Harvard University Press, 1976), p. 7.
29. Apuleius, *The Golden Ass* 5–6, in Nels Bailkey, *Readings in Ancient History: Thought and Experience from Gilgamesh to St. Augustine*, 4th ed. (Lexington, Mass.: Heath, 1992), p. 441.
30. Lucretius, *On The Nature of the Universe* 1.95, trans. Ronald Latham (Baltimore: Penguin, 1951), p. 30.
31. Cicero, *De Legibus* 1.4. 14–6.20.
32. Seneca, *Epistles* 41, quoted in Chester G. Starr, *Civilization and the Caesars: The Intellectual Revolution in the Roman Empire* (New York: Norton, 1965), p. 228.
33. Pliny, *Natural History* 2.14.117–118, trans. H. Rackham, Loeb Classical Library, Vol. 1 (Cambridge, Mass.: Harvard University Press, 1989), pp. 259, 261.
34. Pliny the Younger, *Letters* 6.16–20.
35. Galen, "On Prognosis," in Thomas W. Africa, *Rome and the Caesars* (New York: Wiley, 1965), p. 217.
36. Livy, *Roman History* 1.1, trans. Aubrey de Sélincourt, in *Livy: The Early History of Rome* (Baltimore: Penguin, 1960), p. 34.

5

The tombs of the First Emperor, 210 B.C.E., have yielded most of the surviving art from that period in China. The more than 6000 figures, including these terra cotta warriors, were not discovered until 1974 in one of the greatest archeological discoveries in history.

Classical China

From Origins to Empire,
Prehistory to 220 C.E.

Chapter Contents

As in other parts of the world, there were tool-using humanoids some 600,000 to 800,000 years ago on the Chinese subcontinent. They lived in a vast watershed drained by three river systems that rise close together on the high Tibetan plateau and flow eastward to the Pacific. Three mountain systems also rise in the west, diminishing in altitude as they slope eastward between the river systems. The Huang Ho (Yellow River), traditionally known as "China's Sorrow" because of the misery caused by its periodic flooding, crosses the North China plain. In this area, the original homeland of Chinese culture, the climate is like that of western Europe, with an agriculture based on wheat and millet. The Yangtze River and its valley form the second river system. South of this valley lie the subtropical rice-growing, silk, and tea lands of South China, the home of ancient cultures that were destroyed or transformed by Chinese expansion from the north. Here the Hsi (West) River, converging on present-day Guangzhou (Canton), forms the third major river system.

Within the Chinese subcontinent, geographers have identified at least eight different ecosystems, ranging from the semitropical southeast, receiving more than 4 feet of rain each year, to the desertlike northwest, which gets less than 4 inches of rain annually. Separated by mountains, deserts, and seas from the rest of the world, the Chinese developed independent of the other world centers and spread a unified culture along the river valleys over a greater land area than any other civilization. The same geographical context of easily penetrated frontiers and a fragmented land gave the Chinese a legacy of political disunity.

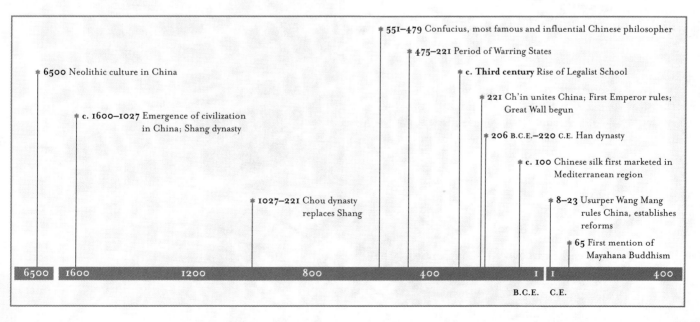

- 6500 Neolithic culture in China
- c. 1600–1027 Emergence of civilization in China; Shang dynasty
- 1027–221 Chou dynasty replaces Shang
- 551–479 Confucius, most famous and influential Chinese philosopher
- 475–221 Period of Warring States
- c. Third century Rise of Legalist School
- 221 Ch'in unites China; First Emperor rules; Great Wall begun
- 206 B.C.E.–220 C.E. Han dynasty
- c. 100 Chinese silk first marketed in Mediterranean region
- 8–23 Usurper Wang Mang rules China, establishes reforms
- 65 First mention of Mayahana Buddhism

6500   1600   1200   800   400   I   I   400
B.C.E.   C.E.

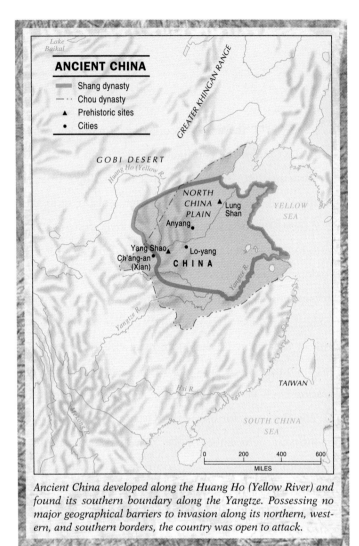

ANCIENT CHINA
- ▬ Shang dynasty
- ‐‐‐ Chou dynasty
- ▲ Prehistoric sites
- ● Cities

Ancient China developed along the Huang Ho (Yellow River) and found its southern boundary along the Yangtze. Possessing no major geographical barriers to invasion along its northern, western, and southern borders, the country was open to attack.

6500 B.C.E. In each region, climate and rainfall dictated which crops could be grown. Each crop imposed its own demands on settlement patterns and land use, especially the need to find artificial means of raising water in the south and the use of horses and other pastoral animals in the north. The evidence indicates that China's Neolithic culture, which domesticated the pig, cultivated millet, and produced silk, originated independent of that in the Near East.

The people of China's last Neolithic culture, called Lung Shan, lived in walled towns throughout North China. The walls of their towns, located along the rivers, sheltered the townfolk from aggressive bands of nomadic Chinese, living in a horse-raising economy, who remained in the foothills and plains. While the towns made institutional and technological advances, especially in the area of defense, the nomadic bands created their own effective weapons. The tension between the settled communities and the invading bands had a decisive effect on the development of Chinese civilization and politics.

The Chinese Neolithic urban centers shared the commercial and religious activities of other world Neolithic centers. But in China the consistent outside threat led to the development of a military elite to defend the population and ultimately the establishment of a system of war leaders who would become kings. The fabled Hsia dynasty actually existed and flourished for some three centuries before it was replaced by the Shang in the seventeenth century B.C.E.

Despite China's huge size—larger than the United States—the threat of invasion from the north was always present. Invaders brought challenges that altered the development of China's civilization and introduced important political concepts. But throughout this vast land, the Chinese pursued a life of settled agriculture, following a system that began in the seventh millennium B.C.E.

New discoveries reveal a unified civilization in the river valleys as early as the beginning of the third millennium B.C.E. Archaeologists have also found evidence of common political life and writing earlier than 1750 B.C.E., which have proved that dynasties once thought legendary actually did exist.

Neolithic China

A series of recently discovered sites confirms the presence of Neolithic settlements in China around

Neolithic bowls, c. 8000–2000 B.C.E. These Neolithic bowls testify to the advanced craftmanship of "preliterate" times.

The Creation of China, to the Fifth Century B.C.E.

Shang was originally the name of a dominant tribe whose leaders replaced the Hsia as the overlords of the tribal leaders in North China. From the archaeological evidence of their capitals it is evident that the kings, victorious war leaders, had enormous power. They could demand the work of a large number of laborers and craftsmen to build their palaces and tombs. The most important testimony to Shang rule were the walled, protected cities to which the less powerful tribal leaders had to come to pay tribute. As their political and military fortunes varied, the rulers moved their capitals frequently during the six centuries of Shang rule (c. 1600–1027 B.C.E.). The last capital was at modern Anyang.

China's Bronze Age began about 2000 B.C.E., and during the Shang dynasty the Chinese developed a sophisticated bronze metallurgy. They used bronze to make elaborate ceremonial and drinking vessels (the Shang leaders were notorious for their drinking bouts) and weapons. Not only were the bronze productions practical, but they were also works of art with both incised and high-relief designs.

The Shang people used a system of writing so advanced that it probably originated before their rule, under the Hsia, although no earlier documents have yet been found. It was based on 3000 pictographic characters, some of which are still in use today. These characters stand for individual words rather than sounds and consist of recognizable representations of everyday objects and ideographs expressing ideas such as walking. The Chinese were the only people in East Asia to devise their own, original written language; the Chinese pictographs and ideographs served as the foundation for the written languages of other people in East Asia, including the Koreans and the Japanese.

Most Shang writing is found on thousands of "oracle bones," fragments of animal bones and tortoise shells. Usually, these contained written questions for the ancestral spirits, who were believed to be closely tied to their living descendants as members of the family group. The living would ask the dead such questions as "Will the king's child be a son?" and "If we raise an army of 3000 men to drive *X* away from *Y*, will we succeed?" The shell or bone would then be heated in a fire, and the resulting cracks would be interpreted as an answer to the question.

Later, as the state and its activities grew more complex, the kings had to oversee not only fighting but also taxing and governing. The leaders needed to record their decisions and to transmit them to their often distant subjects. These tasks were done by scribes, who became increasingly useful to the kings. Later the

Preimperial History

before 1600 B.C.E.	Hsia (Xia)
c. 1600–1027 B.C.E.	Shang
1027–770 B.C.E.	Western Chou (Zhou) (traditional)
770–221 B.C.E.	Eastern Chou (Zhou)
770–476 B.C.E.	Spring and Autumn period
475–221 B.C.E.	Warring States period

scribes would grow in power to become trusted officials who would defend the monarch's power when the kings were off fighting the almost continual wars.

Religion played the key connective role in the maintenance of social order. The hereditary kings that ruled Shang China acted as the sole link between the people and the chief forces in the spirit world. The kings had limited earthly political power because they were compelled by tradition to rule with the consent of the "Council of Great and Small." But only the king could worship and make humble petitions for favors to the chief deity in heaven (the *T'ien*), considered the ancestor of the king's own clan. The oracle bones reveal that the kings often appealed to the ancestral spirits in order to overcome the opposition of the

This bronze mask was discovered at Anyang, in eastern China, in the tomb of a ruler of the Shang dynasty, one of the earliest periods of Chinese history for which we have archaeological evidence.

Council. Unlike the common people, the kings and nobles had recorded ancestors and belonged to a clan. They were the descendants in the male line from a common ancestor whom they worshipped. To win the aid or avoid the displeasure of the spirits, both animals and humans (prisoners of war) were sacrificed, and a beerlike liquor was poured on the ground.

The lesser levels of society each had their local gods, to whom requests to guarantee good harvests and long life were addressed. The peasants belonged to no clans, and there is no evidence that they worshipped their ancestors. Instead, their gods were the fundamental forces of nature, such as rivers, mountains, earth, wind, rain, and the stars and planets.

During the Shang period a special group of Chinese became skilled in the use of magic, with which they attempted to manipulate the two conflicting forces of the world. They called these two opposed but complementary forces *yang* and *yin*. *Yang* was associated with the sun and all things male, strong, warm, and active. *Yin* was associated with the moon and all things female, dark, cold, weak, and passive. In later ages Chinese philosophers—all male—would employ these concepts to require the obedience and passivity that was expected of women.

The power of the kings and nobles rested on their ownership of the land, their monopoly of bronze metallurgy, their chariots, and the kings' religious functions. We can see proof of the power of the Shang kings and their nobles in their imposing buildings, military superiority, and tombs. They often entered into battle across North China and for centuries gained victory by using chariots, a potent technological advantage. After death, they were buried in sumptuous tombs along with their chariots and still-living servants and war captives.

Peasants might be legally free but had little mobility. They rarely owned land and worked plots periodically assigned to them by royal and noble landowners. They collectively cultivated the fields retained by their lords. Farming methods were primitive, not having advanced beyond the Neolithic level. Bronze was used for weapons, not tools or implements, and the peasants continued to reap wheat and millet with stone sickles and till their allotted fields with wooden plows.

The Chou Dynasty: The "Feudal" Age

Shortly after 1030 B.C.E. the Chou (Zhou) tribe came out of the west and overthrew the Shang dynasty, who, the Chou charged, had failed to rule fairly and benevolently. The Chou leader announced that the god of heaven *(T'ien)* had given him a mandate to replace the Shang. This was more than a convenient justification of the seizure of power. It introduced a new aspect of Chinese thought: that the cosmos is ruled by an impersonal and all-powerful Heaven, which sits in judgment over the human ruler, who continues to be the link between Heaven's commands and human fate.

The Chou was a powerful western frontier tribe that took advantage of the opportunities of the wealth and increasing weakness of Shang rule, much as the Macedonians would be drawn into Greece 500 years later. Given their military strength, the other Chinese tribes wisely switched their loyalty to the Chou, who went on to establish a dynasty that lasted for almost 900 years (c. 1027–221 B.C.E.), the longest in Chinese history.

Spread out over most of North China and the Yangtze valley, the very size of the Chou domain made it impossible to be ruled directly from the center. The Chou kings set up what Europeans two millennia later would call a feudal system of government (see Chapter 9). In this system the kings gave local authority and land to relatives and powerful nobles. These 50 or so people entered into a type of contract with the king in which they would hold their land and authority dependent on the king's will: in return they were to fight for him. Sometimes these subordinates (later called *vassals*) received hereditary power and property; others might have to have the contract renewed with each new generation or monarch. Under this system, peasants and women had little or no standing.

The early Chou kings were strong leaders who kept the allegiance of their vassals while fighting off attacks on the frontiers. However, after two centuries, complacency set in, and a succession of weak kings led to a reduction in the central throne's power: taking advantage of advances in military technology, the vassals became more independent.

By the eighth century B.C.E. the vassals no longer went to the Chou capital for investiture by the Son of Heaven, the title the Chou king had adopted. As the Chou monarchs became weaker, court officials increased their influence. Under the feudal politics of the Chou, bureaucratic documentation became ever more complex, as the center had to define its relations with the more than 50 major dependencies and continually changing foreign contacts. The kings' scribes, clerks, and officials wrote the documents that defined hierarchy and order and mastered the political precedents that the military men needed to exercise legitimate authority. As the state became more complex, the qualifications for state servants became more specific. Now the officials of the state, along with the nobles, could gain rank, land, wealth, and an assured future for their family.

The remnants of Chou royal power disappeared completely in 771 B.C.E. when an alliance of disloyal vassals and barbarians destroyed the capital and killed the king. Part of the royal family managed to escape eastward to Lo-yang, however, where the dynasty survived for another five centuries (until around 250 B.C.E.) doing little more than performing state religious rituals as the Sons of Heaven. Seven of the stronger feudal princes gradually conquered their weaker neighbors. In the process they assumed the title *wang* ("king"), formerly used only by the Chou ruler, and began to end the feudal rights of their own vassals and establish centralized bureaucracies.

Warfare among these emerging centralized states was incessant, particularly during the two and one-half centuries known as the period of Warring States (475–221 B.C.E.). By 221 B.C.E. the ruler of the Ch'in, the most advanced of the seven Warring States, had conquered all of his rivals and established a unified empire of which he was the absolute ruler.

The art of horseback riding, common among the nomads of central Asia, greatly influenced later Chou China. In response to the threat of mounted nomads, rulers of the Warring States period began constructing increasingly complex defensive walls. Inside China itself, the swifter and more mobile cavalry replaced the chariots, and the infantry adapted to new conditions by wearing tunics and trousers adopted from the nomads.

Chou Economy and Society

Despite its political instability, the Chou period is unrivaled by any later period in Chinese history for its material and cultural progress. These developments led the Chinese to emphasize the vast difference between their own high civilization and the nomadic ways of the "barbarians" beyond their frontiers. This distinction was proudly kept until the twentieth century, as the Chinese belief in their cultural superiority came to be viewed by non-Chinese as insufferably arrogant.

During the sixth century B.C.E. the Chinese mastered the use of iron and mass-produced cast iron objects from molds, which were in wide use by the end of the third century B.C.E. (The first successful European attempts at casting iron were not made until the end of the Middle Ages.) The ox-drawn iron-tipped plow, together with the use of manure and the growth of large-scale irrigation and water-control projects, led to a more dependable and productive food supply and greater population growth.

The Chou understood the necessity to build canals to improve their realm's economy and communication. The canals made it possible to move food and useful items dependably over long distances. Commerce and wealth grew rapidly. At the beginning of the Chou dynasty, brightly colored shells, bolts of silk, and ingots of precious metals were used as forms of exchange; by the end of the dynasty, small round copper coins with square holes had taken their place.

Under the Chou dynasty, merchant and artisan classes played an economically prominent, if not socially recognized, role as wealth spread beyond the nobles and court servants. Indicative of the rise in the general economic level, chopsticks and finely lacquered objects, today universally considered as sym-

Bronze vessels, such as this one from the early tenth century B.C.E., were designed to contain water, wine, meat, or grain used during the sacrificial rites in which the Shang and Chou prayed to the spirits of their ancestors. Animals were a common motif of ritual bronzes.

bols of Chinese and East Asian culture, were in general use by the end of the period.

Social divisions and consciousness became highly developed under Chou political feudalism and remained until modern times. During the first half of the Chou era, the king and the aristocracy became increasingly separated from the mass of the people on the basis of land ownership and family descent. The social hierarchy came to be more precisely defined, for centuries locking people into their particular social stratum with little or no hope of "moving up."

The core units of aristocratic society were the elementary family, the extended family, and the clan, held together by patriarchal authority and ancestor worship. Marriages were formally arranged unions between families. The customs of the nobles can be compared in only the most general way to those of Europe's feudal nobility, especially when the Chou system began to fall apart (see Chapter 9).

Social changes came with the weakening of the Chou in the fifth century B.C.E. and the division of the land between the remnants of the Chou and a number of independent principalities. With the weakening of the political center, the rigid social hierarchy changed. Money played a more important role, and land came more and more to be transferred by either sale or purchase and less and less by hereditary transfer from generation to generation of the nobility. Once land, the prime measure of wealth and status, could be bought and sold, the rich of whatever rank could become part of the economic, if not social, elites. It can be argued that these changes did not constitute true social mobility, but it did signal the end of the political feudalism of the early Chou and the social system that accompanied it.

This economic and political transformation threatened the traditional, idealized hierarchy. Teachers and philosophers, longing for the "good old days" of social stability, played an important role in defining and teaching the values that would dominate Chinese society into the twentieth century. They found a willing audience among the people who had the most to gain from order and hierarchy, the clerks and officials who increased their influence, wealth, and legal privileges during the Chou dynasty.

One of the social values that emerged during this time was that society was held together by a complex code of what Europeans would later call chivalry, *li*, practiced in both war and peace. It symbolized the traits of the most noble warrior, and men in the elite classes devoted years to its mastery. As Chou China disintegrated, the early kings came to be seen as the most ideal and most representative part of the system. At a time when disorder and social upheaval dominated the land, this nostalgia for the imagined past led to the conceptualizing of an entire hierarchical social order developed around an idealized monarch, with each inferior in the descending scale owing respect and obedience to his superior. Referred to in Chinese chronicles as the *Spring and Autumn Annals*, this schema is the justification for order and discipline. As we will see, Confucius and his disciples codified the rules of how a just society should function during a time of strife.

The peasant masses stood outside of this feudal hierarchy. They were economically subjected to control by "an interlocking oligarchy of government officials, landed gentry, and rural moneylenders," although they remained "legally free to buy and sell land or change their occupation." Unfortunately, they were "bound to the land they cultivated by a number of economic factors."[1] They were in effect tied to their villages—the great majority of the population worked as tenants of noble landholders or moneylenders, paying one-tenth of their crop as rent. Despite the increased agricultural production resulting from large-scale irrigation and the ox-drawn iron-tipped plow, the peasants had difficulty eking out an existence. Some were forced into debt slavery. A major problem in the Chinese economy, evident by late Chou times, was that the majority of farmers worked fields so small that they could not produce a crop surplus to tide them over periods of scarcity. Their poverty drove them even further down in the Chinese social structure.

The Philosophical Schools

The continual battles among the feudal lords during the period of Warring States (475–221 B.C.E.) destroyed the relative stability of the Shang and early Chou dynasties. The values and habits based on the traditions of an orderly society disappeared from Chinese life. In the next three centuries, some great teachers and philosophers thought deeply about the nature of humanity and the problems of society. They created a range of philosophies on "how man should live" that went from the extremes of living for society to living for one's own soul. These teachers and philosophers have shaped Chinese society ever since.

Confucianism: Rationalized Hierarchy

The first, most famous, and certainly most influential Chinese philosopher and teacher was K'ung-fu-tzu ("Master K'ung, the Sage," 551–479 B.C.E.), known in the West as Confucius after Jesuit missionaries to China in the seventeenth century latinized his name. He was just one in a line of teachers who tried to explain the universe and his people's role in it. Unlike some thinkers in the West, the Chinese teachers and thinkers did not spend as much time on abstract concepts—there are no Chinese equivalents of Plato or Aristotle. Only a few teachers "felt called to identify a system that lay behind the operation of the universe; others were moved to formulate a means of sustaining the corporate life of a community, . . . even supporting the rule of a government." Their thoughts "concerned the behavior of man to man and the organization of his government, rather than the framework within which concepts should be defined."[2]

Confucius's disciples believed that their master composed or edited the Five Confucian Classics—two books of history and one book each on poetry, divination (predicting the future through supernatural means), and ceremonies—which were in large part a product of the early Chou period. But the only work that can be accurately attributed to Confucius is the *Analects* ("Selected Sayings"), a collection of his responses to his disciples' questions.

Confucius, who belonged to the lower aristocracy of a minor state, Lu, was more or less a contemporary of the Buddha in India, Zoroaster in Persia, and the early philosophers of Greece. Like the Buddha and Zoroaster, Confucius lived in a troubled time—an age of political and social turmoil—and his prime concern, like theirs, was the improvement of society and the maintenance of order. To achieve this goal, Confucius did not look to the gods and spirits for assistance; he accepted the existence of Heaven *(T'ien)* and spirits, but he insisted it was more important "to know the essential duties of man living in a society of men." "We don't know yet how to serve men," he said; "how can we know about serving the spirits?" And, "we don't yet know about life, so how can we know about death?" He advised a ruler to "respect the ghosts and spirits but keep them at a distance" and "devote yourself to the proper demands of the people." Confucius and his disciples tried to freeze a social hierarchy into an ethical

Through the ages, Confucius became idealized as the genial authority to whom one could look for instruction on "how man should live."

framework, to stabilize society into a complex network of respect bestowed and respect expected, whether between father and son or between ruler and noble.

This goal was more than an academic exercise. It was a response to a time in which violence between communities and a breakdown of tradition within communities threatened the Chinese civilization. Teachers and philosophers sought to explain to their students and followers a way to understand that the disorder in which they lived was part of a larger, eternal scheme, that there was an "operation of the world," "an integrated system" that "brought about the movement seen in the heavens and on earth." Further,

> *Kings and emperors who wished to establish a permanent regime that their sons and grandsons would inherit relied on intellectual support to demonstrate that their call for obedience and exercise of temporal power were legitimate. Theories of empire and statecraft . . . provide for an acceptable explanation of how a monarch had received his charge to rule.[3]*

Thus during this period of the Warring States,

> *it was becoming desirable, or even necessary, to place the requirements of an ordered, civilized society within*

the framework of the single organic universe and to prescribe ideal forms of conduct that would distinguish Chinese from those less fortunate mortals who lived beyond the pale.[4]

Confucius filled the need for the definition of this "single organic universe." He believed that the improvement of society was the responsibility of the ruler and that the quality of government depended on the ruler's moral character: "The way *(Tao)* of learning to be great consists in shining with the illustrious power of moral personality, in making a new people, in abiding in the highest goodness." Confucius's definition of the Tao as "moral personality" and the "highest goodness" was in decided contrast to the old premoral Tao, in which gods and spirits, propitiated by offerings and ritual, regulated human life for good or ill. Above all, Confucius's "new way" meant a concern for the rights of others, the adherence to a type of Golden Rule: when a disciple asked, "Is there any saying that one can act on all day, every day?" Confucius replied, "Perhaps the saying about consideration: 'Never do to others what you would not like them to do to you.'"

Although Confucius called himself "a transmitter and not a creator," his redefinition of Tao and his teachings produced an ethical program for this world, by this world. He was, in effect, putting new wine into old bottles. He did the same thing with two other key terms, *li* and *chün-tzu*. *Li*, meaning "honorable behavior," was the chivalric code of the constantly fighting *chün-tzu*, the hereditary feudal "noblemen" of the Chou period. As refined and reinterpreted by Confucius, *li* came to embody such ethical virtues as righteousness and love for one's fellow humans. The *chün-tzu*, under the influence of the new definition of *li*, became "noble men," or "gentlemen," whose social origins were not important. As Confucius said, "The noble man understands what is right; the inferior man understands what is profitable." Confucius's teachings have had a greater and longer-lasting influence on China, and much of East Asia, than those of any other philosopher.

Taoism: Intuitive Mysticism

A second philosophical reaction to the troubled times of the late Chou period was the teaching of Lao-tzu ("Old Master"), a semilegendary figure who was believed to have been a contemporary of Confucius. As with Confucius, the key term in Lao-tzu's teaching is *Tao*, from which his philosophy takes its name. But whereas Confucius defined Tao as a rational standard of ethics in human affairs, Lao-tzu gave it a metaphysical, transcendental meaning: the course of nature, the natural and inevitable, all-regulating order of the universe.

The goal of Taoism, like that of Confucianism, is a happy life. Lao-tzu believed that this goal could be achieved by living a life in conformity with nature, retiring from the chaos and evils of contemporary Warring States society and shunning human institutions and

Mencius on Human Nature

Lao Tzu said: "The nature of man may be likened to a swift current of water: you lead it eastward and it will flow to the east; you lead it westward and it will flow to the west. Human nature is neither disposed to good nor to evil, just as water is neither disposed to east nor west." Mencius replied: "It is true that water is neither disposed to east nor west, but is it neither disposed to flowing upward nor downward? The tendency of human nature to do good is like that of water to flow downward. There is no man who does not tend to do good; there is no water that does not flow downward. Now you may strike water and make it splash over your forehead, or you may even force it up the hills. But is this in the nature of water? It is of course due to the force of circumstances. Similarly, man may be brought to do evil, and that is because the same is done to his nature."

From W. Theodore de Bary, ed., *Sources of Chinese Tradition* (New York: Columbia University Press, 1960), pp. 102–103.

opinions as unnatural and artificial "outside things." Thus at the heart of Taoist thought is the concept of *wu-wei*, or "nonaction"—a manner of living that, like nature itself, is nonassertive and spontaneous. Lao-tzu pointed out that in nature all things work silently; they fulfill their function, and after they reach their bloom, they return to their origins. Unlike Confucius's ideal gentleman, who is constantly involved in society in order to preserve and better it, Lao-tzu's sage is a private person, an individualist, accepting life's burdens.

Taoism is a revolt not only against society but also against the intellect's limitations. Intuition, not reason, is the source of true knowledge; and books, Taoists said, are "the dregs and refuse of the ancients." One of the most famous Taoist philosophers, Chuang-tzu (fourth century B.C.E.), who made fun of Confucianists as tiresome busybodies, even questioned the reality of the world of the senses. He said that he once dreamed that he was a butterfly, "flying about enjoying itself." When he awakened he was confused: "I do not know whether I was Chuang-tzu dreaming that I was a butterfly, or whether now I am a butterfly dreaming that I am Chuang-tzu."

Anecdotes and allegories abound in Taoist literature, as in all mystical teachings that deal with subjects that are difficult to put into words. (As the Taoists put it, "The one who knows does not speak, and the one who speaks does not know.") But Taoist mysticism is more philosophical than religious. It does not aim to extinguish the personality through the union with the Absolute or God. Rather, its aim is to teach how one can obtain happiness in this world by living a simple life in harmony with nature.

Confucianism and Taoism became the two major philosophies that shaped Chinese thought and civilization. Although these rival schools frequently sniped at each other, they never became mutually exclusive outlooks on life. Taoist intuition complemented Confucian rationalism; during the centuries to come, Chinese were often Confucianists in their social relations and Taoists in their private life.

Mencius's Contribution to Confucianism

The man whose work was largely responsible for the emergence of Confucianism as the most widely accepted philosophy in China was Mencius, or Meng-tzu (372–289 B.C.E.). Born a century after the death of Confucius, Mencius added important new dimensions to Confucian thought in two areas: human nature and government.

Whereas Confucius had only implied that human nature is good, Mencius emphatically insisted that all people are innately good and tend to seek the good just as water tends to run downhill. But unless people strive to preserve and develop their innate goodness, which is the source of righteous conduct, it can be corrupted by the bad practices and ideas existing in the environment. Mencius taught that the opposite of righteous conduct is selfishness, and he attacked the extreme individualism of the Taoists as a form of selfishness. He held that "all men are brothers."

The second area in which Mencius elaborated on Confucius's teaching was politics. Mencius and his followers emphasized the key role of traditions and memories as a guide to life. In their lessons they distinguished between good kings, who ruled benevolently, and the rulers of his day (the period of Warring States), who governed by force and spread violence and disorder. Because good rulers of the past were guided by ethical standards, he said, they behaved benevolently toward the people and provided for their well-being. Unlike Confucius, who did not question the right of hereditary kings to rule, Mencius said that the people have a right to rebel against bad rulers and even kill them if necessary, because they have lost the "mandate of Heaven."

As we have seen, this concept had been used by the Chou to justify their revolt against the Shang. On that occasion the concept had a religious meaning, being connected with the worship of Heaven, who supported the ruler as the Son of Heaven. Mencius,

Legalism: The Theories of Han Fei Tzu (d. 233 B.C.E.)

When the sage rules the state, he does not count on people doing good of themselves, but employs such measures as will keep them from doing any evil. If he counts on people doing good of themselves, there will not be enough such people to be numbered by the tens in the whole country. But if he employs such measures as will keep them from doing evil, then the entire state can be brought up to a uniform standard. Inasmuch as the administrator has to consider the many but disregard the few, he does not busy himself with morals but with laws.

. . . Therefore, the intelligent ruler upholds solid facts and discards useless frills. He does not speak about deeds of humanity and righteousness, and he does not listen to the words of learned men.

Those who are ignorant about government insistently say: "Win the hearts of the people." If order could be procured by winning the hearts of the people, then even the wise ministers Yi Yin and Kuan Chung would be of no use. For all that the ruler would need to do would be just to listen to the people. Actually, the intelligence of the people is not to be relied upon any more than the mind of a baby. If the baby does not have his head shaved, his sores will recur; if he does not have his boil cut open, his illness will go from bad to worse. However, in order to shave his head or open the boil someone has to hold the baby while the affectionate mother is performing the work, and yet he keeps crying and yelling incessantly. The baby does not understand that suffering a small pain is the way to obtain a great benefit.

. . . The sage considers the conditions of the times . . . and governs the people accordingly. Thus though penalties are light, it is not due to charity; though punishment is heavy, it is not due to cruelty. Whatever is done is done in accordance with the circumstances of the age. Therefore circumstances go according to their time, and the course of action is planned in accordance with the circumstances.

. . . Now take a young fellow who is a bad character. His parents may get angry at him, but he never makes any change. The villagers may reprove him, but he is not moved. His teachers and elders may admonish him, but he never reforms. The love of his parents, the efforts of the villagers, and the wisdom of his teachers and elders—all the three excellent disciplines are applied to him, and yet not even a hair on his shins is altered. It is only after the district magistrate sends out his soldiers and in the name of the law searches for wicked individuals that the young man becomes afraid and changes his ways and alters his deeds. So while the love of parents is not sufficient to discipline the children, the severe penalties of the district magistrate are. This is because men become naturally spoiled by love, but are submissive to authority. . . .

That being so, rewards should be rich and certain so that the people will be attracted by them; punishments should be severe and definite so that the people will fear them; and laws should be uniform and steadfast so that the people will be familiar with them. Consequently, the sovereign should show no wavering in bestowing rewards and grant no pardon in administering punishments, and he should add honor to rewards and disgrace to punishments—when this is done, then both the worthy and the unworthy will want to exert themselves.

From W. Theodore de Bary, ed., *Sources of Chinese Tradition* (New York: Columbia University Press, 1960), pp. 141–147.

however, secularized and humanized the "mandate of Heaven" by equating it with the people: "Heaven hears as the people hear; Heaven sees as the people see." By redefining the concept in this way, Mencius made the welfare of the people the ultimate standard for judging government. Indeed, he even told rulers to their faces that the people were more important than the rulers were. Mencius did believe that all people were morally equal and that the ruler needed the consent of the people, but he was clearly the advocate of benevolent monarchy rather than popular democracy.

Legalism

By the end of the Warring States period in the third century B.C.E., as the Ch'in arose in western China, another body of thought emerged. It came to be called the School of Law, or Legalism. It had no single founder, as Confucianism and Taoism did, nor was it ever a school in the sense of a teacher leading disciples. What it did have in common with Confucianism and Taoism was the desire to establish stability in an age of turmoil, to strengthen the king at the expense of all other elements of society.

The Legalists emphasized the importance of harsh and inflexible law as the only means of achieving an orderly and prosperous society. They believed that human nature was basically bad and that people acted virtuously only when forced to do so. Therefore, they argued for an elaborate system of laws defining fixed penalties for each offense, with no exceptions for rank, class, or circumstances. Judges were not to use their own conscience in estimating the gravity of the crime and arbitrarily deciding on the punishment. Their task was solely to define the crime correctly; the punishment was provided automatically by the code of law.

Since the enforcement of law required a strong state, the immediate goal of the Legalists was to enhance the power of the ruler at the expense of other elements, particularly the nobility. Their ultimate goal was the creation of a centralized state strong enough to unify all China and end the chaos of the Warring States period. The unification of China in 221 B.C.E. by the Ch'in was largely the result of putting Legalist ideas of government into practice.

The Early Empires

221–206 B.C.E.	Ch'in (Qin)
206 B.C.E.–8 C.E.	Earlier (Western) Han
8–23 C.E.	Reign of Wang Mang
23–220 C.E.	Later (Eastern) Han

The First Chinese Empire

Two dynasties, the Ch'in (Qin) and the Han, unified China and created a centralized empire. The Ch'in dynasty collapsed soon after the death of its founder, but the Han lasted for more than four centuries. Together these dynasties transformed China, but the changes were the culmination of earlier developments during the Warring States period.

Rise of Legalist Ch'in

Throughout the Warring States period there was a widely shared hope that a king would unite China and inaugurate a great new age of peace and stability. Whereas the Confucians believed that such a king would accomplish the task by means of his outstanding moral virtue, the Legalists substituted overwhelming might as the essential element of effective government. The political philosophy of the Legalists—who liked to sum up and justify their doctrine in the two words "It works"—triumphed, and no state became more adept at practicing that pragmatic philosophy than the Ch'in.

The rise to preeminence of the Ch'in state began in 352 B.C.E., when its ruler selected Lord Shang, a man imbued with Legalist principles, to be chief minister. Recognizing that the growth of Ch'in power depended on a more efficient and centralized bureaucratic structure than could exist under feudalism, Lord Shang undermined the old hereditary nobility by creating a new aristocracy based on military merit. He also introduced a universal draft beginning at approximately age 15. As a result, chariot and cavalry warfare, in which the nobility had played the leading role, was replaced in importance by masses of peasant infantry equipped with iron weapons.

Economically, Lord Shang further weakened the old landowning nobility by abolishing the peasants' attachment to the land and granting them ownership of the plots they tilled. Thereafter the liberated peasants paid taxes directly to the local state, thus increasing its wealth and power. These reforms made Ch'in the most powerful of the Warring States.

China United

Nearly a century after Lord Shang, another Legalist prime minister helped the king of Ch'in prepare and carry out the conquest of the other Warring States, bring an end to the powerless Chou dynasty in 256 B.C.E., and unite China in 221 B.C.E. The king then declared himself the "First August Supreme Ruler" (Shih Huang-ti) of China, or First Emperor, as his new title is usually translated—a title that would endure until 1911. He also enlarged China—a name derived from the word Ch'in—by conquests in the south as far as the South China Sea. He stated that his dynasty would last 10,000 generations; it lasted 15 years.

The First Emperor moved the leading members of the old nobility to the capital, where they could be closely watched. To block rebellion, he ordered the entire civilian population to surrender its weapons to the state. A single harsh legal code, which replaced all local laws, was so detailed in its provisions that it was said to have been like "a fishing net through which even the smallest fish cannot slip out." The population was organized into groups of ten families, and each person was held responsible for the actions of all the members of the group. This structure ensured that all crimes would be reported; it also increased loyalty to the state at the expense of loyalty to the family.

The entire realm, which extended into South China and Vietnam, was divided into 48 provinces, administrative units drawn to erase traditional feudal units and to assist direct rule by the emperor's centrally controlled civil and military appointees. To destroy the source of the aristocracy's power and to permit the emperor's agents to tax every farmer's harvest, private ownership of land by peasants, promoted a century earlier in the state of Ch'in by Lord Shang, was decreed for all of China. Thus the Ch'in Empire reflected emerging social forces at work in China—the peasants freed from serfdom, the merchants eager to increase their wealth within a larger political area, and the new military and administrative upper class.

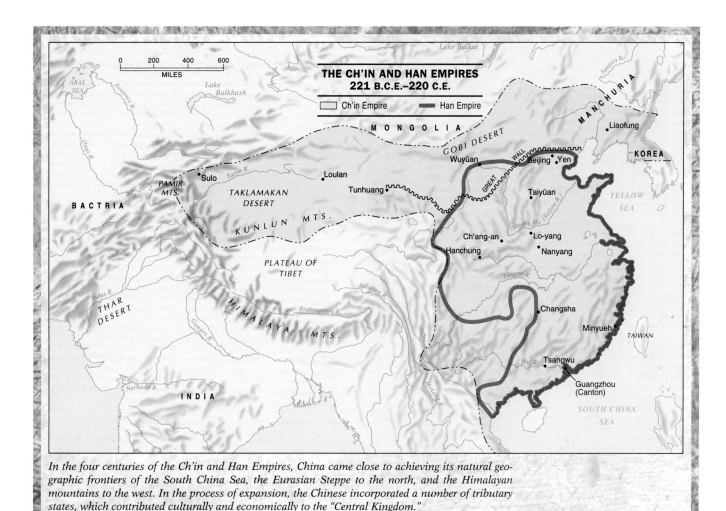

THE CH'IN AND HAN EMPIRES
221 B.C.E.–220 C.E.
☐ Ch'in Empire   ▬ Han Empire

In the four centuries of the Ch'in and Han Empires, China came close to achieving its natural geographic frontiers of the South China Sea, the Eurasian Steppe to the north, and the Himalayan mountains to the west. In the process of expansion, the Chinese incorporated a number of tributary states, which contributed culturally and economically to the "Central Kingdom."

Among the many public works of the First Emperor's short reign—all constructed by forced labor—were 4000 miles of highways and thousands of miles of canals and waterways, one of which connected the Yangtze to the Hsi River and Guangzhou. The written language was standardized, as were weights and measures and even the length of axles so that cart wheels would fit the grooves cut in the highways. Although the First Emperor, like some Warring States rulers before him, built walls to impede the incursion of nomadic tribes from central Asia, it is no longer believed that he built the 1400-mile Great Wall of China. In its present form the Great Wall was mainly the work of the sixteenth-century Ming dynasty.[5]

The First Emperor tried to enforce intellectual conformity and to cast the Ch'in Legalist system as the only natural political order. He suppressed all other schools of thought, especially the Confucians, who idealized Chou feudalism by stressing the obedience of sons to their fathers, of nobles to the lord, and of lords to the king. To break the hold of the past,

the emperor put into effect a Legalist proposal requiring that all privately owned books reflecting past traditions be burned and that "all . . . who raise their voice against the present government in the name of antiquity be beheaded together with their families." He created a new cultural elite of state-appointed teachers who would give an approved reading of the traditions and lessons of history. This set in motion the precedent that "imperial governments would henceforth insist that approved texts and suitable interpretations would be used for this purpose and that teaching would be conducted along recognized lines."[6]

Near the Ch'in capital at Ch'ang-an (Xian), the First Emperor employed over half a million laborers to construct a huge mound tomb for himself and, nearby, three large pits filled with life-size terra cotta figures of his imperial guard. The mausoleum has not been excavated, but the partial excavation of the pits revealed some 7500 soldiers aligned in military formation. Amazingly, each head is a personal portrait—no two faces are alike.

Representations of the First Emperor's army, such as this life-size terra cotta (literally "baked earth") warrior found in his tomb, testify to the grandeur of his reign.

When the First Emperor died in 210 B.C.E. while on one of his frequent tours of inspection, he was succeeded by an inept son who was unable to control the rivalry among his father's chief aides. Ch'in policies had alienated not only the intellectuals and the old nobility but also the peasants, who were subjected to ruinous taxation and forced labor. Rebel armies rose in every province of the empire, some led by peasants, others by aristocrats. Anarchy followed, and by 206 B.C.E. the Ch'in dynasty had disappeared. But the Chinese Empire itself, which Ch'in created, would last for more than 2000 years (until 1912, when China became a republic), the longest-lived political institution in world history.

At issue in the fighting that continued for another four years was not only the question of succession to the throne but also the form of government. The peasant and aristocratic leaders, first allied against Ch'in, became engaged in a ruthless civil war. The aristocrats sought to restore the oligarchic feu-

dalism of pre-Ch'in times. Their opponents, whose main leader was Liu Pang, a peasant who had become a Ch'in general, desired a centralized state. In this contest between the old order and the new, the new was the victor.

The Han Dynasty: The Empire Consolidated

In 206 B.C.E. the peasant Liu Pang defeated his aristocratic rival and established the Han dynasty. Named after the Han River, a tributary of the Yangtze, the new dynasty had its capital at Ch'ang-an. It lasted for more than 400 years and is traditionally divided into two parts: the Earlier Han (206 B.C.E.–8 C.E.) and the Later Han (23–220 C.E.), with its capital at Lo-yang. In time and importance, the Han corresponded to the late Roman Republic and early Roman Empire; ethnic Chinese still call themselves "men of Han."

The empire and power sought by Liu Pang and his successors were those of the Ch'in, but they succeeded where the Ch'in had failed because they were moderate and gradual in their approach. Liu Pang reestablished for a time some of the vassal kingdoms and feudal states in regions distant from the capital. He reduced peasant discontent by momentarily lowering

One of the major reasons for the continuity of Chinese civilizations through the millennia is the role played by women in perpetuating the value structure and passing it on to the next generation.

taxes and reducing forced labor. Later, around 100 B.C.E., the Han established a road system that made it possible for a person to go from Beijing to Guangzhou on foot in 56 days, or 32 days on horseback.

But the masterstroke of the Han emperors was to enlist the support of the Confucian intellectuals. They provided the empire with an ideology that would last until 1912, replacing the Ch'in's extreme legalistic ideology of harsh punishment and terror. The emperors recognized that an educated bureaucracy was necessary for governing so vast an empire. To appeal to the scholar-gentry (the landowner-bureaucrats), they lifted the ban on the Confucian classics and other Chou literature, and the way was open for a revival of intellectual life that had been suppressed under the Ch'in. The result was called Han Confucianism.

In accordance with Legalist principles, now tempered by Confucian insistence on the ethical basis of government, the Han emperors established administrative organs staffed by a salaried bureaucracy with as many as 20 levels to rule their empire. Talented men entered government service through an examination system based on the Confucian classics. Confucius's emphasis on loyalty as the most important duty—son to father within the family, minister to king within the state—pleased the Han and all later emperors. The highest level of bureaucracy made positions hereditary in the family.

The examinations were theoretically open to all Chinese men except merchants. (The Han inherited both the Confucian bias against trade as an unvirtuous striving for profit and the Legalist suspicion of merchants, who put their own interests ahead of those of the state and society.) The bureaucrats came from the landlord class because wealth was necessary to obtain the education needed to pass the examinations. Consequently, the earlier division of Chinese society between aristocrats and peasants became a division between peasants and landowner-bureaucrats.

Wu Ti and the Pax Sinica

After 60 years of consolidation, the Han Empire reached its greatest extent and development during the long reign of Wu Ti ("Martial Emperor"), from 141 to 87 B.C.E. To accomplish his goal of territorial expansion, he raised the peasants' taxes but not those of the great landowners, who remained virtually exempt from taxation. In addition, he increased the amount of labor and military service the peasants were forced to contribute to the state. Further, he imposed a state monopoly on the sale of iron and salt and banned the export of metal goods and female stock animals.

In conventional wisdom, people came to be placed in one of four vocations, in descending order: scholars, farmers, craftsmen, and tradesmen. This was more of a social than an economic arrangement. The merchants worked closely with the farmers and craftsmen to sell everything from food and alcoholic beverages to wagons and hardware. Trade and manufacturing became essential elements of communal life. Even though merchants were social inferiors, they became richer than individuals in the other castes. The traditional officials resented them more and more but could not block them because the tradesmen's wealth grew from their trade in what could be called daily goods. In fact, the state found trade to be useful in buying off the invading steppe tribes.

The Martial Emperor justified his expansionist policies in terms of self-defense against Mongolian nomads, the Hsiung-nu, known later to the West as the Huns. Their attacks had caused the First Emperor to construct a wall to obstruct their raiding cavalry. To outflank the nomads in the west, Wu Ti extended the wall and annexed a large corridor extending through the Tarim River basin of central Asia to the Pamir Mountains, close to Bactria. This corridor has ever since remained a part of China.

Wu Ti failed in an attempt to form an alliance with the Scythians in Bactria, but his envoy's report of the interest shown in Chinese silks by the peoples of the area was the beginning of a commercial exchange between China and the West. This trade brought great profits to Chinese merchants and their colleagues in the West.

Wu Ti also outflanked the Hsiung-nu in the east by the conquest of southern Manchuria and northern Korea. In addition, he completed the conquest of South China, begun by the Ch'in, and he added northern Vietnam to the Chinese Empire. Chinese settlers moved into all the conquered lands. As the armies of the Roman Republic were laying the foundation of the Pax Romana in the West, the Martial Emperor was establishing a Pax Sinica ("Chinese Peace") in the East.

Han Decline

Wu Ti's conquests led to a fiscal crisis. As costs increased, taxes increased, and the peasants' burdens led them to revolt once again. The central government had to rely more and more on local military commanders and great landowners for control of the population, giving them great power and prestige at its own expense. This cycle of decline after an initial period of increasing prosperity and power has been the pattern of all Chinese dynasties. During the Han this "dynastic cycle," as Western historians of China call it, led after Wu Ti's death to a succession of mediocre rulers and a temporary usurpation of the throne (8–23 C.E.) that divided the Earlier from the Later Han.

The usurper, Wang Mang, the Confucian chief minister of the court, united Confucian ethics with Legalist practice. Like his contemporary in the West, the Roman emperor Augustus, his goal was the rejuvenation of society by employing the power of the state. By Wang Mang's day the number of large tax-free estates had greatly increased while the number of taxpaying peasant holdings had declined. This inequity was a by-product of the private land ownership that under the Ch'in had replaced the old communal use of the land. Rich officials and merchants were able to acquire the lands of impoverished peasant-owners, who became tenants paying exorbitant rents.

More and more peasants fell behind in their rents and were forced to sell themselves or their children into debt slavery. To remedy this situation and increase the government's tax income, Wang Mang abolished debt slavery and decreed that the land was the property of the nation and should be portioned out to peasant families, who would pay taxes on their allotments.

Wang Mang also tried to solve the long-standing issue of inflation. This problem had greatly increased after Wu Ti found himself in financial difficulties, debased the coinage, and set maximum prices for basic commodities. Wang Mang tried to stabilize prices by a program called "leveling" in which the government bought surplus commodities when prices fell and sold them when scarcity caused prices to rise. (In 1938 a chance reading of Wang Mang's leveling proposal inspired the "ever-normal granary" program of the American New Deal.)[7]

Wang Mang's remarkable reform program failed. As is the case with so many radical changes, the conservative bureaucracy was unequal to the difficult administrative task. The powerful landowners rebelled against the ruler who proposed to confiscate their land. Although Wang Mang rescinded his reforms, he was killed by the rebels in 23 C.E. The conflict of landlordship and tenancy, along with the concentration of power of great families, became—and remained—a major problem in Chinese history.

The Later Han dynasty never reached the heights of its predecessors. Warlords who were members of the rich landowner class seized more and more power, and widespread peasant rebellions (one band was led by "Mother Lu," a woman skilled in witchcraft) sapped the state's resources. Surviving in name only during its last 30 years, the Han dynasty ended in 220, when the throne was usurped by the son of a famous warlord. Three and a half centuries of disunity and turbulence followed—the longest period of strife in China's long history, often called China's Middle Ages, as in Europe after the fall of the Roman Empire. But China eventually succeeded where Europe failed: in 589 the Sui dynasty united China again. With a few exceptions, it has remained united to this day.

In the Confucian hierarchy, tradespeople ranked at the bottom of the social scale. Yet as economic and political conditions changed in the second and first centuries B.C.E., they came to play a prominent role.

Han Scholarship, Art, and Technology

Politically and culturally, the relation of the Han to the Chou paralleled that of ancient Rome to Greece. Politically, the disunity of Greece and the Chou was followed by the imperial unity and administrative genius of the Romans and the Han. Culturally, just as the Romans owed a great debt to the Greeks, so did the Han to the Chou. Furthermore, Greek and Chou intellectual creativity was not matched by the Romans and the Han.

Scholarship flourished under the Han, but it was mainly concerned with collecting and interpreting the classics of Chinese thought produced in the Chou period. As the basis of education for prospective bureaucrats, Wu Ti established an imperial university in 124 B.C.E.; a century later it had about 3000 students. The Han scholars venerated Confucius, who moved in the popular imagination from being a teacher, a man like any other, to the ideal thinker and a being regarded as in some ways divine. Confucianism became the official philosophy of the state. Great respect for learning, together with the system of civil service examinations based on the Five Confucian Classics, became fundamental characteristics of Chinese civilization.

Han scholars started another scholarly tradition with their historical writings. Their antiquarian interest in researching the past produced a comprehensive history of China, the *Historical Records (Shih Chi)*. This huge and highly detailed work of 130 chapters begins with the Hsia dynasty and discusses the Han emperors and the reign of Wu Ti. Scholars appreciate the work's freedom from superstition and its careful weighing of the evidence. Proof of its independent nature can be seen in the fact that Wu Ti castrated the book's author for defending a general that Wu Ti had dismissed. In the Later Han a scholar wrote the *History of the Han*, about the Earlier Han, and thereafter it became customary for each dynasty to write the official history of its immediate predecessor.

A fundamental belief of Chinese historiography is that "during the period of remotest antiquity a golden age existed of sage-rulers who governed a happy and contented people." There is no "beginning" for Chinese historians, such as Christ for the Christian world or the Hegira for the Muslims. "Events are dated either according to their occurrence within a recurring sixty-year cycle (with each year having its own appellation) or according to their position within the reigns of successive rulers."[8] The Chinese believed that the successes and failures of the past provided guidance for one's own time and for the future. As stated in the *Historical Records*, "Events of the past, if not forgotten, are teachings about the future." The state-sponsored Chinese historians wrote to affirm the intimate and unchanging and essential link—the emperor—between the heavenly order and politics, caught up in a predictable cycle. By contrast, Greek historians such as Herodotus and Thucydides wrote "to face and reconcile themselves to the fact that . . . permanence is impossible" and change is necessary in human affairs.[9]

Archaeological investigation was used as an aid to the writing of history. One scholar anticipated modern archaeologists by more than a thousand years in classifying human history by "ages": "stone" (Old Stone Age), "jade" (New Stone Age), "bronze," and "the present age" when "weapons are made of iron."[10]

Another monument to Han scholarship was the world's first dictionary, *Shuo Wen* ("Words Explained"), produced during Wu Ti's reign. It listed the meaning and pronunciation of more than 9000 Chinese characters.

In contrast to Han scholarship, Han art was clearly creative. The largely decorative art of the past, which served a religious purpose, was replaced by a realistic pictorial art (foreshadowed earlier by the individually sculpted soldiers buried near the First Emperor's tomb) portraying ordinary life. The result was the first great Chinese flowering of sculpture, both in relief and in the round. Some of the finest examples of this realistic secular art are the models of the tall and spirited horses that Wu Ti imported from Bactria. The Han greatly admired these proud "celestial" and "blood-sweating" horses from the West, and their artists brilliantly captured the beasts' high spirit.

This bronze horse is a masterpiece in fluidity and motion. The artist who produced it at the beginning of the Common Era understood the musculature, coordination, and spirit that enable horses to achieve great speed. In this work of art, the only contact the horse has with the earth is the right rear hoof, which is placed on a flying swallow.

This brocade mitten, dating from the first or second century C.E., was unearthed in 1959 from a site in Sinkiang.

During the Han period China surpassed the level of technological development in the rest of the world. Notable inventions included a primitive seismograph capable of indicating earthquakes several hundred miles away; the use of water power to grind grain and to operate a piston bellows for iron smelting; the horse collar, which greatly increased the pulling power of horses; paper made from cloth rags, which replaced cumbersome bamboo strips and expensive silk cloth as a writing surface; and the humble but extremely useful wheelbarrow. By the end of the first century B.C.E., the Han Chinese had recognized sunspots and accurately determined the length of the calendar year, an example of the high level gained in their mathematical and observational astronomy.[11]

Popular Taoism and Buddhism

By the time the First Emperor united China and ended the Warring States period in 221 B.C.E., a popular form of Taoism had emerged. Popular Taoism was a religion of spirits and magic that provided the spiritual comfort not found in the abstract philosophical nature of Taoism or Confucianism. Its goals were long life and personal immortality. These goals were to be achieved not so much as a reward for ethical conduct but through magical charms and spells and by drinking an "elixir of immortality." The search for such an elixir, which was thought to contain the vital forces of nature, led to an emphasis on diet and to the culinary excellence for which the Chinese are famous.

Popular Taoism also became a way to express peasant discontent. In 184 C.E., in one of many such uprisings throughout China's history, the Yellow Turbans led a widespread peasant revolt inspired by Taoist followers of the now-deified Lao-tzu. Over 300,000 rebels destroyed much of China and greatly contributed to the anarchy that fatally weakened the Later Han dynasty.

The breakdown of the political and social order during the Later Han also produced an upsurge in philosophical Taoism. Educated Chinese began to turn inward in their thinking, discouraged with Confucianism and its concern for society.

Mahayana Buddhism, first mentioned in China in 65 C.E., provided another answer to the need for religious assurance. It was brought to China by missionaries and traders through central Asia. About 148 C.E. a Buddhist missionary established a center for the translation of Buddhist writings into Chinese at the Later Han capital. However, relatively few Chinese were attracted to the religion during this period. Buddhism's great attraction of converts and influence on Chinese culture came after the fall of the Han dynasty, when renewed political turmoil made its emphasis on otherworldly salvation appealing to the great majority of Chinese.

China and Foreign Trade

Chinese leaders had ambivalent feelings about trade with foreigners. On the one hand, they did not want to provide them with the means to become richer or the technology to become stronger. But to ensure stability on the northern frontier and with their central Asian neighbors, the Chinese engaged in trade, especially in silk. In return they received the horses and woolen goods they needed. Although this trade directly contradicted the belief in the need for self-sufficiency, the government began to actively promote the silk business in the first century B.C.E. Some of the caravans carrying silk reached the Mediterranean basin via middlemen along the Silk Road.

In 138 B.C.E. the Han emperor Wu Ti sent an envoy to Bactria to seek allies against the Hsiung-nu. Although the envoy failed to secure an alliance, the information he brought back amounted to the Chinese discovery of western Eurasia. Intrigued above all by his envoy's report indicating great interest in

Discovery Through Maps
An Ancient Chinese Map

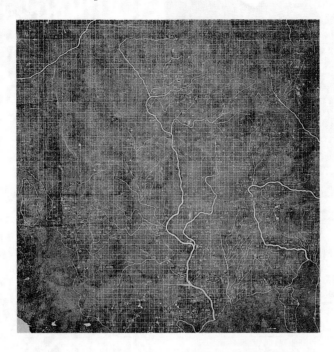

Young civilizations, like young human beings, tend to concentrate solely on themselves, with little idea of the outside world beyond their immediate surroundings. A sense of context can be gained only with experience, wisdom, and—sometimes—humility. The person who made this ancient map had little idea of what lay beyond but revealed considerable knowledge of what is in the center.

Because we are used to a level of great precision, thanks to modern cartography, it is easy to overlook the subtlety of this map. Where are the longitude and latitude lines? Which way is north? What is the scale of this map—how can we know distances from place to place? This 4000-year-old map shows us the three major facts of life for the time: rivers and where they run, mountains, and provinces that paid tribute to the emperor.

As we saw in Chapter 2, rivers served as the centers for the developments of the great civilizations after the Neolithic era. They provided transportation, food, fertilization for lands during the annual floods, and—unfortunately—access for invaders. This map shows the Huang Ho (Yellow) and the Yangtze, not as we would recognize them from a map, but as they must have looked to someone traveling along them without any reference to a larger context. It is an interesting experience to try to draw a map of the world as we know it from the paths we actually traverse and not from the majesty and exactitude of a satellite-verified image. After attempting such an exercise, we can appreciate even more this ancient map of China.

Chinese silks and his description of the magnificent horses, Wu Ti resolved to open trade relations with his western neighbors. His armies pushed across the Pamir Mountains to a location close to Alexandria Eschate (Khojend), founded by Alexander the Great as the northern limit of his empire. Shortly after 100 B.C.E. silk began arriving in the Mediterranean basin, conveyed by the Parthians. Wealthy private merchants carried on this trade, which required large outlays of capital. They organized their cargoes into

caravans of shaggy packhorses and two-humped Bactrian camels. When the Chinese soon moved back across the Pamirs, the Kushans of India became their middlemen, selling the silk to the Parthians and later to Western merchants coming by sea to India.

It was not until about 120 C.E. that the Parthians allowed some Western merchants to cross their land. The information they brought back about the Chinese was used by Ptolemy in constructing his map of the world. During the first and second centuries

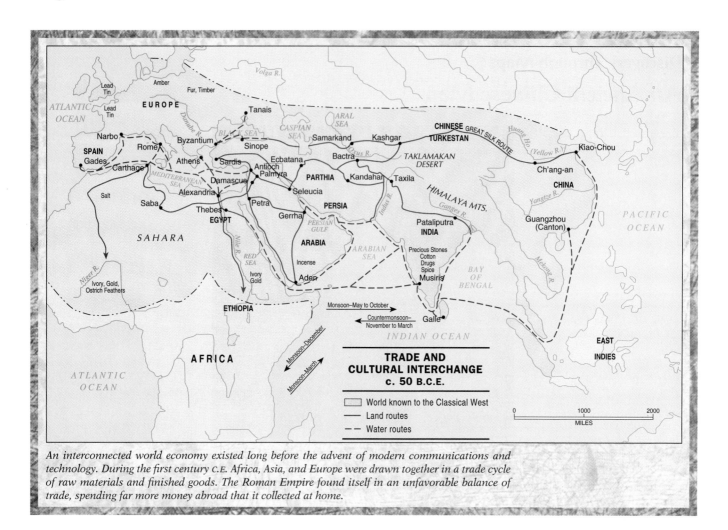

An interconnected world economy existed long before the advent of modern communications and technology. During the first century C.E. Africa, Asia, and Europe were drawn together in a trade cycle of raw materials and finished goods. The Roman Empire found itself in an unfavorable balance of trade, spending far more money abroad that it collected at home.

C.E.—the prosperous years of the Pax Romana—the peoples of the Roman Empire had a voracious appetite for Chinese silk, which the Romans believed was produced from the leaves of trees and which was sold in the market quarter of Rome. In 166 C.E., according to the Chinese *History of the Later Han Dynasty,* some merchants from Ta Ch'in ("Great Ch'in," the Chinese name for Rome), claiming to represent "King Antun" (the emperor Marcus Aurelius Antoninus), arrived in South China by sea across the Bay of Bengal and around the Malay peninsula.

To satisfy the Roman world's insatiable appetite for luxury goods, trade with the East grew immensely in the first two centuries of the Common Era. But because such Roman exports as wool, linen, glass, and metalware to the East did not match in value Rome's imports of silk, spices, perfumes, gems, and other luxuries, the West suffered seriously from an adverse balance of trade. Gold and silver had to be continually exported to Asia. Late in the first century C.E., Pliny estimated that China and Arabia drained away annually at least 100 million sesterces (the daily wage of an unskilled Roman laborer was 4 sesterces).

For the Chinese, trade with what would come to be Europe was the least important aspect during the Han dynasty and continued to be so until the nineteenth century. During the Han there would be no close ties between China and the West. Indochina, Korea, Japan, India, and the lands to the north all came together in the next millennium to form the first global trading zone, in conjunction with the Arab markets, and to enrich and stimulate China.[12]

Conclusion

Despite often cataclysmic disasters during their formative period, the Chinese did not lose their relish for life. They reacted to human suffering not by pursuing a long and arduous religious quest but by instituting ambitious innovations in all aspects of society, from philosophy to economics. Throughout, the power of the state retained its theoretical focus toward the amelioration of social evils and the relief of distress. This was the ever-changing product of two of the main ingredients in the Chinese tradition—Confucianism, with its concern for a humane society, and Legalism, with its stress on the power of the state, always modified by the underlying, unified civilization.

And that unified civilization did for China what the Judeo-Christian tradition with its ethical monotheism, Greece with its individual pursuit of truth and beauty, and Rome with its laws and institutions did for Europe—erect the fundamental frame of identity, in which all other activities take place.

Suggestions for Reading

John K. Fairbank, *China: A New History* (Harvard University Press, 1992), is an up-to-date survey by an eminent authority. Among other general histories of China are Witold Rodzinski, *The Walled Kingdom: A History of China from Antiquity to the Present* (Free Press, 1984); Jacques Gernet, *A History of Chinese Civilization,* 2nd ed. (Cambridge University Press, 1982); Arthur Cotterell, *China: A Concise Cultural History* (Murray, 1988); and John K. Fairbank, *China: Tradition and Transformation,* rev. ed. (Houghton Mifflin, 1989). For insightful contributions on a variety of topics in Chinese history, see Derk Bodde, *Essays on Chinese Civilization* (Princeton University Press, 1981).

For a brilliant series of interpretations on Chinese civilization, see Michael Loewe, *The Pride That Was China* (St. Martin's Press, 1990). Arthur Waldron, *The Great Wall of China: From History to Myth* (Cambridge University Press, 1990), cuts through popular views of the wall (both Chinese and Western) and presents a multifaceted study of the importance of walls in China and their construction.

Fuller accounts of the periods covered in this chapter are Michael Loewe and Denis C. Twitchett, eds., *The Ch'in and Han Empires, 221 B.C.–A.D. 220* (Cambridge University Press, 1986); Kwang-Chih Chang, *The Archaeology of Ancient China,* 4th ed. (Yale University Press, 1987), and *Shang Civilization* (Yale University Press, 1982); René Grousset, *The Rise and Splendour of the Chinese Empire* (Bles, 1952); and Michael Loewe, *Everyday Life in Early Imperial China* (Harper & Row, 1965). Arthur Cotterell, *The First Emperor of China: The Greatest Archaeological Find of Our Time* (Holt, Rinehart and Winston, 1981), is a well-illustrated popular account of the founder of the Ch'in dynasty and the archaeological discoveries at his tomb.

Benjamin Schwartz, *The World of Thought in Ancient China* (Harvard University Press, 1985), is an authoritative fresh view. See also Frederick W. Mote, *Intellectual Foundations of China,* 2nd ed. (McGraw-Hill, 1989); Fung Yulan, *A Short History of Chinese Philosophy* (Free Press, 1966); Arthur Waley, *Three Ways of Thought in Ancient China* (Stanford University Press, 1983); and Marcel Granet, *The Religion of the Chinese People* (Harper Torchbooks, 1975). W. Theodore de Bary, ed., *Sources of Chinese Tradition* (Columbia University Press, 1960), is an outstanding collection of translations with valuable commentaries. On science and invention, see Robert Temple, *The Ge-* *nius of China: 3,000 Years of Science, Discovery, and Invention* (Simon & Schuster, 1986), and Christopher Cullen, *Astronomy and Mathematics in Ancient China: The Zhou bi su an jing* (Cambridge University Press, 1996). On the fine arts, see Michael Sullivan, *The Arts of China,* 3rd ed. (University of California Press, 1984), and Wen Fong, ed., *The Great Bronze Age of China* (Metropolitan Museum of Art/Knopf, 1980).

Robert E. Wheeler, *Rome Beyond the Imperial Frontiers* (Greenwood, 1972) is a study of Rome's trade with the East. See also L. Boulnois, *The Silk Road* (Allen & Unwin, 1963).

Suggestions for Web Browsing

Ancient Dynasties
http:// www-chaos.umd.edu/history/ancient1.html
Images and text present a view of early China, from prehistory to the era of the Warring States, 221 B.C.E.

China the Beautiful
http://www.chinapage.com/chinese.html
Extensive site exploring the art, calligraphy, poetry, literature, and music of China throughout its lengthy history.

Ancient China
http://www.wsu.edu:8080/~dee/ANCCHINA/ANCCHINA.HTM
Chinese history from 4000 to 256 B.C.E., with details about philosophy and culture.

Notes

1. Derk Bodde, "Feudalism in China," in *Essays on Chinese Civilization,* ed. Charles Le Blanc and Dorothy Borei (Princeton, N.J.: Princeton University Press, 1981), pp. 85–86.
2. Michael Loewe, *The Pride That Was China* (New York: St. Martin's Press, 1990), pp. 98–99.
3. Ibid., p. 99.
4. Ibid.
5. Arthur Waldron, *The Great Wall of China: From History to Myth* (Cambridge: Cambridge University Press, 1990).
6. Loewe, *Pride That Was China,* p. 106.
7. W. Theodore de Bary, *East Asian Civilizations: A Dialogue in Five Stages* (Cambridge, Mass.: Harvard University Press, 1988), p. 19.
8. Bodde, "Feudalism," pp. 154, 245.
9. R. G. Collingwood, *The Idea of History* (New York: Galaxy Books, 1956), p. 22.
10. Kwang-Chih Chang, *The Archaeology of Ancient China,* 4th ed. (New Haven, Conn.: Yale University Press, 1987), p. 5.
11. Christopher Cullen, *Astronomy and Mathematics in Ancient China: The Zhou bi su an jing* (Cambridge: Cambridge University Press, 1996).
12. See Loewe, *Pride That Was China,* ch. 18.

*Indian stone carving showing
Buddists worshipping the site be-
neath the Bodhi tree, where the
Buddha gained Enlightenment
(Bodhi).*

Adoration of the Bodhi Tree, India, Amaravati Satavahana period, 2nd century. Stone relief, 80 × 57.1
cm. The Cleveland Museum of Art, Purchase from J. H.
Wade Fund, 1970.43

Ancient India

From Origins to 300 C.E.

Chapter Contents

The Indian subcontinent since ancient times has functioned as a matrix for networks of trade and culture. It has been the target of conquerors and empire builders and the origination point of philosophical and artistic trends that have radiated outward along the land-based routes linking Asia with Europe and the seaborne routes connecting South Asia to Africa, the Middle East, Southeast Asia, and East Asia. The civilizations of classical India have had a profound effect that endures to this day on the arts, literature, religion, and philosophical beliefs of the world.

The subcontinent called India was a land of sometimes dense settlement as early as the Stone Age, dating back 500,000 years. An area diverse in climate, geography, language, and ethnicity, it was a primarily village-based agricultural society and remains so today. In the ancient times discussed here, India produced an extensive riverine civilization in the northwest that ultimately declined, absorbed tribes of immigrating Indo-Europeans (Aryans) who became dominant, generated a second wave of urbanization in the east that matured into a vast empire embracing most of the subcontinent, and again absorbed several waves of invasion and immigration from the northwest. Synthesizing the social ideas and the philosophical and religious beliefs and practices of the immigrant Indo-Europeans and the indigenous Dravidians, India developed three major religious traditions during this time, Hinduism, Jainism, and Buddhism, the last of which spread far beyond the bounds of India to become a pan-Asian and today global religion.

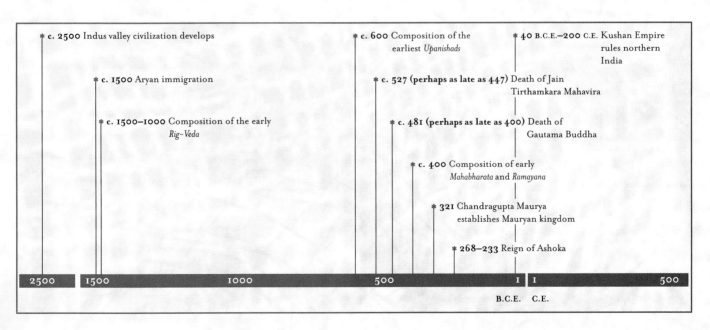

- ✶ c. 2500 Indus valley civilization develops
- ✶ c. 1500 Aryan immigration
- ✶ c. 1500–1000 Composition of the early *Rig-Veda*
- ✶ c. 600 Composition of the earliest *Upanishads*
- ✶ c. 527 (perhaps as late as 447) Death of Jain Tirthamkara Mahavira
- ✶ c. 481 (perhaps as late as 400) Death of Gautama Buddha
- ✶ c. 400 Composition of early *Mahabharata* and *Ramayana*
- ✶ 321 Chandragupta Maurya establishes Mauryan kingdom
- ✶ 268–233 Reign of Ashoka
- ✶ 40 B.C.E.–200 C.E. Kushan Empire rules northern India

| 2500 | 1500 | 1000 | 500 | I | I | 500 |

B.C.E.   C.E.

India comprises an area comparable to Europe in size and internal diversity. And like Europe, the regions and peoples of India came to be roughly divided into two major language groups, the Indo-European in the north and the Dravidian in the south; each group embraces a number of separate languages. In the centuries between 1500 B.C.E. and 300 C.E. the emerging Hindu cultural synthesis gave the subcontinent a general cultural unity similar to the unity afforded to Europe by the spread of the Christian religion in the first millennium C.E.

In this chapter we trace the important threads of Indian history to the third century C.E., a time when the Pax Romana in the West was coming to an end and when India was poised for the rise of another great empire in the north, the classical Hindu empire of the Guptas. This period was the formative age of Indian civilization, when its basic institutions and cultural patterns were determined.

Early India

Sometime before 2500 B.C.E. a counterpart of the civilizations that had emerged along the Tigris and Euphrates and the Nile appeared along the Indus River in India. Among its major cities, Mohenjo-Daro, located north of Karachi in present-day Pakistan, is believed to have been one of the largest Bronze Age cities of the world. Around the time that the Indus valley civilization collapsed, the Indo-European migrants known as Aryans began to move into the subcontinent from the Iranian plateau (about 1500 B.C.E.). The Aryans became the dominant social and cultural group in the subcontinent, though they assimilated much from the indigenous peoples of northern India. Their Vedic religion, cultivated by their seers and priests (Brahmins), became the foundation for much of the later cultural development of the entire subcontinent.

Geography of India

The term *India* is used here to refer to the entire subcontinent, an area encompassing the modern nations of Pakistan, India, Nepal, Bhutan, Bangladesh, and Sri Lanka. It is a large, irregular diamond, the lower sides of which are bounded by the warm waters of the Indian Ocean and the upper sides of which are bounded by the mountain walls of the Himalayas on the north and several smaller ranges on the west. The highest mountains in the world, the Himalayas, and their western counterparts divide India from the rest of Asia, making it a discrete subcontinent. Through the Khyber Pass and other mountain passes in the northwest and across the Indian Ocean have come the armed conquerors, restless tribes, merchants,

and travelers who did much to shape India's turbulent history.

In addition to the northern mountain belt, which shields India from arctic winds, the subcontinent comprises two other major geographical regions. In the north is the great plain (which came to be known as Hindustan after the Muslim invasions), extending from the Indus valley to the Bay of Bengal. It spans the watersheds of two great river systems, the Indus and the Ganges, which have their sources in the Himalayas. South of this great plain, and separated from it in the west by the Vindhya mountain range, rises a semiarid plateau, the Deccan ("southland"). This plateau rises up about 2000 feet above sea level in the Western Ghats ("steps") along India's western peninsular coast and then slopes gently downward to the shallow Eastern Ghats along India's eastern ocean shore.

India's climate and the rhythms of Indian life are governed by the dry northeast monsoon wind of the winter and the wet southwest monsoon wind of the summer. Most parts of India receive most of their rainfall during the summer and autumn months of the southwest monsoon, which blows in from the Arabian Sea. The Western Ghats cause the summer monsoon to drop most of its rain on the thin Malabar Coast, making it one of the wettest areas of the globe but also giving much of the western Deccan its semi-

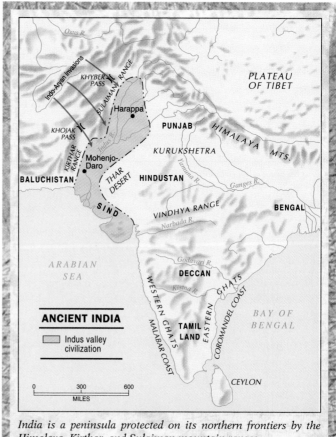

India is a peninsula protected on its northern frontiers by the Himalaya, Kirthar, and Sulaiman mountain ranges.

arid climate. The eastern side of the Deccan fares better from the summer monsoon.

It is in western Hindustan, now part of the state of Pakistan, that India's earliest civilization arose. This area is made up of an alluvial plain (called the Punjab, "land of the five rivers") watered by the upper Indus and its tributaries and the region of the lower Indus (called Sind, from *sindhu*, meaning "river," and the origin of the terms *Hindu* and *India*).

The Indus Civilization, c. 2500–1500 B.C.E.

The rise of civilization in the Indus valley around 2500 B.C.E. duplicated what had occurred in Mesopotamia nearly a thousand years earlier. In both areas Neolithic farmers lived in food-producing villages situated on the hilly flanks of large river valleys. These settlements spread out along the river valleys, capitalizing on their abundant water and fertile soil. Here they developed the more complex way of life we call a civilization. Some of these farming villages had grown into large cities with as many as 40,000 inhabitants by 2300 B.C.E. Excavations of two of these cities, Mohenjo-Daro in Sind and Harappa in the Punjab, have provided much of our knowledge of the Indus valley civilization, but its sites were widely dispersed across the whole of northwestern India. Reaching its height in the centuries around 2000 B.C.E., the Indus valley civilization produced highly organized towns and uniform weights, measures, and pottery.

Although Mohenjo-Daro and Harappa were 400 miles apart, the Indus River made possible the main-tenance of a uniform administration and economy over the entire area. The cities were carefully planned, with straight paved streets intersecting at right angles and an elaborate drainage system with underground channels. The spacious two-storied houses of the well-to-do contained bathrooms and were constructed with the same type of baked bricks used for roads. A script employing some 400 pictographic signs has not yet been deciphered. The only known use of the script was on engraved stamp-seals, which may have been used for identification or to mark property.

The economy of the Indus civilization, like that of Mesopotamia and Egypt, was based on irrigation farming. Wheat and barley were the chief crops, and the state collected these grains as taxes and stored them in huge granaries. The importance of agriculture explains the presence of numerous mother goddess figurines, representing fertility. Such figures are also found in various forms throughout the Mediterranean world. For the first known time in world history, chickens were domesticated as a food source during the Indus civilization, and cotton was grown and used in making textiles. The spinning and weaving of cotton remains one of the subcontinent's chief industries.

Copper and bronze were used for tools and weapons, but the rarity of weapons suggests that warfare was uncommon. Trade was sufficiently well organized to obtain needed raw materials—copper, tin, silver, gold, and timber—from the mountain regions to the west. There is also evidence of active trade contacts with Mesopotamia, some 1500 miles to the west, as early as 2300 B.C.E. (the time of Sargon of Akkad).

The ruins at Mohenjo-Daro are still impressive more than four millennia after the city was established.

For centuries the Indus valley civilization flourished. Excavations at Mohenjo-Daro, however, show clearly that decline set in about 1700 B.C.E., when a series of great floods caused by earthquakes altered the course of the Indus and apparently severely affected the settlements along it. Harappa to the north appears to have suffered a similar fate. The invaders who came through the northwest passes around 1500 B.C.E. may have contributed to the disappearance of the Indus valley civilization, but their role in that process is unclear.

The Aryan Immigration and the Early Vedic Age, 1500–1000 B.C.E.

The semibarbaric migrants, who called themselves Aryas ("noble people," to distinguish themselves from the indigenous people), moved through the mountain passes onto the Indus plains. They spoke an early form of Sanskrit, an Indo-European language, and formed the easternmost wave of the great Indo-European migrations of the second millennium B.C.E., whose profound effects on the ancient world we have noted in earlier chapters. The Aryans were basically a pastoral people who counted their wealth in cattle, but they were also effective warriors whose leaders fought from horse-drawn chariots.

In the first five or six centuries after their arrival in India, the Aryans moved slowly eastward, settled throughout the Punjab, took up agriculture from the indigenous peoples, and came to dominate the whole area socially and culturally. Indigenous populations of the subcontinent, the majority of whom may well have belonged to the ethnolinguistic group called Dravidian, were either conquered and assimilated by the Aryans or driven south into the Deccan. The Aryans referred to these darker-skinned but more civilized people as *Dasas*, "savages," a term that later came to mean "slaves."

During these centuries the Aryans worshipped their gods with sacrificial rituals that were accompanied by specially composed "verses of praise and adoration," *ric* verses, which would be recited together in "hymns." The *ric* verses and the hymns they made up were regarded as the sacred compositions of inspired seers (the Brahmins), who could see the gods and understood their ways and were thus able to compose verses that could influence the gods to favor and bless Aryan men and their families. Over a thousand such hymns were gathered together in the *Rig-Veda*, a collection that has been memorized and used in worship continuously for over three thousand years. (*Veda* means "knowledge," a reference to the Brahmin's knowing all the hymns by memory.) Thanks to the *Rig-Veda* we know more about the Aryans than we know about their Indus civilization predecessors, for whom only archaeological evidence survives.

The early Aryan religion involved making sacrificial offerings of grain, cakes, dairy products, and animals to the gods, who embodied and controlled the forces of what we today call "nature," in return for

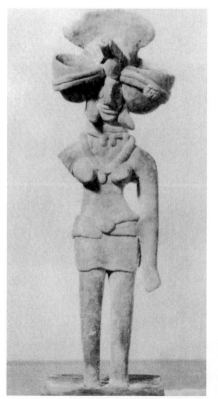

Excavations at Mohenjo-Daro have unearthed mother goddess figurines and stamp seals. The female figure, with her elaborate headdress, may well be a symbol of fertility. The seal shown below features a humped Indian bull. Such figures, suggesting male potency, were prominent in Indus art. The writing on the seals, a pictographic script employing about 250 symbols and 400 characters, remains undeciphered.

Rig-Veda: Creation and the Kinds of Men

The Purusha Sutra of the *Rig-Veda* provides the first suggestion in ancient Vedic texts of the notion of the *varnas*, the idea that humankind is divided into four classes and their differences are based in Creation itself. The four classes are priests *(Brahmins)*, rulers and warriors *(Rajanyas* or *Kshatriyas)*, herders and merchants *(Vaishyas)*, and the low-class workers or servants *(Shudras)*. Purusha (the "primordial cosmic man") serves as the victim in the cosmic sacrifice from which the universe originates.

The sacrificial victim, namely Purusha, born at the very beginning, they [the gods] sprinkled with sacred water upon the sacrificial grass. With him as oblation, the gods performed the sacrifice, and also the *Sadhyas* [a class of semidivine beings] and the *rishis* [ancient seers].

From that wholly offered sacrificial oblation were born the verses and the sacred chants. . . . From it the horses were born and also those animals who have double rows of teeth; cows were born from it, from it were born goats and sheep.

When they divided Purusha, in how many different portions did they arrange him? What became of his mouth, what of his two arms? What were his two thighs and his two feet called?

His mouth became the brahmin; his arms were made into the rajanya; his two thighs the vaishyas; from his two feet the shudra was born.

The moon was born from his mind, from the eye the sun was born; from the mouth Indra and Agni [Vedic gods], from the breath the wind was born.

From the navel was the atmosphere created, from the head the heaven issued forth; from the two feet was born the earth and the quarters [the cardinal directions] from the ear. Thus did they fashion the worlds.

. . . With this sacrificial oblation did the gods offer the sacrifice. These were the first norms [dharma] of sacrifice. These greatnesses reached to the sky wherein live the ancient *Sadhyas* and gods.

From Ainslie T. Embree, ed., *Sources of Indian Tradition*, Vol. 1, 2nd ed. (New York: Columbia University Press, 1988), pp. 18–19.

such material gains as long life, health, many offspring, victory in war, and life in the "bright place in the sky" (heaven). The god worshipped most in the *Rig-Veda* was Indra, storm-god and patron of warriors, who is described as leading the Aryans in destroying the forts of the Dasas. Virile and boisterous, Indra personified the heroic virtues of the Aryan warrior aristocracy as he drove his chariot across the sky, wielded his thunderbolts, ate the meat of sacrificed bulls and buffaloes by the score, and quaffed entire lakes of the stimulating ritual drink *soma*.

Next to Indra in popularity was Agni, the benevolent god of fire, who performed many services for the mobile Aryans, not least of which was conveying their ritual offerings up to the other gods. Another major Aryan god was Varuna, the sky-god. Viewed as the king of the gods, he lived in a great palace in the heavens where one of his associates was a sun-god, Mitra, known as Mithras to the Persians and, a thousand years later, widely worshipped in the Roman Empire. Varuna was the guardian of *rita*, the "right order of things." *Rita* is both the cosmic law of nature (the regularity of the seasons, for example) and the customary tribal law of the Aryans.

The *Rig-Veda* is the earliest surviving Indo-European work of literature, and it gives some insight into the institutions and ideas of the Early Vedic Age. Each tribe was headed by a war leader called *raja*, a word closely related to the Latin word for king, *rex*. (Latin and Sanskrit are both Indo-European lan-

guages.) Like the early kings of Sumer, Greece, and Rome, the *raja* was only the first among equals. Two tribal assemblies, one a small council of the great men of the tribe and the other a larger gathering of the heads of families, approved his accession to office and advised him on important matters.

The hymns in the *Rig-Veda* mention three social classes, the Brahmins, the Kshatriyas (nobility), and the Vaishyas (commoners). Aryan peoples elsewhere, such as the Romans and the Celts, seem to have had a similar social structure. A fourth class, the Shudras, the non-Aryan conquered population of workers and serfs, was then added at the bottom of the social scale. In one of the later hymns of the *Rig-Veda*, these four social classes are mapped out on the body of the Cosmic Man, Purusha.

The Later Vedic Age, c. 1000–600 B.C.E.

Most of our knowledge about the years between 1000 and 500 B.C.E. derives from two great bodies of literature: religious texts the Brahmins composed during this period—three later *Vedas*, Vedic ritual encyclopedias called *Brahmanas*, and the early *Upanishads*, Brahmin texts teaching a mystical way to gain personal beatitude—and various texts composed in the bustling new period that displaced the Vedic age, including the early texts of Buddhism, a new anti-Brahmin and anti-Vedic religion; a manual on royal government called the *Arthashastra;* and two epics that first articulated the religious and cultural synthesis that is called Hinduism today, the *Mahabharata* and the *Ramayana.* All these texts tell us a great deal about religious and philosophical thought during this time, but what we know of this period's political, social, and economic institutions we must glean from religious texts or infer from the convergence of the archaeological record with the later texts.

By about 1000 B.C.E. the Aryans had occupied the critical territory that lies between the Indus watershed and the Ganges watershed. During the Later Vedic Age they continued their movement both to the east, passing into the Doab ("land of two rivers") between the Yamuna and the Ganges and on down the Ganges valley, and to the south, toward the Vindhya Mountains. The area between the two watersheds came to be known as Kurukshetra ("the field of King Kuru"), and it became the sacred heartland of the Aryans in the Later Vedic Age. Kurukshetra was the site of the fabled Bharata war (the story of which is told in the *Mahabharata*), and many other battles critical to the history of India over the next 3000 years were fought in this vicinity. The sense of space, particularly sacred space, is very important in Indian thought; and the ways such spaces have been articulated remain a critical factor in Indian politics today (see Chapter 36).

This era seems to have been a golden age for the Brahmins and their Vedic religion. During this period some of the hymns of the *Rig-Veda* were set to melodies (called *samans*) collected in a separate *Veda* called the *Sama-Veda.* Other parts of the *Rig-Veda* were formed into the prayers of the *Yajur-Veda.* Different families of Brahmins would specialize in learning one or the other of these three *Vedas;* spectacularly large *soma* sacrifices developed that employed Brahmins of each kind. A fourth *Veda,* the *Atharva-Veda,* was formed from a large collection of sacred formulas that, when correctly uttered, were supposed to solve many of life's mundane problems: baldness, impotence, skin rashes, and so on.

As the number of Brahmin priests and *Vedas* increased, the focus of Vedic religion shifted from the gods to the power of the sacrifice itself, and especially to the holy energy contained in the sacred words of the different Vedic songs, chants, recitations, and prayers. The Brahmins' perfect singing or chanting of Vedic verses (now called *mantras*) came to be regarded as the embodiment of the sacred energy at the heart of the ritual—the energy, called *brahman,* that kept the world going, the energy that had brought the world into being.

The Brahmins composed, now in prose rather than verse, a whole new kind of text, the *Brahmanas,* which explained the philosophy of the rituals and the background meaning and use of the Vedic mantras

employed in the rituals. During the Early Vedic Age sacrifice had been a means of influencing the gods in favor of the offerer; now in the later Vedic Age the Brahmins regarded sacrifices to the gods as working automatically to produce the good results people wanted, provided that the ritual was performed exactly right. The sacrifices brought long life, many sons, victory over one's enemies, general prosperity, and heaven; they made the world a good place for all beings. Since only the priests possessed the knowledge to perform the complex and lengthy rites of sacrifice (a few of which could last for months), and since the slightest variation in ritual was thought to bring harm to the people and the land, the Brahmins gained great prestige and power.

By the beginning of the Later Vedic Age the Aryans had acquired iron metallurgy, which may have reached India via the Middle East. As in other parts of the world, iron-based tools and weapons increased the potential for agricultural exploitation of the land and made warriors with access to the technology more deadly and effective. These developments set the stage for the development in the eastern Ganges valley of cities, territory-based kingdoms, standing armies, and stronger institutions of kingship. Although some Indian kingdoms in this period were oligarchic republics, most were ruled by rajas, *maharajas* ("great kings"), or *samrajas* ("universal kings," as some called themselves). Despite the preservation of advisory councils of nobles and priests, the kings' powers were greater than those of the tribal leaders of the earlier period. They now lived in palaces and collected taxes—in the form of goods from the villages—in order to sustain their courts and armies. The cities that arose were often administrative centers connected with a palace, and some were also commercial centers.

Dramatic Developments in Religion and Culture, 600–320 B.C.E.

Out of all these new political and economic developments came dramatic cultural changes that after 600 B.C.E. elevated an entirely different kind of religion to highest status and eventually gave rise to whole new religions that challenged Brahmin hegemony and created important new institutions. The first of these developments was the composition of the earliest *Upanishads* around 600 B.C.E. The second was the rise of the new non-Vedic, even anti-Vedic, monastic religions of Jainism and Buddhism sometime in the fifth century B.C.E.

Around 600 B.C.E. a radical minority of Brahmins embraced ascetic and mystical religious ideas and

Developments in Culture and Religion in India

c. 600 B.C.E.	Earliest *Upanishads*
c. 527 (perhaps as late as 447) B.C.E.	Death of Mahavira
c. 481 (perhaps as late as 400) B.C.E.	Death of Gautama Buddha
c. 300 B.C.E.	Jainism gains support in North and South India

practices (early forms of *yoga,* "spiritual discipline," usually involving some kind of meditation) that ultimately rejected the goals and means of Vedic ritual religion and the settled village and family life that Vedic religion presumed. Some of these radical mystics recorded the *Upanishads,* which taught "secret, mystical understandings" of the human body, the breath, the mind, and the soul. The most important of these understandings was the assertion that the light of consciousness within a person was nothing less than the undiluted energy of *brahman,* the eternal, sacred creative energy that is the source and the end of all that exists (tantamount to God in monotheistic religions).

Most of the *Upanishads* taught that all things that exist—from the most sublime ideas a person could think to the hardest, densest, crudest forms of matter—came from brahman and eventually returned to brahman, which is the only permanent reality. Beyond these ideas, the *Upanishads* taught a way for ethically pure, worthy persons (usually only Aryans, but not necessarily just Brahmins) to immerse themselves into brahman, which the *Upanishads* described as unsurpassably blissful. These ideas gained great power after their presentation in the *Upanishads;* a relatively tiny minority of people followed this yoga (most Aryans continued to avail themselves of Brahmin priests and Vedic rituals), but the basic ideas, values, and meditative techniques came to be regarded as the supreme form of Brahmin religion.

In addition to these mystical ideas, the *Upanishads* introduced the idea of the transmigration of the soul, which was entirely new in Brahmin thought. (Some scholars have speculated that this idea was part of the culture of some of the indigenous Indians, but there is no solid evidence of this.) As with most other Indo-European peoples, the Vedic Brahmins had thought that people live only once and that the fate of their soul is determined in that one

life. (The same general idea is found in all three of the Western Abrahamic religions, Judaism, Christianity, and Islam.) Vedic Aryans hoped to live up in the heavens with the sky-gods after their death. In the *Brahmanas,* the idea was put forward that a person's deeds (especially ethically significant deeds, and sacrificial offerings in particular) stayed with him or her in the form of an unseen power that would act after that person's death and condition the fate of the departed soul. A deed or action was called *karman* in Sanskrit, and the unseen power of past deeds was called *karman* as well (*karma* in contemporary English).

The latest *Brahmana* texts sometimes express a fear that people "die again"—the accumulation of their good works, their good karma, supports them in heaven when they die, but the karma gets used up keeping the soul in heaven, and the soul then "dies" again, in heaven. This fear leads directly to the idea that when the soul dies in heaven, it descends to earth, reincarnated in another body. This new person lives and dies, and the soul goes to heaven once again, if the earthly actions of this latest lifetime have been good (that is, if they conformed with the law, or *dharma,* as revealed in the *Vedas*). Bad deeds, bad karma, lead the soul to hell.

Eventually, rebirth in subhuman forms of life was seen as a natural consequence of violating dharma; after living a life as some kind of animal, a soul automatically moves up the ladder of life forms toward an eventual human incarnation because animals cannot violate dharma. The rebirth of the soul in a new body is called *samsara,* and the *Upanishads* regarded continual, unending samsara as a dreary prospect. The *Upanishads* taught that good deeds, including Vedic rituals, could do nothing more for a person than provide a temporary spell in heaven between incarnations. Bad deeds, of course, had far more unpleasant consequences; but worse than either hell or heaven was the prospect of living, acting, and dying over and over, forever without end. In the face of this bleak prospect, the *Upanishads* said the only truly good thing to do is try to escape perpetual samsara (escape from samsara was called *moksha*) and gain the immortality of reimmersing oneself in *brahman.* Gaining moksha involves permanently escaping from karma, from samsara, and from all the pain and suffering encountered in countless lives. According to the *Upanishads,* the only effective way to gain moksha is to accomplish the reimmersion of oneself into brahman. By permanently immersing oneself in brahman through meditation, a person dissolves the soul back into the holy oneness that is its ultimate source and end. The soul has "returned home"—its journey through samsara is over.

The *Upanishads* depict the first Indian gurus wandering in the forests as ascetics; there they

The Jains on the Souls in All Things

The Jains, like the Buddhists, believe in conquering desire as a way of achieving Enlightenment and escaping from the cyle of rebirth. But the Jains emphasize the existence of souls in all living things. All beings experience pleasure, pain, terror, and unhappiness. Hence Jain texts reveal a heightened sensitivity to the pain man can inflict by harming all things, animate and inanimate. This verse passage is taken from a Jain text depicting the speech of a prince trying to persuade his parents to allow him to take up a life of religion.

*From clubs and knives, stakes and maces, breaking
 my limbs,
An infinite number of times I have suffered without
 hope.
By keen edged razors, by knives and shears,
Many times I have been drawn and quartered, torn
 apart and skinned.
Helpless in snares and traps, a deer,
 I have been caught and bound and fastened, and
 often I have been killed.
A helpless fish, I have been caught with hooks and
 nets;
An infinite number of times I have been killed and
 scraped, split and gutted.
A bird, I have been caught by hawks or trapped in
 nets,
Or held fast by birdlime, and I have been killed an
 infinite number of times.*

*A tree, with axes and adzes by the carpenters
An infinite number of times I have been felled,
 stripped of my bark, cut up, and sawn into
 planks.
As iron, with hammer and tongs by blacksmiths
An infinite number of times I have been struck
 and beaten, split and filed. . . .
Ever afraid, trembling in pain and suffering,
I have felt the utmost sorrow and agony. . . .
In every kind of existence I have suffered
Pains that have scarcely known reprieve for a
 moment.*

From Ainslie T. Embree, ed., *Sources of Indian Tradition,* Vol. 1, 2nd ed. (New York: Columbia University Press, 1988), pp. 62–63.

meditated and taught their disciples. One of them summed up their quest as follows:

*From the unreal lead me to the real!
From darkness lead me to light!
From death lead me to immortality!*

The Jains, Defenders of All Beings

One of the two non-Vedic religions that emerged in this period, Jainism, is the "most Indian" religion of India. The Jains contributed to all of India (and today to the rest of the world) the unique ethical claim that the most important duty of a person is to cause no harm or pain to any being that can feel pain (this ethical value is called *ahimsa,* "nonviolence"). The Jains made this duty the center of their ideal of ethical behavior. The Buddhists readily agreed with the Jains about ahimsa, and they too stressed its central importance. Many, but not all, Brahmins and their followers eventually did likewise.

The most significant figure in Jain belief is Mahavira, the faith's last great teacher. His name means "the greatest of fierce, tough, heroic men" (*vira* is related to such English words as *virile*). He is called the Jina ("victor," "conqueror"), and his followers are called Jainas (those who "follow the Jina"), hence the

Western name Jainism for the religion as a whole. According to Jain tradition, Mahavira was a Kshatriya prince who at the age of 30 renounced the world—his home and family and all property and status that went with them.

For over a dozen years Mahavira followed the teachings of the earlier religious teacher Parshvanatha, whom Jainism regards as the twenty-third of the *tirthamkaras* ("ford-makers," who aid their followers in crossing the swirling flood of *samsara,* the cycle of rebirth). For these 12 years Mahavira wandered naked from place to place, lived on handouts, engaged in meditation, debated with other men also on holy quests, observed celibacy, and engaged in various painful ascetic practices in order to purify his *jiva* ("soul") of past karma. Nudity was a form of asceticism because it invited the painful ridicule of ordinary people. In his thirteenth year of asceticism Mahavira escaped the bondage of all his past karma.

Mahavira gained a great reputation as a wise and holy man, attracting many followers. At the age of 80 he died after deliberately seating himself in the posture of meditation with the intention of never moving again. This deliberate form of death by inaction is seen not as an act of suicide but as the most heroic and ascetic form of nonaction humanly possible. For those whose souls are still fouled with karma, this mode of death was regarded as highly purifying, and many Jain saints have died this way throughout history.

The Jains accept the reality of samsara and karma and regard moksha to be the only sensible goal to pursue in life; but their way of pursuing moksha was very different from that of the Brahmins of the *Upanishads*. The path to moksha that Mahavira preached centers on the practice of asceticism, although one does not have to practice the most rigorous forms to be considered a pious Jain. To gain moksha a Jain must sooner or later, in this life or a future life, renounce the world and become a wandering monk or nun. But a person may be a pious lay Jaina, supporting the monks and nuns with handouts of food, clothing, and shelter and living a life that conforms to the Jain ethic (which emphasizes nonviolence but also forbids liquor, sex outside of marriage, lying, and stealing) until he or she is convinced that the time for renunciation has come. The practice of nudity gradually died out over the centuries.

Jainism places a special emphasis on the idea that all beings (including plants, insects, and minerals) have souls and experience pain. Thus causing pain to any other sentient beings is the biggest source of the worst possible karma. Jain texts, for example, explain in graphic detail the suffering caused to the tiny beings living in wood when it is cast upon the fire. While it is inevitable that a believer will cause pain (by drinking water and the beings that are in it, for example), a person should avoid such destructive acts as much as possible. Jains who practice their faith most rigorously gently sweep the path before them with a broom as they walk, to avoid stepping on living things; they may tie cloths over their mouths to avoid inhaling any small creatures in the air.

Mahavira was the final tirthamkara of the current age of the world. Jains believe he was the twenty-fourth and last great tirthamkara in a long series of wise and powerful men who had shown people how to purify their souls and permanently separate them from the evils of perpetual samsara. Mahavira lived in the sixth or fifth century B.C.E. Jains believe he died in 527 B.C.E., but modern, non-Jain historians believe that date is too early.

In connection with their belief that Mahavira was only the last of twenty-four tirthamkaras, Jains believe that time revolves in endless cycles like a great cosmic wheel. In every era tirthamkaras like Mahavira are born to teach the doctrines of Jainism to humanity. Every era consists of millions of years. The Jains also believe that when a soul gains moksha and escapes the cycle of rebirth forever, it ascends to the topmost point of the universe, where it exists in complete purity forever. This differs dramatically from the idea of the *Upanishads* that every individual's soul is completely submerged into brahman, the single "soul" of the whole universe.

Socially, Jainism rejected the sacredness of the *Vedas* and thereby rejected the social stratification that assigned preeminence to the Brahmins. Interestingly, Jainism was the first Indian religion formally to allow women to become renouncers and pursue moksha as nuns. With some reluctance the Buddha belatedly allowed Buddhist laywomen to become nuns; and although some Hindu women did renounce the world from time to time, the Hindu dharma (Sacred Law) never formally sanctioned their doing so.

In the centuries after Mahavira the number of Jains has always been significant but never tremendously large. In spite of always being a minority religion in India, however, the Jains have consistently exerted greater influence than their numbers would lead anyone to expect. By 300 B.C.E. Jainism had gained significant political recognition in various kingdoms of North and South India. Also, because the ethics of their religion basically forbade farming for pious lay followers of the Jina (because tilling the soil kills so many small creatures), lay Jains were usually merchants living in cities. Lay Jains often became wealthy and often poured much of their wealth into the support of their religion. As a result, the Jain religion has contributed a great number of learned Jain scholars and libraries to India's cultural history.

The Middle Way of Gautama Buddha

About the same time that Mahavira lived, another ascetic and monastic religion arose in northern India. This religion, Buddhism, became tremendously popular and important in India and remained influential there for many centuries. It also spread outside India to all of Asia and today continues its expansion around the globe. Buddhism had some basic similarities to Jainism, but its root ideas were profoundly different. Both religions derive from the life and teachings of a great man; both stress the humanity of their teacher and do not rely on gods or divine rites to pursue the highest goal of life; both developed extensive monastic institutions in which many celibate men and women lived in spiritual communities, supported by a devoted laity. But there is a very archaic quality to many Jain doctrines, due probably to the fact that the Jain religion was never taken up by people outside of India. Buddhist doctrines, by contrast, seem very modern in certain ways, which may in part account for Buddhism's appeal to non-Indian peoples, including Europeans and Americans in the twentieth century.

Whereas Jainism stresses purification of the soul and ascetic pain and its leader is described in military terms as a "great hero" and "victor," Buddhism's founder was a man whose leadership was the result of his "waking up," having his understanding boosted to a higher level of insight. The word *buddha* means basically "someone who has awakened from sleep." Buddhists see the Buddha's Great Awakening *(Bodhi)* as the greatest discovery of the truth of life that has ever been made. As Jains follow Mahavira's soldierly example, Buddhists seek to use the Buddha's example and his teachings so that they too may wake up and realize the benefits of Awakening (often also called Enlightenment).

The man who became the Buddha was born Siddhartha Gautama, a prince of the Shakyas, whose small oligarchic state was located at the foot of the Himalayas. As with many of the world's great figures, the traditional accounts of the Buddha's life contain many legends and miracles. Accordingly, Gautama was conceived when his mother dreamed one night that a white elephant entered her right side. Later the baby was born from her right side, and right after birth the baby stood up and announced that this would be his last life. Seers predicted that Gautama would become either a great king or a great sage who would see four special sights of human suffering—a sick man, an old man, a dead man, and an ascetic holy man seeking to escape suffering—after which he would renounce the world and discover a way to relieve the world's suffering. The traditions tell us that Gautama's father, King Shuddodana, raised him in bounteous luxury and went to great lengths to prevent the prince from ever seeing the sick, the old, or the dead.

In the prince's twenty-ninth year, however, all his father's protections proved vain in the face of fate: on three separate occasions the prince happened to see a sick man, an old man, and a dead man. He was deeply moved and troubled to learn, from his chariot driver, that all people suffer these ghastly problems. He then happened to see a wandering ascetic who was in quest of moksha, and this encounter made him think very deeply about pursuing freedom from life's suffering himself. To his father's great disappointment, Gautama decided to follow that ascetic's example. He renounced his wealth and position, forsaking his wife and child.

Gautama studied meditation for a year with two different teachers, abandoning both after a while because their doctrines were not sufficient. Then, like Mahavira, he took up the most painful and demanding forms of asceticism and practiced them with great determination and devotion. Gautama almost died from this fasting and self-torture, and after five years he concluded that the end of suffering lay in changing the mind but that ascetic practices only weakened the mind.

Gautama left his ascetic companions, who ridiculed him for his "weakness," walked down to a river and had his first bath in five years, and sat down under an expansive banyan tree (the Indian fig tree) to rest in the cool shade. (Asceticism was regarded as a kind of purifying heat by ancient Indians.) Gautama was then offered a refreshing meal by a rich woman who offered a special meal once a year to the spirit of that tree. Clean, refreshed, and reinvigorated by food, Gautama was vibrantly awake as night fell. He sat up meditating all through the night; as the night progressed, his mind examined the world and its workings, and he came to understand more and more the fundamental causes for all that happens. Shortly before the dawn he attained the key insights for understanding and then eliminating suffering, but not, according to legendary tradition, before the demon Mara (Death) and his daughters Greed, Lust, and Anger did all in their powers to prevent his grasping the truth.

Gautama summarized the truth to which he "woke up" during this Great Awakening as the Four Noble Truths, which succinctly express the entire system of Buddhist thought. The religious way of life to which the Four Noble Truths lead is often called the Middle Way—it is the way of life that is in between the normal human life of sensation, desire, and action, on the one hand, and harsh asceticism, on the other. The Middle Way involves the moderate asceticism of renunciation, celibacy, and the Buddhist monastic way of life as opposed to the much more rigorous asceticism of Indian groups such as the Jains. The whole philosophy, which the Buddha taught to others, and the religious way of life to which those ideas lead is referred to in Buddhism as the Dharma. (The root sense of *dharma* for Hindus is "religious law" or "religious good deeds leading to a good afterlife"; Dharma, for Buddhists, has a broader meaning.)

Buddha's Four Noble Truths are these:

1. Suffering dominates our experience.
2. The cause of suffering is desire or craving.
3. It is possible to extinguish suffering by extinguishing its cause, thereby attaining *nirvana* (*nirvana* originally referred to a fire's going out; the Buddha's idea was to let the fire of desire go out by depriving it of its normal fuel).
4. The Noble Eightfold Path leads to the extinction of desire—that is, it leads to nirvana.

The Noble Eightfold Path consists of pursuing the following eight ideals:

1. *Right views*—the intellectual conviction that the Four Noble Truths are "the Truth"
2. *Right resolve*—the decision to act according to the Four Noble Truths
3. *Right speech*—having words be governed by the Five Moral Precepts of right conduct: do not harm

any living being (ahimsa); do not take what is not given to you; do not speak falsely; do not drink intoxicating drinks; do not be sexually unchaste

4. *Right conduct*—having deeds, like words, be governed by the Five Moral Precepts
5. *Right livelihood*—conducting oneself ethically even in earning a living; hence such occupations as farming, soldiering, prostitution, and tavern-keeping are disallowed
6. *Right effort*—following the path with all one's heart and energy by renouncing the world and becoming a monk or nun
7. *Right mindfulness*—a form of meditation that eventually produces "wisdom"; wisdom undermines desire because the wise person no longer sees his or her own self as particularly important in the world
8. *Right concentration*—a form of meditation that uses trances to make the nonrational and unconscious layers of the person completely calm and tranquil

Buddhism claims that desire is extinguished and nirvana attained when steps 7 and 8 of the path have been perfected—that is, when the person on the path has the wisdom to see that he or she is just one more sentient being among many and is no more valuable or important than any other (this removes the natural instinct to fight for success and even survival) and when "concentration meditation" has stilled all the powerful impulses and drives that condition every sentient being's mind. A person who has reached this nirvana of desire simply looks at his or her own condition at any given moment as "what is" and does not wish it to be otherwise, is not driven to improve it, does not envy anyone else, and does not suffer (physical pain may be present, but the person who has reached nirvana is dissociated from it and simply sees it as one more fact of the situation of the moment). Nirvana is a happy, friendly state (in which the Buddha lived for 45 years after his Awakening), but it is not an "altered state" of consciousness and certainly not a paradise or any kind of heavenly world.

Since in Buddhist thought the essential element of action is the desire to get something for oneself, a person who has extinguished desire no longer performs actions, even if his or her body may be going through the motions. In other words, such a person accumulates no karma and has escaped the round of samsara. For Buddhists this nirvana amounts to gaining moksha. As for the question of what comes after the devotee escapes the cycle of rebirth, the Buddha told his followers that the question could not be answered and was pointless anyway. Such a question "tends not to edify"; that is, it does not contribute to the one important goal. The only important thing a person can do in life is deal with suffering.

Dressed in a simple yellow robe, with begging bowl in hand, Gautama wandered through the plain of the Ganges, speaking with everyone (regardless of social class) and attracting disciples to a growing community (called the Sangha) of monks walking the Path. He taught many sermons (the Sutras) and laid down the Rules specifying many details of the monks' daily life (the Vinaya, analogous to the much later Rule of St. Benedict). Resisting at first, Buddha eventually acquiesced to demands that women be allowed to renounce the world and pursue the path and its advanced meditations on a full-time basis as nuns. Buddhist history states that while the Buddha lived, it was relatively easy to accomplish the nirvana of desire and suffering and that a great number of disciples actually did so.

At last, 80 years old and enfeebled, the Buddha was invited by a poor blacksmith to a meal. According to legend, the food included tainted mushrooms, but Gautama ate the meal rather than offend his host. Later in the day the Buddha had severe pains, and he knew death was near. Calling his disciples together, he gave them this parting message: "Be ye lamps unto yourselves. Be a refuge to yourselves. Hold fast to the truth as to a lamp. Look not for refuge to anyone beside yourselves." The Buddha had instructed that his body be burned. His followers, according to legend, quarreled over possession of his ashes, which were divided into eight parts and ensconced in shrines called *stupas*. There are now stupas all over South Asia. In spite of the Buddha's emphasis on correct understanding and on changing oneself through one's own efforts, his followers developed a profound affection for him and were very attached to him. After his death (even to some extent during his life) many of his followers saw him as a true holy man and believed that mere contact with him would somehow benefit them. What the Buddha taught is a philosophy, but the movement we call Buddhism is a religion.

The Buddha, the Dharma he taught, and the Sangha, the community of Buddha's followers, are regarded by Buddhists as the Three Precious Jewels. People did, and still do, officially become members of the Sangha by publicly declaring that they "take shelter in the Buddha, take shelter in the Dharma, and take shelter in the Sangha." As in the Jain religion, the majority of the community are laypeople who live in the world until they sense the time is right to take the sixth step of the path, right effort, and become a monk or a nun. (In some Buddhist countries, lay Buddhists often make short retreats to a monastery for instruction from the monks and practice in meditation.) In addition to restricting their speech, conduct, and livelihood by the Five Moral Precepts, they cultivate the virtues of generosity, friendliness, and compassion. Only people with great amounts of good karma ever hear the Buddhist teachings; people with even better accumulations of karma understand those teachings when they hear them; people with more good karma actually reach the path; and only those with more good karma possess the courage and determination actually to become a monk or a nun. In the end one does not want any karma at all, good or bad, but whatever good karma a lay Buddhist accumulates will help carry that person further along the Path in this or a future life.

Buddhists who became monks or nuns donned the yellow (or orange) robe worn by all renouncers in India except the Jains (who wore white if they wore anything). Unlike their Hindu and Jain counterparts—who usually lived alone or in small assemblies without any Rule—Buddhist renouncers created the world's first monastic communities, in which people pursuing spiritual goals lived together under strict rules. Often the Buddhists lived in caves that rich lay Buddhists had cut into the sides of mountains or rock cliffs. Their only possessions were their sandals, robe, and begging bowl. They ate only one meal a day and ate only what they had begged as a handout. Periodically all the monks in a given area recited together all the rules of monastic life, and anyone who had violated any rule was required to make a public confession. Four sins warranted permanent expulsion from the community: fornication, stealing, murder, and making false claims of one's spiritual attainments. Large parts of the day were given over to the two kinds of meditation, and monks who had accomplished nirvana were known as *arhats* ("worthy ones").

The Buddha was a critic of all religious and philosophical thinkers who came before him in India. He censured the *Vedas* and the rites of the Brahmins, considered the *Upanishads* wrong about brahman, and thought Mahavira's religion of ascetic purification futile. The Buddha took an agnostic stance on what really might lie beyond this world; he claimed that we, as finite, conditioned beings, had no way of knowing anything about infinite, unconditioned beings. He thought that anyone, regardless of social status, could gain nirvana, but he did not try to change Indian society. Though Sudras and women were admitted to Buddhist monasteries, those monasteries tended to mirror the structures and habits of the larger Indian society.

As with Mahavira, there is great uncertainty about exactly when the man who became the Buddha died. Buddhists have traditionally taught that he died in 526 B.C.E. Modern, non-Buddhist historians believed for many decades that 481 B.C.E. was a more accurate date. Current historical scholarship is energetically reconsidering this date and pushing it down toward 400 B.C.E. Whatever the exact dates of Gautama Buddha and his contemporary Mahavira, both lived and taught in eastern India as powerful new kingdoms were in the process of turning into the Mauryan Empire (inaugurated about 320 B.C.E.).

The Mauryan Empire and Its Aftermath, 320 B.C.E.–300 C.E.

The Aryan invaders of India had established 16 major kingdoms and tribal oligarchies in northern India, stretching from modern Pakistan to Bengal. Then a new invader appeared over the mountains of the northwest, preparing the way for the establishment of the first Indian empire. Celebrated in the legends of East and West alike, his name was Alexander. Continuing his conquest of the Persian Empire (see Chapter 3), Alexander the Great in 326 B.C.E. brought his phalanxes into the easternmost Persian province in the Indus valley, defeating local Punjabi rulers. When his weary troops refused to advance further eastward into the Ganges plain, Alexander constructed a fleet and explored the Indus to its mouth. From there he returned overland to Babylon while his fleet skirted the coast of the Arabian Sea and reached the Persian Gulf.

After Alexander's death in 323 B.C.E., the empire he had built so rapidly quickly disintegrated, and within two years his domain in the Punjab had completely disappeared. He had, however, opened routes between India and the West that would remain in use during the following Hellenistic and Roman periods, and by destroying the petty states in the Punjab, he facilitated—and perhaps inspired—the conquests of India's own first emperor.

Chandragupta Maurya, India's First Emperor

A new era began in India in 321 B.C.E., when Chandragupta Maurya seized the state of Magadha in the Ganges valley. Chandragupta conquered northern

The Mauryan Empire

326 B.C.E.	Alexander the Great invades India
321 B.C.E.	Chandragupta seizes Magadha
305 B.C.E.	Chandragupta defeats Seleucus
268–233 B.C.E.	Reign of Ashoka
c. 185 B.C.E.	Brahmin-led revolt against last Maurya emperor

India and founded the Mauryan dynasty, which endured until about 185 B.C.E. At its height the empire included all the subcontinent except the extreme south.

India's first empire reflected the imperial vision of its founder. Chandragupta created an administrative system of remarkable efficiency. He was also a brilliant general. In 312 B.C.E. Seleucus, the general who had inherited the major part of Alexander the Great's empire, crossed the Indus in an attempt to regain his predecessor's Indian conquests. But in 305 B.C.E. Chandragupta soundly defeated him, and Seleucus ceded all territories east of Kabul to the Indian monarch in return for an alliance and 500 war elephants.

Life in the Mauryan Empire

Seleucus's ambassador to the court of Chandragupta, whose name was Megasthenes, wrote a detailed account of India, fragments of which have survived. They give a fascinating picture of life in the empire. Chandragupta's capital, Pataliputra (known today as Patna), covered 18 square miles and was probably the largest city in the world. Outside its massive wooden walls was a deep trench used for defense and the disposal of sewage.

The remarkably advanced Mauryan Empire was divided and subdivided into provinces, districts, and villages whose headmen were appointed by the state. The old customary law, preserved and administered by the Brahmin priesthood, was superseded by an extensive legal code that provided for royal interference in all matters. A series of courts, ranging from the village court presided over by the headman to the emperor's imperial court, administered the law. So busy was Chandragupta with the details of his highly organized administration that, according to Megasthenes, he had to hear court cases during his daily massage.

Two other factors struck Megasthenes as important in the adminstration of the empire. One was the professional army, which he reports was an enormous force of 700,000 men, 9000 elephants, and 10,000 chariots. The other was the secret police, whose numbers were so large that the Greek writer concluded that spies constituted a separate class in Indian society. Chandragupta, fearing conspiracies, was said to have lived in strict seclusion, attended only by women who cooked his food and in the evening bore him to his apartment, where they lulled him to sleep with music.

Of course, the historian cannot take literally the details or the numbers in Megasthenes' account. They were impressionistic and designed to create certain effects on his audience at home. Ambassadors had limited knowledge of and exposure to the daily lives of kings, and stories of rulers and their female companions are often myths based on hearsay and conjecture. Furthermore, the counts of armies, especially of one's enemies, tended to be inflated. Nonetheless, it is clear that Megasthenes was impressed by the urban development, political organization, and military force of Chandragupta's empire.

Another source of information on Chandragupta's reign is a remarkable book, the *Arthashastra,* or *Treatise on Material Gain,* written by Kautilya as a guide for the king and his ministers. Kautilya, said to be Chandragupta's chief adviser, exalted royal power as the means of establishing and maintaining "material gain," meaning political and economic stability. The great evil, according to the *Arthashastra,* is anarchy, such as had existed among the small warring states in northern India. To achieve the aims of statecraft, Kautilya argued, a single authority is needed who will employ force when necessary.

The *Arthashastra* is an early example of a whole genre of literature, sometimes called "mirrors for princes," that provided advice to monarchs on the best and most effective ways to rule. Later examples are found in the Middle East and Europe—for example, the medieval Persian work of Qai Qaus and that of the Renaissance author Machiavelli. Machiavelli, like Kautilya, would advocate deception or unscrupulous means to attain desired ends. The *Arthashastra* remains in print today and has been translated into many languages. Modern leaders have been known to consult its pages.

The Mauryan state also controlled and encouraged economic life. Kautilya's treatise, which is thought to reflect much actual practice, advises the ruler to "facilitate mining operations," "encourage manufacturers," "exploit forest wealth," "provide amenities" for cattle breeding and commerce, and "construct highways both on land and on water." Price controls are advocated because "all goods should be sold to the people at favorable prices," and foreign trade should be subsidized: "Shippers and traders dealing in foreign goods should be given tax exemptions to aid them in making profits." Foreign trade did flourish, and in the bazaars of Pataliputra were displayed goods from southern India, China, Mesopotamia, and Asia Minor. Agriculture, however, remained the chief source of wealth. Irrigation and crop rotation were practiced, and Megasthenes states that there were no famines. In theory, all land belonged to the state, which collected one-fourth of the produce as taxes.

Ashoka, India's Greatest King

Following Chandragupta's death, his son and grandson expanded the Mauryan Empire southward into the Deccan peninsula. His grandson, Ashoka (d. 233 B.C.E.), the most renowned of all Indian rulers, how-

Ashoka left a written record of his reign inscribed on rocks and stone pillars all over the Mauryan Empire.

ever, was more committed to peace than to war. His first military campaign was also his last; the cruelty of the campaign horrified him, and he resolved never again to permit such acts of butchery. Ashoka converted to Buddhism and became a dedicated proponent of nonviolence (ahimsa). The story of Ashoka's horror at the carnage of war is similar in some ways to the account of Yudhishthira in the *Mahabharata*, which also relates a king's remorse in the aftermath of battle.

Throughout his empire, Ashoka had his edicts carved on rocks and stone pillars. They remain today as the oldest surviving written documents of India and are especially valuable for appreciating the spirit and purpose of Ashoka's rule. For example, they contain his conception of the duty of a ruler:

> He shall . . . personally attend the business . . . of earth, of sacred places, of minors, the aged, the afflicted, and the helpless, and of women. . . . In the happiness of his subjects lies his happiness.[1]

Although Ashoka made Buddhism India's state religion, he did not persecute the Brahmins and Hindus but proclaimed religious toleration as an official policy:

> The king . . . honors every form of religious faith . . . ; whereof this is the root, to reverence one's own faith and never to revile that of others. Whoever acts differently injures his own religion while he wrongs another's.[2]

Ashoka was a successful propagator of his faith. He supported the building of temples and stupas all over his empire, and the remains of many are still standing. He sent Buddhist missionaries to various lands—the Himalayan regions, Tamil Land (India's far south), Sri Lanka (Ceylon), Burma, and even as far away as Syria and Egypt, transforming Buddhism from a small Indian sect to an aggressive missionary faith. Modern Indians revere his memory, and the famous lion on the capital of one of his pillars has been adopted as the national seal of the present Indian republic.

Fall of the Mauryan Empire

Almost immediately after Ashoka's death in 233 B.C.E., the Mauryan Empire began to disintegrate. The last emperor was assassinated about 185 B.C.E. in a palace revolution led by a Brahmin priest. Once again the subcontinent was politically fragmented. Northern India was overrun by a series of invaders, and the south broke free from northern control.

The sudden collapse of the powerful Mauryan state and the grave consequences that ensued have provoked much scholarly speculation. Some historians have believed that the fall of the Mauryans can be traced to a hostile Brahmin reaction against Ashoka's patronage of Buddhism. Others believe that Ashoka's inclination toward nonviolence curbed the military ardor of his people and left them vulnerable to invaders. More plausible explanations for the fall of the Mauryan state take into account the transportation and communications problems facing an empire that spanned most of the Indian subcontinent, the difficulty of financing a vast army and bureaucracy, and the intrigues of discontented regional groups within the empire.

In fact, one might argue that political division is a more natural state for large multiethnic, multilingual landmasses with diverse terrain; empires that endure and unite vast expanses of territory are the exception. No one person could directly rule all of the subcontinent; like the later Roman and Ottoman Empires elsewhere, the Mauryan kingdom survived through a combination of talented leadership, economic success, flexible rule, and delegated authority.

Bactrian Greeks and Kushans

The Mauryan Empire was the first of two successful attempts to unify India in ancient times. The second—the work of the Gupta dynasty (c. 320–550

C.E.)—will be described in Chapter 12. In the five centuries between these two eras of imperial splendor, a succession of foreign invaders entered from the northwest and added new racial and cultural elements to the Indian scene.

The first of the new invaders of India were Greeks from Bactria. They were descendants of the soldiers settled there by Alexander the Great to serve his empire in the East. After Alexander, Bactria continued as a province of the Seleucid Empire, a bastion against the attacks of nomadic tribesmen from the north and a center for trade with India to the southeast. The decline of the Seleucid Empire allowed the Bactrian Greeks to establish an independent kingdom about 245 B.C.E.

In 183 B.C.E., two years after the death of the last Mauryan emperor of India, the fourth Bactrian king, Demetrius, crossed the Hindu Kush mountains as Alexander had done 150 years earlier and occupied the northern Punjab. From his base at Taxila, Demetrius and his successors ruled Bactria and the entire Punjab (modern Afghanistan and northern Pakistan).

The Greeks in India established the farthest outpost of Hellenism in the Hellenistic Age. Demetrius and his successors came closer than any Hellenistic ruler to realizing Alexander's supposed goal of a union of races. Their cities were not artificial Greek enclaves in a hostile land, like Alexandria in Egypt and Antioch in Syria. The Indian peoples were enrolled as citizens, a bilingual coinage was issued bearing Greek inscriptions on one side and Indian on the other, and at least one king, Menander, became a Buddhist.

But soon after 150 B.C.E. Bactria was overrun by nomadic tribesmen. Thereafter, Greek rule in the northern subcontinent steadily declined until the last remnants disappeared late in the first century B.C.E. Hordes of nomadic peoples, migrating out of central Asia, replaced the Greeks in Bactria and northwestern India. First to arrive were the Indo-European Scythians, who had been pushed out of central Asia by other Indo-European nomads known in Chinese sources as the Yueh-chih. In their turn, the Yueh-chih occupied Bactria, and about 40 C.E. they crossed the Hindu Kush and conquered the Punjab. The Kushans, as the Yueh-chih were called in India, expanded eastward to the middle Ganges valley and southward perhaps as far as the borders of the Deccan.

In contrast to the highly centralized Mauryan Empire, the Kushan state was more like a loose federation—its kings were overlords rather than direct rulers—yet it gave northern India two centuries of peace and prosperity. The Kushan kingdom acted as a hub for trade routes linking India, China, and the West. Its greatest ruler, Kaniska (fl. c. 120 C.E.), produced a multicultural coinage that employed Chinese, Greek, Persian, Hindu, and Buddhist devices.

Kaniska gained fame as a patron of the arts and of a new form of Buddhism called Mahayana.

Emergent Hinduism and Buddhism, 200 B.C.E.–300 C.E.

Hinduism and Buddhism were not static or fixed in time; they were evolving during the classical era. In the years 200 B.C.E. to 300 C.E. the religion called Hinduism was formulating a synthesis and meeting the challenge of Buddhism. Buddhism in turn split into two distinct strands of interpretation. These developments were set in the context of an Indian social order that was wedded to village life, caste hierarchies, and a household based on the extended family.

Village, Caste, and Family

In the Later Vedic Age, the three pillars of traditional Indian society—the autonomous village, caste, and the joint or extended family—were established. India has always been primarily agricultural, and its countryside is still a patchwork of villages. The ancient village was made up of joint families governed by a headman and a council of elders. Villages enjoyed considerable autonomy; the raja's government hardly interfered at all as long as it received its quota of taxes.

As noted earlier, Hindu society came to be divided into four classes, or *varnas*—Brahmins (priests), Kshatriyas (nobles), Vaishyas (commoners), and Shudras (workers or servants)—known in the West as the *caste system*. Within the framework of these four varnas (or castes) society was perceived as divided into thousands of subgroups, or *jatis* (literally, "species"), each with a special social, occupational, or religious character. For example, occupational groups of merchants or shopkeepers formed many jatis within the Vaishya caste. Those whose occupations were the most menial and degrading—scavengers, sweepers (who remove human waste), and tanners (because they handle the carcasses of dead animals)—also formed numerous jatis but were perceived as outside and beneath the people of the four varnas. These outcasts were called Untouchables because their touch was considered defiling to members of the other castes.

The third pillar of Indian society was the three-generation household, a patriarchal system. In these households seniority brought status to both men and women. Sons were subordinate to their fathers, and young wives were subordinate to their mothers-in-law. When a woman married, she went from the house of her father to the house of her husband's father. Children were considered the property of the father, not the mother. When the patriarch died, his authority was transferred to his eldest son, but his property was divided equally among all his sons. Women were subordinate to men and required a male protector: father, husband, brother, or son. They could not inherit property, nor could they participate in sacrifices to the gods; their presence at the sacrifice was considered a source of pollution.

The emphasis placed on communal interests rather than on the individual is a common denominator of the three pillars of Indian society. Thus Indian society has always been concerned with stability, respect for elders, and family and group solidarity.

The Hindu Synthesis

Hinduism is not one single doctrine. It is an array of highly diverse beliefs that include the various texts of the Vedic Age, pre-Aryan Indian practices, and an evolving set of deities and rituals. Essential to Hinduism are the beliefs in the cycle of birth, death, and

The serene and reclining god Vishnu is shown here in a sculpture from a sixth-century C.E. Hindu temple. Beneath Vishnu are the five Pandavas, heroes of the Mahabharata, *and their shared wife, Draupadi. Draupadi, along with Sita, stands as a model of Hindu womanhood: virtuous, honorable, and strong.*

rebirth (samsara) and a society structured by caste. Beings may be born as humans in various jatis or as lesser creatures, depending on their actions in the previous life. A believer who accumulates good actions ascends in the hierarchy of beings in subsequent births and may ultimately escape rebirth and be absorbed into brahman.

Three Traditions of Worship and Theology: Vishnu, Shiva, and Devi

The Brahmin priests incorporated Upanishadic thought into their teaching. In doing so they gave the caste system additional religious support by linking it to karma and the process of reincarnation. The priests made individual salvation, now a conspicuous part of Indian religion, dependent on the uncomplaining acceptance of one's position at birth and the performance of one's dharma, which varied by caste. In this schema, a person was born into a caste and died in that caste. Marriage outside one's caste was forbidden. Of course, in practice, as in all religious systems, social reality did not always match normative religious ideals. Marriages did cross caste lines, and some groups did apparently change caste over time.

The Upanishadic doctrine of salvation by absorption of the individual soul into brahman, however, was too intellectual and remote for the average person to grasp fully. Thus devotion to personal savior gods also emerged, becoming an important element in Hinduism. This devotion centered on anthropomorphic deities with rich personalities and long histories.

The major Vedic gods gradually faded into the background, and three basically monotheistic gods emerged as paramount in Hinduism: Vishnu, Shiva, and Devi, the Goddess (sometimes called Kali). Brahma, the personification of brahman, never acquired the standing and popular following achieved by these other three, a position they continue to maintain. Vishnu, Shiva, and Devi evolved from Vedic and indigenous Indian origins, and each came to be regarded by one or several different traditions as the uniquely supreme and holy God, creator of the universe. The theologies of Vishnu and Shiva were already well developed by about 200 B.C.E.; that of the Goddess was not fully developed until some time later. As with all great theological traditions, the theologies of these gods did not remain static and fixed over the ensuing centuries.

In the old Vedic pantheon of the Aryans, Vishnu was a relatively minor god associated with the sun. He then developed into a pacific father-god, comforter, and savior who works continuously for the welfare of humanity. "No devotee of mine is lost" is Vishnu's promise. His followers believe that he has appeared in nine major "descents" in human form to save the world from disaster. (A predicted tenth descent has yet to happen.) Two of Vishnu's incarnations are described in the great Indian epics, as Krishna in the *Mahabharata* and as Rama, the hero of the *Ramayana*. Rama saves the human race from the oppressions of a great demon, rules for many years in the city of Ayodhya, and then returns to the "City of the Gods," resuming the form of Vishnu.

Shiva, the other great popular god of classical and modern Hinduism, evolved from a minor Aryan Vedic god who was the guardian of healing herbs but whose arrows also brought disease. It is possible that another prototype of Shiva was a pre-Aryan fertility god who was worshipped in the cities of the Indus civilization. Shiva is often associated with phallic symbols. His spouse, Parvati, is the earliest expression in the Brahmin texts of a powerful female goddess who was eventually recognized as a separate deity in her own right (under other names) and elevated to the status of a unique supreme and holy divinity, the eternal source and end of the universe.

Shiva's followers believe he is superior to the gods Brahma and Vishnu. He personifies the cosmic force of change that destroys in order to build anew; he is often depicted with a necklace of skulls. Some representations show Shiva as the Lord of Dancers; the rhythm of his dance is that of a world continuously forming, dissolving, and re-forming. He also exemplifies another major characteristic of Hinduism, the reconciliation of extremes: violence and passivity, eroticism and asceticism. Shiva is portrayed as remaining unmoved in meditation for years on end. When he emerges from his meditations, however, he is often lustful and violent.

As noted, Shiva's wife, Parvati (followed by Vishnu's wife, Lakshmi), marked the first appearance in Hinduism of a powerful female divinity. Archaeological and other evidence suggests that goddesses were worshipped in India from the time of the Indus valley civilization. But only toward the Gupta period did fully developed theologies of a supreme Goddess, Devi (the word *devi* simply means "goddess"), begin to appear. As with the development of Shiva and Vishnu, the development of Devi involved the fusion of numerous local deities into a single complex figure. The Goddess presents two faces to the world: she is a tender mother to her devotees and a ferocious warrior to those who threaten her devotees. Called "Mother" or "Bestower of Food" (Annapurna) in her benevolent moods, she can also be "the Black One" (Kali), wearing a necklace of the skulls of her victims, or Durga, a many-armed warrior riding on the back of a lion to do battle with demons when angry. As the creative power of the universe (similar to the Vedic idea of brahman), she is referred to as Shakti ("Power," "Creative Energy"), and theologies focused on Devi as the Supreme Being of the universe are referred to as Shaktism.

As mentioned earlier, there is no centralized authority in Hinduism. The resulting "flexibility" makes Hinduism seem extremely complicated to outsiders

Vishnu and his consort, Lakshmi, recline upon the serpent Shesha floating on the waters of creation. Emerging out of Vishnu's navel is a lotus which serves as a throne for the god Brahma, who creates the world.

Lakshmi, Vishnu's consort and goddess of prosperity, beauty, and precious things, emerged from the foam of the ocean. This statuette was found half a world away in the ruins of ancient Pompeii in Italy, thus demonstrating the extent of trade in Indian cultural objects and ideas in the first century C.E.

who are used to more highly defined religious traditions. One aspect of this flexibility is that many versions of the theology and mythology of these deities are mixed together. For example, worshippers of Shiva often recognize Vishnu as an important and exalted creature fashioned by Shiva but who in no way rivals Shiva's divine supremacy. Worshippers of Vishnu often fit Shiva into their theology in similar ways. They also eventually included the Buddha as one of Vishnu's incarnations, and in modern times some have incorporated the Christians' Jesus into these theologies. Today many Hindus worship Jesus as a divine incarnation, but they do so as Hindus in Hindu ways and are not Christian converts.

Most Hindus today are devotees of either Vishnu or Shiva and their respective incarnations. But animals (especially the cow), vegetation, water, and even stones are also worshipped by some as symbols of the divine. Over time literally thousands of deities, demigods, and lesser spirits came to form the Hindu pantheon, the world's largest.

Because the authority to teach normative ideas in Hinduism was vested in the Brahmins as a class, Hinduism is probably the world's most flexible religion. Brahmins were present in villages and towns throughout the subcontinent, and many local ideas and practices were "normalized" as "compatible with the *Vedas.*" Hinduism possesses no canon, such as the Bible or the Qur'an; no single personal founder, such as Christ or Muhammad; and no precise body of authoritative doctrine. Hindu beliefs vary dramatically, but people remain "Hindu" as long as they observe the rules of their caste. Depending on one's intellectual and spiritual needs and capacities, Hinduism offers transcendental philosophies or devotional adherence to a savior god such as Vishnu. From its earliest origins, it has exhibited an unusual organic quality of growth and adaptation and is, by definition, a religious synthesis of highly diverse ritual and belief.

The Epics

The *Mahabharata*, composed in verse, contains over 75,000 stanzas, the longest work of literature in the world. It tells the tale of an all-encompassing war between rival sets of cousins, the Pandavas and the Kauravas. They are fighting for the throne of the Bharata kingdom, in the upper Ganges plain in the region of modern Delhi. But this great battle, lasting 18 days, was ultimately construed as a cosmic struggle between virtue and evil, a battle to set the world right.

As in the Greek *Iliad*'s account of the Trojan War, the *Mahabharata* presents a dramatic tale of heroism, vengeance, and sacrifice in which the gods directly intervene in the affairs of men. In the great Indian epic, however, it is duty that must govern the actions of kings; only through war will the proper order of the universe be restored. When the war is over and the victorious Pandavas view the horrendous slaughter of their sons, cousins, teachers, and friends, Yudhishthira, the intended king, is so shocked and horrified by the carnage that he refuses to accept the throne and wishes to retreat into the forest. Eventually, however, he is persuaded to become king. It is not his own desires or wishes that Yudhishthira must follow but his duty.

The *Mahabharata* was shaped and embellished over time. It was incorporated into royal sacrificial ritual, and a long succession of priestly editors added many long passages on religious duties, morals, and statecraft. One of the most famous additions is the *Bhagavad-Gita* ("The Lord's Song"), a philosophical dialogue that stresses the performance of duty (dharma) and the overcoming of passion and fear. It is still the most treasured piece in Hindu literature. *Dharma*, whose broad meaning is "moral law" and is often translated as "virtue," had by this time replaced the earlier Vedic term *rita*, which, as noted earlier, originally referred to customary and cosmic law.

The dialogue in the *Bhagavad-Gita* takes place between Arjuna, the greatest warrior of the Pandava brothers, and Krishna, an incarnation of the god Vishnu who takes human form and acts as Arjuna's charioteer. Arjuna is shaken by the prospect of killing his kinsmen. But Krishna, who gradually reveals himself as no ordinary charioteer, instructs Arjuna that he must give up worldly desire and personal attachment and devote himself to discipline and duty. In so doing he will be able to attain freedom, overcome despair, and act according to his dharma, fulfilling his role in the cosmic struggle. Krishna tells Arjuna:

"Knowledge is obscured
by the wise man's eternal enemy
which takes form as desire,
an insatiable fire, Arjuna.
The senses, mind, and understanding
are said to harbor desire;
with these desire obscures knowledge
and confounds the embodied self.
Therefore, first restrain
your senses, Arjuna,
then kill this evil
that ruins knowledge and judgment."[3]

The universal appeal of Arjuna's internal struggle and Krishna's advice has made the *Bhagavad-Gita* a world classic; it has been translated into many languages. Once Arjuna realizes that he is receiving advice from a god, he wants to know more. He asks Krishna to reveal himself in all his majesty. Krishna obliges the unwitting Arjuna by giving him a "divine eye"; but Arjuna is unnerved by the terrible vision of world-devouring time, of the whole universe inscribed in the god's body. He expresses his awe, and Krishna takes mercy on him and reverts to his human form.

The other great Hindu epic, the *Ramayana*, has been likened to the Greek *Odyssey*. It recounts the wanderings of the banished prince Rama and his faithful wife Sita's long vigil before they are reunited and Rama gains his rightful throne. In the course of time, priestly editors transformed this simple adventure story into a book of devotion. Rama, like Krishna in the *Bhagavad-Gita,* was an incarnation of the great god Vishnu. He was viewed as the ideal ruler: truly virtuous, mighty, a man who exemplifies "proper conduct and is benevolent to all creatures. Who is learned, capable, and a pleasure to behold."[4] Sita emerged as the perfect woman, devoted and submissive to her husband. Her words were memorized by almost every Hindu bride:

Car and steed and gilded palace,
vain are these to woman's life;
Dearer is her husband's shadow
to the loved and loving wife.

In the *Ramayana*, Sita is abducted by the demon Ravana, thus launching another cosmic battle between the forces of good and evil. Rama, though victorious, is dishonored because Ravana had touched his wife and taken her to his palace. He feels compelled to repudiate Sita; her abduction is viewed as a rape even though she rejected Ravana's advances. One of the most moving scenes of the *Ramayana* is that in which the loyal Sita proposes to immolate herself (sati) rather than live separated from her lord. The gods save her from the flames, thus allowing Rama honorably to take her back. But years later, wagging tongues revive the question of her "tainted" virtue, and the heroine is once again prompted to prove her purity. The figure of Sita endures as an emblem of ideal Hindu womanhood. In the Indian nationalist struggles of the twentieth century, Sita served as a symbol of femininity and of the nation itself.

Counting Time

There are many ways to understand a civilization: through its art, its buildings, its political systems, its religions, its gender relations. One interesting way to envision a people is to examine its imaginings of time. Past societies have counted time in diverse ways, and those ways then shape the people's myths. Christians and Muslims, for example, trace their histories from a creation that includes the first man, Adam. Then each faith begins counting time from the life of its particular savior or prophet, Jesus and Muhammad, respectively. Of the three great religious traditions that emerged earlier in India, Jainism and Buddhism also focus on the lives of particular holy men who taught the way of Enlightenment. But the belief in reincarnation, shared by Hindus, Buddhists, and Jains, makes Indian notions of time radically different from those of traditions in which humans have only one lifetime. In the Indian traditions, humans can and will have thousands of lifetimes. The question "What comes after death?" is intimately linked to the imagining of time.

Hindu civilization is unique among ancient world civilizations in its crafting of a particularly grand and elaborate scheme for counting time. There

The *Ramayana:* The Trial of Sita

After Rama rescues Sita from her captor, the demon Ravana, he is overjoyed to see her but tormented by the shame of knowing she was touched by another. The doubt thus cast upon her virtue forces him to repudiate her. Devastated at this rejection by her lord, Sita nevertheless proudly answers in her own defense and demands that a pyre be built on which she can immolate herself. The ideas of sexual purity and honor expressed here are not limited to the society of classical India. They are common in many traditional societies and continue to influence gender relations in the present day.

Rama speaks to his beloved: Oh illustrious Princess, I have re-won thee and mine enemy has been defeated on the battlefield; I have accomplished all that fortitude could do; my wrath is appeased; and the insult and the one who offered it have both been obliterated by me. . . . As ordained by destiny the stain of thy separation and thine abduction by that fickle-minded titan has been expunged by me, a mortal. . . . [But] a suspicion has arisen, however, with regard to thy conduct, and thy presence is as painful to me as a lamp to one whose eye is diseased! Henceforth go where it pleaseth thee, I give thee leave, O Daughter of Janaka. O Lovely One, the ten regions are at thy disposal; I can have nothing more to do with thee! What man of honor would give rein to his passion so far as to permit himself to take back a woman who has dwelt in the house of another? Thou hast been taken into Ravana's lap and he has cast lustful glances on thee; how can I reclaim thee, I who boast of belonging to an illustrious House [family]?. . . .

Sita replies: Why dost thou address such words to me, O Hero, as a common man addresses an ordinary woman? I swear to thee, O Long-Armed Warrior, that my conduct is worthy of thy respect! It is the behavior of other women that has filled thee with distrust! Relinquish thy doubts since I am known to thee! If my limbs came in contact with another's it was against my will, O Lord, and not through any inclination on my part; it was brought about by fate. That which is under my control, my heart, has ever remained faithful to thee. . . . If despite the proofs of love that I gave thee whilst I lived with thee, I am still a stranger to thee, O Proud Prince, my loss is irrevocable. . . . Raise a pyre for me, O Saumitri, this is the only remedy for my misery! These unjust reproaches have destroyed me, I cannot go on living! Publicly renounced by mine husband, who is insensible to my virtue, there is only one redress for me, to undergo the ordeal by fire!

From *The Ramayana of Valmiki*, trans. Hari Prasad Shastri, Vol. 3 (London: Shanti Sadan, 1970), pp. 336–337.

are many Indian creation myths, and these stories merged and shifted over time. One common notion of the creation and destruction of the universe is that time is counted in eras *(mahayugas).* Just as individuals die and then are reborn, at the end of each era the world dissolves and then reemerges to begin a new era. Each era consists of one complete cycle of four ages: the Golden Age (1,440,000 human years), in which all beings are good and all life is comfortable; the Age of Trey (1,080,000 human years), in which some evil appears along with some suffering and difficulty in life; the Age of Deuce (720,000 human years), in which there is more evil, pain, and suffering; and the Age of Dissolution (360,000 human years), in which evil, pain, and distress predominate in human life. Before and after each age are "twilight periods" of varying length that altogether add another 720,000 years to the length of a whole cycle.

This vast expanse of human time, however, is nothing compared to the life of the god Brahma. One thousand mahayugas make up only one day in his existence, which lasts for 100 years of 360 days each; and as each Brahma dies, a new one is born from an egg that grows within brahman. In this Hindu cosmology, there have already been billions of Brahmas. Accord-

ing to certain ancient Hindu texts, the world is currently in an Age of Dissolution; in other words, we are approaching the end of a mahayuga and the halfway point in the current day of the current Brahma.

Theravada and Mahayana Buddhism

Buddhism reached a great peak of influence and power in India in the third century B.C.E. It maintained a lofty and important position for several hundred years after that and survived in India until it was exterminated in the thirteenth century C.E. in the aftermath of the Muslim invasions. One reason for its enduring presence in India for over 1600 years was that it rejuvenated itself powerfully with an expansive, liberal "Great Vehicle" *(Mahayana)* movement that began to flower about 100 B.C.E. Mahayana Buddhism stressed that pious Buddhists should imitate the Buddha directly by trying to relieve others' suffering with the message of the Dharma. They should do this rather than merely seek their own personal beatitude as arhats.

Whereas the arhat was the ideal Buddhist in the earlier Sangha, the Mahayana argued that the ideal Buddhist was a *bodhisattva,* a person who will eventually become a Buddha, someone who will spread the light of the Dharma. The ideal bodhisattva, according to the Mahayana, is a Buddhist saint who so zealously seeks to eliminate the sufferings of others that, going beyond the example even of Gautama, he postpones his own entry into the final nirvana (that is, one's final death after accomplishing nirvana) in order to act as a compassionate and loving helper to all others who are still suffering within samsara. The Mahayana movement criticized the older forms of Buddhism as a "Lesser Vehicle" *(Hinayana)* because, it said, the ideal of the arhat was a selfish one. Further, said the Mahayana, older forms of Buddhism were mired in a literal-minded sort of Buddhist philosophy, whereas the Mahayana was "sophisticated" and truly profound. One school of older Buddhism continued to thrive in India, Theravada, the so-called Doctrine of the Elders.

The Brahmins launched a countermovement in the second century B.C.E. that picked up several important elements of Buddhism's appeal. The Brahmin countermovement flowered as "Hinduism," and this new "Hinduism" played a major role in giving rise to the Mahayana Buddhist rejuvenation. Brahmins and their followers gradually won back political and economic support from Buddhists, but Buddhism survived in India until the thirteenth century.

Both the older Theravada and the newer Mahayana Buddhism spread outside of India and thrived in all parts of Asia. Buddhism was brought to Sri Lanka by missionaries sent there by the Mauryan emperor Ashoka around 250 B.C.E. After 100 B.C.E. Buddhists spread the Dharma beyond the boundaries of the subcontinent into China and central, western, and southeastern Asia. In those areas it took permanent root, establishing Buddhist societies, states, and monasteries that function to this day. Today the older form of Buddhism survives only in Sri Lanka and Southeast Asia, and the Mahayana is absent there; Mahayana survives in Tibet, Korea, Japan, and China. The translation of the very numerous books of the Buddhist scriptures from Sanskrit into Chinese took place during the second, third, and fourth centuries C.E., an intellectual achievement as fascinating as it is staggering. A small revival of Buddhism occurred in Maharashtra, India, in the 1930s when the Untouchable leader Dr. B. R. Ambedkar led a mass conversion of Untouchables to Buddhism so that they might escape the oppression of Hindu Untouchability.

Buddhist Sculpture and Architecture

Indian thought and art would have a profound effect on the Western world. The most lasting Western influence on India in the Classical Age was the influence of Greek art on Buddhist sculpture. Before the Kushan period, Indian artists were influenced by the

This seated Buddha from Gandhara shows Hellenistic influence in the modeling of the clothing, features, and, hair; the elongated earlobes, heavy-lidded eyes, mark on the forehead, knot of hair, and expression of deep repose are Indian.

Seated Buddha, from Gandhara, Pakistan. Kushan period, 2nd–3rd century. Dark gray schist, H. 36" × W. 22½". Seattle Art Museum, Eugene Fuller Memorial Collection, 33.180. Photo: Paul Macapia.

Buddha's prohibitions against idolatry, and they refrained from portraying the Buddha in human form. His presence was indicated by symbols only, such as his footprints, his umbrella, or the tree under which he attained Enlightenment. Beginning in the first century C.E., however, the Buddha himself was portrayed in numerous statues and reliefs. Most of these early Buddha figures come from Gandhara, the center of the Kushan Empire and the earlier Greco-Bactrian kingdom.

The primary inspiration for this Gandharan Buddhist art came from Mahayana Buddhism, which viewed the Buddha as a savior. This devotional form of Buddhism needed images for worship, and figures of the Buddha as a bodhisattva savior, as well as of many bodhisattva saints, were produced in large numbers. Mahayana Buddhism and Greco-Buddhist images of the Buddha, both of which developed in the Kushan Empire, spread together throughout eastern Asia.

A second inspiration for Gandharan art came from Greece. Apparently Hellenistic sculptors and craftsmen migrated to Gandhara via the central Asian trade routes. The result was an execution of Indian themes through the use of Greek artistic techniques.

The magnificent buildings of the Mauryan emperors have disappeared. All that remain are Buddhist stupas, the dome-shaped monuments that were used as funeral mounds to enshrine the relics of the Buddha and Buddhist saints or to mark a holy spot. Originally made only of earth, more elaborate mounds were later fashioned out of earth faced with brick and surrounded by railings and four richly carved gateways of stone. On top of the dome was a boxlike structure surmounted by a carved umbrella, the Indian emblem that symbolizes the Buddha's princely birth. As centuries passed, the low dome was heightened in some areas into a tall, tapered structure more like a tower. Later, when Buddhism spread to other countries, the stupa type of architecture went along. Its gateway was widely copied, and the stupa itself may have been the prototype of the multistoried Buddhist pagodas that are common in East Asia today.

South India

Like many other regions of the globe, India can be divided culturally into north and south. Although the south was often dominated by northern conquerors, in general its civilizations developed in a fashion distinct from those of the north. Before the rise of the Gupta Empire in the fourth century C.E., the vast tableland of South India—the Deccan—and its fertile coastal plains remained outside the main forces of political change in the north, except for the 150 years of Mauryan imperial rule. The Dravidian peoples of this area, with their dark skin and small stature, differed in appearance, language, and culture from the Aryan-speaking peoples of the north. Gradually, however, as Brahmin priests and Buddhist monks infiltrated the south, Hinduism and Buddhism were grafted onto the existing Dravidian culture.

Politically, the south remained divided into numerous warring states. Prominent among them were three well-developed Tamil (an old Dravidian language) kingdoms in the southern third of the Deccan peninsula. Under the patronage of some of these kings, the Tamil language developed a classically exquisite literature in the first few centuries of the Common Era. This tradition, known as the Sangam ("Academy") tradition, was based in the old city of Madurai in Tamil Nadu ("Tamil Land"), and it produced several anthologies of poetry, several unique epics, and a superb handbook of language and poetics. Love was an important theme in the Tamil poetry:

> As a little white snake
> with lovely stripes on its young body
> troubles the jungle elephant
>   this slip of a girl
>   her teeth like sprouts of new rice
>   her wrists stacked with bangles
>   troubles me.[5]

By the first century B.C.E., Tamil Nadu had become an intermediary in the maritime trade extending eastward to the East Indies and westward to the Hellenistic kingdoms. Indeed, a major factor that distinguishes South India from North India is the former's orientation toward the sea. On the east and west coasts of southern India, ports developed that became important entrepots for the East-West trade

Sanchi is a third-century B.C.E. site in central India that contains Buddhist monastic complexes and large stupas like this one with its carved gateway and umbrella-like summit decoration. Such stupas, supposed to contain relics of the Buddha, were built and patronized by King Ashoka.

and important points of cultural contact with foreign states and peoples.

The Meeting of East and West: Networks of Exchange

In the centuries immediately preceding and following the birth of Christ, the great civilizations of the world—Indian, Chinese, and Roman—were connected by a complex network of commercial, intellectual, and diplomatic exchanges. Although these contacts began to decline in the third century C.E., they were never entirely cut off. Travelers and monks from China visited the holy sites in India, the monsoons carried merchants to and fro across the Indian Ocean, and the goods and ideas of the East continued to enhance and alter the societies of the Mediterranean world.

Beyond the Indian Frontiers

The era of Mauryan hegemony coincided with the rule of the Han dynasty in China and the Roman Empire in the West. These empires provided the commercial anchors in a chain of intercommunicating states that stretched across Eurasia from the Pacific to the Atlantic. While Rome experienced the prosperous years of the Pax Romana during the first and second centuries C.E., Indian merchants supplied goods to the Roman entrepots in the Middle East. South Asian ports acted as staging points for the Chinese silk and Indian cottons in demand in the West. Indian traders exchanged textiles for African gold and ivory and traded rice, oils, precious woods, jewels, and spices in the ports of the Arabian Sea.

After Alexander's death, India maintained trade contacts with the Seleucid and Ptolemaic kingdoms of the Hellenistic Age over two routes, one by land and the other by sea. The most frequented route was the caravan road that extended from Asia Minor and Syria, crossed Mesopotamia, and then skirted the Iranian plateau to either Bactra or Kandahar before crossing the Hindu Kush to reach Taxila in South Asia. The sea route that linked the Eastern and Western worlds extended from China and Southeast Asia across the Bay of Bengal to India and Sri Lanka and thence across the Indian Ocean to the Red Sea ports or to the head of the Persian Gulf. From those two waterways, goods then proceeded overland and via the Mediterranean to the Middle East and into Africa and Europe.

The courts of kings and seats of imperial power were great points of consumption for the goods of the East-West trade. The Mauryan and Kushan kings developed the trade passing through northern India in order to provide the foreign commodities that em-

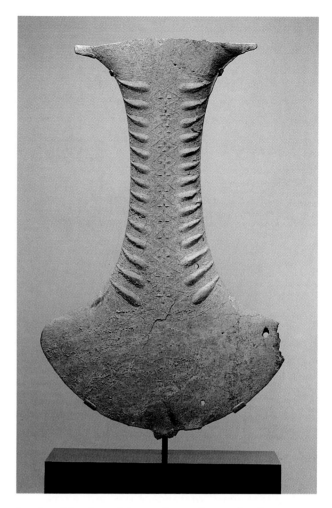

South and Southeast Asia were famous for metalworking. Bronze objects used for practical and ceremonial purposes were widely traded throughout the Indian Ocean region.

Vessel in the Form of an Ax. Bronze. The Metropolitan Museum of Art, Purchase, George McFadden Gift and Edit Perry Chapman Fund, 1993. (1993.525) Photograph by Bruce White © 1993 The Metropolitan Museum of Art.

bellished their palace life. The Roman appetite for luxury goods from India and Southeast Asia—ivory, pearls, spices, dyes, and cotton—greatly stimulated that trade. Rulers vied to control and tax this lucrative commerce.

But no monarch, however great, could maintain control over the whole vast expanse of territory crossed by these trade routes. There were always middlemen. The Parthians, whose kingdom extended from the Euphrates to the borders of Bactria, levied heavy tolls on the caravan trade. The Kushans acted as middlemen for the Chinese silk trade, selling the silk to the Parthians and later to Western merchants coming by sea to India. The Sabaean Arabs of southwestern Arabia seized the Red Sea route at Aden and were in control of much of the Mediterranean world's overseas trade with India. From Aden, the Sabaeans sent Indian goods north by caravan to Petra, which grew rich as a distribution point to Egypt via Gaza and to the north via Damascus.

Discovery Through Maps

The World, Including India, According to Ptolemy, c. 150 C.E.

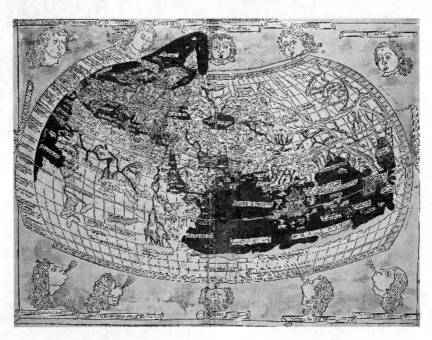

Ptolemy (90–168 C.E.) is well known for his contributions to mathematics and astronomy, but he was also a famous geographer. His work illustrates the fact that people's notions of the world come both from within and from without. South Asian society is a case in point. Indians have apparently been producing maps for more than 2000 years. But with the exception of a few incised potsherds and ancient sculptures, no known examples of distinctively Indian cartography survive from the period covered in this chapter. Later Indian cartography, such as an eleventh-century Jain cosmological map carved in stone, suggests what earlier Indian images of the cosmos may have looked like. (Such images were often markedly different from those produced by Western cartographers.) But at present all we have are out-siders' visions of India, such as the second-century world map of Ptolemy, whose geographical vision remained influential into the sixteenth century.

Ptolemy's *Geography* described four systems of map projection. His description of the world, as seen in this reconstruction, drastically shortens the Indian peninsula from north to south. It imagines an unknown land south of the Indian Ocean, which is depicted as landlocked. Ptolemy's vision of the world spread with copies of his maps along the land and seaborne trade routes linking the Roman world and India. Ultimately it affected the mapmaking of Indian cartographers. The influence of Ptolemy's geography is just one instance of the bilateral exchange of culture and ideas that accompanied the flow of trade in this era.

So great was the demand and so lucrative the trade in Indian goods that the Roman emperor Augustus Caesar broke the hold of the Parthian and Arab middlemen on the Eastern trade, establishing direct commercial connections by sea with India. By 1 B.C.E. he had gained control of the Red Sea, forcing the Sabaeans out of Aden and converting the city into a Roman naval base. Ships were soon sailing from Aden directly to India across the Arabian Sea, blown by the monsoon winds.

From May to October the monsoon blows from the southwest across the Arabian Sea; between No-vember and March the countermonsoon blows from the northeast. Thus direct round-trip voyages, eliminating middlemen and the tedious journey along the coasts, could be made in eight months. Strabo, a Greek geographer during the time of Augustus, stated that 120 ships sailed to India every year from Egyptian ports on the Red Sea.

When Augustus became head of the Roman world, the Tamil and Kushan rulers sent him congratulatory embassies. At least nine other embassies from India visited the Roman emperors, and Roman-Indian trade flourished. Indian birds (particularly talking parrots, costing more than human slaves) became the pets of wealthy Roman ladies, and Indian animals (lions, tigers, and buffaloes) were used in the wild beast shows of Roman emperors. In view of these contacts, we can understand why Ptolemy's second-century map of the world shows considerable knowledge of the geography of India.

During the first century C.E., when Roman-financed ships reached the rich markets of southern India and Sri Lanka, Christianity may have accompanied them. Indian Christians today claim that their small group of about 2 million was founded by St. Thomas, one of Jesus' original 12 disciples, who may have sailed to India about 50 C.E. Thus the trade routes carried more than goods. They bore travelers, envoys, pilgrims, and missionaries. In an era when the Buddhist philosophy of India was spreading east and south into China and Southeast Asia, the Christian philosophy spawned in the Middle East was carried across the seas to India. Although Christian proselytizing met with very limited success in India, Buddhism made remarkable progress as it spread beyond the boundaries of the subcontinent.

The Balance of Trade

The balance of trade between East and West from ancient times until the early modern era tended to favor the East. As noted in Chapter 5, although Western trade with the East grew immensely in the first two centuries C.E., Roman exports such as wool, linen, glass, and metalware to the East did not match in value Rome's imports of silk, spices, perfumes, gems, and other luxuries. To make up the difference, gold and silver had continually to be exported to Asia. The discovery of large hoards of Roman coins in India seems to support claims that the Romans had to pay cash for some significant portion of their Indian goods.

Beginning in the third century, contacts between the East and the West gradually declined. India entered a period of change and transition after the Mauryan Empire fell, the Kushan Empire in northeast India collapsed, and the Han dynasty in China was overthrown. At the Western end of the trade routes, the Roman Empire's power was also circumscribed and the hegemony of the Romans challenged. These political upheavals disrupted cultural and commercial interchange but did not eliminate it entirely.

Conclusion

During India's formative age, three major religions were evolving on the subcontinent. Hinduism became the dominant social and religious force in India, with its notions of dharma allocated by caste.

Jainism fostered the notion of ahimsa (nonviolence), which would play a powerful role in the twentieth-century Indian independence movement. Buddhism challenged the Brahmin order and spread beyond the frontiers of India, ultimately to become a world religion. The great bulk of Indian thought seeks not to challenge the existing social order but to explain and justify it; duty (dharma) dominates. Individual rights and desires in this world are ideally overshadowed by the requirements of eternal salvation, and freedom means escape from the cycle of birth, death, and rebirth.

India is today the heir of one of the longest-living civilizations in the world. By the beginning of the third century C.E., this civilization had produced a set of religious, philosophical, and literary traditions that endures to the present day. Television broadcasts of the *Ramayana* and the *Mahabharata* have been enormously successful in India in recent years. In India, Rama and Sita remain as significant models for the virtuous male and female. Although the caste system has been challenged by the nation-state politics of modern India, it remains an essential element of Hindu identity: shaping social convention, determining political allegiance, and providing a framework for the practice of religion.

Suggestions for Reading

Romila Thapar, *A History of India*, Vol. 1 (Penguin, 1966), is an old standard for ancient India; a more recent one is Herman Kulke and Dietmar Rothermund, *A History of India* (Routledge, 1986). Stanley A. Wolpert, *A New History of India*, 5th ed. (Oxford University Press, 1997), is a brief but comprehensive history of ancient and modern India. Still valuable as an introduction to all aspects of pre-Islamic Indian civilization is A. L. Basham, *The Wonder That Was India*, rev. ed. (Sedgwich & Johnson, 1967); see also William W. Tarn, Frank Lee Holt, and M. C. J. Miller, *The Greeks in Bactria and India*, 3rd ed. (Ares, 1984); Mortimer Wheeler, *The Indus Civilization*, 3rd ed. (Cambridge University Press, 1968); and Emil Lengyel, *Asoka the Great: India's Royal Missionary* (Watts, 1969).

The standard geographical work is Joseph Schwartzberg, ed., *A Historical Atlas of South Asia*, 2nd ed. (Oxford University Press, 1992). On seafaring and India's trade, see Kenneth MacPherson, *The Indian Ocean* (Oxford University Press, 1998), and C. G. Simkin, *The Traditional Trade of Asia* (Oxford University Press, 1968). Robert E. Wheeler, *Rome Beyond the Imperial Frontiers* (Greenwood, 1972), is a study of Rome's trade with the East. See also L. Boulnois, *The Silk Road* (Allen & Unwin, 1963).

Edward Conze, *A Short History of Buddhism* (Allen & Unwin, 1980), is a good introduction. See also Edward J. Thomas, *The Life of Buddha as Legend and History* (Routledge, 1975); Richard H. Robinson, Willard L. Johnson, and Sandra A. Wawrytko, *The Buddhist Religion: A Historical Introduction*, 4th ed. (Wadsworth, 1996); T. W. Rhys Davids, trans., *Buddhist Suttas* (Dover, 1969); and John S. Strong, *The Experience of Buddhism* (Wadsworth, 1995).

On Hinduism, Basham's *Wonder That Was India* provides a good introduction; a concise treatment is Thomas Hopkins, *The Hindu Religious Tradition* (Dickenson, 1971); more informed by recent scholarship is Gavin Flood, *An Introduction to Hinduism* (Cambridge University Press, 1996); still good in many ways is Robert C. Zaehner, *Hinduism* (Oxford University Press, 1966). See also Ainslie Embree, ed., *Sources of Indian Tradition*, Vol. 1 2nd ed., (Columbia University Press, 1988); Wendy O'Flaherty, *Hindu Myths* (Penguin, 1975); and Padmini Sathianadhan Sengupta, *Everyday Life in Ancient India*, 2nd ed. (Oxford University Press, 1957). Also recommended are Pratima Bowes, *The Hindu Religious Tradition* (Routledge, 1978), a forceful statement of Hindu dynamic creativity until the Middle Ages; and Sarvepali Radhakrishnan, *The Hindu View of Life* (Allen & Unwin, 1980). W. Theodore de Bary, ed., *Sources of Indian Tradition* (Columbia University Press, 1958), contains a wide range of important texts with illuminating introductions.

On Indian literature, see *The Rig-Veda*, trans. Wendy O'Flaherty (Penguin, 1986); *Upanishads*, trans. Patrick Olivelle (Oxford University Press, 1996); and *The Laws of Manu*, trans. George Bühler (Dover, 1969). For the *Mahabharata*, see J. A. van Buitenen, ed. and trans., *The Mahabharata*, 3 vols. (University of Chicago Press, 1973–1978), and the theatrical adaptation by Jean-Claude Carrière, *The Mahabharata* (Harper & Row, 1985). The scholarly edition of the *Ramayana* is Robert P. Goldman et al., trans., *The Ramayana of Valmiki: An Epic of Ancient India*, 7 vols. (Princeton University Press, 1984–1998). See also Nigel Frith, *The Legend of Krishna* (Schocken, 1976). Tamil literature can be sampled in A. K. Ramanujan, trans., *The Interior Landscape: Love Poems from a Classical Tamil Anthology* (Indiana University Press, 1975); and R. Parthasarathy, *The Cilappatikāram* (Columbia University Press, 1993).

On Indian art, see Benjamin Rowland, *The Art and Architecture of India: Buddhist, Hindu, Jain*, 3rd ed. (Penguin, 1970); John Marshall, *The Buddhist Art of Gandhara* (Cambridge University Press, 1960); Heinrich Zimmer, *The Art of Indian Asia* (Princeton University Press, 1960); and W. G. Archer, *The Loves of Krishna in Indian Painting and Poetry* (New York: Grove Press, n.d.).

Suggestions for Web Browsing

Itihaas: Chronology—Ancient India
http://www.itihaas.com/ancient/index.html

Lengthy chronology of ancient India, 2700 B.C.E. to 1000 C.E.; most entries include subsites with text and images.

India
http://www.dc.infi.net/~gunther/india/medieval.html

Site discussing the history, sites and monuments, and classical texts of India, 600 B.C. to 1256 C.E.

Jainism
http://www.cs.colostate.edu/~malaiya/jainhlinks.html

Extensive site discusses the principles, traditions, and practices of Jainism and includes numerous related links.

The Buddhist Age, 500 B.C.E. to 319 C.E.
http://www.stockton.edu/~gilmorew/consorti/1cindia.htm#religdone

Text and images detail Buddha's life, the Four Truths, and the evolution of Buddhism. Related links offer analyses of Buddhist texts and a lengthy list of primary texts.

Hinduism
http://www.bcca.org/~cvoogt/Religion/hindu.html

Web page offering a number of sites about Hinduism, including a discussion of Veda, the Vedic culture, and its meaning in today's world, and excerpts from the Bhagavad-Gita *and the* Rig-Veda.

The *Ramayana*: An Enduring Tradition
http://www.maxwell.syr.edu/maxpages/special/ramayana/

The Ramayana *is one of the most important literary and oral texts of South Asia. This extensive site from Syracuse University offers both a short and complete story of Rama, history, images, and maps.*

Notes

1. Quoted in Vincent Smith, *The Oxford History of India* (Oxford: Oxford University Press, 1958), p. 131.
2. Quoted in Charles Drekmeier, *Kingship and Community in Early India* (Stanford, Calif.: Stanford University Press, 1962), p. 175.
3. *The Bhagavad-Gita*, trans. Barbara Stoler Miller (New York: Bantam, 1986), pp. 46–47.
4. *The Ramayana of Valmiki*, Vol. 1, trans. Robert P. Goldman (Princeton, N.J.: Princeton University Press, 1984), p. 121.
5. From *The Interior Landscape: Love Poems from a Classical Tamil Anthology*, trans. A. K. Ramanujan (Bloomington: Indiana University Press, 1975), p. 54.

The Middle Ages

After the "fall" of Rome, the great classical tradition was carried on for another thousand years without interruption in Constantinople, or "New Rome." Until it fell in 1453 the Byzantine Empire acted as a buffer for western Europe, staving off attack after attack from the east and projecting its civilization throughout eastern Europe and Russia.

The culminating series of attacks, resulting in the collapse of the empire, was launched by the adherents of Islam—a dynamic way of life developed by the followers of Muhammad, an eloquent prophet who instilled in his people a vital sense of their destiny to rule in the name of Allah. With unbelievable swiftness the followers of the Prophet became rulers of the Near East, swept across North Africa and surged into Spain, and expanded eastward to the frontiers of China.

The Muslims, the great middlemen of medieval times, shuttled back and forth across vast expanses, trading the wares of East and West and acting as the conveyors of culture, including their own. Throughout most of the Middle Ages the East outshone the West even as Constantinople and Baghdad outdazzled in material magnificence and intellectual and artistic triumphs the capitals of western Europe.

In Europe, after the decline of the Roman Empire, a painful search for stability began. Centuries of confusion followed until Charlemagne established a new "Roman" empire. This ambitious experiment was premature, however, and after its collapse a new system had to be created—one that would offer at least a minimum of security, political organization, and law enforcement. Under this system, called feudalism, the landed nobility acted as police force, judiciary, and army. Crude as it was, feudalism served to mitigate the chaos that followed the fall of Charlemagne's empire.

Yet the feudal system was inherently rural and rigid, and by the eleventh century new forces were at work. Shadowy outlines of new kingdoms—Germany, England, France, and Spain—began to emerge under the direction of vigorous monarchs. Europe went on the offensive, ejecting the Muslims from the southern part of the Continent, breaking Muslim control of the Mediterranean, and launching crusades to capture Jerusalem from the "infidels." The closed economy of the feudal countryside gave way before the revival of trade and communications, the growth of towns, the increased use of money as a medium of exchange, and the rise of a new class in society—the bourgeoisie.

Amidst all of this change, the greatest stabilizing force in Europe during the medieval period was the church. With the authority that stemmed from its vital spiritual service, the church provided the nearest approach to effective and centralized supervision of European life. The church was also the chief patron of poets and artists; its monasteries were repositories for precious manuscripts, and it fostered a new institution of learning—the university.

At the same time that Europe was experiencing dynamic cultural growth, sub-Saharan Africa was undergoing similar transformations. Indeed, Africans had created vibrant civilizations centuries before Europeans ventured beyond their coastal water. Africa gave birth to some of the earliest civilizations, Egypt and Nubia. Africans, however, lived in a variety of social and political systems, ranging from small-scale communities in which families met most of their own needs to large kingdoms, with hereditary rulers, elaborate bureaucracies, and extensive trading networks.

During the ten centuries commonly referred to as the Middle Ages in the West, great civilizations in India and China experienced their greatest flowering. In Gupta India the government was stable, and science and the arts flourished. Under the rule of the T'ang and Sung dynasties, Chinese life was enriched by notable creativity. Later, Mongol conquerors, beginning with Genghis Khan, put together the largest empire in the world, stretching west from China as far as Russia and Mesopotamia. Influenced greatly by China, the proud and independent Japanese developed a unique culture pattern characterized best by the *samurai*, the knight, and *bushido*, the code of the warrior.

The two American continents also created civilizations long before European explorers ventured across the Atlantic. As with their African counterparts, the American civilizations followed a sequence similar to that experienced in Eurasia. Agriculture became more diversified and with its increasing food surpluses was capable of supporting large cities, highly skilled crafts, expanding commerce, complex social structures, and the emergence of powerful states.

Just as theologians through the centuries have fought to understand Christ's message, so too have artists struggled to capture his image. This powerful mosaic of Christ at the Church of Chora in Istanbul was created in the first part of the fourteenth century. Its beauty and spirituality speak to all: believers and nonbelievers alike.

Christianity and the New Christian Romes

Byzantium, Eastern Europe, and Russia, 325–1500

At the same time that Caesar Augustus was laying the foundations of Rome's imperial greatness, Christianity was emerging in the distant Roman province of Judea. The contrast between the grandeur, power, and arrogance of the Romans and the poverty, idealism, and humility of the early Christians could not have been more dramatic.

Three centuries later, despite Diocletian's reforms, the western part of the Roman Empire faced extinction. Throughout the Mediterranean basin, Christianity flourished, especially in the East. After 325 the empire survived in Byzantium as a new, self-proclaimed Christian Rome, the "Second Rome."

Until the fifteenth century, the Byzantines first cooperated and after the eighth century competed in all areas with the Catholic Church, which gained strength after Rome "fell." Rome and Constantinople split eastern Europe into Roman Catholic and Orthodox zones in their combative missionary work, establishing the bases for centuries of Christians killing Christians. When the Ottoman Turks took Constantinople in 1453, the Russians proclaimed the new Christian Rome to be Moscow, the "Third Rome," the arena for the playing out of God's divine plan, the end of the world, and the second coming of Christ. The Russians affirmed that Moscow was the Third Rome, and there would be no other.

After Diocletian, ambitious Christian leaders ruled through the powerful fusion of Roman political, social, and military precedents with symbolism and

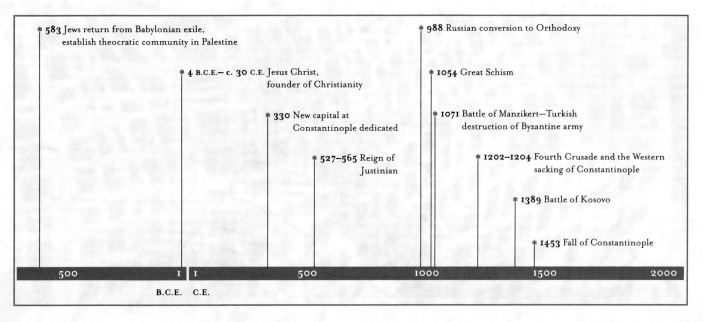

* **583** Jews return from Babylonian exile, establish theocratic community in Palestine

* **4 B.C.E.– c. 30 C.E.** Jesus Christ, founder of Christianity

* **330** New capital at Constantinople dedicated

* **527–565** Reign of Justinian

* **988** Russian conversion to Orthodoxy

* **1054** Great Schism

* **1071** Battle of Manzikert—Turkish destruction of Byzantine army

* **1202–1204** Fourth Crusade and the Western sacking of Constantinople

* **1389** Battle of Kosovo

* **1453** Fall of Constantinople

500 | I | I | 500 | 1000 | 1500 | 2000

B.C.E.   C.E.

Christianity. Not until the development of modern political ideologies after the French Revolution did a more potent combination of theories and symbols help governments motivate and dominate their people.

The Rise and Triumph of Christianity

Following the conquests of Alexander the Great in the Near East, the Ptolemies and then the Seleucids ruled Palestine. After the Jews returned from exile in Babylonia in 538 B.C.E. (see Chapter 2), they created in Palestine a theocratic community based on God's law as recorded by Moses in the *Torah* and contained in the *Pentateuch*, the first five books of the Old Testament. Later they added to this record the teachings of the prophets and the writings of priests and scholars.

Jewish Foundations

Jewish religious life centered on the Temple at Jerusalem, which echoed with the cry "Hallelujah" ("Praise Yahweh") in thanksgiving for Yahweh's gracious dealings with his people. The most powerful figure there was the high priest, who was assisted by the Sanhedrin, the high court for the enforcement of the law. Since there was no distinction between civil and religious law, the jurisdiction of the Sanhedrin covered all aspects of Jewish life.

Jewish groups outside Palestine were linked by spiritual bonds to the Temple and to a law they be-

The Rise of Christianity

4 B.C.E.	Birth of Jesus Christ
c. 30 C.E.	Execution of Jesus Christ
c. 33	Paul begins spreading Christian doctrine
40–70	Writing of the Gospels
c. 65	Peter and Paul executed in Rome
325	Council of Nicaea
340–430	Great church fathers: Jerome, Ambrose, Augustine
440–461	Pontificate of Leo I, the Great
1054	Great, final schism between the Eastern and Western Church

lieved to be divinely inspired. But the Jews of the Diaspora, those who could not return to Palestine after the Babylonian exile, met in local *synagogues* (from the Greek word for "assembly") for public worship and instruction in the Scriptures. Eventually, the synagogue became the heart of Judaism, and it influenced the forms of worship in the Christian churches and the Muslim mosques.

During the Hellenistic Age, Greek influences were constantly at work among the Jews. Most Jews outside Palestine spoke Greek, and a Greek translation of the Hebrew Scriptures, called the *Septuagint* (from the Latin for "seventy"), was produced in Alexandria in the third century B.C.E. Greek influences, however, contributed to factionalism among the Jews in Judea. A radical, extremely pious group came to blows with the aristocratic pro-Greek Sadducees, as they came to be called, who were favored by the Seleucid rulers of Palestine.

In 168 B.C.E this internal conflict gave the Seleucid king, Antiochus IV, an opportunity to intervene and attempt to Hellenize the Jews. He ordered their Temple dedicated to the worship of Zeus. Viewing this decree as a desecration, the Jews rebelled. Under the leadership of Judas Maccabaeus, they rededicated the Temple to Yahweh and in 142 B.C.E. won their independence from the Seleucids. Although Judas and his immediate successors took the title of high priest, later members of the family claimed to be kings. In time these rulers became worldly and corrupt; factionalism flared up again, resulting in persecution and bloodshed.

It was in the midst of a civil war that the Roman legions first made their appearance. Pompey, who was then completing his pacification of Asia Minor and Syria, took advantage of the plea for assistance from one of the factions and ended the civil war in 63 B.C.E. He made Judea subject to the Roman governor of Syria. Eventually, Herod the Great, a half-Jewish, half-Arab leader from Edom, just south of Judea, rose to power as a tool of the Romans. Appointed by Mark Antony, Herod served as king of Judea from 37 to 4 B.C.E. He erected a magnificent palace, a theater, and a hippodrome, and he rebuilt the Temple on a lavish scale. To the Jews, however, Herod remained as a detested usurper who used Judaism as a matter of expediency.

Soon after Herod's death, Judea became a minor Roman province ruled by governors called *procurators*. The best-known procurator was Pontius Pilate, who ruled from 26 to 36 C.E. and under whose government Jesus was crucified. The Jews themselves remained unhappy and divided under Roman domination. For centuries the prophets had taught that God would one day, when righteousness prevailed, create a new Israel under a God-anointed leader, the Messiah. Many Jews lost hope in a political Messiah and an earthly kingdom and instead conceived of a spiritual Messiah who would lead all the righteous, including the resurrected dead, to a spiritual kingdom.

Development of Jewish Religious Thought

Through centuries of suffering, captivity, and subjugation, the Jews had been taught by a succession of prophets and priests to hold their covenant with Yahweh and to safeguard their religious inheritance. In the centuries just preceding and following the birth of Christ, the Sadducees, Pharisees, and Essenes pursued that inheritance in different ways. These theological complexities mirrored cultural, social, and economic differences within the Jewish community.

The aristocratic Sadducees, who controlled the office of high priest, stood for strict adherence to the Torah. The more numerous Pharisees believed that with divine guidance, human beings could modify and amend the law. They accepted belief in personal immortality and the kingdom of heaven. From their ranks came the *rabbis,* scholars who expounded the law and applied it to existing conditions. The "oral law" developed by the Pharisees became the core of the later *Talmud,* the great commentary on Jewish law that laid down a detailed code of daily living for Jews. After the destruction of the Temple and the end of the high priesthood, the rabbinical schools of the Pharisees ensured that Judaism would endure.

The discovery of the Dead Sea Scrolls in 1947 added to modern knowledge of the Essenes, the probable base of the Christian faith. While exploring caves around the desolate western shore of the Dead Sea, two Bedouin boys came across several clay jars containing long manuscripts wrapped in linen. Many more scrolls were later found in other caves. Nearby were the ruins of a monastery built by the Essenes, a militant communal group, "to separate themselves," as the scrolls state, "from the abode of perverse men." Occupied between the second century B.C.E. and 68 C.E., the monastery was destroyed by the Romans during the great Jewish revolt of 66–70 C.E. (see p. 174). Prior to its destruction, the Essenes hid their manuscripts in the caves. Some scrolls are portions of the Old Testament dating from the first century B.C.E. The scrolls that describe the Essene sect in that era have been said to constitute "a whole missing chapter of the history of the growth of religious ideas between Judaism and Christianity."[1]

The Essenes' founder, a shadowy figure known as the Righteous Teacher, suffered persecution and perhaps martyrdom late in the second century B.C.E. His followers considered themselves the true remnant of God's people, preached a "new covenant," and awaited the time when God would destroy the pow-

The partially unrolled Thanksgiving Scroll, one of the Dead Sea Scrolls, preserved at the Hebrew University in Jerusalem, is composed of religious hymns that poetically develop the Essenes' theological doctrines.

ers of evil and inaugurate his kingdom. Similar views concerning the transition from the "Old Age" to the "New Age" were held by many other Jews and later by Christians. Some scholars have attached much significance to common elements in the beliefs and practices of the Essenes and the early Christians. John the Baptist, who baptized Jesus and whom Jesus viewed as the herald of a message from God, may have been a member of the Essene sect.

The Life and Teaching of Jesus

Whatever its parallels with the Essene sect, including baptism and communal meals, the Jewish sect that became Christianity bears the unmistakable imprint of the personality of its founder, Jesus of Nazareth. According to the biblical accounts pieced together from the four Gospels, he was born in Bethlehem during Herod's reign; therefore, he must have been born by the time of Herod's death in 4 B.C.E. rather than in the year that traditionally begins the Christian or Common Era, 1 C.E. After spending the first years of his adult life as a carpenter in the village of Nazareth, Jesus began a three-year mission, preaching love for one's fellow human beings and urging people to turn away from sin because "the kingdom of heaven is near" (Matthew 4:17).

Reports of Jesus' teaching and his "mighty works" miracles such as casting out demons, healing the sick, raising the dead, and walking on water spread among the Jews as he and his 12 apostles traveled from village to village in Palestine. When he came to Jerusalem to observe the feast of the Passover, huge crowds greeted him enthusiastically as the promised Messiah. But Jesus preached a spiritual, not an earthly, kingdom, and when some of the radicals saw that he had no intention of leading a nationalistic movement against the Romans, they turned against him. Other attacks on him were as much social and political as theological. His enemies included the moneylenders, whom he had denounced; the Pharisees, who resented his repudiation of their minute regulations of daily behavior; the people who considered him a disturber of the status quo; and some who saw him as a blasphemer of Yahweh.

Betrayed by Judas, one of his apostles, Jesus was condemned by the Sanhedrin for blasphemy "because he claimed to be the Son of God" (John 19:7). Before the procurator Pontius Pilate, however, Jesus was charged with treason for claiming to be the king of the Jews:

> "Are you the king of Jews?" he [Pilate] asked him. . . . Jesus answered, "My kingdom does not belong to this world; if my kingdom belonged to this world, my followers would fight to keep me from being handed over to the Jews. No, my kingdom does not belong here. . . . You say that I am a king. I was born and came into the world for this one purpose, to speak about the truth. Whoever belongs to the truth listens to me." (John 18:33–38)

Pilate was a professional Roman official. He wanted to maintain the calm and ordered province so desired by his masters in Rome. The theological controversy did not matter to him, but the possibility of massive civil disorder did. Jesus was condemned to the death that Rome inflicted on enemies of the state: crucifixion after a brutal whipping.

The End of the Jewish Polity, 66–70 C.E.

In the generation after Jesus' crucifixion, a group of ardent Jewish nationalists, known as Zealots, called for the use of force to drive the Romans out of "God's land." The atmosphere had been poisoned by incidents such as the following, reported by the contemporary Jewish collaborationist historian Josephus:

> The people had assembled in Jerusalem for the Feast of Unleavened Bread [Passover], and the Roman cohort stood on guard over the Temple colonnade, armed men always being on duty at the feasts to forestall any riot-

ing by the vast crowds. One of the soldiers pulled up his garment and bent over indecently turning his backside towards the Jews and making a noise as indecent as his attitude. This infuriated the whole crowd, who noisily appealed to Cumanus [the procurator] to punish the soldier, while the less restrained of the young men and the naturally tumultuous section of the people rushed into battle, and snatching up stones hurled them at the soldiers. Cumanus, fearing the whole population would rush at him, sent for more heavy infantry.[2]

In 66 C.E. violence erupted into war after the Zealots massacred a small Roman garrison at Jerusalem. After a five-month siege of Jerusalem in 70 C.E., Titus, son of the emperor Vespasian, laid waste to most of the city. Only a small part of the Temple complex, what came to be called the "Wailing Wall," remained standing. It was later prophesied that a third Temple would be erected there when the Messiah came. The Dome of the Rock, a mosque built by the Muslims, has occupied the site since the eighth century C.E. The wholesale destruction of Jerusalem in 70 C.E. marked the end of the Hebrew state, although the fortress of Masada near the Dead Sea held out for two more years. The Jewish dream of an independent homeland was to remain unrealized for almost 19 centuries, until the State of Israel was proclaimed in 1948.

The Work of Paul

With Jesus' death it seemed as though his cause had been exterminated. No written message had been left behind, and his few loyal followers were disheartened. Yet his martyrdom gave impetus to the new religion he inspired. Word soon spread that Jesus had been seen alive after his crucifixion and had spoken to his disciples, giving them solace and reassurance. At first there were few converts in Palestine, but the Hellenized Jews living in foreign lands, in contact with new ideas and modes of living, were less firmly committed to traditional Jewish doctrines. The new faith first made real headway among the Jewish communities in such cities as Damascus, Antioch (where its followers were first called "Christians" by the Greeks), Corinth, and Rome.

The followers of Jesus, like their master, had no thought of breaking away from Judaism. They sought only to pursue the inheritance of their faith spiritually and ethically. Because they adhered to the requirements of the Jewish law, their new message did not easily attract non-Jews. Paul removed this obstacle through his more liberal and cosmopolitan preachings. Because of his influence, he has been called the second founder of Christianity.

Born Saul, of Jewish ancestry but a Roman citizen by birth, and raised in the cosmopolitan city of Tarsus, in Asia Minor, Paul possessed a wide knowledge of Greek culture. He was also a strict Pharisee who considered Christians to be traitors to the sacred law and took an active part in their persecution. One day about 33 C.E., while traveling to Damascus to squelch the Christian community there, Saul had an experience that changed his life. He explained:

As I was traveling and coming near Damascus, about midday a bright light suddenly flashed from the sky around me. I fell to the ground and heard a voice saying to me, "Saul, Saul! Why do you persecute me?" "Who are you, Lord?" I asked. "I am Jesus of Nazareth, whom you persecute," he said to me. The men with me saw the light but did not hear the voice of the one who was speaking to me. I asked, "What shall I do, Lord?" and the Lord said to me, "Get up and go into Damascus, and there you will be told everything that God has determined for you." (Acts 22:6–10)

Saul, henceforth known by the Roman name Paul, turned from being a persecutor into the greatest of Christian missionaries.

Paul taught that Jesus was the Christ (from the Greek *Christos,* "Messiah"), the Son of God, and that he had died to atone for the sins of all people. Only faith in the saving power of Jesus Christ was necessary for the salvation of Jews and Gentiles (non-Jews) alike. Adherence to the complexities of the Jewish law was unnecessary.

A man is put right with God only through faith in Jesus Christ, never by doing what the Law requires.... So there is no difference between Jews and Gentiles, between slaves and freemen, between men and women; you are all one in union with Christ Jesus. (Galatians 2:16, 3:28)

After covering 8000 miles teaching and preaching, Paul was put to death in Rome about 65 C.E., the same year as Peter, founder of the church at Rome during the reign of Nero. By this time Christian communities had been established in all important cities in the East and at Rome. Paul performed a very important service to these infant communities of believers by instructing them, either through visits or letters, in the fundamental beliefs of the new religion. He served as an authority by which standardization of belief could be achieved.

Reasons for the Spread of Christianity

The popular mystery religions that the Romans had embraced from Greece and the Near East during the troubled last century of the Republic gave spiritual

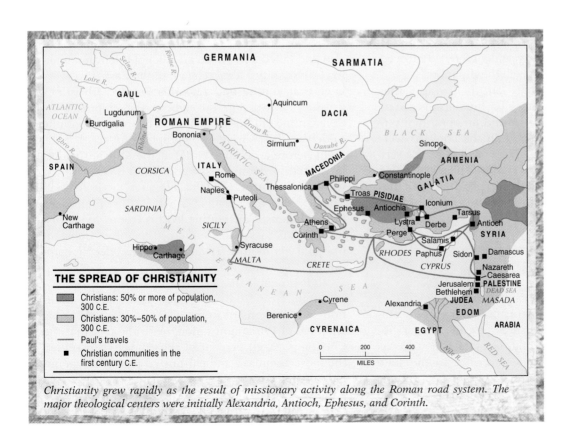

Christianity grew rapidly as the result of missionary activity along the Roman road system. The major theological centers were initially Alexandria, Antioch, Ephesus, and Corinth.

satisfaction not provided by Rome's early ritualistic forms of worship. These mystery religions included the worship of the Phrygian Cybele, the Great Mother *(Magna Mater);* the Egyptian Isis, sister and wife of Osiris; the Greek Dionysus, called Bacchus by the Romans; and the Persian sun-god Mithras, the intermediary between humans and Ahura-Mazda, the great Lord of Light, whose sacred day of worship was called Sunday and from whose cult women were excluded. Common to all the mystery religions were the notions of a divine savior and the promise of everlasting life.

Followers of these mystery cults found Christian beliefs and practices familiar enough to convert easily to the new faith. But Christianity had far more to offer than the mystery religions did. Its founder was not a creature of myth, like the gods and goddesses of the mystery cults, but a real person whose lofty ethical teachings were preserved in detail in a unique record, the New Testament, which also included accounts of his death and resurrection as the divine incarnation of God. Shared with the Jews was the concept of a single omnipotent God, the jealous yet loving God of the Hebrew Scriptures, now the God of all humanity. Moreover, Christianity was a dynamic, aggressive faith. It upheld the equality of all people—rich and poor, slave and freeborn, male and female. Women were among Jesus' audiences, and Paul's letters give much evidence of women active in the early church. One of Jesus' helpers was Mary Magdalene, the repentant prostitute. According to the so-called Gnostic Gospels, which the church declared heretical in the early fourth century and ordered destroyed, "Christ loved her more than all the disciples."[3]

Christianity taught that God, the loving Father, had sent his only Son to atone for human sins and offered a vision of immortality and an opportunity to be "born again," cleansed of sin. Its converts were bound together by faith and hope, and they took seriously their obligation of caring for orphans, widows, and other unfortunates. The courage with which they faced death and persecution impressed even their bitterest enemies.

Persecution of the Christians

The Roman government tolerated any religion that did not threaten the safety or tranquillity of the empire. Christianity, however, was perceived as a subversive danger to society and the state. Christians as monotheists refused to offer sacrifice to the state cults on behalf of the emperor—not even a few grains of incense cast upon an altar. Offering sacrifice to the state cults was considered an essential patriotic rite uniting all Roman subjects in common loyalty to the imperial government. For Christians, however, there

was only one God: they could sacrifice to no others. In the eyes of many Roman officials, this attitude branded them as traitors.

To the Romans, the Christians were a secret antisocial group forming a state within a state—"walling themselves off from the rest of mankind," as a pagan writer observed. Many were pacifists who refused to serve in the army, and all were intolerant of other religious sects and refused to associate with pagans or take part in social functions that they considered sinful or degrading.

During the first two centuries after Jesus' crucifixion, persecution of Christians was sporadic and local, such as that at Rome under Nero. But during the late third and fourth centuries, when the empire was in danger of collapse, three organized efforts were launched to suppress Christianity throughout the empire. By far the longest and most systematic campaign against the Christians, who now comprised perhaps one-tenth of the population, was instigated by the emperor Diocletian from 303 to 311. He stringently imposed the death penalty on anyone who refused to sacrifice to Roman gods. But the inspired defiance of the Christian martyrs, who seemed to welcome death, could not be overcome. "The blood of the martyrs is the seed of the church" became a Christian rallying cry.

Official Recognition and Acceptance

In 311 the emperor Galerius recognized that persecution had failed and issued an edict of toleration making Christianity a legal religion in the East. Two years later Constantine and Lucinius granted Christians freedom of worship throughout the empire. Why Constantine did this is a question historians continue to debate. His Christian biographers assert that the night before a decisive battle at the Milvian Bridge, he looked to the night sky and saw a cross with the words *Hoc vinces* ("By this, conquer") written on it. The next day, after a night in which Christ appeared in his dreams, Constantine led his troops to victory, raising the cross as his symbol. Thereafter, Constantine and his mother, Helena, remained deeply committed to Christianity.

It is probable that his decision to move the political capital from Rome to the East to escape the traditions and factions of Rome also played a role in his embrace of Christianity, along with the fact that the Christians, at 20 percent of the empire, constituted the most organized and galvanized part of the population. His actions at the Council of Nicaea (see p. 179) as a self-proclaimed "thirteenth apostle" showed that the Christian Church was to be his state church. He waited until just before his death to be baptized, and all of his successors but one were Christian.

This colossal head of Constantine captures the emperor's vision of himself as a man in close contact with God.

The sole exception was Julian the Apostate (361–363), a military hero and scholar who had been raised a Christian but then renounced his faith and sought to revive paganism. But Julian did not persecute the Christians, and his efforts to revive paganism failed.

The emperor Theodosius I (379–395) made Christianity the official religion of the empire. Henceforth paganism was persecuted, and even the Olympic Games were suppressed. One famous victim of this persecution *by* Christians was the philosopher Hypatia, who in 415 was killed by a Christian mob in Alexandria. By the age of 25 she had become famous throughout the eastern half of the empire as a lecturer on Greek philosophy. Her popularity and beauty aroused the resentment of Cyril, the archbishop of Alexandria, who had already led a mob in destroying the homes and businesses of the city's Jews. He now incited the mob to abduct Hypatia. She was dragged into a nearby church and hacked to death.

Church Organization

Viewing the present world as something that would end quickly with the imminent second coming of Christ and the last judgment of the living and the dead, the early Christians saw no need to build a formal religious bureaucracy. But after it became clear that the second coming would not be immediate, a church organization emerged to manage the day-to-day business of defining, maintaining, and spreading the faith.

At first there was little or no distinction between laity and clergy. Traveling teachers visited Christian communities, preaching and giving advice. But the steady growth in the number of Christians made necessary special church officials who could devote all their time to religious work, clarifying the body of Christian doctrine, conducting services, and collecting money for charitable purposes.

The earliest officials were called *presbyters* ("elders") or *bishops* ("overseers"). By the second century the offices of bishop and presbyter had become distinct. Churches in villages near the main church, which was usually located in a city, were administered by *priests* (a term derived from *presbyter*), who were responsible to a bishop. Thus evolved the *diocese*, a territorial administrative division under the jurisdiction of a bishop. The bishops were recognized as the direct successors of the apostles and, like them, the guardians of Christian teaching and traditions.

A number of dioceses made up a *province*. The bishop of the most important city in each province enjoyed more prestige than his fellows and was known as an *archbishop* or *metropolitan*. The provinces were grouped into larger administrative divisions called *patriarchates*. The title of *patriarch* was applied to the bishop of such great cities as Rome, Constantinople, and Alexandria.

The bishop of Rome rose to a position of preeminence in the hierarchy of the church. At first only one of several patriarchs, the Roman bishop gradually became recognized as the leader of the church in the West and was given the title of *pope*, from the Greek word for "father." Many factors explain the emergence of the papacy at Rome. As the largest city in the West and the capital of the empire, Rome had an aura of prestige that was transferred to its bishop. After political Rome had fallen, religious Rome remained. When the empire in the West collapsed in the fifth century, the bishop of Rome emerged as a stable and dominant figure looked up to by all. The primacy of Rome was fully evident during the pontificate of Leo I, the Great (440–461), who provided both the leadership that saved Italy from invasion by the Huns and the major theoretical support for papal leadership of the church, the Petrine theory. This doctrine held that since Peter, whom Jesus had made leader of the apostles, was the first bishop of Rome, his authority over all

This World or the Other World

Six years after Alaric's sacking of Rome in 410, Rutilius Namatianus, a man still faithful to his pagan past, retired as prefect of the city of Rome and returned by sea to his home in Romanized Gaul. Passing a Christian monastery on the shore, he recalls that a young man of great promise, because of some "madness," had left "the lands and company of men" to become a monk and was now "buried here alive."

And in the middle of the water rises
The isle of Gorgon, with the Pisan coast
On one side, that of Cyrnos on the other.
And opposite, a rock that held for me
A memory of lately suffered loss:
A man of my own city, buried here
Alive; a youth of noble ancestors
And matching them in marriage and estate.

At least, he was. A madness came upon him
To leave the lands and company of men
And go to exile and ignominy
Among the shades. Poor, superstitious fool,
To think uncleanliness is godliness
And bring more savage torments on himself
Than heaven in its anger could devise.

Paulinus of Nola (c. 355-431) provides an answer to Rutilius's anguished question "Why?" The governor of a Roman province before he was 30, Paulinus gave up his post and his vast estates in Gaul, Spain, and Italy to become a humble Christian priest at Nola, in Italy.

Not that they beggared be in mind, or brutes,
That they have chosen their dwelling place afar
In lonely places: but their eyes are turned
To the high stars, the very deep of Truth.
Freedom they seek, an emptiness apart
From worthless hopes: din of the marketplace,
And all the noisy crowding up of things,
And whatsoever wars on the divine,
At Christ's command and for His love, they hate;
By faith and hope they follow after God,
And know their quest shall not be desperate,
If but the Present conquer not their souls

With hollow things: that which they see they spurn
That they may come at what they do not see,
Their senses kindled like a torch, that may
Blaze through the secrets of eternity.
The transient's open, everlastingness
Denied our sight; yet still by hope we follow
The vision that our minds have seen, despising
The shows and forms of things, the loveliness
Soliciting for ill our mortal eyes.
The present's nothing: but eternity
Abides for those on whom all truth, all good,
Hath shone, in one entire and perfect light.

From Peter D. Arnott, *The Romans and Their World* (New York: St. Martin's Press, 1970), p. 310; and Helen Waddell, *Medieval Latin Lyrics* (London: Constable, 1929), p. 35.

Christians was handed on to his successors at Rome. The church in the East, insisting on the equality of all the apostles, never accepted the Petrine theory. In the West, the Roman Catholic Church served as the "midwife" of Europe as the next stage of history emerged from the ruins of classical Rome.

Pagan writers saw imperial Rome's fall as the consequence of abandoning ancient gods. St. Augustine (354–430), at the time bishop of Hippo in *The City of God*, argued against this point of view and asserted that history unfolds according to God's design. Rome's fall was part of the divine plan, "the necessary and fortunate preparation for the triumph of the heavenly city where man's destiny was to be attained." The Christians, against whom Diocletian launched his most savage attacks, survived, prospered, and laid their claim to the future. They spread their doctrines along the Roman communications links, established their command posts in the Roman administrative centers, and converted Roman citizens to their faith.

Foundations of Christian Doctrine and Worship

While the administrative structure of the church adapted to changing conditions in the West, a combination of theologians and churchly politicians defined and systematized Christian beliefs, sometimes by arbitrary means. This process of fixing Christian doctrine, or *dogma*, began with Paul, who stressed Jesus' divinity and explained his death as an atonement for the sins of all humanity.

In time, differences of opinion over doctrinal matters caused many controversies. One of the most important was over a belief called Arianism. At issue was the relative position of the three persons of the Trinity: God the Father, God the Son, and God the Holy Spirit. The view that Father and Son were equal was vigorously denied by Arius (256–336), a priest from Alexandria. He believed that Christ logically could not fully be God because he was not of a substance identical with God and, as a created being, was not coeternal with his creator. The controversy became so serious that in 325 the emperor Constantine convened the first ecumenical church council to resolve the problem. This Council of Nicaea was the first of nine "world" councils in early church history. With Constantine presiding, the council branded Arian belief a *heresy*—an opinion or doctrine contrary to the official teaching of the church—and Christ was declared to be of the same substance as God, uncreated and coeternal with him. This mystical concept of the Trinity, essential to the central Christian doctrine of the *incarnation*—God becoming man in Christ—received official formulation in the Nicene Creed. However, Arius's views found acceptance among the Germans, and his version of the doctrine of the Trinity was adopted throughout Europe and North Africa.

The liturgy of the early churches was plain and simple, consisting of prayer, Scripture reading, hymns, and preaching. Early Christians worshipped God and sought salvation through individual efforts. Following the growth of church organization and proclamation of official dogma, however, the church came to be viewed as the indispensable intermediary between God and humans. Without the church, the individual could not hope for salvation.

The development of the church's dogma owed much to the church fathers of the second through fifth centuries. Since most of them were intellectuals who came to Christianity by way of Neo-Platonism and Stoicism, they maintained that Greek philosophy and Christianity were compatible. Because reason (*logos* in Greek) and truth came from God, "philosophy was a preparation," wrote Clement of Alexandria (d. 215), "paving the way toward perfection in Christ," the latest and most perfect manifestation of God's reason. Thus Christianity was viewed as a superior philosophy that could supersede all pagan philosophies and religions.

In the West three church fathers stood out. The scholarship of Jerome (340–420) made possible the church-authorized translation of the Bible into Latin. In a revised form, it is still the official translation of the Roman Catholic Church. Jerome, who was canonized for his work, also justified Christian use of the literature and learning of the classical world. Why should not the Christian take what was good from the pagans, he argued, since the Hebrews had taken "spoil" from Egypt when they fled from Egyptian bondage (Exodus 3:22)?

Another of the church fathers, St. Ambrose (340–397), resigned his government post to become bishop of Milan, where he employed his great administrative skills to establish a model bishopric. By criticizing the actions of the strong emperor Theodosius I and forcing him to do public penance, Ambrose was the first to assert the church's superiority over the state in spiritual matters.

St. Augustine was the most important of all the church fathers. At the age of 32, as he relates in his *Confessions*, one of the world's great autobiographies, he found in Christianity the answer to his long search for meaning in life. Before, he had shared the doubts of men "who rush hither and thither, to this side or that, according as they are driven by the impulse of erratic opinion." Now, "by the pity, mercy, and help of God," he had come to anchor in Christianity. "What man shall teach another to understand this?" Augustine asked. No one can teach him; he must come to it on his own after much travail: "This must be asked of you, sought in you, knocked for at you; thus only shall it be received, thus shall it be found, thus shall it be opened to us."[4] Here Augustine echoes the views expressed by many church fathers, that "Christians are not born but made." He blended classical logic and philosophy with Christian belief to lay the foundation of much of the church's theology.

The Regular Clergy

The secular clergy moved through the world (*saeculum*) administering the church's services and communicating its teachings to the laity. But another type of clergy also arose: the regular clergy, so called because they lived by a rule (*regula*) within monasteries. These monks sought seclusion from the distractions of this world in order to prepare themselves for the next. In so doing, they helped preserve and spread the heritage of the classical world along with the faith.

The monastic way of life was older than Christianity, having existed among the Essenes. Christian ascetics, who had abandoned worldly life to live as hermits, could be found in the East as early as the third century C.E. They pursued spiritual perfection by denying their physical feelings, torturing themselves, and fasting. In Syria, for example, St. Simeon Stylites sat for 33 years atop a 60-foot-high pillar. A disciple then beat his record by three months.

In a more moderate expression of asceticism, Christian monks in Egypt developed a monastic life in which, seeking a common spiritual goal, they lived together under a common set of regulations. St. Basil (330–379), a Greek bishop in Asia Minor, drew up a rule based on work, charity, and a communal life that still allowed each monk to retain most of his independence. The Rule of St. Basil became the standard system in the eastern church.

In the West the work of St. Benedict (c. 480–543) paralleled St. Basil's efforts in the East. About 529

Benedict led a band of followers to a high hill between Rome and Naples, named Monte Cassino, where they erected a monastery on the site of an ancient pagan temple. For his monks Benedict composed a rule that gave order and discipline to western monasticism. Benedictine monks took three basic vows—of poverty, chastity, and obedience to the *abbot,* the head of the monastery. The daily activities of the Benedictine monks were closely regulated: they participated in eight divine services, labored in fields or workshops for six or seven hours, and spent about two hours studying and preserving the writing of Latin antiquity at a time when illiteracy was widespread throughout western Europe. Benedictine monasticism was to be the most dynamic civilizing force in medieval Europe between the sixth and twelfth centuries.

Women played an important role in monastic Christianity. In Egypt an early-fifth-century bishop declared that 20,000 women—twice the number of men—were living in desert communities as nuns. In the West several fourth-century biographies of aristocratic women describe how they turned their villas and palaces into monasteries for women of all classes and remained firmly in control of their institutions. These communities became famous for their social and educational services, in addition to providing a different way of life for women who sought alternatives to the usual pattern of marriage, motherhood, and subordination to men.

Byzantium: The Shining Fortress

Constantine the Great had carefully selected the site of his new Roman capital in 325. He chose a site on the frontier of Europe and Asia, dominating the waterway connecting the Mediterranean and Black Seas and protected on three sides by cliffs. The emperors fortified the fourth side with an impenetrable three-wall network. In the first two centuries Visigoths, Huns, and Ostrogoths unsuccessfully threatened the city. In the seventh, eighth, and ninth centuries first Persians, then Arab forces, and finally Bulgarians besieged but failed to take Constantinople. The fortress city withstood all assaults, with the exception of the Fourth Crusade, until 1453.

Constantinople survived more than a thousand years because of the security and wealth provided by its setting. The city was a world trade center that enjoyed the continuous use of a money economy—in contrast to the barter system found in the West after the fifth century. Its wealth and taxes supported a strong military force and financed an effective gov-

	Byzantium
325	Constantine the Great establishes capital in Constantinople (city dedicated May 11, 330)
361–363	Reign of Julian the Apostate
527–565	Reign of Justinian
c. 590	Slavic invasions begin
610–641	Heraclius saves Constantinople, defeats Persians
674–678; 717	Arab seiges of Constantinople
842-1071	Golden Age of Byzantium
1071	Byzantine defeat at Manzikert
1096	First Crusade
1204	Fourth Crusade; Byzantium disappears until 1261
1354	Turks begin to settle in Europe
1453	Fall of Constantinople, end of East Roman Empire

ernment. The city built excellent sewage and water systems that permitted an extremely high standard of living. Food was abundant, with grain from Egypt and Anatolia and fish from the Aegean. Constantinople could feed a million people at a time when it was difficult to find a city in Europe able to sustain more than 50,000.

Unlike Rome, Constantinople had several industries producing luxury goods, military supplies, hardware, and textiles. Until Justinian's reign (527–565), all raw silk had been imported from China, but after silkworms were smuggled out of China about 550 C.E., silk production flourished and became a profitable state monopoly. The state paid close attention to business, controlling the economy through a system of guilds to which all tradesmen and members of professions belonged; setting wages, profits, work hours, and prices; and even organizing bankers and doctors into compulsory corporations.

This security and wealth encouraged an active political, cultural, and intellectual life. The widespread literacy and education among men and women of various segments of society would not be matched in Europe until eighteenth-century Paris. Whether in its Latin, Roman phase, which lasted to the seventh century, or in its Greek, Byzantine phase, which continued to 1453, the empire remained a shining fortress, attracting both invaders and merchants.

The Latin Phase

The eastern capital had to fight for its life against the same invaders who eventually brought down the Roman Empire in the West. However, the dream of reclaiming the Mediterranean basin and reestablishing the empire to its former glory did not die until the end of the reign of Justinian. Aided by his forceful wife, Theodora, and a corps of competent assistants, he made long-lasting contributions to Byzantine and Western civilization but gained only short-term successes in his foreign policy.

In the 520s and 530s Justinian carried out a massive project of urban renewal throughout the empire after earthquakes devastated much of his realm. He strengthened the walls defending Constantinople and built the monumental Hagia Sophia, which still stands. Forty windows circle the base of its dome, producing a quality of light that creates the illusion that the ceiling is floating.

Justinian also reformed the government and ordered a review of all Roman law. This project led to the publication of the Code of Justinian, a digest of Roman and church law, texts, and other instructional materials that became the foundation of modern Western law. Following Constantine's example, he saw himself as the thirteenth apostle and participated actively in the religious arguments of his day.

Justinian's expensive and ambitious projects triggered massive violence among the political gangs of Constantinople, the circus crowds of the Greens and the Blues.[5] Since ancient times, competing factions formed groups throughout the Mediterranean, push-

Hagia Sophia remains intact today, and visitors can share the awe of the Russians who visited the structure in the tenth century and said, "We knew not whether we were in heaven or on earth."

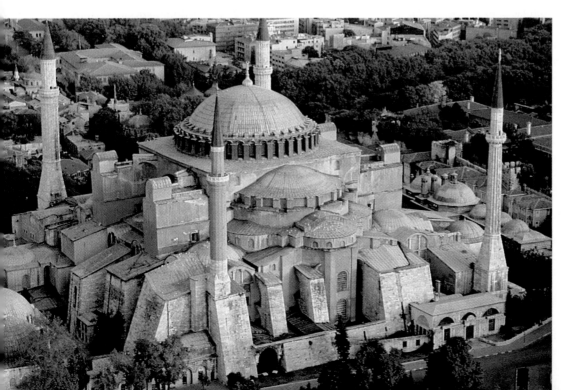

Hagia Sophia (Church of the Holy Wisdom) in Constantinople is considered the architectural masterpiece of the Byzantine Empire. The crowning glory of the church, built during Justinian's reign, was its huge dome, abutted at both ends by a half-dome. The mosaics, painted over when the Ottomans captured the city in 1453, have now been partially restored. The four minarets were added in the fifteenth century.

Discovery Through Maps

A Sixth-Century Map: The Madaba Mosaic

During the first part of Justinian's reign a series of earthquakes shattered buildings around the eastern Mediterranean. The emperor, who had a full treasury, embarked on a massive reconstruction program that adhered to a classical style that was copied all over the empire, even in places that had not suffered from natural disasters. One of the most impressive results of this architectural explosion was Hagia Sophia Church in Constantinople (see p. 181). Another, more subtle but equally revealing, was the Madaba mosaic map, found in present-day Jordan.

Just as Hagia Sophia spoke volumes about the wealth and power of the Christian church, this map, roughly 50 feet by 18 feet, gives remarkable detail about the eastern part of the empire. More than 150 places in present-day Israel, Jordan, Saudi Arabia, Syria, Lebanon, and part of Egypt—the area of the 12 biblical tribes, or the boundaries of Canaan promised to Abraham—are identified, along with an accurate portrayal of the roads, rivers, deserts, seas, and mountains of the region. Unlike modern maps, which are constructed with a north-south orientation, this map points to the east—toward the altar. The importance of a town can be seen by the way it is described—a small town is depicted as having a small church, whereas the unique qualities of the larger places such as Jerusalem are given more elaborate representations.

There are also other details, such as precise illustrations of places mentioned in the Bible, palm trees to indicate oases, and points at which to cross rivers on foot or by ferry boat. It is obvious that the mosaic map profited from the accounts of travelers. The care with which the unique qualities of various sites are illustrated shows that the map had more than just a decorative function: it was also to be used by Christians making pilgrimages—both those from the West and locally.

ing for their own economic, social, and religious goals. Much like contemporary urban gangs, they moved about in groups and congregated at public events. Arguments over the nature of the Trinity divided the Blues and Greens and sparked fights in the streets. A general dislike of Justinian's wife, Theodora, the daughter of a circus animal trainer—a background that made her a virtual untouchable in polite society—provided another point of contention. Her enemies believed that she behaved in an outrageous manner, espoused a heretical variant of Christianity, and had too much control over her husband.

In Constantinople the circus took place in the Hippodrome, a structure that could hold 80,000 spectators. It served as the location for contests of various types, such as chariot races, and the Blues and the Greens could usually be found backing opposing drivers. Usually, the gangs neutralized each other's efforts. In 532, however, the Blues and the Greens joined forces to try to force Justinian from the throne. The so-called Nika rebellion, named after the victory cry of the rioters, almost succeeded. We know from Procopius's *Secret Histories* that Justinian was on the verge of running away until Theodora stopped him and told the frightened emperor:

> *I do not choose to flee. Those who have worn the crown should never survive its loss. Never shall I see the day when I am not saluted as empress. If you mean to flee, Caesar, well and good. You have the money, the ships are ready, the sea is open. As for me, I shall stay.*[6]

Assisted by his generals, the emperor remained and bloodily put the rebellion down.

Justinian momentarily achieved his dream of reestablishing the Mediterranean rim of the Roman Empire. To carry out his plan to regain the half of the empire lost to the Germanic invaders, Justinian first had to buy the neutrality of the Persian kings who threatened not only Constantinople but also Syria and Asia Minor. After securing his eastern flank through diplomacy and bribery, he took North Africa in 533 and the islands of the western Mediterranean from the Vandals.

The next phase of the reconquest was much more exhausting. Like warriors before and after him, he had a difficult time taking the Italian peninsula. He gained his prize from the Ostrogoths after 20 years, but at the cost of draining his treasury and destroying Rome and Ravenna. Ironically, the people against whom he fought had as great a love for Roman institutions and traditions as Justinian did. His generals also reclaimed the southern part of Spain from the Visigoths, but no serious attempt was ever made to recover Gaul, Britain, or southern Germany.

By a decade after Justinian's death, most of the reconquest had been lost. The Moors in Africa, Germanic peoples across Europe, and waves of nomadic tribes from Asia threatened Byzantium's boundaries. Ancient enemies such as the Persians, who had been bribed into a peaceful relationship, returned to threaten Constantinople when the money ran out, setting in motion a half-century-long battle. In addition, the full weight of the Slavic migrations came to be felt. Peaceful though they may have been, the primitive Slavs severely strained and sometimes broke the administrative links of the state. Finally, the empire was split by debates regarding Christian doctrine. The stress of trying to maintain order under these burdens drove two of Justinian's successors insane.

Heraclius: The Empire Redefined

Salvation appeared from the west when Heraclius (610–641), the Byzantine governor of North Africa, returned to Constantinople in 610 to overthrow the mad emperor Phocas (602–610). When Heraclius

The old Roman tradition of the Mediterranean as "Mare Nostrum" ("Our Sea") died hard for Justinian. Twenty years of fighting allowed one last glimmer of the old days, but exhausted his army and his treasury. A half century after his reign, the western holdings would be lost, and the East Roman Empire would be redefined around an Anatolian, not a Mediterranean, base.

This mosaic from the Church of San Vitale at Ravenna, Italy, features the empress Theodora and her attendants.

arrived in the capital, conditions were so bad and the future appeared so perilous that he considered moving the government from Constantinople to Carthage in North Africa.

The situation did not improve soon for the Byzantines. The Persians marched seemingly at will through Syria, took Jerusalem—capturing the "true cross"—and advanced into Egypt. The loss of Egypt to the Persians cost Constantinople a large part of its grain supply. Two fierce Asiatic invaders, the Avars and the Bulgars, pushed against Byzantium from the north. Pirates controlled the sea lanes, and the Slavs cut land communication across the Balkans. Facing ultimate peril, the emperor abandoned the state structure of Diocletian and Constantine.

Heraclius instituted a new system that strengthened his armies, tapped the support of the church and the people, and erected a more efficient, streamlined administration. He determined that the nucleus of the empire would be Anatolia (Asia Minor, the area of present-day Turkey) and that the main source of fighting men for his army would be the free peasants living there rather than mercenaries. Instead of the sprawling realm passed on by Justinian, Heraclius designed a compact state and an administration conceived to deal simultaneously with the needs of government and the challenges of defense.

This system, the *theme* system, had been tested when Heraclius ruled North Africa. Acting on the lessons of the past four centuries, he assumed that defense was a constant need and that free peasant soldiers living in the *theme* ("district") they were defending would be the most effective and efficient force. He installed the system in Anatolia, and his successors then spread it throughout the empire over the next two centuries. Heraclius's scheme provided sound administration and effective defense at half the former cost.[7] As long as the *theme* system, with its self-supporting, landowning, free peasantry endured, Byzantium remained strong. When the *theme* system and its free peasantry were abandoned in the eleventh century, the empire became weak and vulnerable.

Heraclius fought history's first holy war, what Muslims would later call a *jihad*, to reclaim Jerusalem. During the 620s he applied some of the lessons of Hannibal's mobile warfare to attack Persian strength and took the enemy heartland. In 626 Heraclius stood ready to strike the final blow and refused to be drawn away by the Avar siege of Constantinople. He defeated the Persians at Nineva, marched on to Ctesiphon, and finally—symbolic of his victories—reclaimed the "true cross" and returned it to Jerusalem in 630.

He was unable to savor his victory for long, because the Muslims' advance posed an even more dangerous threat to Byzantium. They took Syria and Palestine at the battle of Yarmuk in 636. Persia fell in 637, Egypt in 640. A millennium of Greco-Roman rule in the eastern Mediterranean ended in a mere five years. Constantinople's walls and the redefined Byzantine state withstood the challenge, enduring two sieges in 674–678 and 717. Both times the capital faced severe land and naval attack. The Byzantines triumphed by using new techniques such as Greek fire and germ warfare. Greek fire was the medieval equivalent of napalm. It caught fire on contact with water and stuck to the hulls of the Arabs' wooden ships. At the same time, the Byzantines faced the serious threats of the Bulgarians—continuing their four-century-long pressure on Constantinople—and the Slavs. Heraclius's successors built on his strong foundations by extending the *theme* system and protecting the free peasants—a source of taxes and soldiers.

Iconoclasm and Schism

From Constantine on, the Byzantine emperors played active roles in calling church councils to debate the questions concerning the nature of Christ and his relationship with the Father and the Holy Spirit. In a Caesaropapist structure, an Orthodox Christian doctrine had to be established as a base to deal with both the secular and spiritual opponents of Constantinople. During times of war, such as the Persian invasions during Heraclius's reign, the combined force of church and state provided great strength. At other times, as in the eighth century, when arguments raged between Rome and Constantinople over the use of icons and the propagation of their particular branches of the faith, the emperor's mixing in matters of faith hurt the East Roman state.

When Constantinople faced a three-sided invasion from the Arabs, Avars, and Bulgarians in 717, another powerful leader, Leo the Isaurian (717–741), came forward to turn back the invaders. Over the next decade Leo rebuilt the areas ruined by war and strengthened the *theme* system. He reformed the law, limiting capital punishment to crimes involving treason. He increased the use of mutilation—a less extreme option than execution—for a wide range of common crimes.

Leo took seriously his role as religious leader. He vigorously persecuted heretics and Jews, decreeing that the latter group must be baptized. In 726 he launched a theological crusade against the use of *icons,* pictures and statues of religious figures such as Christ and the saints. He was concerned that icons played too prominent a role in Byzantine life and that their common use as godparents, witnesses at weddings, and objects of adoration went against the Old Testament prohibition of the worship of graven images. Accordingly, the emperor ordered the army to destroy icons. The destruction of the icons caused a violent reaction in the western part of the empire, especially in the monasteries. The government

The Byzantine navy coupled its prowess in battle with the secret and powerful weapon known as Greek fire, depicted here in a fourteenth-century manuscript illumination.

responded by mercilessly persecuting the *iconophiles* ("icon lovers"). The eastern part of the empire, centered in Anatolia, supported destruction of icons *(iconoclasm)*. By trying to remove what he saw to be an abuse, Leo split his empire in two and drove a deeper wedge between the church in Rome and the church in Constantinople.

In Byzantium the religious conflict over destruction of the icons had far-reaching cultural, political, and social implications. Pope Gregory II condemned iconoclasm in 731. Leo's decision to attack icons stressed the fracture lines that had existed between East and West for the past four centuries, typified by the linguistic differences between the Latin West and Greek East.[8] As Leo's successors carried on his religious and political policies, Pope Stephen II turned to the north and struck an alliance with the Frankish king, Pepin, in 754. This was the first step in a process that a half century later would lead to the birth of the Holy Roman Empire and the formal political split of Europe into East and West.

There was a brief attempt under the regent, later empress, Irene (797–802), in 787, to restore icons. In 797 she gained power after having her son, the rightful but incompetent heir, blinded in the very room in which she had given him life. She then became the first woman to rule the empire in her own name. She failed to win widespread support for her pro-icon policies; nor could she put together a marriage alliance with the newly proclaimed western emperor, Charlemagne, a union that would have brought the forces of East and West together. As Irene spent the treasury into bankruptcy, her enemies increased. Finally, in 802 they deposed her and sent her into exile on the island of Lesbos.[9]

The iconoclastic controversy and Irene's ineptitude placed the empire in jeopardy once again. Her successor, Nicepherus (802–811), after struggling to restore the bases of Byzantine power, was captured in

battle with the Bulgarians in 811. Khan Krum beheaded Nicepherus in July and turned his skull into a drinking mug. The iconoclasts had made a comeback, but this phase of image-breaking lacked the vigor of the first, and by 842 the policy was abandoned.

The clash over the icons marked the final split between East and West. Eastern emperors were strongly impressed by Islamic culture, with its prohibition of images. The emperor Theophilus (829–842), for example, was a student of Muslim art and culture, and Constantinople's painting, architecture, and universities benefited from the vigor of Islamic culture. This focus on the East may have led to the final split with the West, but, by the middle of the ninth century, it also produced an East Roman state with its theological house finally in order and its borders fairly secure.

Byzantium's Golden Age, 842–1071

For two centuries, a period coinciding roughly with the reign of the Macedonian dynasty (867–1056), Byzantium enjoyed political and cultural superiority over its western and eastern foes. Western Europe staggered under the blows dealt by the Saracens, Vikings, and Magyars, and the Arabs lost the momentum that had carried them forward for two centuries. Constantinople enjoyed the relative calm, wealth, and balance bequeathed by the *theme* system and promoted by a series of powerful rulers. The time was marked by the flowering of artists, scholars, and theologians as much as it was by the presence of great warriors.

During this Golden Age, Constantinople made its major contributions to eastern Europe and Russia. Missionaries from Constantinople set out to convert the Bulgarians and Slavic peoples in the 860s and in the process organized their language, laws, aesthetics, political patterns, and ethics as well as their religion. But these activities did not take place without competition. Conflict marked the relationship between the Byzantine and Roman churches. A prime example of this conflict was the competition between Patriarch Photius and Pope Nicholas I in the middle of the ninth century.

Photius excelled both as a scholar and as a religious leader. He made impressive contributions to universities throughout the Byzantine Empire and worked to increase Orthodoxy's influence throughout the realm. Nicholas I was Photius's equal in ambition, ego, and intellect. They collided over the attempt to convert the pagan peoples, such as the Bulgarians, caught between their spheres of influence.

Khan Boris of Bulgaria—who was as cunning and shrewd as Photius and Nicholas—saw the trend toward conversion in Europe that had been develop-

The empress Irene, the only woman to rule the Byzantine Empire in her own right, attempted in 787 to restore icons. In 802 she was deposed and exiled to Lesbos.

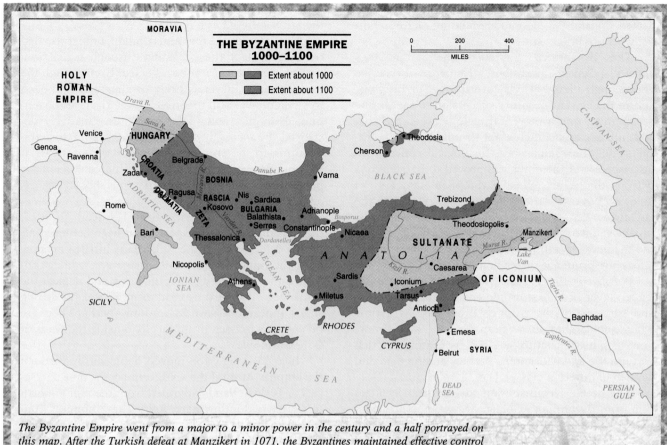

The Byzantine Empire went from a major to a minor power in the century and a half portrayed on this map. After the Turkish defeat at Manzikert in 1071, the Byzantines maintained effective control of only a small fringe of Anatolia. In the Balkans, the new Serbian, Bulgarian, and Hungarian states grew to become powerful, even though the Byzantines claimed control over the region.

ing since the sixth century and realized the increased power he could gain with church approval of his rule. He wanted his own patriarch and church and dealt with the side that gave him the better bargain. From 864 to 866 Boris changed his mind three times over the issue of which holy city to turn to. Finally, the Byzantines gave the Bulgarians the equivalent of an autonomous (independent) church, and in return, the Bulgarians entered the Byzantine cultural orbit. The resulting schism proclaimed between the churches in 867 set off a sputtering sequence of Christian warfare that continued for centuries.[10]

The work of the Byzantine missionary brothers Cyril and Methodius was more important than Bulgarian ambitions or churchly competition. The men were natives of Thessalonica, a city at the mouth of the Vardar-Morava water highway that gave access to the Slavic lands. Versed in the Slavic language, the two led a mission to Moravia, ruled by King Rastislav. He no doubt wanted to convert to Orthodoxy and enter the orbit of distant Constantinople in order to preserve as much independence for his land as he could in the face of pressure from his nearby

powerful German neighbors. Cyril and Methodius carried the faith northward in the vernacular. Cyril adapted Greek letters to devise an alphabet for the Slavs, and the brothers translated the liturgy and many religious books into the Slavic language. Although Germanic missionaries eventually converted the Moravians, the work of Cyril and Methodius profoundly affected all of the Slavic peoples.

Byzantium continued its military as well as its theological dynamism. Arab armies made repeated thrusts, including one at Thessalonica in 904 that led to the loss of 22,000 people. But during the tenth century a decline in Muslim combativeness, combined with the solidity of Byzantine defenses, brought an end to that chapter of conflict. Basil II (963–1025), surnamed *Bulgaroctonus,* or "Bulgar slayer," stopped Bulgarian challenges for more than a century at the battle of Balathista in 1014. At the same time, the Macedonian emperors dealt from a position of strength with western European powers, especially where their interests clashed in Italy. Western diplomats visiting the Byzantine court expressed outrage at the benign contempt with which the eastern emperors treated them. But the attitude merely reflected Constantinople's understanding of its role in the world.

The Byzantines continued their sometimes violent political traditions. Emperor Romanus Lecapenus I (920–944) was overthrown by his sons, and in the eleventh century succession to the throne degenerated into a power struggle between the civil and military aristocracies. Yet through all the political strife, the secular and theological universities flourished, and the emperors proved to be generous patrons of the arts. Basil I (867–886) and Leo VI (886–912) oversaw the collection and reform of the law codes. Leo, the most prolific lawgiver since Justinian, sponsored the greatest collection of laws of the medieval Byzantine Empire, a work that would affect jurisprudence throughout Europe. Constantine VII Porphyrogenitus (912–959) excelled as a military leader, lover of books, promoter of an encyclopedia, and surveyor of the empire's provinces. At a time when scholarship in western Europe was almost nonexistent, Constantinople society featured a rich cultural life and widespread literacy among men and women of different classes.

The greatest contribution to European civilization from Byzantium's Golden Age was the preservation of ancient learning, especially in the areas of law, Greek science and literature, and Platonic and Aristotelian philosophy. Whereas in the West the church maintained scholarship, the civil servants of Byzantium perpetuated the Greek tradition in philosophy, literature, and science. Byzantine monasteries produced many saints and mystics but showed little interest in learning or teaching about this would.

Decline and Crusades

Empires more often succumb to internal ailments than to external takeovers. This was the case with the Byzantine Empire. As long as Constantinople strengthened the foundations laid by Heraclius—the *theme* system and reliance on the free soldier-peasant—the empire withstood the military attacks of the strongest armies of the time. When the Byzantine leaders abandoned the pillars of their success, the state succumbed to the slightest pressure.

Inflation and ambition ate away at the Heraclian structure. Too much money chased too few goods during the Golden Age. Land came to be the most profitable investment the rich could make, and the landowning magnates needed labor. Rising prices meant increased taxes. The peasant villages were collectively responsible for paying taxes, and the rising tax burden overwhelmed them. In many parts of the empire, villages sought relief by placing themselves under the control of large landowners, thus taking themselves out of the tax pool and lowering the number of peasant-soldiers. Both the state treasury and the army suffered as a result.

Until Basil II, the Macedonian emperors had tried to protect the peasantry through legislation, but the trend could not be reversed. Even though the free peasantry never entirely disappeared and each free person was still theoretically a citizen of the empire, economic and social pressures effectively destroyed the *theme* system. An additional factor contributing to the empire's decline was the growth of the church's holdings and the large percentage of the population taking holy orders, thus becoming exempt from taxation.

For 50 years following Basil II's death in 1025, the illusion that eternal peace had been achieved after his devastation of the Bulgarians in 1014 encouraged the opportunistic civil aristocracy, which controlled the state, to weaken the army and neglect the provinces. The next time danger arose, no strong rulers appeared to save Byzantium—perhaps because no enemies massed dramatically outside the walls of Constantinople.

Instead, a new foe moved haphazardly through the empire. Around the sixth century the first in a series of Turkish bands migrated from the region north of China to southwestern Asia. These nomads converted to Islam and, moving westward, fought first with and then against the Persians, the Byzantines, and the Arabs. When the Seljuq Turk leader Alp Arslan (the "Victorious Lion") made a tentative probe into the empire's eastern perimeter near Lake Van in 1071, the multilingual mercenary army sent out from Constantinople fell apart even before fighting began at Manzikert. With the disintegration of the army, the only thing that could stop the Turks' march for the next decade was the extent of their own ambition and energy.

Byzantium lost the heart of its empire, and with it the reserves of soldiers, leaders, taxes, and food that had enabled it to survive for four centuries. From its weakened position, the empire confronted Venice, a powerful commercial and later political rival. By the end of the eleventh century the Venetians had achieved undisputed trading supremacy in the Adriatic and turned their attention to the eastern Mediterranean. The Byzantines also faced the challenges of the Normans, led by Robert Guiscard, who took the last Byzantine stronghold in Italy.

In 1081 a politically astute family, the Comnenians, claimed the Byzantine throne. In earlier times, with the empire at its strongest, these new rulers might have accomplished great things. But the best they could do in the eleventh and twelfth centuries was to play a balance-of-power game between East and West. In 1096 the first crusaders appeared, partly in response to the Council of Clermont, partly in response to the lure of gold and glory (see Chapter 8).

Alexius Comnenus (1081–1118) had appealed to Pope Urban II for help against the Turks, but he did not bargain on finding a host of crusaders, including the dreaded Normans, on his doorstep. Alexius quickly got the crusaders across the Straits of Bosporus and Dardanelles, where they won some battles that allowed the Byzantines to reclaim land lost in the previous 15 years.[11]

Subsequent crusades, however, did not bring good relations between East and West, whose churches had excommunicated each other in 1054. The envy and hatred and frustration that had been building up for some time finally erupted during the Fourth Crusade. The Venetians had control of the ships and money for this crusade and persuaded the crusaders to attack the Christian city of Zadar in Dalmatia—a commercial rival of Venice and Constantinople—before going on to the Holy Land. Venice wanted a trade monopoly in the eastern Mediterranean more than a fight with the Muslims. Constantinople itself was paralyzed by factional strife, and for the first time an invading force captured the city, laying it waste. A French noble described the scene:

> *The fire . . . continued to rage for a whole week and no one could put it out. . . . What damage was done, or what riches and possessions were destroyed in the flames, was beyond the power of man to calculate. . . . The army . . . gained much booty; so much, indeed, that no one could estimate its amount or its value. It included gold and silver, table-services and precious stones, satin and silk, mantles of squirrel fur, ermine and miniver, and every choicest thing to be found on this earth. . . . So much booty had never been gained in any city since the creation of the world.[12]*

The Venetians made sure they got their share of the spoils—such as the bronze horses now found at St. Mark's Cathedral in Venice—and played a key role in placing a new emperor on the throne. The invaders ruled Constantinople until 1261. The Venetians put a stranglehold on commerce in the region and turned their hostility toward the Genoese, who threatened their monopoly.

The empire's last two centuries under the final dynasty, the Paleologus (1261–1453), saw the formerly glorious realm become a pawn in a new game. Greeks regained control of the church and the state, but there was precious little strength to carry on the ancient traditions. Byzantine coinage, which had retained its value from the fourth through the eleventh centuries, fell victim to inflation and weakness. The church, once a major pillar to help the state, became embroiled in continual doctrinal disputes. Slavic peoples such as the Bulgarians and the Serbs under Stephen Nemanja (1168–1196) and Stephen Dushan (1331–1355), who had posed no danger to the empire

The Crusades, viewed from the western perspective as an epoch of bravery, were for the Byzantines and the Arabs a time of barbaric invasions. The crusaders not only failed in the long term to reclaim the Holy Land but also failed to stem the Islamic advance. By the sixteenth century, Turkish forces would be threatening Vienna.

in its former strength, became threats. After Mongol invasions in the thirteenth century destroyed the exhausted Seljuq Turks, a new more formidable foe—the Ottoman or Osmanli Turks—appeared.

The Ottomans were one of the groups of elite warriors, the *ghazis*, on the northwestern frontier of Anatolia. They participated in the complex political and diplomatic relations in the Aegean area in the wake of the Fourth Crusade and were ready to take advantage of the weakened Byzantine Empire. Blessed after 1296 with a strong line of male successors and good fortune, the Ottomans rapidly expanded their power through the Balkans. They crossed the Straits into Europe in 1354 and moved up the Vardar and Morava valleys to take Serres (1383), Sofia (1385), Niš (1386), Thessalonica (1387), and finally Kosovo from the South Slavs in 1389.

The Turks' overwhelming infantry and cavalry superiority gave them their military victories. But their administrative effectiveness, which combined strength and flexibility, solidified their rule in areas

As the Turks patiently advanced in the Balkans in the 1380s, the usually feuding Slavs finally united at the battle of Kosovo. After a long day of valiant fighting, which saw both the Turkish Sultan and the Serbian king die, the Ottomans emerged victorious—with control of the Balkans for the next five centuries. For the Balkan Slavs, especially the Serbs, the memory of the battle of Kosovo would be passed from generation to generation to be used by politicians in the 1990s as a tragedy to unite a people for a better day.

they conquered. In contrast to the Christians, both Roman and Byzantine, who were intolerant of theological differences, the Turks allowed monotheists or any believers in a "religion of the book" (the Bible, Torah, or Qur'an) to retain their faith and be ruled by a religious superior through the *millet* system, a network of religious ghettos.

In response to the Ottoman advance, the West mounted a poorly conceived and ill-fated crusade against the Turks. The confrontation at Nicopolis on the Danube in 1396 resulted in the capture and slaughter of 10,000 knights and their attendants. Only the overwhelming force of Tamerlane (Timur the Magnificent), a Turco-Mongol ruler who defeated the Ottoman army in 1402, gave Constantinople and Europe some breathing space.

The end for Constantinople came in May 1453. The last emperor, Constantine XI, and his force of 9000, half of whom were Genoese, held off 160,000 Turks for seven weeks. Finally, with the help of Hungarian artillerymen, the Turks breached the once im-penetrable walls of the depopulated city. After 1123 years, the shining fortress fell.[13]

Eastern European and Russian Romes

Following in the wake of the Germanic tribes' westward march, the dominant people of eastern Europe, the Slavs, spread from the Pripet marshes west to the Elbe, east to the Urals, north to Finland, and south to the Peloponnesus. As they settled throughout eastern and central Europe from the sixth through the ninth centuries, they absorbed most of the original inhabitants of the region. This mixing of peoples produced the resulting blends of nations that make up the present-day complexity of eastern Europe and Russia.

The geography of eastern Europe contributed to the diversity of the region's population. The climatic extremes range from arctic cold to Mediterranean

Eastern Europe and Russia

c. 700–1014	First Bulgarian Empire
865–870	Bulgarian conversion to Orthodoxy
867	First "Russian" attack on Constantinople
862–867	Cyril and Methodius's mission to the Moravians
c. 900	Serb conversion to Orthodoxy
925	First Croat state, conversion to Catholicism
988	Russian conversion to Orthodoxy
988–1240	Kiev Rus'
1169–1389	Serbian Empire
1197–1393	Second Bulgarian Empire
1220–1242	Mongol invasions in Russia and eastern Europe
1240–1480	Mongol domination of Russia
1300s–1400s	Reemergence of Wallachia and Moldavia
1389	Battle of Kosovo
1450–1468	Albanian state under Skanderbeg
1462–1505	Reign of Ivan III, the Great

mildness. The soil varies from the rich topsoil of the Ukraine and the Danubian plain to the rocky dryness of the Dinaric Alps. Waterways include both the scenic though commercially useless rivulets of Greece and the broad and powerful Vistula and Danube Rivers. Some of the lands have no access to the sea; others, such as Greece, are blessed with fine harbors. The particular scope of climate, soil, and water access dictated the economic possibilities of each nation.

Like that of eastern Europe, Russia's history is largely a product of its geography. The vast expanse of land combined with a comparatively small population has made the domination of the peasants by the landed interests—both individuals and state—one of the continuing themes in Russian history. Russia's difficulty in gaining access to the sea has had important economic and cultural consequences, stunting the growth of a merchant class and encouraging the formation of an inward-looking population.

Russia's waterways have played a key role in the development of the country. The rivers, which flow

north or south across the land, have served as thoroughfares for trade and cultural exchange as well as routes for invasion. Unconnected to the western European region, the rivers dictated a line of communication that led early Russian traders to Constantinople rather than to the West. The Volkhov and Dnieper network tied together the Varangians (also known as the Vikings) and the Greeks through Russia, while the Volkhov and Volga system reached toward central Asia.

Russian historians stress that the interaction of the forest and steppe zones must be considered in order to understand the country. The forest provided protection, a means to make a living through fur-trapping and honey-gathering, and a chance to escape the pressures of the central authorities. The extremely rich topsoil of the steppe zone provided agricultural wealth, political control, and a grass-lined highway for nomadic invaders. Where the two come together is where much of early Russian history took place. It is within this geographical framework that the Russian nation developed, with the arrival—six centuries B.C.E.—of Asiatic tribes following the steppe belt and crossing Russian territory.

The Peoples of Eastern Europe

From the sixth through the ninth centuries the Slavs hunted and traded—usually forest products such as furs, honey, and wax. They also farmed, using the "slash and burn" method of cutting down the forests, tilling the land until it was exhausted, and then moving on. With the exception of the Bulgarians, they formed themselves into male-dominated peasant tribal units, based on blood relations. The clan elders chose from their ranks a leader who would meet with other clan leaders to elect a person to coordinate activities throughout the district. From the ranks of the clan would come the local officials, priests, and tax and military payments.

Compared to the wealth and sophistication of the Byzantines, the Slavs' economic and social lives were primitive, and their political and military structures were weak. Outsiders—Byzantines, Germans, Magyars, Mongols, or Turks—often ruled the various Slavic groups. Each outside ruler imposed a distinctive set of cultural, economic, political, and social traits on the Slavic group it dominated. The rulers' religion was the key means through which these distinctive traits were imposed, leading to tragic divisions in the Slavic peoples, such as those that erupted in Bosnia and Herzegovina in the 1990s.

Eastern Europeans who found themselves in the Roman sphere—the Poles, Czechs, Slovaks, Hungarians, Slovenes, and Croats—joined a cultural community that stretched from the Bug River to the Straits of Gibraltar to Iceland. Common threads uniting this

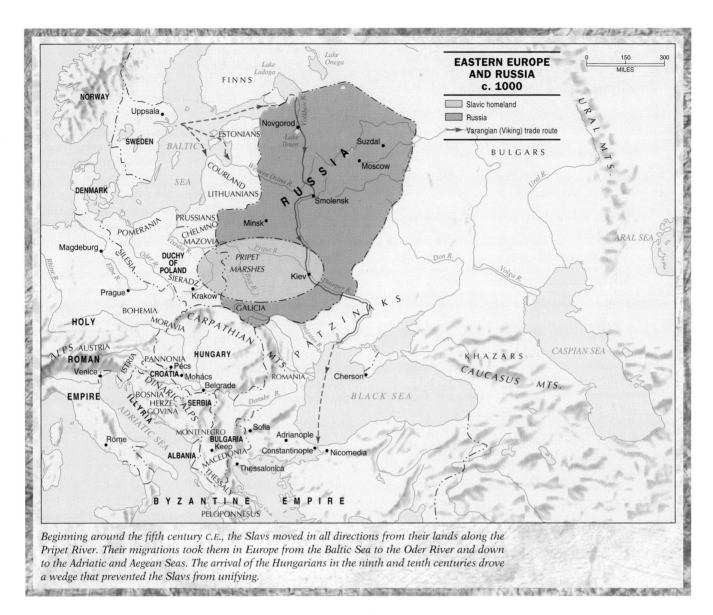

Beginning around the fifth century C.E., the Slavs moved in all directions from their lands along the Pripet River. Their migrations took them in Europe from the Baltic Sea to the Oder River and down to the Adriatic and Aegean Seas. The arrival of the Hungarians in the ninth and tenth centuries drove a wedge that prevented the Slavs from unifying.

community were the Latin language and a belief in papal authority. German monks and priests carried the Roman faith to this area, and they were followed and sustained by a Germanic population movement, the *Drang nach Osten* ("drive to the east"). Hungary, Bohemia, and Poland experienced a golden age of cultural and economic development in the fourteenth century, when their originating dynasties—respectively, the Arpad, Premysl, and Piast dynasties—died out and were replaced by new political and cultural elites. Universities were established in Prague (1348), Krakow (1364), and Pecs (1369), and scholars in those schools partook of the humanist movement of the fifteenth century.

The Hungarians were defeated by the Ottoman Empire at Mohacs (1526), and their land was divided into three zones, the larger part controlled directly by the Turks. Despite this, people in the Roman Catholic orbit shared in the great formative developments of Western civilization: the Renaissance, the Reforma-

tion, the Scientific Revolution, the Capitalist Revolution, the Enlightenment, the French Revolution, and the Industrial Revolution. They also participated directly in the classic developmental process of western Europe of feudalism, the development of the modern state system, and the growth of pluralistic society.

Eastern Europeans who came into the Byzantine, Orthodox orbit during the ninth and tenth centuries—the Bulgarians, Serbs, Montenegrins, Romanians, and Russians—heard the liturgy in their native language, worshiped under a decentralized religious structure, and remained culturally separated from western Europe. These Orthodox Christians lived at various times under the domination of the Mongols or the Turks, two despotic Asiatic powers that permitted the practice of the Orthodox religion but controlled political behavior. The combination of Byzantine autocracy and oriental despotism led to the growth of authoritarian states that did not encourage the pluralistic societies and multifaceted creativity found in western Europe. In fact, before the imposition of Ottoman control, each of the Balkan people would have a moment of glory—the two Bulgarian Empires, the Serbs under Stephen Nemanja and Stephen Dushan—in which it would create its own image of Byzantium. However, in Russia a formidable civilization emerged that by the fifteenth century claimed to be the Third Rome.

Kiev Rus'

In the sixth century C.E. the eastern Slavs began moving out of the area near the Pripet marshes. The various clans went as far north as the White Sea, as far east as the Urals, and to the region south of Kiev. (Kiev Rus' describes the Kievan phase of Russian history, especially the introduction of a stronger Ukrainian historiographical tradition. The apostrophe is for a diacritical mark in the writing of the word Rus' in Russian and Ukrainian.) To the north, around Lake Ilmen, the Slavs established a number of trading towns such as Novgorod, from which they founded other trading bases. By the ninth century they had accumulated sufficient wealth to attract the attention of the Varangians, who came down from the Baltic to dominate the trading routes, especially those going from the Dvina to the Dnieper to Constantinople.

Russian history is said to begin with the entry of the Varangians into eastern Slavic affairs in the 860s. One of the key controversies in Russian history revolves around the question of the Varangians' role. Did they impose themselves on the Slavs and form them into their first political units, or were the Varangians invited in by the already sophisticated, though feuding, Slavic tribes? The so-called Norman controversy can best be addressed by noting that the Slavs, like most other Europeans, fell under the wave of the northern invaders but within two generations assimilated them and incorporated their capabilities.

The Varangian Oleg (c. 882–913) established his seat of government at Kiev, at the transition point between the forest and steppe zones. During the tenth century Oleg and Sviatoslav (964–972) created a state that was the equal of contemporary France. Oleg took control of both Kiev and Novgorod and, with the strength gained, launched an attack on Constantinople. Sviatoslav carried Kievan power to the Danube and the lower Volga. He fell victim to the knives of Asiatic invaders, the Patzinaks. However, he left a state strong enough to endure almost a decade of internal power struggles.

The most important ruler in the Kievan phase of Russian history was Vladimir, who overcame his brothers to dominate his country from 980 to 1015. Vladimir learned his political lessons dealing with the Byzantines, and he consolidated his power in Kiev. At first he based his rule on the pagan party and

erected statues to gods such as Perun (the god of thunder) and Volos (the god of wealth). He made peace with the Volga Bulgars to the east and worked with the Byzantines against the Bulgarians in pursuit of his diplomatic and political goals.

Vladimir acknowledged the fact that the nations surrounding him were converting to one organized religion or another: the Poles and Hungarians to Roman Catholicism, the Khazars to Judaism, the Volga Bulgars to Islam, and the Bulgarians to Orthodoxy. His grandmother, the shrewd and skillful Olga, had accepted Orthodox Christianity from Constantinople in 956, as had other members of his family. During the 980s Vladimir sent observers to judge the various religious alternatives. According to the *Russian Primary Chronicle*, they visited Hagia Sophia at Constantinople in 988 and were impressed with the power and wealth of the city. The observers recommended that Vladimir choose the Orthodox faith.

The story, though interesting, ignores the many concrete advantages Vladimir derived from his decision. As part of the negotiation package, Vladimir agreed to help the Byzantine emperor Basil against his enemies. In return he would receive the hand of the emperor's sister in marriage upon converting to Orthodoxy. After a successful campaign, Basil delayed in carrying out his part of the bargain. Vladimir moved quickly to make his point and marched into the Crimea and took the Byzantine city of Cherson. The Kiev-Byzantine arrangements were finally carried out in 990. Vladimir, now a member of the Byzantine royal family, brought his country into the Byzantine, Orthodox orbit. Even before "becoming a saint," the *Chronicle* tells us, he destroyed the pagan statues, converted his many concubines to nuns, and forced his people to become Christians.[14] Eventually the Russians gained their own church, received their own metropolitan, and adapted Byzantine ritual, theology, and monastic practices to their own use. They also applied Byzantine governmental theories to their own social hierarchy.

After Vladimir, few great monarchs ruled during the Kievan period of Russian history. Instead, political fragmentation began to intensify. During the reign of Yaroslav the Wise (1019–1054), the Kievan state reached its high point, and it was the cultural and economic equal of any government in Europe. Yaroslav undertook major building projects, revised the law code, and promoted the growth of the church. He formed a dynastic alliance with Henry I of France. Unfortunately, Kiev did not long maintain its prestigious position. Yaroslav introduced a principle of succession based on the *seniority* system, passing the rule of Kiev from brother to brother in a given generation before the next generation would have its chance. This practice is in contrast with the Western one of *primogeniture,* under which rule is handed

The Acceptance of Christianity

Russia's conversion to Orthodoxy was a fundamental step in the division of Europe between East and West. This excerpt from the *Russian Primary Chronicle* explains how the decision was made.

6494 (986). Vladimir was visited by Volga Bulgars of Mohammedan [Muslim] faith. . . . Then came the Germans, asserting that they came as emissaries of the Pope. . . . The Jewish Khazars heard of these missions, and came themselves. . . . Then the Greeks sent to Vladimir a scholar. . . .

6495 (987). Vladimir summoned together his vassals and the city elders, and said to them, "Behold, the Volga Bulgars came before me urging me to accept their religion. Then came the Germans and praised their own faith; and after them came the Jews. Finally the Greeks appeared, criticizing all other faiths but commending their own, and they spoke at length, telling the history of the whole world from its beginning. . . ."

. . . The Prince and all the people chose good and wise men to the number of ten, and directed them to go first among the Volga Bulgars and inspect their faith. The emissaries went their way, and when they arrived at their destination they beheld the disgraceful actions of the Volga Bulgars and their worship in the mosque; then they returned to their own country. Vladimir then instructed them to go likewise among the Germans, and examine their faith, and finally to visit the Greeks. They thus went into Germany, and after viewing the German ceremonial, they proceeded to Tsargrad [Constantinople], where they appeared before the Emperor. . . .

Thus they returned to their own country, and the Prince called together his vassals and the elders. Vladimir then announced the return of the envoys who had been sent out, and suggested that their report be heard. He thus commanded them to speak out before his vassals. The envoys reported, "When we journeyed among the Volga Bulgars, we beheld how they worship in their temple, called a mosque, while they stand ungirt. The Volga Bulgar bows, sits down, looks hither and thither like one possessed, and there is no happiness among them, but instead only sorrow and a dreadful stench. Their religion is not good. Then we went among the Germans, and saw them performing many ceremonies in their temples; but we beheld no glory there. Then we went on to Greece, and the Greeks led us to the edifices where they worship their God, and we knew not whether we were in heaven or on earth. For on earth there is no such splendor or such beauty, and we are at a loss how to describe it. We only know that God dwells there among men, and their service is fairer than the ceremonies of other nations. . . ." Then the vassals spoke and said, "If the Greek faith were evil, it would not have been adopted by your grandmother Olga, who was wiser than all other men." Vladimir then inquired where they should all accept baptism, and they replied that the decision rested with him. . . .

By divine agency, Vladimir was suffering at that moment from a disease of the eyes, and could see nothing, being in great distress. The Princess declared to him that if he desired to be relieved of this disease, he should be baptized with all speed, otherwise it could not be cured. . . . The Bishop of Kherson, together with the Princess' priests, after announcing the tidings, baptized Vladimir, and as the Bishop laid his hand upon him, he straightway received his sight. Upon experiencing this miraculous cure, Vladimir glorified God, saying, "I have now perceived the one true God." When his followers beheld this miracle, many of them were also baptized.

From *The Russian Primary Chronicle*, trans. Samuel H. Cross, in *Harvard Studies and Notes in Philology and Literature*, Vol. 12 (Cambridge, Mass.: Harvard University Press, 1953), pp. 183–213 passim. Reprinted by permission.

down to the eldest son of the ruler. Within two generations, the seniority system led to the political breakup of Kiev, although the city maintained its theoretical superiority within Russia.

Kiev also came under attack from both east and west and suffered as well from the economic decline of Constantinople. Under Vladimir Monomakh (1113–1125), Kiev reemerged briefly as a center of power, but a half century of decline soon followed. Competing centers arose at Suzdal; Galicia, where the local aristocracy dominated; Vladimir, where the

prince emerged all-powerful; and Novgorod, where the assembled citizens—the *veche*—were the major force. Even before the Mongols totally destroyed the city in 1240, Kiev's era of prominence was effectively over.

Novgorod, Moscow, and the Mongols

For more than two centuries, from 1240 to 1480, Mongols dominated Russia, and during that time much of the land was cut off from contact with the outside world. During this period a new center of power, Moscow, emerged to serve for most of the time as collector of tribute for the Mongol court. New internal markets developed, and the Orthodox church, unhampered by the Mongols, grew in strength and influence. The Russian city of Novgorod also managed to carry on despite the oriental overlord.

Novgorod had come under the control of the Varangians in the ninth century, but in 997 the citizens received a charter granting them self-government, and for the next five centuries this *veche* elected its own rulers. The city boasted an aggressive and prosperous merchant class, which exploited the region from the Ural Mountains to the Baltic Sea and held its own against German merchants from the Baltic area. Novgorod was the equal of most of the cities found along the Baltic and North Seas. In the middle of the thirteenth century, Alexander Nevsky, the prince of Novgorod, led his fellow citizens in struggles to repel the Teutonic Knights and the Swedes. A few years later he showed exceptional diplomatic skill in paying homage to the Mongols, even though they had halted 60 miles outside the city and left Novgorod untouched. At a time when the rest of Russia suffered mightily under the first phase of Mongol domination, the *veche*-elected oligarchy continued to rule Novgorod.

The city's wealth and traditions permitted the *veche* to rule. The citizens elected their princes and forced them to sign a contract setting out what they could and could not do. In the words of a typical document between ruler and city, the citizens could show their prince "the way out" if he failed to live up to the terms of his agreement. The prince could act as a leader of Novgorod only when he remained within the city's limits. The city's method of government permitted the rise of class divisions that led to more than 20 major outbreaks of violence in the thirteenth and fourteenth centuries. Changes in trade routes in the fifteenth century led to a decline in Baltic commerce, and Novgorod came to depend on Moscow for its grain supply. That dependence, in addition to the class conflict, weakened Novgorod, and in 1478 Moscow absorbed the town.

The obscure fortress town of Moscow, first mentioned in the records in 1147, came to be the core of the new Russia. Even before the Mongol invasion, a large number of Slavs moved toward the north and east, and this migration continued for centuries as that frontier offered opportunities for the oppressed. Moscow was well placed along a north-south river route in a protective setting of marshes and forests.

One of Alexander Nevsky's sons, Daniel, founded the Grand Duchy of Moscow, and he and subsequent rulers inherited Nevsky's ability to get along with the Mongols. As the Moscow princes skillfully acknowledged their inferior position to the Mongol khans,

who sought tribute and recruits, the Muscovites improved their political position in relation to the other Russians by attempting to monopolize the tax collection function for the Mongols, with notable success. In addition, at the beginning of the fourteenth century they made sure that the seat of the Russian Orthodox Church would be in Moscow, a reflection of the city's prestige.[15]

In the first century after the Mongol invasion, the Muscovite princes showed a great deal of ambition and ability, albeit in a sometimes unattractive way. For example, during his reign (1328–1341) Ivan I Kalita (whose surname means "moneybags"), greatly increased the wealth and power of his city by aggressive tax collection practices.

On the surface, the fourteenth century appeared to be a time of decline, of Mongol domination and gains by the European states at Russian expense along the western boundary. The reality, however, was that Russia was laying foundations for its future with Moscow as the country's religious and political center. In 1380 Dmitri Donskoi (1359–1389) defeated the Mongols at Kulikovo. Although Mongol strength was far from broken, the Russian victory had great symbolic significance.

Civil war and invasions threatened the Moscow-based country throughout the fifteenth century. Finally, Ivan III (1462–1505) made major strides to build the modern Russian state. He took Novgorod and two years later ceased acknowledging Mongol domination. He then began to advance toward the south and east against the Turks and Mongols, setting in motion a drive that lasted for centuries.

In developments of considerable symbolic importance, the Russians embraced many elements of the Roman tradition. Ivan III married the niece of the last East Roman emperor, an alliance arranged by the pope. Russians espoused the theory that Moscow was the Third Rome, the logical successor to Constantinople as the center of Christianity. In 1492 (the year 7000 in the Orthodox calendar and the beginning of a new millennium), the Muscovite metropolitan, Zosima, stated that Ivan III was "the new Emperor Constantine of the new Constantinople Moscow." Zosima for the first time called Moscow an imperial city. Philotheus of Pskov expounded the theory of Third Rome in full detail in the 1520s.[16] Ivan began to use the title *tsar* ("caesar") and adopted the Roman two-headed eagle as the symbol of the Russian throne.

Ivan opened the doors to the West ever so slightly. He established diplomatic relations with a number of European powers. He brought in Italian technicians and architects such as Aristotele Fieravanti and Pietro Antonio Solari to work on the churches, palaces, and walls of the Kremlin—the vastly expanded site of the original fortress that was the center of the town three

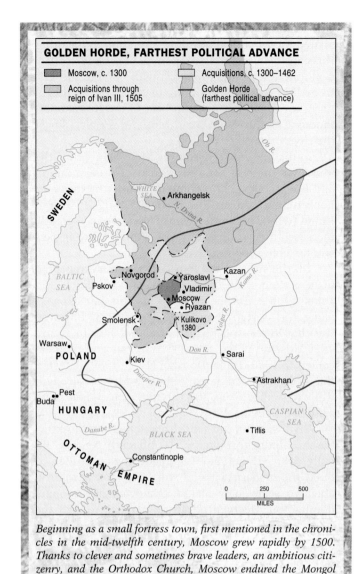

GOLDEN HORDE, FARTHEST POLITICAL ADVANCE

■ Moscow, c. 1300
□ Acquisitions, c. 1300–1462
▨ Acquisitions through reign of Ivan III, 1505
— Golden Horde (farthest political advance)

Beginning as a small fortress town, first mentioned in the chronicles in the mid-twelfth century, Moscow grew rapidly by 1500. Thanks to clever and sometimes brave leaders, an ambitious citizenry, and the Orthodox Church, Moscow endured the Mongol occupation to emerge as the self-proclaimed "Third Rome."

centuries earlier. The Italian artistic tradition had no lasting cultural impact on Russia, but use of Italian artists nonetheless signified an awareness of the West. In recognition of the need to establish a standing army, Ivan began the difficult process of building up a modern state structure and increased restrictions on the Russian peasants. During the fifteenth century Ivan was the equal of his western European colleagues Henry VII of England and Louis XI of France. After three centuries, the Russians were back in touch with Europe.[17]

Conclusion

The Christians grew from a small and despised band of believers whose leader had been crucified to be-

come the most notable survivors of the West Roman Empire. Their spiritual message spread rapidly through the crisis-ridden Mediterranean world after the second century and came to be the foundation for powerful forces. By the sixth century the foundations for the papacy's spiritual and political power had been laid in the West. Pope Leo the Great acquired the moral leadership of the West by successfully protecting Rome from the Huns. Political fragmentation after 476 allowed the papacy to achieve independence and laid the groundwork for the doctrine of the supremacy of the church over the state in spiritual matters, a theory implied by St. Augustine in *The City of God*. The church would serve as the frame on which modern Europe would emerge, weaving together Greco-Roman culture and the strengths of the Germanic peoples, their institutions, and their values.

In the East, Constantine had proclaimed Constantinople the first Christian capital and himself the "thirteenth apostle." For the next 1200 years, after the decline of the Roman Empire in the West, Byzantium preserved and enlarged the heritage of Western civilization, Christianized much of eastern Europe, and held off Persian and Arab assaults. During its millennium of existence the eastern empire enjoyed eight centuries of economic, intellectual, political, and military dominance. Perhaps its longest-lasting effect was on the Slavs, especially the Russians.

From the fourth through the ninth centuries, as the Slavs moved to their new homelands, they came under the influence of dominant outside forces. In Russia and the Balkans, Byzantine patterns and traditions shaped their lives. To the north the Roman Catholic faith, carried by the Germans, helped define national characteristics.

After its initial Kievan phase, in which Vladimir made the choice to follow East Roman precedents, the Russians remained under Mongol domination even when Russia's political and religious center moved to Moscow. When the Russians regained their independence in the fifteenth century, they redefined their polity in Roman and Christian terms, claiming the legacy of the fallen city of Constantinople.

The Christian faith, with its origins in spirituality, humility, and love and its founder who preached a heavenly kingdom, played a historical role not foreseen by its earliest adherents. Christianity fueled a spiritual and secular force based in Rome that would serve as the bridge between the classical and modern worlds. In the East powerful emperors in Constantinople and Moscow used Orthodox Christianity to buttress their own power. It matters little whether the politicians of Rome, Constantinople, and Moscow were pious or hypocritical in governing their new

Christian realms. Their embrace of Christ's message profoundly altered the form, if not the substance, of Christianity.

Suggestions for Reading

J. H. Hexter, *The Judaeo-Christian Tradition*, 2nd ed. (Yale University Press, 1995), is a brief but valuable survey of the evolution of ancient Judaism and Christianity. On the late ancient history of the Jews, see Elias Bickerman, *From Ezra to the Last of the Maccabees: Foundations of the Post-Biblical Judaism* (Schocken, 1949), and D. S. Russell, *The Jews from Alexander to Herod* (Oxford University Press, 1967).

Since their discovery a half century ago, the Dead Sea Scrolls have been the subject of much academic intrigue and infighting. Access to them has been limited, but finally Martin Abegg and Edward Cook used computer technology to reconstruct the bits and fragments that were available, and the results can be found in Michael Owen Wise, ed., with Martin G. Abegg and Edward Cook, *The Dead Sea Scrolls: A New Translation* (Harper/SanFrancisco, 1996). Another version, Geza Vemez, ed., *The Complete Dead Sea Scrolls in English* (Allen Lane, 1997), is impressive but incomplete.

Howard Clark Kee and Carter Lindberg, *Understanding the New Testament*, 5th ed. (Prentice Hall, 1997), is highly recommended. See also Edgar J. Goodspeed, *A Life of Jesus* (Greenwood, 1950); Michael Grant, *Saint Paul* (Scribner, 1976); and Rudolf Karl Bultmann, *Primitive Christianity in Its Contemporary Setting* (Meridian, 1956), on the beginnings of Christianity. J. W. C. Wand, *A History of the Early Church to A.D. 500*, 4th ed. (Methuen, 1975), and Henry Chadwick, *The Early Church* (Penguin, 1969), are excellent surveys of the first five centuries of church history. For a look at Jesus as a social critic and the "Jewish Socrates," see John D. Crossan, *Jesus: A Revolutionary Biography* (HarperCollins, 1994). See also Cyril Richardson, *Early Christian Fathers* (Macmillan, 1970); the superb biography by Peter Brown, *Augustine of Hippo* (University of California Press, 1969); Harold B. Mattingly, *Christianity in the Roman Empire* (Norton, 1967); Ramsay MacMullen, *Paganism in the Roman Empire* (Yale University Press, 1981), and *Christianizing the Roman Empire* (Yale University Press, 1984); and Charles N. Cochrane, *Christianity and Classical Culture: A Study of Thought and Action from Augustus to Augustine* (Galaxy, 1960). On early monasticism, see Helen Waddell, trans., *The Desert Fathers* (University of Michigan Press, 1957), and Peter Brown, *The Making of Late Antiquity* (Harvard University Press, 1978). See also Eusebius, *The History of the Church from Christ to Constantine* (Penguin, 1994). Ramsay MacMullen gives a thorough treatment of the spread of Christianity after 100 in *Christianizing the Roman Empire (100–400)* (Yale University Press, 1984), and Judith Herrin covers the early stages of the church's growth from the perspective of Constantinople in *The Formation of Christendom* (Princeton University Press, 1987).

Two works by Arnold Hugh Martin Jones, *The Decline of the Ancient World* (Longman, 1977), and *The Later Roman Empire, 284–602: A Social, Economic, and Administrative Survey*, 2 vols. (Johns Hopkins University Press, 1986), are indispensable. An excellent short introduction to Byzantium is Steven Runciman's classic, *Byzantine Civilization* (Meridian, 1969). Joan M. Hussey, *The Byzantine World* (Greenwood, 1982), is clear and lively. For an exhaustive treatment of life in Byzantium, see *The Cambridge Medieval History*, Vol. 4

(Cambridge University Press, 1966, 1967). George Ostrogorsky, *History of the Byzantine State* (Rutgers University Press, 1957), provides the best institutional overview. John W. Barker, *Justinian and the Later Roman Empire* (University of Wisconsin Press, 1966); Robert Browning, *Justinian and Theodora* (Praeger, 1971); and Glanville Downey, *Constantinople in the Age of Justinian* (University of Oklahoma Press, 1968), give complementary analyses of the sixth century. Joan M. Hussey, *The Orthodox Church in the Byzantine Empire* (Oxford University Press, 1986), is the best introduction in English to the development of the eastern variant of Christianity. Romilly Jenkins, *Byzantium: The Imperial Centuries* (Vintage, 1969), is a beautifully written treatment of medieval Byzantium. Francis Dvornik, *The Photian Schism: History and Legend* (Rutgers University Press, 1970), and *The Slavs in European History and Civilization* (Rutgers University Press, 1970), address the matters of conversion. Charles M. Brand, *Byzantium Confronts the West, 1180–1204* (Harvard University Press, 1968), and Donald E. Queller, ed., *The Latin Conquest of Constantinople* (Wiley, 1971), describe the tragedy of the Crusades for Byzantium and complement Steven Runciman's three-volume *History of the Crusades* (Penguin, 1965). Donald Nicol, *The Last Centuries of Byzantium* (St. Martin's Press, 1972), discusses the empire in its state of weakness. The best treatment of Byzantium at its peak is Michael Agold, *The Byzantine Empire, 1025–1204* (Longman, 1985).

D. Talbot Rice, *Art of the Byzantine Era* (Oxford University Press, 1962), gives a competent overall assessment of the eastern empire's aesthetics. Andre Grabar, *Byzantium* (Thames & Hudson, 1966), is a beautifully illustrated and thorough discussion of art and architecture before 600. Harry J. Magoulias, *Byzantine Christianity: Emperor, Church, and the West* (Wayne State University Press, 1982), and Timothy Ware, *The Orthodox Church* (Penguin, 1993), are two sophisticated surveys.

George Vernadsky, *Kievan Russia*, 2nd ed. (Yale University Press, 1973), is detailed and authoritative. G. Fedotov, *The Russian Religious Mind: Kievan Christianity, the Tenth to the Thirteenth Centuries* (HarperTorchbooks, 1975), notes the impact of Orthodoxy on Russian civilization. The works cited in notes 6, 12, and 14 (see p. 198) are useful primary readings. John Fennell, *The Crisis of Medieval Russia, 1200–1304* (Longman, 1983), and Robert O. Crummey, *The Formation of Muscovy, 1304–1613* (Longman, 1987), are two first-rate analyses of the first phases of Russian history. Oscar Halecki, *Borderlands of Western Civilization* (Ronald Press, 1952), gives the outlines of eastern European history, especially the northern region. For samples of primary sources, see Serge A. Zenkovsky, ed., *Medieval Russia's Epics, Chronicles, and Tales* (Penguin, 1994).

Suggestions for Web Browsing

Byzantium Studies on the Internet
http://www.bway.net/~halsall/byzantium.html
Byzantine Art
http://www.bway.net/~halsall/images.html
This site includes many images of icons, monasteries, Ravenna, and Hagia Sophia; it details Byzantine life in Jerusalem and offers links to related Web sites.

Historical Tour of Jerusalem: Byzantine Period
http://gurukul.ucc.american.edu/TED/hpages/jeruselum/byzantin.htm
Short history of Jerusalem, from 324 to 638 C.E., including an image and discussion of the Madaba mosaic showing the Jerusalem Gate.

Women in Byzantium
http://www.wooster.edu/ART/wb.html

Extensive bibliography of primary and secondary sources regarding women in Byzantium.

Byzantium Through Arab Eyes
http://www.fordham.edu/halsall/source/byz-arabambas.html

An original account of a mission to Constantinople by an Arab ambassador in the late tenth century.

Notes

1. Edmund Wilson, *The Scrolls from the Dead Sea* (New York: Oxford University Press, 1955), p. 60.
2. Josephus, *The Jewish War,* trans. G. A. Williamson (Baltimore: Penguin, 1970), p. 136.
3. Mary Kinnear, *Daughters of Time: Women in the Western Tradition* (Ann Arbor: University of Michigan Press, 1982), p. 55.
4. St. Augustine, *Confessions* 13.38, trans. E. B. Pusey.
5. Alan Cameron, *Circus Factions: Blues and Greens at Rome and Byzantium* (Oxford: Clarendon Press, 1976), pp. 310–311.
6. Procopius of Caesarea, *History of the Wars,* Vol. 1, 24:36–38, trans. S. R. Rosenbaum, in Charles Diehl, *Theodora: Empress of Byzantium* (New York: Ungar, 1972), pp. 87–88.
7. George Ostrogorsky, *History of the Byzantine State,* trans. Joan M. Hussey (New Brunswick, N.J.: Rutgers University Press, 1957), pp. 86–90.
8. Andreas N. Stratos, *Byzantium in the Seventh Century,* Vol. 1, trans. Marc Oglivie-Grant (Amsterdam: Hakkert, 1968), pp. 37–39.
9. Romilly Jenkins, *Byzantium: The Imperial Centuries,* A.D. *610–1071* (New York: Vintage Books, 1969), pp. 90–104.
10. Francis Dvornik, *The Photian Schism: History and Legend* (New Brunswick, N.J.: Rutgers University Press, 1970).
11. For an eastern perspective, see Amin Maalouf, *The Crusades Through Arab Eyes* (New York: Schocken, 1985).
12. Geoffrey de Villehardouin, *The Conquest of Constantinople,* in M. R. B. Shaw, *Chronicles of the Crusades* (Baltimore: Penguin, 1963), pp. 79, 92.
13. Steven Runciman, *The Fall of Constantinople* (Cambridge: Cambridge University Press, 1965).
14. *The Russian Primary Chronicle,* trans. Samuel H. Cross and O. P. Sherbowitz-Wetzor (Cambridge: Mediaeval Academy of America, 1953), pp. 110–118.
15. John Fennell, *The Crisis of Medieval Russia, 1200–1304* (London: Longman, 1983).
16. Robert O. Crummey, *The Formation of Muscovy, 1304–1613* (New York: Longman, 1987), p. 135.
17. Donald Treadgold, *The West in Russia and China,* Vol. 1 (Cambridge: Cambridge University Press, 1973), pp. 2–4.

The bejeweled front cover of the Lindau Gospels, a work dating from the third quarter of the ninth century, is an example of Carolingian art. The Celtic–Germanic metalwork tradition has been adapted to the religious art produced during the era of Charlemagne. The main clusters of semiprecious stones adorning the gold cover have been raised so that light can penetrate beneath them to make them glow.

The Church in the Middle Ages

Religion and Learning in Medieval Europe, 500–1500

As we have seen in Chapter 4, the Roman Empire in the third and fourth centuries became increasingly unable to provide political stability, economic security, and social confidence to its people. The newly organized church gradually emerged as one of the mainstays of order and authority.

The Church in the Early Middle Ages

In addition to offering comfort and hope in times of great challenge, the Christian Church steadily established its authority as a powerful institution exercising growing political, economic, and social strength.

The Early Medieval Papacy, 600–1000

Chapter 7 examined the growth in the authority of the bishops of Rome, the popes. Often the early popes were looked to for political as well as spiritual guidance in troubled times. During the pontificate of Gregory I, the Great (590–604), the papacy aggressively began to assert its political as well as spiritual authority. After his election as pope, Gregory assumed the task of protecting Rome and its surrounding territory from the Lombard threat. Gregory was the first pope to act as actual ruler of a part of what later became the Papal States.

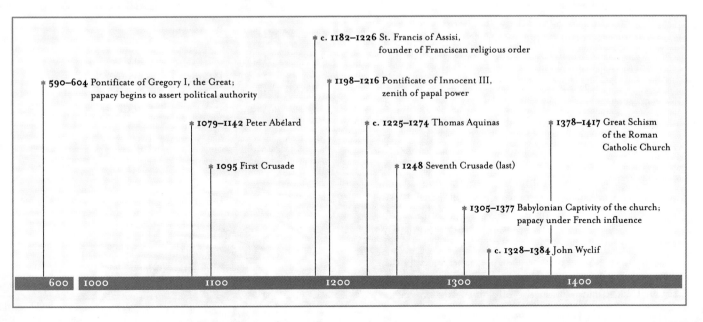

* c. 1182–1226 St. Francis of Assisi, founder of Franciscan religious order

* 590–604 Pontificate of Gregory I, the Great; papacy begins to assert political authority

* 1198–1216 Pontificate of Innocent III, zenith of papal power

* 1079–1142 Peter Abélard

* c. 1225–1274 Thomas Aquinas

* 1378–1417 Great Schism of the Roman Catholic Church

* 1095 First Crusade

* 1248 Seventh Crusade (last)

* 1305–1377 Babylonian Captivity of the church; papacy under French influence

* c. 1328–1384 John Wyclif

| 600 | 1000 | 1100 | 1200 | 1300 | 1400 |

Gregory also laid the foundation for the papal machinery of church government. The pattern of church government that Gregory established in England—bishops supervised by archbishops, who reported to the pope—became standard.

The task of establishing papal control of the church and extending the pope's temporal authority was continued by Gregory's successors. In the eighth century English missionaries transferred to Germany and France the pattern of papal government they had known in England; the Donation of Pepin, a sizable grant of territory in Italy given to the pope by the Merovingian king (see Chapter 9), greatly increased the pope's temporal power by creating the Papal States.

Missionary Activities of the Church

The early Middle Ages was a period of widespread missionary activity. By spreading Christianity, missionaries aided in the merging of Germanic and Roman cultures. One of the earliest Christian missionaries was Ulfilas (c. 311–383), who spent 40 years among the Visigoths and translated most of the Bible into Gothic. Missionary activities in Ireland resulted in the founding of numerous monasteries; in the late sixth and seventh centuries a large number of monks from these Irish monasteries went to Scotland, northern England, the kingdom of the Franks, and even Italy as missionaries to renew the faith and erase the effects of worldly corruption. Irish monks also eagerly pursued scholarship, and their monasteries became storehouses for priceless manuscripts.

The Preservation of Knowledge

After the fall of Rome, learning did not entirely die out in western Europe; the knowledge of the classical world was preserved through the efforts of a number of concerned intellectuals. Seeing that the ability to read Greek was quickly disappearing, the sixth-century Roman scholar Boethius determined to preserve Greek learning by translating all of Plato and Aristotle into Latin. Unjustly accused of treachery by the emperor, Boethius was thrown into prison, where he wrote *The Consolation of Philosophy* while awaiting execution; this work became a medieval textbook on philosophy.

Cassiodorus, a contemporary of Boethius, devoted most of his life to the collection and preservation of classical knowledge. By encouraging the monks to copy valuable manuscripts, he was instrumental in making the monasteries centers of learning. Following his example, many monasteries established *scriptoria*, departments concerned exclusively with copying manuscripts.

During the early Middle Ages most education took place in the monasteries. In the late sixth and seventh centuries, when the effects of the barbarian invasions were still being felt on the Continent, Irish monasteries provided a safe haven for learning. There men studied Greek and Latin, copied and preserved manuscripts, and, in illuminating them, produced masterpieces of art. The *Book of Kells* is a surviving example of their skill.

An outstanding scholar of the early Middle Ages, the Venerable Bede (d. 735) followed the Irish tradition of learning in a northern English monastery. Bede's most famous work, the *Ecclesiastical History of the English People*, remains one of the most important sources for early British history.

Church Dominance, 1000–1300

During the High Middle Ages the church became more involved in the structure of society and, of necessity, more concerned with temporal affairs. Eventually the church overcame its conflicts with secular powers and emerged as a dominant political as well as spiritual force in European life.

Monastic Reform

A religious revival, often called the "medieval reformation," began in the tenth century and reached full force in the twelfth and thirteenth centuries. The first far-reaching manifestation of the revival was the reformed Benedictine order of monks at Cluny, in present-day France, founded in 910. The ultimate goal of the Cluniac reformers was to free the entire church from secular control and subject it to papal authority. Some 300 Cluniac houses were freed from lay control, and in 1059 an attempt was made to rid the papacy itself of secular interference by the creation of the college of cardinals, which elected the pope.

Monastic Reform and the Investiture Controversy

910	Benedictine monastery at Cluny founded
1059	College of cardinals founded
1073–1085	Pontificate of Gregory VII; struggle over lay investiture
1077	Emperor Henry IV begs forgiveness at Canossa
1091–1153	St. Bernard of Clairvaux, founder of the Cistercian religous order

Even the papacy was affected by the call for reform. The most aggressive advocate of church reform in the High Middle Ages was Pope Gregory VII (1073–1085), who claimed unprecedented power for the papacy. In 1075 Gregory VII formally prohibited lay investiture (bestowal of the symbols of the churchman's office by a secular official such as a king) and threatened to excommunicate (expel from the Roman Catholic Church) any layman who performed it. This act virtually declared war against Europe's rulers, as lay investiture had been employed since the emperor Constantine's time. The climax to the struggle occurred in Gregory's clash with the German emperor Henry IV (see Chapter 9).

Late in the eleventh century a second wave of monastic reform produced several new orders of monks, among which were the Cistercians. The Cistercian movement received its greatest impetus from the efforts of St. Bernard of Clairvaux, also in present-day France (1091–1153). This order's abbeys were situated in solitary places, and their strict discipline emphasized fasts and vigils, manual labor, and a vegetarian diet. Their churches contained neither stained glass nor statues, and Bernard denounced the beautification of churches in general as unnecessary distraction.

The Papacy's Zenith: Innocent III

Under Innocent III (1198–1216) a new type of administrator-pope emerged and papal power reached its zenith. Unlike Gregory VII and other earlier reform popes, who were monks, Innocent and other great popes of the late twelfth and thirteenth centuries were lawyers trained in the newly revived and enlarged church, or canon, law.

So successful was Innocent III in asserting his temporal and spiritual supremacy that many states formally acknowledged they were subordinate to the pope. In the case of King John of England, a struggle developed over the election of the archbishop of Canterbury, and Innocent placed England under interdict (see below for definition) for five years and excommunicated John. Under attack from his barons, John capitulated to Innocent by becoming his vassal (subordinate), receiving England back as a fief (feudal estate), and paying him an annual monetary tribute. Innocent forced Philip Augustus of France to take back as his queen the woman he had divorced with the consent of the French bishops. As for the Holy Roman Empire, Innocent intervened in a civil war between rival candidates for the throne, supporting first one and then the other. Innocent finally secured the election of his ward, the young Hohenstaufen heir Frederick II, who promised to respect papal rights.

At Canossa, the penitent Henry IV pleads with Abbot Hugh of Cluny and Countess Matilda of Tuscany to intercede with Pope Gregory VII to rescind Henry's excommunication.

Church Administration

The universality and power of the church rested not only on a systematized, uniform religious creed but also on the most highly organized administrative system in the West. Special emissaries called *legates*, whose powers were superior to those of the local churchmen, carried the pope's orders throughout Europe.

The church was ahead of secular states in developing a system of courts and a body of law. Canon law was based on the Scriptures, the writings of the church fathers, and the decrees of church councils and popes. But the papacy's chief weapons to support its authority were spiritual penalties. The most powerful of these was excommunication. A person who was excommunicated was deprived of the sacraments of the church and condemned to hell.

Interdict was also a powerful instrument. Excommunication was directed against individuals, but interdict suspended all public worship and withheld most sacraments in the realm of a disobedient ruler. Pope Innocent III successfully applied or threatened the interdict 85 times against disobedient kings and princes.

Heresy

Heresy, the belief in doctrines officially condemned by the church, once again became a concern in the High Middle Ages. Numerous spiritual ideas flourished particularly in the newly revived towns, where changing social and spiritual needs went largely unheeded by old-style churchmen. This fertile ground produced many heresies, among which the Albigensian and Waldensian were major ones.

The Cathari ("pure") or Albigensians—so called because Albi in southern France was an important center—regarded the world as the battleground for the opposing forces of good and evil. They denounced many activities of the state and the individual, even condemning marriage for perpetuating the human species in this sinful world. The Albigensians rejected the church as an institution because it too was a part of the earth and thereby inherently evil.

The Waldensians derived their name from Peter Waldo, a merchant of Lyons who gave his wealth to charity and founded a lay order, the Poor Men of Lyons, to serve the needs of the people. He had parts of the New Testament translated into French, believed that laymen could preach the Gospel, and denied the effectiveness of the sacraments unless administered by worthy priests.

For ten years Innocent III tried to reconvert these heretical groups. Unsuccessful, he instigated a crusade against the prosperous and cultured French region of Toulouse where the Albigensians were attacked in 1208. The crusade began with horrible slaughter to the cry of "Kill them all—God will know his own." Soon the original religious motive was lost in a selfish rush to seize the wealth of the accused. In time the Albigensian heresy was destroyed, along with its flourishing culture of southern France, and the Waldensians were scattered.

In 1233 a special papal court called the Inquisition was established to cope with the rising tide of heresy and to bring about religious conformity. Those accused were tried in secret without the aid of legal counsel. Those who confessed and renounced heresy were "reconciled" with the church on performance of penance. Those who did not voluntarily confess could be tortured. If torture failed, the prisoners could be declared heretics and turned over to the secular authorities, usually to be burned at the stake.

Franciscans and Dominicans

As a more positive response to the spread of heresy and the conditions that caused it, Innocent III approved the founding of the Franciscan and Dominican orders of *friars* ("brothers"). Instead of living in remote monasteries, the friars of these orders moved among the people, ministering to their needs, preaching the Gospel, and teaching in the schools.

The Franciscans were founded by St. Francis of Assisi (c. 1182–1226), who rejected riches and spread the gospel of poverty and Christian simplicity. Love of one's fellow human beings and all God's creatures, even "brother worm," was basic in the Rule of St. Francis, which was inspired by Jesus' example.

The second order of friars was founded by St. Dominic (1170–1221), a well-educated Spaniard who had fought the Albigensians in southern France. There he decided that to combat the strength and zeal of its opponents, the church should have champions who could preach the Gospel with the dedication of the apostles. The friar-preachers of Dominic's order dedicated themselves to preaching as a means of maintaining the doctrines of the church and of converting heretics.

The enthusiasm and sincerity of the friars in their early years made a profound impact on an age that had grown increasingly critical of the worldliness of the church. But after they took charge of the Inquisition, became professors in the universities, and served the papacy in other ways, the friars lost much of their original simplicity. Yet their message and zeal had done much to provide the church with moral and intellectual leadership at a time when such leadership was badly needed.

The Crusades

The Crusades, a series of campaigns that began toward the end of the eleventh century, were a remarkable expression of European self-confidence and expansion in the High Middle Ages. The church was instrumental in beginning these efforts to recapture the Holy Land from Muslim control. But by the conclusion of the crusading era, the church, and the papacy in particular, had suffered a serious loss of prestige largely because of its actions related to the crusading movement.

The Call for Crusades

For hundreds of years peaceful pilgrims had been traveling from Europe to worship at the birthplace of Jesus. But during the eleventh century Christian pilgrims to the Holy Land became especially concerned when the Seljuk Turks, new and fierce converts to Islam, took over Jerusalem from the more tolerant Abbasid Muslims.

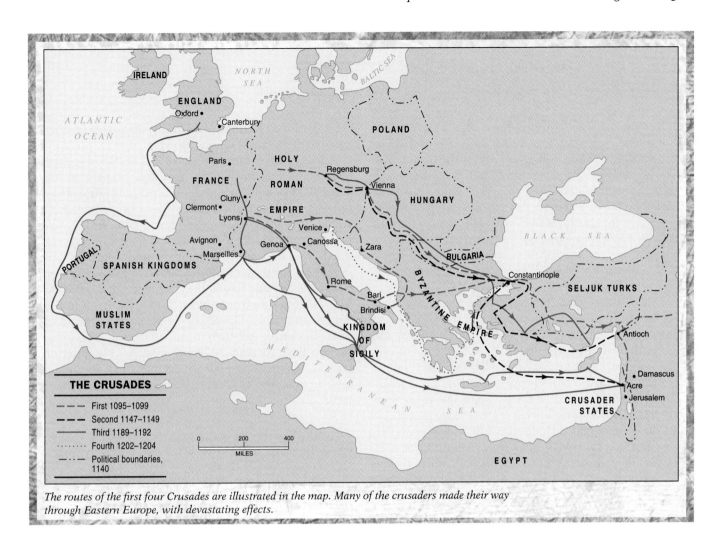

THE CRUSADES

- - - First 1095–1099
— — Second 1147–1149
——— Third 1189–1192
·········· Fourth 1202–1204
—··—·· Political boundaries, 1140

The routes of the first four Crusades are illustrated in the map. Many of the crusaders made their way through Eastern Europe, with devastating effects.

In 1095 Pope Urban II proclaimed the First Crusade to regain the Holy Land. Preaching at the Council of Clermont in that year, he called on Christians to take up the cross and strive for a cause that promised not merely spiritual rewards but material gain as well. Following Urban's appeal, there was a real and spontaneous outpouring of religious enthusiasm. The word *crusade* itself is derived from "taking the cross," after the example of Christ.

The Crusading Expeditions

From the end of the eleventh century through the thirteenth, seven major crusades, as well as various small expeditions, warred against the Muslims, whom the crusaders called Saracens. The First Crusade, composed of feudal nobles from France, parts of Germany, and Norman Italy, marched overland through eastern Europe to Constantinople. Expecting the help of skilled European mercenaries against the Seljuks, the emperor Alexius Comnenus was shocked when confronted by a disorderly mob of crusaders and quickly directed them out of Constantinople to fight the Turks. This First Crusade was the most successful of the seven; with not

more than 5000 knights and infantry, it overcame the resistance of the Turks, who were no longer united. It captured Jerusalem and a narrow strip of land stretching from there to Antioch, which became known as the Latin Kingdom of Jerusalem, and over which crusaders and Islamic armies continued to battle until the region was finally retaken by the Muslims in 1291.

The fall of Jerusalem in 1187 to the Muslims, reinvigorated under the leadership of Saladin, the sultan of Egypt and Syria, provoked the Third Crusade in 1189. Its leaders were three of the most famous medieval kings—Frederick Barbarossa of Germany, Richard the Lion-Hearted of England, and Philip Augustus of France. Frederick drowned in Asia Minor, and, after many quarrels with Richard, Philip returned home. Saladin and Richard remained to fight but finally agreed to a three-year truce and free access to Jerusalem for Christian pilgrims.

The Fourth Crusade (1202–1204) was a disaster from a religious perspective. No kings answered the call of Pope Innocent III, and the knights who did participate were unable to pay the Venetians the agreed-on transport charges. The Venetians persuaded the crusaders to pay off their debts by capturing the Christian

The First Crusade: The Fall of Jerusalem

This selection describes the fall of Jerusalem during the First Crusade in 1099, as witnessed by the author, a Frankish knight.

During this siege, we suffered so badly from thirst that we sewed up the skins of oxen and buffaloes, and we used to carry water in them for the distance of nearly six miles. We drank the water from these vessels, although it stank, and what with foul water and barley bread we suffered great distress and affliction every day, for the Saracens used to lie in wait for our men by every spring and pool, where they killed them and cut them to pieces; moreover they used to carry off the beasts into their caves and secret places in the rocks.

Our leaders then decided to attack the city with engines, so that we might enter it and worship at our Saviour's Sepulchre. . . . On Friday at dawn we attacked the city from all sides but could achieve nothing, so that we were all astounded and very much afraid, yet, when that hour came when our Lord Jesus Christ deigned to suffer for us upon the cross, our knights were fighting bravely on the siege tower. . . . All the defenders fled along the walls and through the city, and our men went after them, killing them and cutting them down as far as Solomon's Temple, where there was such a massacre that our men were wading up to their ankles in enemy blood.

At last, when the pagans were defeated, our men took many prisoners, both men and women, in the Temple. They killed whom they chose, and whom they chose they saved alive. After this our men rushed round the whole city, seizing the gold and silver, horses and mules, and houses full of all sorts of goods, and they all came rejoicing and weeping from excess of gladness to worship at the Sepulchre of our Savior Jesus, and there they fulfilled their vows to him. Next morning they went cautiously up on to the Temple roof and attacked the Saracens, both men and women, cutting off their heads with drawn swords. No-one has ever seen or heard of such a slaughter of pagans, for they were burned on pyres like pyramids, and no-one save God alone knows how many there were.

From Rosalind Hill, ed., *Gesta Francorum* (London: Nelson, 1962). Reprinted by permission of Oxford University Press, Oxford.

---

town of Zara on the Adriatic coast, which had long proved a successful rival to Venetian trading interests. Then, in order to eliminate Byzantine commercial competition, the Venetians pressured the crusaders to attack Constantinople itself. After conquering and sacking the great city, the crusaders set up the Latin Empire of Constantinople and forgot about recovering the Holy Land.

The thirteenth century produced other crusading failures. The boys and girls participating in the Children's Crusade of 1212 fully expected the waters of the Mediterranean to part and make a path from southern France to the Holy Land, which they would take without fighting, but instead thousands of them were sold into slavery by the merchants of Marseilles. The Seventh Crusade was the last major attempt to regain Jerusalem; the crusading movement ended in 1291 when Acre, the last stronghold of the Christians in the Holy Land, fell to the Muslims.

The Crusader States

Four crusader states, with the kingdom of Jerusalem dominant, were established along the eastern Mediterranean coast as a result of the crusading movement. By the time Jerusalem fell to Saladin in 1187, however, only isolated pockets of Christians remained, surrounded by Muslims. The crusader states were able to cling to survival only through frequent delivery of supplies and manpower from Europe.

The crusader states were defended primarily by three semimonastic military orders: the Templars, or Knights of the Temple, so called because their first headquarters was on the site of the old Temple of Jerusalem; the Hospitalers, or Knights of St. John of Jerusalem, who were founded originally to care for the sick and wounded; and the Teutonic Knights, exclusively a German order. Combining monasticism and militarism, these orders served to protect all pilgrims and to wage perpetual war against the Muslims.

Significance of the Crusades

Even though the Crusades failed to achieve their permanent objective, they were more than mere military adventures. Much of the crusading fervor carried over to the European efforts against the Muslims in Spain and the Slavs in eastern Europe. The Crusades crucially weakened the Byzantine Empire and accelerated its fall. And although the early Crusades strengthened the moral leadership of the papacy in Europe, the misadventures of the later Crusades, together with the church's preaching of Crusades against Christian heretics and political opponents,

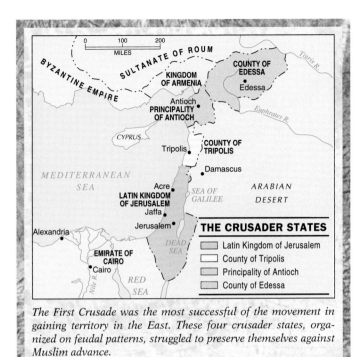

The First Crusade was the most successful of the movement in gaining territory in the East. These four crusader states, organized on feudal patterns, struggled to preserve themselves against Muslim advance.

weakened both the crusading ideal and respect for the papacy.

Contact with the East through the crusading movement widened the scope of many Europeans, ended their isolation, and exposed them to an admirable civilization. And the Crusades did influence the reopening of the eastern Mediterranean to Western commerce, a factor that in itself had an effect on the revival of cities and the emergence of a money economy in the West.

Thought and Culture During the High Middle Ages

In addition to a decline in the general level of education, interest in intellectual matters decreased rapidly in the period following the fall of the Roman Empire and the establishment of the early Germanic kingdoms. And even among the intellectual community that did survive, a controversy raged over the value of studying subjects not directly pertinent to the church. A significant effort to revitalize learning and the arts had been undertaken by Charlemagne (768–814), and his efforts produced what has become known as the Carolingian Renaissance. Charlemagne's efforts to increase literacy and preserve the arts met with great success, but the weakness of later Carolingian rulers somewhat limited the lasting results of his reform.

The Revival of Learning

Prior to the twelfth century, most schools in Europe were under the control and direction of the church.

But when the schools run by monasteries started limiting admissions to students who were preparing for careers in the church, an important development in education took place. Students interested in professions outside the church increasingly sought to attend schools administered by cathedrals. Although still dominated by churchmen and centered around a religion-focused curriculum, the cathedral schools gradually expanded their subject offerings to attract students intending to pursue secular careers.

Interest in studying the classical literature of pagan Greece and Rome further broadened the curriculum. Much of this interest can be attributed to increasing European contacts with the Arab world, through the crusading movement and also through increasing commercial activity. The rebirth of classical learning in the twelfth century produced unprecedented numbers of students flocking to the schools.

Origin of European Universities

The development of professional studies in law, medicine, and theology led to the rise of universities, which soon eclipsed the monastic and cathedral schools as organized centers of learning. Originally the word *university* meant a group of persons possessing a common purpose. The term referred to a guild of learners, both teachers and students, similar to the craft guilds, with their masters and apprentices. In the thirteenth century the universities had no campuses and little property or money, and the masters taught in hired rooms or religious houses. If the university was dissatisfied with its treatment by the townspeople, it could move elsewhere. The earliest universities—at Bologna, Paris, and Oxford—were not officially founded, but in time popes or kings granted them and other universities charters of self-government. These charters gave legal status to the universities and rights to the students, such as freedom from the jurisdiction of town officials.

Scholasticism

Most medieval thinkers did not think of truth as something to be discovered by themselves; they saw it as already existing in authoritative Christian and pagan writings of antiquity. By employing reason (through the use of logic or dialectic), scholars of the twelfth and thirteenth centuries attempted to understand and express truth through this logical process of explanation. Since this task was carried out largely in the schools, these scholars are known as Scholastics, and the intellectual method they produced is called Scholasticism.

Each scholar formed his own judgments and sought to convince others. This activity led to much debate on a range of subjects. Most famous was the argument over universals known as the nominalist-realist controversy. This philosophical controversy

The Hereford Map, c. 1290

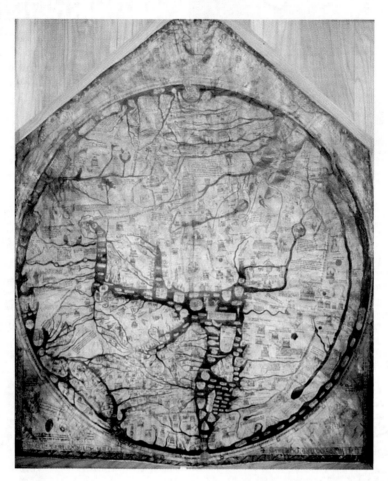

The Hereford Map, the largest of its kind to have re-mained in excellent condition for 700 years, is now preserved in the cathedral of Hereford, England. It is thought that this map was copied in large detail from another, older map, which was in turn copied from a Roman map perhaps dating to the first century of the Common Era. The entire skin of a calf had to be specially prepared for the writing and illustration of the Hereford Map. Calfskin prepared in this special manner is called *vellum*, from the Latin word for "calf."

The map bears an inscription by its author, Richard of Haldingham and Lafford, in the bottom right corner. Such inscriptions are very unusual on medieval maps. Names and descriptions on the map are written in Latin and in the Norman dialect of French. The circle of the world is surrounded by the ocean. At the center of the world is the holy city of Jerusalem, for it was often thought in the Middle Ages that Jerusalem's religious significance indicated its centrality in the world. Mesopotamia is represented at the top of the Hereford Map, in keeping with medieval custom sanctioned by the church. Note the rep-resentation of the Tower of Babel (Turrus Babblus) to the immediate "north" of Palestine, and Paradise placed at the very top of the map. To the right of Palestine is Egypt, which the mapmaker has included in Asia.

Experts think that mapmakers in the late Middle Ages probably did not know as much about geography as sailors and merchants engaged in overseas trade and commerce and may have lagged in their geographical knowledge by as much as 200 years. Such a lag would perhaps explain the lack of a more accurate depiction of Africa and Europe.

The Hereford Map may have been originally intended as a decorative background for an altar. That might account for much of the Christian symbolism displayed on the map and even its basic orientation. Another possibility is that the map was intended to be a teaching device to aid a largely illiterate and provincial populace in understanding both the world and the Christian faith. The Hereford mapmaker was a teacher as well as a cartographer, explaining the world as he illustrated it.

centered on the question of whether universal ideas—beauty, truth, and justice, for example—had a reality other than what existed in people's minds as abstract notions. The realists held that these universal ideas did have a reality, but the nominalists believed that the universal ideas were nothing more than names *(nomina)* used to identify abstract concepts.

The Contribution of Abélard

The extreme and often sterile views of nominalists and realists frustrated the brilliant Peter Abélard (1079–1142), a popular teacher at the cathedral school of Notre Dame in Paris. Abélard's great contribution to medieval thought was an approach called *conceptualism,* his solution to the nominalist-realist controversy. Abélard believed that universals, while existing only in the mind as thoughts or concepts, are nevertheless valid (real) since they are the product of observing the similar qualities that exist in a particular class of things. Thus by observing many chairs and sitting in them, we arrive at the universal concept "chair."

In addition to redefining the purpose of Scholastic thought, Abélard perfected Scholastic method. Like others before him, Abélard emphasized the importance of understanding. However, Abélard's predecessors had begun with faith; Abélard started with doubt. One must learn to doubt, he insisted, for doubting leads to inquiry, and inquiry leads to the truth.

Women and Learning in the High Middle Ages

In the early Middle Ages, and especially after the eighth century, the convents of Europe served as centers of learned activity for a select group of aristocratic and middle-class women who pursued an intellectual life as well as one devoted to religion. But outside of the convents, a life devoted to scholarship was almost impossible for a medieval woman; the church taught that a woman should be either a housewife or a virgin in service to her God, and rarely was it possible for a woman to write, compose, or create in such a society.

Nevertheless, intellectual achievements by some exceptional medieval women were possible. One such remarkable woman was Hildegard of Bingen (1098–1179), the leader of a community of Benedictine nuns in Germany. Hildegard wrote a mystical work describing her visions, which she began to receive at the age of 42. She was also a skilled composer, writing many hymns for her nuns to sing. She wrote a morality play and also several scientific works, which cataloged nearly 500 plants, animals, and stones, assessing their medicinal value.

Hildegard's Vision, *from* Scrivas *by Hildegard of Bingen, c. 1142–1152. Hildegard, a remarkable scholar, musician, and mystic, is shown in this illustrated manuscript receiving divine inspiration while a scribe awaits her words.*

New Knowledge and the Task of Reconciliation

In the twelfth century Western scholars flocked to Spain and Sicily to translate Muslim editions of classical literature. As a result of these translations a great number of new ideas, particularly in science and philosophy, were introduced to Western scholars. Algebra, trigonometry, and Euclid's *Geometry* became available, and Arabic numerals, including the symbol for zero, made possible the decimal system of computation. Physics was based on Aristotle's theory of four elements (water, earth, air, and fire) and on his theories of dynamics—doctrines that took centuries to disprove. Chemistry was also based on Aristotelian concepts, mixed with magic and alchemy. Like Muslim alchemists, Europeans tried in vain to convert base metals into gold and silver and to obtain a magic elixir that would prolong life; in both cases the attempts did much to advance true findings in the field of chemistry.

Because of the emphasis on authority and the influence of the church, the medieval atmosphere was not conducive to free scientific investigation. An exception to this subservience to authority was the English Franciscan Roger Bacon (1214–1292), who introduced the notion of "experimental science" and boldly criticized the deductive "logic chopping" used by Scholastic thinkers. Bacon never doubted the authority of the Bible or the church—his interest lay only in natural science—yet his superiors considered him dangerous because of his criticism of Scholastic thought.

By the thirteenth century learned Muslim commentaries on the medical works of Galen and Hippocrates and on Aristotle's biology were available in the West. This knowledge, coupled with new discoveries and improved techniques, made medieval doctors more than just barbers who engaged in bloodletting. Yet the overall state of medical knowledge and practice was, by current standards, still primitive.

As his writings became known, Aristotle became "the philosopher" to medieval students, and his authority was generally accepted as second only to that of the Scriptures. But because the church's teachings were considered infallible, Aristotle's ideas, as well as those of other great thinkers of antiquity, had to be reconciled with religious dogma. Using logical approaches, the Scholastic thinkers of the thirteenth century undertook this task of reconciliation.

Scholasticism reached its high point with Thomas Aquinas (c. 1225–1274). In *Summa Theologica* this brilliant Italian Dominican dealt with the great problems of theology, philosophy, politics, and economics. Aquinas's goal was to reconcile Aristotle with church dogma—in other words, the truths of natural reason with the truths of faith. There can be no real contradiction, he argued, since all truth comes from God. In case of an unresolved contradiction, however, faith won out because of the possibility of human error in reasoning.

The Decline of Scholasticism

The assumption that faith and reason were compatible was vigorously denied by two Franciscan thinkers, Duns Scotus (d. 1308) and William of Occam (d. c. 1349), who elaborated on Aquinas's belief that certain religious doctrines are beyond discovery by the use of reason. They argued that if the human intellect could not understand divinely revealed truth, it could hope to comprehend only the natural world and should not intrude on the sphere of divine truth.

After the thirteenth century, Scholasticism increasingly lost influence, for its adherents were obsessed with theological subtleties, discouraged independent thought, and in general lost touch with reality. But it should be remembered that the Scholastics sought to compile and then to interpret the vast body of Christian and pagan knowledge left to them by an earlier civilization. In terms of their needs and objectives—an intelligible and complete synthesis of faith, logic, and science—the Scholastics were extremely successful.

The theologian Thomas Aquinas was influenced by Aristotle (lower left) and Plato (lower right) as well as early Christian thinkers, shown above him, The Islamic philosopher Averroës is illustrated as vanquished at his feet.

Arts and Letters in the Middle Ages

Throughout the Middle Ages, Latin served as an international language. This common tongue provided much of the cohesion of the era, for virtually all the crucial communications of the church, governments, and schools were in Latin. Not all Latin dealt with religious and philosophical subjects; the poetry of twelfth- and thirteenth-century students, known as Goliardic verse, proclaimed the pleasures of the good life.

Vernacular Literature: Dante and Chaucer

By the twelfth century, more literature in the vernacular, or native, tongues began to appear, with the epic

Interior view of the Cathedral of St. Pierre at Angoulême, a typical example of Romanesque architecture. The cathedral's ribbed-groin vaults are derived from the Roman intersecting vaults. As shown in the drawing, the ribbed vault is made up of arches that span the sides of a square bay, with groin vaults crossing diagonally from corner to corner.

as the earliest form. The greatest of the French epics, known as *chansons de geste* ("songs of great deeds"), is the late-eleventh-century *Song of Roland*, which tells of the heroic deeds and death of Count Roland in the Pyrenees as he defended the retreat of Charlemagne's army. The great Spanish epic *Poema del Mio Cid* is a product of the twelfth century. These stirring epic poems, with their accounts of prowess in battle, mirror the warrior virtues of early chivalry—the code of conduct developed by the nobility to bring some sophistication and culture to their social conduct.

The vernacular was also used by two of the greatest writers of the period, Dante and Chaucer. Combining a profound religious sense with a knowledge of Scholastic thought and the Latin classics, the Italian Dante Alighieri (1265–1321) wrote the *Divine Comedy*, an allegory of medieval man (Dante) moving from bestial earthliness (hell) through conversion (purgatory) to a spiritual union with God (paradise).

In the *Canterbury Tales*, Geoffrey Chaucer (c. 1340–1400), revealed a cross section of contemporary English life, customs, and thought through personality profiles and stories told by 29 religious pilgrims who assembled in April 1387 at an inn before journeying to the shrine of St. Thomas à Becket at Canterbury.

Medieval Architecture and Sculpture

In the eleventh century a tremendous architectural revival occurred, marked by a return to building in stone rather than in wood, as had been common during the early Middle Ages. At a much later date the term *Romanesque* came to be applied to this new style because, like early Christian architecture, it was based largely on Roman models. Although details of structure and ornamentation differed with locality, the round arch was a standard Romanesque feature. Romanesque cathedrals emphasized symmetry, massive stone walls, small windows, and plain interiors.

In the twelfth and thirteenth centuries Gothic architecture replaced the older Romanesque style. The architects of the Gothic-style cathedral developed vaults with pointed rather than round arches. These vaults replaced the heavy barrel vault and, combined with the use of flying buttresses to distribute weight more evenly, allowed the use of large stained-glass windows set into the walls. The light loftiness of the Gothic interiors was a welcome improvement over the dark, somber interiors of the Romanesque churches.

Most Romanesque and Gothic sculpture served an architectural function by being carved into the

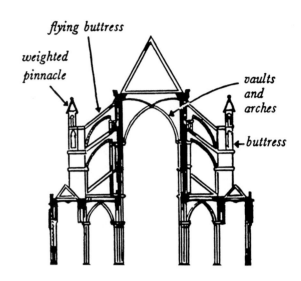

The effect of the fully developed Gothic style, as shown in this interior view of Amiens Cathedral, is one of awesome but ordered intricacy. The drawing is a cross section of the cathedral. Vaults, arches, buttresses, and weighted pinnacles were important structural elements in the Gothic style of architecture.

total composition of a church. To use sculpture to the best architectural advantage, the artist often distorted the subject to achieve a particular effect. Like sculpture, medieval painting in the form of stained-glass windows was an integral part of the architecture.

What the cathedral was to religious life, the castle was to everyday living. Both were havens, and both were built to endure. The new weapons and techniques of siege warfare, which the crusaders brought back from the Holy Land, necessitated more massive castles. By the thirteenth century castle building in Europe had reached a high point of development. The towers were rounded, and bastions stood at strategic points along the walls. The castle as a whole was planned in such a skillful manner that if one section was taken by attackers, it could be sealed off from the remaining fortifications. Whole towns were fortified in the same way, with walls, watchtowers, moats, and drawbridges.

Toward the end of the Middle Ages there was less need for fortified towns and castles. At the same time, the wealth from the revival of trade and increased industry encouraged the development of secular Gothic architecture. Town halls and guildhalls, the residences of the rich, and the chateaux of the nobility all borrowed the delicate Gothic style from the cathedrals.

Decline of the Medieval Church, 1300–1500

The period of the papacy's greatest power—the twelfth and thirteenth centuries—reached its apex with the pontificate of Innocent III, who exerted his influence over kings and princes without challenge. The church then seemed unassailable in its prestige, dignity, and power. Yet that strength soon came under new attack, and during the next two centuries the process of disintegration accelerated.

Decline of the Church

1294–1303	Pontificate of Boniface VIII
1302	*Unam Sanctam*
1305–1377	Popes at Avignon; Babylonian Captivity of the church
1378–1417	Great Schism of the Roman Catholic Church
1414	Council of Constance

Pope Boniface VIII, *Unam Sanctam*

Unam Sanctam (1302), written to Philip IV of France by Pope Boniface VIII, is one of the most extreme statements of papal superiority and one of the final assertions of the temporal power of the church in an age growing more distant from effective political power exercised by the pope.

We are compelled, our faith urging us, to believe and to hold—and we do firmly believe and simply confess—that there is one holy catholic and apostolic church, outside of which there is neither salvation nor remission of sins. . . . In this church there is one Lord, one faith and one baptism. . . . This church, moreover, we venerate as the only one, the Lord saying through His prophet: "Deliver my soul from the sword, my darling from the power of the dog." He prayed at the same time for His soul—that is, for Himself the Head—and for His body—which body, namely, he called the one and only church on account of the unity of the faith promised, of the sacraments, and of the love of the church. . . . Therefore of this one and only church there is one body and one head—not two heads as if it were a monster:—Christ, namely, and the vicar of Christ, St. Peter, and the successor of Peter. . . . We are told by the word of the gospel that in this His fold there are two swords,—a spiritual, namely, and a temporal. . . . Surely he who denies that the temporal sword is in the power of Peter wrongly interprets the word of the Lord when He says: "Put up thy sword in its scabbard." Both swords, the spiritual and the material, therefore, are in the power of the church; the one, indeed, to be wielded for the church, the other by the church; the one by the hand of the priest, the other by the hand of kings and knights, but at the will and sufferance of the priest. One sword, moreover, ought to be under the other, and the temporal authority to be subjected to the spiritual. . . . *Indeed we declare, announce and define, that it is altogether necessary to salvation for every human creature to be subject to the Roman pontiff.* The Lateran, Nov. 14, in our 8th year. As a perpetual memorial of this matter.

From Ernest F. Henderson, ed. and trans., *Select Historical Documents of the Middle Ages* (London: Bell, 1912), pp. 435–437.

Papal power was threatened by the growth of nation-states, which challenged the church's temporal power and authority. Rulers opposed papal interference in state matters. In addition, the papacy was criticized by reformers, who had seen earlier reform movements transformed from their original high-minded purposes to suit the ambitions of the popes, and by the bourgeoisie, whose pragmatic outlook fostered growing skepticism, national patriotism, and religious self-reliance. During the fourteenth and fifteenth centuries, these challenges to papal authority were effective, and papal influence rapidly declined.

Boniface VIII

Pope Boniface VIII (1294–1303) was an outspoken advocate of papal authority. When Boniface boldly declared in the papal bull *Unam Sanctam* (1302) that "subjection to the Roman pontiff is absolutely necessary to salvation for every human creature," King Philip IV of France demanded that the pope be brought to trial by a general church council. In 1303 Philip's henchmen broke into Boniface's summer home at Anagni to arrest him and take him to France to stand trial. Their kidnapping plot was foiled when the pope was rescued by his friends. Humiliated, Boniface died a month later, perhaps from the shock and physical abuse he suffered during the attack.

The Avignon Papacy

But Philip's success was as complete as if Boniface had actually been dragged before the king to stand trial. Two years after Boniface's death, a French archbishop was chosen pope. Taking the title of Clement V, he never went to Rome but instead moved the papal headquarters to Avignon in southern France, where the papacy remained under French influence from 1305 to 1377. During this period, the so-called Babylonian Captivity of the church, papal prestige suffered enormously. Most Europeans believed that Rome was the only suitable capital for the church. Moreover, the English, Germans, and Italians accused the popes and the cardinals, the majority of whom were now also French, of being instruments of the French king.

The Avignon papacy gave support to critics who were attacking church corruption, papal temporal claims, and the apparent lack of spiritual dedication. Increasing their demands for income from England, Germany, and Italy and living in splendor in a newly built fortress-palace, the Avignon popes expanded the papal bureaucracy, added new church taxes, and collected the old taxes more efficiently. These actions provoked denunciation of the wealth of the church and a demand for its reform.

The Great Schism of the Roman Catholic Church

When the papacy paid attention to popular opinion and returned to Rome in 1377, it seemed for a time that its fortunes would improve, but the reverse proved true. In the papal election held the following year, the college of cardinals elected an Italian pope. A few months later the French cardinals declared the election invalid and elected a French pope, who returned to Avignon. The church was now in an even worse state than it had been during the Babylonian Captivity. During the Great Schism (1378–1417), as the split of the church into two allegiances was called, there were two popes, each with his college of cardinals and capital city, each claiming universal sovereignty, each sending forth papal administrators and taxing Christians, and each excommunicating the other. The nations of Europe gave allegiance as their individual political interests prompted them.

The Great Schism continued after the original rival popes died, and each camp elected a replacement. Doubt and confusion caused many Europeans to question the legitimacy and holiness of the church as an institution.

The Conciliar Movement

Positive action came in the form of the Conciliar Movement. In 1395 the professors at the University of Paris proposed that a general council, representing the universal church, should meet to heal the schism. A majority of the cardinals of both factions accepted this solution, and in 1409 they met at the Council of Pisa, deposed both popes, and elected a new one. But neither of the two deposed popes would give up his office, and the papal throne now had three claimants.

The intolerable situation necessitated another church council. In 1414 the Holy Roman Emperor assembled at Constance the most impressive church gathering of the period. By deposing the various papal claimants and electing Martin V as pope in 1417, the Great Schism was ended and a single papacy was restored at Rome.

Failure of Internal Reform

The Conciliar Movement represented a reforming and democratizing influence in the church. But the movement was not to endure, even though the Council of Constance had decreed that general councils were superior to popes and that they should meet at regular intervals in the future. Taking steps to preserve his position, the pope announced that to appeal to a church council without having first obtained papal consent was heretical. Together with the inability of later councils to bring about much-needed reform

and with lack of support for such councils by secular rulers, the restoration of a single head of the church enabled the popes to discredit the Conciliar Movement by 1450. Not until almost a century later, when the Council of Trent convened in 1545, did a great council meet to reform the church. But by that time the church had already irreparably lost many countries to Protestantism.

As the popes hesitated to call councils to effect reform, they failed to bring about reform themselves. The popes busied themselves not with internal problems but with Italian politics and patronage of the arts. The issues of church reform and revitalization were largely ignored.

Wyclif and Hus

Throughout the fourteenth century the cries against church corruption became louder at the same time that heretical thoughts were being publicly voiced (see Chapter 14). In England, a professor at Oxford, John Wyclif (c. 1320–1384), attacked not only church abuses but also certain of the church's doctrines. Wyclif taught that the church should be subordinate to the state, that salvation was primarily an individual matter between humans and God, that transubstantiation—the belief that a miracle actually occurs during the Mass, by which bread and wine actually are transformed into Jesus' body and blood—as taught by the church was false, and that outward rituals and veneration of relics were idolatrous. He formed bands of "poor priests," called Lollards, who spread his views, and he provided the people with an English translation of the Bible, which he considered the final authority in matters of religion. Although Wyclif's demands for reform did not succeed, the Lollards spread a more radical version of Wyclif's ideas until the movement was driven underground early in the next century.

In Bohemia, where a strong reform movement linked with the resentment of the Czechs toward their German overlords was under way, Wyclif's doctrines were popularized by Czech students who had heard him lecture at Oxford. In particular, his beliefs influenced John Hus (c. 1369–1415), a preacher in Prague and later rector of the university there. Hus's attacks on the abuses of clerical power led him to conclude that the true church was composed of a universal priesthood of believers and that Christ alone was its head.

Alarmed by Hus's growing influence, the church excommunicated him. Summoned to the Council of Constance to stand trial for heresy, Hus was promised safe conduct. But he refused to change his views, and the council ordered him burned at the stake. This action made Hus a martyr to the Czechs, who rebelled against both the German emperor and the church. In the sixteenth century the remaining Hussites merged with the Lutheran movement in frustration with a church deaf to their protests.

Conclusion

Religion was largely molded and directed by the church throughout most of the Middle Ages. Through the growing strength of the papacy and because of the timely reform influences originating in the monastic orders, the power of the church as a religious and political force increased steadily in the High Middle Ages. But through a combination of corruption and misuse of power by church officials, the generally negative impact of the crusading movement, the assertiveness of monarchs and the growth of nationalistic interests in the states of Europe, and reforming sentiment within the church itself, the church in the later Middle Ages fell from its position as the sole source of religious authority and as a political power able to rival European nation-states.

Arts and learning in the early Middle Ages were almost completely in the hands of the church, which deserves credit for preserving the learning of antiquity in the dark ages of disorder and invasion. Religious themes and styles continued to dominate medieval literary work until vernacular literature, inspired by such creative forces as Dante and Chaucer, became an acceptable and popular form of expression near the end of the Middle Ages.

Suggestions for Reading

For good general surveys on the church and theology in the Middle Ages, see David Knowles, *The Evolution of Medieval Thought* (Helicon Press, 1962), and *Christian Monasticism* (McGraw-Hill, 1969). See also Gerd Tellenbach, *The Church in Western Europe from the Tenth to the Early Twelfth Century* (Cambridge University Press, 1993); Ian Stuart Robinson, *The Papacy, 1073–1198* (Cambridge University Press, 1990); Stephen E. Ozment, *The Age of Reform, 1250–1550* (Yale University Press, 1980); and Jaroslav J. Pelikan, *The Christian Tradition: Vol. 3. The Growth of Medieval Theology* (University of Chicago Press, 1978).

C. H. Lawrence, *Medieval Monasticism: Forms of Religious Life in Western Europe in the Middle Ages* (Longman, 1984); Malcolm Lambert, *Medieval Heresy: Popular Movements from the Gregorian Reform to the Reformation*, 2nd ed. (Blackwell, 1992); and Geoffrey Barraclough, *The Medieval Papacy* (Norton, 1968), are good examinations. Also see Archibald R. Lewis, *Nomads and Crusaders*, A.D. *1000–1368* (Indiana University Press, 1991); Jonathan Riley-Smith, ed., *The Oxford History of the Crusades* (Oxford University Press, 1997), Malcolm Billings,

The Cross and the Crescent (Sterling, 1987); Amin Maalouf, *The Crusades Through Arab Eyes* (Schocken, 1985); and Malcolm C. Barber, *The Trial of the Templars* (Cambridge University Press, 1993). Also excellent is David Nirenberg, *Communities of Violence: Persecution of Minorities in the Middle Ages* (Princeton University Press, 1996).

See John A. Burrow, *The Ages of Man: A Study in Medieval Writing and Thought* (Oxford University Press, 1989), for an outstanding review of medieval literature, as well as Judith M. Bennett, *Women in the Medieval English Countryside: Gender and Household in Brigstock Before the Plague* (Oxford University Press, 1989); Georges Duby, *The Age of Cathedrals: Art and Society, 980–1420* (University of Chicago Press, 1981); and Nancy G. Siraisi, *Medieval and Early Renaissance Medicine* (University of Chicago Press, 1990). See also C. H. Haskins, *The Rise of Universities* (Cornell University Press, 1965), and Gordon Leff, *Paris and Oxford Universities in the Thirteenth and Fourteenth Centuries: An Institutional and Intellectual History* (Wiley, 1968).

Good accounts of later church history are Ozment's *Age of Reform;* Gordon Leff, *Heresy in the Middle Ages*, 2 vols. (Barnes & Noble, 1967); Kenneth B. McFarlane, *John Wycliffe and the Beginnings of English Nonconformity* (Penguin, 1972); and Matthew Spinka, *John Hus: A Biography* (Princeton University Press, 1968).

Suggestions for Web Browsing

Medieval Studies
http://www.georgetown.edu/labyrinth/Virtual_Library/
 Medieval_Studies.html

The WWW Virtual Library for Medieval Studies, a part of the Labyrinth project at Georgetown University, offers numerous links categorized by national cultures and by artistic genre.

Medieval Women Home Page
http://www.media.mcmaster.ca/mw2.htm

Interdisciplinary exploration of the life of women in the late Middle Ages.

Women Writers of the Middle Ages
http://www.millersv.edu/~english/homepage/duncan/medfem/
 medfem.html

A collection of both secular and religious works authored by medieval women.

Medieval Science Page
http://members.aol.com/McNelis/medsci_index.html

A great site for anyone interested in medieval medicine and astronomy.

Gregorian Chant Home Page
http://silvertone.princeton.edu/chant.html/

Medieval Gregorian chant is sung, and its music theory is discussed.

Avignon Papacy, 1305–1378
http://www.humnet/cmrs/faculty/geary/instr/students/pope.htm

A very complete site dealing with the Babylonian Captivity of the church. Both literary and artistic materials are presented.

An English view of the battle of Agincourt. The English victory at Agincourt, like those at Crécy and Poitiers, are attributed in part to the well-disciplined English longbowmen.

The Birth of Europe
Politics and Society in the Middle Ages

The absence of the political unity and military security once provided by the Roman Empire was increasingly obvious in the fourth and fifth centuries in western Europe. As the centralization of the old Roman order collapsed and Germanic chieftains seized what lands and rights they could, very slowly the civilization of Rome evolved into a culture that melded Roman and Germanic institutions into a distinctly European pattern of life.

A New Empire in the West

In the blending of Roman and Germanic customs and institutions, the Franks played a particularly important role. Not only was the kingdom of the Franks the most enduring of the early Germanic states established in the West, but it became, with the active support of the church, the first significant kingdom of Europe that attempted to replace the Roman Empire in the West.

The Kingdom of the Franks Under Clovis

Before the Germanic invasions of the fourth century, the Franks lived close to the North Sea; late in the fourth century they began to move south and west into Roman Gaul. By 481 they occupied the northern part of Gaul as far south as the old Roman city of Paris, and in that same year Clovis I of the Merovingian dynasty became ruler of one of the small Frankish kingdoms. By the time of his death in 511, Clovis had united the Franks into a single kingdom that stretched south to the Pyrenees.

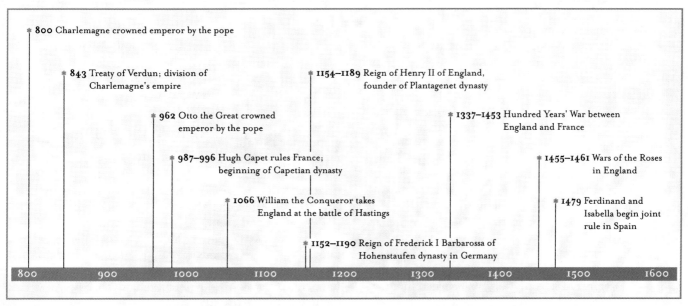

* **800** Charlemagne crowned emperor by the pope

* **843** Treaty of Verdun; division of Charlemagne's empire

* **962** Otto the Great crowned emperor by the pope

* **987–996** Hugh Capet rules France; beginning of Capetian dynasty

* **1066** William the Conqueror takes England at the battle of Hastings

* **1152–1190** Reign of Frederick I Barbarossa of Hohenstaufen dynasty in Germany

* **1154–1189** Reign of Henry II of England, founder of Plantagenet dynasty

* **1337–1453** Hundred Years' War between England and France

* **1455–1461** Wars of the Roses in England

* **1479** Ferdinand and Isabella begin joint rule in Spain

800   900   1000   1100   1200   1300   1400   1500   1600

The Merovingians and the Carolingians

481–511   Clovis unites Franks; beginning of Merovingian dynasty

714–741   Charles Martel mayor of the palace

732   Charles defeats Muslims at Tours

741–768   Pepin the Short mayor of the palace

751   Pepin crowned king of the Franks; beginning of Carolingian dynasty

768–814   Reign of Charlemagne

800   Charlemagne crowned emperor by the pope; beginning of Carolingian Empire

814–840   Reign of Louis the Pious

843   Treaty of Verdun divides Carolingian Empire

Clovis was an intelligent manipulator of alliances and a cunning diplomat who also used religion for political gain. He was converted to Christianity perhaps through the influence of his Christian wife, was baptized together with his whole army, and then became the only Orthodox Christian ruler in the West, since the other Germanic tribes were either still pagan or followers of Arian Christianity (the heresy that maintained that Jesus was not equal to the Father and thereby not completely divine). This conversion of the Franks to Roman Christianity ultimately led to a close alliance of the Franks and the papacy.

Decline of the Merovingians, Rise of the Carolingians

Clovis's sons and grandsons extended Frankish control south to the Mediterranean and east into Germany. But quickly the Merovingian dynasty began to decay. The Germanic tradition of treating the kingdom as personal property and dividing it among all the king's sons resulted in constant and bitter civil wars. Most important, Merovingian kings proved themselves incompetent and ineffectual. Soon the Frankish state broke up into three separate kingdoms; in each, power was concentrated in the hands of the chief official of the royal household, the mayor of the palace, a powerful noble who hoped to keep the king weak and ineffectual. The Merovingian rulers became puppets—"do-nothing kings."

The kingdom of the Franks gained strength when Charles Martel became mayor of the palace (or the king's court) in 714. His military skill earned him the surname Martel, "the hammer." Charles was respon-

sible for introducing a major innovation in European warfare. To counteract the effectiveness of the quick-striking Muslim cavalry, Charles recruited a force of professional mounted soldiers. He rewarded his soldiers with land to enable each of them to support a family, equipment, and war horses. With such a force, now aided by their use of the stirrup, Charles Martel won an important victory over the Muslim cavalry at Tours in 732.

Charles's son, Pepin the Short (741–768), legalized the power already being exercised by the mayors of the palace by requesting and receiving from the pope a decision that whoever exercised the actual power in the kingdom should be the legal ruler. In 751 Pepin was elected king by the Franks; the last Merovingian was sent off to a monastery, and the Carolingian dynasty came to power. In 754 the pope reaffirmed the election of Pepin by personally anointing him as king of the Franks.

Behind the pope's action was his need for a powerful protector against the Lombards, who had conquered the Exarchate of Ravenna (the center of Byzantine government in Italy) and were demanding tribute from the pope. Following Pepin's coronation, the pope secured his promise of armed intervention in Italy and his pledge to give the Exarchate to the papacy, once it was conquered. In 756 a Frankish army forced the Lombard king to withdraw, and Pepin gave Ravenna to the pope. The so-called Donation of Pepin made the pope a temporal ruler over the Papal States, a strip of territory that extended diagonally across northern Italy.

The alliance between the Franks and the papacy affected the course of politics and religion for centuries. It furthered the separation of the Roman from the Greek Christian Church by giving the papacy a dependable Western ally in place of the Byzantines, previously its only protector against the Lombards.

Charlemagne: Enlightened Conqueror

Under Pepin's son Charlemagne (Charles the Great), who ruled from 768 to 814, the Frankish state and the Carolingian dynasty reached the height of power. Although he was certainly a successful warrior-king, leading his armies on yearly campaigns, Charlemagne also tried to provide an effective administration for his kingdom. In addition, he had great appreciation for learning; his efforts at furthering the arts produced a revival in learning and letters known as the Carolingian Renaissance.

Charlemagne sought to extend his kingdom southward against the Muslims in Spain. He crossed the Pyrenees and eventually drove the Muslims back to the Ebro River and established a frontier area known as the Spanish March, centered near Barcelona. French immigrants moved into the area, later called Catalonia, giving it a character culturally distinct from the rest of Spain.

Charlemagne: A Firsthand Look

Einhard was the emperor Charlemagne's secretary and biographer. The following is an excerpt from Einhard's *Life of Charlemagne.*

Charles was large and strong, and of lofty stature, though not disproportionately tall (his height is well known to have been seven times the length of his foot); the upper part of his head was round, his eyes very large and animated, nose a little long, hair fair, and face laughing and merry. Thus his appearance was always stately and dignified, whether he was standing or sitting; although his neck was thick and somewhat short, and his belly rather prominent; but the symmetry of the rest of his body concealed these defects. His gait was firm, his whole carriage manly, and his voice clear, but not so strong as his size led one to expect. His health was excellent, except during the four years preceding his death, when he was subject to frequent fevers; at the last he even limped a little with one foot. Even in those years he consulted rather his own inclinations than the advice of physicians, who were almost hateful to him, because they wanted him to give up roasts, to which he was accustomed, and to eat boiled meat instead. In accordance with the national custom, he took frequent exercise on horseback and in the chase, accomplishments in which scarcely any people in the world can equal the Franks. He enjoyed the exhalations from natural warm springs, and often practiced swimming, in which he was such an adept that none could surpass him; and hence it was that he built his palace at Aix-la-Chapelle, and lived there constantly during his latter years until his death. He used not only to invite his sons to his bath, but his nobles and friends, and now and then a troop of his retinue or bodyguard, so that a hundred or more persons sometimes bathed with him. . . .

. . . Charles was temperate in eating, and particularly so in drinking, for he abominated drunkenness in anybody, much more in himself and those of his household; but he could not easily abstain from food, and often complained that fasts injured his health. He very rarely gave entertainment, only on great feast-days, and then to large numbers of people. His meals ordinarily consisted of four courses, not counting the roast, which his huntsmen used to bring in on the spit; he was more fond of this than of any other dish. While at table, he listened to reading or music. . . .

. . . Charles had the gift of ready and fluent speech, and could express whatever he had to say with the utmost clearness. He was not satisfied with command of his native language merely, but gave attention to the study of foreign ones, and in particular was such a master of Latin that he could speak it as well as his native tongue; but he could understand Greek better than he could speak it. He was so eloquent, indeed, that he might have passed for a teacher of eloquence. He most zealously cultivated the liberal arts, held those who taught them in great esteem, and conferred great honors upon them. He took lessons in grammar of the deacon Peter of Pisa, at that time an aged man. Another deacon, Albin of Britain, surnamed Alcuin, a man of Saxon extraction, who was the greatest scholar of the day, was his teacher in other branches of learning. The King spent much time and labor with him studying rhetoric, dialectics, and especially astronomy; he learned to reckon, and used to investigate the motions of the heavenly bodies most curiously, with an intelligent scrutiny. He also tried to write, and used to keep tablets and blanks in bed under his pillow, that at leisure hours he might accustom his hand to form the letters; however, as he did not begin his efforts in due season, but late in life, they met with ill success.

From Samuel Epes Turner, trans., *Life of Charlemagne by Einhard* (Ann Arbor: University of Michigan Press, 1960), pp. 50–57.

Charlemagne conquered the Bavarians and the Saxons, the last of the independent Germanic tribes, on his eastern frontier. Even farther to the east, the empire's frontier was continually threatened by the Avars, Asiatic nomads related to the Huns, and the Slavs. In six campaigns Charlemagne nearly eliminated the Avars and then set up his own military province in the Danube valley to guard against any future advances by eastern nomads. Called the East March, this territory later became Austria. Like his father Pepin, Charlemagne was involved in Italian politics. The Lombards resented the attempts of the papacy to expand civil control in northern Italy. At the request of the pope, Charlemagne attacked the Lombards in 774, defeated them, and named himself their king.

One of the most important events in Charlemagne's reign took place on Christmas Day, 800. In the previous year the Roman nobility had removed the pope from office, charging him with corruption. But Charlemagne came to Rome and restored the pope to his position. At the Christmas service, as Charlemagne knelt before the altar, the pope placed a crown on his head while the congregation shouted: "To Charles Augustus crowned of God, great and pacific Emperor of the Romans, long life and victory!"

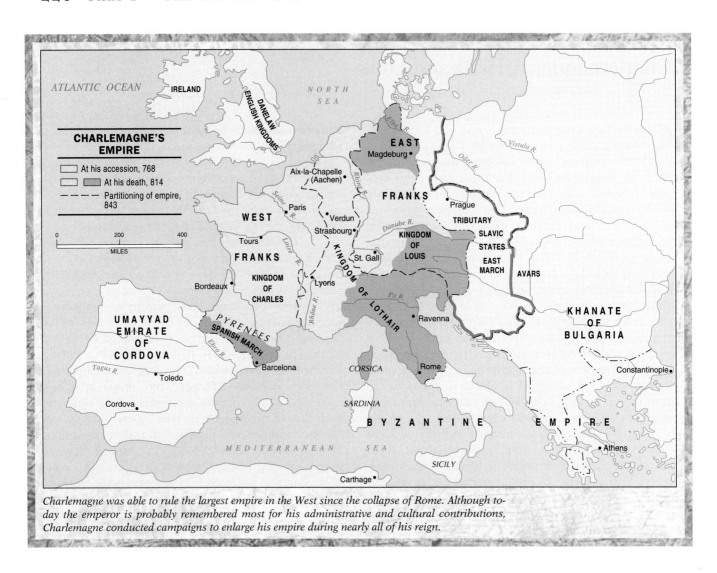

CHARLEMAGNE'S EMPIRE

☐ At his accession, 768

☐ ☐ At his death, 814

- - - Partitioning of empire, 843

0   200   400
MILES

Charlemagne was able to rule the largest empire in the West since the collapse of Rome. Although to-day the emperor is probably remembered most for his administrative and cultural contributions, Charlemagne conducted campaigns to enlarge his empire during nearly all of his reign.

This ceremony demonstrated that the memory of the Roman Empire still survived as a meaningful tradition in Europe and that there was a strong desire to reestablish political unity. In fact, Charlemagne had named his capital at Aix-la-Chapelle (Aachen) "New Rome" and contemplated taking the title of emperor in an attempt to revive the idea of the Roman Empire in the West.

The extent of Charlemagne's empire was impressive. His territories included all of the western area of the old Roman Empire except Africa, Britain, southern Italy, and the majority of Spain. Seven defensive provinces, or marches, protected the empire against hostile neighbors.

The Carolingian territories were divided into some 300 administrative divisions, each under a count *(graf)* or, in the marches along the border, a margrave *(markgraf)*. In addition, there were local military officials, the dukes. In an effort to supervise the activities of local officials, Charlemagne issued an ordinance creating the *missi dominici*, the king's envoys. Pairs of these itinerant officials, usually a bishop and a lay noble, traveled throughout the

realm to check on the local administration. So that the *missi* were immune to bribes, they were chosen from men of high rank, they were frequently transferred from one region to another, and no two of them were teamed for more than one year.

Charlemagne's Legacy

Charlemagne is considered one of the most significant figures of early European history. He extended Christian civilization in Europe, set up barriers to prevent invasions of the Slavs and Avars, and created a state in which law and order were again enforced after three centuries of disintegration. His patronage of learning began a cultural revival that later generations would build on, producing a European civilization distinct from the Byzantine to the east and the Muslim to the south.

Charlemagne's empire was not long-lived, however, for its territories were too vast and its nobility too divisive to be held together after the dominating personality of its creator was gone. Charlemagne had no standing army; his foot soldiers were essentially the old Germanic war band summoned to fight by its war leader. The king did not have a bureaucratic administrative machine comparable to that of Roman times. The Frankish economy was agricultural and localized, and there was no system of taxation adequate to maintain an effective and permanent administration. Under Charlemagne's weak successors, the empire collapsed in the confusion of civil wars and devastating new invasions. Progress toward a centralized and effective monarchy in Europe ended with Charlemagne's death.

When he died in 814, Charlemagne was succeeded by his only surviving son, Louis the Pious, a well-meaning but ineffective ruler. Louis, in accordance with Frankish custom, divided the kingdom among his three sons, and bitter rivalry and warfare broke out among the brothers even before Louis died in 840.

In 843 the three brothers met at Verdun, where they agreed to split the Carolingian lands among themselves. Charles the Bald obtained the western part of the empire and Louis the German the eastern; Lothair, the oldest brother, retained the title of emperor and obtained an elongated middle kingdom, which stretched 1000 miles from the North Sea to central Italy.

The Treaty of Verdun contributed to the shaping of political problems that continued into the twentieth century. Lothair's middle kingdom soon collapsed into three major parts: Lorraine in the North; Burgundy; and Italy in the South. Lorraine included Latin and German cultures and, although it was divided in 870 between Charles and Louis, the area was disputed for centuries. Lorraine became one of the most frequent battlegrounds of Europe.

Europe Under Attack

During the ninth and tenth centuries, coinciding with the collapse of the Carolingian Empire, western Europe came under attack by Scandinavians from the North and Muslims from the South, while the Magyars, a new band of Asiatic nomads, conducted destructive raids on central Europe and northern Italy. Christian Europe was hard pressed to repel these warlike newcomers, who were more threatening to life and property than the Germanic invaders of the fifth century.

From bases in North Africa, Muslim adventurers in full command of the sea plundered the coasts of Italy and France. In 827 they began the conquest of Byzantine Sicily and southern Italy. From forts erected in southern France they penetrated far inland to attack merchant caravans in the Alpine passes. What trade still existed between Byzantium and western Europe, except for that undertaken by Venice and several other Italian towns, was now al-

This gold bust of Charlemagne was made in the fourteenth century and is housed now in the treasury of the Palace Chapel of Charlemagne in Aachen, Germany. The reliquary bust contains parts of the emperor's skull.

most totally cut off, and the Mediterranean Sea came under almost complete Muslim control.

The most widespread and destructive raids, however, came from Scandinavia. Swedes, Danes, and Norwegians—collectively referred to as Vikings—began to move south. Overpopulation and a surplus of young men are possible reasons for this expansion, but some scholars suggest that these raiders were defeated war bands expelled from their homeland by the emergence of strong royal power. The Vikings had developed seaworthy ships capable of carrying 100 men, powered by long oars or by sail when the wind was favorable. Viking sailors had also developed expert sailing techniques; without benefit of the

This wooden animal head dating from the early ninth century is the terminal of a post of a buried Viking ship found at Oseberg, in southern Norway. The carving combines realistic details with the imaginative use of abstract geometric patterns derived from metalwork.

compass, they were able to navigate by the stars at night and the sun by day.

The range of Viking expansion reached as far as North America to the west, the Caspian Sea to the east, and the Mediterranean to the south. Between 800 and 850 Ireland was raided repeatedly. Many monasteries, the centers of the flourishing Irish Celtic culture, were destroyed. The Icelandic Norsemen ventured on to Greenland and, later, to North America. Other raiders traveled the rivers of Russia as merchants and soldiers of fortune and founded the nucleus of a Russian state. Danes raided Britain and the shores of Germany, France, and Spain. By 840 they had occupied most of Britain north of the Thames. They devastated northwest France, destroying dozens of abbeys and towns. Unable to fend off the Viking attacks, the weak Carolingian king accepted the local Norse chieftain as duke of a Viking state, later called Normandy. Like Viking settlers elsewhere, these Northmen, or Normans, became Christian converts and eventually played an important role in shaping the future of medieval Europe.

Feudalism

Europe's response to the invasions of the ninth and tenth centuries was not uniform. By 900 the Viking occupation of England had initiated a strong national reaction, which soon led to the creation of a united British kingdom. Germany in 919 repelled the Magyar threat through the efforts of a new and able line of kings who went on to become powerful European monarchs. But Viking attacks on France accelerated the trends toward political fragmentation. Since the monarchy could not hold together its vast territory, small independent landowners surrendered both their lands and their personal freedoms to the many counts, dukes, and other local lords in return for protection and security. The decline of trade further strengthened the position of the landed nobility, whose large estates, or manors, sought to become economically self-sufficient. In addition, the nobility became increasingly dependent on military service rendered by a professional force of heavily armed mounted knights, many of whom still lived in the house of their noble retainers in return for their military service.

In most parts of western Europe, where an effective centralized government was entirely absent, personal safety and security became the primary concerns of most individuals. Historians have used the term *feudalism* to apply to the individual and unique political and social patterns resulting from political decentralization and the resulting attempts to ensure personal security.

Feudalism can be described as a system of rights and duties in which political power was exercised locally by private individuals rather than through the bureaucracy of a centralized state. In general, western European feudalism involved three basic elements: (1) a personal element, called *lordship* or *vassalage*, by which one nobleman, the *vassal*, became the follower of a stronger nobleman, the *lord*; (2) a property element, called the *fief* or *benefice* (usually land), which the vassal received from his lord to enable him to fulfill the obligations of being a vassal; and (3) a governmental element, the private exercise of governmental functions over vassals and fiefs.

Theoretical Feudal Hierarchy

In theory, feudalism was a vast hierarchy. At the top stood the king, and all the land in his kingdom belonged to him. He kept large areas for his personal use (royal or crown lands) and, in return for the military service of a specified number of mounted knights, invested the highest nobles—such as dukes and counts (in Britain, earls)—with the remainder. Those nobles, in turn, in order to obtain the services of the required number of mounted warriors owed to the king, parceled out large portions of their fiefs to lesser nobles. This process, called *subinfeudation,* was continued in theory until the lowest in the scale of vassals was reached—the single knight whose fief was just sufficient to support one mounted warrior.

By maintaining the king at the head of this theoretical feudal hierarchy, this custom kept the traces of monarchy intact. Although some feudal kings were little more than figureheads who were less powerful than their own vassals, the tradition of monarchy was retained.

Relation of Lord and Vassal: The Contract

Personal bonds between lord and vassal were sometimes formally recognized. In the ceremony known as *homage,* the vassal knelt before his lord, or *suzerain,* and promised to be his "man." In the *oath of fealty* that followed, the vassal swore on the Bible or some other sacred object that he would remain true to his lord. Next, in the ritual of *investiture,* a lance, a glove, or even a clump of dirt was handed to the vassal to signify his jurisdiction over the fief. As his part of the contract, the lord was usually obliged to give his vassal protection and justice. In return, the vassal's primary duty was military service. In addition, the vassal could be obliged to assist the lord in rendering justice in the lord's court. At certain times, as when the lord was captured and had to be ransomed, the lord also had the right to demand special money payments, called *aids.*

The Early Medieval Economy: Manorialism

The economy of the early Middle Ages reflected the localism and self-sufficiency of life that resulted from an ineffective central government in Europe. The economic and social system based on the manors, the great estates held by the nobles, was referred to as *manorialism.*

The manor usually varied in size from one locality to another; a small one might contain only about a dozen households. Since the allotment of land to each family averaged about 30 acres, the smallest manors probably had about 350 acres of land suitable for farming, not counting meadows, woods, wasteland, and the lord's *demesne*—the land reserved for the lord's use alone. A large manor might contain 50 families in a total area of 5000 acres.

The center of the manor was the village, in which the thatched cottages of the peasants were grouped

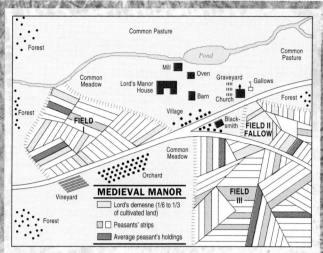

The manor, the self-contained economic unit of early medieval life, operated on a system of reciprocal rights and obligations based on custom. In return for protection, strips of arable land, and the right to use the nonarable common land, the peasant paid dues and worked on the lord's demesne. Under the three-field system, one-third of the land lay fallow so that intensive cultivation did not exhaust the soil.

together along one street. Around each cottage was a space large enough for a vegetable patch, chicken yard, haystack, and stable. An important feature of the landscape was the village church, together with the priest's house and the burial ground. The lord's dwelling might be a fortified house or a more modest dwelling.

Distribution of the Land

Every manor contained arable and nonarable land. Part of the arable land was reserved for the lord and was cultivated for him by his serfs; the remainder was held by the villagers. The nonarable land, consisting of meadow, wood, and wasteland, was used in common by the villagers and the lord.

From one-sixth to one-third of the arable land was given over to the lord's demesne. The arable land not held in demesne was allotted among the villagers under the open-field system, whereby the fields were subdivided into strips. The strips, each containing about an acre, were separated by narrow paths of uncultivated land. The serf's holding was not all in one plot, for all soil throughout the manor was not equally fertile, and an attempt was made to give each of the villagers land of the same quality. Each tenant was really a shareholder in the village community, not only in the open fields but also in the meadow, pasture, wood, and wastelands.

Wooded land was valuable as an area to graze pigs, the most common animal on the manor. Tenants could also gather dead wood in the forest, but cutting down green wood was prohibited unless authorized by the lord.

Medieval Farming Methods

It is difficult to generalize about agricultural methods, because differences in locality, fertility of soil, crop production, and other factors resulted in a variety of farming approaches. Farming as practiced in northwestern Europe was characterized by some common factors. The implements the peasants used were extremely crude; the plow was a cumbersome instrument with heavy wheels, often requiring as many as eight oxen to pull it. (By the twelfth century the use of plow horses had become common.) Other tools included crude harrows, sickles, beetles for breaking up clods, and flails for threshing.

Inadequate methods of farming soon exhausted the soil. The average yield per acre was only 6 to 8 bushels of wheat, one-fourth the modern yield. In classical times farmers had learned that soil planted continually with one crop rapidly deteriorated. As a counteraction they employed a two-field system: half of the arable land was planted while the other half lay fallow to recover its fertility. Medieval farmers learned that wheat or rye could be planted in the autumn as well as in the spring. As a result, by the ninth century they were dividing the land into three fields, with one planted in the fall, another in the spring, and the third left lying fallow. This system not only kept more land in production but also required less plowing in any given year.

Under the manorial system, women of the aristocracy exercised great authority. Often the lord of the manor's wife was placed in charge of managing the manor's accounts and storehouses. She often stood in for her husband in his absence and supervised the peasants and even the courts of justice.

Peasant women usually had to endure backbreaking labor. Peasant women cooked, cleaned, made clothing, maintained the animals, milked cows, made butter and cheese, brewed ale and beer, and nurtured the gardens. Women assisted the men during planting and harvesting seasons and with any seasonal or special projects endorsed by the lord. The sexes were treated fairly equally on the lower social levels in the Middle Ages—there was not much difference in the demanding lifestyle all had to endure.

Administration of the Manor

Although the lord might live on one of his manors, each manor was usually administered by such officials as the steward, the bailiff, and the reeve. The steward was the general overseer who supervised the business of all his lord's manors and presided over the manorial court. It was the bailiff's duty to supervise the cultivation of the lord's demesne; collect rents, dues, and fines; and inspect the work done by the free peasants (freemen) and the nonfree peasants (serfs). The reeve was the "foreman" of the villagers, chosen by them and representing their interests.

Freemen often lived on the manor, although they constituted only a small portion of its population. Freemen were not subject to the same demands as the serfs. The freeman did not have to work in the lord's fields himself but could send substitutes. Serfs, however, were bound to the manor and could not leave without the lord's consent. Serfdom was a hereditary status; the children of serfs were attached to the soil, just as their parents were.

The lord of the manor was bound by custom to respect certain rights of his serfs. So long as they paid their dues and services, serfs could not be evicted from their hereditary holdings. Although a serf could not appear in court against his lord or a freeman, he could appeal to the manor court against any of his fellows. To the serfs, the manor was the center of their very existence, but to the lord, the manor was essentially a source of income and subsistence.

The Life of the Peasants

On the manors of the Middle Ages, the margin between starvation and survival was narrow, and the life of the peasant was not easy. Famines were frequent; warfare was a constant threat; and grasshoppers, locusts, caterpillars, and rats repeatedly destroyed the crops. Men, women, and children alike had to toil long hours in the fields.

Home life offered few comforts. The typical peasant dwelling was a cottage with mud walls, clay floor, and thatched roof. The fire burned on a flat hearthstone in the middle of the floor; unless the peasant was rich enough to afford a chimney, the smoke escaped through a hole in the roof. The window openings had no glass and were stuffed with straw in the winter. Furnishings were meager, usually consisting of a table, a kneading trough for dough, a cupboard, and a bed, often either a heap of straw or a box filled with straw, which served the entire family. Pigs and chickens wandered about the cottage continually; the stable was often under the same roof, next to the family quarters.

The peasants, despite their hard, monotonous life, enjoyed a few pleasures. Wrestling was popular, as were cockfighting, a crude type of football, and fighting with quarter-staves, in which contestants stood an excellent chance of getting their heads

Both peasant men and women toiled in the fields. Here women reap with sickles, while behind them a man binds the sheaves.

bashed in. Dancing, singing, and drinking were popular pastimes, especially on the numerous holy days and festivals promoted by the church.

The High Middle Ages, 1000–1300

The High Middle Ages witnessed the full development of earlier medieval civilization. In this era European monarchies struggled to emerge from the decentralized feudal organization. The church rose to great heights of power and authority. The revival of trade and the rebirth of towns altered the economy of Europe and sped the end of manorialism. And this period gave birth to developments in art, architecture, and literature that stand as some of the most significant achievements in European civilization.

Feudalism was a system founded on the decentralization of authority; the king was often no more than a figurehead in the feudal order. But gradually the monarchs of most European states sought to increase their powers at the expense of their feudal nobility. Through such efforts, several of which took centuries to bear results, national monarchies began to take form on the European continent.

The Capetians and the Beginnings of France

In France, by the beginning of the tenth century, more than 30 great feudal princes were vassals of the king, but they gave him little or no support. When the last Carolingian, Louis the Sluggard, died in 987, the nobles elected one of their number, Hugh Capet, count of Paris, as his successor. The territory that Hugh Capet (987–996) actually controlled was a small feudal county, the Île-de-France, extending from Paris to Orléans. The royal lands were surrounded by many large duchies and counties, such as Flanders, Normandy, Anjou, and Champagne, which were fiercely independent.

The major accomplishment of the first four Capetian kings was their success at keeping the French crown within their own family and at slowly expanding their influence. With the support of the church, the Capetians cleverly arranged for the election and coronation of their heirs. For 300 years the House of Capet never lacked a male heir.

The reign of the fifth Capetian king, Louis VI (1108–1137), known as "the Fat," saw an expansion of Capetian strength. Determined to crush the barons who defied royal authority, he captured their castles and in many cases tore them down. Louis made his word law in the Île-de-France, established a solid

Nation-Building in France

987–996	Reign of Hugh Capet
1108–1137	Reign of Louis VI
1180–1223	Reign of Philip II Augustus
1226–1270	Reign of Louis IX
1285–1314	Reign of Philip IV, the Fair

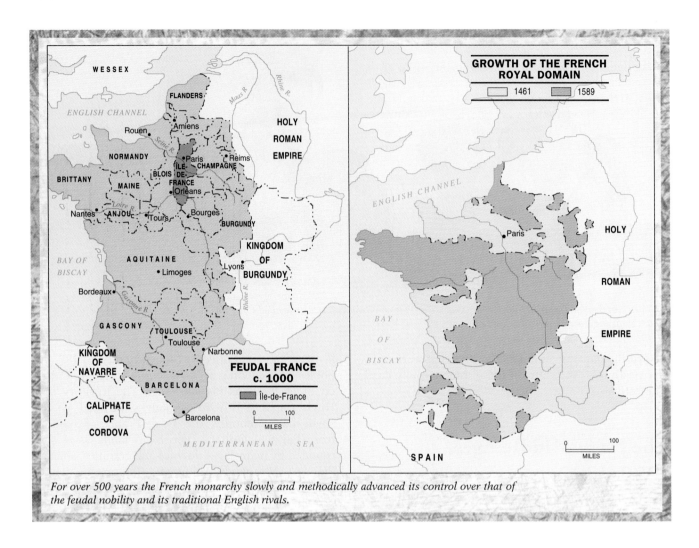

For over 500 years the French monarchy slowly and methodically advanced its control over that of the feudal nobility and its traditional English rivals.

base from which royal power could be extended, and increased the prestige of the monarchy so much that the great duke of Aquitaine agreed to marry his daughter Eleanor to Louis's son. Unfortunately, Eleanor's behavior so scandalized Louis's pious son that the marriage was annulled, and Aquitaine passed to Eleanor's second husband, Henry II of England.

Philip II Augustus

The first great expansion of the royal domain was the work of Philip II Augustus (1180–1223). Philip's great ambition was to seize from the English kings the vast territory they held in France. He made little progress against Henry II, except to encourage his sons, Richard the Lion-Hearted and John, to revolt. Philip took Normandy, Maine, Anjou, and Touraine from John, and by doing so he tripled the size of the French royal domain.

Philip also greatly strengthened the royal administrative system by devising new agencies for centralized government and tapping new sources of revenue, including a money payment from his vassals

instead of military service. Salaried officials, called bailiffs, were given military, political, and judicial responsibilites by the king. Special administrative departments were established: the *parlement*, a supreme court of justice; the chamber of accounts, or royal treasury; and the royal or privy council, a group of advisers who assisted the king in the conduct of the daily business of the state.

After the brief reign of Philip II's son Louis VIII, France came under the rule of Louis IX (1226–1270), better known as St. Louis. Louis's ideal was to rule justly, and in so doing he became one of the most beloved kings of France. The king believed himself responsible only to God, who had put him on the throne to lead his people out of a life of sin. Just, sympathetic, and peace-loving, Louis IX convinced his subjects that the monarchy was the most important agency for ensuring their happiness and well-being.

Height of Capetian Rule Under Philip IV

The reign of Philip IV, known as Philip the Fair (1285–1314), culminated three centuries of Capetian rule. The opposite of his saintly grandfather, Philip was a man of violence and cunning. Aware that anti-Semitism was growing in Europe in the wake of the Crusades, he expelled the Jews from France and confiscated their possessions.

Philip's need for money also brought him into conflict with the last great medieval pope. Boniface VIII refused to allow Philip to tax the French clergy and made sweeping claims to supremacy over secular powers. But Philip IV would not tolerate papal interference, and the result was the humiliation of Boniface, a blow from which the influence of the medieval papacy never recovered. In domestic affairs, the real importance of Philip's reign lay in the king's ability to increase the power and improve the organization of the royal government. Philip's astute civil servants, recruited mainly from the middle class, sought to make the power of the monarch absolute.

Philip enlarged his feudal council to include representatives of the third "estate" or class, the townspeople. This Estates-General of nobles, clergy, and burghers was used to obtain popular support for Philip's policies, including the announcement of new taxes. Philip did not ask the Estates-General's consent for his tax measures, and thus this body did not acquire a role in decisions affecting taxation.

England to 1300

After the Romans withdrew from England in the fifth century, Germanic tribes known as Angles and Saxons invaded the island of Great Britain and divided it among more than a dozen tribal kingdoms, and the overlordship of the island was held in turn by the different rulers. (Soon after their arrival, the Angles and Saxons intermixed to become essentially one tribal group, the Anglo-Saxons.) In the ninth century the kingdom of Wessex held the dominant position. Its king, Alfred the Great (871–899), was confronted with the task of turning back the Danes, who overran all the other English kingdoms. Alfred defeated the Danes and forced them into a treaty whereby they settled in the region called the Danelaw and accepted Christianity.

Alfred's successors were able rulers who conquered the Danelaw and created a unified English monarchy. Danes and Saxons intermarried, and soon most differences between the two peoples disappeared. After 975, however, the power of the central government lagged. In 1016 the Anglo-Saxons were again overrun by the Danes, and King Canute of Denmark extended his rule to include England and Norway.

Canute proved to be a wise and civilized king and was well liked by his Anglo-Saxon subjects because he respected their rights and customs. But Canute's

Nation-Building in England

871–899	Alfred the Great rules Wessex
1016–1035	Reign of Canute
1066	Battle of Hastings
1066–1087	Reign of William the Conqueror
1154–1189	Henry II begins Plantagenet dynasty
1189–1199	Reign of Richard I, the Lion-Hearted
1199–1216	Reign of John I
1215	Magna Carta
1272–1307	Reign of Edward I

empire fell apart after his death in 1035, and in 1042 the English crown was secured by the Anglo-Saxon Edward the Confessor. Although noted for his devotion to religion, Edward was a weak ruler who had little control over the powerful earls who had taken over most of the king's authority in their territories.

William the Conqueror and the Norman Conquest

Edward the Confessor died without an heir, and immediately William, duke of Normandy, claimed the English throne based on a questionable hereditary right and on the assertion that Edward had promised him the crown. An outstanding statesman and soldier, William as duke of Normandy had subdued his rebellious vassals and established an effective centralized feudal state.

William and his army of 5000 men crossed the English Channel to enforce the Norman claim to the English throne. On October 14, 1066, the duke's mounted knights broke through the English infantry at Hastings, and William became king in England, where he began to introduce the Norman style of feudal organization. The new king retained some land as his royal domain and granted the remainder as fiefs to royal vassals called *tenants-in-chief*. In return for their fiefs, the tenants-in-chief provided William with a number of knights to serve in the royal army. From all the landholders in England, regardless of whether they were his immediate vassals, William exacted an oath that they would "be faithful to him against all other men." Both the tenants-in-chief holding fiefs directly from the king and the lesser vassals owed their first allegiance to William.

In line with his policy of controlling all aspects of the government, William redesigned the *witan*, the

Discovery Through Maps

The Danelaw: When Half of England Was Viking

As part of the Treaty of Wedmore, a boundary was drawn across England from London to Mersey. South of this line the laws and customs would be those of the English, under the rule of the king of Mersey. The land to the north and east of this line would be under Viking rule, with Scandinavian laws and customs. This Viking part of England became known as the Danelaw.

Although the Danelaw was brought back under English control within 50 years, Scandinavian cultural influences continued to be important there for many generations. Even today there are vestiges of the time when this area was distinct from England. The strongest reminder is modern English: the words, phrases, and grammar rules of Anglo-Saxon were altered by speakers of Old Norse, the tongue of the Vikings, and more than 600 loan words—including *egg*, *knife*, and *die*—entered the English language. Dialects in the Danelaw developed differently from those in other parts of the island, and even today the residents of the old Danelaw lands pride themselves on the distinctions in their manner of speaking. Arts and crafts were influenced as well, typified by the merging of Norse and Anglo-Saxon design in the Anglo-Norse cross and the design of gravestones.

The Bayeux tapestry, a woolen embroidery on linen, dates from the eleventh century. Over 230 feet long, it depicts events in the Norman conquest of England in 1066, accompanied by a commentary in Latin and surrounded by a decorative border portraying scenes from fables and everyday life.

council that had elected and advised the Anglo-Saxon kings. The new Norman ruler changed its title to the great council—the *Curia Regis,* or king's court—and converted it into a body composed of his tenants-in-chief. The great council met as a court of justice for the great barons and as an advisory body in important matters.

William also dominated the English church. He appointed bishops and abbots and required them to provide military service for their lands. Although he permitted the church to retain its courts, he denied them the right to appeal cases to the pope without his consent. Nor could the decrees of popes and church councils circulate in England without royal approval.

William II, who succeeded his father in 1087, was an ineffective king who inspired several baronial revolts before being shot in the back—accidentally, it was said—while hunting. Succeeding him was his brother, Henry I (1110–1135), a more able monarch who easily put down the only baronial revolt that challenged him.

Although the great council occasionally met to advise Henry, a small permanent council of barons grew in importance. From it, specialized branches of government gradually appeared. The *exchequer,* or court of accounts, supervised the collection of royal revenue and greatly expanded with the revival of a money economy. The well-trained "barons of the exchequer" also sat as a special court to try cases involving revenue.

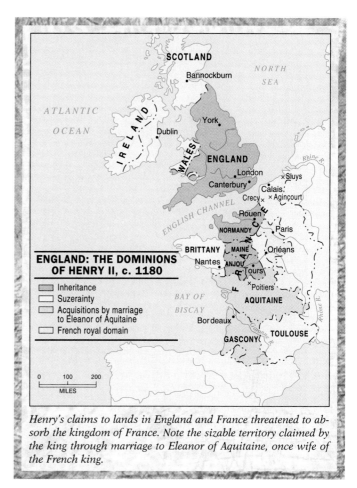

ENGLAND: THE DOMINIONS OF HENRY II, c. 1180

- Inheritance
- Suzerainty
- Acquisitions by marriage to Eleanor of Aquitaine
- French royal domain

Henry's claims to lands in England and France threatened to absorb the kingdom of France. Note the sizable territory claimed by the king through marriage to Eleanor of Aquitaine, once wife of the French king.

Henry II

Almost 20 years of civil war followed Henry's death. But the monarchy was strengthened by Henry's grandson, Henry II (1154–1189), the founder of the Plantagenet, or Angevin, dynasty. As a result of his inheritance (Normandy and Anjou) and his marriage to Eleanor of Aquitaine, the richest heiress in France, Henry's possessions extended from Scotland to the Pyrenees. Henry's great military skill and restless energy were important assets to his reign. He quickly recaptured the lands of his grandfather and began rebuilding the power of the monarchy in England.

Henry's chief contribution to the development of the English monarchy was to increase the jurisdiction of the royal courts at the expense of the feudal courts. His efforts produced significant results. Itinerant justices on regular circuits were sent out once each year to enforce the "King's Peace." Henry's courts also used the jury system to settle private lawsuits; circuit judges handed down quick decisions based on evidence sworn to by a jury of men selected because they were acquainted with the facts of the case.

Henry's judicial reforms stimulated the growth of the common law—one of the most important factors in unifying the English people. The decisions of the royal justices became the basis for future decisions made in the king's courts and became the law common to all English people.

Thomas à Becket

Although Henry strengthened the royal courts, he was not as successful in regulating the church courts. When he appointed his trusted friend Thomas à Becket archbishop of Canterbury, the king assumed that the cleric could easily be persuaded to cooperate, but Becket proved stubbornly independent in upholding the authority of the church courts over the king's. After a number of disagreements in which Becket defended the independence of the English church from royal authority, Henry was reputed to have remarked that he would be relieved if someone would rid England of the troublesome Becket. Responding to this angry remark, four knights went to Canterbury and murdered Becket before the high altar of the cathedral. Popular outrage over this murder destroyed Henry's chances of reducing the power of the church courts.

The Successors of Henry II

Henry's many accomplishments were marred by the mistakes of his successors. Having no taste for routine

A detail from the Carrow Psalter depicts the murder of Thomas à Becket by the knights of Henry II in Canterbury Cathedral. One knight has broken his sword over the archbishop's head.

The Martyrdom of Thomas Becket, Carrow Psalter, MS W. 34 f. 15v. The Walters Art Gallery, Baltimore.

tasks of government, Richard the Lion-Hearted (1189–1199) spent only five months of his ten-year reign in Britain, which he regarded as a source of money for his overseas adventures. Richard's successor, his brother John (1199–1216), was an inept and cruel ruler whose unscrupulousness cost him the support of his barons, at the time he needed them most, in his struggles with the two ablest men of the age, Philip II of France and Pope Innocent III. As feudal overlord of John's possessions in France, Philip declared John an unfaithful vassal and his claims to lands in France illegitmate. John only feebly resisted, and after losing more than half his possessions in France, he became involved in a struggle with Innocent III that ended in John's complete surrender. In the meantime the king alienated the British barons, who rebelled and in 1215 forced him to agree to the Magna Carta, a document that bound the king to observe all feudal rights and privileges. Although in later centuries people looked back on the Magna Carta as one of the most important documents in the history of political freedom, to the English nobility of John's time the Magna Carta did not appear to break any new constitutional ground. It was essentially a feudal agreement be-

tween the barons and the king, the aristocracy and the monarchy. Two great principles were contained in the charter: the law is above the king, and the king can be compelled by force to obey the law of the land.

The Origins of Parliament

The French-speaking Normans commonly used the word *parlement* (from *parler*, "to speak") for the great council. Anglicized as *parliament*, the term was used interchangeably with *great council* and *Curia Regis*. Modern historians, however, generally apply the term to the great council only after 1265, when its membership was radically enlarged. Parliament first became truly influential during the reign of Edward I (1272–1307), one of England's most outstanding monarchs. Beginning with the so-called Model Parliament of 1295, Edward followed the pattern of summoning representatives of shires and towns to meetings of the great council. In calling parliaments, Edward had no intention of making any concession to popular government; rather, he hoped to build popular consensus to support his own policies.

Early in the fourteenth century the representatives of the knights and the townsmen, called the Commons, adopted the practice of meeting separately from the lords. This resulted in the division of Parliament into what came to be called the House of Commons and the House of Lords. Parliament, particularly the Commons, soon discovered its power as a major source of revenue for the king. It gradually became the custom for Parliament to exercise this power by withholding its financial grants until the king had redressed grievances, made known by petitions. Parliament also presented petitions to the king with the request that they be recognized as statutes (laws drawn up by the king and his council and confirmed in Parliament). Gradually, Parliament assumed the right to initiate legislation through petition.

Expansion Under Edward I

Edward I was the first English king who was determined to be master of the whole island of Great Britain—Wales, Scotland, and England. In 1284, after a five-year struggle, English law and administration were imposed on Wales, and numerous attempts were made to conquer the Scots, who continued to offer Edward serious resistance up to the time of his death.

The Reconquista and Medieval Spain

Unification in Spain took a different course from that in either France or England. Customary rivalry between the Christian feudal nobles and

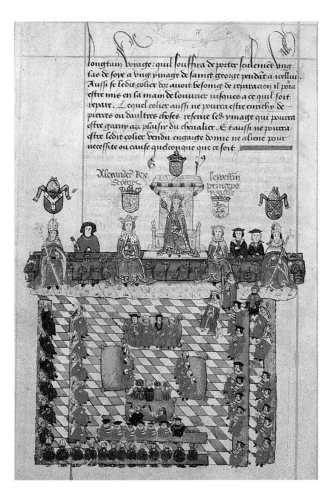

Edward I at a session of Parliament. Edward was the first monarch to give real standing to the institution of Parliament and to expand it to include representatives of the shires and boroughs.
Windsor Castle, Royal Library; © Her Majesty Queen Elizabeth II.

royal authority was complicated by another element: religious fervor. Unification of Christian Spain was not thought possible without the expulsion of the Muslims, with their foreign religion and culture.

During the long struggle to drive the Muslims from Spain, patriotism blended with fierce religious devotion. This movement became known as the *Reconquista*—the reconquest of Spain from Muslim control. As early as the ninth century, northern Spain became caught up in religious zeal centering around the shrine at Santiago de Compostela, reputed to be the burial site of the apostle St. James. In 1212 at Las Navas de Tolosa, the Christian Spaniards achieved a decisive victory over the Muslims. A few years later they captured first Cordova and Seville. The conquest of Seville effectively doubled the territory of the Spanish kingdom. From the end of the thirteenth century, when the Reconquista slowed, until the latter part of the fifteenth century, Muslim political control

was confined to Granada. Until the fifteenth century, the Christian victors usually allowed their new Muslim subjects to practice their own religion and traditions. Muslim traders and artisans were protected because of their economic value, and Muslim culture—art in particular—was often adapted by the Christians.

Disunity in Germany and Italy

When the last Carolingian ruler of the kingdom of the East Franks, Louis the Child, died in 911, the great German dukes elected the weakest of their number to hold the title of king. But an exceptionally strong ruler inherited the throne in 936—Otto the Great (936–973), duke of Saxony and founder of the Saxon dynasty of kings. Otto attempted to gain control of the great dukes by appointing his own relatives and favorites as their rulers. As an extra precaution he appointed counts as supervising officials who were directly responsible to the king.

Through alliance with the church, Otto constructed a stronger German monarchy. The king promised protection to the bishops and abbots and granted them a free hand over their vast estates; in return the church furnished the king with the advisers, income, and troops that he lacked. Otto himself appointed German bishops and abbots; since their offices were not hereditary, he expected that their first obedience was to the king.

Otto also ended the Magyar invasions, thereby enhancing his claim that the king, not the dukes, was the true defender of the German people. In 955 Otto crushed a Magyar army at Lechfeld. The surviving Magyars settled in Hungary, and by 1000 they had accepted Christianity.

Otto the Great wanted to establish a German empire, modeled after Roman and Carolingian examples. The conquest and incorporation of the Italian peninsula into that empire were Otto's primary objectives. He proclaimed himself king of Italy, and in 962 he was crowned emperor by the pope, whose Papal States were threatened by an Italian duke. No doubt Otto thought of himself as the successor of the imperial Caesars and Charlemagne; in fact, his empire later became known as the Holy Roman Empire. But Otto also needed the imperial title to legitimize his claim to Lombardy, Burgundy, and Lorraine, which had belonged to the kingdom of Lothair, the last to hold the title of emperor. Otto and his successors became deeply involved in Italian politics and sometimes preoccupied with Italy to the neglect of their German subjects. The negative effects of the German obsession with Italy were apparent in the reign of Otto III (983–1002), who promoted "the renewal of the Roman Empire." Ignoring Germany, the

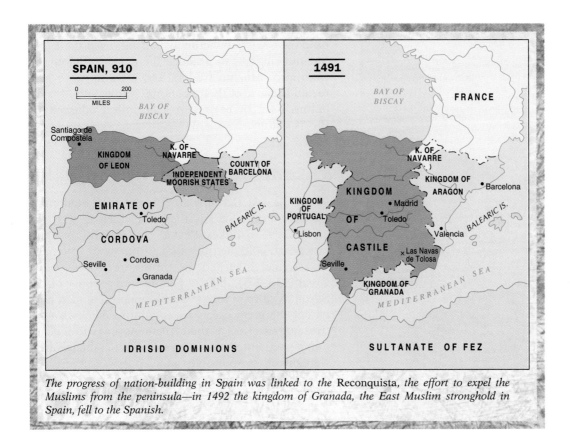

SPAIN, 910

0   200
MILES

BAY OF
BISCAY

Santiago de
Compostela

KINGDOM
OF LEON

K. OF
NAVARRE

COUNTY OF
BARCELONA

INDEPENDENT
MOORISH STATES

EMIRATE OF

Toledo

BALEARIC IS.

CORDOVA

Seville   • Cordova

• Granada

MEDITERRANEAN SEA

IDRISID DOMINIONS

1491

BAY OF
BISCAY

FRANCE

K. OF
NAVARRE

KINGDOM OF
ARAGON

• Barcelona

KINGDOM
OF
PORTUGAL

KINGDOM
OF
CASTILE

• Madrid

Toledo

Valencia

BALEARIC IS.

• Lisbon

Seville

× Las Navas
de Tolosa

MEDITERRANEAN SEA

KINGDOM OF
GRANADA

SULTANATE OF FEZ

The progress of nation-building in Spain was linked to the Reconquista, *the effort to expel the Muslims from the peninsula—in 1492 the kingdom of Granada, the East Muslim stronghold in Spain, fell to the Spanish.*

real source of his power, he made Rome his capital, built a palace there, and styled himself emperor of the Romans.

Despite the distractions in Italy, the Saxon rulers were the most powerful in Europe. They had permanently halted Magyar advances and, by utilizing the German church as an ally, reduced feudal fragmentation in their homeland. They also fostered economic progress. German eastward expansion had begun, and the Alpine passes had been freed from Muslim control and made safe for Italian merchants.

The Salian Emperors

The Saxon kings were succeeded by the Salian dynasty, which ruled from 1024 to 1125 and whose members also tried to establish a centralized monarchy. Under the emperor Henry IV (1056–1106) the monarchy reached the height of its power, but it also experienced a major reverse. The revival of a powerful papacy led to a bitter conflict with Henry, centering on the king's right to appoint church officials who were also his most loyal supporters. This disagreement between state and church culminated in Henry's begging the pope's forgiveness at Canossa in 1077. This conflict, the Investiture Controversy, resulted in the loss of the

monarchy's major sources of strength: the loyalty of the German church, now transferred to the papacy; the support of the great nobles, now openly rebellious and insistent on their "inborn rights"; and the chief material base of royal power, the king's lands, which were diminished by grants to nobles who would stay loyal to the monarchy only if such concessions were made.

The Holy Roman Empire

962	Otto the Great crowned emperor by the pope
1056–1106	Reign of Henry IV
1152–1190	Frederick I Barbarossa begins Hohenstaufen dynasty
1212–1250	Reign of Frederick II
1273	Election of Rudolf of Habsburg as German emperor
1356	Golden Bull
1493–1519	Reign of Maximilian I

The Holy Roman Empire, in its infancy in 1000, was united under the Saxon's emperors, but unity was challenged by strong and independent feudal nobles opposed to the emperor's efforts to rule other than in name only.

The second emperor of the new Hohenstaufen dynasty, Frederick I Barbarossa ("Redbeard"), who ruled from 1152 to 1190, also sought to force the great nobles to acknowledge his overlordship. To maintain his hold over Germany, Frederick needed the resources of Italy—particularly the income from taxes levied on the wealthy northern Italian cities. Encouraged by the papacy, these cities had joined together in the Lombard League to resist him. Frederick spent about 25 years fighting intermittently in Italy, but the final result was failure: opposition from the popes and the Lombard League was too strong. Frederick did, however, succeed in marrying his son to the heiress of the throne of the kingdom of Naples and Sicily.

Barbarossa's grandson, Frederick II (1212–1250), was a remarkable individual. Orphaned at an early age, Frederick was brought up as the ward of Innocent III, the most powerful medieval pope. With the pope's support, Frederick was elected emperor in 1215, one year before Innocent's death. Frederick sacrificed Germany in his efforts to unite Italy under

his rule. He transferred crown lands and royal rights to the German princes in order to win their support for his Italian wars. Born in Sicily, he remained devoted to the southern part of his empire. He shaped his kingdom there into a vibrant state. Administered by paid officials who were trained at the University of Naples, which he founded for that purpose, his kingdom was the most centralized and bureaucratic in Europe.

As long as he lived, this brilliant monarch held his empire together, but it quickly collapsed after his death in 1250. In Germany his son ruled ineffectively for four years before dying, and soon afterward Frederick's descendants in Sicily were executed when the count of Anjou, brother of Louis IX of France, was invited by the pope to annihilate what remained of what he called the "viper breed of the Hohenstaufen."

The Holy Roman Empire never again achieved the brilliance it had enjoyed during the reign of Frederick Barbarossa. Later emperors usually did not try to interfere in Italian affairs, and they ceased going to Rome to receive the imperial crown from the pope. In German affairs the emperors no longer even attempted to assert their authority over the increasingly powerful nobles.

Revival of Trade and Towns

Even though manorialism sought to secure economic self-sufficiency, an increase in trade and commercial activity in Europe was obvious before the tenth century. A northern trading zone, centered on Flanders, extended from the British Isles to the Baltic Sea. By 1050 Flemish artisans were producing woolen cloth of fine quality and in great demand. Baltic furs, honey and forest products, and British tin and raw wool were exchanged for Flemish cloth. From the south by way of Italy came oriental luxury goods—silks, sugar, and spices.

Trade Routes and Trade Fairs

The opening of the Mediterranean to European trade was instrumental in increasing trade and commerce. In the eleventh century Normans and Italians broke the Muslim hold on the eastern Mediterranean, and the First Crusade revived trade with the Near East. The easiest route north from the Mediterranean was to Marseilles and up the Rhône valley. Early in the fourteenth century an all-sea route connected the Mediterranean with northern Europe via the Strait of Gibraltar. The old overland route from northern Italy

A fifteenth-century illustration of the fair of Lendit, held every June in a field outside Paris. Here the bishop of Paris gives his blessing to the fair.

through the Alpine passes to central Europe was also reused.

Along the main European trade routes, lords set up fairs, where merchants and goods from Italy and northern Europe met. During the twelfth and thirteenth centuries the fairs of Champagne in France functioned as the major clearinghouse for this international trade.

Factors in the Revival of Towns

The resurgence of trade in Europe was a prime cause of the revival of towns; the towns arose because of trade, but they also stimulated trade by providing greater markets and by producing goods for the merchants to sell. Rivers were also important in the development of medieval towns; they were natural highways on which articles of commerce could be easily transported.

Another factor contributing to the rise of towns was population growth. In Britain, for example, the population more than tripled between 1066 and 1350. The reasons for this rapid increase in population are varied. The ending of bloody foreign invasions and, in some areas, the stabilization of feudal

society were contributing factors. More important was an increase in food production brought about by the cultivation of wastelands, clearing of forests, and draining of marshes.

Medieval towns were not large by modern standards. Before 1200 no European town contained 100,000 inhabitants, and a town of 20,000 was considered very large. Since the area within the walls was at a premium, towns were more crowded than the average modern city. Shops were even built on bridges, and buildings were erected to seven or more stories. Each additional story of a house often projected over the street, so that it was often possible for persons at the tops of houses opposite one another to touch hands. Streets were crowded, narrow, and noisy.

Merchant and Craft Guilds

In each town the merchants and artisans organized themselves into guilds. There were two kinds of guilds: merchant and craft. The merchant guild ensured a monopoly of trade within a given locality. All foreign merchants were supervised closely and made

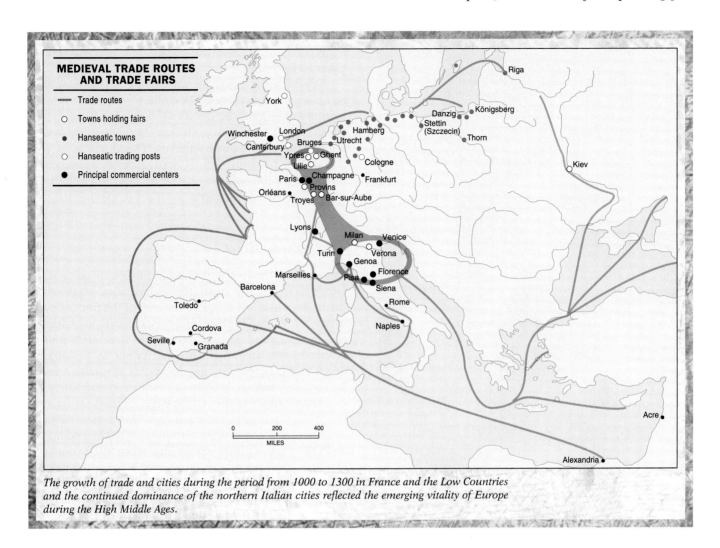

MEDIEVAL TRADE ROUTES AND TRADE FAIRS

—— Trade routes
○ Towns holding fairs
● Hanseatic towns
○ Hanseatic trading posts
● Principal commercial centers

The growth of trade and cities during the period from 1000 to 1300 in France and the Low Countries and the continued dominance of the northern Italian cities reflected the emerging vitality of Europe during the High Middle Ages.

to pay tolls. Disputes among merchants were settled at the guild court according to its own legal code. The guilds also tried to ensure that the customers were not cheated: they checked weights and measures and insisted on a standard quality for goods. To allow only a legitimate profit, the guild fixed a "just price," which was fair to both producer and customer.

With the increase of commerce in the towns, artisans and craftspeople in each of the medieval trades—weaving, cobbling, tanning, and so on—began to organize as early as the eleventh century. The result was the craft guild, which differed from the merchant guild in that membership was limited to artisans in one particular craft.

The general aims of the craft guilds were the same as those of the merchant guilds: the creation of a monopoly and the enforcement of trade rules. The guild restricted the number of its members, regulated the quantity and quality of the goods produced, and set prices. It also enforced regulations to protect the consumer from poor workmanship and inferior materials.

The craft guild differed from the merchant guild in its recognition of three distinct classes of workers: apprentices, journeymen, and master craftsmen. The apprentice was a youth who lived at the master's house and was taught the trade thoroughly. Although the apprentice received no wages, all his physical needs were supplied. Apprenticeship commonly lasted seven years. When the apprentice's schooling was finished, the youth became a journeyman. He was then eligible to receive wages and to be hired by a master. At about age 23, the journeyman sought admission into the guild as a master. To be accepted he had to prove his ability. Some crafts demanded the production of a "master piece," for example, a pair of shoes that the master shoemakers would find acceptable in every way.

The guild's functions stretched beyond business and politics into charitable and social activities. A guild member who fell into poverty received aid from the guild. The guild also provided financial assistance for the burial expense of its members and looked after their dependents. Members attended social

A guild master judges the work of two craftsmen, a mason and a carpenter.

meetings in the guildhall and periodically held processions in honor of their patron saints.

Acquiring Urban Freedom

The guilds played an important role in local government. Both artisans and merchants were subject to the feudal lord or bishop in whose domain the city stood. The citizens of the towns came to resent their overlord's collecting tolls and dues as though they were serfs. The townspeople demanded the privileges of governing themselves—of making their own laws, administering their own justice, levying their own taxes, and issuing their own coinage. The overlord resisted these demands for self-government, but the towns were able to win their independence in various ways.

One method was to become a *commune*, a self-governing town. The merchant guilds took the lead in acquiring charters of self-government for the towns. Sometimes a charter had to be won by revolt; in other circumstances it could be purchased, for a feudal lord was always in need of money. By 1200 the Lombard towns of northern Italy, as well as many French and Flemish towns, had become self-governing communes.

Where royal authority was strong, a town could be favored as "privileged." In a charter granted to the town by the monarch, the inhabitants won extensive financial and legal powers. It was also generally given the right to elect its own officials. The king was usually willing to grant such a charter, for it weakened the power of the nobles and won for the monarch the support of the townspeople.

The Bourgeoisie

Attracted by the freedom of town life, many serfs attempted to escape from the manor and establish themselves in a town. Partly because of the frequency of such escapes, lords of manors came to rely less and less on serfdom and often freed their serfs and induced them to remain on the manor as tenants. Some lords accepted money payments as a substitute for the serf's former obligations of labor and produce.

The triumph of the townspeople in their struggle for greater self-government meant that a new class had evolved in Europe—a powerful, independent, and self-assured group whose interest in trade was to revolutionize social, economic, and political history. The members of this class were called burghers and came to be known as the *bourgeoisie*. Kings began to rely more and more on them in combating the power of the feudal lords, and their economic interests gave rise to an early capitalism.

The Later Middle Ages, 1300–1500

Europe saw many changes during the later Middle Ages, some constructive, some disastrous. Distructive wars and suffering produced by disease and famine took a massive toll on the population. At the same time, political and cultural changes that would have lasting effects on European civilization were under way.

The Black Death and Economic Depression

The twelfth and thirteenth centuries had been an era of growth, but in the fourteenth and fifteenth centuries the economy leveled off and then stagnated. By 1350 the Continent was in the grips of a great economic depression, which lasted almost a century.

Henry Knighton, "The Devastation of England"

The plague raged throughout England and was especially harsh in London, where nearly two-thirds of the residents perished. The following account was written by Henry Knighton, a clergyman in Leicester, who was a boy in 1348 but who had an abundance of direct information.

Then the grievous plague penetrated the seacoasts from Southampton, and came to Bristol, and there almost the whole strength of the town died, struck, as it were, by sudden death; for there were few who kept their beds more than three days, or two days, or half a day; and after this the fell death broke forth on every side with the course of the sun. There died at Leicester in the small parish of St. Leonard more than 380; in the parish of Holy Cross, more than 400; in the parish of St. Margaret of Leicester, more than 700; and so in each parish a great number. Then the bishop of Lincoln sent through the whole bishopric, and gave general power to all and every priest, both regular and secular, to hear confessions, and absolve with full and entire episcopal authority except in matters of debt, in which case the dying man, if he could, should pay the debt while he lived, or others should certainly fulfill that duty from his property after his death. Likewise, the pope granted full remission of all sins to whoever was absolved in peril of death, and every one could choose a confessor at his will.... And there were small prices for everything on account of the fear of death. For there were very few who cared about riches or anything else; for a man could have a horse, which before was worth 40 *s.*, for 6 *s.* 8 *d.*...Sheep and cattle went wandering over fields and through crops, and there was no one to go and drive or gather them, so that the number cannot be reckoned which perished in the ditches and hedges in every district, for lack of herdsmen; for there was such a lack of servants that no one knew what he ought to do....Wherefore many crops perished in the fields for want of some one to gather them; but in the pestilence year, as is above said of other things, there was such abundance of grain that no one troubled about it....

From Edward Potts Cheyney, ed., *Readings in English History Drawn from the Original Sources* (Boston: Ginn, 1908), pp. 255–256.

One symptom of economic stagnation was social unrest and tension. Common working people, many of whom resented the restrictions of the guild system, organized themselves to protect their interests against the guild masters and rich merchants. Peasant unrest in Britain and France erupted into full-scale revolts.

A major cause of the slump was the arrival in Europe of the Black Death, a bubonic plague from Asia carried by fleas on rats. The Black Death struck Europe in 1347 and intermittently thereafter for the next two centuries, decimating and demoralizing society. It is estimated that about one-third of the European population was wiped out. Hardest hit were the towns; within five years the population of Florence, for example, fell from 114,000 to about 50,000. Coupled with the devastation wrought by the Black Death was the destruction and death caused by the Hundred Years' War between France and England.

By 1450 the effects of economic depression and stagnation had begun to ease. A period of great economic expansion was at hand, promoted by a new style of strong monarchy and stimulated by European geographical discovery and expansion over the face of the globe.

The Progress of Late Medieval Politics

The late Middle Ages witnessed the accession of strong monarchs in several of the emerging nation-states of Europe, all of whom put national political and economic interests ahead of submission to papal power. These monarchs sought to break forever the power of the papacy and the feudal nobility in their countries. Some succeeded in doing so; others met with less than total success.

Germany: The Early Habsburgs

After the fall of the Hohenstaufens, Germany lapsed more and more into political disunity. In 1273 the imperial crown was given to the weak Count Rudolf (1273–1291) of the House of Habsburg, a name derived from Habichtsburg ("Castle of the Hawk"), the family's home in northern Switzerland. During the remainder of the Middle Ages, the Habsburgs had amazing success in territorial acquisition; Rudolf himself acquired Austria through marriage, and thereafter the Habsburgs ruled their holdings from Vienna.

At first, victims of the plague were laid to rest in coffins. Later as the plague raged through Europe, mass burials were the only way to keep up with the rapidly increasing number of dead.

In 1356 the German nobility won another significant victory in their efforts to avoid the creation of a powerful monarchy. The Golden Bull, a document that served as the political constitution of Germany until early in the nineteenth century, established a procedure by which seven German electors—three archbishops and four lay princes—chose the emperor. The electors and other important princes were given rights that made them virtually independent rulers, and the emperor could take no important action without the consent of the imperial feudal assembly, the Diet, which met infrequently.

From 1438 until 1806, when the Holy Roman Empire disintegrated, the Habsburgs held the imperial crown almost without interruption. Maximilian I (1493–1519) helped make the Habsburgs the most important royal family in sixteenth-century Europe by marrying Mary of Burgundy, heiress of the rich Low Countries, and by marrying his son to the heiress of Spain.

Inspired by the accomplishments of other contemporary European monarchs, Maximilian attempted to strengthen the monarchy. His program for a national court system, army, and taxation was frustrated by the German princes who insisted on guarding what they called "German freedom." The emperor continued to be limited in power; nor was the empire successful in establishing an imperial treasury, an efficient central administration, or a standing army.

Spain: Ferdinand and Isabella

In 1479 Isabella of Castile and Ferdinand of Aragon began a joint rule that united the Iberian peninsula except for Granada, Navarre, and Portugal. The "Catholic Majesties," the title the pope conferred on Ferdinand and Isabella, set out to establish effective royal control in all of Spain. The Holy Brotherhood, a league of cities that had long existed for mutual protection against unruly nobles, was taken over by the crown, and its militia was used as a standing army and police force. The powerful and virtually independent military orders of knights, which had emerged during the Reconquista, were also brought under royal control.

"One King, One Law, One Faith"

Ferdinand and Isabella believed that the church should be subordinate to royal government. By tactful negotiations the Spanish sovereigns induced the pope to give them the right to make church appointments in Spain and to establish a Spanish court of Inquisition largely free of papal control.

In this romantic Flemish tapestry, Ferdinand and Isabella reign in splendor, attended by richly costumed courtiers and ladies-in-waiting.

The Spanish Inquisition confiscated the property of most Jews and Muslims and terrified the Christian clergy and laity into accepting royal absolutism as well as religious orthodoxy. Although the Inquisition greatly enhanced the power of the Spanish crown, it also caused many people to flee Spain and the threat of persecution. About 150,000 Spanish Jews, mainly merchants and professional people, fled to the Netherlands, England, North Africa, and the Ottoman Empire. Calling themselves Sephardim, many of these exiles retained their Spanish language and culture into the twentieth century.

Another manifestation of Spanish absolutism, defined by Isabella herself as "one king, one law, one faith," was the intentional neglect of the *Cortes* of Castile and Aragon. These representative assemblies, having emerged in the twelfth century, never were allowed by the monarchy to take an effective position as legislative bodies.

One of the most dramatic achievements of the Catholic Majesties was the conquest of Granada in

1492, the same year that Columbus claimed the New World for Spain. Before Ferdinand died in 1516, a dozen years after Isabella, he seized the part of Navarre that lay south of the Pyrenees. This acquisition, together with the conquest of Granada, completed the unification of the Spanish nation-state.

Results of Spanish Unification

Royal absolutism and unification, coupled with the acquisition of territory in the New and Old Worlds, made Spain the strongest power in sixteenth-century Europe. But centuries of fighting against the Muslims left a legacy of hatred and excessive national pride. Religious fervor was generated as a means to an end, and the result was a heritage of religious bigotry and the end of the tolerance, intellectual curiosity, and sense of balance that had been characteristic of Muslim culture in Spain. Spanish contempt for the Muslims fostered scorn for many activities in which the "unbelievers" had engaged, especially commerce and agriculture. This attitude hampered Spanish development in subsequent centuries.

Crisis in England and France

Nation-making in both England and France was greatly affected by the long conflict that colored much of both nations' history during the fourteenth and fifteenth centuries. In both lands the crisis of war led to a temporary resurgence of the feudal nobility at the expense of the king. But increasing anarchy and the continuing misery of war stimulated nationalistic feelings and a demand for strong rulers who could guarantee law and order. By the late fifteenth century the English and French kings were able to resume the task of establishing the institutions of the modern nation-state.

The Hundred Years' War

The Hundred Years' War had its origins in a fundamental conflict between the English and the French monarchies. The English kings wanted to regain the large holdings in France that had been theirs in the days of Henry II. But the French kings were determined not only to keep what had been taken from John of England but also to expand their holdings. Their ultimate goal was a centralized France under the direct rule of the monarchy at Paris.

Another cause was the clash of French and English economic interests in Flanders. This region was falling more and more under French control, to the frustration of both the English wool growers who supplied the great Flemish woolen industry and the English king, whose income came in great part from duties on wool.

The immediate excuse for open conflict was a dispute over the succession to the French throne. In 1328, after the direct line of Capetian succession ended, Philip VI of the House of Valois assumed the throne. But the English king, Edward III, maintained that he was the legitimate heir, and warfare resulted. Interrupted by several peace treaties and a number of truces, the devastating Hundred Years' War stretched from 1337 to 1453.

The first years of warfare witnessed impressive English victories. At the naval battle of Sluys (1340) the English gained command of the English Channel and thus were able to send their armies to France at will. England won a series of great battles—at Crécy (1346), Poitiers (1356), and Agincourt (1415), where the French lost some 7000 knights, including many great nobles, and the English only 500. In the aftermath of Agincourt, large portions of France fell to the English.

The English armies were much more effective than those of the French. With no thought of strategy, the French knights charged the enemy at a mad gallop and then engaged in hand-to-hand fighting. But the English had learned more effective methods. Their greatest weapon was the longbow. Six feet long and made of special wood, the longbow shot steel-tipped arrows that were dangerous at 400 yards and deadly at 100. The usual English plan of battle called for the knights to fight dismounted. Protecting them was a forward wall of bowmen just behind a barricade of iron stakes planted in the ground to slow the enemy's cavalry charge. By the time the French cavalry reached the dismounted knights, the remaining few French were easily killed.

English military triumphs stirred English pride and what we now think of as nationalism—love of country, identification with it, and a sense of difference from (and usually superiority to) others. However, nationalism was stirring in France also. The revival of French patriotism is associated with Joan of Arc, who inspired a series of French victories. Moved by inner voices that she believed divine, Joan persuaded the timid French ruler, Charles VII, to allow her to lead an army to relieve the besieged city of Orléans. Clad in white armor and riding a white horse, she inspired confidence and a feeling of invincibility in her followers, and in 1429 Orléans was rescued from what had seemed certain conquest. Joan was ultimately captured by the enemy, found guilty of bewitching the English soldiers, and burned at the stake. But the martyrdom of the Maid of Orléans seemed a turning point in the long struggle. Also, France's development of a permanent standing army and the greater use of gunpowder began to transform the art of war. English resistance crumbled as military superiority now turned full circle; the English longbow was outmatched by French artillery. Of the vast territories they had once controlled in France, the English retained only Calais when the war ended in 1453.

Aftermath of the War in England

The Hundred Years' War exhausted England and fueled discontent with the monarchy in Parliament and among the common people. Richard II (1377–1399), the last Plantagenet king, was unstable, cruel, power-hungry, and firm in his belief that the king should oversee the lives and property of his subjects. His seizure of the properties of Henry, the duke of Lancaster, led to a revolt in which Henry was victorious.

Henry IV established the Lancastrian dynasty, which ruled England from 1399 to 1461. The king was given the support of Parliament, which had deeply resented Richard's autocratic reign and was determined that its authority should not again be ignored. Hard pressed for money to suppress revolts at home and to carry on the war in France, the Lancastrian kings became more and more financially dependent on Parliament.

A fifteenth-century portrait of Joan of Arc in battle dress. After leading the French to victory at Orléans in 1429, she was captured by the English, tried and convicted of witchcraft and heresy, and burned at the stake in 1431. The French king, Charles VII, whose kingdom she had helped save, did nothing to rescue her.

Baronial rivalry to control both Parliament and the crown flared up during the reign of the third Lancastrian king, Henry VI (1421–1471). When Henry went completely insane in 1453, the duke of York, the strongest noble in the kingdom, became regent. Two years later full-scale civil war broke out between the House of York and the supporters of the Lancastrians. The struggle became known as the Wars of the Roses; the white rose was the symbol of the Yorkists, and the red rose that of the House of Lancaster. In 1461 the Yorkists succeeded in having their leader, Edward IV, crowned king. Within ten years Edward was able to subdue the nobles and win the support of the English middle class, who saw a strong monarchy as the only alternative to anarchy. Edward's power became practically absolute.

The leadership of the House of York ended in 1483 when Edward IV died, leaving two young sons as his heirs. Their uncle bribed and intimidated Parliament to declare his nephews illegitimate and to give him the throne as Richard III. The two boys were imprisoned in the Tower of London, where they were secretly murdered. The double murder caused the kingdom to suspect the involvement of King Richard, and support grew for the claim of Henry Tudor to the throne. Henry defeated Richard in battle at Bosworth Field in 1485 and thereby became Henry VII, the first of the Tudor dynasty.

Henry VII and the Tudor Dynasty

During Henry VII's reign (1485–1509), the English monarchy reclaimed the support of the people. Henry's attention to the domestic affairs of the kingdom, his efficient administration, and his vigorous efforts to increase royal revenues strengthened the monarch's hold on power and his popularity with the commoners. The "new monarchy" in England restored order, promoted trade at home and abroad, and provided a sense of security. The king won the support of the people of middle rank, the burghers and landed gentry, who provided the basis of his power. Henry VII always worked through Parliament, where his wishes were generally honored.

France After the Hundred Years' War

The Hundred Years' War left France with a new national consciousness and royal power that was stronger than ever. In 1438 Charles VII established effective influence over the church in France by decreeing that it should be controlled by a council of French bishops whose appointment was to be regulated by the monarch. Furthermore, the *taille*, a land tax voted during the war to support a standing army, became permanent, making the king financially inde-

Henry Tudor, who ruled England as Henry VII, was the first of the Tudor line. His victory over Richard III in Bosworth Field in 1485 ended the rule of the House of York.

pendent of the Estates-General. Financial matters were kept firmly under royal control.

After the war, the astute and ruthless Louis XI (1461–1483) continued the process of consolidating royal power. A tireless worker completely lacking in scruples, Louis XI earned himself the epithet the "universal spider" because of his constant intrigues. In his pursuit of power he used any weapon—violence, bribery, treachery—to obtain his ends. The "spider king" devoted his reign to restoring prosperity to his nation and to reducing the powers of the noble families still active and ambitious after the long war. Like Henry VII in England, Louis XI was one of the "new monarchs" who worked for the creation of a subject-sovereign relationship in their kingdoms, replacing the old feudal ties of personal fidelity.

Conclusion

During the period known as the early Middle Ages (500–1000), the focus of European civilization shifted from the Mediterranean to France. The conversion of Clovis to Christianity and the subsequent Frankish alliance with the papacy united the most energetic of the Germanic tribes with the greatest existing force for civilization in western Europe, the church. The foundation of a new Europe was established by Charlemagne, but his empire depended too heavily on the forceful personality of its founder and did not survive his successors.

After the Carolingian collapse, feudal systems of organization evolved to meet the turbulent conditions of the time. Manorialism became the economic system through which most of the population provided for its needs. Self-sufficiency and economic isolation provided the most secure means of survival. But the expansion of trade and commerce and the revival of urban life altered the traditional isolation of the manor and helped bring about economic expansion.

The High Middle Ages (1000–1300) and later Middle Ages (1300–1500) witnessed significant change and political development in all the states of Europe. In England, William the Conqueror secured a unified kingdom in 1066, and later kings made progress in keeping the nobility under control and in building the machinery of royal administration. In France, each of the many counties and duchies that constituted the feudal kingdom had to be subordinated and brought within the framework of royal authority. It took the French kings three centuries to accomplish what William the Conqueror had done in one generation.

The political evolution of both England and France was affected by the Hundred Years' War. In England, the power of Parliament was increased, and the upsurge in the power of the nobility led to the Wars of the Roses, which ended finally with the accession of the Tudor dynasty; in France, royal power was consolidated under Louis XI, and his abilities in government made possible further progress in national unification.

Nation-making in Spain was unique, since the ambitions of the monarchy were combined with the religious fervor of a Crusade. In the mid-eleventh century the Christian Spanish states began the Reconquista in earnest, but not until the end of the fifteenth century was the task completed. In Germany, the kings dissipated their energies by seeking to establish an empire that encompassed Italy and Sicily. In the later Middle Ages Germany remained divided and weak; there national unification would not be achieved until the nineteenth century.

Suggestions for Reading

Robert Bartlett, *The Making of Europe: Conquest, Colonization, and Cultural Change, 950–1350* (Princeton University Press,

1993); Harry S. L. B. Moss, *The Birth of the Middle Ages, 395–814* (Oxford University Press, 1962); and Richard W. Southern, *The Making of the Middle Ages* (Yale University Press, 1992), are excellent surveys of the early Middle Ages. Margaret Deanesly, *History of Early Medieval Europe from 476 to 911* (Barnes & Noble, 1959); John Hine Mundy, *Europe in the High Middle Ages, 1150–1309*, 2nd ed. (Addison-Wesley, 1991); Malcolm C. Barber, *The Two Cities: Medieval Europe, 1050–1320* (Routledge, 1992); and Joseph R. Strayer, *Western Europe in the Middle Ages*, 3rd ed. (Waveland, 1991), are also excellent. On Frankish history, see Suzanne Wemple, *Women in Frankish Society: Marriage and the Cloister, 500–900* (University of Pennsylvania Press, 1981), and Peter Munz, *Life in the Age of Charlemagne* (Capricorn, 1971). See also Friedrich Heer, *Charlemagne and His World* (Macmillan, 1975). Johannes Brondsted, *The Vikings* (Penguin, 1965); Gwyn Jones, *A History of the Vikings* (Oxford University Press, 1991); and Gabriel Turville-Petre, *The Heroic Age of Scandinavia* (Greenwood, 1976), are outstanding works on Viking society.

For economic and social history, see "The Agrarian Life of the Middle Ages" in *The Cambridge Economic History of Europe*, Vol. 1, 2nd ed. (Cambridge University Press, 1967); Georges Duby, *Rural Economy and Country Life in the Medieval West* (University of South Carolina Press, 1968); George G. Coulton, *The Medieval Village* (Johns Hopkins University Press, 1991); Robert Fossier, *Peasant Life in the Medieval West* (Blackwell, 1988); and Eileen Power, *Medieval People* (Smith, 1993), all worthwhile accounts of rural life and the manorial system. See also Frances Gies and Joseph Gies, *Women in the Middle Ages* (HarperPerennial, 1980), *Life in a Medieval Village* (HarperPerennial, 1991), *Marriage and Family in the Middle Ages* (Harper Perennial, 1989), and *A Medieval Family: The Pastons of Fifteenth-Century England* (HarperCollins, 1998). Other good studies are Georges Duby, *Medieval Marriage* (Johns Hopkins University Press, 1991); Barbara A. Hanawalt, *Growing Up in Medieval London* (Oxford University Press, 1993); Marjorie Rowling, *Life in Medieval Times* (Perigee, 1979); Shulamith Shahar, *Childhood in the Middle Ages* (Routledge, 1992); Tania Bayard, ed., *A Medieval Home Companion: Housekeeping in the Fourteenth Century* (HarperCollins, 1992); David Herlihy, *Opera Muliebria: Women and Work in Medieval Europe* (McGraw-Hill, 1990), and Georges Duby, *The Three Orders* (University of Chicago Press, 1981).

On Germany in the Middle Ages, see Geoffrey Barraclough, *The Origins of Modern Germany* (Capricorn, 1963), and Robert E. Herzstein, ed., *The Holy Roman Empire in the Middle Ages: Universal State or German Catastrophe?* (Heath, 1966). Peter Munz, *Frederick Barbarossa: A Study in Medieval Politics* (Cornell University Press, 1969), and Thomas Curtis van Cleve, *The Emperor Frederick II of Hohenstaufen, Immutator Mundi* (Oxford University Press, 1972), are interesting biographies. See also Franz Bäuml, *Medieval Civilization in Germany* (Praeger, 1969).

On French history, see Robert Fawtier, *The Capetian Kings of France: Monarchy and Nation, 987–1328* (St. Martin's Press, 1969); John Bell Henneman, ed., *The Medieval French Monarchy* (Krieger, 1973); and Margaret Wade Labarge, *Saint Louis* (Macmillan, 1968). G. O. Sayles, *The Medieval Foundations of England* (Barnes, 1968), and Christopher N. L. Brooke, *From Alfred to Henry Third, 871–1272* (Norton, 1961), are valuable surveys on English history. See also Frank Merry Stenton, *Anglo-Saxon England*, 3rd ed. (Oxford University Press, 1971), the standard account; D. P. Kirby, *The Making of Early England* (Schocken, 1968); and Edmund King, *Medieval England, 1066–1485* (Salem House, 1989).

Joseph F. O'Callaghan, *A History of Medieval Spain* (Cornell University Press, 1983), and J. H. Elliot, *Imperial Spain, 1469–1716* (Penguin, 1963), are standard works. See also

Gabriel Jackson, *The Making of Medieval Spain* (Harcourt Brace, 1972); Ramon Menendez Pidal, *The Cid and His Spain* (Cass, 1971); and Felipe Fernandez-Armesto, *Ferdinand and Isabella* (Taplinger, 1975).

On the later Middle Ages, see Robert S. Gottfried, *The Black Death: Natural and Human Disaster in Medieval Europe* (Free Press, 1983); Christopher Allmand, *The Hundred Years' War* (Cambridge University Press, 1988); Denys Hay, *Europe in the Fourteenth and Fifteenth Centuries*, 2nd ed. (Addison-Wesley, 1989); Edward Potts Cheyney, *The Dawn of a New Era, 1250–1453* (HarperTorchbooks, 1966); Robert E. Lerner, *The Age of Adversity: The Fourteenth Century* (Cornell University Press, 1967); and Daniel Waley, *Later Medieval Europe: From St. Louis to Luther* (Longman, 1985).

Suggestions for Web Browsing

Medieval Studies
http://www.georgetown.edu/labyrinth/Virtual_Library/
   Medieval_Studies.html

The WWW Virtual Library for Medieval Studies, a part of the Labyrinth project at Georgetown University, offers numerous links categorized by national cultures and by artistic genre.

Netserf: The Internet Connection for Medieval Resources
http://netserf.cua.edu

A comprehensive site for resources on many aspects of medieval history, from archaeology and art to law and philosophy.

Internet Medieval Sourcebook
http://www.fordham.edu/halsall/book.html

Extremely helpful site containing original course materials from medieval authors and secondary sources dealing with a large variety of medieval subjects.

Middle Ages
http://www.learner.org/exhibits/middleages/

This site, under the direction of the Annenberg/CBS Project, features information and exhibits illustrating what daily life was really like during the Middle Ages.

Medieval Women
http://www.georgetown.edu/labyrinth/subjects/women/
   women.html

Site details the individual lives and works of medieval women, including Hildegard of Bingen; women rulers and creators; and the impact of the Crusades on women, in addition to numerous general resources.

Women Writers of the Middle Ages
http://www.fordham.edu/halsall/source/byz-arabambas.html

Site offers biographies and images and includes an extensive bibliography.

World of the Vikings
http://www.viking.org/viking.html

This well-indexed site provides links to almost everything there is to know about these medieval seafarers—their everyday life, their travels, their influence.

The Plague
http://www.brown.edu/Departments/Italian_Studies/dweb/
   plague/plague.html

Offers links detailing the origins, causes, effects, and literary influence of the Black Death.

The Dome of the Rock, a Muslim edifice from the seventh century, is built above the Temple Mount in Jerusalem, the site of Solomon's Temple. According to tradition, the site is also the place where Muhammad ascended into heaven on his "Night Journey." Intricate mosaic decoration covers the outer walls of the building.

Islam

From Its Origins to 1300

Chapter Contents

Arabia was the birthplace of the Islamic religion; and the Arabic language was the "tongue of the angels," since God chose to reveal himself through that vehicle to Muhammad, the prophet of the faith. Arabia became the center of the Islamic world and the source of renewal and inspiration for the faithful believers throughout an expanding Islamic Empire.

One of history's most dynamic movements began in the Arabian peninsula, an area of deserts, high temperatures, and exposed frontiers. The geographical conditions encouraged nomadic tribes and strong individualism, not large, settled civilizations with overbearing governments. Much of the interior of Arabia remained isolated, but the peninsula was crossed by trade routes that brought commerce, religious influences, and sometimes military domination from the world beyond. From out of this region between Asia, Europe, and Africa emerged Muhammad, to whom Allah chose to speak.

Muhammad became the prophet of a religion that shaped every aspect of individual and community life: from diet to politics, from family relations to law, from prayer to conquest. Within one century, the power of Islam would be felt from the Indian Ocean to the Atlantic; it would transfigure age-old religious, intellectual, and political patterns.

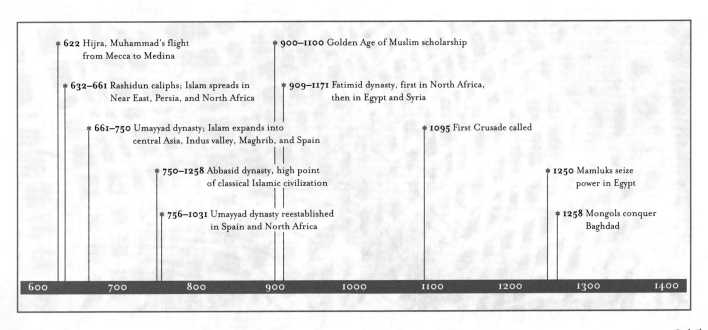

* **622** Hijra, Muhammad's flight from Mecca to Medina

* **632–661** Rashidun caliphs; Islam spreads in Near East, Persia, and North Africa

* **661–750** Umayyad dynasty; Islam expands into central Asia, Indus valley, Maghrib, and Spain

* **750–1258** Abbasid dynasty, high point of classical Islamic civilization

* **756–1031** Umayyad dynasty reestablished in Spain and North Africa

* **900–1100** Golden Age of Muslim scholarship

* **909–1171** Fatimid dynasty, first in North Africa, then in Egypt and Syria

* **1095** First Crusade called

* **1250** Mamluks seize power in Egypt

* **1258** Mongols conquer Baghdad

600   700   800   900   1000   1100   1200   1300   1400

Arabia Before the Prophet

The Arabian peninsula is one-third the size of the continental United States. Most of its land is desert; rainfall is scarce, vegetation is scant, and very little of the land is suitable for agriculture. Arabia before the birth of Muhammad was a culturally isolated and economically underdeveloped region. In the relatively more fertile southwestern corner of the peninsula, however, several small Arab kingdoms once flourished in the area now known as Yemen. The most notable of these early kingdoms, Saba' (the biblical Sheba), existed as early as the eighth century B.C.E. and lasted until the third century C.E., when it was taken by the Himyarites from the south.

Aided by the domestication of the camel and the expanding trade in frankincense and spices, these kingdoms became prosperous; they formed part of a commercial network of kingdoms within and beyond the Arabian peninsula. In the north of Arabia, several kingdoms were able to establish contacts with the Byzantine and the Persian (Sassanid) Empires as early as the fifth century C.E. Among the most notable of these small kingdoms were Nabataea in northwestern Arabia, which dominated Arabian trade routes until the Romans annexed the kingdom in the second century C.E., and the realm of the Lakhmids in the northeast, whose prominence was greatest around 250 to 600 C.E., until the kingdom was destroyed by the Sassanids. But in the interior of Arabia, a vast desert dotted sparsely with oases, a nomadic life based on herding was the only successful existence.

The Bedouin

The desert nomads, or *Bedouin*, lived according to ancient tribal patterns; at the head of the tribe was the male elder, or *shaykh*, elected and advised by the heads of the related families comprising the tribe. These men claimed authority based on family connections and personal merit. Tribes tended to be made up of three-generation families employing a gendered division of labor. The Bedouin led a precarious existence, moving their flocks from one pasture to the next, often following set patterns of migration. Aside from maintaining their herds, these nomads traded animal products for goods from the settled areas. They also relied on plunder from raids on settlements, on passing caravans, and on one another.

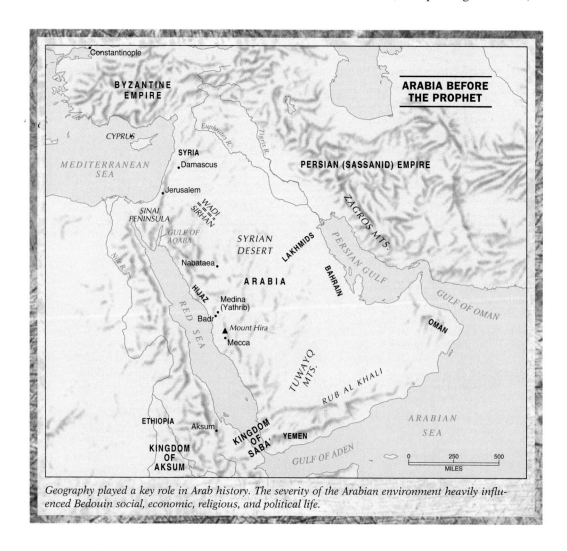

Geography played a key role in Arab history. The severity of the Arabian environment heavily influenced Bedouin social, economic, religious, and political life.

Their nomadic existence, its hardships, and the beauty of the desert landscape are all celebrated in the poetry of pre-Islamic Arabia.

The Bedouin enjoyed a degree of personal freedom unknown in more agrarian and settled societies. They developed a code of ethics represented in the word *muru'a*, or "manly virtue." Far from being abrasive and rough, men proved *muru'a* through grace and restraint, loyalty to obligation and duty, a devotion to do what must be done, and respect for women. The tribe shared a corporate spirit, or *'asabiyya*, which reflected the shared interests and honor of the tribe.

Although Bedouin society was patriarchal (dominated by the senior males), women enjoyed a great degree of independence. They engaged in business and commerce and could sometimes wed men of their own choosing. However, as in all traditional agricultural societies, women were under the protection of men, and the honor of the tribe was vested in the sexual honor of the women. The relative freedom of the Bedouin sprang from the realities of life in the desert, as did their values and ethics. One rule of conduct was unqualified hospitality to strangers. A nomad never knew when the care of a stranger might be essential to provide the necessary water and shade to save his or her own life.

The Bedouin of the seventh century did not have a highly structured religious system. They apparently looked at life as a brief time during which to take full advantage of daily pleasure. Ideas of an afterlife were not well defined or described. The Bedouin were animists; they worshipped a large number of gods and spirits, many of whom they believed to inhabit trees, wells, and stones. Each tribe had its own gods, sometimes symbolized by sacred stones.

The Bedouin of the Arabian interior led a relatively primitive and isolated existence, but it was not in their herding camps that the message of Islam was first spoken. In the Arabian cities along the trade routes, the people came into contact with traders and travelers who brought a complex mix of artistic, religious, and philosophical influences. Among these were the monotheistic beliefs of Judaism and Christianity. Some parts of Arabia were greatly influenced by the neighboring and more highly sophisticated cultures of Byzantium, Sassanid Persia, and Ethiopia. It was out of this more urban and commercial context that the early Islamic state would emerge.

Early Mecca

On the western side of the Arabian peninsula, along the Red Sea, is a region known as the Hijaz, or "barrier." The Hijaz extends along the western coastal plain from Yemen in the south to the Sinai peninsula in the north. One of the oases in the Hijaz is Mecca, set among barren hills 50 miles inland from the sea. This site had several advantages: Mecca possessed a well (the Zamzam) of great depth, and two ancient caravan routes met there. One route ran from Africa through the peninsula to Iran and central Asia, and another, a southeast-northwest route, brought the spices of India and Southeast Asia to the Mediterranean world.

A second significant advantage for Mecca was its importance as a religious sanctuary. An ancient temple, an almost square structure built of granite blocks, stood near the well of Mecca. Known as the *Ka'ba* ("cube"), this square temple contained the sacred Black Stone. According to tradition, the stone, probably a meteorite, was originally white but had become blackened by the sins of all those who touched it. Later Muslim historians would attribute the building of the Ka'ba to the prophet Abraham or even to Adam. The Ka'ba itself was draped with the pelts of sacrificial animals and supposedly held the images and shrines of 360 gods and goddesses. For centuries the Ka'ba had been a holy place of annual pilgrimage for the Arab tribes and a focal point of Arabic culture and ritual practice. As a pilgrimage site, it also brought prestige and wealth to the tribes who controlled the city of Mecca.

By the sixth century, Mecca was controlled by the Quraysh tribe, whose rulers organized themselves into an aristocracy of merchants and wealthy businessmen. The Quraysh engaged in lucrative trade with Byzantium and Persia, as well as with the southern Arabian tribes and the kingdom of Aksum across the Red Sea in what is now Ethiopia. In addition, a number of annual merchant fairs, such as one usually held at nearby Ukaz, were taken over by the Quraysh to extend the economic influence of Mecca. The Quraysh were also concerned with protecting the religious shrine of the Ka'ba, in addition to ensuring that the annual pilgrimage of tribes to the holy place would continue as a source of revenue for the merchants of the city.

Muhammad, Prophet of Islam

Into this environment at Mecca was born a man who would revolutionize the religious, political, and social organization of his people. Muhammad (c. 570–632) came from a family belonging to the Quraysh. An orphan, he suffered the loss of both his parents and his grandfather, who cared for him after his parents' death. He was then raised by his uncle, Abu Talib, a prominent merchant of Mecca. His early years were spent helping his uncle in the caravan trade. Even as a young man, Muhammad came to be admired by his fellow Meccans as a sincere and honest person, who earned the nickname al-Amin, "the trustworthy." When he was

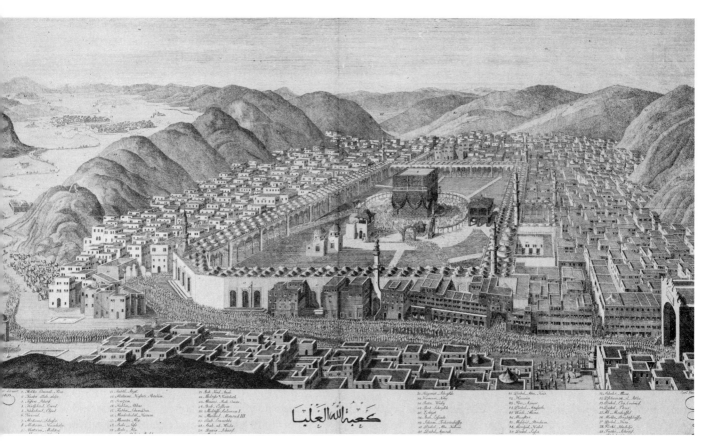

كعبة الله العليا

This engraving depicts the city of Mecca with, at its center, the Ka'ba, a square building of stone draped with black cloth that became the focal point of Muslim worship. Each year Muslims make the pilgrimage to celebrate their unity and to worship at this most sacred shrine of Islam. The site itself has been greatly expanded, and the number of pilgrims has dramatically increased since the time of the prophet Muhammad.

about 25 years old, he accepted employment from a wealthy widow, Khadija, whose caravans traded with Syria. He later married Khadija and began to take his place as a leading citizen of Mecca. Muhammad's marriage to Khadija was a long and happy one that produced two sons, who both died as infants, and two daughters. The younger, Fatima, would play an important role in the future of the fledgling Islamic state.

The Early Islamic State

622   The Hijra, Muhammad's migration from Mecca to Medina

630   The Prophet returns and takes control of Mecca, Ka'ba consecrated to Allah

632   Death of the Prophet

632–661   Rule of the first four caliphs: Abu Bakr, Umar, Uthman, Ali

638   Muslim armies take Jerusalem

651   Defeat of the Sassanids in Persia

Biographies of the Prophet, written after his death by his followers, describe him as a handsome, large man with broad shoulders and black, shining eyes, a man who was reserved and gentle but possessed of impressive energy. Tradition relates that Muhammad was an introspective man. Often he would escape from Meccan society, which he considered too materialistic and irreligious, and spend long hours alone in a cave on nearby Mount Hira. During these hours of meditation, Muhammad searched for answers to the metaphysical questions that many thoughtful people have pondered. Muhammad's meditations sometimes produced nearly total mental and physical exhaustion. During one such solitary meditation, Muhammad heard a call that was to alter history. This initial communication from heaven came in the form of a command:

> *Recite! In the name of your Lord, who created all things, who*
> *created man from a clot [of blood].*
> *Recite! And your Lord is Most Bounteous*
> *Who teaches by the Pen,*
> *teaches man that which he would not have otherwise known.* (Qur'an 96:1–5)

The collected revelations given to Muhammad are known as the *Qur'an* (or *Koran*), an Arabic word meaning "recitation" or "reading." The revelations that continued to come over the next 20 years or so were sometimes terse and short, at other times elaborate and poetic. The early revelations did not immediately persuade Muhammad that he was a messenger of God. In fact, his first reactions were fear and self-doubt. Anxious about the source and nature of his revelations, he sought the comfort and advice of Khadija.

As the revelations continued, Muhammad was persuaded that he had been called to be a messenger of divine revelation. He began to think of himself and his mission as one similar to those of prophets and messengers who had preceded him in announcing the existence of the one God, Allah. Allah, *"the* God," was the same God worshipped by the Christians and Jews, but Allah had now chosen Muhammad to be his last and greatest prophet to perfect the religion revealed earlier to Abraham, Moses, the Hebrew prophets, and Jesus. The religion Muhammad preached is called *Islam,* which means "submission" to the will of God. The followers of Islam are called *Muslims,* those who submit to God's law.

Muhammad's Message and Its Early Followers

At first Muhammad had little success in attracting followers in Mecca. The early message Muhammad brought to the Arabs was strong and direct: that Allah was one and majestic, all-powerful and demanding of the faith of his followers. Furthermore, Allah decreed that his followers be compassionate, ethical, and just in all their dealings:

> *In the name of Allah, the most Beneficent, the Most Merciful*
> *by the night as it enshrouds*
> *by the day as it illuminates*
> *by Him Who created the male and female*
> *indeed your affairs lead to various ends.*
> *For who gives [of himself] and acts righteously, and conforms to goodness,*
> *We will give him ease.*
> *But as for him who is niggardly deeming himself self-sufficient and rejects goodness,*
> *We will indeed ease his path to adversity.*
> *Nor shall his wealth save him as he perishes*
> *for Guidance is from Us*
> *and to Us belongs the Last and First.* (Qur'an 92:1–14)

Muhammad was able to win the early support of some of his relatives and close friends. His first converts were his wife, his cousin Ali, and Abu Bakr, a leading merchant of the Quraysh tribe who was highly respected for his integrity. Abu Bakr remained the constant companion of the Prophet during his persecution and exile and later succeeded him as the leader of Islam. But opposition to Muhammad's message was very strong, especially from Mecca's leading citizens. Many thought Muhammad was an ambitious poet attempting to pass on his own literary creations as the word of God. Others believed him to be possessed by demons. Muhammad challenged the status quo; his strong monotheism threatened the polytheistic beliefs of Mecca and the people who obtained their income from the pilgrims to the Ka'ba. Many of Muhammad's early converts were among the poorest of the city's residents, and Mecca's leading citizens feared the possibility of social revolution.

Since Muhammad was himself a member of the Quraysh tribe, its leaders first approached his uncle Abu Talib to persuade his nephew to stop preaching. Next they tried to bribe Muhammad with the promise of a lucrative appointment as an official. When he rejected such offers, actual persecution of Muhammad's converts began, and the Quraysh attempted a commercial and social boycott of the Prophet's family. During this time of trial, Abu Talib and Khadija both died, and Muhammad's faith and resolution were greatly tested. But inspired by the spirit and example of earlier prophets such as Abraham and Moses, who were also tested and persecuted, Muhammad persevered in his faith and continued his preaching.

The Hijra

To the north of Mecca is the city of Medina, which was then called Yathrib. The residents of Medina were somewhat familiar with monotheistic beliefs, in part because of the Jewish community in residence there. While visiting Mecca, some pilgrims from Medina judged Muhammad to be a powerful and influential mediator and invited him to come to Medina to settle differences among that city's tribal chiefs. As opposition to his message increased in Mecca, Muhammad sent some of his followers to take up residence in Medina in order to escape persecution. Finally, Muhammad and Abu Bakr fled Mecca when it became known that the Quraysh intended to kill the Prophet. They were followed, but escaped, the story goes, by hiding in a narrow cave whose entrance was quickly covered by a spider's web. The Quraysh pursuers saw the web and passed on, thinking that the cave had been abandoned for a long time.

The *Hijra* (or *Hegira*), Muhammad's "migration" from Mecca to Medina, took place in September in the year 622. The event was such a turning point in the history of Islam that 622 is counted as year 1 of the Islamic calendar. It marked the beginning of the Islamic state. In Medina, the Prophet met with entirely different circumstances from those in his birthplace. Muhammad's leadership turned Medina (*Madinat al-Nabi,* the "City of the Prophet") into the major center of power in the Arabian peninsula.

This Turkish manuscript illustration depicts one of the incidents said to have occurred during the Hijra. As the Prophet and his companion, Abu Bakr, were fleeing Mecca for Medina, one of their pursuers was thrown from his horse. Muhammad forgave the man for persecuting him, and Abu Bakr presented him with a written pardon. The Prophet, as in this illustration, is often shown veiled and with a halo of fire.

The Community at Medina

Muhammad was received in Medina as a leader and a spiritual visionary. There, he and his followers set about the establishment of the Muslim *umma* (community). This new community established relations with the Medinan tribes, including the Jewish and Christian residents. Those who did not choose to accept Muhammad's faith were allowed to continue their way of life, since Christians and Jews were thought to be "people of the Book" to whom God had made himself known through earlier prophets. Ultimately, however, the Prophet's new polity came into conflict with some of the Jewish tribes of Medina and expelled them. This conflict illustrates the tension between the expansionist political policies and generally tolerant religious policies of the new state.

Muhammad and his followers became steadily more aggressive in their attempts to win converts to Islam. The word *jihad*, meaning "struggle," was ap-plied to the early efforts of the *umma* to win converts and conquer territory. Military encounters with the opponents of Islam began in 624, with the battle of Badr. Muhammad defeated a stronger Quraysh troop from Mecca, and the victory reinforced the resolve of the new religion's followers. Succeeding battles established the Muslims as the dominant force in Arabia, and a truce with Mecca was arranged, under which the Muslims could visit the holy city.

Return to Mecca

In 630 Muhammad returned to take control of the city of Mecca and to cleanse the Ka'ba of idols. The temple itself, together with the Black Stone, was preserved as the supreme religious center of Islam and rededicated to the One God, Allah. It is to this shrine that all devout Muslims, if able, make pilgrimage during their lifetime. Muhammad urged unbelievers and his old enemies to accept Islam and become part of the *umma*. By 632 almost all of the Arabian peninsula had (at least nominally) accepted Islam, and Muhammad had even sent ambassadors to the neighboring Byzantine and Persian Empires to announce the new religion and encourage converts. Clearly, Muhammad did not regard Islam as a religion solely of the Arabs. Like Christianity, and unlike Judaism, Islam was a universal religion with a missionary spirit.

The Death of Muhammad

Muhammad died on June 8, 632, in Medina. Muslims at first refused to accept his death but were reassured by Abu Bakr, who recited this verse from the Qur'an: "Muhammad is only a messenger: many are the messengers who have died before him; if he dies, or is slain, will you turn back on your heels?" (3:144).

Muhammad had no surviving son and had not designated a successor. On the day of his death, his close companions solved the question of leadership of the faithful by agreeing on the election of Abu Bakr, who became the first successor, or *caliph* (from the Arabic *khalifa*). Abu Bakr could not really replace Muhammad, the last prophet. However, as caliph, he was regarded as the head of the Islamic *umma;* he combined the roles of religious leader and head of state. Abu Bakr and his three successors in the office, Umar, Uthman, and Ali, are often referred to as the *Rashidun*, the "Rightly Guided" caliphs.

The significance of Muhammad to the birth and growth of Islam is impossible to overestimate. The Prophet and his message inspired his followers to create and work for the betterment of a society united by the Islamic faith. Ideally, tribal loyalties were replaced by loyalty to the *umma* and faith in the One God, who chose to speak to his people in their own language through a messenger who was also one of their own.

Soon after Muhammad's death, his followers began to collect and codify his teachings and actions.

The result of their efforts was the *hadith,* or reports of the sayings and activities of Muhammad. The hadith have become an important source of values and ethical paths of behavior for the Islamic world. The *sunna*, the custom or practice of the Prophet, is grounded in the hadith and serves as a pattern for a model way of life to be imitated by the faithful.

Islamic Faith and Law

Islam places great emphasis on the necessity of obedience to God's law in addition to faith. The Qur'an is the fundamental and ultimate source of knowledge about Allah. This holy book contains both the theology of Islam and the patterns of ethical and appropriate conduct to which a Muslim must subscribe. Included in the Qur'an are some basic concepts that the Islamic community holds in common as fundamental to the faith.

The Qur'an

Muslims believe that the Qur'an contains the actual word of God as it was revealed to Muhammad through divine inspiration. These revelations to the Prophet took place over a period of more than 20 years. Before Muhammad's death, many of these messages were written down. Muhammad himself began this work of preservation, and Abu Bakr, as caliph, continued the process by compiling revelations that up to that time had been memorized by the followers and passed on by word of mouth. A complete written text of the Qur'an was produced some years after Muhammad's death, with particular care taken to eliminate discrepancies and record only one standard version. This "authorized" edition was then transmitted to various parts of the new Islamic Empire and used to guide the faithful and assist in the conversion of unbelievers. The text of the Qur'an has existed virtually unchanged for nearly 14 centuries.

This Qur'an leaf from the eighth or ninth century illustrates the formality and elegance of the Kufic form of Arabic calligraphy. In various styles, calligraphy served as a major decorative art form throughout the Islamic world; it was both art and worship.

Islamic manuscript, 8th–9th century. Purchase F30.60. Freer Gallery of Art and Arthur M. Sackler Gallery, Smithsonian Institution.

The Qur'an

The Qur'an is one of the most significant of all religious works and one of the world's most beautiful works of literature. The following is a selection celebrating God's creation, from sura 23, titled "The Believers." It illustrates Islam's connection, through the prophets Moses and Jesus, to the sacred texts and beliefs of Judaism and Christianity. But it also points out the Islamic doctrine that God has no son.

In the name of Allah, the Beneficent, the Merciful.
Successful indeed are the believers
Who are humble in their prayers,
And who shun vain conversation,
And who are payers of the poor-due;
And who guard their modesty—
Save from their wives or the [slaves] that their right
*   hands possess, for then they are not blameworthy,*
But whoso craveth beyond that, such are transgres-
*   sors—*
And who are shepherds of their pledge and their
*   covenant, and who pay heed to their prayers.*
These are the heirs
Who will inherit Paradise. There they will abide.
Verily We created man from a product of wet earth;
Then placed him as a drop [of seed] in a safe lodg-
*   ing;*
Then fashioned We the drop a clot, then fashioned
*   We the clot a little lump, then fashioned We the*
*   little lump bones, then clothed the bones with*
*   flesh, and then produced it as another creation.*
*   So blessed be Allah, the Best of Creators!*
Then lo! after that ye surely die.
Then lo! on the Day of Resurrection ye are raised
*   [again].*
And We have created above you seven paths, and We
*   are never unmindful of creation.*
And We send down from the sky water in measure,
*   and We give it lodging in the earth, and lo! We are*
*   able to withdraw it.*
Then We produce for you therewith gardens of date-
*   palms and grapes, wherein is much fruit for you*
*   and whereof ye eat;*
And a tree that springeth forth from Mount Sinai
*   that groweth oil and relish for the eaters.*
And lo! in the cattle there is verily a lesson for you.
*   We give you to drink of that which is in their bel-*
*   lies, and many uses have ye in them, and of them*
*   do ye eat;*

And on them and on the ship we are carried.
Then We sent Moses and his brother Aaron with Our
*   tokens and a clear warrant*
Unto Pharaoh and his chiefs, but they scorned
*   [them] and they were despotic folk.*
And they said: Shall we put faith in two mortals like
*   ourselves, and whose folk are servile unto us?*
So they denied them, and became of those who were
*   destroyed.*
And We verily gave Moses the Scripture, that haply
*   they might go aright.*
And We made the son of Mary and his mother a
*   portent, and We gave them refuge on a height,*
*   a place of flocks and water-springs.*
O ye messengers! Eat of the good things, and do
*   right. Lo! I am Aware of what ye do.*
And lo! this your religion is one religion and I am
*   your Lord, so keep your duty unto Me.*
Say: In Whose hand is the dominion over all things
*   and He protecteth, while against Him there is no*
*   protection, if ye have knowledge?*
They will say: Unto Allah [all that belongeth]. Say:
*   How then are ye bewitched?*
Nay, but We have brought them the Truth, and lo!
*   they are liars.*
Allah hath not chosen any son, nor is there any
*   God along with Him; else would each God have*
*   assuredly championed that which he created,*
*   and some of them would assuredly have over-*
*   come others. Glorified be Allah above all that*
*   they allege.*
Knower of the invisible and the visible! and exalted
*   be He over all that they ascribe as partners [unto*
*   Him]!*

From Marmaduke William Pickthall, *The Meaning of the Glorious Koran: An Explanatory Translation* (London: Unwin Hyman/HarperCollins). Reprinted by permission.

The Qur'an was intended to be recited aloud; anyone who has listened to the chanting of the Qur'an can testify to its beauty, melody, and power. Much of the power of the Qur'an comes from the experience of reciting, listening, and feeling the message. The Qur'an is never to be translated from the Arabic for the purpose of worship because it is believed that translation distorts the divine message. But over time, the Qur'an was indeed translated into many languages to facilitate scholarship and the spread of the Islamic message. As Islam spread, so too did the Arabic language. Arabic replaced many local languages as the language of administration, and gradually, some of the conquered territories adopted Arabic as the language of everyday use. The Qur'an remains the basic document for the study of Islamic theology, law, social institutions, and ethics. It forms the core of Muslim scholarship, from law and grammatical inquiry to scientific and technical investigation.

The Tenets of Islamic Faith

Monotheism is the central principle of Islam. Muslims believe in the unity or oneness of God; there is no other God but Allah, and this belief is proclaimed five times daily as the believers are called to prayer with these words:

God is most great. I testify that there is no God but Allah. I testify that Muhammad is the Messenger of Allah. Come to prayer, come to revelation, God is most great! There is no God but Allah.

Allah is the one and only God, unchallenged by other false divinities and unlike all others in the strength of his creative power. All life—all creation—is the responsibility of Allah alone. His nature is described in many ways and through many metaphors:

Allah is the light of the heaven and the earth. . . . His light is as a niche wherein is a lamp. The lamp is in a glass. The glass is as it were a shining star. [The lamp is] kindled from a blessed tree, an olive neither of the East nor of the West, whose oil would almost glow forth [of itself] though no fire touched it. Light upon light, Allah guided unto His light whom He will. And Allah speaketh to mankind in allegories, for Allah is Knower of all things.

[This lamp is found] in houses which Allah hath allowed to be exalted and that His name shall be remembered therein. Therein do offer praise to Him at noon and evening. (Qur'an 24:35–36)

Islam also recognizes the significance and the contributions of prophets who preceded Muhammad. From the beginnings of human history, Allah has communicated with his people either by the way of these prophets or by written scriptures:

Lo! We inspire thee as We inspired Noah and the Prophets after him, as We inspired Abraham and Ishmael and Isaac and Jacob and the tribes, and Jesus and Job and Jonah and Aaron and Solomon and as We imparted unto David the Psalms. (Qur'an 4:164)

Twenty-eight such prophets are mentioned in the Qur'an as the predecessors of Muhammad, who is believed to have been Allah's final messenger. Muhammad is given no divine status by Muslims; in fact, Muhammad took great care to see that he was not worshipped as a god.

The creation of the universe and all living creatures within it is the work of Allah; harmony and balance in all of creation were ensured by God. In addition to humans and other creatures on the earth, angels exist to protect humans and to pray for forgiveness for the faithful. Satan, "the Whisperer," attempts to lead people astray, and mischievous spirits called *jinn* can create havoc for believers and unbelievers alike.

These illustrations from a sixteenth-century Persian manuscript depict scenes from the lives of the prophets: Jesus multiplying the loaves and fishes, and the staff of Moses transformed into a dragon.

Noah's Ark. Islamic manuscripts often depict the prophets with halos of fire.

Men and women are given a special status in the pattern of the universe. They can choose to obey or to reject Allah's will and deny him. Allah's message includes the belief in a Day of Resurrection when people will be held responsible for their actions and rewarded or punished accordingly for eternity. The Qur'an graphically describes heaven and hell. Those who have submitted to Allah's law—the charitable, the humble, and the forgiving—and those who have preserved his faith shall dwell in the Garden of Paradise, resting in cool shade, eating delectable foods, attended by "fair ones with wide, lovely eyes like unto hidden pearls," and hearing no vain speech or recrimination but only "Peace! Peace!" This veritable oasis is far different from the agonies of the hell that awaits sinners, the covetous, and the erring. Cast into a pit with its "scorching wind and shadow of black smoke," they will drink boiling water and suffer forever.

The Five Pillars

Islam is united in the observance of the Five Pillars, or five essential duties that all Muslims are required

to perform to the best of their abilities. These obligations are accepted by Muslims everywhere and thus serve further to unite the Islamic world. The first obligation is a basic *profession of faith,* by which a believer becomes a Muslim. The simple proclamation *(shahada)* is repeated in daily prayers. Belief in the One God and imitation of the exemplary life led by his Prophet are combined in the profession of faith.

Prayer (salat) is said five times a day, when Muslims are summoned to worship by the *muezzin,* who calls them to prayer from atop the minaret of the mosque *(masjid,* "place of prostration"). During prayer Muslims face Mecca and in so doing give recognition to the birthplace of Islam and the unity of the Islamic community. Prayer can be said alone, at work, at home, or in the mosque.

A Muslim is required to give *alms (zakat)* to the poor, orphans, and widows and to assist the spread of Islam. The payment of alms is a social and religious obligation to provide for the welfare of the *umma.* Muslims are generally expected to contribute annually in alms a percentage (usually 2.5 percent) of their total wealth and assets.

Muslims are requested to *fast (sawm)* during the holy month of Ramadan, the ninth month of the Islamic lunar calendar. From sunrise to sunset, adult Muslims in good health are to avoid food, drink, tobacco, and sexual activity. Finally, every Muslim able to do so is called to make a *pilgrimage (hajj)* to Mecca at least once in his or her lifetime, in the twelfth month of the Islamic year. The focus of the pilgrimage is the Ka'ba and a series of other sites commemorating events in the lives of the prophets Muhammad and Abraham. The *hajj* emphasizes the unity of the Islamic world community and the equality of all believers regardless of race or class.

Islamic Law

Islam is a way of life as well as a religion, and at its heart is the *Sharia,* the law provided by Allah as a guide for a proper life. The Sharia is based on the Qur'an and hadith; it gives the believers a perfect pattern of human conduct and regulates every aspect of a person's activities. God's decrees must be obeyed even if humans are incapable of understanding them, since the Sharia is greater than human reason. Those who study, interpret, and administer the Sharia are called *ulama,* "those who know." These men emerged, in the era after the Prophet's death, as religious scholars and leaders who administered the institutions of worship, education, and law. But there is no priesthood in Islam; all believers are equal members of the community.

Islamic law, then, permeates all aspects of human conduct and all levels of activity, from private and personal concerns to those involving the welfare of the whole state. The Sharia became the universal law of the Islamic lands. In practice it worked in conjunction with the decrees of rulers and with customary laws that varied from region to region. Family law, set forth in the Qur'an, is based on earlier Arab tribal patterns. Islamic law emphasizes the patriarchal nature of the family and society. Marriage is expected of every Muslim man and woman unless physical infirmity or financial inability prevents it. Muslim men can marry non-Muslim women, preferably Christians or Jews, since they too are "people of the Book," but Muslim women are forbidden to marry non-Muslim men. This law reflects the notion, common in traditional societies, that the children "belong" to the father and his family. Thus the children of a Muslim father and non-Muslim mother would be Muslims. The Qur'an had the effect of improving the status and opportunities of women, who could contract their own marriages, keep and maintain their own dowries, and manage and inherit property (unlike many Western Christian women at that time).

The Qur'an allows Muslim men to marry up to four wives, but only if each wife is treated with equal support and affection. Many modern-day Muslims interpret the Qur'an as encouraging monogamy. Polygamy, in any case, is not required; it is a practice that may have arisen to provide protection and security in early societies, where women may have outnumbered men because of the toll of constant warfare.

Islamic law is considered to be God's law for all humankind, not only for the followers of Islam. Non-Muslim citizens of the Islamic state were called *dhimmis;* they received protection from the state and paid an extra head tax called the *jizya.* The Sharia courts were open to *dhimmis,* who could also appeal to juridical authorities, such as rabbis or priests, within their own communities. Islamic law designated certain dress markers for *dhimmis* and forbade them from corrupting Muslims (with wine, for example) and from ostentatious religious displays.

Thus in addition to its theology, Islam offers to its believers a system of government, a legal foundation, and a pattern of social organization. The Islamic *umma* was and is an excellent example of a theocratic state, one in which power ultimately resides in God, on whose behalf political, religious, and other forms of authority are exercised. Ideally, the role of the state is to serve as the guardian of religious law. Islamic monarchs ruled in the name of Allah and called on the Sharia law to legitimize their rule. Of course, as the Islamic state evolved, some rulers were more pious than others. Some came into conflict with the *ulama* over matters of law. But all Muslim kings, like all Christian kings in this era, claimed to be defenders of their faith.

The Early Islamic Dynasties

661   Umayyad dynasty established; Damascus becomes capital

680   Muhammad's grandson Husayn killed by Umayyads at Karbala in Iraq

711   Tariq ibn Ziyad invades Spain from North Africa

750   Abbasids defeat the Umayyads and establish a new dynasty

756   Umayyads set up a new dynasty in Spain; Córdoba later becomes capital

786–809   Reign of Abbasid caliph Harun al-Rashid

909–1171   Fatimid Shi'ite dynasty in North Africa, Egypt, and Syria

1055   Seljuk Turks gain control of Baghdad but leave Abbasid caliph in place

1095   First Crusade mobilized

1250   Mamluk kingdom established in Egypt, will endure until 1517

1258   Mongols conquer Baghdad and kill Abbasid caliph, ending Abbasid dynasty

The Spread of Islam

The Islamic state expanded very rapidly after the death of Muhammad through remarkable successes in the form of military conquest and conversion. Immediately after the Prophet's death in 632, Caliph Abu Bakr continued the effort to abolish polytheism among the Arab tribes and also to bring all of Arabia under the political control of Medina. The Muslim polity succeeded in strengthening its power throughout the Arabian peninsula and even began to launch some exploratory offensives north toward Syria.

Expansion Under the First Four Caliphs

Under the first four caliphs (632–661), Islam spread rapidly. The wars of expansion were aided by the devotion of the faithful to the concept of *jihad.* Muslims are obliged to extend the faith to unbelievers and to defend Islam from attack. The original concept of *jihad* did not include aggressive warfare against non-Muslims, but Muslims whose interpretation of the Qur'an allowed them such latitude sometimes waged

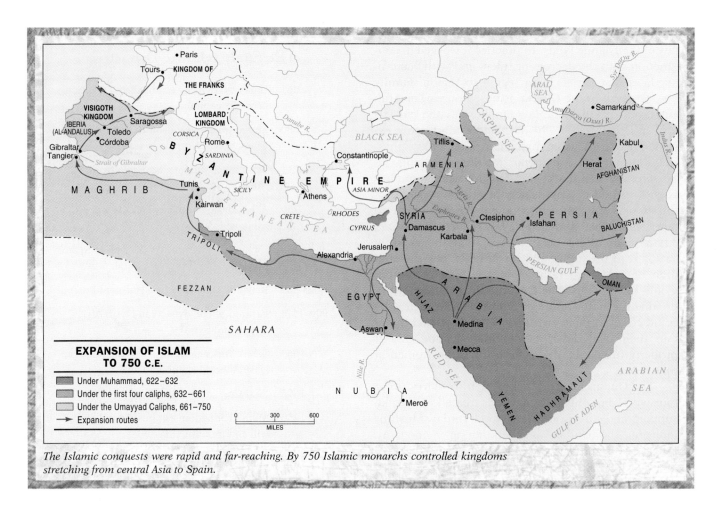

EXPANSION OF ISLAM TO 750 C.E.

- Under Muhammad, 622–632
- Under the first four caliphs, 632–661
- Under the Umayyad Caliphs, 661–750
- → Expansion routes

The Islamic conquests were rapid and far-reaching. By 750 Islamic monarchs controlled kingdoms stretching from central Asia to Spain.

"holy war." *Jihad* was responsible in part for Islam's early conquests beyond the Arabian peninsula.

Political upheavals occurring outside of Arabia also aided the Islamic cause. Early Muslim triumphs in the Near East can be accounted for in part by the long series of wars waged between the Byzantine and Persian (Sassanid) Empires to the north, which left both sides exhausted and open to conquest. In addition, the inhabitants of Syria and Egypt, alienated by religious dissent and resenting the attempts of the Byzantine Empire to impose its brand of Christianity on the population, sought freedom from Byzantine rule. The Arabs combined use of camels for long distance travel and swift horses for the attack was extremely effective. In 636 Arab armies conquered Syria and occupied the city of Damascus. Jerusalem was taken in 638. The Muslims then won Iraq from the Persians and in 651 defeated the last Sassanid ruler, thereby ending the 400-year-old Persian Empire. Most of Egypt had fallen with little resistance by 646, and raids had begun into the lands the Muslims called the Maghrib, in North Africa west of Egypt and north of the Sahara. Within 30 years of Muhammad's death, Islam had become the dominant faith of a vast empire connecting western Asia with the Mediterranean and Africa. This area possessed a cer-

tain cultural unity under Islam, but it was politically divided.

The new Islamic territories were governed with remarkable efficiency and flexibility. The centralization of authority typical of effective military organization aided in the incorporation of new peoples. Unbelievers in the conquered territories became increasingly interested in the new religion and accepted Islam in great numbers. In addition to the power of the religious message of Islam, the imposition of a head tax on all non-Muslims and some restrictions on unbelievers' holding political office encouraged many to become converts. Accounts of the coercive imposition of Islam on conquered peoples are inexact: Jews and Christians outside Arabia enjoyed toleration because they worshiped the same God as the Muslim, and many non-Muslims were active participants in the Islamic state and prospered financially and socially.

Islam was and remains one of the most effective religions in overcoming the potential barriers of race and nationality. In the early days of the spread of Islam, apart from a certain privileged position allowed Arabs and the Prophet's earliest supporters, distinctions were mostly those of economic and political rank. The new religion converted and included peoples of many ethnic origins and cultures. This egalitarian ideal of Islam undoubtedly aided its rapid and successful expansion.

Defining the Community

All Muslims shared belief in the unity of God and the practice of the Five Pillars. But Islamic civilization, like other traditions, was marked by debate and conflict over the interpretation of the law. As Islamic law was codified and as the Islamic state expanded, four main schools of legal interpretation emerged. Scholars struggled with questions of faith and reason, just as their Christian counterparts did. Inspired in part by the spiritual thought and practices of India, Islam also developed a set of mystical traditions that challenged the orthodoxy of the *ulama*. In the political realm, not long after the death of the Prophet, the new Islamic state underwent a crisis that split the community over the question of political authority.

Islam's first three caliphs—Abu Bakr (632–634), Umar (634–644), and Uthman (644–656)—were chosen in consultation with the elders and leaders of the Islamic community, setting a pattern for selecting the caliph exclusively from the Quraysh tribe of Mecca. When Uthman was assassinated by a fellow Muslim, the ensuing struggle for power ultimately split the community into two major divisions, Sunni and Shia. The Shi'ites believed that only descendents of the Prophet could command authority in the Islamic state. Because Muhammad had no surviving sons, his bloodline passed through his grandsons, the sons of his daughter Fatima and her husband Ali, the fourth caliph. Thus for the Shi'ites, the first three caliphs before Ali had been usurpers. Ali and his descendents were the only legitimate heads of the community, *imams*, who were believed to have a special knowledge of the inner meaning of the Qur'an. The Sunnis, rather than insist on a caliph who was a direct descendant of the Prophet, accepted the first three caliphs and upheld the principle that the caliph owed his position to the consent of the Islamic community. The Sunnis argued that they followed the *sunna* of the Prophet, the patterns of behavior modeled on Muhammad's life.

The Shi'ites (or Shia) did not refute the validity of the *sunna*, but they insisted on the Qur'an as the sole and unquestioned authority on the life and teachings of the Prophet. Though originally an Arab party, the Shia in time became a more widespread Islamic movement that stood in opposition to the ruling Umayyad dynasty. That the Shia remained, in general, a minority and opposition party in part explains the evolution of its doctrine of opposition to political authorities. Notwithstanding the several major Shi'ite dynasties in Islamic history, Sunni Muslims have remained numerically dominant. Some 85 percent of the modern world's Muslims are Sunnis, although large Shi'ite communities exist, particularly in Iran, Iraq, and Lebanon.

Umayyad Rule

Ali and his followers were opposed first by Muslims under the leadership of Muhammad's widow and favorite wife Aisha, daughter of Abu Bakr, and later by the forces of Muawiya, the governor of Syria and a relative of the third caliph. The power struggle for leadership in the Muslim community thus erupted into civil war. In 661, after Ali was assassinated, Muawiya proclaimed himself caliph, made Damascus his capital, and founded the Umayyad dynasty, which lasted until 750. In this manner the Umayyads made the caliphate in fact, although never in law, a hereditary office rather than one chosen by election.

The Umayyads expanded the borders of Islam, but not with the spectacular successes of the years immediately after Muhammad's death. The Umayyads held Cyprus, Rhodes, and several Aegean islands, which served as bases for naval attacks on the Byzantine Empire. The Byzantines successfully defended Constantinople against persistent Umayyad attacks, and the Islamic advance toward eastern Europe was checked for the first time. The Umayyads established garrisons in central Asia to further their conquests northward across the Oxus River and southwest into India. Westward across North Africa, Umayyad armies were eventually victorious. The Berbers, a nomadic tribal people inhabiting the Maghrib, initially resisted stubbornly but eventually converted to Islam. The Berbers then aided the Umayyad armies in expanding across the Strait of Gibraltar into the weak Visigoth kingdom in Spain. General Tariq ibn Ziyad led an army across the strait into Spain in 711 (according to legend, the name *Gibraltar* is derived from Jabal Tariq, or "Mountain of Tariq"). After the kingdom of the Visigoths swiftly crumbled, the Muslims were able to make conquests throughout the Iberian peninsula, which they called *al-Andalus*.

The Muslims in Spain seem never to have had serious intentions of expanding their territorial holdings across the Pyrenees into what is now France, but they did engage in seasonal raids to the north. One such raiding party was defeated by Charles Martel near Tours in 732 in a battle that later Europeans exaggeratedly portrayed as a decisive blow to Muslim expansion in Europe. But the Byzantines indeed delivered such a blow: in 717 the Byzantine emperor, Leo III, won a major victory over the Muslims that halted the Umayyad advance into eastern Europe. To the east the Umayyads successfully extended their rule into central Asia; by the middle of the eighth century they could claim lands as far east as

The Early Islamic Conquests

Traditional Western historiography used the rhetorics of medieval Christian writers to portray the early Islamic conquests as sweeping and brutal. The following two excerpts from the Arabic chronicle of al-Tabari (839–923) suggest that wisdom, mercy, and rhetorics of intimidation all played a role in the early Islamic conquests. The Qur'an enjoined mercy as well as warfare, and Abu Bakr's rules of war suggest that the wise conqueror did not kill the citizens and livestock of the lands he wished to rule.

Abu Bakr on the Rules of War (632)

Oh People! I charge you with ten rules; learn them well!

Do not betray, or misappropriate any part of the booty; do not practice treachery or mutilation. Do not kill a young child, an old man, or a woman. Do not uproot or burn palms or cut down fruitful trees. Do not slaughter a sheep or a cow or a camel, except for food. You will meet people who have set them-selves apart in hermitages; leave them to accomplish the purpose for which they have done this. You will come upon people who will bring you dishes with various kinds of food. If you partake of them, pronounce God's name over what you eat. You will meet people who have shaved the crown of their heads, leaving a band of hair around it. Strike them with the sword. Go, in God's name, and may God protect you from sword and pestilence..

The Arab general Khalid ibn al-Walid's letters to the Persians offer mercy in exchange for submission, but they follow up that offer with a challenge.

Letters to the Persians (633)

In the name of God, the Merciful and the Compassionate.

From Khalid ibn al-Walid to the kings of Persia.

Praise be to God who has dissolved your order, frustrated your plans, and split your unanimity. Had he not done this to you, it would have been worse for you. Submit to our authority, and we shall leave you and your land and go by you against others. If not, you will be conquered against your will by men who love death as you love life.

In the name of God, the Merciful and the Compassionate.

From Khalid ibn al-Walid to the border chiefs of Persia.

Become Muslim and be saved. If not, accept protection from us and pay the jizya. If not, I shall come against you with men who love death as you love to drink wine.

From Bernard Lewis, *Islam*, Vol. 1 (Oxford: Oxford University Press, 1987), pp. 213–214.

Turkestan and the Indus valley. To celebrate the enduring power of Islam in the 690s the Umayyads built the Dome of the Rock in Jerusalem on the site of the Jewish Temple. This sacred shrine is built around an enormous rock where, according to tradition, God asked Abraham to sacrifice his son Isaac. A monumental building, it reflected the power of the dynasty and its god; its interior is decorated with Qur'anic inscriptions. The Dome of the Rock has endured to the present day and has become a major site of struggle over Muslim and Jewish claims to the city they both consider holy.

The mainstay of the Umayyad dynasty's power was the ruling class, composed of an Arab military aristocracy. The Arabs formed a privileged class greatly outnumbered by non-Arab converts to Islam. Many of these converted peoples had cultures much more highly developed than that of the Arabs, and the economic and cultural life of this Islamic empire came to be dominated by these non-Arab Muslims,

called *mawali*, or "affiliates." Because they were not Arab by birth, they were treated to a certain extent as citizens of inferior status. They were granted fewer privileges and received less from the spoils of war than the Arabs. Resentment grew steadily among some of the non-Arab Muslims who objected to their inferior status as a violation of the Islamic laws advocating equality. Eventually the resentment of the *mawali* and the opposition of the Shi'ites, who had been forced from power on the accession of Muawiya, helped bring about the downfall of the Umayyads.

Hostility to the Umayyads was also inflamed in 680 when an Umayyad troop massacred Husayn, the second son of Ali, and his followers at Karbala in Iraq. The killing of the grandson of the Prophet was an affront to the Islamic community. The event introduced the theme of martyrdom in Shi'ite tradition around which opposition party unity could be mobilized. To this day, a "passion play" commemorating

Husayn's death is a dramatic and important element in Shi'ite ceremonial in many communities.

The Abbasid Era, Zenith of Classical Islamic Civilization

A new dynasty, the Abbasid, was founded when a rebel army, with Shi'ite support, defeated the Umayyads. The first Abbasid caliph was Abu al-Abbas, a descendant of Muhammad's uncle Abbas. His dynasty ruled most of the Muslim world from 750 to 1258 and built the city of Baghdad in 762 as a symbol of its wealth, power, and legitimacy. The Abbasids owed their initial support and successes in part to the discontent of the non-Arab Muslims, many of whom had become prominent leaders in Islam's cities.

The fall of the Umayyad dynasty marked the end of Arab domination within Islam. The Arab "aristocracy" had led the forces of conquest during the great period of Islamic expansion, but over time, as the new dynasties established themselves, the dominant status previously held only by Arab soldiers was shared with non-Arab administrators, merchants, and scholars.

Traditional Arab patterns of tribal organization and warfare gave way to patterns of military organization and governance based on the imperial traditions of the conquered lands. The new Abbasid polity fostered economic prosperity, the growth of town life, and the promotion of the merchant class. The Abbasid caliph forecast that Baghdad would become the "most flourishing city in the world"; indeed, it rivaled Constantinople for that honor, situated as it was on the trade routes linking East and West. Furthermore, Abbasid patronage of scholarship and the arts produced a rich and complex culture far surpassing that in western Europe.

The founding of the new capital at Baghdad shifted Islam's center of gravity to the province of Iraq, whose soil, watered by the Tigris and Euphrates Rivers, had nurtured the earliest civilizations. Here the Abbasid caliphs set themselves up as potentates in the traditional style of the ancient East (particularly Persia) so that they were surrounded by a lavish court that contrasted sharply with the simplicity of the lifestyle of the Prophet and the first caliphs. One historian described the amazement of the Byzantine envoys who, on entering the Abbasid court, found a magnificent tree of silver and gold, with singing birds, also of silver and gold, perched in its leaves. The Abbasids were also great patrons of scholarship; in Baghdad they founded one of the great medieval libraries, the House of Wisdom.

The Abbasid dynasty marked the high point of Islamic power and civilization. The empire ruled by the Abbasid caliphs was greater in size than the Roman Empire at its height; it was the product of an expansion during which the Muslim state assimilated peoples, customs, cultures, learning, and inventions on an unprecedented scale. This Islamic empire, in fact, drew from the resources of the entire known world.

Abbasid power, however, did not go unchallenged, even in the Muslim world. While the Abbasids ruled in Baghdad, rival dynasties established their sovereignty in other areas that had been incorporated into the Islamic state during the early conquests. Members of the deposed Umayyad dynasty established a new dynasty in Muslim Spain in 756 and eventually set up a glorious court in Córdoba, famous for its scholarship and patronage of the arts. In Egypt the Fatimids established a Shi'ite ruling house and developed a formidable navy that dominated the eastern Mediterranean. To bolster their legitimacy, the Fatimids claimed descent from the Prophet's daughter, Fatima, hence the name of the dynasty. They, too, founded a new and glorious capital at Cairo, where they established al-Azhar, the famous institution of Islamic learning that has attracted scholars from throughout the Muslim world since the tenth century. Thus the eighth to the twelfth centuries were not only the period of the classical glory of the Islamic state but also an era during which rulers in three different Muslim capitals all claimed the title "caliph." This political division stood in contrast to the Islamic world's civilizational unity, which was based on the universal Sharia law and the spread of the Arabic language.

Trade, Industry, and Agriculture

From the eighth century to the twelfth, the Muslim world enjoyed enormous prosperity. In close contact with three continents, merchants from the Islamic lands could move goods back and forth from China to western Europe and from Russia to central Africa. The absence of tariff barriers within the empire and the tolerance of the caliphs, who allowed non-Muslim merchants and craftsmen to reside in their territories and carry on commerce with their home countries, further facilitated trade. The presence of such important urban centers as Baghdad, Cairo, and Córdoba stimulated trade and industry throughout the Muslim world; the courts of the monarchs were great consumers of textiles, foodstuffs, arts, and crafts.

The cosmopolitan nature of Baghdad was evident in its bazaars, which contained goods from all over the known world. There were spices, minerals, and dyes from India; gems and fabrics from central Asia; honey, furs, and wax from Scandinavia and Russia; and ivory and gold from Africa. Muslim trade increased with Southeast Asia, and a large Muslim trading community established itself in the Chinese

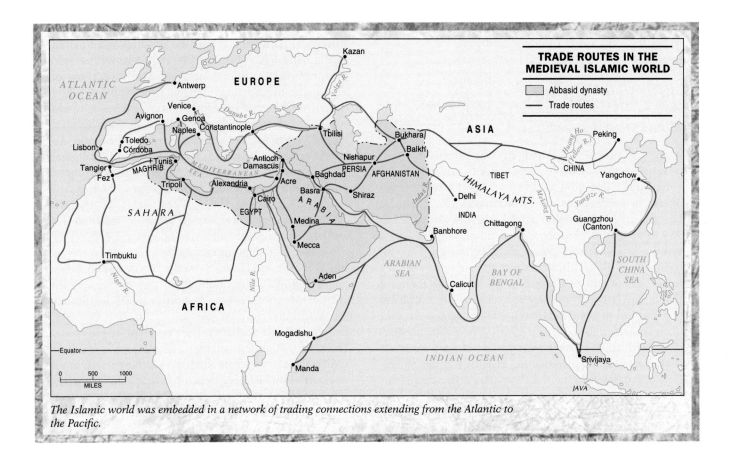

TRADE ROUTES IN THE
MEDIEVAL ISLAMIC WORLD
Abbasid dynasty
Trade routes

The Islamic world was embedded in a network of trading connections extending from the Atlantic to the Pacific.

port of Guangzhou (Canton). One bazaar in Baghdad specialized in goods from China, including silks, musk, and porcelain. In the slave markets Muslim traders bought and sold Scandinavians, Mongolians from central Asia, and Africans. Joint-stock companies flourished along with branch banking organizations, and checks (an Arabic word) drawn on one bank could be cashed with commercial agents throughout this vast network of traders.

Muslim textile industries turned out excellent cottons (muslins) and silks. The steel of Damascus and Toledo, the leather of Córdoba, and the glass of Syria became internationally famous. Notable also was the art of papermaking, learned from the Chinese. Under the Abbasids, vast irrigation projects in Iraq increased cultivable land, which yielded large crops of fruits and grains. Wheat came from the Nile valley, cotton from North Africa, olives and wine from Spain, wool from eastern Asia Minor, and horses from Persia.

By the tenth century Islam was also making inroads into Africa south of the Nile and the Maghrib. Trade routes through the Sahara brought spices, leather work, and eventually slaves from the south to the northern coast, and in return caravans from the north brought luxury goods, salt, and the Islamic religion to the early African kingdoms of Ghana and Mali. Commercial agents and missionaries carried Islam along the sea routes to central and southeastern African ports such as Mogadishu and Manda and to South and Southeast Asia.

The Spectacular Reign of Harun al-Rashid

Just as the Abbasid caliphate was the most celebrated Islamic dynasty, so the rule of Harun al-Rashid (786–809), hero of the tales of *The Arabian Nights*, was the most spectacular of the Abbasid reigns. A contemporary of Charlemagne, who had revived the idea of a Roman Empire in the West (see Chapter 9), Harun was surely the more powerful of the two and the ruler of the more advanced culture. The two monarchs were on friendly terms, based on self-interest. Charlemagne wanted to exert pressure on the Byzantine emperor to recognize his new imperial title. Harun saw Charlemagne as an ally against the Umayyad rulers of Spain, who had broken away from Abbasid dominion. The two emperors exchanged embassies and presents. The Muslim sent the Christian rich fabrics, aromatics, and even an elephant named Abu-Lababah, meaning "the father of

In the Muslim world, merchants transported goods by both land and sea. Camels carried merchants and goods on the overland routes, as shown in this manuscript illumination from the thirteenth century (above left). Sound vessels with space for both passengers and cargo, like the Indian ship depicted in this Iraqi manuscript from 1238 (above right), and reliable navigation techniques facilitated the sea trade.

intelligence." Another gift, an intricate water clock from Baghdad, seems to have been regarded as miraculous in the West.

Relations between the Abbasid caliphate and the Byzantine Empire were never very cordial, and conflicts often broke out along the shifting borders that separated Christian and Muslim territories. Harun al-Rashid once responded to a communiqué from the Byzantine emperor with the following answer:

In the name of God, the Merciful, the Compassionate. From Harun, Commander of the Faithful, to Nicepherus, the dog of the Greeks, I have read your letter, you son of a she-infidel, and you shall see the answer before you hear it.

This response was followed up with Abbasid raids on Byzantine possessions in Asia Minor.

In the days of Harun al-Rashid, Baghdad's wealth and splendor equaled that of Constantinople, and its chief glory was the royal palace. With its annexes for officials, the harem, and eunuchs, the caliph's residence occupied one-third of the city of Baghdad. The caliph's audience chamber was the setting for an

elaborate ceremonial, which mirrored that of the Byzantines and Persians. Such court ceremonial was designed to impress the Abbasid citizens with the justice, power, and magnificence of the caliph and to intimidate foreign envoys.

Challenges to Abbasid Authority

In the tenth century a movement of migration and conquest out of central Asia began that would have a dramatic impact on the political and cultural configuration of the central Islamic lands. By the early eleventh century Turkish peoples had moved from central Asia into the Abbasid lands, where, over time, they converted to Islam. One group, the Seljuks, after annexing most of Persia, gained control of Baghdad in 1055 and subjugated Iraq. Subsequently, they conquered Syria and Palestine at the expense of the Fatimids and proceeded to take most of Asia Minor from the Byzantines. The Seljuks permitted the Abbasids to retain nominal authority, in part to secure political legitimacy for their reign, but they themselves ruled the state. By the time of the First

Crusade in 1095, which was provoked in part by the Seljuk advances, the Abbasid dynasty had lost much of its power and status in the Islamic world.

Seljuk dominance of much of the old Abbasid Empire was later challenged by the arrival of Turco-Mongol invaders from the northeastern steppes of central Asia. Early in the thirteenth century Genghis Khan succeeded in uniting the animistic, tribal horsemen of Mongolia and conquering much of China and Russia; he and his successors moved on to eastern and central Asia (see Chapter 12) and ultimately conquered Persia and Iraq. In 1258 a grandson of Genghis Khan captured Baghdad and had the caliph executed. Unlike the Seljuks, the Mongols were contemptuous of the caliph and felt no need to preserve an Abbasid successor as a figurehead to secure their legitimacy. Not only did the Abbasid dynasty come to an end, but so did most of the vast irrigation system that had supported the land. The dynasty established there by the Mongols survived for almost a century, but the Mongol invaders were eventually acculturated and absorbed into the local population.

Egypt was "saved" from the Mongol advance by the Mamluks (1250–1517). The Fatimids had been replaced by one of their own commanders, Salah al-Din, who established a new dynasty, the Ayyubids (1169–1252). Famed in the West as Saladin, it was Salah al-Din who took Jerusalem from the crusaders. The Ayyubids were in turn overthrown by their own elite "slave" guard, called *mamluks*. *Mamluk* literally means "slave," but these men were not slaves in the sense of people of low status who did menial tasks. Taken as captives or purchased as young men in the slave market, they were trained in the military and political arts to serve their commanders. They were converted to Islam and hence could not be held as true slaves. Indeed, they often wielded great power and wealth. After overthrowing the Ayyubids and founding their own ruling group, they formed the elite military caste of Egypt. It was the Mamluks who stopped the Mongol advance in Syria and later ejected the last of the crusaders in 1291. They ruled in Egypt and Syria until 1517, claiming the title "Protector of the Holy Places" as a result of their governance of Mecca, Medina, and also Jerusalem, the three holy cities of Islam.

Islamic Culture

The attainments of the Muslims in the intellectual and artistic fields can be attributed not only to the genius of the Arabs but also to the peoples who embraced Islam in Persia, Iraq, Turkey, Syria, Egypt, North Africa, and Spain. Muslim learning benefited both from Islam's ability to absorb other cultures and

from the native talents of the Islamic peoples. Under Abbasid rule a great synthesis of culture and scholarship emerged, strands of which were then transmitted by traveling scholars, traders, and missionaries throughout the known world from the Mediterranean to the Indian Ocean.

The cosmopolitan spirit permeating the Abbasid dynasty supplied the tolerance necessary for a diversity of ideas, so that the science, philosophies, and literatures of ancient Greece and India alike received a cordial reception in Baghdad. Under Harun al-Rashid and his successors, the writings of Aristotle, Euclid, Ptolemy, Archimedes, Galen, and other great Greek philosophers and scientific writers were translated into Arabic. This knowledge, together with the teachings of the Qur'an, formed the basis of Muslim learning, which was in turn transmitted to scholars in Europe and Asia. In addition to being valuable transmitters of learning, Muslim scholars made many original contributions to science and the arts

Advances in Medicine

The years between 900 and 1100 can be regarded as the golden age of Muslim learning. This period was particularly significant for its medical advances. Muslim students of medicine were by all measures far superior to their European contemporaries. Muslim cities had excellent pharmacies and hospitals, where physicians received instruction and training. Muslim scholars perfected surgical techniques, figured out the mode for the spread of the plague, and described the course of many diseases.

Perhaps the greatest Muslim physician was the Persian Abu Bakr Muhammad al-Razi (d. 925), better

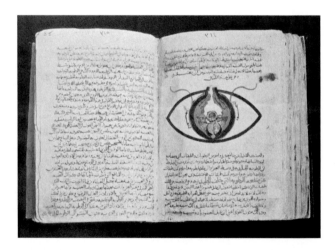

Husayn ibn Ishaq's Book of the Ten Treatises on the Eye *shows the Islamic scientist's outstandingly accurate understanding of the anatomy of the eye. Written in the tenth century, the work was still standard in the thirteenth century, when the copy shown here was made.*

known in the West as Rhazes. Chief physician in Baghdad, he wrote more than 100 medical treatises in which he summarized Greek medical knowledge and added his own clinical observations. His most famous work, *On Smallpox and Measles,* is the first clear description of the symptoms and treatment of these diseases.

The most influential Muslim medical treatise is the vast *Canon of Medicine,* in which the great scholar Ibn Sina, or Avicenna (d. 1037), systematically organized all Greek and Muslim medical learning. In the twelfth century the *Canon* was translated into Latin. It was so much in demand in the West that it was issued 16 times in the last half of the fifteenth century and more than 20 times in the sixteenth, and it continued in use until the modern era.

Progress in Other Sciences

Muslim physicists were also highly creative scientists. Al-Hasan ibn al-Haytham, or Alhazen (d. 1038), of Cairo, developed optics to a remarkable degree and challenged the theory of Ptolemy and Euclid that the eye sends visual rays to its object. The chief source of all medieval Western writers on optics, Alhazen interested himself in optical reflections and illusions and examined the refraction of light rays through air and water.

Although astronomy continued to be strongly influenced by astrology, Muslim astronomers built observatories, recorded their observations over long periods, and achieved greater accuracy than the Greeks in measuring the length of the solar year and in calculating eclipses. Interest in alchemy—the attempt to change base metals into precious ones and to find the magic elixir for the preservation of human life—produced the first chemical laboratories and caused attention to be given to the value of experimentation. Muslim alchemists prepared many chemical substances (sulfuric acid, for example) and developed methods for evaporation, filtration, sublimation, crystallization, and distillation. The process of distillation, invented around 800, produced what was called *al-kuhl* ("the essence"), or alcohol, a new liquor that brought its inventors great honor in some circles.

In mathematics the Muslims were indebted to the Hindus as well as to the Greeks. From the Hindus came arithmetic, algebra, the zero, and the nine signs known in the West as Arabic numerals. From the Greeks came the geometry of Euclid and the fundamentals of trigonometry, which Ptolemy had established. Two Muslim mathematicians made significant contributions: al-Khwarizmi (d. c. 844), whose *Arithmetic* introduced Arabic numerals and whose *Algebra* first employed that mathematical term, and Omar Khayyám (d. c. 1123), the mathematician, as-

tronomer, and poet whose work in algebra went beyond quadratics to cubic equations. Other Islamic scholars developed plane and spherical trigonometry.

In an empire that straddled continents, where trade and administration made an accurate knowledge of lands imperative, the science of geography flourished. The Muslims added to the geographical knowledge of the Greeks, whose treatises they translated, by producing detailed descriptions of the climate, manners, and customs of many parts of the known world. Developments in mapping went hand in hand with the progress of Arab seafaring, which aimed at exploiting commercial possibilities along the seaborne routes of trade.

Islamic Literature and Scholarship

To Westerners, Islamic literature may seem somewhat alien. Early Western literary styles tried to emphasize restraint and simplicity, but Muslim writers have long enjoyed literature that makes use of elegant expression, subtle combinations of words, and fanciful and even extravagant imagery.

Westerners' knowledge of Islamic literature tends to be limited to *The Arabian Nights* and the poetry of Omar Khayyám. The former is a collection of often erotic tales told with a wealth of local color. Although it professedly covers different facets of life at the Abbasid capital, the story is in fact often based on life in medieval Cairo. *The Arabian Nights* took the literary influences of India and Persia, combined them with conventions of Arabic literature, and passed them on to the West, where they can be seen in the works of Chaucer and Boccaccio. These tales present an interesting combination of the courtly and the vulgar. The fame of Omar Khayyám's *Rubáiyát* is due at least in part to the musical (though rather free) translation of Edward FitzGerald. The following stanzas indicate the poem's beautiful imagery and gentle resignation:

A Book of Verses underneath the Bough,
A Jug of Wine, a Loaf of Bread—and Thou
Beside me singing in the Wilderness—
Oh, Wilderness were Paradise enow!

Some for the Glories of This World; and some
Sigh for the Prophet's Paradise to come;
Ah, take the Cash, and let the Credit go,
Nor heed the rumble of a distant Drum! . . .

The Moving Finger writes; and, having writ,
Moves on: nor all your Piety nor Wit
Shall lure it back to cancel half a Line,

Nor all your Tears wash out a Word of it.
And that inverted Bowl they call the Sky,
Whereunder crawling coop'd we live and die,
Lift not your hands to It for help—for It
As impotently moves as you or I.[1]

Discovery Through Maps

An Islamic Map of the World

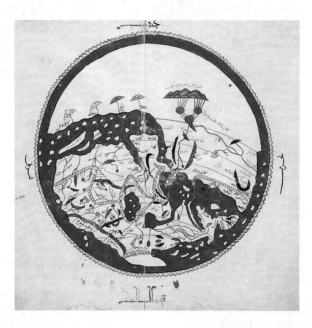

Which way is up? We tend to take the orientation of maps for granted, with north as up. For example, American world maps often depict the United States at the center and north at the top. But not all maps make those same assumptions. The world map of al-Idrīsī, an Arab geographer, is a case in point. Al-Idrīsī's map is oriented, as was common in Arab maps of his time, with south at the top. It is centered on the world of his own experience, the sacred city of Mecca in Arabia and the civilized realm of the Mediterranean. The map includes several distinctive features typical of this type of medieval map. The world is shown as an island encircled by a world sea. The extent of Africa is unknown; it is depicted as a giant mass occupying the upper half of the map. The Americas are not included at all.

Al-Idrīsī was born in Morocco in 1100. Educated in Córdoba, he began his travels as a youth and ended up at the cosmopolitan court of King Roger of Sicily around 1138. There the king asked him to construct a world map complete with written commentary. In collaboration with other scholars, al-Idrīsī crafted the map, which was engraved on silver, around the year 1154. Although the original is lost, there are various manuscript versions of al-Idrīsī's world map, one of which is shown here. The Arab scholar's map was very influential and widely copied in Europe and Asia for centuries after his death in 1165. Al-Idrīsī's map suggests one type of medieval worldview, and his life confirms the notion that cartographers were a valuable commodity in the Afro-Eurasian courts of the time.

Turn the map upside down and see if you can identify the Mediterranean Sea, the Arabian Peninsula, and the Maghrib.

The same rich imagery characterizes much Islamic prose, but *The Arabian Nights* and the *Rubáiyát* merely hint at the breadth and diversity of Islamic literature. As the first important prose work in Arab literature, the Qur'an set the stylistic pattern for all Arabic writers. With classical Arabic then "fixed" in the Qur'an, Muslim writers, spurred on by the generosity of the Islamic kings, produced a great corpus of literature. Arabic and then Persian were the languages of high culture. Poetry contests were a standard of the early Islamic courts, where the poets who contrived the most beautiful or wittiest verses received honors and rich rewards. Poetry was also used for satire. Poets used pointed verse to wound or defame their rivals, and kings used the talents of their poets to send insulting messages to their enemies.

Muslim philosophy, essentially Greek in origin, was developed and modified by Islamic scholars. Like the medieval Christian philosophers (see Chapter 8), Muslim thinkers were largely concerned with

Ibn Sina's Path to Wisdom

Ibn Sina, the famous Muslim philosopher who died in 1037, recorded the progress of his education. His dilligence, but not his pride, might in some ways serve as a model for modern students. As a young boy, Ibn Sina began his education in religion and the sciences. He remembers himself as a determined and independent student who had little patience with or respect for some of his teachers. By the time he was 16, his education was already far-reaching. Ibn Sina was raised in Bukhara, an important center of Islamic learning in central Asia. There, he writes:

I was put under teachers of the Qur'an and of letters. By the time I was ten I had mastered the Qur'an and a great deal of literature, so that I was marvelled at for my aptitude. . . . My father sent me to a certain vegetable-seller who used the Indian arithmetic, so that I might learn it from him. Then, there came to Bukhara a man called Abu 'Abd Allah al-Natili who claimed to be a philosopher; my father invited him to stay in our house, hoping I would learn from him also. I had already occupied myself with Muslim jurisprudence, attending Isma'il the Ascetic; so I was an excellent enquirer, having become familiar with the methods of expostulation and the techniques of rebuttal according to the usages of the canon lawyers. . . . Whatever problem he [al-Natili] stated to me, I showed a better mental conception of it than he. So I continued until I had read all the strightforward parts of Logic with him; as for the subtler points, he had no acquintance with them. From then onwards I took to reading texts by myself; I studied the commentaries, until I had completely mastered the science of Logic. Similarly with Euclid I read the first five or six figures with him, and thereafter undertook on my own account to solve the entire remainder of the book. . . . I now occupied myself with mastering the various texts and commentaries on natural science and metaphysics, until all the gates of knowledge were open to me. Next I desired to study medicine, and proceeded to read all the books that have been written on this subject. Medicine is not a difficult science, and naturally I excelled in it in a very short time, so that qualified physicians began to read medicine with me. I also undertook to treat the sick, and methods of treatment derived from practical experience revealed themselves to me such as baffle description. At the same time I continued between whiles to study and dispute on law, being now sixteen years of age.

From A. J. Arberry. *Aspects of Islamic Civilization* (Ann Arbor: University of Michigan Press, 1967), pp. 136–137.

reconciling Aristotelian rationalism and religion. Some sought to harmonize Platonism, Aristotelianism, and Islam. The philosopher Ibn Sina (980–1037) sought to extract what was purely Aristotelian from later additions and to articulate the truths of Islam in terms of Aristotelian logic. His work had a profound effect on Islamic philosophy and was widely read in the West, where it was translated into Latin in the twelfth century.

Another great Islamic philosopher, Ibn Rushd, or Averroës (d. 1198), lived in Córdoba, where he was the caliph's personal doctor. He is famous for his marvelous commentaries on Aristotle. Ibn Rushd rejected the belief in the ultimate harmony between faith and reason along with all earlier attempts to reconcile Aristotle and Plato. He argued that parts of the Qur'an were to be taken metaphorically, not literally. But most human beings, according to Ibn Rushd, were unable to understand either philosophy or the metaphorical meanings of the Qur'an.

In contrast, Moses Maimonides, Ibn Rushd's contemporary who was also born in Muslim Spain, sought, in his still influential *Guide to the Perplexed*, to harmonize Judaism and Aristotelian philosophy. St. Thomas Aquinas, who in the next century undertook a similar project for Christianity, was influenced by these earlier attempts to reconcile faith and reason.

Islamic historiography found its finest expression in the work of Ibn Khaldun of Tunis (d. 1406), who has been called the "father of sociology." Ibn Khaldun wrote a large general history dealing particularly with human social development, which he held to be the result of the interaction of society with the physical environment. He delineated guidelines for the writing of history and ridiculed earlier historical writing, saying it was often full of stupid or thoughtless errors. Ibn Khaldun defined history in this manner:

It should be known that history, in matter of fact, is information about human social organization, which itself is identical with world civilization. It deals with such conditions affecting the nature of civilization as, for instance, savagery and sociability, group feelings, and the different ways by which one group of human beings achieves superiority over another. It deals with royal authority and . . . with the different kinds of gainful occupations and ways of making a living, with the sciences and crafts that human beings pursue as part of their activities and efforts, and with all the other institutions that originate in civilization through its very nature.[2]

Ibn Khaldun conceived of history as an evolutionary process, in which societies and institutions change continually. He traveled widely in the Islamic world, serving as a judge and scholar in the courts of the Mamluks and other rulers. When he beheld the city of Cairo, he described it as a pinnacle of Islamic civilization, full of shops, gardens, scholars, and institutions of higher learning.

The Sufis

As Islamic civilization produced traditions of scholarship and philosophy, it also produced a tradition of mysticism that came to be a significant factor in the spread of Islam throughout the world. The Arabic word *tasawwuf,* "mysticism," is related to the word *suf,* for the coarse woolen clothes some of the early mystics wore. The early *Sufis* were lone ascetics who practiced physical and spiritual discipline in order to transcend the material world and gain a special kind of closeness to Allah. Later, Sufi orders were founded, where the devotees practiced rules of discipline, followed the path shown them by a spiritual master or *shaykh,* divorced themselves to some extent from the community, and developed rituals that ranged from the simple to the elaborate. There are many similarities between some of the Sufi orders and the medieval monastic orders of Christian Europe. To be a Sufi, however, one does not need to join a spiritual order; many Sufis live and work in the community. What is essential to Sufism is the belief in following a path of discipline that leads to mystical communion with Allah.

The early Muslim mystics expressed their desire for union with God in a language of love, longing, and ecstasy. This longing came to be embodied in the mystical poetry of Sufis like the famous Jalal al-Din Rumi (1207–1273), who compared the Sufi to a man "drunk with God." The *dhikr,* collective repetition of the name of God, sometimes accompanied by rhythmic movements and breathing, became part of Sufi practice as a way of both glorifying God and transcending the distractions of the body and the world. In their quest for communion with God, the Sufis also ran afoul of Islamic orthodoxy, because their beliefs and practices were sometimes considered extreme or blasphemous.

In the ninth century, Sufis began systematically to write down the ways of the path. Communion with God meant the losing of self, however briefly. That losing or merging of self with God smacked of polytheism to many members of the *ulama.* Thus the Sufis were accused of claiming to be divine and of believing they were above the law. In 922 al-Hallaj, a famous teacher and Sufi in Baghdad, was executed for blasphemy after he claimed "I am the Truth." Al-Hallaj had also alienated the authorities by claiming that the *hajj,* the pilgrimage to Mecca, was not necessary, because the Sufi could pursue the pilgrimage to God from his own room. The pathos of the death of al-Hallaj is graphically described in the words of his servant, Ibrahim ibn Fatik, who wrote that al-Hallaj asked Allah to forgive those who were preparing to kill him:

> *Then he was silent. The Headsman stepped up and dealt him a smashing blow which broke his nose, and the blood ran onto his white robe. The mystic al-Shibli, who was in the crowd, cried aloud and rent his garment, and Abu Husayn al-Wasiti fell fainting, and so did other famous Sufis who were there, so that a riot nearly broke out. Then the executioners did their work.*[3]

Al-Hallaj gave the Sufi community in Baghdad a martyr. But in the end, the message of Sufism was too powerful and compelling for Islamic orthodoxy to ignore. Sufis were very effective in spreading the message of Islam beyond its Middle Eastern heartlands. In South and Southeast Asia, Sufi asceticism and belief in mystical communion found resonances in the ascetic and mystical practices of those areas and aided the conversion of non-Muslims to Islam. By the end of the Abbasid era, Sufism had been brought into the mainstream of Islamic thought as a result of its widespread appeal and through the systematic efforts of scholars like al-Ghazali (1058–1111), who legitimized the Sufi way as an acceptable path toward God. Sufism remains a powerful tool in the spread of Islam. In the United States today, Rumi's poetry remains popular, and American college students may get their first taste of Islam through the words of Sufi masters.

Art and Architecture

Religious attitudes played an important part in shaping Islamic art. Because the Prophet warned against idols and their worship, there was a prohibition against pictorial representation of human and animal figures; that prohibition, however, was not always obeyed. The effect of this injunction was to encourage the development of stylized and geometrical designs. Islamic art, like other artistic traditions, borrowed extensively to forge a new and unique synthesis. Artists and craftspeople followed chiefly Byzantine and Persian models, but central Asian, South Asian, and African motifs were also integrated into Islamic styles.

The Muslims excelled in the fields of architecture and the decorative arts. That Islamic architecture can boast of many large and imposing structures is not surprising; monumental building was a natural extension of the power and glory of the Islamic dynasts who wanted to celebrate their own power and glorify God. In time, original styles of building evolved; the great mosques embody such typical features as domes, arcades, and minarets, the slender towers from which the faithful are summoned to prayer. The horseshoe arch is another graceful and familiar feature of Muslim architecture.

On the walls and ceilings of their buildings, the Muslims gave full rein to their love of ornamentation and beauty of detail. The Spanish interpretation of the Islamic tradition is particularly delicate and elegant. A superb artistic example of the sophistication and wealth of the Muslim world is the Alhambra, built between 1248 and 1354 by Muslim kings in Granada, Spain. Some authorities consider it the apogee of Muslim architecture.

Restricted in their subject matter, Muslim craftspeople conceived beautiful patterns from flowers and geometrical figures. The Arabic script, one of the most graceful ever devised, was often used as a decorative motif. Muslim decorative skill also found expression in such fields as carpet and rug weaving, brass work, and the making of steel products inlaid with precious metals.

Conclusion

The great power of Islam's message enabled the fragmented Arab tribes to unify and expand across three continents in an astoundingly brief period. During the reigns of the first four caliphs and the century of dominance by the Umayyad dynasty, great gains were made in conquering new territories and peoples. But the Umayyad dynasty was based on a ruling hierarchy of Arabs, and the resentment of the non-Arab Islamic community helped establish the Abbasid dynasty in a new caliphate in Baghdad. The Abbasid Empire provided the security, patronage, and institutional framework for a great cultural synthesis. Its capital at Baghdad was also a major center in an expanding network of international trade.

During the early Abbasid period Islam reached new heights of geographical expansion and cultural achievement, extending from Spain to eastern Asia. As in all traditional empires of the time, agriculture provided the base for the economy of the Abbasid state. Its unparalleled prosperity evolved from a combination of successful agriculture, trade, and industry. But the Abbasids were not able to maintain an integrated empire; despite its relative religious unity, the great empire broke up into smaller Muslim states.

Muslims made many significant contributions in science, literature, and philosophy. Muslim intellec-

The ultimate stage of refinement of Moorish architecture, which combines Spanish and Islamic elements, is the Alhambra in Granada, the last Islamic stronghold in Spain during the Middle Ages. Slender, rhythmically spaced columns and arches covered with an intricate design of molded stucco frame the Court of the Lions, the most luxurious portion of the palace.

tual life was in large part the product of a genius for synthesizing varying cultural traditions, and the diffusion of this knowledge was a tremendous factor in the rediscovery of classical learning and the emergence of the Renaissance in Europe.

Islam remains an extremely powerful force in the world. The Islamic community today is made up of leading industrialized societies as well as nations just emerging from colonialism. The message of faith and unity under Islam is a powerful influence that will continue to play a significant part in world politics. Islam faces the new era as one of the world's most influential religious and social forces. Present-day

Muslims still derive great meaning from the teachings of Muhammad and the community he and his disciples constructed.

Suggestions for Reading

Major scholarly surveys are Marshall Hodgson, *The Venture of Islam: Conscience and History of a World Civilization*, 3 vols. (University of Chicago Press, 1974), and Albert Hourani, *A History of the Arab Peoples* (Warner, 1992). See also Philip K. Hitti, *The Arabs: A Short History* (Regnery, 1996), an excellent abridgment of a scholarly general history; and H. A. R. Gibb, *Mohammedanism: A Historical Survey*, 2nd ed. (Oxford University Press, 1969). See also the clear introduction to Islam by John L. Esposito, *Islam: The Straight Path*, 3rd ed. (Oxford University Press, 1998); and C. Brockelmann, *History of the Islamic Peoples* (Capricorn, 1948).

W. Montgomery Watt, *Muhammad: Prophet and Statesman* (Oxford University Press, 1974), is a brief account of the Prophet's life and teachings. See also Maxime Rodinson, *Mohammed* (Vintage, 1974); Karen Armstrong, *Muhammad: A Biography of the Prophet* (HarperCollins, 1992); Frederick Mathewson Denny, *An Introduction to Islam*, 2nd ed. (Macmillan, 1996); and Martin Lings, *Muhammad: His Life Based on the Earliest Sources* (Inner Traditions International, 1983). For an interpretation and translation of the Qur'an, see Marmaduke William Pickthall, ed., *The Meaning of the Glorious Koran: An Explanatory Translation* (Knopf, 1993). For primary source selections in translation, see James Kritzeck, *Anthology of Islamic Literature* (Meridian, 1975). John Renard, *Islam and the Heroic Image* (University of South Carolina Press, 1994), is an excellent introduction to heroic Muslim personalities.

On the early development of Islam, see Fred Donner, *The Early Islamic Conquests* (Princeton University Press, 1981); J. J. Saunders, *History of Medieval Islam* (Routledge, 1990); and Dominique Sourdel, *Medieval Islam*, trans. J. Montgomery Watt (Routledge, 1983). For an evaluation of the Umayyad period and its importance, see G. R. Hawting, *The First Dynasty of Islam* (Southern Illinois University Press, 1986).

On the impact of the Crusades, see Malcolm Billings, *The Cross and the Crescent* (Sterling, 1987); Amin Maalouf, *The Crusades Through Arab Eyes* (Schocken, 1985); and Francesco Gabrieli, *Arab Historians of the Crusades* (University of California Press, 1969).

Reynold A. Nicholson, *A Literary History of the Arabs* (Cambridge University Press, 1969), traces the growth of Arab thought and culture through its literature, as does H. A. R. Gibb, *Arabic Literature*, 2nd ed. (Oxford University Press, 1974). See also Philip K. Hitti, *Makers of Arab History* (Torchbooks, 1964), and D. Talbot Rice, *Islamic Art* (Praeger, 1974).

Suggestions for Web Browsing

Internet Islamic History Sourcebook: Muhammad and Foundations
http://www.fordham.edu/halsall/islam/islamsbook .html Muhammad and Foundations—to 632 C.E.

Extensive on-line source for links about the early history of Islam, including a biography of Muhammad and the many aspects of Islam, including the role of women.

Islam and Islamic History in Arabia and the Middle East: The Message
http://www.islamic.org/Mosque/ihame/Sec1.htm
Islam and Islamic History in Arabia and the Middle East: The Golden Age
http://www.islamic.org/Mosque/ihame/Sec7.htm

Extensive site details the origins of Islam and provides information and images about Muhammad, the Hijra, the Qur'an, Arabic writing, science and scholarship, Arabic literature, and Arabic numerals.

The Qur'an
http://islam.org/mosque/arabicscript/1/1.htm
The entire text of the Qur'an, with audio.

Islamic and Arabic Arts and Architecture
http://www.islamicart.com/

A rich and attractively designed general site, with information and images regarding architecture, calligraphy, and textiles. Includes a glossary of terms and names of important artists and architects. A subsite offers a portfolio of shrines and palaces including the Ka'ba, the Mosque of the Prophet Muhammad, the Dome of the Rock, and the Alhambra.

Notes

1. *Rubáiyát of Omar Khayyám*, trans. Edward FitzGerald, stanzas 12, 13, 71, and 72.
2. Ibn Khaldun, *The Muqaddimah: An Introduction to History*, Vol. 1, trans. Franz Rosenthal (London: Routledge & Kegan Paul, 1958), p. 71.
3. John Williams, ed., *Islam* (New York: Braziller, 1962), p. 142.

chapter

II

Cattle played a vital role in the political, economic, social, and religious life of many African cultures. This picture is of a Nuer cattle camp in the modern nation of Sudan.

The African Genesis

African Civilizations to 1500

At the same time that other world civilizations were experiencing dynamic cultural growth, sub-Saharan Africa was undergoing similar transformations. Northern Africa had given birth to some of the earliest civilizations, Egypt and Nubia. But the peoples of the entire continent developed a variety of social and political systems, ranging from small-scale communities in which families and lineages met most of their own needs to large kingdoms with hereditary rulers, elaborate bureaucracies, and extensive trading networks.

The image of Africa as a collection of societies that were isolated, unchanging, and unaware of developments in other parts of the world is erroneous. African cultures emerged from their own experiences and traditions; adapted to changing situations; adopted new ideas, innovations, and technologies; and developed extensive relations with one another through trade, diplomacy, migration, and marriage. They created interregional networks to exchange goods such as salt, iron, and pots, and they traded with other continents. The trans-Saharan trade linked West Africa to the Mediterranean; the Indian Ocean trade tied East Africa to Arabia, Persia, and Asia; and the Red Sea served as a bridge connecting Ethiopia to the Mediterranean and the Indian Ocean.

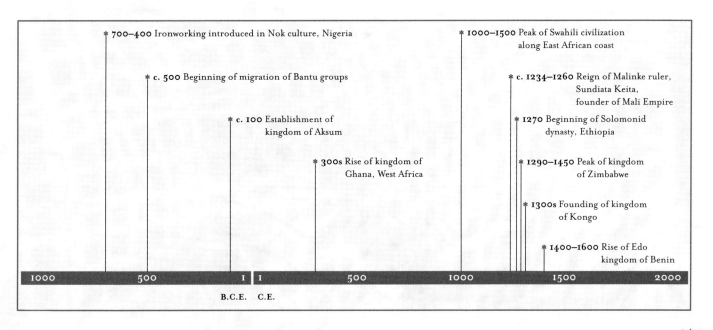

700–400 Ironworking introduced in Nok culture, Nigeria

c. 500 Beginning of migration of Bantu groups

c. 100 Establishment of kingdom of Aksum

300s Rise of kingdom of Ghana, West Africa

1000–1500 Peak of Swahili civilization along East African coast

c. 1234–1260 Reign of Malinke ruler, Sundiata Keita, founder of Mali Empire

1270 Beginning of Solomonid dynasty, Ethiopia

1290–1450 Peak of kingdom of Zimbabwe

1300s Founding of kingdom of Kongo

1400–1600 Rise of Edo kingdom of Benin

1000   500   I | I   500   1000   1500   2000

B.C.E.   C.E.

The African Environment

Ignorance of African geography and environment has contributed greatly to prevailing misconceptions about African culture and history. Many Americans, for instance, have thought of the continent as an immense "jungle." In reality, more than half of the area south of the Sahara consists of grassy plains, known as *savanna*, whereas "jungle," or tropical rain forests, takes up just 7 percent of the land surface.

Physical Environment

The most habitable areas have been the savannas, their grasslands and trees favoring both human settlement and long-distance trade and agriculture. The northern savanna, sometimes called the Sudan (not to be confused with the modern nation of Sudan), stretches across the continent just south of the central desert, the Sahara. Other patches of savanna are interspersed among the mountains and lakes of East Africa and another belt of grassland that runs east and west across southern Africa, north and east of the Kalahari Desert.

Between the northern and southern savannas, in the region of the equator, is dense rain forest. Although the rain forest is lush, its soils are poor because torrential rains cause soil erosion and intense heat leaches the soil of nutrients and burns off humus or organic matter that is essential for soil fertility. The rain forests also harbor insects that carry deadly diseases. Mosquitoes transmit malaria and yellow fever, and the tsetse fly is a carrier of sleeping sickness to which both humans and animals such as horses and cattle are susceptible.

Because of Africa's often harsh and fragile environments, Africans accumulated sophisticated knowledge of what food crops to grow in particular areas and how to manage their environments and sustain a living from marginal or poor soils. Permanent cultivation was a luxury that few African farmers were able to practice. A more prevalent approach in sparsely populated areas was shifting, or "slash and burn," cultivation. Farmers knew that they could stay on a piece of land for a few growing seasons before soils were exhausted. Thus every growing season they would clear land with iron hoes and machetes and fertilize it by burning natural vegetation such as brush and tree leaves for ash. Usually after two to three years, a family had to move on and start the cycle in another area. Shifting agriculture was especially necessary in the rain forests, where, as noted, heavy rainfall and high temperatures produced very poor soils.

Farmers also relied on other strategies, such as bush fallow and intercropping. Bush fallow means letting a field rest for a number of years to restore its fertility before cultivating it again. Intercropping in- volves growing plants that complement each other side by side. For instance, legumes such as peanuts and beans were introduced because they converted nitrogen from the air and spread it to other plants.

General Cultural Patterns

Although African societies are remarkably diverse, they often have common values, belief systems, and aesthetic styles that are reflected in their family and kinship relations and political, economic, religious, and cultural institutions.

Africans place great importance on family and kinship ties. The primary unit of social organization is the extended family, which includes not only parents and children but also a network of wives and relatives—grandparents, aunts, uncles, and cousins. Relations within families are based on descent patterns. Most African societies are patrilineal, with descent traced through the father to his sons and daughters who belong to their father's kin group. When a woman married, she became part of her husband's kin group and usually no longer shared in the economic resources of her father's group.

About 15 percent of African societies are matrilineal, in which descent is passed through the mother's side of the family through a mother's brother. In matrilineal societies, when a man married, he usually went to live at his wife's family homestead and had to work for her family for a number of years. In these societies women lived with their own kin and had at least some independent access to economic resources such as land. Many of the matrilineal societies are found in forest areas with poor soils. Because farming required large numbers of laborers, an advantage of matrilineal relationships is that they can bring together a wide network of families who can contribute laborers to agricultural production.

Families also played an important role in decisions about marriages. Marriage was not solely a private issue between a bride and a groom but was a uniting of two larger groups, such as families or clans. Strict rules stipulated whether a person could marry outside a clan or lineage. Marriage was typically accompanied by an exchange of *bridewealth*, the husband's payment of money, goods, services, or cattle to his new wife's family. Bridewealth gave a husband certain domestic rights—to establish a homestead with his wife, to use his bride's labor in his household and fields, and to attach their offspring to his kinship group. Bridewealth also cemented a social relationship between a husband and his wife's family. If a wife could not bear children or deserted her husband, her parents had to return the bridewealth. This gave the wife's family a vested interest in preserving the marriage.

Another characteristic of African societies is that they accepted *polygyny*, a man's marrying more than one wife. Although a minority of men actually took a second wife, polygyny was seen as a necessity because of high infant mortality, the need for more manpower in farming, and the desire to express status and wealth.

The family household was the foundation for building larger identities and communities—one's *lineage* contained people who could trace their descent to a common ancestor, and one's *clan* contained many lineages or people who shared kinship. Within a society, lineages and clans could be used to mobilize people for self-defense and work parties, to allocate rights to land, to raise bridewealth, and to perform religious rituals. African societies also contained groups of people who were not bound by kinship and who created larger social identities. These were secret societies that often guarded medicines, performed ritual activities, and organized defense and cohorts of people of roughly the same age who had gone through rites-of-passage ceremonies such as circumcision.

The lineage and clan also provided the basis for political units, ranging from the most basic to the largest kingdoms. Many African societies were formed without chiefs, rulers, or centralized political institutions and operated at the village level. These are known as "stateless" societies. Authority was usually vested in a group of elders or senior members of families and lineages who conferred to work out approaches to common concerns such as deciding when to plant and to harvest, whether to move or migrate, and how to resolve disputes within a community or handle conflicts with other communities. In these egalitarian societies, reaching a consensus was an essential part of the decision-making process.

Other African societies developed slowly into chiefdoms and kingdoms that incorporated larger populations, featured elaborate hierarchies and extensive bureaucracies, and engaged in long-distance trade with other states. Even though kingdoms could be made up of many lineages or clans, they were usually dominated by one. These kingdoms were governed by hereditary rulers who wielded religious as well as political power. However, their tendencies to abuse their power were often held in check by councils and courts.

Women played influential roles in decision making. Some states had women rulers, and the king's mother (the queen mother), his wife (the queen), and his sisters were often powers behind the throne. On occasion women served as officials and advisers, religious leaders, and even soldiers. Women were prominent in religious rituals, serving as priestesses, healers, and diviners.

Work within communities was carried out by families and kinship groups. However, specific tasks were usually determined by sex and age. Women were primarily responsible for maintaining the homestead, cultivating the fields, preparing the food, and running local markets, while men took the lead in building houses, constructing paths and roads, clearing fields, raising livestock, hunting, and conducting long-distance trade. Work parties consisting of agemates of one or both sexes could be mobilized for communal tasks such as harvesting and planting, clearing fields, weeding, threshing, and housebuilding. Although men usually controlled technological advances such as ironworking and blacksmithing, there were exceptions to this practice. Among the Pare of eastern Africa, women were given the responsibility for gathering and smelting iron.

An important aspect of the African heritage was its value system, which shaped all aspects of life. Paramount were a profound awareness of human interdependence and an appreciation for communal harmony and unity within the family and the larger society. The African conception of land ownership, for instance, stressed that individuals had the right to cultivate untilled land but that they could not sell or rent the land to others or pass it on to their children. Land was held in trust by the larger community.

Religion permeated the everyday experiences of Africans and was an integral part of their social and political life. Specific religious beliefs and institutions varied from society to society, but several tenets were shared. Most African societies had a belief in a high god or creator that was usually remote and rarely concerned with the everyday affairs of humans. Therefore, Africans were more directly engaged with other divinities, such as nature and ancestral spirits that maintained an active interest in the affairs of the living and could intercede for humans with the high god. Political leaders were often imbued with ritual authority to approach the ancestors, who provided legitimacy to the moral order and reinforced political authority.

As individuals and as communities, Africans were concerned with identifying the causes of illness and disasters such as drought, crop failures, and plagues. One way of explaining misfortune was that the high god or the ancestors were unhappy with the actions of humans. Thus people sought the goodwill of the ancestors with prayers and ritual offerings and sacrifices at shrines. Africans also attributed misfortune to witches, who wielded evil powers and inflicted suffering on people. Those afflicted by witchcraft appealed to specialists such as diviners to diagnose the sources of evil and provide remedies for them.

Some African religious systems were extremely complex, with elaborate priesthoods and cults. The Yoruba traditionally had four levels of spiritual beings. At the top was the supreme being, Oludumare, who was served by his subordinate gods on the second level. The secondary gods had their own priests, who presided over temples and shrines. Then came the ancestors, known as Shango. Finally, there were

Many African religious ceremonies featured masked male dancers. In this photo of the Dogon people of West Africa, the masked dancers performing at a funeral ceremony are driving the spirit of the dead person from its home. The dancers also act out the Dogon myth explaining how death entered the world through the disobedience of young men.

the nature spirits found in the earth, mountains, rivers, and trees.

Like the ancient Mayas in Central America, Africans were remarkably skilled and sensitive artists, particularly in sculpture, which they used to record historical events. They carved expertly in wood, ivory, and soapstone. They also fashioned statues from baked clay and cast them in bronze. An innovative technique was the *cire perdue* (lost wax) technique, which involved making a cast of the object in wax, covering it with clay, and then melting the wax and replacing it with molten bronze. The famous bronze statuary of Benin, which drew on a long tradition of metalworking in the region of present-day Nigeria, compares in craftsmanship and beauty with the best work of the European Renaissance. Other specific artistic traditions, producing naturalism and symbolism in a rich tapestry of styles, flourished in many African cultures.

The Peopling of Africa

Africa was the cradle of humankind. Dating back to 4 million years ago, the fossil remains of the earliest hominid forms, such as *Australopithecus afarensis* and *Homo habilis,* have been found exclusively in the grasslands and woodlands of eastern and southern

Africa (see Chapter 1). Likewise, the earliest skeletal remains of *Homo erectus* have been found near Lake Turkana in East Africa. The tools it used bear a remarkable similarity to the tool kit of *H. erectus* in Asia and Europe. This evidence, as well as the trail of fossil evidence, leads to the conclusion that *H. erectus* spread to southern, western, and northern Africa and then migrated out of Africa through the Arabian peninsula to the Near East, Europe, and Asia.

Early African Civilizations

10,000–6000 B.C.E.	Aquatic Age
c. 4000 B.C.E.	Domestication of food crops in central Sudan
c. 3100 B.C.E.	Beginning of unification of Upper and Lower Egypt
c. 3000 B.C.E.	Sahara region begins changing into desert
c. 730 B.C.E.	Kushite conquest of Egypt
c. 700 B.C.E.	Spread of knowledge of iron-working from Egypt to Kush

The earliest fossil evidence for *Homo sapiens* also comes from eastern and southern Africa. However, this evidence has not resolved the debate whether *H. sapiens* originated on the African continent and spread to other continents or whether it developed independently elsewhere. However, recent testing involving mitochondrial DNA supports the argument for an African origin for *H. sapiens*. Because mitochondrial DNA is passed on only through a mother to her offspring, it is not affected by gene mixing from both parents. Thus by comparing mitochondrial DNA samples from individuals around the world and calculating the rate of mutations, geneticists have traced human ancestors back to a hypothetical "Eve," a woman they believe lived in East Africa some 200,000 years ago.

During the late Stone Age, human communities in Africa were small bands of foragers who based their existence on hunting wild animals and gathering wild plants. Their technology was relatively simple but effective. Small bands of hunters, armed with bows and arrows with stone barbs treated with poisons, tracked down and killed the small and large game that roamed the plains of Africa. While hunting was conducted by men, gathering was mainly carried out by women. With a tool kit of digging sticks, gourds, and carrying bags, they "collected a variety of wild fruits, nuts, and melons, and dug up edible roots and tubers from the ground."[1] For many small groups, hunting and gathering satisfied all their dietary requirements and remained a preferred way of life long after the invention of agriculture.

Foraging groups added more protein to their diets by fishing in rivers and lakes and gathering shellfish. This was done by groups along the Nile River 15,000 to 20,000 years ago. From 10,000 B.C.E. to 6000 B.C.E, the northern half of Africa went through a wet phase known as the Aquatic Age. The region that is now the Sahara was actually a savanna of grassland and woodland, with an abundance of rivers and lakes. Lake Chad, for instance, formed part of a large inland sea. By fashioning bone harpoons and fishnets, people lived off the rich aquatic life. Around 3000 B.C.E. an extended dry phase set in and the vast barren area that we know now as the Sahara began to form. This dry period was likely a major stimulus for the invention of agriculture in West Africa as communities began experimenting with crop agriculture to supplement their diets. They began growing barley, wheat, and flax with simple tools such as digging sticks and wooden hoes.

In the past it was widely assumed that sub-Saharan African communities acquired agriculture by diffusion from Nile civilizations, but more recent scientific investigations have shown that plant domestication began independently in four regions: the Ethiopian highlands, the central Sudan, the West African savanna, and the West African forests. In all cases African farmers adapted crops suited to particular environments that were tested over long periods of

Before the Sahara became a desert, the region was home to pastoralists who herded cattle, sheep, and goats. On a plateau at Tassili n-Ajjer in the central Sahara, these pastoralists left an impressive array of wall paintings depicting their lifestyles and the wild animals that roamed the region. In this painting from the Tassili frescoes, women ride oxen as their community migrates to a new settlement.

time. For instance, around 3000 B.C.E. in the grasslands of the Ethiopian highlands, farmers began cultivating teff (a tiny grain), finger millet, *noog* (an oil plant), sesame, and mustard. In the forests they planted *ensete* (a bananalike plant) and coffee. Around 1000 B.C.E. wheat and barley were imported from across the Red Sea. In the central Sudan agricultural communities producing sorghum, millet, rice, cowpeas, and groundnuts began appearing as far back as 4000 B.C.E. In the West African forests, oil palms, cowpeas, and root crops such as yams were produced.

Africans also began to use domesticated animals about the same time as they adopted agriculture. The earliest evidence of livestock is from the western Egyptian desert about 8000 B.C.E. Cattle, sheep, goats, and pigs were introduced from western Asia to

Egypt and North Africa and then spread much later to western, eastern, and southern Africa. Because these animals were vulnerable to diseases carried by the tsetse fly in the rain forests, they thrived primarily in the savannas and woodland areas with less rainfall.

The other major breakthrough for sub-Saharan African cultures was the introduction of ironworking. Although bronze and copper toolmaking had developed in western Asia, the technology had not spread to sub-Saharan Africa. This was not the case with iron technology, which reached sub-Saharan Africa by two routes. The first was from Egypt to Nubia in the seventh century B.C.E. and then southward to other parts of Africa. Iron technology also appeared in West Africa about the same time, apparently brought south across the Sahara by Berbers, in contact with Phoenician or Carthaginian traders.

Two of the earliest centers of iron smelting were at Meroë, in the Nubian kingdom of Kush, and Nok, situated on the Jos plateau in central Nigeria. Located on the Nile River in a region rich in iron ore deposits, Meroë became well known in the fourth century B.C.E. for iron smelting and making iron tools and weapons that were key to the kingdom's success. Huge iron slag heaps still exist around the ruins of Meroë.

Archaeologists have dated ironworking sites at Nok from 700 to 400 B.C.E. Although some contend that ironworking was an independent invention at Nok, other ironmaking sites of about the same time period have recently been identified in Mauritania, southern Mali, and central Nigeria. Nevertheless, it is clear that Nok had one of the earliest ironworking sites. The Nok workers' preheating techniques and their ability to produce steel with a high carbon content were equal to those of Egypt and Rome. The Nok population included ironsmiths, craftspeople, and artists, who produced terra-cotta sculptures of remarkable realism that were strikingly similar to later art forms among the Yoruba kingdoms of Ife and Benin.

Iron production in most African societies usually took place in the dry months when rain and floods were not disruptive and agriculture was less intensive. Because their products were highly valued and could be exchanged for animals and food, ironworking specialists were persons of wealth and status. Magical, ritual, and spiritual powers were often attributed to them. In some societies the ironworking craft assumed such ritualistic significance that the furnaces were hidden in secluded places. African furnaces in the 900s were capable of generating higher temperatures than those in Europe before the 1700s.

Ironworking allowed African societies to make the leap from stone to metal tools. Iron tools such as hoes, knives, sickles, spear heads, and axes made a

significant difference in clearing forests and thick vegetation for agriculture, in hunting, and in waging war. When combined with the introduction of agriculture and pastoralism, the knowledge of ironworking contributed to population growth, craft specializations, trade between communities, and more complex political and economic systems. Ironworking also spurred migrations such as the spread of Bantu groups throughout eastern, central, and southern Africa.

Bantu Dispersion

One of the striking features of many African societies from central to eastern to southern Africa is that their languages (called Niger-Congo) and cultures have many similarities. How these societies—known as Bantu ("people")—came to spread over this vast area is a question that has long vexed scholars.[2]

Authorities generally agree that the original homeland for Bantu speakers was an area in present-day Cameroon near the Nigerian border. However, they are still not sure what prompted Bantu groups to start migrating from their homeland. One explanation relates to environmental changes—as the Sahara region dried up, small groups were forced to move

This stylized terra-cotta head, dating from about 500 B.C.E., is an outstanding example of a sculpture from the Nok culture of central Nigeria. The head, which has a human face, was probably used for religious purposes.

southward in search of new areas to farm and fish. Another explanation is that the acquisition of iron-working gave Bantu groups access to iron tools that they could use in clearing the thicker vegetation of the forest regions.

Using archaeological and linguistic data, historians have had some success in reconstructing the complex movements of Bantu groups. Around 500 B.C.E, bands of Bantu began slowly moving out of their original homeland. These Bantu groups had common lifestyles—they lived in scattered homesteads and villages and farmed root crops, foraged for food, and fished. One stream moved south into the equatorial rain forests of west central Africa and settled in present-day Angola and Namibia. Their agriculture relied heavily on root crops and cultivating palm trees. The other stream moved east and eventually settled in the area east of Lake Victoria in East Africa. There they came into contact with Cushitic-speaking peoples that had migrated from the Ethiopian highlands. The Bantu adopted their mixed farming practices—growing cereal crops such as millet and sorghum and herding cattle, sheep, and goats.

From that point, wherever Bantu groups migrated, they searched for areas that had enough summer rainfall to support cereal cultivation and their animal herds. As soils were not rich and could not support farmers for long periods, Bantu groups practiced slash-and-burn agriculture. The need to move on after two or three years in an area may explain why some Bantu groups, after spreading throughout East Africa, migrated southward, along tributaries of the Congo River, through the equatorial rain forest to present-day southern Congo and Zambia, where they settled in the savannas and woodland areas. Others migrated south, crossing the Zambezi and Limpopo Rivers by the fourth century of the Common Era.

As Bantu communities moved into eastern and southern Africa, they also acquired knowledge of ironworking and adopted new food crops such as the banana and the Asian yam, brought to Africa by sailors from Malaysia and Polynesia who settled on the island of Madagascar several thousand years ago. The banana in particular became a staple food and a source of mash for beer in the moist regions of Africa.

Throughout their migrations, Bantu societies came into contact with hunting and gathering groups. Although some scholars have portrayed the Bantu as a superior culture that overwhelmed hunting and gathering groups, recent scholarship has shown that the relationship was complex and not one-sided. At the same time that Bantu were practicing agriculture and pastoralism, they relied on foraging for subsistence and turned to hunting and gathering bands for assistance and knowledge of

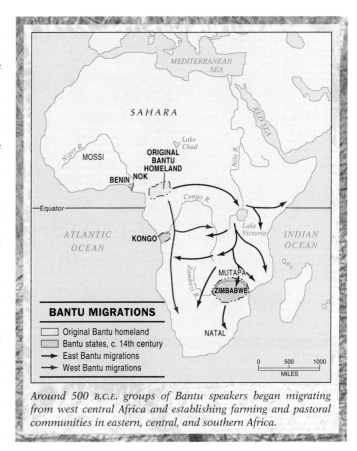

BANTU MIGRATIONS
☐ Original Bantu homeland
▨ Bantu states, c. 14th century
➝ East Bantu migrations
➝ West Bantu migrations

Around 500 B.C.E. groups of Bantu speakers began migrating from west central Africa and establishing farming and pastoral communities in eastern, central, and southern Africa.

local conditions. In addition, hunters and gatherers married into Bantu groups or attached themselves to Bantu groups for periods of time.

Ethiopia and Northeastern Africa

Situated along and inland from Africa's Red Sea coast, Ethiopia has been one of Africa's most enduring and richest civilizations. Indeed, the region between the Nile River and the Red Sea had been recognized as a major source of trade goods several thousand years before the kingdom of Ethiopia came into existence. To the Egyptians the area was known as the Land of Punt, and from the Fifth Dynasty (c. 2494–2345 B.C.E.) on, Egypt's rulers regularly sent expeditions to trade for frankincense, myrrh, aromatic herbs, ebony, ivory, gold, and wild animals. The Egyptian queen Hatshepsut's funerary temple recorded a major expedition that she sent to Punt around 1470 B.C.E. However, historians have not been able to pinpoint Punt's location precisely or reconstruct the inner workings of its political system.

Around 800 B.C.E. traders from Saba', a kingdom on the southwestern Arabian peninsula, crossed the Red Sea, first founding trading settlements on the Eritrean coast and later a kingdom, Da'amat. The Sabaeans tapped into the ivory trade in the interior

Aksum and Ethiopia

c. 800 B.C.E.   Sabaean traders establish trading settlements on the Eritrean coast

320–350 C.E.   Reign of Ezana, king of Aksum

c. 350   Aksum conquers Kush

700–800   Aksum's control of Red Sea trade ended by Persian and Muslim forces

c. 1185–1225   Reign of Lalibela, emperor of the Ethiopian Zagwe dynasty; beginning of construction of rock churches

c. 1314–1344   Reign of Amde-Siyon, emperor of Ethiopia

1434–1468   Reign of Zara Yakob, emperor of Ethiopia

highlands, but because they were also proficient at farming in arid environments, they interacted well with farming communities of the coastal interior. The Sabaean language was similar to the Semitic languages spoken in the area, and a language called Ge'ez evolved that became the basis for oral and written communication of the elites.

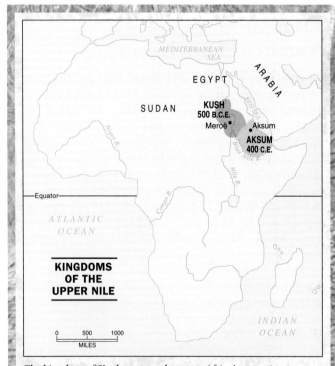

The kingdom of Kush was northeastern Africa's preeminent power until the rise of Aksum in the third and fourth centuries C.E.

By the start of the Common Era, a new state, Aksum, emerged to dominate the Red Sea trade. Taking advantage of its location between the Mediterranean and the Indian Ocean, Aksum developed extensive trading ties with Ptolemaic Egypt and the Roman Empire as well as Asia as far as Sri Lanka and India. Aksum also controlled trade with its interior, exporting ivory and exotic items such as tortoise shells and rhinoceros horns and even slaves in exchange for cloth, glassware, and wine. Aksum's capital, also called Aksum, was a major entrepot for the trade with the interior, while its bustling seaport, Adulis, prospered as the middleman for trade between the Mediterranean and the Indian Ocean. Monsoon winds dictated the rhythm of Indian Ocean trade. After July, when the summer monsoon winds were favorable, Adulis's traders set forth on their journeys. They returned in October when the prevailing winds reversed direction.

By the third and fourth centuries C.E., Aksum was at its zenith as a trading power, conquering its rival, Meroë, on the Nile, and replacing Rome as the dominant trading power on the Red Sea. Aksum minted its own coins with Greek inscriptions, something that only a handful of other states, such as Persia and Rome, were doing.

Aksum's best-known ruler was Ezana (320–350), who converted to Christianity toward the end of his reign, about the same time as the Roman emperor Constantine the Great. Some historians contend that Ezana conveniently converted to strengthen trading relations with the Greek-speaking world. Two Syrian brothers, Frumentius and Aedisius, have been credited with winning over Ezana to the Christian faith. Shipwrecked on the Red Sea coast, the brothers were brought to Aksum's royal court as slaves when Ezana was a child. Frumentius became an influential figure in the royal court, serving as main adviser to Ezana's mother, the queen regent. Following Ezana's conversion, Frumentius was chosen Aksum's first bishop, and Christianity was made the official state religion. Subsequently, the head of the Ethiopian church (abuna) was traditionally chosen by Coptic church leaders in Egypt, even after Muslims gained control over Egypt.

Although Aksum's court language remained Greek, Ge'ez assumed a new prominence as the language of the Ethiopian church. The Old and New Testaments were translated into Ge'ez, which, much like Latin in the Catholic Church, became the primary language of literature and the liturgy. Several centuries after Ezana's conversion, a group of Syrian monks called the Nine Saints played a major role in spreading Christianity among rural people. The Nine Saints were known for their belief in the Monophysite doctrine, which held that Christ's human and divine qualities were inseparable.

The key to Aksum's continued prosperity was maintaining control over Red Sea trade. In the early sixth century Aksum invaded Yemen to protect its trading interests as well as a Christian community persecuted by Jews. However, the Aksumites' influence in the Arabian peninsula ended later in the century when a Persian expeditionary force ousted them. Then, in the eighth century, Islamic expansion totally removed Aksum as a trading force in the Red Sea. Aksum's rulers were forced to migrate to the central highlands of the interior, where their rule continued to be plagued by conflict and warfare. There they mixed with a Cushitic-speaking people, the Agaw, who were assimilated into Aksum's political elite and also converted to Christianity.

This new nobility formed the core of the new Zagwe dynasty that took over in the mid-twelfth century. The Zagwes stressed their continuity with the Aksumite political order by claiming that they were descendants of Moses and encouraging the faithful to make pilgrimages to Jerusalem and Palestine. In this regard, the most enduring cultural expressions of the Zagwe dynasty were its churches, the most famous of which are the 11 awe-inspiring rock-hewn cathedrals of Roha, commissioned by the legendary Emperor Lalibela (c. 1185–1225). These impressive architectural feats, with ornate decorations and intricate workmanship, drew on Byzantine, Greek, and Roman motifs.

Lalibela's reign was the high point of Zagwe rule. His successors were unable to maintain the kingdom, and a new dynasty, the Solomonids, assumed power in 1270. Like the Zagwes, the Solomonid emperors (each known as *negus*, or "king of kings") legitimized their rule by claiming a direct tie to the Aksumite past. In their royal chronicle, the *Kebre Negast* ("Glory of the Kings"), they gave an epic account of their dynasty's direct descent from the Old Testament's King Solomon. The tale related how Makeda, the queen of Sheba (Saba') had visited Solomon to learn his techniques of rule. Instead, Solomon had seduced Makeda, who bore him a son, Menelik. When Menelik later visited his father's court, he tricked Solomon and spirited the Ark of the Covenant out of Israel to Ethiopia. This story was interpreted as a sign of the covenant God was establishing with Ethiopia. Thus to the kings of the Solomonid dynasty it was an article of faith that they were directly descended from Solomon.

To avoid the same fate as the Zagwes, the Solomonid rulers set strict rules to ensure orderly successions. To insulate royal princes from palace infighting and forming alliances with nobles in the countryside, the first Solomonid emperor, Yikunno-Amlak, took the bold step of placing the princes in a remote retreat, Mount Geshen (the "mountain of the kings"). The princes lived a comfortable but monastic existence, totally isolated from the outside world. Many of them followed an ascetic life, absorbed in religious issues and gaining reputations as accomplished writers of Ge'ez poetry and composers of sacred music. When an emperor died without a designated heir, the princes provided a pool of candidates for the throne.

The first Solomonid rulers concentrated on consolidating their rule over the central highlands of Ethiopia

Ethiopia's Emperor Lalibela oversaw the construction of 11 churches carved out of red volcanic rock at Roha. Shaped in the form of a Greek cross, the Church of St. George was an impressive architectural feat. Workers chipped away at the stone until they reached 40 feet down and then molded the church and hollowed out its interior.

A characteristic art form of Ethiopia is wall murals. In this painting the bishop of Aksum confers a blessing on the emperor of Ethiopia at the Cathedral of St. Mary of Zion. When Zara Yakob became emperor in 1434, he chose to be crowned in Aksum because he wanted to link the monarchy with the historical prestige of that kingdom.

and refrained from carrying out aggressive wars of expansion. These goals changed dramatically during the reign of Emperor Amde-Siyon (c. 1314–1344), who conquered territories to the west and toward the coast and who led his armies against Muslim principalities to the south and east. Amde-Siyon's campaigns against the Muslims were aimed not only at securing control of trade routes but also at putting pressure on the Muslim rulers of Egypt to allow the Coptic church to send a new bishop to Ethiopia. Amde-Siyon was so successful in vanquishing his opponents that an Arab historian reported, "It is said that he has ninety-nine kings under him, and that he makes up the hundred."[3] The powers of the Ethiopian monarchy were at their greatest during the reign of Zara Yakob (1434–1468), who resurrected the tradition of kings' being crowned at the ancient capital of Aksum. He fended off Muslim rivals, stamped out doctrines threatening Christianity, strengthened the Ethiopian church, and reorganized the bureaucracy. He also initiated a tentative alliance with the pope against the Muslims.

Within his immediate environs Zara Yakob ruled as an absolute monarch, surrounded by hundreds of courtiers and servants. To consolidate his rule, he dismissed provincial governors and replaced them with his own daughters and other female members of his family. When he held audiences at his court, he was positioned behind a curtain and communicated through a royal spokesman. When he traveled about his kingdom, his subjects had to avert their eyes on the penalty of death.

Because of the conquests of emperors such as Amde-Siyon and Zara Yakob, Ethiopia's rulers had to govern a diverse kingdom of many ethnic, linguistic, and religious backgrounds. They achieved this goal through the feudal relationships they established with their nobles and by promoting the expansion of the Ethiopian church. Until Gondar was designated as the capital in the seventeenth century, Ethiopian emperors did not have a centralized bureaucracy or a fixed capital for more than a few decades at a time. Rather they created a mobile court of family members, high officials, soldiers, priests, and retainers that moved regularly around the kingdom. This mobile court allowed the emperor to show off his power as well as encourage trade with outlying regions and to collect tribute from all his subjects. Mobile courts encamped in areas for up to four months, but they put such a strain on local resources that they were not encouraged to return for many years.

The emperor had to be constantly on guard against potential revolts against his authority. Although he allowed local rulers to remain in power, he strategically placed military garrisons around the kingdom. Moreover, because all land was owned by the emperor, he had the power to grant *gults*, or fiefs, to nobles for their loyalty and to soldiers who distinguished themselves in his service. The emperor could dismiss nobles as easily as he could create them.

In return the landholders had to pay tribute to the emperor and to contribute soldiers to his army. The emperor also imposed taxes on imports and exports. The nobles lived off the taxes or tribute—such as grain, labor service, or cattle—they collected from peasant farmers. Tribute cattle were called "burning" because the cows were branded or "touched with fire" before they were handed over. Peasants were also expected to support any soldiers living in their area.

The Ethiopian church became an extension of the Solomonid rulers, who renewed it and actively promoted its expansion throughout the empire. Clerics, who had previously led ascetic lives more concerned with their personal salvation, were now expected to play active roles in spreading the Christian faith. Priests recruited from monasteries were commissioned to establish churches and evangelize in newly conquered territories. Emperors also granted the church extensive estates and sponsored monastic schools. The schools, mostly for boys, primarily attracted students from families of the priesthood and

Emperor Zara Yakob's Coronation and His Concern for the Church

This fifteenth-century ruler of Ethiopia pulled the central administration together after a long period of feudal decentralization. His several daughters assisted in the task by taking over provincial governments.

When our King Zara [Yakob] went into the district of Aksum to fulfil the law and to effect the coronation ceremony according to the rites followed by his ancestors, all the inhabitants, including the priests, came to meet him and welcomed him with great rejoicing; the chiefs and all the soldiers of Tigre were on horseback carrying shield and lance, and the women, in great numbers, gave themselves up, according to the ancient custom, to endless dancing. When he entered the gates of the town the King had on his right and left the governors of Tigre and Aksum who, according to custom, both waved olive branches. . . . After arriving within the walls of Aksum the King had gold brought to him which he scattered as far as the city gate on the carpets spread along his route. This amount of gold was more than a hundred ounces. . . .

On the twenty-first of the month of Ter [January 16] the day of the death of our Holy Virgin Mary, the coronation rite was carried out, the King being seated on a stone throne. This stone, together with its supports, is only used for the coronation. There is another stone on which the King is seated when he receives the blessing, and several others to the right and left on which are seated the twelve chief judges. There is also the throne of the metropolitan bishop.

While at Aksum the Emperor made a number of regulations for the church.

During his stay at Aksum our King regulated all the institutions of the church and ordered that prayers which had up to that time been neglected should be recited each day at canonical hours. For this purpose he convened a large number of monks and founded a convent, the headship of which he entrusted to an abbot with the title of Pontiff of Aksum,

who received an extensive grant of land called Nader. The King accomplished this work through devotion to the Virgin Mary and to perpetuate his own memory and that of his children and his children's children. He summoned some catechists and presented to the church a great number of ornaments and a golden ewer, revived all the old traditions, spread joy in these places, and returned thence satisfied.

Zara Yakob also founded churches and regulated religious affairs in other provinces.

Arriving in the land of Tsahay in Amhara, he went up a high and beautiful mountain, the site of which he found pleasing; at the top of this mountain and facing east he found a wall which had been raised by his father, King Dawit, with the intention of erecting a shrine. His father, however, had not had the time to complete the work, in the same way that the ancient King David, who planned to build a temple to the Lord, could not accomplish his task which was completed by his son Solomon. Our king Zara Yaqob fulfilled his father's intention by building a shrine to God on the west of the mountain. Everyone, rich and poor alike and even the chiefs, were ordered to carry the stones with the result that this edifice was speedily erected. They embellished this locality, which underwent a great transformation; two churches were built there, one called Makana Gol and the other Dabra Negwadgwad. The King attached to them a certain number of priests and canons to whom he gave grants of land. He also founded a convent and placed in it monks from Dabra Libanos, whom he endowed in a similar manner.

From Richard K. Pankhurst, ed., *The Ethiopian Royal Chronicles* (Oxford: Oxford University Press, 1967), pp. 34–36.

the royal elite. Although these policies may have revived the church, they also made the church intimately identified with imperial power and unable to develop deep roots among the common people.

This was a period of the blossoming of the arts in which priests played a leading role. They produced innumerable biblical translations, theological treatises, biographies of saints, historical chronicles, illuminated manuscripts, and mural paintings.

Zara Yakob's reign was a high point in the Ethiopian kingdom's history. His successors did not

have the skills to hold the kingdom together, and the Solomonid dynasty went into a decline. Provincial officials and nobles seized on the weakness of the emperor to refrain from paying taxes and build up their own power. The Oromo, a pastoral people, began challenging Ethiopian control of the highland areas, and Muslims stopped sending tribute. Muslim states also grew restive. Under the military leadership of Ahmad al-Ghazi Ahmad Gran, the state of Adal launched a holy war against the Christian kingdom in 1527 that continued until 1543 when Ahmad was killed in battle.

Empires of the Western Sudan

The savanna of the western Sudan has been characterized by the long-standing trans-Saharan trade between the western savanna and the Mediterranean coast. Large camel caravans made regular trips across the dangerous desert carrying North African salt in exchange for West African gold. To the Berbers who organized these caravans, the bend of the Niger River offered a secure watering and resting place. Here they found people who had conducted local trade for centuries before the caravans came, who knew the savanna well, and who could acquire gold from distant places. Their resulting control of the lucrative gold and salt trade brought great accumulations of wealth and was a key factor in the rise of major West African kingdoms.

Before the formation of these kingdoms, there was already a thriving interregional trade among the savanna communities. Archaeological evidence shows that in the ninth century B.C.E. some savanna communities began harnessing the floodwaters of the Niger River and started raising livestock and cultivating cereals. They formed settlements of 800 to 1000 people. That the villages they lived in were unwalled and in open areas is an indication that relations between communities were mostly peaceful and cooperative. However, between 600 and 300 B.C.E. the pattern changed as villages erected walls and retreated to more remote and defensible sites—an indication that they were responding to external threats, possibly from nomadic Berbers that roamed the Sahara and occasionally raided savanna societies.

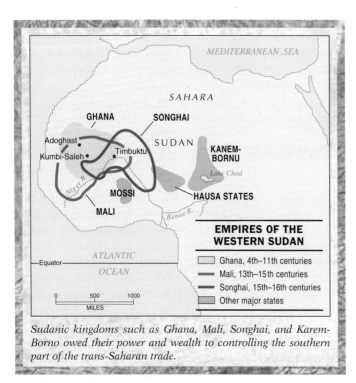

Sudanic kingdoms such as Ghana, Mali, Songhai, and Karem-Borno owed their power and wealth to controlling the southern part of the trans-Saharan trade.

West African Sudanic Kingdoms

c. 250 B.C.E.	Jenne-jeno on Niger River settled
c. 100–40 B.C.E.	Camel introduced to trans-Saharan trade
c. 900 C.E.	State of Kanem founded
1000–1200	Hausa city-states founded
1076	Almoravid attack on Ghana
c. 1200–1235	Reign of Sumaguru, Sosso king
1300–1400	Rise of kingdom of Oyo
1307–1337	Reign of Mansa Musa in Mali
1352	Visit of Berber geographer Ibn Battuta to Mali
1464–1492	Reign of Sunni Ali, Songhai emperor
1493–1528	Reign of Askia Muhammad, Songhai emperor
1591	Morocco invades Songhai

One of the earliest urban settlements, Jenne-jeno, was begun around 250 B.C.E. Situated on an inland delta of the Niger River, Jenne-jeno was ideally located because it was surrounded by water during the rainy season and was much safer for trade than other settlements. Over time, Jenne-jeno became an interregional trade center for farmers, herders, and fishermen that long predated any involvement in the trans-Saharan trade. Jenne-jeno exported food via the Niger to points to the east.

Although the Sahara was not easy to traverse, it was not impenetrable. As early as 1000 B.C.E. Carthaginians, Romans, and perhaps Greeks began establishing several routes across the Sahara for their horse- and ox-drawn chariots. One route stretched from Libya and Tunisia through the Fezzan, while the other connected Morocco to Mauritania. Trade declined with the collapse of the Roman Empire in the fourth century C.E. but was revived several centuries later, first by the Byzantine Empire and then by Arabs.

The camel, introduced from the Middle East in the first century B.C.E., became the main conveyor of goods in the trans-Saharan trade. As pack animals camels had several advantages over horses and oxen. Carrying loads of 250 to 300 pounds, camels could travel extended distances with little water. However, they were slow and inefficient. Averaging about 20 to 30 miles a day, they took about two months to cross the Sahara. Moreover, attendants had to load and unload their cargo once or twice each day, and much of the provisions were used to feed attendants. Whatever the camel's liabilities, its introduction boosted the volume of trade. The camel remained an essential part of the trans-Saharan trade until the twentieth century, when it was replaced by the automobile.

Ghana

The earliest of the Sudanic kingdoms, first known as Aoukar or Wagadu, later took the name of its war chief, Ghana (not to be confused with the modern nation of the same name). It arose on the upper Niger during the fourth century C.E. as a loose federation of village-states, inhabited by Soninke farmers. This set a pattern for future kingdoms of the savanna as a lineage or a clan asserted its authority over other groups.

The introduction of ironworking allowed the Soninke farming communities to form larger political systems. In the face of drier conditions, they applied iron tools to improving agricultural production and devised iron swords and spears to conquer neighboring groups. They also used these weapons to fend off Saharan nomads who grazed their animals in the Sahel (the southern fringe of the Sahara) and occasionally raided Soninke communities.

By about 800 C.E. Ghana had established itself as a powerful kingdom able to exact tribute from vassal states in the region. Although agricultural production contributed to Ghana's wealth, it was the expanding trans-Saharan trade with Europe and the Mediterranean world that gave Ghana even more influence. From their strategic position on the upper Niger River, the Soninke were well positioned as middlemen to barter the salt produced from the Taghaza salt mines in the Sahara, the gold coming from Bambuk, and kola nuts and slaves captured from areas south of the savanna.

Ghana's king controlled the supply of gold within his kingdom and claimed every gold nugget coming into the country, leaving ordinary citizens the right to buy and sell only gold dust. The king was reputed "to own a gold nugget so large that he could tether a horse to it." In addition, taxes were levied on every load of goods entering and leaving the country.

Ghana's gold was actually mined in Bambuk, a region eight days' journey to the west of Ghana's capital, Kumbi-Saleh, from the beds of the Senegal and Faleme Rivers. Ghana's rulers did not have direct control over Bambuk, and the persons who worked the goldfields jealously guarded information about where and how they produced the gold. They devised a strategy for negotiating with Mande traders without actually coming into direct contact with them. Al Masudi, a noted Arab traveler, described this "silent trade" around 950:

> They have traced a boundary which no one who sets out to them ever crosses. When the merchants reach this boundary, they place their wares and cloth on the ground and then depart, and so the people of the Sudan come bearing gold which they leave beside the merchandise and then depart. The owners of the merchandise then return, and if they are satisfied with what they have found, they take it. If not, they go away again, and the people of the Sudan return and add to the price until the bargain is concluded.[4]

Traders avidly sought salt from the trans-Saharan trade because it was a crucial element in diets and a preservative for foods and skins. It was also a scarce commodity in savanna communities. A certain amount of salt could be extracted from vegetable matter or from soil, but not enough to satisfy the requirements of savanna communities. However, in the Sahara there were large salt deposits, the best known at Taghaza, in the middle of the Sahara, about a three-week journey from both Mediterranean and Sudanese trading centers. Salt was quarried in huge 200-pound slabs, loaded on camels, and transported to trading centers like Timbuktu, where they were distributed to other places.

Another item that featured in the trade was kola nuts, which were primarily grown in the forest areas to the south of the savanna. Used to quench thirst, kola nuts were consumed mainly in the drier savanna. They did not become a major staple of the trans-Saharan exchange.

Slaves were the final component of the trans-Saharan trade. Although slavery was an established practice in some, though not all, sub-Saharan African societies, it took many shapes and forms. A common practice was for a family to send a family member—usually a child or a young adult—to serve

Introduced from the Middle East in the first century B.C.E., the camel was the main transporter of goods in the trans-Saharan trade between North Africa and the West African savanna.

in another household to pay off a debt or some other obligation (such as compensation for a crime) or to raise food in times of famine. In those cases, slaves were integrated into a master's family. Servile status could be of limited duration, and the slave would be sent back home as soon as the debt was repaid.

With centralized kingdoms such as Ghana and, later, Mali, slaves were bought and sold in trading transactions and were called on to perform a variety of roles—as servants, farm laborers, porters, traders, and soldiers. Most household slaves were women and children; slave women were often selected as marriage partners or concubines because a man did not have to pay bridewealth for them. Their children had all the rights of free persons.

Slave warriors had a privileged status; they could serve in high capacities as military officers, administrators, and diplomats in a king's court. Slave soldiers were the mainstays of armies and were used in raids to kidnap and capture more slaves. Most slaves were kidnapped or captured in raids on weaker communities by the stronger savanna states, especially in the forest region to the south. Muslim law enjoined Muslims from enslaving other Muslims, but this was not always observed when raiding parties were sent out.

Although savanna kingdoms created their own internal trade in slaves, the trans-Saharan slave trade was fueled primarily by demands from North African Mediterranean states. Slaves were typically taken in caravans, where they were exchanged for salt and horses. In Senegambia in the mid-fifteenth century, 9 to 14 slaves could fetch one horse, while in Kanem-Bornu a horse would cost 15 to 20 slaves. In later centuries some slaves, especially those sold in Libya, were traded on to the eastern Mediterranean, the Italian peninsula, and other southern European areas. From the eighth century, when the trade was initiated, to the early twentieth century, an estimated 3.5 to 4 million slaves were taken across the Sahara.[5]

The 1200-mile journey across the desert was as perilous as the trans-Atlantic slave trade's infamous Middle Passage. Many slaves lost their lives to the harsh conditions. The majority of slaves were women who worked as domestic servants in royal households and courts or were designated as concubines. Male slaves were pressed into service in the salt mines and as caravan porters, agricultural labor, and soldiers. Because many slaves were manumitted or died of diseases and because so few children were born in captivity, there was a constant demand for more slaves to be sold on the market.

To reconstruct the histories of the Sudanic kingdoms, historians draw heavily on the accounts of Arab geographers, travelers, holy men, and scholars. One Arab chronicler, al-Bakri, described Ghana at its peak in 1067. He noted that the army was some 200,000 strong, with many contingents wearing chain mail. The king, who had not converted to Islam, was considered divine and able to intercede with the gods. He appointed all officials and served as supreme judge. His government was organized under ministers, with one responsible for his capital, Kumbi-Saleh. Princes of tributary states were held hostage at his court. When the king appeared in public, he was surrounded by highborn personal retainers holding gold swords, horses adorned with gold cloth blankets, and dogs wearing gold collars.

Ghana's capital, Kumbi-Saleh, was situated on the edge of a crop-growing area and had 15,000 to 20,000 residents. The capital was really two towns, 6 miles apart. One was a large Soninke village, in which the king and his retinue lived. Close to the village was a sacred grove where traditional religious cults were practiced. The other town was occupied by Muslim merchants. The merchants' town had 12 mosques, two-story stone houses, public squares, and a market. Besides the traders, the town was also home to religious and legal scholars. Ghana's king relied on literate Muslims as treasurer, interpreters, and counselors. However influential the Muslims were, Ghana's king had to make sure that his own religious leaders were regularly consulted and that he participated in shrine and other religious activities. The first king to convert to Islam did not do so until after the Almoravid invasion.

Following Ghana's conquest of Adoghast, a Sanhaja Berber trading center, Sanhaja Berbers had rallied around an Islamic revivalist movement called the Almoravid and attacked Ghana in 1076. Although it is still a subject of debate whether the Almoravid attack was a full-scale invasion or a series of raids, Ghana had to give up Adoghast and its dominance over trade. Ghana's dominance over the gold trade was further weakened when the Bure goldfield opened up on the Niger River.

Mali

In the early thirteenth century Ghana's rule was ended by an uprising led by Sumaguru (c. 1200–1235) of the Sosso, who were related to the Soninke. Oral traditions characterize Sumaguru as a tyrant who wielded magical powers over his people. Sumaguru was overthrown in 1235 by Sundiata of the Malinke Keita clan, who forged an alliance of Malinke clans and chiefdoms for that purpose. Lengthy wars followed in which Sundiata's army defeated and killed Sumaguru and routed the Sosso. Sundiata's army then embarked on campaigns of conquest throughout the territory that had been Ghana.

Eventually Sundiata's Malinke created a vast empire called Mali that stretched from the Atlantic south of the Senegal River to Gao on the middle

Niger River. Mali gained control of the desert gold trade and the gold-producing regions of Wangara and Bambuk. When gold replaced silver in 1252 as the main currency in Europe, West Africa became Europe's leading supplier of gold. Several tons of gold were produced annually. Two-thirds of it was exported, while the rest was kept for conspicuous display by Mali's ruling elites.

The kingdom of Mali was at the height of its power and prosperity during the reign of Sundiata's nephew, Mansa (king) Musa (1307–1337). Musa was perhaps the most widely known sub-Saharan African ruler throughout western Asia and Europe. He was a great soldier who consolidated his kingdom's control over a vast domain. Malian and Arab merchants carried on trade with the Mediterranean coast, particularly with Algeria, Tunisia, Egypt, and the Middle East.

Mansa Musa ruled over a state more efficiently organized than the relatively crude European kingdoms of the time. On the north and northeast were loosely held tributary kingdoms of diverse populations, including some Berbers. To the south were more closely controlled tributary states, under resident governors appointed by the king. Elsewhere, particularly in the cities, such as Timbuktu, provincial administrators governed directly in the king's name and at his pleasure. Mali's central government included ministries for finance, justice, agriculture, and foreign relations.

A devout Muslim, Musa lavishly displayed his wealth and power on a pilgrimage he took to Mecca in 1324–1325. His retinue included thousands of porters and servants and a hundred camels bearing loads of gold. In Egypt he spent so lavishly and gave away so much gold that its value in that country plummeted and did not recover for a generation:

This man spread upon Cairo the flood of his generosity. . . . So much gold was current in Cairo that it ruined the value of money. Let me add that gold in Egypt had enjoyed a high rate of exchange up to the moment of their arrival. But from that day onward, its value dwindled. That is how it has been for twelve years from that time, because of the great amounts of gold they brought to Egypt and spent there.[6]

When he returned to his kingdom, Musa brought along an architect who designed mosques in Gao and Timbuktu as well as an audience chamber for Musa's palace. Musa sent students to study at Islamic schools in Morocco. They returned to found Qur'anic schools, the best known of which was at Timbuktu.

Mansa Musa's pilgrimage also caught the attention of Muslim scholars. Among them was the Berber geographer and traveler Ibn Battuta, who visited Mali in 1352 during the reign of Musa's brother,

Mansa Sulayman (1336–1358). Battuta's account is one of the key sources for understanding the kingdom of Mali. He was favorably impressed by Mali's architecture, literature, and institutions of learning but was most laudatory about its law and justice, which guaranteed that no person "need fear brigands, thieves, or ravishers" anywhere in the vast domain. Battuta praised the king's devotion to Islam but was disappointed that so many subjects of Mali were not Muslims. He noted also that the unveiled women were attractive but lacking in humility. He was astounded that they might take lovers without arousing their husbands' jealousy and might discuss learned subjects with men. Battuta was describing the trading center of Walata. He might have been equally impressed with other Malian trading cities, including Adoghast, Kumbi-Saleh, Gao, and Timbuktu.

As Mali's empire grew, Islam became an important unifying element among the political and commercial elite. Key agents for the spread of Islam were Mande traders known as Dyula or Wangara, who settled in towns and villages along the main trade routes that connected every section of western Africa. Although they were largely responsible for the trade in such items as gold and kola nuts, they were Muslim teachers as well. Wherever they went, they became the lifeblood of small Muslim communities, establishing Qur'anic schools and arranging for the faithful to make pilgrimages to Mecca. Although at this time Muslims were not actively converting people in the countryside, they did so in the region known as Senegambia. Despite the devoutness of kings like Musa and the presence of Muslim traders in many areas, Islam was mainly a religion of court and commerce. Most people in the countryside were faithful to their traditional religious beliefs. Even kings and chiefs who were Muslims had to pay homage to traditional religious rituals.

After Mansa Musa's death, his successors found the large empire increasingly difficult to govern. They were plagued by dynastic disputes, raids by desert nomads such as the Tuaregs and Sanhaja, and the restlessness of tributary states. One of the rebellious states was Songhai, centered around the bend of the Niger. Songhai had been in existence for many centuries before it was absorbed into the Malian Empire in the thirteenth century, and its principal city, Gao, was an entrepot for trade with the Maghrib and Egypt. Before the end of the fifteenth century, Songhai had won its independence, and within another century it had conquered Mali.

Songhai

Songhai became the largest of the Sudanic empires, reaching its zenith during the reigns of Sunni Ali (1464–1492) and Askia Muhammad (1493–1528).

Discovery Through Maps
The Catalan Atlas

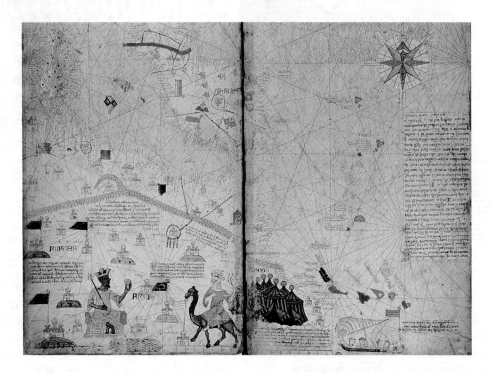

The Catalan Atlas of 1375 was probably drawn by Abraham Cresques (1325–1387), one of a group of Jewish cartographers residing on the Mediterranean island of Majorca. The Catalan Atlas was done for their patron, King Pedro III of Aragon, who presented it to Charles V of France in 1381.

The Catalan Atlas was a *portolano,* or sea chart; it featured radiating *rhumb lines* that noted compass directions. Because the atlas was designed for mariners, it was more concerned with coastlines and harbors and showed detailed knowledge of the Mediterranean and Black Seas. Land areas, by contrast, included very few features. The atlas's depiction of Asia drew heavily from Marco Polo's travels a half century before, and the description of the West African Sudan relied on contacts with a group of Moroccan Jews who had intimate knowledge of the trans-Saharan trade.

One of the 12 leaves of the atlas covered West Africa and featured three inscriptions. The first marked a gap in the Atlas Mountains through which traders passed on their way to the lands south of the Sahara. The inscription reads: "Through this place pass the merchants who travel to the land of the Negroes of Guinea." The second inscription is of a Tuareg trader mounted on a camel: "All this region is occupied by people who veil their mouths; one only sees their eyes. They live in tents and have caravans of camels. There are also beasts called Lemp from the skins of which they make fine shields." The cartographer clearly believed that the inhabitants of the Sudan

were Muslims, as evidenced by the domes that identified Muslim centers such as Timbuktu and Gao. Finally there is the depiction of Mali's king, Mansa Musa, who is holding a huge gold nugget as he awaits the arrival of the Tuareg trader. The inscription beside him reads: "This Negro lord is called Musa Mali, lord of all the Negroes of Guinea. So abundant is the gold which is found in his country that he is the richest and most noble king in all the land." A half century before the Catalan map was drawn, Mansa Musa had lavishly displayed his wealth on a pilgrimage to Mecca. In Egypt he spent lavishly and gave away great quantities of gold. The story of his pilgrimage had such an impact on the Arab and European worlds that they gave an exaggerated prominence to Mansa Musa as a ruler and his kingdom as a source of gold.

Some of the geographical details on the map are wrong. For instance, the mapmaker placed a large lake that does not exist in the middle of the Sudan below the figure of Mansa Musa. One river (the Senegal) is shown flowing out of this lake into the Atlantic, while another river (the Niger) flows eastward and eventually connects to the Nile.

The Catalan Atlas was designed to encourage Europeans to establish commercial ties with other parts of the world. To Europeans, who were seeking sources to finance their trade with India, China, and the Spice Islands, establishing direct contact with the goldfields of the West African Sudan was a tantalizing prospect that the Catalan Atlas encouraged.

Mali, as Described by Ibn Battuta

Ibn Battuta (1304–1368) was a famous Muslim traveler in the Near and Far East, as well as in Africa. He was the only medieval commentator who visited every land under Muslim rule.

The sultan of Mali is Mansa Sulayman, *mansa* meaning sultan, and Sulayman being his proper name. He is a miserly king, not a man from whom one might hope for a rich present. He held a banquet in commemoration of our master [the sultan of Morocco] to which the commanders, doctors, judge and preacher were invited, and I went along with them. Reading desks were brought in and the Koran was read through, then they prayed for our master and also for Mansa Sulayman. When the ceremony was over, I went forward and saluted Mansa Sulayman. The judge, the preacher, and Ibn al-Faquih told him who I was and he answered them in their tongue. They said to me "The sultan says to you 'Give thanks to God,'" so I said, "Praise be to God and thanks under all circumstances."

When I withdrew the sultan's hospitality gift was sent to me. Ibn al-Faquih came hurrying out of his house barefooted, and entered my room saying "Stand up; here comes the sultan's gift to you." So I stood up thinking that it consisted of robes of honour and money, and lo! it was three cakes of bread, and a piece of beef fried in native oil, and a calabash of sour curds. When I saw this I burst out laughing and thought it a most amazing thing that they could be so foolish. . . .

On certain days the sultan holds audiences in the palace yard, where there is a platform; this they call the *pempi*. It is carpeted with silk and has cushions placed on it. Over it is raised the umbrella, which is a sort of pavilion made of silk, surmounted by a bird in gold, about the size of a falcon. The sultan comes out of a door in a corner of the palace, carrying a bow in his hand and a quiver on his back. On his head he has a golden skull-cap bound with a golden band. His usual dress is a velvety red tunic, made of the European fabrics called *mutanfas*. The sultan is preceded by his musicians who carry gold and silver guimbris [two-stringed guitars], and behind him come three hundred armed slaves. He walks in a leisurely fashion . . . and even stops from time to time. On reaching the *pempi*, he stops and looks around the assembly, then ascends it in the sedate manner of a preacher ascending a mosque-pulpit. As he takes his seat the drums, trumpets, and bugles are sounded. Three slaves go out at a run to summon the sovereign's deputy and the military commanders, who enter and sit down. Two saddled and bridled horses are brought, along with two goats, which they hold to serve as a protection against the evil eye.

The negroes are of all people the most submissive to their king and most abject in their behavior before him. They swear by his name, saying *Mansa Sulayman ki* [the Emperor Sulayman has commanded]. If he summons any of them while he is holding an audience in his pavilion, the person summoned takes off his clothes and puts on worn garments, removes his turban and dons a dirty skull-cap, and enters with his garments and trousers raised knee-high. He goes forward in an attitude of humility and dejection, and knocks the ground hard with his elbows, and stands with bowed head and bent back listening to what he says. If anyone addresses the king and receives a reply from him, he uncovers his back and throws dust over his head and back, for all the world like a bather splashing himself with water. . . . Sometimes one of them stands up before him and recalls his deeds in the sultan's service, saying, "I did so-and-so on such a day" or "I killed so-and-so." Those who have knowledge of this confirm his words, which they do by plucking the cord of the bow and releasing it with a twang.

From Rhoda Hoff, ed., *Africa: Adventures in Eyewitness History* (New York: Walck, 1963), pp. 11–12.

Sunni Ali is remembered for his military exploits. His armies ventured out on constant campaigns of conquest, largely to the west along the Niger in what had been Mali's heartland, and captured the trading centers of Timbuktu, Walata, and Jenne-jeno.

After Sunni Ali died, his son ruled for a few months before Askia Muhammad, who came from Sunni Ali's slave officer corps, deposed him. Askia Muhammad set about consolidating and reorganizing the whole empire. Although his armies seized control of the Taghaza saltworks in the Sahara, their attempts to expand control over the Hausa states to the east were not successful.

Askia Muhammad created a centralized bureaucracy to manage finances, agriculture, and taxation, appointed administrators (usually relatives) to oversee newly created provinces, and built up a professional army featuring a cavalry of chain-mailed horsemen and an enlarged fleet of canoes, which constantly patrolled the Niger.

Unlike Sunni Ali, a former Muslim who expelled Muslim scholars from Timbuktu, Askia Muhammad

The Sankore mosque is the oldest surviving mosque in West Africa. Its pyramidlike minaret rises above the city of Timbuktu, the center of Islamic culture in the kingdom of Mali.

became their benefactor. During his reign Timbuktu, Jenne-jeno, and Walata achieved recognition as centers of Islamic scholarship. The Sankore mosque in Timbuktu became so renowned that a contemporary Arab traveler noted that more profits were being made from selling books and manuscripts there than from any other trade.

Like Mansa Musa, Askia Muhammad made a much publicized pilgrimage to Mecca. Traveling in 1497 with a large group of pilgrims, he brought thousands of gold pieces, which he freely distributed as alms to the poor and used to establish a hostel in Mecca for pilgrims from the western Sudan. Muhammad was not just expressing his faith; he was also drumming up trade with Songhai and shoring up his credentials with Muslims throughout his far-flung empire. On his return trip he won the recognition of the Egyptian caliph, an important distinction for any Muslim ruler.

Although a son deposed Askia Muhammad in 1528 and the kingdom was weakened by internal rivalries, Songhai remained a savanna power until 1591, when Morocco's King Ahmad al-Mansur launched an invasion of Songhai to prevent European rivals from gaining access to Sudanese gold. Taking offense at Songhai's refusal to pay a tax on salt from the Taghaza mines, al-Mansur sent a con-

tingent of 4000 mercenaries to secure control over the Sudanic goldfields. Many died in the harsh march across the Sahara, but the survivors, armed with arquebuses (guns mounted on a forked staff) and muskets, proved superior to the spears, swords, and bows and arrows of Songhai's soldiers. Although Morocco's impact was fleeting, Songhai was not able to recover, and the empire fragmented into many smaller kingdoms.

Kanem-Bornu and the Hausa States

In the central Sudan, which stretches from the bend of the Niger to Lake Chad, the Muslim kingdoms of Kanem and Bornu and the Hausa city-states were the dominant political actors. Kanem, which lay to the northeast of Lake Chad, had been formed around 900 C.E. when groups of nomadic pastoralists unified and established the Sayfuwa dynasty. In the Sayfuwas' as in other Sudanic states, power and wealth were based on control of the Saharan trade. The main trade route cut through the central Sahara to the Fezzan and on to Tripoli and Egypt. Because Kanem was too far away from any sources of gold, its rulers exported ivory, ostrich feathers, and especially war captives from societies to the south. In return Kanem received horses that its rulers used to create a cavalry that fueled further raiding. Under Mai (king) Dunama Dibalemi (1210–1248), Kanem boasted a cavalry of 40,000 horsemen.

In the fourteenth century one of Kanem's tributary states, Bornu, became a power in its own right, organizing its own trade and refusing to pay tribute to Kanem. During this period Kanem's rulers were challenged by another clan and by the deterioration of their pasturage. About 1400 the Sayfuwa dynasty decided to move its capital from Njimi to Bornu, where they gained access to new trading networks. At first they paid tribute to Bornu, but during the sixteenth century Kanem's leaders gradually took over and began carrying out raids over an extensive area. Their rule was based on tribute and their ability to tax peasants and levy customs on trade. They established good relations with the Ottoman rulers of Tripoli and imported firearms and contracted Turkish mercenaries to train Bornu's army.

To the west of Kanem and Bornu a group of Hausa city-states had been founded by nomadic cattle-keepers and farmers between 1000 and 1200. A common feature of Hausa villages was wooden stockades for protection. When villages grew into larger towns, they were also surrounded by large walls.

The Hausa city-states became important political and economic forces in the fifteenth century, at the same time as Islam became an important part of the trading and merchant class and the political elite. All of the Hausa states were centralized, with a king and council making decisions. They relied on cavalries to maintain their power and to raid for the slaves who labored on the large royal farms. To undermine lineages who were contesting for power, the rulers of Kano appointed slaves to important state offices, as treasurer, and as palace guards. Kano was noted for its textiles, dyed cloth, and leatherwork. Other significant Hausa city-states were Katsina, an important terminus for the trans-Saharan trade; Zazzau, a supplier of slaves to Hausa states and to North Africa; and Gobir, which traded with Songhai and Mali. However, some of the Hausa states still had to pay tribute to Songhai to the west and Kanem and Bornu to the east. The Hausa states usually coexisted peacefully, although Kano and Katsina carried on a periodic war for almost a century.

West African Forest Kingdoms

Between the savanna grasslands and the Atlantic was forest land. Some of the forests were extensions of the savannas and were suitable for extensive human settlements; closer to the coast were rain forests that required considerable energy to clear for settlement and cultivation. The rain forests were also the home of the tsetse fly, the carrier of sleeping sickness, which prevented the herding of highly susceptible livestock.

Most forest societies were built around villages and small chiefdoms sustained by agriculture and hunting. Root crops such as yams and later cassava were the main staples. Although they did not approach the same size as the savanna empires, some of these small chiefdoms merged and formed vibrant kingdoms.

In southwestern Nigeria a Yoruba city-state, Ife, emerged around the eleventh century C.E. According to oral traditions, the Yoruba god of the sky, Olorun, had sent a founding ancestor, Oduduwa, to establish Ife. Anyone who subsequently made a claim to the kingship of Ife or other Yoruba states had to trace descent from Oduduwa.

To the southeast of Ife was the Edo kingdom of Benin, which rose to prominence in the fifteenth and sixteenth centuries. Benin's prosperity was based not only on commerce with the Hausa states, trading food, ivory, and kola nuts for copper and possibly salt, but also on the strength of its fishing communities on the Niger delta.

Benin was ruled by hereditary kings, known as *obas,* who maintained large, well-trained armies. Advising the king was the *ozama,* a council composed of hereditary leaders who represented the main Edo lineages. They acted as a restraint on the *oba*'s powers until a thirteenth-century *oba* named Ewedo undermined the *ozama*'s powers by creating a court of men who were not members of the royal elite and who were given nonhereditary titles.

Benin remained a minor state until the rule of Oba Ewuare, who usurped the throne by killing his younger brother in 1440. He took over in a period of instability following the conquest of Benin by a neighboring state. Ewuare ensured that his line would succeed him by arranging that his heir be added to the *ozama* council.

Noted for his magical and healing powers, Ewuare was famous for rebuilding the capital, surrounded by a wall and featuring a broad avenue. He constructed an extensive royal palace that provided quarters for his family as well as for advisers, guilds of craftsmen, and servants. All of his freeborn subjects were expected to spend a period in the service of the palace. During Ewuare's three decades of rule, his armies expanded Benin's borders, conquering some 200 towns and extending Benin's influence far to the north and to coastal regions to the east and west. However, Ewuare and his successors did not tightly control their empire. Although *obas* placed loyal officials in subject territories, they gave local rulers autonomy as long as they paid tribute on a regular basis.

The Yoruba kingdoms of Benin and Ife were noted for their bronze, brass, and copper castings dating from the twelfth to the fifteenth centuries. This photo is of a brass casting of an Ife oni *(ruler) and was probably used in a funeral ceremony.*

Other states developed along the forest fringe of the northern savanna. Most of them profited from the long-distance Saharan trade through the Hausa states to the north, but all remained relatively isolated from Sudanic culture. In the Niger River region, the kingdom of Oyo emerged in the fourteenth century. The kings (alafins) of Oyo presided over a complex of palace councils, subkings, secret organizations, and lineage organizations at the village level. The alafins' wealth was built on their control of a slave labor force that they placed on royal farms. Oyo's rise as a regional power was due to its cavalry, assembled with horses traded from the savanna. Because horses did not survive in the tsetse-infested forests, the cavalry was most effective in the open savannas to the southwest of Oyo.

All of these forest states are noted for their artistic achievements. Yoruba artisans created sculptures in bronze, copper, brass, and terra-cotta. Most of these artworks were used in religious contexts, as funereal pieces placed in tombs to honor ancestors and in temples. These objects showed continuity with the artistic styles of earlier civilizations such as the Nok culture of central Nigeria.

Swahili City-States in East Africa

The East African or Swahili coast has also been part of a much wider economic network, the Indian Ocean trading system, for the past 2000 years. However, unlike the trans-Saharan trade, which opened up extensive trade to the south of the desert, trade along the East African coast, with some exceptions, did not have the same impact on the East African interior until the nineteenth century.

The historical and cultural development of the East African coast was intimately linked to the creation of a coastal culture that dates to 100 B.C.E. to 300 C.E. with the arrival of Bantu-speaking communities along the coast north of the Tana River. They took advantage of the fertile soils and forests along the coast to pasture their animals and to raise a great variety of food crops. They also found the creeks, rivers, lagoons, mangrove swamps, and seas ideal for fishing. Although Bantu farmers relied on subsistence agriculture and fishing, they began to expand their local and regional trading contacts and eventually linked up with merchants from the Arabian peninsula and the Persian Gulf.

The language that evolved on the coast and islands was Swahili, which was based on a Bantu language spoken on the Kenyan coast. Indeed, the word Swahili is taken from an Arabic word sawahil, meaning "coast." As the language evolved, it adopted Arabic loan words.

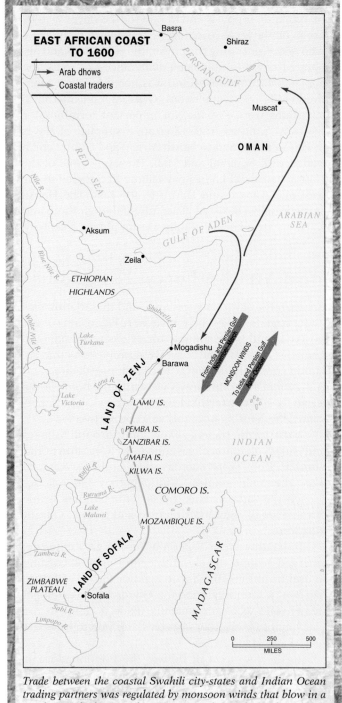

Trade between the coastal Swahili city-states and Indian Ocean trading partners was regulated by monsoon winds that blow in a southwesterly direction between November and March and in a northeasterly direction between April and October.

The earliest known record of the East African trade is *The Periplus of the Erythrean Sea*, a navigational guide written in Greek around the first century C.E. The *Periplus* chronicles shipping ports of the Red Sea and the Indian Ocean and identifies a string of market towns on the "Azanian" (East African) coast that actively participated in the Indian Ocean trade, especially with Arabia. The most important was a port named Rhapta. Market towns exported such goods as ivory, rhinoceros horn, copra, and tortoise shells in exchange for iron tools and weapons, cloth, glass, and grain.

The Indian Ocean trade continued between 300 and 1000, but it was given a great stimulus by the spread of Islam and the settling of Muslims from Arabia and the Persian Gulf along the East African coastline. Muslims intermixed with African communities and helped expand trading links with the Arab world. An Arab traveler described this trade on a visit to the "land of Zanj" (the East African coast) in 916:

> *The land of Zanj produces wild leopard skins. The people wear them as clothes, or export them to Muslim countries. They are the largest leopard skins and the most beautiful for making saddles. . . . They also export tortoise-shell for making combs, for which ivory is likewise used. . . . There are many wild elephants in this land but no tame ones. The Zanj do not use them for war or anything else, but only hunt and kill them for their ivory. It is from this country that come tusks weighing fifty pounds and more. They usually go to Oman, and from there are sent to China and India.*[7]

Arab boats or dhows made the Indian Ocean trade possible. They had the ability to cross the Indian Ocean three times as fast as a camel could cross the Sahara, and they could carry a thousand times as much. The dhows' lateen sails made it possible for sailors to take advantage of seasonal monsoon winds in the Indian Ocean that blow in a southwesterly direction between November and March and northeasterly between April and October. As with the Red Sea trade, the monsoon winds governed the trading calendar. It took about a month for a dhow to make

the 2000-mile journey from East Africa to the Persian Gulf, and the traders had to carry out their business according to the favorable winds or they could not transport their goods at all. Along the East African coast itself, however, it was possible to move between the islands at most times of the year.

Swahili civilization flourished between 1000 and 1500, when perhaps as many as 100 city-states, many of them on offshore islands, sprang up along the 1800-mile stretch from Mogadishu to Sofala on the Mozambique coast. Most were short-lived, but some—such as Malindi, Pemba, Pate, Mombasa, Mafia, and Kilwa—thrived for centuries.

Kilwa had the advantage of a good supply of fresh water and several natural harbors that could handle large ships. But it became the wealthiest of the city-states because of its near monopoly over gold exported from the Zimbabwe interior. Kilwa's merchants claimed a sphere of influence over the East African coast from Kilwa southward to Sofala on the Mozambique coast, where they established an outpost to facilitate the gold trade with Africans from the interior.

The Swahili city-states were never part of an empire, nor were they dominated by any one of the city-states. Indeed, they usually competed fiercely with one another. At times one city might exact tribute from its neighbors or a number of states might federate in time of war. However, commercial competition made such cooperation difficult to maintain and curtailed political expansion on the African mainland, where kingdoms like Great Zimbabwe played one coastal city against another.

Within the city-states, political institutions were controlled exclusively by a Muslim commercial elite.

The Arab dhow was the primary transporter of trade goods in the Indian Ocean. The dhow's lateen sails made it possible to navigate the monsoon winds that dictated the direction of trade at different times of the year.

Although they provided the capital, skills, and boats for their piece of the Indian Ocean trade, they always remained in the shadow of the Indian Ocean trading powers. Most of the Swahili commercial elite were descendants of Arabs and Africans. However, they often claimed that they were descendants of Shirazi Persians. This connection is highly unlikely. Because the Persian Empire had once been an Indian Ocean trading power, Swahili elites probably manufactured a connection to the Persians who settled along the coast many centuries earlier.

The governments of the city-states were usually headed by monarchs or sultans, assisted by merchant councils and advised by holy men or royal relatives. Although the sultans were typical Muslim rulers in most respects, the common order of succession was according to matrilineal rules. When a sultan died at Kilwa, Pate, or any of numerous other cities, the throne passed to one of the head queen's brothers.

As the Muslim Middle East became the commercial center of Eurasia, the maritime trade of the Swahili cities figured significantly in the commercial networks of three continents. Gold, ivory, and slaves were the main exports. Other products commonly exported were hides and skins, rhinoceros horns, spices, and grain, in exchange for cloth, beads, porcelain, incense, glass, cloth, and perfume. Kilwa became the major port for gold sent through Egypt to Europe. Iron ore, exported from Malindi and Mombasa, supplied the iron industries of India. Slaves were shipped to the Arabian peninsula and Cambay, the capital of Gujarat, in India. There they served as domestic slaves or, as in southern Iraq, as laborers draining marshes. Mangrove tree poles were exported throughout the southern Persian Gulf as materials for house construction.

In the early 1400s a Chinese fleet under the command of admiral Zheng He visited Swahili towns such as Malindi and Mombasa, bearing porcelain, silks, lacquerware, and fine art objects and exchanging them for ivory, rhinoceros horns, incense, tortoise shell, rare woods, and exotic animals such as ostriches, zebras, and giraffes. Zheng He's ships also took back African envoys, who stayed at the Chinese court for several years.

Swahili civilization was an urban culture that reflected a well-entrenched hierarchy dominated by the commercial elite. Some towns, such as Mombasa and Lamu, were densely settled; in others, settlements were dispersed. The towns were the preserves of the commercial elite, who lived in houses made of wood and coral blocks. Some of the homes were two or three stories high and reflected the wealth, status, and rank of their owners. Most towns also had a central mosque, a Qur'anic school, a marketplace, a palace, and government buildings.

With the exception of the most loyal household slaves, the Swahili traders were the only ones who

In the early 1400s the Chinese commissioned seven expeditions to visit all the lands of the Indian Ocean to promote trade. A Chinese fleet under the command of admiral Zheng He visited some of the Swahili towns and took back several envoys from Malindi who brought along a giraffe as a gift to the Chinese court in 1414. The presentation of this giraffe was memorialized in a tapestry.

lived inside the walled cities. Most slaves slept outside the city in houses with mud walls and palm-matted roofs. They came into the city to work every day. Because the towns were not self-sufficient, they relied on the farmers and fishermen on the mainland for foodstuffs and meat.

Swahili masons and craftsmen were celebrated for building ornate stone and coral mosques and palaces, adorned with gold, ivory, and other wealth from nearly every major port in southern Asia. Perhaps because it borrowed architectural styles from the Middle East, Kilwa impressed the famous Muslim scholar-traveler Ibn Battuta in 1331 as the most beautiful and well-constructed city he had seen anywhere. Archaeological excavations have confirmed this evaluation, revealing the ruins of enormous palaces, great mansions, elaborate mosques, arched walkways, town squares, and public fountains. The Husuni Kubwa palace and trade emporium at Kilwa, built on the edge of an ocean cliff, contained over 100 rooms, as well as an eight-sided bathing pool in one of its many courtyards.

Kingdoms of Central and Southern Africa

By the third century C.E. central and southern Africa had been settled by migrating groups of Bantu farmers who lived in scattered homesteads or small villages and subsisted on cereal crops and animal herds.

Around 1000 C.E. some of these societies began to grow in size and complexity. This was very evident south of the Zambezi River, where states formed with ruling elites that displayed their wealth through their cattle herds. They accumulated cattle through a variety of means—raids, tribute, death dues, court fines, and bridewealth exchanges for marriages. Cattle exchanges through marriages and loans gave ruling

families the opportunity to establish broader social and political networks with other powerful families. Cattle herds also financed their participation in regional trading networks and links with the Indian Ocean economy.

A common feature of the ruling elites of these new states was that they built walls, dwellings, palaces, and religious centers made of stone. Throughout present-day eastern Botswana, northern South Africa, eastern Mozambique, and Zimbabwe, archaeologists have identified more than 150 political centers. An early state was Mapungubwe, situated south of the Limpopo River. Mapungubwe's rulers lived in stone residences on a hilltop, while commoners lived in their traditional settlements in the surrounding valley. The elites maintained their privileged status through their control over cattle herds, the trade in such metals as tin, copper, iron, and gold, and the hunting of elephants for ivory. Tin, copper, and iron were traded regionally, but ivory and gold were designated primarily for the expanding trade with the Indian Ocean coast. Mapungubwe peaked during the thirteenth century, but its main settlement had to be abandoned soon thereafter because farmers were not able to sustain production when a climatic changed produced a colder, drier environment.

Mapungubwe's successor was Great Zimbabwe ("houses of stone"), centered on a well-watered plateau north of the Limpopo. Its grandeur as a state is symbolized by its imposing granite structures, left after its rulers were forced to move northward to the

Constructed in the thirteenth century by the Muslim sultans of Kilwa, the Great Mosque was built from coral blocks. In the mosque's center, its arches supported a domed ceiling.

Zambezi. Extending over 60 acres and supporting about 18,000 residents, the complex at Great Zimbabwe contained many structures built over several centuries. At its center was a large complex of stoneworks where the political and religious elite lived. The most impressive structure was the Great Enclosure, which likely served as the royal family's main residence. Over 800 feet in circumference, the Great Enclosure was built without mortar and featured massive freestanding walls 12 feet thick and 20 feet high. Undoubtedly, Great Zimbabwe's rulers intended their monumental architecture to enhance their power and prestige among their subjects.

Zimbabwe's king presided over an elaborate court and administration. His key advisers included the queen mother and a ritual sister, a half-sister who was appointed when a king was installed. She had to give her consent to decisions made by the royal council before they could be enacted, she kept the ritual medicines that protected the well-being of the king, and she had considerable input into the choice of a new king.

Zimbabwe's rulers combined political and sacred power. Great Zimbabwe contained a rainmaking shrine, where its rulers prayed for abundant rainfall. On a nearby hillside was a temple where they prayed and offered sacrifices to the high god Mwari and the ancestors to ensure the fertility of the land and the prosperity of the people. Within the temple were placed stone sculptures of birds with human attributes. The birds played symbolic roles as God's messengers, mediating between God and man and the spirits of royal ancestors.

Great Zimbabwe's political elite based their power on their vast cattle herds as well as the control of regional trade, particularly copper and gold. The principal sources of gold were located on the plateau west of Great Zimbabwe. Women and children were responsible for mining most gold, which they did during the dry season, when they could take time off from their farming responsibilities. They sank narrow shafts as deep as 100 feet, brought the ore to the surface, crushed it, and sifted out the gold in nearby streams. Although some of the gold was fashioned into ornamental bangles and jewelry for Zimbabwe's rulers, most of the gold was transported as a fine powder for the external trade with the coastal Swahili cities, especially Kilwa, whose prosperity depended on its ties to Zimbabwe. Besides gold, ivory and animal skins were traded for glass beads, Indian cloth, ceramic vessels from Persia, and blue-and-white porcelain from China.

Great Zimbabwe's zenith was between 1290 and 1450. A common explanation for its sudden collapse is environmental degradation. The land could no longer support large numbers of people living in a

The Great Enclosure was Great Zimbabwe's most impressive structure and likely served as the royal family's main residence. Over 800 feet in circumference, the Great Enclosure was built without mortar and featured massive, freestanding granite walls 12 feet thick and 20 feet high.

concentrated area. However, this interpretation is not supported by data showing that rainfall actually increased around that time. A more likely explanation for the kingdom's decline is the rise to prominence of two of its former tributary states: Torwa to the northwest and Mutapa to the north.

Oral tradition relates that Mutapa's founder was Nyatsimbe Mutota, who Great Zimbabwe's rulers had sent north to search for an alternative source of salt. He founded the Mutapa kingdom in the well-watered Mazoe valley south of the Zambezi River. By 1500 Mutapa's ruler, the *mwene mutapa* ("conqueror"), and his army held sway over a vast part of the upper Zimbabwe Plateau. The *mwene mutapa* did not adopt the stone building traditions of Great Zimbabwe. Instead, he lived in a palace complex within a wooden palisade. With his family, military, bureaucracy, and representatives of tributary chiefdoms, he ruled over a federation of tributary states through governors that he appointed. They paid tribute in the form of agricultural produce, iron, cattle, and especially gold, which was still the mainstay of the trade with the East African coast.

Another notable kingdom in west central Africa was Kongo, located in a fertile agricultural area near the Atlantic coast at the mouth of the Congo River. It was formed in the fourteenth century when a petty prince named Wene led a migration, married into the local ruling family, and began developing a loose federation of states. Wene took the title of *Manikongo* ("lord of Kongo"). However, as kings of Kongo centered their political rule at their capital, Mbanza Kongo, they developed a centralized state. By the time the Portuguese arrived in the late fifteenth century, Kongo had already developed a sophisticated political system. The king, who had a professional army resident at his capital, appointed officials, usually close relatives, as his provincial administrators. The Kongo kingdom also controlled interregional trade, exchanging its cloth, woven from fibers of the raffia palm, for salt and seashells from neighboring societies.

Conclusion

By 1500 C.E. Africans had successfully adapted to the harsh challenges of Africa's environment by creating a diverse range of communities and states. Critical turning points in the histories of African cultures occurred with the introduction of agriculture, herding, and ironworking. These developments spurred population growth, migrations, craft specialization, trade between communities, and more complex political and economic systems. Most Africans in 1500 still lived in scattered homesteads and small communities and earned their livelihoods from farming, herding, and hunting. However, because of trading relations with one another and with other continents, Africans began to establish kingdoms and empires in all parts of the continent. Egypt, Kush, Aksum, Ethiopia, Ghana, Mali, Oyo, Benin, and Great Zimbabwe are some of the major civilizations that dominated eras of Africa's history.

While Africans created their own distinct cultures and traditions, they carried on vigorous commercial, technological, and intellectual exchanges with the cultures of the Indian Ocean region, Europe, the Near East, and Asia, largely through Muslim intermediaries. The kingdom of Aksum became a major Red Sea power, serving as a bridge between the Mediterranean and the Indian Ocean. The Swahili city-states on the East African coast and the states of the Zimbabwe Plateau carried on extensive relations with Indian Ocean trading networks. West African savanna kingdoms created the most extensive trading network through their position overseeing trade between North Africa, the savanna, and forest regions to the south.

Although most Africans remained faithful to their traditional religious beliefs and practices, many in certain areas converted to Christianity and Islam. Ethiopia's rulers firmly established Christianity as their kingdom's state religion, and some rulers and traders in the West African savanna, in northeastern Africa, and along the Swahili coast adopted Islam. However, until the eighteenth century Islam remained primarily a religion of court and commerce in sub-Saharan Africa.

Suggestions for Reading

The best detailed coverage of African history can be found in two multivolume series, each containing chapters by leading scholars: *The Cambridge History of Africa* and *The UNESCO General History of Africa*. This chapter has drawn on vols. 1–3 of the former and vols. 1–4 of the latter. Among other general surveys of African history are Robert W. July, *Precolonial Africa: An Economic and Social History* (Scribner, 1975) and *A History of the African People*, 4th ed. (Waveland Press, 1992); Roland Oliver and J. D. Fage, *A Short History of Africa*, 4th ed. (Facts on File, 1989); Philip Curtin et al., eds., *African History: From Earliest Times to Independence*, 2nd ed. (Longman, 1995); Kevin Shillington, *History of Africa* (St. Martin's Press, 1995); Elizabeth Isichei, *A History of African Societies to 1870* (Cambridge University Press, 1997); and Joseph Harris, *Africans and Their History*, 2nd ed. (Penguin, 1998). The best general reference works on early African history are John Middleton, ed., *Encyclopedia of Africa South of the Sahara*, 4 vols. (Scribner, 1997), and Joseph Vogel, *Encyclopedia of Precolonial Africa: Archaeology, History, Languages, Cultures, and Environment* (AltaMira Press, 1997). General works that examine Africa's history with a disciplinary focus are Ralph Austen, *African Economic History: Internal Development and External Dependency* (Heinemann, 1987), and James Newman, *The Peopling* of *Africa: A Geographic Interpretation* (Yale University Press, 1995). A general introduction to early African urbanization is R. W. Hull, *African Cities and Towns Before the European Conquest* (Norton, 1976).

Studies on African archaeology and the African Iron Age include Thurstan Shaw, *The Archaeology of Africa: Foods, Metals, and Towns* (Routledge, 1993) and *Nigeria: Its Archaeology and Early History* (Thames & Hudson, 1978); J. Desmond Clark, *From Hunters to Farmers: The Causes and Consequences of Food Production in Africa* (University of California Press, 1984); Randi Haaland and Peter Shinnie, *African Iron Working, Ancient and Traditional* (Oxford University Press, 1985); Peter Schmidt, *The Culture and Technology of African Iron Production* (University Press of Florida, 1996) and *Iron Technology in East Africa: Symbolism, Science, and Archaeology* (Indiana University Press, 1997); Roland Anthony Oliver and Brian M. Fagan, *Africa in the Iron Age, c. 500 B.C. to A.D. 1400* (Cambridge University Press, 1975); Roland Anthony Oliver, *The African Experience* (HarperCollins, 1991); David W. Phillipson, *African Archaeology*, 2nd ed. (Cambridge University Press, 1993); Christopher Ehret and Merrick Posnansky, eds., *The Archaeological and Linguistic Reconstruction of African History* (University of California Press, 1982); Graham Connah, *African Civilizations: Precolonial Cities and States in Tropical Africa* (Cambridge University Press, 1987); and Eugenia Herbert, *Iron, Gender, and Power: Rituals of Transformation in African Societies* (Indiana University Press, 1993).

On Nubia and Ethiopia, see William Y. Adams, *Nubia: Corridor to Africa* (Princeton, 1977); Mohammed Hassen, *The Oromo of Ethiopia: A History, 1570–1860* (Red Sea Press, 1994); Steven Kaplan, *The Beta Israel (Falasha) in Ethiopia: From Earliest Times to the Twentieth Century* (New York University Press, 1994); Yuri M. Kobishchanov, *Axum* (Pennsylvania State University Press, 1979); Stuart C. Munro-Hay, *Aksum: An African Civilization of Late Antiquity* (Edinburgh University Press, 1991); Tadesse Tamrat, *Church and State in Ethiopia, 1270–1527* (Oxford University Press, 1972); Richard K. Pankhurst, *A Social History of Ethiopia: The Northern and Central Highlands from Early Medieval Times to the Rise of Emperor Tewodros II* (Red Sea Press, 1992); and Harold Marcus, *A History of Ethiopia* (University of California Press, 1994).

General works on West Africa include A. G. Hopkins, *An Economic History of West Africa* (Longman, 1973), and J. F. Ajayi and Michael Crowder, eds., *History of West Africa*, 3rd ed., Vol. 1 (Longman, 1985). The Sudanic kingdoms of West Africa are treated in Nehemia Levtzion, *Ancient Ghana and Mali* (Methuen, 1973); George Brooks, *Landlords and Strangers: Ecology, Society, and Trade in Western Africa, 1000–1630* (Westview Press, 1993); and E. W. Bovill, *The Golden Trade of the Moors* (Oxford University Press, 1968). The Sundiata epic of the Malian Empire is recorded in D. T. Niane, *Sundiata: An Epic of Old Mali* (Longman, 1995). An excellent study on Muslim scholars in the Sudan is Elias Saad, *Social History of Timbuktu: The Role of Muslim Scholars and Notables, 1400–1900* (Cambridge University Press, 1983). Two important collections of primary documents on West Africa are Nehemia Levtzion, *Medieval West Africa Before 1400: Ghana, Takrur, Gao (Songhay), and Mali as Described by Arab Merchants and Scholars* (Markus Wiener, 1998), and Said Hamdun and Noel Q. King, eds., *Ibn Battuta in Black Africa* (Markus Wiener, 1997).

The East African coast and Swahili city-states are well covered in Christopher Ehret, *An African Classical Age: Eastern and Southern Africa in World History, 1000 B.C. to A.D. 400* (University Press of Virginia, 1998); John Middleton, *The World of the Swahili: An African Mercantile Civilization* (Yale University Press, 1992); Ali Mazrui and I. B. Sharif, *The Swahili: Idiom and Identity of an African People* (Africa World Press, 1994); Derek Nurse and Thomas G. Spear, *The Swahili: Reconstructing*

the History and Language of an African Society, 800–1500 (University of Pennsylvania Press, 1985); Randall Pouwels, *Horn and Crescent: Cultural Change and Traditional Islam on the East African Coast, 800–1900* (Cambridge University Press, 1987); B. A. Ogot and J. A. Kieran, eds., *Zamani: A Survey of East African History*, 2nd ed. (Longman, 1974); G. S. P. Freeman-Grenville, *The East African Coast* (Oxford University Press, 1962); John Sutton, *A Thousand Years of East Africa* (Thames & Hudson, 1990); and H. Neville Chittick, *Kilwa: An Islamic City on the East African Coast* (British Institute in Eastern Africa, 1974).

A record of the earliest written documentation on the Swahili coast is G. W. B. Huntington, ed., *The Periplus of the Erythrean Sea* (Haklyt Society, 1980). Chinese contacts with East Africa are examined in Louise Levathes, *When China Ruled the Seas: The Treasure Fleet of the Dragon Throne, 1405–1433* (Oxford University Press, 1996), and Teobaldi Filesi, *Le Relazioni della Cina con l'Africa nel Nedio-Evo* (Giuffre, 1975).

The best general studies on early central and southern African history are David Birmingham, ed., *History of Central Africa to 1870* (Cambridge University Press, 1981), and Martin Hall, *The Changing Past: Farmers, Kings, and Traders in Southern Africa* (Philip, 1987). The kingdom of Great Zimbabwe is extensively treated in D. N. Beach, *The Shona and Zimbabwe, 900–1850* (Heinemann, 1980); Peter Garlake, *Great Zimbabwe* (Thames & Hudson, 1973); Thomas N. Huffman, *Symbols in Stone: Unravelling the Mystery of Great Zimbabwe* (Witwatersrand University Press, 1987) and *Snakes and Crocodiles: Power and Symbolism in Ancient Zimbabwe* (Witwatersrand University Press, 1996); and Joseph Vogel, *Great Zimbabwe: The Iron Age in South Central Africa* (Garland, 1994). Richard Elphick, *Kraal and Castle: Khoikhoi and the Founding of White South Africa* (Yale University Press, 1977), remains the classic study of Khoikhoi history. Detailed studies of central and eastern African states are Jan Vansina, *Paths in the Rainforest: Toward a History of Political Tradition in Equatorial Africa* (Currey, 1990); Joseph Miller, *Kings and Kinsmen: Early Mbundu States in Angola* (Clarendon Press, 1976); and David Schoenbrun, *A Green Place, a Good Place: Agrarian Change, Gender, and Social Identity in the Great Lakes Region to the 15th Century* (Heinemann, 1998).

Suggestions for Web Browsing

Internet African History Sourcebook
http://www.fordham.edu/halsall/africa/africasbook.html

> *Extensive on-line source for links about the history of ancient Africa, including the kingdoms of Ghana, Mali, and Songhai.*

Art of Benin
http://www.si.edu/organiza/museums/africart/exhibits/
    beninsp.htm

> *Site of the Smithsonian Institution's National Museum of African Art displays art objects from the kingdom of Benin before Western dominance.*

Great Zimbabwe
http://www.mc.maricopa.edu/academic/cult_sci/anthro/
    lost_tribes/zimbabwe/intro.html

> *A 23-slide series, with commentary, that will take you through the ruins of Great Zimbabwe in southern Africa.*

Notes

1. Kevin Shillington, *History of Africa* (New York: St. Martin's Press, 1989), p. 10.

2. The latest synthesis of research on Bantu migrations is Jan Vansina, "A Slow Revolution: Farming in Subequatorial Africa," *Azania*, 29–30 (1994–1995), pp. 15–26.

3. Al Omari, quoted in Tadesse Tamrat, "The Horn of Africa: The Solomonids in Ethiopia and the States of the Horn of Africa," in D. T. Niane, ed., *UNESCO General History of Africa: Africa from the Twelfth to the Sixteenth Century* (Berkeley: University of California Press, 1984), p. 435.

4. Joseph Vogel, *Encyclopedia of Precolonial Africa: Archaeology, History, Languages, Cultures, and Environment* (Walnut Creek, CA: AltaMira Press, 1997), p. 490.

5. Ralph Austen, "Slave Trade: Trans-Saharan Trade," in Seymour Drescher and Stanley Engerman, eds., *A Historical Guide to World Slavery* (Oxford: Oxford University Press, 1998), p. 368.

6. Al Omari, quoted in Vogel, *Encyclopedia of Precolonial Africa*, p. 492.

7. Al Masudi, quoted in G. S. P. Freeman-Grenville, *The East African Coast* (Oxford: Oxford University Press, 1962), pp. 15–17.

The Growth and Spread of Asian Culture, 300–1300

Before and After the Mongol Conquests

Chapter Contents

The millennium between 300 and 1300 was a time of preservation, consolidation, and innovation for the ancient Asian civilizations. Some earlier values and institutions were reaffirmed so effectively that characteristic Hindu and Chinese culture patterns have endured until today despite frequent invasions of both homelands. Alongside that cultural continuity, however, emerged new syntheses combining the cultural patterns of the indigenous peoples with those of new waves of invaders. Each civilization produced significant contributions to the world's common culture. India made remarkable advances in mathematics, medicine, chemistry, textile production, and literature, and Buddhism continued its dramatic spread to East and Southeast Asia. China excelled in political organization, scholarship, and the arts, at the same time producing such revolutionary technical inventions as printing, gunpowder, and the mariner's compass. Maritime trade flourished as Arab, Jewish, and Indian traders crisscrossed the Indian Ocean to the west of the subcontinent while Indian and Southeast Asian traders plied the waters to the east as far as China and Japan.

Growth in the old Asian centers led naturally toward outward cultural diffusion and a varied exchange of goods, philosophies, literatures, and fashions with bordering civilizations. In Southeast Asia these arose from increasing contacts with India and China through trade, missionary efforts, colonizing, and conquest. First Korea and then Japan imported cultural bases from China. Similarly,

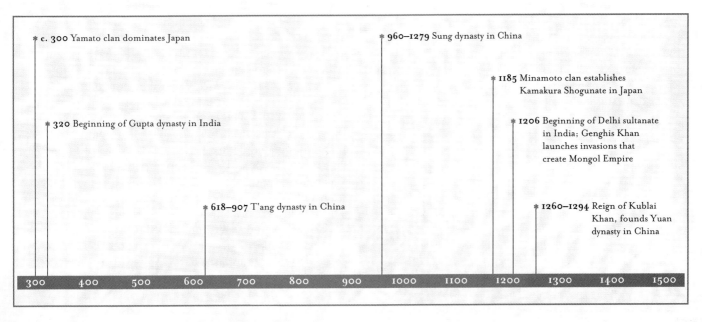

* **c. 300** Yamato clan dominates Japan

* **320** Beginning of Gupta dynasty in India

* **618–907** T'ang dynasty in China

* **960–1279** Sung dynasty in China

* **1185** Minamoto clan establishes Kamakura Shogunate in Japan

* **1206** Beginning of Delhi sultanate in India; Genghis Khan launches invasions that create Mongol Empire

* **1260–1294** Reign of Kublai Khan, founds Yuan dynasty in China

| 300 | 400 | 500 | 600 | 700 | 800 | 900 | 1000 | 1100 | 1200 | 1300 | 1400 | 1500 |

nomads of central Asia—Turks, Uighurs, Mongols, and numerous other steppe peoples—engaged in a vigorous exchange with China and India (often assimilating the cultural patterns of those civilizations) as merchants, subjects, or conquerors. Their states, culminating in the great Mongol Empire of the thirteenth and fourteenth centuries, facilitated the passing of those influences to the peoples of the Middle East and Europe.

India's Politics and Culture

India's cultural renaissance culminated in the fourth and fifth centuries as the Gupta dynasty emerged and attempted to recapture the territorial and cultural grandeur of the Mauryas. The Gupta era marks the end of what has been termed India's Classical Age. Its monarchs gained control over northern India while fostering traditional religions, Sanskrit literature, and indigenous art. Hindu and Buddhist culture also spread widely throughout Southeast Asia in this period.

The Gupta state began its rise in 320 with the accession to power of Chandra Gupta I (not related to his earlier Mauryan namesake). His son Samudra Gupta (c. 335–375) and grandson Chandra Gupta II (c. 376–414) were successful conquerors, extending the boundaries of an original petty state in Maghada until it included most of northern India, from the Himalayas to the Narmada River and east to west from sea to sea. Within this domain the Gupta monarchs developed a political structure along ancient Mauryan lines, with provincial governors, district officials, state-controlled industries, and an imperial secret service. This centralized system, however, was effective only on royal lands, which were much less extensive than in Mauryan times. With a smaller bureaucracy, the Gupta rulers depended on local authorities and communal institutions, raising revenues primarily through tribute and military forces by feudal levy.

Marriage alliances aided the Guptas' rise to power. Chandra Gupta I married a princess from the powerful Licchavi clan; his coins show the king and his queen, Kumaradevi, on one side and a lion with his queen's clan name on the other. Chandra Gupta II gave his daughter, Prabhavati Gupta, in marriage to

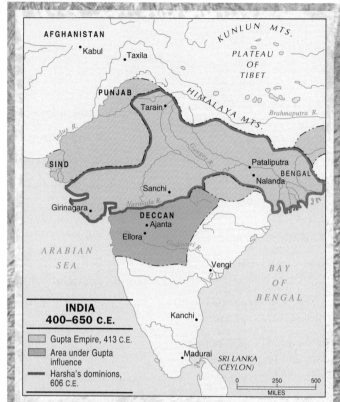

The Guptas extended their rule over northern and central India but never managed to control the southern peninsula.

Rudrasena II, king of the powerful Vakataka dynasty in central India. Rudrasena died after a short reign, and his wife then took control of his kingdom for about 20 years as regent for her minor sons. The two kingdoms remained closely tied even after her death.

Peace and stable government under the later Guptas increased agricultural productivity and foreign trade. Flourishing commerce with Rome in the last decades of the fourth century brought a great influx of gold and silver into the Gupta Empire. Indian traders were also active in Southeast Asia, particularly in Burma, Vietnam, and Cambodia, where they contributed to emerging civilizations. India's resulting prosperity was reflected in great public buildings and in the luxuries of the elite, particularly at the Gupta court.

Although the Gupta rulers generally favored Hinduism, they practiced religious pluralism, patronizing and building temples for Hindus, Buddhists, and Jains. The Brahmins provided the Guptas with religious legitimacy, and the Guptas rewarded them with significant grants of land. Hinduism dominated the subcontinent. The Hindu revival of this period brought a great upsurge of devotion to Vishnu and Shiva. This religious fervor was reflected in a series of religious books, the *Puranas*, which emphasized the compassion of the personal gods. The *Puranas* are a collection of myths, philosophical dialogues, ritual prescriptions, and dynastic genealogies; their tales of the gods were popular.

Gupta India

320	Accession of Chandra Gupta I
c. 335–375	Reign of Samudra Gupta
c. 376–414	Reign of Chandra Gupta II
510	Huns seize northwest India; Gupta Empire collapses

Fa-Hsien: A Chinese Buddhist Monk in Gupta India

Fa-Hsien is an important source on India around 400 C.E. A Buddhist monk, he left China as a pilgrim to India in search of Buddhist texts and was gone for 14 years. When he returned, he translated various Indian works and wrote the account of his travels. Fa-Hsien's story and long arduous journey on foot illustrate both the spread of Buddhism from India to China and the draw that the Indian heartland had on Buddhists abroad. Here he describes Pataliputra (modern Patna), where Ashoka once reigned. The festival illustrates the amalgamation of Buddhist and Hindu ritual and suggests the joyous nature of some urban religious celebrations. Fa-Hsien's account of hospitals gives us some insight into the quality medical care available even to the poor.

By the side of the tower of King Ashoka is built a monastery belonging to the Great Vehicle [Mahayana Buddhism], very imposing and elegant. There is also a temple belonging to the Little Vehicle [Theravada Buddhism]. Together they contain about 600 or 700 priests; their behavior is decorous and orderly. . . . Of all the kingdoms in Mid-India, the towns of this country are especially large. The people are rich and prosperous; they practice virtue and justice. Every year on the eighth day of the second month, there is a procession of images. On this occasion, they construct a four-wheeled [vehicle], and erect upon it a tower of five stages, composed of bamboos lashed together, the whole being supported by a center post resembing a large spear with three points, in height twenty-two feet or more. So it looks like a pagoda. They then cover it with fine white linen, which they afterward paint with gaudy colors. Having made figures of the *devas* [gods], and decorated them with gold, silver, and glass, they place them under canopies of embroidered silk. Then at the four corners [of the car] they construct niches in which they place figures of Buddha in a sitting pos-

ture, with a Bodhisattva [a Buddha in the making] standing in attendance. There are perhaps twenty cars thus prepared and differently decorated. During the day of the procession both priests and laymen assemble in great numbers. There are games and music, whilst they offer flowers and incense. . . . Then all night long they burn lamps, indulge in games and music, and make religious offerings. Such is the custom of all those who assemble on this occasion from the different countries round about. The nobles and householders of this country have founded hospitals within the city, to which the poor of all countries, the destitute, cripples, and the diseased may repair. They receive every kind of requisite help gratuitously. Physicians inspect their diseases, and according to their cases order them food and drink, medicine or decoctions, everything in fact that may contribute to their ease. When cured they depart at their convenience.

From Samuel Beal, ed., *Buddhist Records of the Western World*, translated from the Chinese of Hiuen Tsiang (629) (Delhi: Oriental Books, 1969), pp. lvi–lvii.

Among their legends, for example, is a recounting of the deeds of the goddess Durga and her fight against the buffalo demon. By promoting the devotional Hinduism reflected in these tales, the Gupta monarchs gained great favor among all classes of their subjects.

Much of our knowledge of Gupta society comes from the journal of a Chinese Buddhist monk, Fa-Hsien, who traveled in India for 14 years at the opening of the fifth century. Fa-Hsien was primarily interested in Buddhism in India, but he did occasionally comment on social customs. He reported the people to be happy, relatively free of government oppression, and inclined toward courtesy and charity. He mentions the caste system and its associations with purity and impurity, including "untouchability," the social isolation of a lowest class that is doomed to menial labor.

Gupta Art and Literature

Indian art of the Gupta period depicts a golden age of classical brilliance, combining stability and serenity with an exuberant love of life. The Gupta artistic spirit is well expressed in the 28 monasteries and temples at

Ajanta, hewn out of a solid rock cliff and portraying in their wall frescoes not only the life of Buddha but also life in general: lovers embracing, beds of colorful flowers, musicians, and dancers. These sculptures reveal the beauty of the human form, attesting to the notion of Gupta artists that the divine is not separate from the human, nor the spirit from the body. The various incarnations of Vishnu and the deeds of the goddess Durga were also common subjects of Gupta sculpture.

The Gupta era was also a golden age for literature, written in Sanskrit, the ancient language of the Brahmins. Authors supported by royal patronage poured forth a wealth of sacred, philosophical, and dramatic poetic and prose works, including fables, fairy tales, and adventure stories featuring a wide range of characters—thieves, courtesans, hypocritical monks, and strange beasts. The *Panchatantra* is a manual of political wisdom employing animal tales to advise the king on proper rule. A most renowned literary figure of this era was India's greatest poet and dramatist, Kalidasa, who wrote (apparently) at the court of Chandra Gupta II. His best-known work in the West is *Shakuntala*, a great drama of lovers separated by adversity for many years and then by chance reunited. The play is full of vivid imagery and a loving sympathy for nature.

Gupta Scholarship and Science

The Gupta era brought a great stimulus to learning. Brahmin traditions were revitalized, and Buddhist centers, which had spread after the Mauryan period, were given new support. The foremost Indian university, founded in the fifth century, was at Nalanda. Accomplishments in science were no less remarkable than those in art, literature, scholarship, and philosophy. The most famous Gupta scientist was the astronomer-mathematician Aryabhatta, who lived in the fifth century. He elaborated (in verse) on quadratic equations, solstices, and equinoxes, along with the spherical shape of the earth and its rotation. Other Hindu mathematicians of this period popularized the use of a special sign for zero, passing it on later to the Arabs. Mathematical achievements were matched by those in medicine. Hindu physicians sterilized wounds, prepared for surgery by fumigation, performed cesarean operations, set bones, and were skilled in plastic surgery. They used drugs then unknown in the West, such as chaulmoogra oil for leprosy, a treatment still used in the twentieth century. With these accomplishments in pure science came many effective practical applications by Gupta craftsmen, who made soap, cement, superior dyes, and the finest tempered steel in the world.

New Political Configurations

Gupta hegemony began to collapse in the second half of the fifth century with an invasion of the Huns from the north and a long war for succession. After 497 Guptas ruled only in parts of northern India. In 510 the Huns—who had already successfully invaded Persia and Europe—seized northwestern India, which once again became attached to a central Asian empire. Hun rule did not endure, but it helped prompt the migration of more central Asian tribesmen into India and precipitated a period in which India was generally divided into regional kingdoms rather than more expansive empires like that of the Guptas. The central Asian tribesmen also intermarried with local populations to produce a class of fighting aristocrats known as Rajputs. These fierce warriors carved out kingdoms among the Hindu states of northern India.

In the seventh century the unity of northern India was revived for a short while by Harsha, a strong Hindu leader. In six years he reconquered much of what had been the Gupta Empire, restoring order and partially reviving learning. However, Harsha failed in his bid to conquer the Deccan, and no ruler would again do so until 1206. Harsha left no heir when he died in 647, and regional kingdoms again prevailed.

The period of the regional kingdoms was not a sterile one. In this era the great Hindu philosopher

Shankara (c. 788–820) brilliantly argued a nondualist mystical philosophy based on the Upanishads; regional literatures, especially in Tamil in the south, flourished; and Brahmins and Buddhist monks continued to carry their religious and cultural ideas to Southeast Asia and China. Their crucial role in the "Indianization" of Southeast Asia is reflected in the great temples there. It is also reflected in the Chinese sources that note 162 visits of Buddhist monks from the fifth to the eighth centuries.[1]

The Chola kingdom on India's southwestern coast played a significant role in the commercial and cultural exchange with Southeast Asia as well. Chola rulers in the eleventh century exchanged embassies with China, Sumatra, Malaya, and Cambodia; Chola fleets took Sri Lanka (Ceylon) and challenged the power of the Southeast Asian kingdom of Shrivijaya. When a Chola king conquered Bengal, he ordered the defeated princes to carry the holy water of the Ganges River to his new capital to celebrate his victory.

Muslims in India

The prophet Muhammad founded an Arab Muslim state in Arabia in the seventh century; soon the Arab conquerors had defeated the Sassanids in Persia and Muslim armies arrived at the boundaries of the Indian subcontinent. In 712 an Arab force seized Sind, a coastal outpost in northwestern India, an early signal of the Muslim invasions to come 30 years later. Other Muslim states were established across the northern mountains in Persia and central Asia.

In the year 1000 the Muslim sovereign Mahmud of Ghazni launched a series of campaigns into northwestern India. He gained a reputation as a destroyer for his 17 campaigns, over the course of 25 years, that devastated northern India. One notable episode during these campaigns was Mahmud's destruction of Shiva's large temple complex in Gujarat and the slaughter of its defenders who, according to legend, numbered 50,000 men. These campaigns of pillage rather than conquest made Mahmud a name that to the present day evokes powerful emotions among Hindus. Mahmud is also known for the famous scholars at his court, among them Firdawsi, who wrote the great epic Persian poem the *Shahnamah*, and al-Biruni, author of a major history of India. When Mahmud died, it was more than a century before new Muslim armies attacked the subcontinent.

The date 1206 stands out as the next significant marker of Muslim conquest in India. In the same year that the Mongol Genghis Khan mobilized his campaigns of conquest and expansion, the general Qutb ud-Din Aibak seized power as sultan at Delhi. Qutb ud-Din had been a commander in the army of the Afghan ruler Muhammad of Ghur, who seized Delhi from the Rajputs in 1192. Qutb ud-Din founded a new dynasty and was followed on the throne by his son-in-law, Iltutmish,

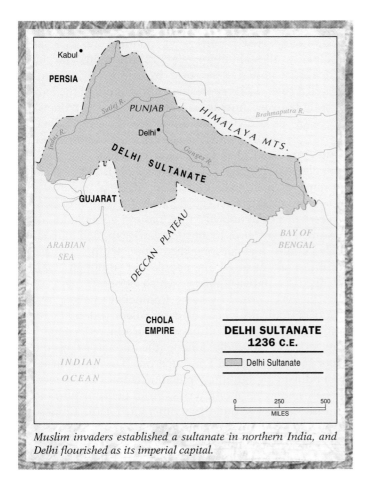

Muslim invaders established a sultanate in northern India, and Delhi flourished as its imperial capital.

and by the latter's daughter, who ruled for three years. Iltutmish had himself formally consecrated in 1229 as sultan of Delhi by a representative of the Abbasid sultan in Baghdad. Even though the Abbasid sultan wielded

little power at this time, he was still a source of Islamic legitimacy for South Asian Muslim rulers. Less than 30 years later the Abbasid caliphate would fall prey to the Mongol descendants of Genghis Khan.

At the peak of its power in the thirteenth century, the Delhi Sultanate held not only the north but also part of the Deccan Plateau in the south. When Sultan Ala ud-Din invaded the Deccan, he called himself the "Second Alexander," a title that was emblazoned on his coins. The Delhi Sultanate also managed to ward off the Mongol invaders who seized the Punjab, thus avoiding the fate of Persia and Iraq. Delhi under the sultanate emerged as a great imperial capital. Patrons of the arts, builders of splendid monuments, and proponents of philosophy, the Delhi sultans held an uneasy rule over the majority Hindu populace. By the middle of the fourteenth century, they had lost control of the south (upon the rise of the Vijayangar Empire in 1346) and were hard pressed by various Hindu and Muslim challengers. Although experiencing brief periods of revival, the regime continued to decline internally before it was destroyed by the Turco-Mongol Timur (Tamerlane) in 1398. Timur's army wrought such destruction in Delhi that in his autobiography he denied responsibility and blamed the slaughter on his soldiers.

Muslim rule in India brought some cultural integration as local lords and warriors were incorporated into the new Muslim court. Some Hindus found emotional appeal in the Muslim faith, which had no caste system, or sought to lighten their taxes and qualify for public service by converting to Islam. Others formed new religious groups synthesizing aspects of Hinduism and Islam—for example, Sikhism. Another typical example of cultural integration was the

India is famous for its rock-carved temples. This is the Kailasanatha Temple at Ellora, dedicated to Shiva and dating to approximately 765 C.E.

spread of Urdu, a spoken Indian language incorporating Persian, Arabic, and Turkish words.

Cultural synthesis, however, could not eliminate Hindu-Muslim contention over polytheism, religious images, and closed castes. Many aristocratic Hindu leaders desperately resisted Islam, often suffering cruel persecution. Unlike the Mongol invaders in the Middle East who became Islamized and adopted the high culture of the Persian courts, the Muslim invaders of the subcontinent assimilated only certain aspects of Hindu civilization. Religion and caste remained significant barriers to assimilation, and the Delhi Sultanate remained a Muslim military-administrative class that ruled over a predominantly Hindu, caste-divided population. The same would be true for the Muslim Mughuls who ruled over India in a later age (see Chapter 17).

Chinese Continuity: T'ang and Sung

Like India, China was also divided into north and south and experienced an invasion of conquerors from beyond its northern frontiers toward the year 1300. In contrast with India and medieval Europe, however, China achieved both political and cultural continuity between the sixth and thirteenth centuries. Political unity was attained briefly under the Sui dynasty (589–618), consolidated under the T'ang (618–907), and maintained precariously under the Sung (960–1279). Despite periods of internal disruption, this political system, re-created from Han precedents, survived repeated invasions and civil wars. Its stability resulted from a common written language; an ancient family structure, guided by mature and conservative-minded matriarchs; an enduring Confucian tradition; and a Chinese elite of scholar bureaucrats who shared power while contending for dominance. Their efforts promoted a flowering of Chinese culture during the expansionist T'ang period, when China was the largest state in the world, and during the ensuing economic prosperity of the Sung.

Before the T'ang Dynasty

Following the fall of the Han Empire in 220, China suffered three centuries of disorder and division. Various nomadic peoples, mainly Huns (Hsiung-nu) and Turks (Yueh-chih), pillaged northern China, setting up petty states. These states were administered mostly by Chinese, and the invaders gradually absorbed Chinese culture. Central and southern China escaped these intrusions and enjoyed relative prosperity and population growth, both resulting from an influx of northern émigrés, in addition to increasingly productive rice cultivation. This growing economy supported a series of political regimes at Nanking, all maintaining classical traditions and the idea of a united state ruled by a "son of heaven." Such a ruler was responsible for maintaining the harmony between humans and nature; he was empowered by his knowledge and practice of right conduct.

During turbulent times in the fourth century, the old Confucian ideal of a balanced social order was challenged by the rapid spread of Buddhism in China. It provided comfort in times of crisis. Its promise of salvation (particularly for common people), its special appeal to the natural compassion of women, its offer of monastic security to men in troubled times, and its long incubation within Chinese culture all ensured its popularity. Although challenged by native Taoism (which adopted many of its ideas), scorned by some Confucian intellectuals, and periodically persecuted by rulers jealous of its strength, Buddhism ultimately won adherents among its critics, especially among the monarchs of the north, including the Sui emperors. They patronized Buddhism by building splendid temples and generously endowing monasteries. From the fourth to the ninth centuries Buddhism interacted with Chinese religious and philosophical traditions to create a complex new synthesis of ideas and art.

The two Sui monarchs, tempered in the rough frontier wars of the north, reconquered all of China, ending nearly four centuries of political fragmentation. They established an imperial military force and a land-based militia, centralized the administration, and revived a civil service recruited through an examination system. They also started building a waterway, which would later become the famous Grand Canal, to link the rice-growing Yangtze basin with northern China. However, their unpredictable cruelty, oppression, and conscription of labor for the

T'ang and Sung China

618–907	T'ang dynasty
c. 692–712	Reign of Empress Wu
713–756	Cultural flowering under Emperor Hsuan-tsung
960–1279	Sung dynasty
1005, 1042	Sung sign treaties of subordination with Khitan Mongols
1115	Sung court flees south to escape invading Jürchen; Chin dynasty established in north

canal led to a great rebellion that ended the dynasty; nevertheless, the Sui emperors deserve much credit for later T'ang successes.

Political Developments Under the Rising T'ang Dynasty, 618–756

During the early T'ang period to 756, China attained a new pinnacle of glory. The first three emperors subjugated Turkish central Asia, made Tibet a dependency, and conquered Annam (northern Vietnam). Along with territorial expansion came great economic, social, and cultural advances. Ironically, these gains resulted largely from the emperors' commitment to Confucianism, with its deference to civilian over military values.

This era of growth and grandeur was marked by the extraordinary reign of the able Empress Wu, a concubine of the second and third emperors, who controlled the government for 20 years after the latter's death, torturing and executing her political opponents but also firmly establishing the T'ang dynasty. She greatly weakened the old aristocracy by favoring Buddhism and strengthening the examination system for recruiting civil servants. Moreover, she decisively defeated the Koreans, making Korea a loyal vassal state. Largely because she was a woman and a usurper, she found little favor with some Chinese historians and politicians, who emphasized her vices, particularly her many favorites and lovers. Her overthrow in 712 ended an era of contention and ushered in a new age of cultural development in the long reign of Emperor Hsuan-tsung (713–756).

T'ang rulers perfected a highly centralized government, utilizing a complex bureaucracy organized in specialized councils, boards, and ministries, all directly responsible to the emperor. Local government functioned under 15 provincial governors, aided by subordinates down to the district level. Military commanders supervised tribute collections in semiautonomous conquered territories. Officeholders throughout the empire were, by the eighth century, usually degree-holders from government schools and universities who had qualified by passing the regularly scheduled examinations. These scholar-bureaucrats were steeped in Confucian conservatism but were more efficient than the remaining minority of aristocratic hereditary officials. One notable T'ang institution was a nationalized land register, designed to check the growth of large estates, guarantee land to peasants, and relate their land tenure to both their taxes and their militia service. Until well into the

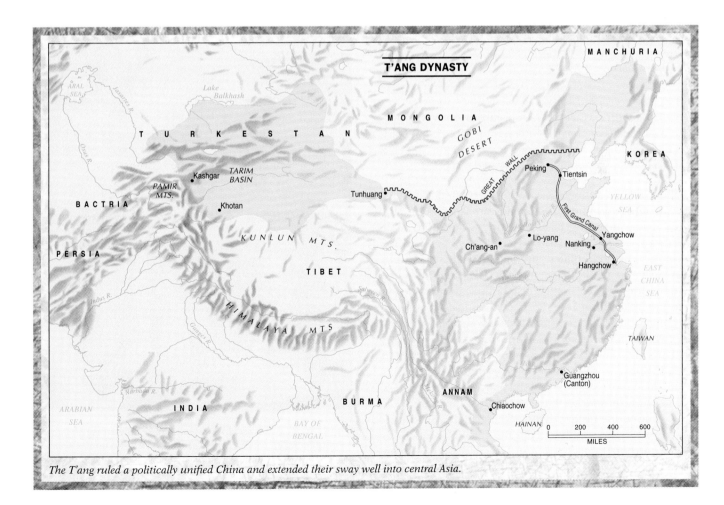

The T'ang ruled a politically unified China and extended their sway well into central Asia.

Empress Wu, the only woman to rule China in name as well as in fact. A royal concubine to two emperors, she usurped the imperial throne and assumed the special title of "Holy Mother Divine Imperial One." As a young girl, Wu studied music and the Chinese classics; as empress, she sponsored the writing of biographies of famous women.

eighth century, when abuses began to show, the system worked to merge the interests of state and people.

T'ang Economy and Society

The T'ang economy was carefully regulated. The government maintained monopolies on salt, liquor, and tea, using licensing in an attempt to prohibit illicit enterprises. In conducting its business, it issued receipts, which circulated among merchants and were antecedents of the paper money that came into use under the Sung. The state also built roads and canals to facilitate commerce. Perhaps the most technically remarkable of these projects was the magnificent Grand Canal, stretching some 650 miles between Hangchow and Tientsin, a great waterway for trade and transport. Other typical government enterprises included post houses and restaurants for travelers and public granaries to ensure against famine.

Economic productivity, both agricultural and industrial, rose steadily during the early T'ang period. The introduction of tea and wet rice from Annam turned the Yangtze area into a vast irrigated food bank and the economic base for T'ang power. More

food and rising population brought increasing manufactures. Chinese techniques in the newly discovered craft of papermaking, along with iron casting, porcelain production, and silk processing, improved tremendously and spread west to the Middle East.

Foreign trade and influence increased significantly under the T'ang emperors in a development that would continue through the Sung era. Chinese control in central Asia facilitated trade along the old overland silk route; but as porcelain became the most profitable export and could not be easily transported by caravan, it swelled the volume of sea trade through Southeast Asia. Most of this trade left from southern ports, particularly from Guangzhou (Canton), where more than 100,000 aliens—Indians, Persians, Arabs, and Malays—handled the goods. Foreign merchants were equally visible at Ch'ang-an, the T'ang capital and eastern terminus of the silk route.

Although largely state-controlled and aristocratic, T'ang society was particularly responsive to new foreign stimuli, which it swiftly absorbed. A strongly pervasive Buddhism, a rising population, and steady urbanization fostered this cross-cultural exchange. Many city populations exceeded 100,000, and four cities had

During the T'ang era, foreign trade and travel affected the character of Chinese art, while technological advances in ceramics led to the development of fine porcelain. Chinese porcelain then became a highly prized trade good. This glazed earthenware figure depicts a Bactrian camel from west central Asia.

more than a million people; the capital at Ch'ang-an was the largest city in the world. Merchants clearly benefited from this exchange, but despite their wealth, merchants were still considered socially inferior. They often used their wealth to educate their sons for the civil service examination, thus promoting a rising class of scholar-bureaucrats. The latter, as they acquired land, gained status and power at the expense of the old aristocratic families. Conditions among artisans and the expanding mass of peasants improved somewhat, but life for them remained hard and precarious.

In the early T'ang era, elite women had been considered sufficiently equal socially to play polo with men. By the eighth century, however, T'ang legal codes had imposed severe punishments for wifely disobedience or infidelity to husbands. New laws also limited women's rights to divorce, inheritance of property, and remarriage as widows. Women were, however, still active in the arts and literature. Although some wielded influence and power at royal courts, many were confined to harems, a practice without precedent in Chinese traditions. This subordinate position was only partly balanced by the continued high status and authority of older women within the families.

T'ang Literature, Scholarship, and the Arts

A fresh flowering of literature occurred during the early T'ang period. It followed naturally from a dynamic society, but it was also greatly furthered by the development of papermaking and the invention, in about 600, of block printing, which soon spread to Korea and Japan. Movable type, which would later revolutionize Europe, was little used in East Asia during this period because Chinese writing was done in characters representing whole words. Printing helped meet a growing demand for the religious and educational materials generated by Buddhism and the examination system.

T'ang scholarship is best remembered for historical writing. Chinese of this period firmly believed that lessons from the past could be guides for the future. As an early T'ang emperor noted, "By using a mirror of brass, you may . . . adjust your cap; by using antiquity as a mirror you may . . . foresee the rise and fall of empires."[2] In addition to universal works, the period produced many studies of particular subjects. History itself came under investigation, as illustrated by *The Understanding of History*, a work that stressed the need for analysis and evaluation in the narration of events.

Writers produced works of all types, but poetry was the accepted medium, composed and repeated by emperors, scholars, singing courtesans, and common people in the marketplaces. T'ang poetry was marked by ironic humor, deep sensitivity to human feeling, concern for social justice, and a near-worshipful love of nature. Three of the most famous

among some 3000 recognized poets of the era were Po Chu, Tu Fu, and Li Po. The last, perhaps the greatest of them all, was an admitted lover of pleasure, but he could pinpoint life's mysteries, as in the following poetic expression of a statement by the Taoist philosopher Chuang Tzu (fl. c. 369–286 B.C.E.):

> *Chuang Tzu in a dream*
> *became a butterfly,*
> *And the butterfly became*
> *Chuang Tzu at waking.*
> *Which was the real—the*
> *butterfly or the man?[3]*

The T'ang literary revival was paralleled by movements in painting and sculpture. The plastic arts, dealing with both religious and secular subjects, became a major medium for the first time in China. Small tomb statues depicted both Chinese and foreign life with realism, verve, and diversity. These figures—warriors, servants, and traders—were buried with the dead and believed to serve them in the afterlife. Religious statuary, even in Buddhist shrines, showed strong humanistic emphases, often juxtaposed with the naive sublimity of Buddhas carved in the Gandaran (Greek Hellenistic) style of northwestern India. Similar themes were developed in T'ang painting, but the traditional preoccupation with nature prevailed in both the northern and southern landscape schools. The most famous T'ang painter was Wu Tao-tzu, whose landscapes and religious scenes were produced at the court of the emperor Ming Huang in the early eighth century.

In the T'ang dynasty, earthenware models of people and objects, like this one of traders with a bullock and cart, were buried with the dead. Such objects were believed to be useful in the afterlife.
Bullock and cart, T'ang Dynasty, 7th–8th century. Pottery with green and brown glazes, H. 16" × L. 20 1/4". Seattle Art Museum, Eugene Fuller Memorial Collection, 37.17. Photo: Paul Macapia.

Fashions in female beauty change from place to place and over time. Around the sixth century, slim elegant earthenware figures of Chinese females showed the influence of dress styles from central Asia and Persia. By the early-seventh-century T'ang dynasty, foreign fashions were all the rage among the upper classes. In the eighth century, however, the slim female and tight wraps gave way to voluptuous female figures (again depicted in earthenware images) in loose gowns. These figures are thought to be modeled after Yang Guifei, the hefty favorite concubine of T'ang emperor Hsuan-tsung (713–756). Yang Guifei is represented in various artworks from the T'ang court. T'ang China is not the only place and era in world history where the ample woman, rather than her gaunt sister, represented health, prosperity, and sexuality—the height of feminine beauty.

T'ang Decline

After the middle of the eighth century, T'ang China began an era of decline. The Uighur Turks gained control of Mongolia. Meanwhile, as the fiscal system weakened under attack from various vested interests, military governors took over control of outlying provinces. One of them, a former court favorite named An Lu-shan, marched on Ch'ang-an in 755; he was a protégé of the emperor's favorite concubine, Yang Guifei. The aged emperor Hsuan-tsung, while fleeing for his life from the capital, was forced by his troops to approve the execution of Yang Guifei, who had dominated his court. According to legend, he died of sorrow less than a month later.

An Lu-shan's rebellion was put down after seven years, but the ensuing disruption was so extensive that the late T'ang emperors never recovered their former power. Following a breakdown of the old land registration system, revenues declined and peasants rebelled against rising taxes. Falling revenues brought deterioration of the state education establishment and a corresponding drop in administrative efficiency. The government further alienated some groups by seizing Buddhist property and persecuting all "foreign" religions. At the capital, weak emperors lost their authority to eunuchs who had originally been only harem servants. Finally, in 907, a military commander killed all the eunuchs and deposed the last T'ang emperor.

Political Developments During the Sung Era, 960–1279

Even as the T'ang dynasty ended, it prepared a way for the Sung. South China, under T'ang rule, had developed an expanding economy. The T'ang collapse permitted a commercial expansion that in turn generated much of the Sung's remarkable cultural achievement, but not before China endured a period of disruptions. For a half century after the fall of the T'ang dynasty, China experienced political division, at times approaching anarchy. During this period of five dynasties in the north and ten kingdoms in the south, attacks by "barbarian" raiders from the north alternated with internal conflicts among contending warlords. One military leader of the northern Chou staged a palace coup and founded the Sung line in 960. He and his successor reunited the country, although certain frontier provinces and the tributary areas held by T'ang rulers were never regained.

Although they were northern conquerors, the early Sung emperors soon abandoned their military aggressiveness in order to win economic support in the south. Most of the remaining aristocratic officials were replaced by military officers or their sons, as soon as they could qualify for office in a newly regenerated educational and examination system. Within a half century these former soldiers had been absorbed into a Confucian scholar-bureaucracy that became an even more powerful elite than had prevailed under the T'ang. In the process, state policy became concentrated on civilian concerns rather than foreign affairs.

Lacking an effective military and plagued with internal bureaucratic dissension, Sung ministers faced continuous threats along their northern and western frontiers. Their weak defenses provoked raids and invasions from neighboring kingdoms, notably that of the Khitan Mongols (907–1127). When their military efforts failed, the Sung ministers turned to diplomacy, ultimately agreeing, in 1005 and 1042, to pay tribute in silk and silver for peace and protection while acknowledging Sung subordination to the Khitan ruler. The process was repeated a century later when a nomadic people from Manchuria, the Jürchen (1115–1234), destroyed the Khitan regime, established the Chin ("golden") dynasty, and invaded the northern Sung territories, taking the capital at K'ai-feng. The Sung court fled in panic to Nanking and later set up a new capital at Hangchow, thus bringing to an inglorious end the Sung effort to govern a united China. After a decade of indecisive war, a treaty in 1141 stipulated new tribute levies of silk and silver on the Sung. It also prescribed that the Chin monarch be addressed as "lord" and the Sung emperor as "servant" in all official communications. The subordination of the Sung was thus formalized in language and in goods.

Along with such troubles, the Sung rulers faced an ambiguous situation at home. The country experienced unprecedented economic and cultural ad-

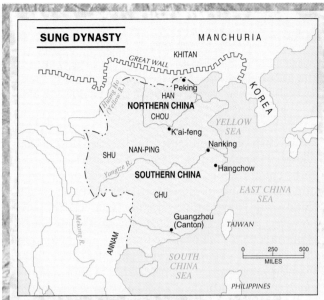

The Great Wall did not protect Sung China from invasions from the north. The Khitan Mongols from central Asia and the Jürchen nomads from Manchuria in turn attacked and subordinated the Sung.

vances, particularly after being reduced to only southern China, and turned increasingly toward oceanborne commerce. But this dearly purchased prosperity brought many internal problems. Spreading affluence encouraged selfish individualism and weakened loyalties among all classes. Paying tribute and suffering tax evasion by the wealthy, the state experienced mounting budgetary deficits, while rising taxes produced peasant unrest. In the late eleventh century, even before the country was divided, the emperor called on an eminent statesman, Wang An-shih, to meet this crisis. Wang sponsored a program that enforced state-controlled interest rates on agricultural loans, fixed commodity prices, provided unemployment benefits, established old-age pensions, and reformed the examination system by stressing practical rather than literary knowledge. Although these measures brought some improvements, they evoked fanatical opposition from scholars, bureaucrats, and moneylenders. In the next generation most of the reforms were rescinded.

The humiliating treaty with the Chin in 1141 was followed by a period of steeper political decline, particularly under the "dim-witted" emperor Ning-tsing (1194–1224) and his lecherous successor Li-tsung (1224–1264). Intrigues of court women paralyzed the central government; high taxes, official injustice, and criminal disorder destroyed public morale; and Mongol armies, moving against the Chin, foreshadowed an inevitable and fast-approaching disaster.

Memorial on the Crop Lands Measure

Wang An-shih wrote this proposal in 1069. It was presented by a government commission to Emperor Shen-tsung, who applied it first in a few provinces. Later it was extended to other areas. The proposal aims in part to relieve farmers from having to take loans at high rates and having to pay loans back in times of bad harvests. Note how the proposal points out abuses and tries to redress them; it ends by invoking the memory of past kings who ruled benevolently, thus urging the current monarch to do the same.

The cash and grain stored in the Ever-Normal and the Liberal-Charity granaries of the various circuits, counting roughly in strings of cash and bushels of grain, amount to more than 15,000,000. Their collection and distribution are not handled properly, however, and therefore we do not derive full benefit from them. Now we propose that the present amount of grain in storage should be sold at a price lower than the market price when the latter is high; and that when the market price is low, the grain in the market should be purchased at a rate higher than the market price. We also propose that our reserves be made interchangeable with the proceeds of the land tax and the cash and grain held by the Fiscal Intendants, so that conversion of cash and grain may be permitted whenever convenient.

With the cash at hand, we propose to follow the example set by the crop loan system in Shensi province. Farmers desirous of borrowing money before the harvest should be granted loans, to be repaid at the same time as they pay their tax, half with the summer payment and half with the autumn payment. They are free to repay either in kind or in cash, should they prefer to do so if the price of grain is high at the time of repayment. In the event disaster strikes, they should be allowed to defer payment until the date when the next harvest payment would be due. In this way not only would we be prepared to meet the distress of famine, but, since the people would receive loans from the government, it would be impossible for the monopolistic houses to exploit the gap between harvests by charging interest at twice the normal rate.

Under the system of Ever-Normal and Liberal-Charity granaries, it has been the practice to keep grain in storage and sell it only when the harvest is poor and the price of grain is high. Those who benefit from this are only the idle people in the cities.

Now we propose to survey the situation in regard to surpluses and shortages in each circuit as a whole, to sell when grain is dear and buy when it is cheap, in order to increase the accumulation in government storage and to stabilize the prices of commodities. This will make it possible for the farmers to go ahead with their work at the proper season, while the monopolists will no longer be able to take advantage of their temporary stringency. All this is proposed in the interests of the people, and the government derives no advantage therefrom. Moreover, it accords with the idea of the ancient kings who bestowed blessings upon all impartially and promoted whatever was of benefit by way of encouraging the cultivation and accumulation of grain.

From *Sources of Chinese Tradition*, comp. W. Theodore de Bary, Wing-tsi Chan, and Burton Watson (New York: Columbia University Press, 1963), pp. 475–476.

Sung Economic and Social Conditions

Economic efficiency was certainly Sung China's redeeming strength. Although the government maintained some monopolies and taxed trade moderately, it built great water-control projects, aided intensive agriculture, and otherwise loosened control over individual enterprise. Consequently, rice production doubled within a century after 1050, and industry grew rapidly, pouring out the finest silk, lacquer wares, and porcelain for home and foreign markets. Sung economic advances were furthered by such technical innovations as water clocks, paddleboats, seagoing junks, the stern post rudder, and the mariner's compass. It was also in this era that the Chinese developed the first explosive projectile weapons. The resulting commercial expansion prompted banks to depend on paper currency and specialized commercial instruments. Trade with the outside world, formerly dominated by foreigners, was taken over by the Chinese, who established trading colonies throughout East Asia.

The Sung economic revolution exerted tremendous foreign influence abroad. Paper money, dating from the eleventh century in the south, was soon copied in the Khitan state and issued by the Chin government in 1153; its use then spread steadily in all directions. Other Sung economic innovations appeared quickly along the Asiatic coast from Japan and Korea to the East Indies, where Chinese merchants were immigrant culture carriers. Sung technology also spread to India, the Middle East, and

This scroll painting is attributed to the Sung dynasty emperor-artist Hui-tsung but may have been produced by an artist in his court. It portrays richly dressed palace women beating and preparing silk. An ineffectual ruler, Hui-tsung is best remembered as a painter, calligrapher, and patron of the arts.

Court Ladies Preparing Newly Woven Silk, Emperor Huizong (attributed to), r. 1101–1125. Chinese; Northern Song Dynasty, early 12th century. Handscroll; ink, color and gold on silk. 27.0 × 145.3 cm. Museum of Fine Arts, Boston, Chinese and Japanese Special Fund.

even Europe. From China, Europe acquired metal horseshoes, the padded horse collar, and the wheelbarrow. Chinese mapping skills, along with the compass and the stern post ship rudder, helped prepare the way for Europe's age of expansion. Later, gunpowder and movable type, both pioneered in Sung China, arrived in Europe via Asian intermediaries.

Profound and rapid change brought many tensions to Sung society. Some arose from urban expansion in a population that swelled from 60 to 115 million, a percentage increase of more than twice the world average. Crowded living and rising economic competition undermined the family, weakened old values, and lessened loyalty to the state. Before the Mongol threat in the thirteenth century, people in the south tended to feel safe from nomad attack, but they were increasingly concerned about their personal freedom, social advancement, psychological satisfaction, and amusement. Social changes during the Sung era, however, did little to affect the class structure. Merchants, no matter how wealthy, could not replace the dominant scholar-bureaucrats, who continued to hold power and land.

Although lower-class women gained the freedom to conduct some businesses and court women continued to exercise power indirectly, Sung affluence and competition helped erode Buddhist compassion and revive the Confucian doctrine of rigid male dominance. Particularly among the elite classes, these changes brought new restrictions for most women. Usually betrothed by their fathers, they lived in near-servile status within their husbands' families, producing children and providing social decoration. The binding of little girls' feet, as preparation for this sterile adult life, became common under the Sung, as

did female infanticide, restriction on remarriage of widows, and harsh legal penalties, including death, for violating the accepted code of prescribed wifely conduct.

Sung Philosophy, Literature, and Art

The rapidly changing Sung society was reflected in a personalizing of philosophy, literature, and art. Writers explored the lives of individual subjects. Artists, while remaining interested in nature, depicted its beauty in more varied styles, all involving greater attention to objectivity and employing a lighter touch than was typical of the T'ang era. Serious thinkers turned increasingly toward humane as opposed to political morality, despite the lingering Confucian influence.

A prevailing social insecurity and the political debate over Wang An-shih's humanitarian reforms led to major philosophical dissension. Most reformers claimed that their proposals were based on Confucian principles, but the reforms were nevertheless strongly opposed by the majority of Confucian scholars, who were part of the established bureaucracy. Buddhist and Taoist spokesmen generally opposed the government, increasing the conflict. Thus the fragile compromise between Buddhism and Confucianism achieved during the T'ang period was placed under severe strain. Ultimately, these problems were resolved by a new compromise known as Neo-Confucianism, which was to become the intellectual foundation for Chinese thought until the twentieth century.

Chu Hsi (1130–1200), the greatest of the Neo-Confucian synthesizers, was a brilliant scholar and

A painting from the Sung dynasty showing the poet Li Po in repose. Li Po's poetry is renowned for its exquisite imagery, rich allusions, and beautiful cadence.

chemistry, zoology, botany, and cartography. Sung algebra was also the most advanced in the world.

Sung aesthetic expression was more secular and less introspective than that during the earlier era of Buddhist influence. This outlook encouraged versatility; as during the later European Renaissance, the universal man—public servant, scholar, poet, or painter—was the ideal. The most famous female Chinese poet, Li Ch'ing-chao (b. 1181), whose work was enthusiastically promoted by her scholar husband, wrote her uniquely personalized verse in the southern Sung period. Another well-known poet of nature and gardens was the traveling scholar-bureaucrat and reporter Fan Changda (1126–1193). Historical and philosophical works reflected the main literary interests of the time, but the traditional love of nature was still displayed in landscape painting, which reached a peak under the Sung. Artists gave more attention to detail and were therefore more precisely naturalistic than T'ang painters, although the latter were often more imaginative.

The Emergence of Japan

The rise of Japan after the sixth century was part of a much larger process in which a number of new fringe cultures developed rapidly in the shadows of the old major civilizations. In Europe, Africa, southeastern and central Asia, Korea, and Japan, these civilizations

respected commentator on the Confucian classics. His teaching sought to reconcile the mystical popular faiths of Buddhism and Taoism with Confucian practicality. Like his near-contemporary in Europe, St. Thomas Aquinas, Chu Hsi synthesized faith and reason; but unlike Aquinas, Chu's highest priority was disciplined reason. He believed that people are naturally neither good nor bad but are inclined either way by experience and education. The universe, according to Chu, is a self-generating and self-regulating order to which humans may adjust rationally. Faith and custom, however, are necessary supports for reason and proper training.

Chu Hsi contended that self-cultivation required the extension of knowledge, best achieved by the "investigation of things." As a consequence, Neo-Confucianism was accompanied by significant advances in the experimental and applied sciences. Chinese doctors, during the period, introduced inoculation against smallpox. Their education and hospital facilities far surpassed anything in the West. In addition, there were notable achievements in astronomy,

Ma Yüan, Bare Willows and Distant Mountains. Ma Yüan was one of the two leading painters of the southern Sung dynasty, the other was Hsia Kuei. Their style of landscape painting, known as the Ma-Hsia school, followed a prescribed formula: a foreground, a middle ground, and a far ground, each separated by mist, which gave the paintings a light, ethereal quality. The delicate tranquillity of this small fan painting is disturbed only by the red seals placed there by a Ming collector.

Ma Yuan, Chinese, active 1190–1235; Southern Song Dynasty, *Bare Willows and Distant Mountains.* Round fan mounted as album leaf; ink and light color on silk, 23.8 × 24.2 cm. Museum of Fine Arts, Boston. Special Chinese and Japanese Fund.

Japan

c. 300	Yamato clan dominates central Japan
552	Buddhism introduced to Japan
645	Taika reforms
794–1185	Heian period
995–1027	Regency of Fujiwara Michinaga
1185	Soldier-statesman Yoritomo establishes Kamakura Shogunate

were able to appropriate the cultural values and commodities of the more highly developed civilizations and integrate them with their own cultural patterns. In its early evolution, for example, Japan borrowed much from China, but this cultural raw material was mixed and reworked into a new Japanese pattern.

Geographical, Ethnic, and Historical Backgrounds

Much that is distinctive in Japanese culture has resulted from geographical conditioning, which provided harsh challenges but maximum national security. The inland sea surrounded by the islands of Kyushu, Shikoku, and Honshu, with their lush and beautiful sheltered plains, was the center of Japanese civilization until the twelfth century. Yet even this area, along with the other 3000 islands of the archipelago, has frequently experienced earthquakes and typhoons. Location was the most important early factor in Japan's evolution; approximately 200 miles of water separate the highly populated islands from the mainland. Isolated as they were during their early history, the Japanese were secure enough to experiment with new ways while retaining a deep attachment to their land and its traditional culture.

Ethnically, the Japanese are of mixed origins, a result of many prehistoric migrations from the mainland, by way of Korea and Southeast Asia, through the island chain to the south. The resulting common ethnic community was predominantly Mongoloid, though darker than Asian mainland types. The language was derived from the basic Altaic family of northern Asia, which also produced Mongol and Korean variations. As the Japanese population expanded and moved north, after the third century C.E., it began exterminating and absorbing the Ainu, a people of less developed culture, who had first occupied the area. This process has continued into the modern era.

In ancient times numerous small warring states, each ruled by a hereditary chieftain who claimed

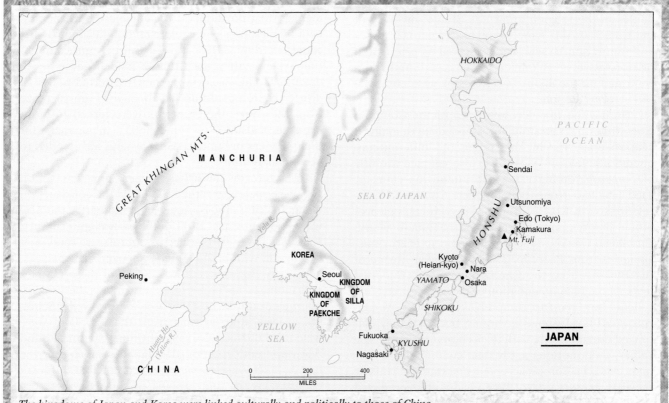

The kingdoms of Japan and Korea were linked culturally and politically to those of China.

descent from a tribal deity, occupied the mountainous Japanese islands. According to Japanese folklore, one of these chieftains named Jimmu ("Divine Warrior"), a descendant of the sun goddess, began the current line of Japanese emperors in 660 B.C.E. Current scholarship places the date later, after migrants from the southern Korean state of Paekche began conquering western Kyushu in the third century C.E. One of their leaders, a fighting queen called Jingo, began a process of unification, with diplomatic and military support from Paekche. During this "tomb period" of war and confusion, which lasted through the fourth century, the Yamato clan emerged as the ruling power in Kyushu, then advanced its conquests east and north, ultimately attacking the Ainu in Honshu.

Early Japanese society resembled others in transition from nomadism to a settled way of life. Dependent on peasant agriculture and centered in villages, it was organized in clans on a kinship basis. Years of war and conquest, however, divided the clans along class lines; members of the top clans enjoyed special privileges, wielded political power, and collected taxes. These nobles constituted a military aristocracy, famous for its archery, iron swordplay, horsemanship, and a code stressing courage, discipline, honor, and pride. Despite this military emphasis, early Japanese society was largely matriarchal, as evidenced by the raising of children in the wives' families, the relative social equality of women, their frequent queenly roles, and the prevalence of female deities in the religion known as Shinto, or "Way of the Gods." In this simple worship of natural forces and family spirits, war leaders served as priests and priestesses; later, as Yamato power grew, Shinto concentrated on the divine ancestress of the clan as the protector of the state.

During the first few centuries of the Common Era, while the Yamato clan extended its domain in central Japan, its chieftain imposed tribute on conquered native clan leaders. He also claimed the title of emperor, forcing vassals to attend his court or send hostages from their families. Continued close relations with Korea through the sixth century promoted progress and awareness of the outside world. Buddhism was introduced into Japan in 552 by missionaries from Paekche. They brought an image of the Buddha from the Korean king, some Buddhist texts, and a recommendation of the new faith as "excellent" but "hard to comprehend." At first Yamato rulers did not respond favorably, but soon they embraced the new faith, with its accompanying Chinese values, even more fervently than contemporary German tribes in Europe accepted Christianity. Thus as the sixth century ended, Japan had about completed its period of early transition and was ready to assume its role as a civilized Asian state.

The Taika Reforms

The first long step in this direction came in 645, when the emperor's government imposed a sweeping program of change, embodied in legal edicts known as the Taika reforms. The new policy was a direct result of rising interest in Korean and Chinese culture, which began after 552 with migrating Korean Buddhists. The Korean influx was markedly increased by refugees after Paekche was absorbed by the neighboring kingdom of Silla in 663. Because Silla had been an ally of China for years, the Japanese feared an attack from the victors in Korea and saw a need to strengthen their defenses. These concerns, along with the expanding Korean influence, generated interest in reforms to protect the country.

The new program was revealed in 645 as the Yamato regime deliberately established a centralized absolutism modeled on T'ang China. A group of young Japanese, including eight Paekchean scholars recently returned from China, seized power to proclaim a new order, hailing the Yamato ruler as *Tenno*, or "Heavenly Emperor." The resulting Taika ("Great Change") reforms asserted the absolute authority of the monarch at the expense of the former clan chieftains. The reformers also established a centralized bureaucracy, a legal code, a tightly controlled provincial system, a standing army, and a land tax similar to that of the T'ang.

From the beginning, differences between Japanese and Chinese societies required drastic adjustments. Most positions in the Japanese bureaucracy, held by members of the old clan nobility, quickly became hereditary. Recruitment through an examination system, after the Chinese model, never developed in Japan. Because the newly asserted power of direct taxation could not be effective at any distance from the court, the emperors were forced to grant tax-exempt estates to some nobles in payment for their services or support. Such estates also tended to become hereditary.

The reforms nevertheless had a great impact on Japanese society, not the least being the construction of Japan's first city, Nara, as a capital where the new ways could flourish. Built in the early eighth century, Nara was carefully planned as a miniature version of Ch'ang-an, with broad streets, imposing new palaces, and many Buddhist edifices. Some of these temples and monasteries still survive as among the best remaining examples of T'ang architectural style. Scholars, priests, and artisans from the mainland were welcomed at Nara. Carriers of Chinese culture found ready apprentices among the Japanese, including the first Japanese historians, who recorded, in Confucian contexts, myths and legends of the past that supported the emperor's right to his throne as a descendant of the sun goddess.

The Great Buddha at Nara, Japan. This 1200-year-old bronze image is Japan's largest Buddha. Its face is approximately 16 feet long. Such Buddhas are dramatic evidence of Buddhism's successful spread into East Asia.

A New Japanese Order: The Heian Period, 794–1185

A re-created Japanese cultural and political system, part traditional, part Chinese, part imperial, and primarily feudal, came into being during the Heian period. In 794 a Confucian-trained emperor built a new capital at Heian-kyo (now called Kyoto and modeled, like Nara, on Ch'ang-an) to free himself from the growing political power of the Buddhist clergy; here the imperial court remained for over a thousand years, until 1868. During the next three and a half centuries, "peace and tranquillity" (a literal translation of *Heian-kyo*) generally characterized Japanese life. The era of Chinese-inspired reforms was over. Imperial authority weakened, and a court aristocracy flourished without much political power. What was left of central government came under the domination of the Fujiwara family, and local lords in the provinces became virtually independent.

By the tenth century the Fujiwara family was accepted as the source of hereditary regents, who ruled the country for figurehead emperors, a system continued, in various forms, to the present. Fujiwara Michinaga, who held dominion over the court from 995 to 1027, was the brother of two empresses and the father of four, the uncle of two emperors, the grandfather of two more, and the great-grandfather of another. Controlled by such a web of family connections and influence, the Heian court functioned in accordance with its own stately rhythms. The sacred emperor performed his ceremonial duties, some Shinto and some Buddhist. Fujiwara women, as imperial consorts, produced future emperors. Mon-

archs were pressured to retire to Buddhist monasteries when their male heirs, usually as little boys, were old enough to perform the prescribed rituals. As maternal uncles or grandfathers of the child-sovereigns, Fujiwara regents managed affairs until the emperors matured and abdicated in turn.

While the Fujiwara, the puppet emperors, and effete court nobles played their formal roles at Heian-kyo, political power was shifting toward the provinces, where local lords were becoming independent governors and military commanders. Some of the strongest and most adventurous lords organized campaigns against the Ainu, seizing and colonizing territories with their followers. A network of feudal relationships, linking land grants with pledges of personal loyalty and service, developed among these provincial nobles and their subordinates, often completely outside imperial authority. The *bushi* (warrior) lords and their mounted *samurai* retainers generated a primitive value system, the Code of *Bushido*, which stressed courage, endurance, discipline, and loyalty unto death. The long-range effect of the Bushido tradition among Japanese men was recognized by many American soldiers in World War II.

Culture of the Heian Period

The court at Heian-kyo produced an artificial culture, largely imported from China. Behind this facade of Chinese traditions and aristocratic pretensions, however, the Japanese by the tenth century had developed a cultural perspective quite distinct from China's. Although also nature lovers, the Japanese were much less scholarly than the Chinese and more moved by intuitive preferences for balance, restraint, delicate precision, and economy. Indeed, "cultivation of the little" has been identified as a characteristic Japanese culture trait, which may have resulted from people living closely together on small secluded islands.

Perhaps the most obvious signs of Chinese influence were the temples. Generally, they followed the characteristic T'ang style and were adorned lavishly with both imported and Japanese statues of the Buddha, executed in bronze or wood and showing the typical benign expression of the Gandaran school. Surviving temples include the Horyuji at Nara and the Phoenix Hall of the Byodoin at Uji, not far from Kyoto. The latter features perfect symmetry, extravagant decoration, and striking contrasts of white and bright red. Although symbolizing the Buddhist paradise, it also expresses the Japanese penchant for harmony between a subject and its natural setting. The hall stands beside a pond, its reflection creating an inverse picture of the building in the water.

Painting developed from Chinese models but, like architecture, soon showed a distinctive Japanese

A fine example of architecture during the Heian period in Japan is Phoenix Hall, near the modern city of Kyoto. The building shows the influence of Chinese style.

flavor. Buddhist themes predominated at first, but later artists chose subjects drawn from everyday life. The new Japanese style, known as *Yamato-e*, was noted for its use of bright colors and for filling in finely sketched outlines. It was often used in decorating sliding doors and screens, but it was most commonly seen in picture scroll illustrations for literary works.

Heian literature, while reflecting clearly the aristocratic life of its setting, was even more independent of Chinese influence than the other arts. Most Japanese intellectuals were men, trained to write in Chinese characters that could not easily express Japanese syllables or thought. Upper-class Japanese women were not as well educated in Chinese and therefore wrote in a phonetic script, expressing Japanese sensitivities in poems, diaries, and novels. These works contained analyses of personal feeling that had no precedents in Chinese literature. The finest example is undoubtedly *The Tale of Genji*, a long novel by Lady Murasaki (c. 978–1031), who depicted her narrow court life with great psychological profundity and aesthetic appreciation for human emotion. As Lady Murasaki explained in the words of her hero, Genji, an author does not write only to tell

a story but also to express an "emotion so passionate that he can no longer keep it shut up in his heart" or "let it pass into oblivion."[4]

Well before Lady Murasaki, in the early eighth century, the countryside beyond Heian-kyo had begun producing its own literature. The *Manyoshu*, a collection of some 4000 poems, reflects a fresh outpouring of the native Japanese spirit in treating the old religion, the brevity of life, love of nature, and appreciation of friends. These short poems have never been surpassed in equating natural phenomena and human emotion, clinching each point in typical Japanese fashion with a twist of thought at the end of a set syllabic sequence.

The Kamakura Shogunate

Cultural development continued past the thirteenth century in directions set during the Heian era, but the Fujiwara regency disintegrated much sooner as the result of warfare among the noble clans. In 1185, after a long struggle still celebrated in Japanese historical fiction, movies, and television, a clique dominated by the Minamoto clan emerged victorious. Its leader, an outstanding soldier-statesman named Yoritomo, forced

A portrait of Lady Murasaki, courtier and author of the romantic novel The Tale of Genji, *the great classic of Japanese literature.*

the emperor to grant him the title of *shogun* ("supreme commander") and established a capital at Kamakura. Subsequent shoguns paid utmost respect to the emperors and governed at a discreet distance from the imperial court at Heian-kyo. Nevertheless, the shoguns, not the emperors, were the real rulers of Japan.

The Kamakura Shogunate was a superfeudal order, designed to control an earlier one created by the Fuji-wara court. It employed constables and stewards in every province but still relied on a complex web of personal obligations among local aristocrats and their common adherence to the Code of Bushido. The prevailing values were extended to women, who were now expected to bear hardships with Spartan endurance, to fight and, if necessary, to die beside their husbands. Their lives became much harder, but they could hold

A thirteenth-century wooden statue of Minamoto Yoritomo, Japan's first shogun.

The artistic style of the Kamakura period in Japan emphasized strength and realism, as is evident in this battle scene. The scroll is from a series illustrating the Heiji Monogatari, *an epic narrative describing the rise and fall of the Taira clan, rivals of the Minamoto, the eventual victors and founders of the Kamakura Shogunate. The* Heiji Monogatari *chronicles events from the winter of 1159–1160 when the Taira temporarily defeated the Minamoto.*

Battle Scene, Kamakura period, 14th century. Section of handscroll mounted as a hanging scroll; ink, color, and touches of gold paint on paper, H. 14" × W. 17 1/4". Seattle Art Museum, Eugene Fuller Memorial Collection, 48.173. Photo: Paul Macapia.

the rights of a vassal and inherit property under the code. Kamakura noblewomen were often successful administrators. One of the ablest was Masako, Yorimoto's widow, also known as the "nun-shogun," who became the power behind the next ruler after her husband died.

The Mongol Impact

Debate continues over what sparked the Mongol invasions: population pressure, military capability, or the inspiration of an ambitious warlord. Regardless of cause, the impulse of the Mongols altered the course of history for much of the world. In the second half of the thirteenth century, a militaristic and well-organized Mongol horde moved out of central Asia to attack China, India, the Middle East, and Europe. The Mongols, horse- and sheep-raising nomads and formidable mounted warriors, spread terror among their enemies and conquered cities and trade routes on the way to establishing a world empire. Beginning with their great conqueror, Genghis Khan

(1162–1227), they claimed that they were destined by "heaven" to subdue all peoples. The greatest of all the khans repeated this injunction as an order to his successors. They responded using their unprecedented organizational skills to launch large-scale military operations throughout Eurasia. They seized Persia, toppled the Islamic Abbasid caliphate in Baghdad, established their rule in Russia and China, and sacked the imperial city of Delhi in India.

In China and the Middle East, the invaders were assimilated into the well-established cultures they conquered. In the subcontinent the invaders were ultimately turned back. And in Russia they established *khanates* (territories ruled by khans) that would endure down to the early modern era. The Mongols have often been represented as destroyers par excellence, sacking cities, disrupting trade, and building towers of the heads of their conquered foes. But holding sway in old and new imperial cities in Eurasia, the Mongols also fostered trade and diplomatic activity, patronized the arts, promoted religious tolerance, and provided security and postal service on the

The Mongols

1162–1227	Genghis Khan establishes Mongol Empire in central Asia
1229–1241	Reign of Ögedei; Mongols take northern China and Russia
1258	Mongol Hülegü takes Baghdad, ends Abbasid caliphate
1260–1294	Rule of Great Khan Kublai, who establishes Yuan dynasty in China
c. 1275	Marco Polo arrives at Kublai's court

roads of a series of interlinked kingdoms extending from China to Europe.

Nomads of Central Asia

The Mongols were part of an old and developing nomadic tradition on the steppes of central Asia. Prior to their conquests, they had ranged widely there, pitching their black felt tents, pasturing their animals, and fighting the elements much like other peoples who had terrorized settled Eurasian populations since the fourth century B.C.E. Their chiefs contended to be the "first among equals," their decisions were made by councils of warriors, and their women enjoyed a high degree of freedom, respect, and influence. It was a proud tradition and one that Genghis

Khan ordered maintained, a charge honored in Mongol law into the fourteenth century.

Mongol society on the steppes fostered a mixture of values, combining primitive superstitions and the fierce ruthlessness of fighting men with a crude democratic equality. The ruling khans held almost unlimited authority, but criminal penalties were enforced equally regardless of one's status. Polygamy was practiced among the warriors, but not all marriages were polygamous, and marital fidelity was enforced equally for men and women. Wives sometimes rode and fought beside their husbands; in a harsh environment where raiding and warfare were common, women as well as men had sometimes to defend the hearth and livestock. But usually Mongol women, as in most traditional societies, confined their activities to domestic affairs. In addition to caring for children, they milked the mares and made all clothing. They were also responsible for many tasks required by their nomadic life, such as breaking camp, loading the ox wagons, and driving animals on the march. There was a gendered division of labor, but within its context women were honored and afforded a rough approximation of social equality.

As was true of their central Asian predecessors, the Mongols held military advantages in their superior cavalry tactics and mobility. Once the conquests began, their disadvantages were that their numbers were relatively few and that they had to depend on the bureaucratic skills of the conquered peoples to run their empire. This situation changed steadily as civilization spread on the steppes of central Asia after the sixth century. Over time the Mongol conquerors were sedentarized and acquired the languages, religions,

Two views of Mongols as seen by their contemporaries. Left is a Persian miniature showing Mongols preparing food at their tents. Right is a Chinese painting of a mounted Mongol archer.

cultural patterns, and administrative skills of the civilizations they conquered.

An earlier precedent for invasions out of central Asia came from the Turkic peoples, who had figured in Eurasian history for a thousand years before the emergence of the Mongols. Originating in the Altai Mountains, near the Orkhon River north of Tibet, they had begun attacking northwestern China in the third century C.E. and continued to be mentioned in Chinese annals as the Yueh-chih, a branch of the Hsuing-nu (Hun) frontier barbarians. As some Turks began living in cities after 500, they were noted for their skills as ironworkers. According to the Chinese, in the sixth century the Turks produced the first written language among the peoples of central Asia; the oldest surviving Turkish records date from 200 years later, by which time the Turks had established their first steppe empire.

Between the sixth and eighth centuries, Turkic and Chinese regimes competed for control of the steppes. With Chinese support, the first Turkish Empire emerged in 552 and extended its dominion over much of central Asia. Internal dissension caused it to split briefly into eastern and western khanates, followed by submission of the eastern khanate to China and ultimately conquest under the early T'ang emperors. Later, as the T'ang regime weakened, a revived Turkish Empire dominated the steppes (684–734), only to succumb again to internal weaknesses. Although maintaining many old tribal institutions, these states had central bureaucracies and appointed provincial officials, as did many petty Turkic monarchies in border areas.

During and after their imperial experiments, the Turks absorbed and transmitted much of the culture from their more advanced neighbors. Trade, religion, and warfare facilitated the process. Eastern Turks borrowed early from China, adopting Buddhism and converting their western kinsmen in far distant Ferghana. After the eighth century, when the Abbasid caliphate brought Islam to the steppes, Turkic invaders launched conquests in the Middle East and India. There were several waves of migration and conquest, lasting into the fifteenth century, out of central Asia and into the settled territories of Eurasia. Such incursions most often brought short-term disaster to occupied regions, but they effected a great synthesis of peoples and cultures and ultimately led to the establishment of Turkic regimes from India to the Middle East (see Chapter 17).

For more than five centuries before the Mongol conquests, this process had been growing in intensity. Westward and to the north of the Chinese frontiers, a series of large states, partially urbanized but still containing nomadic or seminomadic populations, rose and fell. Among them were the Uighur Empire of the ninth century and the Tangut state. Both of these regimes prospered by providing protection and transport for the overland trade with China, which continued to grow. For many peoples of central Asia—Turks, Uighurs, Tanguts, Tibetans, Mongols, and a host of

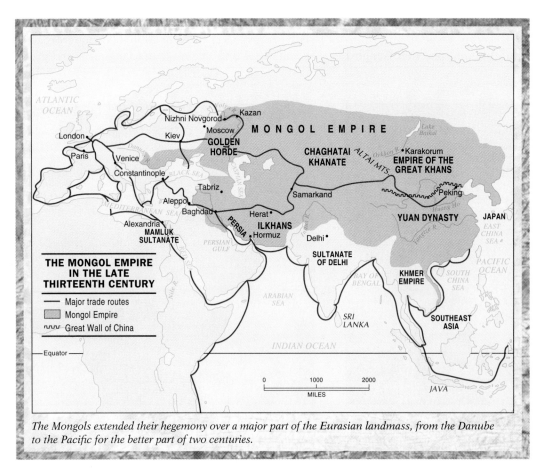

The Mongols extended their hegemony over a major part of the Eurasian landmass, from the Danube to the Pacific for the better part of two centuries.

others—trade, especially the silk trade, was one of many stimuli that turned their attention toward the outside world in the thirteenth century.

Formation of the Mongol Empire

At the opening of the thirteenth century, the Mongols began their whirlwind campaign of conquests and empire building. Within less than a century they had subdued most populations from the Pacific to the Danube, terrorized the rest, and gained luxuries beyond their imaginings. The Mongols also established what has been called the *Pax Mongolica*, which permitted more trade and travel across Eurasia than the world would see again until the seventeenth century. This was the largest empire ever known, comparable in geographical area only to the twentieth-century Soviet Union.

Like all large empires in an era of primitive transportation and communications, however, when it extended far beyond its central administrative centers it began to weaken even as it was being formed and extended. Like the Roman, Mauryan, and Abbasid Empires, the Mongol Empire required the delegation of authority, shared power, and reliance on provincial governors with considerable autonomy to keep it intact. It is also the case, as demonstrated by the reign of Aurangzeb in India, that empires are difficult to hold together once they expand past the distance that a ruler's army can march in a single campaign season. Thus empires like the Mongol are exceptional and notable for the fact that they did not collapse quickly.

Mongol successes, against such great odds, owed much to the guiding genius who launched his people into history. The son of a minor Mongol chief, he was born around 1162 and named Temüjin, or "Man of Iron." When Temüjin's father was killed by enemies, the young warrior was forced into a lonely exile on the steppe, where he nursed his ambitions though barely managing to survive. Using cunning, courage, brutality, and patience through subsequent years, he gathered followers, persevering through tribal wars and forming a new confederacy. Ultimately, a convocation of all the tribes in 1206 recognized him as Genghis Khan, "Oceanic Ruler" of the Mongols.

During the first stage of empire building, to 1241, the Mongols concentrated on the steppe and its less developed border areas. Genghis subordinated the Uighur and Tangut, conquered the Chin capital in northern China, seized Turkestan and Afghanistan, and invaded Persia. After his death in 1227, the campaigns halted and the Mongol forces reassembled in Mongolia to elect Genghis's designated successor, his son Ögedei (1229–1241). Under the new khan the Mongols seized northern China, occupied Russia, and invaded eastern Europe. When Ögedei died, the succession to the khanate was contested. During that time his widow ruled as regent; again in 1248 there was a period of female rule after Güyük Khan died.

In their second phase of conquest the Mongols extended their domain into every civilized area of Eurasia, but as the empire grew larger, its unity became increasingly harder to maintain. Between 1251 and 1259, during the reign of the Grand Khan Möngke, a grandson of Genghis Khan, Mongol armies conquered eastern Tibet (1252) and Korea (1258) while the horde led by Möngke's brother, Hülegü, toppled the Abbasid caliphate, absorbing every subsidiary state in Persia, Palestine, and Syria. Unlike the Seljuk Turks before them, who had also conquered Baghdad but retained the Abbasid caliph to legitimize their rule, the Mongols killed the caliph in 1258, thus effectively ending the classical era of Islamic rule. Hülegü's campaign reflected the newly cosmopolitan nature of the Mongol army; it included a contingent of Chinese catapult operators. Hülegü also had Chinese physicians at his court.

The end of Möngke's reign marked a climax in Mongol expansion. In 1260 the Mongol tide was stopped by the Mamluk army in Syria. This defeat was followed by bloody contention among rival Mongol khans. Kublai Khan (1260–1294) emerged as dominant, but after 1264 the empire broke up into four parts under only nominal central administration: China under Kublai, where he established the Yuan dynasty; the Chaghatai khanate in western Turkestan; the Golden Horde in Russia and the western steppe area; and Hülegü's line, the Ilkhans, in Persia and Iraq. Some Mongol advances occurred when Kublai, another grandson of Temüjin, completed the conquest of southern China and major areas of Southeast Asia in the 1270s and 1280s, but attempted naval attacks against Japan (1281) and Java (1293) were complete failures.

Because they were so few in number, the Mongols often relied on terror to control conquered peoples, particularly during the early conquests. One of Genghis Khan's "old guard" is supposed to have suggested that all of northern China be depopulated and the land used for pasturage. The Mongols were especially noted for abuses by their official envoys, traveling with rapacious entourages through subdued territories. Mongol commanders also regularly imposed mass murder, torture, and resettlement on resisting populations. In Baghdad, for example, Hülegü, Möngke's younger brother, was said to have executed hundreds of thousands of men, women, and children, sparing only some skilled craftsmen and Christian victims of the Muslims, whom he hoped to recruit as allies. The accompanying destruction of the irrigation system almost ruined Mesopotamian agriculture. Such ruthless policies were modified somewhat by Möngke, who issued reforms aimed at lessening Mongol excesses and restoring economic productivity. Yet even under more benign Mongol rule, the population in Kublai's China dropped, according to some figures, from 100 million to less than 70 million.

A Mamluk Officer in Hülegü's Camp

After the Mongols seized the Abbasid capital in Baghdad, the khan, Hülegü, marched on Syria and Egypt. The Muslim Mamluk regime based in Cairo managed to stop the troops at the battle of Ayn Jalut, but the Mongol advance terrified populace and palace alike. In these scenes, al-Sarim, an officer of the Mamluk king, visits the enemy camp while it is laying seige to Aleppo and describes the khan. In effect, al-Sarim became a member of the Mongol's court, but he retained his Mamluk loyalties. Note the roles that honor and magnanimity play in these encounters and the deference granted to the khan's wife. Mongol women often held positions of great influence and sometimes ruled as regents for their minor sons.

When he sent for me and I appeared before him, I saw before me a king of majestic demeanor, high distinction, and great dignity, of short stature, with a very flat nose, a broad face, a loud voice, and compassionate eyes. The ladies sat at his side with the lady Doquz Khatun sitting at his left. . . .

Hülegü asks al-Sarim to bring his Mamluk lord, al-Malik al-Ashraf, to see him, and al-Sarim does so. The Mamluk chief stands terrified before the Mongol khan.

Doquz Khatun looked at al-Malik al-Ashraf and then looked toward Hülegü and said, "This is a fine young man and the knight of the Muslims. That is how kings should be." Then Hülegü looked back at her smiling and said, "Yet we are the kings before whom these kings stand on foot, humbled and in fear of our power." While all this was happening, al-Malik al-Ashraf stood in front of Hülegü, not knowing what fate would do with him. Then Hülegü raised his head and said, "Ashraf, choose what gift you will." And al-Malik al-Ashraf kissed the ground three times. Al-Sarim said: "Ask him to give you the tower of the Citadel [of Aleppo] in which are your mother, and two sisters, your daughters, the wives of the kings, and the daughters and wives of al-Malik al-

Nasir. If you do not ask for this tower now, on this very night the Mongols will capture the Citadel of Aleppo and the womenfolk of the Muslim kings will become slave-girls of this lady Doquz Khatun." Al-Malik al-Ashraf asked, "Will he not kill me?" I answered, "The Mongols do not kill those who are with them as guests."

So al-Malik asked Hülegü for the tower.

This angered Hülegü, who looked downward and said, "Ask for something else." But al-Malik al-Ashraf remained silent. Then Doquz Khatun looked at King Hülegü and said to him, "Are you not ashamed? A man like this king asks you for that tower and you refuse it to him. By God, if he had asked me for Aleppo, I would not have refused it for he is the knight of the Muslims." Hülegü said, "But I only refused it to him for your sake, so that the daughters and wives of the kings may be your slaves." Then she said, "I declare them free before Almighty God and for the sake of Malik al-Ashraf." Thereupon Hülegü granted al-Malik al-Ashraf what he asked, and al-Malik al-Ashraf kissed Hülegü's hand three times.

From Bernard Lewis, ed. and trans., *Islam*, Vol. 1 (Harper & Row, 1974), pp. 89–96 passim.

The Mongol Imperial Structure

Although they were three generations beyond nomadism, Mongol rulers of the mid-thirteenth century were forced to learn quickly how to organize and operate the largest imperial state that had ever existed. Its ethnic diversity was demonstrated at Möngke's court, where official communications had to be prepared in many languages, including Persian, Uighur, Chinese, Tibetan, Arabic, and Tangut. For this complex imperial structure, the methods of the steppes were obviously no longer effective and had to be integrated with those of more experienced conquered bureaucrats.

The ultimate base of authority in the sprawling Mongol territories was military power. Its nucleus was a cavalry force of potentially 130,000 Mongols. For campaigns, the Mongol horsemen were augmented by larger forces, including infantry and siege troops, recruited from the native peoples. Many came as part of the tribute payments from submitting monarchs. Like other conquerors, the Mongols incorporated local war-

riors and governors into their military and administrative systems as long as these men were willing to submit to Mongol rule. Mongol persuasion and diplomacy were effective enough to draw large contingents, who performed well under precise Mongol discipline and organization and shared in the booty of further conquests. Thus the Mongols who conquered northern China in 1241 used more than 97,000 Chinese conscripts, and Hülegü's host before Baghdad numbered 300,000 soldiers. These numbers, of course, are taken from contemporary sources and cannot necessarily be taken literally. Estimates of the size of armies (even today) are often exaggerated to instill fear or inspire awe.

Central administration and internal stability reached a developmental climax in the notable reforms of Möngke's reign. The original empire, divided among descendants of Temüjin's four sons, with one recognized as supreme, was pulled closer together under Möngke's regime. Although he conducted a cruel purge of suspected opponents, Möngke revised the law code of Genghis Khan to accommodate native cultural differences and meet practical needs. He minted coins, issued paper currency, collected taxes in money, and perfected a census system as a basis for taxes and military service. His decrees lessened abuses in the famous Mongol courier service and the thousands of post stations that now radiated in all directions from the capital at Karakorum. To support military operations, his state industries mined ores and produced arms. Other measures regularized trade tolls, improved roads, and provided for the safety of travelers, especially merchants. These reforms encouraged support from subject peoples, many of whom were now employed in the khan's service.

Despite the complex Mongol regimes in Mongolia, Russia, the Middle East, and China, much government within the empire continued to be conducted by vassal monarchs, such as those in Bulgaria or Siam. These subordinate rulers were required to proclaim their submission publicly, leave hostages with the khans, pay annual tribute, and provide troops for military campaigns. A Mongol agent, assigned to the court of each dependent monarch and supported by an occupying military force, approved all policies before they were implemented. In return, tributary rulers who served the khans loyally were guaranteed political security, honored publicly, and rewarded with lavish gifts.

China Under the Mongols

During the reign of Kublai as Grand Khan (1260–1294), China gained new significance in the Mongol system. Although Kublai successfully maintained his titular authority over the subkhanates, he moved his capital from Karakorum to Peking; proclaimed himself the founder of a new Chinese dynasty, the Yuan; and turned attention primarily to his Chinese territories. This new emphasis on the eastern end of the empire contributed directly to the decentralization of Mongol power after Kublai's succession.

For much of our knowledge about China in this era, we are indebted to the Venetian traveler Marco Polo. As a youth he had accompanied his father and uncle, two Venetian merchants who journeyed eastward to Kublai's court, arriving there about 1275. Polo served the khan about 17 years as a trusted administrator before returning home. His fabulous story, dictated to a fellow prisoner of war in Genoa, reported the wondrous world of Cathay (China)—its canals, granaries, social services, technology, and such customs (strange to much of Europe) as regular bathing. His detailed descriptions of the wealth of the khan's court are awe-inspiring. It is no wonder that Polo's contemporaries considered him a braggart and a colossal liar. Polo's account, like many histories, is an interesting mix of fact and fantasy based on impressionistic observations and

A manuscript illumination from Marco Polo's journal depicts the Great Khan riding in a palanquin (an enclosed litter) borne by elephants. Kublai used this mode of travel because he was afflicted with gout. The artist seems not to have been very familiar with elephants, since these look rather like a cross between a boar and a dog.

Marco Polo on Mongol Military Prowess

One of the most famous of world travelers, the Venetian Marco Polo here describes the battle order and provisions of the Mongol army under Kublai Khan. Of course, there is always a fine line between myth and reality in such accounts, and we cannot take literally Marco Polo's account of ten-day rides sustained by the blood of a warrior's mount. Like other observers, however, Polo was impressed with the stamina of the Mongol warriors and astounded at their horsemanship. He calls the Mongol troops "Tartars."

You see, when a Tartar prince goes forth to war, he takes with him, say, one hundred thousand horses. Well, he appoints an officer to every ten men, one to every hundred, one to every thousand, and one to every ten thousand, so that his own orders have to be given to ten persons only, and each of these ten persons has to pass the orders only to another ten, and so on; no one having to give orders to more than ten. And every one in turn is responsible only to the officer immediately over him; and the discipline and order that comes of this method is marvelous, for they are a people very obedient to their chiefs. Further, they call the corps of one hundred thousand men a *Tuc;* that of ten thousand they call a *Toman;* the thousand they call *Miny;* the hundred *Guz;* the ten *On.* And when the army is on the march they have always two hundred horsemen, very well mounted, who are sent a distance of two marches in advance to reconnoitre, and these always keep ahead. They have a similar party detached in the rear, and on either flank, so that there is a good lookout on all sides against a surprise. When they are going on a distant expedition they take no gear with them except two leather bottles for milk, a little earthenware pot to cook their meat in, and a little tent to shelter them from rain. And in case of great urgency they will ride ten days on end without lighting a fire or taking a meal. On such an occasion they will sustain themselves on the blood of their horses, opening a vein and letting the blood jet into their mouths, drinking till they have had enough, and then staunching it.

They also have milk dried into a kind of paste to carry with them; and when they need food they put this in water, and beat it up till it dissolves, and then drink it. It is prepared in this way: they boil the milk, and when the rich part floats on the top they skim it into another vessel, and of that they make butter; for the milk will not become solid till this is removed.

Then they put the milk in the sun to dry. And when they go on an expedition, every man takes some ten pounds of this dried milk with him. And of a morning he will take a half pound of it and put it in his leather bottle, with as much water as he pleases. So, as he rides along, the milk paste and the water in the bottle get well churned together into a kind of pap, and that makes his dinner.

When they come to an engagement with the enemy, they will gain the victory in this fashion. They never let themselves get into a regular medley, but keep perpetually riding round and shooting into the enemy. And as they do not count it any shame to run away in battle, they will sometimes pretend to do so, and in running away they turn in the saddle and shoot hard and strong at the foe, and in this way make great havoc. Their horses are trained so perfectly that they will double hither and thither, just like a dog, in a way that is quite astonishing. Thus they fight to as good purpose in running away as if they stood and faced the enemy, because of the vast volleys of arrows that they shoot in this way, turning round upon their pursuers, who are fancying that they have won the battle. But when the Tartars see that they have killed and wounded a good many horses and men, they wheel round boldly, and return to the charge in perfect order and with loud cries: and in a very short time the enemy are routed. In truth they are stout and valiant soldiers, and inured to war. And you perceive that it is just when the enemy sees them run, and imagines that he has gained the battle, that he has in reality lost it; for the Tartars wheel round in a moment when they judge the right time has come. And after this fashion they have won many a fight.

From *The Travels of Marco Polo* (New York: Grosset & Dunlap, 1931), pp. 79–81.

probably prompted by the desire to entertain as well as inform a specific audience, but his descriptions, particularly of trade goods, are meticulous.

Yuan China strongly resembled the picture presented under earlier dynasties, with some exceptions. The country was governed mainly by foreigners: Mongols at the top, other peoples of central Asia on the next rung, northern Chinese in lower positions, and southern Chinese almost completely excluded from of-

fice. Kublai retained the traditional ministries and local governmental structure. Generally, Mongol law prevailed, but the conquerors were often influenced by Chinese legal precedents, as in the acceptance of brutal punishments for loose or unfaithful women. Most religions were tolerated unless they violated Mongol laws. According to Polo, the state insured against famine, kept order, and provided care for the sick, the aged, and the orphaned. To the awed Venetian, the

Yuan state appeared fabulously wealthy, as indicated by the khan's 12,000 personal retainers, bedecked in silks, furs, fine leathers, and sparkling jewels.[5]

In its cultural preferences, the Yuan court reverted to Chinese traditions. At first, Taoism and Confucianism were subordinated to Buddhism, but both revived during Kublai's reign. Chinese drama remained popular, influenced somewhat by the dance of central Asia. Interest in drama encouraged the development of classical Chinese opera, a combination of singing, dancing, and acting, which reached maturity in the Yuan period. Some of the most influential Chinese painters were also producing at this time, and the novel emerged as a reflection of Chinese concerns. An example is *Romance of the Three Kingdoms*, a long and rambling tale set in late Han times but written in the fourteenth century.

Pax Mongolica: Relinking East and West

During the century of the Mongol Peace, when much of Eurasia was unified to some degree and pacified by Mongol armies, East and West were in closer communication than ever before, even in Han and Roman times. Hosts of missionaries, traders, and adventurers continued to journey to and from Asia, Africa, and Europe, taking advantage of the security provided by the Pax Mongolica and hoping to benefit from the prosperity and patronage of the Mongol courts. These travelers describe the opulence of the Mongol courts, especially the gold brocade used to make court garments and to line the insides of the spectacular Mongol reception tents, some of which could hold over a thousand men.

Even before the Polos, Christian missionaries had proceeded eastward, encouraged by hopes of converting the Mongols and, more important, gaining allies against the Muslims. John of Plano Carpini, dispatched by Pope Innocent IV, visited the Great Khan in 1246 but failed to convert the ruler or enlist him as a papal vassal. In fact, the khan sent him home with a letter demanding that Europe's monarchs submit to him and that the pope attend the khan's court to pay homage. Later, a Flemish Franciscan, William of Rubruck, visited Möngke's court in 1254 and 1255 and met with similar results; but another Franciscan, John of Monte Corvino, attracted thousands of converts between his arrival in Peking in 1289 and his death in 1322. Meanwhile, Mongol religious toleration had drawn Nestorian Christians into central Asia and Buddhists into the Middle East.

In addition to the missionaries, swarms of other people responded to the Mongol interest in foreign knowledge and goods. One was Guillaume Boucier, a Parisian architect, who trekked to Karakorum, where he constructed a palace fountain capable of dispensing four different alcoholic beverages. Other adventurers, equally distinct, moved continuously on the travel routes. Between 1325 and 1354, Ibn Battuta, the famous Muslim globe-trotter from Morocco, visited Constantinople, every Middle Eastern Islamic state, India, Sri Lanka, Indonesia, and China. In Hangchow he encountered a man from Morocco whom he had met before in Delhi. Some travelers went the opposite way. Rabban Sauma, a Nestorian monk from central Asia, traveled to Paris; and a Chinese Christian monk from Peking, while in Europe as an envoy from the Persian khan to the pope, had audiences with the English and French kings.

Eurasian traders—Persians, Arabs, Greeks, and western Europeans—were numerous and worldly-wise travelers. They were enticed by Mongol policies that lowered tolls in the commercial cities and provided special protection for merchants' goods. A Florentine document, published about 1340, described conditions on the silk route as

> *perfectly safe whether by day or night. . . . Whatever silver the merchants carry . . . the lord of Cathay takes from them . . . and gives . . . paper money . . . in exchange . . . and with this money you can readily buy silk and whatever you desire to buy and all the people of the country are bound to receive it.*[6]

Land trade between Europe and China, particularly in silk and spices, increased rapidly in the fourteenth century. The main western terminals were Nizhni Novgorod, east of Moscow, where the China caravans made contact with merchants of the Hanseatic League, a coalition of German merchant companies; Tabriz, in northeastern Persia, which served as the eastern terminal for Constantinople; and the Syrian coastal cities, where the caravans met Mediterranean ships, mostly from Venice.

Expanding land trade along the old silk route did not diminish the growing volume of sea commerce. Indeed, the Mongol devastation of Middle Eastern cities provided a quick stimulus, particularly to the spice trade, which was partly redirected through the Red Sea and Egypt to Europe. Within a few decades, however, the Mamluk monopoly in Egypt drove prices up sharply, and the European demand for cheaper spices helped revive overland trade. By now, however, the southern sea route was thriving for other reasons. The Mongol conquest of China had immediately opened opportunities to Japanese and Malayan sea merchants, causing a modest commercial revolution. Later, after the government in China stabilized and became involved in the exchange, the volume of ocean trade between northeastern Asia and the Middle East surpassed that of Sung times.

The Mongol Legacy

Although their conquests were often accompanied by horrifying slaughter and wrought considerable havoc, Mongol control also promoted stability. The

Gog and Magog in the Ebstorf Mappamundi

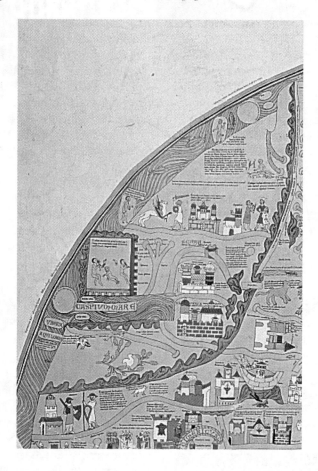

Maps depict more than geographical observations; they tell us the beliefs and imaginings of the people who produce them and reflect the point of view of the mapmaker. Historically, when people lacked a clear picture of far-off lands, they employed fantastic stories to describe what lay beyond their own known world. Like myths and folktales, maps from different eras illustrate some of the ways that societies have imagined apparently "strange" or "foreign" lands. We have seen that there was considerable commercial and intellectual exchange among Europe, India, China, and central Asia in the years 300–1300 C.E. Nonetheless, the "Orient" remained a mysterious place in the imagination of many Westerners, a sometimes frightening place inhabited by strange creatures.

The thirteenth-century Ebstorf Mappamundi (map of the world), discovered in a Benedictine monastery in Germany, presents a geographical vision that combines Christian historiography, geographical observation, biblical mythology, the legends of Alexander the Great, and ancient tales of beastlike races inhabiting the "ends of the earth." It incorporates the idea of Gog and Magog, the homelands of apocalyptic destroyers, drawn from the New Testament (Revelation 20:7–8), into the description of the territory of northeastern Asia, the Mongol territory to the north of the Caucasus Mountains. On medieval Christian maps Gog and Magog were equated with barbarian races, with the Ten Lost Tribes of Israel, and with the armies of the Anti-Christ. According to legend, these ferocious peoples had been trapped by Alexander the Great, who built a great wall to contain them; they would break out at the end of time and overwhelm civilized societies. On the Ebsdorf map the people of Gog and Magog are tribes of savages who are shown eating human body parts and drinking blood. They are walled off in the far northeast of the world. Their identification with the Tartars suggests the fear of Turco-Mongol invaders that pervaded the mapmaker's society in the thirteenth century. Given the striking success of the Mongols' conquests in this era, it is no wonder that they came to be associated with Gog and Magog. Gog and Magog also appear on the twelfth-century Islamic world map of al-Idrīsī (see Chapter 10).

Mongols encouraged trade and borrowed freely from old established civilizations, while their commercial contacts spread knowledge of explosives, printing, medicine, shipbuilding, and navigation to the West. In the Middle East they furthered art, architecture, and historical writing. To China they brought Persian astronomy and ceramics, plus sorghum, a new food from India. The Mongol era also saw great commercial and population growth in Japan and Southeast Asia. Not least important was a new awareness of the wider world, which the Mongols gave to a Europe on the brink of global exploration.

While creating the largest empire in history and decisively affecting Eurasian history, like other conquerors the Mongols could not create an enduring unified empire. Logistic realities and the diverse territories conquered and cultures absorbed meant that the Mongol polity had of necessity to be divided in various ways. The Yuan regime declined rapidly after Kublai's death as the economy became more oppressive and the Mongol aristocracy weakened. A great rebellion, beginning in southern China, ultimately ended the dynasty. After the Chinese reconquered most of Mongolia and Manchuria, many northern Mongols reverted to nomadism. Others, on the western steppes, were absorbed into Turkic states.

Genghis Khan himself may have had the last word on the fleeting glory of empires. According to the Mongol history, written in Persian, of Rashid al-Din, Genghis had this to say about success and memory:

> *"After us, our posterity will wear garments of sewn gold, partake of fatty and sweet delicacies, sit well-formed horses, and embrace beauteous wives. [But] they will not say '[all] these things our fathers and brothers collected,' and they will forget us in this great day."*[7]

Conclusion

During the centuries following the collapse of Rome in the West, significant cultural revivals occurred in Asia. First India and then China experienced golden ages when old political structures were restored and social systems were revitalized in accordance with traditional values. In India the Gupta era brought a lasting synthesis of Hindu thought, along with notable advances in painting, architecture, literature, drama, medicine, and the physical sciences. China perfected its administrative structure while further developing its characteristic Confucian philosophy, poetry, landscape painting, and practical technology. Each civilization served as a culture bank, preserving and extending knowledge.

Over the centuries, cultural diffusion gained increasing momentum throughout Eurasia. From both India and China, goods and cultural patterns spread through migrations, invasions, missionary activities, and trade to Southeast Asia, Japan, the Asian steppes, and Europe. The result was a third wave in the civilizing process. The first wave had washed over the Near East before 500 B.C.E.; the second brought great empires in China, India, and the Mediterranean basin; the third dramatically affected the evolution of civilizations in Southeast Asia and Japan while contributing significantly to the emergence of another in western Europe.

Steppe nomads played an increasingly important role in this period of Eurasian history. Many remained nomad warriors, attacking and pillaging the high civilizations on their frontiers. Others adopted civilized ways, shifting from herding to farming, living in cities as craftspeople or traders, and assimilating the high courtly cultures of the conquered peoples. The steppe peoples in turn brought their military ethos, tactics, and modes of organization to the cities of China and Persia. This development was climaxed by the Mongols, who developed a vast network of imperial cities connected by trade routes and fostering an expansive exchange of goods, embassies, ideas, and cultural patterns that in turn created a medieval "world system" in the era "before European hegemony."[8]

Suggestions for Reading

Two standard treatments of the Gupta era are Sir Percival Spear, *India: A Modern History*, rev. ed. (University of Michigan Press, 1972), and R. C. Majumdar and A. D. Pulsaker, eds., *The Classic Age*, Vol. 3 of *The History and Culture of the Indian Peoples* (Bharatiya Vidya, 1954). Reliable and informative recent surveys include Hermann A. Kulke, *A History of India* (Routledge, 1998); Tej Ram Sharma, *The Political History of the Imperial Guptas* (Concept, 1989); and Stanley Wolpert, *A New History of India*, 5th ed. (Oxford University Press, 1997). Steven Warshaw, *India Emerges* (Diablo, 1987), is a concise and readable paperback for the student and general reader. B. H. Gokhale, *Samudra Gupta* (Asia, 1962), is an interesting biography. A special treatment of women is A. S. Altekar, *The Position of Women in Hindu Civilization*, 3rd ed. (Sundar Lal Jam/Motilal Banarsidass, 1962). For a well-illustrated account of Indian influences on the art of neighboring countries, see Benjamin Rowland, *The Art and Architecture of India* (Penguin, 1971).

Among the best general histories of China for the T'ang and Sung periods are William Scott Morton, *China: Its History and Culture* (Lippincott/Crowell, 1980); Witold Rodzinski, *A History of China*, 2 vols. (Pergamon, 1979); and Charles O. Hucker, *China's Imperial Past* (Stanford University Press, 1975). John K. Fairbank, *The United States and China*, 4th ed. (Harvard University Press, 1983), is a highly readable treatment that goes well beyond the scope of its title to give a brief survey of Chinese history. Others deserving mention are Wolfram Eberhard, *A History of China* (University of California Press, 1977); John Meskill, *An Introduction to Chinese Civilization* (Heath, 1973); Raymond Dawson, *Imperial China* (Hutchinson, 1972); and Hilda Hookham, *A Short History of China* (St. Martin's Press, 1970). A readable paperback is Steven Warshaw, *China Emerges* (Diablo, 1987).

For complete coverage of Chinese technology and engineering, see Joseph Needham, *Science and Civilization in China* (Cambridge University Press, 1954) and *Clerks and Craftsmen in China and the West* (Cambridge University Press, 1970). See also Robert Temple, *The Genius of China* (Simon & Schuster, 1989). A new and comprehensive work on Chinese painting is *Three Thousand Years of Chinese Painting* (Yale University Press, 1998); Esther Yao, *Chinese Women Past and Present* (Idle House, 1987), provides complete coverage of social conditions and important personalities.

The T'ang historical background is ably presented in Arthur F. Wright, *The Sui Dynasty* (Knopf, 1978), and in Woodbridge Bingham, *The Founding of the T'ang Dynasty* (Octagon, 1975). Arthur F. Wright and Dennis Twitchett provide special insights in *Perspectives on the T'ang* (Yale University Press, 1973). The significance of the T'ang examination system is depicted in David McMullen, *State and Scholars in T'ang China* (Cambridge University Press, 1988). A classic study of T'ang decline is Edwin G. Pulleyblank, *The Background of the Rebellion of An Lu-shan* (Greenwood, 1955). Charles Hartman, *Han Yu and the T'ang Search for Unity* (Princeton University Press, 1986), describes the famous philosopher's efforts to synthesize meaning from traditional values during the late T'ang troubles.

Interesting and revealing special studies of the Sung period include Jing-shen Tao, *Two Sons of Heaven* (University of Arizona Press, 1988); Winston W. Lo, *An Introduction to the Civil Service System of Sung China* (University of Hawaii Press, 1987); and Thomas H. C. Lee, *Government, Education, and the Examinations in Sung China, 960–1278* (St. Martin's Press, 1985). Other excellent special studies are James M. Hargett, *On the Road in Twelfth Century China* (Steiner Verlag, 1989), and Richard L. Davis, *Court and Family in Sung China* (Duke University Press, 1986).

George B. Sansom, *A History of Japan*, 3 vols. (Stanford University Press, 1958–1963), is still the best exhaustive work in English. Also valuable are John K. Fairbank et al., *East Asia: Tradition and Transformation* (Houghton Mifflin, 1989); Eric Tomlin, *Japan* (Walker, 1973); Mikiso Hane, *Japan: A Historical Survey* (Scribner, 1972); and Edwin Reischauer, *Japan: The Story of a Nation* (Knopf, 1970). Other noteworthy surveys include R. H. P. Mason, *A History of Japan* (Tuttle, 1987), and Steven Warshaw, *Japan Emerges* (Diablo, 1987). Three penetrating special studies of early Japan are Wontack Hong, *Relationship Between Korea and Japan in the Early Period* (Ilsimsa, 1988); Jonathan E. Kidder, *Early Buddhist Japan* (Praeger, 1972); and Peter Judd Arensen, *The Medieval Japanese Daimyo* (Yale University Press, 1979). Rose Hempel, *The Golden Age of Japan* (Rizzoli, 1983), is a study of Japanese art and architecture in the Heian period.

For a scholarly study of the Turkic peoples, including the Mongols, see Peter Golden, *An Introduction to the History of the Turkic Peoples* (Harrassowitz, 1992). Luc Kwanten, *Imperial Nomads: A History of Central Asia, 500–1500* (University of Pennsylvania Press, 1979), is a superb study of the nomadic steppe peoples, including Turks, Uighurs, Uzbeks, and Mongols. It has been ably augmented by two later works on Mongol life and conquests: David Morgan, *The Mongols* (Blackwell, 1986), and Thomas T. Allsen, *Mongol Imperialism* (University of California Press, 1987). Other standard treatments of the Mongol impact are Rene Grousset, *The Empire of the Steppes* (Rutgers University Press, 1970); Eustace D. Phillips, *The Mongols* (Praeger, 1969); John J. Saunders, *History of the Mongol Conquests* (Barnes & Noble, 1971); and Bertold Spuler, *The Mongols in History* (Praeger, 1971). Paul Ratchnevsky, *Chingiz Khan: His Life and Legacy* (Blackwell, 1993), is a good updated social biography of the great conqueror. See also Adam Kessler, *Empires Beyond the Great Wall: The Heritage of Genghis Khan* (Natural History Museum of Los Angeles County, 1992).

An excellent study of networks of trade and communication in the Mongol era is Janet Abu-Lughod, *Before European Hegemony: The World System, A.D. 1250–1350* (Oxford University Press, 1989). Thomas Allsen looks at the textile trade of the Mongol era in *Commodity and Exchange in the Mongol Empire* (Cambridge University Press, 1997). A sound treatment of the Pax Mongolica is presented in G. F. Hudson, *Europe and China* (Gordon, 1976). On early relations between the Chinese and the Mongols, see H. D. Martin, *The Rise of Genghis Khan and the Conquest of North China* (Octagon, 1971). Charles Halperin, *Russia and the Golden Horde* (Indiana University Press, 1987), looks at the Mongol impact on Russia. Two works by L. Olschki, *Marco Polo's Precursors* (Johns Hopkins University Press, 1943) and *Marco Polo's Asia* (University of California Press, 1960), provide complete accounts of the long-range trade leading to Polo's mission. A readable biography is Henry Hart, *Marco Polo, Venetian Adventurer* (University of Oklahoma Press, 1967). Frances Wood, *Did Marco Polo Go to China?* (Westview, 1996), is a provocative look at the famous traveler.

The best recent accounts of the Yuan regime in China are Elizabeth E. West, *Mongolian Rule in China* (Harvard University Press, 1989); Morris Rossabi, *Kublai Khan: His Life and Times* (University of California Press, 1987); and John D. Langlois, *China Under Mongol Rule* (Princeton University Press, 1981). On Persia in this era, see David Morgan, *Medieval Persia, 1040–1797* (Longman, 1988), and Richard Frye, *Islamic Iran and Central Asia, 7th–12th Centuries* (Variorum, 1979).

Suggestions for Web Browsing

Itihaas: Chronology—Medieval India
http://www.itihaas.com/medieval/index.html

> *Extensive chronology of medieval India, 1000 C.E. to 1756 C.E.; most entries include subsites with text and images.*

Medieval India
http://www.dc.infi.net/~gunther/india/medieval.html

> *Site discussing the history, sites and monuments, and classical texts of medieval India, 600 B.C.–1526 C.E.*

Chinese Empire
http://www.wsu.edu:8080/~dee/chempire/chempire.htm

> *Chinese history from 256 B.C.E. to 1300 C.E., with details about philosophy and culture.*

Ancient Japan
http://www.wsu.edu:8080/~dee/ancjapan/ancjapan.htm

> *Web site on ancient Japan includes political, religious, and cultural history, details about women and women's communities, and a portfolio of art from the era.*

Empires Beyond the Great Wall: The Heritage of Genghis Khan
http://www.pinc.com/khan/khan.html

> *A rich site offering a biography of Genghis Khan and information about the history and culture of the Mongol Empire.*

Notes

1. Hermann Kulke and Dietmar Rothermund, *History of India*, 3rd ed. (London: Routledge, 1998), p. 147.
2. Quoted in H. H. Gowen and H. W. Hall, *An Outline History of China* (New York: Appleton, 1926), p. 117.
3. *The Works of Li Po*, trans. Shigeyoshi Obata (New York: Dutton, 1950), no. 71.

4. Quoted in Ryusaku Tsunoda et al., eds., *Sources of Japanese Tradition* (New York: Columbia University Press, 1958), pp. 181–182.

5. Marco Polo, *Tht Travels of Marco Polo* (New York: Grosset & Dunlap, 1931), pp. 30, 133–149.

6. Quoted in G. F. Hudson, *Europe and China* (Boston: Beacon Press, 1931), p. 156.

7. Thomas Allsen, *Commodity and Exchange in the Mongol Empire* (Cambridge: Cambridge University Press, 1997), p. 12.

8. This system is lucidly outlined in Janet Abu-Lughod, *Before European Hegemony: The World System,* A.D. *1250–1350* (Oxford: Oxford University Press, 1989), which delineates the networks of exchange characterizing this era.

*The Cliff Palace of the Anasazi,
Mesa Verde National Park,
Colorado, is among the important
Anasazi ruins to be found in the
southwestern United States.*

The Americas to 1492

Chapter Contents

At the same time that medieval Europe was experiencing dynamic cultural growth and Africa south of the Sahara was undergoing its own rich evolution, the Americas were creating their own civilizations half a globe away. The American civilizations followed a social sequence similar to that experienced in Africa and Eurasia. Agriculture became more diversified, and as food supplies increased, the culture became more and more able to support large cities, highly skilled crafts, expanding commerce, complex social structures, and the emergence of powerful states.

What is unique about the development of the American civilizations is their having evolved in complete isolation from the rest of the world. The most noteworthy were the civilizations of the Mayas in Yucatán and Guatemala, the Aztecs in central Mexico, and the Incas in Peru. The Mayas are especially famous for their mathematics, solar calendar, and writing system, which has only recently been deciphered. The Aztecs and Incas conquered large populations and governed extensive states. Each civilization produced distinctive customs, values, art, and religion, much of which have become part of the Latin American heritage.

Spanish adventurers who invaded these civilizations were repelled by Amerindian religious sacrifices but astonished by the wealth, grandeur, technical efficiency, urban populations, and institutional complexity they saw in Mesoamerica and Peru. For example, Tenochtitlán, the Aztec capital, with its 150,000

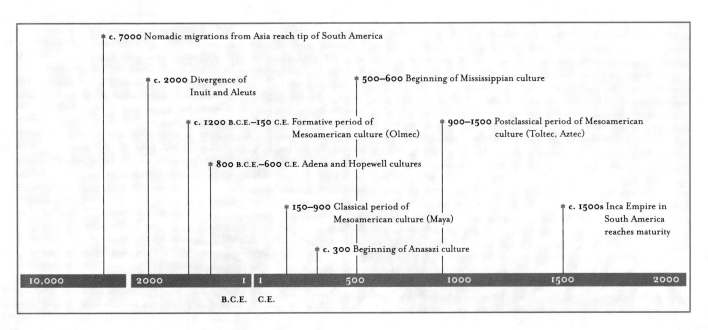

* **c. 7000** Nomadic migrations from Asia reach tip of South America

* **c. 2000** Divergence of Inuit and Aleuts

* **500–600** Beginning of Mississippian culture

* **c. 1200 B.C.E.–150 C.E.** Formative period of Mesoamerican culture (Olmec)

* **900–1500** Postclassical period of Mesoamerican culture (Toltec, Aztec)

* **800 B.C.E.–600 C.E.** Adena and Hopewell cultures

* **150–900** Classical period of Mesoamerican culture (Maya)

* **c. 1500s** Inca Empire in South America reaches maturity

* **c. 300** Beginning of Anasazi culture

| 10,000 | 2000 | I | I | 500 | 1000 | 1500 | 2000 |

B.C.E.   C.E.

inhabitants, was larger and probably cleaner than any European city of its time. Yet this high level of social accomplishment had been attained without iron, draft animals, an alphabet, or known contacts with other high civilizations.

To the north, hundreds of Amerindian tribes developed diverse social patterns, languages, and economic pursuits as they adapted to the differing environmental challenges they faced. Around 3000 B.C.E. Amerindians in the southwestern part of present-day Florida founded villages along the coast in which they enjoyed a rich diet of fish, shellfish, grains, and berries and adhered to a sophisticated religious system that included the burial of the dead in funeral mounds. Recent archaeological finds indicate that still earlier, in the present-day state of Washington, Amerindians founded villages with their own unique cultures and economic activities.

Because of the complex and immense landmass—3000 miles across and 5000 miles from north to south—in which they found themselves, the Amerindians to the north never attained the centralized power or wealth of the Mayas, Aztecs, and Incas. However, they left behind a rich legacy of archaeological sites that indicate their sophistication and flexibility. Unfortunately, in their diversity lay conflict, and the Amerindians were often their own worst enemy.

Origins of Americans and Their Cultures

All American cultures can be traced back to nomadic migrations from Asia to Alaska, across the Bering Strait land bridge. During the Pleistocene epoch, coinciding with the last great ice age, humans established themselves in Siberia, where they built subterranean shelters and hunted mammals. The most recent ice advance, beginning some 65,000 years ago, locked up immense amounts of global water and lowered sea levels, creating a land bridge that enabled Paleolithic hunters to follow their quarry into the New World, as the Americas came to be known. As increasing global temperatures melted the ice and raised water levels, the bridge slowly disappeared, around 10,000 years ago, after an estimated 30,000 years of sporadic human migrations. From Alaska those generations of early Amerindian peoples moved east and south, reaching southern Mexico by 20,000 years ago, Chile some 2500 years later, and the tip of South America by about 7000 B.C.E. Over this protracted period they split into eight major ethnolinguistic groups and hundreds of subgroups and adapted to numerous physical environments.

The development of agriculture in the Mexican highlands, along the Peruvian coastal plain, and in what is now the southwestern United States caused a profound modification of Amerindian culture after 7000 B.C.E. Not only did this development occur considerably later than in the Near East, but the plants that were domesticated were also different from those in other parts of the world. Wheat, barley, and rye did not exist in the New World; instead, the Amerindians domesticated squash, beans, fruits, and peppers. They also domesticated animals—not the cattle, sheep, or horses of the Old World, but alpacas and llamas in the Andes. The major agricultural impact came with the cultivation of maize (corn), shortly before 5000 B.C.E., in the Tehuacán valley of Mexico. From this center, maize culture spread widely. After 1000 B.C.E. it became the staple food for hundreds of societies, from the Mississippi valley to the Argentine pampas. Although the resulting sociopolitical impact was slow, it was decisive; the Aztec and Inca Empires, which so awed the Spanish *conquistadores* after 1500, were based largely on maize economies.

Beyond these mature civilizations, cultural levels varied widely among more than 75 million Amerindians at the end of the fifteenth century. Some cultures, like that of the famous Mound Builders of the Mississippi valley, borrowed heavily from Mexico; Cahokia, an obvious capital and trade center near contemporary St. Louis, Missouri, housed approximately 10,000 people during the thirteenth century. Less complex peasant cultures north of the Rio Grande ranged from the Pueblo of the southwest to the large Iroquois Confederacy of the eastern woodlands. In South America, protocivilizations had risen along the north coast and near the mouth of the Amazon. Simpler peasant societies developed on Caribbean islands, in the South American pampas, and in Chile. Most other Amerindians—probably a majority of them—were still hunters and gatherers. These included the Eskimos, Mesolithic seminomads of the Pacific Northwest; jungle tribes such as the Jivaro of the upper Amazon; and the peoples of Tierra del Fuego, at the southern tip of South America.

Despite their isolation, Amerindian cultures, including the mature civilizations, followed a pattern of development similar to those in Eurasia and

New World Civilizations

2500s B.C.E.–400s C.E.	Olmec
300s–900s C.E.	Mayas
900s–1200s C.E.	Toltecs
1100s–1500s C.E.	Incas
1300s–1500s C.E.	Aztecs

Africa. This phenomenon has been described as "parallel invention." New World societies had evolved certain customs, such as the wearing of ear or lip plugs. They were also limited by their dependence on maize cultivation, with its special demands, as well as by their lack of iron, horses, other common domesticated animals, and an alphabet. Yet they differed little from Old World cultures in their progression from Paleolithic hunting and food-gathering to Mesolithic semifixed communities to Neolithic food production and settled communal life and thence to urban centers and the emergence of political states. They also displayed common traits with other civilizations in their theocratic systems, sun cults, and human sacrifices. Like the African cultures, they were in transition from matriarchal to patriarchal institutions, although further advanced in this process. Finally, a common belief in divine monarchy among Aztecs and Incas was also typical of many other peoples in the ancient riverine civilizations of the Old World.

Emerging Civilizations in Mesoamerica

The term *Mesoamerica* applies to Mexico and Central America, home to a matrix of related cultures. The region varies greatly in geomorphology, climate, and vegetation. Two mountain ranges run through northern Mexico to join a central highland block in the region of the Valley of Mexico. The Pacific coastal region is relatively narrow while that on the Atlantic side is wide. The north and west have dry lands with sparse vegetation; the south and east are marked by tropical rain forests and savannas.

Despite these physical differences, the early Mesoamerican cultures were unified by their economic interdependence, since no one region was self-sufficient. They shared a complex calendar, hieroglyphic writing, bark paper, deerskin books, team games played with balls of solid rubber, chocolate bean money, widespread upper-class polygamy, large markets, and common legends (a popular one featured a god-man symbolized by a feathered serpent).

To facilitate our study of developing Mesoamerican culture, we may conveniently divide its history into three main periods: formative (to 150 C.E.), classical (150–900), and postclassical (900–1492).

The Formative Period

For a millennium after 1500 B.C.E., Mesoamerican villages evolved steadily toward larger urban communities. They fostered the development of pottery making, weaving, feather working, and masonry. As population increased and a more complex division of labor evolved, priests came to dominate govern-

ments, but merchants enjoyed social status as they conducted trade among the temple cities. In time the common culture, known as the Olmec, centered in five geographical areas. One was in the Oaxaca region of western Mexico; another was in the inland Valley of Mexico; a third straddled the present Mexican-Guatemalan border; and a fourth (the later Mayan) arose in the southern highlands and lowlands of Yucatán, Honduras, and Guatemala. The fifth and at the time most significant area spread over some 125 miles of the eastern Mexican coast and its hinterlands, near present-day Veracruz. It was largely parent to the others.

Since 1920 this Olmec culture, revealed through archaeological remains, has astounded experts by its revealed wealth, technical efficiency, and artistic sensitivity. Among many Olmec sites, the oldest, at San Lorenzo, had great stone buildings and pyramids, dating from 1200 B.C.E. The culture is perhaps best known for its colossal heads and its fine jade carving, featuring jaguars. It had already attained maturity when San Lorenzo was destroyed by invaders about 900 B.C.E.; another ceremonial center at La Venta, in Tabasco, assumed leadership until it collapsed six centuries later.

Scattered throughout the Olmec heartland were some 350,000 people, living in relatively sparsely

A magnificent monumental stone head from the Olmec Center at San Lorenzo. Some scholars have suggested that these massive heads are portraits of rulers.

Ranging from the lowland and jungles of Central America to the arctic cold of the Andes, the civilizations of Central and South America exhibited a rich and sophisticated diversity.

populated ceremonial trading centers and their supporting villages. Labor and stone for the massive construction projects, jade for carving, luxury goods, raw materials for the crafts, and food were brought to the centers often from distant places. These goods were probably not the spoils of conquest; Olmec society left little evidence of war or violence, although military operations would have been conducted to protect trading missions. Merchants were bestowed a social status second only to the ruling priestly classes, which governed by enjoying respect and exploiting fear rather than relying on force. The general theocratic orientation is reflected most clearly in the great temple mounds; in the huge stone conical pyramid at

La Venta, rising some 100 feet; and in the characteristic carved statuary that represented Olmec cultism.

Olmec influence permeated most of Mesoamerica. A few independent Olmec centers may have been established in central Mexico, but it was probably more common for a number of Olmec priests and traders to live among native populations, conducting religious rites and arranging for the transport of goods to the homeland. Such enclaves were typical of regions as distant as the Pacific coast of Central America. In other places, such as the Oaxaca valley to the west, the southwestern Mexican highlands, or the southern Mayan regions, Olmec influence was more indirect, possibly resulting from trade or Olmec marriage into local elites. By such varied means, Olmec foundations were laid for the religion, art, architecture, and characteristic ball games—and possibly for the calendars, mathematics, and writing systems— of later Mesoamerican civilizations, including the Mayan and the Aztec.

The Classical Period in Northern Mesoamerica

After the fall of La Venta, Olmec prestige waned, but high civilizations continued to flourish. By the second century C.E., development had progressed to a point of florescence known as the classical period, which would last until the tenth century. This was literally a golden age, when written communication, complex time reckoning, a pantheon of gods, interregional trade, and a 40-fold population increase over the Olmec period affected most of Mesoamerica. Hundreds of communities raised great buildings, decorated them with beautiful frescoes, produced pottery and figurines in large quantities, and covered everything with sculptures. Although classical Mayan culture of the Yucatán lowlands is perhaps best known, we will begin our look at the classical period by viewing other notable northern sites in the Valley of Mexico and Oaxaca.

Teotihuacán, in the northeastern valley, generated the most notable classical culture outside of Yucatán. At its peak about 500 C.E., it was the sixth largest city in the world, with a population of 125,000 to 200,000. Three and a half miles long and nearly 2 miles wide, it was laid out in a grid of sorts and paved with a plaster floor on which clusters of impos-

ing edifices were erected. This ceremonial center is dominated by the temple-pyramids dedicated to the moon and the sun. The first pyramid was truncated to provide for a temple with a broad step ascending from a wide rectangular court. Running south is a long ceremonial axis, and adjacent to it the Pyramid of the Sun. Also truncated, it measures 650 feet at the base and rises in four terraces to 213 feet above the valley floor. The interior contains more than a million cubic yards of sun-dried bricks, and the exterior was once faced entirely with stone. As with other pyramids throughout Mesoamerica, these structures, with their ceremonial staircases, led to temples at the summit where rites and sacrifices were offered to the gods.

Teotihuacán was noted for its specialized craftspeople, who came from all over Mexico and occupied designated quarters of the city. Its streets were studded with bustling markets, where all types of goods were available from foreign as well as local sources. This wealth permitted a governing elite of priests, civil officials, military leaders, and merchants to enjoy great luxury. Over other states, including some among the lowland Mayas, Teotihuacán exerted a powerful influence, arising mainly from its cultural reputation, social connections, and commercial advantages. When necessary, it used its formidable military power to enforce trade and tribute agreements.

Another impressive classical center in Mexico was located at Monte Alban in the Oaxaca valley. In 200 B.C.E. it already had a population of 15,000, and its fortifications dominated the valley. In Teotihuacán's era, this concentration of temples, pyramids, and shrines was a theocratic state, still drawing

The colossal Pyramid of the Sun rose above the metropolis of Teotihuacán. Measuring 650 feet at its base and 213 feet high, the structure is more than four times larger than the Great Pyramid of Cheops in Egypt.

tribute from adjacent hill settlements and a valley population of over 75,000 people. Although developed on a smaller scale than Teotihuacán, Monte Alban produced a similar pattern of external trade, class differentiation, elaborate religious architecture, artistic creativity, writing, and time reckoning. It derived most of its art styles from Teotihuacán and some from the Mayas but synthesized both in its own traditions. Politically, it remained independent through the classical era, although its elite sought the luxury goods and favor of Teotihuacán.

Classical Mayan Civilization

While Teotihuacán and Monte Alban flourished, Mayan peoples farther south in Yucatán and Guatemala produced the most splendid cultural achievements of the classical era and perhaps of Amerindian societies in any time. Artistic and intellectual activity rose to new heights in more than 100 Mayan centers, each boasting temples, palaces, observatories, and ball courts. Although it borrowed from Teotihuacán before the latter's decay in the eighth century C.E., Mayan civilization subsequently cast a brilliant light over the whole of Mesoamerica.

The earliest Mayas are thought to have migrated from the northwest coast of California to the Guatemalan highlands during the third millennium B.C.E. From that homeland, Yucatec- and Cholian-speaking peoples settled the northern and central lowlands, respectively, between 1500 B.C.E. and 100 C.E. Mayan villages developed steadily, many becoming ceremonial centers by the start of the Common Era. In the highlands, Kaminaljuyu had by then developed architecture and primitive writing under the influence of Oaxaca and Teotihuacán. But in the early classical period, before 550 C.E., Tikal, in the central lowlands, assumed Mayan leadership as it traded with Teotihuacán and allied itself with Kaminaljuyu. The fall of Teotihuacán brought temporary confusion, soon followed by the glorious renaissance of the late classical era at Tikal, Palenque, Yaxchilán, Uxmal, and other Mayan centers.

Mayan communities were supported by productive economies, based on agriculture but heavily involved in handicrafts and long-distance trade. In soil sometimes nearly barren, with some exceptions in the highlands, Mayan farmers used intensive agriculture, clearing, irrigating, and terracing to raise squash, chili peppers, and many other crops, including maize—which supplied 80 percent of their food. Mayan metalwork, cotton cloth, and chipped stone implements were traded widely, carried in large dugout canoes along the rivers and the Atlantic coast. Exchange was facilitated by the use of common goods as media of exchange, including cocoa beans, polished beads, salt, and lengths of cotton cloth.

Mayan society in this period was a bewildering mixture of old and new. An ancient kinship system prevailed among all classes, with lands assigned and controlled by the clans. Matriarchal values persisted, as indicated by some queens who retained power and influence. Women were generally respected, held some legal rights, and did some of the most important work, such as weaving. The shift toward patriarchy, however, was definite and unmistakable, as was indicated in priorities accorded men in most social situations, such as being served first by women at meals. A more fundamental change involved the rise of social classes. Hereditary male nobles and priests were in most positions of authority and power, but craftspeople and merchants enjoyed more privileges and status than was formerly believed by experts on Mayan society. Slaves did most of the hard work, particularly in the continuous heavy construction of ceremonial buildings. They were also subject to religious sacrifice, although this was far less common than among the Aztecs later.

Each Mayan center was governed by a hereditary priest-king, usually considered to be a descendant of a god. He was assisted by a council of priests and nobles. His government levied taxes, supervised local government in outlying villages, and administered justice. It also was responsible for conducting foreign relations and making war. This last point is worth

A high-caste Mayan woman working at the loom. One end of the loom is attached to the woman's waist; the other is fastened to a tree trunk. Weaving was considered a noble occupation.

stressing. The Mayas were not very successful in large-scale military operations because their armies were drawn mainly from the nobility and therefore limited in size. Nevertheless, they were equal to other Mesoamericans in their warlike propensities; they could wield their stone-bladed weapons as ferociously as the Aztecs. Indeed, as time passed and cities vied for supremacy, warfare became increasingly common. In the process, some centers remained independent, but most joined loosely organized leagues, based on common religious traditions, royal marriages, or diplomatic alignments.

Religion permeated all phases of Mayan life. Like the later Aztecs, the Mayas saw life as a burden and time as its measure, and they deified many natural phenomena, particularly the heavenly bodies, as powers to be appeased by human pain and suffering. Public bloodletting was part of normal ritualistic worship. Human sacrifice, usually accomplished by decapitation, was common, although not obsessive, and war to obtain prisoners for sacrifice was sometimes waged. The dominance of religion over everyday life is further illustrated by the general interpretation of law as religious principle and taxation as religious offerings. Economic value derived as much from the religious sanctity of a thing as from its material utility or scarcity. Moreover, education was aimed primarily at training priests; reading and writing were considered necessary religious skills, and mathematics and astronomy were valued mainly because they were required in scheduling ceremonies honoring the gods. Despite their many intellectual accomplishments, the Mayas were far more ritualistic than scientific.

The two most significant achievements of the Mayas were their calendar and their writing system. Neither of these was original, but both were more efficient than those of earlier Mesoamerican peoples. The Mayan astronomers, using only naked-eye observation, far surpassed their European contemporaries. Their constant scanning of the heavens allowed the Mayas to perfect a solar calendar with 18 months of 20 days each and a five-day period for religious festivals. Using an ingenious cyclical system of notation known as the "long count," they dated events of the distant past for accurate record keeping and the scheduling of astronomical observations. Their notational mathematics, based on 20 rather than 10 as in the decimal system, employed combinations of dots and bars in vertical sequences, to indicate numbers above 20. For nonnumerical records, they combined pictographic and glyphic symbols, which have recently been deciphered sufficiently to reveal specific historic events and their human dimensions.

These remarkable accomplishments in mathematics, astronomy, and writing were more than matched by the magnificent Mayan art and architecture. The plaza of each Mayan community was marked by at least one pyramid, topped by a temple. The one at Tikal towered to 229 feet, 16 feet higher than the Pyramid of the Sun at Teotihuacán. With their terraced sides and horizontal lines, Mayan pyramids demonstrated a prevailing sense of proportion. The highly stylized sculpture decorating their terraces is regarded by some authorities as the world's finest, even though the Mayan sculptors accomplished their intricate carving with only stone tools. The Mayas also developed mural painting to a high level of expression. Even their lesser arts, such as weaving, ceramics, and jewelry making, reveal a greater aesthetic sense, subtlety of design, and manipulative skill than similar work in numerous other high civilizations.

The Postclassical Era in Mesoamerica

Mesoamerica's classical artistic florescence ended during the eighth and ninth centuries. The causes, not yet fully uncovered, have been generally attributed to overpopulation, internal struggles, and fierce Chichimec invasions from the North. Amid the accompanying disturbances, urban populations dwindled, and most of Teotihuacán's residents scattered in all directions, even into the Mayan lands. But there was no complete collapse; trade continued on a large scale, and the expanded use of writing indicated more social complexity and interstate competition, which contributed to intensified political conflict. Consequently, the age produced a new cultural mode, with heavier emphases on militarism, war, and gods thirsting for human blood. Among many smaller but thriving city-states, in addition to the dying Teotihuacán, were the Mayan polities of Tikal, Chichén Itzá, and Mayapán. Farther north, the Oaxacan centers were still flourishing after the tenth century, as were Atzcapotzalco, Xochicalio, and Cholula, with its colossal pyramid.

The Toltecs

Most prominent of all these centers was Tollan, the Toltec capital. Toltec history is unclear before 980, when Topiltzin, a legendary king, founded the city and created a new power in the Valley of Mexico. His subjects were a mixture of Chichimecs and former urbanites of the area, who may have served for a while as peacekeepers in the north. Over the next two centuries the city became a great urban complex of 120,000 people, a hub of trade, and the center of an evolving Toltec confederacy, which assumed the leading role formerly played by Teotihuacán. Meanwhile,

Tollan's future was shaped by a struggle for power between Topiltzin and his enemies. The king had early adopted the Teotihuacán god Quetzalcoatl, who opposed human sacrifice; but followers of the traditional Toltec war-god, Tezcatlipoca, ultimately rebelled and forced Topiltzin into exile. The victorious war cult took over, steadily expanding its hegemony, by conquest and trade, into an empire stretching from the Gulf of Mexico to the Pacific, including some Mayan cities of the south.

The tumultuous political conditions of the early postclassical period finally brought disaster to the Toltecs. Failing crops and internal dissension caused great outward migrations from Tollan and abandonment of the capital at the end of the twelfth century. Shortly after, the city was burned by Chichimecs. For two centuries thereafter, Mesoamerica was a land of warring states and constantly forming and dissolving federations. Some cultural continuity, however, was maintained by peoples in the Oaxaca valley, notably the Zapotecs, whose culture was as old as the Olmec. Although they struggled constantly with neighboring peoples for supremacy and survival, the Zapotecs produced towns, temples, ball courts, and art, which helped preserve Mesoamerican traditions for later times.

As Toltec militarism spread from central to southern Mexico, it left the less developed Mayan highlands relatively undisturbed but brought decline and reorientation to the old lowland centers, such as Tikal. Severe droughts also drove migrants into northern Yucatán, where a developing cistern technology provided more water. At Chichén Itzá, in the tenth century, a cosmopolitan Mexican-Mayan military elite established tributary hegemony and maintained a trading network, by land and sea, throughout the southern region. From the early thirteenth into the fifteenth century, Mayapán was a fortified center, defended by Mexican mercenaries and maintaining leverage over subkingdoms by holding hostages from dependent royal families. Trade continued to grow, along with population, among the postclassical Mayas; but art, cultural pursuits, and even architecture deteriorated. The Spaniards were later to describe the Mayan people as fiercely independent, bloodthirsty, and, like the Aztecs, inclined to sacrifice war captives' hearts on their gods' altars.

The Aztecs

Arising in the confusion of the late postclassical era, the Aztec Empire, in less than two centuries, came to dominate central Mexico from coast to coast. Cortés and his Spanish adventurers were utterly amazed by the monumental architecture, teeming markets, and dazzling wealth of the Aztec capital at Tenochtitlán; they did not realize that Aztec culture, despite its material prosperity and political power, was a relatively recent and somewhat crude version of earlier and more mature civilizations. The Aztecs, like the

This deer effigy vessel, which comes from the Toltec culture is an example of the only glazed pottery produced in the ancient Americas. The pottery, known as "plumbate ware" although it does not contain lead, was imported from non-Toltec artisans located on the Pacific coast near the Mexico-Guatemala border and traded to all major Toltec sites. Incised on each side of the deer's body is a spear thrower. The head and legs are hollow, with openings on the bottom.

Deer Effigy, Vessel, Mexico. "Plumbate" earthenware. The Saint Louis Art Museum. Gift of Morton D. May.

Discovery Through Maps

Toltec Map of a Mayan City

This map of a Mayan city from the Temple of the Warriors in Chichén Itzá, in present-day Yucatán, provides a number of details of life in Mesoamerica. On its surface, it is a portrayal of a scouting party of Toltecs observing the town from their boats. They are the ultimate outsiders, seemingly ignored by the people on land and even by the fish, crabs, and turtles of the river.

But there is more than just the normal earthly plant, animal, and human life in this map. To the upper right is the god Quetzalcoatl (the Feathered Serpent), not a distant abstraction but a presence in everyday life, a factor to be acknowledged and sacrificed to, who may choose one group over the other.

By the middle of the ninth century, the Mayan civilization went into a decline for reasons that are still uncertain. What we do know is that the Toltecs came down from Mexico and filled the power vacuum. The Toltecs' base was near present-day Mexico City, and they dominated Central America between the tenth and twelfth centuries. That this is a Toltec map can be seen by the fact that the warriors attributed their success to the Cloud Serpent, Mixcoatl, and his son Quetzalcoatl, who occupies a place of honor in this map. The militaristic Toltecs ruled through a series of armed orders, like those depicted in the boats. They were eventually supplanted by the Aztecs.

Toltecs before them, retained much of their old barbarism while freely borrowing from their neighbors and victims. The most significant example of this borrowing was their hydraulic agriculture. It was the major factor by which they increased population in the Valley of Mexico to more than a million people, living in some 50 city-states.

The Aztecs' story really begins with the founding of the capital at Tenochtitlán; their earlier history is

quite obscure. They evidently migrated from the north into central Mexico some time before 1200. For a while they were dominated by other peoples, including the Toltecs. About 1325 they settled on an island in Lake Texcoco (the site of present-day Mexico City), later connecting their new town to the mainland by causeways. In its later days Tenochtitlán was an architectural wonder. The Aztecs built a dam to control the lake level, completed a freshwater aqueduct, and created floating artificial islands where irrigated fields supplied food for the capital. Within the imperial metropolis, beautiful avenues, canals, temples, and monuments symbolized increasing Aztec power, particularly after the early fifteenth century.

The Aztec Empire began assuming a recognizable form about that time. During the early decades at Tenochtitlán, the Aztecs had fought as tributaries of Atzcapotzalco, the dominant city-state in the valley. In 1370 they accepted a king of assumed Toltec lineage. For decades they won victories and prospered in concert with their overlords, but in 1427 they rebelled, forming a "triple alliance" with nearby Texcoco and Tlacopán, which defeated Atzcapotzalco and became the major power in the region. For the Aztecs, these events brought great change. Internally, they shifted power from the old clan leaders to a rising military aristocracy. Externally, they started a series of conquests and trading agreements. Thus arose a new imperial order, shared at first by the other two allies but increasingly dominated by Tenochtitlán. The reigns of the Aztec kings Itzcoatl (1427–1440) and his nephew, Montezuma I (1440–1468), ushered in this new era of rising centralism and expansion. It was still in progress under the ninth monarch, Montezuma II (1502–1520), at the time of the Spanish conquest.

As the empire expanded, so did the state-controlled economy. Its base was agricultural land, particularly anchored floating plots installed on the lake after the 1430s. Most were built by the government. Some were allotted to the clans (calpulli) for distribution to families. Others were developed as estates for the monarch and the nobility; the latter were worked by resident tenants under government supervision. Rising agricultural production supported not only the engineering, dredging, stonework, and carpentry required for heavy construction but also a plethora of crafts, turning out weapons, cloth, ceramics, featherwork, jewelry, and hundreds of other goods. Porters from distant places backpacked over mountains to the markets of the valley. A later Spanish observer reported that the great market at Tlateloco, serving Tenochtitlán, attracted 25,000 people daily.

Conquest and accumulating wealth modified the ancient social structure. The old calpulli developed into city wards, identified largely by occupational specialties. By 1500 most calpulli families were headed by men. Women could inherit property and divorce their husbands but were confined mostly to household tasks, except for midwives, healers, and prostitutes. Kinship still promoted social cohesion, but class status provided major incentives. The appointed nobility (pipiltin), along with the priests, held both power and social status, but were burdened with heavy responsibilities. Moreover, they held appointed rather than hereditary posts, although they could inherit property. Commoners could be made nobles by performing superior service, particularly in war. Craftspeople and merchants paid taxes but were exempt from military service; some long-distance merchants (pochteca) served the government as diplomats or spies in foreign states. Peasants worked their plots and served in the army; nonmembers of calpulli were tenants. Their lot was hardly better than that of the numerous slaves, except for the latter's potential role as ceremonial sacrifice victims.

Official documents of the period and other written accounts focus mainly on Mesoamerican social and political elites and conditions in the imperial capitals. However, recent archaeological studies throw fresh light on the lives of the Aztec common people and conditions in the provinces. Surveys of settlement patterns show that Aztec society experienced one of the most significant population explosions of premodern times. In the Valley of Mexico, the heartland of the Aztec Empire, population increased from 175,000 in the early Aztec period (1150–1350) to almost 1 million in the late period (1350–1519). This pattern of growth was duplicated elsewhere in the empire. To cope with this population explosion, the environment was altered: farmers built dams and canals to irrigate cropland, constructed terraced stone walls on hillsides to form new fields, and drained swamps outside Tenochtitlán to create raised fields (chinampas), and with these changes emerged new villages and towns.

Excavations of rural sites near modern Cuernavaca disclose that provincial society was much more complex than previously thought. Commoners evolved a thriving marketing system whereby craft goods produced in their homes were exchanged for a variety of foreign goods. Houses at these sites were small, built of adobe brick walls supported on stone foundations. These houses were furnished with mats and baskets and had a shrine with two or three figurines and an incense burner on one of the walls. In this region the household production of cotton textiles was the major craft. All Aztec women spun and wove cloth, which provided garments, constituted the most common item of tribute demanded by the state, and served as currency in the marketplaces for obtaining other goods and services. In addition to textiles, some residents made paper out of the bark of the wild fig tree, used to produce books of picture-writing and to burn in ritual offerings.

According to written sources, Aztec commoners were subject to the nobles, who possessed most of the land and monopolized power in the polity. But new archaeological excavations show that the commoners were relatively prosperous and enterprising people whose market system operated largely beyond state control. "There is no evidence to suggest that nobles controlled craft production or exchange. The people of the provinces managed to achieve a degree of economic success through channels unconnected to the state and unreported in the official histories of the Aztecs."[1]

The Aztec polity included subordinated allies and 38 provinces. The latter were taxed directly; most of the former paid tribute in some form; and all were denied free foreign relations. This polyglot empire was headed by a hereditary despot, the proclaimed incarnation of the sun-god. His household was more lavish than many in Europe and swarmed with servants. A head wife supervised the concubines and scheduled their assignments, but Aztec queens rarely engaged in court intrigues or offered advice to the emperor, for he usually ruled without concern for other opinions. He was assisted in his official duties by a chief minister and subordinate bureaucracies for war, religion, justice, treasury, storehouses, and personnel. The capital and each province were administered directly by governors, most of whom were descended from former kings. They collected taxes, held court, arranged religious ceremonies, regulated economic affairs, and directed police activities. In addition, urban guilds, villages, and tribes had their own local officials. Vassal states were governed under their own laws but observed by resident Aztec emissaries. This whole system was defended by a large military organization, comprising allied forces, local militias, and an imperial guard of elite troops.

Aztec religion developed from the worship of animistic spirits, symbolizing natural forces seeking balance while in constant conflict. A pessimistic obsession with human futility also dominated the Aztec worldview, perpetuating the common Mesoamerican belief that the gods required human blood to sustain life. Thus as they assembled their empire, the Aztecs came to envision their sun deity, Uitzilopochtli, as a bloodthirsty war god with an appetite for warriors captured in battle. In every city, the Aztecs built pyramids, topped by its two temples to the sun deity and Tlaloc, god of rain. Here they honored Uitzilopochtli in great public ceremonies, when bloodstained priests at the high altars tore out the living hearts of victims and held them up, quivering, to the sun. One such ceremony in 1487 lasted four days and accounted for 80,000 victims. The need for such victims forced continuing conquests and later weakened the state as it faced the Spanish threat.

Comparing the Aztecs and Mayas with the Romans and Greeks can be an interesting theoretical exercise. The Aztec calendar, mathematics, and writing were derived mainly from Mayan sources, somewhat the way that Roman philosophy and science were based on Greek models. Although Aztec culture spawned skilled sculptors, painters, and craftspeople who produced in great numbers, they lacked the imagination of the Mayas, whom they indirectly

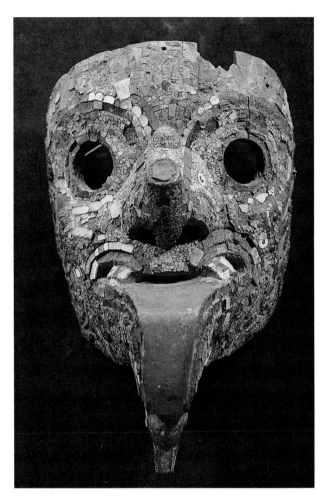

Xototl, the Aztec god of death, depicted as a skeleton. In Aztec religion, the benevolence of the gods was ensured through human sacrifice.

copied, just as Roman artists largely imitated their Greek predecessors. Similarly, both Roman and Aztec cultures were characterized by respect for discipline, practicality, directness, and force. Each was highly skilled in engineering, as attested, for example, by their aqueducts and other feats for furnishing copious amounts of water to their respective capitals. They also shared a militaristic ethos and powerful standing armies.

The Inca Empire

Both the Mayan and Aztec states were less complex than the great Inca Empire in the Andean highlands of South America. Upon reaching full maturity in the early 1500s, it extended 3500 miles between Ecuador and Chile, including almost impassable mountain ranges that separate the upper Amazon forests from the Pacific. The empire contained at least 10 million people in 200 ethnolinguistic groups. It was six times the size of France. The capital, Cuzco, which had an estimated 200,000 inhabitants, was governed in a more centralized way than any city in Europe at the time. The Incas produced fine art and architecture, and were superb engineers, but their major achievement was imperial organization. In this respect they compared favorably with the Romans and the Chinese.

Although it rose very rapidly just before the Spanish conquest, Inca civilization evolved from ancient cultural foundations. Ceremonial and commercial centers had existed on the Peruvian coastal plain well before the Common Era. About 600 C.E. cities began rising in the highlands of the interior. During the next two centuries, tributary kingdoms drew together formerly isolated ceremonial centers of the Peruvian highlands. Some of the resulting states exercised control over the plain, along with territories in what are now Bolivia and Chile. Two kingdoms had capitals at Huari and Tiahuanaco, south central Peru. When these states collapsed in the tenth century, they were succeeded by independent agrarian towns, which were nearly consumed by continuous warfare. A completely different situation developed along the northern coast, where the kingdom of Chimu fostered a high civilization, marked by extensive irrigation, rising population, centralized government, public works, high craft production, widespread trade, and an expanding tributary domain. This polity was conquered and its culture absorbed by the Incas in 1476.

Amid ruthless struggles in the highlands, the Incas created their state in the late medieval era. According to their own legends, these "children of the sun" settled the Valley of Cuzco, in the heartland of the Andes, about 1200 C.E., having migrated from the south, possibly from the region of Tiahuanaco. During the next hundred years they were a simple peasant people, organized by kinship in clans (*ayllu*), living in villages, and worshipping their an-

Machu Picchu, a natural fortress on a narrow ridge between two mountains, was built by the Incas probably after 1440. When the last Inca ruler died, the fortress was abandoned and lost until its rediscovery in 1911.

An Aztec "calender stone," which once stood on the platform of the Great Pyramid at Tenochtitlan.

cestors. To strengthen their unity and better protect themselves in constant wars for survival, they formed a monarchy, developed their military, and began taking over territory near Cuzco. In this competition they were only moderately successful during the reigns of the first seven kings, to the early fifteenth century.

Like the Aztec state at almost the same time, the Inca polity began a climactic period of rapid development with a memorable series of rulers. Viracocha (d. 1438), the eighth emperor, turned his ragtag army into a formidable fighting machine, conquered adjoining territories, and instituted a divine monarchy, with his lineage accepted as descendants of the sungod. His son, Pachacuti (1438–1471), a reformer, religious leader, and builder, has been called "the greatest man ever produced by the American race."[2] He began arduous campaigns to the north and south, notably against Chimu. Topa Yupanqui (1471–1493), Pachacuti's son and successor, who commanded the Inca armies after 1463, completed the annexation of Chimu and extended the empire south into central Chile. The next emperor, Huayna Capec (1493–1527), completed the subjugation of Ecuador, put down rebellions, and attempted to impose order, although the empire was seething with internal discontent when the Spaniards arrived in 1532.

Despite internal problems, intensified by the steep slopes and harsh weather of the Andes, the Incas demonstrated rare technical skills in fashioning their civilization in difficult and often dangerous circumstances. They were master engineers, carrying water long distances by canals and aqueducts, building cities high in the Andes, and constructing networks of roads along the coast and through the mountains, along with suspension bridges and interconnecting valley roadways. All were designed to knit together a vast region that in the Inca Empire covered some 380,000 square miles.

Recent excavations have revealed new evidence about the Incas' sophisticated knowledge of canals and irrigation systems. Canals are difficult to construct: if the slope is too narrow, the canal silts up; if it is too steep, its sides erode. Inca engineers devised different canal shapes to control the water's speed and prevent its velocity from ruining the canal. One "intervalley" canal carried water to a city from 60 miles away; it was only one of many networks, involving thousands of feeder canals, that stretched for hundreds of miles. These hydraulic techniques have been described as deserving to stand with Egypt's pyramids and China's Great Wall as among the world's greatest engineering feats. With irrigation canals constructed far removed from the water's source, the Incas farmed 40 percent more land than is achieved today. But if skills fail, land can quickly return to desert conditions. We have yet to learn what caused the destruction or abandonment of these canal systems—was it human or environmental agencies, or both?

Hydraulic feats were matched by sophisticated organizational skills. To link the empire together, Inca leaders established a communication service, using state-built roads, runner-messengers, rest houses, and smoke signals. Governing by means of a divide-and-rule technique, they appealed wherever possible to traditional prejudices among conquered peoples, perpetuating feuds, courting native leaders, settling colonies of subjects among their enemies, and generally provoking disunity among potentially rebellious areas. They also relied on a common official language and the cult of divine monarchy to unify their own people, particularly the elite. Every part of their system was fitted together in a highly disciplined and integrated whole. Before the Incas, few other states had succeeded so effectively in regimenting millions of people over such great distances and against such formidable obstacles.

Like all civilized peoples, the Incas faced the problem of population expansion and a limited food supply. They solved it well enough to support large military, bureaucratic, and priestly establishments by developing what economists call a command economy. They used no money, no credit, and very little trade beyond local barter. The state planned all economic operations and kept all accounts. Government assigned to families the land to be worked; local family heads, under government supervision, directed workers who produced the crops and saw that harvests were brought to state warehouses. Labor taxes provided work done on public projects, the nobles' estates, and royal lands. A similar approach was used in manufacturing, with craftspeople producing in local guilds, noble households, and palace workshops.

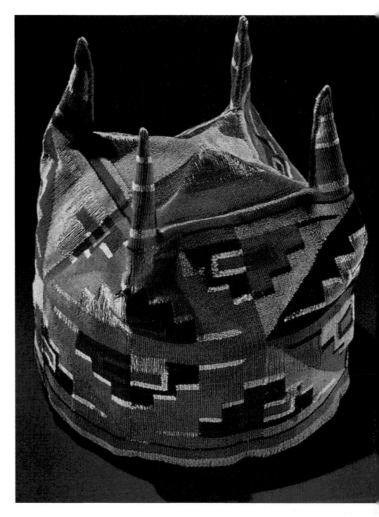

Thanks to the extremely dry Peruvian climate, fine intact examples of early Mesoamerican textiles have survived. This embroidered mantle from the central coast of Peru is from the late intermediate period (c. 1000–1400). Rows of geometric human figures, embroidered in reversals of red and yellow, adorn a sheer tan cotton backing. Miniature human figures fill the interstices between the rows of the large figures.

From its storehouses, the government distributed goods to individuals, to the military, and to government projects. In the process, it built roads, operated hospitals, and maintained schools. All property, even the nobles' land, was state-owned and assigned, except for distinctly personal possessions, including some luxury goods owned by the privileged classes.

This state-controlled economy functioned by way of a precisely defined class structure, built on the lingering kinship tradition. Commoners were kept loyal and disciplined by identifying the state with their ancient *ayllus*. Inca nobles maintained respect because they were all related directly or indirectly to the royal lineage and therefore shared the divine mandate to rule. They held the highest positions in government, the army, and the priesthood. A notch lower were lesser aristocrats and nobles among conquered peoples, who held local offices, up to subgovernors in the provinces. The two upper classes made up a privileged elite. Trained in special schools, they were identified by luxuries in food, dress, and housing. They were also exempted from taxes and cruel punishments. At the third level were common workers. They were generally confined to their villages; their work was prescribed; their dress and food were restricted; and government checked even the cleanliness of their houses. Commoners were thus little better off than the lowest class of slaves, who were taken as war captives and assigned to serve the upper classes.

The shift from kinship toward class division was accompanied by a decline of matriarchal values. Upper-class women shared some social status with their husbands, and all women could inherit property when they were widowed; but they were generally subordinated and exploited. Indeed, a fifteenth-century royal decree prohibited women from testifying in court because they were by nature "deceitful, mendacious, and fainthearted."[3] Female commoners worked in the fields, while women of all classes were expected to keep house, mind the children, and serve the needs of men. Many were concubines or surplus wives, the number depending on the husbands' wealth and status. The most beautiful and intelligent young girls were drafted as "chosen women." Some would become "virgins of the sun," serving as nuns and weavers in the temple workshops; others would become concubines of the emperor or nobles; a few would be sacrificed. All were honored as servants of the state.

All authority in the Inca state originated with the hereditary divine emperor, who exercised the power of life and death over all his subjects. He was usually aloof, even with his own immediate family, although he might, if he chose, delegate authority to the queen (his full sister after 1438) or take advice from his mother. With its thousands of servants and concubines, his court was a magnificent display of wealth and power. It was also the locus of a central government that included agencies for rituals (religion), war, treasury, accounts, and public works. The chief ministers were advisers to the Imperial Council, consisting of the emperor and four viceroys, who governed the four provinces. Each province, about the size of New York State, was divided into approximately 40 districts, under subgovernors and their assistants. Authority in the districts was further subdivided, ultimately into units of ten families. Officials at each level reported regularly to superiors and were subject to frequent inspections. This system regulated every aspect of life, including labor, justice, marriage, and even morals.

The power of the ruler depended largely on an excellent military system, which featured compulsory service. Instructors in the villages trained peasant boys for the army; the most promising were marked for advancement when they were called to active service in their twenties. They served for two years before retiring to the labor reserve and militia. The army was or-

ganized in units of 10, 50, 100, 1000, and 10,000, under officers who held complete authority over subordinates. A combat force of 200,000, with support units, was always under arms. It was supplied from military storehouses throughout the country and garrisoned in mighty stone fortresses, each with independent water sources. Troops from these centers ruthlessly suppressed any resistance to the regime.

A second base for Inca authority was religion. As the empire grew, its priests appropriated the gods of conquered peoples and included them in a vast pantheon, headed by the Inca sun-god. For example, the virgins of the sun, with their ceremonies and temples, evolved from an earlier moon goddess cult among matrilinear societies. War victims would on occasion be sacrificed to the sun, as would some children of "chosen women." In later times the servants of an emperor, as well as his favorite concubines, were sent with him, at his death, to serve him in the hereafter. To emphasize the emperors' divinity and symbolize the state's continuity, dead emperors were mummified, seated on thrones in their sacred palaces, and attended by living servants, wives, and priests. On public occasions these grotesque figures were paraded before the people, who bowed before them in reverence. Such ceremonies were conducted by a clerical establishment of 4000 priests in the capital and many scores of thousands more throughout the country.

There was a remarkable exception to this religious mind-set in the person of the emperor Pachacuti. A highly successful military leader who largely laid the empire's foundation by consolidating the area around Cuzco and annexing the rich Titicaca basin, this multitalented innovator established Quechua as the administrative language (it is today the most widely spoken Indian language in the Americas), reformed the calendar, introduced methods of terracing the hillsides and extending irrigation, and created an efficient public service. Although regarded as a direct descendant of the sun-god, Pachacuti asked himself how the sun could be the supreme deity since it never rested but revolved endlessly around the earth. He concluded that the sun was itself a messenger sent by a more powerful being who from his place of rest could illuminate and command the world. This must be the universal Creator, Viracocha ("Lord"), who governed the sun and had brought into being all other deities. And in his honor the emperor constructed a temple in Cuzco. But as in the case of Akhenaton, his conceptual forerunner in Egypt, Pachacuti's nascent monotheism did not prevail; later rulers continued to sacrifice victims to the sun-god—though not to the extent practiced by the Aztecs.

Order and security were dominant values in Inca cultural expression, and neither aesthetic concerns nor philosophical speculation received much attention. As we have seen, religious innovation was given short shrift, and any theorizing was subordinated to the practicalities of a state cult and the morality of

Father Bernabé Cobo, "Pachacuti, the Greatest Inca"

This selection is from Chapter 12 of Father Bernabé Cobo's *History of the Inca Empire*. Cobo relied on Indian legends and contemporary Indian testimony, as well as earlier Spanish writings.

Viracocha Inca left four sons by his principal wife; they were called Pachacuti Inca Yupanqui, Inca Roca, Tupa Yupanqui, and Capac Yupanqui. The first one succeeded him in the kingdom, and concerning the rest, although they were lords and grandees, nothing is said. Pachacuti married a lady named Mama Anahuarque, native to the town of Choco, near Cuzco, and he founded a family that they call Iñaca Panaca. This king was the most valiant and warlike, wise and statesmanlike of all the Incas, because he organized the republic with the harmony, laws, and statutes that it maintained from that time until the arrival of the Spaniards. He injected order and reason into everything; eliminated and added rites and ceremonies; made the religious cult more extensive; established the sacrifices and the solemnity with which the gods were to be venerated, enlarged and embellished the temples with magnificent structures, income, and a great number of priests and ministers; reformed the calendar; divided the year into twelve months, giving each one its name; and designated the solemn fiestas and sacrifices to be held each month. He composed many elegant prayers with which the gods were to be invoked, and he ordered that these prayers be recited at the same time that the sacrifices were offered. He was no less careful and diligent in matters pertaining to the temporal welfare of the republic; he gave his vassals a method of working the fields and taking advantage of the lands that were so rough and uneven as to be useless and unfruitful; he ordered that rough hillsides be terraced and that ditches be made from the rivers to irrigate them. In short, nothing was overlooked by him in which he did not impose all good order and harmony; for this reason he was given the name of Pachacuti, which means "change of time or of the world"; this is because as a result of his excellent government

things improved to such an extent that times seemed to have changed and the world seemed to have turned around; thus, his memory was very celebrated among the Indians, and he was given more honor in their songs and poems than any of the other kings that either preceded him or came after him.

After having shown himself to be so devoted to the sun and having taken the care just mentioned that all worship him in the same way that his ancestors had done, one day Pachacuti began to wonder how it was possible that a thing could be god if it was so subject to movement as the Sun, that it never stops or rests for a moment since it turns around the world every day; and he inferred from this meditation that the Sun must not be more than a messenger sent by the Creator to visit the universe; besides, if he were God, it would not be possible for a few clouds to get in front of him and obscure his splendor and rays so that he could not shine; and if he were the universal Creator and lord of all things, sometimes he would rest and from his place of rest he would illuminate all the world and command whatever he wished; and thus, there had to be another more powerful lord who ruled and governed the Sun; and no doubt this was Pachayachachic. He communicated this thought to the members of his council, and in agreement with them, he decided that Pachayachachic was to be preferred to the Sun, and within the city of Cuzco, he built the Creator his own temple which he called Quishuarcancha, and in it he put the image of the Creator of the world, Viracocha Pachayachachic.

From *History of the Inca Empire*, trans. and ed. Roland Hamilton from the holograph manuscript in the Biblioteca Capitular y Colombina de Sevilla, © 1979. Reprinted by permission of the University of Texas Press.

power—treason and cowardice were considered the worst sins. The Incas had no written records and seem to have lacked even the picture-writing of Mesoamerica. Instead they relied on oral traditions, supplemented by mnemonic devices such as the system of knotted strings called the *quipu*. These oral traditions would have been dealt a lethal blow by the Spanish conquest. "The result is that our knowledge of the intangible features of Inca civilization, literature, laws and so on, is very imperfect, and we are cut off almost completely from those of pre-Inca ones."[4]

The Inca lunar calendar was inaccurate and provided no starting point for the identification of historical events. Although the Incas were excellent craftspeople, capable of producing fine pottery and metalwork in copper and gold, their most striking technical and cultural accomplishments were in engineering and massive architecture. Without using mortar, they fitted immense slabs of stone into temple and fortress walls. This efficiency is still exhibited in existing roads, bridges, terraced fields, and stone fortresses.

The Amerindians of North America

The movies have reinforced the fallacy that all Indians constituted a single type with a common lifestyle. The mounted, warbonneted warrior of the plains has too often been considered the archetype of the "Red Man." Yet early European settlers found the North American Indians as diverse as the Europeans themselves. Two hundred distinct North American languages have been classified, and numerous physical differences in the continent's inhabitants have been identified. Amerindian societies presented a wide spectrum of variation: from small bands of hunter-gatherers and farmers to well-organized states. A similar diversity was found in their arts and crafts; various regions excelled in basketry, metalwork, weaving, sculpture, totem-carving, and boatmaking.

Amerindians north of the Rio Grande did not produce the massive technological and governmental achievements of the Mesoamericans. As Paleolithic and Neolithic societies, their populations were much smaller and consequently did not create large cities, with their complex division of labor and urban way of life. They had survived by hunting and fishing until

knowledge of food raising spread north from Mesoamerica. Agriculture's effect on those regions where it could be practiced was the same as elsewhere in the world: more stable settlements in which men cleared the fields and women tended the crops. Marked demographic growth, with accompanying large village or town centers, occurred in the Rio Grande, Ohio, Mississippi, and St. Lawrence valleys.

The Iroquois of the Northeast Woodlands

Europeans arriving in what is now upper New York State found various groups speaking dialects of a common Iroquoian language. They had created a distinctive culture by 1000 C.E. and subsequently formed the League of the Five Nations. They used the metaphor of the longhouse, their traditional communal dwelling, to describe their political alliance: the Mohawk along the Hudson were the "keepers of the eastern door," adjoined in sequence by the Oneida, Onondaga, and Cayuga, with the Seneca "keepers of the western door." When the Tuscarora joined in the early eighteenth century, the confederacy became known as the Six Nations. The warlike Iroquois even-

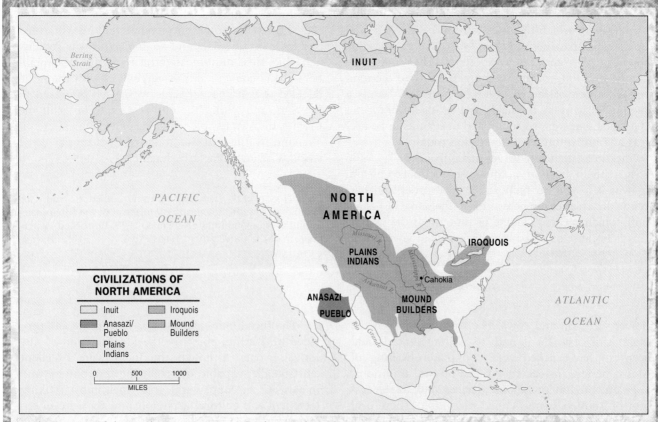

In the vastness of the North American continent, the varied environmental challenges led to the development of hundreds of different Indian tribes—more than 250 alone in the present-day state of California.

tually extended their control from the Great Lakes toward the Atlantic by subjugating the nomadic, food-gathering Algonkian people.

The Iroquois had the advantage of being agriculturists with permanent villages. Some of these had several hundred residents and extensive fields where maize, beans, squash, and tobacco were grown. Weirs were built across streams, and smokehouses preserved joints of game. Related families lived in the longhouses, "long rectangular buildings . . . protected by high wooden palisades. Women played a notable part; they owned the homes and gardens, and, since descent was through the female, chose the leaders. If the men chosen did not give good leadership, they could be replaced."[5]

The Adena and Hopewell Cultures of the Ohio Valley

In the area of present-day Kentucky and Ohio, important Amerindian settlements took root between 800 B.C.E. and 600 C.E. Known generally as the Adena and Hopewell cultures, these Amerindians developed ways of life and social patterns from the Missouri River to the Appalachians and from the Great Lakes to the Gulf of Mexico.

The two groups developed differing ways to construct their homes: the Adena chose to live in circular houses made out of poles and covered with mats and thatched roofs, while the Hopewell built round or oval houses with more protective roofs made of skins, bark from trees, and a combination of thatch and clay. They had a sophisticated view of the after-

life, as can be seen in the effort they took to bury their dead. The Adena interred their deceased in vast cone-shaped mounds of earth, sometimes 500 feet around. Sometimes the dead were cremated, and the ashes were placed in the mounds along with all sorts of relics such as carved stone tablets, pipes smoked during religious ceremonies, and jewelry. The Hopewell did the same, but on a larger scale for the more distinguished members of their families.

Along with the impressive burial mounds, archaeologists have found indications of other projects indicating the combined efforts of hundreds of people in addition to a substantial investment of wealth. At Newark, Ohio, for example, the ceremonial site covers 4 square miles. Such enterprises indicate a long period of relative peace, generations remaining in the same place, and a substantial level of wealth. That these took place before the introduction of the planting of corn is significant. Archaeologists think that the Hopewell and Adena cultures survived on a diet of fish, game, nuts, and other plant life. They have also found indications of contacts with tribes across North America. Whether through trading or tribute, the Ohio valley tribes had access to metals and goods found only in the Rocky Mountain area and shells from the Gulf coast. They had mastered the manufacture of tools, pottery, and copper jewelry.

The Mississippian Culture

In the sixth century C.E. another major Amerindian culture made its appearance in the area just east of present-day St. Louis. Archaeologists are still investi-

The Great Serpent Mound in Ohio is a rich repository of the North American Indian life centered in the Adena culture. Active between 500 B.C.E. and 100 C.E., the Indians of the Adena culture had a well-developed village life and traded with other peoples from Canada to the Gulf of Mexico.

gating the origins and extent of this culture from the various burial sites, the most important of which is that at Cahokia, Illinois. Unlike the Adena and Hopewell cultures, the Mississippian culture lived in houses made out of thin pieces of wood (laths) covered with clay—so-called *wattle-and-daub houses*. These took various shapes in the large villages of the area. So influential was this culture that it came to dominate most of the region west of the Mississippi.

The Mississippian peoples benefited from mastering the raising of maize, beans, and squash, and they tied their religion to the planting and harvesting cycles. Their burial mounds took the form of flat-topped pyramids, arranged around a central square. In the most developed regions, fortresslike palisades surrounded the site. The Cahokia complex was constructed over a period of nearly three centuries (c. 900–c. 1150). The centerpiece of the Cahokia site is a pyramid with a base of more than 18 acres, reaching a height of almost 100 feet. This is only one of more than 80 such mounds to be found at Cahokia, a village more than 6 miles long. There was no set burial practice for the Mississippian culture—remains have also been found in cemeteries, in urns, and under the floors of houses.

After the thirteenth century the peoples in the Mississippian culture passed a highly complex religion along from generation to generation—an indication of their stability, continuity, and sophistication. The extent of their wealth enabled them to construct temples filled with ceremonial objects such as large stone scepters and copper plates. Their religion used symbols such as the cross, the sun, arrows surrounded by semicircles, a sunburst, and—most intriguing—an outstretched hand with an eye in the palm. The art that derived from the religion featured portrayals of gods based on animals, rattlesnakes with feathers and wings, and people portrayed as birds. Vessels found at the sites indicate the presence of human sacrifice: jars with human faces painted on them and portrayals of the heads of sacrificed victims. These are indications that not only adults but also infants were given up to the higher deity the Mississippi culture believed controlled their lives.

The Mogollon, Hohokam, and Anasazi Cultures of the Southwest

The southwestern Amerindian cultures lived in the most environmentally challenging part of the continental United States, the dry and rocky regions of present-day Utah, Arizona, New Mexico, and Colorado. In response to their surroundings, they produced the most advanced levels of technology and agriculture. The Mogollon, Hohokam, and Anasazi grew maize, beans, and squash, each group evolving its own techniques. The homes of each group were built out of adobe brick or other techniques of masonry, sometimes on extremely challenging sites. Each group also produced pottery that could rank in beauty with any in the world.

The Mogollon culture lasted almost 1600 years, from around 300 B.C.E. to 1350 C.E. in southwestern New Mexico. Its people built their homes low to the ground along the tops of ridges. Their villages were built around large underground buildings used for religious ceremonies and as pit houses until the eleventh century; thereafter they built these structures at ground level. Because of the constant threat of drought, they developed a diversified economy based on hunting, gathering, and farming. Relatively isolated, they saw little need to change over the centuries.

The Hohokam culture grew along the valleys of the Salt and Gila Rivers. Its architecture was similar to that of the early Mogollon, except the Hohokam built not just ceremonial structures but also their homes inside underground pits. Perhaps learning from the Mesoamerican cultures, the Hohokam constructed an impressive network of canals, some more than 30 miles long, 6 to 10 feet deep, and 15 to 30 feet wide. The existence of these canals proves the existence not only of wealth but also of substantial social organization. The Hohokam also borrowed their religion, their burial practices, and even some of their games from the Mesoamericans.

Deriving from these two cultures was the Anasazi, which appeared around 300 C.E. Of the three cultures, the Anasazi had the most sophisticated and most impressive architecture and the largest area of influence—from the Idaho-Utah border to the Gulf of California. Early on they built their homes in the shape of beehive-shaped domes made out of logs held together by a mudlike mortar. They grew maize and made pottery, like the Mississippian culture, and stored both in warehouselike structures. Around 700 C.E. they took their economic development one step further by beginning the manufacture of cotton cloth. Their technological genius is apparent from their use of two forms of irrigation: runoff by building dikes and terracing hills and subsoil by constructing sand dunes at the base of hills to hold the runoff of the sometimes torrential rains. Their lives revolved around their religion, with ceremonies to placate the gods to hold off storms and to ensure fertility.

The Anasazi are best known today for their architectural accomplishments. Around the eleventh century they began to construct cities, with houses built in the shapes of squares, ells, and semicircles. They used all of the available materials to build these settlements; with wood, mud, and stone, they erected cliff dwellings and the equivalent of terraced apartment houses. One such structure, with some 500 living units, was the largest residential building in the North America until the completion of an apartment

The features on this artifact, thought to be a stabilizer for a spear shaft, illustrate the closeness of the Eskimo (Inuit and Aleut) peoples to their Mongoloid forebears.

house in New York in 1882. The disappearance of the Anasazi around 1300 remains a mystery. It is believed that a combination of a long drought, internecine conflicts, and the arrivals of the Navajo and the Apache led to their demise.

The Navajo, the Apache, the Mandan

Three other groups of Amerindians established their presence before the arrival of Europeans. The Navajo, the largest tribe in the United States, came down from the north to the Southwest sometime in the eleventh century. There they borrowed extensively from the indigenous cultures.

A century or so later, the Apache, who speak a language close to that of the Navajo, arrived and by the end of the 1500s lived in parts of the present states of Arizona, Colorado, and New Mexico. They too were heavily influenced by the cultures present there.

Finally, the Mandan, who based their economy on fur trading and hunting, came to the vast valley of the Missouri River from east of the Mississippi in the late 1300s. They filled in the final empty spaces on the map of North America, and by 1500 Amerindians lived across the length and breadth of what would become the United States, a long time before the New World would be "discovered" by Christopher Columbus.

The Far North: Inuit and Aleuts

The appearance of the Inuit, also known as the Eskimos, is shrouded in controversy. Some observers assert that they descended from ancient seagoing peoples; others believe that they developed their culture in Alaska after the last ice age. They speak much the same language as the Aleuts, whose origins are similarly unclear. It is accepted that the two groups split

apart more than 4000 years ago and that they are tied more closely to Asians than the Amerindians are.

The Aleuts stayed largely in the area that is now known as the Alaskan peninsula, the Aleutian Islands, and the far eastern portion of Russia. The Inuit spread along the area south of the Arctic Circle from the Bering Strait across the top of Canada to Greenland. Both peoples lived by hunting and fishing. The Aleuts hunted sea lions, otters, and seals from *kayaks*—small boats made of a wood frame over which skins were stretched. The Inuit showed more flexibility, hunting both sea and land animals, fishing in fresh and salt water. Their diet was based primarily on the caribou, musk-ox, walruses, and whales. They used the kayak too, but supplemented it with canoes and dogsleds. Their greatest accomplishment in seafaring vessels was the *umiak*, from which they harpooned whales.

By about 100 C.E. the Inuit had established large villages; one of the biggest, with around 400 homes, was near Nome, Alaska. To counter the arctic cold, they dug as much as 20 inches into the permafrost to erect their homes, covered with poles and sod. In settlements such as that near Nome, archaeologists have found large structures for the performance of religious rites, led by shamans who claimed to be able to heal diseases and wounds.

Conclusion

Before the coming of the Europeans, the Americas produced a rich variety of highly sophisticated and complex civilizations in response to the varied environmental challenges and opportunities of the Western Hemisphere. Some of these groups made the transition from food hunting to food raising, and some did not.

In Central and South America agriculture supplied the sustenance to support growing populations. This in turn led to the establishment of villages and then cities and finally far-flung states. More food and more wealth also produced leisure and priestly classes who had the time to think about religion, literature, art, architecture, mathematics, and astronomy.

In North America environmental conditions were harsher and did not permit an equivalent accumulation of agricultural surpluses found in Central and South America. Some Indian tribes remained hunter-gatherers. Others established settled villages and complex civilizations, but without the wealth, power, or sophistication of Mesoamerica.

Unfortunately, a combination of European diseases and technology would decimate and subjugate the peoples of the Americas after the fifteenth century. Although they fought bravely against overwhelming odds, the Indians would have to struggle to maintain their cultural identities in the centuries to come.

Suggestions for Reading

A sound in-depth introduction to indigenous cultures in the New World is Alvin M. Josephy, ed., *America in 1492* (Knopf, 1992). See also Robert Wauchope's *Indian Background of Latin American History* (Knopf, 1970). The three following comparative studies are well worth attention: George Collier, ed., *The Inca and Aztec States, 1400–1800* (Academic Press, 1982); Geoffrey W. Conrad and Arthur A. Demarest, *Religion and Empire: The Dynamics of Aztec and Inca Expansionism* (Cambridge University Press, 1984); and Alfred Sundell. *A History of the Aztec and the Maya and Their Conquest* (Collier Books, 1967).

Among the most informative works on pre-Columbian Mesoamerica are Ross Hassig, *War and Society in Ancient Mesoamerica* (University of California Press, 1992); Richard A. Dieh and Janet C. Berlo, eds., *Mesoamerica After the Decline of Teotihuacán* (Dumbarton Oakes, 1989); Michael D. Coe, *Mexico*, 3rd ed. (Thames & Hudson, 1986); and Robert R. Miller, *Mexico* (University of Oklahoma Press, 1989). See also Shirley Gorenstein, *Not Forever on Earth: The Prehistory of Mexico* (Scribner, 1975); Kenneth Pearce, *The View from the Top of the Temple* (University of New Mexico Press, 1984); Jacques Soustelle, *The Olmecs: The Oldest Civilization in Mexico* (University of Oklahoma Press, 1985); and Joseph W. Whitecotton, *The Zapotecs: Princes, Priests, and Peasants* (University of Oklahoma Press, 1984).

For informative studies on the Mayas, see Michael D. Coe, *The Maya* (Thames & Hudson, 1987); Norman Hammond, *Ancient Maya Civilization* (Rutgers University Press, 1982); and John S. Henderson, *The World of the Ancient Maya* (Cornell University Press, 1981). Special insights into the Mayan experience are provided in Jeremy A. Sobloff, *A New Archeology and the Ancient Maya* (Scientific American Library, 1990); Linda Schele and David Friedel, *A Forest of Kings* (Morrow, 1990); and Ralph Witlock, *Everyday Life of the Maya* (Dorset, 1987).

Works that reveal the private as well as the public life of the Aztecs include Jane S. Day, *Aztec: The World of Montezuma* (Robert Rinehart, 1992); Richard Townshend, *The Aztecs* (Thames & Hudson, 1992); Inga Clendinnen, *Aztecs* (Cambridge University Press, 1991); Francis F. Berdan, *The Aztecs* (Chelsea House, 1989); Alfonso Caso, *The Aztecs, People of the Sun* (University of Oklahoma Press, 1988); and Nigel Davies, *The Aztecs* (University of Oklahoma Press, 1989). An older acclaimed work, Burr Cartwright Brundage, *A Rain of Darts* (University of Texas Press, 1972), is still valuable. For special studies on Aztec political institutions and development, see Susan Gillespie, *The Aztec Kings* (University of Arizona Press, 1989), and Ross Hassig, *Aztec Warfare: Imperial Expansion and Political Control* (University of Oklahoma Press, 1988). For an interesting description of social conditions, see Rudolf van Zantwijk, *The Aztec Arrangement: The Social History of Pre-Spanish Mexico* (University of Oklahoma Press, 1985), and June Nash, "The Aztecs and the Ideology of Male Dominance," *Signs* 4 (1978), pp. 349–362.

On the Incas, Ian Cameron, *Kingdom of the Sun God* (Facts on File, 1990), deserves special attention. Bernabé Cobo, *A History of the Inca Empire* (University of Texas Press, 1979), is still considered sound and complete. Another long-respected anthropological approach to pre-Columbian Andean culture is J. Alden Mason, *Ancient Civilizations of Peru* (Penguin, 1988). It is supplemented by Richard W. Keating, *Peruvian Pre-History* (Cambridge University Press, 1988). Other standard works include Loren McIntyre, *The Incredible Inca and Their Timeless Land* (National Geographic, 1978), and Alfred Metraux, *The History of the Incas* (Schocken, 1970). Excellent depictions of the Inca command economy can be found in Jonathon Haas et al., *The Origin and Development of the Andean State* (Cambridge University Press, 1987); Frank Solomon, *The Native Lords of Quito in the Age of the Incas: The Political Economy of the North-Andean Chieftains* (Cambridge University Press, 1986); and John V. Murra, *The Economic Organization of the Inca State* (JAI Press, 1980).

Suggestions for Web Browsing

Mesoweb, including Illustrated Encyclopedia of Mesoamerica
http://www.mesoweb.com/

> *Mesoweb is devoted to ancient Mesoamerica and its cultures: the Olmec, Mayas, Aztecs, Toltecs, Mixtecs, Zapotecs, and others.*

University of Pennsylvania Museum of Archaeology and Art: Mesoamerica
http://www.upenn.edu/museum/Collections/mesoamerica.html

> *A history of Mesoamerican culture as reflected by the many artifacts in the university's museum.*

National Museum of the American Indian
http://www.si.edu/activity/planvis/museums/aboutmai.htm

> *Web site of the Smithsonian Institution's National Museum of the American Indian offers a look at one of the finest and most complete collections of items from the indigenous peoples of the Western Hemisphere.*

Arctic Studies Center
http://nmnhwww.si.edu/arctic/

> *Smithsonian Institution site dedicated to the study of Arctic peoples, culture, and environments includes numerous images, as well as audio and video segments of dance and discussion.*

Notes

1. Michael E. Smith, "Life in the Provinces of the Aztec Empire," *Scientific American*, September 1997, p. 83.
2. Clements Markham, in Edward Hyams and George Ordish, *The Last of the Incas* (New York: Simon & Schuster, 1963), p. 99.
3. Ibid., p. 88.
4. G. H. S. Bushnell, *Peru* (London: Thames & Hudson, 1960), p. 30.
5. J. Wreford Watson, *Social Geography of the United States* (New York: Longman, 1979), p. 25.

3

The Transition
to Modern Times

So far we have encountered a number of societies that emphasized the group at the expense of the individual—societies such as ancient Egypt or medieval Europe. In other societies, such as classical Greece, individualism counted for more than collectivism. During the period that historians speak of as early modern times, the interests and rights of the individual were again in the ascendant in the West. By the end of the fifteenth century the medieval ideal of universal political unity had been shattered as national monarchies gained supremacy in England, France, and Spain. Despite opposition from popes and nobles, vigorous monarchs in these countries succeeded in their attempts at nation-making—a process that fostered and was in turn supported by a growing national consciousness among the common people.

In the realm of thought, Italian scholars known as humanists discovered in the manuscripts of ancient Greece and Rome the same emphasis on individual freedom that was rapidly gaining momentum in their own day, and with this spirit of individualism sprang up an unashamed delight in the beauties and joys of life. The creative vigor of the Italian Renaissance in literature, thought, and the fine arts surged throughout Europe, resulting in one of the most fruitful epochs in human cultural history.

Carried into the religious sphere, the resurgence of individualism shattered the universal supremacy of the church and gave rise to the religious diversity of the modern Western world. The followers of Luther, Calvin, and Zwingli substituted the authority of the Scriptures for that of the Roman church and interposed no priestly mediator between the individual and God. The Roman church, which launched a vigorous reform movement of its own, nevertheless continued to be a potent force.

The economic structure of western Europe went through a Commercial Revolution in early modern times. The quickening of town life abetted the rise of a new and forceful middle class, whose members were the chief supporters of the system of economic individualism known as capitalism. Furthermore, overseas expansion stimulated trade, increased wealth, and introduced to European markets an abundance of products previously scarce or unknown. The barter economy of the Middle Ages was superseded by one of money, banks, and stock exchanges, and Europe rapidly became the economic center of the world.

For the kingdoms of Europe, the Ottoman conquest of Constantinople in 1453 signaled a catastrophe. However, the Ottomans symbolized a new Muslim world emerging between the eastern Mediterranean and Indonesia. In that vast territory three new empires held sway for centuries. Geographically, this world was centered in Persia, under its Shi'ite Safavid dynasty. Culturally, it was influenced by Persian, Arab, and Byzantine courtly traditions. To the east the magnificent Mughul Empire emerged on the frontiers of Hindu and Confucian polities. Militarily, this Muslim world was dominated by the forces of the Ottoman Empire, far stronger than those of any country in Europe at the time. Warfare often prevailed among these contending states; but they also shared the same Islamic faith, steppe antecedents, and Persian art traditions. They would later be challenged and supplanted by European states also seeking dominion in the midst of a global economic revolution. But in the sixteenth century Asian empires held primacy of place in the contest for world power, controlling the land and seaborne routes of the East-West trade.

For China, geography and demography had dictated that it would be impossible to have the Central Kingdom remain isolated and arrogant into the modern age. The Ming rulers tried their best after their first half century to pursue a conservative policy of noninvolvement with other peoples and succeeded in bringing some stability to China. However, toward the seventeenth century their inability to reform and the arrival of all manner of outsiders—invading forces and merchants alike—spelled an end to their nearly three-century-long run.

Korea and Japan were the two major recipients of the Chinese example and closeness. Korea rested under the immediate gaze of its immense neighbor yet managed to construct a unique and powerful nation. Japan, blessed with its island position, had the unparalleled advantage of picking and choosing the currents and influences it would receive. To the south and southeast a complex mosaic of nations grew, formed from Indian, Chinese, and Muslim influences. Never able to achieve regional dominance, each of them had a moment of hegemony and added to the rich Asian cultural picture.

A broad view of Michelangelo's
majestic painting of the Sistine
Chapel in the Vatican. This great
artist portrayed hundreds of figures
on a ceiling of several thousand
square yards. Michelangelo is
widely regarded as the most influential artist who ever lived. "Until
you have seen the Sistine Chapel,"
wrote German poet Goethe, "you
have no adequate conception
of what man is capable of
accomplishing."

The Renaissance in Italy and Northern Europe

*Renaissance Thought and Art,
1300–1600*

Chapter Contents

In Italy during the fourteenth and fifteenth centuries, thinkers and artists began to view the thousand years that had passed since the fall of Rome as the "Dark Ages," a time of stagnation and ignorance, in contrast to their own age, which appeared to them enlightened and beautiful. They called themselves *humanists*—scholars who were dedicated to the recovering, study, and transmission of the intellectual and cultural heritage of Greece and Rome. They exuberantly said that they were participating in an intellectual and artistic revolution sparked by a renaissance ("rebirth") of the values and forms of classical antiquity. Modern historians have accepted the term *Renaissance* as a convenient label for this exciting age of intellectual and artistic revival, which continued through the sixteenth century. But since the Renaissance had deep roots in the Middle Ages, which also made rich contributions to civilization, in what ways can the Renaissance be said to signify a true "rebirth"?

First of all, there was an intensification of interest in the literature of classical Greece and Rome. This Classical Revival, as it is called, was the product of a more worldly focus of interest—a focus on human beings and life as an end in itself rather than as a temporarily occupied stop on the way to eternity. Renaissance scholars searched the monasteries for old Latin manuscripts that had been unappreciated and largely ignored by medieval scholars, and they translated previously unknown works from Greek into Latin, the common language of scholarship. In

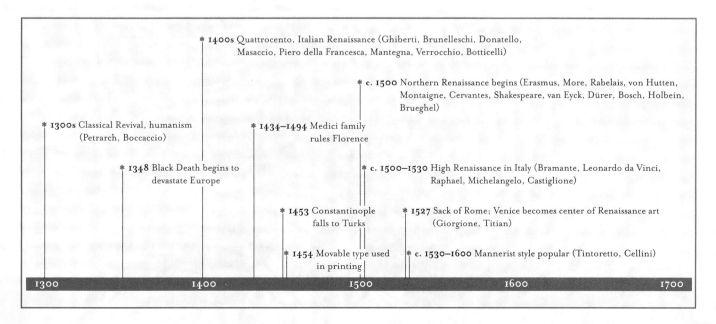

* **1400s** Quattrocento, Italian Renaissance (Ghiberti, Brunelleschi, Donatello, Masaccio, Piero della Francesca, Mantegna, Verrocchio, Botticelli)

* **c. 1500** Northern Renaissance begins (Erasmus, More, Rabelais, von Hutten, Montaigne, Cervantes, Shakespeare, van Eyck, Dürer, Bosch, Holbein, Brueghel)

* **1300s** Classical Revival, humanism (Petrarch, Boccaccio)

* **1434–1494** Medici family rules Florence

* **1348** Black Death begins to devastate Europe

* **c. 1500–1530** High Renaissance in Italy (Bramante, Leonardo da Vinci, Raphael, Michelangelo, Castiglione)

* **1453** Constantinople falls to Turks

* **1527** Sack of Rome; Venice becomes center of Renaissance art (Giorgione, Titian)

* **1454** Movable type used in printing

* **c. 1530–1600** Mannerist style popular (Tintoretto, Cellini)

1300   1400   1500   1600   1700

this manner the humanists greatly added to the quantity of classical literature that had entered the mainstream of Western thought since the Middle Ages. Second, while Renaissance scholars found a new significance in classical literature, artists in Italy were stimulated and inspired by the study and imitation of classical sculpture and architecture.

But the Renaissance was not a mere cult of antiquity, a looking backward into the past. The humanists of the Renaissance were the forefathers of the modern world, enthusiastically widening the horizon of human interests. Renaissance culture exhibited a strong belief in the worth of the individual and the individual's ability to think and act as a free agent. The Renaissance spirit was admirably summed up by the Florentine humanist Leon Battista Alberti when he declared, "Men can do all things if they will."

In some respects every age is an age of transition, but it may be fair to state that the Renaissance marked one of the major turning points in Western civilization. The dominant institutions and thought systems of the Middle Ages were in decline; Scholasticism, church authority, and conformity were constantly questioned. Instead a culture that depended on individualism, on skepticism, and ultimately on science was taking its place.

The Renaissance originated in the cities of central and northern Italy. We shall begin with a description of the new secular interests and values that arose in these urban centers, then note the relationship between these urban interests and the Classical Revival and flowering of art, and conclude with a discussion of the spread of the Renaissance as it crossed the Alps to France, Germany, and England. Ultimately it was in England that the underlying optimism and dynamism of the entire Renaissance period was epitomized by Shakespeare:

> O, wonder!
> How many goodly creatures are there here!
> How beauteous mankind is! O brave new world,
> That has such people in 't![1]

The Italian Renaissance

The culture of the Italian Renaissance was not created in a vacuum. Historians today find a clue to the intellectual and aesthetic changes of the age in economic, social, and political change.

Emergence of the Italian City-States

During the High Middle Ages, a new economy and a new society emerged in western Europe (see Chapter 9). Commerce and a money economy revived, towns arose and became self-governing communes, and townspeople constituted a new middle class, the bourgeoisie. Although Italy had been one of the leaders in these twelfth- and thirteenth-century developments, during the next two centuries the region moved dramatically ahead of the rest of Europe.

During the fourteenth and fifteenth centuries the city-states of northern and central Italy experienced a tremendous growth in population and expanded to become small territorial states. These included the Papal States, where the restored authority of the popes crushed the independence of many little city-states in central Italy. Feudalism had died out in Italy during the twelfth and thirteenth centuries.

Unlike the French nobility, who spent their time participating in the vigorous court life of their fellow nobles, the Italian nobles moved to the cities and joined with the rich merchants to form a patrician ruling class. Together they successfully fought off the intervention of the German emperors Frederick Barbarossa and Frederick II. By 1300 nearly all the land of northern and central Italy was owned by profit-seeking urban citizens who produced for city markets. In the large export industries, such as woolen cloth (it employed 30,000 in Florence), a capitalistic system of production was emerging—the "putting out" system in which the merchant-capitalist retained ownership of the raw material and paid others to work it into the finished product. Additional great wealth was gained from commerce, particularly the import-export trade in luxury goods from the East. So much wealth was accumulated by these merchant-capitalists that they turned to moneylending and banking. From the thirteenth to the fifteenth centuries, Italians monopolized European banking (Florence had 80 banking houses by 1300). It is no wonder that in this prosperous, worldly Italian society, money transformed values and became a new virtue, celebrated in poetry:

> Money makes the man,
> Money makes the stupid pass for bright, . . .
> Money buys the pleasure-giving women,
> Money keeps the soul in bliss, . . .
> The world and fortune being ruled by it,
> Which even opens, if you want, the doors of paradise.
> So wise he seems to me who piles up
> What more than any other virtue
> Conquers gloom and leavens the whole spirit.[2]

These economic and political successes made the Italian upper-class groups strongly assertive, self-confident, and passionately attached to their city-states.

This map illustrates Europe in the time of the Italian and Northern Renaissance, as well as some of the cities which served as centers for artistic and humanist activities during the period.

Literature and art reflected their self-confidence. Poets described them as riding "self-assuredly through the streets"; every major sculptor and painter produced their portraits, sometimes tucked away in corners of religious paintings; and architects affirmed their importance by constructing their imposing palaces—the *palazzi* of the Medici, Rucellai, Pitti, Strozzi, and Pazzi families, for example, still standing in Florence.

Furthermore, the humanists provided them with a justification for their efforts. The humanists' focus on individuals and society, along with their insistent theme of the "dignity of man," was entirely in keeping with the outlook, manners, and accomplishments of the dominant urban groups. These groups embraced new and more secular art and values, both largely alien to the church-dominated culture of the Middle Ages.

Renaissance Patrons

Political leaders and the wealthy merchants, bankers, and manufacturers conspicuously dis-

played their wealth and bolstered their own importance and that of their cities by patronizing artists and humanists. Most of these artists and scholars were provided with governmental, academic, and tutorial posts.

Renaissance artists enjoyed the security and protection offered by their patrons and the advantage of working exclusively on commission. Artists knew where their finished work would be displayed—in cathedral, villa, or city square. This situation contrasts with some later periods, when artists painted as they wished and then attempted to sell the work to anyone who would buy it.

Among the most famous patrons were members of the Medici family, champions of the lower classes, who ruled Florence for 60 years (1434–1494). Under their leadership Florence was in name a republic, but the Medici family completely dominated the state. Lorenzo de' Medici, who was the first citizen of Florence from 1469 until his death in 1492, carried on his family's proud

Discovery Through Maps

The Power and Glory of Renaissance Venice

Maps can be designed to illustrate much more than the physical features of the subject; they can also serve as propaganda—a vehicle to enhance the image of a particular city or state. For example, examine this representation of the Italian Republic of Venice in the mid-sixteenth century, painted by Ignazio Danti (1536–1586), a local member of the Dominican order. Danti depicts a sophisticated and glorious metropolis, proud of its wealth and power. Over the city hovers its symbol, the lion, clutching in its paws a scroll acclaiming the past glory of the city and the perpetual prosperity and honor that is its due.

The purpose of this map was not to render geographical assistance but rather to promote the power and glory of its subject city in the hope of attracting commerce—a beautiful and impressive piece of cartographic propaganda.

The classic example of the Renaissance nobleman, statesman, and patron of the arts was the Florentine Lorenzo de' Medici, known as Lorenzo the Magnificent. Under his patronage and guidance, Florence became the leading city of the Italian Renaissance, renowned for the splendor of its buildings and lavish support for the arts.

traditions and added so much luster to Florence that he became known as Lorenzo the Magnificent. When he added up the principal expenditures made by his family between 1434 and 1471 for commissions to artists and architects, as well as for charities and taxes, and it came to the astounding total of 663,755 gold florins, he remarked: "I think it casts a brilliant light on our estate and it seems to me that the monies were well spent and I am very well pleased with this."[3]

The Renaissance popes—with few exceptions as worldly as their fellow citizens—were lavish patrons who made Rome the foremost center of art and learning by 1500. What Pope Nicholas V (1447–1455) said of himself applies to most of the Renaissance popes through the pontificate of Clement VII (1523–1534), who was a member of the Medici family: "In all things I have been liberal: in building, in the purchase of books [the Vatican Library is still one of the world's greatest], in the constant transcription of Greek and Latin manuscripts, and in the rewarding of learned men."

Humanism and the Classical Revival

During the Middle Ages the writers of antiquity had been interpreted within the framework of Christian religion and often cited as authorities to bolster

The popes' building program was in large measure responsible for Rome's superseding Florence as the center of artistic activity during the High Renaissance. The greatest builder, Julius II (1503–1513), commissioned Bramante to begin the new St. Peter's and had Michelangelo paint the Sistine Chapel while Raphael decorated adjoining rooms in the Vatican.

church dogma. Although many aspects of antiquity were avoided because of their disturbingly pagan quality, the clergy did make use of pagan literature that could be interpreted allegorically and given a Christian meaning. Consequently, the true nature of the classical legacy was generally distorted or obscured. But in Italy in the fourteenth and fifteenth centuries there emerged a new spirit of humanism, a movement that sought to recapture the learning and culture of ancient Greece and Rome.

The Classical Revival

In fourteenth-century Italy a new perspective on life began to evolve and a fresh appreciation of classical literature emerged. As successors to a small group of medieval teachers of grammar and rhetoric, the representatives of this new movement called themselves *humanists,* a name derived from the *studia humanitatis,* or "humanistic studies," as Roman authors termed a liberal or literary education. Writing in praise of the *studia humanitatis,* an early Italian humanist identified them as studies that "perfect and adorn man."

Medieval Scholastic education had emphasized logic, science, and professional training in law, medicine, and theology at the expense of the arts, the literary side of the curriculum. Hence the Scholastics had centered their attention on Aristotle's *Logic, Metaphysics,* and scientific writings and on other an-

cient works on astronomy, medicine, and mathematics. The humanists, however, reflecting urban society's interest in the problems and values of human living, reversed this medieval emphasis and called attention to the importance of an education in the humanities—history, grammar, rhetoric, poetry, and moral philosophy. The humanists avoided the sciences because, as Petrarch—the first of the great Italian humanists—wrote:

> *They help in no way toward a happy life, for what does it advantage us to be familiar with the nature of animals, birds, fishes, and reptiles, while we are ignorant of the nature of the race of man to which we belong, and do not know or care whence we come or whither we go?*[4]

Thus despite the fact that both the humanist and the Scholastic looked to the past and respected its heritage, they differed widely in their choice of the ancient material to be revered.

Humanists and Scholastics also differed in the manner in which they saw themselves in relation to the writers of ancient times. Whereas the Scholastics always felt inferior to the ancients and looked up to them as child to parent or pupil to teacher, humanists saw themselves as equal to the ancients and boldly hailed them as individual to individual and friend to friend. At the beginning of his *Divine Comedy,* Dante describes medieval reliance on the authority of the ancients in allegorical terms: Dante (symbolizing medieval man) is lost in the "dark wood" that is this life until he is rescued by Virgil (a favorite medieval symbol of ancient wisdom), who thereafter guides him along the right path. "Losing me," Virgil is made to say to Dante, "ye would remain astray."

The noticeably different attitude of the humanists was expressed by Niccoló Machiavelli (1469–1527), a Florentine politician, diplomat, and political theorist. In his strictly secular and realistic treatise on politics, *The Prince* (1513), Machiavelli wrote of his regard for classical learning: "I enter the ancient courts of the men of antiquity. Received with affection by them, . . . I do not hesitate to hold conversation with them and to inquire the reason for their actions. They, in their humanity, reply to me."[5] It was in this spirit that Petrarch wrote his *Letters to Ancient Authors,* addressing Homer, Plato, Cicero, and others in familiar terms and sharing with them his own thoughts and experiences. This feeling of equality with ancient authors was also behind the humanists' practice of filling their own writings with apt quotations from the classics. The humanists' purpose, however, differed from that of the Scholastics, who also quoted extensively from the ancients. As the French humanist Montaigne explained in his essays, he quoted the ancients not because he agreed with them but because they agreed with him.

Petrarch and Boccaccio

The "father of humanism" is a title given to Francesco Petrarca, better known as Petrarch (1304–1374), by later Italian humanists because he was the first to play a major role in making people conscious of the attractions of classical literature. Distressed by the condition of society in fourteenth-century Italy—political and social unrest, the decline of the church, the shortcomings of Scholasticism—and resentful of being forced by his father to study law at Bologna, Petrarch found consolation and escape in the literature of ancient Rome. As he explained later in his *Letter to Posterity,* "In order to forget my own time I have constantly striven to place myself in spirit in other ages." And in the same vein, "Nothing that we suffer but has happened to others before us."

In 1327 he met and fell in love with Laura. Little is known of Laura other than that she was married. Inspired by his love for her, Petrarch wrote sonnets that show him to be one of the greatest lyric poets of all time. His portrayal of Laura represents a fresh approach. Earlier poets had woven about their heroines an air of courtly love and religious idealization, which made the characters quite unreal. Petrarch's Laura was a flesh-and-blood creature whom all readers could recognize as human. Petrarch praised her

A miniature portrait of Petrarch from his illuminated manuscript of Remedies Against Fortune. *In keeping with a classical tradition, Petrarch composed many letters—which he edited for publication—that were in effect literary essays expressing his own attitudes and humanistic concerns.*

chastity, which had withstood his advances. And even though he wrote that she had "mocked, despised, scorned" him "with an air of haughty disdain," he forever viewed her as an ennobling influence on his life.

The ancient writers' attitude toward life struck a sympathetic chord in Petrarch. In *On the Secret Conflict of My Cares,* Petrarch has an imaginary conversation with St. Augustine that forcibly brings out the conflict between his new worldly interests and those of traditional Christianity. St. Augustine accuses Petrarch of pursuing false goals: "What are you doing, poor little man? What are you dreaming?" Petrarch concludes that although St. Augustine's arguments cannot be refuted, he will not renounce his chosen path: "The care of mortal things must come first in mortal minds."

This inner conflict between Petrarch's concern for "mortal things" and his loyalty to the traditional Christian ideal of self-denial and otherworldliness exemplifies the transitional position Petrarch, and humanism, occupied in Western culture. He could not accept a lessening of an individual's importance or a reduction of one's mental horizons. Thus he condemned the rigidity and empty logic of Scholasticism and the narrow limits of medieval education. He took as his motto a line from the Roman dramatist Terence: "I am a man, and nothing human do I consider alien to myself." Petrarch was not a careful scholar and never learned Greek, yet he gave humanism its first great impetus.

Another celebrated early humanist was the Florentine Giovanni Boccaccio (1313–1375), who began his career as a writer of poetry and romances. In 1348 the horrible Black Death struck—it wiped out nearly two-thirds of Florence's population. Boccaccio used this event to establish the setting of his masterpiece, the *Decameron.* To escape the pestilence, his characters—three young men and seven young women—seek seclusion in a country villa, where they while away the time telling stories. Boccaccio injected the hundred tales of the *Decameron,* based on medieval *fabliaux* and chivalric romances, with a new and different spirit. Recounted by sophisticated city-dwellers, the tales satirize the follies of knights and other medieval types and clearly express the contempt that had developed for the old and by then dying ideals of feudalism. Many tales are bawdy and even scandalous—a charge Boccaccio sought to refute:

> *Some of you may say that in writing these tales I have taken too much license, by making ladies sometimes say and often listen to matters which are not proper to be said or heard by virtuous ladies. This I deny, for there is nothing so unchaste but may be said chastely if modest words are used; and this I think I have done.*[6]

The *Decameron* offers a wealth of anecdotes, portraits of flesh-and-blood characters, and vivid (although one-sided) glimpses of Renaissance life.

Zeal for the Study of Greek Literature

Petrarch had tried without success to learn Greek. Not until Greek scholars arrived in Italy from Constantinople were competent instructors available. Manuel Chrysoloras, the first of these scholars, came to Venice in 1393, sent by the Byzantine emperor to secure help against the Turks. Three years later he was invited to Florence, where he remained for three years as a teacher of Greek language and literature. Leonardo Bruni (1370–1444) tells how he took this opportunity to throw himself enthusiastically into the study of Greek.

Chrysoloras the Byzantine, a man of noble birth and well versed in Greek letters, brought Greek learning to us. When his country was invaded by the Turks, he came by sea, first to Venice. The report of him soon spread, and he was cordially invited and besought and promised a public stipend, to come to Florence and open his store of riches to the youth. I was then studying Civil Law, but . . . I burned with love of academic studies, and had spent no little pains on dialectic and rhetoric. At the coming of Chrysoloras I was torn in mind, deeming it shameful to desert the law, and yet a crime to lose such a chance of studying Greek literature; and often with youthful impulse I would say to myself: "Thou, when it is permitted thee to gaze on Homer, Plato and Demosthenes, and the other poets, philosophers, orators, of whom such glorious things are spread abroad, and speak with them and be instructed in their admirable teaching, wilt thou desert and rob thyself? Wilt thou neglect this opportunity so divinely offered? For seven hundred years, no one in Italy has possessed Greek letters; and yet we confess that all knowledge is derived from them. How great advantage to your knowledge, enhancement of your fame, increase of your pleasure, will come from an understanding of this tongue? There are doctors of civil law everywhere; and the chance of learning will not fail thee. But if this one and only doctor of Greek letters disappears, no one can be found to teach thee." Overcome at length by these reasons, I gave myself to Chrysoloras, with such zeal to learn, that what through the wakeful day I gathered, I followed after in the night, even when asleep.

From Henry Osborn Taylor, ed., *Thought and Expression in the Sixteenth Century*, Vol. 1 (New York: Macmillan, 1920), pp. 36–37.

The *Decameron* closed Boccaccio's career as a creative artist. Largely through the influence of Petrarch, whom he met in 1350, Boccaccio gave up writing in Italian and turned to the study of antiquity. He began to learn Greek, composed an encyclopedia of classical mythology, and went off to monasteries in search of manuscripts. By the time Petrarch and Boccaccio died, the study of the literature and learning of antiquity was growing throughout Italy.

The search for manuscripts became a mania, and before the middle of the fifteenth century, works by most of the important Latin authors had been found. The degree of difference between humanist and Scholastic is indicated by the ease with which the early humanists recovered the "lost" Latin literary masterpieces: they were found close at hand in monastic libraries, covered by the undisturbed dust of many centuries. The books had always been there; what had been largely lacking was an appreciative audience of readers. In addition to these Latin works, precious Greek manuscripts were brought to Italy from Constantinople after it fell to the Turks in 1453.

Civic Humanism

For the humanists of the fifteenth century—the "civic humanists," as they are called—humanism became the foundation of a course of study designed not for pure contemplation, as it was for Petrarch, but as an educational program outlining what was relevant and useful in the classics for the leaders of the Italian city-states. One of them warned against letting literature "absorb all the interests of life. . . . For the man who surrenders himself entirely to the attractions of letters or speculative thought perhaps follows a self-regarding end and is useless as a citizen or prince." Whereas Petrarch wrote of the "much sweetness and charm" he found in the writings of his "dear friend" Cicero "when the difficulties of life are pressing on me so sharply and inexorably," the civic humanists honored Cicero more for his emphasis on moral philosophy and rhetoric (the art of persuasion) and his commitment to public affairs. They found the ancient historians, notably Livy and Plutarch, especially valuable. "The careful study of the past," wrote one of the humanists, "enlarges our foresight in contemporary affairs."

Revival of Platonism

During the late fifteenth century many humanists gravitated to Platonic and Neo-Platonic philosophy as a result of both their lack of interest in the Aristotelian emphasis on natural science and their search for a classical philosophy that stressed moral purpose and religious and even mystical values. A factor in this revival was the study of Plato in the original Greek, particularly at Florence where Cosimo de' Medici, one of the great patrons of the Renaissance, founded the informal club that came to be known as the Platonic Academy. Its leader, Marsilio Ficino (1433–1499), who always kept a candle burning before a bust of Plato, made the first complete Latin translation of Plato's works.

Ficino sought to synthesize Christianity and Plato, much as St. Thomas Aquinas had done with Aristotle. In his principal work, appropriately titled *The Platonic Theology*, Ficino viewed Plato as essentially Christian and Plato's "religious philosophy" as a God-sent means of converting intellectuals. He coined the expression "Platonic love" to describe an ideal, pure love, and this concept found its way into Renaissance literature and art.

Ficino's disciple, Pico della Mirandola (1463–1494), was driven by an insatiable appetite for knowledge. In addition to Latin and Greek, he learned Hebrew and Arabic in order to read everything he possibly could. At age 23 he announced to the world that he knew everything and invited all interested scholars to join him in Rome (expenses paid) for a public debate on 900 theological and philosophical propositions. (The pope considered some propositions heretical and forbade the debate.) As an introduction to his list of propositions, Pico composed "Oration on the Dignity of Man," an essay that remains one of the most glowing tributes to the human race in all Renaissance writing. With youthful exuberance he wrote, "There is nothing to be seen more wonderful than man. . . . To him it is granted to have whatever he chooses, to be whatever he wills."

Aristotelianism

Despite its great attraction for many humanists, Platonism still had a powerful rival in Aristotelianism. Concerned chiefly with natural science, logic, and metaphysics, Aristotelian commentators continued to dominate teaching in the Italian universities.

The most influential Aristotelians were the Latin Averroists, followers of the Muslim philosopher Averroës (see Chapter 10). The Averroists followed Aristotle in teaching that matter is eternal and in denying the immortality of the soul. Since such views were contrary to the biblical story of creation and the belief in personal immortality, the Averroists advocated the doctrine of "double truth"—a truth in philosophy need not be valid in religion.

By the fifteenth century the University of Padua had become the center of Aristotelianism, which reached its peak in the next century. By championing a secular rationalism that kept philosophy separate from theology, its followers maintained an environ-

Pico della Mirandola, the brilliant humanist who was recognized as a genius. (This medal was produced in the year following his death.) Before he died at age 31, he had been influenced by the fiery sermons of Savonarola, the puritanical reformer of society and the church. In 1494, the year Pico died, Savonarola gained control of Florence and ruled it for four years as the Kingdom of God.

ment necessary for the triumph of scientific thought in the seventeenth century. Some of the pioneers of that "scientific revolution" (see Chapter 21) were connected with Padua. Copernicus studied there before publishing his *Revolutions of the Heavenly Spheres* in 1543; the anatomist Vesalius, whose revolutionary *Fabric of the Human Body* appeared in the same year, was a professor there; and the astronomer and physicist Galileo lectured there early in the next century. Ironically, the experimentalism that Aristotelianism encouraged was destined to overthrow Aristotle's own theories in physics and other fields of science.

Evaluation of Humanism

In the meantime, the humanists continued to downgrade science as sterile, and they did not teach it in the schools they established. Their educational goal, which is still the goal of a liberal education, was the cultivation of the mind both for individual happiness and for equipping a person to play a worthy role in society.

To the humanists we owe the modern ideal of the well-rounded person, the versatile, accomplished, socially assured citizen of the world. Called by the humanists the *uomo universale* ("complete man"), such a person was the subject of eagerly read books on correct social behavior that were produced during the Renaissance.

The most famous book on Renaissance manners, published in 1528, was *The Courtier* by Baldassare

Castiglione (1478–1529), which was soon translated into French, German, English, and Spanish and which established a model for the Renaissance gentleman. To Castiglione good manners and social skills were essential to the ideal courtier because women now played a freer and more active role in polite society, to which they added such feminine refinements as music and dancing.

In the judgment of a modern feminist historian "There was no renaissance for women . . . during the Renaissance."[7] In truth, there were a good number of Renaissance women who were highly educated, read the classics in Greek and Latin, painted with great skill, and produced literature of merit. Most of these women were the daughters and wives of privileged aristocrats, and educational opportunities were provided them so that they would make better companions and conversationalists for their husbands. Many talented women lacked access to further training or patronage necessary to pursue a professional career—a path in life that was not yet considered proper for a woman of high status, whether she possessed extraordinary talent or not.

The courtier must please the ladies as well as the prince; he must master the social graces. But Castiglione's central idea was that a courtier's true worth was more in keeping with his strength of character and excellence of intellect than with his hereditary social position. Well read in the classics but no isolated scholar, the courtier should be a well-rounded individual, capable in the arts of both war and peace.

Reviving the ancient ideal of a healthy mind in a sound body, Renaissance educators and writers stressed the importance of exercise and sports and took their inspiration from ancient Greek examples of leisure—running, track and field events, and wrestling. But not every sport was thought acceptable: in 1531 an English author of a book on manners wrote that football (in reference to a game much like the modern sport of rugby) ought to be avoided by all gentlemen because there is in it "nothing but beastly furie and exstreme violence; whereof precedeth hurte, and consequently rancour and malice do remaine."[8]

Although we owe the humanists a debt of gratitude for reintroducing Latin and Greek literature into the mainstream of Western thought, theirs was otherwise a closed culture whose boundaries had been set by ancient Greece and Rome. Their course was to re-travel old ground, not to explore uncharted territory. The humanists resented the centuries separating them from the golden days of antiquity. Unfortunately, this viewpoint resulted in their dislike of the best works (Dante excepted) produced in the Middle Ages.

The cult of classical letters gave rise to another defect. By the late fifteenth century the humanists' passion for writing Latin prose in imitation of Cicero's graceful, eloquent, and polished style had become a dangerous obsession. One famous humanist,

who was also a cardinal of the church, even hesitated to read St. Paul's epistles for fear they might corrupt his Latin style. A reaction in favor of the native language resulted; Castiglione and Machiavelli, for example, chose to write in the vernacular, Italian.

The humanist men of letters contributed nothing new to philosophy or to science and did little or no original thinking. Nevertheless, they did contribute indirectly to the coming scientific revolution. Their search for Roman and Greek manuscripts resulted in the recovery of more ancient scientific writings than were available to medieval scholars. These were at hand later when the interests of scholars turned decisively toward science. (Copernicus's heliocentric theory of planetary motion, for example, came from his reading of ancient authors.) Furthermore, modern critical scholarship began with the humanists' emphasis on verified facts. They compared manuscripts in order to eliminate errors and establish authentic texts. In their writings they exposed historical myths and eliminated supernatural causes. This critical and objective outlook would be of great value in later scientific research.

Italian Renaissance Art

Outside Italy during the fourteenth and fifteenth centuries, there was a continuation of "Gothic" art—in painting and sculpture, the same emphasis on realistic detail; in architecture, an elaboration of the Gothic style.

Fourteenth- and fifteenth-century Italy, however, saw innovations that culminated in the classic High Renaissance art of the early sixteenth century. All

Major Artists of the Italian Renaissance

c. 1266–1337	Giotto: *Life of the Virgin, Life of St. Francis, Life of St. John the Baptist*
1401–1428	Masaccio: *Tribute Money, Trinity, St. Peter*
1447–1510	Botticelli: *Judith and Holofernes, St. Sebastian, Birth of Venus*
1452–1519	Leonardo da Vinci: *Adoration of the Magi, The Last Supper, La Gioconda* (Mona Lisa)
1475–1564	Michelangelo: Ceiling of the Sistine Chapel, *Moses, Pietà, David*
c. 1477–1576	Titian: *The Venus of Zerbine, The Allegory of Marriage, Venus and Adonis*

these were the products of a new society centered in rich cities, the humanist spirit in thought and religion, and a revived interest in the classical art of Greece and Rome.

Transitional Period in Painting

The greatest figure in the transitional painting of the fourteenth century was the Florentine painter Giotto (c. 1266–1337), who it was said "achieved little less than the resurrection of painting from the dead." While earlier Italian painters had copied the unreal, flat, and rigidly formalized images of Byzantine paintings and mosaics, Giotto observed from life and painted a three-dimensional world peopled with believable human beings dramatically moved by deep emotion. He humanized painting much as Petrarch humanized thought and St. Francis, whose life was one of his favorite subjects, humanized religion. Giotto initiated a new epoch in the history of painting, one that expressed the religious piety of his lay patrons and their delight in images of everyday life.

Quattrocento Painting, Sculpture, and Architecture

The lull in painting that followed Giotto's death in 1337, during which his technical innovations were retained but the spirit and compassion that make him one of the world's great painters were lost, lasted until the beginning of the *quattrocento* (Italian for "four hundred," an abbreviation for the 1400s). In his brief lifetime the Florentine Masaccio (1401–1428) completed the revolution in technique begun by Giotto. As can be seen in his few surviving paintings, Masaccio largely mastered the problems of perspective, the anatomical naturalism of flesh and bone, and the modeling of figures in light and shade *(chiaroscuro)* rather than by Giotto's sharp line. Masaccio was also the first to paint nude figures (Adam and Eve, in his *Expulsion from Eden*), thus reversing the trend of Christian art, which since its beginnings in late Roman times had turned its back on the beauty of the human form. Masaccio died in debt in Rome, having received few commissions in Florence. Apparently, his work was too austere and short on elegance to attract many patrons.

Inspired by Masaccio's achievement, most quattrocento painters constantly sought to improve technique. This search for greater realism culminated in such painters as Andrea Mantegna (1431–1506) and Piero della Francesca (c. 1420–1492). Mantegna's painting of the dead body of Christ lying on a marble slab clearly shows the results of his lifelong study of perspective. His group portrait of the family of his chief patron, the Gonzaga duke of Mantua, is done "in the grand manner" and reflects the self-assurance of the Renaissance elite.

Masaccio, Expulsion from Eden. *Masaccio's mastery of perspective creates the illusion of movement as the angel drives Adam and Eve from Paradise.*

Piero della Francesca's approach to painting was scientific and intellectual. His zeal to reduce perspective to a mathematical science—he wrote a book on the subject—led him to neglect motion. The figures in his *Discovery and Proving of the True Cross*, showing Constantine's mother, Helena, discovering the cross used for Christ's crucifixion, are as still as if hewn out of marble. Piero's restrained, undramatic, unemotional, and mathematically precise paintings bring to mind the abstract painting of our own time.

Whereas Masaccio's successors in the second half of the fifteenth century were intent on giving their figures solidity and resolving the problem of three-dimensional presentation, the Florentine Sandro Botticelli (1447–1510) proceeded in a different direction, abandoning the techniques of straightforward representation of people and objects. Botticelli used a sensitive, even quivering line to stir the viewer's imagination and emotion and to create a mood in keeping with his more subtle and sophisticated poetic vision. This unconventional artist was associated with the Platonic Academy at Florence, where the Christian faith was fused with pagan mythology. Thus although his *Birth of Venus* depicts the goddess of love rising from the sea, there is little that is human or material about her ethereal figure. Like the Virgin Mary, she has become the symbol of a higher kind of love—divine love. The allegory is reinforced by making the winds that blow Venus onto the shore look like Christian angels.

Progress was also being made in sculpture, and it, like painting, reached stylistic maturity at the beginning of the quattrocento. Like the humanists, the sculptors found in ancient Rome the models they were eager to imitate; they too saw what seemed related to their own experience and aspirations.

In his second pair of bronze doors for the baptistery in Florence, Lorenzo Ghiberti (1378–1455) achieved the goal he had set for himself: "I strove to imitate nature as closely as I could, and with all the perspective I could produce." These marvels of relief sculpture, which resurrected the form and spirit of Roman sculpture and architecture and drew from Michelangelo the declaration that they were worthy to be the gates of paradise, depict skillfully modeled human figures—including some classically inspired nudes—which stand out spatially against architectural and landscape backgrounds.

Although Ghiberti was a superb craftsman, he was less of an innovator than his younger contemporary in Florence, Donatello (1386–1466), who visited Rome to study the remains of antique sculpture. Divorcing sculpture from the architectural background it had in the Middle Ages, Donatello produced truly freestanding statues based on the realization of the human body as a functional, coordinated mechanism of bones, muscles, and sinews, maintaining itself against the pull of gravity. His *David* was the first bronze nude made since antiquity, and his equestrian statue of the army commander Gattamelata, clad in Roman armor, was the first of its type done in the Renaissance. The latter clearly reveals the

Botticelli, The Birth of Venus. *The last great Florentine painter of the early Renaissance, Botticelli did most of his best work for Lorenzo de' Medici and his court. In* The Birth of Venus, *Botticelli blends ancient mythology, Christian faith, and voluptuous representation.*

After winning the commission to design the bronze doors for the baptistery in Florence, Ghiberti spent most of his life making the 28 panels for the doors. This panel illustrates the biblical story of Joseph.

influence of classical models and was probably inspired by the equestrian statue of the emperor Marcus Aurelius in Rome.

More dramatic than either of these equestrian statues is that of the Venetian general Bartolomeo Colleoni, the creation of Andrea del Verrocchio (1435–1488). A versatile Florentine artist noteworthy as a sculptor, a painter, and the teacher of Leonardo da Vinci, Verrocchio designed the statue of Colleoni to permit one of the horse's forelegs to be unsupported—a considerable achievement. The posture and features of the famous general dramatically convey the supreme self-confidence and even arrogance of Renaissance public figures.

Renaissance architecture, which even more than sculpture reflects the influence of ancient Roman models, glorifies the worldly success of its patrons. It began with the work of Filippo Brunelleschi (1377–1446). As a youth Brunelleschi accompanied Donatello to Rome, where he employed measuring stick and sketchbook to master the principles of classical architecture. Returning to Florence, Brunelleschi constructed there the uncompleted dome of the cathedral, the first dome to be built since Roman times. Although strongly influenced by classical architecture, Brunelleschi's buildings in Florence,

which include churches and palaces, were not just copies of Roman models. Employing arcades of Roman arches, Roman pediments above the windows, and Roman columns and other decorative motifs, Brunelleschi re-created the Roman style in a fresh and original manner. So began the Renaissance style of architecture that, with many modifications, has lasted to the present time.

The High Renaissance, 1500–1530

By the time of the High Renaissance in Italy, when painting, sculpture, and architecture all reached a peak of perfection, the center of artistic activity had shifted from Florence to Rome. The popes were lavish patrons, and the greatest artists of the period worked in the Vatican at one time or another. It did not seem inconsistent to popes and artists to include representations of pagan mythological figures in the decorations of the papal palace, and so the Vatican became filled with secular as well as religious art.

The great architect of the High Renaissance was Donato Bramante (1444–1514) from Milan. Bramante's most important commission came in 1506 when Pope Julius II asked him to replace the old basilica of St. Peter, built by the emperor Constan-

In Verrocchio's equestrian statue of the condottiere *(professional soldier) Bartolomeo Colleoni, the spirit of the military leader is captured in the face, which is individual and very human, rather than classical.*

Donatello, David. *"The questing genius of Donatello led him in many directions and established him, both for his contemporaries and for all time, as the dominant sculptor of his century."*[9]

tine, with a monumental Renaissance structure. Bramante's plan called for a centralized church in the form of a Greek cross surmounted by an immense dome. His design for St. Peter's exemplifies the spirit of High Renaissance architecture—to approach the monumentality and grandeur of Roman architecture. In Bramante's own words, he would place "the Pantheon on top of the Basilica of Maxentius." Bramante died when the cathedral was barely begun, and it was left to Michelangelo and others to complete the work. Michelangelo's dome influenced the design of most major domes until the beginning of the twentieth century.

The painters of the High Renaissance inherited the solutions to such technical problems as perspective space from the quattrocento artists. But whereas the artists of the earlier period had been concerned with movement, color, and narrative detail, painters in the High Renaissance attempted to eliminate nonessentials and concentrated on the central theme of a picture and its basic human implications. By this process of elimination, many High Renaissance painters achieved a "classic" effect of seriousness and serenity and endowed their work with idealistic values.

Leonardo da Vinci, Raphael, and Michelangelo

The great triad of High Renaissance painters consists of Leonardo da Vinci, Raphael, and Michelangelo. An extraordinary man, Leonardo da Vinci (1452–1519) was brilliant in a variety of fields: engineering, mathematics, architecture, geology, botany, physiology, anatomy, sculpture, painting, music, and poetry. Unfortunately, because he loved the process of experimentation more than seeing all his projects through to completion, few of the projects Leonardo started were ever finished.

A superb draftsman, Leonardo was a master of soft modeling in light and shade and of creating groups of figures perfectly balanced in a given space. But in addition to an advanced knowledge of technique, what makes Leonardo one of the great masters is his deep psychological insight into human nature. As he himself expressed it, "A good painter has two chief objects to paint, man and the intention of his soul."

One of Leonardo's most famous paintings is *La Gioconda*, known as the Mona Lisa, a portrait of a woman whose enigmatic smile captures an air of tenderness and humility. Another is *The Last Supper*, a study of the dramatic impact of Christ's announcement to his disciples, "One of you will betray me." When he painted this picture on the walls of the refectory of Santa Maria delle Grazie in Milan, Leonardo was experimenting with the use of an oil medium combined with plaster, which unfortunately was unsuccessful. The painting quickly began to disintegrate and has had to be repainted several times.

The second of the great triad of High Renaissance painters was Raphael (1483–1520). By the time he was summoned to Rome in 1508 by Pope Julius II to aid in the decoration of the Vatican, Raphael had

St. Peter's Basilica, Rome. After Michelangelo took charge of the construction of the basilica, he modified Bramante's original plan. For the dome Bramante had planned a stepped hemisphere similar to the dome of the Pantheon. Michelangelo redesigned the dome to add a high drum and strongly projecting buttresses accented by double columns. Later a long nave was added to the front of the church, giving it the form of a Latin, rather than a Greek, cross.

Da Vinci, La Gioconda. *Leonardo da Vinci was a painter, sculptor, architect, inventor, scientist, writer, and musician. His portrait of Mona Lisa, perhaps the most famous portrait ever painted, seems to express the artist's feelings about the mystery of human existence.*

absorbed the styles of Leonardo and Michelangelo. His Stanze frescoes in the Vatican display a magnificent blending of classical and Christian subject matter and are the fruit of careful planning and immense artistic knowledge. Raphael possessed neither Leonardo's intellectuality nor Michelangelo's power, but his work has an appealing serenity, particularly evident in his lovely portraits of the Madonna (Mary, the mother of Jesus). Most critics consider him the master of perfect design and balanced composition.

The individualism and idealism of the High Renaissance have no greater representative than Michelangelo Buonarroti (1475–1564). Stories of this stormy and temperamental personality have helped shape our definition of a genius. Indeed, there is something almost superhuman about both Michelangelo and his art. His great energy enabled him to paint for Julius II in four years the entire ceiling of the Vatican's Sistine Chapel, an area of several thousand square yards, and his art embodies a superhuman ideal. With his unrivaled genius for rendering

Leonardo da Vinci, The Last Supper. *In early Renaissance art, architecture sometimes overpowered the figures, but here the architectural details are subordinate to the figures. The main opening in the rear wall, for example, acts as a halo for Christ's head.*

Raphael, Madonna of the Chair. *Along with Michelangelo and da Vinci, Raphael is recognized as one of the three masters of the High Renaissance. Raphael combined the qualities of the other two artists to create a style that is lyrical and dramatic.*

the human form, he devised a wealth of expressive positions and attitudes for his figures in scenes from Genesis. Their physical splendor is pagan, but their spirit is Christian. The *Creation of Adam* depicts God, with the unborn Eve under his left arm, instilling the divine spark of the soul into the body of Adam.

Michelangelo considered himself first and foremost a sculptor, and this *uomo universale*, who also excelled as poet, engineer, and architect, was undoubtedly the greatest sculptor of the Renaissance. The glorification of the human body, particularly the male nude, was Michelangelo's great achievement. Fired by the grandeur of such newly discovered pieces of Hellenistic sculpture as the Laocoön group and strongly influenced by Platonism with its dualism of body and soul, he displayed the classical influence in such works as his *David*. This masterpiece, commissioned in 1501 when he was 26, expressed his idealized view of human dignity and majesty. Succeeding Bramante as chief architect of St. Peter's in 1546, Michelangelo designed the great dome and was still actively creative as a sculptor when he died, almost in his ninetieth year, in 1564. He had long outlived the High Renaissance.

The Venetian School

Following the sack of Rome in 1527 during the Italian Wars, the rich trading city of Venice became the center of art. This wealthy, sophisticated urban center produced a secular rather than a devotional

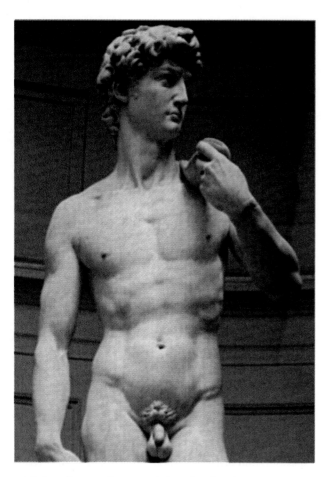

Michelangelo, David. *To Michelangelo, the Florentine painter, sculptor, poet, and architect, sculpture was the noblest of the arts. The large marble statue of the biblical David was commissioned in 1501 to stand in Florence as a symbol of the city, its government, and its culture.*

they tell no story. Viewers are left free to extract their own meaning from them.

The paintings of Titian (c. 1477–1576), who was probably born in the same year as his friend Giorgione but outlived him by 65 years, are less subtle and poetic. His Venuses, for example, are buxom Venetian models—mature, opulent, and sex-conscious. During his long working life he proved himself the master of every kind of subject ranging from religion to pagan mythology and including portraits of royalty and the self-satisfied upper class, for which he was most famed among his contemporaries. With his robust sensuousness and view of all things in terms of light and color, Titian is the type-figure of the Venetian painter, and his work has influenced many generations of modern painters.

Mannerism: The "Anti-Renaissance" Style

In 1494 the French king Charles VIII crossed into Italy with an army of 40,000 men and inaugurated the Italian Wars that lasted until 1559 and turned Italy into a battleground for the powerful new monarchies of France and Spain. While Italians were losing control of their destiny, Machiavelli in *The Prince* lamented his native land as being "more a slave than the Hebrews, more a servant than the Persians, more scattered than the Athenians; without head, without government; defeated, plundered, torn asunder, overrun; subject to every sort of disaster."[10]

In 1527 the unruly army of Charles V, Spanish king and German emperor, sacked Rome, the major center of High Renaissance patronage and culture, and its many artists, writers, and scholars fled the city.

Such unsettling developments, added to the Protestant and Catholic Reformations (see Chapter 15), produced a radical change of outlook on life. The earlier optimistic emphasis on the dignity of man was replaced by a pessimistic belief in man's evil nature—one of the basic assumptions in Machiavelli's *Prince*. Michelangelo, who as we noted had outlived the High Renaissance, expressed a similar pessimism in the tortured figures of his late sculptures and his painting *The Last Judgment* which was painted on a wall of the Sistine Chapel in the 1530s after the sack of Rome and more than 40 years after his glorious *Creation of Adam* on the ceiling. "Led by long years to my last hours," Michelangelo wrote, "too late, O world, I know your joys for what they are. You promise a peace which is not yours to give."

From about 1530 to the end of the sixteenth century, Italian artists responded to the stresses of

school of painting. Most Venetian artists were satisfied with the here and now; though they sometimes painted Madonnas, they more often painted wealthy merchants and proud doges (magistrates), attired in rich brocades, jewels, and precious metals. The sensuousness of the Venetian painting of this period is evident in the artists' love of decoration, rich costumes, striking nude figures, and radiant light and color. It has been said that whereas earlier painting consisted of drawing and coloring, at Venice color and light became paramount ingredients of painting.

The first master of the Venetian High Renaissance was Giorgione (1477–1510), who like Botticelli rejected the quattrocento concern to be scientific and realistic and substituted a delicate and dreamily poetic lyricism. Common to all of his paintings is a mood of languor and relaxation that is called *Giorgionesque*. The lyrical grace of his *Sleeping Venus*, for example, is devoid of erotic overtones. His paintings are fanciful idylls that have no narrative content—

background, standing beside a gigantic and purpose-less column, is absurdly tiny.

Contemporaries of Tintoretto (1518–1594) had good reason to call him "the thunderbolt of painting." His *Abduction of the Body of St. Mark*, depicting the legend that three Venetians stole the body of their patron saint from Alexandria during a storm, replaces the harmony, proportion, balance, and idealized reality of the High Renaissance with dramatic force and movement, violent contrast in light and color, imbalanced composition, and crowded figures in uneasy and agitated poses. The upholders of the pure classical tradition who opposed the innovations of the Mannerists considered Tintoretto's work to be marred by careless execution and eccentric taste. One of them wrote that "had he not abandoned the beaten track but rather followed the beautiful style of his predecessors, he would have become one of the greatest painters seen in Venice."

The outstanding Mannerist sculptor was the braggart Benvenuto Cellini (1500–1571). Both his sculpture and his famous *Autobiography* reflect his violent and corrupt age's rejection of artistic and moral standards. (He boasts of the number of

Tintoretto, Abduction of the Body of St. Mark. *The leading proponent of the Mannerist style in Venice, Tintoretto combined strong use of light and shade with a gift for dramatic storytelling.*

Parmigianino, Madonna with the Long Neck. *Parmigianino's smooth, elongated, languid figures embody an ideal of unearthly beauty and perfection that bears little resemblance to real human beings. Characteristic of Mannerist painting are huge discrepancies in scale, here shown by the tiny figure of the prophet beside the gigantic column.*

the age in a new style called Mannerism. Consciously revolting against the classical serenity and poise of High Renaissance art, Mannerist artists sought to express their own inner vision—often, like Michelangelo in his later years, their doubts and indecisions—in a manner that evoked shock in the viewer.

Typical are the paintings of Parmigianino, who returned to his native Parma from Rome after it was sacked, and the Venetian Tintoretto. Parmigianino's *Madonna with the Long Neck* (1535) shows no logic of structure. One cannot tell whether the distorted figure of the Madonna is seated or standing. Her cloak billows out in defiance of gravity, and her child seems to be slipping off her lap. The prophet in the

Cellini, Saltcellar of Francis I. *The utilitarian purpose of the condiment dish is subordinate to its lavish decoration. Neptune, god of the sea, guards the boat-shaped salt container while a personification of Earth watches over the pepper. Figures around the base represent the four seasons and the four parts of the day. The intricacy of the design is a showcase of the sculptor's virtuosity.*

personal enemies he has killed and quotes a pope as excusing him on the ground that "men like Benvenuto, unique in their profession, stand above the law.") His work, like the gold cup decorated with enamel and precious stones now in the Metropolitan Museum of Art in New York, consists largely of similar elegant, showy trifles, which Michelangelo described as "snuff-box ornaments."

Mannerist architects developed the Jesuit style, named for the new Jesuit Order that first sponsored it in its Gesù (Jesus) Church in Rome (c. 1575). The classical components of Renaissance architecture were manipulated to achieve anticlassical effects. Columns and pilasters were paired for greater richness, curved lines ending in volutes replaced straight lines, and statues were often fixed to upper stories and roofs. The parts were arranged to form a climax in the center and fused into one complex pattern.

Tintoretto's *Abduction of the Body of St. Mark* pictures both the old architecture and the new. In the left background is a typical Renaissance building with its repetition of the same pattern; the whole is no greater than the sum of its parts. To the rear is a Jesuit-style structure whose effect is much more than the sum of its parts—to leave out any part would destroy its essential unity.

The Mannerist Jesuit style prefigures the fully developed baroque architecture of the seventeenth cen-

tury, just as the Mannerist style of Tintoretto—and El Greco (d. 1614) in Spain a generation later—prefigures baroque painting (see Chapter 15). There is no clear dividing line between the Mannerism of the sixteenth century and the baroque of the seventeenth.

Renaissance Music

In contrast to the simple single-voiced, or monophonic, music—called plainsong or Gregorian chant—of the early Middle Ages, the later medieval composers of church music wrote many-voiced, or polyphonic, music. Polyphony often involved a shuttling back and forth from one melody to another—musical counterpoint. By the fifteenth century as many as 24 voice parts were combined into one intricately woven musical pattern. The composers of the High Renaissance continued to produce complicated polyphonic music but in a calmer and grander manner. Compared with the style of his predecessors, that of the Flemish composer Josquin des Prés (c. 1440–1521), the founder of High Renaissance music, "is both grander and more simple . . . and the rhythms and forms used are based on strict symmetry and mathematically regular proportions. Josquin handled all technical problems of complicated constructions with the same ease and sureness one finds in the drawings of Leonardo and Raphael."[11] Also

Gesù Church, Rome. The Mannerist Jesuit style in architecture is characterized by a deliberate contradiction of classical rules and a conscious effort to produce an effect of discord and strain rather than harmony and repose, the ideals of Renaissance style.

during the sixteenth century, instruments such as the violin, spinet, and harpsichord developed from more rudimentary types.

The Renaissance in Italy stimulated various new forms of secular music, especially the madrigal, a love lyric set to music. Castiglione in *The Courtier* insists that the ability to sing, read music, and play an instrument was essential for gentlemen and ladies. In addition to the Italian madrigal, French *chansons* and German *Lieder* added to the growing volume of secular music.

The Northern Renaissance

The Italian Renaissance had placed human beings once more in the center of life's stage and infused thought and art with humanistic values. In time these stimulating ideas current in Italy spread to other areas and combined with developments par-

ticular to the other countries of Europe to produce a French Renaissance, an English Renaissance, and so on.

Throughout the fifteenth century the enrollment records of Italian universities listed hundreds of northern European students. Though their chief interest was the study of law and medicine, many were influenced by the intellectual climate of Italy with its new enthusiasm for the classics. When these students returned home, they often carried manuscripts—and later printed editions—produced by classical and humanist writers. By this time Scholasticism had declined into uncreative repetition and logical subtleties, and both literate laymen and devout clergy in the north were ready to welcome the new outlook of humanism.

The Influence of Printing

Very important in the diffusion of the Renaissance and later in the success of the Reformation was the

Major Figures in the Northern Renaissance

c. 1395–1441   Jan van Eyck (painter): *Man with the Red Turban, Wedding Portrait*

c. 1466–1536   Desiderius Erasmus (humanist and scholar): *The Praise of Folly, Handbook of the Christian Knight*

1471–1528   Albrecht Dürer (painter): *Adam and Eve, The Four Apostles, Self-Portrait*

1478–1535   Sir Thomas More (humanist and diplomat): *Utopia*

c. 1483–1553   François Rabelais (writer): *Gargantua* and *Pantagruel*

1488–1523   Ulrich von Hutten (humanist and poet)

1547–1616   Miguel de Cervantes (writer): *Don Quixote*

1564–1616   William Shakespeare (playwright and poet): *Julius Caesar, Romeo and Juliet, King Lear*

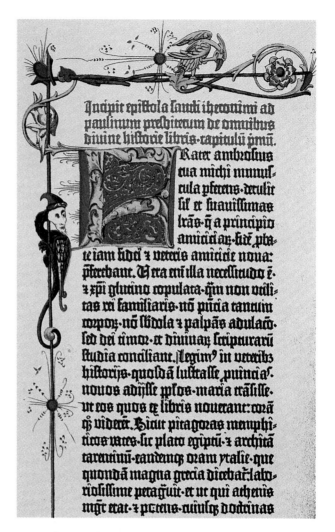

Facsimile copy of a page from the Gutenberg Bible, the Book of Genesis. With the development of printing, learning was no longer the private domain of the church and those few persons wealthy enough to own hand-copied volumes.

invention of printing in Europe. The essential elements—paper and block printing—had been known in China since the eighth century. During the twelfth century the Spanish Muslims introduced papermaking to Europe; in the thirteenth Europeans, in close contact with China (see Chapter 12), brought knowledge of block printing to the West. The crucial step was taken in the 1440s at Mainz, Germany, where Johann Gutenberg and other printers invented movable type by cutting up old printing blocks to form individual letters. Gutenberg used movable type to print papal documents and the first printed version of the Bible (1454).

Soon all the major countries of Europe possessed the means for printing books. In 1465 two Germans brought printing to Italy, and within four years the works of eight classical authors (including Cicero, Livy, Virgil, Pliny, and Caesar) had been printed there. In all of Europe during the remainder of the century an estimated 40,000 titles were published. It is said that the prices of books sank to one-eighth of their former cost, thus placing books within the reach of many people who formerly had been unable to buy them. In addition, pamphlets and controversial tracts soon began to circulate, and new ideas reached a thousand times more people in a relatively short span of time. In the quickening of Europe's intellectual life, it is difficult to overestimate the effects of the printing press. Without printing it is doubtful that a German writer at the end of the fifteenth century could have made the exaggerated boast that "once upon a time Germany was poor in wisdom, power, and wealth; now it is not only equal to others in glorious work, but surpasses loquacious Greece, [and] proud Italy."

Erasmus and Northern Humanism

The intellectual life of the first half of the sixteenth century was dominated by the Dutch humanist Desiderius Erasmus (c. 1466–1536). Although born in Rotterdam, he passed most of his long life elsewhere—in Germany, France, England, Italy, and especially Switzerland. The most influential and cosmopolitan of the northern humanists, he corresponded with nearly every prominent writer and thinker in Europe and personally knew popes, emperors, and kings. He was *the* scholar of Europe, and his writings were eagerly read everywhere.

Perhaps the most famous and influential work by Erasmus was *The Praise of Folly*, a satire written in 1511 at the house of the English humanist Sir Thomas More. Folly, used in the Middle Ages as a synonym for human nature, is described by Erasmus as the source not only of much harmless enjoyment in life but also of many things that are wrong and need correcting. A historian has described the work in these words:

> *At first the book makes kindly and approving fun of the ways of action and the foibles and weaknesses of mankind. It is not mordant, only amused. But gradually from fools innocent and natural and undebased, it passes to those whose illusions are vicious in their setting and results.*[12]

Among such are merchants ("they lie, swear, cheat, and practice all the intrigues of dishonesty"), lawyers ("they of all men have the greatest conceit of their own abilities"), Scholastic philosophers ("that talk as much by rote as a parrot"), and scientists ("who esteem themselves the only favorites of wisdom, and look upon the rest of mankind as the dirt and rubbish of the creation"). Most roughly handled are the clergy, in particular monks ("impudent pretenders to the profession of piety") and popes, cardinals, and bishops ("who in pomp and splendor have almost equaled if not outdone secular princes"). Although his satire is indeed harsh, Erasmus was himself balanced, moderate, and intolerant only of bigotry, ignorance, greed, and violence.

The Praise of Folly illustrates a significant difference between the northern humanists and their Italian predecessors. Most Italian humanists—the civic humanists—spoke to and for the upper-class elements in their city-states. They urged political leaders to become more statesmanlike, businessmen to become more generous with their wealth, and all to become more moral. They did not dissent or speak out in opposition; in urging the elite groups to assume their responsibilities, they were actually trying to defend, not condemn, them. Italian humanism "centered on the liberality or parsimony of princes, on the moral worth of riches, and on the question of how to define true 'nobility.'"[13] By contrast, the northern humanists, like Erasmus in *The Praise of Folly*, spoke out against a broad range of political, social, economic, and religious evils. They faced reality and became ardent reformers of society's ills.

The northern humanists also went further than the Italians in broadening their interest in ancient literature to include early Christian writings—the Scriptures and the works of the church fathers. This led them to prepare new and more accurate editions of the Scriptures (Erasmus's Greek edition of the New Testament became famous and was used by Martin Luther, the founder of Protestantism) and to compare unfavorably the complexities of the church

Portrait of Erasmus by Hans Holbein the Younger. Erasmus's scholarly achievements include a Greek edition of the New Testament and editions of the writings of St. Jerome and other early church fathers. Erasmus is best known, however, for his popular works, especially The Praise of Folly.

in their own day with the simplicity of early Christianity. Since they held that the essence of religion was morality and rational piety—what Erasmus called the "philosophy of Christ"—rather than ceremony and dogma, it is not surprising that the church became a major target of their reforming zeal.

Sir Thomas More's *Utopia*

The most significant figure in English humanism was Sir Thomas More (1478–1535), a good friend of Erasmus. More is best known for his *Utopia*, the first important description of an ideal state since Plato's *Republic*. In this extraordinarily realistic work, More criticized his age through his portrayal of a fictitious sailor who contrasts the ideal life he has seen in Utopia (the "Land of Nowhere") with the harsh

Humanism in the North: Erasmus, *The Praise of Folly*

In 1521 Martin Luther, a respected German friar, broke with the Catholic Church, triggering the so-called Protestant Reformation. Luther and his followers were reacting against abuses and corruption in the Catholic system. Many other Catholics chose to stay true to the church while speaking out against its foibles and follies at the time. One was Desiderius Erasmus. This learned churchman and humanist criticized many of his fellow Catholics for losing sight of the true purpose of Christian life, which he believed to be the imitation of Christ. Monks, priests, intellectuals—all were fair targets for Erasmus's keen mind and satirical pen. In this selection, Erasmus addresses his readers through the voice of Folly.

As for the theologians, perhaps it would be better to pass them over in silence, "not stirring up the hornets' nest," and "not laying a finger on the stinkweed," since this race of men is incredibly arrogant and touchy. For they might rise up en masse and march in ranks against me with six hundred conclusions and force me to recant. And if I should refuse, they would immediately shout "heretic." For this is the thunderbolt they always keep ready at a moment's notice to terrify anyone to whom they are not very favorably inclined....

In all these there is so much erudition, so much difficulty, that I think the apostles themselves would need to be inspired by a different spirit if they were forced to match wits on such points with this new breed of theologians. Paul could provide a living example of faith, but when he said, "Faith is the substance of things to be hoped for and the evidence of things not seen," his definition was not sufficiently magisterial. So too, he lived a life of perfect charity, but he neither distinguished it nor defined it with sufficient dialectical precision in the first epistle to the Corinthians, chapter 13....

Almost as happy as the theologians are those men who are commonly called "religious" and "monks"—though both names are quite incorrect, since a good part of them are very far removed from religion and no one is encountered more frequently everywhere you go. I cannot imagine how anything could be more wretched than these men, if it were not for the many sorts of assistance I give them. For even though everyone despises this breed of men so thoroughly that even a chance meeting with one of them is considered unlucky, still they maintain a splendid opinion of themselves. First of all, they consider it the very height of piety to have so little to do with literature as not even to be able to read. Moreover, when they roar out their psalms in church like braying asses (counting their prayers indeed, but understanding them not at all)...

Now what shall I [Folly] say about those who find great comfort in soothing self-delusions about fictitious pardons for their sins, measuring out the times in purgatory down to the droplets of a waterclock, parceling out centuries, years, months, days, hours, as if they were using mathematical tables? Or what about those who rely on certain little magical tokens and prayers thought up by some pious impostor for his own amusement or profit? They promise themselves anything and everything: wealth, honor, pleasure, an abundance of everything, perpetual health, a long life, flourishing old age, and finally a seat next to Christ among the saints, though this last they don't want for quite a while yet—that is, when the pleasures of this life, to which they cling with all their might, have finally slipped through their fingers, then it will be soon enough to enter into the joys of the saints. Imagine here, if you please, some businessman or soldier or judge who thinks that if he throws into the collection basket one coin from all his plunder, the whole cesspool of his sinful life will be immediately wiped out. He thinks all his acts of perjury, lust, drunkenness, quarreling, murder, deception, dishonesty, betrayal are paid off like a mortgage, and paid off in such a way that he can start off once more on a whole new round of sinful pleasures.

From Desiderius Erasmus, *The Praise of Folly*, trans. Clarence H. Miller (New Haven, Conn.: Yale University Press, 1979).

conditions of life in England. More's denunciations centered on the new acquisitive capitalism, which he blamed for the widespread insecurity and misery of the lower classes. More felt that governments

> *are a conspiracy of the rich, who, in pretence of managing the public, only pursue their private ends, . . . first, that they may, without danger, preserve all that they have so ill acquired, and then, that they may engage the poor to toil and labor for them at as low rates as possible, and oppress them as much as they please.*[14]

In Utopia, by contrast, no one is in want because the economy is planned and cooperative and because property is held in common. Utopia is the only true commonwealth, concludes More's imaginary sailor:

> *In all other places, it is visible that while people talk of a commonwealth, every man only seeks his own wealth: but there, where no man has any property, all men zealously pursue the good of the public.... In Utopia, where every man has a right to every thing, they all know that if care is taken to keep the public*

stores full, no private man can want any thing; for among them there is no unequal distribution, so that no man is poor, none in necessity; and though no man has anything, yet they are all rich; for what can make a man so rich as to lead a serene and cheerful life, free from anxieties; neither apprehending want himself, nor vexed with the endless complaints of his wife?[15]

More was the first of the modern English socialists, but his philosophy should not be considered a forerunner of modern socialism. His economic outlook was a legacy from the Middle Ages, and his preference for medieval collectivism over modern economic individualism was consistent with his preference for a church headed, in medieval style, by popes rather than by kings. This view prompted Henry VIII, who had appropriated the pope's position as head of the Church of England, to execute More for treason.

Rabelais's *Gargantua and Pantagruel*

One of the best-known French humanists was François Rabelais (c. 1483–1553). A brilliant, if coarse, lover of all life from the sewers to the heavens, Rabelais is best remembered for his novel *Gargantua and Pantagruel*. Centering on figures from French folklore, this work relates the adventures of Gargantua and his son Pantagruel, genial giants of tremendous stature and appetite, to whom were credited many marvelous feats.

With much burlesque humor—hence the term *Rabelaisian*—Rabelais satirized his society while putting forth his humanist views on educational reform and inherent human goodness. He made powerful attacks on the abuses of the church and the shortcomings of Scholastics and monks, but he also had no patience with overzealous Protestants. What Rabelais could not stomach was hypocrisy and repression, and for people guilty of these offenses he reserved his strongest criticism. He bid his readers to flee from that

rabble of squint-minded fellows, dissembling and counterfeit saints, demure lookers, hypocrites, pretended zealots, tough friars, buskin-monks, and other such sects of men, who disguise themselves like masquers to deceive the world. . . . Fly from these men, abhor and hate them as much as I do, and upon my faith you will find yourself the better for it. And if you desire . . . to live in peace, joy, health, making yourselves always merry, never trust those men that always peep out through a little hole.[16]

Ulrich von Hutten: German Humanist and Patriot

One of the outstanding German humanists was Ulrich von Hutten (1488–1523). His idealism combined a zeal for religious reform and German nationalist feelings. This member of an aristocratic family, who wanted to unite Germany under the emperor, led a tumultuous life as a wandering Greek scholar and satirist. He supported Luther as a rallying point for German unity against the papacy, to which he attributed most of his country's ills. Hutten reflected the tensions and aspirations of the German people in the early years of the Protestant revolt against the papacy (see Chapter 15).

Montaigne's Essays

The last notable northern humanist was the French skeptic Michel de Montaigne (1533–1592). At age 38, he gave up the practice of law and retired to his country estate and well-stocked library, where he studied and wrote. Montaigne developed a new literary form and gave it its name—the *essay*. In 94 essays he set forth his personal views on many subjects: leisure, friendship, education, philosophy, religion, old age, death. He did not pretend to have the final answer to the subjects he discussed. Instead, he advocated open-mindedness and tolerance—rare qualities in the sixteenth century, when France was racked by religious and civil strife.

Montaigne condemned the empty scholarship and formalism into which humanism and humanistic education had largely degenerated by the end of the sixteenth century. "To know by heart is not to

Michel de Montaigne, author of the Essays. *Montaigne retired from the business world while in his thirties to reflect on and write about humanity's problems.*

know; it is to retain what we have given our memory to keep," he wrote. He added:

> Our tutors never stop bawling into our ears, as though they were pouring water into a funnel; and our task is only to repeat what has been told us. I should like the tutor to correct this practice. . . . I want him to listen to his pupil speaking in his turn.[17]

Montaigne's final essay, "Of Experience," which developed the thought that "when reason fails us we resort to experience," is an acknowledgment of the shortcomings of humanism and a foreshadowing of the coming triumph of science.

Cervantes's *Don Quixote*

In the national literatures that matured during the northern Renaissance, the transition from feudal knight to Renaissance courtier finds its greatest literary expression in a masterpiece of Spanish satire, *Don Quixote de la Mancha,* the work of Miguel de Cervantes (1547–1616). By Cervantes's time, knighthood had become an anachronism, though its accompanying code of chivalry still retained its appeal. It remained for a rationalist like Cervantes to expose the inadequacies of chivalric idealism in a world that had acquired new and intensely practical aims. He did so by creating a sad but appealing character to serve as the personification of an outmoded way of life.

Don Quixote, the "knight of the woeful countenance," mounted on his "lean, lank, meagre, drooping, sharp-backed, and raw-boned" steed Rozinante, sets out in the Spanish countryside to right wrongs and uphold his lady's honor and his own. In his misadventures he is accompanied by his squire, the much less gallant but infinitely more realistic Sancho Panza, whose peasant wisdom and hard-grained common sense serve as a contrast to the impracticality of his master's chivalric code. Tilting at windmills, mistaking serving wenches for highborn ladies and inns for castles, and lamenting the invention of gunpowder as depriving brave knights of a chance to win immortality, Don Quixote is, on the surface at least, a ridiculous old man whose nostalgia for the "good old days" is a constant source of grief to him. But the story represents a superb satire directed against the outworn ideology of the Middle Ages; in particular, it laughed the ideal of chivalric romance into the world of make-believe.

And *Don Quixote* is still more. Cervantes instilled in his main character a sadness born in large measure of the author's own career of frustrated hopes and ambitions. As a result, Don Quixote becomes more than a romantic lunatic; he serves to embody the set of ideals that each of us would like to see realized but that we must compromise in a world in which we must often serve other interests.

Title page from the 1605 English translation of Don Quixote *by Cervantes. In its parody of chivalric romances,* Don Quixote *represents a great change from the outworn concepts of the Middle Ages to the ideology of a newer age, one much more complex and practical.*

Secular Drama

Like Greek drama, medieval drama developed out of religious ceremonies. A complete divorce of church and stage did not occur until the middle of the fifteenth century, when the Renaissance era of drama began in Italian cities with the performance of ancient Roman comedies. In the following century appeared the *commedia dell'arte,* reflections of everyday life in vulgar and slapstick fashion, usually improvised by the players from a plot outline.

As secular dramas grew in popularity, theaters were built as permanent settings for their presentations. Great ingenuity was shown in the design of elaborate, realistic stage scenery as well as in lighting and sound effects. Theaters embodying these innovations only gradually appeared outside Italy. Not until 1576 was the first public theater erected in London; three years later a similar theater was constructed in Madrid.

Imitating the ancient models they admired, French and Italian writers followed what they believed were the rigid conventions of the classical drama and to a large extent catered to the tastes of the aristocracy. By contrast, Spanish and English playwrights created a theatrical environment that was at once more socially democratic, more hospitable to national themes, and less concerned with classical models.

William Shakespeare

The reign of Queen Elizabeth I (1558–1603) climaxed the English Renaissance and produced such a galaxy of talented writers that one would have to go back as far as Athens in the fifth century B.C.E. to find an age as rich with literary genius. Strongly influenced by the royal court, which served as the busy center of intellectual and artistic life, these writers produced works that were intensely emotional, richly romantic, and often wildly extravagant in spite of all their poetic allusions to classical times.

The supreme figure in Elizabethan literature and perhaps in all Western literature is William Shakespeare (1564–1616). His rich vocabulary and poetic imagery were matched by his turbulent imagination. He was a superb lyric poet, and numerous critics have judged him the foremost sonnet writer in the English language.

Shakespeare wrote 37 plays—comedies, histories, tragedies, and romances. His historical plays reflected the patriotic upsurge experienced by the English after the defeat of the Spanish Armada in 1588. For his comedies, tragedies, and romances, Shakespeare was content in a great majority of cases to borrow plots from earlier works. His great strength lay in his creation of characters—perhaps the richest and most diversified collection conceived by the mind of one man—and in his ability to translate his knowledge of human nature into dramatic speech and action. Today his comedies still play to enthusiastic audiences: *The Taming of the Shrew, As You Like It, A Midsummer Night's Dream,* and *The Merchant of Venice* are but a few. But it is in his tragedies that the poet-dramatist runs the gamut of human emotion and experience.

Shakespeare possessed in abundance the Renaissance concern for human beings and the world around them. Hence his plays deal first and foremost with the human personality, passions, and problems. In such works as *Romeo and Juliet, Measure for Measure,* and *Troilus and Cressida,* the problems of love and sex are studied from many angles. Jealousy is analyzed in *Othello,* ambition in *Macbeth* and *Julius Caesar,* family relationships in *King Lear,* and a man's struggle with his own soul in *Hamlet.* Shakespeare's extraordinary ability to build every concrete fact and action on a universal truth makes his observations as applicable today as when they were first presented at

the Globe Theater. Small wonder that next to the Bible, Shakespeare is the most quoted of all literary sources in the English language.

Northern Painting

Before the Italian Renaissance began to influence the artistic circles of northern Europe, the painters of the Low Countries—modern Belgium, Luxembourg, and the Netherlands—had been making significant advances on their own. Outstanding was the Fleming Jan van Eyck (c. 1395–1441), whose work has been called the "full flowering of the spirit of the late Middle Ages," for he continued to paint in the realistic manner developed by medieval miniaturists. Van Eyck also perfected the technique of oil painting, which enabled him to paint with greater realism and attention to detail. In his painting of the merchant Arnolfini and his wife, for example, he painstakingly gives extraordinary reality to every detail, from his own image reflected in the mirror in the background to individual hairs on the little dog in the foreground.

Jan van Eyck, Wedding Portrait. *The painting of a merchant named Arnolfini and his pregnant bride is extraordinary for its meticulously rendered realistic detail. Van Eyck painted exactly what he saw—he "was there," as his signature on the painting says (Johannes de Eyck fuit hic). The painting is also filled with symbolism; the dog, for instance, stands for marital fidelity.*

Jan van Eyck, The Arnolfini Portrait, 1434. NG 186. © National Gallery, London.

The first German painter to be influenced deeply by Italian art was Albrecht Dürer (1471–1528) of Nuremberg. Dürer made more than one journey to Italy, where he was impressed both with the painting of the Renaissance Italians and with the artists' high social status—a contrast with northern Europe, where artists were still treated as craftsmen, not men of genius. His own work is a blend of the old and the new; thus his engraving *Knight, Death, and the Devil* fuses the realism and symbolism of the Gothic with the nobility of Verrocchio's equestrian statue of Colleoni. In his own lifetime and after, Dürer became better known for his numerous engravings and woodcuts, produced for a mass market, than for his paintings.

Another famous German painter, Hans Holbein the Younger (1497–1543), chiefly painted portraits and worked abroad, especially in England. His memorable portraits blend the realism and concern for detail characteristic of all northern painting with Italian dignity.

Two northern painters who remained completely isolated from Italian influences were Hieronymus Bosch (1480–1516) and Pieter Brueghel the Elder (c. 1525–1569). Brueghel retained a strong Flemish flavor in his portrayal of the faces and scenes of his native land. He painted village squares, landscapes, skating scenes, and peasants at work and at leisure just as he saw them, with a reporter's eye for detail.

Very little is known about the Dutch master Bosch other than that he belonged to one of the many puritanical religious sects that were becoming popular at the time. This accounts for his most famous painting, *The Garden of Delights,* a triptych whose main panel is filled with innumerable naked men and women reveling in the sins of the flesh. The smaller left panel, by contrast, depicts an idyllic Garden of Eden, while the right panel portrays a nightmarish hell filled with frenzied sinners undergoing punishment. Bosch was a stern moralist whose obsession with sin and hell reflects the fears of his contemporaries, which contributed to the religious movement to be described in the next chapter—the Reformation.

Conclusion

In the Middle Ages people had thought and acted primarily as members of a community—a manor, a guild, or, above all, the universal community represented by the Roman Catholic Church. But gradually individuals began to attach importance to themselves and to develop an interest in worldly things for their own sake. This new individualistic and secular spirit, the period in which it became prominent, and the ways in which it manifested itself in art, literature, and learning, are called the Renaissance.

The change took place earliest in the cities of fourteenth- and fifteenth-century Italy, and its intellectual and artistic aspects were linked to the practical activities of Renaissance civic life. Its intellectual manifestation, known as humanism—a movement that sought to recapture the learning and culture of ancient Greece and Rome—resulted in a revival of classical literature and learning; it led citizens to seek out and imitate what was relevant and useful in the classics. Scholars eagerly searched for ancient manuscripts and introduced the literature of Greece and Rome into contemporary life. Italian humanists also laid the foundation for modern scholarship. Thus they helped prepare the way for modern science, even though they themselves generally avoided the subject.

Artists, too, reflected the new human-centered view of the world. The extent to which the Italian Renaissance sculptors, architects, and painters succeeded remains one of the glories of Western civilization. But the "anti-Renaissance" art called Mannerism, which arose during the last two-thirds of the sixteenth century after the peak of perfection

The first German painter influenced by the Italian style was Albrecht Dürer. His engraving The Knight, Death, and the Devil *is typical of his combination of the new style (the knight on his charger echoes Verrocchio's statue of Colleoni) with medieval Gothic realism and subject matter.*

Albrecht Dürer, *The Knight, Death and the Devil,* 1513. Engraving, 9 11/16" × 7 9/16". The Brooklyn Museum of Art, New York. Gift of Mrs. Horace OP. Havemeyer.

had been reached in the High Renaissance, has also of late received much favorable attention. Long dismissed as the "grotesque Renaissance" and described as "variations on ugliness," in the twentieth century the appearance of such styles as surrealism and expressionism led to a new understanding and appreciation of Mannerism. The Mannerist period is also regarded as one of invention and exploration out of which arose the baroque style of the seventeenth century.

In the sixteenth century the stimulating ideas current in Italy spread beyond the Alps and combined with local developments to produce renaissances in France, England, and elsewhere. Although influenced by Italian models, thought and art beyond the Alps also developed in distinctive ways. These developments included the invention of printing from movable type, the impact of the reforming zeal of the northern humanists on society, some of the great classics of European national literature, and achievements in painting that blended late medieval Gothic realism with Italian Renaissance dignity.

Suggestions for Reading

Margaret Aston, *The Fifteenth Century: The Prospect of Europe* (Norton, 1979); Peter Burke, *The Italian Renaissance: Culture and Society in Renaissance Italy* (Princeton University Press, 1987); and Jonathan W. Zophy, *A Short History of Renaissance and Reformation Europe*, 2nd ed. (Prentice Hall, 1998), are first-rate introductions to the Renaissance period.

Jacob Burckhardt, *The Civilization of the Renaissance in Italy*, 2 vols. (Torchbooks, 1958), first published in 1860, inaugurated the view that the Italian Renaissance of the fourteenth and fifteenth centuries was a momentous turning point in the history of Western civilization. The editors of this edition maintain that Burckhardt's major interpretations remain valid. For other excellent interpretations, see John Hale, *The Civilization of Europe in the Renaissance* (Touchstone, 1994); De Lamar Jensen, *Renaissance Europe: Age of Recovery and Reconciliation*, 2nd ed. (Heath, 1992); and Lisa Jardine, *Worldly Goods: A New History of the Renaissance* (Bantam, 1996).

Several excellent accounts dealing with the individual Italian city-states include Giovanni Tabacco, *The Struggle for Power in Medieval Italy* (Yale University Press, 1990); David Waley, *The Italian City Republics* (Addison-Wesley, 1988); John Norwich, *A History of Venice* (Vintage, 1989); and Charles Stinger, *The Renaissance in Rome* (Indiana University Press, 1985). Christopher Hibbert, *Florence: The Biography of a City* (Norton, 1993), focuses on the Renaissance period and serves as a guidebook as well as a history. See also Melissa Bullard, *Lorenzo il Magnifico: Image and Anxiety, Politics and Finance* (Oxford University Press, 1994); Christopher Hibbert, *Florence* (Morrow, 1990); and Alison Brown, *The Medici in Florence: The Exercise of Language and Power* (Penguin, 1992).

Paul O. Kristeller, *Renaissance Thought: The Classic, Scholastic, and Humanist Strains* (Torchbooks, 1961), and Paul O. Kristeller and Michael Mooney, eds., *Renaissance Thought and Its Sources* (Columbia University Press, 1979), are both excellent introductions. See also E. B. Fryde, *Humanism and Renaissance Historiography* (Harvard University Press, 1983); Roberto Weiss, *The Renaissance Discovery of Classical Antiquity*

(Blackwell, 1988); Donald R. Kelley, *Renaissance Humanism* (Twayne, 1991); Charles Edward Trinkaus, *The Scope of Renaissance Humanism* (Indiana University Press, 1983); and Brian P. Copenhaver, *Renaissance Philosophy* (Oxford University Press, 1992). Katharina M. Wilson, ed., *Women Writers of the Renaissance and Reformation* (University of Georgia Press, 1987), is an excellent study of a neglected subject. See also Paul F. Grendler, *Schooling in Renaissance Italy* (Johns Hopkins University Press, 1989); Nicholas Mann, *Petrarch* (Cornell University Press, 1984); and Margaret F. Rosenthal and Catherine R. Stimpson, *The Honest Courtesan: Veronica Franco, Citizen and Writer in Sixteenth-Century Venice* (University of Chicago Press, 1992). Sebastian de Grazia, *Machiavelli in Hell* (Princeton University Press, 1989), is an excellent biography.

Frederick Binkerd Artz, *From the Renaissance to Romanticism: Trends in Style in Art, Literature, and Music, 1300–1830* (Unversity of Chicago Press, 1962), is a good overall view of the arts. Also recommended are Peter Murray and Linda Murray, *The Art of the Renaissance* (Thames & Hudson, 1985), and Michael Levey, *Early Renaissance* (Penguin, 1978) and *High Renaissance* (Penguin, 1975), which contain many illustrations of paintings; see also Lorne Campbell, *Renaissance Portraits: European Portrait-Painting in the 14th, 15th, and 16th Centuries* (Yale University Press, 1991); Joachim Poeschke, *Donatello and His World: Sculpture of the Italian Renaissance* (Abrams, 1993); Norman E. Land, *The Viewer as Poet: The Renaissance Response to Art* (Pennsylvania State University Press, 1994); and John White, *Art and Architecture in Italy, 1250–1400*, 3rd ed. (Yale University Press, 1993). Bernard Berenson, *Italian Painters of the Renaissance* (Cornell University Press, 1980), and Rudolf Wittkower, *Architectural Principles in the Age of Humanism* (Norton, 1971), are two classics of art history. See also Roberta J. M. Olsen, *Italian Renaissance Sculpture* (Thames & Hudson, 1992); Charles Seymour Jr., *Sculpture in Italy, 1400–1500* (Yale University Press, 1994); and David Thompson, *Renaissance Architecture: Patrons, Critics, Luxury* (St. Martin's Press, 1993).

On the northern Renaissance, see Charles G. Nauert Jr., *Humanism and the Culture of Renaissance Europe* (Cambridge University Press, 1995); Elaine V. Beilin, *Redeeming Eve: Women Writers of the English Renaissance* (Princeton University Press, 1987); Lisa Jardine, *Erasmus, Man of Letters* (Yale University Press, 1993); Max M. Reese, *Shakespeare: His World and His Work* (Oxford University Press, 1980); Jeffrey Chips Smith, *German Sculpture of the Later Renaissance, c. 1520–1580: Art in an Age of Uncertainty* (Princeton University Press, 1994); and Carl C. Christensen, *Art and the Reformation in Germany* (Yale University Press, 1979).

Suggestions for Web Browsing

Renaissance Art
http://online.anu.edu.au/ArtHistory/renart/pics.art/Part1.html

One of the very best and most comprehensive sites for reproductions of the major paintings, works of sculpture, and architecture from the Renaissance. An amazing resource of the study of Renaissance art.

WebMuseum, Paris: Italian Renaissance (1420–1600)
http://www.hipernet.ufsc.br/wm/paint/tl/it-ren/

A useful site for anyone interested in the art of the Italian Renaissance, especially the work of Leonardo da Vinci, Raphael, and Michelangelo.

Florence in the Renaissance
http://www.mega.it/eng/egui/epo/secrepu.htm

A history of the Florentine Republic, with details about the city's influence on Renaissance culture.

Sistine Chapel
http://christusrex.org/www1/sistine/0-Tour.html

Photo collection depicting all facets of the Sistine Chapel, including 18 images of Michelangelo's ceiling.

Michelangelo
http://www.michelangelo.com.br/

Featuring the works of the artist beautifully illustrated and annotated. An outstanding site.

The Louvre
http://www.paris.org/Musees/Louvre

Web site for one of the world's greatest museums offers many paths to some of the most beautiful Renaissance art in existence.

Image Gallery: Renaissance
http://www.lycos.com/cgi-bin/
pursuit?que...&fs=parent&cat=image_gallery

This site displays the greatest works of Renaissance art by artist. A very comprehensive collection.

Creative Impulse: Renaissance
http://history.evansville.net/renaissa.html

The University of Evansville's outstanding series of sites on Western civilization includes this compendium of art, history, and descriptions of daily life and culture. Includes one of the very best compilations of other sites dealing with the Renaissance.

Medieval and Renaissance Fact and Fiction
http://www.angelfire.com/mi/spanogle/medieval.html

A useful guide to Web resources for students interested in the history, culture, and literature of the Renaissance.

Northern Renaissance Art Web
http://pilot.msu.edu/~cloudsar/nrweb.html

A collection of links for exploring the artists and literature of the northern Renaissance.

Notes

1. *Tempest*, act 5, scene 1, lines 182–185.
2. Quoted in Lauro Martines, *Power and Imagination: City-States in Renaissance Italy* (New York: Knopf, 1979), p. 83.
3. Quoted in ibid., p. 243.
4. Quoted in John Herman Randall Jr., *The Making of the Modern Mind* (Boston: Houghton Mifflin, 1976), p. 213.
5. Letter to Francesco Vettori; see Allan H. Gilbert, *The Letters of Machiavelli* (New York: Capricorn Books), p. 142.
6. Richard Addington, trans., *The Decameron of Giovanni Boccaccio* (New York: Garden City, 1949), p. 559.
7. Joan Kelly, quoted in Bonnie S. Anderson and Judith Zinsser, *A History of Their Own: Women in Europe from Prehistory to the Present*, Vol. 1 (New York: Harper & Row, 1988), p. xvii.
8. Sir Thomas Elyot, *The Book of the Governor*, quoted in Eugene F. Rice, *The Foundations of Early Modern Europe, 1460–1559* (New York: Norton, 1970), p. 88.
9. Eric Newton, *European Painting and Sculpture*, 4th ed. (New York: Penguin, 1956), pp. 139–140.
10. Allan H. Gilbert, trans., *Machiavelli: The Prince and Other Works* (Chicago: Packard, 1941), p. 177.
11. Frederick Binkerd Artz, *From the Renaissance to Romanticism: Trends in Style in Art, Literature, and Music, 1300–1830* (Chicago: University of Chicago Press, 1962), p. 102.
12. Henry Osborn Taylor, ed., *Thought and Expression in the Sixteenth Century*, Vol. 1 (New York: Macmillan, 1920), p. 175.
13. Martines, *Power and Imagination*, p. 208.
14. From the 1684 translation by Gilbert Burnet, in *Introduction to Contemporary Civilization in the West: A Source Book*, Vol. 1 (New York: Columbia University Press, 1946), p. 461.
15. Ibid., p. 460.
16. Quoted in Taylor, *Thought and Expression*, pp. 328–329.
17. Montaigne, "Of the Education of Children," in Donald M. Frame, trans., *The Complete Works of Montaigne* (Stanford, Calif.: Stanford University Press, 1957), p. 112.

The transition from papal religious domination in the thirteenth century to control by kings and states brought with it a pandemic of violence that touched all ages, classes, and nations. That Pieter Brueghel the Elder understood the nature of his times can be seen when he placed the biblical account of the Death of the Innocents (Matthew 2:16) in the context of sixteenth-century Europe. By placing Herod's order to kill all children under the age of 2 in a contemporary setting, Brueghel captured the mindless slaughter justified by the political and religious zealots of his age.

The Christian Reformations and the Emergence of the Modern Political System

Faith and State in Europe, 1517–1648

Chapter Contents

Whennnn the men and women of the late Middle Ages who lived north of the Mediterranean and west of Russia had occasion to think about the world outside their villages, they believed they lived in Christendom. By the middle of the seventeenth century, people living in that part of the world referred to it as Europe. The change from Christendom to Europe, from a community based on faith to an allegiance imposed by the state, brought with it much death, suffering, and destruction in the 150 years after Luther first made his stand at Wittenberg. Not until the twentieth century would Europeans experience greater carnage.

This transition from the medieval to the modern world brought with it the first national liberation struggle—the Dutch; new banks, insurance companies, and stock markets—the rise of modern capitalism; the first modern, elite cadre dedicated to redefining the truth and imposing it throughout the world—the Jesuits; and the Habsburgs' attempt to eradicate not only the Bohemians but also their civilization after 1620—the first modern genocide. The faithful knew that the Almighty had moved in the life of his people since the world had begun, but in this century and a half kings and clerics used the name of God to justify the slaughter of anyone who opposed them. Not since the Crusades had the Christians gone to battle with such bloodthirsty results. Then it was against the so-called infidel. Now it would be against each other, until finally in 1648 the Europeans grew tired of the combat and sought refuge in the rules of the modern state system and absolutist kings.

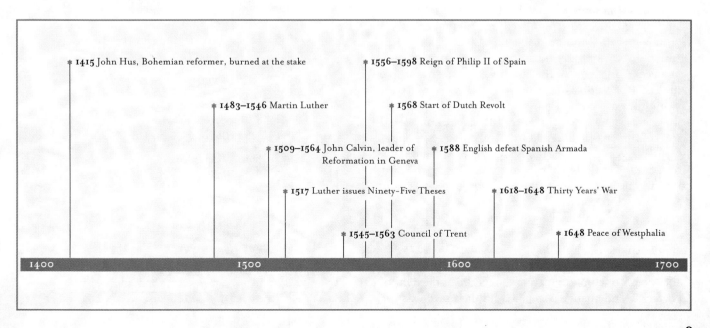

| 1400 | 1500 | 1600 | 1700 |

- **1415** John Hus, Bohemian reformer, burned at the stake
- **1483–1546** Martin Luther
- **1509–1564** John Calvin, leader of Reformation in Geneva
- **1517** Luther issues Ninety-Five Theses
- **1545–1563** Council of Trent
- **1556–1598** Reign of Philip II of Spain
- **1568** Start of Dutch Revolt
- **1588** English defeat Spanish Armada
- **1618–1648** Thirty Years' War
- **1648** Peace of Westphalia

This chapter traces the tortured path of the transition between the age of faith and the age of the state. Faith is the believer's link with God, an individual and mystical force. The state is an artificial creation: an institution erected by human beings that has a monopoly over the right to tax and use force within a defined boundary. The tragic mixture of the faith of an individual such as Martin Luther and the blunt instrument that is the modern state is the subject of this chapter.

The Protestant Reformation in Germany

Luther had no intention of setting the spark that launched this century and a half of conflict. Born in 1483, the son of an ambitious and tough Thuringian peasant turned miner and small businessman, he was raised by his parents under a regime of Christian love and the attendant harsh physical discipline that would affect his way of dealing with the world after 1521. Like many young boys of his time, he enjoyed the sometimes earthy and profane humor of his peasant society. Unlike many of his friends, he, like St. Augustine, distrusted his passionate nature and became obsessed with fear of the devil and an eternity in hell. Until 1517, Luther's pursuit of his salvation was an intensely personal one, with little regard to the larger context of discontent in which he lived.

The Context for Change

As we saw in Chapter 8, the plague, famine, and warfare of the fourteenth and fifteenth centuries brought Europe brutally down from the mountaintop of the High Middle Ages. Institutions such as the papacy and the established nobilities suffered greatly. The Roman Catholic Church's prestige plummeted after Philip the Fair's kidnapping of Pope Boniface and the split between Rome and Avignon—with even, for a time, three popes. Almost continuous warfare destroyed a large part of the nobility of western Europe, and the new nobles created to replace the old warriors were more often bureaucrats than soldiers. The plague and its periodic, dreadful visitations would for centuries keep Europe from reaching its population levels of around 1300. Fewer people meant a tax loss for the various kings, and those people who survived found themselves able to move more easily from the former feudal contracts to become wage laborers in the countryside or workers and artisans in the cities. All of these factors contributed to a potentially explosive situation.

Crisis and change were not new in Europe. But the means of communicating the nature and extent of the crisis and change was new, and the result was the force of mobilized public opinion. The printing presses since their European introduction in the mid-fifteenth century had already spewed out 6 million publications in more than 200 European towns. There were more and better-educated people with a thirst to read these books, which dealt largely with religious themes. Although 90 percent of the population remained rural, cities increased considerably in size and number, swelled by the people coming from the countryside to make a living. And in the cities in the north of Europe, lending libraries were established to make books available to those who could not buy them.

Life in these cities became increasingly difficult as the social problems of urban growth outran the resources of the Catholic Church to deal with them. Many a city-dweller was a peasant who had just arrived and was cut off from his family and village. Such a person would try to adjust to the strange and new ideas and gasped to see his pocketbook emptied as the Catholic Church charged its fees, the feudal nobles claimed their tolls, and the entrenched interests blocked his chances of getting work. The country

Religious Reforms and Reactions

1415	John Hus, Bohemian reformer, burned at the stake
1437–1517	Cardinal Ximenes, carried out reforms of Spanish Catholic Church
c. 1450	Revival of witchcraft mania in Europe
1452–1498	Savonarola, attempted religious purification of Florence
1483–1546	Martin Luther
1484–1531	Ulrich Zwingli, leader of Swiss Reformation
1491–1556	Ignatius Loyola, founder of Society of Jesus (Jesuits)
1509–1564	John Calvin, leader of Reformation in Geneva
1515–1582	St. Teresa of Avila, founder of Carmelite religious order
1517	Luther issues Ninety-Five Theses
1521	Luther declared an outcast by the Imperial Diet at Worms
1534–1549	Pontificate of Paul III
1545–1563	Council of Trent
1561–1593	Religious wars in France

Discovery Through Maps

The Road to Eternity

In the fifteenth and sixteenth centuries, Christians, such as Martin Luther, lived in an environment characterized by disorder and death. As Europe struggled out of the disaster of the recurring plagues, wars, and the breakdown of law and order, life was a tenuous thread between birth and judgment.

Flemish artist Jan van Eyck (d. 1441) did most of his work during the first half of these tumultuous times. In his paintings he made a breakthrough from the formulaic elegance and unnecessary complications of the Gothic style to go to the heart of the human condition. In his travels about Europe he witnessed the fragility of life in the towns where the plague had just made its reappearance, in the bodies of people killed by highway robbers, and in the joy of the birth of a child and the tragedy of the all-too-often death of its mother.

In this altarpiece entitled *The Last Judgment*, painted by van Eyck, we see the only cartography that mattered to believers—the vertical distances between heaven and hell at the Last Judgment. Here, in the upper portion, we have those judged or yet to be judged. Below, pictured in agonizing detail, is hell in all of its awful terror.

As Luther was concerned with his soul, traumatized by his lustful impulses, so too were other Europeans who knew—from paintings such as this—what awaited them on their final journey through time.

Jan van Eyck, *The Last Judgment* (one of two panels), tempera and oil on canvas, transferred from wood. 22¼" × 7¾". The Metropolitan Museum of Art, Fletcher Fund, 1933. Photograph © 1998 The Metropolitan Museum of Art.

person faced a society of grasping merchants, suspicious craftspeople, and poor townsfolk, and more often than not the newcomer would end up among the other starving and out-of-work ex-peasants outside city walls.

The beginning of the sixteenth century marked the end of the relatively favorable situation women had enjoyed in the Middle Ages. The new emphasis on wage labor and competition from men limited their opportunities for outside work. They could get some part-time employment as field laborers, but it paid very little. They also continued to face male resentment against their entry into the economy and nearly complete exclusion from craft guilds. Their bargaining power was further limited because they outnumbered men in most cities, a situation that helped flood the job market while limiting them in finding security with husbands. Later in the century the number of single women rose even more noticeably when thousands were widowed in religious wars.

A sure indicator of the tortured nature of the era was the witchcraft mania that spread over Europe. The idea of witches as agents of evil had been present in the pre-Christian era but had weakened by the end of the thirteenth century. Its revival after 1450 was sudden and fanatical. Accused witches were usually tried in religious courts, both Catholic and, later, Protestant, where many were tortured until they confessed. Over 100,000 of these unfortunates were prosecuted, and many were executed by strangling, drowning, burning, or beheading. Seven out of ten victims were women, nearly half of them widows; most were old and eccentric. Punishment was justified by their alleged alliance with the devil and their threat to the true faith. Supposedly, they had gone over to Satan's side because women were portrayed as being weak and innately evil, as indicated by the biblical account of Eve's role in corrupting Adam. Throughout history, a time of uncertainty has always encouraged the search for scapegoats.

Economic dislocation accompanying the development of capitalism, even this early, added to the crisis of the time, especially among the peasantry. A new global economy brought high rates of inflation and shifting trade routes. The decline of the importance of the Hanseatic League, the Mediterranean, and the routes connecting the two hurt the economy of central Europe. Further, the shifting of work to laborers in the surrounding villages—cottage industry—ruined many old guild industries while swelling the ranks of the urban unemployed. Large-market agriculture weakened the peasants' traditional rights, subjected them to rents beyond their resources, and drove them from the land into the towns, where they joined the idle and the impoverished. The poor and out-of-work often directed their anger against the Catholic Church because it was a visible source of authority and it was rich. The profit motive overshadowed the church's canon law, which stressed compassion and a "just price."

Political Conditions

If Luther's search for salvation had taken place at a time only of social and economic distress, he would have remained just another agonized Christian in his own quest. At the beginning of the sixteenth century, the modern state system was in its formative stages, and the political currents of his time gave Luther's message a powerful medium of expression across central Europe after 1517.

The papacy's political power had been in a continual decline since the thirteenth century. In the cities north of the Alps and east of France, local elites fought both the Catholic clergy and the excluded lower classes for political control. In the country, nobles, local clergy, cities, and state rulers were often engaged in many-faceted political struggles. Kings and their lesser-titled feudal counterparts in the German states competed for supremacy within their realms with the popes and their major political allies of the Habsburg dynasty. The main issues here involved control of taxes and fees, the courts, the law, public support, and military power, but significant economic interests were also at stake. The Catholic Church owned vast properties and collected fortunes in tithes, fees, and religious gifts, controlling by some estimates between a fifth and a fourth of Europe's wealth—all coveted by secular rulers, who hoped to increase their wealth by taking over the church's functions and property.

In the first half of the sixteenth century, the Habsburgs, personified by Charles V, ruled a global empire. Because of fortunate marriage alliances and convenient deaths of competitors in the previous two generations, Charles was king of Spain and its world empire, Bohemia, and Hungary; sovereign over the Netherlands, Burgundy, Austria, Styria, Milan, Naples, and Sicily; and titular head of the Holy Roman Empire. But his far-flung holdings and conflicts with the Turks and the French left him little time to look after the church. The empire, including 2000 independent lesser nobles, 66 autonomous cities, over 100 imperial counts, and 30 secular princes, was loosely governed by the Imperial Diet, which functioned primarily to protect the independence of the princes and cities. With its 70 quasi-independent bishoprics and its close ties with the emperor, the church was naturally an object of resentment within the Diet.

The Catholic establishment faced even more serious political difficulties with the new independent monarchies of western Europe. During the fifteenth century, English, French, and Spanish rulers began freeing themselves from traditional restrictions and gaining independence from the papacy. In Spain, Charles V's maternal grandparents, Ferdinand and Isabella, made taxation of the church a major revenue source and the Inquisition a political tool for removing enemies of the monarchy. French kings by the mid-fifteenth century had won the right of clerical appointment and used it to control their church. In England the Tudor dynasty after 1485 co-opted the nobility and raised new revenues; the break with Rome under Henry VIII would climax a long and bitter struggle between English kings and the papacy over appointments and church incomes.

No longer able to prevail over secular rulers by its religious authority alone, the papacy fared badly in an era of power politics in foreign relations. Free Italian cities, such as Venice and Florence, had helped generate the new balance of power diplomacy, but it soon involved the peninsula in a desperate struggle between the Habsburg and Valois (French) dynasties that lasted from the 1490s to 1559. The Papal States became a political pawn. The papacy's weaknesses were exploited by the troops of Charles V when they sacked Rome in 1527.

Wyclif, Hus, and the Humanists

Before 1517, political notions were not an important part of Luther's life. The confusion and corruption in the Catholic Church affected him far more. As one of his century's finest theologians, he knew that it had taken seven councils and eight centuries to arrive at an agreed-on definition of Christianity and that thereafter the church had fought continuously against heretics—people who disagreed with that prescribed definition of the faith. Adding to the theological disputes during and after the fourteenth century was a widespread argument about the role and pretensions of the papacy. There were also German and Dutch mystics who sought direct spiritual communion with God outside the Catholic Church's hierarchy.

Theologians in England and Bohemia during the 1300s advanced the issues Luther would advocate more than a century later. John Wyclif (1328–1384), the son of a minor Yorkshire nobleman, studied at Balliol College, Oxford, and stayed on there as a professor. He gained a solid foundation in mathematics and optics, but his major contribution lay in theology. Wyclif lived and worked at a time of the weakened Catholic Church and rejected the French-dominated papacy and the popes' desire to exercise power inside England. Strongly influenced by the writings of St. Augustine, Wyclif emphasized the primacy of the Bible in the life of a Christian. He believed that God directly touched each person and that the role of the popes was of minor importance. In fact, the kings had a higher claim on their subjects' loyalty, and the monarchs themselves were accountable only to God, not the pope. Wyclif believed that the church itself, and not the Catholic hierarchy, is the true community of believers. He even went so far as to question the validity of some of the sacraments. Toward the end of his life, Wyclif was attacked by the papacy, and after his death he was declared a heretic. In 1428 his remains were taken from consecrated ground and burned, and his ashes were thrown into a river. In the church's eyes, this act condemned his soul to perpetual wandering and suffering and destroyed the possibility that Wyclif's followers could preserve any parts of his body as relics.

But the influence of Wyclif's writings took root in England through a group he helped organize called the "poor priests," later known as the Lollards. The Welshman William Tyndale (1494–1536) encountered Wyclif's ideas at Oxford and later at Cambridge during his study of Hebrew, Greek, and Latin. He began a translation of the Bible into English but was unable to publish it in England during the 1520s. He went to Germany, where he found a publisher and also met Luther. For the rest of the decade he continued his work of translation and tried to send his published New Testament to England. His books arrived before Henry VIII's creation of the new Protestant Church, and the bishop of London ordered around 18,000 copies to be burned. Finally, he was imprisoned in Antwerp in 1535, was found to be a heretic, and was strangled and burned on the orders of Charles V in 1536. The following year Parliament decreed that an English Bible be published and placed in each church. That text, supervised by one of his colleagues, was essentially the same as Tyndale's translation. In a certain sense, the seeds that Wyclif had planted bore fruit.

The Englishman deeply influenced events in Bohemia and the rest of central Europe. Bohemian students studying at Oxford took his writings back to Prague in the late fourteenth century, where they were translated by John Hus (c. 1370–1415), an im-

poverished but brilliant student at the Charles University in Prague. In 1402, after rising to become the dominant figure at his university, he began to give sermons in the Czech language that soon attracted groups as large as 3000 people to the Bethlehem Chapel. He preached that the Bible is the only source of faith and that every person has the right to read it in his own language. Like Wyclif, Hus preached against clerical abuses and the claim of the church to guarantee salvation. This message became more explosive because it was linked with his criticism of the excesses of the German-dominated church at a time of a growing Czech nationalist movement. In his preaching he openly acknowledged his debt to Wyclif and refused to join in condemning him in 1410. Hus was later excommunicated and called to account for himself at the Council of Constance in 1415. Even though he had been given the assurance of safe passage, he was seized and burned at the stake as a heretic, and his ashes were thrown into the Rhine. His death led to the Hussite wars (1419–1437) in which the Czechs withstood the crusades preached against them. The Bohemians maintained their religious reforms until their defeat by the Habsburgs in the Thirty Years' War.

During the fifteenth century, humanist reformers believed that abuses in the Catholic Church resulted largely from misinterpretation of Scripture by late medieval Scholastic philosophers and theologians. The Scholastics had seen reason as God's greatest gift, permitting man to understand the nature of good and evil. For example, St. Thomas Aquinas, perhaps the best-known Scholastic, tried in his *Summa Theologica* to reconcile Aristotle's logic with church teaching. Unfortunately, during Luther's time Scholastic logic was employed to rationalize many ritualistic and mechanical paths to salvation: good works earned credits against sins; popes could dispense grace through indulgences; the clergy were direct representatives of God and therefore only they could minister the sacraments. These and other similar propositions all reinforced the idea that salvation required services from the Roman Church and the clergy more than piety or faith.

Northern humanists like Erasmus ridiculed later Scholasticism as pedantic; other critics, such as the Augustinian monks, saw the Scholastics as presumptuous and worldly. Following the teachings of St. Augustine, they believed man to be such a depraved sinner that he could be saved not through "good works" but only through personal repentance and faith in God's mercy. Augustinians accepted only Scripture as religious truth; they denied emphatically that the clergy held the keys to heaven; and they condemned all changes from the early primitive church, including veneration of relics, celibacy of the clergy, priests as intermediaries, the necessity of most sacraments, and the infallibility of the pope. They believed that faith was more important than the Scholastics' manipulated power of reason.

Martin Luther found great comfort in the teachings of the humanists and the Augustinians. After four years of law study at Erfurt University, young Martin disappointed his father by entering an Augustinian monastery at age 22, following what was to him a miraculous survival in a violent thunderstorm. Even as a monk, however, Luther was tormented by what he saw as his sinful nature and the fear of damnation. Then, in his mid-thirties, he read St. Paul's Epistle to the Romans and found freedom from despair in the notion of justification by faith:

> *Then I grasped that the justice of God is that righteousness by which through grace and sheer mercy God justifies us through faith. Thereupon, I felt myself to be reborn and to have gone through open doors into paradise.[1]*

As an Augustinian, Luther entered into abstract religious debates that became more spirited because of the widespread problems of the church in central Europe. Critics' doctrinal arguments came to be tied to complaints that the church hierarchy, particularly at the highest levels, had been seriously infected by the lust for power, profit, and sensual pleasures, at the expense of spiritual concerns. Each critic had his list of specific abuses, but most agreed that some priests were so ignorant that they could not read the Scriptures or conduct the Mass; others, even some popes, took mistresses, fathered children, and paid money for forgiveness; and many clergymen, despite their vows of poverty, lived extremely well, enjoying fine wines, rich foods, and superb art. These elements of corruption had been present for centuries, but Luther was still shocked by what he saw when he made a journey to Rome.

The buying and selling of church offices and charging fees to give comfort through a variety of theologically questionable ceremonies to superstitious parishioners angered the critics. A very profitable venture was the sale of supposedly sacred relics, including reputed bones of the saints, vials of mystically preserved blood from Christian martyrs, and other items such as shrouds and pieces of the true cross. There were so many pieces of the "true cross," one critic remarked, that a navy could well be built from them.

The practice that outraged Luther and brought him openly to oppose the Roman Catholic Church was the sale of indulgences. Theoretically, these were shares of surplus grace, earned by Christ and the saints and available for papal dispensation to worthy souls after death. Originally, indulgences were not sold or described as tickets to heaven. By the sixteenth century, however, papal salesmen regularly peddled them as guarantees of early release from purgatory.

Luther's Stand

There are moments in history when the actions of a single person will link all of the prevailing and contrasting currents of an era into an explosive mixture. In Wittenberg on October 31, 1517, Martin Luther issued his celebrated Ninety-Five Theses, calling for public debate on issues involving indulgences and other related theological questions.[2] The ensuing controversy, which soon raged far beyond Wittenberg, split all of western Christendom and focused and strengthened the social, economic, and political contradictions of the time. Luther's act and its repercussions affected not only the German princes and the Holy Roman Emperor but all other states in Europe as well.

Conditions in Germany help explain the impact of Luther's protest, but his powerful personality is also a compelling factor. His immediate adversary in 1517 was a Dominican monk named Johan Tetzel, commissioned by the pope to sell indulgences. This was part of a large undertaking by which Leo X hoped to finance completion of St. Peter's Cathedral in Rome. Tetzel used every appeal to crowds of the country people around Wittenberg, begging them to aid their deceased loved ones and repeating the slogan "A penny in the box, a soul out of purgatory."[3] Luther and many other Germans detested Tetzel's

This map illustrates the geographical patterns of the Protestant Reformation. Lutheranism spread through German-speaking areas along the Baltic Sea but rarely crossed the Rhine River. The spread of Calvinism defies linguistic explanations.

In this sixteenth-century satirical engraving, Johan Tetzel, mounted on a donkey, blessed by the dove of peace, and aided by angels, arrives to sell indulgences. He was reputed to have said that "as soon as coin in coffer rings, the soul to heaven springs."

methods and his Roman connections. The reformer also rejected Tetzel's Dominican theology, which differed from Augustinian beliefs.

Luther's statements were soon translated from Latin into German and published in all major German cities. They denied the pope's ability to give salvation and declared that indulgences were not necessary for a contrite and repentant Christian. The resulting popular outcry forced Tetzel to leave Saxony, and Luther was almost immediately hailed as a prophet, directed by God to expose the pope and a grasping clergy. His message was so well received because it combined a passionate loyalty to religious traditions and a pragmatic acceptance of social change. It satisfied those who wanted a return to simple faith; it also appealed to those, like the humanists, who fought church abuses and irrationality. Luther's message also provided an outlet for German resentment against Rome, and it gave encouragement to princes seeking political independence.

At first, however, Luther proceeded cautiously, as a reformer rather than a revolutionary. Despite such caution, he was soon in trouble. Although Rome was not immediately alarmed, the Dominicans levied charges of heresy against their Augustinian competitor. Having already begun his defense in a series of pamphlets, Luther continued in 1519 by debating the eminent theologian John Eck (1486–1543) at Leipzig. There Luther denied the infallibility of the pope and church councils, declared the Scriptures to be the sole legitimate doctrinal authority, and proclaimed that salvation could be gained only by faith. The next year, Luther was excom-

municated by the pope. Charles V, only recently crowned emperor and aware of Luther's growing following among the princes, afforded the rebellious monk an audience before the Imperial Diet at Worms in 1521, where Luther publicly refused to recant any of his stated principles. The Diet finally declared him an outcast. But by this time his message had spread by the 300,000 copies of his 30 works printed between 1517 and 1520, and he was a German hero.

Soon afterward, as he left Worms, Luther was secretly detained for his own protection in Wartburg Castle by Elector Frederick of Saxony, his secular lord. When the pope issued a decree requiring that he renounce his heretical views, Luther burned the document—unlike the unfortunate Hus, who himself was

Martin Luther and the Wittenberg Reformers, *by Lucas Cranach the Younger. That Martin Luther (left) and other Protestant reformers did not suffer the same fate as John Hus a century earlier was largely due to the political support of rulers such as the Elector Frederick of Saxony (center).*

Lucas Cranach the Younger, German, 1515–1586, Martin Luther and the Wittenberg Reformers (1926.55) c. 1543, oil on panel, 27⅜ × 15⅝ in. (72.8 × 39.7 cm.) The Toledo Museum of Art; Toledo, Ohio; Purchased with funds from the Libbey Endowment, Gift of Edward Drummond Libbey.

Martin Luther at the Diet of Worms

In April 1521, Emperor Charles V called the Imperial Diet into session to hear Luther's defense of statements against church teachings and the papal authority. Luther's refusal to recant resulted in his being put under an imperial ban aimed at enforcing the pope's bull of excommunication.

Most Serene Lord Emperor, Most Illustrious Princes, Most Gracious Lords . . . I have thought and written in simplicity of heart, solely with a view to the glory of God and the pure instruction of Christ's faithful people. . . .

Your Imperial Majesty and Your Lordships; I ask you to observe that my books are not all of the same kind.

There are some in which I have dealt with piety in faith and morals with such simplicity and so agreeably with the Gospels that my adversaries themselves are compelled to admit them useful, harmless, and clearly worth reading by a Christian. . . . If I should begin to recant here, what, I beseech you, should I be doing but condemning, alone among mortals, that truth which is admitted by friends and foes alike, in an unaided struggle against universal consent?

The second kind consists in those writings levelled against the papacy. . . . If then I recant these, the only effect will be to add strength to such tyranny, to open not the windows but the main doors to such blasphemy, which will thereupon stalk farther and more widely than it has hitherto dared. . . .

The third kind consists of those books which I have written against private individuals. . . . But it is not in my power to recant them, because that recantation would give that tyranny and blasphemy an occasion to lord over those whom I defend and to rage against God's people more violently than ever. . . .

And so, through the mercy of God, I ask Your Imperial Majesty, and Your Illustrious Lordships, or anyone of any degree, to bear witness, to overthrow my errors, to defeat them by the writings of the Prophets or by the Gospels; for I shall be most ready, if I be better instructed, to recant any error, and I shall be the first in casting my writings into the fire. . . .

Thereupon the Orator of the Empire, in a tone of upbraiding, said that this answer was not to the point, and that there should be no calling into question of matters on which condemnations and decisions had before been passed by Councils. He was being asked for a plain reply, without subtlety or sophistry, to this question: Was he prepared to recant, or no?

Luther then replied: Your Imperial Majesty and Your Lordships demand a simple answer. Here it is, plain and unvarnished. Unless I am convicted of error by the testimony of Scripture or (since I put no trust in the unsupported authority of Pope or of councils, since it is plain that they have often erred and often contradicted themselves) by manifest reasoning I stand convicted by the Scriptures to which I have appealed, and my conscience is taken captive by God's word, I cannot and will not recant anything, for to act against our conscience is neither safe for us, nor open to us.

On this I take my stand. I can do no other. God help me. Amen.

From Henry Bettenson, ed., *Documents of the Christian Church* (New York: Oxford University Press, 1963), pp. 280–283.

burned for lack of a protector for having said many of the same things a century earlier.

At Wartburg Luther set his course for life as he began organizing an evangelical church distinct from Rome. He also translated the Bible from Latin into German and composed the sermons that would be repeated in hundreds of Lutheran pulpits all over Germany and Scandinavia. Soon he was able to leave Wartburg. He took off his clerical habit in 1523 and two years later married a former nun, Katherine von Bora, who bore him six children, raised his nieces and nephews, managed his household, secured his income, entertained his colleagues, and served as his supportive companion.

As his church grew and sustained its independence, Luther became more confident and strident, pouring verbal abuse on his enemies in 156 works published between 1530 and 1535. His attacks against Jews, Catholics, and even other Protestants became increasingly violent and vulgar in his old age. He died in 1546, pleased to see his church firmly established but disappointed by its meager spiritual accomplishments.

The Lutheran Church

Although he denounced much of the formality and ritual of the Catholic Church, Luther spent much of his time after the Diet of Worms building a new church for his followers. It reflected his main theological differences with Rome but kept many traditional ideas and practices. These were not always dictated by Luther or by the Protestant rulers among the princes; in many cases former Catholic congregations organized themselves into Lutheran churches and influenced secular authorities to go along. Luther was protected by Elector Frederick, who was above all a practical politician.

The fundamental principle of the Lutheran creed was that salvation occurred through faith, that Christ's sacrifice alone could wash away sin. This departed from the Catholic doctrine of salvation by faith and good works, which required conformance to prescribed dogma and participation in rituals. Along with the Lutheran emphasis on faith went belief in an all-powerful and all-knowing God beyond the rational understanding of depraved human sinners. A Christian, according to Luther, could experience God and gain salvation only through personal faith in Christ and the revealed word of the Scriptures.

Following these basic tenets, Lutheranism rejected much of the Catholic ritual. It abandoned all sacraments not mentioned in the New Testament, retaining only baptism and the Eucharist. The Catholic Mass became the Lutheran Communion, involving all who attended services and requiring no priestly blessing to transform the bread and wine into Christ's body and blood, which in Lutheran theory automatically "coexisted" with the wafer and the wine. Other changes included church services in German instead of Latin, an emphasis on preaching, the abolition of monasteries, and the curtailment of formal ceremonies foreign to the personal experiences of ordinary people.

The Lutheran Church claimed to be a "priesthood of all believers" in which each person could receive God directly or through the Scriptures. This required accurate translation of the Bible from Greek and Roman sources, a humanist achievement that Luther hailed, but he saw no absolute need for clerical mediation between a Christian and God. Ordained clergymen and lay members were equally responsible for keeping the faith, helping others, and saving their own souls. Luther saw a clerical hierarchy as at best a necessary evil. Having denied papal infallibility and Catholic clerical privileges, he followed the same principles in dealing with his own hardworking and often impoverished preachers.

Luther's ideas on marriage and Christian equality promised women new opportunities, which were only partly realized. He stressed the importance of wives as marriage partners for both the clergy and the laity. Contrary to Catholic doctrine, he even condoned divorce in cases of adultery and desertion. During the 1520s his views drew numerous women, including his own wife, to Wittenberg, where they found refuge from monasteries or Catholic husbands. Some Lutheran women became wandering preachers, but they evoked protests from male ministers and legal prohibitions from many German municipal councils, including those of Nuremberg and Augsburg. Although teaching that women were equal to men in opportunities for salvation and in their family roles, in his later writings Luther described them as subordinate to their husbands and not meant for the pulpit.

Despite his prejudices against hierarchies, Luther established a church organization as well as a doctrine. Each congregation was charged with disciplining its members in the faith and maintaining schools, with approved catechisms (summaries of religious principles), for the moral and religious education of children. At first each congregation conducted its own affairs, but by the late 1520s Luther saw a need for a governing bureaucracy to maintain unity of faith and combat ignorance of the Scriptures. This led to a central committee in Saxony whose members visited and instructed the congregations. Ultimately, each of the four Saxon districts was put under a superintendent. This Saxon system became the model for subsequent Lutheran state churches in Germany and Scandinavia.

More than has been commonly realized, this early Lutheranism was a religion of resignation and suffering. Luther believed that the end of the world was near at hand, a time when the devil would reign supreme before the day of final judgment. In this "end-time," Christians would be required to endure the most intense miseries as testimony of their faith. They would resist when that faith was threatened, but in other ordinary secular affairs they were obliged to obey authority. Thus Lutheranism recognized two main spheres of human obligation: the first and highest was to God; the other involved a subordinate loyalty to earthly governments, which also existed in accordance with God's will.

The Political Orientation and Effects of Lutheranism

Luther's idea of "two kingdoms," one of God and one of the world, fit well with contemporary political conditions, winning him support from German and Scandinavian rulers while wedding his movement to dynastic nationalism. Although he was sincere in his anticipation of the end-time, he was also aware of the need to protect his church, which he achieved by political cooperation with the elector of Saxony and other German Protestant princes. Under pressure in the 1530s he even wrote and spoke for armed resistance in what he regarded as holy causes. Thus the Lutheran political orientation helped shape emerging national monarchies.

Because his church depended on Saxon electors to protect him from execution and to give him money, Luther was naturally inclined to identify his religion with secular authority. He was also innately conservative, fearful of "the mob" and full of genuine respect for divinely appointed rulers. Although his pleas for equal treatment of children diminished the practice of primogeniture and fragmented Protestant states, Luther strongly supported their rulers. He accepted state churches that enforced the true faith, advocated government efforts to punish idleness while aiding the deserving poor, and favored mercantilist control of the economy to effect communal welfare and enhance state power.

Luther's political orientation was more clearly revealed in 1522 and 1523 during a rebellion of German knights. Seeing themselves ruined by decaying manorialism, these lesser nobles sought an alliance with the emperor against their common enemies: Rome, the princes, and the free cities. Led by ultranationalists such as Ulrich von Hutten and Franz von Sickingen, they attacked the archbishop of Trier while proclaiming their Lutheranism. When Lutheran support was not forthcoming, the rebellion was quickly crushed. Luther took no part in the struggle but was embarrassed by opponents who claimed his religion threatened law and order.

A better example of Luther's political and social conservatism was provided by a general revolt of peasants and discontented townsmen in 1524 and 1525. Encouraged by Lutheran appeals for Christian freedom, the rebels drew up petitions asking for religious autonomy. One group, led by a former Luther ally, Thomas Muntzer (1489–1525), proclaimed that direct revelation was superior to biblical authority. Other demands called for ending serfdom, tithes, enclosure of common lands, excessive rents, high taxes, and harsh punishments. At first Luther expressed sympathy for the requests, particularly for each congregation's right to select its own pastor. Then, as violence erupted throughout central Germany in April and May 1525, imperial and princely troops crushed the rebel armies, killing an estimated 90,000 insurgents. Luther had advised rebel leaders to obey the law as God's will; when they turned to war, he penned a virulent pamphlet, *Against the Thievish and Murderous . . . Peasants.* In it he called on the princes to "knock down, strangle, . . . stab, . . . and think nothing so venomous, pernicious, or Satanic as an insurgent."[4] By this policy he guaranteed his princely support but lost his earlier appeal to the lower classes in country and town.

His alliance with German princes and city councils marked a turning point in the Lutheran political orientation and in its rising success. After this time Lutheran pamphleteers placed heavier emphasis on discipline in church and society. Luther posed as a religious adviser to rulers and often told them what they wanted to hear, as when he approved Philip of Hesse's bigamous marriage. Converted rulers often accepted his advice to their own disadvantage, as when they refused Catholic benefices for their sons or willed away their family lands among many quarreling heirs. In the main, however, Lutheranism aided state-building by ending the Catholic dominance of law, courts, and revenues while providing popular religious support for government. In return Lutheranism was favored by numerous patrician urban oligarchies and by a coterie of Protestant princes. Often the benevolent authorities were women, such as Elizabeth, duchess of Brunswick (1510–1558). These earthly lords provided Luther with respect, political concessions, and security from Catholic persecution. Without them, his life and his movement would have been doomed.

This dependence was soon very evident as the movement precipitated a struggle for religious control in Germany between the emperor and the Lutheran princes. When Catholics sought to impose conformity in Imperial Diets during the late 1520s, Lutheran leaders drew up a formal protest (hence the appellation *Protestant*). After this Augsburg Confession (1530) was rejected, the Lutheran princes organized for defense in the Schmalkaldic League. Because Charles V was preoccupied with the French and the Turks, open hostilities were minimized, but a sporadic civil war dragged on until after Luther's death in 1546. It ended at the Peace of Augsburg in 1555, when the imperial princes were permitted to choose between Lutheranism and Catholicism in their state churches, thus increasing their independence of the emperor. In addition, Catholic properties confiscated before 1552 were retained by Lutheran principalities, which provided a means for financing their policies. Although no concessions were made to other Protestant groups, such as the Calvinists, this treaty shifted the European political balance against the empire and the church.

Outside Germany, Lutheranism furnished a religious stimulus for developing national monarchies in Scandinavia. There as in Germany, rulers welcomed not only Lutheran religious ideas but also the chance to acquire confiscated Catholic properties. They were especially glad to have ministers preaching obedience to constituted secular authority. In Sweden, Gustavus Vasa (1523–1560) used Lutheranism to lead a successful struggle for Swedish independence from Denmark. In turn, the Danish king, who also ruled Norway, issued an ordinance in 1537 establishing the national Lutheran Church, with its bishops as salaried officials of the state. Throughout eastern Europe, wherever there was a German community, the Lutheran church spread—for a brief time even threatening the supremacy of the Catholic Church in Poland and Lithuania.

The Protestant Reformation in England

England was affected by the crises and changes of the fourteenth and fifteenth centuries along with the rest of Europe. And English theologians such as John Wyclif played an active role in the intellectual and theological debates of the High Middle Ages and after. During the fifteenth century, as on the Continent, there was an active underground church, the Lollards, in which laypeople, especially women, played an important role. Unlike central Europe, England was one of the new "Atlantic states" characterized by national monarchies, centralized authority, and greater independence from the papacy. The Tudor dynasty adapted itself to the new conditions after the Hundred Years' War with France and the devastating Wars of the Roses, which depopulated the traditional nobility. During this time of difficult transition it was necessary that each king and queen raise a strong and healthy heir to ensure the continuity of the Tudor dynasty and the strength of England.

Henry VIII (1509–1547) became the heir to the English throne when his brother, Arthur, died in 1502. It had not been expected that he would be king, and his education ran to that of a true Renaissance man: he showed talent in music, literature, philosophy, jousting, hunting, and theology. Not only did he become the king of England on his father's death in 1509, but he also soon married the woman who had been his brother's wife, thus continuing the dynastic alliance with Spain. Henry was a devout Roman Catholic who gained the title "Defender of the Faith" from the pope for a pamphlet he wrote denouncing Luther and his theology. But as one of the strongest kings in a century of powerful monarchs (Charles V, Philip II, Francis I, Sultan Suleiman, Ivan IV, and eventually Henry's own daughter, Elizabeth I), he knew that his primary duty was to ensure his dynasty's continuity and with it his nation's well-being.

Henry's immediate problem in the 1520s was the lack of a male heir. After 11 years of marriage, he had only a sickly daughter and an illegitimate son. His queen, Catherine of Aragon (1485–1536), after four earlier pregnancies, gave birth to a stillborn son in 1518, and by 1527, when she was 42, Henry had concluded that she would have no more children. His only hope for the future of his dynasty seemed to be a new marriage with another queen. This, of course, would require an annulment of his marriage to Catherine. In 1527 he appealed to the pope, asking for the annulment.

Normally, the request would probably have been granted; the situation, however, was not normal. Because she had been the wife of Henry's brother, Arthur, Catherine's marriage to Henry had necessitated a papal dispensation, based on her oath that the first marriage had never been consummated. Now Henry professed concern for his soul, tainted by living in sin with Catherine. He also claimed that he was being punished, citing a passage in the Book of Leviticus that predicted childlessness for the man who married his dead brother's wife. The pope was sympathetic and certainly aware of an obligation to the king, who had strongly supported the church. However, granting the annulment would have been admission of papal error, perhaps even corruption, in issuing the dispensation. Added to the Lutheran problem, this would have doubly damaged the papacy.

A more formidable problem for Henry was Catherine. She was a cultured Spanish woman, a respected consort, and a devoted wife, who had successfully conducted a war against Scotland when he was campaigning in France and had borne their failured attempts to produce a son with admirable Christian patience. Henry recognized her strong character in his daughter, Mary (1516–1558), whom he appointed princess of Wales and heir apparent in the absence of a prince. As late as the mid-1520s, he sought Catherine's companionship and her counsel. Henry soon learned, however, that Catherine would never accept an annulment, and he was afraid she might lead a rebellion against him. As the aunt of Charles V, whose armies occupied Rome in 1527, she was also able to exert considerable pressure on the pope.

Despite these difficulties, Henry could hope for success in his appeal to the pope. He was vigorous, handsome, and popular. Any conflict with Rome was in accord with national pride, often expressed in traditional resentment against Roman domination. Late medieval English kings had challenged the popes over church appointments and revenues. More than a century and a half before Luther, Oxford professor John Wyclif had denounced the false claims of popes and bishops. In more recent times, English Christian humanists, such as Sir Thomas More, had criticized the artificialities of Catholic worship. Thus when the pope delayed a decision, Henry was relatively secure in his support at home.

The Political Reformation

During the three years after 1531, when Catherine saw him for the last time, Henry took control of affairs. Sequestering his daughter and his banished wife in separate castles, he forbade them from seeing each other. He also intimidated the clergy into proclaiming him head of the English church "as far as the law of Christ allows," extracted from Parliament the authority to appoint bishops, and designated his willing tool, Thomas Cranmer (1489–1556), as archbishop of Canterbury. In 1533 Cranmer pronounced Henry's marriage to Catherine invalid, at the same time that he legalized his union with Anne Boleyn, a lady of the court who was carrying his unborn child, the future Elizabeth I. Cruelly, Henry even forced his daughter Mary to accept him as head of the church and admit the illegality of her mother's marriage—by implication acknowledging her own illegitimacy. Parliament also ended all payment of revenues to Rome. Now, having little other choice, the pope excommunicated Henry, making the breach official on both sides.

Amid a marked anti-Catholic campaign in the 1530s, Henry secured the Anglican establishment, which became an engine for furthering royal policies, with his henchmen controlling every function, from the building of chapels to the wording of the liturgy. Former church revenues, including more than 40,000 pounds sterling per year from religious fees alone, poured into the royal treasury. In 1539 Parliament completed its seizure of monastery lands and the wealth of pilgrimage sites such as Canterbury Cathedral, selling some for revenue and dispensing others to secure the loyalties of crown supporters. Meanwhile, Catholics suffered. Dispossessed nuns, unlike monks and priests, could find no place in the new church and were often reduced to despair. One, the famous "holy maid of Kent," who dared to rebuke the king publicly, was executed, as were other Catholic dissidents including former chancellor Sir Thomas More and the saintly Bishop Fisher of Rochester. And later there were Protestant martyrs. Perhaps the most notable was Anne Askew, a woman of Lincolnshire, who was tried before a church court for heresy and so confounded her judges that she became a legend. She was nevertheless burned in 1546, a year before Henry died.

The new Anglican Church, however, brought about little change in doctrine or ritual. The Six Articles, Parliament's declaration of the new creed and ceremonies in 1539, reaffirmed most Catholic theology except papal supremacy. Henry, in his later years, after the decapitation of Anne Boleyn on charges of adultery in 1536 (ironically, the year of the death of Catherine of Aragon), grew increasingly suspicious of popular Protestantism, which built on the centuries-old bases established by Wyclif and others and was spreading into England and Scotland from the Continent. He refused to legalize clerical marriage, which caused great hardships among many Anglican clergymen, including some bishops, and their wives.

Henry finally gained a male heir with his third wife, Jane Seymour, who died giving birth to Edward VI in 1537. His final three wives reflected the religious politics of the time. He married the homely Anne of Cleves in 1539 to consolidate an alliance with Lutheran princes but divorced her the next year. His fifth wife, Catherine Howard, was put forward by the party displeased by the rapid pace of the English Reformation, but she was decapitated two years later in 1542 on charges of adultery. The sixth, Catherine Parr, was sympathetic to the reformers and narrowly escaped the king's displeasure by humbly appealing to his vanity.

The Turmoil of Extremes

In the decade after Henry's death, religious fanaticism brought social and political upheaval. For six

Holbein's portrait of Henry VIII, painted in 1542, shows a man sure of himself in his royal setting. He had by this time broken with Rome, married six times in pursuit of a legitimate male heir, and turned England into a major naval power. What the portrait does not show is all of the suffering and discord he left in his wake.

years during growing political corruption, extreme Protestants ruled the country and dominated the frail young king, Edward VI (1547–1553). When Edward died in 1553, Mary Tudor came to the throne and strove to restore Catholicism until her death in 1558.

In Edward's reign the government was controlled by the Regency Council, dominated first by the duke of Somerset and then after 1549 by his rival, the duke of Northumberland. While the council members furthered their own ambitions, many parishes were engulfed by a wave of radical Protestantism, which weakened religious traditions. Foreign refugees contributed to the unrest, although many were led by English sympathizers like Catherine Willoughby, duchess of Suffolk, and other Protestant court ladies. Starting slowly under Somerset and moving faster under Northumberland, the government sought political support by courting the religious dissidents. It repealed the Six Articles, permitted priests to marry, replaced the Latin service with Cranmer's English version, and adopted the Forty-Two Articles, an embodiment of extreme Protestantism. Such policies frightened Catholics, but there were only two religious burnings, neither involving Catholics.

Harsh persecutions of Protestants marked the reign of Mary Tudor. Although known in Protestant history as "Bloody Mary," the new queen possessed many admirable qualities, including dignity, intelligence, compassion, and a strong moral sense, but she was handicapped by a religious obsession and by her hopeless love for her Catholic husband, Philip II, king of Spain, who married her in 1554, courteously abandoned her soon after, and returned only once, briefly, to ask her aid in furthering his diplomacy. At first successful in putting down rebellion, Mary squandered her early popularity by imposing her will on a divided people. This involved restoring the Catholic church service, proclaiming papal authority, forging a Spanish alliance, and burning 300 Protestants, including Cranmer and two other bishops. Most victims, however, were of the middle and lower classes; 55 of these were women, and two were blind girls. Mary died pitifully, rejected by her husband and people but unmoved from her determined hope to save English Catholicism. Leaving no heir, she was compelled to name Elizabeth, her half-sister, as her successor.

The Protestant Reformation in Switzerland, France, and the Rhine Valley

A very different variety of church reforms took place in Switzerland, France, and the Rhine valley. The leaders of these reforms were conscious of the state, but not dominated by it, as the Anglicans were. Like the Lutherans, they were also concerned for the salvation of their souls, but in a much more doctrinal and often vindictive way. Calvinism was the most popular and the most conservative of these, but there were many others, including multiple forms of Anabaptism. All of them went farther than Lutheranism and Anglicanism in rejecting Catholic dogma and ritual. They were also marked by their fanaticism in pursuing objectives. Generally, they were opposed to monarchy, but their position did not become very apparent until they were deeply involved in religious wars after 1560, when they often found themselves under attack by both the Catholics and the Lutherans.

Popular Protestantism arose early in Switzerland, where many of the same conditions found in Germany favored its growth. During the late medieval period the country prospered in the growing trade between Italy and northern Europe. Busy Swiss craftsmen and merchants in such cities as Zurich, Bern, Basel, and Geneva suffered under their Habsburg overlords and by papal policies, particularly the sale of indulgences. In 1499 the Confederation of Swiss Cantons won independence from the Holy Roman Empire and the Habsburgs. To many Swiss this was also a first step in repudiating outside authority.

The Swiss Reformation began in Zurich, shortly after Luther published his theses at Wittenberg. It was led by Ulrich Zwingli (1484–1531), a scholar, priest, and former military chaplain, who persuaded the city council to create a regime of clergymen and magistrates to supervise government, religion, and individual morality. Zwingli agreed with Luther in repudiating papal in favor of scriptural authority. He simplified services, preached justification by faith, attacked monasticism, and opposed clerical celibacy. More rational than Luther, he was also more interested in practical reforms, going beyond Luther in advocating additional grounds for divorce and in denying any mystical conveyance of grace by baptism or communion; both, to Zwingli, were only symbols. These differences proved irreconcilable when Luther and Zwingli met to consider merging their movements in 1529.

As Zwingli's influence spread rapidly among the northern cantons, religious controversy separated north from south, rural from urban areas, and feudal overlords, both lay and ecclesiastical, from towns within their dominions. When in the 1520s Geneva repudiated its ancient obligations and declared its independence from its local bishop and the count of Savoy, the city became a hotbed of Protestantism, with preachers swarming in from Zurich. Zwingli was killed in the resulting religious war of 1531; the fighting ended quickly in a peace that permitted each Swiss canton to choose its own religion.

John Calvin

Hoping to ensure the dominance of Protestantism in Geneva after the religious wars, local reformers invited John Calvin (1509–1564) to Geneva. Calvin arrived from Basel in 1536. His preaching ultimately won enough followers to make his church the official religion. From Geneva the faith spread widely in all directions after the early 1540s.

Calvin was an uncompromising French reformer, a formidable foe of the ungodly but a caring colleague and minister to humble believers. His mother had died while he was still a child. He had been partly alienated from his father, and a friend of the family sent him to the University of Paris when he was 12. There he began studying theology but later transferred to Orléans, where he took up law. He read some humanist writings, talked to Lutherans, experienced a personal conversion, broke with the church (1534), was suspected of heresy by the authorities, and ultimately fled to Basel. There in 1536 he published the first edition of his *Institutes of the Christian Religion,* an extremely influential theological work that transformed the general Lutheran doctrines into a profoundly rational legal system based around the concept of predestination. It also earned Calvin his invitation to Geneva.

His original plan for a city government there called for domination by the clergy and banishment of all dissidents. This aroused a storm of opposition from both Anabaptists—who believed in adult baptism and separation of church and state—and from the more worldly portion of the population, and Calvin was forced into exile. At Strasbourg he associated with other reformers who helped him refine his ideas and urged him to take a wife. In 1539 he married Idellete de Bures, a sickly widow with two children. She came back to Geneva with him in 1541, when his party regained power. Henceforth, as Protestant refugees packed the city, Idellette managed Calvin's household, took in friends and refugees, nursed him through frequent headaches, tried unsuccessfully to bear his children, and left him bereft when she died in 1549.

Calvin's second regime at Geneva after 1541 involved a long struggle with the city council. His proposed ordinances for the Genevan Church gave the clergy full control over moral and religious behavior, but the council modified the document, placing all appointments and enforcement of law under its jurisdiction. Although recognizing the Bible as supreme law and the *Institutes* as a model for behavior, it did not always act on recommendations from the Consistory, Calvin's supreme church committee. For the next 14 years Calvin fought against public criticism and opposition in the council. He gradually increased his power, however, through support from a stream of Protestant refugees who poured into the city. His influence climaxed after a failed "revolt of the godless" in 1555. From that year until his death in 1564, he dominated the council, ruling Geneva with an iron hand, within the letter but not the spirit of the original ordinances.

Particularly in that later period, the Consistory apprehended violators of religious and moral law, sending its members into households to check every detail of private life. Offenders were reported to secular magistrates for punishment. Relatively light penalties were imposed for missing church, laughing during services, wearing bright colors, dancing, playing cards, or swearing. Religious dissent, however, brought much heavier punishment. The council frequently approved Consistory recommendations by banishing offenders for blasphemy, mild heresies, adultery, or suspected witchcraft. Magistrates sometimes used torture to obtain confessions and often executed heretics, averaging more than a dozen an-

nually as early as the 1540s. Michael Servetus (1511–1553), a Spanish theologian-philosopher and refugee from the Catholic Inquisition, was burned for heresy because he had denied the doctrine of the Trinity.

Calvinism and Its Impact

Before 1555 Calvinism was not a major Protestant movement; indeed, the Peace of Augsburg made no concessions to Calvinist regimes. Yet even that early, when it had gained official status only in Switzerland and the quasi-French state of Navarre, Calvinism exerted its own special appeal and unique impact. Although it shared with Lutheranism a strong dislike of Scholastic theology and a stringent dogmatism, it also perpetuated Calvin's respect for rational precision and his belief in education, along with his will to aggressive resistance whenever the danger of political suppression outweighed his natural inclination to cooperate with secular authorities. Such typical ambiguities between Calvinism and Lutheranism led to differences in theology and politics that helped generate a gulf between the two that has never been bridged.

These differences in theology were subtle but distinct. Calvin accepted Luther's insistence on justification by faith; like Luther, he saw Christian life as a constant struggle against the devil, and he expected a coming divine retribution, an end-time, when God would redress the evils increasing on every side. Calvin also agreed with Luther in seeing God's power as a relief for human anxiety and a source of inner peace. Both reformers believed man to be totally depraved, but Calvin placed greater emphasis on this point, at the same time emphasizing God's immutable will and purpose. If Calvinism, to human minds, seemed contradictory in affirming man's sinful nature and his creation in God's image, this only proved that God's purposes were absolutely beyond human understanding. For depraved humans God required faith and obedience, not understanding.

God's omnipotence was Calvin's cardinal principle. He saw all of nature as governed by a divinely ordained order, discernible to man but governed by laws that God could set aside in effecting miracles as he willed. Carried to its logical conclusion, such ideas produced Calvin's characteristic doctrine of predestination. Since God is all-powerful and all-knowing, he must also know who are to be saved and who are to be damned eternally. The human purpose, then, is not to win salvation, for this has already been determined, but to honor God. Calvin did not profess to know absolutely who were God's chosen, but he believed that some tests might be at least partly successful in identifying the elect: a moral life, a public

John Calvin on God's Omniscience and Predestination

This selection from Calvin's most famous work summarizes one of the two most significant points in his theology. The other was justification by faith.

Of the Eternal Election, by Which God Has Predestined Some to Salvation, and Others to Destruction.

The predestination by which God adopts some of the hope of life, and adjudges others to eternal death, no man who would be thought pious ventures simply to deny; but it is greatly cavilled at, especially by those who make prescience its cause. We, indeed, ascribe both prescience and predestination to God; but we say that it is absurd to make the latter subordinate to the former. When we attribute prescience to God, we mean that all things always were, and ever continue, under his eye; that to his knowledge there is no past or future, but all things are present, and indeed so present, that it is not merely the idea of them that is before him (as those objects are which we retain in our memory), but that he truly sees and contemplates them as actually under his immediate inspection. This prescience extends to the whole circuit of the world, and to all creatures. By predestination we mean the eternal decree of God, by which he determined with himself whatever he wished to happen with regard to every man. All are not created on equal terms, but some are preordained to eternal life, others to eternal damnation; and, accordingly, as each has been created for one or other of these ends, we say that he has been predestined to life or to death. This God has testified, not only in the case of single individuals; he has also given a specimen of it in the whole posterity of Abraham, to make it plain that the future condition of each nation was entirely at his disposal. . . .

We say, then, that Scripture clearly proves this much, that God by his eternal and immutable counsel determined once for all those whom it was his pleasure one day to admit to salvation, and those whom, on the other hand, it was his pleasure to doom to destruction. We maintain that this counsel, as regards the elect, is founded on his free mercy, without any respect to human worth, while those whom he dooms to destruction are excluded from access to life by a just and blameless, but at the same time incomprehensible judgment. In regard to the elect, we regard calling as the evidence of election, and justification as another symbol of its manifestation, until it is fully accomplished by the attainment of glory. But as the Lord seals his elect by calling and justification, so by excluding the reprobate either from the knowledge of his name or the sanctification of his Spirit, he by these marks in a manner discloses the judgment which awaits them. I will here omit many of the fictions which foolish men have devised to overthrow predestination. There is no need of refuting objections which the moment they are produced abundantly betray their hollowness. I will dwell only on those points which either form the subject of dispute among the learned, or may occasion any difficulty to the simple, or may be employed by impiety as specious pretexts for assailing the justice of God.

From "Institutes of the Christian Religion," in Harry J. Carroll et al., eds., *The Development of Civilization* (Glenview, Ill.: Scott, Foresman, 1970), pp. 91–93.

profession of faith, and participation in the two sacraments of baptism and communion.

In Calvin's grand scheme, as laid out precisely in the *Institutes*, his church served to aid the elect in honoring God and preparing the elect for salvation. As communities of believers, congregations were committed to constant war against Satan. They also functioned to spread the Word (Scripture), educate youth, and alleviate suffering among the destitute. Ministers of the church were responsible for advising secular authorities on religious policies and resisting governments that violated God's laws. Within the church, ministers were elected by congregations, under the guidance of experienced pastors, convened in official sessions. Each congregation was required to live by central doctrines but permitted variations in

ritual and ceremony arising from local traditions. Regional elected *synods*, or councils, decided common policies and judged alleged violations by individual churches.

Calvin was particularly ambivalent in his views on government. He believed that all rulers were responsible to God and subject to God's vengeance. But throughout the 1540s, when he was hoping to gain the support of monarchs, he emphasized the Christian duty of obedience to secular authorities. Even then, however, he advised rulers to seek counsel from church leaders, and he ordered the faithful, among both the clergy and the laity, to disregard any government that denied them freedom in following Christ. Although willing to support any political system that furthered the true faith, Calvin always preferred rep-

By the 1560s most of the Rhône valley in France had fallen under Calvinist domination. This painting illustrates a Protestant service in Lyons, France, in 1564. Note that men and women are separated and the believers are seated according to their importance in the town.

resentative government. Later, as a surging Calvinism faced widespread royal opposition, this prejudice remained as a distinct threat to absolute monarchy.

Another ambiguity in Calvin's social thought involved his attitude toward women. Unlike Catholic theologians, he did not cast women in an inferior light. In his mind men and women were equally full of sin, but they were also equal in their chances for salvation. As he sought recruits, Calvin stressed women's right to read the Bible and participate in church services, a promise that attracted women to his movement. At the same time he saw women as naturally subordinate to their husbands in practical affairs, including the conduct of church business. Without female patron saints or priestly confessors, they were now expected to seek protection and moral discipline from their spouses.

Before the Peace of Augsburg, Calvinism made its greatest gains in France, the reformer's own homeland. His message there attracted numerous ambitious nobles and many members of the urban middle classes, who had begun to feel alienated from both church and state. Missionaries from Geneva recruited thousands of these people in a national system of congregations and synods. A large proportion were

women, who worked diligently, not only converting their husbands and families but also founding religious schools, nursing the sick, and aiding the poor. Many educated aristocratic women also promoted the growth of Calvinism. One of them was Margaret of Angoulême, queen of Navarre (1492–1549) and sister of the French king. She often petitioned her brother on behalf of Protestantism and kept reformers at her court, where Calvin was sheltered at one time. Her daughter Jeanne d'Albret (1528–1572), who became queen in 1549, established Calvinism in Navarre. Calvinism also enlisted many French dissident nobles, particularly among the Bourbons, who hoped to use Calvinist support in claiming the French throne. They were part of the aristocratic Huguenot (French Calvinist) clique that included Admiral de Coligny, Jeanne d'Albret, and the Bourbon prince, Louis of Conde.

Calvinism made gains elsewhere but did not win political power. In Italy the duchess of Ferrara copied the Navarre church service for her private chapel while harboring Calvinist refugees; Zofia Olesnicka, the wife of a Polish noble, endowed a local Calvinist church. Strasbourg in the 1530s was a free center for Protestant reformers such as Matthew Zell and his

Margaret of Navarre, a supporter of Protestantism, was the author of the Heptameron, *a collection of tales modeled on Boccaccio's* Decameron.

wife, Katherine, who befriended many Calvinist preachers, including Martin Bucer, a missionary to England during the reign of Edward VI. In the same period John Knox spread the Calvinist message in Scotland. Such efforts, however, were most significant in preparing for later aggressive action.

Anabaptism and the Protestant Sects

Even more extreme than Calvinism were many divergent Protestant splinter groups, each pursuing its own "inner lights." Some saw visions of the world's end, some advocated a Christian community of shared wealth, some opposed social distinctions and economic inequalities, some—the Anabaptists—repudiated infant baptism as a violation of Christian responsibility, and some denied the need for any clergy. Most of the sects emphasized biblical literalism and direct emotional communion between the individual and God. The majority of them were indifferent or antagonistic to secular government; many favored pacifism and substitution of the church for the state.

Women were prominent among the sects. They were usually outnumbered by men, but female sect members in the sixteenth century were marked by their biblical knowledge, faith, courage, and independence. They helped found religious communities, wrote hymns and religious tracts, debated theology, and publicly challenged the authorities. Some preached and delivered prophecies, although such activities were soon suppressed by male ministers. More women than men endured torture and suffered martyrdom. Their leadership opportunities and relative freedoms in marriage, compared to women of other religions, were bought at a high price in hardship and danger.

Persecution of the sects arose largely from their radical ideas, but Catholics and other Protestants usually cited two revolutionary actions. Some radical preachers took part in the German peasants' revolt of the 1520s and shared in the savage punishments that followed. In 1534 a Catholic army besieged Münster, a German city near the southern Netherlands, where thousands of recently arrived Anabaptist extremists had seized control and expelled dissenters. Facing its desperate fate, the regime of saints confiscated property, institutionalized polygamy, and planned to convert the world. John of Leyden, a former Dutch tailor who claimed divine authority, headed a terrorist regime during the final weeks before the city fell. Its defenders suffered horrible tortures and executions.

Among the most damaging charges against the Münster rebels was their reputed sexual excesses and the dominant role played by women in this immorality. Such charges were mostly distortions. The initiation of polygamy, justified by references to the Old Testament, was a response to problems arising from a shortage of men, hundreds of whom had fled the city. Many other men were killed or injured in the fighting. Thus the city leaders required women to marry so that they could be protected and controlled by husbands. Most Anabaptist women accepted the requirement as a religious duty. Although some paraded through the streets, shouting religious slogans, the majority prepared meals, did manual labor on the defenses, fought beside their men, and died in the fighting or at the stake. Most of the original Münster women, however, fiercely resisted forced marriage, choosing instead jail or execution.

For more than a century, memories of Münster plagued the Protestant sects. They were almost immediately driven underground throughout Europe. Their persecution continued long after they had abandoned violence. In time they dispersed over the Continent and to the New World as Mennonites, Quakers, and Baptists, to name only a few denominations. For obvious reasons, voices of the radicals were among the first raised for religious liberty. Their negative experience with governments made them even more suspicious of authority than the Calvinists were. In both the Netherlands and England, they participated in political revolutions and helped frame the earliest written demands for constitutional government, representative institutions, and civil liberties.

Two Edicts Issued by the Elders of Münster

In mid-1534 the Anabaptist regime in the German city of Münster reached its most extreme, as reflected to some extent by these decrees relating to private life and public behavior.

Although all of us in this holy church of [Münster], in whose hearts the law and the will of God are inscribed by the finger of God . . . should readily fulfill them, we, twelve elders of the nation, shall nevertheless summarize them briefly in a list in order that the new state may be protected so that each one may see what to do and what not to do. . . .

The Scripture directs that those who are disobedient and unrepentant regarding several sins shall be punished with the sword:

1. Whoever curses God and his holy Name or his Word shall be killed (Lev. 24).
2. No one shall curse governmental authority (Ex. 22, Deut. 17), on pain of death.
3. Whoever does not honor or obey his parents (Ex. 20, 21) shall die.
4. Servants must obey their masters, and masters must be fair to their servants (Eph. 6).
5. Both parties who commit adultery shall die (Ex. 20, Lev. 20, Matt. 5).
6. Those who commit rape, incest, and other unclean sexual sins should die (Ex. 22, Lev. 20). . . .
7. Avarice is the root of all evil (I Tim. 6).
8. Concerning robbery, you shall not steal (Ex. 20, Deut. 27): Cursed be he who narrows his neighbor's boundary.
9. Concerning fraud and overcharging (I Thess. 4): The Lord will judge this.
10. Concerning lying and defamation (Wisd. [of Sol.] 1): A lying mouth destroys a soul.
11. Concerning disgraceful speech and idle words (Matt. 12): Men must account for every idle word they speak, on the Day of Judgment.
12. Concerning strife, disputes, anger, and envy (Gal. 5, I John 4): Whoever hates his brother is a murderer.
13. Concerning slander, murmuring, and insurrection among God's people (Lev. 19): There shall be no slanderer or flatterer among the people.

. . . Whoever disobeys these commandments and does not truly repent, shall be rooted out of the people of God, with ban and sword, through the divinely ordained governmental authority.

The elders of the congregation of Christ in the holy city of [Münster], called and ordained by the grace of the most high and almighty God, desire that the following duties and articles be faithfully and firmly observed by every Israelite and member of the house of God.

1. What the Holy Scriptures command or prohibit is to be kept by every Israelite at the pain of punishment.
2. Everybody is to be industrious in his vocation and fear God and his ordained government. Government authority does not carry the sword in vain, but it is the avenger of evildoers. . . .
6. Every day from seven to nine o'clock in the morning and from two to four o'clock in the afternoon, six elders are to sit in the market at the appointed place and settle all differences with their decisions. . . .
9. In order to keep the proper order concerning the administration of good, the food-masters are every day to prepare dishes of the kind as was hitherto customary for the brothers and sisters. These are to sit modestly and moderately at separate tables. They must not demand anything apart from what is served to them. . . .
30. A baptized Christian is not to converse with any arriving person or pagan stranger and is not to eat with him, lest there arise the suspicion of treacherous consultation. . . .

From Lowell H. Zuck, ed., *Christian and Revolution* (Philadelphia: Temple University Press, 1975), pp. 95–97.

The Catholic Counter-Reformation

The era of the Protestant Reformation was also a time of rejuvenation for the Roman Catholic Church. This revival was largely caused by the same conditions that had sparked Protestantism. Many sincere and devout Catholics had recognized a need for reform through-

out the fifteenth century, and they had begun responding to the abuses in their church before Luther acted at Wittenberg. Almost every variety of reform opinion developed within the Catholic Church. Erasmus, More, and other Christian humanists provided an impetus for Luther but refused to follow him out of the Catholic Church. In a category of his own was Savonarola (1452–1498), a Dominican friar, ardent puritan, and mystic, who ruled Florence during the last four years before his death. This "Catholic Calvin" consistently invoked the wrath of God on worldly living and sinful luxuries, criticizing the pope and the clergy in terms more caustic than Luther's. At the other extreme, on the side of the establishment, was Cardinal Ximenes (1437–1517) in Spain, who carried out his own Reformation by disciplining the clergy, encouraging biblical studies, and instilling a new spirit of dedication into the monastic orders.

After the Protestant revolt began, the primary Catholic reformer was Pope Paul III (1534–1549). Coming into office at a time when the church appeared ready to collapse, Paul struggled to overcome the troubled legacy of his Renaissance predecessors and restore integrity to the papacy. Realizing that issues raised by the Protestants would have to be resolved and errors corrected, he attacked the indifference, the corruption, and the vested interests of the clerical organization. In pursuing these reforms he appointed a commission, which reported the need for correcting such abuses as the worldliness of bishops, the traffic in benefices (church appointments with guaranteed incomes), and the transgressions of some cardinals. Their recommendations led Paul to call a church council, an idea that he continued to press against stubborn opposition for more than ten years.

When Paul died in 1549, he had already set the Roman Church on a new path, although his proposed church council had only begun its deliberations. Perhaps his greatest contribution was his appointment of worthy members to the college of cardinals, filling that body with eminent scholars and devout stewards of the church. As a result of his labors, the cardinals elected a succession of later popes who were prepared, intellectually and spiritually, to continue the process of regeneration.

New Troops for the Faith

The spirit of reform was reflected in a number of new Catholic clerical orders that sprang up in the early sixteenth century. Among these were the Theatines, a body of devoted priests who worked to regenerate faith among the clergy. The Capuchins, a revived Franciscan brotherhood, became known for preaching and ministering to the poor and the sick. Societies of women also furthered reform. Some of these, such as the Sisters of the Common Life and the Beguines, continued their work of charity and nursing among the poor from the medieval period into the sixteenth century. The Ursuline order of teaching nuns, founded by St. Angela Merci (1474–1540), educated girls in morality and the faith. Even more renowned were the Carmelites, founded by St. Teresa of Avila (1515–1582), whose determination and selfless devotion became legendary. She inspired mystical faith and reforming zeal in written works, such as *Interior Castle* and *The Ladder of Perfection*. Her Carmelite nuns were models of Christian

The devotional works and personal example of St. Teresa of Avila, mystic and visionary, inspired the rebirth of Spanish Catholicism. In 1970 she was proclaimed a doctor of the church, the first woman to be so honored. The sculpture here, The Ecstasy of St. Teresa *(1645–1652), is by the Italian baroque artist Giovanni Bernini.*

charity and compassion who helped restore the pride and integrity of the church.

The most significant of the new orders was the Society of Jesus, whose members are known as Jesuits. It was founded by Ignatius Loyola (1491–1556), a Spanish nobleman and former soldier. While recovering from battle wounds in 1521, he experienced a religious vision similar to the one that transformed Luther. Loyola then became a wandering pilgrim, a self-styled religious teacher, and the author of *Spiritual Exercises*, a work of great psychological insight and Christian inspiration. In 1524 he launched his society at the University of Paris; 16 years later Pope Paul gave it official authorization.

Organized along military lines, with Loyola as general and the pope as commander in chief, the Jesuits were an army of soldiers, sworn to follow orders and defend the faith. As preachers, teachers, confessors, organizers, diplomats, and spies, they took the field everywhere, founding schools and colleges, serving as missionaries on every continent, and working their way into government wherever possible. Their efforts were probably most responsible for the decided check that Protestantism received after the 1560s. They zealously defended Catholicism in France and may be accurately credited with saving Poland and southern Germany for the church. Jesuit missions overseas also helped Spain and Portugal develop their empires. Jesuits played prominent roles after the Council of Trent in reinforcing uniformity and discipline on the church as it faced the Protestant challenge.

The Council of Trent

Pope Paul's reform initiatives were given impetus by the great multinational church council, the first since 1415, which met in three sessions between 1545 and 1563 in the northern Italian city of Trent. Devoting much attention to the external struggle against Protestantism, the council also sought to eliminate internal abuses by ordering changes in church discipline and administration. It strictly forbade absenteeism, false indulgences, selling church offices, and secular pursuits by the clergy. Bishops were ordered to supervise their clergies—priests as well as monks and nuns—and to fill church positions with competent people. The Council of Trent also provided that more seminaries be established for educating priests while instructing the clergy to set examples and preach frequently to their flocks.

Rejecting all compromise, the Council of Trent retained the basic tenets of Catholic doctrine, including the necessity of good works as well as faith for salvation, the authority of church law and traditions, the sanctity of all seven sacraments, the use of only Latin in the Mass, and the spiritual value of indulgences, pilgrimages, veneration of saints, and the cult of the Virgin. The council also strengthened the power of the papacy. It defeated all attempts to place supreme church authority in any general council. When the final session voted that none of its decrees were valid without papal approval, the church became more than ever an absolute monarchy.

The full significance of Trent became evident after the 1560s, when the Catholic reaction to Protestantism acquired new vigor and militancy. Having steeled itself within, the church and its shock troops, the Jesuits, went to war against Protestants and other heretics. The new crusade was both open and secret. In Spain, Italy, and the Netherlands, the Inquisition more than ever before became the dreaded scourge of Protestants and other heretics. Jesuit universities trained scholars and missionaries, who served as both priests and organizers in Protestant countries, such as England. Many died as martyrs, condemned by Protestant tribunals; others suffered similar fates, meted out by pagan authorities in America or Asia. Consequently, Protestantism made no more significant gains in Catholic lands after Trent. Indeed, the geographical scope of Catholicism expanded, particularly overseas.

In this uncompromising and bloody conflict of faiths, women on the Catholic side were both unappreciated heroines and victims. Out of 41 heretics executed in Spain during 1559, some 26 were women. Other Catholic women in Protestant lands faced frustrating problems; some dispossessed nuns, with no place to go were the most stubborn holdouts against secularizing the monasteries. An order of Jesuit nuns became quite active, though it never received papal approval. Their efforts, however, alarmed church leaders. The Council of Trent reaffirmed the prohibition against women preachers; after Trent, the church forced the Ursulines into convents. Catholic prejudice against the female orders is best illustrated by the ordeal of St. Teresa, who struggled for years and was even brought before the Inquisition before her Carmelites were approved.

Impact on the Arts: Mannerism, Baroque, and Rococo

There was no cultural uniformity across Europe from 1500 to 1650, a period of religious and political unrest. By then the Renaissance spirit was beginning to be transformed in Italy but was reaching a climax elsewhere in Europe. Each aspect of the Protestant Reformation had its particular view on the nature and purpose of art. The Counter-Reformation, after the Council of Trent, also polarized European thought and produced spectacular cultural developments. Sometimes reviving religious sensitivities were accompanied by perplexing uncertainties. In other instances lingering Renaissance values coexisted with Protestant Puritanism to fit a middle class and not a noble set of tastes. Such incongruities were indications of a cultural transition, like that in political and social affairs, between medieval and early modern times.

In art and architecture the post-Renaissance transition was reflected in a new style called Mannerism (see Chapter 14). Mannerist painters rejected Renaissance balance and harmony by defying perspective, using asymmetrical designs, and creating bizarre lighting effects. Perhaps the greatest of them was El Greco (1547–1614), who was born in Crete,

The Arts

1472–1553	Lucas Cranach
c. 1525–1569	Pieter Brueghel the Elder
1547–1614	El Greco
1557–1612	Giovanni Gabrieli
1557–1640	Peter Paul Rubens
c. 1564–c. 1638	Pieter Brueghel the Younger
c. 1565–1609	Michelangelo da Caravaggio
1573–1631	John Donne
1598–1680	Giovanni Bernini
1600–1660	Baroque era in art
1606–1669	Rembrandt van Rijn
1608–1674	John Milton

studied in Italy, and settled in Spain. He is known for his imaginative but morbidly ascetic treatment of religious themes, using *chiaroscuro* (strong contrasts of light and shade). Andrea Palladio (1518–1580) exemplified the style in architecture with his Villa Rotonda near Venice, which displays an exaggerated magnificence in its grouping of four identical temple facades on the sides of a square-domed building.

Like art and architecture, trends in music reflected the transition of the era. Both in Italy and in the north, music developed new complexities in keeping with a spirit of gaiety and respect for aesthetic beauty. This was evident in the increase of chordal writing, in the great expansion of tonal ranges, and in the emergence of new secular forms, like the chanson and the madrigal, which often had poetic lyrics. At the other extreme, church music also became very popular. Protestant hymn writing and singing were given high priorities by the reformers. Luther's hymn "A Mighty Fortress Is Our God" is only one example; many others were composed by women, who found this religious outlet when they were prohibited from preaching. Catholic church music was also revolutionized after the Council of Trent ruled that it be less complex and more appealing. The new spirit, simple but emotionally powerful, was well expressed in the masses of Giovanni Palestrina (1525–1594), who has been called the first Catholic church musician.

After about 1600 European culture generated a new artistic style, the baroque. Taken literally, the term means "irregular" and is generally applied to the dynamic and undisciplined artistic creativity of the seventeenth century. At first the baroque style grew out of the Catholic pomp and confidence accompanying the Roman Reformation. Later as the style spread north it became popular at royal courts, where it symbolized the emerging power of the new monarchies. Wherever it showed itself, the baroque approach was likely to exhibit power, massiveness, or dramatic intensity, embellished with pageantry, color, and theatrical adventure. Without the restraints of the High Renaissance or the subjectiveness of Mannerism, it sought to overawe by its grandeur.

Baroque painting originated in Italy and moved north. One of its Italian creators was Michelangelo da Caravaggio (c. 1565–1609), whose bold and light-bathed naturalism impressed many northern artists. The Italian influence was evident in the works of Peter Paul Rubens (1557–1640), a well-known Flemish artist who chose themes from pagan and Christian literature, illustrating them with human figures involved in dramatic physical action. Rubens also did portraits of Marie de' Medici and Queen Anne, at the

El Greco, The Dream of Philip II. *The characteristic art of the seventeenth century was a consciously anti-Renaissance style called Mannerism, which reached its greatest achievements in the works of El Greco, "the Greek." Born in Crete and trained first as a painter of icons, El Greco traveled to Venice and Rome, where he studied the works and techniques of the Italian Renaissance masters. He settled finally in Toledo, Spain. His works combine elements of the Byzantine tradition and Italian Renaissance and Mannerist styles, infused with the intense emotional spiritualism of the Spanish Counter-Reformation.*

French court of Louis XIII. Another famous baroque court painter was Diego Velázquez (1599–1660), whose canvases depict the haughty formality and opulence of the Spanish royal household. A number of Italian women were successful baroque painters, including Livonia Fontana (1552–1614), who produced pictures of monumental buildings, and Artemesia Gentileschi (1593–1652), a follower of Caravaggio.

While the baroque style was profoundly affecting most of Europe, the Dutch were perfecting their own unique artistic genre. It grew directly from their pride in political and commercial accomplishments, emphasizing both the beauty of local nature and the solidity of middle-class life. Dutch painting was sober, detailed, and warmly soft in the use of colors, particularly yellows and browns. Almost every town in the Netherlands supported its own school of painters who helped perpetuate the local traditions. Consequently, many competent artists arose to meet the demand for this republican art.

Only a few painters among hundreds can be cited here. The robust Frans Hals (1580–1666) em-

Peter Paul Rubens, Descent from the Cross. *The muscular figures convey a sense of both physical power and passionate feeling. The elements of the work combine to form a composition of tremendous dramatic force.*

Frans Hals, Malle Babbe *(c. 1650). Hals's technique consisted of economical brushwork, using a few vigorous strokes. The work has the immediacy of a sketch, but in reality it was done with careful precision over a period of hours, not minutes.*

ployed a vigorous style that enabled him to catch the spontaneous and fleeting expressions of his portrait subjects. He left posterity a gallery of types, from cavaliers to fishwives and tavern loungers. His most successful follower, whose works have often been confused with those of Hals, was Judith Leyster (1609–1660), a member of the Haarlem painters guild with pupils of her own. Somewhat in contrast, Jan Vermeer (1632–1675) exhibited a subtle delicacy. His way of treating the fall of subdued sunlight on interior scenes has never been equaled.

Towering above all the Dutch artists, and ranking with the outstanding painters of all time, was Rembrandt van Rijn (1606–1669). While reflecting the common characteristics of his school, he produced works so universally human that they not only expressed Dutch cultural values but also transcended them. His canvases show tremendous sensitivity, depicting almost every human emotion except pure joy. This omission arose partly from his own troubled consciousness and partly from his republican, Calvinist environment. Nevertheless, his work furnished profound insights into the human enigma. He has been called the "Dutch Baroque da Vinci."

Baroque architecture, like painting, was centered in Italy, from whence it permeated western Europe. The most renowned architect of the school in the sev-

Rembrandt van Rijn, Self-Portrait. *The Dutch artist Rembrandt was one of the most gifted painters of all time. His self-portrait, painted late in his life, perfectly captures the simple dignity and quiet resignation of age.*

enteenth century was Giovanni Bernini (1598–1680). He designed the colonnades outside St. Peter's Basilica, where his plan illustrates the baroque style in the use of vast spaces and curving lines. After Bernini, hundreds of churches and public buildings all over Europe displayed the elaborate baroque decorativeness in colored marble, intricate designs, twisted columns, scattered cupolas, imposing facades, and unbalanced extensions or bulges. Stone and mortar were often blended with statuary and painting; indeed, it was difficult to see where one art left off and the other began.

The seventeenth century also brought baroque innovations in music. New forms of expression moved away from the exalted calmness of Palestrina and emphasized melody, supported by harmony. Instrumental music, particularly for the organ and violin, gained equal popularity for the first time with song. Outstanding among baroque innovations was opera, which originated in Italy at the beginning of the century and quickly conquered Europe. The new form combined many arts, integrating literature, drama, music, and painting in elaborate stage settings.

Literature of the baroque age before 1650 showed a marked decline from the exalted heights of the northern Renaissance. Even before 1600, however, Puritanism and the Counter-Reformation in-

clined many writers toward religious subjects. In England this trend continued into the next century and was augmented by a flood of political tracts during the civil war. Religious concerns were typical of the two most prominent English poets, John Donne (1573–1631) and John Milton (1608–1674). Milton's magnificent poetic epic *Paradise Lost* was planned in his youth but not completed until 1667. French literature during the early 1600s was much less memorable. The major advance came in heroic adventure novels, pioneered by Madeleine Scudéry (1608–1701). Most other French writers, influenced by the newly formed French Academy, were increasingly active in salon discussions but were more concerned with form than with substance.

Baroque art and literature somewhat ambiguously expressed the values of this time. In keeping with the prevailing social atmosphere of warring states and their famous rulers, the baroque style emphasized power and grandeur, along with the heroic and the bizarre. But despite its masculine values, the baroque style glorified women in the abstract, at a time when ordinary women were losing social status. This apparent contradiction might be explained by the dominant contemporary roles of famous queens, powerful female regents, and aristocratic salon hostesses.

Wars of Religion and Emergence of the Modern State System

After the 1560s, religious fanaticism, both Protestant and Catholic, combined with pragmatic politics to form a combustible mixture. Sometimes religious conflict caused the reshaping of the old political system to justify movements against royal authority. More often it popularized centralized monarchies, whose rulers promised to restore order by wielding power. Despite pious declarations, kings and generals in this period conducted war with little regard for moral principles; indeed, as time passed they steadily subordinated religious concerns to dynastic ambitions or national interests. This change, however, came slowly and was completed only in 1648 after Europe was thoroughly exhausted by the human suffering and material destruction of religious wars.

Although it ended a short war in Germany, the Peace of Augsburg (1555) failed to end politicoreligious conflict. Even before Calvin died in 1564, his movement was spreading rapidly in France, Scotland, Germany, Poland, Bohemia, and Hungary. The Council of Trent launched a formidable counteroffensive, led by the Jesuits and supported by the Spanish and Austrian Habsburgs, against all Protestants.

Religious and Political Wars

1556–1598	Reign of Philip II of Spain
1558–1603	Reign of Elizabeth I of England
1568	Revolt in the Netherlands
1571	European forces defeat Turks at Lepanto
1572	Massacre of St. Bartholomew's Eve in Paris
1581	Dutch United Provinces declare independence from Spain
1585–1642	Cardinal Richelieu (holds power in France, 1624–1642)
1587	Dutch Republic formed
1588	English defeat Spanish Armada
1589–1616	Reign of Henry IV of France, beginning of Bourbon dynasty
1598	Edict of Nantes guarantees Protestant rights in France
1611–1632	Reign of Gustavus Adolphus in Sweden
1618–1648	Thirty Years' War
1648	Peace of Westphalia

England narrowly avoided the religious civil wars that ended the Valois line in France, the Spanish Netherlands exploded in religious rebellion, and the militant Catholic Reformation suppressed Protestantism in eastern Europe. For decades the politics of religion dominated politics within every European state.

The Spanish Habsburgs' Drive for Dominance

Although it was a relatively small, underdeveloped, and sparsely populated country of 8 million people, Spain under Philip II (1556–1598) was considered the strongest military power in Europe. Seven centuries of resistance against the Arabs during the Reconquista (see Chapter 9) had formed a chilvalric nobility that excelled in the military arts, if not business. This tradition, in addition to the promise of empire, saw the rigidly disciplined Spanish infantry absorb neighboring Portugal and then fan out around the world as *conquistadores* and bring back silver in seemingly unlimited quantities from America. Working in tandem with the army was the Spanish church, with its courts of the Inquisition, which

had earlier banished the Jews and were now being used to eliminate the Moors and Spanish Protestantism. Yet an overworked and overextended bureaucracy and a weak financial, communications, and industrial infrastructure placed the victories gained by the army and the church on a weak foundation.

Philip willingly took on the Habsburgs' global burdens of maintaining Catholic orthodoxy, fighting the Turks, and imposing his will on his troublesome European neighbors. This responsibility was part of Philip's inheritance from his father, Charles V, whose long reign ended in 1556 when he abdicated his imperial throne and entered a monastery. At that time Charles split his Habsburg holdings. His brother Ferdinand, who had governed Austria, Bohemia, and Hungary for Charles, acquired official control of these lands when he was elected Holy Roman Emperor in 1558. Philip received Naples, Sicily, Milan, the Netherlands, Spain, and a vast overseas empire, which was much more lucrative than his father's imperial domain in Germany. Indeed, the division of Habsburg lands appeared to be a blessing for Philip, allowing him to shed his father's worrisome "German problem" and concentrate more effectively on his Spanish realm.

Philip was an obedient, hardworking son and took his father's advice very seriously. A slightly built, somber, and stolid man, he was almost completely absorbed by his awesome official obligations. Charles had warned him about becoming too intimate with subordinates and particularly against trusting or depending on women. Philip heeded this advice. Although he was involved briefly with mistresses, none of them influenced his judgment or policies. The same could be said about his four wives: Maria of Portugal, Mary of England, Elizabeth of France, and his niece, Anne of Austria, all of whom he married for political reasons. Except for Mary, they bore his children but ate at his table only during official banquets. Elizabeth was his favorite, as were her daughters, to whom he wrote notes of tender and loving concern. However, such revelations of his inner feelings were very rare.

Philip made skillful use of his role as defender of the Catholic faith. Although the church owned half the wealth of the country and used the Inquisition to wipe out Protestant and Muslim "heresies," Philip used church policies to enforce Spanish traditions, arouse patriotism, increase his popularity, and strengthen the state. He was by no means a tool of the papacy; indeed, like his father, he defied more than one pope, carefully weighing the costs of papal proposals, particularly military ones, against their benefits. He denied the pope jurisdiction over Spanish ecclesiastical courts, ignored objectionable papal decrees, defied the Council of Trent on clerical appointments in Spanish territories, and fought the Je-

THE HABSBURGS IN EUROPE AFTER THE PEACE OF AUGSBURG, 1555

Spanish Habsburgs
Austrian Habsburgs
Boundary of the Holy Roman Empire

The inherent logic of balance-of-power politics is readily evident in this map showing the extent of Hapsburg—both Spanish and Austrian—holdings.

suits when they challenged his authority. Though a dedicated Catholic and an opponent of heresy, Philip saw the church as an arm of his government and expected its cooperation in return for his support.

Throughout his long reign Philip tried with only moderate success to be an absolute monarch. His councilors, appointed as advisers more than as administrators, submitted most decisions for his resolution. In the Escorial, the cold and somber palace he built north of Madrid, he labored endlessly, reading and annotating his councilors' documents. His attention was directed mainly to Castile, where he nearly achieved complete mastery, issuing royal edicts as law and using the Cortes (the traditional assembly of estates) as a device for measuring public opinion rather than as a legislative body. But such pretensions of centralized government were without much meaning in other parts of Spain. There, as well as in the Netherlands and Italy, proud noble families dominated the assemblies, jealously guarding their privileges and often opposing royal viceroys. They were aided by the weight of tradition, by poor communications, and—in the eastern Spanish kingdoms of Aragon and Catalonia—by the fact that those regions

were so poor it was not worth the effort for Philip to impose strict, centralized rule.

The backward Spanish sociopolitical system caused Philip many economic problems. Tax-exempt nobilities, comprising under 2 percent of the people, owned 95 percent of nonchurch land; the middle classes, overtaxed and depleted by purges of Jews and *Moriscos* (Spanish Muslims), were diminished; and the peasants were so exploited that production of food, particularly grains, was insufficient to feed the population. The use of arable lands for the nobles' sheep runs aggravated the situation. State regulation of industry and trade further limited revenues and forced primary reliance on specie from America, which ultimately brought ruinous inflation. When his income failed to meet expenses, Philip borrowed at rising interest rates. In 1557 and 1575 he had to suspend payments, effectively declaring national bankruptcy.

Revolt of the Netherlands

Philip's centralized rule encouraged some unity in Spain; the Netherlands, with its own traditions, was immediately suspicious of its foreign king. His efforts to enforce Catholic conformity provoked resistance, which ultimately led to the first successful rebellion against a major European monarchy.

This outcome could have been expected. The Netherlands ("Low Countries") at the time also included modern Belgium, Luxembourg, and small holdings along 200 miles of a marshy northern coast, an area not open to easy conquest. The geography promoted strong local nobilities but also relatively independent peasants and townsmen. Even in medieval times cities were centers of rapidly expanding commerce; of the 300 walled towns in 1560, some 19 had populations over 10,000 (England had only three or four that size), and Antwerp was the commercial hub of northern Europe. A resulting independent spirit found early expression in the Reformation, first with Lutheranism, then with Anabaptism, and finally with Calvinism after the 1550s. Charles V had suppressed Protestantism and sporadically burned heretics, but his status as a native son allowed him to preserve a precarious political stability before 1556.

Charles's heavyset, hard-riding daughter, Margaret of Parma (1522–1586), was Philip's first regent for the Netherlands. Like her father, she was also a native of the region who understood her subjects. She was an able administrator, but Philip wasted this asset by ordering her to combat heresy with the Inquisition, a policy that drove the leading nobles from her council and brought increasingly threatening popular protests. For years Philip ignored Margaret's frantic appeals for leniency before finally permitting her to dismiss the hated Cardinal Granville from her government. Despite this belated concession, public clamor against the execution of Protestants continued; the so-called Calvinist Fury in 1566 terrorized Catholics and desecrated 400 churches.

Although the public reaction to these Calvinist outrages provided new support for Margaret, Philip was unimpressed. He dispatched the duke of Alva to the Netherlands with 10,000 Spanish troops, a great baggage train, and 2000 camp followers. Alva removed Margaret from her regency and clamped a brutal military dictatorship on the country. By decree he centralized church administration, imposed new taxes, and established a special tribunal, soon dubbed the Council of Blood, to stamp out treason and heresy. During Alva's regime between 1567 and 1573, at least 8000 people were killed, including the powerful counts of Egmont and Horne. Women and children were often victims. In 1568 one woman was executed because she had refused to eat pork, and an 84-year-old woman whose son-in-law had aided a heretic was condemned at Utrecht. In addition to such atrocities the Catholic terror deprived 30,000 people of their property and forced 100,000 to flee the country.

By 1568 Alva's excesses had provoked open rebellion, led by William of Orange (1533–1584), nicknamed William the Silent. He was a wealthy noble, with holdings in Germany and France as well as in the Low Countries provinces of Holland and Brabant. Born of Lutheran parents, he had been raised a Catholic at the court of Charles V. He had served Charles as an official before 1556 and participated in the abdication ceremony that made Philip king. William only reluctantly became a rebel. His gradual ideological transformation is illustrated by his four marriages. The first two, before 1561, were for status and convenience; the last two, after 1577, were to Charlotte de Bourbon and Louise de Coligny, both leading Huguenots who served him as committed partners in a religious cause.

Until 1579 William persevered through terrible adversities. Constant early defeats left him impoverished and nearly disgraced, but in 1572 the port of Brielle fell to his privateers, the "sea beggars," an event that triggered revolts throughout the north. Soon thereafter William cut the dikes near Zeeland, mired down a weary Spanish army, and forced Alva's recall to Spain. The continuing war was marked by savage ferocity, such as the sack of Antwerp by mutinous Spanish soldiers (1576). At the Spanish siege of Maestricht (1579), women fought beside their men on the walls, and Spanish soldiers massacred the population, raping women first before tearing some limb from limb in the streets. That same year in the Pacification of Ghent, Catholics and Protestants from the 17 provinces united to defy Philip, demand the recall of his army, and proclaim the authority of their traditional assembly, the States General.

Unfortunately for the rebel cause, this unity was soon destroyed by religious differences between militant northern Calvinists and Catholic southerners, particularly the many powerful nobles. The Spanish commander Alexander Farnese exploited these differences by restoring lands and privileges to the southern nobles. He was then able to win victories that induced the ten southern provinces to make peace with Spain in 1579. The Dutch, now alone, proclaimed their continued resistance to Spanish persecution and in 1581 declared their independence from Spain. They persisted after William was assassinated in 1584, while the Spanish continued their war on heresy, hanging, butchering, burning, and burying alive Protestants who would not renounce their faith. This cruelty lasted until a truce was negotiated in 1609.

Religious Wars in France

Although frustrated in the Netherlands, Philip did not face his father's French problem. By the Treaty of Cateau-Cambrésis in 1559, France gave up claims in

Italy and the Netherlands. This humiliating surrender to the Habsburgs marked a definite turning point in French history. With its government bankrupt, its economy nearly prostrate, and its people disillusioned, France lost its leverage in foreign affairs as internal dissension encouraged by Philip wasted the country during the next four decades.

Beneath the prevailing religious contention was another bitter struggle between the haves and the have-nots. High prices, high rents, and high taxes drove the lower classes to riot and rebel against urban oligarchies, noble landlords, and government tax collectors. The social unrest continued sporadically throughout the sixteenth century. It brought no improvement of conditions for suffering peasants and town artisans, but it did badly frighten the wealthy nobles, merchants, and bankers, whose mildly divergent interests were unified by threats from below.

By the 1560s Calvinism had become a major outlet for the frustrations of the discontented. Although outlawed and persecuted earlier, the movement grew rapidly during the decade. It converted approximately 15 percent of the population, most of whom were of the lower urban middle class; however, the leadership came mainly from the nobility, 40 to 50 percent of whom accepted Calvinism. Their motives varied; although many were sincerely religious, most pursued political ends. Even among lesser nobles Calvinism promised military employment, political prominence, and a way for redirecting popular discontent. The movement's potential popular support was particularly appealing to contenders for the throne among the high nobility. In 1559 the Huguenots held a secret synod in Paris that drew representatives from 72 congregations and a million members. Admittedly a distinct minority, they were well organized, with articulate spokesmen and competent military leadership.

Religion and the politics of the high nobility were closely joined after 1559, when King Henry II died, leaving the crown to his sickly 15-year-old son, who became Francis II. The young queen was Mary Stuart (later Mary, queen of Scots), whose uncles, the brothers Guise, assumed control of the government. Their most ambitious opponent was Antoine de Bourbon, a prince by blood and the husband of Jeanne d'Albret, the Calvinist queen of Navarre. The Montmorency family was also opposed to the Guises and was in the process of turning Protestant. Faced with this challenge, the Guises naturally claimed to be champions of the Catholic cause.

Francis died in 1560 and was succeeded by his 9-year-old brother, Charles IX. The real power behind the throne, however, was his mother, Catherine de' Medici. She was a most able woman, single-minded, crafty, ready to use any means but also open to compromise, and determined to save the throne for one of her three sons, none of whom had produced a male heir. Exploiting the split between the Guises and their enemies, she assumed the regency for Charles. She then attempted through reforms of the church to reconcile the differences between Catholics and Protestants. In this endeavor she was unsuccessful, but she retained her tenuous control, using every political strategy, including a squadron of highborn women who solicited information by seducing powerful nobles.

Religious war erupted in 1561; supported by substantial Spanish financial and military interventions, it lasted through eight uneasy truces until 1593. Fanaticism evoked the most violent and inhumane acts on both sides, as destructive raids, assassinations, and torturous atrocities became commonplace. Catherine maneuvered through war and uneasy peace, first favoring the Guises and then the Bourbons. In 1572, fearing that the Huguenots were gaining supremacy, she projected a Guise plot that resulted in the murder of some 10,000 Huguenots in Paris. This Massacre of St. Bartholomew's Eve was a turning point in decisively dividing the country. The final "war of the three Henries" in the 1580s involved Catherine's third son, Henry III, who became king upon the death of Charles IX in 1574. The king's rivals were Henry of Guise and the Protestant Henry of Navarre. When the other two Henries were assassinated, Henry of Navarre proclaimed himself king of France in 1589. Spain would have little to fear from France for the next half century.

Elizabethan England, 1558–1603

For most of the sixteenth century, Spain built its European foreign policies on the base of an English alliance. Despite Henry's breaking his marriage with Catherine of Aragon, the Spanish ambassadors did not give up their efforts to keep England in their camp. For the better part of his reign, Philip had to deal with England's most outstanding monarch, Elizabeth I.

Elizabeth, a superb imagemaker, projected the picture of a country united behind a national church even as her government suppressed Catholicism, put down a northern rebellion, and avoided serious troubles with Scotland or Ireland. Elizabeth dealt with potential dangers from the great Catholic powers, Spain and France, by playing them against each other. Such successes were the natural result of her wisdom and courage. This image only partly reflected reality. The "Protestant Queen" privately detested Protestantism. Her support for Scottish and Dutch rebels violated her fervent inner belief in absolute monarchy. Her celebrated coy approach in encouraging but ultimately denying prospective royal suitors, despite the diplomatic advantages of the practice, often ran counter to her emotional inclinations, throwing her into rages against her advisers.

She was almost incapable of making lasting decisions. But unlike Catherine de' Medici, she had learned from Tudor politics to compromise and discount personal attachments. Consequently, England became her family and her primary interest. She was especially skilled at judging people, dealing with foreign diplomats in their own language, and projecting charisma in public speeches. With these talents she was able to bring the English people a new sense of national pride. In fact, in contrast to France, England seemed to have achieved relative peace and prosperity in the second half of the sixteenth century.

Elizabeth's earliest immediate danger emerged in Scotland, where Mary of Guise was regent for her daughter Mary Stuart, queen of both France and Scotland. French troops in Scotland supported this Catholic regime. Because Mary Stuart was also a direct descendant of Henry VII of England, she was a leading claimant for the English throne and a potential rallying symbol for Catholics who hoped to reestablish their faith in England. These expectations were diminished in 1559 when a zealous Calvinist named John Knox (1505–1572), fresh from Geneva, led a revolt of Scottish nobles. Aided by English naval forces, which Elizabeth delayed and only reluctantly approved, the Scots broke religious ties with Rome, established a Presbyterian (Calvinist) state church, and drove out the French soldiers. Temporarily, Elizabeth had averted disaster.

Another serious problem loomed in Ireland, where Spanish and papal emissaries used old grievances over taxes and religion to arouse uprisings against English rule. James Maurice, an Irish leader in the southwest, began a series of revolts in 1569. Eight years later the pope helped raise troops and money for Maurice on the Continent. An expedition in 1579 to aid the Irish rebels was ruthlessly suppressed, but fighting dragged on for four more years. In 1601 a more serious Irish rebellion, aided by 3000 Spanish troops, cost Elizabeth a third of her revenues up to her death in 1603. Although never directing a successful Irish policy, she managed to escape catastrophe by stubborn persistence.

Her innate pragmatism was most beneficial in quieting English sectarian strife. She despised Puritans and favored rich vestments for the clergy, but she thoroughly understood the practical necessity of securing Protestant political support. Moving firmly but slowly, Elizabeth re-created a nominal Protestant national church but one similar to her father's. It confirmed the monarch as its head, recognized only baptism and communion as sacraments, rejected relic veneration, conducted services in English, and avoided other controversial Protestant tenets. It also retained the old organization, under bishops and archbishops, along with much of the Catholic ritual.

This "Elizabethan compromise" in religion was acceptable to most of the English people.

The queen's policy lessened religious controversy and persecution but failed to end either completely. Nonconformists attacked the establishment in sermons and pamphlets; some, like the Presbyterian minister Thomas Cartwright, were jailed by church courts. Catholics faced more severe persecution and were therefore even more determined and daring. A network of Jesuit priests operated throughout the country, particularly in the north and west, secretly conducting Masses and working with a Catholic political underground. Women played prominent roles among dissidents of both extremes. Protestants, like the duchess of Suffolk and Lady Russell, steadily pressured the queen; Catholic women were the most effective allies of the Jesuits, as evidenced by Margaret Clitherow, who died under torture in 1586 rather than deny her faith.

While dealing with this internal dissension, Elizabeth faced a serious danger from abroad. In 1568 Mary Stuart was forced into exile by her Protestant subjects and received in England by her royal cousin. Although kept a virtual prisoner, she became involved in a series of Catholic plots, which appeared even more dangerous after the pope excommunicated Elizabeth in 1570. Philip of Spain aided the plotters but still hoped to enlist Elizabeth's cooperation in helping him create a Catholic hegemony in Europe.

Despite all her troubles, Elizabeth's reign showed marked economic improvement. By careful financial management, her governments reduced debt and improved the national credit. A new coinage helped make London the financial center of Europe after the collapse of Antwerp. Monopolies granted to joint-stock companies promoted foreign trade and brought specie into the country. Parliamentary acts of 1563 and 1601 standardized laws governing conditions for artisans and relief of the poor. Such positive actions, along with an economy expanding with foreign trade, stimulated agriculture, manufacturing, coal mining, and shipbuilding. By the end of Elizabeth's reign in 1603, England was the most prosperous state in Europe.

If Philip had not assumed the burden of Catholic Orthodoxy, fighting the Turks, and dominating Europe, he could have left well enough alone and compromised with the Dutch, taken pleasure in the self-destructive French civil wars, and continued a patient long-term policy toward England. But he did not have that luxury. His responsibilities and sense of Spain's power drove him to take military action.

The Spanish Bid for Supremacy

Philip's earlier wars against Turkey promoted his image as the Catholic champion, boosted Spanish morale, and revived the traditional national pride in defending the faith. When Cyprus, the last Christian stronghold in the eastern Mediterranean, fell to the Turks in 1570, Philip responded to the pope's pleas and formed a Holy League to destroy Turkish naval power. Spanish and Venetian warships, together with smaller squadrons from Genoa and the Papal States, made up a fleet of over 200 vessels, which drew recruits from all over Europe. In 1571 the Holy League's fleet and the Turkish navy clashed at Lepanto, off the western coast of Greece. The outcome was a decisive victory for Christian Europe; Ottoman sea power would never again be a major threat to Christendom, and Spain could deploy its resources to northwest Europe.

Philip's diplomatic efforts, particularly his marriage to Mary Tudor in 1558, his next marriage to Isabel of Valois in 1560, and his clumsy efforts to court Queen Elizabeth, brought no lasting influence over English or French policies. Indeed, English captains were preying on Spanish shipping in the Atlantic, and Dutch privateers, with English and Huguenot support, were diminishing the flow of vital supplies to northern Europe. In 1580, after nine years of frustration in the Netherlands, Philip launched the first phase of his new offensive policy, using military force to validate his claim to the Portuguese throne. As king of Portugal he gained control of the Portuguese navy and Atlantic ports, where he began assembling an oceangoing fleet, capable of operations against the Dutch and English in their home waters.

Tensions increased in 1585 when Philip signed an alliance with the Guises and sent troops into France. To prevent such an outcome, Elizabeth had been encouraging assorted French dukes to think that she might turn Catholic and marry one of them. She was now especially fearful of a Franco-Spanish invasion from the Netherlands. To delay it she sent token military forces to the Dutch and French Protestants, in addition to the financial aid she was already providing. By 1586 Philip's policies were about to precipitate a major war.

Philip's last hope for an easy solution to his problems was dashed in 1587. Pressed by the pope and the English Catholic exiles, he had tried for years to use Mary Stuart to overthrow Elizabeth, regain England for Catholicism, and seize control of the country, but Mary's complicity in a plot against Elizabeth's life was discovered. Elizabeth, reluctantly convinced that Mary alive was more dangerous than Philip's final frustration, finally signed the death warrant. Mary's execution confirmed Philip's earlier decision that England had to be conquered militarily. In pursuing this end, Philip planned a "great enterprise," an invasion of England blessed by the pope.

The Spanish strategy depended on a massive fleet, known as the Invincible Armada. It was ordered to meet a large Spanish army in the southern Nether-

lands and land this force on the English coast. But in 1588, when the Armada sailed for Flanders, Dutch ships blocked the main ports, preventing the convoying of troops to the Spanish galleons, which could not enter shallow waters. Philip's project was then completely ruined when the smaller and more maneuverable English ships, commanded by Sir Francis Drake, defeated the Armada in the English Channel. A severe storm, the famed "Protestant wind," completed the debacle. After a long voyage around Scotland, the Armada limped back to Spain, having lost a third of its ships. Contrary to English expectations, defeat of the Armada brought no immediate shift of international power. While Spain built new ships and successfully defended its sea lanes, neither side gained dramatic victories. All the major combatants were exhausted, a factor that largely explains the Bourbons' acquisition of the French crown and continued Dutch independence through the 1590s. Lingering war brought new opportunities for France and the Netherlands but only a strength-draining stalemate for England and Spain.

The Balance Sheet of Spanish Failure

During the last decade of Philip's life, his multiple failures foreshadowed the decline of his country. He

An English view of the Spanish Armada shows the pope and the devil plotting the Spanish invasion of England. The engraving is dated 1620.

encountered rebellion in Aragon, quarreled with Pope Clement VIII over recognizing the Bourbons, and sent two more naval expeditions against England, both of which were scattered by storms. In 1598 he gave the southern Netherlands to his favorite daughter, Isabel, and her husband, Archduke Albert, an Austrian Habsburg. Then, before he died in 1598, Philip had to make peace with France. He left Spain bankrupt for the third time during his reign, having wasted the country's considerable resources and sacrificed its future to his dynastic pride. The same poor judgment was even more pronounced in his successor, Philip III (1598–1621), who was lazy, extravagant, and also frivolous. His henchmen increased the already prevalent graft and inefficiency.

Elizabeth experienced similar difficulties. Sea raids on Spanish shipping continued and returned some profits, yet all the grand projects failed, including a fiasco in 1596 when an English naval force, commanded by the earl of Essex, plundered Cadiz but missed the Spanish treasure fleet. Land campaigns in France and the Netherlands, in addition to a continuing rebellion in Ireland, depleted Elizabeth's carefully husbanded resources. When asked for grants, Parliament insisted on debating constitutional questions and hearing Puritan demands for reform of the church. While the old queen grew crotchety, muttering about cutting off heads, the country needed peace. But peace did not come until a year after her death in 1603.

The Dutch, meanwhile, were stumbling toward independence, fearing the advancing Spanish tide in the south, pleading for English or French Protestant aid, and stubbornly persevering. Their declaration of 1581, while displaying what could be interpreted later as democratic rhetoric, reflected more concern for aristocratic privilege and national survival. After failing to find a suitable French or English monarch, the Dutch created a republic in 1587 and held on to sign a truce with Spain in 1609. As time passed, their growing maritime trade and naval power guaranteed their security.

The post-Armada stalemate was most beneficial to war-torn France. With the death of the last Valois claimant in 1589, the Bourbon Protestant king of Navarre was proclaimed king of France as Henry IV. This act threw the Catholic Holy League into a fanatical antiroyalist frenzy and encouraged Philip's military intervention in France to support his daughter's claim to the throne. But English aid and Henry's willingness to turn Catholic led to Philip's withdrawal and the Peace of Vervins in 1598. To pacify the Huguenot minority Henry then issued the Edict of Nantes, which guaranteed the Huguenots some civil and religious rights while permitting them to continue holding more than a hundred fortified towns. Henry thus achieved peace, but the French economy was prostrated, and powerful Protestant armed forces within the country challenged royal authority.

The Thirty Years' War: The Austrian Habsburgs' Quest for Central European Hegemony

By 1600 Spain's golden age had ended, but the religious and political strife of dynasties and nations would continue with even greater intensity. Despite the weakening of Spain, some nations still feared a Habsburg resurgence from the Vienna throne, while other dynasties sought to win more territories and power. Moreover, the increasing number of Calvinists and proponents of the Catholic Counter-Reformation were still looking toward a complete victory for "true religion" in central Europe. Now in the early 1600s they faced severe economic depression, along with intensified conflict in every sphere of human relations. It was a time of disruption and frustration, and a deepening sense of crisis gripped the Continent.

The first few decades of the century brought a marked decline to the European economy, even before the advent of open warfare. Prices continued to fall until about 1660, reversing the inflation of the 1500s. International trade declined, as did Spanish bullion imports from Central and South America. Heavy risks on a falling market caused failures among many foreign trading companies; only the larger houses, organized as joint-stock companies, were able to survive. European industry and agriculture also fell on hard times; urban craftspeople saw their wages drop, and peasants faced increasing exploitation.

Tensions accompanying economic depression added to those arising from continuing religious differences. Calvinism was becoming a formidable force, having become official in Scotland and the Netherlands while achieving an uneasy toleration in France. It was also spreading in eastern Europe and Germany. In England, soon after James of Scotland succeeded Elizabeth, both Anglicans and the more radical sects feared the southward march of Scottish Presbyterianism. A similar tension prevailed in the Dutch Republic, where a militant movement for Calvinist uniformity strove to wipe out all other churches. But the most dangerous area was in Germany, which had directly experienced an increasingly militant Counter-Reformation since the Peace of Augsburg.

Although absolute monarchy was already a recognizable ideal and a dominant trend in the early seventeenth century, every royal house from England to Russia was insecure. The usual threat was posed by nobles defending their traditional privileges. In England and the Netherlands, however, where commercial development was most advanced, nobles tended to support central authority against the urban commercial classes. Theoretical opposition to absolutism, based on monarchs' contractual responsibilities to their subjects, had gained some widespread popularity during the early religious wars. It was particularly common among radical Protestants, but the same theme had even been expressed among extreme royalists, such as the French Guises who opposed Henry IV.

France best illustrates developing absolutism during the period. Henry IV and his hardheaded chief minister, the duke of Sully (1560–1641), produced a balanced budget and a treasury surplus in little more than a decade. At the same time, Henry ended the nobles' control of hereditary offices and council seats. This royalist centralization was temporarily disrupted in 1610 when Henry was assassinated, but the queen, Marie de' Medici (1573–1642), served as regent for her young son Louis XIII until 1617. Like her distant relative Catherine, Marie had survived a tragic marriage to play a dominant role in French affairs. Her peace policy toward Spain and her successful defenses, both military and diplomatic, kept the Huguenots and the great nobles in check, thus securing the succession. Meanwhile, she negotiated a marriage between Louis and the Habsburg princess Anne of Austria.

When he was 15, the new king seized power from his mother. For the next 13 years, after he restored her to his council, they continued their duel for power. Marie favored a pro-Spanish and Catholic policy; Louis, following the advice of his famous minister, Cardinal Richelieu (1585–1642), saw the Habsburgs and the papacy as the main threats to French interests. Richelieu finally prevailed, and Marie was banished in 1631, after which she continued to conspire with Spain and the French Catholic party. Inside France, Richelieu worked relentlessly to increase the king's power. He organized a royal civil service, restricted the traditional courts, brought local government under royal agents *(intendants)*, outlawed dueling, prohibited fortified castles, stripped the Huguenots of their military defenses, and developed strong military and naval forces.

Absolutism elsewhere in Europe was moving in the same general direction but with less success. The Swedish Vasa dynasty, supported by a strong national church and an efficient army, was building an empire involving Finland, the Baltic states, parts of Poland, and Denmark. In Germany many of the princes, particularly the Hohenzollerns of Brandenburg, hoped to become independent absolute monarchs. As was true of earlier Habsburgs, the Holy Roman Emperor Ferdinand II (1619–1637) struggled to concentrate his control over Austria, Hungary, and Bohemia, while extending his limited authority in Germany at the expense of the princes. Other rulers, including those in England, Spain, Russia, and

The power behind the throne of Louis XIII. Cardinal Richelieu was chiefly responsible for the direction of the government, including France's involvement in the Thirty Years' War.

Phillipe de Champaigne, c. 1637. Cardinal Richelieu. NG 1449. © National Gallery, London.

Poland, faced determined local opposition as they sought to centralize power.

This political contention within states was accompanied by rising international tensions. Although the European power balance in 1618 resembled that of the 1500s, it was much less fixed. The Habsburgs still evoked counteralliances, but their vulnerability was now greater, not only because Spain was weakening but also because other states—France, the Netherlands, and Sweden—were growing more powerful. Under these circumstances European revolt against Habsburg dominance became almost inevitable. A general awareness of the coming conflagration was perhaps the most important single source of European insecurity.

The Habsburgs' High Tide to 1630: The Bohemian and Danish Phases of the Thirty Years' War

The Thirty Years' War, fought between 1618 and 1648, was a culmination of all these related religious and political conflicts. Almost all of western Europe except England was involved and suffered accordingly. Wasted resources and manpower, along with disease, further checked economic development and curtailed population expansion. Germany was hit particularly hard, suffering population declines in some areas. Despite the terrible devastation, neither Protestantism nor Catholicism won decisively. What began as a religious war in Bohemia and the German principalities turned into a complex political struggle involving the ambitions of northern German rulers, the expansionist ambitions of Sweden, and the efforts of Catholic France to break the "Habsburg ring."

Despite the general decline of Habsburg supremacy in Spain, the early years of the war before 1629, usually cited as the Bohemian and Danish phases, brought a last brief revival of Habsburg prospects. The new Habsburg emperor, Ferdinand II, who had been raised by his mother as a fanatical Catholic, was determined to intensify the Counter-Reformation, set aside the Peace of Augsburg, and literally wipe out Protestantism in central Europe. For a time he almost succeeded.

Ferdinand's succession came amid severe political tension. Spreading Calvinism, in addition to the aggressive crusading of the Jesuits, had earlier led to the formation of a Protestant league of German princes in 1608 and a Catholic counterleague the next year. The two had almost clashed in 1610. Meanwhile, the Bohemian Protestants had extracted a promise of toleration from their Catholic king, the earlier Holy Roman Emperor Rudolf II (1576–1612). In 1618 the Bohemian leaders, fearing that Ferdinand would not honor the promise, threw two of his officials out a window after heated discussions—an incident known as the "defenestration of Prague." When Ferdinand mobilized troops, the Bohemians deposed him and offered their throne to Frederick, the Protestant elector of the Palatinate, in western Germany.

In the short Bohemian war that followed, Frederick was quickly overwhelmed. At the urging of his wife, Elizabeth, the daughter of James I of England, Frederick had reluctantly accepted the Bohemian crown. But while he and Elizabeth held court in Prague, no practical military support came from England, the Netherlands, or the Protestant German princes. Ferdinand, in contrast, deployed two superb armies, one from Spain and the other from Catholic Bavaria. In 1620 Frederick's meager forces were scattered at the battle of the White Mountain, near Prague. Afterward, the hapless Bohemian monarch and his queen fled the country, ultimately settling at The Hague, in the Netherlands, where they continued to pursue their lost cause. Ferdinand gave their lands to Maximillian of Bavaria, distributed the holdings of Bohemian Protestant nobles among Catholic aristocrats, and proceeded to stamp out Protestantism in Bohemia. Of the some 3.2 million Bohemians in 1618, mostly Protestants, all that remained 30 years later were less than a million people, all Catholics.

War began again in l625 when Christian IV (1588–1648), the Lutheran king of Denmark, invaded Germany. As duke of Holstein and thus a prince of the empire, he hoped to revive Protestantism and win a kingdom in Germany for his youngest son. Christian was luckier than Frederick had been in attracting support. The Dutch reopened their naval war with Spain, England provided subsidies, and the remaining independent German Protestant princes, now thoroughly alarmed, rose up against the Catholics and the emperor. All of these renewed efforts were in vain. Ferdinand's new general, Albert von Wallenstein, defeated the Protestants in a series of brilliant campaigns. By 1629 Christian had to admit defeat and withdraw his forces, thus ending the Danish conflict with another Protestant debacle.

Their successful campaigns of the 1620s gave the Habsburgs almost complete domination in Germany. Using the army raised by Wallenstein in Bohemia, Ferdinand reconquered the north. In 1629 he issued his famous Edict of Restitution, restoring to the

By the simplicity and starkness of his portrayal, the French artist Jacques Callot captured, in a series of 24 etchings, the senseless tragedy of the Thirty Years' War. The dangling bodies in this plate dramatized the tenuousness of life in turbulent times.

Catholics all properties lost since 1552. This step seemed to be only the first step toward eliminating Protestantism completely and creating a centralized Habsburg empire in Germany.

The Swedish and French Phases and the Balance of Power, 1630–1648

Fearing the Counter-Reformation and the growing Habsburg power behind it, threatened European states resumed the war in 1630. As it rapidly spread and intensified, religious issues were steadily subordinated to power politics. This was evidenced by the phases of the conflict usually designated as the Swedish (1630–1635) and the French (1635–1648), because these two countries led successive anti-Habsburg coalitions. Ultimately, their efforts were successful. By 1648 the Dutch Republic had replaced Spain as the leading maritime state and Bourbon France had become the dominant European land power.

Protestant Swedes and French Catholics challenged Ferdinand's imperial ambitions for similar political reasons. Although Gustavus Adolphus (1611–1632), the Swedish king, wanted to save German Lutheranism, he was also determined to prevent a strong Habsburg state on the Baltic from restricting his own expansion and interfering with Swedish trade. A similar desire to liberate France from Habsburg encirclement motivated Cardinal Richelieu. He offered Gustavus French subsidies, for which the Swedish monarch promised to invade Germany and permit Catholic worship in any lands he might conquer. Thus the Catholic cardinal and the Protestant king compromised their religious differences in the hope of achieving mutual political benefits.

Gustavus invaded Germany in 1630 while the Dutch attacked the Spanish Netherlands. With his mobile cannons and his hymn-singing Swedish veterans, Gustavus and his German allies won a series of smashing victories, climaxed in November 1632 at Lützen, near Leipzig, where Wallenstein was decisively defeated. Unfortunately for the Protestant cause, Gustavus died in the battle. Meanwhile, a Dutch army in Flanders advanced toward Brussels, where Philip II's aging daughter Isabella was still governing. Aware of her subjects' desperate need for peace, Isabella began negotiations, but the news from Lützen raised Habsburg hopes in Vienna and Madrid. Subsequently, Isabella was removed, a Spanish army was dispatched to Germany, and Wallenstein was mysteriously murdered. This Habsburg flurry brought no significant victories but led to the compromise Peace of Prague in 1635 between the emperor and the German Protestant states.

The situation now demanded that France act directly to further its dynastic interests. Thus a final French phase of the war began when Richelieu sent French troops into Germany and toward the Spanish borders. He also subsidized the Dutch and Swedes while recruiting an army of German Protestant mercenaries. France continued limiting Protestantism within its borders but gladly allied with Protestant states against Spain, Austria, Bavaria, and their Catholic allies. The war that had begun in religious controversy had now become pure power politics, completing the long political transition from medieval to modern times.

Sweden's warrior-king Gustavus Adolphus is portrayed here at the battle of Breitenfeld in 1631.

Hardships in a German Town During the Thirty Years' War

This account of disaster and suffering by a refugee from Calw, who returned to find his "beloved town" in "ashes and rubble," illustrates the terrible havoc experienced by ordinary German people during the conflict.

During the pillage of Calw by Croat Imperial troops in September [1634] I never totally forsook my flock and only sought to escape from falling into the hands of the enemy. I joined a band of women and children soon amounting to more than 200 people. Like ants we scurried over hills and rocks. The beneficial influence of Heaven helped us continuously throughout this time. If we had bad weather we would have fared even worse than we did.

After it became known that the town [Calw, in Württemberg] had been burnt down, we escaped to Aichelberg, a rough place. We had agreed among ourselves where each of us should hide but since our presence had been betrayed to the enemy, we were barely able to escape a quarter of an hour before we would have been totally ruined. At this the enemy became angry and vented his wrath upon the richest peasant in the place, who after hideous torture was burnt along with his house. . . .

Since the enemy was also active in these parts, . . . we decided to make an attempt to ask the victor for mercy. But to our further consternation we had to flee once again into the hills where no one could readily follow us. From there we wandered around, divided into smaller bands, and on the 15 September alone with my nephew John Joshua and son Gottlieb I hid in the deep Lauterback valley near the stream in a barn on the fields. We spent the night calmly and also the next one.

Since our lodging was moved to another barn where a certain Peter Schill, whom I must praise for his great honesty among the wood-folk, provided us with food and drink, our lack of caution led us back to Gernsbach where we scarcely avoided falling into the

net of the enemy. As we lived scattered about all the secret places on Obertsrot, Hilpertsau, Reichtal, Weissenbach, Langenbrand and elsewhere, the hue and cry was raised after us and huntsmen were hired who knew the forests to track us down with their dogs. We saw them in the distance and became heartily dispirited, but also took a serious warning from the event.

I finally arrived at a peasant's place where the wife was nearing her childbirth, and I had a sleepless night since three hours before dawn I had climbed over the peaks of the hills, gone through hill and dale and eventually arrived back at my own vineyard where I had placed my little son Ehrenreich, and in which farm we now spent our exile. I found my little son much weakened and unable to stand cold and hunger. The Lord took him and released his spirit into the freedom of Heaven on the 20 September. But shortly before this I had already left. We were called back in a letter from our friends, since everything, as far as the times allowed, was back in order, which accorded with the enemy's own best interest.

When I saw my beloved town of Calw in ashes and rubble—it was however not the first time that I had seen a town in ruins—I felt a cold shudder and I brooded repeatedly on that which I neither can nor wish to repeat now. What struck me most deeply was that long ago I had already prophesied the calamity, and that my prophecy had now come true in as much as it had also included me.

From Gerhard Benecke, ed., *Germany in the Thirty Years' War* (London: Edward Arnold, 1978). Reprinted by permission of Hodder & Stoughton, Ltd.

For 13 more years the seemingly endless conflict wore on. France's allies, the Swedes and northern Germans, kept Habsburg armies engaged in Germany, while French armies and the Dutch navy concentrated on Spain. In 1643 the French won a decisive battle at Rocroi, in the southern Netherlands. Next they moved into Germany, defeating the imperial forces and, with the Swedes, ravaging Bavaria. When Richelieu died in 1642, he had already unleashed forces that would make the Bourbon dynasty supreme in Europe.

For all practical purposes the war was over, but years of indecisive campaigning and tortuous negotiations delayed the peace. The French held to rigid demands, despite the deaths of Richelieu in 1642 and Louis XIII in 1643. Richelieu's protégé, Cardinal Mazarin (1602–1661), continued to conduct diplomacy for Queen Anne, now ruling as regent for her son, the future Louis XIV. In the past she had been lazy, indiscreet, and suspected of conspiring with her Spanish relatives, but she now consistently supported her minister's hard line through budget crises and popular unrest. French intransigence was partially nullified, however, by a conciliatory Swedish approach after Queen Christiana, the daughter of Gustavus Adolphus, succeeded to the throne in 1644. A horde of peace emissaries met that year at Westphalia. Even then Spain and France could reach no

Exhausted Europeans finally agreed to put an end to the Thirty Years' War with the Treaty of Westphalia. This agreement put an end to Habsburg ambitions in central Europe, marked the emergence of France as the major continental power, and removed religion as a factor in interstate relations. It also laid the foundations for modern international law.

agreement, but a settlement for the empire was finally completed in 1648.

The Peace of Westphalia

The Peace of Westphalia is among the most significant pacts in modern European history. It ended Europe's torturous journey to the doubtful comforts of the modern state system. Even so, it did not yet establish universal peace; the war between France and Spain lasted another 11 years, ending only at the Peace of the Pyrenees in 1659.

The peace agreement at Westphalia signaled a victory for Protestantism and the German princes while almost dooming Habsburg imperial ambitions: France moved closer to the Rhine by acquiring Alsatian territory, Sweden and Brandenburg acquired

lands on the Baltic, and the Netherlands and Switzerland gained recognition of their independence. The emperor was required to obtain approval from the Imperial Diet for any laws, taxes, military levies, and foreign agreements—provisions that nearly nullified imperial power and afforded the German states practical control of their foreign relations. Their German religious autonomy, as declared at Augsburg, was also reconfirmed, with Calvinism now permitted along with Lutheranism. In addition, Protestant states were conceded all Catholic properties taken before 1624.

In its religious terms the treaty ended the dream of reuniting Christendom. Catholics and Protestants now realized that major faiths could not be destroyed. From such intuitions a spirit of toleration would gradually emerge. Although religious uniformity could be imposed within states for another century, it would not again be a serious issue in European foreign affairs until the end of the twentieth century.

The Peace of Westphalia is particularly notable for confirming the new European state system. Henceforth states would customarily shape their policies in accordance with the power of their neighbors, seeking to expand at the expense of the weaker and to protect themselves—not by religion, law, or morality, but by alliances against their stronger adversaries. Based on the works of the Dutch jurist Grotius, the treaty also instituted the international conference as a means for registering power relationships among contending states, instituted the principle of the equality of all sovereign states—as seen today in the General Assembly of the United Nations—and put into practice the tools of modern diplomacy such as extraterritoriality and diplomatic immunities.

Both Spain and Austria were weakened, and the Austrian Habsburgs shifted their primary attention from central to southeastern Europe. German disunity was perpetuated by the autonomy of so many of the microstates. France emerged from this time as the clear winner, the potential master of the Continent. The war also helped England and the Netherlands. No matter the condition of the surviving states, their future relations would be based on the pure calculus of power, both military and economic.

Conclusion

In many ways the Protestant Reformation and Catholic Counter-Reformation helped create the modern world. By breaking the religious monopoly of European Catholicism, Lutheranism and Anglicanism assisted the growth of northern European national monarchies. Later the puritan values and "work ethic" of Calvinism helped justify the activities of the middle classes. By the 1570s the Catholic Counter-Reformation had checked the spread of Protestantism, and the Roman Church emerged strengthened to protect and advance itself in Europe and carry its message around the globe.

The century and a half after Luther's stand at Wittenberg was an era of wrenching change for Europe. At the opening of the period most people were still imbued with the medieval concern for salvation, which gave meaning to the religious issues of the Protestant Reformation and Catholic Counter-Reformation. In the century after the Peace of Augsburg (1555), the nature of state competition changed. Initially long and exhaustive religious wars and civil wars dominated the Continent. Later secular political concerns became increasingly evident. But whether the wars were for faith or for state, or a combination of the two, the period until the Treaty of Westphalia ended the Thirty Years' War was the bloodiest century Europe would endure until the twentieth. Finally, the modern political structure emerged. Europeans now lived, for better or worse, in a world of nation-states dominated by secular concerns.

Suggestions for Reading

Steven B. Ozment, *The Age of Reform* (Yale University Press, 1980), is excellent for social and political as well as religious topics. Among older but still sound general treatments are Hans J. Hillerbrand, *The World of the Reformation* (Scribner, 1973), and the classic by Roland H. Bainton, *The Reformation of the Sixteenth Century*, rev. ed. (Beacon Press, 1985). On the impact of John Hus, see Thomas A. Fudge, *The Magnificent Ride: The First Reformation in Hussite Bohemia* (Ashgate Press, 1998).

The general background of the Reformation is covered well in Steven E. Ozment, *Protestants: The Birth of a Revolution* (Doubleday, 1992). Criticism of the church by northern humanists is ably described in John Huizinga, *Erasmus and the Age of the Reformation* (Princeton University Press, 1984). See also the debate between the humanists and the Scholastics in Erika Rummel, *The Humanist-Scholastic Debate in the Renaissance and Reformation* (Harvard University Press, 1988). On social conditions in the Reformation era, see R. Po-chin Hsia, *The German People and the Reformation* (Cornell University Press, 1988). The Protestant urban movement in microcosm is treated in Susan C. Karent-Nunn, *Zwickau in Transition, 1500–1547: The Reformation as a Force for Change* (Ohio State University Press, 1987). The sad plight of women in the era is treated in Susan Cahn, *The Industry of Devotion* (Colgate University Press, 1987); Mary E. Wiesner, *Working Women in Renaissance Germany* (Rutgers University Press, 1986); and Retha M. Warnicke, *Women of the English Renaissance and Reformation* (Greenwood, 1983).

The old standard biography by Roland H. Bainton, *Here I Stand: A Life of Martin Luther* (Abingdon-Cokesbury, 1950), is still moving and interesting. For an interesting contrast, compare Erik H. Erikson, *Young Man Luther* (Norton, 1962), and also Mark U. Edwards, *Luther's Last Battles* (Cornell University Press, 1983), which presents a portrait of an aging, prejudiced, and politically motivated reformer. The reformer's personal struggles are vividly depicted in Heiko A. Oberman, *Luther: Between God and the Devil* (Yale University Press, 1989). On the political and social implications of Lutheranism, see Paula Fichtner, *Protestantism and Primogeniture in Early Modern Germany* (Yale University Press, 1989); Abraham Friesen, *Thomas Muentzer, a Destroyer of the Godless* (University of California Press, 1990); and William J. Wright, *Capitalism, the State, and the Lutheran Reformation: Sixteenth-Century Hesse* (Ohio University Press, 1988).

Ulrich Gabler gives a thorough background of Ulrich Zwingli's place in history in his *Huldrych Zwingli: His Life and Work* (Clark, 1995). William J. Bouwsma, *John Calvin* (Oxford University Press, 1988), is a scholarly portrayal of Calvin's human side, emphasizing his inner conflict against the humanistic trend of his time. Another competent study, based on primary materials, is George R. Potter and Mark Greengrass, *John Calvin* (St. Martin's Press, 1983). See also T. H. L. Parker, *John Calvin* (Lion, 1987); Alexandre Ganoczy, *The Young Calvin* (Westminister, 1987); and François Wendel, *Calvin* (Baker,

1996). Rewarding special studies of Calvinism include Mark Greengrass, *The French Reformation* (Blackwell, 1987); Jane Dempsey Douglas, *Women, Freedom, and Calvin* (Westminister, 1985); and Willem Balke, *Calvin and the Anabaptist Radicals* (Eerdmans, 1981). Calvin's political orientation is also thoroughly explored in Ralph C. Hancock, *Calvin and the Foundations of Modern Politics* (Cornell University Press, 1989). A useful handbook for understanding Calvin's contributions is T. H. L. Parker, *Calvin: An Introduction to His Thought* (John Knox Press, 1995).

The context for the English Reformation is provided by Richard H. Britnell in *The Closing of the Middle Ages: England, 1471–1529* (Blackwell, 1997). Two solid and informative accounts of English society and the Anglican Reformation are J. J. Scarisbrick, *The Reformation and the English People* (Blackwell, 1984), and Robert S. Feuerlicht, *The Life and World of Henry VIII* (Crowell-Collier, 1970). See also Peter Lake and Maria Dowling, *Protestantism and the National Church in the Sixteenth Century* (Croom Helm, 1987). G. J. R. Parry, *A Protestant Vision* (Cambridge University Press, 1987), is a thoughtful interpretation of William Harrison's Puritan theology. See also Caroline Litzenberger, *The English Reformation and the Laity: Gloucestershire, 1540--1580* (Cambridge University Press, 1998). On the roles played by Tudor women, see Margaret P. Hannay, *Silent but for the Word* (Kent State University Press, 1985), and Carolly Erickson, *Bloody Mary* (Doubleday, 1978). Paul Hogrife has also produced two volumes on the subject: *Tudor Women* (Iowa State University Press, 1975) and *Women of Action in Tudor England* (Iowa State University Press, 1977).

On the "left wing" of Protestantism, see Peter C. Clasen, *Anabaptism: A Social History* (Cornell University Press, 1972), and E. Belfort Bax, *The Rise and Fall of Anabaptism* (Kelley, 1970). A good more recent treatment of Anabaptism is a collection of essays edited by James M. Stayer, *The Anabaptists and Thomas Münzer* (Kendall Hunt, 1980).

John C. Olin places the Catholic response in perspective in *The Catholic Reformation: From Savonarola to Ignatius Loyola* (Fordham University Press, 1993). Nicholas S. Davidson, *The Counter-Reformation* (Blackwell, 1987), and Michael A. Mullett, *The Counter-Reformation and the Catholic Reformation in Early Modern Europe* (Methuen, 1984), are among the recent works on the Catholic revival. A sympathetic Catholic account is in P. Janelle, *The Catholic Reformation* (Bruce, 1963). Also worth noting is James Brodrick, *The Origin of the Jesuits* (Greenwood, 1971).

Two excellent overall surveys of this Reformation period are Robert Bireley, *Religion and Politics in the Age of the Counter-Reformation* (University of North Carolina Press, 1981), and Helmut G. Koenigsberger, *Early Modern Europe, 1500–1789* (Longman, 1987). See also Trevor Henry Aston, ed., *Crisis in Europe, 1560–1660* (Harper Torchbooks, 1974), and Perez Zagoren, *Rebels and Rulers, 1500–1660* (Cambridge University Press, 1982). Helga Mobius, *Women of the Baroque Age* (Schram, 1984), provides good detail, particularly on women painters, but is less scholarly and more superficial in its generalizations.

Four sound studies of Spain during the period are John Lynch, *Spain Under the Habsburgs*, Vol. 1, *Empire and Absolutism, 1516–1598* (New York University Press, 1984); Reginald Trevor-Davis, *The Golden Century of Spain, 1501–1621* (Greenwood, 1984); Robert James Weston Evans, *The Making of the Habsburg Monarchy, 1550–1700* (Oxford University Press, 1984); and Henry A. F. Kamen, *The Golden Age of Spain* (Humanities Press, 1988). John H. Elliott, *Spain and Its World* (Yale University Press, 1989), is a collection of excellent previously published essays. The classic treatment of the Armada is Garrett Mattingly, *The Armada* (Houghton Mifflin, 1988). Of the spate of books that appeared to commemorate the four

hundredth anniversary of the legendary battle, Peter Kemp, *The Campaign of the Spanish Armada* (Facts on File, 1988), is perhaps the most readable. Peter Pierson, *Commander of the Armada* (Yale University Press, 1989), is a biography of the ill-fated Spanish admiral Medina Sidonia.

The best-known account of the Dutch rebellion is Pieter Geyl, *The Revolt of the Netherlands* (Barnes & Noble, 1958). Noel G. Parker, *The Dutch Revolt* (Cornell University Press, 1977), and John C. Cadoux, *Philip of Spain and the Netherlands* (Archon Books, 1969), are two excellent older studies. For background of the rebellion, see Jonathan I. Israel, *The Dutch Republic and the Hispanic World, 1606–1661* (Oxford University Press, 1986), and James D. Tracy, *Holland Under Habsburg Rule* (University of California Press, 1990). Simon Schama, *The Embarrassment of Riches: An Interpretation of Dutch Culture in the Golden Age* (Knopf, 1987), and Charles R. Boxer, *The Dutch Seaborne Empire* (Penguin, 1989), depict the republic's problems at the apex of its struggle for power and wealth. The social backgrounds are treated in Sherrin Marshall, *The Dutch Gentry, 1500–1650: Family, Faith, and Fortune* (Greenwood, 1987). See also J. L. Price, *Culture and Society in the Dutch Republic During the Seventeenth Century* (Columbia University Press, 1974). Cicely V. Wedgewood, *William the Silent* (Norton, 1968), is a superb biography. See also Guido Marnef, *Antwerp in the Age of Reformation* (Johns Hopkins University Press, 1996).

French society and politics during the whole era are ably treated in Robert Briggs, *Early Modern France, 1560–1715* (Oxford University Press, 1977), and Mack P. Holt, ed., *Society and Institutions in Early Modern France* (University of Georgia Press, 1991). Henry Heller, *Iron and Blood: Civil Wars in Sixteenth-Century France* (McGill-Queen's University Press, 1991), and George D. Balsama, *The Politics of National Despair* (University of Washington Press, 1978), describe the catastrophic religious wars. This tragic time is also reflected in Frederick J. Baumgartner's readable biography, *Henry II, King of France* (Duke University Press, 1988). Robert M. Kingdon presents a Catholic view in *Myths About the Saint Bartholomew's Day Massacres, 1572–1576* (Harvard University Press, 1988). On the early seventeenth century, see Victor L. Tapie, *France in the Age of Louis XIII and Richelieu* (Cambridge University Press, 1984). The best biographies for this later period are A. Lloyd Moote, *Louis XIII* (University of California Press, 1989); Ruth Kleinman, *Anne of Austria* (Ohio State University Press, 1985); and Elizabeth Warwick's two controversial but interesting studies, *Louis XIII: The Making of a King* (Yale University Press, 1986) and *The Young Richelieu* (University of Chicago Press, 1983). The role of French Protestantism in both eras is clearly depicted in George A. Rothrock, *The Huguenots: A Biography of a Minority* (Nelson Hall, 1979).

An outstanding survey of English social history is J. A. Sharpe, *Early Modern England: A Social History, 1550–1760*, 2nd ed. (Arnold, 1997). On the growing social and political awareness of English women in the sixteenth and seventeenth centuries, see Katherine A. Henderson and Barbara McManus, *Half Humankind: Contexts and Texts of the Controversy About Women in England, 1540–1640* (University of Illinois Press, 1985), and Mary Prior, ed., *Women in English Society, 1500–1800* (Methuen, 1985).

Excellent general interpretations of Elizabethan England are presented in Arthur Bryant, *The Elizabethan Deliverance* (St. Martin's Press, 1982), and David B. Quinn and A. N. Ryan, *England's Sea Empire, 1550–1642* (Allen & Unwin, 1983). A creditable but less creative work that gives broad coverage of Elizabethan experience is Stephen White-Thomson, *Elizabeth I and Tudor England* (Bookwright Press, 1985). Other biographies worth consulting include Anne Somerset, *Elizabeth I* (Knopf, 1991); Jasper G. Ridley, *Elizabeth: The Shrewdness of Virtue* (Viking, 1988); Allison Plowden, *Elizabeth Tudor and*

Mary Stuart (Barnes & Noble, 1984); and J. Mary Wormald, *Mary, Queen of Scots* (Philip & Son, 1988). For studies of Elizabethan politics and diplomacy, see Joel Hurstfield, *Elizabeth I and the Unity of England* (Harper Torchbooks, 1967); Charles Wilson, *Queen Elizabeth and the Revolt of the Netherlands* (University of California Press, 1970); and a pair of companion volumes by Richard B. Wernham, *Before the Armada: The Emergence of the English Nation, 1485–1588* (Norton, 1972) and *After the Armada: Elizabethan England and the Struggle for Western Europe,* rev. ed. (Oxford University Press, 1984). A noteworthy special work on Elizabethan women is Susan Cahn, *The Transformation of Women's Work in England, 1500–1600* (Columbia University Press, 1987).

For discussion of the baroque artistic style in its historical setting, see Michael Kitson, *The Age of Baroque* (Haslyn, 1966), and Victor L. Tapie, *The Age of Grandeur: Baroque Art and Architecture* (Praeger, 1961). Three excellent relevant biographies are Henry Bonnier, *Rembrandt* (Braziller, 1968); Christopher White, *Rembrandt and His World* (Viking, 1964); and Andrew M. Jaffe, *Rubens and Italy* (Cornell University Press, 1977). On Mannerism, see Arnold Hauser, *Mannerism* (Knopf, 1965), and Linda Murray, *The High Renaissance and Mannerism* (Oxford University Press, 1977).

A good new study of the Thirty Years' War is Ronald Asch, *The Thirty Years' War: The Holy Roman Empire and Europe, 1618–1648* (St. Martin's Press, 1997), which adds to, but does not replace, Cicely V. Wedgewood's classic *The Thirty Year's War* (Anchor Books, 1961). Joseph Polisensky discusses the by-products of the war in *War and Society in Europe, 1618–1648* (Cambridge University Press, 1978). Michael Roberts, *Sweden's Age of Greatness* (St. Martin's Press, 1973), gives good coverage of both the political and military events in this conflict.

Suggestions for Web Browsing

Internet Medieval History Sourcebook: Protestant and Catholic Reformations
http://www.fordham.edu/halsall/sbookly.html#Protestant Reformation

http://www.fordham.edu/halsall/sbookly.html#Catholic Reformation

Extensive on-line source for links about the Protestant and Catholic Reformations, including primary documents by or about precursors and papal critics, Luther, and Calvin and details about the Reformations themselves.

Martin Luther
http://www.wittenberg.de/e/seiten/personen/luther.html

This brief biography of Martin Luther includes links to his Ninety-Five Theses and images of related historical sites.

Tudor England
http://tudor.simplenet.com/

Site detailing life in Tudor England includes biographies, maps, important dates, architecture, and music, including sound files.

Lady Jane Grey
http://users.wantree.com.au/~halligan/ladyjane/index.html

A biography of the woman who would be queen of England for nine days and a general history of the time.

Peace of Westphalia
http://www.yale.edu/lawweb/avalon/westphal.htm

Complete text of the peace treaties that together made up the Treaty of Westphalia (1648), which ended the Thirty Years' War.

Notes

1. Quoted in Roland H. Bainton, *Here I Stand: A Life of Martin Luther* (New York: Abingdon-Cokesbury Press, 1950), p. 54.
2. Luther probably never posted his theses on the church door at Wittenberg. See H. G. Halle, *Luther* (New York: Doubleday, 1980), pp. 177–178.
3. Quoted in Heiko A. Oberman, *Luther: Between God and the Devil* (New Haven, Conn.: Yale University Press, 1982), p. 190. See also pp. 187–188.
4. Quoted in Harold Grim, *The Reformation Era* (New York: Macmillan, 1968), p. 17.

Marketplace at Antwerp.
*In the sixteenth century, Antwerp
was the leading city in inter–
national commerce. As many
as 500 ships a day docked in its
bustling harbor, and as many as
1000 wagons arrived each week
carrying the overland trade.*

The Global Impact of European Expansion and Colonization, 1492–1660

Chapter Contents

During the fifteenth century Europe began a process of unprecedented expansion, affecting all areas of the world but most decisively the Americas and Africa. This was actually part of a worldwide development of civilizations, encompassing those of the Aztecs, the Incas, Africans, the western Europeans, and the Japanese, as well as others around the Eurasian fringes. The process was furthered by improved navigational technology and the resulting expansion of trade that encouraged long sea voyages by Arabs, Japanese, and Chinese. But only the Europeans succeeded in linking all the continents in a new global age, when their sea power, rather than land-based armies, would become a determining force in empire building.

European successes overseas were obviously related—both as cause and as effect—to salient trends in the European transition from medievalism. The Crusades and the Renaissance stimulated European curiosity; the Reformation produced thousands of zealous missionaries seeking foreign converts and refugees seeking religious freedom; and the monarchs of emerging sovereign states sought revenues, first by trading with the Orient and later by exploiting new and less developed worlds. Perhaps the most permeating influence was the rise of European capitalism, with its monetary values, profit-seeking motivations, investment institutions, and consistent impulses toward economic expansion. Some historians have labeled this whole economic transformation the Commercial

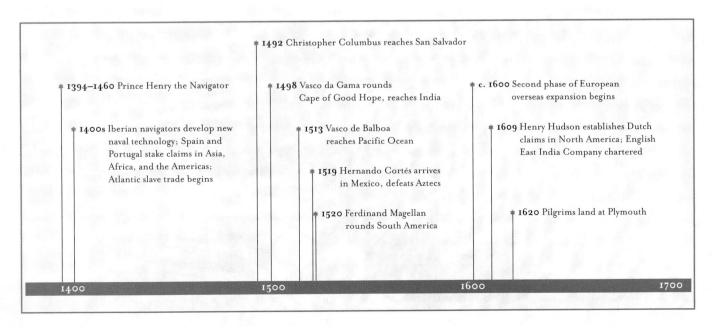

1492 Christopher Columbus reaches San Salvador

1394–1460 Prince Henry the Navigator

1400s Iberian navigators develop new naval technology; Spain and Portugal stake claims in Asia, Africa, and the Americas; Atlantic slave trade begins

1498 Vasco da Gama rounds Cape of Good Hope, reaches India

1513 Vasco de Balboa reaches Pacific Ocean

1519 Hernando Cortés arrives in Mexico, defeats Aztecs

1520 Ferdinand Magellan rounds South America

c. 1600 Second phase of European overseas expansion begins

1609 Henry Hudson establishes Dutch claims in North America; English East India Company chartered

1620 Pilgrims land at Plymouth

1400   1500   1600   1700

Revolution. Others have used the phrase to refer to the shift in trade routes from the Mediterranean to the Atlantic. Interpreted either way, the Commercial Revolution and its accompanying European expansion helped usher in a modern era, largely at the expense of Africans and Amerindians.

Europe's Commercial Revolution developed in two quite distinct phases. The second and climactic one, after 1600, was centered in the Netherlands, England, and to some extent France. It fostered a maritime imperialism based more on trade and finance than the more directly exploitative systems of Portugal and Spain during their earlier "golden age" in the first phase.

The Iberian Golden Age

The two Iberian states launched the new era in competition with each other, although neither was able to maintain initial advantages over the long term. Portugal lacked manpower and resources required by an empire spread over three continents. Spain wasted its new wealth in continuous wars while neglecting to develop its own economy. In 1503 Portuguese pepper cost only one-fifth as much as pepper coming through Venice and the eastern Mediterranean.[1] Within decades gold and silver from the New World poured into Spain. Iberian bullion and exotic commodities, flowing into northern banks and markets, provided a major stimulus to European capitalism. This early European impact abroad also generated

Spanish Exploration and Expansion

1470–1541	Francisco Pizarro
1474–1566	Bartolomé de Las Casas
1479	Treaty of Alcacovas
1494	Treaty of Tordesillas
1509–1515	Alfonso de Albuquerque serves as eastern viceroy of Portugal
1510–1554	Francisco de Coronado
1510	Portuguese acquire Goa, in India
1531	Pizarro defeats Incas in Peru
c. 1550	Spanish introduce plantation system to Brazil
1565	St. Augustine founded, first European colony in North America

great cultural diffusion, promoting an intercontinental spread of peoples, plants, animals, and knowledge that the world had never seen before. But it also destroyed nascent Amerindian states and began a weakening of those in Africa at a time when civilizations were approaching maturation in both places.

Conditions Favoring Iberian Expansion

A number of conditions invited Iberian maritime expansion in the fifteenth century. Muslim control over the eastern caravan routes, particularly after the Turks took Constantinople in 1453, brought rising prices in Europe. At the same time the sprawling Islamic world lacked both unity and intimidating sea power, and China, after 1440, had abandoned its extensive naval forays into the Indian Ocean. These conditions encouraged Portugal and Spain to seek new sea routes to the East, where their centuries-old struggle with Muslims in the Mediterranean might be continued on the ocean shores of sub-Saharan Africa and Asia (and where they also drained the wealth from ports of those distant lands).

During the 1400s Iberian navigators became proficient in new naval technology and tactics. Having adopted the compass and the astrolabe, they learned to tack against the wind, thus partly freeing themselves from hugging the coast on long voyages, particularly when sailing home from West Africa. The Iberians, especially the Portuguese, were also skilled cartographers and chartmakers. But their main advantages lay with their ships and naval guns. The stormy Atlantic required broad bows, deep keels, and complex square rigging for driving and maneuvering fighting ships. Armed with brass cannons, such ships could sink enemy vessels without ramming or boarding at close range. They could also batter down coastal defenses. Even the much larger Chinese junks could not match the maneuverability and firepower of European ships.

A strong religious motivation augmented Iberian naval efficiency. Long and bitter wars with the Moors had left the Portuguese and Spanish with an obsessive drive to convert non-Christians or destroy them in the name of Christ. Sailors with Columbus recited prayers every night, and Portuguese seamen were equally devout. Every maritime mission was regarded as a holy crusade.

For two centuries Iberians had nursed their religious prejudices against Muslims by hoping for a new Christian crusade in concert with Ethiopia. The idea originated with twelfth-century crusaders in the Holy Land; it gained strength later with Ethiopian migrants at Rhodes, who boasted of their king's prowess against the infidels. Thus arose the myth of "Prester John," a mighty Ethiopian monarch and potential European ally against Mongols, Turks, and

Using ships like these broad-beamed carracks, the Portuguese controlled much of the carrying trade with the East in the fifteenth and sixteenth centuries.

Muslims. In response to a delegation from Zara Yakob, the reigning emperor, a few Europeans visited Ethiopia after 1450. These and other similar contacts greatly stimulated the determination to find a new sea route to the East, which might link the Iberians with the legendary Ethiopian king and bring Islam under attack from two sides.

This dream of war for the cross was sincere, but it also served to rationalize more worldly concerns. Both Spain and Portugal experienced dramatic population growth between 1400 and 1600. The Spanish population increased from 5 to 8.5 million; the Portuguese more than doubled, from 900,000 to 2 million, despite a manpower loss of 125,000 in the sixteenth century.[2] Hard times in rural areas prompted migration to cities, where dreams of wealth in foreign lands encouraged fortune seeking overseas. Despite the obvious religious zeal of many Iberians, particularly among those in holy orders, a fervent desire for gain was the driving motivation for most migrants.

The structures of the Iberian states provided further support for overseas expansion. In both, the powers of the monarchs had been recently expanded and were oriented toward maritime adventure as a means to raise revenues, divert the Turkish menace, spread Catholic Christianity, and increase national unity. The Avis dynasty in Portugal, after usurping the throne and alienating the great nobles in 1385, made common cause with the gentry and middle classes,

who prospered in commercial partnership with the government. In contrast, Spanish nobles, particularly the Castilians, were very much like Turkish aristocrats, who regarded conquest and plunder as their normal functions and sources of income. Thus the Portuguese and Spanish political systems worked in different ways toward similar imperial ends.

Staking Claims

During the late fifteenth century both Portugal and Spain staked claims abroad. Portugal gained a long lead over Spain in Africa and Asia. But after conquering Grenada, the last Moorish state on the Iberian peninsula, and completely uniting the country, the Spanish monarchs turned their attention overseas. The resulting historic voyage of Columbus established Spanish claims to most of the Western Hemisphere.

The man most responsible for the brilliant exploits by the Portuguese was Prince Henry (1394–1460), known as "the Navigator" because of his famous observatory at Sagres, where skilled mariners planned voyages and recorded their results. As a young man in 1411, Henry directed the Portuguese conquest of Ceuta, a Muslim port on the Moroccan coast, at the western entrance to the Mediterranean. This experience imbued him with a lifelong desire to divert the West African gold trade from

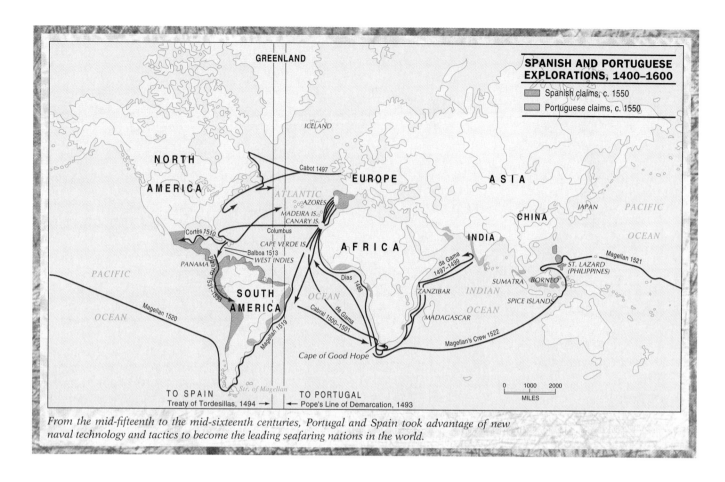

From the mid-fifteenth to the mid-sixteenth centuries, Portugal and Spain took advantage of new naval technology and tactics to become the leading seafaring nations in the world.

Muslim caravans to Portuguese ships. He also shared the common dream of finding Ethiopian Christian allies against the Turks. Such ideas motivated him for 40 years as he sent expeditions down the West African coast, steadily charting and learning from unknown waters.

Before other European states began extensive explorations, the Portuguese had navigated the West African coast to its southern tip. Henry's captains claimed the Madeira Islands in 1418 and the Azores in 1421. They had explored the Senegal River by 1450 and then traced the Guinea coast during the next decade. After Henry's death in 1460 they pushed south, reaching Benin in the decade after 1470 and Kongo, on the southwest coast, in 1482. Six years later Bartolomeu Dias rounded southern Africa, but his disgruntled crew forced him to turn back. Nevertheless, King John II of Portugal (1481–1495) was so excited by the prospect of a direct route to India that he named Dias's discovery the "Cape of Good Hope."

Spain soon challenged Portuguese supremacy. The specific controversy was over the Canary Islands, some of which were occupied by Castilians in 1344 and others by Portuguese after the 1440s. The issue, which produced repeated incidents, was ultimately settled in 1479 by the Treaty of Alcacovas, which recognized exclusive Spanish rights in the Canaries but

banned Spain from the Madeiras, the Azores, the Cape Verdes, and West Africa. Spanish ambitions were thus temporarily frustrated until Columbus provided new hope.

Christopher Columbus (1451–1506), a Genoese sailor with an impossible dream, had been influenced by Marco Polo's journal to believe that Japan could be reached by a short sail directly westward. Although he underestimated the distance by some 7000 miles and was totally ignorant of the intervening continents, Columbus persistently urged his proposals on King John of Portugal and Queen Isabella of Spain, who was captivated by Columbus's dream and became his most steadfast supporter until her death in 1504. Having obtained her sponsorship, Columbus sailed from Palos, Spain, in three small ships on August 3, 1492. He landed on San Salvador in the West Indies on October 12, thinking he had reached his goal. In three more attempts he continued his search for an Asian passage. His voyages touched the major Caribbean islands, Honduras, the Isthmus of Panama, and Venezuela. Although he never knew it, he had claimed a new world for Spain.

Columbus's first voyage posed threats to Portuguese interests in the Atlantic and called for compromise if war was to be averted. At Spain's invitation the pope issued a "bull of demarcation,"

An engraving that shows Columbus landing at Hispaniola. Columbus made four voyages to the New World but died believing that the islands he explored were off the coast of China.

establishing a north-south line about 300 miles west of the Azores. Beyond this line all lands were opened to Spanish claims. The Portuguese protested, forcing direct negotiations, which produced the Treaty of Tordesillas (1494). It moved the line some 500 miles farther west. Later explorations showed that the last agreement gave Spain most of the New World but left eastern Brazil to Portugal.

The Developing Portuguese Empire

Through the first half of the sixteenth century, the Portuguese developed a world maritime empire while maintaining commercial supremacy. They established trading posts around both African coasts and a faltering colony in Brazil, but their most extensive operations were in southern Asia, where they drove Muslims from the Indian Ocean and dominated the spice trade of the East Indies.

Two voyages at the turn of the sixteenth century laid the foundations for the Portuguese Empire in America and the Orient. In 1497 Vasco da Gama (1469–1524) left Lisbon, Portugal, in four ships, rounding the Cape of Good Hope after 93 days on the open sea. While visiting and raiding the East African ports, da Gama picked up an Arab pilot, who brought the fleet across the Indian Ocean to Calicut, on the western coast of India. When he returned to Lisbon in 1499, da Gama had lost two ships and a third of his men, but his cargo of pepper and cinnamon returned the cost of the expedition 60 times over. Shortly afterward Pedro Cabral (1468–1520), commanding a large fleet on a second voyage to India, bore too far west and sighted the east coast of Brazil. The new western territory was so unpromising that it

was left unoccupied until 1532, when a small settlement was established at São Vicente. In the 1540s it had attracted only some 2000 settlers, mostly men, although a few Portuguese women came after the arrival of the lord protector's wife and her retinue in 1535. The colony served mostly as a place to send convicts in the sixteenth century. By 1600 it had only 25,000 European residents.

Brazil was neglected in favor of extensive operations in the Indian Ocean and Southeast Asia. The most striking successes there were achieved under Alfonso de Albuquerque, eastern viceroy from 1509 to 1515. He completed subjugation of the East African sultanates and established fortified trading posts in Mozambique and Zanzibar. After a decisive naval victory over an Arab fleet (1509), Albuquerque captured Hormuz, thus hampering Arab passage from the Persian Gulf. In 1510 the Portuguese acquired Goa on the west coast of India; it became a base for aiding Hindus against Indian Muslims and conducting trade with the interior. The next year a Portuguese force took Malacca, a Muslim stronghold in Malaya, which controlled trade with China and the Spice Islands, through the narrow straits opposite Sumatra.

Although dominant in Indonesia, the Portuguese were mostly supplicants on the Asian mainland. They acquired temporary influence in Laos and Cambodia but were expelled from Vietnam and enslaved in Burma. Their arrogance and violence caused them to be banished from Chinese ports in 1522 and 1544. The Chinese gave them strictly regulated trading rights in Macao in 1557; from then until they were expelled at the end of the Ming dynasty, the Portuguese in China conformed to the law, serving as traders, advisers, and missionaries. In Japan after the 1540s they prospered by selling guns to the warring *daimyo* (feudal barons). Jesuit missionaries converted thousands of Japanese. But as Japan approached political unity, conditions for Europeans grew steadily worse until all Europeans were forced out in the 1630s.

Long before this expulsion the Portuguese Empire had begun to decline. It did not have the special skills or fluid capital required by a global empire and had become dependent on the bankers and spice brokers of northern Europe for financing. This deficiency was magnified by Albuquerque's failure to recruit women from home who might have produced a Portuguese governing elite in the colonies. To make matters worse, the home population dropped steadily after 1600. Thus the relatively few Portuguese men overseas mated with local women. Most were concubines, prostitutes, or slaves—regarded generally as household pets or work animals. These conditions contributed largely to a decided weakening of morale, economic efficiency, and military power. After the turn of the seventeenth century the Portuguese lost ground to the Omani Arabs in East Africa, the Spanish in the Philippines, and the Dutch in both hemispheres. Despite a mild later revival, their empire never regained its former glory.

The Growth of New Spain

While Portugal concentrated on Asian trade, Spain won a vast empire in America. Soon after 1492, Spanish settlements sprouted in the West Indies, most notably on Hispaniola and Cuba. By 1500, as the American continents were recognized and the passage to Asia remained undiscovered, a host of Spanish adventurers—the *conquistadores*—set out for the New World. From the West Indies they crossed the Caribbean to eastern Mexico, fanning out from there in all directions, toward Central America, the Pacific, and the vast North American hinterlands.

In Mexico the Spaniards profited from internal problems within the Aztec Empire. In the early 1500s unrest ran rampant among many recently subdued tribes, who were forced to pay tribute and furnish sacrificial victims for their Aztec overlords. Montezuma II, the Aztec emperor, professed a fear that the Spaniards were followers of the white-skinned and bearded Teotihuacán god, Quetzalcoatl, who had been exiled by the Toltecs because he forbade human sacrifice and had promised a return from across the sea to enforce his law. Whether this was Montezuma's true belief or not, the legend probably added to the widespread resentment already verging on rebellion.

In 1519 Hernando Cortés (1485–1574) arrived from Cuba with 11 ships, 600 fighting men, 200 servants, 16 horses, 32 crossbows, 13 muskets, and 14 mobile cannons. Before marching against the Aztec capital, he destroyed his ships to prevent his men from turning back. In a few battles the Spanish horses, firearms, steel armor, and tactics produced decisive victories. Exploiting the Quetzalcoatl legend and the Aztec policy of taking sacrificial victims, Cortés was able to enlist Amerindian allies. As the little army marched inland, its members were welcomed, feasted, and given Amerindian women, including daughters of chiefs, whom Cortés distributed among his men. One woman, Malinche, later christened Doña Marina, became a valuable interpreter as well as Cortés's mistress and bore him a son. She helped save him from a secret ambush at Cholula; it had been instigated by Montezuma, who otherwise delayed direct action as Cortés approached Tenochtitlán, accompanied by thousands of Amerindian warriors.

In that city of more than 150,000 people, Cortés became a guest of Montezuma, surrounded by a host of armed Aztecs. Undaunted, Cortés implemented his preconceived plan and seized the Amerindian ruler in the man's own palace. Malinche then informed Montezuma, as if in confidence, that he must cooperate or die. The bold scheme worked temporarily, but soon the Aztecs rebelled, renounced their emperor as a traitor, stoned and killed him when he tried to pacify them, and ultimately drove a battered band of terrified Spaniards from the city in the narrowest of

An illustration from the Codex Azacatitlán of the Spanish arriving in Mexico. Standing next to Cortés is Malinche, the Aztec woman who served as his interpreter.

Cortés Meets Montezuma

After arriving in Tenochtitlán, Cortés wrote this famous report in a long letter to Charles V, the Spanish monarch. Such descriptions of fabulous wealth in the New World were major causes of Spanish adventuring overseas.

The next day after I had arrived in this city, I left, and having gone half a league, I reached another causeway, leading out into the lake a distance of two leagues to the great city of Temixtitan, which stands in the midst of the said lake. This causeway is two lances broad, and so well built that eight horsemen can ride abreast; and, within these two leagues, there are three cities, on one and the other side of the said highway, one called Mesicalsingo, founded for the greater part within the said lake, and the other two, called Niciaca, and Huchilohuchico, on the other shore of it, with many of their houses on the water.

The first of these cities may have three thousand families, the second more than six thousand, and the third four or five thousand. In all of them, there are very good edifices, of houses and towers, especially the residences of the lords and chief persons, and the mosques or oratories, where they keep their idols. These cities have a great trade in salt, which they make from the water of the lake, and from the crust of the land which is bathed by the lake, and which they boil in a certain manner, making loaves of salt, which they sell to the inhabitants in the neighbourhood.

I followed the said causeway for about half a league before I came to the city proper of Temixtitan. I found at the junction of another causeway, which joins this one from the mainland, another strong fortification, with two towers, surrounded by walls, twelve feet high with castellated tops. This commands the two roads, and has only two gates, by one of which they enter, and from the other they come out. About one thousand of the principal citizens came out to meet me, and speak to me, all richly dressed alike according to their fashion; and when they had come, each one in approaching me, and before speaking, would use a ceremony which is very common

amongst them, putting his hand on the ground, and afterwards kissing it. . . . There is a wooden bridge, ten paces broad, in the very outskirts of the city, across an opening in the causeway, where the water may flow in and out as it rises and falls. This bridge is also for defence, for they remove and replace the long broad wooden beams, of which the bridge is made, whenever they wish; and there are many of these bridges in the city, as Your Highness will see in the account which I shall make of its affairs.

Having passed this bridge, we were received by that lord, Montezuma, with about two hundred chiefs, all barefooted, and dressed in a kind of livery, very rich, according to their custom, and some more so than others. They approached in two processions near the walls of the street, which is very broad, and straight, and beautiful, and very uniform from one end to the other, being about two thirds of a league long, and having, on both sides, very large houses, both dwelling places, and mosques. Montezuma came in the middle of the street, with two lords, one on the right side, and the other on the left, one of whom was the same great lord, who, as I said, came in that litter to speak with me, and the other was the brother of Montezuma, lord of that city Iztapalapan, whence I had come that day. All were dressed in the same manner, except that Montezuma was shod, and the other lords were barefooted. Each supported him below his arms, and as we approached each other, I descended from my horse, and was about to embrace him, but the two lords in attendance prevented me, with their hands, that I might not touch him. . . .

From *Hernando Cortés, His Five Letters of Relation to the Emperor Charles V,* in Harry J. Carroll et al., eds., *The Development of Civilizations,* Vol. 1 (Glenview, Ill.: Scott, Foresman, 1970), pp. 56–57.

escapes. Later, having regrouped and gained new Amerindian allies, Cortés wore down the Aztecs in a long and bloody siege during which some Spanish prisoners were sacrificed in full view of their comrades. Finally, after fearful slaughter, some 60,000 exhausted and half-starved defenders surrendered. Most tribes in central Mexico then accepted Spanish rule; many who resisted were enslaved.

Tenochtitlán, rebuilt as Mexico City, became the capital of an expanding Spanish empire. *Conquistadores* steadily penetrated the interior, but the fierce

Mayas of Yucatán and Guatemala were not subdued until the 1540s. By then settlements had been established throughout Central America. The first colony in North America was founded at St. Augustine, on Florida's east coast, in 1565. Meanwhile, numerous expeditions, including those of Hernando de Soto (1500–1542) and Francisco de Coronado (1510–1554), explored what is now California, Arizona, New Mexico, Colorado, Texas, Missouri, Louisiana, and Alabama. Spanish friars established a mission at Santa Fe in 1610, providing a base for

Antonio Pigafetta, "Magellan's Last Fight"

This firsthand account, recorded by an Italian crew member, describes the skirmish with inhabitants of the Philippine island of Mactan, where Magellan was killed in April 1521.

On Friday the 26th of April, Zula, the chief of this island of Mactan, sent one of his sons to present two goats to the Captain, and to tell him that [he would send him everything that he had promised but that he could not send it] because of the other chief, Cilapulapu, [who] did not want to obey the king of Spain, [and asked] that on the following night he send him but one boatload of men to help him and fight him. The Captain General decided to go there with three boats. And for a long time the others begged him not to go there, but like a good captain, he did not want to abandon his allies. At midnight sixty men armored with cuirasses and sallers left with the Christian king, the prince and some of the chieftains in twenty or thirty boats. And three hours before daylight they reached Mattan. . . . When day came, our men leaped into the water up to their thighs, forty-nine of them, and thus they waded more than two bowshots before they came to dry land. . . . When they arrived on land, these people had made three sections of more than one thousand and fifty persons. And as soon as they realized that [Magellan's men] were coming, two sections attacked their flanks, and the other their front. When the Captain saw this, he divided his men into two groups and thus they began to fight. The musketeers and the bowmen shot from a distance for almost a half hour in vain, able only to penetrate the shields made of thin planks that they carried on their arms. The Captain shouted to cease firing, but they did not cease firing. [When the natives saw that we were firing muskets without any result] they cried out determined to stand firm. And when the muskets were fired, they shouted all the louder and would not keep still, but jumped hither and yon, covered with their shields shooting so many arrows and hurling bamboo lances, charred pointed stakes, stones and mud at the

Captain that he could scarce defend himself. When the Captain saw this he sent some men to burn their houses to frighten them. And when they saw their houses burning they were all the more fierce, and they killed two of our men near the houses, and twenty or thirty burned. And so great a number came upon us that they pierced the right leg of the Captain with a poisoned arrow, wherefor he ordered that they gradually retreat, and they would follow them, and six or eight remained with the Captain. These people aimed only at their legs because they were not covered with armor. And they had so many spears, darts and stones that [Magellan's soldiers] could not withstand them, and the artillery of the fleet was so far away that it could not help them. And our men withdrew to the shore, fighting all the while, even up to their knees in water, and they recovered their own spears four or five times in order to throw them at us. They recognized the Captain and so many assailed him that twice they knocked his sallet from his head. And he, like a good knight, continued to stand firm with a few others, and they fought thus for more than an hour and refused to retreat. An Indian threw his bamboo spear into his face and he immediately killed him with his own spear and it remained in [the Indian's] body. And the Captain tried to draw his sword and was able to draw it only half way, because he had been wounded in the arm with a spear. When our men saw this they turned their backs and made their way to the ships, still pursued with lances and darts until they were out of sight, and they killed [the Europeans'] guide.

From Paula S. Paige, trans., *The Voyage of Magellan: The Journal of Antonio Pigafetta* (Englewood Cliffs, N.J.: Prentice Hall, 1969). Used by permission of the publisher and the William L. Clements Library.

later missions. All these new territories, known as New Spain, were administered from Mexico City after 1542.

The viceroyalty of Mexico later sponsored colonization of the Philippines, a project justified by the historic voyage of Ferdinand Magellan (1480–1521). Encouraged by the exploits of Vasco de Balboa (1479–1519), who had crossed Panama and discovered the Pacific Ocean in 1513, Magellan sailed from Spain in 1520, steered past the ice-encrusted straits at the tip of South America, and endured a 99-day voyage to the Philippines, where he was killed by in-

habitants of Mactan Island. Only one of Magellan's five ships completed this first circumnavigation of the world, but the feat established a Spanish claim to the Philippines. It also prepared the way for the first tiny settlement of 400 Mexicans at Cebu in 1571. By 1580, when the capital at Manila had been secured against attacking Portuguese, Chinese, and Moro fleets, the friars were beginning conversions that would reach half a million by 1622. The colony prospered in trade with Asia but remained economically dependent on annual galleons from Mexico. Here as in Mexico, Spanish males, as a tiny elite, spawned a mixed-race population in liaisons with Filipino and Chinese women.

The Development of Spanish South America

As in Mexico, the Spanish exploited unique opportunities in their process of empire building in Peru. Just as they arrived, the recently formed Inca state was torn by a bitter civil war between two rival princes. This war, which soon destroyed nearly every semblance of imperial unity, was also a major factor in the surprisingly easy triumph of a handful of Spanish freebooters over a country of more than 10 million people, scattered through Peru and Ecuador in hundreds of mountain towns and coastal cities.

Francisco Pizarro (1470–1541), the son of an illiterate peasant, was the conqueror of Peru. After two earlier exploratory visits, he landed on the northern coast in January 1531 with a tiny privately financed army of 207 men and 27 horses. For more than a year he moved south, receiving some reinforcements as he plundered towns and villages. Leaving a garrison of 60 soldiers in a coastal base, he started inland in September 1532 with a Spanish force of fewer than 200. About the same time, word came that Altahualpa, one of the contending princes, had defeated the other in battle. Pizarro now posed as a potential ally to both sides. At Cajamarca he met and captured Altahualpa, slaughtering some 6000 unarmed retainers of the Inca monarch. He next forced Altahualpa to fill a room with silver and gold, including the imperial throne. Then, having collected the ransom, Pizarro executed his royal prisoner and proclaimed Manco, the young son of Altahualpa's dead brother, as emperor. Thus upon arriving in Cuzco with their puppet ruler, the Spaniards were welcomed as deliverers and quickly secured tentative control of the country.

For two more decades political anarchy reigned in Peru, while *conquistadores* fought, explored, and plundered. Manco, after suffering terrible indignities from the Spaniards, led a rebellion that lasted for 26 years after his final defeat and execution in 1544. The period was marked by an obsessive Spanish rape of the country, along with cruel persecution of its Amerindian population, and by ruthless contention, involving every degree of greed and brutality, among the conquerors. Meanwhile, marauding expeditions moved south into Chile and north through Ecuador into Colombia. Expeditions from Chile and Peru settled in Argentina, founding Buenos Aires. *Conquistadores* and Amerindian women produced a new *mestizo* (Spanish-Indian) population in Paraguay. Despite this dynamic activity, there was no effective government at Lima, the capital, until the end of the sixteenth century.

Along with brutality, Spaniards in the postconquest era also demonstrated unprecedented fortitude and courage. Pizarro's Spaniards were always outnumbered in battle. They faced nearly unendurable torments, including scorching heat, disease-carrying insects, air too thin for breathing, and cold that at times could freeze a motionless man into a lifeless statue. Amid the terrible hardships of this male-dominated era, both Amerindian and Spanish women played significant roles. As in Mexico, Amerindian women were camp-following concubines; like them, some Spanish women prepared food, bore children, and when necessary fought beside the men. Some women were present on all the pioneering ventures, and others were direct participants in the terrible sacrifices of the civil wars.

By 1600 the two viceroyalties of Mexico and Peru were well established, governing over 200 towns with a Spanish and mestizo population of 200,000. Nevertheless, the empire was already in decline. Peruvian silver, the main source of Spanish wealth, was either running out or requiring very expensive mining operations; the Amerindian labor force was depleted, and African slaves were both scarce and expensive. Spain's deteriorating home economy and waning sea power presented even more serious problems.

Iberian Systems in the New World

European expansion overseas after the fifteenth century brought revolutionary change to all the world's peoples, but the Iberian period before 1600 was unique in its violence and ruthless exploitation. Not only were highly organized states destroyed in the New World, but whole populations were wiped out by European diseases, shock, and inhumane treatment. This tragic catastrophe was accompanied by a decided change in the racial composition of Iberian America as an influx of African slaves, along with continued Spanish and Portuguese immigration, led to a variegated racial mixture, ranging through all shades of color between white and black. Fortunately, the Amerindian population began recovering in the mid-1600s, and their cultures, combining with Iberian and African, formed a new configuration, to be known later as Latin American.

The General Nature of Regimes

Iberian regimes in America faced serious problems. Their vast territories, far greater than the homelands, contained nearly impassable deserts, mountains, and jungles. Supplies had to be moved thousands of miles, often across open seas. Communications were difficult, wars with indigenous peoples were

The arrival of the Spanish and Portuguese in America led to a mixing of three cultures: European, African, and Amerindian. This painted wooden bottle, done in Inca style and dating from about 1650, shows the mix. The three figures are an African drummer, a Spanish trumpeter, and an Amerindian official.

frequent, and disease was often rampant. Such conditions help explain, if not justify, the brutality of Iberian imperialism.

With all their unique features, Iberian overseas empires were similar to Roman or Turkish provinces: they were meant to produce revenues. In theory, all Spanish lands were the king's personal property. The Council of the Indies, which directed the viceroys in Mexico City and Lima, advised him on colonial affairs. The highborn Spanish viceroys were aided (and limited) by councils (*audiencias*), made up of aristocratic lawyers from Spain. Local governors, responsible to the viceroys, functioned with their advisory councils (*cabildos*) of officials. Only the rich normally sat in such bodies; poor Spaniards and mestizos had little voice, even in their own taxation. Most taxes, however, were collected by Amerindian chiefs (*caciques*), still acting as rulers of Amerindian peasant villages.

Portuguese Brazil was less directly controlled than the Spanish colonies. It languished for years under almost unrestricted domination of 15 aristocratic "captains" who held hereditary rights of taxing, disposing lands, making laws, and administering justice. In return, they sponsored settlement and paid stipulated sums to the king. This quasi-feudal administration was abandoned in 1548. When Philip II became king of Portugal in 1580, he established munic-

ipal councils, although these were still dominated by the hereditary captains.

Iberian Economies in America

Both the philosophies and the structures of the Iberian states limited colonial trade and industry. Most Spanish and Portuguese immigrants were disinclined toward productive labor. With few exceptions, commercial contacts were limited to the homelands; Mexican merchants fought a steadily losing battle to maintain independent trade with Peru and the Philippines. Local trade grew modestly in supplying the rising towns, some crafts developed into large-scale industrial establishments, and a national transport system, based on mule teams, became a major Mexican industry. So did smuggling, as demand for foreign goods rose higher and higher.

Agriculture, herding, and mining silver, however, were the main economic pursuits. The early gold sources soon ran out, but silver strikes in Mexico and Peru poured a stream of wealth back to Spain in the annual treasure fleets, convoyed by warships from Havana to Seville. Without gold to mine, many Spanish aristocrats acquired abandoned Amerindian land, raising wheat, rice, indigo, cotton, coffee, and sugarcane. Cattle, horses, and sheep were imported and bred on ranches in the West Indies, Mexico, and Argentina. Brazil developed similar industries, particularly those related to sugar, livestock, and coffee. Iberian economic pursuits in America were potentially productive, revealing numerous instances of initiative and originality, but they were largely repressed by bureaucratic state systems.

Before 1660, plantations were not typical for agriculture in Iberian America, although they were developing in certain areas. Portugal had established sugar plantations on its Atlantic islands (Madeiras, Cape Verde, and São Tomé) before introducing the system into Brazil around 1550. The Spanish tried plantations in the Canaries, later establishing them in the West Indies, the Mexican lowlands, and Central America and along the northern coasts of South America. Even in such areas, which were environmentally suited for intensive single-crop cultivation, it was not easy to raise the capital, find the skilled technicians, and pay for the labor the system required.

The perpetual labor problem was solved primarily by the use of Amerindians, but African slaves were imported early and were coming in greater numbers by the late sixteenth century. Some 75,000 slaves were in the Spanish colonies by 1600; more than 100,000 more arrived in the next four decades. In Brazil, slave importing boomed after 1560, with annual figures surpassing 30,000 in the early 1600s. Some slaves were brutally oppressed as laborers in the mines, and others sweated on Spanish or Brazil-

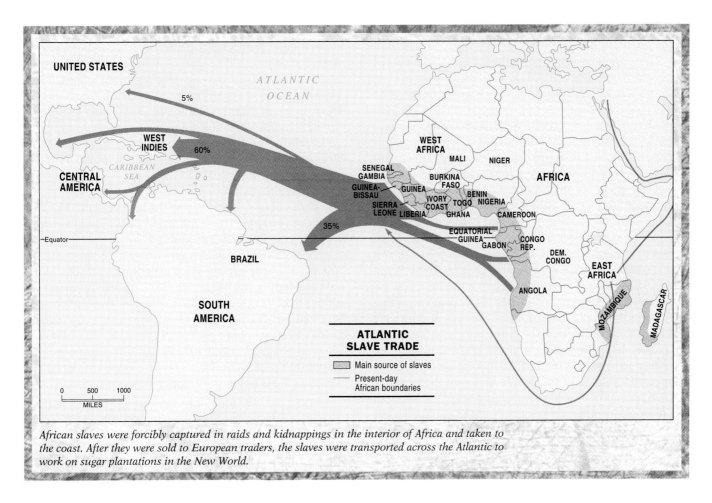

ATLANTIC
OCEAN

UNITED STATES

5%

WEST
INDIES   60%

CARIBBEAN
SEA

CENTRAL
AMERICA

Equator

BRAZIL

SOUTH
AMERICA

35%

WEST
AFRICA   MALI   NIGER

SENEGAL
GAMBIA   BURKINA
GUINEA-   FASO   AFRICA
BISSAU   GUINEA
SIERRA   IVORY   BENIN
LEONE   LIBERIA   COAST   TOGO   NIGERIA
GHANA   CAMEROON
EQUATORIAL
GUINEA   CONGO
GABON   REP.
DEM.
CONGO   EAST
AFRICA
ANGOLA

MOZAMBIQUE   MADAGASCAR

**ATLANTIC
SLAVE TRADE**

Main source of slaves

Present-day
African boundaries

0   500   1000
MILES

African slaves were forcibly captured in raids and kidnappings in the interior of Africa and taken to the coast. After they were sold to European traders, the slaves were transported across the Atlantic to work on sugar plantations in the New World.

ian plantations, but they were the exceptions during this period. Slaves were also teamsters, overseers, personal servants, and skilled artisans. Particularly in the Spanish colonies, a good many earned their freedom, attaining a social status higher than that of Amerindian peasants. Free blacks, both men and women, operated shops and small businesses. Prostitution was understandably common among black and mulatto women, a profession encouraged by the sexual exploitation of female slaves as concubines and breeders.

Iberian Effects on Amerindian Life

The Spanish and Portuguese brought terrible disaster to most Amerindians. Having seen their gods mocked and their temples destroyed, many accepted Christianity as the only hope for survival, as well as salvation, while toiling for their Iberian masters. Some died from overwork, some were killed, and others simply languished as their cultures disintegrated. The most dangerous adversity was disease—European or African—to which Amerindians had no immunities.

Epidemics arrived with Columbus and continued throughout the sixteenth century. Smallpox on Hispaniola in 1518 left only 1000 Amerindians alive

there. Cortés carried the pox to Mexico, where it raged while he fought his way out of Tenochtitlán. From Mexico the epidemic spread through Central America, reaching Peru in 1526. It killed the reigning emperor and helped start the civil war that facilitated Pizarro's conquest. Following these smallpox disasters in the 1540s and 1570s, a wave of measles, along

Amerindian slaves work a Spanish sugar plantation on the island of Hispaniola. Spanish treatment of the Amerindians was often brutal.

with other successive epidemics, continued depleting the population.

Depopulation of Amerindians was caused in part by their enslavement, despite disapproval by the Catholic Church and the Spanish government. The worst excesses came early. Original settlers on Hispaniola herded the gentle Arawaks to work like animals; they soon became extinct. A whole indigenous population of the Bahamas—some 40,000 people— were carried away as slaves to Hispaniola, Cuba, and Puerto Rico. Cortés took slaves before he took Tenochtitlán; other Amerindians, captured in Panama, were regularly sent to Peru. Before Africans arrived in appreciable numbers, the Portuguese organized "Indian hunts" in the forests to acquire slaves.

Another more common labor system in the Spanish colonies was the *encomienda*. This system was instituted in Mexico by Cortés as a way of using Amerindian caciques to collect revenues and provide labor. It was similar to European feudalism and manorialism, involving a grant that permitted the holder (*encomiendero*) to take income or labor from specified lands and the people living on them. Many *encomienderos* starved and lashed their Amerindian laborers, working men and women to exhaustion or renting them to other equally insensitive masters. Amerindian women on the *encomiendas* were generally used as sex slaves by the owners and the caciques, who served as overseers. Abuses became so widespread and Amerindian complaints so insistent that the system was slowly but steadily abandoned after the 1550s.

The change resulted largely from efforts by the Dominican friar Bartolomé de Las Casas (1474–1566), who protested the cruel treatment of Amerindians and persuaded Charles V that they should hold the same rights as other subjects. These led to the New Law of 1542, which ended existing *encomiendas* upon the death of their holders, prohibited Amerindian slavery, and gave Amerindians full protection under Spanish law. Most of these provisions, however, were rescinded when the law evoked universal protest and open rebellion in Peru. Although later governors gradually eliminated *encomiendas*, many Amerindians were put on reservations and hired out as contract laborers under the direction of their caciques and local officials (*corrigodores*). This practice eliminated some of the worst excesses of the *encomiendas*, but corrupt officials often exploited their wards, particularly in Peru.

Such physical hardships were matched by others of a psychological nature, which were almost equally damaging to Amerindians. The Spaniards insisted on forcing Christian conversion even while they raped and destroyed, as Pizarro did before executing Altahualpa. Except when they used Amerindian authorities to support their regimes, the Spaniards went out of their way to insult, shame, and degrade their unfortunate subjects. In the new social milieu, Amerindians were constantly reminded of their lowly status, unworthy of human consideration. Cortés, for example, passed off Malinche to one of his captains; Pizarro forced Manco, while still an ally, to give his young Inca queen to the conqueror. Such indignities, repeated by the hundreds among both Spanish and Portuguese, left many Amerindians demoralized to the point of utter despair.

Their distress was alleviated to some extent by missions, established by the Dominican and Jesuit religious orders. These afforded Amerindians the most effective protection and aid. Las Casas led the way in founding such settlements, where Amerindians were shielded from white exploitation, instructed in Christianity, and educated or trained in special skills. The prevailing philosophy in the missions stressed patient persuasion, "as rain and snow falls from heaven, not . . . violently . . . like a sudden shower, but gradually, with suavity and gentleness."[3] Large mission organizations developed in Brazil, Venezuela, Paraguay, and upper California. But even

Moved by the simplicity and gentle nature of the Amerindians, Bartolomé de Las Casas launched a vigorous campaign to ensure their protection. His Apologetic History of the Indies *(1566) is an indictment of the Spaniards' harsh treatment of the Amerindians.*

the Amerindians protected by the missions died rapidly in this alien way of life.

Although most Amerindians were demoralized by their misfortunes, some resisted. In Yucatán and Guatemala, where the Mayas did not believe the Spaniards were gods, bloody fighting lasted until the 1540s. About that time a revolt on the Mexican Pacific coast was put down with great difficulty by the Spaniards. As the silver mines opened in northern Mexico into the 1590s, the Chichimecs, relatives of the Apaches, conducted a border war, using horses and captured muskets. In Peru an Inca rebellion, led first by Manco, was subdued only in 1577. The most stubborn resistance came from the Araucanians of southern Chile, who fought the Spaniards successfully until the close of the sixteenth century.

The full Iberian impact on Amerindian culture is difficult to assess, although there can be no denying that it was disastrous. A conservative estimate of Amerindian population losses puts the proportion at 25 percent during the era to 1650, but some recent figures place losses much higher, up to 95 percent of the pre-1492 total of 100 million.[4] Signs of mental deterioration were also evident in prevalent alcoholism, which began among Amerindians shortly after the conquest. The social ills of many Amerindians in Latin America have endured, arising from their cultural alienation in a modern world not of their own creation.

Spanish Colonial Society and Culture

Spanish colonial society was stratified but somewhat flexible. A small elite of officials and aristocrats contended over politics, policy toward subject peoples, and foreign trade. Merchants and petty officials were on a lower social level but above mestizos, mulattos, and *zambos* (Indo-Africans). Amerindians were considered incompetent wards of the home government, and African slaves were legally designated as beneath the law, but there were numerous individual exceptions. Many Amerindians went from their rural homes to the towns, mines, or haciendas; some caciques enjoyed wealth and privilege; and a few established Amerindian families retained their nobility as early Spanish allies. Similarly, some African slaves were craftspeople, overseers, or privileged personal servants; others acquired freedom and became prosperous merchants; still others escaped slavery, organized free communities, and successfully defended their independence.

Women in Spanish America played ambiguous roles, reflecting the traditional ideal of male superiority mitigated by a dynamic society. They were excluded from male contacts throughout childhood, educated in cloistered schools to become wives and mothers, married in their teens to further family in-

terests, and legally subordinated to their husbands. Those who did not marry, particularly women of the upper classes, usually entered convents. There was, however, another side to the story. Spanish law guaranteed a wife's dowry rights, a legal protection against the squandering of her wealth, and leverage to limit her husband's activities. The courts recognized separations and at times even granted annulments in cases of wife abuse. Women, particularly widows, operated businesses and held public office. Some were wealthy, powerful, and even cruel *encomienderas*, supervising thousands of workers. Whatever their special roles, Iberian matrons defended religion, sponsored charities, dictated manners, and taught their children family values. They civilized the empires conquered by their men.

Both the unique environment and the mix of peoples shaped Spanish colonial culture toward a new distinctive unity. From southwestern Europe came its aristocratic government, disdain for manual labor, a preference for dramatic over precise expression, and ceremonial Catholic Christianity. From Amerindian traditions came characteristic foods, art forms, architecture, legends, and practical garments like the poncho and serape, as well as substantial vocabulary. From Africa came agricultural knowledge, crafts, and animal husbandry. By 1650 this characteristic colonial culture was being preserved in its own universities, such as those at Lima and Mexico City, both founded more than a century earlier.

The Portuguese Impact on Africa

Unlike the Spanish in America, the Portuguese came to Africa as traders rather than settlers. Their original goal was to find a way around Muslim middlemen who controlled the trans-Saharan caravan trade and to gain direct access to the fabled goldfields of West Africa. Muslim kingdoms of the Sudan, such as Mali, Kanem-Bornu, and the Hausa states, dominated trade in the West African interior and were reluctant to open up their trade to Europeans. When Portugal sent envoys to Mali in the late fifteenth century, the king of Mali claimed that he had never heard of the king of Portugal. Therefore, the Portuguese concentrated their efforts on establishing commercial bases along the West African coast.

The Portuguese in West Africa

Africa was not of primary importance to the Portuguese, especially after they opened up sea routes to Asia. Thus they selectively established links with African states where they could trade for goods of

The Portuguese and Africa

1482   Portuguese establish Fort Elmina on Gold Coast; Portuguese reach kingdom of Kongo

1506–1543 Reign of Nzinga Mbemba, king of Kongo

1506   Portuguese seize Sofala

1571   Portuguese establish colony of Angola

1607   King of Mutapa kingdom signs treaty with Portugal

1698   Portuguese driven from East African coast by Omani Arabs

value such as gold, which could be traded anywhere in the world, and slaves, which were initially taken to southern Portugal as laborers. The first bases of operation for Portuguese seafarers were at Cape Verde, Arguin, and Senegambia. The latter two places afforded opportunities to trade with African states that had trading links with the Sudanic kingdoms.

The Portuguese finally located a place close to a source of gold when they arrived on the Gold Coast (present-day Ghana) in 1471. There they found Akan states carrying on a vigorous trade to the north through Muslim Dyula traders. In a short time the Portuguese crown established a profitable relationship with Akan leaders, exchanging copper, textiles, and later cowrie shells for gold. From their fort at Elmina ("the mine"), established in 1482, the Portuguese exported close to a ton of gold annually for the next half century.

The Portuguese also initiated contacts with the kingdom of Benin, located in the forests of southwestern Nigeria. The kings of Benin, called *obas*, had governed their land since the eleventh century. When the Portuguese arrived, Benin possessed a formidable army and was at the peak of its power. Edo, the walled capital, was a bustling metropolis with wide streets, markets, and an efficient municipal government. The huge royal palace awed Europeans who chanced to see it, although the Portuguese—and later the Dutch—were generally prohibited from living in the city. The few European visitors who gained entrance were amazed by Benin's metalwork, such as copper birds on towers, copper snakes coiled around doorways, and beautifully cast bronze statues. Portuguese visitors were occasionally invited to attend court, and the obas sent emissaries to Lisbon. In the early 1500s the oba Ozuola admitted Catholic missionaries to the kingdom. Although they converted several of Ozuola's sons and high-ranking officials, their influence ended at Ozuola's death.

Portugal believed that it could manipulate Benin's rulers to extend Portuguese trade over a much wider area, but the obas did not regard trade with the Portuguese as a vital necessity and did not allow them to establish a sizable presence in the kingdom. The obas controlled all transactions, and Portuguese traders duly paid taxes, observed official regulations, and conducted business only with the obas' representatives.

The Portuguese traded brass and copper items, textiles, and cowrie shells for pepper, cloth, beads, and slaves. Because Benin did not have access to sources of gold, the Portuguese took the slaves from Benin and traded them for gold with the Akan states, which needed laborers for clearing forests for farmland. However, in 1516, Benin decided to curtail the slave trade and offered only female slaves for purchase.

This saltcellar from Benin depicts a Portuguese sailor sighting land from the crow's nest of his ship.

Although effectively limited in Benin, Portuguese traders operated among nearby coastal states, where they gained some political influence. They were particularly successful in the small kingdom of Warri, a Niger delta vassal state of Benin. Shortly after 1600 the Warri crown prince was educated in Portugal and brought home a Portuguese queen. Warri supplied large numbers of slaves, as did other nearby states, which were now competing fiercely with one another. Before long even Benin would accept dependence on the trade in order to control its tributaries and hold its own against Europeans.

The Portuguese and the Kongo Kingdom

Farther south, near the mouth of the Congo River, the Portuguese experienced their most intensive involvement in Africa. Portuguese seafarers found the recently established Kongo kingdom of several million people, ruled by a king who was heavily influenced by the queen mother and other women on his royal council. Kongo's king, Nzinga Nkuwu, saw the Portuguese as a potential ally against neighboring African states. In the 1480s he invited the Portuguese to send teachers, technicians, missionaries, and soldiers. His son, Nzinga Mbemba (1506–1543), who converted to Catholicism in 1491, consolidated the control of the Catholic faction at his court, making Portuguese the official language and Catholicism the state religion. He encouraged his court to adopt European dress and manners while changing his own name to Don Afonso. Many friendly letters subsequently passed between him and King Manuel of Portugal.

This mutual cooperation did not last long. While the Portuguese were prepared to assist Afonso's kingdom, their desire for profits won out over their humanitarian impulses. Portuguese traders, seeking slaves for their sugar plantations at São Tomé and Principe, ranged over Kongo. By 1530 some 4000 to 5000 slaves were being taken from Kongo annually. No longer satisfied with treaty terms that gave them prisoners of war and criminals, they ignored the laws and bought everyone they could get, thus creating dissension and weakening the country. Driven to despair, Afonso wrote to his friend and ally Manuel: "There are many traders in all corners of the country. They bring ruin.... Every day, people are enslaved and kidnapped, even nobles, even members of the King's own family."[5] Such pleas brought no satisfactory responses. For a while Afonso tried to curb the slave trade; he was shot by disgruntled Portuguese slavers while he was attending Mass. Afonso's successors were no more successful, and Portuguese slavers operated with impunity throughout Kongo and in neighboring areas.

The Portuguese crown also turned its attention to the Mbundu kingdom to the south of Kongo. In 1520 Manuel established contact with the Mbundu king, Ngola. However, when the Portuguese government agreed to deal with Ngola through Kongo, São Tomé slavers were given a free hand to join with Mbundu's rulers to attack neighboring states. Using African mercenaries known as *pombeiros* equipped with firearms and sometimes allied with feared Jaga warriors, the slavers and their allies began a long war of conquest. In the last stages of this war they met the stubborn resistance of Queen Nzinga of Mbundu, a former ally who finally broke with the Portuguese and rallied her kingdom against them.

In 1571 the Portuguese crown issued a royal charter to establish the colony of Angola, situated on the Atlantic coast south of the Kongo kingdom. Although Portugal had ambitious plans to create an agricultural colony for white settlement and to gain control over a silver mine and the salt trade in the interior, Angola was never a successful venture. Few settlers immigrated, and Angola remained a sleepy outpost, consisting of a handful of Portuguese men, even fewer Portuguese women, a growing population of Afro-Portuguese, and a majority of Africans. The colony functioned primarily as a haven for slavers. By the end of the sixteenth century 10,000 slaves were flowing annually through Luanda, Angola's capital.

The Portuguese in East Africa

Portuguese exploits in East Africa were similar to those in Kongo and Angola. The African states of the east were much weaker than those in West Africa. The Swahili city-states along the coast north of the Zambezi River were divided and militarily impotent. They were tempting targets for Portuguese intervention because they were strategically well located for trade with Asia.

Although the Swahili people scorned the bad manners, unclean habits, and tawdry trade goods of the Portuguese, they had been prosperous and peaceful for so long that they could not effectively defend themselves against a ruthless Portuguese naval force that plundered from Kilwa to Mombasa. At Mombasa Portuguese sailors broke into houses with axes, looted, and killed before setting the town afire. The sultan of Mombasa wrote to the sultan of Malindi: "[They] raged in our town with such might and terror that no one, neither man nor woman, neither the old or the young, nor even the children, however small, was spared to live."[6]

To control commerce the Portuguese built fortified stations from which they attempted to collect tribute and maintain trade with the interior. An early station at Mozambique became the main port of call for vessels on the Asia route. In the 1590s the

Afonso Appeals to the King of Portugal

This is an excerpt from a long letter, written by a Kongo schoolboy who was a scribe for Don Afonso, the converted and disillusioned king of Kongo. The rest of the letter, dated October 5, 1514, contains many more complaints against Portuguese treachery and villainy.

We ask your Highness to demand of Fernão de Melo why he imprisoned our Dom Francisco, and why he did not allow him to proceed on your Highness' ships to the place we sent him, out of love—for your Highness had sent word that we should despatch 20 or 30 youths of our kin. And we sent our son to your Highness, so that he could present all the slaves and goods we were remitting—and Fernão de Melo did not wish to let him go, but kept him there on his island, with a stick in his hand, making him beg for the love of God—and likewise our nephews—for which reason we are keenly sorrowful. And as to the flesh, we feel much pain, because he is the fruit of our loins; but as to the soul, it grieves us not, for we sent our son to search for the things of God and learn them, and thus all the travails of the world that visit him, while he searches for the faith of our Lord Jesus Christ and learns it, we take to be blessings, and suffer them for the love of our Lord God, for He will ever remember us.

And now we beg of your Highness that, for the love of our Lord Jesus Christ, that you will not forsake us, nor allow the loss of the fruits of Christianity growing in our kingdom—for we can do no more, and have but one mouth to preach and instruct. We have already married, and all the nobles near us have been married—but those who are afar off do not want to be married, because of the evil examples they see every day, and they do not wish to obey us. So we ask your Highness to help us, so that we can make them get married. And if your Highness does not wish to help us in the spiritual realm, we will kiss your royal hands and ask that you send us five or six ships to take us and our sons and relatives, so that we will not witness so great a perdition. . . .

We shall not write more to your Highness because we would have need of a whole ream of paper to relate all the imbroglios that occur here, but Dom Pedro will give your Highness a detailed account of everything. And if anything in this letter be badly written, we ask pardon, because we do not know the styles of Portugal. And we write this with one of our schoolboys, for we do not dare to use any of the [Portuguese] men who are here, for those who best know how to write are guilty of one misdeed or another.

We would kiss the royal hands of your Highness if you would write a letter, on your own behalf, to the *Moynebata* Dom Jorge, and another to the *Moinepanguo*, who are the principal lords in our kingdom, in which your Highness would thank them for being good Christians, and also send them two priests, in addition to those sent to us, so that in their own churches they can say mass, hear confessions, and teach all the things pertaining to God's service. Your Highness should realize that these two lords live a good 80 or 90 leagues distant from us, and each of them has his own church wherein to see God. In both places we have put two schoolboys to teach them [the lords], and their sons and relatives. In this way we have begun the work there and may reap a great harvest. So now let your Highness see if you can complete it, for our powers are thinly spread out and that is all that we can do—but if they can have priests, to say mass to them and confess them, it will be of great merit and they will be strengthened.

From William H. McNeill and Mitsuko Iriye, eds., *Modern Asia and Africa* (New York: Oxford University Press, 1971), pp. 68–71.

Portuguese built a fort at Mombasa, hoping to intimidate other cities and support naval operations against Turks and Arabs in the Red Sea. Such efforts diminished the coastal trade but failed to achieve any military objectives. When Omani Arabs drove the Portuguese from the Swahili coast in 1698, a proverb captured Swahili sentiment: "Go away, Manuel [the king of Portugal], you have made us hate you; go, and carry your cross with you."[7]

On the southeast coast the Portuguese were lured by the gold trade with the Zimbabwean plateau. The Portuguese seized Sofala in 1506, diminishing the role of Muslim traders and positioning themselves as the middlemen for the gold trade with the coast. After establishing trading settlements along the Zambezi River at Sena and Tete, the Portuguese developed a close relationship with the Karanga kingdom of Mutapa, which received Portuguese traders and Catholic missionaries. This relationship soured when the king of Mutapa ordered a Jesuit missionary to be killed in 1560. In the 1570s the Portuguese retaliated by sending several expeditionary forces up the Zambezi to take over the gold mines. These adventures ended disastrously as drought, disease (especially

Discovery Through Maps

Sebastian Munster's Map of Africa

Born in Hesse, Germany, and educated at Heidelberg University, Sebastian Munster (1489–1552) established a reputation as a professor of Hebrew and mathematics at Heidelberg long before involving himself in mapmaking. A master of Latin and Greek as well as Hebrew, he published a Hebrew Bible and dictionary before settling in 1529 at Basel, the home of Switzerland's oldest university and a center of geographers and cartographers.

Munster became involved in maps through his interest in Ptolemy (90–168 C.E.), the celebrated astronomer, geographer, and mathematician of Alexandria, Egypt, whose theories about the universe influenced the European and Arab worlds for many centuries. Around 1400 Ptolemy's *Guide to Geography* was published in Florence as the first atlas of the world. Drawing on his linguistic skills, Munster translated his own version of Ptolemy's *Geography* from Greek into German and published four editions of it between 1540 and 1552.

Ptolemy's volume shaped Munster's views when he began creating his own atlas of the world. First published in 1544, Munster's *Cosmographia Universalis* went through 46 editions and was translated into six languages over the next century. It was the first collection to feature individual maps of Europe, Asia, the Americas, and Africa.

Munster's map of Africa relied not only on Ptolemy but also on Portuguese and Arab sources. However, it still contained many errors. Like the Catalan Atlas, Munster's map showed a mountain chain stretching across much of North Africa. The source of the Nile was identified far to the south. Based on the assumption that the Senegal and Niger Rivers in West Africa were connected, a river was shown flowing westward to the Atlantic.

The *Cosmographia* was also a descriptive geography, providing an accompanying narrative and drawings of prominent figures, the customs and manners of societies, and the products, animals, and plants of regions. Munster's Africa map showed a lone human figure that bore no resemblance to Africans and a large elephant at the southern end of the continent. His rendering of Africa conformed to Dean Swift's satirical lines:

So Geographers in Africa-Maps
With Savage-Pictures fill their Gaps;
And o'er unhabitable Downs
Place Elephants for want of Towns.

malaria), and African resisters decimated the Portuguese forces.

However, a series of internal rebellions and wars with neighboring states later forced Mutapa's rulers to turn to the Portuguese for assistance. In 1607 they signed a treaty that ceded control of the gold mines to the Portuguese. For the rest of the century the Portuguese regularly intervened in Mutapa's affairs until the forces of Mutapa and a rising power, Changamire, combined to expel the Portuguese from the Zimbabwean plateau.

Along the Zambezi River the Portuguese crown granted huge land concessions (prazos) to Portuguese settlers (prazeros) who ruled them as feudal estates. Over time, the prazeros loosened their ties with Portugals officials and became virtually independent. In the absence of Portuguese women, prazeros intermarried with Africans and adopted African culture.

Ethiopia also attracted Portugal's attention. The tale of Prester John, the mythical Ethiopian Christian monarch who held the Muslims at bay, had long captivated Portugal's monarchs. Thus they responded positively when the Ethiopian empress Eleni made diplomatic overtures in 1513. However, a projected alliance was not completed for many years. In 1541 some 400 Portuguese musketeers helped the Ethiopian army defeat a Muslim army that had almost taken over the kingdom. The following year Muslim forces rallied and defeated a Portuguese force, killing its commander, Christopher da Gama, Vasco's son. Although the Ethiopians later pushed the Muslims out, Portuguese involvement with Ethiopia remained at a low level.

For the rest of the sixteenth century the primary European presence in Ethiopia was that of Catholic priests. Ultimately, a Spanish Jesuit delegation won favor with the Ethiopian royal family and secretly converted Emperor Susenyos (1604–1632). However, the zealous policies of Bishop Alphonso Mendez, head of the mission after 1625, led to rebellion and the emperor's abdication. Mendez tried to Catholicize the Ethiopian orthodox faith by reordaining Ethiopian priests, reconsecrating the churches, and banning circumcision. Susenyos's son, Fasilidas, responded by expelling the Jesuits. Ethiopia's rulers retreated from direct contacts with Europe and concentrated on consolidating their hold over the country.

The Portuguese impact on Africa was not as immediately disastrous as Spanish effects on the New World. The Portuguese did not have the manpower or arms to dictate the terms of trade with most African states. However, they did inflict severe damage in Kongo, Angola, Zimbabwe, and the Swahili city-states. Their most destructive involvement was the slave trade. By the end of the sixteenth century the Portuguese had moved an estimated 240,000 slaves from West and Central Africa; 80 percent were transported after 1575. These trends foreshadowed much greater disasters for African societies in the seventeenth and eighteenth centuries as the Atlantic slave trade expanded.

Beginnings of Northern European Expansion

European overseas expansion after 1600 entered a second phase, comparable to developments at home. As Spain declined, so did the Spanish Empire and that of Portugal, which was tied to Spain by a Habsburg king after 1580 and plagued with its own developing imperial problems. These conditions afforded opportunities for the northern European states. The Dutch between 1630 and 1650 almost cleared the Atlantic of Spanish warships while taking over most of the Portuguese posts in Brazil, Africa, and Asia. The French and English also became involved on a smaller scale, setting up a global duel for empire in the eighteenth century.

The Shifting Commercial Revolution

Along with this second phase of expansion came a decisive shift in Europe's Commercial Revolution. Expanding foreign trade, new products, an increasing supply of bullion, and rising commercial risks created new problems, calling for energetic initiatives. Because the Spanish and Portuguese during the sixteenth century had depended on quick profits, weak home industries, and poor management, wealth flowed through their hands to northern Europe, where it was invested in productive enterprises. Later it generated a new imperial age.

European markets after the sixteenth century were swamped with a bewildering array of hitherto rare or unknown goods. New foods from America included potatoes, peanuts, maize (Indian corn), tomatoes, and fish from Newfoundland's Grand Banks. In an era without refrigeration, imported spices, such as pepper, cloves, and cinnamon, were valued for making spoiled foods palatable. Sugar became a common substitute for honey, and the use of cocoa, the Aztec sacred beverage, spread throughout Europe. Coffee and tea from the New World and Asia would also soon change European social habits. Similarly, North American furs, Chinese silks, and cottons from India and Mexico revolutionized clothing fashions. Furnishings of rare woods and ivory and luxurious oriental carpets appeared more frequently in the homes of the wealthy. The use of American tobacco became almost a mania among all classes, further contributing to the booming European market.

Imported gold and, even more significant, silver probably affected the European economy more than all other foreign goods. After the Spaniards had looted Aztec and Inca treasure rooms, the gold flowing from America and Africa subsided to a respectable trickle; but 7 million tons of silver poured into Europe before 1660. Spanish prices quadrupled, and because most new bullion went to pay for imports, prices more than tripled in northern Europe. Rising inflation hurt landlords who depended on fixed rents and creditors who were paid in cheap money, but the bullion bonanza ended a centuries-long gold drain to the East, with its attendant money shortage. It also increased the profits of merchants selling on a rising market, thus greatly stimulating northern European capitalism.

At the opening of the sixteenth century, Italian merchants and moneylenders, mainly Florentines, Venetians, and Genoese, dominated the rising Atlantic economy. The German Fugger banking house at Augsburg also provided substantial financing. European bankers, particularly the Fuggers and the Genoese, suffered heavily from the Spanish economic debacles under Charles V and Philip II. As the century passed, Antwerp, in the southern Netherlands, became the economic hub of Europe. It was the center for the English wool trade as well as a transfer station, drawing southbound goods from the Baltic and Portuguese goods from Asia. It was also a great financial market, dealing in commercial and investment instruments. The Spanish sack of the city in 1576 ended Antwerp's supremacy, which passed to Amsterdam and furthered Dutch imperial ventures.

Meanwhile, northern European capitalism flourished in nearly every category. Portuguese trade in Africa and Asia was matched by that of the Baltic and the North Atlantic. Northern joint-stock companies pooled capital for privateering, exploring, and commercial venturing. The Dutch and English East India companies, founded early in the seventeenth century, were but two of the better-known stock companies. In England common fields were enclosed for capitalistic sheep runs. Throughout western Europe, domestic manufacturing, in homes or workshops, was competing with the guilds. Large industrial enterprises, notably in mining, shipbuilding, and cannon casting, were becoming common. Indeed, the superiority of English and Swedish cannons caused the defeat of the Spanish Armada and Catholic armies in the Thirty Years' War.

The Dutch Empire

By 1650 the Dutch were supreme in both southern Asia and the South Atlantic. Their empire, like that of the Portuguese earlier, was primarily commercial; even their North American settlements specialized in fur trading with the Indians. They acquired territory where necessary to further their commerce but tried

Dutch Exploration and Expansion

1576	Sack of Antwerp; Amsterdam becomes commercial hub of Europe
1595	First Dutch fleet enters East Indies
1609	Henry Hudson explores Hudson River
1621	Dutch form West India Company
1624	Dutch found New Amsterdam on Manhattan Island
1641	Dutch drive Portuguese out of Malacca

to act pragmatically in accordance with Indian cultures rather than by conquest. Unlike the Spanish and the Portuguese, the Dutch made little attempt to spread Christianity.

Systematic Dutch naval operations ended Iberian imperial supremacy, beginning in 1595 when the first Dutch fleet entered the East Indies. Dutch captains soon drove the Portuguese from the Spice Islands. Malacca, the Portuguese bastion, fell after a long siege in 1641. The Dutch also occupied Sri Lanka and blockaded Goa, thus limiting Portuguese operations in the Indian Ocean. Although largely neglecting East Africa, they seized all Portuguese posts on the west coast north of Angola. Across the Atlantic, they conquered Brazil, drove Spain from the Caribbean, and captured a Spanish treasure fleet. Decisive battles off the English Channel coast near Kent (1639) and off Brazil (1640) delivered final blows to the Spanish navy. What the English began in 1588, the Dutch completed 50 years later.

Trade with Asia, the mainstay of the Dutch Empire, was directed by the Dutch East India Company. Chartered in 1602 and given a monopoly over all operations between South Africa and the Strait of Magellan, it conserved resources and tended to eliminate costly competition. In addition to its trade and diplomacy, the company sponsored explorations of Australia, Tasmania, New Guinea, and the South Pacific. With a capital concentration larger than that of most states, it could easily outdistance its European rivals.

The Dutch Empire in the East was established primarily by Jan Pieterszoon Coen, governor-general of the Indies between 1618 and 1629 and founder of the company capital at Batavia in northwestern Java. At first he cooperated with local rulers in return for a monopoly over the spice trade. When this involved him in costly wars against local sultans as well as their Portuguese and English customers, Coen determined to control the trade at its sources. In the ensuing numerous conflicts and negotiations, which out-

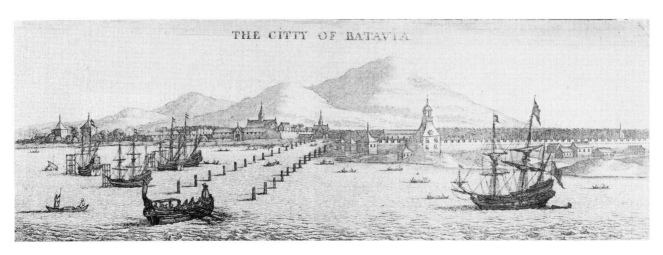

THE CITTY OF BATAVIA

Batavia (present-day Djakarta), on the island of Java, became the headquarters of the Dutch East India Company when the Dutch ousted the Portuguese and took command of the East Indies trade in the seventeenth century.

lasted Coen, the Dutch acquired all of Java, most of Sumatra, the spice-growing Moluccas, and part of Sri Lanka. They began operating their own plantations, supplying pepper, cinnamon, sugar, tea, tobacco, and coffee to a fluctuating world market.

Although commercially successful in Asia, the Dutch were not able to found flourishing colonial settlements. Many Dutchmen who went to the East wanted to make their fortunes and return home; those willing to stay were usually mavericks, uninterested in establishing families but instead pursuing temporary sexual liaisons with female slaves or servants. For a while after 1620 the company experimented with a policy of bringing European women to the Indies, but such efforts were abandoned when the venture failed to enlist much interest at home or in the foreign stations. Consequently, the Dutch colonies in Asia, as well as those in Africa, the Caribbean, and Brazil, remained primarily business ventures with little racial mixing, compared with the Iberian areas.

After resuming war with Spain in 1621, the Dutch formed their West India Company, charged with overtaking the diminishing Spanish and Portuguese holdings in West Africa and America. The company wasted no time. It soon supplanted the Portuguese in West Africa; by 1630 it had taken over the slave trade with America. After driving the Spanish from the Caribbean, the Dutch invited other European planters to the West Indies as customers, keeping only a few bases for themselves. The company then launched a successful naval conquest of Brazil, from the mouth of the Amazon south to the San Francisco River. In Brazil the Dutch learned sugar planting, passing on their knowledge to the Caribbean and applying it directly in the East Indies.

Dutch settlements in North America never amounted to much because of the company's commercial orientation. In 1609 Henry Hudson (d. 1611), an Englishman sailing for the Dutch, explored the river named for him and established Dutch claims while looking for a northwest passage. Fifteen years later the company founded New Amsterdam on Manhattan Island; over the next few years it built a number of frontier trading posts in the Hudson valley and on the nearby Connecticut and Delaware Rivers. Some attempts were made to encourage planting by selling large tracts to wealthy proprietors *(patroons)*. Agriculture, however, remained secondary to the fur trade, which the company developed in alliance with the Iroquois tribes. This arrangement hindered settlement; in 1660 only 5000 Europeans were in the colony.

The French Empire

French exploration began early, but no permanent colonies were established abroad until the start of the seventeenth century. The country was so weakened by religious wars that most of its efforts, beyond fishing, privateering, and a few failed attempts at settlement, had to be directed toward internal stability. While the Dutch were winning their empire, France was involved in the land campaigns of the Thirty Years' War. Serious French empire building thus had to be delayed until after 1650, during the reign of Louis XIV.

Early French colonization in North America was based on claims made by Giovanni da Verrazzano (1485–1528) and Jacques Cartier (1491–1557). The first, a Florentine mariner commissioned by Francis I in 1523, traced the Atlantic coast from North Carolina to Newfoundland. Eleven years later Cartier made one of two voyages exploring the St. Lawrence River. These French expeditions duplicated England's claim to eastern North America.

British and French Exploration and Colonization

1485–1528   Giovanni da Verrazzano

1491–1557   Jacques Cartier

1497–1498   John Cabot establishes English claims in North America

1567–1635   Samuel de Champlain

1605   French establish base at Port Royal, in Nova Scotia

1607   First English colony in North America founded at Jamestown

1627   British conquer Quebec

1629   Puritans settle near Boston

1632–1635   English Catholics found colony of Maryland

1642   Montreal established

French colonial efforts during the sixteenth century were dismal failures. They resulted partly from French experiences in exploiting the Newfoundland fishing banks and conducting an undeclared naval war in the Atlantic against Iberian treasure ships and trading vessels after 1520. In 1543 Cartier tried and failed to establish a colony in the St. Lawrence valley. Other such failures included a French colony in Brazil, terminated by the Portuguese (1555–1557), and an aborted Huguenot settlement in Florida (1562–1564). No more serious efforts were made until 1605, when a French base was established at Port Royal, on Nova Scotia. It was meant to be a fur-trading center and capital for the whole St. Lawrence region. Mapping of the coast was immediately begun, but the site was temporarily abandoned when its fur monopoly was canceled by the French government. The fort was restored after 1610, but it barely survived attacks by Amerindians and the English.

Three years after the founding of Port Royal, Samuel de Champlain (1567–1635), who had been an aide to the governor of the Nova Scotia colony, acted for a French-chartered company in founding Quebec on the St. Lawrence. The company brought in colonists, but the little community was disrupted in 1627 when British troops took the town and forced Champlain's surrender. Although the fort was returned to France by a treaty in 1629, when Champlain came back as governor, growth was slowed by the company's emphasis on fur trading, the bitterly cold winters, and skirmishes with Indians. Only a few settlers had arrived by Champlain's death in 1635, and just 2500 Europeans were in Quebec as late as 1663. Nevertheless, Montreal was established in 1642, after which French trapper-explorers began penetrating the region around the headwaters of the Mississippi.

An early drawing shows the arrival of the first French colonists in North America, brought by Cartier on his third voyage in 1541, against a map of the St. Lawrence estuary. The colony soon failed. (The map is drawn so that north is at the bottom of the drawing rather than at the top.)

Elsewhere the French seized opportunities afforded by the decline of Iberian sea power. They acquired the isle of Bourbon (Réunion) in the Indian Ocean (1642) for use as a commercial base. In West Africa they created a sphere of commercial interest at the mouth of the Senegal River, where they became involved in the slave trade with only slight opposition from the Dutch. Even more significant was the appearance of the French in the West Indies. They occupied part of St. Kitts in 1625 and acquired Martinique and Guadeloupe ten years later. Because the sugar boom was just beginning, the French islands would soon become very profitable. However, fierce attacks by warlike Caribs limited economic development in this era before 1650.

The English Empire

In terms of power and profit, English foreign expansion before 1650 was not impressive. Like French colonialism, it was somewhat restricted by internal political conditions, particularly the poor management and restrictive policies of the early Stuart kings, which led to civil war in the 1640s. A number of circumstances, however, promoted foreign ventures. The population increased from 3 to 4 million between 1530 and 1600, providing a large reservoir of potential indentured labor; religious persecution encouraged migration of nonconformists; and surplus capital was seeking opportunities for investment. Such conditions ultimately produced a unique explosion of English settlement overseas.

During the sixteenth century English maritime operations were confined primarily to exploring, fishing, smuggling, and plundering. English claims to North America were registered in 1497 and 1498 by two voyages of John Cabot, who explored the coast of North America from Newfoundland to Virginia but found no passage to Asia. For the next century English expeditions sought such a northern passage, both in the East and in the West. All of them failed, but they resulted in explorations of Hudson Bay and the opening of a northeastern trade route to Russia. From the 1540s English captains, including the famous John Hawkins of Plymouth, indulged in sporadic slave trading in Africa and the West Indies, despite Spanish restrictions. Subsequent raids against Spanish shipping by English "sea dogs," like Sir Francis Drake, helped prepare for the later dramatic defeat of the Armada.

After failures in Newfoundland and on the Carolina coast, the first permanent English colony in America was founded in 1607 at Jamestown, Virginia. For a number of years the colonists suffered from lack of food and other privations, but they were saved by their dauntless leader, Captain John Smith (1580–1631), whose romantic rescue by the Indian princess Pocahontas (1595–1617) is an American legend. Jamestown set a significant precedent for all English colonies in North America. By the terms of its original charter, the London Company, which founded the settlement, was authorized to supervise government for the colonists, but they were to enjoy all the rights of native Englishmen. Consequently, in 1619 the governor called an assembly to assist in governing. This body would later become the Virginia House of Burgesses, one of the oldest representative legislatures still operating.

Shortly after the founding of Jamestown, large-scale colonization began elsewhere. In 1620 a group of English Protestants known as Pilgrims landed at Plymouth. Despite severe hardships, they survived, and their experiences inspired other religious dissenters against the policies of Charles I. In 1629 a number of English Puritans formed the Massachusetts Bay Company and settled near Boston, where their charter gave them the rights to virtual self-government. From this first enclave, emigrants moved out to other areas in present-day Maine, Rhode Island, and Connecticut. By 1642 more than 25,000 people had migrated to New England, laying the foundations for a number of future colonies. Around the same time (1632–1635), a group of English Catholics, fleeing Stuart persecution, founded the Maryland colony. These enterprises firmly planted English culture and political institutions in North America.

Life in the English settlements was hard during those first decades, but a pioneering spirit and native colonial pride was already evident. Food was scarce, disease was ever-present, and Amerindians were often dangerous. Yet from the beginning, and more than in other European colonies, settlers looked to their future in the new land because they had left so little behind in Europe. Most were expecting to stay, establish homes, make their fortunes, and raise families. The first Puritans included both men and women; a shipload of "purchase brides" arrived in 1619 at Jamestown to lend stability to that colony. This was but the first of many such contingents, all eagerly welcomed by prospective husbands. In addition, many women came on their own as indentured servants.

Anglo-American colonial women faced discrimination but managed to cope with it pragmatically. They were legally dependent on their husbands, who controlled property and children; a widow acquired these rights, but it was not easy to outlive a husband. Hard work and frequent pregnancies—mothers with a dozen children were not uncommon—reduced female life expectancies. Nevertheless, many women developed a rough endurance, using their social value to gain confidence and practical equality with their husbands, although some did this more obviously than others. This independent spirit was revealed by Anne Hutchinson (1591–1643), who left

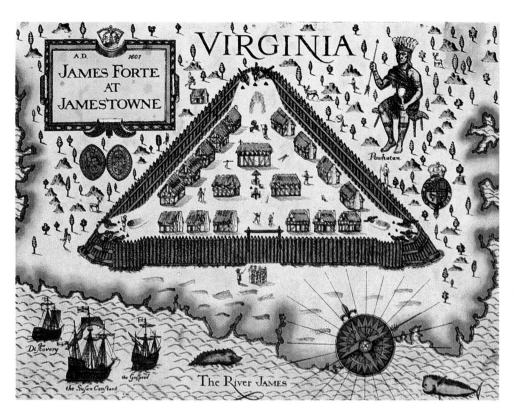

View of Jamestown in 1607 drawn by John Hull. Surrounded by water on three sides, the marshy peninsula on the James River seemed easy to defend and thus an ideal location for the Jamestown fort. By 1614 there were "two faire rowes of howses" protected by a palisade.

Massachusetts and founded a dissenting religious settlement in Rhode Island. Another freethinker was Anne Bradstreet (c. 1612–1672), who wrote thoughtful poetry, although painfully aware that men considered her presumptuous.

The English government considered the rough coasts and wild forests of North America less important in this period than footholds in the West Indies and Africa, where profits were expected in planting and slave trading. Therefore, a wave of English migrants descended on the West Indies after the Dutch opened the Caribbean. In 1613 English settlers invaded Bermuda, and by the 1620s others had planted colonies on St. Kitts, Barbados, Nevis, Montserrat, Antigua, and the Bahamas. Tobacco planting was at first the major enterprise, bringing some prosperity and the promise of more. The white population expanded dramatically, especially on Barbados, which was not subject to Carib Indian attacks. There the English population increased from 7000 to 37,000 in seven years. As yet, however, there were few African slaves on the English islands, although some were already being imported for the sugar plantations.

Meanwhile, English slaving posts in West Africa were beginning to flourish and English adventurers were starting operations in Asia. Captain John Lancaster took four ships to Sumatra and Java in 1601, returning with a profitable cargo of spices. His voyage led to the founding of the British East India Company, which was chartered in 1609. But expansion outside of the Caribbean was difficult because

the Dutch were uncooperative. In the Moluccas, for example, they drove out the English in the 1620s, after repeated clashes. The English fared better in India. By 1622 the British East India Company had put the Portuguese out of business in the Persian Gulf. Subsequently, the English established trading posts on the west coast of India at Agra, Masulipatam, Balasore, and Surat. The station at Madras, destined to become the English bastion on the east coast, was founded in 1639.

Conclusion

Between 1450 and 1650, the era of the early Commercial Revolution, Europeans faced west toward a new world and initiated a new age of oceanic expansion. In the process they stimulated capitalistic development, found a sea route to Asia, became more familiar with Africa, began colonizing America, and proved the world to have a spherical surface. For most of the period Spain and Portugal monopolized the new ocean trade and profited most from exploiting American wealth, following precedents set by earlier Eurasian empires. Only after 1600, when leadership shifted toward the Dutch, French, and English, did European colonialism show signs of developing in new directions.

Overseas expansion exerted a tremendous effect on European culture and institutions. Spain's political predominance in the sixteenth century was

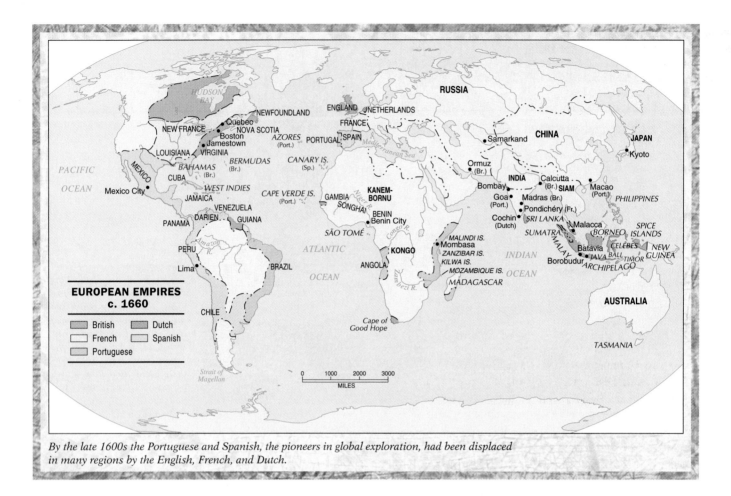

By the late 1600s the Portuguese and Spanish, the pioneers in global exploration, had been displaced in many regions by the English, French, and Dutch.

largely bought with American treasure, and Spain's quick decline was mainly caused by the influx of American bullion, which inflated Spanish money and discouraged Spanish economic development. Northern European capitalism, developing in financial organization, shipbuilding, metalworking, manufacturing, and agriculture, brought a new vitality to northern economies in response to Spanish and Portuguese purchasing power. Economic advantages also contributed to Protestant victories in the Thirty Years' War. This first age of the Commercial Revolution increased northern European confidence and initiative in preparation for later world dominance.

In the New World the European impact was both dramatic and tragic. Spanish *conquistadores* and Portuguese captains nearly destroyed native peoples and subjected most of the survivors to terrible hardships, indignities, cultural deprivations, and psychological injuries. The plight of Latin American peasants today began in Spanish and Portuguese imperial policies of the sixteenth century. Yet the balance sheet is not all negative. The Spanish and Portuguese in America generated a new cultural synthesis, blending European, Amerindian, and African elements to produce a richness and variety not present in any of the parent cultures. This integration was largely accomplished by racial mixing, which created a new Latin American stock in the Western Hemisphere.

The European impact on Africa was less apparent at the time but perhaps more damaging in the long run than what happened to the Amerindians of Latin America. When the Portuguese began exploring the African coastline, they were more concerned with scoring quick profits through gold exports than with establishing stable, long-term relationships with African states. Moreover, with the exception of Angola or landed estates along the Zambezi River, the Portuguese did not have the manpower or resources to conquer or influence the political affairs of African states. However, as the Atlantic slave trade increased, the Portuguese and leaders of African states became bound up in a destructive process that would reach its tragic climax in the next few centuries.

In Asia the European impact before 1650 was mixed. Sri Lanka and the Spice Islands of the Malay archipelago, which were vulnerable to sea attack, came under domination, direct or indirect, and were exploited by the Portuguese and the Dutch. Elsewhere in Asia the European influence was present but less obvious. The Portuguese were run out of

China twice before they came to respect Chinese law, and other Europeans fared worse. All were ultimately excluded from Japan. Southern India was not entirely open, as the Portuguese found by the end of the period. In the main, Turks, Arabs, Chinese, Japanese, Thais, and Vietnamese felt superior to Europeans and were usually able to defend their interests with effective action.

Suggestions for Reading

An excellent work, which covers the whole subject of European exploration and colonization, is Geoffrey V. Scammell, *The First Imperial Age: European Overseas Expansion, 1400–1700* (Unwin Hyman, 1989). See also the two classic studies, Charles E. Nowell, *The Great Discoveries and the First Colonial Empires*, rev. ed. (Greenwood, 1982), and Samuel Eliot Morison, *The European Discovery of America*, in two volumes: *The Northern Voyages* (Oxford University Press, 1971) and *The Southern Voyages* (Oxford University Press, 1974). A briefer but still reliable and interesting volume along the same lines is Samuel Eliot Morison, *The Great Explorers* (Oxford University Press, 1978). A number of other surveys are well worth consulting: Geoffrey V. Scammell, *The World Encompassed: The First European Maritime Empires, c. 800–1650* (University of California Press, 1981); Louis B. Wright, *Gold, Glory, and Gospel* (Atheneum, 1970); Daniel Devine, *The Opening of the World: The Great Age of Maritime Exploration* (Putnam, 1973); and Daniel J. B. Boorstin, *The Discoverers* (Random House, 1985).

For more pointed analyses of early European imperialism, see Carlo M. Cipolla, *Guns, Sails and Empires*, rev. ed. (Sunflower University Press, 1985); William H. McNeil, *Plagues and People* (Doubleday, 1977); Eric R. Wolf, *Europe and the People Without History* (University of California Press, 1982); and Nicholas Canny and Anthony Pagden, *Colonial Identity in the Atlantic World* (Princeton University Press, 1989).

Two time-tested secondary sources on the Iberian New World are H. Hering, *A History of Latin America* (Knopf, 1968), and Stanley J. Stein and Barbara H. Stein, *The Colonial Heritage of Latin America* (Oxford University Press, 1970). To these may be added a number of excellent later studies: Tzvetan Todorov, *The Conquest of America* (Harper & Row, 1984); Lyle N. McAlister, *Spain and Portugal in the New World, 1492–1700* (University of Minnesota Press, 1984); and Mark A. Burkholder, *Colonial Latin America* (Oxford University Press, 1989). For penetrating studies of Latin American social conditions, see two edited collections by Louisa Hoberman and Susan M. Socolow, *Cities and Society in Colonial Latin America* (University of New Mexico Press, 1986) and *The Countryside in Colonial America* (University of New Mexico Press, 1996). The complex issues relating to slavery and plantations are ably identified and evaluated in W. R. Aykroyd, *Sweet Malefactor: Sugar, Slavery, and Human Society* (Heinemann, 1967); Eric Williams, *From Columbus to Castro*, rev. ed. (Random House, 1984); and Herbert S. Klein, *African Slavery in Latin America and the Caribbean* (Oxford University Press, 1988). On the ambiguous status of women, see Ann M. Pescatello, *Power and Pawn: The Female in Iberian Families* (Greenwood, 1976), and Asuncion Lavin, ed., *Latin American Women* (Greenwood, 1978).

A general overview of Spanish empire building in America is provided in Colin M. MacLachlan, *Spain's Empire in the New World* (University of California Press, 1988). Three earlier works are also worth attention: Oskar H. K. Spate, *The Spanish*

Lake (University of Minnesota Press, 1979); J. H. Parry, *The Spanish Seaborne Empire* (Knopf, 1971); and Charles Gibson, *Spain in America* (Harper Torchbooks, 1968). Gianni Granzotto, *Christopher Columbus* (University of Oklahoma Press, 1988), reveals the world of Columbus and a personalized account of his exploits. Other works on Columbus and his voyages are David Henige, *In Search of Columbus: The Sources for the First Voyage* (University of Arizona Press, 1991); Joseph Schnaubelt and Frederick Van Fleteren, *Columbus and the New World* (Long, 1998); and John Yewell, Chris Dodge, and Jan De Surey, *Confronting Columbus: An Anthology* (McFarland, 1992).

On the whole subject of Spanish campaigns in the New World, William H. Prescott, *The Conquest of Mexico* (Bantam, 1964) and *The Conquest of Peru* (Mentor, 1961), are readable abridgments of memorable and dramatic historical classics. See also Frederick A. Kirkpatrick, *The Spanish Conquistadores* (Meridian, 1962); Ross Hassig, *Mexico and the Spanish Conquest* (Longman, 1994); and James Muldoon, *The Americas in the Spanish World Order: The Justification for Conquest in the Seventeenth Century* (University of Pennsylvania Press, 1994). Luis Martin, *Daughters of the Conquistadores* (Southern Methodist University Press, 1989), documents the significant role of women in the grueling process, and Nathan Wachtel, *Vision of the Vanquished* (Barnes & Noble, 1977), shows the Amerindians' views of their new masters. On the Spanish conquest of Mesoamerica, see Inga Clendinnon, *Ambivalent Conquest: Maya and Spaniard in Yucatán, 1517–1570* (Cambridge University Press, 1989); Kenneth Pearce, *The View from the Top of the Temple* (University of New Mexico Press, 1984); T. R. Fehrenbach, *Fire and Blood: A History of Mexico* (Da Capo, 1995); Jon M. White, *Cortés and the Downfall of the Aztec Empire* (Carrol & Graf, 1989); Maurice Collis, *Cortés and Montezuma* (Clark, 1994); and Hugh Thomas, *Conquest: Montezuma, Cortés, and the Fall of Old Mexico* (Simon & Schuster, 1993). Good coverage of the Spanish campaigns in Peru is provided in Bernabé Cobo, *History of the Inca Empire* (University of Texas Press, 1979); Ian Cameron, *The Kingdom of the Sun God* (Facts on File, 1990); Susan Ramirez, *The World Upside Down: Cross-Cultural Contact and Conflict in Sixteenth-Century Peru* (Stanford University Press, 1996); and Rafael Gabai, *Francisco Pizarro and His Brothers: The Illusion of Power in Sixteenth-Century Peru* (University of Oklahoma Press, 1997).

For more focused treatments of the colonial development of New Spain, see Peggy K. Liss, *Mexico Under Spain* (University of Chicago Press, 1984), and James M. Lockhart, *Spanish Peru, 1532–1600* (University of Wisconsin Press, 1968). On political, economic, and social conditions, see Jonathan I. Israel, *Race, Class, and Politics in Colonial Mexico* (Oxford University Press, 1975); Leslie B. Simpson, *The Encomienda in New Spain*, 3rd ed. (University of California Press, 1982); Ross Hassig, *Trade, Tribute, and Transportation in the Sixteenth-Century Political Economy of the Valley of Mexico* (University of Oklahoma Press, 1985); and William I. Sherman, *Forced Native Labor in Sixteenth-Century Central America* (University of Nebraska Press, 1979). The following works effectively depict the racial and cultural synthesis in colonial Mexico: Colin MacLachlan and James E. Rodriguez, *The Forging of the Cosmic Race* (University of California Press, 1980); S. L. Cline, *Colonial Culhacán, 1580–1600: A Social History of an Aztec Town* (University of New Mexico Press, 1986); Jacques Lafaye, *Quetzalcoatl and Guadalupe: The Formation of Mexican National Consciousness* (University of Chicago Press, 1987); and Edward Murguca, *Assimilation, Colonialism, and the Mexican American People* (University Press of America, 1989).

Three respected works on Portuguese exploration and colonization are Samuel Eliot Morison, *Portuguese Voyagers to America in the Fifteenth Century* (Octagon, 1965); Charles R.

Boxer, *Four Centuries of Portuguese Expansion* (University of California Press, 1969); and Malyn Newitt, *The First Portuguese Colonial Empire* (Humanities Press, 1986). On the Portuguese in Asia, see Gerald R. Crone, *The Discovery of the East* (St. Martin's Press, 1972); K. M. Matthew, *History of Portuguese Navigation in India* (South Asia Books, 1987); and Charles R. Boxer, *The Christian Century of Japan* (University of California Press, 1974). On Portugal's policies in America, see E. Bradford Burns, *A History of Brazil* (Columbia University Press, 1970), and Dagmar Schaeffer, *Portuguese Exploration in the West and the Formation of Brazil, 1450–1800* (Brown, 1988). For Portugal's impact on Africa, see Malyn Newitt, *Portuguese Settlement on the Zambesi* (Longman, 1973). An interesting and informative biography is Elaine Sanceau, *Henry the Navigator* (Archon Books, 1969).

For the best treatment of developing African culture during the era of European expansion, see works cited in Chapter 11, particularly Robert W. July, *A History of the African People* (Scribner, 1980). The calamities accompanying Portuguese policies in west central Africa are graphically described in John Thornton, *Kingdom of the Kongo* (University of Wisconsin Press, 1983), and Anne Hilton, *The Kingdom of Kongo* (Oxford University Press, 1985). On early slavery and the slave trade, see Barbara Solow, ed., *Slavery and the Rise of the Atlantic System* (Cambridge University Press, 1991); Charles R. Boxer, *Race Relations in the Portuguese Colonial Empire*, rev. ed. (Greenwood, 1985); and Patrick Manning, *Slavery and African Life* (Cambridge University Press, 1990).

A good survey of Dutch imperial development is Charles R. Boxer, *The Dutch Seaborne Empire* (Penguin, 1989). See also Charles R. Boxer, *The Dutch in Brazil* (Archon Books, 1973); Pieter Geyl, *The Netherlands in the Seventeenth Century* (Barnes & Noble, 1961); and Charles Wilson, *The Dutch Republic* (McGraw-Hill, 1968).

A sound treatment of French colonialism in America is William J. Eccles, *France in America* (Michigan State University Press, 1990). See also John Hopkins Kennedy, *Jesuit and Savage in New France* (Archon Books, 1971), and George W. Wrong, *Rise and Fall of New France* (Octagon Books, 1970).

Angus Calder, *Revolutionary Empire* (Dutton, 1981), is a sweeping study of expanding English culture from the fifteenth to the eighteenth century. Barry Coward, *The Stuart Age* (Longman, 1984), deals effectively with expansion but also provides significant English economic, social, and political backgrounds. See also John Bowle, *The Imperial Achievement* (Little, Brown, 1974), and William Abbot, *The Colonial Origins of the United States* (Wiley, 1975). Carl Bridenbaugh, *Vexed and Troubled Englishmen* (Oxford University Press, 1968), provides a penetrating analysis of perspectives among English colonists. For excellent special studies, see Alden T. Vaughn, *Captain John Smith and the Founding of Virginia* (Little, Brown, 1975);

Grace Woodward, *Pocahontas* (University of Oklahoma Press, 1980); and Cyril Hamshere, *The British in the Caribbean* (Harvard University Press, 1972).

Suggestions for Web Browsing

Age of Discovery
http://www.win.tue.nl/cs/fm/engels/discovery/#age

> *An excellent collection of resources that includes text, images, and maps relating to the early years of European expansion.*

Internet Medieval History Sourcebook: Exploration and Expansion
http://www.fordham.edu/halsall/sbook1z.html

> *Extensive on-line source for links about Western exploration and expansion, including primary documents by or about da Gama, Columbus, Drake, and Magellan.*

Columbus Navigation Home Page
http://www1.minn.net/~keithp/

> *Extensive information regarding the life and voyages of Christopher Columbus.*

Internet African History Sourcebook
http://www.fordham.edu/halsall/africa/africasbook.html

> *Extensive on-line source for links about African history, including primary documents about the slave trade and by people who opposed it, supported it, and were its victims.*

Notes

1. Daniel J. B. Boorstin, *The Discoverers* (New York: Random House, 1985), p. 178.
2. Colin McEvedy and Richard Jones, *Atlas of World Population History* (New York: Penguin, 1978), pp. 100–103.
3. Quoted in H. Hering, *A History of Latin America* (New York: Knopf, 1968), p. 173.
4. For the conservative estimate, see McEvedy and Jones, *Atlas of World Population*, pp. 272–273. For the higher estimate, see Patrick Manning, *Slavery and African Life* (New York: Cambridge University Press, 1978), p. 31.
5. Quoted in David Killingray, *A Plague of Europeans* (New York: Penguin, 1973), p. 20.
6. Quoted in Robert Rotberg, *A Political History of Tropical Africa* (New York: Harcourt Brace, 1965), pp. 85–86.
7. Quoted in John Middleton, *The World of the Swahili: An African Mercantile Civilization* (New Haven, Conn.: Yale University Press, 1992), pp. 46–47.

Islam shares the story of Adam and Eve with Christianity and Judaism, with certain variations. In this Persian manuscript Adam rides a dragonlike serpent and Eve rides a peacock; these two beasts facilitated the entrance of Iblis [Satan] into the Garden of Eden.

Detail. Freer Gallery of Art and Arthur M. Sackler Gallery Archives Smithsonian Institution.

The Islamic Gunpowder Empires, 1300–1650

Chapter Contents

B y the fourteenth century the waves of migration and conquest out of central Asia that had established the Mongol Empire and altered the political configurations of the Islamic world were mostly over. Late in that century a new conqueror called Timur began a campaign that ravaged northern India, Persia, Iraq, and Anatolia; but his empire was not enduring. In the fifteenth and sixteenth centuries, however, three great Turkic empires gained preeminence in the old Mongol and Byzantine domains. The Ottoman, Safavid, and Mughul Empires flourished on the bases of preexisting civilizations, Turco-Mongol military organization, and enhanced firepower; in the process they also crafted a new cultural synthesis. These empires are sometimes called the "gunpowder empires" because, like their European counterparts, they incorporated gunpowder weaponry into their traditional military systems. All three formed parts of a vast trading network reaching from the Pacific to the Atlantic. At the same time that the Ming Chinese (see Chapter 18) were launching voyages that reached the East African coast, the Ottoman Turks were building an empire in the eastern Mediterranean that in the sixteenth century would dominate the region and challenge the Portuguese in the Indian Ocean.

Europeans were active in Asia during this period but exerted relatively little influence. Awed by the wealth and power of Muslim empires, they were generally held in disdain by Asian elites, who considered their own cultures superior. Akbar, the great Mughul emperor, referred to the "savage Portuguese" at his court,[1]

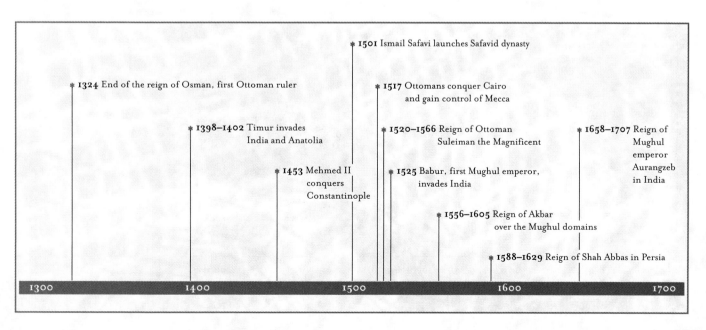

* **1501** Ismail Safavi launches Safavid dynasty

* **1324** End of the reign of Osman, first Ottoman ruler

* **1517** Ottomans conquer Cairo and gain control of Mecca

* **1398–1402** Timur invades India and Anatolia

* **1520–1566** Reign of Ottoman Suleiman the Magnificent

* **1658–1707** Reign of Mughul emperor Aurangzeb in India

* **1453** Mehmed II conquers Constantinople

* **1525** Babur, first Mughul emperor, invades India

* **1556–1605** Reign of Akbar over the Mughul domains

* **1588–1629** Reign of Shah Abbas in Persia

| 1300 | 1400 | 1500 | 1600 | 1700 |

453

Ottoman sultans regarded European envoys as suppliants, and the Safavid shah kept English merchants waiting for weeks while he attended to more important matters.

These were the dominant Asian empires that aspired to world power in this era. They would later be challenged and supplanted by European states also seeking dominion in the midst of a global economic revolution. But in the sixteenth century Asian empires held primacy of place in the contest for world power, controlling the land and sea routes of the East-West trade.

New Polities in Eurasia

For the kingdoms of Europe, the Ottoman conquest of Constantinople in 1453 signaled a catastrophe: the end of the Eastern Roman Empire and a disruption in established commercial patterns. Preachers and writers in Europe depicted the Ottoman victories as a type of divine punishment for the sins of Christendom. Even more significant, the Ottomans symbol-

ized a new Muslim world emerging between the eastern Mediterranean and Southeast Asia. In that expansive territory, the three new empires held sway for centuries. Geographically, this world was centered in Persia, under its Shi'ite Safavid dynasty. Culturally, it was influenced by Persian, Arab, and Byzantine courtly traditions. To the east, the magnificent Mughul Empire emerged on the frontiers of Hindu and Confucian polities. Militarily, this Muslim world was dominated by the forces of the Ottoman Empire, which were far more formidable than those of any country in Europe at the time. War often raged among these contending states. Nevertheless, they shared the Islamic faith, common steppe antecedents, and Persian art traditions.

Background: The Steppe Frontier

After the mid-fourteenth century, tumultuous conditions in central Asia helped generate the Muslim empires to the south. The fragmented Mongol Empire left the steppe politically divided into states that dis-

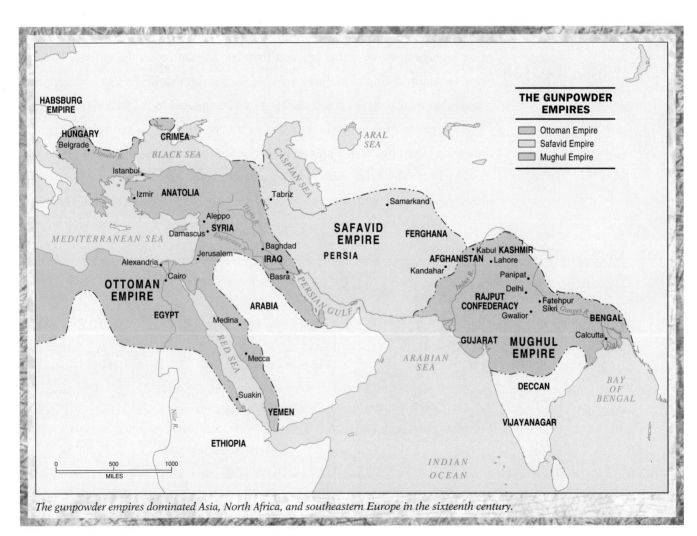

The gunpowder empires dominated Asia, North Africa, and southeastern Europe in the sixteenth century.

solved and re-formed in new combinations. While the old khanates survived for a while, war was almost continuous along the southern steppe frontier, from the Crimea to China.

The continuing steppe influence was well illustrated by the quick rise and collapse of the Timurid Empire at the close of the fourteenth century. Timur the Lame, the "Tamerlane" celebrated in Western literature, who claimed descent from Genghis Khan, rose to power during the 1370s as an *emir* (commander) in the Chaghatai khanate of central Asia. In his quest to restore the original Mongol Empire, Timur led whirlwind campaigns through the western steppe, the Crimea, Persia, and Anatolia. He crushed Ottoman resistance and carted the defeated Ottoman sultan, Bayezid I, off across Anatolia in a cage, subjecting him to ridicule. Timur terrorized northern India and was planning to invade Ming China when he died in 1405. But once Timur's army withdrew, the leaders who had submitted to him were less likely to comply with his demands. A conqueror's real domains were those from which he could collect taxes and levy troops.

For more than a century after Timur had resurrected the spirit of Genghis Khan, a dream of universal empire lingered in the minds of his descendants, real or imagined, among the many Turco-Mongol rulers in northern Persia and Transoxiana to its east. The Ottoman sultans, who had established their hegemony in Asia Minor before Timur's time and only barely survived his onslaught, were not direct heirs of his traditions, but they too aspired to the conquests and prestige of Genghis Khan and Alexander the Great. Russia and particularly northern India, where Muslim regimes took hold after Timur's armies devastated Delhi in 1398, were also sites of a renewed struggle for power.

Drastic change marked the steppe frontier after the late fifteenth century as populations settled around cities and firearms moderated the advantages of tribal cavalry. Indeed, the Uzbeks, who seized most of Transoxiana in this era, were among the last steppe conquerors. Like their predecessors, they were integrated into the courtly cultures of the lands they conquered. But long after the Uzbek conquest, old nomadic traditions continued to shape the rituals and military ethos of Turco-Mongol dynasties.

The Ottoman Empire

The most powerful of the new Muslim empires was that of the Ottoman Turks. Centered in Anatolia, its military might cast long shadows over southeastern Europe, western Asia, and North Africa. In the middle of the sixteenth century the Ottoman patrimony stretched from Hungary to Ethiopia and from the borders of Morocco to Arabia and Iraq.

This miniature painting depicts the envoy of Timur at the court of the Ottoman sultan Bayezid I. The sultan is surrounded by his courtiers, with pages to his right and janissaries, arquebusiers, and officials in the foreground. Bayezid looks imposing, but he was defeated and killed by Timur.

The origin myth of the Ottomans suggests the unique role that both the central Asian warrior traditions and Sufi Islam played in the legitimation of kingship. The founder of the Ottoman line was called Osman. According to legend, he was a valiant young warrior, fighting as a Seljuk subordinate on the frontiers of the Byzantine Empire in the late thirteenth century. Osman had, as a warrior must, a good horse, a strong arm, and a loyal companion. He fell in love

The Ottomans

c. 1281   Osman establishes the Ottoman dynasty

1453   Ottomans capture Constantinople

1517   Sultan Selim conquers Cairo, becomes Protector of the Holy Cities

1520–1566   Reign of Suleiman the Magnificent, Ottoman Golden Age

with the daughter of a revered Sufi *shaykh* and asked for her hand in marriage. Her father refused; but that night the *shaykh* dreamed that he saw the moon descending on his sleeping daughter, merging into her breast. From this union grew a huge and imposing tree that spread its branches over many lands and many flowing streams. When he awoke, the *shaykh* decided to approve the marriage.

Dreams play an important role in Middle Eastern literatures, and many kings took the interpretation of dreams seriously. The legend of the *shaykh's* dream linked the warrior tradition to the mystical religious authority of the Sufis, thus legitimizing Osman's rule. His dynasty, like the tree, did endure and expand to control many and prosperous territories. As the dynasty grew more powerful, the Ottomans also falsified a genealogy linking them to the prophet Muhammad. This Ottoman claim, like Timur's claim to be a descendent of Genghis Khan, also lent an aura of legitimacy to their rule. The Ottomans were not the first or the last family to imagine for themselves illustrious ancestors. Osman's line was spectacularly successful; it ruled for over six centuries, from the late thirteenth century until World War I.

Osman's successors won independence from their Seljuk Turk overlords and gradually conquered the surrounding principalities. They had gained control over most of Asia Minor when Timur's army invaded Anatolia, defeated the Ottomans, and forced a half century of internal restoration. Then two remarkable sultans resumed the Ottoman conquests.

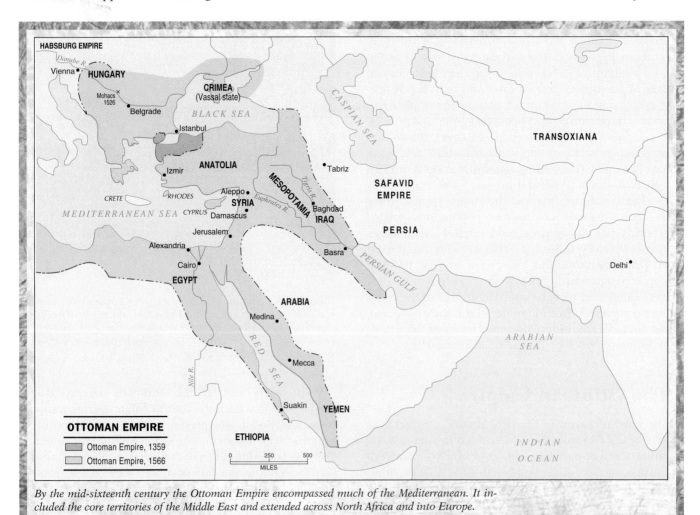

By the mid-sixteenth century the Ottoman Empire encompassed much of the Mediterranean. It included the core territories of the Middle East and extended across North Africa and into Europe.

Discovery Through Maps
The World Map of Piri Reis

Western historiography has highlighted Europeans' "discovery" of the New World. But the Age of Discovery produced many visions of the world, only some of which were preoccupied with the Americas. Ottoman cartographers were interested in the Americas, although Ottoman ambitions for conquest were directed primarily eastward to Asia. Mapping in this era was intimately associated with the objectives of merchants and sailors, and the most famous of Ottoman cartographers was a skilled sea captain named Piri Reis. Like other members of the Ottoman military-administrative class, Piri Reis was a man of diverse talents. In 1517, when his sovereign, Sultan Selim, conquered Cairo, Piri Reis presented him with a parchment map of the world, only part of which survives. The segment reproduced here shows the Atlantic Ocean, the western shores of Africa and Europe, and the eastern shores of South and Central America. Piri Reis map incorporates elaborate illustrations of ships, kings, wildlife, and mythical creatures. It depicts strange tales (like the sailors who landed on a whale's back, mistaking it for an island, at top left) and gives nautical distances. The cartographer provided a list of 20 Western and Islamic sources he consulted, including a map of Christopher Columbus. Piri Reis's map suggests the currents of shared knowledge that linked the scholars, merchants, and sailors of Asia, Africa, and Europe at this time. The boundaries of scholarship were fluid, and learned men eagerly sought out new information. Cartographers like Piri Reis benefited from and contributed to the knowledge assembled by peoples of many nations and religions.

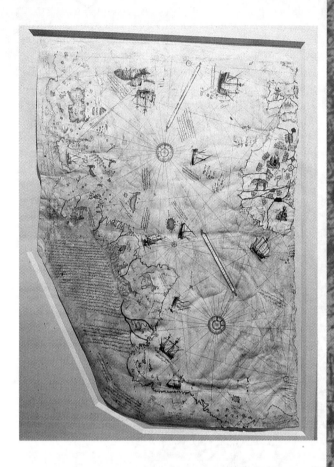

For the sailor or merchant, any map that was more accurate, regardless of its provenance (Portuguese, Ottoman, Christian, Muslim), was a tool for ensuring a more successful and safer journey.

The first, Mehmed II (second reign 1451–1481), took Constantinople, Romania, and the Crimea. The second, Selim I (1512–1520), annexed Kurdistan, northern Iraq, Syria, and Egypt. Mehmed's conquests terrorized European Christendom and brought the Ottoman state considerable wealth and prestige. The sultan repopulated Constantinople, now called Istanbul, using a combination of tax breaks and forced population transfers. The declining but intrepid old warrior was planning new campaigns when he died.

Mehmed's son, Bayezid II, acquired further territories and built up a powerful fleet. Then Selim's conquest of Egypt and Arabia brought added prestige: control of another great imperial capital, Cairo, and claim to the title Custodian of the Holy Cities (Mecca and Medina), coveted by all Muslim monarchs. It also gave him control over the wealth and grain of Egypt and all the Mediterranean outlets of the eastern trade in spices, textiles, and jewels. Under Selim, the Ottoman navy dominated the eastern Mediterranean.

Ottoman power increased under Selim's only son, Suleiman (1520–1566). This determined campaigner soon became the most feared ruler among a generation of monarchs that included Henry VIII of England, Francis I of France, and Charles V of Spain. Suleiman's estimation of his own supremacy is illustrated in a letter to the French monarch in which Suleiman claimed glorious and elaborate titles but addressed Francis simply as "King."

Suleiman extended all his borders, particularly those touching Habsburg lands in Europe. After taking Belgrade in 1521 and the island of Rhodes from the Knights of St. John in 1522, he invaded Hungary in 1526 with 100,000 men and 300 artillery pieces. At Mohacs the Turks won an overwhelming victory, slaughtering thousands of Hungarian nobles and their king. Hungary was then integrated into the Ottoman Empire. Suleiman continued threatening Habsburg interests and European commerce in the Mediterranean. Meanwhile, his forces took Iraq from the Safavids, thus acquiring access to the Persian Gulf. This monarch, who built the great wall around Jerusalem that is still standing today, claimed to be "Lord of the two lands and two seas." His conquests provoked conflicts with the Portuguese in the Red Sea and Indian Ocean. The Portuguese imagined taking Mecca to chastise the "heathen" Ottomans, but no such attack ever materialized.

Terms Integral to the Ottoman Empire

Bey:	Ottoman provincial governor
Darwish:	a Sufi
Devshirme:	special Ottoman levy of non-Muslim boys destined for the janissary corps and palace service
Dhimmi:	non-Muslim subject of a Muslim state
Emir:	commander (same as amir)
Janissaries:	Ottoman elite infantry corps armed with gunpowder weapons
Jizya:	special head tax charged to non-Muslim subjects of Muslim states
Kadi:	(same as qadi) Islamic judge; member of the ulama
Pasha:	Ottoman military commander (governor) of high rank
Sharia:	Islamic law
Sipahi:	Ottoman "feudal" cavalry
Timar:	a type of military "fief" assigned to members of the Ottoman "feudal" cavalry in return for military service
Ulama:	Muslim religious authorities; men versed in the religious sciences and the law

Suleiman responded harshly to challenges to his authority. He executed his own favorite son and a grandson who rebelled against him. The sultan lived amid pomp and splendor exceeding that of Louis XIV's France. An army of servants awakened, bathed, dressed, and entertained him. At meals, each course was served on silver, gold, and fine porcelain, while a physician stood by, ready to minister instantly against poisoning. In the hours between waking and sleeping, Suleiman met with advisers and petitioners, read, or listened to music. For amusement he watched wrestling matches and listened to court poets and jesters. Trained in the fine art of goldsmithing, Suleiman also wrote poetry and had a keen interest in maps. Foreign ambassadors, such as those from the French king or Habsburg emperor, had to prostrate themselves before the sultan, an indication of the perceived balance of power. European observers commented on the intimidating nature of a visit to Suleiman's court where thousands of massed troops would stand for hours in absolute silence. In Europe he was known as Suleiman the Magnificent; in the Ottoman Empire he was called Suleiman the Lawgiver.

The Empire Under Suleiman

Suleiman governed the mightiest state of his day. Extending from Poland to Yemen and from Persia to Tripoli, it included 21 provinces and many linguistic and ethnic groups, such as Magyars, Armenians, Bosnians, Albanians, Greeks, Tartars, Kurds, Arabs, Copts, and Jews. "Multiculturalism," often thought of

An illuminated tughra *of Sultan Suleiman. The* tughra *was the sultan's signature, used to validate imperial documents and mark coinage. It included the sultan's name and his father's name and designated the sultan as "eternally victorious." The palace employed hundreds of artists, including the designers who fashioned and illuminated such beautiful* tughras.

Tughra, (calligraphic emblem) of Suleiman the Magnificent, Sultan of Turkey (1520–1566); from an imperial edict. Ink, colors, and gold on paper. The Metropolitan Museum of Art, Rogers Fund, 1938. (38.149.1) Photograph © 1986 The Metropolitan Museum of Art.

as a twentieth-century concept, was in fact typical of the various large agrarian empires of this age. Economically, Suleiman's empire was nearly self-sufficient, with expanding production and flourishing trade. It produced grain surpluses that gave the Ottomans considerable leverage in the Mediterranean region, where grain shortages were endemic. The Ottoman dominions produced annual revenues greater than those available to any contemporary European monarch.

Power in such a far-flung empire could never be absolute. The sultan delegated authority to local governors and to his top military-administrative officials *(pashas)*. Rule in distant provinces, like Egypt, was more flexible and less direct. Conquered lands closer to the capital were given to Ottoman "fief" holders *(sipahis)*, who were expected to bring cavalry contingents for military campaigns. At other times they lived on their lands *(timars)*, administering local affairs, collecting taxes, and keeping order. Unlike European feudal lords, they were not usually local residents and were often away in distant wars. Provincial governors *(pashas* or *beys)* were drawn from the higher-ranking Ottoman commanders. All members of this governing class were thus heavily dependent on the sultan, who might suddenly change their assignments or cancel their holdings. By Suleiman's reign, the political power of the *sipahis* over their *timars* had been partly usurped by the sultan's central bureaucracy. It functioned under a *vizir*, or chief minister, with a host of subordinate officials. The top officials met regularly as the sultan's council *(divan)* to advise the ruler, but his word was law and he might even execute his own ministers.

The Ottomans developed a unique "slave" *(kul)* system that was a major factor in their success. The system was based on a levy *(devshirme)* of boys from the non-Muslim subjects of the empire; it functioned as a special type of "human tax" on the Balkan provinces. These boys were brought to the capital, converted to Islam, and taught Turkish. Most of them went to the *janissaries*, the famed elite Ottoman infantry corps that was armed with gunpowder weapons. They formed the backbone of the formidable Ottoman armies. The smartest and most talented of the boys, however, were sent to the palace to be educated in literature, science, the arts, religion, and military skills. These boys, when they reached maturity, were given the highest military and administrative posts in the state. Ideally, the *kul* system provided the state with a group of expert administrators who, because they had been separated from their families and homes, would remain loyal to the sultan, to whom they owed everything. These "slaves," rather than occupying the lowest level of the social order, controlled much of the wealth and power in

European writers and their audiences were fascinated by the Ottoman harem and often depicted it in exaggerated erotic terms. This engraving from a seventeenth-century French history of the Ottoman palace imagines the sultan taking his bath attended by naked harem women. In fact, this image is pure fantasy; both sexuality and reproduction in the harem were tightly controlled.

Ottoman society. Many of the buildings they endowed are still standing today.

Western literature has produced an exotic, erotic image of the Ottoman sultan's *harem* (the sacred area of the palace, or of any home, forbidden to outsiders). But much of this image is a myth produced by the overactive imaginations or hostile sentiments of European men inspired by the prospect of several hundred women in one household. In fact, sexuality in the palace was tightly controlled. Like women in other traditional patriarchal societies, most Ottoman women had to work in the fields and towns. Only the women of the elite classes could be fully veiled and secluded. In the palace, the harem women were arranged in a rigid hierarchy much like that of the

Evliya Çelebi, "An Ottoman Official's Wedding Night"

Marriages in the Ottoman administrative system were often arranged to link powerful families, consolidate wealth, and secure loyalty. Love matches were also made, but sometimes officials were forced into marriages at the sultan's command. That was the fate of Melek Ahmed Pasha, who after the death of his beloved first wife was forced to marry the elderly and intransigent Fatma Sultan, daughter of Sultan Ahmed I. This passage, in which Ahmed tells his tale of woe to the chronicler Evliya Çelebi, suggests that marriage to a princess, however prestigious, could be burdensome. It also illustrates the consumption of goods by royal households and the power and status of royal women, who could supersede the wishes of influential men.

As soon as I entered the harem, having uttered a *besmele* [invocation of God's name], I saw her. Now I am supposed to be her husband, and this is our first night—she ought to show me just a little respect. She just sat there stock still, not moving an inch. I went up and kissed her hand.

"Pasha," she says, "welcome."

"God be praised that I have seen my sultan's smiling beauty," say I, and I shower her with all sorts of self-deprecating flatteries. Not once does she invite me to sit down. And she puts on all kinds of virginal airs, as though she weren't an ancient crone who has gone through twelve husbands!

The first pearl from her lips is this: "My dear pasha, if you want to get along with me, whether you are present at court or absent in some government post, my expenses are 15 purses each and every month. Also I owe my steward, Kermetçi Mustafa Agha, 100 purses: pay my debt in the morning. And every year I get six Marmara boatloads of firewood . . . ." (She continued with a long list of expenses.)

Now her stewardess and treasuress and ladies in waiting and, in short, 300 or more women came to kiss my hand and stand there in rows. "Well, my dear pasha, these are my servants of the interior. I also have as many

or more manumitted slave girls on the exterior. Together with children and dependents, they total 700 souls. You will provide all of them with their annual stipend of silk and gauze and brocade and broadcloth. And you will pay the annual stipend of my halberdiers and cooks and gardeners and coachmen and eunuchs and *begs*, as well as those serving them, numbering 500 people. And if you don't—well, you know the consequence!"

Melek Ahmed replied: "I swear by God, my sultan," say I, "that I have just returned from the Transylvania campaign. I am a vizir who fights the holy war. In that campaign I had 7,000 men to feed. I spent 170,000 goldpieces and 600 purses. I even had to sell quite a lot of equipment and arms and armor and helmets and to borrow money from the janissary corps. . . . I am unable to bear such expenses."

After this "wedding night" Melek prayed for death and complained that he had been asked to "feed the state elephant." He vowed never to see Fatma Sultan again.

From Robert Dankoff, trans., *The Intimate Life of an Ottoman Statesman, Melek Ahmed Pasha (1588–1662), as Portrayed in Evliya Çelebi's Book of Travels* (Albany: State University of New York Press 1991), pp. 260–263.

men; each was paid according to her rank. Most of the women were not destined for the sultan's bed; instead they were married to the sultan's officers to create further ties of loyalty to the palace. A select few were chosen to bear the sultan's heirs.

The harem women wielded power because of their wealth, their connections, and their proximity to the sultan. The most powerful among them was the sultan's mother (the *valide sultan*), not his wife. The *valide sultans* participated actively (although behind the scenes) in court politics. Petitioners, including pashas, applied to these high-ranking women to intercede on their behalf with the sultan. Some *valide sultans* even served a diplomatic function, corresponding with European rulers like the Venetian doge, Catherine de' Medici in France, and Queen Elizabeth in England.

Religion was an integral part of government and society. But as in other Muslim lands, the religious authorities (*ulama*) did not run the government; they were subordinated to the state and the sultan. The

grand mufti, as head of the Islamic establishment, was also the chief religious and legal adviser to the sultan. The sultan approved religious appointments and might dismiss any religious officer, including the grand mufti. A corps of learned religious scholars represented the sultan as judges (*kadis*), dispensers of charities, and teachers. Non-Muslims were regarded as inferior but were granted a significant degree of legal and religious toleration through government arrangements with their religious leaders, who were responsible for their civil obedience.

Non-Muslim subjects (*dhimmis*) lived under their own laws and customs, pursuing their private interests within limits imposed by Islamic law and Ottoman economic needs. For tax purposes, Ottoman society was divided between taxpaying subjects and the military-administrative class. The non-Muslim subjects, as in other Islamic lands, had to pay an additional head tax.

In the Ottoman system, proximity to the sultan was the primary avenue to power, and membership in the royal household or military class brought with it the highest status in society. But pashas, palace women, muftis, and members of the palace staff jockeyed for positions of power and formed alliances to advance their own interests. Harem politics, illustrated in Suleiman's reign by the contending influences of his mother and his wife, have often been blamed for weakening the Ottoman state. In fact, however, the factors that compromised Ottoman power were much more complex. Continued conquests produced serious communication and transportation problems, and long wars and failure to pay the troops on time caused rebellions in the ranks. Religious contention, provoked by the rise of the Shi'ite Safavids in Persia, also threatened the empire.

Another important factor in Ottoman politics was the fact that the eldest son had no automatic claim to the throne. The sultan's sons thus contended to succeed him, sometimes producing extended periods of interregnum. That was the case with Bayezid II, whose sons got tired of waiting for him to die and launched a civil war to determine who would sit on the throne in his stead. Once a prince established himself as sultan, he would often have his brothers executed, a grim task designed to ensure the stability of the state and avoid further struggles. A wise prince would try to gain the favor of the janissary corps, for their support might make or break him.

Artistic Production

Ottoman success resulted in a vigorous cultural renaissance, most evident in monumental architecture and decorative tile work. Mehmed II rebuilt his decaying capital, from sewers to palaces. His monumental Fatih Mosque and great Topkapi Palace, with its fortress walls, fountains, and courtyards, were models of the new Ottoman style, which was influenced by the Byzantine artistic tradition. The palace was divided into three courts that reflected Ottoman concepts of power and space. The outer court was for public affairs, as well as stable and kitchen facilities. The second court provided a dividing line between the public and private life of the sultan. There the sultan met with diplomats and built his library. The inner court was reserved for the sultan and his intimates, a place for relaxation and privacy. Suleiman surpassed Topkapi's splendor with the beautiful and elegant Suleimaniye, his own mosque and mausoleum. These were but three architectural wonders among thousands scattered throughout the empire.

In addition, the period was marked by wondrous productions in the realms of decorative arts. Calligraphy could take the form of birds or boats in official documents. Elaborate calligraphy and stunning painted tiles decorated Ottoman mosques and buildings. For example, Suleiman added luminous tiles to the Dome of the Rock in Jerusalem. Ottoman high

An engraving of the sixth emperor of the Turks, Sultan Murad III (r. 1574–1595).

culture also produced a great outpouring of scholarship and literature, mostly following Persian traditions but reflecting a unique Ottoman synthesis. Poets and historians vied for the attentions—and rewards (silver, sable furs, robes of honor, even houses)—of the sultan. Both often signed themselves as humble beggars or "slaves" of the sultan. Some achieved remarkable rank and success; others left the palace disheartened and poor.

Challenges to Ottoman Supremacy

Beginning in Suleiman's reign, cheap silver from the Americas and a population increase led to rising inflation, rebellions, and military mutinies, all of which weakened the government. None of the eight sultans who followed Suleiman before 1648 could duplicate

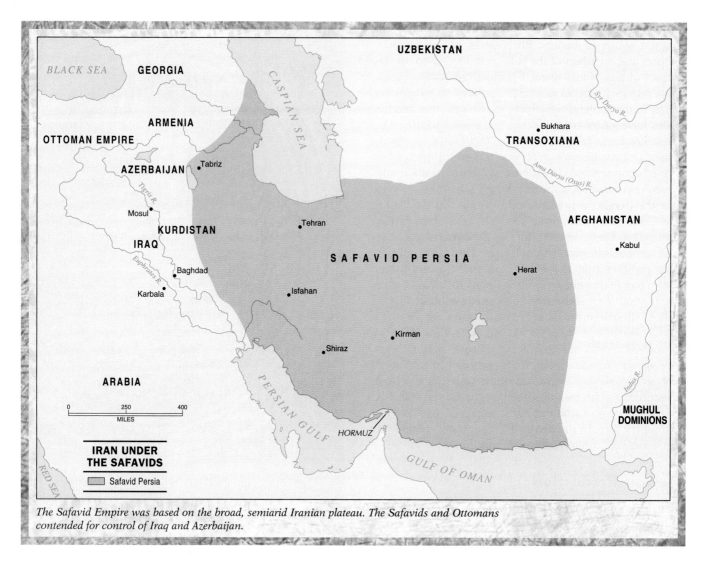

The Safavid Empire was based on the broad, semiarid Iranian plateau. The Safavids and Ottomans contended for control of Iraq and Azerbaijan.

his successes. Selim II was known as "the drunkard"; another sultan gained notoriety by having 19 of his brothers killed on his accession. Increasingly, the sultans did not themselves lead their troops into battle. Other problems plaguing Suleiman's successors were losses to the Russians and Habsburgs in Europe, stalemated wars with Persia, and the end of Ottoman naval supremacy in the Red Sea. Nonetheless, the period between 1566 and 1650 should be viewed as one of reorganization and retrenchment rather than decline. The Ottoman Empire was adjusting to newly emerging global configurations of power and commerce, and Ottoman armies still managed to gain important victories in this era, notably the reconquest of Iraq by Murad IV (1623–1640) in 1638.

With Suleiman's death the Ottoman Empire passed its zenith, but it remained a significant contender for power in the Euro-Asian sphere well into the eighteenth century. It dominated the overland trade with Asia, thus contributing decisively to European maritime expansion. Moreover, the sultans moderated Portuguese domination of the Indian Ocean, ultimately aiding the Dutch and English seaborne empires in the East while humbling their Habsburg rivals in Europe.

The Safavid Empire in Persia

The Safavid dynasty had its origins in an Islamic Sufi (mystical) order founded by Safi al-Din (c. 1252–1334). One of Safi's descendants, Shah Ismail (1501–1524), gathered an army of devoted followers and began a series of campaigns that united Persia, conquered Iraq, and posed a formidable challenge to the Ottomans on their eastern frontiers. Ismail was only 14 when he seized his first territories. Although such precocity may seem unusual today, it was common enough in this era for the sons of powerful men to be trained to fight and rule while still boys.

Ismail was not only a successful military commander; he was also the head of a Shi'ite Muslim sect. Contemporary accounts portray him as a charismatic leader whose army thought him invincible. They followed him into battle crying *"Shaykh, Shaykh!"* The Safavid troops wore red headgear with 12 folds to commemorate the 12 Shi'ite imams (descendants of the prophet Muhammad); because of this headgear they were called "redheads."

Ismail angered the Ottoman sultan by sending missionaries and agitators to stir up the sultan's

The Coming of Ismail Safavi Foretold

Histories and legends of famous leaders and religious figures often recount the ways in which the coming of these men was predicted or foretold. In this selection, from an anonymous Persian manuscript, the story is told of a Sufi mystic named Dede Mohammad. This Sufi, or *darwish*, while returning from a pilgrimage to Mecca, becomes separated from his caravan in the desert. Dying of thirst, he is rescued by a mysterious youth who takes him to a magnificent encampment in a flowering plain. There he sees a veiled prince, whom he does not realize is the Twelfth Imam, a descendant of the Prophet revered by the Shi'ite Muslims. In this vision, the Twelfth Imam girds and sends forth the young Ismail Safavi, thus legitimizing his reign to the Shi'ites.

After his rescue, Dede Mohammad . . . walked by the young man's side, until they came to a palace, whose cupola outrivaled the sun and moon. . . . Golden thrones were arranged side by side, and on one of the thrones a person was seated whose face was covered by a veil. Dede Mohammad, placing his hand on his breast, made a salutation, whereupon an answer to his salutation came from the veiled one, who having bidden him be seated, ordered food to be brought for him. The like of this food he had never seen in his life before. . . . As soon as he had finished his repast, he saw that a party of men had entered, bringing a boy of about fourteen years of age, with red hair, a white face, and dark grey eyes; on his head was a scarlet cap. . . . The veiled youth then said to him, "Oh! Ismail, the hour of your 'coming' has now arrived." The other replied: "It is for your Holiness to command." . . . His Holiness, taking his belt three times lifted it up and placed it on the ground again. He then, with his own blessed hands, fastened on the girdle and taking [Ismail's] cap from his head, raised it and then replaced it. . . . His Holiness then told his servants to bring his own sword which, when brought, he fastened with his own hands on the girdle of the child. Then he said, "You may now depart." [The Arab youth then guided Dede Mohammad back to his caravan, and the Sufi asked his guide who the veiled prince was.] He replied, "Did you not know that the prince you saw was no other than the Lord of the Age?" When Dede Mohammad heard this name he stood up and said: "Oh! youth, for the love of God take me back again that I may once more kiss the feet of His Holiness, and ask a blessing of him, perchance I might be allowed to wait on him." But the youth replied: "It is impossible. You should have made your request at first. You cannot return. But you can make your request where you will, for His Holiness is everywhere present and will hear your prayers."

From E. Dennison Ross, "The Early Years of Shah Ismail," *Journal of the Royal Asiatic Society* (1896), pp. 328–331.

subjects on the Ottoman eastern frontiers. He also launched a sometimes violent campaign to convert the Sunni Muslims of his domain to Shi'ite Islam. Because Persia had been predominantly Sunni, he had to import Shi'ite scholars and jurists from the Arab lands, like Syria and Iraq. Under the Safavid shahs, Persia became overwhelmingly Shi'ite, as it is today.

Power is acquired not only on the field of battle but also in the arenas of reputation and diplomacy. Legends grew up around the youthful leader Ismail because of his many and rapid conquests. He was also supposed to have received the secret knowledge of the Safavi mystical order, passed down from his brother as he lay dying. Hence he had a powerful aura of both political and religious legitimacy. European rulers, including the Portuguese king and the pope, were inspired by the accounts of Ismail's victories and the rumors of his quasi-divine prowess. Hoping that the Safavids would help them defeat the Ottomans, who were Sunni Muslims, they sent envoys to the young shah. Ismail had some interest in exploring possibilities with European powers, but he was apparently more interested in European artillery and defeating the Ottomans than in a Christian-Shi'ite alliance.

Rulers used envoys to intimidate, placate, or try to gain information about foreign powers. The Portuguese, for example, thought of the Safavids as barbarians. Their envoy to Ismail was instructed to brag to the Safavids about the fine Portuguese horses, table service, and women. When in 1510 Ismail defeated Shaibani Khan, the Uzbek ruler in central Asia, he had the Khan's skull gilded and made into a drinking cup. He sent an envoy with the grisly trophy, along with a taunting message, to the Ottoman sultan, Bayezid II. Of course, being an envoy in this era was often dangerous, especially for the bearers of rude messages. The Ottoman sultans often imprisoned Safavid envoys, and messengers to the Safavid court were sometimes detained or abused. When Ismail sent another arrogant message to the Mamluk sultan in Egypt (before the Ottoman conquest), the latter was so enraged that he sponsored a poetry contest to see which of his poets could write the most insulting reply in verse. But he did not harm Ismail's messenger because he was afraid of a Safavid invasion.

The Ottomans were intimidated by Ismail's early successes. In 1514, however, they soundly defeated Ismail's forces on the frontier between Anatolia and Persia. This victory is often attributed to the fact that the Ottomans had more and better gunpowder weaponry. Demoralized, Ismail withdrew to his palace, having lost his reputation for invincibility. After his death, the Safavids fought a series of long wars against the Ottomans to the west and the Uzbeks to the east.

None of his successors wielded the same charismatic religious power as Ismail. They were kings, not *shaykhs* (holy men), even though Ismail's son Tahmasp still claimed the headship of the Safavid order. Still, the next hundred years of Safavid rule were characterized by a consolidation of state power, lavish patronage of the arts, and an exploration of diplomatic and commercial relations with Europe. European merchants visited the shah's court, trying to gain access to the coveted Iranian silk trade, but they met with little success. Tahmasp ruled for half a century (1524–1576), despite having to contend with foreign invasions, religious factionalism, and power struggles among the tribal leaders. The Safavids, with the aid of European renegades, developed their gunpowder weaponry but never to the same extent as the Ottomans. Nor did they imitate the elaborate "slave"-based hierarchy and infantry corps (janissaries) that became the basis for Ottoman success. In Persia, the tribal leaders and their cavalry-based militaries retained their position of power.

The Reign of Abbas the Great

The reign of Shah Abbas (1588–1629) is considered a "golden age" of Safavid power, comparable to that of Suleiman in the Ottoman Empire. Ascending the throne at the age of 17, Abbas ultimately became a pragmatic politician, a wise statesman, a brilliant strategist, and a generous patron of the arts. During his reign, Persia acquired security, stability, and a reputation for cultural creativity, symbolized by the shah's splendid new capital at Isfahan.

Abbas directed much of his attention to the threat posed by an Ottoman-Uzbek alliance, which had almost destroyed his country. He held his holy men in political check but labored to project an image of Shi'ite piety. He reorganized his government and army, creating a personal force of "slaves" of the royal household. This force acted as a counterweight to the ambitious and often unruly tribal chiefs. Within the army, Abbas increased his artillery and musket forces, relying less on traditional cavalry. During the 1590s he slowly recovered territory lost by his less adept predecessors.

Persia prospered under Abbas. The government employed thousands of workers, and the palace was a great consumer of luxury goods, foodstuffs, and other commodities. Government monopolies, particularly in silk, promoted various crafts. Hundreds of new roads, bridges, hostels, and irrigation projects promoted agriculture, encouraged trade, and swelled urban populations. These projects also enhanced the prestige of the ruler. Contemporaries noted that a person could travel from one end of the empire to another in safety, without fear of bandits. That was a significant claim in an age when merchants traveled at their own risk, often with large retinues of armed guards.

A commercial agreement with the British subsequently led to the forcible ejection of the Portuguese from Hormuz, in the Persian Gulf, a most significant development that permitted direct export of Persian silk to Europe by sea, thus avoiding Ottoman tolls on the overland routes. The silk trade was so lucrative that merchants on both sides conspired to get the shipments through, even when the Safavids and the Ottomans were at war. Persia was an important center in the networks of East-West trade. Its silk was in such demand in Europe that Venetian, French, and other traders would wait in the Syrian entrepots for the caravans of Persian silk to come in. They negotiated with local agents, trying to outbid each other for the rights to purchase each incoming load. One Venetian observer stated that a merchant would willingly pluck out his own eye to triumph over a competitor.

Persia at this time was one of the primary cultural centers of the world. It was a conduit to the West not only for the goods but also for the spiritual and literary influences of India. Meanwhile, Sufi Muslim missionaries traveled to South and Southeast Asia, transmitting their own ideas and bringing a synthesis of mystical ideas and practices back to the Islamic heartlands. Persia's fine arts—ceramics, tapestries, and carpets—were eagerly sought from Alexandria to Calcutta. Persian literary forms, particularly the exquisite imagery of Persian poetry, were imitated at both the Ottoman and Mughul courts, even by the rulers themselves. Persian painters explored realist styles and erotic themes. They were recruited abroad, as were two émigrés, Khwaja Abdus Samad and Mir Sayyid Ali, who founded the famous Mughul school of painting in India.

Major Middle Eastern courts housed large workshops of artists, sometimes numbering in the hundreds. The Safavid shahs paid their painters to produce lavish manuscripts like the *Epic of Kings (Shahnamah)*, a long rhyming poem by Firdawsi. Ismail commissioned a wondrous illustrated version of the *Shahnamah* that was not finished in his lifetime. When the Ottomans conquered the Persian capital of Tabriz, they carried back many of the Safavid artists as a valuable part of the booty.

Persian architecture, with its jewel-like colors, intricate geometric and floral patterns, luxurious gardens, and artificial streams, exerted considerable in-

A school scene from a Safavid manuscript painted around 1540 at Tabriz. Not all miniatures were devoted to the exploits of kings or legendary heroes. More mundane matters like education, building projects, and funerals were also sometimes depicted. This scene illustrates some of the beauty, color, and style of Safavid painting.
Mir Sayyid-Ali, Safavid dynasty, 16th century. Freer Gallery of Art and Arthur M. Sackler Gallery Archives, Smithsonian Institution.

fluence on the architecture of the Islamic world. Abbas made the capital at Isfahan a showcase for these artistic and architectural talents. One of the largest cities of its time, Isfahan had a million inhabitants. Its public life centered around a broad square (used for assemblies and polo matches), the palace compound, a huge bazaar, and the main mosque. Five hundred years later the beauty of Abbas's surviving monuments still inspires awe in visitors.

The Mughul Empire in South Asia

The Safavid and Ottoman states were contemporaries of the mighty Mughul Empire in India. It too was ruled by a Turkic dynasty. But unlike the Ottoman sultans and Safavid shahs, the Mughuls ruled a population that was predominantly Hindu rather than Muslim. That fact marked the Mughul Empire indelibly and helped craft its distinctive character.

The Mughuls

1525	Babur invades India
1556–1605	Reign of Akbar, Mughul Golden Age
1632	Shah Jahan commissions the Taj Mahal
1658–1707	Reign of Aurangzeb, reasserts Islamic orthodoxy

Origins

The Ottoman Empire emerged out of a warrior principality in what is now Turkey, and the Safavid Empire was established by a Sufi boy-king who commanded both political and religious authority in Persia. The origin of the Mughul Empire was different from these; one might say it was founded by a determined prince in search of a kingdom.

Miniatures were not painted solely for artistic expression; they also suggested relationships. In this Mughul painting of Shah Jahangir and the Safavid Shah, Jahangir's artist portrayed his master as big and powerful, dominating his rather puny-looking Safavid rival. The monarchs stand on the globe, but Jahangir's lion is much more imposing than Abbas's lamb. The angels supporting the rulers' halo show the influence of European art motifs on Mughul imagery.

Mughal painting, c. 1620. (F45.9a) Freer Gallery of Art and Arthur M. Sackler Gallery Archives, Smithsonian Institution.

The establishment of the Mughul Empire was not the first instance of Muslim contact with the diverse but predominantly Hindu population of India. Muslim merchants and Sufi mystics had traveled to India from the Islamic heartlands for many centuries. From the seventh century onward Muslim rulers extended the frontiers of Islam eastward to the borders of South Asia. Then a Turkic warrior, Mahmud of Ghazna (c. 971–1030), gained control of Khurasan in western Persia and Afghanistan and seized control of northern India. He destroyed the Hindu temple of Shiva in Gujarat. Muslim sultanates were established on the west coast of India, and the Muslim Delhi Sultanate ruled in the thirteenth and fourteenth centuries until Timur's invasion. Thus by the sixteenth

century, much of South Asian society had become familiar with Islamic culture and political power.

India is a land of many peoples, many languages, and diverse terrain. At the beginning of the sixteenth century it was politically fragmented. The Delhi Sultanate, having spawned a number of independent contending Muslim states, had been partially resurrected under the Lodi Afghan dynasty. The Rajput Confederacy held sway in the northwest, the Vijayangar Empire controlled much of southern India, and a string of commercial city-states held sway along the southwestern coast. Although many rulers had aspired to unite the entire subcontinent, that goal remained daunting.

Early in the sixteenth century a new conqueror cast his eye on India. The adventurous Turco-Mongol ruler of Kabul, Babur, "the Tiger" (1483–1530), was a descendant of both Timur and Genghis Khan. Babur did not begin his career in India. He inherited the Afghan principality of Ferghana and twice conquered the Timurid capital at Samarkand before losing everything to the Uzbeks. He and his troops finally seized the throne of Kabul in 1504.

Babur is a striking historical figure because, unlike many rulers of his time, he compiled his memoirs.

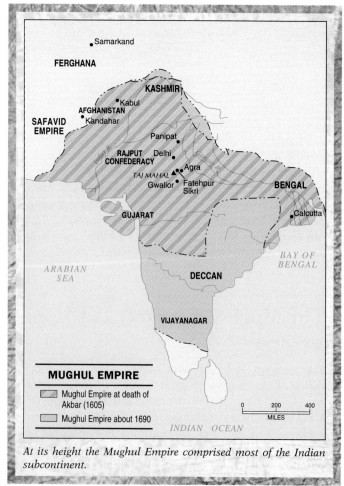

MUGHUL EMPIRE

▨ Mughul Empire at death of Akbar (1605)

▧ Mughul Empire about 1690

At its height the Mughul Empire comprised most of the Indian subcontinent.

Babur, conqueror of northern India, surveying the spectacular rock-cut Hindu sculptures at Urwa fortress in Gwalior, from an illustrated manuscript of Babur's memoirs. Babur ordered these sculptures defaced.

They are a tale of triumphs and losses that reveal Babur as a straightforward narrator who built gardens wherever he went, paid careful attention to geography, was solicitous of his mother, and seemed to enjoy good wine and a good fight. He also loved to compose and declaim poetry. Babur's memoirs tell of rhinoceros hunts and military relations. He notes, rather ruefully, that he had sworn to give up drink when he reached the age of 40 but now felt compelled to drink out of anxiety because he was already 39. Armed with Turkish artillery, this intrepid warrior mobilized an invasion in 1525, winning decisive battles against the Afghan Sultanate at Delhi and the Rajput Confederacy. Babur was not impressed with Indian culture. He

criticized native dress, religion, and the failure of Indians to have running water in their gardens.

> *Hindustan is a place of little charm. There is no beauty in its people, no graceful social intercourse, no poetic talent or understanding, no etiquette, nobility or manliness. . . . There are no good horses, meat, grapes, melons, or other fruit. There is no ice, cold water, good food or bread in the markets.*[2]

Like many travelers, Babur tended to find his own culture superior to those of other peoples. He did, however, admire the Indian systems of numbers, weights, and measures and the country's vast array of craftsmen. Speaking as a prospective ruler, he could not help but remark that "the one nice aspect of Hindustan [India] is that it is a large country with lots of gold and money."[3] When Babur died, soon after the conquest, the hard-living and thoughtful ruler had laid the foundations for a Mughul empire that would dominate most of the subcontinent and endure into the eighteenth century.

Babur was succeeded by his able but erratic son Humayun. After ten years of rule during which he expanded Mughul domains, Humayun was overthrown by his vassal Sher Khan. He then fled to the Safavid court of Tahmasp in Persia. The Safavid shah welcomed Humayun. It was always useful for monarchs of the time to shelter in their courts the sons or rivals of neighboring kings. Such refugees could prove useful; they gave rulers leverage against their enemies. Rulers also demanded that vassals send their sons to reside at court; it was a practical way to ensure the loyalty of subordinates.

In 1555 Shah Tahmasp helped Humayun regain his kingdom, no doubt presuming that Humayun would prove a significant ally on the Safavids' eastern frontiers. But Humayun died shortly thereafter in a fall down his library steps, perhaps a fitting end for a learned man but a rather ignominious one for a warrior.

The Reign of Akbar

Humayun's son Akbar (1556–1605) was 14 years old when he succeeded his father, about the same age as Shah Ismail when he commenced his reign. During a half century of rule Akbar united northern India, advanced against the sultanates in the south of the subcontinent, and presided over a glorious courtly culture. Akbar ruled an empire more populous than those of the Ottoman sultan and the Persian shah; Mughul subjects numbered between 100 and 150 million.

Unlike Ismail, Akbar did not immediately consolidate his power. Initially, he was controlled by a regent. As often happens when a prince comes to power at an early age, powerful men in the court used the prince's youth to advance their own influence and objectives. By the age of 20, however, Akbar took charge and began a determined campaign of conquest that would continue into his old age.

This Mughul potentate was the counterpart of Suleiman in the Ottoman Empire and Shah Abbas in Safavid Persia. His reign is associated with military might, prosperity, and patronage of the arts at a spectacular level. At 13 Akbar led troops in battle; in his thirties he challenged an enemy commander to personal combat; in late middle age he still hunted wild animals with sword and lance. Akbar's concern for morality and social justice was indicated by his advice to a son: "Avoid religious persecution; be strong but magnanimous; accept apologies, sincerely given."[4]

A significant aspect of Akbar's reign is that he adapted the Islamic state to the conditions of ruling a non-Muslim population. In so doing, he promoted cultural synthesis, incorporated Hindus into the inner workings of government, and showed himself to be a pragmatic monarch. He married a number of Rajput princesses and made alliances with Hindu families, taking the men into his service. The mother of his heir, Jahangir, was a Hindu. He also abolished the *jizya*, the special head tax on non-Muslims. This decision may seem like a simple matter, but the *jizya* was a standard of Islamic rule and had been institutionalized in the Sharia Islamic law. By abolishing it, Akbar gave notice to his Hindu subjects that they were granted a more equitable position vis-à-vis the Muslims, who constituted the ruling class.

Akbar also stopped taxing Hindu pilgrims, financed the construction of Hindu temples, and forbade Muslims to kill or eat the cow, which was sacred to Hindus. These measures alienated the *ulama* (the Muslim religious authorities) and the diverse Muslim elite of Turks, Afghans, Mongols, and Persians but won new support among the majority. Akbar, however, also initiated certain measures designed to force Hindu practice into compliance with Islamic law; he issued decrees outlawing Hindu child marriages and *suttee* (the self-burning of widows), two reforms that violated Hindu traditions.

Akbar's tolerance in public administration was matched by his pursuit of knowledge and personal explorations of various religious faiths. He was devoted to certain Sufi *shaykhs* and launched at his court a "house of worship," a forum for religious discussion to which he invited Muslims, Christians, Jews, Jains, Hindus, and Zoroastrians. In 1582 Akbar proclaimed a new cult, the *Din-i Ilahi*, or "Divine Faith," which centered on Akbar himself and was highly influenced by Zoroastrianism. The new creed gained few adherents, but it further antagonized the *ulama* and demonstrated Akbar's religious eclecticism.

The Mughul State and Its Culture

One of the great accomplishments of the Mughul Empire was its establishment of a highly organized and intrusive central administration. In many ways like that of the Ottomans, it was designed to produce a consistent supply of taxes and troops for the government and to manage distant provinces. Akbar's military administrators, about two-thirds of whom were foreign-born Muslims, were organized in military ranks and paid salaries according to the number of soldiers they commanded. Promotion for these military administrators, who were called *mansabdars*, was ideally based on merit. Their ranks were open to Hindus, and their positions were not hereditary like those of European nobles. Like the Ottoman *kul* system, the *mansabdar* system was designed to produce loyalty to the state. Officials, in turn, were now made more dependent on the emperor. Like the Ottomans and Safavids, Akbar drew conquered foes into his service as long as they offered their submission. In this way he took advantage of the military expertise of defeated commanders.

In the early seventeenth century the Mughul Empire was the wealthiest state in the world, with revenues ten times greater than those of France. Cities were numerous and large by European standards. Akbar's capital at Agra, for example, housed 200,000 people—twice the population of contemporary London. In the towns and villages, many industries flourished, particularly cotton textiles, which were exported to most of Asia and Africa. The majority of subjects were Hindu peasants. One-third to one-half of their produce, paid in land taxes, supported the army and kept the administrative elite in considerable luxury.

The early Mughul period saw a new Hindu-Muslim cultural synthesis, well illustrated in literature. Beginning with Babur, each emperor considered himself a poet, a scholar, and a collector of books. Akbar himself could not read, but he founded a great library housing over 20,000 illustrated manuscripts. The Mughuls used their wealth to patronize the arts. Their literature was cosmopolitan, reflected a fresh originality, and was expressed in a variety of languages, including Turkish, Persian, Hindi, Arabic, and Urdu (an Indo-Persian fusion).

Despite the Muslim prohibition of representational figures, human or animal, painting developed rapidly as an art in the early Mughul period. Akbar had studied art as a child under Abdus Samad and Mir Sayyid Ali, two Safavid court painters whom Humayan brought to Kabul and later took to India. Akbar's royal studio employed over a hundred artists, mostly Hindus, who created works of great variety including miniatures of courtly life and large murals for Akbar's palaces.

The royal studio produced beautiful illustrated manuscripts requiring many painters and many years to complete. Foremost among these is the spectacular *Hamzanamah*, which includes 1400 illustrations on cloth. Akbar also sponsored illustrated versions of Babur's memoirs and of the great Sanskrit epics the *Mahabharata* and the *Ramayana*. The Mughul school of painters under Jahangir, Akbar's son, produced wonderful animal and bird imagery, developed new strains of sensual and realist representation, and expertly incorporated motifs of European painting into Mughul art.

The most imposing symbols of Mughul glory are to be seen in architecture. Fusing Persian and Indic styles, it featured the lavish use of mosaics, bulbous domes, cupolas, slender spires, lofty vaulted gateways, and formal gardens, all carefully harmonized. Akbar's major building project was his palace complex at Fatehpur Sikri. Akbar wanted to build his new palace on a site dedicated to a famous Sufi holy man, Shaykh Salim Chishti. But Fatehpur Sikri became a monument to man's vanity and lack of planning. Akbar's court abandoned the complex (which took 15 years to build) after only 14 years because the water supply was inadequate. But visitors still marvel at the red sandstone blocks of the monumental fortress, which were hewn so precisely that they needed no fasteners or mortar.

Akbar's son Jahangir and his grandson Shah Jahan continued the tradition of monumental building. The latter replaced Akbar's sandstone buildings at Delhi with new ones of marble. At Agra Shah Jahan erected the famous Taj Mahal, a tomb for his favorite wife, Mumtaz Mahal, who died while giving birth to her fifteenth child. This elaborate tomb, set in beautiful gardens, took over 20 years to build. Its luminous white marble, beautiful tracery of semiprecious stones, and elegant lines make the Taj Mahal one of the best-known buildings in the world today.

Akbar's Successors: Contesting the Hindu-Muslim Synthesis

Like most empires, the Mughul polity fared best when its administration was relatively tolerant, its treasury full, and its military successful. Jahangir (1605–1627) and Shah Jahan (1628–1658) continued Akbar's policies of relative tolerance. Jahangir was learned and artistically sensitive, but he was also a wastrel, a drunkard, and a drug addict, without the strength to make decisions or conduct policy. He lost Kandahar to the Persians. Shah Jahan launched three unsuccessful campaigns to retake Kandahar, a disastrous thrust into central Asia, four costly invasions of the Deccan, and an extravagant expedition to oust a Portuguese enclave on the Indian coast. To compensate for these military expeditions, Shah Jahan had to raise land taxes, thus oppressing the peasantry.

The tension between Mughul tolerance and Muslim rule culminated in the seventeenth century with Akbar's great-grandsons, Dara Shikoh and Aurangzeb (1658–1707). Dara Shikoh took Akbar's tolerance one step further. He was a devoted Sufi and wrote his own mystical works; he also studied Hindu mysticism. In the end this prince's attempt to find a middle

In 1632 the Mughul emperor, Shah Jahan, commissioned the building of the resplendent Taj Mahal as a memorial to his late wife. Tall minarets surround a central dome, and a reflecting pool perfectly mirrors the white marble building, one of the glories of Mughul architecture.

ground between Islam and Hinduism provoked a violent response from the empire's Muslims and from his brother, Aurangzeb. Dara Shikoh was his father's favorite, but in the battle to succeed Shah Jahan, Aurangzeb was victorious. Charging his brother with apostasy, Aurangzeb marched him through the streets of Delhi in humiliation and had him executed.

Both Sufi orders and the *ulama* opposed the ecumenicalism of Akbar and Dara Shikoh. When Aurangzeb gained the throne, he was determined to restore Sunni orthodoxy to the Mughul dominions. He reimposed the *jizya* and enforced the Sharia with a vengeance. Many Hindu temples were destroyed during his reign, and his intolerance and rigid orthodoxy weakened the Mughul hold on its diverse Hindu populations.

The Mughul Social Order

As already noted, Mughul society comprised a series of hierarchies based on a Hindu majority and a predominantly Muslim ruling class. The vast majority of the populace, as in China, the Middle East, and Europe, consisted of illiterate peasants who provided the bulk of the empire's revenue through agricultural taxes. Wealth was an important factor in determining status, but it was not the primary factor. A merchant could be very wealthy but could not achieve the same status as a member of the elite military-administrative class. Among Hindus, status was intimately linked to caste.

Mughul society, like most societies, was also patriarchal; it allocated family, religious, and political dominance to men. This system of male dominance is often attributed to Islam, but patriarchy predated Islam in India, as it did in the Middle East. In general, it would be more accurate to say that Islam both reinforced preexisting patriarchal structures and improved the position of women by forbidding female infanticide and granting women inheritance rights. In India under Islamic rule, the position of women derived from a synthesis of Hindu custom and Islamic law. Despite Akbar's reform-minded decrees, *suttee* and child marriages continued. Formal education of females, as in most societies, was practically nonexistent, except in a few affluent or learned families.

These practices must, of course, be understood in their temporal and social contexts. In Hindu society, as in Muslim society, in which marriage is considered a preferred state (especially for women), early marriage age acted to prevent the girl's sexual purity from being compromised or questioned. By social convention, women needed male protectors, and when a woman married, she left the protection of her father or brother and became part of her husband's household. By placing herself on her hus-

The birth of a prince in the Mughul harem. This unusual scene shows the numerous female attendants of the princely court and suggests the ceremonial significance of such an event.
Birth of a Prince from an illustrated manuscript of the Jahangir-nama, Bishndas (Attributed to), Northern India, Mughul, about 1620. Opaque watercolor on paper, 24.1 × 17 cm. Museum of Fine Arts, Boston, Francis Bartlett Donation of 1912 and Picture Fund.

band's funeral pyre, a Hindu woman gained honor in the eyes of the community. She also escaped the dilemma of being left without a protector (especially if she had no sons) and becoming a social burden.

As for female education, we should remember that the overwhelming majority of people, in all the world civilizations of this era, were illiterate. Only certain of the elites could read, and even many people of rank, like Akbar, were illiterate. Men's and women's roles were considered complementary, not equal. Because men were expected to perform the political, religious, and administrative tasks that required literacy, formal education tended to be reserved for men.

Networks of Trade and Communication

The gunpowder empires emerged in a set of interconnected regions that were in turn imbedded in even more extensive networks of trade and communication. The primitive nature of transport and communications technology limited the flow of goods, knowledge, and information. But all three circulated in ways that might seem surprising, given that the only ways to get from one place to another were on foot, on animal-back, or aboard oared and sailing vessels. Despite these limitations, scholars traveled from one court to another, enjoying the patronage of Ottoman, Safavid, or Mughul kings and sharing literary, artistic, and legal traditions. The royal courts consumed prodigiously and supported the exchange of goods and culture on a grand scale. Mehmed II had his portrait painted by the famous Italian painter Bellini. Babur brought Persian artists into India, and the Safavid court imported Arab jurists. Rulers in all three empires drank from Chinese porcelain cups.

The Ottoman, Safavid, and Mughul Empires derived most of their income from agriculture. But trade was their second source of wealth. None of these empires invented the trading routes. Rather, they emerged and expanded across a set of well-established commercial networks linking urban centers. They inherited these networks from their predecessors and competed with rival kingdoms to monopolize goods and collect commercial taxes. To understand how these empires worked, we must abandon the notion of modern boundaries that are marked, fixed, and defended. Rulers could not control frontiers absolutely; instead they defended and taxed key routes, fortresses, and cities. The porous nature of borders encouraged tax evaders. If officials demanded high taxes along one route, merchants might shift to another route. If taxes were collected by the camel-load, merchants stopped their beasts outside of town and repacked in order to have fewer loads.

In this context of flexible boundaries, trading communities developed that facilitated the flow of goods from one place to another. Although the Ottomans fought long wars with both Christian states in Europe and Muslim competitors in Persia and Egypt, trade among these regions was seldom squelched for long. The furs of Muscovy flowed south into the empire and the gold of Africa came north. Jewish merchants traded copper to Arab merchants who sold it to South Asian traders in return for cotton, jewels, and spices.

Many great trading centers were scattered throughout the territories of the gunpowder empires. Babur described the emporium of Kabul, located between Persia and India, as receiving merchant caravans of 15,000 or 20,000 pack animals carrying slaves, textiles, sugar, and spices. Kabul channeled the trade of China and India westward in exchange for goods coming eastward from the Ottoman and Safavid realms.

The merchants in turn served an information function. Because communication technologies were so limited, rulers used travelers of all sorts to gain knowledge about the rest of the world. Scholars, Sufis, traders, envoys, and spies all served this purpose. Monarchs used envoys as spies, and their rivals tried to control information by keeping visiting envoys sequestered and by intimidating them with military displays. Response to another ruler's challenge could never be swift because it was often months or years before a monarch received a reply or news about his envoy's fate.

Outside these channels of communication, relations between the gunpowder empires and European or East Asian states were still quite limited. Only the Ottomans had resident consuls from some of the European states in their capital. In this era the balance of trade was tipped very much in favor of the East, with eastern goods flowing into Europe and cash flowing back. European imports, with the exception of certain kinds of textiles, were negligible by comparison.

Conclusion

In the three and a half centuries before 1650, Europe still lagged behind Asia in many respects. No European state, not even the polyglot empire of Charles V, could compare in manpower and resources with the realms of Suleiman or Akbar. Europeans were impressed by the resources and taxation capabilities of the Ottoman governing system. Opportunities for minorities and toleration for dissenting religions were greater in the Muslim countries than in Europe. Asian cities were usually better planned, more tastefully adorned with works of art, and even better supplied with water and with sewage disposal.

Europe's advantages, which began to be more apparent after the beginning of the seventeenth century, were most evident in the realm of technology, specifically in the production of field artillery and ocean-going ships. These technical assets helped certain of the European states gain leverage in a new age, when powerful states would depend on strategic control of sea lanes and world markets. But in the period from 1300 to 1650 it was the gunpowder empires that tended to dominate, using their resources and militaries to become the great imperial powers of that age.

Suggestions for Reading

On Inner Asia and Turkic groups, see Peter Golden, *An Introduction to the History of the Turkic Peoples* (Harrassowitz, 1992). Luc Kwanten, *A History of Central Asia: Imperial Nomads, 500–1500* (University of Pennsylvania Press, 1979), is an illuminating study of a subject long neglected in standard texts. See also David Morgan, *The Mongols* (Blackwell, 1986). More on the steppe background for other civilizations in this period can be found in Gavin Hambly, ed., *Central Asia* (Delacorte, 1969); William H. McNeil, *Europe's Steppe Frontier* (University of Chicago Press, 1964); and John Joseph Saunders, *The Muslim World on the Eve of Europe's Expansion* (Prentice Hall, 1966). The Saunders work also presents coverage of high Muslim civilizations in southern Asia. On Timur and his times, see Beatrice Manz, *The Rise and Fall of Tamerlane* (Cambridge University Press, 1989).

The Ottoman Golden Age is ably depicted in Halil Inalcik, *The Ottoman Empire* (Praeger, 1973); Norman Itkowitz, *The Ottoman Empire and the Islamic Tradition* (University of Oklahoma Press, 1980); Stanford Shaw, *A History of the Ottoman Empire*, 2 vols. (Cambridge University Press, 1976); and M. A. Cook, ed., *A History of the Ottoman Empire to 1730* (Cambridge University Press, 1976). On Sultan Suleiman, see Metin Kunt and Christine Woodhead, eds., *Süleyman the Magnificent and His Age* (Longman, 1995). The harem is covered in Leslie P. Peirce, *The Imperial Harem* (Oxford University Press, 1993). On Ottoman artistic production, see Esin Etil, *The Age of Sultan Suleyman the Magnificent* (Abrams, 1987). A captivating and revealing biography is Franz Babinger, *Mehmed the Conqueror and His Time* (Princeton University Press, 1978); a primary source on the subject is Tursun Beg, *The History of Mehmed the Conqueror*, trans. Halil Inalcik and Rhoads Murphey (Bibliotheca Islamica, 1978). For effects of the Ottomans on Europe, see Paul Coles, *The Ottoman Impact upon Europe* (Harcourt Brace, 1968); C. Max Kortepeter, *Ottoman Imperialism During the Reformation* (New York University Press, 1972); and Peter Sugar, *Southeastern Europe Under Ottoman Rule, 1354–1804* (University of Washington Press, 1977).

On medieval Persia, see Ann Lambton, *Continuity and Change in Medieval Persia* (Persian Heritage Foundation, 1988), and David Morgan, *Medieval Persia, 1040–1479* (Longman, 1988). See also Roger Savory, *Iran Under the Safavids* (Cambridge University Press, 1980). Coverage in English of the Safavid period is still limited; an old standard is Percy M. Sykes, *A History of Persia* (Gordon, 1976), first published in 1938.

The standard popular survey of Indian history, with brief coverage of the Mughul period, is Stanley A. Wolpert, *A New History of India*, 5th ed. (Oxford University Press, 1997). The Mughul system is ably described in John F. Richards, *The Mughul Empire* (Cambridge University Press, 1996); Douglas E. Streusand, *The Formation of the Mughal Empire* (Oxford University Press, 1990); Shireen Mooson, *The Economy of the Mughal Empire* (Oxford University Press, 1987); and Neelan Chandler, *Socio-Economic History of Mughal India* (Discovery, 1987). For studies of individual emperors, see A. S. Beveridge, *The History of Humayun* (B. R. Publishers, 1989), and Bamber Gascoigne, *The Great Moghuls* (Harper & Row, 1971). A well-known biography of Akbar is J. M. Shelat, *Akbar* (Bharatiya Bidya Bhavan, 1964). See also Michael Naylor Pearson, *The Portuguese in India* (Cambridge University Press, 1988); Charles R. Boxer, *The Portuguese Seaborne Empire, 1415–1825* (Knopf, 1969); and A. J. R. Russell-Wood, *The World on the Move: The Portuguese in Africa, Asia, and America, 1415–1808* (New York: St. Martin's Press, 1992).

On networks of trade, see K. N. Chaudhuri, *Asia Before Europe* (Cambridge University Press, 1990); Michael Naylor Pearson, *Merchants and Rulers in Gujarat* (University of California Press, 1976); and James Tracy, *The Rise of Merchant Empires: Long-Distance Trade in the Early Modern World, 1350–1750* (Cambridge University Press, 1990), which, however, bypasses the Ottoman Empire entirely. All of these works focus on South Asia. For a broader study, see Philip Curtin, *Cross-Cultural Trade in World History* (Cambridge University Press, 1992). On Mediterranean and Persian Gulf trade, see Eliyahu Ashtor, *Levant Trade in the Later Middle Ages* (Princeton University Press, 1983); Robert S. Lopez, *Medieval Trade in the Mediterranean World*, trans. Irving W. Raymond (Columbia University Press, 1990), a collection of documents; Daniel Goffman, *Izmir and the Levantine World, 1550–1650* (University of Washington Press, 1990); and Niels Steensgaard, *The Asian Trade Revolution of the Seventeenth Century* (University of Chicago Press, 1973).

Suggestions for Web Browsing

Islam and Islamic History in Arabia and the Middle East
http://www.islamic.org/Mosque/ihame/Sec11.htm
http://www.islamic.org/Mosque/ihame/Sec12.htm
http://www.islamic.org/Mosque/ihame/Sec13.htm

> *Related sites detailing the enormous legacy of the early Islamic civilization, a history of Mongol destruction and Mamluk victory, and the rise of the Ottoman Empire.*

Ottoman Page
http://www.xnet.com/ottoman/

> *Site dedicated to classical Ottoman history, 1300–1600, offering numerous links to other sites.*

Topkapi Palace
http://www.ee.bilkent.edu.tr/~history/topkapi.html

> *A guide to Topkapi Palace, with numerous images of the palace rooms and grounds and its phenomenal artifacts, including portraits of the sultans, manuscripts, clothing, porcelains, and armaments.*

Internet Islamic History Sourcebook: The Persians
http://www.fordham.edu/halsall/islam/islamsbook.html

> *Links to a variety of documents detailing the rise and spread of the Safavid Empire.*

Mughul Monarchs
http://rubens.anu.edu.au/student.projects/tajmahal/mughal.html

> *A detailed introduction to the Mughul dynasty and the city of Agra, whose images emphasize the superb architecture of the time.*

Notes

1. Vincent A. Smith, *Akbar, the Great Mogul*, 2nd ed. (Mystic, Conn.: Verry, 1966), p. 522.
2. Zahiruddin Muhammad Babur, *Baburnama*, trans. and ed. Wheeler Thackston (New York: Oxford University Press, 1996), pp. 350–351.
3. Ibid., p. 351.
4. Quoted in Bamber Gascoigne, *The Great Moghuls* (New York: Harper & Row, 1971), p. 128.

Ming China and National Development in Korea, Japan, and Southeast Asia, 1300–1650

Chapter Contents

Chinese historians from the beginning wrote the history of their country as a series of consecutive dynastic waves—as one dynasty would exhaust itself, another would form in the yin-yang dialectic of ocean and earth. Sometimes the change from one dynasty to the next would be brutal and ugly, but the underlying rhythm of China seemed undisturbed. The sheer vastness of the subcontinent, ranging from the arctic cold of Manchuria to the equatorial lushness of Malaysia, with its diverse populations, could be seen as pale imitations of the Central Kingdom. Ming China, viewed from the West during the period between 1300 and 1650, fits the image of the Central Kingdom—sublimely independent and superior to all outside forces.

But that image is not accurate. Throughout its history, China did not develop in a vacuum. It has been shaped by its neighbors, just as it has shaped its neighbors. A vast network of roads and sea lanes promoted the movement of people, plants and animals, technologies, thoughts, and institutions. The Chinese genius made itself felt in the synthesis the underlying civilization made with each of these outside influences. This capacity to co-opt potentially destructive forces kept Chinese civilization alive and fresh until the eighteenth century. Whether it was from the nomadic tribes continually pressuring from the north, the Indian missionaries coming into China from the west, or the trade and resources coming from the south, China profited.

The noun *China* is used to indicate the actual territory ruled by the central government at a given time. More important is the adjective *Chinese,* which applies to the region dominated by the culture and civilization of China—a much larger area.

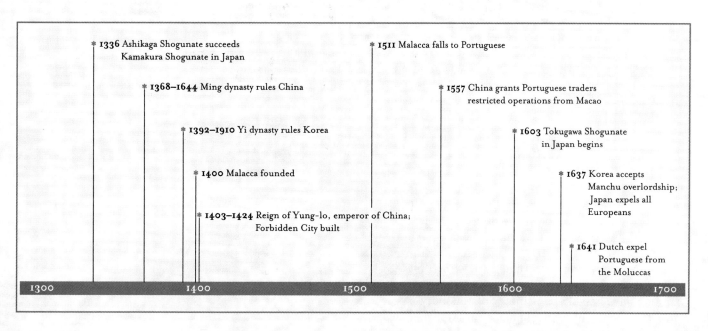

- **1336** Ashikaga Shogunate succeeds Kamakura Shogunate in Japan

- **1368–1644** Ming dynasty rules China

- **1392–1910** Yi dynasty rules Korea

- **1400** Malacca founded

- **1403–1424** Reign of Yung-lo, emperor of China; Forbidden City built

- **1511** Malacca falls to Portuguese

- **1557** China grants Portuguese traders restricted operations from Macao

- **1603** Tokugawa Shogunate in Japan begins

- **1637** Korea accepts Manchu overlordship; Japan expels all Europeans

- **1641** Dutch expel Portuguese from the Moluccas

1300   1400   1500   1600   1700

The Chinese civilization deeply affected the development of Korea, which was under direct Chinese rule for four centuries; Vietnam, which was under Chinese central power for more than a millennium; Japan, which was a cultural satellite for three centuries; and Mongolia, central Asia, Tibet, and Southeast Asia for varying lengths of time. This chapter discusses the development and mutual influences of China, Korea, Japan, and Southeast Asia during what in Europe was known as the late Middle Ages.

China: Political Recovery and the Ming Dynasty

The Mongol-imposed Yuan regime declined rapidly after Kublai's death in 1294 (see Chapter 12). Taxation became more oppressive, and peasant discontent grew. In addition, there were not enough Mongols to carry on the actual governing of the country, so they had to trust foreigners to oversee the Chinese officials. Even Marco Polo had earlier worked for a while in that capacity. Further, the traditionally nomadic Mongol soldiers—the only ones permitted to bear arms—did not take well to serving in permanent posts and lost much of their toughness and discipline. In the 39 years after Kublai's death and the installation of the last Mongol sovereign in 1333, the disorder that prevailed can be seen in the fact that there were eight emperors on the throne. Rising inflation stemming from the higher prices accompanying the expansion of trade and bureaucratic breakdown weakened the base of Yuan power. Finally, a peasant-nationalist rebellion sparked by famine began in southern China in 1352. Sixteen years later the Chinese put an end to the foreign dynasty.

One of the new leaders was a young Buddhist monk, Chou Yuan-Chang, who would rule under the name of Hung-wu. The Ming era, which he began, lasted to 1644. Although the Ming were perhaps less memorable then the earlier Han or T'ang, they stabilized the government and defended their homeland against invasion for the better part of three centuries. For most of the era the country prospered and fostered cultural creativity. Generally, however, the emperors followed pre-Mongol models, except for resisting innovation and trying to block out foreign influences.

The Early Ming Era

The new dynasty showed some potential for creativity before the early fifteenth century. Hung-wu (1368–1398) was aided by his able consort, the legendary Empress Ma, in establishing an efficient Chinese regime. Hung-wu's son, known as Yung-lo (1403–1424), further strengthened the regime and moved the capital back to Peking. These first two emperors restored the examination system and the traditional law, harshly punishing violators but respecting the rights of individuals, even Mongols who

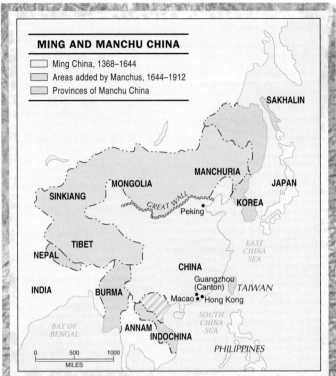

After the first two Ming emperors consolidated and expanded their rule, the rest of the dynasty remained content with the extent of their realm. The Manchus, who would take power in the second half of the seventeenth century, would greatly expand the Central Kingdom.

accepted Ming rule. Hung-wu and Yung-lo also initiated a degree of local autonomy and fostered traditional education while keeping firm control of national government and the military. In addition, they carried on vast economic reconstruction projects: reforestation, water projects, and repopulation.

Policy in the first two reigns reflected a definite interest in the wider world. Both emperors fought successful campaigns against the Mongols, and Yung-lo forcibly reannexed Annam. The Ming government encouraged foreign trade with Japan, Southeast Asia, and India, officially promoting cotton production, introduced earlier from the West, as a new staple export. Yung-lo regularly sent diplomatic and commercial

Ming China

1368–1398	Reign of Hung-wu
1405–1433	Naval expeditions led by Cheng Ho
1472–1529	Wang Yang-ming, philosopher
1644	Founding of Manchu dynasty
1683	Fall of Taiwan

missions to neighboring states and encouraged Chinese migration into the Malay Archipelago. In 1405 Yung-lo set in motion a series of naval expeditions led by Cheng Ho that ended in 1433. With some ships exceeding 500 tons and carrying crews of 700, the Chinese flotillas visited Sumatra, India, the Persian Gulf, Aden, and East Africa. There they exchanged porcelains and pottery for ivory, ostrich feathers, and exotic animals, such as zebras and giraffes. China had already penetrated the Indian Ocean while Portuguese captains were still cautiously exploring the Atlantic coast of Morocco. After the last voyage, Chinese emperors never again sponsored such pathbreaking journeys, but instead rested content within their own Central Kingdom.

Thereafter the Ming emperors were more concerned about recovering the past than pioneering the future. They rallied support by using popular prejudices against the Mongols and the Chinese elite who had served the foreign oppressors. In the process they tried to build a welfare state, funded by heavily taxing the wealthy people who had not supported them and managed by former peasants and tradesmen, instead of the old scholar-bureaucrats. Despite their attempts at some change, the emperors perpetuated many old bureaucratic sources of corruption and weakness. The excesses of court eunuchs, male children sold by their parents to be castrated for court service, continued. Eunuchs had served as court advisers and servants since the Chou dynasty. Continuing destructive Mongol raids, compounded by Japanese pirate attacks along the coast, brought other problems. Consequently, economic revival remained only moderate, population stayed low, and revenues declined while expenditures rose.

The Ming tendency to perpetuate misfortune by clinging to tradition is well illustrated by the declining status of women in this era. This trend had been steady under the Sung and Yuan dynasties, but it reached a new low under the Ming. Foot binding, for example, was most common in the Ming period, when middle-class families hoping to be accepted into the governing elite emulated it. Similarly, legal recognition of concubinage encouraged a traffic in young virgins from poor families. Concubine brokers bought them and then supplied wealthy merchants and officials. Another indication of the new social atmosphere is provided by the increase in suicides and self-mutilations among widows seeking to show grief or prove their loyalty to dead husbands. By the mid-seventeenth century, 8600 Ming widows killed themselves, compared with 359 under the Yuan and 150 under the Sung.

Ming Society and Culture in the Sixteenth Century

As time passed, Chinese rulers became even more resistant to innovation. Yet this inflexibility, so common

Portrait of Hung-wu, the first emperor of the Ming dynasty.

among a long line of "do nothing" emperors, generated an aura of stability through most of the 1500s, when Chinese culture was a model for East Asia. Sixteenth-century European visitors were impressed by Chinese courtesy, respect for law, confidence, and stately ceremonies. They saw material prosperity in the bustling markets, stone-paved roads, and beautiful homes of Ming officials. The elaborate Ming examination system, with its proclaimed principle of advancement on merit, often evoked favorable surprise. But European commentators were perhaps most lavish in praising Chinese justice; one concluded that China was "one of the best-governed" countries "in the entire world."[1] Such recognized superiority, along with the resulting Chinese satisfaction, was a major obstacle to progress in the later Ming period.

The Ming respect for learning was most evident in the production of vast multivolume collections, including 1500 local histories and a dry but famous medical work, *The Outline of Herb Medicine*, which took 30 years to complete. In this spirit, during the reign of Yung-lo there was an attempt to create an enormous library containing all of the works of

Polygamy in a Ming Household

This selection reveals the kind of competition and petty jealousy that could develop in a middle-class family with multiple wives.

Now that she was the favorite, Lotus became more and more intent on having her own way. She was never at peace.... One day, in a bad mood over nothing, she upbraided her maid Plum.... That morning she had risen earlier than usual to help Moon, the principal wife, get ready for a funeral. She had been so tired she took a nap, and was just going back to her own suite. On her way there she ran into Jade, the third wife.

"Why are you looking so worn out?" Jade asked.

"Don't ask me! I had to get up early," Lotus replied, then added, "Sister, where are you coming from?"

"I stopped at the kitchen."

"Did the one there tell you anything?"

"No, not that I can think of."

... She and Jade sat down and passed some time doing needlework. After finishing the tea and cakes Plum and Chrysanthemum set out, they decided to play a game of chess. But no sooner had their game become exciting than Hsi-men was announced and entered the room....

When Jade asked about Moon, Hsi-men said she would be coming later in the sedan chair and that he had sent two servant boys to meet her. He sat down next to them and asked, "What were your stakes in this game?"

"Oh, we were just playing for the fun of it," Lotus answered.

"Then let me challenge you each to a game. Whoever loses forfeits a tael of silver to pay for a party."

"But we don't have any money with us," Lotus objected.

"Never mind. You can give me a hairpin as security."

First he played with Lotus and she lost. He began to reset the pieces for a game with Jade, but Lotus suddenly tipped over the board, causing the chessmen to fall in a jumble. Then she ran out of the room and into the garden.

Hsi-men chased her and found her picking flowers. "What a spoilsport! You run away because you lost, my lovable little oily-mouth," he called to her, panting....

Their diversions were soon interrupted by Jade who called, "Moon has just returned. We'd better go."

Lotus broke loose from Hsi-men and said she would talk to him more later. Then she hurried after Jade to pay her respects to Moon.

Moon asked them, "What makes you two so merry?"

"Lotus lost a tael of silver playing chess with the master, so she will have to host a party tomorrow," Jade answered. "You must come."

Moon smiled and Lotus soon took her leave. She rejoined Hsi-men in the front suite and had Plum light some incense and draw a hot bath so that later they could amuse themselves like a couple of fish.

Although Moon was Hsi-men's principal wife, her ill-health usually kept her from fulfilling all the duties of the mistress of the house. Grace, the second wife, performed most of the social duties such as paying visits and receiving guests, and handled the household budget. Snow, the fourth wife, took charge of the servants and was the chief cook. Wherever Hsi-men was in the house, if he wanted something to eat or drink, he would send his request to Snow via one of the maids of the lady he was visiting.

From the novel *Chin P'ing Mei* (1610), in Patricia B. Ebrey, ed., *Chinese Civilization and Society: A Sourcebook* (New York: Macmillan, 1981), pp. 167–168.

ancient Chinese literature and an encyclopedia on which more than 3000 scholars worked. There were, however, more dynamic intellectual developments, encouraged by the increased printing of books and by the growth of education in private academies preparing students for public examinations. A pragmatic influence against orthodox Neo-Confucianism was provided by the soldier, poet, and philosopher Wang Yang-ming (1472–1529), who taught that knowledge is intuitive and thought is inseparable from action.

Some Ming literature deviated from classical poetic styles. Written in colloquial language, novels describe ordinary life, often including explicit pornography. Three of the best-known novels date from the sixteenth century. *Monkey* is a rollicking semisatirical tale about a Buddhist monk traveling to India with his pig and a monkey, which had led an earlier human life. The partly pornographic *Chin P'ing Mei* recounts a pharmacist's romantic adventures. Perhaps the best-read work is *All Men Are Brothers*, the story of an outlaw band, like Robin Hood's merry men, who robbed the rich to help the poor. Travel literature and adventures found great acceptance among the merchant classes.

Playwrights from the south dominated Chinese drama, which had a golden age of its own during the Ming period. Plays ran sometimes to ten acts, developing intricate plots and subplots with unexpected endings. Music became more prominent on the stage as solos, duets, and even entire choirs alternated with the spoken word in performances.

Ming artists and architects produced great quantities of high-quality works but generally lacked originality. The horizontal lines of the Forbidden City, the imperial family's area of temples and palaces, dating from 1403 to 1424, illustrate the period's values of acceptance, balance, and formalism. In Ming painting, slight exceptions from the norm are found in the free naturalistic landscapes of Shen Chou (1427–1509) and his most talented pupil, Wen Cheng-ming (1470–1559). The great later Ming painter Tung Ch'i-ch'ang (1555–1636) was noted for the formal discipline of his brush strokes. By far the period's major artistic achievement was its porcelains, decorated in "Ming blue" under the glaze. They were copied unsuccessfully from Japan to Holland but were prized everywhere, especially in the sultan's court at the Topkapi Palace in Istanbul.

Porcelain vase featuring the distinguishing blue underglaze of the Ming dynasty.
Prunis Vase (Meiping) with Blossoming Lotus: Fahug Ware. Porcelain with polychrome glazes, H. 37.5 cm. China, Jiangxi Province, Jingdezhen kilns, late 15th century, Ming dynasty. The Cleveland Museum of Art, 1994, Bequest of John L. Severance, 42.716.

Ming Decline

Despite many signs of early vigor, the Ming regime steadily weakened after the middle of the fifteenth century. This decline resulted largely from dynamic changes that the emperors and their courtiers tried to ignore while restricting foreign contacts. Ultimately, the government was beset with serious difficulties on every side, and its own decadence prevented it from responding to the challenges. In the later years of the Ming, eunuchs controlled most of the state power and were content to play the competing clans one against the other. The traditional scholar-bureaucrats found themselves frozen out of their usual positions of influence and pursued their interests through a series of secret societies.

Economic and social signs of decline were particularly evident in the late 1500s. Population had expanded rapidly, from less than 75 million in 1400 to over 150 million.[2] This rising human flood swelled the number and size of market towns, particularly in the heavily populated south. The overflow of determined emigrants poured into Indonesia and the Philippines. Trade expanded voluminously within the country, and smuggling increased along the coasts, despite desperate government attempts to prevent it. Portuguese traders, banned in 1517, were permitted restricted operations from Macao after 1557. Soon

This subtle work, Whispering Pines on a Mountain Path, *painted by Tang Yin (1470–1523) embodies the artistic ideals of the Ming dynasty.*

A sixteenth-century engraving of Macao shows Portuguese ships anchored at the port.

foreign foods, goods, and money, especially Spanish silver, disrupted the economy and contributed to inflation. These changes drew the gentry and peasants into the towns, away from rising land taxes. They became prosperous but discontented members of a middle class that was increasing even faster than the burgeoning general population. Urban unrest and inflation were only two of the converging problems facing later Ming emperors. Technical progress lagged, and production failed to supply the rising population.

Corruption, waste, conservatism, and bureaucratic inertia prevailed at every level of government and especially in the military. The armed forces had doubled in size by the end of the sixteenth century, but they were badly equipped and generally poorly led. The army suffered a serious drop in morale as disorder increased throughout the country: hordes of pirates ravaged the coasts, while Mongol attacks brought near-anarchy along the Great Wall. There was an almost complete breakdown in confidence in the battles with the Japanese, who used gunpowder weapons against Chinese swords and spears in the 1590s. Japanese assaults on Korea, however, were rebuffed.

Local governors and commanders, rather than the imperial government, were largely responsible for limited successes in dealing with these misfortunes. One such leader in southwestern China was the famous female general Ch'in Liang-yu, whose troops put down local rebellion and restored order. Known for her bravery and strength of character, she was also a refined woman who wrote elegant poetry. The central administration meanwhile nearly ceased to function. Most emperors were prisoners of the highly formalized system and puppets of their eunuch ministers, who generally pursued their own interests in directing policies increasingly frivolous and unrealistic.

Until about 1650 China seemed to influence Europe more than Europe influenced China, but the Western impact, viewed in historical perspective, was perhaps greater than it appeared at the time. Its most visible signs were the Portuguese ships and traders at

Macao, the few Portuguese artillerymen employed against the Manchus, and the Jesuit advisers in Peking, who followed Father Matteo Ricci to the Ming court after 1601. The Jesuits were not very successful missionaries, converting only some 100,000 Chinese, a tiny fraction of the population. But Jesuit treatises on the practical sciences, such as medicine, shipbuilding, and metal casting, were widely read and highly valued. Even more lasting effects came with European trade and Western food crops, which helped weaken Chinese values and expand an increasingly contentious population.

In the summer of 1644, after attempting to kill his oldest daughter and succeeding only in cutting off her arm, the last Ming emperor, Ch'ung-cheng (1627–1644), hanged himself in his imperial garden, leaving a pitiful note to indicate his shame in meeting his ancestors. An insurgent government had already formed to the west in Szechwan, another rebel army was approaching Peking, and only a few Portuguese mercenaries and some imperial guards remained nominally loyal. But neither of the Chinese countermovements would succeed. As the Ming regime collapsed, Manchu forces crossed the northern borders. By 1683 a Manchu emperor controlled the whole country.

Korea: The Restless Satellite

Korea, China's northeastern satellite, clung resolutely to its own identity. It had survived for centuries by periodically accepting tributary status under Chinese emperors and adapting imported Chinese culture, much of which it passed on to Japan. The country had been united again by the founder of the Koryo dynasty (918–1392), who gave Korea its name. Koryo kings adopted the Sung Chinese imperial bureaucratic structure as well as its examination system. They were particularly zealous in promoting Neo-Confucian learning. Korean presses, using movable type, were printing scholarly treatises by the eleventh century. The government also organized many basic industries, for which it imported Chinese technology.

As in the past, however, little was done for the common people. While popular unrest and aristocratic contentions prevailed, the Mongols overran the country and dominated it until 1368. Korean monarchs became virtual puppets of Yuan emperors. The nation was then divided between those who courted the conquerors and those who resented the heavy Yuan taxes and manpower levies.

The Beginning of the Yi Dynasty

When the Yuan regime was overthrown in China, Korean military leaders seized power, dispossessing the old landed aristocrats of the Koryo establishment

Discovery Through Maps

A Korea-Centered View of the World

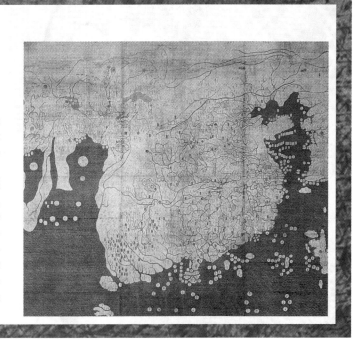

By the way they portray their homeland in relation to their neighbors, mapmakers make a statement about their love of their country and their capacity to see themselves from an accurate perspective.

Unlike modern mapmakers, who are constrained through centuries of observations, satellite photos, and projections to render accurately the comparative sizes of the recorded landmasses, the Korean mapmaker centuries ago faced no limits in his presentation. Korea assumes continental dimensions in this map, and Japan shrivels away to a distant, puny archipelago. Thus, the cartographer served his countrymen with a reassuring, if false, image of Korea's strength.

and redistributing their lands among scholar-bureaucrats who supported the rebellion. In 1392 the military leader Yi Song-gye was recognized as the first king of the new Yi dynasty, which lasted until 1910.

Like the Ming rulers to whom they paid tribute, early Yi monarchs carried out a revolution against elitists of the old regime. They created a new land register, abolished feudal relations in the armed forces, eliminated many Buddhist privileges, made Confucianism the state religion, and created a new bureaucracy made up of military leaders and scholars. In foreign affairs the new dynasty began territorial expansion into Manchuria and conducted successful operations against Japanese coastal pirates.

Improved communications, better agricultural techniques, and new inventions in the crafts brought rising economic productivity. The manufacture of cotton cloth, learned from China, also stimulated trade. Such economic growth increased the number of craftspeople and merchants, although most were employed in government monopolies.

The early Yi promised more than they delivered. In less than a century a new centralized administration entrenched a class of privileged Neo-Confucian bureaucrats who were as corrupt, inefficient, and overbearing as those in Ming China. With their growing power came higher taxes and service requirements for common people, most of whom were peasant tenants, and more than a third were still slaves. These conditions touched off popular uprisings, which the government brutally suppressed.

As in China, the Neo-Confucian revival brought more difficulties for women. Up through the tenth century they had enjoyed near-equality with men

King Sejong of Korea (1419–1450), a member of the Yi dynasty. During his reign Korea reached the height of cultural achievements, and the modern boundaries of the country were fixed. Sejong is also credited with the creation of the Korean phonetic, or Han'gul, alphabet.

This stoneware wine pitcher from the twelfth-century Koryo dynasty of Korea features a celadon glaze and inlaid white and black slip.

in property, inheritance, and marriage rights. Silla rulers had often been women. After the Koryo period, however, new laws severely restricted women's legal rights and prohibited them from participating in games, attending feasts, appearing in public unveiled, or even walking alone outside their homes.

The early Yi period brought a mild upsurge of cultural expression, particularly in literature. Treatises produced by the scholarly ruling class were often dull, but some showed genuine respect for rational learning. These scholarly efforts helped promote practical curricula in the academies, a Korean alphabet, and the development of metal-casted type for printing. Government presses published an increasing number of works in various literary forms. Some of these were prose compositions on mundane subjects, but poetry, stressing love of nature, personal grief, and romantic love, became quite popular. Many lyric poets were women. Less initiative was evident in the other arts, however. Painting, jewelry, calligraphy, sculpture, and architecture generally followed Chinese models, resulting in many creditable works, though most lacked originality. Only in ceramics did the Koreans equal the Chinese.

The end of the Ming era brought troubled times to Korea. Factionalism plagued the government, as too many bureaucrats competed for too few positions. Then, as Ming protective power waned, the Japanese invaded in 1592 with a force of 200,000 soldiers supported by 9000 sailors. The invaders hoped to use Korea as a base against China. Disaster was temporarily averted by Korean armored "tortoise boats," which cut supply lines of the invading forces. In 1597 the Japanese tried again, unsuccessfully, to take Korea. Deliverance was not assured until the death of Hideyoshi, the Japanese shogun, in 1598. The seven years of war diminished Korea's wealth and inflicted terrible hardships on its people. King Kwang-haegun (1608–1623) made determined efforts to rebuild the country, but they came too late.

After aiding Ming China in war against the Manchus, Korea was invaded, ultimately defeated, and forced to accept Manchu overlordship in 1637. Thousands of Koreans, held hostage by the Manchus, suffered great cruelty and privation before they could be ransomed. Many Korean families rejected female members who had been sexually violated and therefore dishonored.

Japan: From Feudal Conflicts to the Tokugawa Shogunate

The disastrous fate of Ming China was not repeated in Japan as it was in Korea. During the fifteenth century the Japanese central government lost almost all of its power to great local lords, the *daimyo*, who fought among themselves for control of the country. Their wars actually stimulated the economy and temporarily opened Japan to foreign influences. Later Japan isolated itself, not from a sense of superiority or a desire to ignore the outside world, but in order to achieve political stability.

The End of Central Power

The rising daimyo, strangely enough, prepared the way for their own decline. Greatly weakened by resisting Mongol invasions in 1274 and 1281, the Kamakura government faced an uprising against the shogun in favor of the emperor. For some 60 years Japan was caught up in civil strife as supporters of the emperor and the shogun claimed authority, each supported by contending forces. In 1336 the dominant force proclaimed the Ashikaga Shogunate the successor to the Kamakura, but the new regime soon lost control of its vassals. The daimyo in time assumed complete authority over each of their lands, not only raising armies but also taxing and issuing laws.

By the late 1400s their sporadic fighting had become protracted and full-scale. When civil war broke out between rival Ashikaga houses in 1467, more than 250,000 men were soon in combat around Kyoto. Intensified by the use of firearms, the conflagration spread throughout the country and lasted, with brief lapses, for over a century; it reduced the number of daimyo from roughly 260 in 1467 to 45 in 1580.

KOREA AND JAPAN BEFORE 1500

MANCHURIA

MING EMPIRE
(CHINA)

HOKKAIDO

KOREA

HONSHU

JAPAN Kamakura

Peking

Seoul

Kyoto
Nara

SHIKOKU

KYUSHU

Nanking

Hangchow

RYUKYU ISLANDS

OKINAWA

TAIWAN

0   200   400
MILES

Korea found itself trapped between the Chinese and Japanese and subject to the Mongol invasions of the thirteenth century. The Japanese were protected by their fortified islands and strong armies and maintained control over Kyushu, Shikoku, and Honshu.

Along with political instability, the period brought economic growth and dynamic social change. The daimyo were so occupied with their wars that they were forced to be more lenient with merchants who paid taxes and with some peasants who served in mercenary armies. Needing weapons, supplies, and money, the daimyo sought to foster trade, build towns, and encourage industry. Agricultural production also continued to rise, as it had done since the thirteenth century. Rising food production increased population, spurred city growth, and encouraged social mobility. Despite such spotty prosperity, many common laborers and peasants worked hard for an insecure existence. These conditions spurred the growth of mystical religions, such as Zen Buddhism and other evangelical cults, which stressed street preaching, congregational worship, and salvation in the next world.

The interests that impelled the daimyo toward trade with China and Korea led them as well toward Europeans. Because Portuguese captains could best supply efficient firearms and help foster profitable enterprises, the daimyo competed for Portuguese fa-

vor. After 1544 various daimyo concluded commercial agreements with the Portuguese, who took over most trade with the mainland, exchanging Japanese silver and copper for Chinese silks. After 1580 Portuguese operations transformed Nagasaki from a tiny fishing village to one of the largest ports in Asia, while the Spanish, English, and Dutch could be found in the ports of Hirado, Nagoya, and Kyushu.

Behind the traders came the missionaries, who were generally welcomed by daimyo eager to establish commercial contacts. Francis Xavier began preaching near Kyoto in 1549; by 1600 he and his Jesuit brothers had converted 300,000 Japanese, including some influential daimyo of Kyushu. The Jesuits worked closely with Portuguese merchants, sometimes acting as commercial agents among the local potentates.

The Tokugawa Shogunate

Between 1560 and 1598 two powerful warlords, Oda Nobunaga and his able commander Toyotomi Hideyoshi, gained control over the daimyo. Nobunaga in 1573 set aside the last of the Ashikaga shoguns, put down the Buddhist military orders, and drove the powerful Mori family from central Japan. Hideyoshi, who succeeded to the regency in 1584, completed the conquest of the daimyo. This former peasant without formal education and training in the higher forms of Japanese culture was extraordinarily intelligent, as could be seen in his military and political policies.

In his pursuit of a strong central power he disarmed the populace and ended all feudal grants of political authority. He made all levels sacrifice for the "greater good." As the feudal lords lost their power, the peasants were tied to the earth and forced to turn over two-thirds of their harvest to the state. Hideyoshi turned increasingly to the merchant classes, which he favored, for both support and taxes. To solidify his control, he separated the warrior samurai from the local landed interests and nationalized their service. With this base thus fortified in the decade after 1590, Hideyoshi warred against Korea and China, hoping to gain Christian support for a religious crusade. When these hopes were not realized and his campaigns failed, he began sporadic persecution of Christians, executing 26 of them in 1597.

After Hideyoshi died in 1598, the country lapsed again into civil war. Within a few years, however, Hideyoshi's former ally in eastern Japan, Tokugawa Ieyasu, became the strongest warlord. He won the decisive battle of Seikigahara in 1600 and soon had himself appointed shogun. Although his son Hidetada succeeded him in 1605, Ieyasu continued to exercise the real power until his own death in 1616. Seven years later his grandson Iemitsu became shogun, holding the office until 1651. By that time the Tokugawa Shogunate was firmly established; it would shape Japanese culture for the next two and a half centuries. The shoguns always remained the subjects of the emperor. They ruled with the aid of a council and had the responsibility to maintain order throughout all of Japan. They also commanded the unified forces of the country should a foreign threat occur, carried on relations with foreign powers, and generally decided the issues of war and peace.

Ieyasu, shrewd, patient, and ruthless, was one of the most successful rulers in Japanese history. Conditioned by the cruel uncertainties of the civil wars, he was both modest and unprincipled. To obtain favor with Nobunaga, he murdered his own wife and compelled a son to commit suicide. He won many battles by treachery. Yet his personal philosophy extolled self-criticism, quiet patience, and humble bearing. Above all, he displayed an iron determination to achieve political security for himself, his family, and his country.

The Tokugawa government was a model of efficient centralized feudalism. As in the past, the emperor symbolized national unity while the shogun held the real power over the fiscal and military affairs. The daimyo remained as local governors, paying tribute to the capital, but bureaucratic regulations and inspections increasingly limited their powers. From the beginning, all were required to attend court, leaving close relatives as hostages when they were at home. This system, so similar to that of the Muslim empires, was much more successful. A major weakness, however, was the government's conservative response to a rapidly expanding economy.

Economic and Social Changes: The Western Factor

Political stability and government projects led directly to a burgeoning Tokugawa economy before the end of Iemitsu's reign. An official system of levees, canals, and dams provided drainage and irrigation for new arable lands; another government network of roads, post houses, and messengers brought agricultural products to flourishing towns. Various industries, especially cotton cloth manufacturing, provided a mass of consumer goods for exchange. Although foreign trade was limited after Ieyasu's time, its regulated flow from the port of Osaka made that city into a great financial center.

Tokugawa society was a medley of contrasts. Along with its expanding economy came a great swelling of population, which would rise by 32 percent during the seventeenth century, from 22 to 29 million.[3] Much of this rising human tide would congregate in cities such as Osaka, Kyoto, Edo (Tokyo), and other castle towns of the earlier warring states. There a rising merchant class began to supersede the old daimyo lords and their fighting retainers, the samurai. Members of the latter class were still honored as they rode the social momentum of the recent civil wars, but they had been reduced to an ornamental petty aristocracy of state mercenaries. Lacking real purpose or practical judgment and addicted to their own amusement, many became indebted to moneylenders and merchants, who profited from samurai misfortunes. Perhaps the two least favored groups were peasants and aristocratic women. The former were still heavily taxed, recruited for labor services, and subject to heavy discipline in their villages. The latter, unlike middle-class women, were victims of the prevailing Neo-Confucian code, which relegated wives to an inferior status as untrustworthy wards of their fathers and husbands.

The early Tokugawa period brought a rapid increase and then a dramatic end to most European influence. At first Ieyasu tolerated Christianity in the hope of maintaining good relations and foreign trade. In his own pursuit of trade Ieyasu issued more than 300 patents permitting Japanese to trade in the first third of

As a defense measure, the Tokugawa government outlawed the building of bridges across major rivers. Thus the rivers were crossed by palanquin, *an enclosed litter that men bore on their shoulders by means of poles. Or one might cross the river on the back of a human porter.*

Ando Hiroshige, c. 1832. Abe River near Fuchu, woodblock print. Honolulu Academy of Arts, Gift of James A. Michener, 1978 (17,235).

Father Xavier's Difficulties as a Missionary in Sixteenth-Century Japan

This is from one of Father Xavier's letters, written in 1549 to friends in India. Note references to recent wars of the daimyo.

I went on with Joam Fernandez to Amanguchi.... The city contains more than ten thousand households.... We found many here, both of the common people and of the nobility, very desirous to become acquainted with the Christian law. We thought it best to preach twice a day in the streets and cross roads, reading out parts of our book, and then speaking to the people about the Christian religion. Some of the noblemen also invited us to their houses, that they might hear about our religion with more convenience. They promised of their own accord, that if they came to think it better than their own, they would unhesitatingly embrace it. Many of them heard what we had to say about the law of God very willingly; some, on the other hand, were angry at it, and even went so far as to laugh at what we said. So, wherever we went through the streets of the city, we were followed by a small crowd of boys of the lowest dregs of the populace, laughing at us and mocking us with some such words as these: "There go the men who tell us that we must embrace the law of God in order to be saved, because we cannot be rescued from destruction except by the Maker of all things and by His Son! There go the men who declare that it is wicked to have more than one wife!"

...We had spent some days in this office of preaching, when the king, who was then in the city, sent for us and we went to him. He asked us wherever did we come from? why had we come to Japan? And we answered that we were Europeans sent thither for the sake of preaching the law of God, since no one could be safe and secure unless he purely and piously worship God and His Son Jesus Christ, the Redeemer and Saviour of all nations. Then the king commanded us to explain to him the law of God. So we read to him

a good part of our volume; and although we went on reading for an hour or more, he listened to us diligently and attentively as long as we were reading, and then he sent us away. We remained many days in the city, and preached to the people in the streets and at the cross roads. Many of them listened to the wonderful deeds of Christ with avidity, and when we came to His most bitter death, they were unable to restrain their tears. Nevertheless, very few actually became Christians.

Finding, therefore, that the fruit of our labours was small, we went on to Meaco, the most famous city in all Japan. We spent two months on the road, and passed through many dangers, because we had to go through countries in which war was raging. I say nothing of the cold of those parts, nor of the roads so infested by frequent robberies. When we arrived at Meaco, we waited for some days that we might obtain leave to approach the king, and ask of him to give us permission to publish the divine law in his kingdom. But we found all ways of access to him altogether closed. And as we discovered that the edicts of the king were generally thought little of among the princes and rulers, we laid aside our design of obtaining from him any such licence, and I determined to sound and try the minds and dispositions of the people themselves, so as to find out how disposed that city was to receive the worship of Christ. But as the people were under arms, and under the pressure of a severe war, I judged that the time was most inopportune for the preaching of the Gospel....

From William H. McNeill and Mitsuko Iriye, eds., *Modern Asia and Africa* (New York: Oxford University Press, 1971), pp. 15–17.

the seventeenth century. The ships ranged from 300 to 800 tons in size and ventured to Taiwan, China, and the Strait of Malacca. Quarters for Japanese sailors were erected in Manila, Haiphong, Phnom Penh, and Indonesia. Despite the arrogance of Spanish Franciscan missionaries, he also tried to negotiate a commercial agreement with the Spanish, but they refused to admit Japanese ships into Philippine or Mexican ports. Ieyasu was also alienated by the desperate intrigues of recently arrived Dutch and English merchants, who consistently outmaneuvered his own merchants. Finally, in 1635 he forbid all Japanese to go abroad, on pain of death.

At the same time, in 1612, 1613, and 1614 Ieyasu issued edicts prohibiting Christianity. Thousands of

loyal Japanese Christians suffered martyrdom during succeeding years, hundreds being crucified. A climax came in 1637 when a popular revolt, led by some Christian daimyo, was put down. Japan then expelled all Europeans except for one regulated Dutch station at Nagasaki. In 1639 he cut all relations with Portugal and Spain. When in 1640 the Portuguese negotiators ignored his order and came back to Nagasaki, he burned their vessels, executed 61 of them, and sent the 13 crew members back to Macao. The Chinese were also limited to their own quarters in Nagasaki after 1635. Ieyasu saw the Christians and the foreigners as disturbers of the public order he was bound by his role as shogun to uphold.

Cultural Expressions

As with the European Renaissance, which was a unique variation on its classical heritage, Japanese culture in this period continued to accent its peculiar identity within Chinese forms. It also expressed the curious duality of Japanese society: a striving for calm serenity and a contrasting lusty vitality, as shown in explicit literature, massive architecture, and brilliant color. Although often obscured by tradition, these latter characteristics became increasingly evident in the Tokugawa era.

During the late Ashikaga period, Zen Buddhism spread from the great monasteries to impress thought and art with respect for things elegantly simple. Its best-known expressions were flower arranging, landscape gardening, and the famous tea ceremony, with its accented restraint and quiet contemplation. Zen also influenced painting as artists strove through the discipline of their brush strokes and the austerity of their subject matter to demonstrate that "less is more" in artistic creativity. The most enduring literary vehicle of the period was the Noh, a traditional form of lyric drama that combined stately mimetic dancing, music, and song. All such pursuits continued to be popular, particularly among the elite, into the Tokugawa era.

The era of political unification, however, brought new cultural emphases. In his mania for discipline, Ieyasu promoted Neo-Confucianism at his court, hoping to achieve emancipation from Buddhist thought. Similarly, the Momoyama period in Japanese art, the age from Nobunaga to Iemitsu, was often marked by ostentation and flamboyance, resembling in its own contexts the contemporary European baroque. It was most obvious in architecture, particularly in massive stone castles. Hideyoshi's famous fortress at Osaka, for example, had 48 towers; the base of the central tower was 75 feet high, and the main structure rose another 102 feet. Within the castles, other arts were displayed in wild profusion, featuring woodcarving, sliding doors, folding screens, and brilliantly colored walls. Paintings were often grandiose, in keeping with the pretensions of the castle lords. To this showy melange early haiku poetry, with its 17-syllable verses, added its own version of traditional sensitivity and measured elegance.

The Competing States of Southeast Asia

Situated on the main sea route between East Asia and the Indian Ocean and divided geographically into diverse subregions, Southeast Asia had long been an area of contending states. Most of the region had managed to escape prolonged, direct Mongol occupation. Although much of the culture came from elsewhere in Asia, particularly from India and China, each country was fiercely committed to its own interests. This nationalism frequently involved war in defense of independence or attempted conquest of neighboring states, which were usually held in contempt.

As Southeast Asia approached the modern era after 1300, difficulties increased with the weakening of the influence of the Khmer and the decline of the civilization of Angkor. The Mongols, who temporarily received tribute from the mainland and parts of Java, seriously disrupted all existing governments. Throughout there were ruinous petty wars, often based on Hindu-versus-Buddhist conflicts, each of which suffered individually under Muslim expansion. Finally, Muslim regimes replaced many traditional Hindu states in Indonesia, which also felt the effects of European empire building, first by the Portuguese and then by the Dutch. Before 1650, however, the total European impact on the mainland was negligible.

Burma and the Thais

In the first millennium of the Common Era, the region of present-day Burma remained an ethnically diverse region under Chinese domination divided into a number of small principalities. Around 1050 a process of political unification began under the Burmese, a group of people who moved to the south from the Tibetan frontier. This movement was shattered by the Mongol invasions of the 1280s. The process of unification recommenced after 1287, culminating in the dominance of the Tongoo kingdom in the fifteenth and sixteenth centuries.

Advancing to the south during the Mongol invasions were the Thais, a group of people from Yunnan already strongly influenced by Chinese culture and civilization. Once in Indochina the Thais also absorbed the richness of the Indian civilization. In the middle of the thirteenth century, during the Sukhothai kingdom (1220–1349), they founded a series of strong settlements in Indochina, displacing the indigenous Khmer and Burmese populations. The Sukhothai were later overthrown by the Ayutthaya kingdom, which lasted from 1350 to 1782 and had periods of regional dominance. After the Mongol withdrawal, a strong Thai state rose to fill the vacuum and came to control the greater part of Indochina by 1394.

Under King Bayinnaung in the 1550s and 1560s Burma briefly absorbed Laos and conquered Siam (Thailand) with an army estimated at 500,000, the largest ever assembled in Southeast Asia. Bayinnaung's capital at Pegu was a nucleus of Buddhist culture, a thriving commercial center, and the site of

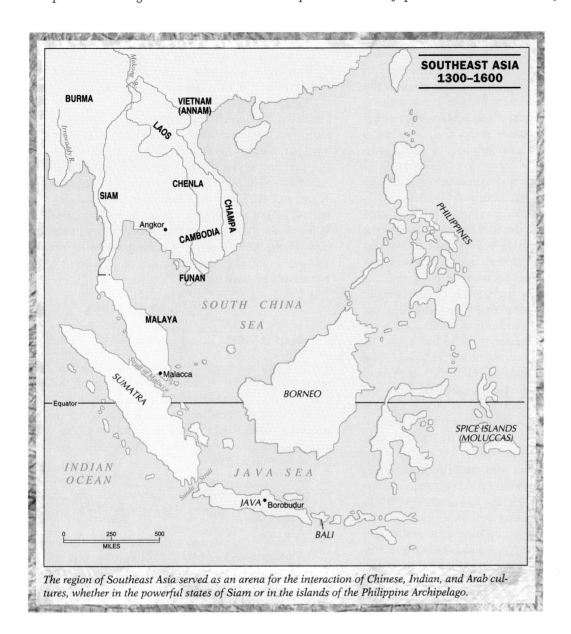

The region of Southeast Asia served as an arena for the interaction of Chinese, Indian, and Arab cultures, whether in the powerful states of Siam or in the islands of the Philippine Archipelago.

his wondrous palace, which was roofed in solid gold. But his successor wasted resources in unsuccessful invasions of Siam. Later the Thai state gained supremacy, humbling Cambodia and Burma after 1595 and profiting from commercial alliance with the Dutch.

Vietnam

During the fifteenth century Vietnam completely overshadowed its neighbors. Rulers of the early Le dynasty after 1428 drove out the Chinese and absorbed Champa while threatening Laos, Cambodia, and Burma. These three nations were all in decline; indeed, Burma had broken into a number of feudal domains. A slight exception to the general trend was the little Thai polity under King Trailock (1448–1488), who was partly successful in creating an efficient army and establishing a civil administra-

tion. By the end of the fifteenth century the Vietnamese, along with the Thais, momentarily controlled the Indochinese peninsula.

Indonesia

Islam expanded into Indonesia in a gradual and generally peaceful manner and achieved a great success in the fourteenth and fifteenth centuries. Sufi Muslim missionaries were drawn to the area by the expanding India-China trade, particularly when Chinese interests waned in the decade after 1424. Many local rulers embraced Islam to gain independence from the great Hindu state of Madjapahet on Java; others sought a share of Indian commerce. The Muslims built on the framework of the Madjapahet maritime empire, which extended throughout the island chain from Sumatra to Bali. The trading power easily accepted and dealt with foreigners, among them the large number of Chinese who immigrated and large number of merchants from Egypt, Persia, Arabia, and western India. These Muslims mixed easily with the populations of the port cities. As the power of the Javan empire weakened, the influence of Islam grew. Muslim sailors—either pirates or traders, depending on the circumstances—came to control the various straits between the islands and set up their own states.

The indigenous population came quite naturally to adopt Islam, as the local princely families intermarried with the Muslims in alliances bringing the power and legitimacy of the first to the wealth of the second. An especially strong point in the mass conversion to Islam in the sixteenth century came in the former Hindu areas: the equality of all people as taught by Muhammad pleased the local people caught in the chains of the caste system. At the same time, the Islamic clerics adapted their faith to some of the local customs and beliefs. From this base in Indonesia, Islam spread throughout present-day Malaysia, the Moluccas, and the Philippines. Only Bali remained relatively untouched by the Islamic advance.

The rising Muslim commercial center of Malacca, on the Malay coast opposite Sumatra, best illustrates the entry of Islam into Southeast Asia. Founded in 1400 under the protection of China, its rulers became Muslims, won independence from Siam, and built a Muslim empire of commercial vassal states in the region. Before 1511, when it fell to the Portuguese, Malacca was the busiest port in Asia, linking China and the Moluccas with India and Africa. Its growing success paralleled Muslim expansion through western Indonesia to the Philippines in the sixteenth century.

Arrival of the Europeans

In Southeast Asia, mainland governments generally maintained their independence against the Europeans. Portuguese missionaries, at first active in Vietnam, were expelled by the end of the period. Portuguese traders and mercenary soldiers served everywhere, but they were usually controlled. Some were enslaved in Burma; only in weakened Cambodia and Laos did they acquire significant political influence. By the seventeenth century the Portuguese were giving way to the Dutch, who courted the Vietnamese in only partially successful efforts to monopolize trade with Siam and Burma.

Well before 1650 Europeans were becoming very active in Indonesia. The Portuguese tried to use Malacca as a base for dominating trade in the region, but Muslim confederacies forcefully ejected them from Java and Sumatra and limited their operations in the Moluccas. In the late 1500s Portugal was allied with Spain when the latter acquired a foothold in the Philippines. The Spanish established a colonial capital at Manila and converted the country to Christianity. But the Spanish presence failed to protect the Portuguese from European competition.

Dutch newcomers quickly took control of the Moluccas and expelled the Portuguese in 1641. Soon after, the Dutch concluded a long war in Java by forcing upon the sultans a treaty that guaranteed a Dutch commercial monopoly in return for native political autonomy. Thereafter, Dutch plantation agriculture began undermining Indonesian economies. By the second half of the century the Dutch had replaced the Muslims as the most powerful merchants in the region. From then on, Europe's demands for the spices and riches of the region would be satisfied by the merchants of Amsterdam.

Conclusion

The geography and demographics of China had dictated that it would be impossible to maintain a Central Kingdom, isolated and arrogant, for long. The Ming tried their best after their first half century to pursue a conservative policy of noninvolvement with other peoples and succeeded in bringing some stability to China. However, toward the seventeenth century their inability to reform and the arrival of all manner of outsiders—invaders and merchants alike—spelled an end to their nearly three-century-long run.

Korea and Japan were the two major recipients of the Chinese example and closeness. Korea rested under the immediate gaze of its immense neighbor yet managed to construct a unique and powerful nation. Japan, blessed with its island position, had the unparalleled advantage of picking and choosing the currents and influences it would receive. To the south and southeast, a complex mosaic of nations grew, formed from Indian, Chinese, and Muslim influences. Never able to achieve regional dominance, each of them had a moment of hegemony and remained to add to the rich and varied cultural picture that Asia remains.

Suggestions for Reading

Among the best general histories of China are William Scott Morton, *China: Its History and Culture* (McGraw-Hill, 1982); Witold Rodzinski, *A History of China*, 2 vols. (Pergamon, 1979); and Charles O. Hucker, *China's Imperial Past* (Stanford University Press, 1975). Others deserving mention are Wolfram Eberhard, *A History of China* (University of California Press, 1977); John Meskill, *An Introduction to Chinese Civilization* (Heath, 1973); Raymond Dawson, *Imperial China* (Hutchinson, 1972); and Hilda Hookham, *A Short History of China* (St. Martin's Press, 1970). A recent readable paperback is Steven Warshaw, *China Emerges* (Diablo, 1987). For complete coverage of Chinese technology and engineering, see Joseph Needham, *Clerks and Craftsmen in China and the West* (Cambridge University Press, 1970). Esther Yao, *Chinese Women Past and Present* (Idle House, 1987), provides complete coverage of social conditions and important personalities.

Morton's *China: Its History and Culture* provides excellent broad coverage of the Ming era. See also a special study by Albert Chan, *The Glory and Fall of Ming China* (University of Oklahoma Press, 1982). Ray Huang, *1587, A Year of No Significance* (Yale University Press, 1981), is noteworthy for its penetrating case study of late Ming weaknesses. A commendable special study of the early Ming period is Bruce Swanson, *The Eighth Voyage of the Dragon: A History of China's Quest for Sea Power* (Naval Institute, 1982). Other scholarly but readable treatments of the Ming era are available in the Hucker, Dawson, and Hookham works cited earlier.

On Korea, see Carter J. Eckert et al., *Korea, Old and New* (Harvard University Press, 1990); Andrew C. Nahm, *Introduction to Korean History and Culture* (Hollym International, 1993); and James Palais, *Politics and Policy in Traditional Korea* (Council of East Asian Studies, 1991). Yung-Chung Kim, *Women of Korea* (Ewha Women's University, 1979), provides a readable and informative treatment of the period.

George B. Sansom, *A History of Japan*, 3 vols. (Stanford University Press, 1958–1963), is still the best exhaustive work in English. Also valuable are John K. Fairbank, *East Asia: Tradition and Transformation* (Houghton Mifflin, 1973); Eric Tomlin, *Japan* (Walker, 1973); Mikiso Hane, *Japan: A Historical Survey* (Scribner, 1972); and Edwin Reischauer, *Japan: The Story of a Nation* (Knopf, 1970). Noteworthy recent surveys include R. H. P. Mason, *A History of Japan* (Tuttle, 1987), and Steven Warshaw, *Japan Emerges* (Diablo, 1987). Rose Hempel, *The Golden Age of Japan* (Rizzoli, 1983), is the only recent study of Japanese art and architecture in the Heian period. A number of other well-known books are recommended for the period before 1650: Mikiso Hane, *Pre-Modern Japan and Modern Japan* (Westview, 1986); Edwin O. Reischauer and Albert Craig, *Japan: Tradition and Transformation* (Houghton Mifflin, 1989); Chie Nakane, *Tokugawa Japan* (University of Tokyo Press, 1990); John W. Hall et al., *Japan Before Tokugawa* (Yale University, 1981); and William S. Martin, *Japan: Its History and Culture* (McGraw-Hill, 1984). Conrad Totman, *Japan Before Perry* (University of California Press, 1981), which devotes much attention to the early modern period, is well organized despite an awkward periodization framework. Stuart Fewster, *Japan from Shogun to Superstate* (St. Martin's Press, 1988), is informative. Two excellent biographies that mirror the time are Mary Elizabeth Berry, *Hideyoshi* (Harvard University Press, 1982), and Conrad Totman, *Tokugawa Ieyasu* (Heian International, 1983). Mary R. Beard, *The Force of Women in Japanese History* (Public Affairs Press, 1953), is still a reliable source. See also Neil Pedlar, *The Imported Pioneers: Westerners Who Helped Build Modern Japan* (St. Martin's Press, 1991).

Anthony Reid, *Southeast Asia in the Age of Commerce, 1450–1680* (Yale University Press, 1988), supplies brilliant coverage of separate cultures and attempts a synthesis of the whole in terms of affecting Western commercialism. Two older general works are well worth examining: George Coedes, *The Making of Southeast Asia*, 2nd ed. (Allen & Unwin, 1983), and Steven Warshaw, *Southeast Asia Emerges* (Diablo, 1987). In addition, the following standard surveys are still useful: John F. Cady, *Southeast Asia* (McGraw-Hill, 1964); George Coedes, *The Indianized States of Southeast Asia* (East-West Center, 1968); D. G. H. Hall, *A History of Southeast Asia* (St. Martin's Press, 1964); and B. R. Pearn, *An Introduction to the History of Southeast Asia* (Longman, 1963). The best regional treatments may be found in Michael Aung-Thwin, *Pagan: The Origins of Modern Burma* (University of Hawaii Press, 1985); David K. Wyatt, *Thailand: A Short History* (Yale University Press, 1983); David P. Chandler, *A History of Cambodia* (Westview, 1992); Joseph Buttinger, *Oragon Defiant* (Praeger, 1972); Barbara W. Andaya, *A History of Malaysia* (Macmillan, 1985); and John David Legge, *Indonesia* (Prentice Hall, 1965).

Suggestions for Web Browsing

Imperial China: The Ming
http://www.fordham.edu/halsall/eastasia/
    eastasiasbook.html#Imperial China

Map and images pertaining to the Ming dynasty, 1368–1644; a part of the Internet East Asian History Sourcebook.

Exploring Japanese Feudalism
http://www.variable.net/hidden/japan/introduction.html

Site explores in depth the history of Japanese feudalism, including Japan's founding myth, the warrior ethic, and the establishment of the shogunate.

Masterpieces of the Kyoto National Museum
http://www.kyohaku.go.jp/

Numerous images, with descriptions, of the artworks of Japan, Korea, and China.

History of Korea
http://socrates.berkeley.edu/~korea/koryo.html
http://socrates.berkeley.edu/~korea/choson.html

Text and images documenting the Koryo and Choson dynasties of Korea.

Notes

1. Quoted in G. F. Hudson, *Europe and China* (Boston: Beacon Press, 1931), p. 244.
2. Colin McEvedy and Richard Jones, *Atlas of World Population History* (New York: Penguin, 1978), p. 171.
3. Ibid., p. 181.

The Rising European Tide

The story of Europe and the New World in the period from 1650 to 1815 forms one of the most complex chapters in world history. Following the challenge to the ideas and institutions of the Middle Ages posed by the Renaissance, the Reformation, and the great religious wars, the search for principles of order became a consistent theme in the writings of scientists as well as in literature and the fine arts. This search for order also played an important role in the ambitious domestic and foreign ventures of autocratic rulers.

In Western politics the late seventeenth century witnessed the high-water mark of absolutism under Louis XIV of France. But new political concepts rose rapidly to challenge royal prerogatives everywhere. The eighteenth century was the period of revolutions that established the precedents and voiced the ideology that were to become the inspiration for the whole liberal-democratic movement of modern times. These political advances were accompanied, and indeed only made possible, by comparably important progress in thought. Outmoded ideas in economics and politics were attacked. So pervasive were the transformations in thought that they constituted an intellectual revolution known as the Enlightenment. Under the spell of the remarkable achievements of science—capped by the work of Newton—thinkers, writers, artists, and members of polite society sought to express a truly scientific, or at least rational, point of view.

The present owes much to the period from 1650 to 1815. That period provided us with the heart of Western liberal political beliefs; it encouraged religious tolerance and freedom of inquiry, and above all it made the individual's happiness, freedom, and potentialities the focus of attention. All these developments made this period a time of hope for the future of the western world.

There was, however, a disquieting feature. Liberalism and rationalism operated *within* but not *between* states. International affairs were dominated by the competitive state system in which each nation was beholden only to itself and any weak neighbor was a potential victim. In this state of international anarchy, the nations of Europe evolved a balance of power to check the grandiose ambitions of national rulers whose only law was force and to achieve some order in the relations between rival states. Thus a coalition of rival powers thwarted the plans of Louis XIV, of the French revolutionary leaders, and finally of the brilliant and unscrupulous Napoleon, who sought to control all of Europe under the pretext of spreading the ideals of equality and liberty. The discrepancy between benevolence and liberalism, on the one hand, and force and autocracy, on the other, was to become increasingly a paradox of modern civilization.

For the powers of Africa and Asia the late seventeenth and ensuing eighteenth centuries were a period of sometimes gentle and sometimes violent transformation. These states faced a set of challenges prompted by both internal upheavals and external threats. The internal upheavals took the forms of regional conflict, economic turmoil, and population growth. The external threats coalesced around the ambitions of certain European states whose growing military and economic power enabled them to launch wars of expansion to the far corners of the globe.

African and Asian responses to the threats of European imperialism took different forms, from imitation to rejection to compromise. The Japanese, fearful of contamination, attempted complete isolation of their country; Burma, Thailand, and Ethiopia tried similar policies. China cooperated with Western missionaries but cautiously kept them under strict controls. In other places, such as Vietnam, Persia, the Ottoman Empire, parts of Africa, and the Pacific, opinions and policies ran the gamut from outraged rejection to enthusiastic acceptance of European ways. Western influence was most evident by 1800 in some regions of Indonesia and India, where Europeans were courted and imitated as a new ruling class. Although some Asians and Africans remained openly scornful of European culture in the eighteenth century, all were ultimately forced to take Europeans seriously because across southern Asia and along the African coasts, steady European penetration encouraged social disintegration while furthering civil and regional strife—results perhaps best illustrated by the African slave trade.

Louis XIV in Robes of State,
by court painter Hyacinthe Rigaud.
The portrait captures the splendor
of the Grand Monarch, known as
the Sun King, who
believed himself to be the center
of France as the sun was the
center of the solar system.

From Absolutism to the Old Regime

Centralized Power in Europe, 1648–1774

Chapter Contents

In the century and a half after the Treaty of Westphalia (1648), European state power took two different forms. The two nations on the North Sea, Britain and the Netherlands, pursued the choice of limited central power. Poland remained mired in a noble-dominated decentralization that allowed the king of this fourth-largest European power an army of only 10,000 men. Most of the rest of Europe chose the path of centralized power, imitating the absolutist government constructed by Louis XIV in France. Russia took a different approach to central power but by the eighteenth century also followed western European political practices.

Two powerful currents came together after 1648 to favor the choice of the absolutist model: the change in the understanding of nature brought about by scientific discoveries and the immediate benefits of economic and political centralization. This Scientific Revolution (see Chapter 21) began when Copernicus established that the sun was at the center of our part of the universe; absolutism took that conception as an explanation for the natural order of things in politics. It was not accidental that Louis XIV of France referred to himself as the "Sun King," the monarch at the center of the political constellation.

Europeans, both Protestant and Catholic, remained concerned about personal salvation. With the memory of war and social upheaval fresh in their minds, however, they found comfort in the belief in a reasonable universe and in order. In this

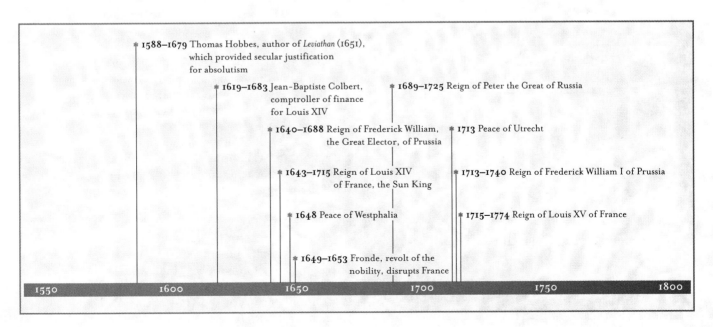

* **1588–1679** Thomas Hobbes, author of *Leviathan* (1651), which provided secular justification for absolutism

* **1619–1683** Jean-Baptiste Colbert, comptroller of finance for Louis XIV

* **1689–1725** Reign of Peter the Great of Russia

* **1640–1688** Reign of Frederick William, the Great Elector, of Prussia

* **1713** Peace of Utrecht

* **1643–1715** Reign of Louis XIV of France, the Sun King

* **1713–1740** Reign of Frederick William I of Prussia

* **1648** Peace of Westphalia

* **1715–1774** Reign of Louis XV of France

* **1649–1653** Fronde, revolt of the nobility, disrupts France

| 1550 | 1600 | 1650 | 1700 | 1750 | 1800 |

chapter we will examine the varieties of centralized states that imposed order, their strengths, their inability to adapt to the demands of a changing world, the wars that would bankrupt them, and their artistic contributions.

Louis XIV, the Sun King: The Model for European Absolutism

The word *absolutism*, which is applied to regimes such as that of Louis XIV (1638–1715, reigned 1643–1715), is somewhat misleading. Despite his grandiose role playing, Louis faced problems arising from preindustrial technology, diverse ethnic groups, local customs, traditional rights, and nobles who still commanded formidable followings, both regionally and nationally. Nor was the move toward centralized monarchy exactly new. Since the late medieval period, rulers had attempted to increase their power at the expense of nobles and the church. In the sixteenth and early seventeenth centuries, however, religious strife blurred political issues and somewhat restricted developing monarchies. After the Peace of Westphalia ended the era of disastrous religious wars, centralized royalist regimes such as that of Louis XIV rapidly gained popularity because they promised to restore order and security.

Along with the postwar obsession for security, economic developments also promoted an increase in monarchical powers. As the Spanish and Portuguese overseas empires declined, the Dutch, Eng-

lish, and French assumed commercial and colonial leadership. Meanwhile, the European economy underwent a second stage of expansion. This Commercial Revolution (see Chapter 16), centered in northern Europe, generated great wealth and increasingly complex capitalistic institutions. Both trends furthered the process of building centralized states to the detriment of the traditional order.

Philosophical Justifications for Absolutism

The prevailing respect for power was most clearly revealed in theoretical justifications for absolute monarchy. Some of these employed the older idea of "divine right," claiming that rulers were agents of God's will. This religious argument was still quite common, but it was now supplemented by new secular appeals to scientific principles.

Bishop Jacques Bossuet (1627–1704), a prominent French churchman and the tutor of Louis XIV's son, produced what was perhaps the classic statement of divine right theory. In *Politics Drawn from Scriptures* (published in 1709), Bossuet declared that

> *the person of the king is sacred, and to attack him in any way is sacrilege. . . . The royal throne is not the throne of a man, but the throne of God himself. . . . Kings should be guarded as holy things, and whosoever neglects to protect them is worthy of death. . . . The royal power is absolute. . . . The prince need render accounts of his acts to no one. . . . Where the word of a king is, there is power. . . . Without this absolute authority the king could neither do good or repress evil.[1]*

Neither Bossuet nor his countryman Jean Bodin (1530–1596) and most early apologists for absolutism advocated unlimited royal power. They thought that monarchs were legally entitled to absolute control over matters of state but were bound to obey God, rule in accordance with natural law, and respect traditional law, particularly individual property rights. Theoretically, these restrictions meant that monarchs could not levy taxes without their subjects' consent. But this requirement and all other legal restraints on the monarch could be set aside during national emergencies. The ruler alone would determine whether his action was legal or appropriate. Subjects, in turn, were bound to accept tyranny while hoping for divine relief in a future world, if not in the current one. One may conclude that the theory promised few practical legal limits to royal powers.

The most penetrating and influential secular justification for absolutism came from the English philosopher Thomas Hobbes (1588–1679), whose political treatise, *Leviathan*, appeared in 1651. The French religious wars, the Thirty Years' War, and the English civil war of the 1640s inclined Hobbes to

---

The Reign of Louis XIV

1638	Birth of Louis XIV
1643	Louis ascends to the throne under the aegis of Cardinal Mazarin
1649–1653	Revolt of the nobles in the Fronde
1661	Death of Mazarin: Louis take personal control
1661–1685	First phase of rule: Colbert installs mercantilism, Louvois reforms army
1670–1713	Four wars of Louis XIV
1685	Revocation of Edict of Nantes
1713	Peace of Utrecht
1715	Death of Louis XIV

view order as the primary social good and anarchy as the greatest social disaster. Unlike Bossuet, he did not see God as the source of political authority. According to Hobbes, people created governments as a protection against themselves because human life was naturally "poor, nasty, brutish, and short." Forced by human nature to surrender their freedoms to the state, people have no rights under government except obedience. The resulting sovereign state could take any form, but—according to Hobbes—monarchy was the most effective in maintaining order and security. Any ruler, no matter how bad, was preferable to anarchy. Monarchs were therefore legitimately entitled to absolute authority, limited only by their own deficiencies and by the power of other states.

Neither Hobbes nor Bossuet described the monarchy of Louis XIV. In an age when rulers enjoyed increasing popular favor, some succeeded in extending their powers and most sought to do so. Louis and his colleagues functioned within institutional systems carried over from the medieval past. Their success or failure depended on their ability to shape old feudal structures into centralized states. In this process none succeeded completely in eliminating aristocratic influence and local tradition as limits to royal authority. Their proclaimed absolutism reflected a trend, rather than an accomplished fact.

Origins of French Absolutism

Although absolutism was not a French invention, it seemed typically French in the later seventeenth century. French armies had recently humbled the Habsburgs at the end of the Thirty Years' War, bringing the Bourbon dynasty to predominance, and Louis XIV continued these military successes, at least for a while. Wealth poured into France from abroad, particularly from sugar plantations in the Caribbean. The magnificent royal palace at Versailles, the luxury of the French court, and the brilliance of French cultural expression dazzled the rest of Europe. It is no wonder that Louis was considered the ultimate in political wisdom or that his political image was widely copied. Like the solar system, then being emphasized in Newtonian physics, France appeared in the European state system as a central sun, surrounded by its orbiting satellites.

The attempted absolutism of Louis XIV followed a long monarchical tradition. Francis I in the early sixteenth century had increasingly subordinated the feudal nobility, created a centralized administration, and waged continuous warfare against his Habsburg enemy Charles V. Religious conflicts of the late 1500s ended the Valois dynasty but only temporarily disrupted the development of French absolutism. Henry IV, the first Bourbon, restored peace and royal authority. Cardinal Richelieu, as minister in the next

Leviathan. *The illustration symbolizes the surrender of individual rights to the government.*

reign, broke the power of the nobility and the independent Protestant cities.

However, for a while in the 1650s the country suffered through a difficult time. It had been nearly bankrupted by the Thirty Years' War, further drained of blood and treasure by conflict with Spain until 1659, and racked by the civil war of the Fronde—a war waged by some of the highest-ranking French nobles against the king—between 1649 and 1653. More than once Louis as a boy narrowly escaped capture by rebel forces. As a result, he became deeply suspicious of the nobility because many Fronde leaders came from that class. He was particularly alienated by court ladies, such as Madame de Longueville, who organized rebel forces, and by his cousin, Mademoiselle de Montpensier, who turned the guns of the Bastille, a royal fortress, against royalist troops. Louis's other nemesis was Cardinal Mazarin (1602–1661), his mother's Italian lover and chief minister, who neglected Louis and ran the government until his death in 1661. The 23-year-old king then took personal control of the state; he never appointed a chief minister once he was in sole possession of power.

The King and His Court

During the remainder of his long reign, Louis worked at projecting an image of himself as the "Grand Monarch." His personal political convictions were clearly revealed in a characteristic statement:

All power, all authority resides in the hands of the king, and there can be no other in his kingdom than that which he establishes. The nation does not form a body in France. It resides entirely in the person of the king.[2]

Louis also claimed authority over the French church and the religion of his subjects, enforcing that authority in contention with both Protestants and the papacy. The king was involved in a long struggle with the pope over revenues. Ultimately, after Bishop Bossuet and a convocation of the French clergy had upheld him, Louis won Rome's approval to collect the income from vacant bishoprics, although he abandoned hope of heading an independent Gallican (French) church. In 1685 he revoked the Edict of Nantes, by which in 1598 Henry IV had granted freedom of worship to Protestant Huguenots. The new law subjected Protestants to torture or imprisonment. Luckily for them but not for France, some 300,000 escaped to other lands, taking with them valuable skills and knowledge.

To symbolize his life-giving presence in the council chamber, Louis had a rising sun painted on his official chair. Today such overbearing egotism might appear as ridiculous as Louis's red-heeled shoes and enormous wig, but these were taken seriously in his time. Louis, in particular, labored very hard. Lingering childhood insecurities produced in him an enormous capacity for work and an absolute dedication to the art of ruling, which he accomplished with remarkable shrewdness.

Louis constantly strove to inspire awe of the monarchy, as was evidenced by his great palace at Versailles, a short distance from Paris. It was set in 17,000 beautifully landscaped acres. The parks and buildings, surrounded by a 40-mile wall, contained 1400 fountains, 2000 statues, and innumerable rooms decorated with marble columns, painted ceilings, costly draperies, mirrored walls, and handcrafted furniture.

A marked characteristic of the court was its loose sexual morality. Here again Louis set the example. Before and after his marriage in 1659 to the Spanish infanta, whom he formally honored but consistently neglected, Louis shared his bed with numerous women, each of whom was designated in her time as "head mistress." The best known among the early ones were the childlike Louise de la Vallière and the sensuous Madame de Montespan. He shared none of his power with them and was extremely wary of their efforts to extract political favors. Louis, after his experience with the women of the Fronde uprising, made a conscious effort to limit female participation in government. Late in life he may have changed slightly, for after his wife died, Louis secretly married Madame de Maintenon, the governess of his illegitimate children. This levelheaded matron offered the

Louis XIV, the Sun King, needed an exalted arena from which to exercise absolute power. In creating Versailles he captivated the imaginations of all of the courts of Europe and set himself above the nobility in France. The architecture, gardens, and court rituals of Versailles were copied across Europe.

With access to Louis XIV being necessary to gain power in France, the king was surrounded by ambitious courtiers and courtesans, such as the witty and beautiful Athénaïs de Montespan and Madame de Maintenon, shown here with her niece.

companionship he had never known, but even she could provoke his ire. He left his stamp on an era when women's limited influence was mainly confined to the boudoir.

The Transmission of Absolute Power

The most striking characteristic of the government of Louis XIV was the decided contrast between central and local functions. In the provinces he had to contend with entrenched local authorities and legal structures, an obstacle that hindered the enforcement of royal edicts and the collection of revenues. At Versailles the situation was quite different. There Louis was the final authority and arbiter of fashion. Theoretically, he made all major decisions. Although this was not actually possible, ministers were responsible directly to him for all their policies, and all their actions were taken in his name. Louis was the supreme lawgiver, the chief judge, the commander of all military forces, and the head of all administration. Central councils and committees of officials discussed policy, but these strictly advisory bodies were concerned primarily with administrative matters. Even in his palace, however, Louis was surrounded by aristocrats who held most of the high positions. Often these were potential claimants to the throne and had to be placated because of their family influence at the court and in the countryside.

The king worked closely with his appointed council and the secretaries who headed major agencies. Subordinate councils supervised ministries and their corps of supporting officials. One such body, the Council of Dispatches, received reports from the *intendants*, who were royal agents in the provinces. They represented the crown to 40,000 local officials, interpreting royal decrees, suggesting actions, and reporting results, although they were largely dependent on the king's appointed noble officials to conduct policies. This system worked generally, but not perfectly, to enforce laws, impose censorship, get favorable action from courts, imprison the king's enemies, and wheedle grants from assembled estates.

The aristocracy through which Louis funneled his power dominated France with clear distinctions precisely defined by law. Hereditary feudal aristocrats

Louis XIV to His Son

This memoir, designed to instruct a young prince who never became king, nevertheless provides revealing insights into Louis's personal rationalizations for his one-dimensional view of government.

I laid a rule on myself to work regularly twice every day, and for two or three hours each time with different persons, without counting the hours which I passed privately and alone, nor the time which I was able to give on particular occasions to any special affairs that might arise. There was no moment when I did not permit people to talk to me about them, provided that they were urgent; with the exception of foreign ministers who sometimes find too favourable moments in the familiarity allowed to them, either to obtain or to discover something, and whom one should not hear without being previously prepared.

I cannot tell you what fruit I gathered immediately I had taken this resolution. I felt myself, as it were, uplifted in thought and courage; I found myself quite another man, and with joy reproached myself for having been too long unaware of it. This first timidity, which a little self-judgment always produces and which at the beginning gave me pain, especially on occasions when I had to speak in public, disappeared in less than no time. The only thing I felt then was that I was King, and born to be one. I experienced next a delicious feeling, hard to express, and which you will not know yourself except by tasting it as I have done. . . .

All that is most necessary to this work is at the same time agreeable: for, in a word, my son, it is to have one's eyes open to the whole earth; to learn each hour the news concerning every province and every nation, the secrets of every court, the mood and the weaknesses of each Prince and of every foreign minister; to be well-informed on an infinite number of matters about which we are supposed to know nothing; to elicit from our subjects what they hide from us with the greatest care; to discover the most remote opinions of our own courtiers and the most hidden interests of those who come to us with quite contrary professions. I do not know of any other pleasure we would not renounce for that, even if curiosity alone gave us the opportunity. . . .

I gave orders to the four Secretaries of State no longer to sign anything whatsoever without speaking to me; likewise to the Controller, and that he should authorise nothing as regards finance without its being registered in a book which must remain with me, and being noted down in a very abridged abstract form in which at any moment, and at a glance, I could see the state of the funds, and past and future expenditure.

The Chancellor received a like order, that is to say, to sign nothing with the seal except by my command, with the exception only of letters of justice, so called because it would be an injustice to refuse them, a procedure required more as a matter of form than of principle. . . . I let it be understood that whatever the nature of the matter might be, direct application must be made to me when it was not a question that depended only on my favour; and to all my subjects without distinction I gave liberty to present their case to me at all hours, either verbally or by petitions. . . .

Regarding the persons whose duty it was to second my labours, I resolved at all costs to have no prime minister; and if you will believe me, my son, and all your successors after you, the name shall be banished for ever from France, for there is nothing more undignified than to see all the administration on one side, and on the other, the mere title of King. . . .

From *A King's Lesson in Statecraft: Louis XIV: Letters to His Heirs*, in Harry J. Carroll et al., eds., *The Development of Civilization*, Vol. 2 (Glenview, Ill.: Scott, Foresman, 1970), pp. 120–121.

retained possession of their lands and manorial courts, where they still controlled peasant affairs. Nobles enjoyed special privileges, such as immunity from regular taxes; they also owned land, exerted a major influence in assemblies local of estates, and held royal appointments to thousands of provincial offices. Many served as army officers and held high positions in the church. A few government officials came from merchant families, many of whom bought their appointments as well as their aristocratic titles, after which they cultivated the manners and pretensions of the elite class.

Through this system of court favorites and old aristocracies, Louis's reign brought the country more order than it had known for a century. Within the limits imposed by tradition, space, and technology, it functioned more effectively in furthering royal interests than any prior regime. In the period until 1685 Louis strengthened his central government while extending his political influence among the local feudal nobility and the urban upper middle classes. In times of crises he might issue edicts and have them obeyed, but he tried to avoid such situations, relying instead on cronyism, bribery, negotiations, and compromise to win cooperation outside of Versailles. Louis also gave or sold titles to his working middle-class officials, known as "nobles of the robe" to differentiate them from the landed "nobles of the sword."

The rest of French society consisted of unprivileged taxpaying commoners, including merchants, craftsmen, and above all peasants. Most peasants owed dues and services to their landlords, although they were no longer bound to the soil as serfs. Commoners, including middle-class townspeople, paid most of the taxes, which were used to finance frequent wars and extravagant royal courts. Peasant landowners usually owed fees and labor dues to local aristocrats. The poorest peasants were hired laborers or vagabonds. Slavery was rare in western Europe, but slaves provided a major labor force on overseas plantations. The status of commoner women did not fall as much or as quickly, but by the late seventeenth century the advent of early capitalism and the decline of domestic economies were excluding them from many industries and enterprises. As will be seen later in this chapter, the misery of "the other 95 percent" constituted a time bomb for absolutism.

Economic and Military Competition

In France during the reign of Louis XIV an alliance paired royal government with wealthy merchant-bankers. The result was a system of national economic regulations known as *mercantilism*, which had originated earlier but was adopted generally by European governments through the late seventeenth century. The trend was accentuated by the expansion of overseas trade, the expenses incurred in wars, and the economic depression of the middle 1600s. France turned to mercantilism in the hope of promoting prosperity and increasing revenues by broadening and unifying controls formerly imposed by towns. Yet all internal regulations, as contrasted with those concerning foreign trade, were usually enforced by local officials.

Louis's comptroller of finance, Jean-Baptiste Colbert (1619–1683), brought French economic self-sufficiency at the expense of Dutch overseas commerce (see Chapter 20). He created a comprehensive system of tariffs and trade prohibitions, levied against foreign imports. French luxury industries—silks, laces, fine woolens, and glass—were subsidized or developed in government shops. The state imported skilled workers and prescribed the most minute regulations for each industry. Colbert also improved internal transportation by building roads and canals. He chartered overseas trading companies, granting them monopolies on commerce with North America, the West Indies, India, Southeast Asia, and the Middle East. The system, named after Colbert, its best-known practitioner, came to be identified with thoroughness.

"Bullionism" was one of system's basic principles. It sought to increase precious metals within a country by achieving a "favorable balance of trade" in which the monetary value of exports exceeded the value of imports. The result was, in a sense, a national profit. This became purchasing power in the world market, an advantage shared most directly by the government and favored merchants. Louis's advisers believed state economic regulation to be absolutely necessary for gaining a favorable balance. They used subsidies, chartered monopolies, taxes, tariffs, harbor tolls, and direct legal prohibitions to encourage exports and limit imports. For the same purpose, French state enterprises received advantages over private competitors.

Because Colbert viewed the world market in terms of competing states, he emphasized the importance of colonial expansion. He regarded colonies as favored markets for French products and as sources of cheap raw materials. Colonial external trade and industries were regulated to exclude foreign competition. Such policies required strong military and naval forces to acquire colonies, police them, and protect them from foreign rivals. These policies often extended beyond commercial competition to war.

French foreign and imperial policy under Louis XIV required a highly efficient war machine. In conducting foreign policy, his most valued prerogative, he identified his personal dynastic interests with those of France. Considering the acquisition of foreign territory as both legitimate and desirable, he pursued his objectives in a competitive game of power politics with other monarchs. His concern for the "balance of power" exemplified the new secular spirit in foreign relations.

Louis's able minister of war, the Marquis de Louvois (1641–1691), revolutionized the French army. In addition to infantry and cavalry, he organized special units of supply, ordnance, artillery, engineers, and inspectors. Command ranks, combat units, drills, uniforms, and weapons were standardized for the first time in Europe. Louvois also improved weaponry by such innovations as the bayonet, which permitted a musket to be fired while the blade was attached. By raising military pay, providing benefits, and improving conditions of service, the war minister increased the size of the army from 72,000 to 400,000, a force larger than all belligerents put together at any one time during the Thirty Years' War. Louvois also improved and expanded the navy. In addition to a Mediterranean galley fleet based at Toulon, the overseas forces by 1683 consisted of 217 men-of-war, operating from Atlantic ports and served by numerous shipyards.

The new navy was also part of Colbert's grand strategy for building an enormous overseas dominion. In the last decades of the seventeenth century the French Empire extended to three continents. In North America fur trappers and missionaries pushed south down the Mississippi. In 1683 when the Marquis de La Salle reached the Gulf of Mexico, he claimed the continental interior for his king, naming it Louisiana. A second area of importance was the West Indies, where a number of French-owned islands, particularly Martinique and Guadeloupe, experienced a booming prosperity. Across the Atlantic, French West African trading posts on the Senegal River supplied slaves for the West Indian sugar plantations. The other areas of interest were in East Africa and southern Asia, where the French had acquired footholds in Madagascar, the Isle of Bourbon (Réunion) in the Indian Ocean, and trading centers at Pondicherry and Chandernagore on the east coast of India.

The Gravitational Pull of French Absolutism

The popular image of Louis XIV as the Sun King symbolized his position in France but also implied that the French system exerted an influence on other European states. Like all such symbolism, the idea was only partly true. As much as it was a response to the French example, royal authority was accepted because it promised efficiency and security, the greatest political needs of the time. Yet French wealth and power certainly generated European admiration and imitation. Countries across the Continent imitated various aspects of the political theater created by Louis in Versailles and also copied the economic and military policies of the Sun King.

The Germanic Satellites

Among the most obvious satellites of the French sun were the numerous German principalities of the Holy Roman Empire. The 1648 Treaty of Westphalia recognized more than 300 sovereign states in the empire. Without serious responsibilities to the emperor and with treasuries filled with the proceeds of confiscated church properties, their rulers struggled to increase their prerogatives and dabble in international diplomacy. Many sought French alliances against the Habsburg emperor; those who could traveled to France and attended Louis's court. Subsequently, many a German palace became a miniature Versailles. Even the tiniest states were likely to have standing armies, state churches, court officials, and economic regulations. The elector of Brandenburg demonstrated the ultimate deference to the French model. Although sincerely loyal to his wife, he copied

Louis XIV by taking an official mistress and displaying her at court without requiring her to perform the duty usually associated with the position.

Scandinavia

The era of the Sun King also witnessed an upsurge of royal authority in Scandinavia. After an earlier aristocratic reaction against both monarchies, Frederick III (1648–1670) in Denmark and Charles XI (1660–1697) in Sweden broke the power of the nobles and created structures similar to the French model. Frederick in 1661 forced the assembled high nobility to accept him as their hereditary king. Later royal edicts proclaimed the king's right to issue laws and impose taxes. A similar upheaval in Sweden (1680) allowed Charles to achieve financial independence by seizing the nobles' lands. Both kingdoms developed thoroughly centralized administrations. Sweden, particularly, resembled France with its professional army, navy, national church, and mercantilist economy. Although Swedish royal absolutism was limited by the nobles in 1718, the Danish system remained into the nineteenth century.

Spain and Portugal: Irregular Orbits

Unlike the Scandinavian and German states, most European governments resembled Louis's system more in their direction of development than in their specific institutions. As agricultural economies became commercialized, changing the developing interests of monarchs and commoners, rulers sought to be free of their feudal councils and exercise more authority. Some states during this period had not developed as far in this direction as France had; others were already finding absolutism at least partly outmoded. Although all felt the magnetic pull of French absolutism, their responses varied according to their traditions and local conditions.

The process is well illustrated by a time lag in the Spanish and Portuguese monarchies. United by Spanish force in 1580 and divided again by a Portuguese revolt in 1640, the two kingdoms were first weakened by economic decay and then nearly destroyed by the costs of the Thirty Years' War and their own mutual conflicts, which lasted until Spain accepted Portuguese independence in 1668. Conditions deteriorated further under the half-mad King Alfonso VI (1656–1668) in Portugal and the feeble-minded Charles II (1665–1700) in Spain.

The nobilities, having exploited these misfortunes to regain their dominant position in both countries, could not be easily dislodged. In Portugal not until the 1680s did Pedro II (1683–1706) restore a semblance of royal authority. His successor, John V

(1706–1750), aided by new wealth from Brazilian gold and diamond strikes, centralized the administration, perfected mercantilism, and extended control over the church. In Spain similar developments followed the War of the Spanish Succession and the granting of the Spanish crown to Louis XIV's Bourbon grandson, Philip V (1700–1746). Philip brought to Spain a corps of French advisers, including the Princess des Ursins, a friend of Maintenon's and a spy for Louis XIV. Philip then followed French precedents by imposing centralized ministries, local intendants, and economic regulations.

The Habsburgs

Aristocratic limits on absolutism, so evident in the declining kingdoms of Portugal and Spain, were even more typical of the Habsburg monarchy in eastern Europe. The Thirty Years' War had diverted Habsburg attention from the Holy Roman Empire to lands under the family's direct control. By 1700 the Habsburgs held the archduchy of Austria, a few adjacent German areas, the kingdom of Bohemia, and the kingdom of Hungary, recently conquered from the Turks. This was a very large domain, stretching from Saxony in the north to the Ottoman Empire in the southeast. It played a leading role in the continental wars against Louis XIV after the 1670s.

Leopold I (1657–1705) was primarily responsible for strengthening the Austrian imperial monarchy during this period. In long wars with the French and the Turks, Leopold modernized the army, not only increasing its numbers but also instilling professionalism and loyalty in its officers. He created central administrative councils, giving each responsibility for an arm of the imperial government or a local area. He staffed these high administrative positions with court nobles, rewarded and honored like those in France. Other new nobles, given lands in the home provinces, became political tools for subordinating the local estates. Leopold suppressed Protestantism in Bohemia and Austria while keeping his own Catholic Church under firm control. In 1687 the Habsburgs were accepted as hereditary monarchs in Hungary, a status they had already achieved in Austria and Bohemia.

In the eighteenth century Maria Theresa (1740–1780) confronted Leopold's problems all over again. When she inherited her throne at the age of 22, her realm, lacking both money and military forces, faced threats from Prussia. In the years after Leopold's time the nobles had regained much of their former power and were rebuilding their dominions at the expense of the monarchy. Known as "Her Motherly Majesty," Maria was a religious and compassionate woman, but she put aside this gentle image to hasten much needed internal reforms. Count Haugwitz, her reforming minister, rigidly enforced new laws that brought provincial areas under more effective royal control.

Despite its glitter and outward trappings, the Habsburg Empire was not a good example of absolutism. Its economy was almost entirely agricultural and therefore dependent on serf labor. This situation perpetuated the power of the nobles and diminished revenues available to the crown. In addition, subjects of the monarchy comprised a mixture of nationalities and languages—German, Czech, Magyar, Croatian, and Italian, to name only a few. Lacking ethnic unity, the various areas persisted in their localism. Even the reforms of Leopold and Maria Theresa left royal authority existing more in name than in fact. Imposed on still functioning medieval institutions, the Habsburg regime was a strange combination of absolutist theory and feudal fact.

Poland: The Last Medieval State

While Habsburg absolutism wavered in an irregular orbit, Poland was in no orbit at all. Local trade and industry were even more insignificant in its economy, the peasants were more depressed, and land-controlling lesser nobles—some 10 percent of the population—grew wealthy by supplying grain for Western merchants. Nobles avoided military service and most taxes; they were lords and masters of their serfs. More than 50 local assemblies dominated their areas, admitting no outside jurisdiction. The national diet (council), which was elected by the local bodies, chose a king who had no real authority. In effect Poland was 50 small and independent feudal estates.

Absolutism in Prussia

The rise of the Hohenzollerns was among the most striking political developments of the era. These relatively unimportant nobles, who once occupied a castle on Mount Zollern in southern Germany, pursued their ambitious policies through marriage, intrigue, religious factionalism, and war. By the early seventeenth century they held lands scattered across northern Germany. The Thirty Years' War was almost disastrous for the Hohenzollerns but conditioned them to austerity, perseverance, and iron discipline.

Two reigns laid permanent foundations for the later monarchy. Frederick William (1640–1688), called "the Great Elector," used his small but well-trained army to win eastern Pomerania at the end of the Thirty Years' War. In the near-anarchy that prevailed in Germany immediately after Westphalia, he reformed the administration in Brandenburg, created a strong army of 30,000 soldiers, intimidated the

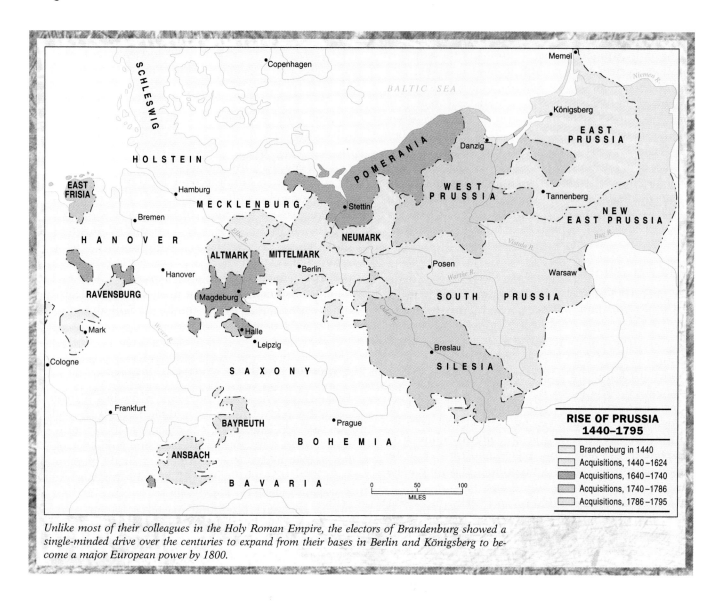

RISE OF PRUSSIA 1440–1795

- Brandenburg in 1440
- Acquisitions, 1440–1624
- Acquisitions, 1640–1740
- Acquisitions, 1740–1786
- Acquisitions, 1786–1795

Unlike most of their colleagues in the Holy Roman Empire, the electors of Brandenburg showed a single-minded drive over the centuries to expand from their bases in Berlin and Königsberg to become a major European power by 1800.

nobles in Prussia and Cleves, and won central control over all three areas. His son Frederick I (1688–1713) exploited Russia's victory over Sweden to annex western Pomerania. As a reward for fighting France, he was also recognized as "King in Prussia" by the Peace of Utrecht in 1713.

After Utrecht, Prussia became a drillyard, with the monarch Frederick William I (1713–1740) as drillmaster. This crusty soldier-king demanded hard work and absolute obedience from his subjects. He once told a group of them, "We are king and master and can do what we like." On another occasion he proclaimed, "I need render account to no one as to the matter in which I conduct . . . affairs."[3] With such unabashed absolutism, he reorganized the government under the so-called General Directory, established a civil service for local administration, created a royal supreme court, taxed the nobles, required the

nobles to train for professional military careers, and built an army of 80,000, considered the best trained and best equipped in Europe. At the end of his reign, the Hohenzollern monarchy was ready for military expansion.

Frederick William I held high hopes for his son Frederick II (1740–1786). The young prince, however, reacted against his Spartan training, secretly seeking escape in music, art, and philosophy. When caught after attempting flight to France, he was forced to witness the beheading of his accomplice and best friend. More years of severe training and discipline brought him in line with his father's wishes but robbed the future king of the capacity for personal feeling. In later years, while retaining his cultural interests and mingling freely with writers and artists, he developed no lasting relationships, particularly not with women. He married early to escape his father's household, then ignored his wife, Elizabeth, subjecting her to a courteous but cold formality. Neither she nor any of his frequent but temporary mistresses could influence his judgment. Neither did he confide in his family after the old king died. Wilhelmina, the sister who had shared his youthful enmity against their father, lost his confidence as they both matured. Such was the price he paid to become a superb administrator, a master of Machiavellian diplomacy, and—as we shall see—the greatest soldier of his day.

In 1780 the Prussia of Frederick II, called "the Great," was regarded as a perfectly functioning absolute monarchy. Stretching some 500 miles across northern Germany between the Elbe and Niemen Rivers, its flourishing population had grown from 750,000 in 1648 to 5 million. For 23 years, between 1740 and 1763, it had waged nearly continuous war, with 200,000 men often in the field. Consequently, the government ran as precisely as an efficient army. Like any good commander, Frederick claimed all ultimate authority. He required rigid discipline and deference to superiors from civilian officials as well as from military officers. Prussian nobles were honored over merchants or nonnoble officials and were permitted complete mastery over their serfs. Frederick's mercantilism stressed tariff protection for agriculture, encouraged industry with government subsidies, imported artisans, and sought economic self-sufficiency as a means of achieving military superiority.

Russian Autocracy

Russia anticipated the trend toward absolutism by two centuries. As we saw in Chapter 7, Ivan III had seized on the Byzantine heritage of the Russian state and his marriage to the niece of the last ruler of Byzantium to proclaim himself as the *tsar* (Russian for "Caesar") and adopted the use of the two-headed eagle as the symbol for the Russian throne. His grandson, Ivan IV (1533–1584), later surnamed "the Terrible," tried to take the next step toward the imposition of a truly imperial, autocratic rule. Ivan was 3 when his father died, and during the next decade he learned to distrust the aristocratic *boyars*, who showed him, his mother, and his tutors no respect as they took advantage of his youth. Once he took power in the late 1540s, he began a series of reforms to put the Russian state on a modern footing. He published a new law code, brought together representatives of the Russian population—the *zemski sobor*—to reform the administration of the land, saw his forces take Kazan and Astrakhan, and opened trade with the West.

As would be the case with the monarchies in western Europe, Ivan faced the opposition of his nobles, the boyars, to his plans to strengthen the central

A portrait of Frederick II of Prussia adorns the lid of this snuffbox. A patron of the arts and sciences as well as an able military leader and administrator, Frederick devoted himself to strengthening his country's military power while he also engaged in the study of philosophy, history, and poetry.

Frederick the Great, *A Political Testament*

In 1752 Frederick published his thoughts on government in A Political Testament. This excerpt is taken from that essay.

Politics is the science of always using the most convenient means in accord with one's own interest. In order to act in conformity with one's interests one must know what these interests are, and in order to gain this knowledge one must study their history and application.... One must attempt, above all, to know the special genius of the people which one wants to govern in order to know if one must treat them leniently or severely, if they are inclined to revolt ... [or] to intrigue....

A well-conducted government must have an underlying concept so well integrated that it could be likened to a system of philosophy. All actions taken must be well reasoned, and all financial, political and military matters must flow towards one goal: which is the strengthening of the state and the furthering of its power. However, such a system can flow but from a single brain, and this must be that of the sovereign. Laziness, hedonism and imbecility, these are the causes which restrain princes in working at the noble task of bringing happiness to their subjects.... A sovereign is not elevated to his high position, supreme power has not been confined to him in order that he may live in lazy luxury, enriching himself by the labor of the people, being happy while everyone else suffers. The sovereign is the first servant of the state. He is well paid in order that he may sustain the dignity of his office, but one demands that he work efficiently for the good of the state, and that he, at the very least, pay personal attention to the most important problems....

You can see, without doubt, how important it is that the King of Prussia govern personally. Just as it would have been impossible for Newton to arrive at his system of attractions if he had worked in harness with Leibniz and Descartes, so a system of politics cannot be arrived at and continued if it has not sprung from a single brain.... All parts of the government are inexorably linked with each other. Finance, politics and military affairs are inseparable; it does not suffice that one be well administered; they must all be.... A Prince who governs personally, who has formed his political system, will not be handicapped when occasions arise where he has to act swiftly; for he can guide all matters towards the end which he has set for himself....

Catholics, Lutherans, Reformed, Jews and other Christian sects live in this state, and live together in peace; if the sovereign, actuated by a mistaken zeal, declares himself for one religion or another, parties will spring up, heated disputes ensue, little by little persecutions will commence and, in the end, the religion persecuted will leave the fatherland and millions of subjects will enrich our neighbors by their skill and industry.

It is of no concern in politics whether the ruler has a religion or whether he has none. All religions, if one examines them, are founded on superstitious systems, more or less absurd. It is impossible for a man of good sense, who dissects their contents, not to see their error; but these prejudices, these errors and mysteries were made for men, and one must know enough to respect the public and not to outrage its faith, whatever religion be involved.

From Frederick the Great, *A Political Testament*, in George L. Mosse et al., comp. and eds., *Europe in Review* (Chicago: Rand McNally, 1962), pp. 110–112.

---

state. After 1560 he launched a full-scale war against them in the *oprichnina*. He declared most of Russia, including Moscow, to be under a martial law, enforced by a group of special forces called the *oprichniki*, masked men of legendary cruelty dressed in black, riding black horses, carrying broomsticks topped with dog skulls. He wanted to replace the old independent boyar class with a service nobility loyal to him. To that end he and his *oprichniki* drove 12,000 families from their lands in the dead of winter. To those who opposed him, Ivan responded with an inventive cruelty that gained him his name. As the terror increased, he lost control of himself, accidentally killing his beloved son and heir to the throne. Finally he achieved his goals, and the terror diminished. When he died in 1584, he was succeeded by his son Fedor, who was totally unequipped to face the challenge of a devastated and discontented land.

For a time Fedor ruled with the advice of his brother-in-law, Boris Godunov, a competent and ambitious boyar. For seven years the country recovered from the trauma through which it had been put by Ivan IV, but in 1591 Ivan's last son, Dmitri, died under mysterious circumstances. When Fedor died in 1598 without an heir, the Rurik line of rulers came to an end. Boris presented himself as the next tsar and received the acclaim of the nobles and church. However, Russia felt the effects of the same famine, eco-

RUSSIA UNDER PETER THE GREAT

From 1696 to 1725 Peter the Great allowed his country only one year of peace. For the rest of his time he radically changed the form and nature of his government in order to pursue war. At the end he had achieved his much desired "Window on the West" on the Baltic.

nomic failure, and discontent that preceded the Thirty Years' War in central Europe. Boris's policies failed to bring the country back to even minimal prosperity. At the same time, plots against him spread throughout the country, and when he died in 1605 there was no agreed successor. Eight years of civil war and Polish intervention, known as the "time of troubles," devastated Russia. Finally, the Russians reunited to drive the Poles out and call a *zemski sobor* in 1613 to choose a new ruling family, the Romanovs.

Between 1613 and 1676 the first two Romanov tsars, Michael and Alexis, integrated most aristocrats into the state nobility and achieved some degree of stability. As in Prussia, the nobles and the government were reconciled in their common exploitation of the serfs through the Code of 1649, which established serfdom, and the primitive agricultural economy encouraged aristocratic independence. Russian ignorance and technical deficiencies, along with a conservative-minded nobility, made the country stagnant in comparison with Western states.

A new era in Russian history began with Peter I, "the Great" (1682–1725). When he was 10 years old, Peter's half-sister Sophia staged a palace coup in which her troops looted the palace, killing many of Peter's maternal uncles. For seven years, while Sophia ruled as regent for Peter and his handicapped half-brother, Ivan, the young co-tsar lived in fear and insecurity. Later Peter roamed the quarter reserved for foreigners, without discipline or much formal education. He recruited and drilled his own guard regiments and learned about boats and Western ways. When he was 16, his mother arranged his marriage to a young noblewoman. From the beginning this was a mismatch; after impregnating his wife, Peter abandoned her within three months. He was now a young giant, weighing 230 pounds and standing 6 feet 8 inches tall, with a temper to match. Fortunately, he also had a sharp mind and boundless energy. Perhaps unfortunately for Russia, he despised Moscow, the traditions of the Russian court, and the culture of his country. In his efforts to westernize

Almost bigger than life for the era in which he lived, the 6-foot 8-inch Tsar Peter the Great remains one of the most controversial figures in Russian history. Liberals see him as a positive force for opening his country to the West. Conservatives see him as a negative factor in Russian history for the same reason.

window on the sea." He achieved this goal in 1703 when he founded St. Petersburg as his future capital on the Baltic. That same year Peter met Marfa Skavronska, a Lithuanian peasant girl who became his mistress, campaign companion, and, after the tsarina's death in a convent, his wife.

Peter's reforms enforced Russian absolutism, in fact as well as in theory. He centralized the government, replacing all representative bodies with an appointed council and appointed ministries. Royal military governors assumed local authority. The Chancery of Police maintained order and collected information from an elaborate spy network. By forcing his nobles to shave their beards and don European-style attire, he conditioned them to accept change and become living symbols of his power over them. They were now required to serve in the army, the government, or industry. Peter also officially abolished the office of patriarch as head of the state church, substituting a synod of bishops, dominated by a secular official, the *procurator*, who represented the tsar. In copying European mercantilism, Peter established factories, mines, and shipyards, importing technical experts along with thousands of laborers. He levied tariffs to protect native industries and taxed almost everything, including births, marriages, and caskets. As revenues increased, he improved the army and navy, both of which were expanded, professionalized, and equipped with efficient Western weapons.

Before and after Peter's time, Russian absolutism reached into the forested wastes of Siberia. Russian Cossacks and fur traders explored this enormous territory between 1580 and 1651. During the seventeenth century it remained a vast game preserve, exploited by the Russian government for its fur. Agents responsible to the Siberian Bureau in Moscow or St. Petersburg governed the relatively peaceful native peoples, collecting tribute from them in furs and a percentage from the profits of chartered companies. Given the financial succession of the tightly regulated fur trade, the government discouraged settlement in Siberia. In the eighteenth century, however, restrictions were lightened and western Siberia, between the Ob and Yenesei Rivers, began attracting colonists; convicts and political prisoners were transported there as well. Some 400,000 settlers had arrived by 1763, but Siberia was largely undeveloped until the late nineteenth century.

After his death in 1725, Peter's policies continued to affect Russian politics through the eighteenth century. The nobles worked constantly to regain their former freedom from the state, while the "old believers," Orthodox Christians who refused to recognize seventeenth-century religious reforms, maintained an "underground existence." Another striking characteristic of the period was the prominence of female rulers. Of

Russia, he would drive a wedge between the elites of the country and the masses that would last through the twentieth century.

After 1689 Peter took control of the country and his life. When Sophia failed in an attempt to become sole ruler, he forced her into a convent, although his brother Ivan remained co-tsar until his death in 1696. Peter amused himself with mistresses and wild drinking parties but continued his pursuit of Western knowledge. His difficulties in wars with the Turks convinced him that he must modernize his army and build a navy. In 1697 he traveled incognito as a member of a great embassy to Poland, Germany, the Netherlands, and England. He worked as a common ship carpenter in the Netherlands, learning Dutch methods firsthand. Back in Moscow, Peter crushed a rebellion of his palace guards with savage cruelty, began extensive reforms, and conducted new wars against the Turks and Swedes in efforts to gain "a

the seven monarchs between 1725 and 1801, only three were men, and they reigned for just six and a half disastrous years. The four tsarinas were Catherine I (1725–1727), Peter's camp-following second wife and the first Russian empress; Anna Ivanovna (1730–1740), daughter of Peter's half-brother, Ivan; Elizabeth (1741–1762), daughter of Peter and Catherine I; and Catherine II (1762–1796), known as "the Great." All tried to continue Peter's policies of turning his country away from its roots toward western Europe. Anna Ivanovna allowed the Baltic Germans too much power, thus alienating their Russian subjects. Elizabeth avoided this mistake while further consolidating the central government and winning new respect in western Europe for Russian military power. She laid the foundations for the long and successful reign of Catherine the Great, whose role as an "enlightened despot" will be discussed in Chapter 21.

Social Challenges for Absolutism

Three major nonpolitical revolutions challenged absolutist regimes in the eighteenth century: a demographic one—Europe's population grew by 58 percent between 1700 and 1800; an agricultural one—the adaptation of rational, scientific methods to food production; and an industrial one (see Chapter 24)—the most important, the use of machines to replace the limited resources of human and animal power. Each of these movements proceeded independently of the others and radically changed global societies while bequeathing a wide range of problems to the centralized powers. The regimes' inability to deal with these issues transformed them from the grandeur of absolute power to the shabby ineptness of the old regime.

The Prevalence of Human Misery

A significant base for popular discontent against government in the eighteenth century was an ever-prevalent misery among the ever-growing numbers of the poor. The various wars destroyed crops, ruined cities, created hordes of starving refugees, and depopulated whole provinces. Armies contributed to prevailing diseases, such as smallpox, typhus, and malaria. Lack of sanitation and the presence of horse manure on roads and streets attracted swarming flies, which spread typhoid and infantile diarrhea among thousands of children. While epidemics of plague spread throughout central Europe, rickets and tuberculosis reflected malnutrition among half the workers, who could not achieve marginal proficiency. Mortality

rates were appalling: Half of the children died before they were 6, one woman in five died in childbirth, and life expectancy was only about 28 years. For a large proportion of Europeans, unemployment, homelessness, grinding poverty, and hunger were inevitable. Indeed, horrible reality could only be escaped on rare affordable occasions in alcohol.

Although sometimes exciting, life in the cities was also miserable for the urban poor, who made up 20 to 40 percent of city populations. Many had come in from the country, seeking survival. Without homes, friends, or steady work, they lived as best they could, toiling at transitory menial jobs, begging, stealing, or selling themselves as prostitutes. Only a social notch higher were the apprentices and journeymen of the decaying craft guilds, who also faced real hardships. The discipline, particularly for apprentices, was difficult, hours were long, and wages were barely enough to buy food. Crowded into filthy quarters, without adequate light, air, or bathing facilities, they lived dull lives conditioned by ignorance, squalor, disease, and crime. Bad as these conditions were, they might always get worse, for as the guilds faced competition, many shops were forced to close, leaving their journeymen to become wandering artisans among the vagabonds on the roads.

Most of these pitiful derelicts were products of the century's most serious social challenge, rural poverty. Despite a general prosperity lasting until about 1770, European peasants suffered severely from ravaging armies and increasing agricultural specialization. High agricultural prices turned aristocrats into aspiring capitalists, willing to gouge their peasants in seeking greater profits. Some nobles, particularly on the Continent, revived and enforced their old manorial rights to fees and services. Others moved in an opposite direction by eliminating the peasants' medieval rights and using hired labor to work their lands. Either way, the peasants lost a substantial amount of their livelihood and were likely to become criminals, vagrants, or part of an alienated subculture. They ceased to be assets to the state—as either taxpayers or soldiers—becoming instead potentially dangerous and expensive liabilities.

Although faring better than the serfs of eastern Europe, western peasants still faced terrible conditions. Some in France were reduced from tenants to laborers when merchants bought up land to profit from rising food prices. Under Louis XV some 30,000 rural vagrants thronged French roads. About 35 percent of the peasants who had managed to acquire land were still paying manorial fees and services to local lords in accordance with feudal law. Earlier these exactions had hurt the peasants' pride more than their chances for survival; when the practice was stepped up during the depression of the 1780s, many lost their lands.

Giacomo Ceruti, Beggar Feeding a Child. *When they had no work, the poor turned to begging. When they could no longer beg, they died. In the painting the beggar and his daughter have found enough to live through one more day.*

Oppressive Conditions for Women

Eighteenth-century society was especially oppressive to women, whose general prospects declined despite some slight gains among those in the upper classes. Rising capitalism diminished work opportunities for all women, but poor widows were hit hardest, as suggested by the number starving in English workhouses. Women died, on the average, five years younger than men, a fact explained largely by the high proportion that died in childbirth. A significant factor was malnutrition, because poor women lacked calcium in their diets and were therefore subject to hemorrhaging. For most women among the rural and urban poor, life was a nightmare of deprivation, suffering, and struggling to survive.

This situation was particularly true for poor country women, as noted by a British writer, Arthur Young, who described a French peasant woman of 28 years who appeared to be 60 or 70. Capitalistic agriculture depressed farm wages, forcing farm laborers to leave the villages in search of work. Women had to stay and eke out support for the children by domestic spinning or weaving. Some went to work in the fields for lower pay and

longer hours than men. As work opportunities diminished, thousands took to the roads, carrying their babies and begging for food. Many died with their children by the roadsides; others joined criminal gangs of robbers or smugglers. The hardiest and the most determined reached the cities, where the best hope for a displaced peasant woman was employment as a cook or maid with a well-to-do family.

In the cities a poor woman's life was not much better than in the villages. The lucky few in household service were paid much less than men, assigned cramped quarters, fed leftovers, and frequently exploited sexually by their masters. Other employment was extremely limited because women were denied membership in most craft guilds. A few could find work outside the guilds, spinning, weaving, sewing, or working leather in starvation-wage sweatshops. Others took dirtier and heavier jobs in the metal trades and in the coalfields, both above and below the ground. Another option, reluctantly chosen by many women, was prostitution. This ancient profession was growing rapidly in every large city, with 50,000 known female prostitutes in London and more than 40,000 in Paris by the late 1700s. Social degradation, venereal disease, and continuous harassment marked their lives as civil authorities allowed them to operate but subjected them to periodic imprisonment.

A vast social chasm separated poor women from those of the wealthy classes; yet even at the top another broad gulf divided the sexes. Royal and noble women exercised considerable political power, but except for numerous ruling monarchs, they operated as satellites of the men they manipulated. Among both aristocratic women and those of the wealthy middle class, many were withdrawn from

Women miners were common in some regions. In this engraving from an eighteenth-century French work, women work at the pit head of a primitive coal mine.

Conditions Among Eighteenth-Century French Peasants

British writer Arthur Young made these observations just before the French Revolution. He saw better conditions elsewhere but was appalled at the backward state of French agriculture and the great gap in living standards between the nobility and the lower classes in the country.

SEPTEMBER 1ST. To Combourg. The country has a savage aspect; husbandry not much further advanced, at least in skill, than among the Hurons, which appears incredible amidst enclosures; the people almost as wild as their country, and their town of Combourg one of the most brutal filthy places that can be seen; mud houses, no windows, and a pavement so broken, as to impede all passengers, but ease none; yet here is a château, and inhabited. Who is this Mons. de Chateaubriand, the owner, that has nerves strung for a residence amidst such filth and poverty? Below this hideous heap of wretchedness is a fine lake, surrounded by well-wooded enclosures. Coming out of Hédé, there is a beautiful lake belonging to Mons. de Blossac, Intendant of Poitiers, with a fine accompaniment of wood. A very little cleaning would make here a delicious scenery. There is a [Château de Blossac], with four rows of trees, and nothing else to be seen from the windows in the true French style. Forbid it, taste, that this should be the house of the owner of that beautiful water; and yet this Mons. de Blossac has made at Poitiers the finest promenade in France! . . .

SEPT. 5TH. To Montauban. The poor people seem poor indeed; the children terribly ragged, if possible worse clad than if with no clothes at all; as to shoes and stockings they are luxuries. A beautiful girl of six or seven years playing with a stick, and smiling under such a bundle of rags as made my heart ache to see her. They did not beg, and when I gave them anything seemed more surprised than obliged. One-third of what I have seen of this province seems uncultivated, and nearly all of it in misery. . . .

JULY 11TH. Pass [Les] Islettes, a town (or rather collection of dirt and dung) of new features, that seem to mark, with the faces of the people, a country not French.

JULY 12TH. Walking up a long hill, to ease my mare, I was joined by a poor woman, who complained of the times, and that it was a sad country. Demanding her reasons, she said her husband had but a morsel of land, one cow, and a poor little horse, yet they had a *franchar* (42 lb.) of wheat, and three chickens, to pay as a quit-rent to one seigneur; and four *franchar* of oats, one chicken and 1 *sou* to pay to another, besides very heavy *tailles* and other taxes. She had seven children, and the cow's milk helped to make the soup. But why, instead of a horse, do not you keep another cow? Oh, her husband could not carry his produce so well without a horse; and asses are little used in the country. It was said, at present, that *something was to be done by some great folks for such poor ones, but she did not know who nor how*, but God send us better, *car les tailles et les droits nous écrasent* [because the *tailles* and other taxes are crushing us]. This woman, at no great distance, might have been taken for sixty or seventy, her figure was so bent, and her face so furrowed and hardened by labour; but she said she was only twenty-eight. An Englishman who had not travelled cannot imagine the figure made by infinitely the greater part of the countrywomen in France; it speaks, at the first sight, hard and severe labour. I am inclined to think, that they work harder than the men, and this, united with the more miserable labour of bringing a new race of slaves into the world, destroys absolutely all symmetry of person and every feminine appearance. . . .

From Arthur Young, *Travels in France*, ed. Constantia Maxwell (Cambridge: Cambridge University Press, 1929), pp. 107 ff.

meaningful work as mothers and homemakers to become social drones, attesting in an ornamental way to the high positions of their husbands. Legally, upper-class wives remained subordinated to their husbands in the disposition of property and rights to divorce; the double standard of marital fidelity remained supreme, both socially and legally. Indeed, despite their improved education and their artistic and literary pursuits, women were still regarded as childlike, irresponsible, and passion-ruled by such eminent eighteenth-century men as Rousseau, Frederick the Great, and Lord Chesterfield. In the council chambers and the countinghouses, it was still a man's world.

Rising Expectations

The eighteenth century brought new wealth (see Chapter 20) and new ideas (see Chapter 21). The wealth brought with it higher living standards for the middle classes as well as opportunities for social display, and the new ideas justified hopes for advancement. Even ordinary people could acquire the muslins and calicoes that permitted them to dress better and thus imitate their social superiors. More products stimulated appetites for even more goods, accenting the acquisitiveness already so common in European society, particularly among the upwardly mobile urban middle classes.

The conspicuous display of wealth, more than birth, came to be associated with social status. Bewigged merchants as well as nobles were resplendent in white silk coats, knee breeches, silk stockings, and gold-braided hats. Young fops, on their way up, might spend the equivalent of $1000 for a single outfit and lose that much more of borrowed money at the gaming tables. Well-to-do women decked themselves out in imported brocades, ostrich feathers, fans, furs, parasols, and silver lace. Home decor featured Persian rugs and imported draperies of chintz and chiffon. There was also a passion for objects from China and Japan—pottery, screens, lacquered trays, and gilded tables.

Although sanitation and living standards among the poor remained terrible, there were some improvements for ordinary citizens above poverty level.

Fantastic hairstyles, like that shown in this engraving, were one of the ways in which members of the French upper class displayed their extravagance.

In a few of the most progressive urban areas, some streets were paved and sewers were constructed. Water was piped to some private mansions, and the number of public bathhouses increased. At the same time, social graces were becoming more refined. Manners, for example, improved somewhat as ordinary middle-class Europeans set their tables with beautiful china and silver, provided napkins, and lifted food with forks rather than fingers. No longer did they throw bones on the floor or use pocketknives to pick their teeth. Eating became an art as well as pure sensual satisfaction.

Such refinements suggested that the comforts and values of the nobility were being shared by the upwardly mobile middle classes. Some 250,000 European families had acquired this status by the middle of the eighteenth century. In France this class constituted about 8 percent of the population and had acquired about 25 percent of the land. The new *bourgeoisie* came to enjoy some privileges formerly confined largely to the aristocracy. Meanwhile, an increasingly large number of individuals were entering the middle class from below. Shopkeepers, petty merchants, and various professionals raised their expectations along with their economic conditions. Very few would actually join the privileged elite, but the unfortunate losers became aware of individual interests, apart from those of caste or dynasty. The rising but excluded middle class enjoyed luxuries while valuing respectability, perhaps resentfully rejecting the flamboyant display so typical of nobilities.

Although largely denied government posts at the higher levels, many members of the new middle class possessed great potential for leadership. They were determined, confident, and often well educated. Many were members of the medical and legal professions, which were striving to earn respect at this time. Because they were somewhat sensitive to their own slights, physicians and lawyers often felt special concerns about public issues. Lawyers, particularly, were familiar with parliamentary procedures and were trained to express themselves clearly. Lower-middle-class leaders were also closer than the nobles to urban workers, with whom they could still share some common experiences and values.

Improving conditions among the middle classes brought some moderate gains for *bourgeois* women. The refinement of manners, a growing concern for fashion, an emphasis on family ties, and a growing concern for religious morality were all reflections of increasing feminine influence. The same family emphasis and middle-class penchant for individualism encouraged women to demand more voice in choosing their husbands; fewer middle-class marriages were negotiated by parents without consulting their offspring. More wealth and leisure also afforded increased opportunities for women's education, as indicated by the large number of new schools for girls, particularly in France and England. As a result, women became more prominent in literary and artistic fields. Educated and fashionable middle-class women often attended or hosted salons, which were centers for intellectual discussion. The salons originated in France but were copied all over Europe.

Privileged Social Orders

Ignoring the mass discontent and middle-class frustrations, the old regimes continued to depend largely on local authorities, military officers, and bureaucrats, drawn almost exclusively from nobilities and wealthy commoners. Governments therefore legalized privilege, conferring social status, political power, and fabulous wealth on a small elite while dooming the masses to grinding poverty. The system cut across class lines. Most of the clergy and nobles were as poor as some peasants, and the great majority of the urban middle classes were denied the leisured comfort of the wealthy bankers and merchants.

The aristocratic nature of the old regimes derived partly from encroachments on royal prerogatives by European nobilities after the Peace of Westphalia. Temporarily checked by such strong monarchs as Louis XIV and Peter the Great, the nobles retained or regained political power in the Habsburg domain, in Germany and Poland. Early in the eighteenth century they did the same in Sweden, Spain, Russia (after Peter's death), and particularly in Louis XV's France.

Europe's old regimes were topped by official ruling classes of high clergy and nobles. Combined, these two privileged orders accounted for less than 2 percent of the total European population; the great magnates, who enjoyed real wealth and power, were concentrated in only 5000 families, among some 4 million titled aristocrats. Most of the true elite lived in city mansions and palaces, far away from their broad acres in the country. For their high incomes, tax immunities, and numerous honors, they contributed almost nothing beyond decoration to church and state.

France provides a good illustration of the system. There the church owned 20 percent of the land and collected returns equal to half those from royal estates. Some of the monies supported education, social work, and charities, but most went to 11,000 of the 130,000 members of the clergy, particularly to 123 bishops and 28 archbishops. Some of their annual incomes exceeded the equivalent of $1 million, but many of the overworked lower clergy existed on $100 a year. Among the 400,000 nobles, only 1000 families were represented at Versailles, where their members held numerous honorific appointments requiring no work. Titled nobles held 20 percent of the land, most by feudal tenures, which permitted them to collect numerous customary fees from their peas-

The ornate staircase and lavishly decorated ceiling of the bishop's palace in Würzburg, Germany, suggest the splendor and luxury enjoyed by the high clergy.

ants. From all such sources, high French nobles probably averaged an annual equivalent of well over $100,000. Many, including some of the royal intendants, were former wealthy nonnobles who had bought their titles or offices.

Conspicuous consumption was typical of the high European nobility, such as the Fitzwilliamses in Ireland, the Newcastles in England, the Schonbrons in Bohemia, the Radziwills in Poland, and the Esterhazys in Hungary. Prince Esterhazy owned about 10,000 acres, including 29 estates, 160 market towns, and 414 villages; his annual revenues exceeded the equivalent of $400,000. With such wealth the magnates built elaborate city dwellings and sumptuous country retreats, filling them with priceless handcrafted furniture, rich tapestries, and fine works of art. While most people scratched for food, the high nobles enjoyed meats, fruits, and rare delicacies that were literally unknown among common people. Generally, the top aristocrats lived lavishly in a fantasy world, marred only by the dull ceremonies accompanying their brilliant but busy social activities.

Beneath this aristocratic superstructure lived millions of European commoners, 80 percent of whom were peasants. Except in Sweden, where their chamber of the diet was confined largely to protests, they were unrepresented in government. Three-fourths were landless, and many were serfs, bound to their villages, not only in Russia, Poland, and Prussia but also in Denmark. Among city-dwellers, only 11 percent were merchants, shopkeepers, artisans, and professionals. This proportion was higher in the Netherlands, England, and northern Italy but generally lower elsewhere, particularly in eastern Europe. At the bottom of urban society was the mass of indigent poor, barely able to survive. Commoners of all economic levels paid most of the taxes. They were subject to legal discrimination in favor of the nobility, from whom they were also separated by differences in education, speech, manners, dress, and social customs.

This general pattern was evident in the French Third Estate. Including some 26 million people, it was more varied in its extremes than the first two estates, the clergy and nobles. At the top were about 75,000 wealthy bankers and merchants who had not bothered to buy titles. Another 3 million urban dwellers consisted largely of shopkeepers, lawyers, doctors, craftsmen, and street people, these last being most prevalent in Paris and port cities. The great mass of commoners in France, as in Europe generally, was the 23 million rural peasants. Most held some property rights to their lands, but many were tenants and about a million were still serfs in 1789. Almost all peasants, serf or free, paid fees to their local nobles. Government taxes were irregular but heavy everywhere; the *taille,* or main land tax, fell heaviest on the class that was least able to pay. French peasants lived better than serfs in eastern Europe or the starving farm laborers of England, but life in a French village was a constant struggle for survival.

Social Discontent

Injustice and misery among women and the poor were obvious sources of discontent, but even more dangerous for old regimes were changing attitudes among the higher classes. A general spirit of change and hope, coupled with the chaotic confusion and inefficiency of most monarchies, aroused general feelings of dissatisfaction, particularly among members of the lower middle class and lesser nobles, who were too numerous to be absorbed into the established system. Even some favored aristocrats showed a casual indifference to royal authority and stubborn determination to defend their privileges. Potential middle-class rebels, particularly lawyers, were well equipped to voice grievances, which they did often by the late 1700s. Although lacking education and opportunities to register direct protests, city workers and peasants sometimes did express their despair in sporadic riots and futile local uprisings.

Because their testimony must be taken from official records, often from the statements of tortured captives, no one can accurately describe peasant attitudes on the Continent. They surely varied from place to place, as did the conditions. Where life was hardest, they regularly resorted to individual acts of violence, such as killing animals or burning outbuildings. Generally, they lacked long-range political objectives but could be aroused en masse by immediate threats to their well-being. Seventy-three peasant rebellions occurred in eighteenth-century Europe, notoriously in Poland (1730s), Bohemia (1775), and the great Pugachev revolt in Russia (1773–1775). Suffering English farm laborers rioted six times between 1710 and 1772. Although generally more docile, French peasants precipitated violent upheavals in 1709, 1725, 1740, 1749, and 1772. Arthur Young recognized their surly attitudes and contempt for authority. In 1789, when they could express grievances to delegates headed for the Estates-General, they were universally bitter against feudal exactions and government taxes.

Urban workers were usually more aggressive and perhaps better informed than peasants but more confused by the complexities of their problems. While their numbers increased with the size of cities, they became alienated from the upper classes by periodic unemployment and inflation. Rioting among workers and the idle poor of the cities was thus quite common, notably in London and Paris. Such outbreaks, however, were more violent than politically significant. Workers did recognize two potential enemies: the capitalist, who contracted for labor and influenced government to eliminate welfare, and the guild, which exploited the journeyman in favor of the master. To combat these enemies, workers occasionally organized in England and France. The organizations were weak, however, and their efforts usually failed for want of leadership.

Middle-class discontent, like that of some peasants, arose more from thwarted expectations than from terrible suffering. Upward mobility, from middle class to aristocracy, was a by-product of economic prosperity all over Europe, particularly in England and France. The movement took many forms—purchase of land and titles, marriage, even reward for personal services of lawyers, doctors, tutors, or governesses. This middle-class struggle for respectability was individually competitive, so long as opportunities were open. But in time, room at the top became limited, as old regimes stabilized and more of the middle class sought to climb the social ladder. At this point ambitious middle-class outsiders became dangerously hostile to the system.

Most dissenting action came from men, but women were also represented among the malcontents. They were regularly involved in local uprisings against the high cost of bread, the introduction of machines to depress labor, and rising taxes. In 1770 a mob of Parisian women left their workplaces to protest the deportation of their vagrant children to the colonies. Such actions were not yet aimed directly against old regimes, but later (as we shall see in Chapter 22) other French and English women would go further to champion women's rights, along with the "rights of man."

More dangerous to monarchical establishments than outside opposition was aristocratic opposition from within. Gains by the nobles in Sweden, Spain, Austria, and even France increased their confidence and whetted their appetites for more power. As old regimes wavered, nobles at the top were frantically determined to maintain their positions; indeed, they professed to believe that they were more legitimate rulers than the kings. This was partly an effort to combat middle-class influence, for nobles were often heavily in debt and feared legal reforms that might require them to pay. At the same time, most lesser nobles resented the court cliques; a few even dreamed of helping the middle classes change the system. Noble opinions were indeed varied, promising weakening support for royal authority but refusing cooperation with kings in curtailing privileges. On this last point nearly all nobles were in total agreement.

The Political Failures of the Old Regimes: An Evaluation

Floating atop the dynamic changes of Europe, the old regimes, especially on the Continent, continued in the first half of the eighteenth century to act in a "business as usual" manner. This led regimes not to adapt to changing conditions, and the result was increasing political weakness and misuse of power. The aristocratic social structure acquired by midcentury the sanctity of tradition, the confidence of long experience, and the insensitivities of old age. Although no longer as typically cruel or exploitative as in the past, its governing classes had become extremely selfish and unresponsive to the larger needs of the countries that supported them in such a rich manner and incapable of understanding the potential opportunities presented by the changes of the century.

French Decline

The absolutists and their supporters—perhaps 2 percent of the population—made an inadequate re-

Old Regime Monarchs		
France	1715–1774	Louis XV
	1774–1792	Louis XVI
Habsburgs	1711–1740	Charles VI
	1740–1780	Maria Theresa
	1780–1790	Joseph II
Prussia	1713–1740	Frederick William I
	1740–1786	Frederick the Great
	1786–1797	Frederick William II
Russia	1730–1740	Anna
	1741–1762	Elizabeth
	1762	Peter III
	1762–1796	Catherine II
Great Britain	1714–1727	George I
	1727–1760	George II
	1760–1820	George III

sponse to the social and economic pressures of the time. After his death in 1715, Louis XIV was succeeded by his 5-year-old great-grandson. Known as "the Well-Beloved," the new king reigned as Louis XV until 1774 but never ruled as a Sun King, partly because of his personal weaknesses but largely because the inflexible institutions of absolutism could not contain or direct the dynamic changes of the eighteenth-century world. In middle age, with most of his royal prerogatives still intact, Louis was openly pessimistic about the future of his dynasty. He might easily have delivered the famous prophecy, stated by his mistress Madame de Pompadour (1721–1764), but usually attributed to him: *"Après moi, le déluge"* ("After me, the flood").

Such royal cynicism reflected the old regime's knowledge that it could do little to control the revolutionary developments of the time. Two centuries of war and foreign expansion had changed the basic way of life for most people and generated high expectations, particularly among the expanding urban middle classes—around 8 percent of the population—who benefited most by the worldwide explosion of foreign trade. Encouraged by the philosophies of the Enlightenment (see Chapter 21), they became more aggressive in improving their position, gaining social recognition, and demanding personal happiness outside the limits imposed by typical monarchical states and their privileged social orders.

Facing such challenges, those states could not respond effectively. They had earlier promised pragmatic compromise, whereby centralized government would maintain the interests of wealthy merchant-bankers and landed aristocrats. By the mid-eighteenth century the system could no longer satisfy its supporters, nor could it absorb any more of the lesser nobles or the excluded middle class as each group grew more numerous. Indeed, with their expensive wars, ballooning debts, outmoded laws, passive bureaucrats, and corrupt officials, the absolute monarchies generally displayed striking political weaknesses and obvious misuses of the powers they managed to wield.

Malfunctioning Governments

Before the eighteenth century, developing absolute monarchies promised to end feudal conventions, correct the abuses of organized religion, and provide national economic security. As the century wore on, most of them not only failed to produce such results but also revealed striking examples of their extravagance, corruption, and inefficiency.

The most obvious weaknesses involved the abuse of state powers or the inability to use them for the public good. Early absolute monarchs had promised to correct abuses in state churches. Such establishments now held great wealth but continued to persecute thousands of dissenting subjects for their religious beliefs. Some kings had vowed to bring their states economic prosperity and security. Under mercantilism their state enterprises and monopolies favored wealthy patrons and throttled trade. Even state military systems were controlled by aristocratic officers, many of whom bought their commissions and commanded local private armies. Even royal provincial agents and judges often existed beside and shared authority with thousands of lingering manorial courts and local officials, operating under the authority of local feudal lords.

Political inefficiency took many other forms. Laws were a perplexing mix of variable local customs, feudal presumptions, and royal decrees. Provincial tolls were imposed on trade within states; on the Rhine River alone there were 38 toll stations between Basel and Rotterdam. Coinage, as well as weights and measures, sometimes differed in adjoining provinces. Overlapping authorities confused courts and officials about their jurisdictions. Public servants avoided responsibilities, fearing they would be blamed for error, a situation that produced bureaucratic delay and elaborate red tape. Every form of bribery, fraud, and distortion characterized governments at every level. Such evils were difficult to combat because legalized privilege was so common.

The general situation is well illustrated by conditions in France. Despite all efforts at centralization, Louis XIV left a chaotic jumble of councils and committees, each with its own expanding network of officials and clerks, whose conflicting claims to authority were barely less perplexing than their fussy procedures. During the next reign the selling of offices became a main source of revenue and patronage. There was no body comparable to the English Parliament for registering public opinion; the French Estates-General was last called in 1614. Government was most deficient in handling revenues, which it attempted to do without budgets, precise accounting, or standard assessments. French local government was even more chaotic. Late medieval districts, with their bailiffs and seneschals, coexisted with ornamental provincial governors and royal intendants who struggled to placate other officials and influence local government after the seventeenth century. Some 360 different legal codes and 200 customs schedules applied in different parts of the country. Attempts to achieve uniformity invariably provoked strong reactions from local interests.

The French government, like some others, was severely damaged by the laziness of King Louis XV, who hated the tedium of governing and was more interested in beautiful women. Well into the 1740s, he left most power in the hands of an able minister, Cardinal Fleury, who had maintained peace and reasonable stability since Louis was a boy. Even in his early reign, however, "mistress power" enlisted the king's fancy; later it influenced his policies. Louis's Polish queen endured a series of rivals who were installed in the palace near the king's bedchamber, granted titles, showered with costly gifts, and paraded by Louis in public. The best known of them was Jeanne-Antoinette Poisson, of nonnoble parentage, who became Madame de Pompadour. She received 17 estates, had a personal staff of 50 attendants, enjoyed nearly unlimited access to the royal treasury, and advised Louis on public policy, particularly during the Seven Years' War. A later famous royal mistress, Madame Du Barry (1743–1793), was another woman of nonnoble origin who played the palace game better than the noble ladies at court, whom she overcame in a series of backbiting struggles for Louis's favor. Until he died in 1774, she reveled in her power, jewels, and luxurious houses. Such behavior earned France a reputation for "petticoat governance."

Other European kings squandered fortunes on mistresses, palaces, courts, and idle aristocrats, thus contributing to their common problem of rising public debt. Their financial difficulties also arose from their military expenses in attempting to protect colonial possessions and play the game of dynastic power politics in Europe. In the late 1700s each of the great continental powers (France, Russia, and Austria) kept standing armies of 250,000 men. Rulers might have borne such heavy expenses if they could have governed by brute force, as former emperors had done, but they were prevented from doing so by their dependence on an international market, which supplied their vital material needs only in exchange for goods, bullion, or credit. Ultimately, they were forced to borrow, putting their states at the mercy of bankers and their own credit ratings. Such financial accountability, almost unknown in the ancient world, placed a serious restriction on monarchical policies in this era.

For France, where the economy was less expansive and commanded less foreign credit, the problem was more serious. Badly weakened by Louis XIV's wars, France averted financial disaster in the 1720s and 1730s only because of Fleury's peaceful foreign policy and reduced military spending. After 1742, however, deficits mounted steadily while France fought three major wars. In 1780 the French debt was so large that interest payments absorbed over half the annual income of approximately $33.8 million. Admittedly, the French debt was not excessive in comparison with Britain's. What the French lacked, however, was the Dutch capital that poured into England. Without adequate foreign credit, France was thrown back on its own resources, which caused a tripling of taxes between 1715 and 1785. The ensuing tax burden, plus the growing anxiety of wealthy government creditors, created the most serious threat to the old regime in France.

Difficulties in Enforcing the State-Controlled Economies

Eighteenth-century monarchs faced many problems in competing with traditional local authorities, but they encountered even more pressing difficulties in enforcing mercantilist regulations. In the sixteenth century merchant-bankers had accepted the system because they shared common interests with kings in combating the Catholic Church and the feudal nobilities. As time passed, however, monarchical states became increasingly more paternalistic and ordered, while capitalism developed spontaneously toward more freedom from state control.

The development, as well as the success, of mercantilism varied widely from East to West. In Prussia and Russia reforms were imposed through state control and worked well, compared with previous attempts; state-imported craftsmen and tools from western Europe continued to improve the economies of both monarchies. Habsburg efforts met with less success because the empire was unable to impose regulations effectively on the aristocracy. Meanwhile, most continental states in western Europe could not easily keep their controlled manufactures competitive in the world market.

In France government regulations favored luxury goods over bulk commodities, which limited French participation in world trade. Reliance on urban guilds created another limitation. These medieval monopolies were given the responsibility for enforcing thousands of minute regulations in every aspect of industry. Government inspectors then sought to monitor the regulatory actions of the guilds. The system, which suffered from vested interests, local politics, corruption, and bureaucratic confusion, provoked periodic confrontations, particularly when it was extended into the countryside. In 1770 the guilds and the French government attempted to stop the domestic production of printed calicoes. More than 16,000 people died in the resulting violent conflicts and subsequent executions. On one day in Valence, 631 offenders were sentenced to the galleys, 58 were put to torture on the wheel, and 77 were hanged. Yet despite all such efforts, printed calicoes continued to be made and sold illegally.

Despite its great promise, European society presented many problems generated by the rising middle classes, crowded cities, dispossessed peasants, rising populations, contrasting cultures, and an expanding world economy. Moreover, that same dynamic society, still more than 70 percent rural, was also still limited by popular ignorance along with its attendant cruelties. All of this complicated the process of governing for old regimes, with their many vested interests and their long-conditioned rigidities.

Breaking the Bank: Diplomacy and War in the Age of Absolutism

Because of dynastic and colonial rivalries, Europeans were constantly involved in conflicts during the age of absolutism. Fighting took place overseas in America, Africa, and Asia—not only against non-Europeans but also in global wars among European colonial powers. At the same time, wars raged on the Continent as dynastic states competed for predominance. While Spain, Sweden, and Poland were declining, Prussia, Russia, and Austria were becoming first-class powers. Along with England's dominance overseas, the last three exerted major influences on the European balance of power.

From Westphalia to Utrecht: The Dominance of France

France was the strongest and most threatening military power in Europe from the Peace of Westphalia (1648) to the Treaty of Utrecht (1713). Louis XIV first dreamed of expanding French frontiers to the Rhine; later he coveted the Spanish crown. Colbert also helped him plan the conquest of a large overseas empire in America, Africa, and Asia. The diplomacy of other European states in the era centered largely on their common efforts to unite against French expansion.

Russian policy was one important exception to this general trend. In early wars with the Turks, Peter the Great took Azov, on the Black Sea. His main target in the later Great Northern War (1709–1721) was Sweden, but his preparatory diplomacy failed when his allies, Denmark and Poland, were quickly defeated by the Swedish warrior-king Charles XII (1697–1712). The Swedes next invaded Russia. They were met with a "scorched earth" withdrawal before being annihilated at Poltava (1709). The war ended in 1721 with Sweden exhausted and Peter gaining a section of the Baltic coast, where he had already begun building his new capital at St. Petersburg.

The three Anglo-Dutch naval wars between 1652 and 1674 showed the balance-of-power principle in one of its more intricate applications. Conflicting commercial and colonial interests of the two maritime states were the immediate issues. At the same time, both belligerents were increasingly aware of danger from a powerful and aggressive France. The Dutch were most directly affected because French expansion toward the northern Rhine threatened the survival of the Netherlands as a nation. To deal with this problem, the Dutch tacitly accepted English maritime supremacy while preparing for an Anglo-Dutch alignment against Louis XIV. Ultimately, the French menace was more decisive than naval action in ending Anglo-Dutch hostilities.

After 1670 Louis was the prime mover in European diplomacy. He fought four major wars, each with overseas campaigns. In the first, Louis claimed the Spanish Netherlands (Belgium). Thwarted by the Dutch and their allies, he next bought off Charles II of England and attacked the Dutch directly. Frustrated again by a combination of enemies, he tried in the 1690s to annex certain Rhineland districts. This time almost all of Europe allied against him and forced him to back down. The climax to these repeated French efforts came between 1701 and 1713, in the War of the Spanish Succession, when Louis sought to secure the Spanish throne for his grandson Philip. Although he finally succeeded in this project, the victory was a hollow one, bought at tremendous cost in lives and resources.

In this most destructive of Louis's wars, women played a major part behind the scenes. In England during the early years, Sarah Churchill, wife of the English supreme commander, the duke of Marlborough, consistently pressured Queen Anne (1702–1714) and members of Parliament for vigorous prosecution of the war. On the other side, at the Spanish court and elsewhere on the continent, Mary of Modena, in exile with her husband, the deposed James II of England, exerted all of her influence to bolster support for France. Other women were most instrumental in bringing peace. Among them were Madame de Maintenon and Princess des Ursins, who helped persuade Louis to drop the idea of uniting the French and Spanish Bourbon monarchies. In England after about 1709, Anne, a patient and plodding monarch but one with at least some common sense, freed herself from Sarah Churchill's influence and guided her ministers toward the Peace of Utrecht.

Louis could not overcome all of the power balanced against him. As France became stronger, it invariably provoked more formidable counteralliances. At first Louis faced Spain, the Netherlands, Sweden, and some German states. In the last two wars England led an alliance that included almost all of western Europe. In this anti-French alignment, Anglo-Dutch commercial rivalry and other traditional prejudices, such as Anglo-Dutch hatred of Spain, were subordinated to the balance-of-power principle.

The Treaty of Utrecht (1713) ushered in a period of general peace, lasting some 30 years. Philip V, Louis's grandson, was confirmed as king of Spain, with the provision that the thrones of France and Spain would never be united. Since Spain had been declining for a century and France was drained financially, the Bourbon succession promised little for French ambitions in Europe. This was particularly true because Spain surrendered the southern Netherlands (Belgium) and its Italian holdings (Naples, Milan, and Sardinia) to the Austrian Habsburgs. In addition, Savoy was ceded to Sicily, which was subsequently traded (in 1720) to Austria for Sardinia. The duke of Savoy was also recognized as king, as was Frederick I of Prussia. The House of Savoy would unify Italy in the nineteenth century, and the Hohenzollerns would accomplish the same for Germany.

By the Treaty of Utrecht almost all the participants except Britain lost more in the wars than they gained. The Dutch had borne the cost of most land fighting against the French; France had been demoralized by a three-front war and a Huguenot uprising, for which it received no tangible compensation except the retention of Alsace; and Spain lost heavily to the Austrian Habsburgs. Britain, by contrast, received the North American properties of Newfoundland and Nova Scotia from France, plus French acceptance of British claims to the Hudson Bay area. Britain also retained the Mediterranean naval bases at Gibraltar and Minorca it took from Spain. Even more important commercially were the concessions permitting Britain to supply Spanish America with slaves and to land one shipload of goods each year at

The Treaty of Utrecht confirmed the expansion of French power in Europe after the half century of wars of Louis XIV, the increased strength of Brandenburg Prussia, and the decline of the Habsburg Empire.

Porto Bello in Panama. These stipulations helped Britain become the leading colonial power.

From Utrecht to Paris: An Unstable Balance

The balance of European power wavered dangerously in the eighteenth century. Prussia and Russia—and even Habsburg Austria—attained great military potential, and each was tempted by power vacuums in Poland and the Ottoman Empire. The situation was complicated by the difficulty in determining which of the Eastern states was the most serious threat and therefore the logical object of counteralliances. To confuse matters further, both Britain and France were absorbed in their growing colonial rivalry, in which Britain was the obvious frontrunner. Major conflicts were on the way.

By 1730 it was apparent that France and Britain would soon clash over their conflicting colonial am-

bitions. Both empires were rapidly increasing their wealth and populations. In the Caribbean, French sugar production had surpassed that of the British, while French slavers were not only supplying their own islands but also challenging British trading privileges in Spanish America, as defined at Utrecht. On the other side of the world, the British and French were also scrambling to obtain influence among the petty rulers of southern India. The two powers, each with Native American allies, were also fighting sporadic little wars in North America. In the preliminary diplomatic testing, French size and military force in Europe were balanced against British financial resources, naval power, and a larger American colonial population.

Conflict began in 1739 over British trade in Spanish America. An English captain testified before Parliament that Spanish authorities had boarded his vessel and cut off his ear, which he displayed wrapped in cotton. The "War of Jenkins's Ear" soon spread, with France immediately offering support to

Spain. Frederick of Prussia, meanwhile, seized Silesia, part of the family holdings of the Habsburg heiress Maria Theresa, who had just succeeded to the Austrian throne. France and Spain now threw in with Frederick, along with the German states of Saxony and Bavaria. Fearful of France, Britain and the Netherlands, now allied with Hanover, joined Austria in 1742. By 1745 Prussia had almost knocked Austria out of the war, but fighting dragged on overseas in North America and India until 1748. The resulting Peace of Aix-la-Chapelle left Frederick with Silesia and the colonial positions of Britain and France about the same as they had been in 1739.

The agreements at Aix-la-Chapelle brought no peace but only a short truce of eight years. During the cessation of hostilities France and Britain prepared to renew their global conflict. At the same time, Maria Theresa, having learned some lessons in international politics and having effected some necessary internal reforms, joined with Tsarina Elizabeth of Russia to negotiate an alliance against Frederick. The Austro-Russian alliance also included Sweden and some German states. Maria Theresa's greatest coup, however, was recruiting France, the old Habsburg enemy, possibly with help from Madame de Pompadour, Louis XV's mistress, who despised Frederick. Prussia was now effectively isolated, but so was Britain, which was more concerned about colonial issues than aggression on the Continent. Britain therefore formed a new alliance with Prussia against France, Russia, and Austria. This swapping of alliances, the famous diplomatic revolu-

tion of the 1750s, was another notable attempt at balance-of-power politics in both the European and world theaters.

Beginning in 1756 war raged relentlessly on three continents—Europe, North America, and Asia (India). Known in American history as the French and Indian War, the conflict in Europe is called the Seven Years' War. Attacked on all sides by three major powers, Frederick marched and wheeled his limited forces, winning battles but seeing little prospect for ultimate victory. He tried without success to buy Madame de Pompadour's influence for peace. Later he described the nearly hopeless predicament, comparing himself to a man assaulted by flies: "When one flies off my cheek, another comes and sits on my nose, and scarcely has it been brushed off then another flies up and sits on my forehead, on my eyes, and everywhere else."[4]

Frederick was saved and the war won by the narrowest of margins when a new pro-Prussian tsar, Peter III, recalled the Russian armies from the gates of Berlin and withdrew from the war. Austria then sued for peace, leaving Frederick with Silesia.

The end of the Seven Years' War in 1763 confirmed the status of Prussia and Russia as great powers and prepared for a new diplomatic order in eastern Europe. Despite its great losses, Prussia gained enormously in prestige; its internal damage would not be revealed until the nineteenth century. Russia regained the military reputation it had achieved under Peter I without winning any striking victories. Austria lost prestige and military strength but man-

To check and maintain the discipline and efficiency of his officers and army, Frederick the Great of Prussia frequently reviewed his troops. Frederick was also a prolific writer, whose complete works were published in 30 volumes. Among his published writings are works addressed to his generals, instructing them on the science of warfare. This painting depicts Frederick, accompanied by his generals, returning to his favorite residence, the rococo Sans Souci Palace at Potsdam, after army field maneuvers.

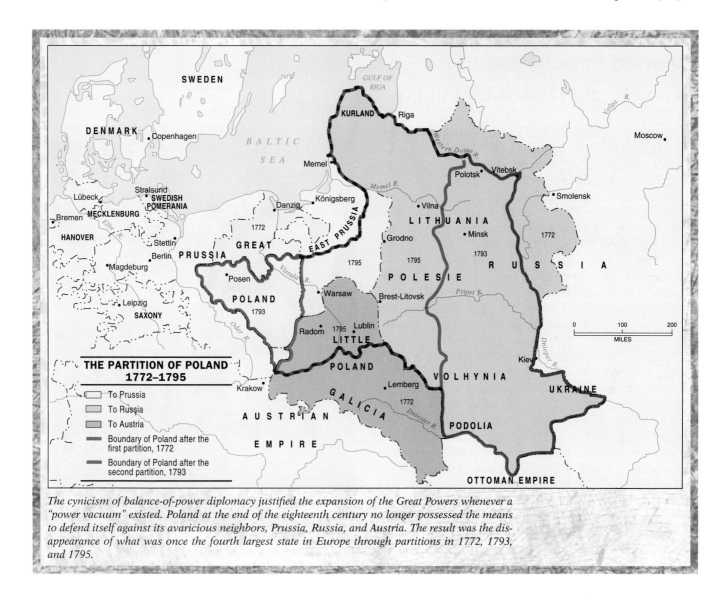

THE PARTITION OF POLAND 1772–1795

☐ To Prussia
☐ To Russia
■ To Austria
— Boundary of Poland after the first partition, 1772
— Boundary of Poland after the second partition, 1793

The cynicism of balance-of-power diplomacy justified the expansion of the Great Powers whenever a "power vacuum" existed. Poland at the end of the eighteenth century no longer possessed the means to defend itself against its avaricious neighbors, Prussia, Russia, and Austria. The result was the disappearance of what was once the fourth largest state in Europe through partitions in 1772, 1793, and 1795.

aged to retain its respectability. The Ottoman Empire and Poland were the real losers in the postwar decades. In 1772 Poland lost half its territory to the Russians, Prussians, and Austrians in a three-way partition, despite Maria Theresa's protestations of remorse. In the 1793 and 1795 Poland was eliminated entirely in two final partitions. The Ottoman Empire, meanwhile, lost the Crimea and most of the Ukraine to the aggressive expansionist policies of Catherine the Great of Russia.

Much more significant than the war's effects on eastern Europe was its impact on Anglo-French colonial rivalry. Britain gained even more than it had at Utrecht, while French colonial hopes were all but destroyed. By the Peace of Paris (1763), France lost to Britain the St. Lawrence valley and the trans-Appalachian area east of the Mississippi. Spain also ceded Florida to Britain, receiving Louisiana west of the Mississippi from France as compensation. In the West Indies, France gave up Granada, Dominica, and St. Lucia. The French kept their main trading sta-

tions in India but were not permitted to fortify them or continue their political ties with local rulers. Yet the British East India Company not only extended its political influence but also acquired Bengal. The Peace of Paris made Britain's the largest, wealthiest, and most powerful empire in the world.

Absolutism in the Arts

This yearning for stability and order was clearly demonstrated in the arts. Earlier, during Europe's era of transitional turbulence, the baroque style had symbolized flamboyant power and restless frustration. Although the forms of baroque art and architecture remained popular, they were overshadowed in this era by a return to traditional classicism. Retaining the baroque deference to power, the revived classical mode emphasized order in its discipline, formality, and balance.

Discovery Through Maps

The Elegant Destruction of Poland

After the century and a half of continentwide upheaval caused by the Reformation, Counter-Reformation, wars of religion, and Thirty Years' War, Europeans sought to impose stability through international law and absolutism. Concepts like "balance of power," *"raison d'état,"* and reason replaced the passions of the religious wars of the sixteenth and the first half of the seventeenth centuries.

This did not mean that peace came to Europe—far from it. War came to be more organized, professional, and limited as state competition took on not only a military but also an economic dimension. In the new arena of 1648 politics, state relations were conducted with almost mathematical precision. States took stock of their strength in terms of population, economic strength, and military power. They ranked themselves and their neighbors and then attacked when it seemed possible, in search of national interest, not religious truth. The wars of Louis XIV sought to gain France its "natural boundaries" of the Pyrenees and the Rhine. The Prussians sought to unify their diverse holdings in north-central Europe. Peter the Great led Russia into war against its neighbors in search of a "Window on the West."

In the last third of the eighteenth century Poland paid the price for its inability to adapt to the modern world. Since the fourteenth century the Polish nobility had tenaciously fought the attempts by their kings to assemble a strong army, preferring often to lose the first battle against invaders while waiting for the nobles to come to the country's defense. Poland after the seventeenth century fell under the influence of the Russians and the Prussians, and not until the 1770s did the Poles try to reform their institutions. It was too late. National interests led Prussia, Russia, and Austria to partition the country in 1772. After the French Revolution broke out, the Russians and Prussians partitioned the country again in 1793 and then, after a doomed national resistance, removed Poland as a state from the map of Europe. The Polish nation

remained divided among the three partitioning powers until 1918.

This engraving by Le Mire is a rather caustic commentary on what was, after all, the murder of a nation state. Here we have Frederick the Great of Prussia, Catherine the Great of Russia, and Maria Theresa of Austria regally carving up Poland while the Polish king, Stanislaus Poniatowski, grabs his crown to keep from losing that too. Le Mire captures the "civilized" nature of post-1648 state relations, in which *raison d'état* imposed no moral or ethical limits.

Classical Literature

Classicism owed much to the aristocratic world, where it flourished. It reflected the growing scientific faith in an ordered universe, and it expressed the political values of strong monarchs, such as Louis XIV, who sponsored many artistic endeavors. Indeed, the French court led Europe's classical revival. Classical literature was perhaps best exemplified in the polished and elegant French dramas of Pierre Corneille (1606–1684), Jean Racine (1639–1699), and Jean-Baptiste Molière (1622–1673). The first two were the great tragedians of the seventeenth century. They followed Aristotle's traditional rules of dramatic unity but produced works noted for psychological insights and beauty of language. Usually borrowing their plots from Greek and

Roman antiquity, they often depicted protagonists as idealized portraits of contemporary courtiers. Molière, an author of witty comedies, contrasted the artificiality of his society with the dictates of moderation and good sense. All three writers were sometimes mildly critical of established institutions, although their criticism was not direct enough to offend patrons.

Classical Architecture and Painting

A similar deference for patronage and authority was revealed in classical architecture and painting. In these areas France also led the way. A state-sponsored culture, begun earlier by Richelieu under Louis XIII in the French Academy, was continued by Louis XIV in academies of architecture, painting, dance, and music. Louis XIV's palace at Versailles, with its horizontal lines, 90-degree angles, and formal gardens, was copied all over Europe. So was the work of French court painters, such as Charles Le Brun (1619–1690), who glorified the Grand Monarch and his society in colorful portraits and panoramic scenes, emphasizing the common values of elegance and order.

Neoclassical Developments in Art and Architecture

The quantity and diversity of artistic works during the period do not fit easily into categories for interpretation, but some loose generalizations may be drawn. Baroque forms were as popular at the start of the eighteenth century as they would be at the end. They were partially supplanted, however, by a general lightening in the rococo motifs of the early 1700s. This was followed after the middle of the century by the formalism and balance of neoclassicism, with its resurrection of Greek and Roman models. Although the end of the century saw a slight Romantic turn, the era's characteristic accent on reason found its best expression in neoclassicism.

In painting, rococo brought a revolt against the "tortured writhing" of the baroque and movements of delightful sensuousness, "like a girl evading her lover."[5] It was full of airy grace and refined pleasures, of delicate jewelry and porcelains, of wooded scenes, artful dances, and women, particularly women in the nude. Rococo painters also specialized in portraiture, showing aristocratic subjects in their idealized finery. The painting of Antoine Watteau (1684–1721) blended fantasy with acute observations of nature, conveying the ease and luxury of French court life. Watteau's successors in France included François Boucher (1703–1770) and Jean Fragonard (1732–1806). Italian painters such as Giovanni Tiepolo (1696–1770) also displayed rococo influences. English painting lacked the characteristic rococo frivolity, but the style affected works by Sir Joshua Reynolds (1723–1792) and Thomas Gainsborough (1727–1788), whose portraits tended to flatter their aristocratic subjects.

In sharp contrast to the robust exuberance and emotionalism of the baroque style was the dainty and delicate decoration of the rococo, the characteristic style of the eighteenth century. The rococo at its best is seen in the works of Antoine Watteau, who often painted scenes of aristocratic society in parklike settings. With the graceful gallantry and gay frivolity of its figures, Les Plaisirs du Bal *(1719) is a typical example of the rococo.*

Eighteenth-century neoclassicism in painting is difficult to separate from some works in the era of Louis XIV. Both Nicolas Poussin (1594–1665) and his student Charles Le Brun had earlier projected order and balance, often in grandiose scenes from antiquity or mythology. Jean Chardin (1699–1779) carried some of this over into the 1700s. The neoclassical approach, however, often expressed a muted respect for reason and order, as well as powerful dissatisfaction with and criticism of established regimes, sometimes in stark realism and sometimes in colossal allegory. Its most typical representative was Jacques-Louis David (1748–1825), whose well-known work, *The Death of Socrates*, illustrates his respect for Greco-Roman tradition. David's revolutionary sympathies are clearly represented in a hostile drawing of Marie Antoinette en route to the guillotine. The best examples of pure realism and social criticism are the London street scenes by the English painter William Hogarth (1697–1764) and the Spanish court portraits of Francisco Goya (1746–1828).

The number of female painters increased during the eighteenth century, but they remained bound by tradition and dependent on public favor. Very few were admitted to academies, where their work might be shown; as a result, they were virtually restricted to still life and portraiture. Among rococo painters, the two best known were Rachel Ruysch (1664–1750), a court painter of flowers in Düsseldorf, and Rosalba Carriera (1675–1757), a follower of Watteau who was admitted to the French Academy in 1720. Three famous female painters who produced grand neoclassical works were limited by their market to flattering portraits. Elisabeth Vigée-Lebrun (1755–1842) and Adelaide Labille-Guiarde (1749–1803) were members of the Academy. But perhaps the most acclaimed of the three was Angelica Kaufmann (1741–1807), a Swiss-born artist who painted in England and Italy.

Neoclassicism also found expression in architecture and sculpture. In architecture it was marked by a return to the intrinsic dignity, simplicity, and elevating tranquillity of ancient Greco-Roman forms. The Madeleine in Paris is a faithful copy of a still-standing Roman temple, and the Brandenburg Gate in Berlin was modeled after the monumental entrance to the Acropolis in Athens. In England, where the classical style had resisted baroque influences, the great country houses of the nobility now exhibited a purity of design, which often included a portico with Corinthian columns. George Washington's home at Mount Vernon is an outstanding example of neoclassicism in colonial America. The trend in sculpture often revived classical themes from Greek and Roman mythology; statues of Venus became increasingly popular. Claude Michel (1738–1814) and Jean-Antoine Houdon (1741–1828) were two French neoclassical sculptors who also achieved notable suc-

Elisabeth Vigée-Lebrun, Madame de Staël as Corinne. *Vigée-Lebrun's flattering portrait style won her the patronage of Marie Antoinette, of whom she painted more than 20 portraits. Vigée-Lebrun fled France at the outbreak of the Revolution and during the Revolutionary years painted portraits of royalty elsewhere in Europe. This portrait is of the French writer Madame de Staël.*

cess with contemporary depictions. Houdon's bust of Voltaire is a well-known example.

Classical Music

At the start of the eighteenth century, music demonstrated typical baroque characteristics. These were evident in instrumental music, especially for the organ and strings. The most typical baroque medium was opera, opulent and highly emotional. The era culminated in the sumptuous religious music of Johann Sebastian Bach (1685–1750), the prolific German organ master and choir director. Bach's equally great contemporary, the German-born naturalized Englishman George Frideric Handel (1685–1759), is known for his grand and dramatic operas, oratorios, and cantatas; he is best known today for his religious oratorio, *The Messiah* (1742).

Composers of the late eighteenth century turned from the heavy baroque style to lighter music of greater simplicity and clarity. A first stage, suggestive of the rococo in art, saw increasing popularity of sonatas, concerti, and chamber music. This trend, along with the muted neoclassicism of increasingly popular formal symphonies, partly eclipsed the appeal of religious music and old baroque-style opera. Plain, often folklike melodies also became common. The new emphases were summarized in the work of the Austrian composers Franz Joseph Haydn (1732–1809) and Wolfgang Amadeus Mozart (1756–1791). Haydn wrote more than 100 symphonies, plus numerous other compositions. Mozart produced more than 600 works, including 41 symphonies, 22 operas, and 23 string quartets. His three most famous operas *(The Marriage of Figaro, Don Giovanni,* and *The Magic Flute)* illustrate the period's musical transition, revealing Mozart's innate conservatism mingled with his depth of human feeling and sympathy for common folk. The transition reached completion in the genius of the German composer Ludwig van Beethoven (1770–1827). The passionate emotion of his sonatas and symphonies expressed a Revolutionary Romanticism that challenged the lingering sedate classicism of his time.

Literature: Classical Poetry and the Arrival of the Novel

The Enlightenment's philosophical orientation toward reason and natural law, generally obscured or ignored in the arts, was more apparent in eighteenth-century literature. To be sure, writers were often concerned with mundane subjects, particularly those related to everyday life and human feelings. But the verbal media of poetry, drama, prose, and exposition, being closely involved in the logic of word selection and grammar, were naturally more receptive than the arts to the much heralded rationalism of the age.

A strong poetic voice in England's Age of Reason was Alexander Pope (1688–1744). In his most famous work, *An Essay on Man* (1733), Pope expressed the optimism and respect for science that marked the era. He described a Newtonian universe in the following often-quoted lines:

All are but parts of one stupendous whole,
Whose body nature is, and God the soul....
All nature is but art, unknown to thee;
All chance, direction, which thou cannot see.
All discord, harmony not understood;
All partial evil, universal good
And, spite of pride, in erring reason's spite,
One truth is clear: Whatever is, is right.[6]

Two other poets deserve mention here. One was the English Countess of Winchelsea (1661–1720), who extolled reason and feminine equality in her verse. The other was the African-born Massachusetts slave Phillis Wheatley (c. 1753–1784), whose rhyming couplets pleaded the cause of natural freedom for the American colonies and for her race.

Reflecting the critical tone of his time, England's famous satirist Jonathan Swift (1667–1745) ridiculed

In Gulliver's Travels, *Jonathan Swift produced one of the outstanding works of satire in world literature. It is written in the form of a travel journal kept by the leading character, ship's physician Lemuel Gulliver. In each of the book's four sections, Gulliver visits a different society and records his observations of the particular group. On the first voyage Gulliver is shipwrecked at Lilliput, a land inhabited by people less than 6 inches tall. In the satire, the diminutive Lilliputians display the pettiness that Swift observes in much of human nature.*

the pettiness of human concerns in *Gulliver's Travels* (1726), wherein Captain Gulliver, in visiting the fictitious land of Lilliput, found two opposing factions: the Big-endians, who passionately advocated opening eggs at the big end, and the Little-endians, who vehemently proposed the opposite procedure.

The novel became a major literary vehicle in this period, catching on first in France and then in England. *Robinson Crusoe* (1719), by Daniel Defoe (1660–1731), described a resourceful man in a true state of nature; it is often called the first modern English novel. A common disdain for irrational customs and institutions was satirized in *Candide* (1759), by François-Marie Arouet, better known as Voltaire (1694–1778). These and other novels satisfied a prevailing demand for clarity and social criticism, but their focus on heroic struggle, sentimental love, and middle-class values foreshadowed Romanticism. Writing along these lines, Samuel Richardson (1689–1761) produced *Pamela* (1740), the story of a virtuous servant girl. Henry Fielding (1707–1754) wrote the equally famous *Tom Jones* (1749), the rollicking tale of a young man's deep pleasures and shallow regrets. Each novel, in its own way, defined natural human morality while appealing to readers' sensitivities.

The shift toward Romanticism climaxed in Germany toward the century's end, mainly in the works of Friedrich von Schiller (1759–1805) and Johann Wolfgang von Goethe (1749–1832). The latter's *Sorrows of Young Werther* (1774), treating a failed love and a tragic suicide, was a typical example.

Literary women found a uniquely promising outlet for their long-ignored talents in the Romantic novel, with its accent on personal feminine concerns and domestic problems. From the multitude of able French and English women novelists, only four may be cited here. Madame de Graffigny (1695–1758) authored the fabulous best-seller, *Lettres d'une Peruvienne* (1730), and Madame de Tencin (1682–1749) wrote *Le Siège de Calais*, a historical novel of love and danger. In England, Fanny Burney (1752–1840) was universally acclaimed after publication of her first novel, *Eveline* (1778), about "a young lady's entrance into the world." Perhaps the most noteworthy English female novelist was Aphra Behn (1640–1689), whose *Oroonoko* (1688) was a plea for the natural man, written long before the works of Defoe and Rousseau.

Spain, and Poland slipped into decline or extinction. France and Austria achieved stability without establishing mastery. Prussia and Russia became major military powers, and Britain began founding a world empire.

On the continent of Europe by the end of the eighteenth century, absolutism was the dominant political trend. But by that time the structural weaknesses of centralized government began to be seen. The incapacity of the kings to impose their theoretically absolute power effectively throughout their lands led to massive corruption. Mercantilism was too slow and rigid to adapt to the changing economic conditions. The aristocracy could not or would not serve as transmitters of royal power and across Europe began a drive to reclaim power they had lost to centralizing kings. The splendor and magnificence of the central courts depleted the countries' treasuries, and the kings' continuous wars drained resources and spread misery. The state religions came to be brittle, dry, and unfeeling to the needs of populations going through the pain of immense social and political change. By the middle of the eighteenth century the absolutist system had come to be known as the *ancien régime*—the old regime—and it did not work.

Conclusion

The period after the Peace of Westphalia brought a significant transition in European history. Following a century of destructive religious wars, Europeans expressed a new longing for stability and order. These desires helped popularize a political system known as absolutism, wherein monarchs greatly increased their internal powers while claiming authority limited only by nature and God. With its control of the economy and the church, its large military establishments, and its rigid class distinctions, absolutism met the psychological needs of the era and also supplied the force to effect some necessary changes. France under Louis XIV was the most representative example of the system. Yet virtually all European states of this period were affected somewhat by absolutism, in theory or in practice.

Absolutism also stamped its impression on international relations. Would-be absolute monarchs conducted war according to secular principles, feeling now more impelled to pursue dynastic or national interests without reference to higher morality or religion. Under these circumstances it seemed that peace and international order could best be achieved by a balance of powers, in which aggressive states would be checked by counteralliances formed against them. Nearly continuous wars in this process between 1650 and 1763 brought varying fortunes to European states. Sweden, the Ottoman Empire,

Suggestions for Reading

For a view of the development of French absolutism to the depths of the Old Regime, see Emmanuel Le Roy Ladurie, *The Ancien Régime: A History of France, 1610–1774*, trans. Mark Greengrass (Blackwell, 1998). General treatments of absolutism may be found in John Miller, *Absolutism in Seventeenth-Century Europe* (St. Martin's Press, 1990), and William Doyle, *The Old European Order* (Oxford University Press, 1978). Revisionist views of absolutism are revealed in Nicholas Henshall, *The Myth of Absolutism* (Longman, 1992), and James B. Collins, *The Fiscal Limits of Absolutism* (University of California Press, 1988). Robert P. Kraynak, *History and Modernity in the Thought of Thomas Hobbes* (Cornell University Press, 1990), is a penetrating study. The political side of absolutism is treated in John Miller, *Bourbon and Stuart: Kings and Kingship in France and England in the Seventeenth Century* (Duke University Press, 1988); and J. H. Shennan, *Liberty and Order in Early Modern Europe* (Longman, 1986).

For economic aspects of the era and the system, see Lars Magnussen, *Mercantilist Economics* (Kluwer, 1993), and Michael Beaud, *A History of Capitalism* (Monthly Review Press, 1983). For foreign trade aspects, see Glenn Joseph Ames, *Colbert, Mercantilism, and the French Quest for Asian Trade* (Northern Illinois University Press, 1996). Mary Fulbrook deals with religion and absolutism in *Piety and Politics: Religion and the Rise of Absolutism in England, Württemberg, and Prussia* (Cambridge University Press, 1984).

Excellent general overviews of the era in France are provided in David L. Rubin, *Sun-King: The Ascendancy of French Culture During the Reign of Louis XIV* (Association of University Libraries, 1992); Victor Mallia-Milanes, *Louis XIV and France* (Macmillan, 1986); and Paul Sonnino, ed., *The Reign of Louis XIV* (Humanities Press, 1990). Perceptions, real and manufactured, of the Sun King can be found in Peter Burke, *The Fabrication of Louis XIV* (Yale University Press, 1994).

Joseph Barry, *Passions and Politics: A Biography of Versailles* (Doubleday, 1972), is a highly personalized account of Louis XIV's glittering world at Versailles. See also Dianna De Marly, *Louis XIV and Versailles* (Holmes & Meier, 1987); Ragnhild Hatton, *Louis XIV and His World* (Putnam, 1972); and Guy Walton, *Louis XIV's Versailles* (University of Chicago Press, 1986). Paris in the seventeenth century is studied in Andrew P. Trout, *City on the Seine: Paris in the Time of Richelieu and Louis XIV* (St. Martin's Press, 1996). French political and social affairs are effectively depicted in Roger Mettam, *Power and Faction in Louis XIV's France* (Blackwell, 1987); William Beik, *Absolutism and Society in Seventeenth-Century France* (Cambridge University Press, 1989); and Jeffrey K. Sawyer, *Printed Poison* (University of California Press, 1992), which deals with pamphlet propaganda in early seventeenth-century France.

Three sound biographies of Louis XIV are John B. Wolf, *Louis XIV* (Hill & Wang, 1972); Olivier Bernier, *Louis XIV: A Royal Life* (Doubleday, 1987); and Louis Marin, *Portrait of the King* (University of Minnesota Press, 1988). Regarding French women of the court, the salons, the markets, and the streets, see Louis Auchincloss, *False Dawn: Women in the Age of the Sun King* (Doubleday, 1984); Carolyn C. Lougee, *Le Paradis de Femmes* (Princeton University Press, 1976); Elborg Forster, ed., *A Woman's Life in the Court of the Sun King* (Johns Hopkins University Press, 1984); and the memoir of Madame de Maintenon, *The King's Way* (Penguin, 1985). See also Charlotte Haldane, *Madame de Maintenon* (Bobbs Merrill, 1970). A study of fashion in the seventeenth- and eighteenth-century France is Daniel Roche, *The Culture of Clothing: Dress and Fashion in the Ancien Régime*, trans. Jean Birrell (Cambridge University Press, 1994).

On French-style absolutism in other countries, see Hajo Holburn, *A History of Modern Germany*, Vol. 1 (Knopf, 1964); Thomas K. Derry, *A History of Scandinavia* (University of Minnesota Press, 1979); Eric Elstob, *Sweden: A Political and Cultural History* (Rowman & Littlefield, 1979); Michael Roberts, *Sweden's Age of Greatness* (St. Martin's Press, 1973); Samuel S. Franklin, *Sweden: The Nation's History* (University of Minnesota Press, 1977); Stuart Oakley, *A Short History of Denmark* (Praeger, 1972); W. Glyn Jones, *Denmark: A Modern History* (Croom Helm, 1986); Henry A. F. Kamen, *Spain in the Later Seventeenth Century, 1665–1700* (Longman, 1980) and *Spain, 1469–1714: A Society in Conflict* (Longman, 1983); John Lynch, *Spain Under the Habsburgs*, Vol 1: *Spain and America, 1598–1700* (New York University Press, 1984); R. A. Stradling, *Philip IV and the Government of Spain, 1621–1665* (Cambridge University Press, 1988); John Lynch, *Bourbon Spain* (Blackwell, 1989); and Harold V. Livermore, *A New History of Portugal* (Cambridge University Press, 1976).

On the less developed absolutism in eastern Europe, see Robert James Weston Evans, *The Making of the Habsburg Monarchy, 1550–1700* (Oxford University Press, 1984); see also Norman Davies, *A History of Poland*, Vol. 1 (Columbia University Press, 1981) and *Heart of Europe: A Short History of Poland* (Oxford University Press, 1986), and Robert N. Bain, *Slavonic Europe* (Arno Press, 1971).

Two excellent short surveys of Prussian history in this period are H. W. Koch, *A History of Prussia* (Longman, 1978), and Otis Mitchell, *A Concise History of Brandenburg-Prussia to 1786* (University Press of America, 1980). For revealing special studies of the Prussian political structure, see Hans Rosenberg, *Bureaucracy, Aristocracy, and Authority: The Prussian Experiment, 1660–1815* (Beacon Press, 1966), and Hubert C. Johnson, *Frederick the Great and His Officials* (Yale University Press, 1975). Christopher Duffy offers a fine analysis of the Prussian army in *The Army of Frederick the Great* (Emperor's Headquarters,

1996). Robert R. Ergang, *The Potsdam Führer* (Octagon, 1972), is a colorful and stimulating portrait of Frederick William I, the founder of Prussian absolutism and militarism. Among the many biographies of Frederick the Great are two excellent ones: Robert B. Asprey, *Frederick the Great* (Ticknor & Fields, 1986); and Mary Kittridge, *Frederick the Great* (Chelsea House, 1987).

Development of the Romanov state is ably described in Otto Hoetzsch, *The Evolution of Russia* (Harcourt Brace, 1966), and W. Bruce Lincoln, *The Romanovs* (Dial, 1981). Sound historical studies of Peter the Great and his impact are Peter B. Putnam, *Peter, the Revolutionary Tsar* (Harper & Row, 1973); V. O. Kliuchevski, *Peter the Great* (Beacon Press, 1984); A. Tolstoy, *Peter the Great*, 2 vols. (Raduga, 1985); Robert K. Massie, *Peter the Great: His Life and World* (Ballantine, 1986); and Henri Troyat, *Peter the Great* (Dutton, 1987).

For interesting studies of the great eighteenth-century Russian empresses who followed Peter, see James F. Brennan, *Enlightened Despotism in Russia: The Reign of Elizabeth* (Lang, 1987), and Robert Coughlan, *Elizabeth and Catherine* (New American Library, 1975). Among excellent biographies of Catherine are Vincent Cronin, *Catherine, Empress of All the Russias* (Morrow, 1978); Leslie Max-Mcguire, *Catherine the Great* (Chelsea House, 1986); and John T. Alexander, *Catherine the Great* (Oxford University Press, 1989). Perspectives on Catherine's impact are provided in Isabel De Madarlaga, *Russia in the Age of Catherine the Great* (Yale University Press, 1981), and Gladys Scott Thomson, *Catherine the Great and the Expansion of Russia* (Greenwood, 1985).

Two useful works are Jeremy Black, *Eighteenth-Century Europe* (St. Martin's Press, 1990), and Matthew Smith Anderson, *Europe in the Eighteenth Century*, 3rd ed. (Longman, 1987). For more interpretive coverage, see Robert Zeller, *Europe in Transition, 1660–1815* (University Press of America, 1988), and for more detailed coverage, see Franco Venturi, *The End of the Old Regime in Europe, 1768–1789*, 3 vols. (Princeton University Press, 1989–1991). National surveys are provided in Louis R. Gottschalk, *Toward the French Revolution* (Scribner, 1973); Dorothy Marshall, *Eighteenth-Century England* (Longman, 1974); and Derek Jarrett, *England in the Age of Hogarth* (Yale University Press, 1986). *Britain in the Age of Walpole* (St. Martin's Press, 1985), edited by Jeremy Black, is a collection of interesting special studies.

William Doyle, *The Old European Order, 1660–1800* (Oxford University Press, 1978), is a superb study, covering all aspects of the Old Regime. See also Catherine B. Behrens, *The Ancien Régime* (Norton, 1989). For general topical treatments of the Old Regime, see Nicholas Henshall, *The Myth of Absolutism* (Longman 1992); J. J. Mangan, *The King's Favour: Three Eighteenth-Century Monarchs and the Favourites Who Ruled Them* (St. Martin's Press, 1991); Rudolf Evans, *The Resurrection of Aristocracy* (Loompanics, 1988); John P. Le Donne, *Absolutism and Ruling Class* (Oxford University Press, 1991); and Catherine B. Behrens, *Society, Government, and the Enlightenment* (Harper & Row, 1985). Intimate biographical insights into the French royal court are presented in Penelope Haslip-Stiebel, *Louis XV and Madame de Pompadour* (Rosenberg & Stiebel, 1990); Joan Haslip, *Madame de Barry: The Wages of Beauty* (Grove-Attic, 1992); and John Hardman, *Louis the Sixteenth* (Yale University Press, 1993). For special treatments of the English social scene, see William B. Willcox, *The Age of Aristocracy, 1688–1830*, 4th ed. (Heath, 1983); John V. Beckett, *The Aristocracy in England* (Blackwell, 1986); and T. H. White, *The Age of Scandal* (Oxford University Press, 1986).

For economic problems facing old regimes, see also Jan de Vries, *The Economy of Europe in an Age of Crisis, 1600–1750* (Cambridge University Press, 1976). Difficulties in regulating the import trade are ably treated in Frederick F. Nicholls, *Hon-*

est Thieves: The Violent Heyday of English Smuggling (Heinemann, 1973), and R. Guttridge, *Smugglers* (Dorset, 1987). The following works depict the adventurous business of piracy: Philip Grosse, *The History of Piracy* (Rio Grande, 1988); Frank Sherry, *Raiders and Rebels: The Golden Age of Piracy* (Morrow, 1987); John Esquemiling, *Buccaneers of America* (Dorset, 1988); and Robert R. Ritchie, *Captain Kidd and the War Against the Pirates* (Harvard University Press, 1989).

Numerous informative works treat the dynamic social trends of the period. On population growth and movement, see Tommy Bengtsson et al., *Pre-Industrial Population Change, the Mortality Decline, and Short-Term Population Movements* (Almquist & Wikrell, 1984). Colin McEvedy and Richard Jones, *Atlas of World Population History* (Penguin, 1978), is also a handy reference for monitoring population growth. On urban growth, see Paul M. Hohenberg, *The Making of Urban Europe, 1000–1950* (Harvard University Press, 1987). Changes in the European class structure are treated in George Rude, *Europe in the Eighteenth Century: Aristocracy and the Bourgeois Challenge* (Harvard University Press, 1985); Jerome Blum, *The End of the Old Order in Rural Europe* (Princeton University Press, 1978); and Colin Mooers, *The Making of Bourgeois Europe* (Verso, 1991). Some obvious social threats to European monarchies are described in M. S. Anderson, *War and Society in Europe of the Old Regime, 1618–1789* (St. Martin's Press, 1988); and Frederick Krantz, *History from Below: French and English Popular Protest, 1600–1800* (Blackwell, 1988). On negative conditions affecting European women, see Marilyn Boxer and Jean H. Quatgaert, *Connecting Spheres: Women in the Western World* (Oxford University Press, 1987).

On French government and classes, see James C. Riley, *The Seven Years' War and the Old Regime in France* (Princeton University Press, 1986); Guy Chaussinand-Nogaret, *The French Nobility in the Eighteenth Century* (Cambridge University Press, 1985); Isser Woloch, *The Peasantry in the Old Regime* (Krieger, 1977); and Elinor G. Barber, *The Bourgeoisie in Eighteenth-Century France* (Princeton University Press, 1975). Government oppression is clearly treated in Robert M. Schwartz, *Policing the Poor in Eighteenth-Century France* (University of North Carolina Press, 1988), and Warren C. Scoville, *The Persecution of the French Huguenots and French Economic Development* (University of California Press, 1960). See also Robin D. Gwynn, *Huguenot Heritage* (Routledge, 1985). On the role of eighteenth-century French women, see Joan Landes, *Women and the Public Sphere in the Age of the French Revolution* (Cornell University Press, 1988). An outstanding study of the crisis of food supply at the end of the Old Regime is Cynthia Bouton, *The Flour War: Gender, Class, and Community in Late Ancien Régime French Society* (Pennsylvania State University Press, 1993).

For good general analyses of international relations in this age of developing power politics, see John B. Wolf, *Toward a European Balance of Power, 1620–1715* (Rand McNally, 1970); Geoffrey Symcox, *War, Diplomacy, and Imperialism, 1618–1763* (Walker, 1974); Theodore K. Rabb, *The Struggle for Stability in Early Modern Europe* (Oxford University Press, 1975); and Derek McKay and H. M. Scott, *The Rise of the Great Powers and the European State System* (Longman, 1983). For more specialized studies, see Carl J. Ekberg, *The Failure of Louis XIV's Dutch War* (University of North Carolina Press, 1979); Michael Roberts, *The Swedish Imperial Experience, 1560–1718* (Cambridge University Press, 1984); and Paul Sonnino, *Louis XIV and the Origins of the Dutch War* (Cambridge University Press, 1989).

Suggestions for Web Browsing

Age of the Sun King (L'Age d'Or)
http://www.geocities.com/Paris/Rue/1663/index.html

Extensive site describing, with text and images, the world of France under Louis XIV.

Internet Modern History Sourcebook: The Ancien Régime
http://www.fordham.edu/halsall/mod/hs1000.html#ancien

Extensive on-line source for links about the Ancien Régime, including primary documents by or about Louis XIV and Cardinal Richelieu and the enlightened despotism of Catherine the Great and Frederick II.

Frederick the Great of Prussia
http://members.tripod.com/~Nevermore/king.html

Extensive site on the king of Prussia and his times.

Russia
http://www.english.upenn.edu/~jlynch/FrankDemo/Places/russia.html

A history of Russia during the time of Peter the Great and Catherine the Great includes information and images regarding geography, politics, people, and places.

Wolfgang Amadeus Mozart
http://kolibri.cosy.sbg.ac.at/personen/mozart/index.html

An extensive biography of Mozart, with images.

Notes

1. Quoted in James Harvey Robinson, *Readings in European History*, Vol. 1 (Boston: Ginn, 1906), pp. 273–275.
2. Quoted in F. Tyler, *The Modern World* (New York: Farrar & Rinehart, 1939), p. 186.
3. Quoted in Robert B. Asprey, *Frederick the Great: The Magnificent Enigma* (New York: Ticknor & Fields, 1986).
4. Quoted in Pierre Gaxotte, *Frederick the Great* (London: Bell, 1941), p. 357.
5. Stephen Jones, *The Eighteenth Century* (New York: Cambridge University Press, 1985), p. 10.
6. George K. Anderson and William E. Buckler, eds., *The Literature of England*, Vol. 1 (Glenview, Ill.: Scott, Foresman, 1958), p. 1568.

Ian Steen, who graphically portrayed daily life in Holland, gave a vivid presentation of The Fishmarket at Leiden *in the mid-seventeenth century. Note the variety of dress and activities Steen describes.*

Limited Central Power in the Capitalist World, 1600–1789

In the century between the Dutch rebellion and the British Glorious Revolution, constitutional government took root in the Netherlands and survived and prospered in England. The Dutch profited from the declining fortunes of the Spaniards and established global trading dominance. Protected by its geography and strengthened by its traditions, England carried on a sometimes bloody argument about its political structure. In both countries rapidly developing commerce and increasing social mobility encouraged a direct transition from feudalism to constitutional government, without a prolonged intermediate stage of centralized monarchy.

The arguments advanced by the Dutch and the English provided the base for the independence movement of another commercial area, the 13 British colonies, to break away in 1776 (see Chapter 21). In the Low Countries and then England, and in the future United States, the notions of individual choice, individual control over property, and political freedom went hand in hand. By 1789 the debate between limited central power and absolutism would be won by the former. As the old regimes in Europe endured their death struggles, the English and the Americans went from strength to strength into the nineteenth century.

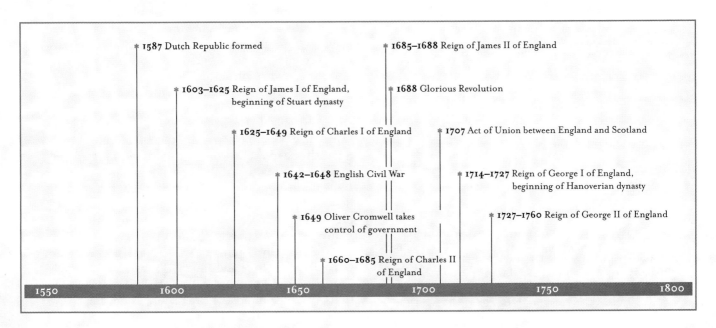

* **1587** Dutch Republic formed

* **1603–1625** Reign of James I of England, beginning of Stuart dynasty

* **1625–1649** Reign of Charles I of England

* **1642–1648** English Civil War

* **1649** Oliver Cromwell takes control of government

* **1660–1685** Reign of Charles II of England

* **1685–1688** Reign of James II of England

* **1688** Glorious Revolution

* **1707** Act of Union between England and Scotland

* **1714–1727** Reign of George I of England, beginning of Hanoverian dynasty

* **1727–1760** Reign of George II of England

| 1550 | 1600 | 1650 | 1700 | 1750 | 1800 |

The Dutch Golden Age, 1581–1660

The Dutch blazed the trail to modernity in Europe in the first half of the seventeenth century, a period described as a time of an "Embarrassment of Riches."[1] They staged the first modern national liberation struggle; conducted the first modern guerrilla war; set up the first modern republic; established the first modern banks, insurance companies, and stock markets; created the first modern capitalist agriculture; and were among the first to practice recycling. After a long and tenacious struggle against the Spaniards, they went on to establish a global trading network that gave them the highest quality of life in Europe. Unfortunately, their lack of military power led to their being dominated by the English in the 1660s. But their precedent-setting contributions established the foundations of modern political and economic life in the West.

The Dutch Republic

The end of the Thirty Years' War in 1648 brought official independence to the Dutch Republic, but its actual freedom had long since been an established fact. Defeat of the Armada in 1588 bought the Dutch time in which to accumulate resources, create an efficient army, and drive out the Spaniards. After the sack and blockade of Antwerp in 1576, most industry and banking moved north to Amsterdam, which became the leading port and financial center in northern Europe.

The Dutch, meanwhile, developed a unique federal government, combining urban and local councils to limit executive power. They established a Protestant state church but only sporadically imposed the rigid religious uniformity advocated by extreme Calvinists. Although the system was identified with the abstract ideal of popular sovereignty in the Dutch independence declaration of 1581 (which was implemented in 1587), this aristocratic polity of burghers and nobles only vaguely resembled a modern democracy. The Dutch system, however, was the first successful major challenge to monarchy in western Europe, and it did provide a precedent for many later democratic institutions.

Perhaps the most striking feature of the Dutch system was its decentralized structure. The republic was a federal union of sovereign states, each with absolute control of its revenues and able to veto any act of the States General (federal assembly). Theoretically, each provincial governor, or *stadtholder*, was merely a military commander, dependent on the assembly for men and supplies. Each of the seven United Provinces of the Netherlands made public decisions in its own assembly, which represented the nobles and the cities in varying proportions. Within the cities, politics was made by councils, whose members sat by inherited rights and usually represented the wealthy merchant and bankers. Urban government, however, was a practical partnership between rich burghers and less affluent craftsmen. The latter held minor administrative posts and maintained peace through their service in the militias.

Concentration of power in any one office or individual was limited by this interaction of classes. Their differences were accented by their separate interests and by their indirect exercise of power, outside government and often outside the law itself. Wealthy urban merchants dominated the town councils, but their power was balanced against that of the nobles in the provincial assemblies. The merchants were also checked by differences within their own class and by dependence on the urban militias. All three classes needed one another to maintain industry and commerce, on which their prosperity depended. Because none of the three major blocs could achieve absolute control by itself, all regulations were lax, and individuals enjoyed more freedom than citizens elsewhere in Europe did.

The Dutch Republic outdistanced contemporary monarchies in creating the first northern European empire overseas. Between 1609 and 1630, while at war with Spain and Portugal, the Dutch navy broke Spanish sea power, drove the Portuguese from the Moluccas of Southeast Asia, and dominated the carrying trade of Europe. In this same period the republic acquired Java, western Sumatra, the spice-producing Moluccas of Indonesia, and part of Sri Lanka. The Dutch East India Company took over most European commerce with ports between the Cape of Good Hope and Japan. Elsewhere, the Dutch acquired the Portuguese West African slaving stations, conquered most of Brazil, and established New

The Dutch Republic

1568	Revolt in the Netherlands
1576	Sack of Antwerp
1581	Dutch United Provinces declare independence from Spain
1581–1584	William I (the Silent) stadtholder
1587	Dutch Republic formed
1619	End of republican power; overthrow of John Oldenbarnveldt
1652–1674	Anglo-Dutch naval wars

Discovery Through Maps

Seventeenth-Century Amsterdam

The "golden age" of Dutch history occurred in the seventeenth century. Not only did the Netherlands successfully rebel against Spain, but they also went on to become a global trading power and the financial center of Europe. Because they were among the first to escape from feudalism, they established the first stock market, modern bank, and insurance company as Amsterdam offered the highest standard of living to all levels of society. The tolerant Dutch received refugees from all over Europe and served as the intellectual, scientific, and artistic center of Europe. It is not surprising that the Dutch also led Europe in cartography.

Dutch maps were not only accurate but also works of art, as can be seen in this map of Amster-

dam, which was made from an overhead perspective, from the *Toonneel der Steden* by Joan Blaeu. Framing the walled cities are well-defined fields, the agricultural basis for Dutch prosperity. At the center one can see the city walls with their projections affording a clear view of any potential invaders who dared approach the city. Then the port, with its seagoing vessels and warehouses, is clearly laid out. Almost unchanged in the more than three centuries since this map was drawn is the core of the city, with its network of canals and bridges. One could take this map and use it today to walk around central Amsterdam.

Amsterdam (on the lower part of Manhattan Island) in North America. Dutch commercial and colonial predominance ended after 1650, but the Dutch Asian empire lasted into the twentieth century.

Emergence of the Dutch Monarchy

The internal Dutch power balance shifted during the early seventeenth century. Republicans, representing

the great urban merchants, supported religious toleration, limited central authority, and peace. The monarchists, representing a majority of the urban lower classes and the nobles, especially the House of Orange, wanted a Calvinist state church, strong stadtholders, a large army, and an aggressive foreign policy against the Habsburgs. Until 1619 the republicans held power, but their leader, John Oldenbarnveldt (1547–1619), was ultimately overthrown and

A prosperous East Indies trader poses with his wife on a hill near the port of Batavia (now Djakarta, Indonesia).

executed after a royalist uprising. Between 1619 and the Peace of Westphalia, the country was ruled by domineering stadtholders, who conducted the war against Spain and acquired a status approaching that of European kings.

As successful military leaders, the Dutch stadtholders appealed to popular loyalties. The House of Orange supplied so many successive stadtholders that the office became virtually hereditary in the family. By the 1640s stadtholders were addressed as "Your Highness" and intermarried with European royalty, including the English Stuarts. They created a political machine that controlled some provincial systems. Arguing for efficiency, they gained the right to name their councilors as working ministers. From 1618 to 1647 and again from 1672 to

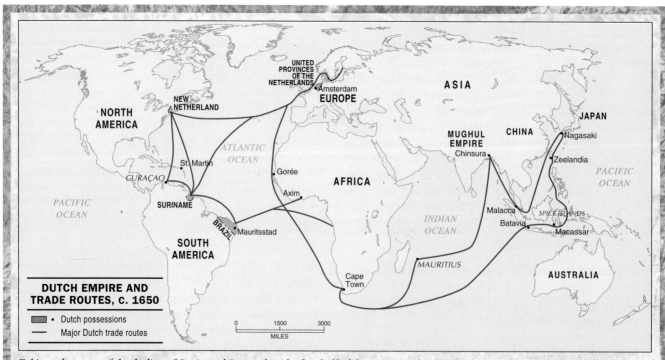

DUTCH EMPIRE AND TRADE ROUTES, C. 1650

- Dutch possessions
— Major Dutch trade routes

Taking advantage of the decline of Spain and Portugal in the first half of the seventeenth century, the Netherlands—one of the smallest states in Europe—established a global trading network.

1703, monarchists controlled the state. In the latter period William III built a highly efficient army and centralized administration.

In the mid-seventeenth century the Dutch Republic enjoyed prosperity and power far beyond its limited population base and territory. During the interval between the decline of Spain and the rise to dominance of modern France and England, the Dutch enjoyed naval, commercial, and colonial supremacy. This predominance, of course, could only be temporary. The small, disputatious Netherlands had not enough people or defensible boundaries to afford long-term competition with France in Europe or with England overseas. But even as a secondary power, which it was destined to become after 1650, it remained economically progressive, culturally advanced, and a pioneer in developing constitutional government. Because of its liberal system, it became the refuge for many of Europe's finest scientists and philosophers.

The English Debate

Between the death of Queen Elizabeth in 1603 and the Glorious Revolution in 1688, the English carried on a fundamental debate about the nature of government. At base were the question of the control of property, the role of law, the nature of the state, and the notion of sovereignty. The Stuart dynasty and its allies upheld the centrality of the monarch as the fundamental principle of government. Arrayed against them were individuals who saw the nation's will as expressed through Parliament as the primary principle of government. The Stuarts saw their legitimacy in birth and "the natural order of things," while the parliamentary forces referred to four centuries of legal traditions and practices.

Political Contentions Under the Early Stuarts in England

While mainland Europe suffered through the Thirty Years' War, England faced serious domestic stress under the first two Stuart kings. Conflict between the first, James I, and his English subjects began immediately after he came to the throne in 1603, but the wily monarch avoided any real constitutional crisis. This fate fell to his son Charles I, who succeeded his father in 1625. During the next 15 years, misguided royal policies produced steadily mounting opposition, until the country stood at the brink of civil war.

Admittedly, the early Stuart kings inherited formidable problems. English Puritans and other radical Protestants had become more vocal in their protests during the last years of Elizabeth's reign; they now sought to pressure the new monarch, who

England: From Stuart Ambition to Parliamentary Power

1603	James VI of Scotland becomes James I of England
1625	Charles I becomes king of England
1628	Petition of Right
1629	Charles I dissolves Parliament
1640	Short Parliament; Long Parliament convenes
1642–1648	Civil war
1649	Charles I executed
1649–1660	Various attempts at a Puritan Commonwealth
1660	Charles II restored to the English throne
1670	Secret Treaty of Dover between France and England
1685	James II becomes king of England
1688	Glorious Revolution
1689	William II and Mary II come to the throne of England
1702–1714	Queen Anne, the last of the Stuarts
1714	George I of Hanover becomes king of England

had earlier accepted a Presbyterian state church in his native Scotland. Economic difficulties were even more of a problem to James. At a time when administrative and military costs were escalating, peace with Spain in 1604 left a debt of 100,000 pounds sterling as well as an end to privateering, a state-supported piracy, which had netted handsome profits for many London shipowners and financiers. The state had no army, a navy in decline, no paid bureaucracy, and diminishing sources of revenue except what could be coaxed from reluctant Parliaments. To make matters worse, falling wages, rising population, and gentry seizure of common lands were alienating thousands of unemployed laborers in both town and country.

James, a cousin of Elizabeth and the son of Mary Stuart, had learned his lessons well in 36 years as king of Scotland. He was rational and learned and a fervent believer in monarchical divine right. He also hated parliaments and Presbyterians but recognized the need for taking what "can be" over what "should be" in political affairs. This ability to compromise reflected a sound administrative sense, which allowed him to hold power despite his natural tendencies toward extravagance and self-indulgence.

During his English reign (1603–1625), James maintained a shaky stability while tentatively pursuing unpopular policies. In 1604 he attended a conference of radical Protestants at Hampton Court and denied their demands for abolition of the episcopal system, relying for support on majority public opinion. Later he threatened to chase all extreme Calvinists from the land and succeeded in chasing some, the Pilgrims, to the Netherlands.

He was not very successful with Parliament. The problems here were mostly financial, involving rejection of his revenue proposals. He dismissed his first parliament in 1611. The second sat for only two months in 1614. James then ruled by decree without Parliament until 1621, when he ended another session by personally entering the House of Commons and rejecting proposals to limit his prerogatives. In the 1620s he defied public opinion by favoring a Spanish marriage for Charles and later arranging the marriage of the heir apparent to the French princess Henrietta Marie, who brought her Catholic confessor to England. But even then, at the apex of his unpopularity, James was able to manipulate his last parliament of 1624, winning acclaim as well as a substantial grant by declaring war against Spain.

The political skills of James were noticeably missing during the next reign. Charles was a loyal friend, devoted husband, and loving father, who was honest, conscientious, and serious in meeting his royal responsibilities. He was also shy, lacking in personal appeal, and stubborn, a procrastinator, a committed royalist ideologue, and a poor judge of people. This combination of qualities, generating strong words and weak actions, ultimately spelled disaster for him.

The constitutional crisis, avoided by James, grew steadily under Charles. After enduring many stormy debates with Parliament, he accepted the famous Petition of Right in 1628. This document affirmed ancient English rights by securing parliamentary approval of taxes, abolishing arbitrary imprisonment, ending the quartering of soldiers with citizens, and prohibiting martial law in peacetime. But Charles's cooperative attitude was only temporary. From 1629 to 1640 he ruled without Parliament, alienating much of English society, particularly the Puritan church reformers and the gentry. In England, Archbishop Laud, the king's Anglican adviser, forced absolute conformity by whipping, mutilating, and jailing Protestant dissidents. The policy backfired in Scotland. When Laud tried to force the Anglican prayer book on the Scottish kirk (church), the Scots rebelled and invaded England in 1640. Charles was forced to conclude a humiliating peace by paying the invaders to withdraw.

Charles I's marriage to Henrietta Marie was a controversial issue in seventeenth-century England. Chosen by his father James I, the French princess arrived in London accompanied by her Catholic confessor.

After agreeing to buy off the Scots, Charles called Parliament to raise the money and secure his future finances. When it insisted on debating other issues, this "Short Parliament" was dismissed after it sat for little more than three weeks. The government then resorted to forceful measures; it imprisoned dissidents, imposed more illegal taxes, forced loans from merchants, and impressed men for the army, measures that made the situation only worse. Finally, desperate for funds and facing mounting public hostility, the king called what would become known as the "Long Parliament," because it sat through 20 years of constitutional debate and civil war. It immediately began limiting the king's powers. Led by the dauntless Puritan John Pym, Parliament imprisoned Laud; executed the earl of Strafford, Charles's hated chief minister; provided for its own regular meetings; abolished the superlegal royal courts of Star Chamber and High Commission; and eliminated taxes levied without its consent.

Civil War and Republican Interregnum

Contention between Charles and Parliament moved steadily toward a climax during 1641 and 1642. In October 1641, rebellion in Ireland precipitated a crisis over financing and controlling an army to quell the revolt. Charles went to Parliament with 400 soldiers, expecting to arrest Pym and four other opposition members, but they had already escaped into London. In January he left the capital for York, and Parliament took the unprecedented action of declaring, without royal approval, its legal authority over national military forces.

Charles then began gathering troops in the north before raising his standard at Nottingham in August. Fighting had already started at numerous places, including South Molton in Devonshire, where a mob of men and women, armed with rocks, clubs, and muskets, resisted royalist troops in the town square. The struggle thus begun would last another seven years; for a decade the government would alternate between a republic and a monarchy, but the prospects for English absolutism were doomed forever.

The royalists, or "cavaliers," were primarily countrymen, familiar with horses and weapons. Their officers were experienced noblemen, such as the dashing Prince Rupert, Charles's nephew and son of Elizabeth, the dethroned queen of Bohemia. The parliamentary forces included many townsmen, although some commanders, like the incompetent earl of Essex, were aristocrats. Therefore, at first the royalist forces were successful, until the rebels turned to extreme measures. They made alliance with the Scots, reorganized their forces into a national army, and enlisted popular support by appeals to radical Protestantism. In 1646, after defeating the royalists decisively at Marston Moor (1644) and Naseby (1645), they accepted Charles from the Scots, who had taken him prisoner. After four long years, the war now seemed to be over.

Almost immediately, however, new conflicts arose between Parliament and its army. Conservative Presbyterians in Parliament, fearful of radical Protestantism in the ranks, were anxious to demobilize the army. This goal brought a rabid reaction among the troops, who refused to go home without their pay, some 2.75 million pounds sterling in arrears. During the spring and summer of 1647 the military units elected "agitators" (leaders) and a general Army Council. At this stage most officers, including the leading commanders Oliver Cromwell (1599–1658) and Lord Fairfax (1612–1671), supported the men. In August Fairfax brought the army into London, where it intimidated members by marching by the parliamentary chambers. While encamped in city suburbs during the fall, the army leadership also sponsored a series of council debates on issues of concern to the common soldiers.

Some rebels in the army advocated truly democratic reforms. Their most striking proposals originated with a civilian group known as "Levellers" because they advocated reforms to favor the common people. They were led by the former army officer "honest John Lilburne" (1614–1657). Beginning in 1647 Levellers aided the near-mutinous agitators in producing a number of documents, each known as an "agreement of the people." These early written democratic constitutions proposed that the English government be organized as a republic, with a one-house legislature elected by broad manhood suffrage. They did not advocate votes for women, but women were active in the movement, writing, speaking, organizing, and, like Elizabeth Lilburne, suffering hardships when their men were in jail. The program did, however, propose civil and religious liberties for all citizens. The Levellers and their "agreements" anticipated modern democratic theory.

As it turned out, the radical dream was only a side issue in maneuvers for power among the Presbyterian Parliament, the conservative army officers, and the radical soldiers. When Charles escaped in November and began negotiations with the Scots, the officers suppressed the mutineers, shooting some of the Leveller leaders and imprisoning others. Although Charles managed to renew the war, he lost his last battle at Preston in August 1648. Again the officers professed to consider the radical program while they tried unsuccessfully to extract a promise from Charles to free Protestant churches from state control. Finally resorting to force, they again outlawed the Levellers while sending Colonel Pride and some soldiers to purge Parliament of 143 Presbyterian opponents. The remaining "Rump Parliament" under the dominance of Oliver Cromwell then abolished the House of Lords, executed the king after a perfunctory trial, and declared England a republic.

After the disruptions and bloodshed of the English Civil War, there were many people on the parliamentary side who viewed Oliver Cromwell as he is depicted here, as the savior of England.

For the next 11 years Cromwell's military regime was able to perpetuate itself in different forms. At first the Rump and a Council of State, dominated by Cromwell, governed the country while crushing all resistance in Scotland and Ireland. In 1653 more contention between Rump politicians and the council resulted in dissolution of the token Parliament and creation of a thinly veiled dictatorship. A new constitution, the Instrument of Government, written by Cromwell's henchmen, assigned him extensive powers as Lord Protector. Two years later Cromwell finally dismissed the Instrument's impotent Parliament and instead ruled through military governors. His regimes during the interregnum were able to increase trade and raise respect for England abroad, but they were never popular, a fact attested to by the continued life of the radical movements, which enlisted popular support and required government countermeasures until after the mid-1650s.

Despite ultimate radical failures, the period of the civil war and the interregnum brought significant changes to England. Constitutionally, it curtailed the powers of the crown and confirmed Parliament's control of finances, thereby decisively checking the Stuart trend toward absolutism. At the same time, the royalist defeat expanded opportunities for business and for imperial expansion under Cromwell. England effectively challenged the naval and maritime supremacy of the Dutch in the 1650s while beginning to develop the world's leading empire.

The Restoration

Initially, almost everyone welcomed the new ruler, Charles II (1660–1685), called back from exile in France and restored to the throne, with his lavish court and his mistresses. But Charles, the cleverest politician of the Stuart line, exploited this common desire for normality to avoid the terms of his restoration, which bound him to rule in cooperation with Parliament. The period from 1660 to 1688 would be marked by increasingly severe struggles between the Stuarts and Parliament.

Charles worked hard to move the country toward absolutism. With the help of his favorite sister, Henrietta Anne, who had married Louis XIV's brother, he negotiated the secret Treaty of Dover, which bound him to further English Catholicism and aid the French in war against the Dutch. In return Charles received subsidies from France that made him almost independent of Parliament. He then used all his deceit and cunning to create a political machine. This precipitated a political crisis, forcing him to back down. Ultimately, he dismissed four Parliaments. After 1681 Charles governed without Parliament, taking advantage of a strong desire among the propertied classes to avoid another civil war.

After the monarchy was restored in 1660, Parliament did not back down in its debate with the last two Stuart kings. The Whig opposition, which represented the desires of the lesser landowners and their business allies in the cities, forced a resignation from Charles II's first minister, imprisoned the second, excluded the king's Catholic supporters from public office, and provided individuals with legal security against arbitrary arrest and imprisonment. The struggle between crown and Parliament created a serious political crisis during the last years of his reign.

Charles's brother James II (1685–1688) proved to be an even more determined absolutist. Like Charles, he was an admirer of Louis XIV and a Catholic. His wife, Mary of Modena, had been persuaded by the pope to marry James as a holy commitment to save England for Rome. Having been repeatedly insulted by Protestants at Charles's court, she was now fanatically determined to accomplish her mission. James was quite willing to cooperate. Early in his reign he suppressed an anti-Catholic rebellion in southwestern England. With his confidence thus buttressed, he attempted to dominate the courts; maintain a standing army, largely commanded by Catholics; take over local government; and return the English church to Catholicism. Most of this was done in defiance of the law while Parliament was not in session.

His actions caused such universal opposition that James was forced to call a new Parliament, which he tried to pack with his supporters, but local officials would not cooperate. Finally, when his wife gave birth to a prince who was widely regarded as a potential Catholic king, parliamentary leaders and Protestant aristocrats met and offered the crown to the former heir Mary Stuart, the Protestant daughter of James by an earlier marriage. Mary accepted the offer with the provision that her husband, William of Orange, be coruler. Then William landed with an efficient Dutch army, defeated James, and forced him to flee into exile. This "Glorious Revolution" ultimately pushed England far in the direction of limited monarchy.

The Establishment of Democratic Precedents

Eighteenth-century revolutionaries looked back with respect to the 1640s when the English Parliament, after struggling to maintain its rights through two reigns, fought a civil war, executed a king, and established a republic. For one brief period, revolutionary soldiers had even proposed a democratic system, guaranteed by a written constitution. Although this effort failed and the republic ultimately produced an unpopular dictatorship, it could never destroy the traditional popular ideal of limited monarchy, functioning in cooperation with a representative Parliament.

After William forced James into exile in France, he accepted Parliament's conditions for his kingship, enacted as the famous Bill of Rights. This declaration provided as follows:

1. The king could not suspend laws.
2. No taxes would be levied or standing army maintained in peacetime without the consent of Parliament.
3. Sessions of Parliament would be held frequently.
4. Freedom of speech in Parliament would be assured.
5. Subjects would have the right of petition and be free of excessive fines, bail, or cruel punishments.
6. The king would be a Protestant.

This document has exerted tremendous influence on developing constitutional governments, as evidenced in the first ten amendments to the Constitution of the United States.

Other parliamentary acts supplemented the Bill of Rights and consolidated the Revolution. In 1689 the Mutiny Act required parliamentary approval for extending martial law more than one year. Although Catholics were subjected to harsh new restrictions and non-Anglican Protestants were still excluded from public office, the Toleration Act (1689) gave all Protestants freedom of worship. In 1693, when Parliament failed to renew the customary Licensing Act, the country achieved practical freedom of the press. Finally, in the Act of Settlement in 1701, Parliament prescribed a Protestant succession to the throne and barred the monarch from declaring war, removing judges, or even leaving the country without parliamentary consent.

The Glorious Revolution permanently limited the English monarchy, guaranteed important legal rights, and helped popularize the ideal, if not the practice, of popular sovereignty. For these reasons it provided a model for Locke and hope for Voltaire and Montesquieu. Yet in many respects it was neither glorious nor revolutionary; it certainly did not establish democracy, for after 1688 the country continued to be governed by a minority of merchants and landowners.

Eighteenth-Century British Politics

After 1688, the landed gentry—functionally a lower aristocracy of landed capitalists with a variety of economic interests—gained almost complete control of the House of Commons. From their base in the Whig alliance they shaped state policy through a prime minister and a cabinet system that became responsible to Parliament, not the king. The gentry made government a closed system, putting members of their class into most of the public offices, lucrative positions in the Anglican church, and commissioned ranks in the army and navy. These privileges were shared only with the few remaining nobles (220 in 1790) who sat in the House of Lords.

Development of the Cabinet System

After the reign of William and Mary, English leaders looked to the German principality of Hanover for the next monarchs. The first two Hanoverian kings, George I (1714–1727) and George II (1727–1760), were so ignorant of the English language and politics that they had to rely on chief advisers (prime ministers) who could maintain support in Parliament. Sir Robert Walpole (1676–1745) first held this post, managing a Whig political machine. Walpole insisted that the entire ministry (cabinet) should act as a body; single members who could not agree were expected to resign. Later he learned the practicality of resigning with his whole cabinet when they could not command a parliamentary majority. This pragmatically developed system of cabinet government and ministerial responsibility provided the constitutional machinery needed to apply the principles of the Glorious Revolution while permitting Parliament to avoid awkward conflicts with royal authority.

Behind the cabinet and Parliament was a tight organization controlled by the upper classes. Membership in the House of Commons consisted mostly of landowners and wealthy merchants who represented an electorate of only some 6000 voters. Two representatives were elected from each county by the lesser

Purchasing a Seat in the English Parliament

These selections are from the letters of Lord Chesterfield (1767) and the memoirs of Sir Samuel Romilly (1807).

Bath, December 19, 1767

My Dear Friend,

... In one of our conversations here, this time twelve-month, I desired him to secure you a seat in the new Parliament; he assured me he would; and, I am convinced, very sincerely; he said even that he would make it his own affair; and desired I would give myself no more trouble about it. Since that, I have heard no more of it; which made me look out for some venal borough: and I spoke to a borough-jobber, and offered five-and-twenty hundred pounds for a secure seat in Parliament; but he laughed at my offer, and said, that there was no such thing as a borough to be had now; for that the rich East and West Indians had secured them all, at the rate of three thousand pounds at least; but many at four thousand; and two or three, that he knew, at five thousand. This, I confess, has vexed me a good deal; and made me the more impatient to know whether Lord Chatham had done anything in it; which I shall know when I go to town, as I propose to do in about a fortnight; and, as soon as I know it, you shall. To tell you truly what I think, I doubt, from all these nervous disorders, that Lord Chatham is *hors de combat,* as a Minister; but do not even hint this to anybody. God bless you!

(Signed) Chesterfield

[June 27th, 1807]

I shall procure myself a seat in the new Parliament, unless I find that it will cost so large a sum, as, in the state of my family, it would be very imprudent for me to devote to such an object, which I find is very likely to be the case. Tierney, who manages this business for the friends of the late administration, assures me that he can hear of no seats to be disposed of. After a Parliament which has lived little more than four months, one would naturally suppose, that those seats which are regularly sold by the proprietors of them would be very cheap; they are, however, in fact, sold now at a higher price than was ever given for them before. Tierney tells me that he has offered 10,000 pound sterling for the two seats of Westbury, the property of the late Lord Abingdon, and which are to be made the most of by trustees for creditors, and has met with a refusal. 6000 pounds sterling and 5500 pounds sterling have been given for seats with no stipulation as to time, or against the event of a speedy dissolution by the King's death, or by any change of administration. The truth is, that the new Ministers have bought up all the seats that were to be disposed of, and at any prices. ...

This buying of seats is detestable; and yet it is almost the way in which one in my situation, who is resolved to be an independent man, can get into Parliament. To come in by a popular election, in the present state of the representation, is quite impossible; to be placed there by some great lord, and to vote as he shall direct, is to be in a state of complete dependence; and nothing hardly remains but to owe a seat to the sacrifice of a part of one's fortune. It is true that many men who buy seats, do it as a matter of pecuniary speculation, as a profitable way of employing their money: they carry on a political trade; they buy their seats, and sell their votes. For myself, I can truly say that, by giving money for a seat, I shall make a sacrifice of my private property, merely that I may be enabled to serve the public. I know what danger there is of men's disguising from themselves the real motives of their actions; but it really does appear to me that it is from this motive alone that I act. ...

From *A Source-Book of English History,* ed. Elizabeth K. Kendall (New York: Macmillan, 1912), pp. 302–305.

"freeholders," but these were usually preselected by the most wealthy families. Of more than 400 members from the boroughs, or towns, the majority were named by prominent political bosses. The duke of Newcastle, for example, held estates in 12 counties, was Lord Lieutenant in three, and literally owned seven other seats in Commons. The same system also determined votes in Parliament. Other bases of power were public offices, army commissions, and appointments in the church. Local magnates squeezed out a wide variety of concessions from the king's ministers, who framed policies in accordance with the system.

English politics, so dynamic in the mid-1600s, became stagnant by the end of George II's reign in 1760. Potential leaders were available in the middle class, whose members were most conscious of defects in the English structure, but they were ignored. Although they loaned the money or paid the taxes that supported governments, they were everywhere excluded from political participation. In England the House of Commons was dominated by the gentry and the House of Lords by the nobles. Self-perpetuating cliques monopolized local government. The middle class had wealth without responsibility, intelligence without authority, and ability without recognition. But despite all of the manipulation and corruption, the system functioned well enough to hold England together during the extraordinarily complex eighteenth century without recourse to a revolution. The tradition of English politics of "evolution, not revolution" was in place.

George III and the Crisis in England

The next Hanoverian king, George III (1760–1820), did not play the role of puppet to Parliament that his two predecessors had. First he alienated many commercial and colonial interests by opposing an aggressive policy toward France. Then he began implementing powers never claimed by his Hanoverian predecessors, who had been virtual captives of Whig politicians. In only a few years, using lavish bribes and patronage (methods developed earlier by Walpole), George's ministers eroded Whig influence and gained control of Parliament. By 1770 they had filled the House of Commons with their supporters, known as "the King's Friends" (Tories). During his first 12 years as the head of government, his policies made enemies and produced a determined opposition party.

Parliamentary opposition merged with popular agitation in the person of John Wilkes (1725–1797), a wealthy member of the Commons and publisher of a newspaper, the *North Briton*. Wilkes became an outspoken critic of the king's policies. When the government imprisoned him, he posed as the champion of civil liberties; despite preliminary victories in court, he was ultimately forced into exile. Returning from France in 1768, he was again elected to the Commons and again thrown into jail. Once freed and elected mayor of London, Wilkes became the central figure in a great public clamor as the spokesman for the dissident middle and lower classes. Briefly, in the early 1770s, the movement raised a mild threat of revolution when some of his followers were killed in clashes between protesters and government troops.

This trouble at home was less serious, in the long run, than that provoked in the American colonies. George Grenville (1712–1770), the king's chief minister after 1763, devised a comprehensive plan to settle problems in North America left after the Seven Years' War. He forbade colonial settlement beyond the Appalachians, put Indian affairs under English superintendents, established permanent garrisons of English troops for maintenance of order on the frontiers, issued orders against smuggling, sent an English fleet to American waters, assigned English customs officials to American ports, and had Parliament impose new taxes on the colonies to pay for their defense. The Sugar Act of 1764 increased duties on sugar, wines, coffee, silk, and linens; and the Stamp Act of 1765 required that government stamps be placed on practically every kind of American document, from college diplomas to newspapers. That same year, the Currency Act prohibited the issuance of paper money in the colonies. Grenville's program aroused an almost universal colonial protest, allied in spirit with Wilkes's movement in England.

The Forces of Change

Dynamic economic and social forces challenged all European governments in the eighteenth century. Absolutist states, as we saw in Chapter 19, were unable to cope with these changes because they were too static and inefficient. The Dutch and English governments proved more able to adapt to the steadily changing nature of their societies. But in the eighteenth century the rate of change was so rapid that the process itself seemed unique, almost revolutionary. Every part of Europe, from Britain past the Russian borders, to the colonies around the world, and every social class, from peasants to the most tradition-bound nobles, felt the insecurity and restlessness inherent in the social transformation. Governments with sufficient flexibility survived these changes; those that could not adapt were weakened or destroyed.

Expanding Capitalism

The primary force driving change was an energetic capitalistic economy developing so rapidly that it could hardly be controlled or even predicted. Absolutism had risen earlier on waves of steady economic expansion, but these waves were now so strong that they tossed the political ships about and determined their direction, no matter how the kings might try to steer them. Capitalism generated new economic pursuits that developed almost spontaneously outside of established institutions.

It also created unprecedented increases in the volume of trade by dealing both in precious goods and bulk commodities. Eastern Europe and the Baltic supplied grains, timber, fish, and naval stores while western Europe supplied manufactures for its outlying regions and overseas trade. Dutch, English,

The Rise of Capitalism

1600	English East India companies formed
1602	Dutch East India Company
1609	Bank of Amsterdam opens
c. 1688	Lloyds of London begins operation
1694	Bank of England is chartered
1698	London Stock Exchange opens
1724	Paris Bourse is established

and French merchant-bankers controlled shipping and credit. Plantation agriculture in the tropics, particularly the cultivation of Caribbean sugar, produced the greatest profits for overseas commerce. The African slave trade, along with its many supporting industries, also became an integral part of the intercontinental system. The New World economy widened European horizons while contributing to European wealth. New foods such as potatoes, yams, lima beans, tapioca, and peanuts became part of the European diet. Tropical plantation crops such as rice, coffee, tea, cocoa, and sugar ceased to be luxuries.

These new markets and resources contributed greatly to the development of modern capitalistic institutions. As the volume rose, great public banks chartered by governments replaced earlier family banks like the Fuggers of Augsburg. The Bank of Amsterdam (1609) and the Bank of England (1694) are typical examples. Such banks, holding public revenues and creating credit by issuing notes, made large amounts of capital available for favored enterprises.

Building on this seventeenth-century foundation, four new conditions produced the commercial boom of the eighteenth century. First, government demand for goods reached astronomical heights as huge standing armies and navies required mountains of food, clothing, arms, and ammunition. Second, a rising European population created another expanding market, demanding bulk commodities, while the attendant declining mortality allowed businessmen to live longer and amass more profits for investment. Developing plantation agriculture in tropical colonies provided a third stimulus to foreign trade. Finally, Brazilian gold and diamond strikes raised prices and encouraged all European business after the 1730s.

The resulting economic changes brought promising but sometimes disturbing results. As wealth increased beyond all expectations, investment and production rose accordingly in textiles, coal, iron, and shipbuilding. With enterprises growing larger, partnerships and joint-stock companies began replacing individually owned companies, as had happened earlier in foreign trade. Specialization, at the same time, became common in new phases of wholesaling and retailing operations.

Expansion and increasing complexity were accompanied by a steady monetary inflation. Wages, for example, increased far less than food prices, thus depressing the condition of workers. Nobles on the Continent who received fixed fees from their peasants and English landlords who had leased their fields on long-term contracts were hurt badly. Conversely, landowners who rented to short-term tenants or received payment in kind profited, as did other capitalistic investors, who became wealthy from the general increase in the cost of goods. At times their profits soared in a wildly speculative "boom and bust" market.

International trade was the most obvious indicator of European business prosperity. An even larger trade with overseas areas encouraged the formation of East India Companies in Austria and Prussia as clones of their older and better-known English, Dutch, and French counterparts. The resulting trade in sugar, silk, cotton, tobacco, and various luxury products generated whole new European industries. Perhaps more of an impact came from the African slave trade, centered in Liverpool and Bordeaux, which reached its peak during the eighteenth century. Altogether, the total foreign trade of Britain and

Modern capitalism made its appearance in the Netherlands and England in the seventeenth century. Banking changed dramatically during this time.

France increased by some 450 percent. (The Dutch, in imperial decline, experienced a notable decrease.)

The Growth of Free Enterprise

Prosperity threatened mercantilist systems. As opportunities for profit increased, capitalists searched for profits outside state-sponsored enterprises and even the legal limits set by governments and traditions. Some of these endeavors were deliberate efforts to evade the law; others—perhaps most—were responses to opportunity. This rising free enterprise capitalism, as distinct from mercantilist state capitalism, was evident in every phase of the eighteenth-century economy.

A rising demand for food encouraged the trend in agriculture. Soaring food prices lured surplus capital into land and improvements. This was most typical of England, but the agricultural boom, on a slightly smaller scale, extended to France, the Dutch Republic, the Low Countries, Prussia, and even the wine producers of Italy and Spanish Catalonia. Wherever it developed, capitalistic agriculture emphasized efficiency and profits, which usually required procedures that did not fit in with the traditional cooperative methods and servile labor of rural villages.

Four Englishmen pioneered the movement. Jethro Tull (1674–1741) carefully plowed the land planted in neat rows using a drill he invented and kept the plants well cultivated as they grew to maturity. Viscount Charles Townshend (1674–1738), nicknamed "Turnip Townshend," specialized in restoring soil fertility by such methods as applying clay-lime mixtures and planting turnips in crop rotation. Robert Bakewell (1725–1795) attacked the problem of scrawny cattle. Through selective breeding he was able to increase the size of meat animals and also the milk yields from dairy cows. Another Englishman, Arthur Young (1741–1820), an ardent advocate for the new agriculture, made lecture tours throughout Europe and recorded his observations (see Chapter 19). He popularized the advantages of well-equipped farms and economical agricultural techniques and did much to free European agriculture from the less productive methods of the past.

New agricultural techniques demanded large capital investment and complete control of the land. Common fields, where villagers shared customary rights, could not be cultivated with the new methods. The land needed to be drained, irrigated, fertilized, and cultivated by scientific methods. Selective stock-breeding could not be practiced with an unregulated community herd. Landlords and investors who wanted to use the new methods brought about a devastating destruction of traditional society by trying to fence or enclose their acres. By outright purchase, foreclosure, suit, fraud, or even legislation (enclosure laws), they tried to free their lands from old manorial restrictions, particularly from traditional rights to community use of the commons.

The gentry used its position of political dominance to improve their economic position, especially in the countryside. Although English manorial fees and services were abolished in the seventeenth century, many villages had retained their medieval rights to pasturage and fuel gathering on the commons. These rights were lost to enclosures. From 1750 until the end of the century, 40,000 to 50,000 small farms disappeared into large estates under the Enclosure Acts. Some of the peasants forced from the land went to the cities, some became agricultural laborers at pitifully poor wages, and others went into parish poorhouses, which were soon overflowing. This movement was strongest in England but also was seen on the Continent. Inflation and buyouts in France, particularly in the north, drove many peasants from the land, but they were so important as taxpayers that the government managed to restrict the movement. Consequently, French landlords were still complaining about manorial restrictions in the late 1780s. But in England, the gentry—unlike many of their colleagues on the Continent—had already embraced capitalism and were powerful in Parliament: They were able to pass 2000 enclosure laws between 1760 and 1800.

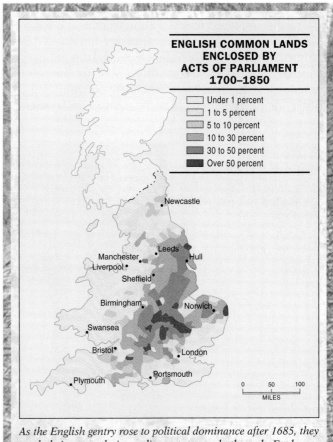

ENGLISH COMMON LANDS ENCLOSED BY ACTS OF PARLIAMENT 1700–1850

- Under 1 percent
- 1 to 5 percent
- 5 to 10 percent
- 10 to 30 percent
- 30 to 50 percent
- Over 50 percent

As the English gentry rose to political dominance after 1685, they used their strength in parliament to push through Enclosure Acts, shutting the peasantry out from access to common lands.

In industry the movement toward free enterprise produced the so-called domestic system, which involved contractual arrangements between capitalistic brokers and handworkers. Brokers supplied materials to the workers in their homes and later collected the products, to be sent through another stage of finishing or sold directly on the market. The system became common in industries where demand was high, profits were large, and capital was available. Domestic manufacturing moved early to the country, away from the regulations imposed by city guilds. The advantages and disadvantages were those associated with unregulated industry. Contracts were freely negotiated and prices were usually low, but capitalists and consumers faced considerable risks. Workers, particularly women and children, were easier to exploit than the guilds were.

Domestic industry was common all over western Europe after 1500, reaching a climax of growth in the eighteenth century. Although most typical of England, it also developed rapidly in northern France, the Low Countries, and southern Germany. It was involved in all essential processes of the woolen industries, notably spinning, weaving, fulling, and dyeing. The system also spread among other textile industries, such as linens and cottons, which provided a decided stimulus to the trend in the 1700s. Other industries affected were silk, lace, leather, paper, glass, pottery, and metals. By 1750 English domestic manufacturing employed over 4 million workers.

The career of Ambrose Crowley illustrates the domestic system in the infant English iron industry. Crowley started as a blacksmith who worked as a guildsman in Greenwich, where he accumulated a little capital. Around 1680 he moved to a small Durham village and built a domestic organization for the large-scale production of hardware. By 1700 the village had become a thriving town of 1500 workers. Crowley, who rented them their houses and supplied some of their tools as well as ore and fuel, employed most of them. The village produced nails, locks, bolts, hammers, spades, and other tools, which Crowley marketed elsewhere. A wealthy and respected citizen, he was knighted in 1706.

British industry benefited from the political system in place. Because most guild monopolies had passed with the seventeenth century, domestic industry faced few legal obstacles, but it did experience frequent functional crises. Despite widespread business prosperity, wages failed to keep up with the steady inflation. Between 1756 and 1786 wages rose by 35 percent but food prices increased by more than 60 percent. Workers also had to accept periodic unemployment, even in good times. They were thus inclined to resist the wage system and agitate for state intervention against low wages and high prices. Their bitter discontent was expressed in violent riots, most notably in 1765 and 1780.

Joint-stock companies were drastically reoriented in the late seventeenth century. Companies, such as the Dutch and English East India Companies, pooled the resources of many investors. In the late seventeenth century, exchanges for buying and selling stock were becoming common, as were maritime insurance companies. Lloyds of London, the most famous of these insurers, began operations about 1688. Originally, they were exclusive monopolies, both in their areas of operation and in their limited number of stockholders. They were generally criticized, and their trading rights were regularly violated by competitors and smugglers.

In major cities, guilds dominated jobs and quality control from settings such as depicted in The Syndics of the Cloth Guild, *painted by Rembrandt.*

Daniel Defoe on the Cloth Market at Leeds

The author of *Robinson Crusoe* also wrote on other subjects. This is a revealing picture of preindustrial capitalism in England.

Early in the morning, tressels are placed in two rows in the street, sometimes two rows on a side, cross which boards are laid, which make a kind of temporary counter on either side, from one end of the street to the other.

The clothiers come early in the morning with their cloth; and, as few bring more than one piece, the market-days being so frequent, they go into the inns and public-houses with it, and there set it down.

At about six o'clock in the summer, and about seven in the winter, the clothiers being all come by that time, the market bell at the old chapel by the bridge rings; upon which it would surprise a stranger, to see in how few minutes, without hurry, noise, or the least disorder, the whole market is filled. . . .

As soon as the bell has ceased ringing, the factors and buyers of all sorts enter the market, and walk up and down between the rows, as their occasions direct. Some of them have their foreign letters of orders, with patterns sealed on them, in their hands; the colours of which they match, by holding them to the cloths they think they agree to. When they have pitched upon their cloth, they lean over to the clothier, and, by a whisper, in the fewest words imaginable, the price is stated; one asks, the other bids; and they agree or disagree in a moment. . . .

If a merchant has bidden a clothier a price, and he will not take it, he may go after him to his house, and tell him he has considered of it, and is willing to let him have it; but they are not to make any new agreement for it, so as to remove the market from the street to the merchant's house.

The buyers generally walk up and down twice on each side of the rows, and in little more than an hour all the business is done. In less than half an hour you will perceive the cloth begin to move off, the clothier taking it up upon his shoulder to carry it to the mer-chant's house. At about half an hour after eight the market bell rings again, upon which the buyers imme-diately disappear, the cloth is all sold; or if any re-mains, it is carried back into the Inn. . . .

Thus you see—10,000 or 20,000 worth of cloth, and sometimes much more, bought and sold in little more than an hour, the laws of the market being the most strictly observed that I ever saw in any market in *England*.

If it be asked, How all these goods at this place, at *Wakefield*, and at *Halifax*, are vended and disposed of? I would observe,

First, that there is an home-consumption; to sup-ply which, several considerable traders in *Leeds* go with droves of pack-horses, loaden with those goods, to all the fairs and market-towns almost over the whole island, not to sell by retail, but to the shops by wholesale. . . .

There are others, who have commissions from *London* to buy, or who give commissions to factors and warehousekeepers in *London* to sell for them, who not only supply all the shop-keepers and whole-sale men in London, but sell also very great quantities to the merchants, as well for exportation to the *Eng-lish* colonies in *America*, which take off great quanti-ties of the coarse goods, especially *New England, New York, Virginia, &c.* as also to the *Russia Merchants* . . . .

The third sorts are such as receive commissions from abroad, to buy cloth for the merchants chiefly in *Hamburg*, and in *Holland, &c.* These are not only many in number, but some of them very considerable in their dealings, and correspond with the farthest provinces in *Germany*.

From Daniel Defoe, *Tour Through Great Britain, 1724–1725*, in Elizabeth K. Kendell, ed., *Source-Book of English History* (New York: Macmillan, 1912), pp. 321–324.

Under pressure, the British East India Company and similar firms steadily liberalized their policies until ul-timately most stocks were sold on the open market. Sales of stock greatly increased opportunities for in-vestment and multiplied the number of joint-stock companies. By 1715 more than 140 existed in England. This situation also encouraged a huge, speculative bull market on stock exchanges, which sprang up in tav-erns and coffeehouses all over western Europe. The London Stock Exchange opened in 1698 and the Paris Bourse in 1724; both were involved in the mania of speculation that collapsed the South Sea and Missis-sippi Companies in 1719–1720. Despite these disasters, such institutions become necessary to the private sec-tor of Europe's economy in the early 1700s.

Banking performed a similar necessary role. In a sense, the banks of Sweden, Amsterdam, and London were examples of state operation; their directors were often government advisers, authorized to perform semiofficial functions such as issuing notes and fi-nancing public debts. In another sense, however, these institutions became integral parts of the free market economy, providing the necessary credit for business enterprise while creating their own nonofficial

Underlying the commercial expansion of the seventeenth century was the skilled labor of workers such as those shown here, in the 1705 engraving by Franz Phillipp Florin, producing linen cloth in Nuremberg.

commercial methods and institutions. Moreover, smaller banks developed within the private monetary and credit systems. The first English country bank was founded as a private enterprise in 1716 at Bristol; by 1780 there were 300 in the country.

Major insurance companies, banks, and stock exchanges formed an integrated institutional system, functioning in a free international market. Their standardized procedures became so complicated that ordinary people could not understand them. That strange new world of business enterprise, unlike the political world, was not controlled directly by anyone, not even by the power of concentrated capital. Goods and credit, commodity prices and wages, monetary values and stock quotations all interacted according to their own laws, which could be studied but not accurately predicted. Participants learned then, as they learn now, that capitalism is a dangerous game in which the number of losers may far outnumber the number of winners.

Trade and Public Finance: The French and the English

Difficulties in industry were mild compared with those in foreign trade and public finance. France and England attempted the careful control of external commerce, but the increased volume and consequent promise of rich profits from such enterprise encouraged widespread smuggling. No government of a coastal state was sufficiently wealthy to police a long and irregular coastline. Moreover, the coast guards, port authorities, and customs officials charged with enforcing trade restrictions were usually so corrupt that they were ineffective. Thus despite feeble efforts to stop it, illegal trade flowed with growing pressure through rotten and fragile mercantilist sieves, violating increasingly complicated commercial laws. To meet this problem, governments resorted to private contractors, often granting immunity from the laws as payment for enforcing the regulations. The resulting monopolies assumed and usually abused government authority.

British controls were probably more successful than the French or the Spanish, but they were extremely costly in the long run. A great body of officials—more than 1250 in London alone—cost the government more than the amounts they were supposed to save in revenues. In the second half of the eighteenth century the government imposed stricter controls over the trade of the American colonies. As a result, smugglers took over much of the English coastline, and the colonies were pushed toward armed rebellion.

Smuggling was big business in the colonies, where it exceeded legal trade in the 1700s. West Indian planters of all nationalities conducted illicit commerce with English colonial merchants. New England timber and manufactures were regularly exchanged for French molasses, which was then made into rum and smuggled into Europe. Half the trade of Boston in 1750 violated British laws; Rhode Island and Pennsylvania merchants grew rich supplying the French during the Seven Years' War; and 80 percent of all tea used in the English colonies before 1770 came in free of duties. In addition, large quantities of tobacco were landed illegally in England with the connivance of Virginia and Carolina planters.

Smuggling was just as common in Europe, where every seacoast swarmed with illegal traders. Families grew wealthy in the business, and fathers trained their sons to maintain their enterprises. Contraband runners and government agents engaged in a continual civil war, using intelligence operations, pitched battles, and prepared sieges. Systematic enforcement was almost impossible because officials were bribed or personally involved, witnesses refused to testify, and juries often acquitted offenders caught in the act. During their classic era after the Seven Years' War, English smugglers operated openly in almost all English west coastal ports, including Bristol and Liverpool. On the other side of the country, desperate smuggling cliques roamed Kent, Sussex, and East Anglia. One of these, the notorious Hawkhurst gang of 500 armed men, forced farmers to store smuggled goods. The booty was then moved under armed convoys from depot to depot and on to waiting London merchants. When the government attempted to stop this traffic, a near civil war resulted, but smuggling was not appreciably curtailed.[2]

Public finance was a serious problem even for Britain, the most commercially advanced state in Europe. In 1700, after war with France, the state debt reached 13 million pounds sterling and was secured by the Bank of England. The public debt continued to rise, despite the government's efforts in the 1720s to eliminate it with profits from its overseas trading monopoly,

the South Sea Company. Unfortunately, following a wild speculation in South Sea stock, the venture failed. Succeeding colonial wars with France drove the debt still higher. By 1782 it had risen to 232 million pounds. Britain was very wealthy and could therefore carry this tremendous burden rather easily, but the debt nevertheless contributed to internal political unrest.

Population Increase

This second stage of capitalist revolution was both cause and result of powerful social turbulence, marked by urbanism, migration, and an unprecedented population explosion. The number of people in Europe increased more than 58 percent, from about 118 million in 1700 to 185 million a century later; some 50 million of this increase came after 1750. Population growth during the era was much higher in Europe than in Asia or Africa; in fact, it had never been as rapid before and has never been exceeded since.

Nearly every part of Europe experienced this tremendous expansion between 1650 and 1800. The English population rose from 5 million to over 9 million; that of Russia increased from 17 to 36 million; and the French population rose from 21 to 28 million. Other areas, which had earlier seen declines, posted gains: The Spanish population rose from 7.5 million to 11 million, while that of Italy expanded from 11 to 19 million.[3]

Population growth was intimately related to the social turbulence of the time. In the past, historians have emphasized rising life expectancy (falling death rates) as the cause. They have attributed this lower mortality to an improved social environment, involving such conditions as cleaner clothes and dishes, made possible by the new textile and pottery industries; better water and sewage facilities, following wider use of iron piping; and better medical treatment, particularly in reducing infant mortality. Other recent studies have suggested, however, that a major cause for population growth was rising fertility in response to more productive agriculture and increasing food supplies, which also encouraged rural people to marry earlier and have more children to work the land. Whatever the cause, population expansion triggered major social changes, including rising economic demand, the growth of cities, an increasing labor surplus, vagabondage, and extensive migration.

As the population increased, people moved in all directions. Some, like the Swiss and Irish, became foreign mercenaries. Others, like 300,000 French Huguenots, moved to escape religious persecution: 40,000 of them settled in England, and 20,000 of the most skilled went to Prussia. Both the Prussian and Russian governments regularly imported specialized craftsmen. German peasants by the thousands also went east to acquire land in Hungary or Russia. And the New World enticed many: In the eighteenth century more than 750,000 English and 100,000 Irish settlers arrived in North America, the largest national contingents of a European migration to the Americas that numbered more than 2 million people.

Life in the Americas varied widely among the Spanish, Portuguese, French, and English colonists, but in all colonies the frontier atmosphere encouraged self-reliance and optimism. Upward mobility was everywhere much more possible than in Europe at the time. This was particularly true in the English American colonies, where Benjamin Franklin could become rich after beginning life penniless and Thomas Jefferson, the son of a poor backcountry farmer, could marry into a wealthy family.

The adventurous spirit that had developed overseas returned to Europe in the eighteenth century. Europeans were fascinated by the cultures of foreigners, whether Chinese, Africans, or Native Americans. Everything American excited great curiosity, particularly after midcentury when regular mail service brought Europe into closer contact with the colonies. Americans and British merchants developed strong ties based on common profits. Americans frequented certain London coffeehouses, and some former Americans won election to Parliament. Retiring employees of the British East India Company, many of whom had risked everything on making their fortunes in India and had succeeded beyond their wildest dreams, aroused tremendous interest. Their country estates excited widespread wonder and envy.

Mass Discontent

Migration overseas was accompanied by rising urban populations, although cities were home to only 10 percent of Europe's total in 1800. Only slight increases occurred in eastern Europe, notably in Prussia and Austria, but the trend was especially pronounced in the West, the main area of commerce and finance. Most affected were the English towns and cities, where populations generally grew faster than those of rural areas. There, as on the Continent, population increased most decisively in commercial centers that were involved in foreign trade.

The scope and significance of the trend may be quickly illustrated by a few figures. London's population rose from 400,000 to over 800,000 between the Peace of Utrecht (1713) and the French Revolution (1789). Other English cities, such as Bristol, Norwich, Liverpool, Leeds, Halifax, and Birmingham, which had been country towns in the 1600s, became medium-sized cities of between 20,000 and 65,000 inhabitants. On the Continent the population of Paris reached 750,000 by 1789, and the number of residents in Bordeaux, Nantes, Le Havre, and Marseilles all increased appreciably. Amsterdam, the nucleus of the Dutch urban cluster, increased from 200,000 residents in 1670 to 250,000 in 1800. Farther east were other expanding cities—Hamburg, Frankfurt, Geneva, Vienna, Berlin; the last two each had more than 100,000 inhabitants in the eighteenth century. In no city did the basic services of police, health, and employment keep pace with the increase in population.[4]

Cities, of course, were the breeding grounds of ideas and contention. There were books and newspapers, coffeehouses, sailors from foreign lands, and varied populations, exchanging views and challenging prejudices. Violent spectacles, such as animal baiting and cockfighting, provided common amusements. Urban life was not only exciting; it was also more impersonal, dangerous, and frustrating. Using every kind of trick and deceit, a large criminal element flourished in the streets. Mobs were easily formed and more easily aroused, particularly in London and Paris, which regularly faced riots in the eighteenth century. Unlike the relatively placid inhabitants of rural villages, city-dwellers thrived on danger, diversity, and unpredictability. One person in three in the cities was unemployed in the eighteenth century. While the unemployed men sought relief in the proliferating gin mills of London, many women had no choice but to practice prostitution to feed their children.

William Hogarth cast a critical and unsparing eye on the desperate conditions of the poor in London during the eighteenth century. In Gin Lane *he depicted the alcoholism that allowed the poor to escape the misery of their lives.*

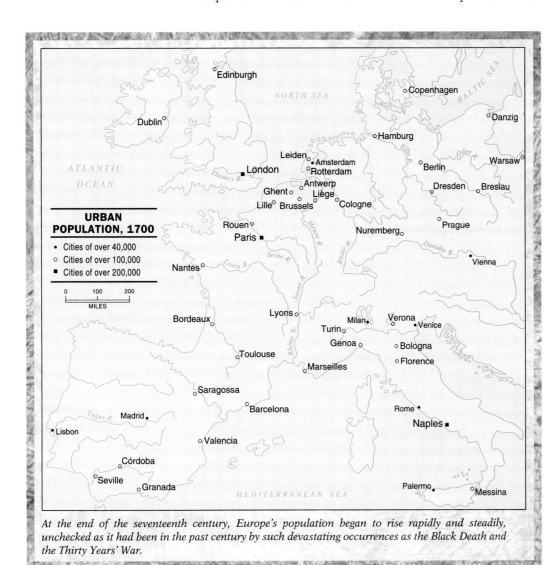

At the end of the seventeenth century, Europe's population began to rise rapidly and steadily, unchecked as it had been in the past century by such devastating occurrences as the Black Death and the Thirty Years' War.

Responses to the plight of the urban and rural poor were crude and cruel. It was felt that the way to eliminate vagrancy was through punishment. The approach was similar to the brutal beating of military delinquents, the condemning of criminals to galley slavery, or the confinement of debtors on rotting prison ships. For the poor, similar punitive solutions were sought in the British parish workhouses and the French "beggar depots." At the end of the century the English workhouses held 100,000 inmates, compared with 230,000 in the French depots. Both systems, like others all over Europe, perpetuated abominable living conditions while denying hope for the unfortunate victims. In England the workhouses were favored by some large landowners, who welcomed cheap labor supplied by the state. Other taxpayers opposed the cost of improving the workhouses and tried to push vagrants into other parishes. Even a pregnant woman or one with a sick child might be given a few pennies and turned away.

Ultimately, the government built larger workhouses for fewer parishes, attempting to spread the cost of poverty relief. Such policies destroyed the initiative of the poor and conditioned them to seek public assistance.

The simmering pressure of the discontent of the multitudes could be denied for a while, but in the 1770s and 1780s across Europe, mass outbreaks of violence and finally revolution would be the price to be paid.

Conclusion

The Dutch and the English went against the absolutist trends of their days, with differing results. The Netherlands emerged under the political, financial, military dominance of the British, while England proceeded to build a world empire. But in each case these examples of limited government provided a different political alternative for those who had become disaffected with absolutism. When the British succeeded in ousting the Stuarts in 1688, the resulting political and theoretical doctrines established the precedent for the American Revolution a century later.

The limited central powers proved able to ride the waves of change that swept the globe in the eighteenth century. Even though the political process was not marked by idealism in England, the diversity of the goals of the political elites provided a suitable framework to absorb the demographic, financial, and social changes that affected the country during the century.

Suggestions for Reading

Jonathan I. Israel, *The Dutch Republic and the Hispanic World* (Oxford University Press, 1986), and Charles R. Boxer, *The Dutch Seaborne Empire* (Penguin 1989), discuss the world trading empire of the Dutch. Social backgrounds are treated in Sherrin Marshall, *The Dutch Gentry, 1500–1650: Family, Faith, and Fortune* (Greenwood, 1987). See also J. L. Price, *Culture and Society in the Dutch Republic During the Seventeenth Century* (Columbia University Press, 1974). On the decisive conflict with the English, see J. R. Jones, *The Anglo-Dutch Wars of the Seventeenth Century* (Addison-Wesley, 1996).

On the reigns of the first two Stuart monarchs and the English civil war, see Maurice Ashley, *The English Civil War* (St. Martin's Press, 1990); Christopher Hibbert, *Cavaliers and Roundheads: The English Civil War* (Scribner, 1993); Derek Hirst, *Authority and Conflict in England, 1603–1658* (Harvard University Press, 1986); and David Underdown, *Revel, Riot, and Rebellion: Politics and Culture in England, 1603–1660* (Oxford University Press, 1985). A recent book on the radical fringe is David Petegorsky, *Left-Wing Democracy in the English Civil War: Gerrard Winstanley and the Digger Movement* (Sutton Alan, 1997). For backgrounds of the civil war, see Ann Hughes, *The Causes of the English Civil Wars* (St. Martin's Press, 1991); Perez Zagoren, *The Court and the Country* (Atheneum, 1970); Graham Perry, *The Golden Age Restored: The Culture of the Stuart Court* (St. Martin's Press, 1981); R. Malcolm Smuts, *Court Culture and the Origin of a Royalist Tradition in Early Stuart England* (University of Pennsylvania Press, 1987); and Thomas Cogswell, *The Blessed Revolution: English Politics and the Coming of the War* (Cambridge University Press, 1989). Two relatively light biographies of Charles I are Charles Carlton, *Charles I, the Personal Monarch*, 2nd ed. (Routledge, 1995), and Pauline Gregg, *King Charles I* (University of California Press, 1984). For special studies on the civil war, see Christopher Hill, *The World Turned Upside Down* (Viking, 1972); G. E. Aylmer, *Rebellion or Revolution? England, 1640–1660* (Oxford University Press, 1986); and John P. Kenyon, *The Civil Wars of England* (Knopf, 1988). Among interesting studies of radicalism are Jerome Friedman, *Blasphemy, Immorality, and Anarchy: The Ranters and the English Revolution* (Ohio University Press, 1987); F. D. Dow, *Radicalism in the English Revolution, 1640–1660* (Blackwell, 1985); and Henry Noel Brailsford, *The Levellers and the English Revolution* (Stanford University Press, 1961). On conditions facing women, see Margaret George, *Women in the First Capitalistic Society* (University of Illinois Press, 1988). For a broad selection of contemporary accounts of the civil war, see

John Eric Adair, *By the Sword Divided: Eyewitness Accounts of the English Civil War* (Sutton Alan, 1998).

For English political developments under the later Stuarts, see Maurice Ashley, *England in the Seventeenth Century* (Penguin, 1975). Among the best treatments of Charles II and his problems are Kenneth H. D. Haley, *Politics in the Reign of Charles II* (Blackwell, 1985), and James R. Jones, *Charles II: Royal Politician* (Unwin Hyman, 1987). On James II and the Glorious Revolution, see Maurice Ashley, *James II* (University of Minnesota Press, 1977); John Childs, *The Army, James II, and the Glorious Revolution* (St. Martin's Press, 1981); and K. Merle Chacksfield, *The Glorious Revolution, 1688* (Wincanton, 1988). See also David Ogg, *England in the Reigns of James II and William III* (Oxford University Press, 1984), and David S. Lovejoy, *The Glorious Revolution in America* (Wesleyan University Press, 1987).

Dorothy Marshall, *Eighteenth-Century England* (Longman, 1974), presents excellent general background on the workings of the aristocratic parliamentary system. A sound biography of the first Hanoverian monarch is Ragnhild Hatton, *George I* (Harvard University Press, 1978). See also the following works dealing with Hanoverian society and politics: John Cannon, ed., *The Whig Ascendancy* (St. Martin's Press, 1981); Michael A. Reed, *The Georgian Triumph* (Routledge, 1983); Paul Langford, *Walpole and the Robinocracy* (Chadwyck-Healey, 1986); and S. Hopewell, *Walpole and the Georges* (Wayland, 1987).

Michel Beaud, *A History of Capitalism* (Monthly Review, 1983), gives a brief but sound account of the major thrust toward capitalism. Volumes 2 and 3 of Immanuel Wallenstein, *The Modern World System*, titled *Mercantilism and the Consolidation of the World Economy* (Academic Press, 1980) and *The Second Era of Great Expansion of the Capitalist World Economy* (Academic Press, 1988), respectively, are excellent for fine details but hard going for beginners. See also Carlo M. Cipolla, *Before the Industrial Revolution* (Norton, 1980); Katrina Honeyman and Goodman Jordan, *Gainful Pursuits: The Making of Industrial Europe* (London: Arnold/Routledge, 1988); and Liana Vardi, *The Land and the Loom: Peasants and Profits in Northern France, 1680–1800* (Duke University Press, 1993).

Dynamic European economic growth is strongly emphasized in Fernand Braudel, *Civilization and Capitalism*, Vol. 2: *The Wheels of Commerce* (Harper & Row, 1986); Nathan Rosenberg and L. E. Birdzell Jr., *How the West Grew Rich* (Basic Books, 1986); and Andre G. Frank, *World Accumulation, 1492–1789* (Monthly Review, 1978). See also Gunnar Persson, *Economic Growth in Pre-Industrial Europe* (Blackwell, 1988). On capitalistic development in England, see Ralph Davis, *The Rise of English Shipping in the Seventeenth and Eighteenth Centuries* (David & Charles, 1972); James A. Yelling, *Common Field and Enclosure in England, 1450–1750* (Archon, 1977); and John J. McCusker, *The Economy of British America, 1607–1789* (University of North Carolina Press, 1986).

Roy Porter, *English Society in the Eighteenth Century* (Penguin, 1983), and J. C. D. Clark, *English Society, 1688–1832* (Cambridge University Press, 1985), provide excellent accounts of the social scene in England. Robert W. Malcolmson focuses on life among the working classes in *Life and Labor in England, 1700–1780* (St. Martin's Press, 1981). For conditions in the country, see Leonard Martin Cantor, *The Changing English Countryside, 1400–1700* (Routledge, 1987), and Pamela Horn, *Life and Labour in Rural England, 1760–1850* (Macmillan, 1987). See also Peter Earle, *The Making of the English Middle Class* (University of California Press, 1989). Some indication of English social problems may be gained from Leslie A. Clarksin, *Death, Disease, and Famine in Pre-Industrial England* (St. Martin's Press, 1975), and J. C. D. Clark, *Revolution and Rebellion:*

State and Society in England in the Seventeenth and Eighteenth Centuries (Cambridge University Press, 1986). Problems facing English women are defined in Bridget Hill, *Eighteenth-Century Women* (Unwin Hyman, 1987).

Suggestions for Web Browsing

Internet Modern History Sourcebook: Mercantile Capitalism
http://www.fordham.edu/halsall/mod/modsbook03.html#
    Mercantile Capitalism

Internet Modern History Sourcebook: Reflections on the Trade and the New Economy
http://www.fordham.edu/halsall/mod/modsbook03.html#
    Reflections on the Trade and the New Economy

On-line sources for numerous documents about the expanding global power of the Dutch and the British.

Trade Products in Early Modern History
http://www.bell.lib.umn.edu/Products/Products.html

University of Minnesota site chronicles the development of global trade, in particular, by the Dutch and the British, as they search for a variety of products, from beaver to tulips, from coffee to tobacco.

Dutch Trade
http://www.delief.org

A fascinating site on the extension of Dutch trade to Japan traces the voyage of five ships that left Rotterdam in 1598 in the search to open the Asian market. Includes maps, descriptions, links, and images.

The Glorious Revolution of 1688
http://www.lawsch.uga.edu/~glorious/index.html

The site includes a range of documents and images regarding the important legal and political precedents set in motion by the Glorious Revolution of 1688.

George Frederick Handel
http://www.npj.com/homepage/territowe/gfhport.html

Entry into the world of the composer George Frederick Handel. Here one can find portraits, pictures of locale, music, and links to other sources.

Notes

1. See the superb book by Simon Schama *The Embarrassment of Riches: An Interpretation of Dutch Culture in the Golden Age* (New York: Vintage, 1997).
2. Neville Williams, *Contraband Cargoes* (Hampden, Conn.: Shoe String Press, 1961).
3. Colin McEvedy and Richard Jones, *Atlas of World Population History* (New York: Penguin Books, 1978), passim.
4. Jan de Vries, *The Economy of Europe in an Age of Crisis, 1600–1700* (New York: Cambridge University Press, 1976), pp. 87–88; William Doyle, *The Old European Order* (Oxford: Oxford University Press, 1978), pp. 28–33; Jonathan D. Chambers, *Population, Economy, and Society in Preindustrial England* (New York: Oxford University Press, 1972), pp. 115–121.

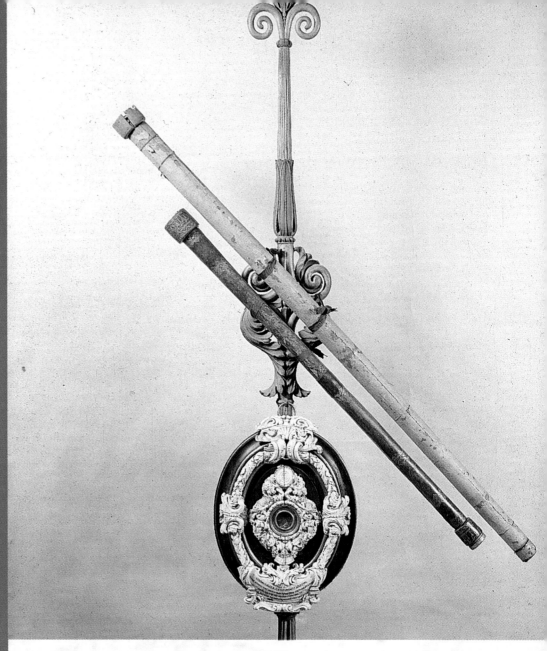

With these telescopes, Galileo was able to make the transition from mathematically verified considerations on the nature of the universe to observational confirmation of Copernicus's views.

The Scientific Revolution and the Enlightenment
New Ideas and Their Consequences

Chapter Contents

Since the beginning of the Western tradition, thinkers have inquired into the fundamental nature of the world and all of its phenomena. The Ionian Greeks, the Hellenistic Greeks, the Romans, the Arab scientists, and the Scholastics all asked the same questions and came up with a variety of answers. When the Polish scholar Copernicus wanted to affirm mathematically the church's position on the nature of the heavens, he was simply another in a 2000-year-old line of questioning individuals. But when his findings—which contradicted the accepted position—appeared, they were *printed*, and they found a ready and numerous audience in the humanists of Europe. Others picked up his thoughts, tested them in different ways, expressed their findings mathematically, and came up with their own contributions to natural law.

People like John Locke asked the same fundamental questions and applied scientific reason to society, politics, and religion in an attempt to stop the abuses of the *ancien régime*. In Scotland and France thinkers like Hume and Smith and Montesquieu and Voltaire looked at the old way of living and applied the test of reason to what they saw and in so doing created the Enlightenment. Their legacy was the notion of human happiness as a natural right, the separation of powers, and the role of the social critic to shine the light of his genius to expose fraud and corruption to a larger world. Even some of the rulers of Europe wanted to apply the new findings to their realms; they became known as "enlightened despots." Locke symbolized the age, and it is his words and his ideas, flowing through Jefferson's pen, that began the American Declaration of Independence.

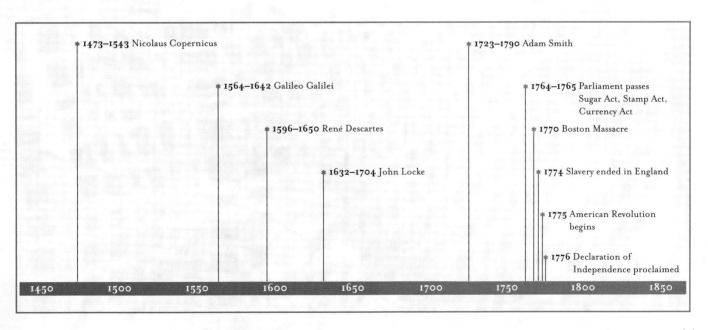

* **1473–1543** Nicolaus Copernicus
* **1564–1642** Galileo Galilei
* **1596–1650** René Descartes
* **1632–1704** John Locke
* **1723–1790** Adam Smith
* **1764–1765** Parliament passes Sugar Act, Stamp Act, Currency Act
* **1770** Boston Massacre
* **1774** Slavery ended in England
* **1775** American Revolution begins
* **1776** Declaration of Independence proclaimed

1450 1500 1550 1600 1650 1700 1750 1800 1850

Revolution in Science: The Laws of Nature

During the time of the religious upheavals of the early sixteenth century, the Polish astronomer and Aristotelian scholar Nicolaus Copernicus (1473–1543) investigated the old geocentric theory that assumed that the sun, the planets, and the stars all circled the earth. He had pursued this question out of a purely intellectual interest and an admiration for Ptolemy. In preparation for his work Copernicus had studied at the great centers of Renaissance learning—Bologna, Rome, and Padua—and when he returned to Poland, he set out to affirm and perfect the Ptolemaic system. His research, however, led him to disprove Ptolemy's assertions, and he published *On the Revolutions of the Heavenly Spheres* in Nuremberg in 1543. His rediscovered heliocentric theory—Aristarchus had arrived at the same conclusion in the second century B.C.E.—postulated the sun as the center, around which the planets moved, a theory directly opposed to the traditional Ptolemaic explanation accepted by most Christians for the rhythm of day and night and the apparent movement of heavenly bodies. The Catholic Church attacked his findings as heretical (and placed his book on the Roman Catholic Church's Index of Forbidden Books in 1616); Luther and Melanchton also ridiculed him.

Copernicus offered his idea as a merely mathematical theory. By the end of the century, however, Tycho Brahe (1546–1601), a Danish astronomer, aided by his sister, Sophia (1556–1643), had recorded hundreds of observations that pointed to difficulties in the Ptolemaic explanation. Brahe even attempted, without much success, to find a compromise between the Ptolemaic and Copernican systems by postulating that the planets moved about the sun while the latter orbited the earth. This proposition raised even more problems and therefore met with little acceptance.

Brahe's data were used by his one-time assistant, the brilliant German mathematician Johannes Kepler (1571–1630) to support the Copernican theory. While working mathematically with Brahe's records on the movement of Mars, Kepler was ultimately able to prove that the planet did not move in a circular orbit but in an ellipse. He also discovered that the paces of the planets accelerated when they approached the sun. From this he concluded that the sun might emit a magnetic force that directed the planets in their courses. The idea was not yet confirmed by a mathematical formula, but that would soon be achieved by Newton, using Kepler's hypothesis. Even in his own time, however, Kepler's laws of planetary motion almost completely undermined the Ptolemaic theory.

During the early seventeenth century, growing acceptance of the heliocentric theory precipitated an intellectual crisis affecting organized Christianity, particularly the Catholic Church. Medieval Catholicism had accepted Aristotle on physics and Ptolemy on astronomy. The church now felt its reputation and authority challenged by the new ideas. Both Copernicus and Brahe had evaded the issue by purporting to deal only in mathematical speculations. Kepler and others of his time became increasingly impatient with this subterfuge. The most persistent of these scientific rebels was the Italian mathematician-physicist Galileo Galilei (1564–1642).

Galileo discovered more facts to verify the Copernican theory. But, as he wrote to Kepler:

Up to now I have preferred not to publish, intimidated by the fortune of our teacher Copernicus, who though he will be of immortal fame to some, is yet by an infinite number (for such is the multitude of fools) laughed at and rejected.[1]

In 1609 Galileo made a telescope with which he discovered mountains on the moon, sunspots, the satellites of Jupiter, and the rings of Saturn. Having published his findings and beliefs, he was constrained by the church in 1616 to promise that he would "not hold, teach, or defend" the heretical Copernican doctrines. After another publication, he was again hauled before a church court in 1633 and forced to make a public denial of his doctrines. Galileo was thus defeated—he would not be pardoned by the church for nearly 360 years—but the heliocentric theory would win common acceptance by the end of the century.

New Ways of Thinking

Copernicus was a man who sought to prove a medieval assertion independently. When his research did not support the commonly accepted theory, he printed his own ideas. In so doing, he ushered in the modern age of science and participated in creating the scientific method. As it was developed in the seventeenth century, this methodology involved a combination of two approaches, each depending on reason, with differing applications. The deductive approach started with self-evident truths and moved toward complex propositions, which might be applied to practical problems. It emphasized logic and mathematical relationships. The inductive approach started with objective knowledge of the material world, from which proponents of induction sought to draw valid general conclusions. In the past the two procedures had often been considered contradictory. Early European astronomers were dependent on both kinds of reasoning.

Discovery Through Maps

The Heliocentric Cosmos of Copernicus

From the first person who walked across the mountain pass that had delimited his world to the views from satellites hovering thousands of miles above the equator, humans have drawn new maps to express their changing perspectives. Nothing made Europeans rethink their perspectives more than the discoveries of the Polish scientist Copernicus. He was not the first to postulate a sun-centered cosmic system. Among others, the Hellenistic Greeks in Alexandria had advanced the concept of the sun at the center of our planetary system with the planets revolving around it in the third century B.C.E.

Ptolemy, another Greek astronomer, disagreed and embellished on Aristotle's theory that the earth was at the center of the universe. This fit in nicely with the emerging Christian church's theology. After all, if God created man in his image, why would God place him anywhere else but the center of the system? Thus a tidy closed system came to be the conventional wisdom, with the earth surrounded by crystallized rings containing the moon, sun, planets; hovering outside the last ring were, of course, God and the angels.

Medieval observers noted obvious flaws in this explanation, but the clever thinkers of the church devised satisfactory refutations of the contradictions. In the 1490s Nicolaus Copernicus left his home in Torun and journeyed to the Polish university town of Krakow, where he became caught up in the debate about the nature of the universe. In the next decade in Krakow and then at the University of Bologna he pursued his study of astronomy. He returned to a post at a church in Frauenburg, where for the next 30 years he worked on making the church's view on the nature of the universe simpler, yet mathematically precise.

The more he worked, the less he could defend Rome's position, and finally in 1543, in a book dedicated to Pope Paul III, he advanced his hypothesis of a sun-centered (heliocentric), not human-centered (homocentric) universe. It was criticized by the church and by Martin Luther and was suspected by most of the astronomers of the time. But by the end of the century the Copernican hypothesis had been verified, and Europeans began to look to charts such as this one by Andreas Cellarius portraying the heliocentric cosmos. The universe had been turned upside down.

René Descartes (1596–1650), the French philosopher-mathematician, initiated a new critical mode of deduction. In his *Discourse on Method* (1627), Descartes rejected every accepted idea that could be doubted. He concluded that he could be certain of nothing except the facts that he was thinking and that he must therefore exist. From the basic proposition "I think, therefore I am," Descartes proceeded in logical steps to deduce the existence of God and the reality of both the spiritual and material worlds. He ultimately conceived of a unified and mathematically ordered universe that operated as a perfect mechanism. In Descartes' universe, supernatural processes were impossible; everything could be explained rationally, preferably in mathematical terms.

Descartes' method was furthered by discoveries in mathematics, and the method in turn popularized study of the subject. Descartes' work coincided with the first use of decimals and the compilation of logarithmic tables, which reduced by half the time required to solve intricate mathematical problems. Descartes himself developed analytical geometry, permitting relationships in space to be expressed in algebraic equations. Using such equations, astronomers could represent the movements of celestial bodies mathematically. Astronomers were further aided later in the century when Isaac Newton

One of the giants of the Scientific Revolution, René Descartes devised a new, critical mode of deduction, which he presented in his Discourse on Method.

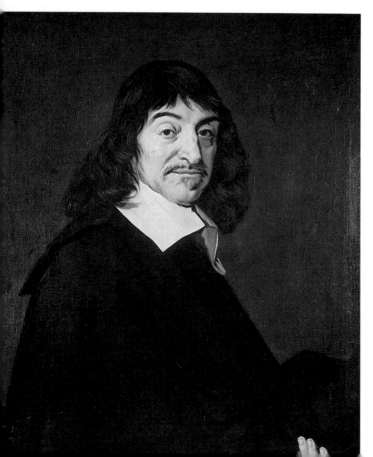

(1642–1727) in England and Gottfried Wilhelm Leibniz (1646–1716) in Germany independently perfected differential calculus, the mathematics of infinity, variables, and probabilities.

Another great early contributor to the theory of scientific methodology was the Englishman Francis Bacon (1561–1626). At a time when traditional modes of thought were crumbling, Bacon advocated the use of reason for interpreting human sensory experiences. His approach emphasized the use of systematically recorded facts derived from experiments to produce tentative hypotheses. When these were tested and verified by continued experiments, he believed they would ultimately reflect fundamental laws of nature. Bacon's ideas, outlined in his *Novum Organum* (1626), were the first definitive European statement of inductive principles.

The inductive approach became even more effective with the invention and perfection of scientific instruments. Both the telescope and the microscope came into use at the start of the seventeenth century. Other important inventions included the thermometer (1597), the barometer (1644), the air pump (1650), and the accurate pendulum clock (1657). With such devices, scientists were better able to study the physical world.

The Newtonian Universe

Great as the contributions of Galileo and Kepler were, their individual discoveries had not been united into one all-embracing principle that would describe the universe as a unit. Both Copernicus and Galileo—the first through mathematical speculation and the second through observation—had been dimly aware of a universal force in material nature. But the final proof was established later by Isaac Newton, who became a professor of mathematics at Cambridge University in the 1660s.

The notion of gravitation occurred to Newton in 1666, when he was only 24. According to his later account, he was sitting in a contemplative mood under an apple tree when a falling apple roused him to wonder why it, and other objects, fell toward the center of the earth and not sideways or upward. A flash of insight suggested to him a drawing power in matter that was related to quantity and distance. In his *Principia* (1687), Newton expressed this idea precisely in a mathematical formula. The resulting law of gravitation states that all material objects attract other bodies—inversely, according to the square of their distances, and directly—in proportion to the products of their masses. Hundreds of observations soon verified this principle and at the same time increased the credibility of scientific methods.

Newton had not only solved the astronomical problems defined by Kepler and Galileo but had also

The Widening Scope of Scientific Discovery

In the two centuries after Copernicus advanced the heliocentric theory, European scientists laid the theoretical foundations for the study of physiology, astronomy, physics, chemistry, and biology.

- *Astronomy:* The astronomer-mathematician Pierre Laplace (1749–1827) demonstrated that apparent inconsistencies, such as comets, are also governed by mathematical laws and developed the nebular hypothesis, which maintains that our sun, once a gaseous mass, threw off the planets as it solidified and contracted.
- *Biology:* Antonie van Leeuwenhoek (1632–1723) discovered protozoa, bacteria, and human spermatozoa. Robert Hooke (1635–1703), an Englishman, described the cellular structure of plants.
- *Chemistry:* Robert Boyle (1627–1691) was the first to distinguish between chemical compounds and mixtures. On the basis of his many experiments he devised a crude atomic theory, superseding the "four elements" and "four humors" of medieval alchemists and physicians. Boyle also investigated fire, respiration, fermentation, evaporation, and the rusting of metals. Joseph Priestley (1733–1804) isolated ammonia, discovered oxygen, and generated carbon monoxide. Along with the discovery of hydrogen (1766) by the Englishman Henry Cavendish (1731–1810), Priestley's work furnished an explanation of combustion. Antoine Lavoisier (1743–1794) proved that combustion is a chemical process involving the uniting of oxygen with the substances consumed. He also showed that respiration is another form of oxidation. Such discoveries led him to define the law of conservation: "Matter cannot be created or destroyed." Much of the credit for Lavoisier's scientific success should go to his wife, Marie-Anne (1758–1836), whom he married when she was 14 and educated in his laboratory. She assisted with all his major experiments, took notes, kept records, illustrated his books, and published her own papers. After he died on the guillotine during the French Revolution, she edited and published a compilation of his works.
- *Physics:* Galileo defined the law of falling bodies, demonstrating that their acceleration is constant, no matter what their weight or size. His experiments also revealed the law of inertia: A body at rest or in motion will remain at rest or continue moving (in a straight line at constant speed) unless affected by an external force. In addition, he showed that the path of a fired projectile follows a parabolic curve to earth, an inclination explained later by the law of gravitation. Galileo made additional notable discoveries through his studies of the pendulum, hydrostatics, and optics. His work was clarified by two professors at the University of Bologna, Maria Agnesi (1718–1799) in mathematics and Laura Bassi (1700–1778) in physics. Christiaan Huygens (1629–1695), along with Newton, developed a wave theory to explain light. Otto von Guericke (1602–1668) proved the material composition of air. His experiments showed that air could be weighed and that it could exert pressure, both properties in accordance with Newton's law.
- *Physiology:* Anatomist Andreas Vesalius (1514–1564), in *On the Fabric of the Human Body* (1543), gave detailed drawings of the body. William Harvey (1578–1657) described the human circulatory system, tracing the flow of blood from the heart through the arteries, capillaries, and veins and back to the heart.

confirmed the necessity of combining the methods advocated by Descartes and Bacon. Although the *Principia* used mathematical proofs, these were tested by observation. Newton insisted that final conclusions must rest on solid facts; he further contended that any hypothesis, no matter how mathematically plausible, must be abandoned if not borne out by observation or experimentation.

Newton also confirmed the basic premise of modern science that all nature is governed by laws. Indeed, his own major law was applicable to the whole universe, from a speck of dust on earth to the largest star in outer space. The magnitude of this idea—the concept of universal laws—was exciting and contagious. Within decades it had spread throughout the Western world and had been applied in every area, including human relations.

The Popularity of Science

Science, long suspect among the leaders of society and particularly the church, had now become respectable. By the beginning of the eighteenth century, scientists were invited to the best salons, and scientific academies

Antoine Lavoisier, working closely with his wife Marie-Anne, proved that combustion is a chemical process involving the uniting of oxygen with the substances consumed.

gained public support as they sprang up all over Europe. The most famous were the Royal Society of London, chartered in 1662, and the French Academy of Science, founded in 1664. Most academies published journals that circulated widely. Scientists and would-be scientists carried on voluminous correspondence, developing a cosmopolitan community with its own language, values, and common beliefs.

Rising enthusiasm on the public fringes of the scientific community was matched by a fervor among leaders of society. Frederick the Great in Prussia and Benjamin Franklin and Thomas Jefferson in America dabbled in scientific experiments, as did hundreds of other nobles, wealthy merchants, and progressive craftsmen. Support for academies was merely one form of public endorsement. Kings endowed observatories, cities founded museums, well-to-do women helped establish botanical gardens, and learned societies sponsored well-attended lectures. Scientists became respected heroes. Giordano Bruno, the Italian philosopher-scientist, was burned for heresy in 1600 by the Inquisition, and Galileo was hounded by persecutors through his most productive years; but Newton received a well-paying government position. He was lionized and knighted during his lifetime, and when he died in 1727, he was buried at Westminster Abbey.

To a great extent, especially among scientific-minded artisans and some entrepreneurs, science was a practical tool, ensuring profit and material progress. Since Bacon's time, some had foreseen a great future when science would solve many problems in agriculture and medicine. By the 1700s, scientific knowledge was being applied to draining mines, pumping water,

irrigating fields, drying textile fibers, producing gunpowder, manufacturing pottery, and building ships, as well as improving navigation. John Smeaton (1724–1792), the English perfector of the atmospheric steam engine, was a member of a scientific society, as was James Watt (1736–1819), the Scottish mechanic who invented the classic and more efficient steam engine with a double-action piston capable of driving a wheel. Watt's engine was only one of many scientific innovations that ushered in the Industrial Revolution of the late eighteenth century.

Most significant, the Newtonian revolution prepared the way for new conceptions of human purposes and goals. Although Newton himself was a staunch Anglican conservative who saw his science as demonstrating God's omnipotence and furthering social stability, many people in the future would think differently. As they looked toward the stars, each moving regularly through infinite space, they would no longer consider the universe as stage equipment created by God for the human drama of sin and salvation. Matter and motion, the fundamental realities of this strange new cosmos, everywhere acted impersonally, without discernible human purpose. In all of this the individual was apparently insignificant, but some thinkers sensed more human potential than had been formerly promised by Christian free will. Indeed, if God were not directly determining human affairs, human reason might learn the natural laws and bring about unlimited human progress.

The Enlightenment

On the same boat that carried Princess Mary of Holland to England in February 1689 after the Glorious Revolution (see Chapter 20), a rather more modest person traveled. In his bags John Locke carried the manuscripts of two works that he had written during his six years in exile in Amsterdam. Born in 1632, Locke had experienced in his youth all of the turmoil and ferment of the English civil war. His father was an ardent Puritan, a notary who served as a captain in the army defending Parliament. At Oxford Locke was interested for a while in all of the arguments of the Cromwell years but soon grew tired of the constant disputes and welcomed the calm of the Restoration. He continued his studies in medicine and the development of his own philosophy, deeply affected by the works of Descartes.

Later, however, he began to work with Lord Ashley, the count of Shaftesbury, whose unsuccessful plots against the Stuarts led him to seek exile in Holland—the place of refuge for all Europe—and with him went Locke. Amsterdam was the center of European thought in those days, made more intellectually alive by the influx of French Huguenots, Jews, Bohemian refugees, and others. There he pursued his studies in an atmosphere that was violently against the Catholic Church and absolutism. He became close to William of

Major Works of the Enlightenment

1690	John Locke, *An Essay Concerning Human Understanding, Second Treatise on Civil Government*
1721	Baron de Montesquieu, *Persian Letters*
1734	Voltaire, *Philosophical Letters Concerning the English Nation*
1739	David Hume, *A Treatise of Human Nature*
1740	Samuel Richardson, *Pamela*
1748	David Hume, *An Enquiry Concerning Human Understanding;* Baron de Montesquieu, *The Spirit of the Laws*
1751–1772	Denis Diderot, *Encyclopédie*
1759	Voltaire, *Candide*
1762	Jean-Jacques Rousseau, *Émile; The Social Contract*
1764	Cesare Beccaria, *Crimes and Punishment*
1781	Immanuel Kant, *Critique of Pure Reason*
1784	Immanuel Kant, *What Is Enlightenment?*
1795	Marquis de Condorcet, *The Progress of the Human Mind*
1798	Thomas Malthus, *An Essay on the Principles of Population*

start of the eighteenth century. This reasoning sought to create a science of man, which would solve human problems, just as other sciences were beginning to reveal secrets of nature. At first the movement was confined to scholars, theologians, and conservative men of affairs, who opposed any threat to existing institutions. But after about 1760, as new ideas were conceived and spread in print among the middle classes, the movement generated a more radical version that logically supported the need for social and political change.

The most fundamental concepts of the Enlightenment, held by its conservative and radical proponents alike, were faith in nature and belief in human progress. Nature was seen as a complex of interacting laws governing the universe. The individual human being, as part of that system, was designed to act rationally. If free to think, the doctrine assumed, people would naturally seek happiness for themselves; and reason would show them that this goal could best be attained through the well-being of others. Accordingly, both human virtue and happiness required freedom from needless restraints, including many imposed by the state or the church. Enlightenment thinkers also passionately believed in education as the path toward future improvement. Indeed, they thought society could become perfect if people were given opportunities and were free to use their reason.

The early conservative Enlightenment movement was centered in England. It was largely a product of

Orange, the leader of the Dutch, and gave him a copy of a work justifying the revolt of Parliament. This work was finally published in 1690 as the *Second Treatise on Civil Government*. Its goals were to destroy absolute monarchy and to refute the theory of divine right.

Locke's *Second Treatise* attempted to support the new English political system by grounding it on the natural laws of psychology, economics, and politics. This justification of the Glorious Revolution of 1688 became the clarion call and rationale for every revolution for the next three centuries. In passing from his studies of Descartes, medicine, and the natural world to espousing the right of revolution in the Western world, Locke charted the transition from the Scientific Revolution to the Enlightenment and beyond.

The Age of Reason: English and Dutch Phases

Most Western writers and artists were aware that they lived in a new intellectual age, one that many philosophers called the Age of Reason. Its principles were based on Newtonian science, which dominated thinking at the

After his study of medicine and exile in the Netherlands, John Locke laid the foundations for modern democratic government, including the American Declaration of Independence, in his writings.

Herman Verelst, Portrait of John Locke. By Courtesy of the National Portrait Gallery, London.

Scientific advances and Enlightenment contributions came from all parts of Europe, from Königsberg in East Prussia to Rome to Glasgow.

the Glorious Revolution, when a group of Whig politicians, having secured control of Parliament and thereby Parliament's control of the king, tried to consolidate its hold on power and avoid further political disturbance. Newton himself identified with this group. He hoped that his system of nature would influence the public to respect political authority and strengthen belief in a God who ruled the stars and the solar system, as well as human beings.

At the same time, a secret society including the intellectual and business elites of England, the Masonic movement, encouraged by the Whig government, began organizing and pleading the cause of English limited monarchy on the Continent, where France was a major rival and a wartime enemy until 1713. By then the early English Enlightenment had reached maturity and was beginning to spread abroad.

A new radical version of the Enlightenment movement soon developed on the Continent. Many dissident English Whigs who had fled to Holland under the later Stuart kings and had failed to gain control of government after the Glorious Revolution, collaborated with

French Huguenots, who were exiled from France after Louis XIV revoked the Edict of Nantes. This latter group included Pierre Bayle (1647–1706), the French skeptic. Both French and English dissidents, led by the Anglo-Irish freethinker John Toland (1670–1772), were also influenced by Baruch Spinoza (1632–1677), a Jewish intellectual and the greatest Dutch philosopher, who accepted Newton's astronomy but denied Newton's contention that God controlled nature as a separate force. Spinoza taught that God existed in all of nature, which therefore ruled itself by its own laws. Such ideas, which developed into arguments against both state churches and monarchies, were spread slowly over the Continent by an underground press, financed by the radical Dutch Huguenots and many antiestablishment Masonic lodges.

The French Philosophes and the Radical Enlightenment

The Enlightenment remained largely moderate as it permeated French high society. Its leading proponents were known as *philosophes,* although the term cannot be literally translated into English as "philosophers." The *philosophes* were mostly writers and intellectuals who analyzed the evils of society and sought reforms in accordance with the principles of right reason and existing institutions. Their most supportive allies were *salonières,* socially conscious and learned women such as the Marquise du Châtelet (1706–1749), Voltaire's mistress, who translated Newton, and Madame de Tencin, whose natural son, Jean d'Alembert (1717–1783), was assistant editor of Diderot's *Encyclopédie.* The *salonières* regularly entertained *philosophes* in their salons, at the same time sponsoring their literary works, artistic creations, and new political ideas. By midcentury the *salonières,* their salons, and the *philosophes* had made France once again the intellectual center of Europe.

Two leading lights among the *philosophes* were the Baron de Montesquieu (1688–1755), a judicial official as well as a titled nobleman, and François-Marie Arouet, better known as Voltaire. Montesquieu was among the earliest critics of absolutist society. His *Persian Letters* (1721), purportedly from an Oriental traveler describing irrational European religious customs and behavior, delighted a large reading audience. His other great work, *The Spirit of Laws* (1748), expressed his main political principles, including checks and balances as safeguards of liberty.

More than any of the *philosophes,* Voltaire personified the skepticism of his century toward traditional religion and the injustices of the old regimes. His early exile in England converted him to Newtonian science and freedom of expression. With a caustic pen, he turned out hundreds of histories, plays, pamphlets, essays, and novels, as well as an estimated correspondence of 10,000 letters, including many to Frederick the Great of Prussia and Catherine the Great of Russia. Always he employed his wry wit in crusading for rationalism and reform of abuses. Even in his own time his reputation became a legend among kings as well as literate commoners.

Voltaire had many disciples, imitators, and critics among the *philosophes,* but his only rival in spreading the Enlightenment was a set of books, the French *Encyclopédie,* edited by Denis Diderot (1713–1784). Begun in 1751 and completed in 1772, it contained 28 volumes and more than 70,000 articles on every conceivable subject, many of which emphasized the supremacy of the new science, denounced superstition, expounded the merits of human freedom, exposed the evils of the slave trade, and denounced unfair taxes. It featured thousands of treatises on practical subjects dealing with agriculture, industry, and medicine, as well as others on art, architecture, literature, and philosophy. Authors included tradesmen and mechanics, along with professors and scientists.

During his lifetime, Voltaire went from being the subject of abuse by petty French nobles to being an internationally known celebrity, welcome at all the courts of Europe such as that of Frederick II.

The last volumes of the *Encyclopédie* became public just as the Enlightenment was producing discernible splits away from its earlier moderation. Unlike Newton's God, who not only supervised nature but also might decree miracles, the new God of Spinoza, an impersonal deity of immutable natural laws, was steadily gaining credibility. More extreme French materialists such as the Baron Paul Henri d'Holbach (1723–1789), Claude Helvetius (1715–1771), Julien de La Mettrie (1709–1751), and Étienne de Condillac (1715–1780) went further than Spinoza, using Newton's law and Locke's psychology to deny any reality except matter, reduce all thought to mere sensation, deny the soul's existence, and disclaim knowledge of any deity. At the other extreme, another argument subordinated reason to feeling as a way to truth and emphasized the natural goodness of human beings, which had been perverted in the past by inhumane institutions. Such new versions of the Enlightenment, even though pointing in different directions, were easily used against authorities by popular journalists, who appealed first to an alienated middle class and later, in the 1780s, to an awakening world of cafés, workshops, and city streets, particularly in Paris.

Perhaps the best known *philosophe* and the forerunner of many later radicals was that eccentric proponent of Romantic rebellion, Jean-Jacques Rousseau (1712–1778). Although believing in the general objectives of the Enlightenment, Rousseau distrusted reason and science. He gloried in human impulse and intuition, trusting emotions rather than thought, the heart rather than the mind. This emphasis was also true of his social criticism. His early rejections by polite society encouraged both contempt for old regimes and professed admiration for "noble savages," who lived completely free of law, courts, priests, and officials. In his numerous writings, Rousseau spoke passionately as a rebel against all established institutions. The most famous of his works, *The Social Contract* (1762), was Rousseau's indictment of absolute monarchy. It began with the stirring manifesto: "Man is born free, but today he is everywhere in chains."

Enlightenment Thought and Women

But few Enlightenment thinkers said "woman is born free." The Enlightenment thinkers disagreed on the place of women in the natural order of things. Although a few of them advocated extending the doctrine to include females, such voices were in the minority. Nevertheless, some women, even before the issue was raised forcefully during the French Revolution, staked their claims under the widely acclaimed laws of nature.

Although she was a monarchist and a follower of Descartes rather than Locke, Mary Astell (1666–1731) claimed legal equality for women on the basis of their innate rationality in her *Serious Proposal to the Ladies* (1694). This clarion call was not repeated for decades, but its echoes were manifest in the writings of English women such as Mary Montague (1689–1762), Catherine Macaulay (1731–1791), and Mary Wollstonecraft (1759–1797) during the eighteenth century. In France a number of *salonières*, including Madame de Puisseux (1720–1798) and Madame Gaçon-Dufour (1753–1835), wrote books defending their sex. Outside the salons, between 1761 and 1775, the *Journal des Dames*, a magazine edited by women, preached freedom, progress, and women's rights.

Before the French Revolution, the question of women's status in society did not concern many leading philosophers. Rousseau represented most of them when he described the ideal woman's proper role as housekeeper, mother, and quiet comforter of her husband, who was responsible for her protection

Mary Wollstonecraft participated fully in the English Enlightenment and was one of the founders of the English feminist movement.
John Opie, Portrait of Mary Wollstonecraft Godwin, c. 1797. Courtesy of the National Portrait Gallery, London.

and moral instruction. A few thinkers disagreed. Both Hobbes and Locke mildly questioned the idea that women were naturally subordinate to men. D'Alembert thought female limitations resulted from women's degradation by society, and Montesquieu saw absolute monarchy as the cause for women's lack of status. But the Marquis de Condorcet (1743–1794) was the only *philosophe* who made a special plea for feminine equality. In his *Letter of a Bourgeois of New Haven* (1787), he claimed that women's rationality entitled them to full citizenship, including the right to vote and hold public office. For the most part, however, his voice went unheard.

International Responses to the French Enlightenment

In the late eighteenth century the French Enlightenment exerted a powerful influence on Western civilization. Many young upper-class Englishmen visited France to complete their education. Among them were three leading English thinkers: Adam Smith (1723–1790), the Scottish father of modern economics; David Hume (1711–1776), the best-known English skeptic; and Jeremy Bentham (1748–1832), the founder of utilitarian philosophy. Another famous English rationalist was the historian Edward Gibbon

(1737–1794), whose *Decline and Fall of the Roman Empire* markedly criticized early Christianity, among many other things. Many English political radicals after 1770, including Joseph Priestley (1733–1804), Richard Price (1723–1791), and Thomas Paine (1737–1809), were greatly affected by French thought. Paine, who figured prominently in the American and French Revolutions, was also a leader in English radical politics.

The reforming doctrines of the radical Enlightenment spread over Europe and also reached the New World. A leading spokesman in Germany was Moses Mendelssohn (1729–1786), who wrote against dogmatism and in favor of natural religion. In Italy the humanist philosopher Cesare Beccaria (1738–1794) pleaded for humanitarian legal reforms. The Enlightenment was popular among the upper classes in such absolutist strongholds as Prussia, Russia, Austria, Portugal, and Spain. French ideas were read widely in Spanish America and Portuguese Brazil. In the English colonies Locke and the *philosophes* were known to Benjamin Franklin (1706–1790), Thomas Jefferson (1743–1826), Mercy Warren (1728–1814), and Abigail Adams (1744–1818).

Faith or Reason?

By the late eighteenth century, organized religion in Europe faced serious problems. The previous centuries of religious upheaval had produced many contending sects and lessened the unquestioning faith of medieval times. Overseas expansion and the resulting contacts with non-Christian religions led to the same result, as did the growing effectiveness of biblical scholarship. State churches, by often supporting corrupt regimes, also lowered respect for traditional Christianity. In addition to all these assaults was the earlier religious persecution of scientists, followed by the impact of the Newtonian revolution. The contrast between the orderly universe described by scientists and the relative chaos of human society was indeed shocking. Although many "enlightened" thinkers still believed that mystical religion was needed to pacify the credulous masses, such savants now began seriously reconsidering their religious ideas and institutions.

For such early thinkers as Descartes and Spinoza, the major theoretical problem was reconciling the mechanistic, self-regulating universe with the traditional belief in an all-powerful God. Descartes solved this problem for himself by dividing all reality between mind and matter. According to Descartes, both realms were governed by a divine will, but they appeared disconnected to human beings. Through science, human reason could accurately comprehend material reality; through faith and theology, the mind might know, directly from God, truths beyond the

world that is apparent to the senses. Thus Descartes, a loyal Catholic, sought to reconcile the old and the new. In contrast, his Dutch pupil, Spinoza, saw mind and matter as dual parts of nature, which was one with God. This pantheistic theory revealed God directly in every natural process, leaving no need for theology or supernatural revelation.

Another early school of religious theory tried to reconcile scientific law with God's free will by subordinating the former to the latter. Newton believed God could set the laws aside and perform miracles if they were needed. Locke, by contrast, argued that some apparent miracles, as described in the Bible, were actually explicable by laws not known at the time of occurrence. Such rationalistic supernaturalism was used by a number of Whig Anglican clergymen known as *latitudinarians*. They included John Tilloston (1630–1694), an archbishop of Canterbury, and Samuel Clarke (1675–1729), a chaplain to Queen Anne. Another approach, that of Thomas Reid (1710–1796), a Presbyterian minister, was to accept both science and Scripture and dissolve in common sense all philosophic conflicts remaining to plague the mind.

The most popular religious belief of the late Enlightenment was Deism. This belief involved a clear break with traditional Christianity, although most Deists accepted Jesus Christ as a great moral teacher. Deists believed in God as an impersonal force, the "master clockwinder" of the universe. Although some accepted the idea of an afterlife, Deists attached no significance to emotional faith as a means to salvation. They based all moral reliance on the individual's reason and conscience. Their common convictions also included rejection of miracles, disbelief in Christ's divinity or his virgin birth, and direct communion with God without need for church or clergy. Nature was the Deists' church, and nature's laws were their Bible. Their number included John Toland, Thomas Woolston (1679–1731), and Thomas Paine in England; Voltaire, Diderot, and d'Alembert in France; and Thomas Jefferson, Ethan Allen (1738–1789), and Elihu Palmer (1764–1806) in the English American colonies. Benjamin Franklin was a Deist as a youth but later gave up the commitment because he considered it politically impractical.

Deism was popular but somewhat logically inconsistent. If the universe operated automatically, how could people possess free will and assume moral responsibility? What material evidence indicated an afterlife? Such questions led some thinkers to religious skepticism and even atheism. Joseph Priestley, who was trained as an English minister and considered himself a Christian theologian, denied that the soul could exist apart from the body. David Hume, in his *Treatise on Human Nature* (1739), questioned the existence of both God and heaven, at the same time delivering a damaging blow against Deism. The most extreme views were professed in France, particularly in Holbach's circle. In *The System of Nature* (1770), Holbach denied the existence of God or any human purpose in the universe. Only a minority of Enlightenment thinkers, however, held such ideas.

Despite such differences among the details of belief, rationalist leaders of the Enlightenment were in almost perfect agreement on one point: They championed religious freedom of conscience. In addition, most were participants in a continuing struggle against alleged abuses of organized religion. Hundreds of their writings, especially those of Voltaire and the *philosophes*, depicted churches and priests as part of a vast conspiracy aimed at perpetuating tyranny. Their crusade for separating church and state was thus particularly threatening to absolutism.

Critiquing Mercantilism: The Physiocrats and Adam Smith

Natural law, a basic concept of the Enlightenment, was applied most consistently and effectively in economic arguments against absolutism. By the eighteenth century, developing capitalism clearly indicated the stimulus of profit to individual incentive. This realization, coming with the Scientific Revolution, strongly suggested that capitalism had outgrown mercantilism, with its state assistance and accompanying controls. The new economic philosophy contended that the free play of economic forces would automatically ensure the greatest prosperity.

Such ideas were expressed in the late 1600s but promoted more effectively by the *physiocrats,* a group of economic thinkers in eighteenth-century France. Their leading spokesman was François Quesnay (1694–1774), the personal physician to Louis XV, who also wrote for the *Encyclopédie.* Originally, Quesnay and his followers opposed Colbert's policy of subordinating agriculture to government-controlled industry. This narrow emphasis later developed into a comprehensive theory based on natural law. Quesnay, for example, compared the circulation of money to the circulation of blood. He likened mercantilist controls to tourniquets, which shut off a life-giving flow. Quesnay also denounced the mercantilist theory of bullionism, arguing that prosperity depended on production, not gold and silver in the royal treasury. According to another physiocrat, Robert Turgot (1720–1781), selfish profit-seeking in a free market would necessarily result in the best service and the most goods for society.

The most influential advocate of the new economic theory was a leader in the Scottish Enlightenment, Adam Smith, a professor of moral philosophy

Even though modern capitalism was well in place a century before his birth, Adam Smith wrote the definitive work on the functioning of the market.

at Glasgow University, who had visited France and exchanged ideas with the physiocrats. In 1776 Smith published *An Inquiry into the Nature and Causes of the Wealth of Nations,* in which he set forth his ideas. The work has since become the Bible of classical economic liberalism, extolling the doctrine of free enterprise or *laissez-faire* economics.

Smith was indebted to the physiocrats for his views on personal liberty, natural law, and the role of the state as a mere "passive policeman." He argued that increased production depended largely on division of labor and specialization. Because trade increased specialization, it also increased production. The growing volume of trade, in turn, depended on each person's being free to pursue individual self-interest. In seeking private gain, each individual was also guided by an "invisible hand" (the law of supply and demand) in meeting society's needs. As he wrote:

> It is not from the benevolence of the butcher, the brewer, or the baker that we expect our dinner, but from their reward to their own interests. We address ourselves not to their humanity, but to their self-love.

Smith regarded all economic controls, by the state or by guilds and trade unions, as injurious to trade. He scoffed at the mercantilist idea that the wealth of a nation depended on achieving a surplus of exports, amassing bullion, and crippling the

Adam Smith on Labor and Self-Interest

The final portion of this excerpt is perhaps the most often quoted. It is based on Bernard Mandeville's *Fable of the Bees,* first published in 1705.

This division of labor, from which so many advantages are derived, is not originally the effect of any human wisdom which foresees and intends that general opulence to which it gives occasion. It is the necessary, though very slow and gradual, consequence of a certain propensity in human nature which has in view no such extensive utility: the propensity to truck, barter, and exchange one thing for another.

Whether this propensity be one of those original principles in human nature, of which no further account can be given; or whether, as seems more probable, it be the necessary consequence of the faculties of reason and speech, it belongs not to our present subject to inquire. It is common to all men, and to be found in no other race of animals, which seem to know neither this nor any other species of contracts. Two greyhounds, in running down the same hare, have sometimes the appearance of acting in some sort of concert. Each turns her toward his companion, or endeavors to intercept her when his companion turns her toward himself. This, however, is not the effect of any contract, but of the accidental concurrence of their passions in the same object at that particular time. . . . When an animal wants to obtain something either of a man or of another animal, it has no other means of persuasion but to gain the favor of those whose service it requires. A puppy fawns upon its dam, and a spaniel endeavors by a thousand attractions to engage the attention of its master who is at dinner, when it wants to be fed by him. Man sometimes uses the same arts with his brethren, and when he has no other means of engaging them to act according to his inclinations, endeavors by every servile and fawning attention to obtain their good will. He has not time, however, to do this upon every occasion. In civilized society he stands at all times in need of the co-operation and assistance of great multitudes, while his whole life is scarcely sufficient to gain the friendship of a few persons. In almost every other race of animals each individual, when it is grown up to maturity, is entirely independent, and in its natural state has occasion for the assistance of no other living creature. But man has almost constant occasion for the help of his brethren, and it is in vain for him to expect it from their benevolence only. He will be more likely to prevail if he can interest their self-love in his favor, and show them that it is for their own advantage to do for him what he requires of them. Whoever offers to another a bargain of any kind proposes to do this. Give me that which I want, and you shall have this which you want, is the meaning of every such offer; and it is in this manner that we obtain from one another the far greater part of those good offices which we stand in need of. It is not from the benevolence of the butcher, the brewer, or the baker that we expect our dinner, but from their regard to their own interest. We address ourselves not to their humanity, but to their self-love, and never talk to them of our own necessities, but of their advantages. Nobody but a beggar chooses to depend chiefly upon the benevolence of his fellow citizens. Even a beggar does not depend upon it entirely. The charity of well-disposed people, indeed, supplies him with the whole fund of his subsistence. But though this principle ultimately provides him with all the necessities of life for which he has occasion, it neither does nor can provide him with them as he has occasion for them. . . .

From *Adam Smith: The Wealth of Nations*, ed. Bruce Mazlish. Copyright ©, 1961, 1989. Reprinted by permission of Macmillan Publishing Company.

economies of other countries. In Smith's view, trade should work to the benefit of all nations, which would follow if trade were free. In such a natural and free economic world, the prosperity of each nation would depend on the prosperity of all. He also saw colonies as potential economic drains on a colonial power.

A number of other thinkers in the late eighteenth century combined or elaborated the ideas of Smith and the physiocrats. In France, Holbach repudiated mercantilism, arguing that free trade would permit one nation to supply the deficiencies of another. Jeremy Bentham, in England, followed Smith in developing his idea of utilitarianism "as the greatest good for the greatest number," but he denied that economic equality would promote happiness because it would destroy incentive and limit production. Other commentators, such as Richard Price and Benjamin Franklin, suggested that rising wealth naturally increased the population, except in new lands where resources were almost unlimited. In one way or another, such propositions implied the basic idea that economic controls were futile or damaging to society.

Enlightenment of the Heart: Philosophical, Religious, and Humanitarian Movements

The Enlightenment was primarily a rational movement, but some of its proponents emphasized feeling as well. After about 1760, there was a general reaction against the major tenets of the materialistic Enlightenment. One form of the reaction came in philosophy with a new idealism, in opposition to earlier prevailing matter and motion explanations. Another form was an emotional religious revival, which won back many wavering Protestants and Catholics. A third form of the reaction replaced reason with religion as the justification for humanitarian reforms. These movements stressed emotion and faith over empirical reason but continued the Enlightenment's accent on individual liberty.

Newton's vision of celestial mechanics, Locke's reduction of knowledge to the mind's organization of experiences gained through the senses, and the literal interpretation of these ideas by materialistic atheists such as Holbach and La Mettrie evoked strong opposition. One opposing theory was that of skepticism of David Hume. Even more significant was a current of Platonic idealism in England, flowing from Mary Astell in the late 1600s through the writings of Bishop George Berkeley (1685–1753). Berkeley denied the possibility of knowing anything definite about the world external to the senses and the mind; in his view, internal mental impressions included vague suppositions about material reality, along with direct revelations from God. These extreme forms of idealism were modified, made more reasonable, and rendered much more widely acceptable by the German philosopher Immanuel Kant (1724–1804).

Kant, a professor at the University of Königsberg, was thoroughly antagonized by the skeptical and materialistic extremes of the Enlightenment. While appreciating science and dedicated to reason, he worked to shift philosophy back to a more sensible position without giving up much of its newly discovered rational basis. His theories, contained primarily in the *Critique of Pure Reason* (1781), ushered in a new age of philosophical idealism. Kant agreed with Locke on the role of the senses in acquiring knowledge of the material world but insisted that sensory experience had to be interpreted by the mind's internal nature. Thus certain ideas—the mind's categories for sorting and recording experiences—were a priori; that is, they existed before the sensory experience occurred. Typical innate ideas of this sort were width, depth, beauty, cause, and God; all were understood, yet none was learned directly through the senses. Kant concluded, as Descartes had, that some truths were derived from material objects not through the senses but through pure reason. Moral and religious truths, such as God's existence, could not be proved by science yet were known to human beings as rational creatures. Reason, according to Kant, could go beyond the mere interpretation of physical realities.

These insights, according to Kant, had certain practical applications to the lives of both individuals and society. In 1785 his *Fundamental Principles of the Metaphysics of Morals* explained the "categorical imperative," which could serve as a moral guide. The rational mind, according to Kant, must always judge an action wrong or immoral if it cannot be accepted as a universal law governing all human behavior. Commission of such an act must cause some pull at the conscience to create some inner discomfort to the person involved. Avoiding such discomfort requires the use of individual free will. The same maxim would apply to lawmaking for society as a whole and suggests Rousseau's concept of general will, which may have influenced Kant's thinking on the subject.

In Kant's philosophical system, pure reason, the highest form of human endeavor, was as close to intuition as it was to sensory experience. It proceeded from certain subjective senses, which were built into human nature. The idea of God derived logically from the mind's penchant for harmony. The human conscience, according to Kant, might be developed or be crippled by experience, but it originated in the person's thinking nature. Abstract reason, apart from science and its laws, was a valid source of moral judgment and religious interpretation. Thus Kant used reason to give a philosophical base to mystical religion.

Religious rationalism, despite its appeal to intellectuals, provoked considerable religious reaction. Part of this came from English theologians such as Bishop Joseph Butler (1692–1752) and William Paley (1743–1805), both of whom defended Christianity and challenged Deism on its own rational grounds. Even more significant was a widespread emotional revival, stressing religion of the heart rather than the mind.

The new movement, known as Pietism, reached full development in England after 1738 when the brothers John Wesley (1703–1791) and Charles Wesley (1708–1788), along with George Whitefield (1714–1770), began a crusade of popular preaching in the Church of England. The Anglican Pietists discarded traditional formalism and stilted sermons in favor of a glowing religious fervor, producing a vast upsurge of emotional faith among the English lower classes. In February 1739 Whitfield preached to 200 miners from on top of a coal tip; the following days thousands of people arrived to hear his words. Breaking out of the ordinary venues for religion, the Wesleys and Whitefield were called "Methodists," at first a term of derision. Later the term came to be the respected and official name for the new movement. After John Wesley's death in 1791, the Methodists officially left the Anglican church to become the most important independent religious force in England.

On the Continent, Lutheran Pietism, led by Philipp Spener (1635–1705) and Emanuel Swedenborg (1688–1772), followed a pattern similar to that of Methodism. Swedenborg's movement in Sweden began as an effort to reconcile science and revelation; after his death it became increasingly emotional and mystical. Spener, in Germany, stressed Bible study, hymn singing, and powerful preaching. The Moravian movement sprang from this background. Under the sponsorship of Count Nicholaus von Zinzendorf (1700–1760), it spread to the frontiers of Europe and to the English colonies in America.

The "Great Awakening," a tremendous emotional revival carried across the Atlantic from the European movements, was sustained by Moravians, Methodists, Baptists, and Quakers. It swept the colonial frontier areas of North America from Georgia to New England in the late eighteenth century. Women played prominent roles in this activity, organizing meetings and providing auxiliary services, running charities and providing religious instruction. Among the Quakers, women were often ministers and itinerant preachers. One was Jemima Wilkinson (1752–1819), leader of the Universal Friends; another was Ann Lee (1736–1784), who founded Shaker colonies in New York and New England.

By the 1780s, religious rationalism and Pietism were effectively balanced against each other. Their proponents disagreed passionately on religious principles but agreed on the issue of religious freedom. Both rationalists and Pietists were outside the state churches; both groups feared persecution and recognized the flagrant abuses of religious establishments. The two movements were therefore almost equally threatening to state churches and governing regimes.

One dominant characteristic of the early Enlightenment—the concern for individual human worth—was given new impetus by religion in the reaction against reason. The demand for reform and the belief in human progress were now equated with traditional Christian principles, such as human communality and God's concern for all people. Religious humanitarianism shunned radical politics and ignored the issue of women's rights, despite the movement's strong support among women. It did, however, seek actively to relieve human suffering and ignorance among children, the urban poor, prisoners, and slaves. This combination of humanitarian objectives and Christian faith was similar in some ways to the rational Enlightenment but markedly different in its emotional tone and religious justifications.

Notable among manifestations of the new desire to help others was the antislavery movement in Eng-

The English reformer John Howard was one of the first advocates of using prisons to rehabilitate their inmates, not to brutalize them.

land. A court case in 1774 ended slavery in that country. From then until 1807, a determined movement sought abolition of the slave trade. Its leader was William Wilberforce (1759–1833), aided by Hannah More (1745–1833) and other Anglican Evangelicals, along with many Methodists and Quakers. Wilberforce repeatedly introduced bills into the House of Commons that would have eliminated the traffic in human bodies. His efforts were rewarded in 1807 when the trade was ended, although he and his allies had to continue the struggle for 26 more years before they could achieve abolition in the British colonies.

Religious humanitarians enforced other movements that had been pushed by the rationalist Enlightenment. For example, the movements for both legal reform and prison reform were supported by religious groups before 1800. Universal education, extolled by rationalist thinkers, also aroused interest among the denominations. The Sunday School movement, particularly in England, was a forerunner of many private and quasi-public church schools. Finally, concern for the plight of slaves, coupled with rising missionary zeal, increased popular efforts to improve conditions for indigenous peoples in European possessions overseas.

Though not as openly political as other movements of the Enlightenment, the new humanitarianism played a significant part in weakening absolutism. It contributed to a spirit of restlessness and discontent while encouraging independent thought, particularly as it improved education. Its successful campaign against the slave trade also struck a direct blow at the old mercantilist economies, which depended so heavily on plantation agriculture overseas. In time the missionaries would also prove to be the most consistent enemies of colonialism.

The Political Critique: Absolutism as an Irrational Institution

Although proponents of the moderate Enlightenment were not revolutionaries and most favored monarchy and an aristocratic social order, they were avid reformers. In this role they developed a tightly organized philosophy, purportedly based on scientific principles and contradicting every argument for absolute monarchy as it generally existed in the eighteenth century. The case against absolutism, as presented by the *philosophes* and their foreign sympathizers, ultimately condemned divine right monarchy, hereditary aristocracies by birth, state churches, and mercantilism. Each was found to be irrational, unnatural, and therefore basically unsound.

The thinkers in the Enlightenment saw the arbitrary policies of absolute monarchs as violations of innate rights, which are required by human nature. The most fundamental part of this nature was reason, the means by which people learned and realized their potential. Learning, as described by Locke in his *Essay Concerning Human Understanding* (1690), consisted entirely of knowledge gained through the senses, interpreted by reason, and stored in memory. Locke admitted no internal sources of knowledge; he insisted that the mind at birth is like a blank piece of paper, on which experience writes. Later thinkers took this idea further than Locke wanted to go, seeing the absence of innate ideas as an indication that moral judgments were only the mind's response to pleasure or pain. Whether this was true, or whether the mind was guided by what the Scottish moderate Thomas Reid called "common sense," the individual was primarily a thinking and judging being who required maximum freedom to operate effectively. The best government, therefore, was the government that ruled least. This argument for human freedom was the heart of the antiabsolutist case.

One fundamental indictment against absolutism was its lack of human concern and moral purpose. Maintaining order by forcing or frightening people into conformity, according to the argument, destroyed the innate human potential for moral judgment. The social environment was thus responsible for corrupting people, who were naturally good, that is, they possessed an ethical potential, in reason, for identifying their own interests with the common welfare. From this precept it followed that removing corrupting social influences could perfect people. For example, Beccaria insisted that unjust and irrational laws should be changed so that they would teach morality and not just punish those who were caught. Prisons, argued the English reformer John Howard (1726–1790), should rehabilitate criminals, not brutalize them. Beccaria, Howard, and other eighteenth-century rationalists believed that humanitarian reforms, in accordance with nature's laws, would lead to unlimited human progress. Their message was voiced effectively by Condorcet, that most idealistic of the *philosophes*, in his *Progress of the Human Mind* (1795). Behind Condorcet's humanitarianism was a passionate faith in human freedom. Thinkers in the Enlightenment saw the arbitrary policies of absolute monarchs as violations of innate rights, which are required by human nature.

Political freedom, like religious freedom, depended ultimately on government, the source of most restrictions or coercion. For this reason political principles in the case against absolutism were fundamental to all others. They were developed in two main categories: ideas concerning individual rights and ideas concerning the organization of government. Both categories involved efforts that were directed at securing individual freedom against unnatural abuses of authority.

According to Locke and most political theorists of the Enlightenment, government existed to maintain order, protect property, defend against foreign enemies, and protect the natural rights of its people. This idea contradicted the divine right theory, which was held by most reigning monarchs in the seven-

One of the most charismatic figures in the history of Christianity, John Wesley spent nearly a half century preaching his message to nontraditional audiences, making his Methodist church the most independent religious force in England.

teenth and eighteenth centuries. Locke, along with many other Enlightenment thinkers including Rousseau, answered the divine right doctrine with the opposing theory of a social contract.

He agreed with Hobbes that the base of power was the people. But instead of seeing people as nasty and brutish, Locke saw that an existence in a free and equal society would bring out the best in human beings, as long as their property was defended and they lived in a state of reason. Locke asserted that people voluntarily came together to form governments for the protection of their basic rights, and it was the consent of the people—and that alone—that gave legitimacy to a government. He did not invent the concept of the social contract—the Huguenots in France had discussed it a century earlier. Hobbes had used the contract idea to justify royal authority; as we have seen, Locke turned Hobbes's argument around in his *Second Treatise on Government*, contending that political systems were originally formed by individuals for defense of their natural rights to life, freedom, and property, against local or foreign enemies. Such individuals voluntarily ceded to government the responsibility for protecting their natural rights. In this transaction, government's authority was derived from the governed. It was not absolute but was limited to performing the functions for which it was constituted. When its authority was used for other purposes, the contract was broken and the people were justified in forming another government.

As insurance against abuses of political authority, theorists of the Enlightenment generally advocated the separation of powers. Locke, for example, proposed that kings, judges, magistrates, and legislatures should share authority and thus check one another. Spinoza also stressed the need for local autonomy and a locally based militia to guard against power concentrated in a central government. Montesquieu, although somewhat skeptical about natural laws and Locke's version of the social contract, advocated the separation of powers in his *Spirit of the Laws,* as did most of the other *philosophes.*

Political freedom and guarantees for human rights were common goals, but ideas concerning the ideal form of government varied considerably. The majority of the *philosophes* were not necessarily opposed to monarchy, despite their rejection of the divine right principle. Voltaire and Montesquieu believed that rule by a "benevolent despot," aided by an aristocracy of integrity and talent, was the most likely way to attain desirable reforms. A few monarchs were inspired by this revived Platonic ideal of the philosopher king, but the results of their policies did not always match their principles.

Perhaps the most popular form of government, particularly during the early Enlightenment, was constitutional monarchy on the English model. Locke, of course, was the recognized spokesman for the Glorious Revolution and the limited English monarchy established by Parliament. Both Voltaire and Diderot were very much impressed with the English system as they understood it. Montesquieu praised it as a practical balance of traditional forces, which secured liberty without sacrificing order.

Concern for internal order was typical of most political thought in the Enlightenment. Both Locke and Voltaire, to name only two well-known examples, advocated that political power be confined to property owners. This, they believed, would secure sound government against the irresponsible masses, at the same time holding open opportunities for intelligent and industrious citizens. Presumably, those with the most to lose from anarchy could best be trusted with political rights. Such ideas also squared with the English parliamentary system, dominated as it was by landed property owners.

Only a few proponents of the Enlightenment believed in democracy as a form of government. Like their more conservative colleagues, they were afraid of mob action but even more afraid of monarchs, aristocrats, and large centralized polities. They saw the ballot box as another check on arbitrary government and regarded political rights, particularly the franchise, as the ultimate security for personal liberty. Because democratic ideas were so uncommon, they were often qualified in their expression. In America, for example, Thomas Jefferson suggested that common men should be represented in government, but he also accepted the property-based franchise. He harmonized the apparent contradiction by arguing that most small farmers in reality own land. Other vague democratic references, sometimes contradictory, appeared in the political writings of Bentham, Priestley, Price, Paine, and Wollstonecraft.

Since the late eighteenth century Rousseau has been somewhat mistakenly considered the great democrat among the French *philosophes*. Admittedly, he respected the republican institutions of his native Geneva, but he did not think them appropriate for a large state such as France. Along with Diderot, he also exalted the "general will" as representing the interests of the community or nation over the selfish interests of individuals. By general will, however, Rousseau meant not majority rule but the social contract as expressed in generally accepted law. This law, he thought, should secure each individual's freedom, up to the point where it threatened the freedom of others. Rousseau did not clearly oppose democracy, but he was more interested in the abstract idea of legal equality. His so-called democracy was most evident in his general opposition to monarchy, hereditary aristocracy, and polite society.

These differences over forms of government were inconsequential compared with the points of political agreement among thinkers of the Enlightenment. All of them rejected the idea of divine right monarchy

John Locke on the Origin of Government

In this passage Locke presents his assumptions about human adversities in "a state of nature," which led to the cooperative forming of states and made all governments logically responsible to their citizens.

Men being, as has been said, by nature all free, equal, and independent, no one can be put out of this estate, and subjected to the political power of another, without his own consent. The only way by which any one divests himself of his natural liberty and puts on the bonds of civil society is by agreeing with other men to join and unite into a community for their comfortable, safe, and peaceable living one amongst another, in a secure enjoyment of their properties, and a greater security against any that are not of it. This any number of men may do, because it injures not the freedom of the rest; they are left as they were in the liberty of the state of nature. When any number of men have so consented to make one community or government, they are thereby presently incorporated, and make one body politic, wherein the majority have a right to act and conclude the rest.

For when any number of men have, by the consent of every individual, made a community, they have thereby made that community one body, with a power to act as one body, which is only by the will and determination of the majority. For that which acts any community being only the consent of the individuals of it, and it being necessary to that which is one body to move one way, it is necessary the body should move that way whither the greater force carries it, which is the consent of the majority. . . . And therefore we see that in assemblies empowered to act by positive laws, where no number is set by that positive law which empowers them, the act of the majority passes for the act of the whole, and of course determines, as having by the law of nature and reason the power of the whole.

And thus every man, by consenting with others to make one body politic under one government, puts himself under an obligation to every one of that society, to submit to the determination of the majority, and to be concluded by it; or else this original compact, whereby he with others incorporates into one society, would signify nothing, and be no compact, if he be left free and under no other ties than he was in before in the state of nature. For what appearance would there be of any compact? What new engagement if he were no farther tied by any decrees of the society, than he himself thought fit, and did actually consent to? This would be still as great a liberty as he himself had before his compact, or any one else in the state of nature hath, who may submit himself and consent to any acts of it if he thinks fit. . . .

Whosoever therefore out of a state of nature unite into a community must be understood to give up all the power necessary to the ends for which they unite into society, to the majority of the community, unless they expressly agreed in any number greater than the majority. And this is done by barely agreeing to unite into one political society, which is all the compact that is, or needs be, between the individuals that enter into make up a commonwealth. And thus that which begins and actually constitutes any political society is nothing but the consent of any number of freemen capable of a majority to unite and incorporate into such a society. And this is that, and that only, which did or could give beginning to any lawful government in the world. . . .

From John Locke, *Second Treatise on Government*, in *Sources of British Political Thought*, ed. Wilfrid Harrison (New York: Macmillan, 1956), pp. 55–57.

and considered monarchs to be the public servants of their peoples and to be obligated to maintain natural rights for all. These rights to life, liberty, and property, as construed by the *philosophes* and their friends abroad, seriously threatened absolutist systems.

It was Locke who made the most forceful political statement. In a state of nature, said Locke, people have two powers: to do what is necessary for the preservation of their rights and to respect the rights of others. These two powers naturally devolved into the legislative and the executive functions; of the two, the legislative function was the more important, for it was here where people maintained their dignity. The executive power was inferior to that of the legislature. It could not enslave or destroy any right or go against the foundations of the laws of nature. If it did so, the people had the right to overthrow it.

The Failure of Monarchical Reform

All politics is involved in the answer to the question "What is human nature?" Hobbes and the absolutists, and their descendants, found humanity vile and unworthy. The people of the Enlightenment found humanity decent and perfectible and thus provided the modern world with notions of liberty. The absolutists who read and agree with the Enlightenment writings tried to bridge the gap between their royal prerogatives and the teachings of the Enlightenment. The "enlightened despots" who tried to do this, and the French monarchs—who employed thinkers of the Enlightenment—failed to solve the paradox.

As old regimes faltered after the middle of the eighteenth century, an urgent need to respond to the problems of the day challenged the rulers of major European states. Neither the nobles nor the clergies, despite their high social status and political power, could provide necessary leadership because they were committed to protecting their privileges, particularly immunity from taxation, which threatened the financial security of most countries. Responding to the literature of the Enlightenment, action by the enlightened despots did bring some curtailment of mercantilism, peasant exploitation, and government repression and seemed to offer a belated best hope for solving the problem. This hope, however, soon proved to be inadequate.

The French Debacle

The necessity for monarchical leadership was well understood in France, where the theory of benevolent or enlightened despotism originated. The proponents were mostly French middle-class intellectuals, such as Voltaire and Diderot. Their writings were widely read in many European courts in a continued deference to French ideas, which were considered to be the latest in intellectual fashion. Their appeal, however, was more than a literary fad because the need for forceful royal action was so pressing that it could hardly be ignored.

The last Bourbon kings in France before the Revolution, Louis XV and his grandson Louis XVI (1774–1792) responded halfheartedly to these reforming ideas. Although he was almost indifferent to affairs of state and dozed through his council meetings, Louis XV abolished serfdom on royal lands, tried twice to tax the nobles, and attempted to curtail the special privileges of the traditional courts, particularly the most aristocratic *parlement* (court) of Paris. Each attempt led to years of controversy between the government and the nobles; in each instance Louis ultimately gave up the fight.

Louis XVI was well-meaning but poorly educated, lazy, and shy. Avoiding government business, he spent his happiest hours in a workshop, tinkering with locks. His child bride, the frivolous Habsburg princess Marie Antoinette, furnished him with no wisdom or practical support. Although dimly aware

Enlightened Despotism

1740–1780	Reign of Maria Theresa of Austria
1740–1786	Reign of Frederick II of Prussia
1762–1796	Reign of Catherine the Great of Russia
1780–1790	Reign of Joseph II of Austria

of problems, Louis was no more successful than his grandfather. The clamor of the nobles forced him to abandon proposals for eliminating the more undeserved pensions and levying a very modest tax on all landed property.

"Enlightened Despotism" Outside France

Unlike the later Bourbons, some eighteenth-century kings earned recognized historical reputations—some generated by themselves—as "enlightened despots." Perhaps the major figure in this "monarch's age of repentance" was Frederick II of Prussia, known as "the Great," who became a model ruler during the second half of his reign. An avowed admirer of Voltaire, Frederick in his writings popularized the ideal monarch as the "first servant of the state," the "father of his people," and the "last refuge of the unfortunate."[2] "Old Fritz," as his subjects called him, was slavishly committed to his principles. He left his bed at 5 each morning and worked until dark, reading reports, supervising, traveling, listening to complaints, and watching every aspect of government.

Under Frederick, Prussia was considered the best-governed state in Europe. Within only a few years it recovered economically from the terrible ravages of war, largely through the state's aid in distributing seed, livestock, and tools. Frederick lessened the burdens of serfs on crown estates, imported new crops, attracted skilled immigrants, opened new lands, and tried to promote new industries, such as silk and other textiles. He codified the law and reorganized the courts, along with the civil service. Following ideas he had learned from French philosophy, he established civil equality for Catholics, abolished torture in obtaining confessions from criminals, decreed national compulsory education, and took control of the schools away from the church. Until he died in 1786, Frederick worked diligently at improving Prussia.

His achievements, nevertheless, were more despotic than enlightened, and his successes were matched by some failures. Although Frederick played the flute, wrote French poetry, and corresponded with Voltaire, his reforms were continuations of his father's mercantilism rather than adjustments to changes in his time. His monetary policy caused inflation, and this, along with his support of state monopolies, seriously hurt many Prussian merchants. Frederick's agricultural program avoided abolition of serfdom. His use of French tax farmers precipitated civil disorders, and his consistent appointment of aristocrats as officials helped exclude the middle class from government. Even his religious and educational reforms were marred by official discrimination against Jews and failure to provide necessary funds for schools. Frederick's approach succeeded so well because it came at a time when mercantilism still worked in Prussia. It left much to be done later, when social change would require different policies.

Frederick's contemporary, Catherine II of Russia, was also known in her time as an enlightened despot and as "the Great." Having learned the politics of survival at the Russian court, she had conspired with palace guards to kill her erratic husband, Peter, and have herself declared tsarina in 1762. She was a ruth-

Even though Catherine II spoke of governing Russia in accordance with Enlightenment principles, the condition of the Russian peasant reached its lowest point during her reign.

less Machiavellian in foreign affairs, with far more lovers than many male monarchs. She also was a sensitive woman who appreciated the arts, literature, and the advantages of being considered enlightened. She corresponded with Voltaire and gave Diderot a pension. The latter even stayed at her court for a year, meeting with her daily for private discussions on intellectual subjects, including improvements for her empire.

Catherine's reign brought considerable enlightenment and social progress to St. Petersburg society. She subsidized artists and writers, permitted publication of controversial works, established libraries, patronized galleries, and transformed the capital city with beautiful architecture. Catherine also founded hospitals and orphanages, notably those providing foundling children with improved education, one of her main interests. During the decade after 1775 she tried to start a national system of elementary and secondary schools. In that same year she began a reorganization of local government, including the cities, one of many administrative reforms that literally demilitarized civil administration in the empire by turning it over to her partners in assassination, the nobility. She secularized church land, restricted the use of torture, and won acclaim for her much publicized orders to a royal commission charged with modernizing and codifying Russian laws.

Catherine's program, however, like Frederick's, was limited in scope and significance. Almost every reform had been attempted or suggested earlier and enhanced royal authority. For example, rigid state control and political indoctrination of the curriculum was fixed in the new educational system. Local government after 1775 was controlled by aristocratic landowners, while aristocrats in the commission sabotaged the much heralded legal reforms. Such deference to the aristocracy was typical of Catherine's later internal policies following the disastrous peasant revolt of the 1770s, when the nobles' hysteria forced her to issue a charter giving them freedom from taxes, release from compulsory government service, and guaranteed ownership of their serfs. The reaction thus begun was continued during the French Revolution, when Catherine reversed most of her earlier stated liberal opinions and imposed severe censorship. Her political legacy was a rigid autocracy, based on support from an aristocratic elite infected by Western liberal ideals.

The most radical of the would-be benevolent despots was Joseph II (1780–1790), the son of Maria Theresa and her successor as Habsburg ruler of Austria. He was intelligent and well educated; indeed, Catherine called him "the most solid, profound, and best-informed mind I have ever met." He was also completely converted to the principles of the new philosophers. "I have made philosophy the legislator of my empire," he wrote to a friend in 1781, shortly after his accession.[3] During his whole reign he fancied

Catherine the Great Assumes Power in Russia

Catherine became empress in 1762 in a coup that overthrew her estranged husband, Peter III. This selection is from her own written account of the episode.

I was sleeping calmly at Peterhof at 6 o'clock in the morning.... The day had been a very disturbing one for me as I knew all that was going on. [Suddenly] Alexius Orlov enters my room and says quite gently: "It is time to get up; all is ready for your proclamation. ..." I dressed myself quickly without making my toilet and got into the carriage which he had brought with him....

Five versts [about 3 miles] from the town I met the elder Orlov with the younger Prince Bariatinsky. Orlov gave up his carriage to me, for my horses were done up, and we got out at the barracks of the Ismailovsky Regiment. [At the gates] were only twelve men, and a drummer, who began sounding an alarm, when the soldiers came running out, kissing me, embracing my hands and feet and clothes, and calling me their deliverer. Then they began swearing allegiance to me. When this had been done, they begged me to get into the carriage, and the priest, cross in hand, walked on in front. We went [first] to the [barracks of the] Semenovsky Regiment, but the regiment came marching out to meet us, crying, Vivat! Then we went to the church of Kazan, where I got out. Then the Preobrazhensky Regiment arrived, crying, Vivat! "We beg your pardon," they said to me, "for being the last. Our officers stopped us, but here are four of them whom we have arrested to shew you our zeal. We want what our brothers want." Then the horse-guards arrived frantic with joy, I never saw anything like it, weeping and crying at the deliverance of their country.... I went to the new Winter Palace where the Synod and the Senate were assembled. A manifesto and a form of oath were hastily drawn up. Then I

went down and received the troops on foot. There were more than 14,000 men, guards and country regiments. As soon as they saw me they uttered cries of joy which were taken up by an innumerable crowd. I went on to the old Winter Palace to take [my] measures and finish [the business,] there we took counsel together, and it was resolved to go to Peterhof, where Peter III was to have dined with me, at their head. All the great roads had been occupied and rumours came in every moment....

Peter III abdicated, at Oranienbaum, in full liberty, surrounded by 5000 Holsteiners, and came with Elizabeth Vorontsov, Gudovich and Ismailov to Peterhof, where, to protect his person, I gave him five officers and some soldiers.... Thereupon I sent the deposed Emperor to a remote and very agreeable place called Ropsha, 25 versts [about 16 miles] from Peterhof, under the command of Alexius Orlov, with four officers and a detachment of picked, good-natured men, whilst decent and convenient rooms were being prepared for him at Schlusselburg. But God disposed otherwise. Fear had given him a diarrhoea which lasted three days and passed away on the fourth; in this [fourth] day he drank excessively, for he had all he wanted except liberty. Nevertheless, the only things he asked me for were his mistress, his dog, his Negro and his violin; but for fear of scandal and increasing the agitation of the persons who guarded him, I only sent him the last three things....

From Warren B. Walsh, comp. and ed., *Readings in Russian History* (Syracuse, N.Y.: Syracuse University Press, 1948), pp. 185–187.

himself a royal voice of reason, fighting for human progress against ignorance, superstition, and vice.

Joseph's reign was an explosion of reform effort that threatened to blow down much of the old aristocratic Habsburg structure. He proposed to simplify Catholic services, abolish the monasteries, take over church lands, remove religion from education, and grant civil equality to Protestants and Jews. Attacking the ancient landed establishment head on, he planned to tax the nobles, abolish entail of their lands, and free the serfs. With increasing revenues, he hoped to finance national education, balance the budget, and improve opportunities for industry and trade. The whole undertaking would be consolidated and regulated under a comprehensive code of laws.

Despite their theoretical benefits, Joseph's endeavors aroused a storm of protest, lasting through the reign and bringing him practical failure. For all of his interest in progress, Joseph was a hardheaded and narrow-minded autocrat, determined to build a state on an Enlightenment model. His administrative reforms were aimed not only at higher efficiency but also at centralized government over all the multicultured Habsburg territories. His attempted unification of administration seriously alienated the Hungarians and provoked revolts in the Low Countries, Bohemia, and the Tyrol. Peasants were angry because he subjected them to compulsory military service, the clergy harangued against him, and the nobles conspired to hinder the conduct of government at every

Joseph II

Joseph's brand of enlightened despotism, as well as his inflexibility and his jealousy of more renowned monarchs, is revealed in this private letter, written in the 1780s.

To Tobias Philip, Baron von Gebler, Bohemian and Austrian Vice-Chancellor, March 1785

Mr. Vice-Chancellor,— The present system of taxation in my dominions, and the inequality of the taxes which are imposed on the nation, form a subject too important to escape my attention. I have discovered that the principles on which it is founded are unsound, and have become injurious to the industry of the peasant; that there is neither equality, nor equity, between the hereditary provinces with each other, nor between individual proprietors, and therefore it can no longer continue.

With this view I give you the necessary orders to introduce a new system of taxation, by which the contribution, requisite for the wants of the state, may be effected without augmenting the present taxes, and the industry of the peasant, at the same time, be freed from all impediments.

Make these arrangements the principal object of your care, and let them be made conformably to the plan which I have proposed, particularly as I have nominated you President of the Aulic Commission, appointed for that purpose.

Adieu, Gebler! Hasten every thing that brings me nearer to the accomplishment of my plans for the happiness of my people, and, by your zeal, justify the respect which they have always had for your services.

From Harry J. Carroll et al., eds., *The Development of Civilization*, Vol. 2 (Glenview, Ill.: Scott, Foresman, 1970), pp. 142–143.

level. He died in 1790, painfully aware of his unfulfilled ideals.

There were other, less well-known enlightened despots during the period. One was Joseph's brother Leopold of Tuscany, who was not only enlightened but also flexible and practical. Without throwing his little country into turmoil, he abolished the Inquisition and reformed the penal code, according to the principles of Italian humanist philosopher Cesare Beccaria. Another successful enlightened despot was Charles Frederick of Baden, who freed the serfs, promoted agrarian development, and achieved the fiscal regularity to make his little country a prosperous German state. Gustavus III of Sweden seized power from the nobles by force. He then reorganized the justice system, abolished torture, reformed agriculture, made taxes more equitable, improved education, decreed religious toleration, and established freedom of the press. Unfortunately, he was assassinated. Charles III of Spain crushed the Jesuits, simplified the legal system, improved education, and balanced the budget, but he was a cruel tyrant.

Even with all their good intentions and achievements, benevolent despots proved incapable of rooting out the deep-seated problems of the old regimes. Most of them underestimated the need for change and overestimated the durability of their traditional systems. All were dependent on, and therefore prisoners of, outmoded aristocratic orders. They were also usually limited by chaotic administrative systems and mounting public debts. They were hopelessly squeezed between a static past and a dynamic future.

The American Revolution

The legacy of the constitutional experiments and the intellectual tools of the Enlightenment came together across the Atlantic in North America. English settlers had come to America for commercial reasons, in search of religious freedom, to seek political refuge, and to better their lot in life. Soon people from other European nations arrived, and the culture began to take on an identity of its own. The North American colonies got caught up in the world struggle that was the Seven Years' War; the view from London was that they should pay higher taxes to ensure their own defense. The problem was made more severe with the accession of King George III (1760–1820), who was a confirmed believer in divine right monarchy.

The Decision to Rebel

Pressure from England helped bring the revolutionary movement to the moment of action. And within a decade after passage of the Stamp Act of 1765, Britain faced open rebellion in its American colonies. The resulting conflagration was also a civil war, with many colonists remaining loyal to the crown. Indeed, Benjamin Franklin's son was a Loyalist leader and the last royal governor of New Jersey. Most colonists were probably apolitical, intent on their own affairs, but a vocal majority of the politically minded, whether New England merchants, Virginia planters, urban intellectuals, or simple farmers, formed an angry and determined opposition. Their outlook combined Locke's political ideas with a spirit of rough

By granting equality to Jews and Protestants, abolishing monasteries, and freeing the serfs, the Habsburg Emperor Joseph II was the most radical of the Enlightened Despots.

frontier independence; it was also nationalistic in its dawning awareness that many English ways were foreign to American needs and values.

John Adams (1735–1826), looking back on the Revolution, was well aware of this maturing American nationalism. He wrote:

> *But what do we mean by the American Revolution? Do we mean the American war? The Revolution was effected before the war commenced . . . in the minds and hearts of the people. . . . This . . . was the real American Revolution.*[4]

From almost the beginning, the American colonies had developed in a direction different from England's. Most Puritan (Calvinist) settlers in New England opposed the early Stuart kings; at the Restoration, a host of rebels fled to America. Many Catholics, favored by the later Stuarts and persecuted at home after the Glorious Revolution, came to the colonies, particularly to Maryland. By 1775 some 40 percent of the colonial population was of non-English stock, mostly from Ireland and southern Germany. After 1750 a popular party in Massachusetts opposed British ways, particularly British attempts to restrict colonial manufacturing, dictate terms for colonial foreign trade, and influence the actions of colonial legislatures.

Experience in self-government conditioned colonial development. Except for an unsuccessful attempt at colonial domination under James II, England had steadily relaxed controls. This trend was particularly typical of relations between the colonies and the home government under the corrupt and static Whig oligarchy, whose leaders became proponents of stability as they gained power. Preoccupied by more pressing political concerns, they allowed the colonists relative freedom to conduct their own affairs. In contrast, radical political opinion, driven deep underground in England after 1649, ran much nearer to the surface in America, where Locke's later emphasis on the social contract appealed to people who had created their own governments in the wilderness and who were somewhat suspicious of a distant king. By 1763 only Maryland and New Hampshire had not attained practical autonomy, and even they were well on their way when the shooting began in 1775.

Colonial political thought was shaped as much by growth and mobility as by historical circumstances. Over 2 million discontented Europeans arrived in the eighteenth century. They formed a vast lower class of indentured servants, tenants, and manual workers, sharply differentiated from wealthy New England merchants or southern planters. Many other immigrants, mainly the Scotch-Irish, pushed toward the frontiers and settled on free or cheap western land. Its easy availability fostered the idea of property as an individual's birthright, so that Prime Minister George Grenville's restriction on westward migration after 1763 aroused general resentment against an assumed

English effort to monopolize land for a privileged aristocracy. Land speculators condemned the policy as a violation of free enterprise and at the same time found an ambiguous common interest with craftsmen, merchants, and planters, who felt themselves dominated and exploited by British mercantilism.

The Peace of Paris of 1763 that ended the Seven Years' War, followed by the Grenville program, brought all the major differences between Britain and the colonies into focus. With foreign enemies out of Canada and Florida, new land beckoned colonists who no longer felt the need for British protection. They naturally abhorred new taxes and trade controls required by rising imperial costs. British troops, under the circumstances, were regarded as oppressors rather than defenders or peacekeepers. To make matters worse, a general economic depression, reflecting British postwar financial difficulties in the late 1760s, hit most colonial economies hard, particularly that of New England.

Contentions between the home government and the colonies deteriorated into open civil war by 1775 and complete separation by the following year. This result was not planned, hoped for, or even foreseen by the colonists. More than 20 percent of them remained loyal to Britain, and no more than one-sixth of the male population ever took up arms. The true rebels consisted largely of the merchants, smugglers, and large landowners who were most hurt by the new British policies, supported by doctrinaire leaders of aroused urbanites and small farmers. Although not originally committed to independence, both groups dreamed of a future America as a center of power, prosperity, and freedom.

The first colonial protests came with the Grenville program, when the Sugar Act prompted arguments against taxation without representation in colonial newspapers and pamphlets. These reactions were mild, however, in comparison with those following the Stamp Act. Colonial assemblies in Massachusetts and New York denounced the law as "tyranny," and a "Stamp Act Congress" meeting in New York petitioned the king to repeal the law. Mob actions occurred in a number of places, but they were less effective than boycotts of English goods, imposed by 1000 colonial merchants. Soon hundreds of English tradesmen were petitioning Parliament, pleading that the taxes be rescinded. They were in 1766, although Parliament issued a declaration affirming its absolute right to legislate for the colonies.

Having repealed the Stamp Act, Parliament almost immediately enacted other revenue measures. Charles Townshend (1725–1767), the new chancellor of the exchequer, had Parliament levy duties on imported paint, paper, lead, wine, and tea. Other laws decreed that admiralty courts, which functioned without juries, should sit in specified ports and enforce all trade regulations. In response, some Boston merchants, mainly

Economic conflicts between the British and their colonists escalated into violence at the Boston Massacre.

the habitual smugglers, generated lively protests. The big wholesalers, who saw renewed boycotts of British goods as a means for reducing their overstocked warehouses, joined them. Samuel Adams (1722–1803), the main radical leader, whipped up anti-British feeling on Boston streets. This culminated on March 5, 1770, when soldiers fired into an unruly mob, killing five people. Some lesser American merchants began to waver, but nonimportation agreements had cut British imports by 50 percent and induced Parliament to repeal most duties on the very day of the Boston Massacre.

For a while the colonies seemed angry but pacified, until Lord North (1732–1792), the king's new chief minister, persuaded Parliament to grant a two-thirds cut in duties on East India Company tea delivered to American ports. Because the company could thus undersell smugglers and legitimate tea merchants, both of these groups again resorted to political radicalism. The tea was turned away from most American ports. In what became known as the Boston Tea Party, Sam Adams's "patriots," thinly disguised as Indians, stole onto a ship and dumped its load of tea into the harbor. Parliament retaliated with the "Intolerable Acts," which closed the port of Boston, revoked the Massachusetts Charter, and provided that political offenders be tried in England.

The Revolutionary War

By September 1774 the Boston crisis had created a revolutionary climate. Representatives of 12

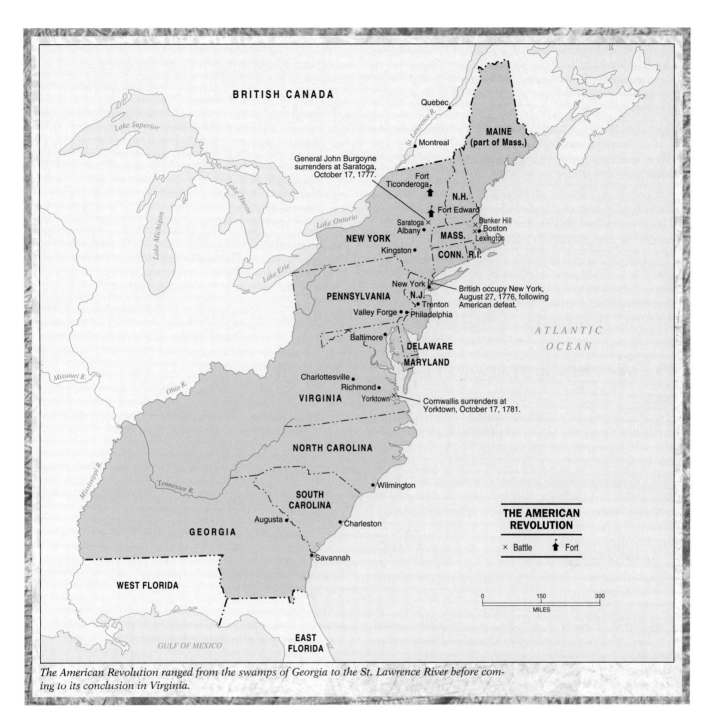

The American Revolution ranged from the swamps of Georgia to the St. Lawrence River before coming to its conclusion in Virginia.

colonies, meeting in the First Continental Congress at Philadelphia, denounced British tyranny, proclaimed political representation to be a natural right, and made plans for armed resistance. In April of the next year, the explosive situation around Boston finally led to a conflict between British regulars and the Massachusetts militia at nearby Lexington and Concord in which eight Americans and 293 English soldiers were killed. Those "shots heard round the world" marked the beginning of the American Revolution.

The war begun at Lexington and Concord lasted eight years. British troops, besieged in Boston, failed

to break out in June 1775 at Bunker Hill. Shortly afterward, General George Washington (1732–1799) accepted command of American forces from the recently convened Second Continental Congress. Long after the British had abandoned Boston in March 1776, his outnumbered and ill-provisioned troops fought defensive battles for survival, an ordeal climaxed at Valley Forge, in Pennsylvania, in the desolate winter of 1777–1778, when the ragged American army almost disintegrated from cold, hunger, and desertion. It was a time, in Thomas Paine's words, "to try men's souls," but it was also a time for dreams of renewed liberties and new opportunities.

The turning point of the war came in October 1777. Having occupied New York and Philadelphia, the British tried to split the country with an army moving south from Canada. Its crushing defeat at Saratoga, in upper New York, effected a diplomatic revolution. France, which had been a cautious and unofficial supplier, now entered the war on the American side and soon persuaded its Spanish ally to do the same. The Dutch followed in a desperate effort to save their American trade. With its sea power thus countered, the British pulled their two main armies back to defensive positions in New York and Virginia. The war reached its conclusion in the southern campaigns in 1781, when French and American troops, aided by the French fleet, forced the British commander, Lord Cornwallis (1738–1805), to surrender at Yorktown, Virginia. This defeat, along with many threats abroad, caused the British to recognize the Americans' independence in the Treaty of Paris (1783).

Creating a Nation: The Logic of Locke

While the war continued, American political leaders were forming a new nation. Paine's *Common Sense,* published early in 1776 as an emotional plea for liberty, inflamed popular passions and helped convince the American Congress to break with England. In June a congressional committee drafted a formal statement of principles. The resulting Declaration of Independence, written by Thomas Jefferson, first announced the creation of the United States. In claiming for every individual "certain unalienable rights . . . to life, liberty, and the pursuit of happiness," it also used typical natural law theory in a direct appeal to radical opinion.

An angrier radicalism born of army wages not paid and taxes incurred among poor civilians marked the late war years. Economic depression and other hardships created suspicions of the highborn and wealthy leaders who were so prominent in national government. This localism was evident in the Articles of Confederation, a national constitution finally ratified by the states in 1781. It stipulated that taxation, control of trade, and issuance of money all be left to the sovereign states, each represented by one vote in Congress. Major decisions required the assent of nine states, and amendments required unanimous agreement of all 13. Although Congress could make war and peace, maintain armies, and conduct Indian affairs, it was financially dependent on the states for these functions. The system was designed to protect liberties against a distant central government dominated by an upper class.

More obvious signs of populism came in new state governments. Their constitutions, often ratified in town meetings, called for the separation of executive, judicial, and legislative powers. Bills of rights typically guaranteed freedom of speech, press, and religion. Property requirements for voting were considerably lowered. Many great Loyalist estates were also divided into smallholdings, and 11 of the 13 states severed church-state ties. Although such innovations were often more public commitments to theory than drastic institutional changes, they did indicate more political participation by the common people, particularly those from the western backcountry in every state.

The 1780s, under the Articles of Confederation, brought serious postwar problems. With so much power distributed among the states, the national government was severely hampered in negotiating commercial treaties with foreign states, maintaining adequate military forces, promoting internal economic development, and maintaining domestic order. While the states contended with one another, former soldiers and impoverished civilians demanded back pay, pensions, land, and cheap paper money to pay their debts. In Massachusetts a former army officer named Daniel Shays (1747–1825) even led a brief rebellion. George Washington and other national leaders, convinced that the prevailing disunity and disorder threatened property as well as the nation's survival, urged a reconsideration of the Articles. Their efforts led to a convening of delegates from 12 state legislatures, who met in Philadelphia from May to September 1787.

The Constitution of the United States

Because few radicals attended the convention, its delegates were concerned primarily with protecting property and strengthening the union. The arguments of the framers of the Constitution were expressed in a series of newspaper articles that came to be known collectively as the *Federalist Papers.* In these essays, people such as Alexander Hamilton and James Madison debated the future power of the United States government, its presidency, the legislature, civil rights, and the powers to be left to the states.

Almost immediately, the framers gave up amending the Articles of Confederation and began work on a new constitution. By allowing each state equal representation in the Senate, the upper house of Congress, they compromised a conflict between large and small states. Another divisive issue was resolved by allowing slaveholding states to count 60 percent of their slaves in the population on which their allocation of seats in the lower house of Congress would be based. With these two questions settled, the convention's work progressed rapidly.

A fundamental principle of the completed Constitution was Montesquieu's separation of powers. It was revealed in the carefully defined distinction between powers granted to the national and state governments and even more specifically in the division of functions among the branches of the central government. Congress was to make the laws, the president was to execute them, and the courts were to interpret them. The president could veto laws passed by Congress, but the latter, by a two-thirds vote, could override a presidential veto. The Supreme Court later expanded its original charge of interpreting laws to interpreting the Constitution itself, thus acquiring the right to declare any law "unconstitutional."

In recognizing the principle of popular sovereignty, the Constitution was similar to the Articles of Confederation; it differed in its centralization of government and in its securities against disorder. Proclaiming itself the supreme law of the land, the Constitution specifically prohibited the states from coining money, levying customs duties, and conducting foreign diplomacy. The president, as chief executive, commanded the national military forces, an arrangement that could protect against popular unrest and disorder. Most of the delegates to Philadelphia favored property qualifications for voting, an idea that they abandoned only because it was politically impractical. They indicated their distrust of democracy, however, by avoiding the direct popular election of senators and presidents: senators would be chosen by the legislature of their particular state while the president would be chosen by a separate, electoral college.

The process of ratifying the Constitution precipitated a great political debate. Congress, dominated by so-called Federalist proponents, ignored the amending provisions of the Articles and appealed directly to the states. Anti-Federalists, who opposed ratification, were alarmed but were generally overwhelmed by arguments from the wealthier, more articulate, and better-educated Federalists, who supported the Constitution. By promising written guarantees of individual liberties—the later Bill of Rights, the first ten amendments to the new Constitution—the Federalists ultimately won the required nine states, and the Constitution was formally adopted on July 2, 1788. Three years later the first ten amendments were added, guaranting freedom of religion, speech, and the press and protecting the people against arbitrary government. Thus the radicals left a lasting legacy, despite the Federalist triumph.

From Theory to Reality

After winning their greatest victory, the Federalists dominated American politics for more than a decade. In 1789 George Washington was elected to the first of his two four-year terms as president under the terms of the Constitution. His administration imposed a high tariff, chartered a national bank, paid public debts at face value, negotiated a commercial treaty with England, and after 1794 opposed the French Revolution. Ironically, some French revolutionaries, such as the Marquis de Lafayette (1757–1834), who had helped win American independence, were bitterly denounced by American leaders a decade later.

The war for American rights and liberties left much unfinished business. For decades after 1783 the right to vote was restricted to propertied white male citizens. Flagrantly omitted were the common

The effectiveness of the work done by the Constitutional Convention can be seen by the fact that the United States still follows its provisions, only slightly amended, more than two centuries later.

people, women, African Americans, and Native Americans, all of whom were denied full civil equality, freedom, and human justice despite their important contributions to the American cause.

The war brought special hardships to American women. On the frontier they faced savage massacres, torture, and enslavement. In eastern areas both Loyalist and rebel women risked rape and pillage by enemy soldiers. Most women hated the war because it left them with heavy responsibilities in the absence of their husbands, yet a majority accepted their fate with quiet courage. Many helped promote the Revolution. Some wrote anti-British plays and pamphlets, others published newspapers, and more organized boycotts against British goods. On both sides they served as spies and couriers. Over 25,000 women moved on foot behind the armies, carrying their baggage and their children. In camp, they cooked, washed, and cared for their men, sometimes foraging after battles among enemy dead for clothing and ammunition. A few saw combat, like the legendary Continental Army wives Mary Hayes (Molly Pitcher) and Margaret Corbin, who continued to fire their husbands' artillery pieces after the men fell in battles at Fort Washington (1776) and Fort Monmouth (1778), respectively. The most famous female fighter in the Revolution was Deborah Sampson, an orphaned Connecticut schoolteacher who donned men's clothes and served for more than a year in Washington's army before she was discovered and honorably discharged.

Despite their sacrifices, American women gained few new rights or privileges. They remained disenfranchised, legally subordinated to their husbands in the disposition of property, and practically denied the possibility of divorce. Reacting against these conditions, two students of Enlightenment thought, Abigail Adams and Mercy Warren, urged their husbands to promote legal and political equality for women during the Revolution. For a while a mild feminism was publicly expressed; the New Jersey constitution of 1776 gave women the vote, and its election law of 1790 permitted local boards to enfranchise women. But general indifference to the nascent women's movement led the New Jersey legislature to end female suffrage in 1807.

Like women, African Americans played major roles during the war. The freedom and equality of "all men," a goal implied in the Declaration of Independence, ran counter to the interests of southern planters, who constantly feared black rebellion. In response to this fear, blacks were at first banned from military service, despite the embarrassing facts that many free blacks had supported the Stamp Act protests and that Crispus Attucks, a runaway slave turned sailor, had been the first American killed in the Boston Massacre. But when the British promised freedom to slave recruits and the supply of white American volunteers dwindled, Congress began enlisting blacks, thereby promising slaves their freedom. Even before they could be legally recruited, black soldiers fought valiantly at Lexington, Concord, and Bunker Hill, and they participated in every major battle afterward. They also served at sea, even on Virginia ships, but they were never admitted to the Virginia militia or to any military forces of Georgia or the Carolinas, although a contingent of Santo Domingo blacks under French command fought the British at Savannah.

Outside the Deep South a strong black emancipation movement developed during and immediately after the revolutionary era. While more than 100,000 former slaves escaped to Canada, to the Indians, or to British sanctuary ships, many blacks, both free and slave, exploited the rhetoric of the Revolution to petition for their freedom and equality. Such petitions were supported by a growing number of white dissidents among Quakers and political activists, such as James Otis (1724–1783), Thomas Paine, Benjamin Rush (1745–1813), and Benjamin Franklin. In response, every state limited or abolished the slave trade; many owners, even in the South, freed their slaves; six state constitutions (Vermont, Connecticut, Rhode Island, Pennsylvania, New York, and New Jersey) abolished slavery; and practical legal emancipation was achieved in New Hampshire and Massachusetts. Free blacks in Massachusetts won the vote in 1783, a precedent slowly adopted by other free states.

Such gains, however, were offset by losses. Many blacks that had been promised their freedom were enslaved by their former masters and even by their new British friends. Laws against slavery were not always enforced. Even in the northern states, emancipation was often legally delayed for decades, so that in 1810 there were still more than 35,000 slaves in New York, New Jersey, and Pennsylvania. The conservative reaction of the 1790s, stimulated by debates in the Constitutional Convention, and the invention of the cotton gin, which gave a new impetus to cotton planting, confirmed the South's emotional commitments to slavery. American slaves after the 1790s were further from the rights of "all men" than they had been before the Revolution. This injustice was the ultimate cause for a subsequent bloody and tragic civil war.

Another shameful abandonment of human rights affected Native Americans. Between 1700 and 1763, thousands of white settlers poured into Indian lands west of the mountains. The result was bloody warfare, marked by barbarous atrocities on both sides. Looking to the British for protection, most of the tribes fought against Americans during the Revolution, only to have their territories put under control of their enemies in the peace of 1783. Protracted negoti-

Even though only a third of the Americans actively supported the Revolution, large numbers of African Americans and women gave their lives to the struggle. Unfortunately, after victory was gained, they did not gain full participation in the new country.

ations with the American government led to more surrenders and numerous treaties, all of which were broken as the flood of white land speculators and settlers moved westward. In desperation, the Indians attempted unification and a hopeless resistance. Subsequently, their Ohio federation was crushed in 1794 at the battle of Fallen Timbers; at about the same time, the Cherokee union in the South collapsed. During the preceding 18 years the Cherokees alone had lost 40,000 square miles of territory. In the same period, all Indian populations east of the Mississippi fell by more than 45 percent. By 1800 enforced living on land set aside for Indians was already promoting the disintegration of Native American cultures.

International Impact of the American Revolution

Even with its shortcomings, the American Revolution exerted a tremendous influence in the world at large. The new republic, promising freedom guaranteed by a written social contract, seemed to validate principles of the Enlightenment for literate peoples everywhere. It soon generated a wave of revolutionary sentiment throughout western Europe.

The trend was evident even in England. Before the Revolution, a number of influential Englishmen, notably Edmund Burke (1729–1797), championed the American cause in Parliament, and English radical reformers, like Major John Cartwright (1740–1824), welcomed American independence. Pro-American enthusiasm languished when the war began, but it revived when American fortunes improved after Saratoga. In 1779 pro-American reform societies sprang up in London and in rural Yorkshire. The more radical London society grew into a national association, with delegates drawn from county organizations, imitating the American town meetings, state conventions, and Congress. The association welcomed American independence while calling for parliamentary reform.

More drastic changes occurred in Ireland, chafing after centuries of religious persecution and economic exploitation under English rule. During the war Henry Gratton (1746–1820) and Henry Flood (1732–1791), two leaders of the Irish Protestant gentry, exploited British weakness to obtain concessions. Having created an Irish militia, supposedly to protect the coasts against American or French attacks, they then followed American precedents. In February 1782 a convention at Dublin, representing 80,000 militiamen, demanded legislative independence. The English Parliament subsequently agreed that a new Irish legislature could make its own laws, subject only to a veto by the English king. Ireland thus acquired a status denied the American colonies in 1774.

Ireland's spirited response to the Revolution was more than matched in the Netherlands, where a pro-American middle-class movement and lawless urban mobs nearly rendered the government impotent and ruined the Dutch economy. Because William V, the stadtholder and a relative of the English royal family, was unjustly blamed for the nation's misfortunes, radical propaganda during the 1780s subjected his government to the most violent abuse. Organized uprisings in 1785 and 1787 forced William to leave his capital. For a brief period in the ensuing civil war, "patriots" held most of the country. The revolt was suppressed only when William's brother-in-law, the king of Prussia, sent 20,000 troops.

In France revolutionary refugees from Holland found a congenial atmosphere decisively affected by American ideas. To French philosophical radicals, the American Revolution proved their principles; to Frenchmen in the establishment, it promised a new and favorable diplomatic alignment against Britain. Consequently, dissenting ideas were no longer confined to learned treatises but appeared everywhere in pamphlets, in newspapers, and in the theater. Aristocratic vanities and even royal formalities suddenly became subjects for humorous comment; but, as one French noble observed, no one "stopped to consider the dangers of the example which the New World set to the Old."

Conclusion

Copernicus asked the fundamental questions about whether or not the earth moved, repeating a process of inquiry that went back to the Ionian Greeks. When, after extensive mathematical calculations, he established the heliocentric theory, his findings were published, to be read and challenged. As others improved on his findings and established the natural laws that defined the motion of the planets, scientific inquiries became widely admired. The surprising discoveries of astronomers produced a new view of the individual's place in the universe; their perspective was apparently proved mathematically by Sir Isaac Newton in the law of gravitation. His laws, along with the other laws of science, suggested that human reason operated effectively only when it was interpreting sensory experience. Material reality was accepted by some thinkers as the only reality. Therefore, the natural laws affecting human society were also considered basically materialistic. Respect for Enlightenment philosophy, many of whose early participants contributed to the Scientific Revolution, was largely derived from the successes and popularity of science.

Within this political context, the eighteenth-century Enlightenment brought a new vision of the future to European civilization. Its proponents thought they had discovered a simple way to achieve perpetual human happiness. They sought to deliver people from irrational restraints so that they might act freely in accordance with a universal human nature. On the one hand, their writings promised that pursuit of self-interest would benefit society; on the other, it promised that a free human reason would produce sound moral judgments. In other words, individual freedom furthered the operation of natural laws. Believing they had learned these laws, eighteenth-century rationalists thought they had found the secret of never-ending progress.

Although the *philosophes* and their prototypes outside of France were not revolutionaries, their ideas promised to undermine absolutism in all of its phases. Deism questioned the necessity of state churches and clergies. The physiocrats, Adam Smith, and other early economic liberals demonstrated the futility of mercantilism. The Enlightenment's political principles substituted the social contract for divine right while emphasizing the natural human rights of political freedom and justice. Each of these ideas denied the absolute authority of monarchs.

As the eighteenth century progressed, an opposing reaction countered this cold materialism without affecting the fundamental objectives of the Enlightenment. Idealistic philosophy and Pietism both challenged the purely scientific view of human cognition, emphasizing that intuition and faith are human capabilities as natural and as essential to truth as reason. Ultimately, idealism and Pietism merged with the humane concerns of rational philosophy to produce a new humanitarianism, which accented both reason and sentimentality but also continued the eighteenth-century concern for human freedom. Together with the rationalism of the Enlightenment, the reaction against reason before 1800 also challenged absolutism's domination of the human body, mind, and spirit.

The ideas of the Enlightenment did not rest imprisoned in abstractions. They were applied by both the monarchs of the times and the English colonists in the New World. The monarchs found they could not graft the ideas based on freedom and reason on trunks built on authority and dogma. The Americans, however, found in the writings of the Enlightenment a vocabulary for victory in their Revolution.

Suggestions for Reading

Good general surveys of intellectual developments during the early modern period in Europe may be found in two standard works that are still worth consulting: Jacob Bronowski and Bruce Mazlish, *The Western Intellectual Tradition from*

Leonardo to Hegel (Torchbooks, 1962), and Crane Brinton, *The Shaping of Modern Thought* (Smith, 1968). Excellent coverage of general background is provided in William Doyle, *The Old Order in Europe* (Oxford University Press, 1978).

Colin A. Ronan, *Science: Its History and Development Among the World's Cultures* (Facts on File, 1982), is a comprehensive treatment of the revolutionary developments of the seventeenth and eighteenth centuries. Two other useful general surveys of scientific achievements during the period are Rupert A. Hall, *The Revolution in Science, 1500–1750* (Longman, 1983) and Robert B. Downs, *Landmarks in Science* (Libraries Unlimited, 1982). For the social implications of science, see Tore Frangamur et al., *The Quantifying Spirit in the Eighteenth Century* (University of California Press, 1990), and Margaret C. Jacob, *The Cultural Meaning of the Scientific Revolution* (Temple University Press, 1988). See also Jerry Weinberger, *Science, Faith, and Politics: Francis Bacon and the Utopian Roots of the Modern Age* (Cornell University Press, 1985). Mary Ornstein, *The Role of Scientific Societies in the Seventeenth Century* (Arno, 1975), is the classic study of this important subject. Overdue recognition of early women scientists is provided in Margaret Alic, *Hypatia's Women in Science Heritage: A History of Women in Science* (Beacon Press, 1986).

On the origins of scientific theory, see Nicholas Jardine, *The Birth of the History and the Philosophy of Science* (Cambridge University Press, 1988). Relatively recent books deal with the special contributions of Descartes and Bacon. On Descartes, see Tom Sorrel, ed., *Descartes* (Oxford University Press, 1987). For Bacon, see Charles Whitney, *Francis Bacon and Modernity* (Yale University Press 1986) and Peter Urbach, *Francis Bacon's Philosophy of Science* (Open Court, 1987).

Among the best interpretive biographies of the great astronomers are John Louis Emil Dreyer, *Tycho Brahe* (Dover, 1963); Arthur Koestler's study of Kepler, *The Watershed* (University Press of America, 1984); Stillman Drake, *Galileo* (Hill & Wang, 1980); and Ernan McMullin, *Galileo, Man of Science* (Scholar's Bookshelf, 1988). On Newton, see Gale E. Christianson, *In the Presence of the Creator* (Free Press, 1984), and Richard S. Westfall, *Never at Rest* (Cambridge University Press, 1983).

Achievements in biology and chemistry are covered in the many biographical works. Two good ones are Robert G. Frank, *Harvey and the Oxford Physiologists* (University of California Press, 1980), and Peter Alexander, *Qualities and Corpuscles: Locke and Boyle on the External World* (Cambridge University Press, 1985). On Lavoisier, see Wilda C. Anderson, *Between the Library and the Laboratory* (Johns Hopkins University Press, 1984).

Solid surveys of the Enlightenment are presented in Robert Anchor, *The Enlightenment Tradition* (University of Pennsylvania Press, 1987), and Roy Porter, *The Enlightenment* (Humanities Press, 1990). On the intellectual origins of the movement, see Alan Kors and Paul J. Korshin, eds., *Anticipation of the Enlightenment in England, France, and Germany* (University of Pennsylvania Press, 1987). Special themes are treated in Donald C. Meil et al., eds., *Man, God, and Nature in the Enlightenment* (Colleagues Press, 1989); Henry May, *The Divided Heart* (Oxford University Press, 1991); and Daniel Brewer, *The Discourse of Enlightenment in Eighteenth-Century France* (Cambridge University Press, 1993). See also Richard B. Sher and Jeffrey R. Smitten, eds., *Scotland and America in the Age of the Enlightenment* (Princeton University Press, 1990).

French and American colonial women who played roles in the Enlightenment are ably credited in Joan B. Landes, *Women and the Public Sphere in the Age of the French Revolution* (Cornell University Press, 1988); Samia I. Spencer, *French Women and the Age of Enlightenment* (Indiana University Press, 1984); Margaret Hunt and Margaret Jacob, *Women and the Enlighten-*

ment (Haworth, 1984); Linda K. Kerber, *Women of the Republic* (University of North Carolina Press, 1980); and Mary Beth Norton, *Liberty's Daughters* (Little, Brown, 1980).

The following biographical studies are recommended: Peter Gilmour, *Philosophers of the Enlightenment* (Barnes & Noble, 1990); Lewis S. Feuer, *Spinoza and the Rise of Liberalism* (Transaction Books, 1987); Otis E. Fellows, *Diderot* (Twayne, 1977); Danthony Flew, *David Hume: Philosophy of Moral Science* (Blackwell, 1986); John W. Yolton, *John Locke* (Blackwell, 1985); Norman Hampson, *Montesquieu, Rousseau, and the French Revolution* (University of Oklahoma Press, 1983); Judith N. Shklar, *Montesquieu* (Oxford University Press, 1987); A. J. Ayer, *Voltaire* (Random House, 1986); Maurice Cranston, *Jean-Jacques: The Early Life of Jean-Jacques Rousseau, 1712–1754* (Penguin, 1987); Jean Starobinski, *Jean-Jacques Rousseau: Transparency and Obstruction* (University of Chicago Press, 1988); and James J. Hoecher, *Joseph Priestley and the Idea of Progress* (Garland, 1987).

On the French economic assault on absolutism, see Elizabeth Fox-Genovese, *The Origins of Physiocracy* (Cornell University Press, 1976). Adam Smith's significance is clearly indicated in R. H. Campbell, *Adam Smith* (St Martin's Press, 1985); Robert Boyden Lamb, *Property, Markets, and the State in Adam Smith's System* (Garland, 1987); and Maurice Brown, *Adam Smith's Economics: Its Place in the Development of Economic Thought* (Routledge, 1988).

Religious issues in the Enlightenment are discussed in John W. Yolton, *Philosophy, Religion, and Science in the Seventeenth and Eighteenth Centuries* (University of Rochester Press, 1990). The opposite orientation is revealed in Joseph P. Wright, *The Skeptical Philosophy of David Hume* (University of Minnesota Press, 1983), and in Timothy A. Mitchell, *David Hume's Anti-Theistic Views* (University Press of America, 1986). For the more typical trend, see Kerry S. Walters, *The American Deists* (University of Kansas Press, 1992). Margaret C. Jacob, *The Radical Enlightenment* (Allen & Unwin, 1981), also deals with religion, along with republicanism and the prevailing radical influence of Freemasonry in the eighteenth century.

For the political impact, see *The Political Thought of John Locke* (Cambridge University Press, 1983); Ruth W. Grant, *John Locke's Liberalism* (University of Chicago Press, 1987); and James Tully, *A Discourse on Property: John Locke and His Adversaries* (Cambridge University Press, 1980). See also Thomas L. Pangle, *Montesquieu's Philosophy of Liberalism* (University of Chicago Press, 1989), and Peter Gay, *Voltaire's Politics*, 2nd ed. (Yale University Press, 1988).

On Rousseau as a political thinker, see Robert Wokler, *Social Thought of J. J. Rousseau* (Garland, 1987). Rousseau's ambiguous views on democracy are given special attention in James Miller, *Rousseau, Dreamer of Democracy* (Yale University Press, 1984).

The radical Enlightenment produced a thin stream of feminism, which is described in the following works: Ruth Perry, *The Celebrated Mary Astell* (University of Chicago Press, 1986); Alice Browne, *The Eighteenth-Century Feminist Mind* (Wayne State University Press, 1987); and Moira Ferguson and Janet Todd, *Mary Wollstonecraft* (Twayne, 1984).

Kant's reinterpretation of the Enlightenment is thoroughly covered in Ernest Cassirer, *Kant's Life and Thought* (Yale University Press, 1981). For special emphases on aspects of Kant's thought, see Robert Hahn, *Kant's Newtonian Revolution in Philosophy* (St. Martin's Press, 1988); and James Booth, *Interpreting the World: Kant's Philosophy of History and Politics* (University of Toronto Press, 1987).

David S. Lovejoy, *Religious Enthusiasm and the Great Awakening* (Prentice Hall, 1969), captures the spirit of Pietism and religious humanitarianism. Among works on Methodism, two excellent ones are Vivian Hubert Howard Green, *John Wesley*

(University Press of America, 1987) and Tim Dowley, *Through Wesley's England* (Abingdon, 1988). Charles Pollock, *Wilberforce* (St. Martin's Press, 1978), is an excellent biography of the great English emancipator.

On the pros and cons of monarchical reform, see Geoffrey Bruun, *The Enlightened Despots* (Holt, Rinehart and Winston, 1967); John G. Gagliardo, *Enlightened Despotism* (Crowell, 1967); and James F. Brennan, *Enlightened Despotism in Russia* (Lang, 1987). Excellent biographies of Frederick the Great and Catherine the Great are noted in the Suggestions for Reading at the end of Chapter 19.

The mid-eighteenth-century background for revolution is provided in a number of pertinent studies. For England, see Peggy Liss, *Atlantic Empires: The Network of Trade and Revolution, 1713–1826* (Johns Hopkins University Press, 1983), and Alan Rogers, *Empire and Liberty* (University of California Press, 1974). For biographical insights into both extremes of the English political spectrum, see Reginald James White, *The Age of George III* (Walker, 1968); Richard Pares, *King George III and the Politicians* (Oxford University Press, 1988); and Louis Kronenberger, *The Extraordinary Mr. Wilkes* (Doubleday, 1974). See also Bernard Bailyn, *The Peopling of British North America* (Vintage, 1988).

Robert Leckie, *George Washington's War* (HarperCollins, 1992), and Page Smith, *A New Age Now Begins: A People's History of the American Revolution*, 2 vols. (Penguin, 1989), are detailed and colorful narratives. Other good general histories of the American Revolution include Bruce Lancaster, *The American Revolution* (Hill & Wang, 1985); and John R. Alden, *A History of the American Revolution* (Da Capo, 1989). For contrasting views on the nobility of the American struggle, compare Robert Middlekauff, *The Glorious Cause* (Oxford University Press, 1985), with Norman Gelb, *Less than Glory* (Putnam, 1984), and John William Tebbel, *Turning the World Upside Down* (Orion Books, 1993).

Thomas Ladenburg, *The Causes of the American Revolution* (Social Science Education, 1989), is a useful study aid. Among the best other studies on the genesis of the Revolution are Richard B. Morris, *Founding of the Republic* (Lerner, 1985); Douglas Edward Leach, *Roots of Conflict* (University of North Carolina Press, 1986); James A. Henretta and Gregory H. Nobles, *Evolution and Revolution: American Society, 1600–1820* (Heath, 1987); and Bernard Bailyn, *The Ideological Origins of the American Revolution* (Belknap Press, 1992). A treatment accenting expansionism as a cause is Marc Egnal, *A Mighty Empire: The Origins of the American Revolution* (Cornell University Press, 1988).

Ronald Hoffman and Peter J. Albert have edited *Women in the Age of the American Revolution* (University of Virginia Press, 1989), a collection of pertinent essays on the hardships and heroics of women in the Revolution. See also Anne Voth, *Women in the New Eden* (University Press of America, 1983); Walter Hart Blumenthal, *Women Camp Followers of the American Revolution* (Ayer, 1974); Elizabeth Ellet, *The Women of the American Revolution*, 3 vols. (Corner House, 1980).

Suggestions for Web Browsing

Galileo Project
http://es.rice.edu/ES/humsoc/Galileo/

A hypertext source of information about the life and work of Galileo Galilei and the science of his time.

Scientific Revolution
http://history.hanover.edu/early/science.htm

The home page of the Galileo Project, offering a variety of helpful resources on the Scientific Revolution.

Internet Modern History Sourcebook: The Scientific Revolution and the Enlightenment
http://www.fordham.edu/halsall/mod/hs1000.html#scirev

Extensive on-line source for links about the Scientific Revolution and the Enlightenment, including primary documents by or about Copernicus, Kepler, Galileo, Descartes, Adam Smith, and John Locke.

Military History: American Revolution (1775–1783)
http://www.cfcsc.dnd.ca/links/milhist/usrev.html

Site lists links on the biographies of Washington and Paine, battles, museums, reenactments, literature, and other aspects of the era.

Women in the American Revolution
http://www.carleton.ca/~pking/arbib/z.htm

Bibliography providing insight into the role of women during the American Revolution.

Notes

1. Quoted in Stillman Drake, *Galileo at Work* (Chicago: University of Chicago Press, 1978), p. 41.
2. Quoted in James Harvey Robinson and Charles A. Beard, *Readings in European History*, Vol. 1 (Boston, Ginn and Co., 1908), pp. 202–205.
3. Quoted in E. Neville Williams, *The Ancien Régime in Europe* (New York: Harper & Row, 1970), p. 424.
4. Quoted in Clinton L. Rossiter, *The First American Revolution* (New York: Harcourt Brace, 1956), prefatory note.

The storming of the Bastille as seen by a participant, a certain Monsieur Cholat.

The French and Napoleonic Revolutions and Their Impact on Europe and the Americas, 1789–1825

Chapter Contents

In the 1760s divine right monarchy and aristocratic society were accepted as normal in the Western world, even if the nature of both institutions had radically changed. After 1800 civil liberties and constitutions became the norm. This transformation was produced by the conjuncture of a number of dynamic forces. Developing European capitalism, expanding population, growing cities, and a rising middle class had destabilized the old regimes by 1750. The "test of reason," the fundamental Enlightenment message, helped advocates of change focus their arguments and make them more powerful. Each of these trends—economic, social, and intellectual—came together at a time when colonial wars plunged England and France deeper into debt. The American Revolution, an early result of these conditions, led to a much more comprehensive French upheaval. These were but the two most dramatic examples of the resulting revolutionary wave that rolled over much of western Europe and the Americas from 1776 to 1825.

The French and Napoleonic revolutions would give later generations a new set of values and guides for taking and exercising power. They critically weakened all old regimes, identified freedom with progress in the popular mind, and ultimately projected democracy, as well as emotional nationalism and horrible new forms of war, into the nineteenth century. For most societies before World War I, the revolutions provided a special heritage. In Europe and the Americas—indeed, throughout the rest of the world today—the love of liberty, brotherhood, and equality and the willingness of revolutionaries to die for these ideals remain powerfully alive.

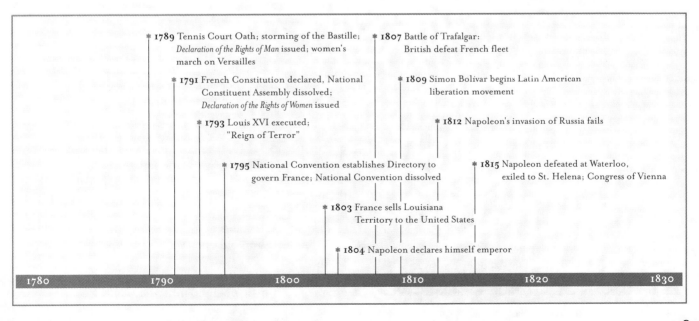

* **1789** Tennis Court Oath; storming of the Bastille; *Declaration of the Rights of Man* issued; women's march on Versailles

* **1791** French Constitution declared, National Constituent Assembly dissolved; *Declaration of the Rights of Women* issued

* **1793** Louis XVI executed; "Reign of Terror"

* **1795** National Convention establishes Directory to govern France; National Convention dissolved

* **1803** France sells Louisiana Territory to the United States

* **1804** Napoleon declares himself emperor

* **1807** Battle of Trafalgar: British defeat French fleet

* **1809** Simon Bolivar begins Latin American liberation movement

* **1812** Napoleon's invasion of Russia fails

* **1815** Napoleon defeated at Waterloo, exiled to St. Helena; Congress of Vienna

1780   1790   1800   1810   1820   1830

The French Revolution

France in 1789 was the center of Europe, the most populous and cultured state of the time, with its thousand-year-old social, political, and economic structure. During the next ten years it would live through a total political and social revolution that swept away traditional systems in three stages: moderate, radical, and finally conservative. After the Revolution had run its bloody course, one could see that the revolutionaries had applied a variety of principles of the Enlightenment in ways the original authors could not have foreseen. Their unanticipated legacy would give Napoleon the resources he needed to dominate the Western world until 1815.

Versailles and the Estates-General: May–June 1789

The process of revolution by default proceeded quickly toward its long-delayed climax during the summer of 1789. Louis XVI, who had succeeded his grandfather in 1774, was intelligent but lacked initiative. Without any help from his frivolously extravagant queen, Marie Antoinette (1755–1793), Louis managed in one way or another to alienate most of his subjects through indecision and bad political judgment. This lapse of leadership led first to discord in top echelons of authority and then to violent mob action, which dominated all subsequent political decisions.

Between Louis's succession in 1774 and 1789, his finance ministers faced continuously rising national deficits. The debt ultimately reached an equivalent of $6 billion (in 1999 dollars), with interest payments absorbing half of annual revenues. Because loans to cover shortfalls were becoming almost impossible to raise, the government in 1787 and 1788 sought help from Assemblies of Notables (prominent nobles and high churchmen). But these bodies refused gifts or taxes without audits of royal accounts and other fiscal reforms. Louis then forced the courts (*parlements*) to register new laws authorizing more taxes and loans. The crisis was intensified by poor harvests caused by spring floods in 1788 and then devastating hailstorms in July 1788 that destroyed the second planting. France endured the second coldest winter of the century in 1788–1789. Merchants holding stocks of grain drove the price of bread up to the highest level in 75 years. By the spring of 1789 the country was seething with unrest, and the government was out of money once again.

With no other recourse, Louis now bowed to the Notables and agreed to call the Estates-General, the nation's medieval representative assembly, which had not met since 1614. The Notables saw the Estates-General meeting as a way to leverage more advantages from the king in return for their support to end the financial crisis. By blindly pursuing their narrow interests in the decade before 1789, they lit the fuse leading to the revolutionary explosion that destroyed their millennium-old position of superiority in French society.

During the spring of 1789, amid feverish excitement but little open hostility among the estates,

---

The French Revolution

August 1788	Louis XVI announces meeting of Estates-General to be held May 1789
May 5, 1789	Estates-General convenes
June 17, 1789	Third Estate declares itself the National Assembly
June 20, 1789	Oath of the Tennis Court
July 14, 1789	Storming of the Bastille
July 20, 1789	Revolution of peasantry begins
August 26, 1789	*Declaration of the Rights of Man and Citizen*
October 5, 1789	Parisian women march to Versailles, force Louis XVI to return to Paris
February 1790	Monasteries, convents dissolved
July 1790	Civil Constitution of the Clergy
June 1791	Louis XVI and family attempt to flee Paris, are captured and returned
April 1792	France declares war on Austria
August 10, 1792	Storming of the Tuileries
September 22, 1792	Revolutionary calendar implemented
January 1793	Louis XVI executed
July 1793	Robespierre assumes leadership of Committee of Public Safety
1793–1794	Reign of Terror
1794	Robespierre guillotined
1799	Napoleon overthrows the Directory and seizes power

electors of each order—the clergy (the First Estate); the nobles, a diverse group of which perhaps 5 percent were in the truly ancient families (the Second Estate); and commoners (the Third Estate)—met in 40,000 assemblies to select representatives. A few women participated among the clergy and nobles, but the 4.3 million electors in the Third Estate were all males, aged 25 or older, who paid the head tax. They nevertheless included most peasants, urban craftsmen, merchants, and professionals, comprising a much larger number of voters than those holding the parliamentary franchise in Britain.

After the French delegates were elected, they compiled lists of reform proposals, the *cahiers*. The Third Estate requested a national legislature, a jury system, freedom of the press, and equitable taxes; there was no mention of overthrowing the monarchy or eliminating the aristocracy. The delegates themselves were not revolutionaries, but most were moderate reformers. Of the more than 1100 delegates in the three orders, about 90 of 285 nobles were more or less sympathetic to the views of the bourgeoisie and 205 of 308 clergy were from nonnoble families. The 621 members of the Third Estate included 380 lawyers, 85 businessmen, and 64 landowners; 267 were officeholders.

Once the Estates-General convened on May 5 at Versailles, the economic question—the issue that had led the king to call the Estates-General—was instantly forgotten. The Third Estate insisted that voting should be by head rather than by chamber, because it had more members than the other two estates combined. Voting by head had already been adopted in some regional assemblies, and the principle had been requested in a large majority of the *cahiers*. During weeks of wrangling on this issue, some members of the clergy joined the Third Estate. On June 17 the Third Estate declared itself the national legislature and invited members of the other estates to attend its sessions. Two days later most of the clergy voted to accept the invitation. Then on June 20, when members found their meeting hall closed, ostensibly to prepare for the king's upcoming address, delegates of the Third Estate moved a half-mile to a court for indoor tennis *(jeu de paume)*, where they solemnly swore not to disband until they had produced a French constitution. Later, after defying a royal order to reconvene separately, they declared themselves the National Constituent Assembly of France—a group legally elected to write a constitution.

At this point the delegates had declared—and won—a revolution in principle, but their full understanding of the process or even their commitment to it would develop only with time. Few members among the middle-class majority were merchants seeking free trade. Many were landowners, officeholders, or judges; many others were disappointed at not yet becoming nobles. Liberal aristocrats were willing to give up some privileges, including their manorial fees and tax immunities, in return for enlightened reforms that would improve the administration of government. Die-hard support for the Old Regime was concentrated primarily among the relatively impoverished local "nobles of the sword" and the traditional peasants from remote communities.

Locked out of their meeting hall on the king's orders, aroused delegates to the Estates-General, primarily members of the Third Estate, convened at a nearby indoor tennis court, where they swore the historic "Tennis Court Oath." The painting is by Jacques-Louis David.

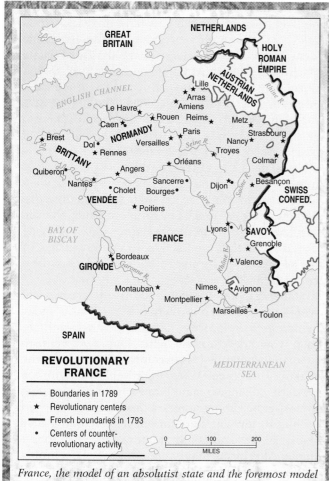

France, the model of an absolutist state and the foremost model of an "old regime," shocked and then threatened its neighbors with its thoroughgoing revolution in the five years after 1789.

Suffering and Explosion in Paris and the Provinces: July–August 1789

Another factor, however, was already exerting its powerful influence. Economic depression in the late 1780s, particularly rising bread prices in the cities, prompted unrest and violence among more than 20 million desperate French workers and peasants. This unfocused force of frustration and violence would for the next five years constantly overwhelm the plans and goals of the various governments' leaders.

Although grudgingly accepting the National Assembly on June 27, Louis tried to placate the nobles by bringing in 18,000 troops to the vicinity of Versailles. Middle-class members of the Assembly, near panic in fear of military intervention and a bloody popular response, appealed for popular support. In Paris the forces of public order were in a confused

state as many of the soldiers, especially among the *gardes-françaises,* who were supposed to protect stocks of grain and weapons, refused to follow the orders of their officers. As the contradictory rumors swirled in from Versailles on the morning of July 14, Parisians broke into military storerooms and took an estimated 30,000 rifles and cannons with little or no resistance. Later that day an estimated 100,000 Parisian shopkeepers, workers, and women demolished the Bastille in Paris, as well as similar buildings in other cities in France. The significance of the action was not in the prisoners they liberated—a small group of obscure nobles. This medieval fortress had served as the most visible symbol of the Old Regime, and its fall clearly demonstrated the rapidly growing popular defiance. Paris became an independent city with its own middle-class council and its own National Guard.

Meanwhile, other urban uprisings and peasant violence in the country consolidated the Assembly's position, so long as it was not overwhelmed by the suppressed violence of centuries. As for the king, he had completely lost control and even comprehension of events, as can be seen by the entry he made in his journal for July 14, the day of the fall of the Bastille: *"Rien."* ("Nothing.")

The most dramatic action of the Assembly occurred on the night of August 4, 1789. By then order had been restored in the cities, but peasants all over France were still rising against their lords—burning, pillaging, and sometimes murdering—in desperate efforts to destroy records of their manorial obligations. Faced with this violence and at first undecided between force and concessions, the Assembly ultimately chose concessions. Consequently, on that fateful night, nobles and clergy rose in the Assembly to renounce tithes, serfdom, manorial duties, feudal privileges, unequal taxes, and the sale of offices. The Old Regime, which had evolved over ten centuries, legally disappeared in a few hours. This was the real French Revolution.

A climax to the summer upheaval came in October. Louis tried to delay taking official action to carry out the Assembly's decrees of August 4, and he was anxiously awaiting the arrival of a trusted regiment from Flanders. Meanwhile, angry Parisians marched and rioted in the streets. Two months later, on October 5, after the Flanders regiment had arrived, some 6000 women, many of them armed, marched to Versailles, accompanied by the National Guard under Lafayette. It was symbolic of the disconnection between Louis XVI and the events of his country that no preparation had been made to anticipate the arrival of this group. He had been out hunting, and to his surprise, he was met by a deputation of six women who presented their demands. In the face of this confrontation the king signed the decrees of August 4. Other women entered the hall where the Assembly was sitting, disrupted proceedings, and forced an adjournment. The next day, after a mob stormed the palace and killed some guards, the king and his family returned to Paris as virtual prisoners, their carriage surrounded by women carrying pikes on which were impaled the heads of the murdered bodyguards.

Moderate Phase of the Revolution: August 1789–September 1791

To define its political principles and set its course, the Assembly issued the *Declaration of the Rights of Man and Citizen* on August 26. Intended as a preamble to a new constitution, it proclaimed human "inalienable rights" to liberty, property, security, and resistance to oppression. It also promised free speech, press, and religion, consistent with public order. Property was declared inviolate unless required for "public safety," in which case the owner was to receive "just compensation." All (male) citizens were to be equal before the law and eligible for public office on their qualifications. Taxes were to be levied only by common consent. Other accents on civil equality and property rights indicated the document's middle-class orientation.[1]

Shortly after the march on Versailles, the Assembly achieved some political stability by declaring martial law, to be enforced by the sometimes dependable National Guard. During the next two years the Assembly's leaders followed the Enlightenment principles and the statements of the *Declaration* in attempting to reorganize France. Because most came from the middle class, with a preponderance of lawyers and a sprinkling of nobles, they were committed to change but also determined to keep order, protect property, and further their special interests. Thus as they achieved their goals, they became increasingly satisfied and conservative. Good harvests and the lowering of food prices also favored them.

One thing remained constant during the revolutionary year of 1789: France was bankrupt. And this financial distress remained one of the new government's most immediate concerns. The Assembly attempted to solve the problem by seizing church properties and using them as a base for new issues of paper currency, the *assignats*. Members also voted to eliminate tithes, largely in an attempt to placate Catholic peasants. Some would have gone further, but many were reluctant to abolish the state church completely, believing that it could be controlled and used to help defend property. Consequently, the Assembly decreed a "Civil Constitution of the Clergy," which made all clericals salaried public servants, abolished all archbishoprics, and reduced the number of bishoprics. Monastic orders were simply dissolved. Incumbent churchmen were required to swear loyalty to the nation, but only seven bishops and half the clergy conformed. The remainder became bitterly hostile to the government and exerted great influence, particularly among the peasants.

A contemporary print of Parisian women advancing on Versailles on October 5, 1789, shows the determined marchers carrying pikes and dragging an artillery piece. The following day the king and the royal family were returned to Paris, and the women were hailed as heroines of the Revolution.

Discovery Through Maps
France Triumphant

Liberty, equality, brotherhood—powerful as these ideological functions may have been, the French drive to European dominance between 1789 and 1814 owed its success more to the force of the French armies. Even before Napoleon came to power, the French armies had rearranged the map of Europe, as can be seen in this engraving from the Bibliothèque Nationale in Paris.

Before the Revolution, the French armies were the most advanced in Europe, with the most sophisticated training, doctrine, and technology. Within three years of the Revolution, many noble officers had been defeated or had left to serve foreign armies, giving a new crop of bright, young, aggressive generals the opportunity to lead. In August 1793 the Committee of Public Safety that ruled France appointed Lazare Carnot to place the army on a new footing. He decreed the full mobilization of all able-bodied men in the *levée en masse* and demanded that the rest of the country work to support the armed forces. An ideologically driven mass army with minimal training proved to be more than enough to defeat the old-style mercenary armies of the opposition.

In October 1794 General Charles Pichegru (third from left) entered Holland and took Amsterdam the next year. At the same time, the French captured the Dutch fleet. The general in the center, Jean-Victor Moreau, holds a map showing Hapsburg holdings in Austria and Italy, symbolic of his string of victories over Austrian forces. Notice the tamed Austrian eagle looking sullenly down on the scene. On the far left is General Lazare Hoche, who put down pockets of resistance in Brittany.

This image, made by Jean-Baptiste Poirson, was well received in France as a testimony to the return of France to continental dominance after a difficult series of wars. As for those who the French defeated, *tant pis*—so much the worse for them.

Understandably, the Assembly's economic policies were aimed at winning middle-class support. It therefore assured payment to holders of government bonds, secured not only by impending sales of confiscated church lands but also by lands taken from nobles who had fled the country. Most of this property was sold to middle-class speculators, who resold it to wealthy land-grabbers and social climbers; very little of it was ever acquired by peasants. The Assembly also abolished all internal tolls, industrial regulations, and guilds, thus throwing open to all the chance to work in the arts and crafts. It banned trade unions and decreed that wages be set by individual bargaining. Except for a few re-

Declaration of the Rights of Man and Citizen

This moderate middle-class document of the French Revolution was inspired by the American Declaration of Independence. Notice, however, that it differs slightly in its precise mention of property rights.

The National Assembly recognizes and declares, in the presence and under the auspices of the Supreme Being, the following rights of man and citizen.

1. Men are born and remain free and equal in rights. Social distinctions can be based only upon the common good.

2. The aim of every political association is the preservation of the natural and imprescriptible rights of man. These rights are liberty, property, security, and resistance to oppression. . . .

4. Liberty consists in the power to do anything that does not injure others; accordingly, the exercise of the natural rights of each man has no limits except those that assure to the other members of society the enjoyment of these same rights. These limits can be determined only by law.

5. The law can forbid only such actions as are injurious to society. Nothing can be forbidden that is not forbidden by the law, and no one can be constrained to do that which it does not decree.

6. Law is the expression of the general will. All citizens have the right to take part personally, or by their representatives, in its enactment. It must be the same for all, whether it protects or punishes.

7. No man can be accused, arrested, or detained, except in the cases determined by the law and according to the forms which it has prescribed. Those who call for, expedite, execute, or cause to be executed arbitrary orders should be punished; but every citizen summoned or seized by virtue of the law ought to obey instantly. . . .

8. The law ought to establish only punishments that are strictly and obviously necessary, and no one should be punished except by virtue of a law established and promulgated prior to the offense and legally applied.

9. Every man being presumed innocent until he has been declared guilty, if it is judged indispensable to arrest him, all severity that may not be necessary to secure his person ought to be severely suppressed by law.

10. No one should be disturbed on account of his opinions, even religious, provided their manifestation does not trouble the public order as established by law.

11. The free communication of thoughts and opinions is one of the most precious of the rights of man; every citizen can then speak, write, and print freely, save for the responsibility for the abuse of this liberty in the cases determined by law.

12. The guarantee of the rights of man and citizen necessitates a public force; this force is then instituted for the advantage of all and not for the particular use of those to whom it is entrusted.

13. For the maintenance of the public force and for the expenses of administration a general tax is indispensable; it should be equally apportioned among all the citizens according to their means.

14. All citizens have the right to ascertain, by themselves or through their representatives, the necessary amount of public taxation, to consent to it freely, to follow the use of it, and to determine the quota, the assessment, the collection, and the duration of it. . . .

16. Any society in which the guarantee of the rights is not assured, or the separation of powers not determined, has no constitution.

17. Property being a sacred and inviolable right, no one can be deprived of it, unless a legally established public necessity evidently requires it, under the condition of a just and prior indemnity.

From *Europe in Review,* ed. George L. Mosse et al. (Chicago: Rand McNally, 1962), pp. 162–164.

maining controls on foreign trade, the Assembly applied the doctrines of Adam Smith and the physiocrats, substituting free competition for economic regulation.

The Assembly also dashed some high hopes for French women. The early Revolution enlisted many, not only from the poor rioting Parisians of the shops and markets but also from those of the middle class, whose salons were political centers. Other women were already prominent in the political clubs of the era. Etta Palm d'Aelders, a Dutch activist, formed a women's patriotic society and even proposed a female militia. In addition, some women were involved in a strong feminist movement, a cause taken up by the *Amis de la Verité* ("Friends of Truth"), an organization that regularly lobbied the Assembly for

Women's political clubs were centers of discussion and debate during the Revolution. This painting shows women reading and discussing the decrees of the Convention.

free divorce, women's education, and women's civil rights. Its pleas, however, were largely ignored.

The Assembly's Enlightenment ideology clashed with its rising conservatism on the issue of policy toward the French West Indies. News from France in 1789 brought violent altercations on Santo Domingo and Martinique, where planters, merchants, poor whites, mulattoes, and slaves evaluated the Revolution according to their diverse interests. Planters in the Assembly differed on trade policies and colonial autonomy but concurred in their fanatic defense of slavery and their opposition to civil rights for free mulattoes. Meanwhile, mulattoes in France spread their pamphlets and petitioned the Assembly, supported by the *Amis des Noirs* ("Friends of the Blacks"), whose supporters also angrily attacked slavery in the Assembly hall. The chamber was left divided and nearly impotent. It first gave the island governments complete control over their blacks and mulattoes; then, yielding to the radicals, it granted political rights to mulattoes born of free parents. Finally, as civil war racked the islands, it bowed to the planters and repealed its last measure in September 1791.

After two years of tedious controversy, the Assembly finally produced the Constitution of 1791, which made France a limited monarchy. It assigned the lawmaking function to the single-chambered Legislative Assembly, which would meet automatically every two years. Louis became a figurehead, allowed to select ministers and temporarily veto laws but denied budgetary control or the right to dismiss the legislature: He had fewer powers than the new American president, George Washington. He could also be legally deposed. In addition, the constitution created an independent and elected judiciary and completely reorganized local government on three levels—departments, districts, and communes—with elected officials relatively free of supervision from Paris. De-

spite implications in the *Declaration,* only male citizens who paid a specified minimum of direct taxes acquired the vote—millions could not vote. Property qualifications were even higher for deputies to the Assembly and national officials. Women were made "passive citizens," without the vote, but marriage became a civil contract, with divorce open to both parties. Other individual rights under a new law code were guaranteed to all citizens, including Jews, according to the principles of the *Declaration.*

On September 30, 1791, the Assembly dissolved itself after denying its members reelection to the new legislature. It had passed more than 2000 laws that combined to end feudalism, serfdom, an irrational provincial system, conflicting courts, sale of offices, and absolute monarchy itself. It had not, however, made all citizens equal, even before the law, a point repeatedly emphasized by radical agitators and their followers among the angry street people of Paris.

The Drift Toward Radicalism: September 1791–June 1793

For more than a year before the new constitution was completed, the moderate conservative Assembly, which wanted to protect property rights and middle-class advances, had come under the increasing pressure of radicals, who wanted to carry out fundamental political and social reforms. Despite all efforts of the National Guard, unrest in the country and mob action in the cities disturbed the uneasy peace. Particularly in Paris after the spring of 1790, radical members of the Assembly played on popular fears and suspicions, encouraged by condemnations of the Revolution from émigré nobles and foreign royalists. Tensions within France were further aggravated by secret efforts by the king and queen to enlist foreign support. In June 1791, when the king—who opposed the state loyalty oath imposed on the clergy—and his family were caught trying to flee the country, the situation deteriorated. People in favor of a republic called for Louis to be removed. Angry crowds gathered, and the Guard fired on them, killing 15 people. The resulting wave of discontent would continue to intimidate national lawmakers, shaping their policies for the next three years.

In this charged atmosphere, the new and inexperienced Legislative Assembly met on October 1, 1791. Its prospects during the fall were not promising. The sullen king continued his secret plotting with foreign supporters while a 20 percent drop in the value of *assignats*—the currency of the French revolutionary government, based on the value of seized property and other "national goods"—alarmed middle-class investors. Public opinion in the cities became more radical as the popular press mounted a virulent and often vulgar campaign against Louis and the Assembly and crowds in Paris and the port cities cursed the government. On the other side, opponents of the Revolution began to act against it. Full-scale revolts threatened to erupt among Catholic peasants in Vendée, Avignon, Brittany, and Mayenne. The divisions and apprehensions of the country were naturally reflected in the Assembly.

At first the delegates formed themselves into three groups whose location in the meeting hall provided the political vocabulary for the future: conservatives to the right of the podium, moderates in the center, and liberals to the left. In Paris in 1791 the delegates on the right supported the limited monarchy; the undecided—roughly half of the delegates— were in the center; and on the left was a diverse group split by their geographical origins—for example, the Girondins from the southwest of the country and the Jacobins from Paris—and political goals, united only by their distrust for the king and his supporters. A majority could agree only on their repudiation of the Declaration of Pillnitz (August 1791), in which the Austrian and Prussian rulers called for European intervention to save the French monarchy.[2]

The Girondists exploited this foreign threat in emotional appeals that rallied the center behind a war to "save the Revolution." Debate gave way to action as the country slipped toward armed conflict during the spring of 1792. The stage was set in February, when Austria and Prussia formed an alliance, a move accented in March when the young and aggressive Francis II (1768–1835) succeeded his comparatively liberal father as Holy Roman Emperor. Louis and his queen, Marie Antoinette, were now hopeful for a war that might set them free. The Girondists savored their newfound dominance, which gave them control of the ministry in March. The Jacobins under Georges-Jacques Danton (1759–1794) and Maximilien Robespierre (1758–1794) argued against entering a war, noting that in France's condition war would harm the Revolution and end government economic aid for the common people.

There was a moment of general elation when France declared war on Austria and Prussia in April. But despair soon set in when it became obvious that revolutionary enthusiasm was no match for Austrian and Prussian military discipline. There were too few trained French recruits, led by too few dependable officers, and the armies soon retreated in disorder amid mass desertions from an invasion of the Austrian Netherlands. Only the enemy's caution and concern about Russia advancing from the east prevented a complete French disaster. French despair, however, turned to mass determination in July when the Prussian duke of Brunswick, who commanded the invading armies, issued a threat to destroy Paris if the French royal family was harmed.

In the wake of the military collapse and the Prussian threat, the Girondist rabble-rousers in the Assembly began to lose their support and came under the attack of Danton, the Jacobin deputy prosecutor for the Paris Commune. Danton was an enormous brute of a man with a voice of commanding power who mesmerized angry street audiences when he denounced the king as a traitor to France and those who did not share Jacobin views as fools or worse. On August 10 an incited throng of Parisians, women as well as men, broke into the palace, terrorized the royal family, massacred the Swiss guards, and looted the premises. There followed the Jacobin-directed "September Massacres" in which under the continual pressure of the mob, the Paris Commune seized power from the Legislative Assembly, deposed the king, and executed some 2000 suspected royalists and priests who did not support the Revolution. As there was no longer a king, it was necessary to call for a new national constitutional convention with members elected by universal male suffrage to prepare the way for a new government. The Jacobin pogrom spread throughout France, even after September 22, when the new National Convention declared France a republic.

Two days earlier a revitalized French army defeated the Prussians at Valmy, in northern France. This victory fused radicalism with nationalism as French armies began successful advances in the Austrian Netherlands, the Rhineland, and Savoy. Confirmed by their victory in November, the Convention declared universal revolutionary war by promising "fraternity to all peoples who wish to recover their liberty" and ordered inhabitants of occupied countries to accept revolutionary principles.[3] Led by Danton; the lawyer Robespierre, a fanatical follower of Rousseau; and Jean-Paul Marat (1743–1793), publisher of a violent paper that consistently denounced traitors, the radical Jacobins were now riding a rising tide. But the Girondists, despite their continued enthusiasm for the war, were now the conservatives of the Convention. They had become mainly the spokesmen for wealthy middle-class provincials, who advocated clemency for the king. On this major issue, the execution of Louis XVI, the Jacobins finally triumphed by one vote—despite foreign ambassadors' bribes—and Louis and Marie Antoinette were led to the guillotine on January 21, 1793.

Early French military advances had alarmed European capitals, but the execution of Louis XVI and his queen proved to be the decisive factor in turning all of Europe against France. Britain, Austria, Prussia, Spain, the Netherlands, and Sardinia formed the First Coalition in February and March 1793. Coalition forces soon expelled French troops from the Austrian Netherlands (Belgium) and Germany, after which France was invaded at a half-dozen places around its borders. In the ensuing military crisis, the Convention initiated a nationwide effort to raise a new levy of 300,000 men, from quotas assigned to every unit of local government. Lazare Carnot (1753–1823), the republic's minister of war, reorganized the armed forces by opening promotion to all ranks and meshing volunteers with old-line units. His efforts, along with a national patriotic response, brought a hard-won but belated stability.

As in the previous year, threats from abroad generated a climactic internal crisis during the spring of 1793. Execution of the king spurred full-scale civil war in Brittany and the Vendée as peasant armies, led by royalist émigrés and supplied by British ships, fought regular battles against troops of the Republic. Meanwhile in Paris worsening hunger among the poor opened the breach between Jacobins and Girondists wider. Again furious mobs entered the Convention hall, protesting food prices and demanding price controls. Such a measure was pushed through the Convention in April by the Enragés, an extremist faction of the Jacobins led by the radical journalist Jacques Hébert (1755–1794). When the Girondists staged uprisings in Marseilles, Lyons, Bordeaux, and Toulon, left-wing Jacobins in the Paris Commune called another armed mob into the Convention on May 31, 1793, and purged that body of any remaining Girondists. Others throughout France, wherever the Convention still retained authority, were arrested or driven into hiding.

Jacques-Louis David, The Death of Marat *(1793). David's painting extols Marat as a martyr of the Revolution.*

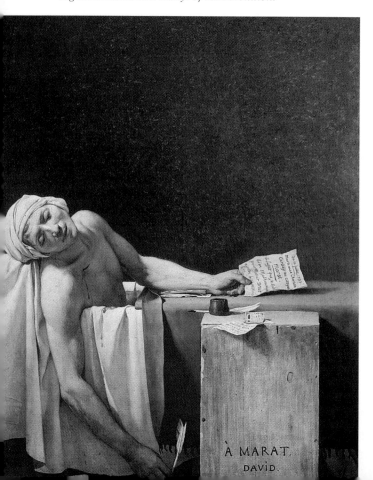

The Jacobin Republic

The Convention was now a "rump" council of the most extreme Jacobins, and their power was secured only after July 12 when Charlotte Corday (1768–1793), a young Girondist sympathizer, came to Paris from Caen and murdered Marat. He had been an adored leader of the Enragés, and his death infuriated the street people, including a contingent of revolutionary women who cursed Corday as they followed her to the guillotine. The general anti-Girondist mania brought the Convention under the domination of Robespierre, who remained in power until the late spring of 1794. During that time, revolutionary France, in a convulsion of patriotic violence, reorganized itself, suppressed internal strife, drove out foreign invaders, and catapulted the radical Jacobin party to a pinnacle of power.

The regime achieved its success largely through rigid dictatorship and terror. The 12-member Committee of Public Safety, headed first by Danton and after July by Robespierre, decided security policies. Subordinate committees were established for the departments, districts, and communes. These bodies deliberately forced conformity and used neighbors to inform on neighbors and sons and daughters to testify against their parents. Suspected traitors were brought to trial before revolutionary tribunals, with most suspects receiving quick death sentences. Between September 1793 and July 1794 some 25,000 victims were dragged to public squares in carts—the famous *tumbrels*—and delivered to the guillotines. Ultimately, the Reign of Terror destroyed most of the revolutionaries, including the Girondists (September 1793), the Dantonists (April 1794), and Robespierre himself (July 1794).

While it lasted, the Jacobin dictatorship was remarkably efficient in its war efforts as it mobilized all of France to fight and changed the nature of European warfare. The Convention made all males between 18 and 40 eligible for military service, a policy known as the *levée en masse* ("mass conscription"), which ultimately produced a force of 800,000, the largest standing army ever assembled in France. Its officers were promoted on merit and encouraged to exercise initiative. Soldiers were lionized in public festivals and provided with special entertainments, while 300 civilian commissars monitored morale and combat readiness. Between 1793 and 1795 these French citizen armies put down all internal rebellions while fighting a series of remarkably successful

As revolutionary justice condemned an increasing number of people to death after 1791, the guillotine provided an efficient means to decapitate the guilty. The advocates of using the guillotine proclaimed it to be humane because the only thing the condemned would feel would be a "slight breeze at the back of the neck." Here the head of Louis XVI is being shown to the crowd.

campaigns against foreign invaders as well. They regained all lost French territory, annexed Belgium, and occupied other areas that extended to the Rhine, the Alps, and the Pyrenees, thus gaining in two years the "natural frontiers" that Louis XIV had dreamed about. By 1794 Prussia and Spain had left the coalition and the Netherlands had become a French ally. Only Britain, Austria, and Sardinia remained at war with France.

Despite their stated beliefs in free enterprise as an ideal, the Jacobins created a war economy, which operated under extensive controls. Government agencies conscripted labor and took over industries, directing them to produce large quantities of uniforms, arms, medical supplies, and equipment. In Paris alone, 258 forges made 1000 gun barrels a day. Reacting to bread riots and the revolutionary women's condemnation of monopolists and speculators, the Convention imposed price controls, rationing, and fixed wages while issuing currency without reference to bank reserves or market demand. The government also punished profiteers, used the

property of émigrés to relieve poverty, sold land directly to peasants, and freed the peasants from all compensatory payments to their old lords.

Many other changes reflected a strange combination of reason and fanaticism. The regime prohibited all symbols of status, such as knee breeches, powdered wigs, and jewelry. It abolished titles; people had to be addressed as "citizen" or "citizeness." Streets were renamed to commemorate Revolutionary events or honor revolutionary heroes. The calendar was reformed by dividing each month into three weeks of ten days each and giving the months poetic new names; July, for example, became Thermidor (hot) to avoid referring to the tyrant Julius Caesar. The Revolution took on a semireligious character in ceremonies and fêtes, which featured attractive young women as living symbols for reason, virtue, and duty. Along with these changes came a strong reaction against Christianity: Churches were closed and religious images destroyed. For a while "Worship of the Supreme Being" was substituted for Roman Catholicism, although in 1794 religion became a private matter.

Colonial problems, which had confounded the National and Legislative Assemblies, were met head-on by the Jacobin Convention. The grant of citizenship to free blacks and mulattoes of the islands in 1792 had drawn the mulattoes to the government side, but their armies, enlisted by the governors, faced determined insurrection from royalists and resentful escaped slaves. Sometimes the two anti-Convention forces were united with support from Spain or the British. In the late spring of 1793 the harried governor of Santo Domingo issued a decree freeing all former slaves and calling on them to join against foreign enemies. His strategy narrowly averted a British conquest. Subsequently, the Convention received a delegation from Santo Domingo and heard a plea for liberty from a 101-year-old former slave woman. The chamber responded by freeing all slaves in French territories and giving them full citizenship rights.

In this satirical print, Robespierre, having executed all others during the Terror, guillotines the executioner. In fact, it was Robespierre who was guillotined, in the summer of 1794.

Unfortunately, the revolutionary women in France were not so successful. A few, such as Olympe de Gouges (1748–1793), author of the *Declaration of the Rights of Women* (1791), had earlier advocated feminist reforms. Most politically conscious women, however, were so caught up in the general principles of the Revolution that they paid little attention to gender issues. At first they were welcomed as supporters by the radical Jacobins, until the latter gained power; then the Jacobins regarded revolutionary women as troublemakers. In October 1793 the Convention refused to hear a group of women who wanted to protest violations of the Constitution. During the next six months the government repressed women's societies and imprisoned the leaders, including de Gouges; later it sent her to the guillotine for her alleged royalist sympathies. Although the Jacobin legislature accented such policies by denying women the vote, it did improve their education, medical care, and property rights.

Because they regulated the economy and showed concern for the lower classes, the Jacobins have often been considered as forerunners of socialism. The Constitution of 1793, which was developed by the Convention but suspended almost immediately because of the war, does not support this interpretation. It did provide public assistance for the poor and aided the unemployed in seeking work, but it also guaranteed private property, included a charter of individual liberties, confirmed the Constitution of 1791's accent on local autonomy, and provided for the Central Committee, appointed by the departments. The greatest difference, in comparison with the Constitution of 1791, was the right to vote, which was granted to all adult males. Although the Jacobin constitution indicated a concern for equality of opportunity, it also revealed its authors as eighteenth-century radical liberals who followed Rousseau rather than Locke.

Conservative Reaction and the End of the Terror

The summer of 1794 brought a conservative reaction against radical revolution. With French arms victorious everywhere, rigid discipline no longer seemed necessary, but Robespierre, still committed to Rousseau's "republic of virtue," was determined to continue the Terror. When he demanded voluntary submission to the "general will" as necessary for achieving social equality, justice, and brotherly love, many practical politicians among his colleagues doubted his sanity. Others wondered if they would be among those next eliminated to purify society. They therefore cooperated to condemn him in the Convention. In July 1794 his enemies sent him to the guillotine with 20 of his supporters, amid great celebration.

Robespierre's fall ended the Terror and initiated a revival of the pre-Jacobin past. In 1794 the Convention eliminated the Committee of Public Safety; the next year it abolished the revolutionary tribunal and the radical political clubs and freed thousands of political prisoners. It also banned women from attendance in the Convention hall, an act that symbolized the return to a time when women's political influence was confined to the ballroom, the bedroom, and the salon. Indeed, as the exiled Girondists, émigré royalists, and nonconforming priests returned to France, Parisian politics moved from the streets to the drawing rooms of the elite, such as that of the former courtesan Madame Tallien (1773–1835), which became a center of high-society gossip and political intrigue. Outside Paris, by the summer of 1795, armed reactionary "white" terrorists roamed the countryside, seeking out and murdering former Jacobins. Everywhere the earlier reforming zeal and patriotic fervor gave way to conservative cynicism.

There was to be one last gasp of idealism in response to the widespread economic distress and human suffering among the Parisian poor. François-Noël Babeuf (1760–1797) was a radical journalist and a true believer in the spirit of the Enlightenment who expected utopia from the Revolution. To its success he sacrificed his worldly goods and his family: His wife and children went hungry while he moved in and out of jails. An earlier follower of Robespierre, he later condemned his former mentor as a traitor to the principle of equality. According to Babeuf, liberty was not possible while the rich exploited the poor; the solution had to be a "society of equals," where the Republic would guarantee efficient production and equitable distribution of goods. Babeuf's nascent socialism, so out of tune with his times, was suppressed in May 1796, along with his attempted uprising. At his trial, despite his heroic oratory, the loving support of his long-suffering wife, and a self-inflicted stab wound, he was condemned and sent to the guillotine.

Before it dissolved itself in 1795, the Convention proclaimed still another constitution and established a new political system known as the Directory, which governed France until 1799. The new government was headed by an executive council of five members (directors) appointed by the upper house of a bicameral (two-house) legislature. Assemblies of electors in each department selected deputies to the two chambers. These electors were chosen by adult male taxpayers, but the electors themselves had to be substantial property owners. Indeed, they numbered only some 20,000 in a total population of more than 25 million. Government was thus securely controlled by the upper middle classes, a condition also evident by the return to free trade.

The Directory was conspicuously conservative and antidemocratic, but it was also antiroyalist. A Bourbon restoration would have also restored church and royalist lands, which had been largely acquired by wealthy capitalists during the Revolution. Politicians who had participated in the Revolution or voted for the execution of Louis XVI had even greater reason to fear restoration of the monarchy. In pursuing this antiroyalist path at a time when royalist principles were regaining popularity, the government had to depend on the recently developed professional military establishment. More than once between 1795 and 1797, army action protected the government against royalists and radicals. The Directory also encouraged further military expansion, hoping to revive patriotic revolutionary fervor. Except for young military officers such as Napoleon Bonaparte, bureaucrats, members of the landowning middle classes, merchants in large cities, and some professionals, the majority of people in 1796 were worse off than they had been two decades before. But the Directory paid little attention to the majority of people and protected its own.

The Napoleonic Revolution

Even as a student, Napoleon considered himself a man of destiny, and he worked hard to construct the image he wanted to project to the future. As soon as the ship carrying him to exile in St. Helena set sail in 1815, his partisans and detractors began a debate over his career that continues to the present day. Whatever the viewpoint of the participants in that debate, all agree that few people have as decisively affected their times and set in motion developments that so profoundly altered the future as Napoleon Bonaparte.

Napoleon the Corsican

Revolutions favor the bright, the ambitious, and the lucky. Napoleon Bonaparte (1769–1821) had all three qualities in abundance. He was born on Corsica to a low-ranking Florentine noble family in 1769, the year after control of that island passed from Genoa to France. At the age of 10 his father placed him in the military academy at Brienne. Six years later he received his officer's commission. At the beginning of the French Revolution he was a 20-year-old officer doomed to a mediocre future by his family's modest standing and the restrictions of the Old Regime. Ten years later, he ruled France. The Revolution gave him the opportunity to rise rapidly, thanks to his intelligence, ability, charm, and daring.

A potent mixture of eighteenth-century rationalism, Romanticism, and revolutionary politics dominated his thought. He learned constantly, reading the classics, absorbing Enlightenment tracts, and talking

The Reign of Napoleon

1799	Napoleon establishes consulate, becomes First Consul
1801	Napoleon reestablishes relations with pope, restores Roman Catholic hierarchy
1802	Plebiscite declares Napoleon First Consul for life
1804	Napoleon proclaims himself emperor of the French
1806	Continental System implemented
1808–1814	France engages in Peninsular War with Spain
June 1812	Napoleon invades Russia
September 1812	French army reaches Moscow, is trapped by Russian winter
1813	Napoleon defeated at Leipzig
March 1814	Napoleon abdicates and goes into exile on island of Elba
March 1815	Napoleon escapes Elba and attempts to reclaim power
June 15, 1815	Napoleon is defeated at Waterloo and exiled to island of St. Helena

to people who could teach him. As an outsider from Corsica, he was tied to no particular faction in France and pursued his own interests with a fresh point of view. He drew close first to the men of 1789, then to the Jacobins, and later to the Directory. Never did he allow control of his fate to escape from his own hands, pragmatically choosing whatever political, social, or religious option that could serve his goals.[4]

He never doubted that fate had chosen him to accomplish great things. Equipped with a vast reserve of energy to match his enormous ego, Napoleon worked and studied ceaselessly, running on very little sleep until his later years. He was disciplined in his use of time and gifted in public relations skills. He pitched his messages and dreams to all levels of society and had the ability to inspire and gain the maximum sacrifice from his nation and his armies.

The Opportunist

Napoleon arrived at the right time—a generation earlier or later, the situation would not have allowed

him to gain power. He took advantage of the gutting of the old officer class by the revolutionary wars and the Jacobins to rise quickly to a prominent position from which he could appeal to the Directory. That self-interested group of survivors asked the Corsican to break up a right-wing uprising in October 1795. The following year the Directory gave Napoleon command of the smallest of the three armies sent to do battle with the Austrians.

The two larger forces crossed the Rhine on their way to attack the Habsburgs while, as a diversionary move, Napoleon's corps went over the Alps into Italy. Contrary to plan, the main forces accomplished little while Napoleon, intended as no more than bait, crushed the Sardinians and then the Austrians in a brilliant series of campaigns. As he marched across northern Italy he picked off Venice and was well on the road to Vienna when the Austrians approached him to make peace. Without instructions from his government, Napoleon negotiated the Treaty of Campo Formio (1797) and returned home a hero.

After considering an invasion of Britain in the first part of 1798—a cross-Channel task he deemed impossible—Napoleon set out with the Directory's blessing to strike at Britain's economy by attacking its colonial structure. He would invade Egypt, expose the weakness of the Ottoman Empire, and from there launch an attack on India. The politicians were as much impressed by this grand plan as they were relieved to get the increasingly popular Napoleon out of town. He successfully evaded the British fleet in the Mediterranean, landed in Egypt, and took Alexandria and Cairo in July. The British admiral, Horatio Nelson (1758–1805), found the French fleet and sank it at Aboukir on August 1, 1798. Even though their supply lines and access to France were cut off, Napoleon's forces fought a number of successful battles against the Turks in Syria and Egypt.[5]

However, the fact remained that the French armies were stranded in Egypt and would be forced to remain there until 1801, when a truce allowed them to come home. This development would normally be regarded as a defeat, yet when Napoleon abandoned his army in August 1799, slipped by the British fleet, and returned to Paris, he was given a frenzied, triumphant homecoming. In public appearances he adopted a modest pose and gave addresses on the scientific accomplishments of the expedition, such as the finding of the Rosetta Stone, a discovery that provided the first clue in the deciphering of Egyptian hieroglyphics.

Napoleon, his brothers, and the Abbé Sieyès—the former vicar general and author of the important 1789 pamphlet "What Is the Third Estate?"—sought to take advantage of the political crisis surrounding the Directory. Second Coalition, consisting of Russia, Great Britain, Austria, Naples, Portugal, and the Ot-

This heroic portrait by Antoine-Jean Gros shows the 27-year-old Napoleon leading his troops at the battle of Arcola in northern Italy in November 1796.

toman Empire, threatened France from the outside, while a feverish inflation ravaged the economy domestically. Various political factions courted Napoleon, whose charisma made him seem the likely savior of the country. In the meantime, he and his confederates planned their course. They launched a clumsy, though successful, coup in November 1799 and replaced the Directory with the Consulate. The plotters shared the cynical belief that "constitutions should be short and obscure" and that democracy meant that the rulers rule and the people obey.

The takeover ended the revolutionary decade. France remained, in theory, a republic, but nearly all power rested with the 31-year-old Napoleon, who ruled as First Consul. Still another constitution was written and submitted to a vote of the people. Only half of the eligible voters went to the polls, but an overwhelming majority voted in favor of the new constitution: 3,011,007 in favor versus 1,562 against.[6]

New Foundations

Ten years of radical change made France ready for one-man rule, but of a type much different from that exercised by the Bourbon monarchy. The events of 1789 had overturned the source of legitimate political power. Now it came not from God but from the people. The social structure of the Old Regime was gone and with it the privileges of hereditary and created nobility. The church no longer had financial or overt political power. The old struggles between kings and nobles, nobles and bourgeoisie, peasants and landlords, and Catholics and Protestants were replaced by the rather more universal confrontation between rich and poor.

There had been three attempts to rebuild the French system in the ten years of revolution: the bourgeois-constitutional efforts to 1791, the radical programs to 1794, and the rule to 1799 by survivors who feared both the right and the left. Although each attempt had failed, each left valuable legacies to the new France. The first attempt established the power of the upper middle classes; the second showed the great power of the state to mobilize the population; and the third demonstrated the usefulness of employing former enemies in day-to-day politics.

Ever the pragmatic tactician, Napoleon used elements from the Old Regime and the various phases of the Revolution to reconstruct France. He built an autocracy far more powerful than Louis XVI's government. He took advantage of the absence of the old forms of competition to central power from the nobility and the feudal structure that had been destroyed in the name of liberty, equality, and brotherhood. He used the mercantile policies, military theories, and foreign policy goals of the Old Regime, the ambitions of the middle class, and the mobilization policies of the Jacobins. All he asked from those who wished to serve him was loyalty. Defrocked priests, renegade former nobles, reformed Jacobins, small businessmen, and enthusiastic soldiers all played a role. His unquestioning acceptance of the ambitious brought him popularity because ten years of constant change had compromised most politically active people in some form of unprincipled, immoral, or illegal behavior.

Napoleon built his state on the *philosophes'* conception of a system in which all French men would be equal before the law. The Revolution destroyed the sense of personal power of a sovereign and substituted what the British historian Lord Acton would later in the century call the "tyranny of the majority." The French state accordingly could intervene more effectively than ever before, limited only by distance and communication problems.[7]

The mass democratic army created by the total mobilization of both people and resources was one of the best examples of the new state system. A revolutionary society had fought an ideological war, and the experience changed the nature of combat forever. Because advancement and success were based on valor and victory, rather than bloodlines or privilege, the army profited from the new social structure and sought to preserve and extend it. The army best

symbolized the great power of the French nation unleashed by the Revolution. Many of the economic
and diplomatic problems that preceded the Revolution remained, but Napoleon's new state structure
provided inspired solutions.

Taking advantage of his military supremacy,
Napoleon gained breathing space for his domestic reforms by making peace with the Second Coalition by
March 1802. He then set about erecting the governing structure of France, which remained virtually intact into the 1980s. He developed an administration
that was effective in raising money, assembling an
army, and exploiting the country's resources. His centralized government ruled through prefects, powerful
agents in the provinces who had almost complete
control of local affairs and were supported by a large
police force. He then established a stable monetary
policy based on an honest tax-collecting system,
backed by up-to-date accounting procedures. The
Bank of France that he created remains a model of
sound finance.

Napoleon knew that the country he ruled was
overwhelmingly Catholic and that national interest
dictated that he come to terms with the papacy.
Through the Concordat of 1801 with Pope Pius VII
the pope gained the right to approve the bishops
whom the First Consul appointed to the reestablished Catholic Church. The state permitted seminaries to be reopened and paid priests' salaries. Pius regained control of the Papal States and saw his church
recognized as the religion of the majority in France.
The church thus resumed its position of prominence,
but without its former power and wealth.

Napoleon viewed education as a way to train useful citizens to become good soldiers and bureaucrats,
and he pursued the development of mass education
by trying to increase the number of elementary
schools, secondary schools, and special institutes for
technical training. The schools were to be used to
propagandize the young to serve the state through
"directing political and moral opinion." Overarching
the entire system was the University of France, which
was more an administrative body to control education than a teaching institution. Napoleon had neither the time nor the resources to put mass education
in place during his lifetime, although he did gain immediate success in training the sons—but rarely the
daughters—of the newly arrived middle classes to become state functionaries.[8]

Perhaps Napoleon's greatest accomplishment
came in the field of law. Building on reforms begun
ten years earlier, he assembled a talented team of
lawyers to bring order to the chaotic state of French
jurisprudence. At the time he took power the country
was caught in the transition from 366 separate local
systems to a uniform code. By 1804 the staff had
compiled a comprehensive civil law code (called the
Code Napoléon after 1807) that was a model of precision and equality when compared to the old system.
The code ensured the continuation of the gains made
by the middle classes in the previous decade and emphasized religious toleration and abolition of the
privileges held under the old order. Unfortunately,
the code perpetuated the inferior status of women in
the areas of civil rights, financial activities, and divorce. Nonetheless, it has served as the basis for law
codes in many other countries.

The price France paid for these gains was rule by
a police state that featured censorship, secret police,
spies, and political trials, which sent hundreds to
their deaths and thousands into exile. Order did prevail, however, and for the first time in a decade it was
safe to travel the country's roads. Napoleon also reduced the "representative assemblies" to meaningless
rubber stamps. Liberty, equality, and brotherhood
meant little in a land where the First Consul and his
police could deny a person's freedom and right of association because of a perceived intellectual or political conflict.

To consolidate all of the changes, Napoleon proclaimed himself emperor in December 1804. Fifteen
years after the outbreak of the Revolution, France
had a new monarch. In a plebiscite the nation approved the change by 3,572,329 to 2,579.[9] As
Napoleon took the crown from Pope Pius VII, who
had come from Rome for the occasion, and crowned
himself, the First French Republic came to an end.

Napoleon as Military Leader

War had been France's primary occupation since
1792, and on the whole it had been a profitable enterprise. The French had gained much land and money,
as well as the opportunity to export the Revolution.
Napoleon's reforms helped make his country even
stronger in battle. At the end of 1804 Napoleon embarked on a series of campaigns designed to show
France's invincibility. A key to French success was the
emperor himself, who employed his own remarkable
genius to lead his strong and wealthy country.

Napoleon brought intellectual strength, sensitivity to mood and opportunity, and bravery to the task
of making war. He had been trained in the most advanced methods of his day, and he had better, more
mobile artillery and more potent powder to blow
holes through the enemy's lines. He worked well with
a talented command staff, to which he gave much responsibility to wield their divisions as conditions
dictated. Finally, he was the ultimate leader. Whether
as lieutenant, general, First Consul, or emperor,
Napoleon inspired masses of soldiers in a dramatic
way. At the same time, he mobilized the home front
through the use of the press and skillfully written
dispatches.

Beneath this imagemaking, the supreme commander was extremely flexible in his use of resources, always changing his tactics. He was pragmatic, moved rapidly, and lived off the land. He won the loyalty of his men by incentives and rewards, not brutal discipline. He set many military precedents, among them the use of ideological and economic warfare as well as the rapid simultaneous movement of a large number of military columns. These columns could quickly converge on a given point with devastating results, breaking the will of the enemy. Finally, he personally led his troops into battle, exposing himself to incredible dangers with little regard for his own safety.[10]

His nemesis was Great Britain, and during 1803 and 1804 he prepared a cross-Channel invasion, but the inability of the French navy to control the Channel and the formation of the Third Coalition (Great Britain, Russia, Austria, and Sweden) forced him to march eastward. In October 1805 Admiral Nelson and the British ended Napoleon's hopes of dominating the seas by destroying the joint French-Spanish fleet at the battle of Trafalgar.

France did far better on land, gaining mastery over the Continent by the end of 1807. Napoleon totally demoralized the Third Coalition in battles at Ulm (October 1805) and Austerlitz (December 1805).

He then annihilated the Prussians, who had entered the conflict in the battles at Jena and Auerstadt (October 1806). He occupied Berlin, where he established the Continental System, a blockade of the Continent that was an effort to defeat Britain by depriving it of trade with the rest of Europe. Finally, in June 1807 he defeated the Russians at the battle of Friedland and forced Tsar Alexander I to sign the Tilsit Treaty in July. This treaty, ratified on a raft anchored in the middle of the Nieman River, brought the two major land powers of Europe together in an alliance against Britain.

At the beginning of 1808 Napoleon stood supreme in Europe, leading France to a dominance it had never experienced before and has not experienced since. Several of his relatives occupied the thrones of nearby countries. The rest of the continent appeared to be mere satellites revolving around, this time, around a Napoleonic sun.[11]

Napoleon's Revolution in Europe

As he achieved his military goals, Napoleon set in motion a chain reaction of minirevolutions that had a profound impact on the rest of the century. British sea power stood in the way of France's total domination of the Continent. Even though the British econ-

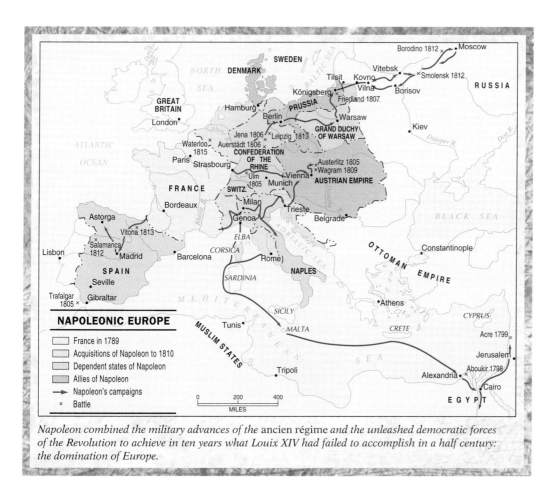

Napoleon combined the military advances of the ancien régime *and the unleashed democratic forces of the Revolution to achieve in ten years what Louix XIV had failed to accomplish in a half century: the domination of Europe.*

omy suffered under the impact of the Continental System (exports dropped by 20 percent, with a resultant cutback in production and rise in unemployment), the damage was not permanent. The Continental System inadvertently contributed to Britain's economic development by forcing it to industrialize quickly as it sought new markets and methods. Safe behind their wall of ships, the British turned out increasing quantities of goods as they passed through the early phases of industrialization.

Napoleon's armies carried French ideological baggage and institutional reforms across the Continent. Even though the emperor consolidated the Revolution in a conservative way in France, he broke apart his opponents' fragile social and governmental structures when he marched across the Rhine. Napoleon consciously spread the messages of liberty, equality, and brotherhood with all of the antifeudal, antiprivilege, and antirepressive themes inherent in the revolutionary triad. Where the French governed directly, they used the Code Napoléon and the reformed administrative practices. After 1815 the changes may have been repressed by the restored governments, but they set precedents that bore fruit throughout most of Europe by 1848.

The French presence triggered a hostile wave of nationalistic resentments. Many Europeans saw Napoleon as an imperialist, and the people he had "emancipated" began to realize that they had exchanged an old form of despotism for a new one. By posing as the champion of the Revolution, Napoleon sowed the seeds of the opposition that would work against him later, especially in Prussia. With the exception of the Poles, who had labored under Russian dominance and now served Napoleon well, the rest of Europe reacted against the French yoke.

The most significant rebellion took place in Portugal and Spain. Napoleon's entry into those countries to topple the passive Bourbons and strengthen the leaky Continental System was uncharacteristically shortsighted. The emperor had a serious fight on his hands in the Peninsular War that followed. Guerrilla uprisings soon broke out, supported by a British expeditionary force and supplies. These bloody wars tied down 200,000 to 300,000 French troops over a period of five years and drained the French treasury. The invasion of Spain also prompted a series of uprisings in the New World that gave birth to modern Latin American history.

The social and political changes the French triggered in Germany were equally profound. When he redrew the map of Europe after his victories, Napoleon destroyed the remnants of the Holy Roman Empire and in so doing erased 112 states of that ancient league. Only six of the former 50 free cities retained their status. Further, by changing the territorial arrangements of other areas, he reduced the

number of German political units from more than 300 to 39. All over Germany a wave of nationalism stirred the politically conscious population and prepared the way for the liberation movement. Prussia in particular underwent a rebirth after 1806 to enable it to compete with France, and many German nationalists thereafter began to look to Berlin for strength and leadership. Prussian reform politicians such as Baron Heinrich vom und zum Stein (1757–1831) and Prince Karl von Hardenberg (1750–1822) initiated a program of social change that included the abolition of serfdom (without turning land over to the peasants), a degree of self-government in the cities, and emancipation of the Jews. Although Napoleon had limited the Prussian army to 42,000 men, the Berlin authorities undermined this restriction by a subterfuge: As soon as one army was trained, it was placed on reserve, and a new army was called up for training. In this way Prussia managed to build a force of 270,000 men. These efforts gained the support of Prussian intellectuals who used education as a means of nationalistic propaganda. In fact, the University of Berlin, founded in 1810, became a strong center for national movements.[12]

The Invasion of Russia and Napoleon's Downfall

Opposition to Napoleon grew in both Austria and Russia. After the valiant but unsuccessful campaigns against the French in 1809, culminating in the bloody battle of Wagram, Vienna became a docile, though unreliable, ally. Napoleon's marriage to Marie Louise, the daughter of Francis I of Austria, proved to be only a tenuous tie between the French emperor and the Habsburgs. In Russia the Tilsit Treaty had never been popular, and the economic hardships brought on by the Continental System made a break in the alliance virtually inevitable. By the end of 1810 France and Russia prepared to go to war against each other.

Napoleon understood the shaky base on which his dominance rested. Involvement in Spain had drained France. The Continental System was not working against Britain. Alexander I proved to be an increasingly undependable ally. Finally, after two years of preparations, Napoleon launched a massive invasion of Russia in 1812 to put an end to at least one of his problems.

The emperor prepared carefully for his attack on Russia. Food supply would be a major problem for the 611,000 troops—half of them non-French—in the first and second lines of the invasion because his forces would be too large to live off the land. Furthermore his army took with them over 200,000 animals, which required forage and water. The invasion force delayed its march until late June to ensure that the Russian plains would furnish sufficient grass to feed

An engraving commemorating the signing of the Treaty of Tilsit by Napoleon and Tsar Alexander I of Russia after the French defeated the Russians at the battle of Friedland in June 1807. The two monarchs conducted their negotiations on a lavishly equipped barge moored midstream in the Nieman River. The peace they concluded failed to last, and Napoleon's invasion of Russia in 1812 did not end as successfully for the French as the battle of Friedland had.

the animals. The massive and well-thought-out preparations for the invasion nevertheless proved inadequate to the problems posed by the 600-mile march from the Nieman River to Moscow.

Although Napoleon's 12-nation army made almost constant headway, the Russian forces remained intact. Outnumbered nearly three to one, the tsar's armies, under the leadership of General Barclay de Tolly (1761–1818) and later General Mikhail Kutuzov (1745–1813), continually retreated into the vastness of their land rather than face almost certain defeat at the hands of the invaders. Employing what is known as a scorched earth policy, the retreating Russians destroyed everything of possible use to Napoleon's forces. The tsar's troops also continually harassed the advancing columns and threatened the French supply lines. When the Russians finally stood their ground at Borodino (September 7, 1812), the effects of distance and disease had taken their toll among the French, and the numbers of the opposing forces were nearly equal. After a brutal conflict in which 75,000 of the total 200,000 combatants were left dead or wounded, the road to Moscow was open to the victorious French.

The Russian campaign was both a success and a failure for Napoleon. The French did gain their objective—the city of Moscow—but the Russians refused to surrender. Shortly after the French occupied Moscow, fires broke out, destroying three-fourths of the city. After spending 33 days in the burned shell of the former capital waiting in vain for the tsar, 400 miles north in St. Petersburg, to agree to peace, Napoleon gave orders to retreat. He left the city on October 19. To remain would have meant having his lines cut by winter and being trapped with no supplies. His isolation in Moscow would have encouraged his enemies in Paris. Leaving the city, as it turned out, condemned most of his men to death.[13]

As the remnants of Napoleon's forces marched west in October and November, they were forced to retrace virtually the same route they had used in the summer. They suffered starvation, attacks by partisans, and the continual pressure of Kutuzov's forces. Thousands perished daily, and by the end of November only about 100,000 of the original force had made their escape from Russia. Thirteen years earlier Napoleon had abandoned an army in Egypt to return to Paris; in November 1812 he abandoned another army, this time in Russia, and returned home to pursue his fortunes.

Russia, which had stood alone against the French at the beginning of 1812, was soon joined by Prussia, Austria, and Britain in 1813 and 1814 in what came to be known as the War of Liberation. While British armies under the duke of Wellington (1769–1852) helped clear the French forces out of Spain, the allied troops pushed Napoleon's forces westward. A combination of Napoleon's genius and the difficulties in coordinating the allied efforts prolonged the war, but in October 1813 the French suffered a decisive defeat at Leipzig in the Battle of the Nations, one year to the day after Napoleon had fled Moscow.

The allies sent peace offers to Napoleon, but he refused them, pointing out that "you sovereigns who were born to the throne may get beaten 20 times, and yet return to your capitals. I cannot. For I rose to power through the camp."[14] After Leipzig the Napoleonic empire rapidly disintegrated, and by the beginning of 1814 the allies had crossed the Rhine and invaded France. At the end of March, the Russians, Austrians, and Prussians took Paris. Two weeks later Napoleon abdicated his throne, receiving in return sovereignty over Elba, a small island between Corsica and Italy.

Napoleon arrived in Elba in May and established rule over his 85-square-mile kingdom. He set up a ministate, complete with an army, a navy, and a court. He soon exhausted the possibilities of Elba and in February/March 1815 he eluded the British fleet and returned to France to begin his campaign to regain power "within one hundred days." His former subjects, bored with the restored Bourbon, Louis XVIII, gave him a tumultuous welcome. Napoleon entered Paris, raised an army of 300,000 men, and sent a message to the allies gathered to make peace at Vienna that he desired to rule France and only France. The allies, who were on the verge of breaking up their alliance, united, condemned Napoleon as an enemy of peace, and sent forces to France to put him down once and for all.

Napoleon on His Place in History

In conversations with the Comte de Las Cases shortly after his arrival at St. Helena, Napoleon clearly expressed his notion of his place in history.

I closed the gulf of anarchy and cleared the chaos. I purified the Revolution, dignified Nations and established Kings. I excited every kind of emulation, rewarded every kind of merit, and extended the limits of glory! This is at least something! And on what point can I be assailed on which a historian could not defend me? Can it be for my intentions? But even here I can find absolution. Can it be for my despotism? It may be demonstrated that the Dictatorship was absolutely necessary. Will it be said that I restrained liberty? It can be proved that licentiousness, anarchy, and the greatest irregularities, still haunted the threshold of freedom. Shall I be accused of having been too fond of war? It can be shown that I always received the first attack. Will it be said that I aimed at universal monarchy? It can be proved that this was merely the result of fortuitous circumstances, and that our enemies themselves led me step by step to this determination. Lastly, shall I be blamed for my ambition? This passion I must doubtless be allowed to have possessed, and that in no small degree; but at the same time, my ambition was of the highest and noblest kind that ever, perhaps, existed—that of establishing and of consecrating the empire of reason, and the full exercise and complete enjoyment of all the human faculties!"

And here the historian will probably feel compelled to regret that such ambition should not have been fulfilled and gratified! Then after a few moments of silent reflection: "This," said the Emperor, "is my whole history in a few words."

From *Memoirs of the Life, Exile, and Conversations of the Emperor Napoleon,* ed. Emmanuel de Las Cases (New York: Eckler, 1900).

At the battle of Waterloo on June 18, 1815, the duke of Wellington, supported by Prussian troops under Field Marshall Gebhard von Blücher (1749–1819), narrowly defeated Napoleon. The vanquished leader sought asylum with the British, hoping to live in exile in either England or the United States. But the allies, taking no chances, shipped him off to the bleak South Atlantic island of St. Helena, 5000 miles from Paris. Here he set about writing his autobiography. He died of cancer in 1821 at the age of 51.

Even with the brief flurry of the One Hundred Days, Napoleon had no hope of re-creating the grandeur of his empire as it was in 1808. The reasons for this are not hard to find. Quite simply, Napoleon was the heart and soul of the empire, and after 1808 his physical and intellectual vigor began to weaken. Administrative and military developments reflected this deterioration as Napoleon began to appoint sycophants to positions of responsibility. Further, by 1812 the middle classes on which he depended began suffering the economic consequences of his policies. The Continental System and continual warfare made their effects deeply felt through decreased trade and increased taxes. Even though some war contractors profited, the costs of Napoleon's ambitions began to make Frenchmen long for peace.

Outside France, the growth of nationalistic resistance on the Continent worked against the dictator, who first stimulated it by exporting the call for liberty, equality, and brotherhood. Equally important, the 25 years of French military superiority disappeared as other nations adopted and improved on the new methods of fighting. Finally, the balance-of-power principle made itself felt. France could not eternally take on the whole world.

Napoleon and the Americas

The forces generated by the French Revolution and Napoleon deeply affected the Americas in the 50 years after 1776. The former English colonies south of Canada had gained their independence with French assistance, and the new government had close relations with Paris until the outbreak of France's revolutionary wars, when President George Washington proclaimed neutrality. To the south, the toppling of the Spanish throne in 1808 set in motion a 15-year wave of revolutions.

The United States of America

When trade relations with the British began to improve in the 1790s, the French waged an undeclared war on American shipping, taking over 800 ships in the last three years of the decade. This, in addition to the undiplomatic activities of the French embassy, deeply affected the emerging party politics of the young country. Meanwhile, southern slaveholders were deeply suspicious of the French policies toward slavery in their colonies in the Caribbean.

The United States benefited from one aspect of Napoleon's activities. In the seventeenth century French explorers had laid claim to the region between the Mississippi River and the Rocky Mountains, naming it Louisiana in honor of their king. They ceded the region to the Spanish in 1763 and then took it back at the beginning of the nineteenth century. The French had never surveyed the full extent of the area and had no hope of exploiting it in the near future. As a way to block the British and the Spaniards and to make sure the port of New Orleans would remain in at least neutral hands, Napoleon sold Louisiana for $15 million to the United States in 1803. Thomas Jefferson had to take some distinctly unconstitutional steps to buy the land, but by so doing, the Louisiana Purchase doubled the land area of the new country and set a precedent for land acquisition and expansion.

Latin American Revolutions

The French overthrow of the Spanish Bourbons in 1808 encouraged revolts that created 13 republics in Spanish America over the next 16 years. The charismatic leader who stepped into the void was Simón Bolívar (1783–1830), hailed as the Liberator of South America. After completing his rationalist education in Paris during the last years of the Directory, Bolívar returned to his native Venezuela to exploit colonial resistance to the Napoleonic takeover of Spain in 1808. Napoleon, convinced after the disaster at Trafalgar that transatlantic ambitions were pointless, left the Spanish colonial empire to its own complex fate.[15]

Loyal at first to the deposed Spanish Bourbons and newly filled with refugees from the parent country, Spain's colonies soon began to entertain the idea that they had their own destinies to fulfill as new nations. The American-born elite of European blood, the Creoles, were especially attracted to the prospect of expelling the controlling *peninsulares*, Spaniards of European birth who usually returned to Spain after a profitable term of colonial service.[16]

Bolívar stepped into this situation by issuing a series of inflammatory and visionary messages calling for the liberation of Venezuela and Gran Colombia (modern-day Colombia, Panama, Ecuador, and Venezuela). From this base he hoped to expand the liberation movement to include all of Spanish South America. Spanish loyalist forces frequently defeated him, yet he kept fighting and made use of skills as an orator and as a tactician. He eventually forced the remnants of the Spanish military and administrative personnel to go home. He proposed a constitution that favored the elite of the new nations, a document much like the one written by the Directory. He dreamed of an independent continent, the north made up of the nation-states of Venezuela, Colombia, Ecuador, Peru, and Bolivia, but he ran afoul of liberal critics and local loyalties and eventually died in exile in British Jamaica.

Argentina, Uruguay, and Chile were liberated in comparable fashion by the stoic, Spanish-educated Creole officer José de San Martín (1778–1850), a man

Simón Bolívar and his army battle the Spanish at Araure in Venezuela. Although the Spanish were better trained and equipped, Bolívar led his soldiers with such personal valor that he managed to liberate four countries.

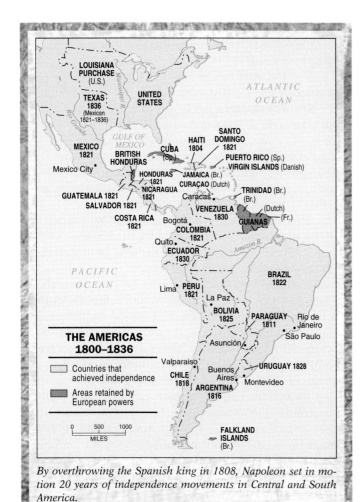

By overthrowing the Spanish king in 1808, Napoleon set in motion 20 years of independence movements in Central and South America.

The revolution was actually begun by an enlightened provincial Creole priest, Miguel Hidalgo (1753–1811), who on September 16, 1810, issued a call for universal freedom (the date is celebrated in Mexico today as the *Dia del Grito*, the Day of the Call). Hidalgo led his ragged army of Indians and idealists to the gates of Mexico City but hesitated to take the city, fearing the bloodbath that would follow. Although Hidalgo was condemned by the colonial bishops and executed for treason six months after his uprising began, his cause was taken up by others, including José María Morelos (1765–1815), a radical *mestizo* (mixed-blood) parish priest who became an effective guerrilla leader. Finally, in August 1821, the last Spanish viceroy recognized the independence of Mexico, whose ruling classes promptly fell to squabbling over the constitution.

While men of ideas argued, military opportunists took power. Two would-be Napoleons, Augustín de Iturbide (1783–1824) and Antonio López de Santa Anna (1794–1876), dominated politics for the next quarter century, at the end of which Mexico lost the northern half of its territory to the United States. Iturbide, a Creole landowner and officer who had fought as a Spanish loyalist until 1816, became emperor of Mexico for a turbulent ten-month reign in 1822–1823. Santa Anna, who emulated Napoleon's opportunism more successfully than he did many of the Frenchman's other qualities, became president or dictator of the Mexican republic 11 times between 1833 and 1855. His career as a military leader included several disastrous incidents, notably his humiliating defeat and capture by Texan rebels at San Jacinto in April 1836, six weeks after he had exterminated their comrades at the secularized Franciscan mission in San Antonio known as the Alamo and a month after he had mercilessly massacred Texan prisoners at Goliad.[17]

The Social and Economic Consequences of the Revolutions

The social and economic consequences of the Latin American revolutions were far different from those in North America and Europe. The area was much poorer and more divided. The new nations of Latin America quickly fell to the commercial dominance of the British Empire. Their economies, exploited by speculators in North America and Europe, have been subject to drastic fluctuations ever since, based as they are on exportation of raw materials. The conditions of the Indian population declined as the new liberal regimes confiscated the large landholdings of the religious orders, which had served to insulate the surviving Indians from direct confrontations with the Europeans' economic and technological dominance. As in every country since the Reformation where

as austere and reserved as Bolívar was flashy and outgoing. The two could never forge an alliance, partly because of personality differences and partly because of San Martín's preference for a constitutional monarchy like Britain or like France under the Constitution of 1791. The Spanish colonies he had freed rejected his desires, but the Portuguese in Brazil accepted them. King John VI of Portugal had fled his country in 1807 and for the next 14 years ruled the Portuguese Empire from Rio de Janeiro. Returning to Lisbon in 1821, the king left his son Dom Pedro as regent of Brazil. Impatient with the reactionary behavior of the Lisbon government, Pedro declared himself emperor of an independent Brazil, which he and then his son Pedro II ruled as a constitutional monarchy for nearly 70 years.

The Mexican Revolution began earlier and produced more extreme consequences than its South American counterpart. The Mexican middle class was even smaller than that of the rest of Spanish America and far more conservative. Between 1808 and 1810 anti-Bonapartist sentiment shifted to a general rejection of the European monarchy in Creole circles throughout the viceroyalty of New Spain.

church property was bought up by the monied classes, the local population was reorganized into a new labor force more profitable to the new owners. In this case the owners simply reorganized the Indian communities into a labor force and drove the unproductive and the mestizos off the land. This movement in some countries has continued in one form or another to the present day.

The Latin American church, staffed largely by *peninsulares*, was shattered by the national revolutions. When reconstituted with greatly reduced property and clerical personnel, the church desperately sought to win the protection of the more conservative elements in the Creole elite by opposing liberalism in any form. Since the church had been the exclusive instrument of education and social welfare before liberation and since the ruling classes showed little interest in providing for the continuation of schools, orphanages, and relief for the lower classes, the misery of the Latin American poor grew more acute throughout the nineteenth century.

The legal and social standing of women rose momentarily and then fell, as it did in France. Individual Creole women, such as Bolívar's astute mistress, Manuela Sanches, made major contributions to the revolution, but the adoption of the Napoleonic Code in the 1820s had the same impact on women's legal status in South America as it did in Europe at the same time.

It can be argued that in the wake of Napoleon's deposing the Spanish Bourbons, Latin America suffered a decline in political stability and internal economic health. The peasants and urban laborers of Indian and mixed-blood descent, the culture-shaping church, and women of all classes paid a heavy price for liberation from the Spanish and Portuguese overlords. The sole group to gain was the secular, male Creole leadership. Nevertheless, what Napoleon had destroyed was gone, and no serious attempt was made to restore the old colonial regime. In the Monroe Doctrine, proclaimed in 1823, the United States guaranteed the political independence of the new nations of Latin America, at least in theory. For the Latin Americans, more important for blocking the old empires from returning was the actual force of the British Navy.

The Vienna Settlement and the Concert of Europe

Once Napoleon was "safely" exiled to Elba, representatives of all the European powers except the Ottoman Empire gathered in September at Vienna. They had the imposing task of building a new political and diplomatic structure for Europe after a quarter century of wars and revolutions. The factor that had brought the British, Prussians, Austrians, and Russians together—Napoleon—was gone, and wartime unity dissolved into peacetime pursuit of self-interest.

The Allied Dilemma: Putting Humpty Together Again

Work went slowly during the ten-month span of the Congress of Vienna. The leaders who gathered at Vienna—Lord Castlereagh of Great Britain, Count von Hardenberg of Prussia, Prince Klemens von Metternich of Austria, Tsar Alexander I of Russia, and Prince Charles-Maurice de Talleyrand of France—met in small secret conferences to decide the future of Europe. Metternich came to dominate the conference, as much by his diplomatic skills as by his ability to impress on the participants the need for stability.

The Congress dealt with numerous issues: the status of France, the new political boundaries, the response to liberal and national attitudes sweeping the continent, the fate of the powers who had lost territory during the previous 25 years, and the future of dispossessed dynasties. The solutions proposed were moderate. France was allowed to return to its 1792 boundaries; however, after Napoleon's return and the One Hundred Days, the allies cut back the boundaries and imposed penalties. They virtually ignored the democratic, liberal, and nationalistic forces in favor of a more traditional solution to the upheavals of the previous 25 years.[18]

The events since 1789 had drastically altered the map of Europe. For example, the 1000-year-old Holy Roman Empire had disappeared. In an attempt to restore some balance, the Congress followed four principles: legitimacy, encirclement of France, compensation, and balance of power. The Congress ruled that royal houses that had been expelled, such as the Bourbons in France, Spain, and Naples, the House of Savoy in Sardinia-Piedmont, and the House of Orange in the Netherlands, would be placed back on their thrones. The redrawn map of Europe resembled the 1789 configuration, except that the Holy Roman Empire remained dissolved. In its place were the 39 states of the German Confederation, dominated by Austria. The redrawing of boundaries created a protective belt of states around France to make future aggression more difficult. The principle of compensation ensured that no important power suffered a loss as the result of the Congress's work. Austria was compensated for the loss of land in the Low Countries by gaining territory in Italy and along the Adriatic. Sweden received Norway in return for permitting Russia to keep Finland.

The desire to construct an effective balance of power remained at the center of the Congress's

Metternich on His Political Principles

In the aftermath of the Napoleonic age, waves of change threatened the structure erected at the Congress of Vienna. Prince Klemens von Metternich of Austria had a precise notion of what was happening.

Kings have to calculate the chances of their very existence in the immediate future; passions are let loose, and league together to overthrow everything which society respects as the basis of its existence; religion, public morality, laws, customs, rights, and duties, all are attacked, confounded, overthrown, or called in question. The great mass of the people are tranquil spectators of these attacks and revolutions, and of the absolute want of all means of defense. A few are carried off by the torrent, but the wishes of the immense majority are to maintain a repose which exists no longer, and of which even the first elements seem to be lost.

Having now thrown a rapid glance over the first causes of the present state of society, it is necessary to point out in a more particular manner the evil which threatens to deprive it, at one blow, of the real blessings, the fruits of genuine civilisation, and to disturb it in the midst of its enjoyments. This evil may be described in one word—presumption; the natural effect of the rapid progression of the human mind towards the perfecting of so many things. This it is which at the present day leads so many individuals astray, for it has become an almost universal sentiment.

Religion, morality, legislation, economy, politics, administration, all have become common and accessible to everyone. Knowledge seems to come by inspi-

ration; experience has no value for the presumptuous man; faith is nothing to him; he substitutes for it a pretended individual conviction, and to arrive at this conviction dispenses with all inquiry and with all study; for these means appear too trivial to a mind which believes itself strong enough to embrace at one glance all questions and all facts. Laws have no value for him, because he has not contributed to make them, and it would be beneath a man of his parts to recognise the limits traced by rude and ignorant generations.

Power resides in himself; why should he submit himself to that which was only useful for the man deprived of light and knowledge? That which, according to him, was required in an age of weakness cannot be suitable in an age of reason and vigour amounting to universal perfection, which the German innovators designate by the idea, absurd in itself, of the Emancipation of the People! Morality itself he does not attack openly, for without it he could not be sure for a single instant of his own existence; but he interprets its essence after his own fashion, and allows every other person to do so likewise, provided that other person neither kills nor robs him.

From *Memoirs of Prince Metternich, 1815–1829*, Vol. 3, trans. Mrs. Alexander Napier (New York: Scribner, 1881).

---

attention. Each nation had its own idea of what constituted a proper balance, and soon the British and the Austrians found themselves arrayed against the Russians and the Prussians. Russia's ambitions in Poland almost broke up the conference because Britain feared that an enlarged Russia threatened the balance. Prussia wanted all of Saxony, which justified Austria's fears of the growing Berlin-based state. While the four wartime allies split, the clever French representative Talleyrand negotiated a secret treaty binding the French, Austrians, and British to pledge mutual assistance to restrain the Russians and Prussians. Russia and Prussia eventually reduced their demands for land in Poland and Saxony, and the sought-after balance of power was achieved.

Although the Congress has been criticized for ignoring the democratic impulse in Europe, it has been praised for crafting a general settlement of a

complex series of problems, especially compared to the work of the vengeful allies at Versailles after World War I.[19] The representatives were not totally, blindly reactionary, however; many of the changes of the previous 25 years were retained. The 40 years of general peace that followed, flawed though they may have been, are testimony to the success of Metternich and his colleagues in gaining stability. But by ignoring the forces of change expressed in the new ideologies, the representatives at Vienna ensured the ultimate failure of the system they created.

The Congress System and the Search for Stability

The Vienna negotiators set out to coordinate their policies to maintain stability. The first proposal for

This cartoon, La Balance Politique, *lampoons the balance-of-power politics played out at the Congress of Vienna. Here Castlereagh places money on the scales opposite the king of Prussia and Metternich. At right, Tsar Alexander I confers with Talleyrand.*

postwar consultation was symbolic and quixotic. In the fall of 1815 Tsar Alexander I proposed the formation of a "Holy Alliance" to be based on "the precepts of justice, Christian charity, and peace." No one was quite sure what the tsar meant by this pact, but every ruler in Europe signed it except the British king, the Turkish sultan, and the pope. Castlereagh dismissed the Holy Alliance as "a piece of sublime mysticism and nonsense." In November 1815 Austria, Prussia, Russia, and Britain signed the Quadruple Alliance, which became the Quintuple Alliance when France joined in 1818. Under this agreement the powers pursued their goals through what came to be known as the Congress System, a concert of the European powers to maintain order, peace, and stability by keeping an eye on France and maintaining the balance of power. This was the first truly functional experiment in collective security.

The Congress System's dedication to the 1815 status quo was challenged in 1820 and 1821 by nationalistic and liberal revolts in Germany, Greece, Spain, Italy, and Latin America. The most violent revolutions occurred in Spain and Italy. Spanish liberals rebelled against the misgovernment of the restored Bourbon king, Ferdinand VII, and their insurrection spread to the army, which mutinied. The general uprising that followed forced the king to give in to the liberals' demands for a constitution and representative government. The Spaniards' success sparked rebellions in Naples and Sicily, governed by the Neapolitan Bourbon king, Ferdinand I. The Italian revolt ran much the same path as that in Spain, and with much the same result: a constitution based on the Spanish model.

Metternich arranged for the Congress allies to meet at Troppau in 1820, Laibach in 1821, and

Verona in 1822 to deal with the uprisings. Ferdinand I came to Laibach, supported Congress System intervention, and reneged on granting a constitution; Austrian troops invaded Italy and placed him back on his throne. In 1822 the Congress allies met to consider the Spanish problem, and the French volunteered to restore the status quo. They sent their armies in to crush the liberals. The repression of the revolts in Spain and Italy marked the high point of the Congress System's success.

Britain began its withdrawal from the Continent into "splendid isolation" in 1820, and the ardent support of British liberals for the 1821 Greek revolt against the Turks further weakened London's interest in cooperating with its former allies. When the Congress System discussed restoring the Spanish king's authority in Latin America, the British objected. Further, U.S. President James Monroe warned the Europeans in 1823 that their intervention into the Western Hemisphere would be regarded as an unfriendly act. By the middle of the decade the Congress System had withered to an Austrian-Russian alliance in which Metternich set the agenda and the Russians acted as the policeman of Europe.

Prince Klemens von Metternich, portrait by Sir Thomas Lawrence. At the height of his powers during the Congress of Vienna, Metternich was largely responsible for the balance of European power agreement worked out at the Congress.

Conclusion

The elements that combined to create the stormy events of May–August 1789 included bad weather and failed harvests that drove up the price of bread for the already suffering French people, nobles' ambitions to regain power lost to the king since 1614 by calling a session of the Estates-General at Versailles, a Third Estate mobilized by middle-class intellectuals and lawyers during the preparations for the Estates-General, and an inept and grief-stricken king who saw power pass quickly from his hands in May and June. All of the pent up frustrations with the old regime broke free in July with the destruction of a symbol of the old system, the Bastille, on July 14 in Paris and similar events in other towns and cities and a bloody monthlong uprising in the provinces by the peasantry. By the time the group gathered at Versailles declared the old regime legally dead on the night of August 4, the revolution had acquired a momentum that would not stop until 1794, when various groups would attempt to harness the flood through constitutions and ideological statements. After the decapitation of Louis XVI, the redefinition of the country by the Jacobins, and the execution of Robespierre, a lull set in for five years.

Then Napoleon Bonaparte powered and redefined the Revolutionary wave after 1799. By 1804 he had established the basic institutional structure of France for the next two centuries, and by 1807 he had defeated all of his European enemies. He spread the values of the French Revolution as his armies marched through Europe, even as he stifled them in France. Through his military and political policies he set in motion the major social and political upheavals that dominated the nineteenth century. By his foreign policies he inaugurated modern Latin American history and enabled the United States to double in size. He rearranged the Holy Roman Empire and set in motion the development of modern Germany. The breadth and nature of his conquests sparked the growth of modern nationalism throughout the Continent—especially in central and eastern Europe. His economic policies changed the flow of capital and stimulated industrialization in Britain and economic reform throughout Europe. When the victorious allies met at Vienna in 1814 to impose a new order—the so-called Concert of Europe—they recognized there was no way they could turn the clock back to 1789.

It was obvious to them that the French and Napoleonic revolutions brought great changes to the entire Western world. They abolished serfdom and feudal privileges, curtailed racial and ethnic discrimination, created a uniform system of local government, started legal reforms that would culminate in the Napoleonic Code, abolished slavery in the colonies, established the standardized metric system, and stimulated urbanization. The ideal, if not the practice, of constitutional government had been rooted in the French mind. Moreover, French armies, even before 1800, scattered abroad the seeds of liberalism, constitutionalism, and even democracy. The most striking result of the Revolution in its own time was its violent disturbance of old orders: from Buenos Aires to St. Petersburg, nothing would ever be the same again.

Through his wars and foreign policies Napoleon broadcast the revolution that had occurred in France to the world and made necessary a wholesale redrawing of political boundaries both in Europe and the Americas. The French emperor changed the nature of warfare and increased the efficiency and reach of state power. For a quarter century the monarchies of Europe faced the battering ram of revolutionary energies, and by 1815 the framers of the Vienna settlement had to admit that Europe could not be returned to its pre-1789 condition.

Suggestions for Reading

François Furet gave a powerful reinterpretation of the whole revolutionary epoch in *The French Revolution, 1770–1814*, trans. by Antonia Nevill (Blackwell, 1996). An exhaustive and readable treatment of the emerging French Revolution is Franco Venturi, *The End of the Old Regime in Europe, 1776–1789*, 2 vols. (Princeton University Press, 1991). Robert Rosswell Palmer's classic, *The World of the French Revolution* (Harper & Row, 1971), also examines French eighteenth-century developments in broad perspective. The coming of the Revolution is described in a number of other thoughtful works: William Doyle, *Origins of the French Revolution* (Oxford University Press, 1980); Michel Vovelle, *The Fall of the French Monarchy* (Cambridge University Press, 1984); and Georges Lefebvre, *The Coming of the French Revolution* (Princeton University Press, 1989). A fundamental examination of the nature of the Revolution is provided in T. C. W. Banning, *The French Revolution: Class War or Culture Clash?* (St. Martin's Press, 1998).

Among the best general surveys of the French Revolution are Olivier Bernier, *Words of Fire, Deeds of Blood: The Mob, the Monarchy, and the French Revolution* (Little, Brown, 1989); William Doyle, *The Oxford History of the French Revolution* (Oxford University Press, 1989); J. F. Bosher, *The French Revolution* (Norton, 1988); M. J. Sydenham, *The French Revolution* (Greenwood, 1985); and James M. Thompson, *The French Revolution* (Blackwell, 1985). Christopher Hibbert, *The Days of the French Revolution* (Morrow, 1981), complements any survey with its colorful accounts of selected major events. For revisionist views, see Colin Lucas, *Rewriting the French Revolution* (Clarendon, 1991), and Eric J. Hobsbawm, *Echoes of the Marseillaise: Two Centuries Look Back at the French Revolution* (Rutgers University Press, 1990).

An important work on the Revolution in the provinces is John Markoff, *The Abolition of Feudalism: Peasants, Lords, and Legislators in the French Revolution* (Pennsylvania State University Press, 1996). Lynn A. Hunt, *Politics, Culture, and Class in the French Revolution* (Methuen, 1986), focuses on the total dynamics of the great upheaval. Timothy Tackett examines the transition made by those who were at Versailles and then went on to form the National Assembly in *The Deputies of the French National Assembly and the Emergence of a Revolutionary Culture (1789–1790)* (Princeton University Press, 1996). On the significance of class hostilities and mob psychology, see Peter Jones, *The Peasantry in the French Revolution* (Cambridge University Press, 1988); Allan I. Forrest, *The French Revolution and the Poor* (St. Martin's Press, 1981); and George F. E. Rude, *The Crowd in the French Revolution* (Greenwood, 1986). Lynn A. Hunt turns attention toward the cities in *Revolution and Urban Politics in Provincial France, 1786–1790* (Stanford University Press, 1978). On the marshaling of public opinion, see Hugh Gough, *The Newspaper Press in the French Revolution* (Lyceum, 1988), and Michael L. Kennedy, *The Jacobin Clubs in the French Revolution* (Princeton University Press, 1988). The role of the revolutionary army is ably depicted in Samuel Scott, *The Response of the Royal Army to the French Revolution* (Clarendon Press, 1978); Jean-Paul Bertaud, *The Army of the French Revolution: From Citizen Soldiers to Instrument of Power* (Princeton University Press, 1989); and Alan Forrest, *The Soldiers of the French Revolution* (Duke University Press, 1990). For glimpses of the chronological development of the Revolution, see Georges Lefebvre, *The Great Fear* (Vintage, 1973); Marc Bouloiseau, *The Jacobin Republic, 1791–1794* (Cambridge University Press, 1984); Carol Blum, *Rousseau and the Republic of Virtue: The Language of Politics in the French Revolution* (Cornell University Press, 1986); Stanley Loomis, *Paris in the Terror* (Richardson & Slierman, 1986); and Martyn Lyons, *France Under the Directory* (Cambridge University Press, 1975).

On the part played by women in the Revolution, see Linda Kelley, *Women of the French Revolution* (David & Charles, 1988); Joan B. Landes, *Women and the Public Sphere in the Age of the French Revolution* (Cornell University Press, 1988); Samia I. Spencer, *French Women and the Age of the Enlightenment* (Indiana University Press, 1984); and Winifred Stephens, *Women of the French Revolution* (Dutton, 1922).

For issues relating to blacks, see Edward S. Seebes, *Anti-Slavery Opinion in France During the Second Half of the Eighteenth Century* (Greenwood, 1969); Shelby McCloy, *The Negro in France* (University of Kentucky Press, 1961); Mitchell Garret, *The French Colonial Question, 1789–1791* (Negro Universities Press, 1970); and Anna J. Cooper, *Slavery and the French Revolutionists* (Milleau, 1988).

The following biographical studies of French personalities in the revolutionary era are recommended: Robert R. Palmer, *Twelve Who Ruled* (Princeton University Press, 1970); James M. Thompson, *Leaders of the French Revolution* (Blackwell, 1988); John Mills Whitham, *Men and Women of the French Revolution* (Ayer, 1982); Vincent Cronin, *Louis and Antoinette* (Morrow, 1975); Bernard Fay, *Louis XVI* (Regnery, 1968); Olivier Bernier, *Lafayette: Hero of Two Worlds* (Dutton, 1983); Norman Hampson, *Danton* (Holmes & Meier, 1978); Louis R. Gottschalk, *Jean-Paul Marat* (University of Chicago Press, 1967); David P. Jordan, *The Revolutionary Career of Maximilien Robespierre* (Free Press, 1985); and James M. Thompson, *Robespierre and the French Revolution* (English Universities Press, 1970).

For short-term impacts of the Revolution, see Robert R. Dozier, *For King, Constitution, and Country* (University of Kentucky Press, 1983), which shows the reaction of British conservatives. The radical reaction is revealed in H. T. Dickenson, *British Radicalism and the French Revolution, 1789–1814* (Blackwell, 1985), and Seamus Deane, *The French Revolution and Enlightenment in England, 1789–1832* (Harvard University Press, 1988). The long-term effects are recognized in Geoffrey Best, *The Permanent Revolution: The French Revolution and Its Legacy, 1789–1989* (University of Chicago Press, 1989). An important reconsideration of the 1792–1794 period is Patrice L.

R. Higonnet, *Goodness Beyond Virtue: Jacobins During the French Revolution* (Harvard University Press, 1998).

Napoleon has attracted the attention of a broad range of historians. See, for example, Pieter Geyl, *Napoleon: For and Against* (Humanities Press, 1974). Felix M. Markham, *Napoleon and the Awakening of Europe* (Collier, 1965), is a convenient introduction to the period. The best surveys dealing with Napoleon's activities are Robert B. Holtman, *The Napoleonic Revolution* (Lippincott, 1967), and Owen Connelly, *French Revolution/Napoleonic Era* (Holt, Rinehart and Winston, 1979). Connolly's *Blundering to Glory* (Scholarly Resources, 1987) gives a less positive account of Napoleon. See also Jean Tulard, *Napoleon: The Myth of the Saviour* (Weidenfeld & Nicholson, 1984). The controversy surrounding Napoleon's death in 1821 is dealt with by Ben Weider and Sten Forshufvud in *Assassination at St. Helena Revisited* (Wiley, 1995).

The military art of the era is well described in Gunther Rothenberg, *The Art of Warfare in the Age of Napoleon* (Indiana University Press, 1978). David G. Chandler's *The Campaigns of Napoleon* (Macmillan, 1966), is comprehensive and well written. One of Napoleon's opponents receives excellent coverage in Elizabeth Longford, *Wellington: The Years of the Sword* (Harper & Row, 1969). Leo Tolstoy's *War and Peace* gives incomparably vivid coverage of the 1812 campaign. For a complete bibliographic reference, see Donald D. Howard, ed., *Napoleonic Military History* (Garland, 1986).

Gerhard Brunn's *Europe and the French Imperium* (Harper, 1938) is a classic. See also essays in Hajo Holborn's *Germany and Europe: Historical Essays* (Doubleday, 1971) for insights into the French emperor's impact in central Europe. Hans Kohn's *Prelude to Nation-States: The French and the German Experience, 1789–1815* (Van Nostrand, 1967) is useful.

The French influence on the Americas is reviewed in Alexander de Conde, *The Quasi-War: The Politics and Diplomacy of the Undeclared War with France, 1797–1801* (Scribner, 1966). R. A. Humphreys and John Lynch edited a useful series of essays and primary documents in *The Origins of the Latin American Revolutions, 1808–1826* (Knopf, 1965). See also Irene Nicholson, *The Liberators: A Study of Independence Movements in Spanish America* (Praeger, 1969), for an essential volume in understanding the revolutionary period. The first chapters of David Bushnell and Neill Macaulay, *The Emergence of Latin America in the Nineteenth Century* (Oxford University Press, 1988), provide essential social, economic, and political background.

Harold Nicolson, *The Congress of Vienna: A Study of Allied Unity, 1812–1822* (Compass, 1961), is a civilized analysis of diplomatic interaction and a good companion to Henry A. Kissinger, *A World Restored: Metternich, Castlereagh, and the Problems of Peace, 1812–1822* (Sentry, 1957). Excellent on the general background to the period are Arthur James May, *The Age of Metternich, 1814–1848* (Holt, Rinehart and Winston, 1967); Eric J. Hobsbawm, *The Age of Revolution: Europe, 1789–1848* (Vintage, 1996); and Jacob L. Talmon, *Romanticism and Revolt: Europe, 1815–1848* (Harcourt Brace, 1967).

Suggestions for Web Browsing

French Revolution
http://otal.umd.edu/~fraistat/romrev/frbib.html

Lists several major Web sites and a selected general bibliography dedicated to the French Revolution.

French Revolution
http://www.hs.port.ac.uk/Users/david.andress/frlinks.htm

Provides a broad range of links and includes numerous images related to the French Revolution.

Marie Antoinette
http://www2.lucidcafe.com/lucidcafe/library/95nov/
antoinette.html

A short biography of the queen, with related Web sites offering portraits, geneology, and life at Versailles.

La Marseillaise
http://acc6.its.brooklyn.cuny.edu/~phalsall/sounds/
marseille.ra

Offers both French and English text, and—with Real Audio—a symphonic rendition of the rousing anthem.

Napoleon
http://www.ping.be/napoleon.series/general_info/online.html

Site provides extensive bibliographic and general historical information about Napoleon and his times.

Military History: Napoleonic Wars (1800–1815)
http://www.cfcsc.dnd.ca/links/milhist/nap.html

Canadian Forces College site lists links on the biographies of Napoleon and Nelson, campaigns and battles, museums, naval operations, and reenactments.

Notes

1. George L. Mosse, ed., *Europe in Review* (Chicago: Rand McNally, 1962), pp. 162–164.
2. For the text of Leopold's Declaration of Pilnitz, issued August 27, 1791, see John Hall Stewart, *A Documentary Survey of the French Revolution* (New York: Macmillan, 1951), pp. 223–224.
3. Ibid., p. 181. Quotation is from the Convention's decree of November 19, 1792.
4. Herbert Butterfield, *Napoleon* (New York: Collier Books, 1977), pp. 20–25.
5. Gunther E. Rothenberg, *The Art of Warfare in the Age of Napoleon* (Bloomington: Indiana University Press, 1980), pp. 31–45.
6. Owen Connelly, *French Revolution/Napoleonic Era* (New York: Holt, Rinehart and Winston, 1979), p. 214.
7. George Lefebvre, *The French Revolution: From 1793 to 1799*, Vol. 2, trans. J. H. Steward and J. Friguglietti (New York: Columbia University Press, 1964), pp. 259–317.
8. Connelly, *French Revolution/Napoleonic Era*, pp. 226–237.
9. Ibid., p. 221.
10. Robert B. Holtman, *The Napoleonic Revolution* (New York: Lippincott, 1967), pp. 38–40.
11. Rothenberg, *Art of Warfare*, pp. 42–52.
12. Hajo Holborn, *Germany and Europe: Historical Essays* (New York: Doubleday, 1971), p. 9.
13. For a view from the Russian side, see Michael and Diana Josselson, *The Commander: A Life of Barclay de Tolly* (Oxford: Oxford University Press, 1980).
14. H. A. L. Fisher, *A History of Europe*, Vol. 3 (Boston: Houghton Mifflin, 1936), p. 891.
15. C. K. Webster, "British, French, and American Influences," in R. A. Humphreys and J. Lynch, eds., *The Origins of the Latin American Revolution, 1800–1826* (New York: Knopf, 1967), p. 78.
16. David Bushnell and Neill Macaulay, *The Emergence of Latin America in the Nineteenth Century* (New York: Oxford University Press, 1988), pp. 3–9.
17. Ibid., pp. 55–82.
18. Gerhard Brunn, *Europe and the French Imperium* (New York: Harper, 1938), p. 38.
19. L. C. B. Seaman, *From Vienna to Versailles* (New York: Harper & Row, 1963), p. 8.

In the rigidly structured Japanese society, rich merchants could not use their wealth to buy power or influence. Instead, they spent their money on luxuries and pleasure in Ukiyo ("the floating world"), a hidden culture where the emphasis was on fads and pleasure. Art made for the floating world, like this picture of a courtesan and her attendants, was known as Ukiyo-e ("pictures of the floating world").

Africa, Asia, and European Penetration, 1650–1815

Chapter Contents

The late seventeenth and the ensuing eighteenth centuries were a period of sometimes gentle and sometimes violent transformation for the powers of Africa and Asia. These states faced a set of challenges prompted by both internal upheavals and external threats. The internal upheavals took the forms of regional conflict, economic turmoil, and population growth. The external threats coalesced around the ambitions of certain European states whose growing military and economic power enabled them to launch wars of expansion to the far corners of the globe. Taking advantage of Iberian decline in the 1600s, northern Europeans demonstrated a new efficiency in exploiting the markets and influencing political affairs on other continents. This emergence of northern European dominance was furthered by the Enlightenment, which encouraged interest in foreign lands; by European capitalism, which transformed the economies of Europe, Africa, and Asia alike; by developments in weapons technology; and by increasing European—notably British—naval power. European imperialism was not limited to colonization, as in the Americas. It also took the forms of coastal conquest (practiced by the Portuguese in an earlier era), economic control of foreign production and infrastructure, and cultural imperialism through the capturing of Asian and African minds, markets, and mores. One of the most significant ways in which European states like Britain and France began to alter African and Asian cultures in this era was through the Europeanization of language and education.

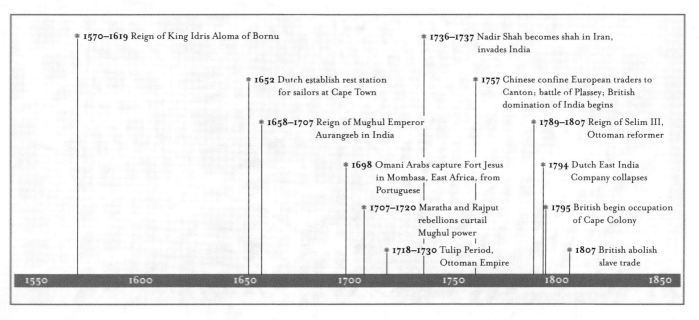

- ★ **1570–1619** Reign of King Idris Aloma of Bornu
- ★ **1652** Dutch establish rest station for sailors at Cape Town
- ★ **1658–1707** Reign of Mughul Emperor Aurangzeb in India
- ★ **1698** Omani Arabs capture Fort Jesus in Mombasa, East Africa, from Portuguese
- ★ **1707–1720** Maratha and Rajput rebellions curtail Mughul power
- ★ **1718–1730** Tulip Period, Ottoman Empire
- ★ **1736–1737** Nadir Shah becomes shah in Iran, invades India
- ★ **1757** Chinese confine European traders to Canton; battle of Plassey; British domination of India begins
- ★ **1789–1807** Reign of Selim III, Ottoman reformer
- ★ **1794** Dutch East India Company collapses
- ★ **1795** British begin occupation of Cape Colony
- ★ **1807** British abolish slave trade

1550 1600 1650 1700 1750 1800 1850

African and Asian responses to the threats of European imperialism took different forms, from imitation to rejection to compromise. Many feared that European dominance would undermine traditional social and religious values and subvert governments and economies. The Japanese, fearful of contamination, attempted complete isolation of their country. Burma, Thailand, and Ethiopia tried similar policies in dealing with presumptuous Jesuit missionaries or unprincipled European soldiers of fortune. China cooperated with the Jesuits but cautiously kept them under strict controls. In other places, such as Vietnam, Persia, the Ottoman Empire, parts of Africa, and the Pacific, opinion and even official policy fluctuated between outraged rejection and enthusiastic acceptance of European ways. Such divisiveness was most evident by 1800 in some regions of Indonesia and India, where Europeans were courted and imitated as a new ruling class. Although some Asians and Africans remained openly scornful of European culture in the eighteenth century, all were ultimately forced to take Europeans seriously.

At the end of the period, large areas of the world were still free of European political domination, but their continued independence was becoming more doubtful. Even in East Asia, where China and Japan were strong states with deep-rooted traditions and magnificent cultural achievements, changes brought by Europeans caused serious internal problems. Across southern Asia and along the African coasts, steady European penetration encouraged social disintegration while furthering civil and regional strife, results perhaps best illustrated by the African slave trade. Elsewhere, Europeans were already conquering and exploiting less politically organized societies. The Russian movement across Siberia, the English and French forays into Polynesia, and Dutch advances in Indonesia and southern Africa, continued a process similar to earlier Spanish exploits in the Western Hemisphere. The way was thus prepared for European mastery over Asia and Africa in the nineteenth century.

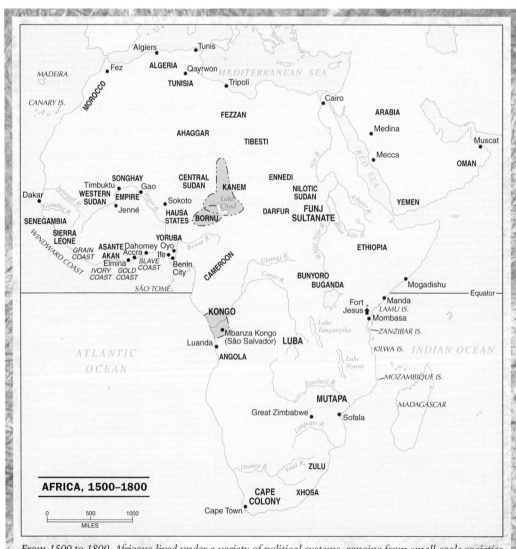

From 1500 to 1800, Africans lived under a variety of political systems, ranging from small-scale societies to expansive monarchies. Powerful kingdoms emerged in every region.

Sub-Saharan Africa

Africans and Dutch Settlement in South Africa

When the Dutch began settling in southern Africa in the mid-seventeenth century, they encountered a mix of African societies that had populated the region for many centuries. The earliest inhabitants of South Africa were San hunters and gatherers and Khoikhoi pastoralists. These were followed by Bantu-speaking farmers who crossed the Limpopo River around the third century of the Common Era.

As they migrated into different parts of the land, the Bantu-speaking societies divided into two streams. The Nguni (Swazi, Zulu, and Xhosa) settled to the east of the Drakensberg mountain range and spread down the Indian Ocean coast as far south as the Great Fish River. As this strip of land was hilly and well watered by rainfall coming off the ocean, Nguni families established scattered homesteads and formed small clan-based chiefdoms. Although splits in ruling families were common, as long as land was plentiful, factions could break away and form their own chiefdoms. The other Bantu-speaking group, the Sotho/Tswana, populated the drier, rolling plains west of the Drakensberg Mountains. Because the grasslands were sparse, Sotho/Tswana cattle-keepers managed their scarce resources by clustering in vil-

Africa, 1500–1800

1441	Portuguese capture first slaves off West African coast in transatlantic slave trade
c. 1581–1663	Queen Nzinga, ruler of Ndongo kingdom, Angola
1632–1667	Reign of Ethiopian Emperor Fasilidas
1685	Portuguese invade kingdom of Kongo
1713	British obtain right to sell slaves in Spanish ports
1672–1727	Reign of Moroccan Sultan Mulay Ismail
c. 1717	Death of Asante King Osei Tutu, West Africa
1725	Fulani Muslims launch jihad in Futo Jalon, West Africa
1779	First Xhosa-European war in eastern Cape, South Africa
1780s	Peak decade of transatlantic slave trade

lages and pasturing their cattle in outlying areas. Those nearest the Kalahari Desert created extensive villages, some containing as many as 10,000 to 15,000 people.

Small groups of Khoikhoi and San inhabited the southwestern Cape. The Khoikhoi were the first to make contact with European seafarers. In the late sixteenth century, Portuguese and English ships on the long voyage to India and southeast Asia began making the harbor at Table Bay a regular stopover for rest and replenishment. Because they needed a reliable source of fresh meat, Europeans depended on the Khoikhoi, who were usually willing to part with their old and sick cattle, in exchange for iron, copper, tobacco, and beads.

The English and Portuguese were followed by the Dutch East Indies Company, which founded a permanent settlement at Table Bay in 1652. Because the company's primary goal was providing meat, fruits, and vegetables for its employees, its first governor, Jan van Riebeeck, had strict instructions to avoid friction and win the cooperation of the Khoikhoi. Only a few years later, however, the company made several fateful decisions that led to clashes with Khoikhoi bands.

Because their fruit and vegetable gardens did not yield enough, in 1657 the company allowed some of its soldiers to establish their own farms a short distance from the main company settlement. Because the company still depended on its cattle trade with the Khoikhoi, it imported slaves from elsewhere to work the farms. The first batches of slaves came from western and central Africa, but thereafter the company turned to the Indian Ocean for most. The majority of slaves came from Mozambique and Madagascar, while the rest were brought over from India, Malaya, and Indonesia.

Over the next 150 years the Dutch colony, populated by Dutch, German, French Huguenot, and Scandinavian settlers, developed a distinctive character. Company officials and personnel made up an elite at Cape Town; a second group included slaveholders whose plantations in the Cape Town vicinity produced fruit and wine; and a third group, the Boers (*boer* is the Dutch word for "farmer"; the settlers did not begin calling themselves Afrikaners until the late nineteenth century), consisted of migratory pastoralists. By 1800 there were about 21,000 Europeans in the colony, compared to a slave population of about 25,000.

The gradual expansion of company farms into the interior alarmed the Khoikhoi, who saw their grazing lands threatened by Dutch takeover. As wars broke out with Khoikhoi groups in the Cape peninsula, the Dutch settlers steadily began conquering Khoikhoi territory farther and farther from the company settlement.

Boer families lived a pastoral lifestyle, relying largely on their own resources and preferring infrequent contact with company officials in Cape Town. Boer men believed that it was their birthright to stake out farms of around 6000 acres apiece. They expected their sons to claim other farms of the same size, usually at the expense of indigenous people. By 1800 the Boers had extended the colony's boundaries 300 miles north and 500 miles east along the Indian Ocean coast.

For most of the eighteenth century Khoikhoi and San bands resisted Boer expansion by carrying on guerrilla skirmishing. The Khoikhoi and San groups who wanted to maintain their autonomy migrated farther into the interior; others, who lost their herds, supplemented the slave population as servants or apprentices to Boers. White settlers began to refer to Dutch-speaking Khoikhoi and San, freed slaves, and mixed-race servants as "Cape Coloureds."

The Boers' first contacts with Xhosa chiefdoms were at the Great Fish River in the early 1700s. Although they had worked out a mutually beneficial trading relationship, as more Boers moved into Xhosa territory, conflicts erupted, largely over land and cattle. The first war between the two groups broke out in 1779. Over the next century eight more were to take place between Xhosa chiefdoms and Europeans. Unlike the small Khoikhoi and San bands, which lacked unity, Xhosa farmers outnumbered the Boers and lived in chiefdoms prepared to defend their land vigorously. Moreover, the Boers' advantage in armaments was slight. Two wars between Xhosa and Boers ended in stalemates broken only by the entrance of the British into the Cape in 1795.

When France invaded the Netherlands in 1795, the British responded to an appeal by the Dutch royal house and colonized the Cape. Controlling the sea route around the Cape of Good Hope also allowed the British to protect the passage to India. After handing control of the Cape back to the Dutch in 1803, the British returned several years later and established a dominant presence in the Cape and southern Africa for the next century. The British were primarily interested in increased commercial ties with the Cape by expanding wine and wool production. The British relationship with European farmers who actively participated in the market economy was more amicable than with Boer cattle-keepers, who kept their involvement in the market economy to a minimum. Throughout the nineteenth century British strategic and economic interests would repeatedly clash with the desires of Boer pastoralists to maintain their independent lifestyle.

The Atlantic Slave Trade

While the Dutch and the British were establishing a foothold on the southern tip of the African continent,

Europeans were also becoming increasingly active in the Atlantic slave trade, which combined to create a huge international complex of enterprises involving the economies of four continents. The western Saharan coast was the setting for the beginning of the Atlantic slave trade in 1441. To win the favor of Prince Henry the Navigator, a Portuguese sea captain kidnapped one man and one woman. The slave trade reached its peak three centuries later as a major component in the rapidly expanding capitalism of northern Europe. Because it was conducted in partnerships between Africans and Europeans, the trade was a less obvious short-term danger to African interests than the migrating Dutch settlers in South Africa, but it posed a more serious long-term threat.

The full historical significance of the trade can best be understood if it is viewed in its broader setting. Europe's economy at the time derived large profits from bulk plantation commodities such as sugar, tobacco, and coffee. The most productive European plantations, which were located in the West Indies, depended primarily on slave labor from West Africa. Thus slaving ports, including Liverpool in England and Bordeaux in France, became thriving centers of a new prosperity. Related industries, such as shipbuilding, sugar refining, distilling, and textile and hardware manufacturing, also flourished. All contributed much to the development of European capitalism and ultimately to the Industrial Revolution.

Northern Europe's commercial impetus reached West Africa in the middle of the seventeenth century. The Portuguese, after losing the whole Atlantic coast to the Dutch, won back only Angola. For a while the Dutch nearly monopolized the trade, operating from Elmina on the Gold Coast. The English subsequently established footholds there at Cormantin and Cape Castle; by 1700 they had seven other posts in the area. The French, meanwhile, acquired St. Louis on the Senegal in the north, which allowed them to control most trade as far south as the Gambia River. In the resulting triangular competition, the Dutch faced constant pressure from their two rivals but maintained their dominance from a dozen strong Gold Coast forts.

By 1700 England was challenging Dutch predominance. Having defeated the Dutch at sea in the late 1600s, Britain next defeated France in the War of the Spanish Succession. At the ensuing Peace of Utrecht in 1713, Britain obtained the right to sell 4800 slaves each year in Spanish ports. Another advantage after 1751 was the British shift from a monopolistic chartered company to an association of merchants, which increased incentives by opening opportunities for individual traders. Finally, in the continuing Anglo-French colonial wars of the eighteenth century, the British fleet consistently hampered French operations. For these reasons, by 1785 the British were

Elmina Castle, in Ghana, was built by the Portuguese in 1482 to facilitate the slave trade. Occupation passed to the Dutch in 1637.

transporting thousands more slaves from West Africa than all of their competitors combined.

Despite this regional competition among Europeans, they conducted trade locally as a black-white partnership, largely on African terms. Rulers such as Queen Auguina, a British ally on the Gold Coast in the eighteenth century, not only enforced their authority but eagerly took profits from regular port fees, rents on the slave stockades (called *barracoons*), and a contracted percentage on the sale of slaves. Ordinary subjects were also active traders. Some conducted slaving expeditions to the interior, while others found work as guides, clerks, or interpreters. Thus arose a class of Westernized blacks and mulattoes. Many adopted European dress, and a few were lionized in Europe or became Christian missionaries. For example, Mae Aurelia Correia, the African wife of a Portuguese army captain posted to Portuguese Guinea, supplemented her husband's meager wages by venturing into the slave trade as well as establishing peanut plantations that relied on slave labor. Most white traders were not so successful. Plagued by an unhealthy climate and surrounded by suspicious inhabitants, they led short and dreary lives in their remote exiles.

Most slaves awaiting shipment in West African barracoons had been kidnapped or taken in war, although some were sold to pay off debts, as punishment for breaking laws, or by relatives in times of famine and hunger. Only a few were seized directly by white raiders. Slaves were usually forcibly marched to the coast in gangs, chained or roped together, and worn down by poor food, lack of water, unattended illnesses, and brutal beatings. Once in the barracoons, where they might stay for months, they were stripped and examined for physical defects by ship doctors and then displayed before captains who were looking to buy their cargoes. The bargaining was hard and complex as slaves were exchanged for beads, alcohol, cloth, and especially firearms.

About twice as many men as women were enslaved and shipped abroad. The traditional explanation for this imbalance is that men brought the highest prices in overseas markets because they could cope with the physical demands imposed on plantation laborers. But recent research has shown that women were just as likely to be assigned the harshest field work and that they fetched roughly the same prices as men. An important reason more women slaves were kept in Africa was that they were more desired as domestic slaves in royal households and as agricultural laborers.

After the barracoons, slaves met a worse nightmare on the ships. Women were usually huddled together on an open deck; male slaves were packed together, side by side, in lower decks, each allotted a space 16 inches wide by 30 inches high. When some slaves refused to eat, a special device, the "mouth opener," was used to force-feed them. Some slaves jumped into the sea while being exercised; those who contracted diseases were frequently thrown overboard. Mutinies were common and were punished with savage brutality. One women mutineer on a British ship in the early 1800s was hoisted by her thumbs, whipped, and slashed with knives, in view of other slaves, until she died. Understandably, the mortality rate on slave ships exceeded 12 percent, not counting those who died after landing. Yet these conditions did not shake the Christian faith of some slavers. "This day," British slave trader John Newton confided to his journal in 1752, "I have reason . . . to beg a public blessing from Almighty God upon our voyage. . . ." After four voyages, however, Newton underwent a dramatic conversion and left slaving for the ministry. His legacy is his moving hymn of atonement, "Amazing Grace."

The era after the Peace of Utrecht has been termed the slave century. Between 1600 and 1700, when the slave-trading companies were mostly state-chartered monopolies, some 1.5 million slaves were carried across the Atlantic. During the next century, when much more trade was being conducted by individual captains outside the forts, more than 6 million slaves were landed in the Americas. The trade peaked

A Slave's Memoir

Olaudah Equiano captured the misery of transported slaves in his *Travels*.

One day, when all our people were gone out to their work as usual and only I and my dear sister were left to mind the house, two men and a woman got over our walls, and in a moment seized us both, and without giving us time to cry out or make resistance they stopped our mouths and ran off with us into the nearest wood. Here they tied our hands and continued to carry us as far as they could till night came on, when we reached a small house where the robbers halted for refreshment and spent the night.

The first object which saluted my eyes when I arrived on the coast was the sea, and a slave ship which was then riding at anchor and waiting for its cargo. These filled me with astonishment, which was soon converted into terror when I was carried on board. I was immediately handled and tossed up to see if I were sound by some of the crew, and I was now persuaded that I had gotten into a world of bad spirits and that they were going to kill me. Their complexions too differing so much from ours, their long hair and the language they spoke (which was very different from any I had ever heard) united to confirm me in this belief. Indeed such were the horrors of my views and fears at the moment that, if ten thousand worlds had been my own, I would have freely parted with them all to have exchanged my condition with that of the meanest slave in my own country. When I looked around the ship too and saw a large furnace or copper boiling and a multitude of black people of every description chained together, every one of their countenances expressing dejection and sorrow, I no longer doubted my fate; and quite overpowered with horror and anguish, I fell motionless on the deck and fainted. When I recovered a little I found some black people about me, who I believed were some of those who had brought me on board and had been receiving their pay; they talked to me in order to cheer me, but all in vain. I asked them if we were not to be eaten by those white men with horrible looks, red faces, and loose hair. They told me I was not, and one of the crew brought me a small portion of spirituous liquor in a wine glass, but being afraid of him I would not take it out of his hand.

The stench of the hold while we were on the coast was so intolerably loathsome that it was dangerous to remain there for any time, and some of us had been permitted to stay on the deck for the fresh air; but now that the whole ship's cargo were confined together it became absolutely pestilential. The closeness of the place and the heat of the climate, added to the number in the ship, which was so crowded that each had scarcely room to run himself, almost suffocated us. This produced copious perspirations, so that the air soon became unfit for respiration from a variety of loathsome smells, and brought on a sickness among the slaves, of which many died, thus falling victims to the improvident avarice, as I may call it, of their purchasers. This wretched situation was again aggravated by the galling of the chains, now become insupportable, and the filth of the necessary tubs, into which the children often fell and were almost suffocated. The shrieks of the women and the groans of the dying rendered the whole a scene of horror almost inconceivable. Happily perhaps for myself I was soon reduced so low here that it was thought necessary to keep me almost always on deck, and from my extreme youth I was not put in fetters.

At last we came in sight of the island of Barbados, at which the whites on board gave a great shout and made many signs of joy to us.

From Paul Edwards, ed., *Equiano's Travels: His Autobiography, The Interesting Narrative of the Life of Olaudah Equiano or Gustavus Vassa the African* (London: Heinemann Educational Books, 1967).

---

in the 1780s, when 750,000 Africans were taken from West and Central Africa.

Denmark was the first European state to end the slave trade, but it was Britain's decision to abolish the trade in 1807 that had the most far-reaching consequences. The ideals of the Enlightenment, in addition to crusading humanitarian movements in England, had prepared the way for this act, but even more decisive factors were the declining profitability of Britain's Caribbean plantations, a rise in the price of slaves, and pressures from British industrialists, who found it more profitable to invest in wage labor in European factories than in the sugar plantations. Although a British squadron did patrol the Atlantic after 1807, looking for slavers, the slave trade was not immediately affected. However, West Africans began making adjustments to their trading relations with the outside world.

There was more to the Atlantic exchange than the trafficking in human beings. Africa's population was

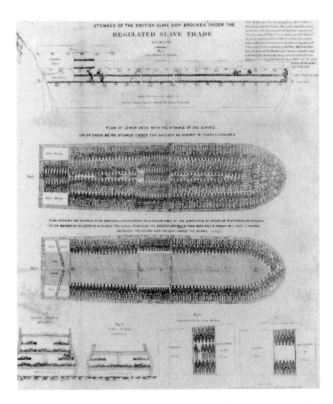

This diagram shows how slaves were packed into cargo holds for the notorious Middle Passage to the Americas. The plan was a model of efficiency as slave traders sought to maximize profits by filling their ships up to and beyond capacity.

still expanding despite the devastation of the slave trade. New foods imported from the Americas, such as manioc (cassava), which could be grown in poor soils, and maize (corn), soon became staples because they could contribute many more calories to people's diets than other mainstays, such as sorghum and millet. Europeans also introduced oranges, lemon, limes, pineapples, groundnuts (peanuts), and guavas to the African continent. In return, yams (sweet potatoes, which were the main provision for slaves on slave ships), sorghum, plantains, bananas, and melegueta pepper ("grains of paradise") made their way from Africa to the Americas.

Whatever its unintended consequences, the Atlantic slave trade was a degrading experience for all the Europeans, Arabs, and Africans who participated in it. An estimated 12 million people were lost to Africa through the Atlantic slave trade over three centuries, and this number does not include the hundreds of thousands of slaves who died en route from their point of capture to the slave ports, in the cramped barracoons, and in the "floating tombs" that transported slaves to the New World.

African States and the Atlantic Slave Trade

African states along the Atlantic coast faced the choice of whether to participate in the Atlantic slave

trade or not. Some African rulers refrained from any involvement, while others saw the slave trade as an opportunity to amass more power through the acquisition of firearms and horses. An example was the Yoruba kingdom of Oyo, situated inland on the savanna. Drawing on revenues derived from the slave trade, the Oyo *alafin* (king) traded for horses from the north and assembled a cavalry that conquered the savanna region to the southwest all the way to the coast. Oyo's royal farms were tilled by slaves captured in warfare and the Sahelian slave trade, but as Oyo's rulers tapped into the Atlantic trade, surplus slaves were sold to European traders in exchange for firearms, cloth, and cowrie shells, which were a widespread form of currency in West Africa.

The *alafin* was not an absolute ruler. He governed with the advice of a seven-man council of state, the *oyo mesi*, and they in turn were overseen by a secret society of religious and political notables. If the *alafin* lost the backing of his counselors, they could force him to commit suicide. A turning point in Oyo's history came in the late eighteenth century when a senior counselor in the *oyo mesi* usurped power from the *alafin*. This set off a period of instability and internal revolts by tributary states and Muslims that led to Oyo's collapse by the 1830s.

Of all the West African states, Dahomey, located west of the Oyo kingdom, was even more affected by the slave trade. Although a tributary state to Oyo for many years, Dahomey managed to maintain its autonomy, and in the mid-seventeenth century it became a major power in its own right as its authoritarian rulers created a highly centralized state. Power revolved around the king, who passed his throne directly to his eldest son and appointed local chiefs who did not come from an established lineage.

The slave trade and every aspect of the economy were rigidly monopolized by the royal elite. Everyone was required to perform military service, even women, who provided an elite palace guard and who in the early nineteenth century served as a key regiment in major wars against Dahomey's rivals, including Oyo. As a way of balancing power with male officials, the king allocated offices and responsibilities to the 5000 to 6000 women (including slaves) known as *ahosi* who served the royal court. Although the legal status of female slaves was fixed, they were allowed to accumulate wealth and to assume many roles, including managing the king's resources, trading, owning private property, and serving as soldiers and ministers of state. Because of their unquestioned loyalty to the throne, female slaves were regularly appointed to the highest offices, including that of the queen mother, who did not have to be related to the king.

Another prominent regional state was Asante, a kingdom founded by Akan peoples in the gold-producing forests of the Gold Coast interior. Akan peoples had

Discovery Through Maps

The African Coast: The Dangers of Seafaring

Despite advances in navigational instruments, sails, and tactics, Portuguese seafaring expeditions around the African coast were often dangerous. This watercolor from a rare manuscript on navigation depicts Portuguese seamen shipwrecked off the coast of Africa being rowed to safety.

Shipwrecks were caused not only by rough weather and heavy seas but also by inexperienced and incompetent sea captains, poorly maintained ships and pumps, and rotten sails and rigging. Sailing conditions were especially treacherous off the southeastern Africa coast, where stormy seas and gales sank many ships. The survival of the seamen, passengers, and slaves who made it ashore was dependent on the goodwill of the Africans they encountered.

The experiences of the passengers of the São Tomé, which sank in stormy conditions in 1589 near the Indian Ocean island of Mauritius, were not unusual. After landing in a small boat on the African coast near St. Lucia Bay, the 100 survivors began walking up the coast. Although they were attacked by one African group, they were treated hospitably by other communities, who gave them food and shelter. When they heard about a settlement of Portuguese ivory traders, they set off to find them. However, a number of their party died of fever en route, and the survivors who finally reached the traders still had to wait another year before a ship arrived to take them to Portugal.

formed states based on the trade in gold, kola nuts, and slaves to the north and gold, slaves, and ivory to the Portuguese on the coast. But in the late seventeenth century the Akan states were absorbed into the Asante kingdom, founded by *Asantehene* (king) Osei Tutu (d. 1717). Ruling from his capital at Kumasi, Osei Tutu transformed a loose confederation into a centralized state and adopted the Golden Stool as the unifying symbol of Asante kingship. When Osei Tutu died in battle, his successor, Opoku Ware (c. 1720–1750), extended Asante's dominion to the savanna regions in the north and to the fringes of the forests in the south.

The southwest coast, from the Bight of Biafra to the Cunene River, was no less affected by the slave trade, as the Portuguese remained an intrusive presence. In the early seventeenth century several kings of Kongo attempted to contain Portuguese involvement in their affairs, but they were thwarted by internal rivalries within their kingdom. When civil war broke out, the Portuguese seized the opportunity to invade Kongo

in 1685, leaving the central government in shambles and fragmenting the kingdom into ministates. By 1800 European influences there were hardly discernible, and the once proud kingdom was only a distant memory.

The Angolan hinterland suffered an even worse fate, despite the heroic efforts at resistance by the Ndongo kingdom's Queen Anna Nzinga (c. 1581–1663). In 1622 she negotiated a treaty with Portuguese officials that opened her kingdom to Catholic missionaries and to Portuguese slavers in return for Portuguese recognition of her rule and the freeing of Ndongo chiefs taken captive by the Portuguese. However, when Ndongo's relations with the Portuguese ruptured, Anna Nzinga allied her kingdom with Jaga warrior bands and led a spirited guerrilla war against the Portuguese for many decades.

However, the Portuguese eventually conquered Ndongo and other kingdoms. When Brazil's sugar plantations required massive numbers of slave laborers in the 1600s, the Portuguese, operating from their coastal ports of Luanda and Benguela, turned Angola into a vast slave-hunting preserve. Armed bands of Portuguese mercenaries regularly intervened in conflicts in African kingdoms, while the kingdoms of Kasanje, Matamba, and Ovimbundu assisted the Portuguese by trading or raiding for slaves in remote inland areas.

African State Formation in Eastern and Northeastern Africa

During the eighteenth century strong new kingdoms arose in the south central and eastern sections of Africa. Like elsewhere in Africa, Portuguese intervention in that region proved equally calamitous. In the seventeenth century Portuguese settlers in Sena and Tete in the Zambezi River valley had intervened to support the *Mwene Mutapa* (king) in a civil war within the Mutapa state; they won concessions from the king to extend trading fairs and gold-mining operations in the Zimbabwean highlands. When the *Mwene Mutapa* then attempted to curb Portuguese adventurers, they deposed him and installed a "more pliant successor."

The fragmentation of the Mutapa kingdom created a power vacuum on the Zimbabwean plateau. Young men who lacked cattle to start their own homesteads joined the armies of wealthy patrons who were contesting for power. The most successful of these warlords was Dombo (d. 1695), who took the title *Changamire*. In the late seventeenth century his *Rozvi* soldiers conquered the remnants of Mutapa and other kingdoms in the region. Then Dombo's army turned its attention to the Portuguese, expelling them from the trading fairs. Thereafter, the Portuguese were allowed to trade in the interior only through African agents.

The Portuguese presence in the Zambezi River valley was restricted to the *prazos*, huge estates run by Portuguese settlers *(prazeros)* who over time intermarried with Africans and assimilated into local African cultures. When they failed to eke out a living from agriculture, the *prazeros* became warlords whose slave armies exacted tribute from clients and hunted elephants for the ivory trade.

In East Africa most states remained small, except in the region west of Lake Victoria, where two kingdoms, Bunyoro and Buganda, vied for power. Bunyoro dominated a confederation based on village-based chiefdoms that paid tribute to Bunyoro and contributed regiments for cattle raids against neighboring societies. Bunyoro's economy was based on hunting, herding, and agriculture. In the late eighteenth century Buganda, a rival kingdom to the northwest of Lake Victoria, was formed by clans, most likely to protect themselves against Bunyoro's raids. Buganda's king *(kabaka)* allocated lands to territorial chiefs and distributed land to lesser chiefs. Buganda's staple food was the banana, which had a

Shown seated on a servant, Queen Nzinga of the Ndongo kingdom of Angola negotiated a treaty with the Portuguese in 1622.

high caloric yield and thrived in the rich, fertile soils bordering Lake Victoria. The banana could be produced on an annual basis, unlike the shifting cultivation practiced in most savanna regions of Africa. Because cattle did not thrive within Buganda's borders, Buganda's regiments regularly carried out cattle raids in neighboring chiefdoms to the west.

While new states were rising in East Africa, the oldest African polity, the kingdom of Ethiopia, was fragmenting. The troubles began when Emperor Susneyos (c. 1575–1632) invited Pedro Paez, a Spanish Jesuit, to serve as an adviser, teacher, and diplomat. Susneyos privately converted to Catholicism in 1612, but when he publicly announced his switch a decade later, he incurred the wrath of the Ethiopian church. The dispute was brought to a head when Paez's successor as bishop attacked the powerful Ethiopian church. Susneyos was forced to abdicate in favor of his son Fasilidas (c. 1632–1667), who expelled the Jesuits from Ethiopia.

From that point on, Ethiopia's trading relationships with Europe and the Ottoman Empire declined, but slaves, coffee, and salt were still exported through the Nile valley and the Red Sea. After founding his capital around 1635 at Gonder, north of Lake Tana, Fasilidas began reshaping the monarchy, continuing his father's policy of outmaneuvering his rivals by integrating the Muslim Oromo into his nobility. When he intervened in a theological dispute over Christ's human and divine qualities, he further alienated the Ethiopian church establishment and Amhara nobles. But he did win additional popular support among the Oromo.

Fasilidas's policies reduced Gonder's power, as the nobles expanded their personal fiefdoms around the kingdom and the Oromo asserted their autonomy. In effect Gonder's emperors became local potentates. One exception was Iyasu II (c. 1730–1755), who ruled with the support of his astute mother, Mentewab, who served as his queen mother. An

Buganda, a kingdom situated west of Lake Victoria, became a regional power in the late eighteenth century. A wide avenue led to the royal palace at its capital, Rubaga.

Oromo, she brought many of her ethnic group into the court and the army. But following Iyasu's reign, civil war erupted, and Ethiopia's monarchy was unable to restore its authority for another century. Between 1769 and 1855 nobles entrenched their power, at the expense of a series of powerless emperors who reigned in Gonder.

Islamic Africa

At the end of the eighteenth century, Islam remained a vibrant force in certain regions of Africa. Muslim West Africa was beginning to experience a cultural revival and was expanding its following beyond traders and rulers. It was carried by a wave of Islamic religious zeal, which arose on the Senegal River and spread east across the savanna regions to Guinea and the Hausa states and to the upper Nile. In East Africa, however, Islam remained a coastal religion with limited appeal beyond the Swahili city-states.

Meanwhile, across the continent in the west, Morocco was under the control of a dynasty that established itself in 1631 and remains in power today. Sultan Mulay Ismail (1672–1727), a canny and successful ruler, corresponded with Louis XIV of France and sent an ambassador to the court of Charles II in England. His uncontested power was based on a large standing army, including a force of black slaves who were recruited or captured in the Sudan as children and trained for specialized tasks. The sultan proved himself an exceptionally competent administrator, a wily military commander, and a patron of the arts. Morocco's economy was based on

a combination of agriculture, trade, and privateering, although its piratic activity was minor compared to that of Algiers and Tunis. Under Mulay Ismail's successors Morocco prospered. It was not integrated into the Islamic heartlands but remained connected to them by long-standing traditions of commercial and intellectual exchange. Each year Moroccan pilgrims and scholars made their ways by land and sea to the shrines of Mecca and to the great academic institutions of the Middle East.

In the West African savanna region, Muslim states had languished as the trans-Saharan gold trade declined after 1650. The Moroccan conquest in 1591 had broken the Songhay Empire into many rival small kingdoms, but as Moroccan administrators intermarried with local people, their ties with Morocco weakened. The Moroccans themselves were displaced by the Tuaregs, another group of desert invaders, in 1737.

The region around Lake Chad was the center of one of the region's most important states, Kanem-Bornu, which became an important center of Islamic learning. The high point of Bornu's power was during the reign of *Mai* (king) Idris Aloma (c. 1542–c. 1619). After being exposed to the wider Muslim world on a pilgrimage to Mecca, he imported firearms from North Africa and employed Turkish musketeers and advisers to command his army. To lessen the possibility of revolt, which had plagued his predecessors, he placed trusted allies rather than close relatives in key positions around his kingdom. For over a century Kanem-Bornu exerted a stabilizing force in the region around Lake Chad, but its power steadily waned during the eighteenth century. By that time the Hausa city-states, notably Kano, Katsina, and Gobir, were becoming prominent as they profited from the expanding trade in slaves now moving across the central Sahara to the Mediterranean.

Meanwhile, new Muslim states were rising in the western and eastern extremities of the region: Fulani-Tukolor kingdoms along the Senegal River in the west and the sultanates of Tonjur, Fur, and Funj in the region south of Egypt. In the west Islam launched a series of successful crusades led by Fulani holy men, who criticized the lax moralities and heretical policies of West African Muslims, particularly the rulers. The Fulani were cattle-keepers who by the fifteenth century had spread across the West African savanna, often pasturing their herds in regions controlled by farming societies. In the highlands of Futa Jalon, the Fulani chafed at their rulers' taxation and restrictions on pasture land, and in 1725 they joined with Muslim traders and clerics to launch a jihad that eventually brought the area under Muslim and Fulani domination. Because of the war, slave raiding increased, and many captives were sold to European slavers at the Senegal and Gambia coast. In Futa Toro on the Senegal River, other Fulanis joined with Tukolor Muslims to wage another jihad and form a Muslim-ruled kingdom.

In East Africa Islam was largely restricted to the coastal area, despite the fact that two centuries of Portuguese tyranny were brought to an end in 1698 after a three-year siege of Fort Jesus by Omani Arabs. The Portuguese retreated to their bases in southern Mozambique, but their expulsion did not bring peace and stability to the Swahili states. They fought among themselves and, except for Zanzibar, against their new Muslim overlords. Despite these conflicts, commerce expanded and population grew. Most trade was in slaves, particularly with the French, who were developing plantations on their Indian Ocean islands of Mauritius and Réunion. This was the era when a distinct Swahili identity developed along the coast and the maturing Swahili language, a blend of Bantu languages and Arabic, produced its earliest poetry.

Challenges to the Muslim World Order

By the seventeenth century the Muslim world stretched from the Atlantic to the Pacific. In a millennium, the spread of Islam from Arabia had indeed been phenomenal. But Muslim polities, from North Africa to Indonesia, experienced a general weakening after 1700. As European states perfected their military power and asserted their dominance over the routes of the maritime trade from East to West, Muslim sovereigns had to grapple with the notion that the eighteenth-century world was no longer centered in Istanbul, Isfahan, and Cairo. For the Ottoman sultans, who for centuries had terrorized European armies and dictated the terms of trade, that ideological adjustment was not easily made. Even in the great Islamic empires, economic changes, vested interests, failure to adapt new technologies, and prolonged warfare drained state treasuries and made it difficult for traditional rulers to restructure their empires and compete with the emergent powers of Europe.

Ottoman Reorganization and Reform

The early seventeenth century in the Ottoman Empire was marked by a series of rebellions, one culminating in the deposition and execution of the ill-starred Sultan Osman II in 1622. Although the empire was still vast and powerful, it had lost the glory of the Golden Age associated with the reign of Süleiman the Magnificent. Many explanations have been advanced for the weaknesses of the empire in this time period: corruption, the intrigues of harem women, keeping princes in the harem instead of sending them out to govern and fight in the provinces. Although these were factors, the more telling reasons were changes in the global economy (linked to late-sixteenth-century inflation and population growth), competition among the various pasha households for position and prestige, and the reorganization required when the empire reached the limits of its expansion.

The Ottoman Empire was surprisingly large and surprisingly long-lived—far surpassing, for example, the Ming Empire in China, the Mughul Empire in India, and the Roman Empire in the West. No empire of any duration can remain static, and the institutions of the Ottomans had to change over time. As the ranks of the janissary corps were inflated, as the *timar* "fiefs" of the traditional cavalry became hereditary, and as a state based on expansion and conquest exhausted its resources fighting long wars on two fronts, the empire began to take a different form from the one it had in the days of Mehmed the Conqueror. All of these changes occurred in the context of a global economy that was shifting due to transatlantic discoveries and the rise of oceanic merchant empires like those of the Dutch and the English.

The Age of the Köprülü Vezirs

Mehmed IV became sultan in 1648, facing rampant inflation, a Venetian blockade of the Dardanelles, rebellion in the provinces, and a violent struggle among palace factions, including his mother, Turhan Sultan, and her rival, the old Valide Sultan Kösem. In 1651 Turhan ended Kösem's long-term dominance of the harem by having her strangled, but the sultan remained

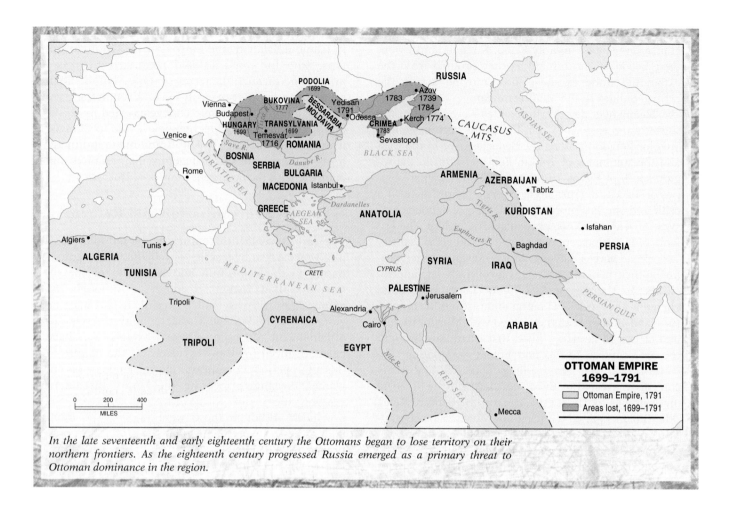

In the late seventeenth and early eighteenth century the Ottomans began to lose territory on their northern frontiers. As the eighteenth century progressed Russia emerged as a primary threat to Ottoman dominance in the region.

enmeshed in factional politics. This internal strife was compounded by a vehement struggle between groups of conservative *ulama* and Sufis, contending for spiritual authority and influence in the capital. By 1656 Istanbul was in a panic as the Venetians vanquished the Ottoman fleet in the Dardanelles, provincial rebels (*celalis*) seized much of eastern Anatolia, and food supplies became scarce. In the midst of this crisis the empire required drastic measures and found a man willing to take such measures in the person of a 79-year-old pasha named Mehmet Köprülü (1586–1661).

Mehmed Köprülü suppressed the rebels in the provinces and broke the Venetian blockade of the Dardanelles. He used the sweeping powers granted him by the sultan to quell opposition and gain some control over the military. For two generations Köprülü and members of his family served as reformist *vezirs* (high Ottoman officials), attempting to bring some power back into the hands of the central government. They launched campaigns against Austria and Poland, took Crete, and reformed taxes. They also struck thousands from the rolls of the janissaries, which had become bloated with nonmilitary men who collected pay but did not fight. The prob-

lems of the empire, however, were not solved: conscription had depopulated the countryside, and Russia was emerging as a major threat to the north. "Tax farms" (the right to collect taxes in return for large advance payments), which the government sold to finance its wars, were becoming hereditary. The empire thus entered the next century in a precarious military and economic state.

The Tulip Period

The eighteenth century for the Ottomans is framed by a period of literary and artistic florescence at its beginning and a period of concerted military reform at its end. The century began inauspiciously, with a massive revolt in the capital that deposed the sultan and brought Ahmed III (1703–1730) to the throne. During his reign the Ottomans were successful in battle against Russia but lost decisively to the Austrians. In 1718 Ibrahim Pasha became grand vezir and under his influence Ahmed launched a program of building, entertainments, and patronage of the arts that was later called the Tulip Period because of the fashion for extravagant gardens. Tulips were the

Images of women appeared more frequently in eighteenth-century Ottoman miniatures. This late-eighteenth-century work depicting childbirth in the harem also illustrates the influence of European fashions in ladies' dress styles. While the midwife delivers the child, a cradle stands by to receive it.

rage, and rare varieties sold for fabulous sums. Ibrahim supervised the building of a pleasure palace for the sultan called the "Place of Happiness," a model for other palaces and their luxurious lifestyles.

In the Tulip Period, Ottoman elites became great consumers of European, particularly French, styles in fashion and decor; European artists were imported. Yirmisekiz Chelebi Mehmed, sent to Paris by Ibrahim, sent back reports on French zoos, gardens, women, publications, and shops as well as on arms and military schools. It was an era when the Ottomans became highly conscious of the need to emulate Western military tactics and technology and the fashions of the French court were perceived as an appropriate model for emulation. The luxuries of the

Tulip Period were celebrated in verse by poets, such as Nedim (d. 1730), who were experimenting with new styles: "This year, border your crimson shawl in mink, / And if the tulip cups are lacking, bring wine cups in their stead."[1] Also founded by Ibrahim Müteferrika in 1720 was the first Ottoman Turkish language press, producing maps, a dictionary, and works on science, history, and geography. The press had been opposed by some of the religious authorities but was permitted so long as it did not print books on religious subjects. The extravagance of the Tulip Period, however, did not mesh well with the conditions of economic depression and political conflict in which the empire found itself. Ahmed's reign ended as it had begun, with a violent rebellion in the capital that produced prolonged rioting and forced the sultan's abdication.

Eighteenth-Century War, Relations, and Reform

Although the empire still had its share of cultural and military successes, overall the eighteenth century was characterized by the extension of more special commercial privileges (capitulations) to European states, loss of Ottoman territory, and a growing willingness to employ European military advisers, tactics, training methods, and technology. The Ottomans also began sending ambassadors to European courts. The empire had been a dominant power for centuries, and its rulers were generally persuaded of their own cultural superiority. But Ottoman military defeats prompted some Ottoman elites to consider significant military reform in order to duplicate or (they hoped) even surpass the successes of Europe. To that end, Sultan Mahmud I (1730–1754) brought in the French mercenary Comte de Bonneval to help modernize the military; Mustafa III (1757–1774) hired the Hungarian Baron de Tott to revamp his artillery corps and establish a military school; and Abdülhamid I (1774–1789) imported numerous foreign military advisers. All of these attempts were vehemently opposed by the janissary corps.

Throughout the century the Ottomans fought intermittently with European foes and with a series of new military leaders in Persia. The government was entangled, in alliances and competing interests, with Britian, France, Austria, and Russia, all of which had designs on certain segments of Ottoman territory. The Ottomans had already lost Hungary and Transylvania to Austria by the Peace of Carolowitz in 1699, and they surrendered to the Austrian emperor the right to intervene in the affairs of Catholics in Ottoman territory. A series of eighteenth-century wars with Russia culminated in the Treaty of Küchük Kaynarca (1774), under which the Ottomans paid a large indemnity, gave up the Crimea, allowed Russia to interfere in the affairs of Orthodox Christians in the empire, and granted Russia commercial access to the Black Sea. Fortunately for the Ottomans, British and Prussian opposition stalled further Russian advances.

Several factors demonstrate the weakness of Ottoman central control over the provinces. The semi-independent governors *(ayan)* and their private armies challenged the dictates of the palace in the provinces. In Iraq, Egypt, Tunis, Tripoli, and Algeria *mamluk* ("slave"), or janissary, garrisons created their own military regimes, often intermarrying with the local elites and refusing to cooperate with Ottoman decrees. A puritanical religious revival in Arabia (the Wahhabi movement), founded by Muhammad ibn Abd al-Wahhab (1703–1792), joined forces with the Sa'ud family and seized control of Mecca in 1803, an enormous blow to Ottoman prestige. The European powers also aggressively intervened in Ottoman affairs; Austria and Russia stirred up revolts in the Balkans, and in 1798 Napoleon invaded Ottoman Egypt. The Ottoman regime was powerless to stop Napoleon, requiring British assistance to defeat his forces. Although the British destroyed Napoleon's fleet and forced him to flee shortly after the invasion, the French occupation both demonstated Ottoman weakness and left a lasting legacy of scholarship on Egypt produced by Napoleon's entourage.

The Reforms of Selim III

Selim III (1789–1807) is often considered the first major Ottoman reformer, but his reform program was not new. Like several of his eighteenth-century predecessors, he proposed military and tax reforms as avenues to restore the empire to its past glory. Selim opened new technical schools to train officers and modernized arms production. He drastically cut the janissary rolls to get rid of noncombatants, but he mollified the traditional military corps by increasing pay and modernizing barracks. Offending the janissary corps had proved disastrous for various of his predecessors. Most of Selim's efforts and resources, however, went to modernizing the navy and training a "new model" army of 23,000 men called the *Nizam-i Cedid.* It was a European-style infantry corps (with European-style uniforms) composed primarily of Turkish peasants and staffed in part with French officers. But the empire was not yet ready to break the entrenched power of its traditional military forces; Selim was deposed by a janissary uprising in 1807. Eliminating the janissaries was a task that would fall to his successor, Mahmud II (1807–1839). Although Selim's new army was disbanded, his reforms opened up the empire to further European influence, especially in the realm of military training.

Selim III's efforts to reform the Ottoman state were thwarted by the janissaries, who deposed the sultan, imprisoned him, and later assassinated him.

Muslim Polities in Persia

The Safavid Empire in Persia suffered from many of the same problems that afflicted the Ottomans, although Persia was more isolated from the conflicts of the European great powers than the Ottoman Empire was. The tribal confederations in Persia remained powerful throughout the period of Safavid rule, and after the reign of Abbas (1588–1629), the central government's authority was increasingly challenged. However, despite weak rulers and an Ottoman invasion of Iraq, the Safavid Empire remained intact and relatively secure for almost a century after Abbas died. But the eighteenth century would bring in new warlords to rule the Safavid domains and place Persia in a military squeeze between the Russians to the north, the Ottomans to the west, the Mughuls to the east, and the British to the south.

The end of Safavid rule was initiated by an Afghan invasion in 1723 that forced Shah Husein to surrender. Although members of the Safavid family controlled parts of Persia for some years afterward, this invasion effectively ended the dynasty's rule over the region. Both the Russians and the Ottomans capitalized on Safavid distress by invading northern and western Persia. Afghan rule was not destined to last long, however. A new Turkic military commander of the Afahar tribe from eastern Persia allied himself with a Safavid prince and defeated the Afghans. By 1736 Nadir Khan had defeated the Ottomans in an engagement near Tabriz and declared himself Shah. This new warlord reformed the government, reorganized the army, and favored both Sunni and Shia branches of Islam, thereby alienating the Shiite *ulama* and gaining some favor with the Ottomans. By 1747 Nadir had regained lost territories, conquered western Afghanistan, plundered the Mughul capital at Delhi, and extended Persian hegemony over the Uzbeks to the north. But his visions of unifying and ruling a Sunni and Shiite empire came to nought when he was assassinated by his own men.

Persia was once again politically fragmented, but soon—between 1750 and 1779—another tribal warlord, Karim Khan Zand, emerged and gained control over most of the region. Karim Khan's reign was one of relative success and prosperity. He invaded Iraq, raided Ottoman territory, and encouraged trade relations with the British in the Persian Gulf. At his death the country lapsed again into savage contention among tribal leaders. Zand successors ruled parts of Persia until 1794, but the Qajar dynasty, which was to rule until 1924, managed to replace them.

As the century drew to a close, Russia, Britian, and France were all competing for Persian trade, and Persia was drawn more directly into European power politics. An Anglo-Persian defense and commercial treaty in 1800 encouraged the Qajar *shah* (king) to expect aid against Afghanistan and Russia; when this was not forthcoming, he accepted a French military mission to train his troops. This entente collapsed when the French and Russians signed a temporary truce and the British regained the advantage as advisers and commercial partners of the shah.

Indigenous Challenges to the Mughul Empire

The Mughul Empire was one of the world's wealthiest and most powerful states: its rich traditions, art, and literature had conditioned the whole Indian subcontinent. Mughul power culminated in the long reign of Aurangzeb (1659–1707), a period marked by military and administrative success. Aurangzeb's policies, however, directly undermined the imperial order established by the great Akbar. The new emperor, who learned the entire Qur'an by heart, was a champion of Islamic orthodoxy; he destroyed Hindu temples and schools, reimposed the ancient poll tax on Hindus, and dismissed them from government service. Until about 1679, while occupied in securing his northern frontiers, he did not push these policies vigorously; but his later reign brought unyielding persecution. To fight the Marathas, a powerful tribal confederation in the south, Aurangzeb virtually moved his capital to a battle camp in the Deccan, staying in the field and heading an unwieldy host of 500,000 servants, 50,000 camels, and 30,000 elephants, in addition to fighting men. By 1690, after terrible losses, he had overcome most resistance, but the south could not be permanently pacified. Time and again the aging ruler was forced to undertake new campaigns; when he died in 1707, it was in the Deccan.

Aurangzeb neglected architecture, patronage of the arts, and literary activities, although he did sponsor various projects in law and theology. As in the Ottoman Empire, when revenues declined, Aurangzeb employed tax farming to provide quick government income; tax farms enriched corrupt officials at the expense of both Hindu and Muslim peasants. After Aurangzeb died, Mughul authority was further decentralized. A period of civil war ensued until Muhammad Shah (1719–1748) succeeded to the imperial throne. Described by one contemporary as "never without a mistress in his arms and a glass in his hand," this indolent monarch made some effort to placate Hindus, with little practical result. Local Muslim dynasties ruled in the south and in Bengal; the Sikhs, a sect based on a Hindu-Muslim synthesis, became autonomous in the northwest; the Hindu Rajputs, once Mughul allies, began to break away; and the fierce Hindu Marathas, whom Aurangzeb had tried to subdue over a period of 30 years, extended their sway over much of central India. The impotence of the empire was most effectively demonstrated in 1739 when the army of Nadir Shah burned and looted the Mughul capital at Delhi, carrying away the imperial Peacock Throne, which would become a centerpiece of the Persian treasury.

Nadir Shah's invasion was but a prelude to the anarchic conditions that prevailed after Muhammad Shah's death in 1748. Mughul power met major challenges from three directions: the Afghans in the north, the Marathas in the south, and later the British from their base in Bengal in the northeast. When Nadir Shah (1736–1747) was assassinated in 1747, his Afghan troops elevated one of their commanders, Ahmad Khan (1747–1773), to the position of shah. He took the title *Durr-I Durran* ("Pearl of Pearls"), after which his line was called the Durrani. Uniting the Afghans and conquering a vast territory, which comprised eastern Persia, present-day Afghanistan, the major part of Uzbek Turkestan, and much of northwestern India including Kashmir and the Punjab, he established a dynasty that would survive in Afghanistan into the twentieth century. During one campaign in India, Ahmad sacked Delhi (1756), decisively defeating the Marathas and helping open the country to the British. At Panipat in 1761 his Afghans (employing their superior light artillery)

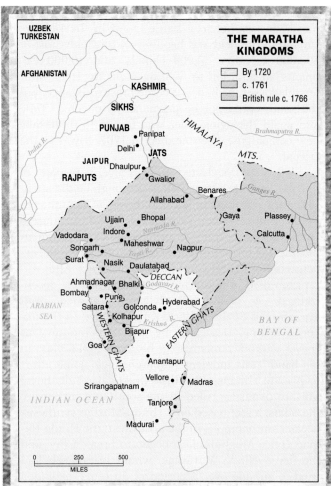

THE MARATHA KINGDOMS

☐ By 1720
☐ c. 1761
☐ British rule c. 1766

UZBEK TURKESTAN

AFGHANISTAN

KASHMIR

SIKHS

PUNJAB
Panipat
HIMALAYA
Delhi
JATS
Brahmaputra R.
JAIPUR
Dhaulpur
MTS.
RAJPUTS
Gwalior
Ganges R.
Benares
Allahabad
Bhopal
Ujjain
Gaya
Plassey
Narmada R.
Vadodara
Indore
Calcutta
Songarh
Maheshwar
Tapti R.
Nagpur
Surat
Nasik
Daulatabad
DECCAN
Ahmadnagar
Bhalki
Godavari R.
Bombay
Pune
Golconda
Hyderabad
ARABIAN SEA
Satara
Krishna R.
WESTERN GHATS
Kolhapur
EASTERN GHATS
BAY OF BENGAL
Bijapur
Goa
Anantapur
Vellore
Srirangapatnam
Madras
INDIAN OCEAN
Tanjore
Madurai

0   250   500
MILES

The indigenous Marathas in the Deccan rebelled against Mughul rule and won many victories against the Mughul kings. In the seventeenth and eighteenth centuries, first the Marathas and then the British posed formidable challenges to Mughul sovereignty.

discipline Shivaji, but the Maratha chief proved illusive, raiding Mughul territory and the prosperous port of Surat on the west coast of India. When Shivaji was called to court to negotiate with the Mughul emperor, Aurangzeb humiliated him. This episode set the stage for a new series of campaigns during which Shivaji bedeviled the Mughul armies and extended his territory in the Deccan.

Shivaji's family had been agriculturalists, not members of the Hindu warrior caste. So to legitimize his rule, Shivaji sent to the holy Hindu city of Varanasi, where he persuaded a distinguished Brahmin to supply him with a warrior (Kshatriya) genealogy and devise ceremonies of Hindu kingship. In these elaborate ceremonies Shivaji offered sacrifices to the gods and received gifts from Brahmins and nobles, thus reviving the notion of Hindu kingship in the subcontinent. In general, Hindu ceremonial was resurrected under the Marathas after long centuries of Muslim Mughul rule. After his death, Shavaji was immortalized in Maratha tales and ballads.

From the base established by Shivaji, various Marathas continued their wars of resistance against the Mughuls, sometimes fragmented by civil war, sometimes losing territory or co-opted by Mughul offers of position and wealth. Shortly after Aurangzeb's death, several Maratha leaders began to expand their territories into Malwa, Gujarat, and Rajasthan. In the second half of the eighteenth century the Marathas gained control over central and north India, reducing the Mughul emperor to the status of puppet ruler. But soon in the north and east they came up against the forces of a new power jockeying for position in the subcontinent, the British East India Company.

The British in India

The Portuguese were the first European power to establish themselves along the coasts of South Asia and exploit the rich commerce of the subcontinent. The Dutch, French, and English followed, and by the seventeenth century all four powers had commercial bases in India. All were attracted by the rich trade in spices and jewels and especially by the wonderful variety and volume of Indian textiles. The Europeans did not often penetrate inland; their commercial ventures were dependent on the elaborate and complex networks of traders, financiers, and middlemen already conducting trade into the interior and along the routes connecting India to China, Southeast Asia, Africa, and the Middle East.

Of the European powers, the Dutch dominated in Southeast Asia, but it was the British who managed to gain ascendancy in South Asia. In 1601 a group of British merchants petitioned Queen Elizabeth to grant them a monopoly over trade with "the East." Although the newly chartered East India Company

crushed a huge Maratha army. But after Ahmad's death in 1772, the Afghans lost power in India, and his sprawling tribal state lapsed into almost continuous civil war.

The Afghans were a serious threat, but it was the Maratha Confederacy in the northwestern Deccan that emerged as the most powerful force to challenge Mughul supremacy. The first great Maratha leader was Shivaji Bhonsle (1630–1680). At the age of 17 Shivaji began to build a small regional state by capturing forts and passes through the Western Ghat mountains. He seized some territory from the kingdom of Bijapur, whose sultan sent an army under the general Afzal Khan to discipline him. Shivaji retreated to one of his hill forts, and in a famous episode, the two generals met to negotiate. Both bore arms, and in close combat Shivaji managed to disembowel Afzal Khan with a "tiger claw" concealed in the palm of his hand. Aurganzeb sent several armies to

claimed a monopoly over all trade between India and Europe, what it actually acquired was a monopoly over all trade between British territory and India. From an early "factory" (commercial office and warehouse) in Surat, the British expanded to bases in Madras, Bombay (ceded to Britian by the Portuguese as a dowry for Charles II's bride), and Bengal (the territory surrounding the mouth of the Ganges river). In 1690 a Company agent acquired a piece of land in the Ganges Delta that the British swiftly developed into the commercial entrepot known as Calcutta. By 1700 the Company had a charter from the Mughul emperor to trade and collect taxes in the area, and by 1750 the population of Calcutta had risen to around 500,000. It was a major port for the Company and for Indian and independent European traders.

The Company used its bases to extend its commercial affairs inland and used its own private army to forge alliances with local rulers. Both sides benefited, although various local lords resisted British incursions. Because the balance of trade was much in favor of India, Britain sent thousands of pounds in silver to pay for its purchases. By 1800 the wealth (especially taxes) generated by the Company's activities provided a substantial portion of Britain's income.

Throughout the 1700s the East India Company became increasingly involved in local politics, building its own domain in Bengal and challenging the authority of the local ruler, Siraj ud-Dawla. In 1756 he retaliated by seizing and plundering Calcutta. The Company then sent a large military force under Robert Clive, who crushed Siraj ud-Dawla's army in the battle of Plassey in 1757. Clive went on to defeat the French and Dutch establishments in Bengal, and by the Treaty of Allahabad in 1765 the Mughul emperor granted the British administrative control of Bengal. The Company thus became an Indian "lord." The British then extended their power inland using a combination of military force and commercial treaty. They gained hegemony over a great circuit of trade from India to China and to England, exchanging Indian opium for Chinese tea (all the rage in England) and English silver for Indian silk. By the end of the century the Mughul ruler Shah Alam II was collecting a British pension and William Jones and other officials were cultivating British interest in Sanskrit classics. The Mughuls could only look on as the British East India Company, employing Indian armies, extended its sway over the subcontinent.

European Encroachments in Eastern Asia

The destructive European impact on African and Middle Eastern lands was matched by a similar process in the outlying areas of East Asia. On the

The British presence in India exerted an increasing influence on the arts. This work of an Indian painter, inscribed in Persian and dated about 1760, depicts an official of the British East India Company smoking a water pipe and receiving an Indian visitor.

mainland and among the islands of Southeast Asia, Europeans continued to intervene, with varying degrees of success, in the chaotic internal affairs of perpetually contending established states. Farther east, on hundreds of Pacific islands, European discovery and exploration resulted in quick revolutions, which tended to demoralize and destroy native cultures.

Southeast Asia

The islands and the mainland of Southeast Asia had contrasting reactions to European influences. The more flexible culture of the archipelago largely succumbed or remained traditional. The stronger mainland states, aware of their vulnerability to China or their immediate neighbors, were sometimes compromised in seeking European aid. A more decisive factor, however, was their warfare for survival and supremacy, in which Thailand and Vietnam were more successful than Burma, Cambodia, and Laos.

The late seventeenth century was a chaotic time for all the mainland states, with the possible exception of tiny Laos. Burma struggled under weak kings, cor-

Not all Indian rulers welcomed the British. A major opponent was Tipu Sultan, called the "Tiger of Mysore," who was finally killed by a British force in 1799. This organ, carved in the shape of a tiger attacking a man in European dress, was seized from Tipu Sultan's court and ended up in an English museum.

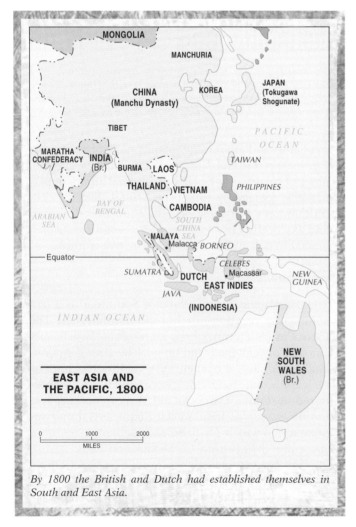

By 1800 the British and Dutch had established themselves in South and East Asia.

rupt ministers, local uprisings, Thai invasions, and Chinese-European competition for advantage. Thailand, meanwhile, faced internal turmoil complicated by Dutch pressure, which encouraged first British and then French attempts to take over the country. Vietnam emerged from savage civil wars as two separate states, North and South. Both became tributaries of Manchu China while trying to avoid granting special concessions to Europeans. These efforts were mainly successful, except for French missionaries, who gained a strong foothold in the southern kingdom. Only Laos, during the long reign of Souligna-Vongsa (1637–1692), enjoyed sustained peace and a degree of good relations with its neighbors.

This situation changed drastically during the eighteenth century. Burma enjoyed a brief revival between 1772 and 1776, when two strong monarchs, Alaungpaya (1752–1759) and his son, Hainbyushin (1763–1776), defeated the Thai, French, British, and Chinese. But this was the apex of Burmese power. In Thailand, after all Europeans were expelled in the early 1700s, a half-Chinese military commander, Paya Taksin, drove out the Burmese invaders, made himself king, and extended Thai influence over Laos, Cambodia, and Malaya. South Vietnam, meanwhile, doubled its territory by expanding into the Mekong valley at the expense of Cambodia. Between 1786 and 1801 it united the country and began eliminating French control of affairs. On the surface, Southeast Asia seemed to be consolidating political power, buttressing traditional institutions, and ending foreign domination. But the stage was nevertheless set for the British conquest of Burma and French moves into Indochina later in the nineteenth century.

Farther south in Indonesia, the European presence was much more compelling and the native resistance much weaker—in part because thousands of migrating Chinese had diluted the Islamic values and loyalties of Muslim societies in the Malay Archipelago. By 1750 the Dutch had subordinated most native dynasties in Malaya, Java, Sumatra, and the other islands. In the process, imported plantation agriculture brought an economic revolution that conditioned much life and labor in the whole area within limits set by European commercial capitalism.

For more than a century a Muslim Malay people known in history as the Bugis challenged Dutch supremacy. Originating on the island of Celebes, the Bugis first won fame as sea rovers and mercenary warriors, serving all sides in the competitive spice trade through the city of Macassar. When the Dutch took Macassar in 1667, the Bugis scattered from Borneo to the Malay Peninsula, where they concentrated at Selangor. Through conquest, intermarriage, and intrigue, they gained control of Jahore, Perak, and Kedah on the mainland while extending their influence to Borneo and Sumatra. The Bugis fought two wars against Dutch Malacca in 1756 and 1784 but were ultimately forced to accept Dutch overlordship.

At the same time, the Dutch were losing ground to the British. With their East India Company facing internal corruption, increasing costs, and mounting competition, the Dutch could no longer maintain their independence amid the rising Anglo-French colonial rivalry. In Asia this rivalry was centered primarily in India, but the British were also expanding their trade through the Malacca Straits and seeking a naval port to counter the French in the Bay of Bengal. In 1786 the British obtained Penang on the Malay coast. Later, when France dominated the Netherlands during the Napoleonic era, Britain temporarily took Malacca and Java. Penang then became a rapidly expanding center of British influence in Malaya.

Europeans on New Pacific Frontiers

Except for Spanish traders and colonists in the Philippines, the Pacific area was almost unknown to Europeans before 1650, but many came during the next century. Some of this contact involved Russian ships cruising southward toward Japan from Kamchatka; at the same time, the French and British penetrated the North Pacific from Polynesia. By the late eighteenth century, when Western ships regularly arrived at Canton (Guangzhou) from Hawaii or other Polynesian islands, East Asians began to feel the Western world crowding in on them.

Russians moved out toward the Pacific in 1632, when they established Yakutsk in eastern Siberia. From there, adventurers drifted down the Lena, first reaching the Arctic and later sailing east to the open Pacific. Their discoveries were ignored until 1728, when Vitus Bering (1680–1741), a Danish navigator sailing for Peter the Great, charted the Bering Strait, which links the Arctic and Pacific Oceans. This discovery opened the North Pacific to Russia during the eighteenth century. Meanwhile, the Russians founded Okhotsk on the Pacific coast opposite the Kamchatka peninsula. At Okhotsk and at other timbered forts in Siberia, Russian governors and their Cossack soldiers exacted tribute in furs from a society of nomadic hunters. Relations between the conquerors and their subjects were not particularly friendly; indeed local populations around the forts were often wiped out by direct violence or European diseases.

Shortly after Bering's expeditions, French and English navigators began their own extensive explorations. The most significant were those of the French noble Louis de Bougainville (1729–1811) and the famous English captain James Cook (1729–1779). Bougainville visited much of southern Polynesia, the Sandwich (Hawaiian) Islands, Australia, New Guinea, and New Britain. Cook's three voyages between 1768 and 1779 went beyond the known waters of the South Pacific to Antarctica and north of Alaska to the Arctic coasts, where Cook made contact with the Russians. Although he was killed in Hawaii on his last voyage, Cook's journals fired European imaginations and encouraged European migration across the Pacific. Botany Bay in eastern Australia, established by the English as a penal colony in 1788, soon became a colony of settlement. Meanwhile, a swarm of Western traders, whalers, missionaries, and beachcombers descended on the South Pacific islands and the North Pacific coasts.

Perhaps the most striking feature of relations between Europeans and Pacific islanders was the contrast in sexual mores and roles. Male islanders, unlike European men, were used to female leadership, if not absolute domination; men were less ambitious and possessive; and sexual indulgence was considered by both men and women as pleasurable but not overly significant. No wonder that Polynesian women in Tahiti or Hawaii, when they learned that sex could be exchanged easily for European goods, descended on each ship at every anchoring. Their preference for iron nails almost caused the ships to be taken apart. In time the crews became so conditioned that they tried to initiate similar transactions in North America, where the women were less interested.

After Cook's time, original cultures in Polynesia rapidly declined as trade goods, rum, and guns

Captain James Cook, Departure from Tahiti

This selection is from Cook's journal on his second voyage into the South Pacific (1772–1775) in a major effort to explore Antarctica.

Thursday 16th. This Morning the Natives came off to the Sloops in their Canoes as usual, after breakfast Captain Furneaux and I paid the Chief a Viset, we found him at his house perfectly easy and satisfied in so much that he and some of his friends came a board and dined with us. . . . Having got a board a large supply of refreshments I determined to put to Sea in the morning and made the same known to the chief who promised to come and take leave of me on board the Ship.

Whilest I was with him [Oreo] yesterday, my Otaheite young man Porio took a sudden resolution to leave me, I have mentioned before that he was with me when I followed Oreo, and of his advising me not to go out of the boat, and was so much affraid at this time that he remaned in the boat till he heard all matters were reconciled, then he came out and presently after met with a young woman for whom he had contracted a friendship, he having my powder horn in keeping came and gave it to one of my people who was by me and then went away; I, who knew that he had found his female friend, took no notice thinking that he was only going to retire with her on some private business of their own, probably at this time he had no other intention, she however had prevailed upon him to remain with her for I saw him no more and to day I was told, that he was married. . . . In the after noon our boats returned from Otaha . . . they made the Circuit of the isle, conducted by one of the Aree's whose name was Boba, and were hospitably entertained by the people who provided them with victuals lodgeing and bed fellows according to the custom of the Country; the first night they were entertained with a Play, the second night their repast was disturbed by the Natives stealing their military Chest, which put them upon making reprisals by which means they recovered the most of what they had lost.

Friday 17th. At 4 o'Clock in Morning we began to unmoor and as soon as it was light Oreo and some of his friends came to take leave, many Canoes also came off with Hogs and fruit, the former they even beged of us to take from them, calling out, Tyu Boa Atoi which was as much as to say, I am your friend take my Hog and give me an ax, but our decks were already so full of them that we could hardly move, having on board the *Resolution* about 230 and on board the *Adventure* about 150. . . .

The Chief and his friends did not leave us till the Anchor was a weigh. At parting I made him a present of a Broad Ax and several other things with which he went away well satisfied. He was extremely desirous to know if, and when I would return, these were the last questions he asked me. After we were out of the Harbour and had made sail we discovered a Canoe conducted by two men following us, upon which I brought to and they presently came a long side with a present of fruit from Oreo, I made them some return for their trouble, dismissed them and made sail to the Westward with the Adventure in company. The young man I got at Otaheite left me at Ulietea two days before we sailed being inticed away by a young Woman for whom he had contracted a friendship. I took no methods to recover him as there were Volanteers enough out of whome I took one, a youth about [17 or 18] years of age who says he is a relation of the great Opoony and . . . may be of use to us if we should fall in with and touch at any isles in our rout to the west. . . .

From John C. Beaglehole, ed., *The Voyage of the* Resolution *and* Adventure, *1772–1775* (Cambridge: Cambridge University Press, 1961), pp. 228–230.

stimulated avarice, status seeking, competition for power, violence, and war. With European help, local rulers—male and female—fought to dominate their islands. Such conflict was particularly true of Hawaii in the decade after 1790, where a Hawaiian chief, Kamehameha, used European ships and cannons to unite the three main islands. Sexual commerce with Europeans also brought syphilis to the islands, blame for which was long disputed by the French and the English. Other European imports included cattle, smallpox, and missionaries. Amid sensual competition and Christian condemnation, the old religion was largely abandoned; whole communities became alcoholic; and other evidences of psychological malaise, such as suicide, became prevalent.

European expansion in the Pacific brought significant changes for civilized East Asia, particularly in maritime commerce. After the middle of the eighteenth century, the British began replacing the Dutch as the major European traders, a trend climaxed by the collapse of the Dutch East India Company in 1794. At Canton the number of British and American ships increased dramatically after 1790. Seeking a product that might be exchanged profitably for Chi-

Captain James Cook charted the coasts of New Zealand, Australia, and New Guinea and the Pacific coast of North America and mapped nearly every island in the Pacific.

nese silk and tea, the British first concentrated on opium from India. When the opium trade created friction with Chinese officials, British merchants began seeking furs, particularly sea otter skins, which were obtained in the North Pacific. Hawaiian ports soon became busy centers for fitting ships and recruiting sailors. By 1815 European expansion into the Pacific had generated a dynamic commercial revolution.

Change and Crisis in East Asia

Among the great states of the East Asian mainland, the European impact was felt less than elsewhere, but it still figured largely in typical problems of the area and the time. Although China and Japan held strong attachments to their traditional values and were the most prosperous and stable of all non-European states, each experienced forceful changes in conflict with their ancient heritages. While struggling to make adjustments, both nations saw their difficulties magnified by an increasing European presence around the western Pacific.

The Rise and Decline of Manchu China

Between 1644, when the Manchu armies took Peking, and the start of the nineteenth century, China

was the most populous country on earth. Its economy grew steadily while its literature, art, and philosophy evoked great admiration from European intellectuals. The Manchu emperors were generally efficient and conscientious; but like many barbarian rulers of the past, they were so awed by Chinese institutions that they were incapable of promoting necessary change. The main problem was not that China was backward—it developed and prospered under the Manchus—but that its progress was much slower than that of the West.

The Manchu system was a unique and highly successful modification of the traditional Chinese institutional structure. Although the conquerors sought to maintain their identity by avoiding intermarriage with Chinese, they retained the Chinese examination system and the privileged scholar-bureaucracy. Manchus and Chinese, working in pairs, conducted government above the provincial level. The most significant innovation was the "banner" system, comprising elite military units, both Manchu and Chinese. Because they were kept distinct from family, tribal, or even geographical identities, the banner companies provided reliable imperial troops. Augmented by Chinese conscripts and foreign tributaries, they extended China's control farther than ever before. Manchu armies subdued Taiwan, Mongolia, Turkestan, and Tibet. The emperors also established tributary control over Korea, North Vietnam, and Burma.

A major contributor to the development of Manchu China was the emperor K'ang-hsi, who reigned longer (1661–1722) than any predecessor. Intelligent, conscientious, and hardworking, he was a brave soldier, an inquisitive scholar, and an able administrator. In six grand tours of the country, he sought to improve local government and promote justice. Always devoted to learning, he encouraged scholarship by sponsoring great research projects. As a commander, he defeated the remaining Ming forces, then directed the long and arduous campaigns that ultimately conquered Mongolia. Unfortunately, he was unable to reform either imperial finance or rural administration, and he refused to encourage foreign trade. In 1717, after the bitter disappointment of having to disinherit his only legitimate son, the old monarch revealed his human weaknesses and concerns in a personal testament. Five years later he died in despair and confusion, without securing future stability by naming a successor. His record, therefore, has been deemed a "mixed legacy."[2]

K'ang-hsi's unresolved problems plagued the next two reigns, as the Manchu regime reached its climax and began to decline. Between 1722 and 1736 the Yung-cheng emperor, one of K'ang-hsi's 19 illegitimate sons, ruthlessly eliminated opposition formed on behalf of his brothers. His dictatorial methods set a dangerous precedent but also lessened corruption

Father Ripa, Family Relations in Manchu China

Father Ripa, an Italian Jesuit missionary, was at the court of the great Manchu emperor K'ang-hsi from 1711 to 1723.

One day as I was talking in my own house with a mandarin [public official] who had come to pay me a visit, his son arrived from a distant part of the empire upon some business relating to the family. When he came in we were seated, but he immediately went down on one knee before his father, and in this position continued to speak for about a quarter of an hour. I did not move from my chair till, by the course of the conversation, I discovered who the person was, when I suddenly arose, protesting to the mandarin that I would stand unless he allowed his son to sit down also. A lengthy contest ensued, the father saying that he would quit his seat if I continued to stand; I myself declaring that it was impossible for me to sit while his son was kneeling; and the son protesting that before his father he must remain on his knees. At last, however, I overcame every scruple, and the mandarin signified to his son by a sign that he might be seated. He instantly obeyed, but he retreated to a corner of the room, where he timidly seated himself upon the edge of a chest. . . .

Chinese women live entirely shut up by themselves in a remote apartment of their houses. Among persons of rank they are seldom allowed to go out, unless it be during the rejoicings of the new year, and even then they are shut up in sedans. They are indeed kept so strictly that they are not allowed to speak even with the father or the brother of their husbands, much less with their uncles, or any other man, however close may be the relationship. . . . And here I will not omit the description of a practice which, while it proves the excellent social order of the Chinese, caused me to smile when I heard of it. If a man, for careless conduct or any other fault, considers it his duty to correct his daughter-in-law, as he cannot, ac-

cording to the custom of the country either enter her room or speak to her, and much less beat her, he summons his son before him, and after reproaching him with the faults of his wife, he bids him prostrate himself, and inflicts a severe flogging upon him. The son then rises upon his knees, and, touching the ground with his forehead, thanks his father for the castigation; after which he goes to his wife, and repeats the correction exactly, giving her the same number of blows that he received from his father.

From their inordinate jealousy arose the custom of crippling the feet of the women, in order to render walking a torment, and induce them to remain at home. I was informed by Chinese that the first who discovered this stratagem was one of their ancient emperors, who purposely hinted that nothing was more beautiful in a woman than to have the smallest feet possible. This imperial opinion being made public throughout China, every husband desired that his wife should be in the fashion, and mothers sought to secure to their daughters an imaginary beauty which it was found could be procured by art. Accordingly, at the tender age of three months, female infants have their feet bound so tightly that the growth of this part of their body is entirely stopped, and they cannot walk without hobbling and limping; and if upon any occasion they endeavour to quicken their pace, they are in danger of falling at every step. . . . In case of marriage, the parties not being able to see each other, it is customary to send the exact dimensions of the lady's foot to her intended, instead of sending him her portrait as we do in Europe.

From Rhoda Hoff, ed., *China: Adventures in Eyewitness History* (New York: Walck, 1965), pp. 63–66.

and prepared the way for the reign of the Ch'ien-lung emperor (1736–1796), the fourth son of Yung-cheng. At first the new ruler was sincere, frugal, and industrious, like his famous grandfather. His early reign was marked by peace at home, victories abroad, a doubling of the empire's territory, expanding wealth, and noteworthy achievements in scholarship and the arts. Unfortunately, these conditions did not last. After about 1770, expensive military campaigns began depleting the treasury. The emperor also instituted a rigorous policy of censorship and book burning. As the eighteenth century ended, government fell into

the hands of a royal favorite, whose corruption and inefficiency coincided with widespread rebellions.

This internal weakening of the Manchu regime was accompanied by increasing problems with foreign affairs. After years of fighting along the Manchurian and Mongolian frontiers, K'ang-hsi negotiated the Treaty of Nerchinsk in 1689. The agreement set the border between Siberia and Manchuria and permitted limited Russian trade in Peking. More specific terms for the Chinese-Russian accord were established by the Treaty of Kiakhta in 1727, when the Russians recognized Chinese sovereignty over

Mongolia. As advisers to the Manchu emperors, Jesuits helped negotiate both of these treaties. They enjoyed considerable status at K'ang-hsi's court, where they preached a version of Christianity consistent with traditional Chinese beliefs, such as ancestor worship. But at the start of the eighteenth century the pope required Chinese Christians to renounce such beliefs. In response, the emperor banned all Christians who complied with the papal order. Henceforth, Catholics and western Europeans were generally regarded with suspicion. In 1757 the Chinese government confined all trade to Canton, where Europeans were forced to deal through a merchant monopoly and corrupt officials. Because of these conditions, Europeans, particularly the British, continually pressed for free trade and regular diplomatic relations.

During Ch'ien-lung's reign China was rapidly approaching the limits of its traditional system. Although Europeans were impressed by the country's order, wealth, and expanding population, which doubled between 1700 and 1800, they saw a facade rather than the country's actual conditions. Chinese agriculture increased in productivity but not enough to feed 300 million people adequately. Consequently, many migrated into the southwestern provinces, North Vietnam, and even across the seas to the Philippines and Java. At home, famine became prevalent as the soil wore out. Peasant uprisings were matched by growing unrest in the southern cities, which were also swelling in size, without increased economic resources. While a few Cantonese merchants, Yangtse salt monopolists, and favored government officials amassed great wealth, Chinese who lived below the elite classes suffered great hardships and injustices.

Despite these problems, the late Manchu emperors held fast to their faith in China's ancient values. K'ang-hsi had been curious about Western medicine, astronomy, and mathematics, without conceding the validity of Western science. After his time, European material advances were noted but neither held in awe nor envied. Both K'ang-hsi and Ch'ien-lung fostered massive scholarly projects in history and philosophy, as their predecessors had done. Thousands of Chinese scholars, who were supported by the state, labored at these compilations while less favored others taught the Confucian classics in government schools or private academies. Their conservatism was demonstrated in a movement that, like its Japanese counterpart, opposed Ming Neo-Confucianism in favor of Confucian principles expounded in the Han period. Thus while China slipped inevitably toward the future, its intellectuals remained preoccupied with the distant past.

Such paralyzing Manchu conservatism is perhaps best illustrated by the social status of women in the eighteenth century. They were held in comparison with men to a stifling Confucian double standard for female self-denial and chastity. Prevailing custom also conditioned most engaged women whose fiancé died to remain single for life, commit suicide, or be buried

The 1689 treaty between Russia and China was the first treaty that China concluded with any Western power. In this contemporary engraving, the Russian ambassador is ceremonially greeted as he arrives for an audience with Emperor K'ang-hsi.

alive with the fiancé. A similar customary conditioning perpetuated the foot binding of upper-class female children, preparing them to be ornamental wives. Early Manchu emperors had forbidden this old Chinese practice, but it was so fashionable and Manchu women were so eager to gain acceptability that the prohibition was generally ignored by the 1700s.

This conservative myopia was typical but not quite universal among writers and artists. Most creative endeavors aimed to please the aristocratic urban classes, who lived artificial lives in their gardens amid their books and paintings. Painters usually followed the classical Sung schools. Traditional drama, having emerged in the Yuan period, remained popular into the nineteenth century. There were, however, some links between Chinese art and the contemporary world. Lacquer and porcelain wares attained such popularity in Europe that they were produced in great quantities to meet foreign demand. Some Chinese painting came to adopt European techniques for achieving perspective. Finally, Chinese literature showed some social concern and attempted realism. *The Dream of the Red Chamber,* an eighteenth-century depiction of a declining aristocratic family, has been widely acclaimed as China's greatest novel.

At the start of the nineteenth century, Manchu China was seemingly in the process of reversing its decline. After 1799, when Ch'ien-lung died, his son Chia-ch'ing (1796–1820) assumed full control of state policy. He immediately responded to the criticism of

Porcelain bowl from Manchu China. During the Manchu era, Chinese potters began to produce two grades of porcelain ware— one for export, designed to satisfy European taste, and a finer grade, "Chinese ware," made for internal, royal use.

Western-oriented intellectuals by executing his father's favorite and by instituting reforms of taxes, imperial finances, and local government. He received indirect aid from the Napoleonic wars in Europe, which turned French and British attentions away from the issue of Chinese trade practices. This lull in foreign pressure was only temporary, however. After 1815, diplomatic contention over the Canton trade and China's internal deficiencies resumed to plague Manchu rulers during the nineteenth century.

Korea, the reluctant Manchu vassal state, experienced problems similar to China's and devised similar solutions. Japanese and Chinese invasions in the early seventeenth century so weakened the scholarly bureaucracy and central government that they could barely function. In the resulting disorder and confusion, the economy developed rapidly, although the population increased by 50 percent; many people suffered, particularly the peasants. Such conditions encouraged new thinking. By the eighteenth century a movement among intellectuals, known as "practical learning," was advocating reforms in government while showing some sympathy for Western Christianity and science. Some of this reform spirit was revealed in the policies of King Yungjo (1724–1776) and his grandson, King Chongjo (1776–1800), who gradually restored some order and efficiency.

Tensions in Japan Under the Mature Tokugawa Shogunate

While much of Asia and Africa absorbed European influences, the Tokugawa regime in Japan seemed unaffected. Deliberately choosing to be isolated from the West, the Japanese acquired an apparent immunity from foreign cultural "viruses." After outlawing Christianity and expelling Europeans, they perfected a remarkably efficient bureaucratic system on traditional social foundations. For two centuries the economy flourished, cities grew, population stabilized, and the standard of living rose. These successes were, however, accompanied by great social tensions, which threatened the political order. At the same time, external stimuli caused some Japanese to advocate foreign ideas, while others reacted emotionally in defense of their sacred heritage.

The Tokugawa system, originally a localized feudal order, became highly centralized in this era. Without the disruption of foreign wars and European support for the *daimyo,* the shoguns turned these great lords into dependent officials and courtiers and transformed the samurai from vassals of their lords into state employees. These changes were largely accomplished by concentrating the warrior class in castle towns and separating them from local control of conscript peasant soldiers. At the same time, the samurai were educated in the Confucian classics, which emphasized civic duties over personal loyalties, as taught in the old Bushido code. Reorientation of the samurai was also furthered by paying them fixed stipends and restricting some of their traditional violent practices, such as feuding or committing honorable suicide *(seppuku)*. With its loyal samurai corps of soldiers, scholars, and bureaucrats, the shogunate became a highly efficient political organization.

Such bureaucratic order naturally lessened flexibility. The official Confucianism stressed loyalty and obedience to authority, but it looked to the past, suspected the future, and resisted most proposed improvements. In practice, it brought all human activity under the shogun's jurisdiction. All of Japanese society was divided into four classes: samurai; peasants, who comprised 80 percent of the population; artisans; and merchants. For each class the state prescribed rules of conduct, including the most trivial and personal. Within each class women were considered servants of their husbands and had their duties prescribed in official edicts. Such ordering of individual behavior remained a widely recognized ideal.

The official disciplinary tone was reflected in an outpouring of cultural expression during this era. Although Buddhism declined generally, its temple schools fostered a rapid expansion of education. Literacy spread rapidly and became almost universal in the cities. The intellectual climate was further improved by a phenomenal increase in book publishing. Samurai scholars produced national histories and Confucian philosophical works to honor Tokugawa accomplishments and provide a basic rationale for state and society. Samurai architects also perpetuated traditional baroque grandeur in castles and public buildings. In painting the samurai influence was represented by the Kano school's synthesis of classical Japanese and Chinese traditions, such as the pictorial essays of the "literati" *(nanga)* painters.

Although the Tokugawa government and society were supposedly prescribed within official limits, the economy underwent dynamic growth and change. In agriculture, land reclamation, improved seeds, better fertilizers, and new tools enabled farmers to double cereal production between 1600 and 1730. Rising wealth in the villages financed many new small industries and generally increased industrial output. A functional road network and a complex money-based financial system gave rise to large capitalistic enterprises centered in the cities, which were rapidly expanding in number and size. With a population of nearly a million, Edo, capital of the shogunate, was the largest city in the world by 1750. The total Japanese population, meanwhile, peaked at approximately 29 million, declining only slightly in the 1700s. This combination of increasing productivity and stable population, unmatched anywhere else in the world,

produced a spirit of enterprise and optimism most evident among the urban classes, especially among commoner women, many of whom were actively involved in hand manufacturing or business.

Increasing wealth, rising expectations, and other unprecedented changes subjected Japanese society to dangerous tensions after the late seventeenth century. Peasants, generally, suffered from high taxes and inflation. Many were alienated from the land and from the upper classes as they became hired laborers or free tenants. The new money economy, while stimulating a desire for luxuries among the samurai, diminished their economic independence and encouraged them to borrow heavily from merchant bankers. Even the *daimyo* had to engage in business to pay for their many social obligations at court. At the same time, their creditors among the urban middle classes were dissatisfied by numerous frivolous demands and penalties imposed by the government on commerce and banking. As such dissatisfaction grew, frequent disorders had to be forcefully repressed.

The government met these problems by alternating between reform and inertia. The first four shoguns ruled wisely and forcefully, but later ones allowed their ministers to make policies, which brought increasing bureaucratic rigidity. While revenues dropped, inflation increased, and respect for authority declined. Some partly successful efforts at reform were attempted by the scholar minister Arai Hakuseki (1709–1716). An even more determined reformer was the eighth shogun, Yoshimune (1716–1745). An honest, sincere, and just statesman, Yoshimune tried to restore traditional morality with the famous Kyoho reforms, which cut expenses, encouraged agriculture, regularized taxes, standardized the diverse feudal laws, and relaxed the ban on foreign technical books. He also ordered the dismissal of nearly half the court ladies, a measure designed to save money and lessen dissension. With such policies, Yoshimune hoped to restore the efficiency of the past, but his policies were only temporary remedies rather than permanent solutions for the country's problems.

Under Yoshimune's successors, conditons deteriorated steadily. His son Ieshige (1745–1760), a semi-invalid with a speech defect, ushered in an era of political decline. The next shogun yielded to his unscrupulous chamberlain, who courted the merchant bankers and attempted to increase revenues and strengthen the regime; but his extravagance and corrupt practices brought economic depression and frequent riots. This commercial policy was reversed by Matsudaira Sananobu, Yoshimune's grandson and chief minister until 1793. A stern traditionalist, he tried unsuccessfully to cut expenses and restore the old samurai values. After he retired, the government drifted aimlessly during the long reign of Shogun Ienari (1787–1837).

While the government floundered, a new urban subculture posed an alternative to official Confucian values. Prosperous urbanites, disillusioned with old-fashioned morality, idealized the "floating world" of irrational sensuality, featuring fine food, alcohol, gambling houses, and brothels. Free love and sexual independence, exemplified by the lifestyles of adventurers, entertainers, and prostitutes, became subjects of a new art and literature, produced in the revolt against samurai morality. Other writings, rejecting artificial themes, evoked appreciation for the realistic or the esoteric. For example, *haiku* poetry, which won great popularity, used 17 syllables in three lines to express clever microcosmic observations on universal themes. A new pictorial art used woodblock printing and vivid colors to portray nature, street scenes, pretty women, and mild erotica.

More threatening to the shogunate than urban alienation was rational criticism from intellectuals. By the end of the eighteenth century, a growing number of people were questioning the shogun's authority. Many of these "nationalists" were militarists who thought that the shogunate had betrayed Japanese traditions. Confucian proponents of "ancient learning" blamed all the trouble on Neo-Confucians, who had strayed from the old texts. Others turned to practical subjects, such as economics, while rejecting the moralistic perspectives of official scholars. After Yoshimune relaxed the ban on foreign non-Christian writings in 1720, "Dutch studies" were pursued widely in medicine, astronomy, and various technical fields. The movement gained momentum as the century passed, indicating that European ideas were significantly involved in the prevailing dissension.

Conclusion

Despite European expansionism, many African and Asian civilizations survived and prospered in this era. Although Dutch settlement in the Cape in South Africa nearly destroyed the Khoikhoi and San cultures, other African societies such as the Xhosa more than held their own against European settlers. Moreover, in East and central Africa, the Rozvi kingdom and Omani Arabs expelled the Portuguese. The transatlantic slave trade took its toll on the inhabitants of western and central Africa, but kingdoms such as Asante, Dahomey, and Oyo all maintained their autonomy and even prospered. In the West African Sudan, Kanem-Bornu and the Hausa states consolidated Muslim dominance, while Fulani Muslims successfully launched *jihads* to spread the faith. Morocco and the Barbary States developed economies based on agriculture, herding, trade, and privateering. Like the recently formed Sikh state, that of

the Marathas remained strong and challenged the military authority of the British in India. France had recently lost influence in Vietnam, which was acutely aware of a revived Thailand. To the north, in East Asia, China persisted in rejecting regular diplomatic relations with European nations, Korea's "practical learning" was producing reforms, and Japan was a convincing example of prosperity with independence.

The independent states of Africa and Asia were, however, facing both internal upheavals and the continuing pressures placed on them by an ascendant and imperialistic Europe. China and Japan were both seriously disturbed by internal tensions. Burma faced a military threat from the British in Bengal. Persia, the Ottoman Empire, and the slave-trading states of western and central Africa were enmeshed in the changes deriving from new global economic configurations and European penetration. In addition to the Cape in South Africa, much of India, Indonesia, Polynesia, and Siberia had felt the direct shock of European conquest.

Whereas the fifteenth and sixteenth centuries had been a time of dominant Asian empires, the seventeenth and eighteenth centuries would constitute an era in which European states became increasingly hegemonic. Britain especially was using its formidable navy to establish a global network of bases and colonies. The Peace of Vienna in 1815 not only brought a decisive British victory over France in Europe but also unofficially ratified the recent rise in British power and influence around the globe: in China, Southeast Asia, India, the Persian Gulf, the eastern Mediterranean, and Africa. With other advantages derived from their phenomenal industrial development, the British prepared to lead the great European scramble for empire in the nineteenth century. It was a scramble that would come at the political, economic, and cultural expense of Africa and Asia.

Suggestions for Reading

The best general treatments of this period in Africa's history are *The Cambridge History of Africa*, vol. 4; *The UNESCO General History of Africa*, vol. 5; Robert July, *A History of the African People*, 5th ed. (Waveland, 1997); Kevin Shillington, *History of Africa*, 2nd ed. (St. Martin's Press, 1995); John Iliffe, *Africans: The History of a Continent* (Cambridge, 1995); and Elizabeth Isichei, *A History of African Societies to 1870* (Cambridge University Press, 1997).

The period of Dutch rule in South Africa is covered in Nigel Worden, *Slavery in Dutch South Africa* (Cambridge University Press, 1985); Robert Shell, *Children of Bondage: A Social History of the Slave Society at the Cape of Good Hope, 1652–1838* (University Press of New England, 1994); Robert Ross, *Cape of Torments: Slavery and Resistance in South Africa* (Routledge & Kegan Paul, 1983); Richard Elphick, *Khoikhoi and the Founding of White South Africa* (Yale University Press, 1985); and

Richard Elphick and Hermann Giliomee, eds., *The Shaping of South African Society, 1652–1840* (Wesleyan University Press, 1989). Good general surveys are Leonard Thompson, *A History of South Africa* (Yale University Press, 1995); Kevin Shillington, *A History of South Africa* (Longman, 1988); T. R. H. Davenport, *South Africa: A Modern History*, 4th ed. (University of Toronto Press, 1991); John D. Omer-Cooper, *History of Southern Africa*, 2nd ed. (Heinemann, 1994); and *Illustrated History of South Africa* (Reader's Digest, 1995). The wars between Europeans and the Xhosa are treated in J. B. Peires, *The House of Phalo* (University of Wisconsin Press, 1981), and Neil Mostert, *Frontiers* (Knopf, 1992).

A comprehensive account of the global slave trade is Stephen Drescher and Stanley Engerman, eds., *A Historical Guide to World Slavery* (Oxford University Press, 1998). Philip Curtin, *The Atlantic Slave Trade: A Census* (University of Wisconsin Press, 1969), is the classic work on the subject. Several general studies are Joseph Inikori and Stanley Engerman, eds., *The Atlantic Slave Trade* (Duke University Press, 1992); Barbara Solow, *Slavery and the Rise of the Atlantic System* (Cambridge University Press, 1991); and Hugh Thomas, *The Slave Trade: The Story of the Atlantic Slave Trade, 1440–1870* (Simon & Schuster, 1997). For the participation of Europeans, see Robert Stein, *The French Slave Trade in the Eighteenth Century* (University of Wisconsin Press, 1980); Johannes M. Postma, *The Dutch in the Atlantic Slave Trade* (Cambridge University Press, 1989); David Eltis, *Economic Growth and the Ending of the Transatlantic Slave Trade* (Oxford University Press, 1987); and Eli Faber, *Jew, Slaves, and the Slave Trade* (New York University Press, 1988). For the effects of the slave trade on Africans, see Paul Lovejoy, *Transformations in Slavery: A History of Slavery in Africa* (Cambridge University Press, 1983); Patrick Manning, *Slavery and African Life* (Cambridge University Press, 1990); Joseph Inikori, ed., *Forced Migration: The Impact of the Export Slave Trade on African Societies* (Africana, 1982); John Thornton, *Africa and Africans in the Making of the Atlantic World, 1400–1680*, 2nd ed. (Cambridge University Press, 1998); and Joseph Miller, *The Way of Death: Merchant Capitalism and the Angolan Slave Trade, 1730–1830* (University of Wisconsin Press, 1988). The role of women in slavery is recounted in Claire Robertson and Martin A. Klein, *Women and Slavery in Africa* (University of Wisconsin Press, 1983); Marietta Morrissey, *Slave Women in the New World* (Kansas University Press, 1989); and Barbara Bush, *Slave Women in Caribbean Society, 1650–1832* (Indiana University Press, 1989). The cultural and crop exchanges between the New World and Africa are covered in Alfred W. Crosby, *The Columban Exchange: Biological and Cultural Consequences of 1492* (Greenwood, 1972), and Herman Viola and Carolyn Margolis, *Seeds of Change: A Quincentennial Commemoration* (Smithsonian Institution Press, 1991).

There are excellent studies of African regions and specific states. Oyo's rise as a major West African state is treated in S. O. Babayemi, *The Fall and Rise of Oyo, c. 1706–1905* (Lichfield, 1990), and Robin Law, *The Oyo Empire, c. 1600–c. 1836: West African Imperialism in the Era of the Atlantic Slave Trade* (Clarendon, 1977). Law has also written on the introduction of the horse in West African societies in *The Horse in West African History* (Oxford University Press, 1980). The Asante kingdom is examined in Ivor Wilks, *Forests of Gold: Essays on the Akan and the Kingdom of Asante* (Ohio University Press, 1993); T. C. McCaskie, *State and Society in Pre-Colonial Asante* (Cambridge University Press, 1995); and J. K. Flynn, *Asante and Its Neighbors, 1700–1807* (Northwestern University Press, 1971). On Dahomey, see Karl Polanyi and Abraham Rotstein, *Dahomey and the Slave Trade* (AMS, 1988), and Patrick Manning, *Slavery, Colonialism, and Economic Growth in Dahomey, 1640–1960* (Cambridge University Press, 1982). Kanem-Bornu's ascendancy as an empire is treated in Augustin Holl, *The Diwan Revisited: Literacy, State Formation, and the Rise of Kanuri Domination (A.D. 1200–1600)* (Columbia University Press, 1998). Hausa states and trade are treated in Paul Lovejoy, *Caravans of Kola: The Hausa Kola Trade, 1700–1900* (Ahmadu Bello University Press, 1980). Portuguese involvement in the Kongo kingdom is examined in Anne Hilton, *The Kingdom of Kongo* (Oxford University Press, 1985), and John Thornton, *The Kingdom of Kongo: Civil War and Transition, 1641–1718* (University of Wisconsin Press, 1983). The Mutapa kingdom is assessed in Stan Mudenge, *A Political History of Munhumutapa, c. 1488–1902* (Zimbabwe Publishing House, 1988). On Central Africa, see David Birmingham and Phyllis Martin, eds., *A History of Central Africa*, 2 vols. (Longman, 1983). On East Africa, see Gideon Were and Derek Wilson, *East Africa Through a Thousand Years* (Africana, 1970). Buganda's history is recounted in Christopher Wrigley, *Kingship and State: The Buganda Dynasty* (Cambridge University Press, 1996).

On Ethiopia, see Arnold H. Jones and Elizabeth Monroe, *A History of Ethiopia* (Clarendon, 1966), and Harold Marcus, *A History of Ethiopia* (University of California Press, 1994). On West Africa, see J. Ajayi and Michael Crowder, eds., *A History of West Africa*, vol. 1 (Longman, 1985).

The North African Muslim revival is treated from various angles in Nehemia Levtzion and John O. Voll, eds., *Eighteenth-Century Renewal and Reform in Islam* (Syracuse University Press, 1987). John S. Trimmingham, *The Influence of Islam upon Africa* (Longman, 1980), is a well-researched treatment of a broad topic. For more limited studies, see the same author's *History of Islam in West Africa* (Clarendon Press, 1959) and *Islam in East Africa* (Clarendon Press, 1964). North Africa is covered in Jamil M. Abun-Nasir, *A History of the Maghrib* (Cambridge University Press, 1975), and Charles A. Julien, *A History of North Africa* (Praeger, 1970). The ambiguous role of women is described in Barbara Calloway, *Muslim Hausa Women in Nigeria* (Syracuse University Press, 1987).

For background on the Middle East in this period, see Marshall Hodgson, *The Venture of Islam*, vol. 3 (University of Chicago Press, 1974). On the Ottoman Empire, see Stanford Shaw, *A History of the Ottoman Empire*, 2 vols. (Cambridge University Press, 1976); M. A. Cook, ed., *A History of the Ottoman Empire to 1730* (Cambridge University Press, 1976); and Roderic H. Davison, *Turkey: A Short History*, 3rd ed. (Eothen Press, 1998). For more specialized studies, see Bruce McGowan, *Economic Life in the Ottoman Empire, 1600–1800* (Cambridge University Press, 1982); and Halil Inalcik, *Studies in Ottoman Social and Economic History* (Variorum, 1985). Ottoman relations with Europe are treated in Charles A. Frazee, *Catholics and Sultans* (Cambridge University Press, 1983); Peter F. Sugar, *Southeastern Europe Under Ottoman Rule, 1354–1804* (University of Washington Press, 1984); and Fatma M. Göçek, *East Encounters West* (Oxford University Press, 1987). A personalized look at English-Ottoman relations is provided in Sonia Anderson, *An English Consul in Turkey: Paul Rycaut at Smyrna, 1667–1678* (Oxford University Press, 1989); and Daniel Goffman, *Britons in the Ottoman Empire* (University of Washington Press, 1998).

The classical work on Persia, still indispensable, is Percy M. Sykes, *A History of Persia* (Gordon, 1976; originally published 1938). See also David Morgan, *Medieval Persia, 1040–1797* (Longman, 1988), and Roger Savory, *Iran Under the Safavids* (Cambridge University Press, 1980). On eighteenth-century Persia, see Lois Beck, *The Qashqa'I of Iran* (Yale University Press, 1986), and for a readable biography as well as a history of the period, see John R. Perry, *Karim Khan Zand* (University of Chicago Press, 1979). Yu Gankovsky, *The History of Afghanistan* (Progress, 1985), throws welcome light on that corner of Asia.

On the Mughul Empire, see John Richards, *The Mughul Empire* (Cambridge University Press, 1996). Stanley Wolpert, *A New History of India*, 5th ed. (Oxford University Press, 1997), is a popular survey that puts the Mughul era in perspective. Percival Spear, *Twilight of the Mughuls* (Cambridge University Press, 1951), is still valuable for its clear focus on Mughul decline. On South Asia in an economic context, see K. N. Chaudhuri, *Trade and Civilization in the Indian Ocean* (Cambridge University Press, 1985) and *Asia Before Europe* (Cambridge University Press, 1990). The following works present more specialized studies on various aspects of the Mughul state and society: Neelan Chaudhary, *Socio-Economic History of Mughal India* (South Asia Books, 1987); S. C. Dutta, *The North-East and the Mughals, 1661–1714* (Stosius, 1984); Robert C. Hallissey, *The Rajput Rebellion Against Aurangzeb* (University of Missouri Press, 1977); Gordon Stewart, *The Marathas, 1600–1818* (Cambridge University Press, 1993); Karl de Schweinitz, *The Rise and Fall of British India* (Routledge, 1989); and Om Prakash, *The Dutch East India Company and the Economy of Bengal, 1630–1720* (Princeton University Press, 1985). For good biographical presentations, see Bamber Gascoigne, *The Great Moghuls*, rev. ed. (Cape, 1987); L. K. Agarwal, *Biographical Account of the Mughal Nobility, 1556–1707* (Coronet, 1985); and Muni Lal, *Aurangzeb* (Advent, 1988).

Among the best general surveys of Southeast Asia in this period are Steven Warshaw, *Southeast Asia Emerges*, rev. ed. (Diablo, 1987), and G. Coedes, *The Making of Southeast Asia*, 2nd ed. (Allen & Unwin, 1983). The beginning of European encroachment is revealed in Anthony Reid, *Southeast Asia in the Age of Commerce, 1450–1680* (Yale University Press, 1988). Good special studies of individual states include Michael Aung-Thwin, *Pagan: The Origins of Modern Burma* (University of Hawaii Press, 1985); Joseph Buttinger, *A Dragon Defiant* (Praeger, 1972); Martin F. Herz, *A Short History of Cambodia* (Praeger, 1958); John D. Legge, *Indonesia* (Prentice Hall, 1965); and Joseph Kennedy, *A History of Malaya* (St. Martin's Press, 1962).

European expansion into the Pacific, in its Russian phases, is traced in John A. Harrison, *Founding of the Russian Empire in Asia and America* (University of Miami Press, 1971), and in Gerhard F. Muller, *Bering's Voyages: The Reports from Russia* (University of Alaska Press, 1988). See also Georg Wilhelm Steller, *Journal of a Voyage with Bering, 1741–1742* (Stanford University Press, 1988). On English exploration, see Lynne Withen, *Captain Cook and the Exploration of the Pacific* (University of California Press, 1989), and Thomas Hoobler and Dorothy Hoobler, *The Voyages of Captain Cook* (Putnam, 1983). More detailed accounts are presented in John Elliot and Richard Pickersgill, *Captain Cook's Second Voyage* (Caliban, 1985), and Sidney Parkinson, *A Journal of a Voyage to the South Seas* (Caliban, 1984). A recent biography of the great English navigator is Alan Blackwood, *Captain Cook* (Watts, 1987). See also W. G. McClymount, *Exploration of New Zealand*, 2nd ed. (Greenwood, 1986).

Traditional Pacific cultures are ably depicted in the following works: Peter S. Brentwood, *The Polynesians* (Thames & Hudson, 1978); Keith Sinclair, *A History of New Zealand*, rev. ed. (Penguin, 1985); David A. Howarth, *Tahiti* (Penguin, 1985); Edwin N. Ferdon, *Early Tahiti as the Explorers Saw It* (University of Arizona Press, 1981); and Elizabeth Bott, *Tongan Society at the Time of Captain Cook's Visits* (University of Hawaii Press, 1983).

Alan Moorehead, *The Fatal Impact* (Harper Collins, 1987), registers the disasters to native cultures that came with the European "invasion of the South Pacific." See also O. H. K. Spate, *Paradise Found and Lost* (University of Minnesota Press, 1988), and Ernest S. Dodge, *Islands and Empires* (University of Minnesota Press, 1976). For specific results on one island, see David A. Howarth, *Tahiti: A Paradise Lost* (Viking, 1984), and Edward H. Dodd, *The Rape of Tahiti* (Dodd, Mead, 1983). The Hawaiian reaction is evident in Richard Tregeskis, *The Warrior King: Hawaii's Kamehameha the Great* (Tuttle, 1973).

A general perspective on China under the Manchus can be gained from Jonathan D. Spence, *The Search for Modern China* (Norton, 1990); Charles O. Hucker, *China to 1850* (Stanford University Press, 1978); and William S. Morton, *China: Its History and Its Culture* (McGraw-Hill, 1982). Lynn Struve, *The Southern Ming, 1644–1662* (Yale University Press, 1984), records the last years of the old dynasty. Jonathan D. Spence, *Ts'ao Yin and the K'ang-hsi Emperor* (Yale University Press, 1988), provides an intimate glimpse of the greatest Manchu ruler. Social conditions under the Manchus are carefully examined in Susan Naquin and Evelyn S. Rawski, *Chinese Society in the Eighteenth Century* (Yale University Press, 1989), and Esther Yao, *Chinese Women, Past and Present* (Idle House, 1983).

The deterioration arising from economic sources is evident in Sinnappah Arasaratnam, *Merchants, Companies, and Commerce on the Coromandel Coast, 1650–1740* (Oxford University Press, 1987); Dean Murray, *Pirates of the South China Coast, 1790–1810* (Stanford University Press, 1987); and George Bryan Souza, *The Survival of Empire: Portuguese Trade and Society in China and the South China Sea, 1630–1754* (Cambridge University Press, 1986).

Andrew C. Nahm, *Tradition and Transformation: A History of the Korean People* (Hollym International, 1988), gives a good account of major Korean developments during the period. See also Isabella Bird, *Korea and Its Neighbors* (Tuttle, 1986); Ki-baik Lee, *A New History of Korea* (Harvard University Press, 1984); and William E. Griffis, *Korea* (AMS, 1971). On the roles of Korean women, see Yung-Chung Kim, *Women of Korea* (Ewha Women's University, 1979), and Laurel Kendall and Mark Peterson, eds., *Korean Women* (East Rock, 1983).

The mature Tokugawa era in Japan is given excellent coverage in Chie Nakano and Shinzaburo Oishi, *Tokugawa Japan* (University of Tokyo Press, 1990); Edwin O. Reischauer and Alfred M. Craig, *Japan: Story of a Nation*, 4th ed. (McGraw-Hill, 1989); Albert C. Danley, *Japan: A Short History* (Wayside, 1989); R. H. P. Mason and J. C. Caiger, *A History of Japan*, rev. ed. (Tuttle, 1997); Mikiso Hane, *Modern Japan* (Westview, 1986); and W. Scott Morton, *Japan: Its History and Culture* (McGraw-Hill, 1984). John H. Wigmore, *Law and Justice in Tokugawa Japan* (Colorado University Press, 1986), reflects the lingering Japanese penchant for authority and discipline. Japanese social turmoil during the period is treated in Anne Walthall, *Social Protest and Popular Culture in Eighteenth-Century Japan* (University of Arizona Press, 1986); Stephen Vlastos, *Peasant Protests and Uprisings in Tokugawa Japan* (University of California Press, 1986); and Herbert P. Bix, *Peasant Protest in Japan, 1590–1884* (Yale University Press, 1986). For Japanese intellectual developments, see Robert N. Bellah, *Tokugawa Religion*, rev. ed. (Free Press, 1985); Herman Ooms, *Tokugawa Religion* (Princeton University Press, 1985); Tetsuo Najita, *Visions of Virtue in Tokugawa Japan* (University of Chicago Press, 1987); and Bob Tadashi Wakaboyashi, *Anti-Foreignism and Western Learning in Early Modern Japan* (Harvard University Press, 1986).

Suggestions for Web Browsing

Internet African History Sourcebook: Impact of Slavery
http://www.fordham.edu/halsall/africa/africasbook.html

> *Extensive on-line source for links about the history of Africa offers short primary documents describing the slave trade and the life of the enslaved peoples in their own words.*

Sub-Saharan African Art Since 1700
http://www.emory.edu/CARLOS/african.gal.html

> *Emory University site displays numerous images from its collection and relates a history of sub-Saharan art and its complex relationship with the West.*

Islam and Islamic History in Arabia and the Middle East: The Coming of the West
http://www.islamic.org/Mosque/ihame/Sec14.htm

A short discussion of the Western influence and domination, from the seventeenth century until 1945.

Internet East Asia History Sourcebook: Western Intrusion
http://www.fordham.edu/halsall/eastasia/eastasiasbook.html

Extensive on-line source for links about the history of East Asia, including primary documents regarding exploration, European imperialism, and the influence of missionaries.

Notes

1. From Walter Andrews et al., trans., *Ottoman Lyric Poetry* (Austin: University of Texas Press, 1997), p. 137.
2. For the full statement, see Jonathan D. Spence, *Emperor of China: A Self-portrait of K'ang-hsi* (New York: Knopf, 1974), pp. 143–151.

The Century of Western Dominance

During the late eighteenth century and throughout the nineteenth, Europeans went through the Industrial Revolution as many types of work done by human and animal power came to be accomplished by machines. The people of Europe made the transition from living in a world centered on agriculture and the land to participating in a society dominated by industries and cities. By the start of the twentieth century economic, scientific, intellectual, cultural, and political conditions were fundamentally different from those that prevailed in 1815.

The rapid and unprecedented changes presented European leaders with both power and peril. They had greater wealth with which to work, but they also had to deal with the middle classes and factory workers who became important actors on the European stage. Europe's intellectuals were equal to the task of developing new ideologies to shape and reflect the changing European world. Nineteenth-century political thinkers and philosophers built on the strong bases of rational social inquiry provided by the Enlightenment. They also took inspiration from the ideals promised by the French Revolution—liberty, brotherhood, and equality—to fuel the fires of liberal, socialist, and nationalist movements. The middle and lower classes had a rich menu from which to select their political programs.

The European states developed a broad variety of governmental structures in response to these material and intellectual developments. The political responses ranged from the gradually changing British democracy to the reactionary Russian autocracy. Each nation in Europe experienced the growth of centralized state power and, ultimately, the voice of the common people in politics, either through revolutions, responses to military events, or rational reform. This revolutionary century strongly tested the European state system. From time to time a major individual, such as Talleyrand, Metternich, Bismarck, Cavour, or Disraeli, would interpret events and opportunities in a sufficiently perceptive manner to take advantage of them. But the outbreak of European war in 1914 would prove that Europe's politicians had run a losing race in trying to keep up with the challenges and changes presented by the times. Nowhere did the leaders fall farther behind than in their failure after 1900 to defend their own best interests in the realm of foreign affairs. The forces of nationalism, militarism, and political and economic competition trapped the politicians in their outmoded alliance systems, which eventually led the continent into a tragic war.

The arrival of the Europeans in all the continents with their advanced technology, developed political ideologies, bureaucratic techniques, and capitalist systems posed severe challenges for the rest of the world. Non-Western peoples faced serious threats to their culture and identity as the Europeans, with few exceptions, possessed sufficient economic and military strength to overwhelm them. There were two major types of European overseas involvement. The most direct method by which the Europeans extended their domination was emigration. Millions of Europeans took part in the greatest transplantation of human beings in history. The other major type of European involvement abroad came in the exploitation of the colonies. In the Middle East, Africa, and South and East Asia—with the notable exception of Japan—the European states established colonies for economic gain. These colonial areas, which were often regarded by the Europeans as unsuited for settlement, were usually governed by a minority of foreign officials and soldiers who controlled the majority of the native peoples.

Despite resistance to the imperialistic takeover by the European states, by the end of the nineteenth century practically all of Africa had been partitioned and placed under European rule. Although China remained technically independent, it was controlled in many areas by the European powers. India fell directly under British control, as did many parts of the Ottoman Empire. Japan was alone in successfully modernizing itself and thus avoided, to a certain extent, being caught in the imperialist net.

The nineteenth century really ended not in 1900 but in 1914 with the outbreak of World War I. The century of European primacy came to a close with this suicidal struggle of the European nations, and the forces that were unleashed during that time of strife were carried throughout the world via the lines of communication spread by the imperialists themselves. The peoples in Asia and Africa would see that the Europeans—who had shown such abilities to scale intellectual mountains and spread their power around the globe—had not found the answer to the basic problem of how to get along with one another.

By serving as the veins and arteries of industry and commerce, the rail-roads assured the successful launch-ing of the second phase of industri-alization and fascinated artists such as French impressionist Claude Monet, who found beauty in a rail-road station, Gare Saint-Lazarre.

Detail. Claude Monet, *The Gare Saint-Lazare,* 1877. Oil on canvas, 80.33 cm. × 98.11 cm. Courtesy of the Fogg Art Museum, Harvard University Art Museums, Be-quest from the collection of Maurice Wertheim, Class of 1906. Photo: David Mathews. © President and Fel-lows of Harvard College, Harvard University.

Foundations of Western Dominance

Industrial, Scientific, Technological, Business, and Cultural Developments, 1815–1914

Chapter Contents

The nineteenth century was the West's time to dominate the globe. In the 99 years from the end of the Napoleonic Wars in 1815 to the outbreak of the First World War in 1914, Europe and its outlying regions imposed themselves on the rest of the world through their industrial productivity, scientific and technological discoveries, and economic power.

The Act of Union of 1707 combined England and Scotland into a unified free market with the richest per capita population in Europe. Thanks to its flexible social structure, liberal economic system, and favorable fiscal and governmental policies, the small island nation was the pioneer in industrialization—the use of new tools and power sources to do work formerly performed by humans and animals—in the making of cotton cloth. As individual spinners and weavers made commonsense changes in their tools, industrialization supplied machines to allow them to make more money from an expanding market. The huge increase in productivity made possible by using machines can be seen in the amount of raw cotton British cloth makers imported in 1760 and 1850: whereas in 1760 they imported a bit over 1000 tons, by 1850 the number had risen to over 222,000 tons. And exports showed a similarly huge increase.

As the nineteenth century progressed, industrialists in other economic sectors used machines to do work formerly performed by humans and animals and saw similar increases. At the same time, the economic structure grew and adapted itself to the new conditions, and Europe's scientists continued to make major advances to open new areas for business. Productive capacity grew geometrically, permitting factories to turn out more and better-quality goods at cheaper prices.

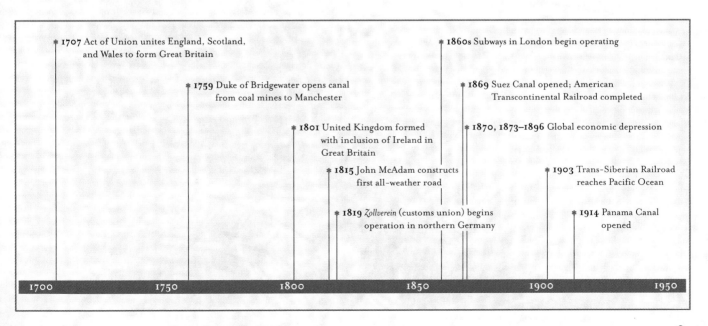

* **1707** Act of Union unites England, Scotland, and Wales to form Great Britain

* **1759** Duke of Bridgewater opens canal from coal mines to Manchester

* **1801** United Kingdom formed with inclusion of Ireland in Great Britain

* **1815** John McAdam constructs first all-weather road

* **1819** *Zollverein* (customs union) begins operation in northern Germany

* **1860s** Subways in London begin operating

* **1869** Suez Canal opened; American Transcontinental Railroad completed

* **1870, 1873–1896** Global economic depression

* **1903** Trans-Siberian Railroad reaches Pacific Ocean

* **1914** Panama Canal opened

| 1700 | 1750 | 1800 | 1850 | 1900 | 1950 |

In fact, the inventors of the new machines changed the everyday lives of people around the world more—for better or for worse—than the French and Napoleonic Revolutions, which touched only social and political structures. The people who devised new tools and new ways to do old jobs set in process the transition from an agrarian to a modern, urbanized society. For those people caught up in the first generation of that transition, there was a terrible cost to be paid.

Industrialization: The First Phase

The transition from a rural agrarian to an urban lifestyle merits applying the term *revolutionary* to the process of industrialization. The incremental steps that led to increased textile production and to the production of other goods in all industries were repeated and continue to be repeated to this day. Liberation from the productive limitations imposed by dependence on human and animal power is the great gift of industrialization.

The Revolution in Making Cloth

Practical people seeing the need for greater output solved the practical problems of increasing production. In the many steps from raw cotton to finished cloth, there were bottlenecks—primarily in making yarn and weaving the strands together. In 1733 John Kay (1704–1764), a spinner and mechanic, patented the first of the great machines, the flying shuttle. This device made it possible for one person to weave wide bolts of cloth by using a spring mechanism that sent the shuttle across the loom. This invention upset the balance between the weavers of cloth and the spinners of yarn: ten spinners were now required to produce the yarn needed by one weaver.

James Hargreaves (d. 1778), a weaver and carpenter, eliminated that problem in 1764 with his spinning jenny, a mechanical spinning wheel that allowed the spinners to keep up with the weavers. Five years later a barber named Richard Arkwright (1732–1792) built the water frame that made it possible to spin many threads into yarn at the same time. Ten years after that, Samuel Crompton (1753–1827), a spinner, combined the spinning jenny and water frame into the water mule, which, with some variations, is still used today. By this time the makers of yarn were outpacing the weavers, but in 1785 Edmund Cartwright (1743–1823) invented the power loom, which mechanized the weaving process. In two generations what had once been a home-based craft became an industry.

The appetite of the new machines outran the supply of cotton. Since most of the material came from the United States, the demand exceeded the capability of the slave-based southern economy to create the supply. The best worker could not prepare more than 5 or 6 pounds of cotton per day because of the problems of removing the seeds. American inventor Eli Whitney (1765–1825), among others, devised the cotton gin, a machine that enabled a worker to clean more than 50 times as much cotton a day. This device coincidentally played a major role in the perpetuation of slavery in the United States for another half century.

Finally, the textile industry became so large that it outgrew the possibilities of its power source: water power. Steam came to drive the machines of industrializing Britain. In the first part of the eighteenth century, mechanic Thomas Newcomen (1663–1729) made an "atmospheric engine" in which a piston was raised by

Skilled workers in an English calico printing works. Most skilled workers, who represented only a small fraction of the workforce, were men; the larger workforce of ordinary factory workers was made up of men, women, and children.

Revolution in the Making of Cotton

1733	John Kay patents flying shuttle
1764	James Hargreaves invents spinning jenny
1769	Richard Arkwright invents water frame
1779	Samuel Crompton invents water mule
1785	Edmund Cartwright invents power loom
c. 1800	Inventions of cotton gin

---

injected steam. As the steam condensed, the piston returned to its original position. Newcomen's unwieldy and inefficient device was put to use pumping water out of mines. James Watt (1736–1819), a builder of scientific instruments at the University of Glasgow, perfected Newcomen's invention. Watt's steam engine was also first used to pump water out of mines. It saved the large amounts of energy lost by the Newcomen engine and led to an increase in coal productivity. After 1785 it was also used to make cloth and drive ships and locomotives. The application of steam to weaving made it possible to expand the use of cloth-making machines to new areas, and after 1815 hand looms began to disappear from commercial textile making, replaced by the undoubted superiority of the cloth-making machines.

These inventors made their contributions in response to the need to solve particular problems. Their machines and the new power sources expanded productivity and transformed society in ways never before imagined.

Britain's Dominance

Industrialization began in Great Britain in the eighteenth century for a number of reasons. Though neither the richest nor the most populous country in western Europe, Britain possessed at virtually all levels of society a hardworking, inventive, risk-taking private sector that received strong support from the government. Industrialization could not begin and grow without individual business owners who took a chance on something new. The British maintained this close tie between private initiative and creative governmental support throughout the eighteenth and nineteenth centuries.

Thanks to early governmental support of road improvements and canal construction, Britain had a better transportation network than any other country in Europe. The British also had mastery of the seas, excellent ports, and a large merchant fleet. They enjoyed the advantage of living safely on their island, away from the carnage of war, even during the Napoleonic conflicts. The chance to industrialize in stable conditions gave them the opportunity to profit from war contracts between 1792 and 1815. They developed their industrial capacity without fear of damage from battle or loss of life. Finally, the Bank of England served as a solid base for economic growth by providing the money and financial stability for English businessmen.

Train of the First Class of Carriages, with the Mail.

Train of the Second Class, for outside Passengers.

Train of Waggons, with Goods, etc., etc.

Train of Carriages with Cattle.

PLATE XX.
TRAVELLING ON THE LIVERPOOL AND MANCHESTER RAILWAY.

The increasing volume of trade between the English industrial towns of Liverpool and Manchester (in the early 1820s the traffic of goods was estimated to be approximately 1000 tons per week) and the demand for a method of transport speedier than the canal led to the building of a railroad between the two towns. Although the original purpose for the railroad was the traffic in goods, passenger traffic soon became important as well.

Probably the most important factor was the relative flexibility of the British social and political systems. Members of the elite, unlike their colleagues on the Continent, pursued their wealth in the new industrial framework with great energy. At the same time, the middle classes, who had no land in the countryside and were excluded from political life until reforms in the second half of the nineteenth century, poured their enthusiasm and inventiveness into developing new businesses and technologies. The rising economic tide eventually included the workers, who benefited from gradual reforms granted to stifle any chance of revolution from below.

The combination of inventiveness, growing markets, governmental support, and social flexibility made Britain the world's dominant economic power until the end of the nineteenth century. Napoleon's interference had hurt British economic growth, but it had also spurred the British to look for new manufacturing methods and markets. Once the wars were over, Britain flooded the Continent and the Americas with high-quality, inexpensive goods. No nation could compete against British efficiency. When Britain began industrializing before 1789, there were isolated areas on the Continent, such as the French Le Creusot works, that could have served as the base for similar growth. However, 26 years of revolution and mercantile policies made that competition impossible.

Industrialized cotton textile production continued to increase in Britain and was supplemented by the arrival of the modern Iron Age. In 1800 Russia and Sweden had exported iron to Britain. By 1815 Britain exported more than five times as much iron as it imported. By 1848 the British produced more iron than the rest of the world combined. As in textile production, a number of inventions in ironmaking appeared in response to problems. Improved refining of brittle cast iron made it more malleable and tough so that it could be used in more products. At the same time, more efficient mining processes for both coal and iron ore were used to ensure a dependable supply of raw materials.

To further help Britain dominate the metals market, in the 1850s Henry Bessemer (1813–1898) developed a process to make steel, a harder and more malleable metal than iron, quickly and cheaply. So effective was the process that between 1856 and 1870 the price of British steel fell to half the amount formerly charged for the best grade of iron. The drastic reduction in price due to innovations in production, a mark of industrialization, had a positive impact on all areas of the economy.

After midcentury, Britain produced more than two-thirds of the world's coal and more than half its iron and cloth. Industrial development encouraged urbanization, and by 1850 more than half of the population lived in cities and worked in industries. The British continued to enjoy the highest per capita income in the world, and the island nation stood head and shoulders above all others in terms of economic and material strength.

The Human Costs of Industrialization

Everywhere it occurred, industrialization drove society from an agricultural to an urban way of life. The old system, in which peasant families worked the fields during the summer and did their cottage industry work in the winter to their own standards and at their own pace, slowly disappeared. In its place came urban life tied to the factory system. The factory was a place where for long hours people did repetitive tasks using machines to process large amounts of raw materials. This was an efficient way to make a lot of high-quality goods cheaply. But the factories were often dangerous places, and the lifestyle connected to them had a terrible effect on the human condition.

The Factory System

In the factory system, the workers worked, and the owners made profits. The owners wanted to make the most they could from their investment and to get the most work they could from their employees. The workers, in turn, felt that they deserved more of the profits because their labor made production possible.

INDUSTRIAL ENGLAND, EARLY NINETEENTH CENTURY

English entrepreneurs established their factories at the beginning of the nineteenth century, not in the traditional population centers such as London, but out of town, close to water power and coal fields and with easy access to markets.

Industrialization and Children

Early industrialization demanded huge sacrifices, especially from children.

Sarah Gooder, Aged 8 Years

I'm a trapper in the Gawber pit. It does not tire me, but I have to trap without a light and I'm scared. I go at four and sometimes half past three in the morning, and come out at five and half past. I never go to sleep. Sometimes I sing when I've light, but not in the dark; I dare not sing then. I don't like being in the pit. I am very sleepy when I go sometimes in the morning. I go to Sunday-schools and read *Reading made Easy*. [She knows her letters and can read little words.] They teach me to pray. [She repeated the Lord's Prayer, not very perfectly, and ran on with the following addition.] "God bless my father and mother, and sister and brother, uncles and aunts and cousins, and everybody else, and God bless me and make me a good servant. Amen. I have heard tell of Jesus many a time. I don't know why he came on earth, I'm sure, and I don't know why he died, but he had stones for his head to rest on. I would like to be at school far better than in the pit."

From *Parliamentary Papers* (1842).

This was a situation guaranteed to produce conflict, especially given the wretched conditions the workers faced in the first stages of industrialization.

The early factories were miserable places, featuring bad lighting, lack of ventilation, dangerous machines, and frequent breakdowns. Safety standards were practically nonexistent, and workers in various industries could expect to contract serious diseases; for example, laborers working with lead paint developed lung problems, pewter workers fell ill to palsy, miners suffered black lung disease, and operators of primitive machines lost fingers, hands, and even lives. Not until late in the nineteenth century did health and disability insurance come into effect. In some factories workers who suffered accidents were deemed to be at fault; and since there was little job security, a worker could be fired for almost any reason.

Woman and Child Labor

The demand for plentiful and cheap labor led to the widespread employment of women and children. Girls as young as 6 years old were used to haul carts of coal in Lancashire mines, and boys and girls of 4 and 5 years of age worked in textile mills, where their nimble little fingers could easily untangle jams in the machines. When they were not laboring, the working families lived in horrid conditions in wretched industrial cities such as Lille, France, and Manchester, England. There were no sanitary, water, or medical services for the workers, and working families were crammed 12 and 15 individuals to a room in damp, dark cellars. Bad diet, alcoholism, cholera, and typhus reduced life spans in the industrial cities.

Children who worked in the English mines were called "hurriers." This illustration of children working in the mines appeared in a book titled The White Slaves of England, *published in 1853.*

An Industrial Town

The terrible life in the industrial towns touched observers such as novelist Charles Dickens, who in his book *Hard Times* described a typical British factory town.

It was a town of red brick, or of brick that would have been red if the smoke and ashes had allowed it; but as matters stood, it was a town of unnatural red and black, like the painted face of a savage. It was a town of machinery and tall chimneys, out of which interminable serpents of smoke trailed themselves for ever and ever, and never got uncoiled. It had a black canal in it, and a river that ran purple with ill-smelling dye, and vast piles of buildings full of windows where there was a rattling and trembling all day long, and where the piston of the steam engine worked monotonously up and down, like the head of an elephant in a state of melancholy madness. It contained several large streets all very like one another, and many small streets still more like one another, inhabited by people equally like one another, who all went in and out at the same hours, with the same sound upon the same pavement, to do the same work, and to whom every day was the same as yesterday and tomorrow, and every year the counterpart of the last and the next.

From Charles Dickens, *Hard Times* (1854).

Simultaneous with, and perhaps part of, the industrialization process was a dramatic increase in illegitimate births and prostitution. Up to midcentury, corresponding to the time of maximum upheaval, at least one-third of all births in Europe were out of wedlock.[1]

Later generations profited from the sacrifices made by the first workers in industrialization. Factory owners came to understand that they could make more profit from an efficient factory staffed by contented and healthy workers. But the costs borne by the first generations making the transition between a family-based rural life and the anonymous cruelty of early industrial cities were immense.

Urban Crises

Industrialization prompted massive growth of European cities in the nineteenth century, as can be seen in the following table.[2]

Nineteenth-Century Urban Growth

City	Population in 1800	Population in 1910
London	831,000	4,521,000
Paris	547,000	2,888,000
Berlin	173,000	2,071,000
Vienna	247,000	2,030,000
St. Petersburg	220,000	1,907,000

In addition, new towns sprang up throughout the Continent and soon reached the level of more than 100,000 inhabitants. Even in agrarian Russia, where 70 percent of the population worked on the land, there were 17 cities of more than 100,000 by the end of the century.

Political leaders faced serious problems dealing with mushrooming city growth. The factory system initially forced families to live and work in squalor, danger, and disease, conditions to be found today in countries undergoing the first stages of industrialization. City leaders had the responsibility to maintain a clean environment, provide social and sanitation services, enforce the law, furnish transportation, and—most serious of all—build housing. They uniformly failed to meet the challenges of growth.

Until midcentury, human waste disposal in some parts of Paris was taken care of by dumping excrement into the street gutters or the Seine River. Not until Baron Georges Haussman (1809–1891) implemented urban renewal in the 1850s and 1860s (see Chapter 25) did the city get an adequate garbage, water, and sewage system. Police protection remained inadequate or corrupt. Other cities shared the same problems to a greater or lesser degree. The new industrial towns that had sprung up were in even worse condition than the older centers.

By the end of the century, however, governments began to deal effectively with urban problems. By 1914 most major European cities began to make clean running water, central heat, adequate street lighting, mass public education, dependable sewage systems, and minimal medical care available for their people.

The Labor Movement

Well before Marx conceived his theories (see Chapter 29), the British economy suffered through a difficult time after the end of the Napoleonic wars. High unemployment struck skilled workers, especially non-

This illustration, Over London—by Rail, *vividly depicts the problems that accompanied urbanization: cramped living spaces, crime, and air and water pollution.*

mechanized loom weavers. In frustration, some of them fought back and destroyed textile machines, the symbol of the forces oppressing them. Strikes, demonstrations, and incidents such as the Peterloo Massacre, August 16, 1819, at St. Peter's Fields, in which soldiers closed down a political meeting, killing 11 and injuring hundreds, vividly expressed the workers' rage. Not until British reformers came forward in the 1820s did the laborers begin to gain some relief.

Their efforts to form labor unions received an important boost in 1825 when the Combination Acts, passed in 1799 against the formation of workers' associations, were repealed. The first unions, such as the half-million-strong Grand National Consolidated Trades Union, were weak and disorganized, split by the gulf between skilled workers and common laborers. Nonetheless, the workers laid the foundations for the powerful unions that defended them by the end of the century.

As industry became more sophisticated and centralized, so did the labor movement. Across Europe the workers could choose anarchist, socialist, or conservative paths to follow. Some unions—the trade or craft unions—centered on a particular occupation. Some found their focus in the various productive stages of an industry, and still others, such as the English Trade Unions Congress, were nationwide and all-encompassing, wielding great power. Whatever the choice, by 1900 unions had made important advances through their solidarity in launching paralyzing strikes.

Although workers could still not negotiate on an equal basis with the owners, they had by 1914 vastly improved their position over that endured by their grandparents. The British movement had 4 million members and was a powerful force; German unions obtained benefits for their members in a broad number of areas, from life insurance to travel. The income gap between rich and poor began to narrow. Working hours were shortened, and living conditions improved. The real wages of workers—that is, the amount of goods that their income could actually buy—increased by 50 percent in the industrial nations in the last 30 years of the nineteenth century.

Industrialization: The Second Phase

The second phase of industrialization brought new products and power sources to the Continent. Increased food production and improved health standards and diet led to a population explosion that promised both economic gains and bureaucratic burdens. The rapid and massive growth of cities brought with it the social problems of urbanization. Workers united to fight for their interests while the middle classes extended their wealth and influence. The actions of both groups changed the nature of social and political life.

Food and Population Increases

Liberated from many of the restraints of the past by the French, Napoleonic, and Industrial Revolutions, most Europeans made the transition from a society based on agriculture to a modern urban society. The spectacular growth of the industrial sector makes it easy to overlook the great strides made in food production during the nineteenth century. Because of the improved global transportation network and better farming methods, the expanding number of city-dwellers had more and better food to eat in 1914 than they had had in 1815.

It is estimated that in 1815, around 60 percent of the money and 85 percent of the people in Europe were tied to farming. These large quantities of capital and labor were not used effectively because the advances made in the Netherlands and Britain in the seventeenth and eighteenth centuries (see Chapter 20) had not spread on the Continent. However, progressive landowners gradually introduced these improved methods when they saw the money to be made by feeding the growing populations of the cities.

By the end of the nineteenth century, farmers on the Continent were plowing new lands and using higher-yielding crop varieties to survive in the world-wide agricultural competition. Industrial nations such as Britain, in which only 10 percent of the population was engaged in farming, imported more than a fourth of its food. Farmers in the Americas, Australia, and New Zealand competed in the cutthroat export market. The peasants of Ireland and southern and eastern Europe were unable to produce efficiently enough to prosper in this new setting. Russia, where the peasantry comprised 70 percent of the population, had to export to bring in foreign capital to finance industrialization. The nation's tsarist minister of finance put it succinctly: "We may go hungry, but we will export."[3]

The expanded food supply supported the growth in European population from 175 million to 435 million.[4] This 130 percent increase between 1800 and 1910 partly disproved the views the British clergyman Thomas Robert Malthus (1766–1834) set forth in his "Essay on Population." Judging from the limited food supply and rapidly increasing population of his own day, Malthus asserted that human reproduction would outrun the earth's ability to produce food. He concluded that the inevitable fate of humanity was misery and ruin, since the number of people would rise geometrically while food supply would grow only arithmetically.[5] What Malthus failed to anticipate was the effects of technological innovation.

A gradual decline in mortality rates, better medical care, more food, earlier marriages, and better sanitary conditions contributed to the population increase. The number of people grew so rapidly in Europe that although 40 million Europeans emigrated throughout the world, the Continent still showed a population increase in a single century that was greater percentagewise than that of the previous 20 centuries. Where the economies were advanced, as in northern and western Europe, the population growth could be absorbed. But in the poorer countries of southern and eastern Europe, the masses faced the choice of Malthusian overcrowding and starvation or emigration.

The Ties That Bind: New Networks

To bring the increased food supply to the growing population, to distribute new resources to larger markets, and to connect augmented capital with essential information, Europeans built the most complete and far-reaching transportation and communication networks ever known. Without rapid and dependable transport and contact, the Industrial Revolution could not have occurred, cities would not have grown, factories could not have functioned, and millions of Europeans would not have been fed. The new networks became the circulatory and nervous systems of Europe.

In 1759 the duke of Bridgewater made a major step forward in water transportation when he built a $7\frac{1}{2}$-mile-long canal from his mines to the city of Manchester. Water transport cut the price of his coal in half and gave Britain a vivid lesson in the benefits of canals. By the 1830s nearly 4000 miles of improved rivers and canals were built, with strong governmental support, making it possible to ship most of the country's products by water. Following the British example, canal building spread through Europe and North America and then to Egypt with the Suez Canal in 1869 and to Latin America with the Panama Canal in 1914. The first project cut the sailing time between London and Bombay, India, by nearly half; the second did away with the need to sail around South America to reach the Pacific Ocean.

Until 1815 most roads were muddy, rutted paths that were impassable during spring thaws and autumn rains. In that year a Scotsman, John McAdam, created the all-weather road by placing small stones in compact layers directly on the road bed. The pressure of the traffic moving over the highway packed the stones together to give a fairly smooth surface. This practical solution cut the stagecoach time for the 160 miles from London to Sheffield from four days in the 1750s to 28 hours in 1820.

Steam-powered vessels replaced the graceful though less dependable sailing ships in ocean commerce. Clipper ships are among the most beautiful objects ever built, but they cannot move without wind. Sturdy, awkward-looking steamships carried larger cargo with greater regularity and thereby revolutionized world trade. The price of American wheat on the European market dropped by three-fourths in the last part of the century, in considerable degree the result of the savings made possible by the large, reliable steamships. Transatlantic passenger and mail services were also improved by the use of steam to power seagoing vessels.

The most important element in the European arterial network was the railroad. Between 1830 and 1860 rails linked every major market in Europe and in the United States. By 1903 the Russians had pushed the Trans-Siberian Railroad to the Pacific Ocean. Railroads cheaply and efficiently carried people and large amounts of material long distances and knit countries and continents closer together. Within cities, urban rail lines and trolleys were widespread by the end of the century; by permitting a wider diffusion of workers, these had an impressive effect on housing and business patterns. In the 1860s London was the first city to establish subways, followed by Budapest in 1896 and Paris in 1900.

Connected with the growth of transportation networks and technological innovation were major improvements in the area of communications. Postal agreements among the various countries made cheap

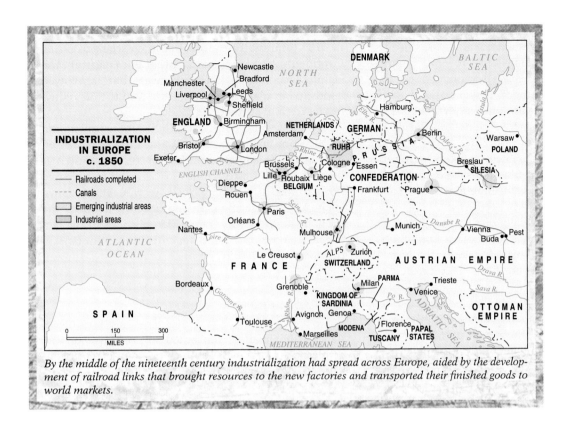

By the middle of the nineteenth century industrialization had spread across Europe, aided by the development of railroad links that brought resources to the new factories and transported their finished goods to world markets.

and dependable mail service possible. The introduction of the postage stamp and improved transportation systems brought astronomical increases in the number of letters and packages mailed after 1850.[6] Starting in the 1840s, the electric telegraph, undersea cable, telephone, wireless telegraph, and typewriter expanded the ability to exchange ideas and information. After the transportation and communications revolutions, no longer would distance be an obstacle. The world became a smaller, if not more unified, place.

Industrialization and Banking Changes on the Continent

The Continent faced many hurdles to economic growth after the Napoleonic wars. Obstacles to mobility, communication, and cooperation among the classes prevented the social structures there from adapting as easily to change as the British had. The farther one traveled to the south and east, the more repressive the structure became. In many parts of the Continent, the restored nobilities reclaimed their power, and they were intellectually, financially, or politically prepared to support industrial development. Fragmented political boundaries, geographical obstacles, and toll-takers along primary river and road systems hampered growth, especially in central Europe. In eastern Europe the middle classes were weaker and more isolated than in the west.

In 1815 the initial stages of industrialization were evident in Belgium, France, and Germany. In Sweden, Russia, and Switzerland there were pockets of potential mechanized production, but these initiatives were tiny compared to Britain's. In 1850 only Belgium could compete with British products in its own markets. There a combination of favorable governmental policies, good transportation, and stability brought some success.

Governments and businesses sent officials and representatives to Britain to try to discover the secrets of industrialization. The British tried to protect their advantage by banning the export of machines and processes and limiting foreign access to their factories. Industrial espionage existed then as now, and competitors from the Continent did uncover some secrets. Britain's success could be studied, components of it stolen, and its experts hired, but no other European country could combine all the factors that permitted Britain to dominate.

After midcentury a long period of peace and improved transportation, as well as strategic government assistance, encouraged rapid economic growth in France and the German states. Population increased 25 percent in France and nearly 40 percent in the Germanies, which provided a larger market and labor supply. Two generations of borrowed British technology began to be applied and improved on; but the two most important developments came in banking and in customs and toll reforms.

After 1815 aggressive new banking houses appeared across Europe, strengthened by the profits they had made by extending loans to governments during the Napoleonic wars. They understood the money to be made investing in new industries, such as railroads, and worked with both governments and major capitalists. Firms such as Hope and Baring in London; the Rothschilds in Frankfurt, Paris, Vienna, and London; and numerous Swiss bankers were representative of the private financiers who had well-placed sources and contacts throughout the state and business communities.[7]

Banking changed radically during this period to satisfy the growing demands for money. Long-range capital needs were met by the formation of investment banks, while new institutions were created to fill the need for short-term credit. The ultimate source of financial liquidity was the middle classes—the thousands of small investors who put their money in banks to make their own profits through interest earned. More money could be gained from the many small investors than from the few rich families who used to dominate banking.

The *Zollverein*

The Germans led the way in the other major development, the *Zollverein* (customs union), which began under Prussian leadership in 1819. This arrangement helped break down the physical and financial barriers imposed at the various state boundaries and in the next 23 years came to include most of central and northern Germany. Instead of the more than 300 divisions fragmenting the Germans in 1800, there was a virtual free trade market, something that Britain had enjoyed since the union of Scotland and England in 1707 (and the European Union created across the Continent at the end of the twentieth century). The significance of the *Zollverein* was that it allowed goods to circulate free of tolls and tariffs, thus reducing prices and stimulating trade.

In the second half of the 1800s, industrialization on the Continent grew rapidly, aided by the increased flow of credit and the elimination of many internal barriers. Tariffs throughout the area fell to a degree not matched until after World War II. Major firms, such as the German Krupp steelworks and the French silk industries, controlled portions of the European market and competed effectively with Britain throughout the world.

Scientific Advances

As industrialization continued to capitalize on the discoveries of the eighteenth century, nineteenth-century scientists made phenomenal advances, preparing for the new technologies of the twentieth century. These allowed the continued domination of the world's technologies and markets by the people of the North Atlantic Community—the area of European-based Western civilization.

Europe's world dominance in basic scientific research continued along the path that began with Copernicus in the 1500s and extended through the eighteenth century. The major difference between the earlier work and modern discoveries was that the effects of the later research had almost immediate and widespread economic applications as well as intellectual and social implications.

The interior of the Krupp steelworks at Essen, Germany, as painted by Otto Bollhagen. Krupp was one of the largest firms in Germany's growing industrial sector.

Scientific Advances

1830–1833 Sir Charles Lyell's *Principles of Geology* popularizes James Hutton's concept of geological time

1847 First law of thermodynamics

1859 Darwin publishes *On the Origin of Species*

1869 Dmitri Mendeleev classifies all known elements into the periodic table

1870–1895 Louis Pasteur makes advances in bacteriology

1880–1910 Robert Koch places immunology on firm footing

1876 Dynamo perfected, based on work of Michael Faraday

1896 Pierre and Marie Curie discover radium

1900–1910 Sir Ernest Rutherford advances electron theory

Darwin and Evolution

In the mid-nineteenth century Charles Darwin (1809–1892) formulated a major scientific theory in *On the Origin of Species by Means of Natural Selection* (1859). This theory of evolution, stating that all complex organisms developed from simple forms through the operation of natural causes, challenged traditionalist Christian beliefs on creation and altered views of life on earth. The theory contended that no species is fixed and changeless. Classical thinkers first stated this view, and contemporary philosophers such as Hegel had used the concept of evolutionary change. In the century before Darwin, other research supported the concept of change, both biological and social.

Darwin built on the work of Sir Charles Lyell (1797–1875) and Jean-Baptiste Lamarck (1744–1829). Lyell's three-volume *Principles of Geology* (1830–1833) confirmed the views of the Scottish geologist James Hutton (1726–1797), who stated that the earth developed through natural rather than supernatural causes. Lyell helped popularize the notion of geological time operating over a vast span of years. This understanding is essential to the acceptance of any theory of biological evolution, based as it is on changes in species over many thousands of generations. Lamarck, a naturalist, argued that every organism tends to develop new organs to adapt to the changing conditions of its environment. He theorized that these changes are transmitted by heredity to the descendants, which are thereafter changed in structural form.

Though he had originally studied medicine at Edinburgh and prepared for the ministry at Cambridge University, Darwin lost interest in both professions and became a naturalist while in his twenties. From 1831 to 1836 he studied the specimens he had collected while on a five-year surveying expedition aboard the ship *Beagle*, which had sailed along the coast of South America and among the Galápagos Islands. The works of his predecessors, in addition to questions that he had about the theories presented in Malthus's "Essay on Population," helped him define his own theory. When Darwin's book finally appeared, it changed many basic scientific and social assumptions.

In his revolutionary work, Darwin constructed an explanation of how life evolves that negated the literal interpretation of the Bible taught in most Christian churches:

> *Species have been modified, during a long course of descent, chiefly through the natural selection of numerous successive, slight, favorable variations; aided in an important manner by the direct action of external conditions, and by variations which seem to us in our ignorance to arise spontaneously.*[8]

His explanation radically affected the views of the scientific community about the origin and evolution of life on the planet. The hypothesis, in its simplified form, states that all existing plant and animal species are descended from earlier and, generally speaking, more primitive forms. The direct effects of the environment cause species to develop through the inheritance of minute differences in individual structures. As the centuries passed, the more adaptable, stronger species lived on, while the weaker, less flexible species died out: the "survival of the fittest." Furthermore, a species may also be changed by the cumulative working of sexual selection, which Darwin regarded as the "most powerful means of changing the races of man."

After the announcement of Darwin's theories, other scientists, such as the German biologist August Weismann (1834–1914) and the Austrian priest Gregor Mendel (1822–1884), worked along similar lines to explore the genetic relationships among living organisms. Weismann proved that acquired characteristics cannot be inherited. Mendel's investigations into the laws of heredity, based on his experiments with the combining of different varieties of garden peas, proved especially valuable in the scientific breeding of plants and animals and demonstrated that the evolution of different species was more complex than Darwin had imagined. Based on their work, biologists hypothesized that there are what would be later called chromosomes that carry the characteristics of an

Discovery Through Maps

World Geological Map, 1849

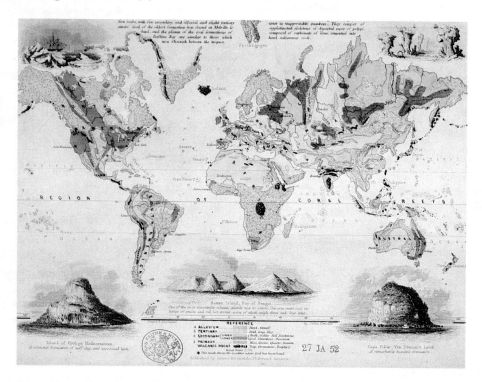

In 1849 James Reynolds published his Geological Map of the World, an exercise in accurate portrayal combined with imagination. Where Reynolds had accurate information, he used the classification systems developed during the eighteenth century and the conventions of geological maps produced in the first part of the nineteenth century. In his maps he used a variety of colors to show the distribution of rocks and soils.

The problem for Reynolds was that there were substantial portions of Asia and Africa that had not yet been systematically explored. He did not let this stop him, however, and filled in the blank areas with extrapolations of what he felt ought to have been there. Reynolds paid particular attention to indicate the location of the Arctic and Antarctic ice packs, volcanic islands, and major coral reefs. It would take another half century before sufficient exploration would permit an accurate map of world geology. Reynolds's confidence shown in this map, as well as the geological atlas and astronomical charts he produced, matched that of his countrymen who went forth to establish the empire for queen and country.

organism. Darwin had hinted at and now further research supported the mutation theory, which states that sudden and unpredictable changes within a chromosome can be transmitted by heredity to produce new species. Scientists began to work with the very fundamental building blocks of life and established the groundwork of contemporary biotechnical research.

Darwin and other investigators carefully researched and cautiously stated their findings. Unlike earlier discoveries, however, their work was widely reported in popular journals and applied by commentators and politicians. The newly ascendant middle classes responded enthusiastically to their understanding of evolutionary theory, finding in it a comfortable reassurance of the "rightness" of their own upward mobility and Europe's dominance in the world (see Chapter 29).

Medicine, Chemistry, and Physics

Important advances in medicine, chemistry, and physics contributed to a population explosion on the Continent and had significant economic implications, further strengthening the bases of Europe's dominance. At the beginning of the nineteenth century, medical practices were making a slow transition away from the indiscriminate use of leeches and bleeding. In the 1840s physicians began to use ether and chloroform to reduce pain during operations. The Scottish surgeon Joseph Lister (1827–1912) developed new antiseptic practices that made major advances against the spread of infection. By 1900 fairly sophisticated and much safer surgical procedures were available.

Probably the most important single advance came with the substantiation of the germ theory of disease by Louis Pasteur (1822–1895) and Robert Koch (1843–1910). During his search for a cure to anthrax—a disease that in the late 1870s destroyed more than 20 percent of the sheep in France—Pasteur established the principle that the injection of a mild form of disease bacterium causes the body to form antibodies that prevent the vaccinated individual from getting the severe form of the particular disease. Koch discovered the specific organisms that caused 11 diseases, including tuberculosis. The work of Pasteur and Koch placed the sciences of bacteriology and immunology on a firm footing and gave promise that the end of such deadly diseases as typhoid and smallpox might be in sight.

Modern chemistry gained its foundations during the nineteenth century, founded on the atomic theory advanced by an English Quaker schoolmaster, John Dalton (1766–1844). In 1869 Russian chemist Dmitri Mendeleev (1834–1907) drew up a "periodic table" in which he classified all known elements according to their weights and properties. From gaps in this table, chemists were able to deduce the existence of undiscovered elements. Other researchers made advances in the field of nutrition and discovered the significance of vitamins. Biochemical research threw light on the presence and function of the ductless (endocrine) glands. Chemotherapy advanced with the discovery of a chemical that could destroy the syphilis bacterium and with procedures that would lead to the discovery of sulfa drugs, penicillin, and other antibiotics.

Revolutionary strides in physics were taken in the areas of electricity and thermodynamics, the first law of which was formulated in 1847. Michael Faraday (1791–1867) prepared the way for the dynamo, a device that made possible changes in communications, the transmission of current over long distances, and the development of the electric motor. The Scottish scientist James Clerk Maxwell (1831–1879) and the German Heinrich Hertz (1857–1894) conducted basic research into the nature of electromagnetic phenomena such as light, radiant heat, and ultraviolet radiation.

Pierre Curie (1859–1906) and his wife, Marie Curie (1867–1934), made major strides toward the discovery of the X-ray and radioactivity. When they extracted radium from uranium ore in 1896, the scientific world became aware of the strength of ra-

Marie Curie, born Manya Skłodowska in Warsaw, Poland, shared with her husband, Pierre, the 1903 Nobel Prize in physics for their work on radioactivity, a term Marie coined in 1898. She won the 1911 Nobel Prize in chemistry for her discovery of radium and polonium and isolation of pure radium. Irène Curie, Marie and Pierre's daughter, shared with her husband, Frédéric Joliot, the 1935 Nobel Prize in chemistry for their work in synthesizing new radioactive isotopes of various elements.

dioactivity. Marie Curie was the first person to be awarded two Nobel Prizes, one in physics and one in chemistry.

At the beginning of the twentieth century the British physicist Ernest Rutherford (1871–1937) helped develop electron theory. It had been postulated that the atom contains particles known as electrons. Rutherford contributed the idea that each atom has a central particle, or nucleus, that is positively charged and separate from the negatively charged electrons. These discoveries destroyed one of the foundations of traditional physics, that matter is indivisible and continuous.

Technological Growth and Advances

Another reason for the Continent's economic emergence was a wide range of new technologies that took advantage of the scientific discoveries to use new materials, processes, and transportation. New competitors began with state-of-the-art factories that allowed them to outproduce Britain, whose older factories were less productive.

Electricity

The basic change in the second phase of industrialization was the use of electricity in all aspects of life. Scientists had discovered electricity's basic principles a century earlier, but it was difficult to generate and transmit power across long distances. When the first dependable dynamo, which changed energy from mechanical into electrical form, was perfected in 1876, it became possible to generate electricity almost anywhere. Inventors, such as the American Thomas A. Edison (1847–1931), began to use the new resource in industry, transportation, entertainment, and the home. Humanity had finally found a source of power that could be transmitted and used easily. The British took the lead in applying electricity to home use. The Germans made the most advanced application of electric technology to industry.

Engines

Another fundamental change came in the use of gas and oil in the newly devised internal combustion engine. Steam power's use was limited by its appetite for huge amounts of fuel and its sheer bulk. Gottlieb Daimler (1834–1900) perfected the internal combustion engine used in most automobiles today. In 1892 Rudolf Diesel invented the engine that bears his name. It burned fuel instead of harnessing the explosions that drove the Daimler engine.

These new developments led directly to the search for and use of petroleum and the beginning of the passenger car industry. By 1914 the making of cars was a key part of the Italian, Russian, German, French, and American economies. Automobile manufacturing called for a number of spin-off industries such as tire, ball-bearing, and windshield manufacturing—the list extends to hundreds of items. Leaving aside the passenger car's economic contribution, the world's cities and people felt the complex impact of this new form of transportation, with consequences such as expanding the range of an individual's world and increased noise levels and pollution that changed the character of urban areas.

Laborsaving Devices

Other new machines also changed the quality of life. Bicycles became commonplace in the 1890s, as did sewing machines, cameras, and typewriters, to name a few items. Never before had people had the ability

to transform ideas almost instantly into products accessible to the average person. This was another dividend of industrialization and a symbol of a rapidly changing Europe.

Economic Bases for Global Dominance

The global economy imposed demands for more money and better management on Europe's firms. Industrialists came to live or die by their efficiency, and efficiency often meant consolidation. Large firms could make more products at a cheaper cost than small firms because they could raise the money to buy the resources, install the newest technology, and train and employ more workers. Large firms carried more political clout than small ones and lobbied for state policies and regulations that favored them. Some firms, such as that of Alfred Nobel (1833–1896), the Swedish industrialist and inventor of dynamite, set up branches in many different countries. Others tried to control an entire market in one country, as the Standard Oil firm of John D. Rockefeller (1839–1937) did in the United States. Whatever the strategy, the gigantic firm became the dominant industrial force.

With the need for more capital, firms began to sell stock to the middle classes. Joint-stock companies were not new, but they had not been favored because if an enterprise failed, the investors were liable for its debts. Britain, followed by other industrial states, adopted statutes, or limited liability laws, that protected investors from business failure. As middle-class wealth increased, more people began to "play the stock market."

New Structures

Businesses developed new strategies to dominate individual sectors of the market. One new development was the *trust*, an arrangement in which a body of trustees held a majority of stock in a given industry and could thereby control wages, prices, and merchandising policies of several companies. Another tactic was the *holding company*, in which a corporation invested in the stock of other companies to gain the type of control it would have with the less formal trust. In Europe these alliances took the form of huge industrial combinations known as *cartels*. The cartel, often secret, controlled prices and markets in fundamentally important goods such as rubber or steel. The ultimate way to dominate an area of business, however, was the *monopoly*, in which one firm gained control of the total economic cycle of a product.

The new generations of industrialists developed more efficient management methods. American engineer Frederick W. Taylor (1856–1912) devised the scientific management system, which recommended breaking down each stage of the industrial process into its most minute segments and studying the efficiency of each step of work to establish the optimum speed of productivity. By 1914 improved methods such as the use of interchangeable parts and the introduction of the assembly line brought productivity to a high level. New production methods and organizational structures were better able to satisfy the seemingly infinite desires of the world market.

The New World Economy

From the fifteenth through the eighteenth centuries, a large part of Europe had expansionist ambitions. Prevailing mercantilist theories encouraged the seeking of colonies and monopolies in overseas trade. A combination of political and economic factors, however, slowed the imperialistic drive in the half century after 1815. Britain's desire for an empire had been diminished after the loss of the 13 American colonies in 1783, and France had lost nearly all of its overseas possessions by the end of the Napoleonic wars. In addition, the laissez-faire school of economics argued against the possession of colonies.

France reignited the drive for a world empire in the 1850s, and the scramble for colonies heated up after 1870. In his six years as British prime minister, Benjamin Disraeli (see Chapter 26) annexed Fiji and Cyprus, fought a war against the Zulus in southeastern Africa, purchased a controlling interest in the Suez Canal, and proclaimed Queen Victoria "empress of India." To a greater or lesser degree France, Germany, the United States, Russia, Belgium, and Italy followed Britain's lead, and the race to carve up the globe was on. It has been estimated that in 1800 fully half of the world was not known to Europeans. By 1900 more land had been explored and acquired by them than in the previous four centuries. The nations of a small northwestern portion of the Eurasian landmass claimed control of 60 percent of the earth's surface.

In 1914 Great Britain, with its far-flung empire, was the world's richest nation. Even though it imported more goods than it exported, it earned nearly a billion dollars a year from overseas investments, shipping fees, and banking and insurance services. Germany had become the Continent's economic giant. Its population had risen from 41 million to 65 million between 1871 and 1910. Close cooperation between government and private industry paid dividends. The state established protectionist tariffs after 1879, supported technical education, and encour-

Assembling magnetos on the assembly line at the Ford Motor Company in Highland Park, Michigan. One worker could assemble a single magneto in 29 minutes; 29 workers, properly arranged, could assemble a magneto in 5 minutes.

aged industrial cartels. France ranked behind Germany in population and industrial output, but it was still an economic power.

In the 50 years before World War I, international trade rose from $7 billion to $42 billion. European nations were by and large their own best customers, even with the tariff barriers that were erected on the Continent after 1879. Europe became the chief supplier of world capital: Britain invested heavily in its empire and the United States; France made huge loans to Russia; and Germany and England extended large loans to the Ottoman Empire. The European economic primacy was felt in the far corners of the world. Soon the Argentinean *gaucho*, the Australian sheep man, and the American cowboy—each a symbol of the free man in the mythology of his own country—and their wives and families were cogs in the global economic machine of constantly circulating raw materials and finished goods.

The international economy tied the world to the rhythms of the booms and busts of Europe. Economic historians differ in their interpretations of the frequency and causes of the stages of economic expansion and contraction in the business cycle. Whether one believes in a ten-year, 20-year, or century-long cycle, the fact remains that economies throughout the world increasingly became extensions of Europe's economic changes.[9] The depression that lasted from 1873 to 1896 is symbolic of the impact of economic events in Europe on the world. Overall, prices fell by roughly 30 percent in all products. Around the world, suffering was severe, especially in areas that depended on the shipment of their raw materials to cities or abroad and that had no control over the price their products could demand. But by 1896 there had been a readjustment, and the period to 1914 was generally prosperous.

Political Implications

The internationalization of the economy placed diplomacy and finances into a common harness. The developing countries needed money to compete in the new world economic system. The indus-

Shrinking national markets sparked the drive for expansion into international markets for manufactured goods. The advertisement for Pears' Soap is inscribed on the rock marking the farthest point of the British advance in the Sudan.

trialized countries looked on the rest of the world as a supplier of labor and raw materials, a market for finished goods, and a place for capital investments.

For creditors, investments abroad fell into three logical groupings. Lenders could purchase the bonds of strong nations—a safe investment but with a low rate of return. They could make loans to underdeveloped countries—a riskier venture but with a much higher rate of return. Finally, the financial powers could put their money into stable countries that needed capital in specialized areas. This choice would ensure a good return on a safe investment. Within these categories were many variations, all of which held the promise of a handsome payoff, usually in both financial and political terms.

For debtors, however, loans could be helpful or devastating, depending on the circumstances. The United States was able to get needed capital with a minimum infringement on its sovereignty. At the opposite extreme was the case of the Ottoman Empire, which received its first loan in 1854. Twenty-two years later the Turks were so deeply in debt that they had to put a major portion of their tax base in foreign hands just to pay the interest. Unlike the Americans, the Turks put just 10 percent of the borrowed funds to productive use. Other countries had similar results. Russia by 1914 had a funded debt of 9 billion rubles, half of which was owed to foreigners. Hungary had to use 10 percent of its gross national product to pay foreign investors to cover loans and interest in the prewar period.[10] Foreign investments of this type were just one facet of the great powers' financial dominance. Economic control implied a profound political impact on the debtor country and represented the most efficient form of domination.

Cultural Reflections of the Age

The increasing wealth and leisure time generated by industrialization vastly enlarged the number of consumers of culture. Artists made the transition from responding to the tastes of the noble courts to the new demands of middle-class audiences attending concerts in vast new halls and viewing art in public galleries. As the classic age of the noble drawing room disappeared, so too did the elites that had dictated the nature and composition of art in the eighteenth century.

Romanticism

The Romantic movement unleashed sensitivities that played a major role in forming the literary, artistic, and musical changes of the nineteenth century. The Romantics' emphasis on the individual is apparent in the novels of Wolfgang von Goethe (1749–1832) and Friedrich von Schiller (1759–1805). Goethe's *Sorrows of Young Werther* (1774) tells the story of a sensitive, feeling, outcast young man who kills himself with the pistol of his rival after failing to gain his true love. Schiller's *Wilhelm Tell* (1804) describes the heroic struggle of the Swiss patriots in their drive for independence against tyranny. Unlike the brittle wit and irony of the authors of the Enlightenment, such as Voltaire, these stories were sentimental and emotional descriptions of people acting in response to overwhelming and impossible social or political dilemmas, who did what their hearts told them was right. It was better to experience a moving young death or to rise up against impossible odds than to look dispassionately and rationally at life.

The Romantic movement's emphasis on the individual created among some of its participants a truly picturesque lifestyle. For every Victor Hugo (1802–1885) who lived a long, full, excessive life, there were artists, writers, and musicians from London to Moscow who "burned the candle at both ends" in brief, passionate, creative lives. To most Romantics such as Keats it was better to live briefly and intensely according to the commandments of the heart than to die old, fat, rich, bored, lecherous, and bourgeois.

The novel came into prominence in the eighteenth century, but it became the dominant literary form of the nineteenth. Writers such as Victor Hugo and Sir Walter Scott (1771–1832) mined the myths and legends of France and Britain, respectively, to write vastly successful works for the ever-expanding middle-class audiences. Hugo's *Notre Dame de Paris* (1831) and Scott's *Ivanhoe* (1819) detailed their nations' past so effectively that both books were imitated, and sequels and imitations continued to appear into the twentieth century. By 1850 a variety of social and psychological themes challenged the historical novel, along with the gently critical works of William Makepeace Thackeray (1811–1863), who through deft characterizations in works such as *Vanity Fair* (1848) poked fun at the *nouveau riche* social climbers that dominated society.

Poets responded far more pointedly to the challenges thrown down by the Napoleonic and Industrial Revolutions. In 1798 two young British poets, William Wordsworth (1770–1850) and Samuel Taylor Coleridge (1772–1834), published a volume of verse called *Lyrical Ballads*. Wordsworth wrote in the preface that poetry was "the spontaneous overflow of powerful feelings recollected in tranquillity." Wordsworth sought to express "universal passions"

Greats of the Romantic Era

Literature

George Gordon, Lord Byron (1788–1824)

Samuel Taylor Coleridge (1772–1834)

Heinrich Heine (1797–1856)

Victor Hugo (1802–1885)

John Keats (1795–1821)

Alexander Pushkin (1799–1837)

Sir Walter Scott (1771–1832)

Percy Bysshe Shelley (1792–1822)

William Wordsworth (1770–1850)

Art and Architecture

John Constable (1776–1837)

Eugène Delacroix (1798–1863)

Joseph M. W. Turner (1775–1851)

Eugène Viollet-le-Duc (1814–1879)

Music

Ludwig van Beethoven (1770–1827)

Hector Berlioz (1803–1869)

Felix Mendelssohn (1809–1847)

Franz Schubert (1797–1828)

Robert Schumann (1810–1856)

Carl Maria von Weber (1786–1826)

and the "entire world of nature" through simple, unladen vocabulary. He stressed the intuitive and emotional contemplation of nature as a path to creativity. In an 1802 sonnet he expressed his love of nature and country:

> *. . . Oft have I looked round*
> *With joy in Kent's green vales; but never found*
> *Myself so satisfied in heart before.*
> *Europe is yet in bonds; but let that pass*
> *Thought for another moment. Thou are free,*
> *My Country! and 'tis joy enough and pride*
> *For one hour's perfect bliss, to tread the grass*
> *Of England once again. . . .[11]*

Eugène Delacroix's illustration for the Prologue of Goethe's Faust *portrays the archfiend Mephistopheles as a winged devil.*

In *Kubla Khan* (1797) and *Rime of the Ancient Mariner* (1798) Coleridge pursued the supernatural and exotic facets of life. His vivid descriptions of distant subjects and nonrational elements of human life served as the precedent for later artists as they examined the areas of fantasy, symbolism, dream states, and the supernatural. The French poet Alphonse de Lamartine (1790–1869) led the way in making the transition from classicism to Romanticism and had an impact across the Continent.

The British poets George Gordon, Lord Byron (1788–1824) and Percy Bysshe Shelley (1792–1822) rebelled against the constraints of their society and expressed their contempt for the standards of their time through their lives and works. Byron gloried in the cult of freedom. When the Greeks rose up against the Turks in 1821, he joined their cause. He died of fever soon after his arrival. Shelley believed passionately that human perfectibility was possible only through complete freedom of thought and action. On the Continent, Heinrich Heine (1797–1856), who was, like Byron, a cutting satirist and, like Shelley, a splendid lyricist, shared their romantic ideals. Heine is best remembered for his *Buch der Lieder,* songs that were put to music by Franz Schubert (1797–1828) and Felix Mendelssohn (1809–1847).

John Keats (1795–1821) was neither social critic nor rebel; for him the worship and pursuit of beauty were of prime importance. In *Ode on a Grecian Urn* (1820) he states:

> *"Beauty is truth, truth beauty"—that is all*
> *Ye know on earth, and all ye need to know.*

Keats advocated for art and beauty's sake in themselves, instead of the classical formulas of an earlier age or the socialist realism of the latter part of the century.

Alexander Pushkin (1799–1837), Russia's greatest poet, liberated his nation's language from the foreign molds and traditions forced on it in the eighteenth century. While serving as the transition between the classical and Romantic ages, Pushkin helped create a truly Russian literature, one that expressed profound depth of his love for his country.

The age of change brought new tendencies to painting as well as to other art forms. There is a great contrast between the precise draftsmanship and formal poses of the classical painters and the unrestrained use of color and new effects of the Romantic artists. Some artists such as the French master Eugène Delacroix (1798–1863) were met with critical resistance. His *Massacre of Chios,* a flamboyant work painted in 1824 upon receiving news of the Turks' slaying of Christians on Chios, was panned by conservative critics as the "massacre of painting."

Lord Byron in Greek dress. One of the leading Romantic poets, Byron lived the life of the Romantic hero he created in his writing. He lived passionately and died tragically of fever in 1824 while fighting with the Greeks against the Turks.
Thomas Phillips, Portrait of George Gordon Byron, 6th Baron Byron, 1835. Courtesy of the National Portrait Gallery, London.

Less flamboyant but equally part of the Romantic transition are the works of the British painter John Constable (1776–1837). Deeply influenced by Romanticism's emphasis on nature, Constable was in some respects the originator of the modern school of landscape painting. His choice of colors was revolutionary, as he used greens freely in his landscape, an innovation considered radical by critics, who favored brown tones. Constable's countryman, Joseph M. W. Turner (1775–1851), sparked controversy with his use of vivid colors and dramatic perspectives, which gave him the ability to portray powerful atmospheric effects.

Around 1830 Romanticism's fascination with the medieval period led to a shift from Greek and Roman architectural models to a Gothic revival, in which towers and arches became the chief characteristics. Sir Walter Scott's romances played a major role in this development, and even his house at Abbotsford was designed along Scottish baronial lines. In France, Eugène Viollet-le-Duc (1814–1879) spearheaded the movement by writing, teaching, and restoring properties under the aegis of the Commission on Historical Monuments. Hugo's *Notre Dame de Paris* popularized the revival with its discussion of fifteenth-century life. For the next few decades, architecture was dominated by styles that looked back especially to the Gothic and rococo styles, which were sometimes combined in aesthetically disastrous presentations.

Realism

Around 1850 artists and writers began responding to the new age in the realist movement. Artists, especially the French, who were among the most notable early proponents of realism, focused on the concrete aspects of life. This led, at the end of the century, to experiments with a range of new forms and structures in the modernist movement. At the same time that these movements were developing, a huge new group of consumers, the lower and middle classes, were becoming participants in the new mass culture. They might find little to admire in the fine arts, but through their buying power and their numbers they would come to have a great effect on large parts of the creative community.

In literature and art as in politics, realism replaced Romanticism after midcentury. To the realists it was no longer enough to be true to one's instincts and emotions. Their job was to faithfully observe and graphically report all aspects of life in a dispassionate, precise manner so as to depict individuals in their proper setting. In this age of change there was much for writers and artists to portray, and a much larger public now had the leisure time and political interests to respond to their work.

Major Writers and Composers at Mid-Century

Literature

Honoré de Balzac (1799–1850)

Anton Chekhov (1860–1904)

Charles Dickens (1812–1870)

Feodor Dostoevski (1821–1881)

Gustave Flaubert (1821–1880)

Thomas Hardy (1840–1928)

Henrik Ibsen (1828–1906)

Henry James (1843–1916)

Harriet Beecher Stowe (1811–1896)

Leo Tolstoy (1828–1910)

Mark Twain (Samuel Clemens) (1835–1910)

Music

Johannes Brahms (1833–1897)

Anton Bruckner (1824–1896)

Frédéric Chopin (1810–1849)

Anton Dvořák (1841–1904)

Gustav Mahler (1860–1911)

Modest Mussorgsky (1835–1881)

Sergei Rachmaninov (1873–1943)

Jean Sibelius (1865–1957)

Bedrich Smetana (1824–1884)

Peter Ilich Tchaikovsky (1840–1893)

Richard Wagner (1813–1883)

Giuseppi Verdi (1813–1891)

The trend toward the realistic novel had been foreshadowed in the work of Honoré de Balzac (1799–1850), the author of a 90-volume *tour de force*, *La Comédie Humaine* (The Human Comedy), which depicts French life in the first half of the nineteenth century. A master of characterization, Balzac described life in such detail that his work is a valuable reference on social history for present-day scholars. Gustave Flaubert (1821–1880) was the first French realist writer. His masterpiece, *Madame Bovary* (1856), exhaustively described how the boredom of a young romantic provincial wife led her into adultery, excess, and ultimately suicide. Émile Zola

(1840–1902) was the leader of the French naturalist school and a prolific author best known for his novel *Germinal* (1885). He also played a major role as the most influential author of his time by mobilizing French public opinion in 1898 to move against the injustices done to Captain Alfred Dreyfus in his open letter to the French president, which opens "J'accuse . . ." ("I accuse") (see Chapter 26).

British novelist Charles Dickens (1812–1870) protested social conditions in his works characterizing the everyday life of the middle classes and the poor. In such works as *Oliver Twist* (1838), *Dombey and Son* (1847–1848), and *Hard Times* (1854) he describes some of the worst excesses of industrial expansion and social injustice. Later, Thomas Hardy (1840–1928), in novels such as *Far from the Madding Crowd* (1874), dealt with the struggle—almost always a losing one—of the individual against the impersonal, pitiless forces of the natural and social environment.

American writers such as Henry James (1843–1916), Samuel Clemens (1835–1910), and Harriet Beecher Stowe (1811–1896) made important contributions to the realist tradition. James tried to catch the "atmosphere of the mind" through an almost clinical examination of the most subtle details. Clemens, better known by his pseudonym, Mark Twain, used humor and accurate descriptions of the American Midwest and Far West to underscore social injustice. Stowe's detailed novel *Uncle Tom's Cabin* (1852) captured American hearts and minds and strongly bolstered the antislavery movement.

The Russian novelists Leo Tolstoy (1828–1910) and Feodor Dostoevski (1821–1881) produced the most developed presentation of the realistic novel. Tolstoy stripped every shred of glory and glamour from war in *War and Peace* (1869) and gave an analytical description of the different levels of society. Dostoevski devised a chilling, detailed view of life in St. Petersburg in *Crime and Punishment* (1866), and his *Brothers Karamazov* (1880) offered a painstaking analysis of Russian life during a period of change.

Drama was deeply influenced by realism, as could be seen in the works of the Norwegian Henrik Ibsen (1828–1906), the Irishman George Bernard Shaw (1856–1950), and the Russian Anton Chekhov (1860–1904). *A Doll's House* (1879), Ibsen's understated yet tension-filled work, assailed marriage without love as immoral. Though his characters are not heroic in their dimensions, Ibsen captures the quiet desperation of normal life. Shaw used satire and nuance to shock the British public into reassessing conventional attitudes. Chekhov's *Cherry Orchard* (1904) dramatized the changes wrought by emancipation of the serfs on the lives of a gentry family. Lacking obvious plot and action, the play depends on day-to-day detail to build a subtle and exhaustive social portrait.

Beethoven and His Successors

Music did not experience the shift in style from Romantic to realistic that art and literature did. Ludwig van Beethoven (1770–1827) served as a bridge between the classical and Romantic periods. However, the regularity of the minuet, the precision of the sonata, and the elegant but limited small chamber orchestra—all forms Beethoven mastered—were not sufficient to express the powerful forces of the age. A comparison of his relatively measured and restrained First Symphony with the compelling and driven Fifth or the lyrical, nature-dominated Sixth dramatically reveals the changes that he underwent. Beethoven was the ultimate Romantic—a lover of nature, passionate champion of human rights, fighter for freedom. Beethoven spoke to the heart of humanity through his music, especially his magnificent Ninth Symphony, the Ode to Joy.

The momentum of the forces that Beethoven set in motion carried through the entire century. Carl Maria von Weber (1786–1826), Hector Berlioz (1803–1869), Robert Schumann (1810–1856), along with Felix Mendelssohn and Franz Schubert, made major contributions in developing the musical repertoire of Europe by midcentury. Thereafter, Johannes Brahms (1833–1897), Anton Bruckner (1824–1896), and Gustav Mahler (1860–1911) made lyrical ad-

In the hands of Beethoven, formal music, which had previously reflected the polished and artificial manners of the salon, became a vehicle for expressing deep human emotions.

vances in composition and presentation. Each made unique use of the large symphony orchestra, and Brahms also composed three exquisite string quartets along with his four massive symphonies.

In addition, many composers turned to their native folk music and dances for inspiration. Beethoven had used native themes, as Schubert and Schumann did in Austria and Germany. Frédéric Chopin (1810–1849), even though he did most of his work in France, drew heavily on Polish folk themes for his mazurkas and polonaises. Jean Sibelius (1865–1957) in Finland, Anton Dvorák (1841–1904) and Bedrich Smetana (1824–1884) in Bohemia-Moravia (the modern Czech Republic), and Russians Peter Ilich Tchaikovsky (1840–1893), Modest Moussorgsky (1835–1881), and Sergei Rachmaninov (1873–1943) all incorporated folk music in their work. This use of folk themes was both pleasingly familiar and aesthetically satisfying to audiences.

Romanticism and nationalism, with their increasing number of enthusiasts, sparked developments in opera during the century. In his fervid Germanic works, Richard Wagner (1813–1883) infused old Teutonic myths and German folklore with typically Romantic characteristics such as emphasis on the supernatural and the mystical. Wagner's cycle of musical dramas known as *Der Ring des Nibelungen* was the culmination of a long and productive career. His descendants still manage the *Festspielhaus*, a theater in Bayreuth, Germany, that he designed and his admirers financed.

The greatest operatic composer of the century was Giuseppi Verdi (1813–1901), who composed such masterpieces as *Aïda, Rigoletto, Il Trovatore,* and *La Forza del Destino*. His operas, along with those of Wagner, form the core of most of today's major opera house repertoires.

The music world rarely dealt with social problems or harsh realism. Its supporters were by and large the newly ascendant middle classes who had benefited from the economic growth triggered by industrialization. They used the wealth derived from their commercial prosperity to finance the building of new opera houses and symphony halls and maintain the composers and orchestras. Major soloists were the idols of their day, as they showed their virtuosity in compositions that made use of Romantic subject matter infused with sentiment and, not infrequently, showmanship such as that shown by Franz Liszt (1811–1886) in his piano concerts or Jenny Lind, the "Swedish Nightingale" (1820–1887), in her recitals. They drew capacity audiences of contented listeners.

Conclusion

In Britain innovators, by eliminating bottlenecks in the making of cotton cloth, overcame the limits of animal and human power and vastly increased output. The island nation possessed the proper balance of population, money, governmental support, internal markets, and a risk-taking entrepreneurial class to accomplish the first revolution in industrialization. The results achieved in textiles were reproduced in iron and steel as Britain came to dominate the world economically by the mid-nineteenth century.

The rapid growth of industrialized cities strained the capabilities of local and national authorities to provide utilities, education, law enforcement, and social services. Industrialization demanded great sacrifices from the first generation of men, women, and children caught up in it, but each successive generation of industrialized society had a much more comfortable life because of those sacrifices.

The second phase of industrialization brought new wealth and a whole new range of products to the Continent and carried the urban problems already experienced in Britain across the Channel. At the same time, new trade and banking systems emerged in response to the economic challenges of industrialization, leading Germany to become the strongest country on the Continent after 1871. Even while nineteenth-century technology was changing the nature of society, scientists were pushing the frontiers of knowledge, preparing the way for the twentieth century and its advantages and disasters.

Scientists made significant discoveries in the fields of biology, chemistry, physics, and medicine, greatly expanding the frontiers of knowledge and technology. Not only did Charles Darwin's work upset the understanding of the development of organisms, but its popularization had immense, if misdirected, social implications. In the second half of the nineteenth century, workers and their supporters responded to the middle-class dominance of the public arena. They struggled, with the help of the socialist parties, for just treatment in the modern, industrial world.

The countries leading the industrial, economic, and scientific growth experienced opportunity and expansion. They possessed not only the tools but also the wealth to impose themselves and their culture on the world. Countries that were not participants in these developments had only two alternatives: to become a resource and customer base for the Europeans or to attempt to resist and be utterly overwhelmed.

Suggestions for Reading

David S. Landes, *The Unbound Prometheus: Technological Change and Industrial Development in Western Europe from 1750 to the Present* (Cambridge University Press, 1969), is a well-written and excellent survey of the entire sweep of industrialization. On Britain specifically, see Thomas S. Ashton, *The Industrial Revolution, 1760–1830* (Oxford University Press,

1997); Peter Mathias, *The First Industrial Nation: An Economic History of Britain, 1700–1914*, 2nd ed. (Routledge, 1988); Phyllis Deane, *The First Industrial Revolution* (Cambridge University Press, 1979); and John Rule, *The Vital Century: England's Developing Economy, 1714–1815* (Longman, 1992). Also recommended is Shepard Bancroft Clough, ed., *Economic History of Europe: Twentieth Century* (Walker, 1968). Charles Singer, *The Late Nineteenth Century, 1850–1900*, vol. 5 in the series *A History of Technology* (Oxford University Press, 1958), is lavishly illustrated and clearly written.

See also W. O. Henderson, *The Industrialization of Europe, 1780–1914* (Harcourt, Brace & World, 1969), and *The Rise of German Industrial Power, 1834–1914* (University of California Press, 1975); J. D. Chambers and G. E. Mingay, *The Agricultural Revolution, 1750–1880* (Schocken, 1966); and Carlo Cipolla, ed., *The Fontana Economic History of Europe: The Emergence of Industrial Societies* (Fontana Books, 1973). Rondo E. Cameron, *France and the Economic Development of Europe, 1800–1914* (Octagon, 1961), gives another perspective, along with Alan S. Milward and S. B. Saul, *The Economic Development of Continental Europe, 1780–1870* (Allen & Unwin, 1973). For a useful survey of German developments, see Theodore S. Hamerow, *Restoration, Revolution, Reaction: Economics and Politics in Germany, 1815–1871* (Princeton University Press, 1958). William Blackwell provides useful background on tsarist developments in *Industrialization of Russia* (Crowell, 1970). For a comparative approach to industrial change in the United Kingdom, Germany, and the United States, see James K. McCraw, ed., *Creating Modern Capitalism: How Entrepreneurs, Companies, and Countries Triumphed in Three Industrial Revolutions* (Harvard University Press, 1998). A useful volume on international economic growth is Sidney Pollard, *European Economic Integration* (Harcourt Brace Jovanovich, 1974). Francis Sheppard, *London, 1808–1970: The Internal War* (University of California Press, 1971), is a fine account of a city experiencing the challenge of growth. A useful guide for research is Peter N. Stearns, ed., *ABC-CLIO Companion to the Industrial Revolution* (ABC-CLIO, 1996).

For the larger context of the first phase of industrialization, see Eric J. Hobsbawn's classic, *The Age of Revolution* (Vintage, 1996). The social impact of industrialization can be seen in the novels of Charles Dickens, especially *Hard Times*. Theodore K. Rabb and Robert I. Rotberg include several selections on the social impact of industrialization in *The Family in History* (Harper Torchbooks, 1973). Two books by Asa Briggs, *Victorian Cities* (Harper & Row, 1968) and *Victorian People* (University of Chicago Press, 1959), are vivid portrayals. Peter N. Stearns, *European Society in Upheaval* (Macmillan, 1967), and William Leonard Langer, *Political and Social Upheaval, 1832–1852* (Harper & Row, 1969), are valuable surveys. Louise A. Tilly and Joan W. Scott, *Women, Work, and Family* (Holt, Rinehart and Winston, 1978), is a seminal work on the change in the work and family life of women wrought by industrialization. For the revolutionary impact of industrialization on the American value structure, see James L. Huston, *Securing the Fruits of Labor: The American Concept of Wealth Distribution* (Louisiana State University Press, 1998).

See Stephen F. Mason, *A History of Sciences* (Collier, 1962), and Rupert Hall and Marie Boas Hall, *A Brief History of Science* (Signet, 1964), for clear and concise surveys of the development of science. The literature on Darwin and his times are voluminous. Darwin's *Origin of Species* and *Voyage of the Beagle* are available in a number of editions. Charles Coulston Gillespie nicely sets the stage for the period in *Genesis and Geology* (Harvard University Press, 1951). Gertrude Himmelfarb, *Darwin and the Darwinian Revolution* (Norton, 1968), and William Irvine, *Apes, Angels, and Victorians: The Story of Darwin, Huxley, and Evolution* (University Press of America, 1983), are ex-cellent studies. Richard Hofstadter, *Social Darwinism in American Thought*, rev. ed. (Beacon, 1992), is a fascinating study of how a subtle theory can be misapplied. René Jules Dubos, *Louis Pasteur, Free Lance of Science* (Da Capo, 1986), is a biography that is sound both as history and literature. Jacob Bronowski, *The Ascent of Man* (Little, Brown, 1974), is a humane and wise overview of the development of science through the ages.

Suggestions for Web Browsing

Plight of Women's Work in the Industrial Revolution in England and Wales
http://home.earthlink.net/~womenwhist/lesson7.html

Site sponsored by Women in World History Curriculum details the working conditions, home life, and other aspects of British women working in the early 1800s.

Child Labor: British History, 1700–1900
http://www.spartacus.schoolnet.co.uk/IRchild.main.htm

Site presents discussions and images related to child labor in Britain, including information about factory reformers, supporters of child labor, life in the factory, and descriptions of personal experiences.

Impressionism
http://www.ticnet.com/gallery/Impress/ravel.mid

General site on Impressionism in both art and music, with link to the WebMuseum, Paris, for further art images and information.

Notes

1. Edward Shorter, "Illegitimacy, Sexual Revolution, and Social Change in Modern Europe," in Theodore K. Rabb and Robert I. Rotberg, eds., *The Family in History* (New York: Harper & Row, 1973), pp. 48–84.
2. Heinz Gollwitzer, *Europe in the Age of Imperialism, 1880–1914* (New York: Harcourt, Brace & World, 1969), p. 20.
3. I. Vyshnegradsky, quoted in William L. Blackwell, *The Industrialization of Russia: A Historical Perspective* (New York: Crowell, 1970), p. 24.
4. Fernand Braudel, *Capitalism and Material Life, 1400–1800* (New York: Harper & Row, 1975), p. 11; William Leonard Langer, "Checks on Population Growth, 1750–1850," *Scientific American* 226 (1972), pp. 92–99.
5. Thomas R. Malthus, "An Essay on Population," in *Introduction to Contemporary Civilization in the West*, vol. 2 (New York: Columbia University Press, 1955), p. 196.
6. Eugen Weber, *A Modern History of Europe* (New York: Norton, 1971), p. 988.
7. Sidney Pollard, *European Economic Integration, 1815–1970* (New York: Harcourt Brace Jovanovich, 1974), pp. 56–62.
8. Charles Darwin "The Origin of Species," in *Introduction to Contemporary Civilization in the West*, Vol. 2 (New York: Columbia University Press, 1955), pp. 453–454.
9. David S. Landes, *The Unbound Prometheus: Technological Change and Industrial Development in Western Europe from 1750 to the Present* (Cambridge: Cambridge University Press, 1969), p. 233.
10. Pollard, *European Economic Integration*, pp. 74–78
11. William Wordsworth, "Composed in the Valley near Dover on the Day of Landing," in Mark van Doren, ed., *Selected Poetry* (New York: Modern Library, 1950).

French painter Eugène Delacroix
captured the idealism and optimism
of the politics of ideology in the first
half of the nineteenth century. In
Liberty Leading the
People (1831), men, women,
and children smash the barricades
of oppression, following their
muse to a better world.

The Politics
of Ideas in the
Western World,
1815–1861

Chapter Contents

In the wake of the forces unleashed by the French Revolution and Napoleon, political thinkers constructed varied responses to the changes through which they were living after 1789. A panoply of "isms"—nationalism, liberalism, conservatism, socialism—came into use in the first half of the nineteenth century. Just as the Romantic artists and philosophers tried to find new ways to express their creativity (see Chapter 24), the political theorists sought new formulas to express their hopes for humanity.

Until 1848 these various "isms" played a decisive role in Western politics. Kings and presidents, legislators and jurists, and revolutionaries held their positions, wrote their programs, and carried out their violence as prescribed by these ideologies. The "isms" gained their greatest success in 1848 when the seeds of "liberty, equality, and brotherhood" bore fruit in the overthrow of many of the governments in Europe. However, their very diversity led to the collapse of the 1848 revolutions.

After the failed revolutions, the language of the "isms" continued to play a role, be it to justify the Machiavellian tactics for the unification of Italy, the oncoming American Civil War, or the British world empire. But they were now coopted, used as post facto explanations for power plays and no longer as value structures for a humane existence.

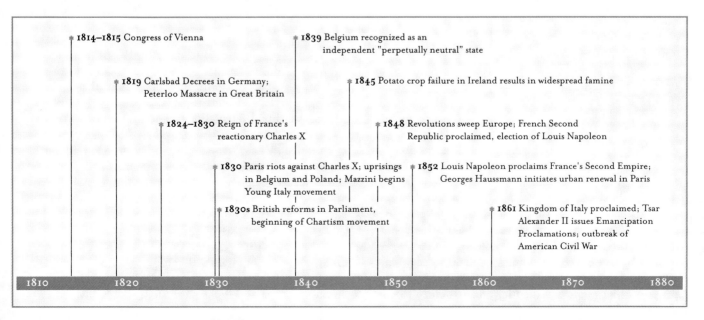

1814–1815 Congress of Vienna

1819 Carlsbad Decrees in Germany; Peterloo Massacre in Great Britain

1824–1830 Reign of France's reactionary Charles X

1830 Paris riots against Charles X; uprisings in Belgium and Poland; Mazzini begins Young Italy movement

1830s British reforms in Parliament, beginning of Chartism movement

1839 Belgium recognized as an independent "perpetually neutral" state

1845 Potato crop failure in Ireland results in widespread famine

1848 Revolutions sweep Europe; French Second Republic proclaimed, election of Louis Napoleon

1852 Louis Napoleon proclaims France's Second Empire; Georges Haussmann initiates urban renewal in Paris

1861 Kingdom of Italy proclaimed; Tsar Alexander II issues Emancipation Proclamations; outbreak of American Civil War

1810   1820   1830   1840   1850   1860   1870   1880

The New Political Vocabulary

The writers, musicians, artists, and philosophers caught up in the Romantic movement at the end of the eighteenth century and the beginning of the nineteenth rebelled against the classicism and the cold logic of the Enlightenment. Instead they stressed an individual's past, uniqueness, emotions, and creativity as the basis for life. The Romantics investigated history, folklore, linguistics, and myths to define their own identity. They revived the Scandinavian sagas, the French *Chanson de Roland,* and the German *Nibelungen* stories. During a time of uncertainty, change, and stress it was both comforting and uplifting to look to the past, even an imagined one. The Romantics' search for their own cultural roots helped give birth to the most powerful and longest-lasting of the new ideologies, nationalism.

Nationalism

Unique conditions in different parts of Europe produced different variants of nationalism. However, common to them all was a populace consciously embracing a common land, language, folklore, history, enemies, and religion. These elements are the ingredients of the nation's and the individual's identity and pull the members into an indivisible unity. Nationalism can exist where there is no state structure and can thrive in a state where a minority nation is repressed. Nationalism, unlike patriotism, does not need flags and uniforms. All that is needed is a historical and emotional unity around which the members of the nation can gather, a unity that defines a shared identity that entails the total cultural and political loyalty of the individual to the nation.

After 1789 this new force dominated the cultural and political activities of France. The spirit of brotherhood projected by the French Revolution united the French people. On the Continent, Romantics reacted against the French and Napoleonic dominance and helped bring people together in nationalistic opposition, especially in Germany. Georg Wilhelm Friedrich Hegel (1770–1831) built on the movement in his lectures and writings at the University of Berlin. For Hegel history was a process of evolution in which the supremacy of primitive instincts would give way to the reign of clear reason and freedom—the "world spirit"—that would be manifested in the state. Hegel believed that the Prussia of his day offered the best example of the state as a spiritual organism, because in Prussia the individual had the greatest "freedom"—defined not as the individual escaping from society but as a condition in which there is no conflict between the individual and society. The Prussian state, in Hegel's eyes, blended the proper proportions of national identity and structure to enable its individuals to gain their greatest growth. His high regard for the state was not shared by most Romantics, but his exaltation of the Prussian state at a time when Germany was still fragmented had a powerful unifying influence. This was the beginning of the belief in the uniqueness and superiority of Germany that had such drastic consequences in the twentieth century.

The research and writings of the Germans Johann Gottfried von Herder (1744–1803) and brothers Jacob (1785–1863) and Wilhelm Grimm (1786–1859) provided historical support and linguistic bases for the Slavic nationalist movements. Herder conceived of a world spirit *(Weltgeist)* made up of component parts of the various national spirits *(Volkgeist).* Each of these national spirits was seen as playing an essential role in the world process, and Herder believed that the Slavs were soon to make an important contribution. The Grimm brothers' philological work aided the literary and linguistic revivals of many Slavic groups

Romantic nationalism in Britain reacted strongly against the human costs of industrialization and the pretensions of the new merchant classes. It focused on the medieval roots of Britain, as well as on movements such as philhellenism (the love of ancient Greece). In France, Spain, Italy, Russia, and other parts of the Continent, the Romantic movement made important contributions to the growth of national identity. In Italy, for example, Giuseppe Mazzini (1805–1872) and Alessandro Manzoni (1785–1873) played important roles in the unification struggle of the country. Romantic nationalism was also found in the writings of history by Leopold von Ranke in Germany, Jules Michelet in France, Frantisek Palacky in Bohemia-Moravia, and George Bancroft in the United States.[1]

Conservatism

The reaction to the French Revolution, especially as expressed by Edmund Burke (1729–1797), provided the basis of nineteenth-century European conservatism. There were many thinkers who did not believe in the revolutionary slogan of liberty, equality, and brotherhood. They did not believe that liberation could be gained by destroying the historically evolved traditions of the Old Regime. Freedom could be found only in order and maintained solely by continual reference to precedents. A legitimate political and social life needed the framework of tradition to survive.

The conservatives did not have faith in the individual, nor did they share the Romantics' love of pure emotion and spontaneity. Beginning with Burke and continuing through the first part of the nineteenth century to the Frenchman Joseph de Maistre

(1753–1821), the Russian Nicholas Karamzin (1766–1826), and the Spaniard Juan Donoso-Cortés (1809–1853), there was a body of intellectuals who found strength, not weakness, in the church and monarchy of the Old Regime; danger, not liberation, in the nationalistic movements; and degradation, not exaltation, in the new Romantic art forms.

Conservatism took many forms during the nineteenth century, ranging from the Romantic to the patriotic to the religious to the secular. Whatever their approach, conservatives stressed the need to maintain order through a constant reference to history. They believed that the welfare and happiness of humanity resided in the slowly evolving institutions of the past. Industrialization and the consequences of the French Revolution severed the connection with the past and were therefore dangerous. The conservatives were backward-looking, finding their standards and values in the proven events of the past, not in the untried reforms of the present.

Liberalism

The rising middle and commercial classes found their interests and ideals best expressed in the doctrine of liberalism. Liberalism affirmed the dignity of the individual and the "pursuit of happiness" as an inherent right. The ideology's roots were set firmly in the eighteenth-century soil of constitutionalism, laissez-faire economics, and representative government. Liberals thought in terms of individuals who shared basic rights, were equal before the law, and used parliament to gain power and carry out gradual reform. In addition, liberals believed that individuals should use their power to ensure that each person would be given the maximum amount of freedom from the state or any other external authority.

In economics liberals followed the views of Adam Smith in his *Wealth of Nations*. They believed in fair competition among individuals responding to the laws of supply and demand with a minimum of governmental regulation or interference. They agreed with Smith that society benefited more from competition among individuals motivated by their self-interest than from governmental regulation. The most intelligent and efficient individuals would gain the greatest rewards, society would prosper, and the state would be kept in its proper place, protecting life and property.[2]

Liberals fought foes from above and below as they translated their ideas into public policy. Nobles and the landed gentry still controlled most countries in Europe, so throughout the century the middle classes fought to gain political power commensurate with their economic strength. While they were trying to increase their own influence, they sought to limit the political base of the emerging working classes. By the end of the century the middle classes had consolidated their control over the industrialized world. This was perhaps the major political achievement of the century.

Liberals were freed from the demands of manual labor and possessed enough wealth to spend their spare time in public pursuits. They had the time and leisure to work in government to control state policy to protect their own interests. They gained sufficient security that they undertook the enactment of social reforms to head off revolution. They became the dominant voices in the press and universities and gained commanding authority over public opinion. The liberals' most important contributions came in the areas of civil rights, promotion of the rule of law, government reform, and humanitarian enterprises.

The main interpreters of liberalism came from Britain, and during the first half of the century Jeremy Bentham (1748–1832) and John Stuart Mill (1806–1873) adapted some liberal theories to modern reality. Bentham devised the concept of utilitarianism, or philosophical radicalism, based on the notions of utility and happiness. He connected these notions by noting that each individual knows what is best for himself or herself and that all human institutions should be measured according to the amount of happiness they give. Bentham built on these two eighteenth-century notions to form the pain-and-pleasure principle. He believed that government's function was to ensure as great a degree of individual freedom as possible, for freedom was the essential precondition of happiness. Utilitarianism in government was thus the securing of the "greatest happiness for the greatest number." If society could provide as much happiness and as little pain as possible, it would be working at maximum efficiency. Bentham recognized what later liberals would eventually espouse—that government would have to work at all levels—but he left no precise prescription as to how to proceed.

Mill spoke more to this issue. He began by noting that in industry the interests of the owners and workers did not necessarily coincide. He proposed the theory that government should, if necessary, pass legislation to remedy injustice, pointing out that when the actions of business owners harm the people, the state must step in to protect the citizenry. He challenged the liberal theory of minimal government interference in the economic life of the nation and pointed out that humanitarianism is more important than profit margin. He accepted that maximum freedom should be permitted in business and that natural law should dictate insofar as possible the relationship of citizens.

He also pointed out that the distribution of wealth depends on the laws and customs of society and that these can be changed by human will. The

John Stuart Mill, "Of the Limits to the Authority of Society over the Individual."

John Stuart Mill, in collaboration with his wife, wrote the classic definition of nineteenth-century liberalism in *On Liberty*. In this extract he defines the claims that society can make on an individual.

What, then, is the rightful limit to the sovereignty of the individual over himself? Where does the authority of society begin? How much of human life should be assigned to individuality, and how much to society?

Each will receive its proper share if each has that which more particularly concerns it. To individuality should belong the part of life in which it is chiefly the individual that is interested; to society, the part which chiefly interests society.

Though society is not founded on a contract, and though no good purpose is answered by inventing a contract in order to deduce social obligations from it, everyone who receives the protection of society owes a return for the benefit, and the fact of living in society renders it indispensable that each should be bound to observe a certain line of conduct towards the rest. This conduct consists, first, in not injuring the interests of one another, or rather certain interests which, either by express legal provision or by tacit understanding, ought to be considered as rights; and secondly, in each person's bearing his share (to be fixed on some equitable principle) of the labours and sacrifices incurred for defending the society or its members from injury and molestation. These conditions society is justified in enforcing at all costs to those who endeavour to withhold fulfilment. Nor is this all that society may do. The acts of an individual may be hurtful to others or wanting in due consideration of their welfare, without going to the length of violating any of their constituted rights. The offender may then be justly punished by opinion, though not by law. As soon as any part of a person's conduct affects prejudicially the interests of others, society has

jurisdiction over it, and the question whether the general welfare will or will not be promoted by interfering with it becomes open to discussion. But there is no room for entertaining any such question when a person's conduct affects the interests of no persons besides himself, or needs not affect them unless they like (all the persons concerned being of full age and the ordinary amount of understanding). In all such cases, there should be perfect freedom, legal and social, to do the action and stand the consequences. . . .

But neither one person, nor any number of persons, is warranted in saying to another human creature of ripe years that he shall not do with his life for his own benefit what he chooses to do with it. He is the person most interested in his well-being. . . .

[The] strongest of all the arguments against the interference of the public with purely personal conduct is that, when it does interfere, the odds are that it interferes wrongly and in the wrong place. . . . There are many who consider as an injury to themselves any conduct which they have a distaste for, and resent it as an outrage to their feelings; as the religious bigot, when charged with disregarding the religious feelings of others, has been known to retort that they disregard his feelings by persisting in their abominable worship or creed. But there is no parity of the feeling of a person for his own opinion and the feeling of another who is offended at his holding it, nor more than between the desire of a thief to take a purse and the desire of the right owner to keep it. And a person's taste is as much his own peculiar concern as his opinion or his purse.

From John Stuart Mill, *On Liberty* (1859).

rights of property and free competition, therefore, should be upheld but within reasonable limits. Mill pointed out that the liberty of the individual is not absolute—a person has the freedom to do as he or she will as long as it does not harm another. But freedom ultimately has to be placed under the wider interests of society.

In the late twentieth century the word *liberalism* has undergone some change in meaning. The term still implies reform, but liberals today advocate an active governmental role in minimizing the extremes of wealth, in balancing the great power enjoyed by business and labor, and in conserving natural resources.

Today's liberals also advocate the state's intervention to help the individual by providing social security and in opposing racial, sexual, and age discrimination.

Socialism

The working classes of Europe, heartened by the French Revolution's call for equality and afflicted by the hardships inherent in the first phase of industrialization, found that socialism best expressed their values and goals. Socialists attacked the system of laissez-faire capitalism as unplanned and unjust. They condemned the increasing concentration of wealth and called for public or worker ownership of business. The nature of the industrial system, dividing worker and owner, also raised serious problems, and socialists insisted that harmony and cooperation, not competition, should prevail.

Socialists believed that human beings are essentially good, and with the proper organization of society there would be a happy future with no wars, crimes, administration of justice, or government. In this perfectly balanced world there would also be perfect health and happiness. As one prophet foretold, "Every man with ineffable ardor, will seek the good of all."[3] Karl Marx (see Chapter 29) later derisively labeled socialists who sought such a world as "Utopians."

The first prominent Utopian socialist was the French noble Claude Henri de Rouvroy, Comte de Saint-Simon (1760–1825). He defined a nation as "nothing but a great industrial society" and politics as "the science of production." He advocated that humanity should voluntarily place itself under the rule of the paternalistic despotism of scientists, technicians, and industrialists who would "undertake the most rapid amelioration possible of the lot of the poorest and most numerous class."[4]

Charles Fourier (1772–1837), another French Utopian, believed that the future society must be cooperative and free. He worked out a communal living unit of 1620 people called a "phalanstery." The members of the group voluntarily chose tasks that appealed to them to do the work needed to ensure the phalanstery's survival. Although his plan was endorsed by many prominent people, attempts made to found cooperative Fourierist communities were unsuccessful. The famous Brook Farm colony in Massachusetts was one such short-lived experiment.

Robert Owen (1771–1858), a successful mill owner in Scotland, was a more practical Utopian socialist. His New Lanark, the site of his textile mills, was a model community. There between 1815 and 1825, thousands of visitors saw rows of neat, well-kept workers' homes, a garbage collection system, schools for workers' children, and clean factories where workers were treated kindly and no children under age 11 were employed. In 1825 Owen moved to the vicinity of Evansville, Indiana, where he established a short-lived community at New Harmony.

Their optimism blinded the Utopians to the nature of humanity and the world in which they lived. Brook Farm and New Harmony were based on the notion that human beings naturally love one another or could be brought to that level. The basic impracticality of the experiments doomed them to failure. However, the notion that capitalism was inherently corrupt and that it was essential to remove the system remained an article of faith for subsequent socialists.

The Search for a Status Quo: Western and Central Europe, 1815–1848

The allies who defeated Napoleon attempted to build an international structure to maintain stability after 1815. Almost immediately, liberal and nationalistic forces tried to change the status quo in Spain, Italy, Greece, and Germany. Until 1848 the efforts of the Russians and the Austrians kept the lid on the boiling pot of political and economic pressures for change. But in that year a wave of revolutions spread across the Continent and put an end to the political momentum generated in the French Revolution of 1789 and the structure created to contain it. The political structure built at the Congress of Vienna could not control the forces of individualism, freedom of thought, pride in nation, and equality under the law that had been unleashed after 1789. Although Europe was at peace by 1815, a new type of upheaval began as the middle and lower classes pursued the unfulfilled promises of the revolutionary era.

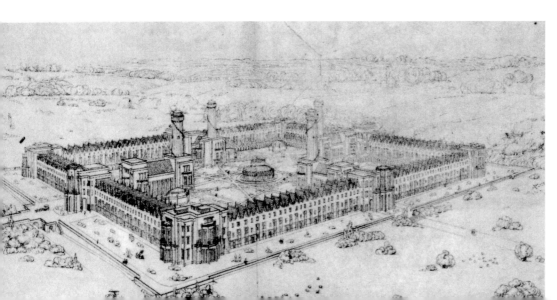

Artist's rendering of Robert Owen's Utopian community at New Harmony, Indiana. Square, fortresslike buildings surround the community's interior gardens and exercise grounds. The community was established in 1825, but internal dissension forced its dissolution three years later.

Revolutionary Outbreaks, 1815–1848

1820–1821	The Germanies, Spain, Italy, Latin America, Greece
1825	Russia
1830	France, Belgium, Poland
1848	France, Prussia, Italy; the Habsburg monarchy: Austria, Bohemia, Hungary, Croatia, Romania

Return of the Bourbons

The restored Bourbon monarch Louis XVIII (1814, 1815–1824) was an unhappy choice for the French throne. The new king, a brother of the guillotined Louis XVI, was ill-equipped to lead France out of a quarter century of revolution and Napoleonic charisma. Dull and unpopular, he had been the target of a Talleyrand epigram that "the Bourbons have learned nothing and forgotten nothing." Nonetheless, he tried to hold the country together by blending elements of the revolutionary period with remnants of the Old Regime. Unfortunately, the mixture helped create the instability that plagued the country throughout the century.

In the July Revolution of 1830, Parisians took to the streets to protest the restrictive laws of Charles X.

Louis began by "granting" his subjects a charter that established a form of constitutional monarchy in which he kept all executive power, controlled law-making, and influenced the makeup of the legislature. The restored Bourbon made little attempt to return to the institutions of the Old Regime and accepted Napoleon's Civil Code, the Concordat with the papacy, and the governmental reforms. For nine years he suffered the fate of moderates trying to navigate between two extremes: he was attacked by both sides. The right wing assailed the charter for giving too much to the middle classes while the liberals and radicals said that he had not gone far enough in his policies. Louis was succeeded by his brother, Charles X (1824–1830), who cared nothing about maintaining political balance.

Charles did not accept any of the changes since 1789. In 1829 he announced that he "would rather saw wood than be a king of the English type." So out of tune was he with the times that in July 1830 he drove the usually submissive legislature to the point that it refused to support his proposed ultraroyalist ministry. When elections went badly for him, he issued a set of laws censoring the press and further limiting the already heavily restricted right to vote. These repressive acts drove liberals, radicals, and their journalist allies to revolt. They barricaded the narrow streets of Paris with overturned carts, boxes, tables, and paving stones. Fighting behind these obstacles and from rooftops, they held off the army. Three days later a less reactionary faction took power after Charles fled across the Channel to exile in Great Britain.

The new government represented the upper middle classes and the landed gentry and stood as a compromise between the republicans—led by the aging Marquis de Lafayette, hero of the American Revolution—and the relatively liberal monarchist supporters of the Orléans branch of the Bourbons. The new king, Louis Philippe (1830–1848), who claimed the title of "citizen king," predictably supported the interests of the wealthy.

Louis Philippe took great pains to present a "bourgeois" image of himself. He received the crown from "the people" and replaced the white Bourbon flag with the revolutionary tricolor. However, Louis Philippe's policies consistently favored the upper bourgeoisie and gentry and shut the workers and middle classes out of the political arena. Of the 32 million French citizens, only 200,000 wealthy male property owners were allowed to vote.

Workers protested that the government was ignoring their interests. Louis Philippe and his advisers were more interested in pursuing a policy of divide and conquer and ignored most suggestions for reform. Restrictive legislation such as the September Laws were passed in 1835 to control the growing radical movement. The government kept control, but under the calm surface, serious pressures were building. By 1848 France faced a serious crisis.

The French Influence in Belgium and Poland

The Paris uprising of 1830 encouraged liberals across the Continent, but only in Belgium were there any lasting results. The Vienna Congress had placed the Belgians under the Dutch crown, but this settlement ignored the cultural, economic, religious, and linguistic differences between the two people. The Belgians were primarily Catholic farmers and workers, some of whom spoke Dutch but most of whom spoke French, whereas the people of the Netherlands were Dutch-speaking Protestant seafarers and traders.

Belgian liberals asked the Dutch king, William I of Orange, to grant them their own administration in August 1830. When he refused, rioting erupted in Brussels, which the Dutch troops were unable to put down. After expelling the troops, the Belgians declared their independence and drew up a liberal constitution. William asked in vain for help from Tsar Nicholas I. The principle of legitimacy as a pretext for intervention was dead. Stalemate ensued until the summer of 1831 when the Belgian national assembly met in Brussels and chose Prince Leopold of Saxe-Coburg-Gotha as king. Eight years later the international status of the new state was settled. Belgium was recognized as a "perpetually neutral" state.

The French rebellion had an impact in Poland, where Poles in and around Warsaw rose up in the name of liberal and national principles. After the Congress of Vienna, Poles in this region gained a special status. The area known as Congress Poland had its own constitution and substantial local autonomy. The winds of change and the repressive tendencies of Tsar Nicholas I combined to push the Poles into rebellion in the winter of 1830–1831. The rebels suffered from internal division, and the numerically and militarily superior Russians crushed them. Their major accomplishment was to tie down the Russian troops, whom Nicholas wanted to send to help the Dutch king, for six months and perhaps save the Belgian revolution.[5]

German and Italian Nationalism

The forces of nationalism influenced central Europe from the tip of Italy through the Habsburg lands of central and eastern Europe to the Baltic Sea. Napoleon had performed a great, though unwitting, service for German and Italian nationalists through his direct governing in the area and also by revising the European map. After 1815 the region knew the positive effects of a different style of governing and was divided into a much more rational set of political units.

Metternich had ensured that the Vienna Congress made Austria the dominant partner in the German Confederation. To preserve his country's dominance both in the Confederation and throughout the Habsburg monarchy he knew that he had to fight continually against nationalism. The currents of Romanticism found forceful expression in the works of German poets and philosophers and in lectures in German classrooms. Nationalism and liberalism found many followers among the young. For example, in a great patriotic student festival that took place in October 1817 (the three hundredth anniversary of the Reformation) at Wartburg, where Luther had taken refuge, liberal students burned reactionary books on a great bonfire to protest their discontent with the status quo. Protests spread both openly and secretly in the *Burschenschaften* (liberal societies). Metternich moved harshly against the students. He pushed the Carlsbad Decrees (1819) through the Diet of the German Confederation. These acts dissolved student associations, censored the press, and restricted academic freedom. However, the decrees failed to stop the forces of liberalism and nationalism, which grew during the next 20 years.

Italy, which Metternich saw as a "geographical expression" and not a nation, also posed special problems. The Congress of Vienna, in accordance with the principles of legitimacy and compensation, had returned Italy to its geographical status of 1789, divided into areas dominated by the Bourbons, the Papal States, and the Austrians. This settlement ignored the fact that in the interim the Italians had experienced more liberty and better government than ever before. The return to the old systems was also a return to high taxes, corruption, favoritism, and banditry.

It was perhaps ironic that this fragmented, individualistic land should produce the most notable Romantic nationalist in Europe, Giuseppe Mazzini. After the Austrians put down the Italian revolutionary movements in 1820 and 1821, Mazzini began to work actively for independence. In 1830 he was implicated in an unsuccessful revolution against the Sardinian royal government and thrown into jail for six months. Once released, he went to London and started a patriotic society that he called Young Italy. This organization sent appeals to students and intellectuals to form an Italian nationalist movement. In the meantime, the reactionary forces weathered nationalist pressures.

Metternich also feared nationalism in the Habsburg realm, a mosaic composed of many different nationalities, languages, and religions. If nationalism and the desire for self-rule became strong among the Magyars, Czechs, southern Slavs, and Italians, the

Mazzini on the Duties of the Individual

Giuseppe Mazzini saw the individual's obligation to the human family to be transcendent.

Your first duties—first as regards importance—are, as I have already told you, towards Humanity. You are men before you are either citizens or fathers. If you do not embrace the whole human family in your affection, if you do not bear witness to your belief in the Unity of that family, consequent upon the Unity of God, and in the fraternity among the peoples which is destined to reduce that unit to action; if, wheresoever a fellow-creature suffers, or the dignity of human nature is violated by falsehood or tyranny—you are not ready, if able, to aid the unhappy, and do not feel called upon to combat, if able, for the redemption of the betrayed or oppressed—you violate your law of life, you comprehend not that Religion which will be the guide and blessing of the future.

From Emilie A. Venturi, *Joseph Mazzini: A Memoir* (1875).

Habsburg Empire would fall apart. Nationalism threatened the Germans who controlled the empire yet constituted only 20 percent of its population.

By understanding the complex and combustible nature of the region in which Metternich exercised his power, one can begin to appreciate his dread of democratic government and nationalism and his obsession with maintaining the status quo. Liberalism and nationalism would destroy his power. In a world that was rapidly industrializing, Metternich's power rested on a backward system. Only in Bohemia and the areas immediately around Vienna was there a middle class. The great majority of the inhabitants were peasants, either powerless serfs, as in Hungary, or impoverished tenant farmers who owed half of their time and two-thirds of their crops to the landlord. Government was autocratic, and the regional assemblies had little power and represented mainly the nobility. The social, political, and economic structures were extremely vulnerable to the winds of change that came in 1848.[6]

1848: The Revolutionary Year

As it had before, France once again opened a revolutionary era, and the events there set a precedent for what was to occur throughout Europe in 1848. The overthrow of the old order came first in Paris in February and then spread to Berlin, Vienna, Prague, Buda, and Pest in March. Never before had France—or Europe—seen such a fragmented variety of political and social pressures at work at the same time. Romantics, socialists, nationalists, middle classes, peasants, and students could all agree that the old structure had to be abandoned, but the ideology espoused by each group envisioned a different path to that goal and a separate view of what the new world should be. Louis Philippe fled Paris, Metternich abandoned Vienna, and the Prussian king, Frederick William IV, gave in. But the movements in France and elsewhere fell apart as soon as they had won because of their diversity, lack of experience, and conflicting ideological goals.

France and the Second Republic

The pressures building since 1830, strengthened by economic depression in 1846 and 1847, erupted in Paris in February 1848 in a series of banquets. In this seemingly harmless social arena, liberals and socialists pushed for an end to corruption and reforms of the electoral system. The government tried to prohibit the banquet scheduled for February 22, and in response the opposition threw up more than 1500 barricades to block the narrow streets of Paris. When violence broke out, republican leaders took the opportunity to set up a provisional revolutionary government and proclaimed the introduction of universal manhood suffrage. Louis Philippe fled to exile in England.

The new government, the Second Republic, had a brief (1848–1851) and dreary existence. Neither the new leaders nor the voters had any experience with representative government. The forces that united to overthrow the king soon split into moderate and radical wings. The first group wanted middle-class control within the existing social order, while the latter faction desired a social and economic revolution. By the summer the new government faced a major crisis over the issue of national workshops sponsored by the socialist Louis Blanc (1811–1882). The workshops were to be the state's means to guarantee every laborer's "right to work." The moderate-dominated government voiced its belief in Blanc's principle of full employment, but the leaders gave the plan's administration to men who wanted to ridicule it. As a result, the workshops became a national joke. Laborers were assigned make-work jobs such as carrying dirt from one end of a park to the other on one day and then carrying it back the next.

The disbanding of the workshops incited a violent insurrection known as the June Days. The unemployed workers raised a red flag as a sign of revolution—the first time that the red flag had been used as a symbol of the proletariat. With the cry of "bread or lead," the demonstrators rebuilt the barricades and tried to overthrow the government. The most bloody fighting Paris had seen since the Reign of Terror gave the insurgents far more lead than bread, and the movement was crushed. After that the bourgeoisie and the workers would be on the opposite ends of the political spectrum.

Germany and the Frankfurt Assembly

The example of the French February revolution quickly crossed the Rhine River and spread to central Europe. At public assemblies throughout Germany, patriotic liberals demanded unification. Rapid changes came with minimal casualties, thanks largely to the humane response of the Prussian King, Frederick William IV. When his subjects erected barricades in Berlin on March 15, he decided to make

concessions rather than unleash further violence and bloodshed. He ordered the regular army troops out of Berlin and tried to make peace with his "dear Berliners" by promising a parliament, a constitution, and a united Germany. Upon learning of this development, the rulers of the other German states agreed to establish constitutional governments and guarantee basic civil rights.

The Frankfurt Assembly opened its first session on May 18. More than 500 delegates attended, coming from the various German states, Austria, and Bohemia. The primarily middle-class membership of the assembly included about 200 lawyers, 100 professors, and many doctors and judges. Popular enthusiasm reached a peak when the assembly's president announced, "We are to create a constitution for Germany, for the whole empire." The assembly deliberated at length over the issues of just what was meant by Germany and what form of government would be best for the new empire. Some debaters wanted a united Germany to include all Germans in central Europe, even Austria and Bohemia. Others did not want the Austrians included, for a variety of religious and political reasons. Another issue of contention was whether the new imperial crown should be given to the Habsburgs in Vienna or the Hohenzollerns in Berlin.

Germany's history changed tragically when the Assembly failed to unite and bring a liberal solution

The artillery attempts to demolish a barricade in this scene of street fighting during an insurrection in Frankfurt in 1848. Like a political plague, revolutions broke out that year in governmental centers that had failed to adapt to new social and economic conditions or had lost the ability to impose force effectively on the people.

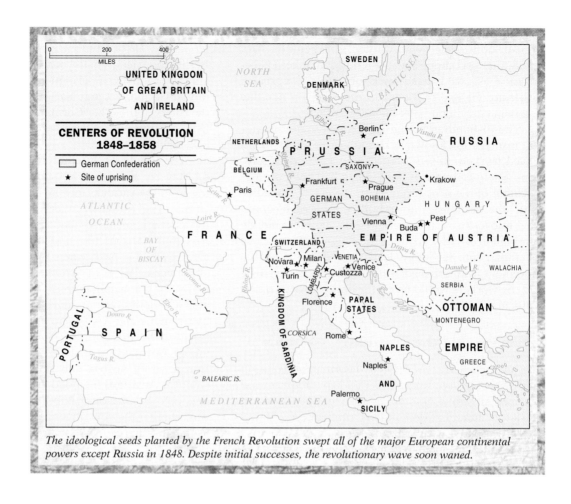

The ideological seeds planted by the French Revolution swept all of the major European continental powers except Russia in 1848. Despite initial successes, the revolutionary wave soon waned.

to political problems. From May to December the Assembly wasted time in splendid debates over nonessential topics. As the participants talked endlessly, they threw away their chance to take decisive action and contributed to the failed dreams of 1848. Gradually, the conservatives recovered from the shock of the spring revolts and began to rally around their rulers, exhorting them to undo the reformers' work. In Prussia the king regained his confidence, the army remained loyal, and the peasants showed little interest in political affairs. The Berlin liberals soon found themselves isolated, and the king was able to regain control.

Even though the antiliberal forces were at full tide, the Frankfurt Assembly continued its work. It approved the Declaration of the Rights of the German People, an inspiring document that articulated the progressive political and social ideals of 1848. In April 1849 the Assembly approved a constitution for a united Germany that included an emperor advised by a ministry and a legislature elected by secret ballot. Austria refused to join the new union.

When the leadership of the new German Reich (nation) was offered to Frederick William, he refused to accept it, later declaring that he could not "pick up a crown from the gutter." After this contemptuous re-

fusal, most of the Assembly's members returned home. Outbreaks against the conservative domination continued, but the Prussian army effectively put them down. Thousands of prominent middle-class liberals fled, many to the United States.

Italy

The news of the revolutions in Paris and Vienna triggered a rash of uprisings on the Italian peninsula. In Sicily, Venice, and Milan revolutionaries demanded an end to foreign domination and despotic rule. In response, King Charles Albert of Sardinia voluntarily granted a new liberal constitution. Other states, such as Tuscany, also issued constitutions. In the Papal States, meanwhile, reform had begun as early as 1846. Absolute government in Italy almost disappeared.

As in the rest of Europe, the liberal and nationalist triumphs and reforms were quickly swept away by the reactionary tide. The Austrians regained their mastery in the north of Italy in July when they defeated Charles Albert at the decisive battle of Custozza. Another defeat a year later forced him to abdicate in favor of his oldest son, Victor Emmanuel II. Austria helped restore the old rulers and systems of government in Italy to their pre-1848 conditions.

The final blow to the Italian movements came in November 1848 when Pope Pius IX, who had begun a program of reform, refused to join in the struggle against Catholic Austria for a united Italy. His subjects forced him to flee from Rome, and the papal lands were declared a republic, with Mazzini as the head. The pope's flight prompted a hostile reaction from conservative Europe, and the French sent in an army to crush the republic in July 1849. When the pope returned to Rome, he remained bitterly hostile to all liberal causes and ideas until his death in 1878.

The Habsburg Monarchy

The events of 1848 took a tragic toll in the Habsburg lands. When the news of the February uprising reached Vienna, Prague, and Budapest, reformers immediately called for change. In Budapest the nationalist liberal Louis Kossuth (1802–1894) attacked the Habsburg ruler's "stagnant bureaucratic system" and spoke of the "pestilential air blowing from the Vienna charnel house and its deadening effect upon all phases of Hungarian life." He demanded parliamentary government for the whole of the empire.

In Vienna Kossuth's speech inspired some Austrian students and workers to demonstrate in the streets. The movement soon gained the force of a rebellion, and the frightened Austrian emperor forced Metternich, the symbol of European reaction, to resign. Meanwhile, the Hungarian Diet advocated a liberal, parliamentary government under a limited Habsburg monarchy. The Vienna-controlled Danubian region, that mosaic of nationalities, appeared to be on the verge of being transformed into a federation.

The empire's diversity soon became mirrored in a characteristic of the revolutionary movements, as the various nationalities divided among themselves. The Hungarians wrote a new constitution that was quite liberal, calling for a guarantee of civil rights, an end to serfdom, and the destruction of special privileges. In theory, all political benefits guaranteed in the constitution were to extend to all citizens of Hungary, including non-Magyar minorities. The emperor accepted these reforms and promised, in addition, a constitution for Austria. He also promised the Czechs in Bohemia the same reforms granted the Hungarians.

By summer the mood suddenly shifted. German and Czech nationalists began to quarrel, and the Magyars began to oppress the Slavic nationalities and Romanians after they in turn demanded their own political independence. Divisions among the liberal and nationalistic forces gave the conservatives in Vienna time to regroup and suggested to them the obvious tactic to follow to regain their former dominance: divide and conquer the subject nationalities. In June demonstrations broke out in the streets of

In this satiric cartoon, Pope Pius IX removes his liberal "savior's" mask to reveal his true nature after his refusal to support the revolution in Italy.

Prague, barricades were thrown up, and fighting began. The Austrians lobbed a few shells, Prague surrendered, and any hope for an autonomous kingdom of Bohemia ended.

In Hungary Kossuth announced that he would offer civil rights, but not national independence, to the minority nationalities under his control. In protest, the South Slavs under the Croat leader Joseph Jellachich (1801–1859) attacked the Magyars, and civil war broke out. The Austrians took advantage of the situation and made Jellachich an imperial general. Following his attack against the Magyars, he was ordered to Vienna, where in October he forced the surrender of the liberals who controlled the capital.

By the end of the year the weak and incapable emperor, Ferdinand I, abdicated in favor of his nephew, Franz Joseph. The Austrians began to repeal their concessions to the Hungarians, arguing that their new emperor was not bound by the acts of his predecessor. The Magyars, outraged by this maneuver, declared complete independence for their country. The Austrians, aided by 100,000 Russian troops sent by Tsar Nicholas I and the leadership of the Croatian general Jellachich, defeated the Hungarians in a bloody and one-sided struggle. In the summer of 1849 Kossuth fled the country, and the Hungarian revolution reached its tragic conclusion.[7]

The Aftermath of 1848: Western and Central Europe to 1861

As western and central Europe regained equilibrium, the idealism of the liberals and socialists lay in ruins. Italian nationalism remained a strong force and bore fruit by 1861. Louis Napoleon III took the opportunity to create his own empire, with remarkable results. And in the Germanies, the center of balance began to tilt from Vienna to Berlin.

Italian Unification

After 1848 the Italian unification movement came to be centered in the kingdom of Sardinia, where the young monarch, Victor Emmanuel II, refused to withdraw the liberal constitution granted by his father. The prime minister, Count Camillo Benso di

Count Camillo Benso di Cavour, the leader of the movement for Italian unification.

Cavour (1810–1861), a liberal influenced by what he had seen in Switzerland, France, and Britain, assumed leadership of the drive to unify the peninsula. After 1852, when he became prime minister, Cavour concentrated on freeing his country from Austrian domination. He knew, however, that Sardinia needed allies to take on the Habsburgs. To that end, in 1855 Sardinia joined Britain and France in their fight against Russia in the Crimean War (see Chapters 27 and 29). This step enabled Cavour to speak at the peace conference after the war, where he stated Italy's desire for unification.

Cavour's presentation won Napoleon III's support, and the two opportunists found that they could both make gains if they could draw the Austrians into war. They agreed that if Cavour could entice the Vienna government into war, France would come to Sardinia's aid and help eject the Austrians from Lombardy and Venetia. In return, France would receive Nice and Savoy from Sardinia. The plan worked to perfection. In April 1859 Cavour lured the Austrians into declaring war. The French and Sardinians defeated them at Magenta and Solferino and drove them out of Lombardy. At the same time, revolts broke out in Tuscany, Modena, Parma, and Romagna. Napoleon was praised and proclaimed as the savior and liberator of Italy.

Upon receiving his share of the agreement, Napoleon III reversed himself and made peace with Austria before the allies could invade Venetia. The massing of Prussian troops on French borders as well as his second thoughts about the implications of a united Italy drove Napoleon to this move. The Sardinians were outraged, but there was little they could do but agree to a peace settlement. The agreement awarded Lombardy to Sardinia; restored the exiled rulers of Parma, Modena, Tuscany, and Romagna; and set up an Italian confederation in which Austria was included.

France's duplicity did not stop Cavour. A year later, appealing to the British, he made major changes in the peace settlement. Plebiscites were held in Tuscany, Modena, and Parma, which voted to join Sardinia. Even with the loss of Nice and Savoy to France, the addition of the three areas made Sardinia the dominant power in the peninsula.

With the consolidation of power in the north, Giuseppe Garibaldi (1807–1882) became the major figure in the unification struggle. This follower of Mazzini, secretly financed by Cavour, led his 1000 tough adventurers, known as the Red Shirts, to conquer Sicily and Naples. He then prepared to take the Papal States. This move prompted Cavour, who feared that a march on the pope's holdings might provoke French intervention, to rush troops to Naples. He convinced Garibaldi to surrender his power to Victor Emmanuel II, thus ensuring Sardinian domination of the unification movement. By November 1860 Sardinia had annexed the former kingdom of Naples and Sicily and all the papal lands, except Rome and its environs.

A meeting at Turin in March 1861 formally proclaimed the existence of the kingdom of Italy, a new nation of 22 million people. But Austrian control of Venetia and the pope's jurisdiction over Rome were problems that remained unsolved until after Cavour's death in 1861. Italy gained Venetia in 1866 by allying with Prussia in the Austro-Prussian war. When the Franco-Prussian war broke out in 1870, the French could do little to help the pope. Italian forces took control of Rome, and in 1871 it became the capital of a unified Italy.

The opportunistic methods used by the Sardinians have been criticized. Cavour made no attempt to hide the true nature of his policies. He once said, "If we did for ourselves what we do for our country, what rascals we should be."[8] He fully understood the rules of the Realpolitik game in the post-1848 state system and played it extraordinarily well.

Italy, united in 1861 and territorially completed by 1870, faced overwhelming problems. The Italians had to deal with economic, political, and cultural differences between the northern and southern parts of the country, a lack of natural resources, and a politically inexperienced population. It also had too many people for its limited economic base.

France and the Second Republic

In France the violence of the June Days moved the conservatives in the countryside and the moderates in the cities to elect Louis Napoleon (1808–1873), nephew of Napoleon I, to the presidency of the Second Republic. Although he had failed miserably in his attempts to overthrow the king in 1836 and 1840, he was sure that destiny intended great things for him. When he came back to Paris after the revolution he was untainted by any involvement in the June Days and appeared to be a unifying force.

The republic's constitution gave strong powers to the president but limited the office to a single term. Louis Napoleon took advantage of the authority given him and his strong majority to fortify his position. He and his conservative allies dominated France for the next two years, becoming strong enough to overthrow the constitution in a coup d'état in December 1851. Louis Napoleon and his allies brutally put down the workers and peasants who opposed the coup and engineered a plebiscite that gave him virtually unanimous support. In 1852 he proclaimed himself Emperor Napoleon III, and the Second Empire replaced the Second Republic.

During its 18-year span the Second Empire accomplished a great deal. Industrialization brought

Italian patriots who sought to unify their country faced major obstacles from the Austrians and the papacy. Thanks to the leadership of Cavour and the uprising led by Garibaldi, the peninsula came to be under one government for the first time since the Roman Empire.

prosperity to France. Production doubled. France supported the building of the Suez Canal, and railway mileage in France increased by 500 percent. The partial legalization of labor unions and guarantee of the right to strike improved workers' conditions. Baron Georges Haussmann transformed Paris in an ambitious urban renewal that featured broad boulevards, unified architecture, modern utilities, and improved traffic flow.

The price for the order and stability needed to build this prosperity came in the form of political control. The government remained, in theory, a parliamentary regime. The emperor's agents rigged the elections to ensure a majority in the powerless legislature for the emperor. The secret police hounded opponents, both real and potential, and the state censored the press, which accordingly rarely reported bad news.

At first the emperor brought glory to France through an interventionist and imperialist foreign policy. He continually claimed to be a man of peace, but he allied with Britain in the Crimean War; supported Cavour, briefly, in Italy; expanded French influence to ensure a foothold in Indochina; raised the

View of the Champs-Élysées after the rebuilding of Paris. In a mere 20 years Baron Georges Haussmann transformed Paris from a city of narrow streets and dark and dirty slums to a beautiful city of broad tree-lined boulevards, open spaces, and small neighborhood parks. Haussmann's renovations had political as well as aesthetic aims; destruction of many small and narrow streets eliminated places where revolutionaries might easily erect barricades, and the wide boulevards permitted the rapid deployment of troops to put down rebellions.

French flag over Tahiti; and penetrated West Africa along the Senegal River. Foreign affairs soured for him in the 1860s when he made an ill-advised attempt to take advantage of the confusion caused by the U.S. Civil War to establish a foothold in the Americas. He placed Maximilian, a Habsburg prince, on the Mexican throne and sent 40,000 troops to support him. Mexican patriots expelled the forces and executed the prince. After 1866 Louis Napoleon met his match in the Prussian Chancellor Otto von Bismarck (1815–1898), when his blundering ambition contributed to a quick Prussian victory over Austria. Finally, in 1870 he gambled on war against Prussia and lost. With this defeat the Second Empire ended (see Chapter 26).[9]

Austria and Prussia to 1861

Conservative forces consolidated control in Vienna after 1848, but the Austrian Habsburgs operated from a weakened position. Their victory over the Hungarians brought only temporary comfort. The collapse of the liberal and nationalistic movements in the Habsburg Empire was followed by a harsh repression that did little to address the basic political problems facing Vienna. Centralizing and Germanizing tendencies stimulated nationalist sentiments in the empire. After their losses to the French and Sardinians in 1859, the Austrians considered moving toward a federal system for their lands. The Hungarians, however, demanded equality with Vienna.

After 1848, with one exception, Prussia went from strength to strength. Facing a different range of problems in a much more unified state, King Frederick William issued a constitution in 1850 that paid lip service to parliamentary democracy but kept real power in the hands of the king and the upper classes. The Berlin court wanted to form a confederation of northern German states, without Austria. This plan frightened the Austrians and made the Russians uneasy as well. A meeting of the three powers at Olmütz in 1850 forced the Prussians to withdraw their plan. Instead, the 1815 German Confederation was affirmed, with Vienna recognized as the major German power. The embittered Prussians returned to Berlin, pledging revenge for the "humiliation of Olmütz."

Despite this diplomatic setback, Prussia gained success in other areas. Berlin kept the Austrians out of the *Zollverein*, the customs union of German states, and fought off their efforts to weaken it. The government, dominated by the nobles, was modern and efficient, especially when compared with that in Vienna. The Prussians extended public education to more of their citizenry than in any other European state. At the start of the 1860s a new ruler, William I (1861–1888), came to power. He had a more permissive interpretation of the 1850 constitution and allowed liberals and moderates the chance to make their voices heard.

Russia and the Obstacles to Reform, 1801–1861

Russia had neither the economic strength nor the social and political flexibility to adapt successfully to the new forces of the nineteenth century. Tsar Alexander I (1801–1825) saw the need for change and understood that the major obstacles to the reform of his empire were its twin foundations: serfdom and autocracy. His grandmother, Catherine II, had educated him in the liberal traditions and assumptions of the Enlightenment, and for the first four years of his reign he aggressively pursued these notions. During his reign he attempted major reforms in the areas of education, government, and social welfare.

Russia, however, possessed neither an inventive and flexible ruling class nor economic wealth. Serfdom, a system that held millions of Russians in its grip, was socially repressive and economically inefficient. The autocratic system was simply inadequate to govern the world's largest state.

Unfulfilled Reformist Dreams

Alexander's experiments with limited serf emancipation, constitutionalism, and federalism demonstrated his desire for change. The tsar was all-powerful in theory, but in reality he depended on the nobles, who in turn gained their wealth from serfdom. Carrying out the necessary reforms would destroy the foundations of Alexander's power. The fact that his father and grandfather had been killed by nobles made him cautious. Further, it was his misfortune to rule during the Napoleonic wars, and for the first 15 years of his reign he had to devote immense amounts of money and time to foreign affairs. His liberal reform plans were never carried through to completion, and not until the 1850s, when it was almost too late, would there be another tsar willing and able to make the fundamental social and political reforms needed to make Russia competitive in the industrializing world.[10]

In the reactionary decade after 1815 reformers fell from favor. However, the open discussion of the need for change in the first part of Alexander's reign, the experiences of the soldiers returning from western Europe, and the activities of the expanding number of secret societies kept the dream of change alive. When Alexander failed to reform, the intensity of the reformers' discussions increased. Alexander died in December 1825, and there was confusion over which of his two brothers would succeed to the throne. The days between his death and the confirmation of his younger brother Nicholas I (1825–1855) gave a small circle of liberal nobles and army officers the chance to advance their ill-defined demands for a constitution. The officers who led this revolt had been infected with liberal French thought. They sought to end serfdom and establish representative government and civil liberties in Russia. On December 26 these liberals led a small uprising in St. Petersburg. This Decembrist Revolt, as it was called, lasted less than a day and could have been put down even earlier had Nicholas been more decisive. This abortive,

ill-planned attempt doomed any chance of liberal or democratic reform in Russia for 30 years.

Nicholas I and the Redefinition of Russia

The Decembrist incident shook Nicholas badly, and throughout his reign he remained opposed to liberal and revolutionary movements. He sponsored "official nationalism," whose conservative foundations were "autocracy, orthodoxy, and nationalism"—the Romanov dynasty, the Orthodox church, and a glorification of the Russian soul. He carried out a thorough policy of censorship that included the screening of foreign visitors, publications, and even musical compositions. The government closely monitored students' activities and curricula in schools and universities. Some 150,000 "dangerous" people were exiled to Siberia. Millions of non-Russians in the empire began to experience limitations on their identities through a forced adherence to Russian customs called "Russification." These activities strengthened Nicholas's immediate control and stopped potential upheaval, but he failed to address adequately the important social and political reforms Russia so badly needed.

Despite his efforts to control intellectual and political currents, Nicholas did not succeed. Reformist activity may have been repressed, but the Russian intellectual circles were creative, tuned as they were to the works of the German philosophers and poets. In the 1840s and 1850s a new breed of intellectuals appeared, thinkers devoted to achieving liberal and socialist political goals. Although they would not make their strength felt until after the 1860s, these thinkers, known as the *intelligentsia*, put down strong roots during Nicholas's reign. Alexander Herzen

When peaceful attempts to settle the Decembrist Revolt failed, Tsar Nicholas ordered troops to fire on the rebels. More than 60 people were killed in the brief fight. Putting down the revolt sounded the death knell for liberal reform in Russia.

(1812–1870) and Michael Bakunin (1814–1876) were the pioneers of this peculiarly Russian movement. Herzen was a moderate socialist who advocated emancipating the serfs, liberalizing the government, and freeing the press. In 1847 he went into exile in London, where he founded his famous paper, the *Kolokol* ("Bell"), ten years later. It was widely read in Russia, supposedly appearing mysteriously on the tsar's table. Bakunin, the father of Russian anarchism, was more radical. He believed that reform of Russia was useless and advocated terrorism. He preached that anarchy—complete freedom—was the only cure for society's ills. He too went into exile in the West.

The Russian intellectuals debated many questions, most important of which was whether Russia should imitate all aspects of European life or pursue its own tradition of Orthodoxy and a single-centered society. The question had been posed since the reign of Peter the Great. The liberal Westerners argued that if Russia wished to survive, it had to adopt basic aspects of the West and renounce much of its own past. The Slavophiles—like other Romantic movements—on the other side of the dialogue, renounced industrial Europe and the modern West, seeing them as materialistic, pagan, and anarchic. They looked to their distant past for guidance for the future.

Nicholas was able to maintain control to the extent that the 1830 and 1848 revolutions had little influence or impact on Russia. Some aspects of industrialization were introduced—for example, the first Moscow–to–St. Petersburg rail line was put into operation. The government appointed commissions to examine the questions of serfdom and reform, but these were extremely secret considerations.[11] Still, basic doubts about Russia's future remained. Dissident intellectuals, economic and social weakness, and autocratic stagnation were indicators that difficult times were in store for the country.

Alexander II and the Great Reforms

Russia's inept performance in the Crimean War (see Chapters 27 and 29) spotlighted the country's weaknesses and the need for reform. When Alexander II (1855–1881) came to the throne, even the conservatives among his subjects acknowledged the need for major change. The new tsar moved quickly to transform the basis of the autocratic structure—the institution of serfdom—but ran into delay from the nobility. Alexander appointed a committee, which after five years of deliberation drew up the Emancipation Proclamation, issued in March 1861. By this reform, 32 million state peasants and 20 million serfs who had no civil rights, could not own property, and owed heavy dues and services to the nobility began the transition to land ownership and citizenship.

The government paid the landlords a handsome price for the land that was to be turned over to the peasants. In return, the peasants had to pay the government for the land over a period of 49 years by making payments through their village commune, the *mir*. The drawn-out nature of the land transfer disappointed the former serfs, who had expected a portion of the lords' lands to be turned over to them without charge. Instead, the peasants were trapped in their village communes, which received and allocated all of the land—much of it poor—and divided it among the various families and paid taxes. Even though they were granted ownership of their cottages, farm buildings, garden plots, domestic animals, and implements, the restrictions placed on the peasants by confining them to their villages constituted a serious problem. New generations of peasants increased the population, but there was no corresponding increase in their share of the land.

The emancipation of the serfs was the single most important event in the domestic history of nineteenth-century Russia. It brought about thoroughgoing reforms of the army, judiciary, municipal government, and system of local self-government. One of the most important reforms came in 1864 when local government was transformed by the *Zemstvo* law. In the countryside the gentry, middle classes, and peasants elected representatives to local boards (*zemstvos*). These boards collected taxes and maintained roads, asylums, hospitals, and schools. The *zemstvos* became perhaps the most successful governmental organizations in Russia.[12]

The United Kingdom

Great Britain did not directly experience the revolutionary upheaval that afflicted the Continent, even though the island nation felt many of the same pressures as France at the same time. The post–Napoleonic War period was the most difficult time for Britain, as the transition back to a peacetime economy and the wrenching changes caused by industrialization made their effects felt. Some traditional workers lost their jobs due to the increasing use of machines, and in response, workers smashed the machines and destroyed some factories. Violence broke out when some working-class groups and radicals pushed for rapid reforms. The worst incident took place in August 1819 in what became known as the Peterloo Massacre. In Manchester a crowd of 60,000 gathered at St. Peter's Fields to push for parliamentary reforms. When the army was sent to disband the meeting, several people were killed and hundreds were injured.

British Flexibility

Britain's ruling class since the 1770s, the Tories were blind to the hardships of the workers. They continued to respond to the long-departed excesses of the French Revolution. Instead of dealing with the misfortunes of the poor and the unemployed, they declared that the doctrine of "peace, law, order, and discipline" should be their guide. To that end, they pushed through a series of repressive acts after 1815 that suspended the Habeas Corpus Act, restricted public meetings, repressed liberal newspapers, and placed heavy fines on literature considered to be dangerous. Massive conflict between the rich and poor appeared inevitable.

The duke of Wellington's failure to acknowledge the need for reforms in the 1830s so aroused the public that the "Iron Duke" and the Conservatives were forced to resign. They were replaced by a more liberal group, the Whigs. The drive toward self-interested changes by the upper classes had begun in the 1820s, led by Robert Peel (1788–1850) and George Canning (1770–1827). These two set in motion the British reform tradition that continued to 1914. When Wellington was voted out of office, Lord Charles Grey (1764–1845), leader of the Whig party, became head of government. In 1832 Grey pushed immediately to reform Parliament.[13]

Britain's political abuses were plain for all to see. Representation in the House of Commons was not at all proportional to the population. Three percent of the people dictated the election of members. The rapidly growing industrial towns such as Manchester and Birmingham—each with more than 100,000 citizens—had no representatives, while other areas, virtually without population, had delegates. After being blocked by aristocratic interests, first in the House of Commons and then in the House of Lords, reform bills responding to these electoral abuses were finally passed. But this occurred only because King William IV threatened to create enough new members of the House of Lords who would vote for the bills in order to pass them. Grey's reform bills did not bring absolute democracy, but they pointed the way toward a more equitable political system.

The Reformist Tide

Beginning in the 1820s, reformers pushed through laws that ended capital punishment for more than 100 offenses, created a modern police force for Lon-

Although Britain escaped the violent revolutions that occurred elsewhere in Europe during the nineteenth century, British critics, like the cartoonist whose work is pictured here, passionately lamented corruption in government and the loss of liberty suffered by British working-class citizens.

don, recognized labor unions, and repealed old laws that kept non-Anglican Protestants from sitting in Parliament. They also passed the Catholic Emancipation Act, which gave Roman Catholics voting rights and the rights to serve in Parliament and most public offices. The reform tide increased in the 1830s and 1840s. Abolitionist pressures brought about the ending of slavery in the British Empire in 1833. Parliament passed laws initiating the regulation of working conditions and hours. In 1835 the Municipal Corporations Act introduced a uniform system of town government by popular elections.

Britain's government was far from being a democracy, and in the 1830s and 1840s a strong popular movement known as Chartism developed. Its leaders summarized the country's needs in six demands: universal manhood suffrage, secret voting, no property qualifications for members of Parliament, payment of Parliament members so that the poor could seek election, annual elections, and equal districts. In 1839, 1842, and 1848 the Chartists presented their demands, backed by more than a million signatures on their petitions. But each time they failed to gain their goals, and the movement declined after 1848. By the end of the century, however, all of their demands, except that for annual parliamentary elections, had been put into law.

Mirroring the ascendancy of the middle classes, economic liberalism became dominant. A policy of free trade came to be favored because, given Britain's overwhelming economic superiority, the country could best profit from that approach. The Corn Laws' protective duties on imported grain, which had favored the gentry since 1815, no longer suited the industrializing British economy. These laws had been designed to encourage exports and to protect British landowners from foreign competition. By the middle of the century the population had grown to such an extent that British farmers could no longer feed the country, and the price of bread rose alarmingly.

The potato crop famine in Ireland in 1845 spotlighted the situation and the need for low-priced food from abroad. Repeal of the Corn Laws made possible the import of cheaper food. Soon Britain abandoned customs duties of every kind. The economy boomed under the stimulus of cheap imports of raw materials and food.

The Irish Problem

One dilemma escaped the solutions of well-meaning reformers, that of the British role in Ireland, which originated in the seventeenth century. The British placed large numbers of Scottish emigrants in the province of Ulster in northern Ireland, which built a strong colony of Protestants—the so-called Orangemen, or Scotch-Irish. In the eighteenth century the British passed a number of oppressive laws against Irish Catholics, re-

Chartists march their Grand Petition, calling for broader voting rights, to the House of Commons in 1842. Parliament rejected the petition, as it had in 1839 and would again in 1848.

Racked by poverty and famine, Ireland was further tormented during the 1840s by the mass eviction of tenant farmers. After the evictions, cottages were burned down at once to prevent other homeless farmers from occupying them.

stricting their political, economic, and religious freedom and effectively taking their lands. Passage of the Act of Union in 1801 forced the Irish to send their representatives to the Parliament in London, not Dublin. A large part of the Irish farmland passed into the hands of parasitic landlords who leased their newly gained lands in increasingly smaller plots to more and more people. Many peasants could not pay their rent and were evicted from the land. The Irish lost both their self-government and their livelihood.

The 1845 potato famine and its aftereffects led to a tremendous decline in population. Hundreds of thousands emigrated to the United States; perhaps as many as 500,000 people died. Between 1841 and 1891 the population fell by more than 40 percent, from 8.8 million to less than 5 million.

The Irish gained a few concessions from the British during the century in the form of the Catholic Emancipation Act (1829) and also received protection from arbitrary eviction for tenants during the Glorious Ministry. The Irish Anglican Church lost its favored position when Roman Catholics were freed of the obligation to pay tax support to a church they did not attend. In the 1880s Irish peasants were given the chance gradually to regain land that had once been theirs.

The United States

The revolutionary movements in Europe during the nineteenth century fought aristocratic domination or foreign rule—or both. The nineteenth-century struggles in the United States were not quite the same. Instead, there were two major related problems. One was the annexation, settlement, and development of the North American continent; the other was slavery. Free land and unfree people were the sources of the many political confrontations that culminated in the Civil War, the greatest struggle of nineteenth-century America.

At the conclusion of its successful revolution in 1783, the United States was not a democracy. When the Constitution of the new nation was ratified, only one male in seven had the vote. Religious requirements and property qualifications ensured that only a small elite participated in government. These restrictions allowed patricians from established families in the South and men of wealth and substance in the North to control the country for nearly half a century.

Democratic Advances

The influence of the western frontier helped make America more democratic. Even before the Constitution was ratified, thousands of pioneers crossed the Appalachian Mountains into the new "western country." In the West, land was to be had for the asking, and social caste did not exist—one person was as good as another. Vigor, courage, self-reliance, and competence counted, not birth or wealth. Throughout the nineteenth century the West was the source of new and liberal movements that challenged the conservative ideas prevalent in the East and South.

Until the War of 1812, democracy grew slowly. In 1791 Vermont had been admitted as a manhood suffrage state, and the following year Kentucky followed

In many regards, Andrew Jackson was the first "people's president," a national leader who looked beyond the demands of the eastern elites to the entire country. Jackson's craggy countenance projects his inner strength and independent spirit.
Memphis Brooks Museum of Art, Memphis, TN; Memphis Park Commission Purchase 46.2.

Territorial Growth of the United States

1803	Louisiana Purchase (part or all of present-day Louisiana, Arkansas, Missouri, Iowa, Minnesota, North Dakota, South Dakota, Nebraska, Kansas, Oklahoma, Colorado, Wyoming, Montana)
1818	British Cession (parts of Minnesota and North Dakota)
1810–1819	Florida Cession (parts of present-day Alabama and Mississippi; all of present-day Florida)
1845	Annexation of Texas (part or all of present-day Texas, Oklahoma, Kansas, New Mexico, Colorado)
1846	Oregon Country (parts of present-day Montana, Idaho, Wyoming; all of present-day Oregon and Washington)
1848	Mexican Cession (part or all of present-day Colorado, New Mexico, Utah, Nevada, Arizona, California)
1853	Gadsden Purchase (parts of present-day New Mexico and Arizona)

suit; but Tennessee, Ohio, and Louisiana entered the Union with property and tax qualifications for the vote. After 1817 no new state entered the Union with restrictions on male suffrage except for slaves. Most appointive offices became elective, and requirements for holding office were liberalized.

Andrew Jackson changed the tone and emphasis of American politics. In 1828 he was elected to the presidency following a campaign that featured the slogan "Down with the aristocrats!" He was the first president produced by the West, the first since George Washington not to have a college education, and the first to have been born in poverty. He owed his election to no congressional clique but rather to the will of the people, who idolized "Old Hickory" as their spokesman and leader.

The triumph of the democratic principle in the 1830s set the direction for political development. With Jackson's election came the idea that any man, by virtue of being an American citizen, could hold any office in the land. Governments widened educational opportunities by enlarging the public school system. With increased access to learning, class barriers became less important. The gaining and keeping of political power came more and more to be tied to satisfying the needs of the people who voted.

Discovery Through Maps

An American View of the World in the 1820s

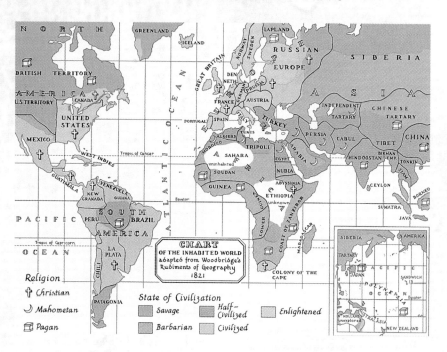

This map, adapted from *The School Atlas to Accompany Woodbridge's Rudiments of Geography*, served to inform students of the status of "civilization" in the world. The color code establishes where the authors believed the various gradations of humanity were: from the "civilized" and "enlightened" to the "savage," with the "barbarians" and "half-civilized" in between. The mapmakers were apparently quite certain that regions where white-skinned Christians were to be found were civilized or at least half-civilized (though they seem to have had their doubts about adherents of Orthodox Christianity in eastern Europe). The people where Islam predominated ranged from half-civilized to barbarian. And much of China, with its four millennia of culture, was classified as barbarian, owing to its "pagan" belief systems.

A complacent arrogance permeates this map, with the area west of the 95th meridian, populated largely by Native Americans, declared to be in a savage state, waiting patiently for Manifest Destiny to bring civilization. Much of Central and South America is admitted to being civilized—but not enlightened. Note also that the cartographer uses Philadelphia as the prime meridian—preferable, he surely thought, to the more traditional but distant Greenwich.

Simultaneous with the growth of democracy came the territorial expansion of the country. The Louisiana Territory, purchased from France for about $15 million in 1803 (see Chapter 22), doubled the size of the United States. In 1844 Americans, influenced by "manifest destiny," the belief that their domination of the continent was God's will, demanded "All of Oregon or none." The claim led to a boundary dispute with Great Britain over land between the Columbia River and 54'40" north latitude. In 1846 the two countries accepted a boundary at the 49th parallel, and the Oregon Territory was settled. The annexation of Texas in 1845 was followed by war with Mexico in 1846. In the peace agreement signed two years later Mexico ceded California, Texas, and the land between the two to the United States. As a result of these acquisitions, by 1860 the area of the United States had increased by two-thirds over what it had been in 1840.

The addition of the new territories forced the issue of whether slavery should be allowed in those areas. Paralleling developments in Great Britain, abolitionists in the United States, particularly in New England, vigorously condemned slavery. Henry Clay's Missouri Compromise of 1820 permitted slavery in Missouri but forbade it in the rest of the Louisiana

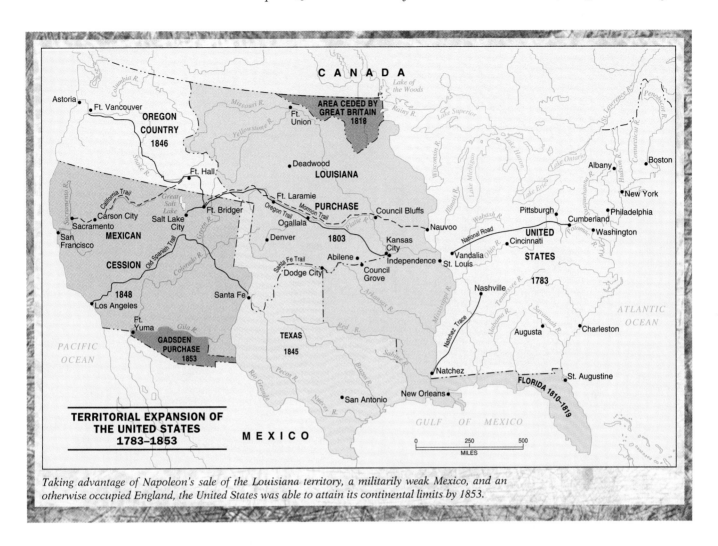

Taking advantage of Napoleon's sale of the Louisiana territory, a militarily weak Mexico, and an otherwise occupied England, the United States was able to attain its continental limits by 1853.

Purchase. This settlement satisfied both sides for only a short time. The antislavery forces grew more insistent. In the senatorial campaigns of 1858, candidate Abraham Lincoln declared:

> A house divided against itself cannot stand. I believe this government cannot endure permanently half slave and half free. I do not expect the Union to be dissolved—I do not expect the house to fall—but I do expect it will cease to be divided. It will become all one thing, or all the other.

Slavery was an important issue; it served as a focus for the differences and tensions separating the North from the South. However, a more fundamental cause of conflict was that in a sense, the two sections had become separate societies. The former was industrial, urban, liberal, and democratic; the latter was mainly agricultural, rural, conservative, and dominated by a planter aristocracy. The South strongly opposed the North's desire for higher tariffs, government aid for new railroads, and generous terms for land settlement in the West. These fundamental differences brought North and South to war. Slavery served as a potent symbol and as a moral irritant.

The United States and the World

From the first, U.S. foreign policy pursued three goals: national security, trade, and the spread of democracy. During its first quarter century, the United States fought a brief naval war with France, became embroiled with Britain in the War of 1812, and sent two expeditions to the Mediterranean to deal with the Barbary pirates. These complications notwithstanding, Americans spent the next century developing their country. Thomas Jefferson summarized the country's foreign policy with these words: "Peace, commerce, and honest friendship with all nations—entangling alliances with none."[14]

Early in the 1820s the policy of noninvolvement was seriously challenged when conservative members of the Quadruple Alliance offered to help the Spanish king regain control of Latin America. Both Britain and the United States viewed this possibility with alarm. George Canning, the British foreign secretary, suggested that his government and the United States make a joint declaration warning against European intervention in South America. U.S. President James Monroe seriously considered the invitation but decided against it.

The exuberance of the American West attracted artists such as George Caleb Bingham. The Jolly Flatboatmen in Port *presents a romantic and idealized vision of what was actually a dangerous and demanding way of life.*

George Caleb Bingham, *The Jolly Flatboatmen in Port,* 1857. The Saint Louis Art Museum, Purchase.

Instead Monroe proclaimed a unilateral doctrine in his message to Congress in December 1823. He warned the European powers against any attempt to impose their system in the Western Hemisphere and also declared that the United States had no intention of interfering in European affairs. In 1823 the United States could "have its cake and eat it too." The shield of the British fleet stood behind the Monroe Doctrine, with or without a formal alliance between Washington and London, and the United States avoided the complications and dangers inherent in European intervention.

It was sometimes difficult to reconcile the desire for isolation with the young country's stated love of freedom; for example, much sympathy was expressed for the Greeks as they fought against Turkish tyranny in the 1820s, but there was little active support. When the country established new foreign contacts, it went across the Pacific. In 1844 the United States made its first treaty with China, opening certain ports to American trade and securing the rights of American merchants and sailors to be tried in American tri-

bunals in China. In 1853 Commodore Matthew Perry visited Japan and, by a show of force, persuaded the Japanese to open some of their harbors to American ships (see Chapter 28). By 1854 the United States was considering the annexation of the Hawaiian Islands, and in 1867 it purchased Alaska from Russia for the amazingly low price of $7.2 million.

Emperor Napoleon III tested the Monroe Doctrine during the Civil War by sending over Maximilian to establish the Mexican Empire. While the war raged, northern protests did little to sway the French. But after 1865 the 900,000 veterans backing up the protests plus the actions of the Mexican patriots forced Napoleon to withdraw his military and financial support. In 1867 a Mexican firing squad executed Maximilian.

Conclusion

The Congress of Vienna dealt with the challenges of liberalism and nationalism as much as it confronted the classic problems of balance of power and compensation. The epidemic of revolutions in the 1820s, 1830s, and 1840s showed that the European patterns laid out in 1815 could not be maintained. In 1848 the legacy of the French Revolution and the process of industrialization combined to overpower the political structures of France, Germany, Italy, and the Habsburg Empire. The 1848 revolutions enjoyed brief, spectacular successes and tragic, lasting failures. The leaders of the revolutions had little or no experience, and they acted under a total infatuation with their ideals. The force of nationalism, so powerful an enemy of autocracy, soon proved to be a fragmenting force among the various liberated nationalities. These factors doomed the idealistic revolutionaries and introduced a new range of political alternatives, such as unification in Italy and the Second Empire in France.

Russia and Britain avoided the revolutionary upheavals of 1848, the first through a policy of repression that failed to respond effectively to its overwhelming problems and the second because of an improving standard of living and a flexible, self-interested middle class. For the rest of the century their paths would diverge as England would grow to establish a world empire while the Russians would struggle with reform and repression until the 1905 Revolution would finally bring an end to autocracy. Across the Atlantic, the United States profited by a massive influx of immigrants and became a leading Western power.

Suggestions for Reading

Important studies of the chief theorists of liberalism are David Lyons, *In the Interest of the Governed: A Study of Bentham's Philosophy of Utility and Law* (Clarendon Press, 1991), and Wendy Donner, *The Liberal Self: John Stuart Mill's Moral and Political Philosophy* (Cornell University Press, 1992). See also Jonathan Beecher, *Charles Fourier: The Visionary and His World* (University of California Press, 1986). A lively survey of the economic thinkers is Robert Heilbroner, *The Worldly Philosophers* (Touchstone, 1970). One of the best studies of European thought remains George L. Mosse, *The Culture of Western Europe: The Nineteenth and Twentieth Centuries*, 3rd ed. (Westview, 1988).

Harold George Nicolson, *The Congress of Vienna: A Study of Allied Unity, 1812–1822* (Compass, 1961), is a classic analysis of diplomatic interaction and a good companion to Henry A. Kissinger, *A World Restored: Metternich, Castlereagh, and the Problems of Peace, 1812–1822* (Sentry, 1957). The following are excellent on the general background to the period: Arthur James May, *The Age of Metternich, 1814–1848* (Holt, Rinehart and Winston, 1967); Eric J. Hobsbawm, *The Age of Revolution: Europe, 1789–1848* (Mentor, 1969); Jacob Leib Talmon, *Romanticism and Revolt: Europe, 1815–1948* (Harcourt, Brace & World, 1967); Peter N. Stearns, *European Society in Upheaval: Social History Since 1750* (Macmillan, 1967); Werner Eugen Mosse, *Liberal Europe: The Age of Bourgeois Realism, 1848–1878* (Harcourt Brace Jovanovich, 1974); and John Weiss, *Conservatism in Europe* (Harcourt Brace Jovanovich, 1977).

A. J. P. Taylor, *The Course of German History* (Capricorn, 1962), is a short, controversial essay on German national history since the French Revolution. Theodore S. Hamerow, *Restoration, Revolution, Reaction: Economics and Politics in Germany, 1815–1871* (Princeton University Press, 1958), remains an important book. Lewis B. Namier, *1848: The Revolution of the Intellectuals* (Oxford University Press, 1992), is critical of the liberals at Frankfurt. Otto Pflanze, *Bismarck and the Development of Germany: The Period of Unification, 1815–1871*, 2nd ed. (Princeton University Press, 1990), is first-rate.

Volume 4 of Alfred Cobban's *History of Modern France* (Penguin, 1970) is a useful survey. For greater detail, see Frederick B. Artz, *France Under the Bourbon Restoration, 1814–1830* (Russell, 1931); T. E. B. Howarth, *Citizen King: The Life of Louis-Philippe* (Verry, 1961); Georges Duveau, *1848: The Making of a Revolution*, trans. Anne Carter (Harvard University Press, 1984); and Frederick Arthur Simpson, *Louis Napoleon and the Recovery of France* (Greenwood, 1975). See also Brison Gooch, *The Reign of Napoleon III* (Rand McNally, 1970).

David Mack Smith, *Mazzini* (Yale University Press, 1996), is a first-rate study of the campaigner for Italian unification. Derek Bayles gives the most thorough coverage of the Italian unification movement in *The Risorgimento and the Unification of Italy* (Allen & Unwin, 1982). Frank Murtaugh explains the reasons behind Sardinia's prominence in *Cavour and the Economic Modernization of the Kingdom of Sardinia* (Garland, 1991). A notion of the complexity of the nationalities question in the Habsburg realm can be found in Peter F. Sugar and Ivo John Lederer, eds., *Nationalism in Eastern Europe* (University of Washington Press, 1969). Barbara Jelavich, *The Habsburg Empire in European Affairs* (Rand McNally, 1969), is an excellent brief history. Carlile Aylmer Macartney, *The Habsburg Empire, 1790–1918* (Weidenfeld & Nicholson, 1968), is thorough but pro-Hungarian. Alan Sked, *The Decline and Fall of the Habsburg Empire, 1815–1918* (Longman, 1989), provides a fresh view of unexpected strengths and weaknesses of the Vienna-based empire.

J. N. Westwood, *Endurance and Endeavour: Russian History, 1812–1992* (Oxford University Press, 1993), is the best new survey, replacing Hugh Seton-Watson, *The Russian Empire, 1801–1917* (Oxford University Press, 1967). Allen McConnell, *Tsar Alexander I* (Cromwell, 1970), remains the best short biography. W. Bruce Lincoln, *In the Vanguard of Reform* (Northern Illinois University Press, 1982), sets the standard for scholarship on Nicholas I. Deep insights into Russian intellectual development are to be found in Nicolas Berdyaev, *The Russian Idea* (Lindisfarne, 1992). The best introductory book on nineteenth-century Russia is Marc Raeff, *Understanding Imperial Russia* (Columbia University Press, 1984).

Two valuable surveys on Britain are Asa Briggs, *The Making of Modern England, 1783–1867: The Age of Improvement* (Torchbooks, 1959), and E. Llewellyn Woodward, *The Age of Reform, 1815–1870* (Oxford University Press, 1962). The tragedy of the Irish famine is thoroughly analyzed in Joel Mokyr, *Why Ireland Starved: A Quantitative and Analytical History of the Irish Economy, 1800–1850* (Allen & Unwin, 1983). David Thomson, *England in the Nineteenth Century, 1815–1914* (Penguin, 1991), and J. B. Conacher, ed., *The Emergence of British Parliamentary Democracy in the Nineteenth Century* (Wiley, 1971), are valuable general accounts.

For a brief and stimulating survey of the first half of U.S. history, see Marcus Cunliffe, *The Nation Takes Shape, 1789–1837* (University of Chicago Press, 1959). Also recommended is Arthur M. Schlesinger Jr., *The Age of Jackson* (Little, Brown, 1988). A good chance to read great literature and fine biography is Carl Sandburg' three-volume biography of *Lincoln* (many editions). A critique of the American scene that has become a classic is Alexis de Tocqueville's *Democracy in America* (many editions). For the economic and social changes taking place in the United States in the first half of the nineteenth century, see James L. Huston, *Securing the Fruits of Labor: The American Concept of Wealth Distribution* (Louisiana State University Press, 1998).

Suggestions for Web Browsing

The Revolution of 1848
http://history.hanover.edu/texts/fr1848.htm

Site includes original source documents from the Revolution of 1848 in France.

Revolutions of 1848
http://www.pvhs.chico.k12.ca.us/~bsilva/projects/revs/1848time.html

Extensive site offers an overview, timeline, biographies, and essays about the revolutions of 1848.

Life of the Tsars
http://www.Alexanderpalace.org/catherinepalace/Alexander.html

Images portraying the luxury of life for the tsars in the nineteenth century.

The Lewis and Clark Expedition
http://www.peabody.harvard.edu/Lewis&Clark/

Lewis and Clark brought back an enormous collection of material, which is housed at the Peabody Museum at Harvard.

Nationalism and Music
http://acc6.its.brooklyn.cuny.edu/~phalsall/sounds/fnlandia.mid

Through articles and sound files, this site discusses how early-nineteenth-century music reflected growing nationalist feelings in Europe.

Notes

1. Peter F. Sugar, "External and Domestic Roots of Eastern European Nationalism," in Peter F. Sugar and Ivo John Lederer, eds., *Nationalism in Eastern Europe* (Seattle: University of Washington Press, 1969), pp. 3–21.
2. Robert L. Heilbroner, *The Worldly Philosophers* (New York: Simon & Schuster, 1972), pp. 40–72.
3. William Godwin, "Political Justice," in Sidney Hook, ed., *Marx and the Marxists: The Ambiguous Legacy* (New York: Van Nostrand, 1955), p. 28.
4. Quoted in Edwin R. Seligman, ed., *Encyclopedia of the Social Sciences*, Vol. 13 (New York: Macmillan, 1935), p. 510a.
5. Norman Davies, *Heart of Europe: A Short History of Poland* (Oxford: Oxford University Press, 1987), pp. 166–167.
6. Barbara Jelavich, *The Habsburg Empire in European Affairs, 1814–1918* (Chicago: Rand McNally, 1969), pp. 21–39.
7. Jorg K. Hoensch, *A History of Modern Hungary, 1867–1986* (London: Longman, 1988), pp. 4–10.
8. Quoted in J. S. Schapiro, *Modern and Contemporary European History, 1815–1940* (Boston: Houghton Mifflin, 1940), p. 222.
9. For vivid characterizations of this period, see Roger L. Williams, *The World of Napoleon III, 1851–1870* (New York: Collier, 1962).
10. See Allen McConnell, *Tsar Alexander I: Paternalistic Reformer* (New York: Crowell, 1970), for a clear treatment of this complex personality.
11. W. Bruce Lincoln, *In the Vanguard of Reform* (De Kalb: Northern Illinois University Press, 1982), pp. 139–167.
12. J. N. Westwood, *Endurance and Endeavour: Russian History, 1812–1986* (Oxford: Oxford University Press, 1987), pp. 79–103.
13. G. Bingham Powell Jr., "Incremental Democratization: The British Reform Act of 1832," in Gabriel A. Almond, Scott C. Flanagan, and Robert J. Mundt, eds., *Crisis, Choice, and Change* (Boston: Little, Brown, 1973), p. 149.
14. Quoted in Foster Rhea Dulles, *America's Rise to World Power, 1898–1954* (New York: Harper & Row, 1955), p. 4.

Following France's defeat in the Franco-Prussian War, the Second Reich of the German Empire was proclaimed on January 21, 1871, in the Hall of Mirrors at the Palace of Versailles outside Paris. (The first Reich was the Holy Roman Empire.) The new emperor, William I, stands on the dais, but the central figure in the painting is the white-coated Otto von Bismarck, the first chancellor of the new empire.

Power Politics in the West, 1861–1914

Chapter Contents

After 1861 Western politics would be built on the basis of *Realpolitik*, realism in politics. Realpolitik disregards theory or idealism and emphasizes the practical application of power to gain state goals, no matter the damage to ethics or morality. The European map changed once again as Bismarck united Germany and the Balkan states struggled to gain national independence. In North America another country centralized using the same methods as those of Realpolitik as the United States of America came together after a bloody and brutal civil war and the devastation of its indigenous population. The United Kingdom, with its control of world markets, its technologies, and its wealth, had the luxury of continuing its dominance in more discreet ways.

All of the Western states engaged in mass participation politics after 1861. They built modern political systems that more or less effectively tapped the resources of their countries while responding more or less efficiently to the demands of their people. Germany, France, the United Kingdom, and the United States were the best at these tasks and dominated Western politics. Russia, Italy, and Austria-Hungary fell behind. Their political infrastructures presented obstacles to effective government. Russia limped along, an autocracy attempting to modernize itself; Italy suffered from regional fragmentation and economic weakness; and Austria-Hungary remained paralyzed by nationalistic discord.

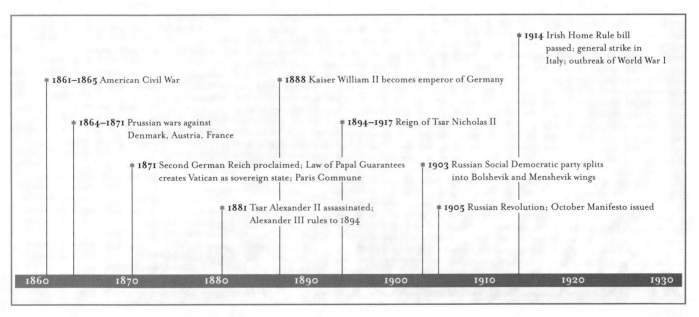

1861–1865 American Civil War

1864–1871 Prussian wars against Denmark, Austria, France

1871 Second German Reich proclaimed; Law of Papal Guarantees creates Vatican as sovereign state; Paris Commune

1881 Tsar Alexander II assassinated; Alexander III rules to 1894

1888 Kaiser William II becomes emperor of Germany

1894–1917 Reign of Tsar Nicholas II

1903 Russian Social Democratic party splits into Bolshevik and Menshevik wings

1905 Russian Revolution; October Manifesto issued

1914 Irish Home Rule bill passed; general strike in Italy; outbreak of World War I

1860   1870   1880   1890   1900   1910   1920   1930

Germany United

A stalemate occurred in 1862 when King William I wanted to strengthen his army but the Chamber of Deputies would not vote the necessary funds. The liberals asserted the constitutional right to approve taxes, while the king equally strongly expressed his right to build up his forces. As the king struggled with this constitutional crisis, he called Otto von Bismarck (1815–1898) home from his post as Prussian ambassador to France and made him prime minister.

Bismarck advised the king to ignore the legislature and collect the needed taxes without the Chamber's approval. Bismarck knew the necessity of armed strength in order to gain Prussia's diplomatic goals. Ironically, his later military victories would gain him the support of many of the liberals whom he had encouraged the king to defy.

Otto von Bismarck

Bismarck's entry on the scene in Berlin strengthened not only the king but also the hopes of all who wanted a united German state. Unification appealed to virtually all segments of German society, from the liberals to the conservatives, such as the historian Heinrich von Treitschke, who stated, "There is only one salvation! One state, one monarchic Germany under the Hohenzollern dynasty."[1] Berlin, through its leadership of the *Zollverein*, sponsorship of the confederation of northern German states, and efficient bureaucracy, was the obvious choice for the capital of a unified German state. With the arrival of Bismarck, the Prussians gained the necessary leadership for unification.

The prime minister was a master of the art of Realpolitik. He had the intelligence to assess the actual state of conditions, the insight to gauge the character and goals of his opponents, and the talent to move

Otto von Bismarck, the "Iron Chancellor," was the shrewd and masterful prime minister of Prussia from 1862 and the first chancellor of the united Germany from 1871 to 1890.

skillfully and quickly. Unlike most of his colleagues, he was a master image maker, so effective that historians have used his epithet "blood and iron" to describe his career. Few statesmen have ever accomplished so much change with such a comparatively small loss of life in a controlled use of war. Bismarck was a master politician who knew that force was the final card to be played, to be used as the servant of diplomacy and not its master.[2]

Some historians have attributed his successes to mere luck, whereas others have deemed them products of genius. An example is his approach to Russia. Bismarck knew that he would have to solidify relations with Russia, and he achieved this in 1863 by promising the Russians that he would aid them in all Polish-related problems. Giving up virtually nothing, he gained a secure eastern flank and proceeded to set up three wars that brought about German unification.

The Danish and Austrian Wars

In 1864 Bismarck invited Austria to join Prussia and wage war on Denmark. The cause of the conflict was

---

Steps to German Unification

1862	Bismarck appointed prime minister
1863	Russian-Prussian accord on Poland
1864	War with Denmark
1866	War with Austria; establishment of North German Confederation
1870	War with France
1871	Proclamation of the Second German Empire (Reich) at Versailles

THE UNIFICATION OF GERMANY
1815–1871

- ☐ Prussia, 1815–1866
- ☐ Annexed by Prussia, 1866
- ☐ Joined Prussia in forming the North German Confederation, 1867
- ☐ Joined with Prussia to form the German Empire, 1871
- ☐ Alsace-Lorraine ceded to German Empire by France, 1871
- ── German Confederation, 1815–1866

The Hohenzollerns, based in Berlin, began the process of linking their widely spread territories in the seventeenth century. Napoleon contributed to a consolidated German state through his rearrangement of the map after his military conquests, and Bismarck completed the unification of Germany by 1871.

the disputed status of two duchies, Schleswig and Holstein, bordering on Prussia and Denmark and claimed by both. The two Germanic powers overwhelmed the modest Danish forces and split the duchies: Austria took Holstein, and Schleswig went to Prussia. With his eastern and northern flanks stabilized, Bismarck set out to isolate Austria.

Italy was already hostile to the Austrians and remained so when Bismarck promised it Venetia in return for its assistance in the future war. He encouraged the French to be neutral by intimating that Prussia might support France should it seek to widen its borders. Severe domestic crises with the Hungarians absorbed Austria, which soon found itself isolated. The Prussian leader provoked war with Vienna by piously expressing alarm at the manner in which the Austrians were ruling Holstein and sending troops into the province. Austria took the bait, entered the war, and was devastated by the Prussians

at the battle of Sadowa. In this Seven Weeks' War, the Prussians avenged the "humiliation of Olmütz" of 1850.

Prussia offered a moderate peace settlement that ended the old German Confederation. In its place Bismarck formed the North German Confederation, with Austria and the southern German states excluded. Prussia annexed several territories, including Hanover, Mecklenburg, and other states north of the Main River, in this penultimate stage in the unification of Germany.

The War with France

After 1867 Bismarck turned his attention westward to France and Napoleon III. The French leader had allowed himself to be talked into neutrality in 1866 because he anticipated a long war between his German

Bismarck and the Ems Dispatch

Bismarck knew how to manipulate public opinion through press leaks and doctored documents. See how he altered the Ems dispatch to achieve his goals vis-à-vis France.

I made use of the royal authorization communicated to me through Abeken, to publish the contents of the telegram; and in the presence of my two guests I reduced the telegram by striking out words, but without adding or altering, to the following form:

After the news of the renunciation of the hereditary Prince of Hohenzollern had been officially communicated to the imperial government of France by the royal government of Spain, the French ambassador at Ems further demanded of his Majesty the King that he would authorize him to telegraph to Paris that his Majesty the King bound himself for all future time never again to give his consent if the Hohenzollerns should renew their candidature. His Majesty the King thereupon decided not to receive the French ambassador again, and sent to tell him through the aide-de-camp on duty that his Majesty had nothing further to communicate to the ambassador.

The difference in the effect of the abbreviated text of the Ems telegram as compared with that produced by the original was not the result of stronger words but of the form, which made this announcement appear decisive, while Abeken's version only would have been regarded as a fragment of a negotiation still pending, and to be continued at Berlin.

After I had read out the concentrated edition to my two guests, Moltke remarked: "Now it has a different ring; it sounded before like a parley; now it is like a flourish in answer to a challenge."

From *Bismarck: The Man and the Statement*, trans. A. J. Butler (1899).

neighbors that would weaken both of them and because he hoped to expand into the neutral state of Belgium. In August 1866 Napoleon approached Bismarck for his share of the fruits of victory, but the German leader refused to agree to French demands. Frustrated and offended, Napoleon III insisted that Prussia approve France's annexation of Luxembourg and Belgium. In a crafty move, Bismarck invited the French envoy to Berlin to put these demands into writing but still avoided giving a definite response.

Four years later Bismarck sent the document to the British in order to gain their sympathy for the upcoming war with the French. After France's active participation in the Crimean War, there was no chance that Russia would come to Napoleon's aid. Bismarck let the Austrians know about France's cooperation with the Prussians during the 1866 war, and Italy was not about to help Napoleon III after his activities in 1859. By 1870 France was isolated. It was simply a question now of Bismarck maneuvering the French into war.

The immediate controversy centered on the succession to the Spanish throne left vacant after a revolution had overthrown the reactionary Queen Isabella. The Spaniards asked Leopold, a Hohenzollern prince, to become the constitutional king of their country. France saw this as an unacceptable extension of Prussian influence, and Leopold withdrew his candidacy. But this was not enough for Paris. The French sent their ambassador to Ems, where the Prussian king was vacationing, to gain from him a pledge that he would not again permit Leopold to seek the Spanish throne. This was not a reasonable request, and the king refused to agree to it. After the interview he directed that a message be sent to Bismarck, describing the incident. Bismarck altered the message of this "Ems dispatch" to give the impression that the French ambassador had insulted the Prussian king and that the king had returned the insult. The rumor was leaked to the press and infuriated both the Germans and the French.

France declared war in July. The two countries' forces appeared to be evenly matched in equipment, but the Germans had a better-trained and more experienced army. In two months the Prussians overwhelmed the French, delivering the crowning blow at the battle of Sedan, where the emperor and his army were surrounded and forced to surrender. Troops of the combined armies of the German states besieged the north of France for four months before the final French capitulation. By the Treaty of Frankfurt, France lost Alsace and a part of Lorraine to Germany and was required to pay a large indemnity. In the Hall of Mirrors at Versailles, the Second Reich was proclaimed, and William I was crowned German emperor. The call for revenge of France's defeat and humiliation became a major issue in French politics.

The New Imperial Structure

Within the brief span of one lifetime, the fragmented German areas of central Europe successfully united under Prussian (Hohenzollern) leadership to challenge Britain for world domination. Bismarck provided the initial genius to bring about unification, but the source of German strength was found in its rapid economic growth, population increase, and efficient political structure. Prussia's success drew the enthusiastic support of prominent businessmen, intellectuals, and artists and the increasing concern of its neighbors.

The Second Reich came into existence at a ceremony in January 1871 in the Hall of Mirrors at the Palace of Versailles. There King William I became emperor *(Kaiser)* of a federal union of 26 states with a population of 41 million. The bicameral (two-house) legislature of the new empire consisted of the *Bundesrat*, representing the ruling houses of the various states, and the *Reichstag*, representing the people through its 397 members elected by male suffrage. Dominant power rested with the emperor, who controlled military and foreign affairs and the 17 votes in the Bundesrat needed to veto any constitutional change. The actual head of government was the chancellor who was appointed by the kaiser and responsible to him only. This arrangement allowed the chancellor to defy or ignore the legislature if it served his purpose. However, he had to operate within the constraints of the federal state structure in which large powers of local government were given to the member states.

Bismarck as Chancellor

As chancellor, Otto von Bismarck built modern Germany on his belief in the inherent efficiency of a state based on one faith, one law, and one ruler. He distrusted institutions that did not fit that tripartite formula—specifically, the Catholic Church and the Socialist party. Bismarck was more constrained in domestic than in foreign affairs. It is not surprising, therefore, that he fared better in foreign matters.

The Catholic political party had sent a large bloc of representatives to the Reichstag in 1871, and these members supported the complete independence of the church from state control, denounced divorce, objected to secular education, and questioned freedom of conscience. Many Catholics strongly supported the new dogma of papal infallibility. Within the Protestant Prussian part of Germany, Bismarck introduced anti-Catholic policies that triggered a conflict known as the *Kulturkampf* (struggle for civilization). These so-called May Laws made it an offense for the clergy to criticize the government, regulated the educational activities of the religious orders, and expelled the Jesuits from the country. The state also required civil marriages and dictated that all priests study theology at state universities. Pope Pius IX declared these acts null and void and told loyal Catholics to refuse to obey them. Many of the

chancellor's laws applied equally to Protestants, who actively protested them.

As opposition spread, Bismarck struck hard at the Catholics, imprisoning priests, confiscating church property, and closing down pulpits. When the tide did not turn in his favor, he realized that he could not afford to create millions of martyrs. Showing his shrewd sense of power, he cut his losses, retreated, and repealed most of the anti-Catholic laws.

The Social Democratic (Marxist) movement posed a greater challenge to Bismarck's rule. The party's founder, Ferdinand Lassalle (1825–1864), rejected violence as a means to gain power and instead advocated working within the existing political structure. After his death the movement retained its nonviolent nature. The party's popularity soared when it was officially established in 1875, and its leaders pushed for true parliamentary democracy and wider-ranging social programs. In 1878 Bismarck used two attempts on the emperor's life as an excuse to launch an all-out campaign to weaken the Social Democrats, even though they had no connection with the assassination attempts. He dissolved extralegal socialist organizations, suppressed their publications, and threw their leaders in jail. Despite these measures, the socialists continued to gain support.

When he failed to weaken the socialists by direct confrontation, the chancellor changed tactics. He decided to undercut them by taking over their program. Through the 1880s he implemented important social legislation that provided wage earners with sickness, accident, and old-age insurance. He sponsored other laws that responded to many of the abuses workers encountered. Still, the Social Democrats continued to grow in size and influence. However, by creating the first welfare state, the pragmatic Prussian chancellor defused a potential revolution.

Kaiser William II

In 1888 William II, the grandson of the emperor, became head of the Reich. Just as Bismarck had dominated European affairs since 1862, the new emperor would play a key role until 1918. Here was a person who advocated a policy of "blood and iron," but without Bismarck's finesse. Where Bismarck knew the limits and uses of force and appreciated the nuances of public statements, William was a militarist and a bully. Serving in a modern age, the new emperor still believed in the divine right of kings and constantly reminded his entourage that "he and God" worked together for the good of the state. With such a contrast in styles, it is not surprising that William saw Bismarck not as a guide but as a threat. He once stated that "it was a question of whether the Bismarck dynasty or the Hohenzollern dynasty should rule."[3] Finally, in March 1890, Bismarck resigned.

Kaiser William II's Naval Ambitions

Kaiser William knew Germany had a grand future, an expanding future. He also wanted Germans to travel on the high seas, to the dismay of the British.

In spite of the fact that we have no such fleet as we should have, we have conquered for ourselves a place in the sun. It will now be my task to see to it that this place in the sun shall remain our undisputed possession, in order that the sun's rays may fall fruitfully upon our activity and trade in foreign parts, that our industry and agriculture may develop within the state and our sailing sports upon the water, for our future lies upon the water. The more Germans go out upon the waters, whether it be in the races of regattas, whether it be in journeys across the ocean, or in the service of the battle-flag, so much the better will it be for us. For when the German has once learned to direct his glance upon what is distant and great, the pettiness which surrounds him in daily life on all sides will disappear.

From C. Edward Gauss, *The German Kaiser as Shown in His Public Utterances* (New York: Scribner, 1915).

At the beginning of the twentieth century Germany presented a puzzling picture to the world. On the one hand, the blustering kaiser made fiery and warlike statements. He encouraged militarism and the belief that *"Alles kommt von oben"* ("Everything comes down from above"). On the other hand, his thoroughly advanced country made great scientific and cultural strides. Observers of German affairs noted that one-third of the voters supported the Social Democrats, an indication of a healthy parliamentary system. A commonly held pride in Germany's accomplishments knit the country together.

More important than William's behavior was the fact that by the beginning of the new century the Germans competed actively in all areas with the British. Although Germany did not outproduce Britain, long-term projections showed that the island nation's growth had leveled out and that in the next generation the Reich would surpass it. The Germans dominated the world market in the chemical and electrical industries and were making strides in other areas. They boasted a more efficient organization of their industries, a higher literacy rate for their workers, better vocational training, and a more aggressive corps of businessmen. German labor unions were less combative than the British, and the government gave more support to industry than Parliament did. When the kaiser demanded a navy the equal of that of England, alarm bells went off in London.

France: The Search for Equilibrium

The defeat of France's Second Empire at Sedan in 1870 gave birth to the Third Republic. The humiliating peace terms, which stripped France of part of Lorraine and all of Alsace and imposed a huge indemnity on the country, created a desire for revenge. The spectacle of the Germans crowning their emperor and proclaiming the Second Reich at Versailles, the symbol of French greatness, left a bitter taste. The stark contrast between the promised grandeur of the Second Empire and the humiliation of 1871 left a legacy of domestic uncertainty and an obsession for revenge against the Germans.

The Third Republic: A Shaky Beginning

Persistent class conflicts, covered over during Louis Napoleon's reign, also contributed to many years of shaky existence before the republic gained a firm footing. A new and overwhelmingly royalist national assembly was elected to construct a new, conservative government after the signing of the peace. This, added to the shock of the defeat, touched off a revolutionary outburst that led to the Paris Commune of 1871.

Parisians had suffered such severe food shortages during the siege of the city that some had been forced to eat rats and zoo animals. When it turned out that their sacrifices had been in vain, republican and radical Parisians joined forces in part of the city to form a commune, in the tradition of the 1792 Paris Commune, to save the republic. The Communards advocated government control of prices, wages, and working conditions (including stopping night work in the bakeries). After several weeks of civil strife, the Commune was savagely put down. Class hatred split France further yet.

Because the two monarchist factions that constituted a majority could not agree on an acceptable candidate for the monarchy, they finally settled on a republic as the least disagreeable form of government. The National Assembly approved the new republican constitution in 1875. Under the new system, members of the influential lower house, the Chamber of Deputies, were elected by direct suffrage. There was also a Senate, whose members were elected indirectly by electoral colleges in the departments. The constitution established a weak executive, elected by the legislature. The ministry exercised real power, but its authority depended on whatever coalition of parties could be assembled to form a tenuous majority in the legislature.

The Boulanger and Dreyfus Affairs

The stormy tenure of the Third Republic was marked by a series of crises, including anarchist violence culminating in a series of bombings in 1893, financial scandals such as the notorious Panama Canal venture that implicated a wide range of leading figures, and lesser scandals. The two most serious threats were the Boulanger and Dreyfus affairs.

The weak and traumatized republic was both threatened and embarrassed by the public cries for vengeance uttered in 1886 by General Georges Boulanger (1837–1891), the minister of war. This charismatic, warmongering figure made a series of speeches, which he ended by emotionally proclaiming: "Remember, they are waiting for us in Alsace." The considerable number of antirepublicans saw him as a man on horseback who would sweep away the republic in a coup d'état, much as Louis Napoleon had done in 1851, and bring back French grandeur. The government finally ordered Boulanger's arrest on a charge of conspiracy, and he fled the country. Later he committed suicide.

The Dreyfus case was far more serious because it polarized the entire country, divided and embittered French opinion by the anti-Semitic fervor it unleashed, and challenged the fundamental ideals of French democracy. Captain Alfred Dreyfus (1859–1935), the first Jewish officer on the French general staff, was accused in 1894 of selling military secrets to Germany. His fellow officers tried him, found him guilty, stripped him of his commission, and condemned him to solitary confinement on Devil's Island, a dreadful convict settlement off the northeast coast of South America. Even with the case supposedly settled, military secrets continued to leak to the Germans, and subsequently a royalist, spendthrift officer named Major Esterhazy was accused, tried, and acquitted.

The case became a cause célèbre in 1898 when the French writer Émile Zola (1840–1902) wrote his famous letter *J'accuse* ("I accuse"), in which he attacked the judge for knowingly allowing the guilty party to go free while Dreyfus remained in jail. The next year Esterhazy admitted his guilt, but by that time the entire country had split into two camps. On the one side were the anti-Dreyfusards—the army, church, and royalists; on the other side were the pro-Dreyfusards—the intellectuals, socialists, and republicans. The case was once again placed under review in the military courts, and even though Esterhazy had confessed, the court continued to find Dreyfus guilty. Finally, the French president pardoned him, and in 1906 the highest civil court in France found him innocent.

Captain Alfred Dreyfus had to pass through this "Guard of Dishonor" each day on his way to the courtroom during his second trial in 1899.

The case had greater significance than just the fate of one man. Those who had worked against Dreyfus, especially the church, would pay dearly for their stand. Many republicans believed that the church, a consistent ally of the monarchists, was the natural enemy of democratic government. They demanded an end to the church's official ties to the state. In 1904 and 1905 the government closed all church schools and rescinded the Napoleonic Concordat. All ties between church and state were formally ended.

After weathering 40 difficult years, by 1914 the Third Republic had gained prosperity and stability. Workers had found their voice in the country as the various trade and local union groups came together in the *Confédération Générale du Travail*, the General Confederation of Labor. Monarchists and other right-wing parties still had considerable influence, although the Dreyfus affair had weakened them.

French republicanism had wide support across the political spectrum. Most French citizens enjoyed basic democratic rights, which they exercised through the extremely complex multiparty political system of the republic. The various ministries that were constructed from the fragile coalitions came and went with bewildering rapidity. Yet France was strong and prosperous, one of only two republics among the world's great powers.

Italy to 1914

Italy's most troubling problem was the question of the papacy, which seriously weakened the state. The pope, the spiritual father of most Italians, refused to accept the incorporation of Rome into the new nation. He called himself the "prisoner of the Vatican," and encouraged—with little effect—his Italian flock not to vote. In an attempt to satisfy the pope, the government in 1871 passed the Law of Papal Guarantees, which set up the Vatican as a sovereign state and allocated the pope an annual sum of $600,000 (roughly the amount of money he had received from his previously held lands). Pius IX rejected the offer, but the state refused to repeal the law.

Despite conflicting and unstable political parties, the new Italian state carried on an impressive program of railroad building, naval construction, and attempts at social and welfare legislation. But major problems remained, especially with the peasantry in the south. Radical political parties made their presence felt after the turn of the century in the form of widespread strikes. In 1900 an anarchist assassinated King Umberto, who had taken the throne in 1878. Change proceeded slowly after that, and not until 1912 did the country gain universal manhood suffrage, a time when there was still widespread illiteracy.

The Italian leaders' ambition to make Italy a world power placed a great burden on the nation. Money spent on the army came at the expense of needed investments in education and social services. National resources were squandered in an unsuccessful attempt to build an empire in Africa.

Up to the beginning of World War I, Italy faced severe economic crises and labor unrest. In June 1914 a general strike spread through the central part of the peninsula. Benito Mussolini, editor of a socialist journal, played a key role in this movement. Attempts to achieve compulsory education, freedom of the press, and better working conditions did little to ease the economic hardships and high taxes that had driven thousands to emigrate to the United States. The south especially suffered, because it had not shared in the industrial gains of the northern part of the country.

The Dual Monarchy

After the Austrians' disastrous defeat by Prussia, Franz Joseph was forced to offer the Hungarians an equal partnership with Vienna in ruling the empire. The offer was accepted, and in 1867 the constitution known as the *Ausgleich* (compromise) was enacted. This document created the Dual Monarchy, in which the Habsburg ruler was both the king of Hungary and the emperor of Austria—defined as the area that was not part of Hungary. Each country had its own constitution, language, flag, and parliament. Ministers common to both countries handled finance, defense, and foreign affairs, but they were supervised by "delegations," which consisted of 60 members from each parliament who did not meet together, except in emergency circumstances. The *Ausgleich* was to be renegotiated every ten years.

By the end of the century the Dual Monarchy contained 12 million Germans, 10 million Hungarians, more than 24 million Slavs, and 4 million Romanians, among other nationalities. Although the Germans of Austria had recognized the equality of the Hungarians, the rest of the nationalities continued to live under alien rule. Now, instead of having to deal with one dominant national group, they had to cope with two. In some cases, as in the prospering, cosmopolitan, and sophisticated area of Bohemia-Moravia, the people wanted an independent state or, at the very least, more rights within the Habsburg realm. Other groups, such as the Serbs, sought the goal of joining their countrymen living in adjacent national states. The nationalities question remained an explosive problem for the authorities in Vienna and Budapest.

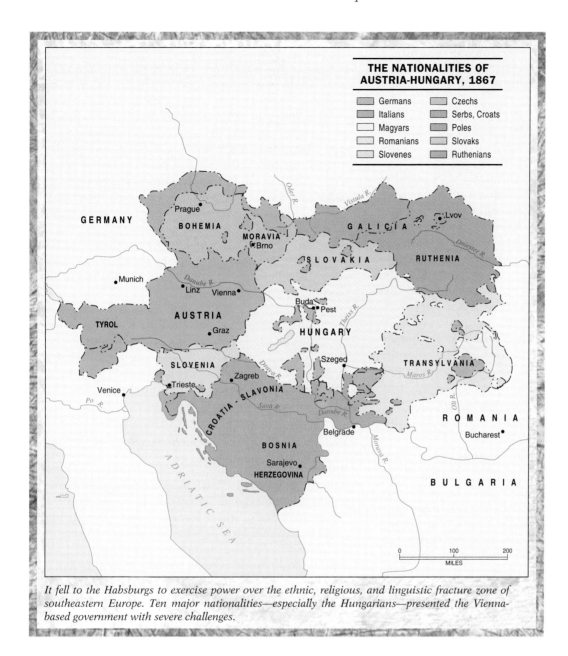

THE NATIONALITIES OF AUSTRIA-HUNGARY, 1867

- Germans
- Italians
- Magyars
- Romanians
- Slovenes
- Czechs
- Serbs, Croats
- Poles
- Slovaks
- Ruthenians

It fell to the Habsburgs to exercise power over the ethnic, religious, and linguistic fracture zone of southeastern Europe. Ten major nationalities—especially the Hungarians—presented the Vienna-based government with severe challenges.

The functioning of the Dual Monarchy was best symbolized by the official banknotes, which were printed in eight languages on one side and in Hungarian on the other. In the Hungarian part of the Dual Monarchy the aristocracy governed under the Kossuth constitution of 1848. The Hungarians refused to share rule with the minorities in their kingdom. A small, powerful landed oligarchy dominated the mass of backward, landless peasants. The conservative leadership carried out a virtual process of Magyarization with their minorities while they continually squabbled with the Austrians.

In the Austrian portion, wealthy German businessmen and the landed aristocracy dominated political life. But even with this concentration of power, the government was much more democratic, especially after 1907, when the two-house legislature was elected by universal manhood suffrage. Here, too, nationalism was a serious problem, and political parties came to be based not on principle but on nationality. Each nationality had to work with the Germans, even though it might detest them. The nationalities frequently disliked one another, and this prevented the formation of any coalitions among them. By 1914 the Austrians had extended substantial local self-government to their subject nationalities, but this concession did little to quiet discontent.

The *Ausgleich* functioned poorly, yet its defenders could still tell themselves that they were, after all, citizens of a "great empire." The Dual Monarchy occupied a strategic geographical location and had enough military strength to be very influential in the Balkans. In addition, the area had great economic potential, with Hungarian wheat, Croatian and

Slovenian livestock, Czech banks and industry, and Austrian commerce. But Franz Joseph ruled over a disjointed conglomeration of peoples who shared only the pretension of being citizens of a great power.

Russia in Reform and Revolution

While Alexander II pushed through the "Great Reforms," the revolutionary movement grew stronger. In the 1850s the nihilist movement developed, questioning all old values, championing the freedom of the individual, and shocking the older generation. At first the nihilists tried to convert the aristocracy to the cause of reform. Failing there, they turned to the peasants in an almost missionary frenzy. Some of the idealistic young men and women joined the movement to work in the fields with the peasants, while others went to the villages as doctors and teachers to preach the message of reform. This "go to the people" campaign was known as the populist, or *narodnik*, movement. Not surprisingly, the peasants largely ignored the outsiders' message.

Revolutionary Response

Frustrated by this rejection, the idealistic young people turned more and more to terrorism. The radical branch of the nihilists, under the influence of Bakunin's protégé Sergei Nechaev (1847–1882), pursued a program of the total destruction of the status quo, to be accomplished by the revolutionary elite. In *Revolutionary Catechism*, Nechaev stated that "everything that promotes the success of the revolution is moral and everything that hinders it is immoral." The soldiers in the battle, the revolutionaries, were "doomed men," having "no interests, no affairs, no feelings, no habits, no property, not even a name."[4] The revolution dominated all thoughts and actions of these individuals.

For the 20 years after his emancipation of the serfs, Alexander suffered under increasing revolutionary attack. It was as though the opposition saw each reform not as an improvement but as a weakness to be exploited. In Poland the tsar had tried to reverse the Russification program of his father and in return saw the Poles revolt in 1863. Would-be assassins made a number of attempts on him, and the violence expanded throughout the 1870s as a number of his officials were attacked by young terrorists such as Vera Zasulich (1851–1919). Finally, Alexander was assassinated in 1881, on the very day he had approved a proposal to call a representative assembly to consider new reforms.

Reaction, 1881–1905

The slain tsar's son, Alexander III (1881–1894), could see only that his father's reforms had resulted in increased opposition and eventually death. Consequently, he tried to turn the clock back and reinstate the policy of "autocracy, Orthodoxy, and nationalism." Under the guidance of his chief adviser, Constantine Pobedonostsev (1827–1907), Alexander pursued a policy of censorship, regulation of schools and universities, and increased secret police activities. Along with renewing Russification among the minorities, he permitted the persecution of Jews, who were bullied and sometimes massacred in attacks called *pogroms*. The tsar may have been successful in driving the revolutionaries underground or executing them, and the nationalities may have been kept in their place, but under Alexander III Russia lost 13 valuable years in its attempt to become economically and politically competitive with western Europe.

Succeeding Alexander was his son, Nicholas II (1894–1917), a decent but weak man. He inherited and retained both his father's advisers and his father's policies. Larger forces overwhelmed him. Industrialization and rural overpopulation exerted a wide range of political pressures, and the autocratic structure could not cope.

Political Alternatives to Autocracy

Russia lacked a tradition of gradual reform and the habits of compromise such as existed in England. After the assassination of Alexander II, the government increasingly used brutal force to keep order. At the same time, it did little to help the people suffering in the transition from an agrarian to an industrial society. The regime worked energetically to eliminate the opposition by placing secret agents among them, launching violent assaults, and carrying on diversionary anti-Semitic activities with bands of thugs called the Black Hundreds.

By attacking the opposition, the tsarist government concentrated on a symptom of Russia's problems, rather than their causes—the repeated failure to carry out effective reform. Despite the best efforts of the tsars to crush all opposition movements, political parties opposing the autocracy flourished.

The Liberal party (Constitutional Democrats, or *Kadets*) wanted a constitutional monarchy and peaceful reform on the British model. Although limited in numbers, because of the elevated social standing of most of their members, the Kadets were a powerful voice for change in Russia.

The much more numerous Social Revolutionaries combined non-Marxist socialism with the *narodnik* tradition and simplistically called for "the whole land for the whole people." These agrarian socialists wanted to give the land to the peasants. However, they lacked a unified leadership and a well-thought-out program.

In this troubled environment, the solutions proposed by Karl Marx attracted a number of supporters. Marx himself did not believe that Russia would be a favorable laboratory for his theories. He expressed surprise when *Das Kapital* was translated into Russian in 1872 but was pleased when he learned of the broad impact of his theories. Not until 1898, however, was there an attempt to establish a Russian Social Democratic party made up of radical intellectuals and politically active workers.

The Russians did not experience the most demanding parts of industrialization until the end of the century and then on a different basis from that of the western European countries. Russia remained an overwhelmingly agrarian society in which the state paid for building factories by using grain produced by the peasants for export on the depressed world market. The Social Democrats looked to Marx to show them the way to a complete social, economic, and political revolution. However, the urban, industrial emphasis of Marx's theories sparked debate over the way in which they applied to Russia. This debate led to fragmentation of the Marxist movement into Bolshevik, Menshevik, Jewish Bund, and Polish factions by 1903 (see Chapter 29).

The Revolution of 1905 and Its Aftermath

As in 1854 at Crimea, a failure in war—this time a "splendid little war" against Japan—exposed the weaknesses of the autocratic tsarist regime (see Chapter 28). Strikes and protests spread throughout the land in response to the military failure in the last days of 1904. On January 22, 1905, the Cossacks opened fire on a peaceful crowd of workers who had advanced on the Winter Palace in St. Petersburg carrying a petition asking for the tsar's help. In response, a general strike broke out, with the strikers demanding a democratic republic, freedom for political prisoners, and the disarming of the police. *Soviets*—councils of workers led by the Social Democrats—appeared in the cities to direct revolutionary activities. Most business and government offices closed, and the whole machinery of Russian economic life creaked to a halt. The country was virtually paralyzed.

After a series of half-measures and stalling in response to strikes and revolutionary activities, the tsar found himself pushed to the wall. Unable to find a dictator to impose order, he was forced to issue the October Manifesto of 1905, which promised "freedom of person, conscience, assembly, and union." A national legislature, the Duma, was to be called without delay. The right to vote would be extended, and no law could be enacted without the Duma's approval. The October Manifesto split the moderate from the socialist opposition and kept Nicholas on the throne,

Russian Political Movements in 1905

Kadets	Liberals
Octobrists	Moderate liberals
Trudoviks	Populist Labour party
Socialist Revolutionaries	Non-Marxist, agrarian-based socialists
Bolsheviks	Revisionist, democratic centralist Social Democrats (Marxists)
Mensheviks	Social Democrats, Marxist fundamentalists
Monarchist right	Supporters of the tsar
Union of Russian People	Extreme right wing, anti-Semitic and antiliberal
Jewish Bund	Marxist Jewish Workers' party

although he was heartbroken for having made the compromise. The socialists tried to start new strikes, but the opposition was now totally split apart.

Most radical forces boycotted the first Duma meeting in the spring of 1906. As a result, the Kadets became the dominant force. Even with this watered-down representation, the tsar was upset by the criticism of the government's handling of the Russo-Japanese War, treatment of minorities, handling of political prisoners, and economic policies. Claiming that the representatives "would not cooperate" with the government, Nicholas dissolved the first Duma. The Russian people turned a cold shoulder to the Kadets' appeals for support. Sensing the decline of political fervor, Nicholas appointed a law-and-order conservative, Peter Stolypin (1862–1911), as prime minister. He assumed emergency powers and cracked down on the radicals.

Unlike previous tsarist appointees, Stolypin knew that changes had to be made, especially in the area of agriculture. Stolypin set up a process to develop a class of small farmers despite Nicholas's lack of support. He pushed through reforms that abolished all payments still owed by the peasants under the emancipation law and permitted peasants to withdraw from the commune and claim their shares of the land and other wealth as private property. He also opened lands east of the Urals to the peasants and extended financial aid from the state. He was well on the way to finding a solution to that most enduring of Russian problems, the peasant problem, before he was assassinated

On January 22, 1905, Russian imperial troops opened fire on a crowd of peaceful demonstrators gathered outside the Winter Palace in St. Petersburg. The day is known in history as Bloody Sunday.

in 1911 by a Socialist Revolutionary, who was also an agent of the secret police.[5]

Despite its reactionary tsar and nobility, Russia took major steps toward becoming a constitutional monarchy in the years after 1905. The nation made great economic and social progress. Industrialization increased and generated new wealth. Increased political and civil rights spawned an active public life. Stolypin's death in 1911, however, deprived the country of needed leadership, and the First World War gave Russia a test it could not pass.

The United Kingdom and Its Dominions

In the mid-1800s an alliance of the landed gentry and the middle classes worked together to dominate the British government and to keep the lower classes "in

their stations." The newly ascendant middle classes believed that political reforms had gone far enough, and the Whig government of Lord Palmerston, who served as prime minister from 1855 to 1865, reflected this view. But the final third of the century would belong to the reforming politicians among the Liberals and Conservatives who had to face the fact that the complacency of government during the "Victorian Compromise" from 1850 to 1865 could not continue. Serious problems plagued the country. Only one adult male in six was entitled to vote. Both parties felt the pressure to make the political system more representative. Both parties also knew that reform must come, and each hoped to take the credit and gain the resultant strength for extending the vote. Thanks to its wealth and adaptability, Britain built a truly democratic political structure by 1914. The state continued to support business even as it became more intimately involved in matters affecting the welfare of its citizens.

Gladstone and Disraeli

Two great statesmen, William Ewart Gladstone (1809–1898), a Liberal, and Benjamin Disraeli (1804–1881), a Conservative, dominated the first part of this period with their policies of gradual reform. They alternated as prime minister from 1867 to 1880. After Disraeli's death, Gladstone prevailed until he retired in 1894. The two leaders came from sharply contrasting backgrounds. The son of a rich Liverpool merchant, Gladstone had every advantage that wealth and good social position could give him. He entered Parliament in 1833 and quickly became one of the great orators of his day. He began as a Conservative, working in the tradition of the Tory reformer Robert Peel. Gradually he shifted his alliance to the newly formed Liberal party in the 1850s and became a strong supporter of laissez-faire economics and worked to keep government from interfering in business. He was far more effective as a political reformer than as a social or economic one.

Disraeli had few of Gladstone's advantages. The son of a Jew who became a naturalized British subject in 1801, Disraeli was baptized an Anglican. He first made a name for himself as the author of the novel *Vivian Grey* (1826). In contrast to Gladstone, Disraeli went from liberalism to conservatism in his philosophy. He stood for office as a Conservative throughout his career and became the leader of the party.

The Liberals' turn came first. In 1866 they introduced a moderate reform bill giving city workers the vote. Some Conservatives opposed it, fearful that increasing the franchise would bring the day of revolution closer. When the proposal failed to pass, political agitation and riots rocked the country. The outbreaks evidently impressed the members of Parliament, and when the Conservatives came to power in 1867, Disraeli successfully sponsored the Second Reform Bill, which added more than a million city workers to the voting rolls. The measure increased the electorate by 88 percent, although women and farm laborers were still denied the vote.

Even though the Conservatives passed the voter reform bill, the new elections in 1868 brought the Liberals back to power, and Gladstone began his so-called Glorious Ministry, which lasted until 1874. With the granting of the vote to the urban masses it became imperative to educate their children. The Education Act of 1870 promoted the establishment of local school boards to build and maintain state schools. Private schools received governmental subsidies if they met certain minimal standards. Elementary school attendance, which was compulsory between the ages of 5 and 14, jumped from 1 to 4 million in ten years.

Other reforms included a complete overhaul of the civil service system. Previously, in both the gov-

In this Punch *cartoon, political rivals William Gladstone (left) and Benjamin Disraeli (right) are ready to sling mud at each other. The cartoon's caption reads, "A Bad Example."*

ernment and the military, appointments and promotions depended on patronage and favoritism. But in 1870 this method was replaced by open examinations. The government also improved the military by shortening enlistment terms, abolishing flogging, and stopping the sale of officers' ranks. Gladstone's government successfully revamped the justice system and introduced the secret ballot. Finally, some restrictions on labor unions' activities were removed. By 1872 the Glorious Ministry had exhausted itself, and Disraeli referred to Gladstone and his colleagues in the House of Commons as a "range of exhausted volcanoes."

Disraeli's government succeeded the Glorious Ministry in 1874, and he stated that he was going to "give the country a rest." He was no stand-pat Conservative, however. He supported an approach known as Tory democracy, which attempted to weld an alliance between the landed gentry and the workers against the middle class. Even during this "time of rest" Disraeli's government pushed through important reforms in public housing, food and drug legislation, and union rights to strike and picket peacefully.

Gladstone returned to power in 1880 and continued the stream of reforms with the Third Reform Bill, which extended the vote to agricultural workers. This act brought Britain to the verge of universal male suffrage. Gladstone also secured passage of the

Employers' Liability Act, which gave workers rights of compensation in case of accidents on the job.

He tried to solve the Irish question, but none of the concessions made up for the lack of home rule, and the Irish patriot Charles Stewart Parnell (1846–1891) began to work actively to force the issue through Parliament. Gladstone introduced home rule bills in 1886 and 1893, but both were defeated. A home rule bill was finally passed in 1914, but by this time the Ulsterites strongly opposed the measure and prepared to resist their forced incorporation into Catholic Ireland. The outbreak of war with Germany postponed civil strife, but it was only a two-year delay until the Easter Uprising of 1916. Not until 1921 did southern Ireland finally gain the status of a British dominion. The home rule bill never went into effect.

The New Liberals

Gladstone's fight for Irish home rule split his party and paved the way for a decade of Conservative rule in Britain (1895–1905). Partly because of foreign and imperial affairs, the Conservatives departed from the reformist traditions of Tory democracy. By 1905 the need for social and political reform again claimed the attention of the parties.

More than 30 percent of the adult male laborers earned a weekly wage equivalent to $7. Such an unacceptably low wage made it impossible to save for periods of unemployment and emergencies. Workers demonstrated their discontent in a number of strikes. Partly in response to the workers' needs and at the prompting of British socialists, the Labour party was founded in 1900, under the leadership of J. Ramsay MacDonald (1866–1937), a self-made intellectual who had risen from humble status, and the Scottish miner Keir Hardie (1856–1915). The Liberals found themselves threatened on both their left and right flanks. They decided to abandon their laissez-faire economic concepts and embrace a bold program of social legislation. The radical Welsh lawyer David Lloyd George portrayed their program thusly: "Four spectres haunt the poor: Old Age, Accident, Sickness, and Unemployment. We are going to exorcise them."[6]

Led by Prime Minister Herbert Asquith, Lloyd George, and the young Winston Churchill, who had defected from the Conservatives, the Liberal party—with the aid of the Labour bloc—put through a broad program. It provided for old-age pensions, national employment bureaus, workers' compensation protection, and sickness, accident, and unemployment insurance. In addition, labor unions were relieved of financial responsibility for losses caused by strikes. Members of the House of Commons, until that time unpaid, were granted a modest salary. This last act allowed an individual without independent wealth to pursue a political career.

The House of Lords tried to block the Liberal reform plan by refusing to pass the 1909–1910 budget, which laid new tax burdens, including an income tax, on the richer classes in order to pay for the new programs. The Liberals and Labour fought back by directly attacking the rationale for the Lords' existence. They argued that a hereditary, irresponsible upper house was an anachronism in a democracy. The result was the Parliament Bill of 1911, which took away the Lords' power of absolute veto. Asquith announced that the king had promised to create enough new peers to pass the bill if needed (a tactic used with the 1832 Reform Bill). The Lords had to approve and thereafter could only delay and force reconsideration of legislation.

By 1914 the evolutionary path to democracy and a modern democratic state structure had been largely completed, except for women's suffrage. In the previous generation some effort had been made to gain the vote for women, to little effect. Women's suffrage was not a concern for the major parties, whose leaders for the most part felt that women's proper place was in the home. At the turn of the century the most effective group working for women's rights was the Women's Social and Political Union (WSPU), whose members were the first to be known as "suffragettes." The founder of the group, Emmeline Pankhurst (1858–1928), first agitated, then disturbed, and then challenged the order and stability of England in the decade before World War I. Pankhurst and her colleagues traveled and worked constantly to make their case, and in 1910 the WSPU abandoned traditional rhetoric in favor of mass marches, hunger strikes, and property damage. In 1913 a young suffragette martyred herself by running in front of the king's horse at the Derby.[7] With the outbreak of the war, the WSPU backed the national effort against the Germans, and finally in 1918 women age 30 and over were granted the vote. Ten years later, they gained equal voting rights with men.

The Dominions

Supporting the United Kingdom as allies, customers, and suppliers of raw materials were its Dominions. The British Dominions became self-governing without breaking their political ties to Great Britain. With the exception of South Africa, these new nations were predominantly British in stock, language, culture, and governmental traditions. In the case of Canada, however, a strong French-speaking minority in Quebec, inherited from the original French regime, persisted and preserved its French heritage. In South Africa, following a confused history of rivalry and war between the British and Dutch settlers, a shaky union was achieved. There were no complications of rival Europeans in Australia and New Zealand, which were settled by the British in the beginning and did not have to adjust to an influx of

Emmeline Pankhurst, in white scarf, at a rally protesting a government unresponsive to women's issues. After 1910 the women's suffrage movement turned increasingly militant.

other Europeans. Both Australia and Canada attained political unity by merging a number of colonies into a single government.

In South Africa, after a bloody war with the Boers ended in 1902, the British extended the right of self-government to the Transvaal in 1906 and to the Orange Free State two years later. The Liberal government in Great Britain permitted the Boer and English states to unite and form the Union of South Africa in 1909. Only seven years after the war, Boer and Briton joined hands to create a new self-governing dominion. The first prime minister of the Union was Louis Botha (1863–1919), who had been a Boer general in the war. Botha's primary purpose was to create neither an English nor a Boer nationality but a blend of the two in a new South African patriotism held together by their shared desire to keep the black majority firmly repressed (see Chapter 27).

The discovery of Australia dates back to the seventeenth century, when Dutch explorers sighted its shores. Captain Cook's South Seas voyage in 1769, however, paved the way for British settlement. In 1788 Britain transported a group of convicts to Australia

and settled them at Sydney. From the parent colony of Sydney, later called New South Wales, five other settlements were founded. Although a majority of the first Europeans in Australia were prisoners, most of them were political prisoners and debtors, rather than hardened criminals. After seven years of servitude, many were liberated and, as "emancipists," became citizens. Quite early in the nineteenth century, many free settlers also came to Australia. They began to protest the dumping of convicts in their new home, and Britain took the first steps to end the practice in 1840. By 1850 the Australian colonies were enjoying a liberal form of self-government. In 1901 the six Australian colonies formed a federal union known as the Commonwealth of Australia, which bears many resemblances to the American system of government.

About 1000 miles from the Australian mainland is a group of islands, two of which are of particular importance. These lonely projections of British influence in the South Pacific constitute the self-governing Dominion of New Zealand. The population of this country, which is slightly smaller than Great Britain in area, is just over 3.3 million. The earliest white

Discovery Through Maps

The British Empire in 1886

In comparison with James Reynolds's comparatively no-nonsense map in Chapter 24, in this map the geography is almost secondary. The map details the global span of Britain's empire and includes an inset showing the much smaller extent of British holdings a century earlier. But the map is almost of secondary importance.

The borders of the map express true pride of empire. Banners at the top proclaim "Freedom," "Frater-nity," and "Federation." Along the left side an Indian chief, a Canadian trapper, and admiring woman, a policeman, and a sailor look out at an Indian elephant and its keeper, the "great white hunter," who with his complacent tiger and his Indian bearer are marching toward Britannia sitting atop the World, surrounded by adoring subjects.

settlers were convicts who had escaped from penal settlements in Australia. The activity of other colonizers forced the British government to assume protection of the islands in 1840, and British agents signed a treaty guaranteeing certain rights, especially land rights, to the original inhabitants, the Maoris.

Canada came into English control in 1763. London tried to ensure the loyalty of the French Canadians by issuing a royal proclamation guaranteeing the inhabitants' political rights and their freedom to worship as Roman Catholics. These guarantees were strengthened in 1774 when the British government passed the Quebec Act, called the "Magna Carta of the French Canadian race." This act reconfirmed the position of the Catholic Church and perpetuated French laws and customs. However, there was no provision for a representative assembly, such as existed in English-speaking colonies.

The period from 1763 to 1867 is known as the formative stage of Canada. A number of developments took place during this period: the growth of the English-speaking population, the defeat of an attempted conquest by the United States, the grant of local self-government, and finally the confederation of Canada into a dominion. Fear of the United States, the need for a common tariff policy, and a concerted effort to develop natural resources led Canadians into confederation. A plan of union, the British North American Act, was approved by the British government and passed by Parliament in London in 1867. This act united Canada into a federal union of four provinces. The new government had some similarities to the political organization of the United States, but it adopted the British cabinet system, with its principle of ministerial responsibility. As a symbol of its connection with Great Britain, provision was made for a governor-general who was to act as the British monarch's representative to Canada.

The new nation encountered many problems from the first. Its vast size caused communication problems, which became even more acute in 1869 when the dominion purchased the territories of the Hudson's Bay Company, extending from present-day Ontario west to the Pacific coast and south to the Columbia River. In 1871 the new colony of British Columbia joined the dominion on the promise of early construction of a transcontinental railroad to link the west coast with eastern Canada. Another disturbing problem was the lack of good relations with the United States. After the Civil War, Irish patriots in the United States, seeking revenge against the British for their treatment of Ireland, launched armed incursions over the border. However, in 1871 the major differences between the two countries were ironed out in the Treaty of Washington, a landmark in the use of arbitration.

The country developed rapidly under the leadership of the dominion's first prime minister, Sir John A. Macdonald (1815–1891), who served from 1867 to 1873 and again from 1878 to 1891. Canadians developed their country through encouraging new industry, building a transcontinental railroad in 1885, and attracting immigrants. Sir Wilfrid Laurier (1841–1919), who served as prime minister from 1896 to 1911, continued Macdonald's work. Between 1897 and 1912 Canada received 2.25 million new citizens, bringing the total population to more than 7 million. Internal restructuring created new provinces out of the former Hudson's Bay Company holdings, so that in 1914 the dominion consisted of nine provinces. At the same time, the country had to deal with the consequences of its rapid growth: labor discontent, corruption, and agrarian unrest. Canada was becoming a mature nation, with all of the accompanying problems of depressions, unequal distribution of wealth, and governmental restraint of business. At the end of the nineteenth century, although Canada was a united political structure, a common Canadianism had not been achieved. The French had no intention of being absorbed by the culture of the majority.

The United States

The Civil War and Its Results

Soon after Abraham Lincoln was inaugurated as president, the slaveholding southern states seceded from the Union and formed the Confederate States of America. The first shot of the Civil War was fired at Fort Sumter, South Carolina, in 1861, initiating the bloodiest war experienced by any Western nation to that time. Four agonizing years of conflict—in which more than half a million men died and basic elements of the Constitution and law were suspended—ended when General Robert E. Lee surrendered to General Ulysses S. Grant at Appomattox Courthouse in Virginia in April 1865. A few days later the nation was stunned by the assassination of President Lincoln, who had just begun his second term.

With the final collapse of the Confederacy before the overwhelming superiority of the Union in manpower, industrial resources, and wealth, the Civil War became the grand epic of American history in its heroism, romance, and tragedy. The victorious North used military occupation to try to force the South to extend voting and property rights to the former slaves. Eventually, this so-called Reconstruction period (1865–1877) was ended by a tacit agreement between the northern industrialists and the southern white leaders that enabled the latter to regain political control and to deprive African Americans of their newly won rights. Later, southerners invoked "Darwinian" arguments to justify their actions in denying full "blessings of freedom" to the former slaves.

Southern politicians deprived African Americans of their voting rights by enacting state laws or employing devices such as poll taxes, literacy tests, property qualifications, and physical threats. Racial segregation in schools, restaurants, parks, and hotels was effectively applied. Laws prohibiting interracial marriage were enacted, and African Americans were generally excluded from unions. Between 1885 and 1918 more than 2500 African Americans were lynched in the United States. As second-class citizens, free but landless, the former slaves essentially formed a sharecropping class, mired in poverty and deprived of educational opportunities. It took more than a century after the Civil War for black Americans to gain a politically equal footing.[8]

As director of agricultural research at the Tuskegee Institute, George Washington Carver derived many new products from southern crops.

"With Malice Toward None": Lincoln's Second Inaugural Address

March 4, 1865, started out dark and rainy. Lincoln spoke only briefly, delivering the shortest inaugural address of any president, before or since. Afterward, as he took the oath of office, the sun came out. Chief Justice Salmon P. Chase, administering the oath, said he hoped that the sunshine would be an "omen of the dispersion of the clouds of war." Indeed it was: the hostilities lasted only a few weeks longer—but they cost Lincoln his life.

At this second appearing to take the oath of the presidential office, there is less occasion for an extended address than there was at the first. Then a statement, somewhat in detail, of a course to be pursued, seemed fitting and proper. Now, at the expiration of four years, during which public declarations have been constantly called forth on every point and phase of the great contest which still absorbs the attention, and engrosses the energies of the nation, little that is new could be presented. The progress of our arms, upon which all else chiefly depends, is as well known to the public as to myself; and it is, I trust, reasonably satisfactory and encouraging to all. With high hope for the future, no prediction in regard to it is ventured.

On the occasion corresponding to this four years ago, all thoughts were anxiously directed to an impending civil-war. All dreaded it—all sought to avert it. While the inaugural address was being delivered from this place, devoted altogether to *saving* the Union without war, insurgent agents were in the city seeking to *destroy* it without war—seeking to dissol[v]e the Union, and divide effects, by negotiation. Both parties deprecated war; but one of them would *make* war rather than let the nation survive; and the other would *accept* war rather than let it perish. And the war came.

One eighth of the whole population were colored slaves, not distributed generally over the Union, but localized in the Southern part of it. These slaves constituted a peculiar and powerful interest. All knew that this interest was, somehow, the cause of the war. To strengthen, perpetuate, and extend this interest was the object for which the insurgents would rend the Union, even by war; while the government claimed no right to do more than to restrict the territorial enlargement of it. Neither party expected for the war, the magnitude, or the duration, which it has already attained. Neither anticipated that the *cause* of the conflict might cease with, or even before, the conflict itself should cease. Each looked for an easier triumph, and a result less fundamental and astounding. Both read the same Bible, and pray to the same God; and each invokes His aid against the other. It may seem strange that any men should dare to ask a just God's assistance in wringing their bread from the sweat of other men's faces; but let us judge not that we be not judged. The prayers of both could not be answered; that of neither has been answered fully. The Almighty has His own purposes. "Woe unto the world because of offences! for it must needs be that offences come; but woe to that man by whom the offence cometh!" If we shall suppose that American Slavery is one of those offences which, in the providence of God, must needs come, but which, having continued through His appointed time, He now wills to remove, and that He gives to both North and South, this terrible war, as the woe due to those by whom the offence came, shall we discern therein any departure from those divine attributes which the believers in a Living God always ascribe to Him? Fondly do we hope—fervently do we pray—that this mighty scourge of war may speedily pass away. Yet, if God wills that it continue, until all the wealth piled by the bond-man's two hundred and fifty years of unrequited toil shall be sunk, and until every drop of blood drawn with the lash, shall be paid by another drawn with the sword, as was said three thousand years ago, so still it must be said "the judgments of the Lord, are true and righteous altogether."

With malice toward none; with charity for all; with firmness in the right, as God gives us to see the right, let us strive on to finish the work we are in; to bind up the nation's wounds; to care for him who shall have borne the battle, and for his widow, and his orphan—to do all which may achieve and cherish a just, and a lasting peace, among ourselves, and with all nations.

From Richard N. Current, ed., *The Political Thought of Abraham Lincoln* (Indianapolis, Ind.: Bobbs-Merrill, 1967), pp. 314–316.

If the causes and consequences of the American Civil War are complex, the all-important result was simple. It settled the issue of whether the United States was an indivisible sovereign nation or a collection of sovereign states. The sacrifice of hundreds of thousands of lives preserved the Union, but the inhuman treatment of African Americans remained.

Development, Abuse, and Reform

The North's victory was a boost for industrialization as well as a result of it, and the economic revolution in the United States that followed was more significant than the conflict itself. Railroads were built across broad prairies, and the first transcontinental line, the Union Pacific, was completed in 1869. Settlers swarmed west, breaking treaties with Native American tribes, altering the environmental balance that supported the lives of the Plains Indians, and destroying the way of life of the original inhabitants of the land.

Between 1850 and 1880 the number of cities with a population of 50,000 or more doubled. The number of men employed in industry increased 50 percent. In 1865 there were 35,000 miles of railroads in the country. By 1900 this was estimated to be about 200,000—more than in all of Europe. In 1860 a little more than $1 billion was invested in manufacturing; by 1900 this figure had risen to $12 billion. The value of manufactured products increased proportionately. In 1870 the total production of iron and steel in the United States was far below that of France and Britain. Twenty years later the United States had outstripped them and was producing about one-third of the world's iron and steel.

In the age of rapid industrialism and materialistic expansion, many who pursued profits lost sight of ethical principles in business and in government. William "Boss" Tweed, the chief of the Department of Public Works for the city of New York, rewarded himself and his friends so lavishly through fraudulent contracts, payments under the table, and other corrupt activities that by 1871 he had driven the city to the brink of bankruptcy. Brought to trial, Tweed was convicted of stealing more than $200 million. Ruthless financiers, such as Jay Gould and Jim Fisk, tampered with the basic financial stability of the nation. The administration of President Ulysses Grant was tainted by scandals and frauds. A new rich class failed to appreciate its responsibilities to society. Corruption was a blatant feature of the new order.

For roughly a century the gospel for the new nation of America had been rugged individualism. As in Europe, governmental interference in business was unwelcome because of the strong belief that individuals should be free to follow their own inclinations, run their own businesses, and enjoy the profits of their labors. In an expanding nation where land, jobs, and opportunity beckoned, there was little to indicate that the system would not work indefinitely. By 1880, however, the end of the frontier was in sight. Free land of good quality was scarce, and the frontier could no longer serve as a safety valve to release the economic and social pressures of an expanding population.

Between 1850 and 1900 the United States became the most powerful nation in the Western Hemisphere, increased its national wealth from $7 billion to $88 billion, established an excellent system of public education, and fostered the spread of civil liberties for its white citizens and other nations. But there were many disturbing factors in the picture. Unemployment, child labor, and industrial accidents were common in the rapidly growing cities. Slums grew and served as breeding places for disease and crime. Strikes, often accompanied by violence, exacerbated the tension between labor and capital.

In response, the wide-ranging Progressive reform movement flourished between 1890 and 1914. This movement was rooted partly in the agrarian protests against big business sparked by the Populists of the Midwest and the South. The Progressives effectively mobilized the middle classes to work to eliminate sweatshops, the exploitation of labor, and the abuse of natural resources.

The success of the Progressive movement was reflected in the constitutions of the new states admitted to the Union and in their introduction of the direct primary, the initiative and referendum, and the direct election of senators. All these measures tended to give the common people more effective control of the government. After the enactment of the Interstate Commerce Act in 1887, which introduced federal regulation over railroads, a steady expansion of governmental regulation of industry began.

Theodore Roosevelt, one of the most flamboyant and effective presidents in the history of the United States, provided cartoonists at the beginning of the twentieth century with almost unlimited possibilities for caricature. Here "T.R." is afflicting the monopolists who dominated the American economy.

As president of the United States from 1901 to 1909, Theodore Roosevelt launched an aggressive campaign to break up the trusts, conserve natural resources, and regulate railroads, food, and drugs. In 1913 President Woodrow Wilson started a militant campaign of reform called the "New Freedom." His administration reduced the tariff because it was too much the instrument of special economic privilege, enacted banking reform with the Federal Reserve Act of 1913, and regulated businesses in the public interest through the Clayton Antitrust Act and the establishment of the Federal Trade Commission, both in 1914.

In 1914 the United States was the richest, most populous, and most influential nation in the West. The country's first census, taken in 1790, counted a population of just under 4 million; by 1910 the number was 99 million. During the nineteenth century more than 25 million immigrants had made their way to America. Since the days of George Washington, the national wealth had increased at least a hundredfold. Once the producer of raw materials only, the United States by 1914 was the world's greatest industrial power, producing more steel than Britain and Germany combined. A single company, United States Steel, was capitalized for $1.46 billion, a sum greater than the total estimated wealth of the country in 1790.

The United States and the World

Foreign affairs were virtually forgotten after the Civil War, and one New York newspaper recommended the abolition of the foreign service. However, as productivity increased, the United States was forced to seek new outlets for its goods, especially now that the frontier had disappeared. Foreign trade increased from $393 million in 1870 to more than $1.33 billion in 1900. During the same period, investments abroad went from virtually nothing to $500 million. American missionary activity greatly expanded in Africa, the Middle East, and Asia. Like their European counterparts, many American leaders were influenced by their misreading of Darwin, especially when it was applied to foreign affairs. The slogan "survival of the fittest" had its followers in the U.S. Congress as well as in the British Parliament, French Chamber of Deputies, and German Reichstag. To be truly great, many argued, the United States must expand and assume a vital role in world politics. This argument was instrumental in the nation's acquisition of a global empire.

Roosevelt the Activist

The United States began building a modern navy in 1883, and by 1890 the buildup had accelerated greatly. Care was taken not to alarm the country, however, and the new ships were officially known as "seagoing coastline battleships," a handy nautical contradiction. When this naval program was initiated, the U.S. Navy ranked twelfth among the powers; by 1900 it had advanced to third place.

The growing international stature of the United States received startling confirmation in a border dispute between Britain and Venezuela in 1895. When Britain delayed before agreeing to submit the issue to arbitration, the State Department of the United States took the initiative and drafted a blunt note to London. The note warned the British that refusal to accept arbitration would have grave consequences. The State Department noted U.S. dominance in the Western Hemisphere and boasted that America's geographical position protected it from European pressures. Britain was preoccupied with the Boers in South Africa, the Germans on the Continent, and the French in the Sudan and thus could not argue too strenuously against the message. They agreed to resolve the dispute through arbitration.

There were signs of the new dynamism in American foreign policy in Asia as well. In 1899 U.S. Secretary of State John Hay initiated the so-called Open Door policy regarding China, an attempt to ensure equal commercial rights for traders of all nations—including, of course, the United States, a latecomer to the China trade. When Chinese patriots fought against the intrusion of foreigners in the Boxer Rebellion, the United States again took the lead in defending its new outward-looking stance (see Chapter 28).

This heightened activity of the United States is best symbolized by the ideas and actions of Theodore Roosevelt. In his terms as president he was one of the leading figures on the world stage. At the request of the Japanese he assumed the role of peacemaker in the Russo-Japanese War. The peace conference, which met in 1905 at Portsmouth, New Hampshire, successfully concluded a treaty, and in 1910 Roosevelt received the Nobel Peace Prize.

Roosevelt was not always a man of peace, however. When he believed the legitimate interests of the United States were at risk, he did not hesitate to threaten or use force. That became very clear in Panama. In 1901 the British conceded to the United States the exclusive right to control any canal that might be dug through the isthmus. For $40 million the United States bought the rights of a private French company that had already begun work on the canal. A lease was negotiated with Colombia, through whose territory the canal would be built, but that country's senate refused to ratify the treaty, claiming the compensation was too small. Roosevelt is reputed to have responded, "I did not intend that any set of bandits should hold up Uncle Sam." The isthmus erupted in revolution, financed with money

President William McKinley on Imperialism

Even the Americans joined the imperialistic race. Unlike the Europeans, who propounded intellectually sophisticated rationalizations, the Americans moved for different, often celestial, reasons. McKinley noted:

I have been criticized a good deal about the Philippines, but I don't deserve it. The truth is, I didn't want the Philippines, and when they came to us, as a gift from the gods, I did not know what to do with them. When the Spanish war broke out, Dewey was at Hongkong, and I ordered him to go to Manila, and he had to; because, if defeated, he had no place to refit on that side of the globe, and if the Dons were victorious they would likely cross the Pacific and ravage our Oregon and California coasts. And so he had to destroy the Spanish fleet, and did it. But that was as far as I thought then. When next I realized that the Philippines had dropped into our lap, I confess that I did not know what to do with them. I sought counsel from all sides—Democrats as well as Republicans—but got little help. I thought first we would take only Manila; then Luzon; then other islands, perhaps all. I walked the floor of the White House night after night until midnight; and I am not ashamed to tell you, gentlemen, that I went down on my knees and prayed Almighty God for light and guidance more than one night.

And one night late it came to me this way—I don't know how it was, but it came: (1) That we could not give them back to Spain—that would be cowardly and dishonorable; (2) that we could not turn them over to France or Germany—that would be bad business and discreditable; (3) that we could not leave them to themselves—they were unfit for self-government—and they would soon have anarchy and misrule over there worse than Spain's was; and (4) that there was nothing left for us to do but to take them all, and to educate the Filipinos, and uplift and civilize and Christianize them, and, by God's grace, do the very best we could by them, as our fellowmen for whom Christ also died. And then I went to bed, and went to sleep, and slept soundly, and next morning I sent for the chief engineer of the War Department (our map-maker), and told him to put the Philippines on the map of the United States (pointing to a large map on the wall of his office); "and there they are, and there they will stay while I am president!"

From George A. Malcolm and Maximo M. Kalaw, *Philippine Government* (Boston: Heath, 1932).

borrowed from American banker and financier John Pierpont Morgan. The new republic of Panama seceded from Colombia in 1903 and promptly concluded a canal treaty with the United States. The canal opened in 1914, on U.S. terms. The United States had moved far from its traditional place on the periphery of world affairs.

Modernism and Popular Culture

Romanticism broke the classical molds and opened the way for diversity in forms, styles, and themes. Romantics followed their emotions, while realists advocated a more objective way of portraying the world by stressing accuracy and precision. By the end of the nineteenth century a new movement, modernism—fragmented, disorganized, and united only in its reaction to the past—came to hold sway among Europe's writers, artists, and musicians.

Modernism freed the writer from all rules of composition and form and all obligations to communicate to a large audience. Poetry was especially affected by this new tendency. Toward the end of the century, in reaction to the demands of realism, French poets Stéphane Mallarmé (1842–1898) and Paul Verlaine (1844–1896) inaugurated the symbolist movement. Poetry rather than prose best fit the symbolists' goal of conveying ideas by suggestion rather than by precise, photographic word-pictures.

In a sense, all modern literature stems from the symbolist movement. By increasing the power of the poet to reach the readers' imagination through expanded combinations of allusion, symbol, and double meaning, symbolism gave new life to the written word. But in exploring new poetic realms and possibilities, the symbolists left behind the majority of readers who had been trained to see clarity, precision, simplicity, and definition as positive aspects of literature.

Modernism freed painters from the need to communicate surface reality. Gustave Courbet (1819–1877) consciously dropped all useless adornments and instead boldly painted the life of the world in which he lived. He was soon surpassed by his countrymen who became preoccupied with capturing color, light, and atmosphere. Artists such as Claude Monet (1840–1926), Édouard Manet (1832–1882),

Edgar Degas (1834–1917), Mary Cassatt (1845–1926), and Pierre-Auguste Renoir (1841–1919) tried to catch the first impression made by a scene or an object on the eye, undistorted by intellect or any subjective attitude. They were called impressionists and worked in terms of light and color rather than solidity of form.

The impressionists found that they could achieve a more striking effect of light by placing one bright area of color next to another without any transitional tones. The also found that shadows could be shown not as gray but as colors complementary to those of the objects casting the shadow. At close range an impressionist painting may seem little more than splotches of unmixed colors, but at a proper distance the eye mixes the colors and allows a vibrating effect of light and emotion to emerge. The impressionists' techniques revolutionized art.

One of the weaknesses of the impressionists' work was that they sacrificed much of the clarity of the classical tradition to gain their effects. Paul Cézanne (1839–1903) addressed that problem. He tried to simplify all natural objects by stressing their essential geometric structure. He believed that everything in nature corresponded to the shape of a cone, cylinder, or sphere. Proceeding from this theory, he was able to get below the surface and give his objects the solidity that had eluded the impressionists, yet he kept the impressionists' striking use of color.

The Dutch artist Vincent van Gogh (1853–1890), while adapting the impressionist approach to light and color, painted using short strokes of heavy pigment to accentuate the underlying forms and rhythms of his subjects. He achieved intensely emotional results, as he was willing to distort what he saw to communicate the sensations he felt. His short life of poverty and loneliness ended in insanity and suicide.

Before 1914 other modernist-inspired forms emerged. French artist Henri Matisse (1869–1954) painted what he felt about an object, rather than just the object itself. He had learned to simplify form partly from his study of African primitive art and the color schemes of oriental carpets. The Spanish artist Pablo Picasso (1881–1974) and others helped develop the school called cubism. Cubists would choose an object, then construct an abstract pattern from it, giving the opportunity to view it simultaneously from several points. Such a pattern is evident in much of Picasso's work, including *Les Demoiselles D'Avignon* (1907).

Modernism affected music as it had affected poetry and art. The French composer Claude Debussy (1862–1918) tried in his music to imitate what he read in poetry and saw in impressionist paintings. He engaged in "tone painting" to achieve a special mood or atmosphere. This device can be heard in his "symphonic poem" *Prelude to the Afternoon of a Faun*, which shocked the musical world when it was first performed in 1894. The impressionist painters had gained their effects by juxtaposing widely differ-

A barrage of hostility greeted Édouard Manet's Luncheon on the Grass *(1863), which juxtaposed the frank nudity of the female model with two clothed male figures. Although the models and the setting seem realistic, Manet was in fact little concerned with subject matter; he believed that the artist's reality lies in the brush strokes and color rather than in the objects represented in the painting. This attitude later coalesced in the "art for art's sake" school of thought.*

A concern for the effects of light and color united the French impressionists, yet each also developed a personal style. Often regarded as the boldest innovator was Claude Monet, who did series of paintings of the same subject, such as Water Lilies *(1906).*

Claude Monet, French, 1840–1926, *Water Lilies*, 1906. Oil on canvas, 87.6 × 92.7 cm., Mr. & Mrs. Martin A. Ryerson Collection, 1933.1157. Copyright © 1999, The Art Institute of Chicago. All rights reserved.

Vincent van Gogh was less interested in the photographic reproduction of nature than in the re-creation of his vision of what he saw, expressed through his use of brilliant, intense, unmodulated color and dynamic brush strokes. The swirling, exploding stars in The Starry Night *(1889), painted at the sanitarium at St. Rémy during one of van Gogh's lucid periods, seem to express the artist's turbulent emotions.*

van Gogh, Vincent. *The Starry Night.* (1889) Oil on canvas, 29 × 36¼" (73.7 × 92.1 cm). The Museum of Modern Art, New York. Acquired through the Lillie P. Bliss Bequest. Photograph © 1999 The Museum of Modern Art, New York.

Not only was Pablo Picasso the most prolific artist of the twentieth century, but he also taught the public over the course of his long life that there was a number of different ways that one could see and portray traditional subjects, as in Les Demoiselles d'Avignon.

Pablo Picasso, Les Demoiselles d'Avignon, Paris (June–July 1907). Oil on canvas, 243.9 × 233.7 cm. The Museum of Modern Art, New York. Acquired through the Lillie P. Bliss Bequest, Photograph © 1999 The Museum of Modern Art, New York.

ent colors. The composers juxtaposed widely separate chords to create similarly brilliant, shimmering effects.

Popular Culture

The urban working and lower middle classes began to be important consumers of the popular cultural products of their countries. With increasing literacy these classes provided a huge audience for publishers. More leisure time and money enabled them to fill the music halls and public sporting arenas. They would rarely be found in the concert halls, art galleries, or serious bookstores. Rather they read the penny press and the dime novel, both of which featured simple vocabulary and easy-to-follow information and plots. The penny press served many functions: to inform, entertain, and sell goods. Sensationalism, whether the confessions of a "fallen woman" or the account of some adventurer, was the main attraction of the dime novel. Comic strips first appeared in central Europe in the 1890s.

There was a level of literature between great novels and the penny press—comforting, light, and entertaining works like those of Scottish author Samuel Smiles (1812–1904). Smiles's *Self Help* (1859) sold 20,000 copies its first year and 130,000 over the next 30 years. Titles of Smiles's other works—*Thrift, Character,* and *Duty*—form a catalog of Victorian virtues. In the United States, Horatio Alger (1834–1899) wrote more than 100 novels following similar themes: virtue is rewarded, the good life will win out in the struggle with temptation, and the heroes—usually poor but pure-hearted youths—will come to enjoy wealth and high honor.

A number of technological advances—coated celluloid film, improved shutter mechanisms, reliable projectors, and a safe source of illumination—were combined to introduce the cinema—motion pictures, or movies—to the world. These developments seem to have come together almost simultaneously in France, Britain, and the United States. The first public motion picture performances took place in Paris in 1895 and soon after in London and New York.

Pioneers in the motion picture industry were the French brothers Auguste and Louis-Jean Lumière. They invented both the color photography process that bears their name and the Cinématographe, an early motion picture camera. This poster is for one of their first films, L'Arroseur Arrosé *(1896).*

Even though another 20 years passed before feature-length films were produced, movies were an immediate success, attracting an infinitely larger audience than live performances could ever reach.

Sports, including football in its North American and European forms, bicycle racing, cricket, baseball, and boxing, captured the popular imagination. Pierre de Coubertin (1863–1937) revived the Olympic Games of ancient Greece in 1896 in Athens. Thirteen nations took part in the event, which instantly caught the international public's imagination.

In the new society of early-twentieth-century Europe, the popular culture of mass literature, movies, and sports played as important a role as high culture did. In a simpler way, purveyors of popular culture communicated values and lessons that bound a nation together much more than the serious writers and artists of the age ever could. The gulf between "high" and "popular" culture has yet to be bridged.

Conclusion

In Prussia, after a period of reaction, a constitutional crisis in 1862 led to the rise to power of Otto von Bismarck and the achievement of German unification by 1871. Thereafter, the Second Reich came to be the most powerful country on the Continent and challenged the United Kingdom for commercial supremacy. The post-1848 generation in France turned to Louis Napoleon in a search for stability and pros-

perity. The French gained both, for a time, at the price of reduced liberty and military and diplomatic defeat in 1870. Thereafter, until 1914, despite the ramshackle nature of the Third Republic and its scandals, France had power and influence. The Italians achieved unification under the leadership of Cavour and Sardinia, but unification did not bring miraculous improvements in the lives of the Italian people. The Habsburg Empire, after nearly 20 years of trying to deal with its fractious nationalities, redefined itself as the Dual Monarchy in 1867. It managed to hold together until the outbreak of World War I.

Russia and Britain avoided the revolutionary upheavals of 1848, the former through a policy of repression that failed to respond effectively to its overwhelming problems and the latter because of an improving standard of living and a flexible, self-interested middle class. For the rest of the century, their paths would diverge as the British would grow to establish a world empire while the Russians would struggle with reform and repression until revolution in 1905 would bring an end to autocracy. Across the Atlantic, the United States profited by a massive influx of immigrants, survived the stresses of the Civil War, and went on to become a leading Western power by 1914.

Never before had the creators of poetry, art, prose, music, and architecture had a greater opportunity to communicate to such a large audience. The cinema and vastly increased publishing facilities held out great opportunity to artists and writers. Unfortunately, by the end of the nineteenth century, the modernist writers, artists, and musicians were seemingly able to communicate only with a finely trained elite. In a sense, what was needed was a new series of classical definitions, forms, and functions on which all classes could agree. But the Romantic drive to individualism, which came to full flower in the century, made that impossible. A century later, the gulf between mass culture and the fine arts remains.

Suggestions for Reading

Otto Pflanze's three-volume *Bismarck and the Development of Germany* (Princeton University Press, 1990) is the most important work on the man and his times. A. J. P. Taylor, *The Course of German History* (Capricorn, 1962), is a short, controversial essay on German national history since the French Revolution. Erich Eyck's balanced *Bismarck and the German Empire* (Norton, 1964) is an essential work. Michael Balfour, *The Kaiser and His Times* (Houghton Mifflin, 1964), describes the impact of William II on Germany and Europe. See also A. Rosenberg, *Imperial Germany: The Birth of the German Republic, 1871–1918* (Oxford University Press, 1970). Fritz Richard Stern, *Gold and Iron: Bismarck, Bleichröder, and the Building of the German Empire* (Random House, 1979), is a fascinating study of the interaction of capital and politics. John C. G. Rohl, *The Kaiser and His Court: Wilhelm II and the Government of Germany*, trans. Terence F. Cole (Cambridge University Press, 1995), corrects some of the more extreme interpretations of the kaiser.

Denise Brogan, *The French Nation: From Napoleon to Pétain, 1814–1940* (Colophon, 1957), is a good survey. See also Brison Gooch, *The Reign of Napoleon III* (Rand McNally, 1970). For the class conflicts with France during the reign of Napoleon III, see Roger V. Gould, *Insurgent Identities: Class, Community, and Protest in Paris from 1848 to the Commune* (University of Chicago Press, 1995). For France after the Franco-Prussian War, Stewart Edwards, *The Paris Commune, 1871* (Quadrangle, 1970), is complemented by Rupert Christiansen, *Paris Babylon: The Story of the Paris Commune* (Penguin, 1996). Gay L. Gullickson gives a new perspective on the Commune in *Unruly Women of Paris: Images of the Commune* (Cornell University Press, 1996). Eric Cahm, *The Dreyfus Affair in French Society and Politics* (Addison-Wesley, 1996), is the best general study of this difficult question. See also John McManners, *Church and State in France, 1870–1914* (Harper & Row, 1972). Michael Burns's important study, *Rural Society and French Politics: Boulangism and the Dreyfus Affair, 1886–1900* (Princeton University Press, 1984), provides a fundamental understanding of the context in which the quixotic general worked. Eugen Weber, *Peasants into Frenchmen* (University of California Press, 1976), and Theodore Zeldin, *France, 1848–1945* (Oxford University Press, 1973–1975), are two brilliant, conflicting, and essential social surveys.

Derek Bayles, *The Risorgimento and the Unification of Italy* (Allen & Unwin, 1982), and Christopher Seton-Watson, *Italy from Liberalism to Fascism, 1870–1925* (Methuen, 1967), give solid background.

A notion of the complexity of the nationalities question in the Habsburg realm can be found in Peter F. Sugar and Ivo John Lederer, eds., *Nationalism in Eastern Europe* (University of Washington Press, 1969). Carl E. Schorske, *Fin-de-Siècle Vienna: Politics and Culture* (Vintage, 1981), is a classical intellectual history of the Dual Monarchy in its decline. Jorg K. Hoensch discusses Hungary's motivations and programs in Chapter 2 of *A History of Modern Hungary* (Longman, 1988).

Barbara Jelavich, *The Habsburg Empire in European Affairs* (Rand McNally, 1969), is an excellent, brief history. Carlile Aylmer Macartney, *The Habsburg Empire, 1790–1918* (Weidenfeld & Nicholson, 1968), is thorough but pro-Hungarian. Alan Sked, *The Decline and Fall of the Habsburg Empire, 1815–1918* (Longman, 1989), provides a fresh view of unexpected strengths and weaknesses of the Vienna-based empire.

Tsarist attempts to compete industrially are discussed in Peter Gatrell, *Government, Industry, and Rearmament in Russia, 1900–1914: The Last Argument of Tsarism* (Cambridge University Press, 1994). Social and political interactions are viewed in Leopold H. Haimson, ed., *The Politics of Rural Russia, 1905–1914* (Indiana University Press, 1979). Jeffrey Burds portrays the important demographic interchange between country and city in *Peasant Dreams and Market Politics: Labor Migration and the Russian Village, 1861–1905* (University of Pittsburgh Press, 1998). Philip Pomper, *Sergei Nechaev* (Rutgers University Press, 1979), remains the best analysis of the ethos of the Russian revolutionary tradition. Donald W. Treadgold gives a solid analysis of Russia's agrarian problems in *The Great Siberian Migration* (Princeton University Press, 1957). Paul Avrich, *The Russian Anarchists* (Norton, 1978), offers a compelling study of the mind-set of a group who could see only violence as a solution. Avrahm Yarmolinsky, *The Road to Revolution* (Collier, 1962), gives an accessible, brief genealogy of the revolutionary movement. Bertram D. Wolfe, *Three Who Made a Revolution* (Scarborough House, 1987), gives a finely crafted study of Lenin, Trotsky, and Stalin. An excellent collection of translated documents giving a firsthand view of the huge changes Russia underwent at this time is found in Gregory L. Freeze, ed., *From Supplication to Revolution* (Oxford University Press, 1988). A well-written and penetrating biography is Louis Fischer, *The Life of Lenin* (Harper & Row, 1965). John D. Klier deals with Russian anti-Semitism in *Imperial Russia's Jewish Question* (Cambridge University Press, 1995).

R. C. K. Ensor, *England, 1870–1914* (Oxford University Press, 1936); G. Kitson Clark, *The Making of Victorian England* (Atheneum, 1967); and George M. Young, *Victorian England: Portrait of an Age* (Galaxy, 1954) are valuable accounts. *Gladstone: A Biography* (Random House, 1997), by 1980s political leader Roy Jenkins, is insightful. Paul Smith, *Disraeli: A Brief Life* (Cambridge University Press, 1996), offers a more accessible approach to the subject than Robert Blake's more thorough *Disraeli* (Anchor, 1969). George Dangerfield, *The Strange Death of Liberal England, 1910–1914* (Capricorn, 1935), describes the inability of the Liberals to deal with major problems. Susan Kent, *Sex and Suffrage in Britain, 1860–1914* (Princeton University Press, 1987), portrays the interconnection between the individual goals of the major suffragettes and the society in which they lived.

Arthur R. M. Lower, *Colony to Nation: A History of Canada* (McClellan & Stewart, 1946), traces the history of Canada from the British conquest to 1850. Bruce Hutchinson, *The Struggle for the Border* (Longman, 1955), provides important coverage of Canadian history. For provocative studies of history and society, see O. H. K. Spate, *Australia* (Praeger, 1968), and Douglas Pike, *Australia* (Cambridge University Press, 1969). See Monica Wilson, ed., *The Oxford History of South Africa* (Oxford University Press, 1969). Also recommended is R. Roux, Edward Roux, and Philip D. Curtin, *Time Longer than Rope: A History of the Black Man's Struggle for Freedom in South Africa* (University of Wisconsin Press, 1964).

Paul H. Buck, *The Road to Reunion, 1865–1900* (Little, Brown, 1937), is a good survey of the consequences of the Civil War. George E. Mowry, *The Era of Theodore Roosevelt* (Torchbooks, 1958), is a skillful characterization. See also Arthur S. Link, *Woodrow Wilson and the Progressive Era* (Torchbooks, 1963). Useful guides to nineteenth-century cultural developments are D. S. Mirsky and Francis J. Whitfield, *A History of Russian Literature* (Vintage, 1958); H. L. C. Jaffe, *The Nineteenth and Twentieth Centuries*, vol. 5 in *The Dolphin History of Painting* (Thames & Hudson, 1969); C. Edward Gauss, *Aesthetic Theories of French Artists: From Realism to Surrealism* (Johns Hopkins University Press, 1949); and H. C. Colles, *Ideals of the Nineteenth and Twentieth Century*, vol. 3 in *The Growth of Music* (Oxford University Press, 1956).

Suggestions for Web Browsing

Nineteenth Century Austria and Germany
http://www.fordham.edu/halsall/mod/modsbook22.html

A rich crossroads of information about nineteenth century Austria and Germany is offered by the Internet Modern History Source Book, which contains documents, maps, and images.

Nineteenth-century Europe in Photos
http://academic.brooklyn.cuny.edu/history/core/pics

Web site providing access to a vast array of historical images of the era.

Benjamin Disraeli
http://vassun.vassar.edu/~vicstud/lockwood.html

Benjamin Disraeli was a controversial figure in British history, as can be seen in the cartoon on this Web site. Links to William Gladstone and the political setting of the time are also found here.

Notes

1. Quoted in Koppel S. Pinson, *Modern Germany* (New York: Macmillan, 1954), p. 116.
2. L. C. B. Seaman, *From Vienna to Versailles* (New York: Harper & Row, 1962), pp. 96–129.
3. Quoted in C. G. Robinson, *Bismarck* (London: Constable, 1918), p. 472.
4. Quoted in Basil Dmystryshyn, ed., *Imperial Russia: A Source Book, 1700–1917* (New York: Holt, Rinehart and Winston, 1967), p. 241.
5. Hans Rogger, *Russia in the Age of Modernisation and Revolution, 1881–1917* (Longman, 1983), pp. 243–247.
6. Quoted in F. Owen, *Tempestuous Journey: Lloyd George, His Life and Times* (London: Hutchinson), p. 186.
7. Emmeline Pankhurst, *My Own Story* (New York: Source Book Press, 1970).
8. Samuel Elliot Morison, *The Oxford History of the American People* (London: Oxford University Press, 1965), p. 793.

John Bull plays the tune while the Khedive dances. This German cartoon, entitled "The Jammering Crocodile," dated 1893, satirizes England's occupation of Egypt.

Africa and the Middle East, 1800–1914

In the eighteenth and nineteenth centuries the countries of Africa and the Middle East underwent a radical restructuring: they faced internal political struggles, the transformation of the world economy, and the military, commercial, and cultural incursions of the Europeans. The economic, technological, and military superiority of certain European states challenged the diverse, complex civilizations of Africa, the Middle East, and Asia and made them targets in the competition for empire.

In sub-Saharan Africa the diversity of kingdoms and societies made a unified political response to the Europeans impossible. By the beginning of the twentieth century Africans found themselves living within political boundaries imposed by the Europeans without regard for the existing ethnic distribution of peoples. They began the painful process of altering their lifestyles to survive in the industrialized world.

In the Middle East politicians and intellectuals discussed ways to keep their empires strong and proposed reforms to enable them to meet the challenges of modernity. The Ottoman Empire at the beginning of the nineteenth century was still large and powerful, but by the end of the century it had faced bankruptcy, territorial losses, and national separatist movements. The Qajar Empire in Persia was similarly weakened by foreign loans and by the military ambitions of Britain and Russia. From North Africa to central Asia the citizens of these traditional, polyglot, multiethnic empires found themselves caught up in the great power rivalries of the new imperialists in Europe.

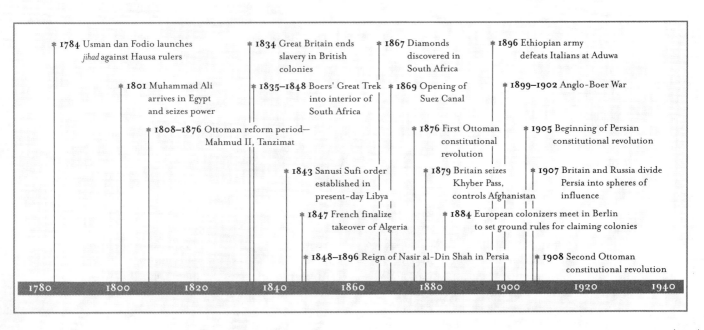

* **1784** Usman dan Fodio launches *jihad* against Hausa rulers

* **1801** Muhammad Ali arrives in Egypt and seizes power

* **1808–1876** Ottoman reform period— Mahmud II, Tanzimat

* **1834** Great Britain ends slavery in British colonies

* **1835–1848** Boers' Great Trek into interior of South Africa

* **1843** Sanusi Sufi order established in present-day Libya

* **1847** French finalize takeover of Algeria

* **1848–1896** Reign of Nasir al-Din Shah in Persia

* **1867** Diamonds discovered in South Africa

* **1869** Opening of Suez Canal

* **1876** First Ottoman constitutional revolution

* **1879** Britain seizes Khyber Pass, controls Afghanistan

* **1884** European colonizers meet in Berlin to set ground rules for claiming colonies

* **1896** Ethiopian army defeats Italians at Aduwa

* **1899–1902** Anglo-Boer War

* **1905** Beginning of Persian constitutional revolution

* **1907** Britain and Russia divide Persia into spheres of influence

* **1908** Second Ottoman constitutional revolution

1780   1800   1820   1840   1860   1880   1900   1920   1940

State Formation and the End of the Slave Trade in Africa

West Africa

In West Africa the political map of the interior savanna changed in the eighteenth century as Fulani Muslim holy men in the western Sudan launched a series of *jihads*. Their efforts inspired Fulani Muslims in the eastern Sudan—the most notable being Usman dan Fodio (1754–1817), son of a Muslim teacher and himself a scholar of some repute. He criticized Muslim Hausa leaders for ignoring Sharia law and for their lax morality. When a Hausa ruler lifted the exemption of Muslims from taxes, Usman mobilized his students, Fulani pastoralists, and Hausa peasants and declared a holy war against Hausa rulers in 1804. Usman's movement succeeded in uniting most of the Hausa states into the centralized Sokoto Caliphate, with a capital at Sokoto on the lower Niger, that encompassed several hundred thousand square miles.

Usman remained a religious leader while his brother Abdullahi and son Muhammad Bello (1781–1837) consolidated the caliphate. Although the Hausa aristocracy was replaced by a Fulani nobility, they allowed Hausa political and religious elites in the emirates a measure of local autonomy as long as they paid an annual tribute and recognized the caliph's political and religious authority. This shift in leadership made little difference to the Hausa peasantry and slaves, who served in households and tilled the fields, or to Hausa traders, who maintained their prosperous links with Tripoli to the north and the Atlantic coast. Their trade items included kola nuts, grain, salt, slaves, cattle, and cloth, which made their way to countries as far away as Egypt and Brazil.

On the West African coast, African societies were adjusting to the gradual winding down of the Atlantic slave trade. Britain, which was responsible for more than half of the slaves exported from Africa, had abolished the slave trade in 1807. Other European nations followed suit in subsequent decades. A British antislavery squadron patrolled the West and East African coasts, intercepting slave ships. Britain and France established colonies in Sierra Leone and Gabon for freed slaves, and the American Colonization Society founded Liberia for slaves freed in the United States who wished to return to Africa. Although the antislavery squadron managed to free about 160,000 slaves, this was a fraction of the overall slave trade. Between 1807 and 1888 a further 1.3 million Africans from West Africa alone were enslaved and shipped overseas.

As the slave trade slowly diminished, African entrepreneurs and European merchants expanded the trade in raw materials supplied to European industry and in finished products sold to Africans. One African export was gum arabic, extracted from acacia trees and used for dyes in European textile factories. Another was palm oil, a key ingredient in soap, candles, and margarine. More important, palm oil was the main lubricant for Europe's industrial machinery before the discovery of petroleum oil.

Along the coast east of the Niger delta, where palm oil was a major export, palm oil production was organized on gender lines: men cut down the nuts from trees, and women extracted the oil. The main beneficiaries of the palm oil trade, however, were not the producers but rulers and merchants. In the Niger River delta, states vying for control of the trade fought a series of wars.

East and Central Africa

East and central Africa were also increasingly drawn into the world economy through long-distance trade. Gold and ivory had long been exported to China and India, but now it was in demand by European middle classes for luxury items such as billiard balls, piano keys, and cutlery handles. Elephant herds paid an enormous price; 33 elephants were slaughtered for every ton of ivory exported. The scourge of slavery also ravaged the region. During the nineteenth century several million people were enslaved. Half of them were sent to southern Arabia, Sudan, and Ethiopia, while the rest ended up on French sugar plantations on the Indian Ocean islands of Mauritius and Réunion; on Brazilian sugar plantations, whose owners found West African slaves too highly priced; and on Arab-run clove plantations on Zanzibar and nearby islands. Zanzibar had become so important to Omani Arabs on the southeastern coast of the Arabian peninsula that Sultan Sayyid Said (1791–1856) transferred most of his court and government there in 1840.

The long-distance trade opened up opportunities for middlemen trading groups. The Yao, Nyamwezi, Afro-Portuguese, Kamba, and Swahili Arabs controlled routes in different parts of the region and recruited thousands of porters for their caravans. The Swahili language increasingly became the lingua franca along trading routes. With imported firearms and slave armies, some of the leading warlords established conquest states based on their control over the slave trade. Mirambo (1840–1884), a Nyamwezi chief, and Tippu Tip (c. 1830–1905), who was of Arab and Nyamwezi parentage, carved out domains east and west of Lake Tanganyika, respectively.

Many African kingdoms such as Rwanda were not dependent on the long-distance trade for their survival. Rwanda was comprised of three main groups: the Twa, who were hunter-gatherers; the Hutu, Bantu-speaking farmers; and the Tutsi, a pastoral Nilotic people who were the latest to immigrate

Discovery Through Maps

Reverend Ashmun's Map of Liberia

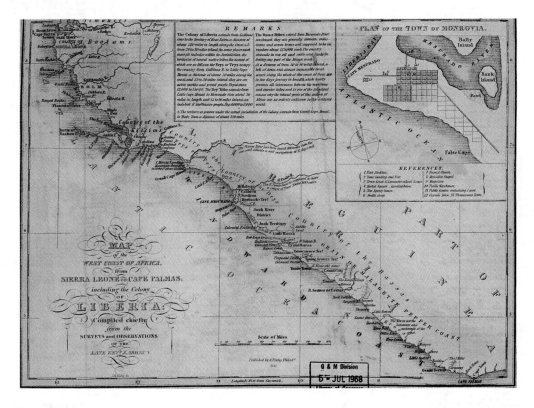

The American Society for Colonizing the Free People of Color of the United States—later shortened to the American Colonization Society (ACS)—was established in 1816 to assist free African Americans who wished to return voluntarily to Africa. The majority of ACS sponsors were supporters of slavery who regarded free blacks as a criminal element and a corrupting influence on slaves; a smaller number were abolitionists who envisioned creating a haven where blacks could enjoy full rights and govern themselves. The American government also backed the ACS because it wanted a place to settle blacks recaptured from slave traders' ships.

In 1820 the first ACS ship, with 86 black colonists and several white agents on board, set sail from New York. However, the settlers had not been prepared for the harsh climate of the West African coast. Their settlement on Sherbro Island in Sierra Leone failed in a short time after the ACS agents and a dozen black colonists died of diseases such as malaria. After ACS agents purchased a strip of land 36 miles long and 3 miles wide for $300 from local Africans at Cape Mesurado, the survivors of Sherbro Island made another attempt at colonization.

A white Methodist missionary, Rev. Jehudi Ashmun, initially played a prominent role in the colony's affairs. Ashmun had accompanied a group of recaptured Africans to the new settlement in 1822, but on arriving and finding the ACS's agents absent, he assumed the position of the ACS's principal agent. Ashmun's tenure, however, was marked by conflict. After settlers charged him with favoritism in allocating town lots, he was forced to leave in 1824. He was allowed to return a short time later, and a system of administration and a constitution were introduced. The territory was called Liberia ("land of the free"), and its main settlement was renamed Monrovia after the American president, James Monroe.

In poor health, Ashmun left Liberia in 1828 and died on his way back to America. This map of Liberia, drawn several years after Ashmun's death, was based on his "surveys and observations" and published with the aim of attracting more settlers. The map details the coastline. However, because the coast and the interior were separated by a dense forest belt, it includes little information about African ethnic groups in the interior. Although the map touted Liberia's coastal area as a healthy environment for settlers and for its agricultural potential, the reality was far different. Liberia was not situated on well-established trade routes. The settlers were inexperienced farmers who lacked the knowledge to cultivate the poor soils. Finally, diseases killed off many of the settlers. Although 4571 settlers arrived in the first two decades of Liberia's existence, the first census in 1843 recorded only 2388 people.

Born of Arab and Nyamwezi parents, Tippu Tip was a warlord who established a state west of Lake Tanganyika to exploit the slave trade.

into the area. Over the centuries Tutsi clans had established a patron-client relationship with Twa and Hutu clans, but the lines between the groups were not clearly drawn. Hutu and Tutsi intermarried and shared a common language, religious beliefs, and cultural institutions, and the distinctions between Tutsi patrons and Hutu clients were often blurred.

However, in the late nineteenth century the Nyiginya, a Tutsi clan led by King Rwabugiri, conquered other Tutsi and Hutu clans. Rwabugiri's state was highly centralized and favored the Tutsi minority, who served as administrators, tax collectors, and army commanders and controlled grazing land. Hutu chiefs were in charge of agricultural lands but tended Tutsi cattle and paid tribute to their Tutsi overlords.

Southern Africa

In the first decades of the nineteenth century African societies in southeastern Africa were swept up in a period of political transformation known as the Mfecane ("the scattering"). Its origins can be traced to in-

creased competition by chiefdoms for grazing land following a series of severe droughts and for control of first the ivory and then the cattle trade with the Portuguese at Delagoa Bay. However, it was the Zulu clan, a minor actor when the Mfecane began, that became the region's most formidable military power.

The Zulu owed their rise in prominence to their king, Shaka (c. 1786–1828). When he was born about 1786, his father was chief of the Zulu clan, which was later part of the Mthethwa confederacy ruled by Dingiswayo (c. 1770s–1816). When Shaka's father rejected his mother, Shaka was forced to spend his childhood among his mother's people. As a young man he enrolled in one of Dingiswayo's fighting regiments. Young men of about 16 to 18 traditionally went to circumcision schools for a number of months to prepare themselves for manhood. Because Dingiswayo needed soldiers who could be called into battle on short notice, he abolished the circumcision schools and enrolled his young men directly into regiments.

Shaka soon distinguished himself as a warrior, and he rose rapidly in Dingiswayo's army. On his father's death in 1815 Shaka assumed the chieftaincy of the Zulu. Several years later, when Dingiswayo's enemies lured him into a trap and killed him, Shaka asserted his leadership of the confederacy. He regrouped his followers and won over others, and eventually he vanquished his opponents. He then be-

African Societies and European Imperialism

1816	Shaka becomes king of Zulu
1824	Basotho king Moshoeshoe moves to mountain fortress Thaba Bosiu
1840	Omani Sultan Said establishes rule in Zanzibar
1876	King Leopold II of Belgium founds International African Association
1879	Zulu army defeats British force at battle of Isandhlwana
1881	Muhammad Ahmad proclaims himself Mahdi in Sudan
1886	Opening of Witwatersrand goldfields
1888	Cecil Rhodes and Barney Barnato found De Beers Diamond Company
1895	Cecil Rhodes launches Jameson raid to overthrow Transvaal government
1898	Confrontation of British and French forces at Fashoda in southern Sudan

gan constructing, primarily by cattle-raiding, a major kingdom between the Phongolo and Tugela Rivers that dominated southeastern Africa.

Shaka was best known for adopting new weapons and battle strategies that revolutionized warfare. He armed the Zulu army with a stabbing spear that was not thrown but used in close fighting. He introduced the buffalo horn formation, which allowed his soldiers to engage an opponent while the horns or flanks surrounded them. He drilled his soldiers so that they could march long distances on short notice. He also transformed his clan into a major kingdom of about 25,000 people by assimilating large numbers of war captives. He created a new hierarchy in which power was centered in his kingship and status was based not on descent but on achievement in the military regiments.

Shaka's repeated raids for cattle and captives throughout the area proved to be his downfall, as his regiments tired of constant campaigns. Several of his half-brothers and one of his generals conspired against him and assassinated him in 1828.

Moshoeshoe was the leader chiefly responsible for creating the Basotho kingdom in the 1820s and 1830s. Renowned for his diplomatic skills, he was able to maintain his kingdom's independence for many decades from Afrikaner and British colonizers.

Using innovative battle tactics and new weapons, the stabbing spear and the buffalo-hide shield, King Shaka transformed the Zulu from a small clan to a major kingdom between 1816 and 1828.

During the Mfecane, refugee groups escaped Shaka's domination by migrating to other parts of the region. Some headed much farther north, adopting Shaka's fighting methods and establishing kingdoms on the Shakan model in Mozambique, Zimbabwe, Malawi, and Tanzania. Still other peoples survived by creating new kingdoms that knit together clans and refugees. One kingdom forged in this way was Moshoeshoe's Basotho kingdom.

The son of a minor chief, Moshoeshoe (c. 1786–1870) gained a reputation as a cattle raider as a young man. Moshoeshoe succeeded his father as refugee groups began streaming into his area. To escape their raids, in 1824 Moshoeshoe moved his small following to an impregnable, flat-topped mountain called Thaba Bosiu. Over the next several decades he creatively built a kingdom that became one of the most powerful in the region. Moshoeshoe accumulated vast cattle herds through raiding, and he won the loyalty of many destitute men by loaning them cattle to reestablish their homesteads. Moshoeshoe married many times to build up political alliances with neighboring chiefs. He also armed his warriors with battle-axes and formed a cavalry using ponies bred for the rugged mountain terrain.

Moshoeshoe is best remembered for his diplomatic skills. He was prepared to fight if necessary, but he preferred to negotiate whenever possible. On many occasions he managed to salvage difficult situations by engaging in diplomacy and exploiting divisions among opponents, especially the rivalry between the Boers and the British. In 1868, toward the end of his life, as Boers were on the verge of destroying his kingdom, Moshoeshoe successfully appealed to the British government for protection.

The Great Trek and British-Afrikaner Relations

As African kingdoms in southern Africa were undergoing a period of transformation, groups of Boers were preparing to escape British control by migrating into the interior of southern Africa. Prompted by the Napoleonic wars, Britain had resumed control over the Cape Colony in 1806 to protect the sea lanes around the Cape of Good Hope. The British were intent on expanding commercial opportunities through wine and wool production; the Boers resented any interference with their pastoral way of life.

Relations between the two groups deteriorated in the next decades. At first the British won Boer approval for a law that tied Khoikhoi servants to white farmers, but after a humanitarian outcry from missionaries over abuses of servants, the British instituted an ordinance giving Khoikhoi farm laborers equal rights. Britain also abolished the slave trade in 1807, driving up the price of slaves, and in 1834 emancipated the slaves. However, this action did not improve

Light and strong, voortrekker *wagons were ideally suited to the rough terrain they were forced to cross. Despite their maneuverability, they could carry a surprising amount of household and other goods. This picture shows a wagon crossing a particularly difficult river.*

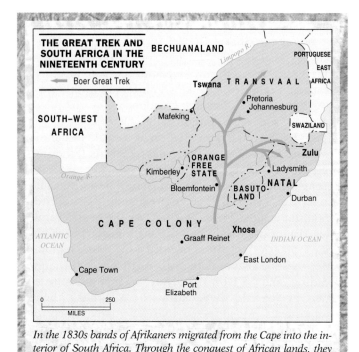

In the 1830s bands of Afrikaners migrated from the Cape into the interior of South Africa. Through the conquest of African lands, they established two republics, the Transvaal and the Orange Free State.

the conditions of former slaves as most of them, unskilled and uneducated, ended up as free but servile labor on white farms. The last straw for the Boers came in 1836 when the British handed back land conquered from Xhosa chiefdoms in a recently completed war.

Seeing their way of life threatened, many Boers decided to escape further British interference by heading for the interior. In the mid-1830s bands of voortrekkers (numbering about 15,000 in all) undertook an epic journey in their ox-drawn wagons to a new country where they could restore their way of life. This Great Trek was comparable to the covered-wagon epic of the American West.

On the high plateau, or *veld*, the Boers established two republics, the Orange Free State and the Transvaal. For the rest of the century they solidified their control by engaging in wars of land conquest against African kingdoms. In the meantime, the British prevented the Boers from having direct access to the Indian Ocean by extending their settlement along the eastern coast north of the Cape and founding the colony of Natal.

The Great Trek did little to resolve the Boers' difficulties. In 1877 Britain created a confederation of the white-ruled states in the region and took over the Transvaal with little resistance from the Afrikaners (the name taken by the Boers about this time). The British attempted to win Afrikaner acceptance by launching offensives against their main African rivals, the Pedi and Zulu kingdoms. Although the Zulus had coexisted peacefully with British and Afrikaners for many decades, the British now perceived them as an obstacle to white control and manufactured a war against the Zulu kingdom. The war started disastrously for the British when, in January 1879, the army of King Cetshwayo (c. 1832–1884) caught a British column by surprise at Isandhlwana and overwhelmed them. A handful of British soldiers survived the battle. Cetshwayo hoped the British would end their aggression following the disaster, but they renewed their efforts and six months later put an end to the Zulu kingdom by carving it into 13 small pieces and exiling Cetshwayo.

This victory did not improve British relations with Transvaal Afrikaners. In 1881 they rebelled against British rule and scored a series of military successes. The British agreed to pull out of the Transvaal, although they still claimed to have a voice in its foreign affairs.

The Mineral Revolution and the Anglo-Boer War

The discovery of diamonds in 1867 on the borders of the Cape Colony and the Orange Free State and of gold in 1886 in the Transvaal were to transform the whole of southern Africa economically and politically.

When the diamond fields were opened up, thousands of black and white fortuneseekers flocked to the area. The mining town of Kimberley sprang up almost overnight. In the first years of the digs there were no restrictions on who could stake claims. But in 1873 European diggers, resentful of competition from blacks, successfully lobbied British officials for a law prohibiting Africans from owning claims. This law set the tone for future laws governing who controlled mineral rights and ownership of the land.

Although Africans were excluded from owning claims, there were few restrictions on their movements and where they lived around the mines. Africans typically came to mine for three to six months and left at a time of their own choosing. This freedom changed as European mine owners sought to prevent diamond thefts and to control black workers by preventing desertion and holding down their wages. In 1885 the mine owners began erecting compounds to house black workers. Throughout their stay at a mine, black workers stayed in the compounds and were allowed out only to work in the mine. The compound system was so effective at controlling black labor that it became a fixture in other mining operations throughout southern Africa.

In the early years of the diamond diggings several thousand people held claims, but by the 1880s ownership of the mines was falling into the hands of fewer and fewer people. In 1888 the two leading magnates, Cecil Rhodes (1853–1902) and Barney Barnato (1852–1897), pooled their resources to found De Beers, a company that controlled 90 percent of diamond production. Over a century later De Beers continues to dominate the diamond industry not only in South Africa but also around the world.

In 1886 gold discoveries on the Witwatersrand ("ridge of the white waters") sparked off another rush. The Witwatersrand gold veins were distinctive because they sloped at sharp angles beneath the earth and required shafts to be sunk at depths of up to 2 miles. The exorbitant costs of deep-level mining as well as of importing skilled labor, mining engineers, and the latest technology required enormous infusions of foreign capital. Profits were hard to sustain, and the main mining houses targeted black wages for cutting costs. They restricted competition for black workers by imposing ceilings on their wages and creating recruiting organizations that eventually developed networks as far north as Zambia and Malawi. The result was a migrant labor system in which tens of thousands of black men came to the mines for six to nine months, while black women stayed home to raise families and look after crops. Another consequence of the mineral discoveries was the extension of railways into the interior of southern Africa.

From 1886 to the end of the century, South Africa's share of world gold production increased from less than 1 percent to over 25 percent. The center of power in the region shifted from Cape Town to Johannesburg, renewing British interest in controlling the Transvaal. Afrikaner leaders were resolute about protecting their independence, but they feared they would be outnumbered when tens of thousands of *uitlanders* (foreigners), mainly English immigrants, flocked to the gold mines. The Transvaal's president, Paul Kruger (1825–1904), was determined that the *uitlanders* would not gain control. As a boy he had joined in the Great Trek. As a young man he led Boer commandos conquering African lands. As head of the Transvaal he was passionately devoted to preserving its independence and the Afrikaners' agrarian way of life.

Kruger's main adversary was Cecil Rhodes, who in 1890 had become prime minister of the Cape Colony. An avowed imperialist, Rhodes now set his sights on bringing down Kruger's republic. He plotted with *uitlanders* in Johannesburg to stage an insurrection. In late 1895 Rhodes's private army, led by Leander Starr Jameson, invaded the Transvaal from

While most black migrant workers in the gold mines were men, black women found employment in the urban areas as domestic servants and washerwomen. A Johannesburg regulation of 1899 stated that "every householder or owner of an erf [a plot of land] may keep in his backyard whatever servants he requires for domestic service."

Transvaal leaders were deeply suspicious that the British had been behind Rhodes's reckless actions. Their fears were heightened when in 1897 the British selected Alfred Milner (1854–1925) as the high commissioner for South Africa. He shared Rhodes's imperialist convictions with a passion. He pressured Kruger to reduce the length of time for *uitlanders* to qualify for citizenship in the Transvaal. Although Milner thought Kruger would make significant concessions under pressure, Kruger was unwilling to meet all of Milner's demands.

War broke out in late 1899. Most observers expected the British army to roll over the heavily outnumbered Afrikaner forces. But Afrikaner soldiers were crack shots and expert horsemen. Knowing every inch of ground on which they fought, they frequently outmaneuvered the British troops by resorting to guerrilla tactics. The British countered by conducting a scorched-earth campaign, burning Afrikaner farms and placing Afrikaner women and children and Africans who worked on their farms in unsanitary concentration camps. About 30,000 Afrikaners (half of them children) and 15,000 blacks perished in the camps from disease and starvation. Among Afrikaners the memory of the deaths fueled animosity against the British for generations.

A bittereinder, *an Afrikaner guerrilla who vowed to fight to the "bitter end" against the British during the Anglo-Boer War.*

neighboring Bechuanaland, but they were quickly captured by Afrikaner commandos. The Jameson raid had dire consequences. Rhodes was forced to resign as prime minister, Afrikaners in the Cape were alienated from the British, the Orange Free State formed an alliance with the Transvaal, and the Transvaal began modernizing its army by importing weapons from Europe.

European Conquest of Africa

In 1870 the European nations controlled only 10 percent of the continent. The two most important holdings were at Africa's geographical extremes: French-administered Algeria in the north and the Boer republics and British colonies in the south. Most of the other European holdings were small commercial ones along the West African coast.

One of the first European leaders to acquire new African territory was King Leopold II of Belgium, who had long dreamed of creating an empire modeled on Dutch holdings in Asia and the Pacific. When the Belgian government was reluctant to acquire colonies, Leopold took the initiative. In 1876 he organized the International African Association (IAA) and brought the explorer Henry Stanley (1841–1904) into his service. The association, composed of scientists and explorers from many nations, was ostensibly intended to serve humanitarian purposes. But the crafty king had less noble motives. He sent Stanley to central Africa on behalf of the association. Stanley brought along hundreds of blank treaty forms and concluded agreements with various African chiefs, few of whom understood the implications of granting sovereignty to the IAA. By 1882 the organization had laid claim to over 900,000 square miles of territory along the Congo River.

Britain's occupation of Egypt and Leopold's acquisition of the Congo moved Chancellor Otto von Bismarck to overcome his indifference to colonies and acquire an African empire for Germany. Beginning in February 1884 Bismarck took just a year to annex four colonies: South-West Africa, Togoland, Cameroon, and German East Africa. However, Bismarck's imperial grab was still firmly rooted in his reading of European power politics. He wanted to deflect French hostility to Germany by sparking French interest in acquiring colonies and to put Germany in a position to mediate potential disputes between France and Britain.

While Bismarck was busy acquiring territory, he was also concerned about preventing clashes between colonizers. In 1884 he called the major European powers together in Berlin to discuss potential problems of unregulated African colonization. The conference paid lip service to humanitarian concerns by condemning the slave trade, prohibiting the sale of liquor and firearms in certain areas, and ensuring that European missionaries were not hindered from spreading the Christian faith. Then the participants moved to much more important matters.

Seeking to avoid competition for territory that could lead to conflict, they set down the ground rules by which the colonizers were to be guided in their search for colonies. They agreed that the area along the mouth of the Congo River was to be administered by Leopold of Belgium but that it was to be open to free trade and navigation. Drawing on precedents beginning in the sixteenth century, when European nations were creating seaborne empires, they decided that no nation was to stake out claims without first notifying other powers of its intention. No territory could be staked out unless it was effectively occupied, and all disputes were to be settled by arbitration. In spite of these declarations, the competitors often ignored the rules. On several occasions, war was barely avoided.

Representatives of 14 nations, including the United States, met in Berlin in 1884 to set new rules to govern their "scramble for Africa." No representative from Africa was invited to participate.

That Was No Brother

Europeans and Africans usually had very different perceptions of the same event. These documents recount two versions of a battle on the Congo River in the 1870s. The first comes from an African chief, Mojimba–recorded by a Catholic priest, Father Joseph Fraessle, several decades after the battle–and the second is by the famed explorer Henry Morton Stanley.

When we heard that the man with the white flesh was journeying down the Lualaba (Lualaba-Congo) we were open-mouthed with astonishment. We stood still. All night long the drums announced the strange news—a man with white flesh! . . . He must have got that from the river-kingdom. He will be one of our brothers who were drowned in that river. All life comes from the water, and in the water he has found life. Now he is coming back to us, he is coming home. . . .

We will prepare a feast, I ordered, we will go to meet our brother and escort him into the village with rejoicing! . . . We assembled the great canoes. We listened for the gong which would announce our brother's presence on the Lualaba. Presently the cry was heard: He is approaching the Lualaba. Now he enters the river! . . . We swept forward, my canoe leading, the others following, with songs of joy and with dancing, to meet the first white man our eyes had beheld, and to do him honor.

But as we drew near his canoes there were loud reports, bang! bang! and fire-staves spat bits of iron at us. We were paralyzed with fright; our mouths hung wide open and we could not shut them. Things such as we had never seen, never heard of, never dreamed of—they were the work of evil spirits! Several of my men plunged into the water. . . . What for? Did they fly to safety? No—for others fell down also, in the canoes. Some screamed dreadfully, others were silent—they were dead, and blood flowed from little holes in their bodies. "War! that is war!" I yelled. "Go back!" The canoes sped back to our village with all the strength our spirits could impart to our arms. That was no brother! That was the worst enemy our country had ever seen.

And still those bangs went on; the long staves spat fire, pieces of iron whistled around us, fell into the water with a hissing sound, and our brothers continued to fall. We fell into our village—they came after us. We fled into the forest and flung ourselves on the ground. When we returned that evening our eyes beheld fearful things: our brothers, dead, bleeding, our village plundered and burned, and the water full of dead bodies. . . .

Now tell me: has the white man dealt fairly by us? Oh, do not speak to me of him! You call us wicked men, but you white men are much more wicked! You think because you have guns you can take away our land and our possessions. You have sickness in your heads, for that is not justice.

At 2 P.M. we emerged out of the shelter of the deeply wooded banks and came into a vast stream, nearly 2,000 yards across at the mouth. As soon as we entered its waters, we saw a great fleet of canoes hovering about in the middle of the stream. . . . We pulled briskly on to gain the right bank, when looking upstream, we saw a sight that sent the blood tingling through every nerve and fiber of our bodies: a flotilla of gigantic canoes bearing down upon us, which both in size and numbers greatly exceeded anything we had seen hitherto!

Instead of aiming for the right bank, we formed a line and kept straight downriver, the boat taking position behind. . . . The shields were next lifted by the noncombatants, men, women and children in the bows, and along the outer lines, as well as astern, and from behind these the muskets and rifles were aimed.

We had sufficient time to take a view of the mighty force bearing down on us and to count the number of the war vessels. There were 54 of them! A monster canoe led the way, with two rows of upstanding paddles, 40 men on a side, their bodies bending and swaying in unison as with a swelling barbarous chorus they drove her down toward us. . . .

The crashing sounds of large drums, a hundred blasts of ivory horns, and a thrilling chant from 2,000 human throats did not tend to soothe our nerves or to increase our confidence. . . . We had no time to pray or to take sentimental looks at the savage world, or even to breathe a sad farewell to it. . . .

The monster canoe aimed straight for my boat, as though it would run us down; but when within fifty yards off, it swerved aside and, when nearly opposite, the warriors above the manned prow let fly their spears and on either side there was a noise of rushing bodies. But every sound was soon lost in the ripping, crackling musketry. For five minutes we were so absorbed in firing that we took no note of anything else; but at the end of that time we were made aware that the enemy was reforming about 200 yards above us.

Our blood was up now. It was a murderous world, and we felt for the first time that we hated the filthy, vulturous ghouls who inhabited it. We therefore lifted our anchors and pursued them upstream along the right bank until, rounding a point, we saw their villages. We made straight for the banks and continued the fight in the village streets with those who had landed.

From Heinrich Schifflers, *The Quest for Africa* (New York: Putnam, 1957), pp. 196–197.

From Henry M. Stanley, *Through the Dark Continent*, Vol. 2 (New York: Harper & Brothers, 1878), pp. 268–273.

The humanitarian guidelines were generally disregarded. The methods used to acquire lands continued in many instances to involve deception of the Africans. European colonists got huge land grants by giving chiefs treaties they could not read and whose contents they were not permitted to understand. In return, African chiefs were plied with bottles of gin, red handkerchiefs, and fancy red costumes. The comparison between the European treaty methods and those of the Americans in negotiations with Native American tribes is all too apparent.

The cultural differences between Africans and Europeans were especially vast regarding their conceptions of land ownership. To most African societies, land was not owned privately by individuals but was vested in their chiefs, who allocated it to their people. When chiefs allocated land or mineral rights to Europeans, they had no idea they were disposing of more than its temporary use. When the Europeans later claimed ownership of the land, Africans were indignant, claiming that they had been cheated. In 1888 Charles Rudd, a representative of Cecil Rhodes, signed a treaty with the Ndebele king Lobengula (c. 1836–1894), in which he was given a monthly stipend and 1000 Martini-Henry rifles in exchange for a concession over minerals and metals. Lobengula was told that the treaty gave Rhodes's company the right to dig a hole in one place, but the treaty actually gave Rhodes unlimited powers.

African leaders who questioned treaty provisions were treated cavalierly. King Jaja (c. 1821–1891) of Opobo, a prosperous trading state in southeastern Nigeria, refused to sign a British treaty unless the wording of clauses on protection and free trade were altered or scrapped. The British agreed to changes, but when the British Consul invited the chiefs to sign the treaty on a ship, they were detained and sent into exile.

The Scrambling of Africa

From the Berlin conference to the First World War, European imperialists partitioned the African continent among themselves, with two exceptions—Liberia, which had been established for freed American slaves, and Ethiopia, which fended off Italian invaders. The colonizers were woefully ignorant about the geography of the areas they colonized. Europeans had knowledge of coastal areas, but nineteenth-century explorers had largely concentrated on river explorations and knew little beyond that. Thus when European statesmen drew boundaries, they were more concerned with strategic interests and potential economic development than with existing kingdoms, ethnic identities, topography, or demography. About half the boundaries were straight lines drawn for simple convenience. As Lord Salisbury, the British prime minister, admitted: "[We] have been engaged in drawing lines upon maps where no white man's foot ever trod, we have been giving away mountains and rivers and lakes to each other, only hindered by the small impediment that we never knew exactly where the mountains and rivers and lakes were."[1]

Shortly after the Berlin conference, King Leopold organized his African territories into his own personal fiefdom, the Congo Free State. He began to exploit the colony's economic resources by granting concessions to private companies, reserving for his own administration an extensive rubber-producing area ten times as large as Belgium. A system of forced labor was introduced, and soon stories of filthy work camps, horrible whippings, and other atrocities leaked out of the "Free State," founded to spread the "blessings" of "civilization." In the face of a rising tide of international outrage, Leopold was forced to turn the state over to the Belgian government in 1908. The conditions of the colony, renamed the Belgian Congo, improved for a short while under the direct administration of the government.

France and Britain were by far the two leading competitors for African territory. The French vision was to create an empire linking Algeria, West Africa, and the region north of the lower Congo River. To achieve their goal the French relied on their military to drive eastward from Senegal and northward from the lower Congo. In West Africa the British concentrated on their coastal trading interests and carved out colonies in Gambia, Sierra Leone, the Gold Coast (Ghana), and Nigeria. But they also scooped up possessions elsewhere. In East Africa they laid claim to Kenya and Uganda, and by 1884 they gained control over a stretch of African coast fronting on the Gulf of Aden. Because it guarded the lower approach to the Suez Canal, this protectorate (British Somaliland) was of great strategic value.

Equally important to British control of Egypt were the headwaters of the Nile, situated in the area known as the Anglo-Egyptian Sudan. The French also had their designs on the area as a bargaining chip to force the British to reconsider their exclusive control over Egypt. The French commissioned Captain Jean-Baptiste Marchand to march a force 3000 miles from central Africa to Fashoda on the White Nile south of Khartoum. In July 1898, several months after Marchand planted a French flag at Fashoda, General H. H. Kitchener successfully led an Anglo-Egyptian force against Muslim forces in control of the Sudan. Then Kitchener turned his attention to Marchand, and their forces faced off nervously at Fashoda. The showdown nearly ended in war. To the British, control of the Nile was a strategic necessity. To the French, it was a matter of national prestige, but they were not prepared to go to war over it, and they withdrew Marchand.

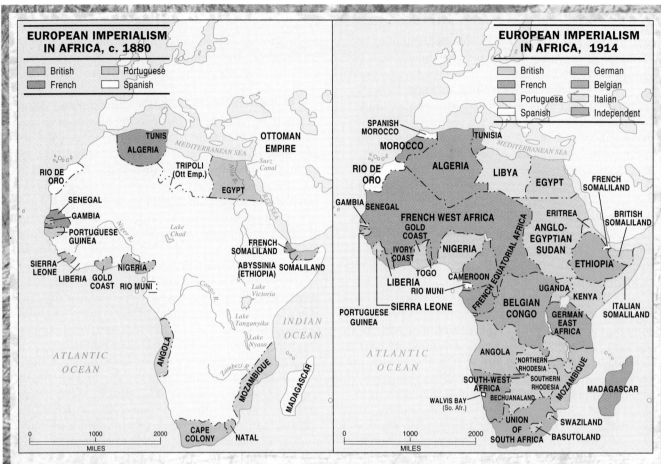

Until the 1880s only a few European countries held colonies in Africa, mostly enclaves on the coast. However, following the Berlin Conference of 1884–1885, European nations moved rapidly to conquer and partition Africa. By World War I, all of Africa, with the exception of Liberia and Ethiopia, was under European domination. Because Europeans were largely ignorant of Africa's interior regions, they drew the boundary lines of their colonies without regard for preexisting states, trading relations, or ethnic ties. This has left an enduring legacy of ethnic strife.

Britain was the principal colonizer in southern Africa. British influence expanded northward from the Cape Colony largely through the personal efforts of the diamond magnate Cecil Rhodes, who dreamed of an uninterrupted corridor of British territory from the Cape of Good Hope to Cairo. When the British government hesitated to claim territory north of the Limpopo River, Rhodes took the initiative. Rhodes had heard the stories that King Solomon's mines were located there, and he thought the area had even more potential than the Witwatersrand goldfields. Lured by a mirage of gold, he poured his personal fortune into founding the British South Africa Company. In 1890 he dispatched a column to settle and, if need be, conquer the area that eventually bore his name, Rhodesia.

Both Portugal and Italy had grandiose visions of empire, but they had to settle for territories the major European powers did not covet. Although the Portuguese had been involved in Africa longer than any of the other European colonizers, their ambition to

unite Mozambique and Angola through a central African corridor was thwarted by Rhodes and British interests. Italy emerged from the scramble for colonies with very little territory. The Italians gained a piece of the Red Sea coast and a slice of barren and desolate land on the Indian Ocean. But these areas were of little value without the rich plateau of Ethiopia in the hinterland. However, their bid to conquer the interior was soundly rebuffed by the Ethiopian army.

European Technology and the African Response to Conquest

The European conquest of most of Africa would not have been possible without advances in European technology. Until quinine was perfected, Europeans setting foot in Africa died in droves from illnesses such as malaria. Advances in military technology gave European armies a decisive advantage in their encounters with African forces. The gunboat allowed European armies to dominate lake and river regions, while the introduction of breechloading rifles and machine guns made it possible for small numbers of European soldiers to defeat much larger African armies, which possessed outmoded muskets.

African states were also at a disadvantage because they did not put up a united front. In the face of European expansion, African states sought to preserve as much of their own autonomy and sovereignty as possible. This response usually prevented them from entering into alliances with other African states to resist a common enemy. Most African societies resisted European conquest at some point, but they first weighed the costs and benefits of European rule and considered whether they should resist, make accommodations, or negotiate with Europeans. They queried European missionaries in their midst for information on the colonizers. They watched developments in neighboring states to see the results of resistance, and they sought advice on the implications of European protection. They assessed their rivalries with neighboring states and the possibility of profit from an alliance with Europeans. They also calculated whether they had the support of their own people. In the East African kingdom of Buganda a Protestant ruling faction sought British allies to maintain an advantage over Muslim, Catholic, and traditionalist rivals.

African states often changed tactics over the course of time. Moshoeshoe's kingdom fought the Boers in the Orange Free State on two occasions, appealed for British protection in 1868 to shield it from Afrikaner rule, fought a war against the Cape government in 1880 after the Cape tried to disarm Sotho warriors, and then invited the British to reestablish colonial rule in 1884.

Despite the disparity in firearms, African states valiantly sustained resistance to European colonizers until World War I. One of the most durable and innovative resistance leaders was Samori Touré (c. 1830–1900), who came from a Dyula trading family in the region of the upper Niger River in West Africa. He built up an army to protect his family's trading interests and then, between 1865 and 1875, created a powerful Islamic kingdom among the Mandinke people that stretched from Sierra Leone to the Ivory Coast. Samori's army could field over 30,000 soldiers and cavalry armed with muskets and rifles, some homemade and some imported from Freetown on the Sierra Leonean coast.

Samori's forces were a formidable opponent when they first clashed with French soldiers probing west from Senegal in 1881. However, the French superiority in weaponry eventually forced Samori to wage a scorched-earth campaign as he moved his

Samori Touré, who built up a powerful kingdom among the Mandinke people of West Africa. After leading a spirited resistance against European colonizers for several decades, he was captured by French soldiers in September 1898.

kingdom eastward. He then had to deal with internal revolts from his new subjects and also with the British, who refused to declare a protectorate over his kingdom. Squeezed between the French and the British, he fought as long as he could before he was captured and exiled by the French in 1898.

Because of their ability to inspire and unite followers, religious leaders often led the resistance to European invaders. In Sudan, Muhammad Ahmad (1844–1885), a Muslim *shaykh* from a village north of Khartoum, proclaimed himself a *Mahdi* ("guided one") in 1881. Muslims believe that in times of crisis a redeemer appears whose mission it is to overthrow tyrannical and oppressive rulers and install just governments in their place. Declaring himself a successor to the prophet Muhammad, Muhammad Ahmad called on people to join him in a *jihad* against the

Crowned emperor of Ethiopia in 1889, Menelik II carried out campaigns of conquest in his region while maintaining his kingdom's autonomy in the face of European imperialism. When Menelik's efforts to keep the Italians restricted to the Red Sea coast failed, he was forced into a military confrontation. Menelik's army routed the Italian forces at Aduwa in 1896.

unbelievers, the Egyptian-appointed administrators who were levying taxes and suppressing a profitable slave trade.

From a base 300 miles southwest of Khartoum, Mahdist forces scored numerous successes against Egyptian forces and laid siege to Khartoum in 1884. Despite last-ditch efforts by British officer Charles Gordon to negotiate with the Mahdi, the Mahdists swept into Khartoum in early 1885, killing Gordon and setting up administration at Omdurman, across the Nile from Khartoum. The Mahdi died a short time later, but his successors founded a Muslim state that lasted until an Anglo-Egyptian force invaded the Sudan in 1898.

African armies scored some victories against European forces, but only one African state, Ethiopia, successfully repulsed European invaders.

In the second half of the nineteenth century, several kings had revived a unified kingdom of Ethiopia, but none was as impressive as Menelik II (1844–1913), the king of Shewa, who was crowned emperor of Ethiopia in 1889. He moved the capital to Addis Ababa and modernized his kingdom by constructing the first railway line and laying telephone lines for communication with provinces. He aggressively expanded Ethiopia's boundaries, more than doubling the size of his kingdom.

At the same time, he kept a wary eye on British, French, and Italian intrigues. In 1889 Italy and Ethiopia signed the Treaty of Wuchale, in which Italy recognized Menelik as emperor of Ethiopia in return for giving the Italians a free hand in a region controlled by one of his rivals. However, the treaty's Italian version stated that Ethiopia had to conduct foreign relations through the Italians, while the Amharic version merely stated that Ethiopia could consult with Italy on foreign matters. When Menelik learned through diplomatic exchanges with Britain and France that Italy was claiming a protectorate over Ethiopia, he denounced the treaty and prepared for an eventual showdown with Italy by importing massive quantities of weapons, many of them from Italy. When the Italians mounted an offensive in Tigré province in 1896, Menelik's army of 100,000 soldiers was more than a match for the 20,000-strong Italian army. The Italians suffered a humiliating defeat at the battle of Aduwa and were forced to recognize Ethiopia's independence and content themselves with their enclave on the Red Sea coast, Eritrea.

The Middle East

At the beginning of the nineteenth century the Middle East consisted primarily of two large and loosely structured empires, the Qajar Empire in Persia and the Ottoman Empire, which included Anatolia, the Arab provinces, and most of North Africa. The Ottoman Empire stretched from the Balkans to Sudan and from the Maghreb to Arabia; the Ottoman sultan could still claim a certain preeminence in the Islamic world based on his position as Protector of the Holy Cities. The Islamic world had for centuries extended well beyond the Middle Eastern heartlands. United by their worship of one god, devotion to the Prophet Muhammad, and adherence to the Sharia Islamic law, Muslims looked to Mecca as the sacred site of pilgrimage. Every year the number of believers traveling to Mecca grew, and by 1900 it is estimated that more than 50,000 Indians and 20,000 Malays were making the *hajj* each year. But the Islamic world had been politically divided since the early centuries of Islam, and Muslim states from Southeast Asia to Morocco pursued their own political agendas with little or no reference to the sovereign who controlled the Islamic heartlands.

Challenges to Ottoman Power

In the sixteenth century the Ottoman administration had been a model of effectiveness. The Ottoman navy dominated the eastern Mediterranean, and Ottoman armies continued to expand the territories of the sultan. The balance of trade was markedly in favor of Asia, with European merchants sending precious coin to procure the goods they wanted from the Ottoman Empire, Persia, and South and Southeast Asia. By the eighteenth century, however, that balance of military and economic power had begun to shift in favor of Europe, where some states were benefiting from industrialization and new military technologies. In this era the Ottoman Empire faced the challenges of decentralizing forces within and vigorous pressure from rivals beyond its boundaries.

Internally, central government power had been weakened by the increasing autonomy of regional governors *(ayan)* in the provinces. These notables mobilized their own provincial forces and resisted or evaded the authority of the central government in Istanbul. In North Africa the local lords had long enjoyed relative autonomy, and by the end of the eighteenth century the Ottomans had little real power in the Maghreb.

The ranks of the janissary corps, the premier Ottoman fighting force, had also become grossly inflated; many of those claiming military pay were performing no military service. So the janissaries, once the front line of Ottoman defense, became a source of rebellion and a drain on the government treasury.

Indeed, the most evident signs of Ottoman weakness were military. The Russians defeated the Ottoman armies, and the empire had to sign the humiliating treaty of Küchük Kaynarca in 1774. Not only did the empire lose territory, but the Russians demanded the right to intervene in the affairs of the Orthodox Christian community in the empire. This concession for the first time granted a foreign state the power to meddle directly in Ottoman affairs. In 1798 Napoleon invaded Ottoman Egypt, and although his stay there was short, his easy victory illustrated the tenuousness of Ottoman control over the North African provinces.

The capitulations, treaties that granted special trade privileges to European states, also weakened both Ottoman and Qajar Empires. In the sixteenth century the Ottoman and Persian sovereigns had dictated the terms of foreign trade. But as their economies weakened, they granted more and more extensive privileges to European traders, which gave states like Britain and France increasing leverage in

The Era of Ottoman Reform

1808–1839	Reign of Ottoman reformer Mahmud II
1839–1876	Tanzimat, Ottoman reform period
1876	First constitutional revolution
1876–1909	Reign of Sultan Abdülhamid
1908	Young Turk Revolution reinstates Ottoman constitution

commercial affairs. As the nineteenth century progressed, European states would extend that influence by granting large loans to Middle Eastern rulers.

Ottoman Reform

To counter these challenges, Sultan Selim III (1789–1806) launched a series of reforms, focusing on the military. He created a new infantry corps composed of Turkish peasants. Selim also opened channels of communication with the European capitals by setting up embassies in London, Paris, Berlin, and Vienna. Ultimately, he was deposed by the janissaries, who resented his new army, but his reign marks the start of an era of Ottoman reform that would last into the early twentieth century.

A much more successful reformer was Sultan Mahmud II (1808–1839). Mahmud restored central authority in the provinces to some degree and cleared the way for military reform by annihilating the janissary corps. He then established a new army, modeled on successful European armies and trained by Prussian and French officers. Mahmud also reformed professional education by opening medical and military schools; the language of instruction was French. Beyond the military sphere, Mahmud's reforms included a restructuring of the bureaucracy, the launching of an official newspaper, and the opening of a translation bureau.

Men trained in the new professional schools and translation bureau would form a new nineteenth-century elite, sometimes called the "French knowers." Able to deal with the European powers on their own terms, these men would both challenge and reform the old Ottoman institutional order. Where French-style uniforms were the symbol of the new military, the frock coat was a symbol of the Europeanization of the civil buraucracy. Mahmud II's reforms were not designed to cast off Ottoman culture and ideology but rather to create systems that would enable the empire to compete with Europe and recoup its status as a world power.

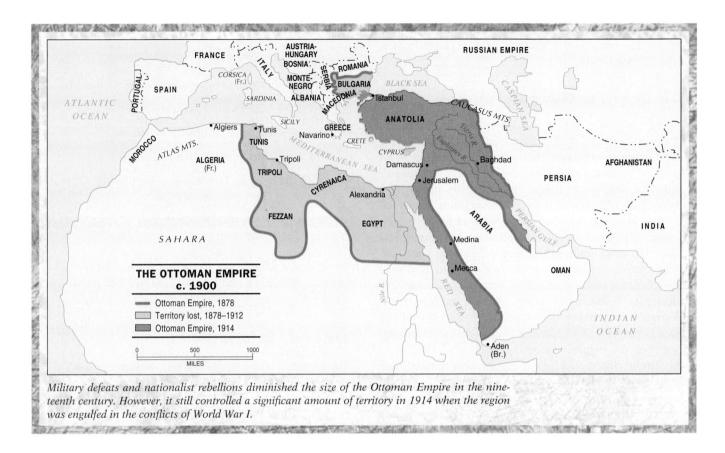

Military defeats and nationalist rebellions diminished the size of the Ottoman Empire in the nineteenth century. However, it still controlled a significant amount of territory in 1914 when the region was engulfed in the conflicts of World War I.

Challenging Ottoman Sovereignty in Europe

Ottoman territorial integrity was challenged in the nineteenth century by a series of separatist movements in the Balkans. The rise of nationalism in Europe and Great Power meddling in Ottoman affairs were both factors in the emergence and evolution of these movements. The Serbs rose in revolt in 1804, followed by the Greeks in 1821, the Romanians in the 1850s, and the Bulgarians in the 1870s.

The Serbs achieved autonomy in 1830 after a long struggle. The Greek Revolt, however, more directly engaged the energies of the Great Powers, who intervened to ensure its success. The Ottomans had crushed the Greek insurrection in its early stages. But Britian, Russia, and France all viewed the rebellion as a focal point in what came to be called the "Eastern Question"—whether the Ottoman Empire would be dismembered, and if so, who would get what.

The Greek Revolt captured the imaginations of European intellectuals who were enamored of the Greek classical tradition and saw the revolt as a romantic instance of the forces of freedom triumphing over the forces of despotism. Although that romanticism had little to do with the ground-level realities of the revolt, it did fuel support for the Greeks in the cities of western Europe. In the end a predominantly British fleet sank the Ottoman navy at Navarino in 1827, and Britain, Russia, and France engineered a treaty to establish an independent Greece.

Russia and Britain would encounter each other again over Ottoman territory, but on opposite sides, in the Crimean War (1854–1856). Britain saved Istanbul from Russian conquest, thereby preserving the balance of power. But by the end of the nineteenth century, Europeans were referring to the empire as the "sick man of Europe" (see Chapter 28), and the Ottomans had lost control over most of their Balkan provinces.

Egypt and the Rule of Muhammad Ali

Egypt had been a province of the Ottoman Empire since its conquest by Sultan Selim the Grim in 1517. By the late eighteenth century, however, Ottoman rule was little more than nominal as Egypt was controlled in fact by local leaders, the heads of Mamluk households. In the nineteenth century Egypt was conclusively detached from Ottoman rule, first by a highly successful Ottoman military commander named Muhammad Ali and then by the British, who seized Egypt as a strategic link to their colonial empire in India.

Muhammad Ali came to power in Egypt in the aftermath of Napoleon's invasion. The French occupation of Egypt was short-lived, although it served to stimulate European interest in Egyptian civilization. When a joint British-Ottoman expedition arrived in Egypt in 1801 to end the French occupation, Muhammad Ali was one of the Ottoman commanders. He established himself as the dominant military leader, filling the power vacuum left by the French departure.

Muhammad Ali destroyed the Mamluks, organized his military along European lines, and built up a new, conscripted peasant army. He founded new professional schools and a government printing press, reorganized the agricultural and taxation systems of Egypt, sent men to study in France, and launched an ambitious program of industrialization. He also undermined the power of the religious establishment, the *ulama*. Muhammad Ali's reforms were more extensive than those of Sultan Mahmud II, but these two contemporaries were both major symbols of Middle Eastern reform.

Once Muhammad Ali consolidated his power, he moved to challenge the Ottoman state directly. Initially, he had defended Ottoman interests by defeating the Wahhabis (a puritanical movement in Arabia that aimed to cleanse Islam of innovations like Sufism) and helping put down the Greek Revolt. But in 1831 he sent his son Ibrahim to invade Syria and Anatolia; Ibrahim marched his armies to within 150 miles of Istanbul.

Here again, Russia, Britain, and France intervened to preserve the Ottoman Empire. In the end Muhammad Ali established an autonomous dynastic state in Egypt where his descendants occupied the throne until the 1950s. His career illustrates the weakness of the Ottoman Empire and its tenuous control over its more distant provinces. European states capitalized on the disruptions caused by Muhammad Ali to negotiate more advantageous commercial agreements with the beleaguered Ottoman sultan, thus undermining the economic foundations of the empire even further.

The Suez Canal

Muhammad Ali's successors pursued parts of his reform programs, with little military or economic success. Egypt benefited from the American Civil War when Egyptian cotton was used to replace the South's cotton exports, which evaporated when the Union blockaded southern ports. But foreign loans and the uncontrolled spending of its rulers left Egypt bankrupt by the 1870s.

The idea of a canal linking the Mediterranean to the Red Sea was not new. The Mamluks, rulers of medieval Egypt, had planned such a canal but lacked the technology to accomplish it. In 1854 the Egyptian ruler, Said, granted a Frenchman, Ferdinand de

Eugène Delacroix, Massacre at Chios *(1824). European liberals and Romantics such as Delacroix supported the Greeks in their struggle for independence from the Turks, who were seen as cruel oppressors.*

Lesseps, a concession to build a canal. De Lesseps was only one among many European entrepreneurs and concessionaires pouring into Egypt at this time to take advantage of building opportunities and commercial privileges.

The Suez Canal was completed in 1869 during the reign of Khedive Ismail (1863–1879). Ismail was committed to the European-style transformation of his realm. But his lavish spending, particularly on his opening ceremonies for the canal, threw Egypt into a financial crisis.

The opening ceremonies were a world event. Ismail commissioned the opera *Aïda* (which was not completed in time) and built special pavilions to house visiting dignitaries. His extravagance dazzled even the jaded aristocrats of Europe. The empress Eugénie of France, a notorious "clothes horse," was said to have taken 250 dresses with her to the affair.

Plagued by financial troubles, Ismail sold Egypt's shares in the canal to Britain for 4 million pounds sterling. The stock was snapped up by Disraeli, the astute

The opening of the Suez Canal in 1869 was an international event attended by numerous heads of state. Lavish spending for this event helped bankrupt Egypt.

prime minister of Great Britain, while the French dithered over whether to buy them. This sale gave Britain virtual control of this essential water link to its South Asian empire. The following year (the same year the Ottoman Empire defaulted on its loans), Egypt was unable to pay the interest on its foreign loans. Britain and France then forced Egypt to accept European control over its debts and hence its economy.

This assertion of foreign control paved the way for a British invasion of Egypt. The British and French forced Ismail to abdicate in 1879; and in 1881 an army officer named Colonel Urabi, of peasant origins, led a military and populist revolt against foreign control in Egypt. He aimed to limit the power of the khedive and to form a national assembly. There was antiforeign rioting in Alexandria, where many Europeans lost their lives. The British, claiming they were acting in the best interests of the Egyptian people, then shelled Alexandria and took Cairo in 1882. Although their occupation was supposedly temporary, they remained until the Egyptian Revolt of 1952 and kept control of the Suez Canal until 1956.

Lord Cromer and the Dinshaway Incident

When the British conquered Egypt, they appointed Sir Evelyn Baring, later named Lord Cromer, to reorganize Egyptian finances, eliminate corruption, improve the cotton industry, and oversee the country's affairs from 1883 to 1907. Cromer was an able administrator who stabilized the Egyptian economy, but his harsh policies and contempt for the Egyptian people earned him the hatred of many and helped galvanize the Egyptian nationalist movement.

Those sentiments are symbolized by an episode in 1906 that came to be called the Dinshaway Incident. The affair began simply with British officers on a pigeon shoot in the countryside. The officers, heedless of the fact that Egyptian villagers kept pigeons for food, pursued their hunt and wounded a villager in Dinshaway, in the Nile delta. In the ensuing scuffle, two officers were wounded, and one subsequently died.

What made this episode famous was the British response. Determined to make an example of Dinshaway,

Egypt was part of the Ottoman Empire for more than 350 years. Although the British conquered Egypt in 1882, the Ottomans still thought of it as their own territory. This Ottoman cartoon, published in Istanbul in 1908, expresses bonds of brotherhood between the Ottoman constitutionalist and the Young Egyptian nationalists who were trying to throw off British imperial rule. As the giant symbol of England leans lazily against the pyramids, the tiny Egyptians do not seem to have much of a chance.

the British punished the whole village. They tried dozens of villagers and publicly hanged four. This incident provoked anger throughout Egypt, prompted the penning of patriotic songs, and gave force to the nationalist movement. The Dinshaway Incident showed that the people in the Middle East, and not just the elites, could be mobilized to protect their own economic security and to resist the inroads of European states.

North Africa West of Egypt

The appellation North Africa suggests a radical separation between Mediterranean and sub-Saharan Africa. But these two areas have long been linked by networks of trade. North Africa is grouped here with the Middle East because it was Islamized during the early Arab conquests and because it was loosely controlled by the Ottoman Empire during the premodern era. West of Egypt, North Africa contained the state of Morocco, ruled by the Filali dynasty since 1631, and three coastal states based on Tunis, Algiers, and Tripoli that were established under Ottoman rule. These latter three dominated the western

Mediterranean for three centuries, remaining nominally under Ottoman control. Semi-autonomous governors, however, exercised the real power in the coastal states, attempting with limited success to subordinate tribal leaders in their hinterlands.

Algiers, Tripoli, and, to a lesser extent, Tunis were corsairing states that collected revenues from pirate activity off their coasts. In the eighteenth century they benefited from treaties with various European states that were willing to pay tribute and gifts in exchange for security for their merchant shipping. That shipping was part of a vast web of seaborne trade that reached from Southeast Asia and China to the American colonies.

When the American colonies gained their independence from Britain, they too negotiated treaties with these "Barbary States" in order to protect the lucrative American trade with North Africa. Sidi Muhammad (1757–1790) of Morocco granted the fledgling United States its first official trading privileges in 1786. The U.S. Congress authorized $40,000 for a treaty and $25,000 annual tribute for Algiers in 1790 and shortly thereafter provided for the building of a navy to gain leverage against the corsair state.

In the nineteenth century, however, European powers began to look to North Africa as an area ripe for conquest. Like Egypt, the rest of North Africa experienced European economic penetration before it suffered actual invasion. That penetration took the form of capitulations, reflecting commercial concessions granted to European states by the Ottomans and the exploitation of North Africa as a market for European goods.

The first target was Algiers. In the 1820s the ruler of Algiers (called the *Dey*) sent ships to aid the Ottomans in putting down the Greek Revolt; he also dealt with internal revolt as Algiers's Berber tribesmen fought against his janissary troops. Meanwhile the French were enmeshed in conflicts with the Dey over fishing rights, piracy, and a debt the French owed Algiers.

In 1827, using the pretext that the Dey had insulted the French consul by publicly hitting him with a fly whisk, France blockaded Algiers. Pursuing France's imperialist agenda, King Charles X then invaded Algiers in 1830. He sent a large army of occupation, but only after 17 years of fierce resistance could Algeria be directly incorporated as an integral part of the French state.

Algiers then became a base for France to extend its influence in North Africa. Tunis remained singularly autonomous of Ottoman rule and in 1861 established its own constitution. An insurrection, which united tribal and urban elements in 1864, led to the bankrupting of Tunis in 1869. Its French, Italian, and British creditors then gained control of the Tunisian economy. Italy coveted the coastal state with its rich agricultural hinterland, but the French stayed those

A Middle Eastern Vision of the West

In 1844 France bombarded Moroccan ports and forced a treaty on the Moroccan sultan, Mulay Abd ar-Rahman. The following year, interested in studying the sources of French power, Morocco sent an embassy to France. One of its members was the scholar Muhammad as-Saffar, who later recorded his impressions of French society. As a distinguished visitor, he tended to travel in elite circles. Muhammad as-Saffar expressed admiration for French military organization, but he was also an astute observer of French culture, as this excerpt shows.

The people of Paris, men and women alike, are tireless in their pursuit of wealth. They are never idle or lazy. The women are like the men in that regard, or perhaps even more so. . . . Even though they have all kinds of amusements and spectacles of the most marvelous kinds, they are not distracted from their work. . . . Nor do they excuse someone for being poor, for indeed death is easier for them than poverty, and the poor man there is seen as vile and contemptible.

Another of their characteristics is a hot-tempered and stubborn arrogance, and they challenge each other to a duel at the slightest provocation. If one of them slanders or insults another, the challenged one has no choice but to respond, lest he be branded a despicable coward for the rest of his life. Then they decide the conditions of the combat—what weapons they will fight with, how it will be done, and the place—and no one in authority interferes with them.

[At dinner the women's dresses] covered their breasts, which were hidden from view, but the rest of their bosom, face and neck were bare and exposed. . . . They bind their waists beneath their dresses with tight girdles which give them a very narrow middle. It is said that they are trained into this [shape] from early childhood by means of a special mold. . . . In the lower part they drape their clothing in such a way that the backside is greatly exaggerated, but perhaps this is due to something they put underneath [bustles].

From Susan G. Miller, trans. and ed., *Disorienting Encounters: Travels of a Moroccan Scholar in France in 1845–1856* (Berkeley: University of California Press, 1992), pp. 153, 158.

---

ambitions by invading in 1881 and making it a protectorate. After that time, much of the country's wealth was siphoned off into French coffers, and most of the population lived in desperate poverty.

From the 1840s to the end of the century, French interests also dominated in Morocco. But Germany was emerging as a significant power in the late nineteenth century and also cast its eye on African territory, including Morocco. France, however, used its established bases in North Africa and its alliance with the British to win this particular standoff. They promised the Germans territory elsewhere in Africa and took over Morocco in 1912. The French left the Moroccan dynasty in place but did not relinquish their hold on the country until 1956.

The Italians, frustrated by the Ethiopians in their ambitions for East Africa, decided to seize a piece of the North African pie. Capitalizing on the disruptions caused by the Ottoman constitutional revolution, they declared war on the Ottoman Empire in 1911 and invaded the area around Tripoli, annexing it in the face of a failed Ottoman defense. The Sanusi order of Sufis, which had great influence in the region, vigorously resisted Italian (and French) expansionism. This order, established in the area in 1843, worked as both an Islamic reform movement and a political force. It would later gain power in the new state of Libya when the colonial powers withdrew.

For the time, however, the early twentieth century saw North Africa, like sub-Saharan Africa, divided among the European imperial powers and incorporated into European empires.

Young Ottomans and Constitutional Reform

The challenges to Ottoman sovereignty, combined with the prospect of a newly emerging "modern" world order, prompted a period of reform known as the *Tanzimat* (reorganization) from 1839 to 1876. New professional schools were opened in the empire, the class of "French knowers" expanded, and a more modern and secular civil bureaucracy was established. The power of the *ulama* was diminished by the legal and educational reforms. The government also tried to ward off separatist sentiments by emphasizing the ideology of Ottomanism, the notion that all Ottoman subjects were equal and should be committed to the preservation of the empire, regardless of ethnicity or religion. Of course, not everyone accepted this ideology, but it did hold sway in the government until the end of the empire.

Out of the reforms of the *Tanzimat* emerged a new civil and military elite, some of whom favored

One type of European penetration into the Ottoman Empire was the opening of textile factories in western Anatolia. The young girls and women who worked in these factories often made relatively good wages, but their work in factories raised moral issues about "unsupervised" women, much as it did in the factories of Europe. These young women workers in a silk-thread factory pose for the camera in 1878.

elements of European culture and more democratic forms of government. Among them, a group of intellectuals and bureaucrats, sometimes called the Young Ottomans, revitalized Ottoman literature and called for a new synthesis that would combine the best elements of traditional Islamic culture with European ideas and technology. These reformers debated issues such as constitutional freedoms, changing the Ottoman calendar and clocks to European time schemes, "modern" schools, and the "woman question," the rights and education of the "modern" woman.

In 1876 a group of these reform-minded elites spearheaded a drive to depose Sultan Abdülaziz and install Western-style constitutional government in the Ottoman Empire. They did not wish to eliminate the monarchy, and the new constitution they proposed left considerable power in the hands of the sultan. But they did want an elected assembly, freedom

of the press, and equality for all Ottomans. The constitutionalists installed a new sultan, Abdülhamid II (1876–1909). But once Abdülhamid consolidated his power, in 1878, he abrogated the constitution and suspended the parliament.

Abdülhamid II and the Young Turk Revolution

Abdülhamid, paradoxically, was both a reformer and an autocrat. He continued many of the trends set in the *Tanzimat* era but controlled opposition through spies, censorship of the press, exile, and imprisonment.

The sultan faced severe challenges on all fronts. Russia declared war on the empire in 1877, resulting in the loss of more Ottoman territory. Britain occupied Egypt and the island of Cyprus. Meanwhile,

Abdülhamid II. Photography was all the rage in the empire during Abdülhamid's reign, and the sultan supported several court photographers. He sent commemorative volumes documenting his reforms and Ottoman progress to heads of state in the United States and Britain. Widespread discontent with his oppressive rule lent strength to the constitutional movement of the Young Turks, who ultimately deposed the sultan in 1909.

the empire, hampered by huge debts that it could not pay, was engaged in trying to redeem its Balkan territories.

Abdülhamid tried to control the centrifugal forces at work on the empire by enhancing central government control, bolstering the military, and establishing closer relations with an increasingly powerful Germany. Kaiser William made two state visits, in 1889 and 1898, including a trip to Jerusalem during which the kaiser, a good politician, declared his friendship with the world's Muslims.

The sultan also fostered the ideology of Pan-Islam to legitimize his reign and mobilize the support of the world's Muslims. His rhetoric of Islamic unity and his claim to be caliph did not necessarily strike a chord among all Muslims. His project for a

Hijaz railway to bring pilgrims from Damascus to Mecca, however, did generate popular support for the sultan, and schoolchildren across the empire contributed their coins to help ensure its success.

But the constitutional ideal in the Ottoman Empire had not been lost, and opposition to the sultan mounted as Abdülhamid entered the third decade of his reign. Outside the empire a group of exiles labored to promote the reinstatement of the constitution. Inside the empire revolutionary sentiments grew among students, bureaucrats, and some members of the military. In 1889 a group of students in the military-medical school founded a secret organization called the Committee for Union and Progress (CUP). This group was instrumental in mobilizing opposition to the regime.

In 1908 a military revolt became the catalyst for the second Ottoman constitutional revolution, known as the Young Turk Revolution. Support for the revolt spread rapidly, and the revolutionaries demanded that Abdülhamid reinstate the constitution. He acceded reluctantly to their demands, elections were held, censorship was suspended, and the Young Turks relegated the sultan to a position of secondary importance. Among the issues debated by the new assembly were rehabilitating the navy, reforming the police, and warding off attacks by the empire's neighbors.

Reactionaries launched a counterrevolution, in which Abdülhamid was implicated, in April 1909; but they were put down by the army. Abdülhamid was promptly deposed, and the CUP came to dominate the Ottoman constitutional regime. Although a new sultan was installed, the revolution marked the end of a centuries-long era of Ottoman monarchical power. The new government remained firmly in the hands of a civilian elite. Discontent simmered in the Arab provinces as the CUP continued the centralizing policies of Abdülhamid. But in general the government and the remaining provinces stayed committed to the empire until World War I.

Qajar Rule and the Tobacco Rebellion

The Ottoman revolution of 1908 was not the only upheaval to transform government and society in the Middle East. In fact, the same tensions among monarchy, foreign intervention, and Western-style constitutional reform that prompted the Young Turk Revolution also provoked a constitutional revolution in Persia two years earlier.

Persia had been controlled by the Qajar dynasty since 1794. After a military defeat by the Russians, in 1828 the Qajar shah was forced to concede extraterritorial rights to Russian merchants and give them special commercial privileges. Soon the British were de-

Young Turks march in triumph after their successful coup and overthrow of Abdülhamid II and his government. Like the sultan, the Young Turks used photography to document the events and successes of their government.

manding similar rights. As the nineteenth century progressed, the Qajars found themselves caught in a military and commercial squeeze play between Russia and Britain.

Foreign incursions reached a climax in the second half of the nineteenth century with the long reign of Nasir al-Din Shah (1848–1896). Unlike the Ottomans or Muhammad Ali, the Qajars remained dependent on the decentralized military power of tribal chiefs to defend Persia. Nasir al-Din implemented some military and educational reforms, but his government remained weak. To bolster his position, the shah negotiated loans, sold concessions to foreign investors, and brought in Russian military advisers to establish a Cossack brigade.

While Russian influence prevailed in the Qajar military, Britain moved to penetrate various spheres of the Persian economy. The British completed a telegraph line from London to Persia in 1870, symboliz-

ing their increased interest in the area. In 1890 Nasir al-Din granted a British group exclusive rights over the entire Persian tobacco industry. This act alienated

The Political Transformation of Persia

1848–1896	Reign of Nasir al-Din Shah
1891	Tobacco Rebellion and boycott
1896–1906	Reign of Muzaffar al-Din Shah
1905	Constitutional revolution begins
1907–1909	Reign of Muhammad Ali Shah
1909	Constitutionalists depose Muhammad Ali Shah

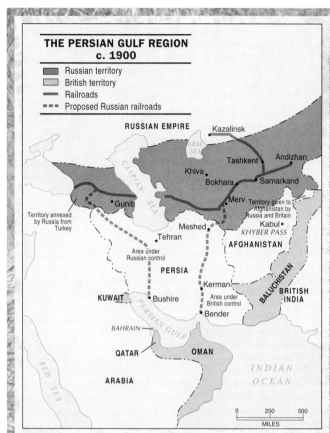

THE PERSIAN GULF REGION c. 1900

- Russian territory
- British territory
- Railroads
- Proposed Russian railroads

RUSSIAN EMPIRE

Kazalinsk

ARAL SEA

Tashkent

Andizhan

Khiva

Bokhara

Samarkand

Merv

Territory annexed by Russia from Turkey

Gunib

Territory given to Afghanistan by Russia and Britain

Meshed

Kabul

KHYBER PASS

Tehran

AFGHANISTAN

Area under Russian control

PERSIA

Kerman

BALUCHISTAN

BRITISH INDIA

KUWAIT

Bushire

Area under British control

Bender

BAHRAIN

PERSIAN GULF

QATAR

OMAN

INDIAN OCEAN

ARABIA

RED SEA

0   250   500
MILES

By the late nineteenth century Britain and Russia were both pressing hard to advance their interests in Persia. Negotiating agreements with local rulers, Britain used the Persian Gulf region as a strategic base for its powerful fleets and as a link to its empire in India.

telegraph lines, established a postal system, and developed trade. Some Persian workers crossed into Russia to work in the Caucasus oilfields. The Russian ministry of finance even set up a bank, The Discount and Loan Bank of Persia, with branches in many parts of the nation. This bank loaned the Persian government 60 million rubles and provided 120 million rubles to Persian merchants to enable them to buy Russian goods.

The British in turn set up the Imperial Bank of Persia in the southeastern part of the country. In 1901 Muzaffar al-Din Shah (1896–1906) granted a British subject a concession for the oil rights to all of Persia except a few northern provinces. This would lead to British control over Persian oil that would continue into the second half of the century. The shah, who made three costly trips to Europe during his short reign, took large foreign loans from the British, the French, and the Russians.

Aiming to dominate the sea routes between Suez and their Indian empire, the British also gained footholds in the Persian Gulf region through treaties with a number of shaykhdoms, including Muscat, Oman, Bahrain, and Kuwait (1899). In 1903 the British foreign secretary issued what has been called a British Monroe Doctrine over the area: "I say it without hesitation, we should regard the establishment of a naval base or a fortified port in the Persian Gulf by any other power as a very grave menace to British interests, and we should certainly resist it by all means at our disposal."[2] Thus the British won the imperialist struggle for control of the Persian Gulf just as France won the struggle for control of the coast of North Africa.

Responding to foreign intervention in Persia, the shah's ineffectual rule, and the growing impetus for representative government, various factions within the nation mobilized a revolt beginning in 1905. This revolution began with a series of protests culminating in a general strike. Mass demonstrations, a strike by the *ulama*, and a massacre of protesters by the Cossack brigade followed in 1906.

The shah succumbed to this pressure and authorized a Constituent National Assembly. Elections were held, and new newspapers flourished in the capital. But Muzaffar al-Din died in 1906, and his successor, Muhammad Ali Shah (1907–1909), soon attempted to overturn the constitutional regime, plunging Persia into civil war. The new shah's tyranny and his use of Russian troops against Persians prompted some members of the *ulama* to send a telegram to the Ottoman sultan, asking for his aid to protect fellow Muslims.

After a bitter struggle, the constitutional forces won and deposed Muhammad Ali Shah in July 1909, installing his 12-year-old son in his place. The nation has had a constitutional government ever since, al-

the merchant classes, who aligned themselves with the Shi'ite *ulama* to launch a rebellion against the shah and the tobacco concession.

The *ulama* in Persia had never been subordinated by the government to the same degree as in the Ottoman Empire. These religious leaders constituted a powerful force for opposition against the government and would be instrumental in the national revolutions of the twentieth century. During the tobacco rebellion of 1891 the *ulama* engineered a countrywide boycott of tobacco, and the shah was forced to cancel the tobacco concession. This boycott not only illustrated the mobilizing power of the Shi'ite clerics, but (like the Dinshaway Incident in Egypt) also pointed up popular discontent over the increasingly intrusive European presence.

The Persian Constitutional Revolution

By the beginning of the twentieth century, parts of northern Persia were under the control of the Russians. Tsarist forces trained the Persian army, put up

though its power was often compromised by the preservation of the monarchy.

The Persian constitutional revolution was watched closely in Istanbul and served as a prelude to the Ottoman revolution, which followed quickly on its heels. The constitutionalists in both empires were inspired by the example of Japan, a modernizing power with a strong military. Japan, more to the point, was an Asian power that had decisively beaten a European power, Russia, in 1905. Finally, the new Persian and Ottoman constitutional regimes faced similar problems and were preoccupied with many of the same issues of modernization, freedom, and reform.

The Great Power Struggle for the East

As so often happens, revolution provided the opponents of the Ottoman and Qajar Empires with opportunities to grab territory. European powers extended their hold on onetime Ottoman lands. Between 1908 and 1913 Austria-Hungary annexed Bosnia and Herzegovina, Greece annexed Crete, and Italy—in the course of a short but difficult war—seized Tripoli and Cyrenaica (northeastern Libya). In 1912 and 1913 the Balkan nations fought two wars, which resulted in the partitioning of Macedonia (see Chapter 28).

In Persia, Russia capitalized on the revolution to occupy territory in the northwest. The British and Russians signed a treaty in 1907 dividing Persia into spheres of influence, with the British claiming powers of intervention in the south and Russia claiming the same powers in the north. These two states held Persia in a great pincers, with the British navy protecting its interests in the Persian Gulf and Russia's powerful armies posing a constant threat to Persian sovereignty in the north.

Persia was not, however, the only object of this competition. Afghanistan, to its east, controlled the Khyber Pass, the most direct land route from Russia to British-controlled India. The country had been divided previously between the Mughul and Persian Empires, but with its mountainous terrain and contending warlords, Afghanistan did not lend itself to unified rule. By the nineteenth century the shah in Kabul, Afghanistan's capital, held tenuous sway over the tribal confederations that controlled the area.

During the first half of the nineteenth century, Persia and Afghanistan were caught up in armed conflicts with the Russians and the British. In an effort to increase their influence in the area and protect India's northern frontiers, the British attempted to install their own handpicked ruler in Afghanistan. The attempt backfired, and the British were forced to retreat. But in 1879 Britain, using its powerful colonial army, seized the Khyber Pass and Kabul and subordinated the Afghan ruler. Between 1881 and

1901 Amir Abdur Rahman consolidated his power over Afghanistan, but Britian retained its hold on Afghanistan's foreign affairs.

Russia, meanwhile, was expanding toward the southeast. Many indigenous peoples, such as the Mongols, Afghans, Turkomans, and Tatars, came within Russia's sphere of influence. Their cities—Samarkand, Tashkent, and Bokhara—became tsarist administrative centers.

Russia's advance was won not only by its army but also by the construction of the Trans-Caspian railway, which at its completion in 1888 reached 1064 miles into the heart of Asia. The Orenburg-Tashkent railway, completed in 1905, stretched 1185 miles farther. Inspired by the feats of both the army and the engineers, some Russian imperialists dreamed of conquering Afghanistan and penetrating India itself. But British pressure blocked Russia's design on Afghanistan, and a British military expedition to Lhasa in 1904 countered Russian influence in Tibet.

By the terms of the Anglo-Russian entente in 1907, Russia agreed to deal with the sovereign of Afghanistan only through the British government. Great Britain agreed to refrain from occupying or annexing Afghanistan so long as the nation fulfilled its treaty obligations. This partnership was, however, only a marriage of convenience brought on by larger pressures in Europe. Neither side wished to alienate the other in the face of the emerging threat of Germany's war machine.

Conclusion

By 1914 European states had established their primacy over Africa and the Middle East. While thousands of Africans worked in European-owned mines, thousands of Persians crossed into Russia to work in tsarist oilfields. While financiers in London, Berlin, and Paris skimmed the profits from the resources of Africa and Asia, European officials and diplomats dictated policy for much of the region. Although the Young Turk and Persian Revolutions brought constitutional governments to the Ottoman and Qajar Empires in the Middle East, only Persia would survive the consuming conflicts of World War I. The Young Turks, engaged in rebuilding the Ottoman Empire, chose to enter the war on the German side and suffered disastrous consequences.

Even before 1914, however, the forces that would eventually remove European dominance in the next half century were at work. In Africa and Egypt various indigenous groups mobilized to throw off the European yoke. In Europe citizens and parliamentary representatives debated the relative costs and benefits of empire and colonies. Many remained committed to social Darwinism, the idea of civilizational hierarchy expressed in the notions of carrying the "white man's burden" of spreading "civilization" to the "lesser peoples." But despite European military, economic, and technological superiority over the Middle East and Africa, the "white man's burden" would become increasingly onerous as the twentieth century progressed and as the conquered peoples mobilized to gain independence and to assert their own cultural identities.

Culture and identity, of course, are not fixed; they are constantly evolving. The period from 1800 to 1914 in the Middle East and Africa was one of particularly intense and rapid cultural change prompted by marked transformations in economic organization and in the technologies of transportation and communications. The effects of such transformations on African and Middle Eastern societies were compounded as those societies were subjugated by or subordinated to European states and economies.

People reacted in different ways to that subordination, depending on their position, class, education, religion, and ethnicity. Some advocated emulation of Europe in order to regain lost powers; others advocated vigorous resistance and adherence to traditional mores; many saw some advantage in compromise, taking technologies and organizational structures from the West while retaining many elements of the old order.

The assertion of European primacy over Africa and the Middle East had dramatic effects. Europeanization altered economic, political, and legal structures. In many cases it radically altered the education systems and even the languages of the conquered territories. French and English culture were adopted to some degree by many subject peoples, especially among the upper and middle classes. Other African and Middle Eastern peoples rejected the imported European traditions or modified them to suit their own needs.

European influence thus created new cultural syntheses. While upper-class ladies in Istanbul sought out French fashions, upper-class European women dressed in "Turkish" style and consumed Orientalist art. In many ways, however, European culture was a veneer applied to powerful local cultural traditions. Islam retained its strength, and European Christian missionaries met with little success in their efforts to convert Muslims in the Middle East. African peoples adapted Christianity to their own rituals. Armed with the technological, intellectual, and political lessons they learned confronting the Europeans, African and Middle Eastern peoples would soon craft new states in the nation-state mold of the new twentieth-century world order.

Suggestions for Reading

Usman dan Fodio's *jihads* and the creation of the Sokoto Caliphate are treated in Mervyn Hiskett, *The Sword of Truth: The Life and Times of the Shehu Usuman dan Fodio* (Northwest-

ern University Press, 1994); Ibrahim Sulaiman, *A Revolution in History: The Jihad of Usman dan Fodio* (Mansell, 1986); and R. A Adeleye, *Power and Diplomacy in Northern Nigeria, 1804–1906* (Humanities Press, 1971). The trans-Saharan slave trade is covered in Elizabeth Savage, ed., *The Human Commodity* (Cass, 1992). The decline of the Atlantic slave trade and the expansion of trade with Europe are traced in Paul Lovejoy, *Slow Death for Slavery: The Course of Abolition in Northern Nigeria, 1897–1938* (Cambridge University Press, 1993), and Robin Law, *From Slave Trade to "Legitimate" Commerce: The Commercial Transition in Nineteenth-Century West Africa* (Cambridge University Press, 1996). The long-distance trade and state formation in eastern Africa is treated in John Iliffe, *A Modern History of Tanzania* (Cambridge University Press, 1979); Abdul Sheriff, *Spices and Ivory in Zanzibar* (Ohio University Press, 1987); and Edward Alpers, *Ivory and Slaves in East Central Africa* (Heinemann, 1975).

John D. Omer-Cooper, *The Zulu Aftermath: A Nineteenth-Century Revolution in Bantu Africa* (Northwestern University Press, 1966), remains the only overview of the Mfecane in southern Africa, while Carolyn Hamilton covers the historiographical debates about the period in *The Mfecane Aftermath: Reconstructive Debates in Southern African History* (Witwatersrand University Press, 1995). Because facts about Shaka's life are the subject of dispute, several writers have examined Shaka's powerful imagery, including Carolyn Hamilton, *Terrific Majesty: The Power of Shaka Zulu and the Limits of Historical Invention* (Harvard University Press, 1998), and Dafnah Golan, *Inventing Shaka: Using History in the Construction of Zulu Nationalism* (Rienner, 1994). John Laband has written a comprehensive treatment of nineteenth-century Zulu history, *The Rise and Fall of the Zulu Nation* (Arms & Armour, 1997). Moshoeshoe's life is treated in biographies by Leonard Thompson, *Survival in Two Worlds: Moshoeshoe of Lesotho* (Oxford University Press, 1975), and Peter Sanders, *Moshoeshoe, Chief of the Sotho* (Heinemann, 1975).

The impact of the end of slavery in South Africa is treated in Nigel Worden and Clifton Crais, eds., *Breaking the Chains: Slavery and Its Legacy in the Nineteenth-Century Cape Colony* (Witwatersrand University Press, 1994). Studies on nineteenth-century South Africa include Timothy Keegan, *Colonial South Africa and the Origins of the Racial Order* (University of Virginia Press, 1996); Peter Delius, *The Land Belongs to Us* (University of California Press, 1984); and Jeff Peires, *The Dead Will Arise: Nongqawuse and the Great Xhosa Cattle-Killing Movement of 1856–7* (Indiana University Press, 1989). An overview of the diamond industry is Stefan Kanfer, *The Last Empire: De Beers, Diamonds, and the World* (Farrar, Straus & Giroux, 1993). The best treatments of the Anglo-Boer War are Peter Warwick, ed., *The South African War* (Longman, 1980), and Thomas Pakenham, *The Boer War* (Random House, 1979).

Studies on the European scramble for Africa include Ronald Robinson and J. Gallagher, *Africa and the Victorians* (St. Martin's Press, 1969); Thomas Pakenham, *The Scramble for Africa* (Random House, 1991); H. L. Wesseling, *Imperialism and Colonialism* (Greenwood Press, 1997); and David Levering Lewis, *The Race to Fashoda: Colonialism and African Resistance* (Henry Holt, 1995). The use of technology to facilitate conquest is treated in Daniel Headrick, *The Tentacles of Progress: Technology Transfer in the Age of Imperialism, 1850–1940* (Oxford University Press, 1988); Michael Adas, *Machines as the Measure of Men: Science, Technology, and Ideologies of Western Dominance* (Cornell University Press, 1989); and Michael Adas, ed., *Technology and European Overseas Enterprise: Diffusion, Adaption, and Adoption* (Variorum, 1996).

The general subject of African resistance to European conquest is comprehensively treated in Robert Rotberg and Ali Mazrui, *Protest and Power in Black Africa* (Oxford University

Press, 1970), and Bruce Vandervort, *Wars of Imperial Conquest in Africa, 1830–1914* (Indiana University Press, 1998). Yves Person has written the authoritative biography of Samori Touré, *Samori: La Renaissance de L'Empire Mandique* (ABC, 1976). Ethiopia's return to a centralized kingdom and its resistance to European conquest is covered in Sven Rubenson, *King of Kings: Tewodros of Ethiopia* (Heineman, 1978); Harold Marcus, *The Life and Times of Menelik II: Ethiopia, 1844–1913* (Red Sea Press, 1995); and Bahru Zewde, *A History of Modern Ethiopia, 1855–1974* (Ohio University Press, 1991).

On the Ottoman Empire in the nineteenth century, see Roderic H. Davison, *Turkey: A Short History*, 3rd ed. (Eothen Press, 1998), for a brief, well-written survey; Bernard Lewis provides the intellectual and cultural context in *The Emergence of Modern Turkey*, 2nd ed. (Oxford University Press, 1968). See also Carter Findley, *Ottoman Civil Officialdom: A Social History* (Princeton University Press, 1989). On the Young Turk revolution, see Feroz Ahmad, *The Young Turks: The Committee of Union and Progress in Turkish Politics, 1908–1914* (Clarendon Press, 1969).

Economic issues are covered in Roger Owen, *The Middle East in the World Economy, 1800–1914* (Methuen, 1981), and Charles Issawi, ed., *The Economic History of the Middle East, 1800–1914: A Book of Readings* (University of Chicago Press, 1975).

A lucid and balanced survey of the "Eastern Question" is J. A. R. Marriott, *The Eastern Question: A Historical Study in European Diplomacy* (Clarendon Press, 1917). L. S. Stavrianos, *The Balkans Since 1453* (Holt, Rinehart and Winston, 1961), provides a treatment of the evolution of the Balkan states in the context of Ottoman rule. A solid study of the evolution of the nation-state in North Africa is Ali Ahmida, *The Making of Modern Libya: State Formation, Colonization, and Resistance, 1830–1932* (State University of New York Press, 1994).

For treatments of the Qajars and the Persian constitutional revolution, see Peter Avery, Gavin Hambly, and Charles Melville, eds., *The Cambridge History of Iran: Vol. 7, From Nadir Shah to the Islamic Republic* (Cambridge University Press, 1968); Edmond Bosworth and Carole Hellenbrand, eds., *Qajar Iran: Political, Social and Cultural Change, 1800–1925* (Mazda,

1992); Janet Afary, *The Iranian Constitutional Revolution, 1906–1911* (Columbia University Press, 1996), which also considers the origins of Iranian feminism; and Ervand Abrahamian, *Iran Between Two Revolutions* (Princeton University Press, 1982).

Suggestions for Web Browsing

Age of European Imperialism: The Partitioning of Africa in the Late Nineteenth Century
http://pw2.netcom.com/~giardina/colony.html

Site discusses the partitioning of Africa and includes an interesting selection of maps tracing the imperial drive in Africa.

End of the Slave Trade in Africa
http://www.fordham.edu/halsall/africa/africasbook.html#
The Impact of Slavery

Documents regarding the termination of slave trade in Africa, from the Internet African History Sourcebook.

Internet Islamic History Sourcebook: Western Intrusion, 1815–1914
http://www.fordham.edu/halsall/islam/islamsbook.html#
The Western Intrusion

Extensive on-line source for links about the history of the Middle East, including short primary documents describing nineteenth-century European imperialism and the end of the Ottoman Empire.

Notes

1. Quoted in N. D. Harris, *Europe and the East* (Boston: Houghton Mifflin, 1926), p. 285
2. *London Times*, Aug. 7, 1890.

The waterfront at Guangzhou (Canton) in a nineteenth-century painting. Guangzhou was the first Chinese port regularly visited by European traders. The Portuguese arrived in 1511, followed by the British in the seventeenth century and the French and Dutch in the eighteenth.

Canton factories, M3156. Oil on glass, post 1780. Peabody Essex Museum, Salem, MA. Photo by Mark Sexton.

Four Faces of Nineteenth-Century Imperialism

Latin America, East Asia, India, and the "Eastern Question"

Chapter Contents

To discuss the nineteenth-century history of the peoples of Latin American, East Asia, India, and the northwestern Ottoman Empire in terms of imperialism invites serious and warranted criticism. As we saw in Chapter 27, African and Middle Eastern civilizations and societies continued at their own pace, momentarily diverted by the arrival of the Europeans during this time. It can be argued that a chapter that focuses on the Western impact in these regions is Eurocentric and places a higher importance on the culture and institutions of the West than on those of these other parts of the world. It can also be asserted that the period of foreign dominance lasted barely half of a century, and its residue is important only in that it created the material and psychological chasm that separates the so-called developed from the lesser developed regions today.

Despite these valid points, we have chosen to discuss Latin America, East Asia, India, and the "Eastern Question" in the nineteenth century as part of the imperialistic phase of the Western state system. Even if the West's direct rule over the larger part of the globe did not last long, the indirect effects of imperialism changed life in all corners of the globe. It also brought the people of the world into closer contact, for better or for worse.

Between 1500 and 1900 the number of European political entities declined from around 500 to around 25,[1] but these remaining competitors in the Great Power game expanded their reach to dominate the globe momentarily. Industrialization gave

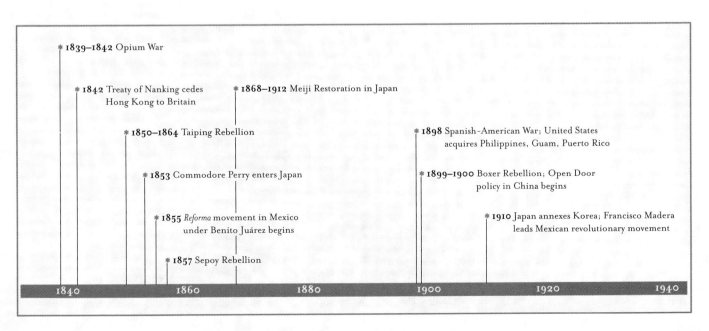

1839–1842 Opium War

1842 Treaty of Nanking cedes Hong Kong to Britain

1868–1912 Meiji Restoration in Japan

1850–1864 Taiping Rebellion

1898 Spanish-American War; United States acquires Philippines, Guam, Puerto Rico

1853 Commodore Perry enters Japan

1899–1900 Boxer Rebellion; Open Door policy in China begins

1855 *Reforma* movement in Mexico under Benito Juárez begins

1910 Japan annexes Korea; Francisco Madera leads Mexican revolutionary movement

1857 Sepoy Rebellion

1840   1860   1880   1900   1920   1940

these states immense material strength, economic power, and technology that affected the everyday lives of their citizens. The states became richer, more powerful, and more effective than ever before. New technology enabled them to intervene in people's lives in new ways. They formed huge conscript armies, increased taxation, established universal education, improved medical and social support services, and installed communications networks. The states initiated activity that fueled Europe's imperialist expansion across the globe.

The greatest population movement in history took place between 1500 and 1914, when millions of Europeans crossed the oceans to make new homes for themselves. The increase in European population from 200 million to 460 million during the nineteenth century provided the pool of 40 million immigrants who crossed the oceans. By 1914 the number of people of European background living abroad totaled 200 million—a figure almost equal to Europe's population a century earlier. At the same time, the slave trade brought vast numbers of West Africans to the Americas. For some 350 years the number transported in the slave trade ran into the millions. All these immigrants, whether voluntary or forced, brought with them their languages, religions, cultures, political institutions, and laws.

Latin America

Throughout Latin America, no matter where it occurred, this demographic invasion posed the challenges of unexplored lands, racial diversity, isolation, and the search for new identities. The middle classes, with their generally liberal politics, dominated, usually at the expense of the indigenous population or the African slaves. Although the challenges were the same, the results were unique to each region. Latin America faced fundamental challenges of racial and social diversity, economic exploitation, and political instability.

Common Denominators

In distinctive ways, each of the new states of Latin America reflected nineteenth-century movements that had originated in western Europe—nationalism, democracy, and imperialism. In addition, they had problems and opportunities that sprang from conditions specific to their environments. One was the assimilation of the tremendous tide of immigrants entering the new lands. But before the settlers and slaves came, vast spaces had to be explored, paths to the interior mapped, and natural resources located. The most famous figure in the exploration of South

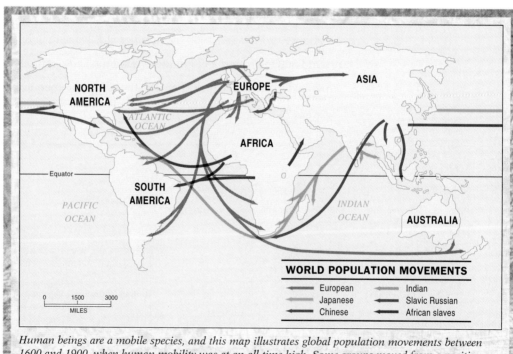

Human beings are a mobile species, and this map illustrates global population movements between 1600 and 1900, when human mobility was at an all-time high. Some groups moved from a position of strength—to increase profits or make their adequate lives better—and some moved because they had to—as slaves or to escape poverty. The flood of Europeans who left the "Old World" for the New in the nineteenth century also contributed to Europe's influence and control over the globe during that period.

America was the German naturalist Alexander von Humboldt, who from 1799 to 1804 explored Mexico, Cuba, and South America. He investigated the valley of the Orinoco River, crossed the Andes, and studied the sources of the Amazon River.

In general, the liberal and egalitarian trends in western Europe eventually took root in Latin America. However, the millions of African slaves taken as prisoners in tribal wars, sold to Europeans, and forcibly transplanted to the Americas initially had little chance to benefit from those ideals. The slave trade in Latin America began shortly after 1502. Because many native Americans died from European diseases such as smallpox and measles, the local population could not fill the mounting demand for labor on the plantations. To meet that demand, the influx of black slaves increased geometrically. The first slaves imported into Brazil arrived in 1538. By 1600 they formed the basis of the economy there, as well as along the Peruvian coast, in Mexico's hot lands, on Hispaniola and Cuba, and in the mines of Colombia. By 1800 the population of Haiti was predominantly black or mulatto, and the African element was substantial in Brazil and Cuba. There were smaller, though still significant, black populations in the Dominican Republic, Panama, Venezuela, and Colombia.

After defeating the native inhabitants in often bloody and vicious wars, the Europeans imposed their economic, political, social, and cultural practices on them. This initially created an almost genocidal situation. In Latin America the indigenous peoples greatly outnumbered the white settlers. Some authorities estimate that the population of Latin America in pre-Colombian days was at least 25 million. A large percentage of these people died following the initial European impact because of disease, war, and famine. In the long run, however, their numbers substantially increased. There was much intermarriage between the Indians and the Europeans. This *mestizo*, or mixed-race, strain, together with the Indians and the African slaves, outnumbered the white population. In the early twentieth century there were estimated to be 20 million Indian, 30 million mestizo, 26 million African and mulatto, and 34 million white people in Latin America. Only in Argentina, Chile, and a few smaller states such as Costa Rica, Cuba, and Uruguay have Europeans remained in the majority.

The Spanish and Portuguese, thanks to 1000 years of contact with the dark-skinned Moorish people and centuries of African explorations, never developed the virulent form of racism that found its way to North America. There was also a difference in the status of the slave in North and South America. In North America the slave was regarded as property, with no legal or moral rights. In Latin America, because of the traditions of Roman law and the Catholic Church, slaves had a legal personality and moral standing.

Even though slave status was generally considered perpetual, gaining freedom was not as difficult in Latin America as in North America. By 1860 free blacks outnumbered slaves two to one in Brazil, at a

This family portrait depicts a mestizo father, a Spanish mother, and their daughter, known as a castiza. Racial mixing was common throughout Latin America.

time when slaves outnumbered free blacks eight to one in the United States. Finally, there has been greater racial mixing in Latin America: the greatest meld of races—red, white, and black—in the history of the world has taken place there. This intermingling went a long way to ease racial tensions.[2]

The Latin Americans generally focused their energies on domestic matters and left world affairs to the larger Western states. The region managed to avoid the cruder imperialistic partitions and outright annexations so evident in Africa, China, and Southeast Asia. This lack of total exploitation owed more to luck than to the virtue of the outside powers. The economic interests of the United States, and to some extent of Britain, coincided with the preservation of the status quo in Latin America. Nationalism burned brightly in each of the Latin American nations, sometimes at the expense of political stability. As we saw in Chapter 21, the eight major administrative divisions in the late colonial era re-formed into 13 republics by 1824—a process frequently accompanied by insurrection, rebellion, and war.

The new nations of Latin America faced a complex of dilemmas that bequeathed a frustrating century of political instability and foreign economic domination. Civil wars, revolutions, and regimes came and went with alarming and costly regularity. Progressive leaders who tried to modernize their countries had to face the opposition of powerful, traditional institutions, massive and complex social problems, and the economic power of the United States and Great Britain.

The Creation of the Latin American States

In the first decades of the nineteenth century, the Latin American colonies pursued an irresistible movement for independence. By 1825 Spanish and Portuguese power was broken in the Western Hemisphere, and nine new political units emerged in Latin America. Mexico, Guatemala, Great Colombia, Peru, Bolivia, Paraguay, Argentina, and Chile were free of Spain, and Brazil had gained its independence from Portugal. Once free of those powers, however, the new nations of Latin America were hampered by European and North American dominance over their economic and political affairs.

For most of the new Latin American nations their first half century was a time of decline and disappointment. The great liberators could not maintain control of the nations they had freed. The liberal, urban Creoles who had begun the independence movements were inexperienced and unable to make the political compromises necessary to govern new countries. They soon lost power to crude military leaders,

or *caudillos*, whose armed gangs struggled for power in a confusing series of upheavals. A growing sectionalism accompanied these coups. Mammoth states broke up into tiny republics, which in turn were threatened by localism.

In part Latin America's problems resulted from the Spanish colonial system that had offered native-born whites little opportunity or responsibility in government. The tradition of autocracy and paternalism was a poor precedent for would-be democratic republics. The emphasis on executive power inspired presidents, generals, landowners, and church officials to wield authority with arrogant disregard for public opinion and representative government.

The colonial economic system, based on raw materials rather than industry, encouraged concentration of land and other forms of wealth in a few hands. The church, with its vast properties, monopoly on education and welfare agencies, and command over cultural life, complicated the politics of every new nation.

In addition, the new states were cursed by problems associated with the wars of independence. Some of the most productive areas were devastated. Hatred and division remained. Many men who had fought the royalists remained armed, predisposed to a life of violence and pillage and likely to group themselves about the *caudillos*, who promised adventure or profit in revolutions.

The final problem facing the new states was that of ethnic disunity. In 1825 there were 15 to 18 million people in the former Spanish Empire. About 3 million of them were whites, the wealthiest and most educated population. That figure remained constant until the last third of the century, when immigration from Europe increased drastically. There were about the same number of mestizos, who scorned the Indians but were not accepted by whites. Their numbers steadily increased, as did their ambition. During the nineteenth century at least half of the population in some states was Indian. Deprived of the small protection once offered by the Spanish crown, they either sank into peonage or lived in semi-independence under their tribal rulers. And in Brazil and most of the Caribbean islands, blacks were a large majority. Conflicts of interest quickly developed between these broad racial groups, particularly between the Creoles and the mestizos. The pernicious effects of these divisive factors were played out in each nation.

Mexico

Despite its promising beginning in 1821, Mexico suffered a half century of turmoil. Iturbide's empire lasted only a few months, to be replaced by a federal republic. In less than ten years, however, a coup brought to power as dictator a preposterous military leader named Antonio López de Santa Anna (1795–1876). Under his notorious rule, the defenders of the Alamo were massacred in 1836 and Mexico's political life was generally debased. His conduct of the war with the United States (1846–1848) humiliated Mexico. The overthrow of this corrupt, incompetent *caudillo* in 1855 brought more thoughtful and circumspect men into politics.

The liberals, under the leadership of Benito Juárez (1806–1872), set out to implement a reform program known as the *Reforma*. They planned to establish a more democratic republic, destroy the political and economic force of the church, and include the mestizos and Indians in political life. A terrible civil war followed their anticlerical measures; it ended in 1861 with Juárez's apparent victory. The European powers invaded when Mexico was unable to meet the payments on its debts owed to foreigners, and a French puppet regime was established. By 1867 popular uprisings and pressure from the United States had driven French troops from Mexican soil.

Juárez again set out to institute the *Reforma*, but the poverty of the country hampered progress. After he died, one of his adherents, Porfirio Díaz (1830–1915), took power. Under Díaz, who served as president from 1877 to 1880 and again from 1884 to 1911, Mexican politics stabilized. Foreign capital entered in large amounts. Factories, railroads, mines, trading houses, plantations, and enormous ranches flourished, and Mexico City became one of the most impressive capitals in Latin America.

Díaz's rule, though outwardly conforming to the constitution, was a dictatorship. If there was much encouragement of arts and letters, there was no liberty. The Indians sank lower and lower into peonage or outright slavery. In spite of the anticlerical laws of the Juárez period, the church was quietly permitted to acquire great wealth, and foreign investors exploited Mexico, creating a long-lasting hatred of foreigners.

Mexico's Struggle for Liberty

1821	Republic declared
1836, 1846–1848	Antonio López de Santa Anna fights United States but loses Mexican-American War
1855	*Reforma* movement begins under Juárez
1864–1867	French puppet government under Maximilian of Habsburg
1877–1880, 1884–1911	Dictatorship of Porfirio Díaz
1910	Mexican revolutionary movement begins under Francisco Madero

In 1910 the critics of Díaz found a spokesman in a frail, eccentric man named Francisco Madero (1873–1913), who undertook to lead a revolutionary movement and surprised the world by succeeding. Madero was murdered in 1913, and Mexico suffered another period of turmoil during which the country was controlled mainly by self-styled local rulers. Still, a determined group was able to organize a revolutionary party and to bring about the only genuine social revolution that Latin America experienced until the World War I.

Argentina

Until the 1970s Argentina was probably the most advanced Spanish-speaking country in the world. It attained this position in a period of sudden growth that followed a half century of sluggishness. Its beginning

Benito Juárez, an Indian from southern Mexico, led the liberal reform group that successfully implemented the reform constitution of 1857. The new constitution curtailed the rights of the military and the church in an effort to break the power of these two influential groups.

as a free nation was promising. Soon, however, the bustling port city of Buenos Aires, whose energetic population sought to encourage European capital and commerce, found itself overawed by the *caudillos*, the great ranchers of the interior, and their retainers, the *gauchos*—the colorful, nomadic cowboys and bandits whose way of life has been romanticized in literature and folklore. The *caudillos* intimidated the supporters of constitutional government in Buenos Aires, and until midcentury Argentina was not a republic but rather a *gaucho* paradise, isolated and ruled by men who wanted to keep European influences out.

In 1852 a combination of progressive elements overthrew the *gaucho* leader. Commerce with Europe was revived, and within ten years Argentina had become a united republic of admirable stability. The constitution was usually observed, and individual rights were respected to a high degree. Immigrants poured in, and soon the population of Argentina became the most European of the New World republics, for it contained few Indians or blacks.

Foreign money, especially British capital, brought about amazing developments; port facilities, railroads, light industry, and urban conveniences were among the most advanced in the world. Buenos Aires became by far the largest and most beautiful city in Latin America, despite its location on a monotonous, flat plain beside a muddy estuary.

The flat plain, or *pampas*, is perhaps the richest land in the world for grass and wheat, and livestock animals have been multiplying there for centuries. The introduction of refrigerated ships around 1880 made it feasible to transport enormous quantities of fresh beef to Britain in exchange for capital and finished goods. About 1900 wheat joined beef as a major Argentine export. This intimate commercial relationship with Britain, which lasted until after World War II, affected nearly every aspect of Argentine life.

Nevertheless, although elite society was dominated by leaders who were pro-British in business and pro-French in culture, a true Argentine nationalism was developing. Along with the growth of this powerful sentiment came demands for more democracy and a wider distribution of wealth.

Brazil

For many years this former Portuguese colony escaped the turbulence and disorders that befell its Spanish-speaking neighbors, probably because it had achieved independence without years of warfare and military dominance and because it enjoyed the continuity and legitimacy afforded by a respected monarchy. The first emperor, Pedro I (1822–1831), promulgated a constitution in 1824, and the accession to the throne of Pedro II in 1840 initiated a period of political liberty and economic and cultural progress that lasted throughout his half-century reign.

Immigrants were attracted to this peaceful land, and foreign investments were heavy but without the massive exploitation that Mexico experienced under Díaz. Economic growth tended to favor the southeastern part of the country at the expense of the great sugar plantations in the tropical north. The abolition of slavery in 1888 hurt the sugar lords economically, and they rose up against the emperor. Joining them were army officers, who resented the civilian nature of Pedro's regime, and a small number of ideological republicans. In 1889 the aging emperor was forced to abdicate.

For nearly ten years the new Federal Republic of Brazil underwent civil wars and military upheavals, much like those experienced by other Latin American countries. Finally, the republic was stabilized with the army in control, and Brazil resumed its progressive course. Foreign capital continued to enter, and immigration from Europe remained heavy. By 1914 Brazil was generally stable and prosperous, with a growing tradition of responsible government.

Other Latin American Nations

Political turmoil, geographical handicaps, and racial disunity all played a part in the development of the other new nations in Latin America. Bolivia, named so hopefully for the Liberator, Simón Bolívar, underwent countless revolutions. Peru's course was almost as futile. The state of Great Colombia dissolved by 1830, and its successors—Colombia, Venezuela, and Ecuador—were plagued by instability and civil wars. Paraguay endured a series of dictatorships, and Uruguay, created in 1828 as a buffer between Argentina and Brazil, long suffered from interventions by those two countries.

An exception to the prevailing pattern of political chaos was the steady growth of the republic of Chile. In 1830 Chile came under the control of a conservative oligarchy. Although this regime proved to be generally enlightened, the country was kept under tight control for a century and was ruled for the benefit of the large landlords and big business.

Central America narrowly escaped becoming part of Mexico in 1822. After a 15-year effort to create a Central American confederation, Guatemala, El Salvador, Honduras, Nicaragua, and Costa Rica asserted their independence. Except for Costa Rica, where whites comprised the bulk of the population, racial disunity delayed the development of national feeling. On the Caribbean island of Hispaniola, the Dominican Republic, after decades of submission to the more populous but equally underdeveloped Haiti, maintained a precarious independence. The other Caribbean islands remained under foreign domi-

Nitrates being loaded at Pisagua, the northernmost nitrate port of Chile. Economic development of the new Latin American republics depended to a large extent on the export trade, especially the export of minerals and other raw materials to the industrial markets of western Europe and the United States. Control of the valuable export trade could occasionally lead to war, as it did in the War of the Pacific (1879–1883) in which Chile defeated Peru and Bolivia for control of the nitrate fields.

nance—British, Dutch, Spanish, or French—and served their European masters as a source of raw materials—especially coffee, sugar, and tobacco—and later as coaling stations for their steam-powered navies.

Foreign Dominance

The Industrial Revolution came into full stride just after the Latin American republics were born. The great industries of western Europe and the United States demanded more and more raw materials and new markets in which to sell finished products. Capital accumulated, and investors eagerly sought opportunities to place their money where they could obtain high rates of interest. This drive for markets, raw materials, and outlets for surplus capital led to classic examples of economic imperialism.

The continual disorder and the lack of strong governments in Latin America gave businesses the opportunity to obtain rich concessions and float huge loans. Many of the Latin American government leaders, brought to power through revolution and interested only in personal gain, often resorted to the vicious practice of selling concessions to foreign corporations for ready cash. Political bosses bartered away the economic heritage of their lands, for Latin America was rich in minerals, oil, and other important resources. Foreign investors sometimes acted in good faith, providing capital at a reasonable rate of interest to Latin

American regimes that, it became apparent, had no intention of fulfilling the contract. On other occasions unscrupulous capitalists took full advantage of officials in ignorant or helpless governments.

Injured foreign investors usually appealed to their government to intercede on their behalf, generating an unending stream of diplomatic correspondence over debt claims. The United States, Great Britain, Germany, France, Italy, and Spain—the chief investor states—would not permit their citizens to be mistreated in their ventures in foreign investments.

In 1902–1903 a dispute between Venezuela and a coalition formed by Germany, Great Britain, and Italy provoked the three European powers into blockading the Latin American country and even firing on some of the coastal fortifications to remind the Venezuelan dictator of his obligations to some of their nationals. U.S. President Theodore Roosevelt at first stood by, watching Venezuela take its punishment. Then he became suspicious of German motives and began to match threat with threat, forcing the Europeans to back down and place the issue into international arbitration.

In 1904 Roosevelt issued the Roosevelt Corollary to the Monroe Doctrine, an addition that was a frank statement that chronic wrongdoing on the part of Latin American governments might force the United States to exercise an international police power. The policy expressed by Roosevelt's pronouncement was picturesquely described as "speak softly, but carry a big stick." The United States established a customs receivership in the Dominican Republic and exercised similar control in Nicaragua and Haiti. The Roosevelt Corollary expanded the Monroe Doctrine from its original purpose of keeping European political interference out of Latin America to enlarging the commercial interests of the United States.

In 1898 the United States had gone to war with Spain over the way the Spaniards ruled Cuba; the mistreatment of the Cubans also affected American commercial interests. Victory in the brief, dramatic, and well-publicized Spanish-American War won the United States recognition as a world power and possession of a conglomeration of islands in the Pacific Ocean as well as in the Caribbean. The United States annexed Puerto Rico and placed the Philippines, which were halfway around the world, under American rule. Sensitive to accusations of imperialism in Cuba, the U.S. government offered Cuba an imperfect, closely tutored independence in which the Cubans were obliged by law to acknowledge the right of the United States to intervene for the "preservation of Cuban independence" and the "maintenance of a government adequate for the protection of life, property, and individual liberty." These and other restrictions on Cuban independence were embodied in the Platt Amendment (1901) to the new

Cuban constitution. Thus the United States established its first American protectorate. Panama soon became another protectorate of the United States (see Chapter 26). Both American business and the local population generally profited from these arrangements.

President Roosevelt oversaw the introduction of what has been called "dollar diplomacy"—the coordinated activities of American foreign investors and the U.S. Department of State to obtain and protect concessions for the investors. From 1890 this policy won for Americans concessions for products such as sugar, bananas, and oil from more than a dozen Latin American republics.

In the face of such activities, the pious assertion that the nations of the Western Hemisphere were "bound by common geography and democratic political ideals" gained little acceptance. The "Colossus of the North," as the Latin American nations referred to the United States, clearly acted in its own self-interest. Sarcastic observers referred to the Pan-American Union, founded in 1889, as "the Colonial Division of the Department of State." By 1914 Latin America's relations with the rest of the world were neither healthy nor comforting. After a century of independence, Latin America still lingered on the margins of international life. Left to shift for itself in the face of a future shaded by U.S. imperialism, Latin America saw only a hard road ahead in its relations with the outside world.

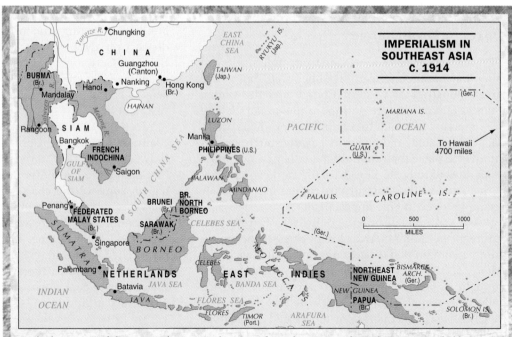

At the beginning of the twentieth century the map of Southeast Asia showed a mixture of old and new imperialisms, with the Dutch still in Indonesia and the British in Brunei. But the new patterns can be seen too with the French in Vietnam, the British in Hong Kong, and the Americans in the Philippines.

Southeast Asia

Throughout Indochina and the islands of the Indian and Pacific Oceans, European investors established a plantation economy to grow coffee, tea, pepper, and other products demanded by the world market in the seventeenth and eighteenth centuries. They also discovered and exploited important mineral deposits. In addition, they attempted to introduce law and order for the purpose of limiting the chronic civil war and banditry that plagued the region. The impact of European ways of life, especially Western education, created a new generation of nationalists. In the Dutch East Indies, French Indochina, and the Philippines, young intellectuals aspired to complete independence for themselves and their countries.

European Incursions

In the eighteenth and nineteenth centuries Great Britain gained control of Sri Lanka (Ceylon), Malaya, and Burma. The first colony, taken from the Dutch in 1796, became one of the most valuable British holdings, producing such prized commodities as tea, rubber, lead, and sapphires. The Malay peninsula, with the island of Singapore at its tip, provided a vantage point from which Britain could dominate the seas surrounding southern Asia and export valuable supplies of tin and rubber. The British conquered Burma in three wars between 1823 and 1885 and annexed it to India.

After a centurylong absence, France returned to Southeast Asia in the nineteenth century. French commercial and religious interests had been established as early as the seventeenth century, but British power in the Indian Ocean prevented France from stabilizing its position at that time. Not until the mid-nineteenth century did France increase its presence in Indochina. Anti-Christian persecutions in the area in 1856 and the fear that Catholicism would be eliminated if France did not go to its aid moved the French to join the British against China and Vietnam.

France took Saigon in 1860 and from that base expanded its influence and power through treaties, exploration, and outright annexation. The French took Hanoi in 1882, governed Cochin China as a direct colony, and held Annam (central Vietnam), Tonkin, and Cambodia as protectorates in one degree or another. Laos too was soon brought under French "protection." By the beginning of the twentieth century France had created an empire in Indochina nearly 50 percent larger than the parent country. Only Siam (Thailand) managed to hold off the French advance and keep its independence.

Late in the sixteenth century the Dutch had taken most of the East Indies from the Portuguese, and in 1602 the Dutch East India Company was organized to exploit the resources of the Spice Islands. In 1798 the company's holdings were transferred to the Dutch crown. For some time the spice trade had been declining, and early in the nineteenth century the Dutch set about raising new products.

In the 1830s the so-called culture system was introduced, under which one-fifth of all native land was set aside to raise crops for the government. One-fifth of all the natives' time was also required to work the lands. As a result, the production of sugar, tobacco, coffee, tea, and other products increased tremendously. In the long run, the culture system gave the islands a prosperous means of raising crops, but it also often deprived the people of sufficient land for their own use. Conditions improved in 1900 when the Dutch abandoned the culture system. Less favorable for the local population were the Dutch neglect of higher education and the failure to prepare the people for eventual self-government.

American Imperialism

While the Europeans were pursuing their interests in the Far East, a new imperial power was emerging in the Pacific—the United States. In 1867 the Americans occupied the Midway Islands and purchased Alaska from the Russians. The next step was in the Hawaiian Islands.

During the nineteenth century Americans and Europeans had developed large sugar plantations on the mid-Pacific islands. The United States poured capital into them, and by 1881 the U.S. secretary

---

U.S. Expansion into the Pacific Rim

1867	Purchase of Alaska; occupation of Midway Islands
1881	Proclamation of American system in mid-Pacific
1893	U.S. marines assisted overthrow of Hawaiian queen
1898	Hawaiian Islands annexed; Spanish-American War brings Philippines, Guam, Wake Island, Cuba, Puerto Rico under U.S. control
1899–1902	Filipino uprising against United States

of state referred to the islands as "part of the American system." In 1893 a revolt, engineered with the assistance of the marines, deposed the Hawaiian queen and set up a republic designed to ensure U.S. control in the islands. Five years later both houses of Congress issued a joint declaration to annex the islands.

The United States' successful war against Spain in 1898 affected both Cuba and the Philippines. In May of that year Admiral George Dewey destroyed the Spanish fleet at Manila and the first American soldiers began operations in the Philippines. By the treaty of December 1898 Spain ceded the Philippines, Guam, and Puerto Rico to the United States. One year later the Americans occupied the small Pacific outpost of Wake Island.

Decline of China

1793	Imperial denial of British request for permanent trade representative
1800–1840	British assist import of opium into China
1839–1842	First Opium War, ended by Treaty of Nanking, which gives Hong Kong to the British
1850–1864	Taiping Rebellion paralyzes China, kills 20 to 30 million people
1856–1858	Second Opium War, ended by Treaty of Tiensin, which opens new ports and confers exterritoriality
1860	*T'ung ch'ih* restoration movement
1860	Russia gains land north of the Amur River in Treaty of Peking
1885	French take Indochina
1886	Macao ceded to Portugal
1894–1895	Sino-Japanese War; Treaty of Shimonoseki forces China to recognize independence of Korea and to give Liaotung peninsula and Taiwan to Japan
1895–1900	China carved into spheres—holdings ceded to United Kingdom, Germany, France, and Russia
1899–1900	Boxer Rebellion
1900	Open Door policy implemented
1912	Republic of China declared by Sun Yat-sen

Some of the liberal Filipino patriots who had rebelled against the Spanish in 1896 assisted the Americans, but they had no wish to exchange one master for another. When it became evident that they would not quickly gain self-rule, fighting broke out. The hostilities that began in 1899 lasted for three years. The ironic spectacle of American forces being used in a second conquest of the Philippines brought about a strong revulsion against imperialism in many quarters of the United States.

American colonial administration in the Philippines, however, proved to be liberal and well intentioned for the most part. In 1913 the legislature became dominantly local, although final authority in the most important matters was still reserved to the U.S. Congress. The Philippine tariff was shaped to favor American trade, and large amounts of capital from the United States were invested in the islands. Increased educational opportunities strengthened the desire for independence among many Filipinos. In their eyes, American government in the Philippines, no matter how efficient or humanitarian, was no substitute for self-government.

By 1900, by virtue of its holdings in Alaska, Hawaii, the Philippines, and various islands in between, the United States dominated the Pacific basin as no other power did. The consequences of this Pacific imperial posture were to become a major and costly constituent of American life in the twentieth century. A massive conflict with Japan, another in Korea, and a tragic war in Vietnam lay in the future. Whether such involvement was essential to American basic interests would become a crucial and painful question.

China: The Central Kingdom

At the end of the 1800s China's 4 million square miles held 450 million people, more than twice the number a century earlier. The ruling dynasty was the Ch'ing, established by Manchus from Manchuria, who in 1644 had superseded the Ming. These descendants of the Mongols appreciated Chinese civilization and adopted a conciliatory attitude toward their subjects. They refused, however, to allow intermarriage with the Chinese, for they realized that only their blood difference kept them from being assimilated and conquered. By and large, however, the Manchus gradually became Chinese in their attitudes and habits.

The Manchu emperors were remarkably successful. The reign of Ch'ien-lung (1736–1795) was a time of great expansion. The Manchus gained Turkestan, Burma, and Tibet. By the end of the eighteenth century Manchu power extended even into Nepal, and the territory under the Ch'ing control was as extensive as under any previous dynasty.

The Perils of Superiority

The prevailing attitude of their own superiority to the cultures of all other peoples was an obstacle to China's leaders. They regarded advances in other parts of the world with contempt rather than admiration. Evidence of China's problems could be found in the eighteenth-century revolts in Taiwan, Kansu, Hunan, Kweichow, and Shantung provinces. China suppressed all of them, but clearly the Central Kingdom faced serious difficulties.

In the first part of the nineteenth century China continued to act imperiously toward foreigners. Merchants from the West came to China in increasing numbers, pursuing their trade in the face of great difficulties. Trade restrictions confined the foreign merchants to Guangzhou (Canton) and the Portuguese colony of Macao. In Guangzhou the Chinese controlled both trade and taxes. In spite of these obstacles, the foreigners made enough profit to compensate for their being treated as inferiors by the Chinese government.[3]

The Manchus would neither recognize nor receive diplomatic representatives of foreign powers. In addition, China knew that the foreigners needed Asian products more than the Chinese required European goods. In 1793 the imperial court responded to the British request for a permanent trade representative in Peking in this manner:

> *To send one of your nationals to stay at the Celestial Court to take care of your country's trade with China . . . is not in harmony with the state system of our dynasty and will definitely not be permitted. . . . There is nothing we lack, as your principal envoy and others have themselves observed. We have never set such store on strange or ingenious objects, nor do we have need of any more of your country's manufactures.[4]*

The Western Attack

The foreigners were especially irritated by the high customs duties the Chinese forced them to pay and by the attempts of Chinese authorities to stop the growing import trade in opium. The drug had long been used to stop diarrhea, but in the seventeenth and eighteenth centuries people in all classes began to use it recreationally. Most opium came from the Ottoman Empire or India, and in 1800 its import was forbidden by the imperial government. Despite this restriction, the opium trade continued to flourish. Privately owned vessels of many countries, including the United States, made huge profits from the growing number of Chinese addicts. The government in Peking noted that

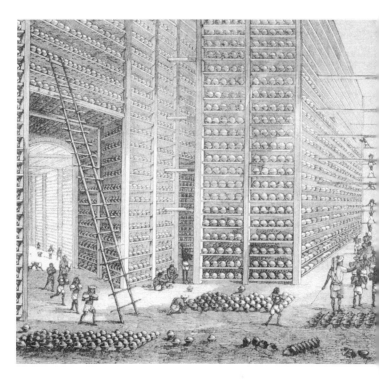

The stacking room at an opium factory in Patna, India. Opium smuggling upset the balance of trade and destroyed China's economy.

the foreigners seemed intent on dragging down the Chinese by encouraging opium addiction.

In the meantime, the empire faced other problems. Corruption spread through the army, and tax farmers defrauded the people. The central bureaucracy declined in efficiency, and the generally weak emperors were unable to meet the challenges of the time. The balance of trade turned against the Chinese in the 1830s, and the British decided to force the issue of increased trade rights. The point of conflict was the opium trade. By the late 1830s more than 30,000 chests of opium, each of which held about 150 pounds of the extract, were being brought in annually by the various foreign powers. Some authorities assert that the trade in opium alone reversed China's formerly favorable balance of trade. In the spring of 1839 Chinese authorities at Guangzhou confiscated and burned the opium. In response, the British occupied positions around the city.

In the war that followed, the Chinese could not match the technological and tactical superiority of the British forces. In 1842 China agreed to the provisions of the Treaty of Nanking. Hong Kong was ceded to Great Britain, and other ports, including Guangzhou, were opened to British residence and trade. It would be a mistake to view the conflict between the two countries simply as a matter of drug control; it was instead the acting out of deep cultural conflicts between East and West.[5]

The French and Americans approached the Chinese after the Nanking Treaty's provisions became

Lin Tse-hsu on the Opium Trade

Lin Tse-hsu saw that the opium trade, which gave Europe such huge profits, undermined his country. He asked Queen Victoria to put a stop to the trade.

After a long period of commercial intercourse, there appear among the crowd of barbarians both good persons and bad, unevenly. Consequently there are those who smuggle opium to seduce the Chinese people and so cause the spread of the poison to all provinces. Such persons who only care to profit themselves, and disregard their harm to others, are not tolerated by the laws of heaven and are unanimously hated by human beings. His Majesty the Emperor, upon hearing of this, is in a towering rage. He has especially sent me, his commissioner, to come to Kwangtung, and together with the governor-general and governor jointly to investigate and settle this matter.

All those people in China who sell opium or smoke opium should receive the death penalty. If we trace the crime of those barbarians who through the years have been selling opium, then the deep harm they have wrought and the great profit they have usurped should fundamentally justify their execution according to law. We take into consideration, however, the fact that the various barbarians have still known how to repent their crimes and return to their allegiance to us by taking the 20,183 chests of opium from their storeships and petitioning us, through their consular officer [superintendent of trade], Elliot, to receive it. It has been entirely destroyed and this has been faithfully reported to the Throne in several memorials by this commissioner and his colleagues.

Fortunately we have received a specially extended favor from His Majesty the Emperor, who considers that for those who voluntarily surrender there are still some circumstances to palliate their crime, and so for the time being he has magnanimously excused them from punishment. But as for those who again violate the opium prohibition, it is difficult for the law to pardon them repeatedly. Having established new regulations, we presume that the ruler of your honorable country, who takes delight in our culture and whose disposition is inclined towards us, must be able to instruct the various barbarians to observe the law with care. It is only necessary to explain to them the advantages and disadvantages and then they will know that the legal code of the Celestial Court must be absolutely obeyed with awe.

We find that your country is sixty or seventy thousand *li* [about 22,000 miles] from China. Yet there are barbarian ships that strive to come here for trade for the purpose of making a great profit. The wealth of China is used to profit the barbarians. That is to say, the great profit made by barbarians is all taken from the rightful share of China. By what right do they then in return use the poisonous drug to injure the Chinese people? Even though the barbarians may not necessarily intend to do us harm, yet in coveting profit to an extreme, they have no regard for injuring others. Let us ask, where is your conscience? I have heard that the smoking of opium is very strictly forbidden by your country; that is because the harm caused by opium is clearly understood. Since it is not permitted to do harm to your own country, then even less should you let it be passed on to the harm of other countries—how much less to China!

From Lin Tse-hsu, *Letter to Queen Victoria* (1839).

known, and in 1844 they gained the same trading rights as the British. The advantages granted the three nations by the Chinese set a precedent that would dominate China's relations with the world for the next century. The "most favored nation" treatment came to be extended so far that China's right to rule in its own territory was limited. This began the period referred to by the Chinese as the time of unequal treaties, a time of unprecedented degradation for China. The humiliation the Central Kingdom suffered is still remembered and strongly affects important aspects of its foreign policy. Meanwhile, the opium trade continued to thrive.

The British and French defeated China in a second opium war in 1856. By the terms of the Treaty of Tientsin (1858) the Chinese opened new ports to trading and allowed foreigners with passports to travel in the interior. Christians gained the right to spread their faith and hold property, thus opening up another means of Western penetration. The United States and Russia gained the same privileges in separate treaties.

The Manchu Empire appeared to be well on the way to political and economic collapse. Three provisions of these treaties caused long-lasting bitterness among the Chinese: extraterritoriality, customs regulations, and the right to station foreign warships in Chinese waters. Extraterritoriality meant that in a dispute with the Chinese, Westerners had the right to be tried in their own country's consular court. Europeans argued that Chinese concepts of justice were more rigid and harsh than those in the West. But the Chinese viewed extraterritoriality as not only humiliating to China's sovereignty but also discriminatory in favor of Western nations. The other two provisions greatly weakened China's fiscal and military structure. After 1860 China was a helpless giant.

China's Response

The Chinese competition with the Westerners had been carried on in military and economic terms. But the basic conflict was in the realm of civilization and values. The Chinese could note the obvious—that the West possessed technological and military superiority. The question they faced was how to adapt the strength of the West to the core of Chinese civilization in order to become able to compete effectively. In Chinese terms, this was the *t'i-yung* concept (*t'i* means "substance," and *yung* means "use").

Combining the two elements presented the severe problem of gaining a proper balance. Those who wanted to keep the old culture opposed those who wanted to modernize the country. In 1860 the *T'ung ch'ih* restoration movement attempted to strengthen the Manchus. Serious attempts were made to preserve Chinese culture while trying to make use of Western technology. Had these attempts at adaptation been carried out in a time of peace, perhaps the Chinese could have adjusted, but China did not enjoy the luxury of tranquillity. The concessions to the "foreign devils" resulted in a great loss of prestige for the Manchus.

More dangerous for the Manchus than the West was the spate of revolts in the north, west, and south of the country. The most tragic was the Taiping Rebellion, which lasted from 1850 to 1864. The uprising, fought to attain the Heavenly Kingdom of Great Peace *(T'ai-p'ing t'ien-kuo),* stemmed from widespread discontent with the social and economic conditions of Manchu rule and the perception of a lack of authority in Peking. The revolt began near Guangzhou and centered on the plans of Hung Hsiu-ch'uan, a person who was driven to desperation by consistently failing the lowest examination to gain entry into the civil service. After contact with American missionaries and some reading of Christian tracts, he came to identify himself as a son of God, Jesus' little brother. His task was to bring salvation to China.

He attracted followers, especially from the poor, and prepared to fight. For ten years he and his forces controlled the southern part of China from Nanking, and he set out to create a new society, totally detached from the traditional Chinese fabric. Hung struck out at vice, Confucianism, private property, and the landlords. By taking on all that was established in China, he ensured his defeat. The Taiping Rebellion was one of the most costly movements in history. It reached into 17 of China's 18 provinces. Estimates of the number of deaths range between 20 and 30 million as the central government brutally repressed the rebels.[6]

After the external buffeting from the West and the internal uprising, the Manchu dynasty limped along for another half century, led by a conservative coalition of Manchu and Chinese officials who advised the empress dowager, Tzu-hsi, who served from 1861 until her death in 1908. Known first as Orchid, then as Yehonala, then as the Yi Concubine, then as Tzu-hsi, and finally as the Old Buddha, she followed the most direct path for a bright and ambitious Manchu female: she entered court circles as a concubine. After receiving the traditional training in court, she honed her political skills. She understood the intricate ceremonial life and mastered the intrigue of palace politics. When the senior concubine failed to give birth to a healthy heir to the throne, Tzu-hsi bore the emperor a strong and healthy child.

Her position as mother of the heir apparent opened the door to power, and during the reigns of the next three emperors she was a dominant power, either as sole or joint regent. She built a network of powerful allies and informers that helped her crush internal revolts and restore a measure of prestige to China during a brief period of tranquillity from 1870 to 1895. She and her circle were so removed from the world that she used funds earmarked for the navy to rebuild her summer house, in honor of her sixtieth birthday. At a time when the Japanese were rapidly modernizing and foreign powers were introducing many forms of new technology in their factories, railroads, and communications, China held to policies based on tradition and custom.

Tzu-hsi, the Empress Dowager or Old Buddha. The central government of China lost power under her rule, as exemplified by the Boxer Rebellion, which erupted toward the end of her reign.

Tzu-hsi, Empress Dowager of China, 1835–1908, Photographs Freer Gallery of Art and Arthur M. Sackler Gallery Archives, Smithsonian Institution.

Carving Up China

During the first wars against the Europeans, the Chinese began the process of ceding territory and spheres of influence to foreigners. By 1860, as a result of the Treaty of Peking, Russia gained the entire area north of the Amur River and founded the strategic city of Vladivostok. In 1885 France took Indochina and Britain seized Burma. In 1887 Macao was ceded to Portugal. China was too weak to resist these encroachments on its borders. But the crowning blow came not from the Western nations but from Japan, a land the Chinese had long regarded with bemused contempt.

Trouble had long brewed between China and Japan, especially over the control of Taiwan and Korea. War broke out in 1894 in a dispute over China's claims on Korea. The brief Sino-Japanese struggle resulted in a humiliating defeat for China. By the treaty of Shimonoseki (1895), China was forced to recognize the independence of Korea and hand over the rich Liaotung peninsula and Taiwan to Japan.

The Chinese defeat was the signal for the renewal of aggressive actions by Western powers, who forced Japan to return the strategic Liaotung peninsula to China. Shortly thereafter, the European powers made their own demands of China. Germany demanded a 99-year lease to Kiaochow Bay and was also given exclusive mining and railroad rights throughout Shantung province. Russia obtained a 25-year lease to Dairen and Port Arthur and gained the right to build a railroad across Manchuria, thereby achieving complete domination of that vast territory. In 1898 Britain obtained the lease of Weihaiwei, a naval base, and France leased Kwangchowan in southern China.

The United States, acting not from any high-minded desires but rather from the fear that American business was being excluded from China, brought a halt, or at least a hesitation, to the process of dismemberment. In 1899 Secretary of State John Hay asked the major powers to agree to a policy of equal trading privileges. In 1900 several powers did so, and the Open Door policy was born.

The humiliation of the defeat by Japan had incensed young Chinese intellectuals, who agitated for liberation from foreign dominance. Led by enlightened and concerned patriots such as Kang Yu-wei, the liberals proposed a wide-ranging series of economic, social, political, and educational reforms, and the young emperor, Tzu-hsi's nephew, approved them. What followed came to be known as the "hundred days of reform."

Tzu-hsi and her advisers encouraged antiforeign sentiment and opposed the patriots' attempts to bring about basic democratic reforms on a Confucianist basis. The reform attempts threatened the interests of Tzu-hsi's supporters, and she came out of retirement in 1898, imprisoned her nephew, and revoked all of the proposed reforms.

After the suppression of the reform movement, a group of secret societies united in an organization known as the Righteous Harmony Fists, whose members were called Boxers in the West. At first they were strongly anti-Manchu, but by 1899 the chief object of their hatred had become the foreign nations who were stripping China of land and power. The Boxers started a campaign to rid China of all "foreign devils." Many Europeans were killed, and their legations at Peking were besieged. In August 1900 an international army forced its way to Peking and released the prisoners. China was forced to apologize for the murder of foreign officials and pay a large indemnity.

By this time even the Old Buddha acknowledged the need for change. After 1901 she sanctioned reforms in the state examination system, education and governmental structure, and economic life; she even approved the drive to end the binding of girls' feet—all to no avail.

Only a decade after the conclusion of the Boxer Rebellion, a revolution broke out all over China, and in 1912 the Republic of China was proclaimed with Sun Yat-sen as president. The revolutionary Chinese leaders knew that there had to be radically different approaches taken in China to allow it to survive and compete. As one official wrote in the 1890s:

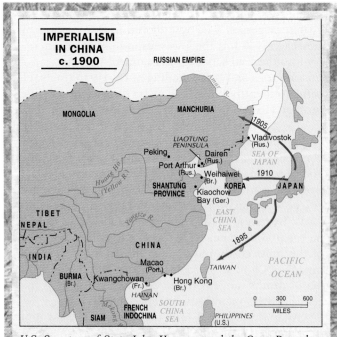

U.S. Secretary of State John Hay proposed the Open Door doctrine to keep the doors of trade open for the Americans, who were too late to profit from the carving up of China.

Discovery Through Maps

Western Designs on China, 1885–1900

PUCK.

THE REAL TROUBLE WILL COME WITH THE "WAKE."

After the Renaissance, European countries increasingly came to be identified with certain animals, which symbolized their respective national characteristics. Russia was the powerful, clumsy bear. The English early on claimed the lion, "the king of beasts," as their symbol. Even though some eighteenth-century Americans wanted the turkey as the national bird, proponents of the eagle won out. Birds served other countries too: the cock for France, the eagle for the Germans, the two-headed eagle for the Austrians. China from earliest days was seen as the dragon.

This American cartoon shows more forcefully and graphically than a "traditional map" the fate of China at the end of the nineteenth century. Behind the polite euphemisms of the Open Door and "spheres of influence" was the cruel reality of the carving up of China.

Western nations rely on intelligence and energy to compete with one another. To come abreast of them China should plan to promote commerce and open minds; unless we change, the Westerners will be rich and we poor. We should excel in technology and the manufacture of machinery; unless we change, they will be skillful and we clumsy. . . . Unless we change, the Westerners will cooperate with each other and we shall stand isolated; they will be strong and we shall be weak.[7]

The Japanese Alternative

Western powers gained effective control of India, Southeast Asia, and China by the end of the nineteenth century. Japan, however, responded to the Western advance in an alert and united manner, successfully adapting elements of strength from the West to the core of its own structures and ways of life.

At the beginning of the eighteenth century Japan was ruled from Edo (now Tokyo), the largest city in the country, by the head of the Tokugawa clan, whose leaders had declared themselves shogun since 1603. As the military dictator with a retinue of feudal lords and warriors, the shogun kept the country united and at peace. The Tokugawa strengthened the feudal framework of unity and stability that helped give Japan the basis for a successful response to the European challenge.

The Japanese emperor, in residence at Kyoto, served as a figurehead with no real function other than as a symbol around which the nation could rally. The Tokugawa ruled the country through their feudal lords, the *daimyo*. These officials in turn governed their regions with the aid of the samurai, the soldiers who also acted as administrators and governed and taxed the peasants. Below the peasants on the social scale were the artisans and merchants who lived in the cities, a reflection of the fact that the Tokugawa saw agriculture as the foundation of politics and society.

The stratified society may well have ensured the power of the Tokugawa, but over a period of two centuries it was tested by peasant uprisings in the countryside and discontent in the cities. The peasant rebellions could be put down by force. But in the cities in the late eighteenth and early nineteenth centuries, remarkable economic growth accompanied rapid urbanization. New social and political forces posed difficulties for the Tokugawa structure. The spread of education and the increase in wealth helped spur the growth of a new urban class drawn from young, aggressive merchants and intellectuals. Those at the lower end of the social scale became wealthier than many of the samurai. These social forces could not be dealt with so easily by the Tokugawa governmental structure.

By the nineteenth century the shogunate lost much of its force and authority. The once efficient government had become lax, especially in the realm of tax collection. Changing conditions in the cities and the flow of Western information from the open port of Nagasaki worked to undermine the traditional system.

The Western Challenge

Both European and American merchants and diplomats tried to open relations with Japan during the first part of the nineteenth century, but even at midcentury foreign traders and missionaries found their ability to move throughout the country greatly limited. Within the country the question of how and when to open up to the West was discussed. European inventions such as the daguerreotype and new manufacturing techniques had already made their appearances. But Japanese policy toward foreigners would not be defined until 1853. On July 7 of that year the U.S. ships under the command of Matthew Perry sailed into Edo Bay.

Perry, with a force of two steam frigates and two sloops-of-war, had been sent by the American government to convince the Japanese that a treaty opening trade relations between the two countries would be of mutual interest. He had been instructed to be tactful and to use force only if necessary. After delivering a letter from the U.S. president, he remained in port ten days. When he departed, he told the authorities in Edo that he would return in a year for an answer. He actually came back eight months later, in February 1854. The Americans returned with more ships before the deadline because they feared that the French or the Russians might gain concessions sooner from the Japanese.

The shogun, after a period of intense debate within his country, agreed to Perry's requests. The Treaty of Kanagawa, the first formal agreement between Japan and a Western nation, was signed. By its terms, shipwrecked sailors were to be well treated and two ports were to be opened for provisioning ships and a limited amount of trade. European traders soon obtained similar privileges, in addition to the right of extraterritoriality.

This contemporary Japanese woodcut records the events surrounding the arrival of Commodore Matthew Perry in Japan in 1853. The panels surrounding the map depict Perry's landing at the seaport of Unaga, an American warship anchored in the harbor, Perry's men on parade, a group of samurai in battle attire, and a sumo wrestling contest.

The entry of the West placed a severe strain on the already weakened Japanese political structure. Antiforeign sentiment grew, even as many Japanese recognized that accommodation with the West was bound to come. Western representatives in Japan were caught in the middle, and there were a number of attacks against them. By 1867, after a time of strife and confusion, Japan reached the point of revolution. European and American fleets had bombarded Kagoshima and Shimonoseki in 1863 and 1864, thereby convincing some of the antiforeign elements of the hopelessness of their position. In 1867 the system of dual government, with the emperor at Kyoto and the shogun at Edo, was abandoned. The capital was moved from Kyoto to Edo, which was renamed Tokyo ("eastern capital").

The Meiji Restoration

The next generation of Japanese leaders accomplished what no other non-Western leaders were able to do—they adapted the Europeans' strengths to their own situation and successfully competed against the West. The new leaders who oversaw the end of the dual-power system were young and most were of samurai origin. They understood the nature of Western power and the threat it posed to their country. They proposed as Japan's best defense the forming of a rich country and a strong military, based on Western technology and institutions adapted to their country's needs. The young emperor, whose rule was known as the *Meiji* ("enlightened government"), reigned from 1868 to 1912. During that time Japan became a dynamic, modern power the West had to recognize as an equal.

Centuries earlier the Japanese had gained a great deal from China. Now they set out to learn from the West the lessons of how to construct an industrialized, bureaucratized state. For the next generation, the results of those lessons would be applied in a broad variety of areas. The voluntary abolition of feudal rights accompanied and facilitated the restoration of the emperor's supreme authority. In 1871 the end of the feudal system was officially announced, although it was far from actual fact. At the same time, the government established a new administrative division and reformed the education and mail systems.

In 1882 a commission went out to study the world's various governmental systems in order to write a new constitution for Japan. The committee members were particularly impressed by Bismarck's German system, and the new constitution proclaimed in 1889 gave the premier a position analogous to that held by the chancellor in Germany. Under the new system the cabinet was responsible to the emperor alone. Only the army and the navy could appoint their respective ministers. Since no statesman could form a

Modern and traditional Japan meet in this 1905 photo. Farmers wheel their carts through the streets while, above them, workers install electric power lines.

cabinet without a war minister, and the army could overthrow any cabinet by simply withdrawing its minister, ultimate control of policies rested with military interests. The constitution provided for a Diet, which wielded financial influence through its refusal power over unpopular budgets in peacetime. Under the new system the emperor, who held sovereign power, was considered "sacred and inviolable."

The Japanese adapted the lessons they learned from the West in other areas. In 1876 national conscription went into effect, and a modern military structure was created. German and French advisers trained army officers while naval officers received their instructions from the British. The government initiated the founding of banks, factories, and business concerns. Later, when they became successful, these establishments were turned over to private ownership and management. Japan also changed to the modern calendar, symbolizing its entry into the modern age.

Ito Hirobumi on the New Japanese Constitution

The Japanese were the only non-Europeans quickly to adopt, choose, and use European concepts successfully for their own purpose. Ito Hirobumi's thoughts on drafting the new Japanese constitution represent one instance of how this system worked.

It was in the month of March 1882, that His Majesty ordered me to work out a draft of a constitution to be submitted to his approval. No time was to be lost, so I started on the 15th of the same month for an extended journey to different constitutional countries to make as thorough a study as possible of the actual workings of different systems of constitutional government, of their various provisions, as well as of theories and opinions actually entertained by influential persons on the actual stage itself of constitutional life. I sojourned about a year and a half in Europe, and having gathered the necessary materials, insofar as it was possible in so short a space of time, I returned home in September 1883. Immediately after my return I set to work to draw up the Constitution. . . .

It was evident from the outset that mere imitation of foreign models would not suffice, for there were historical peculiarities of our country which had to be taken into consideration. For example, the Crown was, with us, an institution far more deeply rooted in the national sentiment and in our history than in other countries. It was indeed the very essence of a once theocratic State, so that in formulating the restrictions on its prerogatives in the new Constitution, we had to take care to safeguard the future realness or vitality of these prerogatives, and not to let the institution degenerate into an ornamental crowning piece of the edifice. At the same time, it was also evident that any form of constitutional régime was impossible without full and extended protection of honor, liberty, property, and personal security of citizens, entailing necessarily many important restrictions on the powers of the Crown. . . .

Another difficulty equally grave had to be taken into consideration. We were just then in an age of transition. The opinions prevailing in the country were extremely heterogeneous, and often diametrically opposed to each other. We had survivors of former generations who were still full of theocratic ideas, and who believed that any attempt to restrict an imperial prerogative amounted to something like high treason. On the other hand there was a large and powerful body of the younger generation educated at the time when the Manchester theory was in vogue, and who in consequence were ultra-radical in their ideas of freedom. Members of the bureaucracy were prone to lend willing ears to the German doctrinaires of the reactionary period, while, on the other hand, the educated politicians among the people having not yet tasted the bitter significance of administrative responsibility, were liable to be more influenced by the dazzling words and lucid theories of Montesquieu, Rousseau, and other similar French writers. A work entitled *History of Civilization*, by Buckle, which denounced every form of government as an unnecessary evil, became the great favorite of students of all the higher schools, including the Imperial University. On the other hand, these same students would not have dared to expound the theories of Buckle before their own conservative fathers. At that time we had not yet arrived at the stage of distinguishing clearly between political opposition on the one hand, and treason to the established order of things on the other. The virtues necessary for the smooth working of any constitution, such as love of freedom of speech, love of publicity of proceedings, the spirit of tolerance for opinions opposed to one's own, etc., had yet to be learned by long experience.

From W. Theodore de Bary, ed., *Sources of Japanese Tradition* (New York: Columbia University Press, 1958). Selections reprinted by permission of the publisher.

Although the Japanese went to the West to find the best ways to modernize their country, they themselves, and not foreigners, made the major changes. Foreigners built the railways, telegraphs, lighthouses, dockyards, and warships. But the authorities in Tokyo initiated a constitution that firmly maintained their control.

Japan's Success

On the surface the Japanese government was liberal and parliamentary. In reality it was ultraconservative, giving the emperor and the cabinet dominant power.

Though Japan was the first Asian nation to achieve a high degree of literacy, education remained the tool of the government, and one of its chief functions was to produce docile servants of the state. The press was subjected to tight control and censorship.

The army was used as a means of instilling conscripts with unquestioning loyalty and obedience to the emperor. In their barracks young soldiers learned that the noblest fate was death on the battlefield. Unlike the Chinese, who revered the scholar most of all, the Japanese admired the soldier—warfare was the supreme vocation. The Japanese were ready to seize the new methods and ideas of the West to serve their own military ends, because it was through a display of military power that the West forced home the notion of its own technological superiority on Asia.

In adopting many of the aspects of the Western state system—universal conscription, professional bureaucracy, mass literacy, state ideology—some Japanese institutions were forced to change. The samurai, who had formerly made their living as warriors or by serving their feudal lords, had to change their lifestyles. Many of them made the transition to the new system effortlessly. The conservative samurai were upset when the government passed a law in 1876 that diminished their financial advantages and also forbade the carrying of swords in public. Civil war broke out in some districts, and the government's forces put down the stubborn samurai and their armies.

The oligarchy that carried out the revolution through which Japan passed was able to keep a fair amount of control. It brought all of the people into the new system in one form or another. It could accomplish such a major revolution with a minimum of turmoil because all the changes occurred within the confines of traditional reverence for the emperor.

Through Shinto, in essence the state religion, the restoration leaders devised the ultimate political and religious ideology. In Shinto the emperor, directly descended from the Sun Goddess, can demand unlimited loyalty to himself. He expresses the gods' will. As a former president of the privy council, Baron Hozumi, wrote:

> The Emperor holds the sovereign power, not as his own inherent right, but as an inheritance from his Divine Ancestor. The government is, therefore, theocratical. The Emperor rules over his country as the supreme head of the vast family of the Japanese nation. The government is, therefore, patriarchal. The Emperor exercises the sovereign power according to the Constitution, which is based on the most advanced principles of modern constitutionalism. The government is, therefore, constitutional. In other words, the fundamental principle of the Japanese government is theocratic-patriarchal-constitutionalism.[8]

The process of industrialization coincided with this fundamental social and political revolution. In its rapid economic growth, Japan faced the same problems of demographic and urban growth the West faced. Social and cultural discontent naturally followed from such a rapid transformation. But the ideological and political structure constructed in the Meiji Restoration was enough to hold the country together while at the same time repelling the Europeans and the Americans.

In the eyes of Western diplomats, Japanese prestige had begun to increase soon after the conclusion of the Sino-Japanese war of 1894–1895. In 1902 Japan scored a diplomatic triumph by allying itself with Great Britain, an alliance viewed by both nations as a deterrent to Russian expansion. When a year later the Russians rebuffed Japanese attempts to negotiate a sphere-of-influence agreement over Korea and Manchuria, the Tokyo government attacked Port Arthur and bottled up Russia's fleet, without a formal declaration of war. The quick series of Japanese victories that followed forced the Russians to agree to the Treaty of Portsmouth in September 1905. Japan gained half the island of Sakhalin, the leaseholds on the Liaotung peninsula and Port Arthur, and various Russian railway and mining rights in southern Manchuria. Japan's paramount position in Korea was also conceded, paving the way for its annexation of that nation in 1910.

Japan's victory in the war with Russia in 1904–1905 astounded the world. Japan had successfully met the challenge of European primacy and was now accepted as a first-class power in its own right.

India

The decline of Mughul power proved to be a great opportunity for the British and French, who through the late seventeenth century and most of the eighteenth competed for dominance in India. They fought through their trading companies and agents who sought local allies. India, like North America, was part of the two European powers' world struggle for empire. The British victory over Bengal in the battle of Plassey (1757) ushered in the British phase of Indian history. Britain's naval supremacy and the superior discipline of its European-led armies enabled Britain to defeat France in 1760. French influence in India soon disappeared.

Dual Control Under the British

The traders became rulers, assuming the dual roles of businessmen and representatives of a sovereign state. Anarchy spread until 1818, when the British East India Company stepped in to become the subcontinent's police force. Some local rulers accepted the company's rule, but others who resisted lost their land. Administration of the subcontinent was divided into two sections: British India was ruled directly by London, while in Indian India the local dynasties ruled under British supervision. The British Parliament, concerned that a profit-seeking company controlled the lives of millions of people, enacted legislation in 1773 and 1784 that gave it power to control company policies and appoint the governor-general, the highest company official in India.

The system of dual control lasted until 1858 and brought several benefits to the peninsula, especially to women. The practice of *suttee* in which widows burned themselves on the funeral pyres of their deceased husbands was prohibited. The company also worked against the practice of killing female infants. Further, steps were taken to end the seclusion of women from society. A secret police force broke up the brutal system of banditry and murder called *thuggee* (from which the English word *thug* is derived). The British also introduced a comprehensive, multilevel educational system.

Rebellion and Reform

In the spring of 1857 a serious rebellion interrupted the flow of liberal reforms. Indian troops, who formed the bulk of the company's armed forces, called *sepoys*, started the uprising when they complained that a new cartridge issued to them was smeared with the fat of cows and pigs. This outraged both the Hindus, for whom the cow was a sacred animal, and the Muslims, who considered the pig unclean. Fortunately for the British, many areas remained loyal or at least calm. But in the affected areas there was fierce fighting, and many lives were lost.

The Sepoy Rebellion marked the final collapse of the Mughuls. The mutineers had proclaimed as their leader the last of the Mughul emperors permitted to maintain a court at Delhi. After the British put down the revolt, they exiled him to Burma. The rebellion

also put an end to the system of dual control under which the British government and the East India Company shared authority. Parliament eliminated the company's political role, and after 258 years the East India Company ended its rule.

Under the new system the governor-general gained additional duties and a new title—viceroy. The viceroy was responsible to the secretary of state for India in the British cabinet. In the subcontinent the British maintained direct control of most of the high positions in government, while Indians were trained to carry out administrative responsibilities in the provincial and subordinate systems. London reorganized the courts and law codes, along with the army and public services. English became the administrative language of the country. Only on rare occasions could native civil officials rise to higher positions in the bureaucracy.

India was governed by and for the British, who viewed themselves as the only people able to rule. In 1900 fully 90 percent of native men and 99 percent of native women were illiterate. Few schools existed at the village level to remedy that situation. The masses of the rural poor paid for the government through taxes on beverages and salt. India provided rich resources and vast markets for the British. In return the British supplied improved health standards, better water systems, and political stability.

The English language and British railroads introduced more unity to the country than it had ever known. But the imperial rulers took advantage of the subcontinent's diversity of religions, castes, and prin-

The storming of the Kashmir Gate at Delhi during the Sepoy Rebellion of 1857.

The "Benefits" of Imperialism

Imperialism provided a previously unattainable standard of living for Europeans, as a letter from a certain Miss Eden, living in British India, proves.

I wish you could see my passage [entry hall] sometimes. The other day when I set off to pay George a visit I could not help thinking how strange it would have seemed at home. It was a rainy day, so all the servants were at home. The two tailors were sitting in one window, making a new gown for me, and Rosina by them chopping up her betel-nut; at the opposite window were my two Dacca embroiderers working at a large frame, and the sentry, in an ecstasy of admiration mounting guard over them. There was the bearer standing upright, in a sweet sleep, pulling away at my punkah [canvas fan]. My own five servants were sitting in a circle, with an English spelling-book, which they were learning by heart; and my jemadar [head of household staff] who, out of compliment to me, has taken to draw, was sketching a bird. [My dog] Chance's servant was waiting at the end of the passage for his "little excellency" to go out walking, and a Chinese was waiting with some rolls of satin that he had brought to show.

From Hilton Brown, ed., *The Sahibs* (London: Hodge, 1948).

cipalities (over 700 separate political units) to rule by a policy of divide and conquer. The British justified their political policies and economic dominance over India by pointing out that they were improving the lives of nearly one-fifth of the human race—almost 300 million people. This rationale could not remove the fact that the contrasts between the European and Asian ways of life in cities like Bombay, Delhi, and Calcutta were as great as the difference between night and day.

Resentment against British rule led to the rapid growth of the Indian nationalist movement. In 1885, with the help of several Englishmen who had Indian political ambitions, the Indian National Congress was formed. The British educational system, although it touched only a minority of the people, served as one of the most potent forces behind the new movement, as the Indians embraced many of the liberal causes popular in England. Especially strong was the drive for women's equality and freedom, away from their traditional position of dependence, in which women's legal standing and power derived from their ties to men.

As Indians learned the history of the rise of self-government in England, their desire for political freedom in their own land grew. The system of British control prevented Indians from rising above a certain level. At the same time, newly educated Indian youths, for social and cultural reasons, disdained manual labor. The result was a pool of thousands of frustrated and unemployed educated Indian youths who turned angrily against the government.

The British responded to the spread of violence with a major shift in policy between 1907 and 1909. They allowed the various provincial legislatures to elect Indian majorities, and an Indian was seated in the executive council of the governor-general. The central government's legislature, however, remained under British control. These concessions satisfied moderates for the time being but did not appease the more radical protesters. In the twentieth century the spirit of nationalism would become even more insistent.

The "Eastern Question"

The Western states dominated Latin America through population transfers and economic influence and East Asia and India through a combination of economic and military power. In dealing with the strategically important territory held by the declining Ottoman Empire, the European powers tried to expand their influence in classic diplomatic-military struggles.

Throughout the nineteenth century the states' power increased enormously. Each tapped into an increasing tax base to finance its expanding ambitions. The German Empire's income, for example, grew from 263 million marks in 1873 to over 1200 million marks in 1909.[9] Other states, even the poorest, registered comparable increases. As the states grew, so did their armies. Military conscription touched the lives of most young men, except in Britain. At the end of the century France and Germany each had nearly 3.5 million men in the field or on reserve, and these soldiers were better and more expensively armed than ever before. Throughout the century the European states looked to the Ottoman Empire and its successors to gain control of key communications routes and markets. Unfortunately, their drive to compete for dominance made it impossible for the European states to devise an answer to the dilemma of what to do with the power vacuum created by the decaying Ottoman Empire—the so-called Eastern Question.[10]

The Balkans Awaken

By the end of the eighteenth century Ottoman power had substantially declined in the Balkans, just at a time when the various peoples began to experience waves of nationalism. In 1799 Sultan Selim III (see Chapter 27) acknowledged the independence of the mountainous nation of Montenegro, after its long and heroic defense of its liberty. Further proof of Ottoman weakness came in 1804 when some renegade Turkish troops in Belgrade went on a rampage, disobeyed the sultan's orders, and forced the Serbian people to defend themselves. This initial act of self-protection blossomed into a rebellion that culminated, after 11 difficult years, when the Serbs gained an autonomous position within the Ottoman Empire.

Turkish weakness attracted both Russian and British interests. Russia had made a substantial advance toward the Mediterranean during the reign of Catherine II. By the Treaty of Küchük Kaynarca (1774) the Russians gained the rights of navigation in the Ottoman waters and the right to intervene in favor of Eastern Orthodox Christians in the Ottoman Empire. The British protested these gains, and in 1791 Prime Minister William Pitt the Younger denounced Russia for its supposed ambitions to dismember the empire. Only the common threat of Napoleon from 1798 to 1815 diverted Great Britain and Russia from their competition in the eastern Mediterranean.

The forces of nationalism in Greece took advantage of the chaotic administration of the Turks in 1821. Unlike the Serbian rebellion, the Greek revolution gained substantial outside support from philhellenic ("admiring Greeks") societies of Great Britain. Even though Metternich hoped the revolt would burn itself out (see Chapter 25), the Greeks were able to take advantage of intervention by the Great Powers to gain their independence.

During the Greek Revolt, the British feared that Russia would use the Greek independence movement as an excuse for further expansion at Turkish expense. The British intervened skillfully, and the Greeks were able to gain their independence without a major Russian advance toward the Straits—the control of which by the Turks blocked their access to the Mediterranean Sea and beyond. Tsar Nicholas I wanted to weaken the Ottoman Empire in order to pave the way for Russia to gain control over the Dardanelles and the Bosporus. So much did he want this expansion of his realm that he set aside his obligations to support the European balance of power. Britain became alarmed at this policy, and the upshot was an agreement in 1827 in which Britain, France,

and Russia pledged themselves to secure Greek independence. Russia eventually defeated the Turks, and in 1829 the Treaty of Adrianople gave the Greeks the basis for their independence while Serbia received autonomy. The Danubian principalities of Moldavia and Wallachia, the basis of the future state of Romania, became Russian protectorates.

By the 1830s it became apparent that the Turks were to be an object of, rather than a subject in, European diplomacy. The sultan's government had few admirers in Europe, but the European powers agreed—at least for the present—to prop up the decaying Ottoman Empire rather than allow one nation to gain dominance in the strategic area.

In 1832 Mehemet Ali, for all intents and purposes the independent governor of Egypt, attacked the sultan, easily putting down the forces of the empire. To prevent the establishment of a new and probably stronger government at the Straits, Nicholas I sent an army to protect Constantinople. The Treaty of Unkiar Skelessi (1833) gave Russia a dominant position over the Turks.

Britain could not tolerate Russia's advantage and for the next ten years worked diplomatically to force the tsar to renounce the treaty and sign a general agreement of Turkish independence. This diplomatic game did little to improve the Ottoman Empire's condition. In 1844, while visiting Britain, Nicholas referred to the empire as a "dying man" and proposed that the British join in a dissection of the body.

The Crimean War

The Crimean War, which lasted from 1853 to 1856, was a major turning point in the course of the Eastern Question. The immediate origins of the war were to be found in a quarrel over the management and protection of the holy places in Palestine. Napoleon III, in a move to gain support from Catholics and the military in France, upheld the Roman Catholics' right to perform the housekeeping duties. On the other side, acting under the terms of the treaty signed in Küchük Kaynarca in 1774, Nicholas stated that the Orthodox faithful should look after the holy places. From this obscure argument the Crimean War eventually emerged, as the Great Powers all intervened in the discussions to protect their interests.

The tsar's ambassador to the Turks tried to use the dispute to improve Russia's position in the region, while the British told the sultan to stand firm against the Russians. After the Russians occupied the Danubian principalities in an attempt to show the Turks the seriousness of their demands, the Turks declared war on the Russians in October 1853. By the next summer the French, Sardinians, and British had joined the Turks. Napoleon III saw the war as a chance to enhance his dynasty's reputation, and the

Sardinians found an opportunity to gain allies in their drive for Italian unification. Under the impact of antitsarist public opinion, the British took steps to stop the Russians. The stated aim of all the allies was, of course, the defense of the sultan.

A combination of the allies' military strength and the tsarist forces' inefficiency stalemated the Russians. Austria, a former close ally of Russia, took advantage of Russia's difficulties to extend Austrian influence into the Balkans. The Russians sued for peace, and the Treaty of Paris (1856) once again attempted to resolve the Eastern Question. Rather than deal with the weakness of the Ottoman Empire, the treaty affirmed its integrity and Great Power status. The Black Sea was to be a neutral body of water, and the Straits were closed to foreign warships. The treaty declared that no power had the right to intervene on behalf of the sultan's Christian subjects. Russian control of the principalities was ended. The Crimean War momentarily stopped the Russian advance into the Balkans and toward the eastern Mediterranean, but the problems posed by the "sick man of Europe" remained. Further, the various Balkan nations became even more inflamed with the desire for self-rule.

The Unanswered Question

In the generation after the Crimean War the problems posed by the disintegrating Ottoman Empire became more severe. To the north the Russians, who could do little militarily in the Balkans during this period of intense internal reforms, broadcast the message of pan-Slavic solidarity to their "Orthodox" brothers in the Balkans. The Austrians, their appetites whetted by their part in the Crimean War, kept a wary and opportunistic eye on developments in the Balkans. British loans to the Turks cut into the Turkish tax base and led to the destruction of the indigenous Ottoman textile industry. In addition, with the completion of the Suez Canal in 1869, the eastern Mediterranean came to be even more essential to British interests. Finally, the Germans began to increase their influence in the area after 1871.

Nationalism further complicated the unresolved Eastern Question. The Bulgarians, who had been under the Turkish yoke since the fourteenth century, started their national revival in the late eighteenth century. By the 1860s they had formed a liberation movement, which was strengthened in 1870 when the Turks gave permission to them to found the Bulgarian Exarchate, a Bulgarian wing of the Greek Orthodox faith. This permitted the Bulgarians to establish their churches wherever there were Bulgarian people, a clear invitation for the expansion of the Bulgarian nation. The Bulgarians took strength from the example of the Romanians, who after centuries of Turkish dominance and a quarter century as a Russian protectorate had gained their independence in 1861, largely as a result of great power influence. Also, during the 1860s the Serbian leader Michael Obrenovich had worked toward a Balkan union against the Turks. Amid this maneuvering and ferment, the Turks were unable to strengthen their rule over areas theoretically under their control.

The crisis came to a head in 1875 when peasants revolted in the district of Bosnia, a Turkish-governed province populated by a religiously diverse group of Slavs. Following this insurrection, Serbia and Montenegro declared war on the Turks. In the summer of 1876 the Bulgarians revolted, but the Ottoman forces put down the rebellion. When highly emotional accounts of the Turkish massacres were published in western Europe, the incident became known as the "Bulgarian horrors" and drew British attention to the Balkans. The pan-Slav faithful in St. Petersburg and Moscow were naturally thrilled at the exploits of their "little brothers," and money and volunteers flowed southward.

The series of nationalistic uprisings in the improperly governed Ottoman provinces had captured the attention of the Great Powers, and by the end of 1875 the Eastern Question was once again the main focus of international diplomacy. The "sick man of Europe" was still strong enough to devastate the Serbs and Montenegrins in battle. The insurgents were forced to sue for peace, a move that drew Tsar Alexander II and the Russians into war with the Ottomans in 1877. After a hard-fought campaign, the Russians broke through early in 1878 and were close to achieving their final goal of taking Constantinople when the sultan sued for peace.

The resulting Treaty of San Stefano in March 1878 recognized the complete independence of Serbia and Romania from theoretical Ottoman sovereignty and reaffirmed Montenegro's independence. A large Bulgarian state was set up, nominally tributary to the Ottoman Empire but actually dominated by Russia. The Straits were effectively under Russian control, as the Bulgarian state would have a coast on the Aegean. The Eastern Question was almost solved by the Russians.

Britain and Austria, however, correctly perceived a major shift of the balance of power in Russia's favor, and the two of them forced a reconsideration of the San Stefano treaty at the Congress of Berlin in June and July 1878. Held under the supervision of Bismarck, the self-styled "honest broker," the congress compelled Russia to agree to a revision of Bulgaria's status. The large state created in March was broken into three parts: the northernmost section would be independent, paying tribute to the Turks, while the other two parts would be under Ottoman

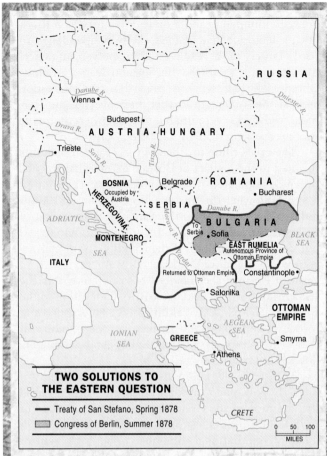

**TWO SOLUTIONS TO
THE EASTERN QUESTION**

—— Treaty of San Stefano, Spring 1878

▨ Congress of Berlin, Summer 1878

In the spring of 1878 the Russians believed that they had imposed their solution to the Eastern Question in the Treaty of San Stefano. The other European powers disagreed and forced a revision of San Stefano in the Congress of Berlin a few months later. Ultimately, the Eastern Question would remain unanswered.

control. Austria got the right to "occupy and administer" the provinces of Herzegovina and Bosnia.

The congress turned back the Russian advance, stymied the national independence movement, and did little to urge Turkey to put its house in order. The Austrian gains caused great bitterness among the Serbs and Russians, a mood that added to the tension in the Balkans. The Eastern Question remained unanswered, and the Balkans remained an arena of local nationalistic conflicts that would appeal to the imperialistic designs of the Great Powers, especially the Russians and the Austro-Hungarian monarchy.

Conclusion

Western imperialism in Latin America, Southeast Asia, China, Japan, and India prompted a variety of reactions. The influx of Europeans and Africans profoundly changed the demographic makeup of Latin America, and the network of states that emerged in the nineteenth century labored under foreign economic

and political domination. Only Siam (Thailand) maintained its independence in southeast Asia, and that only because the French and British wanted a buffer state between their holdings in the region. China suffered a distressing decline in the nineteenth century from its position as the Central Kingdom to a helpless giant split into spheres of influence. The Indians fell under direct British political and economic domination but also gained the tools from the imperial power to use to pursue their eventual independence.

Japan alone was able to adapt and successfully compete with the Western nations. It had a number of advantages, compared to its neighbors. The Japanese culture promoted a rational consideration of Western technological and intellectual advantages that might be useful. It also emphasized hard work, self-sacrifice, loyalty, and the role of the family. Japan's island location helped it resist direct foreign rule. Its leadership in the last third of the century was in the hands of a group of aggressive young officials who embraced the theories and practices of a modern economy. The Japanese brought back from the West the best and most useful elements of a modern economy and applied them to their cultural and social base. The speed with which they accomplished this transformation, barely 40 years after the fall of the shogun, is an impressive indication of the strength of Japanese society. The Japanese defeat of the Russians in 1905 did not alter any basic power relationships, yet it was the first step in a new direction.

The nineteenth century, by and large, saw the West expand its holdings over colonies worldwide, building on sheer technological and economic superiority. At the same time, the foreigners' successes did not fundamentally change the cultural basis of the non-Western peoples. By adapting the strong technology of the West to their own culture, the Japanese provided an example the non-Western world could follow. They set the precedent for other countries that would find their own paths to reassert their self-rule during the course of the twentieth century, after they too had mastered some of the Western tools.

By the end of the century the attention of all the European capitals came to be directed to and dominated by the Eastern Question. It was transformed from a balance-of-power matter to one of small power nationalism and Great Power expansion. The failure to resolve this question would produce an explosive situation that, ironically, would be reproduced in a different context at the end of the twentieth century.

Suggestions for Reading

James R. Scobie, *Revolution on the Pampas: A Social History of Argentine Wheat, 1860–1910* (University of Texas Press, 1964), and Samuel Amaral, *The Rise of Capitalism on the Pampas,*

1785–1870 (Cambridge University Press, 1998), both provide insight into the development of the nineteenth-century prosperity of Argentina. For political developments in Argentina, see Leslie Bethell, ed., *Argentina Since Independence* (Cambridge University Press, 1993). For a remarkable episode in the history of Brazil's independence, see Brian Vale, *Independence or Death! British Sailors and Brazilian Independence, 1822–1825* (Tauris, 1996). For coverage of events in the northern part of the South American continent, see R. L. Gilmore, *Caudillism and Militarism in Venezuela, 1810–1910* (Ohio University Press, 1964).

For events in Central America, see Thomas L. Karnes, *The Failure of Union: Central America, 1824–1960* (University of North Carolina Press, 1961). Michael C. Meyer and William L. Sherman offer a useful, thorough study of Mexico in *The Course of Mexican History* (Oxford University Press, 1995). A view from Mexico of the American advance is found in José António Navarro, *Defending Mexican Valor in Texas: José António Navarro's Historical Writings, 1853–1857* (State House Press, 1996). See also David Bushnell, *The Emergence of Latin America in the Nineteenth Century*, 2nd ed. (Oxford University Press, 1995).

For the impact of the Dutch on the region, see Anne Booth et al., *Indonesian Economic History in the Dutch Colonial Empire* (Yale University Press, 1990). An interesting analysis is provided in Alexander B. Woodside, *Vietnam and the Chinese Model: A Comparative Study of Vietnamese and Chinese Government in the First Half of the Nineteenth Century* (Harvard University Press, 1988). Michael Clodfelter provides an important contribution in *Vietnam Military Statistics: A History of the Indochina Wars, 1772–1991* (McFarland, 1995). Recommended surveys of Southeast Asia are D. G. E. Hall, *A History of Southeast Asia* (St. Martin's Press, 1968), and Harry J. Benda and John A. Larkin, *The World of Southeast Asia* (Harper & Row, 1967).

Li Chien-nung, *The Political History of China, 1840–1928*, trans. Sau-yu Teng and J. Ingalls (Van Nostrand, 1956), is a history of nineteenth-century China. For a good discussion of the transition China faced, see Albert Feuerwerker, ed., *Modern China* (Prentice Hall, 1964). Another useful study of China is Immanuel Hsu, *The Rise of Modern China* (Oxford University Press, 1975). For a recent study of China's response to the West, see David Pong, *Shen Pao and China's Modernization in the Nineteenth Century* (Cambridge University Press, 1994). A key study on China's greatest uprising is Franz H. Michael, *The Taiping Rebellion* (University of Washington Press, 1972). Peter Ward Fay, *The Opium War, 1840–1842* (University of North Carolina Press, 1998), is a fine study. For views on the stresses of the late imperial period, see Daniel H. Bays, *China Enters the Twentieth Century* (Michigan University Press, 1978).

William G. Beasley, *The Modern History of Japan* (Holt, Rinehart and Winston, 1973), is a useful overview. For an investigation into the early contacts between Europe and Asia, see George B. Sansom, *The Western World and Japan* (Knopf, 1974). Thomas Haber, *The Revolutionary Origins of Modern Japan* (Stanford University Press, 1981), and George M. Beckmann, *The Modernization of China and Japan* (Harper & Row, 1962), are essential to an understanding of the Meiji programs. An important recent analysis of the Meiji era is George M. Wilson, *Patriots and Redeemers in Japan: Motives in the Meiji Restoration* (University of Chicago Press, 1992.)

For valuable insights into British rule and its consequences, see Michael Edwardes, *British India, 1772–1947* (Taplinger, 1968), and S. Gopal, *British Policy in India* (Cambridge University Press, 1965). Two good studies of British imperial rule are Philip Woodruff, *The Men Who Ruled India* (St. Martin's Press, 1954), and Jan Morris, *Pax Britannica* (Harcourt Brace Jovanovich, 1980).

Matthew S. Anderson, *The Eastern Question, 1774–1923* (St. Martin's Press, 1966), is the best single-volume treatment of the Balkans dilemma. For the nationalities conflicts in the region, see Barbara Jelavich, *History of the Balkans* (Cambridge University Press, 1983). See also Barbara Jelavich, *Russia's Balkan Entanglements, 1806–1914* (Cambridge University Press, 1991). See also the titles listed for the Ottoman Empire in Chapter 27.

Suggestions for Web Browsing

U.S. Intervention in Latin America
http://www.smplanet.com/imperialism/joining/html

Site offering a wide range of images, movies, and sound bites regarding U.S. intervention in Latin America, particularly the issues surrounding the Panama Canal project.

The Age of Imperialism: Africa and Asia
http://pw2.netcom.com/~giardina/colony.html

An interesting selection of maps tracing the imperial drive in Africa and Asia, with additional sites on the Opium Wars.

Imaging Meiji: Emperor and Era, 1868–1912
http://www.students.haverford.edu/east/meiji/exhibithome.html

Fifty-two wood blocks from a joint exhibition by Haverford, Bryn Mawr, and Swarthmore Colleges describing life during the Meiji era.

Kaiser William and the Partitioning of China
http://h-gtext/kaiserreich/china.htm.

A fascinating selection of documents on Kaiser William II's views on the partitioning of China.

Philippine-U.S. War
http://www.msstate.edu/Archives/History/USA/filipino/filipino.html

Photos and cartoon depicting the takeover of the Philippines by the United States in 1898.

Itihaas: Chronology of Modern India
http://www.itihaas.com/modern/index.html

Extensive chronology of modern India, 1756–1947; most entries include subsites with text and images.

Notes

1. Charles Tilly, "Reflections on the History of European State-Making," in Charles Tilly, ed., *The Formation of National States in Western Europe* (Princeton, N.J.: Princeton University Press, 1975), p. 15.
2. Hubert Herring, *History of Latin America* (New York: Knopf, 1956), p. 97.
3. Kenneth Scott Latourette, *A Short History of the Far East* (New York: Macmillan, 1947), p. 184.
4. Quoted in Franz H. Michael and George E. Taylor, *The Far East in the Modern World* (New York: Holt, Rinehart and Winston, 1956), p. 122.
5. Li Chien-nung, *The Political History of China, 1840–1928*, trans. Sau-yu Teng and J. Ingalls (New York: Van Nostrand, 1956), p. 29.
6. Michael and Taylor, *Far East*, p. 183.
7. Quoted in Ch'u Chai and Winberg Chai, *The Changing Society of China* (New York: Mentor Books, 1962), p. 189.
8. Michael and Taylor, *Far East*, pp. 253–256.
9. Gabriel Ardant, "Financial Policy and Economic Infrastructure of Modern States and Nations," in Tilly, *Formation of National States*, pp. 219–222.
10. See Matthew S. Anderson, *The Eastern Question, 1774–1923* (New York: St. Martin's Press, 1966).

chapter

29

At the turn of the twentieth century, when the Western middle
classes rested complacent in their
superior position in the world and
their belief that "progress" would
ensure their continued dominance,
many of their children became
bored with the smugness of their
parents. One such group, the fu-
turists, had a different vision of the
world, as depicted in Riot in the
Gallery, by the Italian artist
Umberto Boccioni.

The Perils of "Progress"

*Middle-Class Thought and
the Failure of European Diplomacy,
1878–1914*

Chapter Contents

T he middle classes fueled the industrialization, economic transformations, and scientific advances of the nineteenth century. Their newfound wealth, harnessed to the social and legal changes resulting from the French and Napoleonic Revolutions and the reform movements in Britain and the United States, allowed them to control all aspects of Western political life by 1900. Both literate and numerous, they dominated religious, scientific, and cultural affairs, bringing major changes to each area. They were also their own best critics. Two of the most impressive opponents of the middle classes—Marx and Lenin—had impeccable upper-middle-class credentials.

Because of the extent of their triumph, most of the Western middle classes accepted the pseudo-science of the day—social Darwinism and some of the popular racialist theories—to justify their dominant position and to believe that they had entered on the path of irreversible progress. Unfortunately, the middle classes were unable to translate their creativity into the arena of international relations. Their political and foreign policy establishments in Europe reflected the arrogance that accompanied the feelings of superiority and executed a series of blunders that would culminate in World War I.

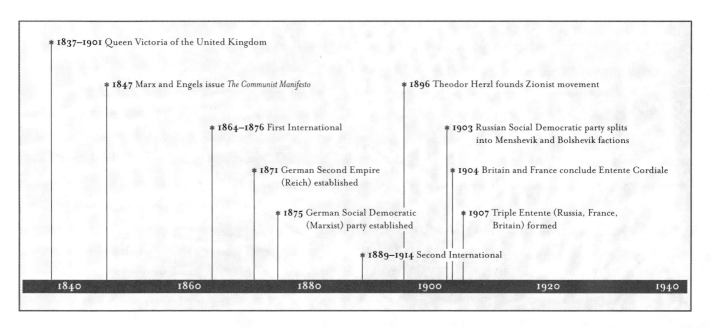

1837–1901 Queen Victoria of the United Kingdom

1847 Marx and Engels issue *The Communist Manifesto*

1896 Theodor Herzl founds Zionist movement

1864–1876 First International

1903 Russian Social Democratic party splits into Menshevik and Bolshevik factions

1871 German Second Empire (Reich) established

1904 Britain and France conclude Entente Cordiale

1875 German Social Democratic (Marxist) party established

1907 Triple Entente (Russia, France, Britain) formed

1889–1914 Second International

| 1840 | 1860 | 1880 | 1900 | 1920 | 1940 |

The Middle Classes and Their Influences

Although it is difficult to give a strict definition of the middle classes, or *bourgeoisie,* it is easier to say who did not belong. Neither factory workers nor peasants nor the aristocracy were included. In general, the farther south and east one went in Europe, the less numerous and weaker the middle classes were.

"Upstairs, Downstairs"

People socially closer to the laboring classes were considered the lower middle classes, while those near the elite formed the upper middle classes. Included in the lower middle classes were skilled artisans, bureaucrats, clerks, teachers, shopkeepers, and clergy. They realized that very little separated them from the laboring masses and were constantly trying to climb socially. Later in the century they benefited most from the compulsory education laws and were avid consumers of the books written by a new wave of authors, the penny-press newspapers, and state propaganda.

The upper middle classes profited the most from industrialization. It was not easy to break into this level of society, but money, taste, and aggressiveness could open the doors for the bankers, factory owners, lawyers, architects, occasional professors, doctors, and high government officials who tried. Once admitted, they gained many of the benefits of the aristoc-

Queen Victoria was a clever and lively woman who was obscured by her stolid appearance and grave demeanor in public. The English monarch's dedication to duty provided stability for her country through an era of massive change.

racy, such as access to the best schools. Thanks to their greater wealth and leisure time, they controlled politics, the press, and the universities.

The English Example

The model for all middle-class people everywhere was the British upper middle class of the Victorian era, named for Victoria (1837–1901), the long-reigning English queen. The Victorian upper middle class was riddled with contradictions. On the surface the Victorians had little doubt about what was right and wrong, moral and immoral, proper and improper. Beneath this surface propriety, however, some members of the leading families pursued debauched lives marked by sexual excesses and drug addiction. One of the prime ministers of the era, William Gladstone, devoted considerable attention to "reforming" prostitutes. At the same time, the Victorian literary establishment concentrated on "cleaning up" Shakespeare's plays and toning down some parts of Gibbon's *Decline and Fall of the Roman Empire* so as not to corrupt the class of

The English, the pioneers of the Industrial Revolution, also established the model of how "proper" middle-class people should live. This family at home embodies an ideal of social and domestic life that was copied wherever in the world a middle class came to exist.

Discovery Through Maps

A Schematic History of Evolution

THE MODERN THEORY OF THE DESCENT OF MAN

Charles Darwin was a cautious man and a fine scientist. That his ideas came to be vulgarized and passed on to an uncritical public in sketches such as this must have caused him considerable distress. But by the turn of the century, this view of "progress" was accepted by a vast majority of people in the West.

Charted here is a map of the distance human beings traveled from the undistinguishable blob at the upper left. The astounding evolution from sharks to marsupials to the European gentleman at the lower right satisfied the middle classes of the Western world in the "rightness" of their comfortable position in life—and dominance in the world.

This view of inevitable northern European superiority was turned into a pseudoscientific mantra by Herbert Spencer (1820–1903), linked to the racist science of the Frenchman Joseph-Arthur de Gobineau (1816–1882), and applied to politics by the likes of the mayor of Vienna, Karl Lueger (1844–1910), and his admirer Adolf Hitler. The holocaust of the twentieth century found its justifications in the fraudulent "science" of the nineteenth.

people in their employ: Britain had more than 2.5 million servants at the century's end—nearly a million people more than farmed the land.

The English middle classes spearheaded crusades against slavery, alcohol, pornography, and child labor and for women's rights. Their efforts led to the passage of a series of reforms limiting the employment of young children, setting maximum working hours for teenagers, and regulating working conditions for women—even when the factory owners argued that such changes were bad for the country because they violated the freedom of contract between worker and employer. The British upper middle class set the complex model of public virtue and private excess to be imitated by their peers around the world.[1]

Middle-Class Christianity

After the Reformation, Christianity continued to be buffeted by serious intellectual, political, and social challenges. The Scientific Revolution and the Enlightenment ate away at the authority of the traditional church. Darwin's theories challenged the traditional Christian view of the origins of the world as presented in the Bible. The Christian churches were reeling under the challenges posed by industrialization and urbanization during the nineteenth century.

This 1895 cartoon satirizes the missionary mania of the age of imperialism. According to the caption, "The Chinaman must be converted even if it takes the whole military and naval forces of the two greatest nations of the world [Great Britain and the United States] to do it."

The demographic changes that resulted from rapid growth of cities forced the church to respond to different audiences facing more difficult problems than those of an earlier, simpler age.

The Protestants endured and adapted, deeply affected by the ambitions and values of the ascending middle classes, especially in the rapidly growing Methodist Church in the United Kingdom and the United States. During the nineteenth century middle-class Protestant missionaries went forth as self-proclaimed messengers of the word of God. Once the Western states began competing for land around the globe, these missionaries often complemented national policy in their religious work. Buttressed by their complacent sense of cultural superiority, they felt justified in undermining the cultures of the peoples with whom they came in contact—especially if that was the price to be paid for "civilization" and the eternal salvation that came with it.

In the Catholic Church, Pope Pius IX (1846–1878), who had become extraordinarily reactionary after having been expelled from Rome in 1848 and after the unification of Italy (see Chapter 25), issued the *Syllabus of Errors* in 1864. This document attacked critics who independently examined matters of faith and doctrine. In 1870 he called a general council of the church to proclaim the doctrine of papal infallibility, which states that when speaking *ex cathedra* ("from the chair") on issues concerning religion and moral behavior, the pope cannot err.

Pius's successor, Leo XIII (1879–1903), a more flexible and less combative pope, helped bring the church into the modern age. In his encyclical *Rerum Novarum* ("Concerning New Things"), issued in 1891, Leo condemned Marxism and upheld capitalism but severely criticized the evils affecting the working classes. By pointing out some of the Christian elements of socialism, Leo placed the church on the side of the workers who were suffering the greatest ills resulting from industrialization. Leo worked to improve relations with Germany, encouraged the passage of social welfare legislation, and supported the formation of Catholic labor unions and political parties.

The Christian Church received a powerful stimulus from the Oxford movement. At the beginning of the nineteenth century a core of spiritual activists at Oxford University, including the future cardinal John Henry Newman (1801–1890), met to defend the church from the various secular and political forces that were besieging it. During the 1830s the group split, some members remaining within the Anglican Church and others, including Newman, joining the Catholic Church. During the rest of the century the Oxford movement brought new life to the church in England through its missionary work, participation in social concerns, and improvement of the intellectual level of the faith. Similar developments occurred across the Continent.

Critique from the Left

The successes and excesses of capitalism drew a powerful reaction from within the middle classes. Utopian socialist thinkers (see Chapter 25) came from the eighteenth-century nobility or early-nineteenth-century elites. After 1850 the most powerful voices against the capitalist, middle-class-dominated world came from Karl Marx (1818–1883), born in Trier, Germany, to bourgeois parents, and from Vladimir Ilich Lenin, the son of a mid-level Russian bureaucrat. Other left-wing protests came from British upper-middle-class intellectuals and the French and German radical bourgeoisie.

Karl Marx and Scientific Socialism

To participate fully in Prussian society, Marx's Jewish parents converted to Protestantism and pushed their son to become a lawyer. Instead of following his parents' wishes, he attended the University of Berlin as a doctoral candidate in philosophy and joined a circle that followed some aspects of Hegel's thought. After finishing his degree, he could not find a university position and so returned to the Rhineland, where he began writing for a local liberal newspaper. The injustices he saw around him and his reading of the French socialists Henri de Saint-Simon and Pierre-Joseph Proudhon led him to concentrate on the economic factors in history and pass from philosophical abstractions to the realities of politics and economics.

In 1845 Marx went to Paris to continue his work; there he met Friedrich Engels (1820–1895), the son of a wealthy German businessman who owned factories in England and Germany. Engels had seen firsthand how workers suffered during the first phase of industri-

EUROPE IN THE MID-NINETEENTH CENTURY

Even with the political changes since 1500, the instability of central and eastern Europe continued to serve as the flashpoint of European politics into the mid-nineteenth century.

alization when he worked at his father's plant in Manchester. In Paris he and Marx spent ten days together sharing their ideas. The two became united in their hatred of what they saw as the inhumane nature of capitalism and spent the rest of their lives attacking it.

Marx was from the start the intellectually dominant partner, but Engels gave him lifelong intellectual, material, and personal support. Marx's radical ideas led to his expulsion by the French in 1845. From there he went first to Belgium and finally to England, where he spent most of his life after 1848.

Almost every day he made his way to the British Museum, where he waged intellectual war on capitalism by doing research for his major works, especially *Das Kapital* ("Capital"). At night he returned home to write, enduring difficult living conditions and the deaths of three of his children in the 1850s. He wrote prolifically, although suffering from boils, asthma, spleen and liver problems, and eyestrain. His constant inability to handle money drove him into fits of rage against his creditors. He was increasingly intolerant of anyone who disagreed with him and became an embittered recluse; yet his vision and theories inspired reformers for the next century and a half. Marx constructed a system that gave the oppressed

an explanation for their difficult position and hope for their future.

A materialistic view of history shaped his approach. He wrote that economic forces drove history. He did not deny the existence or importance of spiritual or philosophical values; nor did he doubt that the occasional genius could alter the flow of events. However, the material aspects of life were much more important. Marx believed that "it is not the consciousness of men which determines their existence, but on the contrary, it is the existence which determines their consciousness." As an economic determinist he believed that when the means of production of a given era changed, the whole social and ideological structure was transformed by the groups who controlled those means of production.

Hegel had written that history is made up of a number of cultural periods, each one the expression of a dominant spirit or idea. After fulfilling its purpose, a given period is replaced by a period of contradictory ideas or values. The original thesis is negated, and that negation is in turn negated once it has run its course. Marx identified the productive forces of society, not culture periods, as the key factor in history. The world was driven by class conflict between those who controlled the means of production and those who did

Karl Marx with his daughter. After being expelled from several European countries, Marx settled in England, where he devoted himself to the development of his theory of scientific socialism.

not, whether master against slave in ancient Greece, patrician against plebeian in Rome, lord against serf in the Middle Ages, noble against bourgeois in early modern times, or capitalist against proletarian in the modern world. History moved in this zigzag pattern through class struggle, a reflection of the Hegelian dialectic. Not until the triumph of the proletariat would this pattern stop: the workers controlling the means of production could not logically engage in class conflict, and hence *communism* would be achieved.

The bourgeoisie, who had erected the new capitalist society by gaining control of the means of production through organizing trade and industry, created its opposition in the proletariat, the class-conscious workers. This latter group would be, according to Marx, "the seeds of the bourgeoisie's own destruction." According to the dialectic, when the workers recognized their true power, they would overthrow the bourgeoisie. Out of this conflict would come the final act of the dialectical process, the classless society in which "each person would work according to his ability and receive according to his need." An interim dictatorship might have to occur, because a number of features of the old order would remain and the proletariat would have to be protected. However, as the classless society evolved, the state would wither away.

Through his research, Marx identified a number of defects that foretold the inevitable overthrow of the bourgeoisie, among them alienation and surplus value. The factory system turned workers into cogs in the larger machine and deprived them of satisfaction in their work. In addition, Marx charged that owners did not pay workers for the value they created. A worker could, for example, produce the necessary economic value to supply one individual's needs in seven hours, but the owner would keep the worker laboring for 12 hours. The owner thereby stole the "surplus value" of five working hours from the worker, in effect robbing the worker of the fruits of his or her work.

Finally, Marx noted that in the capitalist system the rich got richer and fewer and the poor got poorer and more numerous. This produced widespread discontent and increased the impetus toward revolution. Further, the masses would be unable to buy all of the goods they produced, and economic crises of overproduction and unemployment would become the rule. In time, once the bourgeois phase of dominance had run its course, the contradictions between the classes would become so great that the proletariat would rise up and take over the means of production.

Marx was the last of the great Enlightenment universal theorists. As is the case with other ideologists in the rationalist eighteenth-century tradition, he built on the foundations erected by others and made a creative synthesis that has had worldwide appeal. As was also the case with other major thinkers, his thoughts, which were often hypotheses, became frozen in dogma or revised in various countries to take forms he would have had trouble recognizing. It is not surprising that the rapidly changing age in which he lived would outrun many of his projections, especially those concerning the rigidity of the capitalists.

The "Internationals" and European Socialism

Socialist parties, of all varieties, in the second half of the nineteenth century helped advance the workers' movements by providing a theoretical basis and an aggressive public statement of their case. Marx, who spent his life researching and writing in the defense of the workers—even though he had precious little contact with them—organized the International Workingmen's Association, later known as the First International, in London in 1864. The First International included labor activists ranging from English trade unions to eastern European refugees to anarchists to German theorists. Not much came of the First International's efforts because of constant arguing among the factions and Marx's vindictiveness toward other major figures, such as the Russian anarchist Bakunin.

In the three decades after Marx's death in 1883 his theories dominated the European workers' move-

Karl Marx and Friedrich Engels, *Manifesto of the Communist Party*

The *Manifesto* had little effect in the revolutionary year of 1848. However, in the twentieth century it became one of the most widely read tracts in world history.

A spectre is haunting Europe—the spectre of Communism. All the Powers of old Europe have entered into a holy alliance to exorcise this spectre; Pope and Czar, Metternich and Guizot, French Radicals and German police-spies.

The first step in the revolution by the working class is to raise the proletariat to the position of ruling class, to win the battle of democracy.

The proletariat will use its political supremacy to wrest, by degrees, all capital from the bourgeoisie, to centralise all instruments of production in the hands of the State, i.e., of the proletariat organized by the ruling class; and to increase the total of productive forces as rapidly as possible.

In the most advanced countries the following will be pretty generally applicable:

1. Abolition of property in land and application of all rents of land to public purposes.
2. A heavy progressive or graduated income tax.
3. Abolition of all right of inheritance.
4. Confiscation of the property of all emigrants and rebels.
5. Centralisation of credit in the hands of the State, by means of a national bank with State capital and an exclusive monopoly.
6. Centralisation of the means of communication and transport in the hands of the State.
7. Extension of factories and instruments of production owned by the State; the bringing into cultivation of waste lands, and the improvement of the soil generally in accordance with a common plan.
8. Equal liability of all to labour. Establishment of industrial armies, especially for agriculture.
9. Combination of agriculture with manufacturing industries; gradual abolition of the distinction between town and country, by a more equable distribution of the population over the country.
10. Free education for all children in public schools. Abolition of children's factory labour in its present form. Combination of education with industrial production, etc., etc.

When, in the course of development, class distinctions have disappeared, and all production has been concentrated in the hands of a vast association of the whole nation, the public power will lose its political character. Political power, properly so called, is merely the organised power of one class for oppressing another. If the proletariat during its contest with the bourgeoisie is compelled, by the force of circumstances, to organise itself as a class, if, by means of a revolution, it makes itself the ruling class, and, as such, sweeps away by force the old conditions of production, then it will, along with these conditions, have swept away the conditions for the existence of class antagonisms, and of classes generally, and will thereby have abolished its own supremacy as a class.

In place of the old bourgeois society, with its classes and class antagonisms, we shall have an association in which the free development of each is the condition for the free development of all.

From Karl Marx and Friedrich Engels, *Manifesto of the Communist Party* (1848).

ments, though the movements themselves were not united. The French split into three distinct socialist groups. Some British socialists were greatly influenced by the maxims of Christianity, while the socialist Fabian Society—among whose members were the writers George Bernard Shaw, H. G. Wells, and Sidney and Beatrice Webb—pursued a more prosaic political path. With the spread of industrialization, workers and their leaders found important support in Marx's work even in places such as Russia, where Marx had never foreseen his thoughts having any influence.

The Social Democrats—Marxist socialists—made important gains in Germany, forcing Bismarck to make concessions (see Chapter 26). It became the largest party in the country and the strongest socialist party in Europe under the leadership of its founder,

Ferdinand Lassalle. In 1871 there were two socialists in the Reichstag; by 1912 the number had risen to 110.

Because of the widespread impact of Marx's ideas in the social sciences and the labor movement, the period of the Second International (1889–1914) may be called without any exaggeration the "golden age of Marxism."[2] A broad spectrum of thinkers among the 12 million members of the Second International claimed Marx as their inspiration, even though they might differ on the role of the state, the functions of unions, the crisis of capitalism, the role of the proletariat, and even things Marx himself said. There was not a single, monolithic Marxist movement in Europe. Yet despite their doctrinal differences, the Social Democrats in all countries could agree on essentials for the workers: an eight-hour day, the need to

Socialist Internationals (Labor Unions)

1864–1876	International Workingmen's Association (First International)
1889–1914	Second International, Social Democratic (non-Russian remnants remained until 1972)
1919–1943	Third International, Communist (Leninist, also known as the Comintern)
1923–1970s	Fourth International, Trotskyite (formally organized in 1938)

replace standing armies with militias, and a welfare state buttressed by universal suffrage.

The socialist movement strengthened Europe's labor unions, and the workers achieved substantial progress by 1914. Whether by working within the various states' legislatures or by raising the specter of revolution, the socialists helped bring about substantial reforms in the economy, labor practices, civil rights, the courts, and education. They pushed the capitalists to reform, thus ironically avoiding the very apocalyptic revolution forecast by Marx.

Lenin and the Bolsheviks

The person who would eventually apply and implement Marxist theory was Vladimir Ilich Ulyanov (1870–1924), who later took the name Lenin. Born in Ulyanovsk, formerly Simbirsk, a small city along the Volga River, Lenin grew up in the moderate and respectable circumstances provided by his father, a school administrator and teacher.

In 1887 the government arrested and executed Lenin's brother, Alexander, in St. Petersburg on charges of plotting against the life of the tsar. Shortly thereafter Lenin began to master the writings of Marx and to study contemporary Russia. He overcame major obstacles from tsarist officials and passed his law exams at St. Petersburg University without formally attending classes. After 1893 he began to compile theories of tactics and strategy that would form the basis of the Soviet Union throughout its 73-year existence.

In 1895 a court sentenced him to exile in Siberia for his political activities. While in exile he enjoyed complete liberty of movement in the district and could hunt, fish, swim, study, read, and keep up a large correspondence. A political ally, Nadezhda Krupskaia, joined him, and they were married. Later they translated Sidney and Beatrice Webb's *History of Trade Unionism*. When Lenin's exile ended in 1900,

he and Krupskaia went to Switzerland, where they joined other Russian Social Democrats in exile in founding the newspaper *Iskra* ("Spark"), whose motto was "From the Spark—the conflagration."

In applying Marx to Russian conditions, Lenin found it necessary to sketch in several blank spots. Lenin's methods differed greatly from those of western European Marxists, as did his theories. Lenin advocated the formation of a small elite of professional revolutionaries, the "vanguard of the proletariat." These professionals, subject to strict party discipline, would anticipate the proletariat's needs and best interests and lead them through the oxymoronic theory of "democratic centralism."

The Social Democrats met in 1903 in London and split into two wings—the *Bolsheviks* and the *Mensheviks*—over the questions of the timing of the revolution and the nature of the party. (In Russian, *bolshevik* means "majority" and *menshevik* means "minority," the names stemming from a vote on party policies in 1903 when the Bolsheviks did prevail. On most occasions until the summer of 1917, however, the Bolsheviks were in fact in a distinct minority among the Social Democrats.) The two factions differed sharply on strategy and tactics. The Bolsheviks, following Lenin's revisionist views, were prepared to

Lenin, the driving force behind the Russian Revolution from which emerged the Soviet Union, spent years studying Marx's theories and adapting them to conditions in Russia.

move the pace of history along through democratic centralism. The Mensheviks believed that Russian socialism should grow gradually and peacefully in accordance with Marxist principles of development and historical evolution, and they were prepared to work within a framework dominated by bourgeois political parties. They knew that their victory was inevitable, given the historical dialectic, and that the proletariat would play the lead role, assisted by the party. After their split in 1903, the two factions never reconciled.

After 1903 Lenin had little success in changing the political conditions of Russia, beyond affecting the most sophisticated part of the workers' movement. However, he continued to make significant doctrinal contributions. Lenin recommended a socialism whose weapon was violence and whose tactics allowed little long-range compromise with the bourgeoisie. However, he also saw the advantages of flexibility and encouraged temporary deviations that might serve the goals of the working class. He took little for granted and reasoned that the development of class unity to destroy the capitalists among the Russian workers might require some assistance. To that end he refined his notion of the way in which the elite party would function. In revolution the elite party would infiltrate the government, police, and army while participating in legal workers' movements; in government the party would enforce its dictates on the populace with iron discipline.

Lenin looked out at the undoubted strength of the advanced technological nations and marveled at their extension of power. In *Imperialism, the Highest Stage of Capitalism* (1916) he forecast that the modern capitalist states would destroy themselves. He argued that the wages of the workers did not represent enough purchasing power to absorb the output of the capitalists' factories and that the vast amounts of capital that were accumulated could not be invested profitably in the home country. Therefore, the states would engage in an inevitable competition for markets, resources, and capital that would drive them from cutthroat competition to outright war and their ultimate destruction. At that point, he reasoned, his elite party would be ready to pick up the pieces from the blindly selfish powers.

Critique from the Right

The territory opened up by the scientific discoveries of the nineteenth century complemented the ambitions of the middle classes. The optimism generated by science in the laboratory and Europe's advance across the globe supported the commonly held belief in inevitable progress and the bourgeoisie's dominant place in society.

Positivism and Pragmatism

The middle classes took science seriously, and in each of the Western countries popular magazines appeared

Major Figures in Bad Science and Right-Wing Politics

1816–1882	Joseph-Arthur de Gobineau (French)
1820–1903	Herbert Spencer (English)
1840–1910	William Graham Sumner (American)
1844–1910	Karl Lueger (Austrian)
1855–1927	Houston Stewart Chamberlain (English; naturalized German in 1916)

to explain the latest trends to a fascinated world. Every discovery seemed to point to inevitable progress, and a new breed of social scientists, known as the positivists, reinforced that view. Positivism is a mechanistic way of thinking that uses the methods and principles of science to define the laws of a strictly material world that presumably may be scientifically verified.

Auguste Comte (1798–1857), an engineer who was formerly secretary to Saint-Simon, established the foundations for the philosophical approach for positivism in a series of lectures and publications in the 1830s and 1840s. He stated that one could find

Auguste Comte developed the theory of positivism, according to which science is totally objective and value-free.

William Graham Sumner on Socialism

The nineteenth century was the prime age of the "fittest." Darwin's scientific theories were applied to political theory, among many other things. William Graham Sumner saw socialism as retrograde.

The origin of socialism, which is the extreme development of the sentimental philosophy, lies in the undisputed facts which I described at the outset. The socialist regards this misery as the fault of society. He thinks that we can organize society as we like and that an organization can be devised in which poverty and misery shall disappear. He goes further even than this. He assumes that men have artificially organized society as it now exists. Hence if anything is disagreeable or hard in the present state of society, it follows, on that view, that the task of organizing society has been imperfectly and badly performed, and that it needs to be done over again. These are the assumptions with which the so-cialist starts, and many socialists seem also to believe that if they can destroy belief in an Almighty God who is supposed to have made the world such as it is, they will then have overthrown the belief that there is a fixed order in human nature and human life which man can scarcely alter at all, and, if at all, only infinitesimally.

The truth is that the social order is fixed by laws of nature precisely analogous to those of the physical order. The most that man can do is by ignorance and self-conceit to mar the operation of social laws.

From William Graham Sumner, *The Challenge of Facts* (1914).

---

and verify the laws that controlled society in the same way that a scientist discovered physical laws. For Comte humanity was a part of a machine, which possessed neither free will nor a divinely infused spark of life. Comte's goal was to understand the machine and devise a science to discover the laws of history and society. He developed the social science of sociology and stated that when humanity could base itself on science, and not on opinion, harmony would result.

In the United States the American physicist Charles Sanders Peirce (1839–1914) broke new philosophical ground by stressing the role of change and chance in nature and broadly applied Darwinian theory to reinforce the trend away from absolute standards and procedures. In the late 1890s William James (1842–1910) popularized Peirce's approaches in his philosophy of pragmatism. James stated that "an idea is true so long as to believe it is profitable to our lives." In effect the pragmatists rejected any concept of truth or morality as an absolute and favored a more flexible, result-oriented approach. Both positivism and pragmatism fit in well with a social class on its way up.

The New Science and Modern Racism

Darwin's hypotheses were very attractive to the positivists, who, along with their imitators, distorted the British scientist's findings by applying them to areas Darwin never dreamed of discussing—human social, economic, and political activities—to justify the fan-tasies of eternal progress, the dominance of science, the perfectibility of humanity through obedience to the supposedly unchanging laws of society, and the assumption of Anglo-Saxon racial dominance. The social Darwinists, positivists, and others of their kind followed a simplistic approach to the world based on their comforting belief that humanity is but a cog in a machine and that the possibilities of individuals are predetermined by their place in the larger scheme of things.

The most popular social Darwinist was the English philosopher Herbert Spencer (1820 1903), who applied Darwin's theories to all aspects of human social and political life. Spencer had a deep influence in both Europe and the United States. As a convenient doctrine to justify the actions and philosophies of the newcomers at the top of the social and political structure, the middle classes, social Darwinism dominated Western social thought in the late nineteenth century.

The rapid political, social, economic, philosophical, and intellectual changes that shook Europe and the world led to new ways of defining individuals and groups. Even before Darwin publicized his theory of evolution, pseudoscientists such as Joseph-Arthur de Gobineau (1816–1882) laid the foundations of modern racism, justifying the domination of one group over another for "scientific" reasons. Gobineau applied biological theory to politics, regarding nations as organisms. He argued that different races are innately unequal in ability and worth and that the genius of a race depended on heredity, not external factors. Gobineau stated a widely held belief among Europeans that white people alone were capable of cultural creativity and that intermixture with other races would destroy that creativity. Social Darwinist arguments and Gobineau's theories in support of white superiority gave "rational" justifications to blatant bigotry and provided a reassuring sanction for European domination over Asians and Africans.

Supported by the new pseudoscience and the belief that Europeans alone bore the burdens of progress, Western expansion took on a more blatant and bellicose form. In the United States the destruction of the way of life of the Native Americans was "justified" by the demands of the unstoppable tide of progress. Aggressive nationalism based on self-serving theories of superiority was adhered to almost as a religion; it served as a powerful vehicle for politicians to mobilize their constituents. Nationalistic pressures became particularly strong in eastern Europe—especially among the Hungarians and in Romania, Bulgaria, Serbia, and Greece, where political instability and economic underdevelopment created insecure conditions.

One of the manifestations of the identities was the Anglo-Saxon movement. In Britain and Germany writers and speakers presented the case for the superiority of northern Europeans. They stated that world leadership should naturally reside in London and Berlin because the people living there possessed the proper combination of religion, racial qualities, and culture to enable them to dictate the world's future. People as diverse as Kaiser William II and U.S. President Woodrow Wilson shared this outlook.

Another manifestation of a regrouping on the basis of new principles came with the so-called pan-cultural movements. Pan-Slavic movements had begun before 1850. These were based either on the Orthodox Slavs' foundation in Moscow or the Catholic Slavs' center at Prague. In the later part of the century the Russians would use their pan-Slavic movement to expand their influence into the Balkans in pursuit of their "destiny" to create and rule a great Slavic empire. The Pan-Germanic League was organized in Berlin in the 1890s to spread the belief in the superiority of the German race and culture.

Modern Anti-Semitism

Anti-Semitism—systematic hostility toward the Jews—had persisted in Europe since Constantine the Great made Christianity the religion of the Eastern Roman Empire in the fourth century. But the movement attained new strength and vigor in the last part of the nineteenth century. In Germany the historian Heinrich von Treitschke (1834–1896) stated that "the Jews are our calamity." In France anti-Semitism played a significant role in the Dreyfus affair (see

In a work published in 1854, Joseph-Arthur de Gobineau advanced the theory that the Europeans were superior among human beings. The theory would have ominous consequences in the twentieth century.

Chapter 26). In eastern Europe the Jews suffered many injustices; in Russia they were murdered in pogroms (organized massacres). Anti-Semitism became stronger because of the economic dislocation that modernization introduced and of the work of cranks who turned out pseudoscientific tracts and forgeries encouraging bigoted attitudes.

In the first decade of the twentieth century the election of Karl Lueger (1844–1910), who campaigned as mayor of Vienna on an anti-Semitic platform and won, foretold the tragic genocide that would occur later in the century. It was in this atmosphere that the young Adolf Hitler spent some of his formative years, reading racist, social Darwinist, and pan-Germanic tracts.

Jews, in response, expressed a growing desire for a homeland where they would be safe and free. In 1896 the Hungarian Theodor Herzl (1860–1904) founded the movement known as Zionism, promoting the creation of an independent Jewish state in Palestine, the ancestral home of the Jews. The first general congress of Zionists was held in Switzerland in 1897, and so began a small-scale emigration to Palestine, despite the fact that the region had been settled for centuries by Arabs.

The Roots of Fascism

As Marx and Lenin established the foundations of communism and Marxism-Leninism, and as the social Darwinists and racialist writers advocated the superiority of northern and western Europeans, other middle-class thinkers were laying the foundations of

Theodor Herzl founded the Zionist movement to bring to fruition the longing of the Jews of the Diaspora for a homeland in the land of their ancestors, Palestine. He was driven not only by his faith but also by the rabid anti-Semitism that was resurgent in central Europe toward the end of the nineteenth century.

fascism, an ideology that made its appearance in the 1920s in Italy and Germany. Fascism is composed of many elements, all rejecting the middle-class values of the nineteenth century. It is, among other things, antiliberal, anticonservative, antirational, charismatic, nationalist, sometimes racist, and totalitarian.[3]

The decade before and the decade after the turn of the twentieth century saw crushing attacks from all perspectives against the accepted truths of the age. In France Henri Bergson wrote that "vital instinct," not reason, was the most important part of creativity. In Italy Benedetto Croce rebelled against the positivism and rationalism of the age. At the same time that Albert Einstein began to destroy the classic Newtonian universe (see Chapter 30), Sigmund Freud questioned the whole notion of rationality. As the social Darwinists misinterpreted the carefully reasoned hypotheses of Charles Darwin, so did opportunistic political thinkers began to fill the definitional void by advocating a new kind of state based on emotion and charisma.

With the introduction of mass politics came a certain resentment of the classic liberalism that had dominated the nineteenth century. Especially among younger Europeans, this resentment sparked an emotional, often irrational reaction against the values of the older generation and the desire for action—any kind of action. The writings of Friedrich Nietzsche (1844–1900) calling for the dominance of an *Übermensch,* a "superior man" who despised the mediocrity of the bourgeoisie, became popular. In France, Georges Sorel (1847–1922), a retired engineer, stated the need for action and violence to replace parliamentary democracy from a leftish point of view. Sorel advocated the use of violence as a justifiable means to deal with the corruption of bourgeois society and to bring together like-minded people in a common crusade. To Sorel the victims of violence paid the necessary price for progress, and their suffering was more than justified by the advances that brutality could bring.

As the end of the century approached, the notion of the decadence of Western civilization, especially the purported weakening of the white race, was discussed everywhere in Europe. This mode of thinking was especially prevalent in Germany and Austria, and its most influential spokesman was Houston Stewart Chamberlain (1855–1927), who wrote that the blond-haired, blue-eyed "Aryan" (northern Indo-European) had a very special "race soul" whose existence was threatened by Jews.

These thoughts and tendencies found fertile ground in the boredom of the middle classes. Stanley Payne writes that "quite aside from any specific political proclivity, a concern for new approaches and new values—and possibly a new style of life" was fed by this bourgeois boredom. This, plus the growth of a "youth culture" with its roots in the well-to-do middle classes, provided an audience for these ideas. "A

Houston Stewart Chamberlain on the Characteristics of the German Race

Houston Stewart Chamberlain had no doubts about the superiority of the Germans. His views found their way into Hitler's beliefs.

Let us attempt a glance into the depths of the soul. What are the specific intellectual and moral characteristics of this Germanic race? Certain anthropologists would fain teach us that all races are equally gifted; we point to history and answer: that is a lie! The races of mankind are markedly different in the nature and also in the extent of their gift, and the Germanic races belong to the most highly gifted group, the group usually termed Aryan. Is this human family united and uniform by bonds of blood? Do these stems really all spring from the same root? I do not know and I do not much care; no affinity binds more closely than elective affinity, and in this sense the Indo-European Aryans certainly form a family.

Physically and mentally the Aryans are preeminent among all peoples; for that reason they are by right, as the Stagirite [Aristotle] expresses it, the lords of the world. Aristotle puts the matter still more concisely when he says, "Some men are by nature free, others slaves"; this perfectly expresses the moral aspect. For freedom is by no means an abstract thing, to which every human being has fundamentally a claim; a right to freedom must evidently depend upon capacity for it, and this again presupposes physical and intellectual power. One may make the assertion, that even the mere conception of freedom is quite unknown to most men. Do we not see the *homo syriacus* develop just as well and as happily in the position of slave as of master? Do the Chinese not show us another example of the same nature? Do not all historians tell us that the Semites and half-Semites, in spite of their great intelligence, never succeeded in founding a State that lasted, and that because every one always endeavoured to grasp all power for himself, thus showing that their capabilities were limited to despotism and anarchy, the two opposites of freedom?

From Houston Stewart Chamberlain, *Foundations of the Nineteenth Century* (1900).

---

mood of rejection of some of the dominant values of preceding generations had set in. Faith in rationalism, the positivist approach, and the worship of materialism came increasingly under fire. Hostility toward bureaucracy, the parliamentary system, and the drive for 'mere' equality often accompanied this spirit of rejection."[4]

The Failure of European Diplomacy

By 1914 Europeans had many reasons to be optimistic about the future. The growth produced by the previous three generations seemed to support the sturdy belief in progress. There was a substantial amount of unity: Europe was Christian, Caucasian, capitalist, industrialized, and in command of the world. Europeans shared the same vibrant Western traditions, and even the rulers of the various states were all related to one another.

Appearances and Realities

As if to symbolize world changes, there were new ways to organize international communication, defuse conflicts, and maintain peace. As early as 1865 a meeting was held in Paris to coordinate the use of telegraph lines and to establish a unified rate structure. Ten

Major Dates in European Alliances

Central Powers

1879	Dual Alliance (Germany, Austria-Hungary) formed
1882	Triple Alliance (Germany, Austria-Hungary, Italy) formed
1890	Bismarck resigns; Reinsurance Treaty with Russia lapses

Triple Entente

1894	French-Russian Alliance
1890s	Germany decides to build fleet to compete with British navy
1904	Britain and France conclude Entente Cordiale
1907	Russia joins Britain and France to form Triple Entente

years later the Universal Postal Union was set up to handle the world's mail. To protect the rights of authors, an agreement was drawn up in 1886 for an international copyright union.

Scholars and statesmen worked to strengthen international law, the rules of warfare, and the use of arbitration. A significant example of this was the opening of the Hague Conference in 1899. The Russian foreign minister invited the Great Powers to the Dutch city to discuss arms reduction. Although no progress was made on disarmament, the conference did reform the rules of war by improving the treatment of prisoners, outlawing the use of poisonous gas, and defining the conditions of a state of war. In addition, an international court of arbitration, the Hague Tribunal, was established, staffed by an international group of jurists. Appearance before the court was voluntary, as was acceptance of its decisions. The effectiveness of arbitration as a means to solve problems could be seen in the ten years before the war. Various powers signed 162 treaties that pledged the signatories to arbitrate disagreements such as boundary decisions and conflicts over fishing rights.

Alfred Nobel, the Swedish manufacturer of dynamite, personified the contradictions of the age. This international producer of explosives established a peace prize two weeks before his death in November 1896. Andrew Carnegie set up the Carnegie Endowment for International Peace and built a peace palace at The Hague to be used for international conferences. It was finished just weeks before the outbreak of World War I.

All of these developments encouraged believers in progress to envision a peaceful future. They pointed out that all of the wars in the nineteenth century had been generally local and short. They reasoned that if war should break out in the future, the murderous new technologies would ensure that they would not be lengthy or costly. Some social Darwinists asserted that humanity might well evolve beyond the stage of fighting wars altogether. These optimists conveniently ignored the brutal, lengthy, and costly reality of the American Civil War, in many ways the first modern, industrial war. They also ignored the reality that the European state system and military industrial complexes took on a life and momentum of their own.

The End of Bismarck's System

From 1870 to 1890 the German chancellor, Otto von Bismarck, dominated European diplomacy. He built a rational balance-of-power-based foreign policy devoted to the diplomatic isolation of France by depriving it of potential allies. He reasoned that the French would try to take revenge on Germany and regain Alsace and Lorraine, but he knew they could do little without aid from the Austrians or Russians. In 1873

Bismarck made an alliance, known as the Three Emperors' League *(Dreikaiserbund),* with Russia and Austria-Hungary.

Conflicts between the Austrians and Russians in the Balkans soon put a strain on the league, and at the Congress of Berlin (1878) Bismarck was forced to choose between the conflicting claims of Vienna and St. Petersburg. He chose to support Austria-Hungary for a number of reasons, including fear of alienating Great Britain if he backed the Russians. In addition, he felt that he could probably dominate Austria more easily than Russia. This momentous shift paved the way for a new arrangement. In 1879 Bismarck negotiated the Dual Alliance with the Austro-Hungarian monarchy; in 1882 a new partner, Italy, joined the group, which was now called the Triple Alliance.

The choice of Austria over Russia did not mean that Bismarck abandoned his ties with the tsars. In 1881 the Three Emperors' League was renewed. Rivalries between the Dual Monarchy and Russia in the Balkans put an effective end to the arrangement, and the Dreikaiserbund collapsed for good in 1887. Bismarck negotiated a separate agreement with Russia called the Reinsurance Treaty, in which both sides pledged neutrality—except if Germany attacked France or Russia attacked Austria—and support of the status quo.

Under Bismarck's shrewd hand, Germany kept diplomatic control for 20 years. Bismarck chose his goals carefully and understood the states with which he worked. He made every effort to avoid challenging Britain's interests and to continue isolating France. As a result, Germany was not surrounded by enemies. The chancellor kept from alienating Russia while maintaining his ties with Austria.

In the 1890s, however, the rash actions of the new kaiser, William II, destroyed Germany's favorable position. He dismissed Bismarck in 1890, took foreign policy into his own hands, and arrogantly frittered away the diplomatic advantages the chancellor had built up. France had been attempting to escape from its isolation for some time and had begun, through its bank loans, to make important inroads into Russia even before Bismarck retired. When the kaiser allowed the Reinsurance Treaty to lapse, the Russians decided to look elsewhere. France leapt at the chance, after 20 years, to secure a strong ally. In 1894 the Triple Alliance of Germany, Italy, and Austria-Hungary found itself confronted by the Dual Alliance of Russia and France. Germany's worst fears had come to pass: it was now encircled by enemies.

Britain Ends Its Isolation

At the end of the nineteenth century Britain found itself involved in bitter rivalries with Russia in the Balkans and in the Middle East and with France in

Bismarck and the young Kaiser William II meet in 1888. The two disagreed over many issues, and in 1890 William dismissed the aged chancellor.

Africa. During the Boer War all of the Great Powers in Europe were anti-British. However, the supremacy of the British fleet helped discourage intervention. As the new century began, London became concerned that its policy of splendid isolation might need to be abandoned. In these circumstances the most normal place for Britain to turn would be to Germany.

On the surface nothing seemed more natural than that these two dominant European powers should adjust their national interests to avoid conflict. From the 1880s to 1901 both sides made several approaches to investigate an "understanding" between the major sea power, Britain, and the strongest land power, Germany. Tradition and dynastic relations spoke in favor of a closer tie between the two. By 1900 Berlin and London may have competed in economic and imperialistic terms, but they were far from any major strife in any either area.

The two countries could not, however, come together formally. Even though important figures on both sides could see the advantages of an alliance, strong forces worked against this development. Ger-

man and British interests did not match sufficiently to permit equal gain from an alliance. The kaiser's numerous bellicose statements and clumsy actions (such as his meddling in British colonial affairs by sending a telegram to South Africa's president, Paul Kruger, in 1896) offended many British leaders. Germany's expanding influence in the Middle East and the Balkans worried the British, as did Germany's tremendous economic progress.

Most threatening for London was Germany's plan to build a fleet that would compete with Britain's. In 1900 Germany initiated a huge naval program providing for, within a 20-year timetable, a fleet strong enough to keep Britain from interfering with German international goals. The British believed that the German program was aimed directly at them. For the island nation, the supremacy of the Royal Navy was a life-or-death matter. Since food and raw materials had to come by sea, it was crucial that the navy be able to protect British shipping.

Challenged by Germany, Britain looked elsewhere for allies. In 1904 officials from London and

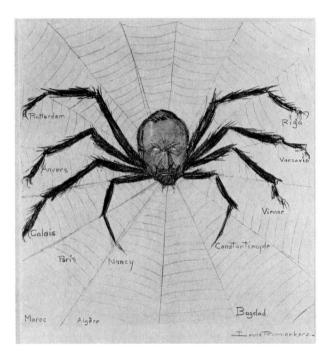

Dutch artist Louis Raemaekers depicted the German kaiser as a spider whose legs reached all parts of Europe and whose predatory eye was cast as far away as Baghdad, Algeria, and Morocco.

Paris began to settle their differences and proclaimed the Entente Cordiale (French for "friendly understanding"), setting aside a tradition of hostility dating back to the Hundred Years' War. The entente and an alliance with Japan in 1902 ended Britain's policy of diplomatic isolation and brought it into the combination that would be pitted against Germany's Triple Alliance. In 1907 London settled its problems with Russia, thereby establishing the Triple Entente. The British made no definite military commitments in the agreements with France and Russia. Theoretically they retained freedom of action, but they were now part of the alliance system.

The North African Crises

In the decade before World War I, Europe experienced a series of crises on its peripheries, none of which vitally threatened the Great Powers' survival individually. However, because of the alliance system, the incidents increased tensions and brought Europe ever closer to war.

The first serious test came in 1905 over Morocco. France sought control of this territory in order to establish a continuous line of dependencies from the Atlantic across the North African coast to Tunisia. Carefully timing their moves, the Germans arranged for the kaiser to visit the Moroccan port of Tangier, where he declared that all powers must respect the independence of the country. The French were forced to give up their immediate plans for taking over Morocco and to agree to

Germany's suggestion that an international conference be called at Algeciras (1906) to discuss the matter.

At this meeting the Germans hoped for a split between the British and French. This did not occur. On the contrary, all but one of the nations in attendance—even Italy—supported France rather than Germany. Only Austria-Hungary remained on the kaiser's side. The conference agreed that Morocco should still enjoy its sovereignty but that France and Spain should be given certain rights to police the area.

In 1911 a second Moroccan crisis escalated tensions. When France sent an army into the disputed territory, ostensibly to maintain order, Germany responded by sending the gunboat *Panther* to the Moroccan port of Agadir. Great Britain came out with a blunt warning that all of its power was at the disposal of France in this affair. A diplomatic bargain was finally struck in which France got a free hand in Morocco and Germany gained a small area in equatorial Africa. The two rival alliances managed to avoid war over Morocco. The illusion of progress was maintained—until the alliance system reached the breaking point in the Balkans.

Conclusion

The middle classes provided the genius, effort, and confidence that propelled Europe to its brief moment in the sun before 1914. They showed far more concern for the well-being of others than the nobility they replaced, but they did not have the comforting restrictions of pre-1789 Europe to protect them from their own excesses. Along with the reform movements and democratic politics they fostered came critics. Karl Marx and his new variety of socialism posed a serious criticism of the bourgeois structure, and in its Russian mode under Lenin communism would come to control a large part of the globe and provide a major challenge to middle-class values and virtues until the end of the twentieth century.

At the other end of the political spectrum, the Western middle classes embraced the new philosophies and scientific discoveries of the age to build a comforting set of beliefs that confirmed their position of dominance. Theories of Anglo-Saxon racial superiority came to be easily accepted, and with them the politics of anti-Semitism. As if bored by their own success, a fringe of the middle classes began to toy with some of the elements that would emerge in the twentieth century as fascism.

It was in the conduct of diplomacy that the perils of progress took their greatest toll. The vastly stronger states operated more and more under their own views of social Darwinism, building huge defense establishments while ignoring important crises such as those around the declining Ottoman Empire.

The Europeans' appetites, egos, and military forces had begun to exceed the terrain left to be taken in the world. The new mass politics, with its popular press, superpatriotic appeals, and blatant aggressivity, could not adapt easily to the new situation. A century of grabbing territory and reprinting maps showing broader swatches of the globe in the national colors had spoiled the Western states and distorted their foreign policies. The results would bring an end to the dominance of the Western tradition.

Suggestions for Reading

On the middle classes in the nineteenth century, see the five volumes of Peter Gay, *The Bourgois Experience: Victoria to Freud* (Norton, 1984–1998). For useful and wise guides to European intellectual history, see George L. Mosse, *The Culture of Western Europe: The Nineteenth and Twentieth Centuries*, 3rd ed. (Westview, 1998), and Franklin L. Baumer, *Modern European Thought: Continuity and Change in Ideas, 1600–1950* (Macmillan, 1977).

A recent study of change in the church in England is Frances Knight, *The Nineteenth-Century Church and English Society* (Cambridge University Press, 1996). On the complex tie between pretense and culture, see Dianne S. MacLeod, *Art and the Victorian Middle Class: Money and the Making of Cultural Identity* (Cambridge University Press, 1996). For a study of a society with a weak middle class, see Harley D. Balzer, ed., *Russia's Missing Middle Class: The Professions in Russian History* (Sharpe, 1996).

Among the immense number of works dealing with Karl Marx, the following are clear and valuable introductions for the student: Isaiah Berlin, *Karl Marx: His Life and Environment*, 4th ed. (Oxford University Press, 1996); George Lichtheim, *Marxism* (Praeger, 1961); and Alexander Balinsky, *Marx's Economics* (Heath, 1970). Edward P. Thompson, *The Making of the English Working Class* (Random House, 1966), remains a classic study of worker adaptation to industrialization. Albert S. Lindemann, *A History of European Socialism* (Yale University Press, 1983), is the best guide to that complex movement. Louis Fischer, *The Life of Lenin* (Harper & Row, 1965), is an objective treatment of the founder of the former Soviet Union.

For background on the rightist critique, see the biographies of Benito Mussolini and Adolf Hitler cited in Chapter 31. Stanley G. Payne, *A History of Fascism, 1914–1945* (University of Wisconsin Press, 1995), is a major contribution to the understanding of fascism. Roger Griffin, ed., *Fascism: An Oxford Reader* (Oxford University Press, 1995), is a superb collection of documents and commentaries. Mike Hawkins's ambitious survey, *Social Darwinism in European and American Thought, 1860–1945: Nature as Model and Nature as Threat* (Cambridge

University Press, 1997), captures both the misunderstanding and the malice of those who made use of Darwin's hypotheses.

Suggestions for Web Browsing

Victorian Web
http://www.stg.brown.edu/projects/hypertext/landow/victorian/victov.html

Brown University's wonderful overview of the Victorian era in England, offering information about all aspects of Victorian life: social context, political context, economics, religion and philosophy, literature, visual arts, and science and technology.

Virtual Victorian Mansion
http://members.aol.com/debsfl/sign.html

One of the most comprehensive Victorian Web site directories on the Internet.

History of Costumes: Nineteenth Century
http://www.siue/edu/COSTUMES/COSTUMES/_INDEX.HTML

Site offers a lively set of images depicting how the various social classes in Europe dressed during the nineteenth century.

Enter Evolution: Theory and History
http://www.ucmp.berkeley.edu/history/evolution.html

An extensive site on evolutionary theory, with brief accounts of many eighteenth-century precursors to Charles Darwin, Darwin himself, and Lamarck, Cuvier, and Malthus.

Marx-Engels Internet Archive
http://www.marx.org/Admin/

Extensive site on both Karl Marx and Friedrich Engels offers biographies, a photo gallery, letters, and additional Web links.

Susan B. Anthony: A Woman's Right to Vote
http://www.fordham.edu/halsall/mod/1873anthony.html

Speech given in 1873 by Susan B. Anthony, one of the strongest advocates of women's rights in the nineteenth century.

Notes

1. J. H. Plumb, "The Victorians Unbuttoned," *Horizon 11*, no. 4 (1969), pp. 16–25. See also Steven Marcus, *The Other Victorians: A Study of Sexuality and Pornography in Mid-Nineteenth Century England* (New York: Basic Books, 1966).
2. Leszek Kolakowski, *Main Currents of Marxism*, trans. P. S. Falla, vol. 2. (Oxford: Oxford University Press, 1978), p. 1.
3. Roger Griffin, *Fascism: An Oxford Reader* (Oxford: Oxford University Press, 1995), pp. 4–9.
4. Stanley G. Payne, *A History of Fascism, 1914–1945* (Madison: University of Wisconsin Press, 1995), ch. 1.

The New Thirty Years' War

W orld War I had been described as a watershed in modern history. It brought to a dramatic close a century of relative peace and ushered in what has been referred to as the Age of Violence. Before 1914 Europe was the center of the world in political influence, cultural creativity, and military and financial power. This small continent ruled a vast colonial structure and with it hundreds of millions of dependent peoples. Ideologically, political liberalism and parliamentary institutions had flourished and multiplied. Democracy, it seemed, was destined to spread all over the globe, and capitalism was the prevailing economic creed, with the middle class its master and chief beneficiary.

The first of the total technological conflicts, the 1914–1918 conflagration, had far-reaching consequences, which include World War II. Because of the fearful price paid by those who endured World War I, people had to believe that a better world would emerge. They were soon disillusioned. Although the statesmen of the victorious Allies championed the democratic and humanistic traditions of Western civilization, their motives in making the peace were often as vindictive and nationalistic as any preparations for war. And although internationalism was activated in the form of the League of Nations, it was given neither the strength nor the support required to bring peace and security during the troubled 1920s and 1930s.

In these years democracy began its struggle with totalitarianism. In war-exhausted Russia, Marxist tenets were embraced by revolutionaries, and a communist society took shape under Lenin. Mussolini and his fascist system gripped Italy, and the most frightening ideology of all, Nazism, grew to terrifying fruition in Germany, where a people embittered by the humiliation of World War I and the Treaty of Versailles staked their future on a madman named Hitler.

By the 1920s and 1930s the non-European world had discovered the concept of nationalism. In the Middle East, Arab national ambitions had flared in 1916 into a revolt against Ottoman rule. The immigration of European Jews to Palestine led to conflict between Arabs and Jews, which was to increase as time passed. The peoples of North Africa, the Middle East, India, southeastern Asia, and Oceania were gathering strength in their battle to oust the Europeans and govern themselves. In the huge colonial area south of the Sahara, Africans were beginning to stir restlessly against European rule. Even China, tradition-bound for centuries, turned to revolution to regain the power and prestige it had lost during the era of imperialism. Although Chiang Kai-shek won an internal power struggle and organized the government, the country remained poor and weak. Meanwhile, Japan embarked on its amazing technological, industrial, and military growth and became a world power.

The economic depression of the 1930s gave the totalitarian movements an opportunity to expand their despotism at home and to launch aggression abroad. From 1931 to 1939, starting with the Japanese invasion of Manchuria, their belligerence mounted. The new dictatorial regimes went from one success to another, glorifying militarism and the potency of the state, regimenting their citizens, and intimidating their neighbors. Appeasement was tried, but the aggression continued. In 1939 the British and French realized that their own nations were next in Hitler's march of conquest and took up arms. With the German invasion of Poland, World War II began. In 1941 the Soviet Union, which had been allied earlier with the Nazis, and the United States, which after the Japanese attack of Pearl Harbor could no longer ignore the mounting tensions abroad, were forced into the struggle. The horrors this global conflict brought were the familiar ones of ruthless enemy occupation, the rigors of battle, and the loss of life and property, and the new ones created by dreadful new weapons and methods of warfare, the organized slaughter of ethnic groups, and the repeated bombing of civilian centers.

The victory of the Grand Alliance in 1945 brought total defeat to Hitler's Third Reich and the fascist states established in Italy by Mussolini and in Japan by Tojo. As in 1919, the victors were confronted with the immense task of rebuilding and reestablishing a great part of the world. This task was made more difficult by the knowledge of the failures of the peace of 1919 and the dismaying realization that World War II was far more encompassing and more destructive than World War I and that a third world war, with the advent of nuclear weapons, indeed might bring about worldwide annihilation.

Winning the War
and Losing the Peace

The Democracies, 1914–1939

Chapter Contents

The West's golden age was brought to an end in 1914 by a combination of forces—militarism, rival alliances, imperialism, secret diplomacy, and narrow, bellicose nationalism. Four years later over 13 million soldiers from around the world lay dead on Europe's battlefields, a generation of the best and bravest. The world economy lost what little equilibrium it had and went into a manic cycle of inflation and depression that devastated nations around the globe. Four empires—the German, Austro-Hungarian, Russian, and Ottoman—either faded away or disappeared entirely. The bitterness created by this war sowed the seeds of World War II a mere 20 years later, leading some historians to refer to this period of global conflicts as the "New Thirty Years' War."

World War I, the "Great War," the war that was to "make the world safe for democracy," left a legacy of physical damage, economic disruption, and doubt that threatened the hard-won liberal victories of the nineteenth century. The horrible costs of the war made the triumph a hollow one for the democratic victors. After the initial taste for revenge had been satisfied, revulsion for war became widespread. The economic dislocation caused by inflation and depression sapped the strength of the middle classes, the traditional defenders of democracy, and paved the way for extremist dictators. The belief in and certainty of progress that had helped fuel Europe's dominance in the nineteenth century were replaced by doubt, cynicism, and an incapacity to deal with aggression.[1]

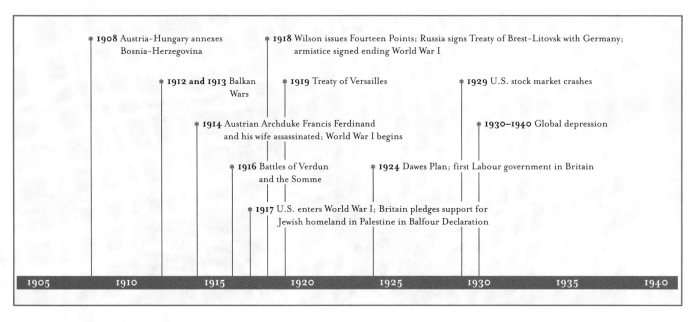

* **1908** Austria-Hungary annexes Bosnia-Herzegovina

* **1912 and 1913** Balkan Wars

* **1914** Austrian Archduke Francis Ferdinand and his wife assassinated; World War I begins

* **1916** Battles of Verdun and the Somme

* **1917** U.S. enters World War I; Britain pledges support for Jewish homeland in Palestine in Balfour Declaration

* **1918** Wilson issues Fourteen Points; Russia signs Treaty of Brest-Litovsk with Germany; armistice signed ending World War I

* **1919** Treaty of Versailles

* **1924** Dawes Plan; first Labour government in Britain

* **1929** U.S. stock market crashes

* **1930–1940** Global depression

1905   1910   1915   1920   1925   1930   1935   1940

World War I

The two rival alliances—the Central Powers of Germany, Austria-Hungary, and Italy and the Triple Entente of the United Kingdom, France, and Russia—came to blows over the Balkans. There the interests of Austria-Hungary and Russia directly collided, and the forces of local nationalism drew the great powers into a military showdown that soon engulfed the Continent.

The Balkan Crises

Austria and Russia had long kept a wary eye on each other's policies in southeastern Europe. During the nineteenth century each country had had an obsessive interest in the Balkan holdings of the Ottoman Empire. Neither side could afford for the other to gain too great an advantage in the area. Throughout the last part of the nineteenth century the two had occasionally disagreed over issues involving Macedonia, railroads, and boundary revisions. In 1908 a crisis erupted that threatened to draw Europe into war. The issue that increased hostility was the Dual Monarchy's annexation of Bosnia and Herzegovina.

The Austro-Hungarian monarchy had administered the two areas since the 1878 Congress of Berlin; thus the annexation actually changed very little. But the Slavs perceived the annexation as humiliating to them and their "protector," Russia. The fact that the Russians, through an ill-considered plan, had initiated the train of events that led to the annexation made the whole affair doubly frustrating for the Slavs.

Russia's foreign minister, Count Izvolskii, had initiated talks with Vienna in 1908 in which Russia would approve the annexation in return for increased Black Sea rights. Bosnia and Herzegovina were annexed, but the Russians never got their part of the bargain. Serbia was outraged by the incorporation of more Slavs into the Habsburg domain and expected its Slavic, Orthodox protector, Russia, to do something about it. The Russians had been badly bruised in their war with Japan and the Revolution of 1905. Aside from making threatening noises, they could do little, especially in the face of Germany's support for Austria-Hungary.

Austro-Hungarian interests in the Balkans were primarily concerned with defense and keeping Serbia under control. The Dual Monarchy was experiencing serious domestic strains as the multinational empire limped along under the terms of the renegotiated *Ausgleich.* Austria-Hungary's pretensions to Great Power status increasingly outdistanced its ability to serve in that role.

Germany's motives in the Balkans were largely strategic in the long term and diplomatic in the short term. The Germans envisioned a Berlin-based political and economic zone stretching from the Baltic Sea to the Persian Gulf. Berlin could not afford to alienate its Austrian ally through lukewarm support.

After 1908 tensions remained high in the Balkans. The Austrians looked to increase their advantage, knowing they had the full support of Germany. Serbia searched for revenge, while Russia found itself backed into a corner. The Russians in the future would be forced to act strongly and encourage aggressive policies on the part of their Balkan allies or lose their position of prestige forever. The 1908 crisis changed relatively few of the major features of the competition for influence in the Balkans, except to limit further the major powers' options.

In 1912 Serbia and its neighbors, including Greece and Bulgaria, formed an alliance with the objective of expelling the Turks from Europe. The First Balkan War began later in the year and came to a quick end with the defeat of the Turks. Each of the Balkan allies had its own particular goals in mind in fighting the Ottomans. When the Great Powers stepped in to maintain the balance, problems arose.

Serbia had fought for a seaport and thought it had gained one with the defeat of the Turks. However, the Italians and Austrians blocked Serbia's access to the Adriatic by overseeing the creation of Albania in the Treaty of London of 1913. Denied their goals, the Serbs turned on their former allies, the Bulgarians, and demanded a part of their spoils from the first war. Bulgaria refused and, emboldened by its successes in the first war, attacked its former allies, starting the Second Balkan War. The Serbs were in turn joined by the Romanians and the Turks. The Bulgarians were no match for the rest of the Balkans and signed a peace that turned over most of the territory that they had earlier gained. The Turks retained only a precarious toehold in Europe, the small pocket from Adrianople to Constantinople.

Had the Great Powers found a way to place a fence around the Balkans and allow the squabbling nations to work out their differences in isolation, the two Balkan wars of 1912 and 1913 would have had little significance. As it was, however, they added to the prevailing state of tension between the two competing alliances, whose policies clashed in the Balkans. In effect, the tail wagged the dog, as the alliances reacted to every flare-up in the turbulent peninsula.

By the end of 1913 no permanent solution had been found to the Balkan problems. Austria was more fearful than ever of Serbia's expansionist desires. Serbian ambitions had grown along with its territory, which had doubled as a result of the recent wars. The Serbian prime minister declared, "The first round is won: now we must prepare the second against Austria." Russia's dreams of Balkan grandeur

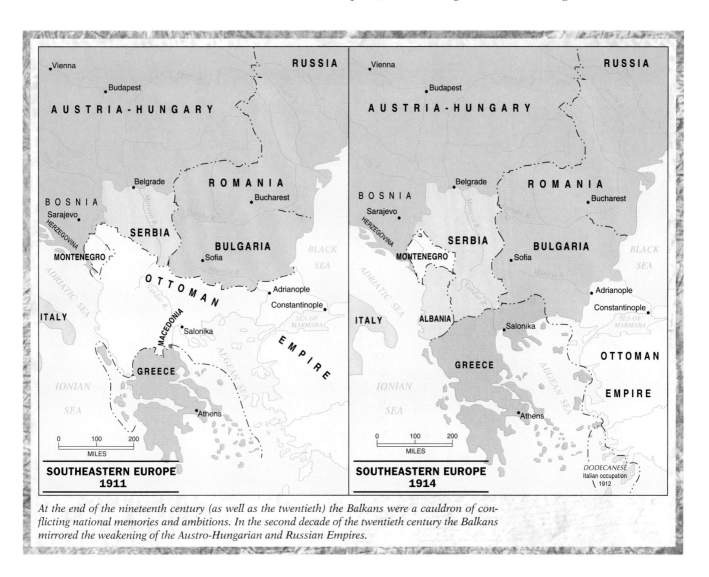

At the end of the nineteenth century (as well as the twentieth) the Balkans were a cauldron of conflicting national memories and ambitions. In the second decade of the twentieth century the Balkans mirrored the weakening of the Austro-Hungarian and Russian Empires.

had not been dashed but only interrupted. The rest of Europe lay divided.

Assassination at Sarajevo

The spark that set off World War I was lit on June 28, 1914, with the assassination of the heir to the Austrian throne, Archduke Francis Ferdinand. The archduke and his wife were visiting the town of Sarajevo, in Bosnia, which his realm had recently annexed. While they were driving through the narrow streets in their huge touring car, a 19-year-old Bosnian student named Gavrilo Princip, one of seven young terrorists along the route, shot them.

Princip had been inspired by propaganda advocating the creation of a greater Serbia and assisted by Serbian officers serving in a secret organization, the Black Hand. The direct participation of the Serbian government was never proved; even so, the Belgrade authorities were likely to have been involved, at least indirectly.

The legal details of the case were lost in Vienna's rush to put an end to the problem of Serbia. Count Leopold von Berchtold, the foreign minister, believed that the assassination in Bosnia justified crushing the anti-Austrian propaganda and terrorism coming from the Serbs. The kaiser felt that everything possible must be done to prevent Germany's only reliable ally from being weakened, and he assured the Austrians of his full support. Berchtold received a blank check from Germany. Vienna wanted a quick, local Austro-Serbian war, and Germany favored quick action to forestall Russian intervention.

On July 23 the Austro-Hungarian foreign ministry presented an ultimatum to the Serbs. Expecting the list of demands to be turned down, Berchtold insisted on unconditional acceptance within 48 hours. Two days later the Austro-Hungarian government announced that Serbia's reply, though conciliatory, was not satisfactory. The Austrians immediately mobilized their armed forces.

Archduke Francis Ferdinand and his wife, Sophie, leave the Senate House in Sarajevo on June 28, 1914. Five minutes after this photograph was taken, Serbian terrorist Gavrilo Princip assassinated them both, triggering World War I.

The Alliances' Inevitable War

The Germans, having second thoughts, urged their ally to negotiate with Russia, which was anxiously following developments. Russia realized that if the Austrians succeeded in humbling the Serbs, Russia's position in the Balkans would suffer irreparably. The French, in the meantime, assured the Russians of their full cooperation and urged full support for Serbia. The British unsuccessfully advised negotiation.

Europe had reached a point of no return: the Austrians had committed themselves to the task of removing a serious opponent, and the Russians could not permit this removal to happen. Neither side would back down, and each had allies ready to come to its aid. Fearful that Serbia would escape from his clutches, Berchtold succeeded on July 27—in part through deception—in convincing the Habsburg emperor that war was the only way out. The next day the Austro-Hungarian Empire declared war against Serbia.

As the possibility of a general European war loomed, Berlin sent several frantic telegrams to Vienna. The German ambassador was instructed to tell Berchtold that "as an ally we must refuse to be drawn into a world conflagration because Austria does not respect our advice."[2] Had the Germans spoken to their ally in such tones a month earlier, war might have been avoided. But Austria's belligerence moved the Russians to act. The tsar ordered mobilization on July 30, 1914.

Germany was caught in a dilemma that Bismarck would never have allowed. Surrounded by potential enemies, the Germans had to move decisively or face defeat. The Russian mobilization threatened them, because in the event of war on the eastern front, there would also be war on the western front. The best plan for Berlin, one that had been worked out since 1905, seemed to be to launch a lightning attack against France, which could mobilize faster than Russia, crush France, and then return to meet Russia, which would be slower to mobilize. To allow Russian mobilization to proceed without action would jeopardize this plan. In the wake of the crisis, the Germans set into effect their long-planned strategy to gain European dominance.

Threatening the generally held views of inevitable progress at the beginning of the nineteenth century were the unanswered Eastern Question in the Balkans and the lingering conflicts over dividing up the prize of North Africa.

On July 31 Germany sent ultimatums to Russia and France, demanding cessation of mobilization from the former and a pledge of neutrality from the latter. Failing to receive satisfactory replies, Germany declared war on Russia on August 1 and on France two days later. On August 2 the German ambassador in Brussels delivered an ultimatum to the Belgian government announcing his country's intention to send troops through Belgium, in violation of the 1839 treaty guaranteeing Belgian neutrality. The Belgian cabinet refused to grant permission and appealed to the Triple Entente for help.

A majority of the British cabinet did not want war, but with the news of the German ultimatum to Belgium, the tide turned. Sir Edward Grey, the British foreign secretary, sent an ultimatum to Germany demanding that Belgian neutrality be respected. Germany refused, and on August 4 Great Britain declared war.

Because Germany and Austria-Hungary were not waging a defensive war, Italy declined to carry out its obligations under the Triple Alliance and for a time remained neutral. In late August Japan joined the al-

lies. Turkey, fearing Russia, threw in its lot with the Central Powers—which by the end of 1914 consisted of Germany, Austria-Hungary, Bulgaria, and Turkey.

Diplomats tried desperately to avert a general war. Through confusion, fear, and loss of sleep, the nervous strain among them was almost unbearable. Many broke down and wept when it became apparent they had failed. Grey himself noted in his autobiography that one evening, just before the outbreak of the war, he watched the streetlights being lit from his office window and remarked: "The lamps are going out all over Europe; we shall not see them lit again in our lifetime."[3]

Total War

Although the terrible struggle that racked the world from 1914 to 1918 was fought mainly in Europe, it is rightly called the First World War. In the sixteenth and seventeenth centuries European powers had competed across the globe; however, never had so many fighters and such enormous resources been brought together in a single conflict. Altogether 27 nations became belligerents, ranging the globe from Japan to Canada and from Argentina to South Africa to Australia.

The Central Powers mobilized 21 million men. The Allies eventually called 40 million men to arms, including 12 million Russians. The two sides were more equally matched than the numbers would indicate, however. Since the Russian divisions were often poorly equipped and ineffectively used, the Allies' apparent advantage was not great. In addition, in the German army the Central Powers boasted superb generalship and discipline. Another advantage was that the Central Powers fought from a central position and were able to transfer troops quickly and efficiently to various fronts.

The Allies had the advantages of greater resources of finance and raw materials. Britain maintained its naval dominance and could draw on its empire for support. In addition, because Germany was effectively blockaded, the United States, even though officially neutral for most of the war, served as a major source of supplies for the Allies.

The warring nations went into battle in a confident mood. Each side was sure of its strength and felt it had prepared carefully. Each nation's propaganda machine delivered reassuring messages of guaranteed victory. All expected that the war would soon be over, concluded in a few decisive battles. It was generally believed that the war would be over by Christmas.

The First Two Years of War

All of the general staffs had been refining their war plans for years. The Germans knew that Allied naval supremacy would cut them off from needed sources abroad. They realized that they were potentially surrounded and that they should strike a quick knockout blow to end the war. Following the plan devised by Chief of the General Staff Alfred von Schlieffen, the Germans aimed to push the Belgians aside and drive rapidly south into France. The plan then called for the German forces to wheel west of Paris, outflank the French forces, and drive them toward Alsace-Lorraine, where they would be met by another German army. Within six weeks the French would be destroyed, caught between the western hammer and the eastern anvil. Meanwhile, a small German force would be holding the presumably slow-moving Russians on the eastern front, awaiting the arrival via the excellent German rail system of the victorious western forces. The plan nearly worked.

The Germans marched according to the plan until they got so close to Paris that they could see the top of the Eiffel Tower. They were hurled back by a bold French offensive through a gap that opened between their armies in the first battle of the Marne,

fought between September 5 and 12. With the assistance of a small British expeditionary force and Parisian taxi drivers who provided transportation, the French then marched north in a race with the Germans to reach and control the vital ports along the English Channel. After much desperate fighting, the enemies established battle positions that stabilized, creating the western front, a solid line of opposing trenches that stretched from the Channel to near Nancy, France.

For the next four years this line of trenches would be the scene of a grisly war of attrition as the Allies and the Central Powers launched desperate attacks hoping to gain the decisive "breakthrough" victory that would end the war. The struggle was made all the more bloody by powerful artillery such as the German's gigantic "Big Bertha," more deadly machine guns, silent and devastating clouds of poison gas, and two new weapons: the tank and the airplane. Single battles along that line of death killed more soldiers than those lost by the North and the South combined during the four years of the American Civil War.

The other part of the German scheme that did not go according to plan was the unexpected speed with which the Russians mobilized. They penetrated deeply into East Prussia and overran the Austrian province of Galicia. However, confused leadership resulted in two catastrophic Russian defeats in East Prussia, and Germany never again in the war faced a serious threat on its eastern frontier.

By the end of 1914 all sides knew that they were trapped in a new type of war, one of horrible consequences. Single battles claimed hundreds of thousands of lives, and the toll during the first few months of the conflict ran as high as 1.5 million dead and wounded.

In 1915 the British attempted a major campaign to force open the Dardanelles, closed by Turkey when it joined the Central Powers. This plan, attributed to Winston Churchill, then first lord of the admiralty, was designed to open up the sea route to Russia, which was badly in need of war supplies, and to take the pressure off the western front. After heroic and costly attacks, Allied Australian and New Zealand troops, known as Anzacs, were forced to withdraw from their landing positions on the Gallipoli peninsula in European Turkey.

Another major Allied setback in 1915 was the defeat of the Russian forces in Poland. More than 1.2 million Russians were killed and wounded, and the Germans took nearly 900,000 prisoners. Although Russia somehow remained in the war and fought well against the Dual Monarchy, it was no longer a concern for the Germans. These defeats generated rising criticism against the tsar's government, and Russian morale deteriorated.

The contrast between the fixed boundary between the Allies and the Central Powers, marked by trenches on the west, and the fluid lines of the eastern front are evident from this map. As much as the Central Powers were blockaded by British control of the North Sea, so too were the Russians blocked by Turkish control of the Dardanelles and the Bosporus and the Germans' control of the Baltic.

Serbia was the next Allied victim. In September 1915 Bulgaria, still aching from its defeat in the Second Balkan War, entered the war on the side of the Central Powers. Surrounded by enemies, Serbia was helpless, and resistance was quickly crushed. The Austrians had finally gained their goal of the previous summer, but in the context of the continental tragedy, this achievement no longer seemed significant.

The Allies' only bright spot in 1915 was Italy's entry into their ranks. Italy had remained neutral in August 1914 when it had defected from the Triple Alliance, of which it had been at best a token member. Italy joined the Allies following promises made in a secret treaty in London that promised the Italians huge concessions of territory once victory had been attained.

Stalemate

The Allies' strategy on the western front was to restrict attacks to a few concentrated assaults in France, thus saving manpower and at the same time concentrating on their naval blockade. Denied badly needed imports, it was assumed, the German war effort would be seriously weakened. Countering this tactic, the German high command under General

These German soldiers, shown here huddled in their trench along the western front, try to find a moment of rest during a lull in the war of attrition.

Falkenhayn launched a massive offensive against the strategic fortress of Verdun in February 1916.

After their defeat in 1871 (see Chapter 26), the French had transformed Verdun into a network of 20 forts with powerful artillery, of which the fort of Douaumont was the most important. Verdun had repulsed the Central Powers' attack in 1914, but the Germans pulled back about 10 miles and set up lines of observation posts and logistical support. So sure were the French of the invincibility of this position that they moved some of their artillery and soldiers to other sites deemed more important. Falkenhayn began in the late autumn of 1915 to build up his strength opposite Verdun, and night after night trains arrived loaded with men and matériel. Bad weather forced the Germans to delay their attack, but finally at 7:15 on the morning of February 21 more than 1000 German cannons along a 6-mile front fired the first of thousands of shells that descended on Verdun in a bombardment that lasted ten hours. Then the

German infantry advanced, equipped with flame throwers. The battered and outnumbered French forces fought back bravely and denied the Germans the rapid victory they had desired, despite losing some fortified positions. This gave the Allies time to throw hundreds of thousands of men into the battle, which would rage into the summer and fall. Falkenhayn, who had gambled all on a quick victory, was replaced by Generals Hindenburg and Ludendorff, who decided to abandon the attack on Verdun. The French reclaimed the forts they had lost by the end of the year. The slaughter brought on by massed artillery and infantry charges between the trenches was horrible. The total loss in the battle of Verdun came to 700,000 men.

To ease the pressure against Verdun, the British army on July 1 began an offensive along the Somme River along the western front. Despite their having fired 2 million shells, the attackers' losses on the first day of the battle were catastrophic: 60 percent of the officers and 40 percent of the soldiers—60,000 men in all. Despite these awesome figures, the attacks—with the British making the first use of tanks in August—continued for three months without any substantial gains. General Haig, stymied by the tenacious German resistance, decided to stop the offensive in November. Total German casualties at the Somme were about 550,000, while the British and French lost about 650,000—a staggering 1.2 million men dead or wounded.

The only major naval engagement of the war, the battle of Jutland (May 31–June 1, 1916), reaffirmed British control of the seas. Taking enormous risks, the Germans maneuvered brilliantly. They could afford to gamble because defeat would in no way worsen their position. The British fleet, however, had to act cautiously and absorbed greater losses. Nevertheless, the Germans finally retreated to their base and remained there for the rest of the war. Only in their submarine warfare did the Germans enjoy success on the high seas during the war.

On the eastern front in 1916 the Russians continued their generally successful campaigns against the Austro-Hungarian forces. But the Germans were always there to save their allies from destruction. Romania, impressed by the Russian victories, finally joined the Allies and launched an attack on the Austrians. After an initial success, the Romanians were soon knocked out of the war by a joint German-Bulgarian invasion.

The Home Front

At the end of 1916, after more than two years of fighting, neither side was close to victory. Instead, the war had turned into a dreary contest of each side trying to bleed the other into submission—a far cry from the glories promised by the propaganda of 1914. War was no longer fought between armies; it was fought between states, and every citizen and office of the state participated.[4]

On the home front, rationing was instituted to ensure sufficient supplies for soldiers at the front. As men went off to fight, women took over their jobs in the workplace. Intensive propaganda campaigns encouraged civilians to buy more bonds and make more weapons. Nations unleashed a barrage of propaganda inciting total hatred of the enemy, belief in the righteousness of the cause, and unquestioned support for the war effort.

Civil liberties suffered, and in some cases distinguished citizens were thrown into prison for opposing the war effort. In Britain, for example, the philosopher and mathematician Bertrand Russell was imprisoned for a short time for his pacifistic views. Governments took over control of their national economies and gambled everything on a victory in which the loser would pay all the expenses incurred in the war. The various states outlawed strikes and rigidly controlled currencies and foreign trade.

Soldiers manning a Vickers machine gun at the Somme in July 1916 wear gas masks as protection against phosgene. The new technology of World War I included increased use of the machine gun and poison gas.

Diary of Private Tom Easton

British enlisted man Tom Easton recorded the horrors of the battle of the Somme in gripping detail.

A beautiful summer morning, though we'd had a bit of rain earlier. The skylarks were just singing away. Then the grand mine went up, it shook the earth for nearly a minute, and we had to wait for the fallout. The whistles blew and we stepped off one yard apart going straight forward. We were under orders not to stop or look or help the wounded. Carry on if you're fit, it was.

Men began to fall one by one. One officer said we were OK, all the machine-guns were firing over our heads. This was so until we passed our own front line and started to cross No Man's Land. Then trench machine-guns began the slaughter from the La Boiselle salient [German positions]. Men fell on every side screaming. Those who were unwounded dare not attend to them, we must press on regardless. Hundreds lay on the German barbed wire which was not all destroyed and their bodies formed a bridge for others to pass over and into the German front line.

There were few Germans, mainly in machine-gun posts. These were bombed out, and there were fewer still of us, but we consolidated the lines we had taken by preparing firing positions on the rear of the trenches gained, and fighting went on all morning and gradually died down as men and munitions on both sides became exhausted.

When we got to the German trenches we'd lost all our officers. They were all dead, there was no question of wounded. About 25 of us made it there.

Yes, as we made our way over the latter stages of the charge, men dropped all around like ninepins. Apart from machine-guns, the German artillery was also very active, great sheets of earth rose up before one. Every man had to fend for himself as we still had to face the Germans in their trenches when we got there.

I kept shouting for my MOTHER to guide me, strange as it may seem. Mother help me. Not the Virgin Mother but my own maternal Mother, for I was then only 20 years of age.

From Michael Kernan, "Day of Slaughter on the Somme," *Washington Post*, June 27, 1976. Copyright © 1976 by the *Washington Post*. Reprinted by permission.

At the beginning of the war, all was flag-waving and enthusiasm. The international socialist movement, whose policy it was to promote international proletarian unity, fell victim to the rabid patriotism that infected the Continent. Workers of one country were encouraged to go out and kill workers of the enemy country in the name of the state. There was great idealism, sense of sacrifice, and love of country. At first there was no understanding of the horror, death, and disaster that comes with modern, industrialized war. The British poet Rupert Brooke caught the spirit in his poem "The Soldier":

> *If I should die, think only this of me:*
> *That there's some corner of a foreign field*
> *That is forever England. There shall be*
> *In that rich earth a richer dust concealed;*
> *A dust whom England bore, shaped, made aware,*
> *Gave, once, her flowers to love, her ways to roam,*
> *A body of England's breathing English air,*
> *Washed by the rivers, blest by suns of home.[5]*

But this early idealism, this Romantic conception of death in battle, gradually changed to one of war weariness and total futility. This growing mood is best seen in the poetry of the young British officer and poet Wilfrid Owen, himself a victim on the western front:

> *What passing-bells for those who die as cattle?*
> *Only the monstrous anger of the guns. . . .*
> *No mockeries for them; no prayers nor bells,*
> *Nor any voice of mourning save the choirs,—*
> *The shrill, demented choirs of wailing shells;*
> *And bugles calling for them from sad shires.[6]*

By the end of 1916 a deep yearning for peace dominated Europe. Sensing this mood, leaders on both sides put forth peace feelers. But these half-hearted overtures achieved nothing. Propaganda was used effectively to continue the war and support for it. The populations of the warring states were made to believe that their crusade was somehow divinely inspired. In reality, the Dual Monarchy and France fought for survival; Russia, German, and Italy all fought to improve their respective positions in Europe; while Britain fought to save Belgium and a renewed balance of power on the Continent.

Allied Fatigue and American Entry

In 1917 British and French military strength reached its highest point, only to fall precipitously. Allied com-

As the men marched off to war, women left their homes to work in war-related industries. These women are working in a British munitions factory.

manders were hopeful that the long-planned break-through might be accomplished, but a large-scale French attack was beaten back, with huge losses. Some French regiments mutinied rather than return to the inferno of "no-man's land" between the trenches. The British sacrificed hundreds of thousands of men without any decisive results in several massive offensives. The Allies also launched unsuccessful campaigns in Italy. Aided by the Germans, the Austrians smashed the Italian front at the battle of Caporetto (1917), an event vividly described by Ernest Hemingway in *A Farewell to Arms*. Italian resistance finally hardened, and collapse was barely averted.

The growing effectiveness of the German submarine menace deepened Allied frustration. By 1917 Allied shipping losses had reached dangerous proportions. In three months 470 British ships fell victim to torpedoes. Britain had no more than six weeks' stores of food on hand, and the supply situation became critical for the Allies. As it turned out, the very weapon that seemed to doom their cause, the submarine, was the source of the Allies' salvation: Germany's decision to use unrestricted submarine warfare brought the United States openly into the war.

The Americans had declared their neutrality in 1914 when President Woodrow Wilson announced that the American people "must be impartial in thought as well as in action." The events of the next two years showed that this would not be the case. American sentiment was overwhelmingly with the Allies from the first. France's help to the colonies in the American Revolution was warmly recalled. Britain and America were closely tied by language, literature, and democratic institutions. Because Britain cut off communications between Germany and the United States, British propaganda and management of the war news dominated U.S. public opinion. Another factor predisposing the United States to the Allied cause was Germany's violation of international law in the invasion of Belgium. This buttressed the widely held view created by the kaiser's saber-rattling speeches that the Germans were undemocratic, unpredictable, and unstable.

These attitudes were reinforced by the fact that the United States had made a substantial investment in the Allied war effort. As the war progressed, it became apparent that the British blockade would permit American trade to be carried on only with the Allies. Before long American factories and farmers were producing weapons and food solely for Great Britain and France. Industry expanded and began to enjoy a prosperity dependent on continued Allied

Steps Toward American Entry into World War I

1914	President Wilson proclaims neutrality "in thought and action"; British blockade Germany—including cable
1914–1917	Allied war bond drive
1915	German submarine sinks *Lusitania*
1916	Wilson reelected under slogan "He kept us out of war"
1916–1917	Increased German submarine activity, plots with Mexico
1917	Wilson asks Congress to declare war on Germany (April 6)

purchases. Between 1914 and 1916 American exports to the Allies quadrupled. Allied bonds totaling about $1.5 billion were sold in the United States in 1915 and 1916. It was quite apparent to the Germans that there was little neutrality on the economic front in the United States.

What triggered the U.S. entry into the war on the Allied side was the German submarine tactics. Blockaded by the British, Germany decided to retaliate by halting all shipping to the Allies. Its submarine campaign began in February 1915, and one of the first victims was the luxury liner *Lusitania*, torpedoed with the loss of more than 1000 lives, including 100 Americans. This tragedy aroused public opinion in the United States. In the fall of 1916 Wilson, campaigning with the slogan "He kept us out of war," was reelected to the presidency. Discovery of German plots to involve Mexico in the war against the United States and more submarine sinkings finally drove Wilson to ask Congress to declare war against Germany on April 6, 1917.

Submarine warfare and a wide range of other causes brought the president to the point of entering the war. Once in the conflict, however, he was intent on making the American sacrifice one "to make the world safe for democracy." Wilson's lofty principles caused a great surge of idealism among Americans.

Germany's Last Drive

The United States mobilized its tremendous resources of men and matériel more rapidly than the Germans had believed possible when they made their calculated risk to increase submarine warfare. Nonetheless, the Central Powers moved to try to gain a decisive victory before U.S. aid could help the Allies.

The fruitless offensives of 1917 had exhausted the British army, and the French had barely recovered from their mutinies. The eastern front collapsed with the February-March revolution in Russia. Eight months later Lenin and the Bolsheviks took power in Russia and began to negotiate for peace. By the Treaty of Brest-Litovsk early in 1918, Russia made peace with Germany, giving up 1.3 million square miles of territory and 62 million people.[7]

Freed from the necessity of fighting on the east, the Germans unleashed a series of major offensives against the west in the spring of 1918. During one of these attacks a brigade of American marines symbolized the importance of U.S. support when they stopped a German charge at Château-Thierry. The Germans made a final effort to knock out the French in July 1918. It was called the *Friedensturm*, the peace offensive. The Germans made substantial gains but did not score a decisive breakthrough. By this time the German momentum was slowing down, and more than a million American "doughboys" had landed in France. The final German offensive was thrown back after a slight advance.

With the aid of U.S. troops, Marshal Ferdinand Foch, the supreme Allied commander, began a counterattack. The badly beaten and continually harassed German troops fell back in rapid retreat. By the end of October German forces had been driven out of France and Allied armies were advancing into Belgium. The war of fixed positions separated by no-man's land was over. The Allies had smashed the trench defenses and were now in open country.

By October 1 the German high command had already urged the kaiser to sue for peace, and three days later the German chancellor sent a note to President Wilson seeking an end to hostilities. Wilson responded that peace was not possible as long as Germany was ruled by an autocratic regime. The German chancellor tried to keep the monarchy by instituting certain liberal reforms, but it was too late. Revolution broke out in many parts of Germany. The kaiser abdicated, and fled to the Netherlands, and a republic was proclaimed.

While Germany was staggering under the continual pounding of Foch's armies, the German allies were suffering even greater misfortunes. Bulgaria surrendered on September 30 and Turkey a month later. Austria stopped its fighting with Italy on November 3. Nine days later the Habsburg Empire collapsed when Emperor Charles I fled Vienna to seek sanctuary in Switzerland.

At five o'clock on the morning of November 11, 1918, in a dining car in the Compiègne Forest, the German delegates signed the peace terms presented by Marshal Foch. At eleven o'clock the same day, hostilities were halted. Everywhere except in Germany, the news was received with an outburst of joy. The world was once more at peace, confronted now with the task of binding up its wounds and removing the scars of combat. Delegates from the Allied nations were soon to meet in Paris, where the peace conference would be held.

The Allied Peace Settlement

In November 1918 the Allies stood triumphant, after the costliest war in history. But the Germans could also feel pleased in 1918. They had fought well, avoided being overrun, and escaped being occupied by the Allies. They could acknowledge they had lost the war but hoped that President Wilson would help them.

In February 1918 Wilson had stated that "there shall be no annexations, no contributions, no punitive damages," and on July 4 he affirmed that every question must be settled on "the basis of the free acceptance of that settlement by the people immediately concerned."[8] As events transpired, however, the losers were refused seats at the peace conference. The leaders of the new German Weimar Republic had no choice but to sign a dictated settlement—an act that simultaneously discredited the republic among the German people and served as the first step toward World War II.

Idealism and Realities

The destructiveness of World War I made a fair peace settlement impossible. The war had been fought on a winner-take-all basis, and now it was time for the Central Powers to pay. At the peace conference the winning side was dominated by a French realist, a British politician, and an American idealist. The French representative was the aged Premier Georges Clemenceau, representing Britain was the Prime Minister David Lloyd George, and the U.S. representative was President Woodrow Wilson. The three were joined by the Italian prime minister, Vittorio Orlando, who attended to make sure his country gained adequate compensation for its large sacrifices. These four men made most of the key decisions, even though most of the interested nations and factions in the world were represented in Paris, except for the Russians.

Clemenceau had played a colorful and important role in French politics for half a century. He had fought continuously for his political beliefs, opposing corruption, racism, and antidemocratic forces. He wanted to ensure French security in the future by pursuing restitution, reparations, and guarantees. Precise programs, not idealistic statements, would protect France.

The two English-speaking members of the Big Three represented the extremes in dealing with the Germans. Lloyd George had been reelected in December on a program of "squeezing the German lemon until the pips are squeaked." He wanted to destroy Berlin's naval, commercial, and colonial position and to ensure his own political future at home. In January 1918 President Wilson had given Congress a list known as the Fourteen Points, describing

The "Big Four" at the Versailles Peace Conference were, left to right, Prime Minister David Lloyd George of Britain, Prime Minister Vittorio Orlando of Italy, Premier Georges Clemenceau of France, and President Woodrow Wilson of the United States. Representatives from Germany were excluded from the negotiating tables. The Big Four became the Big Three when Orlando withdrew abruptly because the conference refused to give Italy all it demanded.

John Maynard Keynes on Clemenceau

Keynes caught the spirit of the peacemakers at Versailles in *The Economic Consequences of the Peace*. His portrait of Clemenceau is especially revealing.

He felt about France what Pericles felt of Athens—unique value in her, nothing else mattering; but his theory of politics was Bismarck's. He had one illusion—France; and one disillusion—mankind, including Frenchmen, and his colleagues not least. His principles for the peace can be expressed simply. In the first place, he was a foremost believer in the view of German psychology that the German understands and can understand nothing but intimidation, that he is without generosity or remorse in negotiation, that there is no advantage he will not take of you, and no extent to which he will not demean himself for profit, that he is without honor, pride, or mercy. Therefore you must never negotiate with a German or conciliate him; you must dictate to him. On no other terms will he respect you, or will you prevent him from cheating you. But it is doubtful how far he thought these characteristics peculiar to Germany, or whether his candid view of some other nations was fundamentally different. His philosophy had, therefore, no place for "sentimentality" in international relations. Nations are real

things, of whom you love one and feel for the rest indifference—or hatred. The glory of the nation you love is a desirable end,—but generally to be obtained at your neighbor's expense. The politics of power are inevitable, and there is nothing very new to learn about this war or the end it was fought for; England had destroyed, as in each preceding century, a trade rival; a mighty chapter had been closed in the secular struggle between the glories of Germany and of France.

Prudence required some measure of lip service to the "ideals" of foolish Americans and hypocritical Englishmen; but it would be stupid to believe that there is much room in the world, as it really is, for such affairs as the League of Nations, or any sense in the principle of self-determination except as an ingenious formula for rearranging the balance of power in one's own interest.

From John Maynard Keynes, *The Economic Consequences of the Peace* (New York: Harcourt, Brace, 1920).

his plan for peace. Wilson wanted to break the world out of its tradition of armed anarchy and establish a framework for peace that would favor America's traditions of democracy and trade. At the peace conference this shy and sensitive man communicated his beliefs with a coldness and an imperiousness that offended his colleagues.

The Great War had not been a "war to end all wars" or a war "to make the world safe for democracy." The United States had hardly been neutral in its loans and shipments of supplies to the Allies before 1917. In fact, during the war the financial and political center of balance for the world had crossed the ocean. The Americans made a rather abrupt shift from debtor to creditor status. The United States had entered the war late and had profited from it, and Wilson could afford to wear a rather more idealistic mantle.

The Europeans had paid for the war with the blood of their young and the coin of their realms. The Allies now looked forward to a healthy return on their investment. The extent of that harvest had long been mapped out in secret treaties, copies of which the Bolsheviks released for the world to see.

Open Covenants, Secret Treaties

Wilson wanted to use his Fourteen Points as the basis for a lasting peace. He wanted to place morality and justice ahead of power and revenge as considerations in international affairs. The first five points were general and guaranteed "open covenants openly arrived at," freedom of the seas in war and peace alike, removal of all economic barriers and establishment of an equality of trade among all nations, reductions in national armaments, and readjustment of all colonial claims, giving the interests of the population concerned equal weight with the claim of the government whose title was to be determined. The next eight points dealt with specific issues involving the evacuation and restoration of Allied territory, self-determination for minority nationalities, and the redrawing of European boundaries along national lines.

The fourteenth point contained the germ of the League of Nations, a general association of all nations whose purpose was to guarantee political independence and territorial integrity to great and small states alike. When Wilson arrived in Europe, the crowds on the streets and the victorious and the defeated nations alike greeted him as a messiah. His program had received great publicity, and its general, optimistic nature had earned him great praise.

The victorious Allies came to Paris to gain the concrete rewards promised them in the various secret treaties. Under these pacts, which would not come to public knowledge until the beginning of 1919, the Allies had promised the Italians concessions that would turn the Adriatic into an Italian sea, the Russians the right to take over the Bosporus and Dardanelles Straits and Constantinople, the Romanians the right to take over large amounts of Austro-Hungarian territory, and the Japanese the right to keep the German territory of Kiaochow in China. In addition, the British and French divided what was formerly Ottoman-controlled Iraq and Syria into their respective spheres of influence. As for Palestine, on November 2, 1917, the British—with the agreement of President Wilson—in the declaration by Lord Arthur James Balfour, stated that "His Majesty's government looks favorably on the establishment of a national home for the Jewish people." Lord Balfour went on to affirm that nothing would be done that would "prejudice the civil and religious rights" of the non-Jewish communities in Palestine.

Wilson refused to consider these agreements, which many of the victors regarded as IOUs now due to be paid in return for their role in the war; but the contracting parties in the treaties would not easily set aside their deals to satisfy Wilson's ideals. Even before the beginning of formal talks—negotiations that would be unprecedented in their complexity—the Allies were split. Lloyd George and Clemenceau discovered early that Wilson had his price, and that was the League of Nations. They played on his desire for this organization to water down most of the 13 other points. They were also aware that Wilson's party had suffered a crushing defeat in the 1918 elections and that strong factions in the United States were drumming up opposition to his program.

The League of Nations

When the diplomats began full meetings, the first issue was the formation of the League of Nations. Wilson insisted that the first work of the conference must be to provide for such a league as part of the peace treaty. After much negotiation, the covenant was approved by the full conference in April 1919. To gain support for the League, however, Wilson had to compromise on other matters. His Fourteen Points were partly repudiated, but he believed that an imperfect treaty incorporating the League was better than a perfect one without it.

The covenant of the League of Nations specified its aims: "to guarantee international cooperation and to achieve international peace and security." To achieve this goal, Article 10, the key section of the document, provided that

> *the Members of the League undertake to respect and preserve against external aggression the territorial integrity and existing political independence of all Members of the League. In case of any such aggression or in case of any threat or danger of such aggression, the Council shall advise upon the means by which this obligation shall be fulfilled.*

The League of Nations was the first systematic and thorough attempt to create an organization designed to prevent war and promote peace. Though ultimately unsuccessful, it was a valiant effort to curb the abuses of the state system while maintaining the individual sovereignty of each member of the community of nations.

The League's main organs were the Council, the Assembly, and the Secretariat. Dominated by the Great Powers, the Council was the most important body. It dealt with most of the emergencies arising in international affairs. The Assembly served as a platform from which all League members could express their views. It could make recommendations to the Council on specific issues, but all important decisions required the unanimous consent of its members, and every nation in the Assembly had one vote.

Two important bodies created by the covenant of the League were the Permanent Court of International Justice and the International Labor Organization (ILO). The first was commonly referred to as the World Court. Its main purpose was to "interpret any disputed point in international law and determine when treaty obligations had been violated." It could also give advisory opinions to the Council or Assembly when asked for them. By 1937 some 41 nations had agreed to place before the World Court most basic international disputes to which they were a party. The ILO was established to "secure and maintain fair and humane conditions of labor for men, women, and children." The organization consisted of three divisions: a general conference, a governing body, and the International Labor Office.

Redrawing German Boundaries

After establishing the League, the diplomats got down to the business of dealing with Germany. France reclaimed Alsace-Lorraine, and plebiscites gave part of the former German Empire to Denmark and Belgium. The French wanted to build a buffer

**THE PEACE SETTLEMENT
IN EUROPE, 1919**

Newly created states
Ceded territories

In the aftermath of World War I, Europe lost four empires—the Russian, Ottoman, Austro-Hungarian, and German—and gained a number of successor states, each unhappy with its new boundaries.

state, made up of former German territory west of the Rhine, to be dominated by France. The Americans and the British proposed a compromise to Clemenceau, which he accepted. The territory in question would be occupied by Allied troops for a period of 5 to 15 years, and a zone extending 30 miles east of the Rhine was to be demilitarized.

In addition, the French claimed the Saar basin, a rich coal-mining area. Although they did not take outright control of the area, which reverted to League administration, they did gain ownership of the mines in compensation for the destruction of their own installations in northern France. It was agreed that after 15 years a plebiscite would be held

in the area. Finally, Wilson and Lloyd George agreed that the United States and Great Britain would, by treaty, guarantee France against aggression.

In Eastern Europe the conference created the "Polish corridor," which separated East Prussia from the rest of Germany, in order to give the newly created state of Poland access to the sea. This raised grave problems, as it included territory in which there were large numbers of Germans. (The land in question had been taken from Poland by Prussia in the eighteenth century.) A portion of Silesia, north of the new state of Czechoslovakia, was also ceded to Poland, but Danzig, a German city, was placed under League jurisdiction. All in all, Germany lost 25,000 square miles inhabited by 6 million people—a fact seized on by German nationalist leaders in the 1920s.

The Mandate System and Reparations

A curious mixture of idealism and revenge determined the allocation of the German colonies and certain territories belonging to Turkey. Because outright annexation would look too much like unvarnished imperialism, it was suggested that the colonies be turned over to the League, which in turn would give them to certain of its members to administer. The colonies were to be known as *mandates,* and precautions were taken to ensure that they would be administered for the well-being and development of the inhabitants. Once a year the mandatory powers were to present a detailed account of their administration of the territories of the League. The mandate system was a step forward in colonial administration, but Germany nevertheless was deprived of all colonies, with the excuse that it could not rule them justly or efficiently.

As the Treaty of Versailles took shape, the central concept was that Germany had been responsible for the war. Article 231 of the treaty stated explicitly:

> *The Allied and Associated Governments affirm and Germany accepts the responsibility of Germany and her allies for causing all the loss and damage to which the Allied and Associated Governments and their nationals have been subjected as a consequence of the war imposed upon them by the aggression of Germany and her Allies.*

Britain and France demanded that Germany pay the total cost of the war, including pensions. The United States protested this demand, and eventually a compromise emerged in which, with the exception of Belgium, Germany had to pay only war damages, including those suffered by civilians, and the cost of pensions. These payments, called *reparations* (implying repair), were exacted on the ground that Germany should bear responsibility for the war.

Although the Allies agreed that Germany should pay reparations, they could not agree on how much should be paid. Some demands ran as high as $200 billion. Finally, it was decided that a committee should fix the amount; in the meantime Germany was to begin making payments. By the time the committee report appeared in May 1921, the payments totaled nearly $2 billion. The final bill came to $32.5 billion, to be paid off by Germany by 1963.

The Allies required Germany, as part of in-kind reparations payments, to hand over most of its merchant fleet, construct 1 million tons of new ship-

ping for the Allies, and deliver vast amounts of coal, equipment, and machinery to them. The conference permitted Germany a standing army of only 100,000 men, a greatly reduced fleet, and no military aircraft. Munitions plants were to be closely supervised.

The treaty also called for the kaiser to be tried for a "supreme offense against international morality and the sanctity of treaties," thus setting a precedent for the Nuremberg tribunals after World War II. Nothing came of this demand, however, as the kaiser remained in his Dutch haven.

Dictated Treaties

Before coming to Paris in April 1919 to receive the Treaty of Versailles, the German delegation was given no official information about its terms. Even though the Weimar government stated that "Germany and its people were alone guilty,"[9] it had no alternative but to sign. The continued blockade created great hardships in Germany, and the Allies threatened an invasion if the Germans did not accept the peace. The treaty was signed on June 28, the fifth anniversary of the assassination of Archduke Francis Ferdinand, in the Hall of Mirrors at Versailles, the same room where the German Empire had been proclaimed. As one American wrote, "The affair was elaborately staged and made as humiliating to the enemy as it well could be."[10]

The Allies imposed equally harsh treaties on Germany's supporters. The Treaty of St. Germain (1919) with Austria recognized the nationalist movements of the Czechs, Poles, and southern Slavs. These groups had already formed states and reduced the remnants of the former Dual Monarchy into the separate states of Austria and Hungary. Austria became a landlocked country of 32,000 square miles and 6 million people. It was forbidden to seek *Anschluss*—union with Germany. Italy acquired sections of Austria, South Tyrol, Trentino (with its 250,000 Austrian

Peace Treaties Ending World War I

Versailles	Germany (1919)
St. Germaine	Austria (1919)
Neuilly	Bulgaria (1919)
Sèvres	Turkey (1920; refused 1923)
Trianon	Hungary (1920)

Germans), and the northeastern coast of the Adriatic, with its large numbers of Slavs.

To complete their control of the Adriatic, the Italians wanted a slice of the Dalmatian coast and the port of Fiume. Fiume, however, was the natural port for the newly created state of Yugoslavia, and it had not been promised to the Italians in 1915. Wilson declared the Italian claim to be a contradiction of the principle of self-determination, and the ensuing controversy almost wrecked the peace conference. The issue was not settled until 1920, when Italy renounced its claim to Dalmatia and Fiume became an independent state. Four years later it was ceded to Italy.

By the Treaty of Sèvres (1920), the Ottoman Empire was placed on the operating table of power politics and divided among Greece, Britain, and France. An upheaval in August 1920 in Constantinople led to the emergence of the Nationalists under Mustafa Kemal, who refused to accept the treaty. Not until July 1923 did Turkey's postwar status become clear in the milder Treaty of Lausanne, which guaranteed Turkish control of Anatolia.

Hungary (Treaty of Trianon, 1920) and Bulgaria (Treaty of Neuilly, 1919) did not fare as well as Turkey in dealing with the Allies. The Hungarians lost territory to Czechoslovakia, Yugoslavia, and Romania. Bulgaria lost access to the Aegean Sea and territory populated by nearly 1 million people, had to pay a huge indemnity, and underwent demilitarization.

The eastern European states that profited from the settlements proved to be useful allies for France in the first 15 years of the interwar period. Those that suffered were easy prey for the Nazis in the 1930s.

Evaluating the Peacemakers

The treaties ending the First World War have received heavy criticism from diplomatic historians, especially when compared with the work of the Congress of Vienna. The peace that emerged brought only weariness, new disagreements, and inflation.

Russia was completely disregarded. The new Bolshevik government (see Chapter 31), in its weak position, indicated a willingness to deal with the West on the issue of prewar debts and border conflicts, if the West would extend financial aid and withdraw its expeditionary forces. The anti-Bolshevik forces in Paris did not take the offer seriously.[11] By missing this opportunity, the Allies took a course that had tremendous consequences for "the long-term future of both the Russian and the American people and indeed of mankind generally."[12]

Many commentators have laid the genesis of World War II just one generation later at the feet of the Paris peacemakers. The opportunism of Orlando and the chauvinism and revenge-seeking of both Clemenceau and Lloyd George brought only short-term satisfaction and long-term disaster to their nations. Other critics point out that the United States' reversion to isolationism doomed the work of the conference. Furthermore, never were any broad plans made for European economic recovery.

Considering the difficult conditions under which it was negotiated, the peace settlement was perhaps as good as could be expected. The delegates were the prisoners of their own constituents, who had themselves been heavily influenced by wartime propaganda. In addition, the diplomats had to deal with the nationalistic pressures and territorial conflicts of the newly formed eastern European nations. Given the costs of the war and the hopes for the peace, it is not surprising that the treaties left a legacy of disappointment for those who won and bitterness for those who lost. Symbolic of the obstacles faced by the statesmen was the fact that while they worked to return order, the globe reeled under the blows of an influenza outbreak that ultimately killed twice as many Europeans as the war did. The epidemic was both a tragic conclusion to the war years and a tragic first step toward the future.

Economic Disasters

One of the most serious problems facing the survivors of World War I was the confused and desperate situation of the European economy. Much of the direct and indirect cost of the war had been covered by borrowing, and now the bills were coming due in a world unable to pay them. The lasting results of the war touched many areas. The conflict altered world trading patterns, reduced shipping, and weakened Europe's former economic dominance. The various peace treaties multiplied the number of European boundaries, which soon became obstacles to the flow of goods, especially in the successor states of the Habsburg monarchy and in Poland. Rail and communications lines had to be reconfigured to reflect the interest of newly created states.

The Costs of the War

It is impossible to give a true accounting of the costs of any war, because there is no way to calculate the contributions that might have been made by the individuals killed in battle. Some 2 to 3 million Russians died, and more perished in the 1918–1921 civil war. Among the other major participants, almost 2 million Germans, over 1.5 million French, close to 1 million English, 500,000 Italians 1.2 million from Austria-Hungary, and 325,000 Turks died in battle. These figures do not count the wounded, whose lives may have been shortened or altered as a result of their injuries. Furthermore, the young paid the highest price: it is estimated that Germany and France each lost over 15 percent of their young men.

Estimates of the financial drain of the war range between $250 billion and $300 billion in early 1920s dollars. These figures do not bring home the depth of the war's impact on trade, shipping, and monetary stability. Belgium, for example, lost over 300,000 houses and thousands of factories, and 15,000 square miles of northeastern France were in ruins. How does one calculate the cost of taking the 75 million men who were mobilized away from their jobs and their homes? How can the mental carnage inflicted on the combatants and their families be measured? No balance sheet can measure the psychological toll of the conflict on the women and children who had to bear the tension of terror of fear and loneliness for their loved ones at the front.

Political institutions felt the effects of the war in different ways. The German, Habsburg, Russian, and Ottoman Empires crumbled and disappeared from the historical stage. Replacing them were uncertain republics or dictatorships. The colonial empires that remained were weakened, and indigenous nationalist movements made substantial progress.

The roots of the economic problems that plagued Europe after the war—agricultural overproduction, bureaucratic regulations, and protectionism—could be seen before 1914. Compounding these factors were the traditional challenges encountered in shifting from a wartime to a peacetime economy, especially that of demobilizing millions of soldiers and bringing them back into the labor market.

The Debt Problem

During the war a radical change had taken place in Europe's economic relationship with the United States. In 1914 the United States had been a debtor nation for the amount of $3.75 billion, owed mostly to Europe. The war totally reversed this situation. The United States lent billions of dollars and sold tons of supplies to the Allies. British blockades kept the United States from being able to deal with the Germans, precluding further profits, but by 1919 Europeans owed the United States more than $10 billion. This tremendous debt posed what economists call a transfer problem. The international obligations could be paid only by the actual transfer of gold or by the sale of goods.

Postwar Economic Events

1919–1923	Inflation (except in Britain and Czechoslovakia)
1922	Great Britain pledges to moderate debt collections
1923–1924	German hyperinflation
1924	Dawes plan for liberalized reparations and loans for German recovery
1929	U.S. stock market crash (October 29)
1930–1940	Great Depression

Complicating the picture, Allied powers in Europe had also lent each other funds, with the British acting as the chief banker, lending more than 1.7 billion pounds sterling. When the Allies' credit dried up, they turned to the United States for financial help. Even though Britain owed huge sums to U.S. financiers, it remained a net creditor of $4 billion because of money owed it by European debtors. France, by contrast, stood as a net debtor of $3.5 billion. In addition to its own war debts, the French government suffered greatly when the Bolsheviks renounced repayment of the tsarist debt, amounting to some 12 billion francs—one-quarter of France's foreign holdings.

Some of the Allies argued that the inter-Allied debts were political, that all of them had, in effect, been poured into a common pool for victory. These people wondered how France's contribution in the lives of its young men could be figured into the equation in terms of francs, dollars, or pounds. They proposed that with victory, all debts should be canceled. The United States, which had gone to Paris with a conciliatory spirit toward Germany in the treaty negotiations, changed its tune when dollars and cents were involved. This attitude was best expressed in a remark attributed to Calvin Coolidge, who expected full repayment, when he said: "They hired the money, didn't they?" Beneath the extremes of these positions were the understandable motives of getting out of paying a huge debt or gaining from the payment of debts owed.

Weimar Germany: Debt, Reparations, and Inflation

Reparations complicated Germany's debt problem and the challenge of converting the country back to a

PASSING THE BUCK.

A British cartoonist's view of the debt and reparations problems following World War I. Germany's inability to pay reparations meant that the Allies were unable to pay their inter-Allied war debts.

on some payments. In response, in January 1923 French troops, supported by Belgian and Italian contingents, marched into the rich industrial district of the Ruhr, undeterred by American and British objections. This shortsighted French move contributed nothing to the solution of Europe's problems and played into the hands of radical German politicians.

Encouraged by the Berlin government, German workers defied the French army and went on strike; many ended up in jail. The French toyed for a while with the idea of establishing a separate state in the Rhineland to act as a buffer between Germany and France. Chaotic conditions in the Ruhr encouraged the catastrophic inflation of the German currency to make up for the loss of exports and to support the striking workers. The value of the mark to the dollar went from 7200 in January 1923 to 160,000 in July to 1 million in August to 4.2 trillion in December. During the worst part of the inflation, the Reichsbank had 150 firms using 2000 presses running day and night to print banknotes. To get out of their dilemma, the Germans made an effective transition to a more stable currency by simply abandoning the old one.[14] The French, in return, gained very little benefit from the occupation.

peacetime economy. In the first three years after the war the German government, like other European states, spent much more than its income. This policy was masked by "floating debts . . . in other words, by the printing press."[13] The mark, which had been valued at 4.2 to the dollar in 1914, went to 75 in July 1921, to 186 in January 1922, to 402 in July, and to 4000 by December of that year. The situation became so serious in the summer of 1922 that Great Britain proposed collecting no more from its debtors—Allied and German alike—than the United States collected from Britain itself. Such "statesmanship" was prompted by the fact that London had gained what it wanted from the peace settlement: Germany's navy was destroyed, Germany's merchant ships were transferred as reparations, and Germany's empire was gone. No more could be squeezed out.

Britain saw that Germany would not be able to meet its reparations payments. Without those payments, the victors would not be able to make their own payments on the inter-Allied debts, especially debts owed to the United States. Although the United States insisted that there was no connection between the inter-Allied debts and German reparations, negotiations were carried on, and debt payment plans were set up with 13 nations. No reductions were made in principal, but in every case the interest rate was radically decreased. Still, the total amount owed came to more than $22 billion.

At the end of 1922 the Germans asked for a delay in their reparations obligations and then defaulted

Inflation in Germany during the 1920s grew so drastic that the German mark became nearly worthless. It was cheaper, for example, to start fires with marks than to use them to purchase kindling.

Alex de Jonge on Inflation in Weimar Germany

Alex de Jonge captured the devastating impact of inflation in Weimar Germany.

Hyperinflation created social chaos on an extraordinary scale. As soon as one was paid, one rushed off to the shops and bought absolutely anything in exchange for paper about to become worthless. If a woman had the misfortune to have a husband working away from home and sending money through the post, the money was virtually without value by the time it arrived. Workers were paid once, then twice, then five times a week with an ever-depreciating currency.

By November 1923 real wages were down 25 percent compared with 1913, and envelopes were not big enough to accommodate all the stamps needed to mail them; the excess stamps were stuck to separate sheets affixed to the letter. Normal commercial transactions became virtually impossible. One luckless author received a sizable advance on a work only to find that within a week it was just enough to pay the postage on the manuscript. By late 1923 it was not unusual to find 100,000 mark notes in the gutter, tossed there by contemptuous beggars at a time when $50 could buy a row of houses in Berlin's smartest street.

A Berlin couple who were about to celebrate their golden wedding received an official letter advising them that the mayor, in accordance with Prussian custom, would call and present them with a donation of money.

Next morning the mayor, accompanied by several aldermen in picturesque robes, arrived at the aged couple's house, and solemnly handed over in the name of the Prussian State 1,000,000,000,000 marks or one half-penny.

From Alex de Jonge, *The Weimar Chronicle: Prelude to Hitler* (New York: New American Library, 1978).

Inflation and Its Consequences

All European nations encountered a rocky path as they attempted to gain equilibrium after the war. Britain had minimal price increases and returned to prewar levels within two years after the signing of the Versailles treaty. On the Continent price and monetary stability came less easily. Only Czechoslovakia seemed to have its economic affairs well in hand.

France did not stabilize its currency until 1926, when the franc was worth 50 to the dollar (one-tenth its value in 1914). In Austria prices rose to 14,000 times their prewar level until stability of sorts came in 1922. Hungary's prices went to 23,000 times prewar level, but this increase is dwarfed by Poland's (2.5 million times prewar level) and Russia's (4 billion times prewar level).

Inflation had massive social and political consequences, most notably in Germany. Millions of middle-class Germans, small property owners who were the hoped-for base of the new Weimar Republic, found themselves caught in the wage-price squeeze. Prices for the necessities of life rose far faster than income or savings. As mothers wheeled baby carriages full of money to bakeries to buy bread, fathers watched a lifetime of savings dwindle to insignificance. Pensioners on fixed incomes suffered doubly under this crisis. The bourgeoisie, the historical champions of liberal politics throughout Europe, suffered blows more devastating than those of war, since inflation stole not only the value of their labor but also the worth of their savings and insurance.

Where the middle classes and liberal traditions were strong, democracy could weather the inflationary storm. But in central Europe, where they were not—especially in Germany, where the inflation was worst—the cause of future totalitarianism received an immense boost. Alan Bullock, a biographer of Adolf Hitler, wrote that "the result of inflation was to undermine the foundations of German society in a way which neither the war nor the revolution of 1918 nor the Treaty of Versailles had ever done."[15]

Temporary Improvements

After 1923 the liberal application of U.S. funds brought some calm to the economic storm. Business was more difficult to conduct because protectionism became more and more the dominant trait of international trade. *Autarky*, the goal of gaining total economic self-sufficiency and freedom from reliance on any other nation, increasingly became the unstated policy of many governments.

Nonetheless, production soon reached 1913 levels, currencies began to stabilize, and the French finally recalled their troops from the Ruhr. Most significant, in September 1924 a commission under the leadership of U.S. banker Charles Dawes formulated a more liberal reparations policy in order to get the entire repayment cycle back into motion. Dawes's plan, replaced in 1929 by the Young plan (named for its principal formulator, U.S. businessman Owen Young), reduced installments and extended them over a longer period. A loan of $200 million, mostly from the United States, was floated to aid German recovery. The Berlin government resumed payments to the Allies, and the Allies paid their debt installments to the United States—which in effect received its own money back again.

Prosperity of a sort returned to Europe. As long as the circular flow of cash from the United States to Germany to the Allies to the United States continued, the international monetary system functioned. The moment the cycle broke down, the world economy headed for the rocks of depression. One economic historian has written:

> In 1924–31 Germany drew some one [billion] pounds [sterling] from abroad and the irony was that Germany, in fact, received far more in loans, including loans to enable her to pay interest on earlier loans than she paid out in reparations, thus gaining in the circular flow and re-equipping her industries and her public utilities with American funds in the processes in the 1920s before repudiating her debts in the 1930s.[16]

Danger Signs

The system broke down in 1928 and 1929 when U.S. and British creditors needed their capital for investments in their own countries. Extensions on loans, readily granted a year earlier, were refused. Even before the U.S. stock market crash on October 29, 1929, disaster was on the horizon.

Few people in America could admit such a possibility during the decade, however. The United States had become the commercial center of the world, and its policies were central to the world's financial health. The United States still had an internal market in the 1920s with a seemingly inexhaustible appetite for new products such as radios, refrigerators, electrical appliances, and automobiles. This expansion, based on consumer goods and supported by a seemingly limitless supply of natural resources, gave the impression of solid and endless growth.

Tragically, the contradictions of the postwar economic structure were making themselves felt. The cornerstones of pre-1914 prosperity—multilateral trade, the gold standard, and interchangeable currencies—were crumbling. The policies of autarky, with high tariff barriers to protect home products against foreign competition, worked against international economic health. Ironically, the United States led the way toward higher tariffs, and other nations quickly retaliated. American foreign trade declined seriously, and the volume of world trade decreased.

There were other danger signals. Europe suffered a population decline. There were 22 million fewer people in the 1920s in the western part of the Continent than had been expected.[17] The decrease in internal markets affected trade, as did the higher external barriers. Around the globe, the agricultural sector suffered from declining prices during the 1920s. At the same time that farmers received less for their products, they had to pay more to live—a condition that afflicted peasants in Europe and Asia and farmers and ranchers in the United States.

In the hopes of reaching a wider market, farmers around the world borrowed money to expand production early in the 1920s. Temporarily, the food surplus benefited consumers, but across the world agricultural interests suffered from overproduction. Tariff barriers prevented foodstuffs from circulating to the countries where hunger existed. By the end of the decade, people in Asia were starving while wheat farmers in Whitman County, Washington, dumped their grain into the Snake River and coffee growers in Brazil saw their product burned to fuel steam locomotives. Many farmers went bankrupt, unable to keep up with payments on these debts. The countryside preceded the cities into the economic tragedy.[18]

The Great Crash

Because of America's central position in the world economy, any development on Wall Street, positive or negative, reverberated around the globe. The United States, with roughly 3 percent of the world's population, produced 46 percent of the globe's industrial output. The country was ill-equipped to use its newfound power. Its financial life in the 1920s was dominated by the activities of daring and sometimes unscrupulous speculators who made the arena of high finance a precarious and exciting world of its own. The businessmen creating this world were not pursuing long-term stability. Their blind rush for profit led to America's crash, which in turn sparked a world disaster.[19] Even before the stock market crash, Wall Street had been showing signs of distress, such as capital shortfalls, excessively large inventories, and agricultural bankruptcies. But nothing prepared financiers for the disaster that struck on October 29, 1929—Black Thursday. By noon Wall Street was caught in a momentum of chaotic fear, and stock prices began plummeting. The end of the trading session halted the initial hemorrhage of stock values, but the damage was done.

John Kenneth Galbraith has written: "On the whole, the great stock market crash can be much more readily explained than the depression that fol-

People, cars, and horses throng Wall Street on October 29, 1929, "Black Thursday," the day of the great stock market crash. With a great many more sellers than buyers participating in the frantic trading on that day, stock prices plummeted, and investors lost billions of dollars within a few hours.

lowed it."[20] Overspeculation, loose controls, dishonest investors, and a loss of confidence in the ever-upward market trend can be identified as causes for the crash. Further causes can be traced to the inequitable distribution of wealth, with the farmers and workers left out while the top 3 percent of Americans grew incredibly rich and irresponsible. Industrial overexpansion was fueled by speculators buying stock "on margin," with insufficient cash backing for the investments. In addition, the government's hands-off policies permitted massive abuses to take place unchecked.

The international impact of the crash can be explained by the involvement in the U.S. market of investors and bankers from a number of countries, the interdependent world economic structure, the peculiar Allied debt and reparations structure, the growing agricultural crisis, and the inadequate banking systems of the world.

Some economics historians believe that the cycle of highs and lows hit a particularly vicious low point in 1929. Crashes had occurred before, but never with such widespread repercussions over such a long period of time. In the United States, stock prices declined one-third overall within a few weeks, wiping out fortunes, shattering confidence in business, and destroying consumer demand. The disaster spread worldwide as American interests demanded payment on foreign loans and imports decreased. The Kredit-Anstalt bank of Vienna did not have enough money to fill demands for funds from French banks and failed in 1931. This set in motion a dominolike banking crisis throughout Europe. Forecasts by Washington politicians and New York financiers that the worst was over and that the world economy was fundamentally sound after a "technical readjustment" convinced nobody. There would be no easy recovery.

The World Depression

By 1932 the value of industrial shares had fallen close to 60 percent on the New York and Berlin markets. Unemployment doubled in Germany, and 25 percent of the labor force was out of work in the United States. The middle classes, which had invested in the stock market, saw their investments and savings wiped out. In nation after nation, industry declined, prices fell, banks collapsed, and economies stagnated. In the western democracies the depression heightened the feelings of uneasiness that had existed since 1918. In other countries the tendency to seek authoritarian solutions became even more pronounced. Throughout the world people feared a future marked by lowered standards of living, unemployment, and hunger.

The middle classes on the Continent, which had suffered from inflation during the 1920s, became caught in a whiplash effect during the depression. Adherence to old liberal principles collapsed in the face of economic insecurity, and state control of the economies increased. Governments raised tariffs to restrict imports and reverted to command economies, an expedient usually reserved for wartime. As conditions deteriorated, fear caused most governments to look no farther than their own boundaries. Under the competing systems of autarky, each nation tried to increase exports and decrease imports.

After almost a century of free trade, modified by a comparatively few protective duties levied during and after World War I, Great Britain finally enacted a high tariff in 1932 with provisions to protect members of its empire. In the United States the Hawley-Smoot Tariff of 1930 increased the value-added duty to 50 percent on a wide variety of agricultural and manufactured imports.

Another technique to increase exports at the expense of others was to depreciate a nation's currency—that is, to reduce the value of its money. When Japan depreciated the yen, for example, a U.S. dollar or British pound could buy more Japanese goods. In effect, lowering the yen reduced the price of Japanese exports. In most cases, however, devaluation brought only a temporary trade advantage. Other nations could play the same game, as the United States did in 1934 when it abandoned the gold standard and reduced the amount of gold backing for the dollar by 40 percent.

The debt problem that grew out of the war worsened during the depression. In 1931 President Herbert Hoover gained a one-year moratorium on all intergovernmental debts. The next year European leaders meeting at Lausanne practically canceled German reparations payments in the hope that the United States would make corresponding concessions in reducing war debts. The Americans, for a variety of domestic financial and political reasons, refused to concede that there was a logical connection between reparations and war debts. As the depression deepened, the debtors could not continue their payments. France refused outright in 1932; Germany after 1933 completely stopped paying reparations; Britain and four other nations made token payments for a time and then stopped entirely in 1934. Only Finland continued to meet its schedule of payments.

Families had at least as many problems in paying their bills as the governments of the world. Factories closed down and laid off their workers. Harvests rotted in the fields as the price of wheat fell to its lowest price in 300 years and other agricultural commodities suffered similar price declines. The lives of the cacao grower along Africa's Gold Coast, the coffee grower in Brazil, and the plantation worker in the Netherlands East Indies were as affected as those of the factory worker in Pittsburgh, Lille, or Frankfurt.

The 1929 crash occurred in an economic framework still suffering from the dislocations of World War I. It began a downturn in the world economy that would not end until the world armed for another global conflict. Whether the depression ended because of World War II or whether the world would have eventually recovered on its own is a question that will always be debated. The weaknesses in American stock market operations were by and large addressed in a series of reforms.

From the major banks to the soup lines in villages, the depression had profound implications for politics. The combination of inflation and depression threatened representative government. Unemployed and starving masses were tempted to turn to dictators who promised jobs and bread. The hardships of economic stability, even in countries where the liberal tradition was strongest, led to a massive increase in state participation in the daily life of the individual.

Politics in the Democracies

During the interwar period, belief in the genius of big business and free market capitalism received a death blow in most quarters, as business itself had to turn more and more to the powers of the state to survive. After 1918 parliamentary government, the foundation of all that the liberals of the nineteenth century had worked for, came under attack everywhere.

For the most part, only in Scandinavia—in Norway, Sweden, and Denmark—did representative government operate smoothly throughout the interwar period. Economic prosperity prevailed throughout

Germans line up for bread and soup during the Great Depression. Similar scenes were common in many other countries, including the United States.

the 1920s, and the depression was less severe than in Britain, France, or the United States. Switzerland, the Netherlands, and Belgium also maintained relatively high standards of living and kept their governments on the democratic road. But in the 20 years after peace came to the West, Britain, France, the United States, and most of the other democracies exhibited lethargy and shortsightedness in the face of fascist aggression.

Britain, 1919–1939

The 1920s was not a tranquil decade for Great Britain. The country endured a number of social and political crises tied to the bitter labor disputes and unemployment that disrupted the nation. Neither Liberals nor Conservatives could do much to alter the flow of events immediately after the war. From 1919 to 1922 David Lloyd George led a coalition, but it broke apart, leading to the division and decline of the Liberals.

From May 1923 to January 1924 Stanley Baldwin led an unsuccessful Conservative government.

Ramsay MacDonald formed the first Labour government and became the first socialist prime minister. For ten months he and his party pursued a program to introduce socialism slowly and within the democratic framework. His move to recognize the newly established Soviet Union (USSR) was controversial. When the London *Times* published the so-called Zinoviev letter, a document in which the Communist Third International supposedly laid out a program for revolution in Britain, the public backlash defeated the Labour government in the October 1924 elections.

For the next five years the Conservatives under Baldwin held power. After renouncing the treaties the Labour cabinet had made with the USSR, the Conservatives set out on a generally unsuccessful and stormy tenure. Britain returned its currency to the gold standard in 1925, a policy that led indirectly to an increase in labor unrest. The government struggled through a coal strike and a general strike in which more than 2.5 million of the nation's 6 million workers walked out. Baldwin reduced taxes on business, but this move did little to remedy the deflationary effect of a return to the gold standard.

In May 1929 Labour under MacDonald won another victory. Once again the Labourites resumed relations with the Soviet Union and attempted their measured socialist program. The effects of the depression, however, condemned MacDonald and his government to failure. In two years exports and imports declined 35 percent and close to 3 million unemployed people roamed the streets. Labour could do little to address the basic causes of the disaster; in fact, no single party could. When MacDonald's government fell in 1931, it was replaced by a national coalition government dominated by the Conservatives. The coalition government initiated a recovery program featuring a balanced budget, limited social spending, and encouragement of private enterprise. By 1933 a substantial measure of prosperity had been regained, and productivity had increased by 23 percent over the 1929 level.

To achieve this comeback, some of what remained of laissez-faire policy was discarded. The government regulated the currency, levied high tariffs, gave farmers subsidies, and imposed a heavy burden of taxation. The taxes went to expanded educational and health facilities, better accident and unemployment insurance, and more adequate pensions. As for the rich, they had a large portion of their income taxed away, and what might be left at death was decimated by inheritance taxes. It was ruefully declared that the rich could hardly afford to live, much less to die.

During the 20 years between the wars, Britain's political parties lacked forward-looking programs. The parties seemed unable to measure up to the demands of a difficult new age. In the empire, demands for home rule grew during the interwar period, especially in India, Sri Lanka, Burma, and Egypt. An ominous trend was the growing antagonism between the Arab inhabitants of mandated Palestine and the Jewish Zionist immigrants. Yet these issues would not come to a crisis until after World War II.

Happier developments could be seen in the attainment of home rule by the Irish Free State (the southern part of Ireland) in 1921 and Britain's recognition in the Statute of Westminster (1931) of a new national status for the dominions (Canada, Australia, New Zealand, and South Africa). Collectively, the four states were then known as the British Commonwealth of Nations and would be held together henceforth only by loyalty to the crown and by common language, legal principles, traditions, and economic interests. Democratic traditions in the dominions did not succumb to the pressures of the depression, even

though they were painfully susceptible to the effects of the world slump.

Interwar France

France suffered from World War I the most of any of the democracies; loss of lives as a proportion of the population and direct property damage were enormous. More than two out of every ten Frenchmen died. Years later the nation, which had historically experienced less rapid population growth than other European states, still felt the war's heavy losses.

Victory did not address any of France's basic political problems. The French labored under much the same political stalemate and social stagnation after 1918 as it had before 1914. The economic impact of the war and the social disruptions that occurred during and after the conflict exacerbated these conditions. A dangerous inflation plagued France and undermined its rather shallow prosperity. The multiparty system hampered the parliamentary structure of the Third Republic, and the governments formed from shaky coalitions. The exhausted country lacked vitality and a sense of national purpose after gaining revenge against the Germans.

After 1919 the British wished to withdraw from continental Europe to look after their imperial interests, and the United States shrank back into isolationism. Working from a dispirited domestic base, France had to bear the burden of overseeing international affairs on the Continent. Overall, with the exception of the counterproductive occupation of the Ruhr, the French carried their duties well in the 1920s. In the next decade, however, France retreated into the so-called Maginot mentality, after the construction of the Maginot line, a supposedly impenetrable line of fortresses to the east.

The depression struck France later than it did other countries, but in some ways the damage was greater. French leadership was no more astute than that of the other democracies before and during the depression. France managed to maintain a false prosperity from the 1920s for a while, partly because of its large gold holdings, but by the early 1930s it suffered much the same fate as the other countries. Tourism dried up, contributing to the already rising unemployment rate and budget deficits. In the face of these problems, the French carried the additional financial burden of rearming to face a renewed German threat.

Ministry after ministry took power, only to collapse a few months later. Citizens became impatient with the government, especially when the press exposed corruption in high places. One of the more shocking scandals was that surrounding the schemes of Alexander Stavisky, a rogue who had bribed officials and cheated French investors out of some 600

German, Italian, and Spanish fascists saw the aerial devastation of a village in the Spanish Civil War as a means to test new methods of warfare. Picasso painted the mural Guernica *to testify to the world what the attack really was: an atrocity inflicted on an innocent population.*

million francs. When the ministry in power in December 1933 refused to authorize an investigation after Stavisky's assumed suicide, thousands of angry citizens took to the streets of Paris in protest. In February 1934 mobs tried to storm the Chamber of Deputies.

The outcome of this affair was a new government, the National Union, a rightist coalition that endured strikes and avoided civil war for the next two years. France was becalmed. The leftists were unable to reorganize their forces quickly to gain control, and the rightists failed to deal with either domestic or foreign problems. In the spring of 1936 the leftist Popular Front took power.

This coalition, under the leadership of Léon Blum (1872–1950), won a national election and set in motion a program to bring socialist reforms to France's struggling economy. Blum's government tried to reduce the domination of the traditional ruling elite over the finances of the country on the one hand, and on the other, to work with the Communists to help block the growing fascist influences. The cooperation with the Communists caused serious problems, including the usual one of how to work with the Soviet-dominated party without being captured by it. Many French voters refused to support the Popular Front for fear that it might commit France to fight against Germany for the benefit of the Soviet Union.

In foreign affairs the Popular Front worked closely with Great Britain and supported the work of the League of Nations. It also attempted to appease Germany, though it remained hostile to Italy. During the Spanish civil war (1936–1939), fearing civil war at home, Blum's government, along with the British, declared neutrality in the face of fascist aggression.

In this atmosphere of social, economic, and international turmoil, Blum was unable to govern successfully. Further, an epidemic of sit-down strikes involving some 300,000 workers embarrassed the government. Gradually, laws introducing a 40-hour workweek, higher wages, collective bargaining, and paid vacations were enacted to satisfy many of labor's demands. In addition, the government extended its control over the Bank of France and instituted a public works program. Blum navigated as best he could, favoring the worker against monopoly and big business while avoiding the totalitarian extremes of fascism and communism. After only a year in office, however, he was forced to resign. The unfavorable trade balance, huge public debt, and unbalanced budget brought down the Popular Front government. France swung back to the right with a government that ended the 40-hour week and put down strikes.

The National Union and the Popular Front mirrored the widening split between the upper and lower classes. The workers believed that the Popular Front's reforms had been sabotaged and that a France ruled by a wealthy clique deserved little or no allegiance. Conversely, some business owners and financiers were horrified at the prospect of communism and openly admired Hitler's fascism. Soviet and German propagandists subtly encouraged the widening of the gulf.

While the French quarreled and France's economic strength declined, Germany—regimented and working feverishly—outstripped France in the manufacture of armaments. There were no leaders to bring France together, and the pieces were in place for the easy and tragic fall of the country to German troops at the start of World War II in the spring of 1940.

Eastern Europe

With the exception of Finland and Czechoslovakia, democratic governments fared poorly in eastern Europe in the interwar period. By 1938 most of the states retained only the false front of parliamentary forms. Real power was exercised by varying combinations of secret police, official censors, armed forces, and corrupt politicians. Except in the western parts of Czechoslovakia and among the Jewish communities, there was a welcoming attitude toward the German National Socialists (Nazis) and their programs.

Most of these countries had an unhappy legacy of oppression by powerful neighbors, minority problems, economic weakness, and peasant societies. Poland, the Baltic states, Finland, Czechoslovakia,

Democracy waned in the uncertain years after World War I as people turned increasingly toward more authoritarian leaders whom they hoped would bring them stability and prosperity.

Yugoslavia, and Albania had not existed as states before 1913. Hungary, Bulgaria, and Austria had been on the losing side in World War I and paid dearly for that alliance in the treaties ending the war. Romania, which had been among the victors, gained large amounts of land and also a number of non-Romanian minorities.

For the first decade after World War I, the small countries of eastern Europe had the opportunity to develop without undue external influence or interference. However, the exclusivist, aggressive, and perhaps paranoid nationalism that dominated each nation thwarted any possibility of regional cooperation. The peace treaties had settled few of the problems plaguing the area and instead constructed a series of arbitrary political boundaries that brought far more conflict than accord. The countries in the region all sought autarkist solutions to their economic problems by erecting huge tariff barriers, which only served to emphasize the states' weaknesses.

Among the eastern European states, Czechoslovakia, with its combination of a strong middle class, accumulation of capital, technology base, and high literacy rate, had the greatest potential for successful democratic government. Four hundred years of Austrian domination had not crushed the Czech national spirit. After the collapse of the Dual Monarchy in November 1918, the Czechs joined with the Slovaks, who had been under Hungarian domination for 1000 years, to establish a republic.

The new state possessed a literate and well-trained citizenry and a solid economic base, and it managed to avoid the roller-coaster ride of inflation in the immediate postwar period. Its solid financial institutions, advanced industry, and a small-farm-based agricultural sector made it an island of prosperity. Like the other eastern European successor states, it had serious minority problems. But of all the new states Czechoslovakia extended the most liberal policies toward minorities. By the time of the depression, Czechoslovakia showed every indication of growing into a mature democratic country. The depression, however, heavily affected the country's export trade and hit especially hard in the textile industry, which was centered in the German-populated Sudetenland. By 1935 the economic blows had made the area ripe for Nazi agitation and infiltration.

After Czechoslovakia, Poland had the best chance of the successor states to form a democratic government. The Poles, however, had to overcome several problems: a border conflict with the Soviet Union, the dilemma of the Polish Corridor to Danzig, minority issues, and the fact that Poland had been partitioned for over a century. When the country was reunited after the war, the Poles chose to imitate the constitutional system of the French Third Republic.

The multiplicity of parties, a weak executive, and the resultant succession of governments led to political paralysis until 1926, when Marshal Josef Pilsudski (1867–1935) led a military revolt against the Warsaw government.

For the next nine years Pilsudski imposed his generally benevolent rule on the country. After his death in 1935, a group of colonels ruled Poland, and they permitted the formation of several protofascist organizations. By the time the Poles turned back toward a more liberal government in 1938, it was too late. For three years they had played up to the Nazis, and now they stood isolated before Hitler's advance.

Problems of geography plagued the Balkan states of Latvia, Lithuania, and Estonia, which came into existence in 1918. The democratic governments of these countries endured much political and economic strife before they eventually gave way to dictatorial forms of government to survive with the Nazis.

The Balkan states of Yugoslavia, Albania, and Greece were buffeted by the ambitions of Italian imperialism, economic upheaval, and political corruption. Disintegration seemed a real possibility for Yugoslavia in the 1920s, but the conglomerate state stubbornly attempted to hold together the six major ethnic groups within its boundaries. King Alexander established himself as dictator in 1929 and ruled until 1934, when he was assassinated by Croatian separatists. Thereafter, the rising Nazi state drew parts of economically depressed Yugoslavia into its orbit, deeply splitting the country. By the end of the 1930s, both Greece and Albania were ruled by dictators.

Romania, another of the Balkan states, gained greatly from World War I, doubling its area and its population. Although the state had great economic potential, the government was unable to impose a stable rule during the interwar period. Severe problems with minorities and peasants and foreign control of the economy foiled the attempts of moderate politicians to rule, until by the 1930s fascist groups wielded a large amount of influence. In 1938 King Carol tried unsuccessfully to counter the pro-Nazi forces in Romania. Two years later the country lost one-third of its territory and population to the Bulgarians, Russians, and Hungarians, and Carol fled to Spain.

Portugal and Spain

During the interwar period, economic problems, aristocratic privilege, and peasant misery worked against successful democratic or parliamentary government in the Iberian peninsula. After the end of World War I, Portugal endured ten years of political indecision until Antonio de Oliveira Salazar (1889–1970), a pro-

fessor of economics, became minister of finance in 1928. After helping straighten out some of the country's financial problems, Salazar became Portugal's premier and virtual dictator. He maintained Portugal's close ties with Britain while lending assistance to right-wing elements in Spain.

None of the political parties could deal adequately with Spain's problems in the 1920s. Revolts and strikes plagued the country until 1931, when the king abdicated and left the country. At the end of the year a new liberal constitution was adopted, and a republic was proclaimed. The new constitution was extremely liberal, but it had the support of neither the left nor the right. Mob violence and the threat of military coups continually harassed the republic.

By 1936 the peasants and workers were beginning to take matters into their own hands. At the same time the military, under Generalissimo Francisco Franco, sought to pursue its own political ends. In July the army made its move and attacked the republican government. This marked the start of a civil war in Spain, a war that in retrospect seems inevitable due to the country's indigenous social antagonisms.[21]

The United States

The United States emerged from World War I as the strongest country in the world. But while other states looked to Washington to continue to play a political and diplomatic role in the world, the U.S. government turned inward, away from the international scene. Americans shelved Wilson's wartime idealism, ignored the League of Nations, and returned to domestic politics. At the same time, however, American businessmen played an active role in international business until 1929: not until the 1980s would a larger percentage of American financial activities take place abroad.

During the 1920s three Republican presidents—Warren G. Harding, Calvin Coolidge, and Herbert Hoover—benefited from the well-being of the country and the generally carefree spirit of the times. Although refusing to join the League of Nations, the United States did participate in the Washington Naval Conference in 1921–1922 to limit the race in warship construction, the Dawes and Young plans for economic stabilization, and the Kellogg-Briand pact (1928) to outlaw war.

Harding's domestic policies were marked by protectionist economics, probusiness legislation, and scandal. After Harding died suddenly in 1923, the widespread corruption of his administration was exposed. His vice president, Coolidge, easily weathered the storm and after his 1924 election advocated high tariffs, tax reduction, and a hands-off policy on federal regulation of business. Only nagging problems in the agricultural sphere detracted from the dazzling prosperity and honest government that marked his administration.

In the 1928 presidential elections, Herbert Hoover—a successful mining engineer who had directed Belgian relief during the war, had been present at the Versailles negotiations, and had overseen the Russian relief plan in the early 1920s—overwhelmed the governor of New York, Alfred E. Smith, the first Catholic to be nominated for president. When Hoover took office in 1929, he had the support of a Republican Congress and a nation enjoying unbounded industrial prosperity. It would be his incredibly bad luck to have to deal with and be blamed for the worst depression the United States has ever experienced.

By 1932 Americans felt the tragic blows of the Great Depression—25 percent unemployment, 30,000 business failures, numerous bank collapses, and a huge number of foreclosed mortgages. Hoover tried unprecedented measures to prop up faltering businesses with government money, devise new strategies to deal with the farm problem, and build confidence among the shaken citizenry. Yet he failed to shift the tide of the depression. Indeed, some observers note that the only force that brought an end to the crisis was the arrival of the World War II.

In the 1932 elections Franklin D. Roosevelt, only the third Democrat elected to the presidency since 1860, defeated Hoover by assembling a coalition of labor, intellectuals, minorities, and farmers—a coalition the Democratic party could count on for nearly a half century. The country had reached a crisis point by the time Roosevelt was inaugurated in 1933, and quick action had to be taken in the face of a wave of bank closings.

Riding with Franklin D. Roosevelt to the Capitol after FDR's victory in the 1932 presidential election, former President Herbert Hoover remained silent and aloof beside the effervescent newly elected president.

Under Roosevelt's leadership the New Deal—a sweeping, pragmatic, often hit-or-miss program—was developed to cope with the emergency. The New Deal's three objectives were relief, recovery, and reform. Millions of dollars flowed from the federal treasury to feed the hungry, create jobs for the unemployed through public works, and provide for the sick and elderly through such reforms as the Social Security Act. In addition, Roosevelt's administration substantially reformed the banking and investment industries, greatly increased the rights of labor unions, invested in massive public power and conservation projects, and supported families who were in danger of losing their homes or who simply needed homes.

The Democrats' programs created much controversy among those who believed that they went too far toward creating a socialistic government and those who believed that they did not go far enough toward attacking the depression. Hated or loved, Roosevelt was in control, and the strength and leadership he provided were unparalleled in the interwar democracies.

Interwar Latin America

The huge wartime demand for Latin American mineral and agricultural products resulted in an economic boom that, with a minor contraction, continued on into the 1920s. However, the area's crucial weakness remained—its economic dependence on only a few products. Among Latin America's 20 republics, Brazil based its prosperity on coffee, Cuba depended on sugar, Venezuela on oil, Bolivia on tin, Mexico on oil and silver, Argentina on wheat and meat, and the various Central American countries on bananas.

Another problem was land distribution. On many large estates conditions resembled medieval serfdom. Because the Catholic Church was a great landowner, certain members of the clergy combined with the landed interests to oppose land reforms.

During the 1920s Mexico spearheaded the movement for social reform in Latin America. A series of governments, each claiming to be faithful to the spirit of the 1910 revolt, sought to gain more control over the vast oil properties run by foreign investors. The government solved the agrarian problem at the expense of the large landowners. These changes were accompanied by a wave of anticlericalism. Under these attacks the Catholic Church lost much property, saw many churches destroyed, and had to work through an underground priesthood for a time.

Mexico exerted a strong influence over other Latin American countries. Between 1919 and 1929 seven nations adopted new, liberal constitutions. In addition, there were growing demands for better economic and social opportunities, a breakdown of the barriers that divided the few extremely rich from the many abysmally poor, and improvements in health, education, and the status of women. Above all there was an increasing desire for more stable conditions.

Because of their dependence on raw-material exports, the Latin American countries suffered a serious economic crisis during the Great Depression. Largely as a result of the disaster, revolutions broke out in six South American countries in 1930.

During the 1930s the "colossus of the north," the United States, attempted to improve its relations with Latin America and to stimulate trade. The Good Neighbor policy, originated in Hoover's administration and begun in 1933, asserted that "no state has the right to intervene in the internal or external affairs of another." Less pious, but more effective, was the $560 million worth of inter-American trade that the new policy encouraged.

Rivalries among industrialized nations for the Latin American market became intense during the 1930s. Nazi Germany concluded many barter agreements with Latin American customers and at the same time penetrated the countries politically by organizing German immigrants into pro-Nazi groups, supporting fascist politicians, and developing powerful propaganda networks. When war came, however, most of Latin America lined up with the democracies.

The Western Tradition in Transition

In the first two decades of the twentieth century, science made great strides, and such figures as Max Planck, Albert Einstein, Ivan Pavlov, and Sigmund Freud enlarged understanding of the universe and the individual. Even before the war, which had dealt a death blow to the nineteenth-century legacy of optimism, these physicists and psychologists pointed out that the old foundations and beliefs on which the European world rested had to be rethought. They and others like them opened new scientific vistas, and after 1918 their work began to have a much wider impact.

In the interwar period, artists too served as observant witnesses and penetrating critics of the difficult age in which they lived. Questioning of the accepted values and traditions of Western civilization increased after 1918.

Science and Society

The British physicist Ernest Rutherford (1871–1937) advanced the theory in 1911 that each atom has a central particle, or nucleus, which is positively charged. Rutherford's argument repudiated the belief that the atom was indivisible. On the Continent dis-

coveries with even greater consequences were being made. German physicist Max Planck (1858–1947) studied radiant heat, which comes from the sun and is identical in nature with light. He found that the energy emitted from a vibrating electron proceeds not in a steady wave, as was traditionally believed, but discontinuously in the form of calculable "energy packages." Planck called each such package a *quantum*, and the *quantum theory* was born. This jolt to traditional physics was to prove extremely valuable in the rapidly growing study of atomic physics.

The scientific giant of the first half of the twentieth century, Albert Einstein (1879–1955), supported Planck's findings. In 1905 Einstein contended that light is propagated through space in the form of particles, which he called *photons*. Moreover, the energy contained in any particle of matter, such as the photon, is equal to the mass of that body multiplied by the square of the velocity of light (approximately 186,300 miles per second). This theory, expressed in the equation $E = mc^2$, provided the answer to many mysteries of physics. For example, questions such as how radioactive substances like radium and uranium are able to eject particles at enormous velocities and to go on doing so for millions of years could be examined in a new light. The magnitude of energy contained in the nuclei of atoms could be revealed. Above all, $E = mc^2$ showed that mass and energy are equatable. In 1906 Einstein formulated his special theory of relativity, which set out a radically new approach to explain the concepts of time, space, and velocity.

Ten years later Einstein proposed his general theory, in which he incorporated gravitation into relativity. He showed that gravitation is identical to acceleration and that light rays would be deflected in passing through a gravitational field—a prediction confirmed by observation of an eclipse in 1919 and by various experiments carried out in the American space programs in the 1960s and 1970s and the Hubble telescope in 1994. The theory of relativity has been subsequently confirmed in other ways as well. The conversion of mass into energy was dramatically demonstrated in the atomic bomb, which obtains its energy by the annihilation of part of the matter of which it is composed.

Einstein's theories upset the Newtonian views of the universe. Einstein's universe is not Newton's three-dimensional figure of length, breadth, and thickness. It is, instead, a four-dimensional space-time continuum in which time itself varies with velocity. Such a cosmic model calls for the use of non-Euclidean geometry. Einstein's theory changed scientists' attitude toward the structure and mechanics of the universe. On a broader scale, his relativistic implications penetrated many of the philosophical, moral, and aesthetic concepts of the twentieth century.

Albert Einstein overturned the Newtonian universe of order and replaced it with his special theory of relativity, which provided new ways to view time and space. He is shown here with his wife.

Planck and Einstein investigated the infinite extent of the external universe, with a massive impact on the state of knowledge. At the same time, the equally infinite extent of the universe known as the mind also began to be studied in greater depth than ever before.

The Russian scientist Ivan Pavlov (1849–1936) gave the study of psychology a new impetus. In 1900 he carried out a series of experiments in which food was given to a dog at the same time that a bell was rung. After a time the dog identified the sound of the bell with food. Henceforth, the sound of the bell alone conditioned the dog to salivate, just as if food had been presented. Pavlov demonstrated the influence of physical stimuli on an involuntary process.

The psychology of "conditioned reflexes," based on Pavlov's work, achieved wide popularity, especially in the United States, as the basis for behaviorism, which considered the human as analogous to a machine responding mechanically to stimuli. Behaviorism stressed experimentation and observational techniques and did much to create relatively valid intelligence and aptitude tests. It also served to strengthen the materialist philosophies of the period.

Probably the most famous and controversial name associated with psychology is that of Sigmund Freud (1856–1939). Placing far greater stress than any predecessor on the role of the unconscious, Freud pioneered the theory and methods of psychoanalysis. This theory is based on the idea that human beings are born with unconscious drives that from the very beginning seek some sort of outlet or expression. Young children often express their drives in ways that violate social conventions for proper behavior. Parents typically forbid these behaviors and punish children for performing them. As a result, many innate drives are *repressed*—pushed out of conscious awareness. Repressed drives, however, continue to demand some kind of expression. Freud believed that many repressed drives were *sublimated,* or channeled into some kind of tolerated or even highly praised behavior.

Freud was particularly interested in psychological disorders, and he treated emotional disturbances by encouraging patients to bring back to the surface deeply repressed drives and memories. By making patients aware of their unconscious feelings, Freud hoped that they would understand themselves better and be able to respond more effectively to the problems they faced. Freud used the techniques of free association and dream interpretation to explore how unconscious feelings might be related to patients' symptoms. He believed that many of his patients' symptoms resulted from repressed sexual and aggressive drives. Freud's theories have had a tremendous influence not only on the science of psychology but also on our culture as a whole, although his theories were falling out of favor as the twentieth century ended.

The Testimony of Artists

Even before the Great War, many of Europe's writers, artists, and musicians had begun to question the generally held faith in European progress. The barbarism and tragedy of the war and its aftermath merely confirmed their perceptions. A whole generation of artists and thinkers cast doubts on their society and the worth of individuals caught in civilization's web. The war had shown to many the fallacies of the old order. Some artists sought release in drugs, oriental religions, or bohemian lifestyles. Other found comfort in ideas drawn from Einstein's relativity theory, which held that nothing in the universe was unchanging, or in Freud's notions of the overwhelming power of the unconscious.

Among writers, Franz Kafka (1883–1924) perhaps best captured the nightmarish world of the twentieth century. In works such as *The Metamorphosis* and *The Trial* he portrayed a ritualistic society in which a well-

Discovery Through Maps

International Air Travel

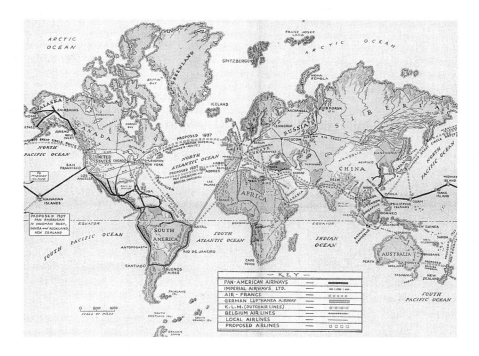

Brothers Orville and Wilbur Wright made the first artificially powered flight by humans at the beginning of the twentieth century; in the generation after that, airplanes would come to play a major role in the fighting of World War I, Charles Lindbergh would make a solo flight across the Atlantic, and commercial firms would inaugurate international air travel.

By 1937 there were six major international airlines: Pan American, based in the United States; Imperial Airways in the United Kingdom; Air France;

Lufthansa in Germany; KLM, the Dutch airline; and the Belgian airline, later known as Sabena. Even during the depths of the Great Depression there was enough business potential that one could fly around the world, using, at times, local carriers such as United Air Lines and American Airlines. Even though there was no regular transatlantic service yet, the Germans were experimenting with the use of the Graf Zeppelin, a helium-filled lighter-than-air dirigible.

organized insanity prevails. Rational, well-meaning individuals run a constant maze from which there is no exit, only more structures. Many sensitive artists and writers cast serious doubt on the Renaissance notion that "man is the measure of all things." The Western world had gone very far off course, and the best that could be hoped for was survival.

Historians worked under the profound influence of Oswald Spengler's *Decline of the West*. The book, finished one year before the defeat of the Central Powers, was more widely quoted than read. In it the German historian traced the life span of cultures, from birth through maturity to death, and identified the symptoms of the West's demise. Other writers expressed a similar fascination with the death of their civilization, but perhaps more significant was that

people in the West knew Spengler's name, just as earlier they had known the names and general messages of Darwin, Freud, and Einstein.

Before 1914 a number of composers had been rebelling strongly against lyrical Romanticism and engaged in striking experimentation. Breaking with the "major-minor" system of tonality, which had been the musical tradition since the Renaissance, some of them used several different keys simultaneously, a device known as polytonality. Outstanding among such composers was Igor Stravinsky (1882–1971), who was less concerned with melody than with achieving effects by means of polytonality, dissonant harmonies, and percussive rhythms. Other composers, such as the Austrian-born Arnold Schoenberg (1874–1951), experimented with atonality, the absence of any fixed key. Schoenberg developed the 12-tone system, an approach in which compositions depart from all tonality and harmonic progressions while at the same time stressing extreme dissonances. Stravinsky's and Schoenberg's music may strike the first-time listener as harsh and unpleasant, but these experiments with polytonality and atonality were symbolic of their time, when the old absolute values were crumbling—a time of clashing dissonance.

Artists all over the world took up abstract, non-representational painting. During the interwar period Pablo Picasso (1881–1973) modified his cubist style and became a public figure through paintings such as *Guernica* (see p. 825), a mural that captures vividly the human horrors of the destruction of a small town in Spain by fascist air forces during that country's civil war. Henri Matisse (1869–1954) continued to exercise a major influence on young painters through his abstract works. Less significant but a useful example of artistic response to the times was the Dada school, which viewed World War I as proof that rationality did not exist and that, therefore, neither did artistic standards. Salvador Dalí (1904–1989) perhaps indicated his convictions about the artistic establishment and the society it represented when he gave a lecture on art while wearing a diver's helmet.[22]

A more lasting movement that came out of the 1920s was surrealism. The proponents of this approach saw the subconscious mind as the vehicle that could free people from the shackles of modern society and lead them to total creative freedom. They felt an affinity with "primitive art" and its close associations with magical and mythological themes. They exalted the irrational, the violent, and the absurd in human experience. French writer André Breton (1896–1966) wrote a manifesto of surrealism in 1924, but the movement had its greatest impact in the visual arts, in the works of such artists as Dalí, Georgio de Chirico (1888–1978), and René Magritte (1898–1967).

Sculpture and Architecture

These two most substantial forms of art went through radical changes during the generation before and after the war. Auguste Rodin (1840–1917) has been called the father of modern sculpture. The realistic honesty and vitality of his work made him the object of stormy controversy during his career. He shared the impressionist painters' dislike of finality in art and preferred to let the viewers' imagination play on his work. Rodin's "rough finish" technique can best be seen in his bronze works, which feature a glittering surface of light and shadow and convey a feeling of immediacy and incompleteness that emphasizes their spontaneous character.

While Rodin was making major contributions in sculpture, architects in Europe were taking advantage of new materials and technologies developed through industrialization to make major improvements in construction. With new resources and methods, architects were able to span greater dis-

The most famous surrealist painter was Salvador Dalí, who sought to express the subjective world of dreams through disturbing and bizarre images like those in The Persistence of Memory *(1931).*

Architectural Pioneers

Alexandre Gustave Eiffel (1832–1923)	Planned and built the tower that bears his name for the 1889 Paris International Exposition
Walter Gropius (1883–1969)	One of founders of the Bauhaus movement; built avant-garde exposition hall in Cologne
Louis Sullivan (1856–1924)	Chicago architect who chose function over form in his skyscrapers
Frank Lloyd Wright (1867–1959)	Greatest twentieth-century American architect

tances and enclose greater areas than had hitherto been possible.

The Great Chicago Fire of 1871 may have leveled much of the city, but it had the beneficial effect of permitting new building on a large scale. A new form of structure emerged—the steel-skeleton "skyscraper," which enabled builders to erect much taller structures, thanks to the perfecting of the elevator. Before, high buildings had required immensely thick masonry walls or buttresses. Now a metal frame allowed the weight of the structure to be distributed on an entirely different principle. Also, the metal frame permitted a far more extensive use of glass than ever before.

Outstanding among the pioneers in this new approach was American architect Louis Sullivan (1856–1924), who did most of his important work in Chicago. Like others, Sullivan saw the value of the skyscraper in providing a large amount of useful space on a small plot of expensive land. He rejected all attempts to disguise the skeleton of the skyscraper behind a false front and boldly proclaimed it by a clean sweep of line. Sullivan had a far-reaching influence on the approach of choosing function over form.

In Europe the French engineer Alexandre-Gustave Eiffel (1832–1923) planned and erected a 984-foot tower for the Paris International Exposition of 1889. Delicately formed from an iron framework, the tower rests on four masonry piers on a base 330 feet square.

In the decade prior to World War I, an "international" style of architecture, which broke sharply with tradition, developed in Germany. This style, which stressed the use of various techniques from the machine age, was particularly well suited to early-twentieth-century industrialization. In 1914 one of the outstanding leaders of this movement,

Walter Gropius (1883–1969), designed an exhibition hall in Cologne that emphasized horizontal lines, used glass, exposed staircases, and did not hide its functionalism. Nearly a century later this hall is still regarded as contemporary. Proponents of this new movement in architecture established a highly influential school of functional art and architecture, the Bauhaus, in 1918.

One of Sullivan's pupils, Frank Lloyd Wright (1867–1959), originated revolutionary designs for houses. One feature of Wright's structures was the interweaving of interiors and exteriors through the use of terraces and cantilevered roofs. He felt that a building should look appropriate on its site; it should "grow out of the land." His "prairie houses," with their long, low lines, were designed to blend in with the flat land of the Midwest. Much of what is today taken for granted in domestic architecture stems directly from Wright's experiments at the beginning of the twentieth century.

Mass Culture

While the creative geniuses of high culture responded in their own ways to the era, purveyors of mass culture made amazing strides to please and entertain a widening audience. Movies became the most popular, most universal art form of the twentieth century. Movie newsreels brought home to millions the immediacy of the rise of Adolf Hitler, the drama of Franklin D. Roosevelt, and the home run power of Babe Ruth.

From the theaters of Main Street, USA, to the private projection rooms of the Kremlin, artists such as Charlie Chaplin became universal favorites. Chaplin's most loved character, the Little Tramp, was an archetypal figure that communicated across all cultures. The tramp's struggle for food and shelter was universal, as was his appeal for freedom and dignity. Despite the odds, he always struggled against the forces of inhumanity, whether the soulless mechanization of the assembly line, as brilliantly shown in *Modern Times* (1935), or jackboot tyranny, as in *The Great Dictator* (1940).

Technology touched the common people in many ways and vastly expanded mass culture. Henry Ford's affordable Model T made automobiles widely accessible and opened up the world to those who cared to drive. In cities, virtually every home had electricity, which powered bright lights, refrigeration, and other conveniences. Radio brought music, drama, and news into millions of living rooms. Politicians quickly learned the usefulness of the new medium; Stanley Baldwin in Britain, Franklin Roosevelt in the United States, and Adolf Hitler in Germany became masters at projecting their personalities and their ideas over the airwaves. The three great networks in

The greatest American architect of the twentieth century, Frank Lloyd Wright adapted the structure, materials, and plan of a building to its natural setting. In the Kaufman House, known as Falling Water, at Bear Run, Pennsylvania (1936), the overhanging concrete slabs blend harmoniously with the rocky ledges, while the interior of the house is a continuous flow of interrelated and interpenetrating areas.

the United States and organizations such as the British Broadcasting Corporation (BBC) in Europe got their start during these years.

The combination of increased leisure time, greater mobility, and improved communications led to the development of the modern "star" system in sports and entertainment. As times became more difficult and front-page news turned grim, Americans, Germans, and French citizens could find some diversion in reading about their boxers—Jack Dempsey, Max Schmeling, and Georges Carpentier. In the United States golfers and baseball stars became better known and better paid than presidents.

Through radio and phonograph records the mass audience discovered jazz, formerly the special pre-serve of black musicians and their audiences. Louis Armstrong and his trumpet and Paul Whiteman and his band became known worldwide. At the same time, Rosa Ponselle, Arturo Toscanini, and other figures from the opera and concert world became celebrities known to millions more than could ever have seen them perform in person.

Conclusion

Germany's rapid economic growth, military buildup, ambitious foreign policy, and inability to control its Austro-Hungarian ally helped bring the normally competitive European economic arena to a crisis in

Charlie Chaplin as the Little Tramp in The Gold Rush *(1925). Chaplin used the new popular art form of the movies as a vehicle for both social commentary and humor. His Little Tramp character became a folk hero whose antics were touched with pathos yet who remained incorrigibly optimistic that one day things would get better.*

the summer of 1914. By violating Belgian neutrality and declaring war on Russia and France, Germany stood clearly as the aggressor in the First World War, a fact for which it was severely punished in the Treaty of Versailles. Its actions had provided the spark to the volatile environment of the aggressive state system and set in motion four years in which the science, wealth, and power of Europe were concentrated on the business of destroying much of what the Continent had accomplished in the previous century.

When the victorious Allies gathered at Paris in 1919 to settle the peace, they did not have the luxury of time, distance, and power the leaders at the Congress of Vienna had enjoyed in 1815. The 1919 peacemakers had endured the most destructive war in history. In this total war, psychological methods were used to motivate all the people of each of the states to hate the enemy, during and after the war. The treaty settled at Versailles produced a mere break in the hostilities.

With all that the Europeans shared, World War I was a conflict that need never have been fought. The Europeans threw away the advantages they had gained since 1815 and set in motion a series of disasters from which they did not recover until the 1960s. The democracies won World War I, and they dictated the peace at Paris, but the peace did not bring them the fruits of victory they so ardently desired. In the West the vanguard of progress since the Middle Ages had been the middle classes. This group, originally small property owners, pursued private enterprise in an urban setting and favored an economy based on minimal governmental interference and free markets. After the war the economic disasters of inflation and the depression depleted the middle classes' economic strength and weakened the democracies' capacity to defend themselves and their allies.

Other basic institutions and assumptions also came under attack. The total mobilization for victory during the war laid the foundations for increased state dominance over society. By the end of the 1930s Bismarck's welfare state had been copied in almost every country in the West. The family's obligation to care for its own members soon passed to society and the state. Whether in the identification card of the French citizen or the social security number of the United States, every adult came to find a tentacle of the state reaching out to insure, support, and protect, while at the same time to tax and restrict.

As if to ignore the political, social, and economic upheaval of the interwar period, scientists came closer to understanding the fundamental nature of the universe. In the course of their discoveries they found the possibility to liberate humanity from its former limits and to destroy it through nuclear weapons. At the same time, the artists, writers, musicians, sculptors, and architects struggled to comprehend and express the nature of the time in which they lived, whether in the dissonance of Schoenberg or the Dada of Dalí. And for the rest of the people in the democracies, mass culture, with its movie stars, athletic heroes, and musical favorites, provided diversion for many, even as it drew criticism from the elite. Mass culture provided release and relief from the stresses of the interwar period.

Suggestions for Reading

The most accessible general study of the war is Martin Gilbert, *The First World War: A Complete History* (Henry Holt, 1996). The standard account on the causes of the war is Fritz Fischer, *Germany's Aims in the First World War* (Norton, 1968). Classic views on the war are to be found in William Leonard Langer, *European Alliances and Alignments, 1871–1890* (Greenwood, 1977) and *The Diplomacy of Imperialism, 1890–1902* (Knopf, 1935), and Sidney B. Fay, *The Origins of the World War* (Macmillan, 1928). Bernadotte Schmidt, *Triple Alliance and Triple Entente* (Fertig, Holt, 1934), is a good introduction. Mark

Ferro examines the broader social and psychological aspects of the origins of World War I, especially the role of manipulated patriotism, in *The Great War, 1914–1918* (Routledge & Kegan Paul, 1993). See also René Albrecht-Carrié, *A Diplomatic History of Europe Since the Congress of Vienna* (Harper & Row, 1973). A good overview of the war's origins is Laurence Lafore, *The Long Fuse: An Interpretation of the Origins of World War I*, 2nd ed. (Waveland Press, 1997).

Specific topics are dealt with by Oron J. Hale, *The Great Illusion, 1900–1914* (Torchbooks, 1971); Vladimir Dedijer, *The Road to Sarajevo* (Simon & Schuster, 1966); Colin Simpson, *The Lusitania* (Harper & Row, 1976); Alan Moorehead, *Gallipoli: Account of the 1915 Campaign* (Harper, 1956); Alistair Horne, *The Price of Glory: Verdun, 1916* (Penguin, 1994); Edgar M. Coffman, *The War to End All Wars: The American Military Experience in World War I* (University Press of Kentucky, 1998); Gerhard Ritter, *The Schlieffen Plan: Critique of a Myth* (Greenwood, 1979); and Gerald D. Feldman, *Army Industry and Labor in Germany, 1914–1918* (Berg, 1992). Paddy Griffith makes sense of the English role on the western front in *Battle Tactics of the Western Front: The British Army's Art of Attack, 1916–1918* (Yale University Press, 1994).

Alexander Solzhenitsyn's *August 1914* (Bantam, 1974) is an important piece of literature describing Russia's entry into the war. Barbara Tuchman, *The Guns of August* (Dell, 1964), is history beautifully written. Paul Fussell captures the brutal nature and impact of the war in *The Great War and Modern Memory* (Oxford University Press, 1977). On the crisis in the French army, see Leonard V. Smith, *Between Mutiny and Obedience: The Case of the French Fifth Infantry* (Princeton University Press, 1994). On the contribution of American women to the First World War, see Letti Gavin, *American Women in World I: They Also Served* (University Press of Colorado, 1993).

See Arthur S. Link, *Wilson the Diplomatist* (Hopkins, 1957), regarding the U.S. president's participation at Paris. Charles L. Mee Jr. captures the aura of Paris during the negotiations in *The End of Order: Versailles, 1919* (Dutton, 1980). Harold G. Nicolson's beautifully written *Peacemaking, 1919* (Houghton Mifflin, 1939) is a fine firsthand account, as is John Maynard Keynes, *The Economic Consequences of the Peace* (Macmillan, 1924). The diplomatic maneuvers behind the creation of the post-Ottoman Levant are examined in David Fromkin, *A Peace to End All Peace: Creating the Modern Middle East, 1914–1922* (Holt, 1989).

The responsibilities of winning the war are discussed in William Laird Kleine-Ahlbrandt, *The Burden of Victory: France, Britain, and the Enforcement of the Versailles Peace, 1919–1925* (University Press of America, 1995). Edward H. Carr, *The Twenty Years' Crisis, 1919–1939* (Harper & Row, 1964), and A. J. P. Taylor, *From Sarajevo to Potsdam* (Harcourt, Brace & World, 1966), give compelling and eloquent coverage of the malaise of the democracies in the interwar period. The problems of peacemaking and the aftermath of Versailles are discussed in F. P. Walters, *A History of the League of Nations* (Oxford University Press, 1952).

Richard Bessel presents a thorough study of the crises of German society in *Germany After the First World War* (Clarendon Press, 1993). The economic situation is well treated in David S. Landes, *The Unbound Prometheus: Technological Change and Industrial Development in Western Europe from 1750 to the Present* (Cambridge University Press, 1969), and Sidney Pollard, *European Economic Integration, 1815–1870* (Harcourt Brace Jovanovich, 1974). See Fritz Ringer, ed., *The German Inflation of 1923* (Oxford University Press 1969), and Gustav Stolper, Karl Hauser, and Knut Borchardt, *The German Economy, 1870 to the Present*, trans. Toni Stolper (Harcourt, Brace & World, 1967), for the view from Berlin. Gerald D. Feldman, *The Great Disorder: Politics, Economics, and Society in the German Inflation* (Oxford University Press, 1997), sustains the view of the fundamental importance of the inflation in the disasters that came later.

John Kenneth Galbraith, *The Great Crash, 1929* (Houghton Mifflin, 1965), is wise and beautifully written. Charles P. Kindelberger, *The World in Depression, 1929–1939*, rev. ed. (University of California Press, 1986), covers the global perspective of the 1930s. Charles S. Maier surveys the social and political consequences of the difficult interwar period in *Recasting Bourgeois Europe: Stabilization in France, Germany, and Italy in the Decade After World War I* (Princeton University Press, 1988). For events in the successor states, see Joseph Rothschild, *East Central Europe Between the Two World Wars* (University of Washington Press, 1974).

Two first-rate biographies of interwar British leaders are David Marquand, *Ramsay MacDonald* (Cape, 1977), and Keith Midlemas, *Baldwin: A Biography* (Macmillan, 1970). John Stevenson provides a good survey of British life between the wars in *Social Conditions in Britain Between the Wars* (Penguin, 1977). For developments in France between the wars, see John T. Marcus, *French Socialism in the Crisis Years, 1933–1936* (Praeger, 1963), and Peter Larmour, *The French Radical Party in the 1930s* (Stanford University Press, 1964). For the United States, see William E. Leuchtenberg, *The FDR Years: On Roosevelt and His Legacy* (Columbia University Press, 1995).

An understanding of the interwar scene can be gained from reading some of the biographies of the participants. See, for example, Albrecht Folsing, *Albert Einstein: A Biography*, trans. Ewald Osers (Viking, 1997); Meryle Secrest, *Frank Lloyd Wright: A Biography* (University of Chicago Press, 1998); Ian Gibson, *The Shameful Life of Salvador Dalí* (Norton, 1998); and Michael Oliver, *Stravinsky* (Phaidon, 1995). Folsing's biography, based on new sources, uncovers the often painful life behind Einstein's earth-shaking discoveries; Secrest sees through Wright's carefully constructed facade; Gibson, a fine art historian, notes that the flamboyant Dalí was driven by a sense of shame; and Oliver places Stravinsky in the full context of great composers. Michael Fitzgerald, *Making Modernism: Picasso and the Creation of the Market for Twentieth-Century Art* (Farrar, Straus & Giroux, 1995), details the pioneering work of Picasso in exploiting the huge market for art among the ever-increasing upper middle classes. To understand the century, the books and stories of Franz Kafka are illuminating—see *The Complete Stories of Kafka* (Schocken Books, 1995).

Suggestions for Web Browsing

The Great War
http://www.pitt.edu/~pugachev/greatwar/ww1.html
Vast site devoted to all aspects of World War I.

World War I
http://www.worldwar1.com/
Another extensive site on all aspects of World War I.

The Great Depression
http://query3.lycos.cs.cmu.edu/wguide/wire/wire
The Lycos U.S. History Guide offers a list of the top 5 percent of Web sites dealing with the Great Depression.

Spanish Civil War
http://www.pitt.edu/~pugachev/greatwar/ww1.html
Extensive site includes links to paintings and posters, maps, history, and poems regarding the Spanish civil war.

Museo Picasso Virtual: On-Line Picasso Project
http://www.tamu.edu/mocl/picasso/

Extensive on-line project, in six languages, offering a tour of the life, family, travels, and works of this twentieth-century master.

Notes

1. Edward H. Carr, *The Twenty Years' Crisis, 1919–1939* (New York: Harper & Row, 1964), p. 224.
2. Quoted by C. J. H. Hayes, *A Political and Cultural History of Modern Europe*, Vol. 2 (New York: Macmillan, 1939), p. 572.
3. Edward Grey, Viscount of Fallodon, *25 Years*, Vol. 2 (New York: Stokes, 1925), p. 20.
4. Frank P. Chambers, *The War Behind the War, 1914–1918* (New York: Arno Press, 1972), p. 473.
5. "The Soldier," in *The Collected Poems of Rupert Brooke* (New York: Dodd, Mead, 1915).
6. "Anthem for a Doomed Youth," in *The Collected Poems of Wilfred Owen.* Copyright © 1963 by Chatto & Windus, Ltd., 1946. Reprinted by permission of New Directions Publishing Corporation and Chatto & Windus on behalf of the estate of Wilfred Owen.
7. Donald W. Treadgold, *Twentieth-Century Russia* (Chicago: Rand McNally, 1959), p. 154.
8. Quoted in Louis M. Hacker and Benjamin B. Kendrick, *The United States Since 1865* (New York: Crofts, 1939), p. 520.
9. Quoted in E. Achorn, *European Civilization and Politics Since 1815* (New York: Harcourt, Brace, 1938), p. 470.
10. Quoted in R. J. Sontag, *European Diplomatic History, 1871–1932* (New York: Century, 1933), p. 392.
11. Louis Fischer, *The Soviets in World Affairs* (New York: Vintage Books, 1960), p. 116.
12. George F. Kennan, *The Decision to Intervene* (Princeton, N.J.: Princeton University Press, 1958), p. 471.
13. A. J. Ryder, *Twentieth-Century Germany: From Bismarck to Brandt* (New York: Columbia University Press, 1973), p. 216.
14. David S. Landes, *The Unbound Prometheus: Technological Change and Industrial Development in Western Europe from 1750 to the Present* (Cambridge: Cambridge University Press, 1969), pp. 361–362; Gustav Stolper, Karl Hauser, and Knut Borchardt, *The German Economy, 1870 to the Present*, trans. Toni Stolper (New York: Harcourt, Brace & World, 1967), p. 83. For a recent analysis of Weimar's social and economic crises, see Richard Bessel, *Germany After the First World War* (New York: Clarendon Press, 1993).
15. Alan Bullock, *Hitler: A Study in Tyranny* (New York: Harper Torchbooks, 1964), p. 91.
16. Sidney Pollard, *European Economic Integration, 1815–1970* (New York: Harcourt Brace Jovanovich, 1974), p. 138.
17. Landes, *Unbound Prometheus*, p. 365.
18. Pollard, *European Economic Integration*, pp. 140–142.
19. William R. Keylor, *The Twentieth-Century World* (Oxford: Oxford University Press, 1984), p. 133.
20. John Kenneth Galbraith, *The Great Crash, 1929* (Boston: Houghton Mifflin, 1961), p. 173.
21. Brian Crozier, *Franco* (London: Eyre & Spottiswoode, 1967), p. 13.
22. A. J. P. Taylor, *From Sarajevo to Potsdam* (New York: Harcourt, Brace & World, 1965), p. 116.

Nazi soldiers round up Jewish men, women, and children in Warsaw for "resettlement" in death camps. Nazi extermination policies led to the deaths of over 6 million Jews and 4 million homosexuals, Gypsies, Slavs, and other "undesirables."

Authoritarian Alternatives

Russia, Italy, and Germany, 1917–1939

World War I and its aftershocks prepared the way for authoritarian rule in Europe. By 1939 dictators ruled the USSR, Italy, and Germany. Using modern technology, they tried to form a new kind of state, described as *totalitarian* by Benito Mussolini in 1925.

Totalitarian regimes are at an opposite pole from democratic governments, which respect laws, representative assemblies, and civil and human rights. Totalitarianism exalts the leader of the state, who uses law and society for the regime's goals. It invades and controls all areas of the individual citizen's life, using propaganda to manipulate the masses. It orchestrates elections to achieve the "democratic fiction" of popular support. When totalitarian rule is perfected, society is atomized so that there is no obstacle between the might of the leader and the individual.[1] Leaders such as Joseph Stalin and Adolf Hitler in the 1930s, Mao Tsetung during the Cultural Revolution in China in the 1960s, and Pol Pot in Cambodia in the 1970s came close to achieving total control, but none of these men succeeded in constructing a lasting totalitarian system.

The costs of war and the incompetence of dual power destroyed the Provisional Government in Russia. The disappointments of the peace and unsettled economic conditions undermined the Italian government and the German Weimar Republic. Even before World War I and the economic upheaval, the political climate in these countries had not been conducive to the development of

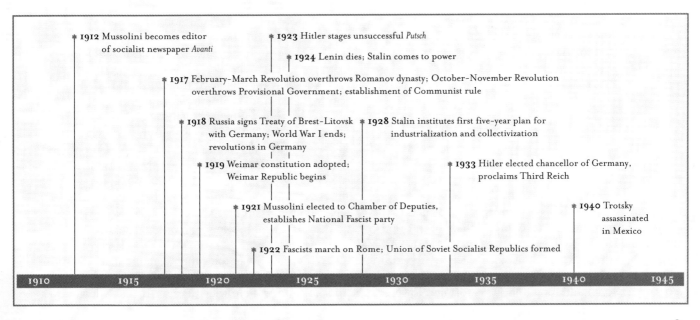

1912 Mussolini becomes editor of socialist newspaper *Avanti*

1923 Hitler stages unsuccessful *Putsch*

1924 Lenin dies; Stalin comes to power

1917 February–March Revolution overthrows Romanov dynasty; October–November Revolution overthrows Provisional Government; establishment of Communist rule

1918 Russia signs Treaty of Brest-Litovsk with Germany; World War I ends; revolutions in Germany

1928 Stalin institutes first five-year plan for industrialization and collectivization

1919 Weimar constitution adopted; Weimar Republic begins

1933 Hitler elected chancellor of Germany, proclaims Third Reich

1921 Mussolini elected to Chamber of Deputies, establishes National Fascist party

1940 Trotsky assassinated in Mexico

1922 Fascists march on Rome; Union of Soviet Socialist Republics formed

1910   1915   1920   1925   1930   1935   1940   1945

839

The self-proclaimed democracies may have won World War I, but they lost the peace. By the end of the 1930s, they were greatly outnumbered by fascist, authoritarian, and communist regimes.

liberal government. The postwar conditions, combined with the exhaustion of the democracies, led to the authoritarian alternative dominating Europe and much of the world by 1939.

Revolution in Russia, 1917 and 1928–1939

The enormous costs of the war set the stage for revolution. Nicholas II and his subjects entered the war in August 1914 in a buoyant and patriotic mood.[2] It took only two months to dampen their initial optimism and to expose the army's weakness and the government's corruption and incompetence. By the middle of 1915 drastic losses (more than 2 million lives that year alone) and food and fuel shortages lowered

morale. Strikes increased among the factory workers during 1916, and the peasants, whose sons were dying in large numbers and whose desire for land reform was being ignored, became discontented.

The tsar and his government did little. Nicholas came more and more under the influence of his wife, Alexandra. She, in turn, had fallen under the control of the "holy man" Rasputin, who had seemingly stopped the bleeding of the tsar's hemophiliac son. Rasputin scandalized Petrograd (the former St. Petersburg) by his influence over Alexandra and by his well-known seductions—he believed that "great sins made possible great repentances"[3] and in pursuit of that goal became one of history's notable sexual athletes.

When Nicholas took the symbolic act of assuming command of his armies in the field—a move that did nothing to help the Russian forces—Alexandra's

Tsar Nicholas and Tsarina Alexandra are surrounded by their daughters (left to right) Marya, Tatiana, Olga, and Anatasia. The young Tsarevich Alexei sits below his parents. The entire family was executed by the Bolsheviks in July 1918.

and Rasputin's power increased. The two capriciously dismissed capable generals and officials, making the government and army even less efficient. In December 1916 a group of Russian nobles tried to kill Rasputin by luring him to an apartment and poisoning him. When the massive amounts of poison had no effect, they shot him and then threw him into the Neva River. According to the autopsy, he finally died by drowning.

The roles of Alexandra and Rasputin in the capital reflected the sad state of the tsarist government in 1917. Under the pressure of war, the Russian economic and political structures dissolved. The tsarina and her associate did not cause the outbreak of the revolution. Rather, "the complex revolutionary situation of 1917 was the accumulated deposit of Russian history, detonated by the explosion of war."[4]

The February–March Revolution of 1917

While politicians, ideologists, and generals acted out their parts in the drama, a spontaneous event from below sparked the 1917 Russian Revolution. In the first part of March (late February in the Julian calendar in use in Russia at the time; all dates will be given according to the Gregorian calendar, which replaced it), a strike broke out in a Petrograd factory. By March 8 sympathy strikes had virtually paralyzed the city. At the same time, a bread shortage occurred, which brought more people into the streets. Scat-

The Russian monk known as Rasputin. Convinced of Rasputin's supernatural powers because of his apparent ability to relieve her son's hemophilia, Tsarina Alexandra came more and more under the influence of the mysterious monk. The name Rasputin, which he acquired during his youth, means "Philanderer."

End of the Romanov Dynasty: The February–March Revolution of 1917

All dates are according to the Gregorian calendar, which replaced the Julian calendar in use in Russia at the time.

March 8   Sympathy strikes paralyze city

March 11   Tsar orders strikers back to work, dismisses Duma

March 12   Army and police disobey orders; Duma declares formation of provisional committee—Provisional Government on March 15; Socialists proclaim formation of Soviet of Workers' Deputies—Soviet of Workers' and Soldiers' Deputies on March 15

March 15   Tsar Nicholas I abdicates, passes power to his brother, Michael

March 16   Michael renounces power, empowerment of Provisional Government

tered fighting broke out between the strikers and protesters on one side and the police on the other.

The tsar ordered the strikers back to work and dismissed the Duma (parliament) on March 11. His orders touched off the revolutionary crisis. The Duma refused to go home, and the strikers defied the government and held mass meetings. The next day the army and police openly sided with the workers.

Three events occurring between March 12 and March 15 marked the end of the old regime. On March 12 the Duma declared the formation of a provisional committee (renamed the Provisional Government on March 15) to serve as a caretaker administration until a constituent assembly could be elected to write a constitution for the future Russian republic. On the same day Marxist socialists in Petrograd formed the Soviet (council) of Workers' Deputies (renamed three days later the Soviet of Workers' and Soldiers' Deputies). Nicholas abdicated on March 15 to his brother Michael, who turned down the throne the next day in favor of the Provisional Government. After more than three centuries in power, the Romanov dynasty ceased to rule.

For the next six months Russia proceeded under a system Leon Trotsky, the great Marxist theoretician and revolutionary, described as "dual power"—the Provisional Government and the Soviet. The moderates and liberals in the Provisional Government quickly produced a program of civil rights and liberties that gave Russia a springtime of freedom in 1917 the likes of which the country had never known before

and would not experience again for 70 years. From the first, however, the Provisional Government was hampered by its temporary nature: it refused to take permanent action on major issues until the constituent assembly, elected by all Russians, could convene.

The Soviet was dominated by the Menshevik wing of the Russian Social Democratic party. The Mensheviks believed, in accordance with Marx's teachings, that a liberal, bourgeois revolution had to run its course. Even though they had greater popular support than the Provisional Government, they refused to take power until what they deemed to be the historically proper moment as defined by Marx's theories. After the fall of the tsar, power passed to those who could not rule or would not rule.

From the first, the dual power system functioned in a contradictory and ineffective way. On March 14 the Soviet issued its first law, Order No. 1, which placed the running of the army on a democratic basis, through a committee structure. Soldiers were to obey only those orders that agreed with the official position of the Soviet, which wanted peace. At the same time, the Provisional Government insisted on carrying out the war, in hopes of gaining the Bosporus, Constantinople, and the Dardanelles.

As the months wore on, the position of moderates in both parts of the system weakened, and all the involved parties became discredited. The Provisional Government put off calling the constituent assembly and thereby deferred any possibility of finding solutions to the problems Russia faced. It continued to pursue the war to "honor its commitments" and to gain the prizes promised in the secret treaties. Reasoning that the liberal, bourgeois phase of history had not run its course in Russia, the Mensheviks refused to take control. The masses who suffered from economic hardships or fought and died on the front lines could find little consolation in either branch of dual power.

By July the liberals and moderates had given up the reins of power. Alexander Kerensky (1881–1970), who was farther to the left and who had been the only real revolutionary in the original cabinet, became the head of the Provisional Government. He was in an impossible situation. Leftists accused the Provisional Government of heartlessly pursuing the war, while rightists condemned it for tolerating too many leftists. In the meantime the Soviet extended its organization throughout Russia by setting up local affiliates. Through the summer, however, the Soviets lacked the forceful leadership they needed to take control of the country.

Lenin's Opportunity and the October–November Revolution of 1917

In 1917 Lenin returned to Russia from exile in Switzerland, intent on giving the revolution the leadership it lacked. He had spelled out his tactics and ideas in the previous decade, and his disciples in Russia, the Bolsheviks, had built up a core of supporters in the factories and the army. As late as December 1916 he had stated that the revolution would not occur within his lifetime. Four months later, working through Swiss contacts and with German assistance, he returned to Russia. The Germans gave him transportation and financial support in the hope that he would cause widespread chaos, forcing Russia to withdraw from the war.

From the moment he stepped off the train in Petrograd on the evening of April 16, Lenin tried to control the revolution. He proposed immediately stopping the war against Germany and starting one against "social oppressors." He called for giving all power to the Soviets and nationalizing all land. He also pushed for calling all Social Democrats, of whatever persuasion, communists. Lenin badly misjudged his audience, and the Mensheviks and Social Revolutionaries rejected his program.

During the summer and fall of 1917 the Provisional Government and the Soviet continued their misgovernment. Kerensky tried to rule through a series of coalitions in which the political balance continually shifted to the left. By the middle of July, after a moderately successful offensive against the Austrians, soldiers began to desert in large numbers rather than face a useless death in World War I. The Russian front, along with the army, disintegrated. In the capital the Mensheviks persisted in refusing to take power through the Soviet: the historical time was not right. As if to match the ineptness of dual power, the Bolsheviks made an ill-conceived attempt to take power. The move backfired, and Lenin was forced to flee in disguise to Finland.

After surviving the Bolshevik crisis, Kerensky faced a new threat from the right when General Lavr Kornilov tried to "help" the government by sending his troops to the capital. Kerensky and the Soviet interpreted this action as a right-wing counterrevolutionary move and mobilized to head it off. Kornilov's ill-advised maneuver failed, and ironically, he weakened the people he wanted to help.

Between March and October 1917 the force of the revolution ground to bits all of Russia's structures and parties, from monarchist to Menshevik. The economic system fell apart as the rhythms of planting and commerce were disrupted by the uproar. To the people caught in this chaos, the moderates' political dreams, the Mensheviks' revolutionary timing, and the Bolsheviks' schemes for the seizure of power were all totally irrelevant.

The actual revolution took place far away from the politicians and "great men." The army withered away as mass desertions and the execution of officers became commonplace. In the countryside the peasants began carrying out land reform on their own, expelling landowners and killing those who would not leave. In the cities workers began to take over factories. The Russian Empire broke apart from internal conflicts, the continued pressure of war, and the rising spirits of the nationalities who had been oppressed for centuries.

Only the Bolsheviks seemed to have an answer to Russia's crisis; even their slogans, such as "Peace, Land, and Bread," reflected what was already happening. Furthermore, they had the discipline and adaptability to take advantage of events. The Mensheviks clung to brittle intellectual formulas, while the Provisional Government continued to dream of Russian control of the Bosporus and Constantinople. Lenin and his colleagues took advantage of the Kornilov debacle and the failure of dual power to form their own revolution.

By October 1917 the Bolsheviks had discarded their slogan, "All Power to the Soviets." Frankly, Lenin, the unchallenged Bolshevik leader, no longer needed these local organizations. After much hesitation, he decided to move on November 6 (October 24 in the Russian calendar). The Bolshevik Military Revolutionary Committee, led by Leon Trotsky and supported by the Communist-dominated crew of the battleship *Aurora*, took control of the communications and police centers in Petrograd. With the exception of sporadic fighting around the Winter Palace, Trotsky's military forces had little trouble. They arrested all members of the Provisional Government who could be found. Kerensky escaped from the capital in a car flying the U.S. flag.

Lenin then found himself leading a party of more than 200,000 people (an increase from 23,600 in February), which claimed control of a state with more than 170 million inhabitants. It was not his individual genius or his plans but rather his discipline and opportunism that enabled him to gain power. He endured the mistakes of April and July to take power. He did not make the revolution, but he did pick up the pieces and profit from the changes brought about by the breakdown of the tsarist government under the pressure of war.

Power, Allied Intervention, and Civil War

The Bolsheviks assumed power over a war-weakened, revolution-ravaged state that was in terrible condition. Lenin's takeover split the Soviet itself when the Mensheviks and the Social Revolutionaries refused to participate. Lenin had a bare majority at the Soviet's first postrevolutionary meeting. In the free elections held in December to form a constituent assembly, the Bolsheviks received just one-fourth of the votes.

The Program of the Provisional Government

The freedom enjoyed by Russia from March to November 1917 was the greatest ever experienced in that country. A major reason for the freedom was the program of the Provisional Government.

Citizens, the Provisional Executive Committee of the members of the Duma, with the aid and support of the garrison of the capital and its inhabitants, has triumphed over the dark forces of the Old Regime to such an extent as to enable it to organize a more stable executive power.

The cabinet will be guided in its actions by the following principles:

1. An immediate general amnesty for all political and religious offenses, including terrorist acts, military revolts, agrarian offenses, etc.
2. Freedom of speech and press; freedom to form labor unions and to strike. These political liberties should be extended to the army insofar as war conditions permit.
3. The abolition of all social, religious, and national restrictions.
4. Immediate preparation for the calling of a Constituent Assembly, elected by universal and secret vote, which shall determine the form of government and draw up the Constitution for the country.

5. In place of the police, to organize a national militia with elective officers, and subject to the local self-governing body.
6. Elections to be carried out on the basis of universal, direct, equal, and secret suffrage.
7. The troops that have taken part in the revolutionary movement shall not be disarmed or removed from Petrograd.
8. On duty and in war service, strict military discipline should be maintained, but when off duty, soldiers should have the same public rights as are enjoyed by other citizens.

The Provisional Government wishes to add that it has no intention of taking advantage of the existence of war conditions to delay the realization of the above-mentioned measures of reform.

From F. A. Golder, ed., *Documents of Russian History, 1914–1917*, trans. E. Aronsberg (New York: Appleton-Century-Crofts, 1927).

Yet such details as democratic representation did not stop Lenin. He proceeded to rule Russia. The Bolsheviks immediately put through decrees to declare peace and settle the land question. In the meantime, his cadres imposed their control over Moscow and the other cities in the country.

Lenin then began to lay the foundations for a single-party dictatorship that endured until 1989. When the Constituent Assembly convened in Petrograd on January 18, 1918, and proved that it would not be a tool for Lenin, the Bolsheviks closed it down at bayonet point the next day. By dissolving the Constituent Assembly, Lenin crushed all remnants of the briefly flowering democracy. This decisive step sealed the fate of the Mensheviks and most other opposition leftist parties. Not for 71 years would there be contested elections, open criticism of the central power, and the possibility of a potential democratic opposition.

Lenin had to make peace with Germany and after two months of negotiations concluded the Treaty of Brest-Litovsk. This agreement drastically reduced the territory under Russian control and made the

centers of government much more exposed to attack. In reality, Lenin sacrificed territory over which he had no control and took his country out of a war it could not fight.

In the late spring the revolutionary government came under attack from the White forces and the Allies. The Whites, a powerful but fragmented group of anti-Bolsheviks, began a civil war that would claim as many casualties in three years as the country had lost in World War I. The Allied Powers sent several expeditionary armies to Russia for the stated purpose of controlling matériel they had sent the former tsarist army. In reality, they helped the Whites. The Allies, still at war with Germany, feared that the Bolsheviks were in a conspiracy with the Germans, especially after the terms of the Brest-Litovsk Treaty became known. They also hoped that if Lenin could be overthrown, the Whites might reopen fighting against the Central Powers. By fall 1918 the Bolsheviks were besieged.

From its new capital at Moscow, the Red (Bolshevik) government took all means to defend the revolution. Lenin's forces reimposed the death penalty (it

Germany took advantage of Russian weaknesses after the 1917 revolution to deprive the revolutionary state of much of its economic base and territory.

Not only did the fledgling Moscow-based communist state face intervention by the Western Allies in 1918, but it also had a war with the newly reunited Polish state over the western borderlands formerly controlled by the tsars.

had been abolished by the Provisional Government) and unleashed a ghastly reign of terror. The Red Army and the Cheka (secret police) systematically destroyed the enemies of the revolution as well as individuals who were only lukewarm in their support of the new regime. Prison camps and repressive terror harsher than any since Ivan IV dominated life in the Russian state. In July 1918 the former tsar and his family, under house arrest since the outbreak of the revolution, were herded into the cellar of the house in which they were being held and were executed. They would not receive their final burial until 1998.

After the Central Powers surrendered in November 1918, Allied intervention in Russia ceased, and the Bolsheviks concentrated their energies against the Whites. Trotsky turned the Red Army into a disciplined, centralized force. The disorganized and dispersed White opposition, whose units ranged from Siberia to the Caucasus to Europe, could not match the Red forces. Taking advantage of their shorter supply lines, ideological unity, and dislike of Allied intervention, the Bolsheviks put an end to White resistance by 1920. The Whites were united on few issues

besides their hatred of the Bolsheviks. After their defeat, nearly a million of them scattered across the globe, eternal émigrés grieving the loss of their country and their dreams.

Theory, Reality, and the State

Lenin had no hesitation about revising Marx's doctrines to fit Russian conditions. He had long opposed all democratic parliamentary procedures, especially the concept of an officially recognized opposition party. He advocated instead a revolutionary "dictatorship of the proletariat" under Bolshevik leadership. The new order would rule in accordance with "democratic centralism," in which the vanguard party would anticipate the best interests of the masses and rule for them.

Lenin altered certain aspects of the Marxist concept of the historical process. He accepted the view that the proletarian-socialist revolution must be preceded by a bourgeois-democratic revolution. He interpreted the March 1917 events as the first democratic revolution and his own coup d'état in November as the second, or proletarian-socialist, revolution. This approach drastically shortened the historical process by which the bourgeois stage was to run its course. Lenin justified dissolving the Constituent Assembly on the grounds that a higher form of democratic principle had now been achieved, making the assembly superfluous. The November revolution had vested all power in the Russian Republic in the people themselves, as expressed in their revolutionary committees, the soviets.

Many orthodox Marxists believed that the state would "wither away" once the dictatorship of the proletariat had eliminated the bourgeoisie. Once in power, however, Lenin found that he had to create a far stronger, more efficient state to govern Russia. The Bolsheviks, as the ultimate democratic centralists, ruled with an iron hand and prepared the way for the totalitarianism of Joseph Stalin.

The state acted in many spheres. In policies reminiscent of Robespierre's tenure during the French Revolution, the new government attacked the church, changed the calendar (adopting the Gregorian and rejecting the Julian system), and simplified the alphabet. The Cheka enforced ideological unity with a level of terror that set the standard for later Soviet secret police organizations. The individual came to be ground down by the all-encompassing power of the state.

In the first six years after Lenin seized power there were three major developments relating to the Communist party, the name adopted by the Bolsheviks in 1918. First, all other parties were suppressed. Second, the function of the party was changed from that of carrying out the revolution to that of governing the country. Third, within the party itself, a small elite group called the Politburo, which set policy, consolidated power in its hands. Among the members of the first Politburo were Lenin, Trotsky, and Stalin. The second major organ of the party was the Secretariat for the Central Committee, which oversaw the implementation of policy into practice.

The state itself came to be known as the Russian Socialist Federated Soviet Republic (RSFSR). As the Moscow-based Communist government extended its authority after the civil war, the jurisdiction of the RSFSR grew. In 1922 the Union of Soviet Socialist Republics (USSR) was formed, consisting of the four constituent socialist republics: the RSFSR, the Ukraine, White Russia (Belorussia), and Transcaucasia.

The Communists had established the first constitution for their government in 1918, but events and growth soon led to the need for a new one, which was adopted in 1924. It set up a system based on a succession of soviets in villages, factories, and cities. This pyramid of soviets in each constituent republic culminated in the All-Union Congress of Soviets at the apex of the federal government. Although it appeared that the congress exercised sovereign power, this body was actually governed by the Communist party, which was in turn controlled by the Politburo.

So great did the authority of the Communist party become over the formation and administration of policy that before Lenin's death in early 1924 that it could be said without exaggeration that party and state were one. Consequently, whoever controlled the

An effective orator, Lenin addresses Russian troops as they prepare to leave for the front in the civil war. Trotsky stands to Lenin's left.

party controlled the state, and in the new Soviet state the key person would be Joseph Stalin.

War Communism and the NEP

Lenin's ability as a politician can be seen in his flexibility between 1917 and 1924. From 1918 to 1921 he tried to apply undiluted Marxist principles to eliminate private ownership of land; nationalize banks, railways, and shipping; and restrict the money economy. This policy, known as *war communism,* was widely unpopular. The peasants, who had just attained their centuries-long goal of controlling their own land, did not like the prospects of collectivization and the surrender of their surplus grain to the state. Many workers did not want to be forced to work in factories. Former managers showed little enthusiasm for running enterprises for the state's benefit.

In the early months of 1920 the new government faced its most dangerous crisis to date. Six years of war and civil strife had left Russia exhausted. Industrial production was 13 percent of what it had been in 1914. Crop failures, poor management, and transportation breakdowns contributed to the disaster. Famine brought more than 20 million people to the brink of starvation. The government was forced to ask for help, and organizations such as Herbert Hoover's American project to bring relief to Russia helped the country through the crisis, but not before some 5 million people died.

Internal chaos plus controversy with Poland over disputed borders further plagued Lenin's government. From 1918 to 1921 other areas of the former Russian empire—Finland, Estonia, Latvia, Lithuania, and Bessarabia—chose to go their own way. In February 1921 sailors at Kronstadt, formerly supporters of the regime, rebelled against the Bolsheviks and were massacred by the Red Army. Lenin said that the revolt "illuminated reality like a flash of lightning,"[5] and chose to make an ideological retreat.

War communism was a total failure. Lenin decided that it was necessary to take one step backward in order to go two steps forward. He explained that Russia had tried to do too much too soon in attempting to change everything at once. He also noted that there had not been a firestorm of complementary communist revolutions sweeping the globe. The outbreaks in Germany and Hungary had been brutally quashed. Russia stood alone. Compromise was necessary to survive, and besides altering his diplomatic front abroad, he recommended a return to certain practices of capitalism, the so-called New Economic Policy, or NEP.

This retreat from war communism lasted from 1921 to 1928 and allowed the Russian state to get on its feet. Peasants were relieved from the wholesale appropriation of grain. After paying a fixed tax, they were permitted to sell their surplus produce in the open market. Private management could once again run firms and factories employing fewer than 20 employees. Workers in state industries received a graduated wage scale. Foreign commerce and technology were actively sought. These compromises proved to be highly beneficial, and the Soviet economy revived.

Ideological purists criticized the policy and pointed out that the *kulaks,* as the ambitious peasants who accumulated property were called, and private businesses profited greatly. Lenin's concessions and compromises gave the Communists time to regroup and recover, and the Russian people gained much-needed breathing space. Lenin emphasized the absolute necessity for the party to "control the commanding heights of the economy." The state continued to manage banking, transportation, heavy industry, and public utilities.

The NEP was Lenin's last major contribution. In broken health since surviving a would-be assassin's bullet in 1918, he worked as much as he could until his death in January 1924. In his 54 years Lenin changed the world's history. He bequeathed to the globe its first Marxist state and provided a base from which his variant of Marxism could spread. He changed the tone and tactics of Marxism, stripping it of much that was humane and tolerant. His defenders claim that such steps were needed to apply a theory intended for industrialized society to an agrarian state. His critics argue that his methods and ideas were merely reflections of his own ego. His tomb in Moscow's Red Square, in which his embalmed body was placed on display, became a shrine where thousands of followers could pay homage to the creator of the Soviet state. Ironically, this secular, atheistic man who led a spartan existence was made by Stalin into a cult figure at the center of a new state religion.

Trotsky Versus Stalin

A weakness of all dictatorships is that there is no well-defined mechanism to pass power from one leader to the next. Lenin was the one person in the party who possessed unchallenged authority and whose decrees were binding. After his death, Leon Trotsky and Joseph Stalin, rivals with conflicting policies and personalities, fought for power.

Leon Trotsky (1879–1940), born Lev Davidovich Bronstein, was a star in the political arena. He was a magnificent, charismatic orator, an energetic and magnetic leader in all areas, and a first-rate intellectual and theoretician. He turned to Marxism as a teenager and, like Lenin, had been exiled to Siberia for his revolutionary activities. He participated in the major events of Russian social democracy. Trotsky was a member of the *Iskra* group of Russian exiles in Zurich, had been present in London in 1903 and opposed Lenin in the Bolshevik-Menshevik split, played a key role in the 1905 Russian Revolution, and was an essential figure in the 1917 Revolutions and the Civil War. His egocentricity and arrogance contrasted sharply with the shrewd and cunning nature of his less colorful but more calculating rival.

Joseph Stalin (1879–1953), born in Georgia as Joseph Vissarionovich Dzhugashvili, labored for the revolution in obscurity. While Trotsky played the star, Stalin worked behind the scenes. Trotsky was a crowd-pleasing orator; Stalin, when he spoke in Russian (his second language—Georgian was his first), was not an inspiring speaker. Admitted to a seminary to be trained for the priesthood, the young Stalin was later expelled for radical opinions. In the years before the revolutions Stalin served the Bolsheviks by robbery to gain funds for the party's organization and propaganda activities. In all ways he faithfully supported Lenin—unlike Trotsky, who had not been a uniformly obedient disciple. Stalin was exiled east of the Urals a number of times before he returned to Petrograd in 1917 to play an active role in the events of that year. He knew his own strengths and weaknesses. He also formed his opinion of Trotsky rather early on, characterizing him in 1907 as "beautifully useless."[6]

After the 1917 revolutions, Stalin did much of the less glamorous organizational work of the party; he was also responsible for dealing with the various nationalities. While others in the Politburo dealt with ideological questions or fought the civil war, Stalin created a network of people—loyal to him alone—who worked in the bureaucratic apparatus and came to be known as *apparatchiks*. With and through them he controlled the bureaucracy. In 1922 *Pravda* ("Truth"), the official party newspaper, carried a brief announcement that the Central Committee had confirmed Stalin as general secretary of the secretariat, a position that became the most powerful in the Soviet Union.

After Lenin's death, Stalin moved to construct a new secular religion for the Soviet Union. Leninism formed in 1924 and remained powerful for more than 60 years. The mark of faith came to be unquestioning loyalty to Lenin. (The city of Petrograd, for example, was renamed Leningrad.) Stalin became Lenin's St. Peter, despite Lenin's criticism of both Trotsky and Stalin in his purported last will and testament. Although written in 1922, it was not widely published until the 1950s.

In the competition with Trotsky, Stalin won because he was the better organizer and the more skill-ful manipulator of people. Staying in the background, Stalin, the modest "helper," played the game of divide and conquer as members of the Politburo fought among themselves. By 1926 party members realized that Stalin had consolidated his position and had the full support of the party apparatus. By the end of that year Trotsky and other opponents were removed from the Politburo. By 1929 Stalin was referred to as the "Lenin of today." Stalin's supporters occupied the key posts in both government and party, and he became the chairman of the Politburo. By 1940 he had eliminated all of the old Bolsheviks, including Trotsky, who was exiled and finally struck down by an assassin in Mexico, on Stalin's orders.

More than just an opportunist or a superbureaucrat, Stalin had his own ideological views on the future of the country. Trotsky and others had believed along with Lenin that the USSR could not survive indefinitely as a socialist island in a capitalist ocean. It was the duty, they held, of Russian Communists to push for revolution elsewhere. Stalin, less a theorist than a political realist, viewed the idea of a world revolution as premature. He correctly noted that Marxism had made little headway outside the USSR, despite the existence of what, from the Marxist standpoint, were advantageous conditions for revolution in Germany and Italy. Stalin called for a new policy of building up socialism in a single state. (Lenin had once hinted at that alternative in 1921.) He put an end to the NEP and began taking "two steps forward"—with brutal and far-reaching results.

Economics and Totalitarianism: Revolution from Above, 1928–1939

Russia had begun industrialization at a late date and from the 1890s on was continuously aware of its backwardness. The drastic destruction of World War I and civil war reversed much of the progress that had been made, and by the late 1920s Stalin was deeply concerned with the country's economic weakness. He ordered a radical overhaul of the entire country and society to make 50 years' progress in ten.

The NEP was scrapped in 1928, and Stalin imposed a series of five-year plans calling for heavy industrialization and collectivization of agriculture. Long working hours and a six-day workweek were instituted in an attempt to revolutionize the Soviet Union's economic structure. For the first time in history, a government truly controlled all significant economic activity through a central planning apparatus.

In the struggle to achieve its goals, the USSR went through what one scholar has called the "totalitarian breakthrough," encompassing "an all-out effort to destroy the basic institutions of the old order and to construct at least the framework of the new."[7]

To drive the entire population along, Stalin strengthened his secret police so that they could force the nation through what would be a decade of convulsive internal struggle. By 1939 Stalin had consolidated his personal dictatorship, at the cost of 10 to 20 million lives.

War on the Peasants

Stalin wanted to transform the peasants into a rural proletariat, raising food on state and collective farms, not on their own plots. He had little doctrinal help from Marx, who had not considered that the revolution he forecast could take place in a peasant-dominated society. Marx left little guidance about what to do with the peasants, beyond mention of collectivized agriculture. He had assumed that capitalism would convert peasants into day laborers before the socialist revolution took place; hence farming would continue, except now the state would own the farms.

Lenin's war communism programs had failed, yet Stalin went back to them as he drew up his guidelines to transform agriculture. The major problem he faced was to convince the peasants to surrender their private lands, which they had finally got in 1917, to the state and collective farms.

Under Stalin's program, the state farms *(sovkhoz)* would be owned outright by the government, which would pay the workers' wages. The collective farms *(kolkhoz)* would be created from land taken from the *kulaks*, farmers who owned implements or employed others, and from the peasants who would voluntarily accept the government's decree to merge their own holdings. *Kolkhoz* members would work the land under the management of a board of directors. At the end of the year each farm's net earnings would be totaled in cash and in kind, and the members would be paid on the basis of the amount and skill of their labor.

The theoretical advantages of large-scale mechanized farming over small-scale peasant agriculture were obvious. In addition, the government intended the reforms to permit the more efficient political education of the peasants. Further, the new programs would liquidate the *kulaks*, successful capitalist farmers who owned more property than their neighbors and who represented a disturbing element on the socialist landscape.

In actual practice, Stalin's collectivization program was a disaster. The vast majority of the peasants disagreed violently with the program. They did not want to give up their land. One of the party leaders, Lazar Kaganovich, noted that "women in the countryside in many cases played the most 'advanced' role in the reaction against collective farms." In one case in a village near Kursk, a government spokesman for collectivization came to convince the peasants to join the movement. The women, led by

Russian children help carry the propaganda for Stalin's campaign for collectivization of agriculture. The banner reads, "Everybody to the collective farm!" These happy faces belie the tragedy resulting from the collectivization program in which millions fell victim to slaughter or starvation.

Stalin and State Terror

Stalin's totalitarianism brought the development of state terror to unparalleled heights. Nadezhda Mandelstam described the nature of the terror.

When I used to read about the French Revolution as a child, I often wondered whether it was possible to survive during a reign of terror. I now know beyond doubt that it is impossible. Anybody who breathes the air of terror is doomed, even if nominally he manages to save his life. Everybody is a victim—not only those who die, but also all the killers, ideologists, accomplices and sycophants who close their eyes and wash their hands—even if they are secretly consumed with remorse at night. Every section of the population has been through the terrible sickness caused by terror, and none has so far recovered, or become fit again for normal civic life. It is an illness that is passed on to the next generation, so that the sons pay for the sins of the fathers and perhaps only the grandchildren begin to get over it—or at least it takes on a different form with them.

The principles and aims of mass terror have nothing in common with ordinary police work or with security. The only purpose of terror is intimidation. To plunge the whole country into a state of chronic fear, the number of victims must be raised to astronomical levels, and on every floor of every building there must always be several apartments from which the tenants have suddenly been taken away. The remaining inhabitants will be model citizens for the rest of their lives—this will be true for every street and every city through which the broom has swept. The only essential thing for those who rule by terror is not to overlook the new generations growing up without faith in their elders, and to keep on repeating the process in systematic fashion. Stalin ruled for a long time and saw to it that the waves of terror recurred from time to time, always on an even greater scale than before. But the champions of terror invariably leave one thing out of account—namely, that they can't kill everyone, and among their cowed, half-demented subjects there are always witnesses who survive to tell the tale.

From *Hope Against Hope: A Memoir,* by Nadezhda Mandelstam, translated from the Russian by Max Hayward. Copyright © 1970 by Atheneum Publishers. Reprinted with the permission of Atheneum Publishers, an imprint of Macmillan Publishing Company.

---

one Praskovia Avdiushenko, approached the stage and said to the spokesmen, "Ah well, come near to us." When he did, she pulled him off the stage, and a major disturbance occurred.[8] When the peasants did not flock to the government's banners, Stalin ordered harsher methods. When the class war between the poor peasants and the *kulaks* did not take place, he sent the secret police and the army to the villages. The transition to collectivization was carried out under some of the most barbarous and brutal measures ever enacted by a government against its own people.

In the tragedy that followed, millions of people, especially in the Ukraine, died from direct attack, from starvation, or in work camps. By a decree in February 1930 the state forced about one million *kulaks* off their land and took their possessions. Many peasants opposed these measures, slaughtering their herds and destroying their crops rather than hand them over to the state. In 1933 the number of horses was less than half the number there had been in 1928, and there were 40 percent fewer cattle and half as many sheep and goats.

In some sections the peasants rebelled en masse, and thousands were executed by firing squads. Villages that failed to capitulate were surrounded by army units that opened fire with machine guns. Official policy resulted in dislocation, destruction of animals and crops, and famine that claimed millions of lives. After nine years of war on the peasants, 90 percent of the land and 100 million peasants were in the collective and state farms.

At the time the atrocities accompanying Stalin's programs were largely overlooked or unknown in the West. Not until World War II was a casualty figure given, and then only casually when Stalin mentioned to British Prime Minister Winston Churchill the loss of around 10 million people. Researchers with access to archives newly opened at the end of the 1990s estimated that the actual figure exceeded 14 million.

The Five-Year Plans

Stalin introduced the system of central planning in 1928. He and his advisers assumed that by centralizing all aspects of the allocation of resources and removing market forces from the economy, they could ensure a swift buildup of capital goods and heavy industries. The five-year plans, which began in 1929, restricted the manufacture of consumer goods and abolished capitalism in the forms permitted under the NEP. Citizens were allowed to own certain types of private property, houses, furniture, clothes, and personal effects. They could not own property that could be used to make profits by hiring workers. The state was to be the only employer.

The first five-year plan called for a 250 percent increase in overall industrial productivity. The state and police turned their entire effort to this goal. Even in the chaos that occurred—buildings were erected to house nonexistent machines, and machines were shipped to places where there were no buildings— growth did take place.

The party cited statistics to prove that the plan had been achieved in four and one-half years. Whether these were accurate or not—and they have been vigorously challenged—Soviet industry and society were totally transformed. The costs were disastrous, but Stalin portrayed the Soviet Union as being in a form of war with the world, and without strength, he pointed out, the USSR would be crushed.

The second five-year plan began in 1933 and sought to resolve some of the mistakes of the first. The government placed greater emphasis on improving the quality of industrial products and on making more consumer goods. The third plan, begun in 1938, emphasized national defense. State strategies called for industrial plants to be shifted east of the Urals, and efforts were made to develop new sources of oil and other important commodities. Gigantism was the key, as the world's largest tractor factory was built in Chelyabinsk, the greatest power station in Dnepropetrovsk, and the largest automobile plant in Gorki.

The plans achieved remarkable results. In 1932 Soviet authorities claimed an increase in industrial output of 334 percent over 1914 levels; 1937 output was 180 percent over that of 1932. But the high volume of production was often tied to mediocre quality, and the achievements were gained only with an enormous cost in human life and suffering and massive damage to the environment. At first the burdensome cost of importing heavy machinery, tools, equipment, and finished steel from abroad forced a subsistence scale of living on the people. These purchases were paid for by the sale of food and raw material in the world's markets at a time when the prices for such goods had fallen drastically.

In the rush to industrialize, basic aspects of Marxism were set aside. The dictatorship *of* the proletariat increasingly became the dictatorship *over* the proletariat. Another ideological casualty was the basic concept of economic egalitarianism. In 1931 Stalin declared that equality of wages was "alien and detrimental to Soviet production" and a "*petit bourgeois* deviation." So much propaganda was used to implant this twist that the masses came to accept the doctrine of inequality of wages as a fundamental communist principle. Piecework in in-

dustry became more prevalent, and bonuses and incentives were used to speed up production. It is ironic that capitalist practices were used to stimulate the growth of the communist economy. Stalin had deviated far from the Marxist maxim of "from each according to his ability, to each according to his need." Until the 1950s centralized planning enabled the Soviets to build a powerful industrial base and survive Hitler's assault. However, by 1991 the centrally planned system collapsed—and with it the USSR.

The Great Purges

During the 1930s Stalin consolidated his hold over the Communist party and created the political system that would last until the ascent to power of Mikhail Gorbachev in 1985. Stalin established an all-powerful, personal totalitarian rule by doing away with all of his rivals, real and potential, in purges. He also took the opportunity to remove all scientific, cultural, and educational figures who did not fit in with his plans for the future. By 1939 Stalin had destroyed what was left of the Russian revolutionary tradition and replaced it with the rule of his people—the apparatchiks—who lived very well in comparison with the rest of the Soviet population.

The long arm of the secret police gathered in thousands of Soviet citizens to face the kangaroo court and the firing squad. All six original members of the 1920 Politburo who survived Lenin were purged by Stalin. Old Bolsheviks who had been loyal comrades of Lenin, high officers of the Red Army, directors of industry, and rank-and-file party members were liquidated. Millions more were sent to forced labor camps. It has been estimated that between 5 and 6 percent of the population spent time in the pretrial prisons of the secret police.

Party discipline prevented party members from turning against Stalin, who controlled the party. The world watched a series of show trials in which loyal Communists confessed to an amazing array of charges, generally tied after 1934 to the assassination of Sergei Kirov, Leningrad party chief and one of Stalin's chief aides. Western journalists reported news of the trials to the world while the drugged, tortured, and intimidated defendants confessed to crimes they had not committed. By 1939 fully 70 percent of the members of the Central Committee elected in 1934 had been purged. Among officers in the armed forces, the purges claimed three of five army marshals, 14 of 16 army commanders, all eight admirals, 60 of 67 corps commanders, 136 of 199 divisional commanders, 221 of 397 brigade commanders, and roughly one-half of the remaining officers, or some 35,000 men. A large portion of the leadership of the USSR was destroyed.

Joseph Vissarionovich Dzhugashvili, fourth from the right in the first row, chose to call himself Stalin (Steel) and came close to gaining totalitarian control of the USSR during the 1930s working through his chosen men of the apparatus the apparatchiks, pictured with him here.

In a sense the purges culminated in Mexico with Trotsky's assassination in 1940. The lessons of the purges were chilling and effective. The way to succeed, to survive, was to be devotedly, unquestioningly, a follower of Joseph Stalin.

Changes in Soviet Society

In the 20 years after 1917, all aspects of Soviet society came under the purview of the party. The atomization of society, a prime characteristic of totalitarian government, did not permit such secret, self-contained, and mutually trusting groups as the family to exist at ease. The party dealt in contradictory terms with various aspects of social life, but by and large the government worked to weaken the importance of the family until 1936. Until that time, after the Revolution, divorces required no court proceedings, abortions were legal, women were encouraged to take jobs outside the home, and communist nurseries were set up to care for children while their mothers worked. Pressure on the family continued under Stalin, but in different ways. Children were encouraged to report to the authorities "antirevolutionary" statements made by their parents.

Women paid a heavy price for the Stalin revolutions in industry and agriculture. In the cities they often did heavy labor, using the same tools and working the same hours men worked and suffering equally from the industrial accidents of the time. In the countryside they carried the burden of laboring on the collective farm, doing all of the work in the home, and doing 80 percent of the work on the private plots,

which provided food for the family and money from sales in the markets. Alarm spread in Moscow at the lack of population growth during the 1930s. By a law of June 27, 1936, intended to strengthen the family unit, it became harder to gain a divorce; abortions were prohibited; and to increase the birth rate, the government held out the promise of subsidies to women: the more children, the larger the subsidy. As one scholar noted in a study of these conditions, "having been mobilized for production, women would henceforth be mobilized for reproduction."[9]

The party did work to upgrade medical care, improve—for a time—the treatment of the more than 100 national groups that made up the USSR, and extend educational opportunities. But even here political goals outweighed humanitarian objectives. Education—almost exclusively in the Russian language—existed primarily to indoctrinate non-Russian pupils with Communist precepts and Great Russian cultural values. Religious persecution was widespread, and the strong wave of anti-Semitism seen at the end of the nineteenth century returned under Stalin. The Orthodox Church lost most of its power in education, and religious training was prohibited, except in the home.

The constitution of 1936 declared, "All power in the USSR belongs to the workers of town and country as represented by the Soviet of Workers' Deputies." Ironically, this document did not mention the Soviet Union's official ideology of Marxism-Leninism and referred only once to the Communist party. On the surface the 1936 constitution affirmed many basic rights, such as free speech, the secret ballot, and universal suffrage, but it was mere window-dressing with no effective application in reality. Secret ballots meant little in a one-party state, and the parliament of the people, the Supreme Soviet, had no power. The Communist party, with a membership of less than 1.5 percent of the total population, dictated the life of every individual.

In the first decade after the 1917 revolutions, intellectuals and artists experienced much more freedom than they would in the 1930s. The party emphasized the tenets of social realism but permitted some innovation. The Bolsheviks initially tolerated and even encouraged writers with independent leanings. Even though a large number of artists and writers fled the country after the revolts, others, including the poets Alexander Blok (1880–1921) and Vladimir Mayakovsky (1893–1930), remained and continued to write. During the NEP and after, cultural life bloomed in many areas, especially the cinema, as can be seen in the works of the great director Sergei Eisenstein (1898–1948). In music, composers Sergei Prokofiev (1891–1953) and Dmitri Shostakovich (1906–1975) contributed works that added to the world's musical treasury, although the latter had to apologize to Stalin for the "bourgeois nature" of one of his symphonies.

Once Stalin gained control, he dictated that all art, science, and thought should serve the party's program and philosophy. Artists and thinkers were to become, in Stalin's words, "engineers of the mind." Art for art's sake was counterrevolutionary. Socialist realism in its narrowest sense was to be pursued. History became a means to prove the correctness of Stalin's policies. As critics and censors tightened their control over artists and scholars, many creators and intellectuals found it safer to hew to the party line. Literary hacks and propagandists gained official favor, churning out what Western critics referred to as "tractor novels." But the citizens of the Soviet Union endured this attempt to transform them into "new Soviet people" and maintained their basic values and identities.

Italy and Mussolini

After entering the war on the Allied side in 1915, the kingdom of Italy joined the peace negotiations with great expectations. The Italians had joined the Allies with the understanding that with victory they would gain Trieste, Dalmatia, Trentino, and some territory in Asia Minor. They came away from Versailles with minor gains, not nearly enough, in their minds, to justify the deaths of 700,000 of their soldiers.

Postwar Italy suffered social and economic damage similar to that of the other combatants. Inflation—the lira fell to one-third of its prewar value—

Mussolini's Rise to Power

1919	Italian discontent with peace treaties
1919–1920	Gabriele D'Annunzio and his followers occupy Fiume
1919–1922	Series of ineffective governments and postwar economic crises
1922	Unsuccessful union antifascist protest; March on Rome; King Victor Emmanuel III asks Mussolini to form a government

and disrupted trade patterns hampered recovery. These ailments worsened the domestic crises the country had been struggling with before the war. There were not enough jobs for the returning soldiers, and unemployed veterans were ripe targets for the growing extremist parties. In some cities residents refused to pay their rent in protest over poor living conditions. In the countryside peasants took land from landlords. Everywhere food was in short supply.

In the four years after the armistice five premiers came and went, either because of their own incompetence or because of the insolubility of the problems they faced. The situation favored the appearance of a strong man, a dictator. Such a man was a blacksmith's son named Mussolini, who bore the Christian name Benito, in honor of the Mexican revolutionary hero Benito Juárez.

Benito Mussolini (1883–1945) grew up in and around left-wing political circles. Although he became editor of the influential socialist newspaper *Avanti* ("Forward") in 1912, he was far from consistent in his views and early on demonstrated his opportunism and pragmatism. When a majority of the Italian Socialist party called for neutrality in World War I, Mussolini came out for intervention. Party officials removed *Avanti* from his control and expelled him from the party. He then proceeded to put out his own paper, *Il Pòpolo d'Italia* ("The People of Italy"), in which he continued to call for Italian entry in the war on the Allied side.

To carry out his interventionist campaign, Mussolini organized formerly leftist groups into bands called *fasci*, a named derived from the Latin *fasces*, a bundle of rods bound around an ax, which was the symbol of authority in ancient Rome. When Italy entered the war, Mussolini volunteered for the army, saw active service at the front, and was wounded. When he returned to civilian life, he reorganized the *fasci* into the *fasci di combattimento* ("fighting groups") to attract war veterans and try to gain control of Italy.

The Path to Power

In the 1919 elections, the freest until 1946, the Socialists capitalized on mass unemployment and hardship to become the strongest party. But the party lacked effective leadership and failed to take advantage of its position.

Although the extreme right-wing groups did not elect a single candidate to the Chamber of Deputies, they pursued power in other ways. The fiery writer and nationalist leader Gabriele D'Annunzio (1863–1938) had occupied the disputed city of Fiume with his corps of followers, in direct violation of the mandates of the Paris peace conference. This defiance of international authority appealed to the fascist movement. D'Annunzio provided lessons for the observant Mussolini, who copied many of the writer's methods and programs, especially D'Annunzio's flare for the dramatic. During his 15-month control of Fiume, D'Annunzio and his followers wore black shirts, carried daggers, and used the so-called Roman salute—raising the right arm in a rigid, ramrod like gesture. Ironically, D'Annunzio and his band were wrong: in antiquity, slaves saluted their masters by raising their right hands; free men shook hands.[10]

The fascists gained the backing of landowning and industrial groups, who feared the victory of Marxist socialism in Italy. Mussolini's toughs beat up opponents, broke strikes, and disrupted opposition meetings in 1919 and 1920 while the government did nothing. Despite these activities, the extreme right-wing politicians still failed to dominate the 1921 elections. Only 35 fascists, Mussolini among them, gained seats in the Chamber of Deputies, while the Liberal and Democratic parties gained a plurality. Failing to succeed through the existing system, Mussolini established the National Fascist party in November.

The Liberal-Democratic government of 1922 proved as ineffective as its predecessors, and the Socialists continued to bicker among themselves. Mussolini's party, however, attracted thousands of disaffected middle-class people, cynical and opportunistic intellectuals, and workers. Frustration with the central government's incompetence, not fear of the left, fueled the fascist rise. One historian has noted, "It was not on political ideas that fascism thrived, but on the yearning for action and the opportunities it provided for satisfying this yearning."[11]

In August 1922 the trade unions called a general strike to protest the rise of fascism. Mussolini's forces smashed their efforts. In October, after a huge rally in Naples, 50,000 fascists swarmed into Rome, and soon thereafter King Victor Emmanuel III invited Mussolini to form a new government. During the next month Mussolini assembled a cabinet composed of his party members and nationalists and gained dictatorial powers to bring stability to the country. The fascists remained a distinct minority in Italy, but by gaining control of the central government they could place their members and allies in positions of power. The October March on Rome ushered in Mussolini's 20-year reign.

Building the Fascist State

The new Italian leader followed no strict ideology as he consolidated his dictatorial rule. He threw out all the democratic procedures of the postwar years and dissolved rival political parties. He and his colleagues ruthlessly crushed free expression and banished critics of their government to prison settlements off Italy's southern coast. They censored the press and set up tribunals for the defense of the state (not the citizens). Although he retained the shell of the old system, the fascist leader established a totally new state.

Mussolini controlled all real power through the Fascist Grand Council, whose members occupied the government's ministerial posts. At one time he personally held no fewer than eight offices. All this activity and centralization of power provided a striking contrast to the lethargy of the four years immediately after the war. Encouraged by the popular support for his regime, Mussolini passed a series of laws in 1925 and 1926 under which the Italian cities lost their freely elected self-governments and all units of local and provincial government were welded into a unified structure controlled from Rome.

Once he had centralized Italian political life, Mussolini pursued the development of his ideology in a pragmatic manner. As one scholar noted, "If he had any principle or prejudice it was against the capitalists, the Church, and the monarchy; all of his life he abused the bourgeoisie."[12] But he would learn to work with all of those elements in his flexible pursuit of power. He once stated in an interview, "I am all for motion."[13] Movement, not consistency and science, marked his ideology.

Early in the 1920s Mussolini, a former atheist, began to tie the church into the structure of his new society. In 1928 he negotiated the Lateran Treaty with church representatives in order to settle the longstanding controversy between Rome and the Vatican. The new pact required compulsory religious instruction and recognized Catholicism as the state religion. Vatican City, a new state of 108 acres located within Rome itself, was declared to be fully sovereign and independent. In addition the state promised the Vatican $91 million. Mussolini gained a measure of approval from devout Italians and the Vatican's support for his fascist government.

Mussolini's economic system, which has come to be known as *state capitalism*, aimed to abolish class conflict through cooperation between labor and capital, by state force if necessary. In communist theory, labor is the basis of society. In fascism, labor and capital are both instruments of the state. The fascists constructed a corporate state, in which the country was divided into *syndicates,* or corporations—13 at first, later 22. Initially, six of these came from labor and an equal number represented capital or management. The thirteenth group was established for the professions. Under state supervision, these bodies were to deal with labor disputes, guarantee adequate wage scales, control prices, and supervise working conditions. After 1926, strikes by workers and lockouts by employers were prohibited.

The pragmatic leader believed that private enterprise was the most efficient method of production: "The state intervenes in economic production only when private enterprise fails or is insufficient or when the political interests of the state are involved."[14] Mussolini liked to claim that his structure embodied a classless economic system that stood as one of fascism's greatest contributions to political theory.

Reflecting the practice of the time, the Italians sought economic self-sufficiency, especially in the areas of food supply, power resources, and foreign trade. Wheat production and hydroelectric-generating capacity both increased, but the drive for self-sufficiency was carried to an unprofitable extreme. The state, in its quest for economic independence, launched many projects to provide for a home supply of products that could be obtained much more cheaply from other nations.

State and Struggle: Mussolini's Legacy

As in the case of the other dictatorships, Mussolini's programs had some worthwhile features, including slum clearance, rural modernization, and campaigns against illiteracy and malaria. The trains *did* run on time, as Mussolini boasted, and the omnipresent Mafia was temporarily dispersed, with many of its more notable figures fleeing to the United States. But these positive achievements were more than outweighed by the ruinous war with Ethiopia (see Chapter 32), excessive military spending, and special benefits to large landowners and industrialists. In 1930 real wages remained low in comparison to the rest of industrialized Europe.

The Great Depression hit Italy later than other countries, but it lasted longer, and its effects were devastating to Mussolini's economy. The 33 percent increase in 1929 gross national product over that of 1914 was soon wiped out, and the old problems of inadequate natural resources, unfavorable balance of trade, and expanding population made the country vulnerable to economic disaster. In 1933 the number

of unemployed reached 1 million, and the public debt soared to an alarming level. Despite a reorganization of the nation in 1934 into 22 government-controlled corporations, a massive public works program, and agricultural reforms, Italy continued to suffer. In the 1930s Italy's fate and future came to be closely tied to that of Germany, whose leaders embraced the ideology haphazardly begun by Mussolini.

Mussolini's fascist ideology built on the cult of the leader, *Il Duce* ("the Great Man") and the all-powerful corporate state. But it was Mussolini's charisma that held the movement together. The Italian dictator asserted that "life for the fascist is a continuous, ceaseless fight" and that "struggle is at the origin of all things."[15] Mirroring the nonintellectual nature of its creator, fascism never had a text, as Marxism did. But its basis was an extreme nationalism that asserted that Italy in its present form was corrupt. Mussolini believed that it was possible to reattain the nation's pure form by rejecting substantial portions of the present age: in his speeches, Mussolini referred constantly to the legacy of the Roman Empire. *Il Duce* and his followers sensed that they lived at a watershed between the tarnished old and the possible gleaming new and that it was their duty to save their nation by bringing in a new breed of man.

Mussolini's movement was antiliberal, characterized by real hatred of the bourgeoisie and all that it created in the nineteenth century. *Il Duce* encouraged a high birthrate but noted that individuals were significant only insofar as they were part of the state. Children

Benito Mussolini, who wanted to portray himself as a man of strength, must have been pleased with Gerardo Dottori's Portrait of the Duce *(1933). The artist, along with others in the futurist movement, longed to escape the mediocrity of the present and looked to the promise of modern technology and the visions of science fiction.*

Military training began early in Mussolini's fascist state. There were youth organizations for every age group over the age of 4.

were indoctrinated with the party line. The movement was also anticonservative, rejecting the traditional role of the monarchy and cynically using the church. Mussolini's party rejected traditional laissez-faire capitalism and the hierarchies that came with it, and in that sense it was socialist. Rather than waiting for the "invisible hand" to furnish the motive force of their country, Italian fascists, as good totalitarians, looked to the state to engineer life at all levels. The Italian fascists were also racists and sought to link up with like-minded people

One of the most ominous acts of Mussolini's fascist regime was the burning of books and other literature deemed "subversive."

around the world. The strength of Mussolini's fascism was that it could be adapted to any ideological or cultural setting, because to be a fascist, one needed only to hate, believe, obey, and fight.[16]

Beneath the talk of struggle and the trappings of grandeur was the reality of Italy. Mussolini was no Stalin or Hitler, and his fascism was a far milder form of totalitarianism than that seen in the USSR or Germany. The Italian people simply defused many of the potentially atrocious elements of his fascist rule. There was no class destruction or genocide in Italy. The Italians, who had endured control by the Goths, the Normans, the French, and the Austrians before unification, were survivors.

The German Tragedy

In the first week of November 1918, as World War I came to a close, revolutions broke out all over Germany. Sailors stationed at Kiel rebelled; leftists in Munich revolted. The kaiser fled to the Netherlands after the authority of his government crumbled. On November 9 the chancellor transferred his power to Friedrich Ebert, leader of the majority party, the Social Democrats, and the new leader announced the establishment of a republic.

Violence spread quickly. The Spartacists, led by Karl Liebknecht and Rosa Luxemburg, who formed the German Communist party at the end of 1918, wanted a complete social and political revolution. Ebert's Social Democrats favored a democratic system in which property rights would be maintained. At the beginning of 1919 the radical and moderate socialists clashed violently. Experiments in revolutionary government in Bavaria and Berlin horrified traditionalists and even the Social Democrats. In the spring a coalition of forces ranging from moderate socialists to right-wing bands of unemployed veterans crushed the leftists and murdered Liebknecht and Luxemburg.

By the end of the year Germany had weathered the threat of a leftist revolution. Meanwhile, the moderate parties triumphed in elections to select a constitutional convention, with the Social Democrats winning the most votes. The constitution they wrote at Weimar and adopted in mid-1919 created some of the problems that would plague the new government.

The liberal document provided for a president, a chancellor who was responsible to the Reichstag, and national referenda. In addition, the constitution guaranteed the rights of labor, personal liberty, and compulsory education for everyone up to the age of 18. Once the new system was put into operation, its weaknesses were readily apparent. The multitude of parties permitted by the constitution condemned the

The Economic Cycle and the Nazis

1919	Transition to peacetime economy, massive unemployment	Formation of National Socialist German Workers' (Nazi) party, drawing from out-of-work soldiers
1923	Peak of Weimar inflation	Munich *Putsch*
1928	High point of economic normalization	Nazis have only 12 seats in the Reichstag
1930	Beginning of Great Depression	Nazis increase seats in Reichstag to 107
1932	Depth of Great Depression	Nazis make strong showing in July elections
1933	Social discontent caused by depression brings increased business support of Nazis	Hitler gains power with 44 percent of deputies, buttressed by Nationalist party's 8 percent

government to function solely by shaky coalitions that often broke apart and forced the president to rule by emergency decree, thus bypassing legal constitutional procedures.

Failure of the Weimar Republic

The new Weimar Republic faced overwhelming obstacles. First, it had to live with the stigma of having accepted the Versailles treaty, with its infamous war guilt clause. The defeatist image, combined with opposition from both right- and left-wing extremists, plagued the Weimar moderates. The myth of betrayal in accepting the Versailles treaty helped Field Marshal Paul von Hindenburg, a stalwart Prussian and war hero, win election to the presidency in 1925. In 1927 he formally renounced the theory of war guilt, a politically popular move but one with little effect on the obligation to pay reparations. Although these payments did not noticeably affect the standard of living after 1925, they continued to be a visible sign of defeat, especially since the money used to pay the victorious Allies had to come from foreign loans.

The Weimar government ruled during an economically chaotic period. The government caused inflation, wiped out savings, and destroyed much of the confidence of the middle class, shaking the resolve of the group on whom the fate of the republic rested. Even after 1923, when the economy took a turn for the better, perceptive observers noted that the new prosperity rested on shaky foundations.

During the five years before the onset of the Great Depression, Germany rebuilt its industrial plant with the most up-to-date equipment and techniques available, becoming the second-ranking industrial nation in the world, behind the United States. Rebuilding, however, was financed largely with foreign loans, including some $800 million from the Americans. In

During the Weimar period in Germany (1918–1933), George Grosz in satirical paintings such as The Pillars of Society *powerfully expressed his scorn for militarism, capitalism, the complacent middle classes, and the corrupt society of his time.*

fact, the Germans borrowed almost twice as much money as they paid out. When the short-term loans came due, the economic bubble burst.

In addition to these economic difficulties, other problems plagued the Weimar government. Many people in Germany still idealized the authoritarian Prussian state. The German general staff and its numerous and powerful supporters were not placed under effective civilian control. Disregarding the Versailles restrictions on military growth, Germany increased its armed forces in the 1920s in cooperation with the Soviet Union, the other European outcast. Probably more dangerous to the Weimar Republic's existence was that group of individuals described by Peter Gay as the *Vernunftrepublikaner,* "rational republicans from intellectual choice rather than passionate conviction." These intellectuals, politicians, and businessmen, who should have been the strength of Weimar, "learned to live with the Republic but they never learned to love it and never believed in its future."[17]

The insecurity of the middle classes was the factor most responsible for the failure of the Weimar Republic. After the war and inflation, what professionals, white-collar workers, and skilled trades people feared most was being dragged down to the level of the masses. Right-wing orators played on such fears and warned that the Weimar Republic could not stop the growth of communism. After 1929, the fear and discontent of the middle classes crystallized around their children, who blamed their parents for the catastrophe of 1918 and the humiliations that followed. German youth, many of them unemployed after 1929, repudiated the Weimar Republic and sought a new savior for their country and themselves. In their rise to power, the Nazis skillfully exploited the fears and hopes of German middle-class youth.[18]

Adolf Hitler

The man who was to "save the fatherland" came from outside its borders. Adolf Hitler (1889–1945) was born in Austria, the son of a minor customs official in the Austro-Hungarian monarchy. A mediocre student and something of a loner during his school days, he went to Vienna in 1908 hoping to become an architect or an artist. When he failed to gain admission to the art institute, he abandoned pursuing a career in art.

In the cosmopolitan capital of Vienna, surrounded by a rich diversity of nationalities and religions, Hitler formed a personal political philosophy. He avidly read pamphlets written by racists who advocated the leader concept and variations of social Darwinism. Hajo Holborn has written that it was on the basis of such "popular and often cranky and murky writings that Hitler formed his original racist and anti-Semitic ideas. [He] derived his ideology from few sources, all of them of a rather low type."[19] Anti-Semitism was a popular political platform, and the city's mayor openly espoused it. Hitler also dabbled in pan-Germanism and Marxist socialism. The swirl of ideas and theories percolated in the brain of the impoverished and aimless young man and furnished him with the motivations and ambitions that drove him forward.

A year before World War I, Hitler moved to Munich, where he earned a meager living by selling his drawings. When the conflict erupted in 1914 he joined a German regiment and was sent to France, where he fought bravely. At the time of the armistice in 1918 he was in a hospital recovering from being blinded in a gas attack. He later said that news of Germany's defeat caused him to turn his face to the wall and weep bitterly.

Following his recovery, Hitler returned to Munich, where he was hired by city authorities to act as a special agent to investigate extremists. In the line of duty he checked on a small organization called the German Workers' party. Hitler became attracted to the group's fervently nationalistic doctrine and agreed with their antidemocratic, anticommunist, and anti-Semitic beliefs. He joined the party and soon dominated it.

In 1920 the party renamed itself the National Socialist German Workers' party, the first two syllables of which are pronounced *"Nazi"* in German. That same year the party founded a newspaper to spread its views; formed a paramilitary organization from out-of-work veterans, the storm troops (*Sturmabteilung*, or SA); and adopted a symbol, the swastika set on a red background. The swastika has been used by many cultures to express the unending cycle of life. The red background symbolized the community of German blood.

More important than the party or its symbol was Hitler, who became widely known for his remarkable powers as a speaker. His ability to arouse and move mass audiences drew large crowds in Munich. Even those who hated all that he stood for were fascinated by his performances. In the early days he would hire a number of beer halls for his adherents and speed from one to the next delivering his emotion-filled message. He called for land reform, the nationalization of trusts, the abolition of all unearned incomes, expansion to include all German-speaking peoples in Europe, and the cancellation of the Versailles treaty. The points of his arguments were less important than the way he delivered them. As the ultimate demagogue, he could package his concepts to fit whatever audience he addressed, and his popularity soared.

In November 1923, at the depth of Germany's inflationary crisis, Hitler staged a *Putsch*, or revolt, in Munich. Poorly planned and premature, the attempt failed. Hitler was sent to prison after his arrest, and there, in comparatively luxurious conditions, he dictated his statement of principles in *Mein Kampf* ("My Struggle"). Far from a literary masterpiece, the work was both an autobiography and a long-winded exposition of Nazi philosophy and objectives.

In *Mein Kampf* Hitler wrote that history is fashioned by great races, of which the Aryan is the finest. The noblest Aryans, according to Hitler, are the Germans, who should rule the world. He charged that the Jews are the archcriminals of all time, that democracy is decadent, and that communism is criminal. He stated that expansion into the Soviet Ukraine and the destruction of France are rightful courses for the Germans, who will use war and force, the proper instruments of the strong, to achieve their goals. The book, initially dismissed as the ravings of a wild man, was widely read in the 1930s. Its sales made Hitler a wealthy man.

Hitler's Chance

Hitler's first attempt to take advantage of economic disaster failed, but he would not fail the second time. After 1930 the *Führer* ("leader") took advantage of the desperate conditions resulting from closed banks, 6 million unemployed, and people roaming the streets for food. Night after night civil and military police battled mobs of rioting communists and Nazis. The depression was "the last ingredient in a complicated witches' brew" that led to Hitler's takeover.[20]

The depression brought on the collapse of the moderates' position in the Weimar government. In the 1930 elections the Nazis increased their number of seats in the Reichstag (the German legislative assembly) from 12 to 107. As conditions grew worse, the hungry and frightened as well as the rich and powerful turned to Hitler. The latter groups feared the communists and saw the Führer as a useful shield against a proletarian revolution.

As the Nazi movement grew in popularity, Hitler's brilliant propaganda chief, Joseph Goebbels, used every communications device available to convert the masses to Nazism. He staged huge spectacles all over Germany in which thousands of storm troopers and the audiences themselves all became supporting players to the star of the drama, Adolf Hitler. Such controlled hysteria was more important than the message Hitler continued to repeat.

Despite Goebbels's work, Hitler lost the March 1932 presidential elections to the aged World War I hero Hindenburg. However, after a strong showing by the Nazis in the July Reichstag elections, Hindenburg, following the advice of his supporters and the business community, asked Hitler to join a coalition government. The Führer refused, demanding instead the equivalent of dictatorial power.

The stalemate led to the dissolution of the Reichstag in September, and for the next two months the

Adolf Hitler's ability to communicate effectively and persuasively with a majority of the German population was a major asset in his rise to power and popularity. Here he is shown (front right) speaking with young members of his Nazi party.

government limped along until a second general election was held. This costly campaign nearly emptied the Nazis' treasury. It was also politically costly in that they lost some of their seats in the Reichstag.

Some observers believed that the Nazis had passed the crest of their power. At this critical point, however, a clique of aristocratic nationalists and powerful industrialists, fearing a leftist revolution, offered Hitler the chancellorship. In January 1933 a mixed cabinet was created with Hitler at the head. Because he did not have a clear majority in the Reichstag, Hitler called another general election for March 5.

The Nazis used all the muscle at their disposal during this campaign. They monopolized the radio broadcasts and the press, and their storm troopers

bullied and beat the voters. Many Germans became disgusted with the strong-arm methods, and the tide definitely swung against the Nazis. Hitler needed a dramatic incident to gain a clear majority in the election.

On the evening of February 27, a fire gutted the Reichstag building. The blaze had been set by a 24-year-old Dutchman, Marinus van der Lubbe, as a statement against capitalism. Apparently acting alone, van der Lubbe gave the Nazis the issue they needed to mobilize their support. Goebbels's propaganda machine went into action to blame the fire on the international communist movement. Uncharacteristically, the propaganda minister overplayed the story, and most of the outside world came to believe that the Nazis themselves had set the fire.

Discovery Through Maps

German Racial Types

As we have seen, maps are created in a number of different formats to guide people from one point to another and to describe physical and geographical features. In pursuit of their pseudoscientific racial theories, the Nazis took it on themselves to establish a different kind of map to enable their followers to chart their way between good Germans and *Untermenschen* (subhumans).

Denying that the term *German* was merely a linguistic designation, Hitler's supporters confronted the complexity of determining what a proper German should look like. This chart, a so-called "race identification table," presents profiles and full-face portrayals of the six purported "German races." The chart was to

enable Nazi supporters to determine at a glance who was and was not a German. No scientist in Germany dared to protest that there was absolutely no scientific basis for charts such as this.

It is a measure of the power Hitler held over his people that his bogus racial theories were widely accepted and that he could get the scientific community to support his ideas. That the German people, either through silent acquiescence or overt enthusiasm, could embrace the genocidal consequences of these theories still stands as one of the most profoundly disturbing legacies of the Third Reich—a legacy seen in the "ethnic cleansing" of Bosnia and Kosovo and in the destruction of the Tutis in Rwanda in the 1990s.

Hitler may not have made much profit from the incident internationally, but he did use it to win the election. The Nazis captured 44 percent of the deputies, a result which—with the 8 percent controlled by the Nationalist party—gave them a bare majority. Quickly, Hitler's forces put through the Enabling Act, which gave the Führer the right to rule by decree for the next four years.

Every aspect of the Weimar government was overturned, legally. The Nazis crushed all opposition parties and put aside the Weimar constitution, which was never formally abolished. Germany for the first time became a unitary national, rather than federal, state. After Hindenburg died in 1934, Hitler became both chancellor and president. As if to put the world on no-

tice that a renewed German force was rising in central Europe, he withdrew Germany from the League of Nations in 1933. Two years later he introduced conscription, in defiance of the Versailles treaty.

Hitler proclaimed his regime the Third Reich, succeeding the First Reich of Otto the Great, which had lasted from 962 to 1806, and Bismarck's Second Reich, from 1871 to 1918. Hitler quickly introduced aspects of his Nazi variant of fascism, which was much more pernicious than Mussolini's. Hitler's ideology united the diverse Germans and expressed resentment against the rapid industrialization that had cut many of the people away from their traditional values. But it was primarily the racist elements of Aryan supremacy and hatred of the Jews that set Nazism apart.

War on the Jews

An essential part of the Nazi ideology was an absolute hatred of the Jews, an element of society the Nazis considered unfit to continue in the new world they envisioned. After crushing all opposition, real and potential, Hitler began to destroy the Jews. When he took power, there were only 500,000 Jews out of a population of 66 million Germans. Since 1880 the number of Jews in the population had been declining and would have continued to do so through assimilation. Hitler, however, proclaimed that Jews were everywhere, plotting to gain control of the world, and he pledged to destroy them. His beliefs reflected his own contempt for the Jews, not any demographic reality.

All Jewish officials in the government lost their jobs, Jews were forbidden to pursue their business and industrial activities, and Jewish businesses were boycotted. Non-Jews snatched up at bargain prices valuable properties formerly owned by Jews. Non-Jewish doctors and lawyers profited when Jewish professionals were forced from their practices. Hitler gained solid supporters among the business and professional classes as he pursued his racist policies. Germans willingly believed that the Jews deserved their fate as the price they had to pay for the Versailles treaty, for the harmful aspects of capitalism, and for internationalism. Half-hearted international protests failed to limit the anti-Semitic policies. Hitler had many fervent supporters both inside and outside Germany.

The Nazis set to building concentration camps; in time these would turn into death camps. In the meantime, the immediate pressures of government policies pushed many Jews into committing suicide. It has been estimated that in 1933 alone, 19,000 German citizens killed themselves and 16,000 more died from unexplained causes.

In 1935 the so-called Nuremberg laws came into force. Marriages between Aryans and non-Aryans were forbidden. Jews (defined as all persons with one-fourth or more Jewish blood) lost their citizenship, and anti-Semitic signs were posted in all public places. (During the 1936 Berlin Olympic Games, these notices were taken down so as not to upset visitors.) Increasingly, there was public mention of the "inferior blood" of the Jews. As the state came to need more and more money for armaments, the Jews would be made to pay. This enterprise reached a climax with vicious attacks on Jews and their businesses and synagogues on November 9, 1938, known as *Kristallnacht*, the "Night of Broken Glass." Nazi sympathizers smashed the windows of 7500 shops and burned 267 synagogues, killing 91 people in the process. The police rounded up 30,000 Jews and sent them to concentration camps. Adding insult to injury, "a fine of one billion marks was imposed on the Jewish community in retaliation for the murder of a German diplomat in Paris."[21]

Attacked, deprived of their citizenship and economic opportunities, and barred from public service, the Jews of Germany, who considered themselves good German citizens, bore the barbaric blows with remarkable resilience. Some, including a number of Germany's best scientific minds, were able to flee the country—a loss that may well have doomed Hitler's efforts in World War II. Most stayed. They, like the outside world, which showed little concern, did not realize that Hitler's true goal was the "Final Solution," the extermination of the Jews. His mad quest, known as the Holocaust, would lead to the deaths of more than 6 million Jews throughout all of Europe and the USSR and at least 4 million others not lucky enough to be "Aryan."

The Nazi Impact on Culture, Church, Education, and Society

Hitler and Goebbels controlled all of the media in the totalitarian Third Reich. A Reich culture cabinet was set up to instill a single pattern of thought in literature, the press, broadcasting, drama, music, art, and the cinema. Forbidden books, including works of some of Germany's most distinguished writers, were seized and destroyed in huge bonfires. The cultural

In his Self-Portrait with a Jewish Identity Card *(1943), Felix Nussbaum visually defines the sheer terror, anxiety, and helplessness felt by Jews under the Third Reich. Nussbaum and his wife were arrested in 1944; both died at the Auschwitz extermination camp.*

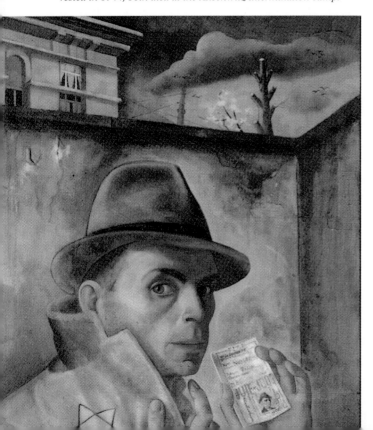

vitality of the Weimar Republic, represented by the likes of Thomas Mann, Erich Maria Remarque, Kurt Weill, and Bertolt Brecht, was replaced by the sterile social realism of the Third Reich.

Religion became entrapped in the totalitarian mechanism. Since Nazism elevated the state above all else, a movement was started to subordinate religion to the Hitler regime. The organized churches originally backed the Nazis warmly, until it became apparent that they were to serve the larger aim of the Aryan cause. The Protestant churches suffered under the Nazi attempt to make them an arm of the state, and several dissident ministers were imprisoned. By the end of the decade the Catholic Church too came under subtle but constant attack.

German universities, once renowned for their academic freedom, became agencies for propagating the racial myths of Nazism and for carrying out far-fetched experiments in human genetic engineering on selected concentration camp inmates. Only good Nazis could go to universities, and professors who did not cooperate with the regime were fired. As Jacob Bronowski wrote, "When Hitler arrived in 1933 the tradition of scholarship in Germany was destroyed, almost overnight."[22]

The state used mass popular education, integrated with the German Youth movement, to drill and regiment boys and girls to be good Nazis. Boys learned above all else to be ready to fight and die for their Führer. The girls were prepared for their ultimate task, bearing and rearing the many babies to be needed by the Third Reich.

When they took power, the Nazis made it clear that they viewed the political and professional activity of women during the Weimar period as a sign of general decadence. Like the other authoritarian states in the 1930s, they declared that the prime role of women was to stay home and bear children—in this case, racially pure German children. As in Stalin's USSR, the state gave subsidies and other financial incentives to large families, and abortion was illegal. However, after 1937, women were first encouraged—and six years later compelled—to contribute to the economy by performing whatever work the state demanded—usually in armaments factories and always at lower wages than received by men. As in Stalin's Soviet Union, the women also had to bear the burden of their housework, carrying a disproportionate share of the workload.

Economic Policies

As in Italy, fascism in Germany revolved around a form of state capitalism. In theory and practice, Nazism retained capitalism and private property. The state, however, rigidly controlled both business and labor. The Nazis dissolved labor unions and enrolled

This painting shows a blissful Nazi family, close to nature, with the blond mother carrying out her duties of bearing and bringing up children for the Third Reich while the sturdy and caring father watches over his nursing baby.

workers and employers in a new organization, the Labor Front. As in Mussolini's corporate state, the right of the workers to strike or of management to call a lockout was denied. The Nazis took compulsory dues from the workers' wages to support Nazi organizations. As a sop, the state set up the "Strength Through Joy" movement, which provided sports events, musical festivals, plays, movies, and vacations at low cost.

The Nazis' ultimate goal was self-sufficiency—autarky—which they would try to reach through complete state control of the economy. They assumed, as the fascists did in Italy, that only the state could ensure the social harmony needed to attain the maximum productive potential for the state's benefit.

The government tried to solve the nation's very serious economic problems by confiscating valuable Jewish property, laying a huge tax load on the middle class, and increasing the national debt by one-third to provide work for the unemployed. To create jobs, the first four-year plan, established in 1933, undertook an extensive program of public works and rearmament. The unemployed were put to work on public projects (especially noteworthy was the system of superhighways, the *Autobahnen*), in munitions factories, and in the army.

Overlapping the first program, the second four-year plan was initiated in 1936. The objective of this plan was to set up an autarkist state. In pursuit of self-sufficiency, substitute commodities—frequently inferior in quality and more costly than similar goods available on the world market—were produced by German laboratories, factories, and mills. The gross national product increased by 68 percent by 1938, but the standard of living did not rise in proportion to the higher economic growth rate. When World War II began in 1939, German industry still produced insufficient munitions, even after Hitler took over the Czech Skoda works. Germany's war economy did not hit its stride until 1942.

By then the economic picture didn't matter. Hitler controlled Germany. How an advanced, "civilized" nation like Germany could have thrown itself willingly under this madman's control is one of history's great questions. Other nations had stronger authoritarian traditions, greater economic problems, and more extreme psychological strain. Some observers maintain that there could have been no Third Reich without this unprecedented demagoguery. That Germany followed the path it did is due solely to the chance juxtaposition of Hitler's personality with the disruptive circumstances of the postwar world.

Conclusion

The Soviet Union, Italy, and Germany each had separate and distinct cultural, social, and political roots that gave unique qualities to their authoritarian governments. However, each of the states shared similar circumstances. Each faced economic upheavals, had weak traditions of liberal rule, and turned up ambitious individuals ready to take command. In the absence of dynamic democratic forces at home, these circumstances produced the interwar government structures of the totalitarian states.

To be sure, the communists and the fascists differed in theory: the fascists used capitalism while the communists opposed it; fascism emphasized nationalism while communism preached internationalism; fascism had a weak dogmatic basis while communism was based on Marx's scientific socialism; fascism made use of religion while communism attacked it. But by 1939 the common interests of the

totalitarian states, fascist or communist, were much more important than the theoretical differences. Although they may have been philosophically separate, in their domination of the individual the totalitarian states were remarkably similar.

But the two authoritarian alternatives bequeated two radically different ideological legacies. Joseph Stalin destroyed the Russian revolutionary tradition and dealt a massive blow to the international communist movement, as can be seen in the works of George Orwell and Arthur Koestler. What survived after World War II had precious little to do with Marx or the NEP of Lenin. Instead, Stalin struggled to impose the failed dreams of war communism until his death in 1953 and left behind a bunch of self-interested apparatchiks who survived through inertia until the 1980s. Mussolini and Hitler, on contrast, left an ideological legacy that remains attractive to a violent minority of disillusioned people throughout the Western world.

Suggestions for Reading

Attempts to analyze the new forms of government in the twentieth century have occupied Hannah Arendt in *The Origins of Totalitarianism* (Harcourt, Brace & World, 1968), Eugene Weber in *Varieties of Fascism* (Krieger, 1982), and C. J. Friedrich and Zbigniew K. Brzezinski in *Totalitarianism, Dictatorship and Autocracy* (Praeger, 1966). Novelist Arthur Koestler has perhaps best captured the essence of the diminution of the individual in *Darkness at Noon* (Signet, 1961).

Orlando Figes provides an excellent perspective of Russia's inability to avoid revolution in *A People's Tragedy: The Russian Revolution, 1894–1924* (Penguin, 1998). Michael Florinsky's analysis of the forces destroying the tsarist regime, *The End of the Russian Empire* (Collier, 1961), is still useful. The best overall survey of Russian history in this century remains Donald W. Treadgold, *Twentieth-Century Russia* (Houghton Mifflin, 1981). A thorough analysis of the infrastructure crisis that doomed the tsarist system is Lars T. Lih, *Bread and Authority in Russia, 1914–1921* (University of California Press, 1990). The best study of the first of the 1917 revolutions is Tsuyoshi Hasegawa, *The February Revolution: Petrograd, 1917* (University of Washington Press, 1981). Alec Nove, *The Soviet Economic System* (Allen & Unwin, 1977), is an essential study. Beatrice Farnsworth and Lynne Viola, eds., *Russian Peasant Women* (Oxford University Press, 1992), is a valuable collection of articles on rural women before and after the revolutions of 1917. See also Wendy Z. Goldman, *Women, the State and Revolution: Soviet Family Policy and Social Life, 1917–1936* (Cambridge University Press, 1993). Important social changes that occurred in the Soviet Union are discussed in H. Kent Geiger, *The Family in Soviet Russia* (Harvard University Press, 1968).

Bertram D. Wolfe, *Three Who Made a Revolution* (Scarborough House, 1987), is a classic study of Lenin, Trotsky, and Stalin. Adam Ulam, *The Bolsheviks* (Macmillan, 1964), gives a clear discussion of the party's development, while Stephen F. Cohen, *Bukharin and the Bolshevik Revolution* (Random House, 1974), provides another perspective. John L. H. Keep dissects the multifaceted and complex actions of the various elements in Petrograd in *The Russian Revolution: A Study in Mass Mobilization* (Norton, 1977). Robert Vincent Daniels, *Red October: The Bolshevik Revolution of 1917* (Beacon Press, 1984), gives scholarly depth to the journalistic enthusiasm of John Reed in *Ten Days That Shook the World* (Vintage, 1960). For a valuable view of the mentality of the postrevolutionary time, see Richard Stites, *Revolutionary Dreams: Utopia, Dreams, and Experimental Life in the Russian Revolution* (Oxford University Press, 1991).

The most detailed analysis of the Russian revolutions and their aftermath is the multivolumed work of Edward H. Carr, *The Russian Revolution* (Pelican, 1966). A discussion of the revolutionary aftermath in the outlying areas appears in Richard E. Pipes, *The Formation of the Soviet Union* (Harvard University Press, 1964). The civil war is nicely outlined in J. F. N. Bradley, *Civil War in Russia, 1917–1920* (Batsford, 1975). George F. Kennan has written the best analysis of Western relations with the young Soviet regime in *Decision to Intervene* (Princeton University Press, 1958) and *Russia and the West Under Lenin and Stalin* (Mentor, 1961). Louis Fischer, *The Soviets in World Affairs* (Vintage, 1960), is a thorough discussion of East-West relations in the 1920s. Sheila Fitzpatrick, *The Russian Revolution, 1917–1932* (Oxford University Press, 1982), is a first-rate analysis that establishes the themes undergirding the Stalinist society that emerged in the 1930s. Isaac Deutscher has written two sharply drawn biographies: *Stalin: A Political Biography* (Vintage, 1961) and *Trotsky* (Vintage, 1965). Placed in the context of Alexander Rabinowitch, *The Bolsheviks Come to Power* (Norton, 1978), Deutscher's biographies provide a compelling description of the generation after 1917.

Robert C. Tucker has compiled the most complete set of analyses of the influence of this century's most powerful man in *Stalinism* (Norton, 1977). For a Russian view of Stalin, see Dmitri Volkogonov, *Stalin: Triumph and Tragedy* (Prima, 1996). The relationship between Marxist ideals and the peasantry is discussed in David Mitrany, *Marx Against the Peasant* (Collier, 1961). For his impact on science, see Nikolai Krementsov, *Stalinist Science* (Princeton University Press, 1997). Stalin's purges are thoroughly analyzed in Robert Conquest, *The Great Terror* (Penguin, 1971). Conquest details the campaign against the peasantry in *Harvest of Sorrow* (Oxford University Press, 1986) and the prison camp system in *Kolyma: The Arctic Death Camps* (Viking, 1978). The most passionate description of the labor camps is Alexander Solzhenitsyn, *The Gulag Archipelago* (Harper & Row, 1973). R. Medvedev approaches the same subject from another perspective in *Let History Judge* (Random House, 1973). The response of some Western intellectuals to events in the Soviet Union is covered in David Caute, *The Fellow Travelers* (Macmillan, 1973). On the traumatic legacy of the time, see Adam Hochschild, *The Unquiet Ghost: Russians Remember Stalin* (Penguin, 1995).

Essential introductions and guides to the complex world of fascism are Stanley G. Payne, *A History of Fascism, 1914–1945* (University of Wisconsin Press, 1995), and Roger Griffin, ed., *Fascism: An Oxford Reader* (Oxford University Press, 1995). Events in Italy are concisely and clearly detailed in Christopher Seton-Watson, *Italy from Liberalism to Fascism, 1870–1925* (Methuen, 1967). A collection of Mussolini's ideas has been compiled in Benito Mussolini, *Fascism: Doctrine and Institution* (Fertig, 1968). A clear and concise study of Italy under Mussolini is Elizabeth Wiskemann, *Fascism in Italy: Its Development and Influence* (St. Martin's Press, 1969). A more detailed discussion of the fascist advance can be found in Adrian Lyttelton, *The Seizure of Power: Fascism in Italy, 1919–1929* (Scribner, 1973).

Weimar Germany's brief time in the sun can be studied in A. J. Ryder, *Twentieth-Century Germany: From Bismarck to Brandt* (Columbia University Press, 1973), and Erich Eyck, *History of the Weimar Republic* (Atheneum, 1962). Two works by Peter Gay, *Weimar Culture* (Torchbooks, 1968) and *Freud, Jews, and Other Germans* (Oxford University Press, 1979), are penetrating studies of a turbulent time. Fritz Stern, *The Politics of Cultural Despair* (University of California Press, 1974), and George L. Mosse, *The Crisis of German Ideology* (Grosset & Dunlap, 1964), are essential to understand the mental underpinnings supporting the rise of Hitler. Andreas Dorpalen, *Hindenburg and the Weimar Republic* (Princeton University Press, 1964), examines the dilemma faced by liberals in the 1920s. J. P. Nettl, *Rosa Luxemburg* (Oxford University Press, 1966), is a fine study of the socialists' dilemma in Germany. The role of propaganda in Hitler's rise to power is studied in Russell G. Lemmons, *Goebbels and Der Angriff: Nazi Propaganda, 1927–1933* (University Press of Kentucky, 1994).

Alan Bullock, *Hitler: A Study in Tyranny* (Torchbooks, 1964), remains the best biography, supplemented by Bullock's *Hitler and Stalin: Parallel Lives* (Vintage, 1993). John Toland, *Adolf Hitler* (Ballantine, 1977), is more readable. William S. Allen, *Nazi Seizure of Power: The Experience of a Single Town, 1930–1935* (New Viewpoints, 1969), makes Hitler's takeover more comprehensible. The challenge to the Christian churches at that time is studied in Jack Forstman, *Christian Faith in Dark Times: Theological Conflict in the Shadow of Hitler* (Westminster/John Knox, 1992). Arthur Schweitzer, *Big Business in the Third Reich* (Indiana University Press, 1977), details the collaboration between capitalism and fascism. Alan D. Beyerchen, *Scientists Under Hitler* (Yale University Press, 1977), shows institutional responses to the Führer. Karl Dietrich Bracher gives a good structural analysis of fascism in operation in *The German Dictatorship* (Praeger, 1970). David Schoenbaum discusses the social effects of the Nazis in *Hitler's Social Revolution: Class and Status in Nazi Germany* (Norton, 1997). Samuel W. Mitcham Jr., *Why Hitler? The Genesis of the Nazi Reich* (Praeger, 1996), gives a thorough, clear analysis of the victory of Hitler in Germany.

Suggestions for Web Browsing

Library of Congress: Soviet Archive Exhibit
http://www.ncsa.uiuc.edu/SDG/Experimental/soviet.exhibit/soviet.archive.html

A magnificent exhibition at the Library of Congress on the Soviet years. Documents on both the foreign and domestic aspects of the USSR, with stunning evidence concerning collectivization.

A USSR Purge Trial
http://art-bin.com/art/omosc20e.html

A transcript from a purge trial. One can see the methods of Andrei Vyshinsky as he grills I. N. Smirnov.

The Italian Fascist Youth Movement
http://www.library.wisc.edu/libraries/dpf/fascism/youth.html

A spectacular collection of images in the Italian Fascist Youth Movement from University of Wisconsin's superb Fascism series, Italian Life Under Fascism.

The Time of Adolf Hitler in Photos and Maps
http://motlc.wiesenthal.com/pages/t030/t003022.html

The Simon Wiesenthal Center provides a rich collection of photos of Adolf Hitler's time in power. With each selection there is interpretive text and maps.

Notes

1. Leonard Schapiro, "Totalitarianism," *Survey*, Autumn 1969.
2. Novelist Alexander Solzhenitsyn captures the mood in *August 1914*, trans. Michael Glenny (New York: Bantam Books, 1974), ch. 7.
3. Bernard Pares, "Rasputin and the Empress, Authors of the Russian Collapse," *Foreign Affairs*, Oct. 1927, p. 140.
4. *The New Cambridge Modern History*, Vol. 12 (Cambridge: Cambridge University Press, 1960), p. 9.
5. J. N. Westwood, *Endurance and Endeavour: Russian History, 1812–1986* (Oxford: Oxford University Press, 1987), p. 276.
6. Isaac Deutscher, *Stalin: A Political Biography* (New York: Vintage Books, 1961), p. 91.
7. Zbigniew M. Brzezinski, "The Nature of the Soviet System," in Donald W. Treadgold, ed., *The Development of the USSR* (Seattle: University of Washington Press, 1964), pp. 6–8.
8. Lynne Viola, "Bab'i i Bunty and the Peasant Worker's Protest During Collectivization," in Beatrice Farnsworth and Lynne Viola, eds., *Russian Peasant Women* (Oxford: Oxford University Press, 1992), pp. 191, 198.
9. Robert Manning, "Women in the Soviet Countryside on the Eve of World War II, 1935–1940," in Farnsworth and Viola, *Russian Peasant Women*, pp. 206–207.
10. Gaetano Salvemini, *The Origins of Fascism in Italy* (New York: Harper Torchbooks, 1973), p. 229
11. Christopher Seton-Watson, *Italy from Liberalism to Fascism, 1870–1925* (London: Methuen, 1967), p. 518
12. Elizabeth Wiskemann, *Fascism in Italy: Its Development and Influence* (New York: St. Martin's Press, 1969), p. 12.
13. Benito Mussolini, *Fascism: Doctrine and Institutions* (New York: Fertig, 1968), p. 38.
14. Wiskemann, *Fascism in Italy*, p. 23.
15. Mussolini, *Fascism*, pp. 35, 38.
16. Roger Griffin, ed., *Fascism: An Oxford Reader* (Oxford, Oxford University Press, 1995), pp. 2–9.
17. Peter Gay, *Weimar Culture* (New York: Harper Torchbooks, 1968), p. 23.
18. See Peter D. Stachura, *The German Youth Movement* (New York: St. Martin's Press, 1981).
19. Hajo Holborn, *Germany and Europe: Historical Essays* (New York: Anchor Books, 1971), p. 222.
20. David S. Landes, *The Unbound Prometheus: Technological Change and Industrial Development in Western Europe from 1750 to the Present* (Cambridge: Cambridge University Press, 1969), p. 398.
21. A. J. Ryder, *Twentieth-Century Germany: From Bismarck to Brandt* (New York: Columbia University Press, 1973), p. 348.
22. Jacob Bronowski, *The Ascent of Man* (Boston: Little, Brown, 1973), p. 367.

Jordan water for the United States. World War I ended the centuries-long dominance of the Ottoman Empire in the Middle East, and the interwar years were marked by colonization, the forging of new nations, and contests for political and economic control of "sacred" space. The Holy Land of Palestine, sacred to Jews, Christians, and Muslims was one of those spaces. In this photo, entrepreneurs, stand next to barrels of water from the Jordan River destined for use in baptizing Christians in New York City.

Emerging National Movements in Asia and Africa, 1920s to 1950s

Chapter Contents

Fifty years of aggressive expansion by the West had spread European ideas, factories, and colonists to much of the world. Those African and Asian societies that were not directly colonized by European powers were nonetheless dramatically influenced by the politics, cultures, and economies of imperialist Western states. It was in the period between the world wars and immediately afterward that many of these societies adopted—or had imposed on them—the nation-state model of political organization. During this period certain African and Asian peoples who had been subordinated to Europe began to gain their political independence.

But European imperialism is only one element, albeit an important one, of the evolution of African and Asian states in this time frame. This era also witnessed a dramatic movement of people from the countryside to the city, with the accompanying social and economic turmoil. The modernization processes that gained momentum in the nineteenth century in the realms of industrialization, education, transportation, and communication remained vigorous. New leaders emerged, and there was a radical transformation in systems of government, law, economics, and traditional social values. While many areas of Africa and the Middle East retained their traditional agrarian economies, others lost or abandoned traditional modes of economic organization. Often this caused dramatic changes in the lives of individuals and families within a single generation.

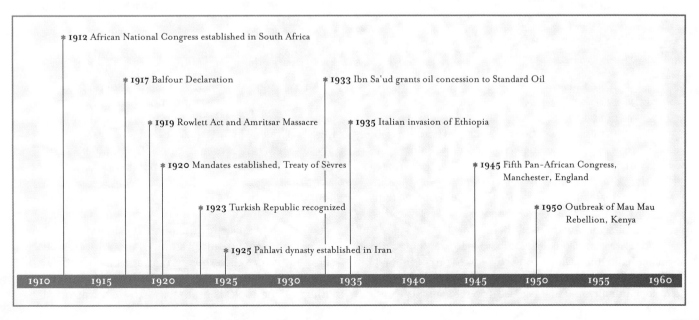

* **1912** African National Congress established in South Africa

* **1917** Balfour Declaration

* **1919** Rowlett Act and Amritsar Massacre

* **1920** Mandates established, Treaty of Sèvres

* **1923** Turkish Republic recognized

* **1925** Pahlavi dynasty established in Iran

* **1933** Ibn Sa'ud grants oil concession to Standard Oil

* **1935** Italian invasion of Ethiopia

* **1945** Fifth Pan-African Congress, Manchester, England

* **1950** Outbreak of Mau Mau Rebellion, Kenya

1910　1915　1920　1925　1930　1935　1940　1945　1950　1955　1960

World War I and its aftershocks strengthened independence movements in Africa and Asia, in part because the power of the dominant imperial states—Britain, France, and Germany—had been diminished by the war. Nationalist campaigns, present in embryonic form in most of the colonies before the war, grew rapidly in virtually all of the European possessions and mandates. Japan emerged as a world power, but by the late 1920s the impact of a depression and a population crisis threatened its democratic institutions. China endured revolution and civil strife as the areas of Southeast Asia pursued independence. India's independence movement gained powerful support under the influence of Mohandas Gandhi and his tactic of nonviolence. Across the Middle East and Africa, nations struggled to redefine themselves and to throw off the yoke of European domination.

Japan

Japan's victory over Russia in the 1904–1905 Russo-Japanese War served notice of the success of the Meiji era reforms. In two generations the island chain had changed from a static, mostly agricultural nation into a modern, highly industrialized state. In the government liberal statesmen tried to strengthen democratic practices. They faced serious problems. The rapidly increasing population strained the nation's limited size and resources. Ten years after World War I, economic pressures combined with a revival of militarism to launch the Japanese toward war and dictatorship.

Authoritarian Victory

From 1889 to 1918 an aristocratic oligarchy of elder statesmen called the *Genro* controlled the Japanese government. By the 1920s most of the patriarchs had passed away and the field of politics was open to new blood. Hara Takashi, the first commoner to hold the post of prime minister, was elected to the office in 1918.

Over the next 12 years Japan seemed to be moving toward the establishment of a democratic, parliamentary government under its new political leaders. However, the liberals faced serious obstacles. There was no widespread tradition of democratic or parliamentary practices in Japan. Japanese society had concentrated wealth and power in the hands of a few families, while the traditional culture encouraged a militaristic system of values. The secret societies and the cult of Shinto favored authoritarianism over liberalism.

Despite these obstacles, liberals in the Japanese parliament, the Diet, showed great promise and courage as they tried to lead the nation away from militant nationalism. They pressed for reforms at home

while criticizing the imperialistic intervention of the Japanese army in Siberia during the Russian civil war. Although the democratic cause suffered a serious setback in 1921 with the assassination of Prime Minister Hara, the liberals continued their work. Passage of the Universal Manhood Suffrage Bill in 1925 strengthened the liberal base. By 1930, after a reactionary interlude, Prime Minister Hamaguchi Yuko established the most liberal government Japan had ever had.

As in Europe, as long as the economy remained strong, the liberals did well. In the 1920s the Japanese built thousands of factories that turned out products enabling Japan to claim a major share of the world textile market and to flood the world with mass-produced, cheap, low-quality goods. Japanese industrialists were quick to adopt modern machine techniques and slow to raise wages. A few giant concerns working together controlled the greater part of the country's wealth.

Prosperity—and by implication the liberals' position—rested on fragile foundations. Japan lacked natural resources, and its population grew at a rapid rate. In 1920 there were more than 55 million inhabitants. Eleven years later there were 65 million people, crowded into a land area smaller than the state of California. By 1932 a million people were being added each year. The Japanese economy had to create 250,000 jobs yearly and find food to feed the growing population. Japan had been paying its way by expanding exports. But between 1929 and 1931 the effects of the Great Depression cut export trade in half. Unemployment soared, leading to wage cuts and strikes. As in Germany on the eve of Hitler's rise to power, frustration became widespread among the younger generation.

In response to the economic crisis, Prime Minister Hamaguchi adopted measured fiscal reforms and a moderate foreign policy. The first approach failed to satisfy the workers, and the second one offended the militarists. Hamaguchi was shot in November 1930 and died the following spring. The assassin's bullets dealt a blow to Japanese liberalism from which it did not recover until after World War II.

A new group of ultranationalistic and militaristic leaders came to power, ruling not through a charismatic leader, as in Germany and Italy, but through a military clique. The members of the clique, who had nothing but contempt for democracy and peaceful policies, terrorized the civilian members of the government, plotted to shelve parliamentary government, and planned to use force on the mainland of China. Their goals were to gain resources for the economy, living space for the population, markets for Japanese goods, and cultural domination throughout Asia. They referred to their program as a "beneficial mission" and called it the "New Order in Asia." The military clique took its first step with the invasion of

Kita Ikki's Plan for Japan

While liberal Europe struggled with the burdens of victory, Japan experimented with a variety of governmental approaches. A radical social and economic concept was enunciated by Kita Ikki, who was executed in 1937.

Suspension of the Constitution: In order to establish a firm base for national reorganization, the Emperor, with the aid of the entire Japanese nation and by invoking his imperial prerogatives, shall suspend the Constitution for a period of three years, dissolve the two houses of the Diet, and place the entire country under martial law.

The true significance of the Emperor: We must make clear the fundamental principle that the Emperor is the sole representative of the people and the pillar of the state. . . .

Abolition of the peerage system: By abolishing the peerage system, we shall be able to remove the feudal aristocracy which constitutes a barrier between the Emperor and the people. In this way the spirit of the Meiji Restoration shall be proclaimed. . . .

The members of the Deliberative Council shall consist of men distinguished in various fields of activities, elected by each other or appointed by the Emperor.

Limitation on private property: No Japanese family shall possess property in excess of one million yen. A similar limitation shall apply to Japanese citizens holding property overseas. No one shall be permitted to make a gift of property to those related by blood or to others, or to transfer his property by other means with the intent of circumventing this limitation.

Nationalization of excess amount over limitation on private property: Any amount which exceeds the limitation on private property shall revert to the state without compensation. No one shall be permitted to resort to the protection of present laws in order to avoid remitting such excess amount. Anyone who violates these provisions shall be deemed a person thinking lightly of the example set by the Emperor and endangering the basis of national reorganization. As such, during the time martial law is in effect, he shall be charged with the crimes of endangering the person of the Emperor and engaging in internal revolt and shall be punished by death.

Limitation on private landholding: No Japanese family shall hold land in excess of 100,000 yen in current market value. . . .

Lands held in excess of the limitation on private landholding shall revert to the state. . . .

Distribution of profits to workers: One half of the net profits of private industries shall be distributed to workers employed in such industries. . . .

Continuation of the conscript system: The state, having rights to existence and development among the nations of the world, shall maintain the present conscript system in perpetuity. . . .

Positive right to start war: In addition to the right to self-defense, the state shall have the right to start a war on behalf of other nations and races unjustly oppressed by a third power. (As a matter of real concern today, the state shall have the right to start a war to aid the independence of India and preservation of China's integrity.)

As a result of its own development, the state shall also have the right to start a war against those nations who occupy large colonies illegally and ignore the heavenly way of the co-existence of all humanity. (As a matter of real concern today, the state shall have the right to start a war against those nations which occupy Australia and Far Eastern Siberia for the purpose of acquiring them.)

From David John Lu, *Sources of Japanese History*, Vol. 2 (New York: McGraw-Hill, 1974). Reprinted by permission of the publisher.

Manchuria in 1931, setting off a sequence of aggression that would lead to World War II.

The Asian Great Power

Despite dramatic domestic institutional and social changes, Japan's goals in China remained remarkably consistent after the Meiji Restoration. In 1914 the Japanese ordered the Germans to remove their warships from the Far East and to surrender Kiaochow in China to them. When the Germans refused to reply to this order, Japan declared war on Germany and seized the territory without consulting China. In 1915 Japan presented China with the Twenty-One Demands, a document whose frank statement of Japan's aims on the Asian continent startled the world.

The Chinese government, weakened by a half century of decline and revolution, could do little but give in to the first 16 demands, reserving the final five for further consideration. By leaking news of the demands to the press, the Chinese attracted the attention

Japan successfully made the transition to a modern industrial economy by 1900. Preserving the traditional monarchy but combining it with a constitutional government and a powerful military, Japan became a model for modernizing Asian states. After World War I no country in East Asia could match its economic and political strength.

of the United States. Washington kept China from falling totally under Japan's domination. Nevertheless, the Chinese had no choice but to recognize Japan's authority in Shantung province and extend Japanese land and rail concessions in southern Manchuria. In 1917 the Allies secretly agreed to support Japanese claims against China in return for Japan's respecting the Open Door policy.

Japan's sphere of economic dominance expanded during the 1920s in Shantung, Manchuria, and southern Mongolia. It also occupied all the former German islands in the North Pacific. The Washington Conference of 1921 acknowledged the Japanese navy as the third most powerful in the world. The signato-ries of the Nine-Power Treaty (United States, Great Britain, France, Italy, Japan, Belgium, Netherlands, Portugal, and China), signed in Washington in 1922, agreed to respect the independence, sovereignty, territoriality, and administrative integrity of China and to respect the Open Door policy.

China: Revolution and Republic

During the nineteenth century China endured one of the darkest periods in its 4,000 years. The old

China in the Early Twentieth Century

1911–1912	Nationwide revolt
1912	Manchu emperor abdicates; Yuan Shih-kai comes to power
1921–1925	Sun Yat-sen president of southern China at Guangzhou
1926–1927	Chiang Kai-shek seizes power in much of China; Kuomintang Nationalist party splits
1931	Mao Tse-tung and others attempt to proclaim a Chinese Soviet Republic

Confucianist, imperial government failed as China lost territory, suffered under the imposition of extraterritoriality, and witnessed its customs and tariffs come under foreign control. The 1898 reform movement and the Boxer Uprising of 1899–1900 were, in effect, two attempts to remove the Manchu dynasty. Thereafter, there were two approaches to change: a constitutionalist attempt to set up representative government and a revolutionary program to overthrow the dynasty.

Sun Yat-sen and Revolution

Sun Yat-sen (1867–1925) proved to be the key figure in the transition from the old to the new China. Born near Guangzhou to a tenant farmer, he received a Western education in Hawaii. He converted to Christianity and in 1892 earned a diploma in medicine in Hong Kong. Soon he became a leader in the Chinese nationalist movement, directing his energies toward the overthrow of the Manchus and the formation of a republic. For his activities he was forced into exile in 1895 and thereafter traveled widely throughout the world seeking political and financial aid from Chinese living abroad. During that period he organized the movement that eventually became the Kuomintang, or Nationalist party.

In 1911 a revolt broke out in China over a foreign loan to finance railways. The outbreak spread like wildfire throughout the country. Yuan Shih-kai (1859–1916), an outstanding northern Chinese military leader with modern ideas, persuaded the imperial clan that the Manchu dynasty was doomed. In 1912 the emperor abdicated, and Yuan was asked to form a republican government. Although a few months earlier a revolutionary assembly in Nanking had elected Sun president of the new republic, he stepped aside in the interest of national unity and the Nanking assembly elected Yuan.

During the next 15 years China went through a period quite similar to the dynastic interregnums that had punctuated its previous history. Trouble broke out in 1913 when Yuan negotiated a large loan with bankers from Britain, France, Germany, and Russia that gave these powers substantial influence in the government of the republic. Resentment over this agreement led to a new rebellion, backed by Sun. Yuan still had control of the army and put down the revolt, forcing Sun to flee to Japan until 1917. Overestimating his strength, Yuan dismissed the parliament and proclaimed the restoration of the monarchy, appointing himself emperor. This act sparked another rebellion, and this time Yuan's prestige evaporated. In June 1916 the now discredited dictator died.

China then entered a period of political anarchy. Warlords heading armies based on local power centers marched across the country seeking control of Peking. Possession of the city was apparently seen as conferring legitimacy on its occupier. For a time China was divided between two would-be governments, one in the north at Peking and the other in the south at Guangzhou. The southern force was composed largely of those who had engineered the

Statesman and revolutionary leader Sun Yat-sen, the organizer of the Kuomintang, is known as the father of modern China.

revolution of 1911–1912. The Guangzhou government elected Sun president in 1921, and he remained there until his death in 1925, unable to unify the country.

Sun's genius was in making revolution, not in governing. His social ideology, however, provided some key elements for twentieth-century Chinese political theory. Sun's *Three Principles of the People*, developed from a series of lectures, became the political manual of the Kuomintang. The three principles are (1) nationalism—the liberation of China from foreign domination and the creation of a Chinese nation-state; (2) democracy—"government by the people and for the people"; and (3) livelihood—economic security for all the people.

In 1923, after failing to obtain aid from the West to overthrow the Peking government, Sun turned to the Soviet Union for advice and assistance. A military and political advisory group arrived, led by Michael Borodin. Under Borodin's guidance, the Kuomintang adopted many of the planks of the program subscribed to by the Soviet Communist party as well as the party's organizational structure.

Chiang Kai-shek's "United" China

Sun's successor as leader of the Kuomintang was Chiang Kai-shek (1886–1975), the son of a minor landlord. Chiang studied at a military academy in Japan before becoming caught up with Sun's vision for a new China. He returned home to take an active part in the revolution. His obvious abilities and loy-

alty attracted Sun's attention, and in 1923 he was sent to Russia for a brief period of training. Before establishing himself as leader of the Kuomintang, he formed a united force and began a drive northward in 1926. Chiang's group encountered little opposition, and by the early spring of the following year they reached the Yangtze valley. However, dissension broke out between the radical and the conservative elements of the Kuomintang, and Chiang crushed the Communists in his ranks when he occupied Shanghai. He went on to create a moderate government at Nanking, and before the end of 1927 public opinion had swung behind his regime.

Chiang continued to purge the leftist elements. The end of the Kuomintang alliance with the Communists was written in blood, when a proletarian uprising in Guangzhou was crushed, with the loss of 5000 lives. The Soviet advisers returned to Moscow and many radicals, including the widow of Sun Yat-sen, were driven into exile. The Chinese Communists fled to the hills and mountains of China.

The 1927 split of the Kuomintang is a major event in modern Chinese history. Not only were Marxist radicals ousted, but many moderate liberals also came under attack. Chiang built his strength on the urban professional, banking, and merchant classes. His government depended for financial support on the foreign bankers of Shanghai. The regime took on a conservative, urban character, far removed from the huge mass of the Chinese people, the peasantry in the countryside.

With his government established at Nanking, Chiang, his armies, and his warlord allies again

Chiang Kai-shek, successor to Sun Yat-sen as leader of the Kuomintang, broke with the Communists in 1927 and set up a new government at Nanking.

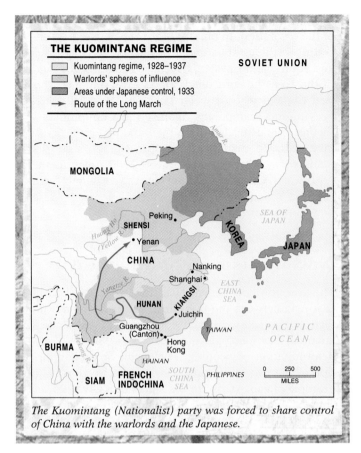

The Kuomintang (Nationalist) party was forced to share control of China with the warlords and the Japanese.

moved north and occupied Peking. China was again united, but it was a unity more in appearance than in fact. While large areas of the country had been conquered by Chiang's forces, other regions came under the Kuomintang by agreement between Chiang and local warlords. In theory the warlords were subordinate to Chiang, but they maintained power in their spheres of influence.

Chinese foreign relations improved during the 1920s. The Nine-Power Treaty guaranteed China's territorial integrity, and China was a member of the League of Nations. The government regained the right to set its own tariffs in 1929 when ten foreign powers gave up or lost the right of extraterritoriality. Partly in response to this development, foreign trade was seven times as great in 1929 as in 1894. In addition, while the liberals were in power in Japan, Tokyo was relatively conciliatory toward China.

Chiang engineered substantial changes in Chinese urban life. More Chinese received education. Linguists championed the use of a new, more colloquial written language, while scholars labored for the adoption of Mandarin (a standardized version of the Peking dialect, used in government affairs) so that people from all parts of China could speak to one another. Social customs changed, and Western dress and folkways appeared. Large cities installed telephones, electric lights, modern water systems, and

movie palaces. The importation of Western conveniences was paid for primarily by the foreign entrepreneurs who controlled most of Chinese industry. Despite efforts at modernization, civil war, a weak currency, and inadequate transportation kept China an underdeveloped nation with pervasive poverty.

A fervent patriot, Chiang unfortunately had little appreciation for the social and economic problems of his nation. Bandits continued to tyrannize the people, and famine in the northwest of the country claimed the lives of millions. Instead of responding to the plight of his nation, Chiang, a Christian whose faith incorporated much from Confucian principles, pursued the moral regeneration of his people through a combination of his religion and his culture—the New Life movement, which he established in the mid-1930s. He would have done better to appreciate the intellectual changes taking place and the social and economic hopes of the peasants.

The New Culture Movement and Chinese Communism

A Chinese intellectual revolution began at Peking University during World War I and spread from there to students all over the country. The first influential voice for this intellectual group was the magazine *New Youth*. This journal transmitted the ideas of students who had returned from universities in the United States and Europe on subjects ranging from Western science to liberalism to socialism. These students wanted to establish a new order and a new set of values to replace much of the old Confucian tradition.

The students became disillusioned with the West after the Versailles peace treaty, which gave Chinese Shantung to Japan. Growing anti-Western sentiment fueled a violent student demonstration on May 4, 1919. A new ideological orientation began in the New Culture movement. Study groups were formed, especially at Peking University, where professors and students began to read Marx and Lenin and to apply their theories to conditions in China. Lenin's analysis of imperialism and his opposition to it struck a responsive chord.

With some guidance from Russian Comintern agents, the first congress of the Chinese Communist party was held in July 1921. A young student at Peking University named Mao Tse-tung was a delegate. About the same time, Chinese worker-students in France established the Young China Communist party in Paris. One of its leaders was Chou En-lai, later premier of the Chinese People's Republic.

Mao Tse-tung (1893–1976) was born in Hunan province, a traditional center of Chinese revolutionary activity. In 1918 he went to Peking University,

Mao Tse-tung has been called the "Stalin of Chinese communism."

where he worked as library assistant under Li Ta-chao, the founder of an important Marxist study group and one of the founders of the Chinese Communist party. Mao began to emerge as a distinctive leader with a new program for revolution when he wrote a report for the Communist party in 1927 about the peasant movement in Hunan. In that document Mao expressed his belief that the revolution must base itself on peasant uprisings, a view that was condemned by the Central Committee of the Chinese Communist party, which closely adhered to the Soviet policy of basing the revolution on the urban proletariat.

Mao led a Hunanese peasant revolt that became known as the Autumn Harvest Uprising. It was crushed, and in May 1928 Mao and other Communist leaders joined forces in the border region of Hunan and Kiangsi provinces. Acutely conscious of peasant needs, Mao organized the peasants in his region into a Chinese "soviet." Other Communist leaders did the same in other regions, and in 1931 delegates from the various local soviets in China met and proclaimed the birth of the Chinese Soviet Republic. Even though Chiang Kai-shek destroyed the Shanghai apparatus of the Communist party, Mao and his colleagues could still claim control of regions containing 9 million inhabitants.

Mao's success as a Communist leader stemmed from his observation that it was the Chinese peasant, not the urban worker, who could be made the agent of the revolution. In pursuit of this objective, Mao encouraged the establishment of farmers' cooperatives and equitable tax systems. He also redistributed land in the areas he controlled. Mao's achievements worried Chiang, who between 1931 and 1934 launched five military campaigns against the Communists—the last one using 1 million men and a German military staff. To avoid annihilation, the Communists made their famous Long March 2000 miles to the northwest. Only a remnant of the original force reached Yenan, in Shensi province, where in 1935 a new Communist stronghold was set up.

Nationalism in Southeast Asia

The drive for independence became stronger in Southeast Asia between the two world wars. Taking advantage of the war-weakened colonialists, local leaders adapted the ideologies of the day—Wilson's "self-determination of peoples," socialism, or a combination of the two—to their campaigns for freedom. The example of Japan's rise to the status of a Great Power showed that the West had no monopoly on harnessing technology and organization to national goals.

Populations grew dramatically in Southeast Asia during the interwar period. From 1930 to 1960 the number of people in Siam, Malaya, and the Philippines increased more than 100 percent; in Indonesia, Burma, and Indochina the number increased more than 50 percent. Population pressures naturally contributed to unrest.

Certain economic trends also characterized most of the region. The imperialist powers continued to exploit their colonies, ignoring the democratic rhetoric they had mouthed during World War I. Europe's draining of the area's resources, coupled with an irregular world market that crashed in 1929, led to increased hardship in much of the region. The Chinese played an increasingly important role as merchants and middlemen in the local economies. In Burma, Indians played the same role. European and Chinese capital investment encouraged a rapid growth in exports of minerals and forest products. In Siam, Indochina, and a few other countries rice production grew more rapidly than population, and as a result the economies became based on rice exports.

Throughout the area the elite became assimilated to European culture as more and more young people went to the "parent countries" to be educated. The masses, however, were barely touched by this process. The result was a growing cultural and social divide between the local leadership and the people at large. With the exception of the United States in the Philippines and Great Britain in Burma and Sri Lanka, none of the imperialist powers undertook to prepare their colonies for eventual self-government, since they had no intention of letting them go.

Indochina

French rule in Indochina was in some ways the least enlightened of all the colonial regimes in Southeast Asia. In 1941, for example, the colonial government had the highest proportion of Europeans in its service of any in the region—some 5100 French officials to 27,000 Indochinese. Four-fifths of the population was illiterate, and of the more than 21 million people, only about 500,000 children received any higher education. French rule was characterized by political oppression, severe economic exploitation, and a rigid and stagnant traditional culture.

Revolution seemed the answer to Vietnam's problems. During World War I over 100,000 Vietnamese laborers and soldiers were sent to France, where many of them came in contact with liberal and radical thinking, which they then brought home. The Vietnam Nationalist party, patterned organizationally and intellectually on the Chinese Kuomintang, was officially outlawed, and by the late 1920s it resorted to terrorism as the only form of political expression open to it.

Communism rapidly became the major revolutionary ideology in the French colony. In 1920 a young Vietnamese calling himself Nguyen Ai Quoc ("Nguyen the Patriot"), later known to the world as Ho Chi Minh (1890–1969), participated actively in the formation of the Communist party in France. In 1930 he organized in Hong Kong what eventually became the Vietnamese (later Indochinese) Communist party. Communist ideas and organization spread throughout Vietnam in the 1930s while the colonial government answered Vietnamese uprisings against French oppression with strong repressive measures. As a result, when World War II began, the Communist party was the major vehicle for the expression of Vietnamese nationalism.

The Philippines

The United States established its form of government in the Philippines on July 4, 1901, under William H. Taft as civil governor of the area. President McKinley declared that the primary aim was to prepare the Filipinos for self-government. The first elections were held in 1907, and by 1913 Filipinos dominated both houses of the legislature, while an American remained as governor-general. By 1935, when the Philippine Commonwealth was inaugurated with a new constitution and the promise of independence within ten years, the islands had developed a complex governmental structure and a sophisticated political life.

Economic developments, however, constricted Philippine independence at the same time that the islands were being prepared for self-rule. Before the outbreak of World War II, four-fifths of Philippine exports went to the United States and three-fifths of its imports came from America. As with most underdeveloped economies, the export trade was dominated by a very few primary products: hemp, sugar, coconuts, and tobacco. Independence, with its accompanying imposition of tariffs, would have been economically difficult. The United States had prevented the development of a colonial-type plantation economy by forbidding non-Filipinos to own plantation lands, but native landlordism was rampant, and the oppressed peasants launched a brief uprising in the mid-1930s.

Dutch East Indies

Unlike other Western imperial powers that loosened controls over their colonies, either through domestic weakness or planned decolonization, the Dutch increased their control in the East Indies. Stretched over 3100 miles of water, the numerous islands of Indonesia were integrated into a unified communications and political system by the Dutch. At the same time, the strict limits put on the power and advancement of native elites led to bitterness and resentment. Dutch imperialism strengthened Indonesian self-consciousness and nationalism.

A Communist party, organized in 1920, attempted unsuccessful uprisings in Java and Sumatra in late 1926 and early 1927. Police repression increased. In 1930 the Dutch attempted to crush the Nationalist party and arrested one of its leaders, Achmed Sukarno (1901–1970), the man who after World War II became the first president of independent Indonesia. The Dutch banned all discussions of any subject that might involve the concept of national independence. Even the name *Indonesia* was censored from official publications.

Siam (Thailand)

In the interwar period, Siam, which changed its name to Thailand in 1939, continued to modernize. Educational improvements, economic growth, and increased political sophistication contrasted sharply, however, with the political and administrative domination of the country by the rather extensive royal family. In 1932 a French-trained law professor led a bloodless coup d'état, and a new constitution was promulgated with the agreement of the king, turning him into a reigning, not ruling, monarch. Since then the country has been ruled by an alliance of army and oligarchy.

Discovery Through Maps

What's in a Name? Siam or Thailand?

Maps nominally show the world "as it really is." But peoples, nations, and boundaries are always evolving, often very quickly. Thus maps tend to depict the world as it used to be or as it was imagined to be. Mapmakers may have a difficult time keeping up with the ways in which states and national identities change. But there are other reasons why maps may reflect different visions of reality. Maps institutionalize points of view, ways of seeing or naming parts of the world. Should a map call a country by the name used by its own people or by the name used by those who buy the map? Western maps, for example, might designate the capital of China as Peking rather than Beijing. Suppose there is a political conflict in some part of the world and the contending parties call their country by two different names. Which name should the mapmaker employ? When a new government comes to power and changes the name of a state, it may take months or even years to change the name on maps, stamps, currency, and textbooks.

The frontispiece of a book published in the United States demonstrates the problems of naming and of demarcating borders in Southeast Asia. This 1941 work by Virginia Thompson is called *Thailand: The New Siam*, reflecting both the old and new names of a country in Southeast Asia. The accompanying map shows Southeast Asia in transition. The name *Siam* was officially changed to *Thailand* in 1939, but two years later this mapmaker thought it wise to include both names on the map. Nor does the map reflect the political realities of the day. In 1941 the borders of Thailand were being contested. In the context of World War II, the Japanese had entered Thailand, and the Thai government was challenging the French in Cambodia. Maps also reflect the progress and losses of imperialism. Thus

this map's designation "French Indo-China" shows the empire that France carved out in Southeast Asia in the nineteenth century. The sweeping title "Netherlands India" across the islands of Sumatra and Borneo suggests the long-term interests and conquests of the Dutch in this region. Compare this map to a current map of Southeast Asia, and to nineteenth century maps, and see how the names and borders have changed.

Burma and Malaya

The Burmese independence movement modeled itself on the tactics practiced by the Indian National Congress, but Buddhism provided the focus for organizational activity. The Young Men's Buddhist Association, formed in 1906, organized the General Council of Burmese Associations in 1921. The General Council brought nationalism to the village level.

British promises after World War I to promote Indian self-government created a similar demand in Burma, which in 1937 was administratively split off from India. A parliamentary system was begun with

a Burmese prime minister under a British governor, who held responsibility for foreign relations, defense, and finance.

No strong nationalist movement developed in Malaya, perhaps because the large ethnic groups living there distrusted one another more than they felt the need to make common cause against the British. The Malays feared Chinese ethnic domination; eventually, the Chinese came to outnumber the Malays themselves. The Chinese were primarily interested in commerce and in developments in China. The Indians, for the most part workers on plantations and in mines, were loyal to India as their homeland.

India: The Drive for Independence

Before 1914, many observers had predicted that in the event of war, Great Britain would find India a serious liability. When hostilities began, however, nearly all anti-British activity in India ceased and thousands of Indian troops were mobilized to fight on the side of their colonial masters the British in the Great War.

Gradual Steps Toward Self-Rule

By 1917 Indian nationalists expected immediate compensation for their loyalty in terms of more self-government. The British, however, pursued a policy stressing gradual development of self-government within the British Empire. To this end, in 1918 a British commission sent to India to study the question of self-government recommended a new constitution. The Government of India Act provided for a system of dual government in the provinces by which certain powers were reserved to the British while the provincial legislatures were granted other, generally lesser, powers.

To Indian nationalists this act represented only a small step toward self-rule. Their frustrations led to open clashes with the British in 1919. At that point the British passed the ill-advised Rowlatt Act, which allowed the police and other officials extraordinary powers in searching out subversive activity. Disgruntled and disheartened by the Government of India Act and the violence that followed, many nationalists demanded sweeping changes. Britain, however, lacked a comprehensive plan to grant independence, and a large segment of British public opinion strongly opposed any such suggestion of the breakup of the empire.

Gandhi and Civil Disobedience

The foremost nationalist leader in India was Mohandas Gandhi (1869–1948). Born of middle-class parents, Gandhi went to London to study law; later he went to South Africa to defend Indians there against the abuses of the planters. Gandhi's encounter with South African discrimination against "nonwhites," transformed him. In South Africa, Indians were subject to numerous legal restrictions that hampered their freedom of movement, prevented them from buying property, and imposed added taxes on them. Gandhi worked aggressively for the legal and political rights of the oppressed. He repudiated wealth, practiced ascetic self-denial, condemned violence, and advocated service to others. He launched a community *(ashram)* that served as a model for living out those principles. With Gandhi as their leader, the Indians in South Africa adopted the tactic of "civil disobedience"—they carried out various protests, refused to work, held mass demonstrations, and marched into areas where their presence was forbidden by law. Through "passive resistance" and noncooperation, Gandhi forced the government to remove some restrictions, thereby attracting worldwide attention.

When he returned to his native land shortly after the outbreak of World War I, Gandhi was welcomed as a hero. Initially, he supported the British in the war effort, but soon he went on the offensive. A crucial factor in his decision was a journey he took in 1917 to Champaran, in Bihar in northeastern India, at the invitation of an impoverished peasant. The peasant had dogged Gandhi's steps until he persuaded him to come and see the terrible conditions of the indigo sharecroppers in his district. Gandhi already had a reputation; his visit alarmed the authorities, who threatened to jail him. But the intrepid lawyer mobilized support and launched a nonviolent campaign for reform and justice for the peasants. Gandhi viewed this episode as seminal. "What I did," he explained, "was a very ordinary thing. I declared that the British could not order me around in my own country."[1]

In India Gandhi founded another ashram based on service, living simply, and self-reliance. He lived there off and on for the rest of his life, but his attention was increasingly turned to agitating for British withdrawal. In response to the Rowlett Act Gandhi launched a campaign of civil disobedience. A mass strike was declared in which all work was to cease and the population was to pray and fast. Gandhi argued that moral force would triumph over physical force.

Contrary to Gandhi's plan, however, riots and violence occurred in some areas. Although the British had forbidden public gatherings, 10,000 to 20,000 Indians assembled in a large walled courtyard in the sacred Sikh city of Amritsar in the Punjab. In an infamous action, known as the Amritsar Massacre, the British general, Reginald Dyer, marched armed soldiers into the courtyard and opened fire without warning on the unarmed crowd. The soldiers mowed down the stampeding men, women, and children, slaughtering 379 and wounding over 1000. Dyer noted afterward that he expected to teach the Indians a lesson and do "a jolly lot of good." Days after the massacre the general exacerbated matters by ordering that all Indians must crawl on all fours as they passed the house of a British schoolteacher who had been assaulted by some rioters. Dyer was forced to resign, but many British colonials supported the bloody suppression of the Amritsar demonstrators.

The massacre inflamed public opinion and prompted Gandhi and other nationalists to intensify their efforts for independence. Congress launched a

Mohandas Gandhi used the weapons of nonviolent protest and noncooperation in his struggle to win independence for India. An immensely popular and beloved leader, Gandhi was called Mahatma, or "Great Soul," by the people of India.

policy of noncooperation with the government in 1920, and Gandhi was arrested in 1922 and sentenced to six years in prison. Gandhi's imprisonment served as a symbol of Indian resistance and earned him the devotion of the Indian people. Gandhi also worked for other goals besides freeing India. He sought to end the drinking of alcohol, raise the status of women, remove the stigma attached to the Untouchables, and bring about cooperation between Hindus and Muslims. In 1927 the Congress demanded full dominion status, the same constitutional equality enjoyed by Canada and Australia. When that demand went unmet, Gandhi began a new campaign of civil disobedience. In a well-publicized "salt march," Gandhi led thousands of men and women to the sea, where he broke British law by panning salt. The British authorities attacked and beat the nonviolent marchers, whose passive resistance, captured on film, presented a picture, at once noble and heartrending, of Indian resolve.

The Continuing Struggle

In 1930 the British arranged a series of roundtable conferences in London. A total of 112 Indian delegates were invited, but with the exception of Gandhi and a few others, all were carefully selected by the British viceroy in India. The British advocated a federal union, which would bring the British provinces and the princely states into a central government. For Gandhi and the other Indian nationalists, the roundtable conferences were a dismal failure. The conferences focused on the division of Indian communities along religious, ethnic, and caste lines and did not seem to move the British any further toward quitting India.

Gandhi's visit to England caused a sensation, and he was in great demand for speeches and visits. As an advocate of nonviolence and self-determination, he attracted like-minded groups and leaders from all over the world. For others he was a curiosity, braving the English winter in his typical garb of loincloth, shawl, and sandals. When Gandhi was invited to visit King George V and Queen Mary for tea, the press had a field day, speculating on what he might wear to the royal occasion. Gandhi dressed in his customary fashion. Later, when someone inquired whether he had had enough on, Gandhi answered with characteristic wit, "The King had enough on for both of us."[2]

The primary moving force in the independence movement was the powerful Indian National Congress, which had become the dominant party for Indian nationalists. Its membership of several million was predominantly Hindu but also included many Muslims and members of other religious groups. The Congress deemphasized communal differences and focused on nationalism and getting the British out of India. Opinion varied on how to get the British out. Gandhi's opposite was Bal Gangadhar Tilak, a firebrand Brahmin who advocated Hindu supremacy and violence to evict the British. But soon after World War I the Congress came under Gandhi's leadership; his personal following among the people was the chief source of the party's tremendous influence. Gandhi transformed the Congress, which had been primarily a highly educated, middle-class organization, into a mass movement that included the peasants. It became the spearhead of nationalist efforts to negotiate with the British for self-rule. It would dominate the Indian elections of 1937 and lead India upon achieving independence in 1947.

Another prominent leader of the Congress was Jawaharlal Nehru (1889–1964), who came from a Brahmin family of ancient lineage. In his youth Nehru had all of the advantages of wealth: English tutors, enrollment in the English public schools of Harrow and later Trinity College, Cambridge, where he obtained his B.A. in 1910. Two years later he was admitted to the bar. On his return to India, however, he showed little interest in practicing law and gradually became completely absorbed in his country's fight for freedom.

A devoted friend and disciple of Gandhi, Nehru could not agree with the older leader's spiritual rejection of much of the modern world. At heart Nehru was a rationalist, an agnostic, an ardent believer in science, and a foe of all supernaturalism. As he himself said: "I have become a queer mixture of the East and the West, out of place everywhere, at home nowhere. Perhaps my thoughts and approach to life are more akin to what is called Western than Eastern, but India calls me."[3] Nehru would later become the first prime minister of independent India. Gandhi and Nehru represented two strands of Indian nationalism. Though their visions of the ideal Indian society differed, they were in agreement that Britain must leave and allow the Indians to govern themselves.

Jawaharlal Nehru, along with Gandhi one of the paramount leaders of Indian nationalism, later served as prime minister of independent India.

The Hindu-Muslim Divide

As Britain's imperial control over India began to loosen, tensions between the Muslim and Hindu communities increased. Many Muslims believed that after independence they would become a powerless minority, the target of Hindu retaliation for centuries of Muslim rule. Some feared that the Hindu-dominated Congress party would have no place for Muslims once the British left India. Thus the conflict that emerged was a struggle for political and cultural survival.

In the early 1930s the Muslim League, a political party, began to challenge the claim of the Indian National Congress to represent all of India. The leader of the Muslim League, Muhammad Ali Jinnah (1876–1948), had originally been a prominent member of the Congress party. Jinnah, once dubbed by Indian nationalists the "ambassador of Hindu-Muslim unity," became alienated by what he considered Hindu domination of the Congress and its claim to be the sole agent of Indian nationalism.

The Muslim League began to advance the "two-nation theory," and in 1933 a group of Muslim students at Cambridge University circulated a pamphlet advocating the establishment of a new state in South Asia to be known as Pakistan. This leaflet was the

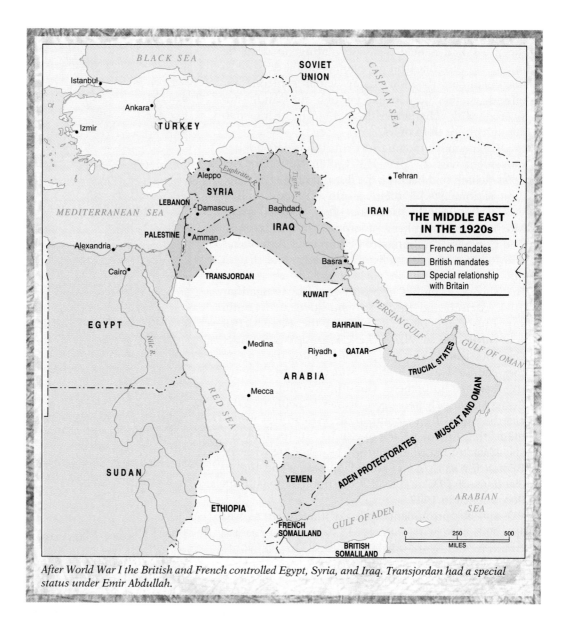

After World War I the British and French controlled Egypt, Syria, and Iraq. Transjordan had a special status under Emir Abdullah.

opening act of a bloody drama. In 1939 the Muslim League emphatically denounced any scheme of self-government of India that would mean majority Hindu rule.

The Middle East Divided

World War I dramatically altered the political, cultural, and geographical configuration of the Middle East. Before the war the Middle East was divided primarily into two large agrarian empires, the Ottoman and the Persian (or Iranian). Most of the North African Muslim states had by this time fallen under the control of European overlords. North Africa's premier cultural center, Egypt, was seized by the British in 1882; France had gained control of Tunis and Algiers; and Italy took parts of Libya from the Ottomans in 1911. After World War I, Persia

(hereafter called Iran), which had remained neutral, maintained its territorial integrity. But the centuries-long rule of the Ottoman Empire in the Middle East was swept away, and its territories were parceled out among the victors. The peoples of the Middle East in the ensuing period can be divided between those who remained independent and those governed by Britain and France. That division would prove critical in the evolution of the modern nation-states of the region.

The War Years

The events of World War I cannot be understood without a grasp of the competing interests involved. There had long been speculation over who might get what when (and if) the Ottoman Empire fell. The Russians coveted a Mediterranean port; the British wished to dominate the area around the

The Middle East Between the Wars

1917	Balfour Declaration
1919	Wafd-led rebellion in Egypt
1920	Mandates set up in conquered Ottoman territory
1923	Saʻd Zaghlul becomes first prime minister of Egypt
1923–1938	Mustafa Kemal Atatürk rules the Turkish Republic
1925	Pahlavi dynasty established in Iran (Persia)
1932	Ibn Saʻud's new state named kingdom of Saudi Arabia

Suez Canal, the sea route to their Indian empire. The French had long-standing connections along the eastern Mediterranean coast, which they aspired to control. The Germans wanted a base in the eastern Mediterranean and some North African territory as well. Perhaps the most hotly contested territory of all was the city of Jerusalem, not a rich or strategic city but sacred to Jews, Christians, and Muslims. Jerusalem had been under Ottoman rule for centuries, but in the early twentieth century a new set of claimants to Jerusalem, the Zionists, had emerged on the world stage.

Prompted by a long-standing military liaison with the Germans and at the urging of Enver Pasha, the Minister of War, the Ottoman Empire joined the Central Powers in the war. The British then used their conquered territory in Egypt as a staging base for military operations. To mobilize support, they also made a series of conflicting agreements concerning the disposition of Ottoman territories. British High Commissioner McMahon in Cairo began correspondence with Sharif Husain of Mecca (1856–1931), guardian of Islam's holy places. The British told Husain that in the event of an Arab revolt against the Ottoman regime, Britain would recognize Arab independence. About the same time, in 1916, Britain, France, and Russia signed the secret Sykes-Picot Agreement. It provided for the division of Syria and Iraq between Britain and France, with Russia receiving parts of Asiatic Turkey. Palestine was to be placed under an international administration.

Believing that the British were promising him an Arab state, Husain launched a revolt in 1916. The

Arab forces were commanded by his third son, Faisal (1885–1933). The Arab Revolt was not particularly large (many Arabs remained loyal to the Ottoman regime), but it was tactically significant and a blow to Ottoman prestige. It also garnered a lot of attention in the Western press, which crafted a romantic adventure story around the exploits of a British officer, T. E. Lawrence (1888–1935), "Lawrence of Arabia," who fought alongside the Arabs.

The Ottoman forces fought valiantly during the war, but the empire was short of money, supplies, and ammunition; it could not match British firepower. When the Ottoman forces were defeated in Syria in October 1918, the Ottoman sultan was forced to sign an armistice. The British allowed Faisal to march into Damascus, the capital of Greater Syria, where he began to set up his own administration. In March 1920 the General Syrian Congress, with high hopes for the birth of a new Arab state, proclaimed Faisal king of Syria.

When Faisal attended the postwar Paris Peace Conference to plead the cause of Arab independence, however, he found he had no real standing. In April 1920 at the San Remo Conference it was decided to turn over all Arab territories formerly in the Ottoman Empire to the Allied powers to be administered as mandates. Syria and Lebanon were mandated to France, Iraq and Palestine to Britain. Husain's dream of a large and independent Arab state was thus short-lived. The French, in line with the Sykes-Picot Agreement, marched troops into Damascus in July 1920 and forced Faisal to relinquish his newly established kingdom.

To mollify their former allies, the British later established Faisal as king of their mandate in Iraq and set up his brother Abdallah as ruler of a desert province based on Amman and carved out of the mandate for Palestine. This new territory was called Transjordan. These two episodes demonstrate the gamelike quality of the partition of the Ottoman Empire. The people of Iraq had no desire for a Hashemite king from Arabia, and there was no logic to the lines drawn around Transjordan except that it was a sparsely populated territory that neither the British nor the Zionists particularly wanted.

The Husain-McMahon correspondence and the Sykes-Picot Agreement were not the only significant promises made during the war. The promise with the broadest ramifications was the Balfour Declaration, which in 1917 promised British support to Zionists in their aspirations for a Jewish "National Home" in Palestine. The Zionist movement, that is the political movement aimed at establishing a Jewish state preferably in the "Holy Land" of Palestine, geared up in the late nineteenth century as the persecution of Jews continued in Russia and anti-Semitism spread

Memorandum of the General Syrian Congress

World War I and its destruction of the old empires paved the way for the rise of Arab nationalism. This memorandum of the General Syrian Congress sounded themes that would be heard throughout the twentieth century. It reflects fear of Zionist encroachments, admiration of the United States as a defender of self-determination, and dismay at the social Darwinistic assumption that the Syrians are among those peoples not yet ready to rule themselves. Despite the desires of the congress, the French soon deposed Emir Faisal as ruler of Syria and took control of the area.

We the undersigned members of the General Syrian Congress, meeting in Damascus on Wednesday, July 2nd, 1919, made up of representatives from the three Zones, viz., the Southern, Eastern, and Western, provided with credentials and authorizations by the inhabitants of our various districts, Moslems, Christians, and Jews, have agreed upon the following statement of the desires of the people of the country who have elected us.

1. We ask absolutely complete political independence for Syria.
2. We ask that the Government of this Syrian country should be a democratic civil constitutional Monarchy on broad decentralization principles, safeguarding the rights of minorities, and that the King be the Emir Faisal, who carried on a glorious struggle in the cause of our liberation and merited our full confidence and entire reliance.
3. Considering the fact that the Arabs inhabiting the Syrian area are not naturally less gifted than other more advanced races and that they are by no means less developed than the Bulgarians, Serbians, Greeks, and Roumanians at the beginning of their independence, we protest against Article 22 of the Covenant of the League of Nations, placing us among the nations in their middle stage of development which stand in need of a mandatory power.
4. In the event of the rejection of the Peace Conference of this just protest for certain considerations that we may not understand, we, relying on the declarations of President Wilson that his object in waging war was to put an end to the ambition of conquest and colonization, can only regard the mandate mentioned in the Covenant of the League of Nations as equivalent to the rendering of economical and technical assistance that does not prejudice our complete independence. And desiring that our country should not fall a prey to colonization and believing that the American Nation is farthest from any thought of colonization and has no political ambition in our country, we will seek the technical and economic assistance from the United States of America, provided that such assistance does not exceed 20 years.
5. In the event of America not finding herself in a position to accept our desire for assistance, we will seek this assistance from Great Britain, also provided that such does not prejudice our complete independence and unity of our country and that the duration of such assistance does not exceed that mentioned in the previous article.
6. We do not acknowledge any right claimed by the French Government in any part whatever of our Syrian country and refuse that she should assist us or have a hand in our country under any circumstances and in any place.
7. We oppose the pretensions of the Zionists to create a Jewish commonwealth in the southern part of Syria, known as Palestine, and oppose Zionist migration to any part of our country; for we do not acknowledge their title but consider them a grave peril to our people from the national, economical, and political points of view. Our Jewish compatriots shall enjoy our common rights and assume the common responsibilities.

From *Foreign Relations of the United States: Paris Peace Conference*, Vol. 12 (Washington, D.C.: U.S. Government Printing Office, 1919), pp. 780–781.

in Europe. In 1897 the World Zionist Organization was founded under the leadership of Theodore Herzl. Following Herzl's death in 1904, leadership of the Zionist movement was assumed by Chaim Weizmann (1874–1952), a Russian Jew who had become a British subject. An intimate intellectual friendship developed between Weizmann and the English statesman Arthur James Balfour (1848–1930), who came to support the Zionist program. That association culminated in the Balfour Declaration, which was designed to mobilize Jewish support for Britain during the war:

His Majesty's Government views with favour the establishment in Palestine of a national home for the Jewish people, and will use their best endeavors to facilitate the achievement of that object, it being clearly understood that nothing shall be done which may prejudice the civil and religious rights of existing non-Jewish communities in Palestine or the rights and political status enjoyed by Jews in any other country.

The sons of Sharif Husain of Mecca were rewarded by the victors for their assistance in World War I. Faisal (seated left), a leader of the Arab Revolt, was first named king of Syria and then king of Iraq after the French forced him out of Damascus. He is shown here with his brothers, Abdullah (center), king of Transjordan, and Ali (right), who briefly ruled the Hijaz.

The carefully worded statement did not specify what the nature of such a Jewish "national home" would be. The population of Palestine, according to British estimates, was only about 9 percent Jewish at the time, but the Balfour Declaration referred to the majority Arab population of Palestine only as "the existing non-Jewish community." Many European and American Jews were fearful that the establishment of a Jewish state would subject them to further discrimination in or even expulsion from their own countries. Nor was the indigenous Jewish population in Palestine necessarily in sympathy with the Zionists, who were considered by many as European outsiders. Nevertheless, the Balfour Declaration provided a great boost to Zionist aspirations in Palestine.

The war and the treaties that followed exacted a high human cost. Besides those killed in the war, thousands of Ottoman citizens starved. The Armenian population was decimated by Ottoman massacres. When the victors divided Ottoman territory, they did so with little consideration for natural ethnic or linguistic affinities. Families were separated and now had to develop new "national" identities; one branch of a family might reside in the new British mandate of Palestine and another in the new country of Transjordan. Over a million Turks and Greeks were uprooted from their homes in forced population transfers after the war. The Young Turk Revolution had imagined a nation based on a multilingual, multiethnic, multireligious citizenship. The new nations and mandates, instead, divided citizens along those same lines.

Mustafa Kemal and the New Secular Model of Turkey

The intention of the victors was to partition the Ottoman lands among the French, the Italians, the British, and the Greeks. The hated capitulations, canceled by the Young Turks, were restored. When the war ended, the sultan dismissed the Ottoman parliament, British warships patrolled the Bosporus and the Dardanelles, and the Greeks occupied Izmir in western Anatolia. The once great Ottoman Empire was dismembered and humiliated.

A group of Ottoman patriots, however, rallied around Mustafa Kemal (1880–1938), hero of the Gallipoli campaign in World War I. After the Ottoman defeat, he had been sent by the sultan to demobilize the Turkish troops in Asia Minor. Disregarding instructions, along with a group of other officers, he reorganized the troops and defied the Allies. From their base in eastern Anatolia and later Ankara these men formed their own government, electing Kemal as president. They upheld self-determination for all peoples, including the Turks, and proclaimed the abolition of all special rights enjoyed by foreigners in Turkey.

Kemal and his forces "liberated" Izmir from the Greeks and gained the support of the new Soviet Union and France. Britain, exhausted by the war, was unwilling to mobilize a major intiative to stop them. Meanwhile Mustafa Kemal established himself in power, abolishing the sultanate and declaring Turkey a republic in 1922. The Allies agreed to a revision of

As president of the Turkish Republic from its beginning until his death in 1938, Mustafa Kemal instituted many civil and cultural reforms. He was called Atatürk, "Father Turk."

the Treaty of Sèvres, and the Treaty of Lausanne, signed in 1923, recognized Turkish sovereignty. The Turkish heartland, Anatolia, remained intact, and no reparations were demanded. Thus Turkey was resurrected as an independent nation-state and escaped the fate of the Arab provinces of the empire, which became mandates under Britain and France.

The circumstances of Turkey's founding gave Mustafa Kemal tremendous power and prestige; he was viewed as the "savior" of the new country. That power and prestige enabled him to dominate Turkish politics and implement a series of radical secularizing reforms. This forceful leader, later called Atatürk, or "Father Turk," established a new democratic constitution, but he regarded autocratic rule under a single political party as a necessary stage in raising his people to the level of education and social well-being that democratic government and parliamentary rule required. Committed to Westernization and secularization, he based his model of progress on the European nation-state.

Atatürk's reforms radically transformed Turkish society. He closed down the popular Sufi orders and the traditional religious schools. Determined to enforce the separation of church and state, he abolished the Islamic Sharia law and replaced it with a civil code based on a Swiss model. Kemal also banned the traditional male headgear, the fez. The fez was a symbol of Ottoman identity, and many Turks resented the antifez law as an

instance of unjust government intervention in people's personal lives and an affront to Islam as well. Atatürk did not try to legislate women's dress, but he did campaign actively for Western-style education and attire for women. In 1935 women were given the vote in Turkey and permitted to run for seats in the national assembly.

Perhaps Atatürk's most drastic reform was changing the Turkish script from the Arabic to the Latin alphabet (the same alphabet used in Britain, France, and the United States). Thousands of teachers had to be trained in the use of the new script; government documents, printing presses, textbooks, newspapers, and street signs had to be changed. The alphabet reform permeated almost all aspects of everyday life; more than any other, this reform decisively divorced Turkey from its past. By the time Atatürk died in 1938, Turkey was a new and different nation.

Iran

Iran remained neutral in World War I, but Qajar rule did not long survive the war. The Russian occupation was ended by the 1917 revolutions, but the British had discovered oil in western Iran shortly before the war and were determined to protect their oil concession. There was widespread antiforeign sentiment in the region, provoked in part by British attempts to dominate Iranian economic and foreign policy. Iran, meanwhile, was economically devastated, and the Qajars could not control the tribal chiefs in their provinces.

Under these chaotic circumstances, Reza Khan, a commander of the nation's Cossack brigade, began a campaign in 1921 to take over the government. By 1925 he had succeeded, persuading the assembly to depose the Qajar shah. The shah was already in Europe, having found it expedient to follow Reza Khan's "suggestion" that he take a "vacation." Reza Khan thus founded a new dynasty, the Pahlavi dynasty. Like Mustafa Kemal in Turkey, the new shah combined a constitutional system with an authoritarian regime. He launched a program of modernizing and secularizing reforms modeled on Kemal's. He adopted a new legal system, thus weakening the power of the *ulama*, and opened the secular Tehran University in 1935.

Reza Shah imposed Western dress for males, but he went even further in 1936, banning the veil for women. This law, and the shah's insistence that his officials bring their wives to mixed-sex entertainments like dinners and balls, caused an uproar. It violated long-standing customs of modesty. Many older women, acccustomed to the veil, were terribly embarrassed and refused to leave the house. Some officials said they would rather divorce or lose their jobs than expose their wives and daughters to the eyes of strange men. Radical reform based on Western models was thus not necessarily welcome; it often violated social custom. Reza Shah was successful in many of his modernizing and economic reforms, but secularization did not succeed in Iran to the same degree that it did in Turkey.

Iran was no longer at the mercy of foreign loans, but neither was it free of foreign intervention. The British-owned Anglo-Iranian Oil Company held a concession dating from 1901 to exploit Iranian oil. In 1933 the shah renegotiated his country's agreement with the company, but Iran still received only 20 percent of the oil revenues. To counteract British influence, the shah cultivated ties with Germany, but when World War II began, Iran remained neutral. Fearful of German intervention, however, Britain and Russia again used military force to intervene in Iranian affairs.

Arabia

Like Turkey and Iran, Arabia remained independent in the aftermath of World War I. The British controlled the Persian Gulf and preserved a series of treaty arrangements with local *shaykhs* along the southern and eastern coasts of Arabia. But the victors saw no particular profit in trying to control the bulk of the Arabian peninsula; its mostly forbidding terrain was sparsely populated, and it had no apparent strategic or natural resource value. Sharif Husain was discredited in the eyes of many Muslims because he had collaborated with the British and proclaimed himself "caliph" after the war. He retained control of the Hijaz after the war, but while his sons ruled in Transjordan and Iraq, he was soon to lose power in Arabia.

The man who would rule Arabia and unite the tribes was Abd al-Aziz ibn Sa'ud (1881–1953). Ibn Sa'ud had seized the city of Riyadh in 1902 and from that base launched a campaign to unify the peninsula under his rule. Like his predecessor a century before, Ibn Sa'ud established himself as both a successful warrior and defender of the puritanical Wahhabi doctrine that aimed to purge Islam of all innovations. In 1924 he captured the holy cities of Mecca and Medina, which have remained under Sa'udi rule ever since. Britain recognized the new king in exchange for his recognition of their special position in the Gulf. The new state was officially named the Kingdom of Saudi Arabia in 1932. Ibn Sa'ud preserved some of the Arabian customs of consultative rule and based his authority on royal decree legitimized by the consent of the *ulama*. His kingdom had no constitution; the law of the land was the Sharia, Islamic law.

Saudi Arabia was impoverished but it was free, unlike most of the Arab provinces. Its economic situation began to change in 1933 when the king granted a concession to the Standard Oil Company (later known as Arabian American Oil). Oil was discovered in 1938 but did not become a significant factor in Arabia until after World War II.

Egypt

Egypt and most of North Africa had been subordinated to European rule before World War I. Nationalist movements were agitating for independence across North Africa, but as in India, Britain and France had no intentions of granting real independence to these conquered territories. That would not be achieved until after World War II.

During the First World War, Egypt was ruled by the British high commissioner and was forced to participate militarily and economically in the war, which caused great hardship. In 1918 some prominent Egyptians, led by Sa'd Zaghlul (c. 1860–1927), formed the *Wafd* ("Delegation") and asked the high commissioner to let them represent Egypt at the Paris Peace Conference. The request was denied. The Wafd then mobilized popular support throughout the country, culminating in widespread rebellion in 1919. Students joined workers demonstrating in the streets for independence. The British put down the demonstrations by force but conceded to popular pressure by allowing Zaghlul and others to attend the peace conference. This series of events began a long period, lasting into World War II during which the Wafd was the dominant party in Egyptian politics.

In 1922 the British declared Egypt independent, but it was a hollow victory for Egyptian nationalists because Britain retained control over defense, foreign affairs, the economy, the Sudan, and the Suez Canal. The capitulations remained in place, and British troops remained in Egypt. In the 1923 elections the Wafd won an overwhelming victory and Zaghlul became the first Egyptian prime minister. The khedive, a descendent of Muhammad Ali, became "king," but England continued to dominate the political life of Egypt. The nature of its position is illustrated by the fact that it forced a mutual defense pact on Egypt in 1936 and reoccupied the country during the Second World War.

One interesting ramification of European influence and educational institutions in Egypt was the emergence of a women's movement. Led by upper-class Egyptian women, often with Western-style educations, the Egyptian Feminist Union was founded in 1923. It took an active role in the nationalist struggle and advocated rights for women: suffrage, education for girls, and marriage reform. The founder of the union, Huda Sha'rawi, is famous for publicly removing her veil in the Cairo train station after returning from a feminist congress in Europe.

Another highly significant movement that began in Egypt in this era and continues to have influence to the present day is the Muslim Brotherhood. The Brotherhood was founded in 1928 by Hasan al-Banna, a teacher and member of the *ulama*. Hasan al-Banna called for the restoration of the Sharia, but the Muslim Brotherhood was not a movement of purification

Egyptian women were active in the struggle for independence and in advocating the rights of women. The streets of Cairo provided the setting for this demonstration, in 1922, in support of the vote for women.

in the same way that the Wahabbi movement in Arabia was. Rather, the Brotherhood was a movement of religious, social, and political reform. It developed social programs such as adult education, job training, and free clinics; it had a special attraction among the poor. With its message of traditional Islamic law and values, combined with social services and respect for modern technology, the Brotherhood had a powerful appeal; chapters rapidly spread beyond the borders of Egypt. The Brotherhood stands as an early and visible example of a modern Islamist movement.

The Mandates

Unlike Egypt and the states of North Africa, the rest of the Arab world had been, at least nominally, under Ottoman control until World War I. The treaties after the war gave Britain the mandates for Iraq and Palestine (out of which Transjordan was carved) and France the mandate for Syria, which it divided into Syria and Lebanon. One historian has called the mandate system "little more than nineteenth-century

imperialism repackaged to give the appearance of self-determination."[4] Mandates were territories considered incapable of self-rule. They were to be governed by "more advanced" nations until such time as they were able to govern themselves.

Iraq was not a country at all but a mandate with a highly diverse population carved out of three Ottoman provinces. For the British, Iraq was a link between their strategic bases in the Persian Gulf and their oil interests in Iran. When the British moved in, Iraqi tribesmen immediately revolted, but the rebellion was aggressively put down and, as noted, the British brought in the outsider Faisal to rule. In 1921 Faisal was crowned king (as the band played "God Save the King"). Britain retained control of the finances and the military, and Iraq was declared a constitutional monarchy. Faisal's government had considerably greater autonomy than the French allowed Syria, and in 1932 Iraq became independent. It was, however, independence with strings attached. Britain retained air bases in the country and had negotiated a 75-year lease to exploit Iraqi oil. During the Second World War, British forces reoccupied the country, a clear reminder that Iraqi freedom was in part a function of British strategic interests.

The French brought in a large military force to enforce their rule in Syria. There they divided the territory in such a way as to emphasize and exacerbate religious and ethnic differences and to privilege the Christian community. Lebanon's population was predominantly Arab but religiously divided among Christians (Maronites were the largest group), Muslims (Sunni and Shi'ite), and Druze (originally a heterodox offshoot of Shi'ite Islam). The French carved Lebanon out of the Syrian mandate in order to set up a majority Christian state that would retain close ties with France even after independence.

The French kept tight control over their mandates, prompting widespread rebellion in Syria from 1925 to 1927. Syria remained without real political representation and without independence until after World War II. Conversely, in Lebanon the French set up a constitutional regime in 1926, but election to office was based on religious affiliation, and France kept control of foreign and military affairs. When the Second World War began, France suspended the constitution. In the end the French withdrew only grudgingly from Syria and Lebanon in 1943. They left Lebanon with a system of religiously based politics that has plagued the new nation ever since.

The Question of Palestine

The mandate for Palestine was unique from the beginning because Palestine was not just another territory, it was the Holy Land, an object of Jewish, Christian, and Muslim fervor and consequently a focus of world attention. The British had to contend with the demands of the Zionists, who felt they had been promised Palestine by the Balfour Declaration, and with the majority Palestinian Arab population, which wanted independence.

The Ottoman government had tried to prevent the Zionists' acquisition of land in Palestine, with little success. Once Palestine became a British mandate, the Jewish population was granted certain privileges—not necessarily because of British sympathy for the Zionists but because the Zionists were Europeans, not "Orientals." Thus they were allowed their own flag, Hebrew was made one of the official languages of the mandate, Jews in service to the British were paid more than Arabs, and the Zionist community, the *Yishuv,* was allowed to arm itself while the Arab community was not. Many of the early Zionists were proponents of socialism, an ideology that manifested itself in the founding of communal farms called *kibbutzim.* In this context it is important to remember that the struggle between the Zionists and the Palestinian Arabs was not primarily a struggle over religion (many of the Zionists were secular Jews, and the Arabs were Muslim, Christian, or secular); it was a struggle over land.

The British failed in trying to balance their own interests with those of the Arabs and Zionists. Unlike other mandates, Palestine never had an assembly or a constitution. Instead the British advanced a series of abortive proposals, trying to satisfy both sides but tending to favor the Zionists. The Arab population was not unified; its leaders lacked connections in Britain and failed to mobilize the same organizational power as the Zionists. The most visible Arab leader was Hajj Amin al-Husayni, the chief Islamic jurist of Jerusalem, but he did not speak for the whole Palestinian community.

Waves of Jewish immigration between 1919 and 1926 seemed to confirm the fears of the Arab population that the British meant to deliver Palestine into the hands of the Zionists. In 1929 Jews and Arabs clashed over activities at the Wailing Wall (a remnant of Solomon's Temple in Jerusalem and part of the sanctuary of the Dome of the Rock, a sacred Muslim shrine). Then the rise of Hitler prompted a dramatic exodus of Jews fleeing Nazi Germany. Many were not Zionists, but restrictive immigration quotas in countries like the United States made Palestine a reasonable option for emigrating Jews. The enormous influx of immigrants between 1933 and 1936 further alarmed the Arab population, prompting a revolt that included demonstrations, rioting, and mass strikes. The revolt was aimed both at the Zionists and at the British administration; the British crushed it after six months but could not crush the frustration and hostility that prompted it.

In 1937 the British Peel Commission found that the mandate could not satisfy its contradictory objectives; it recommended that Palestine be partitioned into an Arab state and a Jewish state. Britain would control a corridor stretching from the Mediterranean to Jerusalem. This recommendation was rejected by both sides; it also prompted another Arab rebellion that lasted until 1939. The rebellion symbolized the intractability of the Palestine question; it was a portent of more violence to come.

Throughout the 1930s the "Palestine question" provoked heated discussion in many parts of the world. Zionists argued that Jews had a historical right to the Holy Land, that they had been promised a state by the Balfour Declaration, and that Jewish colonization constituted a "democratic and progressive" influence in the Middle East. The Palestinians responded that Palestine had been their country for more than a 1000 years and declared that the Balfour Declaration did not bind them because they had not been consulted in its formulation. They asked how any people could be expected to stand idly by and watch an alien immigrant group be transformed from a minority into a majority. For the Palestinians, the Zionists were yet another variety of European imperialism in a particularly virulent form.

With the threat of war looming in 1939, Britain eagerly sought to regain Arab goodwill and thereby strengthen its position in the Middle East. It issued a "white paper" declaring that it was Britain's aim to have as an ally an independent Palestine, to be established at the end of ten years, with guarantees for both Palestinian and Jewish populations. During this ten-year period land sales were to be restricted. Jewish immigration would be limited to 75,000 people over five years; then no more immigration would take place without the consent of the Palestinians. That, of course, was an unfulfillable promise; no one could yet imagine the full extent of Hitler's atrocities. After the war the Zionists would achieve their Jewish state in Palestine, but the Palestine Question would not be resolved.

Colonial Rule in Africa

Once the European nations had completed their conquest of African societies by World War I, they had to figure out how to govern huge colonies with a handful of officials. In 1926 in the Ivory Coast, the French stationed one European official for every 18,000 people, while in southern Nigeria, the British had one for every 70,000. The French, Belgians, Portuguese, and British pragmatically experimented with various policies of administration; whatever their approach, all of them had similar objectives: preserving law and order, quelling disturbances, and spending as little on administration as possible. Thus the common approach was "divide and rule."

The British, through their experience with administering the Muslim Sokoto Caliphate in northern Nigeria, devised a policy of indirect rule or ruling through African traditional authorities. Frederick Lugard, who had commanded the British troops that conquered the caliphate, stayed on as an administrator. An authoritarian figure who instinctively distrusted educated Africans, Lugard found that he had more in common with the conservative Muslim Fulani aristocrats who ruled the caliphate. Thus Lugard favored colonial officials ruling through indigenous political leaders—chiefs and their councils—who were allowed to continue their day-to-day rule with little interference from the British. However, chiefs were expected to observe colonial laws, carry out the directives of colonial officials, and collect taxes. Because they had difficulty balancing their ties to their subjects with their responsibility to their colonial masters, they found themselves making more and more compromises to conform to colonial rules.

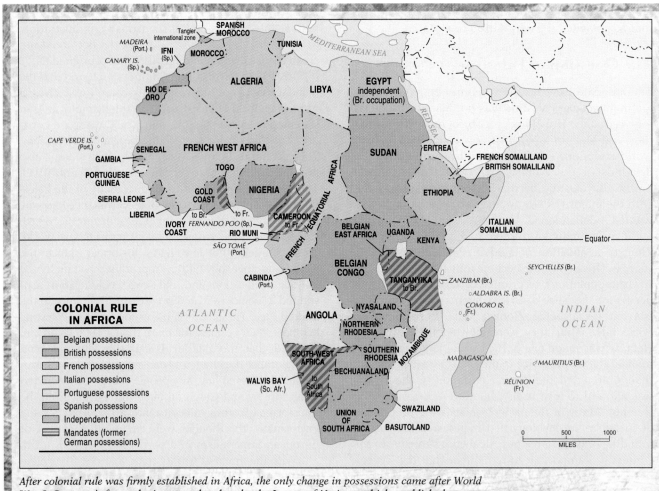

After colonial rule was firmly established in Africa, the only change in possessions came after World War I. Germany's four colonies were placed under the League of Nations, which established a mandate system for other colonizers to administer the territories.

Indirect rule was applied in other British African colonies, even where African societies had structures totally unlike the Sokoto Caliphate. The administrative unit for British rule was the "tribe." For the sake of efficient rule, tribes were arbitrarily created where none had previously existed. The result was an authoritarian structure that barely resembled prior systems of governance. For instance, among the Igbo peoples in southeastern Nigeria, where elders ruled small-scale societies, the British imposed chiefs and issued them warrants to legitimize their authority.

The "warrant chiefs" provoked resentment among their subjects. In 1929 Igbo women in the Oloko district, fearing they were going to be taxed, received written assurances they would not be taxed and had a warrant chief arrested for assaulting a woman. The women's grievances mushroomed into a widespread popular revolt against warrant chiefs and "native" administration in which women attacked jails and released prisoners. Although the British sent in troops to quell the revolt, the women's efforts to reform ruling structures by appointing a council of judges to replace warrant chiefs failed because women could not serve on the courts.

The French had a somewhat different approach to administering their African colonies. Before the scramble for Africa, France had applied the ideals of the French Revolution to a philosophy of assimilation in which selected Africans were immersed in the French language and culture and were treated as French citizens with full political rights. This approach was possible as long as France was governing a small colony like Senegal in West Africa. But once France expanded its holdings in Africa, it was confronted with a large subject population whose cultures were still intact. The French took the attitude that most Africans could not be absorbed into French culture; thus they relied on direct rule that featured a centralized administration. At the top were French officials; below them were layers of African "chiefs" who ruled over villages, districts, and provinces and were primarily responsible for collecting taxes, maintaining law and order, and recruiting forced labor. If a society did not have a chief, the French would select one based on education, administrative ability, and loyalty.

The Portuguese practiced another form of direct rule. Unlike other colonies in Africa, the territories of Angola and Mozambique were constitutionally part of Portugal and were treated as overseas provinces. As the Industrial Revolution in Europe had largely bypassed Portugal under the longtime rule of Antonio Salazar, Portugal based her economic policies on her African possessions' providing the mother country with cheap raw materials and foodstuffs as well as guaranteeing Portuguese manufacturers a profitable market. Colonial governors reported directly to the Salazar government, and provincial and district administrators gradually took over the collection of taxes and the recruitment of forced labor, tasks that had been previously carried out by African police and chiefs.

In theory Portuguese officials believed that they, of all the European colonizers, had the unique ability to create a multiracial society. The reality was far different. The Portuguese created a class of *assimilados* (assimilated people) who were supposed to be treated as equals to Portuguese citizens. To become

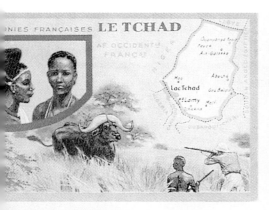

European colonizers created popular images of Africans as uncivilized, lazy savages. In this set of postage stamps issued by the French after World War II, Africans are shown laboring in rural scenes, reinforcing the idea that their productivity and well-being could only be promoted under European supervision.

Africans expressed their images of Europeans through art works. In the car above, an early twentieth-century work from the Congo., a Belgian mining magnate reclines in the back seat while the African chauffeur drives.

an *assimilado*, a person had to become Christian (Roman Catholic); read, write, and speak Portuguese; and "practice a Portuguese lifestyle." The numbers of *assimilados*, however, never amounted to more than 3 percent of the African population. The rest were classed as *indigenas* (indigenous people) and were expected to learn the "dignity of labor" by working on plantations, at public works, and in urban areas. The only way to be exempted from this forced labor system was to be classified as *assimilado* or to seek work as a migrant laborer in neighboring territories. Mozambicans annually supplied over 100,000 members of the labor force for the South African gold mines.

The Colonial Economy

Colonialism imposed a dependent economic relationship between Africa and Europe that continues to shape the economies of independent African nations. Whatever their nationality, European officials shared a common objective: to compel their colonies to produce raw materials for the world market in exchange for finished products from the mother country.

Colonial economies took two forms: colonies where European involvement was direct in the form of plantations, mines, and European settlement, and colonies where Africans with small landholdings grew cash crops such as peanuts, oil palms, cotton, rubber, sisal, coffee, and cocoa for export. Because each colony usually produced one cash crop, the colony's well-being was dependent on the price the crop fetched on the world market. The Gold Coast, for example, soon became the world's leading supplier of cocoa, which inspired a song popular in the 1950s:

If you want to send your children to school, it is cocoa,
If you want to want to build your house, it is cocoa,
If you want to marry, it is cocoa,
If you want to buy cloth, it is cocoa,
Whatever you want to do in this world,
It is with cocoa money that you do it.[5]

The introduction of cash crops was extremely disruptive to African agriculture. Cash crops were often grown on the best land at the expense of other crops; thus overproduction exhausted soils and led to erosion. Colonial officials also favored the interests of African men by granting them the ownership of land on which

African women had the primary responsibility for agriculture. Under colonial rule they were also expected to grow cash crops such as cotton, peanuts, and cocoa for the export market.

cash crops were grown. They reaped the lion's share of any proceeds from sales, while women, who had traditionally been responsible for agriculture, were expected to shoulder the burden of tending the new crops as well as performing their normal duties.

European-run plantations and mining operations also played major roles in the colonial economy. Huge estates and mining concessions were ceded to European and American companies. The Firestone Rubber Company took advantage of minimal rents and no income taxes to establish the largest rubber plantation in the world in Liberia. The Belgian giant Union Minière had a virtual monopoly over the copper-rich southern Congo, while Anglo-American, a South African company, dominated diamond and gold production in southern Africa.

A vast army of migrant laborers was required to run these operations. Because African men were reluctant to leave their families and homes for extended periods, they had to be compelled to seek work in the towns, mines, and plantations through a head tax on all adult men that had to be paid in cash rather than in kind. Besides paying taxes, workers saved their wages to start up their own businesses back home, to acquire imported goods, and to buy cattle to pay bridewealth.

Colonialism also introduced new forms of transportation. Built on the backs of unpaid forced labor, railways were constructed from the coastal ports into the interior to extend trading networks and to facilitate the export of commodities, especially minerals. In areas where white settlers had farms, railways not only exported their products but also deliberately skirted the black reserves that supplied laborers to white farms and mines. While ports and railway towns boomed, railways often undermined established trading networks such as the Hausa trade of northern Nigeria with Tripoli in North Africa and the caravan routes in eastern Africa. Cars and trucks also replaced human porters and animals such as donkeys and horses.

The impact of the colonial economy on different regions was uneven. Coastal areas typically benefited more from roads, railways, and economic development than the interior zones, which stagnated and became the primary sources of migrant laborers for the coast. In southern Africa, where mining was the dominant industry, South Africa became an economic powerhouse because most of the roads and railways were built in a north-south direction that steered regional trade through South Africa.

Social and Religious Change

Colonial rule opened up new avenues of social change for Africans. New trade routes, work sites, and urban centers exposed migrant workers, soldiers, students, teachers, and civil servants to new organizations and associations, music and dance styles, languages, cultures, and idea, values, and faiths.

Both Islam and Christianity won many converts during this period, although in dramatically different ways. In sub-Saharan Africa, Christian missionaries scored few successes before colonial rule. Catholic missionaries who accompanied the Portuguese into Africa had converted some rulers and their courts but had little influence beyond them. In the late eighteenth and early nineteenth centuries a fresh wave of evangelical Christianity stirred many European Protestant denominations to send missionaries to Africa. They believed they had an obligation to spread the Christian faith to African "heathens" and to block Islam; they often saw their missions as working hand in hand with the expansion of European commerce globally.

Although some African leaders perceived the missionaries as positive assets, many questioned whether the missionaries were undermining the leaders' authority and restricted their activities. Thus the few who initially converted to Christianity were on the margins of African society—freed slaves, women fleeing bad marriages, famine victims, war refugees, orphans, and people accused of witchcraft.

The next wave of converts consisted of those who wanted access to technical skills and literacy offered at mission schools. Missionaries often required their students to join their church in order to be admitted to their schools. Because most schooling was at the primary level, few students proceeded on to the handful of secondary schools. Thus high schools such as the École William Ponty in Dakar, Senegal; Achimota in the Gold Coast; and Lovedale in South Africa attracted students from a wide area. Friendships forged at these schools later carried over into anticolonial politics. Those who aspired to university education usually had to go to Europe or America before colleges like Fort Hare in South Africa were established.

Schooling affected avenues of social advancement. Age, family position, ability, and sex had traditionally determined status in African societies, but in the colonial world, whose missions, schools, civil service, and businesses required a literate elite that was fluent in European languages, education and technical skills became a main avenue to personal advancement.

African Christians continually raised probing questions about Christian missions and Christianity. They especially challenged the control of European missionaries over their churches and their attacks on African culture. Some African Christians broke away to form their own independent churches that were carbon copies of missions but featured black leadership. Some Christians also desired to Africanize Christianity by adapting Christian beliefs and rituals to African culture. By the end of the colonial period Christianity was experiencing tremendous growth in the southern two-thirds of the continent, with independent churches leading the way.

Islam had even greater successes in winning new converts. By World War II an estimated half of all Africans were Muslims. Most were Sunni Muslims who lived in the northern third of the continent and along the east coast. Muslim clerics had several advantages over Christian missionaries. They were primarily Africans, not European; they did not demand that their converts give up their customs and cultures; they were not restricted by colonial boundaries; and they were not closely identified with colonial rulers. However, European administrators, once they overcame their initial hostility to Islam, courted some conservative Muslim leaders to maintain law and order and preserve the status quo.

The main agency for spreading Islam was through the mystical Sufi orders or brotherhoods, established to create deeper spiritual bonds between believers and Allah. The Qadiriyya, founded in the twelfth century C.E., was the oldest of the African brotherhoods. It expanded its base in North Africa to northern Nigeria, where it won over the Hausa ruling elite. In Senegal in the 1880s, Shaykh Ahmad Bamba founded the Mourides brotherhood. He instilled in members of his brotherhood the belief that a disciplined work ethic was necessary for salvation. Mourides *shaykhs* encouraged their disciples to participate in peanut production and to use the proceeds to spread Mourides influence.

"New Britains": Kenya and Rhodesia

The few Europeans who lived in French and British colonies in Africa were primarily traders, missionaries, and colonial officials, who did not think of themselves as permanent settlers. Such was not the case in the British colonies of Kenya and Southern Rhodesia, where European settlers found hospitable cli-

Africans who converted to Christianity or attended mission schools were expected to adopt Western dress, culture, language, and values.

mates and staked out extensive land claims at the expense of African societies.

Though located on the equator, Kenya's highland area, at 6000 to 9000 feet above sea level, has a temperate climate that Europeans could tolerate. After conquering African peoples in the region, the British government designated the highlands for white ownership only and encouraged Englishmen and white South Africans to set up farms. The first arrived in 1903; although their numbers were small, they had tremendous influence over British administrators in Nairobi, the capital city. Africans, mostly Kikuyu, who had once tilled the highlands, were classed as squatters and were allowed to farm the land as long as they were needed for labor. In the 1930s thousands of Kikuyu squatters were expelled from white farms and forced to eke out a living in barren reserves or on the streets of Nairobi. This treatment set the stage for a major uprising after World War II.

White settlers in Rhodesia followed a similar path. After conquering Shona and Ndebele kingdoms in several wars in the 1890s, the British South Africa Company (BSAC) turned its attention from a quixotic search for gold to promoting agriculture. White settlers seized additional land from Africans and eventually claimed about half of the country's best land as their own. They were already a potent political force when in 1923 the BSAC gave up administrative control of the colony to the British government. That same year the British gave the largely English settlers a choice of whether they wanted to be incorporated in the Union of South Africa or become a self-governing colony. They chose the latter. In theory the British retained certain powers protecting the rights of the African majority. However, as the Rhodesian parliament passed one discriminatory measure after another based on South African laws, the British did not intervene. The Land Apportionment Act of 1930 divided land into black and white areas. Roads, railways, and towns were placed in the white areas; the blacks, in rural reserves, were expected to pay taxes by selling their labor to white employers. Maize and tobacco farming in white areas became profitable through generous price supports, while black farmers were forced to sell their crops at lower prices.

White Exploitation in the Union of South Africa

At the conclusion of the Anglo-Boer war in May 1902, the British could have dictated a settlement to the Afrikaners and extended full political rights to blacks, but they deferred the issue until self-government was extended to the former Afrikaner republics. Milner, the British high commissioner, set about re-

constructing the devastated former Afrikaner republics, but he scored few successes. His plan for English speakers to outnumber Afrikaners failed because he could not entice many British immigrants to take up farming in South Africa; and his attempt to Anglicize Afrikaners by setting up English-language schools failed when Afrikaners formed their own independent schools.

Once Milner left South Africa in 1905 following a Liberal party electoral victory in Britain, British officials came to a political understanding with Afrikaner leaders and extended self-government to the formed Afrikaner republics, the Orange Free State, and the Transvaal in 1907. The British then moved to unite their four colonies and empowered 30 Afrikaner and English delegates to draft a constitution. Only eight years after a ruinous war, the Union of South Africa became a self-governing dominion in the British Commonwealth.

The first three prime ministers of South Africa were Afrikaners who had led the war against the British. Louis Botha (1863–1919) and Jan Smuts (1870–1950) preached reconciliation with the British, while J. B. M. Hertzog (1866–1942) promoted a separate Afrikaner nationalism. Even though the Afrikaners controlled the government and gained official recognition of their language, Afrikaans, English speakers controlled the civil service and dominated the business sector. Despite the deep rift between Britons and Afrikaners, however, they were prepared to work together to preserve and entrench white domination over South Africa's black majority.

The all-white Parliament passed laws protecting whites and hindering the ability of Africans to advance. With the exception of a small number of African and mixed-race males in the Cape Province who could vote in elections, most blacks were excluded from any role in government. (In 1936 Prime Minister Hertzog's government struck Cape Africans from the voters' roll.) A 1913 law froze the land division between whites and blacks, making it illegal for blacks to buy white land and vice versa. Africans, who comprised over 70 percent of the population, were restricted to reserves that made up about 7 percent of the country. Another 6 percent was later added to the reserves.

In contrast, the government addressed the plight of the numerous unskilled and uneducated whites that lived at or below subsistence level. Ninety percent of these "poor whites" were Afrikaners who, unable to compete on equal terms with blacks, had little choice but to work for pathetically low wages. The government introduced a "civilized labor" policy in the 1920s providing many poor whites with jobs on the railroads, with the post office, and in low-level civil service positions. For every white that won a job, a black had to lose one. The government also reserved supervisory and skilled jobs in the mining industry for whites only. The color bar was extended to most industries and resulted in huge wage disparities. The average wage for Europeans was just under $4 a day, while that for Africans was a little over $3 a week.

African opposition to discriminatory laws was led by the South African Native National Congress, founded in 1912 and renamed the African National Congress (ANC) in 1923. The ANC aimed to bring Africans from all black ethnic groups together in one organization. Led primarily by Africans educated in Christian mission schools, the ANC initially had modest goals. African leaders did not immediately call for black majority rule, but they wanted blacks to be treated as equals with whites and to remove discriminatory laws. They concluded that armed struggle was futile, and they sought change through nonviolent constitutional means.

The ANC's first president was a Congregational minister named John Dube (1871–1946), who became a disciple of the American educator Booker T. Washington while receiving his college education in the United States. After returning to Natal, Dube founded his own school based on Washington's brand of industrial education and modeled after his Tuskegee Institute.

The African challenge to white rule was very restrained until World War II, when tens of thousands of Africans, who streamed into the urban centers like Johannesburg to take up jobs, became involved in protests over housing shortages, high costs of transportation, and pass laws. Sensing this mood of militancy, a younger generation of politicians formed the Youth League within the ANC in 1944 to push their elders to challenge white rule aggressively. Youth Leaguers such as Nelson Mandela, Walter Sisulu, and Oliver Tambo played important roles as resistance leaders for the next half century. In 1949, as the rigid system of racial separation known as *apartheid* was being introduced, Youth Leaguers forced a change of leadership in the ANC and committed the movement to engage in mass protests such as strikes, boycotts, and civil disobedience.

Pan-Africanism

Pan-Africanism grew out of the shared experiences of blacks in many parts of the world in connection with European domination through the slave trade, racism, and colonialism. Although Pan-Africanism's primary aim was to unify and strengthen blacks, its leaders disagreed on who their main audience was. Some Pan-Africanists limited their message exclusively to Africans in sub-Saharan Africa, while others appealed more broadly to Africans throughout the continent or to blacks throughout Africa and the African diaspora, including the Caribbean and the Americas.

In the late nineteenth and early twentieth centuries the leading lights of the Pan-Africanist movement were blacks of the diaspora such as W. E. B. Du

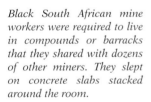

Black South African mine workers were required to live in compounds or barracks that they shared with dozens of other miners. They slept on concrete slabs stacked around the room.

Bois and Marcus Garvey. Born and raised in Massachusetts, Du Bois (1868–1963), an organizer of the National Association for the Advancement of Colored People (NAACP) and editor of its magazine, *The Crisis*, was most comfortable in intellectual circles. He asserted the right of blacks to participate in national governments and advocated the eventual self-rule of African countries. He was a prominent force behind a series of pan-African conferences held in Europe and the United States. One of the congresses, with representatives from 15 countries attending, was convened in Paris in 1919. The congress coincided with the Versailles Peace Conference, and Du Bois urged the gathering to place the former German colonies under an international agency, rather than under the rule of one of the victorious powers, such as Britain.

Du Bois's primary rival in the Pan-Africanist movement was Marcus Garvey (1887–1940), who immigrated from Jamaica to the United States in 1916 and founded the Universal Negro Improvement Association. A charismatic showman, he won a mass following not only in the United States but also in the Caribbean, Great Britain, and many parts of Africa. Rallying his followers around the popular slogan "Africa for the

Crowned emperor of Ethiopia in 1930, Haile Selassie (1892–1975) gained international attention when his country was invaded by Italy in 1935. Haile Selassie's reign extended until 1974, when he was overthrown by a military coup.

Africans," Garvey called for black self-awareness and economic self-sufficiency and Africa's immediate independence. He founded the Black Star shipping line to repatriate blacks to Africa. His activities drew the ire of the American government, which jailed Garvey on tax evasion charges and deported him in 1929. He spent the rest of his life in Jamaica and Britain.

The event that galvanized black opinion throughout the world was the Italian invasion of Ethiopia in 1935. As one of only two African states that survived the scramble for Africa, Ethiopia—and its emperor, Haile Selassie—symbolized Africa's independence and freedom. Ethiopia fell victim, however, to the expansionist designs of the Italian dictator Benito Mussolini, who sought an Italian East African empire and revenge for the Italian defeat at Aduwa in 1896. Using the pretext of a skirmish with Ethiopian troops on the Italian Somaliland border, Mussolini ignored Selassie's calls for international arbitration and marched his troops into Ethiopia. A quarter of a million poorly trained and inadequately armed Ethiopian soldiers were no match for the mechanized Italian army. The Ethiopians, who could field only 13 unarmed planes, were no match for the Italian air force, which had no compunction about using poison gas against their opponent.

The Jamaican-born Marcus Garvey was a fiery Pan-Africanist. After settling in the Harlem neighborhood of New York City in 1916, he won a large black following not only in the United States but throughout the world.

The Awakening of a Pan-African Spirit

Peter Abraham's (b. 1918) autobiography recounts his years growing up in South Africa. Since leaving South Africa in 1940, he has resided in England and Jamaica and has gained acclaim as a novelist. In this passage he relates how he was introduced to African-American music and literature.

I found the Bantu Men's Social Centre on the outer rim of Johannesburg, on the way to Langlaagte and the white mountains of sand that towered beyond it. It was a huge building that stood in its own grounds.

I hesitated uncertainly on the pavement till two well-dressed black men speaking English passed me and went in. I followed them. There was a passage that widened into a rectangular hall. Doors led off to right and left. On the first door on the left was the word: "Secretary." The two men passed that and entered the second door on the left. I knocked on the door marked "Secretary." . . .

From the other side of the huge door that faced the passage came a deep voice, touched with the velvet quality of organ notes, singing a familiar song.

The organ notes stopped. Another, lighter voice, without the magic quality of the first, sang the same words, tried to make them sound the same, but failed. Then the magnificent voice sang a little more of the song. And again the lighter voice repeated it. If only the lighter voice would leave the other alone! Others must have shared my feeling, for a man came out of the door where the two had gone in earlier. He pushed the great door open. I saw part of a huge hall.

"Hlubi, man!" the man called. "The fellows want to hear Robeson. Turn it up!"

"All right."

Black men appeared from everywhere and stood in silence.

That was a black man, one of us! I knew it. I needed no proof. The men about me, their faces, their bearing, carried all the proof. That was a black man! The voice of a black man!

The glorious voice stopped. The men went back to what they were doing. The moment that had given us a common identity was over. Robeson the man had called him. A name to remember, that. I would find out about that man.

"Some voice, heh, son?" a man said to me.

"Yessir!"

"He's an American Negro," the man said, and moved away.

I followed him through the door where the greatest number went. It was a long room, spacious, and with big windows that let in light.

I moved over to the bookshelves. I wanted to touch the books, but held back. Perhaps it was not permitted. Typed slips showed what each shelf held: novels, history, sociology, travel, Africans, political science, American Negro literature . . . I stopped there, American Negro literature. The man had said Robeson was an American Negro.

A man got up and came over. He ran his finger along the American Negro literature shelf and took out a book.

"Excuse me. Can I look at these?"

"Of course," he smiled.

I reached up and took out a fat black book. *The Souls of Black Folk*, by W. E. B. Du Bois. I turned the pages. It spoke about a people in a valley. And they were black, and dispossessed, and denied. I skimmed through the pages, anxious to take it all in. I read:

"For this much all men know: despite compromise, war, struggle, the Negro is not free."

"The Negro is not free." . . . I remembered those "Reserved for Europeans Only" signs; I remembered no white boys ever carried bags at the market or ran from the police; I remembered my long walks in the white sections of the city, and the lavatories, and the park benches, and the tearooms . . . "The Negro is not free."

But why had I not thought of it myself? Now, having read the words, I knew that I had known this all along. But until now I had had no words to voice that knowledge. Du Bois's words had the impact of a revelation.

Elsewhere I read:

I have seen a land right merry with the sun, where children sing, and rolling hills lie like passioned women wanton with harvest. And there in the King's Highway sat and sits a figure veiled and bowed, by which the traveler's footsteps hasten as they go. On the tainted air broods fear. Three centuries' thought has been the raising and unveiling of that bowed human heart, and now behold a century new for the duty and the deed. The problem of the Twentieth Century is the problem of the colour-line.

In the months that followed, I spent nearly all my spare time in the library of the Bantu Men's Social Centre. I read every one of the books on the shelf marked: American Negro literature. I became a nationalist, a colour nationalist, through the writings of men and women who lived a world away from me. To them I owe a great debt for crystallizing my vague yearnings to write and for showing me the long dream was attainable.

Peter Abraham, *Tell Freedom: Memories of Africa* (New York: Knopf, 1966), pp. 222–226.

Ethiopia fell to the Italian advance in May 1936, forcing Haile Selassie to flee to Britain. He had faith that appeals to the League of Nations would lead Britain and France to impose a trade embargo on Italy. But Britain and France were engaged in winning over Mussolini as an ally against Hitler, and Selassie's appeals fell on deaf ears.

The downfall of Ethiopia had a stirring impact on black nationalists all over the world. When Kwame Nkrumah, a Ghanaian nationalist from the Gold Coast newly arrived in London, heard of the invasion, he said, "At that moment it was almost as if the whole of London had declared war on me personally. . . . My nationalism surged to the fore."[6] Groups of blacks in the United States and Britain founded organizations to support the Ethiopian war effort and later began to take on the larger issue of European colonialism.

As World War II was drawing to a close, several hundred black delegates met in Manchester, England, for the Fifth Pan-African Congress. Pan-African veteran Du Bois attended, as well as the Afro-Caribbean organizers of the Manchester congress, C. L. R. James, George Padmore, and Ras Makonnen. However, the most influential participants were Africans such as Nkrumah and Kenya's Jomo Kenyatta, who pressed the congress to adopt resolutions demanding immediate freedom in Africa by any means necessary. They resolved that "if the Western world is still determined to rule mankind by force, then Africans, as a last resort, may have to appeal to force in the effort to achieve Freedom, even if force destroys them and the world."[7] Henceforth the struggle for African independence was to be waged not in European centers of power but in Africa itself.

African Movements for Independence

European colonizers fully expected their rule to extend for the rest of the century, but events of World War II set off forces that accelerated the African nationalist challenge to colonial rule. One change the war brought was that thousands of Africans served as soldiers and laborers in theaters of war in North Africa, Europe, the Middle East, and Asia. As Africans witnessed the collapse of colonial power elsewhere, the myth of European invincibility was punctured. When they returned home to find massive unemployment and rampant inflation, they joined nationalist movements to express their dissatisfaction with colonial rule.

The war also brought about a change in global leadership, as Britain and France were reduced to minor powers and replaced by the United States and the Soviet Union, two countries without colonial possessions in Africa. Moreover, the newly formed United Nations and its Trusteeship Council, which had a responsibility for colonial territories under the old League of Nations, provided a forum for African nationalist leaders to voice their desires for freedom.

India's independence in 1947 also inspired the rest of the colonial world to believe that European rule could not last much longer. Gandhi's use of civil disobedience had a major impact on such prominent African nationalist leaders as Kwame Nkrumah, Julius Nyerere, and Kenneth Kaunda, who applied Gandhi's tactics to win concessions from the British.

World War II was also a dividing line for the types of organizations Africans formed to voice their grievances and concerns. Before the war, groups were established to represent the particular interests of teachers, clerks, clergy, traders, chiefs, and commercial farmers and usually concentrated on local, cultural, or ethnic issues. However, after the war, political movements developed with more ambitious goals that mobilized people on a national level. Their leaders were typically educated in mission and government schools or overseas in Europe and America.

The British colony of Gold Coast set the pace for independence in sub-Saharan Africa. The British believed that the best approach for their colonies was to groom Africans for a gradual takeover of government. They introduced a constitution in 1945 that allowed for a Legislative Council with an African majority that was not directly elected. Several years later a coalition of lawyers, teachers, and businessmen, many with ties to chiefs, formed the United Gold Coast Convention (UGCC) to counter the new constitution. UGCC leaders selected the recently returned Nkrumah as its organizing secretary, but he proved too radical for both the UGCC and British officials.

After Nkrumah formed a rival party, the Convention People's Party (CPP), in 1949, he set out to mobilize a mass following among small traders, unemployed school dropouts, and junior civil servants. When his "Positive Action" campaign sparked off widespread protests, he was jailed. When his party overwhelmingly won elections in 1951 for the Legislative Council, which now allowed for directly elected members, the British recognized the inevitable and released Nkrumah and appointed him leader of government business. After winning several more elections, Nkrumah's party called for independence, and the British granted it in 1957. The former Gold Coast colony became the new nation of Ghana.

Ghana's route to independence set a pattern for the freedom struggle in many other colonies throughout the continent. African nationalist parties won over mass followings and challenged colonial rulers, who initially resisted concessions but finally agreed to transfer power through negotiations.

Although most African nationalist movements favored nonviolent tactics, their protests occasionally escalated into armed rebellion. One place where this happened was the Kenyan highlands, as unrest grew among African squatters working on white farms. In 1950 violence flared up as the Land Freedom Army (popularly known as Mau Mau) attacked white farms and African loyalists that joined home guard units in support of the British. In their forest retreats, the rebels were effective guerrilla fighters, and it took British troops four years to quell the rebellion. Although resistance leaders were drawn from squatters, Africans living in rural reserves, and urban slum-dwellers, the British blamed the uprising on nationalist politicians such as Jomo Kenyatta. They imprisoned him and several hundred others in detention camps for many years. Although the rebels failed to drive white settlers off the land, the costs of the war were so high that British administrators no longer catered to white settler interests. British policy now favored direct negotiations with African nationalist groups, and Kenyatta and others were released from jail to engineer a transfer of power.

Ghana's independence had a catalytic effect on freedom movements in the rest of sub-Saharan African. However, France, Belgium, and especially Portugal were reluctant to follow Britain's lead. They still clung to the belief that their colonies were better off under colonial rule. However, in 1958 President Charles de Gaulle established the French Community, in which France maintained control over economic development and the external and military affairs of its colonies. De Gaulle was so confident that France's African territories preferred to stay under French rule that he offered them a choice in a referendum of joining a French-controlled federation or independence. The only French colony to defy de Gaulle was Guinea, where a trade union leader, Sekou Touré, mobilized his followers to vote against continued French rule. Guinea was granted immediate independence in 1958, although the French punitively pulled out their civil servants and equipment (even ripping out telephones) and refused to offer any economic assistance. However, Guinea's independence was a turning point, and 13 other French colonies in Africa followed suit in 1960. Belgium granted independence to the Congo the same year. Over the next decade most of the other colonies gained their freedom. The exceptions were the Portuguese colonies and the white-ruled states of Rhodesia and South Africa, who resisted any transfer of power to the African majority. Independence in those territories would take much longer and require African nationalist movements to take up arms to force change.

Conclusion

Between the two world wars, imperialism went on the defensive before the rise of nationalism in Asia and Africa. In the opening decades of the twentieth century Japan served as a model of success; it made amazing progress in industrialization and implemented a constitutional government. By 1919 the island nation had become one of the world's leading powers.

Although China was not, strictly speaking, part of the colonial world, in many ways this vast land was under the indirect influence of the Great Powers. Chinese Nationalists, led by Sun Yat-sen, overthrew the Manchu dynasty and established a republic. After years of conflict among rival factions, Chiang Kai-shek consolidated power in the Kuomintang regime. The nascent Chinese Communist movement, under Mao Tse-tung, survived the efforts of the Chinese Nationalists to destroy it.

If Japan was a model of modernization, India was a model of democratic nationalism under the leadership of Mohandas Gandhi. He preached a message of nonviolence and civil disobedience to force Britain to grant a substantial measure of self-government to the Indians. In the Islamic heartlands, one traditional empire, Qajar Persia, maintained its territorial integrity but witnessed the establishment of a new dynasty, a new name, and a program of modernizing reforms. The other, the Ottoman Empire, was broken up in the aftermath of the war and divided among independent states and mandates controlled by Britain and France. Arab nationalists bitterly contested European control in the mandated areas, while Zionists, aspiring to a Jewish homeland, challenged both the British and the indigenous Arab populace for control of Palestine. The mandates in the Arab territories stood in stark contrast to the independent states of Arabia and Turkey, the latter redeemed by Mustafa Kemal Atatürk from the ruins of the Ottoman Empire. In the background of these political struggles a new economic factor, oil, emerged as a resource that would later bring untold riches to some parts of the Middle East. But oil would not become a primary factor in global politics until after World War II.

In Africa black nationalists sought to replace colonial rule with self-government and to bring about the cultural resurgence of a people whose way of life was challenged by Western imperialism. The Pan-African movement primarily attracted a following among intellectuals. Nationalist movements, which gained momentum after World War II, helped capture the independence of the British and French African colonies.

Suggestions for Reading

For an overview, see Paul Thomas Welty, *The Asians: Their Heritage and Their Destiny* (Lippincott, 1973). Thorough coverage of Japan is provided in Edwin O. Reischauer, *Japan: The Story of a Nation*, 3rd ed. (Knopf, 1981), and Takashi Fukutake, *The*

Japanese Social Structure: Its Evolution in the Modern Century, 2nd ed. (University of Tokyo Press, 1989). For a detailed description of how the military extremists undermined parliamentary government in Japan, see Richard Storry, *The Double Patriots: A Story of Japanese Nationalism* (Greenwood, 1973). Economic pressures within Japan are discussed in James Morley, ed., *Dilemmas of Growth in Prewar Japan* (Princeton University Press, 1971).

John K. Fairbank and Kwang-ching Liu, *The Cambridge History of China: Vol. 12, Republican China, 1912–1949* (Cambridge University Press, 1983), is the essential starting point for pre-Mao China. For a solid analysis of the four decades of revolution in China, see Lucien Bianco, *Origins of the Chinese Revolution* (Stanford University Press, 1971). See also Edward Friedman's study on Sun Yat-sen, *Backward Toward Revolution* (University of California Press, 1974); Jonathan D. Spence, *The Search for Modern China*, 2nd ed. (W.W. Norton, 1999). Stuart Schram, ed., *Mao Tse-tung Unrehearsed* (Penguin, 1974), is a good selection of the Chairman's thoughts. D. G. E. Hall, *A History of Southeast Asia* (St. Martin's Press, 1968), and Harry J. Benda and John A. Larkin, *The World of Southeast Asia* (Harper & Row, 1967), provide good general coverage of the area.

For valuable studies of the architects of Indian nationalism, see Louis Fischer, *The Life of Mahatma Gandhi* (New York: Collier Books, 1966); Krishna Kripalani, *Gandhi: A Life* (Verry, 1968); Edward Thomson, *Rabindranath Tagore: Poet and Dramatist* (Greenwood, 1975); and M. C. Rau, *Jawaharlal Nehru* (Interculture, 1975). See also Bal Ram Nanda, *Gokhale, Gandhi, and the Nehrus: Studies in Indian Nationalism* (St. Martin's Press, 1975). Gandhi's own autobiography makes fascinating reading: Mohandas Gandhi, *An Autobiography: The Story of My Experiments with Truth*, trans. M. Desai (Boston: Beacon Press, 1957).

A lucid and balanced survey of the modern Middle East is William Cleveland, *A History of the Modern Middle East* (Boulder: Westview, 1994). Another is Roy Anderson et al., eds., *Politics and Change in the Middle East* (Prentice Hall, 1990). Classical studies of the nature of change in the Islamic world are John Voll, *Islam: Continuity and Change in the Modern World* (Boulder: Westview, 1982), and Albert Hourani, *Arabic Thought in the Liberal Age, 1798–1939* (Oxford University Press, 1970). For a good introduction on the mandate for Palestine, see Charles D. Smith, *Palestine and the Arab Israeli Conflict*, 3rd ed. (New York: St. Martin's Press, 1996). On the years of World War I and the British role, see the interesting account by David Fromkin, *A Peace to End All Peace* (New York: Avon Books, 1988). A short history of the Jewish people is Abba Eban, *My Country* (Random House, 1972). See also Ben Halpern, *The Idea of the Jewish State* (Harvard University Press, 1969). Ann M. Lesch, *Arab Politics in Palestine* (Cornell University Press, 1979), traces the rise of Arab nationalism in Palestine; and a documentary source is Walter Laqueur and Barry Rubin, eds., *The Israel-Arab Reader: A Documentary History of the Middle East Conflict*, 5th ed. (Penguin, 1995).

On the emergence of Turkey and of Mustafa Kemal Atatürk, see Bernard Lewis, *The Emergence of Modern Turkey* (Oxford University Press, 1968), and Feroz Ahmad, *The Making of Modern Turkey* (Routledge, 1993). On Iran in this era, see Ervand Abrahamian, *Iran Between Two Revolutions* (Princeton University Press, 1982). For a nice summary on Egypt, see Afaf Lutfi al-Sayyid Marsot, *A Short History of Modern Egypt* (Cambridge University Press, 1986); on Lebanon, see Kamal Salibi, *A House of Many Mansions* (University of California Press, 1988); and on Syria, see Phillip Khoury, *Syria and the French Mandate, 1920–1945* (Princeton University Press, 1987). For the Iraq mandate, see Peter Sluglett, *Britain in Iraq, 1914–1932* (Ithaca Press, 1976).

The impact of colonial rule in Africa is examined in Adu Boahen, *African Perspectives on Colonialism* (Johns Hopkins University Press, 1987); Crawford Young, *The African Colonial State in Comparative Perspective* (Yale University Press, 1994); and Walter Rodney, *How Europe Underdeveloped Africa* (Howard University Press, 1981). Colonialism's impact on social change is covered in Andrew Roberts, ed., *The Colonial Moment in Africa* (Cambridge University Press, 1986). European women and colonial rule are the subject of Nupur Chaudhuri and Margaret Strobel, eds., *Western Women and Imperialism: Complicity and Resistance* (Indiana University Press, 1992), and the impact of colonial rule on African women is treated in Catherine Coquery-Vidrovitch, *African Women: A Modern History* (Westview, 1997). Europe's image of Africa is presented in Jan Nederveen Pieterse, *White on Black: Images of Africa and Blacks in Western Popular Culture* (Yale University Press, 1992).

South Africa's political history is treated in Nigel Worden, *A History of Modern South Africa* (Oxford University Press, 1995), and William Beinart, *Twentieth-Century South Africa* (Oxford University Press, 1994). Black protest against white rule is examined in Thomas Karis and Gwendolen M. Carter, *From Protest to Challenge: A Documentary History of African Politics in South Africa, 1882–1964* (Hoover Institution Press, 1971).

Rhodesia's system of racial segregation is the topic of Robin Palmer, *Land and Racial Domination in Rhodesia* (Heinemann, 1977). Kenya's twentieth-century history is covered in William Ochieng, ed., *A Modern History of Kenya, 1895–1980* (Evans Brothers, 1989). The Mau Mau rebellion is treated in Greet Kershaw, *Mau Mau from Below* (Ohio University Press, 1996); Wunyabari Malobe, *Mau Mau and Kenya: An Analysis of a Peasant Revolt* (Indiana University Press, 1993); Cora Presley, *Kikuyu Women, the Mau Mau Rebellion, and Social Change in Kenya* (Westview, 1992); and David Throup, *Economic and Social Origins of Mau Mau, 1945–1953* (Ohio University Press, 1988).

The Pan-Africanist movement is assessed in Imanuel Geiss, *The Pan-African Movement* (Methuen, 1974); Ronald Walters, *Pan-Africanism in the African Diaspora: An Analysis of Modern Afrocentric Political Movements* (Wayne State University Press, 1993); and Hakim Adi, ed., *The 1945 Manchester Pan-African Congress Revisited* (New Beacon Books, 1995).

Overviews of the decolonization of Africa are David Birmingham, *The Decolonization of Africa* (Ohio University Press, 1995); John D. Hargreaves, *Decolonization of Africa* (Longman, 1988); and Prosser Gifford and William Roger Louis, eds., *The Transfer of Power in Africa: Decolonization, 1940–1960* (Yale University Press, 1982).

Suggestions for Web Browsing

History: Republic of China, 1912–1949
http://darkwing.uoregon.edu/~felsing/cstuff/republic.html

Numerous documents, and links to other sites, about the people and events of China, 1912–1949, compiled by the Council on East Asian Libraries.

Itihaas: Chronology—Modern India
http://www.itihaas.com/modern/index.html

Extensive chronology of modern India, 1756–1947; most entries include subsites with text and images.

Gandhi
http://amerisoft.net/india/gandhi.htm

An extensive biography of Gandhi with a listing of additional related sites including an audio of a speech.

Internet Islamic History Sourcebook: The Islamic World, 1918–1945

http://www.fordham.edu/halsall/islam/islambook.html#Islamic Nationalism

On-line source for links about the history of the Middle East, 1918–1945.

Internet African History Sourcebook: The Fight for Independence

http://www.fordham.edu/halsall/africa/africasbook.html# The Fight for Independence

On-line source of links about the African struggle for independence. Includes African National Congress: Historical Documents (at ANC.org), which contains a substantial selection of ANC documents, as well as book-length studies of the issues over the past century; and the Manifesto of the Second Pan African Congress, 1922.

Notes

1. Louis Fischer, *The Life of Mahatma Gandhi* (New York: Collier Books, 1966), p. 159.
2. Ibid., p. 285.
3. Jawaharlal Nehru, *Toward Freedom* (New York: Day, 1942), p. 353.
4. William Cleveland, *A History of the Modern Middle East* (Boulder, Colo.: Westview Press, 1994), p. 155.
5. Quoted in William Tordoff, *Government and Politics in Africa*, 3rd ed. (Indiana University Press, 1997), p. 39.
6. Kwame Nkrumah, *Ghana: The Autobiography of Kwame Nkrumah* (London: Nelson, 1957), p. 27.
7. Ali Mazrui and Michael Tidy, *Nationalism and New States in Africa* (London: Heinemann, 1984), p. 22.

President Harry Truman's controversial decision to drop the atomic
bombs at Hiroshima and Nagasaki
in 1945 helped end the war in the
Pacific. However, as nuclear competition between the United States
and the USSR led to devices of
enormously greater destructiveness
than the bombs dropped in 1945,
the mushroom cloud came to symbolize the reality that scientists had
created weapons that could extinguish humanity. Détente between
Moscow and Washington brought a
period of relaxation in the 1980s
and 1990s, but fears of nuclear
proliferation remain.

Western Weakness, Diplomatic Failure, and World War II

In the first decade after World War I, statesmen with global vision made serious attempts to control conflict through international organizations and treaties limiting arms and outlawing war. In the 1930s, however, the competition among states resumed its traditionally violent course. Ambitious dictators made war in Asia, Africa, and Europe, while representatives from the democracies tried to reason with them.

From 1939 to 1945 the Second World War, with its new and horrible technologies, ravaged the globe. Large bombers carried the war to civilians hundreds of miles behind what used to be known as the front lines. Hitler made use of industrial technology to try to exterminate an entire people. Only a massive counterattack by the Allied Powers, capped by the use of the atomic bomb in Japan, brought an end to the fighting.

The Troubled Calm: The West in the 1920s

The aftershocks of World War I overwhelmed the interwar period. The horror, expense, and exhaustion of the tragedy haunted losers and winners alike. A substantial portion of the younger generation had died. Political leadership fell to either the old or the untried. It was in this uncertain environment that the League of Nations began its work.

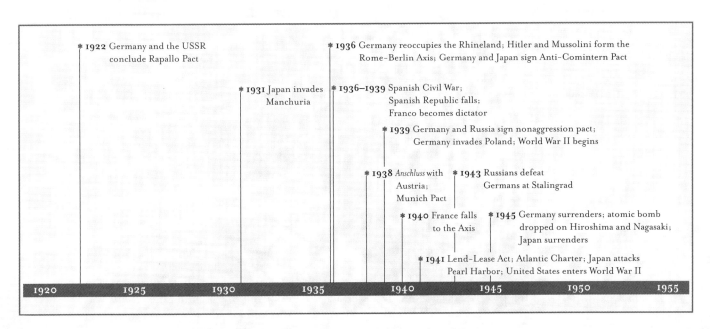

1922 Germany and the USSR conclude Rapallo Pact

1931 Japan invades Manchuria

1936 Germany reoccupies the Rhineland; Hitler and Mussolini form the Rome–Berlin Axis; Germany and Japan sign Anti-Comintern Pact

1936–1939 Spanish Civil War; Spanish Republic falls; Franco becomes dictator

1939 Germany and Russia sign nonaggression pact; Germany invades Poland; World War II begins

1938 *Anschluss* with Austria; Munich Pact

1943 Russians defeat Germans at Stalingrad

1940 France falls to the Axis

1945 Germany surrenders; atomic bomb dropped on Hiroshima and Nagasaki; Japan surrenders

1941 Lend–Lease Act; Atlantic Charter; Japan attacks Pearl Harbor; United States enters World War II

1920   1925   1930   1935   1940   1945   1950   1955

The League of Nations

The League's record from 1919 to 1929 was modest, neither one of failure nor one of triumph. Such threats to peace as disputes between Sweden and Finland and between Britain and Turkey were resolved. When a major power defied the League, however, as in the case of Italy's quarrel with Greece over Corfu, the organization could do nothing. The refusal of the United States, the world's strongest democracy, to join weakened the League's peacekeeping possibilities.

Through no fault of the League's, little progress was made in the field of disarmament. On one occasion, perhaps because of its relative weakness, the Soviet Union proposed complete disarmament. The British delegates, among others, were suspicious of the Communists' sincerity in wanting to surround the world in a "loving embrace."[1] The member states' firmly rooted feelings of mutual distrust and fear of losing sovereignty undermined the League's authority.

However, the League had a distinguished list of accomplishments in other areas. It supervised the exchange and repatriation of prisoners of war and saved thousands of refugees from starvation. It helped Austria, Bulgaria, and Hungary secure badly needed loans. The League also provided valuable services in administering the region of the Saar Basin and the Free City of Danzig. It investigated the existence of slavery in certain parts of the world, sought to stanch traffic in dangerous drugs, and stood ready to offer assistance when disasters brought suffering and destruction.

In the intellectual and cultural realm the League published books and periodicals dealing with national and international problems of all kinds and from its own radio station broadcast important information, particularly in the field of health. Unfortunately, the League's excellent record in these areas has been obscured by its failure to maintain a lasting peace.

The French Quest for Security

Because the United States chose to play a limited role in international affairs and Great Britain returned to its traditional focus on the empire and the Commonwealth, France assumed the leadership of postwar Europe. In 1919 the French pursued a very simple but difficult foreign policy goal: absolute security. Since the Napoleonic grandeur a century earlier, the French had seen their power and authority diminish while German economic and military strength had increased. Twice in 50 years Germany had invaded France, with horrendous results.

France spent much of the postwar decade trying to guarantee its own safety by keeping Germany weak. In the first five years after the armistice the French wanted to impose maximum financial penalties on the Germans. In 1923, assisted by the Belgians, they occupied the Ruhr region in a move that had immense short- and long-range implications (see Chapter 30). Some historians have seen in this act the first step toward World War II because it hardened the German desire for revenge. Even though the Dawes Plan eased the situation, the French attitude divided the former Allies and provided ammunition to German ultranationalists.

The rift between the French and the Germans was papered over in Locarno, Switzerland, in 1925. In the Locarno Pact, Germany, Great Britain, France, and Italy agreed to guarantee the existing frontiers along the Rhine, to establish a demilitarized zone 30 miles deep along the east bank of the Rhine, and to refrain from attacking one another. The problems along France's eastern frontier would be dealt with by international guarantee (although the British dominions stated their disagreement) and U.S. money. Germany received, and accepted, an invitation to join the League of Nations, a symbolic act that seemed to indicate its return to the international community. Still, the Locarno Pact addressed only Germany's western frontier and left unresolved the controversial issues of the territories of the newly formed and contentious nations of eastern Europe. Another well-meaning but ultimately ineffectual agreement was the Kellogg-Briand Pact (1928), developed by U.S. Secretary of State Frank Kellogg and French Foreign Minister Aristide Briand. This pact, eventually signed by 62 nations, outlawed war as an instrument of national policy but omitted provisions to enforce the agreement.

The Paris government had little faith in the Covenant of the League of Nations as a guarantee of France's survival. The French instead depended more and more on their own diplomats. They tried to construct a wall of allies along Germany's eastern frontier that would simultaneously surround the Germans and isolate the Soviet Union. As long as Germany was weak and dependent on Western loans, France could operate as the major diplomatic power on the Continent. But even in the 1920s France lacked the strength or the vision to lead Europe. When Germany and Italy began to flex their muscles in the 1930s, France—even with British help—responded to fascist aggression from a position of weakness.

Soviet and German Cooperation

The Soviet Union and Germany, the two diplomatic outcasts of the 1920s, quickly forged a working relationship that was useful to both of them. The USSR had isolated itself by signing the Treaty of Brest-Litovsk, nationalizing foreign property, and repudiat-

Erich Maria Remarque, *The Road Back*

Erich Maria Remarque, who wrote so eloquently of the horrors of war in *All Quiet on the Western Front,* compellingly expressed the despair and frustration of German veterans in *The Road Back.* He captures the mood that helped Hitler gain power.

Demonstrations in the streets have been called for this afternoon. Prices have been soaring everywhere for months past, and the poverty is greater even than it was during the war. Wages are insufficient to buy the bare necessities of life, and even though one may have the money it is often impossible to buy anything with it. But ever more and more gin palaces and dance halls go up, and ever more and more blatant is the profiteering and swindling.

Scattered groups of workers on strike march through the streets. Now and again there is a disturbance. A rumour is going about that troops have been concentrated at the barracks. But there is no sign of it as yet.

Here and there one hears cries and counter-cries. Somebody is haranguing at a street corner. Then suddenly everywhere is silence.

A procession of men in the faded uniforms of the front-line trenches is moving slowly toward us.

It was formed up by sections, marching in fours. Big white placards are carried before: *Where is the Fatherland's gratitude?—The War Cripples are starving.*

It was no good to go on assuming that a common basis for all the different groups and classes in Germany could be found. The break between them became daily wider and more irreparable. The plebiscite of the Right "against the Young Plan and the war-guilt lie" proved just as unsuccessful as those arranged in former years by the Left, but the poison of the defamatory agitation remained in the body of the community, and we watched its effects with anxiety.

In my own family the political antagonism was growing past endurance. In October Fritz had finished his apprenticeship in an old-established export house, at the precise moment when the firm went bankrupt—a minor incident compared with such events as the breakdown of the Frankfurt General Insurance Company and the Civil Servants' Bank or the enforced reorganization and amalgamation of the Deutsche Bank and the Disconto-Gesellschaft, which all happened in the course of the year and dangerously damaged the whole economic life of Germany. Yet for my brother the bankruptcy of his firm overshadowed all other happenings, since it meant that he lost his job. His three years' training was in vain—there was not a single export firm which was not forced to dismiss as many of its employees as possible.

"Yes, that's just it—millions! If it isn't my fault, whose fault is it? I tell you—your friends, the French, the English, the Americans, all those damnable nations who inflict on us one dishonorable penalty after the other—they are to blame for all this. Before the war the whole world bought German goods. My firm exported to Africa, to the German colonies. Hundreds of thousands we turned over every year. But they have robbed us of our colonies, of all our foreign markets. They have stolen the coal mines in the Saar and in Upper Silesia, they squeeze millions of marks out of our bleeding country. We'll never rise again unless we free ourselves by another war."

"Don't be foolish, Fritz. Things are bad in the whole world."

"I don't care about the world, I care only about Germany, which you and your pacifists have delivered into the hands of our enemies. I despise you, you are not worthy to call yourself a German."

ing foreign debts as well as by espousing its communist ideology internationally. Probably the greatest barrier was the ideological one, as expressed through the activities of the Third Communist International, or Comintern. That body, organized in 1919, was dedicated to the overthrow of capitalism throughout the world.

In the 1920s the Comintern spread communist propaganda, established Communist parties, and infiltrated labor unions and other working-class groups throughout the world. Even after Lenin had given up hope for an immediate world revolution and started to normalize relations with the West, the Comintern encouraged radicals who had broken off from moderate socialist groups to organize Communist parties. Communists of all countries became members of the Comintern, meeting in congresses held in Moscow and setting up committees to coordinate their activities. Communist parties were different from other national political groups because they owed their allegiance to an international organization rather than to the nations in which they resided.

By 1922 the Soviet Union was pursuing a two-pronged foreign policy. One approach used the Communist parties abroad to achieve ideological goals, as in China, where the Communists were active until

Soviet-German Relations, 1917–1939

1917	Germans financially support Bolsheviks
1918	Treaty of Brest-Litovsk
1919–1922	Weimar-Soviet secret joint military agreements
1922	Rapallo Pact formalizes German-Russian cooperation
1926	Rapallo Pact extended five years
1933–1937	Stalin unsuccessfully advocates common front against Germany
1933–1937	Hitler speaks out against USSR, signs Anti-Comintern Pact
1938–1939	Renewed secret negotiations between Moscow and Berlin
1939	USSR-German nonaggression pact

defeated by Chiang Kai-shek in 1927. The other approach worked through normal international channels for traditional economic and diplomatic goals, generally in Europe.

From the time Lenin left Switzerland to return to Petrograd, the Soviet Union enjoyed a mutually advantageous relationship with Germany. At the beginning of the 1920s the two nations carried on secret agreements allowing for joint military training enterprises. Their first major open diplomatic contact came at Rapallo, Italy, in 1922, where they renounced the concept of reparations. In the Rapallo Pact, the Germans and Russians agreed to cooperate in a number of areas. Germany was extremely bitter about the treatment it had received at Versailles; the Soviets had faced Allied intervention during their civil war. It naturally followed that a main feature of the foreign policies of both countries would be either to ignore the Versailles settlement or to escape from its consequences. Both countries shared the ambition to dominate Poland, against whom the USSR had fought at the beginning of the decade.

Although, as Lenin perceptively noted, Russia wanted revolution while Germany sought revenge, the two nations cooperated closely until 1933. Then, after a six-year gap, they cooperated again in the Nazi-Soviet nonaggression pact.

The Weimar government under Gustav Stresemann wanted to rearm but was forbidden to do so by the Versailles treaty. Stresemann backed the cooperation between his government and the Soviet Union to build up German military might. Berlin supplied technical aid to the USSR while German pilots and specialists went on maneuvers in Russia. Even after the proclamation of the so-called spirit of Locarno, the two nations worked with each other. In 1926 the Rapallo Pact was renewed for another five years.

Epoch of the Aggressors

The world found little peace or stability after World War I. Economic and social discontent buttressed by widespread disillusionment with the peace treaties posed grave problems for the victorious Allies. Almost as weak as the defeated powers, France and the United Kingdom had to take on the responsibility for maintaining the peace. The awful toll taken by the Great War convinced the democracies that never again should humanity have to endure such a tragedy. From the point of view of the new aggressors, however, this attitude reflected weakness and cowardice—and opportunity.

Japan Invades Manchuria, 1931

The United States and Britain, however, were alarmed by the growth of Japanese power. By 1931 Japanese investments in China were second only to those of Great Britain, constituting around 35 percent of all foreign investment in China. That same year, responding to perceived population pressures and resource needs, the Japanese military disregarded international treaties and opinions and attacked China. The Japanese invasion of Manchuria was the first step on the road to World War II.

Aggression and Democratic Nonresponse, 1931–1938

1931	Japanese invade Manchuria
1932	Japanese attack Shanghai
1934–1935	Italians invade Ethiopia
1935	Remilitarization of the Rhineland by Germany
1936	Spanish General Francisco Franco rebels against government of republican Spain
1937	Japanese renew advance in China
1938	German *Anschluss* with Austria; dismemberment of Czechoslovakia in the wake of the Munich Accords

Unable to cope with the invader, the Chinese appealed to the League of Nations, which appointed a committee of inquiry in 1933. The committee's report condemned the aggression but at the same time tried not to provoke Japan. The outcome was that the League neither put an end to the aggression nor kept Japan as a member—two years later Tokyo withdrew from the organization.

When the Chinese resorted to an effective nationwide boycott of Japanese goods, the invaders attacked Shanghai in 1932 and began to push deeper into northern China. To slow down the invasion and give themselves a chance in the inevitable struggle, the Chinese agreed to a truce in May 1933 that recognized Tokyo's conquests in Manchuria and northern China.

Despite an undeclared civil war between Chiang Kai-shek's Nationalist forces and the Communist movement led by Mao Tse-tung, China strengthened its position in the face of the Japanese threat. Following Soviet directions, Mao stated that the first objective of all China should be wholehearted resistance against foreign imperialists. A united front between Chiang and Mao was difficult, but in December 1936 and January 1937 the Communists and Nationalists put aside their conflicts, proclaimed a truce, and established a united front against the Japanese. Neither of the parties in the front trusted the other, but both feared the Japanese more.

In 1937 the Japanese, with no official declaration of hostility, renewed their advance and began what would be an eight-year war. After advancing rapidly up the Yangtze River to Nanking, where they committed atrocities, Tokyo's forces captured Peking and proclaimed the "New Order" in eastern Asia. The New Order's objectives were to destroy Chiang Kai-shek's regime, expel Western interests from East Asia, and establish a self-sufficient economic bloc, to include Japan, Manchuria, and China.

The outbreak of war in Europe in 1939 gave Japan a golden opportunity to expand the New Order in China and into the Asian colonies of the Western powers. The Japanese took the island of Hainan in 1939 and, after the fall of France in June 1940, built naval and air bases in Indochina. From there they put pressure on the Netherlands East Indies and the British outposts at Hong Kong and Singapore.

None of the three powers who might have halted the Japanese advance in the 1930s did anything. Britain was in the depths of an economic crisis, France was suffering from political and economic paralysis, and the United States was totally absorbed in fighting the effects of the Great Depression.

Italy Attacks Ethiopia

While Japan pursued old goals in new ways, Italy set out to claim a prize it had failed to take in 1896—

Americans and Europeans are generally aware that the Soviet Union lost more than 20 million people in the Second World War. Fewer are aware, however, that when the Japanese invaded China in 1931, they opened up a series of conflicts that would result in more than 20 million Chinese deaths by 1945. It is hard to comprehend suffering on that scale. Here, in a more limited form, one can see the tragic results of the Japanese invasions.

Ethiopia, one of only two independent states left in Africa. Late in 1934 fighting broke out between the Ethiopians and the Italians, and in the following year, Mussolini's forces invaded the country. Emperor Haile Selassie made a dramatic appearance before the League to appeal for help.

The League tried to arrange for arbitration. Unconvinced by the shameless Italian argument that Ethiopia, not Italy, was the aggressor, the League voted to prohibit shipment of certain goods to Italy and to deny it credit. But the effect of the sanctions was minor because oil—without which no modern army could fight—was not included in the list of prohibited articles. France and Britain gave only lukewarm support to the sanctions because they did not want to alienate Italy. The United States, which had not joined the League, and Germany, which had left it by that time, largely ignored the prohibitions. Only outraged public opinion, moved by newspaper photographs showing barefooted Ethiopians fighting the modern Italian army, drove the governments to even the pretense of action.

Using bombs, mustard gas, and tanks, the Italians advanced swiftly into Ethiopia and crushed Haile Selassie's army. Meanwhile, the German reoccupation of the Rhineland in March helped shift international attention away from the conflict in Africa. The whole sorry story ended in July 1936 when sanctions were removed. Haile Selassie, an emperor without a country, went to live in Britain, the first of several royal exiles who would be forced from their thrones in the next decade.

The Rhineland and the Axis

Soon after taking power, Hitler carried out the revisions the Germans wanted in the Versailles treaty. He also won his country's support by seeking revenge against the Allies. As George F. Kennan noted at the time, "The man is acting in the best traditions of German nationalism, and his conception of his own mission is perhaps clearer than that of his predecessors because it is uncomplicated by any sense of responsibility to European culture as a whole."[2] During his first two years in power Hitler paid lip service to peace while increasing the tempo of rearmament. In March 1935 he negated the disarmament clauses of the Versailles treaty and a year later reoccupied the Rhineland.

The move, which Hitler described as producing the most nerve-racking moments of his life, sent German troops marching boldly into the Rhineland in defiance of the Versailles treaty and the Locarno agreements. The Germans could not have resisted had the British and French moved in response. But London did nothing, and Paris mobilized 150,000 troops behind the Maginot line but did no more. Hitler later confessed that had the French advanced against him, "We would have had to withdraw with our tails between our legs, for the military resources at our disposal would have been totally inadequate for even a moderate resistance."[3]

The League's weak response to the Japanese invasion of China and the Italian attack on Ethiopia combined with the feeble British and French reaction to German reoccupation of the Rhineland encouraged the aggressors and served as a prelude to the formation of the Axis alliance. Until Hitler gained power, Germany had been without close allies. After the Ethiopian crisis and the League sanctions, Italy and Germany began to work more closely together. In 1936 they formalized the friendship in the Rome-Berlin Axis, and one year later Mussolini followed Hitler's lead by withdrawing from the League of Nations.

Japan, the third major member of the Axis, joined forces with Germany in 1936 in the Anti-Comintern Pact. A year later Italy also joined in that agreement, which effectively encircled the Soviet Union. Relations between Moscow and Berlin had cooled after 1934, and the Soviet Union now became the object of anticommunist rhetoric. Many right-wing leaders in the West hoped that the "Red menace" would be taken care of by Hitler and his allies.

All in all, 1936 was a banner year for Hitler. He had gained allies, pleased his own people by remilitarizing the Rhineland, learned the weakness of the democratic powers and the League, and gained international prestige from his successful staging of the Olympic Games. He also found a successful device to distract potential opponents' attention: the Spanish Civil War.

The Spanish Tragedy

By 1936 the five-year-old Spanish republic was disintegrating. It had brought neither prosperity nor stability to Spain. Reactionary forces had tried to gain control of the government while left-wing groups had resorted to terrorism. The liberal approach had failed, and in the summer of 1936 the army revolted against the legal government in Madrid.

General Francisco Franco (1892–1975) commanded the insurgents, who included in their ranks most of the regular army troops. Mussolini strongly backed Franco, and the rightist forces expected a quick victory. However, many groups stood by the republic, and they put up a strong resistance against the insurgents, stopping them at the outskirts of Madrid.

By the end of 1936 each side had gained the backing of a complicated alliance of forces. Franco had the support of the Italians, who sent large numbers of planes, troops, and weapons, and the Germans, who tested their latest military technology against the republicans. The republic gained the support of the Soviet Union, which sent arms, "advisers," and other supplies, as well as a large contingent of disorganized but idealistic antifascist fighters, including a number from Britain and the United States.

The insurgents capitalized on Soviet support for the republic, and Franco pronounced his cause to be strictly an anticommunist crusade—a cunning oversimplification of dubious validity, considering that the communists were never in control of more than a snippet of republican Spain, and that for only a few months in 1938 until Stalin decided to pull his support.[4] While Spain bled, suffering more than 700,000 deaths, outside forces took advantage of the tragic situation for their own selfish purposes.

The democratic powers—Great Britain, France, and the United States—attempted to stay out of the conflict. Britain did not want to risk a Continental war. France suffered from internal divisions that made its leaders fear that their country, too, might dissolve in civil war. The United States declared its official neutrality. Instead of permitting arms to be sent to the recognized, legally constituted republican government, which had the right under international law to purchase weapons for self-defense, Britain and France set up a nonintervention system by which the nations of Europe agreed not to send arms to either side. Only the democracies adhered to this

Members of the Condor Legion raise their arms in the Nazi salute as they pass the reviewing stand during a victory parade in Madrid shortly after the fall of the last republican stronghold, Barcelona, marking the end of the Spanish Civil War. The war in Spain served as a rehearsal for the wider struggle ahead as Germany and Italy came together to support Franco's insurrectionists against the republicans, who received aid in the form of technicians and political advisers from the Soviet Union.

arrangement, which was meant to limit the scope of the conflict. The various dictators continued to send support to their respective sides.

After the last holdout, Barcelona fell in March 1939, and the Spanish republic was no more. Franco, at the head of the new state, gained absolute power, which he held until his death in 1975. The Spanish Civil War was a national catastrophe that left permanent scars on a proud and gallant people.

Appeasement and Weakness

In 1937 Neville Chamberlain (1869–1940) became Britain's prime minister. Years before he took office, the British had tried to achieve détente with the Germans backed by "an efficient bomber air force." Chamberlain tried a new strategy: a defense policy based on a fighter air force and centered solely on protecting Britain. He wanted to make "more positive overtures to Germany to appease her grievances and reach a settlement on the basis not of fear by deterrence but of mutual interests and separate spheres of influence." Chamberlain's name came to symbolize the policy of appeasement, the policy of meeting German demands and grievances without demanding

firm reciprocal advantages; asking instead only for future "mutual understandings."[5]

Chamberlain took the direction of foreign policy on his own shoulders in his attempt to explore every possibility for reaching an understanding with the dictators. He dedicated himself to an effort to ease international tensions despite snubs from those he wished to placate and warnings from his military and foreign policy advisers. He based his policy on the most humane of motives—peace—and on the most civilized of assumptions—that Hitler could be reasonable and fair-minded. By showing good faith and by withdrawing from any possibility of being able to wage war on the Continent, Chamberlain froze himself into a position of having to avoid war at any cost. His policies were strongly supported in Britain and throughout most of the British Commonwealth.

France had shown that it would not move militarily without British backing, and under Chamberlain the entente with France was put on the back burner, a development that hurt French resolve. The democratic world became uneasily aware of its growing weakness in comparison with the dictators. As the European balance of power shifted, the small

After the fall of Barcelona in 1939, thousands of Spanish refugees streamed to the French frontier to escape the fascists.

states began to draw away from the impotent League of Nations.

The prestige of the Axis blossomed. Some nations tried to make deals with Germany and Italy, while others, including the Scandinavian countries and the Netherlands, withdrew into the shelter of neutrality and "innocent isolation." In eastern Europe semifascist regimes became the order of the day, as the states in that unhappy region, with the exception of Czechoslovakia, lined up to get in Germany's good graces. In 1934 Poland had signed a nonaggression pact with Germany. Belgium gave up its alliance with France. In eastern Europe, only Czechoslovakia remained loyal to Paris.

Hitler became increasingly aware of the opportunity presented by Britain's "peace at any price" policy and the decline of the French alliance system. On November 5, 1937, in a meeting at the Reich Chancellery in Berlin that lasted for more than four hours,

Hitler laid out his plans and ideas for the future. According to the notes of the meeting taken by Colonel Friedrich Hossbach, the Führer gave a statement that was to be regarded "in the event of his death, as his last will and testament."

"The aim of German policy," Hitler noted, "was to make secure and to preserve the racial community and to enlarge it. It was therefore a question of space. Germany's future was wholly conditional upon the need for space." The answer to that question was force, which was to be applied in the next six years, because after 1943 German technological and military superiority would be lost. Hossbach noted that "the Führer believed that almost certainly Britain, and probably France as well, had already tacitly written off the Czechs."[6]

Historians still debate the importance of the Chancellery meeting. Hitler's message was not favorably received by the military staff present, since they knew

At the Munich Conference in September 1938, British prime minister Neville Chamberlain (left) and French premier Édouard Daladier (next to him) capitulated to Hitler's demands regarding Czechoslovakia. Italian dictator Benito Mussolini stands to the right of Hitler.

full well that Germany was in no shape to fight. Yet the significance of the message can be found in the wholesale changes in personnel Hitler introduced at the end of 1937 and in the contrast it affords to the views of Chamberlain. The prime minister wanted peace at any price. The Führer wanted space at any price.

Toward Austria and the Sudetenland

When Hitler announced the military reoccupation of the Rhineland in the spring of 1936, he stated, "We have no territorial demands to make in Europe." He lied. By 1938, with the German army growing in strength and the air force becoming a powerful unit, the Führer began to implement one of his foreign policy goals—placing the German-speaking peoples under one Reich. The first step on that path was to unite Austria and Germany in the *Anschluss* ("joining").

In 1934 the Nazis had badly bungled an attempt to annex Austria. Two years later, softening-up operations began again, and by 1938 intense pressure had been levied against Austrian chancellor Kurt von Schuschnigg to cooperate with Berlin. After a stormy meeting with Hitler in February, Schuschnigg restated his country's desire to be independent, although concessions would be made to Germany. He called for a plebiscite in March to prove his point. Outraged at this independent action, Hitler ordered Schuschnigg to resign and to cancel the vote. Both actions were taken, but Hitler sent his forces into Austria anyway.

By March 13, 1938, a new chancellor, approved by Hitler, announced the union of Austria and Germany. After a month in which all opposition was silenced, Hitler held his own plebiscite and gained a majority of 99.75 percent in favor of union. The democratic powers did not intervene to help Austria. In

The Hossbach Memorandum

Two years before the outbreak of World War II, Adolf Hitler recapitulated his goals in a secret meeting. Colonel Friedrich Hossbach took down Hitler's comments.

The aim of German policy was to make secure and to preserve the racial community and to enlarge it. It was therefore a question of space.

The German racial community comprised over 85 million people and, because of their number and the narrow limits of habitable space in Europe, constituted a tightly packed racial core such as was not to be met in any other country and such as implied the right to a greater living space than in the case of other peoples. . . .

Germany's future was therefore wholly conditional upon the solving of the need for space, and such a solution could be sought, of course, only for a foreseeable period of about one to three generations. . . .

The question for Germany ran: where could she achieve the greatest gain at the lowest cost? . . .

Case 1: Period 1943–1945

After this date only a change for the worse, from our point of view, could be expected.

The equipment of the army, navy, and Luftwaffe, as well as the formation of the officer corps, was nearly completed. Equipment and armament were modern; in further delay there lay the danger of their obsolescence. In particular, the secrecy of "special weapons" could not be preserved forever. The recruiting of reserves was limited to current age groups; further drafts from older untrained age groups were no longer available.

Our relative strength would decrease in relation to the rearmament which would by then have been carried out by the rest of the world. If we did not act by 1943–45, any year could, in consequence of a lack of reserves, produce the food crisis, to cope with which the necessary foreign exchange was not available, and this must be regarded as a "waning point of the regime." Besides, the world was expecting our attack and was increasing its counter-measures from year to year. It was while the rest of the world was still preparing its defenses that we were obliged to take the offensive. . . .

Case 2

If internal strife in France should develop into such a domestic crisis as to absorb the French Army completely and render it incapable of use for war against Germany, then the time for action against the Czechs had come.

Case 3

If France is so embroiled by a war with another state that she cannot "proceed" against Germany.

For the improvement of our politico-military position our first objective, in the event of our being embroiled in war, must be to overthrow Czechoslovakia and Austria simultaneously in order to remove the threat to our flank in any possible operation against the West. In a conflict with France it was hardly to be regarded as likely that the Czechs would declare war on us on the very same day as France. The desire to join in the war would, however, increase among the Czechs in proportion to any weakening on our part and then her participation could clearly take the form of an attack toward Silesia, toward the north or toward the west. . . .

The Führer saw case 3 coming definitely nearer; it might emerge from the present tensions in the Mediterranean, and he was resolved to take advantage of it whenever it happened, even as early as 1938.

From *Auswartiges Amt: Documents on German Foreign Policy*, Series D, Vol. 1 (Washington, D.C.: U.S. Government Printing Office, 1949), pp. 29–49.

---

fact, the British ambassador to Germany "had indicated only too clearly that Britain would welcome alteration in Austria's status, if it were done peaceably."[7]

Following his success in Austria, Hitler moved on to his next objective, the annexation of the Sudetenland. This area along the western border of Czechoslovakia was populated mainly by German textile workers who had suffered economically dur-ing the depression. The Sudetenland was also the site of the extremely well-fortified Czech defenses. In September 1938 the Führer bluntly informed Chamberlain that he was determined to gain self-determination for the Sudeten Germans. He charged, falsely, that the Czechs had mistreated the German minorities. In fact, among the eastern European states, Czechoslovakia had the best record in dealing with minority nationalities. But in this affair Britain and

France consistently overlooked both the record of the Prague government and the Czech statesmen themselves.

Chamberlain persuaded French premier Edouard Daladier that the sacrifice of Czechoslovakia would save the peace. When the French joined the British to press the Czechs to accept the Nazi demands, the Prague government had little choice but to agree. Chamberlain informed Hitler of Czechs' willingness to compromise, only to find that the German demands had increased considerably. Angered by the Führer's duplicity, Chamberlain refused to accept the new terms, which included Czech evacuation of some areas and the cession of large amounts of matériel and agricultural goods.

Munich and Democratic Betrayal

The crisis over Czechoslovakia would be the last major international issue decided only by European powers. Symbolically, it would be viewed as a failure that would affect diplomatic decisions for generations to come. On September 28, 1938, Chamberlain received a note from Hitler inviting him to attend a conference at Munich. The following day Chamberlain flew to Germany to meet with Hitler, Mussolini, and Daladier at Nazi headquarters. They worked for 13 hours on the details of the surrender of the Sudetenland. No Czech representative was present, nor were the Soviets—outspoken allies of the Czechs—consulted.

The conference accepted all of Hitler's demands and, in addition, rewarded Poland and Hungary with slices of unfortunate Czechoslovakia. The tragedy for the Czechs brought relief for millions of Europeans, half-crazed with fear of war. But thoughtful individuals pondered whether this settlement would be followed by another crisis. Winston Churchill, who was then in political eclipse in Britain, solemnly warned: "Do not suppose that this is the end. This is only the beginning of the reckoning."[8]

The mounting fears of French and British statesmen were confirmed in 1939. Deprived of its military perimeter, the Czech government stood unprotected against the Nazi pressure that came in March. Hitler summoned Czech president Emil Hacha to Berlin. Subjected to all kinds of threats during an all-night session, Hacha finally capitulated and signed a document placing his country under the "protection" of Germany. His signature was a mere formality, however, for German troops were already crossing the Czech frontier. Not to be outdone, Mussolini seized Albania the following month. The two dictators then celebrated by signing a military alliance, the so-called Pact of Steel.

In response to the taking of Czechoslovakia and violation of the Munich pledges, Britain ended its appeasement policy and for the first time in its history

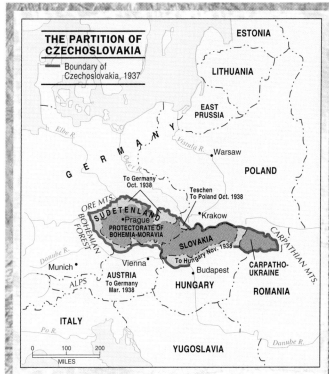

In 1938, Czechoslovakia was a democratic island in an authoritarian sea. When Hitler took advantage of British and French appeasement policies at Munich, he satisfied not only German ambitions, but those of the Poles and the Hungarians, who also received parts of the abandoned country.

authorized a peacetime draft. In Paris, Daladier gained special emergency powers to push forward national defense.

In the United States, isolationism reigned supreme. Between 1935 and 1937, in response to feelings of revulsion stemming from World War I, the U.S. Congress passed neutrality acts that made it unlawful for any nation at war to obtain munitions from the United States. At the same time, in response to events in Ethiopia, in Spain, and along the Rhine, President Franklin D. Roosevelt and the State Department worked quietly to alert the American people to the dangers of the world situation. In October 1937 Roosevelt pointed out that "the peace, the freedom, and the security of 90 percent of the population of the world is being jeopardized by the remaining 10 percent who are threatening a breakdown of all international order and law."[9] The president's call, in this so-called quarantine speech, for "positive endeavors to preserve peace brought forth a hostile reaction from the press and public."[10] Two years later Roosevelt told political leaders that the Germans and Italians could win the next war. His warnings went unheeded, as a significant portion of the American public hoped that the Nazis could do away with the Communists in the Soviet Union.

EUROPE, AUGUST 1939

German Aggression

- Military reoccupation of the Rhineland, 1936
- Seizure of Austria, 1938
- Seizure of Memel, 1939
- Occupation of Sudetenland, 1938
- Seizure of other Czech territory, 1939

Other Territories

- Czech territory annexed by Hungary, 1938–1939
- Italian seizure of Albania, 1939

The extent of Hitler's gains in expanding Germany hegemony by 1939 can be seen here. By using less violence than Bismarck, he took advantage of Allied weakness to become more successful than the old chancellor.

The Nazi-Soviet Pact

The final step on the road to World War II was Germany's attack on Poland. The Treaty of Versailles had turned over West Prussia to Poland as a corridor to the sea. Though 90 percent of the corridor's population was Polish, the Baltic city of Danzig—a free city under a League of Nations high commissioner—was nearly all German. Late in March 1939 Hitler proposed to Poland that Danzig be ceded to Germany and that the Nazis be allowed to occupy the narrow strip of land connecting Germany with East Prussia. Chamberlain, with French concurrence, warned the Nazis that "in the event of any action that clearly

threatens Polish independence," the British would "at once lend the Polish government all support in their power." This was an essentially symbolic gesture, since Poland's location made any useful Western aid impossible.

In the months that followed the Allied warnings, France and Britain competed with Germany for an alliance with Russia. Stalin had closely observed the actions of the democratic powers since Hitler's rise to power. He was aware of the hope expressed in some Western conservative circles that Hitler might effectively put an end to the Soviet regime. Further, he pledged to stay out of a war between "imperialists." He had to make a closely reasoned choice between the two sets of suitors competing for Soviet partnership.

Chamberlain and Daladier had ignored Moscow at Munich, and generally British relations with the Communists were quite cool. Now, with the Polish question of paramount importance, the French and British approaches appeared optimistic to Stalin. In May, Vyacheslav Molotov became the Soviet foreign minister. While Molotov negotiated publicly with the British and French, who sent negotiators not empowered to make agreements, he was also in secret contact with the highest levels in Berlin.

For centuries Germany and Russia had shared a concern over the fate of Poland. They had been able to reach agreement at Poland's expense in the eighteenth and nineteenth centuries. From late 1938 on, Moscow and Berlin pondered yet another division of the country. Negotiations between the two proceeded intensely from June through August 1939. While top-ranking German and Soviet diplomats flew between the two capitals, the lower-ranking mission sent to Moscow by Britain traveled leisurely by boat.

By 1939 Stalin had to choose wisely between the Western democracies, with their spotty record of defending their friends, and Nazi Germany, which could offer him concrete advantages in eastern Europe. On August 21, to the world's great amazement, the Soviet Union and Germany signed a nonaggression pact.

In retrospect, it is not at all surprising that Stalin chose to work with the Nazis. Through this agreement, Stalin gave Hitler a free hand in Poland and the assurance of not having to fight a two-front war. After the British and French guarantees to the Poles in March, Hitler knew that his attack on Poland would precipitate a general European war. The Führer had prepared plans that called for the invasion to begin in August 1939, and thanks to the nonaggression pact, Hitler could attack without fear of Moscow's intervention. Furthermore, he did not believe that Britain and France would dare oppose him.

The nonaggression pact gave the Soviets time to build up strength while the imperialists weakened themselves in war. In addition, the USSR was secretly promised Finland, Estonia, Latvia, eastern Poland, and Bessarabia. Germany would get everything to the west, including Lithuania. The Nazis also got guarantees of valuable raw materials and grain from the Soviets. Ideological differences could be set aside for such a mutually profitable pact.

World War II

When Nazi forces crossed the Polish border early on the morning of September 1, 1939, they set off World War II, the conflict that killed more people more effi-

ciently than any previous war. In all areas the latest scientific and technological advances were placed in the service of a new kind of war that killed civilians as well as soldiers and sailors. New techniques and attitudes revolutionized the field of intelligence. Scientists made major advances in both codemaking and codebreaking. Intelligence-gathering no longer depended on the old cloak-and-dagger stealing of messages and secrets. Now high-altitude aerial reconnaissance aircraft, radar, the first computers, and radio intercepts allowed enemies to find out each others' plans. Among the major advances on the Allied side were the breaking of the Japanese code and the discovery of the German code mechanism. Less than a decade before the war an American statesman had noted that "gentlemen do not read other gentlemen's mail." In the new style of warfare, information meant victory, and the cultured assumptions of an earlier age had to be discarded.

A New Way of War

Tactics and weaponry changed greatly between the two world wars. Tanks and planes had been used in World War I, but the concept of the *Blitzkrieg*, massive mobile mechanized movements and saturation bombings behind the lines, made the weapons far more lethal. The trench warfare of the First World War and the concept of fixed, fortified positions such as the Maginot line built by the French in the 1920s and 1930s proved to be useless.

Mobility was the key—even more so than superior numbers of men and weapons. Better communications, provided by improved radio systems, increased mobility. To strike quickly, in great force, and then to exploit the advantage proved to be the main characteristics of the German successes in 1939 and 1940. The Germans broke through enemy lines by using a large number of tanks, followed by the infantry. Rarely, since Napoleon, had speed and concentrated force been used so effectively.

Complementing increased mobility on the ground was the expanded use of airplanes, which could spread devastating firepower across continents, hundreds of miles behind established battle lines. The new forms of war, however, sparked the inventive genius of the scientists as each technological advance elicited a response—long-range German bombers brought the need for improved radar; improved propeller-driven aircraft set off the development of jet-powered airplanes. No matter how sophisticated the aerial technology became, however, the war proved that with the exception of nuclear weapons, air power alone could not bring an enemy to its knees.

Other innovations appeared during the war— paratroopers, advanced landing crafts, and the German flying bombs such as the V-1 and rockets such as the V-2. Aircraft carriers and amphibious forces played an important part in the war in the Pacific. The Japanese used carriers in their attack on Pearl Harbor, and the Americans used amphibious forces in "island hopping" across the Pacific.

As in World War I, however, military success lay in the ability of the states to mobilize their populations and resources. During World War II governments came to control all aspects of life. But the final, deciding factor was the ability of the individual soldier, following the directions of such brilliant commanders as Rommel or Eisenhower, to apply all of these resources. In the end, all of these factors were overwhelmed by the ultimate scientific and technological accomplishment, the atomic bomb. Ironically, although created to protect state interests, this ultimate weapon could destroy civilization.

Blitzkrieg and *Sitzkrieg*

After staging an "incident" on the morning of September 1, 1939, Nazi troops crossed the Polish frontier without a declaration of war, using the new tactics of the Blitzkrieg (Lightning war). At the same time the German *Luftwaffe* (air force) began to bomb Polish cities. On the morning of September 3 Chamberlain

A German motorized detachment rides through a Polish town badly damaged by Luftwaffe bombs. Poland was unable to withstand Hitler's Blitzkrieg of a combined air and ground attack and fell to the Germans within a month.

sent an ultimatum to Germany demanding that the invasion be halted. The time limit was given as 11:00 A.M. the same day. At 11:15 Chamberlain announced in a radio broadcast that Britain was now at war. France also soon declared war. After 21 years, Europe was once again immersed in war.

The world now had the chance to see the awesome speed and power of Nazi arms. The Polish forces collapsed, crushed between the German advance from the west and, two weeks later, a Soviet invasion from the east. By the end of the month, after a brave but hopeless resistance, the Poles once again saw their country partitioned between the Germans and the Russians.

Britain and France did not try to breach Germany's western defensive line, the Siegfried line along the Rhine. With their blockade and mastery of the seas, they hoped to defeat Hitler by attrition. During the winter of 1939–1940 there was little fighting along the Franco-German frontier. The lull in action came to be referred to as the phony war, or *Sitzkrieg*.

The Soviets took advantage of the lull to attack Finland in November. This campaign revealed to Moscow's embarrassment the Finns' toughness and the Soviet Union's military unpreparedness in the wake of recent purges. After an unexpectedly difficult four-month-long campaign, the immense Soviet Union forced tiny Finland to cede substantial amounts of territory.

"Blood, Toil, Tears, and Sweat"

In the spring of 1940 the Nazi high command launched its attack on western Europe. In its scope, complexity, and accomplishments it was one of the most successful military campaigns ever carried out. In April Nazi forces invaded Norway and Denmark. The Norwegians fought back fiercely for three weeks before being vanquished, and Denmark was taken in even less time. In the second week of May the German armies overran the neutral Netherlands, Belgium, and Luxembourg. The next week they went into northern France all the way to the English Channel. In the process they trapped an Anglo-French army of nearly 400,000 on the beach at Dunkirk.

The reversals in Norway and the Low Countries and the military crisis in France led to Chamberlain's resignation. Winston Churchill (1874–1965) became prime minister of Great Britain. Churchill had uneven success in both his political and military careers. In the 1930s his warnings against Hitler and Mussolini had been largely ignored. He was viewed as a "might-have-been; a potentially great man flawed by flashiness, irresponsibility, unreliability, and inconsistency."[11] Yet in 1940, at the age of 66, Churchill offered qualities of leadership equal to the nation's peril. For the next five years he was the voice and symbol of a defiant and indomitable Britain.

Facing the prospect of the destruction of the British army at Dunkirk, Churchill refused to be publicly dismayed. Appearing before Parliament as the new prime minister, he announced, "I have nothing to offer but blood, toil, tears, and sweat." He prepared his people for a long and desperate conflict, knowing full well that only the Channel, a thin screen of fighter aircraft, and an untried device called radar protected Britain. Churchill's example inspired his people. Hitler had found his match in the area of charismatic leadership.

Hitler hesitated to quash the forces trapped at Dunkirk, thereby allowing time for hundreds of small craft protected by the Royal Air Force to evacuate across the Channel 335,000 soldiers, including more than 100,000 French troops. Military leaders had hoped that they might be able to save 30,000 of the trapped men; now they had 11 times that number. An army had been saved, though it had lost all of its heavy equipment.

After Dunkirk, the fall of France was inevitable. Eager to be in on the kill, Mussolini declared war on France on June 10. Designated as an open city by the French in order to spare its destruction, Paris fell on June 14. As the German advance continued, the members of the French government who wanted to continue resistance were voted down. Marshal Philippe Pétain (1856–1951), the 84-year-old hero of Verdun in World War I, became premier. He immediately asked Hitler for an armistice, and in the same dining car in which the French had imposed armistice terms on the Germans in 1918, the Nazis and French on June 22, 1940, signed another peace agreement. The Germans had gained revenge for their shame in 1918.

France was split into two zones, occupied and unoccupied. In unoccupied France, Pétain's government at Vichy was supposedly free from interference, but in reality it became a puppet of the Nazis. The Third Republic, created in 1871 from the debris of defeat suffered at Germany's hands, now came to an end with a blow from the same country.

A remarkable patriot, Brigadier-General Charles de Gaulle (1890–1970), fled to London and organized the Free French Government, which adopted as its symbol the red cross of Lorraine, flown by Joan of Arc in her fight to liberate France five centuries earlier. De Gaulle worked to keep alive the idea of France as a great power and continued to aid the Allied cause in his sometimes quixotic way throughout the war.

Only Britain remained in opposition to Hitler, and the odds against the British seemed overwhelming. The Nazis planned a cross-Channel assault, while in Buckingham Palace, the queen (the present queen mother) took pistol lessons, saying, "I shall not go down like the others."[12] All Britain had to pin its hopes on was an army whose best equipment was still at Dunkirk, radar, and fast fighter aircraft flown by brave pilots. Churchill's eloquence inspired his people:

> We shall go on to the end.... We shall defend our island, whatever the cost may be, we shall fight on the beaches, we shall fight on the landing grounds, we shall fight in the fields and in the streets, we shall fight in the hills; we shall never surrender.[13]

The Germans sent an average of 200 bombers over London every night for nearly two months in the summer and fall of 1940. They suffered heavy losses to the Royal Air Force, which profited from a combination of superior aircraft, pilots, radar sightings, and visual detection. Yet all through the fall and winter of 1940–1941 Britain continued to be racked by terrible raids. Night bombing destroyed block after block of British cities. Evacuating their children and old people to the north, going to work by day and sleeping in air raid shelters and underground stations at night, Britain's people stood firm—proof that bombing civilians would not break their will.

Mastery of Europe

During the fall and winter of 1940–1941 Hitler strengthened his position in the Balkans, but not without some difficulty. By March 1941 Hungary,

The Nazi air attacks on London in the Battle of Britain caused widespread devastation but failed to bring the city to a halt or destroy the morale of its people. In the background can be seen the unscathed steeple of St. Paul's Cathedral.

WORLD WAR II IN EUROPE, 1939–1945

Axis Powers, August 1939
Extent of Axis control, May 1941
Allies
Neutral nations
→ Axis offenses
→ Allied offenses
⊗ Major battles

Aided by the Nazi-Soviet pact of August 1939, which allowed them to concentrate their fighting on a single front, the Germans, in one of the most successful military campaigns in history, ripped through the Low Countries and France. The Maginot line of defense constructed by the French proved totally useless.

Bulgaria, and Romania had joined the Axis. Hitler had to control the Hungarians and Bulgarians, who were pursuing ancient ambitions for Romanian land. In the process Romania lost a third of its population and territory to its two neighbors. The Romanians emerged, however, as helpful allies for the Germans, and Marshal Ion Antonescu became Hitler's favorite foreign general.

Mussolini, eager to gain some glory for his forces, invaded neutral Greece in October 1940. This thrust proved a costly failure when in December the Greeks successfully counterattacked. The Italians met other defeats in North Africa and Ethiopia, which the British recaptured.

Partly in an attempt to pull Mussolini out of a humiliating position, the Germans in the first four months of 1941 overran Yugoslavia and Greece. Two months of intense aerial and infantry attacks were needed to defeat the Yugoslavs and Greeks, forcing Hitler to spend considerable amounts of men and resources. But when the job was done the Führer had

secured his right flank prior to his invasion of the Soviet Union.

The results of these forays into the Balkans may have been positive for the Axis in the short run. But by going into the Balkans, Hitler delayed his attack on the Soviets by six to eight weeks. This delay, plus inadequate intelligence and bad planning, may have cost him victory on the eastern front. The Germans and the Italians also controlled only the major cities of Yugoslavia. Large bands of resistance fighters and partisans roamed the area, among them Communist forces led by Joseph Tito. Hitler had to leave behind German troops formerly committed to the Soviet invasion and replace them with less effective Bulgarian and Hungarian forces.

By the spring of 1941 nearly all of Europe had come under German control. Only Portugal, Switzerland, Sweden, Ireland, Spain, and Turkey remained neutral. For the Swiss, Swedes, and Spaniards, this was a strange kind of neutrality. The Swiss played an important role as "Germany's central banker." Swiss banks absorbed the accounts of Jews who were in the concentration camps, handled transfers of German looted gold—some of which was gold later melted down from the fillings of the death camp inmates—and financed German purchases of goods from neutral countries. The Swedes permitted German troops to cross their territory for the attack on the USSR, allowed the Germans to use their railroad system, and used their navy to provide escort services for German supply ships. After the German ball-bearing factories were knocked out by Allied aircraft, replacements for that all-important commodity were found in Sweden. Spain under Franco was pro-Nazi, sending 40,000 "volunteers" to fight on the eastern front. Not all the neutrals were as blatant as the Swedes or the Swiss or as pro-German as Franco. The true neutrals were trapped in a difficult position and made the best of their situation. The others profiteered and probably prolonged the war by their activities.[14]

War with the Soviet Union

Hitler and Stalin had signed the nonaggression pact for their own specific, short-term advantages. From the first there was tension and mistrust between the two, and neither side had any illusions about a long-lasting friendship. Stalin had hoped for a much more difficult war in the west among the "imperialists" and had not expected that Hitler would so quickly become the master of Europe.

As early as July 1940 Hitler resolved to attack the Soviets in an operation code-named Barbarossa. In the fall of the year he decided not to invade Britain but instead to pursue his original goal of obtaining living space. During 1941 British and American intelligence experts told Stalin of Hitler's intentions to attack, but the Soviet dictator clung to his obligations under the nonaggression pact. Even while the Nazis were invading in June 1941, shipments of Soviet grain were headed to Germany.

Operation Barbarossa required an enormous amount of effort and resources. Along a battlefront 1800 miles long, 9 million men became locked in struggle. At the outset the Nazi tank units were unstoppable as they killed or captured enormous numbers of Soviet troops. In October Hitler's army neared the center of Moscow (a monument today between the city's Sheremetevo Airport and the Kremlin marks the farthest advance of the German army). A month earlier the Nazis had besieged Leningrad, beginning a two-year struggle in which over 1 million civilians died. The USSR appeared to be on the verge of collapse.

When winter came earlier, and more severely, than usual, the Nazi offensive broke down. Weapons froze, troops were inadequately clothed, and heavy snows blocked the roads. The German attack halted,

For every German soldier who fought on the western front before 1944, 14 fought in the east. The Soviets paid a heavy price for turning back the German advance and deserve the lion's share of the credit for winning the European war.

and in the spring of 1942 the Red Army recovered some territory. One reason the Soviets could bounce back was the success of the five-year plans in relocating industry behind the Urals. Another reason was the sheer bravery and tenacity of the Soviet people. Also, the United States and Britain had begun sending supplies to the USSR.

The United States Enters the War

Following the collapse of France and during the battle of Britain, the American people had begun to understand the dangerous implications of an Axis victory. After Dunkirk, the United States sent arms to Britain, embarked on a rearmament program, and introduced a peacetime draft. The Lend-Lease Act of 1941 empowered the president to make arms available to any country whose defense was thought to be vital to the U.S. national interest. Despite ideological differences, America sent more than $11 billion worth of munitions to the Soviet Union.

To define the moral purpose and principles of the struggle, Roosevelt and Churchill drafted the Atlantic Charter in August 1941. Meeting somewhere in the Atlantic, the two pledged that "after the final destruction of Nazi tyranny," they hoped to see a peace in which "men in all the lands may live out their lives in freedom from fear and want." Though the United States had not yet declared itself at war in the fall of 1941, it was far from neutral.

One event brought the full energies of the American people into the war against the dictators: the Japanese attack on Pearl Harbor on December 7, 1941. Even though Hitler was seen as the most important enemy, it was Japan's expansionist policy that brought the United States into the war.

Alarmed by Tokyo's ambitions for the New Order in Asia and widely published accounts of Japanese atrocities, the United States had failed to renew trade treaties, frozen Japanese funds, and refused to sell Japan war matériel. Despite these measures Japan pursued its expansion. In October 1941 General Hideki Tojo (1884–1948), a militarist, became premier of Japan. On Sunday, December 7, while special "peace" envoys from Tokyo were negotiating in Washington, ostensibly to restore harmony in Japanese-American relations, Japanese planes launched from aircraft carriers attacked the American bases at Pearl Harbor, Hawaii. The stunningly successful attack wiped out many American aircraft on the ground and crippled half of the United States' Pacific fleet.

The following day the United States declared war on Japan; Britain followed suit. The British dominions, the refugee governments of Europe, and many Latin American nations soon joined the American and British cause. Four days later Germany declared war on the United States. On January 2, 1942, the 26 nations that stood against Germany, Italy, and Japan solemnly pledged themselves to uphold the principles of the Atlantic Charter and declared themselves united for the duration of the war.

The Apogee of the Axis

After Pearl Harbor, Japanese power expanded over the Pacific and into Southeast Asia. Tokyo conquered Hong Kong, Singapore, the Netherlands East Indies, Malaya, Burma, and Indochina. The Philippines fell when an American force surrendered at Bataan. The Chinese, however, from their remote inland fortress capital of Chungking, still managed to hold off the Japanese.

The summer of 1942 was an agonizing period for the nations allied against the Axis. A new German offensive pushed deeper into Russia, threatening the important city of Stalingrad. The forces of the gifted German general Rommel menaced Egypt and inflicted a decisive defeat on the British army in Libya. All over the globe the Axis powers were in the ascendancy. But their advantage was to be short-lived.

Japanese expansion in the Pacific was halted by two major American naval victories, the Coral Sea in May and Midway in June. In the first the Americans sank more than 100,000 tons of Japanese shipping

The magazine of the destroyer U.S.S. Shaw *explodes during the Japanese attack on Pearl Harbor, Hawaii, December 7, 1941.*

Discovery Through Maps

U.S. Air Force Survival Maps

We have seen maps scratched on stone, pieced together in a mosaic, and drawn on varieties of vellum and paper. For soldiers fighting in wars, none of these media are useful in the day-to-day hardships of combat in all sorts of weather conditions. So the United States Air Force devised maps printed on silk.

This map of Luzon Island in the Philippines was produced by the Aeronautical Chart Service in April 1944. The inks were waterproof, and the silk was strong—it could be wadded up and shoved in a pocket or even a helmet during battle. All of the major participants produced these maps, but very few of them survived the war.

and stopped the Japanese advance toward Australia. In the second the Americans turned back the advance toward Hawaii by devastating the Japanese carrier force. In both cases the American forces benefited by having broken the Japanese code and intercepting key messages. After these spectacular victories, U.S. marines began the tortuous rooting out of the Japanese at Guadalcanal and driving them back, island by island.

In November 1942 British and American troops landed in North Africa and the British defeated Axis troops at El Alamein in Egypt. By May 1943 all Axis troops in North Africa had been destroyed or captured. In July 1943 the Allied forces invaded and captured Sicily. On the twenty-fifth of that month the whole edifice of Italian fascism collapsed when Mussolini was stripped of his office and held captive. (He was rescued by Nazi agents in September.) In the meantime, the Allies began their slow and bitter advance up the Italian boot. The new Italian government signed an armistice in September 1943, months before Rome was taken in June 1944. Ger-

man resistance in northern Italy continued until the end of the war.

The Russian Turning Point

As important as the victories in the Pacific, North Africa, and Italy were, the decisive campaign took place in Russia. Hitler threw the bulk of his men and resources against the Soviet troops in the hope of knocking them out of the war and of gaining badly needed resources and food supplies. Hitler's strategy and operations along the eastern front constituted one mistake after another.

The Nazis lost a great opportunity to encourage the disintegration of the Soviet Union in 1941 by treating the peoples they encountered as *Untermenschen,* or subhumans. Often the Nazis, far from encountering resistance, would be treated as liberators by the villages they entered as they were given the traditional gifts of bread and salt. Often peasants dissolved the unpopular collective farms in the hope that private ownership would be restored. The

For a decade after the invasion of Manchuria in 1931 the Japanese expanded their control over the region known as the "Greater Far East Asian Co-Prosperity Sphere." Not until the battle of Midway in June 1942 was their momentum broken.

separatist Ukrainians looked forward to German support for reinstituting their state. The Nazi occupation negated all of these potential advantages. The Nazis carried their mobile killing operations of genocide with them, conscripted Slavs for slave labor in Germany, and generally mistreated the population in areas that they occupied.

Hitler's campaign gave Stalin the opportunity to wrap himself in the flag of patriotism. He replaced the ideological standards with those of nationalism and orthodoxy. He even went so far as to announce the end of the Comintern in 1943, an act more symbolic than real. For the first and perhaps the only time, the Communist party and the Soviet people were truly united in a joint enterprise.

The long (September 14, 1942, to February 2, 1943) and bloody battle between the Germans and the Soviets was focused on the strategic industrial city of Stalingrad on the Volga River. Hitler had fanatically sought to take the city, which under the constant pounding of artillery had little of importance left in it. His generals advised him to stop the attempt and retreat to a more defensible line. Hitler refused, and the German Sixth Army of 270,000 men

was surrounded and finally captured in February 1943. A German soldier trapped at Stalingrad wrote in a letter:

> Around me everything is collapsing, a whole army is dying, day and night are on fire, and four men busy themselves with daily reports on temperatures and cloud ceilings. I don't know much about war. No human being has died by my hand. I haven't even fired live ammunition from my pistol. But I know this much: the other side would never show such a lack of understanding for its men.[15]

Along the long front 500,000 German and affiliated troops were killed or taken prisoner. By the autumn of 1943 an army of 2.5 million Germans faced a Soviet force of 5.5 million.

The initiative had definitely passed to the Allies in the European theater. The Germans lost their air dominance, and the American industrial machine was cranking up to full production. By the beginning of 1944 the Germans were being pushed out of the Soviet Union, and in August Soviet troops accepted the surrender of Romania. Bulgaria was next to be liberated by the Soviet Union, while the Allies continued doggedly fighting their way north in Italy. But whereas the western Allies were, in their fashion, fighting the war to its military end, Stalin placed the postwar political objectives in the forefront of his advance into Europe.

An example of the Soviet use of military tactics to gain political goals could be seen in the action around Warsaw in August and September 1944 when the Red Army deferred the capture of the Polish capital to allow the Nazis to destroy potential opponents. The Polish resistance, which was centered in Warsaw and in contact with the exile government in London, had noted the arrival of Soviet forces in Warsaw's eastern suburbs. When the Nazis prepared to evacuate the city, the resistance rose up to claim control of the capital. Since these were non-Communist Poles, Stalin's forces refused to advance to the city, choosing instead to withdraw back across the Vistula River.

During the next five months the Soviets refused to permit the British and the Americans, who wanted to air-drop supplies to the resistance, to land and refuel in the Ukraine. Because the flight to Warsaw from London was too far to make in a round trip, the Allies could not supply the resistance. The Nazis stopped their retreat, returned to Warsaw, and totally destroyed the resistance. Soviet forces then advanced and took the capital in January. Poland was now deprived of many of its potential postwar non-Communist leaders. When the Soviets advanced,

they brought with them their own properly prepared Polish forces, both military and political, to control the country.

Axis Collapse

Following months of intense planning and days of difficult decision making, the Allies on June 6, 1944—D-Day—launched a vast armada of ships that landed half a million men on the beaches of Normandy. The Allied armies broke through the German defenses and liberated Paris at the end of August and Brussels at the beginning of September. The combined forces wheeled toward Germany. After fending off a major German offensive in the Battle of the Bulge in December, the Allies were ready to march on Germany.

It took four more months for the Allies from the west and the Soviets from the east to crush the German Third Reich. By May 1 the battle of Berlin had reached a decisive point, and the Russians were about to take the city. In contrast with World War I, German civilians suffered greatly in World War II. The Allies gained total command of the skies, and for every ton of bombs that fell on English cities, more than 300 tons fell on German towns and cities such as Dresden.

With victory in sight, Stalin, Roosevelt, and Churchill met at Yalta in the Crimea in February 1945 to discuss the peace arrangements. They agreed that the Soviet Union should have a preponderant

This panoramic view of the D-Day invasion shows the land, sea, and air craft preparing for the conquest. The waters are filled with ships as reinforcements and supplies pour ashore; balloon barrages float overhead to protect the ships from low-flying enemy aircraft, while long lines of trucks transport troops and supplies inland.

influence in eastern Europe, decided that Germany should be divided into four occupation zones, discussed the makeup and functioning of the United Nations (a proposed successor to the defunct League of Nations), and confirmed that the Soviets would enter the war against Japan after the defeat of Germany, which they did—two days after the atomic bomb was dropped on Hiroshima. Yalta was the high point of the alliance. After this conference, relations between the Western powers and the Soviets rapidly deteriorated.

The European Axis leaders did not live to see defeat. Mussolini was seized by antifascist partisan fighters and shot to death, and his mutilated body and that of his mistress were hung by the heels in a public square in Milan on April 28, 1945. Hitler committed suicide two days later. His body and that of his mistress, Eva Braun, whom he had just married, were soaked in gasoline and set afire.

President Roosevelt also did not live to see the end of the war. He died suddenly on April 12, 1945, less than a month before the German armies capitulated. The final surrender in Europe took place in Berlin on May 8, 1945, proclaimed by the newly installed president, Harry Truman, as V-E Day, Victory in Europe Day.

The Holocaust

As the Allied armies liberated Europe and marched through Germany and Poland, they came on sites that testified to the depths to which human beings can sink—the Nazi death camps. Nazi Propaganda Minister Joseph Goebbels wrote in his diary on March 14, 1945, that "it's necessary to exterminate these Jews like rats, once and for all. In Germany, thank God, we've taken care of that. I hope the world will follow this example."[16]

He was only too accurate in saying that Germany had "already taken care of that." In Belsen, Buchenwald, Dachau, Auschwitz, and other permanent camps and in mobile killing operations that moved with the armies, Hitler's forces sought to "purify the German race" and to "remove the lesser breeds as a source of biological infection." Working under the efficient efforts of the Gestapo (secret police), led by Chief Heinrich Himmler, and with the aid of hardworking Deputy Chief Reinhard Heydrich, the Nazis set out to gain the "Final Solution" to the Jewish question.

Although preparations had been under way for ten years, the completed plan for the Final Solution came in 1942. More than 3 million men, women, and children were put to death at Auschwitz alone, where more than 2000 people at a time could be gassed in half an hour; the operation could be repeated four times a day. The able-bodied were forced to work until they could work no more, and then they too were gassed. Millions more died from starvation, on diets that averaged 600 to 700 calories a day. Torture, medical experimentation, and executions all claimed a large toll. The victims' eyeglasses were collected,

A gaunt, exhausted Roosevelt, who would live only two months longer, sits between Churchill and Stalin at the Yalta Conference. The discussions at the conference, especially those concerning the establishment of new governments in liberated countries, exposed the mounting tensions that would divide the Allies after the war.

The Nazi Death Camps

Henry Friedlander gave a dispassionate description of the functioning of the Nazi death camps.

The largest killing operation took place in Auschwitz, a regular concentration camp. There Auschwitz Commandant Rudolf Hess improved the method used by Christian Wirth, substituting crystallized prussic acid—known by the trade name Zyklon B—for carbon monoxide. In September, 1941, an experimental gassing, killing about 250 ill prisoners and about 600 Russian POWs, proved the value of Zyklon B. In January, 1942, systematic killing operations, using Zyklon B, commenced with the arrival of Jewish transports from Upper Silesia. These were soon followed without interruption by transports of Jews from all occupied countries of Europe.

The Auschwitz killing center was the most modern of its kind. The SS built the camp at Birkenau, also known as Auschwitz II. There, they murdered their victims in newly constructed gas chambers, and burned their bodies in crematoria constructed for this purpose. A postwar court described the killing process:

Prussic acid fumes developed as soon as Zyklon B pellets seeped through the opening into the gas chamber and came into contact with the air. Within a few minutes, these fumes agonizingly asphyxiated the human beings in the gas chamber. During these minutes horrible scenes took place. The people who now realized that they were to die an agonizing death screamed and raged and beat their fists against the locked doors and against the walls. Since the gas spread from the floor of the gas chamber upward, small and weak people were the first to die. The others, in their death agony, climbed on top of the dead bodies on the floor, in order to get a little more air before they too painfully choked to death.

From Henry Friedlander, "The Nazi Camps," in *Genocide: Critical Issues of the Holocaust,* ed. Alex Grobman and David S. Landes (Los Angeles: Simon Wiesenthal Center, 1983), pp. 222–223.

their hair was shaved off for use in the wig trade, their gold fillings were removed as plunder, and their bodies were either burned or buried.

Thus the captured Jews, along with assorted *Untermenschen* (Gypsies, homosexuals, petty criminals, and conquered non-Aryans), made an economic contribution on their way to extermination. The Nazis did not act alone: they were aided by anti-Semitic citizens in Poland, Romania, France, Hungary, the Baltic States, and the Soviet Union. Few of the more than 4 million Polish Jews survived the war, and similar devastation occurred among Romanian Jewry.

All of this was done with bureaucratic efficiency, coldness, discipline, and professionalism. Himmler believed that his new variety of knights must "make this people disappear from the face of the earth." Had this been done in a fit of insanity and madness by savages, it could perhaps be comprehended. But that it was done by educated bureaucrats and responsible officials from a "civilized" nation made the enterprise all the more chilling and incredible. The question of the complicity of the German people in the Holocaust continues to be raised. For most of the half century after the war it was generally accepted that most of the German people had no precise knowledge of the systematized destruction. The historical debate opened up again after the affirmation by an American scholar in 1996 that the German people were "Hitler's willing executioners."

Within a year serious criticism of this position occurred. The role of the German people in the Holocaust is still a question to be answered, and until it is, it remains possible to believe that perhaps any group of people, given the proper conditions, can commit genocide.[17]

Between 1939 and 1945 the Jewish population in Nazi-occupied Europe decreased from 9,739,200 to 3,505,800. Six million were killed in Nazi gas chambers or in executions, and another 6 million non-Jews fell victim to the Nazi slaughter.[18]

The Atomic Bomb

While the Allied armies finished off the Germans, the Americans from the summer of 1943 advanced toward Japan, capturing on the way the islands of Tarawa, Kwajalein, and Saipan after bloody struggles on sandy beaches. In October 1944, with their victory in the battle of Leyte Gulf, the greatest naval engagement in history, the Allies ended the threat of the Japanese fleet.

The final phase of the war against Japan began to unfold. The Allies took Iwo Jima and Okinawa, only a few hundred miles from Japan. From these bases waves of American bombers rained destruction on Japanese cities. In the China-Burma-India theater, the Chinese with U.S. aid made inroads into areas previously captured by Japan.

American GIs entering the Nazi concentration camps were aghast at what they found. In some camps they forced local Germans to view the piles of Jews who had been murdered before the Allies could liberate them and before the Nazis could burn or bury their bodies—both to make ordinary Germans aware of the unspeakable horror their government had committed and to preclude official denials that the genocide had taken place.

But the decisive developments took place across the Pacific in New Mexico, where by 1945 U.S. scientists, with the help of physicists who had fled central Europe to escape Hitler, invented a new and terrible weapon, the atomic bomb. Based on figures from the island-hopping campaigns, the projected casualty rate for the taking of the main island of Japan ran into the hundreds of thousands.

When the Japanese refused to surrender, an American bomber on August 6 dropped the atomic bomb on the city of Hiroshima. As the mushroom-shaped cloud rose over the city, only charred ruins were left behind. An expanse of approximately 3 square miles, 60 percent of the city, was pulverized. The Japanese government estimated the bomb killed 60,000 people, wounded 100,000, and left 200,000 homeless. Three days later a second bomb was dropped on the city of Nagasaki, with similar results.

The Japanese sued for peace. The surrender ceremony took place aboard the battleship *Missouri* on September 2, 1945, almost six years to the day after Hitler plunged the world into World War II.

Conclusion

When the war was finally over, the living counted the dead. The Germans lost 4.2 million military and civilian dead, while the Western Allies lost 1.5 million. The Soviet Union suffered the greatest losses: close to 25 million citizens. Yugoslavia had the greatest per capita casualty rate—one in every ten. In Asia the census for 1950 showed a loss of some 55 million people, even after a five-year period of recuperation.[19] A meaningful financial accounting for the six years of bloodshed is not possible.

The world went through this carnage to put an end to German, Italian, and Japanese aggression, which came frighteningly close to succeeding in its goal of world dominance. By contrast with the

The Bombing of Hiroshima

Nuclear weapons totally changed the nature and possibilities of warfare. The U.S. Strategic Bombing Survey gave a detached version of what happened at Hiroshima.

At about 0815 there was a blinding flash. Some described it as brighter than the sun, others likened it to a magnesium flash. Following the flash there was a blast of heat and wind. The large majority of people within 3,000 feet of ground zero were killed immediately. Within a radius of about 7,000 feet almost every Japanese house collapsed. Beyond this range and up to 15,000–20,000 feet many of them collapsed and others received serious structural damage. Persons in the open were burned on exposed surfaces, and within 3,000–5,000 feet many were burned to death while others received severe burns through their clothes. In many instances clothing burst into spontaneous flame and had to be beaten out. Thousands of people were pinned beneath collapsed buildings or injured by flying debris. Flying glass particularly produced many non-lethal injuries and the distances at which they occurred are discussed in the following chapter, but the foregoing presentation was necessary for one to appreciate the state of the population immediately after the bomb exploded.

Shortly after the blast fires began to spring up over the city. Those who were able made a mass exodus from the city into the outlying hills. There was no organized activity. The people appeared stunned by the catastrophe and rushed about as jungle animals suddenly released from a cage. Some few apparently attempted to help others from the wreckage, particularly members of their family or friends. Others assisted those who were unable to walk alone. However, many of the injured were left trapped beneath collapsed buildings as people fled by them in the streets. Pandemonium reigned as the uninjured and slightly injured fled the city in fearful panic.

From "The Effects of Atomic Bombs on Health and Medical Services in Hiroshima and Nagasaki," in *The United States Strategic Bombing Survey* (Washington, D.C.: U.S. Government Printing Office, 1948).

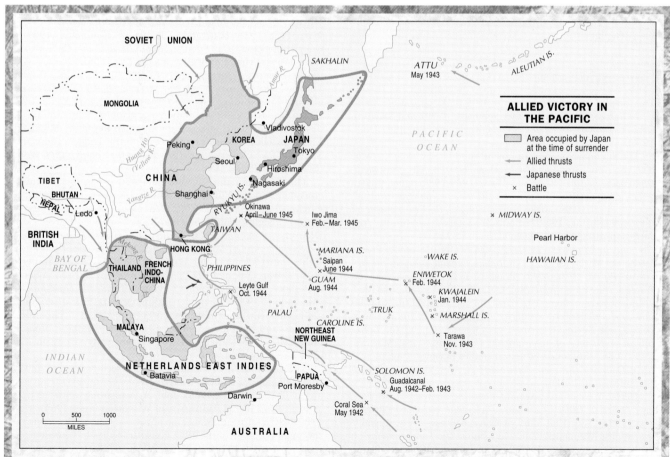

The Pacific theater of World War II saw some of the most savage fighting between Allied forces and the Japanese. So bloody was the conflict during the "island-hopping" phase that the Americans decided to use the atomic bomb to end the war.

First World War, which has spawned many historiographical controversies concerning its causes, there is no doubt that the key figure in the Second World War was Adolf Hitler. He was the essential link, the man whose policies and ideas welded the dictators together.

Unlike the Japanese and the Italians, whose global influence was limited by either geographical or internal problems, Hitler could build on Germany's industrial might and central location to forge a force for world conquest. Historians vary sharply on his goals and motivations. Some see him as a politician playing the traditional game of European power politics in a most skillful way, while others view him as a single-minded fanatic pursuing the plans for conquest laid out in *Mein Kampf*. Between these two extremes are the scholars who believe that the Führer had thought-out long-term goals but pursued them haphazardly as opportunities presented themselves.

Hitler struck the spark that set off the worldwide conflagration. Aiding and abetting his ambitions was the obsessive desire of the democracies for peace. By 1939 the lesson had been learned that appeasement does not guarantee peace, nor does it take two equally belligerent sides to make a war.

Suggestions for Reading

Two helpful introductions to the 1919–1945 period are Laurence Lafore, *The End of Glory* (Lippincott, 1970), and Joachim Remak, *The Origins of the Second World War* (Prentice Hall, 1976).

The diplomacy leading up to and conducted during the war has received extensive study. Hans Gatzke, ed., *European Diplomacy Between the Two Wars, 1919–1939* (Quadrangle, 1972), gives definition to some of the major problems involved in this period. Hans Gatzke, *Stresemann and the Rearmament of Germany* (Norton, 1969), emphasizes interwar continuity. Jon Jacobson discusses four pivotal years in *Locarno Diplomacy: Germany and the West, 1925–1929* (Princeton University Press, 1972). See H. James Burgwyn, *Italian Foreign Policy in the Interwar Period, 1918–1940* (Praeger, 1997), for coverage of Rome's transition from diplomatic frustration to imagined grandeur to complicity with the Germans. For a recent study of one aspect of Moscow's international policies in the interwar period, see Kevin McDermott and Jeremy Agnew, *The Comintern: A History of International Communism* (St. Martin's Press, 1996). Still one of the best studies of Soviet foreign policy is George F. Kennan, *Russia and the West Under Lenin and Stalin* (Mentor, 1961).

Gerhard Weinhard gives a penetrating analysis in *The Foreign Policy of Hitler's Germany: Diplomatic Revolution in Europe, 1933–1936* (University of Chicago Press, 1970). Equally essential is Weinhard's follow-up study, *The Foreign Policy of Hitler's Germany, 1937–1939* (University of Chicago Press, 1980). In *The Nazi Dictatorship* (Arnold, 1985), Ian Kershaw makes the case that Hitler's ideology, from the first, could eventuate only in war. William Leonard Langer and S. Everett Gleason discuss important aspects of U.S. foreign policy in *The Challenge to Isolation* (Smith, 1970). Herbert Feis, *Churchill, Roosevelt, Stalin* (Princeton University Press, 1967), is a classic. For a study of the pressures affecting Franklin Roosevelt as he responded to the European crisis, see Barbara Rearden Farnham, *Roosevelt and the Munich Crisis: A Study of Political Decision Making* (Princeton University Press, 1997). René Albrecht-Carrié traces France's travail in *France, Europe, and the Two World Wars* (Harper & Row, 1961). George F. Kennan, *Memoirs*, vol. I (Bantam, 1969), offers perceptive contemporary observations. Other fine studies on interwar affairs are Étienne Mantoux, *The Carthaginian Peace* (Ayer, 1978), and Sally Marks, *International Relations in Europe, 1918–1939* (St. Martin's Press, 1976). Robert Young, *In Command of France: French Foreign Policy and Military Planning, 1933–1940* (Harvard University Press, 1978), gives needed perspective on France's dilemma.

One of the most discussed aspects of the interwar period is appeasement and the Munich Conference. Keith Middlemas, *The Strategy of Appeasement* (Quadrangle, 1972), gives a balanced survey of this very controversial issue. A study that reveals the multifaceted background of Chamberlain's policy is Gaines Post, *Dilemmas of Appeasement: British Deterrence and Defense, 1934–1937* (Cornell University Press, 1993). Francis L. Loewenheim, ed., *Peace or Appeasement* (Houghton Mifflin, 1965), provides a selection of documents, including the Hossbach Memorandum. Keith Eubank's study, *Munich* (University of Oklahoma Press, 1963), is a good summary.

The Spanish Civil War has also received much scholarly attention. John Coverdale discusses one aspect of the conflict in *Italian Intervention in the Spanish Civil War* (Princeton University Press, 1975) and Rob Wheatley discusses another in *Hitler and Spain: The Nazi Role in the Spanish Civil War, 1936–1939* (University Press of Kentucky, 1989). Gabriel Jackson, *The Spanish Republic and the Civil War, 1931–1939* (Princeton University Press, 1965); Stanley G. Payne, *Spanish Revolution* (Norton, 1970); and Hugh Thomas, *The Spanish Civil War* (Harper & Row, 1977), are all first-rate studies. George Orwell, *Homage to Catalonia* (Harcourt, Brace, 1938), remains a gripping contemporary description of the tragedy of the Spanish Republic. Michael Alpert provides a useful overview of the tragic events in Spain in *A New International History of the Spanish Civil War* (St. Martin's Press, 1998).

The war from the German perspective has to take into consideration the Führer himself, and Robert G. Waite, *The Psychopathic God: Adolf Hitler* (Mentor, 1983), offers fascinating insights into the man's personality. Harold C. Deutsch's, *Hitler and His Germans: The Crisis of January–June 1938* (University of Minnesota Press, 1974), provides good insights into German planning and policies. David Irving, *Hitler's War* (Viking, 1977), is an excellent survey. Albert Speer gives an insider's point of view in *Inside the Third Reich* (Macmillan, 1970). Alexander Dallin, *German Rule in Russia, 1941–1945* (St. Martin's Press, 1957), discusses occupation policies and problems. Albert Seaton, *The Russo-German War, 1941–1945* (Praeger, 1970), is especially strong in its analysis of Soviet strategy.

The diplomacy surrounding Poland is well covered in Anna Cienciala, *Poland and the Western Powers, 1938–1939* (University of Toronto Press, 1968). John A. Armstrong, *Soviet Partisans in World War II* (University of Wisconsin Press, 1964), is a deft analysis of a subtle theater of action. George Bruce gives thorough coverage of the 1944 Polish tragedies in *Warsaw Uprising, 1 August–2 October* (Hart-Davis, 1972). Harrison Salisbury, *The Nine Hundred Days: The Siege of Leningrad* (Harper & Row, 1975), is a heartbreaking story of heroism. The tragic tale of repatriated Soviet citizens is told in Nikolai Tolstoy, *Victims of Yalta* (Hodder & Stoughton, 1978).

Three good books on the Pacific theater are Christopher Thorne, *Allies of a Kind: The United States, Britain, and the War Against Japan* (Oxford University Press, 1978); Gordon W. Prange, *At Dawn We Slept: The Untold Story of Pearl Harbor* (McGraw-Hill, 1981); and Yoshiburo Ienaga, *The Pacific War, 1937–1945* (Pantheon, 1978), which views the war from Japan's perspective.

Other aspects of the war are covered in Anthony Adamthwaite, *France and the Coming of the Second World War, 1936–1939* (Cass, 1977); Maurice Cowling, *The Impact of Hitler: British Politics and British Foreign Policy, 1933–1940* (University of Chicago Press, 1977); Henri Michel, *The Shadow War: European Resistance, 1939–1945* (Harper & Row, 1972); Leila J. Rupp, *Mobilizing Women for War, 1939–1945* (Princeton University Press, 1977); and Len Deighton, *Fighter: The True Story of the Battle of Britain* (J. Cape, 1977). Three books dealing with intelligence activities are Frederick W. Winterbotham, *The Ultra Secret* (Dell, 1979); William Stevenson, *A Man Called Intrepid* (Ballantine, 1976); and Reginald V. Jones, *The Wizard War: British Scientific Intelligence, 1939–1945* (Coward, McCann, 1978).

The Nazis' genocide policies are analyzed in Raul Hilberg, *The Destruction of the European Jews* (Quadrangle, 1961); Karl A. Schleunes, *The Twisted Road to Auschwitz: Nazi Policy Toward German Jews, 1933–1939* (University of Illinois Press, 1970); and Lucy S. Dawidowicz, ed., *A Holocaust Reader* (Behrman House, 1976). See also Dawidowicz, *The War Against the Jews, 1933–1945* (Bantam, 1976). Telford Taylor's memoir, *The Anatomy of the Nuremberg Trials* (Knopf, 1994), is a thorough and compelling discussion of these unprecedented hearings. Daniel Jonah Goldhagen unleashed international controversy with *Hitler's Willing Executioners: Ordinary Germans and the Holocaust* (Knopf, 1996), which implicated almost all Germans as collaborators in genocide. His book has been passionately attacked by a number of scholars, including Norman G. Finkelstein and Ruth Bettina Birn in *A Nation on Trial: The Goldhagen Thesis and Historical Truth* (Henry Holt, 1998).

Nearly all major participants on all sides who survived the war produced memoirs. The classics among them are Winston Churchill's six-volume reminiscence, *The Second World War*, and Charles De Gaulle's *Mémoires*.

Suggestions for Web Browsing

World War II Through Russian Eyes
http://wwiithroughrussianeyes.com

This exhibit from Memphis, Tennesse, depicts World War II as seen through Russian eyes.

Lycos Guide to World War II
http://www.lycos.com/wguide/network/net_969250.html

A rich compilation of web sites regarding all aspects of World War II

Battle of Stalingrad
http://www.massnet.com/wwii.htm

Offers rare photos of this pivotal battle of World War II.

Role of American Women in World War II
http://www.pomperaug.com/socstud/stumuseum/web/
arhhome.htm

This site provides a rich repository of photos, primary interviews, and other materials detailing the role of women on the American side of the war.

D-Day
http://www.nando.net/sproject/dday/dday.html

Extensive site commemorating the fiftieth anniversary of D-Day.

The Holocaust
http://motic.wiesenthal.com/index.html

The Simon Wiesenthal Center provides a wide range of information about the Holocaust.

National Holocaust Museum
http://www.remember.org

Site providing the most exhaustive support for students searching for information on genocide and the Holocaust.

Hiroshima Archive
http://www.kyohaku.go.jp

A poignant research and educational guide for all who wish to expand their knowledge of the atomic bombing of Japan.

Notes

1. Anatole Gregory Mazour, *Russia Past and Present* (New York: Van Nostrand Reinhold, 1951), p. 576.
2. George F. Kennan, *Memoirs* (New York: Bantam Books, 1969), p. 122.
3. John Toland, *Adolf Hitler* (New York: Ballantine Books, 1977), pp. 522, 529.
4. Donald W. Treadgold, *Twentieth-Century Russia* (Chicago: Rand McNally, 1959), pp. 324–325.
5. Keith Middlemas, *The Strategy of Appeasement* (Chicago: Quadrangle Books, 1972), pp. 1, 8.
6. Francis L. Loewenheim, *Peace or Appeasement* (Boston: Houghton Mifflin, 1965), pp. 2, 4.
7. Middlemas, *Strategy of Appeasement*, p. 177.
8. Winston L. S. Churchill, *Blood, Sweat, and Tears* (New York: Putnam, 1941), p. 66.
9. Franklin D. Roosevelt, "Address at Chicago, October 5, 1937," in *The Literature of the United States*, ed. W. Blair, T. Hornberger, and R. Stewart, vol. 2 (Chicago: Scott, Foresman, 1955), p. 831.
10. Ibid., p. 832.
11. S. E. Ayling, *Portraits of Power* (New York: Barnes & Noble, 1963), p. 159.
12. Nigel Nicolson, ed., *Harold Nicolson: The War Years, 1939–1945* (New York: Atheneum, 1967), p. 100.
13. Churchill, *Blood, Sweat, and Tears*, p. 297.
14. James Risen, "U.S. Details 6 Neutral Countries' Role in Aiding Nazis," *New York Times*, June 21, 1998.
15. *Last Letters from Stalingrad*, trans. Franz Schneider and Charles Gullas (New York: Signet Books, 1965), p. 20.
16. Quoted in John Vinocur, "Goebbels in Published 1945 Diary Blames Goring for Nazi's Collapse," *New York Times*, Jan. 3, 1978.
17. See Daniel Jonah Goldhagen, *Hitler's Willing Executioners: Ordinary Germans and the Holocaust* (New York: Knopf, 1996). The most outspoken criticism of Goldhagen's thesis is to be found in Norman G. Finkelstein and Ruth Bettina Birn, *A Nation on Trial: The Goldhagen Thesis and Historical Truth* (New York: Henry Holt, 1998).
18. Raul Hilberg, *The Destruction of the European Jews* (Chicago: Quadrangle Books, 1961); Maurice Crouzet, *Histoire Générale des Civilisations*, Vol. 7 (Paris: Presses Universitaires de France, 1957), pp. 358–359.
19. Simon Kuznets, *Postwar Economic Growth: Four Lectures* (Cambridge, Mass.: Harvard University Press, 1964), pp. 72–76.

From Bipolar Ideology to Global Competition

The political, economic, social, and technological shape of the world changed more dramatically in the three decades following World War II than in any comparable time period in history. Following 1945 three major worlds emerged, each with its distinctive way of life. The Western world comprised most of the Americas, Australia and New Zealand, western Europe, and Japan. Stretching from Berlin through the Soviet Union to Peking was the communist world. The nations of Africa and parts of Asia made up the developing world. The conflicting interests of these three segments have formed much of the story of our time.

At the end of World War II the great nations set about constructing a peace worthy of the sacrifice of millions of lives. An international organization, the United Nations, was created for this purpose. But almost overnight former allies became enemies, former antagonists became allies, and peace became the Cold War. The confrontation between the United States and its allies and the Soviet power bloc threatened world peace. Although on a number of occasions the UN was able to deflect this rivalry, it was powerless to prevent war between these opposing systems. Twice the Western and communist worlds came to the brink of conflict—over Berlin and Cuba.

In the second half of the twentieth century the developing world emerged as the major theater of action. In these countries are the world's fastest-growing populations, its most essential resources, and the most politically explosive situations. All these countries, from richest to poorest, have been affected by decolonization, the Cold War and its conclusion, and the technological revolution. All of them entered the modern era in a period of European dominance that often provoked violent encounters. Many face major economic and demographic issues that find expression in political instability. The drawing of new nation-state boundaries after World War II as imperial powers withdrew from territories like India and Palestine created massive refugee problems and inflamed ethnoreligious tensions in ways that have significantly shaped the destinies of nations in Asia and Africa.

China, the most powerful country in the developing world, participated in Cold War episodes from Korea to Vietnam and fought its own ideological battles before entering a period of rapid modernization after 1978. In the rest of Asia nations freed themselves from the yoke of European dominance but often continued to experience economic dependence. Independence unleashed powerful ethnic and religious antagonisms, many of which remain unresolved. After the British withdrew from the subcontinent, India and Pakistan entered a half century of competition, sometimes peaceful, sometimes hostile. The increasing power of Hindu nationalism has been expressed in communal violence in India, the second most populous nation in the world. In the Middle East the politics of oil have reconfigured global economic relations and split the region very dramatically into haves and have-nots. The Arab-Israeli conflict continues to serve as an epicenter of regional politics while Islamist movements challenge Western-style secular nationalism.

Economic upheavals, more than Cold War tensions, have affected the Latin American states. The region's accumulation of massive debts and its dependence on the export of oil or agricultural products left it at the mercy of the North Atlantic powers. This economic domination provided a rich opportunity for revolutionaries in Cuba and Nicaragua, who fought against the obvious exploitation of the population.

Political changes do not occur in a vacuum. They must be seen in relation to the other factors that shape society. Technology and economics on the one hand and ideological systems on the other play important roles; in addition, the hopes and fears of society's members can be seen in the art, literature, and popular culture of the time. The twentieth century has been remarkable for the rapidity of developments on all these fronts.

The record of the past decades is not a hodgepodge of unconnected events but rather part of a long story and debate. The forces of industrial development have not only accelerated their pace but also engulfed the entire globe. The international character of science and technology, of economic activity, of ideologies, of art, and increasingly of lifestyles has signaled the beginning of a new phase in history. The future of the world remains, as always, under construction, to be determined by its diverse inhabitants.

After Stalin's death, the efficiency of the USSR's police state declined as his successors chose not to exercise his paranoid vigilance. The state security services remained a powerful presence in everyday life, but by the 1970s open protests became common. By 1991 the USSR had withered away.

The Cold War and After

Russia and Eastern Europe, 1945–1999

Chapter Contents

The devastating power of nuclear weapons ensured that the United States and the Soviet Union never directly fought each other during the nearly half century of international tension after World War II, known as the Cold War. However, "proxy wars" fought by their clients and their own occasional intervention cost millions of lives in Asia, Africa, and Latin America. Ironically, Europe, the stage for the previous two hot wars, became caught in the stalemate between the superpowers and enjoyed its longest time of peace in recorded history. Locked in a nuclear standoff, the two systems competed vigorously in every other area, especially economics.

The West's economy had always been more productive than that of the Soviet Bloc. The USSR and its allies suffered drastic damage during the war, and it took the better part of the next decade to recover. This comparatively slow recovery stemmed from the Soviets' decision not to participate in the Marshall Plan for rebuilding wartorn Europe and Moscow's emphasis on regaining security through extensive military spending and building up its own defensive buffer zone under the Warsaw Pact. The Communist nation's centrally planned economic system worked reasonably well when focused on a single, well-defined goal: military buildup. By the mid-1970s the Soviet Bloc had achieved military parity with the West.

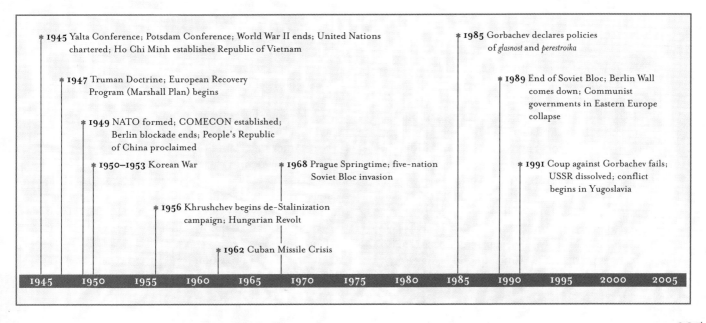

* **1945** Yalta Conference; Potsdam Conference; World War II ends; United Nations chartered; Ho Chi Minh establishes Republic of Vietnam

* **1947** Truman Doctrine; European Recovery Program (Marshall Plan) begins

* **1949** NATO formed; COMECON established; Berlin blockade ends; People's Republic of China proclaimed

* **1950–1953** Korean War

* **1956** Khrushchev begins de-Stalinization campaign; Hungarian Revolt

* **1962** Cuban Missile Crisis

* **1968** Prague Springtime; five-nation Soviet Bloc invasion

* **1985** Gorbachev declares policies of *glasnost* and *perestroika*

* **1989** End of Soviet Bloc; Berlin Wall comes down; Communist governments in Eastern Europe collapse

* **1991** Coup against Gorbachev fails; USSR dissolved; conflict begins in Yugoslavia

| 1945 | 1950 | 1955 | 1960 | 1965 | 1970 | 1975 | 1980 | 1985 | 1990 | 1995 | 2000 | 2005 |

However, the West was presenting challenges beyond those of a military nature. Competition now included all types of technology, economic growth, and quality of life. Citizens of the Warsaw Pact became increasingly aware that their living standards were markedly inferior to those of the West. In response to this discontent, Soviet Bloc leaders were compelled to broaden the goals of their economic system and try to reform it to satisfy their populations. The rigid centrally planned system was put on an exhausting treadmill of reforms, which resulted in little growth in productivity, economic disruption, and confusion among lower-level bureaucrats and managers trying to implement the reforms. The USSR and Eastern Europe found their economic growth rates slowing and their technology becoming obsolete—and consequently losing their military edge. A new round of competition—not only in weapons technology but also in consumer goods, quality of life, and technological progress and innovation—contributed to the breakup of the Warsaw Pact and the end of the Cold War by 1990.

During the 1990s Moscow's relationship with Washington increasingly consisted of maintaining the illusion of Great Power status while being bankrolled and even protected by Washington as the exhausted superpower tried to retain a dominant role in a rapidly changing world. But Moscow was no longer the center of a world empire: the end of the Soviet Bloc and the subsequent breakup of the Soviet Union itself gave birth to more than 20 diverse new nation-states in the territory of the former Warsaw Pact. These states spanned the political spectrum from dictatorship to democracy, the economic spectrum from capitalism to continued central planning, and the spectrum of social conditions from freedom to repression.

The Elusive Peace

After World War II many of the living had reason to envy the dead. Fire bombs and nuclear weapons had depopulated and irradiated parts of Japan. One-fourth of Germany's cities were in rubble, as were many in Italy and central Europe. The war claimed 10 percent of Yugoslavia's population. In China, after 15 years of fighting, survivors faced hunger, disease, civil war, and revolution. Twenty-five million people died in the Soviet Union, and the country lost one-third of its national wealth. Although casualty rates in Britain and France were lower than in World War I, both countries paid dearly in lives and in the ruin that took one-fourth of their national wealth.

Postwar Problems

Europe faced two immediate problems at the end of the war: dealing with Nazi collaborators and resettling millions of labor slaves. In countries that had been occupied by the Germans, victorious resistance groups began to take vigilante justice against those who had worked with the invaders. Across Europe they executed thousands of collaborators. In France alone 800 were sent to their deaths. After the war and into the 1990s, courts sentenced thousands more to prison terms. Eight million foreign laborers who had been exploited as slaves by the Nazis remained to be resettled. By the end of 1945 five million of them had been sent home, including many Soviet citizens who were repatriated against their will. Some of them chose suicide rather than return to Stalin's rule.

In Germany the Allies then began to carry out a selective process of denazification. Some former Nazis were sent to prison, but thousands of others remained free thanks to large-scale declarations of amnesty. Many ex-Nazis were employed by the scientific and intelligence services of each of the Allies. Symbolically, the most important denazification act came at the 1945–1946 trials of war criminals held at Nuremberg. Critics condemned the trials as an act of vengeance, "a political act by the victors against the vanquished." The prosecution stated, however, that the Nazis' crimes were so terrible that "civilization cannot tolerate their being ignored because it cannot survive their being repeated." As Telford Taylor, the American prosecutor of the German general staff, stated, "The gas chambers, mountains of corpses, human-skin lampshades, shrunken skulls, freezing experiments, and bank vaults filled with gold teeth" were the "poisoned fruit" of the tree of German militarism. Taylor brushed aside the generals' arguments that they were "just following orders." He made the point that they still had to exercise moral judgement.[1] An international panel of jurists conducted the proceedings and condemned 12 leading Nazis to be hanged and sent seven to prison for crimes against humanity. The panel acquitted three high officials.

Following the Yalta agreement, the Allies established four occupation zones in Germany: French, British, American, and Soviet. They divided the capital, Berlin, located in the Soviet sector, into four similar parts. The Soviets promised free access from the western zones to Berlin. Growing hostility between the Soviet Union and the United States by the end of the war blocked a comprehensive peace settlement for Germany.

At the Potsdam Conference in the summer of 1945, the Allies set up a council of ministers to draft

After World War II, the bombed-out cities of Europe seemed destroyed beyond repair. In 1947 Winston Churchill described the Continent as "a rubble heap, a charnel house, a breeding ground of pestilence and hate." This photo is of Cologne's central business district as it appeared in 1945.

peace treaties with Berlin's allies. After two years of difficult negotiations, treaties were signed with Italy, Romania, Bulgaria, Hungary, and Finland. In 1951 an accord between the Western powers and the Japanese reestablished Japan as a sovereign state. Austria's position remained in flux until 1955, when a peace treaty was signed and occupation forces were withdrawn.

Not until the signing of the Helsinki Accords in 1975 was a postwar status for Europe acknowledged, and that agreement did not have the force of a binding legal treaty. The diplomatic issues spawned by World War II were finally put to rest in a series of treaties signed by all European parties in the summer of 1990, following the reunification of Germany and the collapse of the Soviet Bloc.

The United Nations

On only one issue, the establishment of an international peacekeeping organization, could the powers agree after the war. Great Britain and the United States laid the foundations for the United Nations in 1941 when they proposed "the establishment of a wider and permanent system of general security" so that "men in all lands may live out their lives in freedom from fear and want." Subsequent meetings in Moscow and Yalta led representatives of 50 governments meeting in San Francisco from April to June 1945 to draft the Charter of the United Nations.

To pursue its goals of peace and an improved standard of living for the world, the UN would work through six organizations: the Security Council, to maintain peace and order; the General Assembly, to function as a sort of "town meeting of the world"; the Economic and Social Council, to improve living stan-

Fearful of letting Germany emerge from its aggression united as after World War I, the victorious Allies partitioned their former enemy in 1945.

dards and extend human rights; the Trusteeship Council, to advance the interests of the colonial peoples; the International Court of Justice, to resolve disputes between nations; and the Secretariat, headed by the secretary-general, to serve the needs of the other organizations. Much of the responsibility for improving the economic and social conditions of the world's people was entrusted to a dozen specialized agencies, such as the International Labor Organization (ILO), the Food and Agricultural Organization (FAO), the World Health Organization (WHO), and the UN Educational, Scientific and Cultural Organization (UNESCO).

The greatest controversy at San Francisco arose over the right of veto in the Security Council. The smaller countries held that it was unjust for the big powers to be able to block the wishes of the majority. But the Big Five—the United States, the Soviet Union, China, France, and Great Britain—affirmed that singly and collectively they had special interests and responsibilities in maintaining world peace and security. The UN Charter therefore provided that the Security Council should consist of 11 members: five permanent members representing the Great Powers and six elected by the General Assembly for a term of two years. These numbers would be increased as the membership of the UN grew. On purely procedural matters a majority of seven votes was sufficient; on matters of substance, all permanent members had to agree.

The UN proved to be more effective than the League of Nations. The UN, like the League, lacks the sovereign power of its member states. However, as was shown in the Korean conflict in the 1950s, the Persian Gulf War in 1991, and subsequent peacekeeping and humanitarian activities in Asia, Europe, and Africa, it has become more wide-reaching in its impact. In 1946 it had 51 members; in 1999 membership stood at 187. Over the years the UN's usefulness has repeatedly been demonstrated despite the difficulties of the Cold War, the strains of massive decolonization, and four Arab-Israeli wars—not to mention an unending series of smaller crises. As was the case with the League, the UN cannot coerce the Great Powers when any of them decides a major national interest is involved.

The Cold War: Part I, 1945–1953

The Soviets and Americans differed in their views on economics, politics, social organization, religion, and the role of the individual. The Nazi threat produced a temporary alliance between the two systems, but by 1943 tension increased over Soviet frustration with the slowness of its allies to open the second front, discontent with being shut out of participation in the Italian campaign, and unhappiness with the amount of U.S. financial assistance.

The Western allies were suspicious of Soviet secrecy. London and Washington gave detailed data on strategy and weapons to Moscow but got little information from the Soviets. Over $12 billion in Lend-Lease aid was sent to the Soviet Union, but its extent and value were not publicly acknowledged by the Soviet Union for four decades.

The breakdown of wartime cooperation soon cooled into the Cold War. From 1945 to 1953 the struggle was centered in Europe and focused on Stalin's attempts to consolidate his hegemony in Eastern Europe.[2]

Postwar Stalinism

Despite the immense destruction it had suffered, the USSR emerged after the war as one of the world's two superpowers. Stalin took seriously his role in building communism and pursuing world revolution. He used the secret police to rid Soviet society of any Western contamination. To achieve military equality with the United States, he launched the fourth five-year plan in 1946, pushing growth in heavy industry and military goods. To increase Soviet output, he imposed double shifts on many workers.

Stalin harshly rewarded the Soviet people for their sacrifices in World War II with a return to the iron repression of the 1930s. In the city of Leningrad (now known by its original name of St. Petersburg), which had lost a million people, streets had been renamed in honor of the war dead. Stalin's bureaucrats ripped down these spontaneous tributes and restored the old, officially approved names.

Huge new factories producing an estimated 80 percent of industrial output sprang up east of a line from Leningrad to Moscow to Stalingrad (now Volgograd). The state lured workers to the new sites with salary increases and other benefits, but much of the need for workers was filled by mass deportation of people to labor camps. Those whose loyalty to Stalin was in the least suspect were sent to a network of camps spread from Siberia to central Asia to the Arctic region. "The economic demand for cheap labour [dictated] the supply of the guilty."[3] Thousands died in the camps from overwork, inadequate food, and the bitter cold.

To rebuild the devastated farming regions Stalin returned to his collectivization policies. Smaller farms became parts of larger units, and the ultimate goal remained to make peasants into members of the rural proletariat, working in "industrialized agriculture." After 1950 the effort was stepped up, but at the cost of discontent and low productivity.

The dictator continued to place his supporters in all important offices, combining "the supreme command of the party with the supreme administration of the state."[4] He made entry into the Communist party more difficult and purged many people who had slipped in through the relaxed membership standards during wartime. The party became a haven for the managerial elite rather than the ideologically pure. The 1946 Supreme Soviet elections dramatized Stalin's political control. The voters were given only one choice for each office. Officials reported that 99.7 percent of the citizens voted; fewer than 1 percent of them crossed out the name of a candidate.

In the early 1950s Stalin lashed out more ruthlessly and unpredictably than ever before as he came to suspect everyone. His half-million-strong security police quashed any sign of dissent, criticism, or free expression. He ordered genocidal attacks on entire peoples, such as the Crimean Tatars. After Stalin removed and later executed the director of national economic planning, there were indications that Stalin was preparing a major purge that would go beyond "elite self-renewal."

In January 1953 the police announced that a "doctors' plot" had been uncovered and charged a group of physicians serving high military and governmental officials with planning to undermine their patients' health. Seven of the nine accused were Jewish, and in some quarters it was feared that an anti-Zionist campaign was in the making. The purge did not occur because on March 5, 1953, Stalin died after a painful illness.

Thus passed one of the most powerful men in world history. He had taken Lenin's revolution and preserved it in Russia and its satellites while exporting it to the world. In a quarter century he remade his society, withstood Hitler's strongest attacks, and emerged from the Second World War as leader of one of the two superpowers. He built the Soviet economic and political systems, which lasted until 1987, and cultivated a group of bureaucratic survivors—the apparatchiks—who ran the country until the advent of Mikhail Gorbachev. In doing all of this, he killed more of his own people than Hitler had.

The Cold War in Eastern Europe to 1953

Soon after the February 1945 Yalta Conference it became clear that Stalin's view of the composition of postwar Eastern Europe was very different from that of Roosevelt and Churchill. As early as April 1, 1945, Roosevelt sent a telegram to Stalin protesting the latter's violation of Yalta pledges. A month later Churchill sent a long message of protest to Stalin in which he concluded:

> *There is not much comfort in looking into a future where you and the countries you dominate . . . are all on one side, and those who rally to the English-speaking nations . . . are on the other. Their quarrel would tear the world to pieces.*[5]

From 1945 to 1948 Stalin carefully expanded his control over the region, working through his allies' domination of the various coalition governments. He had a number of advantages. Most of the local elites had either been killed during the war or been condemned for collaborating with the Nazis. The Communist parties, most of which were underground during the interwar period, had gained public support by leading the resistance to the Nazis after June 1941. Further, the Red Army remained in place to intimidate Eastern Europe.

The Communists occupied the most powerful positions in the coalition governments; opposition parties gained largely symbolic posts. The Communists soon used intimidation and outright force. The Czechs remained free longer than the other Eastern European states. In the 1946 elections the Communists had received only 38 percent of the vote, and they were losing support. In the spring of 1948 the Soviets forced Czechoslovakia to submit to Communist control. By the end of 1948, when the Americans had totally withdrawn from Europe, the governments in Warsaw, East Berlin, Prague, Budapest, Bucharest, Sofia, and Tirana operated as satellites orbiting the political center of Moscow.

Stalin used the Soviet Bloc as a 400-mile-deep buffer against capitalist invasion and as a source to help the USSR rebuild. He blocked any political, economic, or cultural contact with the West. Once his allies gained control, he ordered a purge of the local parties, based on those in the Soviet Union in the 1930s. The main target for the purge was the "national communists," those who were seen as being more loyal to their own nation than to Moscow or Stalin. Overall the purge removed one of every four party members. Many of those eliminated had been loyal Communists since the beginning of the century.

Meanwhile, in the three years after 1945, the four-power agreement on the governing of Germany soon broke apart. In the fall of 1946 Britain and America merged their zones into one economic unit, which came to be known as Bizonia. The French joined the union in 1948. Germany was now split into two parts, one administered by the Western allies and the other by the Soviets and would remain divided until the line between the two powers—dubbed the "Iron Curtain" by Churchill—disappeared in 1990.

The Truman Doctrine

Once the Americans recovered from their post-1945 euphoria, President Truman spelled out his response to perceived Soviet aggression.

The peoples of a number of countries of the world have recently had totalitarian regimes forced upon them against their will. The Government of the United States has made frequent protests against coercion and intimidation, in violation of the Yalta agreement, in Poland, Rumania, and Bulgaria. I must also state that in a number of other countries there have been similar developments.

At the present moment in world history nearly every nation must choose between alternative ways of life. The choice is too often not a free one.

One way of life is based upon the will of the majority, and is distinguished by free institutions, representative government, free elections, guaranties of individual liberty, freedom of speech and religion, and freedom from political oppression.

The second way of life is based upon the will of a minority forcibly imposed upon the majority. It relies upon terror and oppression, a controlled press and ra-

dio, fixed elections, and the suppression of personal freedoms.

I believe that it must be the policy of the United States to support free peoples who are resisting attempted subjugation by armed minorities or by outside pressures.

I believe that we must assist free peoples to work out their own destinies in their own way.

I believe that our help should be primarily through economic and financial aid, which is essential to economic stability and orderly political processes.

From U.S. Congress, *Congressional Record*, 80th Congress, 1st Session (Washington, D.C.: U.S. Government Printing Office, 1947), Vol. 93, p. 1981; U.S. Congress, Senate Committee on Foreign Relations, *A Decade of American Foreign Policy: Basic Documents, 1941–1949* (Washington, D.C.: U.S. Government Printing Office, 1950), pp. 1270–1271.

The Marshall Plan and Containment

The Soviets did not return their armies to peacetime status after 1945. They and their allies challenged the West in Greece, Turkey, and Iran. Britain was too weak to play its former role in the region. The Americans, as they would subsequently do throughout the globe, filled the gap left by the British and French. President Harry Truman responded to Soviet pressure by announcing that the United States would support any country threatened by communist aggression. Soon after this proclamation of the Truman Doctrine in 1947, the United States sent economic and military aid to Greece and Turkey, a move traditionally held to mark the American entry into the Cold War.

It took two years for the United States' wartime goodwill toward the Soviet Union to turn to a paranoid fear of international communism. The Americans, comfortable with their nuclear monopoly, had looked forward to a peaceful postwar world. By the end of 1946 they were angered by Soviet actions in the United Nations, Eastern Europe, and China and by the growth of Communist parties in Western Europe. Conservatives attacked the Yalta agreement as a "sellout" and launched a new "Red scare" campaign. A French observer noted the rapid change in attitude by pointing out that "a whole nation, optimistic and naive, placed its trust in a comrade in arms."[6] Now that comrade was the enemy, and the

United States suddenly felt very vulnerable. And Truman, who felt he could do business with Stalin as one politician to another, changed his mind when he wrote in his journal in November 1946 that there was no difference between the government in Moscow, that of the tsars, or the Hitler regime.[7]

The American diplomat George F. Kennan explained that the correct stance to take toward Stalin's policies was one of containment. In an article titled "The Sources of Soviet Conduct," written anonymously in the July 1947 issue of *Foreign Affairs*, Kennan proposed a "realistic understanding of the profound and deep-rooted difference between the United States and the Soviet Union" and the exercise of "a long-term, patient but firm and vigilant containment of Russian expansive tendencies."[8] This advice shaped U.S. policy throughout Europe.

The policy of containment was first used in Yugoslavia, where a split between Joseph Broz Tito (1891–1980) and Stalin marked the first breach in the Soviet advance. Tito had initiated the ideological break known as national communism. Supported financially by the West, the Yugoslavs were able to survive Stalin's attacks.

The broad economic and political arms of containment came into play. Secretary of State George C. Marshall proposed a plan of economic aid to help Europe solve its postwar financial problems. Western European nations eagerly accepted the Marshall Plan, but the Soviet Union rejected American aid for itself and its bloc. Congress authorized the plan, known as the European Recovery Program, and within four years the industrial output of the recipients climbed to 64 percent over 1947 levels and 41 percent over prewar levels. The European Recovery Act stabilized conditions in Western Europe and prevented the Communists from taking advantage of postwar problems.

Rival Systems

In July 1948, after opposing a Western series of currency and economic reforms in Germany, the Soviets blocked all land and water transport to Berlin from the West. For the next ten months the allies supplied West Berlin by air. They made over 277,000 flights to bring 2.3 million tons of food and other vital materials to the besieged city. Rather than risk war over the city, with the threat of American nuclear weapons, the Soviets removed their blockade in May 1949. In the same month the Federal Republic of Germany came into existence, made up of the three Western allied zones. Almost immediately, the Soviet Union established the German Democratic Republic in the Soviet zone. Germany would remain divided for the next 41 years.

In the spring of 1949 Washington and its allies established the North Atlantic Treaty Organization (NATO), an alliance for mutual assistance. The initial members were Great Britain, France, Belgium, Luxembourg, the Netherlands, Norway, Denmark, Portugal, Italy, Iceland, the United States, and Canada. Greece and Turkey joined in 1952, fol-

lowed by West Germany in 1955. At the beginning NATO was essentially a paper organization. The Americans had disarmed so quickly after World War II that officers left behind in 1949 drew up plans for a retreat behind the Pyrenees in Spain and across the Channel to England in case of a Soviet attack.[9] A year later the Americans crafted their strategic response to the Communists in a document known as NSC-68, which led to the creation of an immense military system and a vast expansion of the newly created Central Intelligence Agency (CIA) to counter the Communist advance anywhere in the world.

In 1955 the Soviets created the Warsaw Pact, which formalized the existing unified military command in Soviet-dominated Eastern Europe. Warsaw Pact members included, in addition to the Soviet Union, Albania, Bulgaria, Romania, Czechoslovakia, Hungary, Poland, and East Germany. The alliance lasted until 1991.

The tension between the rival systems finally snapped in Korea. After Japan's surrender, Korea had been divided at the 38th parallel into American and Soviet zones of occupation. When the occupying troops left, they were replaced by two hostile forces, each claiming jurisdiction over the entire country. On June 25, 1950, North Korean troops crossed the 38th parallel into South Korea. Washington immediately called for a special meeting of the UN Security Council, whose members demanded a cease-fire and withdrawal of the invaders. The Soviet delegate was boycotting the council at the time and was not present to veto the action.

To try to force the Western powers out of Berlin, in July 1948 the Russians imposed a blockade on the city. In response, the Allies organized an airlift to fly in supplies to the city and its beleaguered citizens. In May 1949 the Soviets lifted the blockade.

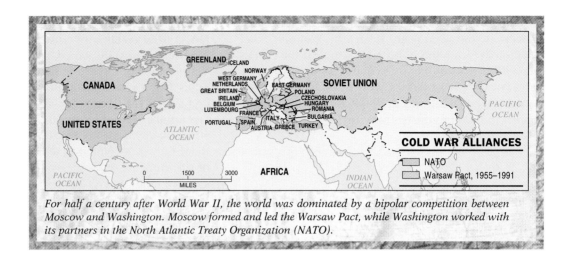

For half a century after World War II, the world was dominated by a bipolar competition between Moscow and Washington. Moscow formed and led the Warsaw Pact, while Washington worked with its partners in the North Atlantic Treaty Organization (NATO).

When North Korea ignored the UN's demand, the Security Council sent troops to help the South Korean government. Three years of costly fighting followed, in what the UN termed a "police action." United Nations forces led by the United States, which suffered over 140,000 casualties, repelled the invaders, who were supported by the USSR and the People's Republic of China. An armistice was signed in July 1953, after Stalin's death in March and a U.S. threat to use nuclear weapons against China.[10] A new border between the two parts of the country was established near the 38th parallel, and South Korea's independence was maintained. The peninsula remained a crisis point into the 1990s.

By 1953 the first phase of the Cold War was over. Both the Soviet Union and the United States possessed terrifying arsenals of nuclear weapons, both competed in all aspects of the Cold War, and both constantly probed for weaknesses in the other's defenses. President Eisenhower in his two terms placed a special emphasis on the development of nuclear arms, and his secretary of state, John Foster Dulles, spoke of "massive retaliation" should the Communists attempt to expand their sphere. On their side,

A U.S. Army howitzer fires on Communist troops in night action during the Korean War. The Cold War erupted into heated conflict in 1950 when North Korean troops invaded South Korea. A cease-fire agreement was reached in 1951, but sporadic fighting continued until an armistice was signed in July 1953. The Korean conflict escalated tensions between the Cold War rivals and sped up the mounting weapons and nuclear arms race between the superpowers.

the Soviets—through an effective spy network and massive investment of resources—soon became the equal of the United States in nuclear weapons. Various types of controlled conflict characterized the next four decades of relations between Moscow and Washington.

The Cold War: Part II, 1953–1962

Stalin's death introduced a period of collective leadership in the Soviet Union. The transition from an all-powerful despot to a clique of competing apparatchiks brought a change to the nature and scope of Soviet foreign policy for the two years after 1953. Nikita Khrushchev dominated global events after 1955, as the Cold War spread throughout Asia, Africa, and Latin America. The introduction of intercontinental ballistic missiles (ICBMs) brought a chilling immediacy to the formation and conduct of foreign affairs.

Khrushchev: The "Uncultured" Man

A committee made up of Lavrenti Beria (secret police), Georgi Malenkov (chief Stalin aide), and Vyacheslav Molotov (foreign affairs) succeeded Stalin. The new rulers issued orders after his death urging the people to guard against enemies and prevent "any kind of disorder and panic." They placed Stalin's embalmed body in the tomb next to Lenin and then relaxed his policies. They dropped the doctors' plot charges, eased censorship, reduced terror, and released many people from prison and the labor camps.

Within three years the initial triumvirate had disappeared, elbowed aside by Nikita Sergeyevich Khrushchev (1894–1971). Khrushchev was a self-made man who rose by his wits and ability. Born of peasant parents, he was a shepherd at 7 and later a

miner and factory worker. He joined the Communist party and quickly rose through its ranks. Like so many of his colleagues, he came to power in the 1930s by taking the jobs of people killed by Stalin and ascended to the Politburo within a few years. By July 1953 he was the first secretary of the party; two years later he led the country.

Educated Soviet citizens viewed Khrushchev as uncultured and uncouth. He delighted in shocking people by his blunt and frequently profane remarks. His crude behavior disguised a subtle, supple, and penetrating mind, which got rapidly to the crux of a problem.

One of Khrushchev's main goals was to reform agriculture. He proposed increasing incentives for the peasants and enlarging the area under production in Soviet Siberia and central Asia—the virgin lands. Between 1953 and 1958 production rose by 50 percent. Thereafter farming in the virgin lands proved to be economically wasteful and environmentally disastrous. These weaknesses, combined with other setbacks, ultimately undermined Khrushchev's position.

De-Stalinization

Khrushchev's greatest contribution to the history of the USSR was to launch the de-Stalinization campaign. In February 1956 at the Twentieth Party Congress he gave a speech titled "The Crimes of the Stalin Era." He attacked his former patron as a bloodthirsty tyrant and revealed many of the cruelties of the purges and the mistakes of World War II. He carefully heaped full responsibility on the dead dictator for the excesses of the past 25 years, removing the blame from the apparatchiks such as himself whom Stalin had placed in power. Khrushchev blamed Stalin's crimes on the dictator's "cult of the personality." The speech shocked every level of Soviet society. In 1961 Stalin's body was removed from the Lenin mausoleum and placed in a grave by the Kremlin wall. His name disappeared from streets and cities; the "hero

Stalin's chief supporters surround the bier at his funeral, March 6, 1953. Left to right, they are Vyacheslav Molotov, Kliment Voroshilov, Lavrenti Beria, Georgi Malenkov, Nikolai Bulganin, Nikita Khrushchev, Lazar Kaganovich, and Anastas Mikoyan. Khrushchev was the victor in the power struggle to succeed Stalin.

Khrushchev's Address to the Twentieth Party Congress

After a quarter century of Stalinist rule, the USSR badly needed a policy change. Khrushchev justified the change on the grounds that Stalin had departed from Leninist norms and pursued the "cult of the personality."

When we analyze the practice of Stalin in regard to the direction of the party and of the country, when we pause to consider everything which Stalin perpetrated, we must be convinced that Lenin's fears were justified. The negative characteristics of Stalin, which, in Lenin's time, were only incipient, transformed themselves during the last years into a grave abuse of power by Stalin, which caused untold harm to our party.

We have to consider seriously and analyze correctly this matter in order that we may preclude any possibility of a repetition in any form whatever of what took place during the life of Stalin, who absolutely did not tolerate collegiality in leadership and in work, and who practiced brutal violence, not only toward everything which opposed him, but also toward that which seemed to his capricious and despotic character, contrary to his concepts.

Stalin acted not through persuasion, explanation, and patient cooperation with people, but by imposing his concepts and demanding absolute submission to his opinion. Whoever opposed this concept or tried to prove his viewpoint, and the correctness of his position, was doomed to removal from the leading collective and to subsequent moral and physical annihilation. This was especially true during the period following the 17th party congress, when many prominent party leaders and rank-and-file party workers, honest and dedicated to the cause of communism, fell victim to Stalin's despotism. . . .

Lenin's traits—patient work with people; stubborn and painstaking education of them; the ability to induce people to follow him without using compulsion, but rather through the ideological influence on them of the whole collective—were entirely foreign to Stalin. [Stalin] discarded the Leninist method of convincing and educating; he abandoned the method of ideological struggle for that of administrative violence, mass repressions, and terror. He acted on an increasingly larger scale and more stubbornly through punitive organs, at the same time often violating all existing norms of morality and of Soviet laws. . . .

During Lenin's life party congresses were convened regularly; always when a radical turn in the development of the party and the country took place Lenin considered it absolutely necessary that the party discuss at length all the basic matters pertaining to internal and foreign policy and to questions bearing on the development of party and government. . . .

Were our party's holy Leninist principles observed after the death of Vladimir Ilyich?

Whereas during the first few years after Lenin's death party congresses and central committee plenums took place more or less regularly; later, when Stalin began increasingly to abuse his power, these principles were brutally violated. This was especially evident during the last 15 years of his life. Was it a normal situation when 13 years elapsed between the 18th and 19th party congresses, years during which our party and our country had experienced so many important events? These events demanded categorically that the party should have passed resolutions pertaining to the country's defense during the patriotic war and to peacetime construction after the war. Even after the end of the war a congress was not convened for over 7 years. . . .

In practice Stalin ignored the norms of party life and trampled on the Leninist principle of collective party leadership.

From U.S. Congress, *Congressional Record*, 84th Congress, 2nd Session (Washington, D.C.: U.S. Government Printing Office, 1956), Vol. 102, pp. 9389–9403.

city" of Stalingrad was renamed Volgograd. Yet the governing structure Stalin had built was carefully preserved, and his protégés remained in place until Mikhail Gorbachev came to power in 1985.

Khrushchev's speech echoed throughout the communist world, sparking uprisings in Poland and Hungary and widening the gulf between China and the Soviet Union. Chinese-Soviet relations soured drastically after 1956, and by 1960 Khrushchev had pulled all Soviet technicians and assistance out of China. During the next decade the split grew still wider as Mao proclaimed himself to be Khrushchev's equal in ideological affairs.

Khrushchev survived an attempt to oust him from power in the summer of 1957, and from then until 1962 he dominated both Soviet and international affairs. During his rule the standard of living in Russia gradually improved, and Soviet scientists made remarkable strides. Khrushchev also initially relaxed the tensions of the Cold War until his pursuit of more aggressive policies in Asia, Africa, and Latin America after 1959 drove the world to the brink of nuclear war.

Discovery Through Maps

Massive Retaliatory Power, 1954

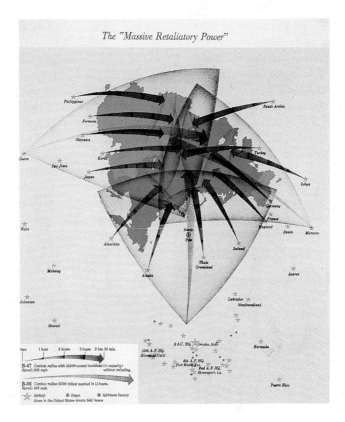

The "Massive Retaliatory Power"

The decisive fact of life for everyone born between 1940 and 1950 was the possibility, perhaps the probability, that a cataclysmic nuclear conflict would bring the end of the human race. Young Americans in school practiced the maneuver of "duck and cover" to protect themselves from incoming warheads; homeowners were encouraged to build bomb shelters, and radio stations broadcast "test emergency warnings."

This is an example of a Cold War map published in *Fortune* magazine in May 1954 after John Foster Dulles, the U.S. secretary of state, announced a new policy based on "massive retaliation." This map was meant to reassure Americans that the major Soviet targets were well covered and that Moscow dare not attack first. This propaganda effort was accompanied by a program to present the Russians as evil to justify the buildup of American arms. Only a few people dared consider that similar maps were circulating in Moscow, showing American targets, and that the likeliest outcome of the retaliation strategy would in fact be mutual destruction.

Peaceful Coexistence

During the transitional period after Stalin's death, Soviet foreign policy shifted from military probing to a more sophisticated approach. When Khrushchev gained control in 1955, he imposed his point of view that nuclear war would be suicidal for all concerned. He returned to the Leninist doctrine of peaceful coexistence and renounced the idea that open war between the socialist and capitalist worlds was inevitable.

Peaceful coexistence ushered in momentarily better relations between Moscow and Washington and led to a summit meeting in Geneva in 1955. Later the Americans refrained from interfering in the Polish and Hungarian crises that erupted in 1956, and Moscow and Washington worked together during the Suez Crisis that same year. Khrushchev visited the United States in 1959. Violence increased in Asia, Latin America, Africa, and the Middle East, however, where the rival systems competed for influence.

Two Soviet technological triumphs in 1957 escalated the tensions between the United States and the USSR. Moscow's scientists put the first artificial satellite, *Sputnik*, into orbit around the earth and began building a powerful fleet of ICBMs. These advances gave the Soviet Union the ability to land a nuclear weapon on U.S. territory in 25 minutes. The Cold War was becoming much more dangerous.

Berlin, which had long been a thorn in the Soviets' side, became the main flash point between the two powers. West Berlin's wealth and freedom stood in sharp contrast to drab, repressive East Berlin. Thousands of East Germany's technical and intellectual elite easily escaped to the West through Berlin. The Soviets, who had tried to drive the West from Berlin in the 1948 blockade, demanded the withdrawal of all Western forces and recognition of Berlin as a "free city." They presumably wanted to bring the whole metropolis under Communist control. The Allies, strengthened in part by the major advances in U.S. rocket power, refused to give in to this demand.

A series of events in the early 1960s brought the superpowers closer to nuclear war. A summit convened in Paris in 1960 broke up angrily when the Soviets shot down an American U-2 reconnaissance plane over Siberia. Khrushchev seized the opportunity to denounce the West and marshaled his forces for a series of provocative moves. He demanded the resignation of UN Secretary-General Dag Hammarskjold who, he believed, opposed the Soviet-backed side in the civil war currently raging in the Congo. The failure of a U.S. attempt to land forces of Cuban exiles at the Bay of Pigs to overthrow Premier Fidel Castro gave Khrushchev another trump card to play.

In the spring of 1961, with John F. Kennedy, a young and inexperienced president, in office, Moscow stepped up all of its pressures around the world. The Soviets again demanded the withdrawal of the Allies from West Berlin. Once again, citing postwar agreements, the West refused to back down. This time the East Germans, acting under Soviet supervision, erected a wall between the two halves of the city, thereby blocking the escape route formerly used by thousands. Tensions also rose in Laos and Vietnam. To a generation of leaders in the United States, students of the lessons of appeasement in Munich a quarter century earlier and of the success of containment, it seemed evident that force had to be met with force.

In October 1962 the world came as close as it ever has to full-scale nuclear war. Three years earlier Fidel Castro had led a successful revolution against the right-wing Cuban dictator Fulgencio Batista. Castro immediately began to transform the island into a communist state. After the failure of the American effort to overthrow him at the Bay of Pigs, the Soviets began to install missiles in Cuba.

To the United States these missiles were a dangerous threat to the Cold War balance of power. Kennedy ordered what was, in effect, a naval block-

Berlin was Europe's flashpoint for the greater part of the Cold War. The Soviet Bloc had failed to win the confrontation during the Berlin Blockade (1948–1949). In 1961, testing the resolve of the new U.S. president, John F. Kennedy, the East Germans erected a wall separating their zone from the sectors controlled by the Western powers. The Berlin Wall was the site of numerous brave and tragic escape attempts until it was torn down in 1989.

ade around Cuba and demanded that Moscow withdraw the offensive weapons. After a few days of "eyeball-to-eyeball" crisis in which one incident might have triggered direct military action between Moscow and Washington, Khrushchev blinked—he ordered the missiles removed in exchange for assurances that the United States would respect Cuba's territory and other concessions.

Having drawn the world to the brink of catastrophe in the Cuban Missile Crisis, Khrushchev moderated his confrontational stance. His perceived blunders in Cuba and failures in agricultural policies led finally to his removal from power. While on vacation in October 1964, he was informed that he had been "released from state duties" and was called back to Moscow. The leader was given a pension and placed under a mild form of house arrest in a comfortable compound outside the capital. He remained largely isolated from the public, writing his memoirs until his death in 1971.

The Vietnam War: 1946–1975

A misreading of the containment doctrine drew the United States into a quagmire in Indochina that would change Americans' views toward their role in the world and their government. After World War II France was forced to grant a measure of autonomy to Cambodia and Laos, its former colonial possessions in Southeast Asia. The status of Vietnam posed a greater problem. In 1945 a nationalist and pro-Communist movement led by Ho Chi Minh had established the independent Republic of Vietnam, usually referred to as the Vietminh regime.

Negotiations between the Vietminh and the French led nowhere, and war broke out in December 1946. The cruel and violent struggle, anticolonial as well as ideological, lasted for nearly eight years. In May 1950 the United States began sending substantial financial and military support to the French. The end came dramatically in 1954 when the French, despite U.S. assistance, surrendered their isolated outpost at Dien Bien Phu, along with 10,000 troops.

In a conference at Geneva later that year a truce line was established at the 17th parallel, to be regarded as a temporary boundary pending nationwide elections. These elections were never held, and instead a new group proclaimed the Republic of South Vietnam, based in Saigon, south of the truce line. Meanwhile, the division between the Vietminh regime in Hanoi and the Saigon government increased. Along with the movement of hundreds of thousands of Roman Catholic Vietnamese refugees from the north came a powerful infiltration of Communist military personnel and matériel from Hanoi.

The United States shipped large numbers of men and weapons to Saigon in an attempt to create a

The Vietnam Tragedy

1945	Ho Chi Minh establishes Republic of Vietnam
1946	French oppose independence; negotiations break down; war begins
1950	U.S. begins sending support to French in Vietnam
1954	French leave Vietnam after defeat at Dien Bien Phu; Geneva Conference divides Vietnam at 17th parallel; elections scheduled
1955	Both sides violate Geneva Accords; United States sends massive support to South Vietnam, establishes Southeast Asia Treaty Organization (SEATO)
1959	Second Vietnamese War begins; National Liberation Front (NLF) established in South, supported by North
1961–1964	U.S. presence increases from 800 to 24,000
1964	"Tonkin Gulf Resolution" places United States fully in support of South Vietnam; Americanization of Vietnam Civil War
1964–1968	American presence grows to more than 500,000 troops
1968	Tet Offensive stopped: military victory, public relations disaster for United States
1973	United States pulls out of Vietnam under Paris Accords
1975	North Vietnam establishes control over entire reunited country

South Vietnamese state capable of holding its own against the Vietminh and their allies in South Vietnam. The military activity on both sides violated the Geneva agreements, but it could be argued that since none of the governments had signed them, they simply were not binding. Washington also sponsored the establishment of the Southeast Asia Treaty Organization (SEATO) to stop the spread of communism into Cambodia, Laos, and South Vietnam.

At first the Americans gave full support to Ngo Dinh Diem, the leading figure of the noncommunist south. He rejected Ho Chi Minh's requests to hold elections throughout all Vietnam under the Geneva agreements because he feared that his government would lose. He also refused to carry out comprehensive land reforms desired by Washington, choosing instead to rely for support on the landlords and the urban middle classes.

At the same time, the Communists, thwarted in their aim to unite North and South by an election, began preperations to undermine Diem's government. This so-called Second Vietnamese War began in 1959. Many peasants, disillusioned with Diem's failure to carry out land reform, tacitly or actively supported the Communist guerrilla effort. In January Hanoi activated the National Liberation Front (NLF), also known as the Viet Cong, to begin open warfare in the South.

Diem, in the face of a rising crisis, became even more autocratic and less inclined to make reforms, perhaps reflecting Washington's shift in policy from President Eisenhower's emphasis on "nation building" to Kennedy's strategy of "counterinsurgency." The NLF threatened to take over the entire government by force, and a coup and Diem's assassination did little to improve the situation. Following a series of short-lived, essentially military governments, Nguyen Van Thieu became president of South Vietnam in 1967.

The Americanization of the War

In 1960 there were only 800 U.S. military advisers in the country. Four years later this figure had risen to 23,000. In August 1964 Washington accused North Vietnam of attacking United States destroyers in the Gulf of Tonkin. At President Lyndon B. Johnson's request, Congress adopted—by a Senate vote of 88 to 2 and a House vote of 416 to 0—a joint resolution approving "all necessary measures . . . to prevent further aggression" and authorized the president to assist South Vietnam in its defense, using military force if required.

Thereafter, the war in all of its aspects became increasingly Americanized. By 1968 there were more than 500,000 U.S. troops in the country. In 1965 the United States started an intensive air campaign against North Vietnam. The aerial campaign failed to intimidate the North Vietnamese and became a subject of bitter controversy in the United States.

Many Americans began to question the U.S. role in Vietnam. Their doubts were sharpened in the early spring of 1968 when the Viet Cong launched the Tet Offensive against the Saigon forces and the Americans. Widely covered by television and print journalists, the offensive turned into a military disaster for the NLF and Hanoi, but the images of death and destruction communicated a notion of helplessness to the American people. The U.S. military victory ironically became a political defeat for President Johnson.

As the number of Americans killed in Vietnam grew, the antiwar movement spread from a few campus radicals to include moderate politicians, suburbanites, and mainstream clergy. The financial costs of the war were enormous, contributing to an inflation that continued throughout the 1970s. The political cost for Lyndon Johnson was equally high: he declined the opportunity to run for reelection in 1968.

During the final months of Johnson's administration, peace talks began in Paris with all interested

The Vietnam War was the first televised war. Images such as this one flooded into American living rooms night after night, and the longer the war dragged on, in the face of repeated official announcements of great victories, the more Americans questioned their nation's participation in the conflict.

parties represented. The Nixon administration continued the talks through more years of frustrating negotiations until in January 1973 an accord was signed. It provided for a cease-fire, the withdrawal of U.S. troops, and the release of all prisoners of war.

Pending elections to be arranged later, Nguyen Van Thieu's South Vietnamese government was to remain in power. An international commission was to be established to investigate cease-fire violations. The Paris Accord contained no provision for the withdrawal of North Vietnamese forces. Once the Americans withdrew, the North Vietnamese continued their advance, and the commission was predictably ineffectual. In early 1975 the Hanoi forces, soon to be the fifth strongest military in the world, began a massive offensive. Deprived of U.S. support, the southern forces fell apart once the northern frontiers were overrun. Saigon was captured in late April and renamed Ho Chi Minh City. Many South Vietnamese fled their homeland, and some 140,000 gained sanctuary in the United States.

For the United States the legacy of the Vietnam conflict was 58,000 lives lost, a financial outlay of at least $146 billion, a society bitterly split, and a host of veterans who were rebuked or ignored. It took a decade for the United States to come to terms with the war. The legacy for Vietnam was a 20-year delay in the Vietminh takeover and incalculable human and material losses.

Repercussions of the U.S. Failure

The United States had expanded the fighting into neutral Cambodia in the spring of 1970, invading it with the goal of cutting North Vietnamese supply lines and driving the Hanoi army from its sanctuaries there. Following the North Vietnamese victory in 1975, Communists took control of Cambodia and Laos. The ruthless and brutal Khmer Rouge regime embarked on a reign of terror in Cambodia, which was renamed Kampuchea. In Phnom Penh, the capital, nearly all the inhabitants—more than 2 million people—were driven into the countryside, regardless of age or infirmity. People in other cities suffered the same fate; many died from sickness or starvation. A new social system of farm units with labor brigades and communal kitchens was set up. The slightest sign of disobedience resulted in death.

The leader of the Chinese-supported Khmer Rouge regime was Pol Pot. His followers murdered thousands of innocent peasants along with "anyone who had been associated with the cities, with foreigners, or with intellectual, business, or technical activities."[11] The regime's goal seems to have been a self-sufficient agricultural society in which most people would have food and shelter but no pay. It is estimated that between 1975 and 1980 as many as 3 mil-

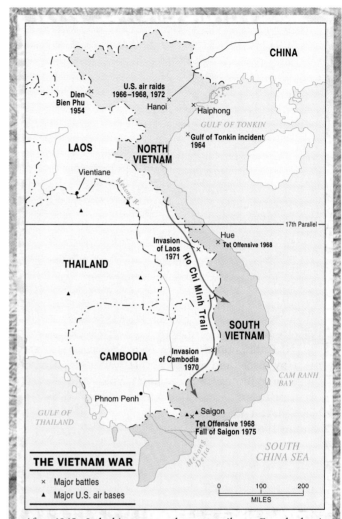

After 1945, Indochina returned temporarily to French dominance. A successful national liberation movement drove the French out in 1954, and thereafter, the United States became increasingly involved in the struggle between Saigon and Hanoi.

lion Cambodians died—"shot, beaten to death, starved, brutalized. Few people in modern times have been subjugated to such barbarism."[12] The Pol Pot regime was overthrown when Vietnamese armies invaded the country. The Cambodians now suffered the ravages of war in addition to continued indiscriminate killings and massacres.

While China supported Pol Pot, the Soviet Union supported the Vietnamese invaders and a Cambodian faction opposed to Pol Pot. Early in 1979 Chinese armies invaded Vietnam, destroying several of its northern towns, but failed to draw Vietnamese armies out of Cambodia. After this brief sortie, the Chinese forces withdrew, and the world gained an appreciation of the military strength of the Vietnamese regime.

Although the situation in Laos was not so chaotic, there also the Vietnamese regime imposed

After the United States withdrew its troops from Vietnam in 1973, many South Vietnamese fled the country. Here a mother and her children struggle across a river to escape the aerial bombardment of their village.

regimentation and abuse on the Laotians, some of whom were sent to "reeducation camps." Many professional people fled the country, and soon the lack of food and deplorable health conditions made Laos's standard of living nearly the lowest in the world.

Until the early 1990s much of Indochina was a confused mass of fleeing refugees. Unwilling to accept Communist rule, thousands of people took to the sea in rickety boats. Many Chinese living in Vietnam were mistreated by the new regime and fled back across the border to China. Great numbers of refugees streamed from Laos and Cambodia to Thailand, Malaysia, Indonesia, and Hong Kong. In addition, thousands of "boat people" drowned at sea in their leaky craft, were attacked by pirates in the South China Sea, or died of thirst and starvation when refused permission to land.

By the end of the 1990s, comparative stability had returned to the region. Normal diplomatic and trade relations were restored between the United States and Vietnam. In Cambodia a massive UN op-

eration stabilized the country and permitted an election in 1993 that included all parties. By 1994 the Khmer Rouge, because of their continued military activities, were expelled from participation in the Phnom Penh government. In 1998, after the death of Pol Pot, the Cambodian government attempted to reach an accord with the Khmer Rouge to bring peace to Cambodia. It would take more time for the Indochinese peninsula to recover from the ravages of a half century of war.

The Cold War: Part III, 1962–1985

Following Khrushchev's "retirement," a classic *apparatchik*, Leonid Brezhnev (1906–1982), dominated the next stage of Cold War and Soviet history. Working with Aleksei Kosygin (1904–1980), he constructed an alliance with the military to deliver support that would enable the USSR to gain military parity with the Americans. This diversion of resources into military spending did little to help the larger economy, which suffered a serious decline at the end of the 1980s. Brezhnev and his colleagues profited from the U.S. involvement in Vietnam to make diplomatic gains despite the entry of China on the international stage as a major power. Ironically, the invasion of Afghanistan in 1979 led the Soviets into a dilemma that was almost a mirror image of the tragedy the United States experienced in Vietnam. As the Vietnam War turned out to be a major turning point for the Americans, the Afghanistan adventure propelled the USSR toward its eventual decline and fall.

The Last of Stalin's Protégés

From 1964 to 1974 Brezhnev and Kosygin split power, Brezhnev acting as general secretary and Kosygin as premier, overseeing sporadic reform attempts. Brezhnev later became president of the country under terms of the 1977 constitution. Serious health problems limited his effectiveness in the last years of his tenure until his death in 1982.

Politics remained based on Stalin's foundations, as modified by Khrushchev. The central planners continued to emphasize industrial growth and slowly increase the supply of consumer goods. In foreign policy the new team pursued peaceful coexistence at the same time that they greatly strengthened the Soviet armed forces. Brezhnev worked closely with military leaders to ensure that they had everything needed to gain equality with the United States in missiles, air, land, and sea forces. During the 18 years of his rule, the Soviet Union built a powerful, global navy to support its foreign policies.

While the USSR gained military parity with the West, its civilian economy ground to a halt. The long-standing agricultural crisis grew worse. The Soviets spent huge amounts to import grain from abroad to cope with food shortages at home. Especially maddening to the Soviet leaders was the extraordinary amount of crops that rotted in the fields or en route to market. Private plots worked by peasants after hours for their own profit, which accounted for only 3 percent of sown land, provided 30 percent of all the table food in the Soviet Union.

The party leaders struggled to deal with low per capita output, poor quality, technological backwardness, transport breakdowns, and widespread corruption. Over the next 20 years, despite numerous reform attempts, the Soviet economy stagnated. The military sector absorbed most economic and technological improvements. Living standards slowly improved, but at a terrific cost. The Soviet Union exacerbated its economic problems by allowing political and ideological considerations to take precedence over productive efficiency.[13]

Brezhnev was succeeded by Yuri Andropov (1914–1984), a railway worker's son who worked his way up the ranks to become Soviet ambassador to Hungary from 1954 to 1957. After putting down the 1956 revolution in Hungary, Andropov returned to Moscow to take a number of increasingly important party and political jobs. In 1967 he became chief of the KGB, the organization that combined the powers and responsibilities of the U.S. FBI and CIA but without the legal restraints affecting those two groups. He remained in that post for the next 15 years. Andropov entered the Politburo in 1973 and seven months before Brezhnev's death became the secretary of the Central Committee. He rose to the top position in the Soviet Union the day after Brezhnev died.

Andropov's jobs put him at the crossroads of all information. He knew the disastrous condition of the USSR's infrastructure. He brought a large number of people from the provinces to work in high party positions in Moscow and set out immediately to increase output, fight corruption, and strengthen the military. He started campaigns to combat alcoholism and cheating and fired people who did not perform up to his standards. However, his own health problems prevailed, and from the summer of 1983 until his announced death in February 1984, Andropov was out of public view.

The last of the Stalin protégés was Konstantin Chernenko (1912–1985), who succeeded Andropov to the posts of first secretary and president. Chernenko had ridden Brezhnev's coattails since the 1950s but had been soundly defeated by Andropov for the top job in 1982. His age and poor health signified that he would be a transition figure between the old guard and a new generation. The strain of leadership almost immediately broke Chernenko's fragile health, and even before his death in March 1985, wholesale changes were taking place in the highest levels of the Soviet government.

Diplomacy and Arms Control Agreements

After 1962 the Soviet Union and the United States moved away from nuclear conflict. Close consultations between the two superpowers, even during proxy wars, helped head off danger. A telephone "hot line," in increasingly sophisticated form, kept the Kremlin and the White House in minute-by-minute contact and helped avoid possible nuclear accidents in the dangerous Vietnamese and Middle Eastern situations. In addition, the USSR saw its options narrow after 1972 with the emergence of China as an independent player in the international game.

The Cuban Missile Crisis convinced leaders in Moscow and Washington of the need to reduce the peril of nuclear war and ushered in a process of complex negotiations dealing with all aspects of the risk of nuclear war. An immediate result of these talks was a limited nuclear test ban treaty negotiated in 1963 and signed on August 5 of that year by Great Britain, the Soviet Union, and the United States. The treaty outlawed the testing of nuclear devices in outer space, in the atmosphere, or underwater. More than 100 nations signed the agreement, although France, China, and India refused to do so. The Latin American Nuclear-Free Zone Treaty was signed in 1968, and treaties and conventions dealing with the nonproliferation of nuclear weapons (1970, 1978) followed.

In 1971 agreements were reached further reducing the risk of nuclear war and updating the hot line. In 1975 a convention dealing with biological weapons and agreements concerning the threat of catastrophic war were signed. In addition, the Mutual Balanced Force Reduction (MBFR) talks began between NATO and the Warsaw Pact to limit conventional forces. These dragged on until the Warsaw Pact dissolved in the 1990s.

The two most important treaties were the Strategic Arms Limitation Talks (SALT I and SALT II). In these negotiations the two superpowers acknowledged, in effect, an equivalence of killing power that led to the capacity for "mutual assured destruction" (MAD). After two years of complicated talks, SALT I was signed by President Richard Nixon and General Secretary Leonid Brezhnev in Moscow in the spring of 1972. SALT I limited the number of ICBMs that each side could deploy for five years and restricted the construction of antiballistic missile systems to two sites in each country to maintain MAD.

Technological advances soon made the limits of SALT I obsolete, as both sides developed the ability to deploy multiple independently targeted reentry vehicles (MIRVs), which vastly expanded the killing power of each missile. At a meeting in Vladivostok in November 1974, President Gerald Ford and Brezhnev established guidelines to deal with the addition of MIRVs that led to the SALT II agreement. Even though considerations such as the Soviet invasion of Afghanistan and domestic politics in each country precluded the formal adoption of SALT II, the attempt to maintain parity continued. Each side charged the other at times with violating the understanding implicit in SALT II, which was eventually signed by President Jimmy Carter and Brezhnev in Vienna in 1979.

Throughout the 1980s Moscow and Washington both adhered to the general framework of SALT II while maneuvering for strategic superiority. The arms control talks were complex, difficult, and subject to frustration as neither side could permit the other to gain the strategic advantage. Thus while negotiations continued in the Strategic Arms Reduction Talks (START) in 1982, so too did full-scale weapons research and espionage. In the first half of the 1980s the USSR upset the balance of force in Europe by placing SS-20 missiles in the territory of its Eastern European allies. The START talks were halted, and the Americans responded by deploying Pershing II and ground-launched cruise missiles, a strategic necessity given NATO's military inferiority in conventional weapons. After Mikhail Gorbachev became Soviet leader, arms talks on all levels resumed and continued under Boris Yeltsin.

The USSR's "Quagmire": Afghanistan

Despite close general cooperation on nuclear weapons talks, Cold War tensions escalated on another front in 1979 when the Soviet Union invaded Afghanistan. Armed coups and assassination had characterized the postwar political history of Afghanistan. After 1945 the Soviet Union extended its influence in the area, the site of the "great game" between tsarist Russia and Great Britain in the nineteenth century.

In 1978 Moscow increased its influence in Kabul by signing a "friendship treaty" with the Afghans. This agreement had little impact outside the capital; neither did postwar efforts by Kabul leaders to introduce changes based on either Western or Marxist models reach very far. The strongly conservative Muslim tribes opposed modernization in almost any form. Finally, in the late 1970s, civil war erupted.

By 1979 it appeared that the government of President Hafizullah Amin, which received support from the USSR, would be toppled by the rebellion. Earlier the Soviets had sent in 5000 military and civilian advisers to assist him. Moscow had made such a large investment that it could not tolerate the loss of its client state. In late December thousands of Soviet troops crossed the border, captured the airport, and stormed the presidential palace in Kabul. They killed their erstwhile ally Amin and installed Babrak Kamal.

Kamal announced that Soviet troops had been invited in to save Afghanistan from imperialist plots fomented by the United States. Few nations accepted this explanation. But coming as it did when U.S. citizens were being held hostage in neighboring Iran, the invasion gave the USSR the chance to dominate this strategic region with little risk of armed opposition. In the next year the USSR gained control of Afghan cities while an assortment of tribal guerrilla forces roamed the countryside. The Soviet advance sputtered to a stop during the next few years.

Moscow had gotten itself caught in a destructive quagmire. The Afghan resistance, lavishly supported by the United States, stalemated the Soviets and their puppets. The one advantage the USSR had in the battlefield—air power—was negated by the Afghan's effective use of the American-supplied Stinger antiaircraft missile. As the decade wore on, Afghanistan became for the USSR what Vietnam had been for the United States: a costly, demoralizing, divisive conflict. Similarly, the cost to the Afghan people was immense. Millions were uprooted, villages were destroyed, and many areas were littered with mines and booby traps. The Soviet Union finally withdrew its forces in 1989. The civil war continued into the 1990s, and Afghanistan returned to its tradition of tribal competition. The difference was that now the firepower available to the combatants was immensely greater.

The End of the Cold War

After Chernenko's death in 1985, a new generation of Soviet leaders came to the fore, led by Mikhail Gorbachev. No less devoted to Marxism-Leninism than the former generation, the new leaders—many of whom had been placed in positions of influence by Andropov—more openly attacked the economic and social problems the USSR faced. Moscow continued to claim that the Soviet Bloc would equal the West in technology by 2000. Technological improvements would not be enough. The centrally planned system, to be competitive in the new global economy, would have to be drastically overhauled to include a free flow of information and flexible responses to incentives and opportunities, both domestic and international.

The Gorbachev Revolution: The Domestic Phase

Mikhail Gorbachev (b. 1931) moved rapidly to take power by implementing a platform based on *glasnost* (openness) and *perestroika* (restructuring) to try to bring new life to the Soviet system. *Glasnost* was Gorbachev's way of motivating the Soviet people to be more creative and work harder. *Perestroika* attempted to remove the structural blocks to modernization. These two themes launched the final act in the de-Stalinization campaign begun by Khrushchev in 1956.

Gorbachev tried to mobilize the support of the cultural and scientific elite by encouraging them to participate in political life. He brought physicist Andrei Sakharov back from internal exile and permitted publication of the works of exiled author Aleksandr Solzhenitsyn, who returned to his native land in 1994. The party relinquished much of its control over culture for the first time since the 1920s. Stalin's total dictatorship over form, content, and aesthetics in the arts—his insistence that artists, writers, and musicians be "engineers of the soul"—had died with him. However, the party maintained its hold on all aspects

of culture and the mass media. *Glasnost* to a large degree brought back to Russia creative freedom that had been absent since the 1917 revolutions.

For the first time the party acknowledged mistakes, such as the Chernobyl nuclear disaster in April 1986. Past tragedies—especially those of the 1930s that had long been common knowledge—were now openly discussed. Gorbachev permitted unprecedented criticism of party and political leaders by the press and television. He sponsored broad reforms in Soviet society, imposing the strongest antialcoholism campaign in history and making the force of the drive felt at the highest levels.

One of the unexpected results of *glasnost* was a revival of separatist movements in the various Soviet republics. People in Estonia, Lithuania, Latvia, Armenia, Azerbaijan, the Ukraine, Moldavia, Kazakhstan, and Georgia declared the supremacy of their laws, institutions, and programs over those of the central government and claimed ownership of resources found within their borders.

Gorbachev originally sought to use *perestroika* to fine-tune the traditional central planning apparatus and party and state procedures, but the total failure of the Stalinist system demanded a more wide-ranging program. By 1990 the depth and severity of the Soviet Union's problems drove Gorbachev to attempt to impose a market economy, reduce the role of the "vanguard party," and alter the governmental structure. The broader scope of *perestroika* sought foreign capital, markets, and technology in order to make the USSR competitive. Gorbachev attempted to rebuild most aspects of the Soviet economic structure, such as its banking system. The result of these efforts was the breakdown of the old central planning structure. It was easier to destroy the old system than to create a new one. Gorbachev, his advisers, and Western experts were shocked at how difficult it was to transplant Western market capitalism onto Communist soil.

Until the summer of 1991, Gorbachev was the undisputed master of the party and the state, putting down rivals with great skill and using public opinion and free elections to neutralize opponents while building a new power base. After being named president in October 1988, he set out to reform that most secret and powerful of all Soviet institutions, the KGB, urging its new leaders to imitate the structure of the American CIA.

Until 1989 the Supreme Soviet was a carefully preselected rubber-stamp body. Real power was concentrated in the Council of Ministers, headed by a prime minister. In elections in March and April 1989 many powerful officials were voted down, even though they had run unopposed. The Congress of People's Deputies, which was to meet annually and be reelected every five years, replaced the old

Supreme Soviet. From the ranks of the Congress came a new Supreme Soviet. Unlike the old Supreme Soviet, which never saw a *no* vote, the Congress and the new Supreme Soviet were outspoken and controversial bodies, even with the guaranteed positions for Communist leaders.

The Communist party posed a special problem for Gorbachev, a dedicated Leninist. He criticized the cumbersome and unresponsive functioning of the organization with its theoretical capstone, the Party Congress, which typically met once every five years and elected the 450-strong Central Committee (300 voting members, 150 nonvoting). The committee, in turn, typically met at least once every six months to consider policies and elect the highest party body, the Politburo, with its 12 voting and eight nonvoting members. From his post as general secretary, Gorbachev could see that the party and its special commissions would not solve the basic problems of the country.

The party had become corrupt and reactionary, concerned more with its privileges than its responsibilities. It was so inflexible that Gorbachev had to diminish its role after the July 1990 party congress. Thereafter, no major political figure sat on the Politburo, with the exception of the Soviet president. The party became subordinate to the state, losing its leading role. Millions gave up their party memberships after 1989, many of them going to work in city and republic governments where there was greater opportunity.

Gorbachev invoked *glasnost* and *perestroika* to jump-start the moribund economy. Although gross domestic product figures continued to indicate that the Soviet economy was the second largest in the world, the reality was that the infrastructure was undermined by outmoded technologies, inefficient factories, a dispirited and underemployed workforce, and environmental disasters. Unlike the Chinese, who had in 1978 started their economic reforms in the countryside so as to ensure an adequate supply of food, Gorbachev relied on a more Leninist, democratic centralist approach and failed miserably. He attacked the Stalinist central planning system with all of its layers of managers and bureaucratic elites that were devoted to fulfilling the plan, not to taking risks to improve profit. Economists spoke openly of letting market forces set prices. Universities stopped the compulsory study of the works of Marx and began instead to feature the rhetoric of American neoconservatives and nineteenth-century English liberals. Gorbachev himself spoke of the fact that the welfare and happiness of the individual would be best served by economic individualism, the free operation of the market, and not the governmentally triggered "groupthink" of Stalinist days.

Admirable though these sentiments might have been, the apparatchiks who still remained in place were now free to pursue their own economic self-interest. Unfortunately, unlike those in a well-functioning market economy, the apparatchiks' interests were not the ones of the larger society. Adam Smith's "invisible hand" became the all too visible hand of corruption. Gorbachev tried to deal with the USSR's systemic problems, not by fine-tuning the incentives within the system, but by firing large numbers of government, industry, military, and party officials, replacing them with younger, more aggressive people

Mikhail Gorbachev and his wife, Raisa, greet a crowd of admirers in 1988. Gorbachev, who came to power in 1985, ushered in a new era of perestroika *(economic restructuring) and* glasnost *(openness) in the Soviet Union. When Gorbachev's policies failed to revive the USSR's stagnant economy but did spark ethnic separatist uprisings in various Soviet republics, admiration for his regime gave way to criticism.*

who he thought could better implement his program. Unfortunately, he faced challenges that demanded more than a lot of new faces. He needed to align the incentives of decision makers with the welfare of the nation. The longer he pursued his program, the smaller his constituency became.

Nagging economic problems and the apparatchiks' stubborn pursuit of their own interests frustrated Gorbachev's plans for reforms and forced him to make continual adjustments in order to hold power. In September 1990 he abandoned a bold plan to bring a market economy to the Soviet Union within 500 days, dashing the hopes of progressives. For the next ten months his former liberal advisers and supporters either resigned or were dismissed from their positions. Rather than give new direction and rethink his plans, Gorbachev continued to respond to his problems by firing people.

Everything went bad at once for Gorbachev. As economic conditions deteriorated, he increased concessions to party hard-liners and bureaucratic opportunists, buying time to hold power. In the spring hundreds of thousands of people marched in the streets of Moscow to protest his retreat from liberalism. In the Baltic republics—Georgia, the Ukraine, and Moldavia—separatist protests increased. Standards of living throughout the nation plummeted.

Domestic problems grew more severe during the summer of 1991. Agriculture faced an estimated grain shortfall of 77 million metric tons in the 1991 harvest, assuming that the crop could even be brought in from the field. The tailspin in which the economy found itself continued to intensify. The Soviet gross domestic product declined more than 11 percent for 1991. Boris Yeltsin (b. 1931), who had been popularly elected president of the Russian Republic in the spring, became an increasingly powerful figure, while rudimentary public opinion polls gave Gorbachev a 7 percent approval rating.

In response to these crises, Gorbachev and republic officials negotiated the Union Treaty, which was to reallocate both authority and resources in the Soviet Union between the USSR government and the various republics. To be signed on August 20, it would have sharply reduced the authority of both the Soviet central power Union and the Communist party.

On August 19, while Gorbachev was on vacation in the Crimea, an eight-man "state emergency committee" made up of leaders of the KGB, the military, the interior department, and other offices of the central government—all appointed by Gorbachev—mounted an attempt to take power. Gorbachev's vice president announced that his leader was ill and that a state of emergency was to be imposed for six months.

The attempted coup was immediately denounced by Yeltsin, who barricaded himself inside the offices of the Russian parliament building in Moscow and instructed all army and KGB units not to obey the coup leaders' orders. The next day 50,000 people turned out in Moscow to face down tanks sent by the central government. Large groups mobilized in Leningrad and Kishinev. Several units of KGB and army forces refused to obey the central command's orders, and the coup began to unravel. By August 21 the crisis was over, and Yeltsin had emerged as the man of the hour.

When Gorbachev returned, he immediately attempted to govern and to follow his old Leninist

On August 19, 1991, Boris Yeltsin, president of the Russian Republic, stood atop an armored carrier in Moscow to read a statement urging people to resist the attempted hard-line coup.

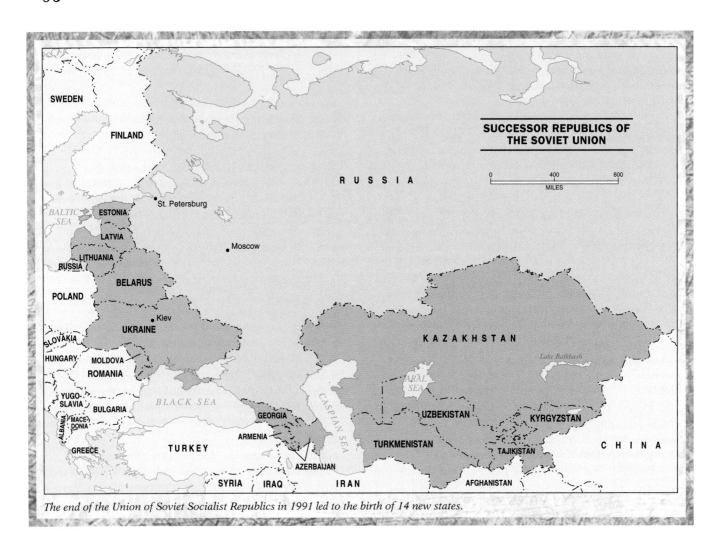

The end of the Union of Soviet Socialist Republics in 1991 led to the birth of 14 new states.

convictions. He soon found that compared to Yeltsin, he had little standing, especially after Gorbachev reiterated his belief that the party was the proper vehicle to carry out reform. Even as the coup leaders languished under arrest or committed suicide, Gorbachev continued to defend the party. Finally, six days after the attempted coup, the reality of the situation became clear. Gorbachev resigned as leader of the Soviet Communist party and recommended dissolution of the Central Committee. Yeltsin claimed control of party archives and KGB records, and across the Soviet Union, in a vast revolution, the Communist party—after 74 years of almost total power—was cut off from all its vanguard roles in running the country. In addition, the party had to surrender its wealth and property to the parliaments of the various republics. Gorbachev remained as president of the Soviet Union, at least until popular elections could be held.

But the union itself would last only four more months. The Baltic republics of Lithuania, Latvia, and Estonia declared their independence and gained diplomatic recognition; Ukraine, Moldavia (now Moldova), Belorussia (now Belarus), and Georgia followed suit.

The USSR ended its 69-year existence on December 21, 1991. It was replaced by a smaller and looser confederation, the Commonwealth of Independent States.

Where Peter the Great had overwhelmed his opposition with sheer power and Stalin had sent his secret police, Gorbachev used *glasnost* and limited force to respond to his growing number of opponents. Ironically, it was the very people he chose who brought him down and his defense of the party and the concepts he embraced that kept him down. His greatest gift to the Soviet people was that through *glasnost* he had removed fear. But the overwhelming problems of a nonfunctional infrastructure remained.

Gorbachev's Contribution to the End of the Cold War

Although Gorbachev's policies largely failed to solve the domestic crises, he made major contributions in the foreign policy arena. In acknowledgment of his accomplishments, he received the Nobel Peace Prize in 1990.

He renounced the Brezhnev doctrine permitting Soviet armed intervention into socialist states. By doing so he allowed the Soviet Bloc and its Warsaw Pact military commitments to disintegrate; in fact, they no longer existed by 1989. He pulled Soviet troops out of Afghanistan in 1989 and worked to bring peace to several hot spots in Africa, including Angola. Most remarkably, he chose not to obstruct the reunification of Germany. He joined in UN resolutions condemning Iraq's takeover of Kuwait in 1990 and cooperated in the alliance's military defeat of the invading forces in 1991.

In arms control Gorbachev brought the process to a logical conclusion. In November 1985 he met with President Ronald Reagan in Geneva to continue the discussion of arms control issues. The two leaders agreed to further consultation, but in the interim both argued forcefully over alleged Soviet violations of the SALT agreements and the U.S. Strategic Defense Initiative (SDI). The SDI was, on paper, a space-deployed system employing the most advanced technologies against nuclear missiles. American negotiators argued that SDI was an attempt to change the nature of arms control from assured destruction to assured defense. The Soviets saw SDI as a technological leap that would upset the weapons parity between the two powers. American domestic opposition and Soviet flexibility defused the SDI issue, and the two powers were able to sign the Intermediate Nuclear Forces (INF) agreement in Washington in 1987. The INF accord set up the destruction of all intermediate- and shorter-range missiles within three years. Further, the treaty would be monitored by on-

site verification, with Soviet and U.S. experts confirming the fulfillment of the treaty's provisions in each other's country.

By the end of the 1980s new talks on strategic long-range weapons were resumed, as were negotiations to shut down plutonium production plants. The MBFR talks, which accomplished more in two months than had been achieved in negotiations over the previous ten years, became moot with the disappearance of the Warsaw Pact as a military force. Clearly, the combination of economic pressures, especially serious in the USSR, and mutual interest brought the superpowers into close accord to control weapons that could destroy the planet. The need to survive and prosper brought the superpowers together on the nuclear weapons issue.

The end of the Cold War removed from the world the nightmare of bipolar nuclear annihilation. The signing of the Strategic Arms Reduction Treaty (START) in July 1991 marked the first step in cutting down the large stockpiles of nuclear warheads on each side. In 1994 Moscow and Washington formally altered the targeting software in their missiles, removing each other's strategic areas from the target list. The two also pledged to work together to fight nuclear proliferation.[14]

Unfortunately, the genie appeared to be out of the nuclear bottle, and even Great Power agreement could not stop proliferation. Some analysts assert that more than 20 countries now have the ability to build and deliver nuclear weapons. In addition,

Early in his first administration, President Ronald Reagan referred to the Soviet Union as the "Evil Empire" and showed little interest in cooperating in any way with Moscow. After the accession of Mikhail Gorbachev, Reagan changed his attitude, and the two men worked closely to ease tensions between the two great powers.

terrible new chemical and biological weapons threaten humanity. Perversely, some commentators have begun to look back on the Cold War with some nostalgia, as a time when there was dependable order.

The Yeltsin Years

After August 1991 Boris Yeltsin emerged as the most important Russian politician. Like other leaders at the end of a revolution, he found that a change in government did not remove the terrible problems facing Russia: inflation, budget deficits, problems with ethnic minorities, privatization, the need for a new infrastructure for international trade and commerce. After eight years, demographic figures graphically indicated that Russia was not solving its problems. By 1998 the average life expectancy for the Russian male had dropped to 57 years—15 years below that for men in the United States and on a par with men in India. In addition, the birthrate plummeted. Another of the demographic crises Russia faced was an infant mortality rate that continues to rise and a population that continues to decline. Cynics observed that Yeltsin's ongoing personal health crises symbolized his country's condition.

Almost immediately Yeltsin had to deal with opposition from the apparatchik-laden Congress of People's Deputies, elected under the old Soviet model. The Congress consistently blocked Yeltsin's attempts to implement a series of market-oriented economic reforms, such as liberalizing prices on most nonfood goods. In addition, Yeltsin faced problems from deputies who accused him of caving in to Western pressures in both domestic and foreign policy. Yeltsin remained personally popular; however, this had little effect on the Congress, which continued to block his initiatives.

Yeltsin's contest with the parliament reached a stalemate in September 1993. When the Congress threatened to take much of his authority away, he responded by dissolving the Congress and calling for new elections in December. He then sent troops to surround the parliament building—the Russian White House—and told deputies that they would have to leave the building by October 4. These actions provoked widespread criticism throughout Russia, and leaders of 62 out of 89 regional councils called for Yeltsin to remove the troops.

On October 3 forces opposing Yeltsin took over the office of the mayor of Moscow and attacked the state television center. To an audience watching these events live on TV, it was remarkable that only 62 people died in the fighting. The next day Yeltsin sent tanks and artillery against the Russian White House and battered the resisters into submission.

Yeltsin's forces and the new constitution barely carried the vote in the December elections, winning enough seats in parliament to prevent the opposition from being able to impeach the president. However, extremists such as Vladimir Zhirinovsky, a nationalist and virulent anti-Semite, attracted the votes of many moderate Russians who resented the conditions that four years of reform had brought them. Zhirinovsky momentarily gained worldwide attention, which he promptly used to espouse the regaining of Russia's boundaries, including reclaiming Alaska.

To maintain power in the face of an extremist coalition that was seemingly held together only by its opposition to Yeltsin, the president took a centrist course, advocating a rebirth of the Great Russian state, damping down essential programs to produce a privatized economy, and distancing himself from the West in foreign affairs—especially the extension of early NATO membership to the former Eastern European states and Western intervention in disintegrating Yugoslavia.

Russia's economy during the Yeltsin years proved unable to make the comparatively rapid change to a market system, as the economies of Poland, the Czech Republic, and Hungary had. The ethnic and social diversity of the continent-sized state made a "cold turkey" transition to the market system difficult. As a result, in the three years after Yeltsin took power, the state tried to meet its problems by printing more money, leading to an inflation in which the worth of the ruble declined from 300 rubles to the dollar in 1992 to over 6000 rubles to the dollar in 1997. Standards of living for many Russians continued to decline, while the few spectacularly wealthy attained a level of living comparable to that of tsarist-era nobles. Inflation and a deepening deficit together kept economic development limited. Still, the West felt that Yeltsin must be kept afloat and that loans made for peace were not nearly as expensive as money spent for war. They had to support Yeltsin, whose vulnerability was further accentuated in February 1994 when his enemies from the 1991 August coup attempt and the 1993 October uprising were freed by parliament.

After periodic crises, some tied to the Asian financial crisis, others to strikes by people who hadn't been paid in months, price levels had stabilized by the end of 1998 and over 20,000 businesses had made the transition to a market-based system. Privately held firms employed more than three-fourths of Russian factory workers. On the positive side, Russia had undergone with a minimum amount of violence a revolution in many ways more profound and widespread than those of 1917. On the negative side, widespread criminal activities and mounting resentment of the economic and social changes provided fertile ground for the enemies of reform. Despite these troubles, Yeltsin remained in office, his power tied to his ability to get along with regional bosses and to attract financial aid from the West.

In the successor states, economic and political developments ranged from the tragic in the Caucasian republics to the corrupt and inefficient in Ukraine. Kiev had nuclear weapons, untapped economic potential, and a disastrously corrupt and inept government. In July 1994 the Western powers offered to loan Ukraine $4 billion and to aid in the rebuilding or replacing of the damaged Chernobyl nuclear power plant. But Ukraine's economy continued to limp along despite a new constitution in 1996 that gave President Leonid Kuchma the power to impose major structural reforms.

Countries such as Moldova took heroic measures to introduce the discipline and quality needed to compete in the international market. However, they faced political, supply, and transportation problems in addition to the Russian army, which was a continual threat. But it was only the imposition of Russian arms that brought a tenuous peace to the Caucasus. Armenians and Azeris battled over control of Nagorno-Karabakh; Georgians and Abkhazians and roving bands of independent mercenaries fought over long-disputed lands. And in the Chechnya region of Russia, a full-scale war between Moscow and Chechen separatists in 1995 and 1996 ended with an armed truce that left the Chechens in control of vital oil and gas pipelines.

The Russians felt susceptible to military actions from their former allies—the so-called *near abroad*—where independent armed forces used some of the most advanced weaponry from the former Soviet army. In the 15 newly independent former Soviet republics, significant minority problems continue. Russia itself can claim 81 percent ethnic Russians, but ethnic Russians make up substantial minorities in many other states, including Ukraine, Kazakhstan, Latvia, and Estonia. It is as much concern for their fellow Russians as for purely defensive reasons that there were more than 120,000 Russian soldiers outside Russia at the beginning of 1995. The Russians wanted to look after their own people while fearing the numerous private armies, some of them stocked with powerful weapons that became available in the wake of the defunct USSR.

Another crisis Russia faced was the environmental pollution left by Soviet defense plants and heavy industry. The residue of nuclear accidents—Chelyabinsk in 1957, Chernobyl (Ukraine) in 1985, Tomsk in April 1993, and a bacteriological warfare plant in Sverdlovsk in 1979—has contributed in some regions to a precipitous decline in living standards and life expectancy rates. Throughout the former Soviet Bloc the nuclear power industry, operating outmoded and potentially dangerous reactors, remained disasters-in-waiting.

The American position, mirroring its previous policy of personalizing its foreign policy toward the former superpower, was to depend on Yeltsin. Of some $68 billion promised in aid from the West in 1992 and 1993, only $20 billion actually arrived. Part of the reason for this failure could be found in bureaucratic inertia and corruption on the Western side and in a lack of infrastructure for any effective use of this aid, except for direct cash transfers for the new elite. Even with the full extent of aid, the legacy of the Soviet centrally planned economy presented problems that might be insoluble. The question remained whether the Russians could develop the political skills of consensus-building and compromise needed to make the changes required to keep Russia from sliding back to another authoritarian model, as it had so often in the past after a time of change. As cynics remarked, "Russia had to move on from its historic questions: What's to be done? Who is to blame?"

Eastern Europe

After consolidating political control over Eastern Europe by 1948, Moscow attempted to organize its allies through the trade organization COMECON. The USSR set up COMECON in 1949 as a response to the Marshall Plan and other Western projects to promote economic growth. In its first decade the organization served Soviet postwar recovery needs. Moscow worked a reverse system of mercantilism on the region, exporting raw materials at high prices and buying back finished goods at low cost. Eastern Europe suffered greatly under this system, and nowhere could the contrast between the capitalist and communist systems be seen more dramatically than in the divided city of Berlin.

In the 1960s and 1970s the Soviet Bloc states began to profit from buying cheap energy supplies from the USSR in return for which they could send goods they could not market to the West. Their standard of living began to improve along with their economic growth rates. However, by the end of the 1970s, COMECON faced a serious crisis. The region fell behind the rest of the world economically because of the rigidity of the centrally planned system used in the Bloc economies and the restrictive bilateral nature of COMECON. Everything had to go through Moscow. Prague and Budapest, for instance, could not work directly to achieve production or trade efficiency. COMECON countries faced far more barriers than the Common Market countries did. Further, each country's currency was nonconvertible; it could be spent only within that country.

Aggravating the situation was the fact that as world energy prices fell in the latter part of the 1980s, the Eastern Europeans were trapped into paying premium prices for Soviet oil and gas. Several Eastern European states borrowed heavily from the West and invested the proceeds unwisely. Far more damaging than these purely fiscal concerns were the environmental disasters spawned by the Soviet-model centrally planned economies. Eastern Europe, as well as the former USSR, was one of the most devastatingly polluted areas in the world. Fifty years of Soviet domination were a terrible burden for the peoples of Eastern Europe.

East Germany

After 1945 Eastern Europe reflected the changes that took place in the USSR. Nowhere was this more evident than in East Germany from 1945 to 1990. Following the organization of the eastern zone of Germany into the German Democratic Republic, Communist authorities broke up large private farms and expanded heavy industry. Thousands of discontented East Germans fled each week to West Germany through Berlin. In June 1953 severe food shortages coupled with new decrees establishing longer working hours touched off a workers' revolt, which was quickly put down. The westward flow of refugees continued, however, until 1961, when the Berlin Wall was constructed.

The wall stopped the exodus of people, and East Germany stabilized. For the next 28 years the country had the highest density of armed men per square mile in the Soviet Bloc and the Communist world's highest economic growth rate. The country's athletes and businesses did well in world competition, and slowly and subtly under Erich Honecker and a new generation of bureaucrats the German Democratic Republic improved relations with West Germany.

Gorbachev's program of liberalization threatened Honecker and his colleagues. After 1988 East German authorities stopped the circulation of Soviet periodicals that carried stories considered to be too liberal. At the same time, analysts noted the slowing economic growth rate of East Germany and the fact that the standard of living in West Germany was far higher. Old facilities, old managers, and old ideas eroded the economy of East Germany.

In September 1989 East Germans looking for a better life again fled by the thousands to the West, this time through Hungary and Czechoslovakia. This exodus, followed by Gorbachev's visit to Berlin in October, helped precipitate a crisis bringing hundreds of thousands of protesters to the streets of Berlin. Honecker was removed in October, and on November 9 the Berlin Wall was breached. Once that symbolic act took place, both East and West Germans began to call for a unified Germany. Press exposés

revealed corruption and scandals among the Communist elite. In the East German elections of March 1990 pro-Western parties won overwhelmingly. By October Germany was reunited, with the first free all-German elections since Hitler took power.[15] Berlin was once again to be the capital of all Germany. Once the thrill of reunification had passed, Germans faced the difficult task of making the two parts of their country into one efficient unit. By 1998 they had made significant progress toward true economic and social unification.

Germany: The European Epicenter of the Cold War

1945	Russians take Berlin; Four Power Agreement on the governing of Germany; quadripartite division of Berlin
1946	Russians begin reneging on economic agreements; British and U.S. zones merged
1947	Truman Doctrine announced; start of containment strategy; Marshall Plan
1948	USSR consolidates control over Eastern Europe, blockades Berlin; French zone merges with British and U.S. zones
1949	NATO established; COMECON established; German Federal Republic (West Germany) established, Konrad Adenauer becomes chancellor; German "economic miracle" begins
1953	Workers revolt in East Germany (German Democratic Republic) over food shortage and increased working hours
1955–1961	USSR demands withdrawal of Western forces; Berlin a "free city"
1961	Khrushchev demands Western withdrawal from Berlin; construction of Berlin Wall; German Democratic Republic sealed off from West
1982–1983	Missile debate
1988	East German leaders begin censoring Russian papers
1989	East Germans flee to West through Czechoslovakia and Hungary; Berlin Wall opened up
1990	Germany reunited

Just as the existence of the Berlin Wall was the most visible reminder of the reality of the Cold War, the destruction of the wall in November 1989 became the most powerful image of the war's end. Here a demonstrator pounds away at the wall as East German border guards standing atop the Brandenburg Gate look on impassively.

Poland

In Poland, as in Yugoslavia, communism acquired a national character after a slow, subtle struggle that broke open in the fall of 1956 following Khrushchev's "Crimes of the Stalin Era" speech. Polish leader Wladyslaw Gomulka set out on a difficult path to satisfy both Moscow and Warsaw, Soviet power and Polish nationalism. Gomulka governed skillfully through the 1960s until 1970, when he fell victim to the pressures of economic discontent and an increasingly corrupt Communist party.

Demonstrations and strikes broke out around the country, and some, such as those at the Baltic port city of Gdansk (formerly Danzig), were bloodily repressed. Gomulka was replaced by Edward Gierek, who throughout the 1970s walked the same narrow line as Gomulka between satisfying Moscow and Poland. Gierek borrowed extensively from the West and made several ill-advised economic decisions. By 1980 Poland was laboring to pay the interest on a foreign debt of $28 billion, and in the summer of 1980 the delicate compromise created by Gomulka and Gierek fell apart in a series of strikes caused by increases in food prices.

A nationwide labor movement, *Solidarnosc,* or Solidarity, came into being. By October around 10 million Poles from all segments of society had joined this movement, which stood for reform, equality, and workers' rights. In many ways Solidarity's programs were protests against the Leninist concept of the party. It was Solidarity's proletarian base that made it so appealing to the world and so threatening to the other Marxist-Leninist leaders of the Soviet Bloc. Unfortunately, the problems that had brought down Gierek remained. A year of Solidarity-dominated government brought no solutions, only continued frustration.

Conflict with the government, now headed by General Wojciech Jaruzelski, appeared inevitable. Solidarity's leader, Lech Walesa—an out-of-work electrician who had been fired for earlier attempts to organize a trade union in Gdansk—showed an instinctive genius for dealing effectively with every element of the Polish spectrum and the Soviet Union. He attempted to maintain a moderate position.

When Walesa's backers pushed him to call for a national vote to establish a noncommunist government, the Jaruzelski government responded with force, in part to maintain itself and in part to avoid Soviet intervention. Jaruzelski declared martial law, and security forces rounded up Solidarity's leaders. Outward shows of protest were squelched within two weeks.

Through the 1980s Communist party morale dipped as membership fell 20 percent. Although banned, Solidarity retained the genuine affection of the Poles and the support of the Roman Catholic Church, headed by Pope John Paul II, a former Polish cardinal. To the embarrassment of the Polish state, Lech Walesa was awarded the Nobel Peace Prize in 1983. The economic situation deteriorated as inflation increased, the standard of living plummeted, and foreign debt soared to $40 billion. The party could not solve the problems it faced, and in desperation it turned to Solidarity, which it had outlawed eight years earlier. The June 1989 elections resulted in an overwhelming victory for the union, and in July it took its place in the Polish parliament, the *Sejm*, as the first opposition party to win free elections in Eastern Europe since 1948. Solidarity won 99 out of 100 seats in the upper house and 161 seats (35 percent) in the lower house—all that was allotted to it in a preparatory roundtable.

In January 1990 Poland decided to adopt a market economy. Even with substantial financial support from the West, the country faced rising unemployment and recession. The strains produced by the shift to a market economy tested even the Solidarity movement, which split into two wings, one led by Mazowiecki Tadeusz, who briefly became prime minister in 1990, and one led by Lech Walesa, who eventually became the president of Poland.

Despite political roadblocks, Poland made amazing success toward privatization and market reforms. Even when Poland's former Communists, now called Social Democrats, took power in 1993, they did not reverse course. Poland stands as one of the success stories in the former Soviet Bloc, with economic growth of 5 percent in 1996, a thriving stock market, and a successful market economy. From 1993 to 1998

foreign investment in Poland more than doubled and the per capita gross domestic product reached nearly $4000, still 20 percent that of Western industrialized countries. Symbolic of Poland's progress was the fact that it was admitted as a full member of the North Atlantic Treaty Organization in 1998.

Czechoslovakia

After the fall of the democratic government in 1948, the Czechoslovak Communist party, the most Stalinist of the European parties, imposed harsh control for 20 years. However, in the spring of 1968 the country's liberal traditions came into the open. Under the influence of Marxist moderates, a new form of communism—"socialism with a human face"—was put into effect by the Slovak leader Alexander Dubček. As in Yugoslavia under Tito, the Czechoslovaks chose not to rebel against Moscow but rather to adapt communism to their own conditions. But in August 1968 the Soviet Union and four Soviet Bloc allies invaded Prague with more than 500,000 troops. Within 20 hours the liberal regime, which advocated policies strikingly similar to those to be supported by Gorbachev 20 years later, was overthrown. The Soviets captured Dubček and took him to Moscow to confront Brezhnev.

The Soviets took their action against Czechoslovakia pursuant to the so-called Brezhnev Doctrine, under which Communist states were obliged to aid their fraternal colleagues against "aggression," even

Under the dynamic leadership of Lech Walesa, Solidarity, the Polish workers' union, grew into a nationwide social movement. In this photo from 1981, Solidarity members carry Walesa on their shoulders to celebrate a Polish supreme court decision upholding the workers' right to stage protest strikes throughout Poland.

Under the leadership of Alexander Dubček in 1968, the Czechoslovak Communist Party sought to reverse 20 years of Stalinist policies by instituting "socialism with a human face." This prompted the nation's invasion, for a variety of geopolitical and ideological reasons, by the joint forces of five socialist nations in August of that year.

when the fraternal colleague does not ask for aid, in order to safeguard the communal gains of the socialist movement. The Soviet-led forces crushed the Czechoslovak reforms to "protect the progress of socialism." Like that of East Germany, the Czech economy by the late 1980s was hampered by outmoded technology, timid leadership, and discredited ideology. The country suffered greatly from polluted air and acid rain, and the population suffered under a declining standard of living.

The wave of change from Moscow caught the Czech party out of place. Dissidents, including president-to-be Vaclav Havel, who in January 1989 had been thrown in jail for human rights protests, found themselves running the country by December. Events in East Germany precipitated the October 1989 events in Prague, when a prodemocracy meeting by over 10,000 demonstrators was savagely broken up. Protests in November met similar results. Still the Czechoslovaks were not deterred. In the "Velvet Revolution" of November 1989 some 200,000 demonstrators in Prague demanded free elections and the resignation of the Communist leaders. Dubček came out of internal exile, and in December Havel became

president, a result confirmed in the June 1990 elections. As in the other Eastern European states, however, the high spirits of the 1989 revolution were soon replaced by the sober realities of repairing the effects of two generations of Communist rule.

Serious political problems and Slovak separatist demands drove Czechoslovakia to split into its constituent parts, the Czech Republic and the Slovak Republic, on January 1, 1993. The Czech Republic suffered little from the dissolution of the 65-year-old federation, but the Slovaks suffered from economic decline and political instability under the rule of the former Communist hard-liner Vladimir Meciar. A year after the split, unemployment in Slovakia exceeded 15 percent, compared to 3.5 percent among the Czechs, and since then the gap between the two countries has widened.

The Czech Republic's economic growth faltered in the 1990s. A combination of corruption and a high trade deficit led to a new government under the Socialists being formed in the spring of 1998. Vaclav Havel remained a stabilizing force. The Czechs, with a $5,600 per capita GDP, also entered NATO and were being considered for membership in the European Union.

Playwright Vaclav Havel, who was soon to become president of Czechoslovakia, hugs former Czech leader Alexander Dubček following the "Velvet Revolution" of November 1989 in which the entire Communist government of Czechoslovakia resigned.

Hungary

After the Stalin purges, the Hungarian Communist party became increasingly inept until October 1956, when discontent with Soviet dominance erupted into revolution. For a week a popular government existed, and Russian troops withdrew from Budapest. When the new government announced its intentions to leave the Warsaw Pact and be neutral, Soviet forces returned and crushed the rebellion. More than 200,000 refugees fled to the West.

Over the next 30 years Janos Kadar (1912–1989) oversaw an initially bloody repression of the revolution and the execution of Hungarian premier Imre Nagy. Later Kadar led a subtle pursuit of a Hungarian variant of communism. In the process the Hungarians gained a higher standard of living than the Soviets, an active intellectual life, and a range of economic reforms. In the mid-1980s, however, the Hungarian economic system, which encouraged

more private initiative and decentralization, ran into difficulties. Hungary's foreign debt and inflation both increased. Gorbachev encouraged the Hungarians to pursue their reforms, sometimes at the discomfort of Kadar, who was gently moved from power in 1987.

In 1989 the Hungarians dismantled the barriers, fences, and minefields between themselves and the Austrians. Hungary imposed the first income tax and value-added tax in Eastern Europe, allowed 100 percent foreign ownership of Hungarian firms, opened a stock market, and set up institutions to teach Western management methods to Hungarian businessmen.

By March 1990 Hungary had installed a multi-party system and was holding free elections, which led to the installation of a right-of-center government led by Joszef Antall and the overwhelming repudiation of the Communists. However, the next four years proved to be frustrating to the Hungarians. Substantial Western investment came in, but the suffering among the poorer population in the country increased.

Tragically, in this area stripped of Jews by the Holocaust, anti-Semitism reemerged as a political force. Anti-Gypsy feelings also intensified. Elections in 1994 resulted in a victory for the Communist Social Democrats, who promised to maintain the free market reforms while extending social justice. Although they fulfilled these promises, a rise in organized crime and growing doubts about the Social Democrats' competence led back to a a right-of-center government in the summer of 1998. Despite substantial foreign debt, Hungary has exhibited impressive governmental and social stability and entered NATO as the third nation from the former Soviet Bloc.

Bulgaria

Bulgaria proved to be a loyal ally of Moscow after 1945, and its standard of living greatly improved. The Bulgarian economy averaged a growth rate of close to 3 percent a year and became increasingly diversified. Todor Zhivkov skillfully followed the Soviet lead and showed flexibility in responding to the early Gorbachev programs, especially the agricultural reforms. Until the autumn of 1989 the party appeared to be conservative and nationalist, as shown in its campaign against the country's Turkish minority (nearly 8 percent of the population) to deprive them of their heritage.

The wave of freedom hit Bulgaria at the end of 1989. Zhivkov was ousted in a party-led coup and replaced by Peter Mladenov. It seemed in the free elections in May 1990 that Mladenov and his allies would be the only party group to make the transition and maintain power in Eastern Europe. But even he was thrown out in July when his role as orchestrator of the Zhivkov coup was noted, and the noncommunist philosopher Zhelyu Zhelev became president.

The Bulgarians avoided making the hard economic choices needed to reform their country, and at the end of 1996 they experienced a virtual economic collapse. Inflation soared, wiping out savings and driving prices up. At the same time, the government proved unable to pay the interest on the foreign debt. The International Monetary Fund has imposed an austerity program on Bulgaria that has caused widespread distress. Local mafias have prospered, conducting black market trade with the various factions in the Yugoslav conflict and serving as a conduit for the international drug trade.

Romania

After the 1960s Romania under Nicolae Ceauşescu was the most independent of the Warsaw Pact countries in foreign policy. Domestically, the country labored under one of the most hard-line and corrupt regimes in the Bloc, whose economic policies of self-sufficiency plunged the standard of living to unprecedented depths. Ceauşescu achieved his goal to become free of foreign debts by the summer of 1989, but at a cruel cost in human suffering.

Ceauşescu, accused by critics of desiring to achieve "socialism in one family," developed the cult of the personality to new heights. While imposing severe economic hardship on the nation, he built grandiose monuments to himself. Protected by his omnipresent secret police, the *Securitate,* he seemed untouchable. But the 1989 wave of democracy spread even to Romania, which was the only country to experience widespread violence during that revolutionary year. Ceauşescu and his wife were taken into custody and executed, thus bringing their dreadful regime to an end.

The Romanian pattern of political corruption continued, and Ion Iliescu manipulated the elections of May 1990 to keep power. Later in the summer, the National Salvation Front made shameless use of miners and former Securitate officials to terrorize its critics. An uneasy equilibrium was attained, but little progress was made to heal the devastating wounds inflicted by the Ceauşescu regime. Under Iliescu the Leninist heritage remained strong in Romania, whose authoritarianism had a chilling effect on the pluralistic tendencies in the region.

Finally in 1996 the neo-Communists lost power when Emil Constantinescu became president. The country faces many of the same problems as neighboring Bulgaria—the need to privatize inefficient state industries, to introduce efficient management methods, and to gain some sort of control over the rampant corruption that plagues its economy. Many Romanians placed high and unrealistic hopes on being invited to join NATO. When that did not happen,

there was a backlash against the West among a segment of the population who support the neo-fascist politics of Vadim Tudor.

Albania

Albania under Enver Hoxha (1908–1985) worked closely with the Soviet Union until 1956. After Khrushchev's denunciation of Stalin, the country switched its allegiance to the Chinese until 1978. For the next decade Albania—the poorest and most backward country in Europe—went its own way in seeming isolation, only reluctantly entering into trade, diplomatic, and sports relations with other nations. Yet even Albania was not immune to the unrest sweeping Eastern Europe in 1989. In the summer of 1990 people desperate to escape the country flocked into foreign embassies, and soon thereafter some 40,000 Albanians fled to Italy and Greece. Democratic elections were held in March 1991, but even there the Albanians marched to their own tune as the Communists carried two-thirds of the vote. Two years later the Democratic party won an overwhelming victory. Albania remained the poorest and most backward country in Europe.

Tragically, the economically inexperienced Albanians flocked to "get rich quick" pyramid schemes that collapsed in December 1996 when those who were in first started to pull their money out. Civil order collapsed in the country as factions gained control of the army's weapons and the country dissolved into regions controlled by local warlords. European intervention led by the Italians brought order, but then Albanians living in Yugoslavian provinces began to rebel against their Belgrade overlords. As the decade came to an end, Albania remained a fragmented nation and a potential tinderbox overwhelmed by the hundreds of thousands of Kosovar Albanians seeking refuge there.

Yugoslavia and After

One of Stalin's major failures after 1945 was in his dealings with Marshal Josip Broz Tito of Yugoslavia. Tito had been a loyal Communist and a good Stalinist in the 1930s. During the war he was an effective resistance leader, surviving attacks from Germans, Italians, and various right-wing factions in Yugoslavia. He had been in close contact with the Western allies and after the war began to receive substantial assistance from them. Tito led the liberation of Yugoslavia from the Nazis and kept the country out of Moscow's orbit.

Stalin noted Tito's independence and from 1946 on sought measures to oppose him. Ethnically divided Yugoslavia overcame its internal divisions and a 10 percent casualty rate during the war to unite behind Tito. The Yugoslav leader's national backing,

Yugoslavia Since 1945

1945 Tito liberates Yugoslavia without Soviet assistance

1946 Stalin opposes Tito's independence from Moscow

1947 Stalin pulls back from supporting Tito-sponsored Communists in Greece

1948 Stalin expels Tito and Yugoslavia from the Soviet Bloc; Tito gains support from the West

1957 Khrushchev reestablishes relations with Yugoslavia

1980 Tito dies; rotating presidency instituted

1989 Serb leader Slobodan Milosevic advocates Serb nationalist cause in Albanian-dominated province of Kosovo; Slovenia begins to make moves to leave Yugoslavia

1991 Slovenia and Croatia declare independence; Macedonia declares independence; Bosnia-Herzegovina declares independence

1991–1995 Three-sided war in Bosnia among Serbs, Croats, and Muslims

1995 Dayton Accords imposed on Bosnian conflict

1997–1999 Kosovo sees repeat of Serb policies in Bosnia

geographical distance from the Soviet Union, and support from the West enabled him to stand firm against increasing Soviet meddling in his country.

Tito became the first national communist, a firm believer in Marxism who sought to apply the ideology within the context of his nation's objective conditions. This position placed him directly against Stalin, who believed that communists the world over must work for the greater glory and support of the Soviet Union. Tito believed that the setting in which ideology was found had to be taken into consideration, pointing out that Lenin had to adapt Marxist doctrine to conditions in Russia. Stalin insisted that Moscow's orders and examples must be slavishly followed. In 1948 Yugoslavia was expelled from the Soviet Bloc. Successfully withstanding Stalin's pressures, including assassination attempts, Tito emerged as a key figure in the development of world communism.

After 1948 the six republics, containing ten ethnic groups, that formed Yugoslavia survived the pressures of national diversity, the political stresses of the bipolar world, and serious economic difficulties. Many observers doubted that the country could survive Tito's death in 1980. However, Yugoslavia remained tenuously united under its unique system of annually rotating the head of state—despite an 80 percent inflation rate and a 30 percent decline in the standard of living.

Ethnic strife among Serbs and Croats and the Albanians of Kosovo finally destroyed the unity of the multinational state in 1991. Armed conflict broke out as the various constituent republics sought to break away from the Serbian-dominated coalition led by Slobodan Milosevic. Slovenia and Croatia won their freedom in June, and Macedonia declared its independence in November 1991, followed by Bosnia-Herzegovina in December. Serbia and tiny Montenegro were all that remained in the Yugoslav "federation."

Serbs, Croats, and Bosnian Muslims fought in a continually shifting multiple-front war to claim what each side saw as its legitimate patrimony. The Bosnian Serbs, inheriting the bulk of the old Yugoslav armed forces' supplies and weapons and backed by Belgrade, gained 70 percent of Bosnia-Herzegovina and in the process became international pariahs. They carried out genocidal attacks—"ethnic cleansing"—on the Bosnian Muslims, who labored under an arms embargo nominally imposed by the West. In reality the Americans tacitly permitted Islamic states to arm the Bosnians.

The Western allies made noises of protest and even got the Russians to share in the token condemnations of the Serbs, but the only tangible Western aid for the Bosnians came from a U.S. airlift, which in its first year made more sorties over the region and dumped more supplies in the general region than the U.S. Air Force supplying Berlin in 1948. NATO forces also launched air strikes and periodically bluffed the Serbs into pulling back from Muslim enclaves such as Sarajevo and Gorazde. Truces and peace plans came and went, resolving nothing, while the West hoped that the economic sanctions against Serbia would finally yield some results. Finally the Western powers, joined by Russia, placed forces in the region, and a negotiated truce was arrived at in 1995 at the unlikely site of Dayton, Ohio. The war had led to the deaths of more than 200,000 people and forced more than 3 million to leave their homes.

A peacekeeping force led by the Americans remains in Bosnia, imposing order on the contesting forces and monitoring the activities of the Belgrade government led by Slobodan Milosevic, elected president of rump Yugoslavia in July 1997. The next year he began to use the ethnic cleansing tactics he had used in Bosnia in the southern province of Kosovo, a province

Although nearly a million refugees fled to the safety of Albania, many thousands lost their lives in the Serb ethnic cleansing campaign.

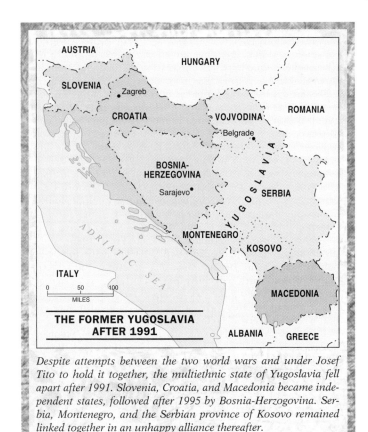

THE FORMER YUGOSLAVIA AFTER 1991

Despite attempts between the two world wars and under Josef Tito to hold it together, the multiethnic state of Yugoslavia fell apart after 1991. Slovenia, Croatia, and Macedonia became independent states, followed after 1995 by Bosnia-Herzogovina. Serbia, Montenegro, and the Serbian province of Kosovo remained linked together in an unhappy alliance thereafter.

which threatened Serb control in some parts of the province. All through 1998 the Belgrade government built up its military and paramilitary presence there. Fearing a repeat of the events in Bosnia at the beginning of the decade, the Western allies in October 1998 and February–March 1999 tried to convince Milosevic to change his tactics through diplomatic means. When he did not, NATO forces began a bombing campaign at the end of March to "degrade" the Yugoslav military forces. What had been a comparative trickle of refugees and sporadic atrocities became a flood of a million people forced from their homes and mass murders. At the same time, the NATO bombing, which was stated to be against Milosevic and his forces and not the Yugoslav people, produced numerous civilian casualties. Thanks to the NATO coalition holding together, the energizing of Russia to support an end to the conflict, and the impact of the bombardments, peace of sorts returned to Kosovo in the middle of June. As the Yugoslavs pulled out of the province, to be replaced by the UN-sponsored peace-keeping forces, the reintegration of the almost 1 million Kosovars who fled the region before the coming winter showed signs of being a difficult task.

Conclusion

In 1989 the Soviet Bloc disintegrated in a revolutionary change not seen since 1848. However, after the fractured shells of the old apparatchik-ridden governments fell, the new states, like those that emerged after the 1848 revolutions, faced all the accumulated

which contains the spiritual center of the Serbs, the battlefield where the Ottoman forces defeated them in 1389. Kosovo's population was 90 percent Kosovar Albanians and after a decade of frustration, some of the Albanians had formed the Kosovo Liberation Army,

problems of the past. Initially, with the exception of the Romanians and the Serbs, the former Soviet Bloc renounced communism.

By the end of 1994, after five years of difficult economic and social transition from centrally planned systems to market-dominated economies, Communists staged a comeback in Hungary, Lithuania, Ukraine, and other parts of the former Soviet realm. The democratic reformers failed for a number of reasons, but the new "reform Communists" were a different breed from the Marxist-Leninist-Stalinist variety that dominated the region for a half century, reflecting the fact that the diplomatic patterns of the 1990s are so different from those of the Cold War.

As the decade comes to an end the region has maintained an impressive calm, with the exception of Yugoslavia and the Caucasus. Given the revolutionary nature of the changes the region has gone through, this is no small accomplishment. However, freedom from Communist rule has not brought the radical improvements so desired by many. Instead, the people of Russia and Eastern Europe know they cannot go back to the old ways and in elections try to choose people they think might benefit their interests. In ten years the region has gone from a rejection of the Communists to a halfhearted embrace of the new generation of leftists and then back to the right. There is no ideological message here, simply a search for prosperity and good government.

Suggestions for Reading

Lynn E. Davis, *The Cold War Begins* (Princeton University Press, 1974), is a thorough account of the origins of the conflict. Perhaps the best overview on the historiographical conflict is Louis J. Halle, *The Cold War as History* (HarperCollins, 1994). Various points of view on American-Soviet relations can be found in Walter La Feber, *America, Russia, and the Cold War* (Wiley, 1976); Paul Y. Hammond, *Cold War and Détente: The American Foreign Policy Process Since 1945* (Harcourt Brace Jovanovich, 1975); and Lawrence S. Wittner, *Cold War America: From Hiroshima to Watergate* (Praeger, 1974). Other studies of note on the Cold War are John C. Donovan, *The Cold Warriors: A Policy-Making Elite* (Heath, 1974); and Herbert S. Dinerstein, *Soviet Foreign Policy Since the Missile Crisis* (Johns Hopkins University Press, 1976). The articles in Charles S. Maier, ed., *The Origins of the Cold War and Contemporary Europe* (Franklin Watts, 1978), constitute a good survey of the opportunities and dangers presented by the Moscow-Washington conflict. Adam Ulam provides a good review of Moscow's policies in *Expansion and Coexistence: Soviet Foreign Policy, 1917–1973* (Holt, Rinehart and Winston, 1974). A penetrating study of the major figures in U.S. foreign policy formation is Walter Isaacson and Evan Thomas, *The Wise Men* (Touchstone, 1997). Robbin F. Laird and Erik P. Hoffman, eds., *Soviet Foreign Policy in a Changing World* (Aldine, 1986), is a solid collection of articles on the dilemmas facing the Soviets. Peter Zwick, *Soviet Foreign Relations: Process and Policy* (Prentice Hall, 1990), spells out the factors shaping Moscow's policies. The Committee on Foreign Affairs' analysis in *Soviet Diplomacy and Negotiating Be-*

havior, 1979–1988: New Tests for U.S. Diplomacy (U.S. Government Printing Office, 1988) gives good insights into Washington's understanding of Soviet diplomacy. Michael R. Beschloss, *The Crisis Years: Kennedy and Khrushchev, 1960–1963* (HarperCollins, 1994), is a well-written work based on recently released documents. The Soviet world at the beginning of the 1990s still labored under the impact of Stalin's policies and accomplishments; Robert C. Tucker, ed., *Stalinism: Essays in Historical Interpretation* (Transaction, 1999), presents the panorama of Stalin's life and policies.

On the Vietnam War, see Stanley Karnow, *Vietnam: A History* (Penguin, 1984). Thomas Powers, *The War at Home* (Grossman, 1973), and Paul Kattenberg, *The Vietnamese Trauma in American Foreign Policy* (Transaction, 1980), deal with the anti–Vietnam War movement. For personal assessments, see Joseph Buttinger, *Vietnam: The Unforgettable Tragedy* (Horizon, 1976); Arthur M. Schlesinger Jr., *The Bitter Heritage: Vietnam and American Democracy* (Premier, 1972); Francis Fitzgerald, *Fire in the Lake* (Vintage, 1989); and George C. Herring, *America's Longest War: The United States and Vietnam, 1950–1975* (Wiley, 1979). The best summary of the tragedy in the Indochina peninsula is Marilyn Young, *The Vietnam Wars, 1945–1990* (HarperCollins, 1994).

Milovan Djilas, *Conversations with Stalin*, trans. Michael B. Petrovich (Harcourt, Brace & World, 1962), gives a vivid firsthand account of Stalin's personality. Khrushchev's tenure is competently covered in Edward Crankshaw, *Khrushchev: A Career* (Viking, 1966), and in Khrushchev's own words in *Khrushchev Remembers* (Ballantine, 1976). Hedrick Smith, *The New Russians* (Random House, 1990), is an outstanding updated classic introduction to the "way things really work." Martin McCauley, ed., *Khrushchev and Khrushchevism* (Macmillan, 1987), presents an all-encompassing study of Khrushchev's time in power. Impressionistic and important is Roy Medvedev, *Khrushchev* (Doubleday, 1983). Elizabeth Valkenier discusses the problems of overextension in *The Soviet Union and the Third World: An Economic Bind* (Praeger, 1983). The Brezhnev years are examined in Archie Brown and Michael Kaser, eds., *The Soviet Union Since the Fall of Khrushchev* (Free Press, 1976). Gail Lapidus examines the difficult lot of women in *Women, Work, and Family in the Soviet Union* (Sharpe, 1982). Frederick Starr's splendid *Red and Hot: The Fate of Jazz in the Soviet Union, 1917–1980* (Oxford University Press, 1983), gives a unique insight into cultural vitality in the "totalitarian" Soviet Union. A work anticipating the disintegration of the USSR is Paul Dibb, *The Soviet Union: The Incomplete Superpower* (Illinois University Press, 1986). Martin Ebon gives essential background to the key figure in Soviet political change in *The Andropov File* (McGraw-Hill, 1983). Marshall Goldman's perceptive book, *Gorbachev's Challenge: Economic Reform in the Age of High Technology* (Norton, 1987), anticipated the crises of the 1990s. A good primer on the "balance of terror" is Ray Perkins Jr., *The ABCs of the Soviet-American Nuclear Arms Race* (Brooks/Cole, 1991). Stephen White, *Gorbachev and After* (Cambridge University Press, 1991), gives a solid account of the dénouement of the Gorbachev revolution.

Eastern European developments through the 1960s can be studied in the surveys by Hugh Seton-Watson, *The East European Revolution* (Praeger, 1961); Ivan Volgyes, *Politics in Eastern Europe* (Dorsey, 1986); and Zbigniew M. Brzezinski, *The Soviet Bloc: Unity and Conflict* (Harvard University Press, 1971). François Fejto, *History of the People's Democracies* (Pelican, 1973), is a solid survey of post-1945 Eastern Europe. Dennis Rusinow, *The Yugoslav Experiment, 1948–1974* (University of California Press, 1977), gives a view of the multinational state to the mid-1970s. Jorg K. Hoensch, *A History of Modern Hungary, 1867–1986* (Longman, 1988), is an objective survey.

Easily the best coverage of the collapse of communism in Eastern Europe is Gale Stokes, *The Walls Came Tumbling Down* (Oxford University Press, 1993).

The Czech crisis of 1968 and after is well covered in Galia Golan, *Reform Rule in Czechoslovakia: The Dubček Era* (Cambridge University Press, 1971). Norman Davies, *Heart of Europe: A Short History of Poland* (Oxford University Press, 1987), gives a short survey of events in that country. Joseph Rothschild, *Return to Diversity: A Political History of East Central Europe* (Oxford University Press, 1989), is a first-rate analysis of life in the last years of the Soviet Bloc; Roger Cohen, *Hearts Grown Brutal: Sagas of Sarajevo* (Random House, 1998), captures the human tragedy of the Yugoslav crises.

Suggestions for Web Browsing

Cold War International History Project
http://cwihp:si.edu/default.html

Offers a wide range of scholarly discussions of the conflict.

National Security Archive
http://www.seas.gwu/edu/nsarchive

Up-to-date revelations of Cold War events based on newly opened archives.

National Security Agency Venona Project
http://www.nsa.gov:8080/docs/verona.html

An in-depth account of the U.S. infiltration of Soviet cryptology, revealing the extent of the USSR's attempts to penetrate the highest levels of the American national security apparatus.

National Security Agency Cuba Missile Crisis
http://www.nsa.gov:808/docs/cuba/index.html

Site reveals the importance of both spies and spy planes in the incident that almost led to a nuclear confrontation.

North Atlantic Treaty Organization (NATO)
http://www.nato.org

Site provides the fundamental documents for the North Atlantic Treaty Organization.

Cable News Network's Series on the Cold War
http://www.cnn.com/SPECIALS/cold.war

Offers a wide range of interviews with participants and never-seen-before photographs.

Brookings Institution's U.S. Nuclear Weapons Study Project
http://www.brook.edu/PROJECTS/NUCWCOST/WEAPONS.HTM

Site offers documents covering the assumptions that nuclear weapons brought "more bang for the buck."

Central Intelligence Agency
http://www.cia.gov

More and more documents detailing CIA doctrines and actions during the Cold War are now declassified and available to the general public.

Russia: How Has Change Affected the Former USSR?
http://www.learner.org/exhibits/russia/

Site sponsored by the Annenberg/CPB Project Exhibits Collection details the enormous changes that have taken place in the former Soviet Union since 1991.

Notes

1. "Obituary, Telford Taylor," *The Economist*, May 30, 1998, p. 95.
2. A useful guide to the historiography of the Cold War can be found in J. L. Black, *Origins, Evolution, and Nature of the Cold War: An Annotated Bibliographic Guide* (Santa Barbara, Calif.: ABC-Clio, 1986).
3. J. P. Nettl, *The Soviet Achievement* (New York: Harcourt, Brace & World, 1967), p. 198.
4. Leonard Schapiro, *The Communist Party of the Soviet Union* (London: Methuen, 1963). pp. 534–535.
5. Winston Churchill, *Triumph and Tragedy* (Boston: Houghton Mifflin, 1953), p. 497.
6. Raymond Aron, "The Foundations of the Cold War," in *The Twentieth Century*, ed. Norman F. Cantor and Michael S. Werthman (New York: Crowell, 1967), p. 157.
7. John Lewis Gaddis, "The Insecurities of Victory: The United States and the Perception of the Soviet Threat After World War II," in *The Truman Presidency*, ed. Michael J. Lacey (Cambridge: Woodrow Wilson International Center for Scholars/Cambridge University Press, 1989), pp. 237, 250–257.
8. David Rees, *The Age of Containment* (New York: St. Martin's Press, 1967), p. 23.
9. Robert Ferrell, "The Formation of the Alliance, 1948–1949," in *American Historians and the Atlantic Alliance*, ed. Laurence Kaplan (Kent, Ohio: Kent State University Press, 1991), pp. 13–14.
10. Joseph L. Nogee and John Spanier, *Peace Impossible, War Unlikely: The Cold War Between the United States and the Soviet Union* (Glenview, Ill.: Scott, Foresman/Little, Brown, 1988), p. 67.
11. Sheldon W. Simon, "Cambodia: Barbarism in a Small State Under Siege," *Current History*, Dec. 1978, p. 197.
12. Robert A. Scalapino, "Asia at the End of the 1970s," *Foreign Affairs* (1980), p. 720.
13. Alec Nove, *The Soviet Economic System* (London: Allen & Unwin, 1977), p. 320.
14. Alvin Z. Rubinstein, *Soviet Foreign Policy Since World War II*, 3rd ed. (Glenview, Ill.: Scott, Foresman, 1988), p. 266.
15. Gale Stokes, *The Walls Came Tumbling Down* (New York: Oxford University Press, 1993), pp. 60–65.

This chapter was written with the assistance of Dr. Daniel Kazmer, Adjunct Professor of Economics, Georgetown University, Washington, D.C.

Si Accettano pagamenti

in EURO

€

SVILUPPA E STAMPA UN RULLINO

VINCI IL TRENTINO

*The arrival of the euro in 1999 as
the currency uniting 11 European
countries was hailed as a first step
toward creating a single economy
capable of rivaling that of the United
States in the twenty-first century.*

The "Developed World" Since 1945

Chapter Contents

I n the first 500 years of the nation-state system, the primary factor in international relations was the ability to project force—military power. Until the 1940s the state that could deliver the most force usually dominated the others. The development of nuclear weapons changed the nature of international power.

The Cold War came to an end, not as the result of a surprise nuclear attack, but because the USSR's social and economic infrastructure crumbled and the United States was undergoing considerable social and economic stress. Power has now come to be defined by a nation's ability to compete effectively in the world's economic arena.

The Modern Global Economy

Even before the defeat of the Axis in World War II, the Allies made plans to avoid the horrendous economic crisis that had followed the First World War. Forty-four nations met in July 1944 at the New Hampshire resort town of Bretton Woods to put the peacetime world economy on a solid footing. Recalling the protectionist lessons of the 1930s, the financial leaders devised plans to ensure a free flow of international trade. Later the Marshall Plan for Europe and the Dodge Plan for Japan provided capital to support reconstruction of the war-torn areas.

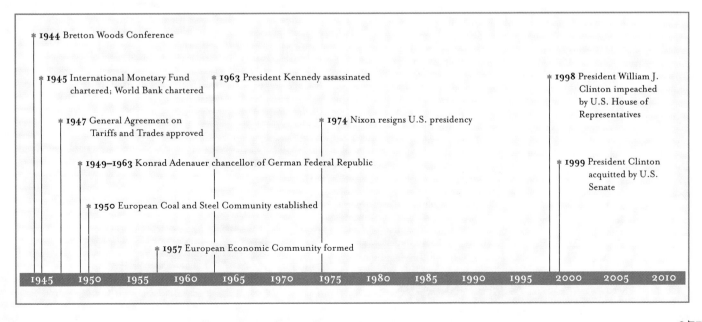

* **1944** Bretton Woods Conference

* **1945** International Monetary Fund chartered; World Bank chartered

* **1947** General Agreement on Tariffs and Trades approved

* **1949–1963** Konrad Adenauer chancellor of German Federal Republic

* **1950** European Coal and Steel Community established

* **1957** European Economic Community formed

* **1963** President Kennedy assassinated

* **1974** Nixon resigns U.S. presidency

* **1998** President William J. Clinton impeached by U.S. House of Representatives

* **1999** President Clinton acquitted by U.S. Senate

1945 1950 1955 1960 1965 1970 1975 1980 1985 1990 1995 2000 2005 2010

A New International Framework

The Bretton Woods Conference created the International Monetary Fund (IMF), chartered in 1945, to restore the money system that had collapsed in previous decades when countries abandoned the gold standard and resorted to export-enhancing devices such as currency devaluation and protectionist measures such as tariffs and quotas. The conference intended that the IMF would oversee a system of fixed exchange rates, founded on the dollar, which could be easily exchanged for gold at the rate of $35 an ounce. The IMF was based on a foundation of currencies paid in by the member states. These deposits served as a world savings account from which a member state could take short-term loans to handle debt payments without having to resort to the disruptive tactics of manipulating exchange rates or devaluation. The standard for the exchange rates among the various currencies was that in existence as of the first day of the Bretton Woods conference. Member countries could not change their currency's values without approval of the IMF. Although the system faced some problems based on the weaknesses of many of the member states' economies after the war, the IMF supported a generation of monetary stability that al-

lowed businesses to pursue their international plans with confidence in a stable market.

The conference also established the International Bank for Reconstruction and Development, more commonly known as the World Bank, chartered in December 1945. In its first ten years the World Bank focused mostly on the rebuilding of Europe. Over the next three decades the bank devoted the bulk of its resources to aiding states undergoing development or rebuilding. In the 1990s the bank became closely involved with states in transition from Communist central planning to Western market economies.

A key development in reforming the world economy was the establishment in 1947 of the General Agreement on Tariffs and Trade (GATT), under U.S. leadership. Having absorbed the lessons of the protectionist and autarkic 1930s, the Allies put together an international institution to set up worldwide rules for business that would give nations the confidence to break down old barriers that blocked free trade. GATT operated through a series of meetings between nations to remove protectionist restrictions. The assurance a nation received for entering the GATT framework was the "most favored nation" clause, which guaranteed that any trade advantage worked out in a nation-to-nation agreement would be automatically shared by all members of GATT.

Buttressing the activities of these international institutions was the economic and strategic self-interest of the world's most powerful nation, the United States. The Marshall Plan supplied most of the capital and technical assistance the Western European states needed for reconstruction. The Marshall Plan funds came with strict conditions: the recipients had to promise to balance their budgets, free prices, fight inflation, establish a stable currency, and eliminate protectionist trade measures. The Dodge Plan played the same role in Japanese recovery that the Marshall Plan played in Europe.[1]

The developed world achieved its present status of wealth and productivity thanks largely to the far-sighted and self-interested American investments in the Marshall Plan and the Dodge Plan and to the structure provided by the Bretton Woods Conference, GATT, and other institutions. Trade grew at a phenomenal annual rate of 7 percent adjusted for inflation in the first quarter century after the war. Even during difficult times, such as the oil embargo mounted by the Organization of Petroleum Exporting Countries (OPEC) in the 1970s and the banking crisis of the 1980s, the postwar international financial structures have proved to be dynamic and creative.

Stalin and his successors, until Gorbachev, chose not to participate in the new world economic structure. While the individual economies of the non–Soviet Bloc countries prospered within the new structure, the economies of the Soviet Bloc states

---

Global Economic Milestones

1944	Bretton Woods Conference plans peacetime economy
1945	International Monetary Fund, World Bank chartered
1947	General Agreement on Tariffs and Trade established
1948	Marshall Plan in Europe and Dodge Plan in Japan established; COMECON instituted in Soviet Bloc
1971	President Nixon takes dollar off gold standard
1973–1974	OPEC oil crisis
1980s	Banking crises in Latin America and Eastern Europe
1987	U.S. Stock market crash
1989	USSR and Soviet Bloc abandon central planning model
1993	World Trade Organization established
1997–1998	Asian economic crisis

stagnated. By the 1980s the economic gap between the two sides forced Moscow and its allies in COMECON to seek admission to the IMF and to GATT. It was apparent that the global political economy had become the most important factor in world relations. Ignoring the world's new economic realities had disastrous consequences for the Soviet Union and its satellites.

Technological Revolutions

Propelling the developed world's economic growth was the exceedingly fruitful work of its scientists and engineers. Atomic energy continued to present its Janus-like face of unlimited energy and great danger, as seen in the disastrous meltdown at Chernobyl, Ukraine, in 1986. Advances in biology and biochemistry produced a similar mixed picture. In 1953 James D. Watson and Francis H. C. Crick revealed a model of the structure of the DNA (deoxyribonucleic acid) molecule, the basic genetic building block. Research stemming from their work brought new insights into processes of heredity and led to the possibility of shaping the future of numerous species, from tomatoes that last longer on the supermarket shelf to shaping human beings to order. Like the problems raised by nuclear power, this capability posed profound social and ethical issues.

The potential for automation in industry was vastly enhanced by the development of the silicon chip. This was a complex miniature electric circuit etched onto a tiny wafer of silicon crystal. One type of chip, the microprocessor, could serve as the "brain" of a computer. Besides being able to carry out computing functions in a very small space, no larger than a thumbnail, it was much cheaper than earlier technology and much more reliable. Microtechnology markedly affected corporate structures and organization, as well as the nature and extent of work. Communications systems became more sophisticated and widely available. In the space of 20 years the personal computer became as common as television sets in the homes and businesses of the developed world. For individuals, everything from financial planning to training to basic communications can now be done on computers. For businesses, inventories can be more effectively monitored, and financial operations have been simplified. These new systems have led to the increased use of robotics in assembly lines, cheaper and more effective than humans for carrying out repetitive work.

By the end of the century all parts of the world were industrializing. There were major petrochemical complexes in the Middle East, automated steel mills in India, computer factories in Brazil, and sophisticated hydroelectric installations in Africa. All around the Pacific Rim, nations big and small experienced technological transformation. A vast network of highways, pipelines, railways, shipping and air lanes, fiber-optic cables, and communications satellites united the world. All of these served the needs of multinational firms and publicly owned enterprises.

Technology in turn transformed agriculture and diet. Food canning and refrigeration, together with the bulk transport of grains, permitted the shipping of perishable goods to all parts of the world. Food production was increased by plant genetics, new managerial methods, and large-scale agribusinesses with machines steadily reducing the number of workers doing menial labor. New business methods

No expert could accurately predict the impact of robotics and computers on the global economy and societies around the world. Even more startling was the Internet's rapid evolution from an obscure network used by scientists working on government projects to a new form of global communications on which millions of ordinary people depend.

and technology made the world a smaller and more profitable place. However, this also made the nations of the world more interdependent than ever before.

Interdependence in a Changing World

After 1945 the world experienced unprecedented economic growth and development and increasing interdependence. But trade flows changed. The international monetary system of exchange rates pegged to the dollar and the fixed price of gold lasted until 1971, when trade imbalances led to gold outflows from major importing nations such as the United States. President Richard Nixon dealt a fatal blow to the Bretton Woods system by severing the link between gold and the dollar. His move opened the way for "floating rates," the determination of exchange rates by market mechanisms.

This policy change aided multinational firms, headquartered in one country but with operations throughout the world, because by shifting operations they could take advantage of exchange rate differences to reduce cost. In response, countries whose economies depended on the export of raw materials began to band together in an attempt to affect the price of their goods, because the price of their goods determined the value of their currency.

The oil embargo of the 1970s imposed by the OPEC countries, originally intended to punish the nations that supported Israel in the 1973 Arab-Israeli war, dealt a serious blow to international stability. Quadrupling their prices, the OPEC nations gained in wealth at the expense of oil-importing nations. Poor oil-importing nations borrowed on international markets to finance their oil purchases. Banks in the United States, Europe, and Japan made substantial loans to countries in Eastern Europe, Latin America, and Africa—whose total debt by the end of the 1970s topped $1.3 trillion. Brazil's debt was nearly $100 billion; Mexico's was close to $90 billion. To ensure their survival, nations such as Brazil, Hungary, and Poland allowed World Bank personnel to impose regulations on domestic economic policy in return for loans, an unprecedented sacrifice of national sovereignty to an international body. Nonetheless, nonpayment by the debtor nations threatened to topple the world's banking structure as it became apparent that these poor nations could not repay their loans. The debt crisis of the 1980s pressed the IMF to the limit. Debts continued to be rescheduled, but the largest debtors showed an ever-declining ability to pay.[2]

This situation, and the world recession of 1978–1985, had different effects on different parts of the globe. Unemployment soared around the world, especially in the less developed countries, which were also plagued with rising population rates. In the United States the recession contributed to huge trade deficits and federal budget deficits. The United States was the first nation to recover from the recession, largely by generating a huge national debt and borrowing heavily from foreigners. A creditor since 1917, the United States now became a debtor nation.

In the late 1980s the United States momentarily lost its financial dominance to the Japanese, who themselves would later be challenged by Asia's "Four Tigers"—South Korea, Taiwan, Hong Kong, and Singapore. New technologies and cheaper labor overseas produced high-quality items that cost less than U.S. manufactured goods. Competition was especially severe for the Americans in the advanced technology and automobile markets until the early 1990s.

The resulting foreign trade deficits increased the desire for protectionist legislation in the 1980s, especially in the United States. Many congressional members argued that Japanese trade restrictions and subsidies harmed U.S. agricultural and technological exports while American markets remained relatively open to foreign imports. The GATT mechanism was pushed to the breaking point. In 1989 the United States invoked Section 301 of the Trade Act of 1974 to levy sanctions against India, Brazil, and Japan for unfair trade practices.

By the end of the 1990s Japan, South Korea, Indonesia, and Malaysia faced serious economic problems as a combination of vastly overvalued real estate investments, currency speculation, and corruption led to a collapse of those countries' currencies and fears of a "meltdown" of the Asian economic system that would threaten the global economy. Once again the IMF stepped into the crisis with its prescriptions of closing down weak banks and businesses, austerity budgets, and fiscal conservatism. Also, the United States plunged billions of dollars into the region to stabilize the situation. The Asian crisis had a damaging effect on the new capitalist economies of the former Soviet Bloc. Russia's inability to take the serious steps to reform its economy and the crooked nature of its economy made the Russian market rickety even before the Asian crisis. Westerners found themselves on the horns of a dilemma: whether to let Russia suffer through its crisis with the possibility that the democratic experiment might fail or to pour more billions of dollars in with the knowledge that most of it would never help most ordinary Russians anyway.

Given the turbulence of the previous half century, however, the foundation established at Bretton Woods allowed the world to avoid the inflation and depression that marked the 1920s and 1930s. The long-running Uruguay Round of the GATT talks, in which the United States worked with 115 other states to update the GATT rules, ended successfully in December 1993. This led to the establishment of the World Trade Organization (WTO), a streamlined approach to continuing the fight against trade barriers that had been successfully waged by GATT since World War II.

The United States Since 1945

The United States emerged from World War II with its landscape unscathed and its economy the most powerful in the world. This wealth enabled the United States over the next 30 years to assume vast global responsibilities such as those involved with the Marshall Plan, the expansion of a broad range of public services demanded by the expanded welfare state, and maintenance of a global military presence. Until 1981 both Democratic and Republic administrations based their policies firmly on the legacy of Franklin D. Roosevelt's New Deal. Politicians who opposed the Roosevelt programs suffered decisive defeats. However, starting in the 1980s, leaders began questioning various aspects of the New Deal to deal with the fact that there were no longer sufficient resources to satisfy such an economically demanding population.

Postwar Leadership

In addition to his foreign policy accomplishments after 1945, Harry Truman, who served as president from 1945 to 1953, continued to crusade for the rights of the "common man" and against the "fat cats" as he extended the New Deal. Republican Dwight David Eisenhower, the former supreme commander of Allied forces in Europe, was twice elected to the presidency with overwhelming victories. He continued, with somewhat less enthusiasm, to oversee the growth of federal programs.

Eisenhower's successor, the Democrat John F. Kennedy, was elected president in 1961 and promised a "New Frontier" spirit for America. While speaking out for programs to aid the poor and minorities, he was unable to deal effectively with Congress. He captured the nation's idealism, especially with the Peace Corps, but his assassination in November 1963 cut his presidency short.

The Crisis of the Presidency

Kennedy's vice president, Lyndon B. Johnson, picked up the burden of the slain chief executive and completed a series of major domestic reforms. Johnson could claim credit for the Civil Rights Act of 1964, the War on Poverty, Medicare, important environmental legislation, and the creation of the Department of Housing and Urban Development. However, major problems such as environmental pollution, de-

American Presidents Since World War II

Harry S Truman (D)	1945–1953
Dwight D. Eisenhower (R)	1953–1961*
John F. Kennedy (D)	1961–1963
Lyndon B. Johnson (D)	1963–1969
Richard M. Nixon (R)	1969–1974
Gerald R. Ford (R)	1974–1977
Jimmy Carter (D)	1977–1981
Ronald Reagan (R)	1981–1989*
George H. W. Bush (R)	1989–1993
William J. Clinton (D)	1993–

*served two full terms

cay of the inner cities, and minority discontent—the crisis of rising expectations—remained unsolved.

In foreign affairs the increasingly unpopular Vietnam conflict (see Chapter 34) plagued Johnson's presidency. The war alone cost more than $30 billion annually, and this outlay, along with expensive domestic programs, fueled the inflation of the 1970s.

The motto "The Buck Stops Here," displayed on Harry Truman's desk, reflected his belief in the authority of the president. Uninformed about confidential government policy when he assumed the presidency in April 1945, Truman presided over the military victories over Germany and Japan ending World War II. Truman contended with two major events following his election in 1948: the Korean War and constant opposition from the Republican party.

In August 1961 the first Peace Corps volunteers to leave the United States arrived in Ghana, where they were to spend two years teaching in Ghana's secondary schools. Peace Corps volunteers provide educational, health care, and agricultural services to help developing countries meet their basic needs.

Congress was hesitant to provide the funds needed to improve conditions for minorities and the inner cities while at the same time conducting a costly war. These priorities angered many Americans, spurring the development of a powerful protest movement, and many average citizens found themselves in deep and serious opposition to their government's policies. The ensuing political turmoil turned especially ugly in 1968 with the assassinations of civil rights leader Martin Luther King, Jr. and of Senator Robert F. Kennedy, brother of the former president, who was close to gaining the Democratic presidential nomination.

The fragmentation of the Democratic opposition led to the 1968 election by a razor-thin margin of Republican Richard M. Nixon, Eisenhower's vice president, who had himself been narrowly defeated by John Kennedy in 1960. Nixon, reelected by a landslide in 1972, shifted toward a more pragmatic philosophy of government. To fight inflation, caused in part by the costs of the Vietnam War and social programs, the administration imposed a wage and price freeze from August to November 1971 and wage and price controls from November 1971 to January 1973. These measures helped reduce the rate of inflation to about 3 percent. But when the administration returned to a free market policy at the end of April 1974, prices began to rise. The oil embargo imposed by the OPEC nations to protest American support of Israel contributed to the rise in inflation rates to 12 percent and a 6 percent unemployment rate.

During this time the Nixon administration concentrated on foreign affairs—especially matters related to ending the war in Vietnam, keeping peace in the Middle East, opening relations with China, and maintaining détente with the Soviet Union. In each area Nixon and his chief adviser, Henry Kissinger, compiled a substantial record of success. However, this record was overshadowed by scandal.

Henry Kissinger, *The White House Years*

Henry Kissinger, who served as secretary of state under Presidents Nixon and Ford, advocated a balance-of-power approach to foreign relations and a policy of détente with the Soviet Union.

In my view, Vietnam was not the cause of our difficulties but a symptom. We were in a period of painful adjustment to a profound transformation of global politics; we were being forced to come to grips with the tension between our history and our new necessities. For two centuries America's participation in the world seemed to oscillate between overinvolvement and withdrawal, between expecting too much of our power and being ashamed of it, between optimistic exuberance and frustration with the ambiguities of an imperfect world. I was convinced that the deepest cause of our national unease was the realization—as yet dimly perceived—that we were becoming like other nations in the need to recognize that our power, while vast, had limits. Our resources were no longer infinite in relation to our problems; instead we had to set priorities, both intellectual and material. In the Fifties and Sixties we had attempted ultimate solutions to specific problems; now our challenge was to shape a world and an American role to which we were permanently committed, which could no longer be sustained by the illusion that our exertions had a terminal point. . . .

But in our deliberations at the Pierre Hotel the President-elect and I distilled a number of basic principles that were to characterize our approach to US-Soviet relations as long as we were in office:

The principle of concreteness. We would insist that any negotiations between the United States and the Soviet Union deal with specific causes of tensions rather than general atmospherics. Summit meetings, if they were to be meaningful, had to be well prepared and reflect negotiations that had already made major progress in diplomatic channels. We would take seriously the ideological commitment of Soviet leaders; we would not delude ourselves about the incompatible interests between our two countries in many areas. We would not pretend that good personal relations or sentimental rhetoric would end the tensions of the postwar period. But we were prepared to explore areas of common concern and to make precise agreements based on strict reciprocity.

The principle of restraint. Reasonable relations between the superpowers could not survive the constant attempt to pursue unilateral advantages and exploit areas of crisis. We were determined to resist Soviet adventures; at the same time we were prepared to negotiate about a genuine easing of tensions. We would not hold still for a détente designed to lull potential victims; we were prepared for a détente based on mutual restraint. We would pursue a carrot-and-stick approach, ready to impose penalties for adventurism, willing to expand relations in the context of responsible behavior.

The principle of linkage. We insisted that progress in superpower relations, to be real, had to be made on a broad front. Events in different parts of the world, in our view, were related to each other; even more so, Soviet conduct in different parts of the world. We proceeded from the premise that to separate issues into distinct compartments would encourage the Soviet leaders to believe that they could use cooperation in one area as a safety valve while striving for unilateral advantages elsewhere. . . .

We would have to learn to reconcile ourselves to imperfect choices, partial fulfillment, the unsatisfying tasks of balance and maneuver, given confidence by our moral values but recognizing that they could be achieved only in stages and over a long period of time.

It was a hard lesson to convey to a people who rarely read about the balance of power without seeing the adjective "outdated" precede it.

From Henry A. Kissinger, *The White House Years.* Copyright © 1979 by Henry A. Kissinger. Reprinted by permission of Little, Brown & Company.

Nixon's vice president, Spiro T. Agnew, resigned under the weight of charges of bribery, extortion, and kickbacks dating from his time as governor of Maryland. (Under the Twenty-Fifth Amendment to the U.S. Constitution, passed just six years earlier, Nixon appointed a new vice president, Gerald R. Ford.) Far more serious, several men connected with Nixon's 1972 reelection campaign were arrested and charged with burglarizing the Democratic party's campaign headquarters at the Watergate, an apartment and hotel complex in Washington, D.C. Citing "presidential confidentiality," Nixon withheld information concerning these activities from a special prosecutor, a grand jury, and the public. When lengthy televised hearings led to the conviction of his closest associates, Nixon lost the confidence of most of the nation. The Judiciary Committee of the House of Representatives in July 1974 voted to recommend impeachment.

An embattled Richard Nixon raises his arms in a victory salute after resigning the presidency on August 9, 1974.

Repudiated and disgraced, Nixon resigned in August. His handpicked successor, Gerald Ford, granted Nixon a full pardon.

The Limited Presidency

Economic problems, including high inflation, high unemployment, and a falling dollar, continued to plague the nation. In 1976 Ford ran against the relatively unknown Jimmy Carter, former governor of Georgia. Carter campaigned on promises to restore trust in government, extend social programs, and improve economic conditions. Carter won the close election, becoming the first president from the Deep South since the Civil War.

Carter inherited the same problems as his predecessors and incurred some new ones. To deal with the crisis in the Middle East, he brought the leaders of Egypt and Israel together at the presidential retreat in Camp David, Maryland. He continued to pursue limitations on nuclear arms. But for many observers, his greatest accomplishment was that he made human rights considerations an operative part of American foreign policy. Domestically, Carter attempted to enact an extremely ambitious program of social and economic benefits while maintaining sufficient military strength. Not surprisingly, spending increased despite the goal of a balanced budget.

Rising fuel prices and declining per capita output exacerbated the economic difficulties. American

helplessness and frustration grew when Iranian militants captured 53 hostages during a takeover of the U.S. embassy in Tehran. The combination of economic problems, the foreign policy crisis surrounding the Soviet invasion of Afghanistan, and the hostage dilemma led to Carter's defeat in November 1980 by Ronald Reagan, former actor and governor of California. As a final snub to Carter, the Iranians released the American hostages just as Reagan took the oath of office in January 1981.

Reagan won the presidency with an overwhelming victory, and he promised to set about reversing a half century of increasing federal involvement in American life by making drastic cuts in federal programs. These cuts were part of his "New Federalism" program to reduce the budget, which also included proposals to cut personal tax rates by 25 percent and to make huge reductions in taxes paid by businesses. The administration also planned to increase military spending substantially. The assumption underlying the policy was that the budget cuts and tax cuts would simultaneously cure inflation and bring about economic growth.

However, the tax cuts were not matched by reduced federal spending. The percentage of gross domestic product spent by government increased during Reagan's first term. By the time he left office in 1988, the federal deficit had soared to unprecedented heights. Inflation rates fell significantly, but interest rates remained high.

The economic problems posed little obstacle to Reagan in the 1984 election, in which he carried 49 of the 50 states. Not even his bitterest critic could deny the effect of his will and personality on the office of president. Observers looked back to Franklin D. Roosevelt to find Reagan's equal as a communicator and master of the legislative process. Reagan won major tax and budget victories in the Democrat-controlled House of Representatives and gained backing in the Senate for such controversial diplomatic initiatives as the sale of sophisticated equipment to Saudi Arabia and the INF treaty. He survived an assassination attempt in March 1981, and this display of stamina and his considerable charm gave him an aura of authority and respect—despite a sometimes shocking lack of mastery of the details of his own programs—that no president since Eisenhower had enjoyed.

Reagan faced a number of foreign policy challenges as a result of the rapid changes occurring as the Cold War wound down. He sent contingents of marines to Lebanon in 1982 to act as part of an international peacekeeping force. A bombing in October 1983 killed 241 marines. This atrocity forced Reagan to withdraw U.S. troops from the area. Relations with Israel cooled when Israeli forces bombed an Iraqi nuclear facility, annexed the Golan heights (wrested from Syria in 1967), and invaded Lebanon.

The aggressive policies of Libyan leader Muammar al-Qadhafi led to conflicts with the United States, which triggered U.S. air attacks on Libya in the spring of 1986. In another controversial move, Reagan sent U.S. naval forces to the Persian Gulf when war between Iran and Iraq threatened to disrupt international oil shipments.

Festering social and economic problems in Latin America erupted into revolutionary movements in El Salvador and Nicaragua. The Reagan administration sent in military advisers and millions of dollars to support the factions it considered "democratic." When Congress withdrew support for the rebels known as the Contras, who were fighting the Sandinista government of Nicaragua, officials in the Reagan administration conspired to carry out illegal maneuvers, including the selling of weapons to supposed moderates in Iran and diverting the proceeds to the Nicaraguan rebels. The "Iran-Contra affair" cast a pall over the last two years of the administration and led to felony convictions for high-ranking Reagan aides.

The Republicans maintained their hold on the White House with the election of George Bush in 1988. The new president failed to maintain the Reagan momentum to extend American influence favorably to affect the development of democracy and free markets in the Soviet Union. Bush instead drew back, choosing to be "prudent" and to consult closely with allies and opponents alike to maintain stability during the enormous changes occurring in Eastern Europe and the Soviet Union during 1989. Bush's major success in foreign policy was his leadership of the anti-Iraq coalition during the Persian Gulf War, mounted after Iraq invaded and annexed neighboring Kuwait. Deftly working through the United Nations and mobilizing a broad coalition, Bush effectively stymied the Iraq government diplomatically and then sent U.S. troops to lead the UN coalition forces in a powerful bombing campaign against Iraq. A 100-hour ground offensive ultimately drove Saddam Hussein's Iraqi forces out of Kuwait. However, for most of Bush's term, the administration responded to foreign events more often with pronouncements and slogans than with carefully thought-out policies.

Bush's administration faced worsening economic problems: a growing budget deficit, productivity declines, balance-of-trade problems, the failure of many savings and loan institutions, and the fear of recession. Makeshift solutions to foreign opportunities, the deficit crisis, and other pressing domestic problems contributed to the president's decline in public opinion polls.

Nagging economic problems helped ensure the 1992 victory of Bill Clinton, who used a succinct catchphrase to keep his campaign staff focused: "It's the economy, stupid!" In his first two years the former Arkansas governor attempted to take the Democratic party to a more centrist position, responding to the conditions in the bond market more than his presumed constituency of labor, the poor, and the disaffected. Despite successes such as gaining U.S. acceptance of the North American Free Trade Agreement (NAFTA), the cloud of earlier personal improprieties and inadequate staff work gave the Clinton administration an image of muddling inefficiency in both domestic and foreign affairs that contributed to a sweeping Republican victory in the 1994 elections, giving the GOP control of both houses of Congress.

Clinton and his advisers learned their lessons from that defeat and moved increasingly to the political center. In the 1996 elections he ran on a program that was ideologically to the right of George Bush's positions in 1992 and easily defeated the Republican candidate, former Senate leader Robert Dole. Clinton benefited from the booming economy, which resulted from a basic overhaul of American management and manufacturing techniques, and the generally peaceful world situation. However, a tawdry scandal plagued the president throughout 1998; after finally admitting to improper behavior and lying to the

Health care reform was a major component of President Bill Clinton's platform. Riders of the president's "Health Security Express" gathered at a rally on Capitol Hill in August 1994. The next month Clinton announced the details of his reform package. Defeat of the plan was a major setback for the president.

American people, Clinton was impeached by the House of Representatives and sent to the Senate for trial. But the economy continued to be strong and no Americans were dying in foreign wars; perhaps that is why the public seemed more embarrassed than embittered by the entire spectacle and greeted his acquittal by the Senate in 1999 with a collective yawn.

Japan: From Defeat to Dominance to Doubt

On August 28, 1945, just three weeks after the atomic bomb was dropped on Hiroshima and Nagasaki, an advance party of 150 Americans, the lead group of a substantial army of occupation, landed in Japan. Supreme Commander General Douglas MacArthur soon arrived to preside over Japan's transition from one military authority to another. The Japanese had successfully recast their infrastructure during the Meiji Restoration. They would make another massive—and successful—adjustment after 1945.

Postwar Japan

The terms of armistice took all territory outside the four main islands away from Japan and imposed complete demilitarization on the Japanese. Key wartime military leaders were placed on trial, and Japanese premier General Hideki Tojo and six of his colleagues were executed. Other militarist governmental and business leaders were blocked from postwar activities. For a while industries were dismantled for reparations, but this practice was soon stopped.

In return the Allies gave aid under the Dodge Plan to rebuild the shattered economy while insisting on democratic institutions in the government and society. The new education system was based on the American pattern of decentralized public schools, with textbooks rewritten to delete militant nationalism. A land reform policy intended to reduce tenancy and absentee landlordism was introduced. Unions gained the right of collective bargaining, and their membership grew rapidly. American authorities tried with limited success to reduce the great concentration of wealth in the hands of monopolistic industries, the *zaibatsu*.

A new constitution, drafted in consultation with the occupation government, came into effect in May 1947. It set up a democratic two-house parliamentary-cabinet system in which the majority party selected the prime minister. Sovereignty rested in the people; the emperor, forced to renounce his divinity, was referred to as the "symbol of state." Voting was no longer dependent on income or sex. War was renounced as a sovereign right, and the maintenance of "land, sea, and air forces, as well as other war potential," was forbidden.

As a result of the Cold War in Europe and the Communist invasion of South Korea in 1950, Japan became the United States' principal ally in the Pacific. Despite Soviet opposition and without the participation of the USSR, a peace treaty was signed in 1951 and went into effect the next year, giving Japan full political independence. A security pact between Japan and the United States allowed Americans to station troops in Japan.

Political and Social Change

Conservatives have consistently, with brief interruptions, controlled the Japanese government. In 1955 two conservative parties merged to form the Liberal Democratic party, which was friendly to the West, favored modest rearmament, and backed the alliance with the United States. Based on professional civil servants and business interests, it was sufficiently strong to endure periodic charges of corruption for the next 38 years. The Socialist party, the major opposition, demanded nationalization of industry, opposed the 1947 security pact, and favored neutrality in foreign affairs. The small Communist party was vocal but weak.

The new system was flexible enough to absorb the radical transformation Japan has experienced in the past half century, although charges of corruption brought the political system to near-paralysis in the mid-1990s. In 1994 alone there were three prime ministers, including a Socialist. After a half century reformers seemed ready to shake off the legacy of the Liberal Democratic party and attack problems in the economy, politics, and society. But the Liberal Democratic party showed considerable tenacity and kept power, leading a coalition government under Prime Minister Ryutaro Hashimoto. However, the economy became stagnant, and a recession was declared in the spring of 1998.

Rapid urbanization posed the greatest social challenges. Rural areas lost population while city populations—and consequent environmental problems—skyrocketed. With more than 23 million people, Mexico City became the largest urban area in the world. The cities of Tokyo, Osaka, and Nagoya occupied only 1 percent of the country's land area but contained over one-fourth of the country's population.

Urban living caused traditional values and attitudes to change. Parental authority and family ties weakened as young married couples, forsaking the traditional three-generation household, set up their own homes. The stresses and strains of urbanization were reflected in student riots and in the appearance, for the first time in Japanese history, of juvenile delinquency. Western influences—seen in fashions, television, sports, and beauty contests and heard in rock music—clashed with the traditional culture. The harmony that characterized industrial concerns disappeared, and guaranteed lifetime employment came increasingly under challenge. Corporate paternalism had to be discarded to satisfy the demands of efficiency. Slowly but surely the communalism that had dominated Japanese life weakened under the impact of economic and cultural individualism.

Perhaps the greatest changes were those affecting women. Before World War II there was little for Japanese women to do outside the family. After 1945 they gained the right to own property, sue for divorce, and pursue educational opportunities. By the end of the 1980s women constituted nearly 50 percent of the nation's workforce, and more than 30 percent of women high school graduates attended postsecondary institutions.

Economic Dominance and Doubt

Japan faced serious obstacles in its path to economic development. It had to import much of the food for its growing population (125 million by 1995) and most of the raw materials for its industries. The Korean War gave Japan an initial boost, as American forces spent lavishly. In 1950 the GDP was $10 billion. The 1973 oil embargo and subsequent price in-

creases hit Japan hard. Inflation skyrocketed, economic growth plunged, and for a while the balance of trade was negative. Japan's business managers made the necessary adjustments for recovery.

By the end of the 1970s the Japanese built half the world's tonnage in shipping and had become the world's biggest producer of motorcycles, bicycles, transistor radios, and sewing machines. The Japanese soon outpaced the United States in automobile production and drove the American domestic television industry virtually out of business. After the October 1987 U.S. stock market slide, Tokyo temporarily became the world financial center, dominating banking.

In the late 1980s the Japanese began to watch uneasily as South Korea, Taiwan, Hong Kong, and Singapore, using the Japanese formula of a strong and disciplined workforce and efficient use of new technology, became effective competitors in the world market. South Korea especially launched a direct challenge to Japan in the high-technology and automotive markets. But the Japanese economy remained one of the world's strongest. Japan's per capita GDP in 1999 was $41,080, compared with $27,590 in the United States.

Yet within two years Japan was speeding toward economic meltdown. A vastly overpriced real estate market (at one time the listed real estate value for Tokyo alone exceeded the value of the entire United States!); a weakening management structure, with a parade of industrial chiefs solemnly apologizing for

Male and female officials of a computer firm in Japan discuss a technical question. Japan passed an equal opportunity law in 1985, widening access to the paid workforce for many Japanese women. Although many women have taken jobs outside the home, their upward progress has been limited as the Japanese tradition of male dominance continues to be strong.

Jean Monnet on European Unity

Jean Monnet was a pioneer in building the foundations for a unified Europe. In a 1953 speech he expressed his hopes for the future, to be attained in 1992.

Mr. President, Ladies and Gentlemen, on behalf of my colleagues . . . and myself, I wish to say how very pleased we are to have this meeting to-day with the members of the Common Assembly and the members of the Consultative Assembly. The co-operation between the Council of Europe and the European Coal and Steel Community has now definitely entered a concrete phase. . . .

In respect of coal and steel, the community has set up a huge European market of more than 150 million consumers, i.e., equal in number to the population of the United States of America. Under the terms of the Treaty, customs duties and quota restrictions have been abolished between Germany, Belgium, France, Italy, Luxembourg and the Netherlands; the principal discriminations in respect of transport have been done away with. . . . The road along which the six countries of the Community have set out is the right road, but we must continue to seek even more zealously ways and means of achieving a more complete understanding with the other countries of Europe. When they have seen and understood, as we have done, what this new and living Europe means for them, they will, one of these days, I hope, themselves join in.

From the Joint Meeting of the Members of the Consultative Assembly of the Council of Europe and of the Members of the Common Assembly of the European Community of Coal and Steel, *Official Report of the Debate*, Strasbourg, June 22, 1953.

running their firms into ruin and committing suicide; and a disastrous series of bad loans brought the nation to the brink of a financial crash. Japan's annualized GDP fell 5.3 percent in the first three months of 1998—and that in a part of the globe that saw the annualized GDP of South Korea, Malaysia, Thailand, and Indonesia, who imitated the Japanese policy of export at any cost, fall by 20 percent in 1997. As the yen continued to decline against the dollar, observers held their breath to see if the Japanese government would take the necessary steps to put its financial structure in shape.[3]

The Western European States

The most significant development in postwar Europe was the progress toward economic integration. The desire for cooperation came from the lessons learned during World War II, taught by visionaries such as the French statesmen Jean Monnet and Robert Schumann. In 1950 Monnet and Schumann put forth a program to create the European Coal and Steel Community to coordinate the supply of those two essential industrial commodities in West Germany, France, Italy, Belgium, the Netherlands, and Luxembourg. Five years later the European Atomic Energy Community was created.

The same six nations that participated in these supranational organizations in 1957 established the European Economic Community (EEC), the Common Market. The organization's goal was to build enduring foundations for the closer union between European peoples. To that end it reduced tariffs among its members and created a great free trade union that became the fastest-growing market in the Western world.

From EEC headquarters in Brussels, a staff of thousands of experts administered the organization's affairs. In the 1950s the income of its members doubled. While the U.S. economy grew at a rate of 3.8 percent, that of France expanded by 7.1 percent, Italy by 8.4 percent, and West Germany by 9.6 percent. During the rest of the decade trade nearly doubled among EEC members. Their factories and power plants hummed with activity, their workforce augmented by more than 10.5 million workers who migrated, many with their families, from southern Europe.

Lagging far behind these advances, Britain became a member of the Common Market in 1973; Ireland and Denmark also joined in that year. The admission of Spain and Portugal in 1986 brought the number to 12. While the member nations jealously guarded their sovereignty, they made substantial strides toward total economic integration. Various advances have been made toward adopting a common passport, setting a basic workweek and holiday policy for all workers, and equalizing welfare benefits.

Europe became a single market, the European Union (EU), at the end of 1992, by an act similar to the 1707 Act of Union between England and Scotland, the Constitution of the United States, and the North German *Zollverein* in the first part of the nineteenth century. Reaching the goal of "Europe 1992" was not easy. Serious controversies over agricultural policy, banking policies, and tax differences had to be overcome. The European leaders worked hard to re-

Discovery Through Maps

The Euro and Its Map

Les faces nationales des pièces de 1 euro

On January 1, 1999, eleven European countries entered into a three-year transition at the end of which they will share a single currency: the euro. The countries involved—France, Belgium, Germany, Luxembourg, the Netherlands, Ireland, Austria, Portugal, Spain, Italy, and Finland—will cease to use their national currencies on June 30, 2002. The euro coins will have on one side a common European face and on the other a design for the particular country in which they will circulate primarily, though they will be acceptable in all participating countries.

Europe will gain an advantage that the United States has had for two centuries: a single currency. No longer will Europeans have to contend with exchange rates and costly currency conversions, and prices throughout Europe will be both more consistent and more competitive for international shoppers. But some older Europeans fear that they may make unwise purchase decisions when spending funds they don't understand, and some patriots feel that giving up their national currency is tantamount to giving up part of their national sovereignty.

assure the rest of the world that their 12-nation market would not be protectionist while they put together the more than 300 directives that would form the laws for the commercial union.

The program entailed opening up the 12 nations' boundaries so that there would be no restriction to the movement of goods and people and the establishment of the "social dimension" to define the "rights of ordinary people in the great market and to help the poorer among them." There was also a more difficult drive toward economic and monetary unity, including a single European currency and central bank. One indication of the EU's success was the introduction of the currency, the euro, in 1999. Economic union also included single standards on electricity, pipeline pressures, safety, and health.

The momentum toward political unity slowed somewhat during the 1990s. Obstacles born of a thousand years of nationalism remained. Unresolved issues included a state's favoring its own industries in the purchase of supplies and equipment, protection of particular industries by sovereign states, and the value-added tax.[4]

Political changes brought challenges of expansion. By 1995 the remaining members of the rival European Free Trade Association—Finland, Austria, Iceland, and Sweden—had gained membership in the EU. Norway voted not to join. The former Soviet Bloc states and Switzerland, Turkey, Malta, and Cyprus sought to establish relationships with "the Fifteen." In light of the problems experienced in integrating the poorer nations of Europe, especially Greece, the EU's leadership was hesitant to extend full membership to the former Soviet Bloc states.

In response to the Common Market's successes, other trade zones were established: NAFTA, which

As the millenium comes to an end, Europe stands on the verge of attaining its greatest unity in history: and with that unity, the possibility of regaining the global dominance it lost in 1914.

linked Canada, Mexico, and the United States; and the Asia Pacific Economic Cooperation (APEC), which included the Pacific Rim states of Australia, Brunei, Canada, China, Hong Kong, Indonesia, Japan, South Korea, Malaysia, New Zealand, the Philippines, Singapore, Taiwan, and the United States.

Great Britain

Great Britain emerged from World War II at the height of its prestige in the twentieth century, but the glow of victory and the glory earned by its sacrifices served only to conceal Britain's dismal condition. The country was in a state of near-bankruptcy. As a result of the war, its investments had drastically declined and huge bills had been run up for the support of British armies overseas. In addition, increases in welfare benefits drained the economy.

After 1945 the London government could not reinstate the delicately balanced formula under which Britain had paid for massive imports of food and raw materials through exports and income from foreign investments, banking, and insurance. The British people, who had paid dearly to defeat the Axis Powers, did not produce the necessary export surplus to restore Britain's wealth. Over the next 40 years they would watch their vanquished enemies become wealthy while they struggled with aging industrial facilities and extremely costly welfare programs.

The Conservatives have dominated British politics since the end of the war, with interludes of Labour rule. The Conservatives oppose nationalization of industry, encourage private enterprise, and favor a reduced social welfare program. Labour supports nationalization of industry and a thorough welfare state. Neither party has been able to find a wholesale cure for the serious ailments afflicting the country.

After the wartime coalition government of Conservatives and Labour, the country held its first peacetime regular election in July 1945, and to the amazement of many, Labourite Clement Attlee defeated wartime leader Winston Churchill. Attlee was a low-key, hardworking, honest politician who came from a comfortable middle-class background. In foreign affairs the Labour government continued to work closely with the United States, while in domestic policy it set out to improve basic living standards while converting to a peacetime economic base. Within two years most major industrial and financial functions had been nationalized. In Britain's mixed economy 80 percent of the workforce was employed by private enterprise. The Labour party suffered, as it would for the next 40 years, from factionalism between its left wing, which was inclined to be anti-American and pro-Russian, and the mainstream.

Weakened by this split, Labour lost the general election in 1951, and the Conservatives began a 13-year span of dominance.

Churchill returned as prime minister until 1955, when he resigned and was succeeded by Anthony Eden. Eden resigned in January 1957 following the Suez Crisis, and Harold Macmillan took the party's leadership until July 1963. During the 1950s economic conditions slowly improved until 1959, when they rapidly deteriorated. Britain went deeply in the red in its balance of payments. By the end of 1960 the economic outlook was grim. The next year the government applied for membership in the Common Market, in the belief that a closer trading association with the Continent would reverse the terrible domestic economic situation. The issue of membership in the EEC split both the Conservative and Labour parties. But debate became moot when French president Charles de Gaulle moved successfully to block Britain's admittance.

The long period of Conservative rule ended in 1964 with the election of a small Labour majority headed by Harold Wilson, who had previously been the youngest cabinet minister in 150 years. Under his leadership Labour made important advances in education, slum clearance, and housing. But the old economic problems remained to plague the government. In 1967 Wilson was forced to devalue the pound sterling. Labour's lackluster performance in the late 1960s led to a victory in the 1970 election for the Conservatives under the leadership of Edward Heath. Heath's only significant achievement was bringing the country into the Common Market. Labor unrest in 1973 and the Arab oil embargo dealt crippling blows to the British economy, and Heath's bland leadership could not save his party from defeat in the 1974 elections. Labour returned once again, led by Wilson, who commanded a narrow majority. Continued industrial unrest, declining production, and alarming inflation led to major changes.

In 1975 Wilson resigned, to be succeeded by James Callaghan, a pragmatic moderate. He warned that "we are still not earning the standard of living we are enjoying. We are only keeping up our standards by borrowing, and this cannot go on indefinitely."[5] During 1976 Britain had to borrow $5.3 billion from ten other countries. Massive cuts were proposed for social services and the armed forces. Many unions denounced this action, but it seemed imperative to all responsible leaders. Callaghan's inability to deal with what one authority called "the most serious challenge in [Britain's] recent history as a liberal democracy" led to yet another change in the spring of 1979.

Margaret Thatcher led her Conservative forces to victory—and herself into the role of Britain's first woman prime minister—by proposing radical

Margaret Thatcher was the first woman to head a major British party (the Conservative party) and the first woman to serve as prime minister of Great Britain, a post she held for 11½ years.

changes in Britain's economic and social programs. Thatcher's success in carrying out her programs gave her overwhelming victories in 1983 and again in 1987. She demanded—and received—sacrifices from her own people, more favorable treatment from the Common Market, and firm backing from the United States. She built a solid political base against a disorganized Labour opposition. From there she proceeded to change the nature of the Conservative party and to attempt to reform British society, until she was removed by her party in 1990 and replaced by John Major, who barely kept power in the 1992 elections.

Major never enjoyed the standing or the success of Thatcher and was ousted by the pragmatic leader of the Labour party, Tony Blair, in 1997. The Conservatives suffered a massive defeat, and Blair found himself in the position to change the basic thrust of the Thatcherite programs. After he had taken control of the Labour party, Blair had effectively neutralized its radical element and later took a centrist path, which pleased British business. In presenting socialism with a capitalist face Blair set a trend in European politics that was followed by Lionel Jospin in France and Gerhard Schroeder in Germany.

Slow economic growth and unemployment were constant problems in the half century after the war. Britain continued to try to find the difficult balance between making an industrial comeback without seriously sacrificing its extensive welfare services. Another serious dilemma was the stark contrast be-

tween the rich southeastern part of the country and the permanently depressed areas of the Midlands, Scotland, and Wales. Friction between Protestants and Catholics remained a flashpoint in Northern Ireland. Racial problems generated by English resentment over the influx of nonwhite British subjects from the Commonwealth defied easy solution. But as the 1990s ended, the United Kingdom and Ireland were both riding an economic wave that drove real GDP beyond $20,000 per capita and gave evidence that the infrastructure problems were finally solved.

France: Grandeur and Reality

While most of France agreed to do the "rational" thing and capitulate to the Nazis in June 1940, Charles de Gaulle urged the government to move to North Africa and continue the struggle. During the war he personified France as a Great Power rather than a humiliated Nazi victim. In a famous broadcast to the French people from his exile in London, de Gaulle declared:

> *Whatever happens, the flame of French resistance must not and shall not die. . . . Must we abandon all hope? Is our defeat final and irremediable? To those questions I answer—No![6]*

After the liberation of Paris in August 1944, de Gaulle was proclaimed provisional president and for 14 months was a virtual dictator by consent. Elections held in October 1945 confirmed that the people wanted a new constitution. Sharp differences, however, developed between de Gaulle and members of the government. The general resigned in January 1946, occupying himself with the writing of his memoirs. In the fall of that year the Fourth Republic was established. Unfortunately, the old confusing patterns of the Third Republic were repeated. Too many parties and too much bickering precluded any significant action; nevertheless, the regime lasted a dozen years.

The Fourth Republic collapsed over the issue of Algeria. Revolt against the French colonial government there began in 1954 and for the next eight years drained French resources. The French population in Algeria, more than a million people, insisted that Algeria be kept French. Army leaders supported them. Plots to overthrow the government in Paris were started. Facing the prospect of a civil war, the ineffectual French government, which had been referred to as a "regime of mediocrity and chloroform," resigned in 1958, naming de Gaulle as president. His new government was granted full power for six months.

De Gaulle had been awaiting his nation's call in his country home. Eager to reenter the political arena, he returned to Paris and oversaw the drafting of a new constitution, this for the Fifth French Republic. The new code was overwhelmingly approved by referendum in September 1958. De Gaulle was named president for seven years and proceeded to make this office the most important in the government. In both the Third and Fourth Republics the legislature had been dominant, but now the president and cabinet held supreme power. During a crisis the executive could assume nearly total power. De Gaulle once commented, "The assemblies debate, the ministers govern, the constituent council thinks, the president of the Republic decides."

De Gaulle ended the Algerian war and shrugged off assassination plots and armed revolts. Then he set forth on his foremost objective to make France a Great Power, to give it grandeur. He noted in his memoirs that "France cannot be France without greatness." For the next seven years he worked to make France the dominant power in Europe, a third force free of either U.S. or Soviet domination. To this end he persisted in making France an independent nuclear power. In 1966 he withdrew French military forces from active participation in NATO, although France remained a consultative member of the alliance. Above all, de Gaulle was opposed to membership in any supranational agency. For this reason, while he tolerated the Common Market, he blocked any attempts to transform it into a political union. Even though he wielded great influence internationally, at home his position weakened.

A serious upheaval of university students and workers' strikes in 1968 further diminished de Gaulle's authority. A national referendum had been called to reorganize the government on a regional basis. De Gaulle unnecessarily made it a vote of confi-

dence. When the referendum failed, he resigned his office and retired to his country estate, where he died 18 months later. His successor was Georges Pompidou, an able administrator who gave evidence of vision in his leadership. When Pompidou died unexpectedly in 1974, the country elected Valéry Giscard d'Estaing as president. A resistance hero and a brilliant student, he had entered government service and become a high-ranking civil servant by the age of 26. The new president initiated a series of important reforms relating to urban growth, real estate, and divorce. He also favored lowering the voting age to 18.

Despite the generally high quality of leadership in France, the country was afflicted by the international economic difficulties relating to the energy crisis and American financial woes after 1973. Problems of inflation and housing shortages helped the rise to power of the Communist and Socialist parties, whose active participation in the wartime resistance had increased their popularity. There was a real possibility that a combined political program by the two parties might lead to a Marxist domination of the government. This did not happen in the elections of March 1978. Nevertheless, the strength of the left was evident and continued to grow in the face of economic problems and discontent with Giscard's personal rule. In May 1981 Socialist leader François Mitterrand was elected president, and 20 years of right-of-center government came to an end.

In June the Socialist party gained a majority in the National Assembly, and Mitterrand set out to reverse two centuries of French tradition by decentralizing the governmental apparatus installed by Napoleon. In addition, he pursued a program to

Indian immigrants in France sewing in a sweatshop. Immigrant workers in European countries took menial jobs. They faced resentment from xenophobic native Europeans.

nationalize some of France's largest business and banking enterprises. Mitterrand's honeymoon did not last long, as the parties to his right began to practice stalling tactics in the Assembly to block his programs. The Communists, who had lost badly in the 1981 elections, received four relatively insignificant seats in the cabinet, in return for which they promised cooperation with the new government. Mitterrand had to deal with the economic problems of slow industrial growth, inflation, and unemployment, and he found these as resistant to solution as Giscard did. By the end of 1985 the economy began to improve. The president lost his majority in elections in March 1986 but regained it in 1988 before losing it again in 1993.

Mitterrand died in 1996 and was succeeded in the elections by the centrist leader Jacques Chirac, who maintained the policy of close cooperation with the United States and moderate domestic government first with prime minister Alain Juppé of his own party and then with the Socialist government headed by Lionel Jospin. France's challenge remains balancing its pride in its culture and way of doing things with the demands of an increasingly internationalized, American-dominated world.

West Germany: Recovery to Reunification

The most dramatic postwar European transformation has been that of West Germany. Recovering from the death, disaster, and destruction of World War II, the Bonn government accomplished political and economic miracles. When the Soviet Bloc disintegrated in 1989, the Bonn government moved rapidly to extend economic aid and work for reunification. By October 1990 unification had been accomplished, justifying the dreams of postwar Germany's most important leader, Konrad Adenauer, who led his country from the status of despised outcast to that of valued Western ally.

Born in 1876, Adenauer entered politics in 1906 as a member of the city council of Cologne. In 1917 he became mayor of the city, holding office until 1933, when the Nazis dismissed him. During Hitler's regime he was imprisoned twice but lived mostly in retirement at home, cultivating his rose garden. After 1945 he entered German national politics, becoming leader of the new Christian Democratic party. With the approval of the Allied occupation authorities, German representatives drafted a constitution for the German Federal Republic, which was ratified in 1949. Adenauer, at the age of 73, became chancellor of West Germany.

In the new democratic government the presidency was made weak, while the real executive, the chancellor, was given specific authority to determine "the fundamental policies of the government." The chancellor was responsible to the Bundestag, a popularly elected legislative body. One of the weaknesses of the Weimar Republic had been the existence of many small parties, leading to unstable multiparty coalitions. In the new government a party, to be recognized, had to win at least 5 percent of the votes in a given election.

Adenauer assumed power when Germany was still an outcast and its economy was in ruins. His one driving obsession was to get his people to work. Taking advantage of the tensions of the Cold War, he succeeded admirably. Under the force of his autocratic and sometimes domineering leadership, the Germans rebuilt their destroyed cities and factories using some $3 billion in Marshall Plan assistance. As early as 1955 West German national production exceeded prewar figures, with only 53 percent of former German territory. Providing the initial economic guidance for this recovery was Adenauer's minister of economics, Ludwig Erhard, a professional economist and a firm believer in laissez-faire economics. Germany's economic growth was accompanied by little inflation, practically no unemployment, and few labor problems.

Adenauer's achievements in foreign affairs were as remarkable as his leadership in domestic affairs. The German Federal Republic gained full sovereignty in 1955. At that same time, West Germany was admitted into the NATO alliance. Adenauer decided to align closely with the West and cultivated close ties with the United States. In 1963 he signed a treaty of friendship with France, ending a centurylong period of hostility. Adenauer expressed his attitude toward foreign affairs when he said, "Today I regard myself primarily as a European and only in second place as a German." It was natural that he brought his nation into Europe's new institutions, the European Coal and Steel Community and the Common Market. Adenauer's great frustration in foreign affairs was his failure to achieve the reunification of Germany.

In 1963, after 14 years in office, Adenauer retired and was succeeded as chancellor by Erhard, who was in turn succeeded by Kurt Kiesinger. The big change in German politics occurred in 1969 with the victory of the Social Democratic party. This moderate, nondoctrinaire socialist party was led by Willy Brandt, who became chancellor. A foe of the Nazis, Brandt had fled to Norway, where he became a member of the resistance after Hitler's conquest. After the war he returned to Germany and became prominent in the Social Democratic party. In 1957 he became mayor of West Berlin, then in 1966 foreign minister in Bonn. Brandt was very active in setting West Germany's foreign policy. He was instrumental in getting Britain into the Common Market, and he tried to improve relations with Eastern Europe and the Soviet Union through *Ostpolitik*, a policy of cooperation with Warsaw Pact nations. In journeys to both Moscow and

Warsaw in 1970 he negotiated a treaty with the USSR renouncing the use of force and an agreement with Poland recognizing its western border along the Oder and Neisse Rivers. A treaty was also signed with East Germany for improving contacts and reducing tensions. These negotiations and others paved the way for the entry of the two Germanies into the United Nations.

Brandt's concentration on foreign affairs led to the appearance of neglect of domestic issues such as inflation and rising unemployment. Important segments of German public opinion attacked him on the policy of *Ostpolitik*. After a spy scandal rocked the government, Brandt resigned in the spring of 1974. Helmut Schmidt, who succeeded him, paid closer attention to domestic affairs.

Under Schmidt's leadership Germany continued its strong economic growth in the wake of the oil embargo. German workers did not suffer the unemployment problems of other countries because of the practice of firing and sending home foreign workers when job cutbacks were needed. Germany's economy in the 1980s was not immune to issues such as foreign trade fluctuations and oil imports. Still, Schmidt, as head of the most powerful Western European nation, had the prestige and record to ensure his victory in the 1980 elections.

In the late 1970s Schmidt had asked the United States to counter the Soviet placement of SS-20 intermediate-range missiles by placing intermediate-range ballistic missiles in Europe, thereby setting off a debate that did not end until 1983. Schmidt faced both the disapproval of antinuclear demonstrators, who did not want the missiles, and the displeasure of conservatives in his country and the United States over German economic ties with the Soviet Union. In the autumn of 1982 political power passed again to the Christian Democratic party, now led by Helmut Kohl.

Into the mid-1990s Kohl's party proved to be a staunch supporter of the United States, in particular of its program to place U.S. intermediate-range missiles in Europe. In the face of strident Soviet protests, Kohl guided a bill through the West German parliament in November 1983 to deploy the missiles. After that success and a strong victory in 1987, Kohl, despite his reputation as a plodding politician, came to play a strong role in European affairs and in relations with the Soviet Union. In the course of his tenure Kohl changed with the times to deal with environmental issues brought forcefully to the public forum by the environmentally focused Green party. He masterfully took advantage of the breakdown of the German Democratic Republic in 1989 to claim the issue of reunification for himself and his party.

By the end of 1994 Kohl had confounded critics who had contempt for his intellect and who thought him politically naive. He overcame all the opposition for election, and his three-party coalition once again

enabled him to remain chancellor. The cost of incorporating East Germany into the republic has been immense and has led to a high unemployment rate, centered in the east, which will need at least another decade to catch up with its neighbors to the west. Yet after a brief downswing, German industries have reformed themselves and are reclaiming parts of the world market, especially in automobiles, that they lost in the 1980s. None of this resurgence helped Kohl in the September 1998 elections, as his center-right coalition was replaced by a center-left coalition headed by the moderate Socialist Gerhard Schroeder.

Italy: Political Instability, Economic Growth

Following the end of Mussolini's regime, Italy voted by a narrow margin to end the monarchy. A new constitution, adopted in 1947, provided for a premier and a ministry responsible to the legislature. The Christian Democratic party—strongly Catholic, pro-Western, and anticommunist—was the leading middle-of-the-road group. Its spokesman and leader was Alcide de Gasperi, whose ministry governed the country from 1947 to 1953. Like Adenauer, de Gasperi was a strong adherent of democracy and supported European unity. Italy joined NATO in 1949 and the Common Market in 1957.

In little more than a decade the Italian economy changed from predominantly agricultural to industrial. For a time, in the late 1950s and early 1960s, industry advanced faster in Italy than in any other part of Europe. In 1960 the output of manufacturing tripled pre-1939 levels, and in 1961 steel production exceeded 1 million tons. By the end of the 1980s Italy ranked among the world's leaders in high-tech industry, fashion, design, and banking. Most economic development occurred in northern Italy around the thriving cities of Turin, Milan, and Bologna.

Southern Italy did not progress as rapidly. Too many people, too few schools, inadequate roads, landlordism, and inefficient, fragmented farms worked by poor peasants were among the problems besetting the area. The government offered help in the form of subsidies, tax concessions, and programs for flood control and better highways, but southern Italy remained a challenging problem.

If the Italian economy was a source of optimism, politics was another story. After de Gasperi's retirement in 1953, politics became increasingly characterized by a series of cabinet crises, shaky coalitions, and government turnovers. Between the end of World War II and the end of the century, Italy had had more than 50 governments.

In the 1970s labor unrest, unemployment, and inflation posed problems that politicians could not deal with, even in coalitions in which the Communist party joined with other factions. For a while terrorism dominated political life. In 1978 the anarchist Red Brigade kidnapped one of Italy's most prominent public figures, former premier Aldo Moro, and assassinated him nearly two months later, leaving his body in a car parked equidistant between the Christian Democratic and Communist party headquarters in Rome. Terrorists spread chaos among business and political leaders. Finally, during the 1980s the government, dominated by Bettino Craxi and Ciriaco de Mita, improved conditions. The terrorist networks were broken, and law enforcement agencies began to combat organized crime in southern Italy and Sicily.

Widespread corruption and inefficiency in the Christian Democratic–dominated system were exposed in a series of trials that reached to the highest levels of Italian society and government in the 1990s. Exposure of the nationwide network of corruption in 1992 sent some of the most powerful Italian leaders to jail, where some committed suicide. Revulsion provoked by the widespread corruption led in 1993 to a reform of the political system from that of a senate based on a proportional system of representation to a scheme in which power went to the group claiming the majority of votes. In 1994 a national election to form the new parliament resulted in victory for the charismatic television businessman, soccer team owner, and right-winger Silvio Berlusconi. Berlusconi's *Forza Italia* ("Let's Go, Italy") coalition included openly fascist politicians. Predictably, within six months Berlusconi's government itself was em-

broiled in crisis, and in 1998 the man himself was sentenced to two years in prison for corruption.

The businesslike late-1990s government of Romano Prodi stabilized the Italian economy and politics, and Italy was one of the first European countries to meet the standards for entry into the euro system.

Portugal

Portugal was an incredibly corrupt monarchy until 1910. The country then became a republic, but its record of internal turmoil continued. Between 1910 and 1930 there were 21 popular uprisings and 43 cabinets. Toward the end of that period the army ousted the politicians and took control of the government. In 1932 the generals called on Antonio de Oliveira Salazar to run the country. This former economics professor, a fervent and austere Catholic, shunned social life and was content to live on a very small salary. He devoted all of his time to running an authoritarian government. The press was censored, and education—in a country in which two-thirds of the population was illiterate—was neglected. Some economic improvement did take place, but the people, who were frozen out of politics, remained poor. In 1955 a five-year program to stimulate the economy was launched, but its gains were canceled out by population increases and the huge costs resulting from wars in Portugal's African colonies.

Salazar retired in 1968 because of ill health, and six years later a group of junior army officers overthrew the government. Serious divisions appeared between the moderate liberal factions and the Communists. In the summer of 1976, however, elections confirmed the victory of the moderate Socialists. A new constitution was enacted, establishing a democratic system. The government faced difficult economic problems. Six hundred thousand refugees from Portuguese Africa had to be absorbed, fueling high unemployment and runaway inflation. After the 1974 revolution, workers had seized many businesses, large farms, and hotels. In most instances private ownership had to be restored under efficient management. During the 1980s political and economic stability returned to the country, led in the latter part of the decade by Mario Soares, ruling through a Socialist coalition. Compared with the rest of Europe, Portugal remained poor, but it has stabilized its economy with a 3 percent inflation rate and increased literacy rates. Much progress had been made.

Spain

In the four decades after World War II, Spain passed from the Franco dictatorship to a rapidly industrial-

Spanish prime minister Felipe Gonzales signs the treaty admitting Spain and Portugal to membership in the Europe Economic Community in June 1985.

izing, modern European state. Franco ruled over an almost ruined country after taking control in 1939. Many of Spain's most talented and productive people had fled, and 700,000 people had died in the civil war. So horrible was the conflict and so great the losses that Franco gained a grudging toleration from the majority of the exhausted population. Those who did not cooperate faced his secret police.

Cold War tensions eased Spain's reentry into the community of nations in the 1950s. The United States resumed diplomatic relations, and Spain became a member of the UN in 1955. The following year the Pact of Madrid provided naval and air bases for the Americans, in return for which Spain received more than $2 billion a year in aid. In the 1960s and 1970s the widespread poverty and backwardness that had long characterized Spain began to diminish. Inspired by the Portuguese revolution of 1974, workers and students began to demonstrate and show their unrest. In the summer of 1975 Franco died. He had named Prince Juan Carlos as his successor, thereby indicating his wish that the monarchy be restored.

The young king was crowned in November 1975, and in his speech of acceptance he promised to represent all Spaniards, recognizing that the people were asking for "profound improvements." In 1976 the reformed government announced amnesty for political prisoners, freedom of assembly, and more rights for labor unions. An orderly general election took place in the spring of 1977. Post-Franco Spain began its parliamentary-monarchy phase with impressive stability. Underneath, deep ideological divisions remained, which decreased over time. The major crisis came in February 1981 when radical elements of the army invaded the parliament building to attempt a coup. It immediately became apparent that there was no support for the coup either from the king, in the military, or among the public at large, and the attempt was brushed aside.

In May 1982 Spain joined NATO—still a controversial decision—and later that year elected Felipe Gonzales of the Socialist party to run the country. Gonzales brought Spain into the Common Market and worked hard to diversify the country's economy. He strengthened his position in the 1986 elections and by 1990 was governing a country attractive to investors in high-tech industries. Gonzales's party became complacent in their years in power and lost the 1996 elections to the Conservatives led by José Maria Aznar, who imposed a strict program of fiscal responsibility on the country

Greece

Greece, since its modern creation in 1821, has rarely enjoyed political stability. From that year until 1945

there were 15 different types of government with 176 premiers, who obviously averaged less than one year in office. Inefficiency in government, economic backwardness, and political crises have continued to plague Greece since 1945. In the Greek civil war (1946–1949) pro-Western forces, who controlled only the major cities, turned back a powerful Communist surge for power and reestablished the monarchy. Greek politicians ignored the complex economic issues affecting the peasants, preferring instead to attempt to regain various islands and territories controlled by Greeks in the long-distant past (these are known as *irredentas*). In the spring of 1967 a group of army colonels seized power. A dictatorship was established that jailed many political figures and harshly punished any criticism of its rule. Many Greeks fled into exile. The military junta made a serious miscalculation in 1974 when it connived to increase Greek authority on Cyprus, a move that led to a Turkish invasion of the island. This blunder led to the junta's downfall.

Thereafter the Greeks created a republic, complete with a new constitution. They applied for membership in the Common Market in 1975 and were admitted in 1981. In its application the government stated that its desire to join the European Economic Community was "based on our earnest desire to consolidate democracy in Greece within the broader democratic institutions of the European Community to which Greece belongs." Since that time Greek leaders have maintained their democratic traditions. In November 1981 the Socialist party, led by Andreas Papandreou, gained power and held it through 1989. He led his party back to power four years later. Papandreou ran on pledges to evict U.S. forces from Greek bases and to move Greek foreign policy away from its Western orientation. In the middle of the decade Papandreou followed traditional Greek irredentist tendencies to mobilize the nation by actively opposing the independence of the former Yugoslav republic of Macedonia on political, economic, and historical grounds.

Yet the Greeks remained active participants in NATO and the Common Market. Like Portugal, Greece is, by European standards, a poor country with a stagnant economy and an inflation rate of 18 percent. In the 1989 elections these factors plus scandals surrounding Papandreou's personal life led to the defeat of the Socialists and the forming of an unlikely coalition made up of the Communist and Conservative parties, which enjoyed a short tenure in power. As the decade came to an end the Greek prime minister, Costas Simitis, walked a political tightrope between nationalist expectations, fired up by the conflicts in Yugoslavia to his north, and the need for sound fiscal policies. The difficult relationship with Turkey, which has plagued the country for most of its existence, remains at the forefront of Greek consciousness.

A Shared Concern: The State of the Environment

Economic success brought with it a number of new concerns for the developed world. Principal among them is the fight against environmental pollution.

The world's financial and political leaders have become increasingly aware of the spread of pollution and the deterioration of the environment. The UN Conference on the Human Environment held in Stockholm in 1972 produced no serious negotiations but did sound the call that environmental problems know no national boundaries. This led to the creation of the UN Environmental Program (UNEP), based in Nairobi, Kenya. Unfortunately, inadequate funding and jurisdictional disputes prevented UNEP

The real question faced by the West at the end of the twentieth century was whether it could live the life of widespread well-being without polluting the planet.

from living up to its expectations. In the 1970s and 1980s a series of conventions relating to the environment were signed, including agreements dealing with pollution from ships, prevention of marine pollution from land-based sources, transboundary air pollution, conservation of migratory species, protection of the Mediterranean Sea from land-based pollution, various regional pollution agreements, and protection of the ozone layer.

In the 1990s it became apparent that vastly more efficient fishing fleets were exhausting the oceans' capacity to replenish their fish. In addition, pollution destroyed traditionally rich fishing grounds such as those in the Black Sea, threatening one of the basic food sources for the globe's rapidly expanding population. In the United States the Environmental Quality Index compiled by *National Wildlife* showed overall declines in the condition of wildlife, air quality, water quality, forests, and the soil.

It was difficult enough to deal with the rate at which modern industry and technology generated by-products that destroyed the environment and the equivalent pace of the planet's forests. But discovery of massive environmental problems in the former Soviet Bloc, especially central Asia, and the abysmal conditions in which the centrally planned economies had left Eastern Europe and Russia overwhelmed planners and reformers.[7] The developed world has yet to work out the conflict between economic development and environmental safety for itself, let alone the peoples of the former Soviet Union and the developing world.

Conclusion

At the end of the twentieth century the United States, Japan, and the Western European states were committed to international cooperation to maintain global economic growth and prosperity. This trend toward cooperation found its basis in the recognition of the benefits gained from the collaborative economic framework established at Bretton Woods and continued thereafter.

The half century after World War II witnessed an unprecedented improvement in living standards in the developed world. This improvement gained from the effective work by leaders of the world's governments to respond in a concerted manner to threats to the common economic well-being. The adoption of a global market mechanism combined with diplomatic and political cooperation ensured that the innovations in technology would be efficiently translated into better products and services at lower cost for the citizens of these countries.

The United States, experiencing its longest-running economic growth cycle, still faces the challenges of making its pluralistic system work. Japan seemingly reached its peak by 1990 and thereafter had to deal with the residue of political, social, and economic problems generated during its rapid rise to power. If Europe can work out the old problems of political and cultural particularism, its economic union holds the promise that in the twenty-first century, as in the nineteenth, economic power will return to the Europeans.

Suggestions for Reading

The Marshall Plan and its impact are well covered in Stanley Hoffman and Charles S. Maier, *The Marshall Plan: A Retrospective* (Westview, 1984), and Michael J. Hogan, *The Marshall Plan: America, Britain, and the Reconstruction of Western Europe* (Cambridge University Press, 1987), which treats the U.S. initiative as a consistent part of an American vision to regain capitalist momentum.

Post-1945 events in the United States are discussed in Jim Heath, *Decade of Disillusionment: The Kennedy-Johnson Years* (Indiana University Press, 1984). Allen J. Matusow, *The Unraveling of America: A History of Liberalism in the 1960s* (Harper & Row, 1984), traces the political results of that shocking decade. At the end of the 1980s, Joseph S. Nye Jr. wrote a magisterial analysis of the United States' role in *Bound to Lead: The Changing Nature of American Power* (Basic Books, 1989). Most of the postwar presidents have produced memoirs. Probably the best and most enjoyable are Harry S Truman, *Memoirs* (Doubleday, 1955–1956). See also Lyndon B. Johnson, *The Vantage Point* (Holt, Rinehart and Winston, 1971), and Dwight D. Eisenhower, *The White House Years* (Doubleday, 1963). Also instructive is Doris Kearns, *Lyndon Johnson and the American Dream* (Harper & Row, 1976).

Edwin O. Reischauer, *Japan: The Story of a Nation* (Knopf, 1974), provides the best general coverage. See also Reischauer, *The Japanese* (Harvard University Press, 1977). Kazuo Kawai, *Japan's American Interlude* (University of Chicago Press, 1979), discusses occupation policies and their impact. Ronald Philip Dore traces one major problem in *Land Reform in Japan* (University of California Press, 1958). John K. Fairbank, Edwin O. Reischauer, and Albert M. Craig discuss the challenges of change in *East Asia: Tradition and Transformation*, rev. ed. (Houghton Mifflin, 1989).

The resurgence of Western Europe is dealt with in J. Robert Wegs, *Europe Since 1945* (St. Martin's Press, 1991). Michael Emerson et al., *The Economics of 1992: The E.C. Commission's Assessment of the Economic Effects of Completing the Internal Market* (Oxford University Press, 1988), is a wise assessment of the challenges and promises of the united Europe. See also Neil McInnes, *The Communist Parties of Western Europe* (Oxford University Press, 1979), and Theodore Geiger, *The Fortunes of the West: The Future of the Atlantic Nations* (Indiana University Press, 1973).

Good accounts of the various Western European countries are David McKie and Chris Cook, eds., *The Decade of Disillusionment: Britain in the 1960s* (St. Martin's Press, 1973); Christopher John Bartlett, *A History of Postwar Britain, 1945–1974* (Longman, 1977); John Darby, *Conflict in Northern Ireland* (Barnes & Noble, 1976); George Dangerfield, *The Damnable Question* (Little, Brown, 1976); Henry Ashly Turner Jr., *The Two Germanies Since 1945* (Yale University Press, 1987); P. A. Allum, *Italy: Republic Without Government* (Nor-

ton, 1974); and Roy C. Macridis, *French Politics in Transition* (Winthrop, 1975). Max Gallo, *Spain Under Franco* (Dutton, 1974), and Paul Preston, ed., *Spain in Crisis* (Barnes & Noble, 1976), study the evolution of that country under Franco. Neil Bruce, *Portugal: The Last Empire* (Halstad, 1975), presents the background of the 1974 revolution.

For pioneering works of environmental concern, see Barbara Ward and René Jules Dubos, *Only One Earth: The Care and Maintenance of a Small Planet* (Penguin, 1973), and Barbara Ward, *The Home of Man* (Norton, 1976). On the profound transformation in women's roles in the twentieth century, see Simone de Beauvoir, *The Second Sex* (Vintage, 1974), and Betty Friedan, *The Feminine Mystique* (Dell, 1977). For a worldwide survey, see Kathleen Newland, *The Sisterhood of Man* (Norton, 1979).

Suggestions for Web Browsing

Vietnam War
http://www.ahandyguide.com/cat1/v/v153.htm
> *Access to a wide variety of testimonies on the Indochinese war can be found here.*

Europe in the 1990s
http://www.nato.int
> *Official documents for the rapidly changing European scene in the 1900s.*

The European Union
http://www.eurunion.org
> *Information on events within the European Union.*

The New European Politics of the 1990s
http://nwl.newsweek.com/nw-srv/inetguide/
    guide_2023877.html
> *A new kind of politics emerged in Europe during the 1990s—the so-called "third way" between traditional socialism and conservatism. Prime Minister Tony Blair exemplifies that path and his career can be traced on the site.*

Changing Relationships Between the United States and Japan
http://www.nichibei.org
> *The relationship between the United States and Japan is a rapidly changing one. This site provides both information and the opportunity for interchange.*

Notes

1. *The Economist*, July 9, 1994, pp. 69–75.
2. For a good summary of international economics and politics at the end of the 1980s, see Walter S. Jones, *The Logic of International Relations* (Glenview, Ill.: Scott, Foresman, 1988), ch. 12–14.
3. "As Japan Goes . . . ," *The Economist*, June 20, 1998.
4. Nicholas Colchester, "Europe's Internal Market: A Survey," *The Economist*, July 8, 1989, insert, pp. 1–52.
5. Michael R. Hodges, "Britain Tomorrow: Business as Usual," *Current History*, Mar. 1975, p. 138.
6. Charles de Gaulle, *The Call to Honor* (New York: Viking, 1955), p. 38.
7. See Murray Feshbach and Alfred Friendly Jr., *Ecocide in the USSR* (New York: Basic Books, 1992).

Nuclear tests by India and Pakistan in 1998 prompted the launching of this hot–air protest balloon, which sails past the Taj Mahal in Agra, northern India.

The Developing World

The Struggle for Survival

Chapter Contents

The developing world comprises three categories of nation-states: the new countries in Asia and Africa created after 1945 when the old European empires disappeared, the nations of Latin America, and the states emerging from old imperial powers like China that were never fully colonized. During the Cold War the developing world served as an arena for competition between Washington and Moscow; some of its leaders were successful in manipulating that contest to their own advantage, and others were not. In addition to the Cold War, population pressure and economic dependence were major factors in the evolution of developing world nations in the second half of the twentieth century.

In the 1990s the vast majority of the nations of the developing world remained trapped by poverty, overpopulation, and the indifference of the developed world. Less than 8 percent of the world's population lived in areas where per capita GDP exceeded $3000. Two-thirds of the world's population lived in areas classified as developing, producing less than one-sixth of the world's output. Various factors accounted for this widespread backwardness: the dominance of a peasant subsistence economy, the residual effects of colonialism, lack of capital, lack of education, rising fuel prices, inflation, and overpopulation. But some nations once considered "developing" no longer fit that designation. The end of the Cold War has signaled a reconfiguring of economies, governments, allegiances, and identity politics that is still being contested.

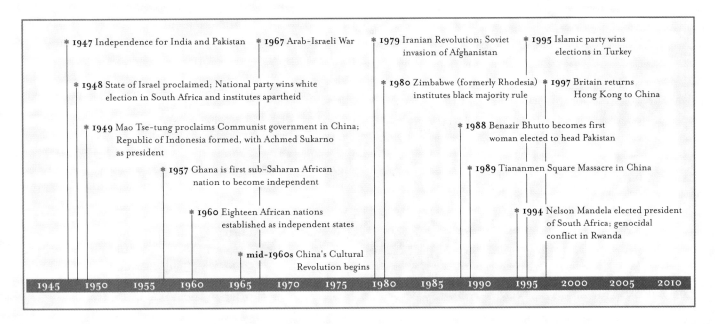

1947 Independence for India and Pakistan

1948 State of Israel proclaimed; National party wins white election in South Africa and institutes apartheid

1949 Mao Tse-tung proclaims Communist government in China; Republic of Indonesia formed, with Achmed Sukarno as president

1957 Ghana is first sub-Saharan African nation to become independent

1960 Eighteen African nations established as independent states

mid-1960s China's Cultural Revolution begins

1967 Arab-Israeli War

1979 Iranian Revolution; Soviet invasion of Afghanistan

1980 Zimbabwe (formerly Rhodesia) institutes black majority rule

1988 Benazir Bhutto becomes first woman elected to head Pakistan

1989 Tiananmen Square Massacre in China

1994 Nelson Mandela elected president of South Africa; genocidal conflict in Rwanda

1995 Islamic party wins elections in Turkey

1997 Britain returns Hong Kong to China

1945　1950　1955　1960　1965　1970　1975　1980　1985　1990　1995　2000　2005　2010

Chinese Revolutions

Between 1927 and 1937 Chiang Kai-shek's Nationalist (Kuomintang) government initiated useful reforms in the cities that, had it not been for Japanese aggression in China, might have expanded to include the rest of the country. But the Nationalists after 1937 lost many of their strongest supporters and most of their prosperous area to Japanese control. By the end of World War II, after eight years of combat, Chiang's government was defeated and worn out. In contrast, the Communists under Mao Tse-tung after the war enjoyed great popularity, control of an area with 90 million people, and a disciplined and loyal army of 500,000.

Civil War in China

Following the victory over Japan, U.S. troops, cooperating with Nationalist forces, recaptured land taken by the Japanese. The Americans helped move Chinese troops to strategic areas such as Manchuria. At the same time, the Soviet Union reclaimed areas formerly controlled by the tsars. During this time Chiang tried unsuccessfully to negotiate a settlement

In 1947, Mao's Communist forces were engaged in a civil war with the Nationalist government's army.

with Mao Tse-tung. In October 1945 heavy fighting broke out between the Nationalist and Communist forces.

For the next three years the United States tried to end the conflict. In December 1945 President Truman defined American policy toward China. The United States regarded the Nationalist regime as the legal government of China; however, because it was a one-party system, it was necessary that full opportunity be given to other groups to participate in a representative government. To that end Truman urged an end to the fighting.

The U.S. Army chief of staff, General George C. Marshall, went to China to implement Truman's policy and to serve as a friendly mediator. Newly appointed as American secretary of state, Marshall returned home in January 1947, his mission a failure. In his final report he blasted extremists on both sides for failing to make peace.

The Communist Victory

Chiang's army—poorly equipped, miserably paid, and suffering low morale—began to disintegrate. The Communists captured city after city, frequently facing only token resistance. Economic problems added to Chiang's military dilemma. The Nationalists had been unable to rebuild the economy after 1945, and inflation soared. The U.S. dollar came to be worth 93,000 Chinese dollars on the black market. Serious riots broke out, and in Shanghai thousands of workers went on strike.

By the end of 1947 the Nationalist forces went into retreat, and in 1948 the Nationalist presence in Manchuria collapsed. The complete defeat of Chiang's armies occurred in 1949 when Mao's "People's Liberation Army" captured the major cities in China. Mao proclaimed the establishment of his government on October 1, 1949, and by the middle of 1950 Mao ruled all of mainland China. Chiang's Nationalists sought refuge on Taiwan, a Chinese island in the South China sea.

Mao and his forces imposed a tightly centralized administration extending to Manchuria, Inner Mongolia, and Chinese Turkestan. In 1950 his armies moved into Tibet. The Peking government continued to seek to regain the traditional holdings of the Central Kingdom, especially the lands gained by Russia during the nineteenth century. Such a policy caused serious problems not only for the Soviet Union but also for Vietnam, Burma, and India.

Mao's policy attracted a large following, calling as it did for a mild program of reform, including the confiscation of large farms, state control of large businesses, protection of small private concerns, rapid industrialization under state control, and increased benefits to labor such as social insurance.

Mao on Communism in China

Mao Tse-tung adapted Marxism to China. After paying tribute to the Soviet Union in a speech delivered in 1949, he stated his goals for the future.

Communists the world over are wiser than the bourgeoisie, they understand the laws governing the existence and development of things, they understand dialectics and they can see farther. The bourgeoisie does not welcome this truth because it does not want to be overthrown.

As everyone knows, our Party passed through these twenty-eight years not in peace but amid hardships, for we had to fight enemies, both foreign and domestic, both inside and outside the Party. We thank Marx, Engels, Lenin and Stalin for giving us a weapon. This weapon is not a machine-gun, but Marxism-Leninism. . . .

The Russians made the October Revolution and created the world's first socialist state. Under the leadership of Lenin and Stalin, the revolutionary energy of the great proletariat and labouring people of Russia, hitherto latent and unseen by foreigners, suddenly erupted like a volcano, and the Chinese and all mankind began to see the Russians in a new light. Then, and only then, did the Chinese enter an entirely new era in their thinking and their life. They found Marxism-Leninism, the universally applicable truth, and the face of China began to change. . . .

There are bourgeois republics in foreign lands, but China cannot have a bourgeois republic because she is a country suffering under imperialist oppression. The only way is through a people's republic led by the working class. . . .

Twenty-four years have passed since Sun Yat-sen's death, and the Chinese revolution, led by the Communist Party of China, has made tremendous advances in both theory and practice and has radically changed the face of China. Up to now the principal and fundamental experience the Chinese people have gained is twofold:

1. Internally, arouse the masses of the people. That is, unite the working class, the peasantry, the urban petty bourgeoisie and the national bourgeoisie, form a domestic united front under the leadership of the working class, and advance from this to the establishment of a state which is a people's democratic dictatorship under the leadership of the working class and based on the alliance of workers and peasants.
2. Externally, unite in a common struggle with those nations of the world which treat us as equals and unite with the peoples of all countries. That is, ally ourselves with the Soviet Union, with the People's Democracies and with the proletariat and the broad masses of the people in all other countries, and form an international united front.

To sum up our experience and concentrate it into one point, it is: the people's democratic dictatorship under the leadership of the working class (through the Communist Party) and based upon the alliance of workers and peasants. This dictatorship must unite as one with the international revolutionary forces. This is our formula, our principal experience, our main programme. . . .

The Communist Party of the Soviet Union is our best teacher and we must learn from it. The situation both at home and abroad is in our favor, we can rely fully on the weapon of the people's democratic dictatorship, unite the people throughout the country, the reactionaries excepted, and advance steadily to our goal.

From Mao Tse-tung, "In Commemoration of the 28th Anniversary of the Communist Party of China, June 30, 1949," in *Selected Works*, Vol. 5 (New York: International Publishers, n.d.), pp. 411–423.

The government that eventually appeared, however, was far more fierce and totalitarian than the reforms might indicate.

Right-wing Americans, influenced by the anti-Communist demagoguery of Wisconsin Senator Joseph McCarthy, charged that liberals and "fellow travelers" (anyone who espoused social aims similar to the Communists') had lost China.[1] U.S. American military aid to China during World War II totaled $845 million; from 1945 to 1949 it came to slightly more than $2 billion. It is extremely doubtful whether additional American military aid to China would have changed the final outcome of the civil war. The bulk of the Nationalist forces had lost the will to fight. Large quantities of American arms sent to Chiang's army were turned over to the Communists by apathetic Nationalist leaders.

Mao's Government

After 1949 Mao used his version of Marxism to change the whole order of Chinese society from its traditional patterns. Tolerating no opposition, he concentrated all power in the Communist party, which was led by the party's Central Committee. This group held all major civil and military positions. The day-to-day work of the Central Committee fell to a smaller Politburo, headed by Mao, the chairman of the republic.

The new government brought both inflation and corruption under control and then began to apply the Soviet model of the 1930s to China. Since more than 70 percent of farmland was owned by 10 percent of the landlords, the government proceeded to confiscate large holdings and redistribute them, temporarily, to landless peasants. Late in 1953 the party stripped the large landowners and even prosperous peasants of their holdings, executing an estimated 2 to 5 million of them in the process. The party then established huge farm collectives. Within three years nearly all peasants had become members of rural collectives in which, although individual land ownership was retained in theory, all labor, farm equipment, and land were pooled.

A Soviet-style five-year plan for economic development in industry was initiated in 1953. The Chinese made impressive advances in heavy industry, and the success of the first plan led to a second five-year plan, which Mao dubbed the Great Leap Forward. The Chinese built on their own experience, rejecting parts of the Soviet model. They launched the Great Leap Forward with a huge propaganda campaign and galvanized millions of urban and rural workers into a frenzied effort to increase tremendously the production of steel, electricity, and coal. Thousands of small backyard furnaces sprang up to produce steel. The Chinese boldly predicted that they would surpass British industrial capacity in 15 years.

In the countryside Mao installed "people's communes." The state created some 26,000 of these units, each averaging 5000 households, or about 25,000 people. The heads of the communes collected taxes and ran schools, child care centers, dormitories, communal kitchens, and even cemeteries in a massive social experiment. Mao tried to convert peasants into a rural proletariat paid in wages. Until the late 1970s all land, dwellings, and livestock reverted to the effective ownership of the communes. During the two decades in which the people's communes functioned, they helped produce improvements in medical care and literacy.

The Great Leap Forward ultimately proved disastrous for China. Central planners erred in allocating resources and capital, and farm production fell. The steel and iron produced in the backyard furnaces turned out to be unusable. At the same time that the Great Leap was failing, the Soviet Union withdrew its technological and financial support. From 1959 to 1961 Chinese industry lacked essential raw materials, and millions of people went without adequate food. Between 1960 and 1962 a combination of bad weather and chaos bequeathed by the failure of the Great Leap resulted in malnutrition and the premature death of between 16 and 30 million people.

Faced with this crisis, the government radically changed its economic policy. In the communes social experimentation and centralized control were relaxed. Working conditions were improved, and private plots in which peasants were allowed to keep or sell the crops and animals they raised were used as incentives to increase agricultural production. Between 1961 and 1964 industry also recovered, and the discovery of petroleum provided new energy sources. China made advances in light industry, espe-

Celebrating the first anniversary of Mao's government in 1950, Chinese workers march through the streets of Peking carrying giant placards depicting their leader.

cially in consumer goods and cotton production. Signs of technological progress included the detonation of a nuclear device in 1964 and of a hydrogen bomb in 1967.

The Cultural Revolution and After

By the early 1960s an ideological schism widened between Mao and some of his longtime comrades. Moderates advocated gradual social change and economic development, while radicals sought to pursue the drastic restructuring of Chinese society. Mao believed, or so it seemed, that many in the party had lost their revolutionary zeal.

In the mid-1960s Mao mobilized the Red Guards, a radical student militia. They attacked the moderates and forced Maoist orthodoxy on party members and populace alike. In all areas, from surgery to nuclear physics and beyond, Mao's words were law. Application of the great leader's wisdom, as contained in the "Little Red Book," *Quotations from Chairman Mao,* was to lead to miraculous achievements. Placing political purity above economic growth, the Red Guards hampered production and research. Their rallies and demonstrations disrupted the entire educational system.

The effects of this so-called Cultural Revolution were dire. By 1967 industrial production had plummeted and basic education and research had ceased; some areas of the country were approaching anarchy. Into this void stepped the People's Liberation Army (PLA), the most important element in Chinese politics until 1985. The PLA brought the Red Guards under control, restored order, and put an end to the excesses of the Cultural Revolution.

Mao's longtime associate, Premier Chou En-lai (1898–1976), restored the country's industrial productivity. The return to political stability was more difficult, but Chou managed to hold the country together while rival factions intrigued for power. Chou removed China from the diplomatic isolation in which it had resided since 1958. He responded to a diplomatic initiative made by the Nixon administration in 1971 and moved closer to the United States, motivated perhaps by the armed border clashes with the Soviet Union that had begun to occur along the Amur River. In addition, China sought to develop its industrial capacity through the use of foreign technology and to bring in foreign currency through both an expanded banking system based in the British crown colony of Hong Kong and the development of a tourist industry.

China Since 1976

After Chou and Mao died in 1976, politicians jockeyed for control with varying intensity. Leading the most militant faction, known as the Gang of Four,

was Mao's widow, Chiang Ching, who was overthrown, disgraced, and brought to a televised show trial in 1980. Her demise paved the way for the advent of a more moderate, pragmatic group of officials led by Deng Xiaoping.

Deng was a political survivor whose roots in the party went back to the 1920s. He endured political exile and the Cultural Revolution to introduce his variant of reform Marxism, in which the party kept control of the "commanding heights" of the economy. Aided by his liberal chief lieutenants, Hu Yaobang and Zhao Ziyang, Deng introduced a pragmatic series of economic reforms.

The first major move to introduce a more market-oriented economy came in the countryside in 1978. The party allowed greater personal profit for the peasants, and this resulted in a vast increase in productivity. China had a grain surplus in six of the next seven years. With an increased food supply and a contented peasantry, Deng in 1985 encouraged the introduction of the free market economy in the cities, with the goal of gaining similar economic gains there. To foster the rapid transformation of the underdeveloped country, Deng permitted the entry of Western experts and technology. Western, especially American, influence grew in the cities in China

During the Cultural Revolution, members of the Red Guard display for public humiliation several Chinese students wearing dunce caps. The Guard denounced the students as leaders of "antirevolutionary" groups.

during the 1980s, along with foreign trade and an influx of other foreigners.

The government continued to keep the cost of medicine low and supplemented wages with accident insurance, medical coverage, day care centers, and maternity benefits. The standard of living in China improved, but the removal of price controls on food and other staple items led to inflation. Even with economic progress, the standard of living in China remained far below the standards in industrialized countries.

The educational system changed drastically under the Communists. In the 1930s only 20 percent of the people had been literate. By the end of the 1980s the figure had risen to 75 percent. Across China a crash program of schooling was initiated, and "spare-time" schools with work-study programs for those unable to attend school full time were established. Thousands of Chinese students emigrated abroad to study, including some 40,000 to the United States.

Deng had worked for the economic liberalization of his country but failed to sponsor similar reform on the political front. Students were the first to express discontent with inflation and corruption in China. In the spring of 1989 students across China demonstrated in honor of the liberal politician Hu Yaobang, who had died in March. The demonstrators went on to criticize Deng's government. The protest reached a climax in May and June when thousands of demonstrators calling for democracy occupied the ceremonial center of modern China, Tiananmen Square in Peking.

The party split over how to deal with the protesters and their supporters, sometimes numbering a million strong. Zhao advocated accommodation, but the hard-line prime minister, Li Peng, called for a crackdown. While the debate went on within the party, the students erected a tall replica of the Statue of Liberty to symbolize their demands for democracy and an end to corruption. By the end of May the students had won the enthusiastic support of the workers and citizens of Peking, Shanghai, and Chengdu. Finally, the party decided what to do about the protesters. In June the People's Liberation Army, using tanks and machine guns, cleared the square and the surrounding area of the student demonstrators. More than 3000 people were killed in the massacre.

By 1990 it was apparent that China would not retreat into another period of diplomatic isolation. Deng had integrated his country too firmly into the world economy for that. Chinese leaders worked skillfully to maintain their commercial relations and to regain two traditionally Chinese areas, Taiwan and Hong Kong, both thriving capitalistic outposts, to help their struggling economy.

The leaders in Peking had already worked out with the British how Chinese authority over Hong Kong would be restored when its lease to Great Britain ran out in 1997. Another major potential source of economic strength lay across the Straits of Formosa in Taiwan, where Chiang and the remnant of his Nationalist forces had fled in 1949. For the next quarter century the United States recognized the Taiwan government, headquartered in Taipei, as the legitimate government of all of China. By 1992 Taiwan's gross national product had reached $210.5 billion, and its 21 million people had an average annual per

A Peking citizen faces down a convoy of tanks rolling down the Avenue of Eternal Peace during the prodemocracy demonstrations in Tiananmen Square in June 1989.

capita income of close to $9300. Mainland China, in contrast, had an estimated GNP of $600 billion and a per capita income of $560 for its 1.15 billion people.

During the 1990s China's export trade expanded dramatically, and foreign economic interests increased their activities in China. Economic ties between the Chinese and the United States grew to such an extent that President Clinton was forced to overlook human rights abuses when he renewed most-favored-nation trading status to China in 1994. Inflationary pressures resulting from rapid economic growth threatened to create major social problems for the Chinese Communist leadership. At the same time, the Chinese continued to construct enterprise zones along the coast in which the most modern technology was used by Chinese businesses working closely with world banking and commercial interests for joint profits.

Somewhat surprisingly, the Communist party remained popular and ever stronger, counting around 52 million members in 1992, even though fewer than 10 percent of those applying for party membership were admitted. When Deng Xiaoping died in 1997, China weathered the transition in leadership and now is poised to become a true world power in the twenty-first century.

On China's periphery, the "Four Tigers"—South Korea, Taiwan, Singapore, and Hong Kong—continued their phenomenal growth. Not only had they successfully competed with Japan in a wide range of high-tech products and automobiles, but they were erecting financial institutions that challenged Japanese banks and investment firms. The Tigers knew, however, that they could not rest on their laurels. China's increasingly aggressive commercial sector and the entry of Indonesia, Malaysia, and India as competitors have made the Pacific Rim a most active arena for business in the final decade of the twentieth century, despite a late 1990s downturn.

Southeast Asia

One of the first indications that the whole structure of European imperialism would quickly collapse came in the late 1940s when Indonesian nationalists demanded a complete break with the Netherlands. An ugly war ensued, and finally in 1949, through UN mediation, the Netherlands East Indies formally became the Republic of Indonesia, achieving nationhood at roughly the same time as the states of India and Israel. Although it is the biggest and potentially richest nation in Southeast Asia, Indonesia has enjoyed little tranquillity since it gained independence.

The state is 87 percent Muslim but encompasses a mixture of many cultures on more than 3000 islands, ranging from Stone Age people to urban pro-

fessionals and intellectuals. Complicating the situation is the prominence of the Chinese minority. Chinese Indonesians, making up less than 3 percent of Indonesia's more than 200 million people, control two-thirds of the nation's economy. Anti-Chinese riots and plots against the central government in Java have arisen in various places.

For the first 15 years after independence, Indonesia experienced declining exports, inflation, and food shortages. Its population increased while its economy declined. A large portion of the blame for this situation rested with Indonesia's flamboyant president Achmed Sukarno. He contracted huge Russian loans for arms, fought a costly guerrilla campaign against Malaysia, confiscated foreign businesses, and wasted money on expensive, flashy enterprises. Sukarno had come to power as a prominent leader in the preindependence nationalist movement. After experimenting with "guided democracy" in the 1950s, he assumed dictatorial power in 1959 and declared himself president for life in 1963.

Muslim students in Indonesia triggered the events that led to Sukarno's downfall. After an attempted Communist coup in 1965, they launched attacks on Indonesians they believed to have Communist connections. The Chinese minority was targeted, and 500,000 to 750,000 people were executed or killed during several months of lawlessness. The army's chief of staff, General T. N. J. Suharto, who put down the coup, became effective head of state and in March 1968 officially became president.

Suharto installed a more Western-oriented government initially, and in return received substantial American aid for the country. He rehabilitated the Indonesian economy and developed highly successful literacy programs. But over the next 25 years Suharto's military regime engaged in several violent incidents. In 1971 and again in 1974 there were serious racial outbursts during which thousands of students went on rampages, looting and damaging Chinese shops and homes. The Indonesians invaded East Timor, the Portuguese half of one of the islands, in 1975 and initiated a savage occupation that led to the death of over 200,000 people. During the 1970s some 30,000 political dissidents were imprisoned, while rampant corruption dominated government, the civil service, and business. Enormous wealth remained concentrated in the hands of a very few individuals.

The end of Suharto's regime was strangely reminiscent of its beginning. Indonesia shared in a radical slowdown of East Asian economies beginning in 1997. As economic discontent simmered, mass demonstrations of Indonesian students turned violent. The students demanded democratization, an end to government corruption, new elections, and the ouster of Suharto. As in the earlier crises, violence was both random and directed at

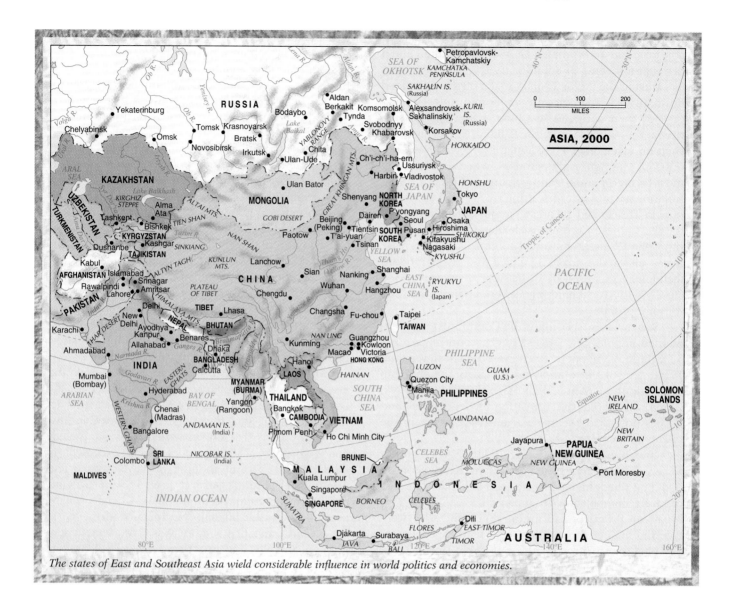

The states of East and Southeast Asia wield considerable influence in world politics and economies.

the economically privileged Chinese minority. Terrified shopkeepers painted notices on the fronts of their buildings saying they were "good Muslims" or Hindus—in other words, not Chinese. In 1998, in the midst of mass protests and widespread looting and burning, Suharto was forced to step down. The Indonesian students celebrated his resignation as a victory over autocracy, but what coalition of forces will replace the cadre in power during Suharto's 32-year rule remains undetermined.

Created out of former British holdings, the Federation of Malaysia was admitted into the British Commonwealth in 1957. In 1963 it became independent and immediately faced Sukarno-sponsored guerrilla attacks. As in Indonesia, a major problem in Malaysia was the country's racial mix and the resulting hostilities. The majority of the population is Malay and Muslim, but the mainly Buddhist Chinese hold the majority of the wealth, and what they do not control is owned largely by the small Hindu Indian

minority. In the late 1960s and early 1970s Malays attacked the other two groups, and ethnoreligious conflicts continue to plague the region.

One of the richest areas in Southeast Asia after the war was Singapore, a city-state roughly three times the size of Washington, D.C. Singapore withdrew from the Federation of Malaysia and declared its independence in August 1965 and after that was dominated by the People's Action party, run by Lee Kuan Yew. Taking advantage of its superb location on the Straits of Malacca, Singapore became one of the richest places in the world. At the end of the 1980s its 2.5 million people generated a GNP of more than $29 billion. What Lee Kuan Yew did not provide in terms of unfettered civil rights—including prohibitions on the sale of chewing gum—he more than made up for in the efficiency and stability of his rule. His successor, Goh Chok Tong, who came to power in 1990, has built on Lee Kuan Yew's policies. In recent years several criminal cases involving foreign nationals have made Singapore the center of a debate over state-enforced order versus individual freedom.

Southeast Asia provides a window on the ways in which ethnoreligious conflicts will play out in the twenty-first century. Like many states in South Asia, the Middle East, and Africa, its newly independent nations are still working out the dynamics of democratic versus authoritarian rule in the contexts of rapidly changing economics and ethnoreligious tensions of long standing. Indonesia alone has the fourth largest population in the world, and most of the world's Muslims live in Southeast Asia, not the Middle East. Thus as in India, religious nationalism is likely to remain a significant and enduring factor in the evolution of Indonesian society.

The Subcontinent

In the Indian subcontinent, the western thrust of the Japanese armies in World War II induced the British government to make substantial concessions to Indian nationalist leaders. In 1942 Britain offered India independence and the option of joining the British Commonwealth when the war ended. During and immediately after the war, tensions between the Muslim and Hindu populations in India, which had been compounded by the British administration, were inflamed. The minority Muslim population was fearful that when the British withdrew, it would be targeted and dominated by the Hindu majority.

Partition

When World War II ended and it became apparent that the British would indeed leave India, the shape the new state would take was vigorously contested. The Indian National Congress, founded in 1885 and the primary Indian nationalist organization, had had great success in the 1936–1937 elections and took the lead in negotiations for independence with the British government. Congress included many Muslim members, but in the late 1930s the Muslim League, guided by onetime Congress member Muhammad Ali Jinnah, began to agitate vigorously for a separate Muslim state. Muslims constituted one-fifth of the population of the subcontinent, and many Muslims feared majority Hindu rule. Gandhi had envisioned an independent India where all communal groups shared in governance and lived in harmony. But India had a long history of ethnic hostilities dating to the violence of the medieval Muslim invasions and exacerbated by centuries of Mughul Muslim rule.

This religious animosity and mistrust; the presence of armed, demobilized soldiers in the countryside; and the insecurity produced by negotiations

over the future nature of the Indian state resulted in communal violence and chaos in some provinces. Lord Mountbatten arrived in India as British viceroy in March 1947 and promptly determined that the date for British withdrawal should be moved up. Although the Muslim League's demand for a separate state called Pakistan did not represent the wishes of all Muslims, Mountbatten was persuaded that India must be partitioned along religious lines. Accordingly, when the British withdrew, they handed over the reins of government to two new sovereign states, India and Pakistan, on August 12, 1947. The new Pakistan consisted, awkwardly, of two chunks of land separated by 1000 miles of Indian territory. Although Jinnah was not satisfied with the land allocated to the new Muslim state, he had little choice but to accept the British division. As it turned out, however, the borders drawn in 1947 would not be final.

Defining the boundaries of the new states was not easily accomplished. For one thing, the British had not directly ruled all of India. Nearly 600 Indian princes were governing about 40 percent of the subcontinent in autonomous or semiautonomous states. These principalities had to be incorporated into the new political entities. The boundary lines of the two new nations, which took months to formalize, also sacrificed existing economic, ethnic, and linguistic affinities in order to ensure religious divisions. Partition radically disrupted commerce, social relations, and people's day-to-day lives.

As the boundaries were drawn, many Indians, fearful of discrimination and communal violence, left their homes: Muslims to migrate or flee to Pakistan and Hindus to the new state of India. Millions became refugees. Hundreds of thousands died in the relocation process or in the riots, killings, and panic produced by the hastily imposed partition. This terrible slaughter is engraved in the memories of the citizens of the two nations and has contributed to the continuation of communal violence. The state of Kashmir, which had an overwhelmingly Muslim population but a Hindu ruler, was attached to India and has been a point of contention between India and Pakistan ever since.

India: The Largest Democracy

Of the long list of states that became independent after 1945, few have retained genuine liberal regimes. Until 1975 the sole outstanding example was India, the world's largest democratically governed state. In its first half century of independence India's government was dominated by the Congress party, which had in turn emerged out of the nationalist struggle in the context of British rule. But as the fledgling nation established itself, new indigenous forces began to percolate to the top, expressing a certain unease with

India After Independence

1947	Independence from Britain
1947–1964	Jawaharlal Nehru prime minister
1966	Indira Gandhi, Nehru's daughter, becomes prime minister
1971	India defeats Pakistan; Bangladesh formed
1975	Indira Gandhi declares emergency, assumes dictatorial powers
1977	Moraji Desai prime minister
1979	Indira Gandhi reelected
1984	Gandhi assassinated; son Rajiv succeeds her
1991	Rajiv Gandhi assassinated
1998	Bharatiya Janata, Hindu nationalist party, wins elections

Western- and British-style government and those who endorsed it. Especially from the late 1970s onward, separatist movements also challenged the notion of Indian unity, posing the threat of a new partition.

After independence, India's parliament functioned with little friction. This success was due to the efforts of a cadre of very skilled and capable men in the Congress party. One of them was Jawaharlal Nehru, the country's first prime minister, who held that office from 1947 to 1964 and was an Anglophile of sorts and an ardent devotee of democratic government. Nehru asserted the power of strong central government while trying to manage the decentralizing tendencies of his large, polyglot, multiethnic state. He sought to maintain close relations with both the Soviet Union and China, often to the discomfort of the United States. Relations with China, however, were compromised by a border conflict that led to a major military action in the first part of the 1960s and acted as a drain on India's economy. Nehru, along with Egypt's President Nasser, was a founder of the Non-Aligned Nations Movement, which aimed to avoid commitment to either the United States or the Soviet Union in the context of the Cold War.

Nehru's daughter, Indira Gandhi (no relation to Mohandas Gandhi), was elected prime minister in 1966. She proved to be less malleable than Congress leaders had expected and moved to consolidate her power and achieve a new political stability for India. Her popularity reached a peak with the defeat of Pak-

istan in a 1971 war that led to the creation of the country of Bangladesh. In 1972–1974, however, India's mildly socialist economy was battered by serious crop failures, food riots, strikes, and student unrest. In the face of mounting opposition, and claiming to act in defense of national unity, Gandhi declared a state of emergency in June 1975 and took over direct control of the government. She jailed 10,000 of her critics, imposed press censorship, and suspended fundamental civil rights.

With the opposition muzzled, the people were exhorted to "work more and talk less." After a year the new order claimed numerous gains, advances in productivity, a drop in inflation, curbs in the black market, and more widespread birth control measures to alleviate India's population pressures. Although Gandhi declared that her drastic measures were only temporary, some critics observed that she was trying to move "from dictatorship to dynasty."

In 1977 Gandhi released political prisoners and announced that national elections would be held. But many Indians had been alienated by her draconian policies, which included forced sterilizations for birth control and the bulldozing of some of the Delhi slums. A coalition of opposition parties defeated Gandhi in the elections and brought Moraji Desai to the prime ministry. Democratic freedoms were restored, but the coalition failed to hold together, and Indian voters returned Gandhi to power in 1979. She promised the country strong leadership, with no more "excesses." For the next four years she pursued a neutral course, reflecting the geopolitical position in which India found itself. India's close ties with the USSR served as a defensive shield against China. The Soviet invasion of Afghanistan constituted an indirect threat to India, but Gandhi refrained from criticizing the action.

Although India achieved a certain economic success and political prominence under Indira Gandhi, it also faced serious ethnic and communal conflicts. In the south and in Sri Lanka the culturally distinct Tamils agitated for independence. In the north the religiously and linguistically distinct Sikhs, who constitute a majority in the state of Punjab, also entertained separatist aspirations.

The Sikh religion dates to the early sixteenth century when the mystic Nanak founded a monotheistic creed that was influenced by both Hinduism and Islam. The Sikhs, whose territories were divided in the 1947 partition, had a golden temple in their sacred city of Amritsar. When Sikh extremists took over and occupied the temple in 1984, Gandhi sent in the army to blast them out. This reckless act was considered a desecration of the Sikh temple and led to an explosion of rioting and violence. In October of that year Gandhi was assassinated by members of her Sikh bodyguard.

Indira Gandhi was succeeded by her son Rajiv, a former pilot and political novice who soon showed a surprising degree of confidence and competence in governing the world's largest democracy, with more than 800 million citizens. Rajiv consolidated his political position and moved India toward a more Westernized, capitalist orientation. Still, the country's widespread poverty and internal divisions, especially the long-standing Kashmir border dispute with Pakistan and the continued challenges of Sikh and Tamil separatism, posed significant problems for Gandhi's administration. He was defeated in elections at the end of 1989 and replaced by V. P. Singh of the National Front party, which proved unable to consolidate its power. In 1991 new elections returned the Congress party to power, but not before Rajiv Gandhi was assassinated by a Tamil separatist.

After independence the Indian government pursued Mohandas Gandhi's ideal of self-sufficiency. It insisted on indigenous control of the economy and emphasized developing the production of consumer goods at home rather than relying on imports. It demanded 51 percent Indian control of foreign companies on its soil, even refusing to let the Coca-Cola Company operate in India unless it shared its secret formula. In these efforts India was relatively successful, developing many locally produced goods. During the first half of the 1990s, however, Indian leaders abandoned many of the socialist foundations of their economic structure and introduced various aspects of the capitalist market economy. Analysts had pointed out during the 1980s that India possessed the largest essentially untapped middle-class market in the world. With the entry of market forces into the country, the Indian economy expanded. The countryside had gained self-sufficiency in the 1970s and 1980s. Now it was the turn of the cities and the business community to become major players in the international economy.

In 1995 P. V. Narasimha Rao was the only prime minister not in the bloodline of the Nehru-Gandhi dynasty to have lasted through the first half of a parliamentary term. Working with his finance minister, Manmohan Singh, and enjoying the total support of the business community, he continued to pursue market reforms. India's economy continued to grow under the changes in the central government in the 1990s.

But the communal hostilities inflamed by partition have not ended half a century after independence. The constitution of India aimed to make all citizens equal before the law. But caste and communal differences were not so readily eradicated. Upper-caste Hindus resisted privileges given by the government to the members of the Untouchable caste. In response, the Untouchables, taking the name *Dalits*, meaning "the oppressed," organized politically. In the 1980s Hindu parties mobilized to make India an indelibly Hindu state.

Hindu-Muslim tensions crystallized around a sixteenth century mosque at Ayodhya, which is said to be the birthplace of the Hindu Lord Ram. Stirred by Hindu nationalist politicians, Hindu militants tore the mosque down by hand in 1992, prompting further intercommunal violence. In the 1996 elections the Hindu nationalist Bharatiya Janata party (BJP), representing business and entrepreneurial interests, won 186 seats in parliament, up from only two seats

Hindu militants attack the mosque at Ayodhya, which became a symbol of Hindu-Muslim conflict in India.

in 1984. In 1998 the BJP won the Indian elections, prompting new fears that Muslims, Sikhs, and other minorities will suffer under Hindu rule. Shortly after coming to power the BJP enhanced its popularity among Indians and sent a message of warning to China and Pakistan when it set off a series of nuclear bomb tests. In so doing India allienated its Western allies but staked its claim as a major power for the next century. India presents a continuing paradox of democratic rule, economic development, and a society polarized by caste and communal politics.

Pakistan

Pakistan's two distant parts had religion in common but not language or culture. When Jinnah, the primary voice for the creation of Pakistan and its constitutional government, died in 1948, the artificially constructed state splintered as each region pursued its own local agenda. Meanwhile Pakistan had to contend with challenges on its borders with India and Afghanistan. In a broader frame, Pakistan joined U.S.-backed alliances to contain the Soviet Union and in return benefited from U.S. aid.

In 1958 General Mohammad Ayub Khan came to power. His regime gave Pakistan reasonable stability and some relief from corrupt politicians, and under his tutelage the country made economic progress. Ten years later, however, pent-up dissatisfaction against corruption in the government led to a new military dictatorship under General Yahya Khan. Regionalism continued to be a major problem. The more prosperous West Pakistan dominated and ex-

ploited East Pakistan, and the East's grievances escalated into riots and threats of secession.

The Pakistani government sent troops into East Pakistan in 1971 in response to an uprising. This attack and the depredations committed by the troops caused an influx of East Pakistani refugees into India. India intervened on behalf of East Pakistan, defeating the central government's forces and encouraging the region to break away. In 1972 East Pakistan became the new state of Bangladesh. Bangladesh, covering an area not much larger than the state of Arkansas, was an instantaneous economic disaster with twice the population density of Japan. The Bangladeshi population in 1990 was 121 million (half the population of the United States), while the per capita GNP was a mere $155. Like Indonesia, Bangladesh is home to a significant percentage of the world's Muslims; the number of Bangladeshi pilgrims journeying to Mecca every year is second only to the number of Indonesians.

A civilian government was reestablished in Pakistan, led by Zulkifar Ali Bhutto (1928–1979), a populist leader who had been educated at universities in Oxford and Berkeley. Throughout the 1970s Pakistan's economic problems persisted, along with its domestic instability. Bhutto, overthrown in 1977 by General Mohammad Zia ul-Haq, was executed in 1979. The new military dictator, who faced widespread opposition, invoked martial law and postponed elections. Like his predecessors, he had to contend with both Indian hostility and potential Soviet intervention. Pakistan retained its traditional alignment with China, while India kept close ties with Moscow.

Supporters hold a picture of Benazir Bhutto, who became the first woman to lead a Muslim nation when she was elected prime minister of Pakistan in 1988. In the October 1993 elections Bhutto and her Pakistan People's party defeated the incumbent prime minister, Nawaz Sharif, and the Pakistani Muslim League.

In 1979 the Iranian Revolution and the Soviet invasion of Afghanistan enhanced the importance of Pakistan's Cold War alliance with the West. Meanwhile a contingent of 36 Islamic foreign ministers meeting in Pakistan condemned the Soviet aggression against the Afghan people. In 1981 a substantial American aid agreement was negotiated, providing for $3.2 billion in arms over a period of six years. Pakistan thereafter served as the American support base for the Afghan resistance.

In 1985 Zia ul-Haq lifted martial law; he was killed in 1988. Bhutto's daughter Benazir, the first woman elected to govern a Muslim nation, succeeded him at the age of 35. She remained in office 20 months until, under pressure from the army, she was dismissed after accusations of incompetence and corruption. She returned to prominence in the early 1990s and serves as an example of both the power of political dynasties in South Asia and the ability of well-placed Muslim women to hold positions of great power.

Like India, Pakistan continues to grapple with the problems of high population growth and uneven economic development. Relations between India and Pakistan remain tense, especially over the issue of Kashmir. In 1998 India asserted its sovereignty and defied Western nations by conducting nuclear tests. Pakistan replied shortly thereafter by exploding its own nuclear bombs, claiming that it had no choice in the face of the Indian nuclear threat. While the United Nations and established nuclear powers like the United States condemned these tests as the beginning of another nuclear arms race, citizens of Pakistan and India celebrated their respective states' tests as symbols of national power and autonomy.

The Middle East

Four major factors conditioned the evolution of the Middle East in the second half of the twentieth century: decolonization, the creation of the state of Israel, the exploitation of oil resources, and the Cold War. Toward the end of the century a fifth element, the growing popularity of Islamist factions (political groups advocating Islamic government), has challenged the established secular governments of Middle Eastern nations.

Decolonization was a gradual process. Although some of the Arab states were granted independence in the interwar period, the mandate powers, Britain and France, retained a significant military and economic presence. During World War II England reoccupied Iraq and used Egypt as a staging ground for its war effort. Only in the generation after the war did all the nation-states of the Middle East truly gain

their independence. In the meantime the arrival of European Jews seeking refuge in the area after the war, Zionist mobilization (which aimed at the establishment of a Jewish state in Palestine), and Great Power political pressure led to the creation of the state of Israel in 1948. This touched off a bitter conflict between the new state and its Arab neighbors, who viewed Israel as a symbol of continued European imperialism in the region. Israel's creation provided a homeland for Jews brutalized by the Holocaust, but it produced an immediate refugee problem as thousands of Palestinian residents fled or were driven from their homes. It also produced the dilemma of how a Westernized state with a significant Muslim and Christian population could also be a Jewish state. Israel was and remains one of the most significant factors in Middle East politics in the twentieth century.

Short years after the creation of Israel, Colonel Gamal Abdel Nasser of Egypt helped lead the revolution that overthrew King Faruq in 1952, made Egypt a republic in 1953, and ended British control over the Suez Canal. Nasser became a hero of Arab nationalism and of the Non-Aligned Nations movement in the context of the Cold War, playing the United States and the Soviet Union against each other. He envisioned Egypt becoming a dominant power in the Arab world, the Muslim world, and Africa; but many of his ambitious modernizing schemes failed, as did his attempt to merge Egypt and Syria into one Arab state. Egypt and Israel formed the two poles around which the Arab-Israeli conflict was to revolve in the decades to come.

The Arab-Israeli Conflict

In 1947, plagued by Zionist terror tactics, Britain referred the question of the mandate for Palestine to the United Nations. The resulting partition plan, which gave most of the territory of Palestine to the Jews, was rejected by the Arab League. As with its precipitous withdrawal from India about the same time, Britain responded to the deteriorating situation in Palestine by announcing the end of the mandate. In the ensuing chaos and civil war, the armed and well-organized Zionist community seized Palestine and proclaimed the independent state of Israel in May 1948.

Conscious of its hostile surroundings, the fledgling Israeli state took steps to become militarily, economically, and politically strong. The success of those efforts became quite evident in 1956 when Nasser nationalized the Suez Canal. As allies of the British and French, the Israelis retaliated and overwhelmed the Egyptians in a war for control of the canal. International pressure applied by the United States, the USSR, and the United Nations forced the

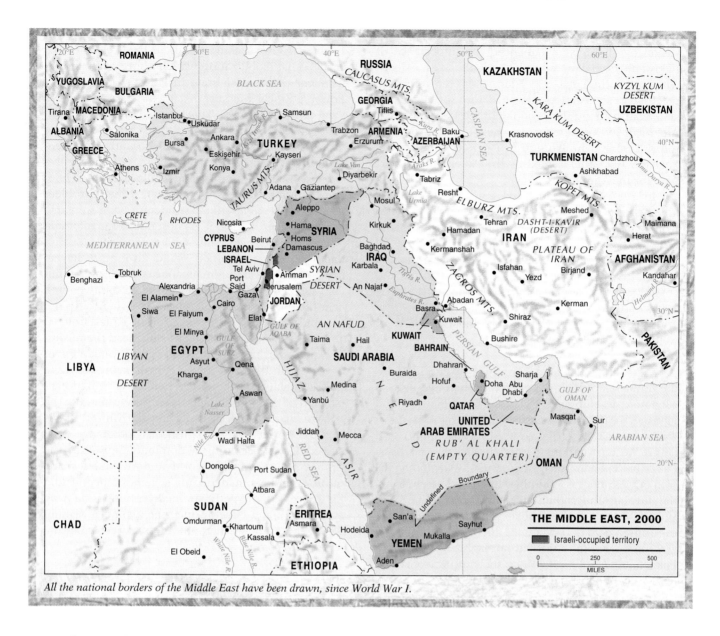

THE MIDDLE EAST, 2000

Israeli-occupied territory

All the national borders of the Middle East have been drawn, since World War I.

Israelis to withdraw from their territorial gains. But Israel's joining the old colonial powers was a slap in the face to the Arab states still smarting from their failure to prevent Israeli statehood in 1948.

The conclusion of this crisis brought only a temporary reprieve from hostilities. In the next decade the issues of Palestinian rights, the existence of the state of Israel, and free access to the Suez Canal monopolized the attention of foreign policy makers in the region, as well as in Moscow and Washington. Nasser sought a military solution to the Arab-Israeli conflict in 1967 by mobilizing his forces and those of the Arab states surrounding Israel, requesting the withdrawal of UN peacekeeping forces, and blockading the Gulf of Aqaba, Israel's access to the Red Sea. Israel retaliated, and within 72 hours Israel had completely overwhelmed and humiliated Nasser and his Arab allies. When a cease-fire was arranged after only six days of fighting, Israel occupied the Sinai penin-

sula, including the east bank of the Suez Canal, East Jerusalem, the West Bank of the Jordan River, and the tactically important Golan Heights inside Syria.

Meanwhile, the Palestinians, disillusioned by the failure of the Arab states to liberate Palestine, began to mobilize to fight Israel on their own. The Palestine Liberation Organization (PLO) was founded in 1964. A secular umbrella organization aiming to establish an independent Palestine, it rejected the idea of an Israeli state. The PLO was given great impetus by the Six-Day War, a triumph for Israel but a disaster for the Palestinians. The conquest of the occupied territories created new waves of refugees and made the Israelis masters over a large and unwilling population. Now Israel had three types of residents: Jewish citizens, Palestinian citizens (Muslim and Christian) with second-class citizenship status, and individuals under military occupation who had no citizen's rights.

The Arab-Israeli Conflict

1948   State of Israel proclaimed; Arab states attack

1956   Israel joins Britain and France in war on
        Egypt for control of Suez Canal

1964   Palestine Liberation Organization (PLO)
        founded

1967   Israel wins Arab-Israeli war (Six-Day War),
        occupies conquered territories; U.N. Resolu-
        tion 242

1973   Egypt and Syria attack Israel (Yom Kippur
        War)

1977   Egyptian president Anwar Sadat talks peace
        in Jerusalem

1978   Camp David Accords

1982   Israel invades Lebanon

1993   Israel and Palestinians negotiate limited au-
        tonomy for the Palestinians

The UN responded to the 1967 war with Resolu-tion 242, which recognized Israel's right to exist but ordered the return of the occupied territories. Argu-ing both that they were essential for the defense of Is-rael and that they constituted part of the Promised Land, the Israelis refused to give up the territories and launched a program of Jewish settlements de-signed to make the newly conquered lands indelibly Jewish. These territories thus became the focal point of an ongoing struggle between Israel, the Palestini-ans, and the surrounding Arab states. The Arab states each pursued their own national agendas and Cold War alliances, but they were united in their opposi-tion to Israel.

As in 1967, a new round of hostilities was pre-ceded by a period of rising tension, characterized by attacks by Arab guerrillas and Israeli counterattacks. The Soviet Union was a major supplier of arms, aid, and technicians to the Arabs. The United States pro-vided arms and aid to some Arab states but commit-ted itself to the existence of Israel, investing billions of dollars a year in aid. That support was a reflection of American perceptions that Israel, as a "Western" state founded by European immigrants, was a nat-ural ally; but it also reflected the support of many Americans for Judeo-Christian tradition and biblical promises of a return to Zion.

Realizing the danger of a Soviet-American con-frontation in the Middle East should a new round of war explode, Britain, France, the United States, and

the USSR explored ways to bring the contending par-ties to agreement. Acceptance of a cease-fire in the summer of 1970 gave some hope for a settlement, but the situation deteriorated a few months later when Israel charged Egypt with cease-fire violations and Nasser died suddenly. On October 6, 1973, the Jewish holy day of Yom Kippur, the Egyptians and Syrians launched a coordinated attack on Israel. For the first few days the Arabs held the initiative, but Israeli forces counterattacked, crossing the Suez Canal into Egypt and driving to within 25 miles of Damascus, the capital of Syria. In some of the most concen-trated armored combat since World War II, 1800 tanks and 200 aircraft were destroyed.

During the fighting the United States organized a large airlift of arms to Israel, and the Soviets re-sponded with troop movements. Soviet and American leaders averted a possible showdown through consul-tations, and the UN arranged a cease-fire. In January 1974 Egypt and Israel signed a pact, providing for mutual troop withdrawals, the return of the east bank of the canal to Egypt, a UN buffer zone, and an ex-change of prisoners. Fighting continued between Is-rael and Syria in the strategic Golan Heights area.

The Yom Kippur War and its spin-offs were costly for the world. Israel spent $5 billion and suf-fered 5000 casualties, in addition to an ever-increas-ing rate of inflation generated by war expenses. Arab casualties were more than five times the Israeli losses. But whereas the Israelis came to a sober real-ization of their demographic and financial limita-tions, the Egyptians came out of this latest war with improved morale.

Oil Politics

As the Cold War was gaining momentum and the state of Israel was establishing itself, a new eco-nomic weapon was emerging in the Middle East. Oil had first been exploited by the British in Iran early in the twentieth century. In 1933 Ibn Sa'ud, sovereign of the newly constituted kingdom of Saudi Arabia, granted an oil concession to the American Oil Company (ARAMCO). Bahrain began exporting oil in 1934 and became the first Gulf state to develop an oil-based economy. Oil was soon discovered in Arabia and in the kingdom of Kuwait (a British protectorate from the end of World War I until 1961).

Saudi Arabia, Kuwait, and the other Gulf states now control 50 percent of the world's proven oil re-serves. But major production did not gear up until af-ter World War II, and foreign companies tended to control the revenues and organization of Middle Eastern oil resources in the 1950s. Their dominance began to change in 1960 when the Organization of Petroleum Exporting Countries (OPEC) was founded

Discovery Through Maps

Borders and Identities: The UN Partition Plan

The borders of new nations can be planned and mapped, but those plans and maps are often radically different from ground-level realities. The United Nations' partition plan for the British mandate of Palestine is a case in point. After World War II, the Zionists in Palestine began aggressively to push for the establishment of a Jewish state. Violence in the mandate, created out of the Ottoman Empire by the treaties of World War I, escalated between 1944 and 1947. Then Britain's foreign secretary, Ernest Bevin, reflecting Britain's loss of control in the area, referred the "Palestine Question" to the United Nations. The UN created a special committee in 1947 that proposed the end of the mandate and its partition into one Arab and one Jewish state, with Jerusalem as a special internationalized city. The proposal was accepted by Zionist leaders and rejected by Arab leaders. After hard lobbying by President Harry Truman, the partition plan passed in the UN General Assembly. But the plan, shown on this map, never became a reality. Britain's planned withdrawal from Palestine caused a panic in the mandate. Zionist forces seized the initiative, gained control of Palestine, and proclaimed an Israeli state on May 14, 1948.

The drawing of borders in the Middle East, for mandates after World War I, and later for nation-states often did not take into account the identities or wishes of the people living there. But the drawing of these borders ultimately did create new national identities, like those of Israelis and Jordanians, residents of newly created states. Others, like the Palestinians, were dispossessed by the new boundary lines and began a struggle for their own nations and "national" identities. The UN partition plan for Palestine was designed by a committee that spent only five weeks in the mandate. It had to take into account the political, religious, and strategic interests and demands of many competing parties outside of Palestine. The re-

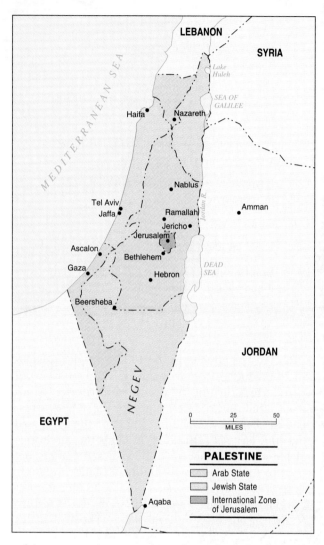

sulting map was an awkward patchwork of divided territories. Over 50 years later the ultimate shape of the map of Israel is still contested. Look at a series of maps of this region beginning in 1900; see how frequently the boundaries have changed.

---

by Iran, Iraq, Kuwait, Saudi Arabia, and Venezuela to gain control over their oil output and pricing. For these states oil began to mean global power. Oil also meant an influx of foreign workers for the petroleum-producing states: Western technical workers, South Asian laborers, and workers from neighboring Middle Eastern states seeking higher wages.

In 1973 OPEC's Arab member states deployed the oil weapon in the aftermath of the October Arab-Israeli war. Saudi Arabia placed an embargo on oil

shipments to the United States, and the Arab oil-producing states cut production, creating panic in the industrialized world and long lines at gas pumps. The embargo symbolized a new balance in systems of world power. It harshly affected the Japanese and the Western Europeans, who respectively received 82 and 72 percent of their oil from the Middle East.

The United States, which imported only 11 percent of its oil supplies from the Middle East, suffered substantial disruption in its economic activity, and a shocked American public began to rail against Saudi "oil shaikhs." The embargo was lifted in 1974, but the industrialized nations had been forced into a greater appreciation of oil as a world-class weapon wielded by states that otherwise had little leverage in world politics.

Egyptian-Israeli Détente

In September 1975 Egypt and Israel reached an agreement by which additional territory in the Sinai peninsula was returned to Egypt and both sides resolved not to resort to force. The United States agreed to provide up to 200 civilian technicians to maintain a precautionary warning system between the two sides. Washington also committed additional arms and financial support to Israel and Egypt (the two largest recipients of U.S. aid).

In late November 1977 President Anwar Sadat initiated a dramatic shift in regional affairs when he flew to Jerusalem to conduct peace talks with Israeli leaders. Sadat, born of a peasant family, had excelled in school and entered the Royal Military Academy. He had worked with other officers to rid Egypt of British domination and in the coup to expel King Faruq. He was a loyal follower of Nasser and succeeded him as president in 1970. Sadat gravitated increasingly into the U.S. sphere, and in 1972 he ordered the 18,000-member corps of Soviet military and technical advisers out of his country. He faced serious problems at home brought on by a faltering economy and a rapidly increasing population. These problems led to severe riots, sparked by runaway inflation. Sadat came to believe that Egypt's most compelling need was for peace and recovery.

The United States strongly supported Sadat's peace overtures, and President Jimmy Carter invited Sadat and Israel's prime minister, Menachem Begin, to meet at Camp David, outside Washington, in September 1978. After intense negotiations, the three leaders produced a framework for peace. Israel agreed to return all the Sinai to Egypt, but no definite agreement was reached on the status of the West Bank, where 1 million displaced Palestinians lived. It was proposed that negotiations should begin to set up an elected self-governing authority for the Palestinians and to end the Israeli military government. The final status of the West Bank, however, remains an issue that more than two decades later has yet to be resolved.

Sadat and Begin received the Nobel Peace Prize in 1978. The Sinai was returned to Egypt and the Suez Canal opened to Israeli ships. In 1980 the two nations opened their borders to each other, exchanged ambassadors, and began air service between the countries. But Sadat was viewed as a traitor in the Arab world, and Egypt was expelled from the Arab League, losing the dominant position in the region that Nasser had secured for it.

Separate Destinies: The Evolution of Turkey and Lebanon

Once nation-states were created in the Middle East, they evolved in very different ways. Some became rich as a result of the exploitation of oil; others

Israeli prime minister Menachem Begin standing beside U.S. president Jimmy Carter, shakes hands with Egyptian president Anwar Sadat. Carter invited Begin and Sadat to a summit meeting at Camp David in September 1978 to work out a peace agreement between Israel and Egypt. This agreement was celebrated in the West, but it failed to produce the hoped-for resolution to the Arab-Israeli conflict.

remained poor. Most developed secular governmental systems; others, like Saudi Arabia, retained the Sharia (Islamic law) as the basis of their political and legal systems. In the Cold War competition between the United States and the Soviet Union, Middle Eastern states chose sides, cultivated alliances, or tried to remain aloof. A good example of the divergent ways in which Middle Eastern states evolved is found in the cases of Turkey and Lebanon. The former became a model of Western-style secularism in the Middle East; the latter was devastated by civil war rooted in religion-based politics and the dislocations caused by the Israeli-Palestinian conflict.

Unlike much of the Middle East, Turkey escaped the fate of becoming a tributary of Britain or France after World War I. Its attainment of independence early in the century and the success of Atatürk's radical secularizing reforms made Turkey a model of sorts for those who envisioned Western-style, secular government as the proper course for Middle Eastern nations. Yet Atatürk's transformation of the institutions of government, education, religion, and law did not eliminate Islam as a powerful force in Turkish society. After Atatürk's death Turkey entered an inevitable period of readjustment, during which it struggled to reach an equilibrium between its religious and cultural traditions on the one hand and the Westernized secularism of Atatürk on the other.

Turkey's first multiparty elections were held in 1946, and in 1950 the opposition Democratic party won a substantial majority of the votes. One of its first acts was to legalize the call to prayer in Arabic, reverting to a traditional practice that Atatürk had outlawed. Over time other aspects of the secularizing policies of Atatürk were moderated, reflecting the religious sentiments of much of the Turkish populace, which is 99 percent Muslim. Despite these changes, however, Atatürk remains a dominant figure in the Turkish public imagination, and the Turkish government, particularly the military, remains committed to secularism.

After World War II both Turkish and Iranian sovereignty were threatened by Soviet expansionism, which drove both states into the U.S. camp. From the late 1940s on, the United States perceived of Turkey and Iran as strategic bulwarks against the Soviet Union and poured military and economic aid into both. Turkey permitted the Americans to establish military bases on its territory and built up its own military with U.S. aid. Although it remained an important ally of the Americans throughout the Cold War period, that relationship was seriously strained when the United States supported Greece in the struggle for the Mediterranean island of Cyprus. Since that time Turkey has explored closer relations with other Middle Eastern states and is seeking to establish itself as a regional power and as a broker in relations between Europe and the newly constituted central Asian republics spun off from the Soviet Union.

Since the 1950s Turkey has retained its secular, democratic, multiparty government, although coups in 1960, 1971, and 1980 each brought interludes of military rule. Turkish society now faces a series of challenges ranging from devastating inflation to an undeclared civil war with elements of its Kurdish population in the eastern provinces to new political challenges mounted by the Islamist parties.

In the 1990s Turks elected their first female prime minister, Tansu Ciller, and their first Islamist prime minister, Necmettin Erbakan. These elections suggest the divergent strains in Turkish politics. The Refah party, which promised a series of Islamic reforms, won substantial victories in 1994 in the major centers of Istanbul and Ankara. This populist party, with its appeal to Islamic values and its vigorous social programs, struck a sympathetic chord, especially among the poor and the millions of rural Turks who have recently migrated to the large urban centers. Refah won the 1995 national elections by a slim margin and ultimately constructed a precarious coalition government with Erbakan as prime minister from 1996 to 1997. But the military, interpreting Refah's successes as a threat to Turkey's secular system of government, maneuvered to oust Erbakan, and in 1998 the Turkish High Court outlawed the Refah party. This latest episode in Turkey's political history illustrates the disillusionment of some Turks with government incompetence, the evolution of Atatürk's Westernizing reforms, and the perceived failures of the United States and Europe to reward Turkey for its allegiance. It also illustrates the continued tension between the secular, Western vision of Mustafa Kemal and the cultural identity of Turkey as a Middle Eastern and Muslim state.

Unlike Turkey, Lebanon became a mandate of the French after World War I, and that era of colonial rule indelibly marked its evolution as an independent state. Lebanon's capital, Beirut, was once one of the most beautiful and most civilized cities in the Middle East, a center for commerce and a crossroads of cultures and religions. But in the 1970s it became an arena in which competing factions played out their ambitions.

First Lebanon became a battleground in the Israeli-Palestinian conflict. The Palestine Liberation Organization (PLO) led by Yassir Arafat had been driven out of Jordan in the early 1970s. It set up its headquarters in Lebanon and stepped up demands for Israeli withdrawal from the West Bank of the Jordan River and the Gaza Strip, both captured by Israel during the 1967 war. The PLO wanted an independent Palestinian state and in pursuit of that goal launched guerrilla raids from its bases in southern Lebanon and encouraged demonstrations to harass Israeli authorities. In response, beginning in 1978, Israel made repeated incursions into Lebanese territory to strike back at the PLO bases.

Civil war added to Lebanon's troubles. This small, ethnically mixed nation, its area slightly less than that of Connecticut, is divided among Muslim, Christian, and Druze factions. The Druze originated as a Shi'ite splinter group in the medieval era; they now constitute a separate religious faction. Syria and Lebanon had been declared independent in 1941, but the French relinquished control only grudgingly and waited five years to withdraw their troops. And when they left, they set the stage for political and religious violence. The Christians held a slight majority in Lebanon, and France wanted to ensure the continuity of that Christian dominance. So they set up a political system for Lebanon based on confessional politics—political office allocated by religious affiliation. Under this system, the various factions maintained a somewhat precarious balance. High Muslim birthrates, in addition to the influx of Palestinians after the creation of Israel, the 1967 Arab-Israeli War, and civil strife in Jordan in the early 1970s, tipped that balance. The Christians, initially supported by Syria, fought the Muslim and Druze factions in the streets of Beirut until an October 1976 cease-fire. The cost was 25,000 dead, thousands more wounded, and sections of the city gutted. The country's once flourishing economy was at a standstill.

In the summer of 1981 PLO forces in southern Lebanon fired rockets into Israel, which responded with massive air attacks on Palestinian strongholds in Beirut. Hundreds of civilians were killed. In the summer of 1982 the Israelis invaded the city, surrounding Muslim-held West Beirut. The PLO evacuated Beirut in September, under the direction of a French, Italian, and U.S. multinational contingent. But after the multinational force departed, the violence resumed; the newly elected president, Bashir Gemayel, a Christian, and 26 of his colleagues were killed by a bomb. In apparent response, Christian militiamen, unchecked by the Israelis, massacred over 1000 Palestinian men, women, and children in two refugee camps.

In the succeeding decade the skeletal outlines of bombed buildings, shadowy videotapes of hostages, and pictures of young and old darting through streets to avoid gunfire made Lebanon a symbol to the world of the costs of civil strife. Many of Beirut's citizens fled during the course of the civil war; others remained hopeful that an equilibrium could once again be reached. Although Beirut has begun to recover, it remains tainted by intercommunal violence and the deep-seated hostilities that the Arab-Israeli conflict has produced.

The Iranian Revolution

Iran, which had served as an area of competition between the British and the Russians since the nineteenth century, became a bone of contention between the United States and the Soviet Union after World War II. Shah Mohammad Reza Pahlavi ascended the Iranian throne in 1941 after the Allies forced his father to abdicate for supporting Germany in World War II. After the war he asked foreign troops to withdraw from his country. But the continued presence of Soviet troops on his borders, the aggressive activities of the Iranian Communist party (Tudeh), and a shared interest in exploiting Iranian oil moved the shah increasingly into the U.S. camp as the Cold War geared up.

In 1953 Iranian premier Mohammad Mosaddeq advocated a set of liberalizing reforms and nationalization of Iranian oil. Mosaddeq directly challenged the shah, who fled the country; but a CIA-supported military coup overthrew Mosaddeq in 1954 and restored the shah to power. For the next 25 years Iran rested firmly within the orbit of the United States, a valuable source of oil and a bulwark against Soviet expansion. In return, the Americans supplied the shah's arsenal.

The shah attempted a rapid modernization of his country, but the so-called White Revolution threatened the integrity of Iranian culture. Pahlavi imagined himself a benevolent father dragging an unwilling Iran into the twentieth century. But many Iranians saw him as brutal dictator and a Western pawn. The presence of over 100,000 foreigners (especially technicians and military advisers), including 47,000 Americans, alienated many Iranians, who perceived the shah as undermining both Islam and Iran's political and economic base. Opposition to the shah's rule spread widely, from militant communists to Shi'ite clergy to discontented nationalists. Inflation angered the business classes and the laborers. Peasants who were disenchanted with the shah's land reforms and who had swelled the ranks of impoverished migrants in the capital city, Tehran, also resented the shah's rule.

The plight of these peasants and their resentment toward the shah, with his fancy palaces, lavish celebrations, and affluent, Westernized retainers, is graphically depicted in children's stories by the Iranian author Samad Behrangi. In one of those stories, a ragged and hungry village boy, who has come to Tehran with his father to find work, describes the neighborhood where the rich Iranians live.

I came to the streets where there wasn't any smoke or dirty smell. The children and adults all had clean, fresh clothing. Their faces shone. . . . Whenever I came to such areas, I thought I was sitting in a theatre and watching a movie. I was never able to imagine what kind of food they ate, how they slept or spoke, or what kind of clothing they wore in such tall, clean houses.[2]

The boy and his father ultimately decide to go home, thinking it better to starve in the village surrounded by family and friends than to starve homeless and alone in the city. The characters in Behrangi's stories symbolized the suffering of many of the Iranian people despite Iran's oil wealth and the shah's Westernizing reforms.

To stem the growing opposition to his regime, the shah launched a reign of terror. The storm broke in January 1978 when large numbers of students demonstrated in the streets. Many were killed and wounded by the shah's troops. Strikes and demonstrations spread throughout the country. The army and secret police (SAVAK) proved helpless in the face of the revolt. In January 1979 the shah fled the country, seeking asylum in the United States, then in Panama, and finally in Egypt, where he died in 1980.

The main objective of the disparate revolutionary factions was to get rid of the shah. Once that task was accomplished, the coalition broke down and the Shi'ite clergy used its organizational apparatus to gain ascendancy. The diffuse and widespread revolution found its focus in the aged Ayatollah Ruhollah Khomeini, a Shi'ite holy man who had been exiled in 1963 for speaking out against the shah. From Iraq and then from Paris he had carried on an incessant propaganda effort directed at the shah's "godless and materialistic" rule. Khomeini's rhetoric struck a sympathetic chord among Iranians offended by the shah's anti-Islamic reforms, ostentatious lifestyle, and "selling out" of Iran's resources to the West. Khomeini returned to Iran to take up the reins of power. He promptly banned Western music on radio and television, "provocative" bathing suits, liquor, and a broad range of other items deemed "un-Islamic." Consolidating his power after the revolution, the Ayatollah retained Iran's constitutional government but based it firmly on the Sharia. He then changed the curriculum and textbooks of Iran's schools to reflect the ideology of the new regime.

Khomeini viewed the United States as the "Great Satan," a symbol of imperialism, materialism, and godlessness. He encouraged the expression of anti-American sentiments. In November 1979 a mob of young Iranians stormed and seized the U.S. embassy and took 53 hostages, whom they held for over a year. This act and other consequences of the revolution alienated Iran from its previously warm relations with Western powers, who were fearful of the implications of Islamic rule and of the potential for desta-

bilization of the Middle East. Iran's regional neighbors were also alarmed at Khomeini's rise to power, fearing that he might export his Islamic revolution. In the aftermath of the revolution, Iraqi leader Saddam Hussein, hoping for a speedy victory over a weakened Iran, attacked Iranian airfields and oil refineries in September 1980. This attack provoked a war that devastated the Iranian economy, already severely disrupted by the revolution. The financial drain of the war helped force the Iranians to release the U.S. hostages in return for the United States' release of Iranian assets frozen in response to the hostage taking.

The Iran-Iraq war dragged on for nearly a decade until an armistice in 1989—brought on by exhaustion. It had been a war of attrition in which both sides suffered enormous losses. The Iranians employed all of their resources, including 12- and 13-year-old boys, in attacks against the well-ensconced but smaller Iraqi army. The Iraqis violated the accepted rules of combat by using chemical weapons and poison gas.

Khomeini died in June 1989, but the idea of Islamic revolution lived on. Iran became a worldwide model for people disenchanted with secularism and interested in new state formations that might combine representative government with traditional religious culture and law.

Toward a New Balance

During the first part of the 1980s Egypt remained an outcast among Arab countries because of its détente with Israel. In October 1981 a small group of Islamic militants assassinated Sadat while he was reviewing a military parade. Shortly before his death, he had ordered a crackdown on the Muslim Brotherhood, which opposed his reconciliation with Israel and Egypt's increasingly secular nature.

Sadat's successor, Hosni Mubarak, pledged to continue Sadat's commitments and welcomed U.S. support in dollars and weapons. During the 1980s Mubarak improved Egypt's relations with other moderate Arab states as he struggled with his country's overwhelming economic problems, brought on by a mushrooming population along the Nile. Mubarak solidified his position and maintained Sadat's foreign policies.

Huge outlays for defense drove Israel's inflation rate to average over 50 percent in the last part of the 1980s. The Israelis came to depend more and more on aid from the United States, whose annual announced subsidies exceeded $3 billion a year. Meanwhile, world and American public opinion became increasingly sympathetic to the Palestinians as their *intifada* (resistance movement) within Israel drew harsh Israeli responses extensively covered on world

Ayatollah Khomeini, Message to the Pilgrims

The following message was written in September 1978 while Khomeini, in exile in Iraq, was preparing to leave for Paris. An appeal for solidarity of all Muslims with the Iranian people in their struggle against the shah, it circulated among those making the sacred pilgrimage to Mecca. It was translated into Arabic, Turkish, Urdu, Malay-Indonesian, French, and English. The Saudi Arabian government was fearful of Khomeini's brand of Islam, and many Muslims felt little affinity for the Ayatollah's Shi'ite beliefs. But Khomeini's call to support oppressed peoples against the forces of imperialism and despotism was calculated to strike a sympathetic chord worldwide among all Muslims suffering under repressive regimes or Western dominance.

Now that it is the season of Pilgrimage to the sacred House of God and Muslims have come from all over the world to visit God's House, it is necessary that they pay attention to one of the most important aspects of this great gathering while they are performing the noble rites of the hajj, and examine the social and political circumstances of the Islamic countries. They must inform themselves of the hardships that their brothers in faith are suffering and strive to relieve those hardships, in accordance with their Islamic and moral duty.... For fifty years Iran, which has about thirty million Muslims, has been in the grip of the Pahlavi dynasty, a self-proclaimed servant of foreign powers. During those fifty dark years, the great people of Iran have been writhing under police repression, suffocation, and spiritual torture.

The Shah has given foreigners all the subterranean wealth and vital interests belonging to the people. He has given oil to America; gas to the Soviet Union; pastureland, forests and part of the oil to England and other countries. The people have been deprived of all the necessities of life and kept in a state of backwardness. The imperialist system has taken control of the army, the education, and the economy of our country....

Now that our people in recent years have awakened, risen up to gain their rights, and cried out against oppression, they have been answered with machine guns, tanks, and cannons. The massacres that have occurred in the cities of Iran in recent months are a cause of shame to history. With the support of America and with all the infernal means at his disposal, the Shah has fallen on our oppressed people, turning Iran into one vast graveyard. General strikes engulf the country.... Martial law has cast its sinister shadow over the people, and his mercenaries and commandoes are busy killing young and old, men and women.

I have not been permitted to continue my activity in any Islamic country, my activity that consists of conveying to the world the cry of my oppressed people. Because I must at all events fulfill my religious and ethical duty, I have been obliged to leave the Islamic world in the hope of alerting human society to the suffering of the oppressed people of Iran.

Now, O Muslims of the world, show concern for the problem of Iran, and convey to the world the cry of thirty million oppressed Muslims. The Most Noble Messenger [the Prophet, Muhammad] (peace and blessings be upon him) is reported to have said: "He who arises in the morning and gives no thought to the affairs of the Muslims is not a Muslim."

O God, I have conveyed the message, and peace be upon those who follow true guidance.

From Ruhollah Khomeini, *Islam and Revolution: Writings and Declarations of Imam Khomeini*, trans. by Hamid Algar. Berkeley: Mage Press, 1980.

---

television. Indeed, from the Iranian Revolution to the Palestinian *intifada* to the Persian Gulf War, television coverage began to play an increasingly influential role in the crafting of Middle Eastern politics.

While committed to Israel's security, the United States, especially during the administration of President George Bush (1989–1993), continued to aid friendly Arab states who opposed Israel. This was particularly the case with Saudi Arabia, the main supplier of American oil imports. The United States sold the Saudis large quantities of sophisticated weapons and sent the U.S. Navy to keep the Persian Gulf oil shipment lanes open during the latter stages of the Iran-Iraq war.

Iraq, a country with immense oil reserves and agricultural potential, had expended huge sums on the war with Iran. Under Saddam Hussein the Iraqis had developed extensive military capabilities. Saddam, whose secular nationalist Ba'th party regime had vigorously suppressed all political opposition in Iraq, imagined himself filling the power vacuum left in the Middle East by Nasser's death. But his aspirations to nuclear power were set back when the Israelis bombed his nuclear reactor in 1981. During the Iran-Iraq war, more than a million people died in the fighting, and the Iraqi leader used chemical weapons on Iraqi Kurdish villagers to intimidate the large Kurdish minority in northern Iraq.

Soon after the Iran-Iraq war ended, Saddam Hussein launched another offensive in the region. In August 1990 Iraqi troops invaded and overran the oil-rich nation of Kuwait. This aggressive act, and its im-

Pro-Iranian Muslims in Lebanon raise their hands in salute to the Ayatollah Khomeini during a symbolic funeral held in Beirut to honor the deceased Iranian spiritual leader. Khomeini had become an important world symbol of self-determination and opposition to Western dominance. For some Muslims he was a hero; many others, however, rejected Khomeini's brand of Islam and found his conservatism, subordination of women, and intrusive moral control unpalatable.

plied threat to Saudi Arabia, produced an immediate response. The fear that if it took the Saudi oilfields, Iraq would control one-third of the global oil reserves moved the UN Security Council to impose a series of strict sanctions on Baghdad. The Soviet Union and the United States, both former patrons of Saddam, lined up in opposition to the Iraqi dictator.

For the next six months the UN, led by a coalition assembled by the United States, increased pressure on Saddam Hussein by imposing sanctions and embargoes on his country. The Iraqi leader received the support of the PLO and Jordan, but much of the Arab world viewed his aggression with fear and anger. When sanctions and embargoes failed to move Iraq to withdraw from Kuwait, an American-led 26-nation coalition (including Egypt, Saudi Arabia, Syria, Turkey, France, Italy, and the United Kingdom) began heavy bombardment of Iraq in January 1991. A month later the allies launched a land offensive that in 100 hours evicted Iraq's soldiers from Kuwait and left the coalition in possession of one-fifth of Iraq. This smashing of Iraq's forces represented a post–Cold War reconfiguration of Middle Eastern al-

liances. Kuwait had been redeemed, but Saddam Hussein remained firmly in power at home. He brutally put down uprisings by Shi'ite groups in the south of Iraq and by Kurds in the north. Hundreds of thousands of Kurds fled and became refugees. Wartime oil spills and oil wells torched by the retreating Iraqis left an ecological disaster in the Gulf region. Saddam continues to resist post-war, U.N.-mandated weapons inspections, and the Iraqis continue to suffer under a prolonged international boycott.

Meanwhile, diplomatic activity in the major capitals of the world prepared the way for conferences that might bring peace to the region. A step in that direction took place in September 1993 when PLO leader Yassir Arafat and Israeli leader Yitzhak Rabin met in Washington to sign an agreement to turn certain parts of the occupied territories over to the Palestinians in return for guarantees of peace for Israel. Secret negotiations had brought the bitter enemies together.

The PLO, isolated from much of its financial support because of its backing of Iraq and challenged by the increasing popularity of Islamist factions, saw the negotiations as perhaps a last chance to maintain a position in the Middle East and gain a foothold for a future Palestinian state. Israel saw an opportunity to construct a peace that would fragment its opponents and bring some relief to an Israeli populace weary of war.

The agreement set up a five-year-long framework of limited autonomy for the Palestinians in Jericho and the Gaza Strip and continuing negotiations for a permanent solution. For the first time Palestinian schools were permitted texts that openly taught their pupils about "Palestine." But the settlement proved largely unworkable. Prime Minister Rabin was later assassinated by an Israeli extremist, and many Palestinians have become disillusioned with their limited gains under the new administration. The Israeli government has refused to alter its policies promoting Jewish settlements in the occupied territories and has stepped up its annexation of Palestinian lands around Jerusalem. Bombings by Palestinian factions in Tel Aviv and Jerusalem have terrified Israelis and helped derail peace negotiations. In 1998 Israelis celebrated 50 years of Israeli statehood, while Palestinians remained frustrated in their hopes for a state. Both peoples remain deeply divided over the limits of Palestinian autonomy and over the future character of the Israeli state.

Islamist Factions

After three generations of independence, some segments of Middle Eastern society have become disillusioned with the promises of Western-style secular na-

Encouraged by U.S. president Bill Clinton, Israeli prime minister Yitzhak Rabin (left), and PLO chairman Yassir Arafat shake hands after the signing of a peace accord in September 1993. The agreement pledged the signatories to strive to achieve a "just, lasting and comprehensive peace settlement." That peace, however, has proved elusive. Rabin was assassinated by an Israeli extremist, and Arafat has failed in his bid to achieve an independent Palestinian state through negotiations.

tionalism. Their hopes for prosperity and freedom under the new national regimes have often failed to materialize, and their frustration has found expression in support for Islamist movements. These movements, which assert the central role of Islam in Middle Eastern culture, politics, and law, are not a new phenomenon. They have their roots in the Islamic reform movements—the Muslim Brotherhood, for example—of the nineteenth and early twentieth centuries. But Islamist factions have been given impetus in recent decades by the success of the Iranian Revolution, the economic failures of secular regimes, and the corruption of moral and family values associated by some Muslims with the importation of Western culture.

In the context of widespread poverty and political strife, some Islamist factions have gained support in the Middle East, particularly among the poor. These factions span a broad range of ideological and political positions. They may advocate a return to "traditional" piety and communal values, a rejection of Western consumerism and cultural imperialism, a more significant role for Islam in schools and government, or a discarding of secular rule altogether. Often they augment their political base of support by providing social services such as adult education, job training, and relief services. The assassination of Sadat in Egypt and the victories of the Refah party in Turkey are indicators of the success of Islamist rhetorics among certain segments of the Middle Eastern populace. So is the popularity of Hamas among Palestinians. Hamas is an Islamist party that rejects Israel and advocates the implementation of Shariah law. It became increasingly popular during

the *intifada* as many Palestinians became disenchanted with PLO leadership.

Most of the governments in the Middle East remain committed to secular rule, as do many citizens of Middle Eastern states. But the successes of Islamist factions in the area are a reflection of a worldwide process of self-examination among peoples suffering from economic deprivation, critical of the systems imposed during the period of Western imperial dominance, and interested in incorporating their own cultural traditions and values more directly into the institutions of government, education, and law.

Africa

In 1945 there were four independent African nations; at the end of the century there were 53 sovereign states. The critical years were from the mid-1950s to the end of the 1960s when dozens of African states won their independence. Africa's postindependence leaders generally embraced Kwame Nkrumah's dictum to "seek ye first the political kingdom." They were optimistic that once they had thrown off the shackles of colonial rule, they could build viable nation-states and tackle the poverty and underdevelopment that gripped the continent. But their optimism was short-lived as they underestimated the long-term impact of the colonial legacy.

One of the most pressing problems the new states faced was how to build and maintain national unity among different and sometimes antagonistic religious, cultural, regional, and ethnic groups. In most cases the new African states were not the

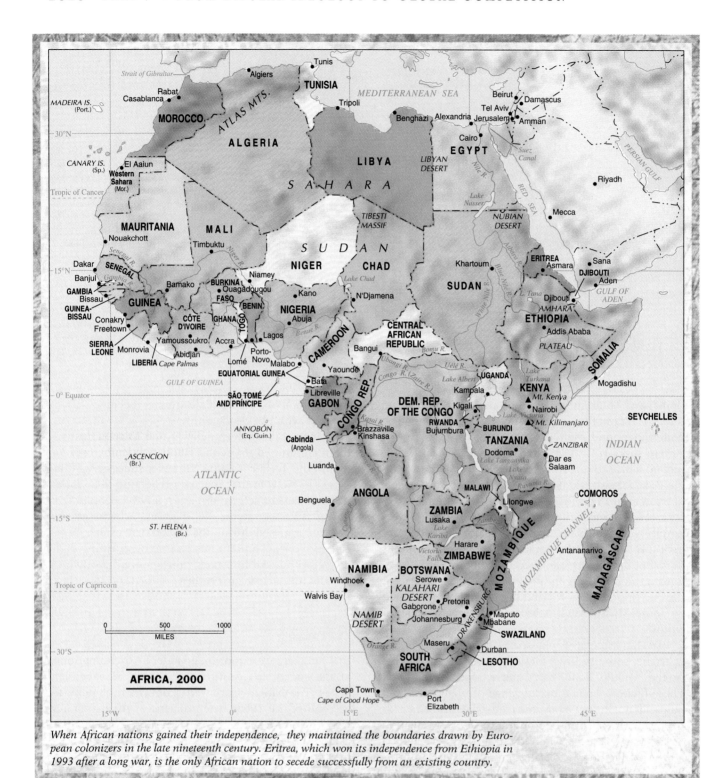

When African nations gained their independence, they maintained the boundaries drawn by European colonizers in the late nineteenth century. Eritrea, which won its independence from Ethiopia in 1993 after a long war, is the only African nation to secede successfully from an existing country.

product of a long historical process such as took place in Europe. Most African boundaries were arbitrary creations of the imperialists and had little relation to the people who lived there. Nigeria, for example, was known as the "linguistic crossroads of Africa" because it encompassed hundreds of diverse ethnic groups, all competing for a share of national resources. However, when African countries founded the Organization of African Unity (OAU) in 1963,

they decided to maintain existing boundaries rather than to open up conflicts by redrawing them.

In most newly independent countries the men who led the freedom struggle took over the reins of power. However, politicians had little experience with running governments, political parties were immature, and civil cultures were weak. The authoritarian governing styles of colonial rulers shaped the outlooks of many politicians, who did not tolerate opposition parties. A democratic culture did not take root, and power became increasingly concentrated in the hands of executive presidents who often proclaimed themselves "president for life." There was little difference between a president's pronouncements and official policy.

However, civilian leaders in many African countries did not last long because soldiers were prepared to stage coups against governments. African armies are generally small, but they have the means to topple civilian governments with ease. Soldiers usually justified a coup by portraying themselves as guardians of the public interest who were saving their country from corrupt and inefficient politicians. As in Nigeria, they also intervened to protect regional interests. More than half of all African states have experienced military takeovers in the past four decades. Between 1952 and 1985 independent African states experienced 54 military coups. A common cycle was for the military to stage a coup, return to the barracks in favor of civilians, and then intervene again. One of the few African states to sustain a multiparty system is Botswana, which succeeded despite living for many decades in the shadow of neighboring white regimes. However, since the end of the Cold War a second wave of independence has swept through Africa. Grassroots people and civic organizations around the continent have stepped up their calls for democratic government, and some promising steps have been made toward implanting democratic rule. Since the late 1980s Africa has witnessed dozens of elections. Some of them have installed genuine democratic governments, while others have been manipulated by autocratic rulers and military officers trying to stay in power.

Another critical part of the colonial inheritance was that independent African nations were saddled with underdeveloped economies that were closely tied to their former colonial rulers. In the 1960s African countries depended on primary products such as minerals and crops for about 80 percent of their exports. That dependence has not changed appreciably since then. Thus the health of African economies is still largely dependent on the prices their raw materials receive in world commodity markets.

Some African nations such as Kenya and the Ivory Coast adopted the view that the capitalist path was the correct path to development and prosperity. They modeled their policies after Western Europe and the United States, encouraged foreign investment and private businesses, and promoted rapid industrialization.

Other African leaders took the attitude that African economies, because of their marginal position in the global economy, were doomed to perpetual underdevelopment and poverty. They tried to break their states' dependency on the West by adopt-

ing socialism and developing close relations with the Soviet Union or China. African socialism typically meant state ownership of public enterprises, mines and industries, and banks and insurance companies, but socialist policies came in many varieties. Some states, such as Ethiopia, Angola, and Mozambique, practiced an orthodox brand of Marxism, while others, such as Tanzania, experimented with a socialism based on African communal values.

Regardless of the path taken, most African economies have not prospered. The nations of Africa import more goods than they export, they have to import food to feed their own citizens, they have not attracted significant amounts of foreign assistance and foreign investment, and they have been plagued by enormous debts to lending institutions. African states devote about four times as much on repaying debts as they do on providing health services. The net result is that most African states had GDPs smaller than the endowments of top Ivy League universities. Thirty-two of the 47 countries classified by the World Bank as "least developed" are in Africa. And the poorer countries are even poorer than they were in the 1960s.

In the first decades after independence most African states remained closely tied to their former colonial rulers economically and politically, leading some observers to charge that independence was really another form of colonialism, or "neocolonialism." Of the former colonizers, France retained a unique status in its former colonies. French culture and language persisted among African elites, and France maintained its financial, technical, and military links. The French military intervened on several dozen occasions to rescue African leaders under fire from their own people. Francophone (French-speaking) African leaders usually paid more attention to their ties with France than to those with the OAU.

By the 1980s African states were shackled with enormous debts, declining standards of living, and sluggish economies. GDP growth rates in the 1980s averaged only 2.1 percent per year, while the population growth rate increased to 3.1 percent per year. As a result, since the mid-1980s African governments have shifted their ties with their former colonial rulers to international lending agencies such as the World Bank and the International Monetary Fund (IMF).

The World Bank and IMF cure for ailing African economies has been Structural Adjustment Programs (SAPs) that compel African governments to promote market economies, liberalize foreign investment codes, and sell off state-owned enterprises to the private sector. More than two-thirds of African countries have adopted SAPs, but the cure has often been worse than the illness. The conditions for loans—currency devaluations, an end to the subsidies of staple foods, and wage freezes—have imposed enormous pressures on governments to carry out highly unpopular policies that have provoked protests. Some countries and individuals have benefited from SAPs, but many others have suffered. Women and children have suffered the most from these policies as various government support programs have been ended.

North Africa

France's two protectorates in North Africa, Tunisia and Morocco, gained independence in a relatively peaceful way in 1956. In sharp contrast stands the transfer of autonomy to Algeria. France had invested millions of dollars in the development of this territory, largely for the benefit of French immigrants who, by 1960, constituted about one-tenth of the population.

Although Algeria was an integral part of France and sent representatives to the French National Assembly, resentment against foreign control grew among the Muslim majority. Following a mounting campaign of violence, revolution broke out in 1958. After four years of savage warfare, whose repercussions brought down the French Fourth Republic, Charles de Gaulle paved the way for Algeria's independence in 1962. Most of the 1 million Europeans left the scarred and battered country for France.

The Front for National Liberation (FLN), which led the independence struggle, together with the armed forces, ruled for the first three decades of Algeria's independence. Abundant oil and natural gas reserves attracted foreign investment and sustained a dramatic expansion of agriculture and industry. In the 1980s a sluggish economy and social unrest forced the government to introduce political reforms and allow the first multiparty elections for local government in 1990. When parliamentary elections were held in 1992, the Islamic Salvation Front (FIS) won an unexpected victory over the FLN. However, the military intervened, voided the elections results, and banned the FIS. General Liamine Zéroual won elections without the FIS participating in 1995, but his government has not been able to reach a settlement with opposition parties or to stanch a bloody war between the military and radical Islamists in which tens of thousands of people have been brutally murdered.

Libya made the transition from Italian colony to independent nation in 1951 following a period of French-British supervision. Inspired by Nasser's revolution in Egypt, a group of young army officers led by Colonel Muammar al-Qadhaffi overthrew the monarchy in 1969. As "leader of the revolution," Qadhaffi has remained Libya's head of state, promoting a *jamahiriya* ("state of the masses") philosophy, a blend of socialist and Islamic ideas. Because he opposed the formation of political parties and parliamentary democracy, Qadhaffi established a government based on people's committees and popular congresses. In 1977 Libya proclaimed itself the Socialist People's Libyan Arab Jamahiriya.

Oil revenues have been the main source of Libya's economic growth, financing industrial development and paying for social programs, housing, health care, and education for many of its citizens. Qadhaffi's regime nationalized all foreign-owned property, but declining oil prices led to the opening up of the private sector in the 1990s.

Libya's oil wealth allowed Qadhaffi to promote an idiosyncratic foreign policy based on pan-Arab nationalism and support for revolutionary movements such as the PLO. Libya's intervention in Middle Eastern and African Affairs has led to confrontations with Western European nations and the United States, which have accused Libya of sponsoring international terrorism. When Libyan agents were implicated after bombs exploded on a Pan American Airlines flight over Lockerbie, Scotland, and a French UTA flight over Niger, the UN imposed a trade and international flight embargo on Libya. The resulting increases in inflation and higher costs of imported goods prompted Libya to pursue close ties with neighboring Egypt and Tunisia. At the same time, Libya, an implacable foe of Israel, broke relations with the PLO for participating in the peace process with Israel.

Middle Africa

Ghana was the first nation south of the Sahara to gain independence. In 1957 Kwame Nkrumah (c. 1909–1972), its prime minister, was the idol of African nationalists for championing African unity, and his newly freed nation was the symbol of freedom and democracy in Africa. But in the year after taking power, Nkrumah began to muzzle the press and imprison the opposition. In 1964 he made Ghana a one-party state. As he developed into an outright dictator, he embarked on ruinous economic policies such as a showy hydroelectric dam and the support of a large military establishment. Nkrumah's controlled press called him the "Great Redeemer" and "His Messianic Majesty," while his economy slid downhill under the weight of extravagant spending and corruption.

In 1966 a group of army officers seized control of the country. Eager to speed economic recovery and restore some semblance of political freedom, the army leaders permitted the return to parliamentary institutions in 1969. Ghana thus became the first African country to return to multiparty government after being under military rule. During the 1970s another military junta staged a coup, but by the end of the decade civilian rule had been restored. In 1981 the military under Flight Lieutenant Jerry Rawlings (b. 1947) resumed control until 1996, when Rawlings was elected president in multiparty elections.

When it gained independence in 1960, Nigeria, Africa's most populous nation, offered the greatest promise of a prosperous and stable future among all new African states. It had several thousand well-trained civil servants, more than 500 doctors, an equal number of lawyers, a substantial body of engineers and urban professionals, and vibrant universities. It was endowed with a variety of important natural resources, especially oil.

Between 1962 and 1966 a series of crises—disputed elections, corruption, and crime waves—undermined the government's stability. In 1966 military officers took control of the country in a bloody coup. The following year Ibo groups in southeastern Nigeria seceded and proclaimed the independent Republic of Biafra. The Nigerian government launched military offensives as well as an economic blockade against the rebel state. Hundreds of thousands, especially children, died of starvation. In 1970 Biafra surrendered and was reincorporated into Nigeria.

After 13 years of military rule, civilian government was restored in 1979, along with a new constitution patterned after that of the United States. Designed to prevent a return of the ethnic and regional feuds that had wrecked the first republic, the new constitution created a federal system providing for the allocation of powers between a central and 19 states governments. However, following a sharp drop in petroleum prices, the military intervened again in 1983 and banned all political parties. In the early 1990s it appeared that the military was preparing to hand over power to civilians. But after newspaper publisher Moshood Abiola was elected president in 1993, the governing military council declared the election results null and void, and jailed Abiola. Following the deaths in 1998 of Abiola in prison and military strongman Sani Abacha, military leaders allowed for elections and a return to civilian rule. It remains to be seen whether the military will refrain from intervening in politics.

Events were equally unfortunate in the former Belgian Congo, a country as large as Western Europe but lacking any ethnic or political unity. In 1959 the Belgians, in the face of general protest and serious rioting, promised independence. When self-government came the next year, 120 political parties representing regional and ethnic interests contested elections. The new government lacked unity and stability. A civil war broke out almost immediately, and Katanga province, which produced 70 percent of the country's mineral wealth, seceded. At the request of the Congolese government, UN peacekeeping forces intervened to restore order and quell the Katanga secession, which they did by 1964.

A passionate advocate of African unity, Kwame Nkrumah was the leader of Ghana's drive for independence from Great Britain and served as its first president from 1957 until his overthrow by the military in 1966.

The government still lacked coherence, and the army commander, General Joseph Mobutu Sese Seko (1930–1997), staged a coup in 1965. He renamed the Congo Zaïre, but his style of rule mirrored that of King Leopold of Belgium a century earlier. Mobutu was a "kleptocrat": he and his elite bilked the mineral-rich country of billions of dollars while leaving their people with one of the lowest per capita incomes in the world. Mobutu cleverly played Cold War politics and won support from the West by portraying himself as a bulwark against communism. When the Cold War ended, Mobutu made halfhearted attempts at negotiating with opposition groups for a democratic constitution. His regime was finally toppled in 1997 by an insurgency led by Laurent Kabila, who was supported by several neighboring states. In

Patrice Lumumba on Achieving Independence

These are excerpts from the Independence Day speech of Patrice Lumumba, the first prime minister of the Congo. His words convey both the emotion of the independence struggle and the unbridled optimism that African leaders had at independence. A year after delivering this speech, Lumumba was abducted and killed.

I ask of you all, my friends who have ceaselessly struggled at our side, that this 30th of June, 1960, may be preserved as an illustrious date etched indelibly in your hearts, a date whose meaning you will teach proudly to your children, so that they in turn may pass on to their children and to their grandchildren the glorious story of our struggle for liberty.

. . . No Congolese worthy of the name can ever forget that it has been by struggle that this independence has been gained, a continuous and prolonged struggle, an ardent and idealistic struggle, a struggle in which we have spared neither our strength nor our privations, neither our suffering nor our blood.

Of this struggle, one of tears, fire, and blood, we are proud to the very depths of our being, for it was a noble and just struggle, absolutely necessary to bring to an end the humiliating slavery which had been imposed upon us by force.

This was our fate during eighty years of colonial rule; our wounds are still too fresh and painful for us to be able to erase them from our memories.

We have known the backbreaking work exacted from us in exchange for salaries which permitted us neither to eat enough to satisfy our hunger nor to dress and lodge ourselves decently, nor to raise our children as the beloved creatures that they are.

We have known the mockery, the insults, the blows submitted to morning, noon and night because we were "nègres." Who will forget that [when speaking] to a Negro one used the familiar term of address, not, certainly, as to a friend, but because the more dignified forms were reserved for whites alone?

. . . We have known the atrocious suffering of those who were imprisoned for political opinion or religious beliefs; exiles in their own country, their fate was truly worse than death itself.

We have known that in the cities there were magnificent houses for the whites and crumbling hovels for the Negroes, that a Negro was not admitted to movie theatres or restaurants, that he was not allowed to enter so-called "European" stores, that when the Negro travelled, it was on the lowest level of a boat, at the feet of the white man in his deluxe cabin. . . .

But all this, however, we who by the vote of your elected representatives are directed to guide our beloved country, we who have suffered in our bodies and in our hearts from colonialist oppression, we it is who tell you—all this is henceforth ended. . . .

Together, my brothers, we are going to start a new struggle, a sublime struggle which will lead our country to peace, prosperity and greatness. Together we are going to establish social justice and ensure for each man just remuneration for his work. We are going to show the world what the black man can do when he works in freedom, and we are going to make the Congo the hub of all Africa. . . . We are going to re-examine all former laws, and make new ones which will be just and noble. We are going to put an end to suppression of free thought and make it possible for all citizens fully to enjoy the fundamental liberties set down in the Declaration of the Rights of Man.

We are going to succeed in suppressing all discrimination—no matter what it may be—and give to each individual the just place to which his human dignity, his work, and his devotion to his country entitle him.

We shall cause to reign, not the peace of guns and bayonets, but the peace of hearts and good will.

And for all this, dear compatriots, rest assured that we shall be able to count upon not only our own enormous forces and immense riches, but also upon the assistance of numerous foreign countries whose collaboration we shall accept only as long as it is honest and does not seek to impose upon us any political system, whatever it may be. . . .

And so, my brothers in race, my brothers in conflict, my compatriots, this is what I wanted to tell you in the name of the government, on this magnificent day of our complete and sovereign Independence.

Our government—strong, national, popular—will be the salvation of this country.

From Leon E. Clark, *Through African Eyes: The Past—The Road to Independence*, 2nd ed., Vol. 1 (Center for International Training and Education, 1991), pp. 222–226.

turn, Kabila has been faced with a rebel force sponsored by several neighbors, Uganda and Rwanda.

Northeastern Africa, known as the Horn of Africa, consisted of Ethiopia, Somalia, and several

small states. It became geopolitically significant after 1945 because of its proximity to the sea lanes of the Red Sea and the Persian Gulf. After Emperor Haile Selassie (1892–1975) returned to Ethiopia following the expulsion of the Italians in 1941, he kept the anachronistic feudal system largely in place. In the 1960s, in the face of student and ethnic protests, the emperor failed to move decisively on land reform or reduce the dominance of his Amhara ethnic group in government. The crisis that led to his downfall began with a famine in 1973 that killed an estimated 200,000 people. Blame was pinned on his government for mismanaging drought relief, and strikes, student unrest, and scandal among the royal family all combined to bring success to a military coup that dethroned the emperor in 1974.

The new military rulers were bitterly divided among moderates and radicals. Following three years of disputes, the radicals led by Mengistu Haile Meriam (b. c. 1937) seized control. Their governing council, the Dergue, immediately set to abolishing the country's feudal system, transforming Ethiopia into a socialist state with a Stalinist one-party system. The council nationalized businesses and land, introduced collective farms, censored the media, imprisoned opponents, and executed at least 10,000 opponents.

The Dergue then turned to addressing a host of secessionist movements in Ogaden, a province adjacent to Somalia, and Eritrea, which had been governed first by the Italians and then by the British until being absorbed into Ethiopia in 1961. Somalia had taken possession of Ogaden in 1977, but the next year the Ethiopians broke with their longtime American allies and signed a treaty with the Soviet Union that gave them $1 billion in aid, 17,000 Cuban troops, and up-to-date weapons. The Ethiopians launched a counteroffensive and pushed the Somalis back.

In the late 1970s the Dergue also became bogged down in protracted wars with Eritrean and Tigrean guerrillas, who were fighting for independence in provinces bordering each other. When Eritrea won its independence in 1993, it was the first case in which an African state successfully seceded.

Mengistu finally began to loosen his tight grip on the country. He reversed disastrous economic policies and moderated his political line. However, his efforts were too little and too late to make any difference. Tigrean rebels toppled his regime in 1991 and have governed the country since then. Relations between Ethiopia and Eritrea have been tense since they clashed over a border dispute in 1998.

In Somalia, where clan rivalries dominated national politics, Siad Barré (b. 1919) maintained himself and his Maréhan clan in power for several decades by manipulating clan rivalries. However, insurgencies, droughts, and refugees contributed to the collapse of the Barré regime in 1991, and a civil war

between clans broke out. Food shortages in the rural areas of southern Somalia led to some 300,000 dying of starvation. Televised pictures of dead and dying infants moved the international community to action, and in 1992 a UN peacekeeping force intervened to facilitate food relief.

However, what started out as a humanitarian crusade ended in disaster when the UN force attempted to disarm warring Somali factions and stabilize the situation. A number of UN and American troops lost their lives attempting to disarm the soldiers of one of the clan leaders, Mohammed Aydeed. The American contingent of the UN force was withdrawn in 1994 and the whole UN forces a year later. Since then unity talks between clan leaders have faltered and no faction or coalition has been able to form a coherent government.

One of the most tragic events in recent African history was the genocide that took place in Rwanda in 1994 as Hutu extremists massacred an estimated 1 million Tutsis. This tragedy had been in the making during the colonial era. German and Belgian colonial officials had reinforced Tutsi dominance over the Hutus by favoring Tutsi chiefs, replacing Hutu chiefs with Tutsi chiefs, and compelling the Hutu to provide forced labor for the colonial economy. Catholic missionaries compounded the problem by catering to the Tutsis and excluding Hutus in their schools.

Antagonisms between the Hutus and the Tutsis intensified. Before Rwanda's independence in 1962, the Tutsi monarchy was deposed and some Hutus took vengeance and massacred thousands of Tutsis. After independence, the Hutu majority took power and excluded Tutsis from political life and discriminated against them. Many Tutsis fled into exile in neighboring states. After 1972 the dominant figure in Hutu politics was a military officer, Juvenal Habyarimana (1936–1994), who seized power in a military coup in 1972 but who won elections from 1983 on.

In 1990 a Tutsi-led rebel force invaded Rwanda from Uganda, sparking off a civil war that forced thousands of refugees to flee the country. Habyarimana and the rebels negotiated a transitional government, but in April 1994, as Habyarimana and the president of Burundi were returning from peace talks, a rocket from an unknown source shot down their plane, killing them both. Hutu extremists who opposed Habyarimana's negotiations with the Tutsi rebels blamed his death on a Tutsi conspiracy. They methodically incited violence against the Tutsis. They mobilized Hutu militia groups, known as *interahamwe* ("those who work together"), and the presidential guard and launched a reign of terror against Tutsis and any Hutu moderates who opposed them. Within a few months their genocidal campaign had killed hundreds of thousands and forced more than

2 million refugees into exile. In the chaos the Tutsi-led rebels seized power and ousted the Hutu-dominated regime. Although many Tutsi and Hutu refugees have returned to Rwanda, the situation is far from stable.

Southern Africa

In southern Africa white-ruled regimes resisted the calls for black majority rule, and African nationalist movements turned to armed struggle to bring about change. Self-governing white regimes in Rhodesia and South Africa dug in their heels and defied the "winds of change" to the north. Portugal clung to its African colonies because they were profitable and enhanced Portugal's prestige in the world and because large numbers of Portuguese, especially the rural poor, had emigrated to the African colonies after World War II. Frustrated by the lack of political change, African nationalist movements launched wars of liberation in the Portuguese colonies in the early 1960s. By 1970 Portugal was committing over 40 percent of its budget and more than 150,000 soldiers to the African insurgencies. A decisive moment came in April 1974 when the Portuguese military, weary of the protracted African wars, revolted against the dictatorship that had ruled Portugal for nearly 50 years. The new military junta quickly con-

African freedom movements produced poster art to publicize their causes. This poster depicts guerrillas of the South West African People's Organization (SWAPO) in Namibia in combat.

cluded settlements with African political movements in Angola, Mozambique, and Guinea-Bissau. The last two gained independence with little difficulty as power was transferred to the leading party.

Freedom for Angola was complicated by superpower rivalries and three Angolan political parties contesting for power. Following the granting of independence in 1975, the parties were supposed to share power in a government of unity, but bloody strife broke out between them. The United States covertly assisted the National Union for the Total Independence of Angola (UNITA), while the Soviet Union and Cuba backed the Movement for the Popular Liberation of Angola (MPLA). When the South African military invaded in support of UNITA, the Cubans sent troops to aid the MPLA. The South Africans pulled back their forces, but a civil war continued between UNITA and the MPLA and their external backers for the next two decades. Despite efforts to resolve the conflict, independent Angola has never known peace.

Zimbabwe, the successor to Rhodesia, also suffered a painful war. In the 1960s some 250,000 whites ruled more than 5 million Africans in Rhodesia. In 1965 the white minority declared its independence from Great Britain, which declared that it would not recognize Rhodesia's independence until full political rights had been granted to the African majority. Britain did not send troops to end the rebellion, but neither a trade embargo imposed by Britain nor economic sanctions levied by the UN could force the whites to give up power. In the early 1970s Britain and Rhodesia negotiated an agreement that would have allowed whites to maintain power indefinitely. But the agreement foundered because African nationalists were virtually unanimous in their opposition to it.

In the mid-1960s African nationalists launched a guerrilla war to overthrow white rule. A decade later the war intensified. Zambia and newly independent Mozambique allowed guerrillas to infiltrate into Rhodesia, while South African troops joined Rhodesian forces in search-and-destroy missions, often crossing the borders into neighboring countries. White leaders struck a bargain with several black leaders that placed blacks in political leadership but protected white privilege and landholdings and allowed whites to maintain control of the civil service, army, and police. Black factions led by Joshua Nkomo (b. 1917) and Robert Mugabe (b. 1924) boycotted the elections held in April 1978 and continued the war. After Britain brought all the parties together for fresh negotiations and brokered a settlement, new elections were held in April 1980, and Mugabe won a decisive victory.

Mugabe has been elected president of the nation, renamed Zimbabwe, in three subsequent elections and has entrenched himself and his political party in firm command of the government. Mugabe changed his ideology from Marxist socialism to market socialism, and he has promoted pragmatic reforms rather than a radical transformation of the economy and society. The most sensitive issue has been the continued control of a small number of white farmers over the best land. On occasion Mugabe's government has expressed its intent to confiscate white farms rather than buying them up.

South Africa was the dominant actor in the region, and its white minority defied the winds of change the longest. In 1948 the Afrikaner-dominated National party won a surprise victory in white elections and began implementing its policies of rigid racial separation known as *apartheid.* Parliament passed hundreds of new laws entrenching inequality. The Population Registration Act separated South Africans according to arbitrary racial classifications. The Group Areas Act segregated residential and business areas in cities along racial lines.

The cornerstone of apartheid was its program of territorial segregation, based on the historical fiction that all racial groups belonged to distinct nations and that Africans belonged to ten "autonomous" states known as Bantustans or homelands. These specious states, carved out of land of little value to white South Africans, were, not surprisingly, poor and underdeveloped, forcing a constant exodus of blacks to find employment on white farms and in urban areas as migrant workers. Those who could not find work and housing and meet other requirements were classed as illegal immigrants and shipped back to the homelands. Millions of people, almost all of them black, were forcibly moved from their homes to achieve the apartheid vision.

In the 1960s the Bantustans were offered self-governing status and, in the mid-1970s, full independence. The first to accept independence in 1976 was Transkei, and three more homelands eventually accepted it, but no country outside of South Africa recognized their independence because recognition meant conceding that Africans were no longer citizens of South Africa.

In the 1970s the government began experimenting with piecemeal reforms to prolong white domination into the next century. In 1978 Prime Minister P. W. Botha (b. 1916), declaring that whites "must adapt or die," urged the repeal of laws prohibiting sexual relations and marriages across the color line and segregating racial groups in public places. In 1984 a new constitution established a tricameral parliament that featured legislative bodies for whites, Indians, and Coloureds (people of mixed-race ancestry) but pointedly left out Africans.

Botha's reforms came too late to satisfy most blacks. Black political groups had waged nonviolent protest campaigns for many decades. Thus when new laws required African women to start carrying passes, 20,000 women of all races marched on the prime minister's offices in Pretoria in 1956 to present petitions. As these and other protests persisted, the government banned the African National Congress (ANC) and a breakaway group, the Pan Africanist Congress, in 1960. Their members responded by forming underground groups and turning to armed struggle. The government ruthlessly clamped down on the opposition, wielding new laws that allowed detention without trial. Many opposition leaders such as Nelson Mandela (b. 1918) were imprisoned for lengthy jail terms, while others were forced into exile to organize resistance from African states to the north.

Resistance was dampened for a few years until black workers and students renewed the protest. The most visible organization was the Black Consciousness movement, which stressed black self-reliance and psychological emancipation from whites, redefined "black" to embrace Coloureds, Asians, and Africans, and rejected collaboration with apartheid institutions such as the homelands. Black Consciousness had a special appeal to black youth, and in 1976 black students rebelled against the government's education policies, which prevented most blacks from acquiring skills. When police and soldiers clamped down on their protests, thousands of youths left the country to take up the armed struggle. The next year security police killed Black Consciousness leader Steve Biko (1947–1977) in jail and banned dozens of groups.

When the ANC and PAC renewed their guerrilla activities, South Africa launched a campaign of destabilization against southern African countries that supported them. To bring regional states into line, the South African government not only applied a variety of economic pressures but also unleashed cross-border raids against ANC bases in neighboring states and supported antigovernment guerrillas in Angola, Mozambique, and Lesotho. The cost of the wars and economic destabilization to southern African countries has been estimated at close to $1 billion.

By the late 1980s South Africa was under pressure on a number of fronts to end apartheid. International economic, arms, and sporting sanctions were hurting and isolating the country. The economy was stagnating, and new government programs were at a standstill. Although the government declared a state of emergency and jailed some 30,000 antiapartheid activists, protests continued. Moreover, time and demographics were on the side of the black majority, whose members were gaining clout in trade unions and the economy. Without a decisive break from its apartheid past, long-term prospects for change without considerable bloodshed looked remote.

Nelson Mandela and Frederik W. de Klerk led the negotiations that brought about an end to white majority rule and elections in South Africa in 1994. Mandela was elected president, and de Klerk served for three years as a deputy vice president.

F. W. de Klerk (b. 1936), who replaced Botha as president in September 1989, broke the logjam in early 1990 by legalizing all banned political parties and freeing Nelson Mandela, the symbolic leader of many South African blacks, from almost three decades of imprisonment. De Klerk, who had not been known as a reformer, and Mandela, the inveterate foe of apartheid, were unlikely partners. However, they and their negotiating teams began the arduous process of dismantling apartheid and preparing the way for the writing of a new constitution. They had to contend with ultra-right-wing whites who disrupted meetings and hoped to polarize the country as well as conservative blacks who wanted to prevent an ANC government. Thousands died in warfare in the area around Johannesburg and Natal as Chief Mangosuthu Buthelezi's Zulu Inkatha Freedom party contested power with the ANC. The violence was fueled by a "third force" of government agents who covertly fomented violence and assassinated government opponents.

Amazingly, the elections of April 1994 proceeded with few problems. The ANC won almost two-thirds of the seats in the new parliament. Mandela was inaugurated as president, and de Klerk was chosen as one of his vice presidents (he stepped down in 1997). A crisis that a decade earlier seemed destined for a tragic end had been resolved through compromise and democratic elections. Mandela's government has concentrated on healing the divisions between whites and blacks and tackling apartheid's legacy of inequality. Housing, health care, land redistribution, education, and water resources are some of the areas the new government is addressing.

While the South African government was undergoing its own transformation, it was moving to grant independence to Namibia in 1990. A German colony until 1919, the area was known as South-West Africa and administered as a mandate by South Africa under the supervision of the League of Nations. Following World War II South Africa treated South-West Africa as one of its provinces and refused to transfer its jurisdiction to the UN, which formally ended South Africa's mandate in 1966. Inhabited by 1 million blacks and 100,000 whites, Namibia contained valuable mineral deposits, but even more important, it served as a buffer against the tide of liberation in black countries to the north.

In 1985 South Africa concluded an agreement with a coalition of blacks and whites for a form of self-rule, but it refused to negotiate with the South-West African Peoples' Organization (SWAPO), which had been waging a guerrilla war from neighboring Angola and Zambia since the late 1960s. The stalemate was broken in the late 1980s when Cuba agreed to withdraw its troops over several years from neighboring Angola. South Africa likewise offered to withdraw and then worked with the United Nations to oversee a transition to independence. Elections were held in 1989 with SWAPO winning nearly 60 percent of the vote. Namibia has maintained its commitment to democracy and has held national and local elections on a regular basis.

Latin America: Reform or Revolt

After World War II Latin America shared many of the problems experienced by the developing countries of the world outside Europe. Formerly competitive

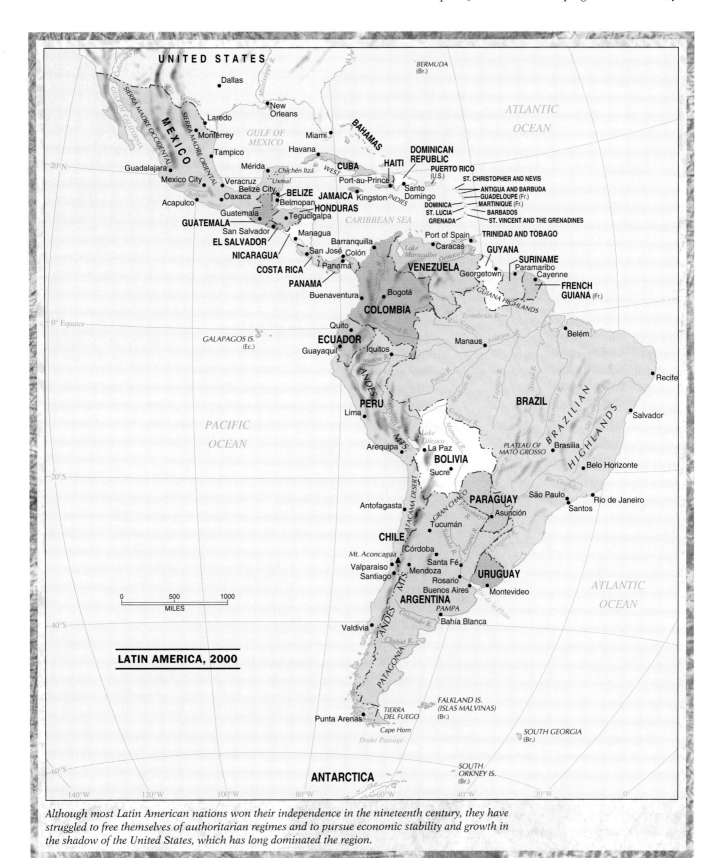

UNITED STATES

Dallas

BERMUDA (Br.)

ATLANTIC OCEAN

New Orleans

Laredo

Monterrey

Miami

BAHAMAS

GULF OF MEXICO

Tampico

Havana

CUBA

HAITI

DOMINICAN REPUBLIC

PUERTO RICO (U.S.)

Guadalajara

Mérida

Chichén Itzá

MEXICO

Mexico City

Veracruz

Belize City

Uxmal

Port-au-Prince

Santo Domingo

ST. CHRISTOPHER AND NEVIS

ANTIGUA AND BARBUDA

GUADELOUPE (Fr.)

MARTINIQUE (Fr.)

Acapulco

Oaxaca

BELIZE

JAMAICA

Kingston

WEST INDIES

DOMINICA

ST. LUCIA

BARBADOS

Guatemala

Belmopan

HONDURAS

GRENADA

ST. VINCENT AND THE GRENADINES

GUATEMALA

Tegucigalpa

CARIBBEAN SEA

TRINIDAD AND TOBAGO

San Salvador

Managua

Port of Spain

EL SALVADOR

Barranquilla

Caracas

GUYANA

NICARAGUA

San José

Colón

VENEZUELA

Georgetown

SURINAME

Paramaribo

Cayenne

COSTA RICA

Panamá

PANAMA

Lake Maracaibo

Orinoco R.

GUIANA HIGHLANDS

FRENCH GUIANA (Fr.)

Buenaventura

Bogotá

COLOMBIA

Quito

Rio Negro

Trombetas R.

Belém

ECUADOR

Iquitos

Manaus

Amazon R.

Recife

Guayaquil

GALAPAGOS IS. (Ec.)

PERU

Lima

BRAZIL

BRAZILIAN HIGHLANDS

Salvador

ANDES MTS.

Lake Titicaca

La Paz

PLATEAU OF MATO GROSSO

Brasilia

Arequipa

Sucre

BOLIVIA

Belo Horizonte

PACIFIC OCEAN

Antofagasta

GRAN CHACO

São Paulo

Rio de Janeiro

Santos

ATACAMA DESERT

PARAGUAY

Asunción

Tucumán

CHILE

Córdoba

Mt. Aconcagua

Santa Fé

Valparaiso

Mendoza

URUGUAY

Santiago

Rosario

Buenos Aires

Montevideo

ARGENTINA

PAMPA

Valdivia

Bahía Blanca

Colorado R.

Chubut R.

ATLANTIC OCEAN

0 500 1000 MILES

LATIN AMERICA, 2000

PATAGONIA

Punta Arenas

TIERRA DEL FUEGO

FALKLAND IS. (ISLAS MALVINAS) (Br.)

SOUTH GEORGIA (Br.)

Cape Horn

Drake Passage

ANTARCTICA

SOUTH ORKNEY IS. (Br.)

Although most Latin American nations won their independence in the nineteenth century, they have struggled to free themselves of authoritarian regimes and to pursue economic stability and growth in the shadow of the United States, which has long dominated the region.

economies such as those of Argentina, Mexico, and Brazil had fallen far behind rapidly advancing areas such as South Korea, Taiwan, and Singapore. Whether in countries of primarily European stock (Argentina, Uruguay, and Chile), dualistic Indian-

Spanish societies (Peru, Bolivia, Ecuador, and Mexico), racially diverse societies such as Brazil and Venezuela, or single-crop economies such as those of Central America, Latin America faced serious problems at the end of the century.

The Perils of the Postwar Era

The period since 1945 witnessed much political instability and social unrest in the region. For example, the only countries with continuously elected governments after 1950 have been those dominated by a single major party. Between 1950 and 1966 a total of 14 governments were forcefully overthrown and dictatorial rule was imposed on more than half the Latin American population. The political instability and the seeds of social upheaval spring from appalling socioeconomic disparities. Despite the region's great natural resources, the average citizen of Latin America is desperately poor. Shantytowns on the edges of large cities house thousands amid filth, disease, hunger, and crime. Life expectancy for Latin American males is around 55 years—17 years less than in North America. Agricultural productivity is inefficient and low. The population increases by about 3 percent yearly. By 1990 the region's population topped 500 million, most living in cities. Educational and health services are insufficient, and literacy rates remain low.

Since 1948 the countries south of the Rio Grande have been aligned with the United States in the Organization of American States (OAS). Dominated by the United States, the OAS sought to prevent Communists from acquiring control in Latin American countries by well-meaning, if incomplete, social and economic aid. In 1959 Fidel Castro rapidly transformed Cuba into a Communist country; afterward his attempts to export his revolution were countered by an OAS boycott.

In Castro's Cuba educational and health standards rose appreciably, as did living conditions among the peasants, who constituted the great majority of the population. The professional and middle classes, however, suffered losses in both living standards and personal liberties, and many hundreds of thousands fled to the United States. Cuba exported sugar to other Communist countries in exchange for major economic subsidies from the Soviet Union. In 1975 some 16 members of the OAS voted to end the embargo, and the United States intimated a desire for détente. This last possibility was made remote with the intervention of thousands of Cuban troops and advisers in Angola and other African countries.

By the mid-1990s global political changes had created new challenges for Castro. Cuba's role overseas ended with peace talks in Angola. The Soviet Union could no longer afford the luxury of propping up Castro's faltering economy and virtually abandoned him. His version of Marxism-Leninism was shared only in North Korea. However, Castro, defying predictions that his regime would quickly collapse, has extended his rule by modifying certain of his policies. He invited Pope John Paul II to pay a state visit in 1998 and allowed Christmas to be celebrated as a public holiday for the first time in three decades. He tolerated some private enterprise, especially in the area of tourism. He eased the impact of the American economic boycott against Cuba by improving trade ties with Latin American, Caribbean, and European nations. Although the American government has generally taken a hostile stance toward Cuba, there are slight differences from one branch of government to another. The U.S. Congress passed the Helms-Burton Act in 1996 to punish non-American businesses operating in Cuba; several years later the Clinton administration eased restrictions on humanitarian assistance and medicines being sent to Cuba.

Until the end of the Cold War, American policy toward Latin America was based on the fear of the spread of communism. After the failure of the American invasion attempt at the Bay of Pigs in Cuba in 1961, President John F. Kennedy initiated the Alliance for Progress to improve the quality of life in Latin American nations. The United States pledged $20 billion, to be matched by the other members of the alliance, but even after 20 years, the alliance had done little to change basic conditions. Oligarchic rule, paternalism, and incompetence hindered economic and political reform. By the mid-1990s Brazil was suffering from a high inflation rate and Mexico remained deeply in debt, paying the interest on foreign loans with difficulty. Rapidly increasing inflation also hampered economic growth. In Brazil there was substantial indication that a large percentage of the foreign loans were not being invested in needed industrialization and regional integration, but were instead being funneled to Swiss banks by top-ranking bureaucrats.

The Yankee Factor

A key element in Latin America is the relationship between the United States and its neighbors. American economic involvement in Latin America has remained massive. American companies continue to employ about 2 million people, pay 25 percent of the region's taxes, and produce one-third of its exports. Softening the imperialist presence are the activities of humanitarian efforts from the Rockefeller Foundation and churches and federal programs of educational, agricultural, and social improvements. In response to the development of the European Union and the possibility of a unified Asian market, the United States pushed for the creation of the North American Free Trade Association, which was put into effect when Canada, Mexico, and the United States

Cuba's socialist policies and an American trade boycott have caused hardships and shortages of basic goods. In this photo from the 1990s, Cubans line up to buy baked goods.

ratified the agreement in 1993. This marked one of the great successes of Mexican president Carlos Salinas and his Institutional Ruling party (PRI). However, from 1995 to 1997 the PRI's control declined as Mexico underwent a severe economic crisis and faced a determined guerrilla movement in Chiapas province. The PRI lost control of Mexico's congress to opposition parties for the first time in over 50 years.

In Chile, the U.S. Central Intelligence Agency used large sums to support the opponents of Chilean president Salvador Allende, an avowed pro-Soviet Marxist. In his hasty efforts to nationalize industry, both domestic and foreign-owned, and to redistribute landholdings, Allende had antagonized many of his own people. His regime came to a bloody end in a 1973 coup. Military leaders ousted the president, who died—perhaps by his own hand—during the

fighting. The new repressive regime, under General Auguste Pinochet, imposed a harsh rule and acted aggressively to curb all opposition, which had been growing since the early 1980s. Pinochet stepped down in 1990 and was replaced by the moderate Patricio Aylwin. Although Pinochet stepped down in 1990 and was succeeded by moderate presidents, he maintained influence as head of the army until his retirement in 1998.

One long-standing source of discord between the United States and Latin America was removed in 1978 when the United States Senate approved the treaty that returned the Panama Canal Zone to the Republic of Panama while safeguarding American interests in the area. This agreement, negotiated over a period of 14 years under four American presidents, was a sign to some that the United States was eager to improve relations with its neighbors. However, there were some excesses the United States would not tolerate: allegations that Panamanian President Manuel Noriega cooperated in drug running and overturned democratic elections moved U.S. President Bush to order an American military invasion of Panama to oust Noriega in December 1989.

In the 1990s the countries of Latin America dealt differently with the economic, social, and political challenges they faced. Many states made the transition from military to civilian rule, although the new democracies remain fragile. Nicaragua carried out a socialist revolution but faced the powerful overt and covert opposition of the United States. In spite of democratic elections in 1990 that led to the defeat of the socialist Sandinista party in Nicaragua, economic and social problems continued to plague the new government. El Salvador struggled through a bloody civil war in which death squads from both right and left brought terror to the countryside. Corruption and a series of poor policy decisions in the early 1990s undermined Brazil's economy. Although the government of President Fernando Cardoso curbed inflation, it has not controlled huge budget deficits and currency devaluations, which have slowed economic growth. Out-of-control inflation destroyed Argentina's economy, though elected officials restored normal democratic politics. Mexico remained stable, despite challenges to its one-party domination, but faced a birthrate that outstripped its economic progress. Although the Colombian government has waged a vigorous war against drug lords, its basic sovereignty has been undermined by drug traffickers and corrupt government officials.

In the Caribbean the British successfully ushered in independence in the West Indies—Jamaica, Trinidad and Tobago, Barbados, and numerous other colonies became sovereign nations. Grenada fell to a leftist government before President Ronald Reagan sent U.S. marines to the island to overthrow the regime in 1983. Unrest continued in Haiti, the poorest country in the Western Hemisphere. President for Life Jean-Claude Duvalier, "Baby Doc," was forced out of office and fled the country in February 1986. In February 1991 Jean-Bertrand Aristide, a Catholic priest, was elected president. Seven months later the army kicked him out. In response, the UN laid an oil and arms embargo on the country, which led to a compromise under which Aristide would be allowed back in the country. When the compromise collapsed, a wave of reprisals and random murders swept the country and led to the frantic exodus of thousands of Haitians on fragile craft to avoid punishment. By autumn 1994, after the coup leaders refused to give in to international demands for Aristide's return, the United States and its Caribbean allies forced the coup leaders out and restored Aris-

tide to power—but only after he agreed not to run for reelection. After Aristide's party's candidate, René Préval, succeeded him as president in 1996, Aristide grew dissatisfied with Préval's performance and formed his own political party.

Conclusion

In the second half of the twentieth century the developing world has emerged as a potentially dynamic theater of action for the next century. These countries hold the world's fastest-growing populations, its most essential resources, and the most politically explosive situations. All these countries, from richest to poorest, have been affected by decolonization, the Cold War and its conclusion, and the technological revolution. All of them entered the modern era in a period of European dominance that often provoked violent encounters. Many face major economic and demographic issues that find expression in political instability. The drawing of new nation-state boundaries after World War II as imperial powers withdrew from territories like India and Palestine created massive refugee problems and inflamed ethnoreligious tensions in ways that have significantly shaped—and continue to shape—the destinies of nations in Asia and Africa.

China, the most powerful country in the developing world, participated in Cold War episodes from Korea to Vietnam and fought its own ideological battles before entering a period of rapid modernization after 1978. In the rest of Asia nations freed themselves from the yoke of European dominance but often continued to experience economic dependence. Independence unleashed powerful ethnic and religious antagonisms, many of which remain unresolved. After the British withdrew from the subcontinent, India and Pakistan entered a half century of sometimes peaceful competition. The increasing power of Hindu nationalism now signals an era of continued communal violence in India, the second most populous nation in the world. In the Middle East the politics of oil have reconfigured global economic relations and split the region very dramatically into haves and have-nots. The Arab-Israeli conflict continues to serve as an epicenter of regional politics, while Islamist movements challenge Western-style secular nationalism.

African nations succeeded in gaining their independence from European colonizers and white-settler regimes in southern Africa. However, they have been plagued by a host of problems in creating viable nation-states—regional and ethnic factionalism, dictators and military coups, Cold War rivalries, lack of trained administrators, and weak physical infrastructures. In addition, despite Africa's abundant natural resources, most African countries are economically underdeveloped and have high rates of poverty. Despite the challenges of independence, some African nations have introduced democratic political systems and policies that have improved their economic performance.

More than Cold War tensions, economic upheavals have affected the Latin American states. The region's accumulation of massive debts and its dependence on the export of oil or agricultural products left it at the mercy of the North Atlantic powers. This economic domination provided a rich opportunity for revolutionaries in Cuba and Nicaragua, who fought against the obvious exploitation of the population.

Suggestions for Reading

John K. Fairbank, Edwin O. Reischauer, and Albert M. Craig discuss the challenges of change in *East Asia: Tradition and Transformation*, rev. ed. (Houghton Mifflin, 1989). Stuart Schram, *Mao Tse-tung* (Penguin, 1966), is good for the formative stages of the leader's life. Richard H. Solomon, *Mao's Revolution and the Chinese Political Culture* (University of California Press, 1971), ties political change to social transformation. Edward F. Rice gives a good summation of Mao's theories in *Mao's Way* (University of California Press, 1975). Roderick MacFarquar, *Origins of the Cultural Revolution* (Oxford University Press, 1983), is first-rate. Changes in the countryside are considered in Jan Myrdal, *Report from a Chinese Village* (Signet, 1969), which discusses political change from a rural perspective. Thomas Raski gives an overall view of economic modernization in *China's Transition to Industrialism* (University of Michigan Press, 1980). See also Immanuel C. Y. Hsu, *China Without Mao: The Search for a New Order*, 2nd ed. (Oxford University Press, 1990). Bruce D. Porter, *The USSR in Third World Conflicts: Soviet Arms and Diplomacy in Local Wars, 1945–1980* (Cambridge University Press, 1984), presents analyses of various episodes of Soviet participation in Third World crises and the changing nature of Moscow's involvements. Franz Ansprenger gives a helpful account of decolonization in *The Dissolution of the Colonial Empires* (Routledge, 1989).

For studies of Southeast Asia, see Michael Leifer, *The Foreign Relations of the New States* (Longman, 1979); Robert N. Kearney, *Politics and Modernization in South and Southeast Asia* (Halstead, 1974); and Robert Shaplan, *A Turning Wheel: The Long Revolution in Asia* (Random House, 1979). On Indonesia, see Wilfred T. Neill, *Twentieth-Century Indonesia* (Columbia University Press, 1973), and Alistair MacDonald Taylor, *Indonesian Independence and the United Nations* (Greenwood, 1975).

Some valuable surveys of modern India include W. Norman Brown, *The United States and India, Pakistan, and Bangladesh* (Harvard University Press, 1972); Stanley Wolpert, *A New History of India*, 5th ed. (Oxford University Press, 1997); and Sugata Bose and Ayesha Jalal, *Modern South Asia: History, Culture, and Political Economy* (Routledge, 1998). A solid biography of Indira Gandhi is Zareer Masani, *Indira Gandhi* (Crowell, 1976). An informative guide to Indian politics is Richard L. Park and Bruce Bueno de Mesquita, *India's Political System* (Prentice Hall, 1979).

A good survey of the Middle East in the late twentieth century is William Cleveland, *A History of the Modern Middle East* (Westview, 1996). See also Malcolm Yapp, *The Near East Since the First World War*, 2nd ed. (Longman, 1996). On Islam in context, see John Voll, *Islam: Continuity and Change in the Modern World* (Westview 1982). The best survey of the Arab-Israeli conflict is Charles D. Smith, *Palestine and the Arab-Israeli Conflict*, 3rd ed. (St. Martin's Press, 1996); see also Ian Bickerton and Carla Klausner, *A Concise History of the Arab-Israeli Conflict*, 3rd ed. (Prentice Hall, 1998). On the United Nations' original partition plan, see Walter Laqueur and Barry Rubin, eds., *The Israeli-Arab Reader: A Documentary History of the Middle East Conflict*, 5th ed. (Penguin, 1995).

Some insightful books on Iran are Rouhollah K. Ramazani, *The Persian Gulf: Iran's Role* (University of Virginia Press, 1972); Said Arjomand, *The Turban for the Crown: The Islamic Revolution in Iran* (Oxford University Press, 1988); and James Bill, *The Eagle and the Lion: The Tragedy of American-Iranian Relations* (Yale University Press, 1988). William Dorman and Mansour Farhang, *The U.S. Press and Iran* (University of California Press, 1987), is an interesting study of the treatment of Iran in the U.S. media. On Turkey, see Feroz Ahmad, *The Making of Modern Turkey* (Routledge, 1993); and Erik Zürcher, *Turkey: A Modern History* (Tauris, 1993).

Soviet participation in the area is spelled out in Jon D. Glassman, *Arms for Arabs: The Soviet Union and War in the Middle East* (Johns Hopkins University Press, 1976). Daniel Yergin, *The Prize* (Touchstone Press, 1991), is a beautifully written and acutely analytical study of the impact of oil on politics and diplomacy in the world.

General studies on contemporary African political and economic development include Claude Ake, *A Political Economy of Africa* (Longman, 1981); Richard Sklar, *African Politics and Problems in Development* (Rienner, 1991); April Gordon and Donald Gordon, eds., *Understanding Contemporary Africa* (Rienner, 1996); William Reno, *Warlord Politics and African States* (Rienner, 1998); William Tordoff, *Government and Politics in Africa*, 3rd ed. (Indiana University Press, 1997); Edmond Keller and Donald Rothchild, eds., *Africa in the New International Order* (Rienner, 1996); Mahmood Mamdani, *Citizen and Subject: Contemporary Africa and the Legacy of Late Colonialism* (Princeton University Press, 1996); Okello Oculi, *Discourses on African Affairs: Directions and Destinies for the 21st Century* (Africa World Press, 1997); and Peter Lewis, *Africa: Dilemmas of Development and Change* (Westview, 1998). Among the best studies on Afro-Marxism is Edmond Keller and Donald Rothchild, eds., *Afro-Marxist Regimes: Ideology and Public Policy* (Rienner, 1987).

Recent developments in specific African countries are covered in Marina Ottaway, ed., *The Political Economy of Ethiopia* (Praeger, 1990); Dawit Wolde Giorgis, *Red Tears: War, Famine, and Revolution in Ethiopia* (Red Sea Press, 1989); Christopher Clapham, *Transformation and Continuity in Revolutionary Ethiopia* (Cambridge University Press, 1988); Kinfe Abraham, *Ethiopia* (Red Sea Press, 1994); Alice Hashim, *The Fallen State: Dissonance, Dictatorship, and Death in Somalia* (University Press of America, 1997); Walter Clarke and Jeffrey Herbst, *Learning from Somalia: The Lessons of Armed Humanitarian Intervention* (Westview, 1997); Anna Simons, *Networks of Dissolution: Somalia Undone* (Westview, 1995); Laurent Kaela, *The Question of Namibia* (St. Martin's Press, 1996); Colin Leys, *Namibia's Liberation Struggle* (Ohio University Press, 1995); Lionel Cliffe, ed., *The Transition to Independence in Namibia* (Rienner, 1994); Paul Beckett and Crawford Young, *Dilemmas of Democracy in Nigeria* (University of Rochester Press, 1997); Wole Soyinka, *The Open Sore of a Continent: A Personal Narrative of the Nigerian Crisis* (Oxford University Press, 1996); and

Christine Sylvester, *Zimbabwe* (Westview, 1991). Mobutu Sese Seko's mismanagement of Zaïre is chronicled in Crawford Young, *The Rise and Decline of the Zaïrian State* (University of Wisconsin Press, 1985). Rwanda's genocide is examined in Fergal Keane, *Season of Blood: A Rwandan Journey* (Viking, 1995), and Gerard Prunier, *The Rwanda Crisis, 1959–1994: History of a Genocide* (Fountain, 1995).

The movement toward democratization in Africa is analyzed in Claude Ake, *Democracy and Development in Africa* (Brookings Institution, 1996); Marina Ottaway, ed., *Democracy in Africa* (Rienner, 1997); Richard Joseph, ed., *State, Conflict, and Democracy in Africa* (Rienner, 1998); and Georges Nzongola-Ntalaja and Margaret Lee, eds., *The State and Democracy in Africa* (Africa World Press, 1998). The liberation struggle in Portugal's African colonies is examined in David Birmingham, *Frontline Struggles in Angola and Mozambique* (Africa World Press, 1992), and David Birmingham and Phyllis Johnson, eds., *A History of Central Africa: The Contemporary Years Since 1960* (Longman, 1998).

Afrikaner politics and the construction of the apartheid system are covered in Heribert Adam and Hermann Giliomee, *Ethnic Power Mobilized* (Yale University Press, 1979); Dan O'Meara, *Forty Lost Years: The Apartheid State and the Politics of the National Party, 1948–1998* (Ohio University Press, 1996); and David Harrison, *The White Tribe of Africa* (University of California Press, 1982). The African challenge to apartheid is treated in Gail Gerhart, *Black Power in South Africa* (University of California Press, 1978), and Thomas Karis and Gail Gerhart, *From Protest to Challenge: A Documentary History of African Politics in South Africa*, vols. 3 and 5 (Indiana University Press, 1997). The ending of apartheid and the transition to democratic rule in South Africa is covered in Allister Sparks, *Tomorrow Is Another Country: The Inside Story of South Africa's Road to Change* (University of Chicago Press, 1996), and Patti Waldmeir, *Anatomy of a Miracle: The End of Apartheid and the Birth of the New South Africa* (Norton, 1997).

General studies on Latin America include E. Bradford Burns, *Latin America: A Concise Interpretive History*, 9th ed. (Prentice Hall, 1994); Peter Winn, *Americas: The Changing Face of Latin America and the Caribbean* (University of California Press, 1995); Brian Blouet, *Latin America and the Caribbean: A Systematic and Regional Survey*, 3rd ed. (Wiley, 1996); Leslie Bethell, ed., *Latin America: Economy and Society Since 1930* (Cambridge University Press, 1998); Will Fowler, ed., *Ideologues and Ideologies in Latin America* (Greenwood Press, 1997); and Gordon Mace and Louis Helanger, eds., *The Americas in Transition: The Contours of Regionalism* (Lynne Rienner, 1999). In the 1990s scholars have focused on the transition from military to civilian governments. Among the key studies are Jorge Dominguez and Abraham Lowenthal, eds., *Constructing Democratic Governance: South America in the 1990s* (Johns Hopkins University Press, 1996); Paul Zagorski, *Democracy vs. National Security: Civil-Military Relations in Latin America* (Lynne Rienner, 1992); Jorge Dominguez and Marc Lindenberg, eds., *Democratic Transitions in Central America* (University Press of Florida, 1997); Rachel Sider, *Central America: Fragile Transition* (St. Martin's Press, 1996); Kurt von Mettenheim and James Malloy, eds., *Deepening Democracy in Latin America* (University of Pittsburgh Press, 1998); John Peeler, *Building Democracy in Latin America* (Lynne Rienner, 1999); and Ivelaw Griffith, *Democracy and Human Rights in the Caribbean* (Westview Press, 1997).

The best general studies on Mexican politics are Roderic Al Camp, *Mexico: Politics in Mexico*, 2nd ed. (Oxford University Press, 1996), and Enrigue Krauze, *Mexico: Biography of Power: A History of Modern Mexico, 1810–1996* (HarperCollins, 1997). Specific studies on Brazil include Susan Kaufman Purcell and Riordan Roett, eds., *Brazil Under Cardozo* (Lynne Rienner, 1997); Wendy Hunter, *Eroding Military Influence in Brazil: Politicians Against Soldiers* (University of North Carolina Press, 1997); Javier Martine-Lara, *Building Democracy in Brazil: The Politics of Constitutional Change, 1985–1995* (St. Martin's Press, 1996); and Michael Hanchard, *Racial Politics in Contemporary Brazil* (Duke University Press, 1999).

Recent works on Cuba are Irving Louis Horowitz and Jaime Suchlicki, *Cuban Communism*, 9th ed. (Transaction, 1998); Miguel Angel Centeno and Mauricio Font, eds., *Toward a New Cuba: Legacies of a Revolution* (Lynne Rienner, 1997); Louis Perez, *On Becoming Cuban: Identity, Nationality, and Culture* (University of North Carolina Press, 1999); G. L. Simons, *Cuba: From Conquistador to Castro* (St. Martin's Press, 1996); and Archibald Miller and John Kirk, eds., *Cuba in the International System: Normalization and Integration* (St. Martin's Press, 1995).

American foreign policy toward Latin America is examined in Lars Schoultz, *Beneath the United States: A History of U.S. Policy Toward Latin America* (Harvard University Press, 1998); Eldon Kenworthy, *America/Americas: Myth in the Making of U.S. Policy Toward Latin America* (Pennsylvania State University Press, 1995); and Walter La Feber, *Inevitable Revolutions: The United States in Central America*, 2nd ed. (Norton, 1993).

Suggestions for Web Browsing

Internet East Asia History Sourcebook: China Since World War II
http://www.fordham.edu/halsall/eastasia/eastasiabook.html#China Since World War II

Extensive on-line source for links about the history of China after 1949.

History: People's Republic of China
http://darkwing.uoregon.edu/~felsing/cstuff/prchist.html

Numerous documents, and links to other sites, about the people and events of China since 1949, compiled by the Council on East Asian Libraries.

Internet Islamic History Sourcebook: The Islamic World Since 1945
http://www.fordham.edu/halsall/islam/islamsbook.html#The Islamic World Since 1945

Extensive on-line source for links about the history of the Middle East since 1945, including country studies, international affairs, and the Israel-Palestine conflict.

Itihaas: Chronology—Independent India
http://www.itihaas.com/medieval/index.html

In-depth chronology of independence; most entries include subsites with text and images.

Internet African History Sourcebook: Modern Africa
http://www.fordham.edu/halsall/africa/africasbook.html#Modern Africa

Detailed on-line source for links about the history of Africa since 1945, including primary documents regarding country studies, continuing imperialism, international affairs, and gender and sexuality.

Internet African History Sourcebook: Latin America
http://www.fordham.edu/halsall/mod/modsbook55.html#
20th Century Latin America

Detailed on-line source for documents regarding specific countries, common themes and issues, and indigenous peoples.

Notes

1. Richard Rovere, *Senator Joe McCarthy* (London: Methuen, 1959), p. 24.
2. Samad Behrangi, *The Little Black Fish and Other Stories,* trans. Eric and Mary Hooglund (Washington, D.C.: Three Continents Press, 1982), p. 37.

Epilogue

Into the Third Millennium

This ninth edition of *Civilization Past & Present* takes us beyond the two thousandth anniversary of the birth of Christ and therefore into the third millennium of the Christian era. In the Bible, the *millennium* related to the prophecy of Christ's reign on earth for 1000 years, envisioned as an era of happiness and good government. Associated with any such era is the concept of an ideal society, or *utopia*. We have referred to some of these in the pages of this book: Plato's *Republic*, Thomas More's *Utopia*, and Francis Bacon's *New Atlantis*.

In contrast to these earlier works about societies where everything is fundamentally good, twentieth-century literature also produced a number of *dystopias*, where things are basically bad. They include Aldous Huxley's *Brave New World* and its disillusionment with Western materialism, George Orwell's *Nineteen Eighty-Four* with its nightmare vision of a future totalitarian state controlled by "Big Brother," and Jacques Ellul's *Technological Society*, where moral and social values are subordinated to the overarching demands of "technique," and human beings have become appendages of mechanistic processes.

What are we to make of this? Is our society fundamentally good and getting better or bad and getting worse? Because we live in a highly complex period of history, although the moral guidelines may still seem straightforward, our social behavior has been anything but simple. At the beginning of the 1990s there was much talk about a "new world order," but few believe that it ushered in any "golden age." Yet if we cannot expect to live in a utopia, the challenge of the twenty-first century is to make sure at least that our actions do not become dystopian. To employ a salutation that reflects our times: "Take care."

"I am like a man standing between two worlds. I look both forward and backward." So spoke the Italian "father of humanism," Francesco Petrarch, who has been described as the "hinge of the door" between two very different societies: the Middle Ages, with its emphasis on faith and collective values, and the Renaissance, with its humanist concerns and focus on individual values. Is it possible that we too are in the midst of a societal shift of historic proportions, one that will become increasingly apparent as we move forward in the coming decades? To determine whether we are also situated at another "hinge of the door," let us emulate Petrarch by looking both backward at our recent past and forward into the emerging shape of the third millennium.

The Twentieth Century in Retrospect

As we leave the twentieth century, we have the opportunity to look back at its evolution, the description of which occupies nearly a quarter of the pages of the ninth edition of *Civilization Past & Present*. It was probably the most tumultuous and creative—and certainly the most populous—century in recorded history. Perhaps its unique characteristic has been to create what the American statesman Wendell Willkie in the 1940s described as "One World" and Marshall McLuhan later termed the "global village"—observations vividly corroborated in photographs of our beautiful but finite planet taken from space. Its decades were responsible for *globalizing* communication networks, air routes, weather systems, scientific and medical discoveries, trade and finance, travel and tourism, sports and movies, and a host of computerized technologies. Sadly, they also witnessed warfare and carnage on a global scale, as well as unprecedented despoliation of our planetary environment. The Chinese have a benediction that they traditionally regarded as something of a curse: "May you live in interesting times." It has indeed been an "interesting" century.

Along with *global*, our language makes increasing use of a number of related terms that give a distinctive quality to our times, terms such as *systemic*, *holistic*, *interconnected*, and *interacting*. Nationalism and independence remain powerful divisive forces in the world, as is seen in the continuation of tragic microconflicts and political devolution around the world. But at the same time in today's increasingly integrated world we find an unprecedented emphasis on internationalism and interdependence in the activities of transnational corporations and intergovernmental agencies. It remains to be seen which force, the centrifugal or the centripetal, will dominate in the next century.

Scientific and Technological Change

More scientists and technologists have worked in the past hundred years than in all previous centuries combined. Together they have revolutionized our understanding of the planet's basic structure and processes. Some of the major scientific breakthroughs occurred early in the century with Planck's quantum mechanics, Einstein's relativity theory, and Heisenberg's uncertainty principle; later decades saw the development of systems and chaos theories. Advances in biology, especially in molecular biology and the significance of the DNA code, have opened the way to genetic engineering in plants and animals, cloning, and the treatment of various human diseases.

Atomic fission created the nuclear age by releasing vast new energy sources for civilian and military purposes. But this has proved to be a two-edged sword. On the one hand, nuclear power gives promise of a seemingly endless source of energy that might be employed, for example, to desalinate ocean waters on a massive scale. On the other hand, atomic bombs destroyed urban populations in Hiroshima and Nagasaki, and an explosion in a nuclear power plant wreaked havoc in Chernobyl and far beyond. Meanwhile, a continuing problem is the safe disposal of ever-growing amounts of spent radioactive nuclear fuel.

A quantum leap in the technological evolution of humanity occurred with the invention of heavier-than-air machines to move into the third, or vertical, dimension, thereby ushering in the space age. This new control capability has had unprecedented global consequences for transportation, politics, and the peace equation and has propelled us in turn into exploring and understanding outer space. And with the invention of computer technology, we now network in the information age and through cyberspace. Electronics enables the factoring and dissemination of an incredible amount of data at the speed of light. Millions of computer terminals make possible the complex activities of large and small businesses, governments, universities, and schools. In short, the computer provides the informational sinews of a global economy and all segments of society.

Political Change

The past century was marked by tensions and competition in two areas: nationalism and ideology. World War I was largely a struggle between competing national ambitions; World War II witnessed a struggle to the death among liberal democracy, fascism, and communism. As the century waned, we again saw nationalist struggles break out in Europe, Asia, and Africa.

For decades after World War II, millions of people living on either side of the Iron Curtain suffered the trauma of the Cold War between antagonists equipped with trillions of dollars' worth of nuclear weapons—a conflict that, by desire or mishap, could have plunged the planet into the holocaust of World War III. In the early 1990s the Cold War ended with the tearing down of the Berlin Wall and the signing of new disarmament agreements. These years also saw the dismantling of the Soviet Union itself. In the ensuing period, marked by regional upheavals such as the Persian Gulf War, conflict in the former Yugoslavia, and genocidal tragedies in central Africa, Americans wondered how long their country, as the only remaining superpower, must bear the primary responsibility for policing the world.

To create a new international institution for advancing peace, the United States and its allies had founded the United Nations, together with a number of specialized agencies to work toward new global economic and social standards and improve health and education in the developing countries. Because of the threat of mutual annihilation posed by nuclear weapons, new means for controlling conflict had to be devised. One such technique was to empower the UN with the role of peacekeeper—a role it has found difficult to fulfill.

Probably the most far-reaching political change since 1945 was the dismantling of colonial empires and their replacement by large numbers of new nation-states in Asia, Africa, and the Middle East. All too often their respective roads to independence and economic viability proved rocky, thereby threatening global stability. Their problems underscored a potentially dangerous threat to all societies, namely, an increasing disparity in living standards between the rich industrial countries and the impoverished developing countries.

Economic Change

Throughout the past century, in times of peace and war alike, national economies continued to expand. Industrialization triumphed in the developed countries of the world. Its success was accompanied by the advent of the "consumer society" and the extension of the "welfare state." Notable, too, was the creation of a truly global economic market, spearheaded by the transnational corporations of these nations. Their penetration into developing countries stimulated the governments of East Asia to establish market economies geared to emulate, on a massive scale, the developed nations' industrial processes and manufacturing of consumer goods. East Asia, led by China, became the world's fastest-growing economic region.

However, in attempting to modernize their economies, many countries in Africa and Latin America embarked on ambitious programs largely financed by borrowing from wealthier nations' financial institutions. The result was a debt crisis; in the 1981–1990 period, interest payments alone became larger than the total debt of developing countries at the beginning of that decade. Meanwhile, the failure of state-controlled economies in the former Soviet Union and other socialist countries in eastern Europe led to wholesale shifts to market economies. These shifts were so abrupt and so lacking in transitional strategy that they caused enormous economic suffering and social unrest.

After decades of unprecedented growth, the economies of the developed world ran into major problems. Postwar expansion enabled governments to embark on publicly funded programs that created the welfare state. In the 1990s, skyrocketing public debt brought into question the affordability and even the value of retaining this welfare state. How to handle the national debt and its implications for maintaining existing standards in education, health, and social assistance became major issues in the United States and other democracies.

Social Change

The greatest population explosion in history occurred in the twentieth century. Concurrent with this demographic explosion was the mass migration to cities on every continent. Urban dynamics also found expression in two other major social movements: universal free public education and universal suffrage. Increasing dependence on specialized skills and scientific knowledge translated into a fundamental need for effective systems of education. The expansion of educational opportunities for women, especially at the postsecondary level, was part of the drive toward gender parity in society.

The urban explosion and way of life were certain to strengthen a globally oriented type of society, given the continuous communication exchanges among all cities. The city is also the center of what has been called the mass society. Here, too, we encounter widespread socioeconomic tensions. In addition, the dynamics of social change gave voice in the 1960s to

a counterculture: rebellion, particularly among the young, against traditional values and the materialism of an acquisitive society. The century had produced a volatile global society.

The Twenty-First Century in Prospect

Let us extrapolate from our present experiences to project foreseeable issues of fundamental importance for our new century. The basic issues we have examined throughout the pages of *Civilization Past & Present* will simultaneously affect global society and the future prospects of our various ways of life. They derive logically from the experiences and behavior of the twentieth century and are intermixed with both promises and perils. In what follows, we set forth these doubled-edged issues in the form of *challenges* confronting all peoples.

Sustaining the Natural Environment

All species depend for survival on the planet's resources, derived from its water, soil, and air. Hence it is logical that ecologists and philosophers alike are discussing whether we humans own the earth and its resources or have the right only to act as its stewards. According to the Haida Indians, "We do not inherit the earth from our fathers; we borrow it from our children." Poets and painters describe its beauty by word and brush; societies are organized on its land. Governments seek to control specific parcels of territory and adjacent waters. Economists devise means to account for its wealth; from time immemorial men and women have labored to sustain their families by harvests from the soil and seas, while technologists invent ever more effective means to obtain and consume the planet's resources.

As a consequence of all these activities, our species' relationship to its global environment has shifted from simple adaptation to progressively more powerful usage and exploitation. Today we see about us the consequences of this exploitation; tomorrow will confront us with prospects and problems challenging human ingenuity to preserve the planet and its myriad inhabitants. In the decades ahead we shall have to cope with at least six major environmental issues.

1. *The population explosion will continue to exert ecological pressures.* To appreciate the magnitude of this issue, we should put it into historical perspective. After hundreds of thousands of years of high birth and death rates, genus *Homo* reached the 1.6 billion mark in 1900. Half a century later, the number rose to

2.5 billion, and it took only another 37 years for it again to double. By 2000 C.E. it had reached 6.25 billion. The planet's human population had virtually quadrupled in one century.

This demographic increase is already slowing down from the twentieth century's unparalleled rate of growth, and some of the developed countries are reaching a steady state. But other regions, including Southeast Asia, sub-Saharan Africa, and Latin America, continue to have such rapid growth that the planet's aggregate numbers could still reach 10 billion by the middle of the twenty-first century and conceivably exceed 12 billion by its end.

2. *Demographic pressures are accelerating the diminution of nonrenewable resources, such as minerals and fossil fuels, and the destruction of many renewable resources.* Fishing stocks in the North Atlantic have become so depleted that scientists warn they may never return to previous levels. Rain forests in Amazonia are being destroyed at the rate of thousands of hectares daily to create new grazing lands that serve, among other purposes, to raise beef for fast-food outlets in the United States. This destruction is doing critical harm to the earth's atmosphere since the rain forests are its principal producers of oxygen. They are also the chief repository of animal species and plants whose daily destruction represents the permanent loss of potential sources of pharmaceutical material for our medicines. In 1998 a global assessment based on more than two decades of field studies found at least one in eight plant species in the world—and nearly one in three in the United States—threatened by extinction. Meanwhile, the current destruction of plants, "the building blocks of our food," continues at an accelerating pace.[1]

3. *Gases released by the use of refrigerants and aerosols have depleted the atmosphere's ozone layer.* This depletion, observed over both the Antarctic and Arctic latitudes, has increased the incidence of skin cancers in numerous countries, and experts predict that a substantial loss of ozone "could have catastrophic effects on human and livestock health and on some life forms at the base of the marine food chain."[2]

4. *Slow but significant atmospheric warming is likely to occur.* Caused by the emission of greenhouse gases, such as carbon dioxide, methane, and chlorofluorocarbons, this could either enhance or impede agriculture. It might be of benefit in cold regions where the growing season is short, but it would reduce crop yields in tropical and subtropical areas where certain crops are already growing near their limit of heat tolerance. In fact, National Oceanic and Atmospheric Administration reported that the 1990s had been the hottest decade on record. Were global warming to precipitate a swelling of the oceans and a melting of polar ice, the results could be catastrophic. Higher sea levels could claim low-lying farmland, such as in Bangladesh and parts of Florida, or even entirely submerge islands in the Indian Ocean and elsewhere.

5. *The lower atmosphere is likely to become increasingly polluted from smog and other harmful substances.* Although this problem is now being alleviated in most developed countries, it will continue to endanger the health of urban populations in the developing nations where economies, such as the Chinese, are rapidly industrializing with little concern for protecting the environment.

6. *All countries will have to carry large economic burdens resulting from environmental problems.* To the long-standing problems of water pollution, depletion of groundwater, and proliferation of hazardous wastes and toxic chemicals must be added two more: acid rain and desertification. Acid rain has threatened lakes and forests over large areas of North America and Europe. Meanwhile, deserts have been advancing on every continent, the worst situation occurring in Africa's Sudano-Sahelian zones. Caused by increasing human population, cattle overgrazing, cultivation of cash crops on unsuitable rangelands, and deforestation, the degradation of land to desertlike conditions has grown at an annual rate of 6 million hectares, while 21 million more hectares provide no economic return.[3]

In an effort to avert any potential environmental disaster, 135 governments held an "Earth Summit" at Rio de Janeiro in June 1992. There they agreed to protect endangered species and act on global warming and adopted an agenda for economic development within a sustainable environment. But most of the recommendations were nonbinding, and when they gathered again in Kyoto in 1998 to confer on protecting the global climate, participants admitted that little had been accomplished. Then, in what seemed a backward step to environmentalists, they agreed that international audits of each country's performance on reducing carbon emissions would not begin until 2008. They also accepted the principle of "carbon trading," giving each country a quota for the amount of carbon dioxide it is allowed to release into the atmosphere each year.

Our ultimate ability to survive as a species depends squarely on our planet's continued environmental viability. And for the first time in history that viability is now in question.

Balancing Population and Resources

The past century's population explosion resulted from two interrelated components: mortality and fertility. The major cause for the spectacular jump in global population has been the rapid fall in death rates as a result of medical advances and increased life expectancy. Birthrates have not declined proportionately, nor have they declined evenly among regions. In this century the populations of the developed nations will reach a steady state, but those of the developing world will continue so as to become about nine times that of the developed world by 2050, in large part because of the high percentage of children who have yet to reproduce. Population control depends in large measure on ethical and religious considerations and on political will. An international population conference held in Cairo in 1994 showed how difficult it will be to mobilize sufficient political consensus to make a substantial difference in reducing global population growth.

The relationship between global population and resources is worsened by the inverse ratio between increasing human numbers and diminishing arable space on which to feed them. In 1000 B.C.E. the planet's estimated 50 million people had available roughly 3 square kilometers per person. A millennium later saw that figure reduced to 0.8 square kilometer, while in 1000 C.E. the earth's 265 million people had little more than half a square kilometer apiece. Since 1500, space per person has been shrinking drastically. If and when global population reaches 11.6 billion later in the twenty-first century, it will be constricted to 0.013 square kilometer per person. Each square would have to provide living space, operate factories, and grow food for 78 persons. But since that area includes polar ice caps, mountain ranges, and deserts, an estimated 200 people would then have to squeeze themselves and their support systems into each habitable square kilometer.[4]

Can the growing human population continue to feed itself? Experts are divided. The optimists—economists and some agricultural scientists—argue that the earth can produce more than enough food for the expected population in 2050 because of technological innovation and continued investment of human capital. Thus the Green Revolution, with its combination of high-yielding hybrid seed, chemical pesticides, and improved water supply, has enabled Asian and Latin American agriculture to keep pace with population growth in the aggregate—although per capita food production declined in Africa. The pessimists, led by environmentalists, regard the situation as a catastrophe in the making. Feeding a growing population can only be done by intensifying farming practices, which, as with the Green Revolution, run counter to ecologically sound aspects of traditional agriculture and cause massive damage by depleting water tables, increasing salinity, reducing soil fertility, and reducing biodiversity.[5] A third position regards the other

two as extremist. The real problem lies in the maldistribution of resources and wealth, and this will continue to be the case until developing countries have greater access to resources and acquire greater freedom of economic initiative.

In the past, the prosperous people of the developed nations thought they could insulate themselves from the poverty and problems in the rest of the world. But developments in recent decades have made the rich and the poor nations mutually vulnerable. Besides their environmental interconnectedness and global population pressures, strains between their respective economic standards will have to be addressed. At present, some 70 percent of the world's income is produced and consumed by 15 percent of its people. Conversely, living standards in Latin America are lower than in the 1970s, and in Africa they have fallen to 1960s levels. We are confronted with a "growing mismatch between where the world's riches, technology, good health, and other benefits are to be found, and where the world's fast-growing new generations, possessing few if any of those benefits, live. A population explosion on one part of the globe and a technology explosion on the other is not a good recipe for a stable international order" because it leads to the crisis posed by the "revolution of rising expectations" among both the haves and the have-nots.[6]

Affecting developed and developing nations alike, the fulfillment of these expectations depends on availability of resources, a high level of employment, and continuing growth of a consumer society. Environmentalists warn that present rates of resource consumption cannot continue indefinitely and that we should already be cutting back for the sake of future generations. This warning strikes at the heart of the free enterprise system as we know it today. The concept of growth has always been considered essential to the structure and behavior of this system, which historically has made spectacular gains producing goods and services and raising living standards. But this growth ethos always assumes that abundant physical resources and energy can continue to satisfy all future requirements, whatever the scale. The new century will test that basic assumption as never before.

Social Changes and Challenges

At the international level, we will have to recognize that in an interdependent world, people everywhere must be treated as equals. Global acceptance of nondiscrimination is critical as population and resource problems build and regions of the developed world cry out for help. Realistic responses will require not only aid and rehabilitation assistance to poorer societies at critical times but also willingness by the richer economies to share a larger proportion of their own resources for the others' long-term development. Given the growing mutual vulnerability of the two great segments of the planet's people, such cooperation will be indispensable in this century to make them mutually viable.

A related factor affecting all nations will be the massive movement of people. Migration has been a phenomenon throughout history, but its present scale is made unique by the speed of the process combined with the density of existing settlements. Among the many millions of migrants are refugees fleeing from political conflicts and civil wars, and these flows will pose mounting social and ethical questions as developed societies formulate their immigration policies.

Another kind of perennial migration is taking place on every continent: from the countryside to the cities, a phenomenon that began in ancient Mesopotamia and made possible the first urban civilization. Today the world is urbanizing as never before, with cities increasing by 170,000 people daily. In 1950 London and New York were the only megacities with populations of 8 million or more. In 2015 there will be 33 megacities, 27 of them in the developing world. The ten largest will range from Mexico City (28.7 million) to Tokyo (18.8 million).[7]

Many chapters in this book attest to the key role of the city in advancing cultural and economic development. The pace of societal advancement can be expected to accelerate as a result of global urbanization. Indeed, the city has been described as a hotbed of creative innovation where key intellectual spillovers occur across a variety of enterprises concentrated in the urban environment.[8] To optimize its unique role, however, tomorrow's city must reform and reorganize itself. It will not be enough to get rid of the *barrios* that surround Latin American cities or rebuild the decaying cores of America's older urban centers. The push of highways, automobiles, and real estate developments into the open country has produced a formless urban sprawl; there is need to return—in concept—to the pedestrian scale of the small town with its familiar individuality. Paradoxically, because all cities will be interconnected in tomorrow's communication superhighway so as to function as components of the global village, "the smallest neighborhood or precinct must be planned as a working model of the larger world."[9] The corporate will of its citizens, aiming at self-knowledge, self-government, and self-actualization, needs to be embodied in the city. In such a social environment, "education will be the center of their activities ... [while] the city itself provides a vivid theater for the spontaneous encounters and challenges and embraces of daily life."[10]

We can expect social change to continue to be marked by "liberation" movements. These are characterized by "rights" that their proponents insist must be recognized as fundamental. One ongoing movement relates to racial and ethnic rights, a second to women's rights. Female emancipation remains a long and difficult struggle around the world. Suffrage was won by most women of the West early in the twentieth century, but their attempts to gain commensurate economic and social rights continue to be protracted, with their gains too often circumscribed or only begrudgingly yielded. "Coming out of the closet" is a familiar phrase associated with a third broad movement: the right of homosexuals to disclose their sexual orientation without being ostracized or denied rights to full economic and social parity.

Related to these broad social changes will be the need to advance the role of education on a global scale. After decades of international efforts to eradicate illiteracy, over a billion adults still cannot read or write, and over 100 million children of primary school age are not able to attend school every year.[11] These problems exist primarily in the developing world, where in the past 30 years the educational gap with the industrialized nations has increased. A close correlation exists among national levels of education, the status of women, and fertility rates. When education is widely available to women, average family size drops sharply, birthrates decline to socially manageable proportions, and health and living standards improve.[12]

In the developed countries, the dynamics of widespread technological change will require the continuing educational upgrading of the workforce, with technical and professional programs geared to both training and retraining. In other words, education is likely to be regarded as a lifelong process for all citizens—not only because of the demands of economies to remain competitive in the global economy but also because of the need for altering and enriching our understanding of why and how the world community is changing and what the privileges and accompanying responsibilities of world citizenry entail.

A historic change is occurring in the accumulation of knowledge and the ability of our educational system to assimilate information and deliver it effectively. Until modern times, humanity suffered from an overall paucity of knowledge, and acquiring knowledge entailed much rote learning at school. Today, in sharp contrast, a plethora of information—and misinformation—bombards us from all directions or is readily accessible from data banks. In fact, we seem to be suffering progressively from information overload and run the risk as societies of becoming so complex as to become dysfunctional.

Before World War II, T. S. Eliot had asked:

> Where is the Life we have lost in living?
> Where is the wisdom we have lost in knowledge?
> Where is the knowledge we have lost in
> information?[13]

His question seems more relevant now than ever. Are today's world citizens controlled by the dictates of the computer and data bank, or are they being empowered to use the new technology creatively so as to solve problems and set meaningful goals? There is much experimentation these days in educational theory and pedagogy as educators recognize that fundamental change is essential if our schools are to cope with tomorrow's many challenges.

Throughout recorded history, human striving and aspirations have been essential elements of problem solving. As the twenty-first century unfolds, what is new is not the existence of problems but humanity's more acute awareness of them and of an impending need to solve them. What is also unique for our times is that these major problems and the challenges they present are truly global in dimension. If they are great, so too are the numbers of people in every society who are deeply concerned about the future prospects of life on earth. This unprecedented awareness bodes well for a creative collective response.

Lest we become complacent, however, we have to ask ourselves: How much lead time do we have to make and then implement critical decisions for a global-scale civilization that is changing at an accelerating rate? The most intelligent planning can be thwarted by sociocultural inertia, by an inherent resistance to basic changes. A large, complex society can be likened to a supertanker whose size and momentum prevent it from coming to a stop for many miles. To pursue this analogy, those concerned about the future have no intention of trying to halt society in its tracks. Even if that were possible, any sudden stop could prove catastrophic. Rather they seek to alert society to be ready to change course. This requires not only charting viable alternative routes but also making sure that all concerned are fully alerted to the need for a change of direction and will accept the new destination. The critical factors here are awareness and timing, because setting a new course cannot wait for the storm that could engulf us if unprepared. We must develop contingency plans well in advance and be ready to act on them.

Suggestions for Reading

Because of the present-day and future orientation of materials in this Epilogue, you may want to consult a broad body of periodicals and journals to obtain up-to-date information regarding developments in the various segments of global culture. The Internet is a readily available and rapidly increasing source of new information in these areas—environmental, economic, political, social, scientific, technological, literary, and aesthetic (architecture, the arts, and music).

A useful introduction to what we may anticipate in the decades ahead as a global community, with its interlinked opportunities and constraints, is set forth lucidly in Paul Kennedy's *Preparing for the Twenty-First Century* (HarperCollins, 1993). This book might be read in conjunction with "A Special Moment in History" (*Atlantic Monthly*, May 1998), in which it is argued that the planet's fate will be determined in the next few decades through our technological, lifestyle, and population choices.

An important and influential assessment of the relationship of ecological and economic factors in a global context was produced in 1987 by the UN Commission on Environment and Development in *Our Common Future* (also known as the "Brundtland Report"); the commission was mandated by the General Assembly to "propose long-term environmental strategies for achieving sustainable development by the year 2000 and beyond." For an annual updating of progress toward a sustainable society, see the Worldwatch Institute Reports, *State of the World*. Consult *Planet Earth: Problems and Prospects* (McGill-Queen's University Press, 1995) for sections on climatic change, world hunger and health, animal impoverishment, and environmental toxicology. A special issue of *Scientific American* (September 1989), titled "Managing Planet Earth," also deals with major threats and challenges.

The powerful impetus provided by contemporary technological innovations in shaping and altering society is discussed from a number of vantage points in Merritt R. Smith and Leo Marx (eds.), *Does Technology Drive History? The Dilemma of Technological Determinism* (MIT Press, 1996); among its topics are technological determinism in American culture, technological momentum, the political and feminist dimensions of technological determinism, and rationality versus contingency in the history of technology. How systems' behavior affects the relationship of technology and society is discussed in Paul A. Alcorn's *Social Issues in Technology* (Prentice Hall, 1997). A *Newsweek Extra* (Winter 1997–1998) explores the power of invention and how an explosion of discoveries has changed our lives in the ways we work, live, fight, and heal.

The accelerating role of transnational corporations and the globalization of national economies have resulted in a large number of studies. These include Richard O'Brien, *Global Financial*

Integration: The End of Geography (Council on Foreign Relations Press, 1992); Richard Barnet and John Cavanagh, *Global Dreams: Imperial Corporations and the New World Order* (Simon & Schuster, 1994); and Jerry Mander and Edward Goldsmith (eds.), *The Case Against the Global Economy—and a Turn Toward the Local* (Sierra Club Books, 1996). The World Bank has published a number of monographs, including *Global Economic Prospects and the Developing Countries* (1993) and *Workers in an Integrating World* (1995). See also United Nations Development Program, *World Development Report, 1992* (Oxford University Press, 1992).

A major overhaul of trends in historiography, past and present, has been undertaken by Joyce Appleby, Lynn Hunt, and Margaret Jacob in *Telling the Truth About History* (Norton, 1994); they provide a fair forum to the advocates of postmodernism but defend with telling arguments the relevance and intellectual integrity of their discipline. In *The Culture of Hope: A New Birth of the Classical Spirit* (Free Press, 1995), Frederick Turner charges the "postmodern cultural establishment" with being philosophically empty and failing to give a satisfying answer to the question of the proper role of the arts in our society. But he revives the vision of a hope-oriented culture in the current convergence of science, art, and religion.

Notes

1. William R. Stevens, *Toronto Globe and Mail,* April 9, 1998.
2. World Commission on Environment and Development, *Our Common Future* (New York: Oxford University Press, 1987), p. 33.
3. Ibid., p. 128.
4. John Kettle, "Population Jump Puts the Squeeze on Space," *Toronto Globe and Mail,* April 23, 1998.
5. Gita Sen, "World Hunger, Livelihoods, and the Environment," in *Planet Earth: Problems and Prospects* (Montreal: McGill-Queen's University Press, 1995), pp. 67–81.
6. Paul Kennedy, *Preparing for the Twenty-First Century* (New York: HarperCollins, 1993), p. 331.
7. "Habitat II," United Nations Conference on Cities, Istanbul, June 1996.
8. Jane Jacobs, *The Economy of Cities* (New York: Vintage Books, 1970); Jane Jacobs, *Cities and the Wealth of Nations: Principles of Economic Life* (New York: Random House, 1984).
9. Lewis Mumford, *The City in History: Its Origins, Its Transformations, and Its Prospects* (New York: Harcourt Brace, 1961), p. 573.
10. Ibid.
11. United Nations Development Program, *Human Development Report, 1992* (New York: Oxford University Press, 1992), p. 2.
12. Kennedy, *Preparing for the Twenty-First Century,* pp. 339–343.
13. T. S. Eliot, choruses from "The Rock," in *The Complete Poems and Plays, 1909–1950* (New York: Harcourt Brace, 1971), p. 96.

Credits

Chapter 1

4 Des & Jen Bartlett/Bruce Coleman; **7** John Reader/Science Photo Library/Photo Researchers, NY; **8** John Reader/Science Photo Library/Photo Researchers, NY; **13** Courtesy of James Mellaart, London; **16R** Art Resource, NY; **16M** Art Resource, NY; **16R** Giraudon/Art Resource, NY; **17** © Adam Woolfitt/ Woodfin Camp & Associates, Inc., New York.

Chapter 2

20 SCALA/Art Resource, NY; **24** Kassite Map of Nippur, Hilprecht Collection of Near Eastern Antiquities, Friedrich-Schiller-Universitäat Jena, Germany; **26** SCALA/Art Resource, NY; **27** Hirmer FotoArchiv, Munich; **30** Pair Statue of Mycerinus and Queen Kha-merer-nebty II, Egypt, Dynasty IV, Giza, Valley Temple of Mycerinus. Museum of Fine Arts, Boston, Harvard-Museum Expedition, 11.1738; **31** © The British Museum, London; **32** Black Star; **34** © The British Museum, London; **35** © The British Museum, London; **36** Hirmer FotoArchiv, Munich; **37L** Fragment of a head of King Sesostris III. The Metropolitan Museum of Art, Carnarvon Collection, Gift of Edward S. Harkness, 1926 (26.7.1394). All rights reserved. The Metropolitan Museum of Art; **37R** © Bildarchiv Preussischer Kulturbesitz, Berlin, 1999. Photo by Margarete Büsing. Staatliche Museen zu Berlin-Ägyptisches Museum; **44** © The British Museum, London; **46** Erich Lessing/ Art Resource, NY; **48** Museo Nazionale, Naples.

Chapter 3

52 Claudia Parks/The Stock Market; **55** © Michael Holford Photographs; **56** Hirmer FotoArchiv, Munich; **57** Art Resource; **60** Art Resource; **63** © The British Museum, London; **67** Courtesy of The Manchester Museum, The University of Manchester; **73** AKG London; **75B** Robert Frerck/Odyssey Productions, Chicago; **75T** Robert Frerck/Odyssey Productions, Chicago; **76L** Kouros, Statue of a youth, c. 610–600 B.C.E. The Metropolitan Museum of Art, New York. Fletcher Fund, 1932. (32.11.1). Photograph © 1993 The Metropolitan Museum of Art; **76M** SCALA/Art Resource, NY; **76R** SCALA/Art Resource, NY; **77** SCALA/Art Resource, NY; **81** Erich Lessing/Art Resource, NY.

Chapter 4

86 Steve Vidler/Leo de Wys Inc.; **90** SCALA/Art Resource, NY; **91** SCALA/Art Resource, NY; **102B** Alinari/Art Resource, NY; **102T** Nimatallah/Art Resource, NY; **104** Bedroom from the Villa of P. Fannius Synistror, Roman Pompeii, 1st century B.C.E. The Metropolitan Museum of Art, Rogers Fund, 1903 (03.14.13). Photograph by Schecter Lee. Photograph © 1986 The Metropolitan Museum of Art; **105** SCALA/Art Resource, NY; **106** SCALA/Art Resource, NY; **111L** © Michael Holford Photographs; **111R** SCALA/Art Resource, NY; **115** SCALA/Art Resource, NY.

Chapter 5

120 Don Hamilton; **122** Christie's Images, Ltd. 1999; **123** Academia Sinica, Taipei; **125** Musée Cernushi, Paris; **127** Corbis/Bettmann; **132L** Laurie Platt Winfrey, Inc.; **132R** Christie's Images, Ltd. 1999; **134** Bronze cowrie-container decorated with weaving scene on lid, unearthed in 1955. The Chinese Exhibition, Nelson Gallery-Atkins Museum, Kansas City, Missouri; **135** Robert Harding Picture Library; **136** Brocade mitten with the characters: Yen Nien Yi Shou, 1st–2nd century A.D. (Eastern Han) Unearthed in 1959 from a site at Niya, Minfeng county in Sinkiang. The Chinese Exhibition, Nelson Gallery-Atkins Musueum, Kansas City, Missouri; **137** Vault Map Collection, Library of Congress.

Chapter 6

140 *Adoration of the Bodhi Tree*, India, Amaravati Satavahana period, 2nd century. Stone relief, 80 × 57.1 cm. The Cleveland Museum of Art, Purchase from the J. H. Wade Fund, 1970.43; **143** © MacQuitty International Collection, London; **144** Pakistan National Museum; **144** Pakistan National Museum; **156** AKG London; **157** British Library/e.t. archive, London; **58** Museo Nazionale, Naples; **161** Seated Buddha, from Gandhara, Pakistan. Kushan period, 2nd-3rd century. Dark gray schist, H. 36" × W. 22½". Seattle Art Museum, Eugene Fuller Memorial Collection, 33.180. Photo: Paul Macapia; **162** Prithwish Neogy; **163** Vessel in the Form of an Ax. Bronze. The Metropolitan Museum of Art, Purchase, George McFadden Gift and Edit Perry Chapman Fund, 1993. (1993.525) Photograph by Bruce White © 1993 The Metropolitan Museum of Art; **164** © Michael Holford Photographs.

Chapter 7

170 Erich Lessing/Art Resource, NY; **173** The "Thanksgiving Scroll" before opening, Dead Sea Scroll. Israel Museum, Jerusalem. The Shrine of the Book; **177** Photo by Duane Preble. Museo dei Conservatori, Rome; **181B** © 95 Harvey Lloyd/The Stock Market; **181T** Marvin Trachtenberg; **182** AKG London; **184** SCALA/Art Resource, NY; **185** The Granger Collection, New York; **186** © The British Museum, London; **189** Bibliothèque nationale de France, Paris; **190** Roger-Viollet/ Gamma Liaison.

Chapter 8

200 The Pierpont Morgan Library/Art Resource, NY; **203** AKG London; **208** The Cathedral Churck of the Blessed Virgin Mary and St. Ethelbert in Hereford, England; **209** Giraudon/Art Resource, NY; **210** SCALA/Art Resource, NY; **211** Marburg/Art Resource, NY; **212** Archives Photographiques, Paris.

Chapter 9

216 Battle of Agincourt, 1415, English with Flemish illuminations St. Alban's Chronicle (late 15th century). Lambeth Palace Library, London, UK/Bridgeman Art Library, London/New York; **222** Universitets Oldsaksamling, Oslo; **221** Art Resource, NY; **225** The British Library, London; **228** Giraudon/Art Resource, NY; **230** The Martyrdom of Thomas Becket, Carrow Psalter, MS W. 34f. 15v. The Walters Art Gallery, Baltimore; **231** Edward I in Parliament, MS 1113. The Royal Collection © 1999 Her Majesty Queen Elizabeth II; **234** Bibliothèque nationale de France, Paris; **236** Master, carpenter and stonemason, 1482. Roy 15 EII f.265. Des Proprietez des Choses/British Library, London, UK/Bridgeman Art Library, London/New York; **238** Bibliothèque Royale Albert, Brussels; **239** Institut Amatller d'Art Hispanic; **240** Giraudon/Art Resource, NY; **241** Portrait of Henry VII by English School (16th century), T31778. Phillips, The International Fine Art Auctioneers, UK/Bridgeman Art Library, London/New York.

Chapter 10

244 Color Day Productions/The Image Bank; **248** The British Library, London; **250** Edinburgh University Library; **251** Islamic manuscript, 8th–9th century. Purchase F30.60. Freer Gallery of Art and Arthur M. Sackler Gallery, Smithsonian Institution; **253L** Courtesy of the Spencer Collection, The New York Public Library, Aster, Lenox and Tilden Foundation; **253R** Qisas al-Anbiya, Moses turns staff into a dragon. Spencer Persian Manuscript, 46, folio 82. Courtesy of the Spencer Collection, The New York Public Library, Aster, Lenox and Tilden Foundation; **254** Qisas al-Anbiya, Jesus performs miracle of loaves. Spencer Collection 46, folio 152v. Courtesy of the Spencer Collection, The New York Public Library, Aster, Lenox and Tilden Foundation; **261L** Bibliothèque nationale de France, Paris; **261R** Bibliothèque nationale de France, Paris; **262** National Library, Cairo; **264** © The Bodleian Library, Oxford, England; **267** SuperStock.

Chapter 11

270 © Betty Press/Woodfin Camp & Associates, Inc.; **274** © Sarah Errington/The Hutchison Library, London; **275** © Erich Lessing/Art Resource, New York ; **276** National Museum, Lagos, Nigeria; **279** © Georg Gerster/Photo Researchers; **280** Marc/Evelyn Berheim/ Woodfin Camp & Associates, New York; **283** Bibliothèque nationale de France, Paris; **286** Bibliothèque nationale de France, Paris; **288** Werner Forman Archive/Art Resource, New York; **290** © Dirk Bakker; **291** AKG London; **292** The National Palace Museum, Republic of China; **293** Marc/Evelyn Berheim/ Woodfin Camp & Associates, New York; **294** Robert Aberman/Werner Forman Archive/Art Resource, New York.

Chapter 12

298 *Krishna Battling the Horse Demon*, Keshi, Terracotta. The Metropolitan Museum of Art, Purchase, Florence and Herbert Irving Gift, 1991. (1991.300) Photograph by Bruce White, Photograph © 1994 The Metropolitan Museum of Art; **303** Robert Ivey/Ric Ergenbright Photography; **306L** Shaanxi Provincial Museum, Xian; **306R** © The British Museum,

London; **307** Bullock and cart, T'ang Dynasty, 7th–8th century. Pottery with green and brown glazes, H. 16" × L. 20¼". Seattle Art Museum, Eugene Fuller Memorial Collection, 37.17. Photo: Paul Macapia; **308** Courtesy of The Schloss Collection, The Bowers Museum of Cultural Art, Santa Ana, CA **311** *Court Ladies Preparing Newly Woven Silk*, Emperor Huizong (attributed to), r. 1101–1125. Chinese; Northern Song Dynasty, early 12th century. Handscroll; ink, color and gold on silk, 27.0 × 145.3 cm. Museum of Fine Arts, Boston, Chinese and Japanese Special Fund; **312L** Tokyo National Museum; **312R** Ma Yuan, Chinese, active 1190–1235; Southern Song Dynasty, *Bare Willows and Distant Mountains*. Round fan mounted as album leaf; ink and light color on silk, 23.8 × 24.2 cm. Museum of Fine Arts, Boston. Special Chinese and Japanese Fund; **315** Black Star; **316** © Kyodo News Service; **317B** Courtesy of Kyoryokukai, The Tokyo National Museum; **317T** Kodansha Ltd., Tokyo; **318** *Battle Scene*, Kamakura period, 14th century. Section of handscroll mounted as a hanging scroll; ink, color, and touches of gold paint on paper, H. 14" × W. 17¼". Seattle Art Museum, Eugene Fuller Memorial Collection, 48.173. Photo: Paul Macapia; **319L** Bibliothèque nationale de France, Paris; **319R** Victoria & Albert Museum, London/Art Resource, NY; **323** Bibliothèque nationale de France, Paris; **326** Special Collections, The New York Public Library.

Chapter 13

330 Randy G. Taylor/Leo de Wys, Inc., New York; **333** Werner Forman/Art Resource, NY; **335** Enrique Franco Torrijos; **336** Museo Nacional de Antropologia, Mexico City; **338** Deer Effigy, Vessel, Mexico. "Plumbate" earthenware. The Saint Louis Art Museum. Gift of Morton D. May; **339** Library of Congress; **341L** SCALA/Art Resource, NY; **342L** Werner Forman Archive/Art Resource, New York; **342R** Ewing Krainen; **343** Lee Boltin; **347** Mark C Burnett, Ohio Historical Society, Columbus/Photo Researchers; **349** Museum of Anthropology and Ethnography in St. Petersburg FL.

Chapter 14

354 Victor Boswell/National Geographic Society Image Collection; **358L** SCALA/Art Resource, New York; **358R** SCALA/Art Resource, New York; **360** © Erich Lessing/Art Resource, New York; **362** © The British Museum, London; **364** © Erich Lessing/Art Resource, New York; **365** SCALA/Art Resource, NY; **366** Alinari/Art Resource, NY; **367L** Alinari/Art Resource, NY; **367R** Alinari/Art Resource, NY; **368L** SCALA/Art Resource, New York; **368R** Art Resource; **369B** SCALA/Art Resource, NY; **369T** SCALA/Art Resource, NY; **370** SCALA/Art Resource, NY; **371L** © Erich Lessing/Art Resource, New York; **371R** Cameraphoto/Art Resource, New York; **372** Kunsthistorisches Museum, Vienna; **373** SCALA/Art Resource, New York; **374** AKG London; **375** Reunion des Musées nationaux; **377** Giraudon/Art Resource, New York; **378** The History of Don Quixote, London, 1620 (t.p.) Special Collections, The New York Public Library; **379** Jan van Eyck, The Arnolfini Portrait, 1434. NG 186. © National Gallery, London; **380** Albrecht Dürer, *The Knight, Death and the Devil*, 1513. Engraving, 9¹¹⁄₁₆" × 7⅝". The Brooklyn Museum of Art, New York. Gift of Mrs. Horace O. Havemeyer, 54.35.6.

Chapter 15

384 © Erich Lessing/Art Resource, New York; **387** Jan van Eyck, *The Last Judgment* (one of two panels), tempera and oil on canvas, transferred from wood. 22¼" × 7¾". The Metropolitan Museum of Art, Fletcher Fund, 1933. Photograph © 1998 The Metropolitan Museum of Art; **391L** Lutherhalle, Wittenberg, Germany; **391R** Lucas Cranach the Younger, German, 1515-1586, *Martin Luther and the Wittenberg Reformers* (1926.55) c. 1543, oil on panel, 27⅞ × 15⅝ in. (72.8 x 39.7 cm.) The Toledo

Museum of Art; Toledo, Ohio; Purchased with funds from the Libbey Endowment, Gift of Edward Drummond Libbey; **397** Erich Lessing/Art Resource, NY; **400** Photo Francois Martin, Geneva. Document BPU; **401** Giraudon/Art Resource, NY; **403** SCALA/Art Resource, NY; **405** SCALA/Art Resource, NY; **406L** SCALA/Art Resource, NY; **406R** *Malle Babbe*, Style of Frans Hals, c. 1650. The Metropolitan Museum of Art, Purchase, 1871 (71.76) All rights reserved. The Metropolitan Museum of Art; **407** English Heritage as Trustees of Iveagh Bequest, Kenwood; **413** © The British Museum, London; **415** Philippe de Champaigne, c. 1637. *Cardinal Richelieu*. NG 1449. © National Gallery, London; **416** Print Collection, Miriam and Ira D. Wallach. Division of Art, Prints and Photographs, the New York Public Library, Astor, Lennox and Tilden Foundations.

Chapter 16

424 Musées royaux des Beaux-Arts de Belgique, Bruxelles-Koninklijke Musea voor Schone Kunsten van Belgie, Brussel; **427** Portuguese Carracks off a Fortified Coast, c. 1520 by Joachim Patinir. National Maritime Museum, London, UK/Bridgeman Art Library, London/New York; **430** Bibliothèque nationale de France, Paris; **434** © The British Museum, London; **436** Hispanic Society of America, New York; **438** The British Museum, London/Werner Forman Archive; **442** Sebastian Münster, Cosmographia, 1540. Vault Map Collection, Library of Congress; **445** The Huntington Library, Art Collections, and Botanical Gardens-San Marino, CA/SuperStock; **447** © A.H. Robins Co. Courtesy Doneiler's Custom Photography.

Chapter 17

452 Detail. Freer Gallery of Art and Arthur M. Sackler Gallery Archives, Smithsonian Institution; **455** The British Library, London; **457** Weltkarte des Piri Reis, 1513; Istanbul, Topkapi Serail-Museum. AKG London; **458** Tughra (calligraphic emblem) of Süleyman the Magnificent, Sultan of Turkey (1520–1566); from an imperial edict. Ink, colors and gold on paper. The Metropolitan Museum of Art, Rogers Fund, 1938. (38.149.1) Photograph © 1986 The Metropolitan Museum of Art; **459** Title page of Baudier's Histoire...empereur des Turcs, 1631. Department of Rare Books and Special Collections, Princeton University Library; **461** Hulton Getty/Liaison Agency; **465** Mir Sayyid-Ali, Safavid dynasty, 16th century. Freer Gallery of Art and Arthur M. Sackler Gallery Archives, Smithsonian Institution; **466** Mughal painting, c. 1620. (F45.9a) Freer Gallery of Art and Arthur M. Sackler Gallery Archives, Smithsonian Institution; **467** The British Library, London; **469** S. Vidler/SuperStock; **470** Birth of a Prince from an illustrated manuscript of the Jahangir-nama, Bishndas (Attributed to), Northern India, Mughal, about 1620. Opaque watercolor on paper, 24.1 × 17 cm. Museum of Fine Arts, Boston, Francis Bartlett Donation of 1912 and Picture Fund.

Chapter 18

474 (Detail) Attributed to Sesshu, Japan, 1420–1506. Muromachi period. Birds and Flowers in a Landscape. Six-fold screen, ink and color on paper, 173.4 × 378 cm. © The Cleveland Museum of Art, Purchase from the J. H. Wade Fund, 1961.204; **477** © Wan-go H. C. Weng, Lyme, NH; **479L** National Palace Museum, Taipei Taiwan; **479R** Prunis Vase (Meiping) with Blossoming Lotus: Fahug Ware. Porcelain with polychrome glazes, H. 37.5 cm. China, Jiangxi Province, Jingdezhen kilns, late 15th century, Ming dynasty. The Cleveland Museum of Art, 1994, Bequest of John L. Severance, 42.716; **481T** Courtesy of the History of Cartography Project. By permission of Ryukoku University Library, Kyoto, Japan; **481B** Korean Cultural Center; **482** National Museum of Korea, Seoul; **484** Ando Hiroshige, c. 1832. *Abe River near Fuchu*, woodblock print. Honolulu Academy of Arts, Gift of James A. Michener, 1978 (17,235).

Chapter 19

492 Hyacinthe Rigaud (1659–1743), *Louis XIV, King of France, Portrait in royal costume*. Oil on canvas, 277 × 194 cm—Inv. 7492. Louvre, Dpt. des Peintures, Paris, France. © Photograph by Erich Lessing/Art Resource, New York; **496** Giraudon/Art Resource, NY; **497** © Photo RMN-D. Arnaudet/G.B; **497** © Photo RMN-D. Arnaudet/G.B; **503** Danish Royal Collection at Rosenborg Castle, Copenhagen; **506** Central Naval Museum, St. Petersburg; **508L** Alinari/Art Resource, NY; **510** Corbis/Bettmann; **518** AKG London; 521 Art Resource, New York; **522** Giraudon/Art Resource, NY.

Chapter 20

528 Jan Steen (1626–1679), *Fishmarket of Leiden*. Stadelsches Kunstinstitut, Frankfurt am Main. Photo: © Ursula Edelmann, Frankfurt am Main; **531** Johannes Blaeu, Toonneel der Steden, 1652. Map of Amsterdam. Library of Congress; **532** Aelbert Cuyp, SK-A-2350, A senior merchant of the Dutch East India Company, presumably Jacob Mathieusen and his wife; in the background the fleet in the roads of Batavia. Rijksmuseum, Amsterdam; **534** Nimatallah/Art Resource, NY; **540** © Michael Holford Photographs; **542** Rembrandt, SK-C-6, The syndics: the sampling officials of the Amsterdam drapers' guild. Rijksmuseum, Amsterdam.

Chapter 21

550 SCALA/Art Resource, NY; **553** The British Library, London; **554** Art Resource; **556** Jacques Louis David/Bulloz; **557** Herman Verelst, Portrait of John Locke. By Courtesy of The National Portrait Gallery, London **559** Corbis/Bettmann; **560** John Opie, Portrait of Mary Wollstonecraft Godwin, c. 1797. Courtesy of the National Portrait Gallery, London; **565** By kind permission of the Earl of Harrowby, Sandon Hall, Stafford, England; **566** From Clark, An Album of Methodist History, Abingdon Press; **570** © Sovfoto/Eastfoto; **573** Austrian National Library, Vienna; **574** © Collection of The New-York Historical Society.

Chapter 22

584 Giraudon/Art Resource, NY; **587** Giraudon/Art Resource, New York; **589** Bulloz; **592** Bulloz; **594** Giraudon/Art Resource, NY; **595** Giraudon/Art Resource, NY; **599** © Erich Lessing/Art Resource, NY; **603** NYPL, Astor, Lenox, and Tilden Foundations, Prints Division; **609R** The Royal Collection © 1999 Her Majesty Queen Elizabeth II.

Chapter 23

614 The Newark Museum/Art Resource, New York; **619** Werner Forman Archive/Art Resource, New York; **621** Library of Congress; **622** Pierpoint Morgan Library/Art Resource, NY; **623** G. Weidenfeld and Nicholson; **624** Peter Newarks' Historical Pictures; **626** *Birth in a Harem*, late 18th century. Los Angeles County Museum of Art, gift of Edwin Binney, 3rd collection of Turkish art; **628** Selim III, Sultan of Turkey (1761–1808) Duchateau, 1792, engraved by Nutter. Mary Evans Picture Library, London; **631** Victoria & Albert Museum, London/Art Resource, New York; **632** Victoria & Albert Museum, London; **635** National Maritime Museum, London; **638** Christie's Images, Ltd. 1999.

Chapter 24

646 Detail. Claude Monet, *The Gare Saint-Lazare*, 1877. Oil on canvas, 80.33 cm × 98.11 cm. Courtesy of the Fogg Art Museum, Harvard University Art Museums, Bequest from the Collection of Maurice Wertheim, Class of 1906. Photo: David Mathews. © President and Fellows of Harvard College, Harvard University; **648** © The British Museum, London; **649** Mansell Collection; **653** Gustav Dore and Blanchard Jerrold, London: A Pilgrimage, Grant & Co. London, 1872; **656** Courtesy Fried Krupp GmbH (Historisches Archiv Fried. Krupp AG); **658** James Reynolds, Geological Map, 1849 NO. 946 (5) By Permission of the British Library, London; **659** Corbis/Bettmann; **661** P833.167. From the Collections of Henry Ford Museum & Greenfield Village; **662** Pear's Soap Ad (African Girl), Illustrated London News, 1899. Mary Evans Picture Gallery; **664L** Bibliothèque nationale de France, Paris; **664R** Thomas Phillips, Portrait of George Gordon Byron, 6th Baron Byron, 1835. Courtesy of the National Portrait Gallery, London; **666** Corbis/Bettmann.

Chapter 25

670 Giraudon/Art Resource, NY; **675** Library of Congress; **76** Bibliothèque nationale de France, Paris; **679** AKG London; **681** © The British Museum, London; **682** Mansell Collection; **684** Roger Viollet/Gamma Liaison; **685** © Sovfoto; **687** Mansell Collection; **688L** Weidenfeld & Nicholson Ltd.; **689** Memphis Brooks Museum of Art, Memphis, TN; Memphis Park Commission Purchase 46.2; **692** George Caleb Bingham, *The Jolly Flatboatmen in Port*, 1857. The Saint Louis Art Museum, Purchase.

Chapter 26

696 Die Proklamierung des Deutschen Kaiserreiches am 18. Januar 1871 im Spiegelsaal von Versailles (Friedrichsruher Fassung). Gemälde von Anton von Werner, 1885. Oil on canvas, 167 × 202 cm. Friedrichsruh, Bismarck-Museum, bildarchiv preussischer kulturbesitz, Berlin; **698** Liaison Agency; **703** Bibliothèque nationale de France, Paris; **708** © Sovfoto; **711** Museum of London; **712** Mansell Collection; **713** Library of Congress; **715** The Granger Collection, New York; **718** Giraudon/Art Resource, NY; **719T** Claude Monet, French, 1840–1926, *Water Lilies*, 1906. Oil on canvas, 87.6 × 92.7 cm., Mr. & Mrs. Martin A. Ryerson Collection, 1933.1157. © 1999, The Art Institute of Chicago. All rights reserved. **719B** van Gogh, Vincent. *The Starry Night*. (1889) Oil on canvas, 29 × 36¼" (73.7 × 92.1 cm). The Museum of Modern Art, New York. Acquired through the Lillie P. Bliss Bequest. Photograph © 1999 The Museum of Modern Art, New York; **720** Pablo Picasso, *Les Demoiselles d'Avignon*, Paris (June–July 1907). Oil on canvas, 243.9 × 233.7 cm. The Museum of Modern Art, New York. Acquired through the Lillie P. Bliss Bequest, Photograph © 1999 The Museum of Modern Art, New York; © 2000 Estate of Pablo Picasso/Artists Rights Society (ARS), New York; **721** Poster for L'arroseur arrosé for Cinématographe Lumière, designed by Auzolle, 1896. Cliché J.- L. Charmet.

Chapter 27

724 W. Wellner in Lushige Blatter. Courtesy Mary Evans Picture Library; **727** Map of Liberia (9 out of 20) from the American Colonization Society Collection. G8882.C6 1830.A8 ACS 2. Library of Congress, Geography and Map Division, Washington, DC; **728** Roger Viollet/Gamma Liaison; **729L** The British Library, London; **730** Mary Evans Picture Library, London; **732L** Africana Museum JPL; **732R** Corbis/Hulton Deutsch; **733** Culver Pictures, Inc.; **737** Roger Viollet/Gamma Liaison; **738** Roger Viollet/Gamma Liaison; **741** Delacroix, Eugene (1798–1860) *The Massacre of Chios, Greek families waiting for death or slavery*. Oil on canvas, 1824. Louvre, Department of Paintings, Paris. © Erich Lessing/Art Resource, New York; **742** Mary Evans Picture Library; **743** The Ottoman Gazette Kalem; **745** Roger Viollet/Gamma Liaison; **746** Corbis/Bettmann; **747** Brown Brothers.

Chapter 28

752 *Canton factories*, M3156. Oil on glass, post 1780. Peabody Essex Museum, Salem, MA. Photo by Mark Sexton; **755** *Castas, De mestizo y española, castiza*. Museo National de Historia; **757** Instituto Nacional de Bellas Artes; **759** From W. H. Russell, A Visit to Chile, 1890; **765** Tz'u-hsi, Empress Dowager of China, 1835–1908, Photographs Freer Gallery of Art and Arthur M. Sackler Gallery Archives, Smithsonian Institution; **767** *Puck*, August 15, 1900. Courtesy of American Heritage; **768** Mariners' Museum, Newport News, Virginia. Carl. H. Boehringer Collection; **769** Keystone-Mast Collection (Ku58130) UCR/California Museum of Photography, University of California, Riverside; **772** Mary Evans Picture Library.

Chapter 29

778 SCALA/Art Resource, NY; **780L** Culver Pictures, Inc.; **781** Culver Pictures, Inc.; **782** Culver Pictures, Inc.; **784** Corbis/Hulton Deutsch; **786** Historical Photos/Stock Montage, Inc.; **787** Corbis/Bettmann; **789** Roger Viollet/Gamma-Liaison; **790** The Granger Collection, New York; **793** Hulton Getty/Liaison Agency.

Chapter 30

798 © 1999 Artists Rights Society (ARS), New York/ADAGP, Paris; **802** Corbis/Bettmann; **806** Corbis/Bettmann; **807** The Trustees of the Imperial War Museum, London; **809** The Trustees of the Imperial War Museum, London; **811** Brown Brothers; **818L** Historical Photos/Stock Montage, Inc.; **818R** Corbis/Bettmann; **821** Corbis/Bettmann; **823** Corbis/Bettmann; **825** © 2000 Estate of Pablo Picasso/Artists Rights Society (ARS), New York. Giraudon/Art Resource, NY; **828** Corbis/Bettmann; **830** Corbis/Bettmann; **832** Dali, Salvador. *The Persistence of Memory* (Persistance de la mémoire). 1931. Oil on canvas, 9½ × 12" (24.1 × 33 cm). The Museum of Modern Art, New York. Given anonymously. Photograph © 1999 The Museum of Modern Art, New York. © 2000 Artists Rights Society (ARS), New York; **834** Art Resource, NY; **835** The Museum of Modern Art/Film Stills Archive, NY.

Chapter 31

838 Corbis/Bettmann; **841T** Corbis/Bettmann; **841B** Corbis/Hulton Deutsch; **846** Corbis/Underwood; **849** © Sovfoto; **852** © Sovfoto; **855** Erich Lessing/Art Resource, NY; **856T** Corbis/Bettmann; **865B** Corbis/Bettmann; **858** bpk Berlin, Nationalgalerie; **860** Popperfoto; **861** Wiener Library, London; **862** Kulturgeschichtliches Museum, Osnabruck (c) Auguste Moses-Nussbaum and Shulamit Jaari. © 2000 Artists Rights Society (ARS), New York/VG Bild-Kunst, Bonn.

Chapter 32

868 The End of the Ottoman Empire, Turkey 1908–1938. A History in Documentary Photographs by Jaques Benoist-Méchin. Published by Swan; **874** Culver Pictures, Inc.; **876** Corbis/Bettmann; **880** Margaret Bourke-White /Life Magazine/Time Warner, Inc.; **881** AP/Wide World Photos, Inc.; **885**

Index

Note: Page numbers preceded by E refer to the Epilogue.

GREENLAND
(KALAALLIT NUNAAT)
(Den.)

ICELAND

UNITED
KINGDOM

IRELAND

FRANC

ALASKA
(U.S.)

CANADA

UNITED STATES

ATLANTIC
OCEAN

SPA

PORTUGAL

AZORES (Port.)

MOROCCO

CANARY IS. (Sp.)

WESTERN SAHARA
(Mor.)

BAHAMAS

DOMINICAN
REPUBLIC

HAITI

PUERTO RICO (U.S.)

ST. KITTS AND NEVIS

ANTIGUA AND BARBUDA

DOMINICA

ST. VINCENT AND THE GRENADINES

BARBADOS

GRENADA

TRINIDAD AND TOBAGO

GUYANA

SURINAME

FRENCH GUIANA (Fr.)

CAPE
VERDE

MAURITANIA

MALI

SENEGAL

THE GAMBIA

GUINEA-BISSAU

GUINEA

SIERRA LEONE

LIBERIA

CÔTE D'IVOIRE

BURKINA FASO

GHANA

HAWAII (U.S.)

Tropic of Cancer

MEXICO

CUBA

JAMAICA

BELIZE

GUADELOUPE (Fr.)

MARTINIQUE (Fr.)

ST. LUCIA

GUATEMALA

HONDURAS

EL SALVADOR

NICARAGUA

COSTA RICA

PANAMA

VENEZUELA

COLOMBIA

PACIFIC OCEAN

Equator

GALÁPAGOS IS.
(Ec.)

ECUADOR

PERU

BRAZIL

WESTERN
SAMOA

AMERICAN
SAMOA (U.S.)

TONGA

FRENCH
POLYNESIA (Fr.)

BOLIVIA

PARAGUAY

Tropic of Capricorn

CHILE

URUGUAY

ATLANTIC
OCEAN

ARGENTINA

0   1,500   3,000 Miles
0   1,500   3,000 Kilometers

**Contemporary
Political Map
of the World**

FALKLAND IS. (U.K.)

Antarctic Circle